seventh edition

MODERN MANAGEMENT

DIVERSITY, QUALITY, ETHICS, AND THE GLOBAL ENVIRONMENT

SAMUEL C. CERTO

Professor of Management
Roy E. Crummer
Graduate School of Business—Rollins College

PRENTICE HALL, Upper Saddle River, New Jersey 07458

To Matthew—the idea person for this book.

Acquisitions Editor: David Shafer
Executive Editor: Natalie Anderson
Development Editor: Ronald S. Librach
Associate Editor: Lisamarie Brassini
Editorial Assistant: Brett Moreland
Editor-in-Chief: James Boyd
Director of Development: Steve Deitmer
Marketing Manager: Sandra Steiner
Production Editor: Lynne Breitfeller
Production Coordinator: David Cotugno
Managing Editor: Carol Burgett
Manufacturing Supervisor: Arnold Vila
Manufacturing Manager: Vincent Scelta
Senior Production Manager: Lorraine Patsco
Senior Designer: Ann France
Design Director: Patricia Wosczyk
Interior Design: A Good Thing
Cover Design: Lorraine Castellano
Composition/Interior Illustrator: Monotype Composition Company, Inc.
Cover Art/Photo: Sharmen Liao, Inc.

Certo, Samuel C.
    Modern management : diversity, quality, ethics, and the global
environment / Samuel C. Certo. — 7th ed.
    p.   cm.
    Includes bibliographical references and index.
    ISBN 0-13-210634-5 (alk. paper)
    1. Management.   2. Industrial management.   3. Social
responsibility of business.   I. Title.
HD31.C4125   1997
658—dc20   96-31857
                                                CIP

Prentice-Hall International (UK) Limited, London
Prentice-Hall of Austrailia Pty. Limited, Sydney
Prentice-Hall Canada, Inc., Toronto
Prentice-Hall Hispanoamericana, S.A., Mexico
Prentice-Hall of India Private Limited, New Delhi
Prentice-Hall of Japan, Inc., Tokyo
Simon & Schuster Asia Pte. Ltd., Singapore
Editora Prentice-Hall do Brasil, Ltda., Rio de Janeiro

Printed in the United States of America

10 9 8 7 6 5 4 3 2

BRIEF CONTENTS

CONTENTS

15 LEADERSHIP   348

16 MOTIVATION   378

17 GROUPS, TEAMS, AND CORPORATE CULTURE   402

18 UNDERSTANDING PEOPLE: ATTITUDES, PERCEPTION, AND LEARNING   428

Part 5 CONTROLLING

19 PRINCIPLES OF CONTROLLING   454

20 PRODUCTION MANAGEMENT AND CONTROL   475

21 INFORMATION AND TECHNOLOGY   506

x   Contents

As it was in the previous six editions of *Modern Management*, the purpose of this text is to prepare students to be managers. Coverage includes a wealth of conventional wisdom related to traditional management challenges. In addition, contemporary management challenges related to such issues as people, diversity, quality, ethics, and the global environment are featured. Overall, this book is carefully crafted to present traditional management concepts, important contemporary management issues, and insights regarding ways that students should handle both in order to ensure organizational success.

The seventh edition of the **Modern Management Learning Package**—which is to say, this text plus its ancillaries—continues a recognized and distinctive tradition in management education. This tradition entails clear, concise, current, and thorough coverage of management concepts. In addition, that tradition features learning materials that are based upon an understanding of and a determination to enhance the student learning process. Only instructional-support materials that contribute to the design and conduct of the highest-quality principles of management courses are included in the package.

Revisions to the **Modern Management Learning Package** have been spirited by a single objective—improving student learning. All revisions reflect a responsiveness to instructor and student insights regarding ways to refashion the package in order to further enhance student learning. Starting with the text, the following sections describe and explain each major component of this revision.

Text: Theory Overview

Decisions about which concepts to include in this text were indeed difficult. Such decisions were heavily influenced by information from accrediting agencies like the American Assembly of Collegiate Schools of Business (AACSB), organizations established by professional managers like the American Management Association (AMA), and organizations established by management scholars like the Academy of Management. Overall, management theory in this text is divided into six main sections:

- Introduction to Management
- Planning
- Organizing
- Influencing
- Controlling
- Topics for Special Emphasis.

Of course, updates of theory and examples have been made extensively in every section. More detailed discussion of content and other revisions to each section follows.

Introduction to Management

This section lays the groundwork necessary for studying management.

- **Chapter 1, Management and Management Careers,** not only exposes students to what management is, but also gives them an understanding of special career issues, such as the progress of women in management, dual-career couples, and the multicultural workforce.
- **Chapter 2, The History of Management,** presents several fundamental but different ways in which managers can perceive their jobs. The work of management pioneers like Frederick W. Taylor, Frank and Lillian Gilbreth, and Henry L. Gantt is highlighted. This edition includes expanded coverage of the human relations movement.
- **Chapter 3, Corporate Social Responsibility and Business Ethics,** discusses the responsibilities that managers have to society and how business ethics applies to modern management. For this edition, a new focus on determining if social responsibility exists in a particular situation has been added.
- **Chapter 4, Managing in the Global Arena,** represents a major new enhancement to this edition. New coverage includes discussion of domestic versus international, multinational, and transnational organizations; expatriates and repatriation; and international market agreements like the European Community (EC) and the North American Free Trade Agreement (NAFTA).

Discussion also extends to the evolving international market agreement among Pacific Rim countries. Note that to better enable students to reflect on global management issues throughout the course, this chapter has been moved from the last section to the first section of this book.

Planning

This section elaborates on planning as a primary management function.

- The section begins with **Chapter 5, Organizational Objectives,** in order to emphasize the set-

ting of organizational objectives as the beginning of the planning process.

- **Chapter 6, Fundamentals of Planning,** presents the basics of planning.
- **Chapter 7, Making Decisions,** discusses the decision process as a component of the planning process. New coverage focuses on group decision processes like brainstorming, the nominal group technique, and the Delphi technique. New coverage also focuses on advantages and disadvantages of having groups make decisions and problems in evaluating group decision process.
- **Chapter 8, Strategic Planning,** highlights Porter's model for industry analysis, the BCG Growth-Share Matrix, the GE Portfolio Matrix, strategy implementation, and strategic control.
- **Chapter 9, Plans and Planning Tools,** discusses various planning tools, such as forecasting and scheduling, that are available to help formulate plans.

Organizing

This section discusses organizing activities as a major management function.

- **Chapter 10, Fundamentals of Organizing,** presents the basic principles of organizing.
- **Chapter 11, Responsibility, Authority, and Delegation,** focuses on ways to organize worker activities.
- **Chapter 12, Managing Human Resources,** discusses hiring and developing people who will make desirable contributions to the attainment of organizational objectives.
- **Chapter 13, Organizational Change and Stress,** focuses on ways in which managers change organizations and highlights some stress-related issues that can accompany such action. Discussion also stresses the definition of stress and the importance of studying and managing stress.

Influencing

This section discusses ways in which managers should deal with people. Reflecting the spirit of AACSB guidelines encouraging more coverage of human factors in the business curriculum, the influencing section has been revised extensively.

- **Chapter 14, Fundamentals of Influencing and Communication,** introduces the topic of managing people, defines interpersonal communication, and presents organizational communication as the primary vehicle that managers use to interact with people.

- **Chapter 15, Leadership,** highlights more traditional concepts like the Vroom-Yetton-Jago leadership model, the path-goal theory of leadership, and the life cycle theory of leadership. Coverage new to this edition includes additional concepts like transformational leadership, coaching, Super-Leadership, and entrepreneurial leadership.
- **Chapter 16, Motivation,** defines *motivation*, describes the motivation process, and provides useful strategies that managers can use in attempting to motivate organization members.
- **Chapter 17, Groups, Teams, and Corporate Culture,** emphasizes managing clusters of people as a means of accomplishing organizational goals. This chapter has been significantly revised to include new coverage of managing teams. Discussion focuses on groups versus teams; virtual teams; problem-solving, self-managed, and cross-functional teams; stages of team development; empowerment; and factors contributing to team effectiveness.
- **Chapter 18, Understanding People: Attitudes, Perception, and Learning,** is new to this edition. Coverage focuses on important characteristics of people that managers must understand. First, the relationship among attitudes, values, and beliefs is described; then the role of attitudes in influencing behavior is discussed. Detailed coverage is also extended to such topics as employee attitudes and key theories about ways in which to change attitudes. The chapter then turns to perception and the perceptual process, including detailed analyses of attribution theory and perceptions of procedural justice. Finally, the concept of learning is studied. The most important theories of learning are covered, including operant and cognitive learning, as are key approaches to the learning process, including goal-setting and reinforcement strategies.

Controlling

This section presents control as a major management function.

- **Chapter 19, Principles of Controlling,** discusses the basics of control.
- **Chapter 20, Production Management and Control,** focuses on the creation of goods and services, paying special attention on automation and production strategies, systems, and processes available to managers.
- In keeping with the spirit of AACSB guidelines, **Chapter 21, Information and Technology,** has been significantly revised to add more coverage of current technology. New coverage emphasizes in-

formation technology by discussing recent developments ranging from E-mail, electronic data interchange, and videoconferencing to the Internet and the World Wide Web. Discussion focuses on becoming a better manager by using technological tools, *not* by understanding the intricacies of technology design.

Topics for Special Emphasis

The last section of *Modern Management* discusses additional issues important to managers operating in today's organization and today's global environment.

- **Chapter 22, Quality: Building Competitive Organizations,** emphasizes building quality through all phases of organizational activity. Discussion focuses on defining *quality*, achieving quality through strategic planning, and describing the management skills necessary to build quality throughout an organization. The ideas of such internationally known quality experts as Philip B. Crosby, W. Edwards Deming, and Joseph M. Juran are highlighted.
- **Chapter 23, Management and Diversity,** defines *diversity*, explains the advantages of promoting diversity in organizations, and outlines ways in which managers can promote diversity. This chapter also discusses some key challenges and dilemmas that managers face in attempting to build a diverse workforce.

TEXT: STUDENT LEARNING AIDS

Several features of this text were designed to make the study of management more efficient, effective, and enjoyable. Following is a list of these features and an explanation of each.

Learning Objectives

The opening pages of each chapter contain a set of learning objectives that are intended as guidlelines for studying the chapter.

Chapter Outlines

The opening pages of each chapter also contain a chapter outline that previews the textual material and helps the reader keep the information in perspective while it is being read.

Chapter Highlights

Chapter highlights are another exciting feature of this text. In essence, highlights are extended examples or "boxes" emphasizing the wide range of ways in which modern managers face contemporary issues in real companies. Each chapter has from 3 to 5 highlights. The highlights program has been significantly revised in this edition and includes the following elements:

- **Spotlights.** Spotlights focus on the following major textual themes: diversity, quality, ethics, and the global environment. At least two Spotlights appear in each chapter, with all topics receiving equivalent emphasis throughout the book. In Chapter 13, for instance, an Ethics Spotlight focuses on the relationship between attitude changes and a responsible approach to job safety at Sonoco Products Company. In the same chapter, a Diversity Spotlight reports on changing attitudes toward disabled workers at McDonald's.
- **People Perspectives.** Each chapter contains one section called People Perspectives, a feature emphasizing how a people issue related to chapter content actually exists in a real organization. Reflecting the spirit of AACSB guidelines, People Perspectives are a continuing theme throughout the text, emphasizing that the fact people issues are both critical to leadership in organizations and related to all facets of management. Thus Chapter 12 features a People Perspective focusing on a program at NationsBank for developing a high-quality child-care program.
- **Cutting Edge.** Each chapter contains one Cutting Edge, a feature emphasizing current management practices in a wide variety of organizations. This feature illustrates recent and exciting actions taken by management to address organizational threats and opportunities. Thus in Chapter 21, a Cutting Edge feature describes the work of Dell Computer's recently organized Internet SWAT team.

Introductory Cases with "Back to the Case" Sections

The opening of each chapter contains a case study that introduces readers to management problems related to chapter content. Detailed "Back to the Case" sections appear throughout each chapter, applying specific areas of management theory discussed in the chapter to the introductory case. All cases involve real companies, ranging from American Speedy Printing Centers and Arkansas Freightways to United Airlines, Polaroid, and Ortho Pharmaceutical. Well over half of the cases in this edition are new or updated.

Internet Appendix

The Internet Appendix is not only new to this edition, but represents an exciting and valuable innovation in the

field of management education. The Internet Appendix is an assortment of Internet-based learning exercises specifically designed to enhance student learning via this text. These exercises are all different, and all are tied to interactive tours for students through actual locations of companies on the World Wide Web. Each text chapter has a corresponding learning-enrichment exercise that is accessed through the website built for *Modern Management*. Exercises are flexible and can be used as the basis for assigned learning activities like group projects for classroom discussion, individual assignments, or voluntary independent-study activities. Additional explanation of the Internet Appendix appears on the inside front and back cover. Become more familiar with the Internet Appendix by visiting **http://www.profcerto.com**

Chapter Internet Icons.

New to this edition, an Internet Appendix icon appears in the materials at the end of each chapter. The icon is accompanied by a reminder that additional study materials related to the chapter are contained in the Internet Appendix and can be used independently by students to enhance their learning about management even if their course does not require such usage.

End-of-Chapter Pedagogy

As in the previous edition of *Modern Management*, several pedagogically useful features are integrated at the end of each chapter:

Action Summaries.

Each chapter ends with an action-oriented chapter summary that allows students to respond to several objective questions that are clearly linked to the learning objectives stated at the beginning of the chapter. Students can check their answers against the answer key at the end of the chapter. This key also lists the pages in the chapter that can be referred to for a fuller explanation of the answers.

Introductory Case Wrap-Up.

Each chapter ends with several questions about the introductory case. These questions provide an additional opportunity to apply chapter concepts directly to the case.

Issues for Review and Discussion.

The concluding pages of each chapter contain a set of discussion questions that test the understanding of chapter material and can serve as a vehicle for study and for class discussion.

Chapter-Ending Cases.

Every chapter of *Modern Management* contains a case that students can analyze, either on their own or as a group activity. *All of these cases are brand-new to this edition of the book.*

Skills Exercise.

In conjunction with each chapter-ending case, there is a brief "Skills Exercise" in which students are given suggested teamwork assignments for further in-depth study.

Additional Features

- *Marginal Notes.* Each chapter contains marginal notes that can be helpful both in initial reading and for review. These notes highlight key terms in each chapter while providing brief definitions for student review.
- *Glossary.* Major terms and their definitions are gathered at the end of the text. Terms appear in boldface type and include references to the text pages on which the discussion of the term appears.
- *Illustrations.* Figures, tables, and photographs depicting various management situations are used throughout the text to help bridge the gap between management theory and real-world facts and figures.

Video Sectional Cases

New to this edition is a series of seven video cases focusing on Lands' End, Inc., a major catalog retailer headquartered in Dodgeville, Wisconsin. Each case includes an 8-10-minute video on some facet of Lands' End operations and is accompanied by appropriate questions that students should explore. The videos were produced specifically for this text and designed to be interesting, engaging, and helpful to students in learning management concepts. One video case corresponds to each major text part and allows students to review and apply major sections of text material. Video cases were purposefully designed to allow instructors to use any or all of the videos in building the management course best suited for their students. Extensive instructional materials are also available to help instructors integrate these video cases into their courses.

1. LANDS' END, INC.—A BRIEF HISTORY: Found at the end of Chapter 1, this Introductory Case reviews the history of the company, defines its core business, and gives general background information that students may find necessary for future case analysis.
2. DOING BUSINESS ABROAD THE LANDS' END WAY: Discusses the expansion of Lands' End into the international market (specifically The United Kingdom and Japan), the strategic decisions involved, and the ways in which cultural differences have been addressed.
3. PLANNING IN THE COMING HOME DIVISION AT LANDS' END: Looks at the plan-

ning and implementation of the decision to expand the Lands' End product line into the home textile (curtains and bedding) market.

4. PRODUCT DEVELOPMENT AT LANDS' END: FROM A FUNCTIONAL TO A TEAM APPROACH: Traces the process of reorganizing the company's structure from one based on functional areas (creative, merchandising, quality, inventory, design, and support) to one based on product teams.

5. LANDS' END: CONTROLLING A MUCH-ENVIED WORK CLIMATE: Examines the innovative and unique corporate culture that makes Lands' End one of "The 100 Best Companies to Work for in America."

6. LANDS' END: GETTING THE PRODUCT OUT TO THE CUSTOMER: Details internal operations from receiving to shipping, explaining how inventory is controlled, orders are processed, and quality assured.

7. GIVING HIGH QUALITY CUSTOMER SERVICE: A FOCAL POINT AT LANDS' END: Explains that, rather than a trend for the 1990's, commitment to quality is a guiding principle for all Lands' End employees. This case discusses how this passion for quality is instilled and how it is maintained.

Each accompanying video was shot on location and includes interviews with each of the case principles as well as additional background material. Each video runs approximately 8 minutes and is accompanied by an extensive teaching note.

Both the author and publisher are grateful to the people at Lands' End and thank them for their openness, cooperation, and honesty.

Additional Teaching Materials

Instructor's Manual.   Includes chapter outlines, case and video notes for Lands' End Inc., and Internet Exercise support.

Electronic Instructor's Manual.   Includes all of the previously mentioned material, plus an option for professors to annotate and add their own material.

Test Item File.   Contains multiple-choice, true/false, essay, and scenario-based questions.

Custom Test for Windows and Macintosh.   Contains all the above test questions plus the option for professors to customize and adapt their own material.

Electronic Transparencies.   Includes over 200 PowerPoint four-color overheads, available on 3.5" disks.

Color Transparencies.   Contains 100 four-color overheads for classroom use taken from the electronic files and produced on high quality mylar.

Experiencing Modern Management.   A student-oriented workbook, including both study activities and over 70 experiential exercises for classroom or home assignment.

Instructor's Manual for Experiencing Modern Management.   Contains answers to study activities questions as well as information on incorporating and facilitating experiential exercises into the classroom.

Lands' End Inc. Video Case Series.   Produced exclusively for this text by Prentice Hall, these six part ending cases and introductory case are enhanced by videos featuring the people involved and additional background information.

ACKNOWLEDGMENTS

The **Modern Management Learning Package** has maintained its popularity and position as a market leader since it was written over two decades ago. Over the years, this package has been used in colleges and universities, as well as in professional management-training programs. It has been translated into foreign languages for distribution throughout the world and has been used by over half a million students.

I have received much recognition for the success of this text. Considerable recognition for the success of this project, however, should be given to valuable contributions made by many of my respected colleagues. I am pleased to recognize the contributions of these individuals and extend to them my warmest personal gratitude for their professional insights, as well as for their personal support and encouragement throughout the life of this project.

Professor Lee A. Graf, Illinois State University, deserves special recognition. As a close personal friend, he has been specially vigilant in helping to keep this text a market leader since the first edition. In this edition, Dr. Graf has made the significant contribution of crafting the sectional video cases on Lands' End. His overall professional competence and instructional insights have made the Lands' End cases a significant contribution to this edition.

Other colleagues have also made important contributions to this text and its ancillaries. I would like to thank these individuals for their dedication and professionalism in making this project all that it can be. These professionals and the contribution that each has made are listed below:

Robert E. Kemper at Northern Arizona University for assistance in the revision of Chapter 20, "Production Management and Control"

Toni Carol King at Binghamton University for assistance in writing Chapter 23, "Management and Diversity"

Maurice Manner at Marymount College for assistance in the revision of Chapter 4, "Managing in the Global Arena"

Richard Ratliff, Shari Tarnutzer, and their colleagues at Utah State University for assistance in the revision of Chapter 22, "Quality: Building Competitive Organizations"

Larry Waldorf at Boise State University for assistance in the revision of Chapter 15, "Leadership"

Michael Carrell of Morehead State University for assistance in the composition of Chapter 18, "Understanding People: Attitudes, Perception, and Learning," which is new to this edition

Teachable Tech of Atlanta, Georgia, for assistance in researching and writing the new chapter-ending cases and skills exercises

In addition, both Prentice Hall and I would like to extend a special thanks to Lisa Mullens, Coordinator of Public Relations at Lands' End, Inc. She did a thorough and thoroughly gracious job of marshaling the resources that Lands' End made available to us in the creation of our seven new video cases.

Every author appreciates the valuable contribution reviewers make to the development of a text project. Reviewers offer that "different viewpoint" that requires an author to constructively question his or her work. I again had an excellent team of reviewers. Thoughtful comments, concern for student learning, and insights regarding instructional implications of the written word characterized the high-quality feedback I received. I am pleased to be able to recognize members of my review team for their valuable contributions to the development of this text:

Chi Anyansi-Archibong, North Carolina A&T State University
Chandler Atkins, Adirondack Community College
James Clinton, University of Northern Colorado
Ronald Courchene, Allegheny Community College
Jim Day, Shawnee State University
Shirley Fedorovich, Embry Riddle Aero University
Carl Gates, Sauk Valley Community College
Richard Gordon, Detroit College of Business
John Heinsius, Modesto Junior College
James Henderson, Kingwood College
John Herrmann, California State University at Long Beach
Eileen Bartels Hewitt, University of Scranton
Lynn Hoffman, University of Northern Colorado
Susan Jackson, New York University

Colleen Jones, Suffolk University
Cheryl Macon, Butler County Community College
Maurice Manner, Marymount College
Malcolm B. McGregor, Ozark Technical Community College
Thomas Meier, West Virginia University
Stephen Mosher, University of North Dakota
Tony Ortega, California State University at Bakersfield
Shari Tarnutzer, Utah State University
Stephen Walter, Davenport College
Warren Weber, California Polytechnic University
Zan Whitman, Tallahassee Community College

As always, I would also like to acknowledge the personal interest and encouragement for this project shown by my colleagues in the Crummer Graduate School of Business at Rollins College. The faculty has been very supportive of this project. In addition, my management colleagues, James M. Higgins, Theodore T. Herbert, and Max R. Richards, have all helped me to validate my professional judgments and crystalize my book concept. I am fortunate indeed to work with a faculty that possess such expertise and high professional standards.

I am deeply indebted to many colleagues and friends at Prentice Hall for their outstanding support, vision, and encouragement throughout the development and publication of this text and its ancillary package. As Acquisitions Editor, David Shafer has been a constant source of innovative ideas and support. His relentless focus on excellence was a driving force throughout all phases of text development. As Senior Development Editor, Ron Librach's careful attention to communicating to students as opposed to simply writing a text for them did not go unnoticed. His writing-oriented suggestions undoubtedly made this text a more effective learning instrument. The invaluable efforts of Lynne Breitfeller and Carol Burgett ensured timely, high-quality text production. Last, but certainly not least, I'd like to thank my friend and colleague Bill Oldsey, President of Prentice Hall Business Publishing for creating an organization in which this text can flourish.

Finally, I cannot imagine publishing a text package of this magnitude without strong and unwavering family support. My wife, Mimi, is undaunting in her encouragement. She has helped me to maintain professional dedication and, more importantly, to become a better person. The debt that I owe her cannot be tallied. The interest that my children, Brian, Matthew, Sarah, and Trevis, show in my work helps me to stay involved and motivated. As an interesting sidenote, Matthew's professional Internet skills served as the catalyst for adding the Internet Appendix to this text. The ideals and values of my father and mother, Sam and Annette, are permanent support guideposts.

part 1

Introduction to Management

MANAGEMENT AND MANAGEMENT CAREERS

STUDENT LEARNING OBJECTIVES

From studying this chapter, I will attempt to acquire:

1. An understanding of the importance of management to society and individuals.
2. An understanding of the role of management.
3. An ability to define *management* in several different ways.
4. An ability to list and define the basic functions of management.
5. Working definitions of managerial effectiveness and managerial efficiency.
6. An understanding of basic management skills and their relative importance to managers.
7. An understanding of the universality of management.
8. Insights concerning what management careers are and how they evolve.

CHAPTER OUTLINE

"We're researching new technologies and trying to form strategic alliances with Xerox and IBM," says a conservatively dressed businessman in a suburban Detroit hotel suite. The speaker's name is Isiah Thomas. *The* Isiah Thomas? Yep, the recently retired point guard of the Detroit Pistons. Thomas has abandoned the hoop for the PC, and he is talking about American Speedy Printing Centers, the company he and his partners acquired last year.

American Speedy Printing Centers is an international chain that offers printing services. As its name implies, American Speedy focuses on providing printing options that are fast, but also reliable and of high quality. The company is very flexible, offering services ranging from printing a student's resumé for getting that first job to binding over a hundred pages for commercial use. Other services offered by American Speedy include faxing, binding, laminating, and copying.

Even before hanging up his shorts, Thomas could often be found in the locker room before practice cruising his Compaq E-20 for his E-mail and for updates on his investments.

"I got some strange looks," Thomas chuckles, describing his teammates' reaction, but he wasn't just showing off. He was determined not to wait until his basketball career was over to start on a future career. He wanted to cash in on his name while it was still before the public. "I believe," he says, "that the leverage you have, the accessibility you have to people while you're playing, is a hundred times greater than when you quit."

Playing professional basketball in the National Basketball Association is one of the most glamorous jobs around. Isiah Thomas' success in the arena of professional basketball is undeniable. Making the switch from NBA player to professional business manager, however, may be the most difficult challenge that he has yet faced.

Former NBA All-Star Isiah Thomas did not wait until his basketball career was over to begin a new career in business. Today, as one of the owner-managers of American Speedy Printing Centers, he focuses his strategic skills on ventures with companies like IBM and Xerox.

what's ahead

As discussed in the introductory case, Isiah Thomas, a highly successful National Basketball Association player, is currently undergoing a career change from professional athlete to professional manager. Not content to simply invest in American Speedy, Thomas is determined to take an active role in managing the company. This chapter is designed to help individuals like Thomas who are on the verge of a career in management to understand the basics of modern management. Management is defined in this chapter through four important features:

1. A discussion of its importance both to society and to individuals.
2. A description of the management task.
3. A discussion of the universality of management.
4. Insights about management careers.

THE IMPORTANCE OF MANAGEMENT

Managers influence all phases of modern organizations. Plant managers run manufacturing operations that produce the clothes we wear, the food we eat, and the automobiles we drive. Sales managers maintain a salesforce that markets goods. Personnel managers provide organizations with a competent and productive workforce. The "jobs available" section in the classified advertisements of any major newspaper describes many different types of management activities and confirms the importance of management (see Figure 1.1).

Our society could neither exist as we know it today nor improve without a steady stream of managers to guide its organizations. Peter Drucker emphasized this point when he stated that effective management is probably the main resource of developed countries and the most needed resource of developing ones.[1] In short, all societies desperately need good managers.

Besides its importance to society as a whole, management is vital to many individuals in society because they earn their livings by being managers. Government statistics show that management positions have increased from approximately 10 percent to approximately 18 percent of all jobs since 1950. Managers come from varying backgrounds and have diverse educational specialties. Many people who originally trained to be accountants, teachers, financiers, or even writers eventually make their livelihoods as managers. Although in the short term, the demand for managers varies somewhat, in the long term, managerial positions can yield high salaries, status, interesting work, personal growth, and intense feelings of accomplishment.

In fact, there is some concern that certain managers are paid *too* much. Consider the results of a 1994 poll by *Forbes* magazine ranking the highest-paid chief executives over the five-year period 1989–1993. Table 1.1 (see page 5) lists the top ten compensation packages as indicated by this poll, the companies that paid them, and the managers who received them.[2]

BACK TO THE CASE

The information just presented furnishes a beginning manager like Isiah Thomas with some insights into the significance of his role as manager. This role is important, not only to society as a whole, but also to himself as an individual. In general, as a manager, Isiah contributes to sustaining and enhancing the standard of living in the United States, and thereby earns corresponding rewards. His company, American Speedy Printing Centers, is making a societal contribution by helping people produce various types of printed materials. If Thomas is successful in forming alliances with organizations like IBM and Xerox, his company's contribution to society as well as his personal returns will probably be considerably magnified.

SR. MANAGEMENT DEVELOPMENT SPECIALIST

We are a major metropolitan service employer of over 5,000 employees seeking a person to join our management development staff. Prospective candidates will be degreed with 5 to 8 years experience in the design, implementation, and evaluation of developmental programs for first-line and mid-level management personnel. Additionally, candidates must demonstrate exceptional oral and written communications ability and be skilled in performance analysis, programmed instruction, and the design and implementation of reinforcement systems.

If you meet these qualifications, please send your résumé, including salary history and requirements to:

Box RS-653
An Equal Opportunity Employer

BRANCH MGR— $30,500. Perceptive pro with track record in administration and lending has high visibility with respected firm.

Box PH-165

AVIATION FBO MANAGER NEEDED

Southeast Florida operation catering to corporate aviation. No maintenance or aircraft sales—just fuel and the best service. Must be experienced. Salary plus benefits commensurate with qualifications. Submit complete résumé to:

Box LJO-688

DIVISION CREDIT MANAGER

Major mfg. corporation seeks an experienced credit manager to handle the credit and collection function of its Midwest division (Chicago area). Interpersonal skills are important, as is the ability to communicate effectively with senior management. Send résumé with current compensation to:

Box NM-43

ACCOUNTING MANAGER

Growth opportunity. Michigan Ave. location. Acctg. degree, capable of supervision. Responsibilities include G/L, financial statements, inventory control, knowledge of systems design for computer applications. Send résumé, incl. salary history to:

Box RJM-999
An Equal Opportunity Employer

FINANCIAL MANAGER

CPA/MBA (U of C) with record of success in management positions. Employed, now seeking greater opportunity. High degree of professionalism, exp. in dealing w/financial inst., strong communication & analytical skills, stability under stress, high energy level, results oriented. Age 34, 11 yrs. exper. incl. major public acctng., currently 5 years as Financial VP of field leader. Impressive references.
Box LML-666

MARKET MANAGER

Major lighting manufacturer seeks market manager for decorative outdoor lighting. Position entails establishing and implementing marketing, sales, and new product development programs including coordination of technical publications and related R & D projects. Must locate at Denver headquarters. Send résumé to
Box WM-214
No agencies please

GENERAL MANAGER

Small industrial service company, privately owned, located in Springfield, Missouri, needs aggressive, skilled person to make company grow in profits and sales. Minimum B.S. in Business, experienced in all facets of small business operations. Must understand profit. Excellent opportunity and rewards. Salary and fringes commensurate with experience and performance. **Box LEM-116**

FOUNDRY SALES MANAGER

Aggressive gray iron foundry located in the Midwest, specializing in 13,000 tons of complex castings yearly with a weight range of 2 to 400 pounds, is seeking experienced dynamic sales manager with sound sales background in our industry. Salary commensurate with experience; excellent benefit package. **Box MO-948**

PERSONNEL MANAGER

Publicly owned, national manufacturer with 12 plants, 700 employees, seeks first corporate personnel director. We want someone to administer programs in:

- Position and rate evaluation
- Employee safety engineering
- Employee training

- Employee communications
- Employee benefits
- Federal compliance

Qualifications: minimum of 3–5 years personnel experience in mfg. company, ability to tactfully deal with employees at all levels from all walks of life, free to travel. Position reports to Vice President, Operations. Full range of company benefits, salary $32,000–40,000. Reply in complete confidence to:

Box JK-236

Figure 1.1 **The variety of management positions available**

THE MANAGEMENT TASK

Besides understanding the significance of managerial work to themselves and society and its related benefits, prospective managers need to know what the management task entails. The sections that follow introduce the basics of the management task through discussions of the role and definition of management, the management process as it pertains to management functions and organizational goal attainment, and the need to manage organizational resources effectively and efficiently.

The Role of Management

Essentially, the role of managers is to guide organizations toward goal accomplishment. All organizations exist for certain purposes or goals, and managers are respon-

Table 1.1	
The Ten Highest-Paid Chief Executives, 1989–1993	
COMPANY/CHIEF EXECUTIVE	5-YEAR* TOTAL COMPENSATION
Walt Disney/Michael D Eisner	$236,771
Travelers/Sanford I Weill	141,605
HJ Heinz/Anthony J F O'Reilly	120,844
US Surgical/Leon C Hirsch	114,346
Fund American/John J Byrne	80,809
Loral/Bernard L Schwartz	64,753
Forest Labs/Howard Solomon	62,819
McCaw Cellular/Craig O McCaw	52,833
Coca-Cola/Roberto C Goizueta	51,896
Conseco/Stephen C Hilbert	51,156

*All dollar amounts in thousands; compensation comprises payments, salary bonuses and stock options.

sible for combining and using organizational resources to ensure that their organizations achieve their purposes. Management moves an organization toward its purposes or goals by assigning activities that organization members perform. If the activities are designed effectively, the production of each individual worker will contribute to the attainment of organizational goals. Management strives to encourage individual activity that will lead to reaching organizational goals and to discourage individual activity that will hinder the accomplishment of those goals. "There is no idea more important to managing than goals. Management has no meaning apart from its goals."[3] Managers must, therefore, keep organizational goals in mind at all times.

Defining Management

Students of management should be aware that the term *management* can be, and often is, used in several different ways. For instance, it can refer simply to the process that managers follow in order to accomplish organizational goals. It can also refer to a

Michael Eisner (standing, second from right) is CEO of Walt Disney Co. In 1993, he set a record by earning total pay of $203,010,590. Are executives worth that much to their employers (that is, stockholders)? Consider the fact that Eisner is shown here announcing Disney's purchase of Capital Cities/ABC Inc. Eisner is thus responsible for engineering a deal that cost Disney stockholders $19.3 billion. Thus he is now being paid to integrate two giant corporations smoothly and thereafter to manage a behemoth company with 85,000 employees.

After taking over as CEO of Eastman Kodak Co. in 1993, George Fisher has sought to focus the company's strategy on its core business—imaging. He realized, for example, that the company's efforts to develop and market new digital-imaging techniques were scattered among various divisions. He has thus moved everyone involved into a single division, which is now headed by a handpicked executive with experience in computer marketing.

Management is the process of reaching organizational goals by working with and through people and other organizational resources.

body of knowledge; in this context, management is a cumulative body of information that furnishes insights on how to manage. The term *management* can also refer to the individuals who guide and direct organizations or to a career devoted to the task of guiding and directing organizations. An understanding of the various uses and related definitions of the term will help you avoid miscommunication during management-related discussions.

As used most commonly in this text, **management** is the process of reaching organizational goals by working with and through people and other organizational resources. A comparison of this definition with the definitions offered by several contemporary management thinkers shows that there is broad agreement that management has the following three main characteristics:

1. It is a process or series of continuing and related activities.
2. It involves and concentrates on reaching organizational goals.
3. It reaches these goals by working with and through people and other organizational resources. (See Table 1.2).

A discussion of each of these characteristics follows.

The Management Process: Management Functions

Management functions are activities that make up the management process. The four basic management activities are planning, organizing, influencing, and controlling.

The four basic **management functions**—activities that make up the management process—are described in the following sections.

Table 1.2
Contemporary Definitions of Management

Management—

1. Is the process by which a cooperative group directs actions of others toward common goals (Massie and Douglas).
2. Is the process of working with and through others to effectively achieve organizational objectives by efficiently using limited resources in a changing environment (Kreitner).
3. Is the coordination of all resources through the processes of planning, organizing, directing, and controlling in order to attain stated objectives (Sisk).
4. Is establishing an effective environment for people operating in formal organizational groups (Koontz and O'Donnell).
5. Entails activities undertaken by one or more persons in order to coordinate the activities of others in the pursuit of ends that cannot be achieved by any one person (Donnelly, Gibson, and Ivancevich).

As CEO of Quantum Health Resources, a diversified health-care services organization providing therapies to individuals affected by chronic and other disorders, Douglas Stickney manages one of America's fastest-growing companies. Stickney sees influencing as one of his major jobs as a manager. Among other things, he likes to encourage employees to communicate more informally; the result, he believes, is a more creative environment for his workforce.

Planning   Planning involves choosing tasks that must be performed to attain organizational goals, outlining how the tasks must be performed, and indicating when they should be performed. Planning activity focuses on attaining goals. Through their plans, managers outline exactly what organizations must do to be successful. Planning is concerned with organizational success in the near future (short term) as well as in the more distant future (long term).[4]

Organizing   Organizing can be thought of as assigning the tasks developed under the planning function to various individuals or groups within the organization. Organizing, then, creates a mechanism to put plans into action. People within the organization are given work assignments that contribute to goal attainment. Tasks are organized so that the output of individuals contributes to the success of departments, which, in turn, contributes to the success of divisions, which ultimately contributes to the overall success of the organization.

Influencing   Influencing is another of the basic functions within the management process. This function—also commonly referred to as *motivating, leading, directing,* or *actuating*—is concerned primarily with people within organizations.* Influencing can be defined as the process of guiding the activities of organization members in appropriate directions. An appropriate direction is any direction that helps the organization move toward goal attainment. The ultimate purpose of influencing is to increase productivity. Human-oriented work situations usually generate higher levels of production over the long term than do task-oriented work situations because people find the latter type of situations distasteful.

Controlling   Controlling is the management function for which managers:

1. Gather information that measures recent performance within the organization.
2. Compare present performance to preestablished performance standards.
3. From this comparison, determine if the organization should be modified to meet preestablished standards.

Controlling is an ongoing process. Managers continually gather information, make their comparisons, and then try to find new ways of improving production through organizational modification.

---

*In early management literature, the term *motivating* was more commonly used to signify this people-oriented management function. The term *influencing* is used consistently throughout this text because it is broader and permits more flexibility in discussing people-oriented issues. Later in the text, motivating is discussed as a major part of influencing.

Management Process and Goal Attainment

Although we have discussed the four functions of management individually, planning, organizing, influencing, and controlling are integrally related and therefore cannot be separated in practice. Figure 1.2 illustrates this interrelationship and also indicates that managers use these activities solely for the purpose of reaching organizational goals. Basically, these functions are interrelated because the performance of one depends on the performance of the others. For example, organizing is based on well-thought-out plans developed during the planning process, and influencing systems must be tailored to reflect both these plans and the organizational design used to implement them. The fourth function, controlling, involves possible modifications to existing plans, organizational structure, or the motivation system used to develop a more successful effort.

To be effective, a manager must understand how the four management functions must be practiced, not simply how they are defined and related. Thomas J. Peters and Robert H. Waterman, Jr., studied numerous organizations—including Frito-Lay and Maytag—for several years to determine what management characteristics best describe excellently run companies. In their book *In Search of Excellence*, Peters and Waterman suggest that planning, organizing, influencing, and controlling should be characterized by: a bias for action; a closeness to the customer; autonomy and entrepreneurship; productivity through people; a hands-on, value-driven orientation; "sticking to the knitting"; a simple organizational form with a lean staff; and simultaneous loose-tight properties.

The information in this section has given you but a brief introduction to the four management functions. Later sections are devoted to developing these functions in much more detail.

Management and Organizational Resources

Organizational resources are all assets available for activation during normal operations; they include human resources, monetary resources, raw materials resources, and capital resources.

Management must always be aware of the status and use of **organizational resources**. These resources, composed of all assets available for activation during the production process, are of four basic types:

1. Human
2. Monetary
3. Raw materials
4. Capital resources

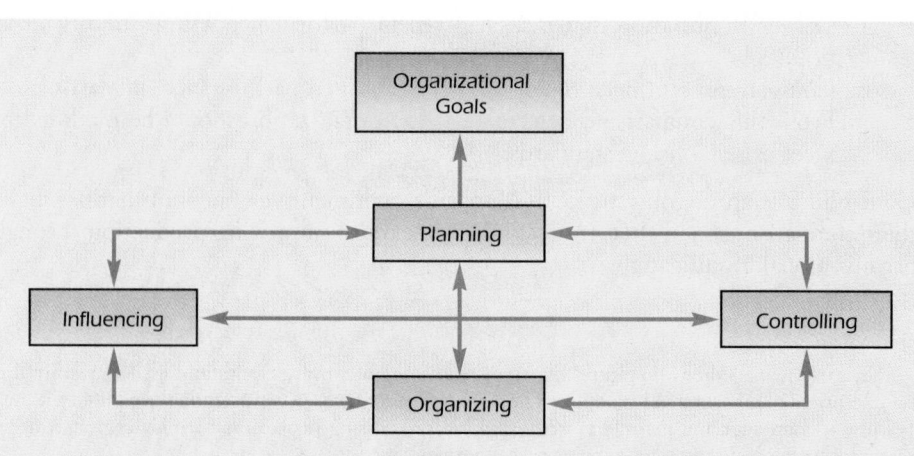

Figure 1.2 Interrelations of the four functions of management to attain organizational goals

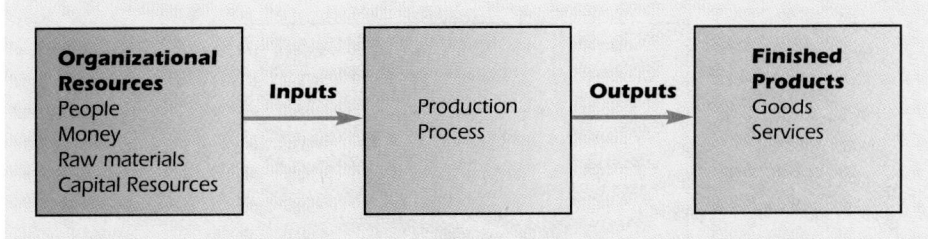

As Figure 1.3 shows, organizational resources are combined, used, and transformed into finished products during the production process.

Human resources are the people who work for an organization. The skills they possess and their knowledge of the work system are invaluable to managers. Monetary resources are amounts of money that managers use to purchase goods and services for the organization. Raw materials are ingredients acquired to be used directly in the manufacturing of products. For example, rubber is a raw material that a company such as Goodyear would purchase with its monetary resources and use directly in the manufacturing of tires. Capital resources are the machines an organization uses during the manufacturing process. Modern machines, or equipment, can be a major factor in maintaining desired production levels. Worn-out or antiquated machinery can make it impossible for an organization to keep pace with competitors.

Managerial Effectiveness   As managers use their resources, they must strive to be both effective and efficient. **Managerial effectiveness** refers to management's use of organizational resources in meeting organizational goals. If organizations are using their resources to attain their goals, the managers are said to be effective. In reality, however, there are degrees of managerial effectiveness. The closer an organization comes to achieving its goals, the more effective its managers are considered to be. Managerial effectiveness, then, exists on a continuum ranging from *ineffective* to *effective*.

Managerial Efficiency   **Managerial efficiency** is defined in terms of the proportion of total organizational resources that contribute to productivity during the manufacturing process.[5] The higher this proportion, the more efficient the manager. The more resources wasted or unused during the production process, the more inefficient the manager. In this situation, *organizational resources* refers not only to raw materials that are used in manufacturing goods or services but also to related human effort.[6] Like management effectiveness, management efficiency is best described as being on a continuum ranging from inefficient to efficient. *Inefficient* means that a very small proportion of total resources contributes to productivity during the manufacturing process; *efficient* means that a very large proportion contributes.

As Figure 1.4 shows, the concepts of managerial effectiveness and efficiency are obviously related. A manager could be relatively ineffective—with the consequence that the organization is making very little progress toward goal attainment—primarily because of major inefficiencies or poor utilization of resources during the production process. In contrast, a manager could be somewhat effective despite being inefficient if demand for the finished goods is so high that the manager can get an extremely high price per unit sold and thus absorb inefficiency costs.

For example, oil companies in Saudi Arabia can probably absorb many managerial inefficiencies when oil is selling at a high price. Management in this situation has a chance to be somewhat effective despite its inefficiency. Thus a manager can be effective without being efficient and vice versa. To maximize organizational success, however, both effectiveness and efficiency are essential.

Managerial effectiveness refers to management's use of organizational resources in meeting organizational goals.

Managerial efficiency is the degree to which organizational resources contribute to productivity. It is measured by the proportion of total organizational resources used during the production process.

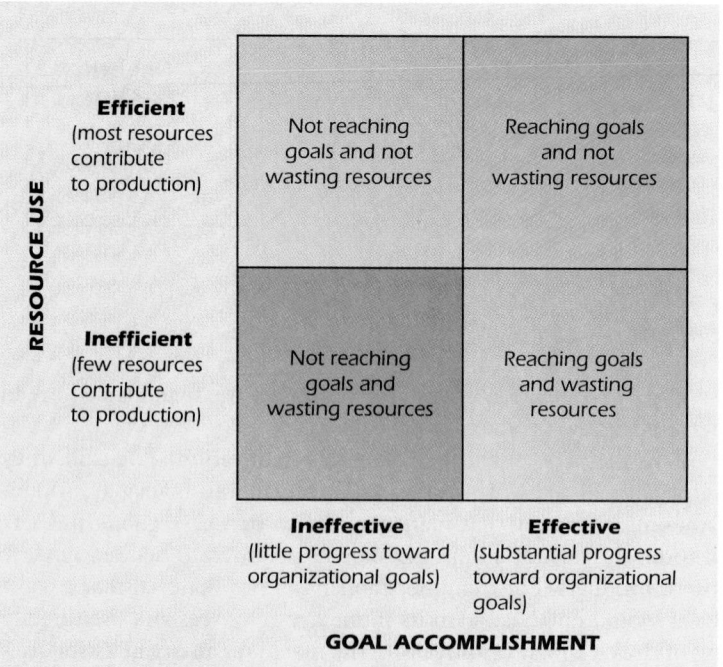

Figure 1.4   Various combinations of managerial effectiveness and managerial efficiency

BACK TO THE CASE   The text contains some specific information on what management is and what managers do. According to this information, Isiah Thomas must have a clear understanding of American Speedy Printing Centers' objectives and guide the organization toward reaching those objectives. This guidance will involve his working directly and indirectly with other top managers and partners within the company as well as with local managers in the printing centers themselves.

Thomas must be sure that planning, organizing, influencing, and controlling are being carried out appropriately within his company. In other words, at American Speedy Printing Centers, managers must outline how jobs are to be performed to reach objectives, assign these jobs to appropriate workers, encourage the workers to perform their jobs, and make any changes necessary to ensure reaching company objectives. As Thomas and other American Speedy Printing Centers managers perform these four functions, they must remember that the activities themselves are interrelated and therefore must be appropriately blended.

The wise use of organizational resources is critical. Thomas must strive to make sure that his company is both effective and efficient—that it reaches company objectives without wasting company resources.

Management Skills   No discussion of organizational resources would be complete without the mention of management skills, perhaps the primary determinant of how effective and efficient managers will be.

According to a classic article by Robert L. Katz, managerial success depends primarily on performance rather than on personality traits.[7] Katz also states that managers' ability to perform is a result of their managerial skills. A manager with the necessary management skills will probably perform well and be relatively successful. One without the necessary skills will probably perform poorly and be relatively unsuccessful.

Katz indicates that three types of skills are important for successful management performance: technical skills, human skills, and conceptual skills.

- **Technical skills** involve using specialized knowledge and expertise in executing work-related techniques and procedures. Examples of these skills are engi-

Technical skills are skills involving the ability to apply specialized knowledge and expertise to work-related techniques and procedures.

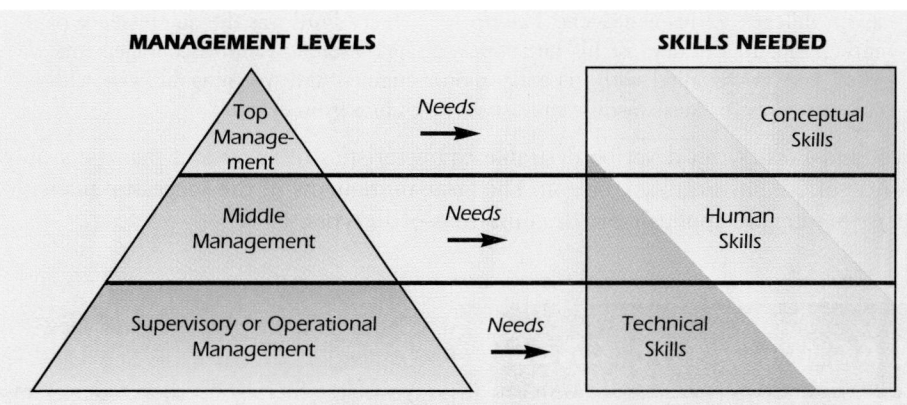

Figure 1.5   **As a manager moves from the supervisory to the top-management level, conceptual skills become more important than technical skills, but human skills remain equally important**

neering, computer programming, and accounting. Technical skills are mostly related to working with "things"—processes or physical objects.

- **Human skills** are skills that build cooperation within the team being led. They involve working with attitudes and communication, individual and group interests—in short, working with people.
- **Conceptual skills** involve the ability to see the organization as a whole. A manager with conceptual skills is able to understand how various functions of the organization complement one another, how the organization relates to its environment, and how changes in one part of the organization affect the rest of the organization.

Human skills are skills involving the ability to build cooperation within the team being led.

Conceptual skills are skills involving the ability to see the organization as a whole.

As one moves from lower-level management to upper-level management, conceptual skills become more important and technical skills less important (see Figure 1.5). The supportive rationale is that as managers advance in an organization, they become less involved with the actual production activity or technical areas and more involved with guiding the organization as a whole. Human skills, however, are extremely important to managers at top, middle, and lower (or supervisory) levels.[8] The common denominator of all management levels, after all, is people.

THE UNIVERSALITY OF MANAGEMENT

Management principles are **universal:** That is, they apply to all types of organizations (businesses, churches, sororities, athletic teams, hospitals, and so on) and organizational levels. Naturally, managers' jobs are somewhat different from one type of organization to another because each organizational type requires the use of specialized knowledge, exists in a unique working and political environment, and uses different technology. However, there are job similarities across organizations because the basic management activities—planning, organizing, influencing, and controlling—are common to all organizations.

Universality of management means that the principles of management are applicable to all types of organizations and organizational levels.

The Theory of Characteristics

Henri Fayol, one of the earliest management writers, stated that all managers should possess certain characteristics, such as positive physical and mental qualities and special knowledge related to the specific operation.[9] B. C. Forbes has emphasized the importance of certain more personal qualities, inferring that enthusiasm, earnestness of purpose, confidence, and faith in their own worthwhileness are primary characteristics of successful managers. Forbes has described Henry Ford as follows:

> At the base and birth of every great business organization was an enthusiast, a man consumed with earnestness of purpose, with confidence in his powers, with faith in the

worthwhileness of his endeavors. The original Henry Ford was the quintessence of enthusiasm. In the days of his difficulties, disappointments, and discouragements, when he was wrestling with his balky motor engine—and wrestling likewise with poverty—only his inexhaustible enthusiasm saved him from defeat.[10]

Fayol and Forbes can describe desirable characteristics of successful managers only because of the universality concept: The basic ingredients of the successful management situation are applicable to organizations of all types.

BACK TO THE CASE   In order to be successful, a relatively low-level manager in Thomas' printing company would generally need, in order of importance, human skills, technical skills, and conceptual skills. As a top manager of the company, Thomas himself would normally need, first, human skills, then conceptual skills, and finally technical skills. In general, as managers at American Speedy Printing Centers move up from low- to middle- and upper-level management positions, they will find that conceptual skills become more important than technical skills.

A manager like Thomas will usually find that as he gains experience in managing, his cumulative managerial experience will be valuable in whatever management position he may hold—either at American Speedy Printing Centers or in some other printing company or even some other business altogether. Thomas will also likely discover that as his personal qualities of enthusiasm, earnestness, confidence, and faith in his own worthwhileness become more pronounced, he will tend to be a more successful manager.

MANAGEMENT Careers

Thus far, this chapter has focused on outlining the importance of management to our society, presenting a definition of management and the management process, and explaining the universality of management. Individuals commonly study such topics because they are interested in pursuing a management career. This section presents information that will help you preview your own management career. It also describes some of the issues you may face in attempting to manage the careers of others within an organization. The specific focus is on career definition, career and life stages and performance, and career promotion.

A Definition of *Career*

A **career** is a sequence of work-related positions occupied by a person over the course of a lifetime.

A **career** is a sequence of work-related positions occupied by a person over the course of a lifetime.[11] As the definition implies, a career is cumulative in nature: As people accumulate successful experiences in one position, they generally develop abilities and attitudes that qualify them to hold more advanced positions. In general, management positions at one level tend to be stepping-stones to management positions at the next higher level.

Career Stages, Life Stages, and Performance

The **exploration stage** is the first stage in career evolution; it occurs at the beginning of a career, when the individual is typically 15–25 years of age, and is characterized by self-analysis and the exploration of different types of available jobs.

Careers are generally viewed as evolving through a series of stages.[12] These evolutionary stages—exploration, establishment, maintenance, and decline—are shown in Figure 1.6, which highlights the performance levels and age ranges commonly associated with each stage. Note that the levels and ranges in the figure indicate what is likely at each stage, not what is inevitable.

Exploration Stage   The first stage in career evolution is the **exploration stage,** which occurs at the beginning of a career and is characterized by self-analysis and the

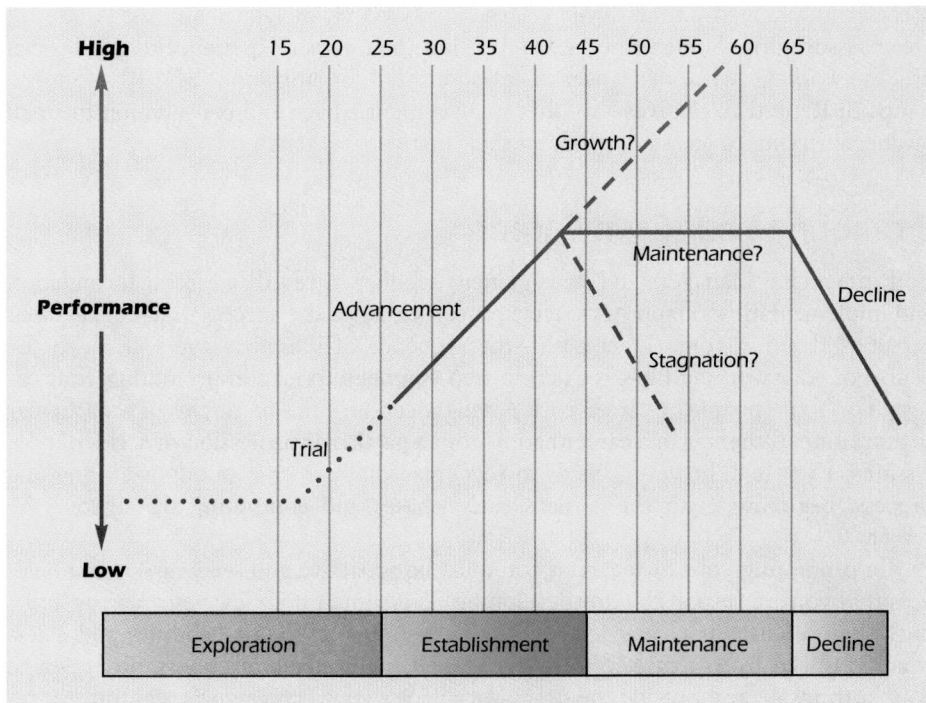

High   15 20 25 30 35 40 45 50 55 60 65

Growth?

Maintenance?

Performance   Advancement

Decline

Stagnation?

Trial

Low

| Exploration | Establishment | Maintenance | Decline |

Figure 1.6   **The relationships among career stages, life stages, and performance**

exploration of different types of available jobs. Individuals at this stage are generally about 15 to 25 years old, and are involved in some type of formal training, such as college or vocational education. They often pursue part-time employment to gain a richer understanding of what a career in a particular organization or industry might be like. Typical jobs held during this stage include cooking at Burger King, stocking at a Federated Department Store, and working as an office assistant at a Nationwide Insurance office.

Establishment Stage
The second stage in career evolution is the **establishment stage,** during which individuals who are about 25 to 45 years old typically start to become more productive, or higher performers (as Figure 1.6 indicates by the upturn in the dotted line and its continuance as a solid line). Employment sought during this stage is guided by what was learned during the exploration stage. In addition, the jobs sought are usually full-time. Individuals at this stage commonly move to different jobs within the same company, to different companies, or even to different industries.

> The **establishment stage** is the second stage in career evolution; individuals of about 25 to 45 years of age typically start to become more productive, or higher performers.

Maintenance Stage
The third stage in career evolution is the **maintenance stage.** In this stage, individuals who are about 45 to 65 years old show either increased performance (career growth), stabilized performance (career maintenance), or decreased performance (career stagnation).

From the organization's viewpoint, it is better for managers to experience career growth than maintenance or stagnation. That is why some companies, such as IBM, Monsanto, and Brooklyn Union Gas, have attempted to eliminate **career plateauing**[13]—defined as a period of little or no apparent progress in the growth of a career.

> The **maintenance stage** is the third stage in career evolution; individuals of about 45 to 65 years of age either become more productive, stabilize, or become less productive.

> **Career plateauing** is a period of little or no apparent progress in the growth of a career.

Decline Stage
The last stage in career evolution is the **decline stage,** which involves people of about 65 years whose productivity is declining. These individuals are either close to retirement, semiretired, or fully retired. People in the decline stage may find it difficult to maintain prior performance levels, perhaps because they have lost interest in their careers or have failed to keep their job skills up-to-date.

As Americans live longer and stay healthier into late middle age, many of them choose to become part-time workers in businesses such as Publix supermarkets and

> The **decline stage** is the fourth and last stage in career evolution; it occurs near retirement age, when individuals of about 65 years of age show declining productivity.

McDonald's or in volunteer groups such as the March of Dimes and the American Heart Association. Some retired executives put their career experience to good social use by working with the government-sponsored organization SCORE—Service Corps of Retired Executives—to offer management advice and consultation to small businesses trying to gain a foothold in their market.

Promoting Your Own Career

Both practicing managers and management scholars agree that careful formulation and implementation of appropriate tactics can enhance the success of a management career.[14] Planning your career path—the sequence of jobs that you will fill in the course of your working life—is the first step you need to take in promoting your career. For some people, a career path entails ascending the hierarchy of a particular organization. Others plan a career path within a particular profession or series of professions. Everyone, however, needs to recognize that career planning is an ongoing process, beginning with the career's early phases and continuing throughout the career.

In promoting your own career, you must be proactive and see yourself as a business that you are responsible for developing. You should not view your plan as limiting your options. First consider both your strengths and your liabilities and assess what you need from a career. Then explore all the avenues of opportunity open to you, both inside and outside the organization. Set your career goals, continually revise and update these goals as your career progresses, and take the steps necessary to accomplish these goals.

Another important tactic in promoting your own career is to work for managers who carry out realistic and constructive roles in the career development of their employees.[15] (The cartoon on this page lightheartedly depicts a manager who is brutally uninterested in the careers of his employees.) Table 1.3 outlines what career development responsibility, information, planning, and follow-through generally include. It also outlines the complementary career development role for a professional employee.

To enhance your career success, you must learn to be *proactive* rather than *reactive*.[16] That is, you must take specific actions to demonstrate your abilities and accomplishments. You must also have a clear idea of the next several positions you are seeking, the skills you need to acquire to function appropriately in those positions, and plans for how you will acquire those skills. Finally, you need to think about the ultimate position you want and the sequence of positions you must hold in order to gain the skills and attitudes necessary to qualify for that ultimate position.

"As this is your proposal, Cosgrove, its failure could mean the end of your career. I think, however, that is an acceptable risk."

From Warren Keith Schilit, "What's the Logic of Strategic Planning?" *Management Review* (November 1988), p. 42. © Leo Cullum, 1991.

Table 1.3

Manager and Employee Roles in Enhancing Employee Career Development

DIMENSION	PROFESSIONAL EMPLOYEE	MANAGER
Responsibility	Assumes responsibility for individual career development	Assumes responsibility for employee development
Information	Obtains career information through self-evaluation and data collection: What do I enjoy doing? Where do I want to go?	Provides information by holding up a mirror of reality: How manager views the employee How others view the employee How "things work around here"
Planning	Develops an individual plan to reach objectives	Helps employee assess plan
Follow-through	Invites management support through high performance on the current job by understanding the scope of the job and taking appropriate initiative	Provides coaching and relevant information on opportunities

Special Career Issues

In the business world of today, there are countless special issues that significantly affect how careers actually develop. Three issues that have had a significant impact on career development in recent years are:

1. Women managers
2. Dual-career couples
3. A multicultural workforce

The following sections discuss each of these factors.

Women Managers   Women in their roles as managers must meet the same challenges in their work environments that men do. However, since they have only recently joined the ranks of management in large numbers, women often lack the social contacts that are so important in the development of a management career. Another problem for women is that, traditionally, they have been expected to manage families and households while simultaneously handling the pressures and competition of paid employment. Finally, women are more likely than men to encounter sexual harassment in the workplace.

As a high-ranking manager at Nickelodeon, Anne Sweeney, who is now CEO of fX Network, worked on joint ventures with David Evans, former president of British Sky Broadcasting, a satellite-TV service run by Rupert Murdoch's News Corporation. When Murdoch needed someone to head fX, a fledgling cable network, Evans recommended Sweeney. Murdoch met Sweeney once and offered her the job.

Interestingly, Tom Peters, author of the aforementioned classic management book *In Search of Excellence*, believes that women may have an enormous advantage over men in future management situations.[17] He predicts that in the late 1990s networks of relationships will replace rigid organizational structures and star workers will be replaced by teams made up of workers at all levels who are empowered to make decisions. Detailed rules and procedures will be replaced by a flexible system that calls for judgments based on a system of key values and a constant search for new ways to get the job done. Strengths often attributed to women—emphasizing interrelationships, listening, and motivating others—will be the dominant virtues in the corporation of the future.

Dual-Career Couples

Because of the growing number of women at work, many organizations have been compelled to consider how dual-career couples affect the workforce.[18] The traditional scenario in which a woman takes a supporting role in the development of her spouse's career is being replaced by one of equal work and shared responsibilities for spouses. This requires a certain amount of flexibility on the part of the couple as well as the organizations for which they work. Today such burning issues as whose career takes precedence if a spouse is offered a transfer to another city and who takes the ultimate responsibility for family concerns point up the fact that dual-career relationships involve trade-offs and that it is very difficult to "have it all."

How Dual-Career Couples Cope. Studies of dual-career couples reveal that many cope with their career difficulties in one of the following ways.[19] The couple might develop a commitment to both spouses' careers so that, when a decision is made, the right of each spouse to pursue a career is taken into consideration. Both husband and wife are flexible about handling home- and job-oriented issues. They work out coping mechanisms, such as negotiating child care or scheduling shared activities in advance, to better manage their work and their family responsibilities. Often dual-career couples find that they must limit their social lives and their volunteer responsibilities in order to slow their lives to a manageable pace. Finally, many couples find that they must take steps to consciously facilitate their mutual career advancement. Organizations that want to retain an employee may find that they need to assist that employee's spouse in his or her career development as well.

A Multicultural Workforce

The term *multicultural* refers to the mix of many different ethnic groups that are already working in business in the United States and will be increasingly in the twenty-first century. Various minority groups are included in the term, among them African-Americans, Hispanics, Asians, Africans, Native Americans, and Caribbean Islanders. The U.S. Department of Labor estimates that almost one-third of new entrants into the labor force in the late 1990s will be members of various minority groups.

Minority groups are underrepresented in management today. The Rutgers University Graduate School of Management and the Program to Increase Minorities in Business found in an often-cited survey that of 400 Fortune 1,000 corporations, less than 9 percent of all managers were members of a minority. One reason for this shortage is that minorities are often not educated in the fields most in demand by businesses: the hard sciences, business administration, and engineering. Many minority members therefore end up in staff rather than line positions and are consequently more likely to be laid off during a downturn. Finally, in some instances, discrimination is responsible for minority workers' being passed over for promotions.

Recruiting Minority Workers. Since more and more new entrants into the labor market are members of various minority groups, it is becoming essential for businesses to recruit talented minority workers. Building community visibility may be the first step companies can take to help minority applicants find them. Arranging internships and career fairs as well as providing financial support are other concrete

The giant chemical company Hoechst Celanese Corporation has attached some real numbers to its workforce-diversity goals. By 2001, for example, it wants a minimum of 34-percent representation of women and minorities at all levels. Hoechst also conducts so-called "salary-equity reviews" to detect pay imbalances that do not result from performance or longstanding seniority standards.

steps a firm can take. Managers can look within the firm for minority employees who can be promoted. Finally, firms may need to conduct their own training and education programs to provide workers with the skills they need to join the ranks of management.

Valuing Diversity.   Instead of looking for people who fit into the existing corporate culture, managers should consider talent in the context of diversity. Some managers are uncomfortable dealing with workers from different backgrounds and different cultures; corporations may need to provide support and reeducation for these managers so they will be sensitive to other cultures. To take one small example, much business jargon in the United States is sports-oriented. A manager who tells an employee from another culture to "play hardball" may not be understood.

Some U.S. businesses are making a concerted effort to attract and promote minorities. A *Black Enterprise* magazine survey listed 25 firms that were rated by African-Americans as good places to work. Among them were Xerox, IBM, Hewlett-Packard, Avon, Philip Morris, AT&T, and Equitable. The multicultural workforce of the 1990s needs a new, more flexible and open style of management to reflect the new mix of backgrounds and cultures.[20]

SPECIAL FEATURES FOR THE REMAINING CHAPTERS

The **law of the situation,** based upon the classic work of Mary Parker Follett, indicates that managers must continually analyze the unique circumstances within their organizations and apply management concepts to fit those circumstances.[21] Managers can understand planning, organizing, influencing, and controlling, but unless they are able to apply these concepts to deal with specific organizational circumstances, their knowledge will be of little value.

SPOTLIGHT, PEOPLE PERSPECTIVES, and CUTTING EDGE are special features in the remaining chapters that provide a wealth of examples on how chapter concepts can be applied to managing organizations. These features have been purposely designed to convey a practical understanding of chapter content by emphasizing the application of management principles by real managers in real organizations. Overall, they offer a rich assortment of applications in top-level to lower-level managerial positions in service, manufacturing, nonprofit, for-profit, and other types of organizations. Additionally, smaller and midsize companies like Courier Publications, Steele's Market, and American Blimp Corporation are highlighted, as well as larger, better-known companies like Harley-Davidson, John Deere, Compaq Computer, and Adidas U.S.A.

The **law of the situation** indicates that managers must continually analyze the unique circumstances within their organizations and apply management concepts to fit those circumstances.

Spotlights

Four types of "spotlights" appear throughout the text to focus attention on four important contemporary management themes: global management, business or corporate ethics, diversity in organizations, and quality in organizations. Each chapter contains at least two SPOTLIGHT features, with all four themes being equally developed throughout the book. Each type of SPOTLIGHT is discussed in the following paragraphs.

Global Spotlight   Modern managers are faced with many challenges involving global business. Some of these challenges involve building organizations in developing countries, fighting foreign competition, developing joint ventures with foreign companies, and building a productive workforce across several foreign countries. This feature illustrates the application of management concepts to meet international challenges.

Ethics Spotlight   Modern managers face the challenge of developing and maintaining social responsibility and ethical practices that are appropriate for their particular organizations. Some challenges involve such issues as settling on who within an organization should perform socially responsible activities, determining the role of ethics in an organization, encouraging ethical behavior throughout the organization, and determining internal funding for socially responsible activities.[22] This feature illustrates the application of management concepts to meet a firm's social responsibility and ethical challenges.

Diversity Spotlight   Modern managers constantly face the challenge of handling situations involving diversity in organizations. *Diversity* is defined as differences in people in such areas as age, gender, ethnicity, nationality, and ability. In essence, today's managers must continually deal with significant variability in the people who interface with the organization. Thus organization members as well as customers may be a mix of African-Americans, Hispanics, Asians, and Native Americans.[23] Or the mix may involve people who are older, women, and the handicapped. This management feature presents practical insights for appropriately building organizational diversity into a resource so that the organization can understand and respond to diversity in its broader environment (e.g., among customers) and thereby enhance its success. In addition, diversity is discussed in Chapter 23, "Management and Diversity."

Quality Spotlight   Contemporary managers, perhaps more than any other generation of managers, face the challenge of developing and maintaining high quality in the goods and services they offer.[24] High-quality products are defined as goods or services that customers rate as excellent. Most management theorists and practicing managers agree that if an organization is to be successful in today's national and international markets, it must offer high-quality goods and services to its customers.

The need to maintain high-quality products has evolved from an issue pertinent to the success of individual businesses to one pertinent to the economic success of the United States. Congress passed the Malcolm Baldrige National Quality Improvement Act in 1987 to encourage business organizations throughout the United States to focus on quality products. . Under this law, annual national quality awards, called the "Malcolm Baldrige National Quality Awards," are granted to the companies that produce products and services of exemplary quality. The Baldrige awards, named after a former U.S. secretary of commerce, are the highest level of national recognition that a company in the United States can receive, and they demonstrate the growing cooperation of business and government to improve the quality of U.S. goods and services.

Virtually every activity a manager performs can have some impact on the quality of goods or services that that manager's organization produces. Developing organiza-

tional objectives, training organization members, practicing strategic management, and designing organization structures—all affect the quality of a company's output. This management feature illustrates how various management activities affect product quality.

You will find it valuable to study all of these management spotlights carefully, for they will help you build realistic expectations about your career as a manager. The cases detailed in the spotlights illustrate that as managers show the ability to solve various organizational problems, they become more valuable to organizations and are more likely to receive the organizational rewards of promotion and significant pay increases.

People Perspectives

PEOPLE PERSPECTIVES concentrates on human issues in organizations. This feature, new to this edition, appears in every chapter of the book to emphasize how crucial managing people is and to illustrate that no management topic exists independent of people issues. In addition, the Influencing section of this text provides an in-depth theoretical look at many people-oriented topics, such as communication, managing teams, and motivation. The PEOPLE PERSPECTIVES throughout complement this theoretical focus by integrating human topics and their application into the entire book.

Cutting Edge

Studying management necessarily involves studying the accumulated wisdom composed of the successful ideas of past as well as recent generations of management researchers and practicing managers. It is well to keep in mind that current management thinking benefits from a rich history of research and practice.

CUTTING EDGE is a special feature of this text that highlights *recent* management research and practice—that is, this feature emphasizes current management research and the innovative ways in which contemporary managers are confronting modern organizational problems. CUTTING EDGE is new to this edition. It appears in each chapter to emphasize the importance of being open to new ideas in management. Some of the companies in this feature are Hewlett-Packard, The Body Shop, John Deere, and NationsBank.

BACK TO THE CASE   Managers at American Speedy Printing Centers, like the managers at any company, are at various stages of career development. To illustrate how the stages of career development might relate to managers at American Speedy Printing Centers, we will focus on one hypothetical manager, Martin Plane.

Plane is a regional manager who oversees five of Isiah Thomas' printing offices. He is 45 years old and is considered a member of the company's middle management.

Plane began his career (exploration stage) in college by considering various areas of study and by holding down several types of part-time positions, including delivering pizzas for Domino's Pizza and working for Scott's, a lawn-care company. He began college at age 18 and graduated when he was 22.

Plane then moved into the establishment stage of his career. For a few years after graduation, he held full-time trial positions in the printing industry as well as in the restaurant and retailing industries. What he learned during the career exploration stage helped him decide what type of full-time trial positions to pursue. At the age of 26, he accepted a trial position as assistant manager in an American Speedy Printing Centers office. While working in this position, Plane decided that he wanted to remain in the printing industry in general, and at American Speedy Printing Centers in particular. From age

27 to age 45, he worked in a number of supervisory and middle-management positions within the company.

Now Plane is moving into an extremely critical part of his career, the maintenance stage. He could probably remain in his present position and maintain his productivity for several more years. However, he wants to advance his career, so he must take a proactive stance and formulate and implement tactics that will enhance his career success. For example, he might seek training to develop certain critical skills, or he might move into a position that is a prerequisite for other, more advanced positions at American Speedy Printing Centers.

In the future, as Plane approaches 65 years of age (the decline stage), it is probable that his productivity at American Speedy Printing Centers will decline somewhat. He may decide to go from full-time employment to semiretirement. Perhaps he will work for American Speedy Printing or another company in the same industry on a part-time advisory basis. Or he may decide to do part-time work in another industry—for example, teach a small-business management course at a nearby college.

Action Summary

Reread the learning objectives below. Each objective is followed by questions. Answering these questions accurately will help you to retain the most important concepts discussed in this chapter. After answering each question, check your answer against the answer key at the end of this chapter. (*Hint:* If you have any doubts regarding the correct response, consult the page whose number follows the answer.)

Circle:	From studying this chapter, I will attempt to acquire:
	1. An understanding of the importance of management to society and individuals.
T, F	a. Managers constitute less than 1 percent of the U.S. workforce.
T, F	b. Management is important to society.
	2. An understanding of the role of management.
a, b, c, d, e	a. The role of a manager is to: (a) make workers happy; (b) satisfy only the manager's needs; (c) make the most profit; (d) survive in a highly competitive society; (e) achieve organizational goals.
T, F	b. Apart from its goals, management has no meaning.
	3. An ability to define *management* in several different ways.
a, b, c, d, e	a. Management is: (a) a process; (b) reaching organizational goals; (c) utilizing people and other resources; (d) all of the above; (e) a and b.
T, F	b. Management is the process of working with people and through people.
	4. An ability to list and define the basic functions of management.
a, b, c, d, e	a. Which of the following is not a function of management: (a) influencing; (b) planning; (c) organizing; (d) directing; (e) controlling.
a, b, c, d, e	b. The process of gathering information and comparing this information to preestablished standards is part of (a) planning; (b) influencing; (c) motivating; (d) controlling; (e) commanding.
	5. Working definitions of managerial effectiveness and managerial efficiency.
T, F	a. If an organization is using its resources to attain its goals, the organization's managers are efficient.
T, F	b. A manager who is reaching goals but wasting resources is efficient but ineffective.
	6. An understanding of basic management skills and their relative importance to managers.
a, b, c, d, e	a. Conceptual skills require that management view the organization as: (a) a profit center; (b) a decision-making unit; (c) a problem-solving group; (d) a whole; (e) individual contributions.
T, F	b. Managers require fewer and fewer human skills as they move from lower to higher management levels.
	7. An understanding of the universality of management.
T, F	a. The statement that management principles are universal means that they apply to all types of organizations and organizational levels.
T, F	b. The universality of management means that management principles are taught the same way in all schools.

8. Insights concerning what management careers are and how they evolve.

T, F   **a.** In general, as careers evolve, individuals tend to further develop job skills but show very little or no change in attitude about various job circumstances.

T, F   **b.** Individuals tend to show the first significant increase in performance during the establishment career stage.

Introductory Case Wrap-Up

"Isiah Thomas: Player to Manager" (p. 2) and its related back-to-the-case sections were written to help you better understand the management concepts contained in this chapter. Answer the following discussion questions about this introductory case to enrich your understanding of the chapter content:

1. Do you think that it will be difficult for Isiah Thomas to become a successful manager? Explain.

2. What do you think you would like most about being a manager? What would you like least?

3. You have just been appointed a regional manager at American Speedy Printing Centers and are responsible for supervising five printing offices in Nashville, Tennessee. List and describe five activities that you think you'll have to perform as part of this job.

Issues for Review and Discussion

1. What is the main point illustrated in the introductory case on American Speedy Printing Centers?
2. How important is the management function to society?
3. How important is the management function to individuals?
4. What is the basic role of the manager?
5. How is *management* defined in this text? What main themes are contained in this definition?
6. List and define each of the four functions of management.
7. Outline the relationship among the four management functions.
8. List and describe five of Peters and Waterman's characteristics of excellent companies, and explain how each of these characteristics could affect planning, organizing, influencing, and controlling.
9. List and define the basic organizational resources managers have at their disposal.
10. What is the relationship between organizational resources and production?
11. Draw and explain the continuum of managerial effectiveness.
12. Draw and explain the continuum of managerial efficiency.
13. Are managerial effectiveness and managerial efficiency related concepts? If so, how are they related?
14. According to Katz, what are the three primary types of skills important to management success? Define each of these types of skills.
15. Describe the relative importance of each of these three types of skills to lower-level, middle-level, and upper-level managers.
16. What is meant by "the universality of management"?
17. What is a career?
18. Discuss the significance of the maintenance career stage.
19. What tips contained in this chapter for promoting the success of a career do you find most valuable? Explain.
20. What does the law of the situation tell you about the success of your management career?

Action Summary Answer Key

1. a. F, p. 3
    b. T, p. 3
2. a. e, p. 4
    b. T, p. 5

3. a. d, pp. 5–7
    b. F, p. 7
4. a. d, pp. 6–8
    b. d, pp. 6–8

5. a. F, p. 9
    b. F, p. 9
6. a. d, pp.10–11
    b. F, pp.10–11

7. a. T, p. 11
    b. F, p. 11

8. a. F, p. 12
    b. T, pp. 12–13

Case Study

Chrysler's Top Gun

More than any other of its current executives, President Robert Lutz personifies Chrysler's image as the brashest of the U.S. Big Three automakers. His flamboyant, often combative personality may have put off his former boss, Lee A. Iacocca, but it has endeared him to Chrysler's current low-key chairman, Robert Eaton. According to *Business Week*, their relationship is a textbook case of opposites attracting. Although it appears that Lutz will never achieve his dream of holding the top office at a U.S. automaker, he respects Eaton. In 1992, when Eaton left General Motors for Chrysler, hand-picked to succeed CEO and Chairman Iacocca, he called Lutz "integral to our success." Ever since then, the two leaders have bonded through their love of fast cars and their wish to see Iacocca retire. Once in control of Chrysler, Eaton approved a five-year product plan and gave his president free rein to execute it.

The son of a Swiss banker, Lutz became a citizen of the United States in 1943, along with his parents. He was captivated at an early age by motorcycles, cars, and planes, and became a fighter pilot in the Marine Corps in 1954. After five years in the service, he went on to earn a B.S. and an M.B.A. at the University of California. From there, he pursued his "need for speed" in the car industry, working first for General Motors as a planner, and later as a GM executive vice president in Europe. In 1971, he left GM to become vice president of sales and director at BMW. Eight years later, he was the head of Ford's European division. In 1982, Lutz returned to the United States as executive vice president for Ford's international operations.

Lutz's career at Ford soured, however, when Ford's European business fell through the floor. Held responsible for the collapse, he returned to Europe to correct it. Two years later, he was back in the United States again, heading Ford's sluggish truck operations. It was then that Lee Iacocca tapped Lutz for the position of executive vice president at Chrysler. Although his relationship with the charismatic Iacocca gradually decayed, Lutz moved up to the position of president in 1991.

By 1996, Lutz had convinced Chrysler's stockholders that he was almost exclusively responsible for boosting Chrysler's U.S. market share two points, to 14.3 percent, during his five-year tenure. Most shareholders tended to agree because of two key changes the tough-minded, dynamic new president had made:

1. He overhauled Chrysler's engineering ranks into skillful, cross-functional teams.
2. He supported daring styling in new performance

models such as the Dodge Intrepid sedan and the Ram pickup.

According to Lutz "I have an unusual ability to direct the product-creation process, sort of a gift," he says. "I'm much like the conductor of a symphony orchestra." Lutz conducted the "Chrysler automotive symphony" in a 180-degree turnaround by helping to create Chrysler's vaunted "platform teams," in which engineers' work was organized around specific models. The team concept eventually came to include marketing, manufacturing, design, and financial personnel as well. Ultimately, product development became faster, cheaper, and more creative, as these cross-functional teams learned to build better-looking, better-performing models.

Widely regarded as the best product-development executive in the automotive industry, Lutz has also been blamed for the questionable quality of Chrysler's cars. While he refuses to acknowledge his company's cars are any lower in quality than other American autos, Lutz does admit that quality has to be Chrysler's major focus in the immediate future. Eaton agrees.

Quality complaints aside, Lutz is highly valued at Chrysler, and neither stockholders, board members, nor Eaton wants to lose him. The company has quietly overlooked its mandatory retirement age of 65 in his case, and extended his contract through 1999. As Lutz puts it, "Reports of my pending retirement have turned out to be greatly exaggerated." Without question, Lutz's dynamic ideas—backed by solid experience, enthusiasm, and success with shareholders—have made him a valuable commodity at Chrysler now and in the years to come.

Questions:

1. In what stage of the career cycle was Robert Lutz in each of the positions he held? What personal skills, interests, and abilities did he call upon in moving through his chosen career path? Explain.
2. What managerial characteristics described in the text are reflected in Robert Lutz? Cite examples from the case study to support your choices.
3. According to the text, "enthusiasm, earnestness of purpose, confidence, and faith in their worthwhileness are primary characteristics of successful managers." Use information about Robert Lutz contained in this case study to support or refute this statement.

Skills Exercise

Despite your lack of managerial experience, you have made it through the initial stages for executive employment and are now getting ready for an interview with Robert A. Lutz. Review the discussion of management functions in the text and prepare for your interview using the following heads: (1) Planning, (2) Influencing, (3) Controlling, and (4) Organizing. Under each head, list experiences that you have had that meet the definition of that managerial function, however broadly, and that you think would appeal to an executive of Lutz's vision and abilities. Review your lists and select the *one* experience that you will discuss in your interview. Write a short description of the experience, highlighting those aspects that you plan to emphasize when you meet Lutz.

The Internet learning materials that accompany this chapter can be found at
http://www.profcerto.com
Additional information can be found on the inside front and back covers of this text.

Lands' End, Inc.
A Brief History

This is the first of seven cases in this book that explore a variety of management-related issues at the well-known direct-retailing company Lands' End. This installment is designed to be a general introduction. You may want to refer to it when you are studying the cases that appear at the end of each part of the book.

Lands' End, headquartered in Dodgeville, Wisconsin, is an international direct merchant of "cut and sewn" products. Through regular mailings of its catalogs, Lands' End provides customers with quality merchandise offered at competitive prices and backed by an unconditional guarantee. In addition to casual and tailored clothing for men, women, and children, the company's products include accessories, shoes, soft luggage, and products for bed and bath.

Founded in 1963 in Chicago by Gary C. Comer, Lands' End initially supplied sailboat hardware and equipment by mail. In the early 1970s, catalogs also featured a sampling of outerwear and casual clothing. In 1977, the company decided to focus its efforts on selling clothing and soft luggage. By 1979, Lands' End had moved to Dodgeville, Wisconsin, expanded the clothing selection in its catalog, and begun to recruit personnel experienced in the areas of fabrics and clothing manufacturing.

Since then, the company has been a leader in the integration of consumer advertising techniques with mail-order practices. In 1981, Lands' End began a national advertising campaign to describe its business philosophy and expand its reputation for quality, value, and service (the Lands' End philosophy is outlined in the inset labeled "Lands' End—Principles of Doing Business"). This campaign introduced the phrase "direct merchant" to illustrate the company's approach to its business.

Lands' End catalogs are known for descriptive product narratives that tell customers everything they could want to know about a garment and its construction. The company's toll-free phone lines to both sales and customer-service departments are open 24 hours a day, 364 days a year. Over 1,000 phone lines handle about 50,000 calls each day—almost 100,000 calls daily in the weeks just prior to Christmas. Eighty-five percent of all orders are placed by phone.

Telephone sales representatives undergo 80 hours of product, customer-service, and computer training when initially hired and 24 hours each year thereafter. So-called "specialty shoppers"—specialists trained to assist on a variety of technical issues—are available 16 hours each day to assist with sizing questions, gift suggestions, and wardrobe coordination. In-stock orders leave Lands' End's Dodgeville distribution center (a structure the size of 16 football fields) the day after they are received. Standard delivery is two business days anywhere within the continental United States (two to three business days for Alaska and Hawaii). Orders placed from the five states surrounding Wisconsin are frequently received in one shipping day. Even when trousers are hemmed (free of charge) to a customer's desired length, shipping is delayed by only one day. Swatches of fabric from catalog garments, replacement of most buttons and belts, and repair of luggage or attaché cases are all free. Monogramming and gift boxing are available at a cost of $5.00.

Lands' End also employs more than 80 quality-assurance personnel—one of the largest in-house staffs in the retail industry. Product managers put back into garments the construction details of old that are commonly left out today and operate on a mandate not to reduce the quality of a garment in order to make it cheaper. Lands' End works directly with some of the best fabric mills and manufacturers in the world. Garments are produced to Lands' End's own quality specifications, not to less stringent industrywide specifications.

Lands' End
Principles of Doing Business

Principle 1: We do everything we can to make our products better. We improve material, and add back features and construction details that others have taken out over the years. We never reduce the quality of a product to make it cheaper.

Principle 2: We price our products fairly and honestly. We do not, have not, and will not participate in the common retailing practice of inflating mark-ups to set up a future phony "sale."

Principle 3: We accept any return, for any reason, at any time. Our products are guaranteed. No fine print. No arguments. We mean exactly what we say: GUARANTEED, PERIOD.

Principle 4: We ship items in stock the day after we receive the order. At the height of the last Christmas season, the longest time an order was in the house was 36 hours, excepting monograms, which took another 12 hours.

Principle 5: We believe that what is best for our customer is best for all of us. Everyone here understands that concept. Our sales and service people are trained to know our products and to be friendly and helpful. They are urged to take all the time necessary to take care of you. We even pay for your call, for whatever reason you call.

Principle 6: We are able to sell at lower prices because we have eliminated middlemen; because we don't buy branded merchandise with high protected mark-ups; and because we have placed our contracts with manufacturers who have proved that they are cost conscious and efficient.

Principle 7: We are able to sell at lower prices because we operate efficiently. Our people are hard-working, intelligent and share in the success of the company.

Principle 8: We are able to sell at lower prices because we support no fancy emporiums with their high overhead. Our main location is in the middle of a 40-acre cornfield in rural Wisconsin.

Lands' End became a public company through an offering of 1.4 million shares of stock on October 3, 1986. In August 1987, shares were split two-for-one. In May 1994, shares were again split two-for-one and are now on the New York Stock Exchange (ticker symbol—*LE*). In fiscal 1995, spread across the United States, Canada, and overseas, there were about 8.2 million Lands' End customers who had made a purchase within the previous 36 months. In 1994, Lands' End sales surpassed those of L.L. Bean Inc., making it the leading specialty-catalog company in the United States. Net income for the fiscal year ending January 27, 1995, was $36.1 million on net sales of $992 million. In addition to its booming U.S. business, the company now does business with customers in 75 countries, with facilities or special licensing agreements in place in Canada, the United Kingdom, Japan, and Germany (see the inset labeled "Lands' End—A Calendar of Significant Events" for more specifics related to the company's international business ventures).

Lands' End
A Calendar of Significant Events

1963—Lands' End, Inc. is founded in Chicago, IL by Gary C. Comer, a former advertising copywriter and avid sailor. The company sold sailboat hardware and equipment by catalog.

1975—First full-color catalog, with 30 pages of sailing gear and two pages of clothing, is distributed.

1977—Selling focus moves toward clothing as 13 of 40 pages are devoted to clothes. Square Rigger® soft luggage is introduced.

1978—Warehouse and phone operations are located in Dodgeville, WI, a rural community located 40 miles southwest of Madison, WI. Toll-free 800 number is operational and first buttondown oxford shirt is sold.

1980—Toll-free phone is operational 24 hours a day.

1985—Lands' End catalog comes out monthly. Big snowstorm hits Dodgeville in the middle of the holiday rush; everyone pitches in to take care of the holiday business (and each other).

1986—Lands' End goes public.

1987—Begin servicing Canadian customers.

1990—Three new specialty catalogs are launched: *Coming Home* (bed and bath), *Lands' End Kids, Beyond Buttondowns* (men's tailored).

1991—Lands' End sends first catalog to customers in the United Kingdom.

1993—Lands' End opens warehouse and phone center in United Kingdom. *Textures* (women's tailored) catalog is introduced.

1994—Lands' End announces from its Japanese offices in Yokohama that it has launched a catalog business in Japan with the initial mailing of its first Japanese-language, yen-denominated catalog. Corporate offices and telephone center (which are staffed by local customer-service representatives) are located in Yokohama.

1995—Lands' End purchases trademark of Willis and Geiger.
   —Lands' End Internet home page debuts in July.
   —First Willis and Geiger catalog is mailed in late August.
1996—Lands' End opens phone center in Germany.

Questions:

1. Discuss the concepts of inputs and the production process as they relate to the transformation of organizational resources into finished products at Lands' End.
2. List three issues in the case that illustrate the ways in which Lands' End management strives for efficiency. Be sure to explain how each issue relates specifically to efficiency as an organizational goal.
3. List three skills that middle managers need to be successful at Lands' End. Why do you regard these skills as important?

2
chapter

THE HISTORY OF MANAGEMENT

"Mickey's Kitchen" at The Disney Store

You want a Mickey Mouse T-shirt and the kids are clamoring for a burger? Well, if you're in or near Montclair, California, The Disney Store has got you covered.

In a shopping mall 40 miles east of Los Angeles, The Disney Store, Inc., has opened Mickey's Kitchen, where you can chow down on french fries shaped like Mickey or Donald or pig out on a Hot Diggity Dog, a meatless Mickey Burger, or the "Soup-a-Dee-Doo-Dah" garden soup.

In typical Disney style, the decor is more elaborate than that of the average burger joint. Diners are seated in one of four themed areas that are mock sound stages—giant friezes, actually, where a famous Disney cartoon is being "filmed." (No actual filming takes place.)

The Montclair Mickey's Kitchen has 190 seats and sells food items priced from 50 cents to $3.45. The menu, which includes more low-fat items than typical fast-food fare, has been fine-tuned many times, but not substantially altered.

Pinocchio's Pizza includes three varieties of pizza: a cheese pizza and a vegetable pizza that sell for $2.75 and a barbecue chicken pizza that costs $2.95.

The PB&J Handwich, a pancake wrapped around a banana half and filled with peanut butter and jelly, has proved popular with children, said Chuck Champlin, spokesman for Disney's consumer products division headquartered in Burbank, California.

For those concerned about fat and calorie content, there is the Goofy Burger, with lean ground beef and a fat content of less than 15 percent, which sells for $1.95 in the adult version and $1.25 in the children's version. The Hot Diggity Dog is a turkey frank that costs $1.50. The meatless Mickey Burger consists of a blend of walnuts, mozzarella, bean curd, and vegetables. Rather than being fried, it is browned under a heat lamp.

Champlin said the lower-fat items aren't meant to be a subtle comment on the typically high-fat American diet but are intended to offer diners a variety of choices. "Our priority is to create fun . . . and the emphasis is to offer really good food with something for everybody."

Disney's restaurant plans do not stop at Mickey's Kitchen. Future restaurant openings include a House of Blues, tied to entertainer Dan Akroyd's House of Blues; a Lario's, featuring the music of singer Gloria Estefan along with Latin food and music; and a Rainforest, featuring live and artificial tropical plants and animals accompanied by thunderstorms.

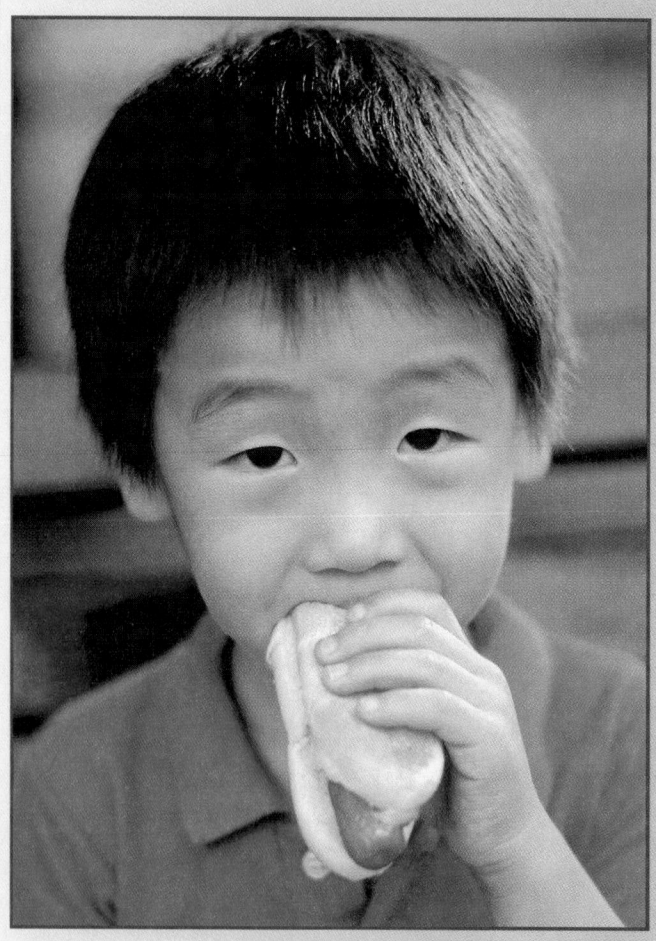

Capitalizing on the popularity of the Disney characters, The Disney Stores, Inc. has opened restaurants called Mickey's Kitchens that offer such fun fare as Hot Diggity Dogs for kids.

what's ahead

There are several ways to approach management situations and to solve related organizational problems. Managers like those running Disney's new Mickey's Kitchen must understand these different approaches if they are to build successful organizations. This chapter explains five approaches to management:

1. Classical
2. Behavioral
3. Management science
4. Contingency
5. System

Chapter 1 focused primarily on defining *management*. This chapter presents various approaches to analyzing and reacting to the management situation, each characterized by a basically different method of analysis and a different type of recommended action.

There has been much disagreement over the years on just how many different approaches to management there are and what each approach entails. In an attempt to simplify the discussion of the field of management without sacrificing significant information, Donnelly, Gibson, and Ivancevich combined the ideas of Koontz, O'Donnell, and Weihrich with those of Haynes and Massie, and concluded that there were three basic approaches to management:[1]

1. The classical approach
2. The behavioral approach
3. The management science approach

The following sections build on the work of Donnelly, Gibson, and Ivancevich in presenting the classical, behavioral, and management science approaches to analyzing the management task. The contingency approach is also discussed as a fourth primary approach, while the system approach is presented as a recent trend in management thinking. It is this last approach that is emphasized in this text.

THE CLASSICAL APPROACH

The **classical approach to management** was the product of the first concentrated effort to develop a body of management thought. In fact, the management writers who participated in this effort are considered the pioneers of management study. The classical approach recommends that managers continually strive to increase organizational efficiency in order to increase production. Although the fundamentals of this approach were developed some time ago, contemporary managers are just as concerned about finding the "one best way" to get the job done as their predecessors were. To illustrate this concern, notable management theorists see striking similarities between the concepts of scientific management developed many years ago and the more current management philosophy of building quality into all aspects of organizational operations.[2]

For discussion purposes, the classical approach to management can be broken down into two distinct areas. The first, lower-level management analysis, consists primarily of the work of Frederick W. Taylor, Frank and Lillian Gilbreth, and Henry L. Gantt. These individuals studied mainly the jobs of workers at lower levels of the organization. The second area, comprehensive analysis of management, concerns the management function as a whole. The primary contributor to this category was Henri Fayol. Figure 2.1 illustrates the two areas in the classical approach.

The **classical approach to management** is a management approach that emphasizes organizational efficiency to increase organizational success.

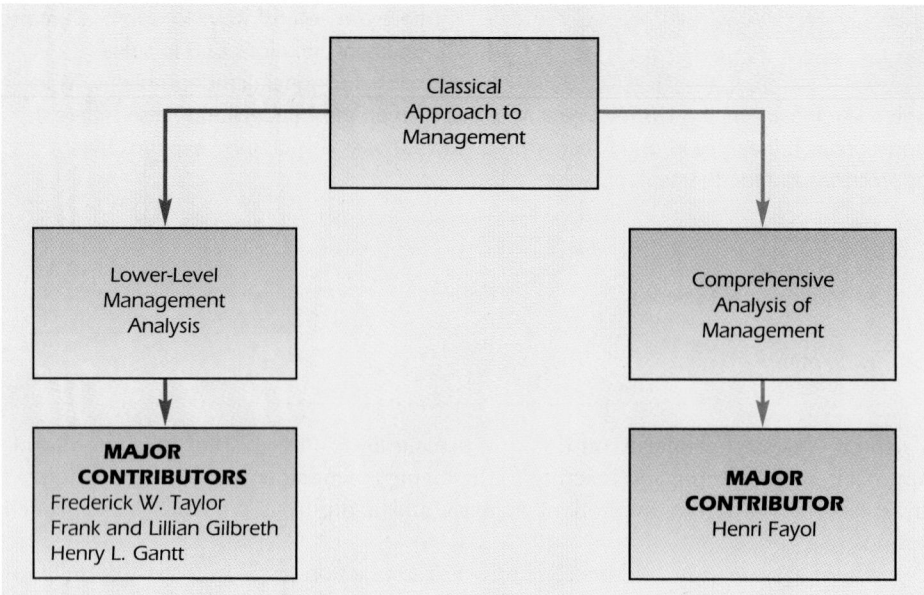

Figure 2.1   Division of classical approach to management into two areas and the major contributors to each area

Lower-Level Management Analysis

Lower-level management analysis concentrates on the "one best way" to perform a task; that is, it asks how a task situation can be structured to get the highest production from workers. The process of finding this "one best way" has become known as the *scientific method of management*, or simply, **scientific management.** Although the techniques of scientific managers could conceivably be applied to management at all levels, the research, research applications, and illustrations relate mostly to lower-level managers. The work of Frederick W. Taylor, Frank and Lillian Gilbreth, and Henry L. Gantt is summarized in the sections that follow.

Scientific management emphasizes the "one best way" to perform a task.

Frederick W. Taylor (1856–1915)   Because of the significance of his contributions, Frederick W. Taylor is commonly called the "father of scientific management." His primary goal was to increase worker efficiency by scientifically designing jobs. His basic premise was that there was one best way to do a job and that that way should be discovered and put into operation.

Work at Bethlehem Steel Co.   Perhaps the best way to illustrate Taylor's scientific method and his management philosophy is to describe how he modified the job of employees whose sole responsibility was shoveling materials at the Bethlehem Steel Company.[3] During the modification process, Taylor made the assumption that any worker's job could be reduced to a science. To construct the "science of shoveling," he obtained answers—through observation and experimentation—to the following questions:

1. Will a first-class worker do more work per day with a shovelful of 5, 10, 15, 20, 30, or 40 pounds?
2. What kinds of shovels work best with which materials?
3. How quickly can a shovel be pushed into a pile of materials and pulled out properly loaded?
4. How much time is required to swing a shovel backward and throw the load a given horizontal distance at a given height?

As Taylor formulated answers to these types of questions, he developed insights on how to increase the total amount of materials shoveled per day. He raised worker

At its new factory in southern Italy, Fiat has made perhaps the most concerted attempt of any Western European manufacturer to improve worker efficiency by getting rid of old ideas and methods. The centerpiece of the new program is training designed to create multiskilled teams composed of engineers as well as production-floor workers. Top-down decision making is a thing of the past, and problems are typically addressed by teams working on the factory floor.

efficiency by matching shovel size with such factors as the size of the worker, the weight of the materials, and the height and distance the materials were to be thrown. By the end of the third year after Taylor's shoveling efficiency plan was implemented, records at Bethlehem Steel showed that the total number of shovelers needed had been reduced from about 600 to 140, the average number of tons shoveled per worker per day had risen from 16 to 59, the average earnings per worker per day had increased from $1.15 to $1.88, and the average cost of handling a long ton (2,240 pounds) had dropped from $0.072 to $0.033—all in all, an impressive demonstration of the applicability of scientific management to the task of shoveling.[4]

DELTA FAUCET COMPANY COMPETES GLOBALLY

GLOBAL SPOTLIGHT

When they saw it was necessary for their company to compete efficiently in the global manufacturing environment, managers at Delta Faucet Company in Chickasha, Oklahoma, focused on automation to find the most efficient ways to perform jobs in Delta's manufacturing plant. Their effort illustrates the scientific approach to management, which emphasizes finding the one best way to do a job—in this case, through the use of machines.

Experts analyzed the assembling and packaging of one of Delta's products, a faucet aerator. An aerator is the part attached to the end of a faucet that increases water pressure by introducing air into the water stream. Delta's aerator consists of six plastic parts that fit together for easy assembly. With the help of the Kingsbury Machine Tool Company, Delta developed a special machine that assembles and packages about 50 aerators per minute. Once assembled and packaged, the aerators are placed on a conveyor belt for distribution to another part of the plant, where they are made ready for shipment. This application of scientific management techniques has enabled Delta to assemble, package, and distribute its aerators more efficiently.

One benefit of Delta's search for the most efficient and effective way to perform each of its jobs is that the company can now compete more effectively in the international marketplace. In fact, finding the "one best way" to do a job is the key to Delta's successful expansion into international markets.≈

Frank Gilbreth (1868–1924) and Lillian Gilbreth (1878–1972)   The Gilbreths were also significant contributors to the scientific method. As a point of interest, the Gilbreths focused on handicapped as well as normal workers.[5] Like other contributors to the scientific method, they subscribed to the idea of finding and using the one best way to perform a job. The primary investigative tool in the Gilbreths' research was **motion study,** which consists of reducing each job to the most basic move-

A **motion study** finds the best way to accomplish a task by analyzing the movements necessary to perform that task.

ments possible. Motion analysis is used today primarily to establish job performance standards. Each movement, or motion, that is used to do a job is studied in terms of how much time the movement takes and how necessary it is to performing the job. Inefficient or unnecessary motions are pinpointed and eliminated.[6]

Frank Gilbreth's experience as an apprentice bricklayer led him to do motion studies of bricklaying. He found that bricklayers could increase their output significantly by concentrating on performing some motions and eliminating others. Table 2.1 shows a simplified portion of the results of one of Gilbreth's bricklaying motion studies. For each bricklaying operation, Gilbreth indicated whether it should be omitted for the sake of efficiency and why. He reduced the five motions per brick listed under "The Wrong Way" to the one motion per brick listed under "The Right Way." Overall, Gilbreth's bricklaying motion studies resulted in a reduction in the number of motions necessary to lay a brick by approximately 70 percent and consequently tripled bricklaying production.

Lillian Gilbreth, who began as her husband's collaborator, continued to research and write on motion studies after his death. She is noted especially for her application of the scientific method to the role of the homemaker and to the handicapped.

Henry L. Gantt (1861–1919)

The third major contributor to the scientific management approach was Henry L. Gantt. He, too, was interested in increasing worker efficiency. Gantt attributed unsatisfactory or ineffective tasks and piece rates (incentive pay for each product piece an individual produces) primarily to the fact that these tasks and rates were set according to what had been done by workers in the past or on somebody's *opinion* of what workers could do. According to Gantt, *exact scientific knowledge* of what could be done by a worker should be substituted for opinion. He considered this the role of scientific management.

Gantt's management philosophy is encapsulated in his statement that "the essential differences between the best system of today and those of the past are the manner in which tasks are 'scheduled' and the manner in which their performance is rewarded."[7] Using this rationale, he sought to improve systems or organizations through task-scheduling innovation and the rewarding of innovation.

Scheduling Innovation.   The Gantt chart, the primary scheduling device that Gantt developed, is still the scheduling tool that is most commonly used by modern managers.[8] Basically, this chart provides managers with an easily understood summary of what work

Table 2.1

Partial Results for One of Gilbreth's Bricklaying Motion Studies

OPERATION NO.	THE WRONG WAY	THE RIGHT WAY	PICK AND DIP METHOD: THE EXTERIOR 4 1INCHES (LAYING TO THE LINE)
1	Step for mortar	Omit	On the scaffold, the inside edge of mortar box should be plumb with the inside edge of the stock platform. On the floor, the inside edge of mortar box should be 21 inches from wall. Mortar boxes should never be over 4 feet apart.
2	Reach for mortar	Reach for mortar	Do not bend any more than absolutely necessary to reach mortar with a straight arm.
3	Work up mortar	Omit	Provide mortar of right consistency. Examine sand screen and keep it in repair so that no pebbles can get through. Keep tender on scaffold to temper up and keep mortar worked up right.
4	Step for brick	Omit	If tubs are kept 4 feet apart, no stepping for brick will be necessary on scaffold. On floor, keep brick in a pile not nearer than 1 foot nor more than 4 feet 6 inches from wall.
5	Reach for brick	Included in 2	Brick must be reached for at the same time that the mortar is reached for, and picked up at exactly the same time the mortar is picked up. If it is not picked up at the same time, allowance must be made for operation.

In Staatsburg, New York, sheet-metal maker PDQ Manufacturing Inc. has been able to meet accelerated schedules by going paperless. For example, electronic blueprints are now sprinted between designers and customers. Soon, CEO Scott Hutchins hopes to speed operations by routing orders simultaneously to both administrative and manufacturing departments. Already, Hutchins has increased annual sales by 67 percent—with fewer workers.

was scheduled for specific time periods, how much of this work has been completed, and by whom it was done.

Special computer software like MacSchedule has been developed to help managers more efficiently and effectively apply the concept of the Gantt chart today.[9] Mac-Schedule allows managers to easily monitor complicated and detailed scheduling issues like the number of units planned for production during a specified period, when work is to begin and to be completed, and the percentage of work that was actually completed during a period. (The Gantt chart is covered in much more detail in Chapter 8.)

Although the Gantt chart is usually thought of as a scheduling device for finding the "one best way"—the most efficient way—to create a work schedule, the following CUTTING EDGE feature describes an innovative adaptation of the chart to help parents find a "one best way" of handling both job and family demands.

LEWIS PLATT DEVELOPS FAMILY-FRIENDLY WORK SCHEDULES AT HEWLETT-PACKARD COMPANY

CUTTING EDGE

Lewis Platt, Hewlett-Packard Company's chief executive officer, is different from most other CEOs of major corporations in one significant way: at one time, he was a working single parent. So Lewis knows very well how parents can be torn apart by the conflicting demands of their jobs and their children.

In response to the need of many workers today to balance job and parenting demands, Lewis is trying to make Hewlett-Packard a more "family-friendly" company—a company that understands and tries to help parents (especially single parents) handle the conflicting demands of work and children. H-P employees therefore have an influential voice in determining when and how they perform their jobs. They have, for example, some choice in determining what hours they will work, and they may do a portion of their work at home.

At a time when the "family-friendly organization" is merely a fashionable notion at most companies, Hewlett-Packard is making meaningful changes that will help people be both good employees and good parents. Whereas other companies conduct therapy sessions for single-parent employees and their managers or provide a call-in service that offers expert advice to single parents with family problems, Hewlett-Packard is actually changing the way it does business so workers do not feel they have to sacrifice their children to their jobs, or vice versa.≈

Rewarding Innovation.   Gantt was more aware of the human side of production than either Taylor or the Gilbreths were. He wrote that "the taskmaster (manager) of

the past was practically a slave driver, whose principal function was to force workmen to do that which they had no desire to do, or interest in doing. The task setter of to-day under any reputable system of management is not a driver. When he asks the workmen to perform tasks, he makes it to their interest to accomplish them, and is careful not to ask what is impossible or unreasonable."[10]

In contrast to Taylor, who pioneered a piece-rate system under which workers were paid according to the amount they produced and who advocated the use of wage-incentive plans, Gantt developed a system wherein workers could earn a bonus in addition to the piece rate if they exceeded their daily production quota. Gantt, then, believed in worker compensation that corresponded not only to production (through the piece-rate system) but also to overproduction (through the bonus system).

As the work of Frederick W. Taylor, Frank and Lillian Gilbreth, and Henry L. Gantt implies, managers should always be looking for the "one best way" to do a job. The following PEOPLE PERSPECTIVES spotlight shows how searching for this "one best way" must consider people working in the organization.

"ONE BEST WAY" CONSIDERS PEOPLE AND TECHNOLOGY AT COURIER PUBLICATIONS

PEOPLE PERSPECTIVES

Courier newspapers serve communities along a 250-mile stretch of the Maine coast. Dave Morse, a top manager at the company, recently decided to focus on using technology to find the "one best way" to publish the newspapers. His initial $250,000 investment in technology earned a return of $500,000 within two years—and he is still adding new equipment. In essence, Morse changed a group of newspapers that were poor performers financially into a profitable business venture for Courier Publications.

Morse's investment gave Courier two important business advantages. First, the company was able to cut labor costs by eliminating 20 full-time workers. Second, the new technology enhanced Courier's ability to track invoices. For example, Courier can now better alert advertisers to bills that will soon be overdue and remind them that early payment will earn them a discount.

Why was Morse so successful in implementing new technology at Courier when other managers have found great worker resistance to technological innovation? Morse realized that his employees were key actors in the success of his technology initiatives. They are, after all, the ones who operate equipment, so they must be motivated and committed to making a technology implementation successful. Managers can build such commitment among their employees by involving them in decisions about the kind of equipment to be purchased and how it should be used. In addition, they must convince employees that any technology initiative will benefit them as individuals as well as the organization. For example, managers can show workers how a technology initiative will help the company become more competitive and therefore more successful, and how this success will contribute to their own job security. ≈

BACK TO THE CASE

The managers of Mickey's Kitchen could use a classical approach to management to stress organizational efficiency—the "one best way" to perform jobs at the restaurant—in order to increase productivity. To take a simplified example, Mickey's Kitchen managers might want to check whether the dispenser used to apply mustard and catsup is of the appropriate size to require only one squirt or whether more than one squirt is necessary to adequately cover the new lean ground beef Goofy Burger bun.

The managers could also use motion studies to eliminate unnecessary or wasted motions by their employees. For example, are Hot Diggity Dogs, french fries, and drinks located for easy insertion into customer bags, or must an employee walk unnecessary steps during the sales process? Would certain Mickey's Kitchen employees work more efficiently through the entire working day if they sat, rather than stood, while doing their job?

The classical approach to management might also guide Mickey's Kitchen managers in scheduling more efficiently. By ensuring that an appropriate number of people with the required skills are scheduled to work during peak hours and that fewer are on during slower hours, managers would maximize the return on their labor costs.

Mickey's Kitchen managers also might want to consider offering their employees some sort of bonus if they reach certain work goals. But managers should make sure that the goals they set are realistic, since unreasonable or impossible goals tend to make workers resentful and unproductive. For example, managers might ask that certain employees reduce errors in filling orders by 50 percent during the next month. If and when these employees reach the goal, Mickey's Kitchen managers could give them rewards like extended work breaks or coupons for free meals.

Comprehensive Analysis of Management

Comprehensive analysis of management involves studying the management function as a whole.

Whereas scientific managers approach the study of management primarily in terms of job design, managers who embrace the comprehensive view—the second area of the classical approach—are concerned with the entire range of managerial performance.

Among the well-known contributors to the comprehensive view are Chester Barnard,[11] Alvin Brown, Henry Dennison, Luther Gulick and Lyndall Urwick, J. D. Mooney and A. C. Reiley, and Oliver Sheldon.[12] Perhaps the most notable contributor, however, was Henri Fayol. His book *General and Industrial Management* presents a management philosophy that still guides many modern managers.[13]

Henri Fayol (1841–1925)   Because of his writings on the elements and general principles of management, Henri Fayol is usually regarded as the pioneer of administrative theory. The elements of management he outlined—planning, organizing, commanding, coordinating, and control—are still considered worthwhile divisions under which to study, analyze, and effect the management process.[14] (Note the close correspondence between Fayol's elements of management and the management functions outlined in Chapter 1—planning, organizing, influencing, controlling.)

The general principles of management suggested by Fayol are still considered useful in contemporary management practice. Here are the principles in the order developed by Fayol, accompanied by corresponding definitional themes:[15]

1. *Division of work.* Work should be divided among individuals and groups to ensure that effort and attention are focused on special portions of the task. Fayol presented work specialization as the best way to use the human resources of the organization.
2. *Authority.* The concepts of authority and responsibility are closely related. *Authority* was defined by Fayol as the right to give orders and the power to exact obedience. *Responsibility* involves being accountable, and is therefore naturally associated with authority. Whoever assumes authority also assumes responsibility.
3. *Discipline.* A successful organization requires the common effort of workers. Penalties should be applied judiciously to encourage this common effort.
4. *Unity of command.* Workers should receive orders from only one manager.
5. *Unity of direction.* The entire organization should be moving toward a common objective, in a common direction.
6. *Subordination of individual interests to the general interests.* The interests of one person should not take priority over the interests of the organization as a whole.

7. *Remuneration.* Many variables, such as cost of living, supply of qualified personnel, general business conditions, and success of the business, should be considered in determining the rate of pay a worker will receive.

8. *Centralization.* Fayol defined *centralization* as lowering the importance of the subordinate role. *Decentralization* is increasing the same importance. The degree to which centralization or decentralization should be adopted depends on the specific organization in which the manager is working.

9. *Scalar chain.* Managers in hierarchies are part of a chainlike authority scale. Each manager, from the first-line supervisor to the president, possesses certain amounts of authority. The president possesses the most authority; the first-line supervisor, the least. Lower-level managers should always keep upper-level managers informed of their work activities. The existence of a scalar chain and adherence to it are necessary if the organization is to be successful.

10. *Order.* For the sake of efficiency and coordination, all materials and people related to a specific kind of work should be assigned to the same general location in the organization.

11. *Equity.* All employees should be treated as equally as possible.

12. *Stability of tenure of personnel.* Retaining productive employees should always be a high priority of management. Recruitment and selection costs, as well as increased product-reject rates, are usually associated with hiring new workers.

13. *Initiative.* Management should take steps to encourage worker initiative, which is defined as new or additional work activity undertaken through self-direction.

14. *Esprit de corps.* Management should encourage harmony and general good feeling among employees.[16]

Fayol's general principles of management cover a broad range of topics, but organizational efficiency, the handling of people, and appropriate management action are the three general themes he stresses. With the writings of Fayol, the study of management as a broad comprehensive activity began to receive the attention it deserved.

Limitations of the Classical Approach

Contributors to the classical approach felt encouraged to write about their managerial experiences largely because of the success they enjoyed. Structuring work to be more efficient and defining the manager's role more precisely yielded significant improvements in productivity, which individuals such as Taylor and Fayol were quick to document.

In the late 1980s, LSG/Sky Chefs, an airline caterer based in Arlington, Texas, reported 1,000 injuries—and 18,000 lost workdays—per year. The company has since instituted a safety-awareness program that also encourages employee initiative and what Henri Fayol called "esprit de corps." Here, for example, employees have taken over morning stretching exercises. Sky Chef also provides rewards to reinforce safe behavior.

The classical approach, however, does not adequately emphasize human variables. People today do not seem to be as influenced by bonuses as they were in the nineteenth century. It is generally agreed that critical interpersonal areas, such as conflict, communication, leadership, and motivation, were shortchanged in the classical approach.

THE BEHAVIORAL APPROACH

The **behavioral approach to management** emphasizes striving to increase production through an understanding of people. According to proponents of this approach, if managers understand their people and adapt their organizations to them, organizational success will usually follow.

The **behavioral approach to management** is a management approach that emphasizes increasing organizational success by focusing on human variables within the organization.

The Hawthorne Studies

The behavioral approach is usually described as beginning with a series of studies conducted between 1924 and 1932 that investigated the behavior and attitudes of workers at the Hawthorne (Chicago) Works of the Western Electric Company.[17] Accounts of the Hawthorne Studies are usually divided into two phases: the relay assembly test room experiments and the bank wiring observation room experiment. The following sections discuss each of these phases.

The Relay Assembly Test Room Experiments
The relay assembly test room experiments originally had a scientific management orientation. The experimenters believed that if they studied productivity long enough under different working conditions (including variations in weather conditions, temperature, rest periods, work hours, and humidity), they would discover the working conditions that maximized production. The immediate purpose of the relay assembly test room experiments was to determine the relationship between intensity of lighting and worker efficiency, as measured by worker output. Two groups of female employees were used as subjects. The light intensity for one group was varied, while the light intensity for the other group was held constant.

The results of the experiments surprised the researchers: No matter what conditions employees were exposed to, production increased. There seemed to be no consistent relationship between productivity and lighting intensity. An extensive interviewing campaign was undertaken to determine why the subjects continued to increase production under all lighting conditions. The following are the main reasons, as formulated from the interviews:

1. The subjects found working in the test room enjoyable.
2. The new supervisory relationship during the experiment allowed the subjects to work freely, without fear.
3. The subjects realized that they were taking part in an important and interesting study.
4. The subjects seemed to become friendly as a group.

The experimenters concluded that human factors within organizations could significantly influence production. More research was needed, however, to evaluate the potential impact of this human component in organizations.

The Bank Wiring Observation Room Experiment
The purpose of the bank wiring observation room experiment was to analyze the social relationships in a work group. Specifically, the study focused on the effect of group piecework incentives on a group of men who assembled terminal banks for use in telephone exchanges. The group piecework incentive system dictated that the harder a group worked as a whole, the more pay each member of that group would receive.

The experimenters believed that the study would show that members of the work group pressured one another to work harder so that each group member would receive more pay. To their surprise, they found the opposite: The work group pressured the faster workers to slow down their work rate. It was the men whose work rate would have increased individual salaries who were being pressured by the group, rather than the men whose work rate would have decreased individual salaries. Evidently, the men were more interested in preserving work group solidarity than in making more money. The researchers concluded that social groups in organizations could effectively exert pressure to influence individuals to disregard monetary incentives.[18]

Recognizing the Human Variable   Taken together, the series of studies conducted at the Hawthorne plant gave management thinkers a new direction for research. Obviously, the human variable in the organization needed much more analysis, since it could either increase or decrease production drastically. Managers began to realize that they needed to understand this influence so they could maximize its positive effects and minimize its negative effects. This attempt to understand people is still a major force in today's organizational research.[19] The cartoon below humorously illustrates how a manager's lack of understanding of an employee results in employee discontent and will perhaps eventually produce a less productive employee. More current behavioral findings and their implications for management are presented in much greater detail in later sections of this text.

The Human Relations Movement

The **human relations movement** is a people-oriented approach to management in which the interaction of people in organizations is studied to judge its impact on organizational success.

Human relations skill is the ability to work with people in a way that enhances organizational success.

The Hawthorne Studies sparked the **human relations movement,** a people-oriented approach to management in which the interaction of people in organizations is studied to judge its impact on organizational success. The ultimate objective of this approach is to enhance organizational success by building appropriate relationships with people. To put it simply, when management stimulates high productivity and worker commitment to the organization and its goals, human relations are said to be effective; and when management precipitates low productivity and uncommitted workers, human relations are said to be ineffective. **Human relations skill** is defined as the ability to work with people in a way that enhances organizational success.

The human relations movement has made some important contributions to the study and practice of management. Advocates of this approach to management have continually stressed the need to use humane methods in managing people. Abraham Maslow, perhaps the best-known contributor to the human relations movement, believed that managers must understand the physiological, safety, social, esteem, and self-actualization needs of organization members. Douglas McGregor, another im-

Cathy Copyright © 1990, Cathy Guisewite. Reprinted with permission of Universal Press Syndicate.

portant contributor to the movement, emphasized a management philosophy built upon the views that people can be self-directed, accept responsibility, and consider work to be as natural as play. The ideas of both Maslow and McGregor are discussed thoroughly in Chapter 16. As a result of the tireless efforts of theorists like Maslow and McGregor, modern managers better understand the human component in organizations and how to appropriately work with it to enhance organizational success.

BACK TO THE CASE Comprehensive analysis of organizations implies that Mickey's Kitchen managers might be able to improve their restaurant by evaluating the entire range of their managerial performance—especially with regard to organizational efficiency, the handling of people, and appropriate management action. For example, Mickey's Kitchen managers should check with their employees to make sure they are receiving orders from only one source—that one manager doesn't instruct an employee to man the french fry station moments before an assistant manager directs the same employee to prepare Pinocchio's Pizzas. Along the same lines, Mickey's Kitchen managers might want to verify that all of their employees are being treated equally—that fry cooks, for example, don't get longer work breaks than order takers.

The behavioral approach to management suggests that Mickey's Kitchen managers should evaluate the impact of workers' feelings and interrelationships on the productivity of the new restaurants. Managers could, for example, try to make the work more enjoyable by allowing their employees to work at different stations (grill, beverage, french fry, cash register, etc.) each day. Managers might also consider creating opportunities for employees to become better acquainted with one another, perhaps through a Mickey's Kitchen employee picnic. In essence, the behavioral approach to management stresses that Mickey's Kitchen managers should recognize the human variable in their restaurants and strive to maximize its positive effects.

THE MANAGEMENT SCIENCE APPROACH

Churchman, Ackoff, and Arnoff define the management science, or operations research (OR), approach as (1) an application of the scientific method to problems arising in the operation of a system and (2) the solving of these problems by the solving of mathematical equations representing the system.[20] The **management science approach** suggests that managers can best improve their organizations by using the scientific method and mathematical techniques to solve operational problems.

The Beginning of the Management Science Approach

The management science, or operations research, approach can be traced to World War II, an era in which leading scientists were asked to help solve complex operational problems in the military.[21] The scientists were organized into teams that eventually became known as operations research (OR) groups. One OR group, for example, was asked to determine which gunsights would best stop German attacks on the British mainland.

These early OR groups typically included physicists and other "hard" scientists, who used the problem-solving method with which they had the most experience: the scientific method. The scientific method dictates that scientists:

1. Systematically *observe* the system whose behavior must be explained to solve the problem.
2. Use these specific observations to *construct* a generalized framework (a model) that is consistent with the specific observations and from which consequences of changing the system can be predicted.

The **management science approach** is a management approach that emphasizes the use of the scientific method and quantitative techniques to increase organizational success.

3. Use the model to *deduce* how the system will behave under conditions that have not been observed but could be observed if the changes were made.
4. Finally, *test* the model by performing an experiment on the actual system to see if the effects of changes predicted using the model actually occur when the changes are made.[22]

The OR groups proved very successful at using the scientific method to solve the military's operational problems.

Management Science Today

After World War II, America again became interested in manufacturing and selling products. The success of the OR groups in the military had been so obvious that managers were eager to try management science techniques in an industrial environment. After all, managers also had to deal with complicated operational problems.

By 1955, the management science approach to solving industrial problems had proved very effective. Many people saw great promise in refining its techniques and analytical tools. Managers and universities alike pursued these refinement attempts.

By 1965, the management science approach was being used in many companies and being applied to many diverse management problems, such as production scheduling, plant location, and product packaging.

In the 1980s, surveys indicated that management science techniques are used extensively in very large, complex organizations. Smaller organizations, however, had not yet fully realized the benefits of using these techniques. Finding ways to apply management science techniques to smaller organizations is undoubtedly a worthwhile challenge for managers in the 1990s and beyond.[23]

QUALITY SPOTLIGHT

BALDRIGE AWARD EXEMPLIFIES QUALITY

Since it was established in 1987, the Malcolm Baldrige National Quality Award has become the sought-after award for quality standards among U.S. businesses. In fact, it is to corporate America what the Oscars are to the motion-picture industry and the Grammys to the music industry.

The Baldrige Award's evaluation of quality in a company includes an examination of both efficiency and effectiveness. The guidelines for award application provide a detailed plan for improving quality in all areas of a company's business.

"The guidelines are outstanding," says James Houghton, chairman and chief executive officer of Corning Glass, which has competed for the award. "We have passed out the guidelines for our divisions and just said, 'If you want to know what quality is all about, take a look at this.' " Corning estimates that its staffers spent 14,000 hours competing for the award.

Six prizes are offered each year, two each for manufacturing and service companies and two for small businesses with fewer than 500 employees. Some past award winners are Motorola, Globe Metallurgical, IBM Rochester, Federal Express, Wallace Company, the Ritz-Carlton Hotel Company, AT&T Universal Card Services, Texas Instruments Defense Systems & Electronics Group, and Granite Rock Company.

The Baldrige Award is administered by the National Institute of Standards and Technology. To apply, a large company must pay a fee of $4,000 and submit responses to over 90 "Areas to Address" on a 75-page questionnaire. A small company pays $1,200 and answers a 50-page questionnaire.

Applications are scored by volunteer examiners, largely from industry. Companies that survive the initial screening enter the second phase of the competition, which includes an on-site visit by four to six examiners who verify information presented in the application.

Finally, application scores and examiners' reports are given to a panel of nine judges who submit their choices to the U.S. secretary of commerce.

Because the process is so detailed and exacting, merely applying for the Baldrige Award forces a company to review its entire operation with an eye to discovering quality weaknesses. Applicants also receive reports from the examiners highlighting strengths and weaknesses in their operations. Former Xerox Chairman David Kearns say that 90 percent of the value of applying for the award lies in that examiners' report. Adds David Luther, Corning Glass' vice president for quality, "It's the cheapest consulting you can ever get."≈

Characteristics of Management Science Applications

Four primary characteristics are usually present in situations in which management science techniques are applied.[24] First, the management problems studied are so complicated that managers need help in analyzing a large number of variables. Management science techniques increase the effectiveness of the managers' decision making in such a situation. Second, a management science application generally uses economic implications as guidelines for making a particular decision. Perhaps this is because management science techniques are best suited for analyzing quantifiable factors such as sales, expenses, and units of production.

Third, the use of mathematical models to investigate the decision situation is typical in management science applications. Models constructed to represent reality are used to determine how the real-world situation might be improved. The fourth characteristic of a management science application is the use of computers. The great complexity of managerial problems and the sophisticated mathematical analysis of problem-related information required are two factors that make computers very valuable to the management science analyst.

Today managers use such management science tools as inventory control models, network models, and probability models to aid them in the decision-making process. Later parts of this text will outline some of these models in more detail and illustrate their applications to management decision making. Since management science thought is still evolving, more and more sophisticated analytical techniques can be expected in the future.

THE CONTINGENCY APPROACH

In simple terms, the **contingency approach to management** emphasizes that what managers do in practice depends on, or is contingent upon, a given set of circumstances—a situation.[25] In essence, this approach emphasizes "if-then" relationships: "If" this situational variable exists, "then" this is the action a manager probably would take. For example, if a manager has a group of inexperienced subordinates, then the contingency approach would recommend that he or she lead in a different fashion than if the subordinates were experienced.

In general, the contingency approach attempts to outline the conditions or situations in which various management methods have the best chance of success.[26] This approach is based on the premise that, although there is probably no one best way to solve a management problem in all organizations, there probably is one best way to solve any given management problem in any one organization. Perhaps the main challenges of using the contingency approach are the following:

1. Perceiving organizational situations as they actually exist.
2. Choosing the management tactics best suited to those situations.
3. Competently implementing those tactics.

Although the notion of a contingency approach to management is not novel, the use of the term itself is relatively new. Moreover, the contingency approach has be-

The **contingency approach to management** is a management approach that emphasizes that what managers do in practice depends on a given set of circumstances—a situation.

Bob Price manages a 7-Eleven store in a suburb of Dallas, Texas. In an effort to speed decision making in its outlets, parent company Southland Corporation has adopted the contingency approach to increase the autonomy of store managers. Now, for example, Price uses a hand-held computer to process data relayed from headquarters; with such data, he will not only calculate his own orders but take into account other factors—from the weather to local special events—that will affect demand in his store.

come a popular discussion topic for contemporary management thinkers. The general consensus of their writings is that if managers are to apply management concepts, principles, and techniques successfully, they must consider the realities of the specific organizational circumstances they face.[27]

THE SYSTEM APPROACH

The **system approach to management** is based on general system theory. Ludwig von Bertalanffy, a scientist who worked mainly in the areas of physics and biology, is recognized as the founder of general system theory.[28] The main premise of the theory is that to understand fully the operation of an entity, the entity must be viewed as a system. A **system** is a number of interdependent parts functioning as a whole for some purpose. For example, according to general system theory, to fully understand the operations of the human body, one must understand the workings of its interdependent parts (ears, eyes, brain, etc.). General system theory integrates the knowledge of various specialized fields so that the system as a whole can be better understood.

The **system approach to management** is a management approach based on general system theory—the theory that to understand fully the operation of an entity, the entity must be viewed as a system. This requires understanding the interdependence of its parts.

A **system** is a number of interdependent parts functioning as a whole for some purpose.

Types of Systems

According to von Bertalanffy, there are two basic types of systems: closed and open. **Closed systems** are not influenced by, and do not interact with, their environments. They are mostly mechanical and have necessary predetermined motions or activities that must be performed regardless of the environment. A clock is an example of a closed system. Regardless of its environment, a clock's wheels, gears, and so forth must function in a predetermined way if the clock as a whole is to exist and serve its purpose. The second type of system, the **open system,** is constantly interacting with its environment. A plant is an example of an open system. Constant interaction with the environment influences the plant's state of existence and its future. In fact, the environment determines whether or not the plant will live.

A **closed system** is one that is not influenced by, and does not interact with, its environment.

An **open system** is one that is influenced by, and is constantly interacting with, its environment.

Systems and "Wholeness"

The concept "wholeness" is very important in general system analysis. The system must be viewed as a whole and modified only through changes in its parts. Before modifications of the parts can be made for the overall benefit of the system, a thorough knowledge of how each part functions and of the interrelationships among the parts must be present. L. Thomas Hopkins suggested the following six guidelines for anyone doing system analysis:[29]

1. The whole should be the main focus of analysis, with the parts receiving secondary attention.
2. Integration is the key variable in wholeness analysis. It is defined as the interrelatedness of the many parts within the whole.
3. Possible modifications in each part should be weighed in relation to possible effects on every other part.
4. Each part has some role to perform so that the whole can accomplish its purpose.
5. The nature of the part and its function is determined by its position in the whole.
6. All analysis starts with the existence of the whole. The parts and their interrelationships should then evolve to best suit the purpose of the whole.

Since the system approach to management is based on general system theory, analysis of the management situation as a system is stressed. The following sections present the parts of the management system and recommend information that can be used to analyze the system.

The Management System

As with all systems, the **management system** is composed of a number of parts that function interdependently to achieve a purpose. The main parts of the management system are organizational input, organizational process, and organizational output. As discussed in Chapter 1, these parts consist of organizational resources, the production process, and finished goods, respectively. The parts represent a combination that exists to achieve organizational objectives, whatever they may be.

The management system is an open system—that is, one that interacts with its environment (see Figure 2.2). Environmental factors with which the management system interacts include the government, suppliers, customers, and competitors. Each of these factors represents a potential environmental influence that could significantly change the future of the management system.

Environmental impact on management cannot be overemphasized. As an example, the federal government, through its Occupational Safety and Health Act (OSHA) of 1970, encourages management to take costly steps to safeguard workers. Many managers believe that these mandated safeguards are not only too expensive but also unnecessary.

The critical importance of managers' knowing and understanding various components of their organization's environments is perhaps best illustrated by the constant struggle of supermarket managers to know and understand their customers. Supermarket managers fight for the business of a national population that is growing by less than 1 percent per year. Survival requires that they know their customers better

> The **management system** is an open system whose major parts are organizational input, organizational process, and organizational output.

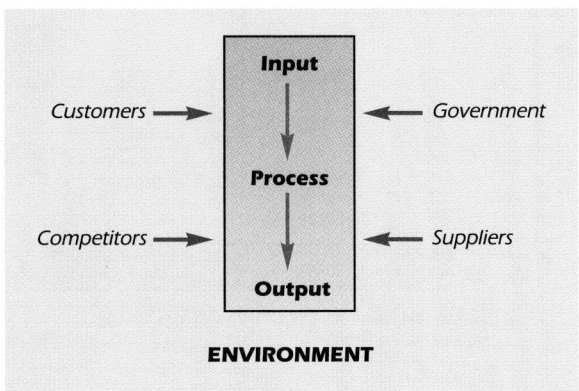

Figure 2.2   The open management system

than the competition does. That is why many food retailers conduct market research to uncover customer attitudes about different kinds of foods and stores. Armed with a thorough understanding of their customers, gained from this kind of research, they hope to win business from competitors who are not benefiting from the insights made possible by such research.[30]

Information for Management System Analysis

As noted earlier, general system theory supports the use of information from many specialized disciplines to better understand a system. This certainly holds true for the management system. Information from any discipline that can increase the understanding of management system operations enhances the success of the system. This is a sweeping statement. Where do managers go to get this broad information? The concise answer: To the first three approaches to management outlined in this chapter.

Thus the information used to discuss the management system in the remainder of this text comes from three primary sources:

1. The classical approach to management.
2. The behavioral approach to management.
3. The management science approach to management.

Triangular management is a management approach that emphasizes using information from the classical, behavioral, and management science schools of thought to manage the open management system.

The use of these three sources of information to analyze the management system is referred to as **triangular management.** Figure 2.3 presents the triangular management model. The three sources of information depicted in the model are not meant to represent all the information that can be used to analyze the management system. Rather, these are the three bodies of management-related information that probably would be most useful to managers analyzing the management system.

A synthesis of classically based information, behaviorally based information, and management science–based information is critical to effective use of the management system. This information is integrated and presented in the five remaining parts of

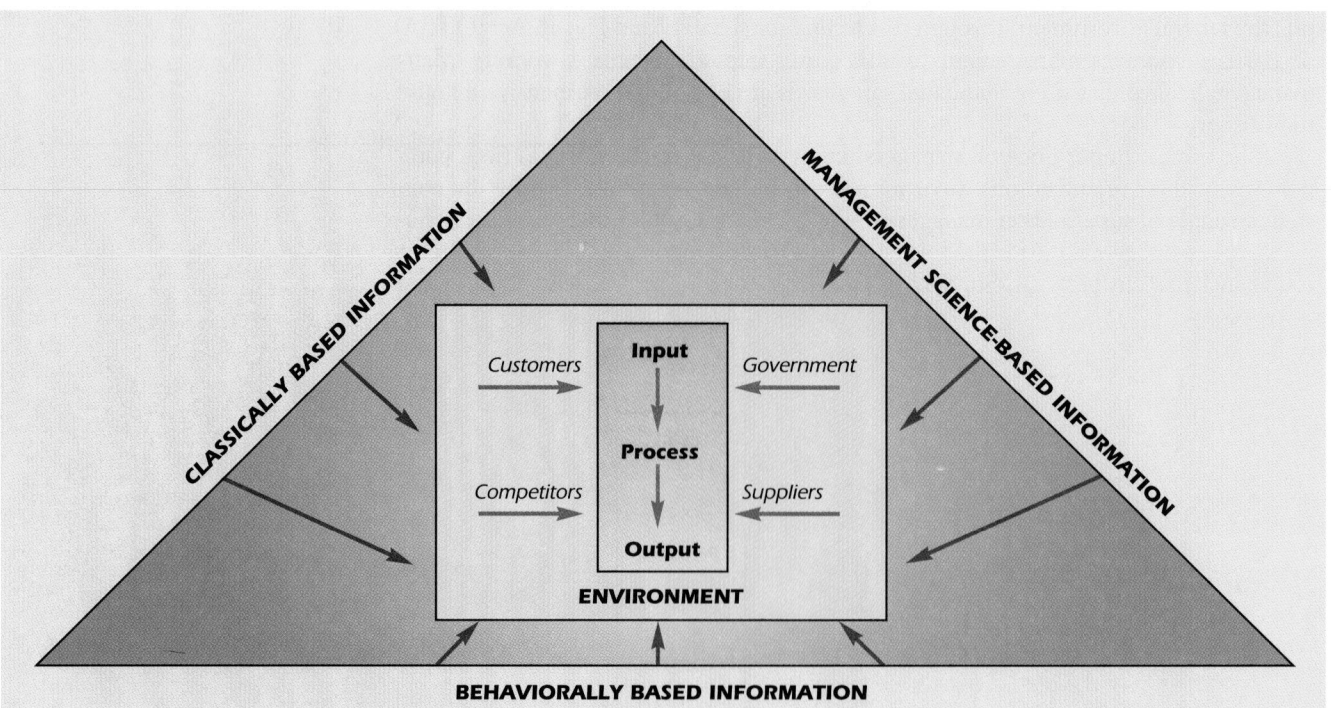

Figure 2.3   Triangular management model

this book. These parts discuss, respectively, management systems and planning (Chapters 5–9), organizing (Chapters 10–13), influencing (Chapters 14–18), controlling (Chapters 19–21), and topics for special emphasis (Chapters 22–23). In addition, some information in these parts of the text is presented from a contingency viewpoint to emphasize the practical application of management principles.

BACK TO THE CASE

Mickey's Kitchen managers could use the management science approach to solve any operational problems that arise. According to the scientific method, Mickey's Kitchen managers would first spend some time observing what takes place in their restaurants. Next, they would use these observations to outline exactly how the restaurants operate as a whole. Third, they would apply this understanding of Mickey's Kitchen operations by predicting how various changes might help or hinder the restaurants as a whole. Before implementing any changes, they would test them on a small scale to see whether they would affect the restaurants as desired.

If Mickey's Kitchen managers decide to follow the contingency approach to management, their actions as managers would depend on the situation. For example, if some customers hadn't been served within a reasonable period because the equipment needed to make PB&J Handwiches had broken down, a Mickey's Kitchen manager probably would not hold employees responsible. But if the manager knew that Handwich equipment had broken down because of employee mistreatment or neglect, his or her reaction to the situation would likely be very different.

Mickey's Kitchen managers could also apply the system approach and view their restaurants as a system—a number of interdependent parts that function as a whole to reach restaurant objectives. Naturally, Mickey's Kitchen would be seen as an open system—one that exists in, and is influenced by, its environment. Major factors within the environment of Mickey's Kitchen would be customers, suppliers, competitors, and the government. For example, if McDonald's, a competitor, significantly lowered its price for hamburgers to a point well below what Mickey's Kitchen was charging for a hamburger, Mickey's Kitchen management might be forced to consider modifying different parts of their restaurant system in order to meet or beat that price.

Action Summary

Reread the learning objectives below. Each objective is followed by questions. Answering these questions accurately will help you retain the most important concepts discussed in this chapter. After answering each question, check your answer against the answer key at the end of this chapter. (*Hint:* If you have any doubts regarding the correct response, consult the page whose number follows the answer.)

Circle: From studying this chapter, I will attempt to acquire:

1. An understanding of the classical approach to management.

T, F   **a.** The classical management approach established what it considered the "one best way" to manage.

a, b, c, d, e   **b.** The process of finding the one best way to perform a task is called: (a) comprehensive analysis of management; (b) the concept of wholeness; (c) the Hawthorne Studies; (d) the management science approach; (e) scientific management.

2. An appreciation for the work of Frederick W. Taylor, Frank and Lillian Gilbreth, Henry L. Gantt, and Henri Fayol.

a, b, c, d, e   **a.** Fayol defines 14 principles of management. Which of the following is *not* one of those principles: (a) scalar chain of authority; (b) esprit de corps; (c) centralization; (d) unity of command; (e) directedness of command.

a, b, c, d, e   **b.** Which of the following theorists assumed that any worker's job could be reduced to a science: (a) Gilbreth; (b) Gantt; (c) Mayo; (d) Fayol; (e) Taylor.

T, F   **c.** Gantt increased worker efficiency by setting standards according to top management's opinion of what maximum performance should be.

3. An understanding of the behavioral approach to management.

T, F   **a.** The behavioral approach to management emphasizes striving to increase production through an understanding of the organization itself.

a, b, c, d, e   **b.** The behavioral approach began with: (a) the Hawthorne Studies; (b) the mental revolution; (c) the Industrial Revolution; (d) motion studies; (e) the Bethlehem Steel Studies.

4. An understanding of the studies at the Hawthorne Works and the human relations movement.

T, F   **a.** The Hawthorne Studies showed a direct relationship between lighting and efficiency.

T, F   **b.** The Hawthorne experimenters found that people were more concerned with preserving the work group than with maximizing their pay.

T, F   **c.** The human relations movement deemphasized the importance of the people component in organizations.

5. An understanding of the management science approach to management.

a, b, c, d, e   **a.** Which of the following is *not* one of the philosophies of the management science approach: (a) managers can improve the organization by using scientific methods; (b) mathematical techniques can solve organizational problems; (c) models should be used to represent the system; (d) individual work is better than teamwork; (e) observation of the system must take place.

T, F   **b.** In the management science theory, models are used to represent reality and then to determine how the real-world situation might be improved.

6. An understanding of how the management science approach has evolved.

a, b, c, d, e   **a.** The management science approach emerged after: (a) World War I; (b) the Civil War; (c) the Korean War; (d) World War II; (e) the 1930s Depression.

T, F   **b.** Although management science was first applied to military problems, it is now applied by companies to diverse management problems.

7. An understanding of the system approach to management.

a, b, c, d, e   **a.** An organization that interacts with external forces is: (a) a closed system; (b) a model; (c) an independent entity; (d) an open system; (e) a contingency.

a, b, c, d, e   **b.** Which of the following is *not* one of the guidelines proposed by Hopkins for doing system analysis according to the concept of wholeness: (a) the whole should be the main focus of analysis; (b) all analysis starts with the existence of the whole; (c) the nature of the part is determined by its position in the whole; (d) each part has some role to perform so that the whole can accomplish its purpose; (e) modifications should be made as problems occur.

8. An understanding of how triangular management and the contingency approach to management are related.

a, b, c, d, e   **a.** The contingency approach emphasizes the viewpoint that what managers do in practice depends overall on: (a) the worker; (b) the situation; (c) the task; (d) the environment; (e) the manager's personality.

a, b, c, d, e   **b.** The three sources of information in triangular management are: (a) input, process, and output; (b) management science, the classical approach to management, and the behavioral approach to management; (c) mathematics, psychology, and sociology; (d) managers, directors, and stockholders; (e) executives, administrators, and supervisors.

Introductory Case Wrap-Up

" 'Mickey's Kitchen' at The Disney Store" (p. 28) and its related back-to-the-case sections were written to help you better understand the management concepts contained in this chapter. Answer the following discussion questions about this introductory case to enrich your understanding of the chapter content:

1. What are three problems that you think the managers of The Disney Store's Mickey's Kitchen will have to solve?

2. What action(s) do you think the managers will have to take to solve these problems?

3. From what you know about fast-food restaurants, how easy do you think it would be to manage Mickey's Kitchen? Explain your answer.

Issues for Review and Discussion

1. List the five approaches to managing.
2. Define the classical approach to management.
3. Compare and contrast the contributions to the classical approach made by Frederick W. Taylor, Frank and Lillian Gilbreth, and Henry L. Gantt.
4. How does Henri Fayol's contribution to the classical approach differ from the contributions of Taylor, the Gilbreths, and Gantt?
5. What is scientific management?
6. Describe motion study as used by the Gilbreths.
7. Describe Gantt's innovation in the area of worker bonuses.
8. List and define Fayol's general principles of management.
9. What is the primary limitation to the classical approach to management?
10. Define the behavioral approach to management.
11. What is the significance of the studies carried out at the Hawthorne Works of the Western Electric Company?
12. Describe the human relations movement.
13. What is the management science approach to management?
14. What are the steps in the scientific method of problem solving?
15. List and explain three characteristics of situations in which management science applications usually are made.
16. Define the contingency approach to management.
17. What is a system?
18. What is the difference between a closed system and an open system?
19. Explain the relationship between system analysis and "wholeness."
20. What are the parts of the management system?

Action Summary Answer Key

1. **a.** T, p. 29
   b. e, p. 29
2. **a.** e, pp. 35–36
   b. e, pp. 30–31
   c. F, p. 32
3. **a.** F, p. 37
   b. a, p. 37
4. **a.** F, p. 37
   b. T, pp. 37–38
   c. F, p. 38
5. **a.** d, p. 39
   b. T, p. 39
6. **a.** d, p. 39
   b. T, p. 40
7. **a.** d, p. 42
   b. e, pp. 42–43
8. **a.** b, p. 41
   b. b, p. 44

Case Study

"Chainsaw Al Dunlap": A New Breed of Manager?

West Point graduate Albert J. Dunlap, former chairman and CEO of Scott Paper Company, claims that the U.S. Military Academy made him "tenacious and very organized." Others say his experience gave him an "in-your-face attitude rare among executives" and made him a valuable hired gun for straightening out troubled companies. Dunlap is known to attack and challenge nearly every premise and person that gets in his sight. Those who interfere with his efforts usually get chewed up by the experience.

Scott Paper is a familiar brand name to the American consumer. Founded by Clarence and Irvin Scott in 1879, the company eventually became the world's largest supplier of toilet tissue, paper napkins, and paper towels. As it matured, however, Scott's profitability suffered and growth stagnated when rival Procter & Gamble took an increasing market share. Between 1960 and 1971, Scott's market share of consumer paper products dropped from 45 to 33 percent. In the period 1990 to 1994, Scott continued to lose market share, and in 1993, the company lost $277 million and saw its credit rating deteriorate.

By 1994, Scott Paper was a moribund bureaucracy. In hiring Al Dunlap, Scott's board of directors signaled its determination to take decisive action. Dunlap initiated changes that would eliminate 11,000 employees (71 percent of headquarters staff, 50 percent of all managers, and 20 percent of hourly workers). He sold off unrelated business units—including publishing papermaker S.D. Warren Company, for $1.6 billion—and slashed spending—the research and development budget alone was cut in half, to $35 million.

Not surprisingly, Dunlap's cost cuts and increased prices achieved immediate bottom-line results. The company's profitability soared, as did the market value of its stock, which rose 225 percent under Dunlap's leadership. Dunlap claimed that by launching new products and selling unprofitable ventures, he had positioned Scott Paper for long-term positive returns for investors. Critics disagreed, seeing Dunlap's moves as constituting a short-term strategy to groom the company for a merger. In the words of one former marketing executive, Dunlap's strategy "became a volume-driven plan to pretty up the place for sale." In fact, on December 12, 1995, Scott share-

holders approved a $9.4 billion merger with Kimberly-Clark Corporation.

As for Al Dunlap, he enjoys his "chainsaw" reputation and believes that his approach is helping to change the norms of corporate behavior. However, according to Peter D. Cappelli, chairman of the management department at the Wharton Business School, "He is persuading others that shareholder value is the be-all and end-all. But Dunlap didn't create value. He redistributed income from the employees and the community to the shareholders."

Nevertheless, the cuts continue. Kimberly-Clark plans to remove 8,000 workers from the combined companies' 60,000 workforce by 1997 and to close Scott's headquarters in Boca Raton, Florida. One former high-level Scott executive believes that the company is now "just a hollow core."

Meanwhile Dunlap walked away with $100 million in salary, bonus, stock gains, and other perks. He offers no apologies for his approach: "I'm not going to apologize for success . . . for all this, for hard work. That's the free-market system." Dunlap does not believe that a business should be run for the stakeholders, such as employees or the communities in which they live, but for the shareholders—period. "Stakeholders are total rubbish," according to Dunlap. "It's the shareholders who own the company. Not enough American executives care about the shareholders."

The real question is whether short-term stockholder gains are good for business down the road. Says Sarah Teslik, executive director of the Council of Institutional Investors in Washington, a watchdog group for big shareholders: "Dunlap holds himself up as a role model,

but any company is apt to have significant stock runup if current costs are reduced by a huge amount. That's no guarantee [Scott] will do well in the future."

On the other hand, some analysts contend that Dunlap has changed corporate America for the better. In a *Financial World* magazine poll, for example, CEOs voted Dunlap "most admired" chief executive officer. Certainly he is now a high-profile business leader who will be sought out by the boards of other troubled companies to enhance shareholder value. It remains to be seen, however, what impact the short-term and long-term consequences of Al Dunlap's management theory will have on corporate America and the American workforce.

Questions:

1. Describe Al Dunlap's management approach. Does it fit any of the classical or modern approaches? Explain. How does it contradict some points in these approaches?
2. Delineate the good points and bad points of a massive downsizing effort such as that undertaken at Scott Paper—as if you were a stakeholder, and then, as if you were a shareholder. Are your two lists different? Explain.
3. What factors were the keys to increased productivity at Scott Paper? How was Dunlap responsible for the company's turnaround?
4. Describe the kind of company that might hire Dunlap next. What goals might its board of directors have? What problems might the company face? What companies in the news today fit your description?

Skills Exercise

You have been assigned to update a management textbook by writing an article on "The Chainsaw Approach to Management." Search the media to discover examples of this management trend to use in your report. Based on

the instances of success or failure that you find in your research, draw some conclusions for the future of corporate America and the U.S. workforce.

 The Internet learning materials that accompany this chapter can be found at
http://www.profcerto.com
Additional information can be found on the inside front and back covers of this text.

CORPORATE SOCIAL RESPONSIBILITY AND BUSINESS ETHICS

STUDENT LEARNING OBJECTIVES

From studying this chapter, I will attempt to acquire:

1. An understanding of the term *corporate social responsibility*.
2. An appreciation of the arguments both for and against the assumption of social responsibilities by business.
3. Useful strategies for increasing the social responsiveness of an organization.
4. Insights on the planning, organizing, influencing, and controlling of social responsibility activities.
5. A practical plan for how society can help business meet is social obligations.
6. An understanding of the relationship between ethics and management.
7. An understanding of how ethics can be incorporated into management practice.

CHAPTER OUTLINE

Introductory Case: Larami Corporation "Super Soaks" Society

Fundamentals of Social Responsibility
The Davis Model of Corporate Social Responsibility
Areas of Corporate Social Responsibility
Varying Opinions on Social Responsibility
Conclusions About the Performance of Social Responsibility Activities by Business

Global Spotlight: DuPont Protects the Environment

People Perspectives: Anita Roddick Influences Body Shop Employees by Communicating Her Position on Social Responsibility

Social Responsiveness
Determining If a Social Responsibility Exists
Social Responsiveness and Decision Making
Approaches to Meeting Social Responsibilities

Diversity Spotlight: Social Responsiveness and the Equal Opportunity Act at Opryland

Social Responsibility Activities and Management Functions
Planning Social Responsibility Activities
Organizing Social Responsibility Activities
Influencing Individuals Performing Social Responsibility Activities
Controlling Social Responsibility Activities

How Society Can Help Business Meet Social Obligations

Business Ethics
A Definition of Ethics

Cutting Edge: The New Management Role Includes Practicing Ethics

Why Ethics Is a Vital Part of Management Practices
A Code of Ethics
Creating an Ethical Workplace

Larami Corporation produced a very hot toy in the summer of 1992. Super Soaker was a high-powered plastic toy gun that shot more water farther than any other toy gun on the market. It was a toy maker's dream—until it turned into a nightmare.

Soon after the toy's introduction, stories of Super Soaker–wielding youths squirting people with water, bleach, ammonia, and urine flooded the offices of lawmakers and police departments around the country. One youth in Boston died, and two others—one in New York, another in New Castle, Pennsylvania—were wounded in shootings triggered by dousings.

The controversy thrust closely held Larami into a dilemma—particularly because the water gun was the company's biggest profit maker. Other companies made similar guns, such as Tyco Toys' Super Saturator, but Larami's Super Soaker was the top-selling water gun by far.

Larami took cover from the controversy by issuing a one-page statement expressing sympathy for the family of the 15-year-old Boston youth who was killed, but noting that violent misuse of the water gun is "something we cannot control." No one in the 50-employee company other than Al Davis, executive vice president, was authorized to speak to the media or public officials. But Mr. Davis, the Philadelphia-based company said, was unavailable for comment.

The then-mayor of Boston, Raymond Flynn, urged retailers to stop selling the gun, and Michigan state Senator Gilbert DiNello introduced a bill to outlaw the toy. In response, Woolworth's and Bradlee's pulled the product off the shelves in some of their stores, and the Sharper Image said it would give to charity the money it made from the sale of the toy guns in its Boston stores. . . .

The Super Soaker came in three models that varied in price from $10 to $30 apiece. It was a best-selling toy, according to NPD Group, a Port Washington, New York, researcher that supplies industry sales figures to the Toys Manufacturers Association and to toy retailers. In fact, analysts estimated that Larami's water gun represented more than 70 percent of the water-gun market. The gun's air compression system, which propelled water as far as 50 feet away, was patented to keep competitors from copying the technology. But that didn't stop others from riding on the wave of this hot toy. For example, Tyco's Super Saturator, a battery-operated gun, was able to shoot water in spurts, lawnmower-style, as far as 35 feet. The Super Saturator, however, wasn't linked to any violent incidents.

Overall, the business attitude toward powerful water guns has been somewhat mixed. By including a miniversion of the Super Soaker water guns in its kids meals, Hardee's Food Systems seemed to be supporting Larami's right to sell this toy gun. On the other hand, by refusing to stock certain types of guns it believed could be dangerous, Toys 'R' Us, the largest toy retailer in the United States, seemed to be saying that only clearly safe toy guns should be manufactured.

The mayor of Boston urged retailers to stop selling the Super Soaker, a high-powered toy water gun, after a 15-year-old youth was killed in an incident involving the toy.

<table>
<tr><td>

what's ahead

</td><td>

The introductory case describes societal efforts to curb sales of a toy gun produced by Larami Corporation. Manage-

</td></tr>
</table>

ment at Larami faced the difficult challenge of making a profit from its Super Soaker while mollifying the public criticism that this toy gun encouraged youth violence that resulted in serious injuries and even death. This chapter presents material that managers such as those at Larami can use to help analyze and handle the dilemma of reaching company objectives while protecting or improving the welfare of society. Specifically, the chapter discusses the following subjects:

1. Fundamentals of social responsibility.
2. Social responsiveness.
3. Social responsibility activities and management functions.
4. How society can help business meet social obligations.
5. Business ethics.

FUNDAMENTALS OF SOCIAL RESPONSIBILITY

The term *social responsibility* means quite different things to different people. For purposes of this chapter, however, **corporate social responsibility** is the managerial obligation to take action that protects and improves both the welfare of society as a whole and the interests of the organization. According to the concept of corporate social responsibility, a manager must strive to achieve societal as well as organizational goals.[1]

> **Corporate social responsibility** is the managerial obligation to take action that protects and improves both the welfare of society as a whole and the interests of the organization.

The amount of attention given to the area of social responsibility by both management and society has increased in recent years and probably will continue to increase in the future.[2] The following sections present the fundamentals of social responsibility of businesses by discussing these topics:

1. The Davis model of corporate social responsibility.
2. Areas of corporate social responsibility.
3. Varying opinions on social responsibility.
4. Conclusions about the performance of social responsibility actions by business.

The Davis Model of Corporate Social Responsibility

A generally accepted model of corporate social responsibility was developed by Keith Davis.[3] Stated simply, Davis' model is a list of five propositions that describe why and how business should adhere to the obligation to take action that protects and improves the welfare of society as well as of the organization:

Proposition 1: Social responsibility arises from social power. This proposition is derived from the premise that business has a significant amount of influence on, or power over, such critical social issues as minority employment and environmental pollution. In essence, the collective action of all businesses in the country determines to a major degree the proportion of minorities employed and the prevailing condition of the environment in which all citizens must live.

Davis reasons that since business has this power over society, society can and must hold business responsible for social conditions that result from the exercise of this power. Davis explains that society's legal system does not expect more of business than it does of each individual citizen exercising personal power.

Proposition 2: Business shall operate as a two-way open system, with open receipt of inputs from society and open disclosure of its operations to the public. According to this proposition, business must be willing to listen to society's representatives concerning what must be done to sustain or improve societal welfare. In turn, society must be willing to listen

to business' reports on what it is doing to meet its social responsibilities. Davis suggests that there must be ongoing honest and open communications between business and society's representatives if the overall welfare of society is to be maintained or improved.

Proposition 3: The social costs and benefits of an activity, product, or service shall be thoroughly calculated and considered in deciding whether to proceed with it. This proposition stresses that technical feasibility and economic profitability are not the only factors that should influence business decision making. Business should also consider both the long- and short-term societal consequences of all business activities before undertaking them.

Proposition 4: The social costs related to each activity, product, or service shall be passed on to the consumer. This proposition states that business cannot be expected to finance completely activities that may be socially advantageous but economically disadvantageous. The cost of maintaining socially desirable activities within business should be passed on to consumers through higher prices for the goods or services related to the socially desirable activities.

Proposition 5: Business institutions, as citizens, have the responsibility to become involved in certain social problems that are outside their normal areas of operation. This last proposition makes the point that if a business possesses the expertise to solve a social problem with which it may not be directly associated, it should be held responsible for helping society solve that problem. Davis reasons that because business eventually will reap an increased profit from a generally improved society, business should share in the responsibility of all citizenry to generally improve society.

BACK TO THE CASE

Social responsibility obliges a business manager to take actions that protect and improve the welfare of society along with the interests of the organization. Management at Larami, as discussed in the introductory case, faces the social responsibility issue of curbing youth violence. Following the logic of Davis' social responsibility model, if the sale of the Super Soaker actually does encourage youths to perform violent acts, Larami management will probably have to address this violence issue by somehow modifying the design of the product and the way it is marketed. The real challenge in this situation is to determine whether the sale of the Super Soaker indeed causes these violent acts. Should Larami management hold itself responsible for contributing to the delinquency of minors simply because some young customers use Super Soakers with violent intent? Larami management must carefully weigh the social costs and benefits of providing society with such toys and then proceed with the course of action that will best benefit society as well as Larami.

The information presented thus far in this chapter also implies that Larami management should seriously listen to society's concerns about the Super Soaker. Perhaps the

Faced with increasingly successful assaults by antismoking forces, the tobacco industry—a $47-billion concern—has retrenched. In the process, it has become a focal point in the debate about the interrelationship between business and society. In one 15-month period, for example, Philip Morris Co. and R.J. Reynolds Tobacco Co. spent $235 million on ads attacking antismoking laws, and in California alone, they have made $10 million in political donations in order to influence votes on pending legislation.

best response to this situation is for Larami management to gather as much information as possible concerning violent acts committed with the Super Soaker and take such steps as redesigning the product or refocusing its marketing to minimize the toy gun's use in any future acts of this nature.

As a consequence of handling this situation, Larami management might acquire special expertise in developing products that not only discourage youth violence but also encourage young people to become a positive force in their communities. This expertise could certainly benefit society if Larami management shared it with businesspeople in other fields. For example, Larami management might be able to help the president of a publishing company publish books that discourage youth violence.

Areas of Corporate Social Responsibility

The areas in which business can act to protect and improve the welfare of society are numerous and diverse. Perhaps the most publicized of these areas are urban affairs, consumer affairs, environmental affairs, and employment practices affairs.

Varying Opinions on Social Responsibility

Although numerous businesses are already involved in social responsibility activities, there is much controversy about whether such involvement is necessary or even appropriate. The following two sections present some arguments for and against businesses performing social responsibility activities.[4]

Arguments *for* Business Performing Social Responsibility Activities

The best-known argument for the performance of social responsibility activities by business was alluded to earlier in this chapter. This argument begins with the premise that business as a whole is a subset of society, one that exerts a significant impact on the way in which society exists. Since business is such an influential member of society, the argument continues, it has the responsibility to help maintain and improve the overall welfare of society. After all, since society puts this responsibility on its individual members, why should its corporate members be exempt from such responsibility?

In addition, some people argue that business should perform social responsibility activities because profitability and growth go hand in hand with responsible treatment of employees, customers, and the community. This argument says, essentially, that performing social responsibility activities is a means of earning greater organizational profit.

Empirical studies, however, have not demonstrated any clear relationship between corporate social responsibility and profitability. In fact, several companies that were acknowledged leaders in social commitment during the 1960s and 1970s—including Control Data Corporation, Atlantic Richfield, Dayton-Hudson, Levi Strauss, and Polaroid—experienced serious financial difficulties during the 1980s.[5] (No relationship between corporate social responsibility activities and these financial difficulties was shown, however.)

Arguments *against* Business Performing Social Responsibility Activities

The best-known argument against business performing social responsibility activities has been advanced by Milton Friedman, one of America's most distinguished economists. Friedman argues that making business managers simultaneously responsible to business owners for reaching profit objectives and to society for enhancing societal welfare sets up a conflict of interest that could potentially cause the demise of business as it is known today. According to Friedman, this demise will almost certainly occur if business is continually forced to perform socially responsible actions that directly conflict with private organizational objectives.[6]

Friedman also argues that to require business managers to pursue socially responsible objectives may, in fact, be unethical, since it compels managers to spend money on some individuals that rightfully belongs to other individuals:

> In a free enterprise, private property system, a corporate executive is an employee of the owners of the business. He has direct responsibility to his employers. That responsibility is to conduct the business in accordance with their desires, which generally will be to make as much money as possible while conforming to the basic rules of society, both those embodied in law and those embodied in ethical custom. . . . Insofar as his actions reduce returns to stockholders, he is spending their money. Insofar as his actions raise the price to customers, he is spending the customers' money.[7]

An example that Friedman could use to illustrate his argument is the Control Data Corporation. Former chairman William Norris involved Control Data in many socially responsible programs that cost the company millions of dollars—from building plants in the inner city and employing a minority workforce to researching farming on the Alaskan tundra. When Control Data began to incur net losses of millions of dollars in the mid-1980s, critics blamed Norris' "do-gooder" mentality. Eventually, a new chairman was installed to restructure the company and return it to profitability.[8]

BACK TO THE CASE There are many different areas of social responsibility in which Larami management could become involved—for example, product line, marketing practices, employee education and support, corporate philanthropy, environmental control, and minority employment. The situation with the Super Soaker is best categorized under the heading of "product line," since society's criticisms focus on how misuse of the product can cause pain, injury, or even death to young people.

Whatever Larami management might do to minimize the bad social effects associated with the Super Soaker would probably result in a short-run decrease in Super Soaker sales, and perhaps even cost the company additional money as management looked for and invested in better ways to manufacture the product. Although at first glance, such action might seem unbusinesslike, performing this type of social responsibility activities could significantly improve Larami's public image and be instrumental in maintaining the company's growth in the long run.

Conclusions about the Performance of Social Responsibility Activities by Business

The preceding section presented several major arguments for and against businesses performing social responsibility activities. Regardless of which argument or combination of arguments particular managers embrace, they generally should make a concerted effort to do the following:

1. Perform all legally required social responsibility activities.
2. Consider voluntarily performing social responsibility activities beyond those legally required.
3. Inform all relevant individuals of the extent to which their organization will become involved in performing social responsibility activities.

Performing Required Social Responsibility Activities   Federal legislation requires that businesses perform certain social responsibility activities. In fact, several government agencies have been established expressly to enforce such business-related legislation (see Table 3.1). The Environmental Protection Agency, for instance, has the authority to require businesses to adhere to certain socially responsible environmental standards. Examples of specific legislation requiring the performance of cor-

Table 3.1

Primary Functions of Several Federal Agencies That Enforce Social Responsibility Legislation

FEDERAL AGENCY	PRIMARY AGENCY FUNCTIONS
Equal Employment Opportunity Commission	Investigates and conciliates employment discrimination complaints that are based on race, sex, or creed.
Office of Federal Contract Compliance Programs	Ensures that employers holding federal contracts grant equal employment opportunity to people regardless of their race or sex.
Environmental Protection Agency	Formulates and enforces environmental standards in such areas as water, air, and noise pollution.
Consumer Product Safety Commission	Strives to reduce consumer misunderstanding of manufacturers' product design, labeling, etc., by promoting clarity of these messages.
Occupational Safety and Health Administration	Regulates safety and health conditions in non-government workplaces.
National Highway Traffic Safety Administration	Attempts to reduce traffic accidents through the regulation of transportation-related manufacturers and products.
Mining Enforcement and Safety Administration	Attempts to improve safety conditions for mine workers by enforcing all mine safety and equipment standards.

porate social responsibility activities are the Equal Pay Act of 1963, the Equal Employment Opportunity Act of 1972, the Highway Safety Act of 1978, and the Clean Air Act Amendments of 1990. The GLOBAL SPOTLIGHT on page 56 discusses DuPont's handling of a clean air issue.

Voluntarily Performing Social Responsibility Activities   Adherence to legislated social responsibilities is the minimum standard of social responsibility performance that business managers must achieve. Managers must ask themselves, however, how far beyond the minimum they should go.

Determining how far to go is a simple process to describe, yet one that is difficult and complicated to implement. It entails assessing the positive and negative outcomes of performing social responsibility activities over both the short and the long term, and then performing only those activities that maximize management system success while making a desirable contribution to maintaining or improving the welfare of society.

Events at Sara Lee Bakery's plant in New Hampton, Iowa, illustrate how company management can voluntarily take action to protect employees' health. Many employees at the plant began developing carpal tunnel syndrome, a debilitating wrist disorder caused by repeated hand motions. Instead of simply having their employees go through physical therapy—and, as the principal employer in the town, watching the morale of the town drop—Sara Lee thoroughly investigated the problem. Managers took suggestions from factory workers and had their engineers design tools to alleviate the problem. The result was a virtual elimination of carpal tunnel syndrome at the plant within a very short time.[9]

Sandra Holmes asked top executives in 560 major firms in such areas as commercial banking, life insurance, transportation, and utilities to state the possible negative and positive outcomes their firms could expect to experience from performing social responsibility activities.[10] Table 3.2 lists these outcomes and indicates the percentage of executives questioned who expected to experience them. Although this information furnishes managers with general insights into how involved their organizations should

Table 3.2

Outcomes of Social Responsibility Involvement Expected by Executives and the Percent Who Expected Them

EXPECTED OUTCOMES	PERCENT OF EXECUTIVES EXPECTING THEM
Positive Outcomes	
Enhanced corporate reputation and goodwill	97.4
Strengthening of the social system in which the corporation functions	89.0
Strengthening of the economic system in which the corporation functions	74.3
Greater job satisfaction among all employees	72.3
Avoidance of government regulation	63.7
Greater job satisfaction among executives	62.8
Increased chances for survival of the firm	60.7
Ability to attract better managerial talent	55.5
Increased long-term profitability	52.9
Strengthening of the pluralistic nature of American society	40.3
Maintaining or gaining customers	38.2
Investor preference for socially responsible firms	36.6
Increased short-term profitability	15.2
Negative Outcomes	
Decreased short-term profitability	59.7
Conflict of economic or financial and social goals	53.9
Increased prices for consumers	41.4
Conflict in criteria for assessing managerial performance	27.2
Disaffection of stockholders	24.1
Decreased productivity	18.8
Decreased long-term profitability	13.1
Increased government regulation	11.0
Weakening of the economic system in which the corporation functions	7.9
Weakening of the social system in which the corporation functions	3.7

become in social responsibility activities, it does not give them a clear-cut indication of what to do. Managers can determine the appropriate level of social responsibility involvement for a specific organization only by examining and reacting to specific factors related to that organization.

GLOBAL SPOTLIGHT

DuPont Protects the Environment

E.I. DuPont de Nemours and Company, a producer of chemical products, is certainly a company whose actions affect the environment at both the national and the international level. When scientists in the early 1970s theorized that certain types of gases—gases used in the production of some of DuPont's products—were contributing to the breakdown of the ozone layer, DuPont encouraged further research and began looking for alternative products. As the evidence that these gases caused ozone depletion became more conclusive, the company stepped up its research efforts so that management would be able to make informed decisions about its products and their impact on the environment. As a company that conducts business in many countries, DuPont wished to assure its customers and concerned citizens throughout the world that it was sensitive to the ozone issue and that it was acting in a socially responsible manner to ensure that its products would not contribute to further deterioration of the ozone layer.

Under the direction of CEO Robert D. Haas, Levi Strauss & Co. has sought to establish fairly rigorous standards for socially conscious behavior in conducting its worldwide operations. For example, its "Aspirations," a set of written guidelines, prohibit Levi's from dealing with suppliers who violate the company's standards for workplace environments. "We are far from perfect," admits Haas. "But the goal is out there, and it's worth striving for."

Critics, however, could argue that DuPont was merely reacting to pressure from stakeholders and/or outside pressures from environmentalists instead of proactively seeking solutions to global environmental problems.≈

Communicating the Degree of Social Responsibility Involvement   Determining the extent to which a business should perform social responsibility activities beyond legal requirements is a subjective process. Despite this subjectivity, however, managers should have a well-defined position in this vital management area and should inform all organization members of that position.[11] Taking these steps will ensure that managers and organization members behave consistently to support the position and that societal expectations of what a particular organization can achieve in this area are realistic.

The following PEOPLE PERSPECTIVES feature shows how Anita Roddick, by clearly stating her position on social responsibility as founder/owner of The Body Shop, clearly encourages her employees to strive to make the company more socially responsible.

ANITA RODDICK INFLUENCES BODY SHOP EMPLOYEES BY COMMUNICATING HER POSITION ON SOCIAL RESPONSIBILITY

PEOPLE PERSPECTIVES

Anita Roddick is the founder of "The Body Shop," a successful chain of cosmetics shops headquartered in Great Britain and spread across the world. Although her company refrains from marketing and advertising, Roddick has been so successful that by age 47 she was the fourth-richest woman in Great Britain.

According to Roddick, her business is about two things: social change and social correctness. She puts these two issues ahead of making a profit.

Roddick is obviously dedicated to operating in a socially correct fashion. Her company has launched projects to save the whales, to end the testing of cosmetics on animals, and to help the homeless. Her new headquarters has natural ventilation and walls filled with ozone-friendly insulation. Moreover, it is built of timber supplied by plantations where new trees are planted as mature trees are harvested.

Given the huge size of her company, Roddick can neither initiate nor implement very many environmentally correct projects at The Body Shop. Instead, she clearly communicates her position on such issues and requires all her employees to spend two

hours a week on volunteer work in their communities. Thus Roddick's employees have a clear mandate to make business decisions that will help The Body Shop make a positive social impact.≈

BACK TO THE CASE Some social responsibility activities are legislated and therefore must be performed by business. Most of this type of legislation, however, is aimed at larger companies. Even though Larami is a significant company in the toy industry, there probably is no existing legislation that would require its management to modify the Super Soaker.

Because Larami is not required by law to modify its Super Soaker for the benefit of society, whatever modifications management might decide to make would be strictly voluntary. In making a decision on modifications, Larami should assess the positive and negative outcomes of such action over both the long and the short term. Then it should make the modifications (if any) that would maximize the success of the company as well as offer some desirable contribution to society. Larami management should let all organization members, as well as the public, know how the company feels about the situation with the Super Soaker and why.

SOCIAL RESPONSIVENESS

The previous section discussed social responsibility, a business' obligation to take action that protects and improves the welfare of society along with the business' own interests. This section defines and discusses **social responsiveness,** the degree of effectiveness and efficiency an organization displays in pursuing its social responsibilities.[12] The greater the degree of effectiveness and efficiency, the more socially responsive the organization is said to be. The next three sections take up the following issues:

1. Determining if a social responsibility exists.
2. Social responsiveness and decision making.
3. Approaches to meeting social responsibilities.

Determining If a Social Responsibility Exists

One challenge facing managers who are attempting to be socially responsive is to determine which specific social obligations are implied by their business situation. Managers in the tobacco industry, for example, are probably socially obligated to contribute to public health by pushing for the development of innovative tobacco products that do less harm to people's health than present products do, but they are not socially obligated to help reclaim shorelines contaminated by oil spills.

Clearly, management has an obligation to be socially responsible toward its stakeholders. **Stakeholders** are all those individuals and groups that are directly or indirectly affected by an organization's decisions.[13] Managers of successful organizations typically have many different stakeholders to consider: stockholders, or owners of the organization; suppliers; lenders; government agencies; employees and unions; consumers; competitors; and local communities as well as society at large. Table 3.3 lists these stakeholders and gives a corresponding example of how a manager is socially obligated to each of them.

Social Responsiveness and Decision Making

The socially responsive organization that is both effective and efficient meets its social responsibilities without wasting organizational resources in the process. Determining exactly which social responsibilities an organization should pursue and then

Social responsiveness is the degree of effectiveness and efficiency an organization displays in pursuing its social responsibilities.

Stakeholders are all individuals and groups that are directly or indirectly affected by an organization's decisions.

Table 3.3

Stakeholders of a Typical Modern Organization and Examples of Social Obligations Managers Owe to Them

STAKEHOLDER	SOCIAL OBLIGATIONS OWED
Stockholders/owners of the organization	To increase the value of the organization.
Suppliers of materials	To deal with them fairly.
Banks and other lenders	To repay debts.
Government agencies	To abide by laws.
Employees and unions	To provide safe working environment and to negotiate fairly with union representatives.
Consumers	To provide safe products.
Competitors	To compete fairly and to refrain from restraints of trade.
Local communities and society at large	To avoid business practices that harm the environment.

deciding how to pursue them are the two most critical decisions for maintaining a high level of social responsiveness within an organization.

Figure 3.1 is a flowchart that managers can use as a general guideline for making social responsibility decisions that enhance the social responsiveness of their organization. This figure implies that for managers to achieve and maintain a high level of social responsiveness within an organization, they must pursue only those social responsibilities their organization possesses and has a right to undertake. Furthermore, once managers decide to meet a specific social responsibility, they must determine the best way to undertake activities related to meeting this obligation. That is, managers must decide whether their organization should undertake the activities on its own or acquire the help of outsiders with more expertise in the area.

As an example of how the guidelines in Figure 3.1 can profitably be used, consider a recent decision made by Radisson Hotels International. Radisson's management determined that the company had an obligation to help to preserve the environment. To proactively meet this obligation, management initiated a new concept called Green Suites. Along with the normally expected suite appointments, Green Suites feature recycled paper goods because Radisson managers believe that by offering its customers recycled paper products, the company can discourage the unnecessary cutting of trees. In order for this decision to be considered truly socially responsible, however, it must actually help to preserve the environment by saving trees and attract customer dollars that will help Radisson Hotels International reach such organizational objectives as making a profit.[14]

Approaches to Meeting Social Responsibilities

Various managerial approaches to meeting social obligations are another determinant of an organization's level of social responsiveness. According to Lipson, a desirable and socially responsive approach to meeting social obligations does the following:[15]

1. It incorporates social goals into the annual planning process.
2. It seeks comparative industry norms for social programs.
3. It presents reports to organization members, the board of directors, and stockholders on social responsibility progress.
4. It experiments with different approaches for measuring social performance.
5. It attempts to measure the cost of social programs as well as the return on social program investments.

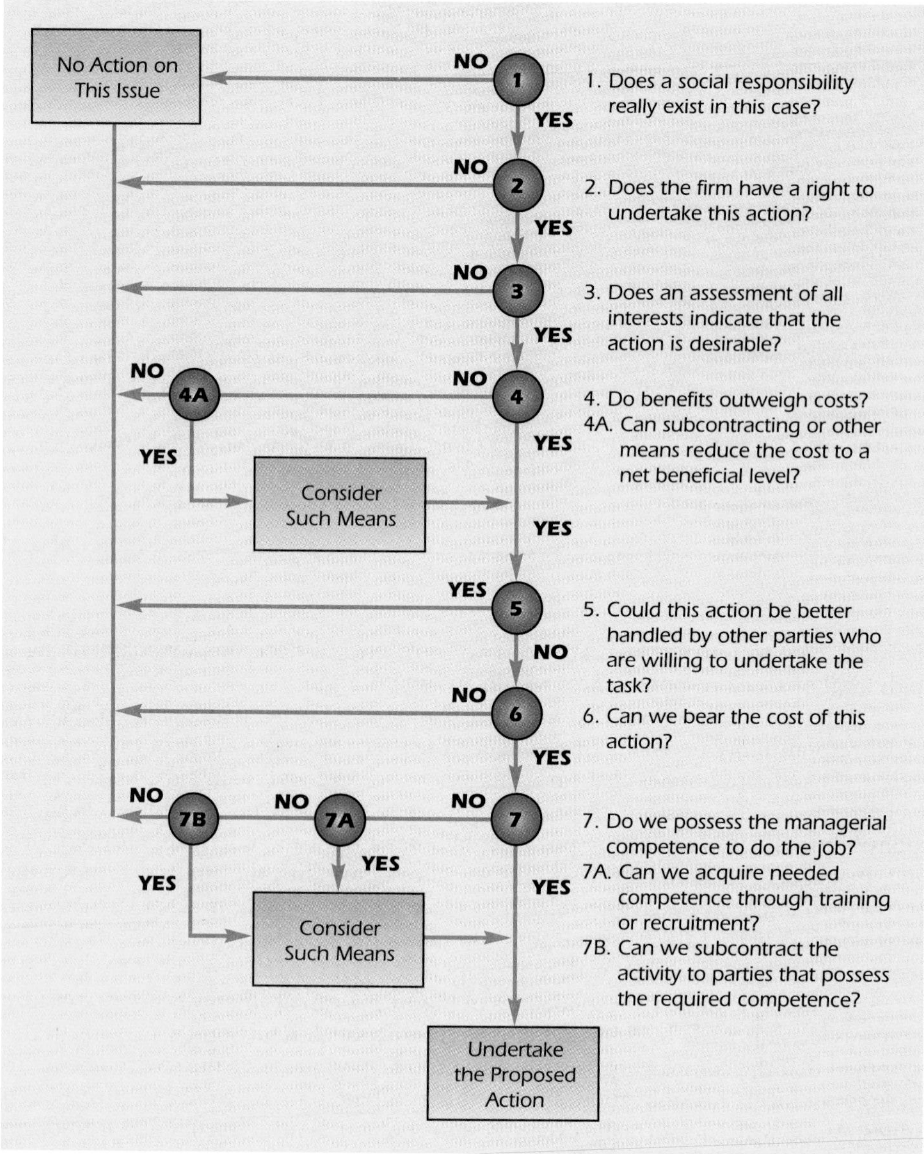

Figure 3.1   Flowchart of social responsibility decision making that generally will enhance the social responsiveness of an organization

The **social obligation approach** is an approach to meeting social obligations that considers business to have primarily economic purposes and confines social responsibility activity largely to conformance to existing legislation.

The **social responsibility approach** is an approach to meeting social obligations that considers business as having both societal and economic goals.

The **social responsiveness approach** is an approach to meeting social obligations that considers business to have societal and economic goals as well as the obligation to anticipate potential social problems and to work actively toward preventing them from occurring.

S. Prakash Sethi presents three management approaches to meeting social obligations:[16]

1. The social obligation approach.
2. The social responsibility approach.
3. The social responsiveness approach.

Each of these approaches entails behavior that reflects a somewhat different attitude toward the performance of social responsibility activities by business. The **social obligation approach,** for example, considers business as having primarily economic purposes and confines social responsibility activity mainly to conformance to existing legislation. The **social responsibility approach** sees business as having both economic and societal goals. The **social responsiveness approach** considers business as having both societal and economic goals as well as the obligation to anticipate potential social problems and to work actively toward preventing them from occurring.

Organizations characterized by attitudes and behaviors consistent with the social responsiveness approach are generally more socially responsive than organizations characterized by attitudes and behaviors consistent with either the social responsibil-

ity or the social obligation approach. And organizations that take the social responsibility approach usually achieve higher levels of social responsiveness than organizations that take the social obligation approach. In other words, as one moves along the continuum from social obligation to social responsiveness, one generally finds management becoming more proactive. Proactive managers do what is prudent from a business viewpoint to reduce liabilities whether such action is required by law or not.

SOCIAL RESPONSIVENESS AND THE EQUAL OPPORTUNITY ACT AT OPRYLAND

DIVERSITY SPOTLIGHT

The Equal Opportunity Act was passed in 1972 to eliminate employment discrimination based upon race, sex, or color. Management's attitude toward performing Equal Opportunity Act social responsibility activities at Opryland illustrates the social responsiveness approach.

The inevitability of having a future workforce characterized by cultural diversity is driving many hotels to aggressively recruit minorities for management-level positions. Such hotels see the careful building of a diverse workforce as a means not only of enhancing worker productivity but also of attracting a more diverse customer base since minorities are a growing segment of their market.

Because the pool of minority candidates for hotel manager positions is relatively small, many hotels and hotel chains are aggressively recruiting. At the Opryland Hotel, for example, the human resource department supports a wide range of special minority recruitment programs. One such program, called INROADS, gives minority college students the financial means to experience four years of hotel-management training. Upon completing such a college program, students are qualified for entry-level management positions in a hotel such as Opryland. Although participating in INROADS will not solve Opryland Hotel's minority recruitment problems in the short run, it will certainly increase the supply of minority candidates to fill the company's management positions in the longer run.≈

BACK TO THE CASE

Larami management should strive to maintain a relatively high level of social responsiveness in pursuing such issues as the one involving the Super Soaker. To do this, managers should make decisions appropriate to the company's social responsibility area and should approach the meeting of those social responsibilities in an appropriate way.

In terms of the Super Soaker situation, Larami management must first decide if the company has the social responsibility to help fight, through the design and marketing of its products, society's problem of youth violence. Assuming that management decides Larami has such a responsibility, the next step is to determine exactly how the company should accomplish the activities necessary to meet this responsibility. For example, can the people presently employed by Larami develop and implement a modified Super Soaker design or a new marketing campaign that would minimize Super Soaker use in violent incidents? Or should management hire independent consultants to recommend and install such product design and/or marketing modifications? Making appropriate decisions of this nature will help Larami management effectively and efficiently meet the company's social obligations.

In terms of finding an approach to meeting social responsibilities that will increase Larami's social responsiveness, management should view its organization as having both societal and economic goals. In addition, Larami managers should attempt to anticipate social problems, such as the one generated by the Super Soaker, and actively work to prevent their appearance.

SOCIAL RESPONSIBILITY ACTIVITIES AND MANAGEMENT FUNCTIONS

This section considers social responsibility as a major organizational activity that should be subjected to the same management techniques used in other major organizational activities, such as production, personnel, finance, and marketing. Managers have known for some time that to achieve desirable results in these areas, they must be effective in planning, organizing, influencing, and controlling. Achieving social responsibility results is no different. The following sections discuss planning, organizing, influencing, and controlling social responsibility activities.

Planning Social Responsibility Activities

Planning was defined in Chapter 1 as the process of determining how the organization will achieve its objectives, or get where it wants to go. Planning social responsibility activities, then, involves determining how the organization will achieve its social responsibility objectives, or get where it wants to go in the area of social responsibility. The following sections discuss how the planning of social responsibility activities is related to the overall planning process of the organization and how the social responsibility policy of the organization can be converted into action.

The Overall Planning Process   The model presented in Figure 3.2 illustrates how social responsibility activities can be handled as part of the overall planning process of the organization. As shown in this figure, social trends forecasts should be performed within the organizational environment along with the more typically performed economic, political, and technological trends forecasts. Examples of social trends are prevailing and future societal attitudes toward water pollution, safe working conditions, and the national education system.[17] Each of the forecasts would influence the development of the organization's long-run plans, or plans for the more distant future, and short-run plans, or plans for the relatively near future.

Converting Organizational Policies on Social Responsibility into Action   A *policy* is a management tool that furnishes broad guidelines for channeling management thinking in specific directions. Managers should establish organizational policies in the social responsibility area just as they do in some of the more generally accepted areas, such as hiring, promotion, and absenteeism.

To be effective, social responsibility policies must be converted into appropriate action. As shown in Figure 3.3, this conversion involves three distinct and generally sequential phases.

- *Phase 1* consists of the recognition by top management that the organization has some social obligation. Top management then must formulate and com-

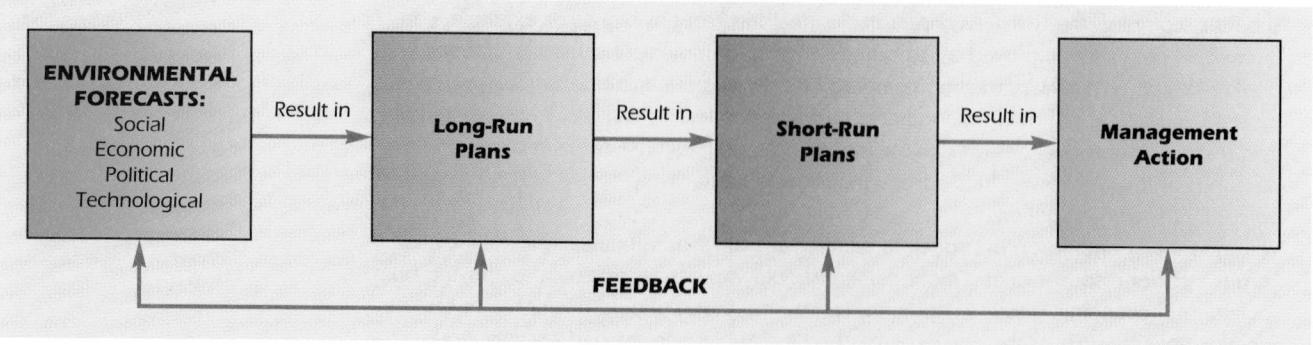

Figure 3.2   Integration of social responsibility activities and planning activities

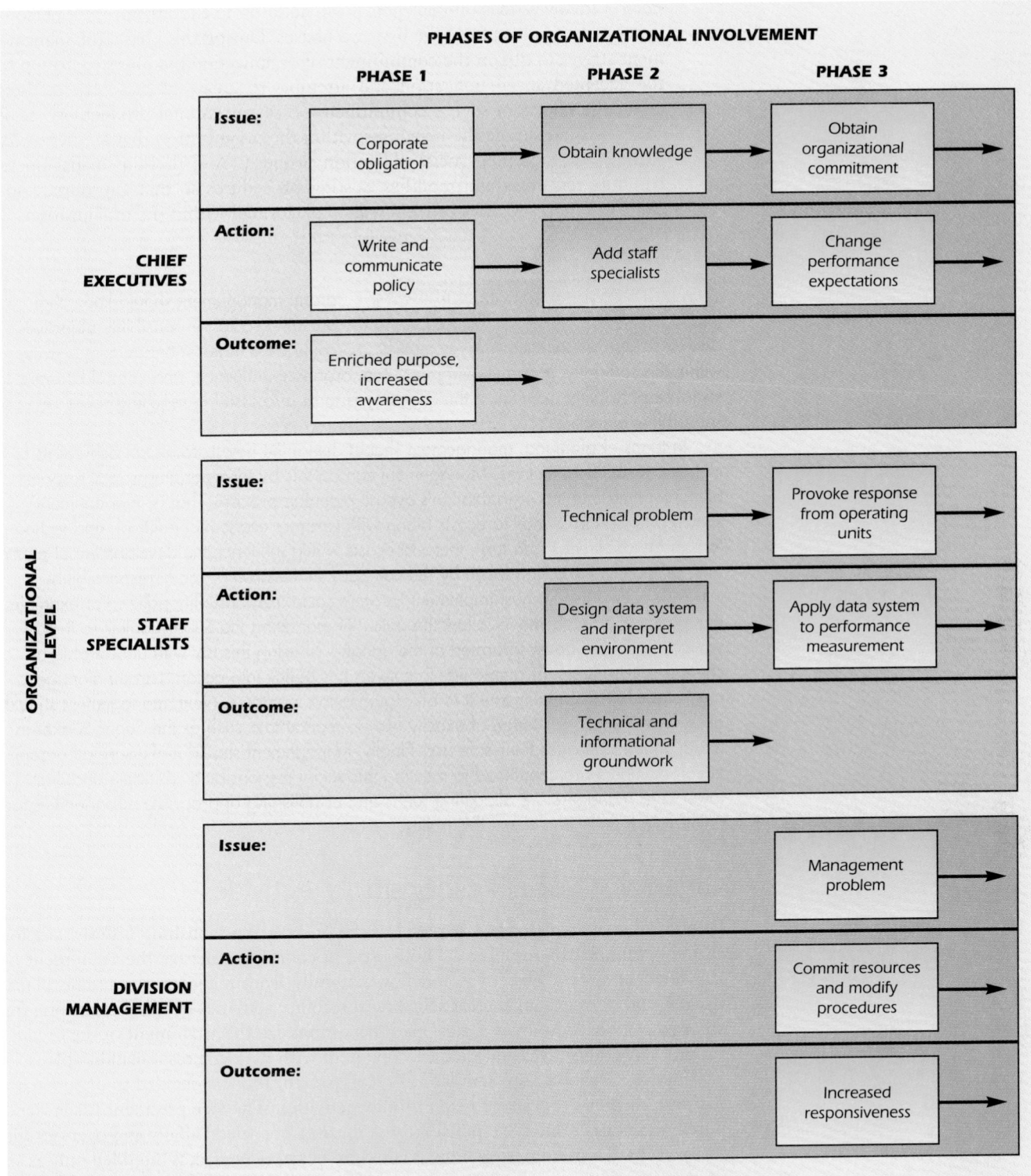

PHASES OF ORGANIZATIONAL INVOLVEMENT

Figure 3.3   Conversion of social responsibility policy into action

municate some policy about the acceptance of this obligation to all organization members.

- *Phase 2* involves staff personnel as well as top management. In this phase, top management gathers information related to meeting the social obligation accepted in phase 1. Staff personnel are generally involved at this point to give advice on technical matters related to meeting the accepted social obligation.

• *Phase 3* involves division management in addition to the organization personnel already involved from the first two phases. During this phase, top management strives to obtain the commitment of organization members to live up to the accepted social obligation and attempts to create realistic expectations about the effects of such a commitment on organizational productivity. Staff specialists encourage the responses within the organization that are necessary to meet the accepted social obligation properly. And division management commits resources and modifies existing procedures so that appropriate socially oriented activities can and will be performed within the organization.

BACK TO THE CASE

Larami management should know that pursuing social responsibility objectives could be a major management activity within the company. Management must plan, organize, influence, and control Larami's social responsibility activities if the company is to be successful in reaching social responsibility objectives.

In terms of planning, management should determine how Larami can achieve its social responsibility objectives. Management can do this by incorporating social responsibility planning into the organization's overall planning process. That is, management should make social trends forecasts along with Larami's economic, political, and technological trends forecasts. In turn, these forecasts would influence the development of plans and, ultimately, the action taken by the company in the area of social responsibility.

Management also must implement Larami's social responsibility policy. For example, management may decide to follow the policy of marketing the Super Soaker so that young people are better informed of the dangers of using this toy with undesirable chemicals like bleach or ammonia. To convert this policy into action, Larami management should first communicate it to all organization members. Next, management should obtain additional knowledge of exactly how to market toys such as the Super Soaker in a way that encourages their safe use. Finally, management should make sure all organization members are committed to meeting this social responsibility objective and that lower-level managers are allocating funds and establishing appropriate opportunities for employees to help implement this policy.

Organizing Social Responsibility Activities

Organizing was discussed in Chapter 1 as the process of establishing orderly uses for all the organization's resources. These uses, of course, emphasize the attainment of management system objectives and flow naturally from management system plans. Correspondingly, organizing for social responsibility activities entails establishing for all organizational resources logical uses that emphasize the attainment of the organization's social objectives and that are consistent with its social responsibility plans.

Figure 3.4 shows how Standard Oil Company of Indiana decided to organize for the performance of its social responsibility activities. The vice president for law and public affairs has primary responsibility in the area of societal affairs and oversees the related activities of numerous individuals. This chart, of course, is intended only as an illustration of how a company might include its social responsibility area on its organization chart. Specific organizing in this area should always be tailored to the unique needs of a company.

Influencing Individuals Performing Social Responsibility Activities

Influencing was defined in Chapter 1 as the management process of guiding the activities of organization members in directions that enhance the attainment of organi-

zational objectives. As applied to the social responsibility area, then, influencing is the process of guiding the activities of organization members in directions that will enhance the attainment of the organization's social responsibility objectives. More specifically, to influence appropriately in this area, managers must lead, communicate, motivate, and work with groups in ways that result in the attainment of the organization's social responsibility objectives.

Controlling Social Responsibility Activities

Controlling, as discussed in Chapter 1, is making things happen as they were planned to happen. To control, managers assess or measure what is occurring in the organization and, if necessary, change these occurrences in some way to make them conform to plans. Controlling in the area of social responsibility entails the same two major tasks. The following sections discuss various areas in which social responsibility measurement takes place and examine the social audit, a tool for determining and reporting progress in the attainment of social responsibility objectives.

Areas of Measurement   Measurements to gauge organizational progress in reaching social responsibility objectives can be taken in any number of areas. The specific areas in which individual companies decide to take such measurements will

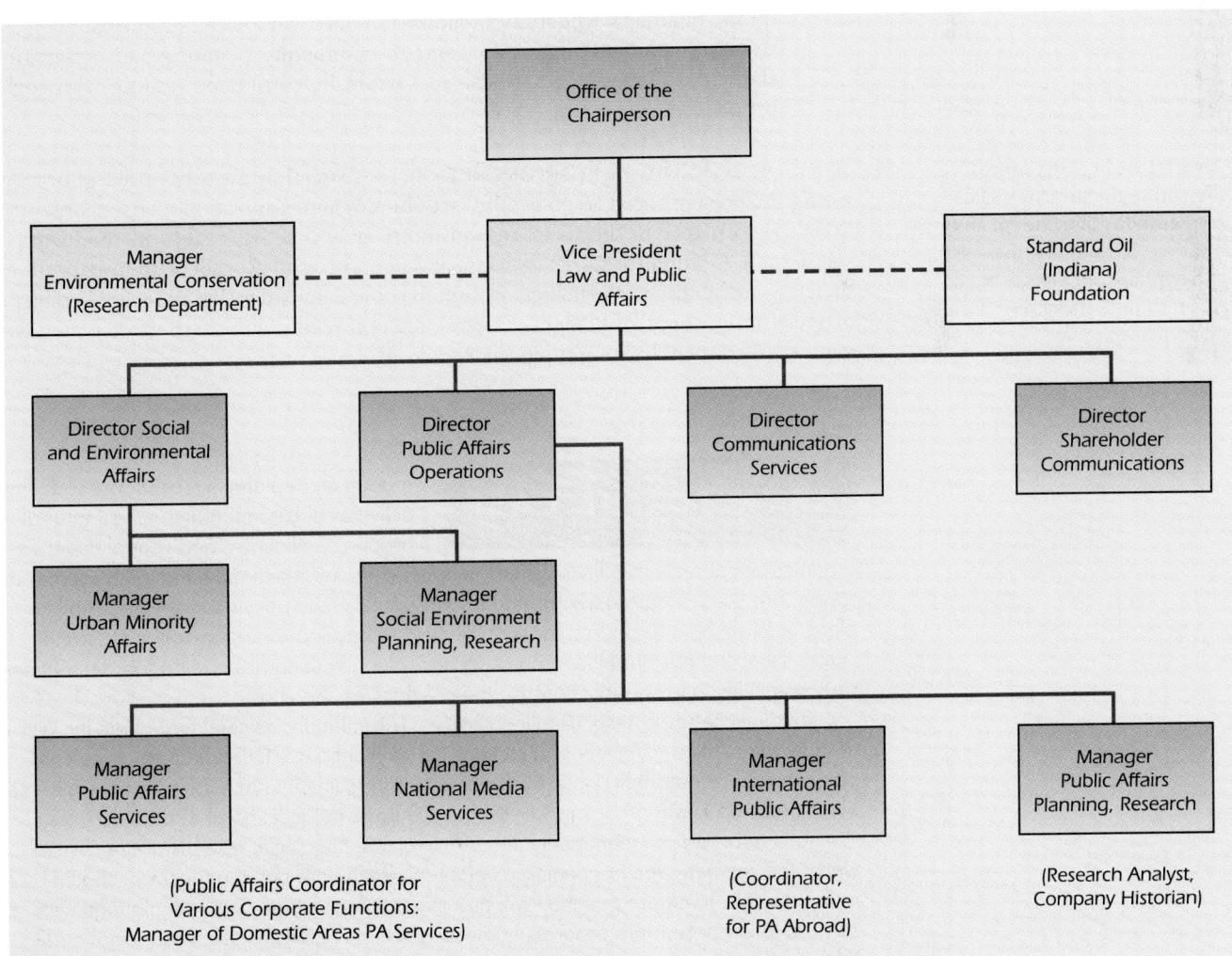

Figure 3.4   How Standard Oil Company of Indiana includes social responsibility in its organization chart

vary according to the specific social responsibility objectives to be met. All companies, however, should probably take social responsibility measurements in at least the following four major areas:[18]

1. *The economic function area.*   A measurement should be made of whether the organization is performing such activities as producing goods and services that people need, creating jobs for society, paying fair wages, and ensuring worker safety. This measurement gives some indication of the economic contribution the organization is making to society.

2. *The quality-of-life area.*   The measurement of quality of life should focus on whether the organization is improving or degrading the general quality of life in society. Producing high-quality goods, dealing fairly with employees and customers, and making an effort to preserve the natural environment are all indicators that the organization is upholding or improving the general quality of life. As an example of degrading the quality of life, some people believe that cigarette companies, because they produce goods that can harm the health of society overall, are socially irresponsible.[19]

3. *The social investment area.*   The measurement of social investment deals with the degree to which the organization is investing both money and human resources to solve community social problems. Here, the organization could be involved in assisting community organizations dedicated to education, charities, and the arts.

4. *The problem-solving area.*   The measurement of problem solving should focus on the degree to which the organization deals with social problems. Such activities as participating in long-range community planning and conducting studies to pinpoint social problems could be considered dealing with social problems.

> A **social audit** is the process of measuring the present social responsibility activities of an organization. It monitors, measures, and appraises all aspects of an organization's social responsibility performance.

The Social Audit: A Progress Report   A **social audit** is the process of measuring the present social responsibility activities of an organization to assess organizational performance in the social responsibility area. The basic steps in conducting a social audit are monitoring, measuring, and appraising all aspects of an organization's social responsibility performance. Although some companies that pioneered concepts of social reporting, like General Electric, are still continuing their efforts, few companies, unfortunately, are joining their ranks.[20]

BACK TO THE CASE   In addition to planning social responsibility activities at Larami, management must also organize, influence, and control them. To organize social responsibility activities, management must determine that all resources at Larami are used in an orderly fashion to carry out the company's social responsibility plans. It might be appropriate for management to develop an organization chart that shows the social responsibility area at Larami, along with corresponding job descriptions, responsibilities, and specifications for the positions on this chart.

To influence social responsibility activities, Larami management must guide the activities of organization members in directions that will enhance the attainment of the company's social responsibility objectives. That is, management must lead, communicate, motivate, and work with groups in ways that encourage the meeting of those objectives.

To control, Larami management must make sure that social responsibility activities within the company are happening as planned. If they are not, management should make changes to ensure that they will occur in the near future. One tool management can use to check Larami's progress in meeting social responsibilities is the social audit. With this audit, management can assess management system performance in such areas as economic functions, quality of life, social investment, and problem solving.

When a local business supports the fund-raising activity in the quality-of-life area. Of course, the value of such activities is difficult to measure quantitatively, both for large and small organizations. Clearly, however, social responsibility is a decision-making area encountered by managers in all organizations, regardless of size.

HOW SOCIETY CAN HELP BUSINESS MEET SOCIAL OBLIGATIONS

Although early in this chapter the point was made that there must be an open and honest involvement of both business and society for business to meet desirable social obligations, the bulk of the chapter has focused on what business should do in the area of social responsibility. This section emphasizes actions that society should take to help business accomplish its social responsibility objectives.

Jerry McAfee, chairman of the board and chief executive officer of Gulf Oil Corporation, says that although business has some responsibilities to society, society also has the following responsibilities to business:[21]

1. *Set rules that are clear and consistent.* This is one of the fundamental things that society, through government, ought to do. Although it may come as a surprise to some, I believe that industry actually needs an appropriate measure of regulation. By this I mean that the people of the nation, through their government, should set the bounds within which they want industry to operate.

   But the rules have got to be clear. Society must spell out clearly what it is it wants the corporations to do. The rules can't be vague and imprecise. Making the rules straight and understandable is really what government is all about. One of my colleagues described his confusion when he read a section of a regulation that a federal regulatory representative had cited as the reason for a certain decision that had been made. "You're right," the official responded, "that's what the regulation says, but that's not what it means."

2. *Keep the rules technically feasible.* Business cannot be expected to do the impossible. Yet the plain truth is that many of today's regulations are unworkable. Environmental standards have on occasion exceeded those of Mother Nature. For example, the Rio Blanco shale-oil development in Colorado was delayed by the fact that the air-quality standards, as originally proposed, required a higher quality of air than existed in the natural setting.

3. *Make sure the rules are economically feasible.* Society cannot impose a rule that society is not prepared to pay for because, ultimately, it is the people who must pay, either through higher prices or higher taxes, or both. Furthermore, the costs involved include not only those funds constructively spent to solve problems, but also the increasingly substantial expenditures needed just to comply with the red-tape requirements. Although the total cost of government regulation of business is difficult to compute, it is enormous. To cite an example, the Commission on Federal Paperwork estimated the energy industry's annual cost of complying with federal energy-reporting requirements at possibly $335 million per year.

4. *Make the rules prospective, not retroactive.* Nowadays, there is an alarming, distressing trend toward retroactivity, toward trying to force retribution for the

past. Certain patterns of taxation and some of the regulations and applications of the law are indications of this trend.

[As a case in point, the U.S. government recently filed a multimillion-dollar lawsuit against Borden Chemicals & Plastics, a company operating in Louisiana and Illinois that produces various chemical products for the construction, industrial, and agricultural markets.[22] The suit alleges that Borden released significant amounts of cancer-causing and other hazardous contaminants into the groundwater at its Louisiana complex. Borden maintains that recent changes to hazardous waste regulations are being applied retroactively to force the company to pay penalties for actions it took before the law existed. Borden charges that this type of action by the government violates the basic concepts of fairness and due process.]

It is counterproductive to make today's rules apply retroactively to yesterday's ball game.

5. *Make the rules goal-setting, not procedure-prescribing.* The proper way for the people of the nation, through their government, to tell their industries how to operate is to set the goals, set the fences, set the criteria, set the atmosphere, but don't tell us how to do it. Tell us what you want made, but don't tell us how to make it. Tell us the destination we're seeking, but don't tell us how to get there. Leave it to the ingenuity of American industry to devise the best, the most economical, the most efficient way to get there, for industry's track record in this regard has been pretty good.

BUSINESS ETHICS

The study of ethics in management can be approached from many different directions. Perhaps the most practical approach is to view ethics as catalyzing managers to take socially responsible actions. The movement to include the study of ethics as a critical part of management education began in the 1970s, grew significantly in the 1980s, and is expected to continue growing into the next century. John Shad, chairman of the Securities and Exchange Commission during the 1980s when Wall Street was shaken by a number of insider trading scandals, recently pledged a $20 million trust fund to the Harvard Business School to create a curriculum in business ethics for MBA students. And television producer Norman Lear gave $1 million to underwrite the Business Enterprise Trust, which will give national awards to companies and "whistle blowers . . . who demonstrate courage, creativity, and social vision in the business world."[23]

The following sections define ethics, explain why ethical considerations are a vital part of management practices, discuss a workable code of business ethics, and present some suggestions for creating an ethical workplace.

A Definition of Ethics

Ethics is our concern for good behavior; our obligation to consider not only our own personal well-being but also that of other human beings.

Business ethics involves the capacity to reflect on values in the corporate decision-making process, to determine how these values and decisions affect various stakeholder groups, and to establish how managers can use these observations in day-to-day company management.

The famous missionary physician and humanitarian Albert Schweitzer defined ethics as "our concern for good behavior. We feel an obligation to consider not only our own personal well-being, but also that of other human beings." This is similar to the precept of the Golden Rule: Do unto others as you would have them do unto you.[24]

In business, **ethics** can be defined as the capacity to reflect on values in the corporate decision-making process, to determine how these values and decisions affect various stakeholder groups, and to establish how managers can use these observations in day-to-day company management. Ethical managers strive for success within the confines of sound management practices that are characterized by fairness and justice.[25] Interestingly, using ethics as a major guide in making and evaluating business decisions is not only popular in the United States but also in the very different societies of India and Russia.[26]

In the past, some management experts expressed the concern that practicing ethics might result in unsound management. As the following CUTTING EDGE feature demonstrates, most management writers now believe that practicing ethics is an integral part of managing.

THE NEW MANAGEMENT ROLE INCLUDES PRACTICING ETHICS

CUTTING EDGE

Modern managers must realize that business and ethics are not contradictory terms. The perception that they are contradictory is based on a dated, unenlightened view of what managers are supposed to do and how they are supposed to act. This outdated view of management assumes that profit maximization is the exclusive purpose of managers and that practicing ethics in the business world would hamper them in fulfilling this purpose.

Ethics theory assumes that managers should focus on other things as well as on profit. This new view of management stresses the need to make managerial decisions in concert with ethical norms and customs prevalent within the organization's environment. It also emphasizes the need for managers to build a foundation of trust and cooperation with employees, customers, and all other members of society who are affected by the organization's activities. The principle underlying these emphases is that managers who act ethically will improve the welfare of society while enhancing the short- and long-run success of the organization.≈

Why Ethics Is a Vital Part of Management Practices

John F. Akers, former chairman of the board of IBM, recently said that it makes good business sense for managers to be ethical. Unless they are ethical, he believes, companies cannot be competitive in either national or international markets. According to Akers:

> Ethics and competitiveness are inseparable. We compete as a society. No society anywhere will compete very long or successfully with people stabbing each other in the back; with people trying to steal from one another; with everything requiring notarized confirmation because you can't trust the other person; with every little squabble ending in litigation; and with government writing reams of regulatory legislation, trying business hand and foot to keep it honest.[27]

While ethical management practices may not be linked to specific indicators of financial profitability, there is no inevitable conflict between ethical practices and making a profit. As Akers' statement suggests, our system of competition presumes underlying values of truthfulness and fair dealing. The employment of ethical business practices can enhance overall corporate health in three important areas: productivity, stakeholder relations, and government regulation.

Productivity   The employees of a corporation constitute one major stakeholder group that is affected by management practices. When management is resolved to act ethically toward stakeholders, then employees will be positively affected. For example, a corporation may decide that business ethics requires it to make a special effort to ensure the health and welfare of its employees. To this end, many corporations have established Employee Advisory Programs (EAPs) to help employees with family, work, financial, or legal problems, or with mental illness or chemical dependency. These programs have even enhanced productivity in some corporations. For instance, Control Data Corporation found that its EPA reduced health costs and sick-leave usage significantly.[28]

Stakeholder Relations   The second area in which ethical management practices can enhance corporate health is by positively affecting "outside" stakeholders such as

suppliers and customers. A positive public image can attract customers who view such an image as desirable. For example, Johnson & Johnson, the world's largest maker of health-care products, is guided by a "Credo" addressed over 50 years ago by General Robert Wood Johnson to the company's employees and stockholders and members of its community (see Figure 3.5).

Government Regulation   The third area in which ethical management practices can enhance corporate health is in minimizing government regulation. Where companies are believed to be acting unethically, the public is more likely to put pressure on legislators and other government officials to regulate those businesses or to enforce existing regulations. For example, in 1995, Texas state legislators held public hearings on the operations of the psychiatric hospital industry. These hearings arose, at least partly, out of the perception that private psychiatric hospitals were not following ethical pricing practices.[29]

A Code of Ethics

A **code of ethics** is a formal statement that acts as a guide for making decisions and acting within an organization.

A **code of ethics** is a formal statement that acts as a guide for how people within a particular organization should act and make decisions in an ethical fashion. Ninety percent of Fortune 500 firms, and almost half of all other firms, have ethical codes.

We believe our first responsibility is to the doctors, nurses, and patients, to mothers and all others who use our products and services.
In meeting their needs everything we do must be of high quality.
We must constantly strive to reduce our costs in order to maintain reasonable prices.
Customers' orders must be serviced promptly and accurately.
Our suppliers and distributors must have an opportunity to make a fair profit.

We are responsible to our employees, the men and women who work with us throughout the world.
Everyone must be considered as an individual.
We must respect their dignity and recognize their merit.
They must have a sense of security in their jobs.
Compensation must be fair and adequate, and working conditions clean, orderly and safe.
Employees must feel free to make suggestions and complaints.
There must be equal opportunity for employment, development, and advancement for those qualified.
We must provide competent management, and their actions must be just and ethical.

We are responsible to the communities in which we live and work and to the world community as well.
We must be good citizens — support good works and charities and bear our fair share of taxes.
We must encourage civic improvements and better health and education.
We must maintain in good order the property we are privileged to use, protecting the environment and natural resources.

Our final responsibility is to our stockholders.
Business must make a sound profit.
We must experiment with new ideas.
Research must be carried on, innovative programs developed and mistakes paid for.
New equipment must be purchased, new facilities provided, and new products launched.
Reserves must be created to provide for adverse times.
When we operate according to these principles, the stockholders should realize a fair return.

Figure 3.5   The Johnson & Johnson Credo

Moreover, many organizations that do not already have an ethical code are giving serious consideration to developing one.[30]

Codes of ethics commonly address such issues as conflict of interest, competitors, privacy of information, gift giving, and giving and receiving political contributions or business. According to a recent survey, the development and distribution of a code of ethics are perceived as an effective and efficient means of encouraging ethical practices within organizations.[31] The code of ethics that Johnson & Johnson drew up to guide company business practices (Figure 3.5) is distributed in its annual report, as well as to employees.

Managers cannot assume that merely because they have developed and distributed a code of ethics, organization members have all the guidelines they need to determine what is ethical and to act accordingly. It is impossible to cover all ethical and unethical conduct within an organization in one code. Managers should view codes of ethics as tools that must be evaluated and refined periodically so that they will be comprehensive and usable guidelines for making ethical business decisions efficiently and effectively.

Creating an Ethical Workplace

Managers commonly strive to encourage ethical practices, not only to be morally correct, but also to gain whatever business advantage that lies in projecting an ethical image to consumers and employees.[32] Creating, distributing, and continually improving a company's code of ethics is one common step managers can take to establish an ethical workplace.

Another step managers can take to create an ethical workplace is to set up a special office or department that is responsible for ensuring the organization's practices are ethical. For example, management at Martin Marietta, a major supplier of missile systems and aircraft components, has established a corporate ethics office as a tangible sign to all employees that management is serious about encouraging ethical practices within the company (see Figure 3.6).

Another way to promote ethics in the workplace is to furnish organization members with appropriate training. General Dynamics, McDonnell Douglas, Chemical Bank, and American Can Company are examples of corporations that conduct train-

To ensure continuing attention to matters of ethics and standards on the part of all Martin Marietta employees, the Corporation has established the Corporate Ethics Office. The Director of Corporate Ethics is charged with responsibility for monitoring performance under this Code of Ethics and for resolving concerns presented to the Ethics Office.

Martin Marietta calls on every employee to report any violation or apparent violation of the Code. The Corporation strongly encourages employees to work with their supervisors in making such reports, and in addition, provides to employees the right to report violations directly to the Corporate Ethics Office. Prompt reporting of violations is considered to be in the best interest of all.

Employee reports will be handled in absolute confidence. No employee will suffer indignity or retaliation because of a report he or she makes to the Ethics Office...

The Chairman of the Corporate Ethics Committee will be the President of the Corporation. The Committee will consist of five other employees of the Corporation, including representatives of the Corporation's operating elements, each of whom will be appointed by the Chairman of the Committee subject to the approval of the Audit and Ethics Committee of the Corporation's Board of Directors.

The Chairman of the Corporate Ethics Committee reports to the Audit and Ethics Committee of the Martin Marietta Corporation Board of Directors.

Figure 3.6   Martin Marietta's Corporate Ethics Statement

In a 1994 lawsuit, wearers of contact lenses charged Bausch & Lomb Inc. with charging wildly divergent prices. In the same year, the Securities and Exchange Commission, following up on a report by **Business Week** *magazine, alleged that B&L's contact division had inflated sales and profits by shipping vast quantities of unneeded lenses at the tail end of 1993. Distributors were told not to worry: They need not pay for the lenses until they had sold them. For more on B&L's failure on a variety of ethics tests, see the case at the end of Chapter 18.*

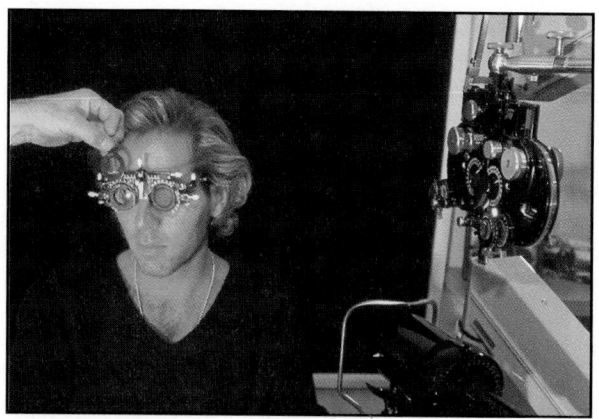

ing programs aimed at encouraging ethical practices within their organizations.[33] Such programs do not attempt to teach managers what is moral or ethical, but rather give them criteria they can use to help determine how ethical a certain action might be. Managers can feel confident that a potential action will be considered ethical by the general public if it is consistent with one or more of the following standards:[34]

1. *The golden rule*. Act in a way you would expect others to act toward you.
2. *The utilitarian principle*. Act in a way that results in the greatest good for the greatest number of people.
3. *Kant's categorical imperative*. Act in such a way that the action taken under the circumstances could be a universal law, or rule, of behavior.
4. *The professional ethic*. Take actions that would be viewed as proper by a disinterested panel of professional peers.
5. *The TV test*. Managers should always ask, "Would I feel comfortable explaining to a national TV audience why I took this action?"
6. *The legal test*. Is the proposed action or decision legal? Established laws are generally considered minimum standards for ethics.
7. *The four-way test*. Managers can feel confident that a decision is ethical if they can answer "yes" to the following questions: Is the decision truthful? Is it fair to all concerned? Will it build goodwill and better friendships? Will it be beneficial to all concerned?

Finally, managers can take responsibility for creating and sustaining conditions in which people are likely to behave ethically and for minimizing conditions in which people might be tempted to behave unethically. Two practices that commonly inspire unethical behavior in organizations are to give unusually high rewards for good performance and unusually severe punishments for poor performance. By eliminating such factors, managers can reduce the pressure on employees to perform unethically in organizations.[35]

BACK TO THE CASE   As indicated earlier, there is at present no legislation requiring Larami management to modify its Super Soaker water gun to address the youth violence problem. Were such legislation to be considered, however, legislators could take certain reasonable steps to help Larami management meet its social responsibilities in this area. For example, any laws enacted should be clear, consistent, and technically feasible to ensure both that Larami management would know what actions were expected of the company and that the technology existed to help them take these actions.

Laws should also be economically feasible, and not be applied retroactively. That is, Larami management should be able to obey the laws without going bankrupt and should

not be penalized for what has happened in the past. Larami management should also be given the flexibility to follow these laws to the company's best advantage. In other words, laws should not require management to follow specific procedures, but rather should set goals and allow the company to devise the most effective and efficient means for achieving those goals.

Ethical management is inclined to consider the well-being of other people. Assuming that Larami management is ethical, then, it will seriously consider any reasonable action to aid society in its efforts to curb youth violence. If, however, Larami significantly reduces the overall appeal of its products to young customers because of management's desire to help curb violence among youths, employees, stockholders, and others who have a legitimate interest in the organization's success will probably consider management's actions to be unethical.

Action Summary

Reread the learning objectives below. Each objective is followed by questions. Answering these questions accurately will help you retain the most important concepts discussed in this chapter. After answering each question, check your answer against the answer key at the end of this chapter. (*Hint:* If you have any doubts regarding the correct response, consult the page whose number follows the answer.)

Circle: From studying this chapter, I will attempt to acquire:

1. An understanding of the term *corporate social responsibility*.

   T,F   **a.** According to Davis, since business has certain power over society, society can and must hold business responsible for social conditions that result from the exercise of this power.

   a,b,c,d,e   **b.** Major social responsibility areas in which business can become involved include all of the following except: (a) urban affairs; (b) consumer affairs; (c) pollution control; (d) natural resource conservation; (e) all of the above are areas of potential involvement.

2. An appreciation of the arguments both for and against the assumption of social responsibilities by business.

   T,F   **a.** Some argue that since business is an influential component of society, it has the responsibility to help maintain and improve the overall welfare of society.

   a,b,c,d,e   **b.** Milton Friedman argues that business cannot be held responsible for performing social responsibility activities. He does *not* argue that: (a) doing so has the potential to cause the demise of American business as we know it today; (b) doing so is in direct conflict with the organizational objectives of business firms; (c) doing so would cause the nation to creep toward socialism, which is inconsistent with American business philosophy; (d) doing so is unethical because it requires business managers to spend money that rightfully belongs to the firm's investors; (e) doing so ultimately would either reduce returns to the firm's investors or raise prices charged to consumers.

3. Useful strategies for increasing the social responsiveness of an organization.

   a,b,c,d,e   **a.** When using the flowchart approach in social responsibility decision making, which one of the following questions is out of appropriate sequential order: (a) Can we afford this action? (b) Does a social responsibility actually exist? (c) Does the firm have a right to undertake this action? (d) Does an assessment of all interests indicate that the act is desirable? (e) Do benefits outweigh costs?

   T,F   **b.** The social obligation approach to performing social responsibility activities is concerned primarily with complying with existing legislation on the topic.

4. Insights on the planning, organizing, influencing, and controlling of social responsibility activities.

   T,F   **a.** Organizational policies should be established for social responsibility matters in the same manner as, for example, for personnel relations problems.

   a,b,c,d,e   **b.** Companies should take social responsibility measurements in all of the following areas except: (a) economic utility area; (b) economic function area; (c) quality-of-life area; (d) social investment area; (e) problem-solving area.

5. A practical plan for how society can help business meet its social obligations.

T,F   **a.** Ultimately, it is the citizens in a society who must finance the social responsibility activities of business by paying higher prices for goods and services or higher taxes or both.

a,b,c,d,e   **b.** The following is *not* one of the responsibilities that society has toward business, as listed by Jerry McAfee: (a) setting rules that are clear and concise; (b) making rules prospective, not retroactive; (c) making rules goal-setting, not procedure-prescribing; (d) making rules that are subjective, not objective; (e) making sure the rules are economically feasible.

6. An understanding of the relationship between ethics and management.

T,F   **a.** The utilitarian principle suggests that managers should act in such a way that an action taken under specific circumstances could be a universal law, or rule, of behavior.

a,b,c,d,e   **b.** Management might strive to encourage ethical behavior in organizations in order to: (a) be morally correct; (b) gain a business advantage by having employees perceive their company as ethical; (c) gain a business advantage by having customers perceive the company as ethical; (d) avoid possible costly legal fees; (e) all of the above.

T,F   **c.** Once developed, a company's code of ethics generally does not have to be monitored or revised for at least two years.

T,F   **d.** Some managers create a special "office of ethics" to show employees the critical importance of ethics.

Introductory Case Wrap-Up

"Larami Corporation 'Super Soaks' Society?" (p. 50) and its related back-to-the-case sections were written to help you better understand the management concepts contained in this chapter. Answer the following discussion questions about this introductory case to enrich your understanding of the chapter content:

1. Do you think that Larami managers have a responsibility to somehow modify the situation involving the Super Soaker so that this product does not encourage youth violence? Explain.

2. Assuming that Larami managers have such a responsibility, under what conditions could they commit the company to assume that responsibility?

3. Assuming that Larami managers have such a responsibility, when would it be relatively difficult for them to get the company to live up to it?

Issues for Review and Discussion

1. Define *corporate social responsibility*.
2. Explain three of the major propositions in the Davis model of corporate social responsibility.
3. Summarize three arguments that support the pursuit of social responsibility objectives by business.
4. Summarize Milton Friedman's arguments against the pursuit of social responsibility objectives by business.
5. What is meant by the phrase *performing required social responsibility activities*?
6. What is meant by the phrase *voluntarily performing social responsibility activities*?
7. List five positive and five negative outcomes a business might experience as a result of performing social responsibility activities.
8. What is the difference between social responsibility and social responsiveness?
9. Discuss the decision-making process that can help managers increase the social responsiveness of their organizations.
10. In your own words, explain the main differences among Sethi's three approaches to meeting social responsibilities.
11. Which of Sethi's approaches has the most potential for increasing the social responsiveness of a management system? Explain.
12. What is the overall relationship between the four main management functions and the performance of social responsibility activities by business?
13. What suggestions does this chapter make concerning the planning of social responsibility activities?
14. Describe the process of turning social responsibility policy into action.
15. How do organizing and influencing social responsibility activities relate to planning social responsibility activities?
16. List and define four main areas in which any management system can take measurements to control social responsibility activities.
17. What is a social audit? How should the results of a social audit be used by management?
18. How can society help business meet its social responsibilities?
19. What is the relationship between ethics and social responsibility?
20. Explain how managers can try to judge if a particular action is ethical.
21. What steps can managers take to make their organizations more ethical workplaces?

Action Summary Answer Key

1. a. T, pp. 51–52
   b. e, p. 53
2. a. T, p. 53
   b. c, pp. 53–54

3. a. a, pp. 59–60
   b. T, p. 60
4. a. T, p. 62
   b. a, pp. 64–65

5. a. T, p. 68
   b. d, p. 68

6. a. F, p. 71
   b. e, p. 71
   c. F, p. 71
   d. T, p. 71

Case Study

Dow Corning: A Question of Legality or Ethics?

Corporate social responsibility can be defined as the managerial obligation to take action to protect and improve both the welfare of society and the interests of the organization. In recent years, the public has placed more importance on corporate social responsibility, and businesses that violate this responsibility have suffered in both the courts and the marketplace.

The dilemma some companies confront in trying to meet their social responsibilities without sacrificing corporate objectives is exemplified by Dow Corning's legal problems over the safety of the company's silicone breast implants. Dow Corning introduced silicone breast-implant products in 1963, and by 1994, the company was enjoying $2.2 billion in annual sales of its line of silicone products. In 1984, however, the company was sued for fraudulently misrepresenting its product, and lost the case. This was only the first of many such suits Dow Corning lost. So far, the company's silicone implant business has cost it more than $1 billion in legal expenses, plunging it into bankruptcy and exposing its parent companies, Dow Chemical Company and Corning, Inc., to legal action as well.

John Swanson was 30 years old when he went to work for Dow Corning in 1966. He moved from the advertising to the industrial marketing department, and then went on to write speeches for CEOs William C. Goggin and Jack S. Luddington. In the mid-1970s, as corporations came under attack for unethical practices both at home and abroad, Swanson was given the task of creating an ethics committee to help Dow Corning measure its social responsibility.

Swanson and his new committee decided to promote the belief that the corporation should behave as if it were constantly in the public view. Meetings were held with managers who were part of Dow Corning's global operations in order to reinforce this decision and to determine ways to implement it. Implementation was considered so successful that by 1984 Swanson was a nationally recognized expert on the subject of corporate ethics. Unfortunately, Swanson's position was undermined when his superiors proved unwilling to allow the

business ethics he preached to take precedence over the corporation's profit objectives in the matter of silicone implants.

Swanson was not a passive bystander during investigations into the ethics of Dow Corning's marketing of its silicone implants. In 1974, his own wife, Colleen, had had breast implants, and almost immediately afterward had developed illnesses for which no doctor could find a cause. It was fully 15 years after the surgery before Colleen Swanson learned of another woman who had also had the Dow implants and was suffering from similar maladies. Eventually, Colleen Swanson had the breast implants removed and filed suit against Dow Corning.

The next chapter in the story occurred in 1989, when the Food and Drug Administration was sued by a consumer group demanding to know the results of studies the FDA had done on the silicone gel used in breast implants. It became apparent that breast implants were not as strictly regulated by the FDA as other health-related products. After several reports concerning the effects of faulty implants appeared in the media, the adverse publicity prompted congressional hearings into the matter.

In December 1990, John Swanson received a memo alleging that some Dow Corning executives were attempting to destroy damaging internal reports on the complications of implant surgery. After an unsuccessful attempt to force the company to investigate these charges, Swanson resigned from Dow Corning to become an ethics consultant.

In 1991, a court awarded $7.3 million to a woman who had sued Dow Corning for damages resulting from her breast implants, and the verdict was upheld on appeal. In January 1992, Dow Corning announced that it was declaring a 45-day moratorium on the sale of breast implants, and in March of that year, the company formally ceased production of the implants. Three years later, a court determined that the corporation was unable to pay the $4.23 billion it estimated was needed to settle all the lawsuits that had been against it, and the company declared bankruptcy. Other health-product manufactur-

ers have also had to contend with a barrage of lawsuits concerning silicone implants. Bristol-Myers Squibb, for example, has spent millions of dollars defending itself. Two other companies named in these lawsuits, Baxter Healthcare and 3M, have also expended large amounts on legal defense.

An interesting issue raised by this ethics struggle is whether so-called mass-tort lawsuits are valid. Such lawsuits are filed by hundreds—even thousands—of plaintiffs charging a company or product with the same violations. They often arise, as in the Dow Corning scenario, after a large settlement is awarded to one plaintiff—what was a trickle of lawsuits becomes an avalanche as the publicity about the defective product snowballs. It is then advantageous—and profitable to lawyers—to combine many suits into one mass-tort lawsuit.

Dow Corning—along with many other companies that fear being bankrupted by a mass-tort action—has pressed lawmakers to pass tort reform measures that will replace mass torts with "common issue" trials. These types of trials would set a limit on a company's liability.

Whatever the outcome of tort reform efforts, many people believe the legal issues in such cases as Dow Corning's are beside the point. For them, the issue is ethics.

Questions:

1. What should a corporation learn from the experiences of Dow Corning? Why was setting up an ethics committee insufficient to monitor social responsibility?
2. How might Dow Corning argue its case using Milton Friedman's argument against corporations assuming social responsibility?
3. Had Dow Corning performed a social audit, what would have been issues raised by the audit and what would have been the likely outcome?
4. What was the final outcome of Dow Corning's behavior? Role-play a conversation among Dow managers in 1963, when the company introduced silicone implants. Could you have convinced them to drop the project? Explain.

Skills Exercise

Based on the definition of *business ethics* given in the text, do you believe that Dow Corning acted ethically or unethically? Explain. Conduct research to create a timeline of events in the Dow Corning case. Analyze the sequence of events and underscore those events that you believe support your opinion. Use your timeline to prepare a short presentation (no more than 5 minutes) of your opinions and the points that support them.

Challenge: If you take the position that Dow Corning acted irresponsibly, analyze the timeline to identify points at which the company acted unethically. In your opinion, what action(s) should the company have taken to prevent—or rectify—any unethical behavior?

The Internet learning materials that accompany this chapter can be found at
http://www.profcerto.com
Additional information can be found on the inside front and back covers of this text.

4
chapter

MANAGING IN THE GLOBAL ARENA

STUDENT LEARNING OBJECTIVES

From studying this chapter, I will attempt to acquire:

1. An understanding of international management and its importance to modern managers.
2. An understanding of what constitutes a multinational corporation.
3. Insights concerning the risk involved in investing in international operations.
4. Insights about those who work in multinational corporations.
5. Knowledge about managing multinational corporations.
6. Knowledge about managing multinational organizations versus transnational organizations.
7. Insights about what comparative management is and how it might help managers do their jobs better.
8. Ideas on how to become a better manager through the study of Japanese management techniques.

CHAPTER OUTLINE

Baskin-Robbins Brings U.S. Ice Cream to Vietnam

Baskin-Robbins, an ice cream company based in Glendale, California, has a strong tradition of high-quality products. Rather than rest on its laurels, however, the company has lately taken several very aggressive steps to broaden its business in a very competitive marketplace.

One of these steps is the recent unveiling of the new Baskin-Robbins line of "Incredibles." These are ice cream cakes produced through a partnership with Sara Lee Corporation. Baskin-Robbins has invested nearly $8 million in advertising for this new product.

In an effort to grow the company, Baskin-Robbins management is also expanding sales at nontraditional store sites. For example, the company is exploring the sale of its new Yogurt Gone Crazy hardpack in coffee shops like Starbucks Coffee. It is also testing ice cream fountains in restaurants like Denny's and Miami Subs.

Perhaps Baskin-Robbins' most aggressive attempt to grow its business, however, involves a business venture in Southeast Asia. By opening a Baskin-Robbins outlet in Ho Chi Minh City, the company has brought American ice cream back to Vietnam. Baskin-Robbins was the first fast-food company to open a store in Vietnam after President Clinton recently lifted a 19-year economic embargo of that country.

According to the manager of the new Vietnamese outlet, Bui Vi Hoanh, the Baskin-Robbins store is attracting about 100 customers a day. This is a significant number of customers since a single-scoop cone sells for 18,000 dong (about $1.60), which is more than a day's wage for the average Vietnamese factory worker. A double-scoop sundae costs about three days' wages.

Ho Chi Minh City was chosen for the store site because it is the most prosperous city in Vietnam and the country's chief tourist destination. Moreover, the older residents of the city remember American ice cream from the 1960s and 1970s, when thousands of U.S. soldiers were stationed there during the Vietnamese War.

The Baskin-Robbins store in Vietnam is risky but potentially highly profitable. Only the future will tell if Baskin-Robbins has made a sound management decision.

In order to grow its business in the international market, Baskin-Robbins has built new stores like this one in Ho Chi Minh City—thus bringing American ice cream to Vietnam after an absence of 19 years.

what's ahead

The introductory case illustrates several aggressive steps that Baskin-Robbins management has taken to maintain the company's competitiveness. The boldest of these steps is opening a store in Vietnam. This move toward expanding the company's international presence is consistent with a worldwide trend in corporate management. This chapter provides insights about the challenge that firms like Baskin-Robbins face in expanding internationally and will give you an overview of the international management arena. The major topics covered are:

1. The need to manage internationally.
2. The multinational corporation and its workforce.
3. Management functions and multinational corporations.
4. Transnational organizations.
5. Comparative management.

MANAGING ACROSS THE GLOBE: WHY?

Most U.S. companies see great opportunities in the international marketplace today.[1] While the U.S. population is growing steadily but slowly, the population in many other countries is exploding. For example, it has been estimated that China, India, and Indonesia together had more than 2 billion people, or 40 percent of the world's population, in 1990.[2] Obviously, such countries offer a strong profit potential for aggressive businesspeople throughout the world.

This potential does not come without serious risk, however. Managers who attempt to manage in a global context face formidable challenges. Some of these challenges are: the cultural differences among workers from different countries, different technology levels from country to country, and laws and political systems that can vary immensely from one nation to the next.

The remaining major sections of this chapter deal with the intricacies of managing in a global context by emphasizing the following:

1. Fundamentals of international management.
2. Categories of organizations by international involvement.
3. Comparative management (with an emphasis on Japanese management).

FUNDAMENTALS OF INTERNATIONAL MANAGEMENT

International management is simply the performance of management activities across national borders. It entails reaching organizational objectives by extending management activities to include an emphasis on organizations in foreign countries. The trend toward increased international management, or *globalization*, is now widely recognized. The primary question for most firms is not *whether* to globalize, but *how* and *how fast* to do so and how to measure global progress over time.[3]

International management can take any of several different forms, from simply analyzing and fighting competition in foreign markets to establishing a formal partnership with a foreign company. AMP, Inc., for example, has been vigorously fighting competition in a foreign market. This company, a manufacturer of electrical parts, headquartered in Harrisburg, Pennsylvania, has achieved outstanding success by gaining significant control over a portion of its multinational market. The company built factories in 17 countries because experience showed management that competitors could best be beaten in foreign markets if AMP actually produced products within those markets. A message recently sent to AMP stockholders by company president William J. Hudson indicates that the company is continuing to make good progress in the international arena. Hudson has promised to persist in his efforts to develop AMP into a "globe-able" organization.[4]

International management is the performance of management activities across national borders

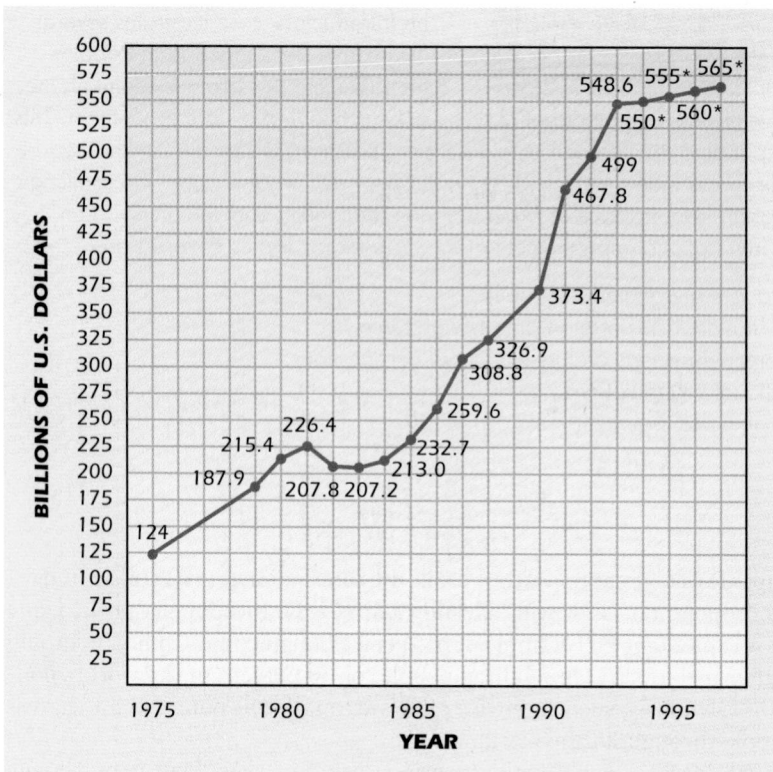

Figure 4.1   Growth in U.S. investment
*(Author forecast based on past data)

An example of a formal international partnership involves Toshiba Corporation and Time Warner. Toshiba Corporation, a Japanese computer manufacturer, and Time Warner, a communications conglomerate that owns a major Hollywood film studio, recently formed a partnership aimed at developing a new technology for presenting movies to consumers. This technology is called digital videodisc (DVD). In a natural division of labor, Toshiba will focus on making the hardware needed to deliver the new technology, and Time Warner will provide the movies to be presented on DVD. Both companies hope the partnership will give them an edge over formidable competitors like Sony.[5]

The notable trend that already exists in the United States and other countries toward developing business relationships in and with foreign countries is expected to accelerate even more in the future. As Figures 4.1 and 4.2 illustrate, U.S. investment in foreign countries and investment by foreign countries in the United States have been growing since 1970 and are expected to continue growing, with only slight slowdowns or setbacks in recessionary periods. As an interesting side note, in the 1990s the growth rate of foreign investment in developing countries like India and China has increased, while the growth rate of foreign investment in the United States, Japan, and the European Community has slowed somewhat.[6] Information of this nature has spurred both management educators and practicing managers to insist that an understanding of international management is necessary for a thorough contemporary understanding of the fundamentals of management.[7]

BACK TO THE CASE   As you read in the introductory case, Baskin-Robbins is a U.S organization that now operates in the global arena. In opening a store in Ho Chi Minh City, Baskin-Robbins, in essence, expanded management activities across the U.S. border into Vietnam. Given the international trend toward greater foreign investments, Baskin-Robbins is likely to continue to emphasize worldwide

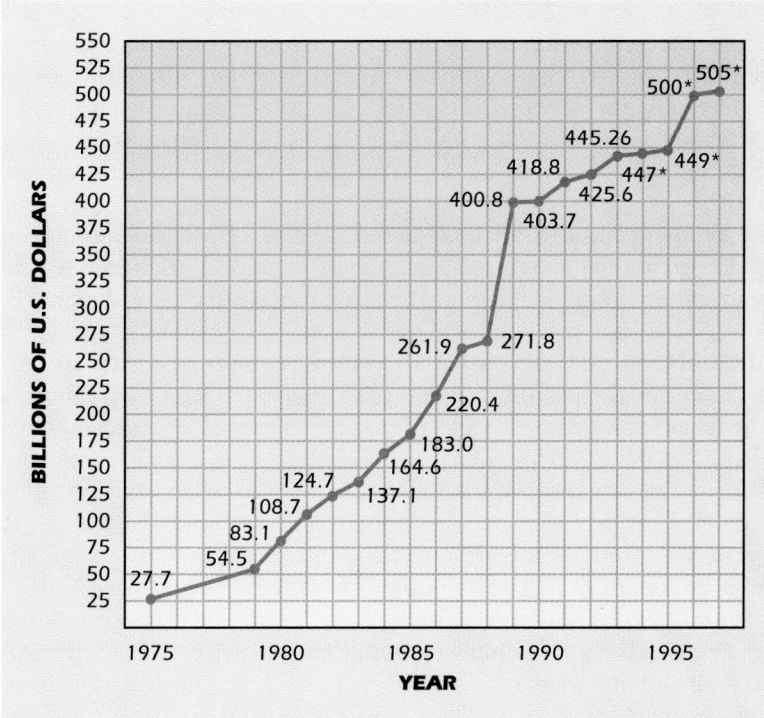

Figure 4.2   Growth in foreign investment in the United States
*(Author forecast based on past data)

expansion and foreign companies will attempt to compete in Baskin-Robbins' market in the United States. It is only a matter of time, for example, until companies like Delta Dairy, an ice cream maker based in Athens, Greece, start expanding to the United States.

CATEGORIZING ORGANIZATIONS BY INTERNATIONAL INVOLVEMENT

A number of different categories have evolved to describe the extent to which organizations are involved in the international arena. These categories are domestic organizations, international organizations, multinational organizations, and transnational or global organizations. As Figure 4.3 suggests, this categorization format actually describes a continuum of international involvement, with domestic organizations representing the least and transnational organizations the most international involvement. Although the format may not be perfect, it is very useful for explaining the primary ways in which companies operate in the international realm.[8] The following sections describe these categories in more detail.

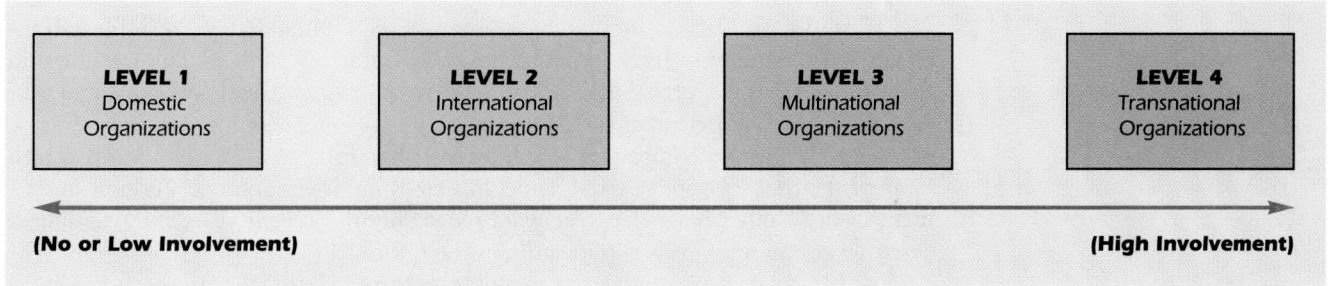

Figure 4.3   Continuum of international involvement

A **domestic organization** is a company that essentially operates within a single country.

Domestic Organizations

Domestic organizations are organizations that essentially operate within a single country. These organizations normally not only acquire necessary resources within a single country but also sell their goods or services within that same country. Although domestic organizations may occasionally make an international sale or acquire some needed resource from a foreign supplier, the overwhelming bulk of their business activity takes place within the country where they are based.

Although this category is not determined by size, most domestic organizations today are quite small. Even smaller business organizations, however, are following the trend and becoming increasingly involved in the international arena.

An **international organization** is a company that is primarily based within a single country but has continuing, meaningful transactions in other countries.

International Organizations

International organizations are organizations that are primarily based within a single country but have continuing, meaningful international transactions—such as making sales and/or purchases of materials—in other countries. Nu Horizons is an example of a small company that can be classified as an international organization. This distributor of electronic goods made mainly by some 40 U.S. manufacturers has about 5,000 customers and is the fastest-growing company in Amityville, New York. Nu Horizons is an international organization because an important part of its business is to act as the primary North American distributor of electronic components made by Japan's NIC electronics company.[9]

In summary, international organizations are more extensively involved in the international arena than are domestic organizations, but less so than either multinational or transnational organizations.

Multinational Organizations: The Multinational Corporation

The *multinational organization*, commonly called the *multinational corporation (MNC)*, represents the third level of international involvement. This section of the text defines the multinational corporation, discusses the complexities involved in managing such a corporation, describes the risks associated with its operations, explores the diversity of the multinational workforce, and explains how the major management functions relate to managing the multinational corporation.

Defining the Multinational Corporation

A **multinational corporation** (**MNC**) is a company that has significant operations in more than one country.

The term *multinational corporation* first appeared in American dictionaries about 1970, and has since been defined in various ways in business publications and textbooks. For the purposes of this text, a **multinational corporation** is a company that has significant operations in more than one country. Essentially, a multinational corporation is an organization that is involved in doing business at the international level. It carries out its activities on an international scale that disregards national boundaries and it is guided by a common strategy from a corporation center.[10]

A list of the ten largest multinationals in this country (see Table 4.1) includes four corporations whose major business is energy: Exxon, Mobil, Texaco, and Chevron. As the table implies, multinational organizations have significant foreign revenues, related profits, and foreign assets.

A list of the 12 largest foreign investments in the United States (see Table 4.2) includes an investment in JE Seagram by Seagram Company Limited, an investment in Shell Oil by Royal Dutch/Shell Group, and an investment in British Petroleum of America by British Petroleum. Other significant investments on the list include those in popularly known companies like Burger King, Pillsbury, Pearle Vision, Smith Corona, Hardee's Food Systems, and Ground Round Restaurants. Foreign investment in the United States has reached a record high in recent years and will almost certainly continue to grow significantly in the future.

Neil H. Jacoby explains that companies go through six stages to reach the highest degree of multinationalization. As Table 4.3 indicates, multinational corporations

Table 4.1

The Effect of Foreign Operations on the Ten Largest U.S. Multinationals

1993 RANK	COMPANY	FOREIGN REVENUE AS PERCENT OF TOTAL	FOREIGN PROFIT AS PERCENT OF TOTAL PROFITS	FOREIGN ASSETS AS PERCENT OF TOTAL ASSETS
1	Exxon	77.3	77.0	56.4
2	General Motors	28.0	91.0	21.3
3	Mobil	67.5	79.8	62.6
4	IBM	59.0	D-D	55.1
5	Ford Motor	30.3	D-P	26.0
6	Texaco	53.5	51.8	39.1
7	Citicorp	64.5	81.3	51.3
8	El du Pont de Nemours	51.4	99.8	37.3
9	Chevron	41.1	67.0	55.2
10	Procter & Gamble	52.1	65.1	40.7

D-D: Deficit to Deficit
D-P: Deficit to Profit
Source: "Getting the Welcome Carpet," *Forbes,* July 18, 1994, p. 276.

can range from slightly multinationalized organizations that simply export products to a foreign country to highly multinationalized organizations that have some of their owners in other countries. According to Alfred M. Zeien, the chief executive officer of Gillette Company, it can take up to 25 years to build a management team with the requisite skills, experience, and abilities to mold an organization into a highly developed multinational company.[11]

In general, the larger the organization, the greater the likelihood it participates in international operations of some sort. Companies such as General Electric, Lockheed, and du Pont, which have annually accumulated over $1 billion from export sales, support this generalization. There are exceptions, however. BRK Electronics, for example, a small firm in Aurora, Illinois, has won a substantial share of world sales of smoke detectors. By setting up local distributors in Italy, France, and England, BRK caused its export sales to climb from $124,000 in one year to $4 million five years later.[12] As noted earlier, an increasing number of smaller organizations are undertaking international operations.

Even small U.S. companies are beginning to participate in international operations. With a little help from a Japanese partner, Petrofsky's International, a St. Louis-based bagel maker, has opened a store in Tokyo.

Table 4.2

The 12 Largest Foreign Investments in the United States

1993 RANK	FOREIGN INVESTOR	COUNTRY	US INVESTMENT	% OWNED	INDUSTRY	REVENUE ($MIL)	NET INCOME ($MIL)	ASSETS ($MIL)
1	Seagram Co Ltd	Canada	El du Pont de Nemours	24	chemicals, energy	32,732	566.0	37,053
			JE Seagram	100	beverages	3,784	180.0	9,182
						36,516		
2	Royal Dutch/Shell Group	Netherlands/UK	Shell Oil	100	energy, chemicals	20,853	781.0	26,851
3	British Petroleum	UK	BP America	100	energy	16,006	NA	18,293
4	Sony Corp	Japan	Sony Music Entertainment	100	music entertainment			
			Sony Picture Entertainment	100	movies	12,195	NA	12,657
			Sony Electronics	100	consumer electronics			
5	Grand Metropolitan	UK	Burger King	100	fast food	5,250		
			Pillsbury	100	food processing	3,700		
			Heublein	100	wines and spirits	1,600	NA	6,131
			Pearle Vision	100	eye care retailing	600		
			Other companies	100	wines and spirits	625		
						11,775		
6	Hanson	UK	Hanson Industries	100	mining, aggregates, chemicals	7,975	758.6	18,700
			Quantum Chemical	100	petrochemicals	2,294	-222.5	4,980
			Smith Corona	48	office supplies	309	-9.0	198
			Ground Round Restaurants	33	restaurant chain	233	5.3	152
			Marine Harvest International	27	food processing	137	9.4	104
						10,948		
7	Tengelmann Group	Germany	Great A&P Tea	53	supermarkets	10,384	4.0	3,099
8	Nestlé	Switzerland	Nestlé USA	100	food processing	8,646	NA	NA
			Alcon Laboratories	100	pharmaceuticals			
	L'Oreal	France	Cosmair	>50	cosmetics	1,347	NA	NA
						9,993		
9	B.A.T. Industries	UK	Brown & Williamson Tobacco	100	tobacco	2,774	NA	NA
			Farmers Group	100	insurance	1,709	508.5	6,999
	Imasco	Canada	Hardee's Food Systems	100	fast food	4,957	NA	843
						9,440		
10	Toyota Motor Corp	Japan	Toyota Motor Mfg	100	automotive	4,000E	NA	NA
			New United Motor Mfg	50	automotive	3,600E	NA	NA
	Nippondenso	Japan	Nippondenso America	100	auto parts	1,800	NA	NA
						9,400		
11	Petroleos de Venezuela	Venezuela	Citgo Petroleum	100	refining, marketing	9,107	162.1	3,866
12	Unilever NV	Netherlands	Unilever United States	100	food processing, personal prods	8,970	NA	8,560
	Unilever Pic	UK						

NA: Not Available

Source: "A Year for the Record Books," *Forbes*, July 18, 1994, p. 2.

Table 4.3					
Six Stages of Multinationalization					
STAGE 1	STAGE 2	STAGE 3	STAGE 4	STAGE 5	STAGE 6
Exports its products to foreign countries	Establishes sales organizations abroad	Licenses use of its patterns and know-how to foreign firms that make and sell its products	Establishes foreign manufacturing facilities	Multinationalizes management from top to bottom	Multinationalizes ownership of corporate stock

U.S. COMPANIES SEND HAZARDOUS WASTE TO MEXICO

ETHICS SPOTLIGHT

The export of hazardous wastes by companies in more developed countries to companies in less developed countries is becoming commonplace. For example, U.S. companies commonly send large quantities of such waste to Mexico for disposal by Mexican companies. Although accidents related to this business could cause extensive environmental damage and even result in a loss of human life, useful international legislation governing the export of hazardous waste is virtually nonexistent.

Perhaps partly because of the absence of such legislation, there is much public controversy over the ethics of the international trade in the disposal of hazardous wastes. Citizens of underdeveloped countries have demonstrated against the disposal of hazardous wastes from developed countries in their areas, insisting that they have a right to a livable environment. They charge that dumping is a form of racism and should be halted immediately.

Managers involved in international hazardous waste disposal should ensure that the interests of domestic and foreign societies are protected along with the interests of their organizations. Although providing such protection is largely voluntary at this time, the evolution of legislation in this area will undoubtedly mandate protections in the future. To cope with the problem, the Japanese have drawn up a 100-year plan, called New Earth 21, that aims at developing ecologically efficient technology that will provide clean energy to the world.≈

Since 1987, Japan's Matsushita Electrical Industrial Co. has opened 13 new subsidiaries in the nation of Malaysia. The company has shown its sensitivity to the large Muslim segment of its workforce by providing special prayer rooms in each plant and permitting two prayer sessions during each shift.

Complexities of Managing the Multinational Corporation

From the discussion so far, it should be clear that international management and domestic management are quite different. Classic management thought indicates that international management differs from domestic management because it involves operating:[13]

1. Within different national sovereignties.
2. Under widely disparate economic conditions.
3. Among people living within different value systems and institutions.
4. In places experiencing the industrial revolution at different times.
5. Often over greater geographical distance.
6. In national markets varying greatly in population and area.

Figure 4.4 shows some of the more important management implications of these six variables and some of the relationships among them. Consider, for example, the first variable. Different national sovereignties generate different legal systems. In turn, each legal system implies a unique set of rights and obligations involving property, taxation, antitrust (control of monopoly) law, corporate law, and contract law. In turn, these rights and obligations require the firm to acquire the skills necessary to assess the international legal considerations. Such skills are very different from those required in a purely domestic setting.

Risk and the Multinational Corporation

Developing a multinational corporation obviously requires a substantial investment in foreign operations. Normally, managers who make foreign investments expect that such investments will accomplish the following:

1. Reduce or eliminate high transportation costs.
2. Allow participation in the rapid expansion of a market abroad.
3. Provide foreign technical, design, and marketing skills.
4. Earn higher profits.[14]

The **parent company** is the company investing in international operations.

The **host country** is the country in which an investment is made by a foreign company.

Unfortunately, many managers decide to internationalize their companies without having an accurate understanding of the risks involved in making such a decision.[15] For example, political complications involving the **parent company** (the company investing in the international operations) and various factions within the **host country** (the country in which the investment is made) could prevent the parent company from realizing the desirable outcomes just listed. Some companies attempt to minimize this kind of risk by adding standard clauses to their contracts stipulating that in the event of a business controversy that cannot be resolved by the parties involved, they will agree to mediation by a mutually selected mediator.[16]

The likelihood of achieving desirable outcomes related to foreign investments will probably always be somewhat uncertain and will certainly vary from country to country. Nevertheless, managers faced with making a foreign investment must assess this likelihood as accurately as possible. Obviously, a poor decision to invest in another country can cause serious financial problems for the organization.

The Workforce of Multinational Corporations

As organizations become more global, their organization members tend to become more diverse. Managers of multinational corporations face the continual challenge of building a competitive business team made up of people of different races who speak different languages and come from different parts of the world. The following sections perform two functions that should help managers build such teams:

1. They furnish details and related insights about the various types of organization members generally found in multinational corporations.

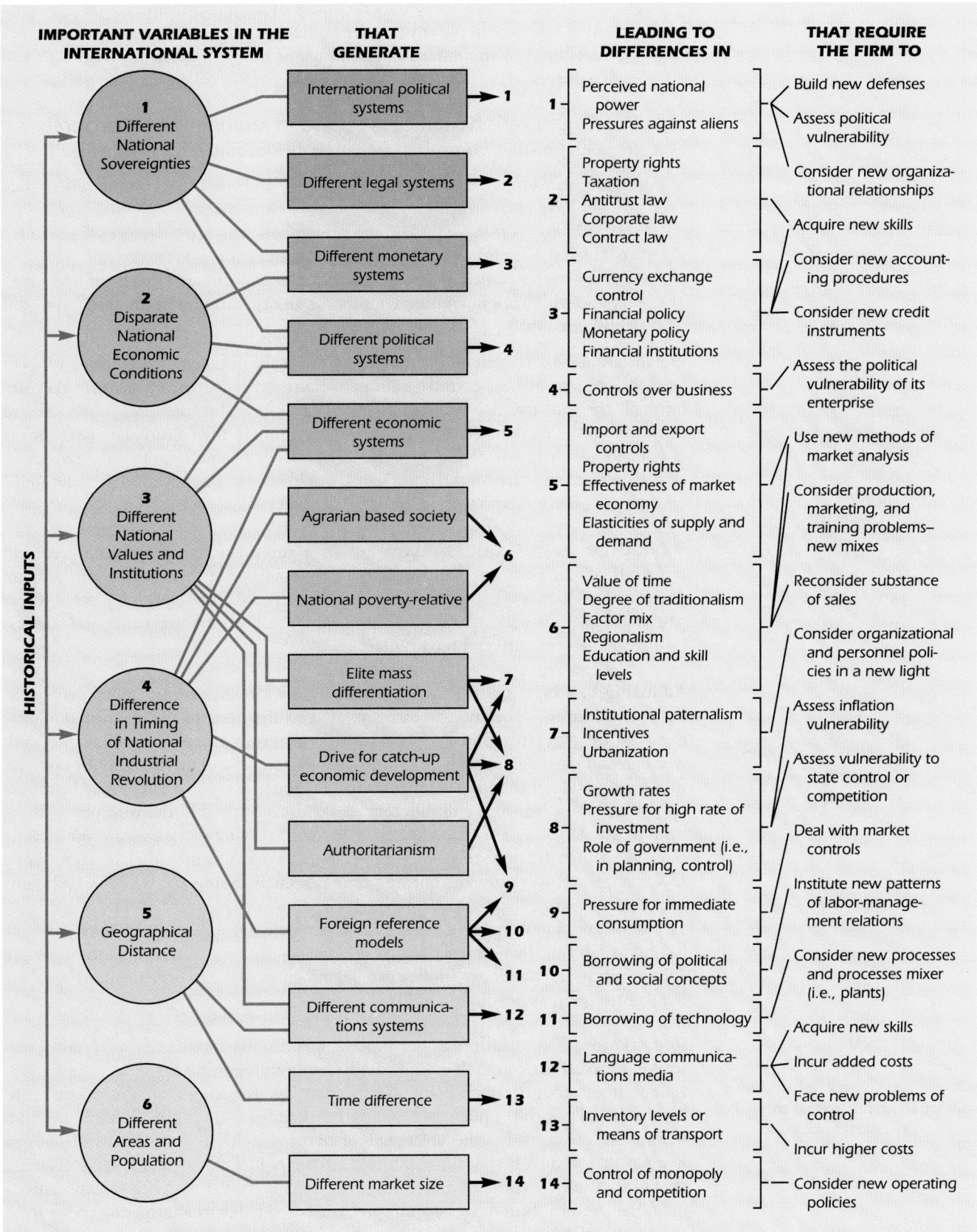

Figure 4.4   Management implications based on six variables in international systems and relationships among them

2. They describe the adjustments members of multinational organizations normally must make in order to become efficient and effective contributors to organization goal attainment and also suggest how managers can facilitate these adjustments.

Types of Organization Members Found in Multinational Corporations

Workers in multinational organizations can be divided into three basic types:

- *Expatriates:* Organization members who live and work in a country where they do not have citizenship.
- *Host-Country Nationals:* Organization members who are citizens of the country in which the facility of a foreign-based organization is located.
- *Third-Country Nationals:* Organization members who are citizens of one country and who work in another country for an organization headquartered in still another country.

Organizations that operate in the global businessplace often employ all three types of worker. The use of host-country nationals, however, is increasing because they are normally the least expensive to employ. Such employees, for example, do not need to be moved to the work location or to undergo training in the culture, language, or tax laws of the country where the organization is doing business. Both expatriates and third-country nationals, on the other hand, would have to be moved to the new country and normally undergo such training.

Workforce Adjustments
Working in a multinational corporation requires more difficult adjustments than working in an organization that focuses primarily on domestic activities. Probably the two most difficult challenges—which pertain to expatriates and third-country nationals rather than to host-country nationals—are adjusting to a new culture and repatriation.

Adjusting to a New Culture.   Upon arrival in a foreign country, many people experience confusion, anxiety, and stress related to the need to make cultural adjustments in their organizational and personal lives. From a personal viewpoint, food, weather, and language may all be dramatically different, and driving may be done on the "wrong" side of the road. From an organizational viewpoint, there may be different attitudes toward work and different perceptions of time in the workplace. To illustrate, the Japanese are renowned for their hard-driving work ethic, while Americans take a slightly more relaxed attitude toward work. On the other hand, in many U.S. companies, working past quitting time is seen as exemplary, while in Germany, someone who works late is commonly criticized.

Members of multinational corporations normally have the formidable task of adjusting to a drastically new organizational situation. Managers must help these people adjust quickly and painlessly so they can begin contributing to organizational goal attainment as soon as possible.

Repatriation is the process of bringing individuals who have been working abroad back to their home country and reintegrating them into the organization's home-country operations.

Repatriation. **Repatriation** is the process of bringing individuals who have been working abroad back to their home country and reintegrating them into the organization's home-country operations. Repatriation has its own set of adjustment problems, especially with people who have lived abroad for a long time. Some individuals become so accustomed to the advantages of an overseas lifestyle that they greatly miss it when they return home. Others idealize their homeland so much while they are abroad that they become disappointed when it fails to live up to their expectations upon their return. Still others acquire foreign-based habits that are undesirable from the organization's viewpoint and that are hard to break.

Managers must be patient and understanding with repatriates. Some organizations provide repatriates with counseling so that they will be better prepared to handle readjustment problems. Others have found that providing employees, before they

leave for foreign duty, with a written agreement specifying what their new duties and career path will be when they return home reduces friction and facilitates the repatriate's adjustment.

The trend toward participating in the international business arena will inevitably result in more and more organization members serving as expatriates. The following PEOPLE PERSPECTIVES feature presents some useful insights into how managers can facilitate the adjustments that expatriate organization members will need to make in their foreign assignments.

HELPING EXPATRIATES TO ADJUST

PEOPLE PERSPECTIVES

As more companies initiate or expand overseas operations, the need to send employees on international assignments will increase. Because many companies use overseas assignments as a means of assessing which employees should be promoted to top-level positions, success in such positions is critically important to both the individual and the organization.

Unfortunately, the success rate in foreign assignments is unimpressive. Up to 40 percent of expatriate employees leave their posts early. The reasons vary, but early termination is generally accompanied by negatives for both the organization and the employee. Each failure to complete a foreign assignment costs companies between $50,000 and $150,000 and usually derails the employee's career.

The primary reason for early termination is that the employee was not properly prepared for the foreign assignment. Poorly prepared expatriates find it very difficult to make the personal and organizational adjustments necessary for success in positions abroad.

Management can take certain steps to better prepare organization members for expatriate positions. For example, organization members who are eligible for expatriate positions should be involved in discussions concerning the challenges of working in another country before they are actually given an international assignment.

Employees chosen for an assignment should be given an early start on learning the language and etiquette of the host country where they will work, as well as the culture and value system of that country.

Finally, management should develop and refine the stress management skills of future expatriates. These employees will undoubtedly encounter high levels of stress related to their new foreign job, and they must know how to manage such stress if they are to be successful organization members.≈

BACK TO THE CASE

As Baskin-Robbins expands internationally, it will become more of a multinational corporation—that is, an organization with significant operations in more than one country. In any company, international management is a complex undertaking. Baskin-Robbins managers will have to learn how to operate successfully within different countries that are geographically separated and that are characterized by different economic conditions, cultures, technology levels, market sizes, and laws. Baskin-Robbins' experience with foreign expansion illustrates the potential rewards available to managers who can handle the complexity of doing business in other countries.

Naturally, management at Baskin-Robbins has tried to minimize the risk of investing in Vietnam. Other managements might see expansion into Vietnam as too risky to attempt at this time because Vietnam is still unstable economically and thus perilous for foreign investors. Moreover, many U.S. managers worry about an unfriendly reception to U.S. business because of the scars left by the Vietnam War.

The United States, however, is now attempting to establish a normal trading relationship with Vietnam, so Baskin-Robbins may have much to gain from being one of the first companies in its industry to establish a presence in Vietnam. Still, the company must be aware that the political situation between the United States and Vietnam can change quickly again. Therefore, Baskin-Robbins management should monitor the political relationship between the two countries constantly so that it can quickly devise a response if the relationship changes.

Baskin-Robbins management has obviously decided that its foreign investment entails a tolerable amount of risk when weighed against the prospect of increased return from operations in Vietnam. Only a significant period of operations in Vietnam will furnish the necessary feedback to determine whether this decision was sound.

Perhaps the most important variable for success in the Vietnamese store is the employees working there. Baskin-Robbins must determine the best combination of expatriates, host-country nationals, and third-country nationals to run the store. Whatever blend of human resources the company ultimately decides upon, management should be sensitive in helping individuals adjust both personally and organizationally to an international situation. In addition, if expatriates are involved in running the store, the company should plan on helping them adjust when they are repatriated.

MANAGEMENT FUNCTIONS AND MULTINATIONAL CORPORATIONS

The sections that follow discuss the four major management functions—planning, organizing, influencing, and controlling—as they occur at multinational corporations.

Planning in Multinational Corporations

Planning was defined in Chapter 1 as determining how an organization will achieve its objectives. This definition is applicable to the management of both domestic and multinational organizations, but with some differences.

The primary difference between planning in multinational versus planning in domestic organizations is in the plans' components. Plans for the multinational organization include components that focus on the international arena, whereas plans for the domestic organization do not. For example, plans for multinational organizations could include the following:

1. Establishing a new salesforce in a foreign country.
2. Developing new manufacturing plants in other countries through purchase or construction.
3. Financing international expansion.
4. Determining which countries represent the most suitable candidates for international expansion.

Components of International Plans   Although planning for multinational corporations varies from organization to organization, the following four components are commonly included in international plans:

- Imports/exports
- License agreements
- Direct investing
- Joint ventures

This section discusses these four components as well as the responses of multinational corporations to international market agreements.

Imports/Exports.   Imports/exports planning components emphasize reaching organizational objectives by **importing** (buying goods or services from another country) or **exporting** (selling goods or services to another country).

Organizations of all sizes do importing and exporting. On the one hand, there are companies like Auburn Farms, Inc., a relatively small producer of all-natural, fat-free snack foods that imports products to be resold. Auburn Farms recently became the exclusive U.S. importer of Beacon Sweets & Chocolates of South Africa. Auburn sees its importing activities as a way of expanding and diversifying.[17] On the other hand, there are extremely large and complex organizations, such as Eastman Kodak, which exports photographic products to a number of foreign countries.[18]

Importing is buying goods or services from another country..

Exporting is selling goods or services to another country.

License Agreements.   A **license agreement** is a right granted by one company to another to use its brand name, technology, product specifications, and so on in the manufacture or sale of goods and services. Naturally, the company to which the license is extended pays some fee for the privilege. International planning components in this area involve reaching organizational objectives through either the purchase or the sale of licenses at the international level.

For example, the Tosoh Corporation recently purchased a license agreement from Mobile Research and Development Corporation to commercialize Mobile's newly developed process for extracting mercury from natural gas. Tosoh, a Japanese firm, will use its subsidiaries in the United States, Japan, the Netherlands, Greece, Canada, and the United Kingdom as bases of operations from which to profit from Mobile's new process.[19]

A **license agreement** is a right granted by one company to another to use its brand name, technology, product specifications, and so on in the manufacture or sale of goods and services.

Direct Investing.   **Direct investing** is using the assets of one company to purchase the operating assets (for example, factories) of another company. International planning in this area emphasizes reaching organizational objectives through the purchase of the operating assets of another company in a foreign country.

A number of Japanese firms have recently been making direct investments in the United States. In fact, many people believe that a new wave of direct Japanese investment in the United States is building. Several large Japanese companies have lately announced plans to expand their U.S. production facilities. These planned direct investments are focused on building competitive clout for Japanese companies in such core industries as autos, semiconductors, electronics, and office products. Lower manufacturing wages and lower land costs in the United States are key attractions for the Japanese firms. For example, since the cost of building a factory was 30 percent cheaper in the United States than in Japan, Ricoh Company recently decided to spend $30 million to start making thermal paper products near Atlanta, Georgia. One of the largest Japanese direct investments in the United States was Toyota Motor Company's

Direct investing is using the assets of one company to purchase the operating assets of another company.

South Korea's LG Electronics Group chose direct investment as the best means of jumping ahead in the competition to develop high-definition TV and multimedia products. In 1995, LG paid $350 million to buy majority control of Zenith Electronics, a U.S. firm whose technologies in both areas are among the world's best.

$900 million expansion of its Georgetown, Kentucky, plant. The lower costs associated with expanding and operating the Georgetown plant were the key reason Toyota decided to make this investment.[20]

An **international joint venture** is a partnership formed by a company in one country with a company in another country for the purpose of pursuing some mutually desirable business undertaking.

Joint Ventures.   An **international joint venture** is a partnership formed by a company in one country with a company in another country for the purpose of pursuing some mutually desirable business undertaking. International planning components that include joint ventures emphasize the attainment of organizational objectives through partnerships with foreign companies.

Joint ventures between car manufacturers are becoming more and more common as companies strive for greater economies of scale and higher standards in product quality and delivery.

General Motors and Suzuki Motor Company recently formed CAMI Automotive as a joint venture to manufacture the Geo Metro, touted as Chevrolet's most affordable car model. General Motors is based in the United States and is known throughout the world for its prowess as an automobile manufacturer. Suzuki is a leading minicar and motorcycle manufacturer based in Japan. General Motors' substantial size and marketing muscle make the joint venture desirable from Suzuki's viewpoint, and Suzuki's international presence through its subsidiaries in Spain, Canada, Australia, New Zealand, Germany, France, Italy, Belgium, the Philippines, Pakistan, and Colombia makes the partnership desirable from General Motors' viewpoint.[21]

Planning and International Market Agreements

In order to plan properly, managers of a multinational corporation or any other organization participating in the international arena must understand numerous complex and interrelated factors that are present within the organization's international environment. Managers should have a practical grasp of such international environmental factors as the economic and cultural conditions, the laws and political circumstances, of foreign countries within which their companies operate.

An **international market agreement** is an arrangement among a cluster of countries that facilitates a high level of trade among these countries.

One international environmental factor impacting strategic planning that has lately received significant attention is the international market agreement. An **international market agreement** is an arrangement among a cluster of countries that facilitates a high level of trade among these countries. In planning, managers must consider existing international market agreements as they relate to countries in which their organizations operate. If an organization is from a country that is party to an international market agreement, the organization's plan should include steps for taking maximum advantage of that agreement. On the other hand, if an organization is from a country that is *not* party to an international market agreement, the organization's plan must include steps for competing with organizations from nations that are parties to such an agreement. The most notable international market agreements are discussed here.

The European Community (EC).   The European Community is an international market agreement first formed in 1958 and dedicated to facilitating trade among member nations. To that end, the European nations in the EC have agreed to eliminate tariffs among themselves and work toward meaningful deregulation in such areas as banking, insurance, telecommunications, and airlines. Longer-term members of the EC are Denmark, the United Kingdom, Portugal, the Netherlands, Belgium, Spain, Ireland, Luxembourg, France, Germany, Italy, and Greece. More recent members include Austria, Finland, and Sweden. Swedish businesses are particularly excited about their country's entrance into the EC since they are sure that membership will ultimately boost exports and encourage foreign investment from other member nations. The significance of the EC as an international environmental factor can only increase, since the number of member countries is expected to grow to over 25 by 2010.[22]

North American Free Trade Agreement (NAFTA).   The North American Free Trade Agreement is an international market agreement aimed at facilitating trade among member nations. Current NAFTA members are the United States, Canada, and Mexico. To facilitate trade among themselves, these countries have agreed to such actions as the phasing out of tariffs on U.S. farm exports to Mexico, the opening up of Mexico to American trucking, and the safeguarding of North American pharmaceutical patents in Mexico.

NAFTA has had significant impact story since its implementation in January 1994. Recent figures show that since the agreement went into effect, there has been a 30 percent increase in U.S. exports to Mexico and a 15 percent increase in Mexican exports to the United States. Trade between the United States and Canada has exploded since NAFTA took effect. As with the EC, the significance of NAFTA as an international environmental factor can only grow in the future as other countries in the Caribbean and South America apply for membership.[23]

The Evolving Pacific Rim.   Countries in the Pacific Rim area are commonly believed to be interested in developing an international market agreement among themselves that is as effective as the EC has proved to be in Europe. The countries categorized as belonging to the Pacific Rim are Japan, China, Malaysia, Singapore, Indonesia, South Korea, Thailand, Taiwan, Hong Kong, the Philippines, New Zealand, Pakistan, Sri Lanka, and Australia. One country on this list, Japan, is presently a world economic power, while others, like Taiwan and South Korea, are making good progress toward that status. The Pacific Rim countries as a group are anxious to develop an international trade agreement that can best serve their particular economic needs.[24]

To sum up, numerous countries throughout the world are already signatories to international market agreements. Moreover, the number of countries that are parties to such agreements will almost certainly grow significantly in the future.

Organizing Multinational Corporations

Organizing was generally defined in Chapter 1 as the process of establishing orderly uses for all resources within the organization. This definition applies equally to the management of domestic and multinational organizations. Two organizing topics as they specifically relate to multinational corporations, however, bear further discussion. These topics are organization structure and the selection of managers.[25]

After the passage of the North American Free Trade Agreement, many economists and public-policy makers have pushed to extend the web of free-trade arrangements to more countries in Latin and South America. As the idea of hemisphere-wide free trade takes hold, ports like this one in Miami are already living off trade with Latin America.

Organization Structure   Basically, *organization structure* is the sum of all established relationships among resources within the organization, and the *organization chart* is the graphic illustration of organization structure.

Figure 4.5 illustrates several ways in which organization charts can be designed for multinational corporations. Briefly, multinational organization charts can be set up according to major business functions the organization performs, such as production or marketing; major products the organization sells, such as brakes or electrical parts; geographic areas within which the organization does business, such as North Amer-

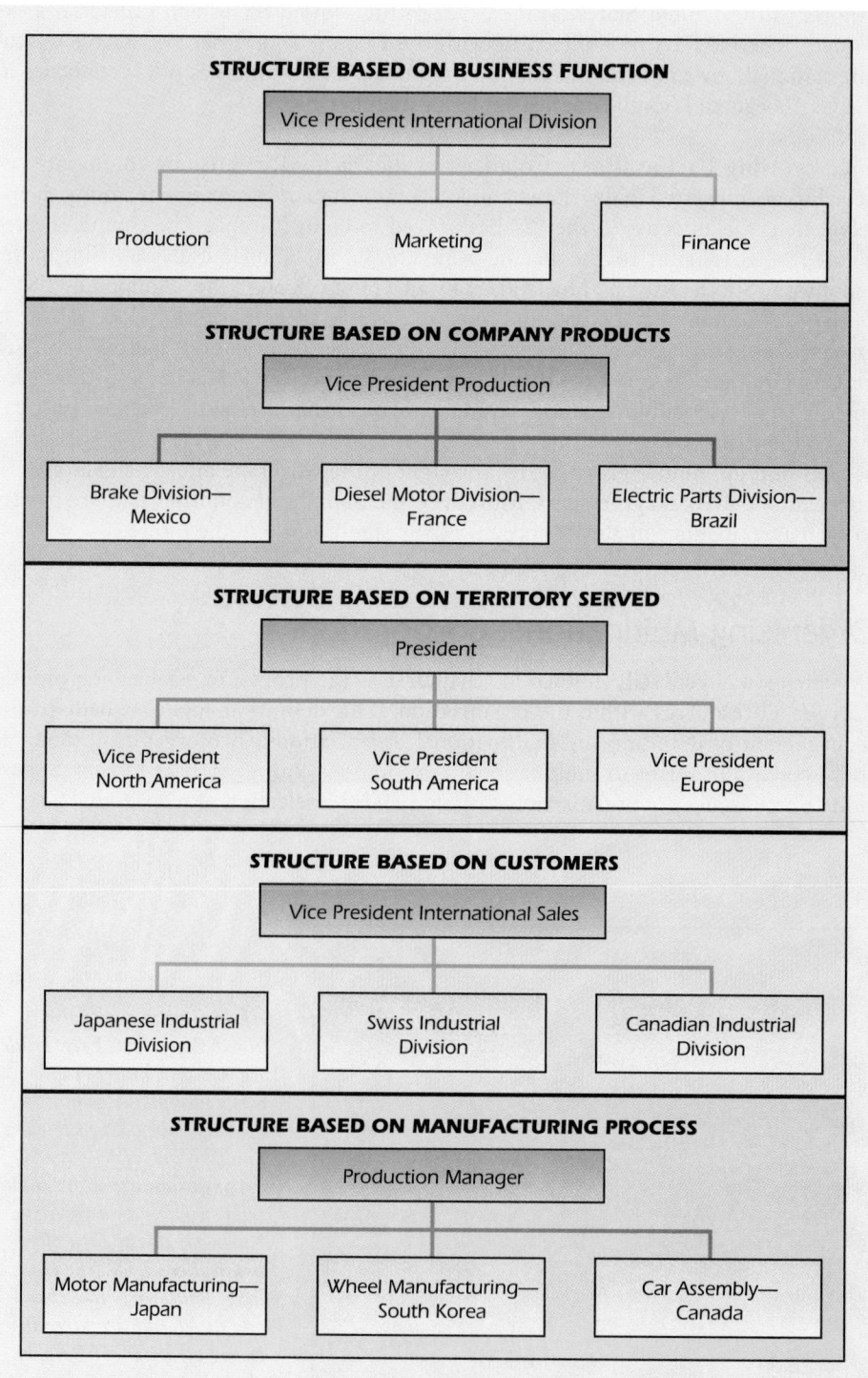

Figure 4.5   Partial multinational organization charts based on function, product, territory, customers, and manufacturing process

ica or Europe; customers the organization serves, such as the Japanese or Swiss; or the way in which the organization manufactures and assembles its products. The topic of organization structure is discussed in much more detail in Chapter 10.

As with domestic organizations, there is no one best way to organize a multinational corporation. Instead, managers must analyze the multinational circumstances that confront them and develop an organization structure that best suits those circumstances.

EUROPEAN ORGANIZATION STRUCTURES ARE BECOMING MORE DIVERSE

DIVERSITY SPOTLIGHT

An organization structure is specifically designed to carry out established organizational plans. Recently, many European firms have been designing organization structures to carry out plans to build more diverse working units. These companies see the fostering of such diversity as essential to becoming top European and global competitors.

One trend reflecting this desire to build more diverse structures is the increased hiring of workers from outside a firm's home country. European human resource directors believe that hiring workers across national borders in Europe is becoming more and more accepted. Nobody knows how significant this trend will be in the future, however, for in order for the trend to benefit European companies, management will have to become competent at handling people from a number of different countries.

Still, several noteworthy European companies are already creating organizational structures that include individuals from various countries. At Mars, Inc., for example, where international transfers are now simply called *transfers*, the general manager is English, the finance manager is French, and the personnel director is Swiss. Another example is Hewlett-Packard of Spain, which has taken concrete steps to incorporate more women professionals from other countries into its organization structure.≈

Selection of Managers
For multinational organizations to thrive, they must have competent managers. One characteristic that is believed to be a primary determinant of how competently managers can guide multinational organizations is their attitude toward how such organizations should operate.

Managerial Attitudes Toward Foreign Operations.   Over the years, management theorists have identified three basic managerial attitudes toward the operations of multinational corporations: ethnocentric, polycentric, and geocentric. The **ethnocentric attitude** reflects the belief that multinational corporations should regard home-country management practices as superior to foreign-country management practices. Managers with an ethnocentric attitude are prone to stereotype home-country management practices as sound and reasonable and foreign management practices as faulty and unreasonable. The **polycentric attitude** reflects the belief that because foreign managers are closer to foreign organizational units, they probably understand them better, and therefore foreign management practices should generally be viewed as more insightful than home-country management practices. Managers with a **geocentric attitude** believe that the overall quality of management recommendations, rather than the location of managers, should determine the acceptability of management practices used to guide multinational corporations.[26]

Advantages and Disadvantages of Each Management Attitude.   It is extremely important to understand the potential advantages and disadvantages of these three attitudes within multinational corporations. The ethnocentric attitude has the advantage of keeping the organization simple, but it generally causes organizational problems because it prevents the organization from receiving feedback from its foreign

The **ethnocentric attitude** reflects the belief that multinational corporations should regard home-country management practices as superior to foreign-country management practices.

The **polycentric attitude** reflects the belief that because foreign managers are closer to foreign organizational units, they probably understand them better, and therefore foreign management practices should generally be viewed as more insightful than home-country management practices.

The **geocentric attitude** reflects the belief that the overall quality of management recommendations, rather than the location of managers, should determine the acceptability of management practices used to guide multinational corporations. The geocentric attitude is considered most appropriate for long-term organizational success.

Japan's Mitsubishi Motors Corporation has been particularly successful in encouraging collaboration in its partnership with Malaysia's state-owned automaker, Proton. Mitsubishi, for example, gave expertise and technical assistance to Proton when it was in its infancy; today, Proton is a $1.2 billion company whose biggest sellers are sedans and subcompacts developed jointly with Mitsubishi.

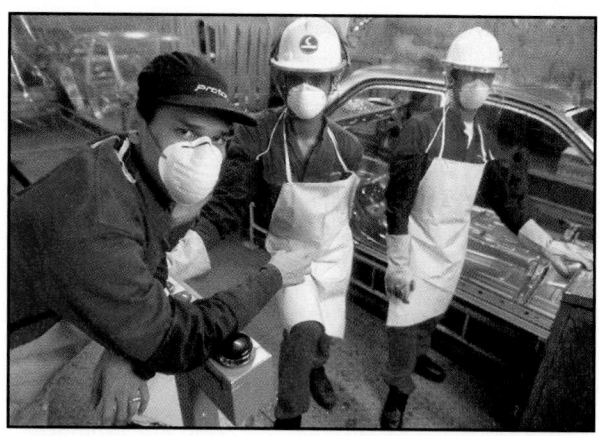

operations. In some cases, the ethnocentric attitude even causes resentment toward the home country within the foreign society. The polycentric attitude permits the tailoring of foreign organizational segments to their cultures, which can be an advantage. Unfortunately, this attitude can lead to the substantial disadvantage of creating numerous foreign organizational segments that are individually run and rather unique, which makes them difficult to control.

The geocentric attitude is generally thought to be the most appropriate for managers in multinational corporations. This attitude promotes collaboration between foreign and home-country management and encourages the development of managerial skills regardless of the organizational segment or country in which managers operate. An organization characterized by the geocentric attitude generally incurs high travel and training expenses, and many decisions are made by consensus. Although the risks from such a wide distribution of power are real, the potential payoffs—better-quality products, worldwide utilization of the best human resources, increased managerial commitment to worldwide organizational objectives, and increased profit—generally outweigh the potential harm. Overall, managers with a geocentric attitude contribute more to the long-term success of the multinational corporation than managers with an ethnocentric or polycentric attitude.

Influencing People in Multinational Corporations

Influencing was generally defined in Chapter 1 as guiding the activities of organization members in appropriate directions through such activities as communicating, leading, motivating, and managing groups. Influencing people in a multinational corporation, however, is more complex and challenging than in a domestic organization.

Culture   The factor that probably contributes most to this increased complexity and challenge is culture. Culture is the total characteristics of a given group of people and their environment. The components of a culture that are generally designated as important are customs, beliefs, attitudes, habits, skills, state of technology, level of education, and religion. As a manager moves from a domestic corporation involving basically one culture to a multinational corporation involving several, the task of influencing usually becomes progressively more difficult.

To successfully influence employees, managers in multinational corporations should:

1. *Acquire a working knowledge of the languages used in countries that house foreign operations.* Multinational managers attempting to operate without such knowledge are prone to making costly mistakes.
2. *Understand the attitudes of people in countries that house foreign operations.* An understanding of these attitudes can help managers design business practices that

are suitable for unique foreign situations. For example, Americans generally accept competition as a tool to encourage people to work harder. As a result, U.S. business practices that include some competitive aspects seldom create significant disruption within organizations. Such practices could cause disruption, however, if introduced into either Japan or the typical European country.

3. *Understand the needs that motivate people in countries housing foreign operations.* For managers in multinational corporations to be successful at motivating employees in different countries, they must present these individuals with the opportunity to satisfy personal needs while being productive within the organization. In designing motivation strategies, multinational managers must understand that employees in different countries often have quite different personal needs. For example, the Swiss, Austrians, Japanese, and Argentinians tend to have high security needs, whereas Danes, Swedes, and Norwegians tend to have high social needs. People in Great Britain, the United States, Canada, New Zealand, and Australia tend to have high self-actualization needs.[27] Thus, to be successful at influencing, multinational managers must understand their employees' needs and mold such organizational components as incentive systems, job design, and leadership style to correspond to these needs.

Controlling Multinational Corporations

Controlling was generally defined in Chapter 1 as making something happen the way it was planned to happen. As with domestic corporations, control in multinational corporations requires that standards be set, performance be measured and compared to standards, and corrective action be taken if necessary. In addition, control in such areas as labor costs, product quality, and inventory is important to organizational success regardless of whether the organization is domestic or international.

Special Difficulties Control of a multinational corporation involves certain complexities. First, there is the problem of different currencies. Management must decide how to compare profits generated by organizational units located in different countries and therefore expressed in terms of different currencies.

Another complication is that organizational units in multinational corporations are generally more geographically separated. This increased distance normally makes it difficult for multinational managers to keep a close watch on operations in foreign countries.

Improving Communication One action successful managers take to help overcome the difficulty of monitoring geographically separated foreign units is to carefully design the communication network or information system that links them. A significant part of this design is requiring all company units to acquire and install similar computer equipment in all offices, both foreign and domestic, to ensure the likelihood of network hookups when communication becomes necessary. Such standardization of computer equipment also facilitates communication among all foreign locations and makes equipment repair and maintenance easier and therefore less expensive.[28]

Transnational Organizations

Transnational organizations, also called *global organizations,* take the entire world as their business arena. Doing business wherever it makes sense is primary; national borders are considered inconsequential. The transnational organization transcends any single home country, with ownership, control, and management being from many different countries. Transnational organizations represent the fourth, and maximum, level of international activity as depicted on the continuum of international involve-

Transnational organizations, also called *global organizations,* take the entire world as their business arena.

ment presented earlier in this chapter. Seeing great opportunities in the global marketplace, some MNCs have transformed themselves from home-based companies with worldwide interests into worldwide companies pursuing business activities across the globe and claiming no singular loyalty to any one country.

Perhaps the most commonly cited example of a transnational organization is Nestlé.[29] Although Nestlé is headquartered in Veney, Switzerland, its arena of daily business activity is truly the world. Nestlé has a very diversified list of products, including instant coffee, cereals, pharmaceuticals, coffee creamers, dietetic foods, ice cream, chocolates, and a wide array of snack foods. Its recent acquisition of the French company Perrier catapulted Nestlé into market leadership in the mineral water industry. Nestlé has over 210,000 employees and operates 494 factories in 71 countries worldwide, including the United States, Germany, Portugal, Brazil, France, New Zealand, Australia, Chile, and Venezuela. Of Nestlé's sales and profits, about 45 percent come from Europe, 35 percent from North and South America, and 25 percent from other countries.

BACK TO THE CASE

Planning is equally valuable to domestic and international companies. The primary difference in planning for Baskin-Robbins as an international rather than a domestic company is reflected in certain components of the company's plans. As an international corporation, Baskin-Robbins needs planning components that focus on the international sector, whereas a totally domestic organization obviously would not need such components. Examples of such components in Baskin-Robbins' case are establishing a partnership with a Vietnamese construction company to build ice cream stores throughout Vietnam, building an ice cream manufacturing facility in Vietnam that could furnish product to Baskin-Robbins' Vietnamese stores as well as prospective stores in nearby countries, choosing additional store locations in other countries, and selling the rights (license agreements) to a foreign company to use the name Baskin-Robbins in selling ice cream.

The organization structure of an international company such as Baskin-Robbins should generally be based on one or more of the important variables of function, product, territory, customers, and manufacturing process. In deciding on an organization structure, Baskin-Robbins managers should consider all of these variables within the situations that confront them, and then design the structure that is most appropriate for those situations.

Over the long term, top management at Baskin-Robbins should try to select for international positions those managers who display geocentric rather than polycentric or ethnocentric attitudes. Such managers would be the most competent at building operating units in other countries and at using the best human resources available. They would also tend to be highly committed to the attainment of organizational objectives.

As Baskin-Robbins becomes more multinational, influencing employees will become more and more complicated. The cultures of people in Vietnam and whatever other countries the company expands into will have to be thoroughly understood by Baskin-Robbins managers of foreign operations. Those who are U.S. citizens will have to acquire a working knowledge of the languages spoken in the various host countries and an understanding of what attitudes and personal needs motivate individuals within the foreign workforce. For instance, the rewards used to motivate Vietnamese workers may need to be very different from the rewards the company uses to motivate U.S. workers.

The control process at Baskin-Robbins should involve standards, measurements, and corrective action where necessary, just as it would in a purely domestic company. But the currency used in Vietnam—and wherever else the company decides to set up foreign operations—will tend to make control more complicated for Baskin-Robbins than for a domestic organization. The geographic distance of its foreign operations from the United States will also complicate control at Baskin-Robbins.

COMPARATIVE MANAGEMENT: AN EMPHASIS ON JAPANESE MANAGEMENT

Perhaps the most popular international management topic today is comparative management. The sections that follow define *comparative management* and provide insights into Japanese management practices that can be of value to U.S. managers.

Defining Comparative Management

Comparative management is the study of the management process in different countries to examine the potential of management action under different environmental conditions. Whereas international management focuses on management activities across national borders, comparative management analyzes management practices in one country for their possible application in another country.[30]

The sections that follow discuss motivation and management practice insights gained from analyzing Japanese management methods. These insights are currently being applied by many U.S. managers.

Comparative management is the study of the management process in different countries to examine the potential of management action under different environmental conditions.

Insights from Japanese Motivation Strategies

The country studied the most from a comparative management viewpoint is Japan. Before World War II, huge industrial conglomerates called *zaibatsus* controlled the Japanese economy. The *zaibatsus* were outlawed after the war, and *keiretsus* emerged to take their place. *Keiretsus* are collections of major business organizations whose managers effectively motivate organization members.[31]

Japanese managers seem to motivate their subordinates by:[32]

1. *Hiring employees for life.* A close relationship between workers and the organization is built through this practice of lifetime employment. Because workers have a guaranteed job, they know that their future will be heavily influenced by the future of the organization; therefore, they are willing to be flexible and cooperative.
2. *Elevating employees to a level of organizational status equal to that of management.* In Japanese factories, employees at all levels wear the same work clothes, eat in the same cafeteria, and use the same rest rooms.
3. *Making employees feel that they are highly valued by management and that the organization will provide for their material needs.* New workers and their relatives attend a ceremony at which the company president welcomes them to the firm. The newcomers often live in company-built housing for several years until they can afford to buy their own housing. Also, employees spend much of their leisure time in company social clubs, and employee weddings and receptions are often held in company facilities. Some Japanese companies even help pay for employees' weddings.

Japanese managers obviously go to great lengths to build positive working relationships with their Japanese employees. In addition, there is some evidence that similar actions have been applied successfully by Japanese managers to motivate American employees at the Nissan plant in Smyrna, Tennessee.

Because the general Japanese culture has been shown to be a significant factor in the success of Japanese management practices, however, managers other countries should imitate Japanese actions only with extreme caution. After all, company actions that satisfy Japanese workers' needs and desires may not satisfy the needs and desires of workers from other countries.[33] Still, managers throughout the world can undoubtedly gain valuable insights about how to motivate workers by studying the motivation tactics used by Japanese managers. At the same time, as the following CUT-TING EDGE feature implies, the personal needs of younger Japanese workers seem to

be changing, so even Japanese managers will probably have to alter their motivational tactics when dealing with the upcoming generation of Japanese workers.

CUTTING EDGE

JAPANESE MANAGERS MAY HAVE TO CHANGE MOTIVATION TACTICS

Over the last several decades, the intense Japanese drive to excel in business has resulted in countless very productive and successful Japanese business organizations. Japanese workers have proved to be some of the most motivated workers in the world.

A recent survey, however, indicates that the tactics used to motivate Japanese workers in the past may not be appropriate for the new generation of workers. The survey queried a number of Japanese nationals who were pursuing their graduate business degrees in the United States—individuals who will be among Japan's top business leaders in the future. The survey's purpose was to investigate the impact of the Japanese lifestyle on Japanese citizens.

Survey results show that although Japanese workers feel a higher obligation toward their companies than American workers do toward theirs, they are not necessarily more satisfied. One implication of this finding is that the collective decision-making and paternalistic management style characteristic of large Japanese corporations creates a noticeable level of undesirable stress in the Japanese workplace.

Survey results also indicate that the personal needs of younger Japanese workers are different from those of older workers. Younger workers have a greater preference for spending less time at work and more time with their friends, for traveling and enjoying leisure activities, than their older counterparts do. Though they recognize that their preferences are causing some disappointment in their elders, young people in Japan want to work less and have more free time available.≈

Insights from Japanese Management Practices: Theory Z

Given the success of such Japanese organizations as Nissan and Toshiba, many U.S. management writers have been carefully analyzing Japanese organizations and comparing them to American organizations with the purpose of making recommendations about how Japanese management practices can be adapted to improve the operation of American organizations.

One such recommendation, called Theory Z, was introduced by William Ouchi in 1981.[34] Theory Z suggests that significant management practices in the United States and Japan be combined into one middle-ground, improved framework. Ouchi studied the following management practices in U.S. and Japanese organizations:

1. The length of time workers were employed.
2. The way decisions were made.
3. Where responsibility existed.
4. The rate at which employees were evaluated and promoted.
5. The type of control tools used.
6. The degree to which employees had specialized career paths.
7. The type of concern shown for employees.

After completing his study, Ouchi made some suggestions for integrating American and Japanese management practices to develop a new, more successful American organization, called a Type Z organization. This Type Z organization is characterized by both the "individual responsibility" of American organizations and the "collective decision making, slow evaluation and promotion, and holistic concern for employees" of Japanese organizations. The length of employment, control, and career path characteristics of Ouchi's proposed Type Z organization are essentially compromises between practices at American and at Japanese organizations.

One idea that U.S. companies have borrowed from Japanese counterparts is the use of technology to speed up the production of specifically demanded products. For example, Baxter Healthcare of Deerfield, Illinois, can now ship a modular medical-supplies factory anywhere in the world, assemble it and get it running in one week, and then move it somewhere else whenever necessary.

Japanese management has spurred U.S. business to consider new approaches to compete with the high standard of industrialization established by Japanese corporations. For example, leading American management consultants are developing and proposing future changes for U.S. managers' consideration in the areas of strategies, organization, group cooperation, and competitive advantage.[35]

BACK TO THE CASE

Managers at Baskin-Robbins should undoubtedly be concerned with comparative management, meaning they should study management practices in foreign operations with the idea of applying the best of them to operations at Baskin-Robbins.

One insight from comparative management studies that Baskin-Robbins managers might want to consider applying within their company has to do with Japanese motivation strategies. Japanese managers seem to be very successful at motivating their workers by elevating the workers to the same status as managers and by convincing the workers that the organization will provide for their material needs. However, because the Japanese culture is very different from other cultures—even in Asia—Baskin-Robbins managers should be careful in applying Japanese motivational strategies to workers in other countries. On the other hand, if Baskin-Robbins opens an ice cream store in Japan, motivation insights acquired from watching successful Japanese store managers operate could prove very valuable.

Another comparative management insight that could be valuable to Baskin-Robbins managers is Theory Z, which suggests blending American and Japanese management practices. Thus, Baskin-Robbins managers might make their company more successful by implementing such strategies as hiring employees for the long term and providing only moderately specialized career paths for workers. If Theory Z is implemented, however, its worth and impact should be carefully monitored, because not enough research has been done to date to validate the theory.

The just-in-time (JIT) inventory strategy, another Japanese concept, could prove to be a valuable inventory control method for Baskin-Robbins. Keeping inventory to a minimum by ordering materials from suppliers only as they are needed for sale could significantly improve organizational performance. Minimizing storage and handling costs related to inventories and engaging only the organizational resources needed to meet customer needs are advantages that Baskin-Robbins could gain by using JIT.

Action Summary

Reread the learning objectives below. Each objective is followed by questions. Answering these questions accurately will help you retain the most important concepts discussed in this chapter. After answering each question, check your answer against the answer key at the end of this chapter. (*Hint:* If you have any doubts regarding the correct response, consult the page whose number follows the answer.)

Circle: From studying this chapter, I will attempt to acquire:

1. An understanding of international management and its importance to modern managers.

   T,F   **a.** To reach organizational objectives, management may extend its activities to include an emphasis on organizations in foreign countries.

   a,b,c,d,e   **b.** The U.S. multinational corporation with the highest foreign revenue as a percent of total revenue in 1993 was: (a) IBM; (b) Citicorp; (c) Exxon; (d) General Motors; (e) Mobil.

2. An understanding of what constitutes a multinational corporation.

   a,b,c,d,e   **a.** According to Jacoby, the first stage in a corporation's multinationalization is when the corporation: (a) multinationalizes ownership of corporate stock; (b) multinationalizes management from top to bottom; (c) establishes foreign manufacturing facilities; (d) establishes sales organizations abroad; (e) exports its products.

   T,F   **b.** In general, the smaller the organization, the greater the likelihood that it participates in international operations of some sort.

3. Insights concerning the risk involved in investing in international operations.

   a,b,c,d,e   **a.** Managers who make foreign investments believe that such investments: (a) reduce or eliminate high transportation costs; (b) allow participation in the rapid expansion of a market abroad; (c) provide foreign technical, design, and marketing skills; (d) earn higher profits; (e) a,b,c, and d.

   T,F   **b.** A manager's failure to understand different national sovereignties, national conditions, and national values and institutions can lead to poor investment decisions.

4. Insights about those who work in multinational corporations.

   a,b,c,d,e   **a.** People who work in multinational corporations are generally categorized as: (a) expatriates; (b) third-country nationals; (c) host-country nationals; (d) all of the above; (e) a and b only.

   T,F   **b.** Personal adjustments that employees of multinational corporations must make can influence how productively they work.

   T,F   **c.** Repatriation is the process of sending an individual out of his or her home country to work for a multinational corporation.

5. Knowledge about managing multinational corporations.

   T,F   **a.** The primary difference between planning in multinational versus domestic organizations probably involves operational planning.

   a,b,c,d,e   **b.** The attitude that regards home-country management practices as superior to foreign-country practices is known as a(n): (a) egocentric attitude; (b) ethnocentric attitude; (c) polycentric attitude; (d) geocentric attitude; (e) isocentric attitude.

6. Knowledge about managing multinational organizations versus transnational organizations.

   T,F   **a.** Generally speaking, a transnational organization transcends any home country, whereas a multinational organization does not.

   T,F   **b.** A multinational organization is basically the same as a transnational organization.

7. Insights about what comparative management is and how it might help managers do their jobs better.

   T,F   **a.** Comparative management emphasizes analyzing management practices in one country to determine how best to counteract the effectiveness of a foreign competitor.

   a,b,c,d,e   **b.** A successful Japanese technique involves copying and improving a competitor's strategy and product. The similar U.S. technique is known as: (a) problem solving; (b) benchmarking; (c) toeing the mark; (d) *keiretsus*; (e) none of the above.

8. Ideas on how to become a better manager through the study of Japanese management techniques.

   T,F   **a.** Since the Japanese have been so successful and there is little relationship between their culture and their success, American management would be wise to immediately implement Japanese management techniques.

a,b,c,d,e   **b.** Which of the following is *not* one of the significant management practices that Ouchi studied in American and Japanese organizations: (a) the length of time workers were employed; (b) the way in which decisions were made; (c) the type of incentive plan used; (d) where responsibility existed within the organization; (e) the rate at which employees were evaluated and promoted.

Introductory Case Wrap-Up

"Baskin-Robbins Brings U.S. Ice Cream to Vietnam" (p. 78) and its related back-to-the-case sections were written to help you better understand the management concepts contained in this chapter. Answer the following discussion questions about this introductory case to enrich your understanding of the chapter content:

1. Do you think that at some point in your career you will become involved in international management? Explain.

2. Assume that you are about to become the manager of a Baskin-Robbins ice cream store in Japan. What challenges do you think will be most difficult for you? Why?

3. Evaluate the following statement: Baskin-Robbins can learn to manage its U.S. operations better by studying how successful competitive operations are managed in other countries.

Issues for Review and Discussion

1. More and more organizations are initiating business ventures in foreign countries. Explain why in detail.
2. Define *international management.*
3. How significant is the topic of international management to the modern manager? Explain fully.
4. What is meant by the term *multinational corporation?*
5. List and explain four factors that contribute to the complexity of managing multinational corporations.
6. Choose an organization and describe how it has become multinational by progressing through two or more stages of Jacoby's six stages of multinationalization.
7. List and define three types of organization members generally found in multinational corporations.
8. Describe personal and professional adjustments that members of multinational corporations generally must make. How should managers respond to employees making such adjustments? Why?
9. What is the difference between direct investing and joint ventures at the international level?
10. What is an international market agreement? Explain how these agreements can impact organization plans.
11. Draw segments of organization charts that organize a multinational corporation on the basis of product, function, and customers.
12. Is there one best way to organize all multinational corporations? Explain your answer fully.
13. What are the differences between ethnocentric, polycentric, and geocentric attitudes? Describe advantages and disadvantages of each.
14. How does culture affect the international management process?
15. Discuss three suggestions that would be helpful to a manager attempting to influence organization members in different countries.
16. What is a transnational organization? How does it differ from a multinational organization?
17. How can comparative management help managers of today?
18. What insights can be learned from Japanese managers about how to motivate people? Should caution be exercised by a Canadian manager in applying these insights? Explain.

Action Summary Answer Key

1. **a.** T, pp. 79–80
   b. c, p. 82
2. **a.** e, pp. 82–83
   b. F, p. 83
3. **a.** e, p. 86
   b. T, p. 86
4. **a.** d, pp. 86–87
   b. t, p. 88
   c. F, p. 88
5. **a.** F, p. 95
   b. b, p. 95
6. **a.** T, pp. 97–98
   b. F, pp. 97–98
7. **a.** F, p. 99
   b. b, p. 99
8. **a.** F, p. 99
   b. c, p. 100

Case Study

A Global Success Story

Robert Goizueta, Coca-Cola's president and CEO since 1981, believes that "soft drinks are very much a local product. I'd love for the Chinese to arrive in New York" he explains, "and say, 'My goodness, they have Coca-Cola here, too,' " The hand-picked protégé of longtime Coca-Cola chairman Robert Woodruff, Goizueta recognized when he became CEO that changes had to be made in the company's way of doing business around the world to overcome the 1970s stagnation in Coca-Cola's growth. In the past, he says, "You'd plant your flag in a new country every time you needed to grow. We ran out of countries, so I had to do something different." In fact, Goizueta was recognized by *Fortune* magazine for his success in enhancing shareholder value—a crucial investment value that showed a significant loss in the ten-year period before he took over.

Atlanta-based Coca-Cola boasts one of the best-recognized logos in the world. Whether he or she speaks Japanese, Hebrew, or Russian, the world traveler knows the product inside the familiar tapered bottle or distinctively labeled can and trusts its consistently high quality. Even five years ago, however, Goizueta believed that Coca-Cola's marketing was flawed. Too much marketing money, he felt, was being devoted to advertising and too little to brand strategy and packaging. So Coca-Cola hired hundreds of new marketers to take a more "holistic" approach to the international market. At the same time, however, Goizueta cautioned a worldwide gathering of Coca-Cola's quality assurance staff about the dangers of change for its own sake. "It's extremely important," he reminded them, "that you show some sensitivity to your past in order to show the proper respect for the future."

Coca-Cola's push into the international market began during World War II, when company president Robert Woodruff announced, "We will see that every man in uniform gets a bottle of Coca-Cola for 5 cents wherever he is and whatever it costs." General Dwight D. Eisenhower, a Coke fancier, agreed. Thus, as competing soft-drink companies watched helplessly, Coca-Cola established bottling plants near every battlefront. By the end of the war, the company had 64 international bottling plants, most of them built at the expense of U.S. taxpayers.

During the Cold War, however, the company faced severe criticism in certain countries as a symbol of American imperialism. For example, efforts were made to drive Coke from the shelves of French stores. "The moral landscape of France," declared the respected French newspaper *Le Monde*, "is at stake." In the end, of course, the company won this and other fights on foreign soil. Coca-Cola was once boycotted by Arabic countries because it had a franchised bottler in Israel, but over time, the company's persistence—and consumer demand— broke down this barrier.

Coca-Cola currently does business in 195 countries, deriving close to 70 percent of its total revenues and 80 percent of its operating profits from outside the United States. In 1994, Coke had revenues exceeding $15 billion and had more than doubled sales from the decade before. Today, the international market remains the key to Coca-Cola's future. With domestic per capita consumption leveling, the global market offers enormous potential.

Goizueta recognizes that Coca-Cola's present success comes from operating in different geographic locations. First, Coke pushed aggressively into foreign markets when the domestic market matured. Indeed, facing just 2 to 4 percent annual growth domestically, Coca-Cola *had* to concentrate on the world market. Coke managers reason that when sales drop in troubled economies like those of Mexico or Argentina, growth in new markets like India or China can create a hedge.

Today, Coca-Cola's International Business Sector is divided into four operating groups: the Greater Europe Group, the Latin America Group, the Middle and Far East Group, and the Africa Group. Moreover, Coke is putting major resources into continued international growth. The company has, for instance, targeted Eastern Europe and China for future expansion and has spent liberally to support business in these sizable markets. In addition, Coke plans a $250 million expansion in Russia. Bottlers in Venezuela anticipate a $200 million expansion, and in Brazil, $2 billion is slated to be spent in the next five years to add vending machines and coolers. Not forgetting the home market, Coca-Cola will also continue to add vending machines and coolers in U.S. gas stations, convenience stores, and grocery stores to help catch up with archrival Pepsi Cola in these areas.

Finally, since 1928, Coca-Cola has supported Olympic Games and athletes—this is the longest continuous support provided by a corporation. Through international and national sponsorship programs, Coke helps finance teams and aspiring athletes in 195 countries. The company has already agreed to continue this worldwide marketing effort through the 1998 Winter Olympic Games in Nagano, Japan, and the 2000 Olympic Games in Sydney, Australia.

The key to Coca-Cola's future success is management's commitment to create value for shareholders. One of its major assets in this effort is the company's "strong

global leadership in the beverage industry in particular and in the business world in general."

Questions:

1. What does Goizueta mean when he says that "soft drinks are very much a local product"? Is Goizueta's vision of a "local" multinational company possible? Explain.
2. Cite evidence to illustrate ways in which Coca-Cola management stresses the company's multinational status.
3. Consider past and current Coca-Cola advertising campaigns. Were these tailored for the international or the domestic market? Explain. How do these campaigns illustrate the concept of a "local" multinational?
4. Would a Coke bought in Atlanta taste the same as one bought in Moscow? Why or why not? What does this say about the company and its commitment to the international market?

Skills Exercise

The four operating groups of Coca-Cola's International Business Sector are the Greater Europe Group, the Latin America Group, the Middle and Far East Group, and the Africa Group. Work with others to create a comparison chart illustrating possible differences in the strategies and priorities of each group. Consider the most likely countries to capitalize on, the product changes or additions that might be necessary to do so, and the most effective marketing campaigns for each group.

The Internet learning materials that accompany this chapter can be found at
http://www.profcerto.com
Additional information can be found on the inside front and back covers of this text.

Doing Business Abroad the Lands' End Way

This is the second of seven cases in this book that explore a variety of management-related issues at the well-known direct-retailing company Lands' End. The first installment (on pp. 24–26) is designed to be a general introduction. You may want to refer to it when you are studying the cases that appear at the end of each part of the book.

International sales are not new to Lands' End. The company first started servicing Canadian customers through its regular U.S. mailings in 1987. But overseas expansion presented completely new challenges and opportunities for a land-locked Midwestern retailer.

Its first real overseas foray was to the United Kingdom less than ten years ago. In the late summer of 1991, Lands' End prepared its first pound-denominated catalog for distribution in the United Kingdom Phone operators handled calls on a contractual basis, and distribution was managed jointly through the company's U.S. facility in Dodgeville, Wisconsin, and a contract U.K. facility.

Although this first venture was a success, it was not without its problems. The first U.K. catalog, for example, was developed by Lands' End copywriters in Dodgeville. Because the company wanted to portray itself as truly American, they wrote in American English rather than the Queen's English. Occasionally, of course, some subtle differences in vocabulary had to be acknowledged. The word *thongs*, for instance, which was meant to refer to *sandals*, translated in the Queen's English as a rather skimpy women's bathing suit. Similarly, to the Brits, the word *pants* does not connote outerwear; *pants* are *underwear*. Finally, note that in England, there is no such word as *diaper bag*. In the United Kingdom, *nappy-bag* is the term of choice. With these and other corrections in place, the first catalog was mailed.

Unfortunately, according to Vice President for International Operations Frank Buettner, once the catalog was out, the language issue was not completely resolved. As catalogs found their way into the hands of potential U.K. customers, the phones began to ring. "Even with the obvious corrections made," recalls Buettner, "the catalog was still written in our English. A number of customers called to let the company know that they would refuse to order from the Lands' End catalog as long as it was written in other than the Queen's English."

To manage linguistic and other problems, in February 1993 Lands' End hired Henry Heavisides, who had previously been with a U.K. mail-order business called Laura Ashley by Post. Heavisides came on board as Managing Director–U.K. and was charged with managing all U.K. marketing and merchandising initiatives. Although he was familiar with the direct-mail business from his previous job, doing business according to the Lands' End formula—which meant applying LE's Principles of Doing Business—would require Heavisides to go through some significant LE indoctrination. According to Buettner:

> In all of our international ventures we try to transplant what we believe has historically made Lands' End so successful—its culture, its principles, its customer focus, how it treats its employees, its way of doing business. I guess we could put it all into two words—"our formula." That formula for success involves all of the above-mentioned components of doing business, including who we are, what we are, and what we stand for. It's not only our outward focus on customer satisfaction, but also our inward caring attitude—to be sure that the needs of organizational members are cared for appropriately.
>
> It was agreed from the very start of our international ventures that we would not compromise any of our principles. Whatever we had done here in the U.S. that had made us successful we would simply transplant into the foreign business culture. For example, when we explained that the copy we wished to have included in newspaper ads should describe, in every detail, the features of a product and even some sections on company history, every British ad agency we worked with told us that we were

crazy, that no one does this, and that such an advertising approach would be a silly waste of both time and money. But we did it anyway, because it's the Lands' End way. And it turned out great.

By August 1993, Lands' End had leased a 60,000-square-foot U.K. telephone and distribution center in the town of Oakham, about 80 miles north of London. From there, the company was able to place merchandise in customers' homes three to four days after an order was received.

By early 1994, Lands' End began to feel that it could do better if it established its own creative staff in the United Kingdom to write the sort of English with which British customers would be comfortable. Obviously, meeting the demands of one's customers need not entail any compromise of a firm's basic principles. Today, according to Buettner, "while Lands' End continues to mail its American English language catalog to 175 countries and continues to do very well, the copy in the U.K. catalog is now developed there using the Queen's English."

Japan was next. Operations got under way in October 1993, and the first catalog was issued in August 1994. Japan, whose population is only slightly less than that of the United States, is—a sizable marketplace. As is now well known, of course, Japanese culture and business practices are quite different from those of the United States. Yet, according to Frank Buettner, "Lands' End's principles for doing business were applied exactly the same way in Japan as they were in the United Kingdom, or for that matter, in the United States." For example, part

Exhibit I (on left): This ad has little copy with many pictures
Exhibit II (on right:) A copy–heavy ad

of Lands' End's early and continuing prospecting for new business in Japan involved the use of newspaper inserts. However, adhering to the LE formula, these one-fold regionalized inserts (that is, different inserts for Tokyo, for Yokohama, and for Osaka) were designed to carry the same message elements as all LE catalog advertising. "They are to include," says Buettner, "detailed information on the product and the company, the company's culture, its principles, its way of doing business, its guarantee, and where to write or call for a catalog." Problems, however, developed with the first insert developed by the Japanese advertising firm that Lands' End had hired to assist with the start-up. Instead of carefully explaining and visually displaying the various quality features of a garment, the first newspaper insert looked like an insert for any other advertiser: Numerous items were advertised, but other than size and color, little detail was provided (see Exhibit 1).

Buettner quickly stepped in to bring the second insert into conformance with the LE formula. "Our catalog and our ads," he stresses,

> are our store. One of the barriers to mail-order shopping anywhere in the world is customers not having the luxury of walking in, touching the garment, feeling it, and trying it on. So we have to make sure that the photography in our catalogs and ads is big, bright, and beautiful—it must capture the tone, the texture, and the essence of what the product is like. Further, the ads must describe fully how the product is made, why our product has an edge over the competition (its special features) and, believe it or not, in some cases even the occasions at which the garment ideally might be worn— for example, "ideal for cool summer evenings." As it turns out, in the first four-page insert designed by our Japanese staff tried to sell more than two dozen products. However, when ascribing to our formula, the revised ad managed to focus on is selling only a half-dozen or so items. (see Exhibit 2)

With one exception, Lands' End newspaper advertising was well received in Japan. The exception? "We actually had no surprises," recalls Buettner,

> until we got to the guarantee, and then no one believed it. This was perhaps our biggest challenge. We didn't realize it at the time, but the single most important factor involved in entering that market—which is also the factor that has set us ahead and apart from other mail-order companies—was our iron-clad guarantee.

Interest in the new American start-up—and its unusual guarantee—eventually led to a nationwide press conference. Because of the stir that Lands' End was causing, all three of Japan's TV channels covered the event. The extensive coverage, explains Buettner,

> was a result of both the press kit we sent out and the fact that in the States, we were the number-one mail-order company in apparel. The Japanese like to be associated with the best. And for us, national coverage from the three stations meant we reached just about everyone. The focus of the press conference was meant to introduce Lands' End, but the Japanese media helped out by comparing us to various Japanese mail-order companies. In fact, they summarized their report with a chart for LE with "yes" marked next to each service guarantee item being compared. The charts for our Japanese competitors, for example, indicated "yes," "no," "no," "no," "yes," "no," "no." Obviously, the message came across clearly to everybody.
>
> However, to defend our iron-clad guarantee and prove that what we were stating was accurate, the Japanese media also asked that we ship a number of our U.S. returns to Japan so that they could be inspected. These included items that were monogrammed and then returned, items that were soiled and torn, and items that were years-old. And, yes, to everyone's surprise, these were returned items that had been replaced or fully refunded. Once we got this message across, we were off and running.

At that point, one of Lands' End's biggest challenges was to get the Japanese staff to do things the LE way. For example, Buettner was surprised to learn that a country so well known for its service orientation actually provided very poor mail-order service. "One of our biggest struggles," He reports:

was getting people in the phone center to understand how we wanted them to deal with customers. When we would say, "This is how we want you to do this," they would say, "No, this is how we do it in Japan. This is the way people are going to expect to be treated, talked to, and handled, so this is how we think it should be done." Getting them to adopt our way of doing business and our service philosophy was a difficult challenge, but we are there now and doing very well with it.

Finally, one accommodation that had to be made for Japanese catalog shoppers relates to payment methods that LE had to be willing to accept. For example, with widespread use of checking accounts and credit cards in the United States, payment is usually made before a product is shipped. In Japan, however, the reverse is true about half the time. Trust, explains Buettner,

plays a significant role in business in Japan. If you want someone to do business with you, you must first earn his or her trust. A handshake goes a lot further than a written contract. However, trust takes on an even different meaning when method of payment is considered. About one-half of our sales in Japan is credit card, the other half some other form of payment—either bank transfers or postal transfers. With these latter forms of payment, we send the product, they try it on and, if they like it, pay for it. Obviously, there is a high degree of trust on our part, too. While this approach may seem a little strange, Lands' End has had very, very minimal problems with these payment methods.

Questions:

1. Applying what you have learned from your text, what can you say about Lands' End's recent internationalization?
2. From everything that you now know about Lands' End, are there any indicators that would suggest that its operations are effective? Efficient? Explain.
3. Is there anything in the case that would suggest that Lands' End specifically employs ethical management practices? Explain.

part 2

Planning

ORGANIZATIONAL OBJECTIVES

Entrepreneur Suffers Growing Pains at Arkansas Freightways

In 1991, Sheridan Garrison got the news that countless entrepreneurs secretly crave: His biggest competition, Jones Truck Lines, had gone out of business. Fast-growing Arkansas Freightways Corporation, which Garrison founded, seemingly stood to make a fortune as hundreds of shippers scrambled to secure a trucker to haul their goods. Garrison quickly signed up as many customers as he could. But instead of a windfall, he got a nightmare.

Overloaded with business, the regional trucking firm's terminals that service hauling to ten states from Texas to Illinois to Tennessee were backed up for days, infuriating old customers. Some took their business elsewhere. The crisis forced the Harrison, Arkansas, concern into costly emergency measures, from paying overtime to renting more trucks. As a result, the company reported a 22 percent drop in net income for the fourth quarter of the year—the first such reversal since Garrison formed the firm in 1982.

The day after Jones failed, Arkansas Freightways was flooded with orders from its former competitor's customers. "They came to us and said, 'Do you want the business we were giving to Jones?'" Mr. Garrison says. "We're pretty aggressive. We weren't going to turn them down."

In 24 hours, Arkansas Freightways' volume rose 20 percent. The extra business would bring the company $40 million in annual revenue, but Garrison soon realized he had taken on more than he could handle. At one point, nearly a quarter of all Arkansas Freightways shipments were running behind schedule, up from 5 percent in normal times. In Dallas and Oklahoma City, two of the company's busiest terminals, shipments that were supposed to be delivered overnight were backed up for days. "That's something I've never experienced before," Garrison says, "and we'd sold ourselves on service."

He rented 500 trailers and farmed out work to other carriers and to the railroads. Employees labored overtime until the company finished hiring 700 more workers. Office personnel, including senior executives, helped out on the docks, and dock workers became drivers.

Some solutions led to new problems. Packing more goods into each shipment meant trucks took longer to load and unload. The trailers that Arkansas Freightways rented not only required more maintenance but also were much larger than the kind the company normally used, further increasing the time needed for loading. It took five months to overcome such obstacles, but Arkansas Freightways seems back on course. Garrison says 97 percent of its shipments are arriving on time, partly with the help of a new mainframe computer that supplies a daily analysis of activity at each of the company's 116 terminals. Profit growth, too, has been restored. In the first quarter, net more than doubled to $1.7 million on a 48 percent increase in sales to $57.7 million.

Management at Arkansas Freightways has earned the respect of the outside world. For several years, the company has been touted as one of the Best 200 Small Companies in America. To continue growing, management plans to expand its trucking services north and farther west. "Arkansas Freightways" now seems too parochial a name for a company with such ambitious growth plans. Almost inevitably, the company will soon be renamed American Freightways.

Trucking companies must be ready to deal with the competitive economic environment. Arkansas Freightways found that it took five months, costly emergency measures, and some creative scrambling to assimilate all the new business that it was able to acquire when a rival trucking firm went out of business.

what's ahead

Managers such as Sheridan Garrison, the chief executive officer of Arkansas Freightways, must recognize that too strong a focus on one organizational objective—like growth, in this case—can cause an organization serious problems. This chapter can help a manager like Garrison gain a broad appreciation of how managers can use objectives to appropriately guide their organizations to success. This chapter discusses the following topics:

1. The general nature of organizational objectives.
2. Different types of organizational objectives.
3. Various areas in which organizational objectives should be set.
4. How managers actually work with organizational objectives.
5. Management by objectives (MBO).

GENERAL NATURE OF ORGANIZATIONAL OBJECTIVES

Definition of Organizational Objectives

Organizational objectives are the targets toward which the open management system is directed. Organizational input, process, and output—topics discussed in Chapter 2—all exist to reach organizational objectives (see Figure 5.1). Properly developed organizational objectives reflect the purpose of the organization—that is, they flow naturally from the organization's mission. The **organizational purpose** is what the organization exists to do, given a particular group of customers and customer needs. Table 5.1 contains several statements of organizational purpose, or mission, as developed by actual companies. If an organization is accomplishing its objectives, it is accomplishing its purpose and thereby justifying its reason for existence.

Organizations exist for various purposes and thus have various types of objectives. A hospital, for example, may have the primary purpose of providing high-quality medical services to the community. Therefore, its objectives are aimed at furnishing this assistance. The primary purpose of a business organization, in contrast, is usually to make a profit. The objectives of the business organization, therefore, concentrate on ensuring that a profit is made. Some companies, however, assume that if they focus on such organizational objectives as producing a quality product at a competitive price,

> **Organizational objectives** are the targets toward which the open management system is directed. They flow from the organization's purpose or mission.
>
> The **organizational purpose** is what the organization exists to do, given a particular group of customers and customer needs.

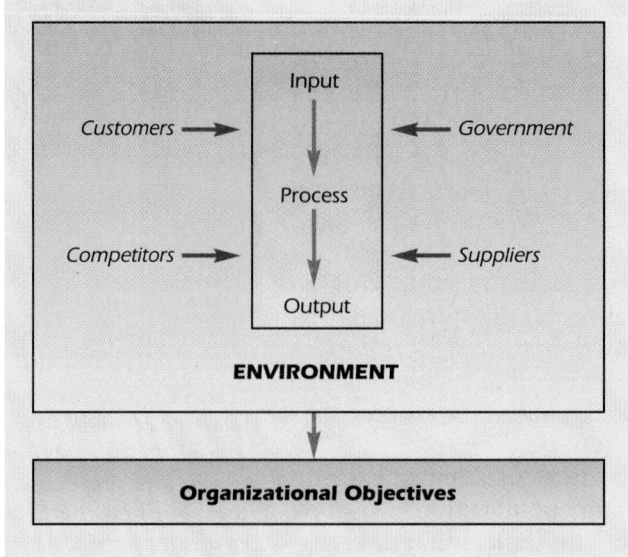

Figure 5.1   How an open management system operates to reach organizational objectives

Table 5.1

Examples of Statements of Organizational Purpose

DuPont	DuPont is a multinational high-technology company that manufactures and markets chemically related products. It services a diversified group of markets in which proprietory technology provides the competing edge.
Polaroid	Polaroid manufactures and sells photographic products based on its inventions in the field of one-step instant photography and light-polarizing products. Utilizing its inventions in the field of polarized light, the company considers itself to be engaged in one line of business.
Central Soya	The basic mission of Central Soya is to be a leading producer and merchandiser of products for the worldwide agribusiness and food industry.
General Portland Cement	It has long been a business philosophy of Central Portland that "we manufacture and sell cement, but we market concrete." The company sees its job as manufacturing top-quality cement and working with customers to develop new applications for concrete while expanding current uses.

profits will be inevitable. For example, although the Lincoln Electric Company is profit oriented, management has stated organizational objectives in these terms:

> The goal of the organization must be this—to make a better and better product to be sold at a lower and lower price. Profit cannot be the goal. Profit must be a by-product. This is a state of mind and a philosophy. Actually, an organization doing this job as it can be done will make large profits which must be properly divided between user, worker, and stockholder. This takes ability and character.[1]

In a 1956 article that has become a classic, John F. Mee suggested that organizational objectives for businesses can be summarized in three points:

1. Profit is the motivating force for managers.
2. Service to customers by the provision of desired economic values (goods and services) justifies the existence of the business.
3. Managers have social responsibilities in accordance with the ethical and moral codes of the society in which the business operates.[2]

Founded in 1987, Outback Steak-houses, based in Tampa, Florida, set as its broad organizational goal capturing the mid range of the casual-dining steakhouse business. In order to maintain stable management and integrate employees into its organizational structure, Outback gives restaurant managers significant ownership stakes, maintains only one layer of management between founders and outlet managers, and permits in-store managers to handle all human resource decisions. Service quality is maintained because staff serve only three tables, and product quality because everything is prepared on site.

Deciding on the objectives for an organization, then, is one of the most important actions managers take. Unrealistically high objectives are frustrating for employees, while objectives that are set too low do not push employees to maximize their potential. Managers should establish performance objectives that they know from experience are within reach for employees, but not within *easy* reach.[3]

ASEA BROWN BOVERI DECIDES ON GLOBAL OBJECTIVES

GLOBAL SPOTLIGHT

An important part of being a manager is deciding on the objectives to formulate for an organization. Management at ASEA Brown Boveri (ABB) has set the organizational objective of expanding its international business.

ABB, winner of R&D magazine's Corporation of the Year award, is a Swiss-Swedish corporation that was established in 1988. It is fast becoming a model for how to manage globally. Already, ABB is the world's largest manufacturer of railway vehicles, the world's leading equipment supplier to the electric power industry, and a major contender in robotics and worldwide pollution control equipment.

One of ABB's secrets in accomplishing its objectives to grow globally is that the company delegates large amounts of authority to managers around the world while maintaining influence over their important decisions regarding the business. Managers at ABB understand that reaching the organization's global objectives involves much more than generating international sales. A company like ABB must use management training sessions to inculcate global management skills in its managers. These skills include the ability to negotiate effectively with people from other cultures, the expertise to interpret market factors in different countries, and the competence to understand foreign politics. Such training will give a company like ABB a labor force that can compete effectively anywhere in the world.≈

Importance of Organizational Objectives

Managers use organizational objectives the way sailors use the North Star—they sight their compass by the objective, and then use it as the means of getting back on track whenever they go astray.[4] Organizational objectives give managers and all other organization members important guidelines for action in such areas as decision making, organizational efficiency, organizational consistency, and performance evaluation.

Guide for Decision Making   A significant part of managerial responsibility is making decisions that influence the everyday operation and existence of the organization and of organization members. Once managers grasp organizational objectives, they know the direction in which the organization must move. It then becomes their responsibility to make decisions that push the organization toward the achievement of its objectives.

Guide for Organizational Efficiency   Because inefficiency results in a costly waste of human effort and resources, managers strive to increase organizational efficiency whenever possible. Efficiency is defined in terms of the total amount of human effort and resources that an organization uses to achieve organizational aims. Therefore, before organizational efficiency can improve, managers must have a clear understanding of organizational goals. Only then will they be able to use the limited resources at their disposal as efficiently as possible.

Guide for Organizational Consistency   Organization members often need work-related directives. If organizational objectives are used as the basis for these directives, the objectives will serve as a guide to consistent encouragement of productive activity, quality decision making, and effective planning.

In 1992, Boeing CEO Frank Shrontz set two efficiency-related goals for his company. First, Boeing would cut costs so dramatically that airlines would find it cheaper to buy new planes than constantly refurbish old ones. Second, Boeing would reduce from 18 months to 8 months the time needed to build a 747 or 767. The purpose of this second goal was to reduce both inventories and the risk entailed by buyers waiting for delivery. At present, Boeing can build most wide-bodied jets inside of ten months.

Guide for Performance Evaluation   Periodically, the performance of all organization members should be evaluated to assess individual productivity and to determine what might be done to increase it. Organizational goals are the guidelines or criteria that should be used as the basis for these evaluations. The individuals who contribute most to the attainment of organizational goals should be considered the most productive organization members. Specific recommendations for increasing productivity should include suggestions about what individuals can do to help the organization move toward goal attainment.[5]

BACK TO THE CASE   The text discussion of organizational objectives gives managers such as Sheridan Garrison, the chief operating officer of Arkansas Freightways, useful insights on how a company can be put on the right track and kept there. The introductory case revealed that Garrison had focused almost solely on one objective—company growth. He used this objective as a guide for making decisions about taking on the business of a failed competitor and promoting organizational consistency regarding how various company terminals should handle this new business. The case implies that in order to achieve his objective of growth, Garrison monitored his terminals in various cities and concentrated on improving their effectiveness in handling new business. From a management viewpoint, these steps he took to pursue and reach his growth objective were logical. Although in the shorter run it is debatable whether Garrison made a sound decision to pursue the growth objective so relentlessly, profits have been restored and even increased at Arkansas Freightways, so in the longer run Garrison's decision seems to have been a sound one.

TYPES OF OBJECTIVES IN ORGANIZATIONS

Objectives in organizations can be separated into two categories: organizational and individual. Recognizing the two categories and reacting appropriately to each are a challenge for all modern managers.

Organizational Objectives

Organizational objectives are the formal targets of the organization and are set to help the organization accomplish its purpose. They concern such areas as organizational efficiency, productivity, and profit maximization.

Y. K. Shetty conducted a study to determine the nature and pattern of corporate objectives as they actually exist in organizations. Shetty analyzed 193 companies in four basic industrial groups: (1) chemicals and drugs, (2) packaging materials, (3) electricity and electronics, and (4) food processing.[6] The results of his study indicate that the most common organizational objectives relate to profitability, growth, and market share. Social responsibility and employee welfare objectives are also common and probably reflect a change in approaches to management activities over a period of years. Still important, but less common objectives, relate to efficiency, research and development, and financial stability.

Individual Objectives

Individual objectives are personal goals that each organization member would like to reach as a result of personal activity in the organization.

Individual objectives, which also exist within organizations, are the personal goals each organization member would like to reach through activity within the organization. These objectives include high salary, personal growth and development, peer recognition, and societal recognition.

It is a problem for management when organizational objectives and individual objectives are incompatible. For example, a professor may have an individual goal of working at a university primarily to gain peer recognition. Perhaps she pursues this recognition primarily by channeling most of her energies into research. This professor's individual objective could significantly contribute to the attainment of organizational objectives if she is at a university whose organizational objectives emphasized research. Her individual objective might contribute little or nothing to organizational goal attainment, however, if she is employed at a teaching-oriented university, because rather than improving her general teaching ability and the quality of her courses—which would be compatible with the teaching university's goals—she would be secluded in the library writing research articles.

One alternative managers have in situations of this type is to structure the organization so that individuals have the opportunity to accomplish their own objectives while contributing to the attainment of organizational goals. For instance, the teaching-oriented university could take steps to ensure that good teachers received peer recognition—by offering an "excellence in teaching" award, for example. In this way, professors could strive for their personal peer recognition goal while simultaneously contributing to the university's organizational objective of good teaching.

Goal Integration

Goal integration is compatibility between individual and organizational objectives. It occurs when organizational and individual objectives are the same.

An objective, or goal, integration model can help managers understand and solve problems related to incompatibility between organizational and individual objectives. Jon Barrett's model, presented in Figure 5.2, depicts a situation in which the objectives in area C are the only individual ones (area A) compatible with organizational objectives (area B). Area C, then, represents the extent of **goal integration.**

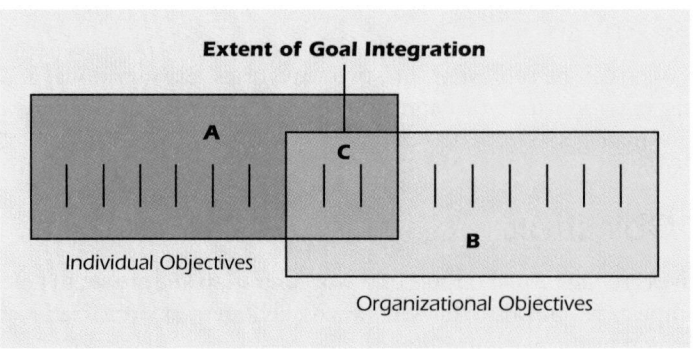

Figure 5.2   Goal integration model

Managers should keep in mind two things about the situation depicted in this figure. First, the individual will tend to work for goals in area C without much managerial encouragement because the attainment of these goals will result in some type of reward the individual considers valuable. Second, the individual will usually not work for goals outside area A without some significant type of managerial encouragement because the attainment of these goals holds little promise of bringing any reward the individual considers valuable. Barrett suggests that "significant types of managerial encouragement" could take any one of the following forms:

1. Modifications to existing pay schedules.
2. Considerate treatment from superiors.
3. Additional opportunities to engage in informal social relationships with peers.[7]

BACK TO THE CASE   Conflict between organizational objectives and individual objectives can spell trouble for an organization. Finding a common ground between these two types of objectives is often difficult. Part of Garrison's success in accomplishing growth at Arkansas Freightways undoubtedly can be attributed to compatibility between organizational and individual objectives. For example, key managers of company terminals as well as drivers at Arkansas Freightways might have individual objectives of national visibility and recognition within the trucking industry. Assuming these employees believe that company growth will contribute to the satisfaction of these two individual goals, they will do all they can to help Garrison achieve the organizational goal of company growth. In this type of situation, a significant degree of goal integration helps management to achieve company growth.

Areas for Organizational Objectives

Peter F. Drucker, one of the most influential management writers of modern times, believed that the very survival of a management system was endangered when managers emphasized only the profit objective because this single-objective emphasis encourages managers to take action that will make money today with little regard for how a profit will be made tomorrow.[8]

Managers should strive to develop and attain a variety of objectives in all areas where activity is critical to the operation and success of the management system. Following are the eight key areas in which Drucker advised managers to set management system objectives:

1. *Market standing.*   Management should set objectives indicating where it would like to be in relation to its competitors.
2. *Innovation.*   Management should set objectives outlining its commitment to the development of new methods of operation.
3. *Productivity.*   Management should set objectives outlining the target levels of production.
4. *Physical and financial resources.*   Management should set objectives regarding the use, acquisition, and maintenance of capital and monetary resources.
5. *Profitability.*   Management should set objectives that specify the profit the company would like to generate.
6. *Managerial performance and development.*   Management should set objectives that specify rates and levels of managerial productivity and growth.
7. *Worker performance and attitude.*   Management should set objectives that specify rates of worker productivity as well as desirable attitudes for workers to possess.
8. *Public responsibility.*   Management should set objectives that indicate the company's responsibilities to its customers and society and the extent to which the company intends to live up to those responsibilities.

According to Drucker, since the first five goal areas relate to tangible, impersonal characteristics of organizational operation, most managers would not dispute their designation as key areas. Designating the last three as key areas, however, could arouse some managerial opposition, since these areas are more personal and subjective. Regardless of this potential opposition, an organization should have objectives in all eight areas to maximize its probability of success.

The information in this section pertains to all the different areas in which managers can establish organizational objectives. The following CUTTING EDGE feature discusses those areas in which setting objectives is most related to the success of a modern organization.

OBJECTIVES AREAS MOST RELATED TO SUCCESS OF MODERN ORGANIZATIONS

CUTTING EDGE

Towers Perrin, a management consulting firm, recently conducted a management survey to determine which are the key areas for setting objectives to ensure business success. Over 300 senior executives at midsize and large companies were asked to rank the three most important areas for establishing organizational objectives.

Customer satisfaction received the highest rating by the executives, with 72 percent ranking this area among the three most important. *Financial performance* and *product and service quality* were next: The first area was mentioned by 60 percent and the second by 41 percent of the executives. *Quality of marketing* received the lowest survey rating—only 15 percent of those surveyed ranked this area within the top three. As a somewhat controversial aside, just 32 percent of the managers ranked *investment in people* within the top three areas and only 28 percent put *people performance* in the top three.≈

WORKING WITH ORGANIZATIONAL OBJECTIVES

Appropriate objectives are fundamental to the success of any organization. Theodore Levitt noted that some leading U.S. industries could be facing the same financial disaster as the railroads faced years earlier because their objectives were inappropriate for their organizations.[9]

Managers should approach the development, use, and modification of organizational objectives with the utmost seriousness. In general, an organization should set three types of objectives:

1. **Short-term objectives:** targets to be achieved in one year or less.
2. **Intermediate-term objectives:** targets to be achieved in one to five years.
3. **Long-term objectives:** targets to be achieved in five to seven years.

The necessity of predetermining appropriate organizational objectives has led to the development of a management guideline called the **principle of the objective.** This principle holds that before managers initiate any action, they should clearly determine, understand, and state organizational objectives.

Establishing Organizational Objectives

Setting objectives is becoming an increasingly important part of a manager's job. Managers today are commonly asked to establish objectives for themselves, their departments, and their employees.[10] The three main steps a manager must take to develop a set of working organizational objectives are:

Short-term objectives are targets to be achieved in one year or less.

Intermediate-term objectives are targets to be achieved within one to five years.

Long-term objectives are targets to be achieved within five to seven years.

The **principle of the objective** is a management guideline that recommends that before managers initiate any action, they should clearly determine, understand, and state organizational objectives.

1. Determine the existence of any environmental trends that could significantly influence the operation of the organization.
2. Develop a set of objectives for the organization as a whole.
3. Develop a hierarchy of organizational objectives.

These three steps are interrelated and usually require input from several people at different levels and operational sections of the organization. Each step is further developed in the paragraphs that follow.

Analyzing Trends

The first step in setting organizational objectives is to list major trends in the organizational environment over the past five years and to determine if these trends have had a noticeable impact on organizational success. Conceivably, the trends could include changing customer needs,[11] marketing innovations of competitors, government controls, and social changes such as decreasing family size. Management should then decide which present and future trends are likely to affect organizational success over the next five years. This decision will determine what kinds of objectives are set at various levels of the organization.

Developing Objectives for the Organization as a Whole

After analyzing environmental trends, management should develop objectives that reflect this analysis for the organization as a whole. For example, the analysis may show that a major competitor has been continually improving its products over the past five years and, as a result, is gaining an increasingly large share of the market. In reaction to this trend, management should set a product improvement objective that will enable the organization to keep up with competitors. This objective would result directly from identification of a trend within the organizational environment and from the organizational purpose of profit. The paragraphs that follow illustrate how management might set financial objectives, product-market mix objectives, and functional objectives for the organization as a whole.

DIVERSITY: OBJECTIVE FOR THE WHOLE ORGANIZATION AT THE DEPARTMENT OF TRANSPORTATION

DIVERSITY SPOTLIGHT   Managers at the Department of Transportation (DOT), a major department within the U.S. government, appreciate the role that a properly managed diverse workforce can play in making an organization successful. In fact, management has set the objective of creating a work environment throughout DOT that fully values and uses the talents and capabilities of all employees, including employees of different cultures and colors.

DOT has taken several specific actions to try to accomplish this diversity objective. Management started out by holding sessions with DOT employees to hear their suggestions on how to create a diversity-sensitive environment. Building upon this employee input, DOT then held a diversity summit that was attended by over 650 department executives from across the country. The purpose of the summit was to pinpoint and explore diversity-related challenges and opportunities that confront DOT today. In addition, DOT assembled a team of human resources management professionals to work full-time on promoting diversity. This team works closely with managers throughout the department to create, plan, and implement diversity initiatives and to ensure that diversity issues are emphasized in all facets of DOT's operations. DOT also publishes a diversity newsletter to explain diversity issues to employees, provide them with information about department initiatives in this area, and suggest how diversity issues should be handled in the workplace.≈

Establishing Financial Objectives.   **Financial objectives** are organizational targets relating to monetary issues. In some organizations, government regulations guide

Financial objectives are organizational targets relating to monetary issues. They are influenced by return on investment and financial comparisons with competitors.

$$\text{Return on Investment} = \frac{\text{Total dollar amount earned}}{\text{Total dollar amount invested to keep organization operating}}$$

$$\text{Return on Investment} = \frac{\$50,000 \text{ (earnings)}}{\$500,000 \text{ (investment)}} = .10 = 10\% \text{ (rate of return)}$$

Figure 5.3 Calculations for return on investment

management's setting of these objectives. Managers of public utility organizations, for example, have definite guidelines for the types of financial objectives they are allowed to set. In organizations free from government constraints, the setting of financial objectives is influenced mainly by return on investment and financial comparisons with competitors.[12]

Return on investment (ROI) is the amount of money an organization earns in relation to the amount of money invested to keep the organization in operation. Figure 5.3 shows how to use earnings of $50,000 and an investment of $500,000 to calculate a return on investment. If the calculated return is too low, managers can set as an overall objective improving the organization's rate of return.

Information on organizational competition is available through published indexes, such as Dun & Bradstreet's *Ratios for Selected Industries*. These ratios reflect industry averages for key financial areas. Comparing company figures with the industrial averages should tell management about the areas in which new financial objectives should be set or the ways in which existing objectives should be modified.[13]

Product-market mix objectives are objectives that outline which products—and the relative number or mix of these products—the organization will attempt to sell.

Establishing Product-Market Mix Objectives. Product-market mix objectives outline which products—and the relative number or mix of these products—the organization will attempt to sell. Granger suggests the following five steps in formulating product-market mix objectives:[14]

1. Examine key trends in the business environments of the product-market areas.
2. Examine growth trends (both market and volume) and profit trends (for the industry and for the company) in the individual product-mix areas.
3. Separate product-market areas into those that are going to pull ahead and those that are going to drag. For promising areas, the following questions need to be asked: How can these areas be made to flourish? Should additional capital, marketing effort, technology, management talent, or the like be injected

His predecessor had insisted that each of the company's operating units remain independent so that they would be more responsive to changing consumer tastes. But when Philip B. Fletcher took over as CEO of ConAgra Inc., a consumer-foods giant based in Omaha, Nebraska, he instituted a program of cost controls that applied to the company as a whole. Thus while he still grants the virtues of independence, he has established executive councils on which division heads meet to discuss ways of sharing such costs as purchasing and warehousing.

into these areas? For the less promising areas, these questions are pertinent: Why is the product lagging? How can the lag be corrected? If it cannot be corrected, should the product be milked for whatever can be regained, or should it be withdrawn from the market?

4. Consider the need or desirability of adding new products or market areas to the mix. In this regard, management should ask these questions: Is there a profit gap to be filled? Based on the criteria of profit opportunity, compatibility, and feasibility of market entry, what are possible new areas of interest in order of priority? What sort of programs (acquisitions or internal development) does the company need to develop the desired level of business in these areas?

5. Derive an optimum yet realistic product-market mix profile based on the conclusions reached in steps 1–4. This profile embodies the product-market mix objectives, which should be consistent with the organization's financial objectives. Interaction while setting these two kinds of objectives is advisable.

Establishing Functional Objectives   **Functional objectives** are targets relating to key organizational functions, including marketing, accounting, production, and personnel. Functional objectives that are consistent with the financial and product-market mix objectives should be developed for these areas. People in the organization should perform their functions in a way that helps the organization attain its other objectives.

> **Functional objectives** are targets relating to key organizational functions. They should be consistent with financial and product-market mix objectives.

BACK TO THE CASE   The information just presented implies that managers such as Garrison should set and strive to achieve objectives other than growth objectives. These additional objectives are in such areas as profitability, market standing, innovation, productivity, physical and financial resources, managerial performance and development, worker performance and attitude, and public responsibility. All should be set for the short, intermediate, and long term.

Before developing such objectives, however, Garrison should pinpoint any environmental trends, such as changes in the cost of gasoline or the growth of competitors, that could influence Arkansas Freightways' operations. Objectives that reflect such environmental trends could then be set for the organization as a whole. These normally would include financial objectives, such as return on investment, as well as product-market mix objectives, such as the length and size of hauls the company will offer.

At 3M Corporation, Scotch-Brite, Never Rust soap pads are just one result of CEO L. D. DeSimone's focusing of short- and long-term objectives squarely on the new product pipeline. He has established, for example, a so-called 30-and-4 standard: 3M must generate 30 percent of its profits from products introduced within the previous four-year period. Within 18 months of their launch, the new Scotch-Brite soap pads captured 22 percent of the $100 million annual U.S. market.

Developing a Hierarchy of Objectives

In practice, an organizational objective must be broken down into subobjectives so that individuals at different levels and sections of the organization know what they must do to help reach the overall organizational objective.[15] An organizational objective is attained only after the subobjectives have been reached.

The overall organizational objective and the subobjectives assigned to the various people or units of the organization are referred to as a **hierarchy of objectives.** Figure 5.4 presents a sample hierarchy of objectives for a medium-sized company.

Suboptimization is a condition wherein subobjectives are conflicting or not directly aimed at accomplishing the overall organizational objective. Suboptimization is possible within the company whose hierarchy of objectives is depicted in Figure 5.4 if the first subobjective for the finance and accounting department clashes with the second subobjective for the supervisors. This conflict would occur if supervisors needed new equipment to maintain production and the finance and accounting department couldn't approve the loan without the company's borrowing surpassing 50 percent of company assets. In such a situation, in which established subobjectives are aimed in different directions, a manager would have to choose which subobjective would better contribute to obtaining overall objectives and should therefore take precedence.

Controlling suboptimization in organizations is part of a manager's job. Managers can minimize suboptimization by developing a thorough understanding of how various parts of the organization relate to one another and by ensuring that subobjectives properly reflect these relations.

A **hierarchy of objectives** is the overall organizational objectives and the subobjectives assigned to the various people or units of the organization.

Suboptimization is a condition wherein organizational subobjectives are conflicting or not directly aimed at accomplishing the overall organizational objectives.

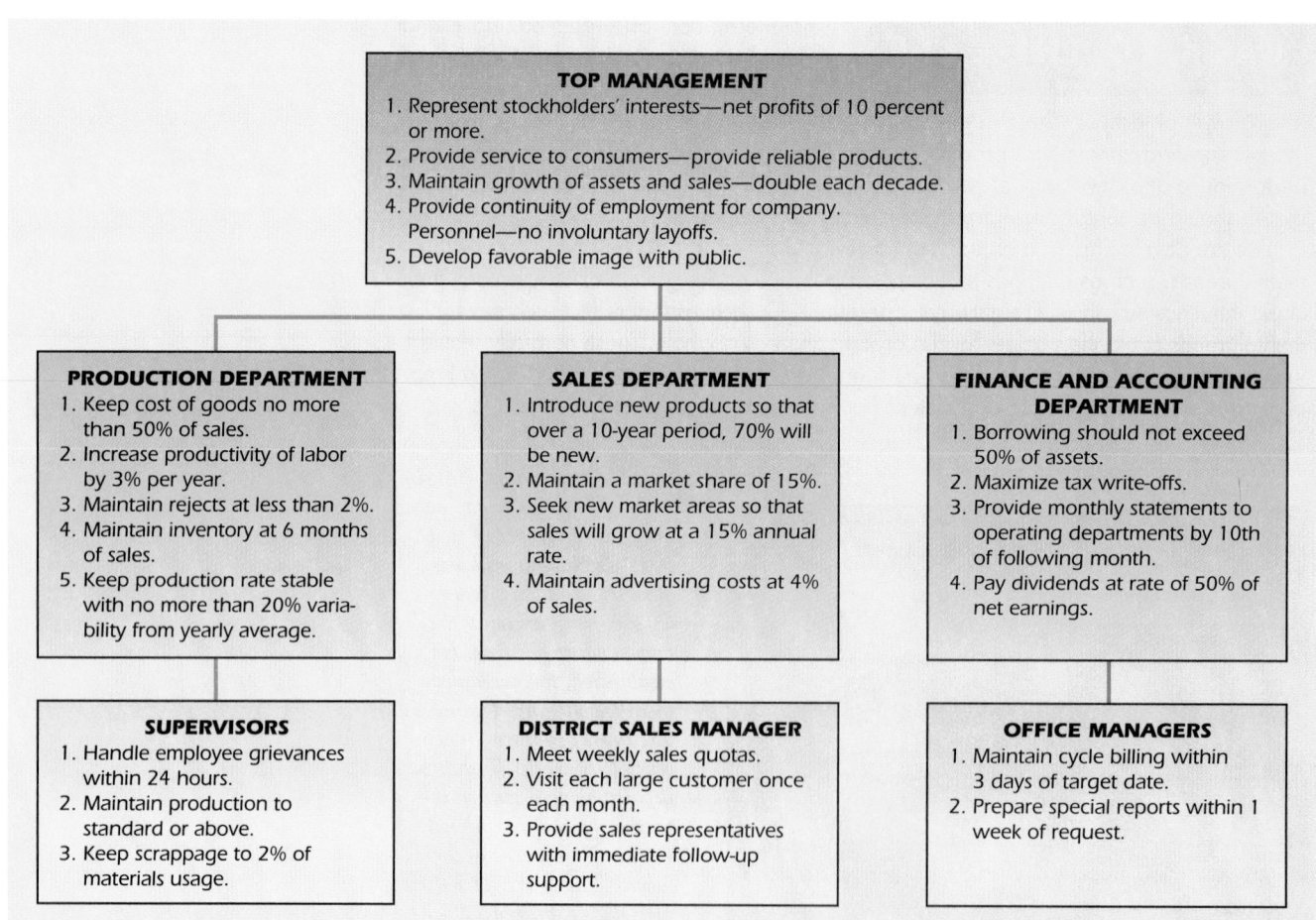

Figure 5.4   Hierarchy of objectives for a medium-sized organization

Guidelines for Establishing Quality Objectives

The quality of goal statements, like that of all humanly developed commodities, can vary drastically. Here are some general guidelines that managers can use to increase the quality of their objectives:

1. *Let the people responsible for attaining the objectives have a voice in setting them.* Often the people responsible for attaining the objectives know their job situation better than the managers do and can therefore help to make the objectives more realistic. They will also be better motivated to achieve objectives they have had a say in establishing. Work-related problems that these people face should be thoroughly considered when objectives are being developed.
2. *State objectives as specifically as possible.* Precise statements minimize confusion and ensure that employees have explicit directions for what they should do. Research shows that when objectives are not specific, the productivity of individuals attempting to reach those objectives tends to fluctuate significantly over time.
3. *Relate objectives to specific actions whenever necessary.* In this way, employees do not have to infer what they should do to accomplish their goals.
4. *Pinpoint expected results.* Employees should know exactly how managers will determine whether or not an objective has been reached.
5. *Set goals high enough that employees will have to strive to meet them, but not so high that employees give up trying to meet them.* Managers want employees to work hard but not to become frustrated.
6. *Specify when goals are expected to be achieved.* Employees must have a time frame for accomplishing their objectives. They then can pace themselves accordingly.
7. *Set objectives only in relation to other organizational objectives.* In this way, suboptimization can be kept to a minimum.
8. *State objectives clearly and simply.* The written or spoken word should not impede communicating a goal to organization members.[16]

Guidelines for Making Objectives Operational

Objectives must be stated in operational terms. That is, if an organization has **operational objectives,** managers should be able to tell if these objectives are being attained by comparing the actual results with the goal statements.[17]

Assume, for example, that a physical education instructor has set the following objectives for his students:

Operational objectives are objectives that are stated in observable or measurable terms. They specify the activities or operations needed to attain them.

1. Each student will strive to develop a sense of balance.
2. Each student will attempt to become flexible.
3. Each student will try to become agile.
4. Each student will try to become strong.
5. Each student will work on becoming powerful.
6. Each student will strive to become durable.

These objectives are not operational because the activities and operations a student must perform to attain them are not specified. Additional information, however, could easily make the objectives operational. For example, the fifth physical education objective could be replaced with: Each student will strive to develop the power to do standing broad jumps the distance of his or her height plus one foot. Table 5.2 lists four basically nonoperational objectives and then shows how each can be made operational.

Table 5.2

Nonoperational Objectives Versus Operational Objectives

NONOPERATIONAL OBJECTIVES	OPERATIONAL OBJECTIVES
1. Imrove product quality.	1. Reduce quality rejects to 2%.
2. Improve communications.	2. Hold weekly staff meetings and initiate a newsletter to improve communications.
3. Improve social responsibility.	3. Hire 50 hard-core unemployed each year.
4. Issue monthly accounting reports on a more timely basis.	4. Issue monthly accounting reports so they are received 3 days after the close of the accounting period.

BACK TO THE CASE

Once managers have set overall objectives for their organization, the next step is to develop a company hierarchy of objectives. The development of this hierarchy entails breaking down the organization's overall objectives into subobjectives so that all organization members know what they must do to help the company reach its overall objectives.

At Arkansas Freightways, a hierarchy of objectives must not include a wide array of objectives. Most employees would understand that the company places a serious emphasis on developing new business and on maintaining terminals and driving schedules that support this growth, and would also know what their particular roles are regarding this emphasis. It is advisable that the company address the setting and accomplishment of objectives in other areas, such as social responsibility, employee welfare, and diversification.

In establishing a hierarchy of objectives, Garrison must be careful not to suboptimize, or establish objectives or subobjectives that conflict with one another. One suboptimization problem at Arkansas Freightways in the past was that growth objectives conflicted with profitability and high-quality service objectives. In many organizations, confusion about what the organizational objectives and subobjectives actually are can make it difficult for managers to recognize suboptimization.

Other guidelines for establishing useful objectives at a company like Arkansas Freightways are making the objectives clear, consistent, challenging, and specific. Perhaps most important of all, organizational objectives should be operational. These are certainly good guidelines for a manager like Garrison to follow in formulating organizational objectives. In addition, if he allows his workers to participate in establishing organizational objectives, Garrison will increase the odds that company objectives are realistic and that organization members are committed to reaching them.

Attainment of Objectives

The attainment of organizational objectives is the obvious goal of all conscientious managers. Managers quickly discover, however, that moving the organization toward goal attainment requires taking appropriate actions within the organization to reach the desired ends. This process is called means-ends analysis.

Means-ends analysis is the process of outlining the means by which various organizational objectives, or ends, can be achieved.

Basically, **means-ends analysis** entails "(1) starting with the general goal to be achieved; (2) discovering a set of means, very generally specified, for accomplishing this goal; and (3) taking each of these means, in turn, as a new subgoal and discovering a more detailed means for achieving it."[18]

Table 5.3 illustrates a means-ends analysis for three sample goals for a hotel: increased market share, financial stability, and owner satisfaction. The goal of increased market share includes two means: good service and employee morale/loyalty. These two means are subgoals that the hotel manager must focus on attaining in order to

Table 5.3		
Sample Goals, Means, and Measures for a Hotel		
Increased market share	Good service	Ratio of repeat business Occupancy Informal feedback
	Employee morale and loyalty	Turnover Absenteeism Informal feedback
Financial stability	Image in financial markets	Price-earnings ratio Share price
	Profitability	Earnings per share Gross operating profit Cost trends Cash flow
	Strength of management team	Turnover Divisional profit Rate of proportion Informal feedback
Owner satisfaction	Adequate cash flow	Occupancy Sales Gross operating profit Departmental profit

reach the goal of increased market share. The last column of the table lists the measures that can be taken to operationalize the subgoals.

Effective managers are aware of the importance not only of setting organizational objectives but also of clearly outlining the means by which these objectives can be attained. They know that means-ends analysis is essential for guiding their own activities as well as those of their subordinates. The better everyone within the organization understands the means by which goals are to be attained, the greater the probability that the goals will be reached.

How to Use Objectives

As stated earlier in the chapter, organizational objectives flow naturally from organizational purpose and reflect the organization's environment. Managers must have a firm understanding of the influences that mold organizational objectives, for as these influences change, so must the objectives themselves. Managers should never look upon objectives as unchangeable directives. In fact, a significant managerial responsibility is to help the organization change objectives when necessary.

MANAGEMENT BY OBJECTIVES (MBO)

Some managers find organizational objectives such an important and fundamental part of management that they use a management approach based exclusively on them. This approach, called **management by objectives (MBO),** was popularized mainly through the writings of Peter Drucker. Although mostly discussed in the context of profit-oriented companies, MBO is also a valuable management tool for nonprofit organizations like libraries and community clubs.[19] The MBO strategy has three basic parts:

1. All individuals within an organization are assigned a specialized set of objectives that they try to reach during a normal operating period. These objectives are mutually set and agreed upon by individuals and their managers.

Management by objectives (MBO) is a management approach that uses organizational objectives as the primary means of managing organizations.

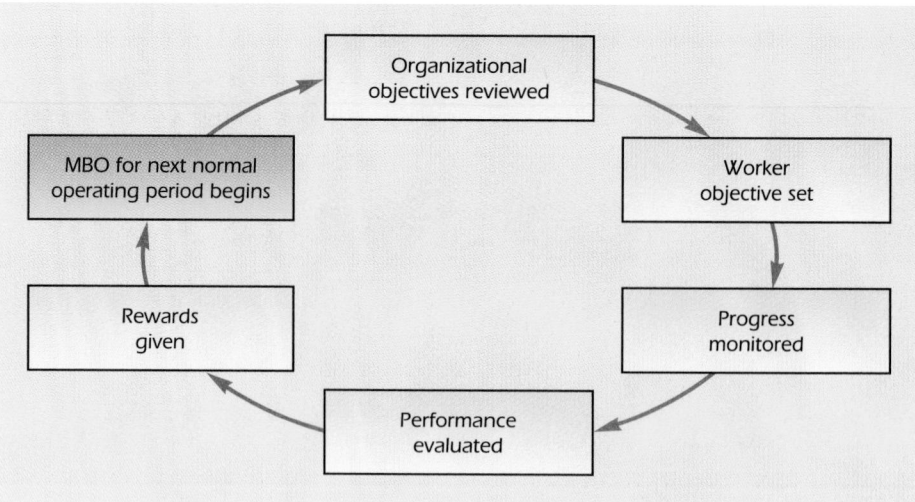

Figure 5.5   The MBO process

2. Performance reviews are conducted periodically to determine how close individuals are to attaining their objectives.
3. Rewards are given to individuals on the basis of how close they come to reaching their goals.[20]

The MBO process consists of five steps (see Figure 5.5):

1. *Review organizational objectives.* The manager gains a clear understanding of the organization's overall objectives.
2. *Set worker objectives.* The manager and worker meet to agree on worker objectives to be reached by the end of the normal operating period.
3. *Monitor progress.* At intervals during the normal operating period, the manager and worker check to see if the objectives are being reached.
4. *Evaluate performance.* At the end of the normal operating period, the worker's performance is judged by the extent to which the worker reached the objectives.
5. *Give rewards.* Rewards given to the worker are based on the extent to which the objectives were reached.

The traditional focus of MBO is on encouraging individuals to accomplish organizational objectives. The following PEOPLE PERSPECTIVES feature emphasizes that MBO can also be used to encourage groups of people to work as a team toward accomplishing organizational objectives.

BUILDING TEAMWORK TO REACH OBJECTIVES AT HARLEY-DAVIDSON

PEOPLE PERSPECTIVES

Teamwork is a commonsense business tool that too many businesses have almost abandoned. In the simplest terms, a team consists of two or more people working to accomplish a common objective. Management by objectives (MBO) can be used to build employees into teams that accomplish organizational objectives.

Take Harley-Davidson, the world-renowned producer of motorcycles. During any operating period, Harley-Davidson has the objective of shipping some agreed-upon number of motorcycles. To reach this shipping objective, however, many sub-goals—like timely purchases of materials, assembly of parts, and assembly testing—must be accomplished. Team-focused MBO at Harley-Davidson requires all employees who have to work together to accomplish an objective to agree collectively

on what subobjectives are necessary to meet the objective and when these subobjectives must be accomplished. Once agreement is reached, each worker's subobjective(s) is listed on paper and all the workers responsible for accomplishing the subobjectives are asked to sign the paper. Thus MBO at Harley-Davidson emphasizes teamwork— individuals coordinating their efforts to accomplish some common objective.≈

Factors Necessary for a Successful MBO Program

Certain key factors are essential to the success of an MBO program. First, top management must be committed to the MBO process and set appropriate objectives for the organization. Since all individual MBO goals will be based on these overall objectives, if the overall objectives are inappropriate, individual MBO objectives will also be inappropriate and related individual work activity will be nonproductive. Second, managers and subordinates together must develop and agree on each individual's goals. Both managers and subordinates must feel that the individual objectives are just and appropriate if each party is to seriously regard them as a guide for action. Third, employee performance should be conscientiously evaluated against established objectives. This evaluation helps determine whether the objectives are fair and if appropriate means are being used to attain them. Fourth, management must follow through on employee performance evaluations by rewarding employees accordingly.

If employees are to continue to strive to reach their MBO program objectives, managers must reward those who do reach, or surpass, their objectives more than those whose performance falls short of their objectives. It goes without saying that such rewards must be given out fairly and honestly. Managers must be careful, though, not to automatically conclude that employees have produced at an acceptable level simply because they have reached their objectives. The objectives may have been set too low in the first place, and managers may have failed to recognize it at the time.[21]

MBO Programs: Advantages and Disadvantages

Experienced MBO managers say that there are two advantages to the MBO approach. First, MBO programs continually emphasize what should be done in an organization to achieve organizational goals. Second, the MBO process secures employee commitment to attaining organizational goals. Because managers and subordinates have developed objectives together, both parties are sincerely interested in reaching those goals.

MBO managers also admit that MBO has certain disadvantages. One is that the development of objectives can be time-consuming, leaving both managers and employees less time in which to do their actual work. Another is that the elaborate written goals, careful communication of goals, and detailed performance evaluations required in an MBO program increase the volume of paperwork in an organization.

On balance, however, most managers believe that MBO's advantages outweigh its disadvantages. Therefore, they find MBO programs beneficial.[22]

BACK TO THE CASE In addition to making sure that an appropriate set of objectives has been developed for an organization, management must clearly outline for employees the means by which these objectives can be attained. Although Garrison may have done this for his company's objective of growth, he apparently did not follow such guidelines when he quickly took on the extra business created by the failure of his biggest competitor, Jones Truck Lines. Growing too fast caused Arkansas Freightways to develop serious problems in the area of delivery schedules.

To avoid the problem of growing too fast in the future, Garrison might want to consider clarifying company growth objectives through a management-by-objectives pro-

gram. In that case, each employee at Arkansas Freightways would develop with her or his manager a set of mutually agreed-upon objectives that focus on company growth. Performance reviews would give employees feedback on their progress toward reaching their growth-related objectives, and the employees who made the most progress would be rewarded accordingly. The MBO process would allow Garrison to see immediately if he was considering a growth-related action that would place too much strain on company resources.

Action Summary

Reread the learning objectives below. Each objective is followed by questions. Answering these questions accurately will help you retain the most important concepts discussed in this chapter. After answering each question, check your answer against the answer key at the end of this chapter. (*Hint:* If you have any doubts regarding the correct response, consult the page whose number follows the answer.)

Circle: From studying this chapter, I will attempt to acquire:

1. An understanding of organizational objectives.
   - T,F   **a.** Organizational objectives should reflect the organization's purpose.
   - a,b,c,d,e   **b.** The targets toward which an open management system is directed are referred to as: (a) functional objectives; (b) organizational objectives; (c) operational objectives; (d) courses of action; (e) individual objectives.

2. An appreciation for the importance of organizational objectives.
   - a,b,c,d,e   **a.** Organizational objectives serve important functions in all of the following areas except: (a) making performance evaluations useful; (b) establishing consistency; (c) increasing efficiency; (d) improving wages; (e) decision making that influences everyday operations.
   - T,F   **b.** Implied within organizational objectives are hints on how to define the most productive workers in the organization.

3. An ability to tell the difference between organizational objectives and individual objectives.
   - a,b,c,d,e   **a.** The following is considered to be an individual objective: (a) peer recognition; (b) financial security; (c) personal growth; (d) b and c; (e) all of the above.
   - a,b,c,d,e   **b.** When goal integration exists: (a) there is a positive situation, desired by management; (b) managers will not see conflict between organizational and personal objectives; (c) the individual will work for goals without much managerial encouragement; (d) additional opportunities to engage in informal social relationships with peers will not be necessary to encourage the individual; (e) all of the above.

4. A knowledge of the areas in which managers should set organizational objectives.
   - a,b,c,d,e   **a.** The eight key areas in which Peter F. Drucker advises managers to set objectives include all of the following except: (a) market standing; (b) productivity; (c) public responsibility; (d) inventory control; (e) manager performance and development.
   - T,F   **b.** Long-term objectives are defined as targets to be achieved in one to five years.

5. An understanding of the development of organizational objectives.
   - a,b,c,d,e   **a.** The following factor would *not* be considered in analyzing trends: (a) marketing innovations of competitors; (b) projections for society; (c) government controls; (d) known existing and projected future events; (e) product-market mix.
   - a,b,c,d,e   **b.** The following factor would *not* be considered in the "developing objectives for the organization as a whole" stage of setting organizational objectives: (a) establishing a hierarchy of objectives; (b) establishing product-market mix objectives; (c) establishing financial objectives; (d) establishing return-on-investment objectives; (e) establishing functional objectives.

6. Some facility in writing good objectives.
   - a,b,c,d,e   **a.** The following is an objective stated in nonoperational terms: (a) reduce customer complaints by 9 percent; (b) make great progress in new-product development; (c) develop a new customer; (d) increase profit before taxes by 10 percent; (e) reduce quality rejects by 2 percent.

T, F   **b.** An example of a good operational objective is: "Each student in this class will try to learn how to manage."

7. An awareness of how managers use organizational objectives and help others to attain the objectives.

T, F   **a.** Means-ends analysis implies that the manager is results-oriented and discovers a set of means for accomplishing a goal.

a, b, c, d, e   **b.** Managers should use the following guidelines in changing objectives: (a) objectives should not be changed; (b) adapt objectives when the organization's environmental influences change; (c) change objectives to create suboptimization as needed; (d) adapt objectives so that they are nonoperational; (e) all of the above are valid guidelines.

8. An appreciation for the potential of a management-by-objectives (MBO) program.

T, F   **a.** Both performance evaluations and employee rewards should be tied to objectives assigned to individuals when the firm is using MBO.

a, b, c, d, e   **b.** A method under which a manager is given specific objectives to achieve and is evaluated according to the accomplishment of these objectives is: (a) means-ends analysis; (b) operational objectives; (c) individual objectives; (d) management by objectives; (e) management by exception.

Introductory Case Wrap-Up

"Entrepreneur Suffers Growing Pains at Arkansas Freightways" (p. 111) and its related back-to-the-case sections were written to help you better understand the management concepts discussed in this chapter. Answer the following discussion questions about this introductory case to enrich your understanding of the chapter content:

1. If you were Garrison, what objectives besides growth would you develop for Arkansas Freightways? Discuss the importance of each objective to the success of the company.

2. Explain how Garrison's preoccupation with growth caused problems for the company. List several of these problems, explain how they were created, and discuss how they could be eliminated in the future.

3. As a manager, what strengths does Garrison have? What weaknesses does he have?

Issues for Review and Discussion

1. What are organizational objectives and how do they relate to organizational purpose?
2. Explain why objectives are important to an organization.
3. List four areas in which organizational objectives can act as important guidelines for performance.
4. Explain the difference between organizational objectives and individual objectives.
5. What is meant by goal integration?
6. List and define eight key areas in which organizational objectives should be set.
7. How do environmental trends affect the process of establishing organizational objectives?
8. How does return on investment relate to setting financial objectives?
9. Define *product-market mix objectives*. What process should a manager go through to establish them?
10. What are functional objectives?
11. What is a hierarchy of objectives?
12. Explain the purpose of a hierarchy of objectives.
13. How does suboptimization relate to a hierarchy of objectives?
14. List eight guidelines a manager should follow to establish quality organizational objectives.
15. How does a manager make objectives operational?
16. Explain the concept of means-ends analysis.
17. Should a manager ever modify or change existing organizational objectives? If no, why? If yes, when?
18. Define *MBO* and describe its main characteristics.
19. List and describe the factors necessary for an MBO program to be successful.
20. Discuss the advantages and the disadvantages of MBO.

Case Study

The Atlanta Committee for the Olympic Games (ACOG): Setting Objectives for an Event and a City

For Atlanta, Georgia, and the 1996 Olympic Committee, the Olympic motto, "Swifter, Higher, Stronger," was more than the objective for world-class competing athletes. It was their objective as well. Beginning in 1987, Billy Payne, a local real estate attorney, worked with city volunteers to convince the International Olympic Committee (IOC) that Atlanta was the best choice to host the centennial summer Olympic Games. In 1990, the IOC gave Atlanta the go-ahead, and the real work began. Considering the estimated $5.1 billion impact of the games on Georgia's economy, organizing was truly a task of Olympian proportions.

First, ACOG created advisory groups and task forces to help meet the city's objectives before, during, and after the games. Working with constituencies that included neighborhood groups affected by the construction of new Olympic venues, specialists in environmental, transportation, and security issues, Olympic sponsors, artists and artisans who will participate in the Olympics Arts Festival, ACOG eventually developed a process for planning and implementing a vast array of projects.

For example, ACOG worked with transportation officials from a wide range of public agencies to detail traffic circulation plans for movement of the Olympic Family, spectators, and the public in and around the "Olympic Ring"—an imaginary transportation circle encompassing Atlanta. The goal of the plan was to use lane restrictions and limited-hour street closings to keep major arteries and streets accessible to the Olympic Transportation System. In addition to the city's current transit buses and drivers, ACOG organized the delivery, preparation, maintenance, and return of a fleet of 2,000 new mass-transit buses borrowed from cities across the United States and hired 4,000 part-time drivers to supplement existing staff. Another 2,000 people—radio dispatchers, route supervisors, park-and-ride attendants,

bus terminal managers, and baggage handlers—were engaged as support personnel. To further its mandate to protect the city's environment, ACOG tapped the American Gas Association to provide a fleet of 250 natural-gas vehicles, necessary infrastructure, and the natural-gas to fuel both the fleet and another 300 natural-gas-powered buses lent to the Olympic Games by municipalities around the nation. It was decided to include the cost of Olympic transportation for spectators in Atlanta in the price of an Olympic ticket.

To achieve the objective of safe and secure games, ACOG organizers brought together the State Olympic Public Safety Operations Task Force, the Georgia Emergency Management Agency, the Georgia National Guard, the CIA, the Bureau of Alcohol, Tobacco, and Firearms, the Immigration and Naturalization Service, the Secret Service, and U.S. Customs. An overall command and control center was established to divide tasks and coordinate the duties of these diverse groups.

From the beginning, construction around Atlanta was planned to have a major beneficial impact on neighborhoods. Olympic housing, the Olympic Stadium, and the Centennial Olympic Park (according to ACOG, the first urban park to be constructed in the nation in 52 years) are legacies of the games that will be part of the city landscape for years to come. At the same time, ACOG was committed to leaving no unwanted legacies—"white elephants" that the city could not maintain or support. Thus, the 1996 Olympics was planned to be the most transient in Olympics history.

To that end, 1 million square feet of tents, 24 miles of fencing, power backup, 4,000 tons of portable air-conditioning units, 1,800 portable toilets, and 186,000 temporary seats were all designed to disappear after the Olympics. Even some substantial construction was built to be torn down. For example, ACOG spent $6.5 million—much less than went into Barcelona's $25 million

track—on a Velodrome track that can be disassembled after the games. A restaurant large enough to serve 3,000 athletes a day was built at the Olympic Village at a cost of less than one-tenth of the expense of a permanent building. According to John Hancock, ACOG's project manager for temporary structures, "We don't need to invest a lot of ACOG's money in owning things that are only going to be used for 16 days, then have a big fire sale later." ACOG's objective was to avoid the chastening experience of Montreal, whose taxpayers are still paying off the construction debt for the 1976 Summer Games.

Georgia Power, the Atlanta Chamber of Commerce, NationsBank, and other Georgia-based groups worked with ACOG to ensure that when the 1996 Olympic Summer Games were over, their legacy would be a powerful and positive one for Atlanta and the state. Almost two-thirds of the world's population watched the 1996 Olympics on television, and thousands of people coordinated their efforts to prove that through hard work and a shared vision, even the most complex goals could be reached.

Questions:

1. List the areas in which ACOG had to set objectives. What factors inherent in the Olympic Games added to the difficulty of meeting those objectives?

2. Select one objectives area and list possible subobjectives. Consider transportation, traffic control, security, and marketing. What diverse groups of people were necessary to carry out these subobjectives? How were their efforts managed?

3. One of ACOG's major objectives was the international promotion of the city of Atlanta, the state of Georgia, and the southeastern United States. Based on your knowledge of these areas both prior to the Olympics and after the games, was ACOG successful in its promotion efforts? Search for news items showing whether or not there has been an ongoing positive impact from the 1996 Olympics. Why or why not has there been such an impact?

Skills Exercise

After six years of planning, ACOG had only 16 days to execute plans whose success was judged by the entire world. How would you evaluate ACOG's plans and the 1996 Olympics? List at least five areas of the games and at least one major objective for each. Grade ACOG on how close it came to reaching each of these objectives on a scale from 1 to 5 (where 5 is outstanding and 1 is poor). Cite specific examples to support your scoring. On the basis of this evaluation, what aspects of ACOG's plans should Olympic planners in Sydney, Australia, imitate for the 2000 Olympics? What aspects should they discard? Why?

The Internet learning materials that accompany this chapter can be found at
http://www.profcerto.com
Additional information can be found on the inside front and back covers of this text.

6
chapter

FUNDAMENTALS OF PLANNING

STUDENT LEARNING OBJECTIVES

From studying this chapter, I will attempt to acquire:

1. A definition of planning and an understanding of the purposes of planning.
2. A knowledge of the advantages and potential disadvantages of planning.
3. Insights on how the major steps of the planning process are related.
4. An understanding of the planning subsystem.
5. A knowledge of how the chief executive relates to the planning process.
6. An understanding of the qualifications and duties of planners and how planners are evaluated.
7. Guidelines on how to get the greatest return from the planning process.

CHAPTER OUTLINE

DuPont Plans to Make Women's Clothes

DuPont is planning to make clothes as well as chemicals. Long known for its plastics and pesticides, the nation's biggest chemical producer now wants to make women's apparel. In less than a year, the company predicts, the first private-label sportswear designed and manufactured by DuPont Company will begin showing up in U.S. department stores and specialty retail chains.

Why would a $40 billion industrial giant decide to get into the rag trade? The new business, DuPont says, can yield a profit. At the same time, it can help boost DuPont's huge synthetic-fiber business.

Entering an arena ruled by the whims of fashion is a "nontraditional" move, DuPont concedes. In fact, its embryonic garment unit has yet to sign up a single customer. And even though the house-label apparel DuPont plans to make is the garment industry's fastest-growing segment, it remains a hotly competitive field.

The fashion game offers "no sure things," says Faye Landes, a Smith Barney footwear-and-apparel analyst. But "if DuPont can get the right designers and deliver the clothes at the right quality and price, they have a shot." She notes that it's relatively easy to enter the fragmented private-label industry and that it's "a business where you can definitely buy expertise."

DuPont's new unit, Initiatives Inc., is doing just that. Donald Linsenmann, former head of DuPont's Lycra spandex business in Europe and now Initiatives president, is interviewing designers and marketers for the unit's office in New York's garment district.

"I don't want people with a background in chemical engineering," says Mr. Linsenmann. "I want people who may have worked for a Liz Claiborne or DKNY."

DuPont notes that it has been a big provider of textile fibers for decades—in 1994, it sold apparel makers and textile companies more than $3 billion of nylon, Lycra spandex, and polyester fibers—and so already works with designers and retailers. "We've got a lot of experience" in apparel, says a spokesman. "Do we have enough experience? Probably not, yet."

Most private-label concerns design clothing, then take orders from retailers and have the garments made in Asia. Initiatives will work with retailers to design house-brand clothing, then contract to have the apparel cut and sewn in Mexico.

Long a supplier of textile fibers for the fashion industry, DuPont is confident that if it can find the right combination of pricing and design, it can break into the world of private-label high fashions.

what's ahead

The introductory case discusses the initiation of a new product line, women's clothes, at DuPont. It leaves the impression that since DuPont has had little experience in manufacturing and selling women's clothing, the challenges of introducing and maintaining a new, successful line of women's clothing will be formidable. Material in this chapter will help managers like the ones at DuPont's Initiatives understand why planning is so important, not only for ensuring the success of a new-product introduction, but also for carrying out virtually every other organizational activity. The fundamentals of planning are described in this chapter. More specifically, this chapter does the following:

1. Outlines the general characteristics of planning.
2. Discusses steps in the planning process.
3. Describes the planning subsystem.
4. Elaborates upon the relationship between planning and the chief executive.
5. Summarizes the qualifications and duties of planners and explains how planners are evaluated.
6. Explains how to maximize the effectiveness of the planning process.

GENERAL CHARACTERISTICS OF PLANNING

This first major part of the chapter is a general introduction to planning. The sections in this part discuss the following topics:

1. A definition of planning.
2. The purposes of planning.
3. The advantages and potential disadvantages of planning.
4. The primacy of planning.

Defining Planning

Planning is the process of determining how the management system will achieve its objectives. In other words, it determines how the organization can get where it wants to go.

Planning is the process of determining how the organization can get where it wants to go. Chapter 5 emphasized the importance of organizational objectives and explained how to develop them. Planning is the process of determining exactly what the organization will do to accomplish its objectives. In more formal terms, planning is "the systematic development of action programs aimed at reaching agreed business objectives by the process of analyzing, evaluating, and selecting among the opportunities which are foreseen."[1]

Planning is a critical management activity regardless of the type of organization being managed. Modern managers face the challenge of sound planning in small and relatively simple organizations as well as in large, more complex ones, and in nonprofit organizations such as libraries as well as in for-profit organizations such as General Motors.[2]

The following PEOPLE PERSPECTIVES feature concerns McDonald's plans to open restaurants across the globe. It describes how McDonald's Corporation is accomplishing this plan largely by focusing on people.

MCDONALD'S ACCOMPLISHES PLANS BY FOCUSING ON PEOPLE

PEOPLE PERSPECTIVES

The McDonald's Corporation is an excellent example of a modern organization that has successfully implemented its plan to reach profit and growth objectives by establishing operations throughout the world. Over the last 12 years, McDonald's profits have more than

tripled, to almost $1.1 billion on revenues of $7.4 billion and companywide sales of over $23 billion from over 14,000 restaurants. The company is delivering world-standardized food, smiles, value, and cleanliness to every continent in the world except Antarctica. McDonald's presently pulls in about 45 percent of its operating income from foreign operations.

How has McDonald's implemented its plan to go global? The plan has been accomplished through a collection of surprisingly simple people-oriented strategies. First, management constantly gathers employees for face-to-face planning-related meetings whose purpose is to encourage people to learn from one another about how to best accomplish organizational plans. Second, management emphasizes the need to understand a country's culture before attempting to do business there. This strategy encourages managers to uncover issues like a society's values and religious beliefs so they can appropriately deal with customers and workers in that society. Finally, McDonald's hires individuals from the country in which operations are established whenever possible. These locals have a firmer understanding of their society than foreign managers could ever hope to acquire and are therefore invaluable implementing McDonald's organizational plans.≈

Purposes of Planning

Over the years, management writers have presented several different purposes of planning. For example, a classic article by C. W. Roney indicates that organizational planning has two purposes: protective and affirmative. The protective purpose of planning is to minimize risk by reducing the uncertainties surrounding business conditions and clarifying the consequences of related management actions. The affirmative purpose is to increase the degree of organizational success.[3] For an example of this affirmative purpose, consider Whole Foods Market, a health-food chain in Texas. This company uses planning to ensure success as measured by the systematic opening of new stores. Company head John Mackey believes that increased company success is not an accident, but a direct result of careful planning.[4] Still another purpose of planning is to establish a coordinated effort within the organization. Where planning is absent, so, usually, are coordination and organizational efficiency.

The fundamental purpose of planning, however, is to help the organization reach its objectives. As Koontz and O'Donnell put it, the primary purpose of planning is "to facilitate the accomplishment of enterprise and objectives."[5] All other purposes of planning are spin-offs of this fundamental purpose.

Planning: Advantages and Potential Disadvantages

A vigorous planning program produces many benefits. First, it helps managers to be future-oriented. They are forced to look beyond their normal everyday problems to project what situations may confront them in the future.[6] Second, a sound planning program enhances decision coordination. No decision should be made today without some idea of how it will affect a decision that might have to be made tomorrow. The planning function pushes managers to coordinate their decisions. Third, planning emphasizes organizational objectives. Since organizational objectives are the starting points for planning, managers are constantly reminded of exactly what their organization is trying to accomplish.

Overall, planning is very advantageous to an organization. According to an often-cited survey, as many as 65 percent of all newly-started businesses are not around to celebrate a fifth anniversary. This high failure rate seems primarily a consequence of inadequate planning. Successful businesses have an established plan, a formal statement that outlines the objectives the organization is attempting to achieve. Planning does not eliminate risk, of course, but it does help managers identify and deal with organizational problems before they cause havoc in a business.[7]

The downside is that if the planning function is not well executed, planning can have several disadvantages for the organization. For example, an overemphasized planning program can take up too much managerial time. Managers must strike an appropriate balance between time spent on planning and time spent on organizing, influencing, and controlling. If they don't, some activities that are extremely important to the success of the organization may be neglected.

Overall, the advantages of planning definitely outweigh the disadvantages. Usually, the disadvantages of planning result from the planning function's being used incorrectly.

Primacy of Planning

Planning is the primary management function—the one that precedes and is the basis for the organizing, influencing, and controlling functions of managers. Only after managers have developed their plans can they determine how they want to structure their organization, place their people, and establish organizational controls. As discussed in Chapter 1, planning, organizing, influencing, and controlling are interrelated. Planning is the foundation function and the first one to be performed. Organizing, influencing, and controlling are all based on the results of planning. Figure 6.1 shows this interrelationship.

BACK TO THE CASE   t is obvious from the information given in the introductory case that DuPont managers must focus heavily on planning if the company's new line of women's clothing is to be successful. The planning process should help DuPont determine such issues as what and when equipment must be purchased to manufacture the new clothing, where the clothing will be manufactured, and how finished clothing will be delivered to customers.

Because of the many related benefits of planning, DuPont managers should make certain that the planning process is thorough and comprehensive. One particularly notable benefit of planning is the probability of increased profits. To gain this and other benefits of planning, however, DuPont managers must see to it that the planning function is well executed, but not overemphasized.

DuPont managers should also keep in mind that planning is the primary management function. Thus, when introducing new products like women's clothing, they should not begin to organize, influence, or control until they have completed the planning process. Planning is the foundation management function upon which all other management functions at DuPont should be based.

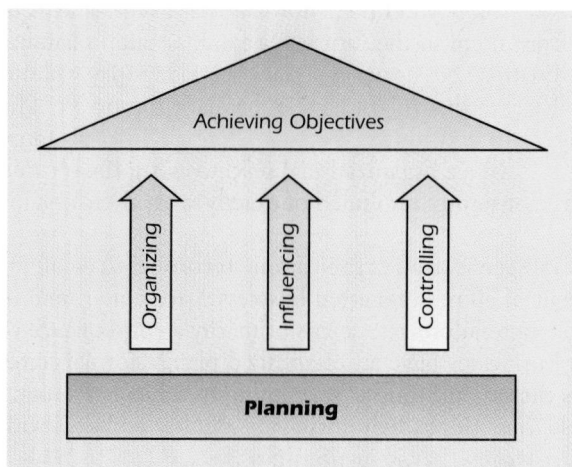

Figure 6.1   Planning as the foundation for organizing, influencing, and controlling

STEPS IN THE PLANNING PROCESS

The planning process consists of the following six steps:

1. *State organizational objectives.*   Since planning focuses on how the management system will reach organizational objectives, a clear statement of those objectives is necessary before planning can begin. In essence, objectives stipulate those areas in which organizational planning must occur.[8] Chapter 5 discusses how the objectives themselves are developed.

2. *List alternative ways of reaching objectives.*   Once organizational objectives have been clearly stated, a manager should list as many available alternatives as possible for reaching those objectives.

3. *Develop premises on which to base each alternative.*   To a large extent, the feasibility of using any one alternative to reach organizational objectives is determined by the **premises,** or assumptions, on which the alternative is based. For example, two alternatives a manager could generate to reach the organizational objective of increasing profit might be: (a) increase the sale of products presently being produced; (b) produce and sell a completely new product. Alternative (a) is based on the premise that the organization can gain a larger share of the existing market. Alternative (b) is based on the premise that a new product would capture a significant portion of a new market. A manager should list all of the premises for each alternative.

4. *Choose the best alternative for reaching objectives.*   An evaluation of alternatives must include an evaluation of the premises on which the alternatives are based. A manager usually finds that the premises on which some of the alternatives are based are unreasonable and can therefore be excluded from further consideration. This elimination process helps the manager determine which alternative would best accomplish organizational objectives. The decision making required for this step is discussed more fully in Chapter 7.

5. *Develop plans to pursue the chosen alternative.*   After an alternative has been chosen, a manager begins to develop strategic (long-range) and tactical (short-range) plans.[9] More information about strategic and tactical planning is presented in Chapters 7 and 8.

6. *Put the plans into action.*   Once plans that furnish the organization with both long-range and short-range direction have been developed, they must be implemented. Obviously, the organization cannot directly benefit from the planning process until this step is performed.

Figure 6.2 shows the sequencing of the six steps of the planning process.

> **Premises** are the assumptions on which an alternative to reaching an organizational objective is based.

CEO Gordon M. Bethune has stated quite clearly his objectives for Continental Airlines: He intends to reduce jobs, costs, and cut-rate fares while simultaneously improving service. The two prongs of the attack may seem contradictory, but Bethune is operating on a specific premise: Continental management, he maintains, can achieve both goals if it becomes more market-savvy and customer-oriented and less willing to let strictly financial considerations dictate marketing decisions.

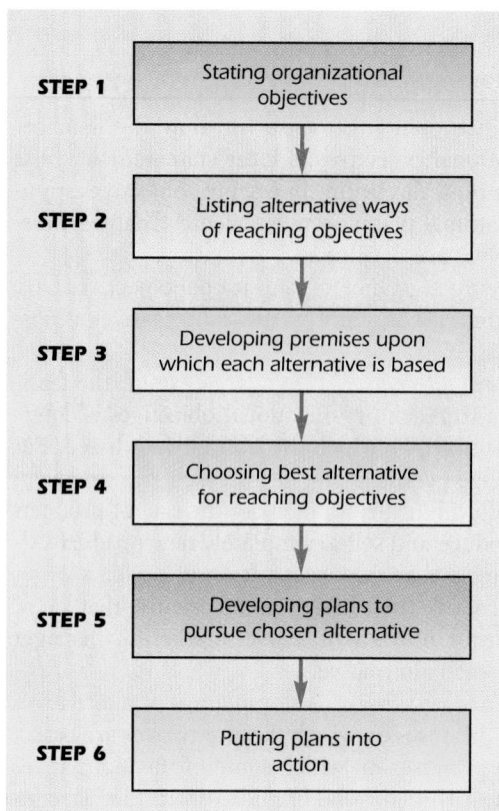

Figure 6.2 Elements of the planning process

THE PLANNING SUBSYSTEM

Once managers thoroughly understand the basics of planning, they can take steps to implement the planning process in their organization. Implementation is the key to a successful planning process. Even though managers might be experts on facts related to planning and the planning process, if they cannot transform this understanding into appropriate action, they will not be able to generate useful organizational plans.

A **subsystem** is a system created as part of the process of the overall management system. A planning subsystem increases the effectiveness of the overall management system.

One way to approach implementation is to view planning activities as an organizational subsystem. A **subsystem** is a system created as part of the process of the overall management system. Figure 6.3 illustrates this relationship between the overall management system and a subsystem. Subsystems help managers organize the overall system and enhance its success.

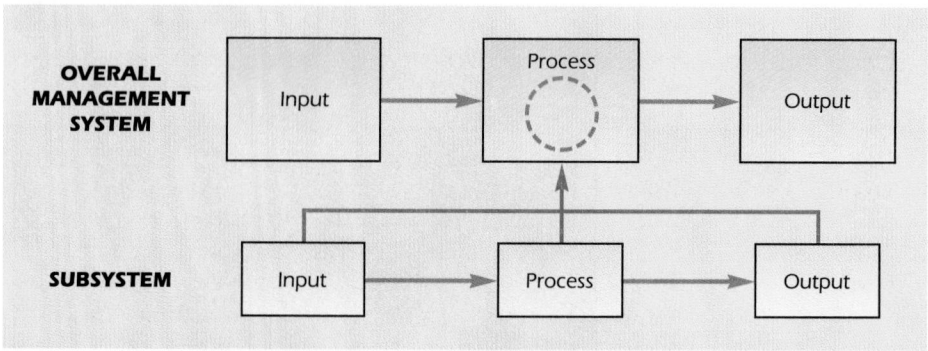

Figure 6.3 Relationship between overall management system and subsystem

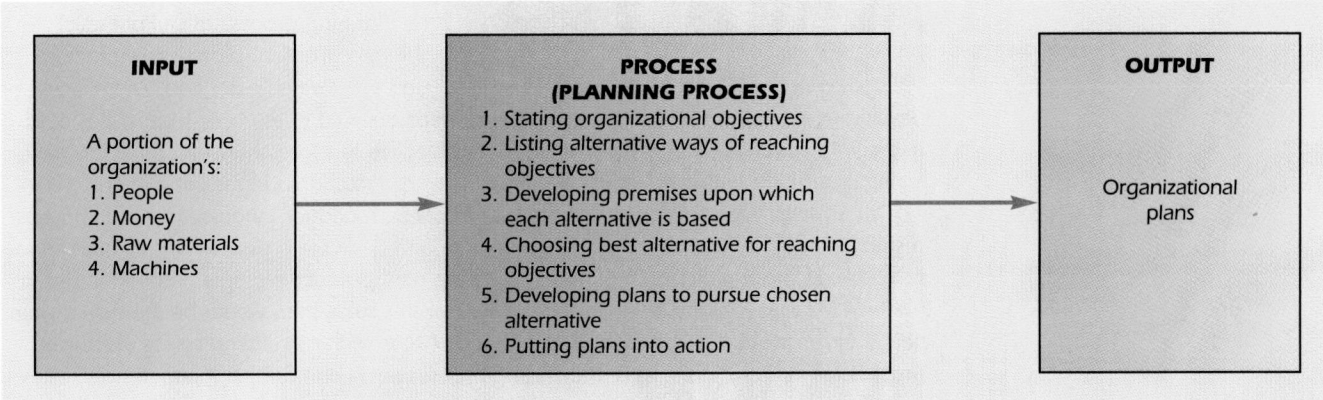

Figure 6.4   **The planning subsystem**

Elements of the Subsystem

Figure 6.4 presents the elements of the planning subsystem. The purpose of this subsystem is to increase the effectiveness of the overall management system by helping managers to identify planning activities within the overall system and to guide and direct those activities.

Obviously, only a portion of organizational resources can be used as input in the planning subsystem. This input is allocated to the planning subsystem and transformed into output through the steps of the planning process.

The Subsystem at Work

How planning subsystems are organized in the industrial world can be exemplified by the rather informal planning subsystem at the Quaker Oats Company and the more formal planning subsystem at the Sun Oil Company.[10]

Quaker Oats Company   At Quaker Oats, speculations about the future are conducted, for the most part, on an informal basis. To help anticipate social changes, Quaker Oats management has opened communication lines with various groups believed to be harbingers of change. The company has organized a "noncommittee," whose members represent a diversity of orientations, to spearhead this activity. They monitor social changes—and thus augment the company's understanding of social change. Many companies throughout the world plan in an informal way, as Quaker Oats does.

Sun Oil Company   Several groups within Sun Oil Company are engaged in formal business planning and forecasting. Operational planning with a five-year horizon is done annually. The planning activity with the longest time horizon takes place within the Sun Oil Company of Pennsylvania, the corporation's refining, transportation, and marketing arm. A centralized planning group, reporting to the vice president of development and planning, is responsible for helping top management set the company's long-term objectives, develop plans to achieve those objectives, and identify future consumer needs and market developments that might indicate business areas for diversification. Current efforts focus on discussions of a series of long-range issues with the executive committee. This planning process is designed to generate a restatement of long-term objectives for the organization.

BACK TO THE CASE

The planning process at DuPont must result in a practical plan to manufacture and sell women's clothing. The process of developing this plan should consist of the six steps outlined in the text. That is, it should begin with a statement of the organizational objective to successfully introduce the new clothing and end with guidelines for putting the organizational plans into action.

To appropriately implement a planning process, managers should view planning as a subsystem of the overall management system and dedicate a portion of organizational resources to organizational planning. Using the new-product example detailed in the introductory case, we would say that the output of this subsystem would be the actual plans needed to introduce the private-label clothing. Areas such as refining a manufacturing process for the new clothing and ensuring that suppliers can furnish the materials necessary to produce it would be emphasized. Naturally, a comprehensive planning effort at DuPont would need to focus on many other organizational areas, such as obtaining funds for the venture and fighting established competitors for a share of the market for private-label women's sportswear.

PLANNING AND THE CHIEF EXECUTIVE

More than two decades ago, Henry Mintzberg pointed out that the top managers—the chief executives—of organizations have many different roles to perform.[11] As organizational figureheads, they must represent their organizations in a variety of social, legal, and ceremonial situations. As leaders, they must ensure that organization members are properly guided toward achieving organizational goals. As liaisons, they must establish themselves as links between their organizations and factors outside their organizations. As monitors, they must assess organizational progress. As disturbance handlers, they must settle disputes between organization members. And as resource allocators, they must determine where resources should be placed to benefit their organizations best.

Final Responsibility

In addition to these many varied roles, chief executives have the final responsibility for organizational planning. As the scope of planning broadens to include a larger portion of the management system, it becomes increasingly important for chief executives to get involved in the planning process.

As planners, chief executives seek answers to the following broad questions:[12]

1. In what direction should the organization be going?
2. In what direction is the organization going now?
3. Should something be done to change this direction?
4. Is the organization continuing in an appropriate direction?

Keeping informed about social, political, and scientific trends is of utmost importance in helping chief executives to answer these questions.

Planning Assistance

Given the necessity to participate in organizational planning while performing other time-consuming roles, more and more top managers have established the position of organization planner to obtain the planning assistance they require. Just as managers can ask others for help and advice in making decisions, so can they involve others in formulating organizational plans.[13]

The chief executive of a substantial organization almost certainly needs planning assistance.[14] The remainder of this chapter assumes that the organization planner is

When she was hired as CEO back in 1989, Sally G. Narodick, who holds advanced degrees in both business and education, was an obvious match for Edmark Corp., a maker of educational materials in Redmond, Washington. Citing research that showed an increase in demand from the children of baby boomers, Narodick steered Edmark in the direction of multimedia consumer software. Today, Edmark has gone beyond products like Millie's Math House to programs that introduce children to such topics as critical-thinking skills and Boolean logic.

an individual who is not the chief executive of the organization, but rather a manager inside the organization who is responsible for assisting the chief executive on organizational planning issues.[15] Where the planner and the chief executive are the same person, however, the following discussion of the planner can, with slight modifications, be applied to the chief executive.

THE PLANNER

The planner is probably the most important input in the planning subsystem. This individual combines all other inputs and influences the subsystem process so that its output is effective organizational plans. The planner is responsible not only for developing plans but also for advising management on what actions should be taken to implement those plans. Regardless of who actually does the planning or what organization the planning is being done in, the qualifications, duties, and evaluations of the planner are all very important considerations for an effective planning subsystem.

Qualifications of Planners

Planners should have four primary qualifications:

- First, they should have considerable practical experience within their organization. Preferably, they should have been executives in one or more of the organization's major departments. This experience will help them develop plans that are both practical and tailor-made for the organization.
- Second, planners should be capable of replacing any narrow view of the organization they may have acquired while holding other organizational positions with an understanding of the organization as a whole. They must know how all parts of the organization function and interrelate. In other words, they must possess an abundance of the conceptual skills mentioned in Chapter 1.
- Third, planners should have some knowledge of and interest in the social, political, technical, and economic trends that could affect the future of the organization. They must be skillful in defining those trends and possess the expertise to determine how the organization should react to the trends to maximize its success. This qualification cannot be overemphasized.
- The fourth and last qualification for planners is that they be able to work well with others. Their position will inevitably require them to work closely with several key members of the organization, so it is essential that they possess the personal characteristics necessary to collaborate and advise effectively. The ability to communicate clearly, both orally and in writing, is one of the most important of these characteristics.[16]

These are the fundamental qualifications that managers who are planners normally must have. The following CUTTING EDGE feature suggests, however, that contemporary organizations are increasingly asking nonmanagerial employees who have other, special qualifications to participate in the planning process.

EMPLOYEES HAVE SPECIAL QUALIFICATIONS FOR FLEXIBILITY PLANNING

Managers continually search for new ways to reduce costs in their organizations. One recently discussed method for lowering costs is to develop and empower more flexible employees.

Flexible employees are those who can do more than one task. Theoretically, a flexible employee is one who can move from job to job, thereby eliminating the organization's need to hire more specialized employees who are not constantly working, yet still must be paid during slack times. Obviously, employee flexibility is a tremendous help in lowering an organization's labor costs and in increasing its productivity, thereby allowing the organization to offer lower-priced products to its customers.

In order for the organization to achieve maximum benefit from employee flexibility, however, managers must permit employees to help plan their own jobs. Employee involvement in job planning is essential because employees know what most jobs entail better than managers do. Thus they have special qualifications for determining what resources jobs require, when work should be performed, and with whom and in what sequence it should be done.

Managers who wish to develop and empower more flexible employees must give subordinates a say in organizing and controlling their jobs. They need to ask employees to help ensure that they have the organizational resources required to do their jobs and to take responsibility for monitoring their own job performance so that necessary improvements to their work situations can be made.

If an organization truly wants employees to become involved in planning, organizing, and controlling their jobs, it must be prepared to reward them for effective involvement. The development, empowerment, and rewarding of flexible employees challenge traditional notions of management, not only because it means doing away with rigid job categories, but also because it demands giving employees a significant voice in the management prerogatives of planning, organizing, and controlling.≈

Duties of Planners

Organizational planners have at least three general duties to perform:[17]

1. Overseeing the planning process.
2. Evaluating developed plans.
3. Solving planning problems.

Overseeing the Planning Process
First and foremost, planners must see that planning gets done. To this end, they establish rules, guidelines, and planning objectives that apply to themselves and others involved in the planning process. In essence, planners must develop a plan for planning.

Simply described, a **plan for planning** is a listing of all of the steps that must be taken to plan for an organization. It generally includes such activities as evaluating an organization's present planning process with the intention of improving it, determining how much benefit an organization can gain from planning, and developing a planning timetable to ensure that all of the steps necessary to plan for the organization are performed by some specified date.

A **plan for planning** is a listing of all the steps that must be taken to plan for an organization. It ensures that planning gets done.

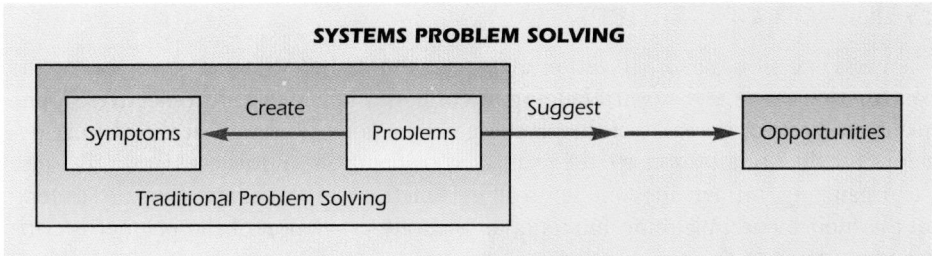

Figure 6.5 Relationships among symptoms, problems, and opportunities that face the planner

Evaluating Developed Plans The second general duty of planners is to evaluate plans that have been developed. They must decide if these plans are sufficiently challenging for the organization, if they are complete, and if they are consistent with organizational objectives. Any developed plans that do not fulfill these three requirements should be modified appropriately.

Solving Planning Problems Planners also have the duty to gather information that will help solve planning problems. Sometimes they find it necessary to conduct special studies within the organization to obtain this information. Effective planners continually evaluate the need for change and improvement. They then recommend what the organization should do to deal with planning problems and forecast how the organization might benefit from opportunities related to solving these problems.[18]

For example, a planner may observe that the organization's production objectives are not being met. This is a symptom of a planning problem. The problem might be that the objectives are unrealistically high, or it could be that the plans developed to achieve the production objectives are inappropriate. The planner must gather information pertinent to the problem and then suggest to management how the organization can solve it and become more successful.

Other symptoms that could signify planning problems are weakness in dealing with competition, declining sales volume, inventory levels that are either too high or too low, high operating expenses, and too much capital investment in equipment.[19] King and Cleland's presentation of the relationships among problems, symptoms, and opportunities is depicted in Figure 6.5.

The discussions of the three duties of the planner—overseeing the planning process, evaluating developed plans, and solving planning problems—were general comments on the planner's activities. The main focus of these activities is to advise management on what should be done in the future and to ensure that the timing of any managerial action is appropriate. A planner, of course, can only recommend. Management may decide not to accept the planner's recommendations.

Like most consumer-products companies, Colgate-Palmolive is immersed in the implementation of plans to extend its activities into international markets. CEO Reuben Mark admits, however, that he must reevaluate some of the company's plans: In its core U.S. market, Colgate-Palmolive has been losing market share and revenue. In particular, detergent brands like Fab and Ajax have gone from 10-percent to 5-percent market share, largely because of increased competition from lower-cost products from companies like Dial Corp.

Evaluation of Planners

Planners, like all other organization members, should be evaluated according to the contribution they make toward helping the organization achieve its objectives.[20] The quality and appropriateness of the planning system and the plans that the planner develops for the organization are the primary considerations in this evaluation. Because the organizing, influencing, and controlling functions of managers all vitally depend on the fundamental planning function, an accurate evaluation of the planner is critically important to the organization.

Objective Indicators

Although the assessment of planners is necessarily somewhat subjective, there are several objective indicators. The use of appropriate techniques is one objective indicator. A planner who uses appropriate techniques is probably doing an acceptable job. The degree of objectivity displayed by the planner is another indicator. The planner's advice should be largely based on a rational analysis of appropriate information.[21] This is not to say that planners should abandon subjective judgment altogether, only that their opinions should be based chiefly on specific and appropriate information.

Malik suggests that a planner is doing a reputable job if the following objective criteria are met:[22]

1. The organizational plan is in writing.
2. The plan is the result of all elements of the management team working together.
3. The plan defines present and possible future business of the organization.
4. The plan specifically mentions organizational objectives.
5. The plan identifies future opportunities and suggests how to take advantage of them.
6. The plan emphasizes both internal and external environments.
7. The plan describes the attainment of objectives in operational terms whenever possible.
8. The plan includes both long- and short-term recommendations.

These eight criteria furnish objective guidelines for evaluating the performance of planners. Management's evaluation of planners should never be completely objective, however. Important subjective considerations include how well planners get along with key members of the organization, the amount of organizational loyalty they display, and their perceived potential.

BACK TO THE CASE Technically, the chief executive officer (CEO) at DuPont is responsible for planning for the organization as a whole and for performing such related time-consuming functions as keeping abreast of internal and external trends that could affect the future of the company. Because planning requires so much time, and because the chief executive officer of DuPont has many other responsibilities within the company, the CEO might want to consider appointing a director of planning.

The director of planning at DuPont would need certain qualities. Ideally, this person would have considerable experience at DuPont, be able to see the company as an entire organization, have the ability to gauge and react to major trends that could affect the company's future, and be able to work well with others. The chief duties of the director of planning would be to oversee the planning process, evaluate developed plans, and solve planning problems. Naturally, the introduction of the company's new line of women's clothing would be an important area of focus for DuPont's director of planning. The evaluation of this person would be based on both objective and subjective appraisals of his or her performance.

MAXIMIZING THE EFFECTIVENESS OF THE PLANNING PROCESS

Success in implementing a planning subsystem is not easily attainable. As the size of the organization increases, the planning task becomes more complicated, requiring more people, more information, and more complicated decisions.[23] Several safeguards, however, can ensure the success of an organizational planning effort:

1. Top-management support.
2. An effective and efficient planning organization.
3. An implementation-focused planning orientation.
4. Inclusion of the right people.

Top-Management Support

Unless top management supports the planning effort, other organization members may not take it seriously. This support is critical in planning for *any* type of organization—small or large, domestic or multinational.[24] Whenever possible, therefore, top management should actively guide and participate in planning activities. If the planner is furnished with the resources needed to structure the planning organization, if planning is a continuing process (not a once-a-year activity), and if people are adequately prepared for the changes that usually result from planning, it will be clear to organization members that top management is solidly behind the planning effort. Above all, the chief executive must give continual and obvious attention to the planning process if it is to be successful. The CEO must not allow concerns about other organizational matters to interfere with giving planning the emphasis it deserves.

TOP MANAGEMENT SUPPORTS ENVIRONMENTAL PROTECTION PLANNING AT SHELL OIL COMPANY

ETHICS SPOTLIGHT

The Shell Oil Company produces and sells various chemical and petroleum products such as gasoline and oil. To ensure that all organization members will take environmental planning seriously, top management at Shell solidly supports such planning within the company.

Shell's top managers began supporting environmental planning several years ago primarily because of the radical change in public attitudes toward the environment in recent decades. The credit for this change in attitude goes largely to the "green groups"—pressure groups that constantly push business as well as society in general to strive to protect the environment. The pro-environment attitude of society has made companies like Shell look upon environmental protection not as a cost, but rather as an investment in the future that will impress present and potential customers. At Shell, environmental planning is a factor in every business venture, and such issues as health, safety, and environmental considerations are fundamental at every planning stage in the development of a project or product.

Shell continues to strive for improved response to accidents involving oil, gas, chemical, and any other business in which it is engaged. The company has developed management guidelines for using environmental audits to determine whether a company activity complies with internal environmental standards.≈

An Effective and Efficient Planning Organization

A well-designed planning organization is the primary vehicle by which planning is accomplished and planning effectiveness is determined. Therefore the planner must take the time to design a planning organization as efficient and effective as possible.

The planning organization should have three built-in characteristics. First, it should be designed to use established management systems within the company. As expressed by Paul J. Stonich:

> Many organizations separate formal planning systems from the rest of the management systems that include organization, communication, reporting, evaluating, and performance review. These systems must not be viewed as separate from formal planning systems. Complex organizations need a comprehensive and coordinated set of management systems, including formal planning systems to help them toward their goals.[25]

Second, the planning organization should be complex enough to ensure a coordinated effort of all planning participants, yet as simple as possible. Although the planning process may require a somewhat large planning organization, the planner should strive to make the complex facets of this planning organization as clear as possible to organization members.

Last, the planning organization should be flexible and adaptable. Planning conditions are constantly changing, and the planning organization must be able to respond to these changing conditions.

Implementation-Focused Planning

Because the end result of the planning process is some type of action that will help achieve stated organizational objectives, all planning should be aimed at implementation.[26] As Peter Drucker points out, a plan is effective only if its implementation helps attain organizational objectives. After a plan is developed, the planner should scrutinize it in light of how it is to be implemented.[27] Ease of implementation is a positive feature that should be built into the plan whenever possible.

The Best-Laid Plans: The Edsel   The marketing plan for the Edsel automobile introduced by Ford in the 1950s is an example of how a sound plan can fail simply because of ineffective implementation.[28] The rationale behind the Edsel was complete, logical, and defensible. Three consumer trends at that time solidly justified the automobile's introduction:

1. The trend toward the purchase of higher-priced cars.
2. A general income increase in the society that resulted in all income groups purchasing higher-priced cars.
3. The trend for owners of lower-priced Fords to trade them in for Buicks, Oldsmobiles, or Pontiacs after they became more affluent.

Conceptually, these trends were so strong that Ford's plan to introduce the larger and more expensive model it called the Edsel appeared virtually risk-free.

Two factors in the implementation of this plan, however, turned the Edsel introduction into a financial disaster for Ford. First, the network of controllers, dealers, marketing managers, and industrial relations managers Ford created to get the Edsel to the consumer was overcomplicated and highly inefficient. Second, because Ford pushed as many Edsels as possible onto the road immediately after introducing the model, consumers found they were buying a poorly manufactured product. In summary, the plan to make and market the Edsel was defensible, but the manufacturing and marketing processes Ford used to implement the plan doomed it to failure.

Inclusion of the Right People

A plan is found to fail unless the planning process includes the right people. Whenever possible, planners should obtain input from the managers of the functional areas for which they are planning. Since these managers are close to the everyday activity

of their segments of the organization, they can provide planners with invaluable information. They should probably also be involved in implementing whatever plan is developed, and should certainly be asked to furnish the planner with feedback on how implementation is working. As a general rule, managers who are to be involved in implementing plans should also be involved in developing the plans.[29]

Input from other individuals who will be directly affected by the plans also can be helpful to planners. Employees should be asked, for example, how various proposed plans will influence the work flow.

Not all organization members can or should be involved in the planning process. The kinds of decisions and types of data needed should dictate the choice of whom to involve in different aspects of planning within an organization.

INCLUDING THE RIGHT PEOPLE IN PLANNING ENHANCES QUALITY AT SUN MICROSYSTEMS

QUALITY SPOTLIGHT

Sun Microsystems, Inc., is an integrated portfolio of businesses that supply computing technologies, products, and services. Its computing solutions include networked workstations and multiprocessing servers, operating system software, silicon designs, and other value-added technologies.

Management at Sun Microsystems has developed a team approach to planning. The planning team, known within the company as the business team, consists of representatives from design engineering, manufacturing, customer service, finance, and marketing. It is used primarily during the introduction of a new product.

The business team follows a very specific process. First, it creates a formal plan for the new-product introduction and submits it to an executive-level committee within the corporation. This plan, known as the Product Initiation Form (PIF), is essentially a business plan for a single new product. Once the executive committee approves a PIF, implementation proceeds by establishing an implementation team, which also consists of a number of individuals representing several different operational areas.

Through this cross-functional deployment of individuals in both business and implementation teams, Sun Microsystems has achieved more effective planning. This improved planning, in turn, has enhanced overall product quality by contributing to more on-time delivery of products, better product designs, and a higher proportion of manufactured products meeting established quality standards.≈

BACK TO THE CASE

A number of safeguards can be taken to ensure that the efforts of the person who has primary responsibility for planning at DuPont will be successful. First, top executives at the company should actively encourage planning activities and demonstrate their support of the planning process. Second, the planning organization designed to implement the planning process should use established systems at DuPont, be only as complex as necessary, and be flexible and adaptable. Third, the entire planning process should be oriented toward easing the implementation of generated plans. Finally, all key people at DuPont should be included in the planning process. With these safeguards, DuPont management should be able to ensure sound planning for future new-product introductions as well as for all other organizational areas.

Action Summary

Reread the learning objectives below. Each objective is followed by questions. Answering these questions accurately will help you retain the most important concepts discussed in this chapter. After answering each question, check your answer against the answer key at the end of this chapter. (*Hint:* If you have any doubts regarding the correct response, consult the page whose number follows the answer.)

Circle   From studying this chapter, I will attempt to acquire:

1. A definition of planning and an understanding of the purposes of planning.

T,F   **a.** The affirmative purpose of planning is to increase the degree of organizational success.

a,b,c,d,e   **b.** The following is *not* one of the purposes of planning: (a) systematic; (b) protective; (c) affirmative; (d) coordination; (e) fundamental.

2. A knowledge of the advantages and potential disadvantages of planning.

a,b,c,d,e   **a.** The advantages of planning include all of the following except: (a) helping managers to be future-oriented; (b) helping coordinate decisions; (c) requiring proper time allocation; (d) emphasizing organizational objectives; (e) all of the above are advantages of planning.

a,b,c,d,e   **b.** The following is a potential disadvantage of planning: (a) too much time may be spent on planning; (b) an inappropriate balance between planning and other managerial functions may occur; (c) some important activities may be neglected; (d) incorrect use of the planning function could work to the detriment of the organization; (e) all of the above are disadvantages of planning.

3. Insights on how the major steps of the planning process are related.

a,b,c,d,e   **a.** The first major step in the planning process, according to the text, is: (a) developing premises; (b) listing alternative ways of reaching organizational objectives; (c) stating organizational objectives; (d) developing plans to pursue chosen alternatives; (e) putting plans into action.

a,b,c,d,e   **b.** The assumptions on which alternatives are based are usually referred to as: (a) objectives; (b) premises; (c) tactics; (d) strategies; (e) probabilities.

4. An understanding of the planning subsystem.

T,F   **a.** A subsystem is a system created as part of the process of the overall management system.

a,b,c,d,e   **b.** The purpose of the planning subsystem is to increase the effectiveness of the overall management system through which of the following: (a) systematizing the planning function; (b) more effective planning; (c) formalizing the planning process; (d) integrating the planning process; (e) none of the above.

5. A knowledge of how the chief executive relates to the planning process.

T,F   **a.** The responsibility for organizational planning rests with middle management.

a,b,c,d,e   **b.** The final responsibility for organizational planning rests with: (a) the planning department; (b) the chief executive; (c) departmental supervisors; (d) the organizational planner; (e) the entire organization.

6. An understanding of the qualifications and duties of planners and how planners are evaluated.

T,F   **a.** The performance of planners should be evaluated with respect to the contribution they make toward helping the organization achieve its objectives.

a,b,c,d,e   **b.** The organizational planner's full responsibilities are: (a) developing plans only; (b) advising about action that should be taken relative to the plans that the chief executive developed; (c) advising about action that should be taken relative to the plans of the board of directors; (d) selecting the person who will oversee the planning process; (e) none of the above.

7. Guidelines on how to get the greatest return from the planning process.

T,F   **a.** Top management should encourage planning as an annual activity.

a,b,c,d,e   **b.** The following is *not* a built-in characteristic of an effective and efficient planning organization: (a) it should be designed to use established systems within a company; (b) it should be simple, yet complex enough to ensure coordinated effort; (c) it should cover an operating cycle of not more than one year; (d) it should be flexible and adaptive; (e) all of the above are characteristics of an effective and efficient planning organization.

Introductory Case Wrap-Up

"DuPont Plans to Make Women's Clothes" (p. 133) and its related back-to-the-case sections were written to help you better understand the management concepts contained in this chapter. Answer the following discussion questions about this introductory case to enrich your understanding of chapter content:

1. What special challenges will DuPont face in planning for its new line of women's clothing? What steps would you take to meet these challenges?
2. Would you have the DuPont CEO or a DuPont planning executive do the planning for the new women's clothing? Why?
3. List three criteria that you would use to evaluate the planning done for DuPont's new women's clothing. Explain why you chose each criterion.

Issues for Review and Discussion

1. What is planning?
2. What is the main purpose of planning?
3. List and explain the advantages of planning.
4. Why are the disadvantages of planning called *potential* disadvantages?
5. Explain the phrase *primacy of planning*.
6. List the six steps in the planning process.
7. Outline the relationships among the six steps in the planning process.
8. What is an organizational subsystem?
9. List the elements of the planning subsystem.
10. How do the many roles of a chief executive relate to his or her role as organization planner?
11. Explain the basic qualifications of an organization planner.
12. Give a detailed description of the general duties an organization planner must perform.
13. How would you evaluate the performance of an organization planner?
14. How can top management show its support of the planning process?
15. Describe the characteristics of an effective and efficient planning organization.
16. Why should the planning process emphasize the implementation of organizational plans?
17. Explain why the Edsel automobile failed to generate consumer acceptance.
18. Which people in an organization typically should be included in the planning process? Why?

Action Summary Answer Key

1. a. T, p. 134
   b. a, p. 134
2. a. c, pp. 135–136
   b. e, pp. 135–136
3. a. c, p. 137
   b. b, p. 137
4. a. T, p. 138
   b. b, p. 138
5. a. F, p. 140
   b. b, p. 140
6. a. T, p. 144
   b. e, p. 144
7. a. F, pp. 145–146
   b. c, pp. 145–146

Case Study

Quaker Oats Focuses on a Planning Problem

According to a 1996 fiscal report in *The Wall Street Journal*, venerable Chicago-based Quaker Oats Company was in the midst of a financial downturn indicating serious planning snafus. In particular, Quaker had lost $47.8 million in the second quarter of 1995, largely because of restructuring charges necessitated by its Snapple division's poor performance and the company's unsuccessful efforts to improve overseas sales. Quaker did not expect 1996 to begin any better.

Quaker Oats opened its doors to customers as the American Cereal Company of Chicago in 1891. Ten years later, the company changed its name to Quaker Oats Company and adopted the Quaker Man as its logo. Creative marketing practices and a powerful sales staff touted the healthful virtues of oatmeal and turned oatmeal cereal into a booming business. By 1911, Quaker had consolidated its mill operations and was ready to diversify, expanding into both animal feed and more gro-

cery items. Acquisitions continued into the 1960s, as Quaker added Aunt Jemima pancake flour, Cap'n Crunch cereal, Fisher-Price toys, restaurants, and candies.

Until 1990, Quaker was still adding new products—everything from clothiers and opticians to Stokely-Van Camp, Gatorade, and Gaines dog food. A prime acquisition was Anderson Clayton & Company, a Houston food-products company that boasted such popular brands as Seven Seas salad dressings, Chiffon margarine, and Igloo ice chests. Then a downturn in 1990 convinced management to refocus the company on food.

Quaker implemented this new strategy by increasing its advertising budget, reformulating its dog foods, and launching new products. Determined to emphasize its core food categories, the company in 1993 sold Sutherland Foods, a British maker of sandwich-filling products, and purchased the Chico-San rice cake brand from Heinz. Then, in 1994, Quaker consolidated manufacturing, cut employment, and purchased Snapple.

Unfortunately, the Snapple deal did not fulfill Quaker's dreams of growth. Quaker had hoped to streamline distribution of its soft-drink products by combining the Snapple delivery system with Gatorade's. However, independent Snapple distributors, armed with ironclad contracts, refused to cooperate. They forced the company to abandon its plans for streamlining. And that was only the beginning of the brand's troubles. Huge inventories of obsolete products and packaging had to be dumped. And where Snapple had once created a cult following by running ads featuring offbeat celebrities, advertising of the brand under Quaker dried up. Competitors PepsiCo and Coca-Cola filled the marketing void with Lipton teas and Fruitopia juice drinks.

Another problem was that Quaker had counted on greater manufacturing synergies, or cooperative activities, but inherited contracts that locked it into unrealistic production levels with independent bottlers. To avoid paying penalties and to straighten out its supply-chain problems, Quaker eventually had to buy out some of these agreements.

Profits, predictably, disappeared for a while, but by the end of 1995, Snapple seemed to be rallying. Although some experts still question whether Snapple can help protect Quaker's market share in the soft-drink business, CEO William D. Smithburg rejects the suggestion that Quaker "bet the farm on a fad": "We certainly believe we bought a brand with legs." Smithburg has several plans to back up his belief:

1. Release a new ad campaign at the beginning of the soft-drink season to maintain Snapple's old quirky image despite its present association with a giant corporation.
2. Promote an under-the-bottle-cap sweepstakes.
3. Update flavors, improve taste, and jazz up the line with sporty new labels.
4. Reduce customer confusion with a new shelf-stocking scheme that separates tea, juice, lemonade, and diet drinks.

Besides solving its marketing problems, Quaker plans to improve Snapple's production systems. To cure production bottlenecks and overcome stocking problems, for instance, Quaker has eliminated one-third of its independent bottlers and introduced a centralized ordering system. Newly streamlined plants will produce a wider range of packaging, including a 32-ounce plastic bottle. Weak distributors will be bought out as Quaker takes additional territories in-house.

Some experts expect Snapple's growth to be slow—about $40 million in earnings in 1996. Others, however, contend that Quaker's global connections give the drink what beverage consultant Tom Pirko of Bevmark calls "colossal prospects." At the same time, of course, Snapple has lost its innovative edge as competitors have moved in with their own healthful teas and fruit juices. Only time will tell if the changes instituted by Quaker management are timely enough to make Snapple rise from the ashes of previous poor planning.

Questions:

1. Classify the plans that Quaker made both before and after it purchased Snapple. Were they "protective"? "Affirmative"? Or were they established to coordinate efforts within the organization? Explain.
2. Use the example of the Quaker Oats Company's purchase of Snapple to illustrate the definition of *planning*.
3. What were Quaker's objectives when it bought Snapple? On what premises were these objectives based? Explain.
4. How would you say Quaker's decision to purchase and support Snapple illustrates planning activities as described in the text? Explain.

Skills Exercise

On the basis of the information given in the case, outline planning steps taken by Quaker Oats in determining to buy Snapple and, later, in attempting to resurrect the failing division. For each area of planning, consider the following questions:

1. What were Quaker's objectives?
2. What alternative did the company decide to pursue?

3. On what premises did Quaker base its choice of alternative?
4. How did Quaker implement its plan?

Now, analyze the plans: What mistakes did Quaker make? At what point in the overall planning process did Quaker management make good choices? Explain. How would you rate Quaker's overall planning process and why would you give it that rating?

The Internet learning materials that accompany this chapter can be found at
http://www.profcerto.com
Additional information can be found on the inside front and back covers of this text.

MAKING DECISIONS

STUDENT LEARNING OBJECTIVES

From studying this chapter, I will attempt to acquire:

1. A fundamental understanding of the term *decision*.
2. An understanding of each element of the decision situation.
3. An ability to use the decision-making process.
4. An appreciation for the various situations in which decisions are made.
5. An understanding of probability theory and decision trees as decision-making tools.
6. Insights about groups as decision makers.

CHAPTER OUTLINE

Introductory Case: Cadillac Decides Whether to Make a Sport-Utility Vehicle

Fundamentals of Decisions
Definition of a Decision
Types of Decisions

Diversity Spotlight: Nonprogrammed Decision at U.S. Office of Personnel Management Includes a Focus on Severely Disabled Workers

The Responsibility for Making Organizational Decisions
Elements of the Decision Situation

Global Spotlight: Executives at United Technologies Detect a Weakness among Japanese Decision Makers

The Decision-Making Process
Identifying an Existing Problem
Listing Alternative Solutions
Selecting the Most Beneficial Alternative

Cutting Edge: Decision Alternatives Should Reflect Organizational Values

Implementing the Chosen Alternative
Gathering Problem-Related Feedback

People Perspectives: Decision at John Deere: Eliminate Problems by Building Employee Involvement

Decision-Making Conditions
Complete Certainty Condition
Complete Uncertainty Condition
Risk Condition

Decision-Making Tools
Probability Theory
Decision Trees

Group Decision Making
Advantages and Disadvantages of Using Groups to Make Decisions
Processes for Making Group Decisions

Think of Cadillac and you think of chrome-encrusted boatlike cars.

Think again.

In a few years, you will likely see Cadillac sport-utility vehicles blasting down the freeway. Cadillac has been actively lobbying its parent company, General Motors Corporation, for approval to make a luxury sport-utility vehicle, and it now appears the division has the support of at least some of GM's directors.

"Cadillac will get a sport-utility vehicle," said a person close to the GM board who didn't want to be named. "There's clearly a need. Cadillac has made its case, and GM's other marketing divisions aren't worried about having another utility vehicle in the family." A spokesman is more circumspect: "We've been evaluating the market and have discovered that as a certain number of potential buyers enter the luxury-car market, they're electing to buy sport utilities."

Of course, to attract buyers of traditional Cadillacs, the new model would have to be one fancy sport-utility vehicle. It would likely have a smooth, carlike ride, flared fenders, tinted side windows, the Cadillac crest up front, and Cadillac's Northstar multivalve engine, according to Lincoln Merrihew of DRI/McGraw-Hill's automotive consulting group. Inside, he added, there would be real wood on the dashboard, a satellite-based navigation system, and probably appliances to refrigerate and heat food.

People close to Cadillac said the vehicle would sell for over $40,000, which is toward the upper end of the price range for such vehicles.

Cadillac's desire to expand into the sport-utility segment of the market is understandable, according to Stephen Girsky, an analyst with PaineWebber. The division wants to appeal to baby-boom-era buyers, who are reaching the age at which they are considering buying expensive vehicles. "Rich people—typical Cadillac customers—are already driving their Chevy Blazers and pickups to their country clubs," Girsky said. "Cadillac may feel like they're losing customers because of this."

General Motors, the maker of Cadillac, has decided to enter the market for sport-utility vehicles. In analyzing information obtained from the marketplace, GM has reason to believe that it can attract a significant segment of people who buy Land Rovers and other sport-utility vehicles.

The introductory case discusses a decision that management at Cadillac is presently evaluating—whether to make a sport-utility vehicle. This chapter presents the specifics of decision making and provides insights about the steps that management at Cadillac might take in deciding whether to enter the highly competitive sport-utility segment of the market. It discusses the following subjects:

1. The fundamentals of decisions.
2. The decision-making process.
3. Various decision-making conditions.
4. Decision-making tools.
5. Group decision making.

These topics are critical to managers and all other individuals who make decisions.

FUNDAMENTALS OF DECISIONS

Definition of a Decision

A **decision** is a choice made between two or more available alternatives.

A **decision** is a choice made between two or more available alternatives. *Decision making* is the process of choosing the best alternative for reaching objectives. Decision making is covered in the planning section of this text, but since managers must also make decisions when performing the other three managerial functions—organizing, influencing, and controlling—the subject requires a separate chapter.

We all face decision situations every day. A decision situation may involve simply choosing whether to spend the day studying, swimming, or golfing. It does not matter which alternative is chosen, only that a choice be actually made.[1]

Managers make decisions affecting the organization daily and communicate those decisions to other organization members.[2] Not all managerial decisions are of equal significance to the organization. Some affect a large number of organization members, cost a great deal of money to carry out, or have a long-term effect on the organization. Such significant decisions can have a major impact, not only on the management system itself, but also on the career of the manager who makes them. Other decisions are fairly insignificant, affecting only a small number of organization members, costing little to carry out, and producing only a short-term effect on the organization.

Types of Decisions

Decisions can be categorized according to how much time a manager must spend in making them, what proportion of the organization must be involved in making them, and the organizational functions on which they focus. Probably the most generally accepted method of categorizing decisions, however, is based on computer language; it divides all decisions into two basic types: programmed and nonprogrammed.[3]

Programmed decisions are decisions that are routine and repetitive and that typically require specific handling methods.

Programmed decisions are routine and repetitive, and the organization typically develops specific ways to handle them. A programmed decision might involve determining how products will be arranged on the shelves of a supermarket. For this kind of routine, repetitive problem, standard-arrangement decisions are typically made according to established management guidelines.

Nonprogrammed decisions, in contrast, are typically one-shot decisions that are usually less structured than programmed decisions. An example of the type of nonprogrammed decision that more and more managers are having to make is whether to expand operations into the "forgotten continent" of Africa.[4] Another example is deciding whether a supermarket should carry an additional type of bread. The manager making this decision must consider whether the new bread will merely stabilize bread sales by competing with existing bread carried in the store or actually increase bread sales by offering a desired brand of bread to customers who have never before bought bread in the store. These types of issues must be dealt with before the manager can finally decide whether to offer the new bread. Table 7.1 shows traditional and modern ways of handling programmed and nonprogrammed decisions.

Programmed and nonprogrammed decisions should be thought of as being at opposite ends of the decision programming continuum illustrated in Figure 7.1. As the figure indicates, however, some decisions are neither programmed nor nonprogrammed, but some fall somewhere between the two.

Nonprogrammed decisions are typically one-shot decisions that are usually less structured than programmed decisions.

NONPROGRAMMED DECISION AT U.S. OFFICE OF PERSONNEL MANAGEMENT INCLUDES A FOCUS ON SEVERELY DISABLED WORKERS

DIVERSITY SPOTLIGHT

The U.S. Office of Personnel Management is in the process of making a nonprogrammed decision concerning whether to employ home-based workers. Recognizing the needs of the diverse workforce of the 1990s, this government office is examining the feasibility of using home-based positions to improve employee recruitment, retention, and other aspects of personnel management.

Home-based workers presently range from entrepreneurs who work for themselves and have multiple clients to people who are regular company employees. Research indicates that home-based employee programs work especially well with severely disabled workers. Such programs have proved not only cost-effective from the company's viewpoint but personally satisfying to workers as well.

Experience shows that planning to ensure that home-based workers fit into the company properly greatly enhances the success of these programs. One area on which such planning should focus is the workstation itself. Home workstations should be equivalent to those designed for in-office employees because furnishing lesser-equipped offices to home-based workers normally causes worker frustration and lower productivity. Planning should also focus on making sure that home-based workers receive initial training and orientation relating to their work role, as well as ongoing contact with support groups to help them handle any problems that might arise as a result of working at home. Finally, planning should ensure that home-based workers receive the same benefits, status, promotion opportunities, and rights as in-office workers.≈

The Responsibility for Making Organizational Decisions

Many different kinds of decisions must be made within an organization—such as how to manufacture a product, how to maintain machines, how to ensure product quality, and how to establish advantageous relationships with customers. Since organizational decisions are so varied, some type of rationale must be developed to stipulate who within the organization has the responsibility for making which decisions.

Table 7.1

Traditional and Modern Ways of Handling Programmed and Nonprogrammed Decisions

	Decision-Making Techniques	
TYPES OF DECISIONS	TRADITIONAL	MODERN

Programmed:
Routine, repetitive decisions
Organization develops specific processes for handling them
	1. Habit
	2. Clerical routine:
	    Standard operating procedures
	3. Organization structure:
	    Common expectations
	    A system of subgoals
	    Well-defined information channels
		1. Operations research:
		    Mathematical analysis models
		    Computer simulation
		2. Electronic data processing

Nonprogrammed:
One-shot, ill-structured, novel policy decisions
Handled by general problem-solving processes
	1. Judgment, intuition, and creativity
	2. Rules of thumb
	3. Selection and training of executives
		1. Heuristic problem-solving techniques applied to:
		    Training human decision makers
		    Constructing heuristic computer programs

The **scope of the decision** is the proportion of the total management system that a particular decision will affect. The broader the scope of a decision, the higher level of the manager responsible for making that decision.

One such rationale is based primarily on two factors: the scope of the decision to be made and the levels of management. The **scope of the decision** is the proportion of the total management system that the decision will affect. The greater this proportion, the broader the scope of the decision is said to be. *Levels of management* are simply lower-level management, middle-level management, and upper-level management. The rationale for designating who makes which decisions is this: the broader the scope of a decision, the higher the level of the manager responsible for making that decision. Figure 7.2 illustrates this rationale.

One example of this decision-making rationale is the manner in which E.I. DuPont de Nemours and Company handles decisions related to the research and development function.[5] As Figure 7.3 shows (see page 158), this organization makes both narrow-scope research and development decisions, such as "which markets to test" (decided by lower-level managers), and broad-scope research and development decisions, such as "authorize full-scale plant construction" (decided by upper-level managers).

The manager who is responsible for making a particular decision, of course, can ask the advice of other managers or subordinates before settling on an alternative. In fact, some managers prefer to use groups to make certain decisions.

Consensus is agreement on a decision by all individuals involved in making that decision.

Consensus is one method a manager can use in getting a group to arrive at a particular decision. **Consensus** is agreement on a decision by all the individuals involved in making that decision. It usually occurs after lengthy deliberation and discussion by members of the decision group, who may be either all managers or a mixture of managers and subordinates.[6]

The manager who asks a group to produce a consensus decision must bear in mind that groups will sometimes be unable to arrive at a decision. Lack of technical skill or poor interpersonal relations may prove insurmountable barriers to arriving at

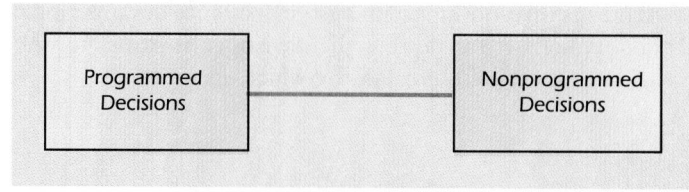

Figure 7.1   Decision programming continuum

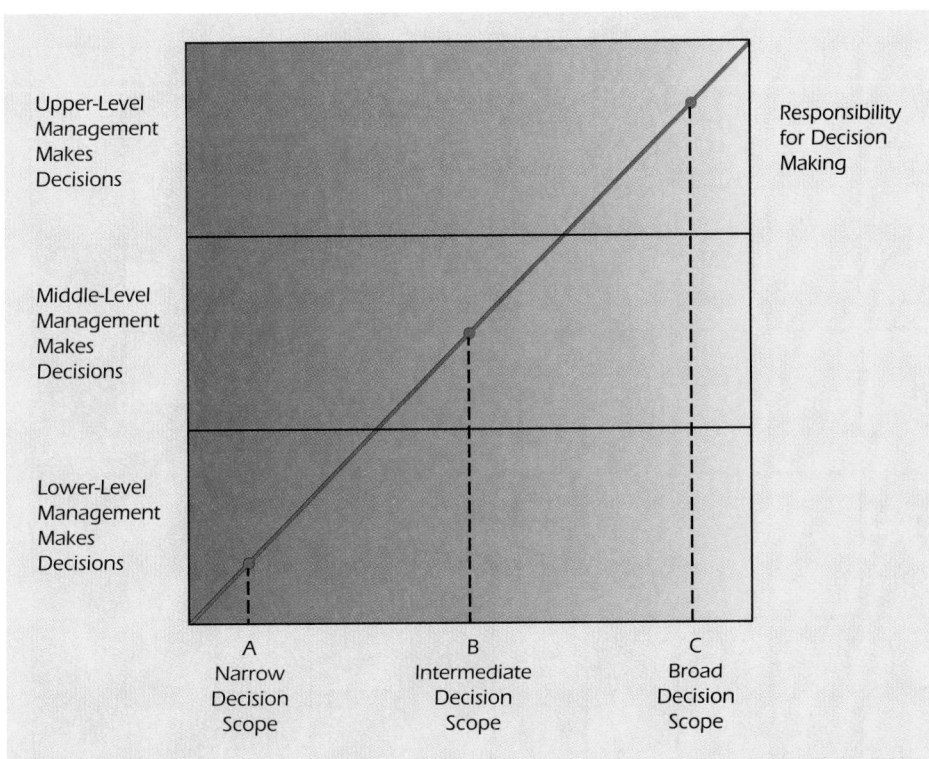

Figure 7.2   Level of managers responsible for making decisions as decision scope increases from A to B to C

a consensus. When a group is stalemated, managers need to offer assistance in making the decision or simply make it themselves.

Decisions arrived at through consensus have both advantages and disadvantages. One advantage of this method is that it focuses "several heads" on the decision. Another is that employees are more likely to be committed to implementing a decision if they helped make it. The main disadvantage of this method is that it often involves time-consuming discussions relating to the decision that can be costly to the organization.

BACK TO THE CASE   Evaluating whether or not to design and manufacture a sport-utility vehicle is definitely a formal decision situation—that is, one that requires management at Cadillac to choose between alternatives that will be costly, significant to the organization as a whole and to the careers of the Cadillac man-

In retail stores, lower-level managers like this manager at Circuit City oversee the stocking of inventory and perform numerous other functions on the floor of the outlet. Sometimes called first-line managers, *they spend a good deal of their time working with and supervising employees who report directly to them. They also interact with suppliers and middle-level managers at home offices.*

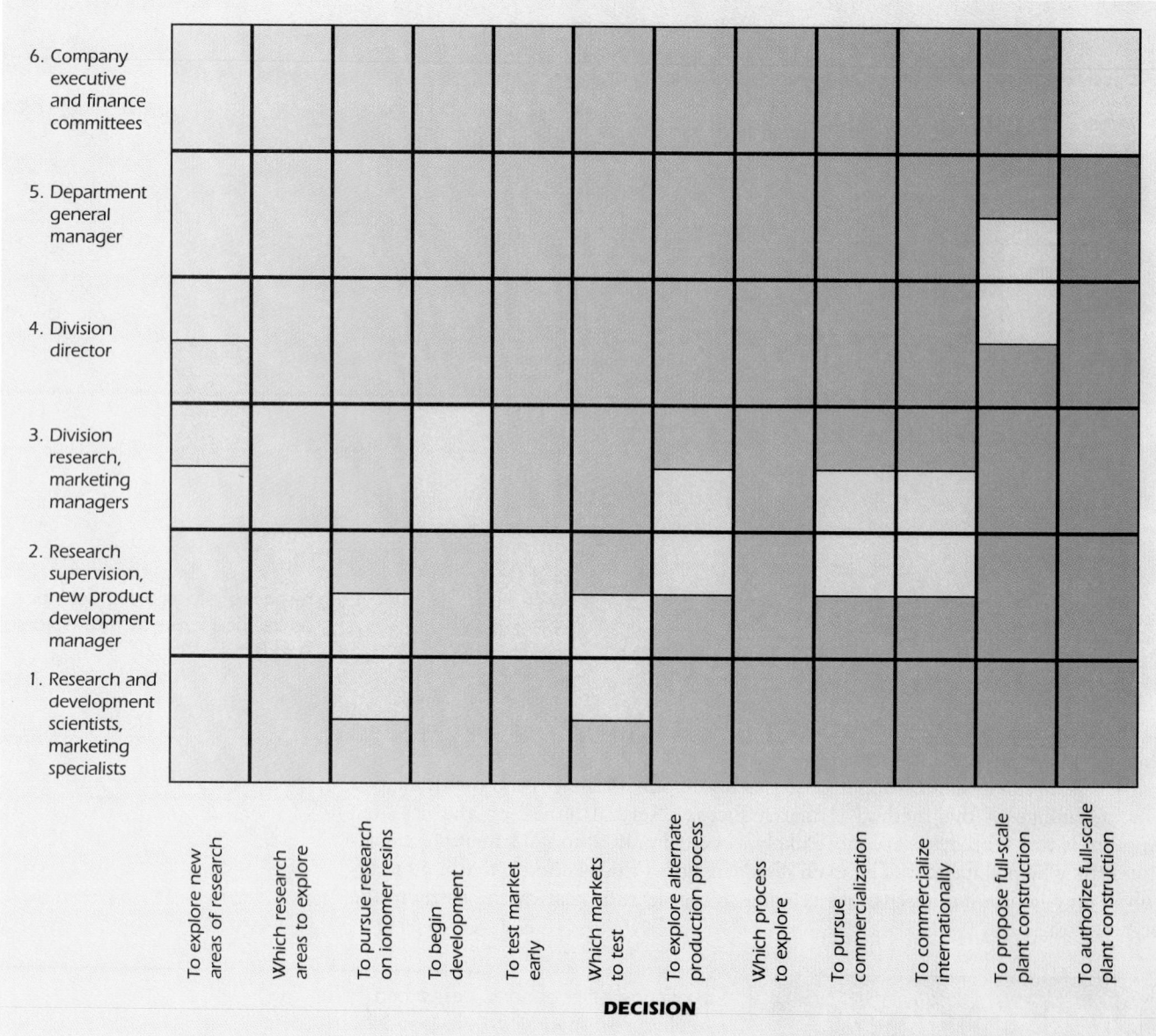

Figure 7.3   How scope of decision affects management level making decision at DuPont

agers making the decision, and that will have a long-term effect on the organization. Since this is a nonprogrammed decision, it will be based more on judgment than on simple quantitative data.

As General Motors' chief executive officer, John F. Smith, Jr., probably has the ultimate responsibility for making such a broad-scope decision—subject, of course, to the approval of his board of directors. This does not mean, however, that Smith has to make the decision all by himself. He has the options of asking for advice from other General Motors managers and of appointing a group of managers/employees to arrive at a consensus decision concerning the production of the sport-utility vehicle.

Elements of the Decision Situation

Wilson and Alexis isolate several basic elements in the decision situation.[7] Five of these elements are defined and discussed in this section.

The Decision Makers   Decision makers, the first element of the decision situation, are the individuals or groups that actually make the choice among alternatives. According to Dale, weak decision makers usually have one of four orientations: receptive, exploitative, hoarding, and marketing.[8]

Decision makers who have a *receptive* orientation believe that the source of all good is outside themselves, and therefore they rely heavily on suggestions from other organization members. Basically, they want others to make their decisions for them.

Decision makers with an *exploitative* orientation also believe that the source of all good is outside themselves, and they are willing to steal ideas as necessary in order to make good decisions. They build their organizations on others' ideas and typically hog all the credit themselves, extending little or none to the originators of the ideas.

The *hoarding* orientation is characterized by the desire to preserve the status quo as much as possible. Decision makers with this orientation accept little outside help, isolate themselves from others, and are extremely self-reliant. They are obsessed with maintaining their present position and status.

Marketing-oriented decision makers look upon themselves as commodities that are only as valuable as the decisions they make. Thus they try to make decisions that will enhance their value and are highly conscious of what others think of their decisions.

The ideal decision-making orientation emphasizes the realization of the organization's potential as well as that of the decision maker. Ideal decision makers try to use all of their talents when making a decision and are characterized by reason and sound judgment. They are largely free of the qualities of the four undesirable decision-making orientations just described.

EXECUTIVES AT UNITED TECHNOLOGIES DETECT A WEAKNESS AMONG JAPANESE DECISION MAKERS

GLOBAL SPOTLIGHT

United Technologies is a company that designs, manufactures, and sells high-technology products, such as radar equipment and rocket motors. Executives at United Technologies think that they have identified a common weakness in Japanese multinational decision makers that Western firms can profitably exploit.

According to United Technologies managers, in most Japanese companies, important corporate decisions regarding activities in foreign operations are made by top-management Japanese nationals who are quick to tell their foreign customers and managers that there is only one way to handle the design or delivery of a product or service—the way it is done in Japan. They seem to base decisions primarily on Japanese business custom at the home office rather than on the elements of the decision situation itself. This tendency makes Japanese operations in foreign countries particularly vulnerable to competition from Western manufacturers that can achieve Japanese standards of excellence in production *and* adjust to local customs and preferences. Through the 1990s, United Technologies intends to strive for those Japanese standards of excellence in production, while treating its foreign managers and partners with respect and defer to their knowledge and ideas.≈

Goals to Be Served   The goals that decision makers seek to attain are another element of the decision situation. In the case of managers, these goals should most often be organizational objectives. (Chapter 5 discusses the specifics of organizational objectives.)

Relevant Alternatives   The decision situation is usually composed of at least two relevant alternatives. A **relevant alternative** is one that is considered feasible for solv-

Relevant alternatives are alternatives that are considered feasible for solving an existing problem and for implementation.

ing an existing problem and for implementation. Alternatives that will not solve an existing problem *or* cannot be implemented are irrelevant and should be excluded from the decision-making situation.

Ordering of Alternatives

The decision situation requires a process or mechanism for ranking alternatives from most desirable to least desirable. This process can be subjective, objective, or some combination of the two. Past experience of the decision maker is an example of a subjective process, and the rate of output per machine is an example of an objective process.

Choice of Alternatives

The last element of the decision situation is the actual choice between available alternatives. This choice establishes the decision as a fact. Typically, managers choose the alternative that maximizes long-term return for the organization.

BACK TO THE CASE   As Cadillac management decides whether to offer a sport-utility vehicle, it must be aware of all the elements in the decision situation. Both the internal and external environments of Cadillac itself and of its parent company, General Motors, must be one focus of the analysis. For example, the decision makers must ask themselves if the company has the financial resources and expertise to diversify into this area (internal environment) and if there is a market for the kind of sport-utility vehicle that Cadillac would offer (external environment). Management's orientation in making this decision would need to be characterized by reason and sound judgment. In addition, management would have to keep General Motors and Cadillac organizational objectives in mind and list relevant alternatives to the development of a sport-utility vehicle. These relevant alternatives—other new products that could be designed and manufactured—might include a new luxury van or a new luxury subcompact. Finally, management should rank these relevant alternatives in order of desirability before choosing which alternative to implement.

THE DECISION-MAKING PROCESS

A decision is a choice of one alternative from a set of available alternatives. The **decision-making process** comprises the steps the decision maker takes to arrive at this choice. The process that a manager uses to make decisions has a significant impact on the quality of the decisions that manager makes. If managers use an organized and systematic process, the probability that their decisions will be sound is higher than if they use a disorganized and unsystematic process.[9]

A model of the decision-making process that is recommended for managerial use is presented in Figure 7.4. In order, the decision-making steps this model depicts are as follows:

1. Identify an existing problem.
2. List possible alternatives for solving the problem.
3. Select the most beneficial of these alternatives.
4. Implement the selected alternative.
5. Gather feedback to find out if the implemented alternative is solving the identified problem.

The paragraphs that follow elaborate upon each of these steps and explain their interrelationships.[10]

This model of the decision-making process is based on three primary assumptions.[11] First, the model assumes that humans are economic beings with the objective

---

The **decision-making process** comprises the steps the decision maker takes to make a decision.

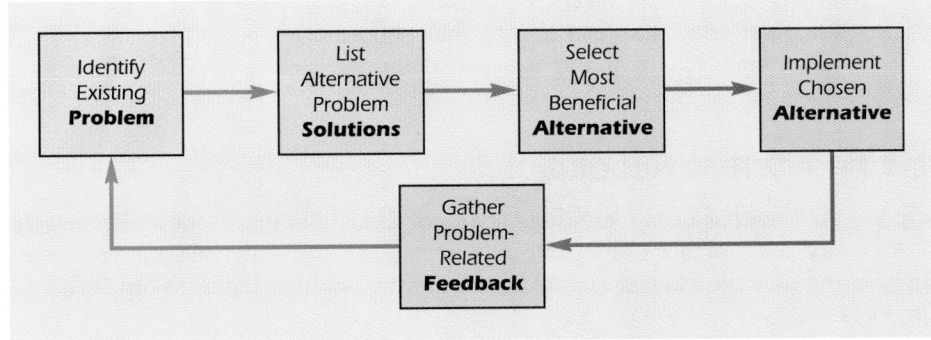

Figure 7.4   Model of the decision-making process

of maximizing satisfaction or return. Second, it assumes that within the decision-making situation all alternatives and their possible consequences are known. Its last assumption is that decision makers have some priority system to guide them in ranking the desirability of each alternative. If each of these assumptions is met, the decision made will probably be the best possible one for the organization. In real life, unfortunately, one or more of these assumptions is often not met, and therefore the decision made is less than optimal for the organization.

Identifying an Existing Problem

Decision making is essentially a problem-solving process that involves eliminating barriers to organizational goal attainment. Naturally, the first step in this elimination process is identifying exactly what the problems or barriers are, for only after the barriers have been adequately identified can management take steps to eliminate them. Several years ago, Molson, a Canadian manufacturer of beer as well as of cleaning and sanitizing products, faced a barrier to success: a free-trade agreement that threatened to open Canadian borders to U.S. beer. Although the borders were not due to open for another five years, Molson decided to deal with the problem of increased beer competition from the United States immediately by increasing production and sales of its specialty chemical products. Within four years, Molson's chemical sales exceeded its beer sales. Essentially, the company identified its problem—the threat of increased U.S. competition for beer sales—and dealt with it by emphasizing sales in a different division.[12]

Chester Barnard has stated that organizational problems are brought to the attention of managers mainly by the following means:[13]

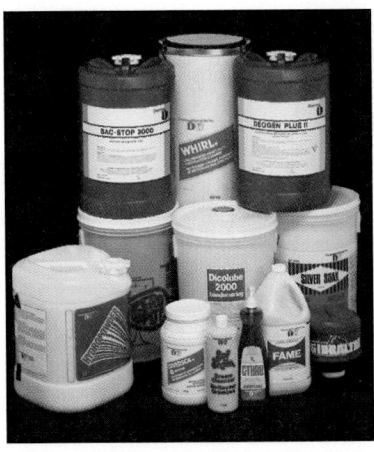

Throughout the United States, the Canadian manufacturer Molson is known almost exclusively by the product that it advertises on American television: its beer. In fact, however, Molson manufactures a very broad line of products, especially chemical cleaning products. Faced with the threat of keener competition from U.S. breweries once NAFTA has eliminated trade barriers, Molson has used its product-line strength to take precautionary steps. In particular, it has already focused its domestic energy on the sales of chemical products, which now enjoy more sales than Molson beers.

1. Orders issued by managers' supervisors.
2. Situations relayed to managers by their subordinates.
3. The normal activity of the managers themselves.

Listing Alternative Solutions

Once a problem has been identified, managers should list the various possible solutions. Very few organizational problems are solvable in only one way. Managers must search out the numerous available alternative solutions to most organizational problems.

Before searching for solutions, however, managers should be aware of five limitations on the number of problem-solving alternatives available:[14]

1. Authority factors (for example, a manager's superior may have told the manager that a certain alternative is not feasible).
2. Biological or human factors (for example, human factors within the organization may be inappropriate for implementing certain alternatives).
3. Physical factors (for example, the physical facilities of the organization may be inappropriate for certain alternatives).
4. Technological factors (for example, the level of organizational technology may be inadequate for certain alternatives).
5. Economic factors (for example, certain alternatives may be too costly for the organization).

Figure 7.5 presents additional factors that can limit a manager's decision alternatives. This diagram uses the term *discretionary area* to depict all the feasible alternatives available to managers. Factors that limit or rule out alternatives outside this area are legal restrictions, moral and ethical norms, formal policies and rules, and unofficial social norms.[15]

Selecting the Most Beneficial Alternative

Decision makers can select the most beneficial solution only after they have evaluated each alternative very carefully. This evaluation should consist of three steps. First, decision makers should list, as accurately as possible, the potential effects of each alter-

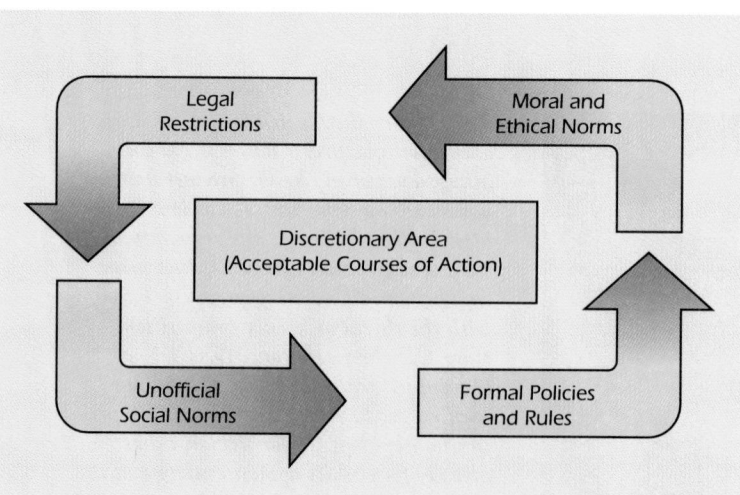

Figure 7.5   Additional factors that limit a manager's number of acceptable alternatives

2. native as if the alternative had already been chosen and implemented. Second, they should assign a probability factor to each of the potential effects, that is, indicate how probable the occurrence of the effect would be if the alternative were implemented.

3. Third, keeping organizational goals in mind, decision makers should compare each alternative's expected effects and the respective probabilities of those effects.[16] After these steps have been completed, managers will know which alternative seems most advantageous to the organization.

The information in this section of the text indicates that a decision alternative should be evaluated primarily for its ability to solve an organizational problem(s). The following CUTTING EDGE feature, however, suggests that decision alternatives should be evaluated not only for their ability to solve an organizational problem(s) but also for their ability to build important organizational values. This is an important new approach in management studies.

DECISION ALTERNATIVES SHOULD REFLECT ORGANIZATIONAL VALUES

CUTTING EDGE

Conventional approaches to decision making focus on generating and evaluating alternatives as means for solving organizational problems. According to more current management thinking, however, alternatives should be evaluated not only as means of solving such problems but also as ways of exemplifying and achieving important organizational values. *Values* here refer to the organization's ideals. In order for such an approach to be feasible, of course, organizational values must be clearly defined and communicated to organization members.

For an instance of how a company uses organizational values in evaluating decision alternatives, consider a recent action at American Telephone and Telegraph Company (AT&T). AT&T's chief financial officer has delineated and distributed to all workers in the financial area a set of core values or ideals they should consider important to the success of operations in that area. Among these values are respect for individuals, the highest standards of integrity, teamwork, innovation, and dedication to helping customers. All decision alternatives being considered within the financial area at AT&T are now to be evaluated not only for their ability to solve some organizational problem(s) but also for their ability to reflect and build on these core values.≈

Implementing the Chosen Alternative

The next step is to put the chosen alternative into action. Decisions must be supported by appropriate action if they are to have a chance of success.

Gathering Problem-Related Feedback

After the chosen alternative has been implemented, decision makers must gather feedback to determine the effect of the implemented alternative on the identified problem. If the identified problem is not being solved, managers need to search out and implement some other alternative.

The text presents the decision-making process essentially as a problem-solving process. The following PEOPLE PERSPECTIVES feature illustrates how top management at John Deere and Company decided to solve significant problems by getting employees more involved in the company.

DECISION AT JOHN DEERE: ELIMINATE PROBLEMS BY BUILDING EMPLOYEE INVOLVEMENT

PEOPLE PERSPECTIVES

Hans W. Becherer, chief executive of John Deere and Company, a firm that manufactures and sells farm equipment, recently faced two significant company problems: (1) the long-term demand for company products was weakening, and (2) competition from other companies was intensifying.

Becherer decided that the best way to deal with these problems was to get employees more involved in the company. For example, assembly-line workers were trained to travel across North America to explain Deere's new products to dealers and farmers. Becherer believed that this action would help the company fight its competition by impressing customers and dealers with the quality of Deere employees and hence its products. Becherer was also convinced that making production workers marketing emissaries for Deere's products would strengthen their commitment to manufacturing only the best products because they would feel more responsible for output once they had developed personal relationships with customers and dealers.

Another move Becherer has taken is to encourage employee involvement in maintaining customer relationships and monitoring product-quality feedback.

As Becherer expands the responsibilities of his employees, he has been careful to step up their training so they will be well prepared for their new roles. Preliminary reports indicate that Becherer's implementation of his decision to involve employees has indeed helped him solve Deere's problems of weakening product demand and increased product competition.≈

BACK TO THE CASE

To illustrate the text material about the decision-making process, we will assume that Cadillac management needs to decide how to increase product safety. Management's first step would be to identify the problem. For example, management must find out if customer injury has been the result of faulty parts, inadequate safety devices, or poor operating instructions. Having identified the problem, management's next step would be to list all possible problem solutions—for example: Can the quality of parts be improved? Can additional safety devices be invented? Would better operating instructions reduce the risk of injury?

After eliminating infeasible solutions, Cadillac management would evaluate all remaining solutions, select one, and implement it. If it turns out that operating instructions are unreliable mainly because of customer error or if it proves too expensive to manufacture better-quality parts, the best alternative would be to create new safety devices for Cadillac products. Management would then have to initiate appropriate action to design and manufacture such devices. Once the safety devices were added, problem-related feedback would be extremely important because management would need to know if the new devices were, in fact, reducing customer injury. If they were not, management would have to decide what other actions should be taken to improve product safety.

DECISION-MAKING CONDITIONS

In most instances, it is impossible for decision makers to know exactly what the future consequences of an implemented alternative will be. The word *future* is the key in discussing decision-making conditions. Because organizations and their environments are constantly changing, future consequences of implemented decisions are not perfectly predictable.

In general, there are three different conditions under which decisions are made. Each of these conditions is based on the degree to which the future outcome of a decision alternative is predictable. The conditions are as follows:[17]

1. Complete certainty.
2. Complete uncertainty.
3. Risk.

Complete Certainty Condition

The **complete certainty condition** exists when decision makers know exactly what the results of an implemented alternative will be. Under this condition, managers have complete knowledge about a decision, so all they have to do is list outcomes for alternatives and then choose the outcome with the highest payoff for the organization. For example, the outcome of an investment alternative based on buying government bonds is, for all practical purposes, completely predictable because of established government interest rates. Deciding to implement this alternative, then, would be making a decision in a complete certainty situation. Unfortunately, most organizational decisions are made outside the complete certainty situation.

> The **complete certainty condition** is the decision-making situation in which the decision maker knows exactly what the results of an implemented alternative will be.

Complete Uncertainty Condition

The **complete uncertainty condition** exists when decision makers have absolutely no idea what the results of an implemented alternative will be. The complete uncertainty condition would exist, for example, if there were no historical data on which to base a decision. Not knowing what happened in the past makes it difficult to predict what will happen in the future. In this situation, decision makers usually find that sound decisions are mostly a matter of chance. An example of a decision made in a complete uncertainty situation is choosing to pull the candy machine lever labeled "Surprise of the Day" rather than the lever that would deliver a familiar candy bar. Fortunately, few organizational decisions need to be made in the complete uncertainty condition.

> The **complete uncertainty condition** is the decision-making situation in which the decision maker has absolutely no idea what the results of an implemented alternative will be.

Risk Condition

The primary characteristic of the **risk condition** is that decision makers have only enough information about the outcome of each alternative to estimate how probable the outcome will be if the alternative is implemented.[18] Obviously, the risk condition lies somewhere between complete certainty and complete uncertainty. The manager who hires two extra salespeople in order to increase annual organizational sales is deciding in a risk situation. He may believe that the probability is high that these two new salespeople will raise total sales, but it is impossible for him to know that for sure. Therefore, some risk is associated with this decision.

> The **risk condition** is the decision-making situation in which the decision maker has only enough information to estimate how probable the outcome of implemented alternatives will be.

The risk condition is a broad one in which *degrees* of risk can be associated with decisions. The lower the quality of information about the outcome of an alternative, the closer the situation is to complete uncertainty and the higher is the risk of choosing that alternative. Most decisions made in organizations have some amount of risk associated with them.

BACK TO THE CASE Should Cadillac managers decide to offer the new sport-utility vehicle, they would next need to decide how to handle competition from other sport-utility products like the Chevrolet Blazer and the Ford Bronco. The decision-making condition for such a situation lies somewhere between complete cer-

tainty and complete uncertainty about the outcome of proposed alternatives. Cadillac management could decide, for example, to lower Cadillac sport-utility prices or to increase advertising to fight off the competition, but there would be no guarantee that such measures would produce the desired results. Management *does* know, however, what kind of action has succeeded in the past in stopping competitors of other products, and thus is not dealing with a complete unknown. Therefore, any decision that Cadillac managers make about handling increased competition would be made under the risk condition. In other words, they would have to determine the outcome probability for each proposed alternative and base their decision on the alternative that appears to be most advantageous.

DECISION-MAKING TOOLS

Most managers develop an intuition about what decisions to make—a largely subjective feeling, based on years of experience in a particular organization or industry, that gives them insights into decision making for that industry or organization.[19] Although intuition is often an important factor in making a decision, managers generally emphasize more objective decision-making tools. The two most widely used such tools are probability theory and decision trees.[20]

Probability Theory

Probability theory is a decision-making tool used in risk situations—situations in which decision makers are not completely sure of the outcome of an implemented alternative. *Probability* refers to the likelihood that an event or outcome will actually occur. It is estimated by calculating an expected value for each alternative considered. Specifically, the **expected value (EV)** for an alternative is the income (*I*) that alternative would produce multiplied by its probability of producing that income (*P*). In formula form, $EV = I \times P$. Decision makers generally choose and implement the alternative with the highest expected value.[21]

An example will clarify the relationship of probability, income, and expected value. A manager is trying to decide where to open a store that specializes in renting surfboards. She is considering three possible locations (A, B, and C), all of which seem feasible. For the first year of operation, the manager has projected that, under ideal conditions, her company would earn $90,000 in Location A, $75,000 in Location B, and $60,000 in Location C. After studying historical weather patterns, however, she has determined that there is only a 20 percent chance—or a .2 probability—of ideal conditions occurring during the first year of operation in Location A. Locations B and C have a .4 and a .8 probability, respectively, for ideal conditions during the first year of operations. Expected values for each of these locations are as follows: Location A—$18,000; Location B—$30,000; Location C—$48,000. Figure 7.6 shows the situation this decision maker faces. According to her probability analysis, she should open a store in Location C, the alternative with the highest expected value.

Probability theory is a decision-making tool used in risk situations—situations in which the decision maker is not completely sure of the outcome of an implemented alternative.

Expected value (EV) is the measurement of the anticipated value of some event, determined by multiplying the income an event would produce by its probability of producing that income ($EV = I \times P$).

Alternative (Locations)	Potential Income	Probability of Income	Expected Value of Alternatives
A	$90,000	.2	$18,000
B	75,000	.4	30,000
C	60,000	.8	48,000
I	x	P	=	EV

Figure 7.6 Expected values for locating surfboard rental store in each of three possible locations

Decision Trees

In the previous section, probability theory was applied to a relatively simple decision situation. Some decisions, however, are more complicated and involve a series of steps. These steps are interdependent; that is, each step is influenced by the step that precedes it. A **decision tree** is a graphic decision-making tool typically used to evaluate decisions involving a series of steps.[22]

John F. Magee has developed a classic illustration that outlines how decision trees can be applied to a production decision.[23] In his illustration (see Figure 7.7), the Stygian Chemical Company must decide whether to build a small or a large plant to manufacture a new product with an expected life of ten years (Decision Point 1 in Figure 7.7). If the choice is to build a large plant, the company could face high or low average product demand, or high initial and then low demand. If, however, the choice is to build a small plant, the company could face either initially high or initially low product demand. If the small plant is built and there is high product demand during an initial two-year period, management could then choose whether to expand the plant (Decision Point 2). Whether the decision is made to expand or not to expand, management could then face either high or low product demand.

Now that various possible alternatives related to this decision have been outlined, the financial consequence of each different course of action must be compared. To adequately compare these consequences, management must do the following:

1. Study estimates of investment amounts necessary for building a large plant, for building a small plant, and for expanding a small plant.

A **decision tree** is a graphic decision-making tool typically used to evaluate decisions involving a series of steps.

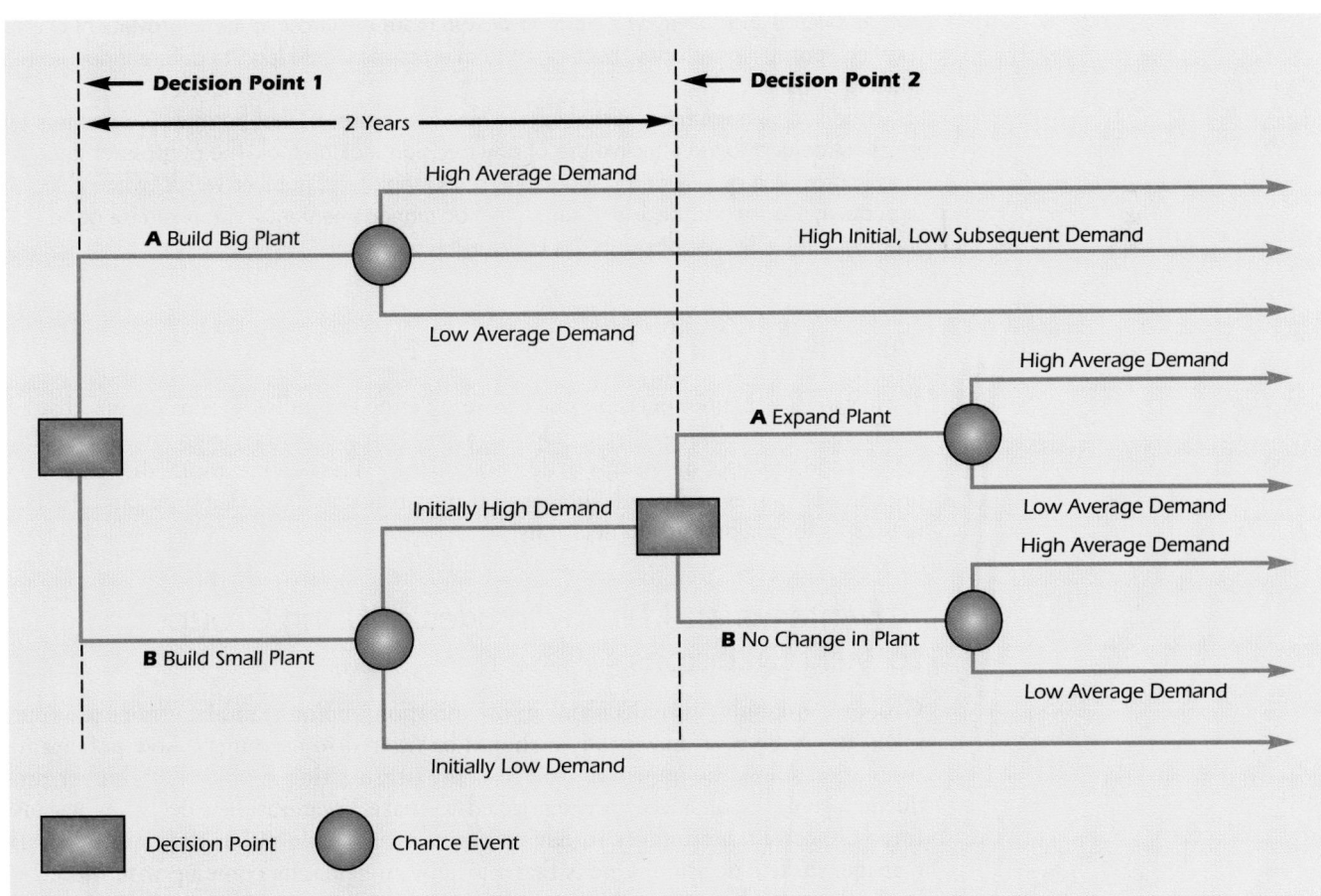

Figure 7.7   A basic decision tree illustrating the decision facing Stygian management

2. Weigh the probabilities of facing different product demand levels for various decision alternatives.
3. Consider projected income yields for each decision alternative.

Analysis of the expected values and net expected gain for each decision alternative helps management to decide on an appropriate choice.[24] *Net expected gain* is defined in this situation as the expected value of an alternative minus the investment cost. For example, if building a large plant yields the highest net expected gain, Stygian management should decide to build the large plant.

BACK TO THE CASE

According to the information in the text, managers at Cadillac have two objective decision-making tools available to help them make better decisions. First, they can use probability theory to obtain an expected value for various decision alternatives and then implement the alternative with the highest expected value. For example, in determining what tactic to use to handle Cadillac's competition from the Ford Bronco, management may see the alternatives as: (1) devoting more resources to making higher-quality automobiles, or (2) initiating more effective advertising for Cadillac's present products. The decision management makes would depend on the projected value of each alternative once implemented.

Second, for decisions involving a series of steps related to each of several alternatives, Cadillac management could use a decision tree to assist in picturing and evaluating each alternative. To take the same example, Cadillac management might reason that to handle the Ford Bronco competition the company needs either to design an entirely new solar-powered sport-utility vehicle or to devote more resources to the improvement of its existing sport-utility vehicles. Each of these alternatives would lead to different decision-making steps.

Cadillac management must always remember, however, that business judgment is an essential adjunct to the effective use of any decision-making tool. The purpose of the tool is to improve the quality of this judgment, not to replace it. In other words, when using probability theory and decision trees, Cadillac management must also exercise good judgment in finally deciding what is best for the company.

GROUP DECISION MAKING

Earlier in this chapter, decision makers were defined as individuals or groups that actually make a decision—that is, choose a decision alternative from those available. This section focuses on groups as decision makers. The two key topics discussed here are the advantages and disadvantages of using groups to make decisions, and the best processes for making group decisions.

Advantages and Disadvantages of Using Groups to Make Decisions

Groups commonly make decisions in organizations.[25] For example, groups are often asked to decide what new product should be offered to customers, how policies for promotion should be improved, and how the organization should reach higher production goals. Groups are so often asked to make organizational decisions because there are certain advantages to having a group of people rather than an individual manager make a decision. One is that a group can generally come up with more and better decision alternatives than an individual can. The reason for this is that a group can draw on collective, diverse organizational experiences as the foundation for deci-

sion making, while the individual manager has only the limited experiences of one person to draw on.[26] Another advantage is that when a group makes a decision, the members of that group tend to support the implementation of the decision more fervently than they would if the decision had been made by an individual. This can be of significant help to a manager in successfully implementing a decision. A third advantage of using a group rather than an individual to make a decision is that group members tend to perceive the decision as their own, and this ownership perception makes it more likely that they will strive to implement the decision successfully rather than prematurely giving in to failure.

There are also several disadvantages to having groups rather than individual managers make organizational decisions. Perhaps the one most often discussed is that it takes longer to make a group decision because groups must take the time to present and discuss all the members' views. Another disadvantage is that group decisions cost the organization more than individual decisions do simply because they take up the time of more people in the organization. Finally, group decisions can be of lower quality than individual decisions if they become contaminated by the group members' effort to maintain friendly relationships among themselves. This phenomenon of compromising the quality of a decision to maintain relationships within a group is referred to as *groupthink* and is discussed more fully in Chapter 17, "Groups, Teams, and Corporate Culture."

Managers must weigh all these advantages and disadvantages of group decision making carefully, factoring in unique organizational situations, and give a group authority to make a decision only when the advantages of doing so clearly seem to outweigh the disadvantages.

Processes for Making Group Decisions

Making a sound group decision regarding complex organizational circumstances is a formidable challenge. Fortunately, several useful processes have been developed to assist groups in meeting this challenge. The following sections discuss three such processes: brainstorming, the nominal group technique, and the Delphi technique.

Brainstorming

Brainstorming is a group decision-making process in which negative feedback on any suggested alternative by any group member is forbidden until all members have presented alternatives that they perceive as valuable.[27] Figure 7.8 shows this process. Brainstorming is carefully designed to encourage all group members to contribute as many viable decision alternatives as they can think of. Its premise is that if the evaluation of alternatives starts before all possible alternatives have been offered, valuable alternatives may be overlooked. During brainstorming, group members are encouraged to state their ideas, no matter how wild they may seem, while an appointed group member records all ideas for discussion.

Brainstorming is a group decision-making process in which negative feedback on any suggested alternative to any group member is forbidden until all group members have presented alternatives that they perceive as valuable.

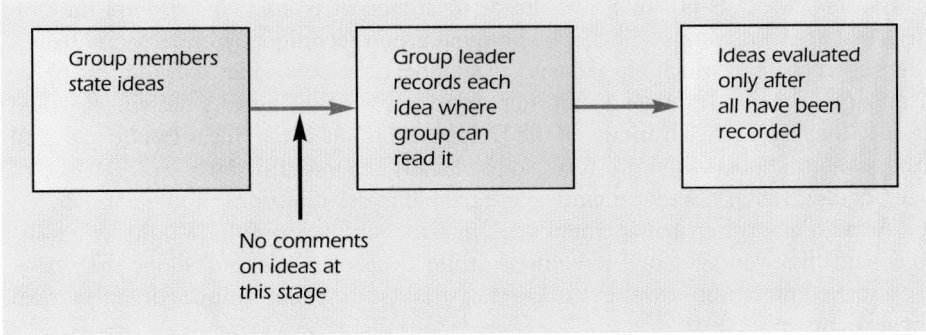

Figure 7.8   The brainstorming process

Armstrong International's David Armstrong has discovered an intriguing method for discouraging the premature evaluation of ideas during a brainstorming session. He allows only one negative comment per group member. Before discussion begins, he hands every member one piece of M&M's candy. Once a member makes a negative comment, he or she must eat the piece of candy. Because a group member is required to have an uneaten piece of candy in order to make a negative comment, members use their sole opportunity to be negative very carefully.[28] Once everyone's ideas have been presented, the group evaluates them and chooses the one that holds the most promise.

Nominal Group Technique

Nominal group technique is a group decision-making process in which every group member is assured of equal participation in making the group decision. After each member writes down individual ideas and presents them orally to the group, the entire group discusses all the ideas and then votes for the best idea in a secret ballot.

The **nominal group technique** is another useful process for helping groups to make decisions. This process is designed to ensure that each group member has equal participation in making the group decision.[29] It involves the following steps:

- **Step 1:** Each group member writes down individual ideas on the decision or problem being discussed.
- **Step 2:** Each member presents individual ideas orally. The ideas are usually written on a board for all other members to see and refer to.
- **Step 3:** After all members present their ideas, the entire group discusses these ideas simultaneously. Discussion tends to be unstructured and spontaneous.
- **Step 4:** When discussion is completed, a secret ballot is taken to allow members to support their favorite ideas without fear. The idea receiving the most votes is adopted and implemented.

The Delphi Technique

The **Delphi technique** is a group decision-making process that involves circulating questionnaires on a specific problem among group members, sharing the questionnaire results with them, and then continuing to recirculate and refine individual responses until a consensus regarding the problem is reached.

The Delphi technique is a third useful process for helping groups to make decisions. The **Delphi technique** involves circulating questionnaires on a specific problem among group members, sharing the questionnaire results with them, and then continuing to recirculate and refine individual responses until a consensus regarding the problem is reached.[30] In contrast to the nominal group technique or brainstorming, the Delphi technique does not have group members meet face to face. The formal steps followed in the Delphi technique are:

- **Step 1:** A problem is identified.
- **Step 2:** Group members are asked to offer solutions to the problem by providing anonymous responses to a carefully designed questionnaire.
- **Step 3:** Responses of all group members are compiled and sent out to all group members.
- **Step 4:** Individual group members are asked to generate a new individual solution to the problem after they have studied the individual responses of all other group members compiled in Step 3.
- **Step 5:** Steps 3 and 4 are repeated until a consensus problem solution is reached.

Evaluating Group Decision-Making Processes

All three of the processes presented here for assisting groups to reach a decision have both advantages and disadvantages. Brainstorming offers the advantage of encouraging the expression of as many useful ideas as possible, but the disadvantage of wasting the group's time on ideas that are wildly impractical. The nominal group technique, with its secret ballot, offers a structure in which individuals can support or reject an idea without fear of recrimination. Its disadvantage is that there is no way of knowing why individuals voted the way they did. The advantage of the Delphi technique is that ideas can be gathered from group members who are too geographically separated or busy to meet face to face. Its disadvantage is that members are unable to ask questions of one another.

As with any other management tool, managers must carefully weigh the advantages and disadvantages of these three group decision tools and adopt the one—or some combination of the three—that best suits their unique organizational circumstances.

BACK TO THE CASE

The material in this section of the text offers insights about how a group at Cadillac could be entrusted with the decision of whether or not to manufacture a sport-utility vehicle. First a decision of this magnitude and importance should probably be made by a group of top managers drawn from many different organizational areas. A group decision would almost certainly be better than an individual decision in this case because a group would have a broader view of Cadillac and the market than any one person in the company would and therefore be more likely to make an appropriate decision. Perhaps the group decision-making process used in this case should be a combination of the three processes discussed in the text. Brainstorming sessions would ensure that all thoughts and ideas related to this crucial decision surface, while the nominal group technique would focus group members on the urgency of making the decision by requiring them to vote on whether or not to make the sport-utility vehicle. The Delphi technique could be used to obtain important input on the decision from experts around the country by asking them to present their written views through a specially designed questionnaire.

Unquestionably, using a group to make this decision will be time-consuming and expensive. Once the decision is made, however, group members will be committed to it, perceive it as their own, and do all in their power to ensure that it is successfully implemented—even if the decision is *not* to offer the new vehicle.

Action Summary

Reread the learning objectives below. Each objective is followed by questions. Answering these questions accurately will help you retain the most important concepts discussed in this chapter. After answering each question, check your answer against the answer key at the end of this chapter. (*Hint:* If you have any doubt regarding the correct response, consult the page whose number follows the answer.)

Circle: From studying this chapter, I will attempt to acquire:

1. A fundamental understanding of the term *decision*.

T,F   a. A decision is a choice made between two or more alternatives.

a,b,c,d,e   b. Decision making is involved in the following function: (a) planning; (b) organizing; (c) controlling; (d) influencing; (e) all of the above.

2. An understanding of each element of the decision situation.

a,b,c,d,e   a. The following type of decision-making orientation involves the belief that the source of all good is outside oneself and that, therefore, one must rely heavily on suggestions from other organizational members: (a) exploitation; (b) hoarding; (c) marketing; (d) natural; (e) receptive.

a,b,c,d,e   b. According to Wilson and Alexis, all of the following are elements of the decision situation except: (a) the ordering of alternatives; (b) the decision makers; (c) the goals to be served; (d) the timeliness of the decision; (e) the relevant alternatives.

3. An ability to use the decision-making process.

a,b,c,d,e   a. After identifying an existing problem, the next major step in the decision-making process is: (a) defining the terminology in the problem statement; (b) listing possible alternatives to solve the problem; (c) investigating possible alternatives to determine their effect on the problem; (d) determining what parties will participate in the problem-solving process; (e) identifying sources of alternatives to solve the problem.

a,b,c,d,e   b. After going through the decision-making process, if the identified problem is not being solved as a result of the implemented alternative, the manager should: (a) attempt to redefine the problem; (b) turn attention to another problem; (c) search out and implement some other alternative; (d) attempt to implement the alternative until the problem is solved; (e) accept the fact that the problem cannot be solved.

4. An appreciation for the various situations in which decisions are made.

T,F   a. The risk condition exists when decision makers have absolutely no idea of what the results of an implemented alternative will be.

T,F   **b.** When operating under the complete uncertainty condition, decision makers usually find that sound decisions are a matter of chance.

      5. An understanding of probability theory and decision trees as decision-making tools.

a,b,c,d,e   **a.** Expected value is determined by using the formula: (a) $EV = I \times P$; (b) $EV = I/P$; (c) $EV = I + P$; (d) $EV = P - I$; (e) $EV = 2P \times I$.

a,b,c,d,e   **b.** In the case of the Stygian Chemical Company, the problem was solved through the use of: (a) executive experience; (b) decision tree technique; (c) queuing theory; (d) linear programming; (e) demand probability.

      6. Insights about groups as decision makers.

T,F   **a.** One disadvantage of using a group to make a decision is that members of the group will feel ownership of the decision.

a,b,c,d,e   **b.** The process for group decision making that involves the use of questionnaires is: (a) brainstorming; (b) nominal group technique; (c) Delphi technique; (d) a and b; (e) all of the above.

Introductory Case Wrap-Up

"Cadillac Decides Whether to Make a Sport-Utility Vehicle" (p. 153) and its related back-to-the-case sections were written to help you better understand the management concepts contained in this chapter. Answer the following discussion questions about this introductory case to enrich your understanding of the chapter content:

1. List three alternatives that Cadillac management might consider in handling Ford Bronco competition *before* deciding whether to offer the new sport-utility vehicle.

2. What information would management need to evaluate these three alternatives?

3. Do you think that you would enjoy making this decision on whether to offer the new sport-utility vehicle at Cadillac? Explain.

Issues for Review and Discussion

1. What is a decision?
2. Describe the difference between a significant decision and an insignificant decision. Which would you rather make? Why?
3. List three programmed and three nonprogrammed decisions that the manager of a nightclub would probably have to make.
4. Explain the rationale for determining which managers in the organization are responsible for making which decisions.
5. What is the consensus method of making decisions? When would you use it?
6. List and define five basic elements of the decision-making situation.
7. How does the receptive orientation for decision making differ from the ideal orientation for decision making?
8. List as many undesirable traits of a decision maker as possible. (They are implied within the explanations of the receptive, exploitative, hoarding, and marketing orientations to decision making.)
9. What is a relevant alternative? An irrelevant alternative?

10. Draw and describe in words the decision-making process presented in this chapter.
11. What is meant by the term *discretionary area*?
12. List the three assumptions on which the decision-making process presented in this chapter is based.
13. Explain the difference between the complete certainty and complete uncertainty decision-making situations.
14. What is the risk decision-making situation?
15. Are there degrees of risk associated with various decisions? Why?
16. How do decision makers use probability theory? Be sure to discuss expected value in your answer.
17. What is a decision tree?
18. Under what conditions are decision trees usually used as decision-making tools?
19. Discuss the advantages and disadvantages of using a group to make an organizational decision.
20. In what ways are brainstorming, the nominal group technique, and the Delphi technique similar? How do they differ?

Action Summary Answer Key

1. **a.** T, p. 154
   b. e, p. 154
2. **a.** e, p. 159
   b. d, pp. 158–160

3. **a.** b, pp. 161–162
   b. c, p. 163
4. **a.** F, p. 165
   b. T, p. 165

5. **a.** a, p. 166
   b. b, pp. 167–168
6. **a.** F, pp. 168–169
   b. c, pp. 169–170

Case Study

The Decision to Change at General Motors Corporation

In 1992, unhappy with the company's direction and continuing operational losses, the executive board of General Motors Corporation made several major decisions to change GM. The positions of chairman and chief executive officer, then held by Robert Stempel, were separated. John G. Smale, former chairman of Procter & Gamble, became "nonexecutive chairman," and, under new guidelines that formalized stronger board oversight, John F. Smith, Jr., became CEO.

Smith, who proved a capable manager, in December 1994 hired Ronald Zarrella, formerly president of Bausch & Lomb, as head of marketing. Zarrella set out to dispel the long-held Detroit belief "that product is everything." Instead, he supported a strategy of emphasizing brand identification. As confirmation of the success of his strategy, Zarrella points to GM's popular Saturn, which has won more praise for its straightforward selling practices and unconventional ads than for its sedans and coupes. Says Lynn Upshaw, executive vice president of brand marketing for Ketchum Worldwide, "It's a nice little car, but what has really made [the Saturn] successful is its different marketing concept."

As part of this strategy of brand-name positioning, GM has adopted a concept known as "needs-based marketing," a brainchild of GM consumer research director Vincent Barabba. Barabba's concept required surveying car buyers on their preferences in order to make cars that fit what *customers* say they need rather than what *engineers* think they should have. According to Zarrella, "Part of this process is to get the decisions made on facts and data instead of emotion and history. Brand management will allow us to do that."

GM has targeted Cadillac, one of its most venerable divisions, to test the effectiveness of these branding decisions. Why Cadillac? According to one observer, "In the luxury-car business, where success hinges on luring affluent younger buyers, General Motors Corporation's Cadillac Motor Car Division is something of an industry joke." Since peaking at 351,000 cars in 1978, Cadillac sales have gone down steadily. In 1995, Cadillac's share of the roughly 1.2-million-unit luxury market stood at a mere 15 percent, down from 24 percent six years earlier.

The solution to this problem is to attract the segment of the luxury market that currently buys Cadillac's chief competitors—Lexus, BMW, and Infiniti. In 1994, this market of 40- to 50-year-old baby boomers accounted for one-third of all luxury car sales; by 2000, that figure will be 40 percent. The targeted market is younger and somewhat wealthier than present Cadillac buyers, and more likely to be college educated and female. In addition, it features very definite "psychographic" characteristics. For example, the average baby boomer was raised on imports and retains a youthful and busy lifestyle in middle age. Baby boomers are confident of their ability to shop and often have no brand loyalty. They expect high quality and reliability from their cars, and tend to avoid what they perceive as the common, the garish, and the excessive.

GM hopes that the new Catera model will solve the problem of Cadillac's sliding sales. True to their new commitment to design for the customer, Cadillac and GM's German subsidiary Opel created in the Catera a car to suit the American market. Confesses Opel engineer Willem Kohl, "We didn't realize you could know so much about your customer and what he wants in a car." Based on the data gathered from Saturn's foray into the market, Cadillac is requiring major changes in the methods that dealers use to sell the Catera. Catera brand manager Dave Nottoli believes the target market will demand "a hassle-free buying experience from a salesperson who is knowledgeable about the product and the competition."

Industry observers acknowledge that although the new Catera is a big improvement, it's only a start. According to David Bradley, an analyst at J. P. Morgan Securities, "If you need 10 steps to get [to targeted market share] this is half a step." Still, Cadillac hopes Catera will firmly establish the company as a viable producer in the minds of luxury-car buyers and thus prepare that market for more of the same from the company in the next century. If its expectations are off, Cadillac may fall completely out of the luxury-car market early in the twenty-first century.

The story of the Catera exemplifies one of the ways in which John Smith has positioned GM for long-term profitability. GM's board of directors has recognized his success. In 1995, it declared itself "free to [separate or recombine the positions of CEO and chairman] any way that seems best for the company." Thus the board voted in early 1996 to recombine the two positions, and Smith assumed both of them.

Questions:

1. List all the decisions described in the story of Cadillac's Catera. How would you categorize each of these decisions? Explain. In your opinion, what decision-making techniques were used by GM's board and management?

2. What internal and external environmental factors influenced GM's decision to build the Catera? Which, do you think, had the greatest influence? Explain.

3. Illustrate the elements of the decision-making process with examples from the story of Catera's development.

4. Under which of the three decision-making conditions do you believe Cadillac's decision to build the Catera was made? Cite statements from the case to support your opinion.

Skills Exercise

What are the benefits and drawbacks of banking on the Catera as a solution to GM's problems? Working with a teammate, spend five to ten minutes brainstorming other possible alternatives to Cadillac's problem of falling market share. Examine each suggested alternative to determine its feasibility. To evaluate your alternatives, list the potential benefits and effects of each one. Then rank the alternatives, including the decision to make the Catera. Based on these rankings, do you think that the Cadillac Catera is a good solution? What might have been better? Defend your choice.

The Internet learning materials that accompany this chapter can be found at
http://www.profcerto.com
Additional information can be found on the inside front and back covers of this text.

8 chapter

STRATEGIC PLANNING

STUDENT LEARNING OBJECTIVES

From studying this chapter, I will attempt to acquire:

1. Definitions of both strategic planning and strategy.
2. An understanding of the strategy management process.
3. A knowledge of the impact of environmental analysis on strategy formulation.
4. Insights about how to use critical question analysis and SWOT analysis to formulate strategy.
5. An understanding of how to use business portfolio analysis and industry analysis to formulate strategy.
6. Insights into what tactical planning is and how strategic and tactical planning should be coordinated.

CHAPTER OUTLINE

Introductory Case: Sea World Plots a New Competitive Course

Strategic Planning

Fundamentals of Strategic Planning

Cutting Edge: Competitive Advantage through "People Development" Strategy

Strategy Management

Ethics Spotlight: Quaker Oats Cashes in on Fitness Fad

People Perspectives: Improving Dependent Care Builds Job Commitment at Bankers Trust Company

Quality Spotlight: Lutheran General Health System's Mission Emphasizes Quality

Tactical Planning

Comparing and Coordinating Strategic and Tactical Planning

Planning and Levels of Management

Sea World Plots a New Competitive Course

Walking through the cavernous passenger loading area of Sea World's new simulator ride one day in May 1992, park president Bill Davis fires a question at one of the ride's testers.

"Is this thing going to work?" he asks, stepping over construction debris.

"I sure hope so," the employee says.

Davis chuckles. While there is considerable cleaning, landscaping, and fine-tuning to be done, he is confident that *Mission: Bermuda Triangle* will be ready for guests May 22, in time for the Memorial Day weekend.

"I rode it three or four times on Monday and it was great," he says. "The one thing we are not going to do is open an attraction that is not ready to open."

Mission: Bermuda Triangle will simulate an underwater dive. Passengers will seemingly plunge a mile below the ocean's surface, where they will view deep-sea flora and fauna and, as their journey continues, learn why the area has been called the "graveyard of the Atlantic." The ride is part of a $48 million complex of new exhibits and improvements planned in 1992 at the Sea World and Busch Gardens park owned by Anheuser-Busch Companies, the St. Louis brewer. *Mission: Bermuda Triangle* is the first ride installed at the Orlando park. In its 19-year history, Sea World has concentrated on marine animal shows rather than edge-of-the-seat experiences.

The new ride is likely to help the park compete against its neighbors, Universal Studios Florida and Walt Disney World, which already have simulator rides, said John Gerner, an attractions consultant in Richmond, Virginia. The ride might also help Sea World attract thrill-seeking teenagers and boost attendance by 5 percent to 15 percent in 1992, Gerner said. Attendance the previous year was 3.9 million.

"Anheuser-Busch knows the value of putting a major thrill ride in its parks," Gerner stated. "It has seen the impact new roller coasters have had" when installed at Busch Gardens parks in Tampa and Williamsburg, Virginia.

Earlier in the week before its debut, the hum of construction machinery could be heard at the new ride and lights flashed off and on as the electrical system was tested. Bright orange and yellow submersibles that were used in undersea exploration are on loan to Sea World from oceanographic institutes, and are on display at the entrance of the ride.

Guests entering the attraction will see a preshow hosted by ABC journalist Hugh Downs. They will then be belted into one of three "submersibles"—the Neptune, Skipjack, or Barracuda. The cabins are attached to motion bases that pitch, shake, and tilt in sync with a film. The motion and video duplicate what people would actually feel on an underwater exploration.

"Early in the ride, it's very smooth, much like you're floating in the water," said Davis, standing near one of the several-ton motion bases. "Then, at the appropriate time, it really starts jostling you. There's a lot of motion."

To ensure that the cabins can withstand constant use, each will be run for a continuous 24 hours before the ride opens to guests, said Rick Waterhouse, the park's vice president of design and engineering.

Sea World is best known for its entertaining and informative marine animal shows and exhibits. In 1992, however, in order to compete with the many theme parks in Orlando and the surrounding area, Sea World made a strategic decision to add simulation rides such as **Mission: Bermuda Triangle**.

what's ahead

The introductory case highlights the new competitive course taken by Bill Davis, president of Sea World, in 1992. Developing a new course of this sort is part of Sea World's strategic planning process. The material in this chapter explains how developing a competitive strategy fits into strategic planning and discusses the strategic planning process as a whole. Major topics include the following:

1. Strategic planning.
2. Tactical planning.
3. Comparing and coordinating strategic and tactical planning.
4. Planning and levels of management.

STRATEGIC PLANNING

If managers are to be successful strategic planners, they must understand the fundamentals of strategic planning and how to formulate strategic plans.

Fundamentals of Strategic Planning

This section presents the basic principles of strategic planning. In doing so, it discusses definitions of both strategic planning and strategy in detail.

Defining Strategic Planning   **Strategic planning** is long-range planning that focuses on the organization as a whole. In doing strategic planning, managers consider the organization as a total unit and ask themselves what must be done in the long term to attain organizational goals. *Long range* is usually defined as a period of time extending about three to five years into the future. Hence, in strategic planning, managers try to determine what their organization should do to be successful three to five years from now. The most successful managers tend to be those who are capable of encouraging innovative strategic thinking within their organization.[1]

Managers may have a problem trying to decide exactly how far into the future they should extend their strategic planning. As a general rule, they should follow the **commitment principle,** which states that managers should commit funds for planning only if they can anticipate, in the foreseeable future, a return on planning expenses as a result of the long-range planning analysis. Realistically, planning costs are an investment and therefore should not be incurred unless a reasonable return on that investment is anticipated.

Defining Strategy   **Strategy** is defined as a broad and general plan developed to reach long-term objectives. Organizational strategy can, and generally does, focus on many different organizational areas, such as marketing, finance, production, research and development, and public relations. It gives broad direction to the organization.[2]

The following CUTTING EDGE feature encapsulates current management theory on developing a strategy that will gain the organization a competitive advantage in the marketplace by focusing on the development of organization members.

> **Strategic planning** is long-range planning that focuses on the organization as a whole.

> The **commitment principle** is a management guideline that advises managers to commit funds for planning only if they can anticipate, in the foreseeable future, a return on planning expenses as a result of the long-range planning analysis.

> **Strategy** is a broad and general plan developed to reach long-term organizational objectives; it is the end result of strategic planning.

COMPETITIVE ADVANTAGE THROUGH "PEOPLE DEVELOPMENT" STRATEGY

CUTTING EDGE

Many management theorists believe that modern managers are having significant difficulty in sustaining a competitive advantage for their organizations because they are ignoring the single most important factor in achieving and maintaining a competitive advantage: peo-

ple. Instead, these managers seem fixated on developing strategies that require enormous investments in technology, research, and state-of-the-art marketing.

Traditional sources of success, such as technology, can still provide a competitive advantage, of course. But to a more significant extent, strategies that focus on organizational culture and the management of people to elicit their best capabilities can provide organizations with an enormous competitive advantage. For example, a simple strategy aimed at developing and maintaining a workforce with competitive skills is critical for most companies. Training programs should aim at producing workers who can use advanced technology and who are also flexible, since their jobs may need to be changed quickly and often so the company can keep up with the competitive demands of a changing marketplace. The most effective strategy in this area will aim at developing employees who have a special competitive skill, such as the ability to do effective and efficient teamwork, that cannot be easily duplicated by a competing organization.≈

Strategy is actually the end result of strategic planning. Although larger organizations tend to be more precise in developing organizational strategy than smaller organizations do, every organization should have a strategy of some sort.[3] For a strategy to be worthwhile, though, it must be consistent with organizational objectives, which, in turn, must be consistent with organizational purpose. Table 8.1 illustrates this relationship between organizational objectives and strategy by presenting sample organizational objectives and strategies for three well-known business organizations.

Strategy Management

Strategy management is the process of ensuring that an organization possesses and benefits from the use of an appropriate organizational strategy. In this definition, an appropriate strategy is one best suited to the needs of an organization at a particular time.

The strategy management process is generally thought to consist of five sequential and continuing steps:[4]

1. Environmental analysis.
2. Establishment of an organizational direction.
3. Strategy formulation.
4. Strategy implementation.
5. Strategic control.

The relationships among these steps are illustrated in Figure 8.1.

Strategy management is the process of ensuring that an organization possesses and benefits from the use of an appropriate organizational strategy.

Table 8.1

Examples of Organizational Objectives and Related Strategies for Three Organizations in Different Business Areas

COMPANY	TYPE OF BUSINESS	SAMPLE ORGANIZATIONAL OBJECTIVES	STRATEGY TO ACCOMPLISH OBJECTIVES
Ford Motor Company	Automobile manufacturing	1. Regain market share recently lost to General Motors. 2. Regain quality reputation that was damaged because of Pinto gas tank explosions.	1. Resize and downsize present models. 2. Continue to produce subintermediate, standard, and luxury cars. 3. Emphasize use of programmed combustion engines instead of diesel engines
Burger King	Fast food	Increase productivity.	1. Increase people efficiency. 2. Increase machine efficiency.
CP Railroad	Transportation	1. Continue company growth. 2. Continue company profits.	1. Modernize. 2. Develop valuable real estate holdings. 3. Complete an appropriate railroad merger.

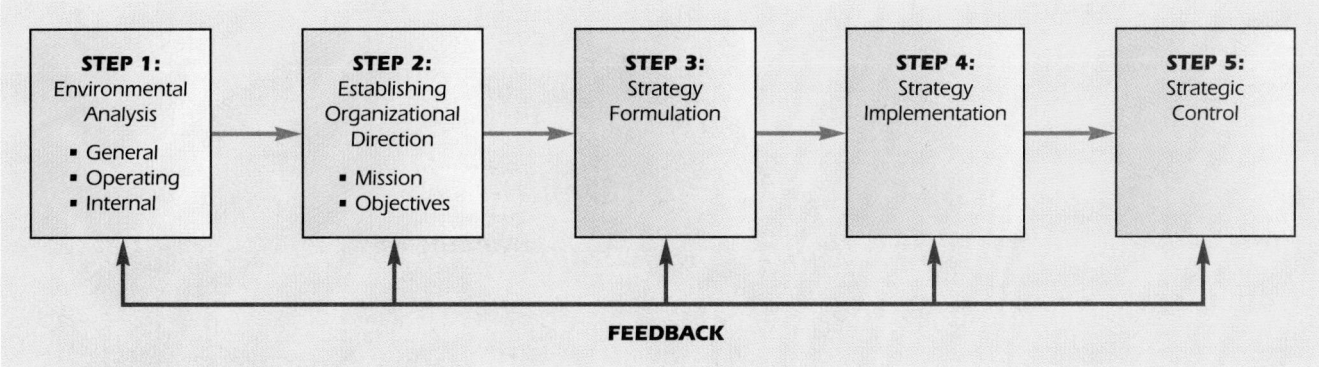

Figure 8.1   Steps of the strategy management process

BACK TO THE CASE In developing a plan to compete with other theme parks, management at Sea World would normally begin by thinking strategically. That is, management should try to determine what can be done to ensure that Sea World will be successful with its theme park at some point three to five years in the future. Obviously, developing a theme park that best suits the marketplace is part of this thinking. Sea World managers must be careful, however, to spend funds on strategic planning only if they can anticipate a return on these expenses in the foreseeable future.

The result of Sea World's overall strategic planning will be a strategy—a broad plan that outlines what must be done to reach long-range objectives and carry out the organizational purpose of the company. This strategy will focus on many organizational areas, one of which will be competing with other theme parks. Once the strategy has been formulated using the results of an environmental analysis, Sea World management must conscientiously carry out the remaining steps of the strategy management process: strategy implementation and strategic control.

Environmental Analysis   The first step of the strategy management process is environmental analysis. Chapter 2 presented organizations as open management systems that are constantly interacting with their environments. In essence, an organization can be successful only if it is appropriately matched to its environment. **Environmental analysis** is the study of the organizational environment to pinpoint environmental factors that can significantly influence organizational operations. Managers commonly perform environmental analyses to help them understand what is happening both inside and outside their organizations and to increase the probability that the organizational strategies they develop will appropriately reflect the organizational environment.

In order to perform an environmental analysis efficiently and effectively, a manager must thoroughly understand how organizational environments are structured. For purposes of environmental analysis, the environment of an organization is generally divided into three distinct levels: the general environment, the operating environment, and the internal environment.[5] Figure 8.2 illustrates the positions of these levels relative to one another and to the organization; it also shows the important components of each level. Managers must be well aware of these three environmental levels, understand how each level affects organizational performance, and then formulate organizational strategies in response to this understanding.

Environmental analysis is the study of the organizational environment to pinpoint environmental factors that can significantly influence organizational operations.

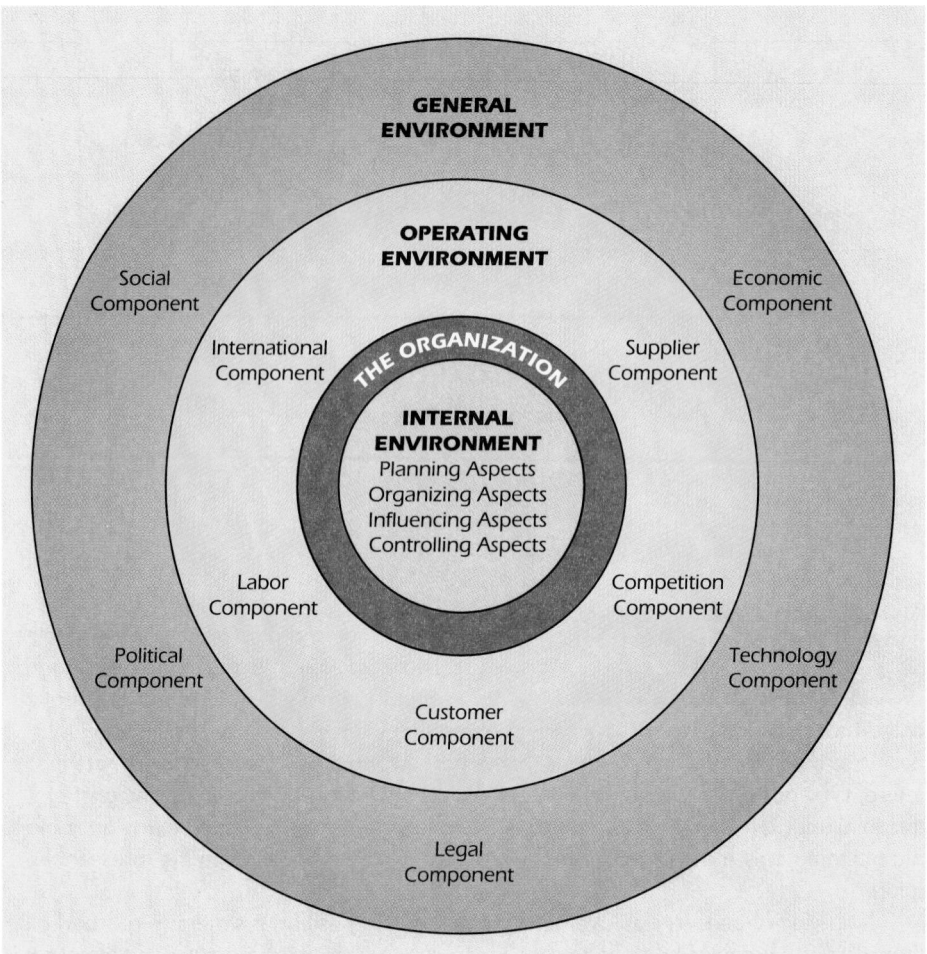

Figure 8.2 The organization, the levels of its environment, and the components of those levels

The **general environment** is the level of an organization's external environment that contains components normally having broad long-term implications for managing the organization; its components are economic, social, political, legal, and technological.

Economics is the science that focuses on understanding how people of a particular community or nation produce, distribute, and use various goods and services.

The General Environment. The level of an organization's external environment that contains components having broad long-term implications for managing the organization is the **general environment**. The components normally considered part of the general environment are economic, social, political, legal, and technological.

The Economic Component. The economic component is that part of the general environment that indicates how resources are being distributed and used within the environment. This component is based on **economics,** the science that focuses on understanding how people of a particular community or nation produce, distribute, and use various goods and services. Important issues to be considered in an economic analysis of an environment are generally the wages paid to labor, inflation, the taxes paid by labor and businesses, the cost of materials used in the production process, and the prices at which produced goods and services are sold to customers.

Economic issues like these can significantly influence the environment in which a company operates and the ease or difficulty the organization experiences in attempting to reach its objectives. For example, it should be somewhat easier for an organization to sell its products at higher prices if potential consumers in the environment are earning relatively high wages and paying relatively low taxes than if these same potential customers are earning relatively low wages and have significantly fewer after-tax dollars to spend.

Naturally, organizational strategy should reflect the economic issues in the organization's environment. To build on the preceding example, if the total amount of after-tax income that potential customers earn has significantly declined, an appropriate organizational strategy might be to lower the price of goods or services to make

Whirlpool exports these refrigerators to Bangkok, Thailand, where it must respond to such demographic factors as local consumption habits and resulting product demands. For reasons of both space and status, for example, many Asian buyers place their refrigerators in their living rooms. Hence Whirlpool's offer of blue and fire-engine-red refrigerators.

them more affordable. Such a strategy should be evaluated carefully, however, because it could have a serious impact on organizational profits.

The Social Component. The social component is part of the general environment that describes the characteristics of the society in which the organization exists. Two important features of a society commonly studied during environmental analysis are demographics and social values.[6]

Demographics are the statistical characteristics of a population. These characteristics include changes in numbers of people and income distribution among various population segments. Such changes can influence the reception of goods and services within the organization's environment and thus should be reflected in organizational strategy.

> **Demographics** are the statistical characteristics of a population. Organizational strategy should reflect demographics.

For example, the demand for retirement housing would probably increase dramatically if both the number and the income of retirees in a particular market area doubled.[7] Effective organizational strategy would include a mechanism for dealing with such a probable increase in demand within the organization's environment.

An understanding of demographics is also helpful for developing a strategy aimed at recruiting new employees to fill certain positions within an organization. Knowing that only a small number of people have a certain type of educational background, for example, would tell an organization that it should compete more intensely to attract these people. To formulate a recruitment strategy, managers need a clear understanding of the demographics of the groups from which employees eventually will be hired.

Social values are the relative degrees of worth that society places on the ways in which it exists and functions. Over time, social values can change dramatically, causing significant changes in how people live. These changes alter the organizational en-

> **Social values** are the relative degrees of worth society places on the manner in which it exists and functions.

Silicon Graphics Inc. of Mountain View, California, has taken advantage of changing Indian social values to open this center in Bangalore, which produces three-dimensional images for diagnosing brain disorders. The pertinent change in Indian social values is one that U.S. companies have recognized there and elsewhere since the 1970s: the shift to knowledge-based labor.

vironment and, as a result, have an impact on organizational strategy. It is important for managers to remember that although changes in the values of a particular society may come either slowly or quickly, they are inevitable. The following ETHICS SPOTLIGHT shows how Quaker Oats responded to changing societal values.

ETHICS SPOTLIGHT

QUAKER OATS CASHES IN ON FITNESS FAD

As values of our society shifted toward exercising to achieve and maintain better physical health, Quaker Oats intensified its marketing of Gatorade, a drink touted as an after-exercise refreshment that effectively and efficiently replaces body nutrients lost through exercise. Quaker Oats, however, has come under some attack for this marketing move because scientific analyses have shown that Gatorade is really no more effective than water in replenishing body fluids. Some might say that it is therefore unethical for Quaker Oats to present Gatorade as a worthwhile product. The company could argue, however, that, as with other image products, merely consuming the drink gives a person an athletic self-image that makes him or her feel better.

Gatorade has the largest share of any product in the so-called sports drink market in the United States and is Quaker Oats' biggest brand. Competitors estimate that Gatorade spends about $100 million a year on marketing the drink. Many companies have tried to win market share from Gatorade, but none have been very successful.≈

The Political Component. The political component is that part of the general environment that contains the elements related to government affairs. Examples include the type of government in existence, the government's attitude toward various industries, lobbying efforts by interest groups, progress on the passage of laws, and political party platforms and candidates. The reunification of Germany and the shift from a Marxist-Socialist government in the Soviet Union in the 1980s illustrate how the political component of an organization's general environment can change at the international level.

The Legal Component. The legal component is that part of the general environment that contains passed legislation. This component comprises the rules or laws that society's members must follow. Some examples of legislation specifically aimed at the operation of organizations are the Clean Air Act, which focuses on minimizing air pollution; the Occupational Safety and Health Act, which aims at ensuring a safe workplace; the Comprehensive Environmental Response, Compensation, and Liability Act, which emphasizes controlling hazardous waste sites; and the Consumer Prod-

Since President Bill Clinton lifted the embargo against trade with Vietnam in February 1994, the communist country in Southeast Asia has ordered an annual average of 300,000 fiber-optic phone lines (plus advanced digital switches)—despite a per capital income of $220. Political factors, it seems, have been overridden by economic factors: Like most of their Third World counterparts, Vietnam's leaders realize that economic progress is dependent on a modern telecommunications infrastructure.

The two Indonesian farm boys posed here with the family television disk actually represent what may be the biggest television market in the world: Asia. U.S. media companies like CNN, Discovery, ESPN, and HBO already broadcast in Indonesia over the host country's Palapa satellite but will soon be using a more powerful satellite launched by a Chinese government consortium. How profound is the advent of such opportunities in the technological component of the international business environment? The president of HBO International has suggested that "Asia may be bigger for us than the U.S."

ucts Safety Act, which upholds the notion that businesses must provide safe products for consumers. Naturally, over time, new laws are passed and some old ones are amended or eliminated.

The Technology Component. The technology component is that part of the general environment that includes new approaches to producing goods and services. These approaches can be new procedures as well as new equipment. The trend toward exploiting robots to improve productivity is an example of the technology component. The increasing use of robots in the next decade should vastly improve the efficiency of U.S. industry.

The Operating Environment. The level of an organization's external environment that contains components normally having relatively specific and immediate implications for managing the organization is the **operating environment.** As Figure 8.2 shows, major components of this environmental level are customers, competition, labor, suppliers, and international issues.

The Customer Component. The customer component is the operating environment segment that is composed of factors relating to those who buy goods and services provided by the organization. Businesses commonly create profiles, or detailed descriptions, of those who buy their products. Developing such profiles helps management generate ideas for improving customer acceptance of organizational goods and services.

The Competition Component. The competition component is the operating environment segment that is composed of those with whom an organization must battle in order to obtain resources. Organizational strategy requires searching for a plan of action that will give the organization an advantage over its competitors. Because understanding competitors is a key factor in developing effective strategy, understanding the competitive environment is a fundamental challenge to management. Basically, the purpose of competitive analysis is to help management comprehend the strengths, weaknesses, capabilities, and likely strategies of existing and potential competitors.[8]

The Labor Component. The labor component is the operating environment segment that is composed of factors influencing the supply of workers available to perform needed organizational tasks. Issues such as skill levels, trainability, desired wage rates, and average age of potential workers are important to the operation of the organization. Another important, but often overlooked, issue is potential employees' desire to work for particular organizations.

The Supplier Component. The supplier component is the operating environment segment that comprises all variables related to the individuals or agencies that provide organizations with the resources they need to produce goods or services. These indi-

The **operating environment** is the level of the organization's external environment that contains components normally having relatively specific and immediate implications for managing the organization.

Suppliers are individuals or agencies that provide organizations with the resources they need to produce goods and services.

viduals or agencies are called **suppliers.** Issues such as how many suppliers offer specified resources for sale, the relative quality of the materials offered by different suppliers, the reliability of supplier deliveries, and the credit terms provided by suppliers are all important to managing an organization effectively and efficiently.

The International Component. The international component is the operating environment segment that is composed of all the factors relating to the international implications of organizational operations. Although not all organizations must deal with international issues, the number that have to do so is increasing dramatically and continually in the 1990s. Significant factors in the international component include other countries' laws, culture, economics, and politics.[9] Important variables within each of these four categories are presented in Table 8.2.

The Internal Environment.   The level of an organization's environment that exists inside the organization and normally has immediate and specific implications for managing the organization is the **internal environment.** In broad terms, the internal environment includes marketing, finance, and accounting. From a more specifically management viewpoint, it includes planning, organizing, influencing, and controlling within the organization.

The **internal environment** is the level of an organization's environment that exists inside the organization and normally has immediate and specific implications for managing the organization.

The following PEOPLE PERSPECTIVES feature describes action that management at Bankers Trust Company, an investment bank, took to improve the organization's internal environment. By offering organization members improved dependent-care opportunities, Bankers Trust enabled its employees to become more committed to their jobs.

Table 8.2

Important Aspects of the International Component of the Organization's Operating Environment

Legal Environment	**Cultural Environment**
Legal tradition	Customs, norms, values, beliefs
Effectiveness of legal system	Language
Treaties with foreign nations	Attitudes
Patent and trademark laws	Motivations
Laws affecting business firms	Social institutions
	Status symbols
Economic Environment	Religious beliefs
Level of economic development	**Political System**
Population	
Gross national product	Form of government
Per capita income	Political ideology
Literacy level	Stability of government
Social infrastructure	Strength of opposition parties and
Natural resources	groups
Climate	Social unrest
Membership in regional economic blocs	Political strife and insurgency
(EEC, LAFTA, etc.)	Government attitude toward foreign
Monetary and fiscal policies	firms
Nature of competition	Foreign policy
Currency convertibility	
Inflation	
Taxation system	
Interest rates	
Wage and salary levels	

IMPROVING DEPENDENT CARE BUILDS JOB COMMITMENT AT BANKERS TRUST COMPANY

PEOPLE PERSPECTIVES

Management at Bankers Trust, an investment bank, evaluated its internal environment a few years ago. One conclusion of the evaluation was that many employees felt high commitment to Bankers Trust in general, and to their jobs in particular, but conflicting family demands were making it difficult, if not impossible, for them to translate that felt commitment into productive action.

During meetings held with employees, management discovered that employees were desperate for some sort of help in handling their dependent-care needs so they could become more reliable and productive workers. They felt that at Bankers Trust work problems took priority over family problems. Management agreed that in the 1980s Bankers Trust, like most other large investment banking houses, had projected an attitude that work must come before family, and that this attitude was highly frustrating to employees who were committed to *both* their jobs and their families.

To help correct this problem in its internal environment, management took several steps aimed at alleviating employee dependent-care demands that conflict with job commitment. For example, an onsite emergency child-care facility was planned for Bankers Trust's Harborside Center in Jersey City, New Jersey, so that employees whose regular child-care arrangements were disrupted for some reason could drop their children off at a company facility and proceed to their jobs without having to worry all day about the needs and safety of their small children. In addition, the company has spent substantial time and capital to create work and family programs aimed at alleviating some of the stress inherent in working while simultaneously raising a family. Management at Bankers Trust has come to see that employees who are relieved of, or who are better trained to handle, family demands will become more productive workers.≈

BACK TO THE CASE   As part of the strategy development process, Sea World management should spend some time analyzing Sea World's general, operating, and internal environments. One environmental factor that would be important to consider is the number of theme parks with which Sea World competes and whether this number will be increasing or decreasing. Other factors management should probably consider as part of the strategic planning process are the strengths and weaknesses of its theme park compared to competing parks, the reasons that people are willing to pay to be admitted to theme parks, and the methods that competitors such as Disney World and Universal Studios are presently using to promote their products to their customers. Obtaining information about environmental issues such as these will increase the probability that any strategy developed for Sea World will be appropriate for its environment and will help the company achieve success in the long term.

Establishing Organizational Direction

The second step of the strategy management process is establishing organizational direction. Through an interpretation of information gathered during environmental analysis, managers can determine the direction in which an organization should move. Two important ingredients of organizational direction are organizational mission and organizational objectives.

Determining Organizational Mission.   The most common initial act in establishing organizational direction is determining an organizational mission. **Organizational mission** is the purpose for which—the reason why—an organization exists. In general, the firm's organizational mission reflects such information as what types of

The **organizational mission** is the purpose for which, or the reason why, an organization exists.

products or services it produces, who its customers tend to be, and what important values it holds. Organizational mission is a very broad statement of organizational direction and is based upon a thorough analysis of information generated through environmental analysis.[10]

A **mission statement** is a written document developed by management, normally based on input by managers as well as nonmanagers, that describes and explains the organization's mission.

Developing a Mission Statement.

A **mission statement** is a written document developed by management, normally based on input by managers as well as nonmanagers, that describes and explains what the mission of an organization actually is. The mission is expressed in writing to ensure that all organization members will have easy access to it and thoroughly understand exactly what the organization is trying to accomplish. Here, for example, is the mission statement of Federal Express:

> Federal Express is committed to our People-Service-Profit philosophy. We will produce outstanding financial returns by providing totally reliable, competitively superior, global air-ground transportation of high-priority goods and documents that require rapid, time-certain delivery. Equally important, positive control of each package will be maintained utilizing real time electronic tracking and tracing systems. A complete record of each shipment and delivery will be presented with our request for payment. We will be helpful, courteous, and professional to each other and the public. We will strive to have a completely satisfied customer at the end of each transaction.

The Importance of Organizational Mission.

An organizational mission is very important to an organization because it helps management increase the probability that the organization will be successful. There are several reasons why it does this. First, the existence of an organizational mission helps management to focus human effort in a common direction. The mission makes explicit the major targets the organization is trying to reach and helps managers keep these targets in mind as they make decisions. Second, an organizational mission serves as a sound rationale for allocating resources. A properly developed mission statement gives managers general, but useful, guidelines about how resources should be used to best accomplish organizational purpose. Third, a mission statement helps management define broad but important job areas within an organization and therefore critical jobs that must be accomplished.[11]

LUTHERAN GENERAL HEALTH SYSTEM'S MISSION EMPHASIZES QUALITY

QUALITY SPOTLIGHT

A mission statement should emphasize the values that are important to a particular organization. The Lutheran General Health System, for instance, has a mission statement that emphasizes quality of services as an important value that managers should use to guide them in managing the organization.

Lutheran General Health System is a multiregional, multicorporate network of health and human service organizations, including the 742-bed Lutheran General Hospital. According to Dr. Richard L. Phillips, chairperson of Lutheran General Health System's board of directors, the board's most important job is to review and define the mission and related core values of the organization as a whole. During the 1980s, each of the company's seven health-care facilities had a separate mission statement and a different strategic direction. As a result, there was very little coordination among the company's operating units in such areas as quality, long-term care, and substance-abuse treatment. Stephen L. Ummel, the company's president and CEO, created an 18-member task force to develop a mission statement that would enunciate important values for the company as a whole. The task force explored the company's core values and drafted a common mission statement for all of Lutheran's operating units, and the company's board approved it. This new mission statement has provided a basis for Lutheran's push toward total quality management in all of its operating units.≈

The Relationship Between Mission and Objectives.   Organizational objectives were defined in Chapter 5 as the targets toward which the open management system is directed. Sound organizational objectives reflect and flow naturally from the purpose of the organization. The organization's purpose is expressed in its mission statement. As a result, useful organizational objectives must reflect and flow naturally from an organizational mission that, in turn, was designed to reflect and flow naturally from the results of an environmental analysis.

Strategy Formulation: Tools

After managers involved in the strategic management process have analyzed the environment and determined organizational direction through the development of a mission statement and organizational objectives, they are ready to formulate strategy. **Strategy formulation** is the process of determining appropriate courses of action for achieving organizational objectives and thereby accomplishing organizational purpose.

Managers formulate strategies that reflect environmental analysis, lead to the fulfillment of organizational mission, and result in the reaching of organizational objectives. Special tools they can use to assist them in formulating strategies include the following:

1. Critical question analysis.
2. SWOT analysis.
3. Business portfolio analysis.
4. Porter's Model for Industry Analysis.

These four strategy development tools are related but distinct. Managers should use the tool or combination of tools that seems most appropriate for them and their organizations.

Critical Question Analysis.   A synthesis of the ideas of several contemporary management writers suggests that formulating appropriate organizational strategy is a process of **critical question analysis**—answering the following four basic questions:[12]

- *What are the purposes and objectives of the organization?* The answer to this question will tell management where the organization should be going. As indicated earlier, appropriate strategy reflects both organizational purpose and objectives. By answering this question during the strategy formulation process, managers are likely to remember this important point and thereby minimize inconsistencies among the organization's purposes, objectives, and strategies.
- *Where is the organization presently going?* The answer to this question can tell managers if the organization is achieving its goals, and if it is, whether the level of progress is satisfactory. Whereas the first question focuses on where the organization should be going, this one focuses on where the organization is actually going.
- *In what kind of environment does the organization now exist?* Both internal and external environments—factors inside and outside the organization—are covered in this question. For example, assume that a poorly trained middle-management team and a sudden influx of competitors in a market are factors in, respectively, the internal and external environments of an organization. Any strategy formulated, if it is to be appropriate, must deal with these factors.
- *What can be done to better achieve organizational objectives in the future?* It is the answer to this question that results in the strategy of the organization. The question should be answered, however, only *after* managers have had an adequate opportunity to reflect on the answers to the previous three questions. Managers cannot develop an appropriate organizational strategy unless they have a clear understanding of where the organization wants to go, where it is going, and in what environment it exists.

Strategy formulation is the process of determining appropriate courses of action for achieving organizational objectives and thereby accomplishing organizational purpose. Strategy development tools include critical question analysis, SWOT analysis, business portfolio analysis, and Porter's Model for Industry Analysis.

Critical question analysis is a strategy development tool that consists of answering basic questions about the present purposes and objectives of the organization, its present direction and environment, and actions that can be taken to achieve organizational objectives in the future.

SWOT analysis is a strategy development tool that matches internal organizational strengths and weaknesses with external opportunities and threats.

SWOT Analysis.   **SWOT analysis** is a strategic development tool that matches internal organizational strengths and weaknesses with external opportunities and threats. (SWOT is an acronym for a firm's **S**trengths and **W**eaknesses and its environmental **O**pportunities and **T**hreats.) SWOT analysis is based on the assumption that if managers carefully review such strengths, weaknesses, opportunities, and threats, a useful strategy for ensuring organizational success will become evident to them.[13]

Business portfolio analysis is the development of business-related strategy based primarily on the market share of businesses and the growth of markets in which businesses exist.

Business Portfolio Analysis.   Business portfolio analysis is another strategy development tool that has gained wide acceptance. **Business portfolio analysis** is an organizational strategy formulation technique that is based on the philosophy that organizations should develop strategy much as they handle investment portfolios. Just as sound financial investments should be supported and unsound ones discarded, sound organizational activities should be emphasized and unsound ones deemphasized. Two business portfolio tools are the BCG Growth-Share Matrix and the GE Multifactor Portfolio Matrix.

The BCG Growth-Share Matrix.   The Boston Consulting Group (BCG), a leading manufacturing consulting firm, developed and popularized a portfolio analysis tool that helps managers develop organizational strategy based upon market share of businesses and the growth of markets in which businesses exist.

A **strategic business unit (SBU)** is, in business portfolio analysis, a significant organizational segment that is analyzed to develop organizational strategy aimed at generating future business or revenue. SBUs vary in form, but all are a single business (or collection of businesses), have their own competitors and a manager accountable for operations, and can be independently planned for.

The first step in using the BCG Growth-Share Matrix is identifying the organization's strategic business units (SBUs). A **strategic business unit** is a significant organization segment that is analyzed to develop organizational strategy aimed at generating future business or revenue. Exactly what constitutes an SBU varies from organization to organization. In larger organizations, an SBU could be a company division, a single product, or a complete product line. In smaller organizations, it might be the entire company. Although SBUs vary drastically in form, each has the following four characteristics:[14]

1. It is a single business or collection of related businesses.
2. It has its own competitors.
3. It has a manager who is accountable for its operation.
4. It is an area that can be independently planned for within the organization.

After SBUs have been identified for a particular organization, the next step in using the BCG Matrix is to categorize each SBU as being within one of the following four matrix quadrants (see Figure 8.3):

- *Stars.*   SBUs that are "stars" have a high share of a high-growth market and typically need large amounts of cash to support their rapid and significant growth. Stars also generate large amounts of cash for the organization and are usually segments in which management can make additional investments and earn attractive returns.
- *Cash Cows.*   SBUs that are cash cows have a large share of a market that is growing only slightly. Naturally, these SBUs provide the organization with large amounts of cash, but since their market is not growing significantly, the cash is generally used to meet the financial demands of the organization in other areas, such as in the expansion of a star SBU.
- *Question Marks.*   SBUs that are question marks have a small share of a high-growth market. They are dubbed "question marks" because it is uncertain whether management should invest more cash in them to gain a larger share of the market or deemphasize or eliminate them. Management will choose the first option when it believes it can turn the question mark into a star, and the second when it thinks further investment would be fruitless.
- *Dogs.*   SBUs that are dogs have a relatively small share of a low-growth market. They may barely support themselves; in some cases, they actually drain off cash resources generated by other SBUs. Examples of dogs are SBUs that produce typewriters or cash registers.

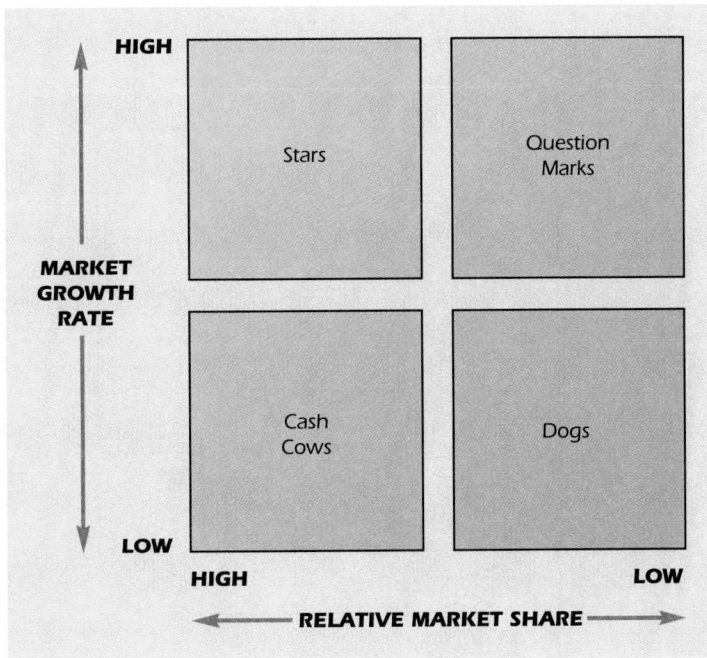

Figure 8.3   The BCG Growth-Share Matrix

Companies such as Westinghouse and Shell Oil have successfully used the BCG Matrix in their strategy management processes. This technique, however, has some potential pitfalls. For one thing, the matrix does not consider such factors as (1) various types of risk associated with product development; (2) threats that inflation and other economic conditions can create in the future; and (3) social, political, and ecological pressures. These pitfalls may be the reason for recent research results indicating that the BCG Matrix does not always help managers make better strategic decisions.[15] Managers must remember to weigh such factors carefully when designing organizational strategy based on the BCG Matrix.

The GE Multifactor Portfolio Matrix. With the help of McKinsey and Company, a leading consulting firm, the General Electric Company (GE) has developed another popular portfolio analysis tool. Called the GE Multifactor Portfolio Matrix, this tool helps managers develop organizational strategy that is based primarily on market attractiveness and business strengths. The GE Multifactor Portfolio Matrix was deliberately designed to be more complete than the BCG Growth-Share Matrix.

Its basic use is illustrated in Figure 8.4. Each of the organization's businesses or SBUs is plotted on a matrix in two dimensions: industry attractiveness and business strength. Each of these two dimensions is actually a composite of a variety of factors that each firm must determine for itself, given its own unique situation. As examples, industry attractiveness might be determined by such factors as the number of competitors in an industry, the rate of industry growth, and the weakness of competitors within an industry; while business strengths might be determined by such factors as a company's financially solid position, its good bargaining position over suppliers, and its high level of technology use.

Several circles appear on Figure 8.4, each representing a company line of business or SBU. Circle size indicates the relative market size for each line of business. The shaded portion of a circle represents the proportion of the total SBU market that a company has captured.

Specific strategies for a company are implied by where their businesses (represented by circles) fall on the matrix. Businesses falling in the cells that form a diagonal from lower left to upper right are medium-strength businesses that should be invested in only selectively. Businesses above and to the left of this diagonal are the strongest and the ones that the company should invest in and help to grow. Businesses

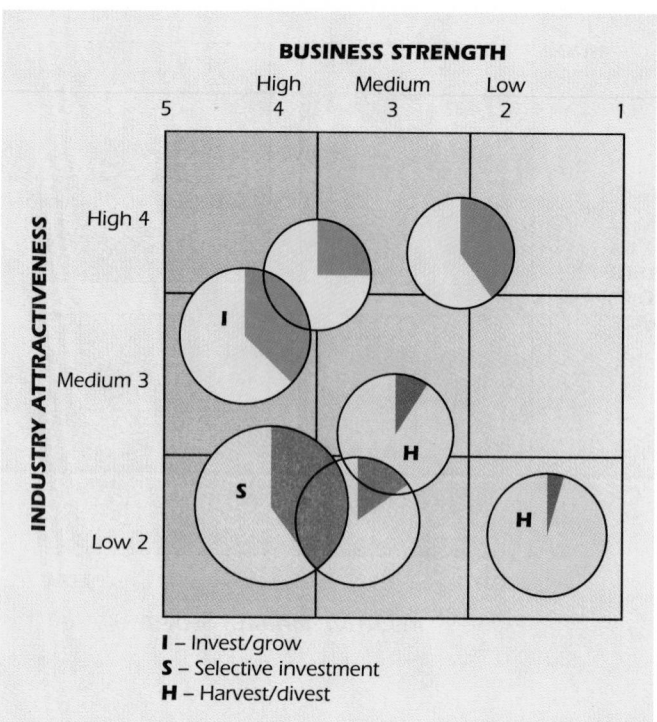

Figure 8.4   GE's Multifactor Portfolio Matrix

in the cells below and to the right of the diagonal are low in overall strength and are serious candidates for divestiture.

Portfolio models are graphic frameworks for analyzing relationships among the businesses of an organization, and they can provide useful strategy recommendations. However, no such model yet devised gives managers a universally accepted approach for dealing with these issues. Portfolio models, then, should never be applied in a mechanistic fashion, and any conclusions they suggest must be carefully considered in the light of sound managerial judgment and experience.

Porter's Model for Industry Analysis.   Perhaps the best-known tool for formulating strategy is a model developed by Michael E. Porter, an internationally acclaimed strategic management expert.[16] Essentially, Porter's model outlines the primary forces that determine competitiveness within an industry and illustrates how those forces are related. The model suggests that in order to develop effective organizational strategies, managers must understand and react to those forces within an industry that determine an organization's level of competitiveness within that industry.

Porter's model is presented in Figure 8.5. According to the model, competitiveness within an industry is determined by the following: new entrants or new companies within the industry; products that might act as a substitute for goods or services that companies within the industry produce; the ability of suppliers to control issues like costs of materials that industry companies use to manufacture their products; the bargaining power that buyers possess within the industry; and the general level of rivalry or competition among firms within the industry. According to the model, then, buyers, product substitutes, suppliers, and potential new companies within an industry all contribute to the level of rivalry among industry firms.

Strategy Formulation: Types

Understanding the forces that determine competitiveness within an industry should help managers develop strategies that will make their companies more competitive within the industry. Porter has developed three generic strategies to illustrate the kind of strategies managers might develop to make their organizations more competitive.

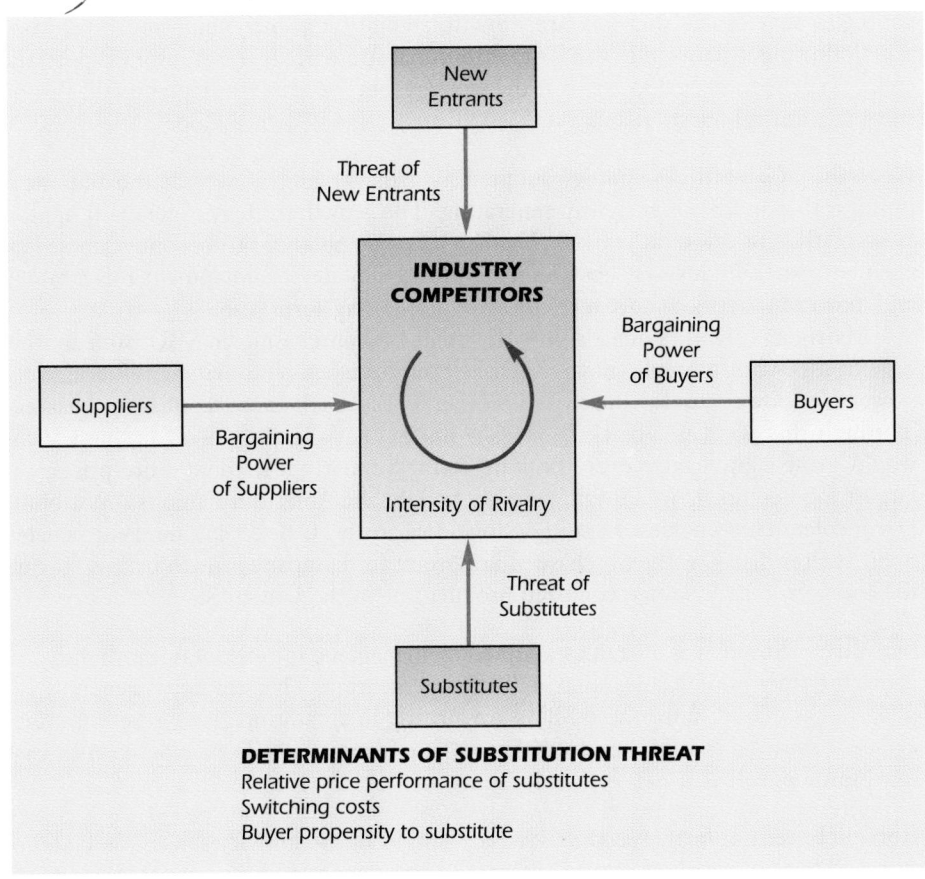

Figure 8.5   Porter's model of factors that determine competitiveness within an industry

Differentiation.   **Differentiation,** the first of Porter's strategies, focuses on making an organization more competitive by developing a product or products that customers perceive as being different from products offered by competitors. Differentiation might consist of uniqueness in such areas as product quality, design, and level of after-sale service. Examples of products that customers commonly purchase because they perceive them as being different are Nike's Air Jordan shoes (because of their high-technology "air" construction) and Honda automobiles (because of their high reliability).

Differentiation is a strategy that focuses on making an organization more competitive by developing a product or products that customers perceive as being different from products offered by competitors.

Cost Leadership.   **Cost leadership** is a strategy that focuses on making an organization more competitive by producing products more cheaply than competitors can. According to the logic behind this strategy, by producing products more cheaply than its competitors do, an organization will be able to offer products to customers at lower prices than competitors can, and thereby increase its market share. Examples of tactics managers might use to gain cost leadership are obtaining lower prices for product parts purchased from suppliers and using technology like robots to increase organizational productivity.

Cost leadership is a strategy that focuses on making an organization more competitive by producing products more cheaply than competitors can.

Focus.   **Focus** is a strategy that emphasizes making an organization more competitive by targeting a particular customer. Magazine publishers commonly use a focus strategy in offering their products to specific customers. *Working Woman* and *Ebony* are examples of magazines that are aimed, respectively, at the target markets of employed women and African-Americans.

Focus is a strategy that emphasizes making an organization more competitive by targeting a particular customer.

Sample Organizational Strategies.   Analyzing the organizational environment and applying one or more of the strategy tools—critical question analysis, SWOT analysis, business portfolio analysis, and Porter's model—will give managers a foundation on which to formulate an organizational strategy. The four common organizational

strategies that evolve this way are growth, stability, retrenchment, and divestiture. The following discussion of these organizational strategies features business portfolio analysis as the tool used to arrive at the strategy, but the same strategies could also result from critical question analysis, SWOT analysis, or Porter's model.

Growth is a strategy adopted by management to increase the amount of business that a strategic business unit is currently generating.

Growth.   **Growth** is a strategy adopted by management to increase the amount of business that an SBU is currently generating. The growth strategy is generally applied to star SBUs or question mark SBUs that have the potential to become stars. Management generally invests substantial amounts of money to implement this strategy, and may even sacrifice short-term profit to build long-term gain.[17]

Managers can also pursue a growth strategy by purchasing an SBU from another organization. For example, Black & Decker, not satisfied with being an international power in power tools, purchased General Electric's small-appliance business. Through this purchase, Black & Decker hoped that the amount of business it did would grow significantly over the long term. Similarly, President Enterprises, the largest food company in Taiwan, recently bought the American Famous Amos brand of chocolate chip cookies. Despite a downturn in the U.S. cookie market, management at President saw the purchase as important for company growth because it gave the company a nationally recognized product line in the United States.[18]

Stability is a strategy adopted by management to maintain or slightly improve the amount of business a strategic business unit is generating.

Stability.   **Stability** is a strategy adopted by management to maintain or slightly improve the amount of business that an SBU is generating. This strategy is generally applied to cash cows, since these SBUs are already in an advantageous position. Management must be careful, however, that in its pursuit of stability it doesn't turn cash cows into dogs.

Retrenchment is a strategy adopted by management to strengthen or protect the amount of business a strategic business unit is currently generating.

Retrenchment.   In this section, *retrench* is used in the military sense: to defend or fortify. Through **retrenchment** strategy, management attempts to strengthen or protect the amount of business an SBU is generating. This strategy is generally applied to cash cows or stars that are beginning to lose market share.

Douglas D. Danforth, the chief executive of Westinghouse, is convinced that retrenchment is an important strategy for his company. According to Danforth, bigger profits at Westinghouse depend not only on fast-growing new products but also on the revitalization of Westinghouse's traditional businesses of manufacturing motors and gears.[19]

Divestiture is a strategy adopted to eliminate a strategic business unit that is not generating a satisfactory amount of business and has little hope of doing so in the future.

Divestiture.   **Divestiture** is a strategy generally adopted to eliminate an SBU that is not generating a satisfactory amount of business and that has little hope of doing so in the near future. In essence, the organization sells or closes down the SBU in question. This strategy is generally applied to SBUs that are dogs or question marks that have failed to increase market share but still require significant amounts of cash.

Strategy implementation, the fourth step of the strategy management process, is putting formulated strategy into action.

Strategy Implementation   **Strategy implementation,** the fourth step of the strategy management process, is putting formulated strategies into action. Without successive implementation, valuable strategies developed by managers are virtually worthless.[20]

The successful implementation of strategy requires four basic skills:[21]

1. *Interacting skill* is the ability to manage people during implementation. Managers who are able to understand the fears and frustrations others feel during the implementation of a new strategy tend to be the best implementers. These managers empathize with organization members and bargain for the best way to put a strategy into action.
2. *Allocating skill* is the ability to provide the organizational resources necessary to implement a strategy. Successful implementers are talented at scheduling jobs, budgeting time and money, and allocating other resources that are critical for implementation.

3. *Monitoring skill* is the ability to use information to determine whether a problem has arisen that is blocking implementation. Good strategy implementers set up feedback systems that constantly tell them about the status of strategy implementation.

4. *Organizing skill* is the ability to create throughout the organization a network of people who can help solve implementation problems as they occur. Good implementers customize this network to include individuals who can handle the special types of problems anticipated in the implementation of a particular strategy.

Overall, then, the successful implementation of a strategy requires handling people appropriately, allocating resources necessary for implementation, monitoring implementation progress, and solving implementation problems as they occur. Perhaps the most important requirements are knowing which people can solve specific implementation problems and being able to involve them when those problems arise.

Strategic Control

Strategic control, the last step of the strategy management process, consists of monitoring and evaluating the strategy management process as a whole to ensure that it is operating properly. Strategic control focuses on the activities involved in environmental analysis, organizational direction, strategy formulation, strategy implementation, and strategic control itself—checking that all steps of the strategy management process are appropriate, compatible, and functioning properly.[22] Strategic control is a special type of organizational control, a topic that is featured in Chapters 19, 20, and 21.

Strategic control, the last step of the strategy management process, consists of monitoring and evaluating the strategy management process as a whole to ensure that it is operating properly.

BACK TO THE CASE   According to the information in the text, after Sea World has performed its environmental analysis, it should determine the direction in which the organization will move to maintain its competitive position. Issues such as adding ride-oriented attractions will naturally surface at this point. Developing a mission statement with related objectives would be a clear signal to all Sea World employees that the new ride attractions play an important role in the organization's future. Sea World managers have several tools available to assist them in formulating strategy. To be effective in this area, however, they must use such tools in conjunction with environmental analysis. One of the tools, critical question analysis, would require management to analyze the purpose of Sea World, the direction in which Sea World is going, the environment in which it exists, and how its goals might be better achieved.

SWOT analysis, another strategy development tool, would require management to generate information regarding the internal strengths and weaknesses of Sea World, as well as the opportunities and threats that exist within its environment. Management would probably classify the products of competitors, such as new movie-related rides and attractions at the Universal Studios theme park in Orlando, as threats—significant factors to be considered in Sea World's strategy development process.

Business portfolio analysis would suggest that Sea World management classify each major attraction (SBU) in the park as a star, cash cow, question mark, or dog, depending on the growth rate of the market interested in the attraction and the market share achieved by the Sea World attraction. By categorizing *Mission: Bermuda Triangle* and the other Sea World attractions as units for SBU analysis, managers could develop growth, stability, retrenchment, or divestiture strategies for each attraction. Sea World managers should use whichever strategy development tools they believe will prove most useful in advancing their objective of determining an appropriate strategy for the development of Sea World's attractions.

To successfully execute whatever strategy is chosen, managers at Sea World must apply their interacting, allocating, monitoring, and organizing skills. In addition, they must be able to improve the strategy management process when necessary.

TACTICAL PLANNING

Tactical planning is short-range planning that emphasizes the current operations of various parts of the organization.

Tactical planning is short-range planning that emphasizes the current operations of various parts of the organization. *Short range* is defined as a period of time extending about one year or less into the future. Managers use tactical planning to outline what the various parts of the organization must do for the organization to be successful at some point one year or less into the future.[23] Tactical plans are usually developed in the areas of production, marketing, personnel, finance, and plant facilities.

Comparing and Coordinating Strategic and Tactical Planning

In striving to implement successful planning systems within organizations, managers must remember several basic differences between strategic planning and tactical planning:

1. Because upper-level managers generally have a better understanding of the organization as a whole than lower-level managers do, and since lower-level managers generally have a better understanding of the day-to-day organizational operations than upper-level managers do, strategic plans are usually developed by upper-level management and tactical plans by lower-level management.

2. Because strategic planning emphasizes analyzing the future and tactical planning emphasizes analyzing the everyday functioning of the organization, facts on which to base strategic plans are usually more difficult to gather than are facts on which to base tactical plans.

3. Because strategic plans are based primarily on a prediction of the future and tactical plans on known circumstances that exist within the organization, strategic plans are generally less detailed than tactical plans.

4. Because strategic planning focuses on the long term and tactical planning on the short term, strategic plans cover a relatively long period of time whereas tactical plans cover a relatively short period of time.

All of these major differences between strategic and tactical planning are summarized in Table 8.3.

Despite their differences, tactical and strategic planning are integrally related. As Russell L. Ackoff states, "We can look at them separately, even discuss them separately, but we cannot separate them in fact."[24] In other words, managers need both tactical and strategic planning programs, and these programs must be closely related to be successful. Tactical planning should focus on what to do in the short term to help the organization achieve the long-term objectives determined by strategic planning.

Table 8.3

Major Differences Between Strategic and Tactical Planning

AREA OF DIFFERENCE	STRATEGIC PLANNING	TACTICAL PLANNING
Individuals involved	Developed mainly by upper-level management.	Developed mainly by lower-level management.
Facts on which to base planning	Facts are relatively difficult to gather.	Facts are relatively easy to gather.
Amount of detail in plans	Plans contain relatively little detail.	Plans contain substantial amounts of detail.
Length of time plans cover	Plans cover long periods of time.	Plans cover short periods of time.

PLANNING AND LEVELS OF MANAGEMENT

Top management of an organization has the primary responsibility for seeing that the planning function is carried out. Although all management levels are involved in the typical planning process, upper-level managers usually spend more time planning than lower-level managers do. Lower-level managers are highly involved in the everyday operations of the organization and therefore normally have less time to contribute to planning than top managers do. Middle-level managers usually spend more time planning than lower-level managers, but less time than upper-level managers. Figure 8.6 shows how planning time increases as a manager moves from lower-level to upper-level management. In small as well as large organizations, determining the amount and nature of the work that each manager should personally handle is extremely important.

The type of planning done also changes as a manager moves up in the organization. Typically, lower-level managers plan for the short term, middle-level managers for the somewhat longer term, and upper-level managers for the even longer term. The expertise of lower-level managers in everyday operations makes them the best planners for what can be done in the short term to reach organizational objectives—in other words, they are best equipped to do tactical planning. Upper-level managers usually have the best understanding of the whole organizational situation and are therefore better equipped to plan for the long term—or to develop strategic plans.[25]

BACK TO THE CASE   In addition to developing strategic plans for Sea World, management should consider adopting tactical, or short-range, plans that would complement its strategic plans. Tactical plans for Sea World should emphasize what can be done within the next year to reach the organization's three- to five-year objectives and to stem competition from other theme parks. For example, Sea World could devote more resources to aggressive short-range marketing campaigns or draw more visitors to the park by enhancing its overall visual attractiveness.

Moreover, Sea World managers must closely coordinate strategic and tactical planning within the company. They must keep in mind that strategic planning and tactical planning are different types of activities that usually involve different people within the organization and therefore result in plans with different degrees of detail. Yet they must also remember that these two types of plans are interrelated. While lower-level managers would be mostly responsible for developing tactical plans, upper-level managers would spend most of their time on long-range planning and developing strategic plans that reflect company goals.

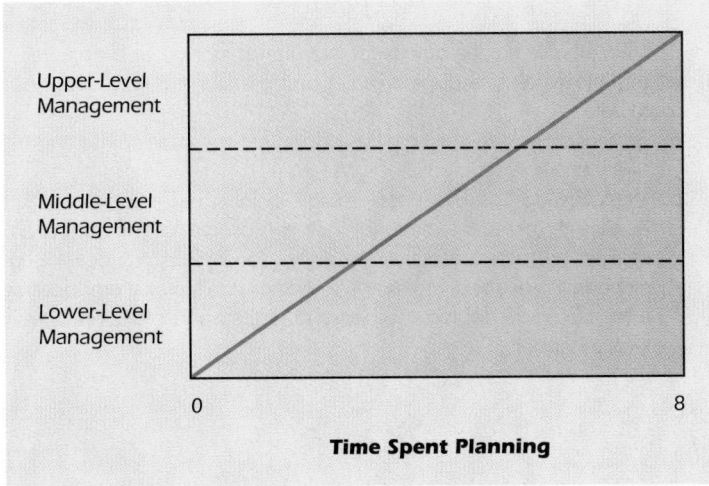

Figure 8.6   Increase in planning time as manager moves from lower-level to upper-level management

Action Summary

Reread the learning objectives below. Each objective is followed by questions. Answering these questions accurately will help you retain the most important concepts discussed in this chapter. After answering each question, check your answer against the answer key at the end of this chapter. (*Hint:* If you have any doubts regarding the correct response, consult the page whose number follows the answer.)

Circle: From studying this chapter, I will attempt to acquire:

1. Definitions of both strategic planning and strategy.

T,F **a.** Strategic planning is long-range planning that focuses on the organization as a whole.

a,b,c,d,e **b.** Strategy: (a) is a specific, narrow plan designed to achieve tactical planning; (b) is designed to be the end result of tactical planning; (c) is a plan designed to reach long-range objectives; (d) is timeless, so the same strategy can meet organizational needs anytime; (e) is independent of organizational objectives and therefore need not be consistent with them.

2. An understanding of the strategy management process.

a,b,c,d,e **a.** Which of the following is *not* one of the steps in strategy management: (a) strategy formulation; (b) strategy implementation; (c) strategy control; (d) environmental analysis; (e) all of the above are steps.

T,F **b.** The steps of the strategy management process are sequential but usually not continuing.

3. A knowledge of the impact of environmental analysis on strategy formulation.

T,F **a.** Environmental analysis is the strategy used to change an organization's environment to satisfy the needs of the organization.

a,b,c,d,e **b.** All of the following are factors to be considered in environmental analysis except: (a) suppliers; (b) economic issues; (c) demographics; (d) social values; (e) none of the above.

4. Insights about how to use critical question analysis and SWOT analysis to formulate strategy.

a,b,c,d,e **a.** The following is *not* one of the four basic questions used in critical question analysis: (a) Where has the organization been? (b) Where is the organization presently going? (c) What are the purposes and objectives of the organization? (d) In what kind of environment does the organization now exist? (e) What can be done to better achieve organizational objectives in the future?

T,F **b.** SWOT is an acronym for "Strengths and Weaknesses, Objectives and Tactics."

5. An understanding of how to use business portfolio analysis and industry analysis to formulate strategy.

a,b,c,d,e **a.** Use of the BCG Matrix requires considering the following factors: (a) types of risk associated with product development; (b) threats that economic conditions can create in the future; (c) social factors; (d) market shares and growth of markets in which products are selling; (e) political pressures.

a,b,c,d,e **b.** To users of the BCG Matrix, products that capture a high share of a rapidly growing market are known as: (a) cash cows; (b) milk products; (c) sweepstakes products; (d) stars; (e) dog products.

T,F **c.** Use of the GE Multifactor Portfolio Matrix requires considering total market size for an SBU but generally not the amount of that market that the SBU has won.

6. Insights into what tactical planning is and on how strategic and tactical planning should be coordinated.

T,F **a.** Tactical plans generally are developed for one year or less and usually contain fewer details than strategic plans.

a,b,c,d,e **b.** The following best describes strategic planning: (a) facts are difficult to gather, and plans cover short periods of time; (b) facts are difficult to gather, and plans cover long periods of time; (c) facts are difficult to gather, and plans are developed mainly by lower-level managers; (d) facts are easy to gather, and plans are developed mainly by upper-level managers; (e) facts are easy to gather, and plans are developed mainly by lower-level managers.

Introductory Case Wrap-Up

"Sea World Plots a New Competitive Course" (p. 176) and its related back-to-the-case sections were written to help you better understand the management concepts contained in this chapter. Answer the following discussion questions about this introductory case to enrich your understanding of chapter content:

1. Is Sea World management's response to its theme park competitors—adding a new ride—a strategic management issue? Explain.

2. State three factors in Sea World's internal environment that management should be assessing in determining the company's organizational direction. Why are these factors important?

3. Using the business portfolio matrix, categorize *Mission: Bermuda Triangle* as a dog, question mark, star, or cash cow. From a strategic planning viewpoint, what do you recommend that Sea World managers do as a result of this categorization? Why?

Issues for Review and Discussion

1. What is strategic planning?
2. How does the commitment principle relate to strategic planning?
3. Define *strategy* and discuss its relationship to organizational objectives.
4. What are the major steps in the strategy management process? Discuss each step fully.
5. Why is environmental analysis an important part of strategy formulation?
6. List one major factor from each environmental level that could have a significant impact on specific strategies developed for an organization. How could the specific strategies be affected by each factor?
7. Discuss the significance of the questions answered during critical question analysis.
8. Explain in detail how SWOT analysis can be used to formulate strategy.
9. What is business portfolio analysis?
10. Discuss the philosophy on which business portfolio analysis is based.
11. What is an SBU?
12. Draw and explain the BCG Growth-Share Matrix.
13. What potential pitfalls must managers avoid in using this matrix?
14. Explain three major differences in using the GE Multifactor Portfolio Matrix to develop organizational strategy as opposed to the BCG Matrix.
15. Draw and explain Porter's model of factors that determines competitiveness within an industry. What is the significance of this model for developing an organizational strategy?
16. List and define four sample strategies that can be developed for organizations.
17. What is tactical planning?
18. How do strategic and tactical planning differ?
19. What is the relationship between strategic and tactical planning?
20. How do time spent planning and scope of planning vary according to management levels?

Action Summary Answer Key

1. a. T, p. 177
   b. c, p. 177
2. a. e, p. 178
   b. F, p. 178

3. a. F, p. 179
   b. e, p. 179
4. a. a, pp. 187–188
   b. F, pp. 188–189

5. a. d, pp. 188–189
   b. d, pp. 188–189
   c. F, pp. 189–190

6. a. F, p. 194
   b. b, p. 194

Case Study

How New Strategies Could Make a Difference at IBM

By the early 1990s, IBM Corporation was clearly in trouble. The company, whose past successes depended on mainframe personal computer (PC) sales, was in need of new direction. Lou Gerstner took command of IBM in April of 1993. His success outside the technology industry indicated the desire of IBM's board of directors to infuse new and productive approaches into the company's operations. From the beginning, Gerstner insisted he had no grand plan to turn IBM around. Instead, he concentrated on three major areas:

- The inefficient size of the company.
- The loss of revenue that resulted when former customers took their business elsewhere.
- A line of products that was lagging behind those of competitors.

Gerstner has received high marks for the management team he assembled. Although most are IBM veterans, two are new to the IBM environment and culture. Jerry York was tapped to reduce IBM's size and to cut back on expenses. The number of employees on the IBM rolls has been slashed by more than 105,000, from a high of 407,080 in 1985 to 301,542 in 1995. High development costs have also hurt IBM. Thus far, York has reduced expenses by $5.6 billion. His eventual goal is to cut $8 billion in expenses. Richard Thoman was a member of Gerstner's team at other consumer-services companies and, like Gerstner, is a former McKinsey consultant. The sound decision to stop selling IBM PCs when a flaw was found in the Intel chip is attributed to him.

Gerstner and his new management team preach the concept of "network-centricity"—that is, basing company plans on computer networks and the products needed to complete this vision of the future. In a sense, this approach is a return to the computing concept of the single mainframe with multiple points of connectivity, for a network-centric environment maintains the computing power of the mainframe while providing the connectivity and communication demanded by individual PC users. The advantage to customers is that they can reap the benefits of the network without making large outlays for mainframe computers and software. Gerstner is counting on IBM's ability to provide outsourcing and systems integration to its corporate customers. Current large corporate customers as well as the burgeoning—and as yet untapped—world of small businesses would benefit from the arrangement. IBM, which currently owns one-third of the world's data-processing centers, would retain ownership and maintenance of the mainframe that would be the center of each network.

A milestone in Gerstner's plan was the purchase of Lotus Development Corporation for $3.5 billion. IBM is betting big money on Lotus Notes, a "groupware" product that lets individuals communicate with others via E-mail and databases. This acquisition fits neatly with Gerstner's plan to free IBM from overdependence on the personal computer. Already, IBM has lost the lead in PC hardware sales to companies like Compaq and new mail-order companies like Dell and Gateway, and its OS/2 PC operating system is unable to compete successfully with Microsoft's Windows.

By and large, Gerstner's strategies have paid off. Most of IBM's product lines are showing not only higher sales but higher revenues as well. Even the mainframe sector has demonstrated growth, although many observers believe that this is not a long-term trend. In any case, customers now perceive IBM as more responsive to their needs, and the financial figures reflect this improvement in customer perception.

In addition to cutting costs and improving customer relations, Gerstner is forging new partnerships with other technology companies to reduce both the costs and time it takes to develop new products. IBM's new partnerships ensure that different perspectives will be incorporated into the product development process. This approach is especially important in the fast-paced world of technology. At the same time, Gerstner's plans capitalize on what made IBM successful in the past. He will use IBM's global presence, excellent consultant resources, and long-standing relationships with corporate customers to deliver solutions in the network-centric environment.

Of course, creating a network-centric plan for the future does not ensure its success. Gerstner must convince current and potential IBM customers that the plan offers important benefits to them. But even before he goes to the customer, he must sell his plan to those within the ranks of IBM who are not eager to abandon IBM's past model of success. The company's future depends on his success in both arenas.

Questions:

1. What struggles does Lou Gerstner face in his plan to make IBM network-centric? Consider internal and external impediments.
2. Must IBM's basic corporate culture change in order to meet Gerstner's goal? Explain.
3. What strengths does IBM possess that make Gerstner's plan achievable? How do Gerstner's strategies incorporate those strengths?

Skills Exercise

Is Gerstner's strategy revolutionary for the technology industry? Search to discover strategic plans for other technology companies—Microsoft, Compaq, Netscape, etc. Look for each company's vision of the future, its major marketing strategies, and its financial track record.

Work with others in the class to compile data into a comparison chart. Predict the winners and losers in the technology field. Will Gerstner's strategies take IBM successfully into the twenty-first century? Why or why not?

The Internet learning materials that accompany this chapter can be found at
http://www.profcerto.com
Additional information can be found on the inside front and back covers of this text.

9 chapter

PLANS AND PLANNING TOOLS

STUDENT LEARNING OBJECTIVES

From studying this chapter, I will attempt to acquire:

1. A complete definition of a plan.
2. Insights regarding various dimensions of plans.
3. An understanding of various types of plans.
4. Insights on why plans fail.
5. A knowledge of various planning areas within an organization.
6. A definition of forecasting.
7. An ability to see the advantages and disadvantages of various methods of sales forecasting.
8. A definition of scheduling.
9. An understanding of Gantt charts and PERT.

CHAPTER OUTLINE

Introductory Case: Fiat Plans Car Production

Plans
Plans: A Definition

Ethics Spotlight: Toyota Uses Philanthropy Plan to Take Aim at General Motors

Dimensions of Plans
Types of Plans

People Perspectives: Program at Wisconsin Power & Light Builds Employee Motivation

Why Plans Fail
Planning Areas: Input Planning

Global Spotlight: Mexico as an Attractive Manufacturing Site

Cutting Edge: Choosing a Plant Site for Manufacturing Network Potential

Planning Tools
Forecasting
Scheduling

Fiat Plans Car Production

Automobile group Fiat, shrugging off the slowdown in European car demand, plans to build a major car plant in Basilicata, southern Italy, and expand and remodel an existing parts factory at Avellino, near Naples.

The decision involves investments totaling five trillion lire ($4.5 billion) over a three-year period.

The Basilicata car plant will produce 1,800 cars a day and employ 7,000 workers, while the Avellino parts plant will be transformed into a factory producing 3,600 engines a day and employing 1,300 people.

The company is going ahead with the plan despite having cut back production because of slack European demand. [Recently,] Fiat doubled the number of workers temporarily laid off to 70,000 as part of a program of plant closures that cut planned output by about 90,000 cars. As a result, Fiat expects to produce about 2,150,000 cars a year worldwide, down from a level of about 2,250,000 sustained in previous years.

Susanne Oliver, European automotive analyst at London brokerage firm Hoare Govett, said the move was unexpected in the current depressed state of the market. "The move is a little bit surprising, given that they have announced production cutbacks. And that in the medium term there is no sign of an upswing in demand," she said.

"Obviously, it takes some years to bring the plants on stream . . . , nevertheless, capacity is being underutilized," she added. The Basilicata plant will have a theoretical capacity of almost 400,000 cars a year, working an average 220 days a year. Avellino could produce 790,000 engines a year.

Fiat will be eligible for hefty state aid on both plants. The company declined to put a figure on the subsidies, but a [spokesperson] said, "We have asked the government for the maximum the law allows—nothing special, but the maximum."

An official of the ministry dealing with Italy's depressed South, the Mezzogiorno, said state grants of 15 percent were available on large productive investments of this type. On this calculation, Fiat could receive a subsidy of about 750 billion lire, though not all funds invested may be eligible.

In addition, soft loans, at 60 percent of prime rate, are available to cover 30 percent of the investment cost, and reductions will also be given on social security payments for workers. Extra subsidies may also be available because the plants are in zones that sustained earthquake damage in 1980.

Fiat, which already has ambitious production plans in Poland, is calculating that European car demand will sustain a further increase in capacity. "We think Europe will continue to absorb cars—maybe not at the record level of the past two to three years, but the market is healthy," a [spokesperson] said.

Despite the slowdown in European car demand, Fiat has invested five trillion lire ($4.5 billion) in auto and parts factories.

what's ahead

The introductory case describes Fiat's plans to build one new plant and to increase the capacity of another. This chapter emphasizes several fundamental issues about plans that should be useful to managers like those at Fiat who are involved in planning. It describes what plans are and discusses several valuable tools that can be used in developing them.

PLANS

The first half of the chapter covers the basic facts about plans. It does the following:

1. Defines what a plan is.
2. Outlines the dimensions of a plan.
3. Lists various types of plans.
4. Discusses why plans fail.
5. Explains two major organizational areas in which planning usually takes place.

Plans: A Definition

A **plan** is a specific action proposed to help the organization achieve its objectives.

A **plan** is a specific action proposed to help the organization achieve its objectives. A critical part of the management of any organization is developing logical plans and then taking the steps necessary to put the plans into action.[1] Regardless of how important experience-related intuition may be to managers, successful management actions and strategies typically are based on reason. Rational managers are crucial to the development of an organizational plan.

ETHICS SPOTLIGHT

TOYOTA USES PHILANTHROPY PLAN TO TAKE AIM AT GENERAL MOTORS

The Toyota Motor Company, a Japanese firm, is one of the largest automobile manufacturers in the world. Toyota's top management has created a philanthropy plan to help the company better compete with General Motors.

Toyota has designed a comprehensive plan for the organization that has both domestic and overseas components. It outlines an enormous undertaking that calls for annual automobile production and sales of more than 6 million units within three to five years. Toyota's president, Shoichiro Toyoda, believing that the world automobile market has plenty of room to grow, is determined to overtake General Motors as the world's largest automaker by the end of this century.

Although GM's output and sales have declined in recent years while Toyota's output and sales have increased, some industry analysts doubt Toyota has the ability to develop a marketing effort that will enable the company to surpass GM. Toyota's management team, however, insists that the company's aspirations to overtake GM are realistic. One reason for Toyota's optimism is the company's philanthropy plan, which channels corporate profits into local communities, enhancing Toyota's public image and thus boosting sales. Over the last few years, Toyota has channeled about 1.5 percent of its profits into philanthropic programs. In the near future, the company's level of philanthropy will probably remain about the same or even increase.≈

Dimensions of Plans

Kast and Rosenzweig identify a plan's four major dimensions as:[2]

1. Repetitiveness
2. Time

  3. Scope
  4. Level

Each dimension is an independent characteristic of a plan and should be considered during plan development.

Repetitiveness   The **repetitiveness dimension** of a plan is the extent to which the plan is used over and over again. Some plans are specially designed for one situation that is relatively short-term in nature. Plans of this sort are essentially nonrepetitive. Other plans, however, are designed to be used time after time for situations that continue to occur over the long term. These plans are basically repetitive in nature.

The **repetitiveness dimension** of a plan is the extent to which the plan is to be used over and over again.

Time   The **time dimension** of a plan is the length of time the plan covers. In Chapter 8, strategic planning was defined as being long-term in nature, while tactical planning was defined as being short-term. It follows, then, that strategic plans cover relatively long periods of time and tactical plans cover relatively short periods of time.

The **time dimension** of a plan is the length of time the plan covers.

Scope   The **scope dimension** of a plan is the portion of the total management system at which the plan is aimed. Some plans are designed to cover the entire open management system: the organizational environment, inputs, process, and outputs. Such a plan is often referred to as a *master plan*. Other plans are developed to cover only a portion of the management system. An example of the latter would be a plan that covers the recruitment of new workers—a portion of the organizational input segment of the management system. The greater the portion of the management system that a plan covers, the broader the plan's scope is said to be.

The **scope dimension** of a plan is the portion of the total management system at which the plan is aimed.

Level   The **level dimension** of a plan is the level of the organization at which the plan is aimed. Top-level plans are those designed for top management of the organization, whereas middle-level and lower-level plans are designed for middle and lower management, respectively. Because all parts of the management system are interdependent, however, plans designed for any level of the organization have some effect on all other levels.

The **level dimension** of a plan is the level of the organization at which the plan is aimed.

Figure 9.1 illustrates the four dimensions of an organizational plan. This figure indicates that when managers develop a plan, they should consider the degree to which it will be used over and over again, the period of time it will cover, the parts of the management system on which it focuses, and the organizational level at which it is aimed.

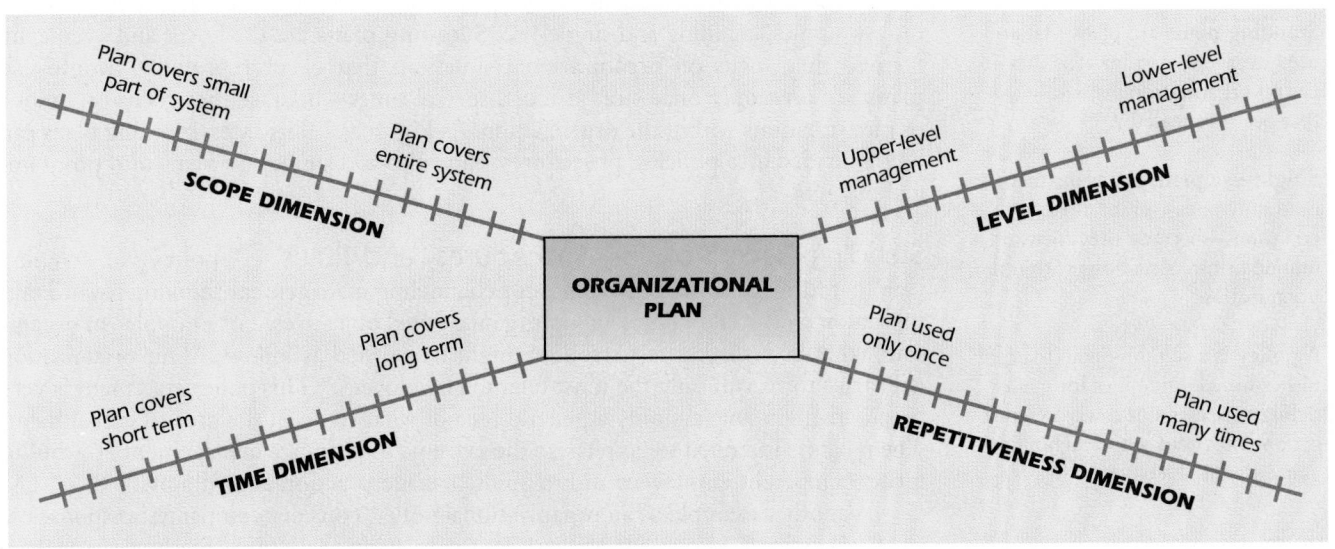

Figure 9.1   Four major dimensions to consider when developing a plan

Engineer Ron Shriver and his Japan-based counterpart Hiroyuki Itoh (second and third from the left, respectively) are celebrating the successful completion of a project to reduce the costs of building the Civic at Honda Motor Co.'s plant in East Liberty, Ohio. The project was a model of both team-based problem solving and creating plans across management levels. Originally, for instance, Shriver and Itoh had formed separate teams, but once they had begun pooling their resources, they were able to gather money-saving suggestions from suppliers and factory workers in both the U.S. and Japan.

BACK TO THE CASE In developing plans for Fiat, management is devising recommendations for future actions. Therefore, plans should be action-oriented—that is, they should state precisely what Fiat is going to do to achieve its goals.

Fiat managers should consider how often the plans it is developing will be used and the length of time they will cover. Will a plan be implemented only once or will it be used over the long term to handle an ongoing issue such as maintaining product quality? A plan to build a new factory would probably not be used more than once and would be designed to cover a specific amount of time.

Fiat managers should consider at which part of the organization to aim the plans they develop and on which organizational level the plans will focus. For example, a plan to cut costs might encompass all Fiat operations, whereas one to improve product quality might affect only one part of the production process. Similarly, a plan to cut costs might be aimed at top-level management, whereas a product quality plan might be aimed toward lower-level management and the auto assemblers themselves. Of course, managers must realize that, because management systems are interdependent, any plans they implement will affect the whole system.

Types of Plans

With the repetitiveness dimension as a guide, organizational plans are usually divided into two types: standing and single-use. **Standing plans** are used over and over again because they focus on organizational situations that occur repeatedly. **Single-use plans** are used only once—or, at most, several times—because they focus on unique or rare situations within the organization. As Figure 9.2 illustrates, standing plans can be subdivided into policies, procedures, and rules and single-use plans into programs and budgets.

Standing Plans: Policies, Procedures, and Rules

A **policy** is a standing plan that furnishes broad guidelines for channeling management thinking toward taking action consistent with reaching organizational objectives. For example, an organizational policy relating to personnel might be worded as follows: "Our organization will strive to recruit only the most talented employees." This policy statement is very broad, giving managers only a general idea of what to do in the area of recruitment. The policy is intended to emphasize the extreme importance management attaches to hiring competent employees and to guide managers' action accordingly.

As another example of an organizational policy, consider companies' responses to studies showing that one out of every four workers in the United States was attacked, threatened, or harassed on the job during a recent 12-month operating period. To deal

Standing plans are plans that are used over and over because they focus on organizational situations that occur repeatedly.

Single-use plans are plans that are used only once—or, at most, several times—because they focus on unique or rare situations within the organization.

A **policy** is a standing plan that furnishes broad guidelines for channeling management toward taking action consistent with reaching organizational objectives.

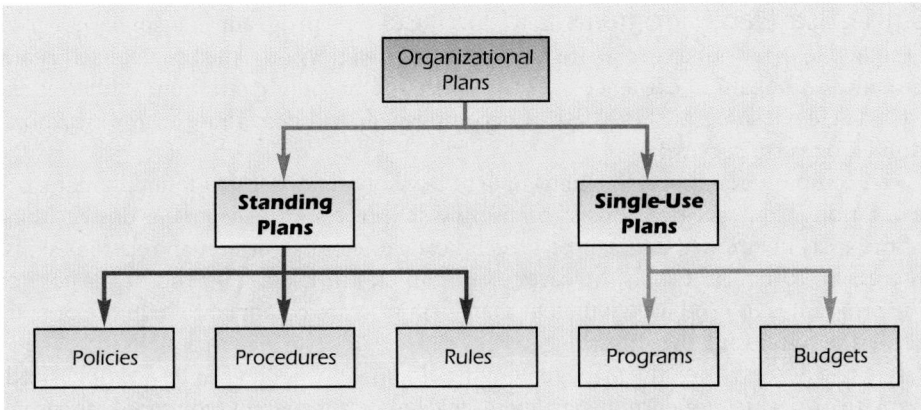

Figure 9.2   Standing plans and single-use plans

with this problem, many managers are developing weapons policies. A sample policy could be: "Management strongly discourages any employee from bringing a weapon to work." This policy would encourage managers to deal forcefully and punitively with employees who bring weapons into the workplace.[3]

A **procedure** is a standing plan that outlines a series of related actions that must be taken to accomplish a particular task. In general, procedures outline more specific actions than policies do. Organizations usually have many different sets of procedures covering the various tasks to be accomplished. Managers must be careful to apply the appropriate organizational procedures for the situations they face, and to apply them properly.[4]

A **rule** is a standing plan that designates specific required action. In essence, a rule indicates what an organization member should or should not do and allows no room for interpretation. An example of a rule that many companies are now establishing is No Smoking. The concept of rules may become clearer if one thinks about the purpose and nature of rules in such games as Scrabble and Monopoly.

Although policies, procedures, and rules are all standing plans, they are different from one another and have different purposes within the organization. As Figure 9.3 illustrates, however, for the standing plans of an organization to be effective, policies, procedures, and rules must be consistent and mutually supportive.

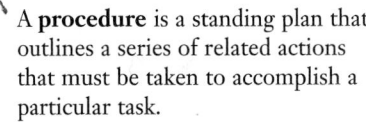

A **procedure** is a standing plan that outlines a series of related actions that must be taken to accomplish a particular task.

A **rule** is a standing plan that designates specific required action.

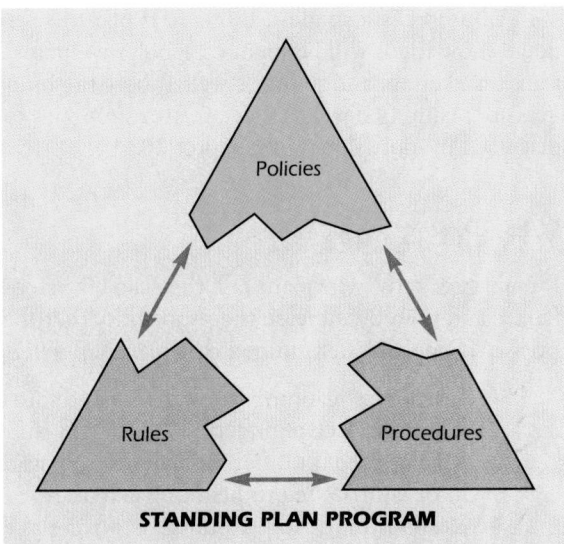

STANDING PLAN PROGRAM

Figure 9.3   A successful standing plan program with mutually supportive policies, procedures, and rules

A **program** is a single-use plan designed to carry out a special project in an organization that, if accomplished, will contribute to the organization's long-term success.

Single-Use Plans: Programs and Budgets

A **program** is a single-use plan designed to carry out a special project within an organization. The project itself is not intended to remain in existence over the entire life of the organization. Rather, it exists to achieve some purpose that, if accomplished, will contribute to the organization's long-term success.

A common example is the management development program found in many organizations. This program exists to raise the skill levels of managers in one or more of the areas mentioned in Chapter 1: technical, conceptual, or human relations skills. Increasing managerial skills, however, is not an end in itself. The end or purpose of the program is to produce competent managers who are equipped to help the organization be successful over the long term. In fact, once managerial skills have been raised to a desired level, the management development program can be deemphasized. Activities on which modern management development programs commonly focus include understanding and using the computer as a management tool, handling international competition, and planning for a major labor shortage by the year 2000.[5]

The following PEOPLE PERSPECTIVES feature describes a program at Wisconsin Power & Light Company that was aimed at building cooperation and motivating organization members to do a good job.

PROGRAM AT WISCONSIN POWER & LIGHT BUILDS EMPLOYEE MOTIVATION

PEOPLE PERSPECTIVES

Management at Wisconsin Power & Light Company decided that it needed a special program aimed at building employee cooperation and motivation. It decided not to engage a consultant, but to undertake the design and implementation of the program itself. Under the direction of Jim Bindl, Wisconsin Power & Light devised a simple reward program that employees like and support, even though it puts $200 of their pay at risk every year.

The program is called Employees Recognizing Employees. Workers at all levels can reward their colleagues immediately for extraordinary cooperation, brilliant ideas, or just plain hard work. At the beginning of each year, 800 employees each get 10 certificates worth $20 apiece. Throughout the year, workers pass these certificates along to other employees as tokens of appreciation for jobs well done. The employee who receives the certificate can choose to redeem it at the end of the year for cash or pass it along to another employee. Initial reviews of the program are very positive, though it is uncertain how long the program will run.≈

A **budget** is a control tool that outlines how funds in a given period will be spent, as well as how they will be obtained.

A **budget** is a single-use financial plan that covers a specified length of time. It details how funds will be spent on labor, raw materials, capital goods, information systems, marketing, and so on, as well as how the funds will be obtained.[6] Although budgets are planning devices, they are also strategies for organizational control. They are discussed in more detail in Chapter 20.

Why Plans Fail

If managers know why plans fail, they can take steps to eliminate the factors that cause failure and thereby increase the probability that their plans will be successful. A study by K. A. Ringbakk determined that plans fail when:[7]

1. Corporate planning is not integrated into the total management system.
2. There is a lack of understanding of the different steps of the planning process.
3. Management at different levels in the organization has not properly engaged in or contributed to planning activities.
4. Responsibility for planning is wrongly vested solely in the planning department.

5. Management expects that plans developed will be realized with little effort.
6. In starting formal planning, too much is attempted at once.
7. Management fails to operate by the plan.
8. Financial projections are confused with planning.
9. Inadequate inputs are used in planning.
10. Management fails to grasp the overall planning process.

Planning Areas: Input Planning

As discussed earlier, organizational inputs, process, outputs, and environment are major factors in determining how successful a management system will be. Naturally, a comprehensive organizational plan should focus on each of these factors. The following two sections cover planning in two areas normally associated with the input factor: plant facilities planning and human resource planning. Planning in areas such as these is called **input planning**—the development of proposed action that will furnish sufficient and appropriate organizational resources for reaching established organizational objectives.

Plant Facilities Planning   **Plant facilities planning** involves determining the type of buildings and equipment an organization needs to reach its objectives. A major part of this determination is called **site selection**—deciding where a plant facility should be located. Table 9.1 lays out several major areas to be considered in plant site selection and gives sample questions that can be asked as these areas are being explored. Naturally, the specifics of site selection will vary from organization to organization.[8]

Input planning is the development of proposed action that will furnish sufficient and appropriate organizational resources for reaching established organizational objectives.

Plant facilities planning is input planning that involves developing the type of work facility an organization will need to reach its objectives.

Site selection involves determining where a plant facility should be located. It may use a weighting process to compare site differences.

Table 9.1

Major Areas of Consideration When Selecting a Plant Site and Sample Exploratory Questions to Be Asked

MAJOR AREAS OF CONSIDERATION IN SITE SELECTION	SAMPLE QUESTIONS TO BE ASKED
Profit	
Market Location	Where are our customers in relation to the site?
Competition	What competitive situation exists at the site?
Operating costs	
Suppliers	Are materials available near the site at reasonable cost?
Utilities	What are utility rates at the site? Are utilities available in sufficient amounts?
Wages	What wage rates are paid by comparable organizations near the site?
Taxes	What are tax rates on income, sales, property, and so on for the site?
Investment costs	
Land/development	How expensive are land and construction at the site?
Others	
Transportation	Are airlines, railroads, highways, and so on accessible from the site?
Laws	What laws related to zoning, pollution, and so on will influence operations if the site is chosen?
Labor	Does an adequate labor supply exist around the site?
Unionization	What is the degree of unionization in the site area?
Living conditions	Are housing, schools, and so on around the site appropriate?
Community relations	Does the community support the organization's moving into the area?

MEXICO AS AN ATTRACTIVE MANUFACTURING SITE

For several years, U.S. companies have been building and running manufacturing plants just across the Mexican border. The mere existence of these plants—called *maquiladoras*—is evidence that Mexico has become an extremely attractive foreign manufacturing site for U.S. firms. The low cost of Mexican labor—significantly less than that in the United States—is the main reason for the success of the *maquiladoras*. Accompanying these lower labor costs, however, are several challenges that U.S. managers of *maquiladoras* must face: In general, the Mexican labor force employed at *maquiladoras* is young, inexperienced, and unskilled; because the labor force comes mainly from rural Mexico, there are significant cultural differences between Mexican workers and U.S. owners or managers; Mexican labor laws are more protective of workers than are U.S. labor laws. As U.S. manufacturers find ways to improve the productivity of the Mexican labor force through special training for young, unskilled workers, they are gaining a real appreciation for Mexican culture and learning to manage effectively within the limits of Mexican labor laws. U.S. manufacturers are meeting the challenges of the *maquiladora* industry, improving the productivity of the Mexican labor force, and making Mexico an even more appealing site for foreign manufacturing plants.≈

One factor that significantly influences site selection is foreign location. Management in a foreign country planning to select a site must deal with such issues as differences among foreign governments in time taken to approve site purchases and political pressures that may slow down or prevent the purchase of a site. For example, Japanese investors who locate businesses in the United States tend to select those states that have low unionization rates, low employment rates, relatively impoverished populations, and the highest possible educational levels under those conditions. Japanese managers believe that these factors enhance the chances of success of Japanese business in the United States.[9]

Many organizations use a weighting process to compare site differences among foreign countries. Basically, this process involves the following steps:

1. Deciding on a set of variables that are critical to obtaining an appropriate site.
2. Assigning each of these variables a weight reflecting its relative importance.
3. Ranking alternative sites according to how they reflect these different variables.

Table 9.2 shows the results of such a weighting process for seven site variables in six countries. In this table, "living conditions" are worth 100 points, and are the most important variable; "effect on company reputation" is worth 35 points, and is the least

ABB Asea Brown Boveri, a Swiss-based manufacturer of engineering products, makes turbine exhaust casings at this factory in Hungary because it can produce casings, turbine blades and rotors, and high-voltage switching gear at about half the cost of making them in Western European plants. These parts are then used in power-plant equipment assembled in Germany and Switzerland. By integrating such factories into its global manufacturing network, ABB has created economies of scale and reduced the prices of some industrial products by 50 percent.

		SITES					
	MAXIMUM VALUE						
CRITERIA	ASSIGNED	Japan	Chile	Jamaica	Australia	Mexico	France
Living conditions	100	70	40	45	50	60	60
Accessibility	75	55	35	20	60	70	70
Industrialization	60	40	50	55	35	35	30
Labor availability	35	30	10	10	30	35	35
Economics	35	15	15	15	15	25	25
Community capability and attitude	30	25	20	10	15	25	15
Effect on company reputation	35	25	20	10	15	25	15
Total	370	260	190	165	220	275	250

Table 9.2

Results of Weighting Seven Site Variables for Six Countries

important variable. The six countries are given a number of points for each variable, depending on the importance of the variable and how well it is reflected within the country. The table shows that, using this particular set of weighted criteria, Japan, Mexico, and France are more desirable sites than Chile, Jamaica, and Australia.

The following CUTTING EDGE discusses a new emphasis in the site selection process—the potential of a site to develop into a manufacturing network.

CHOOSING A PLANT SITE FOR MANUFACTURING NETWORK POTENTIAL

CUTTING EDGE

Traditional wisdom about choosing a plant site emphasizes careful analysis of quantitative data relating to what is happening now and what has happened in the past at the site. Such quantitative data commonly focus on such variables as transportation costs involved in procuring materials and delivering finished products to customers, prevailing wage rates in the area, currency exchange rates (if the site happens to be in a foreign country), and tax rates in the area.

Current thinking about site location stresses that location decisions based primarily on historical quantitative data tend to ignore evolving qualitative factors that can provide significant long-term advantages for an organization. One such qualitative factor is the probability of a site becoming part of a manufacturing network, which is defined as a system of interrelated organizations that cooperate in the manufacturing of a product. It is not necessary that all these organizations be owned by the same company. Some management experts believe that organizations of the future, particularly global ones, will develop most successfully if they become part of a manufacturing network of decentralized, cooperative plants based in large, sophisticated regional markets. Under this system, plants will be smaller and more flexible than the typical plant is today.

In choosing a plant site, then, managers should consider not only present and historical quantitative data but also more future-oriented qualitative issues like the probability that an effective and efficient manufacturing network will grow up and flourish in a region. ≈

Human Resource Planning   Human resources are another area of concern to input planners. Organizational objectives cannot be attained without appropriate per-

sonnel. Future needs for human resources are influenced mainly by employee turnover, the nature of the present workforce, and the rate of growth of the organization.[10]

The following are representative of the kinds of questions personnel planners should try to answer:

1. What types of people does the organization need to reach its objectives?
2. How many of each type are needed?
3. What steps should the organization take to recruit and select such people?
4. Can present employees be further trained to fill future needed positions?
5. At what rate are employees being lost to other organizations?

Human resource planning is input planning that involves obtaining the human resources necessary for the organization to achieve its objectives.

Figure 9.4 shows the human resource planning process developed by Bruce Coleman. According to his model, **human resource planning** involves reflecting on organizational objectives to determine overall human resource needs, comparing these needs to the existing human resource inventory to determine net human resource needs, and, finally, seeking appropriate organization members to meet the net human resource needs.

BACK TO THE CASE

Managers at Fiat would use both standing plans and single-use plans. Standing plans include policies, procedures, and rules, and should be developed for situations that occur repeatedly. For example, Fiat might develop a standing plan that focuses on attaining and maintaining the degree of product quality management considers desirable.

Single-use plans include programs and budgets and should be created to help manage situations that occur once or only rarely. The introductory case implies that Fiat management has worked on a budget for renovating an existing plant in Avellino, Italy. In

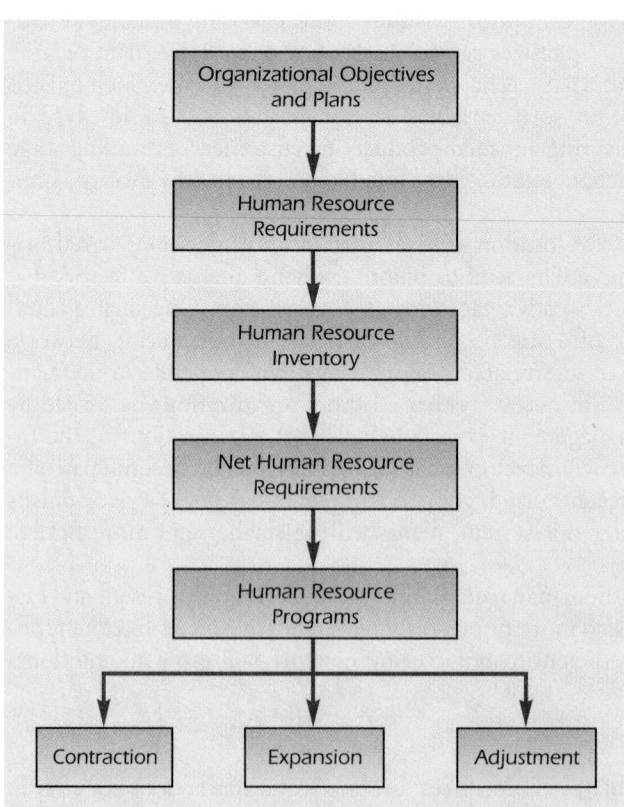

Figure 9.4   **The human resource planning process**

developing such a single-use plan, Fiat managers should make sure they thoroughly understand the reasons plans fail and take steps to avoid those pitfalls.

Planning plant facilities and human resource planning are two other types of planning that managers commonly perform. In Fiat's case, planning plant facilities entails designing the types of factories that the company needs to reach its objectives. The company has developed plans to build a new plant in Basilicata as well as to expand and remodel an existing parts factory near Avellino. Certainly, a strong influence on the decision to develop these plans was the financial support package offered to the company by the Italian government.

Human resource planning involves obtaining or developing the personnel an organization needs to reach its objectives. Fiat management must have considered the numbers and kinds of employees required to run both the new and the renovated factories, and this discussion must inevitably have focused on such issues as when these employees would be needed, how they would be recruited, and how they would be trained appropriately after joining Fiat.

PLANNING TOOLS

Planning tools are techniques managers can use to help develop plans. The remainder of this chapter discusses forecasting and scheduling, two of the most important of these tools.

Planning tools are techniques managers can use to help develop plans.

Forecasting

Forecasting is the process of predicting future environmental happenings that will influence the operation of the organization. Although sophisticated forecasting techniques have been developed only rather recently, the concept of forecasting can be traced at least as far back in the management literature as Fayol. The importance of forecasting lies in its ability to help managers understand the future makeup of the organizational environment, which, in turn, helps them formulate more effective plans.[11]

Forecasting is a planning tool used to predict future environmental happenings that will influence the operation of the organization.

How Forecasting Works   William C. House, in describing the Insect Control Services Company, has developed an excellent illustration of how forecasting works. In general, Insect Control Services forecasts by attempting to:[12]

1. Establish relationships between industry sales and national economic and social indicators.
2. Determine the impact of government restrictions on the use of chemical pesticides will have on the growth of chemical, biological, and electromagnetic energy pest-control markets.
3. Evaluate sales growth potential, profitability, resources required, and risks involved in each of its market areas (commercial, industrial, institutional, governmental, and residential).
4. Evaluate the potential for expansion of marketing efforts in geographical areas of the United States as well as in foreign countries.
5. Determine the likelihood of technological breakthroughs that would make existing product lines obsolete.

Types of Forecasts   In addition to the general type of organizational forecasting done by Insect Control Services, there are specialized types of forecasting, such as economic, technological, social trends, and sales forecasting. Although a complete organizational forecasting process should, and usually does, include all these types of forecasting, sales forecasting is considered the key organizational forecast. A *sales forecast* is a prediction of how high or low sales of the organization's products and/or ser-

vices will be over the period of time under consideration. It is the key forecast for organizations because it serves as the fundamental guideline for planning. Only after the sales forecast has been completed can managers decide, for example, if more salespeople should be hired, if more money for plant expansion must be borrowed, or if layoffs and cutbacks in certain areas are necessary. Managers must continually monitor forecasting methods to improve them and to reformulate plans based upon inaccurate forecasts.[13]

Methods of Sales Forecasting

Modern managers have several different methods available for forecasting sales. Popular methods are the jury of executive opinion method, the salesforce estimation method, and the time series analysis method. Each of these methods is discussed in this section.

Jury of Executive Opinion Method.

The **jury of executive opinion method** is a method of predicting future sales levels primarily by asking appropriate managers to give their opinions on what will happen to sales in the future.

The **jury of executive opinion method** of sales forecasting is straightforward. Appropriate managers within the organization assemble to discuss their opinions on what will happen to sales in the future. Since these discussion sessions usually revolve around hunches or experienced guesses, the resulting forecast is a blend of informed opinions.

A similar, more recently developed forecasting method, called the *delphi method*, also gathers, evaluates, and summarizes expert opinions as the basis for a forecast, but the procedure is more formal than that for the jury of executive opinion method.[14] The basic delphi method employs the following steps:

- *Step 1:* Various experts are asked to answer, independently and in writing, a series of questions about the future of sales or whatever other area is being forecasted.
- *Step 2:* A summary of all the answers is then prepared. No expert knows how any other expert answered the questions.
- *Step 3:* Copies of the summary are given to the individual experts with the request that they modify their original answers if they think it necessary.
- *Step 4:* Another summary is made of these modifications, and copies again are distributed to the experts. This time, however, expert opinions that deviate significantly from the norm must be justified in writing.
- *Step 5:* A third summary is made of the opinions and justifications, and copies are once again distributed to the experts. Justification in writing for *all* answers is now required.
- *Step 6:* The forecast is generated from all of the opinions and justifications that arise from step 5.

Salesforce Estimation Method.

The **salesforce estimation method** predicts future sales levels primarily by asking appropriate salespeople for their opinions of what will happen to sales in the future.

The **salesforce estimation method** is a sales forecasting technique that predicts future sales by analyzing the opinions of salespeople as a group. Salespeople constantly interact with customers, and from this interaction they usually develop a knack for predicting future sales. As with the jury of executive opinion method, the resulting forecast normally is a blend of the informed views of the group.

The salesforce estimation method is considered to be a very valuable management tool and is commonly used in business and industry throughout the world. Although the accuracy of this method is generally good, managers have found that it can be improved by taking such simple steps as providing salespeople with sufficient time to forecast and offering incentives for accurate forecasts. Some companies help their salespeople to become better forecasters by training them to better interpret their interactions with customers.[15]

Time Series Analysis Method.

The **time series analysis method** is a method of predicting future sales levels by analyzing the historical relationship in an organization between sales and time.

The **time series analysis method** predicts future sales by analyzing the historical relationship between sales and time. Information showing the relationship between sales and time typically is presented on a graph, as

Figure 9.5   Time series analysis method

in Figure 9.5. This presentation clearly displays past trends, which can be used to predict future sales.

Although the actual number of years included in a time series analysis will vary from company to company, as a general rule, managers should include as many years as necessary to ensure that important sales trends do not go undetected. At the Coca-Cola Company, for example, management believes that in order to validly predict the annual sales of any one year, it must chart annual sales in each of the ten previous years.[16]

The time series analysis in Figure 9.5 indicates steadily increasing sales for B.J.'s Men's Clothing over time. However, since in the long term products generally go through what is called a product life cycle, the predicted increase based on the last decade of sales should probably be considered overly optimistic. A **product life cycle** is the five stages through which most products and services pass. These stages are introduction, growth, maturity, saturation, and decline.

Product Stages. Figure 9.6 shows how the five stages of the product life cycle are related to sales volume for seven products over a period of time. In the introduction stage, when a product is brand-new, sales are just beginning to build (cellular phones and compact disc players). In the growth stage, the product has been in the marketplace for some time and is becoming more accepted, so product sales continue to climb (personal computers). During the maturity stage, competitors enter the market, and while sales are still climbing, they are climbing at a slower rate than they did in the growth stage (microwave ovens). After the maturity stage comes the saturation stage, when nearly everyone who wanted the product has it (refrigerators and freezers). Sales during the saturation stage typically are due to the need to replace a worn-out product or to population growth. The last product life cycle stage—decline—finds the product being replaced by a competing product (black-and-white televisions).

Managers may be able to prevent some products from entering the decline stage by improving product quality or by adding innovations. Other products, such as scissors, may never reach this last stage of the product life cycle because there are no competing products to replace them.

A **product life cycle** is the five stages through which most products and services pass: introduction, growth, maturity, saturation, and decline.

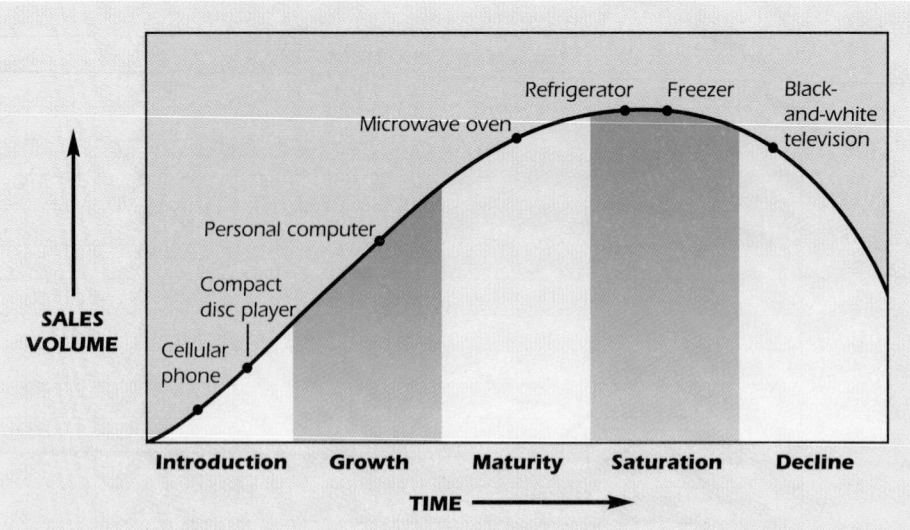

Figure 9.6   Stages of the product life cycle

Evaluating Sales Forecasting Methods   The sales forecasting methods just described are not the only ones available to managers. Other, more complex methods include the statistical correlation method and the computer simulation method.[17] The methods just discussed, however, do provide a basic foundation for understanding sales forecasting.

In practice, managers find that each sales forecasting method has distinct advantages and disadvantages. Before deciding to use a particular sales forecasting method, a manager must carefully weigh these advantages and disadvantages as they relate to the manager's organization. The best decision may be to use a combination of methods to forecast sales rather than just one. Whatever the method or methods finally adopted, the manager should be certain the framework is logical, fits the needs of the organization, and can be adapted to changes in the environment.

BACK TO THE CASE   One of the planning tools available to Fiat management is forecasting, which involves predicting future environmental events that could influence the operation of the company. Although various specific types of forecasting—such as economic, technological, and social trends forecasting—are

Motorola is building this new cellular-phone factory in Tianjin, China, because it was pleasantly surprised by some errors in its market forecasting. Although there is only one phone for every 102 people in China, Motorola forecast slow growth for sales of cell phones and pagers. In the late 1980s, therefore, it kept investment costs down by shipping products from the United States. By 1993, however, sales began increasing 100 percent a year in China—the fastest-growing sector of Motorola's business.

available, Fiat management would probably choose to make sales forecasting its key forecast since that method will predict how high or low sales will be during the time period under consideration. According to the information in the introductory case, Fiat managers made a sales forecast and relied on its results in deciding to construct a new factory and expand an existing one.

In order to forecast sales, Fiat managers could follow the jury of executive opinion method by having company executives discuss their opinions of future sales. This method would be quick and easy to use, and assuming that Fiat executives have a good feel for product demand, it might be as valid as any other method available to the company.

Fiat management might, instead, ask its auto retailers (salesforce) for opinions on predicted sales. Although the opinions of car dealers may not prove completely reliable, these are the people closest to the market who must ultimately sell Fiat's products, so their views are well informed.

Finally, Fiat management could use the time series analysis method and analyze the relationship between sales and time. This method takes into account the cyclical patterns and past history of sales, and assumes the continuation of these patterns in the future without considering outside influences, such as economic downturns, that could cause the patterns to change.

Because each sales forecasting method has both advantages and disadvantages, Fiat management should carefully analyze each of the methods before deciding which method or methods should be used for the organization.

Scheduling

Scheduling is the process of formulating a detailed listing of activities that must be accomplished to attain an objective, allocating the resources necessary to attain the objective, and setting up and following timetables for completing the objective. Scheduling is an integral part of every organizational plan. Two popular scheduling techniques are Gantt charts and the program evaluation and review technique (PERT).

Gantt Charts   The **Gantt chart,** a scheduling device developed by Henry L. Gantt, is essentially a bar graph with time on the horizontal axis and the resource to be scheduled on the vertical axis. It is used for scheduling resources, including management system inputs such as human resources and machines.

Figure 9.7 shows a completed Gantt chart for a work period entitled "Workweek 28." The resources scheduled over the five workdays on this chart were the human

Scheduling is the process of formulating a detailed listing of activities that must be accomplished to attain an objective, allocating the resources necessary to attain the objective, and setting up and following timetables for completing the objective.

The **Gantt chart** is a scheduling tool composed of a bar chart with time on the horizontal axis and the resource to be scheduled on the vertical axis. It is used for scheduling resources.

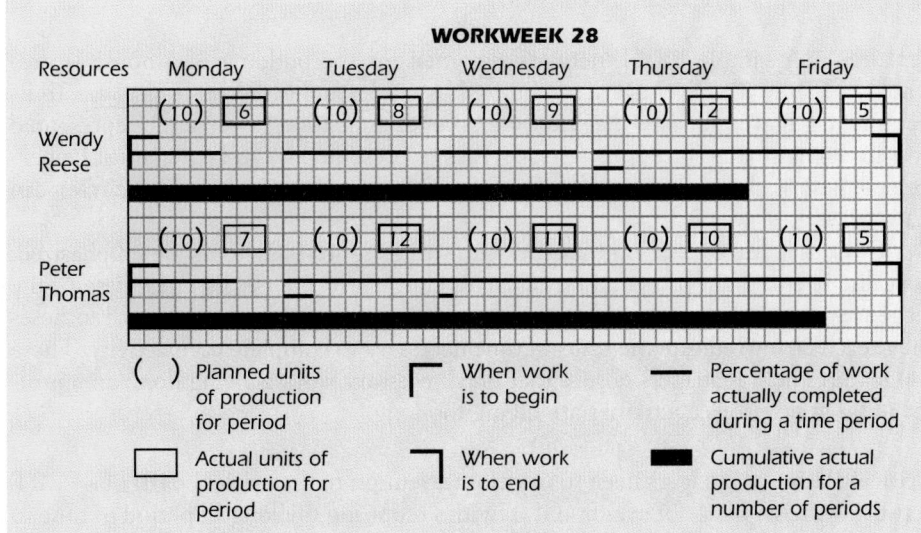

Figure 9.7   Completed Gantt chart

resources Wendy Reese and Peter Thomas. During this workweek, both Reese and Thomas were supposed to produce ten units a day. Note, however, that actual production deviated from planned production. There were days when each of the two workers produced more than ten units, as well as days when each produced fewer than ten units. Cumulative actual production for workweek 28 shows that Reese produced 40 units and Thomas 45 units over the five days.

Features.   Although simple in concept and appearance, the Gantt chart has many valuable managerial uses. First, managers can use it as a summary overview of how organizational resources are being employed. From this summary, they can detect such facts as which resources are consistently contributing to productivity and which are hindering it. Second, managers can use the Gantt chart to help coordinate organizational resources. The chart can show which resources are not being used during specific periods, thereby allowing managers to schedule those resources for work on other production efforts. Third, the chart can be used to establish realistic worker output standards. For example, if scheduled work is being completed too quickly, output standards should be raised so that workers are scheduled for more work per time period.

Program Evaluation and Review Technique (PERT)

The main weakness of the Gantt chart is that it does not contain any information about the interrelationship of tasks to be performed. Although all tasks to be performed are listed on the chart, there is no way of telling if one task must be performed before another can be started. The program evaluation and review technique (PERT), a technique that evolved partly from the Gantt chart, is a scheduling tool that does emphasize the interrelationship of tasks.

The **program evaluation and review technique (PERT)** is a scheduling tool that is essentially a network of project activities showing estimates of time necessary to complete each activity and the sequence of activities that must be followed to complete the project.

Defining PERT.   PERT is a network of project activities showing both the estimates of time necessary to complete each activity and the sequence of activities that must be followed to complete the project. This scheduling tool was developed in 1958 for designing and building the Polaris submarine weapon system. The people who were managing this project found Gantt charts and other existing scheduling tools of little use because of the complicated nature of the Polaris project and the interdependence of the tasks to be performed.[18]

The PERT network contains two primary elements: activities and events. **Activities** are specified sets of behavior within a project, and **events** are the completions of major project tasks. Within the PERT network, each event is assigned corresponding activities that must be performed before the event can materialize.[19]

Activities and events are the primary elements of a PERT network. **Activities** are specified sets of behavior within a project. **Events** are the completions of major project tasks.

Features.   A sample PERT network designed for the building of a house is presented in Figure 9.8. Events are symbolized by circles and activities by arrows. To illustrate, the figure indicates that after the event "Foundation Complete" (represented by a circle) has materialized, certain activities (represented by an arrow) must be performed before the event "Frame Complete" (represented by another circle) can materialize.

Two other features of the network shown in Figure 9.8 should be emphasized. First, the left-to-right presentation of events shows how the events interrelate or the sequence in which they should be performed. Second, the numbers in parentheses above each arrow indicate the units of time necessary to complete each activity. These two features help managers ensure that only necessary work is being done on a project and that no project activities are taking too long.

A **critical path** is the sequence of events and activities within a program evaluation and review technique (PERT) network that requires the longest period of time to complete.

Critical Path.   Managers need to pay close attention to the **critical path** of a PERT network—the sequence of events and activities requiring the longest period of time to complete. This path is called *critical* because a delay in completing this sequence re-

relationship among tasks

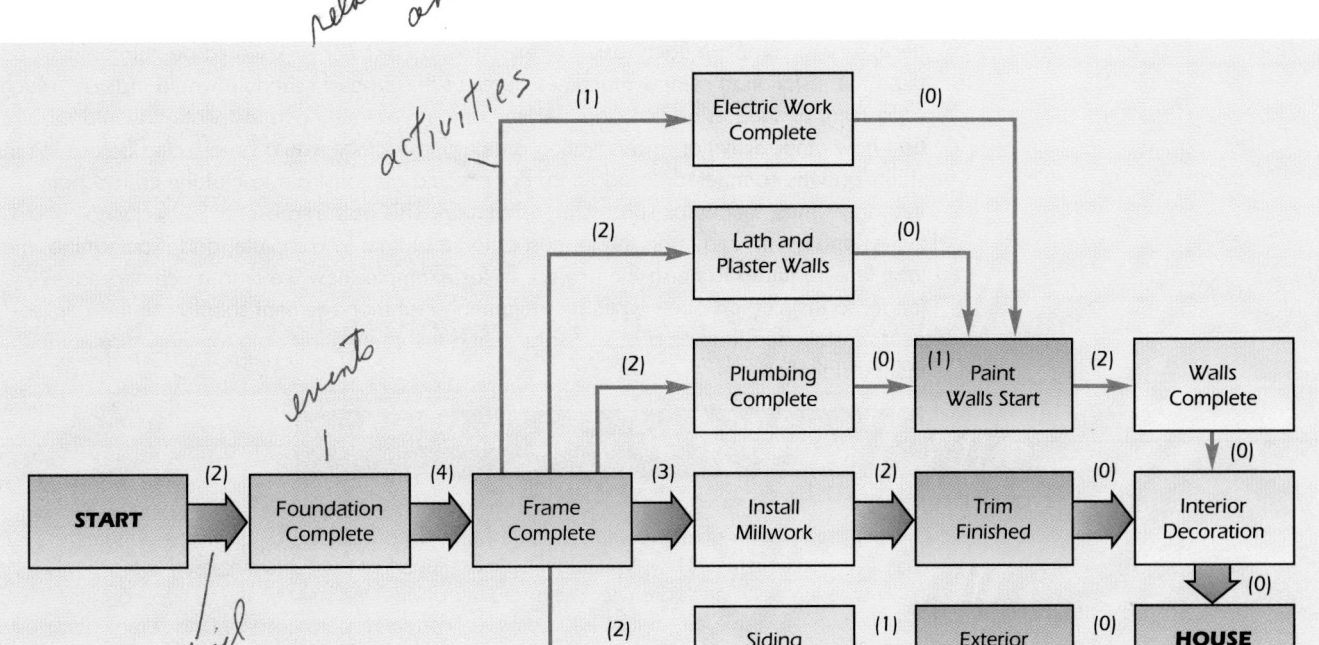

activities

events

critical path

Figure 9.8   PERT network designed for building a house

sults in a delay in completing the entire project. The critical path in Figure 9.8 is indicated by thick arrows; all other paths are indicated by thin arrows. Managers try to control a project by keeping it within the time designated by the critical path. The critical path helps them predict which features of a schedule are becoming unrealistic and provides insights into how those features might be eliminated or modified.[20]

Steps in Designing a PERT Network.   When designing a PERT network, managers should follow four primary steps:[21]

- *Step 1:* List all the activities/events that must be accomplished for the project and the sequence in which these activities/events should be performed.
- *Step 2:* Determine how much time will be needed to complete each activity/event.
- *Step 3:* Design a PERT network that reflects all of the information contained in steps 1 and 2.
- *Step 4:* Identify the critical path.

BACK TO THE CASE   Scheduling is another planning tool available to Fiat management. It involves the detailed listing of activities that must be accomplished to reach an objective. For example, if Fiat's goal is to have all its employees working proficiently on updated equipment in its planned renovated factory within two years, management needs to schedule activities such as installing the equipment, training the employees, and establishing new output standards.

Two scheduling techniques available to Fiat management are Gantt charts and PERT. To schedule employee production output, Fiat managers might want to use Gantt charts—bar graphs with time on the horizontal axis and the resources to be scheduled on the vertical axis. They might also find these charts helpful for evaluating workers' performance and for setting new production standards.

When Fiat managers feel they need to see the relationships among tasks, they should use PERT to develop a flowchart showing activities, events, and the amount of time

necessary to complete each task. For example, a PERT network would be helpful in scheduling the installation of new machines because this type of schedule would indicate which equipment needed to be installed first, the amount of time each installation would require, and how other activities in renovating an existing factory would be affected before the installation was completed. In addition, PERT would demonstrate to Fiat the critical path managers must follow for successful installation. This path represents the sequence of activities and events requiring the longest amount of time to complete, and it determines the total time required to finish the project. If, for example, new welding machinery takes longer to install than other types of equipment, Fiat management should use this component's installation time as a basis for targeting the completion date for the entire equipment installation.

Action Summary

Reread the learning objectives below. Each objective is followed by questions. Answering these questions accurately will help you retain the most important concepts discussed in this chapter. After answering each question, check your answer against the answer key at the end of this chapter. (*Hint*: If you have any doubts regarding the correct response, consult the page whose number follows the answer.)

Circle: From studying this chapter, I will attempt to acquire:

1. A complete definition of a plan.

a,b,c,d,e   **a.** A plan is: (a) the company's buildings and fixtures; (b) a specific action proposed to help the company achieve its objectives; (c) a policy meeting; (d) a projection of future sales; (e) an experiment to determine the optimal distribution system.

a,b,c,d,e   **b.** The following is generally *not* an important component of a plan: (a) the evaluation of relevant information; (b) the assessment of probable future developments; (c) a statement of a recommended course of action; (d) a statement of manager intuition; (e) strategy based on reason or rationality.

2. Insights regarding various dimensions of plans.

T,F   **a.** Most plans affect top management only.

a,b,c,d,e   **b.** The following is one of the four major dimensions of a plan: (a) repetitiveness; (b) organization; (c) time; (d) a and c; (e) b and c.

3. An understanding of various types of plans.

a,b,c,d,e   **a.** Standing plans that furnish broad guidelines for channeling management thinking in specified directions are called: (a) procedures; (b) programs; (c) single-use plans; (d) policies; (e) rules.

a,b,c,d,e   **b.** Programs and budgets are examples of: (a) single-use plans; (b) standing rules; (c) procedures; (d) Gantt chart components; (e) critical paths.

4. Insights on why plans fail.

a,b,c,d,e   **a.** The following is a reason that plans fail: (a) adequate inputs are used in planning; (b) corporate planning is integrated into the total management system; (c) management expects that plans developed will be realized with little effort; (d) management operates by the plan; (e) responsibility for planning is vested in more than just the planning department.

T,F   **b.** The confusion of planning with financial projections will have no effect on the success of plans.

5. A knowledge of various planning areas within an organization.

T,F   **a.** Input planning includes only site selection planning.

a,b,c,d,e   **b.** Personnel planners who reflect on organizational objectives to determine overall human resource needs and compare needs to existing human resource inventory are engaging in a type of planning called: (a) process layout; (b) plant facilities; (c) input; (d) life cycle; (e) delphi.

6. A definition of forecasting.

T,F   **a.** Forecasting is the process of setting objectives and scheduling activities.

a,b,c,d,e   **b.** According to the text, the following product is in the growth stage of the product life cycle: (a) microwave oven; (b) cellular phone; (c) black-and-white television; (d) personal computer; (e) refrigerator.

7. An ability to see the advantages and disadvantages of various methods of sales forecasting.

a,b,c,d,e   **a.** The sales forecasting technique that utilizes specialized knowledge based on interaction with customers is: (a) jury of executive opinion; (b) salesforce estimation; (c) time series analysis; (d) a and b; (e) b and c.

T,F   **b.** One of the advantages of the jury of executive opinion method is that it may be the only feasible means of forecasting sales, especially in the absence of adequate data.

8. A definition of scheduling.

a,b,c,d,e   **a.** Scheduling can best be described as: (a) the evaluation of alternative courses of action; (b) the process of formulating goals and objectives; (c) the process of formulating a detailed listing of activities; (d) the calculation of the break-even point; (e) the process of defining policies.

T,F   **b.** Scheduling is the process of predicting future environmental happenings that will influence the operations of the organization.

9. An understanding of Gantt charts and PERT.

a,b,c,d,e   **a.** The following is *not* an acceptable use of a Gantt chart: (a) as a summary overview of how organizational resources are being used; (b) to help coordinate organizational resources; (c) to establish realistic worker output standards; (d) to determine which resources are consistently contributing to productivity; (e) none of the above (all are acceptable uses of Gantt charts).

a,b,c,d,e   **b.** In a PERT network, the sequence of events and activities requiring the longest period of time to complete is: (a) called the network; (b) indicated by thin arrows; (c) the path that managers avoid; (d) the critical path; (e) eliminated from the rest of the project so the project will not take too long.

Introductory Case Wrap-Up

"Fiat Plans Car Production" (p. 201) and its related back-to-the-case sections were written to help you better understand the management concepts contained in this chapter. Answer the following discussion questions about this introductory case to enrich your understanding of chapter content:

1. Should Fiat's plant facilities planning be related to its human resource planning? Explain.

2. Explain this statement: "The quality of Fiat's decision to build one factory and to expand and renovate another is largely determined by the validity of the company's sales forecast."

3. What sales forecasting method(s) do you think Fiat management should have used as the basis for making its plant facilities decision? Explain.

Issues for Review and Discussion

1. What is a plan?
2. List and describe the basic dimensions of a plan.
3. What is the difference between standing plans and single-use plans?
4. Compare and contrast policies, procedures, and rules.
5. What are the two main types of single-use plans?
6. Why do organizations have programs?
7. Of what use is a budget to managers?
8. Summarize the ten factors that cause plans to fail.
9. What is input planning?
10. Evaluate the importance of plant facilities planning to the organization.
11. What major factors should be involved in site selection?
12. Describe the human resource planning process.
13. What is a planning tool?
14. Describe the measurements usually employed in forecasting. Why are they taken?
15. Draw and explain the product life cycle.
16. Discuss the advantages and disadvantages of three methods of sales forecasting.
17. Elaborate on the statement that all managers should spend some time scheduling.
18. What is a Gantt chart? Draw a simple chart to assist you in your explanation.
19. How can information related to the Gantt chart be used by managers?
20. How is PERT a scheduling tool?
21. How is the critical path related to PERT?
22. List the steps necessary to design a PERT network.

Case Study

Plans and Planning Tools

On February 2, 1996, Congress passed a landmark bill deregulating every aspect of the communications business. Under this bill, cable-TV providers, local phone companies, and long-distance carriers will all be allowed to forage in one another's markets for profits. On the basis of past performance, MCI looks like the heir apparent in this competitive free-for all. But first the company must learn to sell a lot more than long-distance calls. According to UBS Securities analyst Linda B. Meltzer, "It's no longer a question of how large a share of the $75 billion long-distance market you can get. It's a question of how big a share of the $500 billion converged or integrated market [MCI] will get."

MCI has responded to the new telecom opportunities with a series of contradictory starts and stops. For example, the company started and stopped two different wireless strategies and one on-line service effort. CEO Bert C. Roberts, however, contends that his company's erratic activities are evidence of its ultimate strength—the ability to be flexible: "We're quick to move forward and quick to pull back when we have to," says Roberts. Such flexibility, he argues, will enable MCI to conceive and implement a cohesive strategy for the new communications market.

Present MCI strategy concentrates company resources on current industry logic—namely, what *Business Week* magazine describes as: "Offer a single source for long-distance and local calling, video, data, and wireless services, bundle them onto one bill, and customers will come." Through joint ventures, partnerships, resale agreements, and its own initiatives, MCI expects to be able to offer almost every service that can be delivered over both wired and wireless communications systems—satellite TV, Internet connections, and electronic commerce transactions, as well as local, long-distance, and international phone service. "We want to get as many hooks into each of our customers as possible," says CEO Roberts, pointing to revealing MCI studies showing that customers who buy more than one service from a carrier switch carriers 40 percent less often than customers who buy only one service.

In fact, in support of MCI's new "diversify-or-die-mantra," Roberts says that he wants the company to earn 50 percent of its revenues from new ventures by the year 2000. To meet this objective, MCI spent more than $6 billion during the calendar year of 1995, buying everything from a cellular-phone reseller to SHL System-house, a Canadian-based computer systems integrator. MCI has also built fiber links in 25 cities to provide local phone service to business customers.

Above all, the company shocked industry experts when it paid $2 billion for a 13.5 percent stake in News Corporation because the experts could not reconcile this investment decision with known MCI goals and objectives. Early in 1996, however, MCI and News Corporation announced a joint venture that entailed spending $1.3 billion to build a DBS (digital broadcast system) network. Soon afterward, MCI announced another broad alliance, this time with Microsoft Corporation, in which MCI would become the primary distributor of Microsoft's on-line network.

MCI claims to base its "scattershot" strategy on a consistent set of principles. "We buy when there are finite resources and [sell] when there is a glut," says Timothy F. Price, president of MCI's long-distance business. As an example of the first principle, MCI paid $628.5 million for the last available slot for its DBS satellite, despite analysts' protests that the price was twice the value. The second principle influenced MCI to resell wireless services purchased from other suppliers. MCI planners figured that once PCS (Personal Communications Service) networks were built—at high setup costs—there would be a glut of capacity. In support of its plans, MCI paid $190 million in September of 1995 for Nationwide Cellular Services, Inc., a large reseller.

Another strategic MCI tenet is to share the cost of its many ventures in order to spread the risk. To that end, Roberts hopes to take on partners as often as possible—whether Rupert Murdoch (News Corporation), Bill Gates (Microsoft), or British Telecommunications PLC (20 percent owner of MCI since 1994). "I'm not so visionary that I know where all the bucks are going to flow

five years from now," says Roberts. Finally, MCI president Price points to the company's ultimate trump card—and one of the main tenets of its successful planning: killer marketing instincts. "We don't want to dive in ahead of where the customer is," he says. "We just want to move as fast as possible to where they are." According to British Telecom's new president, Peter Bonfield, that won't be a problem: "They are bloody fast. They can turn an idea into a product in a month."

Questions:

1. Characterize the policy by which CEO Bert Roberts runs his company. Do you consider this a strong policy on which to base MCI's future? Explain.

2. Is the plan devised by MCI to take advantage of the new communications environment a *standing plan* or a *single-use plan?* Explain, using definitions and diagrams from the text section entitled "Types of Plans."

3. Describe the forecasting process used by MCI to develop diversification plans. Review the text description of the five actions Insect Control Services took to forecast the future environment of its industry. What forecasting steps do you believe MCI followed in its planning procedures?

4. Consider all the products that MCI now offers from long-distance service to entertainment packages, and place each product on the *product life cycle*. What can MCI do to extend the life of the products on the far end of the curve and bring to maturity those at the beginning of the curve?

Skills Exercise

MCI must implement a number of new programs to meet the needs of the burgeoning communications market. Most of these projects must work together smoothly to provide customers with a bundle of services on one bill. Create a PERT network diagram showing possible sequences that MCI would follow to achieve its objectives. Share these in class and discuss the pros and cons of each of the plans. As a class, design the most beneficial network of activities for MCI.

The Internet learning materials that accompany this chapter can be found at
http://www.profcerto.com
Additional information can be found on the inside front and back covers of this text.

Planning in the Coming Home Division at Lands' End

This is the third case in this book that explores a variety of management-related issues at the well-known direct-retailing company Lands' End. The first installment (on pp. 24–26) is designed to be a general introduction. You may want to refer to it when you are studying the cases that appear at the end of each part of the book.

Beginning in 1989, three new specialty catalogs were launched at Lands' End. While two of these, Lands' End Kids and Beyond Buttondowns (men's tailored), were extensions of the main line in clothing, Coming Home moved Lands' End in a new direction. The Coming Home division markets primarily items for bed and bath. According to managing director Phil Young, the home textile focus was originally envisioned by Lands' End founder Gary Comer and former CEO Dick Anderson in late 1988 or early 1989. "They decided to start a home business," explains Young,

> because they recognized opportunity in the marketplace. The 12 to 13 major mills that had existed in the early 80s were being consolidated—eventually into three major mills. For example, Cannon and Fieldcrest have been consolidated into Fieldcrest-Cannon, Westpoint and Stephens into Westpoint-Stephens, and so forth. As all of this was happening, the major focus in the mills was simply to keep them running—more and more emphasis was placed on efficiency and less and less emphasis on quality. So, just as had been true for Lands' End with apparel, the same opportunity now existed in terms of home textiles. With expertise in both textiles and in cut-and-sew, it was a natural fit for us.

The mission at Coming Home (CH) is quite similar to the main company's: to provide the highest-quality home textiles and exceed customer expectations. "Strategically," says Young,

> we see ourselves in a fairly unique position in the marketplace. Everything we do with our product, with our service, and in positioning the company, relates to building an edge over our competition. Further, to position ourselves successfully in home textiles, we felt that we had to be successful in the bedding market—specifically sheets.

To accomplish this strategic objective—in a sense, to create a better sheet—CH management analyzed the entire sheet market. What they came up with was a sheet with totally unique construction: CH fitted sheets feature 12-inch-deep pockets and a 2-to-1 stretch ratio on the elastic that goes fully around the bed; flat sheets are 6 inches longer than standard sheets so that they stay tucked in. The CH sheet is thus promoted as "the sheet that fits." This approach, says Young,

> provides an edge for all Coming Home products—meeting the needs of the customer. For example, our blankets are 6 inches longer than any other blanket in the industry. We don't want to build in features and bells and whistles that no one really needs. We are trying to make sure that our products and services match the true needs of the customer.

Product development in the Coming Home division goes through several steps. First, the development team identifies what members believe to be a need or an opportunity in the marketplace. Next, they focus on the company mission—to develop the best product for that end use. Then they shop all the major markets and examine the competition. Contact with potential customers is made either informally, through customer comments that are summarized on a monthly basis, or more formally, through focus groups. The resulting information is then analyzed and summarized. Finally, a search is conducted for a vendor with the technical expertise to produce the product in question. Phil Young describes one such vendor search:

> In an effort to maintain our edge in the sheet market, in January of 1993 we began looking for a mill that could produce a sheet of outstanding quality. Our travels took

us to a home-textile show in Europe. We were hoping to identify one of the finest mills in the world and we found one in Switzerland. What they were selling was not appropriate for us, but we worked with them and identified what we were looking for. Their technical people and our product people started developing ideas for samples of various products. We had, I believe, two or three different runs of various weaves. It took a year and a half to bring it to market, but we ultimately created a really fine Swiss sateen. We think it's the finest sheet sold in the United States today.

Wear-testing of developed products is carried out using six to ten Coming Home employees. This process usually includes the product manager for that category, the quality-assurance manager, and the selling team (including the art director and the copywriter). According to Young, "We can only tell our customers, 'It's the best, or it does this or that,' if we've tried it ourselves." In addition, CH will solicit customers to help with wear-testing. In answering customer calls, CH often sends out items free of charge in order to get other feedback.

According to Phil Young, strategic planning in the CH division begins with SWOT Analysis—identifying the strengths, the weaknesses, the opportunities, and the threats.

Then we come up with the top five or so critical issues for the division. One issue is always the "edge." Our just-completed SWOT analysis indicated that our competitors were catching up—chipping away at the "edge." So, to identify all the elements of the edge, we listed the strengths and weaknesses that we have and what we *needed to do* to reinforce that edge. Then we set up a timeline and set some specific goals in order to address everything we had to do in order to stay ahead of the competition.

Coming Home has been fairly successful in the last five years—a fact that has not gone unnoticed by the competitors. "No one," says Young,

has gone the full nine yards, but one major competitor now has what they call an "Ultrafirm Sheet," and another sells a deep-pocket sheet for I believe $3.99. And in service, until recently we were the only home-textile catalog to offer two-business day UPS shipping at no additional charge. In August 1995 another competitor launched a home catalog and they now have picked up on that.

Competition also is copying how we present products in our catalogs. We have a certain way of merchandising our product: We make the product the hero—show the product, focus on the product, and explain in great detail all the benefits of the product. Using this approach, we know that we really have to communicate and establish a rapport with the customer.

As mentioned earlier, once Coming Home management has identified something as a "critical issue," they try to understand exactly what is going on in the marketplace, what the competition is doing, and what has changed in the marketplace. "One thing that we have learned," explains Young,

is that change is a constant. What we had in place before may no longer be appropriate. So we basically do an analysis of competition. Using focus groups (both buyers and nonbuyers), we get a much better idea of what customers really want. Then we put some action steps into place that will permit us to stay one step ahead of the competition. Strategic planning has helped us to be innovative and stay a step ahead.

At the same time, while the planning process at Coming Home is formal, the plans that are actually implemented must be flexible. "When I came to Lands' End eight years ago," Phil Young reports,

I would just go blindly forward to carry out the plan that was in place. Then, one day Gary Comer took me aside and explained how he felt planning implementation should be approached. He is a big sailor and was, I believe, a gold medalist in sailing in the Mexican Olympic games. His explanation of flexibility in planning went something like this. "In any sailboat race, you know where the start and finish are, but when you are racing, things change. So as the wind changes or competition makes a move, you have to change to counter those actions. That is the flexibility that you need to have to execute a plan. You can't just have tunnel vision and say this is the plan we have

in place and this is the way it is going to be. Things are changing daily and weekly and you've got to react and respond to those things."

The point of the story is that change is occurring all the time. You have to balance where you are going and how you are going to get there (which is the plan) with adapting and adjusting to what is happening as you move along. With planning, however, it's not just a knee-jerk reaction to what is happening; it's more of a *proactive* approach. While you may be bouncing back and forth a bit, you have to anticipate where all the bouncing will take you and plan your next step.

Here is an example of what flexibility means at Coming Home. In 1995, plans in the window-treatments area at CH were not working out exactly as anticipated. As Phil Young puts it,

we sort of stepped back, regrouped, and began to prepare for 1996. Home textiles is a $14.8-billion industry, with window treatments $5.5 billion of that. Obviously, window treatments is one area on which we'll be focusing for the coming year—it's quite simply the sheer size of the opportunity.

The window-treatment market is comprised of soft- and hard-window treatments—draperies versus venetian blinds. In the drapery area, there are essentially three types available—ready-made, made-to-measure, and custom-made. That's the way that it's been for a long time. Ready-mades tend to be of lesser quality but are available on order. Made-to-measures are of slightly better quality, manufactured to customer specifications, and require 4 to 6 weeks for delivery. Custom-mades are high quality, typically require the assistance of an interior designer or window expert when ordering, and usually have longer delivery dates.

According to Young, the strategic plan for window treatments at Coming Home in 1996 is to create an entirely new drapery category: in other words, to provide a product and a service that currently are unavailable in window treatments. "If our strategic plan is approved," he explains,

we will be offering window treatments that actually fit the precise dimensions of windows. They will be of custom-made quality in terms of fabrication, they will be in stock, and the customer will be able to order them to virtually any size or dimension. Again, we are able to do this because we can totally eliminate the middleman and the incredible markup that goes along with it. So, now we are looking at the services that will be needed to support our new idea. If we remove the interior decorator from the picture, how will we fill that void? Our plan is to train a dozen or so of our own employees and make them "window experts." In our scheme of things, they will take the place of the interior decorator. While they will not be available 24 hours each day, we will publish their hours.

We know that many customers are willing to do decorating jobs themselves to save money. If we can give the customer the knowledge—explain how to do the job and give them the right product—I think we can be quite successful with this venture.

Does Phil Young expect this new venture to be successful? Yes, but not immediately. "When we get into a business like that," he admits,

we don't really expect it to make a huge profit right away. A product team, led by a product manager, will put together a three-year plan that includes expected sales volume, amount of warehouse space, product assortment, and profit down to the pre-tax level. We may not make money the first or even the second year. But as long as we have a well-thought-out plan to follow and see the potential for profit, we'll invest in it.

Questions:

1. Applying what you have learned from your text, what can you say about planning in the Coming Home division at Lands' End?
2. More specifically, what strategy did Coming Home use for window treatments in 1995? Explain. If its strategic plan is approved, what strategy will CH use in its window-treatments area over the next three years? Which of Porter's three

generic strategies is being used in the window-treatments area at Coming Home to make it more competitive? Explain.

3. From everything that you have read in this case, for what purpose is planning carried out in the Coming Home division at Lands' End, Inc.? Explain.

4. Consider the statement made by LE founder Gary Comer: "So as the wind changes or competition makes a move, you have to change to counter those actions." What basic principle of effective and efficient planning does this philosophy reflect? Explain.

10 chapter

part 3
Organizing

FUNDAMENTALS OF ORGANIZING

STUDENT LEARNING OBJECTIVES

From studying this chapter, I will attempt to acquire:

1. An understanding of the organizing function.
2. An appreciation for the complexities of determining appropriate organizational structure.
3. Insights on the advantages and disadvantages of division of labor.
4. A working knowledge of the relationship between division of labor and coordination.
5. An understanding of span of management and the factors that influence its appropriateness.
6. An understanding of scalar relationships.

CHAPTER OUTLINE

Introductory Case: MCI Communications Organizes to Be More Competitive

A Definition of Organizing
The Importance of Organizing
The Organizing Process
The Organizing Subsystem

Classical Organizing Theory
Structure

People Perspectives: New Organization Chart at Northrop Grumman Helps Managers Explain a Newly Formed Organization

Global Spotlight: Crown Cork & Seal Company Organizes by Territory to Boost International Expansion

Division of Labor

Quality Spotlight: Mercedes-Benz Improves Coordination to Improve Product Quality

Span of Management

Cutting Edge: Flatter Organizations and the New Middle Managers of the 1990s

Scalar Relationships

MCI Communications Organizes to Be More Competitive

MCI Communications Corporation, headquartered in Washington, D.C., provides a wide spectrum of domestic and international voice and data communication services. For residential customers, the company offers long-distance opportunities like PrimeTime and SuperSaver. For business customers, communication opportunities provided by MCI enable businesspeople to strengthen relationships between customers and suppliers and to eliminate the traditional communications barriers of time and distance. MCI is the only telecommunications services company offering a full spectrum of voice, data messaging, and fax services with international capability. Facing vigorous competition and a sluggish economy, the company announced in late 1990 that it was restructuring operations and might lay off 1,500 employees nationwide over the next six months.

The long-distance company decided to revamp operations along commercial and residential lines by setting up a Business Markets unit and a Consumer Markets unit. The business unit has four divisions, pared down from seven. In addition, a newly established Network Services organization will meet new demands of both the business and consumer units.

The streamlining, which gives MCI a structure more like AT&T's, is intended to allow managers to react more swiftly to competition and position the company for growth. The previous structure, with seven regions corresponding to the seven regional Bell companies, has proven unwieldy as AT&T has sharpened efforts to stem further erosion of its share of the long-distance market. That share had dropped to around 70 percent of the $50 billion to $55 billion market by 1990.

Bert C. Roberts, Jr., MCI president, said the reorganization was driven by "our recognition of the changing conditions that most businesses are experiencing" and the demands of a more competitive marketplace. He said that MCI expects to grow more rapidly than the overall market for long-distance service.

AT&T is probably the most formidable competitor standing in the way of MCI's realization of its aggressive growth expectations. AT&T has swept top honors in *Data Communications* magazine's annual reader survey of U.S. long-distance customers. As the nation's largest carrier, AT&T continues to outpace its rivals in both network performance and customer service. If it is to grow significantly, therefore, MCI must directly confront AT&T.

Bert Roberts, CEO of MCI Communications, wants to take advantage of his company's flexibility to expand it. Although MCI now only carries long-distance phone calls, Roberts believes it can become a diversified communications company.

The introductory case describes how MCI is reorganizing in order to be more competitive. Information in this chapter would be useful to a manager like Bert C. Roberts, Jr., who is contemplating organizing issues. This chapter defines organizing and describes the principles of classical organizing theory that can help managers to organize a company.

A DEFINITION OF ORGANIZING

Organizing is the process of establishing orderly uses for all the organization's resources.

Organizing is the process of establishing orderly uses for all resources within the management system. Orderly uses emphasize the attainment of management system objectives and assist managers not only in making objectives apparent but also in clarifying which resources will be used to attain them. A primary focus of organizing is determining both what individual employees will do in an organization and how their individual efforts should best be combined to advance the attainment of organizational objectives.[1] *Organization* refers to the result of the organizing process.

Fayol's Guidelines   In essence, each organizational resource represents an investment from which the management system must get a return. Appropriate organization of these resources increases the efficiency and effectiveness of their use. Henri Fayol developed 16 general guidelines for organizing resources:[2]

1. Judiciously prepare and execute the operating plan.
2. Organize the human and material facets so that they are consistent with objectives, resources, and requirements of the concern.
3. Establish a single competent, energetic guiding authority (formal management structure).
4. Coordinate all activities and efforts.
5. Formulate clear, distinct, and precise decisions.
6. Arrange for efficient selection so that each department is headed by a competent, energetic manager and all employees are placed where they can render the greatest service.
7. Define duties.
8. Encourage initiative and responsibility.
9. Offer fair and suitable rewards for services rendered.
10. Make use of sanctions against faults and errors.
11. Maintain discipline.
12. Ensure that individual interests are consistent with the general interests of the organization.
13. Recognize the unity of command.
14. Promote both material and human coordination.
15. Institute and effect controls.
16. Avoid regulations, red tape, and paperwork.

The Importance of Organizing

The organizing function is extremely important to the management system because it is the primary mechanism managers use to activate plans. Organizing creates and maintains relationships between all organizational resources by indicating which resources are to be used for specified activities and when, where, and how they are to be used. A thorough organizing effort helps managers minimize costly weaknesses, such as duplication of effort and idle organizational resources.

Some management theorists consider the organizing function so important that they advocate the creation of an organizing department within the management system. Typical responsibilities of this department would include developing the following:[3]

At Frito-Lay's Lubbock, Texas, plant, reorganization has meant slashing the number of middle managers, increasing the hourly workforce by 20 percent, and introducing work teams to deal with most daily problems. Now, for example, employees serve on ten-person crews that perform tasks ranging from equipment maintenance to quality control to scheduling their own workloads.

1. Reorganization plans that make the management system more effective and efficient.
2. Plans to improve managerial skills to fit current management system needs.
3. An advantageous organizational climate within the management system.

The Organizing Process

The five main steps of the organizing process are presented in Figure 10.1:[4]

1. Reflect on plans and objectives.
2. Establish major tasks.
3. Divide major tasks into subtasks.
4. Allocate resources and directives for subtasks.
5. Evaluate the results of implemented organizing strategy.

As the figure implies, managers should continually repeat these steps. Through repetition, they obtain feedback that will help them improve the existing organization.

The management of a restaurant can serve as an illustration of how the organizing process works. The first step the restaurant manager would take to initiate the organizing process would be to reflect on the restaurant's plans and objectives. Because planning involves determining how the restaurant will attain its objectives, and orga-

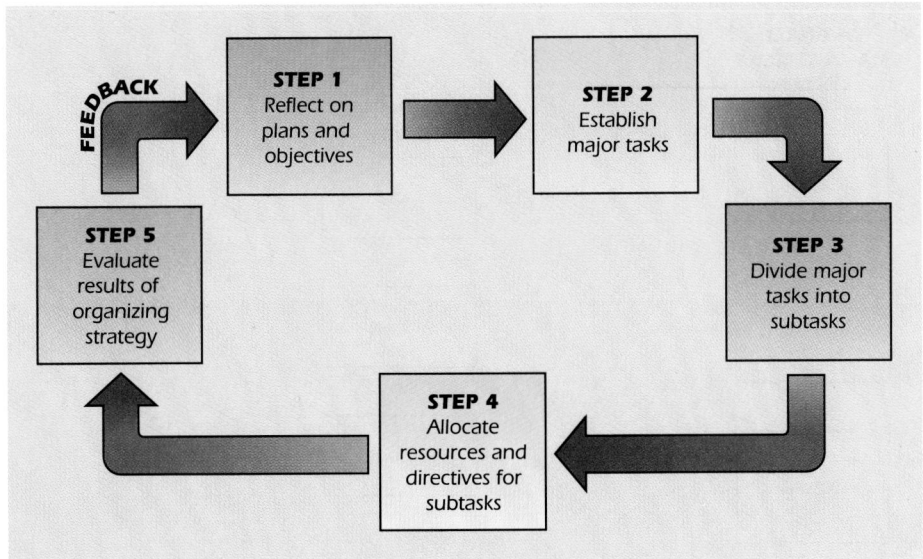

Figure 10.1 The five main steps of the organizing process

At Rock Bottom Restaurants Inc., which is owned by Denver-based Rock Bottom Brewery, the watchword in making many organizational decisions is service quality—management wants its outlets to be perceived as restaurants rather than taverns. Rock Bottom restaurants thus feature an unusual degree of teamwork: Employees back up each other's tables, rotate undesirable shifts, and even have approval before new hires pass probation and join the permanent staff.

nizing involves determining how the restaurant's resources will be used to activate plans, the restaurant manager must start to organize by understanding planning.

The second and third steps of the organizing process focus on tasks to be performed within the management system. The manager must designate major tasks or jobs to be done within the restaurant. Two such tasks are serving customers and cooking food. Then the tasks must be divided into subtasks. For example, the manager might decide that serving customers includes the subtasks of taking orders and clearing tables.

The fourth organizing step is determining who will take orders, who will clear the tables, and what the details of the relationship between these individuals will be. The size of tables and how they are to be set are other factors to be considered at this point.

In the fifth step, evaluating the results of the implemented organizing strategy, the manager gathers feedback on how well the strategy is working. This feedback should furnish information that can be used to improve the existing organization. For example, the manager may find that a particular type of table is not large enough and that larger ones must be purchased if the restaurant is to attain its goals.

The Organizing Subsystem

The organizing function, like the planning function, can be visualized as a subsystem of the overall management system (see Figure 10.2). The primary purpose of the organizing subsystem is to enhance the goal attainment of the general management sys-

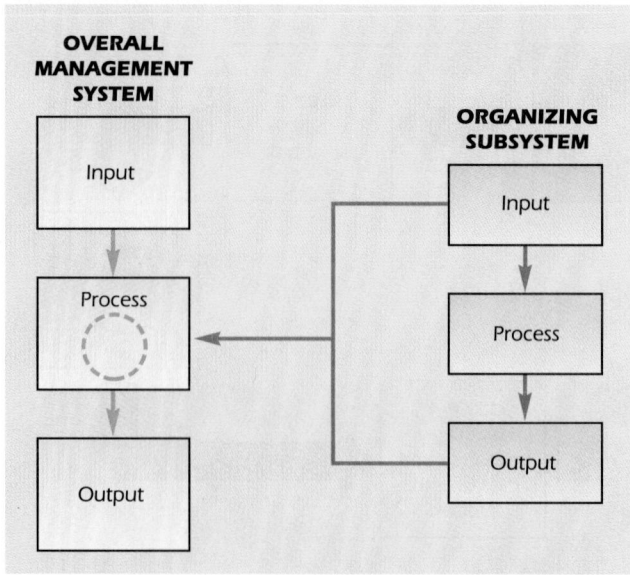

Figure 10.2   Relationships between overall management system and organizing subsystem

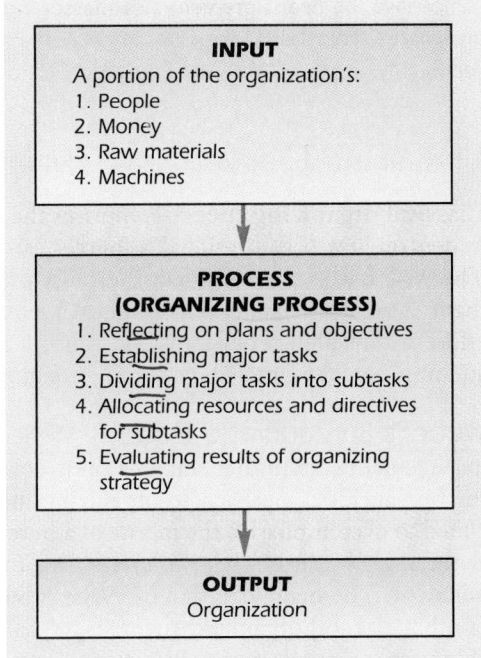

Figure 10.3   Organizing subsystem

tem by providing a rational approach for using organizational resources. Figure 10.3 presents the specific ingredients of the organizing subsystem. The input is a portion of the total resources of the organization, the process is the steps involved in the organizing function, and the output is organization.

BACK TO THE CASE   In contemplating how MCI should be organized, Bert C. Roberts can focus on answering questions aimed at establishing an orderly use of MCI's organizational resources. Because these resources represent an investment on which he must get a return, Roberts' questions should be geared toward gaining information that can be used to maximize this return. Overall, such questions should focus on determining what use of MCI's resources will best accomplish the organization's goals. Some preliminary questions might be as follows:

1. What are MCI's organizational objectives? For example, does MCI want to focus on international markets as well as domestic markets? Does MCI want to grow or to maintain its present size?
2. What plans does MCI have to accomplish these objectives? Is MCI going to open more offices abroad? Are additional training programs being added to enable employees to understand how best to work abroad?
3. What are the major tasks MCI must accomplish to offer message and voice products? For example, how many steps are involved in developing needed fax equipment and making it available to appropriate customers?
4. What resources does MCI have to run its operations? Answers to this question focus on such issues as number of employees, financial resources available, and equipment being used.

Roberts also should begin thinking of devising a mechanism for evaluating whatever organizing strategy he develops. Once the strategy is implemented, he must be able to obtain feedback on how all of MCI's resources are functioning so he can improve his organizing efforts. For example, Roberts may find that in order for MCI to become more

competitive, he needs greater voice-messaging capability in one country than in another and more employees in the Consumer Markets unit. With appropriate feedback, he can continually improve MCI's existing organizational system.

CLASSICAL ORGANIZING THEORY

Classical organizing theory comprises the cumulative insights of early management writers on how organizational resources can best be used to enhance goal attainment. The writer who probably had the most profound influence on classical organizing theory was Max Weber.[5] According to Weber, the main components of an organizing effort are detailed procedures and rules, a clearly outlined organizational hierarchy, and impersonal relationships among organization members.

Weber's Bureaucratic Model   Weber used the term **bureaucracy** to label the management system that contains these components. Although he firmly believed in the bureaucratic approach to organizing, he was concerned that managers were inclined to overemphasize the merits of a bureaucracy. He cautioned that a bureaucracy is not an end in itself, but rather a means to the end of management system goal attainment. The main criticism of Weber's bureaucracy model, as well as the concepts of other classical organizing theorists, is that they give short shrift to the human variable within organizations. In fact, it is recognized today that the bureaucratic approach without an appropriate emphasis on the human variable is almost certainly a formula for organizational failure.[6] Considerable discussion on this variable is presented in Chapters 13 through 18.

The rest of this chapter summarizes four main considerations of classical organizing theory that all modern managers should incorporate into their organizing efforts:

1. Structure
2. Division of labor
3. Span of management
4. Scalar relationships

Structure

In any organizing effort, managers must choose an appropriate structure. **Structure** refers to the designated relationships among resources of the management system. Its purpose is to facilitate the use of each resource, individually and collectively, as the management system attempts to attain its objectives.[7]

Organization structure is represented primarily by means of a graphic illustration called an **organization chart.** Traditionally, an organization chart is constructed in pyramid form, with individuals toward the top of the pyramid having more authority and responsibility than those toward the bottom.[8] The relative positioning of individuals within boxes on the chart indicates broad working relationships, and lines between boxes designate formal lines of communication between individuals.

Authority and Responsibility.   Figure 10.4 is an example of an organization chart. The dotted line is not part of the organization chart but has been added to emphasize the chart's pyramid shape. The position of restaurant manager is at the point of the pyramid, and those positions close to the restaurant manager's involve more authority and responsibility, while those positions farther away involve less authority and responsibility. The locations of positions also indicate broad working relationships. For example, the positioning of the head chef over the three other chefs indicates that the head chef has authority over them and is responsible for their productivity. The lines between the individual chefs and the restaurant manager indicate that formal communication from chef 1 to the restaurant manager must go through the head chef.

Classical organizing theory comprises the cumulative insights of early management writers on how organizational resources can best be used to enhance goal attainment.

Bureaucracy is the term Max Weber used to describe a management system characterized by detailed procedures and rules, a clearly outlined organizational hierarchy, and impersonal relationships among organization members.

Structure refers to the designated relationships among resources of the management system.

An **organization chart** is a graphic representation of organizational structure.

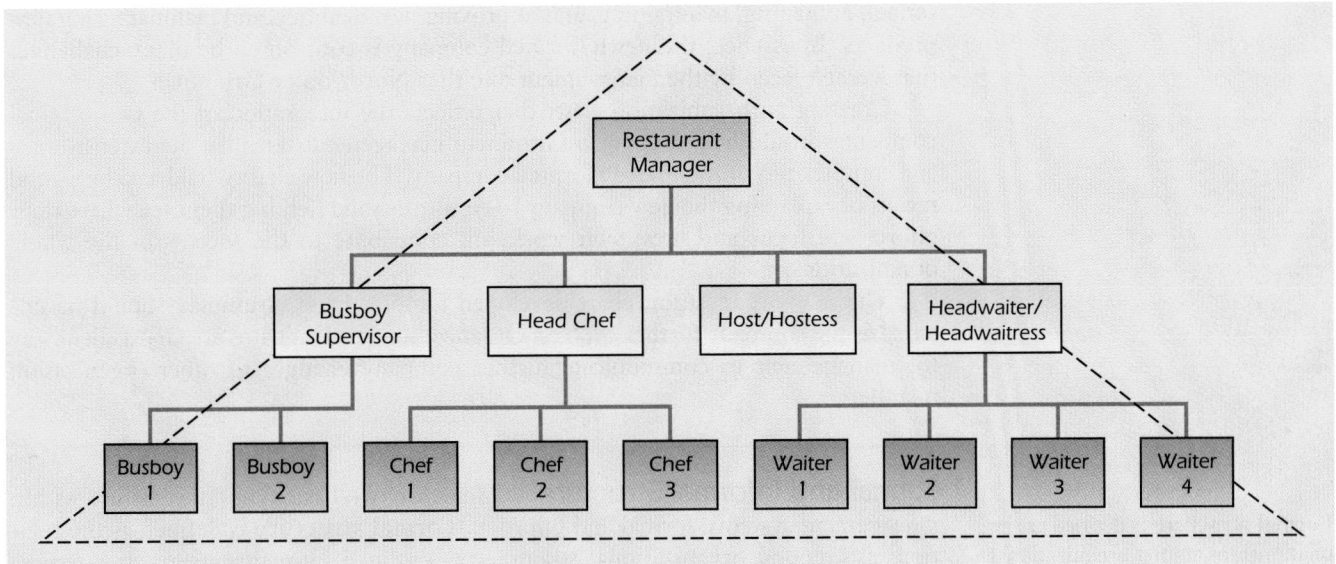

Figure 10.4   Sample organization chart for a small restaurant

Structure and Gender.   Pyramidal organization structures are probably modeled on the hierarchical structure of military command. In the Western world, the structure of organized religion has also been hierarchical, with authority derived from the top. Some researchers have found that women are not comfortable with this type of structure. As more and more women enter the management field, therefore, a new type of structural model may be needed. In *The Female Advantage: Women's Ways of Leadership*, Sally Helgesen postulates that women create networks or "webs" of authority and that women's leadership styles are relational rather than hierarchical and authoritarian. Management writer Tom Peters suggests that these styles are inherently better suited to the new kinds of organizational structures, featuring teamwork and participative management, required for the competitive global environment of the 1990s.[9]

Organization charts help managers achieve such commonly discussed competitive advantages as eliminating red tape and visualizing broad, logical relationships among job areas. The following PEOPLE PERSPECTIVES feature presents a much less discussed advantage of the organization chart: It is a vehicle for communicating the main points of a newly formed or changing organization.

NEW ORGANIZATION CHART AT NORTHROP GRUMMAN HELPS MANAGERS EXPLAIN A NEWLY FORMED ORGANIZATION

PEOPLE PERSPECTIVES   Northrop Corporation's recent multibillion-dollar buyout of Grumman Corporation has resulted in the formation of a giant new aerospace company called Northrop Grumman Corporation. The new company, based in Los Angeles, designs, develops, and manufactures aircraft, aircraft subassemblies, and electronic systems for use in commercial and military aircraft. With 29,800 employees, it is one of about 12 major companies in this industry.

The most obvious result of Northrop's purchase is immediate organization growth. This growth has given rise to such management issues as managing new per-

sonnel, evaluating, maintaining, and improving new facilities, and manufacturing new products. In essence, the newly formed company is confronted by many challenges that weren't faced by the management of either Northrop or Grumman.

Creating an organization chart that reflects the integration of the two original companies would help Northrop Grumman management visualize the extensiveness and complexities of their newly formed company. The new chart would also be a good means of explaining the new company to employees and helping them see where their efforts will focus and how their work will contribute to the success of the whole organization.

The new organization chart developed for Northrop Grumman should be updated as the company further evolves. Organization chart updates are an excellent way for management to communicate further company changes to other organization members.≈

Formal and Informal Structure

Formal structure is defined as the relationships among organizational resources as outlined by management.

Informal structure is defined as the patterns of relationships that develop because of the informal activities of organization members.

There are two basic types of structure within management systems: formal and informal. **Formal structure** is defined as the relationships among organizational resources as outlined by management. It is represented primarily by the organization chart.

Informal structure is defined as the patterns of relationships that develop because of the informal activities of organization members. It evolves naturally and tends to be molded by individual norms and values and social relationships. Essentially, an organization's informal structure is the system or network of interpersonal relationships that exists within, but is not usually identical to, the organization's formal structure.[10] This chapter focuses on formal structure. Details on informal structure are presented in Chapter 17.

Departmentalization and Formal Structure: A Contingency Viewpoint

A **department** is a unique group of resources established by management to perform some organizational task.

Departmentalization is the process of establishing departments within the management system.

The most common method of instituting formal relationships among resources is to establish departments. Basically, a **department** is a unique group of resources established by management to perform some organizational task. The process of establishing departments within the management system is called **departmentalization.** Typically, these departments are based on, or contingent upon, such situational factors as the work functions being performed, the product being assembled, the territory being covered, the customer being targeted, and the process designed for man-

Top management at GE Appliances headquarters in Louisville, Kentucky, uses such technologies as worldwide teleconferencing as more than communications tools: They are in fact one means of recognizing fundamental changes in the organization of today's big businesses. According to many experts, such factors as global markets and advances in communication are forcing businesses to reorganize more radically than at any time since the 1950s, when the multidivision corporation became commonplace.

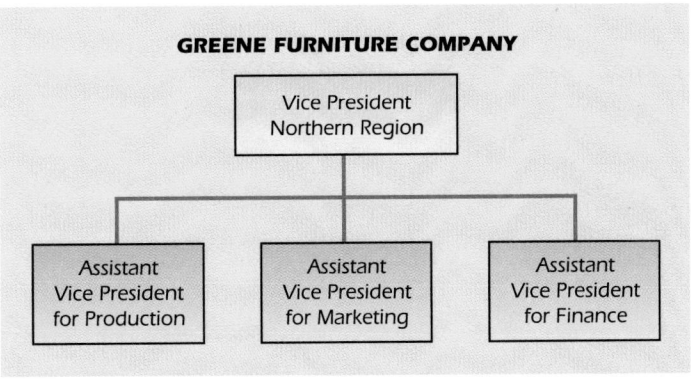

Figure 10.5 Organization structure based primarily on function

ufacturing the product. (For a quick review of the contingency approach to management, see chapter 2.)

Functional Departmentalization Perhaps the most widely used basis for establishing departments within the formal structure is the type of *work functions* (activities) being performed within the management system.[11] Functions are typically divided into the major categories of marketing, production, and finance. Figure 10.5 is an organization chart showing structure based primarily on function for a hypothetical organization, Greene Furniture Company.

Product Departmentalization Organization structure based primarily on *product* departmentalizes resources according to the products being manufactured. As more and more products are manufactured by a company, it becomes increasingly difficult for management to coordinate activities across the organization. Organizing according to product permits the logical grouping of resources necessary to produce each product. Figure 10.6 is an organization chart for Greene Furniture Company showing structure based primarily on product.

Geographic Departmentalization Structure based primarily on *territory* departmentalizes according to the places where the work is being done or the geographic markets on which the management system is focusing. The physical distances can range from quite short (between two points in the same city) to quite long (between two points in the same state, in different states, or even in different countries).[12] As market areas and work locations expand, the physical distances between places can make the management task extremely cumbersome. To minimize this problem, resources can be departmentalized according to territory. Figure 10.7 is an organization chart for Greene Furniture Company based primarily on territory.

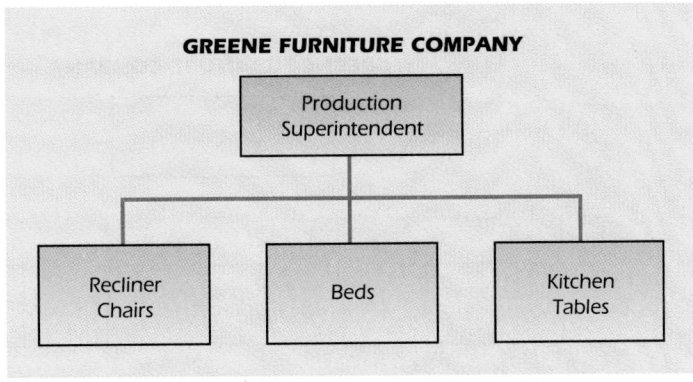

Figure 10.6 Organization structure based primarily on product

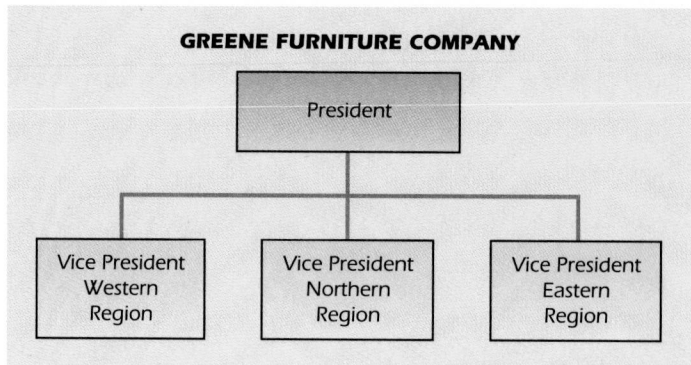

Figure 10.7   Organization structure based primarily on territory

CROWN CORK & SEAL COMPANY ORGANIZES BY TERRITORY TO BOOST INTERNATIONAL EXPANSION

The Crown Cork & Seal Company, headquartered in Philadelphia, Pennsylvania, manufactures and sells a variety of food and beverage packaging containers as well as packaging machinery. The company has designed its structure to ensure its continued international growth.

Crown Cork & Seal has experienced substantial international growth in recent years, virtually doubling its global sales to an estimated $3.8 billion. Today the company has 141 plants in 32 countries. When John F. Connelly took it over in 1956, it had worldwide sales of $100 million and a heavy debt load that brought it close to collapse. By 1962, Crown was relatively debt-free and positioned for growth, with the beverage industry as its main target. To focus organizational resources and efforts on continued organizational growth in the global arena, Connelly restructured the company into two basic divisions: North America and International. Present international efforts focus on Hong Kong, the People's Republic of China, Korea, Venezuela, and Saudi Arabia.≈

Customer Departmentalization   Structure based primarily on the *customer* establishes departments in response to the organization's major customers. This structure, of course, assumes that major customers can be identified and divided into logical categories. Figure 10.8 is an organization chart for Greene Furniture Company based primarily on customers. Greene Furniture obviously can clearly identify its customers and divide them into logical categories.

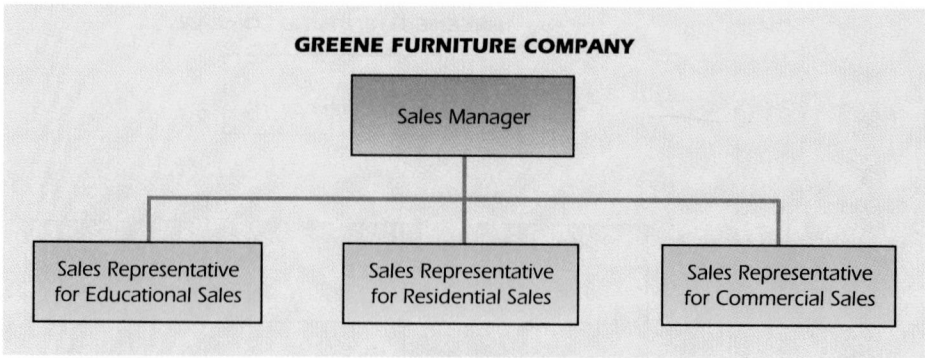

Figure 10.8   Organization structure based primarily on customers

GREENE FURNITURE COMPANY
Production Superintendent
Woodcutting Department
Sanding Department
Gluing Department
Painting Department

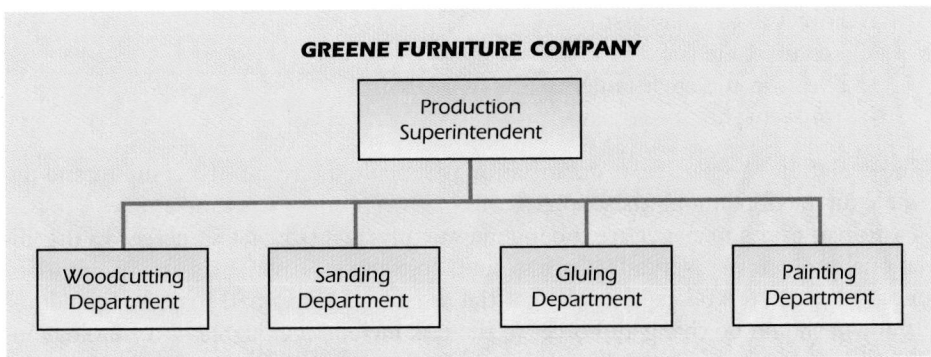

Figure 10.9 Organization structure based primarily on manufacturing process

Manufacturing Process Departmentalization Structure based primarily on *manufacturing process* departmentalizes according to the major phases of the process used to manufacture products. In the case of Greene Furniture Company, the major phases are woodcutting, sanding, gluing, and painting. Figure 10.9 is the organization chart that reflects these phases.

If the situation warrants it, individual organization charts can be combined to show all five of these factors. Figure 10.10 shows how all the factors are included on the same organization chart for Greene Furniture Company.

Forces Influencing Formal Structure According to Shetty and Carlisle, the formal structure of a management system is continually evolving. Four primary forces influence this evolution:[13]

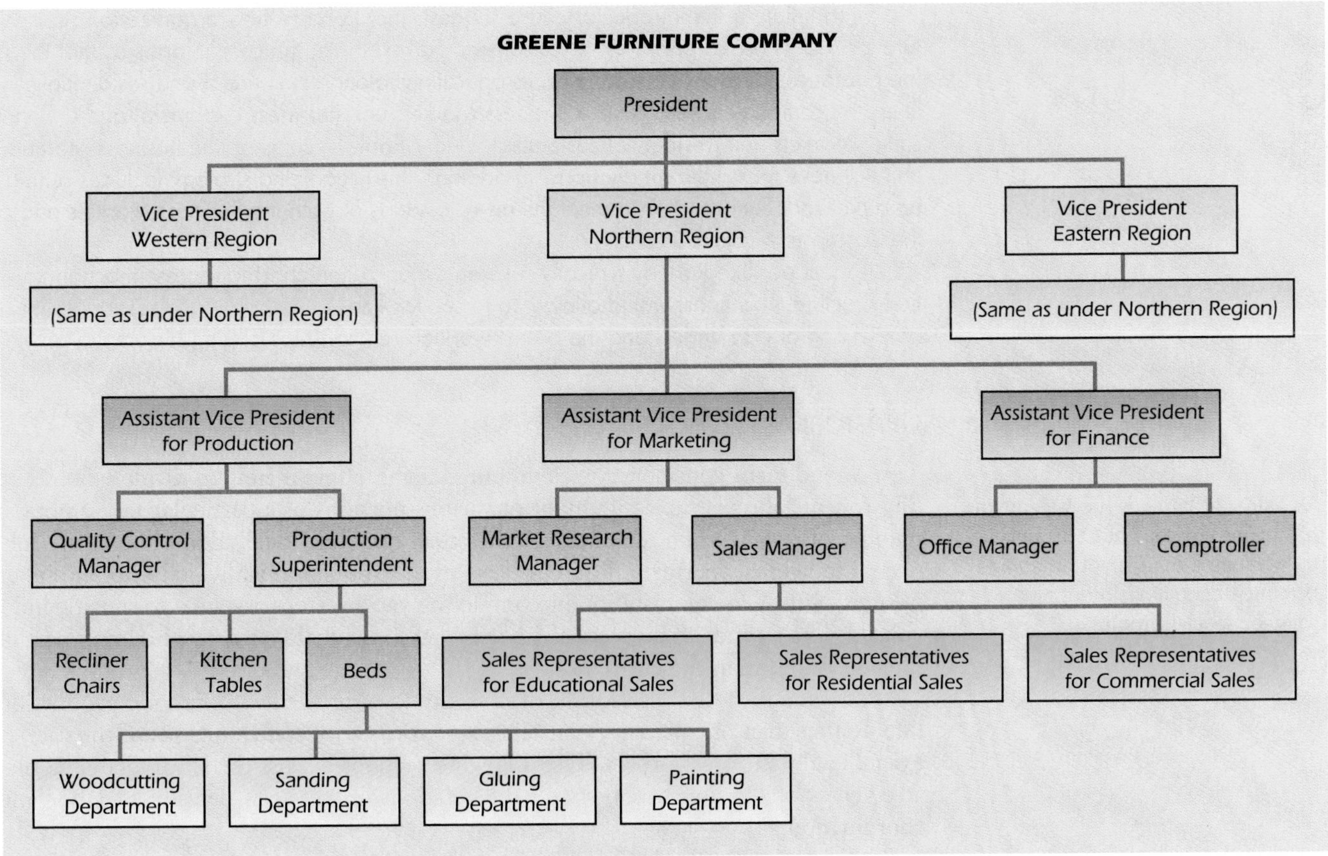

GREENE FURNITURE COMPANY
President
Vice President Western Region
Vice President Northern Region
Vice President Eastern Region
(Same as under Northern Region)
(Same as under Northern Region)
Assistant Vice President for Production
Assistant Vice President for Marketing
Assistant Vice President for Finance
Quality Control Manager
Production Superintendent
Market Research Manager
Sales Manager
Office Manager
Comptroller
Recliner Chairs
Kitchen Tables
Beds
Sales Representatives for Educational Sales
Sales Representatives for Residential Sales
Sales Representatives for Commercial Sales
Woodcutting Department
Sanding Department
Gluing Department
Painting Department

Figure 10.10 Combined organization chart for Greene Furniture Company

1. Forces in the manager.
2. Forces in the task.
3. Forces in the environment.
4. Forces in the subordinates.

The evolution of a particular organization is actually the result of a complex and dynamic interaction among these forces.

Forces in the manager are the unique way in which a manager perceives organizational problems.[14] Naturally, background, knowledge, experience, and values influence the manager's perception of what the organization's formal structure should be or how it should be changed. Forces in the task include the degree of technology involved in performing the task and the task's complexity. As task activities change, a force is created to change the existing organization. Forces in the environment include the customers and suppliers of the management system, along with existing political and social structures. Forces in the subordinates include the needs and skill levels of subordinates. Obviously, as the environment and subordinates change, forces are created simultaneously to change the organization.

BACK TO THE CASE   A manager engaged in an organizing effort should take classical organizing theory into consideration. Of the four major elements of classical organizing theory, the first to be considered is structure. Roberts' considerations regarding the structure of MCI would be aimed at creating working relationships among all MCI employees. To develop an effective organizational structure, he must analyze situational factors in the company, such as functions, products, geographic locations, customers, and processes involved in offering its products to customers.

Information in the introductory case suggests that Roberts' new organization structure for MCI is based primarily on customers. For example, the case informs us that the long-distance company is revamping its operations along commercial and residential lines; the company is setting up a Business Markets unit (business customers) and a Consumer Markets unit (residential customers). Under Roberts' concept, the Business Markets unit will have four different divisions. In addition, his organizing strategy includes setting up a Network Services unit to meet the new demands of both the Business Markets and the Consumer Markets units.

A manager like Roberts typically uses an organization chart to represent organization structure. This chart would allow him to see the lines of authority and responsibility at MCI and also to understand the broad working relationships among his employees.

Division of Labor

Division of labor is the assignment of various portions of a particular task among a number of organization members. Division of labor calls for specialization.

The second main consideration of any organizing effort is how to divide labor. The **division of labor** is the assignment of various portions of a particular task among a number of organization members. Rather than one individual's doing the entire job, several individuals perform different parts of it. Production is divided into a number of steps, with the responsibility for completing various steps assigned to specific individuals. The essence of division of labor is that individuals specialize in doing part of the task rather than the entire task.

A commonly used illustration of division of labor is the automobile production line. Rather than one person assembling an entire car, specific portions of the car are assembled by various workers. The following sections discuss the advantages and disadvantages of division of labor and the relationship between division of labor and coordination.

Advantages and Disadvantages of Division of Labor   Even the peerless physicist Albert Einstein, famous for his independent theorizing, believed that division of labor could be very advantageous in many undertakings.[15] Several explanations have been offered for the usefulness of division of labor. First, when workers specialize in a particular task, their skill at performing that task tends to increase. Second, workers who have one job and one place in which to do it do not lose valuable time changing tools or locations. Third, when workers concentrate on performing only one job, they naturally try to make the job easier and more efficient. Last, division of labor creates a situation in which workers need only to know how to perform their part of the work task rather than the entire process for producing the end product. The task of understanding their work, therefore, does not become too burdensome.

Arguments have also been presented against the use of an extreme division of labor.[16] Essentially, these arguments contend that division of labor focuses solely on efficiency and economic benefit and overlooks the human variable in organizations. Work that is extremely specialized tends to be boring and therefore will eventually cause production rates to go down as workers become resentful of being treated like machines. Clearly, managers need to find a reasonable balance between specialization and human motivation. How to arrive at this balance is discussed in Chapter 16.

Division of Labor and Coordination   In a division-of-labor situation, the importance of effective coordination of the different individuals doing portions of the task is obvious. Mooney has defined **coordination** as "the orderly arrangement of group effort to provide unity of action in the pursuit of a common purpose." In essence, coordination is a means for achieving any and all organizational objectives.[17] It involves encouraging the completion of individual portions of a task in a synchronized order that is appropriate for the overall task. Groups cannot maintain their productivity without coordination.[18] Part of the synchronized order of assembling an automobile, for example, is that seats are installed only after the floor has been installed; adhering to this order of installation is an example of coordination.

Establishing and maintaining coordination may require close supervision of employees, though managers should try to break away from the idea that coordination can only be achieved this way.[19] They can, instead, establish and maintain coordination through bargaining, formulating a common purpose for the group, or improving on specific problem solutions so the group will know what to do when it encounters those problems. Each of these efforts is considered a specific management tool.

Follett's Guidelines on Coordination.   Mary Parker Follett provided valuable advice on how managers can establish and maintain coordination within the organization. First, Follett said that coordination can be attained with the least difficulty through direct horizontal relationships and personal communications. In other words, when a coordination problem arises, peer discussion may be the best way to resolve it. Second, Follett suggested that coordination be a discussion topic throughout the planning process. In essence, managers should plan for coordination. Third, maintaining coordination is a continuing process and should be treated as such. Managers cannot assume that because their management system shows coordination today it will show coordination tomorrow.

Follett also noted that coordination can be achieved only through purposeful management action—it cannot be left to chance. Finally, she stressed the importance of the human element and advised that the communication process is an essential consideration in any attempt to encourage coordination. Employee skill levels and motivation levels are also primary considerations, as is the effectiveness of the human communication process used during coordination activities.[20]

Coordination is the orderly arrangement of group effort to provide unity of action in the pursuit of a common purpose. It involves encouraging the completion of individual portions of a task in an appropriate, synchronized order.

MERCEDES-BENZ IMPROVES COORDINATION TO IMPROVE PRODUCT QUALITY

QUALITY SPOTLIGHT

Improving coordination can improve the effectiveness and efficiency of the workforce in virtually any organization. Mercedes-Benz executives focus on improving coordination to improve product quality.

Although they acknowledge that new competitors such as Lexus and Infinity have made an impact in the upscale automobile market, Mercedes-Benz executives are neither discouraged nor digressing from decades-old organizational objectives. The company remains dedicated to the needs and wants of the upscale-but-unpretentious buyer who is looking for a vehicle that balances style and performance with form and function.

As in the past, the company will compete by remaining firmly committed to improving the overall quality of its products. Klaus-Dieter Vohringer, a member of the Mercedes-Benz top-management team, says the company will demonstrate this commitment to product quality through a plan that focuses on improving coordination among three different manufacturing and assembly plants. This major restructuring of the manufacturing process at Mercedes-Benz is expected to result not only in better product quality but also in more productive uses of existing facilities, quicker responses to changing customers' needs and competitive products, and lowered product costs. According to Vohringer, Mercedes-Benz has developed a sophisticated understanding of its customers over the years. In order to maintain a high level of customer satisfaction, management knows that it must constantly be on the alert for new methods of improving product quality, and is convinced that better coordination in the manufacturing process will help Mercedes-Benz achieve its quality goals.≈

BACK TO THE CASE

In developing the most appropriate way to organize MCI employees, Roberts can reflect on the second major element in classical organizing theory: division of labor. He could decide, for example, that instead of having one person do all the work involved in servicing a business customer, the labor could be divided so that, for each business customer, one person would make the initial contact, another would assess the communication needs of the organization, and a third person would explore the alternative ways MCI offers of meeting those needs. In this way, employees could work more quickly and could specialize in one area of business customer relations, such as assessing business needs or meeting the needs of business customers.

In considering the appropriateness of division of labor at MCI, Roberts might also consider creating a mechanism for enhancing coordination. To do this, however, he would need to have a thorough understanding of various MCI business processes so he could split up various tasks and maintain coordination within the different company divisions. He would also have to stress communication as a prerequisite for coordination, for unless MCI employees continually communicate with one another, coordination will be virtually impossible. Finally, to enhance organizational coordination, Roberts would also have to plan for and take action to maintain such coordination.

Span of Management

The **span of management** is the number of individuals a manager supervises.

The third main consideration of any organizing effort is **span of management**—the number of individuals a manager supervises. The more individuals a manager supervises, the greater the span of management. Conversely, the fewer individuals a man-

ager supervises, the smaller the span of management. The span of management has a significant effect on how well managers carry out their responsibilities. Span of management is also called *span of control, span of authority, span of supervision,* and *span of responsibility*.[21]

The central concern of span of management is to determine how many individuals a manager can supervise effectively. To use the organization's human resources effectively, managers should supervise as many individuals as they can best guide toward production quotas. If they are supervising too few people, they are wasting a portion of their productive capacity. If they are supervising too many, they are losing part of their effectiveness.

Designing Span of Management: A Contingency Viewpoint

As reported by Harold Koontz, several important situational factors influence the appropriateness of the size of an individual's span of management:[22]

- *Similarity of functions:* the degree to which activities performed by supervised individuals are similar or dissimilar. As the similarity of subordinates' activities increases, the span of management appropriate for the situation widens. The converse is also generally true.
- *Geographic contiguity:* the degree to which subordinates are physically separated. In general, the closer subordinates are physically, the more of them managers can supervise effectively.
- *Complexity of functions:* the degree to which workers' activities are difficult and involved. The more difficult and involved the activities are, the more difficult it is to manage a large number of individuals effectively.
- *Coordination:* the amount of time managers must spend synchronizing the activities of their subordinates with the activities of other workers. The greater the amount of time that must be spent on such coordination, the smaller the span of management should be.
- *Planning:* the amount of time managers must spend developing management system objectives and plans and integrating them with the activities of their subordinates. The more time managers must spend on planning activities, the fewer individuals they can manage effectively.

Table 10.1 summarizes the factors that tend to increase and decrease the span of management.

Graicunas and Span of Management

Perhaps the best-known contribution to span-of-management literature was made by the management consultant V. A. Graicunas.[23] He developed a formula for determining the number of *possible* relationships between a manager and subordinates when the number of subordinates is known. **Graicunas' formula** is as follows:

$$C = n\left(\frac{2^n}{2} + n - 1\right)$$

C is the total number of possible relationships between manager and subordinates, and *n* is the known number of subordinates. As the number of subordinates increases arithmetically, the number of possible relationships between the manager and those subordinates increases geometrically.

A number of criticisms have been leveled at Graicunas' work. Some have argued that he failed to take into account a manager's relationships outside the organization and that he considered only *potential* relationships rather than *actual* relationships. These criticisms have some validity, but the real significance of Graicunas' work lies outside them. His main contribution, in fact, was to point out that span of management is an important consideration that can have a far-reaching impact on the organization.

Graicunas' formula is a formula that makes the span-of-management point that as the number of a manager's subordinates increases arithmetically, the number of possible relationships between the manager and the subordinates increases geometrically.

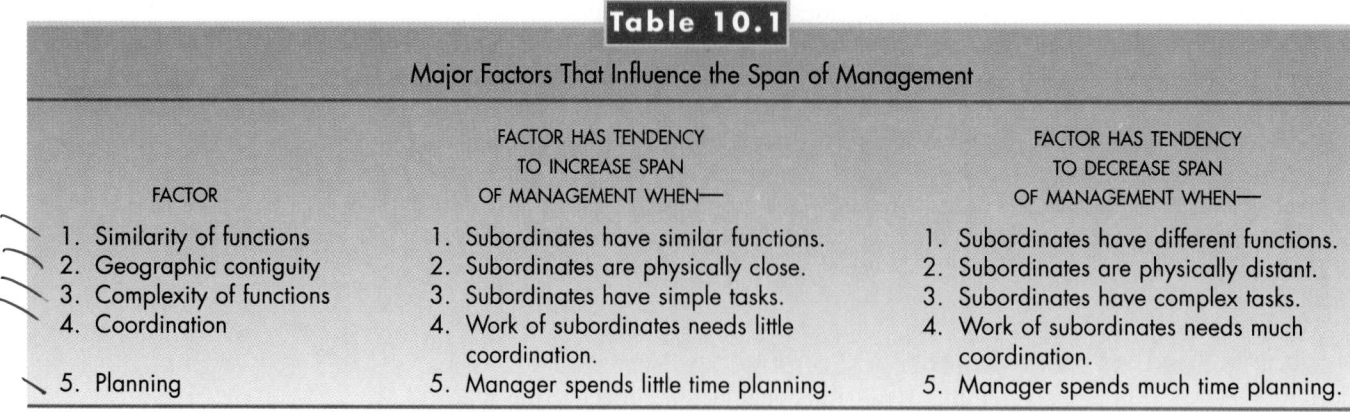

Table 10.1

Major Factors That Influence the Span of Management

FACTOR	FACTOR HAS TENDENCY TO INCREASE SPAN OF MANAGEMENT WHEN—	FACTOR HAS TENDENCY TO DECREASE SPAN OF MANAGEMENT WHEN—
1. Similarity of functions	1. Subordinates have similar functions.	1. Subordinates have different functions.
2. Geographic contiguity	2. Subordinates are physically close.	2. Subordinates are physically distant.
3. Complexity of functions	3. Subordinates have simple tasks.	3. Subordinates have complex tasks.
4. Coordination	4. Work of subordinates needs little coordination.	4. Work of subordinates needs much coordination.
5. Planning	5. Manager spends little time planning.	5. Manager spends much time planning.

A **flat organization chart** is an organization chart characterized by few levels and a relatively broad span of management.

A **tall organization chart** is an organization chart characterized by many levels and a relatively narrow span of management.

Height of Organization Chart   There is a definite relationship between span of management and the height of an organization chart. Normally, the greater the height of the organization chart, the smaller the span of management, and the lower the height of the chart, the greater the span of management.[24] Organization charts with little height are usually referred to as **flat,** while those with much height are usually referred to as **tall.**

Figure 10.11 is a simple example of the relationship between organization chart height and span of management. Organization chart A has a span of management of six, and organization chart B has a span of management of two. As a result, chart A is flatter than chart B. Note that both charts have the same number of individuals at the lowest level. The larger span of management in A is reduced in B merely by adding a level to B's organization chart.

An organization's structure should be built from top to bottom to ensure that appropriate spans of management are achieved at all levels. Increasing spans of management merely to eliminate certain management positions and thereby reduce salary expenses may prove to be a very shortsighted move. Increasing spans of management to achieve such objectives as speeding up organizational decision making and building a more flexible organization is more likely to help the organization achieve success in the long run.[25]

A survey of organization charts of the 1990s reveals that top managers are creating flatter organizational structures than top managers used in the 1980s. The following CUTTING EDGE feature discusses this trend in detail and considers the job of the middle manager in these new flatter structures.

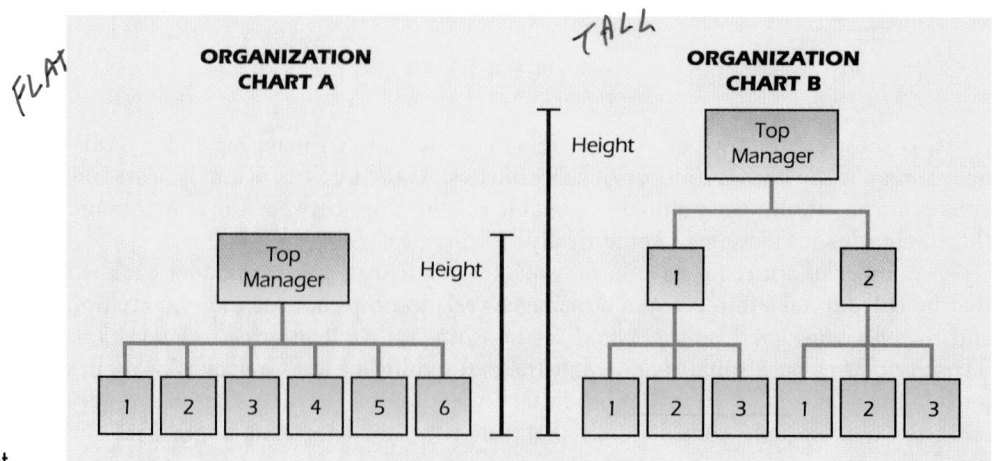

Figure 10.11   Relationship between organization chart height and span of management

Flatter Organizations and the New Middle Managers of the 1990s

CUTTING EDGE

An undeniable trend of the 1990s is to redesign organizations to include fewer and fewer middle managers. This trend is sometimes referred to as *downsizing* or *rightsizing*—reducing the organization structure to an appropriate size. As one example of this trend, the publishing giant Times Mirror recently announced that in order to trim expenses, 1,000 staff members (including middle managers) were being eliminated from its seven newspapers, the most notable of which is the *Los Angeles Times*.

Middle managers in the flatter organization of the 1990s face several challenges generally not encountered by middle managers of the 1980s. First of all, by definition, the flatter organizations include fewer middle managers, so each middle manager will have to manage a greater number of subordinates than before. Second, with more subordinates to manage, it is impossible to do the kind of close supervision that was feasible in the taller organizations of the 1980s. Therefore, middle managers today must involve employees more fully in organizational decision making and build them into functioning, productive teams.

Finally, middle managers confront several challenges that are more urgent today than they were in the 1980s. One is the need to understand global issues as they impact on organizational success. Another is the necessity to learn how to use new information technologies to enhance decision making. Finally, middle managers of the 1990s must have the ability to handle the concerns of a workforce that is far more culturally diverse than ever in our history and one in which women are becoming equal participants with men.≈

Scalar Relationships

The fourth main consideration of any organizing effort is **scalar relationships**—the chain of command. Every organization is built on the premise that the individual at the top possesses the most authority and that other individuals' authority is scaled downward according to their relative position on the organization chart. The lower a person's position on the organization chart, then, the less authority that person possesses.

The scalar relationship, or chain of command, is related to the unity of command. **Unity of command** is the management principle that recommends that an individual have only one boss. If too many bosses give orders, the result will probably be confusion, contradiction, and frustration—a sure recipe for ineffectiveness and inefficiency in an organization. Although the unity-of-command principle made its first appearance in management literature well over 75 years ago, it is still discussed today as a critical ingredient of successful organizations.[26]

Fayol's Guidelines on Chain of Command.   Fayol has indicated that strict adherence to the chain of command is not always advisable.[27] Figure 10.12 explains his rationale. If individual F needs information from individual G and follows the concept of chain of command, F has to go through individuals D, B, A, C, and E before reaching G. The information would get back to F only by going from G through E, C, A, B, and D. Obviously, this long, involved process can be very time-consuming and therefore expensive for the organization.

To avoid this long, involved, expensive process, Fayol has recommended that in some situations a bridge, or **gangplank,** be used to allow F to go directly to G for information. This bridge is represented in Figure 10.12 by the dotted line connecting F and G. Managers should be very careful in allowing the use of these organizational bridges, however, because although F might get the information from G more quickly and cheaply that way, individuals D, B, A, C, and E would be excluded from the com-

Scalar relationships refer to the chain-of-command positioning of individuals on an organization chart.

Unity of command is the management principle that recommends that an individual have only one boss.

A **gangplank** is a communication channel extending from one organizational division to another but not shown in the lines of communication outlined on an organization chart. Use of Fayol's gangplank may be quicker, but could prove costly in the long run.

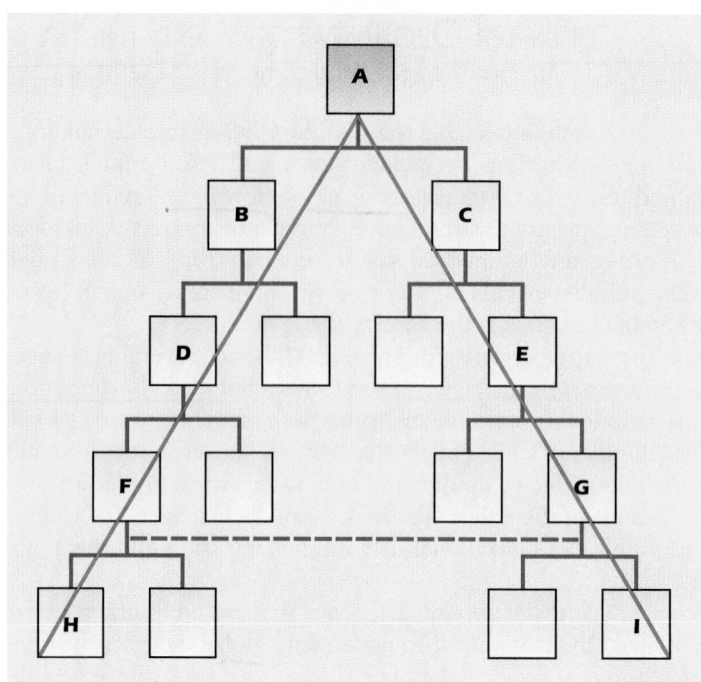

Figure 10.12 Sample organization chart showing that adhering to the chain of command is not advisable

munication channel, and their ignorance might prove more costly to the organization in the long run than would following the established chain of command would. When managers allow the use of an organizational bridge, they must be extremely careful to inform all other appropriate individuals within the organization of any information received that way.

BACK TO THE CASE The last two major elements in classical organizing theory that a manager should reflect on are span of management and scalar relationships. In thinking about span of management, Roberts would focus on the number of subordinates that managers in various roles at MCI can successfully supervise. He might explore several important situational factors, such as similarities among various MCI activities, the extent to which MCI workers being managed are physically separated, and the complexity of various MCI work activities.

For example, Roberts should consider that while signing up a business customer as a long-distance user is fairly simple, installing a special equipment network within a company is much more difficult. Therefore, the span of management for workers doing the signing up should generally be larger than that for those doing the installation. Two other important factors Roberts should take into account when determining spans of management for various MCI managers are the amount of time managers must spend coordinating workers' activities and the amount of time they spend planning. After gathering all this information, Roberts should be quite capable of determining appropriate spans of management for MCI managers.

Action Summary

Reread the learning objectives below. Each objective is followed by questions. Answering these questions accurately will help you retain the most important concepts discussed in this chapter. After answering each question, check your answer against the answer key at the end of this chapter. (*Hint:* If you have any doubts regarding the correct response, consult the page whose number follows the answer.)

Circle: From studying this chapter, I will attempt to acquire:

1. An understanding of the organizing function.

a,b,c,d,e   **a.** Of the five steps in the organizing process, the following is grossly out of order: (a) reflect on plans and objectives; (b) establish major tasks; (c) allocate resources and directives for subtasks; (d) divide major tasks into subtasks; (e) evaluate results of the implemented organizational strategy.

T,F   **b.** Proper execution of the organizing function normally results in minimal duplication of effort.

2. An appreciation for the complexities of determining appropriate organizational structure.

a,b,c,d,e   **a.** The XYZ Corporation is organized as follows: it has (1) a president, (2) a vice president in charge of finance, (3) a vice president in charge of marketing, and (4) a vice president in charge of human resources management. This firm is organized on the: (a) functional basis; (b) manufacturing process basis; (c) customer basis; (d) territorial basis; (e) production basis.

a,b,c,d,e   **b.** All of the following forces are influences on the evolution of formal structure except: (a) forces in the manager; (b) forces in subordinates; (c) forces in the environment; (d) forces in the division of labor; (e) forces in the task.

3. Insights on the advantages and disadvantages of division of labor.

a,b,c,d,e   **a.** Extreme division of labor tends to result in: (a) human motivation; (b) boring jobs; (c) nonspecialized work; (d) decreased work skill; (e) all of the above.

a,b,c,d,e   **b.** The following is *not* a generally accepted advantage of division of labor within an organization: (a) workers' skills in performing their jobs tend to increase; (b) workers need to know only how to perform their specific work tasks; (c) workers do not waste time in moving from one task to another; (d) workers naturally tend to try to make their individual tasks easier and more efficient; (e) none of the above (all are advantages of the division of labor).

4. A working knowledge of the relationship between division of labor and coordination.

T,F   **a.** Effective coordination is best achieved through close employee supervision.

T,F   **b.** Mary Parker Follett contended that managers should plan for coordination.

5. An understanding of span of management and the factors that influence its appropriateness.

a,b,c,d,e   **a.** Of the factors listed, the following would have a tendency to increase (expand) the span of management: (a) subordinates are physically distant; (b) subordinates have similar functions; (c) subordinates have complex tasks; (d) subordinates' work needs close coordination; (e) manager spends much time in planning.

a,b,c,d,e   **b.** The concept of span of management concerns: (a) seeing that managers at the same level have equal numbers of subordinates; (b) employee skill and motivation levels; (c) supervision of one less than the known number of subordinates; (d) a determination of the number of individuals a manager can effectively supervise; (e) a and d.

6. An understanding of scalar relationships.

a,b,c,d,e   **a.** The management concept that recommends that employees should have one and only one boss is termed: (a) departmentalization; (b) function; (c) unity of command; (d) scalar relationship; (e) none of the above.

T,F   **b.** According to Fayol, under no circumstances should a gangplank be used in organizations.

Introductory Case Wrap-Up

"MCI Communications Organizes to Be More Competitive" (p. 237) and its related back-to-the-case sections were written to help you better understand the management concepts contained in this chapter. Answer the following discussion questions about this introductory case to enrich your understanding of the chapter content:

1. Does it seem reasonable that Roberts is attempting to better organize MCI in order to make his organization more competitive? Explain.
2. List all the questions you can think of that Roberts should ask himself in exploring how best to organize MCI.
3. Explain why it would be important for Roberts to ask each of the questions you listed.

Issues for Review and Discussion

1. What is organizing?
2. Explain the significance of organizing to the management system.
3. List the steps in the organizing process. Why should managers continually repeat these steps?
4. Can the organizing function be thought of as a subsystem? Explain.
5. Fully describe what Max Weber meant by the term *bureaucracy*.
6. Compare and contrast formal structure with informal structure.
7. List and explain three factors that management structure is based on, or contingent upon. Draw three sample portions of organization charts that illustrate the factors you listed.
8. Describe the forces that influence formal structure. How do these forces collectively influence structure?
9. What is division of labor?
10. What are the advantages and disadvantages of employing division of labor within a management system?
11. Define *coordination*.

12. Does division of labor increase the need for coordination? Explain.
13. Summarize Mary Parker Follett's thoughts on how to establish and maintain coordination.
14. Is span of management an important management concept? Explain.
15. Do you think that similarity of functions, geographic contiguity, complexity of functions, coordination, and planning influence appropriate span of control in all management systems? Explain.
16. Summarize and evaluate Graicunas' contribution to span-of-management literature.
17. What is the relationship between span of management and *flat* and *tall* organizations?
18. What are scalar relationships?
19. Explain the rationale behind Fayol's position that always adhering to the chain of command is not necessarily advisable.
20. What caution should managers exercise when they use the gangplank Fayol described?

Action Summary Answer Key

1. a. c, pp. 229–230
   b. T, pp. 229–230
2. a. a, pp. 234–235
   b. d, pp. 237–238

3. a. b, p. 239
   b. e, p. 239
4. a. F, p. 239
   b. T, pp. 239–240

5. a.. b, p. 241
   b. d, p. 241
6. a. c, pp. 243–244
   b. F, pp. 243–244

Case Study

Three's a Company at AT&T

In the fall of 1995, AT&T chairman Robert Allen announced that AT&T was separating into three publicly traded global companies. It is the fourth strategic restructuring in AT&T's history, and the biggest corporate reorganization ever in terms of stock market value. Under the terms of the split, AT&T shareowners will receive shares in each of the new companies.

In justifying the decision to reorganize, Allen pointed to transformations in the communications industry resulting from changes in customer needs, in technology, and in public policy. With AT&T at the intersection of all those changes, the restructuring had a single purpose—to give AT&T's businesses the agility to seize the best of new market opportunities. In Allen's view, restructuring was the only logical action for AT&T.

Three problems faced the old corporate giant: size, agility, and stock price. AT&T management realized that only companies would be positioned to take full advantage of the many new opportunities. Before the restructuring, AT&T was one company competing in four segments of information technology: (1) computing, (2) premises equipment, (3) network systems, and (4) communications services. The company had swollen to the point where advantages of size and scope were offset by the time and cost of coordinating and integrating sometimes conflicting business strategies.

At least two of the new companies have one important advantage: Although they are smaller and more focused than the parent company, they are by no means underfinanced. For example, the new AT&T communications group, holding almost 60 percent of the long-distance market, ranks No. 12 on the Fortune 500 list; moreover, its Universal card is the second-largest credit card in the country. In addition, the acquisition of Mc-Caw Cellular Communications in 1994 made AT&T a powerhouse in wireless services, with 80 percent of the wireless market. Finally, with changes brought about by the 1996 telecommunications bill, the company is set to take a bite of the local phone market as well, as it bundles its services into one-stop consumer shopping handled on a single bill.

In Allen's view, restructuring offers shareholders several advantages. For example, each of the main AT&T businesses can follow its individual path, striving to create greater value without worrying about bumping into another AT&T unit along the way. Each can now transfer energy previously expended on coordinating complex strategies across businesses into new offers for customers. Finally, each company can be more responsive to customers and offer shareowners a more focused investment in a high-growth industry, allowing investors to evaluate each company on its own merits

AT&T's voluntary restructuring is regarded by Wall Street as nothing less than miraculous. Shortly after the stunning announcement was made, stocks climbed by a little over 6 points. According to investment experts, the company that had long been synonymous with "Big Business" and the model for vertical integration had divested itself for its own good. Because AT&T is now poised to jump into the newly opened local-phone-service business and to offer integrated services that rival cable companies' services, downsizing may make the company bigger and better than ever.

Of course, such radical restructuring does not come without pain. In early 1996, for instance, Allen announced 40,000 layoffs touching every area of the business: AT&T itself, the communications group; Lucent, the new equipment and research group; and NCR, the computer group. NCR was the company most in trouble at the time of the restructuring. Many observers thought that AT&T's hostile $7.4 billion takeover of NCR in 1991 was too costly. Others have argued that although communications and computers seemed a perfect marriage, integration of the two companies proved too complicated—that AT&T bet too much on synergies that did not materialize.

Many of AT&T's problems in the mid-1990s originated in the breakup of the early 1980s, when AT&T spun off seven regional telephone companies, known as the "Baby Bells." Problems arose when AT&T began to supply competitors and compete with its own customers. For example, loath to enrich a telephone service competitor after deregulation opened new markets, the Baby Bells started to buy new equipment from other suppliers—a major blow to the equipment side of AT&T.

Allen believes the new restructuring will eliminate the problems of internal competition and put all three companies on a clearer path. This CEO, who entered the telephone business in 1957 as a management trainee for Indiana Bell, could never have foreseen as a young manager that telephone companies would someday have to compete with software companies, data providers, cable groups, and broadcasters. But as the definition of communications expanded, he came to believe that restructuring was the only answer and that the three new parts of AT&T will be even greater than the old whole.

Questions:

1. Discuss the problems that Robert Allen and his reorganizing team have identified. Which problems

suggested restructuring? What alternatives might the team have considered? Explain.

2. Create a new AT&T organizational chart based on information given in the case study. Conduct research to find updated information so you can add further areas to the chart. On what principle(s) is this organizational strategy based? Explain.

3. Using information from the text, explain the statement made by one AT&T competitor and customer, Pacific Telesis' Robert I. Barada: "There has always been a cloud in dealing with AT&T. It makes you stop and think when you buy one of their [fiber-optic cable rings], because you know they're installing the same fiber ring in our territory to compete with us. This will take part of that cloud away."

Skills Exercise

Analyze the advantages and disadvantages of chairman Robert Allen's decision to restructure AT&T from the point of view of an investor in the company. Fold a sheet of paper in half lengthwise. On one side list the advantages of corporate giantism (the old AT&T); on the other, list the advantages of downsizing (the new AT&T). Compare and contrast the two sets of advantages. On the basis of your analysis, would you have invested in one or more of the new AT&T companies immediately after the restructuring? Why or why not? Does AT&T's record since the restructuring support or refute your analysis? Explain. Based on your analysis of the success of restructuring, write a short article for new investors, advising them either to buy or to stay clear of the new AT&T stocks.

The Internet learning materials that accompany this chapter can be found at
http://www.profcerto.com
Additional information can be found on the inside front and back covers of this text.

11

chapter

RESPONSIBILITY, AUTHORITY, AND DELEGATION

STUDENT LEARNING OBJECTIVES

From studying this chapter, I will attempt to acquire:

1. An understanding of the relationship of responsibility, authority, and delegation.
2. Information on how to divide and clarify the job objectives of individuals working within an organization.
3. Knowledge of the differences among line authority, staff authority, and functional authority.
4. An appreciation for the issues that can cause conflict in line and staff relationships.
5. Insights on the value of accountability to the organization.
6. An understanding of how to delegate.
7. A strategy for eliminating various barriers to delegation.
8. A working knowledge of when and how an organization should be decentralized.

CHAPTER OUTLINE

Introductory Case: "Famous" Amos: The Organizing Challenge

Responsibility

People Perspectives: Robert Stempel Needed to Know His Job at General Motors

Dividing Job Activities
Clarifying Job Activities of Managers

Authority

Types of Authority

Ethics Spotlight: General Electric Staff Organizes Renovation

Accountability

Diversity Spotlight

Procter & Gamble's Managers Held Accountable for Advancement of Minorities

Delegation

Steps in the Delegation Process
Obstacles to the Delegation Process
Eliminating Obstacles to the Delegation Process
Centralization and Decentralization

Cutting Edge: Steele's Markets Finds Advantages in Centralizing Bakery Functions

"Famous" Amos: The Organizing Challenge

Wally "Famous" Amos, a pioneer of the now burgeoning $450-million-a-year gourmet cookie industry, is an entrepreneur who is famous not only for his delicious chocolate chip cookies but for his upbeat take on life as well. This former William Morris Talent Agency employee, the first African-American ever hired by the agency to be a talent agent, founded his company in 1975 with $24,000 (in exchange for 25 percent of stock) lent by celebrity friends Helen Reddy, her husband Jeff Wald, and singer Marvin Gaye. Amos had been baking cookies since he was a teenager (his Aunt Della got him started), and he regularly used them as a "hook" to charm the producers and other Hollywood executives he met during his 14 years as an agent. People kept telling Amos he should sell his cookies, but it wasn't until his career as an agent took a downturn that he decided he wanted a more stable business of his own to run.

Amos opened his first store, which an artist friend designed, on Sunset Boulevard. He traded in his tailored suits for Hawaiian-style shirts, baggy pants, and a panama hat. Then he had himself photographed and the image put on each package of Famous Amos cookies. For the opening, he sent out 2,500 invitations to the press, and, as a band played, poured champagne and dispensed cookies to his willing publicity pawns. By the next morning, lines were forming outside his door as people tried to become part of L.A.'s latest media event.

The Famous Amos Chocolate Chip Cookie Company quickly grew to include stores in Santa Monica and Hawaii. The company grossed $300,000 in its first year, $4 million in 1979, and $10 million in 1987. Today "fresh-baked" retail outlets are located across the country, and Famous Amos cookies line the shelves of thousands of grocery stores and supermarkets worldwide. Recently, Amos sold his company to Denver real estate investors and entrepreneurs Jeffrey and Ronald Baer.

The outstanding initial success of Famous Amos Cookies was based primarily on the ability of Wally Amos to see a market and to sell his vision. One of the most pressing challenges management must now meet is how to professionally manage the company that has evolved. Successfully organizing the efforts of employees throughout the company is a prerequisite to maintaining and expanding the company Wally Amos founded.

While the Baers are busy running his old company, Wally "Famous" Amos is deeply involved in establishing his new venture—Uncle Noname Cookie Company.

The challenge facing the Famous Amos Chocolate Chip Cookie Company is to organize the efforts of employees throughout the company.

what's ahead

The introductory case describes how Wally Amos initiated and built the Famous Amos Cookie Company into a thriving enterprise, which he later sold to Jeffrey and Ronald Baer. The case ends with the implication that the company has gone beyond the fledgling phase and management must now focus on meeting the normal challenges of an established company if the organization is to continue to prosper. The case indicates that one such challenge is how best to organize the efforts of employees throughout the company. The information in this chapter on organizing the job activities of individuals within an organization should be of great value to managers like the Baers. Three major elements of organizing are presented:

1. Responsibility
2. Authority
3. Delegation

Chapter 10 dealt with applying the principles of organizational structure, division of labor, span of management, and scalar relationships to establish an orderly use of resources within the management system. Productivity in any management system, however, results from specific activities performed by individuals within that organization. An effective organizing effort, therefore, includes not only a rationale for the orderly use of management system resources but also three other elements of organizing that specifically channel the activities of organizational members: responsibility, authority, and delegation.

RESPONSIBILITY

Perhaps the most fundamental method of channeling the activity of individuals within an organization, **responsibility** is the obligation to perform assigned activities. It is the self-assumed commitment to handle a job to the best of one's ability. The source of responsibility lies within the individual. A person who accepts a job agrees to carry out a series of duties or activities or to see that someone else carries them out.[1] The act of accepting the job means that the person is obligated to a superior to see that job activities are successfully completed. Because responsibility is an obligation that a person *accepts*, there is no way it can be delegated or passed on to a subordinate.

Responsibility is the obligation to perform assigned activities.

The Job Description   An individual's job activities within an organization are usually summarized in a formal statement called a **job description**—a listing of specific activities that must be performed by whoever holds the position. Unclear job descriptions can confuse employees and may cause them to lose interest in their jobs. On the other hand, a clear job description can help employees to become successful by focusing their efforts on the issues that are important for their position. When properly designed, job descriptions communicate job content to employees, establish performance levels that employees must maintain, and act as a guide that employees should follow to help the organization reach its objectives.[2]

A **job description** is a listing of specific activities that must be performed to accomplish some task or job.

To emphasize that job descriptions are useful for *every* job in an organization, the following PEOPLE PERSPECTIVES feature illustrates why even the top manager should be given a job description.

ROBERT STEMPEL NEEDED TO KNOW HIS JOB AT GENERAL MOTORS

PEOPLE PERSPECTIVES

Robert Stempel was recently fired from his job as chief executive officer of General Motors. This high-profile firing took place because the world-renowned automobile manufacturer was experiencing low profits, a shrinking market share, and questionable product quality.

There was, however, no guarantee that General Motors would rebound after Stempel's departure.

In reflecting on this and other sudden firings of CEOs, a 32-member Blue Ribbon Commission of the National Association of Corporate Directors recommended that organizations establish job descriptions for their top managers so they and their boards of directors will understand each other from the start. According to the commission, such job descriptions should be used to evaluate the performance of top managers, not only to avert highly publicized firings like Stempel's, but also to enable the organization to make necessary changes before it seriously deteriorates.

The commission recommends that top managers be personally involved in developing their job description so there will be no misunderstandings about their duties and responsibilities. If a board of directors and a top manager agree on exactly what the top manager is being hired to do, appraisals of that top manager's performance should be less controversial.≈

Job activities are delegated by management to enhance the accomplishment of management system objectives. Management analyzes its objectives and assigns specific duties that will lead to reaching those objectives. A sound organizing strategy delineates specific job activities for every individual in the organization. Note, however, that as objectives and other conditions within the management system change, so will individual job activities.

The following three areas are related to responsibility:

1. Dividing job activities.
2. Clarifying job activities of managers.
3. Being responsible.

Each of these topics is discussed in the sections that follow.

Dividing Job Activities

Obviously, one person cannot be responsible for performing all of the activities that take place within an organization. Because so many people work within a given management system, organizing necessarily involves dividing job activities among a number of individuals. Some method of distributing these job activities is essential.

The **functional similarity method** is a method for dividing job activities in the organization.

The Functional Similarity Method
The **functional similarity method** is, according to many management theorists, the most basic method of dividing job activities. Simply stated, the method suggests that management should take four basic interrelated steps to divide job activities in the following sequence:

1. Examine management system objectives.
2. Designate appropriate activities that must be performed to reach those objectives.
3. Design specific jobs by grouping similar activities.
4. Make specific individuals responsible for performing those jobs.

Figure 11.1 illustrates this sequence of activities.

Functional Similarity and Responsibility
At least three additional guides can be used to supplement the functional similarity method.[3] The first of these supplemental guides suggests that overlapping responsibility should be avoided in making job activity divisions. **Overlapping responsibility** refers to a situation in which more than one individual is responsible for the same activity. Generally speaking, only one person should be responsible for completing any one activity. When two or more employees are unclear about who should do a job because of overlapping responsibility, it usually leads to conflict and poor working relationships.[4] Often the job doesn't get done because each employee assumes the other will do it.

Overlapping responsibility refers to a situation in which more than one individual is responsible for the same activity.

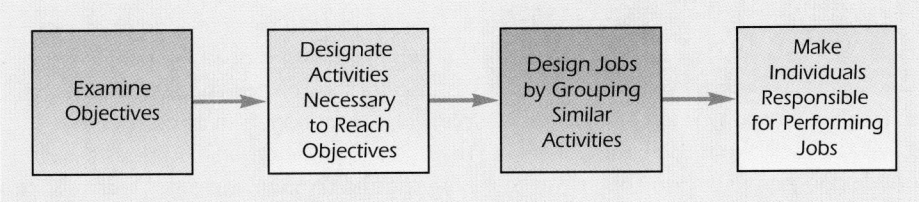

Figure 11.1   Sequence of activities for the functional similarity method of dividing job activities

The second supplemental guide suggests that responsibility gaps should be avoided. A **responsibility gap** exists when certain tasks are not included in the responsibility area of any individual organization member. This results in a situation in which nobody within the organization is obligated to perform certain necessary activities.

The third supplemental guide suggests that management should avoid creating job activities for accomplishing tasks that do not enhance goal attainment. Organization members should be obligated to perform *only* those activities that lead to goal attainment.

The absence of clear, goal-related, nonoverlapping responsibilities undermines organizational efficiency and effectiveness.[5]

When job responsibilities are distributed inappropriately, the organization will have both responsibility gaps and overlapping responsibilities.

The effects of responsibility gaps on product quality are obvious, but overlapping responsibilities also impair product quality. When two (or more) employees are uncertain as to who is responsible for a task, four outcomes are possible:

1. One of the two may perform the job. The other may either forget to or choose not to do the job—and neither of these is a desirable outcome for product quality control.

2. Both employees may perform the job. At the least, this results in duplicated effort, which dampens employee morale. At worst, one employee may diminish the value of the other employee's work, resulting in a decrement in product quality.

3. Neither employee may perform the job because each assumed the other would do it.

4. The employees may spend valuable time negotiating each aspect and phase of the job to carefully mesh their job responsibilities, thus minimizing both duplication of effort and responsibility gaps. Though time-consuming, this is actually the most desirable option in terms of product quality.

Note that each of these outcomes negatively affects both product quality and overall productivity.

A **responsibility gap** exists when certain organizational tasks are not included in the responsibility area of any individual organization member.

In addition to adopting such practices as just-in-time parts delivery and continuous improvement, General Motors' Adam Opel plant in Eisenach, Germany, has increased productivity by experimenting with new forms of job responsibility. Job applicants, for example, are tested for teamwork abilities and trained specifically in the demands of just-in-time operations. Two-thirds of all employees work in teams, and any individual can stop the assembly line to check or correct a defect in quality.

The Baers face the challenge of organizing the activities of all the people working for the Famous Amos Cookie Company. If the company is to continue to be successful, the managers must derive these activities directly from company objectives. The Baers' specific organizing steps should include analyzing company objectives, outlining specific company activities that must be performed to reach those objectives, designing company jobs by grouping similar activities, and assigning these jobs to company personnel. In taking these steps, the Baers must be careful not to create, or allow, overlapping responsibilities, responsibility gaps, or responsibilities for activities that do not lead directly to goal attainment.

Clarifying Job Activities of Managers

Clarifying the job activities of managers is even more important than dividing the job activities of nonmanagers because managers affect greater portions of resources within the management system. Responsibility gaps, for instance, usually have a more significant impact on the management system when they relate to managers than when they relate to nonmanagers.

One process used to clarify management job activities "enables each manager to actively participate with his or her superiors, peers, and subordinates in systematically describing the managerial job to be done and then clarifying the role each manager plays in relationship to his or her work group and to the organization."[6] The purpose of this interaction is to ensure that there are no overlaps or gaps in perceived management responsibilities and that managers are performing only those activities that lead to the attainment of management system objectives. Although this process is typically used to clarify the responsibilities of managers, it can also be effective in clarifying the responsibilities of nonmanagers.

Management Responsibility Guide

A specific tool developed to implement this interaction process is the **management responsibility guide,** some version of which is used in most organizations. This guide helps management to describe the various responsibility relationships that exist in the organization and to summarize how the responsibilities of various managers relate to one another.

The seven main organizational responsibility relationships covered by the management responsibility guide are listed in Table 11.1. Once it is decided which of these relationships exist within the organization, the relationships between these responsibilities can be defined.

> A **management responsibility guide** is a tool that is used to clarify the responsibilities of various managers in the organization.

Responsible Managers

Managers can be described as responsible if they perform the activities they are obligated to perform.[7] Because managers have more impact on an organization than nonmanagers, responsible managers are a prerequisite for management system success. Several studies have shown that responsible management behavior is highly valued by top executives because the responsible manager guides many other individuals within the organization in performing their duties appropriately.

The degree of responsibility that a manager possesses can be determined by appraising the manager on the following four dimensions:

1. Attitude toward and conduct with subordinates.
2. Behavior with upper management.
3. Behavior with other groups.
4. Personal attitudes and values.

Table 11.2 summarizes what each of these dimensions entails.

Table 11.1

Seven Responsibility Relationships Among Managers, as Used in the Management Responsibility Guide

1. *General Responsibility.* The individual who guides and directs the execution of the function through the person accepting operating responsibility.
2. *Operating Responsibility.* The individual who is directly responsible for the execution of the function.
3. *Specific Responsibility.* The individual who is responsible for executing a specific or limited portion of the function.
4. *Must Be Consulted.* The individual whose area is affected by a decision who must be called on to render advice or relate information before any decision is made or approval is granted. This individual does not, however, make the decision or grant approval.
5. *May Be Consulted.* The individual who may be called on to relate information, render advice, or make recommendations before the action is taken.
6. *Must Be Notified.* The individual who must be notified of any action that has been taken.
7. *Must Approve.* The individual (other than persons holding general and operating responsibility) who must approve or disapprove the decision.

BACK TO THE CASE

In organizing employees' activities, the Baers must recognize, for example, that a department manager's job activities, as well as those of his or her subordinates, are a major factor in the company's success. Because the activities of department managers have an impact on all personnel within the department, these activities must be well defined. In addition, within each company division, all department managers' job activities should be coordinated so that departments do not work at cross-purposes. The Baers might choose to use the management responsibility guide process to achieve this coordination of responsibilities across departments.

Overall, for managers within the Famous Amos Cookie Company to be responsible managers, they must perform the activities they are obligated to perform and respond appropriately to their subordinates, their superiors in the company, and their peers in other departments in the division.

Table 11.2

Four Key Dimensions of Responsible Management Behavior

BEHAVIOR WITH SUBORDINATES	BEHAVIOR WITH UPPER MANAGEMENT	BEHAVIOR WITH OTHER GROUPS	PERSONAL ATTITUDES AND VALUES
Responsible managers— 1. Take complete charge of their work groups. 2. Pass praise and credit along to subordinates. 3. Stay close to problems and activities. 4. Take action to maintain productivity and are willing to terminate poor performers if necessary.	Responsible managers— 1. Accept criticism for mistakes and buffer their groups from excessive criticism. 2. Ensure that their groups meet management expectations and objectives.	Responsible managers make sure that any gaps between their areas and those of other managers are securely filled.	Responsible managers— 1. Identify with the group. 2. Put organizational goals ahead of personal desires or activities. 3. Perform tasks for which there is no immediate reward but that help subordinates, the company, or both. 4. Conserve corporate resources as if the resources were their own.

AUTHORITY

Individuals are assigned job activities to channel their behavior within the organization appropriately. Once they have been given specific assignments, they must be given a commensurate amount of authority to perform those assignments satisfactorily.

Authority is the right to perform or command. It allows its holder to act in certain designated ways and to directly influence the actions of others through orders. It also allows its holder to allocate the organization's resources to achieve organizational objectives.[8]

Authority is the right to perform or command.

Authority on the Job
The following example illustrates the relationship between job activities and authority. Two primary tasks for which a particular service station manager is responsible are pumping gasoline and repairing automobiles. The manager has the authority necessary to perform both of these tasks, or he or she may choose to delegate automobile repair to the assistant manager. Along with the activity of repairing, the assistant should also be delegated the authority to order parts, to command certain attendants to help, and to do anything else necessary to perform repair jobs. Without this authority, the assistant manager may find it impossible to complete the delegated job activities.

Practically speaking, authority merely increases the probability that a specific command will be obeyed.[9] The following excerpt emphasizes that authority does not always exact obedience:

> People who have never exercised power have all kinds of curious ideas about it. The popular notion of top leadership is a fantasy of capricious power: the top man [*or woman*] presses a button and something remarkable happens; he [*or she*] gives an order as the whim strikes him [*or her*], and it is obeyed. Actually, the capricious use of power is relatively rare except in some large dictatorships and some small family firms. Most leaders are hedged around by constraints—tradition, constitutional limitations, the realities of the external situation, rights and privileges of followers, the requirements of teamwork, and most of all, the inexorable demands of large-scale organization, which does not operate on capriciousness. In short, most power is wielded circumspectively.[10]

Acceptance of Authority
As Chapter 10 showed, the positioning of individuals on an organization chart indicates their relative amount of authority. Those positioned toward the top of the chart possess more authority than those positioned toward the bottom. Chester Barnard writes, however, that the exercise of authority is determined less by formal organizational decree than by acceptance among those under the authority. According to Barnard, authority exacts obedience only when it is accepted.

In line with this rationale, Barnard defines *authority* as the character of communication by which an order is accepted by an individual as governing the actions that individual takes within the system. Barnard maintains that authority will be accepted only under the following conditions:

1. The individual can understand the order being communicated.
2. The individual believes the order is consistent with the purpose of the organization.
3. The individual sees the order as compatible with his or her personal interests.
4. The individual is mentally and physically able to comply with the order.

The fewer of these four conditions that are present, the lower the probability that authority will be accepted and obedience be exacted.

Barnard offers some guidance on what action managers can take to raise the odds that their commands will be accepted and obeyed. He maintains that more and more of a manager's commands will be accepted over the long term if:[11]

1. The manager uses formal channels of communication and these are familiar to all organization members.
2. Each organization member has an assigned formal communication channel through which orders are received.
3. The line of communication between manager and subordinate is as direct as possible.
4. The complete chain of command is used to issue orders.
5. The manager possesses adequate communication skills.
6. The manager uses formal communication lines only for organizational business.
7. A command is authenticated as coming from a manager.

BACK TO THE CASE The Baers must be sure that all the people in their company who are delegated job activities also receive the authority to give necessary orders and to accomplish their obligated activities. Company managers need to recognize that authority must be accepted if obedience is to be exacted. To increase the probability of acceptance, managers should take care that employees understand internal orders and see these orders as consistent with the objectives of both their own department and the entire company. In addition, employees need to perceive orders as compatible with their individual interests and to see themselves as mentally and physically capable of carrying out the orders.

Types of Authority

Three main types of authority can exist within an organization:

1. Line authority
2. Staff authority
3. Functional authority

Each type exists only to enable individuals to carry out the different types of responsibilities with which they have been charged.

Line and Staff Authority **Line authority,** the most fundamental authority within an organization, reflects existing superior-subordinate relationships. It consists of the right to make decisions and to give orders concerning the production-, sales-, or finance-related behavior of subordinates. In general, line authority pertains to matters directly involving management system production, sales, and finance and, as a result, the attainment of objectives. People directly responsible for these areas within the organization are delegated line authority to assist them in performing their obligated activities.

Whereas line authority involves giving orders concerning production activities, **staff authority** consists of the right to advise or assist those who possess line authority as well as other staff personnel. Staff authority enables those responsible for improving the effectiveness of line personnel to perform their required tasks. Examples of organization members with staff authority are people working in the accounting and human resource departments. Obviously, line and staff personnel must work together closely to maintain the efficiency and effectiveness of the organization. To ensure that line and staff personnel do work together productively, management must see to it that both groups understand the organizational mission, have specific objectives to strive for, and realize that they are partners in helping the organization reach its objectives.[12]

Size is perhaps the most significant factor in determining whether or not an organization will have staff personnel. Generally speaking, the larger the organization,

Line authority consists of the right to make decisions and to give orders concerning the production-, sales-, or finance-related behavior of subordinates.

Staff authority consists of the right to advise or assist those who possess line authority.

the greater the need and ability to employ staff personnel. As an organization expands, it usually needs employees with expertise in diversified areas. Although small organizations may also require this kind of diverse expertise, they often find it more practical to hire part-time consultants to provide it as needed than to hire full-time staff personnel, who may not always be kept busy.

Line-Staff Relationships   Figure 11.2 shows how line-staff relationships can be presented on an organization chart. The plant manager on this chart has line authority over each immediate subordinate—the human resource manager, the production manager, and the sales manager. But the human resource manager has staff authority in relation to the plant manager, meaning the human resource manager possesses the right to advise the plant manager on human resource matters. Still, final decisions concerning human resource matters are in the hands of the plant manager, the person holding line authority. Similar relationships exist between the sales manager and the sales research specialist, as well as between the production manager and the quality control manager.

Roles of Staff Personnel.   Harold Stieglitz has pinpointed three roles that staff personnel typically perform to assist line personnel:[13]

1. *The advisory or counseling role.*   In this role, staff personnel use their professional expertise to solve organizational problems. The staff personnel are, in effect, internal consultants whose relationship with line personnel is similar to that of a professional and a client. For example, the staff quality control manager might advise the line production manager on possible technical modifications to the production process that will enhance the quality of the organization's products.
2. *The service role.*   Staff personnel in this role provide services that can more efficiently and effectively be provided by a single centralized staff group than by many individuals scattered throughout the organization. This role can probably best be understood if staff personnel are viewed as suppliers and line personnel as customers. For example, members of a human resource department recruit, employ, and train workers for all organizational departments. In essence, they are the suppliers of workers, and the various organizational departments needing workers are their customers.

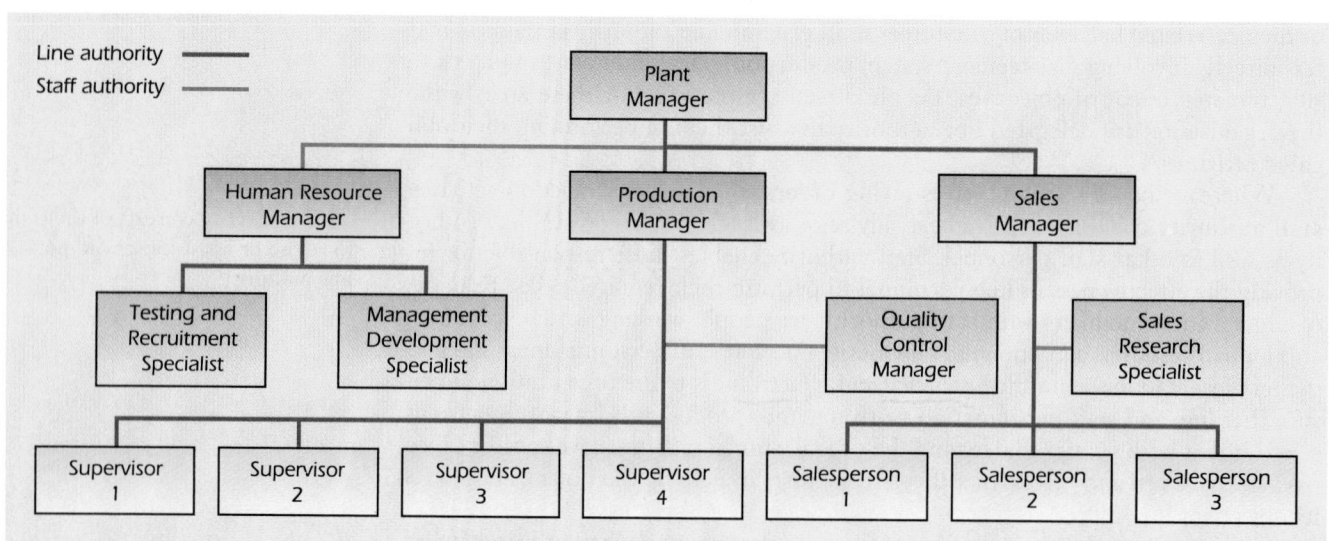

Figure 11.2   Possible line-staff relationships in selected organizational areas

3. *The <u>control</u> role.* In this role, staff personnel help establish a mechanism for evaluating the effectiveness of organizational plans. Staff personnel exercising this role are representatives, or agents, of top management.

These three are not the only roles performed by staff personnel, of course, but they are the major ones. In the final analysis, the roles of staff personnel in any organization should be specially designed to best meet the needs of that organization. In some organizations, the same staff people must perform all three major roles.

GENERAL ELECTRIC STAFF ORGANIZES RENOVATION

ETHICS SPOTLIGHT

At General Electric, not too long ago, a social responsibility project was organized and managed by one of GE's staff personnel, Bob Hess, a marketing specialist. As part of a sales meeting, GE salespeople renovated San Diego's Vincent de Paul–Joan Kroc urban center for the homeless. This project was part of a company program in which tired buildings used by a worthy nonprofit organization are selected to be renovated by GE employees. At the beginning of the renovation day, GE workers formed teams, each with a captain, a safety expert, and a task expert. In about eight hours, the work teams completed 95 percent of the job, renovating space for 400 beds and preparing space for 200 additional beds.

The renovation program at General Electric reflects a very progressive management attitude. Through staff activities, the company has been able to demonstrate its desire and ability to make a worthwhile contribution to society.≈

Conflict in Line-Staff Relationships.   Most management practitioners readily admit that a noticeable amount of organizational conflict centers around line-staff relationships.[14] From the viewpoint of line personnel, conflict is created because staff personnel tend to assume line authority, do not give sound advice, steal credit for success, fail to keep line personnel informed of their activities, and do not see the whole picture. From the viewpoint of staff personnel, conflict is created because line personnel do not make proper use of staff personnel, resist new ideas, and refuse to give staff personnel enough authority to do their jobs.

Sheldon Laube became chief technologist—a staff position that ranks among the 20 most senior management jobs—at the accounting firm of Price Waterhouse in 1989. His first assignment: Make the firm's technology state-of-the-art. The screen in the background—on which each icon corresponds to a database that can be shared with 18,000 other people—is what Laube sees when he boots his computer.

Staff personnel can often avert line-staff conflicts if they strive to emphasize the objectives of the organization as a whole, encourage and educate line personnel in the appropriate use of staff personnel, obtain any necessary skills they do not already possess, and deal intelligently with resistance to change rather than view it as an immovable barrier. Line personnel can do their part to minimize line-staff conflict by using staff personnel wherever possible, making proper use of the staff abilities, and keeping staff personnel appropriately informed.[15]

BACK TO THE CASE

Assuming that a main objective of the Famous Amos Cookie Company is to produce the highest-quality cookie possible, Famous Amos personnel who are directly responsible for achieving this objective should possess line authority to perform their responsibilities. For example, individuals responsible for purchasing ingredients for the cookies must be given the right to do everything necessary to obtain ingredients that will result in the best possible cookies.

Famous Amos may need to hire one or more individuals to assist line personnel. Perhaps these staff personnel could be responsible for advising Famous Amos management on such issues as how consumers rate Famous Amos Cookies relative to a competitor's product (Mrs. Fields' Cookies, for example) and on how employees should be trained to become more productive. Staff responsible for advising line personnel should be delegated the authority to do so.

As in all organizations, the potential for conflict between line personnel and staff personnel would be significant. Famous Amos Cookie Company management should be aware of this potential and encourage both line and staff personnel to strive to minimize it.

Functional authority consists of the right to give orders within a segment of the management system in which the right is normally nonexistent.

Functional Authority

Functional authority consists of the right to give orders within a segment of the organization in which this right is normally nonexistent. This authority is usually assigned to individuals to complement the line or staff authority they already possess. Functional authority generally covers only specific task areas and is operational only for designated amounts of time. Typically, it is possessed by individuals who, in order to meet responsibilities in their own areas, must be able to exercise some control over organization members in other areas.

The vice president for finance in an organization is an example of someone with functional authority. Among his or her basic responsibilities is the obligation to monitor the financial situation of the whole management system. To do so requires having appropriate financial information continually flowing in from various segments of the organization. The vice president for finance, therefore, is usually delegated the functional authority to order various departments to furnish the kinds and amounts of information he or she needs to perform an analysis. In effect, this functional authority allows the vice president for finance to give orders to personnel within departments in which he or she normally cannot give orders.

From this discussion of line authority, staff authority, and functional authority, it is logical to conclude that although authority can exist within an organization in various forms, these forms should be used in a combination that will best enable individuals to carry out their assigned responsibilities and thereby best help the management system accomplish its objectives. When trying to decide on an optimal authority combination for a particular organization, managers should be aware that each type of authority has both advantages and disadvantages. The organization chart illustrated in Figure 11.3 shows how the three types of authority could be combined for the overall benefit of a hospital management system.

Accountability

Accountability refers to the management philosophy whereby individuals are held liable, or accountable, for how well they use their authority or live up to their responsibility of performing predetermined activities.

Accountability refers to the management philosophy whereby individuals are held liable, or accountable, for how well they use their authority and live up to their re-

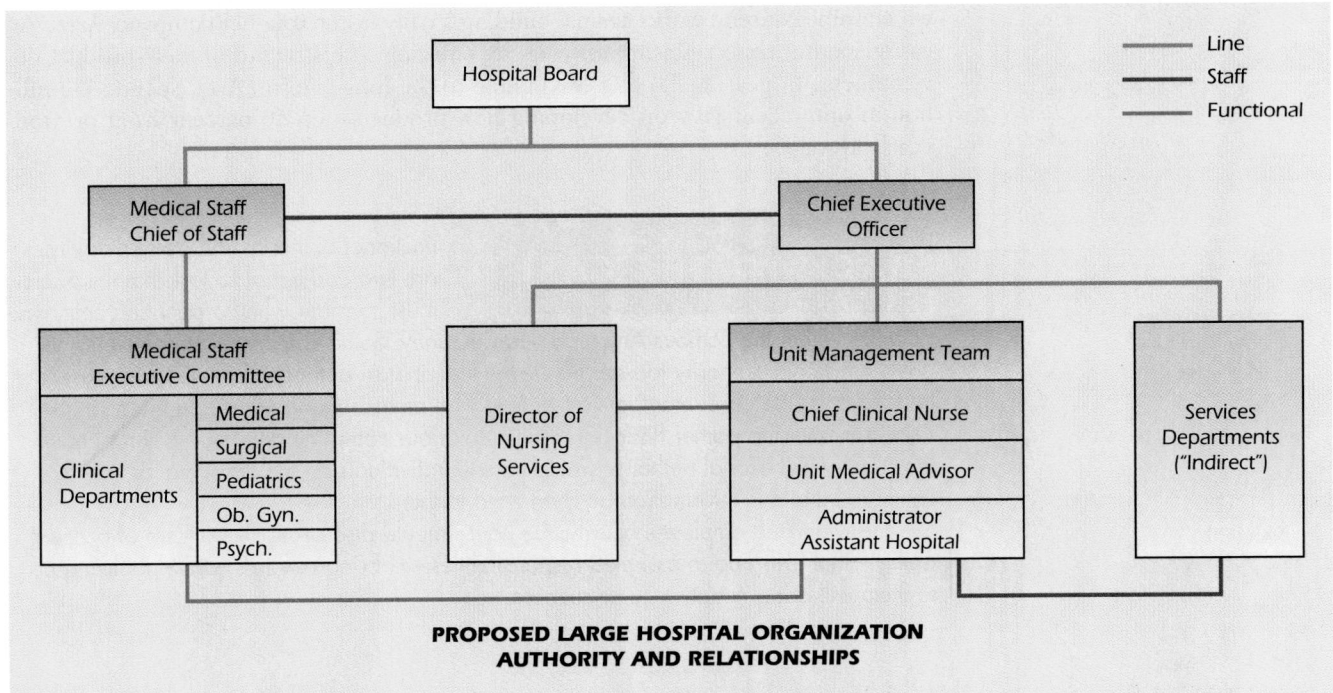

Figure 11.3   Proposed design for incorporating three types of authority in a hospital

sponsibility of performing predetermined activities.[16] The concept of accountability implies that if an individual does not perform predetermined activities some type of penalty, or punishment, is justifiable. The punishment theme of accountability has been summed up by one company executive: "Individuals who do not perform well simply will not be around too long."[17] The accountability concept also implies that some kind of reward will follow if predetermined activities are performed well.

PROCTER & GAMBLE'S MANAGERS HELD ACCOUNTABLE FOR ADVANCEMENT OF MINORITIES

DIVERSITY SPOTLIGHT Organizations commonly hold their managers accountable for performance issues such as earning higher profits, developing new products, and keeping work environments safe. At Procter & Gamble, managers are also held accountable for a more rarely used performance variable: the advancement of minority workers.

Edwin L. Artzt, P&G's chairman, aims to build a tougher, faster, more global organization, and believes that the company must be able to harness the energies of a diverse workforce if this objective is to be accomplished. Hence Artzt has instituted a system to track minority employees' advancement and to hold managers accountable for their progress. P&G's participative approach to decision making, use of teams to accomplish company projects, and formulation and assignment of company goals will be useful only if the company is successful in building its workforce—which will inevitably become progressively more diverse—into a productive, dedicated work unit.

Diversity is not the only accountability issue at Procter & Gamble. Artzt is taking other steps to build a faster, tougher company—demanding, for example, that his managers consistently beat the competition to market with the latest products. Many inside the company think that Artzt is pushing this first-to-market agenda too hard. He is also being criticized for focusing too much on short-term financial results,

which some contend works against building a truly faster, tougher company. Artzt can easily counter this criticism, however, by pointing to his record on new-product development. In gearing Procter & Gamble to the longer term, Artzt spent $400 million in one recent year on developing new products—up 50 percent from previous yearly averages.≈

BACK TO THE CASE   Functional authority and accountability are two additional factors that the Baers must consider when organizing employee activities within the Famous Amos Cookie Company. Some employees may have to be given functional authority to supplement the line or staff authority they already possess. For example, the accountant, a staff person who advises management on financial affairs, may need to gather financial results of various company retail outlets throughout the country. Functional authority would enable individuals on the accountant's staff to command that this information be channeled to them.

In organizing employee activity, the Baers should also stress the concept of accountability—that living up to assigned responsibilities will bring rewards, while not living up to them will bring negative consequences.

DELEGATION

Delegation is the process of assigning job activities and related authority to specific individuals in the organization.

So far in this chapter we have discussed responsibility and authority as complementary factors that channel activity within the organization. **Delegation** is the actual process of assigning job activities and corresponding authority to specific individuals within the organization. This section focuses on the following topics:

1. Steps in the delegation process.
2. Obstacles to the delegation process.
3. Elimination of obstacles to the delegation process.
4. Centralization and decentralization.

Steps in the Delegation Process

According to Newman and Warren, the delegation process consists of three steps, all of which may be either observable or implied.[18] The first step is assigning specific duties to the individual. In all cases, the manager must be sure that the subordinate assigned specific duties has a clear understanding of what these duties entail. Whenever possible, the activities should be stated in operational terms so the subordinate knows exactly what action must be taken to perform the assigned duties. The second step of the delegation process involves granting appropriate authority to the subordinate— that is, the subordinate must be given the right and power within the organization to accomplish the duties assigned. The last step involves creating the obligation for the subordinate to perform the duties assigned. The subordinate must be aware of the responsibility to complete the duties assigned and must accept that responsibility. Table 11.3 offers several guidelines that managers can follow to ensure the success of the delegation process.

Obstacles to the Delegation Process

Obstacles that can make delegation within an organization difficult or even impossible can be classified into three general categories:

1. Obstacles related to the supervisor.
2. Obstacles related to subordinates.
3. Obstacles related to organizations.

Table 11.3

Guidelines for Making Delegation Effective

- Give employees freedom to pursue tasks in their own way.
- Establish mutually agreed upon results and performance standards for delegated tasks.
- Encourage employees to take an active role in defining, implementing, and communicating progress on tasks.
- Entrust employees with completion of whole projects or tasks whenever possible.
- Explain the relevance of delegated tasks to larger projects or to department or organization goals.
- Give employees the authority necessary to accomplish tasks.
- Allow employees access to all information, people, and departments necessary to perform delegated task.
- Provide training and guidance necessary for employees to complete delegated tasks satisfactorily.
- When possible, delegate tasks on the basis of employee interests.

An example of the first category is the supervisor who resists delegating his authority to subordinates because he cannot bear to part with any authority. The cartoon below depicts a different sort of manager—one who delegates simply because he enjoys exercising the power to do so. Two other supervisor-related obstacles are the fear that subordinates will not do a job well and the suspicion that surrendering some authority may be seen as a sign of weakness. Moreover, if supervisors are insecure in their jobs or believe certain activities are extremely important to their personal success, they may find it hard to put the performance of these activities into the hands of others.

Supervisors who do wish to delegate to subordinates may encounter several subordinate-related roadblocks. First, subordinates may be reluctant to accept delegated authority because they are afraid of failing, lack self-confidence, or feel the supervisor doesn't have confidence in them.[19] These obstacles will be especially apparent in subordinates who have never before used delegated authority. Other subordinate-related

Wall Street Journal, March 9, 1990, p. A13.

obstacles are the fear that the supervisor will be unavailable for guidance when needed and the reluctance to exercise authority that may complicate comfortable working relationships.

Characteristics of the organization itself may also make delegation difficult. For example, a very small organization may present the supervisor with only a minimal number of activities to be delegated. In organizations where few job activities and little authority have been delegated in the past, an attempt to initiate the delegation process may make employees reluctant and apprehensive, for the supervisor would be introducing a significant change in procedure and change is often strongly resisted.

Eliminating Obstacles to the Delegation Process

Since delegation has significant advantages for the organization, the elimination of obstacles to the delegation process is important to managers. Among the advantages of delegation are enhanced employee confidence, improved subordinate involvement and interest, more free time for the supervisor to accomplish tasks, and, as the organization gets larger, assistance from subordinates in completing tasks the manager simply wouldn't have time for otherwise. True, there are potential disadvantages to delegation—such as the possibility that the manager will lose track of the progress of a delegated task—but the potential advantages of some degree of delegation generally outweigh the potential disadvantages.[20]

What can managers do to eliminate obstacles to the delegation process? First of all, they must continually strive to uncover any obstacles to delegation that exist in their organization. Then they should approach taking action to eliminate these obstacles with the understanding that the obstacles may be deeply ingrained and therefore require much time and effort to overcome. Among the most effective managerial actions that can be taken to eliminate obstacles to delegation are building subordinate confidence in the use of delegated authority, minimizing the impact of delegated authority on established working relationships, and helping delegatees cope with problems whenever necessary.[21]

Koontz, O'Donnell, and Weihrich believe that overcoming the obstacles to delegation requires certain critical characteristics in managers. These characteristics include the willingness to consider the ideas of others seriously, the insight to allow subordinates the free rein necessary to carry out their responsibilities, trust in the abilities of subordinates, and the wisdom to allow people to learn from their mistakes without suffering unreasonable penalties for making them.[22]

BACK TO THE CASE

To delegate effectively within the Famous Amos Cookie Company, managers must assign specific duties to individuals, grant them corresponding authority, and create in them the awareness that they are obligated to perform these activities.

In encouraging the use of delegation within their company, the Baers must be aware that managers, subordinates, and departments may all present obstacles to the delegation process. They must strongly encourage managers to meet the delegation challenge—that is, to discover which delegation obstacles exist within their work environments and then to take steps to eliminate them. If Famous Amos managers are to be successful delegators, they must be willing to consider the ideas of their subordinates, allow them the free rein necessary to perform their assigned tasks, trust them, and help them learn from their mistakes without suffering unreasonable penalties.

Centralization and Decentralization

There are noticeable differences from organization to organization in the relative number of job activities and the relative amount of authority delegated to subordi-

nates. This is seldom a case of delegation existing in one organization and not existing in another. Rather, the difference is one degree of delegation.

The terms **centralization** and **decentralization** describe the general degree to which delegation exists within an organization. They can be visualized as opposite ends of the delegation continuum depicted in Figure 11.4. It is apparent from this figure that centralization implies that a minimal number of job activities and a minimal amount of authority have been delegated to subordinates by management, whereas decentralization implies the opposite.

The issues practicing managers usually face in this are determining whether to further decentralize an organization and, if that course of action is advisable, deciding how to decentralize.[23] The section that follows presents practical suggestions on both issues.

Decentralizing an Organization: A Contingency Viewpoint
The appropriate degree of decentralization for an organization depends on the unique situation of that organization. Some specific questions managers can use to determine the amount of decentralization appropriate for a situation are as follows:

1. *What is the present size of the organization?*   As noted earlier, the larger the organization, the greater the likelihood that decentralization will be advantageous. As an organization increases in size, managers have to assume more and more responsibility and different types of tasks. Delegation is typically an effective means of helping them manage this increased workload.

   In some cases, however, top management will conclude that the organization is actually too large and decentralized. One signal that an organization is too large is labor costs that are very high relative to other organizational expenses. In this instance, increased centralization of certain organizational activities could reduce the need for some workers and thereby lower labor costs to a more acceptable level.[24]

2. *Where are the organization's customers located?*   As a general rule, the more physically separated the organization's customers are, the more viable a significant amount of decentralization is. Decentralization places appropriate management resources close to customers and thereby makes quick customer service possible. J.C. Penney, for example, decentralized its purchasing activities to give its managers the ability to buy merchandise best suited to customers of their individual stores.[25]

3. *How homogeneous is the organization's product line?*   Generally, as the product line becomes more heterogeneous, or diversified, the appropriateness of decentralization increases. Different kinds of decisions, talents, and resources are needed to manufacture different products. Decentralization usually minimizes the confusion that can result from diversification by separating organizational resources by product and keeping pertinent decision making close to the manufacturing process.

4. *Where are organizational suppliers?*   The location of raw materials needed to manufacture the organization's products is another important consideration.

Centralization refers to the situation in which a minimal number of job activities and a minimal amount of authority are delegated to subordinates.

Decentralization refers to the situation in which a significant number of job activities and a maximum amount of authority are delegated to subordinates.

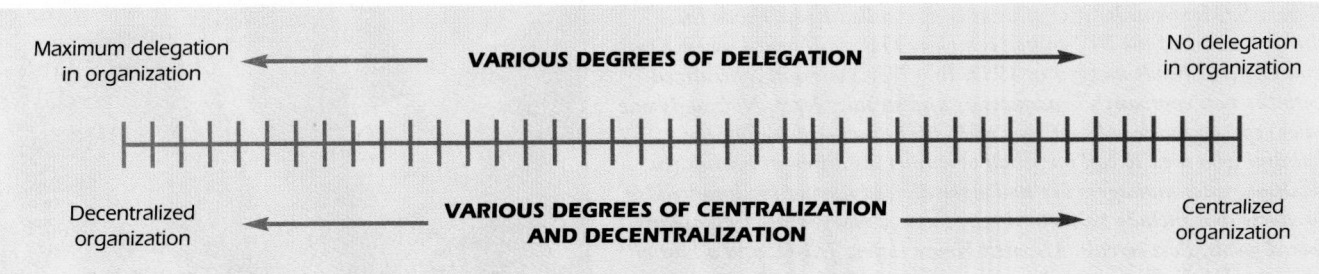

Figure 11.4   Centralized and decentralized organizations on delegation continuum

Time loss and high transportation costs associated with shipping raw materials over great distances from supplier to manufacturer could signal the need to decentralize certain functions.

For example, the wood necessary to manufacture a certain type of bedroom set may be available only from tree growers in certain northern states. If the bedroom set in question is an important product line for a furniture company and if the costs of transporting the lumber are substantial, a decision to decentralize may be a sound one. The effect of this decision would probably be the building of a plant that produces only bedroom sets in a northern state close to where the necessary wood is readily available. The advantages of such a costly decision, of course, would accrue to the organization only over the long term.

5. *Is there a need for quick decisions in the organization?*   If speedy decision making is essential, a considerable amount of decentralization is probably in order. Decentralization cuts red tape and allows the subordinate to whom authority has been delegated to make on-the-spot decisions when necessary. It goes without saying that this delegation is advisable only if the potential delegatees have the ability to make sound decisions. If they don't, faster decision making results in no advantage for the organization. Quite the contrary, the organization may find itself saddled with the effects of unsound decisions.

6. *Is creativity a desirable feature of the organization?*   If creativity is desirable, then some decentralization is advisable, for decentralization allows delegatees the freedom to find better ways of doing things. The mere existence of this freedom encourages the incorporation of new and more creative techniques within the task process.[26]

Depending upon the specific organizational situation, either centralizing or decentralizing organizational activities could be advisable. The following CUTTING EDGE feature illustrates a situation in which centralizing organizational activities proved advantageous.

STEELE'S MARKETS FINDS ADVANTAGES IN CENTRALIZING BAKERY FUNCTIONS

CUTTING EDGE

Before Steele's Markets opened its fourth supermarket, co-owners Bert Steele and Russell Kates realized that they had outgrown the company's 2,500-square-foot central baking facility. The solution was to quadruple the size of the bakery and build it within Steele's warehouse. The facility is now operated as a centralized independent bakery.

Robert S. Morrison is CEO of what is now called Kraft Foods Inc.— the new name of the $17-billion company that was formed when Kraft and General Foods merged in 1989. In 1995, Morrison centralized both the new company's headquarters and its sales force. Now, only one sales representative calls on each of 26,000 stores—instead of the handful who used to call on behalf of numerous different brands. In addition, sales managers are no longer divided among the hundreds of products that include Velveeta cheese, Parkay margarine, Entenmann's baked goods, Post cereals, Maxwell House coffee, Jell-O, and a host of beverage labels. Rather, they are centralized in 300 marketing-support teams, each of whose efforts are focused on one chain of stores.

The new bakery bakes products for all company supermarkets. It runs daily from about 4 A.M. to 11 P.M. and employs between 45 and 50 people, of whom only 4 or 5 are part-time workers. Approximately 300 different bakery products are produced at the facility. Breads account for nearly 13.5 percent of bakery sales at Steele's supermarkets, while rolls contribute almost the same percentage of volume. The largest part of Steele's business, however, is decorated cakes.

Kates favors a centralized facility over separate bakeries in each supermarket for several reasons. First, he believes that central baking gives him a greater opportunity to control the quality of the bakery products in each of his supermarkets. More importantly, centralizing baking activities has helped him ensure the consistency of the products sold within all of his supermarkets. Kates is determined that his company's bakery products will taste the same regardless of the store in which they are sold.≈

Decentralization at Massey-Ferguson: A Classic Example   Positive decentralization is decentralization that is advantageous for the organization in which it is being implemented; negative decentralization is disadvantageous for the organization. To see how an organization should be decentralized, it is worthwhile to study a classic example of an organization that achieved positive decentralization: Massey-Ferguson.[27]

Guidelines for Decentralization.   Massey-Ferguson is a worldwide farm equipment manufacturer that has enjoyed noticeable success with decentralization over the past several years. The company has three guidelines for determining the degree of decentralization of decision making that is appropriate for a situation:

1. The competence to make decisions must be possessed by the person to whom authority is delegated. A derivative of this principle is that the superior must have confidence in the subordinate to whom authority is delegated.
2. Adequate and reliable information pertinent to the decision is required by the person making the decision. Decision-making authority therefore cannot be pushed below the point at which all information bearing on the decision is available.
3. If a decision affects more than one unit of the enterprise, the authority to make the decision must rest with the manager accountable for the most units affected by the decision.

Delegation as a Frame of Mind.   Massey-Ferguson also encourages a definite attitude toward decentralization in its managers. The company's organization manual indicates that delegation is not delegation in name only but a frame of mind that includes both what a supervisor says to subordinates and the way the supervisor acts toward them. Managers at Massey-Ferguson are prodded to allow subordinates to make a reasonable number of mistakes and to help them learn from these mistakes.

Complementing Centralization.   Another feature of the positive decentralization at Massey-Ferguson is that decentralization is complemented by centralization:

> The organization plan that best serves our total requirements is a blend of centralized and decentralized elements. Marketing and manufacturing responsibilities, together with supporting service functions, are located as close as possible to local markets. Activities that determine the long-range character of the company, such as the planning and control of the product line, the planning and control of facilities and money, and the planning of the strategy to react to changes in the patterns of international trade, are highly centralized.

Thus, Massey-Ferguson management recognizes that decentralization is not necessarily an either/or decision and uses the strengths of both centralization and decentralization to its advantage.

Management Responsibilities. Not all activities at Massey-Ferguson are eligible for decentralization. Only management is allowed to follow through on the following responsibilities:

1. The responsibility for determining the overall objectives of the enterprise.
2. The responsibility for formulating the policies that guide the enterprise.
3. The final responsibility for the control of the business within the total range of the objectives and policies, including control over any changes in the nature of the business.
4. The responsibility for product design where a product decision affects more than one area of accountability.
5. The responsibility for planning for the achievement of overall objectives and for measuring actual performance against those plans.
6. The final approval of corporate plans or budgets.
7. The decisions pertaining to the availability and the application of general company funds.
8. The responsibility for capital investment plans.

BACK TO THE CASE Centralization implies that few job activities and little authority have been delegated to subordinates; decentralization implies that many job activities and much authority have been delegated. Managers within the Famous Amos Cookie Company will have to determine the best degree of delegation for their individual situations. For guidelines, they can use the rules of thumb that greater degrees of delegation become appropriate as departments become larger, as retail outlets become more dispersed and diversified, and as the need for quick decision making and creativity increases.

Massey-Ferguson's experience with decentralization provides many valuable insights on what characteristics the decentralization process within the Famous Amos Cookie Company should assume. First, Famous Amos managers should use definite guidelines in deciding whether their situation warrants more decentralization. In general, additional delegation would be warranted within the company as the competence of subordinates increases, as Famous Amos managers' confidence in their subordinates increases, and as more adequate and reliable decision-making information becomes available to subordinates. For delegation to be advantageous for the Famous Amos Cookie Company, managers must help subordinates learn from their mistakes. Depending on their situations, individual Famous Amos managers may want to consider supplementing decentralization with centralization.

Action Summary

Reread the learning objectives below. Each objective is followed by questions. Answering these questions accurately will help you retain the most important concepts discussed in this chapter. After answering each question, check your answer against the answer key at the end of this chapter. (*Hint:* If you have any doubts regarding the correct response, consult the page whose number follows the answer.)

Circle: From studying this chapter, I will attempt to acquire:
1. An understanding of the relationship of responsibility, authority, and delegation.
   T,F a. Responsibility is a person's self-assumed commitment to handle a job to the best of his or her ability.
   a,b,c,d,e b. The following element is *not* an integral part of an effective organizing effort: (a) rationale for the orderly use of management system resources; (b) responsibility; (c) authority; (d) delegation; (e) none of the above (they are all important).
2. Information on how to divide and clarify the job activities of individuals working within an organization.

a,b,c,d,e   **a.** The following is *not* one of the four basic steps for dividing responsibility by the functional similarity method: (a) designing specific jobs by grouping similar activities; (b) examining management system objectives; (c) formulating management system objectives; (d) designating appropriate activities that must be performed to reach objectives; (e) making specific individuals responsible for performing activities.

a,b,c,d,e   **b.** A management responsibility guide can assist organization members in the following way: (a) by describing the various responsibility relationships that exist in their organization; (b) by summarizing how the responsibilities of various managers within the organization relate to one another; (c) by identifying manager work experience; (d) a and b; (e) none of the above.

3. Knowledge of the differences among line authority, staff authority, and functional authority.

a,b,c,d,e   **a.** The production manager has mainly: (a) functional authority; (b) staff authority; (c) line authority; (d) a and c; (e) all of the above.

T,F   **b.** An example of functional authority is the vice president of finance being delegated the authority to order various departments to furnish him or her with the kinds and amounts of information needed to perform an analysis.

4. An appreciation for the issues that can cause conflict in line and staff relationships.

a,b,c,d,e   **a.** From the viewpoint of staff personnel, a major reason for line-staff conflict is that line personnel: (a) do not make proper use of staff personnel; (b) resist new ideas; (c) do not give staff personnel enough authority; (d) a and c; (e) all of the above.

a,b,c,d,e   **b.** From the viewpoint of line personnel, a major reason for line-staff conflict is that staff personnel: (a) assume line authority; (b) do not offer sound advice; (c) steal credit for success; (d) fail to keep line personnel informed; (e) all of the above.

5. Insights on the value of accountability to the organization.

T,F   **a.** Accountability refers to how well individuals live up to their responsibility for performing predetermined activities.

a,b,c,d,e   **b.** Rewarding employees for good performance is most closely related to: (a) simplicity; (b) a clear division of authority; (c) centralization; (d) decentralization; (e) accountability.

6. An understanding of how to delegate.

T,F   **a.** The correct ordering of steps in the delegation process is: assignment of duties, creation of responsibility, and granting of authority.

a,b,c,d,e   **b.** The following are obstacles to the delegation process: (a) obstacles related to supervisors; (b) obstacles related to subordinates; (c) obstacles related to the organization; (d) all of the above; (e) none of the above.

Introductory Case Wrap-Up

"'Famous' Amos: The Organizing Challenge" (p. 250) and its related back-to-the-case sections were written to help you better understand the management concepts contained in this chapter. Answer the following discussion questions about this introductory case to enrich your understanding of the chapter content:

1. What first step would you recommend that the Baers take in organizing the activities of individuals within their company? Why?

2. Discuss the roles of responsibility, authority, and accountability in organizing the activities of individuals within Famous Amos.

3. At this time, do you think that the company should be more centralized or more decentralized? Why?

Issues for Review and Discussion

1. What is responsibility, and why is it so important in organizations?

2. Explain the process a manager would go through to divide responsibility within an organization.

3. What is a management responsibility guide, and how is it used?

4. List and summarize the four main dimensions of responsible management behavior.

5. What is authority, and why is it so important in organizations?

6. Describe the relationship between responsibility and authority.

7. Explain Barnard's notion of authority and acceptance.

8. What steps can managers take to increase the probability that subordinates will accept their authority? Be sure to explain how each of these steps increases that probability.

9. Summarize the relationship that exists between line and staff personnel in most organizations.

10. Explain three roles that staff personnel can perform in organizations.

11. List five possible causes of conflict in line-staff relationships and suggest appropriate action to minimize the effect of these causes.
12. What is functional authority?
13. Give an example of how functional authority actually works in an organization.
14. Compare the relative advantages and disadvantages of line, staff, and functional authority.

15. What is accountability?
16. Define *delegation* and list the steps of the delegation process.
17. List three obstacles to the delegation process and suggest action for eliminating them.
18. What is the relationship between delegation and decentralization?
19. What is the difference between decentralization and centralization?

Action Summary Answer Key

1. a. T, p. 251
   b. e, p. 251
2. a. c, pp. 252–253
   b. d, p. 254

3. a. c, pp. 257–258
   b. T, p. 260
4. a. e, pp. 259–260
   b. e, pp. 259–260

5. a. F, pp. 260–261
   b. e, pp. 260–261

6. a. F, p. 262
   b. d, pp . 262–263

Case Study

Change Agents in Midstream

In today's fast-paced business world, companies need managers who can channel the activities of organization members through efforts that include responsibility, authority, and delegation. Companies that handle these tasks well will very likely see dramatic increases in speed, productivity, and profits.

Unfortunately, middle managers who have the skills to navigate the rapids of change associated with technology shifts, more sophisticated customers, and ever-growing competitors are often unrecognized by top executives, who often prefer more traditional managers. This fact seems to be true even though the consequence of "business as usual" may be failure to accomplish important company objectives.

Top managers must learn to recognize effective change leaders in their company. In a study of middle-manager change agents at organizations from Compaq Computer to the New York City Transit Authority, McKinsey & Company director Jon R. Katzenbach concluded that the most sought-after person in today's workplace is a new breed of middle manager—a focused, determined "maverick" who is willing to break rules if necessary to carry out responsibilities delegated by upper management.

According to Katzenbach, change agents tend to be between 25 and 40 years old and may be either men or women. (In the McKinsey study, about a third of the change agents identified were women.) As a rule, they are more flexible than ordinary general managers and much more people-oriented. In addition, they balance several abilities:

1. They are technically skilled and have the ability to develop and employ personal relationships very successfully.
2. They are tough decision makers who are highly disciplined about performance results.
3. They are capable of energizing people and getting them to focus on one agenda, often finding ways to get more out of people than might be expected.

Typically, however, change leaders are rarely viewed by top management as high-potential company leaders. Katzenbach quoted one CEO as saying, "These are the funny little fat guys with thick glasses who always get the job done." Why does this perception prevail? For one thing, change agents usually do not come out of company training programs or standard business schools. Rather, they are often engineers, accountants, or production-line workers. Generally, they are not found in more traditional organizations dominated by strong role models. They are people who have figured out how to get jobs done by themselves, often by fighting their way out of tough situations. The best of them have developed skills that many more conventional managers simply do not have.

One of the outstanding traits of change agents is the ability to deploy more than one leadership style. They will use whatever works in an existing situation, especially if it helps them get more out of their people. Generally speaking, managers want more than rising financial numbers. Often their greatest satisfaction comes from getting people to do more than they thought they could.

Therefore, change leaders like to use custom measurements that determine both customer and employee reactions. In addition, they instinctively look to people in front-line jobs for help and are generous in sharing the rewards of accomplishment.

Change leaders are also hungry for information from the marketplace. Because they want the facts badly, they will not wait for the system to deliver them. Instead, they go out and get direct feedback from customers and competitiors. In turn, they use their findings to motivate their employees, firing up their desire to beat the competition and increase their own bottom lines—namely, higher salries and greater job security.

Finally, change leaders tend to be problem solvers by nature. And they are more motivated by the results of their solutions than by the recognition those solutions may bring them. They really like delivering results, getting people to stretch. Once they have accomplished one assignment, they want to plunge into another. Over time, they become so confident of their own skills that they are free to focus on results rather than job security.

Katzenbach is quick to point out that a company needs a good mix of managers—from change leaders, who shake things up, to traditional managers who keep things under control. Both, he emphasizes, are needed in today's global business environment.

Questions:

1. Explain how change leaders, as described by Jon Katzenbach, might handle the problems of responsibility gaps and overlapping responsibility.

2. Create job descriptions to suit the talents of a change leader. How would these differ from job descriptions for a more traditional manager? Use this comparison to explain Katzenbach's finding that the people identified as potential change leaders in a company were definitely not the same as the people identified as a "high-potential" leaders.

3. Describe the different sources of authority that change agents use to motivate their people. For example, change agents derive authority from their positions of command and from the relationships that they have with their people. On what other sources do they depend for authority?

4. How do change agents measure accountability? Explain. Is this practice realistic? How does it differ from the norm? Why is it important to a company?

Skills Exercise

Jon R. Katzenbach of McKinsey & Company, a management consultancy firm, believes that "you need a critical mass of change leaders in the middle of an organization for large-scale transformations." He defines that critical mass as roughly one-third of a company's middle managers. Companies facing really rapid change require even a greater percentage of change leaders, while those in rel- atively stable environments need a smaller percentage. Based on your reading, support or refute his assertion. Work with a partner to name companies that might need a greater percentage of change agents. Which companies would need a lower percentage? In class, defend your classifications with findings about each company's environment, objectives, and activities.

The Internet learning materials that accompany this chapter can be found at
http://www.profcerto.com
Additional information can be found on the inside front and back covers
of this text.

12

chapter

MANAGING HUMAN RESOURCES

STUDENT LEARNING OBJECTIVES

From studying this chapter, I will attempt to acquire:

1. An overall understanding of how appropriate human resources can be provided for the organization.

2. An appreciation for the relationship among recruitment efforts, an open position, sources of human resources, and the law.

3. Insights on the use of tests and assessment centers in employee selection.

4. An understanding of how the training process operates.

5. A concept of what performance appraisals are and how they can best be conducted.

CHAPTER OUTLINE

United Airlines' training center in Chicago has recently been packed tighter than an overhead storage bin. To meet its goal of hiring 1,000 flight attendants, United has been herding trainees through its seven-week course, and the crush has forced the nation's largest airline to cram four to a dormitory room, prowl for temporary quarters, and briefly ponder the unthinkable: shipping new hires to a Dallas training center owned by archrival American Airlines. Floored at a doubling in the size of flight-attendant classes, Ursula Georgi, a United trainer since 1991, said, "I've never seen anything like this."

Besides flight attendants, United is adding 500 pilots, 200 mechanics, and 1,200 reservationists. Its Denver personnel office has been so swamped that pilots have helped interview candidates. After all the newcomers settle into their jobs, United's employment will total about 79,000, up 3,000 from the previous year.

Why does United need all of these new people? While rival airlines are shrinking operations and cutting costs, Gerald Greenwald, United's chairman and chief executive since July 1994, is flying against the pack, leading the UAL Corporation unit on a costly—and risky—expansion binge.

The company recently increased by 13 percent the daily flights offered by its new low-fare West Coast Shuttle. In addition, United is emphasizing overseas business as its growth target. The airline has earmarked most of a special $50 million fund to improve its high-fare, international service. It will add 2 passenger-pampering flight attendants to the current 16 on its 747-400s on trans-Pacific flights and will spruce up menus—rescinding earlier cutbacks that eroded its market position.

Meanwhile, United is lobbying hard to win route authority between Chicago and London's Heathrow Airport, the biggest hole in United's overseas network. It also plans to raise capacity 2 percent in the Pacific, with more flights out of Tokyo and Osaka. It is considering requesting new route authorities into China and has been holding investment discussions with fast-growing China Southern Airlines.

Clearly, United must hire new employees to implement its aggressive new plans. Management must be careful, however, not to hire just anybody, but to choose the *right* people.

United Airlines Chicago training center is bustling because United is bucking an industrywide trend by hiring 1,000 new flight attendants, 500 pilots, 200 mechanics, and 1,200 reservationists.

The introductory case discusses an intense effort by United Airlines to hire more flight attendants, pilots, mechanics, and reservationists. The task of hiring not just people, but the *right* people, is an important part of managing human resources. This chapter outlines the process of managing human resources within an organization and illustrates how the hiring of the right employees fits within this process. First it defines appropriate human resources. Then it examines the steps to be followed in providing them.

The emphasis in Chapter 11 was on organizing the activity of individuals within the management system. To this end, responsibility, authority, and delegation were discussed in detail. This chapter continues to explore the relationship between individuals and organizing by discussing how appropriate human resources can be provided for the organization.

DEFINING APPROPRIATE HUMAN RESOURCES

Appropriate human resources are the individuals in the organization who make a valuable contribution to management system goal attainment.

The phrase **appropriate human resources** refers to the individuals within the organization who make a valuable contribution to management system goal attainment. This contribution results from their productivity in the positions they hold. The phrase *inappropriate human resources* refers to organization members who do not make a valuable contribution to the attainment of management system objectives. For one reason or another, these individuals are ineffective in their jobs.

Productivity in all organizations is determined by how human resources interact and combine to use all other management system resources. Such factors as background, age, job-related experience, and level of formal education all play a role in determining how appropriate the individual is for the organization. Although the process of providing appropriate human resources for the organization is involved and somewhat subjective, the following section offers insights on how to increase the success of this process.

STEPS IN PROVIDING HUMAN RESOURCES

To provide appropriate human resources to fill both managerial and nonmanagerial openings, managers follow four sequential steps:

1. Recruitment
2. Selection
3. Training
4. Performance appraisal

Figure 12.1 illustrates these steps.

Recruitment

Recruitment is the initial attraction and screening of the supply of prospective human resources available to fill a position.

Recruitment is the initial attraction and screening of the supply of prospective human resources available to fill a position. Its purpose is to narrow a large field of

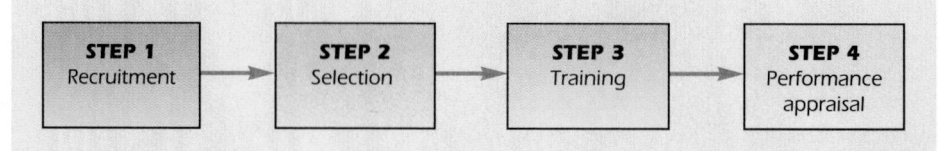

Figure 12.1 **Four sequential steps to provide appropriate human resources for an organization**

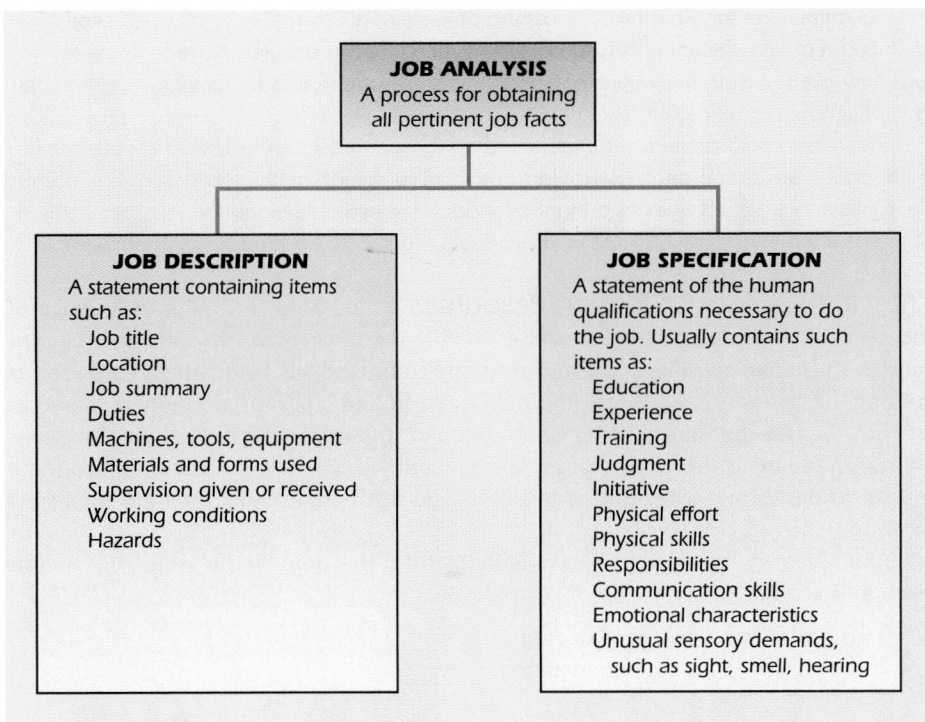

Figure 12.2   Relationship of job analysis, job description, and job specification

prospective employees to a relatively small group of individuals from which someone eventually will be hired. To be effective, recruiters must know the following:

1. The job they are trying to fill.
2. Where potential human resources can be located.
3. How the law influences recruiting efforts.

Knowing the Job

Recruitment activities must begin with a thorough understanding of the position to be filled so the broad range of potential employees can be narrowed down intelligently. The technique commonly used to gain that understanding is known as **job analysis.** Basically, job analysis is aimed at determining a **job description** (the activities a job entails) and a **job specification** (the characteristics of the individual who should be hired for the job). Figure 12.2 shows the relationship of job analysis to job description and job specification.[1]

The U.S. Civil Service Commission has developed a procedure for performing a job analysis. As with all job analysis procedures, the Civil Service procedure uses information gathering as the primary means of determining what workers do and how and why they do it. Naturally, the quality of the job analysis depends on the accuracy of information gathered. This information is used to develop both a job description and a job specification.[2]

BACK TO THE CASE

In hiring new employees for an operation like United Airlines, management must be careful to emphasize not just hiring workers, but hiring the right workers. For United Airlines, appropriate human resources are those people who will make a valuable contribution to the attainment of United's organizational objectives. In hiring flight attendants, reservationists, and mechanics, for example, management should consider taking on only those people who will most help the organization become successful. In finding appropriate human resources, management at United Airlines needs to follow four basic steps: recruitment, selection, training, and performance appraisal.

Job analysis is a technique commonly used to gain an understanding of what a task entails and the type of individual who should be hired to perform that task.

A **job description** is a list of specific activities that must be performed to accomplish some task or job.

A **job specification** is a list of the characteristics of the individual who should be hired to perform a specific task or job.

Recruitment entails the initial screening of individuals available to fill open positions at United. For recruitment efforts to be successful, United's recruiters have to know the jobs they are trying to fill, where potential human resources can be located, and how the law influences recruiting efforts.

Recruiters could acquire an understanding of open positions at United by performing a job analysis. The job analysis would force them to determine the job description of the open position—the activities of a flight attendant, for example—and the job specification of the position, including the type of individual who should be hired to fill that position.

Knowing Sources of Human Resources

Besides a thorough knowledge of the position the organization is trying to fill, recruiters must be able to pinpoint sources of human resources. Since the supply of individuals from which to recruit is continually changing, there will be times when finding appropriate human resources will be much harder than at other times. Human resources specialists in organizations constantly monitor the labor market so they will know where to recruit appropriate human resources and what kind of strategies and tactics to use to attract job applicants in a competitive marketplace.[3]

Sources of human resources available to fill a position can be generally categorized in two ways:

1. Sources inside the organization.
2. Sources outside the organization.

Sources Inside the Organization. The pool of employees within the organization is one source of human resources. Some individuals who already work for the organization may be well qualified for an open position. Although existing personnel are sometimes moved laterally within an organization, most internal movements are promotions. Promotion from within has the advantages of building employee morale, encouraging employees to work harder in hopes of being promoted, and enticing employees to stay with the organization because of the possibility of future promotions. Companies such as Exxon and General Electric find it very rewarding to train their managers for advancement within the organization.[4]

Human Resources Inventory. A **human resource inventory** consists of information about the characteristics of organization members. The focus is on past performance and future potential, and the objective is to keep management up-to-date about the possibilities for filling a position from within. This inventory should indicate which individuals in the organization would be appropriate for filling a position if it became available. In a classic article, Walter S. Wikstrom proposed that organizations keep three types of records that can be combined to maintain a useful human resource inventory.[5] Although Wikstrom focused on filling managerial positions, slight modifications to his inventory forms would make his records equally useful for filling nonmanagerial positions. Many organizations computerize records like the ones Wikstrom suggests to make their human resource inventory system more efficient and effective.

- The first of Wikstrom's three record-keeping forms for a human resource inventory is the **management inventory card.** The management inventory card in Figure 12.3 has been completed for a fictional manager named Mel Murray. It indicates Murray's age, year of employment, present position and the length of time he has held it, performance ratings, strengths and weaknesses, the positions to which he might move, when he would be ready to assume these positions, and additional training he would need to fill the positions. In short, this card contains both an organizational history of Murray and an indication of how he might be used in the future.
- Figure 12.4 shows Wikstrom's second human resource inventory form—the **position replacement form.** This form focuses on position-centered information rather than the people-centered information maintained on the man-

A **human resource inventory** is an accumulation of information about the characteristics of organization members; this information focuses on members' past performance as well as on how they might be trained and best used in the future.

The **management inventory card** is a form used in compiling a human resource inventory. It contains the organizational history of an individual and indicates how that individual might be used in the organization in the future.

The **position replacement form** is used in compiling a human resource inventory. It summarizes information about organization members who could fill a position should it open up.

NAME Murray, Mel	AGE 47	EMPLOYED 1985
PRESENT POSITION Manager, Sales (House Fans Division)		On Job 6 years
PRESENT PERFORMANCE Outstanding—exceeded sales goal in spite of stiffer competition.		
STRENGTHS Good planner—motivates subordinates very well—excellent communication.		
WEAKNESSES Still does not always delegate as much as situation requires. Sometimes does not understand production problems.		
EFFORTS TO IMPROVE Has greatly improved in delegating in last two years; also has organized more effectively after taking a management course on own time and initiative.		
COULD MOVE TO Vice President, Marketing		WHEN 1997
TRAINING NEEDED More exposure to problems of other divisions (attend top staff conference?). Perhaps university program stressing staff role of corporate marketing versus line sales.		
COULD MOVE TO Manager, House or Industrial Fans Division		WHEN 1998 1999
TRAINING NEEDED Course in production management; some project working with production people; perhaps a good business game somewhere.		

Figure 12.3 Management inventory card

POSITION	Manager, Sales (House Fans Division)		
PERFORMANCE Outstanding	INCUMBENT Mel Murray	SALARY $44,500	MAY MOVE 1 Year
REPLACEMENT 1 Earl Renfrew		SALARY $39,500	AGE 39
PRESENT POSITION Field Sales Manager, House Fans		EMPLOYED: Present Job 3 years	Company 10 years
TRAINING NEEDED Special assignment to study market potential for air conditioners to provide forecasting experience.		WHEN READY Now	
REPLACEMENT 2 Bernard Storey		SALARY $38,500	AGE 36
PRESENT POSITION Promotion Manager, House Fans		EMPLOYED: Present Job 4 years	Company 7 years
TRAINING NEEDED Rotation to field sales. Marketing conference in fall.		WHEN READY 2 years	

Figure 12.4 Position replacement form

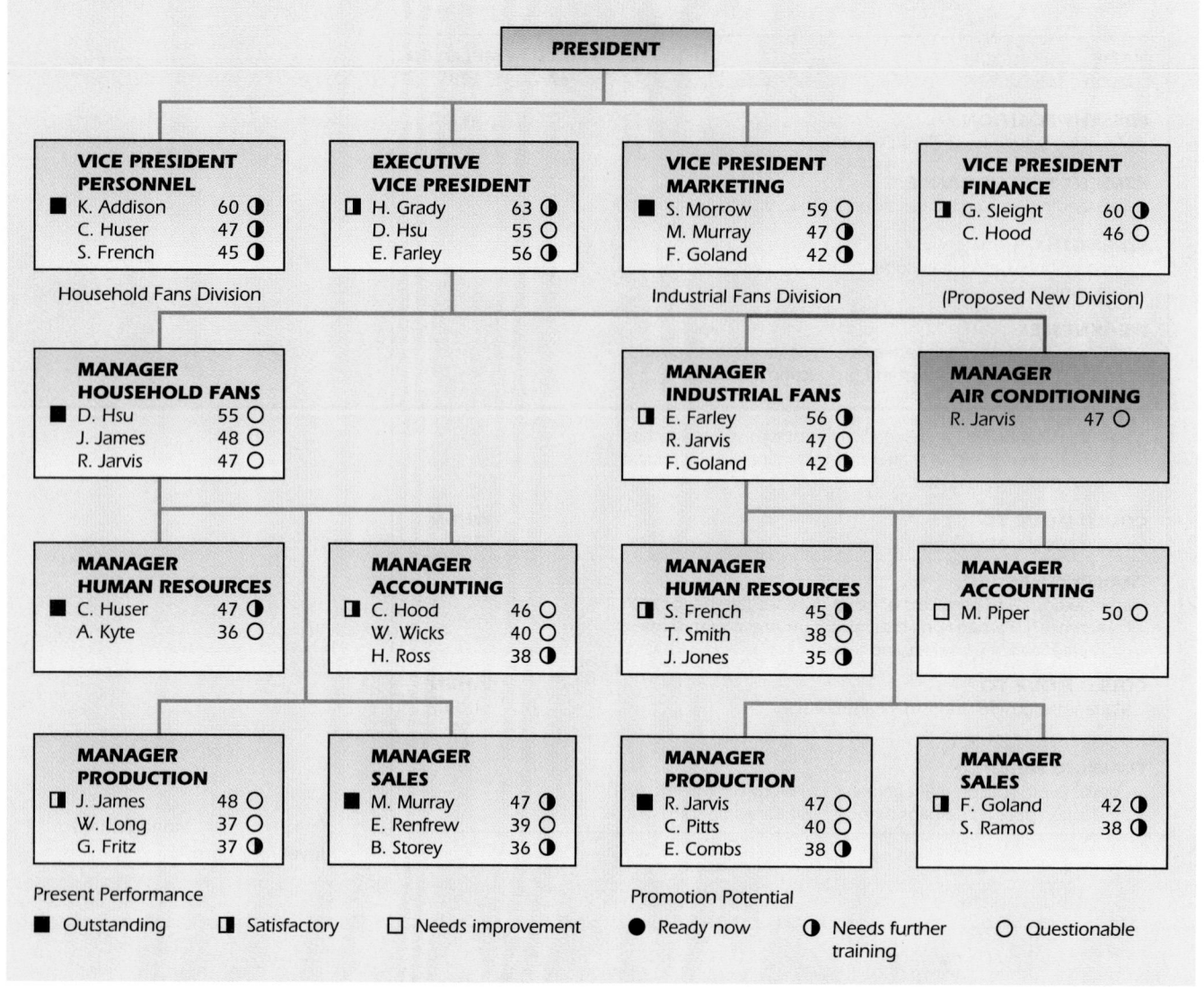

Figure 12.5 Management manpower replacement chart

agement inventory card. Note that the form in Figure 12.4 indicates little about Murray, but much about two individuals who could replace him. The position replacement form is helpful in determining what would happen to Murray's present position if Murray were selected to be moved within the organization or if he decided to leave the organization.

The **management manpower replacement chart** is a form used in compiling a human resource inventory. It is people-oriented and presents a composite view of individuals management considers significant to human resource planning.

- Wikstrom's third human resource inventory form is the **management manpower replacement chart** (see Figure 12.5). This chart presents a composite view of the individuals management considers significant for human resource planning. Note on Figure 12.5 how Murray's performance rating and promotion potential can easily be compared with those of other employees when the company is trying to determine which individual would most appropriately fill a particular position.

The management inventory card, the position replacement form, and the management manpower replacement chart are three separate record-keeping devices for a human resource inventory. Each form furnishes different data on which to base a hiring-from-within decision. These forms help management to answer the following questions:

1. What is the organizational history of an individual, and what potential does that person possess (management inventory card)?
2. If a position becomes vacant, who might be eligible to fill it (position replacement form)?
3. What are the merits of one individual being considered for a position compared to those of another individual under consideration (management manpower replacement chart)?

Considering the answers to these three questions collectively should help management make successful hiring-from-within decisions. Computer software is available to aid managers in keeping track of the organization's complex human resource inventories and in making better decisions about how employees can be best deployed and developed.[6]

Sources Outside the Organization.   If a position cannot be filled by someone presently employed by the organization, management has available numerous sources of human resources outside the organization. These sources include the following:

1. *Competitors.*   One often-tapped external source of human resources is competing organizations. Since there are several advantages to luring human resources away from competitors, this type of piracy has become a common practice. Among the advantages are the following:

   - The individual knows the business.
   - The competitor will have paid for the individual's training up to the time of hire.
   - The competing organization will probably be weakened somewhat by the loss of the individual.
   - Once hired, the individual will be a valuable source of information about how to best compete with the other organization.

2. *Employment agencies.*   Employment agencies help people find jobs and help organizations find job applicants. Such agencies can be either public or private. Public employment agencies do not charge fees, whereas private ones collect a fee from either the person hired or the organization doing the hiring, once the hire has been finalized.

3. *Readers of certain publications.*   Perhaps the most widely used external source of human resources is the readership of certain publications. To tap this source, recruiters simply place an advertisement in a suitable publication. The advertisement describes the open position in detail and announces that the organization is accepting applications from qualified individuals. The type of position to be filled determines the type of publication in which the advertisement is placed. The objective is to advertise in a publication whose readers are likely to be interested in filling the position. An opening for a top-level executive might be advertised in *The Wall Street Journal*, a training director opening might be advertised in the *Journal of Training and Development*, and an educational opening might be advertised in the *Chronicle of Higher Education*.

4. *Educational institutions.*   Many recruiters go directly to schools to interview students close to graduation. Liberal arts schools, business schools, engineering schools, junior colleges, and community colleges all have somewhat different human resources to offer. Recruiting efforts should focus on the schools with the highest probability of providing human resources appropriate for the open position.

Knowing the Law

Legislation has had a major impact on modern organizational recruitment practices. Managers need to be aware of the laws that govern recruitment efforts. The Civil Rights Act passed in 1964 and amended in 1972 created the **Equal Employment Opportunity Commission (EEOC)** to enforce federal laws prohibit-

The **Equal Employment Opportunity Commission (EEOC)** is an agency established to enforce federal laws regulating recruiting and other employment practices.

In Louisville, Kentucky, a program called Job Link has been established by the nonprofit Louisville Private Industry Council. Job Link is a one-stop career center that helps job seekers prepare materials and devise strategies. Applicants with good skills are referred to current employment leads; in other cases, training is provided—for example, an unemployed data-processing clerk may be trained as a systems analyst. Most people find jobs within six weeks.

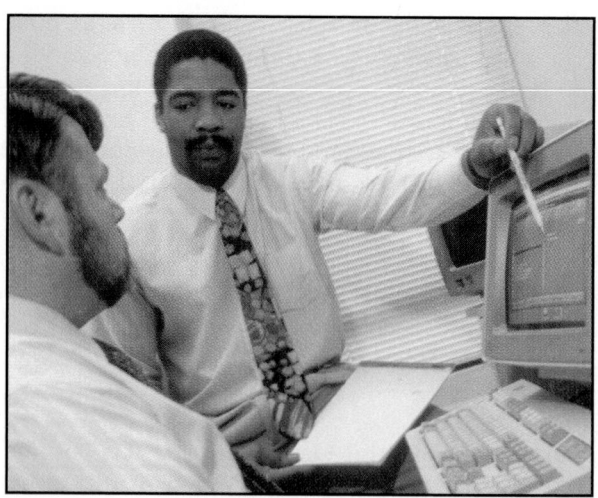

ing discrimination on the basis of race, color, religion, sex, and national origin in recruitment, hiring, firing, layoffs, and all other employment practices. The EEOC report was amended in 1978 to include the Pregnancy Discrimination Act, which requires employees to treat pregnancy, insofar as leave and insurance are concerned, like any other form of medical disability.

Equal opportunity legislation protects the right of a citizen to work and to obtain a fair wage based primarily on merit and performance. The EEOC seeks to uphold this right by overseeing the employment practices of labor unions, private employers, educational institutions, and government bodies.

Affirmative action programs are organizational programs whose basic purpose is to eliminate barriers against and increase employment opportunities for underutilized or disadvantaged individuals.

Affirmative Action. In response to equal opportunity legislation, many organizations have established **affirmative action programs.** Translated literally, *affirmative action* means positive movement: "In the area of equal employment opportunity, the basic purpose of positive movement or affirmative action is to eliminate barriers and increase opportunities for the purpose of increasing the utilization of underutilized and/or disadvantaged individuals."[7] An organization can judge how much progress it is making toward eliminating such barriers by taking the following steps:

1. Determining how many minority and disadvantaged individuals it presently employs.
2. Determining how many minority and disadvantaged individuals it should be employing according to EEOC guidelines.
3. Comparing the numbers obtained in steps 1 and 2.

If the two numbers obtained in step 3 are nearly the same, the organization's employment practices probably should be maintained; if they are not nearly the same, the organization should modify its employment practices accordingly.

Modern management writers recommend that managers follow the guidelines of affirmative action, not merely because they are mandated by law, but also because of the characteristics of today's labor supply.[8] According to these writers, more than half of the U.S. workforce now consists of minorities, immigrants, and women. Since the overall workforce is so diverse, it follows that employees in today's organizations will also be more diverse than in the past. Thus today's managers face the challenge of forging a productive workforce out of an increasingly diverse labor pool, and this task is more formidable than simply complying with affirmative action laws.

Many managers confront special issues related to minority employees after they are hired. The following PEOPLE PERSPECTIVES feature describes one issue pertaining to women employees and explains how NationsBank is responding to it.

As part of its effort to train a future diverse workforce, Merrill Lynch helps schools in cities like multiracial Jersey City, New Jersey, develop programs to teach students the use of computers and financial-services software. Merrill Lynch also provides tutors for grade-school children and sponsors summer internships for high-school students.

NationsBank Helps Women Employees with Child Care

PEOPLE PERSPECTIVES
Many managers are discovering that their women employees need child-care services during working hours. This is an important issue in today's workplace since many managers are finding that the quality of child care employees can obtain for their children has a direct and measurable impact on those employees' productivity.

Companies are responding to the need for high-quality child care for the dependents of their employees out of sheer self-interest. NationsBank Corporation, for example, recently set aside $10 million for a five-year investment in such programs as developing a child-care center within the company and training outside caregivers to be made available for hire by NationsBank employees. This allocation of company funds is not viewed as a charitable donation by NationsBank management. Rather, management sees the $10 million as an investment in productivity, on the theory that by eliminating working parents' concerns about the care their dependents are receiving, the bank will gain more productive employees.

NationsBank decided to focus on child care because of the deplorable conditions in so many child-care facilities today. Many working parents are leaving their children in facilities that are unhealthy and unsafe, and studies show that such poor-quality care threatens children's cognitive and emotional development. A recent study of 400 day-care centers across the United States found that 73.7 percent of them were providing only average care that may compromise children's readiness to learn when they enter school. Another 12.3 percent of the centers studied were rated unacceptable.≈

BACK TO THE CASE
A successful recruitment effort at United Airlines would require recruiters to know where to locate appropriate human resources to fill positions open at the company. These sources could be found both within the company and outside it.

To support its expansion plans, United management must devise ways to obtain appropriate human resources, along with equipment, airport space, and other necessary resources. Maintaining some type of human resource inventory would keep management up-to-date on the possibilities of filling positions from within the organization. This inventory would contain information about (1) the organizational histories and potential of various United employees, (2) the qualifications of employees who are eligible to fill expansion roles, and (3) the relative abilities of various United employees to fill the necessary openings. Some outside sources of human resources that management could tap are competitors (for example, Delta Airlines, Southwest Airlines, and Transworld Airlines),

"*How many times do I have to tell Personnel we want a hip young crowd buying our products, not working for us?*"

public and private employment agencies, the readership of industry-related publications, and various types of educational institutions.

United management must also be aware of how the law affects its recruitment efforts. Under federal law, recruitment practices cannot discriminate on the basis of race, color, religion, sex, or national origin. If United's recruitment practices are discriminatory, the company will be subject to prosecution by the Equal Employment Opportunity Commission.

Selection

Selection is choosing an individual to hire from all those who have been recruited.

The second major step involved in providing human resources for the organization is **selection**—choosing an individual to hire from all those who have been recruited.[9] Selection, obviously, is dependent on the first step, recruitment. The cartoon below lightheartedly points up the importance of selecting the right people for an organization.

Selection is typically represented as a series of stages through which job applicants must pass in order to be hired.[10] Each stage reduces the total group of prospective employees until, finally, one individual is hired. Figure 12.6 lists the specific stages of the selection process, indicates reasons for eliminating applicants at each stage, and illus-

STAGES OF THE SELECTION PROCESS	REASONS FOR ELIMINATION	
Preliminary screening from records, data sheets, etc. Preliminary interview	Lack of adequate educational and performance record Obvious misfit from outward appearance and conduct	Available potential personnel from inside or outside company
Intelligence tests Aptitude tests	Failure to meet minimum standards Failure to have minimum necessary aptitude	
Personality tests Performance references	Negative aspects of personality Unfavorable or negative reports on past performance	Rejection of potential employees
Diagnostic interview	Lack of necessary innate ability, ambition, or other qualities	
Physical examination Personal judgment	Physically unfit for job Remaining candidate placed in available position	Employee

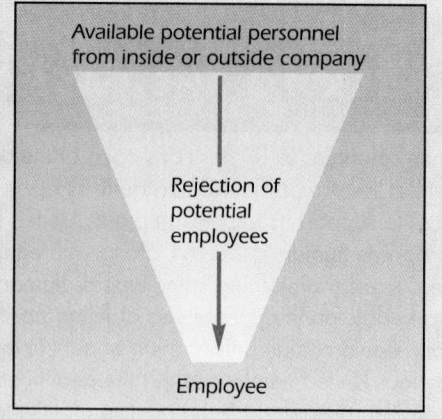

Figure 12.6   Summary of major factors in the selection process

trates how the group of potential employees is narrowed down to the individual who ultimately is hired. Two tools often used in the selection process are testing and assessment centers.

COMPAQ COMPUTER COMPANY'S INTERNATIONAL SELECTION SLIP-UPS

GLOBAL SPOTLIGHT

At times, managers must handle selection mistakes—people who shortly after being hired leave the company voluntarily or are fired. In these cases, recruitment and selection expenses are lost.

Growth at Compaq Computer Company, a computer manufacturer based in Houston, Texas, has been phenomenal in recent years. In 1994, the firm had annual sales of $10.9 billion—up from $7.2 billion in 1993—with $887 million in net profit—up from $462 million in 1993. The company's expansion into international markets has played a major role in its success.

Selection mistakes in the international arena are likely to be more expensive for a company like Compaq than selection mistakes in the domestic arena because foreign assignments are usually more expensive than domestic assignments to set up and maintain. Expenses incurred for employees posted to a foreign country include salary based on the value of the U.S. dollar in that country, housing allowance, cost-of-living adjustments, transportation allowances, and private-school tuition for employees' children.≈

Testing   **Testing** is examining human resources for qualities relevant to performing available jobs. Although many different kinds of tests are available for organizational use, they generally can be divided into the following four categories:[11]

> **Testing** is examining human resources for qualities relevant to performing available jobs.

1. *Aptitude tests.*   Tests of aptitude measure the potential of an individual to perform a task. Some aptitude tests measure general intelligence, while others measure special abilities, such as mechanical, clerical, or visual skills.

2. *Achievement tests.*   Tests that measure the level of skill or knowledge an individual possesses in a certain area are called achievement tests. This skill or knowledge may have been acquired through various training activities or through experience in the area. Examples of skill tests are typing and keyboarding tests.

3. *Vocational interest tests.*   Tests of vocational interest attempt to measure an individual's interest in performing various kinds of jobs. They are administered on the assumption that certain people perform jobs well because they find the job activities stimulating. The basic purpose of this type of test is to select for an open position the individual who finds most aspects of that position interesting.

4. *Personality tests.*   Personality tests attempt to describe an individual's personality dimensions in such areas as emotional maturity, subjectivity, honesty, and objectivity. These tests can be used advantageously if the personality characteristics needed to do well in a particular job are well defined and if individuals possessing those characteristics can be identified and selected. Managers must be careful, however, not to expose themselves to legal prosecution by basing employment decisions on personality tests that are invalid and unreliable. Test validity and reliability are discussed under "Testing Guidelines."[12]

Testing Guidelines.   Several guidelines should be observed when tests are used as part of the selection process. First, care must be taken to ensure that the test being used is both valid and reliable. A test is *valid* if it measures what it is designed to mea-

sure and *reliable* if it measures similarly time after time.[13] Second, test results should not be used as the sole determinant of a hiring decision. People change over time, and someone who doesn't score well on a particular test might still develop into a productive employee. Such factors as potential and desire to obtain a position should be assessed subjectively and used along with test scores in the final selection decision. Third, care should be taken to ensure that tests are nondiscriminatory; many tests contain language or cultural biases that may discriminate against minorities. This third guideline is especially important for managers to remember since the EEOC has the authority to prosecute organizations that use discriminatory testing practices.

Assessment Centers
Another tool often used in employee selection is the **assessment center.** Although the assessment center concept is discussed in this chapter primarily as an aid to selection, it is also used in such areas as human resource training and organization development. The first industrial use of the assessment center is usually credited to AT&T. Since AT&T's initial efforts, the assessment center concept has expanded greatly, and today it is used not only as a means for identifying individuals to be hired from outside an organization but also for identifying individuals from inside the organization who should be promoted. Corporations that have used assessment centers extensively include J.C. Penney, Standard Oil of Ohio, and IBM.[14]

An assessment center is a program (not a place) in which participants engage in a number of individual and group exercises constructed to simulate important activities at the organizational levels to which they aspire.[15] These exercises can include such activities as participating in leaderless discussions, giving oral presentations, and leading a group in solving some assigned problem. The individuals performing the activities are observed by managers or trained observers who evaluate both their ability and their potential. In general, participants are assessed according to the following criteria:[16]

1. Leadership
2. Organizing and planning ability
3. Decision making
4. Oral and written communication skills
5. Initiative
6. Energy
7. Analytical ability
8. Resistance to stress
9. Use of delegation
10. Behavior flexibility
11. Human relations competence
12. Originality
13. Controlling
14. Self-direction
15. Overall potential

An **assessment center** is a program in which participants engage in, and are evaluated on, a number of individual and group exercises constructed to simulate important activities at the organizational levels to which they aspire.

BACK TO THE CASE After the initial screening of potential human resources, United Airlines will be faced with the task of selecting from among those who have been screened the individuals to be hired. Two tools the company could use in this selection process are testing and assessment centers.

After screening potential employees, for example, management might administer aptitude tests, achievement tests, vocational interest tests, or personality tests to see if any of the screened individuals have the qualities necessary to fill a specific job. Before it uses these tests, however, management must make sure that they are both valid and reliable, that they will not be the sole basis on which a selection decision is made, and that they are nondiscriminatory.

Table 12.1

Types and Popularity of Training Offered by Organizations

TYPES OF TRAINING	PERCENTAGE OF SURVEYED COMPANIES THAT OFFER THE TRAINING
1. Management skills and development	74.3
2. Supervisory skills	73.4
3. Technical skills/knowledge updating	72.7
4. Communication skills	66.8
5. Customer relations/services	63.8
6. Executive development	56.8
7. New methods/procedures	56.5
8. Sales skills	54.1
9. Clerical/secretarial skills	52.9
10. Personal growth	51.9
11. Computer literacy/basic computer skills	48.2
12. Employee/labor relations	44.9
13. Disease prevention/health promotion	38.9
14. Customer education	35.7
15. Remedial basic education	18.0

United can also use assessment centers to simulate the tasks necessary to perform jobs people are applying for. Those who perform well on these tasks would generally be more suited to the positions than would those who do poorly. Assessment centers are particularly appropriate for evaluating applicants for flight attendant because simulation of job conditions in this area would give management an excellent idea of how applicants would interact with passengers during flights.

Training

After recruitment and selection, the next step in providing appropriate human resources for the organization is training. **Training** is the process of developing qualities in human resources that will enable them to be more productive and thus to contribute more to organizational goal attainment. The purpose of training is to increase the productivity of employees by influencing their behavior. Table 12.1 provides an overview of the types and popularity of training being offered by organizations today.

The training of individuals is essentially a four-step process:

1. Determining training needs.
2. Designing the training program.
3. Administering the training program.
4. Evaluating the training program.

These steps are presented in Figure 12.7 and are described in the sections that follow.

Training programs are sometimes developed with definite beginning and end points in mind. The following CUTTING EDGE feature describes how Motorola's training of employees focuses on continuous, lifelong learning.

Training is the process of developing qualities in human resources that will enable them to be more productive.

CUTTING EDGE

LIFELONG LEARNING AT MOTOROLA

To increase its competitiveness, Motorola, Inc., has started a training campaign built on the idea of lifelong learning. Training for all Motorola employees is now continuous throughout their entire careers at the company. Under a program conceived by Robert W. Galvin,

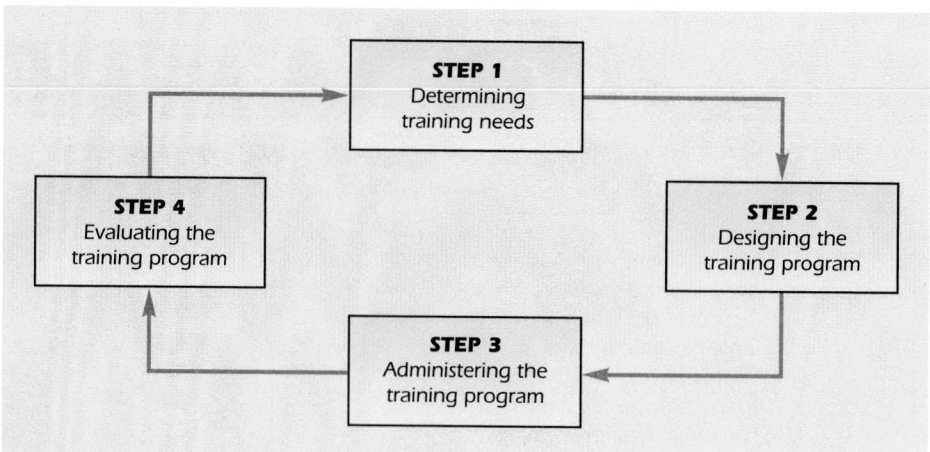

Figure 12.7 Steps of the training process

Motorola will dramatically upgrade the training of all employees, from the factory floor to the corporate office. The goal is a workforce that is disciplined, yet free-thinking.

One area in which the company trains its people is "statistical process control," a method for catching and correcting mistakes made during the manufacturing process. Statistical process control involves determining the rates at which production errors are made and requires the use of arithmetic and even a bit of algebra. Since the company's success depends on how well workers from the shop floor on up are able to use statistical process control, much of Motorola's training effort is concentrated on this area.

In general, Motorola's lifelong learning program links training to job activities that are crucial to the long-run success of the company. For instance, reducing the time it takes to develop new products is vital to the company's competitiveness, so Motorola has designed a special course to teach employees how to speed up the new-product development process.

Motorola's lifelong learning approach is being applied at company facilities in several different countries. Management believes it is essential to establish training consistency across national borders because more than half of Motorola's revenue comes from overseas and this percentage is bound to rise as the company increases foreign production. To promote consistency, translators are used to make certain that Motorola's training courses communicate the same message throughout the world.≈

Training needs are the information or skill areas of an individual or group that require further development to increase the productivity of that individual or group.

Determining Training Needs

The first step of the training process is determining the organization's training needs.[17] **Training needs** are the information or skill areas of an individual or group that require further development to increase the productivity of that individual or group. Only if training focuses on these needs can it be productive for the organization.

The training of organization members is typically a continuing activity. Even employees who have been with the organization for some time and who have undergone initial orientation and skills training need continued training to improve their skills.

Determining Needed Skills. There are several methods of determining which skills to focus on with established human resources. One method calls for evaluating the production process within the organization. Such factors as excessive rejected products, unmet deadlines, and high labor costs are clues to deficiencies in production-related expertise. Another method for determining training needs calls for getting direct feedback from employees on what they believe are the organization's training needs. Organization members are often able to verbalize clearly and accurately

exactly what types of training they require to do a better job. A third way of determining training needs involves looking into the future. If the manufacture of new products or the use of newly purchased equipment is foreseen, some type of corresponding training almost certainly will be needed.

Designing the Training Program   Once training needs have been determined, a training program aimed at meeting those needs must be designed. Basically, designing a program entails assembling various types of facts and activities that will meet the established training needs. Obviously, as training needs vary, so will the facts and activities designed to meet those needs.

BACK TO THE CASE   After hiring new employees, United Airlines must train them to be productive organization members. To train effectively, the company must determine training needs, design a corresponding training program, and administer and evaluate it.

Designing a training program requires that United assemble facts and activities that address specific company training needs. These needs are information or skill areas that must be further developed in United employees to make them more productive. Over the long term, United's training program should focus on established employees as well as on newly hired employees.

As mentioned in the introductory case, United's new hires will fill positions in expansion areas like London, Tokyo, and Osaka. Management should try to learn as much as possible from past training programs that the company operated to support expansion in other foreign cities. Knowing the strengths and weaknesses of these training programs will enable management to design efficient and effective training programs for its newest expansion plans.

Administering the Training Program   The next step in the training process is administering the training program—that is, actually training the individuals selected to participate in the program. Various techniques exist for both transmitting necessary information and developing needed skills in training programs, and several of these techniques are discussed in the sections that follow.

Techniques for Transmitting Information.   Two techniques for transmitting information in training programs are lectures and programmed learning. Although it could be argued that these techniques develop some skills in individuals as well as transmit information to them, they are primarily devices for the dissemination of information.

1. *Lectures.*   Perhaps the most widely used technique for transmitting information in training programs is the lecture. The **lecture** is a primarily one-way communication situation in which an instructor orally presents information to a group of listeners. The instructor typically does most of the talking in this type of training situation. Trainees participate primarily through listening and note taking.

   An advantage of the lecture is that it allows the instructor to expose trainees to a maximum amount of information within a given time period. The lecture, however, has some serious disadvantages:

   > The lecture generally consists of a one-way communication: the instructor presents information to the group of passive listeners. Thus, little or no opportunity exists to clarify meanings, to check on whether trainees really understand the lecture material, or to handle the wide diversity of ability, attitude, and interest that may prevail among the trainees. Also, there is little or no opportunity for practice, reinforcement, knowledge of results, or over-

A **lecture** is primarily a one-way communication situation in which an instructor trains by orally presenting information to an individual or a group.

learning. . . . Ideally, the competent lecturer should make the material meaningful and intrinsically motivating to his or her listeners. However, whether most lectures achieve this goal is a moot question. . . . These limitations, in turn, impose further limitations on the lecture's actual content. A skillful lecturer may be fairly successful in transmitting conceptual knowledge to a group of trainees who are ready to receive it; however, all the evidence available indicates that the nature of the lecture situation makes it of minimal value in promoting attitudinal or behavioral change.[18]

AETNA LIFE & CASUALTY COMPANY TRAINS VIA TV

QUALITY SPOTLIGHT

When Aetna Life & Casualty Company evaluated its employee training program, it found that the key problem was not the quality of the instructors, the tools and styles of program presentations, the content, or even the materials used to supplement the workshops. Instead, Aetna found that the key problem was enabling large numbers of geographically distributed trainees to attend programs conducted at a central location.

Aetna realized that if it wanted to provide high-quality service to its customers, it had to train more than the select few of its employees who were able to travel to the program locations. Aetna's goal was to dramatically increase the number of trained employees, thereby enhancing the quality of the service they could provide to customers. After company executives and training personnel brainstormed ideas for disseminating training more widely, they came up with a plan to offer interactive training via television.

Thus Aetna developed the Aetna Television Network, which links 235 field offices with the home office. The Aetna Television Network enables the company to make its training programs available throughout the country to office locations that previously were unable to take advantage of the programs. As an example, over the past few years, 810 Aetna employees have participated in a business-writing workshop in person, whereas more than 3,000 have participated in the workshop via the Aetna Television Network.

Using television to train employees is gaining in popularity throughout the business world. Television networks allow great flexibility in business training programs. The same workshop can be heard by employees throughout a company at the same time or at different times, as schedules allow. The trend toward using television as a vehicle for increasing the quality of business training should continue to grow in the future.≈

Programmed learning is a technique for instructing without the presence or intervention of a human instructor. Small pieces of information requiring responses are presented to individual trainees, and the trainees determine from checking their responses against provided answers whether their understanding of the information is accurate.

2. *Programmed Learning.* Another commonly used technique for transmitting information in training programs is called programmed learning. **Programmed learning** is a technique for instructing without the presence or intervention of a human instructor.[19] Small parts of information that require related responses are presented to individual trainees. The trainees can determine from checking their responses against provided answers whether their understanding of the information is accurate. The types of responses required of trainees vary from situation to situation, but usually are multiple-choice, true-false, or fill-in-the-blank.

Like the lecture method, programmed learning has both advantages and disadvantages. Among the advantages are that it can be computerized and students can learn at their own pace, know immediately if they are right or wrong, and participate actively in the learning process. The primary disadvantage of this method is that no one is present to answer a confused learner's questions.

As part of its Product Education Program, Fred Meyer, a discount-store chain based in Portland, Oregon, has installed PCs in the lunchrooms of its 133 stores. Here, employees can take advantage of some 200 CD-ROM interactive mini-courses in such subjects as product features and customer-service procedures. Meyer uses training software that was custom-produced by another Portland firm, Graphic Media. Typically, CD-ROM courses present video, audio, and text material and permit users to proceed at their own pace.

Techniques for Developing Skills.   Techniques for developing skills in training programs can be divided into two broad categories: on-the-job and classroom. Techniques for developing skills on the job, referred to as **on-the-job training,** reflect a blend of job-related knowledge and experience. They include coaching, position rotation, and special project committees. *Coaching* is direct critiquing of how well an individual is performing a job. *Position rotation* involves moving an individual from job to job to enable the person to gain an understanding of the organization as a whole. *Special project committees* are vehicles for assigning a particular task to an individual to furnish him or her with experience in a designated area.[20]

Classroom techniques for developing skills also reflect a blend of job-related knowledge and experience. The skills addressed through these techniques can range from technical, such as computer programming skills, to interpersonal, such as leadership skills. Specific classroom techniques aimed at developing skills include various types of management games and role-playing activities. The most common format for *management games* requires small groups of trainees to make and then evaluate various management decisions. The *role-playing format* typically involves acting out and then reflecting on some people-oriented problem that must be solved in the organization.

In contrast to the typical one-way communication of the lecturer, the skills instructor in the classroom encourages high levels of discussion and interaction among trainees, develops a climate in which trainees learn new behavior from carrying out various activities, clarifies related information, and facilitates learning by eliciting trainees' job-related knowledge and experience in applying that knowledge. The difference between the instructional role in information dissemination and the instructional role in skill development is dramatic.[21]

On-the-job-training is a training technique that blends job-related knowledge with experience in using that knowledge on the job.

Evaluating the Training Program

After the training program has been completed, management should evaluate its effectiveness.[22] Because training programs

At Cin-Made Corp., a paper-packaging maker in Cincinnati, Ohio, one program for broadening employees' skills has some employees training in such techniques as statistical process control; in turn, these workers train colleagues with whom they work on teams. Teams also schedule their own production and control their own inventories. Rewards and bonuses are paid from a fund that earmarks 30 percent of the company's pretax earnings.

represent an investment—costs include materials, trainer time, and production loss while employees are being trained rather than doing their jobs—a reasonable return is essential.

Basically, management should evaluate the training program to determine if it meets the needs for which it was designed. Answers to questions like the following help determine training program effectiveness:

1. Has the excessive reject rate of products declined?
2. Are deadlines being met more regularly?
3. Are labor costs per unit produced decreasing?

If the answer to such questions is yes, the training program can be judged as at least somewhat successful, though perhaps its effectiveness could be enhanced through certain selective changes. If the answer is no, significant modification to the training program is warranted.

In a noteworthy survey of businesspeople, 50 percent of respondents thought that their sales per year would be unaffected if training programs for experienced salespeople were halted.[23] This is the kind of feedback management should seek and scrutinize to see if present training programs should be discontinued, slightly modified, or drastically altered to make them more valuable to the organization. The results of the survey just mentioned indicate a need to make significant changes in sales training programs at the companies covered by the survey.

BACK TO THE CASE

After management has determined training needs at United Airlines and designed programs to meet those needs, the programs must, of course, be administered. To administer its training programs, United might choose to use both the lecture technique and the programmed learning technique for transmitting information to trainees. For actually developing skills in trainees, the company could use on-the-job training methods such as coaching, position rotation, and special project committees. For developing skills in a classroom setting, United might use instructional techniques such as role-playing activities. For example, flight attendants could be asked to handle passengers with various kinds of attitudes and families traveling with small children. Their behavior would then be analyzed with an eye to improving attendant-passenger interactions on United flights.

Once a United training program has been completed, it must be evaluated to determine if it met the training need for which it was designed. Training programs aimed at specific motor skills, such as serving food to passengers or maintaining aircraft, are much easier to evaluate than training programs aimed at interpersonal skills, such as improving attendant-passenger relations. The evaluation of any training program at United should, of course, emphasize how to improve the program the next time it is implemented.

Performance Appraisal

Performance appraisal is the process of reviewing past productive activity to evaluate the contribution individuals have made toward attaining management system objectives.

Even after individuals have been recruited, selected, and trained, the task of making them maximally productive within the organization is not finished. The fourth step in the process of providing appropriate human resources for the organization is **performance appraisal**—the process of reviewing individuals' past productive activity to evaluate the contribution they have made toward attaining management system objectives. Like training, performance appraisal—which is also called *performance review* and *performance evaluation*—is a continuing activity that focuses on both established human resources within the organization and newcomers. Its main purpose is to furnish feedback to organization members about how they can become more productive and useful to the organization in its quest for quality.[24] Table 12.2 describes several methods of performance appraisal.

Table 12.2	
Descriptions of Several Methods of Performance Appraisal	
APPRAISAL METHOD	DESCRIPTION
Rating scale	Individuals appraising performance use a form containing several employee qualities and characteristics to be evaluated (e.g., dependability, initiative, leadership). Each evaluated factor is rated on a continuum or scale ranging, for example, from 1 to 7.
Employee comparisons	Appraisers rank employees according to such factors as job performance and value to the organization. Only one employee can occupy a particular ranking.
Free-form essay	Appraisers simply write down their impressions of employees in paragraph form.
Critical-form essay	Appraisers write down particularly good or bad events involving employees as these events occur. Records of all documented events for any one employee are used to evaluate that person's performance.

Why Use Performance Appraisals?   Most U.S. firms engage in some type of performance appraisal. Douglas McGregor has suggested the following three reasons for using performance appraisals:[25]

1. They provide systematic judgments to support salary increases, promotions, transfers, and sometimes demotions or terminations.
2. They are a means of telling subordinates how they are doing and of suggesting needed changes in behavior, attitudes, skills, or job knowledge; they let subordinates know where they stand with the boss.
3. They furnish a useful basis for the coaching and counseling of individuals by superiors.

Handling Performance Appraisals   If performance appraisals are not handled well, their benefits to the organization will be minimal. Several guidelines can assist management in increasing the appropriateness with which appraisals are conducted. The first guideline is that performance appraisals should stress both performance in the position the individual holds and the success with which the individual is attaining organizational objectives. Although conceptually separate, performance and objectives should be inseparable topics of discussion during performance appraisals. The second guideline is that appraisals should emphasize how well the individual is doing the job, not the evaluator's impression of the individual's work habits. In other words, the goal is an objective analysis of performance rather than a subjective evaluation of habits.

The third guideline is that the appraisal should be acceptable to both the evaluator and the subject—that is, both should agree that it has benefit for the organization and the worker. The fourth, and last, guideline is that performance appraisals should provide a base for improving individuals' productivity within the organization by making them better equipped to produce.[26]

Potential Weaknesses of Performance Appraisals   To maximize the payoff of performance appraisals to the organization, managers must avoid several potential weaknesses of the appraisal process. Potential weaknesses include the following pitfalls:[27]

1. Performance appraisals focus employees on short-term rewards rather than on issues that are important to the long-run success of the organization.
2. Individuals involved in performance appraisals view them as a reward-punishment situation.
3. The emphasis of performance appraisal is on completing paperwork rather than on critiquing individual performance.
4. Individuals being evaluated view the process as unfair or biased.
5. Subordinates react negatively when evaluators offer unfavorable comments.

To avoid these potential weaknesses, supervisors and employees should look on the performance appraisal process as an opportunity to increase the worth of the employee through constructive feedback, not as a means of rewarding or punishing the employee through positive or negative comments. Paperwork should be viewed only as an aid in providing this feedback, not as an end in itself. Also, care should be taken to make appraisal feedback as tactful and objective as possible to minimize negative reactions.

BACK TO THE CASE

The last step in providing appropriate human resources at United Airlines is performance appraisal. This step involves evaluating the contributions that United employees make to the attainment of management system objectives. Naturally, the performance appraisal process should focus on recently hired employees who filled expansion positions, but it should also prove useful with more established employees.

In fact, it would be difficult to visualize a United employee who could not benefit from a properly conducted performance appraisal. Such an appraisal would stress activities on the job and effectiveness in accomplishing job objectives. An objective appraisal would provide United employees with tactful, constructive criticism aimed at increasing their productivity. Handled properly, United's appraisals would not be a reward or punishment in themselves, but rather an opportunity for employees to increase their value to the company.

Action Summary

Reread the learning objectives below. Each objective is followed by questions. Answering these questions accurately will help you retain the most important concepts discussed in this chapter. After answering each question, check your answer against the answer key at the end of this chapter. (*Hint:* If you have any doubts regarding the correct response, consult the page whose number follows the answer.)

Circle: From studying this chapter, I will attempt to acquire:

1. An overall understanding of how appropriate human resources can be provided for the organization.

T,F   a. An appropriate human resource is an individual whose qualifications are matched to job specifications.

a,b,c,d,e   b. The term *appropriate human resources* refers to: (a) finding the right number of people to fill positions; (b) individuals being satisfied with their jobs; (c) individuals who help the organization achieve management system objectives; (d) individuals who are ineffective; (e) none of the above.

2. An appreciation for the relationship among recruitment efforts, an open position, sources of human resources, and the law.

a,b,c,d,e   a. The process of narrowing a large number of candidates to a smaller field is called: (a) rushing; (b) recruitment; (c) selection; (d) enlistment; (e) enrollment.

a,b,c,d,e   b. The characteristics of the individual who should be hired for the job are indicated by the: (a) job analysis; (b) job specification; (c) job description; (d) job review; (e) job identification.

3. Insights on the use of tests and assessment centers in employee selection.

a,b,c,d,e   **a.** The level of skill or knowledge an individual possesses in a particular area is measured by: (a) aptitude tests; (b) achievement tests; (c) acuity tests; (d) assessment tests; (e) vocational interest tests.

a,b,c,d,e   **b.** The following guideline does *not* apply when tests are being used in selecting potential employees: (a) the tests should be both valid and reliable; (b) the tests should be nondiscriminatory in nature; (c) the tests should not be the sole source of information for determining whether someone is to be hired; (d) such factors as potential and desire to obtain a position should not be assessed subjectively; (e) none of the above—all are important guidelines.

4. An understanding of how the training process operates.

a,b,c,d,e   **a.** Four steps involved in training individuals are: (1) designing the training program, (2) evaluating the training program, (3) determining training needs, (4) administering the training program. The correct sequence for these steps is:
(a) 1, 3, 2, 4
(b) 3, 4, 1, 2
(c) 2, 1, 3, 4
(d) 3, 1, 4, 2
(e) none of the above

T,F   **b.** The lecture offers learners an excellent opportunity to clarify meanings and ask questions, since communication is two-way.

5. A concept of what performance appraisals are and how they can best be conducted.

a,b,c,d,e   **a.** Performance appraisals are important in an organization because they: (a) provide systematic judgments to support promotions; (b) provide a basis for coaching; (c) provide a basis for counseling; (d) let subordinates know where they stand with the boss; (e) all of the above.

a,b,c,d,e   **b.** To achieve the maximum benefit from performance evaluations, a manager should: (a) focus only on the negative aspects of performance; (b) punish the worker with negative feedback; (c) be as subjective as possible; (d) focus only on the positive aspects of performance; (e) use only constructive feedback.

Introductory Case Wrap-Up

"Getting the Right People for United Airlines" (p. 273) and its related back-to-the-case sections were written to help you better understand the management concepts contained in this chapter. Answer the following discussion questions about this introductory case to enrich your understanding of the chapter content:

1. How important is the training of employees to an organization such as United Airlines? Explain.

2. What actions besides training must an organization such as United take to make its employees as productive as possible?

3. Based upon information in the case, what do you think will be the biggest challenge for United management as it tries to provide appropriate human resources for its expansion plans? Explain.

Issues for Review and Discussion

1. What is the difference between appropriate and inappropriate human resources?
2. List and define the four major steps in providing appropriate human resources for the organization.
3. What is the purpose of recruitment?
4. How are job analysis, job description, and job specification related?
5. List the advantages of promotion from within.
6. Compare and contrast the management inventory card, the position replacement form, and the management manpower replacement chart.
7. List three sources of human resources outside the organization. How can these sources be tapped?
8. Does the law influence organizational recruitment practices? If so, how?
9. Describe the role of the Equal Employment Opportunity Commission.
10. Can affirmative action programs be useful in recruitment? Explain.
11. Define *selection*.
12. What is the difference between aptitude tests and achievement tests?

13. Discuss three guidelines for using tests in the selection process.
14. What are assessment centers?
15. List and define the four main steps of the training process.
16. Explain two possible ways of determining organizational training needs.
17. What are the differences between the lecture and programmed learning as alternative methods of transmitting information in the training program?

18. On-the-job training methods include coaching, position rotation, and special project committees. Explain how each of these methods works.
19. What are performance appraisals, and why should they be used?
20. If someone asked your advice on how to conduct performance appraisals, describe in detail what you would say.

Action Summary Answer Key

1. a. F, p. 274
   b. c, p. 274

2. a. b, p. 274
   b. b, p. 275

3. a. b, p. 283
   b. d, pp. 283–284

4. a. d, p. 285
   b. F, pp. 287–288

5. a. e, p. 291
   b. e, pp. 291–292

Case Study

Why CEOs Are Looking at PEOs

A new industry, sometimes called *employee leasing*, has emerged to help businesses cope with human resource management. Known as *professional employer organizations*, or *PEOs*, these firms have grown from a handful in 1984 to some 2,200 companies, leasing almost 2 million employees and generating $10 billion in revenues, in 1995. PEOs are valuable to all kinds and sizes of businesses. For example, with human capital an increasing cost of doing business, American companies are instituting downsizing programs, typically by eliminating or reorganizing their workforces. PEOs were developed to help companies outsource nonessential tasks related to their human resource needs. PEOs offer businesses two distinct options.

One option provides professional employees for specific projects. For example, a business can tap a pool of experienced executives or skilled workers to replace those lost in downsizing or to staff a special project. This option is particularly attractive to a company that needs engineers for a project that may last only a year or two.

The second option meets the needs of companies that do not want to bear the expense of full-time employees. The PEO can place *all* of the company's current employees on its own payroll, thereby becoming the employer of record and taking legal responsibility for them. The PEO takes care of paychecks, W-2 forms, workers' compensation claims, health insurance matters, personnel placement and safety, and even personnel training. It may even handle EEOC and other government agency matters, maintain a credit union, and manage the company's facilities.

Outsourcing the human resource function is a particularly valuable option for small businesses. A human resource department is often not economically cost-ef-

fective at a company with fewer than 100 employees, yet every company has personnel matters that must be attended to, even if it employs only one person. The business owner, for instance, can easily be overwhelmed by government-mandated policies and practices, often discovering costly regulatory changes after the fact. As much as 25 percent of an employer's time may be taken up by these matters.

PEOs were spawned both by increasing governmental pressures on businesses to remain in compliance with human resource laws and by the need to focus sharply on their core competencies in the face of severe competition. As a specialist, the PEO can administer payrolls in a more cost-effective manner. In the purchase of insurance and related matters, it can pool the employees into larger groups that have more economic clout. Generally, the business owner who uses a PEO saves money and has satisfied personnel whose needs are professionally met in accordance with governmental regulations.

It must be noted, however, that PEOs are neither management consulting firms nor payroll companies. A professional employer organization differs from the first in that it is a continuing on-site presence rather than a periodic advisor. A PEO differs from a payroll company in that it takes care of all other employee needs as well as paychecks. Thus the business owner is freed to concentrate on getting the product out the door. PEOs help businesses lower human resources costs in two ways:

1. Competitive pressures force smaller businesses to provide benefit packages in line with those offered by larger employers. The unique services of PEOs allow these businesses with limited resources to concentrate on developing their strate-

gic strengths with minimum human resources expenditures.

2. Workers' compensation insurance can be an incredibly expensive benefit for certain companies or industries that have unsatisfactory claim histories. With workers' compensation mandated by law, a leasing company is ensured a steady source of motivated prospects.

For these reasons, the growth in PEOs in the next decade should be similar to the growth experienced by the payroll-processing industry in its infancy. From large companies such as AT&T and Delta Airlines to a plethora of smaller companies, PEOs are expanding their client portfolios around the nation. And there's still room for growth. Surveys indicate that PEOs are now used by only 1 percent of the 6.2 million small businesses in the United States. Since 42 percent of all U.S. workers are employed by small businesses, this field is obviously a fertile one for PEOs. Thus the industry should continue to grow well into the next century.

Questions:

1. Does employee leasing diminish workers' loyalty toward a company? Is this a positive or a negative factor for workers? For the company?
2. Would employee leasing be an attractive alternative for Boeing? For Procter & Gamble? Which company would derive the greater benefit from employee leasing? Why?
3. Should employee leasing replace the human resource function in a company? Explain your answer.
4. During a business slowdown, would an employee of a leasing company have a better chance of staying employed than someone working for a large corporation? Explain your answer.

Skills Exercise

PEOs are relatively new to the business world. Conduct research to find PEOs that are operating in your area and contact one of these companies to interview managers about the business. Compile your findings in a business report to share in class.

Suggested questions:

1. How does the PEO find and hire workers?
2. How does the PEO find customers? Through advertising? Networking? Telemarketing?
3. If the company advertises, where and what does it advertise and what does it emphasize in its ads?
4. How does the PEO service its customers? How does it determine fees?
5. How does the cost of the PEO's services compare to the clients' costs of administration, salaries, and benefits?
6. If possible, interview the owner or a manager at a company using the PEO and ask: At what level of hiring did you decide that the PEO's services would enhance your bottom line?

 The Internet learning materials that accompany this chapter can be found at
http://www.profcerto.com
Additional information can be found on the inside front and back covers of this text.

13 chapter

ORGANIZATIONAL CHANGE AND STRESS

STUDENT LEARNING OBJECTIVES

From studying this chapter, I will attempt to acquire:

1. A working definition of *changing an organization*.
2. An understanding of the relative importance of change and stability to an organization.
3. Some ability to recognize what kind of changes should be made within an organization.
4. An appreciation for why the people affected by a change should be considered when the change is being made.
5. Some facility at evaluating change.
6. An understanding of how organizational change and stress are related.

CHAPTER OUTLINE

Michael Dell was less than 20 years old when he founded Dell Computer Corporation, a company specializing in selling computers over the telephone and through the mail. He has endured boom, bust, and bumbles in the volatile personal computer business. He has engineered his first turnaround, and lays claim to the longest tenure of any current chief executive in the industry.

And now, believe it or not, Michael Dell has turned 30 years old.

In place of the brash and boastful whiz kid is a more circumspect adult who this year actually tried to slow Dell Computer Corporation's growth. While admitting to changes in himself and his company, he makes no apologies for learning some lessons the hard way. "The nature of our business is that everything is changing," he says. "I've learned you have to take advantage of change and not let it take advantage of you."

His years of experience show, according to observers of his company. "Maturity is probably the right word," says First Boston analyst Bill Gurley. "Dell used to be a company that kind of lived on the edge." Today it's a conservative $3-billion-a-year business.

And with the wisdom of age, Dell concedes he has made plenty of mistakes. The company suffered big losses in foreign-currency futures and interest-rate derivatives when it tried to generate profits with high-risk investments. In 1993, a noncompetitive notebook line had to be scrapped, bruising the company's reputation. Then, after rushing into retail stores like Wal-Mart and CompUSA, Dell learned his made-to-order manufacturing scheme was too expensive for such low-margin channels and had to pull out.

At one point, he now says, Dell Computer was down to $20 million in cash. "We could have used that up in a day or two. For a company our size, that was ridiculous," he says. "I realized we had to change the priorities of the company."

Inspired by the rapid turnaround at rival Compaq Computer Corporation, Dell set out to build a company under his existing business. He changed and refined organization structure. He overhauled management and adopted formal planning and budgeting processes. Instead of "growth, growth, growth," he says, the company focused on earnings and liquidity.

The company now has $400 million in the bank, leading to speculation—denied by Dell executives—that it may be looking to acquire a rival.

"I think we have good times for our industry, good times for the leading companies, and good times for Dell," Dell says.

Married, with a three-year-old daughter, Dell adds, "I have good balance—a wonderful family and a wonderful business. I don't have any complaints."

Dell Computer CEO Michael Dell has been forced to engineer change at the company that he founded just over a decade ago. Once an organization focused on "growth, growth, growth," Dell is now a more conservative company that keeps a closer eye on its earnings and the cash in its bank accounts.

what's ahead The introductory case describes how Michael Dell, the chief executive officer of Dell Computer Corporation, rescued his sliding company by making some crucial changes. He and other managers who face constant decisions about making changes will ultimately be held accountable for the consequences of those changes. Therefore Dell and other managers who are modifying their organizations should find the discussion of change in this chapter very valuable. The major topics covered in this chapter are as follows:

1. The fundamentals of changing an organization.
2. The factors to consider when changing the organization.
3. The connection between organizational change and stress.

FUNDAMENTALS OF CHANGING AN ORGANIZATION

Thus far, discussion in this "Organizing" section of the text has centered on the fundamentals of organizing, furnishing appropriate human resources for the organization, authority, delegation, and responsibility. This chapter focuses on changing the organization.

Defining "Changing an Organization"

Changing an organization is the process of modifying an existing organization to increase organizational effectiveness.

Changing an organization is the process of modifying an existing organization to increase organizational effectiveness—that is, the extent to which an organization accomplishes its objectives. These modifications can involve virtually any organizational segment, but typically affect the lines of organizational authority, the levels of responsibility held by various organization members, and the established lines of organizational communication. Driven by new technology, expanding global opportunities, and the trend to organizational streamlining, almost all modern organizations are changing in some way.[1]

The Importance of Change   Most managers agree that if an organization is to thrive, it must change continually in response to significant developments in the environment, such as changing customer needs, technological breakthroughs, and new government regulations. The study of organizational change is extremely important because all managers at all organizational levels are faced throughout their careers with the task of changing their organization. Managers who determine appropriate changes to make in their organizations and then implement such changes successfully enable their organizations to be more flexible and innovative. Because change is such a fundamental part of organizational existence, such managers are very valuable to organizations of all kinds.[2]

Many managers consider change to be so critical to organizational success that they encourage employees to continually search for areas in which beneficial changes can be made. To take a classic example, General Motors provides employees with a "think list" to encourage them to develop ideas for organizational change and to remind them that change is vital to the continued success of GM. The think list contains the following questions:[3]

1. Can a machine be used to do a better or faster job?
2. Can the fixture now in use be improved?
3. Can handling of materials for the machine be improved?
4. Can a special tool be used to combine the operations?
5. Can the quality of the part being produced be improved by changing the sequence of the operation?

 - 6. Can the material used be cut or trimmed differently for greater economy or efficiency?
 - 7. Can the operation be made safer?
 - 8. Can paperwork regarding this job be eliminated?
 - 9. Can established procedures be simplified?

Change *versus* Stability

In addition to organizational change, some degree of stability is a prerequisite for long-term organizational success. Figure 13.1 presents a model developed by Hellriegel and Slocum that shows the relative importance of change and stability to organizational survival. Although these authors use the word *adaptation* in their model rather than *change*, the two terms are essentially synonymous.

The model stresses that organizational survival and growth are most probable when both stability and adaptation are high within the organization (number 3 on the model depicted in Figure 13.1). The organization without enough stability to complement change is at a definite disadvantage. When stability is low, the probability of organizational survival and growth declines. Change after change without regard for the essential role of stability typically results in confusion and employee stress.[4]

BACK TO THE CASE   The information in the text suggests how Michael Dell should make decisions concerning changes in Dell Computer's organization structure. He should evaluate all such proposed changes in relation to the degree that they would enable the company to accomplish its objectives. He should understand that if Dell Computer is to have continued success over the long run, significant changes will probably have to be made again and again. In fact, appropriate change is so important to a company like Dell Computer that Dell may want to consider initiating some type of program that would encourage employees to submit their ideas on how to change the company in order to increase its effectiveness. When considering possible changes, however, Dell will have to keep in mind that stability is also essential if his company is to survive and thrive.

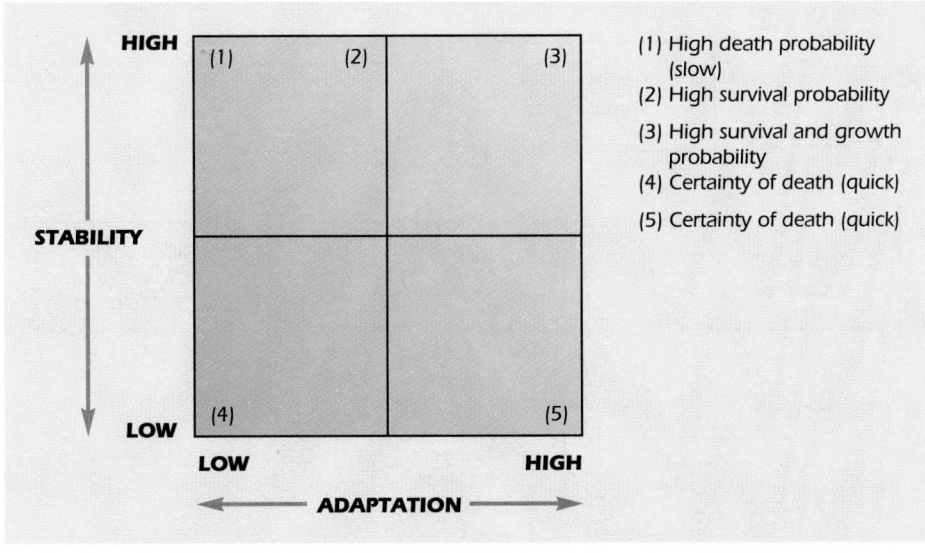

Figure 13.1   Adaptation, stability, and organizational survival

FACTORS TO CONSIDER WHEN CHANGING AN ORGANIZATION

How managers deal with the major factors that need to be considered when an organizational change is being made will largely determine how successful that change will be. The following factors should be considered whenever change is being contemplated:

1. The change agent.
2. Determining what should be changed.
3. The kind of change to make.
4. Individuals affected by the change.
5. Evaluation of the change.

Although the following sections discuss each of these factors individually, Figure 13.2 makes the point that it is their collective influence that ultimately determines the success of a change.

The Change Agent

Perhaps the most important factor managers need to consider when changing an organization is who will be the **change agent**—the individual inside or outside the organization who tries to modify the existing organizational situation. The change agent might be a self-designated manager within the organization or an outside consultant hired because of a special expertise in a particular area. This individual might be responsible for making very broad changes, like altering the culture of the whole organization, or more narrow ones, like designing and implementing a new safety program or a new quality program.[5] Although in some circumstances the change agent will not be a manager, the term *manager* and *change agent* are used synonymously throughout this chapter.

Special skills are necessary for success as a change agent. Among them are the ability to determine how a change should be made, the skill to solve change-related problems, and facility in using behavioral science tools to influence people appropriately during the change process. Perhaps the most overlooked skill of successful change agents, however, is the ability to determine how much change employees can withstand.[6]

A **change agent** is an individual inside or outside the organization who tries to modify an existing organizational situation.

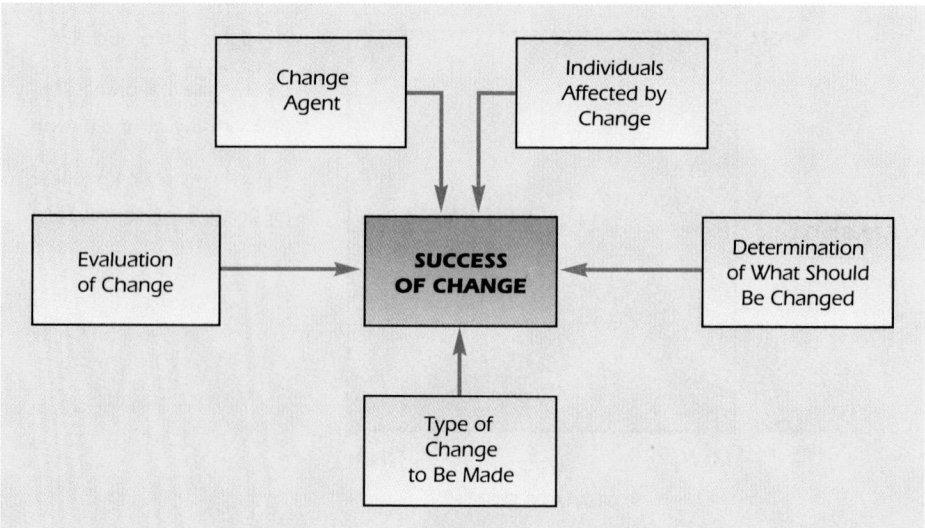

Figure 13.2 The collective influence of five major factors on the success of changing an organization

The change agent for the Eugene (Oregon) Water & Electric Board has been General Manager Randy Berggren. For example, Berggren has instituted more than 60 changes designed to improve the management of customer accounts. In turn, these changes have entailed an entirely new information system, new job descriptions, and revamped human resources procedures for training employees in new technical and interpersonal skills.

Overall, managers should choose change agents who have the most expertise in all these areas. A potentially beneficial change might not result in any advantages for the organization if a person without expertise in these areas is designated to make the change.

BACK TO THE CASE   Michael Dell has taken the main role in deciding what structural changes need to be made in Dell Computer, as well as in implementing the changes. He is, therefore, the change agent for the company. He probably assumed this role because he believes he is the best-suited person at Dell Computer to evaluate the advantages and disadvantages of having one type of structure as opposed to another for the organization.

As change agent, Dell must be able to use behavioral science tools to influence organization members during the implementation of planned change. For example, he must determine how much structural change his employees can withstand, influence them to work together in their new organizational roles, and implement particular changes gradually so that employees are not overwhelmed.

Determining What Should Be Changed

Another major factor managers need to consider is exactly what should be changed within the organization. In general, managers should make only those changes that will increase organizational effectiveness.

It has been generally accepted for many years that organizational effectiveness depends primarily on activities centering around three classes of factors:

1. People
2. Structure
3. Technology

People factors are attitudes, leadership skills, communication skills, and all other characteristics of the human resources within the organization. **Structural factors** are organizational controls, such as policies and procedures. And **technological factors** are any types of equipment or processes that assist organization members in the performance of their jobs.

For an organization to maximize its effectiveness, appropriate people must be matched with appropriate technology and appropriate structure. Thus people factors, technological factors, and structural factors are not independent determinants of organizational effectiveness. Instead, as Figure 13.3 shows, organizational effectiveness is determined by the relationship of these three factors.

People factors are attitudes, leadership skills, communication skills, and all other characteristics of the organization's employees.

Structural factors are organizational controls, such as policies and procedures.

Technological factors are any types of equipment or processes that assist organization members in the performance of their jobs.

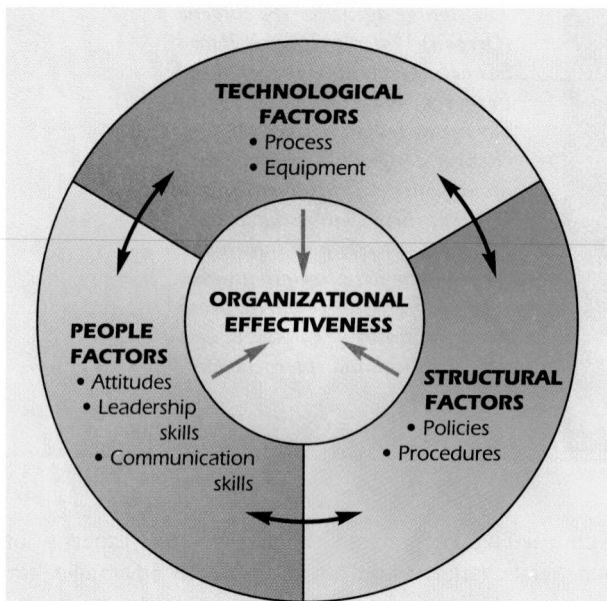

Figure 13.3 Determination of organizational effectiveness by the relationship of people, technological, and structural factors

ETHICS SPOTLIGHT

ATTITUDE CHANGE IS THE KEY TO ESTABLISHING A SOCIALLY RESPONSIBLE POSITION ON JOB SAFETY AT SONOCO

Progressive companies take seriously the challenge to establish a safe working environment for their employees. They are determined to meet this challenge, not only because fewer accidents means a more productive workforce, but also because they recognize their social responsibility to provide a workplace in which employees are reasonably free from harm. The Sonoco Products Company, an organization that produces primarily paperboard packaging, had to change employee attitudes in order to reshape the company into one that is appropriately responsible for job safety.

The Corrugating Department of Sonoco Products Company's Paper Division in Hartsville, South Carolina, celebrated a milestone recently when its employees completed their first year of injury-free work. As a result, the Paper Division received the annual Best Safety Record award from the Southern Pulp & Paper Safety Association. To achieve this record, management had to instill in employees the attitude that job safety is important and worthy of serious attention from everyone at Sonoco. To that end, the company designed and implemented a program called STOP—Safety Training Observation Program—to impress upon employees the importance of job safety and to help them develop safe work habits. STOP was successful because Sonoco management was solidly behind it and spared no effort in pushing the idea that employees and management share responsibility for creating a safe work environment. Once Sonoco employees developed the attitude that a safe workplace is indeed important, actually establishing such an environment became a realistic objective for management.≈

The Kind of Change to Make

The kind of change to make is the third major factor that managers need to consider when they set out to change an organization. Most changes can be categorized as one of three kinds:

`1.` Technological
`2.` Structural
`3.` People

Note that these three kinds of change correspond to the three main determinants of organizational effectiveness—each change being named for the determinant it emphasizes.

For example, **technological change** emphasizes modifying the level of technology in the management system. Because this kind of change so often involves outside experts and highly technical language, it is more profitable to discuss structural change and people change in detail in this text.

Technological change is a type of organizational change that emphasizes modifying the level of technology in the management system.

Structural Change
Structural change emphasizes increasing organizational effectiveness by changing controls that influence organization members during the performance of their jobs. The following sections further describe this approach and discuss matrix organizations (organizations modified to complete a special project) as an example of structural change.

Describing Structural Change.   **Structural change** is change aimed at increasing organizational effectiveness through modifications to the existing organizational structure. These modifications can take several forms:

1. Clarifying and defining jobs.
2. Modifying organizational structure to fit the communication needs of the organization.
3. Decentralizing the organization to reduce the cost of coordination, increase the controllability of subunits, increase motivation, and gain greater flexibility.

Structural change is a type of organizational change that emphasizes modifying an existing organizational structure.

Although structural change must take account of people and technology to be successful, its primary focus is obviously on changing organizational structure. In general, managers choose to make structural changes within an organization if information they have gathered indicates that the present structure is the main cause of organizational ineffectiveness. The precise structural changes they choose to make will vary from situation to situation, of course. After changes to organizational structure have been made, management should conduct periodic reviews to make sure the changes are accomplishing their intended purpose.[7]

Matrix Organizations.   Matrix organizations provide a good illustration of structural change. According to C. J. Middleton, a **matrix organization** is a traditional organization that is modified primarily for the purpose of completing some kind of special project. Essentially, a matrix organization is one in which individuals from various functional departments are assigned to a project manager responsible for accom-

A **matrix organization** is a traditional organizational structure that is modified primarily for the purpose of completing some type of special project.

Intel Corporation, which holds a near-monopoly over the microprocessor chip, still strives to make technological change a key factor in its market leadership. In particular, Intel uses its resources to push technological advancements faster than its competitors, and one of the company's formal goals is to render its own products obsolete before other chipmakers do it.

plishing some specific task.[8] For this reason, matrix organizations are also called *project organizations*. The project itself may be either long term or short term, and the employees needed to complete it are borrowed from various organizational segments.

John F. Mee has developed a classic example showing how a traditional organization can be changed into a matrix organization.[9] Figure 13.4 presents a portion of a traditional organizational structure based primarily on product line. Although this design is generally useful, management might learn that it makes it impossible for organization members to give adequate attention to three government projects of extreme importance to long-term organizational success.

Making the Change to Matrix: An Example.   Figure 13.5 illustrates one way management could change this traditional organizational structure into a matrix organization to facilitate completion of the three government projects. A manager would be appointed for each of the three projects and allocated personnel with appropriate skills to complete the project. The three project managers would have authority over the employees assigned to them and be accountable for the performance of those people. Each of the three project managers would be placed on the chart in Figure 13.5 in one of the three boxes labeled Venus Project, Mars Project, and Saturn Project, and the work flow related to each project would go from right to left on the chart. After the projects were completed, the organization chart would revert to its original design—assuming that design is more advantageous under most circumstances.

There are several advantages and disadvantages to making structural changes such as those reflected by the matrix organization. The major advantages are that such structural changes generally result in better control of a project, better customer relations, shorter project development time, and lower project costs. In addition, matrix organizations are flexible enough to allow managers to shift resources to special projects as needed. The downside is that such structural changes generally create more complex internal operations, which commonly cause conflict, encourage inconsistency in the application of company policy, and result in a more difficult situation to manage.

The advantages and disadvantages of changing a traditional organization into a matrix organization will have different weights according to the situation. One point is clear, however. For a matrix organization to be effective and efficient, organization members must be willing to learn and execute somewhat different organizational roles than they are used to.[10]

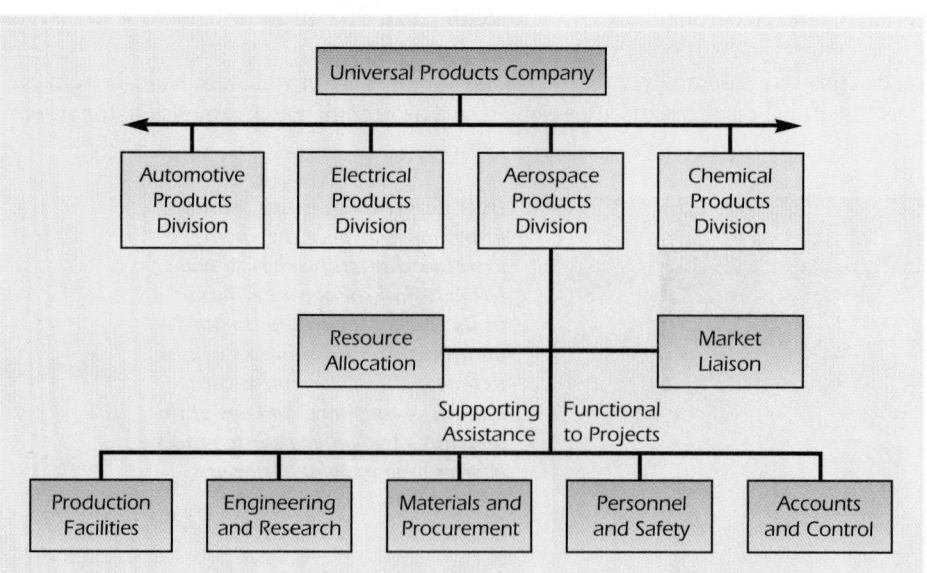

Figure 13.4 Portion of a traditional organizational structure based primarily on product line

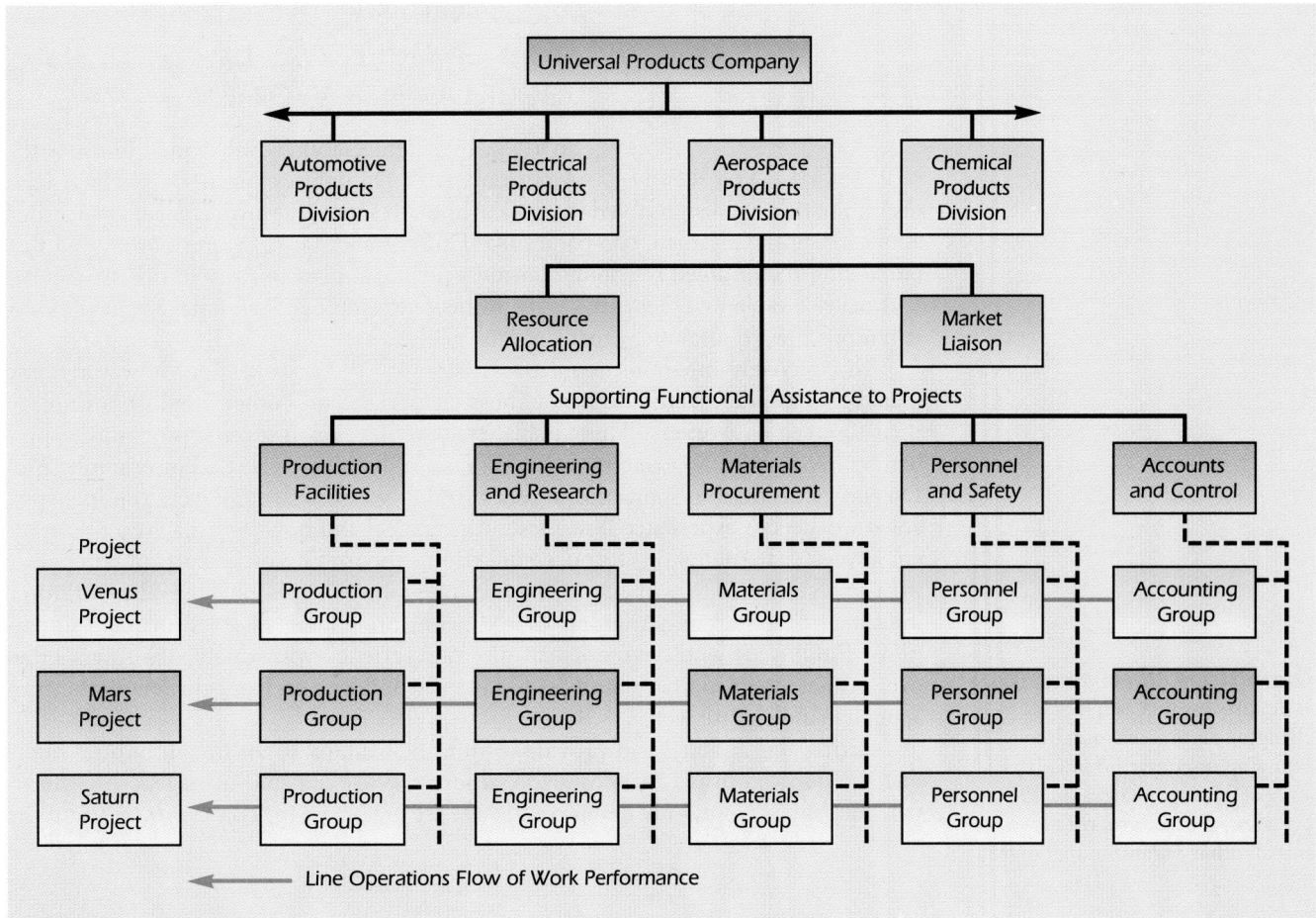

Figure 13.5   Traditional organization chart transformed into matrix organization chart

BACK TO THE CASE   The information in the text indicates that there are three different types of factors that a manager like Michael Dell can change in an organization: technological, people, and structural factors. Dell's actions to change organization design to increase organizational effectiveness would be categorized as a structural change. Other structural changes he is making are adopting a formal planning process and focusing on budgeting. The introductory case provides some evidence that Dell is also focusing on changing people factors within the company—for example, he has overhauled his management team. Although in running Dell Computer Corporation, Michael Dell will inevitably change technology factors from time to time, the case provides no information in this area.

People Change   Although successfully changing people factors necessarily involves some consideration of structure and technology, the primary emphasis is on people. The following sections discuss people change and examine grid organization development, one commonly used means of changing organization members.

Describing People Change: Organization Development (OD).   People change emphasizes increasing organizational effectiveness by changing certain aspects of organization members. The focus of this kind of change is on such factors as employees' attitudes and leadership skills. In general, managers should attempt to make this kind of change when human resources are shown to be the main cause of organizational ineffectiveness.

People change is a type of organizational change that emphasizes modifying certain aspects of organization members to increase organizational effectiveness.

McDonald's Corporation Is Changing the Way Employees Think about Disabled Workers

In 1990, President George Bush signed into law the Americans with Disabilities Act (ADA), which bans discrimination against disabled workers. Although some employers may be concerned about hiring the disabled, companies like DuPont and Target Stores have found that employing the disabled is a sound business practice. Their history in this area shows that many disabled workers are loyal, enthusiastic employees and make valuable contributions toward attaining organizational goals.

To effectively integrate disabled workers into the organization, however, some managers have discovered that they must change the way other employees think of their disabled co-workers. These managers have developed specific programs to prepare employees for appropriate interaction with disabled workers. For example, McDonald's Corporation sponsors awareness training in which employees role-play disabled workers to experience how these workers feel and how they may react to other employees' statements or attitudes concerning them. The experience of companies with a successful history of employing and integrating the disabled into the workforce indicates that awareness training should avoid prejudging disabled people's limitations. Employees who have not had direct experience with disabled workers often overestimate their limitations and consequently buffer them from challenges they can actually handle quite well.

Hiring the disabled can provide significant benefits to an organization. One is that the disabled usually are loyal and productive workers and managers. Another is that consumers commonly develop a deep sense of respect for companies that hire the disabled.≈

Organization development (OD) is the process that emphasizes changing an organization by changing organization members and bases these changes on an overview of structure, technology, and all other organizational ingredients.

Grid organization development (grid OD) is a commonly used organization development technique based on a theoretical model called the managerial grid.

A **managerial grid** is a theoretical model based on the premise that concern for people and concern for production are the two primary attitudes that influence management style.

The process of people change can be referred to as **organization development (OD).** Although OD focuses mainly on changing certain aspects of people, these changes are based on an overview of structure, technology, and all other organizational ingredients.

Grid OD.   One commonly used OD technique for changing people in organizations is called **grid organization development,** or **grid OD.**[11] The **managerial grid,** a basic model describing various managerial styles, is used as the foundation for grid OD. The managerial grid itself is based on the premise that various managerial styles can be described by means of two primary attitudes of the manager: concern for people and concern for production. Within this model, each attitude is placed on an axis,

Pizza Hut pizza is now served in "contract feeders" like this North Carolina high school because Wayne Calloway, CEO of parent PepsiCo, is working to create a "culture of growth." Central to that idea, says Calloway, is people change: getting managers—especially young ones—to break out of old modes of thinking and to develop self-confidence by posting them in places where risk taking and new-business growth are the primary goals.

which is scaled 1 through 9 and is used to generate five managerial styles. Figure 13.6 shows the managerial grid, its five managerial styles, and the factors that characterize each of these styles.

The Ideal Style.   The central theme of this managerial grid is that 9,9 management (as shown on the grid in Figure 13.6) is the ideal managerial style. Managers using this style have a high concern for both people and production. Managers using any other style have lesser degrees of concern for people or production, and are thought to reduce organizational success accordingly. The purpose of grid OD is to change organization managers so they will use the 9,9 management style.

Main Training Phases.   How is a grid OD program conducted? The program has six main training phases that are used with all managers within the organization. The first two phases focus on acquainting managers with the managerial grid concept and assisting them in determining which managerial style they most commonly use. The last four phases of the grid OD program concentrate on encouraging managers to adopt the 9,9 management style and showing them how to use this style within their specific job situation. Emphasis throughout the program is on developing teamwork within the organization.

Some evidence suggests that grid OD is effective in enhancing profit, positively changing managerial behavior, and positively influencing managerial attitudes and values.[12] Grid OD will have to undergo more rigorous testing for an extended period of time, however, before conclusive statements about it can be made.

The Status of Organization Development.   If the entire OD area is taken into consideration, changes that emphasize both people and the organization as a whole

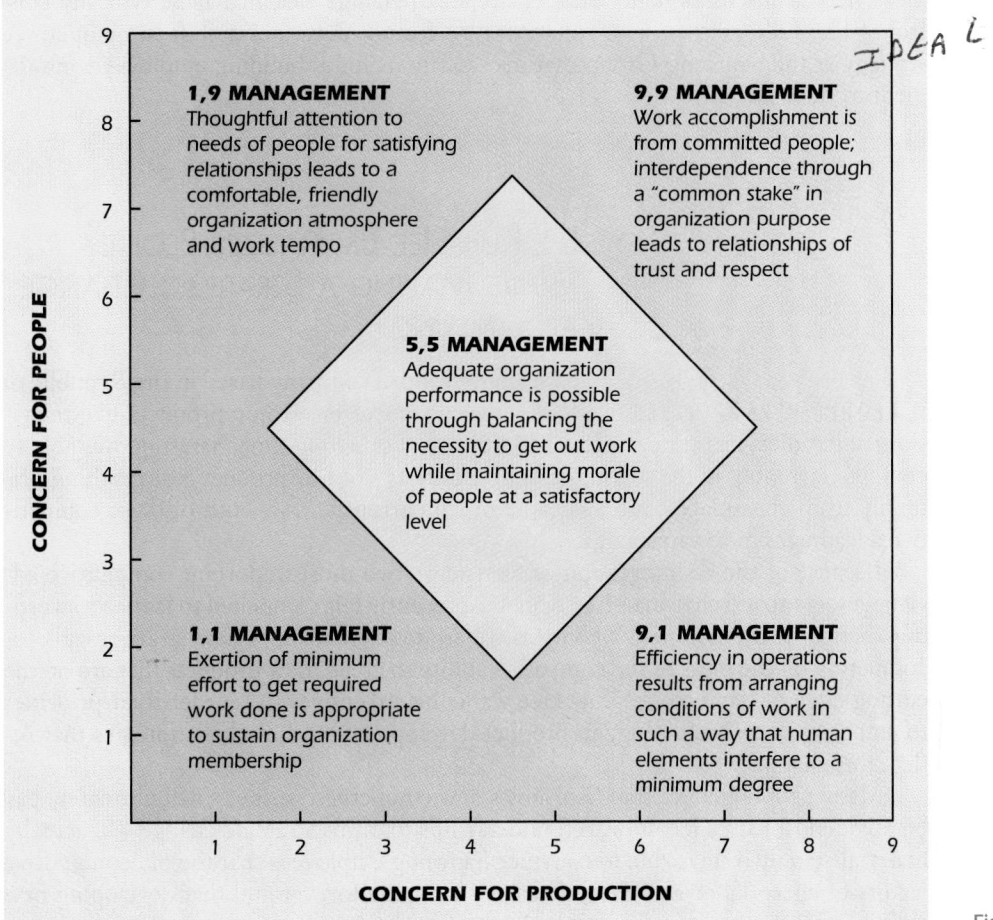

Figure 13.6   The managerial grid

org. development

seem to have inherent strength. There are, however, several commonly voiced weaknesses in OD efforts. These weaknesses are as follows:[13]

1. The effectiveness of an OD program is difficult to evaluate.
2. OD programs are generally too time-consuming.
3. OD objectives are commonly too vague.
4. The total costs of an OD program are difficult to gauge at the time the program starts.
5. OD programs are generally too expensive.

These weaknesses, however, should not eliminate OD from consideration, but rather should indicate areas to perfect within it. Managers can improve the quality of OD efforts by doing the following:[14]

1. Systematically tailoring OD programs to meet the specific needs of the organization.
2. Continually demonstrating exactly how people should change their behavior.
3. Conscientiously changing organizational reward systems so organization members who change their behavior in ways suggested by the OD program are rewarded.

Managers have been employing OD techniques for several decades, and broad and useful applications of these techniques continue to be documented in the more recent management literature. OD techniques are currently being applied not only to business organizations but also to many other types of organizations, such as religious organizations. Moreover, OD applications are being documented throughout the world, with increasing use being reported in countries like Hungary, Poland, and the United Kingdom.[15]

The text discusses many different types of change that managers typically confront. The following PEOPLE PERSPECTIVES feature describes a shift in competitive strategy at the Samsung Group that necessarily includes building employee commitment to the change.

LEE KUN-HEE EMPHASIZES PEOPLE WHILE MAKING A STRATEGIC CHANGE AT SAMSUNG

PEOPLE PERSPECTIVES

Samsung Group, a company based in the Republic of Korea that produces electronic products like televisions and radios, has annual sales of $54 billion. For a long time, Samsung was able to compete favorably in the world market on the basis of low product cost resulting primarily from cheap labor and a cheap Korean currency. Now both of these competitive advantages have vanished.

Because of the disintegration of Samsung's two most important competitive advantages, company chairman Lee Kun-Hee recently felt compelled to launch a sweeping change in the company's competitive strategy. Samsung's new strategy calls for competing on the basis of the company's ability to create new products that are on the cutting edge of technology. Kun-Hee wants his executives to reorder their priorities to emphasize new technology in product development and market strategies that reflect this change.

Many people believe that Samsung's new competitive strategy will ultimately pay big dividends. Kun-Hee, however, understands that this strategic change will actually materialize only if he is able to convince Samsung employees that the old competitive factors of cheap labor and cheap currency are gone forever and that developing new technology–oriented products is the key to future company success.≈

BACK TO THE CASE Michael Dell's organization structure change would not be classified as a people change, for although the people involved in this change must be considered to some extent, the main emphasis is on structural factors.

If, however, once the new organization structure is in place Dell comes to believe that human resource problems are the main cause of organizational ineffectiveness, he will probably plan and initiate an organization development program and use grid OD to modify management styles and produce more cooperative team efforts.

Individuals Affected by the Change

A fourth major factor to be considered by managers when changing an organization is the people who will be affected by the change. A good assessment of what to change and how to make the change will be wasted if organization members do not support the change. To increase the chances of employee support, managers should be aware of the following factors:

1. The usual employee resistance to change.
2. How this resistance can be reduced.
3. The three conditions that usually accompany behavioral change.

Resistance to Change Resistance to change within an organization is as common as the need for change. After managers decide to make some organizational change, they typically meet with employee resistance aimed at preventing that change from occurring.[16] Behind this resistance by organization members lies the fear of some personal loss, such as a reduction in personal prestige, a disturbance of established social and working relationships, and personal failure because of inability to carry out new job responsibilities.

Reducing Resistance to Change To ensure the success of needed modifications, managers must be able to reduce the effects of the resistance that typically accompanies proposed change. Resistance can usually be lowered by following these guidelines:[17]

1. *Avoid surprises.* People need time to evaluate a proposed change before management implements it. Unless they are given time to evaluate and absorb how the change will affect them, employees are likely to be automatically opposed to it. Whenever possible, therefore, individuals who will be affected by a change should be informed of the kind of change being considered and the probability that it will be adopted.
2. *Promote real understanding.* When fear of personal loss related to a proposed change is reduced, opposition to the change is also reduced. Most managers find that ensuring that organization members thoroughly understand a proposed change is a major step in reducing this fear. Understanding may even generate enthusiastic support for the change if it focuses employees on individual gains that could materialize as a result of it. People should be given information that will help them answer the following change-related questions they invariably will have:

- Will I lose my job?
- Will my old skills become obsolete?
- Am I capable of producing effectively under the new system?
- Will my power and prestige decline?
- Will I be given more responsibility than I care to assume?
- Will I have to work longer hours?
- Will it force me to betray or desert my good friends?

3. *Set the stage for change.* Perhaps the most powerful tool for reducing resistance to change is management's positive attitude toward the change. This attitude should be displayed openly by top and middle management as well as by lower management. In essence, management should convey that change is one of the basic prerequisites for a successful organization. Management should also strive to be seen as encouraging change to increase organizational effectiveness, rather than for the sake of trying something new. To reinforce this positive attitude toward change, some portion of organizational rewards should be earmarked for those organization members who are most instrumental in implementing constructive change.

4. *Make tentative change.* Resistance to change can also be reduced if the changes are made on a tentative basis. This approach establishes a trial period during which organization members spend some time working under a proposed change before voicing support or nonsupport of it. Tentative change is based on the assumption that a trial period during which organization members live under a change is the best way of reducing feared personal loss. Judson has summarized the benefits of using the tentative approach:

- Employees affected by the change are able to test their reactions to the new situation before committing themselves irrevocably to it.
- Those who will live under the change are able to acquire more facts on which to base their attitudes and behavior toward the change.
- Those who had strong preconceptions about the change are in a better position to assess it with objectivity. Consequently, they may review and modify some of their preconceptions.
- Those involved are less likely to regard the change as a threat.
- Management is better able to evaluate the method of change and make any necessary modifications before carrying it out more fully.

The Behavioral Side of Change   Almost any change requires that organization members modify the way in which they are accustomed to behaving or working. Therefore managers must not only choose the best people-structure-technology relationship for the organization but also make corresponding changes in such a way that related human behavior is altered most effectively. Positive results of any change will materialize only if organization members alter their behavior as demanded by the change.

Field Theory.   Kurt Lewin, a German social scientist, pioneered the study of field theory. According to Lewin, behavioral change is caused by three distinct but related conditions experienced by an individual:[18]

1. Unfreezing
2. Changing
3. Refreezing

Chevron Oil CEO Kenneth Derr, who cut his workforce by 50,000 when Chevron merged with Gulf in 1984, works to reduce resistance to further change—and to bolster morale in general—by keeping open the lines of communication. For example, Derr and other Chevron executives hold periodic meetings with employees to explain how changes will affect them in such areas as job security and career advancement.

The first condition, **unfreezing,** is the state in which individuals experience the ineffectiveness of their present mode of behavior and become ready to attempt to learn new behaviors that will make them more effective. Often people find it especially difficult to "thaw out" because of positive attitudes they traditionally associate with their past behavior.

Changing, the second of Lewin's conditions, is the state in which individuals, now unfrozen, begin to experiment with performing new behaviors. They try out the new behaviors in the hope that they will increase their effectiveness. According to Edgar Schein, this changing is best effected if it involves both identification and internalization:[19]

- *Identification* is the process in which individuals performing new behaviors pattern themselves after someone who already has expertise in those behaviors— that is, they model themselves after an expert.
- *Internalization* is the process in which individuals performing new behaviors attempt to use those behaviors as part of their normal behavioral pattern—that is, they consistently try to make the new behaviors useful over an extended period of time.

Refreezing, the third of Lewin's conditions, is the state in which individuals see that the new behavior they have experimented with during "changing" is now part of themselves. They have developed attitudes consistent with performing the new behavior and see that behavior as part of their normal mode of operations. The rewards they receive as a result of performing the new behavior are instrumental in refreezing.

Field Theory at Work: An Example. To increase their success as change agents, managers must be able to make changes in such a way that the individuals who are being required to modify their behavior live through Lewin's three conditions. Here is an example:

- A middle-level manager named Sara Clark has gathered information indicating that Terry Lacey, a lower-level manager, must change his memo technique. Clark knows that Lacey firmly believes he can save time and effort by writing out his intracompany memos rather than having them typed, proofread, corrected if necessary, and then sent out. Lacey also believes that an added benefit to this strategy is that it frees his secretary to do other kinds of tasks.
- Clark, however, has been getting regular requests for help in reading Lacey's sometimes illegible handwriting and knows that some of his memos are so poorly written that words and sentences are misinterpreted. Obviously, some change is necessary. As Lacey's superior, Clark could simply mandate change by telling Lacey to write more clearly or to have his memos typed. This strategy, however, might not have enough effect to cause a lasting behavioral change and could result in the additional problem of personal friction between the two managers.
- Clark could increase the probability of Lacey's changing his behavior in a more lasting way if she helps Lacey experience unfreezing, changing, and refreezing. To encourage unfreezing, Clark could direct all queries she receives about Lacey's memos back to Lacey himself and make sure that he is aware of all misinterpretations and resulting mistakes. This should demonstrate to Lacey that there is a need for change.
- Once Lacey recognizes the need for changing the way in which he writes his memos, he will be ready to try alternative memo-writing methods. Clark could then suggest methods to Lacey, taking special care to give him examples of how others write intracompany memos (identification). Over time, Clark could also help Lacey develop the method of transmitting memos that best suits his talents (internalization).
- After Lacey has developed an effective method of writing memos, Clark should take steps to ensure that positive feedback about his memo writing reaches

Unfreezing is the state in which individuals experience the ineffectiveness of their present mode of behavior and become ready to learn new behaviors.

Changing is the state in which individuals begin to experiment with performing new behaviors.

Refreezing is the state in which an individual's experimentally performed behaviors become part of the person.

Lacey. This feedback, of course, will be instrumental in refreezing his new method. The feedback can come from Clark, from Lacey's subordinates and peers, and from Lacey's own observations.

Evaluation of Change

As with all other managerial actions, managers should spend some time evaluating the changes they make. The purpose of this evaluation is not only to gain insights into how the change itself might be modified to further increase its organizational effectiveness but also to determine whether the steps taken to make the change should be modified to increase organizational effectiveness the next time they are used.

According to Margulies and Wallace, making this evaluation may be difficult because the data from individual change programs may be unreliable.[20] Nevertheless, managers must do their best to evaluate change in order to increase the organizational benefits from the change.

Evaluation of change often involves watching for symptoms that indicate that further change is necessary. For example, if organization members continue to be oriented more to the past than to the future, if they recognize the obligations of rituals more readily than they do the challenges of current problems, or if they pay greater allegiance to departmental goals than to overall company objectives, the probability is high that further change is necessary.

A word of caution is needed at this point. Although symptoms such as those listed in the preceding paragraph generally indicate that further change is warranted, this is not always the case. The decision to make additional changes should not be taken solely on the basis of symptoms. More objective information should be considered. In general, additional change is justified if it will accomplish any of the following goals:[21]

1. Further improve the means for satisfying someone's economic wants.
2. Increase profitability.
3. Promote human work for human beings.
4. Contribute to individual satisfaction and social well-being.

BACK TO THE CASE   Michael Dell must realize that even if he formulates a change that would be beneficial to Dell Computer Corporation, his attempt to implement this change could prove unsuccessful if he does not appropriately consider the people who will be affected by the change. For example, if a new structural change requires employees to report to managers they are not used to reporting to, employees may fear that this change will diminish their freedom and decision-making opportunities, and therefore subtly resist it.

To overcome such resistance, Dell could use such strategies as giving employees enough time to fully evaluate and understand the change, demonstrating a positive attitude toward the change himself, and—if resistance is very strong—making the proposed change tentative until it can be fully evaluated. In addition, he would probably find Lewin's unfreezing-changing-freezing theory helpful in implementing the proposed change.

All of Dell's changes at Dell Computer need to be evaluated after implementation to assess whether further organizational change is necessary and whether the process used to make the change might be improved for future use. For instance, evaluation of the change of establishing new retail outlets for Dell products in stores like Wal-Mart showed that such outlets were not profitable and had to be eliminated.

CHANGE AND STRESS

Whenever managers implement changes, they should be concerned about the stress they may be creating. If the stress is significant enough, it may well cancel out the improvement that was anticipated from the change. In fact, stress could result in the organization being *less* effective than it was before the change was attempted. This section defines stress and discusses the importance of studying and managing it.

Defining *Stress*

The bodily strain that an individual experiences as a result of coping with some environmental factor is **stress.** Hans Selye, an early authority on this subject, said that stress constitutes the factors affecting wear and tear on the body. In organizations, this wear and tear is caused primarily by the body's unconscious mobilization of energy when an individual is confronted with organizational or work demands.[22]

> **Stress** is the bodily strain that an individual experiences as a result of coping with some environmental factor.

The Importance of Studying Stress

There are several sound reasons for studying stress:[23]

- Stress can have damaging psychological and physiological effects on employees' health and on their contributions to organizational effectiveness. It can cause heart disease, and it can prevent employees from concentrating or making decisions.
- Stress is a major cause of employee absenteeism and turnover. Certainly, such factors severely limit the potential success of an organization.
- A stressed employee can affect the safety of other workers or even the public.
- Stress represents a very significant cost to organizations. Some estimates put the cost of stress-related problems in the U.S. economy at $150 billion a year. As examples of these costs, many modern organizations spend a great deal of money treating stress-related employee problems through medical programs, and they must absorb expensive legal fees related to handling stress-related lawsuits.

The information in the text indicates that stress can cause heart disease. The following CUTTING EDGE feature provides more recent information on how organization members can foil one of the most dreaded results of heart disease—heart attacks.

DR. RAYMOND BAHR GIVES ADVICE ON HOW TO DERAIL HEART ATTACKS

CUTTING EDGE

Many doctors believe that people who learn to recognize the early-warning signs of heart attacks may be able to prevent heart attacks from occurring. Dr. Raymond Bahr, head of coronary care at St. Agnes Hospital in Baltimore, Maryland, is a leading crusader in heart attack prevention. According to Dr. Bahr, most people know that heart attacks are often preceded by crushing pain. Many people, however, are unaware of other, less publicized early-warning signals of heart attack. The most common of these early warnings are nausea and on-off central chest discomfort.

People experiencing these heart attack signals should go to a hospital immediately. Recent findings confirm that getting to a hospital fast in order to obtain medical treatment is a definite advantage. The hospitals best equipped to handle heart attack victims have board-certified emergency physicians and well-established procedures and systems that afford patients needed care within 30 minutes of entering the hospital.

According to Bahr, although nobody can alter an inherited vulnerability to heart attack, everyone can take steps to prevent a full-fledged heart attack from occurring. Preventive measures include avoiding smoking, maintaining an acceptable blood pressure level, controlling cholesterol levels, and exercising regularly.≈

Managing Stress in Organizations

Because stress is felt by virtually all employees in all organizations, insights about managing stress are valuable to all managers. This section is built on the assumption that in order to appropriately manage stress in organizations, managers must do the following:

1. Understand how stress influences worker performance.
2. Identify where unhealthy stress exists in organizations.
3. Help employees handle stress.

Understanding How Stress Influences Worker Performance
To deal with stress among employees, managers must understand the relationship between the amount of stress felt by a worker and the worker's performance. This relationship is shown in Figure 13.7. Note that extremely high and extremely low levels of stress tend to have negative effects on production. Additionally, while increasing stress tends to bolster performance up to some point (Point A in the figure), when the level of stress increases beyond this point, performance will begin to deteriorate.

In sum, a certain amount of stress among employees is generally considered to be advantageous for the organization because it tends to increase production. However, when employees experience too much or too little stress, it is generally disadvantageous for the organization because it tends to decrease production. The cartoon on page 315 lightheartedly illustrates the profoundly negative effect that too much stress can have on job performance.

Identifying Unhealthy Stress in Organizations
Once managers understand the impact of stress on performance, they must identify where stress exists within the organization.[24] After areas of stress have been pinpointed, managers must then determine whether the stress is at an appropriate level or is too high or too low. Because most stress-related organizational problems involve too much stress rather than too little, the remainder of this section focuses on how to relieve undesirably high levels of stress.

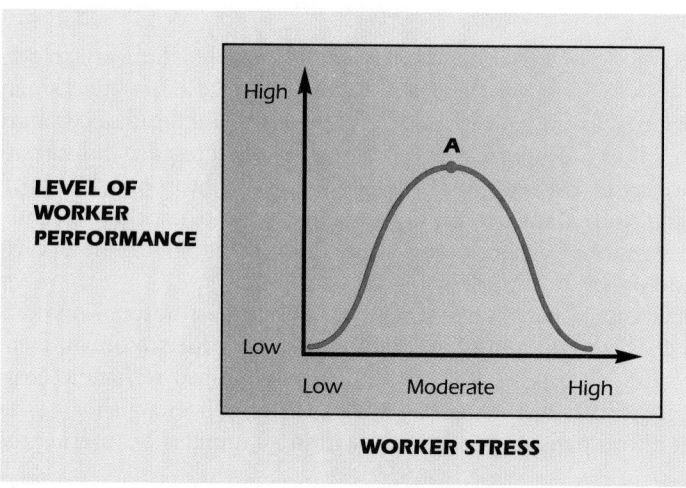

Figure 13.7 **The relationship between worker stress and the level of worker performance**

Keller is a good man but totally lacking in stress-management skills.

Harvard Business Review (July/August 1987), p. 64.
© Lee Lorenz 1989.

Managers often find it difficult to identify the people in the organization who are experiencing detrimentally high levels of stress. Part of the difficulty is that people respond to high stress in different ways, and part is that physiological reactions to stress are hard, if not impossible, for managers to observe and monitor. Such reactions include high blood pressure, pounding heart, and gastrointestinal disorders.

Nevertheless, there are several observable symptoms of undesirably high stress levels that managers can learn to recognize. These symptoms are as follows:[25]

- Constant fatigue
- Low energy
- Moodiness
- Increased aggression
- Excessive use of alcohol
- Temper outbursts
- Compulsive eating
- High levels of anxiety
- Chronic worrying

A manager who observes one or more of these symptoms in employees should investigate to determine if those exhibiting the symptoms are indeed under too much stress. If so, the manager should try to help those employees handle their stress and/or should attempt to reduce stressors in the organization.

Helping Employees Handle Stress

A **stressor** is an environmental demand that causes people to feel stress. Stressors are common in situations where individuals are confronted by circumstances for which their usual behaviors are inappropriate or insufficient and where negative consequences are associated with failure to deal properly with the situation. Organizational change characterized by continual layoffs or firings is an obvious stressor, but many other factors related to organizational policies, structure, physical conditions, and processes can also act as stressors.[26]

Reducing Stressors in the Organization

Stress is seldom significantly reduced until the stressors causing it have been coped with satisfactorily or withdrawn from the environment. For example, if too much organizational change is causing undesirably high levels of stress, management may be able to reduce that stress by improving organizational training that is aimed at preparing workers to deal with job demands resulting from the change. Or management might choose to reduce such stress by refraining from making further organizational changes for a while.[27]

A **stressor** is an environmental demand that causes people to feel stress.

Management can also adopt several strategies to help prevent the development of unwanted stressors in organizations to begin with. Three such strategies follow:[28]

1. *Create an organizational climate that is supportive of individuals.* Organizations commonly evolve into large bureaucracies with formal, inflexible, impersonal climates. This setup leads to considerable job stress. Making the organizational environment less formal and more supportive of employee needs will help prevent the development of unwanted organizational stressors.

2. *Make jobs interesting.* Routine jobs that do not allow employees some degree of freedom often result in undesirable employee stress. If management focuses on making jobs as interesting as possible, this should help prevent the development of stressors related to routine, boring jobs.

3. *Design and operate career counseling programs.* Employees often experience considerable stress when they do not know what their next career step might be or when they might take it. If management can show employees that next step and when it can realistically be achieved, it will discourage unwanted organizational stressors in this area.

IBM is an example of a company that for many years has focused on career planning for its employees as a vehicle for reducing employee stress.[29] IBM has a corporationwide program to encourage supervisors to annually conduct voluntary career planning sessions with employees that result in one-page career action plans. Thus IBM employees have a clear idea of where their careers are headed.

BACK TO THE CASE

Michael Dell should be careful not to create too much stress on organization members as a result of his planned changes because such stress could prove significant enough to cancel out any anticipated improvements from the changes and might eventually result in such stress-related effects on employees as inability to concentrate and to make sound decisions.

Although some additional stress on organization members as a result of Dell's planned changes could enhance productivity at Dell Computer, too much stress could have a negative impact on production. Signs that Dell should look for in employees are constant fatigue, increased aggression, temper outbursts, and chronic worrying.

If Dell determines that his changes have produced undesirably high levels of stress, he should try to reduce the stress either through training programs aimed at better equipping employees to deal with new job demands or by slowing the rate of change.

It would probably be wise for Dell to take action to prevent unwanted stressors from developing as a result of his planned change. In this regard, he could ensure that the organizational climate at Dell Computer Corporation is supportive of individual needs and that jobs resulting from the planned change are as interesting as possible.

Many companies are finding today that if they cannot offer employees security, they can help by offering what employees want next—freedom. Thus American Express not only permits travel agents to work at home but, for workers who want to improve skills and advancement opportunities, offers "career resource centers" like this one at its North Carolina facility.

Action Summary

Reread the learning objectives below. Each objective is followed by questions. Answering these questions accurately will help you retain the most important concepts discussed in this chapter. After answering each question, check your answer against the answer key at the end of this chapter. (*Hint:* If you have any doubts regarding the correct response, consult the page whose number follows the answer.)

Circle: From studying this chapter, I will attempt to acquire:

1. A working definition of *changing an organization*.

T,F **a.** The purpose of organizational modifications is to increase the extent to which an organization accomplishes its objectives.

a,b,c,d,e **b.** Organizational modifications typically include changing: (a) overall goals and objectives; (b) established lines of organizational authority; (c) levels of responsibility held by various organization members; (d) b and c; (e) all of the above.

2. An understanding of the relative importance of change and stability to an organization.

a,b,c,d,e **a.** According to the Hellriegel and Slocum model, the following is the most likely outcome when both adaptation and stability are high: (a) high probability of slow death; (b) high probability of survival; (c) high probability of survival and growth; (d) certainty of quick death; (e) possibility of slow death.

T,F **b.** According to Hellriegel and Slocum, repeated changes in an organization without concern for stability typically result in employees with a high degree of adaptability.

3. Some ability to recognize what kind of changes should be made within an organization.

T,F **a.** Although managers can choose to change an organization in many ways, most changes can be categorized as one of three kinds: (1) people change, (2) goal or objective change, and (3) technological change.

a,b,c,d e **b.** Decentralizing an organization is a structural change aimed at: (a) reducing the cost of coordination; (b) increasing the controllability of subunits; (c) increasing motivation; (d) all of the above; (e) a and b.

4. An appreciation for why the people affected by a change should be considered when the change is being made.

a,b,c,d,e **a.** The following is *not* an example of personal loss that organization members fear as a result of change: (a) possibility of a reduction in personal prestige; (b) disturbance of established social relationships; (c) reduction in overall organizational productivity; (d) personal failure because of an inability to carry out new job responsibilities; (e) disturbance of established working relationships.

T,F **b.** Support for a proposed change may be altered by focusing attention on possible individual gains that could materialize as a result of the change.

5. Some facility at evaluating change.

a,b,c,d,e **a.** Symptoms indicating that further change is necessary are that organization members: (a) are oriented more to the future than to the past; (b) recognize the challenge of current problems more than the obligations of rituals; (c) pay more allegiance to overall company goals than to departmental goals; (d) none of the above; (e) a and b.

T,F **b.** Change is an inevitable part of management and considered so important to organizational success that some managers encourage employees to suggest needed changes.

6. An understanding of how organizational change and stress are related.

T,F **a.** Stress is simply the rate of wear and tear on the body.

T,F **b.** From a managerial viewpoint, stress on employees can be either too high or too low.

T,F **c.** Stressors are the factors within an organization that reduce employee stress.

Introductory Case Wrap-Up

"Michael Dell Faces Constant Change at Dell Computer Corporation" (p. 297) and its related back-to-the-case sections were written to help you better understand the management concepts contained in this chapter. Answer the following discussion questions about this introductory case to enrich your understanding of the chapter content:

1. How complicated was it for Michael Dell to implement the change of establishing new retail outlets for his products? Explain.

2. Do you think that certain Dell Computer employees subtly resisted this change? Why or why not?

3. What elements of this change caused organization members to experience stress, and what could Michael Dell have done to help alleviate this stress? Be specific.

Issues for Review and Discussion

1. What is meant in this chapter by the phrase *changing an organization?*
2. Why do organizations typically undergo various changes?
3. Does an organization need both change and stability? Explain.
4. What major factors should a manager consider when changing an organization?
5. Define *change agent* and list the skills necessary to be a successful change agent.
6. Explain the term *organizational effectiveness* and describe the major factors that determine how effective an organization will be.
7. Describe the relationship between "determining what should be changed within an organization" and "choosing a kind of change for the organization."
8. What is the difference between structural change and people change?
9. Is matrix organization an example of a structural change? Explain.
10. Draw and explain the managerial grid.
11. Is grid OD an example of a technique used to make structural change? Explain.
12. What causes resistance to change?
13. List and explain the steps managers can take to minimize employee resistance to change.
14. Explain the significance of unfreezing, changing, and refreezing for changing the organization.
15. How and why should managers evaluate the changes they make?
16. Define *stress* and explain how it influences performance.
17. List three stressors that could exist within an organization. For each stressor, discuss a specific management action that could be taken to reduce or eliminate the stressor.
18. What effect can career counseling have on employee stress? Explain.

Action Summary Answer Key

1. a. T, p. 298
   b. d, p. 298
2. a. c, p. 299
   b. F, p. 299

3. a. F, p. 301
   b. d, pp. 302–303
4. a. c, p. 309
   b. T, p. 309

5. a. d, p. 312
   b. T, p. 298

6. a. T, p. 313
   b. T, p. 313
   c. F, pp. 314–315

Case Study

Layoffs—The Cost of Doing Business

In 1995, 385,000 American jobs were cut across a broad base of industries—manufacturing, telecommunications, finance and securities, and retailing. From 1990 to 1995, U.S. corporations slashed 2.9 million jobs. The largest of these cuts came in 1993, when IBM cut 60,000 and Sears Roebuck 50,000 workers from their payrolls. On January 2, 1996, AT&T rang in the new year with the announcement that 40,000 workers would be asked to leave as part of its mass restructuring into three separate companies.

According to the American Management Association, however, this trend in corporate downsizing has been slowing. Each year in the period from 1990 to 1992, almost 8 percent of the U.S. workforce was laid off; 1993

saw the highest number of layoffs, with over 8 percent of U.S. workers dismissed. The percentage decreased in 1993–1994, to less than 6 percent; in 1994–1995, just 1 percent of workers lost their jobs because of corporate downsizing.

National statistics, however, do not tell the whole story, especially the human side. AT&T's announced breakup stunned its 300,000 employees. In his announcement speech, AT&T Chairman Robert E. Allen, who has presided over five large workforce reductions in the past eight years, declared that "to the extent we can get in trim, we'll produce better margins, more flexibility and more cash flow to invest in other opportunities." Officials admitted it was impossible to predict when layoffs would end because no one knew how many employees would be required to run the new AT&T. Throughout the company, employees felt the stress of job insecurity.

Two months after the layoffs announcement, the stress hit home as 72,000 managers—about half of AT&T's total administrative staff—were offered buyout packages. Managers were given until the end of December 1996 to decide. The offer was not that "sweet"; in fact, managers who waited to see if they would be among those laid off stood to receive quite similar severance packages. Analysts believe AT&T management decided not to make the buyout too attractive for fear of losing talent that they hoped to capitalize on in their new companies. Only 6,500 managers accepted the buyout prior to the deadline.

On January 2, 1996, Allen announced that "the reduction in our workforce will be the most difficult and painful step we've had to take in this restructuring process. Compassion will be an essential ingredient in the handling of the job cuts. . . ." In an E-mail message to employees, he explained that job reductions "are being driven by changes in our marketplace—changes in customer needs, technology and public policy—not through any fault of the people who will leave."

Whether or not they were included in the first round of layoffs, virtually all AT&T employees have felt the stress of downsizing. Morale is low. In New Jersey, a state where the company is the largest private employer and 6,000 to 7,000 workers were laid off in the beginning of January, entire communities stand to suffer at least a temporary downturn in their economies. According to Don Jay Smith, an AT&T worker in Parsippany, "I think there are a lot of people who are very nervous about this and about their prospects for getting a replacement job. I think most people feel this is pretty much the end of it."

One top AT&T executive, a 36-year veteran and key architect of the 1984 breakup, has decided to leave the company before the new restructuring takes place. In an Associated Press interview, Victor A. Pelson, who will end his AT&T career as chairman of global operations, said, "It's absolutely necessary, but when you go through changes of this sort, there's a tremendous amount of work that has to be done—separation of all kinds of assets, most importantly human assets . . . and I've been through that."

According to *The Wall Street Journal*, insiders fear that years of downsizing have devastated morale at AT&T just when the company needs "an esprit de corps among its workers to attack new markets." Says John Challenger, an employment consultant at Challenger, Gray & Christmas, Inc., a Chicago outplacement firm, "Cutbacks such as these throw the organization into chaos, making it harder for the company that remains to get back on its feet."

Nevertheless, according to Richard Klugman of PaineWebber, corporate moves that hurt employees but benefit stockholders are on the rise: "You [will see] more and more companies . . . take a realistic approach that the shareholders come first and employees are there to serve the shareholders." It seems, therefore, that Americans entering the workforce will have to develop a mind set about their careers that is very different from the mind set their parents had when they were young. White- and blue-collar workers can expect to change jobs six or seven times throughout their careers.

Job insecurity is a stress that afflicts corporate workers at all levels. "Managers used to be impervious to changes in the economy," says Paul Osterman, a human resources professor at Sloan School of Management. "Now, they feel like their world is falling apart, even though they are still better off than most folks."

Questions:

1. Should all American workers feel insecure about their jobs, or are specific areas and types of workers targeted in downsizing? Cite examples to support your opinion.

2. How does AT&T's restructuring plan effect change in the three main classes of organizational factors—people, structure, and technology? Describe how effectiveness might be maximized in each area.

3. Massive layoffs like those at AT&T obviously have a strong effect on the people who lose their jobs, but they also affect employees who remain at the company. List the negative effects of layoffs on remaining human resources. Brainstorm a list of ways in which companies might reduce this negative impact.

Skills Exercise

Conduct a survey in your community to examine corporate downsizing, job security, and company loyalty from the workers' perspective. From the data, can you make generalizations about the workforce? Why or why not?

What factors might be unique to your population? Why? Are opinions divided among specific socioeconomic groups? Explain.

The Internet learning materials that accompany this chapter can be found at
http://www.profcerto.com
Additional information can be found on the inside front and back covers of this text.

Product Development at Lands' End: From a Functional to a Team Approach

This is the fourth case in this book that explores a variety of management-related issues at the well-known direct-retailing company Lands' End. The first installment (on pp. 24–26) is designed to be a general introduction. You may want to refer to it when you are studying the cases that appear at the end of each part of the book.

ON LOCATION!

Prior to March 1994, the creative, merchandising, quality, inventory, and design functions at Lands' End were all grouped into separate departments. Consequently, employees associated with a specific function were generally housed in one specific area. Quality, for example, encompassed half of the first floor of Building 5, design the other half of floor one. Merchandising, inventory, and design occupied the second floor. According to Joan Brown, Vice President for Quality Assurance,

> while we were expected to work together as a team, it really wasn't working very well. Under that set-up, a merchant might have three quality specialists who did fittings and manufacturing for them. Plus, a quality specialist might be working with as many as six different merchants. That arrangement made setting priorities—and just simply communicating—very difficult.

It quickly became apparent that the existing structure made product development far too time-consuming. Thus in September 1993, a group of nine employees (four managers and five vice presidents, including Joan Brown) were assembled to devise ways of cutting the time required to bring products to market. The group's goal was actually twofold: for Lands' End to be able to develop products in a shorter period of time and to improve communication-across functions. "Product development was taking a very long time to get accomplished and communication was poor," admits Joan Brown:

> So with the support of the head of merchandising, we established a team of people to sit down and try to figure out how to better organize. Actually, we didn't even say "to better organize ourselves" because we weren't sure organization was the problem. Our objective was to come up with a way to cut down the time that it takes to develop a product. One of the first things we realized was that we were all grouped into functional silos and didn't have any common goals. Inventory's goal, for example, was to get the product in the building, have it arrive on the receiving dock, and be out the door to the customer. Quality, on the other hand, would stop anything from going out that did not meet its expectations—which ran headlong against the inventory manager's goal. In fact, none of our goals blended.

With a general idea of its objectives in mind, the team began to meet—twice each week, off-site. This effort would be maintained for about six and one-half months and then expanded to a three-day-per-week schedule over the last month or so of the planning period. Admittedly, being away from regular day-to-day duties made the task even more challenging. According to Brown, however, team members enthusiastically accepted the assignment:

> We were supported by top management and were given all the resources and support that were needed. Even though we all knew one another, our first task was to find out more about ourselves and how to work as a team. Finding out our communication styles—for example, controller, analyzer—was a major breakthrough. Then things really began to click.

It soon became clear that cross-functional teams offered the best solution to LE's product-development problems. "Each team," explains Brown,

would have a product category that it would be responsible for (for example, coed knits, luggage, women's knits, and swimwear). It was also agreed that once team members were assigned, they would no longer be shared with other teams. At this point, other members of Lands' End were brought in to help. The next big questions facing the larger group were how many teams would be needed and who would go on what team. So, for a team that we might call men's tailored, we had to decide how many inventory people would be needed, how many quality people, and so forth. Finally, we agreed that instead of each function having its own support person, everybody on the team would share the support person or persons for that team.

Along with the regular meetings of the original team, meetings also were scheduled with vendors who worked with Lands' End and understood the product development process. Site visits to respected companies were also set up. The purpose of both vendor and site visits was to gain a broader perspective on various product-development processes. Lessons from vendors supported the fact that LE's current structure was generating communications problems. Vendors were apparently getting mixed signals from inventory, merchants, and quality. With such mixed signals, they were often unsure as to what was needed from them. As Brown puts it, "We had the team concept in mind prior to talking with vendors, but those discussions helped to confirm the fact that we were making the right decision."

By January 15, 1994, many of the details of the Lands' End reorganization plan were beginning to come together. One goal of the task force was to assign people to teams with the least amount of disruption. For example, explains Brown, "If a person had been the quality person for men's slacks, we would make every attempt to see to it that that person ended up on the men's tailored team."

March 1 was set as the roll-out date for the plan. But as the work of the group progressed, it became clear that there was some apprehension among employees. "We never got to the point," recalls Brown, "where we could talk to people about the reorganization without it causing some concerns. It was the uncertainty associated with the changes that caused apprehension."

A month or so before the plan was to be rolled out, 12 additional people were added to the team. This advisory group was shown the plan, given time to think about it, and asked to come back with questions and reactions. Although a few had reservations about some aspects of the plan, most could see the benefits and were supportive. On March 1, 1994, all 180 or so affected employees were called together and a 45-minute overview of the plan was presented by the CEO and vice chairman. Then, department heads met one-on-one with each person in his or her department. Each individual was given an explanation of where he or she would fit into the new structure. Everyone was also asked to attend other meetings during the day that would provide additional details related to reorganization and the new team concept. Although most people would be functioning in the same or similar capacities, there were, of course, some changes.

Not surprisingly, reorganization meant more than just changes in working relationships. It also meant changes in work locations—work space had to be physically reconfigured to accommodate the team concept. "We decided that we wouldn't dictate how teams should be configured," recalls Brown,

> so we decided to set up two pilot environments. We asked two of the new product development teams to volunteer to occupy the two environments and then let the other teams know what they thought. Over the six-week trial period, other teams were encouraged to talk to these groups and, finally, to vote on their preference. While the idea was a good one, that six-week period was total disruption. In hindsight, the trial teams were a mistake—they unnecessarily kept everybody in a state of flux and just prolonged the transition to teams.

At the same time that physical moves were being made, team-development activities also were initiated. These included a course on perceptive communications and other activities to help team members understand the importance of cooperation.

More than a year now has passed since the team concept was adopted at Lands'

End. The precise impact of the shift from the functional to the team approach on effectiveness and efficiency is yet to be known. Joan Brown, however, is certain that it has had a positive impact: "Time to bring a new product to market has been reduced," she points out,

and communication significantly improved. Even more importantly, everyone associated with the product now has the same goals. Putting people on teams avoids those situations in which the quality person down here is miscommunicating with the merchant upstairs, who is miscommunicating with the vendor by sending out information different from what the quality person or the inventory person wanted to communicate. These kinds of communications problems have, for the most part, been rectified.

What might one of these Lands' End product-development teams look like? Merchandiser Kelli Larke explains what she does as the member of the Adult Sleepwear and Slippers team:

My job as merchant for adult sleepwear and slippers was to manage everything related to product development as well as having total profit and loss responsibility for the products in these categories. The first team member is Dave, the inventory manager. His job is to manage the inventory at the stockkeeping-unit level—ordering sufficient quantities to service the customers' needs. Priscilla is the quality-assurance specialist. She sees that products exceed the customers' expectations in fit, construction, and fabrication.

Ellen is the copywriter and is responsible for presenting products to customers in our catalogs. Carolyn is the art director. She ensures that the product features come across clearly to the customer in photography. Dawn is the team-support member: in short, she provides assistance for all team members.

One of the most positive things about the team environment is what we call the "workroom." This room provides a focal point where we get together to work on product development and catalog presentation. We also have an area to hold team meetings, vendor appointments, and product-fit sessions. To help us visualize the selling concept, we hang catalog layouts in here once they are created. The proximity of all the specialists on the team allows better communication, shortened lead times, more knowledge by all members, and therefore increased customer benefits.

As we have already seen, implementing team concepts has been beneficial, especially to Lands' End customers. According to Joan Brown, however, like all successful and progressive companies, LE continues to look to the future and to anticipate additional change so as to remain a leading direct-mail apparel merchant in the United States: "We realize," says Brown, "that putting people in teams is not the final answer. In fact, it's far from the final answer. This was just one structural change that, undoubtedly, will lead to many other process changes."

Questions:

1. Specifically, what was, and what is now, the basis of departmentation for product development at Lands' End? Draw partial organization charts to support your contentions.

2. Since the time that this book was written, additional changes have been made to the structure of teams at Lands' End. What do you think some of those changes might be?

3. There are three major types of change (technological, structural, and people) that can be made in organizations. Of these, people change is generally the most difficult to carry out because individuals are often sensitive to change. From the information provided in the case, evaluate the effectiveness of people change at Lands' End.

4. Applying what you have learned from the text, what else can you say about organizing at Lands' End?

14
chapter

FUNDAMENTALS OF INFLUENCING AND COMMUNICATION

STUDENT LEARNING OBJECTIVES

From studying this chapter, I will attempt to acquire:

1. An understanding of influencing.
2. An understanding of interpersonal communication.
3. A knowledge of how to use feedback.
4. An appreciation for the importance of nonverbal communication.
5. Insights on formal organizational communication.
6. An appreciation for the importance of the grapevine.
7. Some hints on how to encourage organizational communication.

CHAPTER OUTLINE

Introductory Case: Eaton Managers Concentrate on Influencing People

Fundamentals of Influencing
Defining Influencing
The Influencing Subsystem

People Perspectives: The U.S. Army Teaches Leadership by Teaching Communication

Communication
Interpersonal Communication

Global Spotlight: Compression Labs Sends Messages via Videoconferencing

Interpersonal Communication in Organizations

Cutting Edge: Communicating with Customers at Intel

Quality Spotlight: Enhanced Formal Communication Contributes to Improving Quality at Holiday Inn

Eaton Managers Concentrate on Influencing People

It's 7:30 A.M., time for the morning quiz at Eaton Corporation's factory. Ten union workers, each representing work teams, sit around a boardroom table. "What were our sales yesterday?" asks a supervisor at the head of the table. A worker, glancing at a computer printout, replies that they were $625,275. "And in the month?" From another worker comes the response: $6,172,666.

Eaton may not be a household name, and its products—including gears, engine valves, truck axles and, at Lincoln, Nebraska, circuit breakers—aren't glamorous. But its success in raising productivity and cutting costs throws plenty of doubt on recent hand-wringing about unmotivated American workers and flaccid American corporations.

Getting people to think for themselves—and work in teams—is important to Eaton. The company starts by hiring managers who aren't autocratic and training them to accept encroachments on their authority. Not everyone can hack it: When engineers at Lincoln were evicted from their office enclave and the department was moved out onto the shop floor, the department chief and a colleague quit in protest.

Managers who adjust, however, tend to stay at one plant a long time. The same person has been plant manager at Lincoln since 1980. The Kearney manager, Nebraskan Robert Dyer, is an area native who was hired as a machine operator in 1969, when the plant opened. That, too, isn't unusual: 23 of Lincoln's salaried staff of 57 came up from the rank and file.

Management shares extensive financial data with employees at the two plants to underscore the link between their performance and the factory's. At Kearney, a TV monitor in the cafeteria indicates how specific shifts and departments did the previous day against their cost and performance goals. Lincoln gets the message out via computer printouts. "It gives you a sense of direction," says Ricky Rigg, a metal fabricator, "and makes you appreciate what you do more."

At Kearney, where workers labor amid the noise and heat of hot forged metal, bonuses are based on the entire plant's performance compared with the prior year. In the first quarter, for instance, Kearney topped the year-earlier profit and cost criteria by 7 percent—and workers got a quarterly bonus of 7 percent, or about $500 each. Kearney employees have earned a bonus every quarter since the system was introduced six years ago.

There's noncash recognition as well. On a recent Wednesday, the Kearney plant held a lunchtime barbecue to mark the first shift's 365th consecutive day without any injuries. Plant Manager Dyer and his staff prepared the meal—hamburgers, hot dogs, potato salad, and baked beans—while the first shift chowed down.

"Bob personifies what I look for in a plant manager," says George Dettloff, general manager of Eaton's engine-components division and Robert Dyer's boss. "He manages, but he gives people freedom."

That style was evident a year ago, when Kearney was looking for a human resources manager to replace one who had resigned. A joint labor-management committee of 18 people whittled the field down to 3 candidates. And when it came time for a final decision, Dyer asked the committee to decide on its own.

These team workers at Eaton Corporation are planning and evaluating their own work. The company provides them with the financial information and other data they need to make their own decisions.

n the introductory case, Eaton Corporation's recent success in enhancing company productivity and efficiency is credited largely to how its managers manage people. According to the case, Eaton managers manage by encouraging employees to think for themselves, to make decisions about who is hired at Eaton, and to make changes in the organization that will result in improvements. The information in this chapter emphasizes the value of such managers and offers insights into what additional steps managers might take to guide the activities of organization members in directions that lead to the attainment of management system objectives. The chapter is divided into two main parts:

1. Fundamentals of influencing
2. Communication

FUNDAMENTALS OF INFLUENCING

The four basic managerial functions—planning, organizing, influencing, and controlling—were introduced in Chapter 1. *Planning* and *organizing* have already been discussed; *influencing* is the third of these basic functions covered in this text. A definition of *influencing* and a discussion of the influencing subsystem follow.

Defining *Influencing*

Influencing is the process of guiding the activities of organization members in appropriate directions. *Appropriate directions*, of course, are those that lead to the attainment of management system objectives. Influencing involves focusing on organization members as people and dealing with such issues as morale, arbitration of conflicts, and the development of good working relationships. It is a critical part of a manager's job. In fact, the ability to influence others is a primary determinant of how successful a manager will be.[1]

> **Influencing** is the process of guiding the activities of organization members in appropriate directions. It involves the performance of four management activities: (1) leading, (2) motivating, (3) considering groups, and (4) communicating.

The Influencing Subsystem

Like the planning and organizing functions, the influencing function can be viewed as a subsystem within the overall management system (see Figure 14.1). The primary

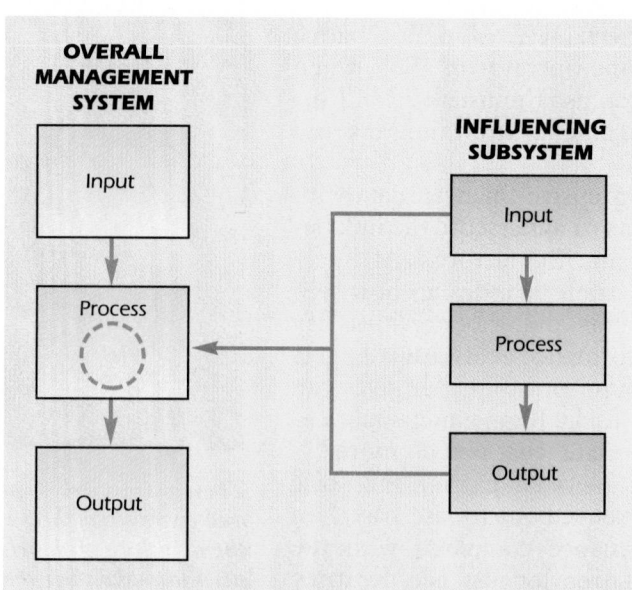

Figure 14.1   Relationship between overall management system and influencing subsystem

purpose of the influencing subsystem, as stated above, is to enhance the attainment of management system objectives by guiding the activities of organization members in appropriate directions.

Figure 14.2 shows the constituents of the influencing subsystem. The input of this subsystem is composed of a portion of the total resources of the overall management system, and its output is appropriate organization member behavior. The process of the influencing subsystem involves the performance of four primary management activities:

1. Leading
2. Motivating
3. Considering groups
4. Communicating

Managers transform a portion of organizational resources into appropriate organization member behavior mainly by performing these four activities.

As Figure 14.2 shows, leading, motivating, and considering groups are interrelated. Managers accomplish each of these influencing activities, to some extent, by communicating with organization members. For example, managers can only decide what kind of leader they need to be after they analyze the characteristics of the various groups with which they will interact and determine how those groups can best be motivated. Then, regardless of the leadership strategy they adopt, their leading, motivating, and working with groups will be accomplished—at least partly—through communication with other organization members.

In fact, all management activities are accomplished at least partly through communication or communication-related endeavors. Because communication is used re-

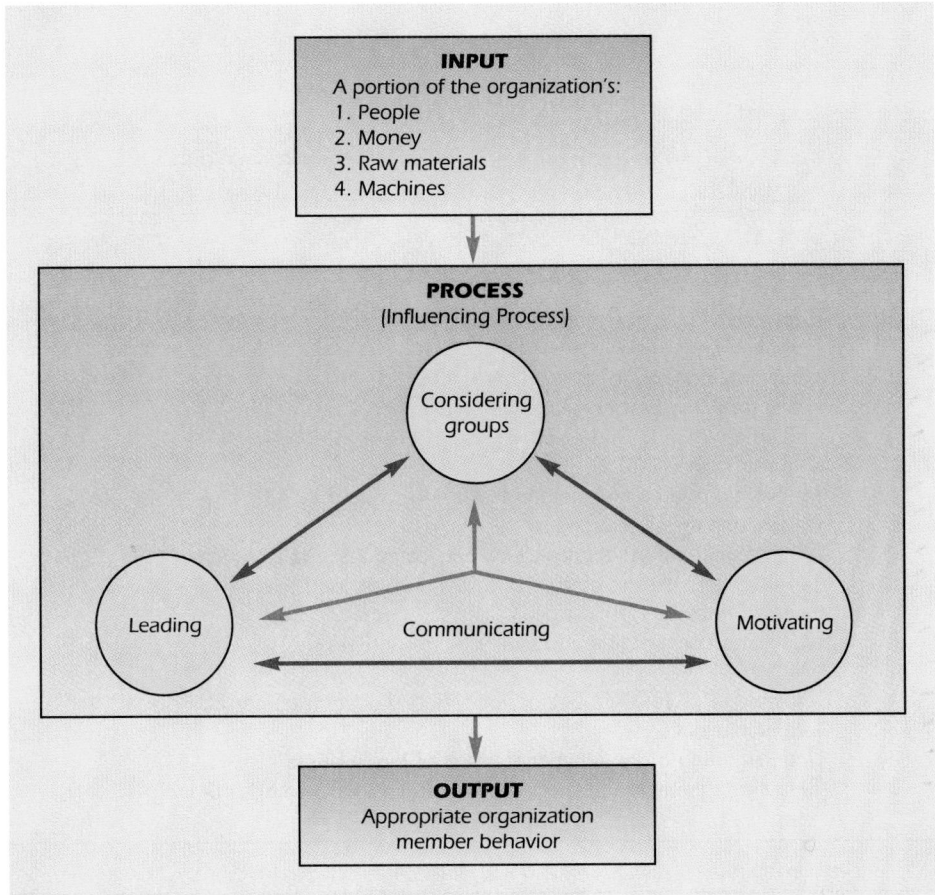

Figure 14.2   **The influencing subsystem**

CEO Anthony O'Reilly (right) of H.J. Heinz Co. is well aware that travel is actually a communications-related aspect of his job. He averages 500,000 frequent-flier miles per year, and although he takes ample advantage of modern communications technology, he also understands the importance of his personal presence as Heinz focuses much of its strategic energy on overseas markets like Europe and, especially, Asia.

peatedly by managers, ability to communicate is often referred to as the fundamental management skill.

A recent survey of chief executives supports this notion that communication is the fundamental management skill. The results, which appear in Table 14.1, show that CEOs ranked oral and written communication skills first (along with interpersonal skills) among the skills that should be taught to management students.

The information in the text indicates that managers lead, at least partly, by communicating with organization members. The following PEOPLE PERSPECTIVES feature explains why the U.S. Army has made teaching communication skills an important part of its leadership training program.

Table 14.1

Chief Executives, Ranking of Skills They Believe Should Be Taught to Management Students

RANK*	KEY LEARNING AREA	FREQUENCY INDICATED
1	Oral and written communication skills	25
1	Interpersonal skills	25
3	Financial/managerial account skills	22
4	Ability to think, be analytical, and make decisions	20
5	Strategic planning and goal setting—concern for long-term performance	13
6	Motivation and commitment to the firm—giving 110%	12
7	Understanding of economics	11
8	Management information systems and computer applications	9
8	Thorough knowledge of your business, culture, and overall environment	9
8	Marketing concept (the customer is king) and skills	9
11	Integrity	7
11	Knowledge of yourself: Setting long- and short-term career objectives	7
13	Leadership skills	6
13	Understanding of the functional areas of the business	6
13	Time management: Setting priorities—how to work smart, not long or hard	1

*1 is most important.

THE U.S. ARMY TEACHES LEADERSHIP BY TEACHING COMMUNICATION

PEOPLE PERSPECTIVES

The U.S. Army claims that it can teach people how to lead. Cadets get their leadership training in Advance Camp, a six-week summer program for officer candidates held at Fort Bragg, North Carolina, and at Fort Lewis, Washington.

One of the issues the Army emphasizes in its leadership training program is communication. Future leaders are taught how to communicate, both orally and in writing. Making presentations to groups is especially stressed.

Other areas emphasized in the Army leadership training program are planning and organizing, technical competence, judgment, sensitivity, and delegation. Physical exercises aimed at building leadership skills include crawling out on a rope to drop 40 feet into water, directing a squad to build a bridge over fast-running water, and leading a squad through obstacles.

In sum, the Army wants officers who can lead intellectually and physically. Thus it emphasizes teaching cadets both intellectual and physical skills to prepare them for their future as officers.≈

BACK TO THE CASE

One of the primary functions of Eaton's management is influencing—guiding the activities of Eaton employees to enhance the accomplishment of organizational objectives. Illustrations in the case give clear examples of how the company influences people through leadership (hiring managers who aren't autocratic), motivation (granting cash and noncash rewards for jobs done well), managing groups (operating work teams to enhance company success), and communicating (giving workers feedback on exactly how well they are doing).

Of all of these influencing activities, communication is the most important. In subsequent back-to-the-case sections, discussion will focus on communication as it relates to Robert Dyer, Eaton's plant manager in Lincoln, Nebraska. As mentioned in the introductory case, Dyer communicates to employees how well the plant is performing, what problems and challenges it faces, and how those problems and challenges will be addressed. Communication, in fact, is the main tool through which he accomplishes his duties as plant manager. Almost any work that Dyer does at Eaton (planning, organizing, or controlling) requires him to communicate with other Eaton employees. In essence, Dyer must be a good communicator if he is to be a successful plant manager.

Communication is discussed further in the rest of this chapter. Leading, motivating, and considering groups are discussed in Chapters 15, 16, and 17, respectively.

COMMUNICATION

Communication is the process of sharing information with other individuals. Information, as used here, is any thought or idea that managers desire to share with other individuals. In general, communication involves one person projecting a message to one or more other people that results in everyone's arriving at a common understanding of the message. Because communication is a commonly used management skill and ability and it is often cited as the skill most responsible for a manager's success, prospective managers must learn how to communicate. To help managers become better interpersonal communicators, new communication training techniques are constantly being developed and evaluated.[2]

The communication activities of managers generally involve interpersonal communication—sharing information with other organization members. The following sections feature both the general topic of interpersonal communication and the more specific topic of interpersonal communication in organizations.

Communication is the process of sharing information with other individuals.

Interpersonal Communication

To be a successful interpersonal communicator, a manager must understand the following:

1. How interpersonal communication works.
2. The relationship between feedback and interpersonal communication.
3. The importance of verbal versus nonverbal interpersonal communication.

How Interpersonal Communication Works

Interpersonal communication is the process of transmitting information to others.[3] To be complete, the process must have the following three basic elements:

> The **source/encoder** is the person in the interpersonal communication situation who originates and encodes information to be shared with another person or persons.

1. *The source/encoder.* The **source/encoder** is the person in the interpersonal communication situation who originates and encodes information to be shared with another person or persons. Encoding is putting information into a form that can be received and understood by another individual. Putting one's thoughts into a letter is an example of encoding. Until information is encoded, it cannot be shared with others. (From here on, the *source/encoder* will be referred to simply as the *source.*)

> A **message** is encoded information that the source intends to share with others.

> The **signal** is a message that has been transmitted from one person to another.

2. *The signal.* Encoded information that the source intends to share constitutes a **message.** A message that has been transmitted from one person to another is called a **signal.**

GLOBAL SPOTLIGHT

COMPRESSION LABS SENDS MESSAGES VIA VIDEOCONFERENCING

The dissemination of messages becomes a greater technical challenge when businesses expand into the international arena. According to Carl Marszewski of Compression Labs, Inc., the increased need to compete with other businesses on the international level has driven organizations to look for new and better ways of projecting communication signals. Compression Labs and a growing number of other organizations are using international videoconferencing—conferences via television—as an economical yet effective way to communicate about topics like new areas for organizational research, reviewing budgets, and overall organizational problem solving.

Unfortunately, problems like a lack of coordination between the United States and other countries have made the process of setting up videoconferences across national borders challenging. But given the effectiveness and efficiency of videoconferencing and the intense competition among firms at the global level, aggressive companies will undoubtedly find ways to overcome these problems. Rapid growth in international videoconferencing is a certainty.≈

New technologies like Intel's Proshare software program are expanding the nature of the encoded signals that can be communicated across today's business environment. An example of what is called liveboard *technology, Proshare permits the coder/sender to draw a picture—say, an order-entry process, an organization chart—that is transmitted over telephone wires to a decoder who will see it immediately.*

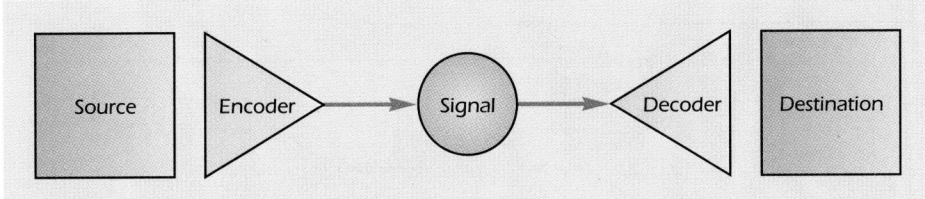

3. *The decoder/destination.* The **decoder/destination** is the person or persons with whom the source is attempting to share information. This person receives the signal and decodes, or interprets, the message to determine its meaning. Decoding is the process of converting messages back into information. In all interpersonal communication situations, message meaning is a result of decoding. (From here on, the *decoder/destination* will be referred to simply as the *destination*.)

The classic work of Wilbur Schramm clarifies the role played by each of the three elements of the interpersonal communication process. As implied in Figure 14.3, the source determines what information to share, encodes this information in the form of a message, and then transmits the message as a signal to the destination. The destination decodes the transmitted message to determine its meaning and then responds accordingly.

A manager who desires to assign the performance of a certain task to a subordinate would use the communication process in the following way: First, the manager would determine exactly what task he or she wanted the subordinate to perform. Then the manager would encode and transmit a message to the subordinate that would accurately reflect this assignment. The message transmission itself could be as simple as the manager's telling the subordinate what the new responsibilities include. Next, the subordinate would decode the message transmitted by the manager to ascertain its meaning and then would respond to it appropriately.

Successful and Unsuccessful Interpersonal Communication.   **Successful communication** refers to an interpersonal communication situation in which the information the source intends to share with the destination and the meaning the destination derives from the transmitted message are the same. Conversely, **unsuccessful communication** is an interpersonal communication situation in which the information the source intends to share with the destination and the meaning the destination derives from the transmitted message are different.

To increase the probability that communication will be successful, the message must be encoded so that the source's experience of the way a signal should be decoded is equivalent to the destination's experience of the way it should be decoded. If this is done, the probability is high that the destination will interpret the signal as intended by the source. Figure 14.4 illustrates these overlapping fields of experience that ensure successful communication.

Barriers to Successful Interpersonal Communication.   Factors that decrease the probability that communication will be successful are called *communication barriers.* A clear understanding of these barriers will help managers maximize their communication success. The following sections discuss both communication macrobarriers and communication microbarriers.

Macrobarriers.   **Communication macrobarriers** are factors that hinder successful communication in a general communication situation.[4] These factors relate primarily to the communication environment and the larger world in which communication takes place. Some common macrobarriers are the following:[5]

The **decoder/destination** is the person or persons in the interpersonal communication situation with whom the source is attempting to share information.

Successful communication refers to an interpersonal communication situation in which the information the source intends to share with the destination and the meaning the destination derives from the transmitted message are the same.

Unsuccessful communication refers to an interpersonal communication situation in which the information the source intends to share with the destination and the meaning the destination derives from the transmitted message are different.

Communication macrobarriers are factors hindering successful communication that relate primarily to the communication environment and the larger world in which communication takes place.

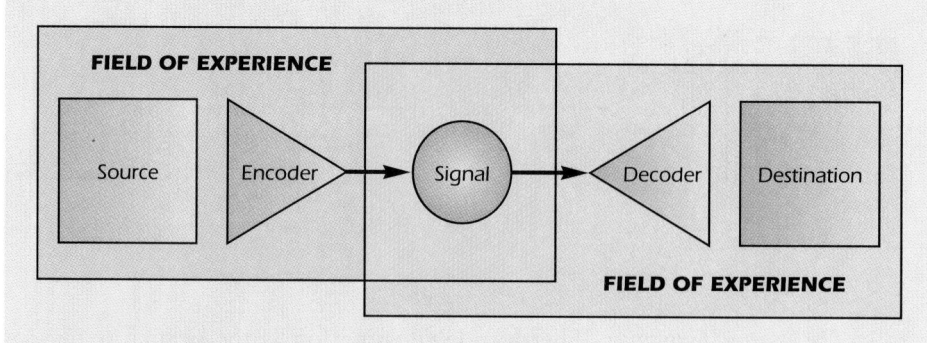

Figure 14.4 Overlapping fields
of experience that ensure
successful communication

1. *The increasing need for information.*   Because society is changing constantly
   and rapidly, individuals have a greater and greater need for information. This
   growing need tends to overload communication networks, thereby distorting
   communication. To minimize the effects of this barrier, managers should take
   steps to ensure that organization members are not overloaded with information. Only information critical to the performance of their jobs should be
   transmitted to them.

2. *The need for increasingly complex information.*   Because of today's rapid technological advances, most people are confronted with complex communication
   situations in their everyday lives. If managers take steps to emphasize simplicity in communication, the effects of this barrier can be lessened. Furnishing
   organization members with adequate training to deal with more technical
   areas is another strategy for overcoming this barrier.

3. *The reality that people in the United States are increasingly coming into contact with
   people who use languages other than English.*   As U.S. business becomes more international in scope and as organization members travel more frequently, the
   need to know languages other than English increases. The potential communication barrier of this multilanguage situation is obvious. Moreover, people
   who deal with foreigners need to be familiar not only with their languages but
   also with their cultures. Formal knowledge of a foreign language is of little
   value unless the individual knows which words, phrases, and actions are culturally acceptable.

4. *The constant need to learn new concepts cuts down on the time available for communication.*   Many managers feel pressured to learn new and important concepts
   that they did not have to know in the past. Learning about the intricacies of
   international business or of computer usage, for example, takes up significant
   amounts of managerial time. Many managers also find that the increased demands training employees makes on their time leaves them less time available
   for communicating with other organization members.

Communication microbarriers
are factors hindering successful
communication that relate primarily to such variables as the communication message, the source, and
the destination.

Microbarriers.   **Communication microbarriers** are factors that hinder successful communication in a specific communication situation.[6] These factors relate directly to such variables as the communication message, the source, and the destination. Among the microbarriers are the following:[7]

1. *The source's view of the destination.*   The source in any communication situation has a tendency to view the destination in a specific way, and this view influences the messages sent. For example, individuals usually speak differently
   to people they think are informed about a subject than to those they believe
   are uninformed. The destination can sense the source's attitudes, which often
   block successful communication. Managers should keep an open mind about
   the people with whom they communicate and be careful not to imply any negative attitudes through their communication behavior.

2. *Message interference.*   Stimuli that compete with the communication message for the attention of the destination are called **message interference,** or noise. An instance of message interference is a manager talking to an office worker while the worker is trying to input data into a word processor. The inputting of data is message interference here because it is competing with the manager's communication message for the office worker's attention. Managers should attempt to communicate only when they have the total attention of the individuals with whom they wish to share information. An amusing example of message interference is depicted in the cartoon above.

3. *The destination's view of the source.*   Certain attitudes of the destination toward the source can also hinder successful communication. If, for example, a destination believes that the source has little credibility in the area about which the source is communicating, the destination may filter out much of the source's message and pay only slight attention to that part of the message actually received. Managers should attempt to consider the worth of messages transmitted to them independently of their personal attitudes toward the source. Many valuable ideas will escape them if they allow their personal feelings toward others to influence which messages they attend to.

4. *Perception.*   **Perception** is an individual's interpretation of a message. Different individuals may perceive the same message in very different ways. The two primary factors that influence how a stimulus is perceived are the destination's education level and the destination's amount of experience. To minimize the negative effects of this perceptual factor on interpersonal communication, managers should try to send messages with precise meanings. Ambiguous words generally tend to magnify negative perceptions.

5. *Multimeaning words.*   Because many words in the English language have several meanings, a destination may have difficulty deciding which meaning should be attached to the words of a message. A manager should not assume that a word means the same thing to all the people who use it.

A classic study by Lydia Strong substantiates this point. Strong concluded that for the 500 most common words in our language, there are 4,070 different dictionary definitions. On the average, each of these words has over 18 usages. The word *run* is an example:[8]

Babe Ruth scored a *run.*
Did you ever see Jesse Owens *run?*
I have a *run* in my stocking.
There is a fine *run* of salmon this year.
Are you going to *run* this company or am I?
You have the *run* of the place.
What headline do you want to *run?*
There was a *run* on the bank today.
Did he *run* the ship aground?

Message interference refers to stimuli that compete with the communication message for the attention of the destination.

Perception is the interpretation of a message by an individual.

I have to *run* (drive the car) downtown.
Who will *run* for president this year?
Joe flies the New York–Chicago *run* twice a week.
You know the kind of people they *run* around with.
The apples *run* large this year.
Please *run* my bathwater.

When encoding information, managers should be careful to define the terms they are using whenever possible, never use obscure meanings for words when designing messages, and strive to use words in the same way their destination uses them.

BACK TO THE CASE   In discussing Robert Dyer's ability to communicate, we are really discussing his ability to share ideas with other Eaton employees. For Dyer to be a successful communicator, he must concentrate on the three essential elements of the communication process. The first element is the source—the individual who wishes to share information with another. In this case, the source is Dyer. The second element is the signal—the message transmitted by Dyer. The third element is the destination—the Eaton employee with whom Dyer wishes to share information. Dyer should communicate with Eaton employees by first determining exactly what information he wants to share, encoding the information, and only then transmitting the message. Communication is complete when his subordinates interpret the message and respond accordingly. Dyer's communication would be termed successful if his subordinates interpreted his messages as he intended.

If Dyer is to be a successful communicator, he must also learn to minimize the impact of numerous communication barriers. These barriers include the following:

1. Eaton employees need to have more information and more complex information to do their jobs.
2. Message interference.
3. Dyer's view of the destination as well as the destination's view of Dyer.
4. The perceptual processes of the people involved in the communication attempt.
5. Multimeaning words.

Feedback and Interpersonal Communication

Feedback is, in the interpersonal communication situation, the destination's reaction to a message.

Feedback is the destination's reaction to a message. Feedback can be used by the source to ensure successful communication. For example, if the destination's message reaction is inappropriate, the source can conclude that communication was unsuccessful and that another message should be transmitted. If the destination's message reaction is appropriate, the source can conclude that communication was successful (assuming, of course, that the appropriate reaction did not happen merely by chance). Because of its potentially high value, managers should encourage feedback whenever possible and evaluate it carefully.[9]

Gathering and Using Feedback.   Feedback can be either verbal or nonverbal.[10] To gather verbal feedback, the source can simply ask the destination pertinent message-related questions; the destination's answers should indicate whether the message was perceived as intended. To gather nonverbal feedback, the source can observe the destination's nonverbal response to a message. Say a manager has transmitted a message to a subordinate specifying new steps that must be taken in the normal performance of the subordinate's job. Assuming there are no other problems, if the subordinate does not follow the steps accurately, this constitutes nonverbal feedback telling the manager that the initial message needs to be clarified.

If managers discover that their communication effectiveness is relatively low over an extended period of time, they should assess the situation to determine how to improve their communication skills. It may be that their vocabulary is confusing to the

destination. For example, a study conducted by Group Attitudes Corporation found that when managers used certain words repeatedly in communicating with steelworkers, the steelworkers usually became confused.[11] Among the words causing confusion were *accrue*, *contemplate*, *designate*, *detriment*, *magnitude*, and *subsequently*.

Achieving Communication Effectiveness.   In general, managers can sharpen their communication skills by adhering to the following "ten commandments of good communication" as closely as possible:[12]

1. *Seek to clarify your ideas before communicating.*   The more systematically you analyze the problem or idea to be communicated, the clearer it becomes. This is the first step toward effective communication. Many communications fail because of inadequate planning. Good planning must consider the goals and attitudes of those who will receive the communication and those who will be affected by it.

2. *Examine the true purpose of each communication.*   Before you communicate, ask yourself what you really want to accomplish with your message—obtain information, initiate action, change another person's attitude? Identify your most important goal and then adapt your language, tone, and total approach to serve that specific objective. Don't try to accomplish too much with each communication. The sharper the focus of your message, the greater its chances of success.

3. *Consider the total physical and human setting whenever you communicate.*   Meaning and intent are conveyed by more than words alone. Many other factors influence the overall impact of a communication, and managers must be sensitive to the total setting in which they communicate. Consider, for example, your sense of timing—that is, the circumstances under which you make an announcement or render a decision; the physical setting—whether you communicate in private or otherwise, for example; the social climate that pervades work relationships within your company or department and sets the tone of its communications; custom and practice—the degree to which your communication conforms to, or departs from, the expectations of your audience. Be constantly aware of the total setting in which you communicate. Like all living things, communication must be capable of adapting to its environment.

4. *Consult with others, when appropriate, in planning communications.*   Frequently, it is desirable or necessary to seek the participation of others in planning a communication or in developing the facts on which to base the communication. Such consultation often lends additional insight and objectivity to your message. Moreover, those who have helped you plan your communication will give it their active support.

5. *Be mindful while you communicate of the overtones rather than merely the basic content of your message.*   Your tone of voice, your expression, your apparent receptiveness to the responses of others—all have a significant effect on those you wish to reach. Frequently overlooked, these subtleties of communication often affect a listener's reaction to a message even more than its basic content. Similarly, your choice of language—particularly your awareness of the fine shades of meaning and emotion in the words you use—predetermines in large part the reactions of your listeners.

6. *Take the opportunity, when it arises, to convey something of help or value to the receiver.*   Consideration of the other person's interests and needs—trying to look at things from the other person's point of view—frequently points up opportunities to convey something of immediate benefit or long-range value to the other person. Subordinates are most responsive to managers whose messages take the subordinates' interests into account.

7. *Follow up your communication.*   Your best efforts at communication may be wasted, and you may never know whether you have succeeded in expressing

your true meaning and intent, if you do not follow up to see how well you have put your message across. You can do this by asking questions, by encouraging the receiver to express his or her reactions, by follow-up contacts, and by subsequent review of performance. Make certain that you get feedback for every important communication so that complete understanding and appropriate action result.

8. *Communicate for tomorrow as well as today.*   Even though communications may be aimed primarily at meeting the demands of an immediate situation, they must be planned with the past in mind if they are to be viewed as consistent by the receiver. Most important, however, communications must be consistent with long-range interests and goals. For example, it is not easy to communicate frankly on such matters as poor performance or the shortcomings of a loyal subordinate, but postponing disagreeable communications makes these matters more difficult in the long run and is actually unfair to your subordinates and your company.

9. *Be sure your actions support your communications.*   In the final analysis, the most persuasive kind of communication is not what you say, but what you do. When your actions or attitudes contradict your words, others tend to discount what you have said. For every manager, this means that good supervisory practices—such as clear assignment of responsibility and authority, fair rewards for effort, and sound policy enforcement—communicate more than all the gifts of oratory.

10. *Last, but by no means least: Seek not only to be understood but also to understand—be a good listener.*   When you start talking, you often cease to listen, at least in that larger sense of being attuned to the other person's unspoken reactions and attitudes. Even more serious is the occasional inattentiveness you may be guilty of when others are attempting to communicate with you. Listening is one of the most important, most difficult, and most neglected skills in communication. It demands that you concentrate, not only on the explicit meanings another person is expressing, but also on the implicit meanings, unspoken words, and undertones that may be far more significant.

Verbal and Nonverbal Interpersonal Communication

Interpersonal communication is generally divided into two types: verbal and nonverbal. Up to this point, the chapter has emphasized **verbal communication**—communication that uses either spoken or written words to share information with others.

Nonverbal communication is the sharing of information without using words to encode thoughts. Factors commonly used to encode thoughts in nonverbal communication are gestures, vocal tones, and facial expressions.[13] In most interpersonal communication, verbal and nonverbal communications are not mutually exclusive. Instead, the destination's interpretation of a message is generally based both on the words contained in the message and on such nonverbal factors as the source's gestures and facial expressions.

Verbal communication is the sharing of information through words, either written or spoken.

Nonverbal communication is the sharing of information without using words.

The Importance of Nonverbal Communication.   In an interpersonal communication situation in which both verbal and nonverbal factors are present, nonverbal factors may have more influence on the total effect of the message. Over two decades ago, Albert Mehrabian developed the following formula to show the relative contributions of verbal and nonverbal factors to the total effect of a message: Total message impact = .07 words + .38 vocal tones + .55 facial expressions. Other nonverbal factors besides vocal tones that can influence the effect of a verbal message are facial expressions, gestures, gender, and dress. Managers who are aware of this great potential influence of nonverbal factors on the effect of their communications will use nonverbal message ingredients to complement their verbal message ingredients whenever possible.[14]

Nonverbal messages can also be used to add content to verbal messages. For instance, a head might be nodded or a voice toned to show either agreement or disagreement.

Managers must be especially careful when they are communicating that verbal and nonverbal factors do not present contradictory messages. For example, if the words of a message express approval while the nonverbal factors express disapproval, the result will be message ambiguity that leaves the destination frustrated.

Managers who are able to communicate successfully through a blend of verbal and nonverbal communication are critical to the success of virtually every organization. In fact, a recent survey of corporate recruiters across the United States commissioned by the Darden Graduate School of Business at the University of Virginia revealed that the skill organizations most seek in prospective employees is facility at verbal and nonverbal communication.

BACK TO THE CASE Employees' reactions to Dyer's messages can provide him with perhaps his most useful tool for honing his communication skills—feedback. He must be alert to both verbal and nonverbal feedback. When feedback seems inappropriate, Dyer should transmit another message to clarify the meaning of his first one. Over time, if feedback indicates that he is a relatively unsuccessful communicator, he should analyze his situation carefully to improve his communication effectiveness. He might find, for instance, that he is using a vocabulary that is generally inappropriate for certain employees or that he is not following one or more of the ten commandments of good communication.

In addition, Dyer must remember that he communicates to others without using words. His facial expressions, gestures, even the tone of his voice, say things to his employees. In most communication situations, in fact, Dyer is sending both verbal and nonverbal messages to Eaton employees. Because a message's impact is often most dependent on its nonverbal components, Dyer must make certain that his nonverbal messages complement his verbal messages.

Interpersonal Communication in Organizations

To be effective communicators, managers must understand not only general interpersonal communication concepts but also the characteristics of interpersonal communication within organizations, or **organizational communication.** Organizational communication directly relates to the goals, functions, and structure of human organizations.[15] To a major extent, organizational success is determined by the effectiveness of organizational communication.

Although organizational communication was frequently referred to by early management writers, the topic did not receive systematic study and attention until after World War II. From World War II to the 1950s, the discipline of organizational communication made significant advances in such areas as mathematical communication theory and behavioral communication theory, and the emphasis on organizational communication has grown stronger in colleges of business throughout the nation since the 1970s.[16] The following sections focus on three fundamental organizational communication topics:

1. Formal organizational communication.
2. Informal organizational communication.
3. The encouragement of formal organizational communication.

Formal Organizational Communication
In general, organizational communication that follows the lines of the organization chart is called **formal organizational communication.**[17] As discussed in Chapter 10, the organization chart depicts

Organizational communication is interpersonal communication within organizations.

Formal organizational communication is organizational communication that follows the lines of the organization chart.

The idea of designing office space around cubicles gained popularity in the 1960s as a means of promoting interpersonal communication. Proponents of cubicles argue that the absence of physical barriers enhances communication and encourages an "egalitarian" atmosphere in the workplace (and reduces construction costs). Critics point to the placement of chairs in cubicle doorways and conversations carried out in hushed voices—the reaction of employees who feel that they need their privacy in order to function.

relationships of people and jobs and shows the formal channels of communication among them.

Types of Formal Organizational Communication.   There are three basic types of formal organizational communication:

1. Downward
2. Upward
3. Lateral

Downward organizational communication is communication that flows from any point on an organization chart downward to another point on the organization chart.

Downward organizational communication is communication that flows from any point on an organization chart downward to another point on the organization chart. This type of formal organizational communication relates primarily to the direction and control of employees. Job-related information that focuses on what activities are required, when they should be performed, and how they should be coordinated with other activities within the organization must be transmitted to employees. This downward communication typically includes a statement of organizational philosophy, management system objectives, position descriptions, and other written information relating to the importance, rationale, and interrelationships of various departments.

Upward organizational communication is communication that flows from any point on an organization chart upward to another point on the organization chart.

Upward organizational communication is communication that flows from any point on an organization chart upward to another point on the organization chart.[18] This type of organizational communication contains primarily the information managers need to evaluate the organizational area for which they are responsible and to determine if something is going wrong within it. Techniques that managers commonly use to encourage upward organizational communication are informal discussions with employees, attitude surveys, the development and use of grievance procedures, suggestion systems, and an "open door" policy that invites employees to come in whenever they would like to talk to management.[19] Organizational modifications based on the feedback provided by upward organizational communication enable a company to be more successful in the future.

Lateral organizational communication is communication that flows from any point on an organization chart horizontally to another point on the organization chart.

Lateral organizational communication is communication that flows from any point on an organization chart horizontally to another point on the organization chart. Communication that flows across the organization usually focuses on coordinating the activities of various departments and developing new plans for future operating periods. Within the organization, all departments are related to all other departments. Only through lateral communication can these departmental relationships be coordinated well enough to enhance the attainment of management system objectives.

The text states that the three basic types of formal communication within an organization are downward, upward, and lateral. The following CUTTING EDGE feature suggests that another type of communication is important to managers: communication with individuals outside the organization.

COMMUNICATING WITH CUSTOMERS AT INTEL

CUTTING EDGE

Andrew S. Grove, the chief executive officer of Intel Corporation, a company that designs, develops, and markets advanced microcomputer components, has long been one of the most admired managers in the business world. Recently, however, critics suggested that he made an enormous blunder after customers found that they had purchased a flawed computer component, the Pentium chip, from Intel. Instead of initiating a program of immediate replacement of the flawed chips with no questions asked, Grove allowed customer dissatisfaction to mount and the company to reap a great deal of bad publicity before he acted.

According to the critics, Grove is so thoroughly focused on enhancing the capability of Intel computer chips that he has trouble seeing much else. They also charge that Intel's lack of response to customer complaints about the Pentium chip betrayed a cavalier arrogance born of Intel's market leadership. Grove himself was characterized as highly insensitive to customers. Many people believe that he will have to reconsider his stubbornly analytical style in dealing with such problems.

Stung by these criticisms, Grove blamed the company's failure to detect the Pentium chip problem on Intel's remoteness from its customers. He now supports maintaining a regular communication system between Intel and its customers to avoid similar disasters in the future.≈

Patterns of Formal Organizational Communication.   By its very nature, organizational communication creates patterns of communication among organization members. These patterns evolve from the repeated occurrence of various serial transmissions of information. According to Haney, a **serial transmission** involves passing information from one individual to another in a series. It occurs under the following circumstances:

> A communicates a message to B; B then communicates A's message (or rather his or her interpretation of A's message) to C; C then communicates his or her interpretation of B's interpretation of A's message to D; and so on. The originator and the ultimate recipient of the message are separated by middle people.[20]

One obvious weakness of a serial transmission, of course, is that messages tend to become distorted as the length of the series increases. Research has shown that message details may be omitted, altered, or added in a serial transmission.

The potential inaccuracy of transmitted messages is not the only weakness of serial transmissions. A classic article by Alex Bavelas and Dermot Barrett[21] makes the case that serial transmissions can also influence morale, the emergence of a leader, the degree to which individuals involved in the transmissions are organized, and their efficiency. Three basic organizational communication patterns and their corresponding effects on the variables just mentioned are shown in Figure 14.5.

A **serial transmission** involves the passing of information from one individual to another in a series.

ENHANCED FORMAL COMMUNICATION CONTRIBUTES TO IMPROVING QUALITY AT HOLIDAY INN

QUALITY SPOTLIGHT

Improving the flow of communication dictated by the organization chart can be of immense benefit to an organization. Holiday Inn discovered that improving the flow of such communication enhanced the quality of customer service throughout the organization.

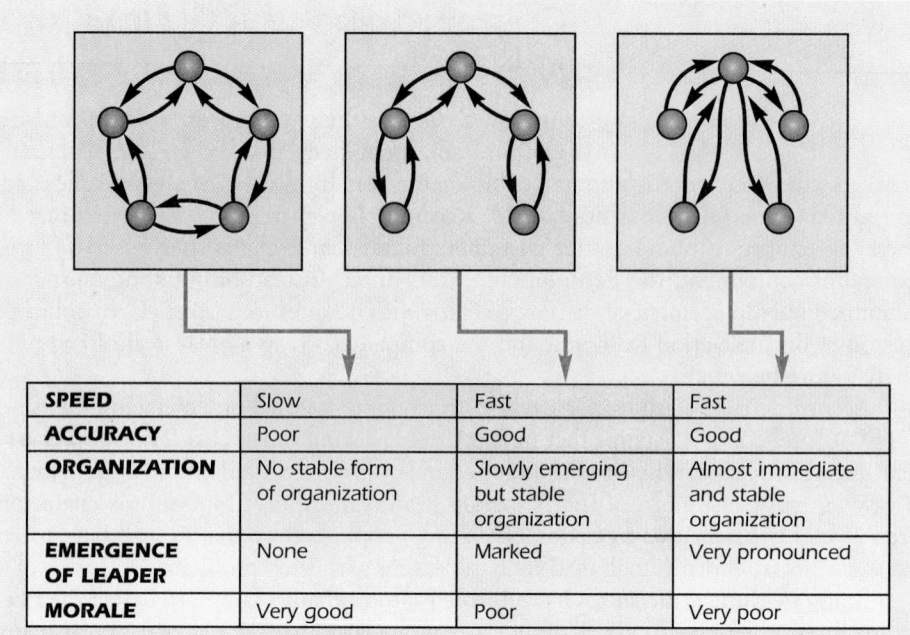

SPEED	Slow	Fast	Fast
ACCURACY	Poor	Good	Good
ORGANIZATION	No stable form of organization	Slowly emerging but stable organization	Almost immediate and stable organization
EMERGENCE OF LEADER	None	Marked	Very pronounced
MORALE	Very good	Poor	Very poor

Figure 14.5   Comparison of three patterns of organizational communication on the variables of speed, accuracy, organization, emergence of leader, and morale

Marketing and product quality were the themes at a recent Holiday Inn Worldwide Franchise Conference. Individual Holiday Inn operators expressed more confidence in the company after it announced it had a new plan to improve customer service as well as customer attitudes toward Holiday Inn by improving Holiday Inn's formal communication system. The company stated it would extend its satellite communication system into Europe to allow for more efficient communication of hotel room rate information between North American and European operations.

Mike Leven, president of the Holiday Inn franchise division, said that franchisees have always depended on Holiday Inn's commitment to maintaining quality service. Company chairman Bryan Langton believes that this focus on quality has helped Holiday Inn outperform the industry in occupancy rates in recent years.≈

BACK TO THE CASE   As a plant manager at Eaton, Robert Dyer must strive to understand the intricacies of organizational communication—that is, interpersonal communication as it takes place within the organization—since this is such an important factor in determining the company's level of success. Dyer can communicate with his people in two basic ways: formally and informally.

In general, Dyer's formal communication should follow the lines on the organization chart. He can communicate downward to, for example, a department head; or he can communicate upward to, for example, George Dettloff, Eaton's engine components division general manager and Dyer's boss, as mentioned in the introductory case. Dyer's downward communication will commonly focus on the activities his subordinates are performing. His upward communication will usually concentrate on how the company is performing. Dyer can get advice on problems and improve coordination by communicating laterally with other plant managers, like the manager of Eaton's Lincoln, Nebraska, plant. He should take steps to ensure that lateral communication also occurs at other organizational levels to enhance planning and coordination within his plant.

Informal organizational communication is organizational communication that does not follow the lines of the organization chart.

Informal Organizational Communication

Informal organizational communication is organizational communication that does not follow the lines of the organization chart.[22] Instead, this type of communication typically follows the pattern of

personal relationships among organization members: One friend communicates with another friend, regardless of their relative positions on the organization chart. Informal organizational communication networks generally exist because organization members have a desire for information that is not furnished through formal organizational communication.

Patterns of Informal Organizational Communication.   The informal organizational communication network, or **grapevine,** has three main characteristics:

1. It springs up and is used irregularly within the organization.
2. It is not controlled by top executives, who may not even be able to influence it.
3. It exists largely to serve the self-interests of the people within it.

Understanding the grapevine is a prerequisite for a complete understanding of organizational communication. It has been estimated that 70 percent of all communication in organizations flows along the organizational grapevine. Not only do grapevines carry great amounts of communication, but they carry it at very rapid speeds. Employees commonly cite the company grapevine as the most reliable and credible source of information about company events.[23]

Like formal organizational communication, informal organizational communication uses serial transmissions. The difference is that it is more difficult for managers to identify organization members involved in these transmissions than members of the formal communication network. A classic article by Keith Davis that appeared in the *Harvard Business Review* has been a significant help to managers in understanding how organizational grapevines spring up and operate. Figure 14.6 sketches the four most common grapevine patterns as outlined by Davis. They are as follows:[24]

1. *The single-strand grapevine.*   *A* tells *B,* who tells *C,* who tells *D,* and so on. This type of grapevine tends to distort messages more than any other.
2. *The gossip grapevine.*   *A* informs everyone else on the grapevine.
3. *The probability grapevine.*   *A* communicates randomly—for example, to *F* and *D.* *F* and *D* then continue to inform other grapevine members in the same way.
4. *The cluster grapevine.*   *A* selects and tells *C, D,* and *F. F* selects and tells *I* and *B,* and *B* selects and tells *J.* Information in this grapevine travels only to selected individuals.

Dealing with Grapevines.   Clearly, grapevines are a factor managers must deal with because they can, and often do, generate rumors that are detrimental to organi-

The **grapevine** is the network of informal organizational communication.

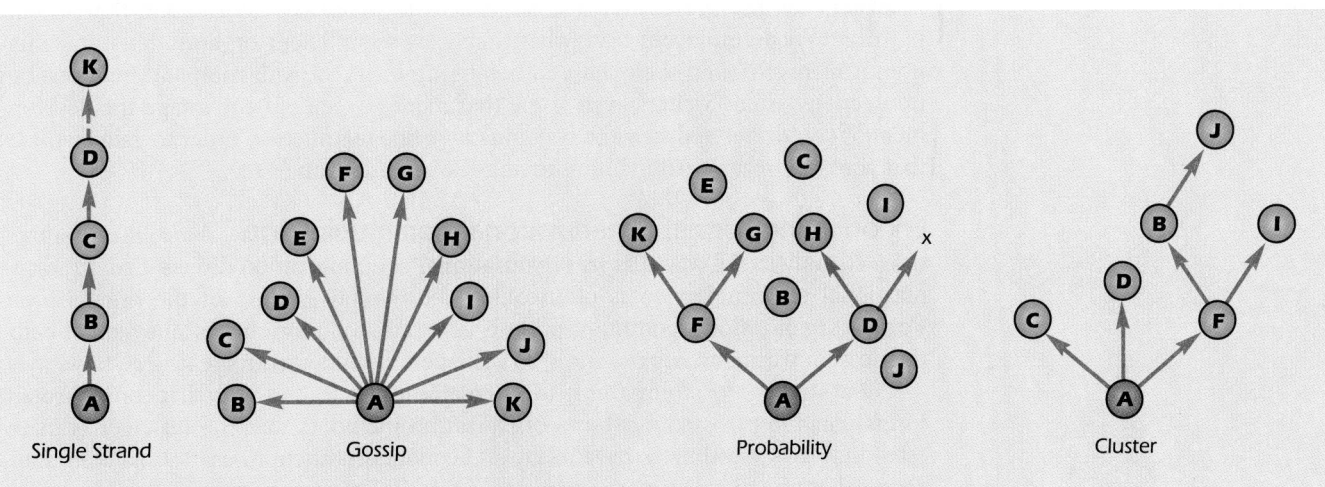

Single Strand   **Gossip**   **Probability**   **Cluster**

Figure 14.6   Four types of organizational grapevines

Table 14.2

Ten Commandments for Good Listening

1. *Stop talking!*
   You cannot listen if you are talking.
   Polonius (*Hamlet*): "Give every man thine ear, but few thy voice."
2. *Put the talker at ease.*
   Help the talker feel free to talk.
   This is often called establishing a permissive environment.
3. *Show the talker that you want to listen.*
   Look and act interested. Do not read your mail while he or she talks.
   Listen to understand rather than to oppose.
4. *Remove distractions.*
   Don't doodle, tap, or shuffle papers.
   Will it be quieter if you shut the door?
5. *Empathize with the talker.*
   Try to put yourself in the talker's place so that you can see his or her point of view.
6. *Be patient.*
   Allow plenty of time. Do not interrupt the talker.
   Don't start for the door or walk away.
7. *Hold your temper.*
   An angry person gets the wrong meaning from words.
8. *Go easy on argument and criticism.*
   This puts the talker on the defensive. He or she may "clam up" or get angry.
   Do not argue: even if you win, you *lose.*
9. *Ask questions.*
   This encourages the talker and shows you are listening.
   It helps to develop points further.
10. *Stop talking!*
    This is the first and last commandment, because all other commandments depend on it.
    You just can't do a good listening job while you are talking.
    Nature gave us two ears but only one tongue,
    which is a gentle hint that we should listen more than we talk

zational success. Exactly how individual managers should deal with the grapevine, of course, depends on the specific organizational situation in which they find themselves. Managers can use grapevines advantageously, to maximize information flow to employees. When employees have what they view as sufficient organizational information, it seems to build their sense of belonging to the organization and their level of productivity. Some writers even argue that managers should encourage the development of grapevines and strive to become grapevine members in order to gain feedback that could be very valuable in improving the organization.[25]

Encouraging Formal Organizational Communication

Since the organization acts only in the way that its organizational communication directs it to act, organizational communication is often called the nervous system of the organization. Formal organizational communication is generally the more important type of communication within an organization, so managers should encourage its free flow.

One strategy for doing this is to listen attentively to messages that come through formal channels. Listening shows organization members that the manager is interested in what subordinates have to say and encourages them to use formal communication channels in subsequent situations. Table 14.2 presents some general guidelines for listening well.

At Walt Disney World Resort, one means of bolstering formal communication is substituting camaraderie and enthusiasm for an overabundance of procedures and policies. Newcomers are exposed immediately to the company culture, and although there are fairly strict rules about dress, hairstyle, and makeup, managers encourage imagination and independence when it comes to dealing directly with guests .

Some other strategies to encourage the flow of formal organizational communication are as follows:

- Support the flow of clear and concise statements through formal communication channels. Receiving an ambiguous message through a formal organizational communication channel can discourage employees from using that channel again.
- Take care to ensure that all organization members have free access to formal communication channels. Obviously, organization members cannot communicate formally within the organization if they don't have access to the formal communication network.
- Assign specific communication responsibilities to staff personnel who could be of enormous help to line personnel in spreading important information throughout the organization.

BACK TO THE CASE

It is virtually certain that there is an extensive grapevine in Dyer's plant—there is one in nearly every organization. Although Dyer must deal with this grapevine, he may not be able to influence it significantly. Eaton employees at his plant, like employees everywhere else, will latch onto a grapevine out of self-interest or because the formal organization has not furnished them with the information they believe they need.

By developing certain social relationships, Dyer could conceivably become part of the grapevine and obtain valuable feedback from it. Also, because grapevines generate rumors that could have a detrimental effect on the success of Dyer's plant, he should make sure that all personnel at his plant receive all the information they need to do their jobs well through formal organizational communication channels, thereby reducing their reliance on the grapevine.

Because formal organizational communication is vitally important to Dyer's plant, he should strive to encourage it by listening intently to messages that come to him over formal channels, supporting the flow of clear messages through formal channels, and making sure that all employees at his plant have access to formal communication channels.

Reread the learning objectives below. Each objective is followed by questions. Answering these questions accurately will help you retain the most important concepts discussed in this chapter. After answering each question, check your answer against the answer key at the end of this chapter. (*Hint:* If you have any doubts regarding the correct response, consult the page whose number follows the answer.)

Circle: From studying this chapter, I will attempt to acquire:

1. An understanding of influencing.

T,F **a.** The influencing function can be viewed as forcing the activities of organization members in appropriate directions.

a,b,c,d,e **b.** The following activity is *not* a major component of the influencing process: (a) motivating; (b) leading; (c) communicating; (d) correcting; (e) considering groups.

2. An understanding of interpersonal communication.

a,b,c,d,e **a.** Communication is best described as the process of: (a) sharing emotion; (b) sharing information; (c) sending messages; (d) feedback formulation; (e) forwarding information.

a,b,c,d,e **b.** The basic elements of interpersonal communication are: (a) source/encoder, signal, decoder/destination; (b) sender/message, encoder, receiver/decoder; (c) signal, source/sender, decoder/destination; (d) signal, source/decoder, encoder/destination; (e) source/sender, signal, receiver/destination.

3. A knowledge of how to use feedback.

T,F **a.** Feedback is solely verbal.

a,b,c,d,e **b.** Robert S. Goyer suggested using feedback: (a) as a microbarrier; (b) as a way for sources to evaluate their communication effectiveness; (c) to ensure that instructions will be carried out; (d) to evaluate the decoder; (e) all of the above.

4. An appreciation for the importance of nonverbal communication.

T,F **a.** In interpersonal communication, nonverbal factors often play a more influential role than verbal factors.

T,F **b.** Nonverbal messages can contradict verbal messages, creating frustration in the destination.

5. Insights on formal organizational communication.

a,b,c,d,e **a.** The following is *not* upward communication: (a) cost accounting reports; (b) purchase order summary; (c) production reports; (d) corporate policy statement; (e) sales reports.

a,b,c,d,e **b.** The primary purpose served by lateral organizational communication is: (a) coordinating; (b) organizing; (c) direction; (d) evaluation; (e) control.

6. An appreciation for the importance of the grapevine.

a,b,c,d,e **a.** The following statement concerning the grapevine is *not* correct: (a) grapevines are irregularly used in organizations; (b) a grapevine can and often does generate harmful rumors; (c) the grapevine is used largely to serve the self-interests of the people within it; (d) some managers use grapevines to their advantage; (e) in time, and with proper pressure, the grapevine can be eliminated.

T,F **b.** The grapevine is much slower than formal communication channels.

7. Some hints on how to encourage organizational communication.

a,b,c,d,e **a.** To encourage formal organizational communication, managers should: (a) support the flow of clear and concise statements through formal channels; (b) ensure free access to formal channels for all organization members; (c) assign specific communication responsibilities to staff personnel; (d) a and b; (e) all of the above.

T,F **b.** Since formal organizational communication is the most important type of communication within an organization, managers must restrict its flow if the organization is to be successful.

Introductory Case Wrap-Up

"Eaton Managers Concentrate on Influencing People" (p. 325) and its related back-to-the-case sections were written to help you better understand the management concepts contained in this chapter. Answer the following discussion questions about this introductory case to enrich your understanding of the chapter content:

1. List three problems that could be caused at Eaton's Kearney plant if Robert Dyer were a poor communicator.

2. Explain *how* the problems you listed in number 1 could be caused by Dyer's inability to communicate.

3. Assuming that Dyer is a good communicator, discuss three ways that he is having a positive impact on Eaton's Kearney plant as a result of his communication expertise.

Issues for Review and Discussion

1. What is influencing?
2. Describe the relationship between the overall management system and the influencing subsystem.
3. What factors make up the input, process, and output of the influencing subsystem?
4. Explain the relationship between the factors that compose the process section of the influencing subsystem.
5. What is communication?
6. How important is communication to managers?
7. Draw the communication model presented in this chapter and explain how it works.
8. How does successful communication differ from unsuccessful communication?
9. Summarize the significance of field of experience to communication.
10. List and describe three communication macrobarriers and three communication microbarriers.
11. What is feedback, and how should managers use it when communicating?

12. How is the communication effectiveness index calculated, and what is its significance?
13. Name the ten commandments of good communication.
14. What is nonverbal communication? Explain its significance.
15. How should managers use nonverbal communication?
16. What is organizational communication?
17. How do formal and informal organizational communication differ?
18. Describe three types of formal organizational communication, and explain the general purpose of each type.
19. Can serial transmissions and other formal communication patterns influence communication effectiveness and the individuals using the patterns? If so, how?
20. Draw and describe the four main types of grapevines that exist in organizations.
21. How can managers encourage the flow of formal organizational communication?

Action Summary Answer Key

1. a. F, p. 326
   b. d, pp. 326–328
2. a. b, pp. 329–330
   b. a, pp. 329–331

3. a. F, p. 334
   b. b, p. 334
4. a. T, p. 336
   b. T, pp. 336–337

5. a. d, p. 338
   b. a, p. 338
6. a. e, pp. 341–342
   b. F, p. 341

7. a. e, p. 342
   b. F, p. 343

Case Study

Communication Services at Chick-fil-A Restaurants

Chick-fil-A, the Atlanta-based chicken restaurant chain, went through some major growing pains in the past 13 years as it changed from an operation predominately located in shopping malls to one that expanded into at least eight different restaurant concepts. Along the way, this close-knit family-owned company doubled its number of locations to over 600.

For the past 30 years, Truett Cathy, the charismatic founder, has held the company together. Corporate communication for most of the company's history was through traditional methods—personal contact, telephone calls, and written memos. Cathy went to considerable effort to ensure that he communicated successfully with his operators, whether through personal appearances at operator get-togethers or through routine visits at company locations.

Chick-fil-A restaurants are not franchises. Owner/operators, who are considered employees by the company, split restaurant profits with corporate headquarters. They are rewarded financially for profitable performance and have the opportunity to add units or move into more profitable markets. This entrepreneurial arrangement serves to motivate direct communication between owner/operators and corporate headquarters.

As the corporation grew, field management consultants became part of the organizational structure. These consultants helped resolve problems and assisted owner/operators in running profitable restaurants according to corporate guidelines. Whenever owner/operators needed assistance, they would simply leave messages at Atlanta corporate headquarters for the field consultants. As operations exploded, however, responses were delayed or even lost because of consultants' heavy travel schedules.

According to Mark Ashworth, Chick-fil-A's manager of communication services, the need for better communication was initially a result of the rapid increase in the number of restaurant units that the corporation owned. Personal contact by headquarters, except at regional workshops and annual meetings, became almost logistically prohibitive. Thus the field consultants' role in effective corporate communication became more imperative. Later, the introduction of new food items and expansion into new markets heightened the need for fresh ideas in communicating quality guidelines.

Chick-fil-A headquarters consequently began expanding its communication procedures to include different kinds of media; soon newsletters, audiotapes, and videotapes were spreading the corporate message. At first, corporate communications were highly decentral-

ized. Not only were employees getting different messages from different people, but messages sometimes lacked relevance and timeliness or were duplicated or poorly implemented. In short, few communications were used to the fullest potential. In addition, production quality was inconsistent, and managers often chose the wrong communication tools to reach intended audiences.

Under Mark Ashworth's direction, corporate communications have not yet become totally centralized, but department managers at Chick-fil-A headquarters have begun to deliver their messages more effectively. Because the communication needs of the owner/operators are sometimes different from those of front-line employees, managers are encouraged to choose from an arsenal of communication programs. Being able to pick the right medium for their message has not only helped people at Chick-fil-A headquarters become better communicators, but has also saved the company money. Managers who once requested only expensive videos are now using other media, such as newsletters or audiotapes, to communicate.

According to Ashworth, even after they switched to more effective media, corporate managers were still doing a lot of one-way communicating with owner/operators. To rectify this situation, voice mail and E-mail were recently added to Chick-fil-A's arsenal of communication tools. Now, says Ashworth, owner/operators are trained to use personal computers to expedite the flow of two-way communications. Field consultants, who are still the front-line communicators, receive messages in a more timely manner as owner/operators communicate with absent colleagues or leave E-mail messages for people at corporate headquarters. Important voice and electronic mail messages are now broadcast immediately, without any of the delays associated with traditional communications methods. The Internet is the next communication tool to be exploited by Ashworth and his colleagues.

Questions:

1. How has communication changed over the corporate life of Chick-fil-A? What precipitated the changes?
2. Define successful communication. Why is the choice of medium so important to successful communication?
3. According to Ashworth, communication at Chick-fil-A is still one-way in many circumstances. Do you consider this a problem? Explain. How is the company attempting to encourage two-way communication and make it more effective. What other ways would you suggest?

Skills Exercise

Based on the information given in the case, diagram the formal communication system at Chick-fil-A. Include the people who must communicate, the reasons for communication at each level, and the types of communica-tion tools available. Does your diagram illustrate a successful system? Where might problems exist? Why? What might be done to solve these problems?

 The Internet learning materials that accompany this chapter can be found at
http://www.profcerto.com
Additional information can be found on the inside front and back covers of this text.

LEADERSHIP

STUDENT LEARNING OBJECTIVES

From studying this chapter, I will attempt to acquire:

1. A working definition of leadership.
2. An understanding of the relationship between leading and managing.
3. An appreciation for the trait and situational approaches to leadership.
4. Insights about using leadership theories that emphasize decision-making situations.
5. Insights about using leadership theories that emphasize more general organizational situations.
6. An understanding of alternatives to leader flexibility.
7. An appreciation of emerging leader styles and leadership issues of today.

Eisner's Leadership Challenge at Disney's New Wild Animal Kingdom

Michael Eisner, chairman of Walt Disney Company, recently announced that he will be building a whole new theme park at Walt Disney World in Orlando, Florida. The new park, called Wild Animal Kingdom, is scheduled to open in 1998.

Visitors entering Disney's Wild Animal Kingdom will find themselves in an exotic garden enveloped by wildlife, waterfalls, and lush greenery.

Crossing the Safari River on a wooden bridge, they'll come upon the hub of the park—a village of shops, artisans, eateries, and street entertainers.

Looming over Safari Village is the park's 14-story Tree of Life. As they move closer to the faux tree, they'll see that the 50-foot-wide fiberglass and plaster trunk and its branches actually are hand-carved animal forms. Around the Tree of Life will be exhibits of small animals. Inside, characters from *The Lion King* will star in a show.

Wild Animal Kingdom is divided into three major sections representing mythological, real, and extinct animals. The fantasy animal area is dedicated to dragons, griffins, unicorns, and other such creatures from fables, fairy tales, and mythology.

Extinction is the theme of Dinoland. There will be a thrill ride that races tourists back through time in an attempt to save animals from extinction. The children's play area is designed to have the feel of an archaeological dig. Disney will use audio-animatronic technology to bring massive dinosaurs to life. Dinoland will also be home to some real reptiles.

The Africa area alone is the size of most typical theme parks. Visitors will ride Jeep-like vehicles for a safari during rainy season, so the roads are always washed out. The vehicles will take guests through a savannah, where they will chase poachers and encounter monkeys, lions, zebras, elephants, gorillas, rhinos, hippos, and crocodiles. There also is a nature trail so people can go on a walk-through expedition.

Many different groups are very excited about Eisner's plans for Disney's Wild Animal Kingdom. Stockholders are excited about the potential financial returns, employees about career opportunities at the theme park, and tourists about the prospect of visiting this exotic new Disney creation. Successfully establishing the new park may well be the most formidable leadership challenge of Michael Eisner's career.

The opening of a whole new theme park at Walt Disney World presents a host of leadership challenges to CEO Michael Eisner, who must satisfy the needs and demands of groups that include stockholders, employees, and customers.

| what's ahead |

Michael Eisner, chairman of the Walt Disney Company, is about to embark on a very ambitious project: building Wild Animal Kingdom, a new Disney theme park. The case ends by noting that this project will be a significant leadership challenge for Eisner. The information in this chapter is designed to be helpful to managers like Michael Eisner who are facing a leadership challenge. The chapter discusses the following topics:

1. How to define leadership.
2. The difference between a leader and a manager.
3. The trait approach to leadership.
4. The situational approach to leadership.
5. Leadership today.
6. Current topics in leadership.

DEFINING *LEADERSHIP*

Leadership is the process of directing the behavior of others toward the accomplishment of objectives.

Leadership is the process of directing the behavior of others toward the accomplishment of some objective. Directing, in this sense, means causing individuals to act in a certain way or to follow a particular course. Ideally, this course is perfectly consistent with such factors as established organizational policies, procedures, and job descriptions. The central theme of leadership is getting things accomplished through people.

As indicated in Chapter 14, leadership is one of the four main interdependent activities of the influencing subsystem and is accomplished, at least to some extent, by communicating with others. It is extremely important that managers have a thorough understanding of what leadership entails. Leadership has always been considered a prerequisite for organizational success. Today, given the increased capability afforded by enhanced communication technology and the rise of international business, leadership is more important than ever before.[1]

Leader versus Manager

Leading is not the same as managing. Many executives fail to grasp the difference between the two and therefore labor under a misapprehension about how to carry out their organizational duties. Although some managers are leaders and some leaders are managers, leading and managing are not identical activities.[2] According to Theodore Levitt, management consists of

> the rational assessment of a situation and the systematic selection of goals and purposes (what is to be done); the systematic development of strategies to achieve these goals; the marshalling of the required resources; the rational design, organization, direction, and control of the activities required to attain the selected purposes; and, finally, the motivating and rewarding of people to do the work.[3]

Leadership, as one of the four primary activities of the influencing function, is a subset of management. Managing is much broader in scope than leading and focuses on nonbehavioral as well as behavioral issues. Leading emphasizes mainly behavioral issues. Figure 15.1 makes the point that although not all managers are leaders, the most effective managers over the long term are leaders.

Merely possessing management skills is no longer sufficient for success as an executive in the business world. Modern executives need to understand the difference between managing and leading and know how to combine the two roles to achieve organizational success. A manager makes sure that a job gets done, and a leader cares about and focuses on the people who do the job. To combine management and leadership, therefore, requires demonstrating a calculated and logical focus on organizational processes (management) along with a genuine concern for workers as people (leadership).[4]

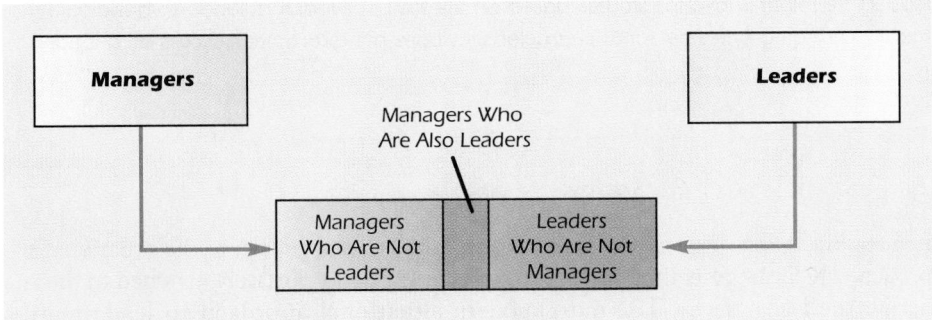

Figure 15.1   **The most effective managers over the long term are also leaders**

THE TRAIT APPROACH TO LEADERSHIP

The **trait approach to leadership** is based on early leadership research that seemed to assume that a good leader is born, not made. The mainstream of this research attempted to describe successful leaders as precisely as possible. The reasoning was that, if a complete profile of the traits of a successful leader could be drawn, it would be fairly easy to identify the individuals who should and should not be placed in leadership positions.

Many of the early studies that attempted to summarize the traits of successful leaders were documented. One of these summaries concludes that successful leaders tend to possess the following characteristics:[5]

1. Intelligence, including judgment and verbal ability.
2. Past achievement in scholarship and athletics.
3. Emotional maturity and stability.
4. Dependability, persistence, and a drive for continuing achievement.
5. The skill to participate socially and adapt to various groups.
6. A desire for status and socioeconomic position.

Evaluations of these trait studies, however, have concluded that their findings are inconsistent. One researcher says that 50 years of study have failed to produce one personality trait or set of qualities that can be used consistently to discriminate leaders from nonleaders.[6] It follows, then, that no trait or combination of traits guarantees that someone will be a successful leader. Leadership is apparently a much more complex issue.

Contemporary management writers and practitioners generally agree that leadership ability cannot be explained by an individual's traits or inherited characteristics. They believe, rather, that individuals can be trained to be good leaders. In other words, leaders are made, not born. That is why thousands of employees each year are sent through leadership training programs.[7]

The **trait approach to leadership** is an outdated view of leadership that sees the personal characteristics of an individual as the main determinants of how successful that individual could be as a leader.

BACK TO THE CASE   According to the material in the text, Michael Eisner, the Disney chairman discussed in the introductory case, should understand that his leadership activities relating to Wild Animal Kingdom involve directing the behavior of organization members so that the new theme park will be successfully established. Eisner should also realize that leading and managing are not the same thing. When managing, he is involved with planning, organizing, influencing, and controlling. When leading, he is performing an activity that is part of the influencing function of management. To maximize his long-term success, Eisner should strive to be both a manager and a leader.

In assessing his ability to lead the new Disney project, Eisner should not fall into the trap of trying to change his personal traits or attitudes to mirror those of successful

leaders he might know, for studies based on the trait approach to leadership indicate that merely changing one's personal characteristics does not guarantee success as a leader.

THE SITUATIONAL APPROACH TO LEADERSHIP: A FOCUS ON LEADER BEHAVIOR

The **situational approach to leadership** is a relatively modern view of leadership that suggests that successful leadership requires a unique combination of leaders, followers, and leadership situations.

Leadership studies have shifted emphasis from the trait approach to the situational approach, which suggests that leadership style must be appropriately matched to the situation the leader faces. The more modern **situational approach to leadership** is based on the assumption that each instance of leadership is different and therefore requires a unique combination of leaders, followers, and leadership situations.

This interaction is commonly expressed in formula form: $SL = f(L,F,S)$, where SL is *successful leadership*, f stands for *function of*, and L, F, and S are, respectively, the *leader*, the *follower*, and the *situation*.[8] Translated, this formula says that successful leadership is a function of a leader, follower, and situation that are appropriate for one another.

Leadership Situations and Decisions

The Tannenbaum and Schmidt Leadership Continuum   Since one of the most important tasks of a leader is making sound decisions, all practical and legitimate leadership thinking emphasizes decision making. Tannenbaum and Schmidt, who wrote one of the first and perhaps most often quoted articles on the situational approach to leadership, stress situations in which a leader makes decisions.[9] Figure 15.2 presents their model of leadership behavior.

This model is actually a continuum, or range, of leadership behavior available to managers when they are making decisions. Note that each type of decision-making behavior depicted in the figure has both a corresponding degree of authority used by the manager and a related amount of freedom available to subordinates. Management behavior at the extreme left of the model characterizes the leader who makes decisions by maintaining high control and allowing subordinates little freedom. Behavior at the extreme right characterizes the leader who makes decisions by exercising little control and allowing subordinates much freedom and self-direction. Behavior in between the extremes reflects graduations in leadership from autocratic to democratic.

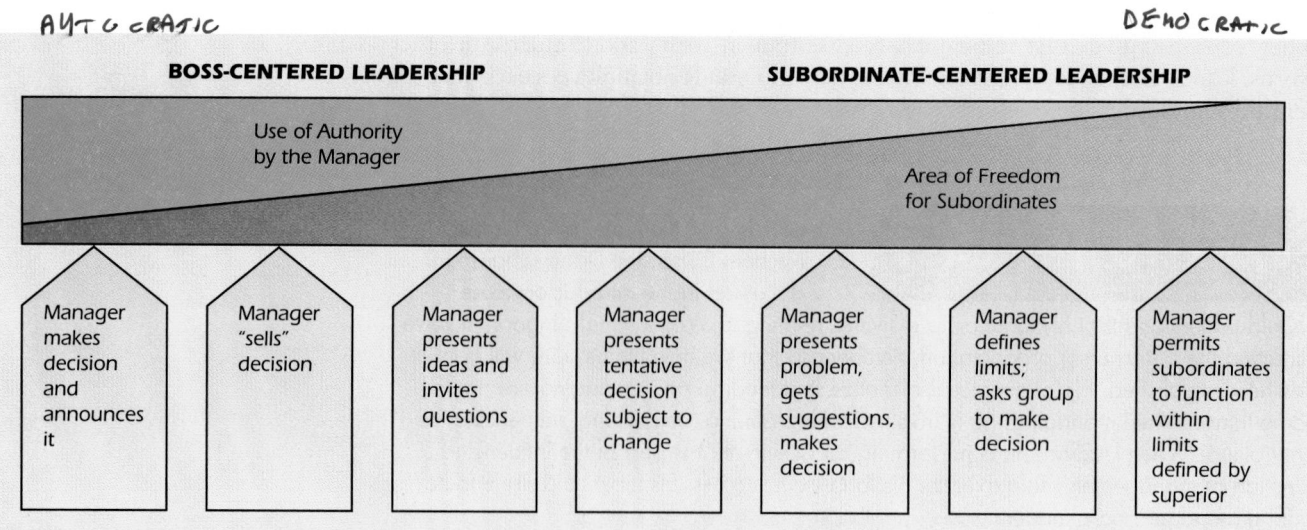

Figure 15.2   Continuum of leadership behavior that emphasizes decision making

Managers displaying leadership behavior toward the right of the model are more democratic, and are called *subordinate-centered* leaders. Those displaying leadership behavior toward the left of the model are more autocratic, and are called *boss-centered* leaders.

Each type of leadership behavior in this model is explained in more detail in the following list:

1. *The manager makes the decision and announces it.*   This behavior is characterized by the manager (a) identifying a problem, (b) analyzing various alternatives available to solve it, (c) choosing the alternative that will be used to solve it, and (d) requiring followers to implement the chosen alternative. The manager may or may not use coercion, but the followers have no opportunity to participate directly in the decision-making process.

2. *The manager "sells" the decision.*   As above, the manager identifies the problem and independently arrives at a decision. Rather than announce the decision to subordinates for implementation, however, the manager tries to persuade subordinates to accept the decision.

3. *The manager presents ideas and invites questions.*   Here, the manager makes the decision and attempts to gain acceptance through persuasion. One additional step is taken, however: Subordinates are invited to ask questions about the decision.

4. *The manager presents a tentative decision that is subject to change.*   The manager allows subordinates to have some part in the decision-making process but retains the responsibility for identifying and diagnosing the problem. The manager then arrives at a tentative decision that is subject to change on the basis of subordinate input. The final decision is made by the manager.

5. *The manager presents the problem, gets suggestions, and then makes the decision.*   This is the first leadership activity described thus far that allows subordinates the opportunity to offer problem solutions before the manager does. The manager, however, is still the one who identifies the problem.

6. *The manager defines the limits and asks the group to make a decision.*   In this type of leadership behavior, the manager first defines the problem and sets the boundaries within which a decision must be made. The manager then enters into partnership with subordinates to arrive at an appropriate decision. The danger here is that if the group of subordinates does not perceive that the manager genuinely desires a serious group decision-making effort, it will tend to arrive at conclusions that reflect what it thinks the manager wants rather than what the group itself actually wants and believes is feasible.

7. *The manager permits the group to make decisions within prescribed limits.*   Here, the manager becomes an equal member of a problem-solving group. The entire group identifies and assesses the problem, develops possible solutions, and chooses an alternative to be implemented. Everyone within the group understands that the group's decision will be implemented.

Determining How to Make Decisions as a Leader   The true value of the model developed by Tannenbaum and Schmidt lies in its use in making practical and desirable decisions. According to these authors, the three primary factors, or forces, that influence a manager's determination of which leadership behavior to use in making decisions are as follows:

1. *Forces in the Manager.* Managers should be aware of four forces within themselves that influence their determination of how to make decisions as a leader. The first force is the manager's values, such as the relative importance to the manager of organizational efficiency, personal growth, the growth of subordinates, and company profits. For example, a manager who values subordinate growth highly will probably want to give group members the valuable experi-

At Rubbermaid, a giant consumer-products company based in Wooster, Ohio, CEO Wolfgang Schmitt has watched as three division heads left the company in an 18-month period; two top executives in international operations, plus several lower-level managers, have also left. Critics attribute the departures to Schmitt's leadership style, which some observers call "autocratic." Rubbermaid, they contend, is losing division presidents and other managers who preferred the greater decision-making freedom granted by Schmitt's predecessor, Stanley C. Gault.

ence of making a decision, even though he or she could make the decision much more quickly and efficiently alone.

2. The second influencing force is level of confidence in subordinates. In general, the more confidence a manager has in his or her subordinates, the more likely that manager's decision-making style will be democratic, or subordinate-centered. The reverse is also true: The less confidence a manager has in subordinates, the more likely that manager's decision-making style will be autocratic, or boss-centered.

3. The third influencing force within the manager is personal leadership strengths. Some managers are more effective in issuing orders than in leading group discussions, and vice versa. Managers must be able to recognize their own leadership strengths and capitalize on them.

4. The fourth influencing force within the manager is tolerance for ambiguity. The move from a boss-centered style to a subordinate-centered style means some loss of certainty about how problems should be solved. A manager who is disturbed by this loss of certainty will find it extremely difficult to be successful as a subordinate-centered leader.

BACK TO THE CASE

The situational approach to leadership affords more insights than the trait approach on how Michael Eisner can successfully establish Wild Animal Kingdom. The situational approach suggests that successful leadership depends on an appropriate combination of three factors:

1. Michael Eisner as a leader.
2. Disney employees as followers.
3. The organizational situation(s) that Eisner faces.

One of the most important activities that a manager like Eisner performs as a leader is making decisions. He can use any number of styles, ranging from authoritarian to democratic, to make decisions. For example, he could unilaterally make a decision to forgo having real animals in the new theme park and install only mechanical animals—in which case he would be an autocratic leader. Or he could decide to generally define the type of theme park being created, discuss these plans with appropriate Disney personnel, and ask them to come up with and implement a mix of animals they think appropriate for Wild Animal Kingdom—in which case he would be a democratic leader. Of course, Eisner could take a less extreme stance—that is, his leadership behavior could fall in the middle of the continuum. He might, for example, tell appropriate Disney personnel what type of theme park is being planned, ask them to suggest what type of animal population should be installed in it, and then make the final decision on the basis of his own ideas and those of his staff.

2. *Forces in Subordinates.*   A manager also should be aware of forces within subordinates that influence the manager's determination of how to make decisions as a leader.[10] To lead successfully, the manager needs to keep in mind that subordinates are both somewhat different and somewhat alike and that any cookbook approach to leading all subordinates is therefore impossible. Generally speaking, however, managers can increase their leadership success by allowing subordinates more freedom in making decisions when:

- The subordinates have a relatively high need for independence. (People differ greatly in the amount of direction they desire.)
- They have a readiness to assume responsibility for decision making. (Some see additional responsibility as a tribute to their ability; others see it as someone above them "passing the buck.")
- They have a relatively high tolerance for ambiguity. (Some employees prefer to be given clear-cut directives; others crave a greater degree of freedom.)
- They are interested in the problem and believe it is important to solve it.
- They understand and identify with the organization's goals.
- They have the necessary knowledge and experience to deal with the problem.
- They have learned to expect to share in decision making. (People who have come to expect strong leadership and then are suddenly told to participate more fully in decision making are often upset by this new experience. Conversely, people who have enjoyed a considerable amount of freedom usually resent the boss who assumes full decision-making powers.)

If subordinates do not have these characteristics, the manager should probably assume a more autocratic, or boss-centered, approach to making decisions.

3. *Forces in the Situation.*   The last group of forces that influence a manager's determination of how to make decisions as a leader are forces in the leadership situation. The first such situational force is the type of organization in which the leader works. Organizational factors like the size of working groups and their geographical distribution are especially important influences on leadership style. Extremely large work groups or wide geographic separations of work groups, for example, could make a subordinate-centered leadership style impractical.

The second situational force is the effectiveness of a group. To gauge this force, managers should evaluate such issues as the experience of group members in working together and the degree of confidence they have in their ability to solve problems as a group. As a general rule, managers should assign decision-making responsibilities only to effective work groups.

The third situational force is the problem to be solved. Before deciding to act as a subordinate-centered leader, a manager should be sure that the group has the expertise necessary to make a decision about the problem in question. If it doesn't, the manager should move toward more boss-centered leadership.

The fourth situational force is the time available to make a decision. As a general guideline, the less time available, the more impractical it is to assign decision making to a group because a group typically takes more time than an individual to reach a decision.

As the situational approach to leadership implies, managers will be successful decision makers only if the method they use to make decisions appropriately reflects the leader, the followers, and the situation.

Determining How to Make Decisions as a Leader: An Update   Tannenbaum and Schmidt's 1957 article on leadership decision making was so widely accepted that the two authors were invited by the *Harvard Business Review* to update their original work in the 1970s.[11] In this update, they warned that in modern orga-

nizations the relationship among forces within the manager, subordinates, and situation had become more complex and more interrelated since the 1950s and that this obviously made it harder for managers to determine how to lead.

The update also pointed out that new organizational environments had to be considered in determining how to lead. For example, such factors as affirmative action and pollution control—which hardly figured in the decision making of managers in the 1950s—have become significant influences on the decision making of leaders since the 1970s.

The Vroom-Yetton-Jago Model

The **Vroom-Yetton-Jago (VYJ) Model of leadership** is a modern view of leadership that suggests that successful leadership requires determining through a decision tree what style of leadership will produce decisions that are beneficial to the organization and accepted and committed to by subordinates.

Another major decision-focused theory of leadership that has gained widespread attention was first developed in 1973 and refined and expanded in 1988.[12] This theory, which we will call the **Vroom-Yetton-Jago (VYJ) Model of leadership** after its three major contributors, focuses on how much participation to allow subordinates in the decision-making process. The VYJ Model is built on two important premises:

- 1. Organizational decisions should be of high quality (should have a beneficial impact on performance).
- 2. Subordinates should accept and be committed to organizational decisions that are made.

Decision Styles. The VYJ Model suggests that there are five different decision styles or ways that leaders can make decisions. These styles range from autocratic (the leader makes the decision) to consultative (the leader makes the decision after interacting with the followers) to group-focused (the manager meets with the group, and the group makes the decision). All five decision styles within the VYJ Model are described in Figure 15.3.

Using the Model. The VYJ Model, presented in Figure 15.4, is a method for determining when a leader should use which decision style. As you can see, the model is a type of decision tree. To determine which decision style to use in a particular situation, the leader starts at the left of the decision tree by stating the organizational problem being addressed. Then the leader asks a series of questions about the problem as determined by the structure of the decision tree until he or she arrives at a decision style appropriate for the situation at the far right side of the model.

Figure 15.3 The five decision styles available to a leader according to the Vroom-Yetton-Jago Model

DECISION STYLE	DEFINITION
AI	Manager makes the decision alone.
AII	Manager asks for information from subordinates but makes the decision alone. Subordinates may or may not be informed about what the situation is.
CI	Manager shares the situation with individual subordinates and asks for information and evaluation. Subordinates do not meet as a group, and the manager alone makes the decision.
CII	Manager and subordinates meet as a group to discuss the situation, but the manager makes the decision.
GIII	Manager and subordinates meet as a group to discuss the situation, and the group makes the decision.
A = autocratic; C = consultative; G = group	

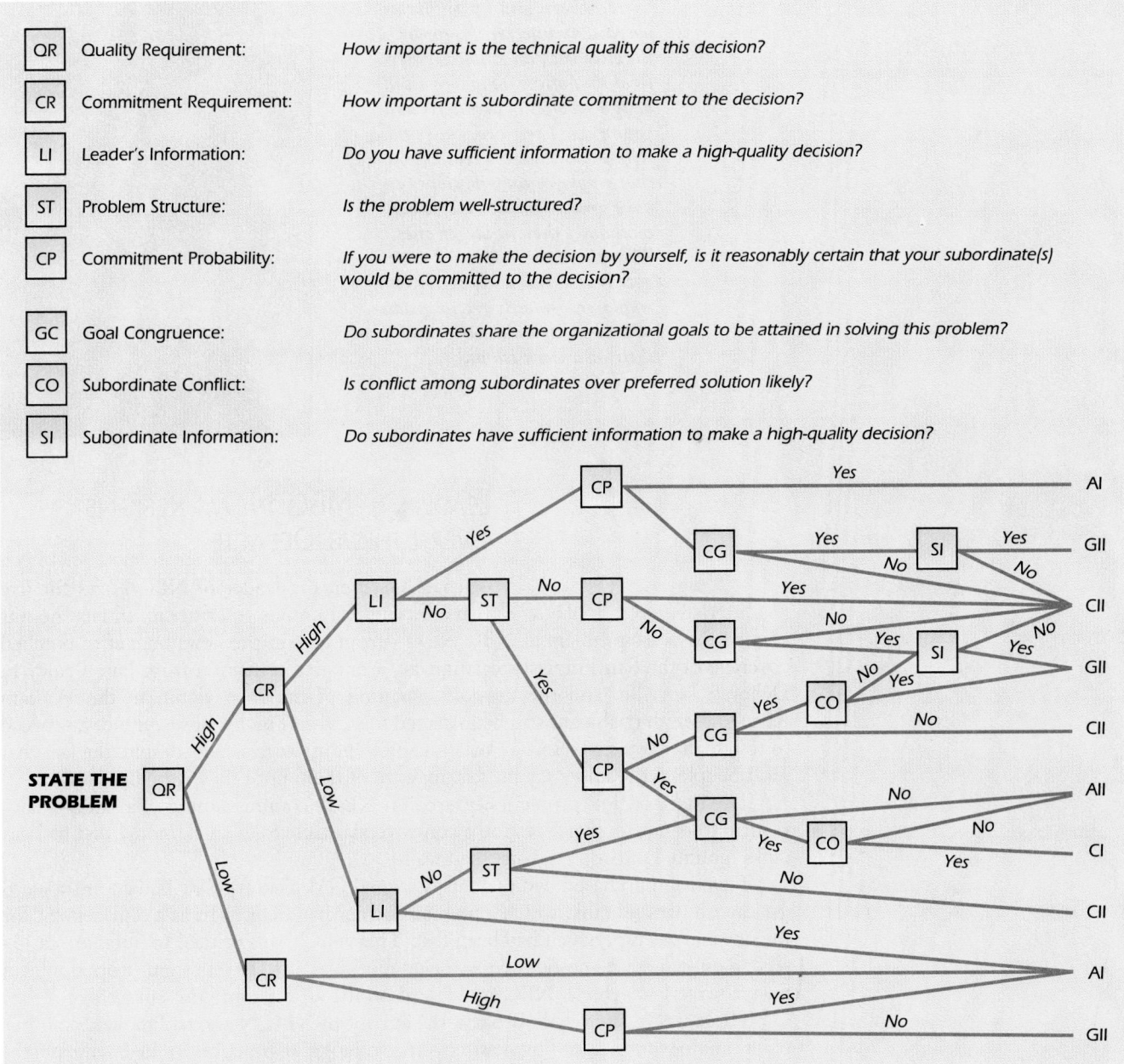

QR	Quality Requirement:	*How important is the technical quality of this decision?*
CR	Commitment Requirement:	*How important is subordinate commitment to the decision?*
LI	Leader's Information:	*Do you have sufficient information to make a high-quality decision?*
ST	Problem Structure:	*Is the problem well-structured?*
CP	Commitment Probability:	*If you were to make the decision by yourself, is it reasonably certain that your subordinate(s) would be committed to the decision?*
GC	Goal Congruence:	*Do subordinates share the organizational goals to be attained in solving this problem?*
CO	Subordinate Conflict:	*Is conflict among subordinates over preferred solution likely?*
SI	Subordinate Information:	*Do subordinates have sufficient information to make a high-quality decision?*

Figure 15.4   **The Vroom-Yetton-Jago Model**

Consider, for example, the very bottom path of the decision tree. After stating an organizational problem, the leader determines that a decision related to that problem has a low quality requirement, that it is important that subordinates be committed to the decision, and it is very uncertain whether a decision made solely by the leader will be committed to by subordinates. In this situation, the model suggests that the leader use the GII decision—that is, the leader should meet with the group to discuss the situation, and then allow the group to make the decision.

The VYJ Model seems promising. Research on an earlier version of this model has yielded some evidence that managerial decisions consistent with the model are more successful than are managerial decisions inconsistent with the model.[13] The model is rather complex, however, and therefore difficult for practicing managers to apply.

Joyce Roberts and Vic Williams operate Architectural Support Services Inc., an Atlanta-based firm that offers computer-aided design services to architects and engineers. Their decision-making style is based on the realization that employee contributions can have greater impact at smaller companies than at larger ones. Thus they have continued to delegate real authority to their young employees—mostly recent graduates who train each other and form their own work teams.

LEADER OF NBC NEWS RESIGNS OVER ETHICAL DEBACLE

ETHICS SPOTLIGHT

Michael Gartner, the leader of NBC News for five years, was never immune to criticism. In fact, he was blamed for every problem at NBC News—from cuts in the news budget to botched coverage of the San Francisco earthquake, a bungled transition from Jane Pauley to Deborah Norville, and the network's naming of the rape victim in the William Kennedy Smith trial—but still he managed to survive. Finally, however, he was forced to resign after two newscasts of questionable validity were aired—despite the fact that most people in the know say he was unaware of them until they were broadcast.

The more critical problem centered on NBC's commissioning of a safety-analysis firm to conduct a crash test on a controversial Chevrolet truck model that had gas tanks mounted outside the truck-bed walls.

This firm purchased two previously owned GM pickups. One had a nonstandard gas cap on the fuel tank, which a previous owner had bent to fit as a replacement for the original gas cap, which had been lost. This vehicle was primed to burst into a 15-second on-camera flame-out by toy rocket motors that were set to ignite upon impact from a driverless vehicle. NBC apologized on the air for using this subterfuge.

Three weeks later, Tom Brokaw, the anchor of NBC News, had to make another public apology for misleading news coverage on logging practices in the Pacific northwest. This incident involved the use of "inappropriate video" on clear-cutting forests. The video showed what was purported to be fish killed by stream damage precipitated by clear-cut logging but, actually, the fish had merely been stunned for testing purposes as part of an environmental study. Moreover, some dead fish shown were videotaped not at the forest in question, but at another location altogether. The clear-cutting damage was filmed in another state and was a result of a forest fire rather than poor logging practices.

A business leader can make several errors in judgment and survive, but making ethical mistakes is catastrophic to one's leadership status. ≈

BACK TO THE CASE

According to the text, in determining how to make decisions about Wild Animal Kingdom, Michael Eisner should consider forces in himself as manager, forces in his Disney subordinates, and forces in the specific organizational situation he faces. Forces within Eisner himself include his ideas about how to lead and his level of confidence in the Disney employees he is leading. If,

for example, he believes that he is more knowledgeable about new theme park design than his staff is, Eisner will be likely to make boss-centered decisions about what steps to take to make this venture successful. Forces within his subordinates, such as their need for independence, their readiness to assume responsibility, and their knowledge of and interest in the issues to be decided, also have an influence on what style of leadership Eisner should adopt. If his staff is relatively independent and responsible and feels strongly that the new Wild Animal Kingdom is important to meeting Walt Disney Company objectives, then Eisner should be inclined to allow his employees more freedom in deciding how to build the new theme park.

Forces within the company to be considered include the number of people making decisions and the problem to be solved. For example, if Eisner's staff is small, he will be more likely to use a democratic decision-making style, allowing his employees to become deeply involved in decisions on how best to build Wild Animal Kingdom. He will also be likely to use a subordinate-centered leadership style if his staff is knowledgeable about what makes a successful new theme park.

The VYJ Model suggests that Eisner should try to make decisions in such a fashion that their quality is high and his followers are committed to them. Doing so requires using a decision tree to determine what decision style (autocratic, consultative, or group) best matches the particular situation he faces.

Leadership Behaviors

The failure to identify predictive leadership traits led researchers in this area to turn to other variables to explain leadership success. Rather than looking at traits leaders should possess, the behavioral approach looked at what good leaders do. Are they concerned with getting a task done, for instance, or do they concentrate on keeping their followers happy and maintaining high morale?

Two major studies series were conducted to identify leadership behavior, one by the Bureau of Business Research at Ohio State University (referred to as the OSU studies), and another by the University of Michigan (referred to as the Michigan studies).

The OSU Studies   The OSU studies concluded that leaders exhibit two main types of behavior:

- **Structure behavior** is any leadership activity that delineates the relationship between the leader and the leader's followers or establishes well-defined procedures that followers should adhere to in performing their jobs. Overall, structure behavior limits the self-guidance of followers in the performance of their tasks, but while it can be relatively firm, it is never rude or malicious.

  Structure behavior can be useful to leaders as a means of minimizing follower activity that does not significantly contribute to organizational goal attainment. Leaders must be careful, however, not to go overboard and discourage follower activity that *will* contribute to organizational goal attainment.
- **Consideration behavior** is leadership behavior that reflects friendship, mutual trust, respect, and warmth in the relationship between leader and followers. This type of behavior generally aims to develop and maintain a good human relationship between the leader and the followers.

Leadership Style.   The OSU studies resulted in a model that depicts four fundamental leadership styles. A **leadership style** is the behavior a leader exhibits while guiding organizational members in appropriate directions. Each of the four leadership styles depicted in Figure 15.5 is a different combination of structure behavior and consideration behavior. For example, the high structure/low consideration leadership style emphasizes structure behavior and deemphasizes consideration behavior.

Structure behavior is leadership activity that (1) delineates the relationship between the leader and the leader's followers or (2) establishes well-defined procedures that the followers should adhere to in performing their jobs.

Consideration behavior is leadership behavior that reflects friendship, mutual trust, respect, and warmth in the relationship between leader and followers.

Leadership style is the behavioral pattern a leader establishes while guiding organization members in appropriate directions.

High

Low structure
High consideration

High structure
High consideration

CONSIDERATION

Low

Low structure
Low consideration

High structure
Low consideration

Low   High ➞
STRUCTURE

Figure 15.5   Four fundamental leadership styles based on structure behavior and consideration behavior

The OSU studies made a significant contribution to our understanding of leadership, and the central ideas generated by these studies still serve as the basis for modern leadership thought and research.[14]

The Michigan Studies

Around the same time the OSU leadership studies were being carried out, researchers at the University of Michigan, led by Rensis Likert, were also conducting a series of historically significant leadership studies.[15] After analyzing information based on interviews with both leaders and followers (managers and subordinates), the Michigan studies pinpointed two basic types of leader behavior: job-centered behavior and employee-centered behavior.

Job-centered behavior is leader behavior that focuses primarily on the work a subordinate is doing.

Job-Centered Behavior.   **Job-centered behavior** is leader behavior that focuses primarily on the work a subordinate is doing. The job-centered leader is very interested in the job the subordinate is doing and in how well the subordinate is performing at that job.

Employee-centered behavior is leader behavior that focuses primarily on subordinates as people.

Employee-Centered Behavior.   **Employee-centered behavior** is leader behavior that focuses primarily on subordinates as people. The employee-centered leader is very attentive to the personal needs of subordinates and is interested in building cooperative work teams that are satisfying to subordinates and advantageous for the organization.

As co-founders and operators of Ben & Jerry's Homemade Inc., Ben Cohen and Jerry Greenfield have become renowned as practitioners of so-called consideration behavior. *For example, they stopped marketing their popular brownie ice cream sandwiches because making them had begun to cause an unacceptable rate of repetitive-stress injuries among their employees.*

The results of the OSU studies and the Michigan studies are very similar. Both research efforts indicated two primary dimensions of leader behavior: a work dimension (structure behavior/job-centered behavior) and a people dimension (consideration behavior/employee-centered behavior). The following section focuses on determining which of these two primary dimensions of leader behavior is more advisable for a manager to adopt.

Effectiveness of Various Leadership Styles

An early investigation of high school superintendents concluded that desirable leadership behavior is associated with high leader emphasis on both structure and consideration and that undesirable leadership behavior is associated with low leader emphasis on both dimensions. Similarly, the managerial grid described in Chapter 13 implies that the most effective leadership style is characterized by high consideration and high structure. Results of a more recent study indicate that high consideration is always preferred by subordinates.[16]

Comparing Styles. One should be cautious, however, about concluding that any single leadership style is more effective than any other. Leadership situations are so varied that pronouncing one leadership style as the most effective is an oversimplification. In fact, a successful leadership style for managers in one situation may prove ineffective in another situation. Recognizing the need to link leadership styles to appropriate situations, A. K. Korman notes in a classic article that a worthwhile contribution to leadership literature would be a rationale for systematically linking appropriate styles with various situations so as to ensure effective leadership.[17] The life cycle theory of leadership, which is covered in the next section, provides such a rationale.

The Hersey-Blanchard Life Cycle Theory of Leadership

The **life cycle theory of leadership** is a rationale for linking leadership styles with various situations so as to ensure effective leadership. This theory posits essentially the same two types of leadership behavior as the OSU leadership studies, but it calls them "task" and "relationships" rather than "structure" and "consideration."

> The **life cycle theory of leadership** is a leadership concept that hypothesizes that leadership styles should reflect primarily the maturity level of the followers.

Maturity. The life cycle theory is based on the relationship among follower maturity, leader task behavior, and leader relationship behavior. In general terms, according to this theory, leadership style should reflect the maturity level of the followers. Maturity is defined as the ability of followers to perform their job independently, to assume additional responsibility, and to desire to achieve success. The more of each of these characteristics that followers possess, the more mature they are said to be. (Maturity here is not necessarily linked to chronological age.)

The Life Cycle Model. Figure 15.6 illustrates the life cycle theory of leadership model. The curved line indicates the maturity level of the followers: Maturity level increases as the maturity curve runs from right to left. In more specific terms, the theory indicates that effective leadership behavior should shift as follows:[18] (1) high-task/low-relationships behavior to (2) high-task/high-relationships behavior to (3) high-relationships/low-task behavior to (4) low-task/low-relationships behavior, as one's followers progress from immaturity to maturity. In sum, a manager's leadership style will be effective only if it is appropriate for the maturity level of the followers.

Exceptions to the Model. There are some exceptions to the general philosophy of the life cycle theory. For example, if there is a short-term deadline to meet, a leader may find it necessary to accelerate production through a high-task/low-relationships style rather than use a low-task/low-relationships style, even if the followers are mature. A high-task/low-relationships leadership style carried out over the long term with such followers, though, would typically result in a poor working relationship between leader and subordinates.

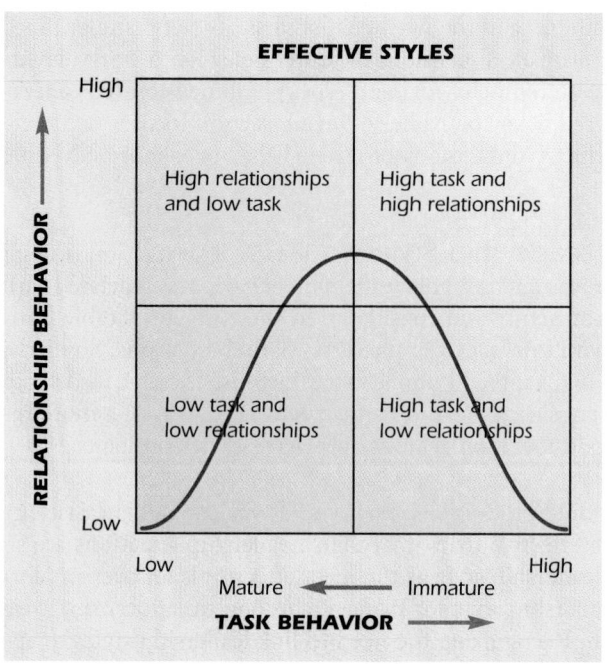

EFFECTIVE STYLES

High relationships and low task

High task and high relationships

Low task and low relationships

High task and low relationships

RELATIONSHIP BEHAVIOR

High

Low

Low   High

Mature ← Immature

TASK BEHAVIOR →

Figure 15.6   The life cycle theory of leadership model

Applying Life Cycle Theory. Following is an example of how the life cycle theory applies to a leadership situation:

- A man has just been hired as a salesperson in a men's clothing store. At first, this individual is extremely immature—that is, unable to solve task-related problems independently. According to the life cycle theory, the appropriate style for leading this salesperson at his level of maturity is high-task/low-relationships—that is, the leader should tell the salesperson exactly what should be done and how to do it. The salesperson should be shown how to make cash and charge sales and how to handle merchandise returns. The leader should also begin laying the groundwork for developing a personal relationship with the salesperson. Too much relationship behavior at this point, however, should be avoided, since it can easily be misinterpreted as permissiveness.

- As time passes and the salesperson gains somewhat in job-related maturity, the appropriate style for leading him would be high task/high relationships. Although the salesperson's maturity has increased somewhat, the leader still needs to watch him closely because he requires guidance and direction at times. The main difference between this leadership style and the first one is the amount of relationship behavior displayed by the leader. Building on the groundwork laid during the period of the first leadership style, the leader can now start to encourage an atmosphere of mutual trust, respect, and friendliness between herself and the salesperson.

- As more time passes and the salesperson's maturity level increases still further, the appropriate style for leading this individual will become high relationships/low task. The leader can now deemphasize task behavior because the salesperson is of above-average maturity in his job and is capable of solving most job-related problems independently. The leader would continue to develop a human relationship with her follower.

- Once the salesperson's maturity level reaches its maximum, the appropriate style for leading him is low task/low relationships. Again, the leader deemphasizes task behavior because the follower is thoroughly familiar with the job. Now, however, the leader can also deemphasize relationship behavior because she has fully established a good working relationship with the follower. At this point, task behavior is seldom needed, and relationship behavior is used pri-

marily to nurture the good working rapport that has developed between the leader and the follower. The salesperson, then, is left to do his job without close supervision, knowing that he has a positive working relationship with a leader who can be approached for guidance whenever necessary.

The life cycle approach more than likely owes its acceptance to its intuitive appeal. Although at first glance it appears to be a useful leadership concept, managers should bear in mind that there is little scientific investigation verifying its worth and therefore it should be applied very carefully.[19]

BACK TO THE CASE

The OSU leadership studies should furnish a manager like Michael Eisner with insights about leadership behavior in general situations. According to these studies, Eisner can choose to exhibit one of two general types of leadership behavior: structure or consideration. He will be using structure behavior if he tells Walt Disney Company personnel what to do—for example, exactly how to design the Tree of Life or animal shelters in the new Wild Animal Kingdom. He will be using consideration behavior if he attempts to develop a more human rapport with his employees by discussing their concerns and becoming friendly with them.

Depending on how much emphasis he gives to each of these behaviors, Eisner's leadership style will reflect a combination of structure and consideration ranging from high structure/low consideration to low structure/high consideration. For example, if Eisner stresses giving orders to employees and deemphasizes developing relationships, he will be exhibiting high structure/low consideration. If he emphasizes establishing a good rapport with his staff and allows its members to function largely independently of him, his leadership style will be termed low structure/high consideration.

Although no single leadership style is more effective than any other in all situations, the life cycle theory of leadership furnishes Eisner with a strategy for using various styles in various situations. According to this theory, he should make his style consistent primarily with the maturity level of the Walt Disney Company organization members he is leading. As Eisner's followers progress from immaturity to maturity, his leadership style should shift systematically according to the following pattern: (1) high task/low relationships behavior to (2) high task/high relationships behavior to (3) high relationships/low task behavior to (4) low task/low relationships behavior.

Fiedler's Contingency Theory

Situational theories of leadership like the life cycle theory are based on the concept of **leader flexibility**—the idea that successful leaders must change their leadership styles as they encounter different situations. Can any leader be so flexible as to span all major leadership styles? The answer to this question is that some leaders can be that flexible, and some cannot. Unfortunately, there are numerous obstacles to leader flexibility. One is that a leadership style is sometimes so ingrained in a leader that it takes years to even approach flexibility. Another is that some leaders have experienced such success in a basically static situation that they believe developing a flexible style is unnecessary.

Leader flexibility is the ability to change leadership style.

Changing the Organization to Fit the Leader.   One strategy, proposed by Fred Fiedler, for overcoming these obstacles is changing the organizational situation to fit the leader's style, rather than changing the leader's style to fit the organizational situation.[20] Applying this idea to the life cycle theory of leadership, an organization may find it easier to shift leaders to situations appropriate for their leadership styles than to expect those leaders to change styles as situations change. After all, it would probably take three to five years to train a manager to use a concept like life cycle theory effectively, while changing the situation that leader faces can be done very quickly simply by exercising organizational authority.

The **contingency theory of leadership** is a leadership concept that hypothesizes that, in any given leadership situation, success is determined primarily by (1) the degree to which the task being performed by the followers is structured, (2) the degree of position power possessed by the leader, and (3) the type of relationship that exists between the leader and the followers.

Table 15.1

Eight Combinations, or Octants, of Three Factors: Leader-Member Relations, Task Structure, and Leader Position Power

OCTANT	LEADER-MEMBER RELATIONS	TASK STRUCTURE	LEADER POSITION POWER
I	Good	High	Strong
II	Good	High	Weak
III	Good	Weak	Strong
IV	Good	Weak	Weak
V	Moderately poor	High	Strong
VI	Moderately poor	High	Weak
VII	Moderately poor	Weak	Strong
VIII	Moderately poor	Weak	Weak

According to Fiedler's **contingency theory of leadership,** leader-member relations, task structure, and the position power of the leader are the three primary factors that should be considered when moving leaders into situations appropriate for their leadership styles:

- *Leader-member relations* is the degree to which the leader feels accepted by the followers.
- *Task structure* is the degree to which the goals—the work to be done—and other situational factors are outlined clearly.
- *Position power* is determined by the extent to which the leader has control over the rewards and punishments followers receive.

How these three factors can be arranged in eight different combinations, called *octants,* is presented in Table 15.1.

Figure 15.7 shows how effective leadership varies among the eight octants. From an organizational viewpoint, this figure implies that management should attempt to match permissive, passive, and considerate leaders with situations reflecting the mid-

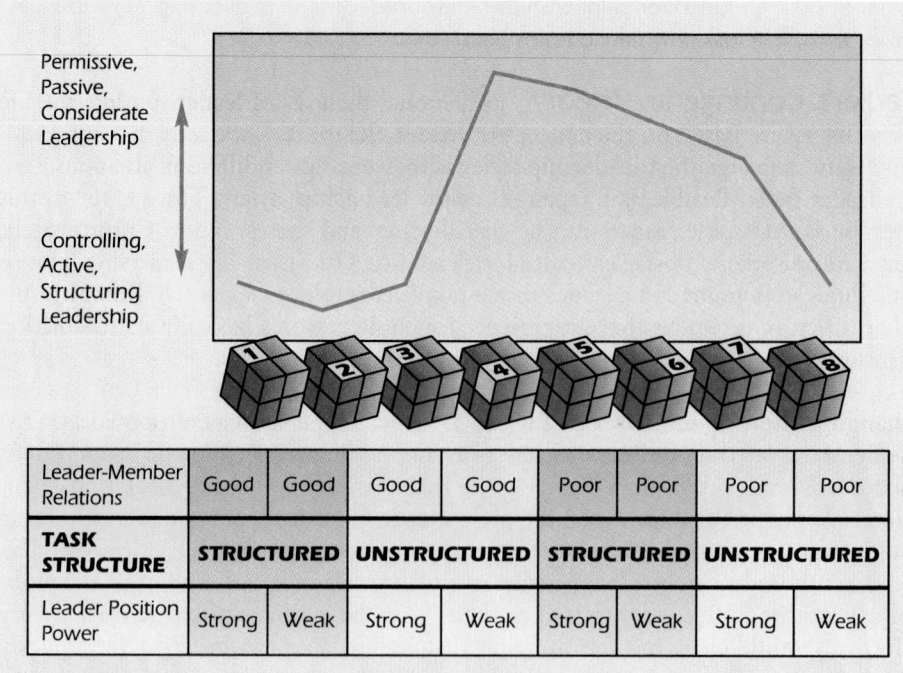

Figure 15.7   How effective leadership style varies with Fiedler's eight octants

dle of the continuum containing the octants. It also implies that management should try to match controlling, active, and structuring leaders with the extremes of this continuum.

Fiedler suggests some actions that can be taken to modify the leadership situation. They are as follows:[21]

1. In some organizations, we can change the individual's task assignment. We may assign to one leader very structured tasks which have implicit or explicit instructions telling him what to do and how to do it, and we may assign to another the tasks that are nebulous and vague. The former are the typical production tasks; the latter are exemplified by committee work, by the development of policy, and by tasks which require creativity.

2. We can change the leader's position power. We not only can give him a higher rank and corresponding recognition, we also can modify his position power by giving him subordinates who are equal to him in rank and prestige or subordinates who are two or three ranks below him. We can give him subordinates who are experts in their specialties or subordinates who depend upon the leader for guidance and instruction. We can give the leader the final say in all decisions affecting his group, or we can require that he make decisions in consultation with his subordinates, or even that he obtain their concurrence. We can channel all directives, communications, and information about organizational plans through the leader alone, giving him expert power, or we can provide these communications concurrently to all his subordinates.

3. We can change the leader-member relations in this group. We can have the leader work with groups whose members are very similar to him in attitude, opinion, technical background, race, and cultural background. Or we can assign him subordinates with whom he differs in any one or several of these important aspects. Finally, we can assign the leader to a group in which the members have a tradition of getting along well with their supervisors or to a group that has a history and tradition of conflict.

Fiedler's work certainly helps destroy the myths that there is one best leadership style and that leaders are born, not made. Further, his work supports the theory that almost every manager in an organization can be a successful leader if placed in a situation appropriate to that person's leadership style. This, of course, assumes that someone in the organization has the ability to assess the characteristics of the organization's leaders and of other important organizational variables and then to match the two accordingly.

Fiedler's model, like all theoretical models, has its limitations. But although it may not provide concrete answers, it does emphasize the importance of situational variables in determining leadership effectiveness. As said earlier, it may actually be easier to change the leadership situation or move the leader to a more favorable situation than to try to change a leader's style.[22]

The Path-Goal Theory of Leadership
The **path-goal theory of leadership** suggests that the primary activities of a leader are to make desirable and achievable rewards available to organization members who attain organizational goals and to clarify the kinds of behavior that must be performed to earn those rewards.[23] In essence, the leader outlines the goals that followers should aim for and clarifies the path that followers should take to achieve those goals and earn the rewards contingent on doing so. Overall, the path-goal theory maintains that managers can facilitate job performance by showing employees how their performance directly affects their reception of desired rewards.

Path-goal theory of leadership is a theory of leadership that suggests that the primary activities of a leader are to make desirable and achievable rewards available to organization members who attain organizational goals and to clarify the kinds of behavior that must be performed to earn those rewards.

Leadership Behavior.   According to the path-goal theory of leadership, leaders exhibit four primary types of behavior:

1. *Directive behavior*. Directive behavior is aimed at telling followers what to do

and how to do it. The leader indicates what performance goals exist and precisely what must be done to achieve them.

2. *Supportive behavior.* Supportive behavior is aimed at being friendly with followers and showing interest in them as human beings. Through supportive behavior, the leader demonstrates sensitivity to the personal needs of followers.

3. *Participative behavior.* Participative behavior is aimed at seeking suggestions from followers regarding business operations to the extent that followers are involved in making important organizational decisions. Followers often help to determine the rewards that will be available to them in organizations and what they must do to earn those rewards.

4. *Achievement behavior.* Achievement behavior is aimed at setting challenging goals for followers to reach and expressing and demonstrating confidence that they will measure up to the challenge. This leader behavior focuses on making goals difficult enough that employees will find achieving them challenging, but not so difficult that they will view them as impossible and give up trying to achieve them.

Adapting Behavior to Situation.   As with other situational theories of leadership, the path-goal theory proposes that leaders will be successful if they appropriately match these four types of behavior to situations that they face. For example, if inexperienced followers do not have a thorough understanding of a job, a manager may appropriately use more directive behavior to develop this understanding and to ensure that serious job-related problems are avoided. For more experienced followers, who have a more complete understanding of a job, directive behavior would probably be inappropriate and might create interpersonal problems between leader and followers.

If jobs are very structured, with little room for employee interpretation of how the work should be done, directive behavior is less appropriate than if there is much room for employees to determine how the work gets done. When followers are deriving much personal satisfaction and encouragement from work and enjoy the support of other members of their work group, supportive behavior by the leader is not as important as when followers are gaining little or no satisfaction from their work or from personal relationships in the work group.

The primary focus of the path-goal theory of leadership is on how leaders can increase employee effort and productivity by clarifying performance goals and the path to be taken to achieve those goals. This theory of leadership has gained increasing acceptance in recent years. In fact, research suggests that the path-goal theory is highly promising for enhancing employee commitment to achieving organizational goals and thereby increasing the probability that organizations will be successful. It should be pointed out, however, that the research done on this model has been conducted mostly on its parts rather than on the complete model.[24]

BACK TO THE CASE   The life cycle theory suggests that Michael Eisner should be flexible enough to behave as the Wild Animal Kingdom situation requires. If he finds it extremely difficult to adopt a flexible style of leadership, however, he should attempt to structure his situation so as to make it appropriate for his style. As suggested by Fiedler, if Eisner's leadership style is high task in nature, he generally will be a more successful leader in situations best described by octants 1, 2, 3, and 8 in Table 15.1 and Figure 15.7. If, however, Eisner's leadership style is more relationship oriented, he will probably be a more successful leader in situations representative of octants 4, 5, 6, and 7. Overall, Fiedler's work provides Eisner with insights on how to reconfigure situations at Walt Disney Company so they will be appropriate for his leadership style.

The path-goal theory of leadership suggests that in establishing Wild Animal Kingdom Michael Eisner should clarify what rewards are available to followers in the organi-

zation and how those rewards can be earned, as well as eliminate barriers to earning the rewards. He can use directive behavior, supportive behavior, participative behavior, and achievement behavior in implementing the path-goal theory.

LEADERSHIP TODAY

Leaders in modern organizations have been confronting many situations rarely encountered by organizational leaders of the past.[25] Today's leaders are often called upon to make massive personnel cuts in order to eliminate unnecessary levels of organizations and thereby lower labor expenses, to introduce work teams in order to enhance organizational decision making and work flow, to reengineer work so that organization members will be more efficient and effective, and to initiate programs designed to improve the overall quality of organizational functioning.

In reaction to these new situations, organizations are emphasizing leadership styles that concentrate on getting employees involved in the organization and giving them the freedom to use their abilities as they think best. This is a dramatically different type of leadership from that known in organizations of the past, which largely concentrated on controlling people and work processes. Figure 15.8 contrasts the "soul" of the new leader with the "mind" of the manager.

The information in this section of the text points up the trend among leaders of today to get employees involved in their organizations and to give them the freedom to make and carry out decisions. The following PEOPLE PERSPECTIVES feature describes how the CEO of Chrysler Corporation involves employees in the organization.

ROBERT EATON GETS PEOPLE INVOLVED AT CHRYSLER

PEOPLE PERSPECTIVES

Chrysler Corporation, a worldwide manufacturer of automobiles, trucks, and sport vehicles, recently experienced earnings of $3.7 billion—up 246 percent—and sales of $52.2 billion—up 20 percent. Both of these figures far surpassed the company's previous records. On the strength of this extraordinary performance, Chrysler paid 91,550 of its 125,825 employees a profit-sharing bonus averaging $8,000, also an all-time high.

Chrysler CEO Robert Eaton attributes the company's recent success to its program of getting employees more seriously involved in company operations. For example, when Chrysler begins to create a new vehicle model or to revamp an old one, a team of about 700 people, comprising employees from engineering, design, manu-

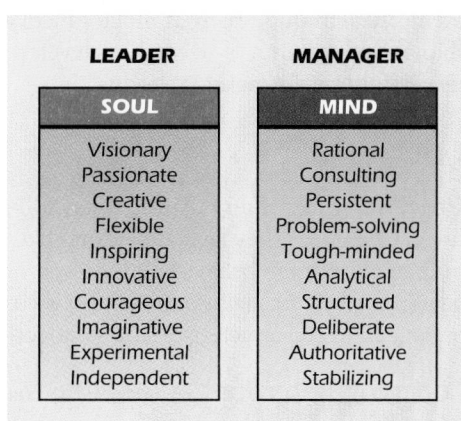

Figure 15.8   Characteristics of the emerging leader versus characteristics of the manager

facturing, marketing, and finance, is formed. A company vice president acts as "godfather" to the group, but all of the actual work is directed by team leaders below that rank, and the team organizes itself as it sees fit.

One of the most significant advantages of this method of operation is that it has greatly reduced the time it takes for Chrysler to get a new product to the marketplace. Once it took the company five years to develop a vehicle concept and to actually begin producing the vehicle. Now, using this new work process that focuses on people involvement, it takes Chrysler only two and a half to three years to begin producing a new vehicle. Moreover, the company projects that its concept-to-market time will shrink further in the future. ≈

Four leadership styles have emerged in recent years to suit these new situations: transformational leadership, coaching, "superleadership," and entrepreneurial leadership.[26] Each of these new styles is discussed in the following sections.

Transformational Leadership

Transformational leadership is leadership that inspires organizational success by profoundly affecting followers' beliefs in what an organization should be, as well as their values, such as justice and integrity.

Transformational leadership is leadership that inspires organizational success by profoundly affecting followers' beliefs in what an organization should be, as well as their values, such as justice and integrity.[27] This style of leadership creates a sense of duty within an organization, encourages new ways of handling problems, and promotes learning for all organization members. Transformational leadership is closely related to concepts like charismatic leadership and inspirational leadership.

Perhaps transformational leadership is receiving more attention nowadays because of the dramatic changes that many organizations are going through and the critical importance of transformational leadership in "transforming" or changing organizations successfully. Lee Iacocca is often cited as an exemplar of transformational leadership because of his success in transforming Chrysler Corporation from a company on the verge of going under into a successful company.

The Tasks of Transformational Leaders

Transformational leaders perform several important tasks. First, they raise followers' awareness of organizational issues and their consequences. Organization members must understand an organization's high-priority issues and what will happen if these issues are not successfully resolved. Second, transformational leaders create a vision of what the organization should be, build commitment to that vision throughout the organization, and facilitate organizational changes that support the vision. In sum, transformational leadership is consistent with strategy developed through an organization's strategic management process.[28]

Managers of the future will continue to face the challenge of significantly changing their organizations, primarily because of the accelerating trend to position organizations to be more competitive in a global business environment. Therefore, transformational leadership will probably get increasing attention in the leadership literature. Although there is much practical appeal and interest in this style of leadership, more research is needed to develop insights about how managers can become successful transformational leaders.

Coaching

Coaching is leadership that instructs followers on how to meet the special organizational challenges they face.

Coaching is leadership that instructs followers on how to meet the special organizational challenges they face. Operating like an athletic coach, the coaching leader identifies inappropriate behavior in followers and suggests how they might correct that behavior. The increasing use of teams has elevated the importance of coaching in today's organizations. Characteristics of an effective coach are presented in Table 15.2.

Coaching Behavior

A successful coaching leader is characterized by many different kinds of behavior. Among these behaviors are the following:

Table 15.2

Characteristics of an Effective Coach

TRAIT, ATTITUDE, OR BEHAVIOR	ACTION PLAN FOR IMPROVEMENT
1. Empathy (putting self in other person's shoes)	*Sample:* Will listen and understand person's point of view. *Your own:*
2. Listening skill	*Sample:* Will concentrate extra-hard on listening. *Your own:*
3. Insight into people (ability to size them up)	*Sample:* Will jot down observations about people upon first meeting, then verify in the future. *Your own:*
4. Diplomacy and tact	*Sample:* Will study book of etiquette. *Your own:*
5. Patience toward people	*Sample:* Will practice staying calm when someone makes a mistake. *Your own:*
6. Concern for welfare of people	*Sample:* When interacting with another person, will ask myself, "How can this person's interests best be served?" *Your own:*
7. Minimum hostility toward people	*Sample:* Will often ask myself, "Why am I angry at this person?" *Your own:*
8. Self-confidence and emotional stability	*Sample:* Will attempt to have at least one personal success each week. *Your own:*
9. Noncompetitiveness with team members	*Sample:* Will keep reminding myself that all boats rise with the same tide. *Your own:*
10. Enthusiasm for people	*Sample:* Will search for the good in each person. *Your own:*

- *Listens closely.* The coaching leader tries to gather both the facts in what is said and the feelings and emotions behind what is said. Such a leader is careful to really listen and not fall into the trap of immediately rebutting statements made by followers.
- *Gives emotional support.* The coaching leader gives followers personal encouragement.[29] Such encouragement should constantly be aimed at motivating them to do their best to meet the high demands of successful organizations.
- *Shows by example what constitutes appropriate behavior.* The coaching leader shows followers, for instance, how to handle an employee problem or a production glitch. By demonstrating expertise, the coaching leader builds the trust and respect of followers.

Superleadership

Superleadership is leading by showing others how to lead themselves. If superleaders are successful, they develop followers who are productive, work independently, and need only minimal attention from the superleader.

In essence, superleaders teach followers how to think on their own and act constructively and independently.[30] They encourage people to eliminate negative

Superleadership is leadership that inspires organizational success by showing followers how to lead themselves.

thoughts and beliefs about the company and co-workers and to replace them with more positive and constructive beliefs. An important aspect of superleadership is building the self-confidence of followers by convincing them that they are competent, have a significant reservoir of potential, and are capable of meeting the difficult challenges of the work situation.

The objective of superleaders is to develop followers who require very little leadership. This is an important objective in the typical organization of today, whose structure is flatter than that of organizations of the past and which therefore has fewer leader-managers. Organizations cannot be successful in such a situation unless their members become proficient at leading themselves.

Entrepreneurial Leadership

Entrepreneurial leadership is leadership that is based on the attitude that the leader is self-employed. Leaders of this type act as if they are playing a critical role in the organization rather than a mostly unimportant one. In addition, they behave as if they are taking the risk of losing money, but will receive the profit if one is made. They approach each mistake as if it were a significant error rather than a smaller error that will be neutralized by the normal functioning of the organization.

Each of these four contemporary leadership styles has received notable attention in recent management literature. Managers should realize that these four styles are not mutually exclusive; they can be combined in various ways to generate a unique style. For example, a leader can assume both a coaching and an entrepreneurial role. Figure 15.9 shows the various combinations of these four leadership styles that a leader can adopt. The shaded portion of the figure represents a leader whose style comprises all four.

This section of the text has described a number of leadership styles aimed at influencing followers to become more committed to organizational objectives. The following CUTTING EDGE feature describes some recent activities of Patricia Gallup, a leader at *PC Connection*, that provide further insights about how a leader can build this kind of follower commitment.

Entrepreneurial leadership is leadership that is based on the attitude that the leader is self-employed.

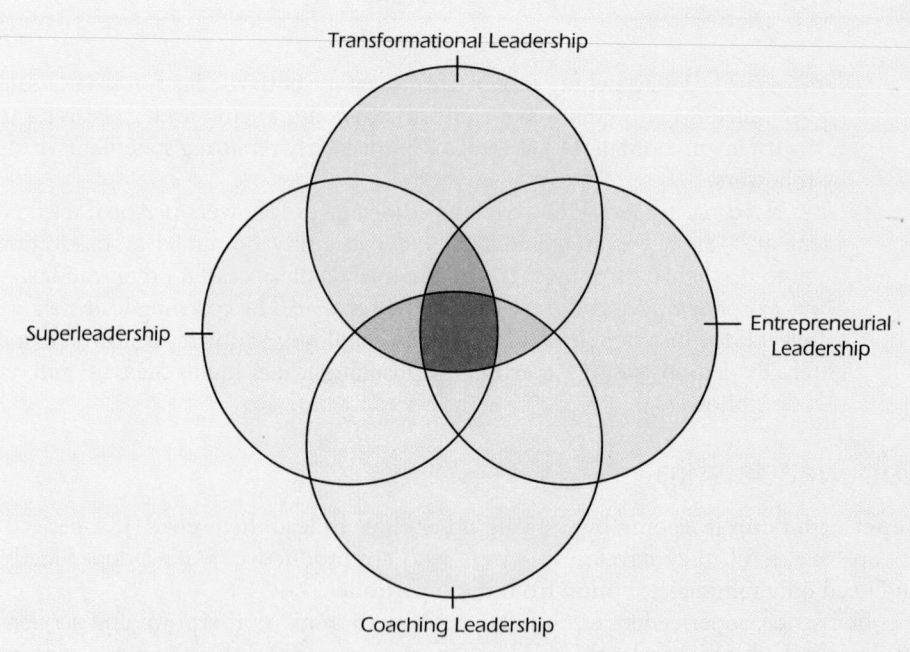

Figure 15.9 **Various combinations of transformational, coaching, superleader, and entrepreneurial leadership styles**

LEADER PATRICIA GALLUP DOESN'T FORGET RECOGNITION OF FOLLOWER EFFORTS

Patricia Gallup, co-founder and CEO of *PC Connection*, a popular computer magazine, is a very successful entrepreneur. She stands out as a leader of organizational vision who has enriched those followers who have helped her achieve that vision.

Gallup understands that offering people money is not the only way to motivate them. She knows that perhaps the simplest, and yet one of the most effective, ways to motivate people is with plain, old-fashioned praise handed out in the right way at the right time. The importance of publicly recognizing a talented, effective employee may seem obvious, but a surprising number of leaders resist praising followers face-to-face and in public, often because they mistakenly believe that people who are well paid should not need any other proof of their value.

The timing of recognition is especially important. When organizational morale is high, followers don't generally need the psychological boost of praise, but when morale is low, recognizing the individual efforts of followers is vital.

Praising the personal accomplishments of followers is an integral part of leadership. This skill, however, requires training and planning. Clumsy or ill-timed praise can be worse than no praise at all. Most importantly, the acknowledgment of effort has to be tailored to the specific situation of the follower—it should not be so general that it is virtually meaningless to the individual. ≈

CURRENT TOPICS IN LEADERSHIP

Two currently popular leadership topics are leadership substitutes and women leaders. Both are discussed in the following sections under the heads "Substitutes for Leadership," "Women as Leaders," and "Ways Women Lead."

Substitutes for Leadership

There are times when leaders do not have to lead or, for one reason or another, cannot lead. In these circumstances, situational substitutes can have as much influence on employees as any leader.

You have probably heard of or observed situations in which the nominal leader—for a number of reasons, including factors beyond the leader's control—had little or no impact on the outcome of a situation. Because so many factors can affect a situation, some people argue that leadership is really irrelevant to many organization outcomes. Under various conditions—for instance, strong subordinates, knowledge of the task, organizational constraints—subordinates may not need or even want leadership.

Substitute leadership theory attempts to identify those situations in which the input of leader behavior is partly or wholly canceled out by characteristics of the subordinate or the organization. Examples: A subordinate may have such high levels of ability, experience, education, and internal motivation that little or no leadership is required or desired; task characteristics may be so routine that the subordinate does not require much, if any, leadership; organizational characteristics such as group cohesion and a high degree of formalization may reduce the need for leadership. Recall, also, from our earlier discussion of life cycle theory the situation in which the leader delegates tasks to highly mature followers in a low-task/low relationship situation.[31]

Throughout this chapter, we have concentrated on a number of factors affecting leadership effectiveness. Much of this attention has centered on leadership characteristics, situations, and leader behavior. Substitute theory tends to downplay the impor-

tance of these dimensions. Why? Meindl and Ehrlich suggest one possible answer: Throughout history, human beings have had a tendency to romanticize leadership, treating it as more important than it actually is.[32] Substitute theory reminds us that—at least in some situations with some people in some organizations—things just seem to get done regardless of the quality of leadership.

Women as Leaders

One can read Stogdill's *Handbook of Leadership* (1974) and find barely any reference to women leaders, except as a subject deserving further research. This is probably because in 1970 only 15 percent of all managers were women. By 1989, this figure had risen to more than 40 percent. By 1995, women will make up about 63 percent of the total workforce. Just how many of these women will become leaders in their companies or industries remains to be seen. Currently, only 3 of every 100 top jobs in the largest U.S. companies are held by women—about the same number as a decade ago. A Labor Department study of the early 1990s concluded that the so-called glass ceiling was keeping women from moving into leadership positions. The "glass ceiling" is the subtle barrier of negative attitudes and prejudices that prevents women from reaching seemingly attainable top-management positions.[33]

Ways Women Lead

Women who have broken through the glass ceiling have found that there is no one mold for effective leadership. In the past, women leaders modeled their leadership styles after successful male managers. Today's women managers, however, often describe their leadership styles as transformational—getting workers to transform or subordinate their individual self-interests into group consensus directed toward a broader goal. This leadership style attributes power to such personal characteristics as charisma, personal contacts, and interpersonal skills rather than to the organizational structure.

Men, on the other hand, are more likely to characterize their leadership as transactional. They see their jobs as involving a series of transactions between themselves and their subordinates. This leadership style involves exchanging rewards for services or dispensing punishment for inadequate performance.[34]

As CEO of clothing manufacturer Warnaco, Linda J. Wachner is the only woman currently heading a Fortune 500 industrial company. She practices a direct approach to both leadership and communication, often gathering marketing data by talking directly with salespeople in retail stores. "When people have a good leader who instills team spirit," she says, ". . . they live in an environment that demands excellence, energy, and keeping up of momentum. . . ."

For James G. Kaiser of Corning, Being Employee-Centered Includes a Focus on Diversity

DIVERSITY SPOTLIGHT

James G. Kaiser is a senior vice president at Corning, Inc. Kaiser is responsible for keeping the Technical Products Division competitive in the global marketplace and for masterminding the strategic planning for his division's operations. In addition, he oversees research and development for new products and is responsible for seeking business partners with whom the company can pursue joint ventures. Lastly, Kaiser is in charge of a series of export and sales offices in several locations.

Kaiser considers himself to be a people-oriented leader. His is an African-American manager who sees his race as an asset in managing people from different cultures because it gives him a broader perspective on the differences among various types of employees. He focuses formally on cultural diversity at Corning largely through the Executive Leadership Council, a group whose mission is to offer guidance and leadership to other up-and-coming African-American executives. As president of Corning's Executive Leadership Council, Kaiser provides minority executives with a network and a discussion forum that help them to understand what the achievement of excellence means within and for the African-American community and how they can personally excel.

Because Kaiser is an African-American leader, it could be argued that he has special insights for advising and helping minority employees to be successful leaders. For their own long-run success, however, leaders like Kaiser must be careful not to become "specialists" who deal with only one culture, but rather "generalists" who develop the skills to successfully manage people from many different cultures.≈

BACK TO THE CASE

Based upon the information in the text, Michael Eisner, in establishing Wild Animal Kingdom, could act as a transformational leader. In that case, he would inspire his followers to focus on achieving organizational objectives by encouraging their ideas, creating in them a sense of duty toward the organization, and urging them to learn and grow. Since Walt Disney is a company undergoing significant changes, a chairman who knows how to exercise transformational leadership would be a great asset.

Three other popular leadership styles also offer Eisner insights about how to lead at Walt Disney Company. As a coaching leader, he could focus on instructing Disney followers on how to meet the special challenges of establishing Wild Animal Kingdom. In the role of a coaching leader, Eisner would listen closely, give employees emotional support, and demonstrate by example what should be done. As a superleader, Eisner would teach employees involved in the new theme park venture how to think and act constructively and independently. As an entrepreneurial leader, he would act much like a self-employed owner of Walt Disney Corporation. He would, for example, behave as if he were personally incurring the risk of making Wild Animal Kingdom profitable and personally benefiting from any profit to be made.

Eisner must remember that all these leadership styles are aimed at getting people involved in the organization and giving them the freedom to use their abilities as they think best. Like all leaders, he should realize that regardless of the type of leadership style he employs, he must earn and maintain the trust of his followers if he is to be successful in the long run.

Action Summary

Reread the learning objectives below. Each objective is followed by questions. Answering these questions accurately will help you retain the most important concepts discussed in this chapter. After answering each question, check your answer against the answer key at the end of this chapter. (*Hint:* If you have any doubts regarding the correct response, consult the page whose number follows the answer.)

Circle: From studying this chapter, I will attempt to acquire:

1. A working definition of leadership.

a,b,c,d,e   **a.** The process of directing others toward the accomplishment of some objective is: (a) communication; (b) controlling; (c) leadership; (d) managing; (e) none of the above.

a,b,c,d,e   **b.** Directing must be consistent with: (a) organizational policies; (b) procedures; (c) job descriptions; (d) none of the above; (e) all of the above.

2. An understanding of the relationship between leading and managing.

T,F   **a.** Leading and managing are the same process.

a,b,c,d,e   **b.** In the relationship between managers and leaders, one could say that: (a) all managers are leaders; (b) all leaders are managers; (c) some leaders are not managers; (d) managers cannot be leaders; (e) management is a subset of leadership.

3. An appreciation for the trait and situational approaches to leadership.

a,b,c,d,e   **a.** The following is true about the conclusions drawn from the trait approach to leadership: (a) the trait approach identifies traits that consistently separate leaders from nonleaders; (b) there are certain traits that guarantee that a leader will be successful; (c) the trait approach is based on early research that assumes that a good leader is born, not made; (d) leadership is a simple issue of describing the traits of successful leaders; (e) none of the above.

a,b,c,d,e   **b.** The situational approach to leadership takes into account: (a) the leader; (b) the follower; (c) the situation; (d) a and b; (e) a, b, and c.

4. Insights about using leadership theories that emphasize decision-making situations.

a,b,c,d,e   **a.** Forces in the manager that determine leadership behavior include: (a) the manager's values; (b) the manager's confidence in subordinates; (c) the manager's strengths; (d) the manager's tolerance for ambiguity; (e) all of the above.

a,b,c,d,e   **b.** Limiting the self-guidance of the follower and specifically defining procedures for the follower's task performance are called: (a) initiating behavior; (b) structure behavior; (c) maturity behavior; (d) consideration behavior; (e) relationship behavior.

T,F   **c.** The VYJ model suggests that a leader should match one of five decision-making styles to the particular situation the leader faces.

5. Insights about using leadership theories that emphasize more general organizational situations.

a, b, c, d, e   **a.** The ability of followers to perform their jobs independently and to assume additional responsibilities in their desire to achieve success is called: (a) maturity; (b) authority; (c) aggressiveness; (d) assertiveness; (e) consideration.

a,b,c,d,e   **b.** Usually upon entrance into an organization, an individual is unable to solve task-related problems independently. According to the life cycle theory, the appropriate style of leadership for this person is: (a) high task/low relationships; (b) high task/high relationships; (c) high relationships/low task; (d) low task/low relationships; (e) none of the above.

T,F   **c.** According to the path-goal theory of leadership, a leader should carefully inform followers of the rewards that are available to them in the organization and then allow them to pick their own methods of earning the rewards.

6. An understanding of alternatives to leader flexibility.

a,b,c,d,e   **a.** According to Fiedler, the three primary factors that should be used as a basis for moving leaders into more appropriate situations are: (a) task behavior, consideration behavior, maturity; (b) maturity, job knowledge, responsibility; (c) the worker, the leader, the situation; (d) leader-member relations, task structure, position power; (e) task structure, leadership style, maturity.

T,F   **b.** Fiedler's studies have proven true the myths that leaders are born, not made, and that there is one best leadership style.

7. An appreciation of emerging leader styles and leadership issues of today.

T,F   **a.** Transformational leaders modify organizations by precisely carrying out strategic plans and emphasizing only slightly the values that followers may have.

a,b,c,d,e   **b.** The coaching leader: (a) listens closely; (b) gives emotional support; (c) shows by example; (d) a and c; (e) all of the above.

T,F   **c.** The superleader and entrepreneurial leadership styles are basically the same.

T,F   **d.** Even though there are situations in which a leader has little or no impact on the outcome, the leader is nevertheless an important part of management.

Introductory Case Wrap-Up

"Eisner's Leadership Challenge at Disney's New Wild Animal Kingdom" (p. 349) and its related back-to-the-case sections were written to help you better understand the management concepts contained in this chapter. Answer the following discussion questions about this introductory case to enrich your understanding of the chapter content:

1. List and define several activities that Michael Eisner might perform as a *manager* building Wild Animal Kingdom. List and de-

fine several that he might perform as a *leader* building the new theme park.

2. Do you feel that Eisner should use a more boss-centered or subordinate-centered leadership style in making decisions about Wild Animal Kingdom? Why?

3. If you were Eisner, would understanding the transformational and the entrepreneurial leadership styles be valuable to you in leading Disney employees to the establishment of Wild Animal Kingdom? Explain fully.

Issues for Review and Discussion

1. What is leadership?
2. How does leadership differ from management?
3. Explain the trait approach to leadership.
4. What relationship exists between successful leadership and leadership traits?
5. Explain the situational approach to leadership.
6. Draw and explain Tannenbaum and Schmidt's leadership model.
7. List the forces in the manager, the subordinates, and the situation that ultimately determine how a manager should make decisions as a leader.
8. How is the VYJ Model similar to Tannenbaum and Schmidt's model? How is it different?
9. What contribution did the OSU studies make to leadership theory?
10. Can any one of the major leadership styles resulting from the OSU studies be called more effective than the others? Explain.
11. Compare the results of the OSU studies with the results of the Michigan studies.
12. What is meant by *maturity* as it is used in the life cycle theory of leadership?
13. Draw and explain the life cycle theory of leadership model.
14. What is meant by *leader flexibility*?
15. Describe some obstacles to leader flexibility.
16. In general, how might obstacles to leader flexibility be overcome?
17. In specific terms, how does Fiedler suggest that obstacles to leader flexibility be overcome?
18. Based upon the path-goal theory of leadership, how would you advise a friend to lead?
19. Describe three challenges that a transformational leader must face.
20. Compare and contrast the coaching leader and the entrepreneurial leader.
21. Describe the leadership style indicated by the shaded portion of Figure 15.9.

Action Summary Answer Key

1. **a.** c, p. 350
   b. e, p. 350
2. **a.** F, p. 350
   b. c, p. 350

3. **a.** c, p. 351
   b. e, p. 352
4. **a.** e, pp. 353–354
   b. b, p. 359
   c. T, pp. 356–357

5. **a.** e, p. 361
   b. a, pp. 361–363
   c. F, p. 363
6. **a.** d, pp. 363–364
   b. F, p. 365

7. **a.** F, p. 368
   b. e, pp. 368–369
   c. F, pp. 369–370
   d. F, p. 371

Case Study

Come Fly the Turbulent Skies

In the highly competitive airline industry, airline company after airline company has crashed owing to lack of controls on costs or has been swallowed up by competitors. Delta Airlines, based in Atlanta, Georgia, is certainly not immune to all the ill winds blowing through the industry but, so far, CEO Ron Allen seems to have kept the company on course.

Traditionally, Delta has promoted from within the company, and Allen is no exception. He entered Delta through the human resources department, became its president in 1982, and took on the mantle of CEO in 1987. As an insider, Allen personally knows the value of making plans and sticking to them, no matter how it might hurt employees in the short run. His loyalty, in short, is to the company shareholder and to the customer. At the same time, however, although Delta is ranked at the head of all domestic airlines, complaints about its customer service have risen sharply. Why? In part, because of cutbacks in frequent-flier benefits, use of fewer flight attendants, and the elimination of meals on the shortest flights.

Originally, Allen depended on such tried measures to ease Delta's financial problems. In 1993, however, he and his management team met daily for a period of six months to develop a long-range plan for the company. Throughout this period, they sought the opinions of middle management and front-line employees on Delta's status. By the end of the half-year planning session, it was obvious that layoffs would have to be instituted to get the company back on a balanced footing. For example, Delta had acquired Western Airlines in 1987, and its employee ranks had risen to 73,533 in 1993. Allen's most difficult leadership decision was to lay off 3,000 employees in a company that had once boasted that it did not know the meaning of the word "layoff." Thousands of other employees left after being offered early-retirement and other company-proposed plans. Since April 1994, Delta has cut its workforce by more than 10,000. As of January 1996, the number of employees was down to 59,000.

At the admitted expense of employee morale and goodwill, Allen pledged to continue cutting operating costs—eliminating the purchase of new aircraft, laying off pilots, and instituting a 5 percent pay reduction across the board. Such cuts led to outsourcing some jobs and reducing some employees to part-time status. Beset by financial woes and boasting the fewest unionized employees in the airline industry, Delta then became a prime target for union organizers. Even though full-time employees at Delta ranked among the highest paid in the industry, their wages and benefits had not risen since 1989.

In effect, employees had taken a 20 percent cut in pay to hold their jobs and keep the company flying.

Meanwhile, Allen's cost cuts worked. In early 1996, he restored the 5 percent pay cut, gave nonunion employees a bonus amounting to 5 percent of their base pay, and brought back 665 customer-service employees who had been laid off. Allen is also reaching out to disaffected employees in other ways. To give them a voice in management, for example, he has created a flight attendants' group. To provide a sense of stability, he has announced that no full-time nonpilot employees will be subject to further layoffs. Many employees welcome Allen's changes and appreciate being given more responsibility—a natural result of running the company with fewer employees.

Of course, some changes are easier to make than others. If Delta is to experience less turbulent flying in the future, it must reach Allen's goal of improving employee morale and customer service. By the end of 1995, Delta had achieved annual cost savings of $1.6 billion—well on its way to its announced $2 billion per year by the end of 1997. It has reevaluated some of its plans and is working to improve its poor on-time record. To upgrade customer service, Delta has built a new $30 million operations center.

Allen continues to have his critics, both in the ranks and outside the firm. He has been taken to task, for instance, for paying large bonuses (totaling $1.3 million) to his executives while Delta is still going through tough times. He counters that the management team he has put together is crucial to the company's long-term success and could easily make more money at another airline.

The competitive atmosphere of the airline industry demands strong leadership. Of the more than 100 airlines that were started after the industry was deregulated in 1978, very few remain flying today. ValuJet, a powerful Delta competitor in the Southeast, is an exception. At first, Allen tried to match ValuJet's discount prices and services, but these moves resulted in a loss of Delta's business customers. So Delta stopped trying to play ValuJet's game—and actually increased sales on ValuJet routes. Allen has learned a valuable lesson in leadership: When you're out in front, lead.

Questions:

1. What situation led to the hard choices that Ron Allen had to make at Delta Airlines? Do these decisions highlight his leadership abilities? Explain.

2. Cite specific points to illustrate Allen's position on the boss-centered and subordinate-centered leadership scale. Is this balance effective in all decision-making situations? Explain.

3. Does Allen fall into one or more of the new categories of leadership: transformational, substitute, superleadership, and/or entrepreneurial? Explain.

Skills Exercise

Is there more than one way to run an airline? In order to create a comparison chart, work with other members of the class to research the leaders of several airline companies. Basing your evaluation on leadership style, effectiveness, and the bottom line, which leaders seem most effective? Why?

 The Internet learning materials that accompany this chapter can be found at **http://www.profcerto.com**
Additional information can be found on the inside front and back covers of this text.

MOTIVATION

STUDENT LEARNING OBJECTIVES

From studying this chapter, I will attempt to acquire:

1. A basic understanding of human motivation.
2. Insights about various human needs.
3. An appreciation for the importance of motivating organization members.
4. An understanding of various motivation strategies.

CHAPTER OUTLINE

American Greetings Motivates through Lateral Moves

With few promotions to give out, companies are trying to motivate employees by shifting them sideways instead of up.

Consider American Greetings Corporation, the Cleveland greeting card and licensing concern. The company recently redesigned about 400 jobs in its creative division and asked workers and managers to reapply. Everyone was guaranteed a position, and no one took a pay cut.

Since the restructuring was completed, employees develop products in teams instead of assembly-line fashion. And they are free to transfer back and forth among teams that make different products, instead of working on just one product line, as they did in the past.

As a result, people who have spent careers specializing in Christmas and Easter cards can now sign up to work on birthday ribbons, humorous mugs, and Valentine's Day gift bags all in the same year. And artists whose only job was choosing dyes now try their hands at illustration and lettering.

"It unleashes a lot of their creative potential," says Dennis Chupa, a division vice president, who engineered the shakeup. Added an employee: "A lot of people think it's a good time to make a change or work for someone different."

The main purpose of the restructuring was to cut production time by as much as half for some products, especially greeting cards that play on fleeting fads. But at the same time, American Greetings addressed an increasingly common problem: how to light fires under workers at a time when few promotions or pay raises are on the horizon.

Unless companies act now, workers whose eyes have glazed over during the recession will leave "so damn fast when the economy turns up that they're going to leave burn marks on the carpet," says Marilyn Moats Kennedy, editor of the newsletter *Kennedy's Career Strategist*. Lateral moves that require new skills may be companies' "only hope" for retaining talent.

Traditionally, lateral moves have smacked of demotion because they derailed what seemed like inevitable promotions. The moves make more sense now that more hands are grabbing for fewer rungs on the corporate ladder. "If the channel above you is clogged, moving sideways can get you out of the traffic jam," says Robert Kelley, a business professor at Carnegie-Mellon University who has written about nontraditional career paths.

The greeting card industry utilizes the diverse talents of many creative individuals. In order to cut production time and to keep employees motivated and creative, American Greetings Corporation recently restructured its operation to allow employees to work in teams and to transfer back and forth between different kinds of products.

Dennis Chupa, the division vice president at American Greetings quoted in the introductory case, has engineered a reorganization of company workers. This reorganization is partially aimed at motivating employees at a time when few company promotions or pay raises are on the horizon. This chapter discusses why managers such as Chupa should focus on motivating workers and how this might be accomplished. It addresses two major topics:

 ↘ 1. The motivation process.
 ↘ 2. Motivating organization members.

The Motivation Process

To be successful in working with subordinates, managers need to acquire a thorough understanding of the motivation process. To this end, the definition of motivation, various motivation models, and theories of people's needs are the main topics of discussion in this section of the chapter.

Defining *Motivation*

Motivation is the inner state that causes an individual to behave in a way that ensures the accomplishment of some goal.[1] In other words, motivation explains why people act as they do. The better a manager understands organization members' behavior, the more able that manager will be to influence subordinates' behavior to make it more consistent with the accomplishment of organizational objectives. In essence, since productivity is a result of the behavior of organization members, motivating organization members is the key to reaching organizational goals.[2]

Several different theories about motivation have been proposed over the years. Most of these theories can be categorized into two basic types: process theories and content theories. **Process theories of motivation** are explanations of motivation that emphasize how individuals are motivated. They focus, essentially, on the steps that occur when an individual is motivated. **Content theories of motivation** are explanations of motivation that emphasize people's internal characteristics. They focus on the need to understand what needs people have and how these needs can be satisfied. The following sections discuss important process and content theories of motivation and establish a relationship between them that should prove useful to managers in motivating organization members.

Process Theories of Motivation

There are four important theories that describe how motivation occurs:

 ↘ 1. The needs-goal theory.
 ↘ 2. The Vroom expectancy theory.
 ↘ 3. The equity theory.
 ↘ 4. The Porter-Lawler theory.

These theories build on one another to furnish a description of the motivation process that begins at a relatively simple and easily understood level and culminates at a somewhat more intricate and realistic level.

The Needs-Goal Theory of Motivation   The **needs-goal theory** of motivation, diagrammed in Figure 16.1, is the most fundamental of the motivation theories discussed in this chapter. As the figure indicates, motivation begins with an individual feeling a need. This need is then transformed into behavior directed at supporting, or

---

Motivation is the inner state that causes an individual to behave in a way that ensures the accomplishment of some goal.

Process theories of motivation are explanations of motivation that emphasize how individuals are motivated.

Content theories of motivation are explanations of motivation that emphasize people's internal characteristics.

The **needs-goal theory** is a motivation model that hypothesizes that felt needs cause human behavior.

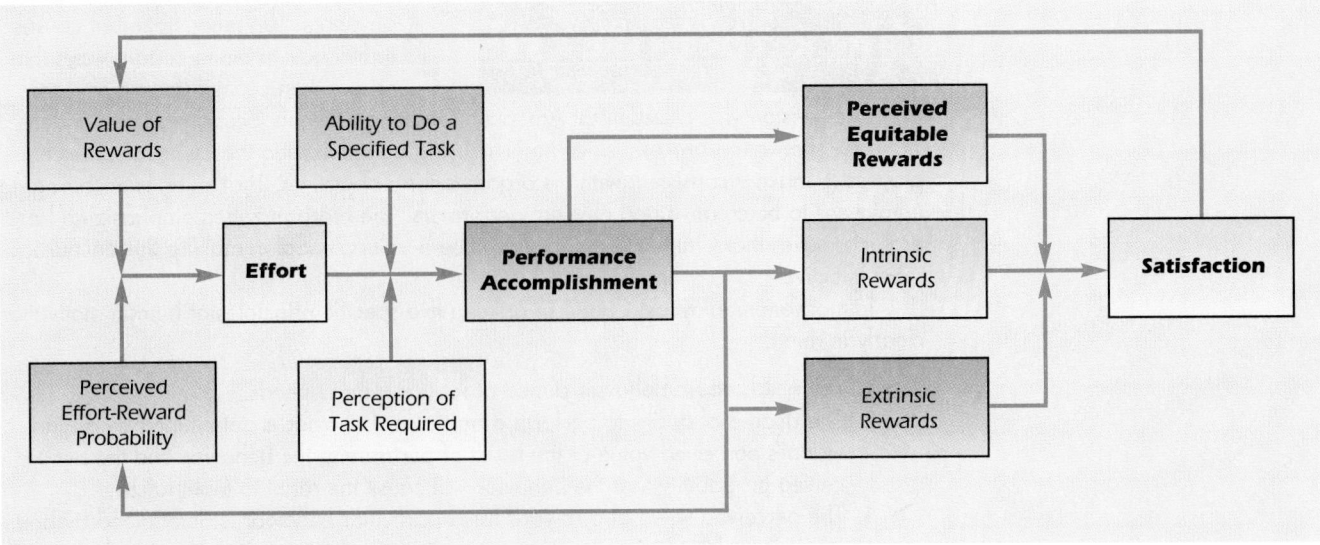

Figure 16.3   The Porter-Lawler theory of motivation

intrinsic reward, however, the manager also receives an extrinsic reward in the form of the overall salary the manager is paid.

2. The extent to which an individual effectively accomplishes a task is determined primarily by two variables: the individual's perception of what is required to perform the task and the individual's ability to perform the task. Naturally, effectiveness at accomplishing a task increases as the perception of what is required to perform the task becomes more accurate and ability to perform the task increases.

3. The perceived fairness of rewards influences the amount of satisfaction produced by those rewards. In general, the more equitable an individual perceives the rewards to be, the greater the satisfaction that individual will experience as a result of receiving them.

The preceding discussion of the Porter-Lawler theory of motivation indicates that rewards are very important in motivating human behavior. The following CUT-TING EDGE feature describes a very novel reward now being offered to employees for outstanding service.

BLIMP RIDES USED AS REWARDS FOR OUTSTANDING PERFORMANCE

CUTTING EDGE

James Thiele, who founded the American Blimp Corporation in 1987, started the company to provide clients with advertising space. Despite all the hype about the high-tech, interactive future of advertising, the blimp—one of advertising's oldest media—seems to be enjoying a revival. The American Blimp Corporation now has ten blimps wafting around the country displaying advertising and plans to build three new blimps a year over the next few years.

Blimps are also being used today for a quite different purpose. Companies are offering blimp rides to employees as rewards for outstanding performance, to customers to influence their buying decisions, and to suppliers as rewards for good service. The gondola, or passenger space, of a blimp can hold up to 13 people, making the blimp a perfect vehicle for transporting small groups.≈

BACK TO THE CASE

Motivation is an inner state that causes individuals to act in certain ways that ensure the accomplishment of some goal. As division vice president at American Greetings, Dennis Chupa seems to understand the motivation process, since he is focusing on influencing the behavior of his employees to make it consistent with his organization's objectives. That is, he is encouraging employees to be creative and efficient performers. The reorganization emphasizing lateral job moves that Chupa designed should be a valuable tool in making this encouragement effective.

To motivate employees, Chupa must keep five specific principles of human motivation clearly in mind:

1. Felt needs cause behavior aimed at reducing those needs.
2. The degree of desire to perform a particular behavior is determined by an individual's perceived value of the result of performing the behavior and the perceived probability that the behavior will cause the result to materialize.
3. The perceived value of a reward for a particular behavior is determined by both intrinsic and extrinsic rewards that result in need satisfaction when the behavior is accomplished.
4. Individuals can effectively accomplish a task only if they understand what the task requires and have the ability to perform it.
5. The perceived fairness of a reward influences the degree of satisfaction generated when the reward is received.

Content Theories of Motivation: Human Needs

The motivation theories discussed thus far imply that an understanding of motivation is based on an understanding of human needs. There is some evidence that most people have strong needs for self-respect, respect from others, promotion, and psychological growth.[7] Although identifying all human needs is impossible, several theories have been developed to help managers better understand these needs:

1. Maslow's hierarchy of needs.
2. Alderfer's ERG theory.
3. Argyris' maturity-immaturity continuum.
4. McClelland's acquired needs theory.

Maslow's Hierarchy of Needs   Perhaps the most widely accepted description of human needs is the hierarchy-of-needs concept developed by Abraham Maslow.[8] Maslow states that human beings possess the <u>five</u> basic needs described below, and theorizes that these five basic needs can be arranged in a hierarchy of importance—the order in which individuals generally strive to satisfy them. The needs and their relative positions in the hierarchy of importance are shown in Figure 16.4.

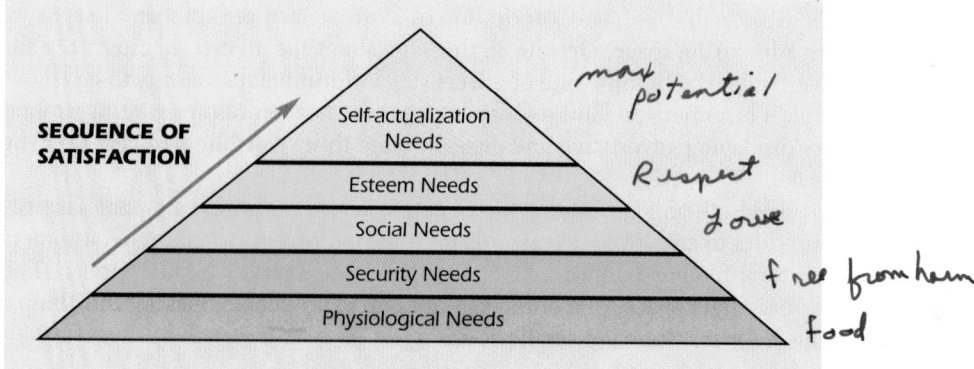

Figure 16.4   Maslow's hierarchy of needs

*In 1995, U.S. sugar farmers orga-
nized to protest the proposed end to
a federal subsidy program that
guaranteed them prices much
higher than the worldwide market
price. While critics of the subsidy
labeled it "corporate welfare,"
sugar producers argued that European producers would dump their
own subsidized sugar on the U.S.
market. They were responding,
then, to protect what they perceived
as a **security need**—in this case, a
buffer against a serious economic
challenge.*

- **Physiological needs** relate to the normal functioning of the body. They include the needs for water, food, rest, sex, and air. Until these needs are met, a
  significant portion of an individual's behavior will be aimed at satisfying them.
  Once the needs are satisfied, however, behavior is aimed at satisfying the needs
  on the next level of Maslow's hierarchy.
- **Security, or safety, needs** relate to the individual's desire to be free from harm,
  including both bodily and economic disaster.

  Traditionally, management has best helped employees satisfy their physiological and security needs through adequate wages or salaries, which employees use to purchase such things as food and housing.
- **Social needs** include the desire for love, companionship, and friendship.
  These needs reflect a person's desire to be accepted by others. As they are satisfied, behavior shifts to satisfying esteem needs.
- **Esteem needs** are concerned with the desire for respect. They are generally
  divided into two categories: self-respect and respect from others. Once esteem
  needs are satisfied, the individual moves to the pinnacle of the hierarchy and
  emphasizes satisfying self-actualization needs.
- **Self-actualization needs** refer to the desire to maximize whatever potential an
  individual possesses. For example, in the nonprofit public setting of a high
  school, a principal who seeks to satisfy self-actualization needs would strive to
  become the best principal possible. Self-actualization needs occupy the highest
  level of Maslow's hierarchy.

The traditional concerns about Maslow's hierarchy are that it has no research
base, that it may not accurately pinpoint basic human needs, and that it is questionable whether human needs can be neatly arranged in such a hierarchy. Nevertheless,
Maslow's hierarchy is probably the most popular conceptualization of human needs to
date, and it continues to be positively discussed in management literature.[9] Still, the
concerns expressed about it should remind managers to look upon Maslow's hierarchy
more as a subjective statement than an objective description of human needs.

Physiological needs are Maslow's
first set of human needs—for the
normal functioning of the body, including the desires for water, food,
rest, sex, and air.

Security, or safety, needs are
Maslow's second set of human
needs—reflecting the human desire
to keep free from physical harm.

Social needs are Maslow's third set
of human needs—reflecting the human desire to belong, including
longings for friendship, companionship, and love.

Esteem needs are Maslow's fourth
set of human needs—including the
desires for self-respect and respect
from others.

Self-actualization needs are
Maslow's fifth, and final, set of human needs—reflecting the human
desire to maximize personal potential.

MASLOW'S HIERARCHY AND JAPANESE, CHINESE, AND U.S. WORKERS

GLOBAL SPOTLIGHT

Research shows that people from different cultures
normally place quite different values on the various
human needs in Maslow's hierarchy. Companies like Motorola and Digital Equipment
International understand the human needs of workers from different cultures.

For an organization to function effectively, its managers must motivate subordinates to take consistent action toward company goals. In global companies like Digital and Motorola, managers are challenged to understand how motivation and the importance of various human needs change from country to country. For example, consider how Maslow's hierarchy of needs might be applied to workers in Japan, China, and the United States. Research indicates that when attempting to motivate Chinese workers, managers should focus on their esteem and social needs. On the other hand, when attempting to motivate Japanese workers, managers should focus more on safety, social, esteem, and self-actualization needs. When attempting to motivate U.S. workers, managers should emphasize their esteem and self-actualization needs.≈

Alderfer's ERG Theory

Alderfer's ERG Theory   Clayton Alderfer responded to some of the criticisms of Maslow's work by conducting his own study of human needs.[10] He identified three basic categories of needs:

1. Existence needs—the need for physical well-being.
2. Relatedness needs—the need for satisfying interpersonal relationships.
3. Growth needs—the need for continuing personal growth and development.

The first letters of these needs form the acronym ERG, by which the theory is now known.

Alderfer's ERG theory is an explanation of human needs that divides them into three basic types: existence needs, relatedness needs, and growth needs.

    Alderfer's ERG theory is similar to Maslow's theory except in three major respects. First, Alderfer identified only three orders of human needs, compared to Maslow's five orders. Second, in contrast to Maslow, Alderfer found that people sometimes activate their higher-level needs before they have completely satisfied all of their lower-level needs. Third, Alderfer concluded that movement in his hierarchy of human needs is not always upward. For instance—and this is reflected in his frustration-regression principle—he found that a worker frustrated by his failure to satisfy an upper-level need might regress by trying to fulfill an already satisfied lower-level need.

    Alderfer's work, in conjunction with Maslow's, has implications for management. Employees frustrated by work that fails to provide opportunities for growth or development on the job might concentrate their energy on trying to make more money, thus regressing to a lower level of needs. To counteract such regression, management might use job enrichment strategies designed to help people meet their higher-order needs.

Argyris' Maturity-Immaturity Continuum

Argyris' maturity-immaturity continuum is a concept that furnishes insights into human needs by focusing on an individual's natural progress from immaturity to maturity.

Argyris' Maturity-Immaturity Continuum   **Argyris' maturity-immaturity continuum** also furnishes insights into human needs.[11] This continuum concept focuses on the personal and natural development of people to explain human needs. According to Argyris, as people naturally progress from immaturity to maturity, they move:

1. From a state of passivity as an infant to a state of increasing activity as an adult.
2. From a state of dependence on others as an infant to a state of relative independence as an adult.
3. From being capable of behaving only in a few ways as an infant to being capable of behaving in many different ways as an adult.
4. From having erratic, casual, shallow, and quickly dropped interests as an infant to having deeper, more lasting interests as an adult.
5. From having a short time perspective as an infant to having a much longer time perspective as an adult.
6. From being in a subordinate position as an infant to aspiring to occupy an equal or superordinate position as an adult.
7. From a lack of self-awareness as an infant to awareness and control over self as an adult.

According to Argyris' continuum, then, as individuals mature, they have increasing needs for more activity, enjoy a state of relative independence, behave in many different ways, have deeper and more lasting interests, are capable of considering a relatively long time perspective, occupy an equal position vis-à-vis other mature individuals, and have more awareness of themselves and control over their own destiny. Note that, unlike Maslow's needs, Argyris' needs are not arranged in a hierarchy. Like Maslow's hierarchy, however, Argyris' continuum is a primarily subjective explanation of human needs.

McClelland's Acquired Needs Theory

Another theory about human needs, called **McClelland's acquired needs theory,** focuses on the needs that people acquire through their life experiences. This theory, formulated by David C. McClelland in the 1960s, emphasizes three of the many needs human beings develop in their lifetimes:

1. The need for achievement *(nAch)*—the desire to do something better or more efficiently than it has ever been done before.
2. The need for power *(nPower)*—the desire to control, influence, or be responsible for others.
3. The need for affiliation *(nAff)*—the desire to maintain close, friendly personal relationships.

The individual's early life experiences determine which of these needs will be highly developed and therefore dominate the personality.

McClelland's studies of these three acquired human needs have significant implications for management.

Need to Achieve.   McClelland claims that in some businesspeople the need to achieve is so strong that it is more motivating than the quest for profits. To maximize their satisfaction, individuals with high achievement needs set goals for themselves that are challenging, yet achievable. Although such people are willing to assume risk, they assess it very carefully because they do not want to fail. Therefore, they will avoid tasks that involve too much risk. People with a low need for achievement, on the other hand, generally avoid challenges, responsibilities, and risk.

Need for Power.   People with a high need for power are greatly motivated to influence others and to assume responsibility for subordinates' behavior. They are likely to seek advancement and to take on increasingly responsible work activities to earn that advancement. Power-oriented managers are comfortable in competitive situations and enjoy their decision-making role.

Need for Affiliation.   Managers with a high need for affiliation have a cooperative, team-centered managerial style. They prefer to influence subordinates to complete tasks through team efforts. The danger is that managers with a high need for affiliation can lose their effectiveness if their need for social approval and friendship interferes with their willingness to make managerial decisions.[12]

McClelland's acquired needs theory is an explanation of human needs that focuses on the desires for achievement, power, and affiliation that people develop as a result of their life experiences.

BACK TO THE CASE   Chupa undoubtedly understands the basic motivation concept that felt needs cause behavior. Before he can have a maximum effect on motivating organization members, however, he must also meet the more complex challenge of thoroughly acquainting himself with the various individual human needs of his employees.

According to Maslow, people generally possess physiological, security, social, esteem, and self-actualization needs arranged in a hierarchy of importance. Argyris suggests that as people mature, they have increasing needs for activity, independence, flexi-

bility, deeper interests, analyses of longer time perspectives, a position of equality with other mature individuals, and control over personal destiny. McClelland believes that the need for achievement—the desire to do something better or more efficiently than it has ever been done before—is a strong human need.

As part of his reorganization efforts, Chupa guaranteed every worker a position with no pay cut. In so doing, he sought to satisfy employees' physiological and safety needs. Other features of Chupa's reorganization, like management development programs and a "best card verse of the month" program, could further motivate his employees by satisfying other needs they might have.

MOTIVATING ORGANIZATION MEMBERS

People are motivated to perform behavior to satisfy their personal needs. Therefore, from a managerial viewpoint, motivation is the process of furnishing organization members with the opportunity to satisfy their needs by performing productive behavior within the organization. In reality, managers do not motivate people. Rather, they create environments in which organization members motivate themselves.[13]

people motivate themselves

As discussed in Chapter 14, motivation is one of the four primary interrelated activities of the influencing function performed by managers to guide the behavior of organization members toward the attainment of organizational objectives. The following sections discuss the importance of motivating organization members and present some strategies for doing so.

The Importance of Motivating Organization Members

Figure 16.5 makes the point that unsatisfied needs can lead organization members to perform either appropriate or inappropriate behavior. Successful managers minimize inappropriate behavior and maximize appropriate behavior among subordinates, thus raising the probability that productivity will increase and lowering the probability that it will decrease.

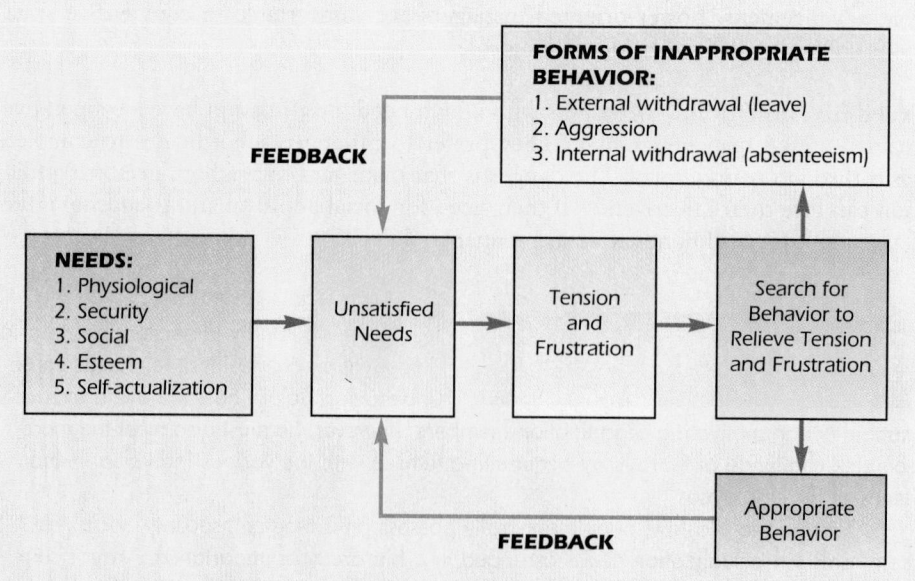

Figure 16.5 Unsatisfied needs of organization members resulting in either appropriate or inappropriate behavior

Strategies for Motivating Organization Members

Managers have various strategies at their disposal for motivating organization members. Each strategy is aimed at satisfying subordinates' needs (consistent with the descriptions of human needs in Maslow's hierarchy, Alderfer's ERG theory, Argyris' maturity-immaturity continuum, and McClelland's acquired needs theory) through appropriate organizational behavior. These managerial motivation strategies are as follows:

— 1. Managerial communication
— 2. Theory X–Theory Y
— 3. Job design
— 4. Behavior modification
— 5. Likert's management systems
6. Monetary incentives
7. Nonmonetary incentives

The strategies are discussed in the sections that follow.

Throughout the discussion, it is important to remember that no single strategy will always be more effective for a manager than any other. In fact, most managers find that some combination of these strategies is most effective in the organization setting.

Managerial Communication   Perhaps the most basic motivation strategy for managers is simply to communicate well with organization members. Effective manager-subordinate communication can satisfy such basic human needs as recognition, a sense of belonging, and security. For example, such a simple managerial action as attempting to become better acquainted with subordinates can contribute substantially to the satisfaction of each of these three needs. To take another example, a message praising a subordinate for a job well done can help satisfy the subordinate's recognition and security needs.

As a general rule, managers should strive to communicate often with other organization members, not only because communication is the primary means of conducting organizational activities, but also because it is a basic tool for satisfying the human needs of organization members.

Theory X–Theory Y   Another motivation strategy involves managers' assumptions about human nature. Douglas McGregor identified two sets of assumptions: **Theory X** involves negative assumptions about people that McGregor believes managers often use as the basis for dealing with their subordinates (for example, the average person has an inherent dislike of work and will avoid it whenever he or she can). **Theory Y** represents positive assumptions about people that McGregor believes

Theory X is a set of essentially negative assumptions about human nature.

Theory Y is a set of essentially positive assumptions about human nature.

For Horst Stormer, director of physical research at AT&T Bell Laboratories, lunch is important to the communication process: He feels that the informal atmosphere, in which managers and employees can bounce ideas off one another without the usual pressure, contributes to teamwork and creativity. Although he does not claim to know precisely what "creativity" is, he is sure that it emerges when people communicate: "Nobody," he admits, "manages creativity. People are what gets managed."

managers should strive to use (for example, people will exercise self-direction and self-control in the service of objectives to which they are committed).[14]

McGregor implies that managers who use Theory X assumptions are "bad" and that those who use Theory Y assumptions are "good." Reddin, however, argues that production might be increased by using *either* Theory X or Theory Y assumptions, depending on the situation the manager faces: "Is there not a strong argument for the position that any theory may have desirable outcomes if appropriately used?" The difficulty is that McGregor had considered only the ineffective application of Theory X and the effective application of Theory Y. Reddin proposes a **Theory Z**—an effectiveness dimension that implies that managers who use either Theory X or Theory Y assumptions when dealing with people can be successful, depending on their situation.

The basic rationale for using Theory Y rather than Theory X in most situations is that managerial activities that reflect Theory Y assumptions generally are more successful in satisfying the human needs of most organization members than are managerial activities that reflect Theory X assumptions. Therefore, activities based on Theory Y assumptions are more apt to motivate organization members than are activities based on Theory X assumptions.

Theory Z is the effectiveness dimension that implies that managers who use either Theory X or Theory Y assumptions when dealing with people can be successful, depending on their situation.

BACK TO THE CASE

Once a manager such as Chupa understands that felt needs cause behavior and is aware of people's different types of needs, he is ready to apply this information to motivating his workforce. From Chupa's viewpoint, motivating employees means furnishing them with the opportunity to satisfy their human needs by performing their jobs. This is a very important notion because successful motivation tends to increase employee productivity. If Chupa does not give his employees the opportunity to satisfy their human needs on the job, they will probably develop low morale. Common signs of low morale in a company are workers who seldom initiate new ideas, go out of their way to avoid tough situations, and strongly resist innovation.

One strategy that the text recommends Chupa follow to further motivate American Greetings workers is to take the time to communicate with his employees. Effective manager-employee communication satisfies employee needs for recognition, belonging, and security. Another strategy he could adopt is based on McGregor's Theory X–Theory Y concept. In following this strategy, Chupa would assume that work is as natural as play; that employees can direct themselves to accomplish organizational goals; that the granting of rewards encourages the achievement of American Greetings objectives; that employees seek and accept responsibility; and that most employees are creative, ingenious, and imaginative. If Chupa manages by such assumptions, it should lead to the satisfaction of many of his employees' needs as defined by Maslow, Argyris, and McClelland.

Job Design   A third strategy managers can use to motivate organization members involves the design of jobs that organization members perform. The following two sections discuss earlier and more recent job design strategies.

Earlier Job Design Strategies.   A movement has long existed in American business to make jobs simpler and more specialized in order to increase worker productivity. The idea behind this movement is to make workers more productive by enabling them to be more efficient. Perhaps the best example of a job design inspired by this movement is the automobile assembly line. The negative result of work simplification and specialization, however, is job boredom. As jobs become simpler and more specialized, they typically become more boring and less satisfying to workers, and, consequently, productivity suffers.

Job Rotation.   The first major attempt to overcome job boredom was **job rotation**—moving workers from job to job rather than requiring them to perform only

Job rotation is the process of moving workers from one job to another rather than requiring them to perform only one simple and specialized job over the long term.

one simple and specialized job over the long term. For example, a gardener would do more than just mow lawns; he might also trim bushes, rake grass, and sweep sidewalks.

Although job rotation programs have been known to increase organizational profitability, most of them are ineffective as motivation strategies because, over time, people become bored with all the jobs they are rotated into.[15] Job rotation programs, however, are often effective for achieving other organizational objectives, such as training, because they give individuals an overview of how the various units of the organization function.

Job Enlargement.   Another strategy developed to overcome the boredom of doing very simple and specialized jobs is **job enlargement,** or increasing the number of operations an individual performs in order to enhance the individual's satisfaction in work. According to the job enlargement concept, the gardener's job would become more satisfying as such activities as trimming bushes, raking grass, and sweeping sidewalks were added to his initial activity of mowing grass. Some research supports the contention that job enlargement does make jobs more satisfying, and some does not.[16] Still, job enlargement programs have generally proved more successful at increasing job satisfaction than have job rotation programs.

A number of other job design strategies have evolved since the development of job rotation and job enlargement programs. Two of these more recent strategies are job enrichment and flextime.

Job Enrichment.   Frederick Herzberg has concluded from his research that the degrees of satisfaction and dissatisfaction organization members feel as a result of performing a job are two different variables determined by two different sets of items.[17] The items that influence the degree of job dissatisfaction are called **hygiene,** or **maintenance, factors,** while those that influence the degree of job satisfaction are called **motivating factors,** or **motivators.** Hygiene factors relate to the work environment, and motivating factors to the work itself. The items that make up Herzberg's hygiene and motivating factors are presented in Table 16.1.

Herzberg believes that when the hygiene factors of a particular job situation are undesirable, organization members will become dissatisfied. Making these factors more desirable—for example, by increasing salary—will rarely motivate people to do a better job, but it will keep them from becoming dissatisfied. In contrast, when the motivating factors of a particular job situation are high, employees usually are motivated to do a better job. In general, people tend to be more motivated and productive as more motivators are built into their job situation.

The process of incorporating motivators into a job situation is called **job enrichment.** Early reports indicated that companies such as Texas Instruments and Volvo had notable success in motivating organization members through job enrichment pro-

Job enlargement is the process of increasing the number of operations an individual performs in a job.

Hygiene, or **maintenance, factors** are items that influence the degree of job dissatisfaction.

Motivating factors, or **motivators,** are items that influence the degree of job satisfaction.

Job enrichment is the process of incorporating motivators into a job situation.

Table 16.1

Herzberg's Hygiene Factors and Motivators

DISSATISFACTION: HYGIENE OR MAINTENANCE FACTORS	SATISFACTION: MOTIVATING FACTORS
1. Company policy and administration	1. Opportunity for achievement
2. Supervision	2. Opportunity for recognition
3. Relationship with supervisor	3. Work itself
4. Relationship with peers	4. Responsibility
5. Working conditions	5. Advancement
6. Salary	6. Personal growth
7. Relationship with subordinates	

grams. More recent reports, though they continue to support the value of job enrichment, indicate that for a job enrichment program to be successful, it must be carefully designed and administered.[18]

Job Enrichment and Productivity.   Herzberg's overall conclusions are that the most productive organization members are those involved in work situations that have both desirable hygiene and motivating factors. The needs in Maslow's hierarchy of needs that desirable hygiene factors and motivating factors generally satisfy are shown in Figure 16.6. Esteem needs can be satisfied by both types of factors. An example of esteem needs satisfied by a hygiene factor is a private parking space—a status symbol and a working condition evidencing the employee's importance to the organization. An example of esteem needs satisfied by a motivating factor is an award given for outstanding performance—a public recognition of a job well done that displays the employee's value to the organization.

QUALITY SPOTLIGHT

APPLE COMPUTER'S JOB ENRICHMENT EXCELS

Apple Computer has attempted to provide both hygiene factors and motivating factors for its employees because company executives firmly believe that highly motivated, satisfied employees produce high-quality products. Apple's job enrichment program serves as a good example of how management can take steps to enrich a work environment.

Creating the right work environment—pleasant but challenging—is the key to encouraging people to be productive at Apple. For example, management has established award systems for employees that incorporate both recognition for jobs well done and opportunities for growth and advancement. In addition, Apple management has made hygiene factors acceptable to employees and takes pride in providing sufficiently generous salaries to its valued workers.

To take one example of the recognition programs at Apple, the company announces new products and projects through the employees who developed them instead of through a public relations office. This announcement process recognizes hardworking employees and makes them feel that they are making valuable contributions to the company. At Apple, rewards and recognition are an ongoing part of company life that helps management ensure the quality of its products, such as the Macintosh and Apple computers.≈

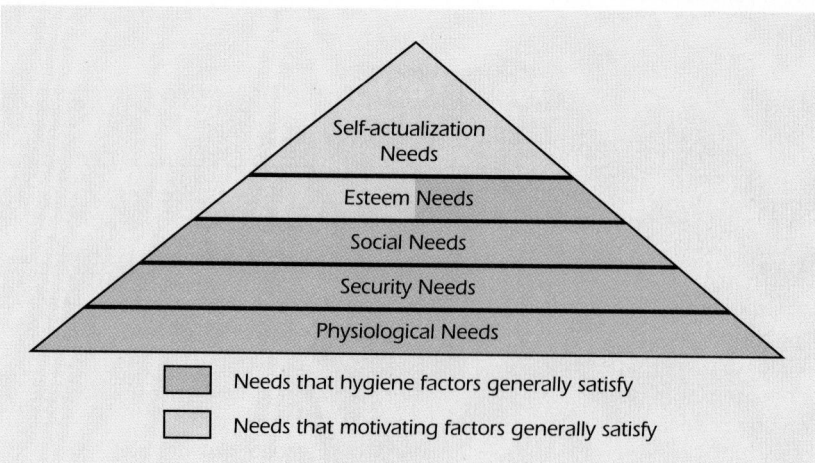

Figure 16.6   Needs in Maslow's hierarchy of needs that desirable hygiene and motivating factors generally satisfy

one line short

Flextime.   Another more recent job design strategy for motivating organization members is based on a concept called *flextime*. Perhaps the most common traditional characteristic of work in the United States is that jobs are performed within a fixed eight-hour workday. Recently, however, this tradition has been challenged. Faced with motivation problems and excessive absenteeism, many managers have turned to scheduling innovations as a possible solution.[19]

The main purpose of these scheduling innovations is not to reduce the total number of work hours, but rather to give workers greater flexibility in scheduling the hours during which they perform their jobs. The main thrust of **flextime,** or flexible working hours programs, is that it allows workers to complete their jobs within a workweek of a normal number of hours that they arrange themselves.[20] The choices of starting and finishing times can be as flexible as the organizational situation allows. To ensure that flexibility does not become counterproductive within the organization, however, many flextime programs stipulate a core period during which all employees must be on the job.

Advantages of Flextime.   Various kinds of organizational studies have indicated that flextime programs have some positive organizational effects. Douglas Fleuter, for example, has reported that flextime contributes to greater job satisfaction, which typically results in greater productivity. Other researchers have concluded that flextime programs can result in higher motivation levels of workers. Because organization members generally consider flextime programs desirable, organizations that have such programs can usually better compete with other organizations in recruiting qualified new employees. (A listing of the advantages and disadvantages of flextime programs appears in Table 16.2.) Although many well-known companies, such as Scott Paper, Sun Oil, and Samsonite, have adopted flextime programs,[21] more research is needed before flextime's true worth can be conclusively assessed.

Flextime is a program that allows workers to complete their jobs within a workweek of a normal number of hours that they schedule themselves.

Table 16.2

Advantages and Disadvantages of Using Flextime Programs

ADVANTAGES	DISADVANTAGES
Improved employee attitude and morale.	Lack of supervision during some hours of work.
Accommodation of working parents.	Key people unavailable at certain times.
Decreased tardiness.	Understaffing at times.
Fewer commuting problems—workers can avoid congested streets and highways.	Problem of accommodating employees whose output is the input for other employees.
Accommodation of those who wish to arrive at work before normal workday interruptions begin.	Employee abuse of flextime program.
Increased production.	Difficulty in planning work schedules.
Facilitation of employees scheduling of medical, dental, and other types of appointments.	Problem of keeping track of hours worked or accumulated.
Accommodation of leisure-time activities of employees.	Inability to schedule meetings at convenient times.
Decreased absenteeism.	Inability to coordinate projects.
Decreased turnover.	

BACK TO THE CASE Chupa can use two major job design strategies to motivate his employees at American Greetings. Through job enrichment, he can incorporate such motivating factors as opportunities for achievement, recognition, and personal growth into jobs. Chupa's program of allowing workers to transfer back and forth among work teams and to work on more than one product is a type of job enrichment because it gives employees opportunities for personal growth. However, for maximum success, hygiene factors at American Greetings—company policy and administration, supervision, salary, and working conditions, for example—must also be perceived as desirable by employees.

Another major job design strategy that Chupa can use to motivate his employees is flextime. With flextime, workers would have some freedom to schedule the beginning and ending of their workdays. Of course, this freedom would have to be limited by such organizational factors as seasonal demand and peak selling seasons.

SKINNER

Behavior modification is a program that focuses on managing human activity by controlling the consequences of performing that activity.

Behavior Modification

A fourth strategy that managers can use to motivate organization members is based on a concept known as behavior modification. As stated by B. F. Skinner, the Harvard psychologist considered by many to be the "father of behavioral psychology," **behavior modification** focuses on encouraging appropriate behavior in controlling the consequences of that behavior.[22] According to the law of effect, behavior that is rewarded tends to be repeated, while that which is punished tends to be eliminated.

Although behavior modification programs typically involve the administration of both rewards and punishments, it is rewards that are generally emphasized because they are more effective than punishments in influencing behavior. Obviously, the main theme of behavior modification is not new.

REWARDS

Positive reinforcement is a reward that consists of a desirable consequence of behavior.

Negative reinforcement is a reward that consists of the elimination of an undesirable consequence of behavior.

Reinforcement. Behavior modification theory asserts that if managers want to modify subordinates' behavior, they must ensure that appropriate consequences occur as a result of that behavior. **Positive reinforcement** is a reward that consists of a desirable consequence of behavior, and **negative reinforcement** is a reward that consists of the elimination of an undesirable consequence of behavior.

If arriving at work on time is positively reinforced, or rewarded, the probability increases that a worker will arrive on time more often. If arriving late for work causes a worker to experience some undesirable outcome, such as a verbal reprimand, that worker will be negatively reinforced when this outcome is eliminated by on-time arrival. According to behavior modification theory, positive reinforcement and negative reinforcement are both rewards that increase the likelihood that a behavior will continue.

Punishment is the presentation of an undesirable behavioral consequence or the removal of a desirable one that decreases the likelihood that the behavior will continue.

Punishment. **Punishment** is the presentation of an undesirable behavioral consequence or the removal of a desirable behavioral consequence that decreases the likelihood the behavior will continue. To use our earlier example, a manager could punish employees for arriving late for work by exposing them to some undesirable consequence, such as a verbal reprimand, or by removing a desirable consequence, such as their wages for the amount of time they are late.[23] Although punishment would probably quickly convince most workers to come to work on time, it might have undesirable side effects, such as high absenteeism and turnover, if it is emphasized over the long term.

Applying Behavior Modification. Behavior modification programs have been applied both successfully and unsuccessfully in a number of organizations. Management at Emery Air Freight Company (now called Emery Worldwide), for example, found that an effective feedback system is crucial to making a behavior modification program successful.[24] This feedback system should be aimed at keeping employees informed of the relationship between various behaviors and their consequences.

Other ingredients of successful behavior modification programs are the following:[25]

1. Giving different levels of rewards to different workers according to the quality of their performances.
2. Telling workers what they are doing wrong.
3. Punishing workers privately in order not to embarrass them in front of others.
4. Always giving out rewards and punishments that are earned to emphasize that management is serious about its behavior modification efforts.

The behavior modification concept is also being applied to cost control in organizations, with the objective of encouraging employees to be more cost conscious. Under this type of behavior modification program, employees are compensated in a manner that rewards cost control and cost reduction and penalizes cost acceleration.[26]

Likert's Management Systems

Another strategy that managers can use to motivate organization members is based on the work of Rensis Likert, a noted management scholar.[27] After studying several types and sizes of organizations, Likert concluded that management styles in organizations can be categorized into the following systems:

- **System 1.** This style of management is characterized by a lack of confidence or trust in subordinates. Subordinates do not feel free to discuss their jobs with superiors, and are motivated by fear, threats, punishments, and occasional rewards. Information flow in the organization is directed primarily downward; upward communication is viewed with great suspicion. The bulk of all decision making is done at the top of the organization.
- **System 2.** This style of management is characterized by a condescending master-to-servant–style confidence and trust in subordinates. Subordinates do not feel very free to discuss their jobs with superiors, and are motivated by rewards and actual or potential punishments. Information flows mostly downward; upward communication may or may not be viewed with suspicion. Although policies are made primarily at the top of the organization, decisions within a prescribed framework are made at lower levels.
- **System 3.** This style of management is characterized by substantial, though not complete, confidence in subordinates. Subordinates feel fairly free to discuss their jobs with superiors, and are motivated by rewards, occasional punishments, and some involvement. Information flows both upward and downward in the organization. Upward communication is often accepted, though at times it may be viewed with suspicion. Although broad policies and general decisions are made at the top of the organization, more specific decisions are made at lower levels.
- **System 4.** This style of management is characterized by complete trust and confidence in subordinates. Subordinates feel completely free to discuss their jobs with superiors, and are motivated by such factors as economic rewards based on a compensation system developed through employee participation and involvement in goal setting. Information flows upward, downward, and horizontally. Upward communication is generally accepted—but even where it is not, employees' questions are answered candidly. Decision making is spread widely throughout the organization and is well coordinated.

Styles, Systems, and Productivity.   Likert has suggested that as management style moves from system 1 to system 4, the human needs of individuals within the organization tend to be more effectively satisfied over the long term. Thus, an organization that moves toward system 4 tends to become more productive over the long term.

Figure 16.7 illustrates the comparative long- and short-term effects of both system 1 and system 4 on organizational production. Managers may increase production

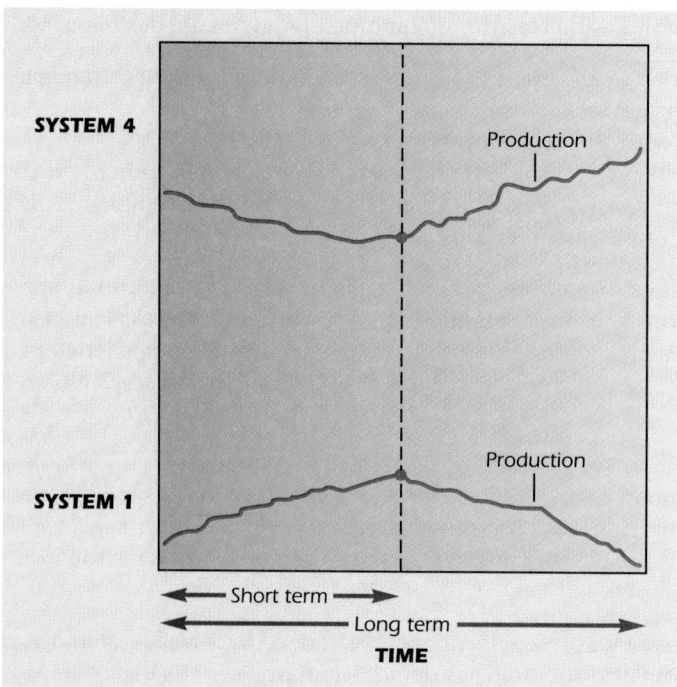

Figure 16.7   Comparative long-term and short-term effects of system 1 and system 4 on organizational production

in the short term by using a system 1 management style, because motivation by fear, threat, and punishment is generally effective in the short run. Over the long run, however, this style usually causes production to decrease, primarily because of the long-term nonsatisfaction of organization members' needs and the poor working relationships between managers and subordinates.

Conversely, managers who initiate a system 4 management style will probably face some decline in production initially, but will see an increase in production over the long term. The short-term decline occurs because organization members must adapt to the new system management is implementing. The production increase over the long term materializes as a result of organization members' adjustment to the new system, greater satisfaction of the human needs of organization members, and the good working relationships that develop between managers and subordinates.

This long-term production increase under system 4 can also be related to decision-making differences in the two management systems. Because decisions reached in system 4 are more likely to be thoroughly understood by organization members than decisions reached in system 1, decision implementation is more likely to be efficient and effective in system 4 than in system 1.

Monetary Incentives   A number of firms make a wide range of money-based compensation programs available to their employees as a form of motivation. For instance, employee stock ownership plans (ESOPs) motivate employees to boost production by offering them shares of company stock as a benefit. Managers are commonly given stock bonuses as an incentive to think more like an owner and ultimately do a better job of building a successful organization. Other incentive plans include lump-sum bonuses—one-time cash payments—and gain-sharing, a plan under which members of a team receive a bonus when their team exceeds a goal. All of these plans link pay closely to performance. Many organizations have found that by putting more of their employees' pay at risk, they can peg more of their total wage costs to sales, which makes expenses more controllable in a downturn.[28]

Mary McConnell is a real estate agent for Taco Bell. Her job includes locating sites for future outlets, arranging purchases, and even securing building permits, and she works under a pay-for-performance system. In one banner year, McConnell closed 45 deals in her North and South Carolina region—thereby earning eight times her base pay. It is little wonder that Taco Bell agents agreed to a 30-percent cut in base pay (to $40,000) in return for a monetary-incentive system: More than half of them now average $100,000 a year.

Nonmonetary Incentives   A firm can also keep its employees committed and motivated by nonmonetary means. For instance, some companies have a policy of promoting from within. They go through an elaborate process of advertising jobs internally before going outside to fill vacancies. Another nonmonetary incentive emphasizes quality, on the theory that most workers are unhappy when they know their work goes to producing a shoddy product.[29]

This section of the text has presented information about providing both monetary and nonmonetary incentives to motivate employees. The following PEOPLE PERSPECTIVES feature implies that nonmonetary incentives can be the more powerful motivator.

JOB SATISFACTION IS A MORE POWERFUL MOTIVATOR THAN MONEY AT MICROSOFT

PEOPLE PERSPECTIVES   Microsoft Corporation is a world-renowned developer of computer software. This is the company that has developed such popular software packages as Microsoft Windows, a computer operating system; Microsoft Word, a word-processing package; and Microsoft Excel, an electronic spreadsheet.

Microsoft has paid its employees exceedingly well over the years. For example, those with more than six years' seniority stand a very good chance of becoming independently wealthy. The typical salaried employee received a grant of 1,500 shares of Microsoft stock in 1982, which, with regular company stock additions, compounded and untouched, was valued at over $5 million in 1995. There are at present at least 10,000 rank-and-file employees in the company who stand to gain over $3 billion altogether simply by exercising their options to buy almost 50 million shares of Microsoft stock.

Despite their incredibly high compensation, which makes many Microsoft employees financially independent, these employees have remained startlingly creative and productive over the years. Just what motivates them to continue to do a superb job when they don't need any more money? According to Mike Murray, the vice president for human resources and administration at Microsoft, the fact that these millionaire employees have remained highly productive proves that providing personally satisfying and interesting jobs is a far more effective motivator over the long run than simply handing out more and more money.≈

BACK TO THE CASE   Chupa can apply behavior modification at American Greetings by rewarding appropriate employee behavior and punishing inappropriate behavior. He would have to use punishment very carefully, however, for if he overuses it, he may destroy his good working relationship with his employees. If a behavior modification program is to be successful, Chupa will have to furnish employees with feedback concerning which behaviors are appropriate and which are inappropriate, reward them differently according to the quality of their performance, tell them what they are doing wrong, punish them privately, and consistently give rewards and punishments when earned.

To use Likert's system 4 management style to motivate employees over the long term, Chupa would have to demonstrate complete confidence in his workers and encourage them to feel completely free to discuss work problems with him. In addition, communication at American Greetings would have to flow freely in all directions within the organization structure, with upward communication generally discussed candidly. Chupa's decision-making process under system 4 would have to involve many employees. He could use the principle of supportive relationships as the basis for his system 4 management style.

No single strategy mentioned in this chapter for motivating organization members would necessarily be more valuable to managers like Chupa than any other of the strategies. In reality, Chupa would probably find that some combination of all of these strategies is most useful in motivating the workforce at American Greetings.

Action Summary

Reread the learning objectives below. Each objective is followed by questions. Answering these questions accurately will help you retain the most important concepts discussed in this chapter. After answering each question, check your answer against the answer key at the end of this chapter. (*Hint:* If you have any doubts regarding the correct response, consult the page whose number follows the answer.)

Circle: From studying this chapter, I will attempt to acquire:

1. A basic understanding of human motivation.

a,b,c,d,e   a. An individual's inner state that causes him or her to behave in such a way as to ensure accomplishment of a goal is: (a) ambition; (b) drive; (c) motivation; (d) need; (e) leadership.

T,F   b. According to the needs-goal theory of motivation, a fulfilled need is a motivator.

a,b,c,d,e   c. The following most comprehensively describes how motivation takes place: (a) the Vroom expectancy theory; (b) the needs-goal theory; (c) the Porter-Lawler theory; (d) all of the above; (e) none of the above.

2. Insights about various human needs.

a,b,c,d,e   a. The following is a rank-ordered listing of Maslow's hierarchy of needs from lowest to highest: (a) self-actualization, social, security, physiological, esteem; (b) social, security, physiological, self-actualization; (c) esteem, self-actualization, security, social, physiological; (d) physiological, security, social, esteem, self-actualization; (e) physiological, social, esteem, security, self-actualization.

a,b,c,d,e   b. According to Argyris, as individuals mature, they have an increasing need for: (a) greater dependence; (b) a shorter-term perspective; (c) more inactivity; (d) deeper interests; (e) youth.

a,b,c,d,e   c. The desire to do something better or more efficiently than it has ever been done before is known as the need for: (a) acceleration; (b) achievement; (c) acclamation; (d) actualization; (e) none of the above.

3. An appreciation for the importance of motivating organization members.

T,F   a. From a managerial viewpoint, motivation is the process of furnishing organization members with the opportunity to satisfy their needs by performing productive behaviors within the organization.

T,F   b. The concepts of motivation and appropriate behavior are closely related.

4. An understanding of various motivation strategies.

a,b,c,d,e   **a.** The following is a Theory Y assumption: (a) the average person prefers to be directed; (b) most people must be threatened and coerced before they will put forth adequate effort; (c) commitment to objectives is a function of the rewards associated with achievement; (d) the average person seeks no responsibility; (e) all of the above.

a,b,c,d,e   **b.** The process of incorporating motivators into the job situation is called: (a) job enlargement; (b) flextime; (c) satisfying; (d) job enrichment; (e) Theory X.

a,b,c,d,e   **c.** Successful behavior modification programs can include: (a) giving rewards and punishments when earned; (b) giving rewards according to performance quality; (c) telling workers what they are doing wrong; (d) punishing workers privately; (e) all of the above.

Introductory Case Wrap-Up

"American Greetings Motivates Through Lateral Moves" (p. 379) and its related back-to-the-case sections were written to help you better understand the management concepts contained in this chapter. Answer the following discussion questions about this introductory case to enrich your understanding of the chapter content:

1. Do you think it unusual for a manager like Chupa to spend a significant portion of his time motivating his workforce? Explain.

2. Which of the needs in Maslow's hierarchy of needs would the restructuring at American Greetings probably help satisfy? Why? If you have omitted one or more of the needs, explain why the reorganization probably would not satisfy those needs.

3. Can Chupa's restructuring succeed in both cutting production time and motivating workers? Explain fully.

Issues for Review and Discussion

1. Define *motivation* and explain why managers must understand it.

2. Describe the difference between process and content theories of motivation.

3. Draw and explain a model that illustrates the needs-goal theory of motivation.

4. Explain Vroom's expectancy theory of motivation.

5. List and explain three characteristics of the motivation process described in the Porter-Lawler motivation theory that are not contained in either the needs-goal theory of motivation or Vroom's expectancy theories.

6. What is the main theme of the equity theory of motivation?

7. What does Maslow's hierarchy of needs tell us about the relationship between personal needs and workplace needs?

8. What concerns have been expressed about Maslow's hierarchy of needs?

9. What are the similarities and differences between Maslow's hierarchy of needs and Alderfer's ERG theory?

10. Explain Argyris' maturity-immaturity continuum.

11. What is the need for achievement?

12. Summarize the characteristics of individuals who have a high need for achievement.

13. Explain "motivating organization members."

14. Is the process of motivating organization members important to managers? Explain.

15. How can managerial communication be used to motivate organization members?

16. Describe Theory X, Theory Y, and Theory Z. What does each of these theories tell us about motivating organization members?

17. What is the difference between job enlargement and job rotation?

18. Describe the relationship of hygiene factors, motivating factors, and job enrichment.

19. Define *flextime* and *behavior modification*.

20. What basic ingredients are necessary to make a behavior modification program successful?

21. In your own words, summarize Likert's four management systems.

22. What effect do Likert's systems 1 and 4 generally have on organizational production in both the short and the long term? Why do these effects occur?

23. List three nonmonetary incentives that you personally would find desirable as an employee. Why would these incentives be desirable to you?

Action Summary Answer Key

1. a. c, p. 380
   b. F, pp. 380–381
   c. c, pp. 382–383

2. a. d, pp. 384–385
   b. d, pp. 386–387
   c. b, pp. 386–387

3. a. T, p. 388
   b. T, pp. 388–389

4. a. c, pp. 389–390
   b. d, p. 391
   c. e, p. 394

Case Study

Why Bart Simpson Flies Western Pacific Airlines

Motivation is the inner state that causes an individual to behave in a way that ensures the accomplishment of some goal. Management policies at Ed Beauvais' new airline, Western Pacific, reflect his belief in the importance of a motivated workforce to a company's bottom line.

Convinced that low-cost, low-fare flights should make for a sound and profitable business, Beauvais spent a year reflecting on what had gone wrong with his previous venture, America West Airlines. He then looked to Oklahoma billionaire Edward Gaylord and oil heiress Margaret Hunt Hill for backing to try again. Beauvais' personal motivation was so convincing that they gave him $5.5 million each. Other investors kicked in an additional $17 million, and $48 million was raised from a public offering. Beauvais was back in business with Western Pacific Airlines.

Western Pacific is a low-cost airline similar in some ways to America West. Beauvais hopes both to borrow successful strategies from his experience with America West and to create new strategies for overcoming the difficulties that brought down his former airline. For one thing, Beauvais has been able to offer an unembellished travel option to potential customers by flying only Boeing 737-300s, thereby simplifying maintenance, training, and inventory control.

One of the mistakes that Beauvais will not repeat with Western Pacific is going head-to-head with Southwest Airlines, the inventors of low-cost airline travel. One of the strategies he hopes will bring success is maintaining routes out of Colorado Springs and only offering routes accessible to the 737s. This strategy gives Beauvais a chance to take advantage of the $5 billion Denver International Airport boondoggle. "Beauvais is right on top of a gold mine," says Michael Boyd, president of Aviation Systems Research Corporation.

Beauvais is counting on such customer- and equipment-based strategies to keep his new airline successful (eight months after Western Pacific began operations, Beauvais' initial $100,000 investment in stock was worth several million dollars). However, he is repeating one important and previously successful strategy—ensuring that his workforce is highly motivated. He strives, for instance, to create an atmosphere of respect and employee involvement. Employees are encouraged to become stockholders and are offered opportunities to buy stock at discounted rates. An owner-employee is more motivated to save the company money and to look for ways to improve service and cut costs, Beauvais figures. Owner-pilots take greater responsibility for their aircraft.

Employees are treated as individuals and encouraged to develop ideas in their own ways. Similarly, managers are instructed to coach, cheer on, and help employees shape their ideas. Employees are encouraged to communicate to all levels of the hierarchy with no fear of reprisals; thus there is a free flow of communication and a near-level playing field at Western Pacific. This open-door policy contributes to a highly motivated staff that is unafraid to speak up and eager to work together for the benefit of the company.

By offering a friendly and creative workplace where employees are allowed to manage themselves, Western Pacific is able to maintain a highly motivated, energetic workforce. Beauvais' flight attendants run contests and crack jokes aboard aircraft bearing pictures of the TV cartoon Simpsons, a 38-foot showgirl, and other images that advertisers pay $800,000 to display. Such goings-on bear out Ed Beauvais' philosophy: "We think folks should have a lot of fun when they fly with us." This approach holds for his employees as well as his customers.

Western Pacific employee benefit programs are designed to encourage employee input; they are people-oriented and employee-friendly. For example, the company offers maternity leave and counseling programs. Job-share and work-at-home programs are under consideration, as are programs to reward attendance with discounted tickets to special events. Another program being considered is a prepayment plan whereby employees may borrow against future salary to purchase big-ticket items, take vacations, or invest.

Such programs existed at American West Airlines, and Beauvais still believes that they are key to a motivated staff and a successful business. "If people enjoy working here, then the bottom line is they will provide the best customer service," says Director of Human Relations Glenn Goldberg.

Questions:

1. How are the process theories of motivation implemented in the Western Pacific model?
2. Use Maslow's hierarchy to identify the needs addressed in Beauvais' approach to employee relations.
3. Would Beauvais be considered a Theory X, Theory Y, or Theory Z manager? Why?
4. Why do you think Beauvais considers his style of management to be critical to the success of the company?

Skills Exercise

Beauvais believes that employees should be given responsibility to perform jobs their own way without seeking management approval. Look for company examples of managerial styles that encourage this sort of freedom. What difficulties does this style of management pose for such businesses? Does the size of the corporation play a role in how much authority is delegated? Do owner-employees tend to develop longer-term relationships with their employers? Write an editorial for a hypothetical company in which you either support or refute plans to open management to employee input.

 The Internet learning materials that accompany this chapter can be found at
http://www.profcerto.com
Additional information can be found on the inside front and back covers of this text.

17 chapter

GROUPS, TEAMS, AND CORPORATE CULTURE

STUDENT LEARNING OBJECTIVES

From studying this chapter, I will attempt to acquire:

1. A definition of the term *group* as used in the context of management.
2. A thorough understanding of the difference between formal and informal groups.
3. Knowledge of the types of formal groups that exist in organizations.
4. An understanding of how managers can determine which groups exist in an organization.
5. An appreciation for what teams are and how to manage them.
6. Insights about managing corporate culture to enhance organizational success.

CHAPTER OUTLINE

Work Groups Are Important to Progress at Rolls-Royce

In Crewe, England, Dennis Jones lifts a long slice of stainless steel and peers down the edge, squinting one eye as if aiming a rifle. He likes what he sees.

The piece is slightly bowed, he explains, to create the illusion from a distance of a straight line, "like a column on the Parthenon." "It's perfect for a Rolls-Royce radiator grill," says Jones, who has built the units for 22 years in a shop at the company's factory here. "We can't afford to make many mistakes," he concedes.

In the early 1990s, however, Rolls-Royce did make some mistakes. Combined with a worldwide recession, a shift in tastes, even among customers for one of the world's ultimate status symbols, caused sales to slip; Rolls lost $54.5 million in 1991.

But by 1995, Rolls-Royce was at least on the threshold of a turnaround. An overall increase in retail sales of 10 percent was above the industry average and included an increase of 25 percent in North and South America. Chief executive Chris Woodwark attributes the improved performance to more focused marketing strategies, the introduction of competitive leasing programs, and greater responsiveness to customer needs. For instance, at the Mulliner Park Ward division, which operates under its own management, engineers work directly with customers to implement special and often unique requirements.

Streamlined operations have made it possible for engineers to respond more quickly to customer requests, and chairman Peter Ward readily admits that Rolls-Royce's improved performance has resulted in part from the adaptation of so-called "lean manufacturing" techniques pioneered by high-volume Japanese automakers.

Over the past several years, Ward has installed a computer-controlled production system, slashed 1,300 jobs, and reorganized workers into Japanese-style teams. Rolls-Royce now has its own version of such Japanese innovations as just-in-time parts delivery and continuous quality improvement.

"We've really gone further than the Japanese," he asserts, adding that some of the moves are only bringing Rolls-Royce closer to its original structure. Before World War II, the car maker used a much more open system, with workers learning a variety of skills and having closer contact with management and engineers. This faded during the 1960s and 1970s, as unions sharply defined workers' tasks and the shop floor became more insulated from the management suite.

Not that any change is easy in a company as tradition-bound as Rolls-Royce, where workers are often second- or third-generation employees. The changes also are grating against Britain's class structure. Workers now routinely get pulled off the floor for "brown-paper sessions," in which engineers and workers sit together, dissecting and critiquing production processes on long sheets of brown paper taped to the wall. Company officials say some of the best worker input still comes, however, from yellow notes stuck on by workers when no one else is around.

Rolls-Royce officials attribute the company's recent turnaround to such factors as more focused marketing strategies, greater responsiveness to customer needs, and more efficient production techniques.

what's ahead

The introductory case highlights the important role that new work groups or teams are playing in solving problems at Rolls-Royce. The material in this chapter should give a manager like Peter Ward, Rolls-Royce's chairman, some insight into the broad area of work group management. This chapter proceeds as follows:

1. It defines groups.
2. Next it discusses the kinds of groups that exist in organizations.
3. Finally, it explains what steps managers should take to manage groups appropriately.

The previous chapters in this section dealt with three primary activities of the influencing function: communication, leadership, and motivation. This chapter focuses on managing groups, the last major influencing activity to be discussed in this text. As with the other three activities, managing work groups requires guiding the behavior of organization members in ways that increase the probability of reaching organizational objectives.

GROUPS

To deal with groups appropriately, managers must have a thorough understanding of the nature of groups in organizations.[1] As used in management-related discussions, a **group** is not simply a gathering of people. Rather it is "any number of people who (1) interact with one another, (2) are psychologically aware of one another, and (3) perceive themselves to be a group."[2] Groups are characterized by frequent communication among members over time and a size small enough to permit each member to communicate with all other members on a face-to-face basis. As a result of this communication, each group member influences and is influenced by all other group members.

> A **group** is any number of people who (1) interact with one another, (2) are psychologically aware of one another, and (3) perceive themselves to be a group.

The study of groups is important to managers because the most common ingredient of all organizations is people and the most common technique for accomplishing work through these people is dividing them into work groups. In a classic article, Cartwright and Lippitt list four additional reasons managers should study groups:[3]

1. Groups exist in all kinds of organizations.
2. Groups inevitably form in all facets of organizational existence.
3. Groups can cause either desirable or undesirable consequences within the organization.
4. An understanding of groups can help managers raise the probability that the groups with which they work will cause desirable consequences within the organization.

KINDS OF GROUPS IN ORGANIZATIONS

Organizational groups are typically divided into two basic types: formal and informal.

Formal Groups

A **formal group** is a group that exists within an organization by virtue of management decree to perform tasks that enhance the attainment of organizational objectives.[4] Figure 17.1 is an organization chart showing a formal group. The placement of organization members in such areas as marketing departments, personnel departments, and production departments involves establishing formal groups.

> A **formal group** is a group that exists in an organization by virtue of management decree to perform tasks that enhance the attainment of organizational objectives.

Actually, organizations are made up of a number of formal groups that exist at various organizational levels. The coordination of and communication among these groups is the responsibility of managers, or supervisors, commonly called "linking pins."

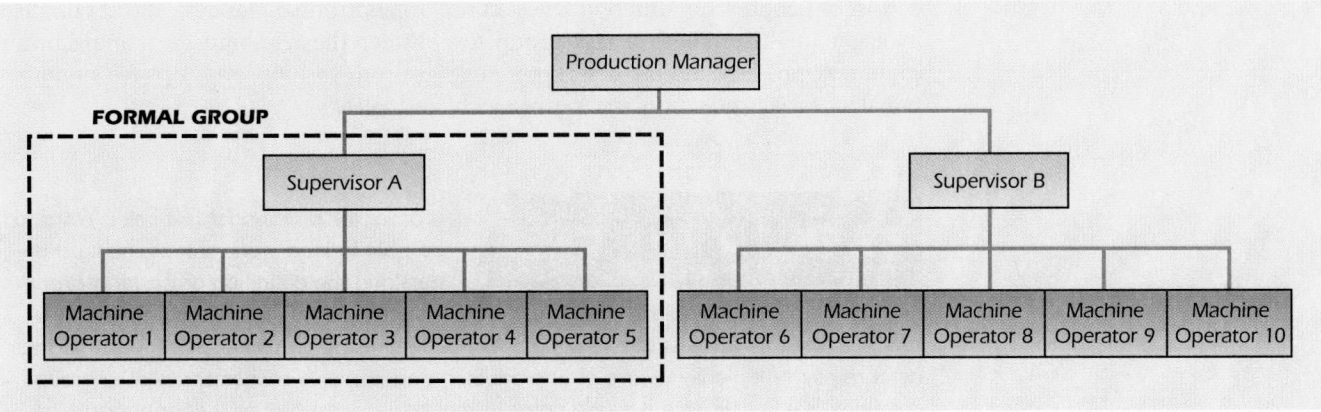

Figure 17.1   **A formal group**

MANAGING A DIVERSE SALESFORCE TAKES SPECIAL INSIGHT AT EQUITABLE

DIVERSITY SPOTLIGHT

An example of a formal group that must be managed in many organizations is a salesforce. According to José S. Suquet, manager of Equitable Life Assurance Company's South Florida agency, managing a salesforce in a multicultural, multiethnic environment requires special insight and understanding. Suquet says that the key to management success is not to overcompensate for cultural diversity, but to be consistent across the board. His experience suggests that regardless of culture, employees need to feel that they are being treated fairly and that managers do not mark "favorites" for special treatment.

Experience also indicates that the first critical step in successfully managing a diverse salesforce is recruiting. Managers should not try to clone themselves, but rather attempt to recruit people who reflect the market—that is, they should struggle to build a salesforce that represents the diverse ethnic market segments the company wishes to penetrate. Building such a salesforce should help to ensure that the organization's salespeople are able to communicate well with customers. To this end, managers should determine the language or languages that salespeople need to speak and be sensitive to customs, jargon, and individual needs that are relevant to a particular organizational situation. When leading a diverse salesforce, managers should also keep in mind that simply because employees have the same ethnic and cultural backgrounds does not automatically mean they will have the same opinions about organizational issues, approach problems in the same way, or be motivated by the same organizational incentives.≈

Formal groups are clearly defined and structured. The next sections discuss the following topics:

1. The basic kinds of formal groups.
2. Examples of formal groups as they exist in organizations.
3. The four stages of formal group development.

Kinds of Formal Groups   Formal groups are commonly divided into command groups and task groups. **Command groups** are formal groups that are outlined on the chain of command on an organization chart. They typically handle routine organizational activities.

Task groups are formal groups of organization members who interact with one another to accomplish most of the organization's nonroutine tasks. Although task groups are usually made up of members on the same organizational level, they can

A **command group** is a formal group that is outlined in the chain of command on an organization chart. Command groups handle routine activities.

A **task group** is a formal group of organization members who interact with one another to accomplish nonroutine organizational tasks. Members of any one task group can and often do come from various levels and segments of an organization.

consist of people from different levels in the organizational hierarchy. For example, a manager might establish a task group to consider the feasibility of manufacturing some new product and include representatives from various levels of such organizational areas as production, market research, and sales.

BACK TO THE CASE

In order for a manager like Peter Ward to be able to lead work groups, he must understand the definition of the term *group* and grasp the idea that there are several types of groups that exist in organizations. A *group* at Rolls-Royce—as at any other organization—is any number of people who interact, are psychologically aware of one another, and perceive of themselves as a group. A company like Rolls-Royce is made up of formal groups (the groups that appear on the company's organization charts) such as the marketing department. Managers of formal groups act as the "linking pins" among departments. The ability of managers at Rolls-Royce to coordinate and communicate with formal groups other than their own, as well as their success in dealing with their own departments, is certainly important to the future success of the company.

At times, managers at Rolls-Royce will form new groups to handle some of the nonroutine challenges the organization faces. For example, management might form a task group on recruitment—that is, choose people from several different departments and put them together to develop new and more efficient company hiring procedures.

Then, of course, Rolls-Royce—like virtually every organization—has informal groups (those that do not appear on the organization chart). Informal groups will be discussed in later back-to-the-case sections.

Examples of Formal Groups

Two formal groups that are often established in organizations are committees and work teams. Committees are the more traditional formal group; work teams have only recently gained acceptance and support in U.S. organizations. Because the part of this text dealing with the managerial function of organizing emphasized command groups, however, the examples here emphasize task groups.

A **committee** is a task group that is charged with performing some type of specific activity.

Committees.   Since a **committee** is a group of individuals charged with performing some type of specific activity, it is usually classified as a task group. From a managerial viewpoint, there are four major reasons for establishing committees:[5]

1. To allow organization members to exchange ideas.
2. To generate suggestions and recommendations that can be offered to other organizational units.
3. To develop new ideas for solving existing organizational problems.
4. To assist in the development of organizational policies.

Committees exist in virtually all organizations and at all organizational levels. As Figure 17.2 suggests, however, the larger the organization, the greater the probability that it will use committees on a regular basis. The following two sections discuss why managers should use committees and what makes a committee successful.

CALVARY HOSPITAL FORMS ETHICS COMMITTEES

ETHICS SPOTLIGHT

A survey conducted at Calvary Hospital in the Bronx, New York, indicated that hospital managers are commonly using committees to help make ethical decisions. Health-care professionals today face many ethical dilemmas. For example, should patients be denied treatment be-

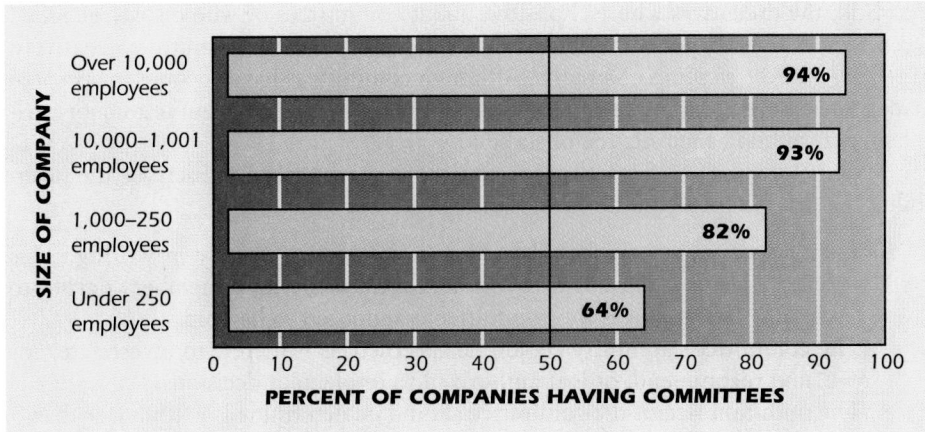

Figure 17.2   **Percent of companies that have committees, by size of company**

cause they cannot afford to pay for it or because they do not have medical insurance? Or: Which patients should receive scarce transplant organs from donors?

To better handle such ethical dilemmas, hospital administrators are establishing ethics committees and to get practical and worthwhile input from these committees, they are asking representatives from many different areas of health care to serve on them—nurses as well as physicians. Nurses are heavily involved in patient care, so their views on ethical questions can be extremely valuable.

The primary purpose of these committees is to help hospital administrators and other health-care professionals ensure that appropriate decisions are made in response to ethical dilemmas. Organization members seem willing to sit on ethics committees because participation allows them to express to management various ethical concerns they have about their work situation.≈

Why Managers Should Use Committees. Managers generally agree that committees have several uses in organizations.

- Committees can improve the quality of decision making. As more people become involved in making a decision, the strengths and weaknesses of various alternatives tend to be discussed in greater detail and the chances of reaching a higher-quality decision increase.
- Committees encourage the expression of honest opinions. Committee members feel protected enough to say what they really think because the group output of a committee cannot be associated with any one member of that group.
- Committees also tend to increase organization members' participation in decision making and thereby enhance the chances of widespread support of decisions. Another result of this increased participation is that committee members satisfy their social or esteem needs through committee work.
- Finally, committees ensure the representation of important groups in the decision-making process. Managers must choose committee members wisely, however, to achieve appropriate representation, for if a committee does not adequately represent various interest groups, any decision it comes to may well be counter to the interests of some important organizational group.

Although executives vary somewhat in their enthusiasm about using committees in organizations, a study reported by McLeod and Jones concludes that most executives favor using committees. The executives who took part in this study said they got significantly more information from organizational sources other than committees, but found the information from committees more valuable than the information from any other source. Nevertheless, some top executives express only qualified support for using committees as work groups, and others had negative feelings toward commit-

tees. Still, the executives who feel positive about committees or who display qualified acceptance of them in general outnumber those who look upon committees negatively.

What Makes Committees Successful. Although committees have become an accepted management tool, managerial action taken to establish and run them is a major variable in determining their degree of success.

PROCEDURAL STEPS. Several procedural steps can be taken to increase the probability that a committee will be successful:[6]

- The committee's goals should be clearly defined, preferably in writing. This will focus the committee's activities and reduce the time members devote to discussing just what it is the committee is supposed to be doing.
- The committee's authority should be specified. Is it merely to investigate, advise, and recommend, or is it authorized to implement decisions?
- The optimum size of the committee should be determined. With fewer than 5 members, the advantages of group work may be diminished. With more than 10 or 15 members, the committee may become unwieldy. Although optimal size varies with the circumstances, the ideal number of committee members for most tasks seems to be from 5 to 10.
- A chairperson should be selected on the basis of ability to run an efficient meeting—that is, the ability to keep committee members from getting bogged down in irrelevancies and to see to it that the necessary paperwork gets done.
- Appointing a permanent secretary to handle communications is often useful.
- The agenda and all supporting material for the meeting should be distributed before the meeting takes place. When members have a chance to study each item beforehand, they are likely to stick to the point and be prepared to make informed contributions.
- Meetings should be started on time, and the time at which they will end should be announced at the outset.

PEOPLE-ORIENTED GUIDELINES. In addition to these procedural steps, managers can follow a number of more people-oriented guidelines to increase the probability that a committee will succeed. In particular, a manager can raise the quality of committee discussions by doing the following:[7]

- *Rephrasing ideas already expressed.* This rephrasing ensures that the manager as well as other people on the committee clearly understand what has been said.
- *Bringing all members into active participation.* Every committee member is a potential source of useful information, so the manager should serve as a catalyst who sparks individual participation whenever appropriate.
- *Stimulating further thought by members.* The manager should encourage committee members to think ideas through carefully and thoroughly, for only this type of analysis will generate high-quality committee output.

Groupthink is the mode of thinking that group members engage in when the desire for agreement so dominates the group that it overrides the need to realistically appraise alternate problem solutions.

GROUPTHINK. Managers should also help the committee avoid a phenomenon called "groupthink." **Groupthink** is the mode of thinking that group members engage in when the desire for agreement so dominates the group that it overrides the need to realistically appraise alternative problem solutions. Groups tend to slip into groupthink when their members become overly concerned about being too harsh in judging one another's ideas and lose their objectivity. Such groups tend to seek complete support on every issue to avoid conflicts that might endanger the "we-feeling" atmosphere.[8]

A **work team** is a task group used in organizations to achieve greater organizational flexibility or to cope with rapid growth.

Work Teams.   **Work teams** are another example of task groups used in organizations. Contemporary work teams in the United States evolved out of the problem-solving teams—based on Japanese-style quality circles—that were widely adopted in the 1970s. Problem-solving teams consist of 5 to 12 volunteer members from different areas of the department who meet weekly to discuss ways to improve quality and efficiency.

Special-Purpose and Self-Managed Teams. Special-purpose teams evolved in the early to middle 1980s out of problem-solving teams. The typical special-purpose team consists of workers and union representatives meeting together to collaborate on operational decisions at all levels. The aim is to create an atmosphere conducive to quality and productivity improvements.

Special-purpose teams laid the foundation for the self-managed work teams that arose in the 1990s, and it is these teams that appear to be the wave of the future. Self-managed teams consist of 5 to 15 employees who work together to produce an entire product. Members learn all the tasks required to produce the product and rotate from job to job. Self-managed teams even take over such managerial duties as scheduling work and vacations and ordering materials. Because these work teams give employees so much control over their jobs, they represent a fundamental change in how work is organized. (Self-managed teams will be discussed in some detail later in this chapter.)

Employing work teams allows a firm to draw on the talent and creativity of all its employees, not just a few maverick inventors or top executives, to make important decisions. As product quality becomes more and more important in the business world, companies will need to rely more and more on the team approach in order to stay competitive. Consider a recent situation at Yellow Freight Systems, a shipping company, whose management was intent on giving its customers excellent service. To address this concern, management established a work team made up of employees from many different parts of the company, including marketing, sales, operations, and human resources. The overall task of the work team was to run an excellence-in-service campaign that management had initiated.[9]

BACK TO THE CASE

Rolls-Royce management could decide to form a committee to achieve some specific goal. A committee might be formed, for example, to offer recommendations on how to enhance the quality of the company's automobiles. This quality committee could encourage various Rolls-Royce departments to exchange quality improvement ideas and generate related suggestions to management. It could also improve Rolls-Royce decision making in general by encouraging honest feedback from employees about quality issues in the organization. Such a committee could be used as well to urge Rolls-Royce employees to participate more seriously in improving the quality of the automobiles made by the company. Finally, the committee could help Rolls-Royce management ensure that all appropriate departments are represented in important quality decisions so that whenever Rolls-Royce takes an action to improve the

This team of engineers at Oracle Corp., the world's second-largest software company, built the successful Video Server—a program that can provide 100 different digitized films to 100 different locations at 100 different times. They also managed to accomplish the feat in about eight weeks—whereas programmers at Microsoft needed more than a year. How? Besides teamwork, suggests one of the team's leaders, "Microsoft programmers need more sleep than we do."

quality of its automobiles, every important angle will be considered, including design, production, marketing, and sales.

While committees *can* be useful, a poorly run committee wastes a lot of time. Therefore, setting up a quality committee at Rolls-Royce management should encourage committee members to take certain steps to enhance the committee's success. For example, the committee should clearly define its goals and the limits of its authority: Is the committee supposed to merely come up with quality improvement ideas, or is it also supposed to initiate a program for implementing those ideas?

The quality committee should not have too few or too many members. Issues such as the need to appoint an administrator to handle communications and a chairperson who works well with people must be addressed. The committee needs a chairperson who can rephrase ideas clearly so that everyone understands them and who can get members to participate in discussions and think about the issues without slipping into groupthink. A company like Rolls-Royce wants its committees to generate original ideas, not a unanimous opinion where major virtue is that it enabled the committee to avoid conflict.

Stages of Formal Group Development

Another requirement for successfully managing formal groups is understanding the stages of formal group development. In a classic book, Bernard Bass suggested that group development is a four-stage process that unfolds as the group learns how to use its resources.[10] Although these stages may not occur sequentially, for the purpose of clarity, the discussion that follows will assume that they do.

The Acceptance Stage.   It is common for members of a new group to mistrust one another somewhat initially. The acceptance stage occurs only after this initial mistrust melts and the group has been transformed into one characterized by mutual trust and acceptance.

The Communication and Decision-Making Stage.   Once they have passed through the acceptance stage, group members are better able to communicate frankly with one another. This frank communication provides the basis for establishing and using an effective group decision-making mechanism.

The Group Solidarity Stage.   Group solidarity comes naturally as the mutual acceptance of group members increases and communication and decision making continue within the group. At this stage, members become more involved in group activities and cooperate, rather than compete, with one another. Members find belonging to the group extremely satisfying and are committed to enhancing the group's overall success.

The Group Control Stage.   A natural result of group solidarity is group control. In this stage, group members attempt to maximize the group's success by matching individual abilities with group activities and by assisting one another. Flexibility and informality usually characterize this stage.

As a group passes through each of these four stages, it generally becomes more mature and effective—and therefore more productive. The group that reaches maximum maturity and effectiveness is characterized by the following traits in its members:

- *Members function as a unit.* The group works as a team. Members do not disturb one another to the point of interfering with their collaboration.
- *Members participate effectively in group effort.* Members work hard when there is something to do. They seldom loaf, even if they have the opportunity to do so.
- *Members are oriented toward a single goal.* Group members work for the common purpose; they do not waste group resources by moving in different directions.
- *Members have the equipment, tools, and skills necessary to attain the group's goals.*

Members are taught the various parts of their jobs by experts and strive to acquire whatever resources they need to attain group objectives.

- *Members ask and receive suggestions, opinions, and information from one another.* A member who is uncertain about something stops working and asks another member for information. Group members generally talk to one another openly and frequently.

BACK TO THE CASE

Managers in companies like Rolls-Royce must be patient and understand that it will take some time for a newly formed group to develop into a productive work unit. Like the members of any new group, the work teams at Rolls-Royce must learn to trust and accept one another, and then to freely communicate and exchange ideas within the group. Once acceptance and easy communication are established, group solidarity and control will naturally follow. In other words, the group members first get involved, then cooperate, and finally work to maximize the group's success.

All this is true as well of the quality committee we used as an example in the previous back-to-the-case section. Rolls-Royce management must be patient and let the quality committee mature before expecting maximum effectiveness and productivity from it. If given time to grow, the committee will likely function as a unit, its members will participate willingly and effectively in committee discussions, and it will reach valuable decisions about what needs to be done to improve the quality of the automobiles that Rolls-Royce produces.

Informal Groups

Informal groups, the second major kind of group that can exist within an organization, are groups that develop naturally as people interact. An **informal group** is defined as a collection of individuals whose common work experiences result in the development of a system of interpersonal relations that extend beyond those established by management.[11]

As Figure 17.3 shows, informal group structures can deviate significantly from formal group structures. As is true of Supervisor A in the figure, an organization member can belong to more than one informal group at the same time. In contrast to formal groups, informal groups are not highly structured in terms of procedure and are not formally recognized by management.

> An **informal group** is a collection of individuals whose common work experiences result in the development of a system of interpersonal relations that extend beyond those established by management.

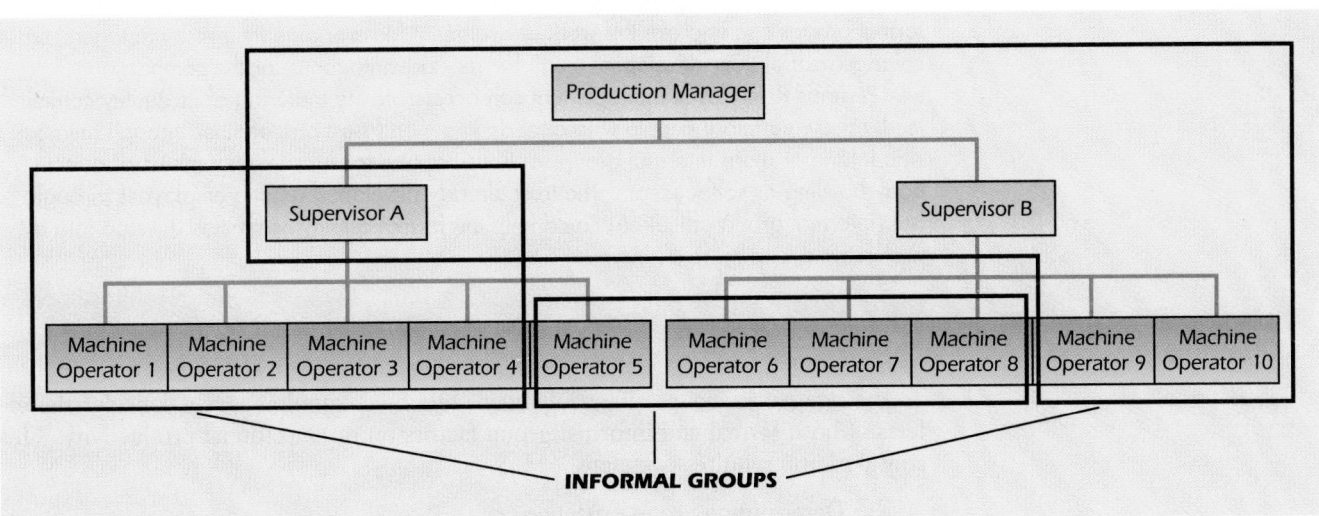

Figure 17.3   Three informal groups that deviate significantly from formal groups within the organization

The next sections discuss the following subjects:

1. Various kinds of informal groups that exist in organizations.
2. The benefits people usually reap from belonging to informal groups.

Kinds of Informal Groups

An **interest group** is an informal group that gains and maintains membership primarily because of a common concern members have about a specific issue.

A **friendship group** is an informal group that forms in organizations because of the personal affiliation members have with one another.

Informal groups generally are divided into two types: interest groups and friendship groups. **Interest groups** are informal groups that gain and maintain membership primarily because of a common concern members have about a specific issue. An example is a group of workers pressing management for better pay or working conditions. Once the interest or concern that instigated the formation of the informal group has been eliminated, the group will probably disband.

As its name implies, **friendship groups** are informal groups that form in organizations because of the personal affiliation members have with one another. Such personal factors as recreational interests, race, gender, and religion serve as foundations for friendship groups. As with interest groups, the membership of friendship groups tends to change over time. Here, however, membership changes as friendships dissolve or new friendships are made.

Benefits of Informal Group Membership

Informal groups tend to develop in organizations because of various benefits that group members obtain:[12]

1. Perpetuation of social and cultural values that group members consider important.
2. Status and social satisfaction that people might not enjoy without group membership.
3. Increased ease of communication among group members.
4. Increased desirability of the overall work environment.

These benefits may be one reason that employees who are on fixed shifts or who continually work with the same groups tend to be more satisfied with their work than employees whose shifts are continually changing.

BACK TO THE CASE ssues pertaining to informal groups could affect the success of formal work groups at Rolls-Royce. Employees sometimes form interest groups because they are concerned about a certain issue. For example, certain minority employees might form a group to enhance their opportunities for professional growth at Rolls-Royce. In addition, employees form friendship groups, which ease communication and increase members' satisfaction in working for a company. Since such informal groups can improve the work environment for everyone involved, managers' encouragement of their development can be very advantageous for the company.

Perhaps Rolls-Royce management can accelerate the maturing of its quality committee by drawing into it people who already know and trust one another through membership in one or more informal groups at Rolls-Royce—for example, members of a company bowling or softball team. The trust already developed among employees through past informal group affiliations could help the formal quality committee develop into a productive group more quickly.

MANAGING WORK GROUPS

To manage work groups effectively, managers must simultaneously consider the effects of both formal and informal group factors on organizational productivity. This consideration requires two steps:

1. Determining group existence.
2. Understanding the evolution of informal groups.

Determining Group Existence

The most important step that managers need to take in managing work groups is to determine what informal groups exist within the organization and who their members are. **Sociometry** is an analytical tool managers can use to do this. They can also use sociometry to get information on the internal workings of an informal group, including the identity of the group leader, the relative status of group members, and the group's communication networks.[13] This information on informal groups, combined with an understanding of the established formal groups shown on the organization chart, will give managers a complete picture of the organization's group structure.

Sociometric Analysis   The procedure for performing a sociometric analysis in an organization is quite basic. Various organization members simply are asked, through either an interview or a questionnaire, to name several other organization members with whom they would like to spend free time. A sociogram is then constructed to summarize the informal relationships among group members. **Sociograms** are diagrams that visually link individuals within the population queried according to the number of times they were chosen and whether the choice was reciprocated.

Applying the Sociogram Model   Figure 17.4 shows two sample sociograms based on a classic study of two groups of boys in a summer camp—the Bulldogs and the Red Devils. An analysis of these sociograms leads to several interesting conclusions. First, more boys within the Bulldogs than within the Red Devils were chosen as being desirable to spend time with. This probably implies that the Bulldogs are a

Sociometry is an analytical tool that can be used to determine what informal groups exist in an organization and who the members of those groups are.

A **sociogram** is a sociometric diagram that summarizes the personal feelings of organization members about the people in the organization with whom they would like to spend free time.

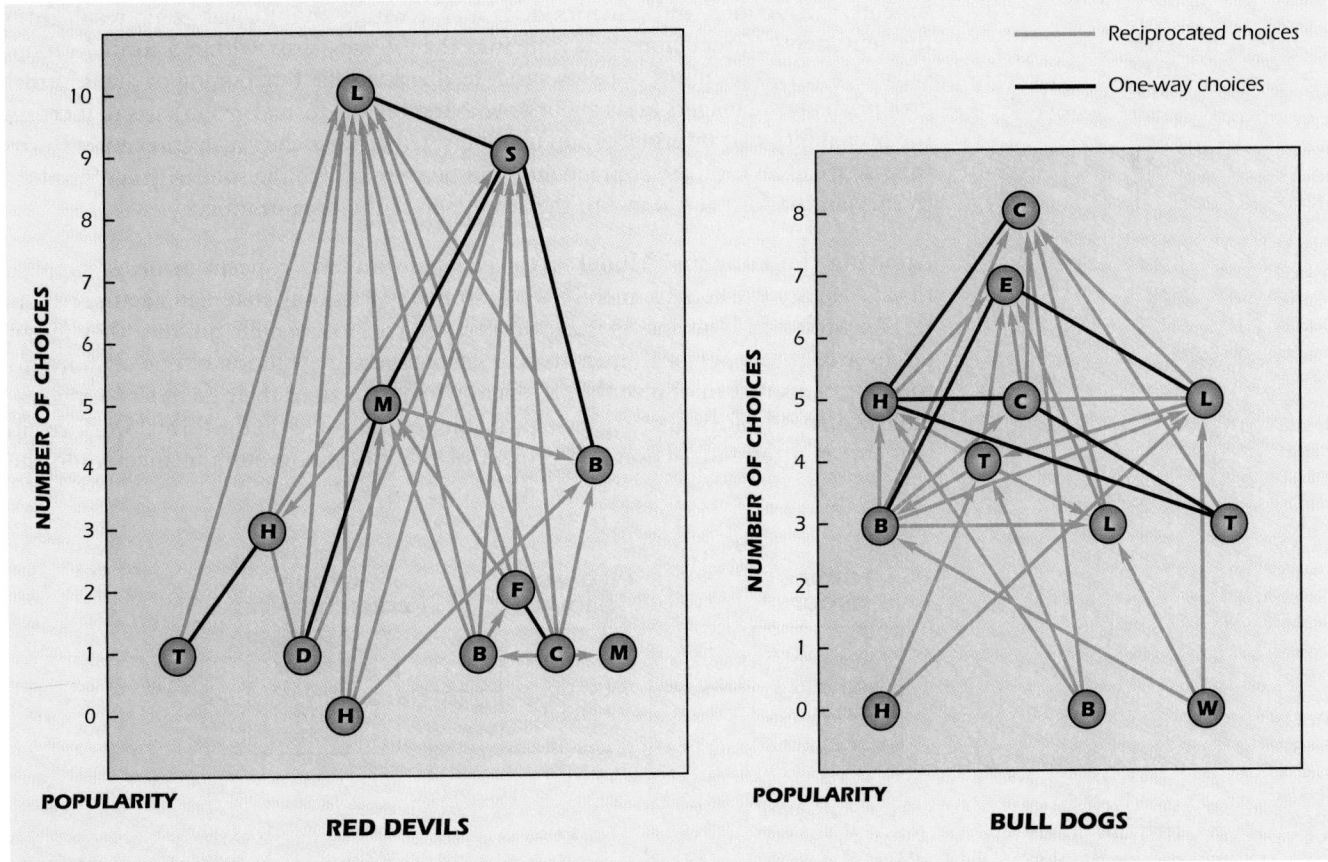

Figure 17.4   Sample sociograms

closer-knit informal group than the Red Devils. Second, the greater the number of times an individual was chosen, the more likely it was that the individual would be the group leader. Thus individuals C and E in Figure 17.4 are probably Bulldog leaders, while L and S are probably Red Devil leaders. Third, communication between L and most other Red Devils members is likely to occur directly, whereas communication between C and other bulldogs is likely to pass through other group members.

Sociometric analysis can give managers many useful insights concerning the informal groups within their organization. Managers who do not want to perform a formal sociometric analysis can at least casually gather information on what form a sociogram might take in a particular situation. They can pick up this information through normal conversations with other organization members as well as through observations of how various organization members relate to one another.

Understanding the Evolution of Informal Groups

As we have seen, the first prerequisite for managing groups effectively is knowing what groups exist within an organization and what characterizes the membership of those groups. The second prerequisite is understanding how informal groups evolve. This understanding will give managers some insights on how to encourage the development of appropriate informal groups that is, groups that support the attainment of organizational objectives and whose members maintain good relationships with formal work groups within the organization.

Homans' Model   Perhaps the most widely accepted framework for explaining the evolution of informal groups was developed by George Homans.[14] Figure 17.5 broadly summarizes his theory. According to Homans, the informal group is established to provide satisfaction and growth for its members. At the same time, the sentiments, interactions, and activities that emerge within an informal group result from the sentiments, interactions, and activities that already exist within a formal group. Given these two premises, it follows that feedback on the functioning of the informal group can give managers ideas about how to modify the formal group so as to increase the probability that informal group members will achieve the satisfaction and growth they desire. The ultimate consequence will be to reinforce the solidarity and productiveness of the formal group—to the advantage of the organization.

Applying the Homans' Model.   To see what Homans' concept involves, suppose that 12 factory workers are members of a formal work group that manufactures toasters. According to Homans, as these workers interact to assemble toasters, they might discover common personal interests that encourage the evolution of one or more informal groups that maximize the satisfaction and growth of their members. Once established, these informal groups will probably resist changes in the formal work group that threaten the satisfaction and growth of the informal group's members. On the

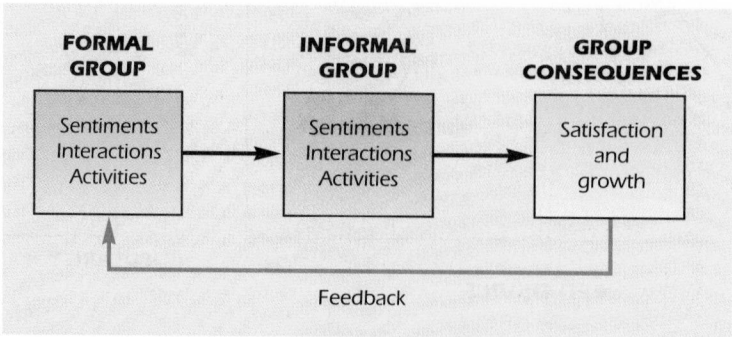

Figure 17.5   Homans' ideas on how informal groups develop

other hand, modifications in the formal work group that enhance the satisfaction and growth of the informal group's members will tend to be welcomed.

BACK TO THE CASE   For a company such as Rolls-Royce to be successful, managers must know how both formal and informal groups affect organizational productivity. Thus they need to determine what informal groups exist and who the group members are, as well as understand how these groups form. Armed with this information, managers can strive to make their work groups more effective.

One analytical tool Rolls-Royce management can use to get information about informal groups within the company is sociometry. That is, managers can design a questionnaire asking their employees whom they spend time with and then construct a sociogram to summarize this information. Of course, managers might choose to do a more casual analysis by simply talking to their employees and observing how they interact with one another.

Rolls-Royce managers should also realize that an organization's formal structure influences how informal groups develop within it. Assume, for example, that in one department at Rolls-Royce there are 30 people working on automobile design. Many of them are interested in sports, have become friends because of this common interest, and work well together as a result. When the department manager needs to make some changes in this design department, he or she should try to accommodate these informal friendship groups to keep their members satisfied. Actions that interfere with this productive friendship group—such as transferring one or more of its members out of the design department—should be taken only for very good reason.

TEAMS

The preceding sections of this chapter discussed groups—what they are, what kinds exist in organizations, and how such groups should be managed. This section focuses on a special type of group: teams. It covers the following topics:

1. The difference between groups and teams.
2. The types of teams that exist in organizations.
3. The stages of development that teams go through.
4. What constitutes an effective team.
5. The relationship between trust and team effectiveness.

Groups *versus* Teams

The terms *group* and *team* are not synonymous. As we have seen, a group consists of any number of people who interact with one another, are psychologically aware of one another, and think of themselves as a group. A **team** is a group whose members influence one another toward the accomplishment of an organizational objective(s).

Not all groups in organizations are teams, but all teams are groups. A group qualifies as a team only if its members focus on helping one another to accomplish organizational objectives. In today's quickly changing business environment, teams have emerged as a requirement for success.[15] Therefore, good managers constantly try to help groups become teams. This part of the chapter provides insights on how managers can facilitate the evolution of groups into teams.

The text has defined "team" and emphasized the difference between a group and a team. The following CUTTING EDGE feature discusses a new type of organizational team made possible by the acquisition of advanced technology by organizations—the virtual team.

A **team** is a group whose members influence one another toward the accomplishment of (an) organizational objective(s).

THE VIRTUAL TEAM—A NEW TYPE OF TEAM IN ORGANIZATIONS

CUTTING EDGE

Virtual teams are organizational teams whose members, though separated by several miles or even continents, are able to work together because they can communicate through modern technology. The technological advancements that have made virtual teams possible include fax machines, E-mail, videoconferencing, and computer software called groupware. The last electronically links team members via computer, allowing them to instantly trade and manipulate information.

Virtual teams are bound to become more prevalent in organizations through the rest of the 1990s and into the next century because of the growing globalization and complication of business. Globalization requires organization members to work together across vast distances, and today's complex business problems demand the attention of the best minds in the organization, regardless of their physical location. The management challenge presented by virtual teams is how to get people to work together as a team even though they cannot meet face-to-face.≈

Types of Teams in Organizations

Organizational teams take many different forms. The following sections discuss three types of teams commonly found in today's organizations: problem-solving teams, self-managed teams, and cross-functional teams.

Problem-Solving Teams

Management confronts many different organizational problems daily. Examples are: production systems that aren't manufacturing products at the desired levels of quality; workers who appear to be listless and uninvolved; and managers who are basing their decisions on inaccurate information.

For assistance in solving such formidable problems, management commonly establishes special teams. A team set up to help eliminate a specified problem within the organization is called a **problem-solving team.** The typical problem-solving team has 5 to 12 members and is formed to discuss ways to improve quality in all phases of the organization, to make organizational processes more efficient, or to improve the overall work environment.[16]

After the problem-solving team reaches a consensus, it makes recommendations to management about how to deal with the specified problem. Management may re-

A **problem-solving team** is an organizational team set up to help eliminate a specified problem within the organization.

Thanks to technology, chief information officer Kevin Parker at investment bank Morgan Stanley is now head of a virtual group of 9,600 people. The group exists because of an "intranet"—an internal corporate web—that connects people at 37 worldwide offices. In New York, for example, employees in the securities division can send 100 pages' worth of data to traders who will receive it before the next morning's opening bell on the Tokyo exchange. Even verbalized buy and sell orders can be digitized and sent over a worldwide voice-messaging system.

spond to the team's recommendations by implementing them in their entirety, by modifying and then implementing them, or by requesting further information to assess them. Once the problem that management asked the problem-solving team to address has been solved, the team is generally disbanded.

Self-Managed Teams

The **self-managed team,** sometimes called a *self-managed work group* or *self-directed team*, is a team that plans, organizes, influences, and controls its own work situation with only minimal intervention and direction from management. This creative team design involves a highly integrated group of several skilled individuals who are cross-trained and have the responsibility and authority to perform some specified activity.

Activities typically carried out by management in a traditional work setting—creating work schedules, establishing work pace and breaks, developing vacation schedules, evaluating performance, determining the level of salary increases and rewards received by individual workers, and ordering materials to be used in the production process—are instead carried out by members of the self-managed team. Generally responsible for whole tasks as opposed to "parts" of a job,[17] the self-managed team is an important new way of structuring, managing, and rewarding work. Since these teams require only minimum management attention, they free managers to pursue other management activities like strategic planning.

Reports of successful self-managed work teams are plentiful.[18] These teams are growing in popularity because today's business environment seems to require such work teams to solve complex problems independently, American workers have come to expect more freedom in the workplace, and the speed of technological change demands that employees be able to adapt quickly. Not all self-managed teams are successful of course. To ensure the success of a self-managed team, the manager should carefully select and properly train its members.[19]

A **self-managed team** is an organizational team established to plan, organize, influence, and control its own work situation with only minimal direction from management.

Cross-Functional Teams

A **cross-functional team** is a work team composed of people from different functional areas of the organization—marketing, finance, human resources, and operations, for example—who are all focused on a specified objective. Cross-functional teams may or may not be self-managed, though self-managed teams are generally cross-functional. Because cross-functional team members are from different departments within the organization, the team possesses the expertise to coordinate all the department activities within the organization that impact its own work.

A **cross-functional team** is an organizational team composed of people from different functional areas of the organization who are all focused on a specified objective.

Once a bastion of top-down management, Texas Instruments Inc. had to make changes when, beginning in the late 1980s, it was hit hard by defense-contract cutbacks and competition. When TI turned to employees for suggestions, the idea of self-managed teams emerged as a productive solution. At TI's Dallas factory, for example, self-managed teams now schedule their own activities, record their own attendance, and even order their own supplies. In one three-year period, sales per employee grew from $88,300 annually to $122,820.

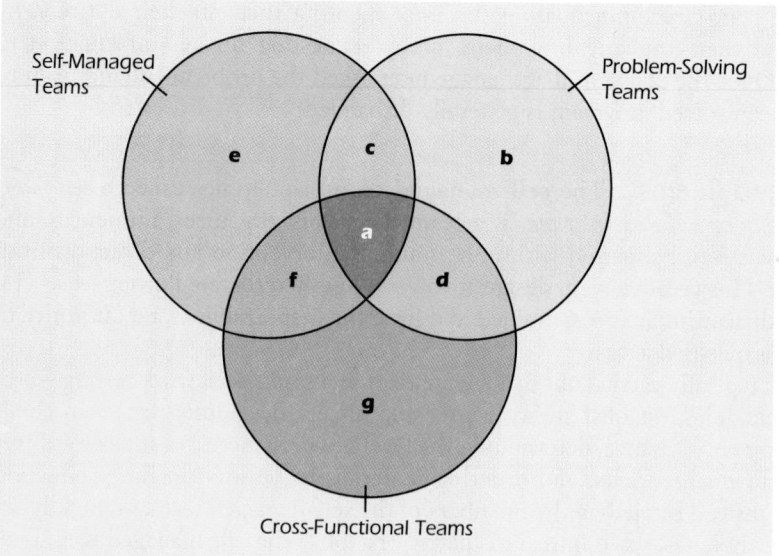

Figure 17.6   Possible team types based on various combinations of self-directed, problem-solving, and cross-functional teams

Some examples of cross-functional teams are: teams established to choose and implement new technologies throughout the organization; teams formed to improve marketing effectiveness within the organization; and teams established to control product costs.[20]

This section discussed three types of teams that exist in organizations: problem-solving, self-directed, and cross-functional. It should be noted here that managers can establish various combinations of these three types of teams. Figure 17.6 illustrates some possible combinations that managers could create. For example, *a* in the figure represents a team that is problem-solving, self-directed, and cross-functional, while *b* represents one that is problem-solving, but neither cross-functional nor self-directed. Before establishing a team, managers should carefully study their own unique organizational situation and set up the type of team that best suits that situation.

The text describes different types of teams that are found in organizations. The following PEOPLE PERSPECTIVES feature illustrates the need for managers to empower work teams if they want them to be successful.

MANAGERS MUST EMPOWER WORK TEAMS

PEOPLE PERSPECTIVES

Empowerment is the granting to teams or individuals the power and authority to do their jobs. It involves far more than merely delegating decision-making authority. Empowerment means releasing organization members to use their total capabilities—all of their knowledge along with their personal influence—to reach objectives. Too many managers simply announce that they are empowering work teams and then fail to create the organizational support structure teams need to function optimally while using their discretion and abilities.

To empower work teams properly, managers must ensure that the teams have complete information relating to their work situation, for without such information, teams will find it impossible to exercise the necessary power and authority to meet organizational goals. Most managers find that to properly empower work teams, they also must see to it that the traditional organizational hierarchy, which is based primarily on individual positions, is gradually replaced by a new structure that emphasizes team functioning. Unless this is done, work teams' progress will be seriously hampered.≈

Stages of Team Development

More and more modern managers are using work teams to accomplish organizational tasks. Simply establishing such a team, however, does not guarantee it will be productive. In fact, managers should be patient when an established work team is not initially productive, for teams generally need to pass through several developmental stages before they become productive. Managers must understand this developmental process so they can facilitate it. The following sections discuss the various stages a team usually must pass through before it becomes fully productive.[21]

Forming   **Forming** is the first stage of the team development process. During this stage, members of the newly formed team become oriented to the team and acquainted with one another. This period is characterized by the exploration of issues related to their new job situation, such as what is expected of them, who has what kind of authority within the team, what kind of people are team members, and what skills team members possess.

The forming stage of team development is usually characterized by uncertainty and stress. Recognizing that team members are struggling to adjust to their new work situation and to one another, managers should be tolerant of lengthy informal discussions exploring team specifics and not regard them as time wasters. The newly formed team must be allowed an exploratory period if it is to become truly productive.

Storming   After a team has formed, it begins to storm. **Storming,** the second stage of the team development process, is characterized by conflict and disagreement as team members become more assertive in clarifying their individual roles. During this stage, the team seems to lack unity because members are continually challenging the way the team functions.

To help the team progress beyond storming, managers should encourage team members to feel free to disagree with any team issues and to discuss their own views fully and honestly. Most of all, managers should urge team members to arrive at agreements that will help the team reach its objective(s).

Norming   When the storming stage ends, norming begins. **Norming,** the third stage of the team development process, is characterized by agreement among team members on roles, rules, and acceptable behavior while working on the team. Conflicts generated during the storming stage are resolved in this stage.

Managers should encourage teams that have entered the norming stage to progress toward developing team norms and values that will be instrumental in building a successful organization. The process of determining what behavior is and is not acceptable within the team is critical to the work team's future productivity.

Performing   The fourth stage of the team development process is **performing.** At this stage, the team fully focuses on solving organizational problems and on meeting assigned challenges. The team is now productive: after successfully passing through the earlier stages of team development, it knows itself and has settled on team roles, expectations, and norms.

During this stage managers should recognize the team's accomplishments regularly, for productive team behavior must be reinforced to enhance the probability that it will continue in the future.

Adjourning   The fifth, and last, stage of the team development process is known as **adjourning.** Now the team is finishing its job and preparing to disband. This stage normally occurs only in teams established for some special purpose to be accomplished in a limited time period. Special committees and task groups are examples of such teams. During the adjourning stage, team members generally feel disappointment that their team is being broken up because disbandment means the loss of personally satisfying relationships and/or an enjoyable work situation.

Forming is the first stage of the team development process, during which members of the newly formed team become oriented to the team and acquainted with one another as they explore issues related to their new job situation.

Storming, the second stage of the team development process, is characterized by conflict and disagreement as team members try to clarify their individual roles and challenge the way the team functions.

Norming, the third stage of the team development process, is characterized by agreement among team members on roles, rules, and acceptable behavior while working on the team.

Performing, the fourth stage of the team development process, is characterized by a focus on solving organizational problems and meeting assigned challenges.

Adjourning, the fifth and last stage of the team development process, is the stage in which the team finishes its job and prepares to disband.

During this phase of team development, managers should recognize team members' disappointment and sense of loss as normal and assure them that other challenging and exciting organizational opportunities await them. It is important that management then do everything necessary to integrate these people into new teams or other areas of the organization.

Although some work teams do not pass through every one of the development stages just described, understanding the stages of forming, storming, norming, performing, and adjourning will give managers many useful insights on how to build productive work teams. Above all, managers must realize that new teams are different from mature teams and that their challenge is to build whatever team they are in charge of into a mature, productive work team.

Team Effectiveness

Earlier in this chapter, teams were defined as groups of people who influence one another to reach organizational targets. It is easy to see why effective teams are critical to organizational success. Effective teams are those that come up with innovative ideas, accomplish their goals, and adapt to change when necessary. Their individual members are highly committed to both the team and organizational goals. Such teams are highly valued by upper management and recognized and rewarded for their accomplishments.[22]

Figure 17.7 sketches the characteristics of an effective team. Note the figure's implications for the steps managers need to take to build effective work teams in organizations. *People-related steps* include:

1. Trying to make the team's work satisfying.
2. Developing mutual trust among team members and between the team and management.
3. Building good communication—from management to the team as well as within the team.
4. Minimizing unresolved conflicts and power struggles within the team.

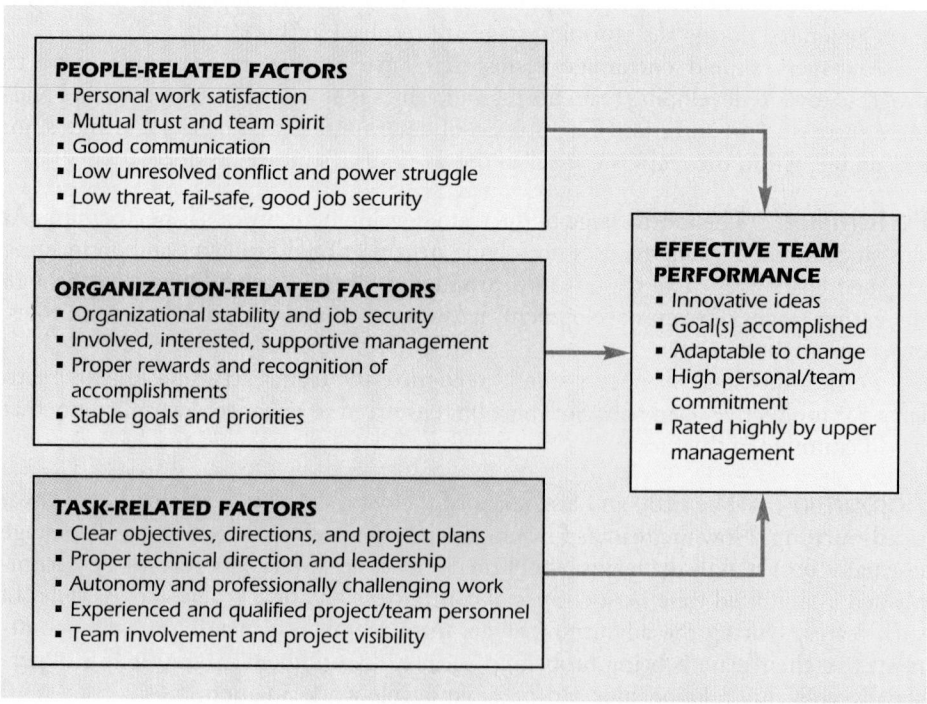

Figure 17.7   Factors contributing to team effectiveness

5. Dealing effectively with threats toward and within the team.
6. Building the perception that the jobs of team members are secure.

Organization-related steps managers can take to build effective work teams include:

1. Building a stable overall organization or company structure that team members view as secure.
2. Becoming involved in team events and demonstrating interest in team progress and functioning.
3. Properly rewarding and recognizing teams for their accomplishments.
4. Setting stable goals and priorities for the team.

Finally, Figure 17.7 implies that managers can build effective work teams by taking six *task-related steps:*

1. Developing clear objectives, directions, and project plans for the team.
2. Providing proper technical direction and leadership for the team.
3. Establishing autonomy for the team and challenging work within the team.
4. Appointing experienced and qualified team personnel.
5. Encouraging team involvement.
6. Building visibility within the organization for the team's work.

Trust and Effective Teams

Probably the most fundamental ingredient of effective teams is trust. Trust is belief in the reliance, ability, and integrity of another. Unless team members trust one another, the team leader, and management, managers may well find that building an effective work team is impossible.[23]

Today there is significant concern that management is not inspiring the kind of trust that is essential to team effectiveness. In fact, subordinates' trust in their managers is critically low, and employee opinion polls indicate that it may well decline even further in the future.

Management urgently needs to focus on reversing this trend. There are many strategies managers can use to build trust within groups:[24]

- *Communicate often to team members.* This is a fundamental strategy. Keeping team members informed of organizational news, explaining why certain decisions have been made, and sharing information about organizational operations are examples of how managers should communicate to team members.
- *Show respect for team members.* Managers need to show team members that they are highly valued. They can demonstrate their respect for team members by delegating tasks to them, listening intently to feedback from the group, and acting on it appropriately.
- *Be fair to team members.* Team members must receive the rewards they have earned. Managers must therefore conduct fair performance appraisals and objectively allocate and distribute rewards. It should go without saying that showing favoritism in this area sows mistrust and resentment.
- *Be predictable.* Managers must be consistent in their actions. Team members should usually be able to forecast what decisions management will make before those decisions are made. Moreover, managers must live up to commitments made to team members. Managers who make inconsistent decisions and fail to live up to commitments will not be trusted by teams.
- *Demonstrate competence.* To build team trust, managers must show team members that they are able to diagnose organizational problems and have the skill to implement solutions to those problems. Team members tend to trust managers they perceive as competent and distrust those they perceive as incompetent.

Corporate Culture

So far, this chapter has focused on managing smaller work groups. This section, in contrast, discusses corporate culture as an important ingredient for managing organization members as a total group.

Corporate culture is a set of shared values and beliefs that organization members have regarding the functioning and existence of their organization. What type of corporate culture is present in any organization can be discovered by studying that organization's special combination of status symbols, traditions, history, and physical environment. A management that understands the significance of all these factors can use them to develop a corporate culture that is beneficial to the firm.

> **Corporate culture** is a set of shared values and beliefs that organization members have regarding the functioning and existence of their organization.

Status Symbols　Looking at the status symbols of an organization—the visible, external signs of social position that are associated with the various positions in the firm—gives an observer a feeling for the organization's social hierarchy. The size and location of an organization member's office, as well as the member's access to executive clubs and reserved parking, indicates the status level of that member's job.

Traditions and History　A firm's history and traditions can determine how workers in that particular firm act on a daily basis. Typically, traditions developed over time let workers know exactly what is expected of them. By developing traditions, therefore, managers can steer the everyday behaviors that go on in an organization.

Physical Environment　The firm's physical environment makes a statement about its corporate culture. For instance, closed offices and few common areas where organization members can meet indicate a closed form of culture. On the other hand, a building with open offices and extensive common areas where employees can interact indicates a more open culture. Management that wants an open culture, then, will see to it that office doors are usually open; management that wants a more formal type of corporate culture will encourage closed office doors.

The Significance of Corporate Culture

The significance of corporate culture for management is that it influences the behavior of everyone within an organization and, if carefully crafted, can have a significant positive effect on organizational success.[25] If not properly managed, however, corporate culture can help doom an organization. Typically, top management and other present or past organizational leaders are the key agents influencing corporate culture.

The current management literature is full of advice about the way managers should handle corporate culture issues. One especially practical and helpful book sug-

The corporate culture at Interval Research in Palo Alto, California, is less a reflection of what the company does (conducting "pure research" on consumer goods and services for the information highway) than of how it goes about it. To build this futuristic kitchen, for example, researchers "collected" samples of people's everyday behavior in the real world. Then they brought it back to the office, where the workday consisted of freewheeling "informances"—informative performances in which staffers "play act" the imagined lives of imaginary consumers.

gests that there are five primary mechanisms to develop and reinforce the desired corporate culture:[26]

- *What leaders pay attention to, measure, and control.* Leaders can communicate very effectively what their vision of the organization is and what they want done by consistently emphasizing the same issues in meetings, in casual remarks and questions, and in strategy discussions. For example, if product quality is the dominant value to be inculcated in employees, leaders may consistently inquire about the effect of any proposed changes on product quality.
- *Leaders' reactions to critical incidents and organizational crises.* The manner in which leaders deal with crises can create new beliefs and values and reveal underlying organizational assumptions. For example, when a firm faces a financial crisis but does not lay off any employees, the message is that the organization sees itself as a "family" that looks out for its members.
- *Deliberate role modeling, teaching, and coaching.* The behaviors of leaders in both formal and informal settings have an important effect on employee beliefs, values, and behaviors. For example, if the CEO regularly works very long hours and on weekends, other managers will probably respond by spending more time at work also.
- *Criteria for allocation of rewards and status.* Leaders can firmly communicate their priorities and values by consistently linking rewards and punishments to the behaviors that concern them. For example, if a weekly bonus is given for exceeding production or sales quotas, employees will recognize the value placed on these activities and focus their efforts on them.
- *Criteria for recruitment, selection, promotion, and retirement of employees.* The kinds of people who are hired and who succeed in an organization are those who accept the organization's values and behave accordingly. For example, if managers who are action oriented and who implement strategies effectively consistently move up the organizational ladder, the organization's priorities will come through loud and clear to other managers.

To influence the type of culture that exists within an organization, a manager must first determine what culture would be appropriate for the organization, and then take calculated and overt steps to encourage the establishment, growth, and maintenance of that culture. Merely allowing a corporate culture to develop without planned management influence can result in an inappropriate culture that limits the organization's success.

BACK TO THE CASE

In managing groups, Rolls-Royce managers must understand that there is a crucial difference between a group and a team. While a group consists of people who interact with one another, are psychologically aware of one another, and think of themselves as a group, a team is a group whose members influence one another toward the accomplishment of organizational goals. Obviously, teams are more desirable from management's point of view, and an important managerial challenge is to turn work groups into teams.

Rolls-Royce management can use problem-solving, self-managed, and cross-functional teams to solve specific organizational problems and to approach organizational issues from a variety of functional perspectives. The choice of teams—or combination of teams—would depend on the specific organizational circumstances.

Once a team is established, Rolls-Royce management must be patient and recognize that teams usually need some time to develop into productive work units. The team development process generally proceeds from an initial forming stage to a fully effective performing stage. Management must understand each stage of the process, help teams progress through the stages, and empower them to do their jobs.

Rolls-Royce managers should strive to develop *effective* teams—teams that generate innovative ideas, accomplish their goals, adapt to change, and are characterized by members who are dedicated both to the team and to the organization. It is essential also that Rolls-Royce managers develop trust within their work teams by keeping team members informed about company events, showing respect for team members, being fair to them, being predictable in their own decision making, and demonstrating to team members that management is capable of solving organizational problems.

If Rolls-Royce wants to capitalize fully on the talents of its employees, management must work not only at turning work groups into effective work teams but also at making such teams a part of the corporate culture. That is, Rolls-Royce organization members must come to share management's belief that effective teams are an important means to the end of company success.

Action Summary

Reread the learning objectives below. Each objective is followed by questions. Answering these questions accurately will help you retain the most important concepts discussed in this chapter. After answering each question, check your answer against the answer key at the end of this chapter. (*Hint:* If you have any doubts regarding the correct response, consult the page whose number follows the answer.)

Circle: From studying this chapter, I will attempt to acquire:

1. A definition of the term *group* as used in the context of management.

T,F   **a.** A group is made up of people who interact with one another, perceive themselves to be a group, and are primarily physically aware of one another.

a,b,c,d,e   **b.** According to Cartwright and Lippitt, it is *not* true to say that: (a) groups exist in all kinds of organizations; (b) groups inevitably form in all facets of organizational existence; (c) groups cause undesirable consequences within the organization, so their continued existence should be discouraged; (d) understanding groups can assist managers in increasing the probability that the groups with which they work will cause desirable consequences within the organization; (e) all of the above are true.

2. A thorough understanding of the difference between formal and informal groups.

T,F   **a.** An informal group is one that exists within an organization by virtue of management decree.

T,F   **b.** A formal group is one that exists within an organization by virtue of interaction among organization members who work in proximity to one another.

3. Knowledge of the types of formal groups that exist in organizations.

a,b,c,d,e   **a.** The type of group that generally handles more routine organizational activities is the: (a) informal task group; (b) informal command group; (c) formal task group; (d) formal command group; (e) none of the above.

a,b,c,d,e   **b.** Managers should be encouraged to take the following steps to increase the success of a committee: (a) clearly define the goals of the committee; (b) rephrase ideas that have already been expressed; (c) select a chairperson on the basis of ability to run an efficient meeting; (d) a and b; (e) a, b, and c.

4. An understanding of how managers can determine which groups exist in an organization.

T,F   **a.** The technique of sociometry involves asking people whom they would like to manage.

a,b,c,d,e   **b.** A sociogram is defined in the text as: (a) a letter encouraging group participation; (b) a diagram that visually illustrates the number of times that the individuals were chosen within the group and whether the choice was reciprocal; (c) a composite of demographic data useful in determining informal group choices; (d) a computer printout designed to profile psychological and sociological characteristics of the informal group; (e) none of the above.

5. An appreciation for what teams are and how to manage them.

T,F   **a.** A cross-functional team can also be a problem-solving team, but it cannot be a self-managed team.

a,b,c,d,e   **b.** Which of the following is *not* a stage of team development: (a) storming; (b) alarming; (c) forming; (d) performing; (e) norming.

T,F   **c.** Trust is probably the most fundamental ingredient of effective teams.

      6. Insights about managing corporate culture to enhance organizational success.

T,F   **a.** The concept of corporate culture usually does not include the set of beliefs that organization members have about their organization and its functioning.

a,b,c,d,e   **b.** Mechanisms that managers can use to influence corporate culture include: (a) what leaders pay attention to; (b) criteria that leaders use to make organizational awards; (c) criteria leaders use to select new employees; (d) all of the above; (e) none of the above.

Introductory Case Wrap-Up

"Groups Are Important to Progress at Rolls-Royce" (p. 403) and its related back-to-the-case sections were written to help you better understand the management concepts contained in this chapter. Answer the following discussion questions about this introductory case to enrich your understanding of the chapter content:

1. What kinds of group would the Japanese-style work teams at Rolls-Royce be classified as? Explain.
2. What advice would you give to a Rolls-Royce manager who is managing such a work team?

Issues for Review and Discussion

1. How is the term *group* defined in this chapter?
2. Why is the study of groups important to managers?
3. What is a formal group?
4. Explain the significance of linking pins to formal groups in organizations.
5. List and define two types of formal groups that can exist in organizations.
6. Why should managers use committees in organizations?
7. What steps can managers take to ensure that a committee will be successful?
8. Explain how work teams can be valuable to an organization.
9. Describe the stages a group typically goes through as it matures.
10. What is an informal group?
11. List and define two types of informal groups in organizations.
12. What benefits generally accrue to members of informal groups?
13. What is the relationship between work teams and informal groups?
14. Are formal groups more important to managers than informal groups? Explain.
15. Describe the sociometric procedure used to study informal group membership. What can the results of a sociometric analysis tell managers about members of an informal group?
16. Explain Homans' concept of how informal groups develop.
17. What is the difference between a group and a team? Is this an important difference for a manager to understand? Why?
18. Discuss how managers can develop effective teams in organizations.
19. What steps can managers take to develop trust in work teams? Is developing this trust important? Why?
20. Define corporate culture. Can managers actually build corporate culture? Explain.

Action Summary Answer Key

1. **a.** F, p. 404
   b. c, p. 404
2. **a.** F, p. 404
   b. F p. 404

3. **a.** d, pp. 405–406
   b. e, p. 408
4. **a.** F, pp. 412–413
   b. b, pp. 412–413

5. **a.** F, pp. 417–418
   b. b, pp. 419–420
   c. T, p. 421

6. **a.** F, p. 422
   b. d, p. 423

Case Study

Whose Turn Is It to Polish the Apple?

On February 2, 1996, Apple Computer installed its fourth new chief—Gilbert Amelio, the CEO credited with turning around failing National Semiconductor Corporation. Amelio describes his turnaround magic in his book *Profit from Experience:* In essence, he creates a simple vision and pulls people together to back it, no matter what it takes. His plan has become known as the "chartreuse strategy" because, in the midst of turning around a division at Rockwell International, Amelio declared that he'd even paint the buildings chartreuse if that would draw people's attention to his insistence on cultural change.

Today the board, shareholders, employees, and customers of Apple are looking to Amelio to transform a floundering operation and rekindle a once-vital organization's hopes and commitments. Amelio certainly has his work cut out for him: Apple's share of the personal-computer market was down to 7.8 percent when he took office. If market share goes any lower, the once brash technological innovator will be merely a niche player.

Amelio makes quick changes, but he is not a slash-and-burn artist. A physicist by training, he has a professorial bent and considerable personal charm. Although Amelio writes in his book that "layoffs are a sign of management failure," some observers believe that he has no choice but to make deep, fast cuts at what many critics consider a "flabby" company. His plans will also end Apple's waffling over broadly licensing Mac technology, reinventing Apple's Internet strategy, and terminating efforts that Amelio believes to be beyond the company's core business.

"The fact is," according to a *Business Week* magazine article, "despite its glowing reputation, Apple has rarely run smoothly—at least not for more than a few years at a time. The pattern of mismanagement that has characterized the company since its inception has caused Apple to bungle critical decisions and waver back and forth between strategies."

This disastrous pattern began with Apple's founders, Steven P. Jobs and Stephen Wozniak. While virtually inventing the PC industry with the Apple II, Jobs and Wozniak also created the renegade Apple corporate culture. Their guiding principles: Do your own thing, defy the pessimists, and ignore the Establishment. The crowning achievement of this attitude was a ground-breaking machine—the "insanely great" Mac—with which users fell in love.

According to a former Apple executive, however, this celebrated corporate culture had a dark side: It was "unharnessed and uncontrolled." Inevitably, this "dark side" led to clashes between Apple's free-wheeling creators and the experienced managers who had been hired to run the company's marketing and finance activities. First, disagreements between the two founders led to Wozniak's withdrawal from Apple. Then the clashes converged in an all-out-battle between remaining founder Jobs and former PepsiCo executive John Sculley over the Mac's ultimate design.

Sculley came out on top. He immediately acted to protect the company with sweeping layoffs. Unfortunately, the rank and file resented the big-company systems that Sculley put in place. The new CEO also had to find a way to retain the dynamic engineers and programmers whose genius had kept Apple generally ahead of the technology curve. The solution: Don't tinker with the culture set in place by Jobs and Wozniak. By and large, that approach worked, but it had certain costs. The glorification of the so-called technical wizards made them difficult to supervise and fostered an atmosphere of arrogance that kept employees at all levels from responding seriously to competition.

Additionally, at least one grapevine joke had it that at Apple, protecting Apple's culture meant allowing an endless search for consensus. No decision was final; "even a vote of 15,000 to 1 can still be a tie." But the joke, it seemed, was ultimately on Apple. Year after year, key decisions were postponed, reversed, or avoided. Asks one former Apple executive, "Why can't somebody just say: 'I'm the leader. This is the way it's going to be. Thanks for the discussion, but if you don't want to do it, leave.' "

Still, Apple's fortunes took a turn for the good, and Sculley turned his attention to R&D. In fact, he took on the role of "techno-visonary," awarding himself the title of Chief Technology Officer in 1990. This was a major mistake. His pet project, the Newton, which was aimed at the needs of a converging computer/communications/media market, was released to widespread ridicule in 1993.

Apple's board didn't laugh. They moved to fire Sculley and replaced him with Michael Spindler, whose no-nonsense attitude toward business seemed like the long-awaited voice of reason in Apple's chaotic culture. Like Sculley, Spindler began with massive layoffs. He also moved the firm toward a new, low-margin business model. The company responded to his strategy with four quarters of strong growth and a rebound in stock price. But Apple's cult of consensus and the new CEO's inconsistency quickly proved a deadly combination. Within a year, Spindler was caught in a cycle of delay, reversal, and missed opportunities.

Now, loyal Mac users, shareholders, employees, and the board all look to Gilbert Amelio to "polish the Apple." He will have to solve the problem of Apple's culture if he is to succeed.

Questions:

1. Describe the corporate culture created at Apple by Jobs and Wozniak. What were the pros and cons of that culture? What could have been done differently to maximize the pros and minimize the cons? Explain.

2. How did the Mac reflect the culture of the company? Discuss "decisions by indecision" made by Apple leadership that caused the Mac to lose its preeminence. Did these decisions reflect problems within Apple's corporate culture? Explain.

3. Examine the five suggestions for leaders who hope to manage corporate culture successfully. Evaluate Apple's management decisions in light of each. What mistakes were made and how could they have been corrected? What advice would you give Amelio?

Skills Exercise

According to many experts, Marco Landi of Apple Europe is a good example for new Apple CEO Amelio to emulate. Landi tripled Apple's European profits by imposing discipline and accountability: "I tried to understand the Apple culture," explains Landi. "I used the good things like entrepreneurialism and innovation and tried to bring in more control and management processes." Research current *Business Profiles* and periodicals to describe the current corporate culture at Apple. Was Amelio's "chartreuse strategy" a success? Was he able to maintain the "good things" at Apple and improve the culture with "more control and management"? Explain.

The Internet learning materials that accompany this chapter can be found at
http://www.profcerto.com
Additional information can be found on the inside front and back covers of this text.

18
chapter

UNDERSTANDING PEOPLE:
ATTITUDES, PERCEPTION, AND LEARNING

STUDENT LEARNING OBJECTIVES

From studying this chapter, I will attempt to acquire:

1. An understanding of employee workplace attitudes.
2. Insights into how to change employee attitudes.
3. An appreciation of the impact of employee perceptions on employee behaviors.
4. Knowledge of employee perceptions of procedural justice.
5. An understanding that adult learners are different from younger students.

CHAPTER OUTLINE

Introductory Case: Reviving Workplace Attitudes

What Are Attitudes?
How Beliefs and Values Create Attitude
Attitude Surveys

People Perspectives: Changing Attitudes toward Surveys

Quality Spotlight: The Success Formula at Nucor Steel

Cutting Edge: We Hire Attitudes!

Perception
Perception and the Perceptual Process
Attribution Theory: Interpreting the Behavior of Others
Perceptual Distortions

Global Spotlight: The Wide, Wide World of Cultural Perceptions

Perceptions of Procedural Justice

Learning
Learning Strategies

Reviving Workplace Attitudes

Claudia Younce, a 43-year-old nurse, considers herself gregarious and positive. She loves mending broken bodies and is passionate about nursing. But off and on between 1991 and 1993, Younce hit an impasse in her career: After the alarm buzzed in the mornings, she'd lie in bed daydreaming about what she'd rather do than go to work. Other symptoms surfaced. She noticed that she didn't chat as often with co-workers. She began to question whether nursing was truly her calling.

"I felt I wasn't getting much from my job," recalls Younce, who works at St. Elizabeth Medical Center, one of the five hospitals in Dayton, Ohio. "I liked my job, but there was something more I needed to be doing." Her experience was hardly unusual. Countless Americans experience times of frustration and dissatisfaction with their jobs and declining work attitudes. During these periods, their productivity usually falls and they perceive no meaning or purpose to their jobs. In fact, many people believe that quitting is the only way to relieve the stress. However, experts warn frustrated employees not to make a major move too quickly.

Experiencing workplace blues—a career low point—is common. The Bureau of Labor Statistics reports that more than 50 percent of workers are unhappy on the job. According to Priscilla Mutter, a career counselor in Dayton, people need to discover the cause of their frustrations in order to make the most of their job.

Employees often believe that managers and co-workers cause their frustrations at work. Yet it's usually their own response to others that creates problems, Mutter says. Once people discover the true source of their concerns, they should look around the company for other opportunities and consider going back to school to gain new skills or a new life interest. Every effort people make to better a work situation usually helps. "Even though work may not have changed, they're proactive and their work seems better," says Mutter. "They're taking charge of their lives and things look a lot brighter."

Claudia Younce, for example, wanted more from her career as a nursing supervisor. She visited two career counselors for advice. After some testing, the first counselor recommended that she consider another career—an idea that didn't sit well with Younce. She then went to Priscilla Mutter, who reinforced her career choice, but suggested that Younce pursue non-work activities to create a balance in her life. More balance, Mutter suggested, would make her job more meaningful.

Younce thus began working with Starfish, a local organization that does volunteer work in developing countries. This summer, she will spend a month teaching nursing in South Africa. "I love to travel and I like helping people," says Younce. "Volunteering gives me something more to look forward to, and it broadens my outlook on life."

Younce also entered graduate school at the University of Cincinnati. Education not only fuels the part of her that loves to learn but also provides a chance to boost her career at the hospital. Now Younce gets out of bed every morning looking forward to work. Although her job responsibilities haven't changed at St. Elizabeth, she has largely healed herself by doing what made her happy. Although most people will never discover that "perfect" job, it's their *attitude* and view of work that *make the difference* in the world.

Career counselor Priscilla Mutter believes that when people encounter frustration in the workplace, they should be "proactive" in seeing their problems as something they can address.

what's ahead n the opening case, Claudia Younce, an employee who had skills and experience to be successful on the job, developed attitudes that negatively impacted her work. The information in this chapter provides insights for managers regarding how to enhance the productivity of organization members like Claudia through an understanding of people. More precisely, this chapter studies people by discussing the following topics:

1. attitudes
2. perception
3. learning

The previous chapters in this section discussed people issues important to managing like influencing and communication, leadership, motivation, and groups and teamwork. This chapter continues the study of people issues important to managing by elaborating upon characteristics of individuals in organizations. Characteristics discussed in the following sections are attitudes, perception, and learning.

WHAT ARE ATTITUDES?

An **attitude** is a predisposition to react to a situation, person, or concept with a particular response.

An **attitude** is a predisposition to react to a situation, person, or concept with a particular response. This response can be either positive or negative. It is a learned reaction—one that results from an individual's past observations, direct experiences, or exposure to others' attitudes. For example, someone may say, "I love baseball," thus communicating to others a general attitude about the sport. Some baseball fans developed their love for the sport while playing it in childhood; direct experience shaped their attitude. Others never played the game but developed a love for the sport by watching games at the ballpark or on television. Still others had friends or family members who influenced their attitudes by communicating their love for the game.

Attitudes are internal and may be largely kept to oneself, or they may be made known to others through overt behaviors. Generally, attitudes have three primary components:[1]

1. *Cognitive:* information and beliefs about a particular person or object.
2. *Affective:* a positive or negative feeling about a particular person or object.
3. *Behavioral:* an intent or desire to behave in a certain way toward a particular person or object.

Again, a conversation among co-workers may help illustrate these differences:

MARIA: Did you hear about the training program that starts next week?
LEX: Yes, I've read several reviews on that software. It may make my job much easier and help me to produce better newsletters and reports.
DAVID: I hate going to training programs and having to learn new software. Just when you really get comfortable with one, they change to a new one.
MARIA: Well, I intend to pick it up as quickly as possible so I can expand my skills and possibly bid for a higher-grade job.

In this brief exchange, Lex communicates one attitude about the specific training program. The information that he has learned about it has given him an attitude of awareness (a cognitive component), but no positive or negative feelings toward the program. David, however, expresses both awareness and a negative attitude (an affective component) toward the training program, probably based on his own past experiences or those of others. Maria not only has knowledge of the program (cognitive) and a positive feeling toward it (affective) but also has decided how she will approach it (a behavioral component).

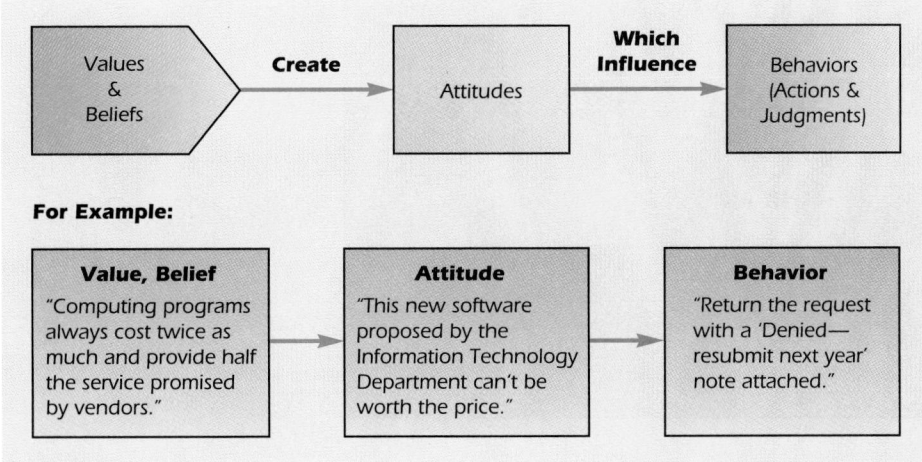

Figure 18.1   Situation: Based on personal attitudes, beliefs and values, a manager decides to deny a request for new software

How Beliefs and Values Create Attitudes

Overall, an individual's attitudes are a result of the beliefs and values held by the individual. **Beliefs** are accepted facts or truths about an object or person that have been gained from either direct experience or a secondary source. For example, what people believe about McDonald's restaurants or the Publisher's Clearinghouse Sweepstakes tends to form their attitudes about each and influences the way they react to each.

Values are levels of worth placed by an individual on various factors in the environment. Values tend to be broad views of life and are influenced by parents, peer groups, and associates. Values tend to guide one's actions and judgments across a variety of situations. Thus a person's workplace values may be defined as those concepts, principles, people, objects, or activities that he or she considers important. Values are those things for which a person may make sacrifices and work hard. In the workplace, such factors as compensation, recognition, and status are often regarded as common values.[2]

One way in which the relationship among attitudes, values, and beliefs can affect people's behavior in the workplace is illustrated in Figure 18.1.[3] For example, direct past experiences or observations of others may have led our hypothetical manager to believe that software vendors usually exaggerate the virtues of their products. In fact, this person has developed a rule of thumb: New office software programs cost twice as much as their initial price (because of add-on charges, upgrades, training expenses, and so forth) and deliver only half the level of promised service. This general belief has led the manager to develop an attitude of distrust toward any new software. When the manager's skepticism is applied to a specific new product, this attitude influences his behavior—he denies the request for the software. We can see that the manager's decision-making process was not objective. Instead, the process was negatively biased because of an attitude—an attitude resulting from general beliefs and values formed by past experiences and observations.

Attitude Surveys

In election years, political candidates spend millions of dollars on public opinion surveys. In addition, the media publishes their own polls on candidates and issues. Why are such surveys done? In the case of the candidate, survey information can be used to plan future campaign strategy. The most important reason for such surveys, however, is that a professionally conducted poll will almost invariably predict the outcome of an

Beliefs are accepted facts or truths about an object or person that have been gained from either direct experience or a secondary source.

Values are the global beliefs that guide one's actions and judgments across a variety of situations.

Its "Intel Inside" campaign made Intel Corporation's Pentium chip a household name among computer-savvy consumers. In November 1994, however, when Intel learned of a minor flaw in its best-selling microprocessor, certain corporate values came up short. In particular, Intel failed to offer no-questions-asked replacements because its corporate culture valued growth and profitability and largely ignored the difficulties involved in marketing high-tech products directly to consumers.

election. Polls tend to be accurate because the people surveyed express *attitudes* on which they are likely to base *behavior*.

Managers also use attitude surveys. Faced with such employee problems as excessive turnover and absenteeism, low productivity, and poor-quality work, they may use surveys to predict employee behavior or determine the sources of existing problems. An attitude-survey program is outlined in the PEOPLE PERSPECTIVES box below. In the workplace, surveys are sometimes called "polling-attitude surveys" or simply "job-satisfaction surveys." In recent years, attitude surveys have gained in popularity because they often determine the sources of employee dissatisfaction. If an employer addresses problem areas identified in attitude surveys, organizational problems like low productivity and poor-quality products can often be reduced, employee morale improved, and productivity increased.

CHANGING ATTITUDES TOWARD SURVEYS

PEOPLE PERSPECTIVES

In 1992, Rich Robinson, the new CEO at Doctors Hospital of Manteco, California, decided that an employee-attitude survey was needed to measure employee satisfaction in a variety of areas. Confidentiality, however, was a must: Employees had recently decertified a union after 32 years of collective bargaining, and labor relations at the hospital were generally better, though tense. To guarantee confidentiality, an outside firm was hired to conduct the survey. Employees mailed completed forms directly to the survey firm.

The survey contained 115 statements about all aspects of the workplace. On each statement, employees expressed their attitudes by choosing one response from a five-point response scale ranging from "strongly agree" to "strongly disagree." The survey contained statements like the following:

1. The people in my work area encourage each other to give their best effort.
2. Considering the skill and effort I put into my work, I am satisfied with my pay.
3. There are significant problems in communication between my department and others.

Robinson made a critical leadership decision when he chose to form an Employee Opinion Survey Committee to oversee the hospital's response to the survey results. The committee was given a free hand in the process. Most importantly, the survey results did not sit on a shelf and gather dust. Instead, the committee reviewed them and identified *problem spots*—items that received "unfavorable" responses of 35 percent or higher. Problem spots included the following:

- Communication
- Career development
- Identifying staffing needs
- Performance evaluations
- Compensation and benefits
- Cafeteria

The committee then developed *action plans* to correct the problems. One plan addressed the barriers to education faced by many employees. For example, employees were receiving 100 percent tuition reimbursement for college courses they took, but because funds were not distributed until the end of a semester, many workers could not afford to participate. The action plan provided up-front tuition payments to employees and even established a loan program to assist with other costs.

The committee communicated its action plans to all hospital personnel so that employees could appreciate the priority the hospital had given the survey. Additional memos and newsletters announced further plans and updated progress.≈

Theory of Reasoned Action   Research indicates that the attitudes employees hold toward their jobs and employers are quite stable over time: Both people with generally positive and people with generally negative attitudes tend to retain them over time.[4] This finding is important to managers because it means they can feel reasonably confident that measuring attitudes is likely to produce useful information.

At the same time, however, changing employees' attitudes toward specific aspects of their jobs is usually a challenging task for management. Researchers generally agree that while attitudes "influence" employee behaviors in the workplace, they are not perfect predictors of behaviors. Thus behavioralists Martin Fishbein and others have developed a model designed to provide a more complete examination of the attitude-behavior relationship. This model, called the **theory of reasoned action**, is summarized in Figure 18.2. According to the model, when a behavior is a matter of *choice*, the best predictor of the behavior is the person's *intention* to perform it. Intention is best predicted from two factors:

The **theory of reasoned action** states that when a behavior is a matter of *choice*, the best predictor of the behavior is the person's *intention* to perform it.

1. The person's attitude toward performing the behavior.
2. The person's subjective norm—the perception that he or she is expected by peers or others to perform a certain behavior.

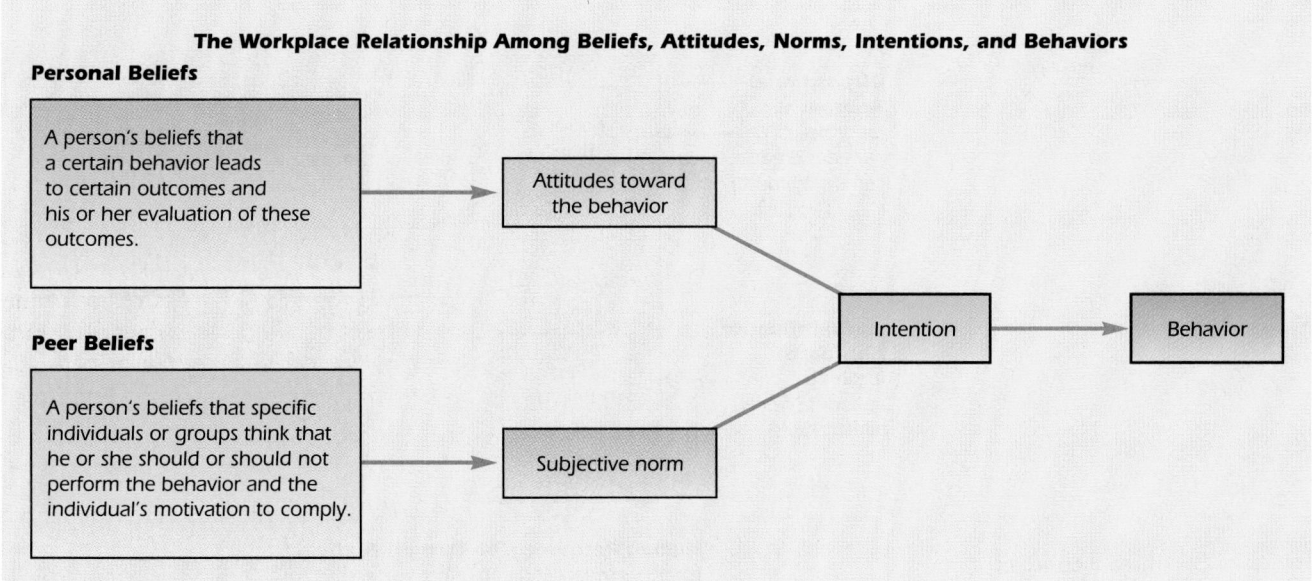

Figure 18.2   **Theory of Reasoned Action**

According to this view, then, attitude is a person's positive or negative feeling toward performing a behavior.

The *reasoned action* model further suggests that a person's attitude can be predicted by his or her belief that a certain behavior will lead to certain outcomes. Also important is the value that the person places on those outcomes. Similarly, a person's subjective norm can sometimes be predicted from his or her belief that other individuals (supervisors, co-workers, friends) think that the person should (or should not) perform a behavior. Not surprisingly, when people have strong beliefs and attitudes about a certain behavior and perceive that it is expected of them, they are more likely to perform it. The reverse, of course, is also true.[5]

Employee Attitudes   Many managers find employee attitudes complex and difficult to understand—and even more difficult to change. What job factors are important determinants of employee attitudes? Academic research and the hands-on experience of managers have produced at least three theories concerning the primary determinants of employee attitudes. (see Figure 18.3)

The first approach focuses on the *design of the job* and stresses such factors as task design, work autonomy, and level of challenge. The second approach stresses *social influence*, assuming that employees' attitudes toward their jobs are affected by the attitudes or beliefs of their peers.

The third theory, called the *dispositional approach*, stresses personal characteristics that are fairly stable over time. This theory holds that people are *generally predisposed* to like or dislike both the overall quality of their jobs and such specific job characteristics as the work itself, supervision, compensation, and work rules. The dispositional approach does not deny potentially positive or negative situational influences—say, changes in supervision, work assignment, job design—but it holds that individuals enter the workplace with predisposed job attitudes formed from past experiences and personal beliefs. Changes such as pay increases, job redesign, and flexible hours can improve job attitudes, at least temporarily, but in the long run, the best predictor of employees' current job attitudes is their prior work attitudes.[6]

Attitude Theory and Reasoned Action.   All three of these attitude theories can be adapted to the theory of reasoned action. Thus a change in job design may alter the general workplace situation to the extent that a worker's beliefs are changed. So-

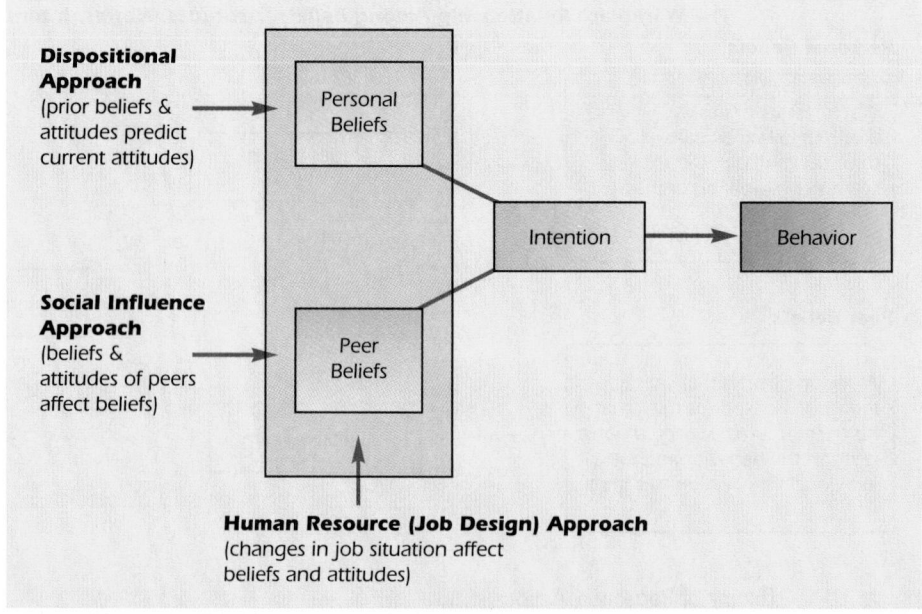

Figure 18.3   **Three theories of job attitudes applied to the theory of reasoned action**

Terry Vitorelo's attitude toward her job at Business Wire, a San Francisco public-relations firm, has changed since she arrived at the company 16 years ago. Then, she admits, she was a "proverbial job-hopper" with little long-term concern about bonuses and benefits. Now vice president of operations, she helps to form a core group of committed managers. The secret to keeping high-quality committed employees, according to Business Wire founder Lorry Lokey, is providing stability and attractive benefits tied to company performance.

cial influence theory would say that the beliefs that predict a person's subjective norm will change when the beliefs and attitudes of the person's peers are changed. Finally, the dispositional approach would argue that a person's own prior beliefs and attitudes are the strongest predictor of job attitudes—and thus of intentions and behaviors while performing a newly designed job.

Changing Attitudes   Behaviors and attitudes can best be predicted by knowing two factors:

1. A person's beliefs.
2. The social norms that influence a person's intentions.

Managers may strive to change attitudes, intentions, and behaviors by changing workplace situations—that is, by changing such work factors as compensation, job design, and work hours. However, they must realize that employee attitudes are both fairly stable over time and slow to change. Thus, selecting employees who come to their positions with positive job attitudes might be the most effective way to build a workforce with a positive attitude.

Human Resource Approach.   Research has also supported a related managerial philosophy often called the *human resource approach* to job satisfaction. Consistently providing personnel activities that are highly valued by employees will in the long run improve attitudes, intentions, and behaviors. This approach typically works because employees' attitudes are favorably affected by their belief that the organization is com-

Among the changes that Motorola wants to see in the workplace attitudes of its employees are greater degrees of independent-mindedness, of equality in proposing creative ideas, and of teamwork in decision making. From its headquarters in Schaumberg, Illinois, to its offices in Honolulu and Tokyo, the company is thus pushing employee training as the key to both greater knowledge and upward mobility.

Table 18.1
Basic Principles of the Human Resource Approach
Providing employee training
Communicating about human resource programs and policies
Helping new employees learn about their job and the company
Providing advancement opportunities within the company
Providing job security
Hiring qualified employees
Having enough people to get the job done
Asking my opinions about how one can improve one's own job
Asking my opinions about making the company successful
Asking for employee suggestions
Acting on employee suggestions

Source: Angelo J. Kinicki, Kenneth P. Carson, and George W. Bohlander, "Relationships between an Organization's Actual Human Resource Efforts and Employee Attitudes," *Group & Organization Management*, June 1992, p. 142.

mitted to providing a positive work environment. Studies have shown that employees who believe that their employer cares about them will reciprocate with more positive attitudes, reduced absenteeism, increased quality and productivity, and greater creative input.[7] Thus the basic principles of the human resource approach, which are listed in Table 18.1, can favorably influence employee attitudes when they are consistently applied by managers.

QUALITY SPOTLIGHT

Nucor Steel

F. Kenneth Iverson is the chief executive officer of Nucor Corporation. Nucor is America's seventh-largest steel company and the only one to consistently make a profit over the past 20 years. Nucor has increased its dividend annually and operated profitably in each quarter since 1968—this is quite an accomplishment in an industry that has lost money overall in more than half of those years. In addition, while the U.S. steel industry has laid off over 300,000 workers and shut down numerous plants in the past two decades, Nucor has not laid off a single worker. According to former U.S. Secretary of Labor Ann McLaughlin, "Every manager who wonders what it will take to compete in the twenty-first century needs to know the Nucor story."

Why has Nucor succeeded while the other U.S. steel firms have struggled? Ken Iverson proudly but without hesitation cites four practices that are directly related to the company's human resources policies:

1. *Employee Teams.* All tasks in Nucor's mills are performed by employee teams. Each team is in charge of complete tasks and receives a production bonus every week in which work standards are exceeded. This program is an excellent example of applied behavior modification with continuous reinforcement.

2. *Levels of Management.* Iverson believes that those closest to the work should make the decisions concerning that work whenever possible. Thus, the greater the autonomy given to teams, the fewer levels of management that are necessary.

3. *Limited Staff.* Iverson also believes that staff tend to obstruct effective work teams. Nucor, therefore, operates 6 steel mills, 6 joist plants, and 2 products divisions with only 22 staff members. All staff are located at the corporate headquarters in Charlotte, North Carolina.

4. *No-Layoffs Policy.* For well over 20 years, Nucor has maintained a no-layoffs policy in an industry that has laid off over 350,000 U.S. workers. During lean times, Nucor prefers a "share the pain" policy. This plan reduces the number of days per week that a team works. In addition, management, including Iverson, also takes a pay reduction.

These principles have helped Nucor build an environment in which autonomous teams of employees strive for maximum productivity—a goal that, if achieved, maximizes bonuses and minimizes interference from management or staff. In addition, the teams have a great deal of job security because of the no-layoffs policy. As a result, Nucor employees have consistently maintained higher levels of productivity and far more positive work attitudes than their counterparts elsewhere in the steel industry.≈

As a practical matter, what does the manager do with the employee who has a "bad attitude"? Unfortunately, managerial experience and research both indicate that changing attitudes is very difficult. Fortunately, a "bad attitude" is often not the problem. Rather, the problem is usually unacceptable *behavior.* Attitude, of course, influences behaviors, as we have seen, but there are two good reasons why managers should not focus too sharply on attitudes:

1. Attitudes are *internal* and therefore cannot be accurately measured or observed.
2. The beliefs, values, and norms that affect attitudes are complex and have been constructed over a lifetime.

Behaviors, on the other hand, are not only observable but can also be documented and measured. Most importantly, managers can deal successfully with unacceptable performance.

Not surprisingly, then, the correct identification, analysis, and resolution of behavioral problems are an important task for managers. Of course, poor attitude or motivation is only one potential cause of unsatisfactory behavior or performance. Determining exactly *why* an employee is performing at an unsatisfactory level is critical because problems cannot be corrected unless their causes are known. Effective managers not only look for performance problems but also recognize that they stem from a variety of causes. Human resource specialists have identified at least four major causes of behavior problems:[8]

1. Lack of Skills. Organizations often place employees in jobs without giving them sufficient training. Once identified, the skills-deficiency problem can be remedied in one of three ways: (a) train the employee to remove the skill deficiency; (b) transfer the employee to a job that better utilizes his or her current skills; (c) terminate the employee.

2. Lack of Positive Attitude. Although there are numerous approaches to attitude and motivation problems, most strategies rest on one seemingly simple axiom: *Determine what the employee needs and offer it as a reward for good performance.* (Yet as most managers know, determining the needs of an employee and providing a corresponding change in job design or work environment is a challenging task.)

3. Rule Breaking. Rule breakers are employees who are occasionally absent or late to work without good reason, who violate dress codes, or who refuse to follow safety procedures. They have the necessary skills and normally do good work, but they disregard the organization's policies and regulations. The most effective approach to this form of behavior is to apply positive discipline. This means providing a written policy of expected behaviors and a written program detailing progressive disciplinary steps (for example, first offense—oral warning; second offense—written warning; third offense—suspension; fourth offense—termination).

4. Personal Problems. A final type of unsatisfactory behavior is associated with the *troubled employee*—one whose personal problems are so significant that they prevent

the employee from performing satisfactorily at work. The troubled employee may suffer from a variety of problems, including emotional illness, financial crisis, alcohol or drug dependency, chronic physical problems, and family unrest.

CUTTING EDGE

WE HIRE ATTITUDES!

Despite increased competition from rival airlines, Southwest Airline's profit for the year ending 1994 was up nearly 64 percent. Moreover, the company's cost per available seat mile for that year was significantly lower than that of its competitors. CEO Herb Kelleher states that employee attitudes have played a vital role in Southwest's success. Kelleher says that from the beginning, he has tried to instill in employees what he calls an "effervescence."

One result is that Southwest workers often go out of their way to amuse, surprise, or otherwise entertain passengers. During delays at the gate, for instance, ticket agents will award prizes to the passenger with the largest hole in his or her sock. Flight attendants have been known to hide in the overhead luggage bins and then pop out when passengers start filing on board. Veteran Southwest fliers looking for a few laughs have learned to pay attention to announcements over the intercom. A recent effort: "Good morning, ladies and gentlemen. Those of you who wish to smoke will please file out to our lounge on the wing, where you can enjoy our feature film, *Gone with the Wind.*"

Clearly, not everyone is cut out to be a Southwest employee. "What we are looking for, first and foremost, is a sense of humor," says Kelleher. "Then we are looking for people who have to excel to satisfy themselves and who work well in a collegial environment. We don't care that much about education and expertise, because we can train people to do whatever they have to do. *We hire attitudes.*"≈

BACK TO THE CASE   Job attitudes are developed internally by each employee. They are shaped by the employee's own values and beliefs as well as by the norms confirmed by the employee's peers. In the introductory case, we saw that employees who developed "bad attitudes" or job burnout could not expect to easily change such situational (external) factors as difficult bosses, frustrating co-workers, or unchallenging work. Instead, they realized they needed to change their own (internal) values and beliefs. Only in that way could they gain greater control over their attitudes and behaviors and generally improve their morale and productivity.

PERCEPTION

The above material focused on individuals by discussing attitudes. This major chapter section continues the discussion of individuals by emphasizing perception. Topics discussed below are as follows:

1. Defining perception and the perceptual process.
2. Attribution theory.
3. Perceptual distortions.

Perception and the Perceptual Process

Perception is the psychological process of selecting stimuli, organizing the data into recognizable patterns, and interpreting the resulting information. The **perceptual process** is the series of actions that individuals follow in order to select, organize, and

---

Margin notes:

Perception is the psychological process of selecting stimuli, organizing the data into recognizable patterns, and interpreting the resulting information.

The **perceptual process** is the series of actions that individuals follow in order to select, organize, and interpret stimuli from the environment.

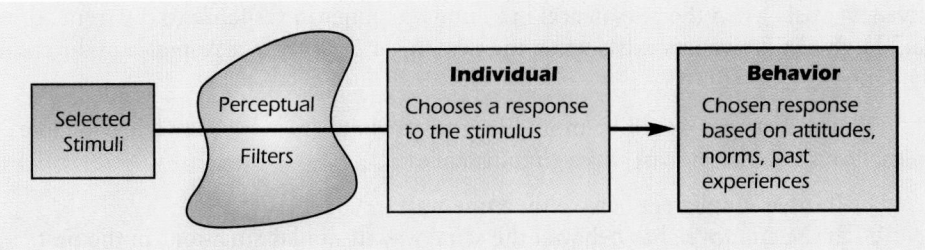

Figure 18.4   **Process of Perception**

interpret stimuli from the environment. Every second of every day individuals are bombarded by countless stimuli through human senses of sight, hearing, touch, smell, and taste. We attend to only a small portion of these stimuli.

Thus, as you can see in Figure 18.4, the perceptual process links the individual with his or her environment. Since we can only select and process a limited number of the stimuli, we are never aware of everything that occurs around us. Moreover, the limited stimuli that we do perceive are subjected to perceptual filters that are largely determined by our past experiences, attitudes, and beliefs. Just as importantly, stimuli that are inconsistent with our predispositions are often ignored or distorted. Thus we can become "close-minded" without realizing it.

Attribution Theory: Interpreting the Behavior of Others

Attribution is the process by which people *interpret* the behavior of others by assigning to it motives or causes. For example, if an employee is routinely late to work, a manager might try to determine the cause of the behavior. Is it lack of motivation or lack of ability? Is it some personal factor or a situational factor such as the way the job is structured or scheduled? The manager may believe that poor attitude is the cause of the behavior and try to motivate the employee to arrive on time. As a rule, managers do *not* consider situational factors. Why? Much of the conflict that occurs between managers and subordinates stems from the tendency of managers to act on their own perception and interpretation of a given situation, which may be quite different from those of subordinates; they may not even coincide with the facts of the situation. Managers can avoid inappropriate attributions in three ways:

1. By making a greater effort to see situations as they are perceived by others.
2. By guarding against perceptual distortions.
3. By paying more attention to individual differences among subordinates.[9]

The underlying assumption of attribution theory is that managers are typically motivated to understand the *causes* of employee behavior. Naturally, they tend to question whether the behavior is the result of internal or external causes. *Internal* causes include attitude or motivation, ability, and lack of knowledge of the desired (correct) behavior. *External* causes include the difficulty of tasks and the actions of others, both of which may exert influence beyond the control of the individual. Research indicates that people generally focus on three factors when making attributions:[10]

1. Consensus: The extent to which they believe that the person being observed is behaving in a manner consistent with the behavior of his or her peers. High consensus exists when the person's actions reflect, or are similar to, the actions of the group; low consensus exists when the person's actions do not.

2. Consistency: The extent to which they believe that the person being observed behaves consistently—in a similar fashion—when confronted on other occasions with the same or similar situations. High consistency exists when the person repeatedly acts in the same way when faced with similar stimuli.

3. Distinctiveness: The extent to which they believe that the person being observed would behave consistently when faced with different situations. Low distinc-

Attribution is the process by which people *interpret* the behavior of others by assigning to it motives or causes.

tiveness exists when the person acts in a similar manner in response to different stimuli. High distinctiveness exists when the person varies his or her response in different situations.

Thus a manager would be more likely to attribute an employee's behavior to external causes under at least three circumstances:

1. If other employees behave the same way.
2. If the employee has behaved the same way in similar situations in the past.
3. If this behavior is highly unusual or distinctive.

Internal causes might be attributed if other employees do not behave in the same manner or if the employee usually behaves in the same manner under most circumstances.

Perceptual Distortions

Managers, like everyone else, make judgments and decisions based on their perceptions. To help ensure that these judgments and decisions are worthwhile, managers must strive to avoid common perceptual distortions, including stereotypes, halo effects, projection, self-serving bias, attribution error, selective perception, and recency. Each of these distortions is discussed below.

Stereotypes

A **stereotype** is a fixed, distorted generalization about members of a group.

A **stereotype** is a fixed, distorted generalization about members of a group. Stereotyping—which often stems from such aspects of diversity as race, gender, age, physical abilities/qualities, social background, and occupation—attributes incomplete, exaggerated, or distorted qualities to individual members of groups. Stereotyping results from the nature of our information-processing tendencies. As human beings, we process information through learned knowledge gained by means of past experience, observation, or contact with other individuals who influence us, such as our family, friends, and co-workers. Stereotyping, therefore, is not generalization. A stereotype is usually *learned* through outside sources rather than through direct individual experiences.

Halo Effect

The **halo effect** results from allowing one particular aspect of someone's behavior to influence one's evaluation of all other aspects of that person's behavior.

When a manager allows one particular aspect of an employee's behavior to influence his or her evaluation of all other aspects of that employee's behavior, the so-called **halo effect** has occurred. For example, the manager who knows that a particular employee always arrives at work early and helps to open the business may let the "halo" of the employee's dependability influence his or her perceptions of the employee in other areas—say, customer relations or products knowledge. Thus even if the employee is only mediocre in these areas, the manager perceives overall strength.

Of course, a negative halo—"devil's horns"—may also affect perceptions. If an accountant performs poorly only when working directly with plant managers on annual budget projects, a supervisor may allow this one negative behavior to cloud his or her judgment of the employee's other behaviors.

The halo problem can be minimized by supervisory training that focuses on the fact that it is not unusual for employees to perform well in some areas and less effectively in others.

Projection

Projection is the unconscious tendency to assign one's own traits, motives, beliefs, and attitudes to others.

The unconscious tendency to assign (project) our own traits, motives, beliefs, and attitudes to others is called **projection.** Consider, for example, a manager who enjoys working as part of a quality-improvement team. This manager may strongly encourage subordinates to join similar teams, and then be disappointed in those who refuse to do so. This classic form of perceptual distortion assumes that others have the same needs and desires as oneself. Not surprisingly, this assumption is rarely accurate.

Self-Serving Bias and Attribution Error

In practice, when asked to identify the causes of an employee's poor performance, managers will usually choose internal causes, such as motivation, ability, or effort, rather than external causes, such as lack of support from others or circumstances beyond the employee's control. This tendency to overestimate internal causes of behavior and underestimate external ones is called **attribution error.** Interestingly, many of the same managers, when asked to identify the causes of their own performance, refer to external causes. This form of perceptual distortion is called **self-serving bias:** the tendency to attribute personal success to internal causes and personal failures to external causes.

Selective Perception

When bombarded with too many external stimuli, people may resort to perceptual filters in order to reduce their awareness of the stimuli. In particular, we tend to attend to stimuli that are consistent with our own motives, beliefs, and attitudes. Thus we are prone to collect information that not only supports our perceptions but also minimizes the emotional distress caused by unfamiliar or troublesome stimuli. This form of perceptual distortion is called **selective perception.**

Recency

For example, let's say that a manager notices a few unusually negative comments in the weekly stack of customer comment cards. However, because the majority of the cards contain positive comments about the service that the manager believes accurately reflect the work of her staff, she ignores the negative messages. A few weeks later, she notices a substantial number of negative comments. An investigation reveals that one newly hired employee is the cause of the negative comments—but this discovery comes too late to prevent negative impressions of the service among a good many customers. What went wrong here? The manager allowed her own perceptions to filter out early information that did not conform to her beliefs. Only later did she seek reliable data to check the accuracy of her perceptions.

Attribution error is the tendency to overestimate internal causes of behavior and underestimate external ones when judging other people's behavior.

The **self-serving bias** is the tendency to overestimate external causes of behavior and underestimate internal ones when judging one's own behavior.

Selective perception is the tendency to collect information that not only supports one's own motives, beliefs, and attitudes but also minimizes the emotional distress caused by unfamiliar or troublesome stimuli.

THE WIDE, WIDE WORLD OF CULTURAL PERCEPTIONS

GLOBAL SPOTLIGHT

On a sea voyage, you are traveling with your wife, your child, and your mother. The ship develops problems and starts to sink. Of your family, you are the only one who can swim, and you can save only one other individual. Whom will you save?

This question was posed to a group of men in Asia and the United States. In the United States, more than 60 percent of respondents said they would save the child, 40 percent the wife, and none the mother. In the Asian countries, 100 percent of respondents said they would save the mother. Their rationale? You can always remarry and have more children, but you can never have another mother.

When doing business overseas, Americans cannot rely only on uniquely American perceptions and behavior patterns. What seems good in one place ("Father is getting to the age where he would probably be happier in the senior citizen home in Arizona") is scandalous in another ("Look at how Americans treat older people—it's awful").

Cross-cultural mistakes can be expensive. For example, many companies spend a minimum of $125,000 per year to employ one U.S. manager in an overseas position. Another less obvious factor is the human cost accrued when someone does poorly or returns early from an overseas assignment. Premature return of an employee and family may cost the company between $50,000 and $200,000 when replacement expenses are included. Mistakes of corporate representatives because of language or intercultural incompetence can jeopardize millions of dollars in negotiations and purchases, sales, and contracts, as well as undermine customer relations. No doubt, managers' cultural ineptitude damages organizational productivity and profitability.

The price of providing employees with education and training for intercultural effectiveness is miniscule compared to the financial losses that can occur because of personnel "faux pas" in cross-cultural business relations. The benefits from developing human resources can be enormous.≈

Perceptions of Procedural Justice

Procedural justice is the perceived fairness of the process used for deciding workplace outcomes such as merit increases and promotions.

Perhaps the most important workplace perception formed by employees, however, is of **procedural justice:** the perceived fairness of the process used for deciding outcomes such as merit increases and promotions. The most important of these processes are performance appraisals, job applicant interviewing systems, pay systems, grievance or dispute-resolution systems, and participative decision making. Most employees continually evaluate not only the fairness of these systems but also their consequences for themselves.

Procedures and Outcomes   Employees actually form separate perceptions about the organization's process for deciding outcomes on the one hand and the consequences on the other hand. *Procedural justice* examines the fairness of the process itself: Are decisions made according to clear standards? Is the process used consistently for everyone? Can I appeal the decision? Will I be able to have input? *Distributive justice*, on the other hand, examines only the outcome of a decision or policy: Did I receive the promotion? Did I get the raise? Research indicates that employees often view these two types of workplace justice quite differently.[11]

Obviously, then, employees expect managers to be fair in making selection and promotion decisions, in assigning tasks and scheduling work, in choosing people for training and promotion opportunities, in conducting performance appraisals, and in making pay decisions. Of all these processes the one most likely to affect attitudes and morale is performance appraisal. Probably because of the highly personal nature of the process, employees are especially sensitive to perceived unfairness in this area. Consequently, they base a large portion of their overall perceptions about procedural justice on their perceptions of performance appraisals.

A history of perceived fairness, therefore, can be a major asset to a manager in shaping employee perceptions of fairness, positive job attitudes, and productive behaviors. The manager with such a history is also often seen as honest, ethical, and trustworthy. Such a manager may, moreover, be judged less harshly when he or she is perceived as having made an unfavorable decision.[12]

Dispute Resolution   Another critical factor in employees' evaluations of fairness is how managers resolve disputes. Experienced managers are likely to use *mediation* techniques—they listen to the points of view of the parties involved, offer resources to help resolve the dispute, and encourage the parties to seek inventive solutions. Managers who resort to formal authority and simply impose their own settlements are less likely to be perceived as fair, regardless of the quality of their decisions.[13]

Employee Responses   How do employees respond to perceptions of unfairness? Those with seniority usually decide that they have invested too many years in the organization either to leave or to cause a disturbance. Instead, they may respond by performing marginally until retirement. Newer employees are more likely to leave for (perceived) better opportunities elsewhere. The costs of unfair employee treatment are difficult to compute. Research has determined that employees' perceptions of unfair treatment are very strong predictors of job absence and turnover—two costly employee behaviors. Other consequences of unfair treatment include lower production quantity and quality, less initiative, diminished morale, lack of cooperation, spread of dissatisfaction to co-workers, fewer suggestions, and less self-confidence. Each result has a substantial organizational cost, whether direct or indirect.[14]

Measuring Employee Attitudes

Considering the effects on the organization of employee responses to perceived unfairness, it is not surprising that managers often try to measure employees' perceptions of their treatment. However, measuring employee feelings is a complex and difficult process. Getting honest answers in interviews and group discussions is hardly assured; the most practical alternative is to use anonymous survey techniques. One advantage of using written questionnaires is that they make it easier to identify the dimensions of perceived unfairness. For example, results of a written survey can be compared across departments, jobs, and supervisors. A survey taken for Lens Lab, Inc., a national chain of eyeglass stores, found, overall, a high level of perceived fairness. However, in two of eight stores, the levels reported were significantly lower on two dimensions—work pace and pay administration. An investigation led to changes in policy and supervision at those stores, which resulted in higher levels of perceived fairness, and higher store profitability, the following year.

BACK TO THE CASE

In the introductory case, we saw that employees often perceive both managers and peers to be sources of their low morale and low productivity, though, many times, these perceptions are not entirely accurate. Rather, employees' perceptions of the workplace change as they gain more direct experiences and become acquainted with the attitudes of other employees. The response of employees to their own changing perceptions largely determines how happy and productive they will be on the job. Those who seek to control their lives and work situations as their perceptions change—like the nurse in the introductory case—will usually be happier and more productive on and off the job.

LEARNING

Learning can be defined as a relatively permanent change in behavior resulting from practice, experience, education, or training. Behavioral change includes the acquisition of skills, knowledge, and ability. In organizations, people learn specific job-related skills, knowledge, and abilities. They also learn about organizational norms—what is expected from them and how things are accomplished. Both of these learning situations affect employee beliefs, attitudes, intentions, and behaviors. This section will focus on two of the traditional approaches to learning that are of particular value in the workplace: operant and cognitive learning.

> **Learning** is a more or less permanent change in behavior resulting from practice, experience, education, or training.

Operant Learning

Operant learning, also called operant conditioning, is based on the belief that behavior is a function of its consequences. If a person perceives that a behavior will lead to a positive consequence, that person will be more likely to repeat the behavior. For example, a salesperson who has taken a client to lunch at a favorite restaurant and has always subsequently received a large order from that client is likely to arrange a similar lunch meeting on the client's next visit. Conversely, if a person perceives that a behavior will likely lead to a negative consequence, that person will be more likely to avoid the behavior. An employee who receives a written disciplinary warning after submitting a report 24 hours late is more likely to submit the report on time next month.

> **Operant learning** is an approach that holds the behavior leading to positive consequences is more likely to be repeated.

Cognitive Learning

The approach theory that focuses on thought processes is known as **cognitive learning.** This theory assumes that human beings have a high capacity to act in a purposeful manner, and so to choose behaviors that will enable them to achieve long-run goals. Thus employees will evaluate the work environment and choose behaviors that will enable them to achieve such goals as pay bonuses, promotions, and recognition.

> **Cognitive learning,** an approach theory that focuses on thought processes, assumes that human beings have a high capacity to act in a purposeful manner, and so to choose behaviors that will enable them to achieve long-run goals.

Goal-Setting Strategies.   Cognitive learning theory is the basis for "goal-setting" strategies and has therefore become the most widely applied learning theory in the business world. Goal setting is the basis for individual incentive plans like commissions or piecework, group-incentive plans, and organizationwide incentive plans like profit sharing and gainsharing. The widespread use of goal setting in organizations is attributed to several advantages these strategies offer:[15]

1. Directed Behavior. Goals help people focus their daily decisions and behaviors in specific ways.

2. Challenges. Individuals are more motivated, and thus achieve higher levels of performance, when given specific objectives instead of such nondirective responses as "keep up the good work."

3. Resource Allocation. Critical decisions involving resources (people, time, equipment, money) are more consistent with organizational goals when goal-setting strategies are used.

4. Structure. The formal and informal organizational structure can be shaped to set communication patterns and provide each position with a degree of authority and responsibility that supports employee and organizational goals.

Basically, goal-setting strategies involve a systematic process wherein managers and subordinates discuss and agree upon a set of specific, jointly determined goals. If the process is functioning effectively, the final result will be a set of goals in keeping with the overall goals of the organization. Moreover, managers will have exact, measurable objectives by which to gauge each subordinate's performance. In this process, feedback on progress is periodically supplied, enabling workers to recognize and make necessary corrections in their work performance. Above all, the link between performance and evaluation and organizational rewards (goals) is made explicitly clear to the subordinate, with emphasis on *what* was achieved and *how.*

Goal Setting and Problem Solving.   Managers use goal setting to correct problems as well as achieve new objectives. For example, if the manager of a video store is told in her annual review that she should "cut down on the total number of employee hours," how will she react? This vague reference to a perceived problem may cause the manager to do any one of a number of things, ranging from laying off several employees (and negatively affecting service) to simply worrying about the suggestion for a few days until it's forgotten. The problem: Her supervisor did not give her a specific measurable goal, require a plan of action, and provide a framework for feedback to see if the plan is working.

Moreover, the manager cannot be sure how achieving the goal (or failure to do so) will directly affect *her*—a necessary link in cognitive learning. Management by ob-

Employees at Monsanto's Luling, Louisiana, plant resisted an incentive plan tied to plantwide performance because they felt that goals were beyond their control. Monsanto, therefore, adjusted the goals and the strategy: Now, bonuses paid to workers like electrical technician Bruce Swaim are tied to the performance of employee groups numbering no more than 50 or 60 people.

jectives (MBO), as discussed in detail in Chapter 6, is perhaps the most common application of goal setting. In an MBO process, the supervisor and store manager would jointly discuss and agree upon a goal such as: "20% reduction of total employee hours per month to be achieved by reducing the number of 10:00 A.M.–5:00 P.M. personnel by 33% under a flextime program. The program is to be developed by the store manager, approved before implementation, and reported on monthly. This goal is one of three that will determine midyear bonuses."

Learning Strategies

Many strategies have evolved that managers can use to enhance the learning of organization members. These strategies are positive strategy, avoidance strategy, escape strategy, and punishment strategy and are discussed further in the following sections.

Reinforcement Strategy

Managers often use the principle of *reinforcement* when attempting to shape employee behavior. Reinforcement is based on operant conditioning theory: It is assumed that employees will repeat behavior that is reinforced or rewarded. Forms of reinforcement may include positive recognition by a supervisor, a "pass" on a checklist training item, or even simple praise ("You've mastered that, so let's move on to something new"). Of course, formal awards and monetary compensation also work. To shape or strengthen employee behavior, the manager can select from any combination of the following four reinforcement strategies:[16]

1. *Positive Reinforcement.* Any stimulus that causes a behavior to be repeated is a positive reinforcer. Common examples of positive reinforcement are praise, recognition, pay, and support. It is essential that the reinforcer directly follow the desired behavior. For example, if a manager witnesses an employee superbly handling an irate customer, immediate praise (or praise offered no later than the end of the day) is much more effective than a comment three months later during a performance appraisal.

2. *Avoidance Strategy.* Behavior that can prevent the onset of an undesired consequence often results from *avoidance learning*. In recent years, for example, many employers have adopted strict policies regarding the use of illegal drugs by employees. Research indicates that such strict "avoidance" policies have contributed to the overall decline in casual drug use, both in organizations and within the larger society. Indeed, one major pharmaceutical firm reported a drop in the number of job applicants testing positive for drug use from 7 percent in 1985 to less than 1 percent ten years later.[17]

3. *Escape Strategy.* When a manager provides an arrangement in which a desired response will terminate an undesired consequence, that manager is using the *escape strategy*. For example, a manager may first set employees the least desired task, such as cleaning and setting up equipment, and inform them that once the equipment has passed inspection, they can move on to a more desirable task.

4. *Punishment Strategy.* When an *undesired* behavior by an employee is followed by an undesired response by management, a punishment strategy is being used. Organizations commonly select such punishment strategies—usually they are called "disciplinary actions"—as oral and written warnings, demotion, suspension, and termination. The primary objective of a disciplinary program is to warn employees that certain undesired behaviors are considered serious enough to invoke discipline. The purpose, of course, is to motivate employees to comply with work rules and performance standards. A second objective is to establish and maintain a climate of respect and mutual trust between employees and managers.

BACK TO THE CASE ▌n the introductory case, employees who experienced morale problems or burnout were able to improve their lives by seeking out learning opportunities. For example, Claudia Younce, the middle-aged nurse, entered graduate school and found that it broadened her outlook and boosted her nursing career.

Action Summary

Read the learning objectives below. Each objective is followed by questions. Answering these questions accurately will help you retain the most important concepts discussed in this chapter. After answering each question, check your answer against the answer key at the end of this chapter. (*Hint:* If you have any doubts regarding the correct response, consult the page whose number follows the answer.)

Circle: From studying this chapter, I will attempt to acquire:

1. An understanding of employee workplace attitudes.
   - T,F   **a.** Attitudes are largely shaped by personal beliefs and values and the norms communicated by others.
   - a,b,c,d,e   **b.** People commonly communicate their attitudes through all the following methods *except:* (a) eyes; (b) body language; (c) thoughts; (d) voice; (e) behavior.

2. Insights into how to change employee attitudes.
   - T,F   **a.** Employee workplace attitudes are fairly stable over time and slow to change.
   - a,b,c,d,e   **b.** Managers should keep in mind that of the following employee characteristics, only one is *external* and thus should be subject to potential disciplinary action: (a) bad attitude; (b) negative intention; (c) poor behavior; (d) inappropriate values; (e) false beliefs.

3. An appreciation of the impact of employee perceptions on employee behaviors.
   - T,F   **a.** Managers can usually correctly attribute poor employee behavior to a lack of motivation.
   - a,b,c,d,e   **b.** When a manager evaluates an employee highly on all aspects of his or her job performance even though, in reality, the employee excels at only one aspect, the manager is guilty of the (a) halo effect; (b) stereotyping; (c) attribution error; (d) selective perception; (e) recency.

4. Knowledge of employee perceptions of procedural justice.
   - T,F   **a.** Employee perceptions of the fairness of the processes used in reaching organizational decisions are often as important as the fairness of the decisions themselves.
   - a,b,c,d,e   **b.** Managers are most likely to be perceived as fair in their dispute-resolution strategy if they: (a) impose their own ideas for a settlement; (b) stay out of all disputes; (c) use mediation techniques; (d) side with one party quickly; (e) refer disputes to the human resource department.

5. An understanding that adult learners are different from younger students.
   - T,F   **a.** Adult learners seek skills and knowledge that they can apply to their work or use to further their careers.
   - a,b,c,d,e   **b.** At Nucor Steel, employees have very positive work attitudes and production records owing to: (a) the use of employee teams; (b) a "no-layoffs" policy; (c) weekly production bonuses; (d) limited levels of staff; (e) all of the above.

Introductory Case Wrap-Up

"Reviving Workplace Attitudes" (p. 429) and its related back-to-the-case sections discuss one of management's greatest challenges—poor job attitudes and burnout on the part of employees. Answer the following discussion questions about this introductory case to enrich your understanding of the chapter content:

1. Do you agree that most employees with "poor attitudes" blame managers and co-workers for their work problems?

2. What are some potentially effective methods, other than those presented in the case, that employees might use to take responsibility for improving their workplace attitude?

3. What services might an employer offer to employees to encourage them to improve their job attitudes?

Issues for Review and Discussion

1. Define *attitude*.
2. Explain how people's own values and beliefs affect their job behaviors.
3. How do employees communicate their job attitudes to their co-workers?
4. In your own words, explain the theory of reasoned action.
5. Why are people with positive job attitudes often the best-liked employees?
6. How would you rate your current ability to maintain a positive attitude when you have a task to perform? Are you satisfied with your ability? How could you improve it?
7. What strategies should managers use in striving to improve employee attitudes?
8. What are the most common sources of unsatisfactory employee performance?
9. Do you really believe that hiring employees who have a positive attitude has been critical to the success of Southwest Airlines?
10. Do employees form mental sets about their managers that are at odds with reality?
11. Why do people "filter out" stimuli that do not match their perceptions?
12. Describe the differences between perceptions of objects and perceptions of people.
13. To provide for more effective communication, what seating arrangement should a manager utilize (around a desk or table) when discussing a behavioral problem with an employee?
14. How common is "attribution error" among managers when they are evaluating employees' behavioral problems?
15. List several employee stereotypes you have heard from co-workers.
16. How can a manager guard against selective perception?
17. Why do employees often form more negative perceptions of the organizations they work for after their first year on the job?
18. Which of the two traditional approaches to learning is more often used in organizations?
19. Describe several effective forms of managerial positive reinforcement.

Action Summary Answer Key

1. a. T, p. 430
   b. c, p. 430

2. a. T, p. 434
   b. c, pp. 434–438

3. a. F, pp. 434–438
   b. a, pp. 440–441

4. a. T, pp. 442–443
   b. c, pp. 442–443

5. a. T, p. 443–444
   b. e, p. 436

Case Study

Sending the Wrong Signal

There is no more disheartening experience for a corporate manager than to see his or her company exposed for wrongdoing by a national publication. Former chairman and CEO Daniel Gill of Bausch & Lomb had such an experience when *Business Week* published an article in October 1995 that accused the company of faked sales invoices, loose accounting practices, and ethics violations.

Rochester, New York–based Bausch & Lomb develops, manufactures, and markets products for the personal health, medical, and optical-care fields. It is widely known for its contact lenses and related products. The company's stock has long been a darling of Wall Street, but after ten years of increasing sales and income, earnings per share plunged in 1995.

Bausch & Lomb's problems did not begin with the *Business Week* article; they began in the field, where Gill's managers got the wrong perception of the company's expectations for them. A very demanding, numbers-oriented manager, Gill expected double-digit annual growth. He focused on the bottom line and quarterly results. Once target goals had been set, he and other top executives at Bausch & Lomb would not accept excuses for shortfalls.

In fact, Gill was known to say, "Make the numbers, but don't do anything stupid." Not surprisingly, since managers generally take their cues from the top, numbers became the key to success. Moreover, management incentives were based on sales targets rather than profitability. As a result, decisions were made to maximize short-term sales figures at the expense of long-run profitability. Ultimately, then, the attitude conveyed to field managers was that cutting corners was an acceptable tactic. Those who were just 10 percent shy of their targets were awarded much smaller bonuses than those who topped their targets. Finally, as field managers aban-

doned sound business practices and made decisions designed to maximize their personal bonuses, the results became costly to the company.

For example, both to perpetuate reported increases and to enhance personal bonuses, managers at B & L's Hong Kong unit inflated sales by faking invoices to real customers for Ray-Ban sunglasses; some of the same glasses were later sold at cut-rate prices to gray-market dealers. Because top management demanded increased sales figures, the attitude of the field managers was to continue the deceit in order to win top management's favor—and, of course, earn higher bonuses. Nor did Bausch & Lomb's problems end with inflated sales figures. The contact lens division shipped products never ordered, forcing distributors to take unnecessary inventory and violating accepted accounting practices. The Miami warehouse operation may have even laundered drug money.

Eventually, further *Business Week* reports alerted the Securities and Exchange Commission, which launched an investigation into the company's accounting procedures. After the investigation, the company instituted the most conservative practices possible. Quarter-end wheeling and dealing stopped, and a new bonus system was instituted to reflect long-term shareholder and corporate goals.

In addition, the board of directors began to take a more active interest in management. By naming William Balderston III, a former executive vice president of Chase Manhattan Bank and a board member since 1989, as chairman of the audit committee, the board hoped to send a strong message to management and to control operating practices. According to Balderston, "We have carefully reviewed the company's recent audits and investigations into assertions regarding sales and accounting practices. While we have no reason to believe there is a systemic problem, we do take any questions about the company's operating methods extremely seriously." Nevertheless, the board made it clear to management that financial controls must be strengthened.

In keeping with these changes, Gill himself had announced that as part of its three-year strategic planning process, Bausch & Lomb would centralize management to gain greater global coordination in core businesses.

On December 13, 1995, however, as a result of both shareholder complaints and the board's loss of confidence, Gill announced his retirement. On December 31, outside director William H. Waltrip took over as interim chairman and CEO.

Although the board claims that Gill's retirement was not forced, some analysts believe that he wanted to stay at Bausch & Lomb to clear his name. He still faces scrutiny by the SEC, and Waltrip has vowed to continue the board's probe. Gill claims to have only a general understanding of what happened, and continues to assert that no Bausch & Lomb executive would have placed numbers ahead of ethical practices. Meanwhile, however, there seems to be a disparity between what senior executives now believe happened and what managers down the line recollect. According to the latter, the signals they perceived gave them a license to commit unethical practices. According to one executive, "Gill blamed the problems on poor decisions by individual division presidents and said the divisions needed closer monitoring. It was like slapping the hands of children when they were really acting on Daddy's orders."

Questions:

1. Did the behavior of Bausch & Lomb's field managers accurately reflect Gill's attitude and company policy? Explain.

2. Did Bausch & Lomb set the correct goals for its field managers? Was there a difference between the goals and managers' perception of them? In your opinion, how could Bausch & Lomb have prevented its field managers from getting the "wrong" perception of what was expected of them?

3. Gill disavowed knowledge of what was happening in the field. Should he have known? Should he have taken responsibility for the events? Might a change in his position have changed the actions of shareholders and the board? Explain.

4. Will changes in Bausch & Lomb's management solve the misperception problem? Explain. In what other ways is the board heading off possible problems?

Skills Exercise

Analyze the misconceptions conveyed by top management at Bausch & Lomb. Create a list of statements and actions that upper-level managers might use with field managers to encourage increased sales or production. Work with a partner to role-play an interaction that could be misinterpreted by managers. Have the class decide if the misperception was the fault of management strategies, faulty communications techniques, or management/employee attitude.

The Internet learning materials that accompany this chapter can be found at
http://www.profcerto.com
Additional information can be found on the inside front and back covers of this text.

Lands' End: Controlling a Much-Envied Work Climate

This is the fifth case in this book that explores a variety of management-related issues at the well-known direct-retailing company Lands' End. The first installment (on pp. 24–26) is designed to be a general introduction. You may want to refer to it when you are studying the cases that appear at the end of each part of the book.

According to employees, "Lands' End is a great place to work." But what makes this so? According to Vice President of Human Resources Kelly Ritchie, many things contribute to this perception: "At Lands' End," she explains,

all employees are treated with dignity and respect. For example, four times each year, everything shuts down (with the exception of a skeleton crew in customer service), so that all employees have the opportunity to hear [CEO] Michael Smith's state-of-the-company addresses. The focus of these all-company quarterly meetings is "how are we doing, what are we doing well, and on which areas do we need to focus?" It's really quite expensive to shut everything down so that virtually all employees have a chance to get feedback from the president, but that's part of our "we're all in this together" philosophy.

A further personal touch, begun by founder Gary Comer and continued today by Michael Smith, is frequent visits paid by the CEO to almost all company units. Says Ritchie:

It's commonplace to see Michael Smith walking through the packing lines, chatting with people in customer relations, or stopping by Reedsburg or the Cross Plains locations. He knows the importance of communications and uses a number of different communication avenues. For example, communication is facilitated by monthly feedback from groups of randomly selected individuals (20–25 per group) at each company location, plus the feedback he gets through monthly lunchtime conversations with employees being honored for 10 years' service to the company. At the honorees' luncheons, Mike Smith might say, "So you've now been here for 10 years. What have we been doing well? What should we be doing differently? What should be changed?" The answers to such questions are especially important because many enhancements or improvements down through the years have come from employees.

From Ritchie's perspective, because people like what they do, like their co-workers, and like the people for whom they work, turnover is low and organizational commitment high: "Turnover of our regular benefitted group," she reports,

is in the single digits—very low for this industry. When people really like what they do, like who they do it with and for, work in facilities that are among the best around, and are fairly paid for their efforts, it would seem almost impossible to not be at least minimally satisfied.

Interestingly, however, this same feeling appears to affect even the part-timer group. We bring people in for the peak holiday season, and when the peak is over in January, hours are reduced or eliminated. Yet these folks are also extremely supportive of Lands' End. Many only want to work to earn money to cover their Christmas expenses during the slow time on the farm and couldn't work during the spring, summer, or fall even if we wanted them to. So we start bringing in the seasonal group in late October or early November. They start collecting paychecks just in time to make purchases for Christmas, and their last paychecks in January and February cover last-minute holiday expenses. Furthermore, like benefitted employees, they and their families can take advantage of employee discounts. They're given work assignments in facilities that are not only functional but also aesthetically appealing, and they're encouraged to participate in everything that goes on in the Activity Center. For benefitted employees, the other specific benefits—health insurance, life insurance—also go a long way toward creating a sense of security.

Lands' End also is different from many other organizations of its size in that it has no dress code. At Lands' End, it is work performance that is important. Beyond that, according to Ritchie, "we just want people to be comfortable at work. Our emphasis is on not how one dresses," she emphasizes,

> but on how one works. In fact, we've talked about companies that have formal dress codes and casual Fridays and wondered if having such a special dress day might not also translate into a more casual focus towards work. We believe that everything at work is important and that job performance really has little to do with dress.

Perhaps most important of all is the respect that people have for each other and the level of responsibility and authority given each and every LE employee. "What has always amazed me in the 10 years I've been with Lands' End," says Ritchie

> —what has kept us the employer of choice—is the respect we each have for one another and the incredible amount of responsibility that each person is given. Right down to our frontline sales reps, everybody has the authority to make whatever decision is necessary to please the customer.
>
> I have first-hand experience with this because a few years back I managed one of our phone centers. Almost daily, sales reps would be asked by customers, "Are you sure you don't need to check with your supervisor before you make that commitment?" And the rep would say, "No, I can give you free shipping," or "Lands' End will pick up that order at our expense because we inconvenienced you," or "I'm going to give you a $25 gift certificate because that should not have happened."
>
> In every employee at every level, we try to instill the idea that they must do whatever is needed to meet the customer's needs. And what happens if they aren't sure what to do and they make a mistake? They're told in advance not to worry about it—that we'll either follow up with an explanation of how to handle such situations in the future or that the mistake (without reference to the individual involved) will become one of the focuses at some future training session.

In fact, Lands' End probably leads the direct-retail industry in proactive approaches to minimizing such customer-service errors. "Employees get all kinds of continuing training," explains Ritchie:

> Guidelines for every type of situation are explained. So, maybe I should back up and say that along with the responsibility we give people goes a lot of job training. For example, before telephone sales reps take their first call, they have received 70-80 hours' training on products, service, and computers. That's really unique in this industry.
>
> The other thing that's unique is our commitment to continuous, proactive training. For example, we provide background on new products or services that will be coming on-line in the future and new computer aids that can assist in serving the customer.

"To pull 1,100 operators off the phones for two hours of training each month in just one of our phone centers," adds Ritchie,

> involves thousands of dollars if you consider just pay. However, when you multiply that times two other phone centers and then add in the other indirect costs, you can see that we have a lot invested. But what we have discovered is that, unlike other companies, by spending the money up front, we have much happier employees, we don't have to spend nearly as much money on the back end on quality checks and, most importantly, we have satisfied customers.

According to Lisa Mullen, Corporate Relations Coordinator, this custom-dominated focus on both customers and employees is not something new. It was in fact a guiding principle of Lands' End founder Gary Comer and then nurtured by his successors. "Although I was not here at the time," explains Mullen,

> it is common knowledge that Gary Comer always believed that if you do what's best for the customer, you won't have to worry about the company—it'll take care of itself. To Mr. Comer, customers were both external and internal. From an external perspective, his philosophy was to do whatever it takes to make the customer happy. How-

ever, the same was true for the internal customer. Since the company was first formed, Gary Comer insisted on all employees sharing in its prosperity. If Lands' End was doing well, he made sure that some of that success was returned to every employee. That sharing of success came in a number of forms. The earliest was establishing an annual bonus, which is still given to every employee, no matter what position or capacity. His view was, "We are all in this together—management doesn't have a lock on ideas: it takes all 8,000 employees to make us successful, and each contributor deserves to benefit in what ever success we have."

In 1987, as the company was reaching an incredible success level, Comer decided it was time to return even more to employees for their loyalty and contributions. According to Randy Adolphs, Activity Center Manager,

> Gary Comer personally donated $8 million for the building of an 80,000-square-foot Activity Center for Lands' End employees. The structure includes an Olympic-size swimming pool, a full-size gymnasium, an 8th-mile indoor track, Wisconsin's largest not-for-profit cafeteria, an aerobics room, state-of-the-art exercise equipment, handball courts, a wellness lab, free over-night laundry service for athletic wear, a locker area, shower and dressing rooms, and computerized check-in and record keeping of everyone's use of the facilities. The computer also can keep track of calories burned, weight gained or lost, and so forth.
>
> The architecture of the structure is such that from almost any location in the building, you have a view of the outdoors. Outdoor facilities, on the other hand, include a soccer field that doubles in the winter as an ice-skating rink, tennis courts, a softball field, horse shoe pits, a golf driving range, and a quarter-mile outdoor walking/jogging/bicycling track (with equipment loaned free-of-charge in the Activity Center).
>
> Seventy-five to eighty percent of the Lands' End population will use the facility during the course of a year. In the summer, 200 to 300 people go through here in a day, and in the winter, that number more than doubles. In fact, a pretty regular group, including CEO Mike Smith, uses the facility at lunch time almost daily. He rarely schedules a lunch-hour meeting so that he can get his "hoops in."

The Activity Center was completed and dedicated in February 1989. Gary Comer had the names of each of the 1,750 benefitted employees hand-painted on tiles, had the tiles fired, and then incorporated them into a pool-side wall, with the inscription:

> These are the names of the people whose daily work and good spirit at Lands' End have made this building possible. It is dedicated to them and their continued good health.

The inscription is signed, "Gary Comer." Comer, recalls Adolphs, "really wanted to do something nice for what he felt were his faithful, hard-working employees—to give something back to them. The company had been a successful venture for him and the spirit of the gesture was simply "The employees deserve it."

Other actions taken by Comer testify to his commitment to his employees and the community. In 1989, for example, he established the Comer Foundation Scholarship Fund. This money assists the children of Lands' End employees in pursuing post-high school educations. Furthermore, in appreciation of the Dodgeville community for its ongoing contributions to the success of Lands' End, the Foundation has funded educational scholarships for graduates of Dodgeville High School, for which it has also provided a computer lab. Through Comer's generosity and commitment, other community projects have also been undertaken. For example, when Dodgeville needed funds to complete a community swimming pool project, Comer was there to help. And when traffic signals were needed at one particularly busy corner in Dodgeville (a town with a population of 3,800), Comer donated the lights. Today the company continues to pay the cost of their operation.

Over the years, while Lands' End has grown and changed, the focus on the customer, both external and internal, has remained constant. Although the Activity Center was originally envisioned primarily as a place in which employees could en-

gage in exercise and athletic activity, today it is used for a much wider range of activities. "It started with a real focus on exercise science and the fitness end of health," explains Adolphs:

> However, over the last number of years, we have shifted our focus more to the total person. Our orientation process now looks at six dimensions of wellness—the physical, social, intellectual, emotional, spiritual, and occupational. Currently, we're trying to use the facility to accommodate all of these dimensions. For example, Garrison Keillor comes in every June and does a great show for all of the employees. A musical group called the Kids from Wisconsin comes in and does Christmas concerts. We do family events such as Halloween parties and Christmas parties and an Easter bunny dance. It's really great; we have all ages involved in these events.
>
> The Red Cross comes in a couple times each year for blood drives, and we're now offering many classes other than those related to athletics. For example, we recently offered classes in basket weaving, copyrighting, and paper making. Massage therapy is going on right now. We have scheduled lunchtime talks on such topics as tips for parenting, stress management, and weight loss. This, of course, is the big difference between our approach and that of health clubs—our approach is designed to involve the whole family.

Questions:

1. Using what you know about Lands' End from this and all other case-related materials that you have read, what influencing-related issues do you believe have significantly contributed to the work climate at Lands' End?

2. According to your text, a firm's corporate culture can be identified by studying its status symbols, its traditions, its history, and its physical environment. Using what you know about Lands' End, is there anything that you would add to your answer for Question 1 to further delineate Lands' End's corporate culture?

3. McGregor believed that the way that people are treated is the way one would expect to find them behaving in the long run (he called this the "self-fulfilling prophecy"). Do you feel that the way employees are treated at Lands' End has had any impact on their attitudes? On their values? Explain.

19
chapter

part 5

Controlling

PRINCIPLES OF CONTROLLING

STUDENT LEARNING OBJECTIVES

From studying this chapter, I will attempt to acquire:

1. A definition of *control*.
2. A thorough understanding of the controlling subsystem.
3. An appreciation for various kinds of control and for how each kind can be used advantageously by managers.
4. Insights into the relationship between power and control.
5. Knowledge of the various potential barriers that must be overcome to implement successful control.
6. An understanding of steps that can be taken to increase the quality of a controlling subsystem.

CHAPTER OUTLINE

Controlling at Polaroid

The Polaroid Corporation, maker of instant cameras and electronic imaging products, has recently been struggling with anemic sales and high production and labor costs. A company financial projection reflecting these factors predicted that the company would have operating losses of over $20 million for the year 1995. (For comparison purposes, the company made $1.4 million on sales of $462.6 million in 1994.)

In response to this negative situation, Polaroid management announced that it was cutting the workforce by up to 5 percent, or 600 people. This action is intended to lower production costs, thereby allowing the company to charge lower prices for its products, on the theory that lower prices will boost company sales.

Management also announced that several other steps would be taken. First, Polaroid will consolidate several of its manufacturing facilities. The end result of this action will be a reduction in the number of company plants. Second, the company intends to speed up its entry into such emerging markets as China, India, and Southeast Asia in order to aggressively pursue new customers and higher sales. Third, Polaroid will put added emphasis on product development. Management is especially stressing getting the most profitable new products to market.

Polaroid management also announced that it is establishing a new inventory control program that will clamp down on the discounts the company has been giving to wholesale distributors and emphasize higher spending on advertising and marketing. The initial reaction to this move is expected to be negative, as wholesalers deplete their existing inventories rather than order new product without the discounts to which they have become accustomed. This will undoubtedly lower Polaroid's sales in the near term, but management anticipates that the long-run impact of the new inventory control program on the company's profitability will be positive.

I. MacAllister Booth, Polaroid's president, believes that all these steps will boost profitability as the company pursues a more focused, aggressive approach to the market. He indicated that streamlining operations would make Polaroid more efficient and, ultimately, more profitable. Some industry analysts agree that the actions planned by Polaroid management are necessary and will eventually lower costs and raise profits. Others, however, are more skeptical about the outcome of the announced actions. They think that Polaroid has many other weaknesses that these steps do not address.

In addition to streamlining operations, Polaroid president I. MacAllister Booth intends to place renewed emphasis on new product development and on speeding new products to market.

what's ahead

The introductory case reports on how management is attempting to deal with high costs, low sales, and low profitability at Polaroid. The management function called *control* can help managers like those at Polaroid eliminate such problems. The material in this chapter explains why eliminating these problems at Polaroid would be controlling at that company, and elaborates on the control function in general. The major topics in this chapter are as follows:

1. The fundamentals of controlling.
2. The controller and control.
3. Power and control.
4. Performing the control function.

THE FUNDAMENTALS OF CONTROLLING

As the scale and complexity of modern organizations grow, so does the problem of control in organizations. Prospective managers, therefore, need a working knowledge of the essentials of the controlling function.[1] To this end, the following sections provide a definition of control, a definition of the process of controlling, and a discussion of the various types of control that can be used in organizations.

Defining *Control*

Control is making something happen the way it was planned to happen.

Stated simply, **control** is making something happen the way it was planned to happen. As implied by this definition, planning and control are virtually inseparable functions.[2] In fact, these two functions have been called the Siamese twins of management. According to Robert L. Dewelt:

> The importance of the planning process is quite obvious. Unless we have a soundly charted course of action, we will never quite know what actions are necessary to meet our objectives. We need a map to identify the timing and scope of all intended actions. This map is provided through the planning process.
>
> But simply making a map is not enough. If we don't follow it or if we make a wrong turn along the way, chances are we will never achieve the desired results. A plan is only as good as our ability to make it happen. We must develop methods of measurement and control to signal when deviations from the plan are occurring so that corrective action can be taken.[3]

Murphy's Law is a lighthearted adage that makes the serious point that managers should continually control—that is, check to see that organizational activities and processes are going as planned. According to Murphy's Law, anything that can go wrong will go wrong.[4] This law reminds managers to remain alert for possible problems, because even if a management system appears to be operating well, it might be eroding under the surface. Managers must constantly seek feedback on how the system is performing and make corrective changes whenever warranted.

Defining *Controlling*

Controlling is the process managers go through to control. It is a systematic effort to compare performance to predetermined standards, plans, or objectives to determine whether performance is in line with those standards or needs to be corrected.

Controlling is the process managers go through to control. According to Robert Mockler, controlling is

> a systematic effort by business management to compare performance to predetermined standards, plans, or objectives to determine whether performance is in line with these standards and presumably to take any remedial action required to see that human and other corporate resources are being used in the most effective and efficient way possible in achieving corporate objectives.[5]

For example, production workers generally have daily production goals. At the end of each working day, the number of units produced by each worker is recorded so

weekly production levels can be determined. If these weekly totals are significantly below weekly goals, the supervisor must take corrective action to ensure that actual production levels equal planned production levels. If, on the other hand, production goals are being met, the supervisor should allow work to continue as it has in the past.[6]

The following sections discuss the controlling subsystem and provide more details about the control process itself.

BACK TO THE CASE

The information in the introductory case supports the notion that high production costs at Polaroid should be categorized as a control problem. In essence, control is making things happen at Polaroid in the way that management planned they should happen. When Polaroid management realized that actual profit levels were falling far below planned levels, it decided to take action to reduce production costs in order to ensure that future profit levels would be more in line with planned profit levels. Polaroid's control, then, must be closely linked to its planning activities.

Going one step further, controlling at Polaroid, as at any company, is the process that management goes through in order to control. This process at Polaroid would include taking steps to compare company performance to predetermined company plans, standards, and objectives for products like instant cameras, and then acting to eliminate problems that are causing any deviations from the standards. The ultimate goal of controlling is to ensure that Polaroid resources are being used in the most effective and efficient way possible to achieve corporate objectives.

The Controlling Subsystem   As with the planning, organizing, and influencing functions described in earlier chapters, controlling can be viewed as a subsystem of the overall management system. The purpose of this subsystem is to help managers enhance the success of the overall management system through effective controlling. Figure 19.1 shows the specific components of the controlling subsystem.

The Controlling Process   As Figure 19.2 illustrates there are three main steps in the controlling process:

1. Measuring performance.

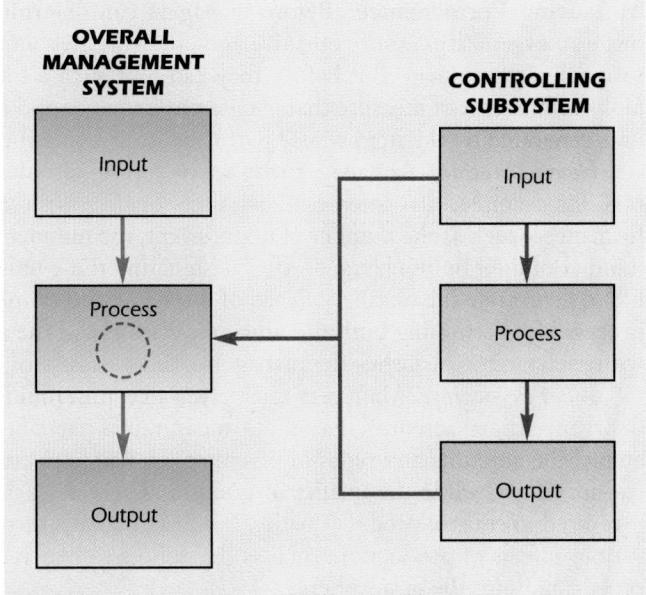

Figure 19.1   Relationship between overall management system and controlling subsystem

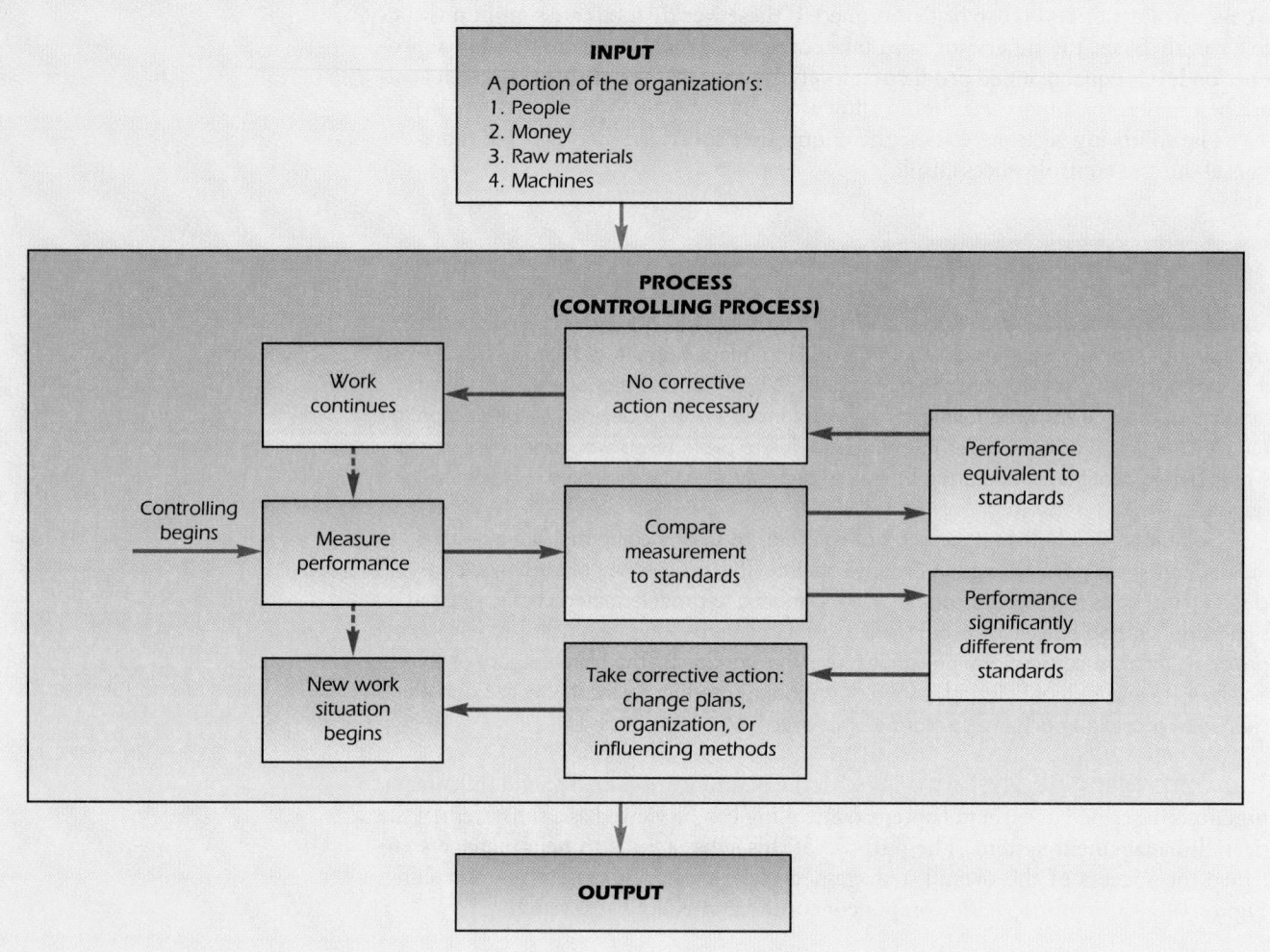

Figure 19.2   The controlling subsystem

2. Comparing measured performance to standards.

3. Taking corrective action.

Measuring Performance. Before managers can determine what must be done to make an organization more effective and efficient, they must measure current organizational performance.[7] But before they can take such a measurement, they must establish some unit of measure that gauges performance and observe the quantity of this unit generated by the item whose performance is being measured.

How to Measure. A manager who wants to measure the performance of five janitors, for example, first must establish units of measure that represent janitorial performance—such as the number of floors swept, the number of windows washed, or the number of light bulbs changed. After designating these units of measure, the manager has to determine the number of each of these units accomplished by each janitor. This process of determining both the units of measure and the number of units associated with each janitor furnishes the manager with a measure of janitorial performance.

What to Measure. Managers must always keep in mind that there is a wide range of organizational activities that can be measured as part of the control process. For example, the amounts and types of inventory on hand are commonly measured to control inventory, while the quality of goods and services being produced is commonly measured to control product quality. Performance measurements can relate as well to various effects of production, such as the degree to which a particular manufacturing process pollutes the atmosphere.

At retail outlets like this Best Buy store in Evanston, Illinois, inventory control often consists of addressing three related issues: (1) the information system gathers data needed to make merchandise decisions; (2) the valuation system determines the worth of merchandise in stock; (3) the analysis system is designed to measure past performance and plan for future activities.

The degree of difficulty in measuring various types of organizational performance, of course, is determined primarily by the activity being measured. For example, it is far more difficult to measure the performance of a highway maintenance worker than to measure the performance of a student enrolled in a college-level management course.

CONTROLLING FINANCES AT EURO DISNEYLAND

GLOBAL SPOTLIGHT

One area in which performance measurements are commonly taken is the financial affairs of an organization. Certified public accountant Judson Green left the Arthur Young accounting firm to join Walt Disney World in Florida. Today he is a senior vice president at Disney who is working at Euro Disneyland outside Paris. The French government has extended unprecedented hospitality to Euro Disneyland by offering favorable land deals, tax breaks, and loans with advantageous payback provisions. In addition, decisions that affect the financial affairs of Euro Disney are commonly made by Green in conjunction with financial people in cities like London and Brussels. In the near future, Disney's focus will shift to developing hotels outside the theme park and initiating the building of a second theme park in Europe. One of Green's major responsibilities is to monitor or measure the effects of all these financial decisions being made for Euro Disney. On the basis of such measurements, he will encourage company actions that meet or exceed profitability standards and discourage actions that do not meet or fall below the standards. In essence, Green is responsible for controlling financial activities at Euro Disney.≈

Comparing Measured Performance to Standards.   Once managers have taken a measure of organizational performance, their next step in controlling is to compare this measure against some standard. A **standard** is the level of activity established to serve as a model for evaluating organizational performance. The performance evaluated can be for the organization as a whole or for some individuals working within the organization.[8] In essence, standards are the yardsticks that determine whether organizational performance is adequate or inadequate.[9]

A **standard** is the level of activity established to serve as a model for evaluating organizational performance.

Studying operations at General Electric will give us some insights into the different kinds of standards managers can establish. GE has established the following standards:

1. *Profitability standards.* In general, these standards indicate how much money General Electric would like to make as profit over a given time period—that is, its return on investment. More and more, General Electric is using computerized preventive maintenance on its equipment to help maintain prof-

itability standards. Such maintenance programs have reduced labor costs and equipment downtime and thereby helped raise company profits.

2. *Market position standards.*   These standards indicate the share of total sales in a particular market that General Electric would like to have relative to its competitors. General Electric's market position standards were set by company chairman John F. Welch, Jr., in 1988, when he announced that henceforth any product his company offers must achieve the highest or second-highest market share compared to similar products offered by competitors or it would be eliminated or sold to another firm.

3. *Productivity standards.*   How much various segments of the organization should produce is the focus of these standards. Management at General Electric has found that one of the best ways of convincing organization members to commit themselves to increasing company productivity is simply to treat them with dignity and make them feel they are part of the General Electric team.

4. *Product leadership standards.*   General Electric intends to assume a leading position in product innovation in its field. Product leadership standards indicate what must be done to attain such a position. Reflecting this interest in innovation, General Electric has pioneered the development of synthetic diamonds for industrial use. In fact, GE is considered the leader in this area, having recently discovered a method for making synthetic diamonds at a purity of 99.9 percent. In all probability, such diamonds will eventually be used as a component of super-high-speed computers.

5. *Personnel development standards.*   Standards in this area indicate the type of training programs General Electric personnel should undergo to develop properly. General Electric's commitment to sophisticated training technology is an indication of the seriousness with which the company takes personnel development standards. Company training sessions are commonly supported by sophisticated technology like large-screen projection systems, computer-generated visual aids, combined video and computer presentations, and laser videos.

6. *Employee attitudes standards.*   These standards indicate what types of attitudes General Electric managers should strive to inculcate in GE employees. Like many other companies today, General Electric is striving to build positive attitudes toward product quality in its employees.

7. *Social responsibility standards.*   General Electric recognizes its responsibility to make a contribution to society. Standards in this area outline the level and types of contributions management believes GE should make. One recent activity that reflects social responsibility standards at General Electric is the renovation of San Diego's Vincent de Paul Joan Kroc center for the homeless accomplished by work teams made up of General Electric employees. These teams painted, cleaned, and remodeled a building to create a better facility for a number of San Diego's disadvantaged citizens.

8. *Standards reflecting the relative balance between short- and long-range goals.* These standards express the relative emphasis that should be placed on attaining various short- and long-range goals. General Electric recognizes that short-range goals exist to enhance the probability that long-range goals will be attained.

Successful managers pinpoint all important areas of organizational performance and establish corresponding standards in each area.[10] For instance, American Airlines has set two very specific standards for appropriate performance of its airport ticket offices: (1) at least 95 percent of the flight arrival times posted should be accurate, meaning that actual arrival times do not deviate more than 15 minutes from posted times; and (2) at least 85 percent of customers coming to the airport ticket counter should not have to wait more than 5 minutes to be serviced.

BACK TO THE CASE Polaroid's management should view controlling activities within the company as a subsystem of the organization's overall management system. For management to achieve organizational control, Polaroid's controlling subsystem must receive an adequate portion of the people, money, raw materials, and machines available within the company.

The process portion of the controlling subsystem at Polaroid requires management to take the following three steps:

1. Measure the performance levels of various productive units.
2. Compare these performance levels to predetermined performance standards for these units.
3. Take any corrective action necessary to ensure that planned performance levels are consistent with actual performance levels.

The introductory case indicates that one area in which Polaroid management needs to develop standards is desired profitability. According to the case, there are two major reasons why Polaroid has been struggling with profitability in recent years: high production costs and low product sales. Because the company is not achieving a desirable level of profits at present, the control actions that management should take in this area would be aimed at lowering production costs and increasing sales competitiveness.

Taking Corrective Action. After actual performance has been measured and compared with established performance standards, the next step in the controlling process is to take corrective action if necessary. **Corrective action** is managerial activity aimed at bringing organizational performance up to the level of performance standards. In other words, corrective action focuses on correcting organizational mistakes that are hindering organizational performance. Before taking any corrective action, however, managers should make sure that the standards they are using were properly established and that their measurements of organizational performance are valid and reliable.

Recognizing Problems. At first glance, it seems a fairly simple proposition that managers should take corrective action to eliminate **problems**—factors within an organization that are barriers to organizational goal attainment. In practice, however, it often proves difficult to pinpoint the problem causing some undesirable organizational effect. Let us suppose that a performance measurement indicates a certain worker is not adequately passing on critical information to fellow workers. If the manager is satisfied that the communication standards are appropriate and that the performance measurement information is both valid and reliable, the manager should take corrective action to eliminate the problem causing this substandard performance.

Recognizing Symptoms. But what exactly is the problem causing substandard communication in this situation? Is it that the worker is not communicating adequately simply because he or she doesn't want to communicate? Or is it that the job makes communication difficult? Or is it that the worker does not have the necessary training to communicate in an appropriate manner? Before attempting to take corrective action, the manager must determine whether the worker's failure to communicate is a problem in itself or a **symptom**—a sign that a problem exists.[11] For example, the worker's failure to communicate adequately could be a symptom of inappropriate job design or a cumbersome organizational structure.

Once the problem has been properly identified, corrective action can focus on one or more of the three primary management functions of planning, organizing, and influencing. That is, corrective action can include such activities as modifying past plans to make them more suitable for future organizational endeavors, making an existing organizational structure more suitable for existing plans and objectives, or restructuring an incentive program to ensure that high producers are rewarded more than low producers. Note that because planning, organizing, and influencing are

Corrective action is managerial activity aimed at bringing organizational performance up to the level of performance standards.

Problems are factors within an organization that are barriers to organizational goal attainment.

A **symptom** is a sign that a problem exists.

CEO Ronald W. Allen has set some goals for Atlanta-based Delta Airlines Inc. that include stemming a tide of red ink and transforming the airline into a low-cost carrier. Cost reduction is at the top of his list of corrective controls but promises to be a difficult challenge. For example, while he wants to lower seat costs from 9.76¢ to 7.5¢ by 1997, he is faced with large wage and benefits packages (Delta pilots average $140,000 annually, as opposed to, say, the $42,000 earned by pilots at low-cost competitor ValuJet).

closely related, there is a good chance that corrective action taken in one area will necessitate some corresponding action in one or both of the other two areas.

This section has discussed corrective action and described its role in the controlling process. The following PEOPLE PERSPECTIVES feature on Toyota Motor Corporation illustrates that corrective action can involve changing organization members so that organizational standards can be more effectively maintained.

TOYOTA TAKES CORRECTIVE ACTION BY CHANGING ITS PRESIDENT

PEOPLE PERSPECTIVES

A stroke that forced the resignation of Tatsuro Toyoda, president of Toyota Motor Corporation, sent shock waves throughout the company. Toyota is Japan's largest automaker and the third largest automaker in the world. Toyota management was highly dissatisfied with the company's share of international automobile sales. In choosing a new president, therefore, management had to decide whether to go with someone who was likely to continue Toyoda's conservative, moderately successful posture or someone who promised to implement a bold new approach to international sales that might achieve the standards management desired.

The company appointed Hiroshi Okuda as president and thereby signaled that it would be "taking off the gloves" in the increasingly vicious arena of international car sales. The 62-year-old Okuda is a gregarious man who loves gambling and late night movies and holds a black belt in judo. In contrast to past Toyota presidents, he openly boasts that he is willing to use any and all company resources to beat competitors. Okuda sees himself as a warrior and, consistent with this image, recently announced that he will speed up new-product development, do whatever it takes to recover lost market share, and hasten Toyota's shift of product manufacturing to overseas locations.

Clearly, upper management at Toyota was convinced that the key to improving international sales was a new and very different type of president. It remains to be seen whether this corrective action was appropriate given Toyota's situation. ≈

BACK TO THE CASE

n taking any corrective action at Polaroid, management must be certain that the action is aimed at organizational problems rather than at the symptoms of those problems. For example, if production costs are too high because workers are not trained well enough to operate their equipment properly, the symptom of high production costs will disappear when action is taken to improve the training of production workers—which is the real problem.

Any corrective action taken at Polaroid must focus on further planning, organizing, or influencing efforts. For example, if production workers are being more carefully trained, how must Polaroid's scheduling of workers change? Will the company still need the same number of production supervisors when workers become more competent as a result of their improved training?

Types of Control

Three types of management control are possible:

1. Precontrol
2. Concurrent control
3. Feedback control

What type is used is determined primarily by the work phase in which the control is needed.

Precontrol
Control that takes place before work is performed is called **precontrol,** or *feed-forward control*.[12] Managers using this type of control create policies, procedures, and rules aimed at eliminating behavior that will cause undesirable work results. For example, the manager of a small record shop may find that a major factor in attracting return customers is having salespeople discuss records with customers. This manager might use precontrol by establishing a rule that salespeople cannot talk to one another while a customer is in the store. This rule is a precontrol because it is aimed at eliminating an anticipated problem: salespeople who are so engrossed in conversations with one another that they neglect to chat with customers about records. In sum, precontrol focuses on eliminating predicted problems.

> **Precontrol** is control that takes place before some unit of work is actually performed.

Concurrent Control
Control that takes place as work is being performed is called **concurrent control.** It relates not only to employee performance but also to such nonhuman areas as equipment performance and department appearance. For example, most supermarkets have rigid rules about the amount of stock that should be placed on the selling floor. The general idea is to display generous amounts of all products on the shelves, with no empty spaces. A concurrent control aimed at ensuring that shelves are stocked as planned could consist of a stock manager's making periodic visual checks throughout a work period to evaluate the status of the sales shelves and, correspondingly, the performance of the stock crew.[13]

> **Concurrent control** is control that takes place as some unit of work is being performed.

Feedback Control
Control that concentrates on past organizational performance is called **feedback control.**[14] Managers exercising this type of control are attempting to take corrective action by looking at organizational history over a specified time period. This history may involve only one factor, such as inventory levels, or it may involve the relationships among many factors, such as net income before taxes, sales volume, and marketing costs.

This section has described feedback control. The following CUTTING EDGE feature discusses how Ford Motor Company uses virtual reality to exercise feedback control over a product that is being "produced" on the computer but not yet on the production line.

> **Feedback control** is control that takes place after some unit of work has been performed.

FORD USES VIRTUAL REALITY AS A FEEDBACK CONTROL TOOL

CUTTING EDGE

Automobile designers and engineers now have something in common with Hollywood directors: they both use computer special-effects technology—one to design movies, the other to develop the cars of the future. Engineers at Ford Motor Company, for instance, are gen-

erating full-size, full-color, photographic-quality holograms of proposed new cars with Hollywood virtual reality technology. These computer images allow Ford to study new vehicle designs without incurring the huge expense of building a clay model or prototype. For example, virtual reality allows designers to create a whole new car and take it for a test drive without ever constructing a physical prototype.

The introduction of virtual reality technology marks the beginning of an exciting new era in the manufacture of automobiles. The computer is permitting the automotive industry to cut the cost of feedback controlling as well as the cost of manufacturing, testing, and improving products. The latest trend is to use the power of computers to reduce even the number of *virtual* prototypes needed by guiding designers into an optimal design at the beginning of the process.≈

BACK TO THE CASE   In controlling at Polaroid, management should use an appropriate combination of precontrol, concurrent control, and feedback control. Precontrol would emphasize the elimination of factors that could cause low annual profitability at Polaroid before the year actually begins. Through concurrent control, management would be able to assess the company's profitability during a particular operating period. Finally, feedback control would enable Polaroid management to control at the end of some operating period. By analyzing a segment of Polaroid's history, management could use feedback control to improve future performance.

An optimal mix of these types of control would certainly help to eliminate profitability problems at Polaroid before they became overwhelming. Polaroid management must be careful, however, not to make the common mistake of emphasizing feedback control to the detriment of concurrent control and precontrol.

FEEDBACK CONTROL INDUCES COSMETIC INDUSTRY TO DEVELOP NEW PRODUCTS FOR DIVERSE POPULATION SEGMENTS

DIVERSITY SPOTLIGHT

For years, the cosmetics industry operated on the assumption that cosmetics sales are not influenced by recessions. As a result, firms like Maybelline Company and Fashion Fair historically developed their company plans with little regard for the U.S. economy.

Through feedback control, however, cosmetics companies recently came to the conclusion that economic downturns indeed influence cosmetics sales. An analysis of operating periods in the early 1990s indicated that the $4-billion-a-year cosmetics market had gone soft and that the main reason was the recession of that time.

Cosmetic firms swing into action to try to reignite cosmetics sales. Feedback control finally made the industry recognize the needs of a previously underserved diverse population—African-American, Asian, Hispanic, and Native American women, who cannot wear mainstream makeup lines because the colors and formulations were developed for white skin. New products developed specifically for such ethnic customers are expected to give this previously "recession-proof" business a boost. Many cosmetics companies are either introducing separate brand lines aimed at ethnic customers or expanding present mainstream product lines to include a greater range of shades to accommodate those customers' coloring. Cosmetics industry consultant Allan Mottus estimates that makeup for women of color accounts for approximately 10 percent of the total market.≈

THE CONTROLLER AND CONTROL

Organization charts developed for medium- and large-sized companies typically contain a position called *controller*. The sections that follow explain the job of the con-

troller and discuss its relationship to the control function and how much control is needed within an organization.

The Job of the Controller

The **controller** (also sometimes called the *comptroller*) is the staff person who gathers information that helps managers control. From the preceding discussion, it is clear that managers are responsible for comparing planned and actual performance and for taking corrective action when necessary. In smaller organizations, managers may also be completely responsible for gathering information about various aspects of the organization and developing necessary reports based on this information. In medium- or large-sized companies, however, the controller handles much of this work. The controller's basic responsibility is to assist line managers with the controlling function by gathering appropriate information and generating reports that reflect this information.[15] The controller usually works with information about the following financial dimensions of the organization:[16]

1. Profits
2. Revenues
3. Costs
4. Investments
5. Discretionary expenses

The sample job description of a controller in Table 19.1 shows that the controller is responsible for generating information managers rely on when exercising the control function. Because the controller is seldom directly responsible for taking corrective action within the organization but instead advises managers on what sort of action to take, the controller position is considered a staff position.

How Much Control Is Needed?

As with all organizational endeavors, control activities should be pursued if the expected benefits of performing such activities are greater than the costs of performing them.[17] The process of comparing the cost of any organizational activity with the expected benefit of performing the activity is called **cost-benefit analysis.** In general, managers and controllers should collaborate to determine exactly how much controlling is justified in a given situation.

Figure 19.3 (see page 467) graphs controlling activity at a certain company over an extended period of time. Note how controlling costs increase steadily as more and more controlling activities are performed. Also note that because the controlling function requires start-up costs, controlling costs are usually greater than the income generated from increased controlling at first. As controlling starts to correct major organizational errors, however, the income from increased controlling eventually equals controlling costs (point X_1 on Figure 19.3) and ultimately surpasses them by a large margin.

As more and more controlling activity is added beyond X_1, however, controlling costs and the income from increased controlling eventually become equal again (point X_2 on Figure 19.3). As more controlling activity is added beyond X_2, controlling costs again surpass the income from increased controlling. The main reason for this last development is that major organizational problems probably were detected much earlier, so most corrective measures at this point are aimed at smaller and less costly problems.

The **controller** is the staff person whose basic responsibility is to assist line managers with the controlling function by gathering appropriate information and generating necessary reports that reflect this information.

Cost-benefit analysis is the process of comparing the cost of some activity with the benefit or revenue that results from the activity to determine the activity's total worth to the organization.

BACK TO THE CASE The job of the controller at Polaroid is to gather information for reports that management can use to take corrective action. The controller does not take any corrective action, but simply advises management as to what actions should be taken.

Table 19.1
Sample Job Description for a Controller in a Large Company

OBJECTIVES
The controller (or comptroller) is responsible for all accounting activities within the organization.

FUNCTIONS
1. *General accounting.* Maintain the company's accounting books, accounting records, and forms. This includes:
   a. Preparing balance sheets, income statements, and other statements and reports.
   b. Giving the president interim reports on operations for the recent quarter and fiscal year to date.
   c. Supervising the preparation and filing of reports to the SEC.
2. *Budgeting.* Prepare a budget outlining the company's future operations and cash requirements.
3. *Cost accounting.* Determine the cost to manufacture a product and prepare internal reports for management of the processing divisions. This includes:
   a. Developing standard costs.
   b. Accumulating actual cost data.
   c. Preparing reports that compare standard costs to actual costs and highlight unfavorable differences.
4. *Performance reporting.* Identify individuals in the organization who control activities and prepare reports to show how well or how poorly they perform.
5. *Data processing.* Assist in the analysis and design of a computer-based information system. Frequently, the data-processing department is under the controller, and the controller is involved in management of that department as well as other communications equipment.
6. *Other duties.* Other duties may be assigned to the controller by the president or by corporate bylaws. Some of these include:
   a. Tax planning and reporting.
   b. Service departments such as mailing, telephone, janitors, and filing.
   c. Forecasting.
   d. Corporate social relations and obligations.

RELATIONSHIP
The controller reports to the vice president for finance.

Polaroid management should determine, with the advice of the controller, exactly how much control is necessary throughout the company—that is, which production costs are most detrimental and how these expenses can be reduced. Management will probably find that controlling costs exceed savings from corrective actions in the beginning because of start-up expenses. But as major production and labor savings are achieved, the benefits from the control activities (enhanced profitability) will exceed their cost. Management should bear in mind throughout the control process that too much control results in a superabundance of paperwork throughout the company and often slows decision making to an undesirable level. In addition, controlling reaches a point of diminishing returns when the major organizational problems have all been successfully tackled and controlling is concentrating on even less significant problems. Beyond a certain point, controlling costs will again exceed savings achieved through corrective actions.

POWER AND CONTROL

To control successfully, managers must understand not only the control process itself but also how organization members relate to it. Up to this point, the chapter has emphasized the nonhuman variables of controlling. This section focuses on power, per-

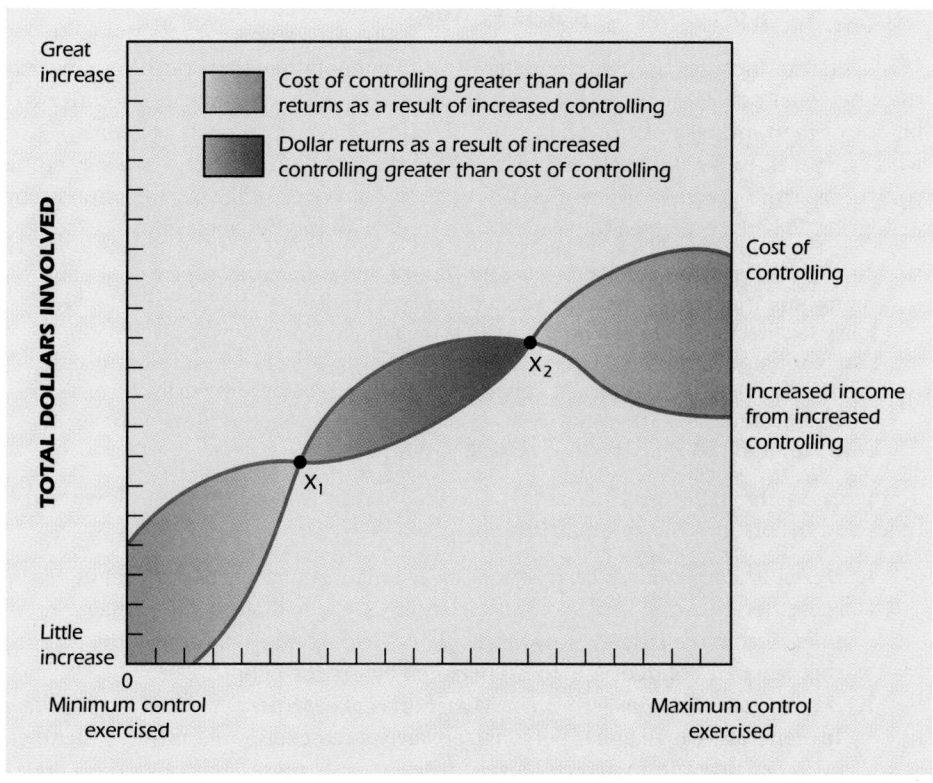

Figure 19.3   Value of additional controlling

haps the most important human-related variable in the control process. The following sections discuss power by:

1. Presenting its definition.
2. Elaborating on the total power of managers.
3. Listing the steps managers can take to increase their power over other organization members.

A Definition of *Power*

Perhaps the two most often confused terms in management are *power* and *authority*. Authority was defined in Chapter 11 as the right to command or give orders. The extent to which an individual is able to influence others so that they respond to orders is called **power.** The greater this ability, the more power an individual is said to have.

Obviously, power and control are closely related. To illustrate, after comparing actual performance with planned performance and determining that corrective action is necessary, a manager usually gives orders to implement this action. Although the orders are issued by virtue of the manager's organizational authority, they may or may not be followed precisely, depending on how much power the manager has over the individuals to whom the orders are addressed.

Total Power of a Manager

The **total power** a manager possesses is made up of two different kinds of power: position power and personal power. **Position power** is power derived from the organizational position a manager holds. In general, a manager moving from lower-level management to upper-level management accrues more position power. **Personal power** is power derived from a manager's relationships with others.[18]

Power is the extent to which an individual is able to influence others so that they respond to orders.

Total power is the entire amount of power an individual in an organization possesses. It is made up of position power and personal power.

Position power is power derived from the organizational position a manager holds.

Personal power is the power derived from a manager's relationships with others.

Steps for Increasing Total Power

Managers can increase their total power by enhancing either their position power or their personal power or both. Position power is generally enhanced by a move to a higher organizational position, but most managers have little personal control over when they will move up in an organization. Managers do, however, have substantial control over the amount of personal power they hold over other organization members. John P. Kotter stresses the importance of developing personal power:

> To be able to plan, organize, budget, staff, control, and evaluate, managers need some control over the many people on whom they are dependent. Trying to control others solely by directing them and on the basis of the power associated with one's position simply will not work—first, because managers are always dependent on some people over whom they have no formal authority, and second, because virtually no one in modern organizations will passively accept and completely obey a constant stream of orders from someone just because he or she is the "boss."[19]

To increase personal power, a manager should attempt to develop the following attitudes and beliefs in other organization members:[20]

1. *A sense of obligation toward the manager.* If a manager succeeds in developing this sense of obligation, other organization members will allow the manager to influence them within certain limits. The basic strategy suggested for creating this sense of obligation is to do personal favors for people.

2. *A belief that the manager possesses a high level of expertise within the organization.* In general, a manager's personal power increases as organization members perceive that the manager's level of expertise is increasing. To raise perceptions of their expertise, managers must quietly make their significant achievements visible to others and build up a successful track record and a solid professional reputation.

3. *A sense of identification with the manager.* The manager can strive to develop this identification by behaving in ways that other organization members respect and by espousing goals, values, and ideals commonly held by them. The following description illustrates how a certain sales manager took steps to increase the degree to which his subordinates identified with him:

> One vice-president of sales in a moderate-sized manufacturing company was reputed to be so much in control of his sales force that he could get them to respond to new and different marketing programs in a third of the time taken by the company's best competitors. His power over his employees was based primarily on their strong identification with him and what he stood for. Emigrating to the United States at age seventeen, this person worked his way up "from nothing." When made a sales manager in 1965, he began recruiting other young immigrants and sons of immigrants from his former country. When made vice-president of sales in 1970, he continued to do so. In 1975, 85 percent of his sales force was made up of people whom he hired directly or who were hired by others he brought.[21]

4. *The perception that they are dependent on the manager.* The main strategy here is to clearly convey the amount of authority the manager has over organizational resources—not only those necessary for organization members to do their jobs but also those organization members personally receive in such forms as salaries and bonuses. This strategy is aptly reflected in the managerial version of the Golden Rule: "He who has the gold makes the rules."

BACK TO THE CASE | f Polaroid managers are to be successful in controlling, they must be aware not only of the intricacies of the control process itself but also of how to deal with employees as they relate to that process. Polaroid managers have to consider the amount of power they hold over organization members—that is,

their ability to get workers to follow orders. Judging from the introductory case, many of the orders managers at Polaroid are likely to issue would relate to implementing better production methods and improved selling techniques.

The total amount of power that Polaroid managers possess comes from both the positions they hold and their personal relationships with other organization members. Polaroid's top managers already have more position power than any other managers in the organization. Therefore, to increase their total power, they would have to enhance their personal power. Top management might attempt to do this by developing the following attitudes in other organization members:

1. A sense of obligation toward top managers.
2. The belief that top management has a high level of task-related expertise.
3. A sense of identification with top management.
4. The perception that they are dependent on top management.

PERFORMING THE CONTROL FUNCTION

Controlling can be a detailed and intricate function, especially as the size of an organization increases. The following two sections furnish valuable guidelines for successfully executing this complicated function. They discuss potential barriers to successful controlling and how to make controlling successful.

Potential Barriers to Successful Controlling

To avoid potential barriers to successful controlling, managers should take action in the following areas.[22]

Long-Term versus Short-Term Production.   A manager, in striving to meet planned weekly production quotas, might be tempted to "push" machines in a particular area so hard they cannot be serviced properly. This kind of management behavior would ensure that planned performance and actual performance are equivalent in the short term, but it might well cause the machines to deteriorate to the point where it is impossible to meet long-term production quotas.

Employee Frustration and Morale.   Worker morale tends to be low when management exerts too much control. Employees become frustrated when they perceive management is too rigid in its thinking and will not allow them the freedom they need in order to do a good job. Overcontrol may also make employees suspect that control activities are merely a tactic to pressure them to work harder and harder to increase production.

Filing of Reports.   Employees may perceive that management is basing corrective action solely on department records with no regard for extenuating circumstances. If this is the case, they may feel pressured to falsify reports so that corrective action pertaining to their organizational unit will not be too drastic. For example, employees may overstate actual production figures to make their unit look good to management; or they may understate the numbers to create the impression that planned production is too high, thereby tricking management into thinking that a lighter workload is justified.

A well-publicized instance of falsifying control reports involved the Federal Aviation Administration (FAA) and Eastern Airlines.[23] The FAA is a government organization charged with controlling airlines' safety. As part of the FAA's controlling process, airline companies must fill out service reports and return them to the FAA for monitoring and evaluation. Before Eastern went out of business, the company and its senior maintenance executives were charged by a federal grand jury with conspiring

to falsify aircraft maintenance records and returning improperly maintained aircraft to passenger service. The indictment charged that on 52 different occasions company managers signed off on, or coerced aircraft mechanics and mechanics supervisors to sign off on maintenance that had not been completed. Management seems to have regarded the falsification of maintenance reports as a way of reducing maintenance costs and thereby boosting Eastern's poor profit performance. In essence, the pressure of poor profits at Eastern Airlines caused certain company managers to falsify service reports, making it impossible for the FAA to properly control the airline company.

Perspective of Organization Members.   Although controls can be designed to focus on relatively narrow aspects of an organization, managers must remember to consider any prospective corrective action not only in relation to the specific activity being controlled but also in relation to all other organizational units.

For example, a manager may determine that actual and planned production are not equivalent in a specific organizational unit because during various periods a low inventory of needed parts causes some production workers to pursue other work activities instead of producing a product. The appropriate corrective action in this situation would seem to be simply to raise the level of inventory, but this would be taking a narrow perspective of the problem. The manager should take a broader perspective by asking the following questions before initiating any corrective action: Is there enough money on hand to raise current inventory levels? Are there sufficient personnel presently in the purchasing department to effect the necessary increase? Who will do the work the production workers are now doing when they run out of parts?

Means Versus Ends.   Control activities are not the goals of the control process; they are merely the means to eliminate problems. Managers must keep in mind throughout the control process that the information gathering and report generating done to facilitate the taking of corrective action are activities that can be justified only if they yield some organizational benefit that exceeds the cost of performing them.

Making Controlling Successful

In addition to avoiding the potential barriers to successful controlling mentioned in the previous section, managers can perform certain activities to make the control process more effective. To increase the quality of the controlling subsystem, managers should make sure that controlling activities take all of the following factors into account.

Specific Organizational Activities Being Focused On.   Managers should make sure the various facets of the control process are appropriate to the control activity under consideration. For example, standards and measurements concerning a line worker's productivity are much different from standards and measurements concerning a vice president's productivity. Controlling ingredients related to the productivity of these individuals, therefore, must be different if the control process is to be applied successfully.

Different Kinds of Organizational Goals.   According to Jerome, control can be used for such different purposes as standardizing performance, protecting organizational assets from theft and waste, and standardizing product quality.[24] Managers should remember that the control process can be applied to many different facets of organizational life and that, if the organization is to receive maximum benefit from controlling, each of these facets must be emphasized.

Timely Corrective Action.   Some time will necessarily elapse as managers gather control-related information, develop necessary reports based on this information, and decide what corrective action should be taken to eliminate a problem. However, man-

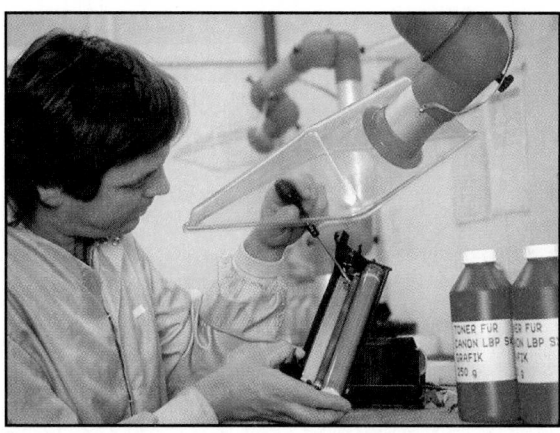

In its efforts to downsize plants like this one in Montpellier, France, IBM Europe encountered an almost continent-wide barrier to operational control: Already facing recessions and unemployment rates of about 10 percent, strong labor unions filed suit in France, Germany, Italy, and Spain. IBM was thus forced to find other solutions. At this plant, for example, about 500 laid-off employees are now working for other companies that have rented or bought space from IBM.

agers should take the corrective action as promptly as possible to ensure that the situation depicted by the information gathered has not changed. Unless corrective actions are timely, the organizational advantage of taking them may not materialize.

Communication of the Mechanics of the Control Process.   Managers should take steps to ensure that people know exactly what information is required for a particular control process, how that information is to be gathered and used to compile various reports, what the purposes of the various reports actually are, and what corrective actions are appropriate given those reports. The lesson here is simple: For control to be successful, all individuals involved in controlling must have a working knowledge of how the control process operates.[25]

BACK TO THE CASE

Polaroid managers must be aware of the potential barriers to successful controlling and know what actions to take to increase the probability that controlling activities will be successful. They must, for instance, do all that they can to raise the probability that any new production techniques introduced will be performed efficiently, effectively, and without resistance.

To overcome potential control-related barriers at Polaroid, management must maintain a proper balance between short-term and long-term objectives, minimize any negative effects controlling may have on the morale of Polaroid employees, eliminate all forces tending to lead to the falsification of control-related reports, adopt a control perspective that appropriately combines narrow and broad organizational focuses, and stress that controlling is a means rather than an end.

To increase the probability that its controlling activities will be effective, Polaroid management must ensure that the various facets of its controlling subsystem are appropriate for company activities, that components of the controlling subsystem are flexible enough to accommodate many purposes, that corrective action is based on timely information, and that the controlling subsystem is understood by all organization members taking part in its operation.

Action Summary

Reread the learning objectives below. Each objective is followed by questions. Answering these questions accurately will help you retain the most important concepts discussed in this chapter. After answering each question, check your answer against the answer key at the end of this chapter. (*Hint:* If you have any doubts regarding the correct response, consult the page whose number follows the answer.)

Circle: From studying this chapter, I will attempt to acquire:

1. A definition of *control*.

a,b,c,d,e **a.** Managers must develop methods of measurement to signal when deviations from standards are occurring so that: (a) the plan can be abandoned; (b) quality control personnel can be notified; (c) the measurement standards can be checked; (d) corrective action can be taken; (e) none of the above.

T,F **b.** Control is making something happen the way it was planned to happen.

2. A thorough understanding of the controlling subsystem.

a,b,c,d,e **a.** The main steps of the controlling process include all of the following *except:* (a) taking corrective action; (b) establishing planned activities; (c) comparing performance to standards; (d) measuring performance; (e) all of the above are steps in controlling.

T,F **b.** Standards should be established in all important areas of organizational performance.

3. An appreciation for various kinds of control and for how each kind can be used advantageously by managers.

a,b,c,d,e **a.** The following is *not* one of the basic types of management control: (a) feedback control; (b) precontrol; (c) concurrent control; (d) exception control; (e) all are basic types.

a,b,c,d,e **b.** An example of precontrol established by management would be: (a) rules; (b) procedures; (c) policies; (d) budgets; (e) all of the above are examples.

4. Insights into the relationship between power and control.

T,F **a.** According to Kotter, controlling others solely on the basis of position power will not work.

a,b,c,d e **b.** The extent to which an individual is able to influence others to respond to orders is: (a) power; (b) sensitivity; (c) authority; (d) communication skills; (e) experience.

5. Knowledge of the various potential barriers that must be overcome to implement successful control.

a,b,c,d,e **a.** A control-related potential barrier to successful controlling is: (a) overemphasizing short-term production as opposed to long-term production; (b) creative employee frustration leading to reduced workplace morale; (c) the falsification of reports; (d) narrowing the perception of organization members to the detriment of the organization; (e) all of the above are potential barriers.

T,F **b.** Control activities should be seen as the means by which corrective action is taken.

6. An understanding of steps that can be taken to increase the quality of a controlling subsystem.

a,b,c,d,e **a.** All of the following are suggestions for making controlling successful *except:* (a) managers should make sure the mechanics of the control process are understood by organization members involved with controlling; (b) managers should use control activities to achieve many different kinds of goals; (c) managers should ensure that control activities are supported by most organization members; (d) managers should make sure that the information on which corrective action is based is timely; (e) all of the above are suggestions.

T,F **b.** The standards and measurements pertaining to a line worker's productivity are much the same as the standards and measurements pertaining to a vice president's productivity.

Introductory Case Wrap-Up

"Controlling at Polaroid" (p. 455) and its related back-to-the-case sections were written to help you better understand the management concepts contained in this chapter. Answer the following discussion questions about this introductory case to enrich your understanding of the chapter content:

1. List four areas in which standards should be developed at Polaroid. Why would standards in these areas be important to company success?

2. Assume that Polaroid has a controller. From what the case tells about this company, describe five important duties of this controller. Be as specific as you can about how the controller's activities relate to this particular company.

3. What kind of power does Polaroid management need to ensure that the new programs aimed at reducing production costs and improving sales will be implemented successfully? Explain.

Issues for Review and Discussion

1. What is control?
2. Explain the relationship between planning and control.
3. What is controlling?

4. What is the relationship between the controlling subsystem and the overall management system?
5. Diagram and explain the controlling subsystem.

6. List and discuss the three main steps of the controlling process.
7. Define the term *standards*.
8. What is the difference between a symptom and a problem? Why is it important to differentiate between the two before taking any controlling action?
9. What types of corrective action can managers take?
10. List and define the three basic types of control that can be used in organizations.
11. What is the relationship between controlling and the controller?
12. What basis do managers use to determine how much control is needed in an organization?
13. What is the difference between power and authority? Describe the role of power in the control process.
14. What determines how much power a manager possesses?
15. How can a manager's personal power be increased?
16. Describe several potential barriers to successful controlling.
17. What steps can managers take to ensure that control activities are successful?

Action Summary Answer Key

1. **a.** d, p. 456
   b. T, p. 456
2. **a.** b, pp. 457–458
   b. T pp. 459–460

3. **a.** d, p. 463
   b. e, p. 463
4. **a.** T, pp. 467–468
   b. a, pp. 467–468

5. **a.** e, pp. 469–470
   b. T, p. 470

6. **a.** c, pp. 470–471
   b. F, pp. 470–471

Case Study

Who Killed Barings Bank?

In February 1995, London-based Barings, an international investment bank with a 200-year tradition of providing financial services throughout the world, died an untimely death following the discovery of a $1.4 billion loss at one of its subsidiaries, Baring Futures Singapore (BFS). Most of that loss was attributed to the questionable dealings of a Singapore-based derivatives trader named Nick Leeson. A month earlier, it had been revealed that Leeson had imperiled Barings by taking large trading positions in Japan's Nikkei Index futures. Examiners also uncovered fictitious accounts Leeson had set up to cover his huge trading losses. But Nick Leeson was not the only cause of the demise of prestigious Barings Bank. Barings' death is an excellent example of the ultimate cost of a lack of management controls.

In Singapore, government-hired auditors "found the fall of Baring Futures Singapore was caused by 'institutional incompetence,' lack of understanding of futures business among senior executives, and a 'total failure of internal controls.'" The report also claimed that Barings CEO Peter Norris and other top officers not only tried to conceal Leeson's unauthorized dealings but also played down their significance.

In early 1993, Leeson had become BFS's general manager. Sometime later, he opened a special account, to conceal unauthorized trading. Leeson is said to have hidden the activity of his special account from his London superiors by creating fictitious accounts to cover huge losses until the market improved. Then, panicked by a continuing plunge in the Tokyo futures market, Leeson according to one source, began "doubling his bets in desperation."

In July and August 1994, an internal audit by Barings officials identified possible control problems at BFS. This report noted that Leeson supervised both the front and back offices at BFS, which allowed him both to make trades and to settle them. At first, Barings management in London did little, if anything, to rectify the situation. It seems that London feared that attempting to control BFS's operations might slow Barings' aggressive global expansion. Moreover, some London executives were too involved with a planned restructuring of BFS and/or intoxicated by their own prospective handsome annual bonuses to question Leeson's methods. Much of the money for those bonuses was generated by the Singapore subsidiary, which had provided almost two-thirds of Barings' total profit for the year. Indeed, Leeson could claim to have made nearly $30 million of the subsidiary's $157 million profit.

Because BFS was expected by London to produce disproportionately large profits from a relatively small capital base, Leeson strove not only to please his bosses but also to boost his own economic and social standing. A report issued later by the Bank of England's Board of Banking Supervisions speculated that had Leeson been successful, "he and his team would have received $24 million in bonuses."

Officials in Singapore claimed that Leeson "dominated the staff at BFS, who did his bidding, sometimes falsifying reports and transferring trades between Barings

accounts." Barings management, however, consistently contended that they had no knowledge of false accounts. This discrepancy, continues the Singapore report, raises the question of how Mr. Leeson had obtained over $1.2 billion from the Barings Group without accounting for it."

It was not until someone noticed BFS's large exposure in future trading positions on the Nikkei Index that alarms began to go off. Fearing that one of BFS's customers might not be able to meet a margin call, London officials in January 1995 instructed BFS to reduce its exposure. Apparently that order was never carried out. The Singapore report later claimed that the large-exposures report submitted by Barings to the Bank of England (BOE), although inaccurate because of Leeson's false reporting, showed that the bank's maximum exposure had already exceeded the BOE's 25 percent large-exposure limit.

In late January 1995, Barings' auditors informed London of an apparent outstanding debt of $86 million due from a New York securities trader. In early February, two London Barings officials were sent to Singapore to look at the purported account receivable. They were unable to meet with Leeson until some 16 days later. After about a half-hour talk on February 23, Leeson left the BFS office and never returned. From his hotel in Kuala Lumpur, Malaysia, the next day, Leeson faxed his resignation to Singapore. Later that day, officials in Singapore discovered information that the $86 million account receivable was a fake.

Two days later, after the discovery of additional losses totaling an estimated $1.4 billion, the London High Court named a panel to manage Barings. Leeson and his wife, on their way to London, were arrested in Frankfurt on March 1. Three days later, a Dutch banking and insurance company, ING, bought Barings, thus ending the bank's 200-year-old tradition as a leading British international investment bank.

Leeson's rogue trading practices precipitated the bank's fall. Lack of control at all levels—by Barings top executives, the Bank of England, and the Singapore government—laid the groundwork for its demise.

Questions:

1. List actions that Nick Leeson took that led to the demise of Barings. When should alarms have triggered control activity at Barings' London headquarters? What may have interfered with the process?
2. How were symptoms of problems at BFS hidden? Were some symptoms readily apparent? Explain. How might Barings' organizational goals have conflicted with control activities and corrective action at BFS?
3. In which areas of control—precontrol, concurrent control, and/or feedback control—was Barings remiss? Explain.
4. Describe Leeson's power at BFS. How did the power he accumulated play a role in circumventing control?

Skills Exercise

Conduct a media search to discover news articles and anecdotes that illustrate control activity at financial institutions. Analyze the information to make generalizations about controls set in place by executives and government agencies to ensure that the kind of problems that led to Barings' collapse will not go unnoticed in the future.

The Internet learning materials that accompany this chapter can be found at
http://www.profcerto.com
Additional information can be found on the inside front and back covers of this text.

20
chapter

PRODUCTION MANAGEMENT AND CONTROL

STUDENT LEARNING OBJECTIVES

From studying this chapter, I will attempt to acquire:

1. Definitions of production, productivity, and quality.
2. An understanding of the importance of operations and production strategies, systems, and processes.
3. Insights into the role of operations management concepts in the workplace.
4. An understanding of how operations control procedures can be used to control production.
5. Insights concerning operations control tools and how they evolve into a continual improvement approach to production management and control.

CHAPTER OUTLINE

Introductory Case: *The Quick Turn at USAir*

Production
Defining Production

Cutting Edge: *Chrysler Uses Teams to Speed Up Production Process*

Productivity

People Perspectives: Characteristics of Japanese Employment Motivate Workers to Improve Productivity

Quality and Productivity

Quality Spotlight: Focusing on Quality at Adidas USA

Automation
Strategies, Systems, and Processes

Operations Management
Defining Operations Management
Operations Management Considerations

Ethics Spotlight: Firestone Exits LaVergne

Operations Control
Just-in-Time Inventory Control
Maintenance Control
Cost Control
Budgetary Control
Ratio Analysis
Materials Control

Selected Operations Control Tools
Using Control Tools to Control Organizations
Inspection
Management by Exception
Management by Objectives
Breakeven Analysis
Other Broad Operations Control Tools

The Quick Turn at USAir

Ed Vilchis is in a hurry. So is his employer, USAir Group, Inc.

A ramp-agent supervisor at the company's Baltimore-Washington airport terminal, Vilchis used to have 45 minutes to see that bags moved off and on planes between flights. These days he and his crews have about half that (see Figure 20.1). "Once that plane rolls in, you basically attack it," says Vilchis, a 17-year USAir veteran. "You load it, fuel it, cater it, push it back, and it's gone."

What's the rush? It's all part of the "quick-turn" strategy being implemented by some U.S. airlines. To improve productivity and lower operating costs, these carriers are trying to cut the time that planes on non-connecting flights stay on the ground. After all, planes earn money flying passengers, not sitting on the tarmac.

The strategy offers flyers one big advantage. Because of delays in boarding, "people were telling us they weren't getting their business done in one day,"

says a USAir spokeswoman. Stripping away amenities such as meals, pillows, and blankets means caterers and cleaners can turn around the flights more quickly and passengers can get where they're going faster, she maintains.

But flyers do lose some amenities, and there are other pitfalls. Some customers don't like the stricter boarding procedures. USAir, for example, has a "10-minute rule," which requires boarding 10 minutes or more before departure time. It also insists that all carry-on luggage fit into a "sizer box" at the gate, which is roughly the size of an overhead compartment. The box is intended to keep passengers from bringing on huge bags and holding up seating.

Some workers grumble about having to move faster. "They're not used to working this hard," says Tim Goodrich, a USAir ground-crew worker in Baltimore. "In the old days, you'd come to work and have 30 or 40 minutes before you did anything. Now, they've got to pick up the pace or get out."

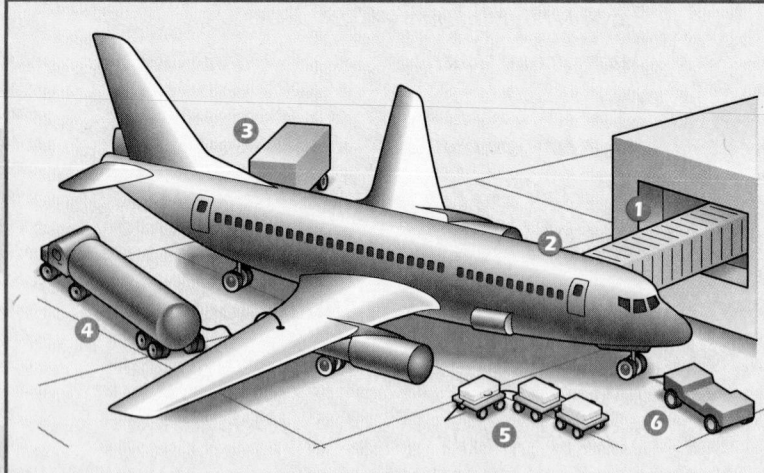

USAir is attempting to cut the turnaround time on some commercial flights from the current 45 minutes to 20 minutes for Boeing 737s. Below is a list of procedures that must be completed before the flight can depart:

1. Ticket agent takes flight plan to pilot, who loads information into aircraft computer. About 130 passengers disembark from the plane.
2. Workers clean trash cans, seat pockets, lavatories, etc.
3. Catering personnel board plane and replenish supply of drinks and ice.
4. A fuel truck loads up to 5,300 gallons of fuel into aircraft's wings.
5. Baggage crews unload up to 4,000 pounds of luggage and 2,000 pounds of freight. "Runners" rush the luggage to baggage claim area in terminal.
6. Ramp agents, who help park aircraft upon arrival, "push" plane back away from gate.

The quick turn at USAir.
Source: USAir Group, Inc., Boeing Co.

what's ahead

The introductory case describes one airline company's attempt to raise productivity. It explains how USAir is shortening the amount of time that its planes stay on the ground between flights by speeding up procedures for preparing a plane for takeoff. This chapter is designed to help managers in a company like USAir increase employee productivity.

This chapter emphasizes the fundamentals of **production control**—ensuring that an organization produces goods and services as planned. The primary discussion topics in the chapter are as follows:

1. Production.
2. Operations management.
3. Operations control.
4. Selected operations control tools.

> **Production control** ensures that an organization produces goods and services as planned.

PRODUCTION

To reach organizational goals, all managers must plan, organize, influence, and control to produce some type of goods or services. Naturally, these goods and services vary significantly from organization to organization. This section of the chapter defines production and productivity, and discusses the relationship between quality and productivity and automation.

Defining *Production*

Production is the transformation of organizational resources into products.[1] In this definition, *organizational resources* are all assets available to a manager to generate products, *transformation* is the set of steps necessary to change these resources into products, and *products* are various goods or services aimed at meeting human needs. Inputs at a manufacturing firm, for example, would include raw materials, purchased parts, production workers, and even schedules. The transformation process would encompass the preparation of customer orders, the design of various products, the procurement of raw materials, and the production, assembly, and (perhaps) warehousing of products. Outputs, of course, would consist of products fit for customer use.

"Production" occurs at service organizations as well. Inputs at a hospital, for instance, would include ambulances, rooms, employees (doctors, nurses, administrators, receptionists), supplies (medicines, bandages, food), and (as at a manufacturer) funds, schedules, and records. The transformation process might begin with transporting patients to the facility and end with discharging them. In between, the hospital would attend to patients' needs (nursing and feeding them, administering their medication, recording their progress). Naturally, the output here is health care.

This section has defined production. The following CUTTING EDGE feature describes a production change recently implemented at Chrysler Corporation. The automaker is using cross-functional teams to speed up a segment of its production process—the interval between developing a new or modified car model and actually producing the model.

> **Production** is the transformation of organizational resources into products.

CHRYSLER USES TEAMS TO SPEED UP PRODUCTION PROCESS

CUTTING EDGE

Chrysler recently reported that annual earnings rose 246 percent, to $3.7 billion, and that sales were up 20 percent, to $52.2 billion. Both of these figures far exceed the company's previous all-time highs. Chrysler paid 91,550 of its 125,825 employees a profit-sharing bonus averaging $8,000, also an all-time high.

CEO Robert Eaton attributes his company's success to management's decision to empower employees as members of teams. Nowadays, when Chrysler begins to create a new model or revamp an old one, it forms a team of about 700 people. Members come from the engineering, design, manufacturing, marketing, and finance departments, and include company specialists of all kinds. A vice president acts as "godfather" to the team, but all of the team's actual work is directed by leaders below that rank and team members organize themselves as they see fit.

One big payoff of this production approach has been speed-to-market. It used to take Chrysler five years to go from concept to production of a new or improved car model. The new team-oriented production process has reduced this time to two and a half to three years. Moreover, company officials believe the time lapse between concept and production will get even shorter in the future.≈

Productivity

Productivity is the relationship between the total amount of goods or services being produced (output) and the organizational resources needed to produce them (input).

Productivity is an important consideration in designing, evaluating, and improving modern production systems. We can define **productivity** as the relationship between the total amount of goods or services being produced (output) and the organizational resources needed to produce them (input). This relationship is usually expressed by the following equation:[2]

$$\text{productivity} = \frac{\text{outputs}}{\text{inputs}}$$

The higher the value of the ratio of outputs to inputs, the higher the productivity of the operation.

Managers should continually strive to make their production processes as productive as possible. It is no secret that over the last 20 years the rate of productivity growth related to production management and innovation in U.S. manufacturing has lagged significantly behind that of countries such as Japan, West Germany, and France.[3] Some of the more traditional strategies for increasing productivity are as follows:

1. Improving the effectiveness of the organizational workforce through training.
2. Improving the production process through automation.
3. Improving product design to make products easier to assemble.
4. Improving the production facility by purchasing more modern equipment.
5. Improving the quality of workers hired to fill open positions.[4]

This section has defined productivity. The following PEOPLE PERSPECTIVES feature describes how the Japanese employment system induces Japanese employees to identify with the company objective of increasing productivity.

CHARACTERISTICS OF JAPANESE EMPLOYMENT MOTIVATE WORKERS TO IMPROVE PRODUCTIVITY

PEOPLE PERSPECTIVES

The Japanese employment system in large corporations is based on two principles that American managers have difficulty endorsing. First, the Japanese system supports employing an individual for a lifetime. Second, it awards pay mainly on the basis of seniority. According to American managers, these employment principles are contrary to free market ideals. Moreover, many U.S. observers believe that, in the long run, the Japanese employment system will be incapable of surviving competition from the "more efficient" hire-and-fire labor systems of the United States and Europe.

American managers' criticisms of the Japanese employment system, however, may be based on a failure to understand it. For example, many American managers mistakenly think that lifetime employment is deeply rooted in the Japanese culture. It is not. In the early days of Japan's industrialization, in fact, most employers generally operated by hire-and-fire rules, and as a result suffered many of the same labor problems that are thought of today as peculiarly Western. A closer look reveals that lifetime employment is not a policy dictated by Japanese culture, but rather one rooted in strong business logic. Japanese managers are convinced that the lifetime employment guarantee is a major reason for the enviable speed with which Japanese corporations are able to introduce productivity-enhancing new technologies. According to these managers, Japanese workers see no personal risk in helping their employers improve productivity because they know that productivity gains will not deprive them of their jobs.≈

Quality and Productivity

Quality can be defined as how well a product does what it is intended to do—how closely it satisfies the specifications to which it was built. In a broad sense, quality is the degree of excellence on which products or services can be ranked on the basis of selected features or characteristics. It is customers who determine this ranking, and customers define quality in terms of appearance, performance, availability, flexibility, and reliability. Product quality determines an organization's reputation.

During the last decade or so, managerial thinking about the relationship between quality and productivity has changed drastically. Many earlier managers chose to achieve higher levels of productivity simply by producing a greater number of products given some fixed level of available resources. They saw no relationship between improving quality and increasing productivity. Quite the contrary. They viewed quality improvement as a controlling activity that took place toward the end of the production process and largely consisted of rejecting a number of finished products that were too obviously flawed to be offered to customers. Under this approach, quality improvement efforts were generally believed to *lower* productivity.

Focus on Continual Improvement. Management theorists have more recently discovered that concentrating on improving product quality throughout all phases of a production process actually improves the productivity of the manufacturing system.[5] U.S. companies were far behind the Japanese in making this discovery. As early as 1948, Japanese companies observed that continual improvements in product quality throughout the production process normally resulted in improved productivity. How does this happen? According to Dr. W. Edwards Deming, a world-renowned quality expert, a serious and consistent quality focus normally reduces nonproductive variables such as the reworking of products, production mistakes, delays and production snags, and inefficient use of time and materials.

Deming believed that for continual improvement to become a way of life in an organization, managers need to understand their company and its operations. Most managers feel they do know their company and its operations, but when they begin drawing flowcharts, they discover that their understanding of strategy, systems, and processes is far from complete. Deming recommended that managers question every aspect of an operation and involve workers in discussion before they take action to improve operations. He maintained that a manager who seriously focuses on improving product quality throughout all phases of a production process will initiate a set of chain reactions that benefits not only the organization but also the society in which the organization exists.

Focus on Quality and Integrated Operations. Deming's flow diagram for improving product quality (Figure 20.2) contains a complete set of organizational vari-

Quality is the extent to which a product reliably does what it is intended to do.

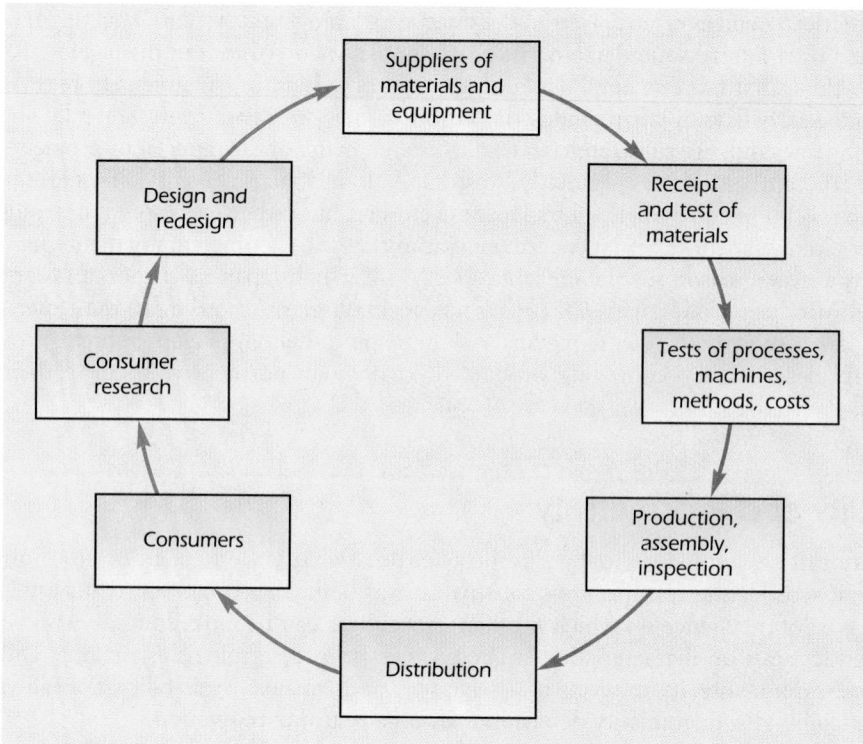

Figure 20.2   Deming's flow diagram for improving product quality

ables. It introduces the customer into the operations process, and introduces the idea of continually refining knowledge, design, and inputs into the process in order to constantly increase customer satisfaction. The diagram shows the operations process as an integrated whole, from the first input to actual use of the finished product; a problem at the beginning of the process will impact on the whole process and the end product. In Deming's scheme, there are no barriers between the company and the customer, between the customer and suppliers, between the company and its employees. Since the process is unified, the greater the harmony among all its components, the better the results will be.

An organization's interpretation of quality is expressed in its strategies. The following sections elaborate on the relationship between quality and production by discussing quality assurance and quality circles as part of organizational strategy.

Quality Assurance

Quality assurance is an operations process involving a broad group of activities that are aimed at achieving the organization's quality objectives.[6] Quality assurance is a continuum of activities that starts when quality standards

Quality assurance is an operations process involving a broad group of activities that are aimed at achieving the organization's quality objectives.

The bad news is that productivity is a little sluggish: General Electric cannot make quite enough Maxus washing machines to keep up with demand. The good news: With 40-percent fewer parts, a larger tub, and a new suspension that reduces both noise and vibration, the Maxus is a high-quality product. GE collected data from both market-research studies and service technicians in order to design its first really new washing machine in over 40 years, and managers attribute productivity snags to predictable but temporary start-up problems.

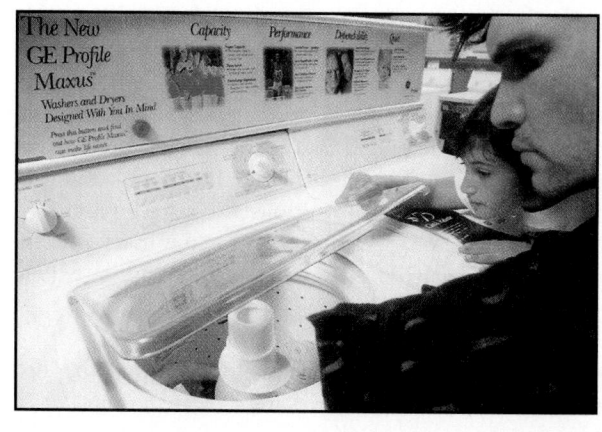

are set and ends when quality goods and services are delivered to the customer. Although the precise activities involved in quality assurance vary from organization to organization, activities like determining the safest system for delivering goods to customers and maintaining the quality of parts or materials purchased from suppliers are part of most quality assurance efforts.

Statistical Quality Control.   Statistical quality control is a much narrower concept than quality assurance. **Statistical quality control** is the process used to determine how many products should be inspected to calculate a probability that the total number of products will meet organizational quality standards. An effective quality assurance strategy reduces the need for quality control and subsequent corrective actions.

Statistical quality control is the process used to determine how many products should be inspected to calculate a probability that the total number of products will meet organizational quality standards.

"No Rejects" Philosophy.   Quality assurance works best when management adopts a "no rejects" philosophy. Unfortunately, such a philosophy is not economically feasible for most mass-produced products. What is possible is training employees to approach production with a "do not make the same mistake once" mind set. Mistakes are costly. Detecting defective products in the final quality control inspection is very expensive. Emphasizing quality in the early stages—during product and process design—will reduce rejects and production costs.

Quality Circles

The recent trend in U.S. organizations is to involve all of a company's employees in quality control by soliciting employees' ideas for judging and maintaining product quality. This trend developed out of a successful Japanese control system known as *quality circles*. Although many U.S. corporations are now moving beyond the concept of the quality circle to the concept of the work team, as discussed in Chapter 17, many of the ideas generated from quality circles continue to be valid.[7]

Quality circles are small groups of workers that meet to discuss a particular project in terms of quality assurance and communicate their solutions to these problems to management directly at a formal presentation session. Figure 20.3 shows the quality circle problem-solving process.

Most quality circles operate in a similar manner. The circle usually has fewer than eight members, and the circle leader is not necessarily the members' supervisor. Members may be workers on the project and/or outsiders. The focus is on operational problems rather than interpersonal ones. The problems discussed in the quality circle may be ones assigned by management or ones uncovered by the group itself.

Quality circles are small groups of workers that meet to discuss quality-related problems on a particular project and communicate their solutions to these problems to management at a formal presentation session.

FOCUSING ON QUALITY AT ADIDAS USA

QUALITY SPOTLIGHT

Adidas USA, Inc., is an athletic apparel company that is best known for its athletic footwear. Recent events at Adidas illustrate that, without proper control aimed at enhancing profit, an organization may not last long enough to have the opportunity to focus on enhancing product quality.

Although Adidas USA lost significant amounts of money in the late 1980s, the company seemed to turn the corner in the early 1990s. It went from a $63 million loss in 1989 to a $2 million profit in 1990. This profit, although small, was highly significant because it was achieved despite an 11 percent drop in revenues, to $249 million. Staff reductions and an emphasis on collecting overdue receivables were important control measures that helped to produce the turnaround in earnings. The company also exercised control by analyzing product lines weekly to assess and increase the contributions to profit that each line was making.

Adidas' chief financial officer, Andrew P. Hines, concedes that these and other cost controls instituted by the company were primarily one-time measures. According

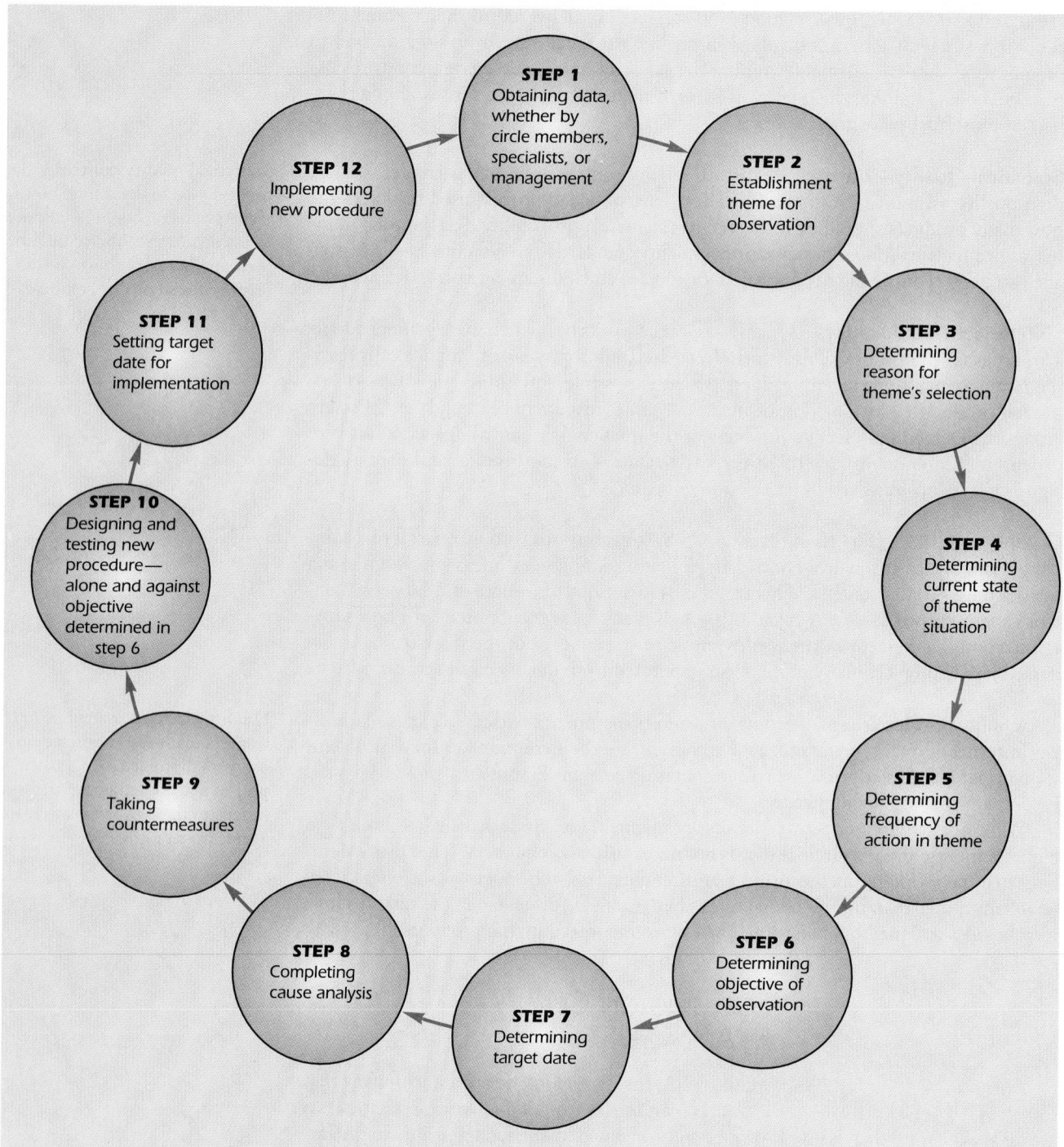

Figure 20.3 The quality circle problem-solving process

to Hines, now that the company is once again profitable, its challenge is to build lasting quality in both its staff and its products. Adidas USA dominated the U.S. market for athletic footwear in the 1970s, but strong competition and internal problems in the 1980s caused its market share to dwindle from more than 60 percent to 4 percent. Hines believes that such new measures as creating a pay-for-performance plan, clarifying and documenting job responsibilities, and instituting critical training programs will allow Adidas to build more quality into its staff and its products.

In 1992, Adidas was acquired by Britain's Pentland Group, which plans to invigorate the Adidas brand name by upgrading products, improving distribution, and signing up more big-name endorsers.≈

Automation

The preceding section discussed the relationship between quality and productivity organizations. This section introduces the topic of automation, which shows signs of increasing organizational productivity in a revolutionary way.[8]

Automation is defined as the replacement of human effort by electromechanical devices in such operations as welding, materials handling, design, drafting, and decision making. It includes robots—mechanical devices built to perform repetitive tasks efficiently—and **robotics**—the study of the development and use of robots.

Over the past 20 years, a host of advanced manufacturing systems have been developed and implemented to support operations. Most of these are automated systems that combine hardware-industrial robots and computers—and software. The goals of new automation include reduced inventories, higher productivity, and faster billing and product distribution cycles. So far, the industrialized Asian countries appear to be doing the best job of making optimal use of company resources through automation.

Robotics is the study of the development and use of robots.

Strategies, Systems, and Processes

According to Kemper and Yehudai, an effective and efficient operations manager is skilled not only in management, production, and productivity but also in strategies, systems, and processes. A *strategy* is a plan of action. A *system* is a particular linking of organizational components that facilitates carrying out a process. A *process* is a flow of interrelated events toward a goal, purpose, or end. Strategies create interlocking systems and processes when they are comprehensive, functional, and dynamic—when they designate responsibility and provide criteria by which to measure output.[9]

BACK TO THE CASE

ncreasing productivity at USAir, as described in the introductory case, is mainly a matter of integrating resources such as people, equipment, and materials to provide better customer service.

Although productivity at USAir was far from disastrous, management seems to have decided that it was necessary to lower operating costs through improved productivity in order to stay competitive in the increasingly combative airline carrier business. USAir's first move to increase productivity has been the "quick-turn" strategy described in the introductory case—taking less time to ready a plane for takeoff after it has landed so customers will have shorter waits for flights. To improve productivity even further, USAir might consider implementing more effective training programs for employees and institut-

In order to win back business that they have lost to trucking companies, Conrail and other railroads have turned to information technology to improve productivity in servicing their customers. Now, for example, Conrail uses specialized database computers to organize and access massive amounts of data about both its own facilities and the different needs of different customers.

ing more selective hiring procedures. In addition, company managers could evaluate the possibility of using robots to further shorten airport turnaround time. This strategy has the added advantage that robots would make fewer errors than humans.

To maintain and improve the quality of customer services like shorter turnaround time, USAir management could establish a quality assurance program that continually monitors services to ensure that they are at acceptable levels. Quality circles could be established to involve employees in the effort to improve customer service in both the specific area of turnaround time and in more general terms.

Operations Management

Operations management deals with managing the production of goods and services in organizations. The sections that follow define *operations management* and discuss various strategies that managers can use to make production activities more effective and efficient.

Defining *Operations Management*

Operations management is the systematic direction (strategy) and control of operations processes that transform resources into finished goods and services; it is getting things done by working with or through other people.

According to Chase and Aquilano, **operations management** is the performance of the managerial activities entailed in selecting, designing, operating, controlling, and updating production systems.[10] Figure 20.4 describes these activities and categorizes them as being either periodic or continual. The distinction between periodic and continual activities is one of relative frequency of performance: Periodic activities are performed from time to time, while continual activities are performed essentially without interruption.

Operations Management Considerations

Overall, *operations management* is the systematic direction and control of operations processes that transform resources into finished goods and services. The concept conveys three key notions:

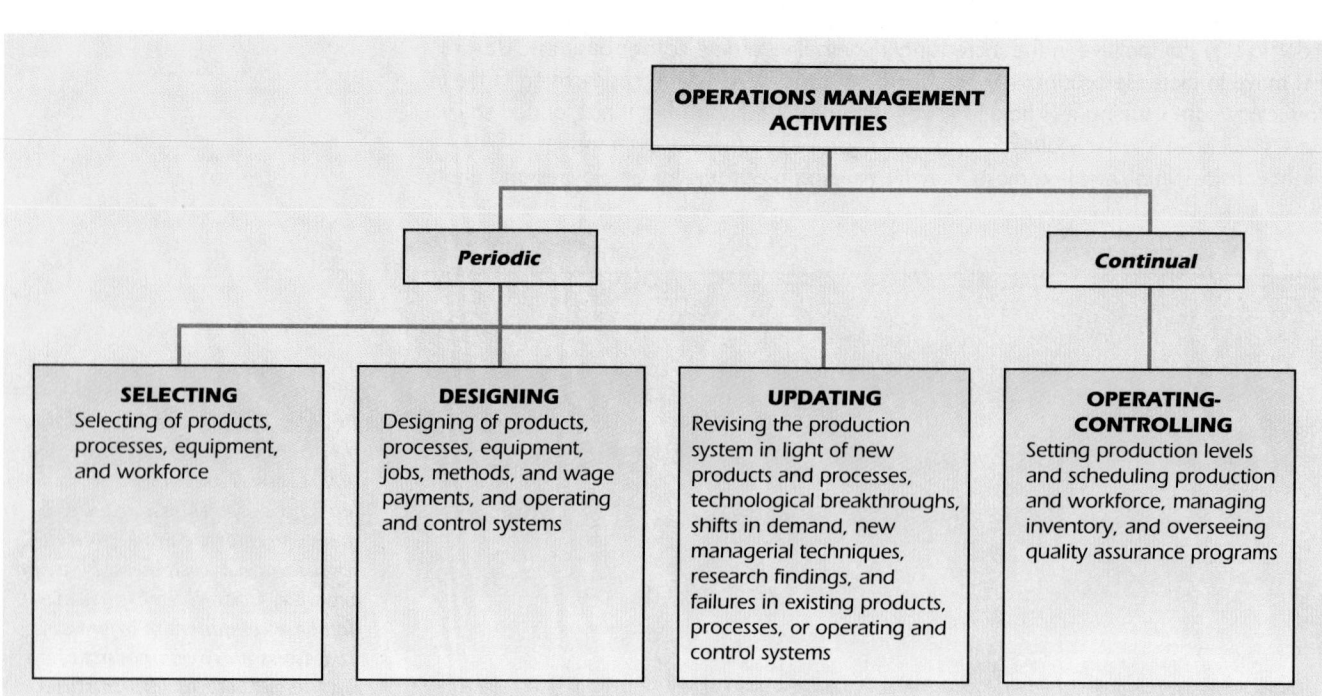

Figure 20.4   Major activities performed to manage production

- Operations management involves managers—people who get things done by working with or through other people.
- Operations management takes place within the context of objectives and policies that drive the organization's strategic plans.
- The criteria for judging the actions taken as a result of operations management are standards for effectiveness and efficiency.

Effectiveness is the degree to which managers attain organizational objectives: "doing the right things." **Efficiency** is the degree to which organizational resources contribute to productivity: "doing things right." A review of organizational performance based on these standards is essential to enhancing the success of any organization.

Operations strategies—capacity, location, product, process, layout, and human resources—are specific plans of action designed to ensure that resources are obtained and used effectively and efficiently. An operational strategy is implemented by people who get things done with and through people. It is achieved in the context of objectives and policies derived from the organization's strategic plan.

Capacity Strategy

Capacity strategy is a plan of action aimed at providing the organization with the right facilities to produce the needed output at the right time. The output capacity of the organization determines its ability to meet future demands for goods and services. *Insufficient capacity* results in loss of sales that, in turn, affects profits. *Excess capacity* results in higher production costs. A strategy that aims for *optimal capacity*, where quantity and timing are in balance, provides an excellent basis for minimizing operating costs and maximizing profits.

Capacity flexibility enables the company to deliver its goods and services to its customers in a shorter time than its competitors. This component of capacity strategy involves having flexible plants and processes, broadly trained employees, and easy and economical access to external capacity, such as suppliers.

Managers use capacity strategy to balance the costs of overcapacity and undercapacity. The difficulty of accurately forecasting long-term demand makes this balancing task risky. Modifying long-range capacity decisions while in production is both hard and costly. In a highly competitive environment, construction of a new high-tech facility might take longer than the life cycle of the product. Correcting overcapacity by closing a plant saddles management with high economic costs and even higher social costs—in the form of lost jobs that devastate both employees and the community in which the plant operates—that will have a long-term adverse effect on the firm.

The traditional concept of economies of scale led management to construct large plants that tried to do everything. The more modern concept of the focused facility has led management to conclude that better performance can be achieved in more specialized plants that concentrate on fewer tasks and are therefore smaller.

Five Steps in Capacity Decisions.   Managers are more likely to make sound strategic capacity decisions if they adhere to the following five-step process:

1. Measure the capacity of currently available facilities.
2. Estimate future capacity needs on the basis of demand forecasts.
3. Compare future capacity needs and available capacity to determine whether capacity must be increased or decreased.
4. Identify ways to accommodate long-range capacity changes (expansion or reduction).
5. Select the best alternative based on a quantitative and qualitative evaluation.

Location Strategy

Location strategy is a plan of action that provides the organization with a competitive location for its headquarters, manufacturing, services and distribution activities. A competitive location results in lower transportation and communication costs among the various facilities. These costs—which run as high as 20

Effectiveness is the degree to which managers attain organizational objectives; it is doing the right things.

Efficiency is the degree to which organizational resources contribute to production; it is doing things right.

Capacity strategy is an operational plan of action aimed at providing the organization with the right facilities to produce the needed output at the right time.

Location strategy is an operational plan of action that provides the organization with a competitive location for its headquarters, manufacturing, services, and distribution activities.

to 30 percent of a product's selling price—greatly affect the volume of sales and amount of profit generated by a particular product. Many other quantitative and qualitative factors are important when formulating location strategy.

Factors in a Good Location.   A successful location strategy requires a company to consider the following major factors in its location study:

- Nearness to market and distribution centers.
- Nearness to vendors and resources.
- Requirements of federal, state, and local governments.
- The character of direct competition.
- The degree of interaction with the rest of the corporation.
- The quality and quantity of labor pools.
- The environmental attractiveness of the area.
- Taxes and financing requirements.
- Existing and potential transportation.
- The quality of utilities and services.

The dynamic nature of these factors could make what is a competitive location today an undesirable location in five years.

ETHICS SPOTLIGHT

FIRESTONE EXITS LAVERGNE

Firestone built a radial truck tire plant in LaVergne, Tennessee, in 1972. After a decade in LaVergne, faced with lower-than-anticipated demand, a hostile local union, and quality problems, Firestone announced that it was planning to sell the plant or to close it down if a buyer could not be found. The company had already shut down 7 of its 17 plants, so it was clear that management meant what it said and workers at the Lavergne plant would lose their jobs. In many observers' eyes, Firestone was reneging on its obligations to the community and to its own employees.

Bridgestone, a Japanese tire maker, was looking to locate in Tennessee. The state had been openly wooing Japanese companies for some time—Nissan was in Smyrna, Komatsu in Chattanooga, Sharp in Memphis, and Toshiba in the tiny town of Lebanon—so Bridgestone had ample reason to believe it would be welcome in Tennessee. Bridgestone sent negotiators to LaVergne to arrange to buy the plant from Firestone, provided they could come to reasonable terms with the union. The union's leadership seemed to view the negotiations as an opportunity to win concessions, not make them. Both sides dug in their heels. Then, in a moment of ill-advised bravado, the local union president told the Japanese that they should go back to Japan. In many observers' eyes, the union was failing to take seriously its obligation to its members and to the community.

Bridgestone's negotiators did go home. Soon the local union's officers were summoned to Akron to meet with Firestone's top management and officers of the International Rubber Workers Union. This meeting between the union and management resulted in an invitation to Bridgestone negotiators to return to the bargaining table. This time both sides made commitments: Bridgestone pledged to recall laid-off workers, and the union agreed to a contract that eased work rules and promised to lobby members for its ratification. The $52 million sale went through.

Firestone's decision to build a plant in LaVergne resulted, many believed, in certain legitimate expectations about how Firestone would behave toward local employees and the community—expectations that were left unstated in the agreement the company made when it located in LaVergne. Bridgestone, on the other hand, has agreed to what many hope will be a long-range ethical commitment to plant workers and the community of LaVergne. The moral is that a successful location strategy requires that a company consider not only major location factors but long-range ethical and cultural factors as well.≈

Product Strategy

Product strategy is an operational plan of action outlining which goods and services an organization will produce and market. Product strategy is a main component of an organization's operations strategy—in fact, it is the link between the operations strategy and the other functional strategies, especially marketing and research and development. In essence, product, marketing, and research and development strategies must fit together if management is to be able to build an effective overall operations strategy. A business' product and operations strategies should take into account the strengths and weaknesses of operations, which are primarily internal, as well as those of other functional areas concerned more with external opportunities and threats.

Cooperation and coordination among its marketing, operations, and research and development departments from the inception of a new product are strongly beneficial to a company. At the very least, it ensures a smooth transition from research and development to production, since operations people will be able to contribute to the quality of the total product, rather than merely attempt to improve the quality of the components. Even the most sophisticated product can be designed so that it is relatively simple to produce, thus reducing the number of units that must be scrapped or reworked during production, as well as the need for highly trained and highly paid employees. All of these strategies lower production costs and hence increase the product's price competitiveness or profits or both.

> **Product strategy** is an operational plan of action outlining which goods and services an organization will produce and market.

Process Strategy

Process strategy is a plan of action outlining the means and methods the organization will use to transform resources into goods and services. Materials, labor, information, equipment, and managerial skills are resources that must be transformed. A competitive process strategy will ensure the most efficient and effective use of these organizational resources.

> **Process strategy** is an operational plan of action outlining the means and methods the organization will use to transform resources into goods and services.

Types of Processes.

All manufacturing processes may be grouped into three different types. The first is the *continuous process*, a product-oriented, high-volume, low-variety process used, for example, in producing chemicals, beer, and petroleum products. The second is the *repetitive process*, a product-oriented production process that uses modules to produce items in large lots. This mass-production or assembly-line process is characteristic of the auto and appliance industries.

The third type of manufacturing process is used to produce small lots of custom-designed products such as furniture. This high-variety, low-volume system, commonly known as the *job-shop process*, includes the production of one-of-a-kind items as well as unit production. Spaceship and weapons systems production are considered job-shop activities.

Organizations commonly employ more than one type of manufacturing process at the same time and in the same facility.

Process strategy is directly linked to product strategy. The decision to select a particular process strategy is often the result of external market opportunities or threats. When this is true, the corporation decides what it wants to produce, then selects a process strategy to produce it. The product takes center stage and the process becomes a function of the product.

The function of process strategy is to determine what equipment will be used, what maintenance will be necessary, and what level of automation will be most effective and efficient. The type of employees and the level of employee skills needed are dependent on the process strategy chosen.

Layout Strategy

Layout strategy is a plan of action that outlines the location and flow of all organizational resources around, into, and within production and service facilities. A cost-effective and cost-efficient layout strategy is one that minimizes the expenses of processing, transporting, and storing materials throughout the production and service cycle.

> **Layout strategy** is an operational plan that determines the location and flow of organizational resources around, into, and within production and service facilities.

Layout strategy—which is usually the last part of operations strategy to be formulated—is closely linked, either directly or indirectly, with all other components of operations strategy: capacity, location, product, process, and human resources. It must target capacity and process requirements. It must satisfy the organization's product design, quality, and quantity requirements. It must target facility and location requirements. Finally, to be effective, the layout strategy must be compatible with the organization's established quality of work life.

A **layout** is the overall arrangement of equipment, work areas, service areas, and storage areas within a facility that produces goods or provides services.[11] There are three basic types of layouts for manufacturing facilities:

> A **layout** is the overall arrangement of equipment, work areas, service areas, and storage areas within a facility that produces goods or provides services.

1. A **product layout** is designed to accommodate high production volumes, highly specialized equipment, and narrow employee skills. It is appropriate for organizations that produce and service a limited number of different products. It is not appropriate for an organization that experiences constant or frequent changes of products.

> A **product layout** is a layout designed to accommodate a limited number of different products that require high volumes, highly specialized equipment, and narrow employee skills.

2. A **process (functional) layout** is a layout pattern that groups together similar types of equipment. It is appropriate for organizations involved in a large number of different tasks. It best serves companies whose production volumes are low, whose equipment is multipurpose, and whose employees' skills are broad.

> A **process (functional) layout** is a layout pattern based primarily on grouping together similar types of equipment.

3. The **fixed-position layout** is one in which the product is stationary while resources flow. It is appropriate for organizations involved in a large number of different tasks that require low volumes, multipurpose equipment, and broad employee skills. A *group technology layout* is a product layout cell within a larger process layout. It benefits organizations that require both types of layout.

> A **fixed-position layout** is a layout plan appropriate for organizations involved in a large number of different tasks that require low volumes, multipurpose equipment, and broad employee skills.

Figure 20.5 illustrates the three basic layout patterns. Actually, most manufacturing facilities are a combination of two or more different types of layouts. Various techniques are available to assist management in designing an efficient and effective layout that meets the required specifications.

Human Resources Strategy

Human resources is the term used for individuals engaged in any of the organization's activities. There are two human resource imperatives:

1. It is essential to optimize individual, group, and organizational effectiveness.
2. It is essential to enhance the quality of organizational life.

A **human resources strategy** is an operational plan to use the organization's human resources effectively and efficiently while maintaining or improving the quality of work life.

> A **human resources strategy** is an operational plan to use the organization's human resources effectively and efficiently while maintaining or improving the quality of work life.

As discussed in Chapter 12, human resource management is about employees—who are the best means of enhancing organizational effectiveness. Whereas financial management attempts to increase organizational effectiveness through the allocation and conservation of financial resources, human resource management (personnel management) attempts to increase organizational effectiveness through such factors as the establishment of personnel policies, education and training, and procedures.

Operational Tools in Human Resources Strategy. Operations management attempts to increase organizational effectiveness by employing the methods used in the manufacturing and service processes. Human resources, one very important factor of operations, must be compatible with operations tasks.

Manpower planning is the primary focus of the operations human resources strategy. It is an operational plan for hiring the right employees for a job and training them to be productive. This is a lengthy and costly process. A human resources strategy must be founded on fair treatment and trust. The employee, not operations, must take center stage.

> **Manpower planning** is an operational plan that focuses on hiring the right employees for a job and training them to be productive.

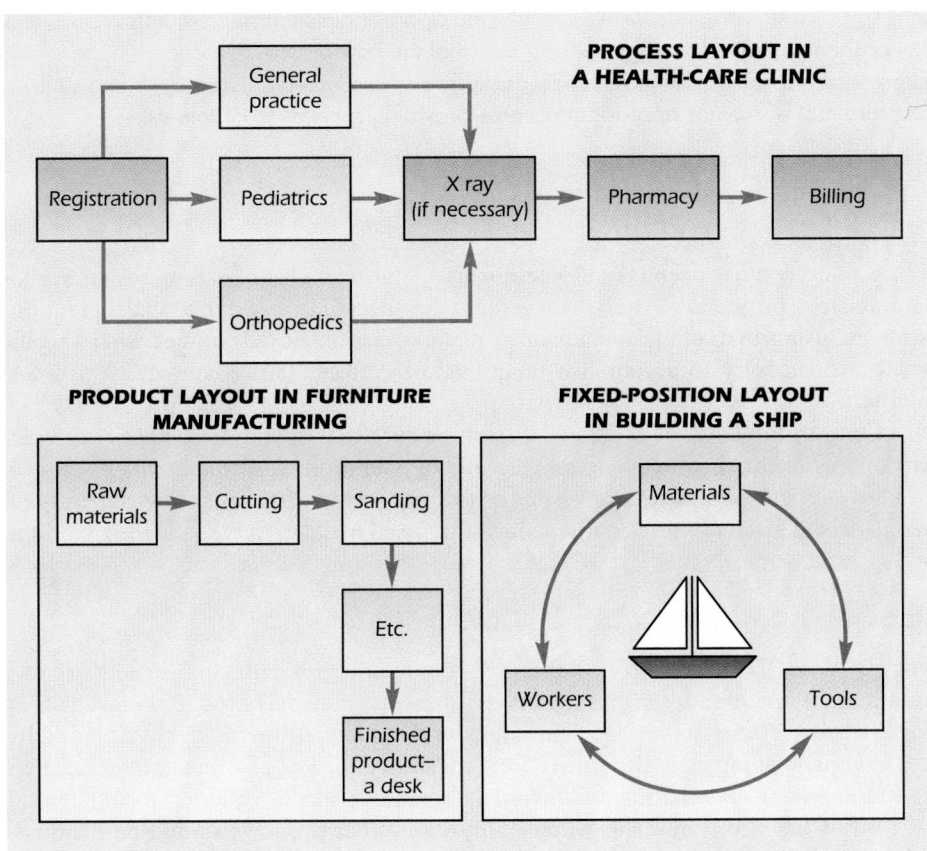

PROCESS LAYOUT IN
A HEALTH-CARE CLINIC

PRODUCT LAYOUT IN FURNITURE
MANUFACTURING

FIXED-POSITION LAYOUT
IN BUILDING A SHIP

Figure 20.5   The three basic
layout patterns

Job design is an operational plan that determines who will do a specific job and how and where the job will be done. The goal of job design is to facilitate productivity. Successful job design takes efficiency and behavior into account. It also guarantees that working conditions are safe and that the health of employees will not be jeopardized in the short or the long run.

Work methods analysis is an operational tool used to improve productivity and ensure the safety of workers. It can be performed for new or existing jobs. **Motion-study techniques** are another set of operational tools used to improve productivity.

Work measurement methods are operational tools used to establish labor standards. These standards are useful for planning, control, productivity improvements, costing and pricing, bidding, compensation, motivation, and financial incentives.

Job design is an operational plan that determines who will do a specific job and how and where the job will be done.

Work methods analysis is an operational tool used to improve productivity and ensure the safety of workers.

Motion-study techniques are operational tools that are used to improve productivity.

Work measurement methods are operational tools that are used to establish labor standards.

BACK TO THE CASE

n attempting to speed up plane turnaround, USAir management is involved in operations management. Most of the issues mentioned in the introductory case pertain to the "periodic updating" segment of operations management activities—revising systems to provide better customer service. USAir's periodic updating should focus on the appropriate use of company resources like ticket agents, caterers, fuel trucks, and ramp agents. Once established, the new operations procedure must be continually monitored by USAir management for both effectiveness—"doing the right things"—and efficiency—"doing things right."

Factors USAir management must consider in making operations decisions are: *capacity strategy,* making sure that the airline has appropriate resources to perform needed functions at appropriate times; *location strategy,* making sure that airline resources are appropriately postured for work when the work must be performed; *product strategy,* making sure that appropriate customer services are targeted and provided; *process*

strategy, making sure that USAir is employing appropriate steps in providing various customer services; *layout strategy,* making sure that the flow of USAir resources in the process of providing customer services is desirable; and *human resources strategy,* making sure that USAir has appropriate people providing services to customers.

OPERATIONS CONTROL

Once a decision has been taken to design an operational plan of action, resource allocations are considered. After management has decided on a functional operations strategy, using marketing and financial plans of action, it determines what specific tasks are necessary to accomplish functional objectives. This is known as *operations control.*

Operations control is an operational plan that specifies the operational activities of an organization.

Operations control is defined as making sure that operations activities are carried out as planned. The major components of operations control are *just-in-time inventory control, maintenance control, cost control, budgetary control, ratio analysis,* and *materials control.* Each of these components is discussed in detail in the following sections.

Just-in-Time Inventory Control

Just-in-time (JIT) inventory control is a technique for reducing inventories to a minimum by arranging for production components to be delivered to the production facility "just in time" to be used.

Just-in-time (JIT) inventory control is a technique for reducing inventories to a minimum by arranging for production components to be delivered to the production facility "just in time" to be used. The concept, developed primarily by the Toyota Motor Company of Japan, is also called "zero inventory" or *kanban*—the latter a Japanese term referring to purchasing raw materials by using a special ordering form.[12]

JIT is based on the management philosophy that products should be manufactured only when customers need them and only in the quantities customers require in order to minimize the amounts of raw materials and finished goods inventories manufacturers keep on hand. It emphasizes maintaining organizational operations by using only the resources that are absolutely necessary to meet customer demand.

Best Conditions for JIT.   JIT works best in companies that manufacture relatively standardized products for which there is consistent demand. Such companies can comfortably order materials from suppliers and assemble products in small, continuous batches. The result is a smooth, consistent flow of purchased materials and assembled products, with little inventory buildup. Companies that manufacture nonstandardized products for which there is sporadic or seasonal demand, however, generally face more irregular purchases of raw materials from suppliers, more uneven production cycles, and greater accumulations of inventory.

Advantages of JIT.   When successfully implemented, JIT enhances organizational performance in several important ways. First, it reduces the unnecessary labor expenses generated by manufacturing products that are not sold. Second, it minimizes the tying up of monetary resources in purchases of production-related materials that do not result in timely sales. Third, it helps management hold down inventory expenses—particularly storage and handling costs. Better inventory management and control of labor costs, in fact, are the two most commonly cited benefits of JIT.

Characteristics of JIT.   Experience indicates that successful JIT programs have certain common characteristics:[13]

1. *Closeness of suppliers.*   Manufacturers using JIT find it beneficial to utilize raw materials suppliers who are based only a short distance from them. When a company is ordering smaller quantities of raw materials at a time, suppliers must sometimes be asked to make one or more deliveries per day. Short distances make multiple deliveries per day feasible.

2. *High quality of materials purchased from suppliers.* Manufacturers using JIT find it especially difficult to overcome problems caused by defective materials. Since they keep their materials inventory small, defective materials purchased from a supplier may force them to discontinue the production process until another delivery from the supplier can be arranged. Such production slow-downs can be disadvantageous, causing late delivery to customers or lost sales.

3. *Well-organized receiving and handling of materials purchased from suppliers.* Companies using JIT must be able to receive and handle raw materials effectively and efficiently. Materials must be available for the production process where and when they are needed, because if they are not, extra costs will be built into the production process.

4. *Strong management commitment.* Management must be strongly committed to the concept of JIT. The system takes time and effort to plan, install, and improve—and is therefore expensive to implement. Management must be willing to commit funds to initiate the JIT system and to support it once it is functioning.

Maintenance Control

Maintenance control is aimed at keeping the organization's facility and equipment functioning at predetermined work levels. In the planning stage, managers must select a strategy that will direct personnel to fix equipment either before it malfunctions or after it malfunctions. The first strategy is referred to as a **pure-preventive maintenance policy**—machine adjustments, lubrication, cleaning, parts replacement, painting, and needed repairs and overhauls are done regularly, before facilities or machines malfunction. At the other end of the maintenance control continuum is the **pure-breakdown policy,** which decrees that facilities and equipment be fixed only after they malfunction.

Most organizations implement a maintenance strategy somewhere in the middle of the maintenance continuum. Management usually tries to select a level and a frequency of maintenance that minimize the cost of both preventive maintenance and breakdowns (repair). Since no level of preventive maintenance can eliminate breakdowns altogether, repair will always be an important activity.

Whether management decides on a pure-preventive or pure-breakdown policy, or on something in between, the prerequisite for a successful maintenance program is the availability of maintenance parts and supplies or replacement (standby) equipment. Some organizations choose to keep standby machines to protect themselves against the consequences of breakdowns. Plants that use special-purpose equipment are more likely to invest in standby equipment than those that use general-purpose equipment.

> **Pure-preventive maintenance policy** is a maintenance control policy that tries to ensure that machine adjustments, lubrication, cleaning, parts replacement, painting, and needed repairs and overhauls will be performed before facilities or machines malfunction.

> **Pure-breakdown (repair) policy** is a maintenance control policy that decrees that machine adjustments, lubrication, cleaning, parts replacement, painting, and needed repairs and overhaul will be performed only after facilities or machines malfunction.

Cost Control

Cost control is broad control aimed at keeping organizational costs at planned levels. Since cost control relates to all organizational costs, it emphasizes activities in all organizational areas, such as research and development, operations, marketing, and finance. If an organization is to be successful, costs in all organizational areas must be controlled. Cost control is therefore an important responsibility of all managers in an organization.

Operations activities are very cost-intensive—perhaps the most cost-intensive of all organizational activities—so when significant cost savings are realized in organizations, they are generally realized at the operations level.

Operations managers are responsible for the overall control of the cost of goods or services sold. Since producing goods and services at or below planned cost levels is their principal objective, operations managers are commonly evaluated primarily on their cost control activities. When operations costs are consistently above planned levels, the organization may need to change its operations management.

At IBM's Raleigh, North Carolina, plant, the key to cost control is tightening up internal operations, especially control over finished goods. The strategy calls not only for getting products to market quickly, building them in sufficient volumes, and pricing them optimally, but also selling them while they are still salable. Whereas IBM was once writing off $700 million per year in obsolete inventory, finished-goods inventory is now down 65 percent; procurement and distribution costs are down 50 percent.

Stages in Cost Control.   The general cost control process has four stages:

1. Establishing standard or planned cost amounts.
2. Measuring actual costs incurred.
3. Comparing planned costs to incurred costs.
4. Making changes to reduce actual costs to planned costs when necessary.

Following these stages for specific operations cost control, the operations manager must first establish planned costs or cost standards for operations activities like labor, materials, and overhead. Next, the operations manager must actually measure or calculate the costs incurred for these activities. Third, the operations manager must compare actual operations costs to planned operations costs, and fourth, take steps to reduce actual operations costs to planned levels if necessary.

Budgetary Control

A **budget** is a control tool that outlines how funds will be obtained and spent in a given period.

As described in Chapter 9, a budget is a single-use financial plan that covers a specified length of time. An organization's **budget** is its financial plan outlining how funds in a given period will be obtained and spent.

In addition to being a financial plan, however, a budget can be the basis for *budgetary control*—that is, for ensuring that income and expenses occur as planned. As managers gather information on actual receipts and expenditures within an operating period, they may uncover significant deviations from budgeted amounts. If that be the case, they should develop and implement a control strategy aimed at bringing actual performance into line with planned performance. This, of course, assumes that the plan contained in the budget is appropriate for the organization. The following sections discuss some potential pitfalls of budgets and human relations considerations that may make a budget inappropriate.

Potential Pitfalls of Budgets   To maximize the benefits of using budgets, managers must avoid several potential pitfalls. Among these pitfalls are the following:

1. *Placing too much emphasis on relatively insignificant organizational expenses.* In preparing and implementing a budget, managers should allocate more time for dealing with significant organizational expenses and less time for relatively insignificant organizational expenses. For example, the amount of time managers spend on developing and implementing a budget for labor costs typically should be much more than the amount of time they spend on developing and implementing a budget for office supplies.

2. *Increasing budgeted expenses year after year without adequate information.* It does not necessarily follow that items contained in last year's budget should be increased this year. Perhaps the best-known method for overcoming this poten-

tial pitfall is zero-base budgeting.[14] **Zero-base budgeting** is a planning and budgeting process that requires managers to justify their entire budget request in detail rather than simply refer to budget amounts established in previous years.

Some management theorists believe that zero-base budgeting is a better management tool than traditional budgeting—which simply starts with the budget amount established in the prior year—because it emphasizes focused identification and control of each budget item. It is unlikely, however, that this tool will be implemented successfully unless management adequately explains what zero-base budgeting is and how it is to be used in the organization. One of the earliest and most commonly cited successes in implementing a zero-base budgeting program took place in the Department of Agriculture's Office of Budget and Finance.

3. *Ignoring the fact that budgets must be changed periodically.* Managers should recognize that such factors as costs of materials, newly developed technology, and product demand change constantly and that budgets must be reviewed and modified periodically in response to these changes.

A special type of budget called a *variable budget* is sometimes used to determine automatically when such changes in budgets are needed. A **variable budget,** also known as a *flexible budget,* outlines the levels of resources to be allocated for each organizational activity according to the level of production within the organization. It follows, then, that a variable budget automatically indicates an increase in the amount of resources allocated for various organizational activities when production levels go up and a decrease when production goes down.

> **Zero-base budgeting** requires managers to justify their entire budget request in detail rather than simply referring to budget amounts established in previous years.

> A **variable budget** (also known as a *flexible budget*) is one that outlines the levels of resources to be allocated for each organizational activity according to the level of production within the organization.

Human Relations Considerations in Using Budgets   Many managers believe that although budgets are valuable planning and control tools, they can result in major human relations problems in an organization. A classic article by Chris Argyris, for example, shows how budgets can build pressures that unite workers against management, cause harmful conflict between management and factory workers, and create tensions that result in worker inefficiency and worker aggression against management.[15] If such problems are severe enough, a budget may result in more harm to the organization than good.

Reducing Human Relations Problems.   Several strategies have been suggested to minimize the human relations problems caused by budgets. The most often recommended strategy is to design and implement appropriate human relations training programs for finance personnel, accounting personnel, production supervisors, and all other key people involved in the formulation and use of budgets. These training programs should emphasize both the advantages and disadvantages of applying pressure on people through budgets and the possible results of using budgets to imply that an organization member is a success or a failure at his or her job.

Ratio Analysis

Another type of control uses ratio analysis.[16] A *ratio* is a relationship between two numbers that is calculated by dividing one number into the other. **Ratio analysis** is the process of generating information that summarizes the financial position of an organization through the calculation of ratios based on various financial measures that appear on the organization's balance sheet and income statements.

The ratios available to managers for controlling organizations, shown in Table 20.1, can be divided into four categories:

1. Liquidity ratios
2. Leverage ratios

> **Ratio analysis** is a control tool that summarizes the financial position of an organization by calculating ratios based on various financial measures.

Table 20.1

Four Categories of Ratios

TYPE	EXAMPLE	CALCULATION	INTERPRETATION
Profitability	Return on investment (ROI)	$\dfrac{\text{Profit after taxes}}{\text{Total assets}}$	Productivity of assets
Liquidity	Current ratio	$\dfrac{\text{Current assets}}{\text{Current liabilities}}$	Short-term solvency
Activity	Inventory turnover	$\dfrac{\text{Sales}}{\text{Inventory}}$	Efficiency of inventory management
Leverage	Debt ratio	$\dfrac{\text{Total debt}}{\text{Total assets}}$	How a company finances itself

3. Activity ratios
4. Profitability ratios

Using Ratios to Control Organizations   Managers should use ratio analysis in three ways to control an organization:[17]

- Managers should evaluate all ratios simultaneously. This strategy ensures that they will develop and implement a control strategy appropriate for the organization as a whole rather than one that suits only one phase or segment of the organization.
- Managers should compare computed values for ratios in a specific organization with the values of industry averages for those ratios. (The values of industry averages for the ratios can be obtained from Dun & Bradstreet; Robert Morris Associates, a national association of bank loan officers; the Federal Trade Commission; and the Securities and Exchange Commission.) Managers increase the probability of formulating and implementing appropriate control strategies when they compare their financial situation to that of competitors in this way.
- Managers' use of ratios should incorporate trend analysis. Managers must remember that any set of ratio values is actually only a determination of relationships that existed in a specified time period (often a year). To employ ratio analysis to maximum advantage, they need to accumulate ratio values for several successive time periods to uncover specific organizational trends. Once these trends are revealed, managers can formulate and implement appropriate strategies for dealing with them.

Materials Control

Materials control is an operational activity that determines the flow of materials from vendors through an operations system to customers.

Materials control is an operations control activity that determines the flow of materials from vendors through an operations system to customers. The achievement of desired levels of product cost, quality, availability, dependability, and flexibility heavily depends on the effective and efficient flow of materials. Materials management activities can be broadly organized into six groups or functions: purchasing, receiving, inventorying, floor controlling, trafficking, and shipping and distributing.

Procurement of Materials.   Over 50 percent of the expenditures of a typical manufacturing company are for the procurement of materials, including raw materials, parts, subassemblies, and supplies. This procurement is the responsibility of the purchasing department. Actually, purchases of production materials are largely automated and linked to a resources requirement planning system. Purchases of all other

materials, however, are based on requisitions from users. The purchasing department's job does not end with the placement of an order; order follow-up is just as crucial.

Receiving, Shipping, and Trafficking.   Receiving activities include unloading, identifying, inspecting, reporting, and storing inbound shipments. Shipping and distribution activities are similar. These may include preparing documents, packaging, labeling, loading, and directing outbound shipments to customers and to distribution centers. Shipping and receiving are sometimes organized as one unit.

A traffic manager's main responsibilities are selection of the transportation mode, coordination of the arrival and departure of shipments, and auditing freight bills.

Inventory and Shop-Floor Control.   Inventory control activities ensure the continuous availability of purchased materials. Work-in-process and finished-goods inventory are inventory control subsystems. Inventory control specifies what, when, and how much to buy. Held inventories buffer the organization against a variety of uncertainties that can disrupt supply, but since holding inventory is costly, an optimal inventory control policy provides a predetermined level of certainty of supply at the lowest possible cost.

Shop-floor control activities include input/output control, scheduling, sequencing, routing, dispatching, and expediting.

While many materials management activities can be programmed, the human factor is the key to a competitive performance. Skilled and motivated employees are therefore crucial to successful materials control.

BACK TO THE CASE   Operations control activities help USAir management make certain that customer services are carried out as planned. *Just-in-time inventory control*, for example, would ensure that pillows, blankets, ticketing materials, and packing materials are available just when customers need them. Putting money into large surpluses of these items would needlessly tie up company resources and reduce company profitability. *Maintenance control* would ensure that equipment (e.g., baggage conveyors) needed to provide customer services is operating at a desirable level. *Cost control* would ensure that USAir is not providing services to customers too expensively. *Budgetary control* would focus on acquiring company resources and using them to provide customer services as stipulated by USAir's financial plan.

Operations control at USAir can also include ratio analysis, or determining relationships between various factors on USAir's income statement and balance sheet to arrive at a good indication of the company's financial position. Through ratio analysis, USAir management could monitor issues like customer services to determine their overall impact on company profitability, liquidity, and leverage. To assess the impact of providing various customer services on the financial condition of USAir, management would track ratios over time to discern trends.

Finally, operations control at USAir would need to include materials control to ensure that materials purchased from suppliers are flowing appropriately from vendors to customers in the form of customer services. For example, the goal of monitoring the drinks, snacks, and meals that caterers are providing to USAir passengers would be to improve the quality of such items in terms of temperature, freshness, and nutritional value.

Selected Operations Control Tools

In addition to understanding production, operations management, and operations control, managers also need to be aware of various operations control tools that are useful in an operations facility. A **control tool** is a specific procedure or technique that

A **control tool** is a specific procedure or technique that presents pertinent organizational information in a way that helps managers to develop and implement an appropriate control strategy.

presents pertinent organizational information in a way that helps managers and workers develop and implement an appropriate control strategy. That is, a control tool aids managers and workers in pinpointing the organizational strengths and weaknesses on which a useful control strategy must focus. This section discusses specific control tools for day-to-day operations as well as for longer-run operations.

Using Control Tools to Control Organizations

Continual improvement of operations is a practical, not a theoretical, managerial concern. It is, essentially, the development and use of better methods. Different types of organizations have different goals and strategies, but all organizations struggle daily to find better ways of doing things. This goal of continual improvement applies not just to money-making enterprises, but to those with other missions as well. Since organizational leaders are continually changing systems and personal styles of management, everyone within the organization is continually learning to live with change.

Inspection

Traditionally, managers believed that if you wanted good quality, you hired many inspectors to make sure an operation was producing at the desired quality level. These inspectors examined and graded finished products or components, parts, or services at any stage of operation by measuring, tasting, touching, weighing, disassembling, destroying, and testing. The goal of inspection was to detect unacceptable quality levels before a bad product or service reached a customer. Whenever a lot of defects were found, management blamed the workers and hired more inspectors.

To Inspect or Not to Inspect.   Today managers know that inspection cannot catch problems built into the system. The traditional inspection process does not result in improvement and does not guarantee quality. In fact, according to Deming, inspection is a limited, grossly overused, and often misused tool. He recommended that management stop relying on mass inspection to achieve quality, and advocated instead either 100 percent inspection in those cases where defect-free work is impossible or no inspection at all where the level of defects is acceptably small.

Management by Exception

Management by exception is a control tool that allows only significant deviations between planned and actual performance to be brought to a manager's attention.

Management by exception is a control technique that allows only significant deviations between planned and actual performance to be brought to a manager's attention. Management by exception is based on the *exception principle*, a management principle that appears in early management literature.[18] This principle recommends that subordinates handle all routine organizational matters, leaving managers free to deal with nonroutine, or exceptional, organizational issues.

Establishing Rules.   Some organizations rely on subordinates or managers themselves to detect the significant deviations between standards and performance that signal exceptional issues. Other organizations establish rules to ensure that exceptional issues surface as a matter of normal operating procedure. Setting rules must be done very carefully to ensure that all true deviations are brought to the manager's attention.

Two examples of rules based on the exception principle are the following:[19]

1. A department manager must immediately inform the plant manager if actual weekly labor costs exceed estimated weekly labor costs by more than 15 percent.
2. A department manager must immediately inform the plant manager if actual dollars spent plus estimated dollars to be spent on a special project exceed the funds approved for the project by more than 10 percent.

Although these two rules happen to focus on production-related expenditures, to detect and report significant rules deviations can be established in virtually any organizational area.

If appropriately administered, the management-by-exception control technique ensures the best use of managers' time. Because only significant issues are brought to managers' attention, the possibility that managers will spend their valuable time working on relatively insignificant issues is automatically eliminated.

Of course, the significant issues brought to managers' attention could be organizational strengths as well as organizational weaknesses. Obviously, managers should try to reinforce the first and eliminate the second.

Management by Objectives

In management by objectives, which was discussed in Chapter 5, the manager assigns a specialized set of objectives and action plans to workers and then rewards those workers on the basis of how close they come to reaching their goals. This control technique has been implemented in corporations intent on using an employee-participative means to improve productivity.

Breakeven Analysis

Another production-related control tool commonly used by managers is breakeven analysis. **Breakeven analysis** is the process of generating information that summarizes various levels of profit or loss associated with various levels of production. The next sections discuss three facets of this control tool:

- 1. The basic ingredients of breakeven analysis.
- 2. The types of breakeven analysis available to managers.
- 3. The relationship between breakeven analysis and controlling.

Basic Ingredients of Breakeven Analysis

Breakeven analysis typically involves reflection, discussion, reasoning, and decision making relative to the following seven major aspects of production:

1. *Fixed costs.* **Fixed costs** are expenses incurred by the organization regardless of the number of products produced. Some examples are real estate taxes, upkeep to the exterior of a business building, and interest expenses on money borrowed to finance the purchase of equipment.
2. *Variable costs.* Expenses that fluctuate with the number of products produced are called **variable costs.** Examples are costs of packaging a product, costs of materials needed to make the product, and costs associated with packing products to prepare them for shipping.
3. *Total costs.* **Total costs** are simply the sum of the fixed and variable costs associated with production.
4. *Total revenue.* **Total revenue** is all sales dollars accumulated from selling manufactured products or services. Naturally, total revenue increases as more products are sold.
5. *Profits.* **Profits** are defined as the amount of total revenue that exceeds the total costs of producing the products sold.
6. *Loss.* **Loss** is the amount of the total costs of producing a product that exceeds the total revenue gained from selling the product.
7. *Breakeven point.* The **breakeven point** is that level of production where the total revenue of an organization equals its total costs—that is, the point at which the organization is generating only enough revenue to cover its costs. The company is neither gaining a profit nor incurring a loss.

Breakeven analysis is a control tool that summarizes the various levels of profit or loss associated with various levels of production.

Fixed costs are expenses incurred by the organization regardless of the number of products produced.

Variable costs are expenses that fluctuate with the number of products produced.

Total costs are the sum of fixed costs and variable costs.

Total revenue is all sales dollars accumulated from selling the goods or services produced by the organization.

Profits are the amount of total revenue that exceeds total costs.

Loss is the amount of the total costs of producing a product that exceeds the total revenue gained from selling the product.

The **breakeven point** is that level of production where the total revenue of an organization equals its total costs.

Types of Breakeven Analysis   There are two somewhat different procedures for determining the same breakeven point for an organization: algebraic breakeven analysis and graphic breakeven analysis.

Algebraic Breakeven Analysis.   The following simple formula is commonly used to determine the level of production at which an organization breaks even:

$$BE = \frac{FC}{P - VC}$$

where—

- BE = the level of production at which the firm breaks even
- FC = total fixed costs of production
- P = price at which each individual unit is sold to customers
- VC = variable costs associated with each product manufactured and sold

In using this formula to calculate a breakeven point, two sequential steps must be followed. First, the variable costs associated with producing each unit must be subtracted from the price at which each unit will sell. The purpose of this calculation is to determine how much of the selling price of each unit sold can go toward covering total fixed costs incurred from producing all products. Second, the remainder calculated in the first step must be divided into total fixed costs. The purpose of this calculation is to determine how many units must be produced and sold to cover fixed costs. This number of units is the breakeven point for the organization.

Say a book publisher faces the fixed and variable costs per paperback book presented in Table 20.2 If the publisher wants to sell each book for $12, the breakeven point could be calculated as follows:

$$BE = \frac{\$88,800}{\$12 - \$6}$$
$$BE = \frac{\$88,800}{\$6}$$
$$BE = 14,800 \text{ copies}$$

This calculation indicates that if expenses and selling price remain stable, the book publisher will incur a loss if book sales are fewer than 14,800 copies, will break even if book sales equal 14,800 copies, and will make a profit if book sales exceed 14,800 copies.

Graphic Breakeven Analysis.   Graphic breakeven analysis entails the construction of a graph showing all the critical elements in a breakeven analysis. Figure 20.6 is such

Table 20.2

Fixed Costs and Variable Costs for a Book Publisher

FIXED COSTS (YEARLY BASIS)		VARIABLE COSTS PER BOOK SOLD	
1. Real estate taxes on property	$1,000	1. Printing	$2.00
2. Interest on loan to purchase equipment	5,000	2. Artwork	1.00
		3. Sales commission	.50
3. Building maintenance	2,000	4. Author royalties	1.50
4. Insurance	800	5. Binding	1.00
5. Salaried labor	80,000		
Total fixed costs	$88,800	Total variable costs per book	$6.00

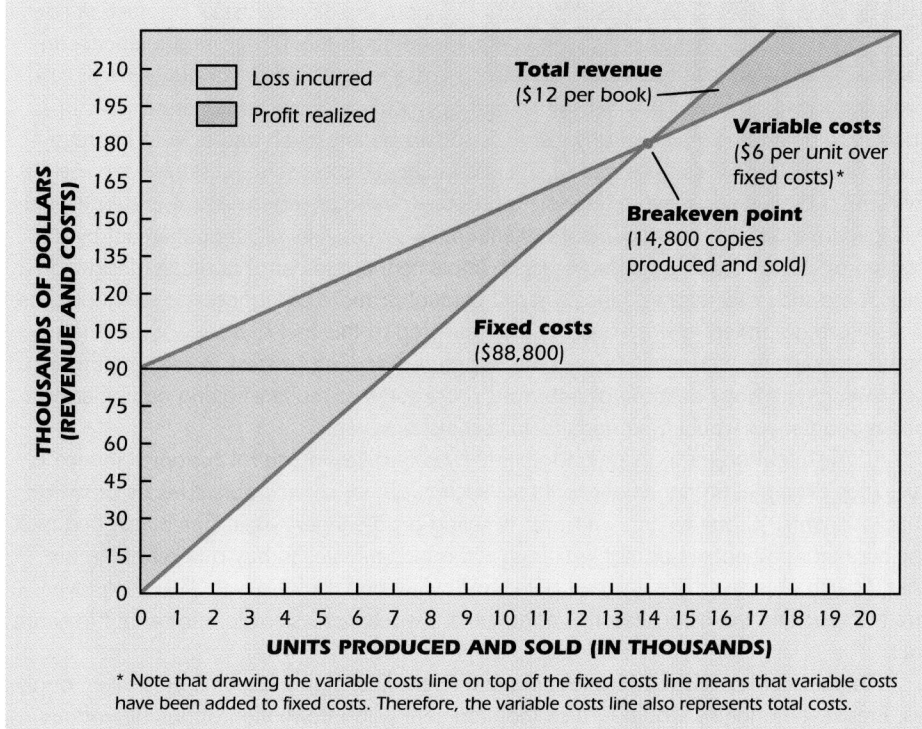

FIGURE 20.6   Breakeven analysis for a book publisher

a graph for the book publisher. Note that in a breakeven graph, the total revenue line starts at zero.

Advantages of Using the Algebraic and Graphic Breakeven Methods.   Both the algebraic and the graphic methods of breakeven analysis for the book publisher result in the same breakeven point—14,800 books produced and sold—but the processes used to arrive at this point are quite different.

Which breakeven method managers should use is usually determined by the situation they face. For a manager who desires a quick yet accurate determination of a breakeven point, the algebraic method generally suffices. For a manager who wants a more complete picture of the cumulative relationships between the breakeven point, fixed costs, and escalating variable costs, the graphic breakeven method is more useful. For example, the book publisher could quickly and easily see from Figure 20.6 the cumulative relationships of fixed costs, escalating variable costs, and potential profit and loss associated with various levels of production.

Control and Breakeven Analysis   Breakeven analysis is a useful control tool because it helps managers understand the relationships between fixed costs, variable costs, total costs, and profit and loss within an organization. Once these relationships are understood, managers can take steps to modify one or more of the variables to reduce deviation between planned and actual profit levels.[20]

Increasing costs or decreasing selling prices has the overall effect of increasing the number of units an organization must produce and sell to break even. Conversely, the managerial strategy for decreasing the number of products an organization must produce and sell to break even entails lowering or stabilizing fixed and variable costs or increasing the selling price of each unit. The exact breakeven control strategy a particular manager should develop and implement is dictated primarily by that manager's unique organizational situation.

BACK TO THE CASE There are several useful production control tools that USAir management can use to ensure that various services are provided to customers as planned. First, management can have customer services inspected to determine which, if any, services should be improved and how to improve them. Second, USAir can use management by exception to control customer services. In this case, USAir workers would handle all routine customer service issues and bring only exceptional matters to management's attention. To successfully use management by exception at USAir, it would be necessary to implement a number of carefully designed rules. One such rule might be that when 5 percent or more of luggage bags handled on a flight are damaged, a baggage handler must report this fact to a supervisor. The supervisor would then carefully inspect the baggage-handling process to see why this is happening—perhaps because of improper procedures or malfunctioning equipment— and management would take steps to correct the situation.

USAir might prefer to use management by objectives to control customer service issues. For example, management could set such customer service objectives as answering a ticket counter phone within five rings, ticketing a passenger within 5 minutes, and making sure that passengers do not wait longer than 30 minutes to buy a ticket at the airport. If such objectives are deemed both worthwhile and realistic, yet USAir employees are not reaching them consistently, management would take steps to ensure that they are met.

Another control tool USAir management might find highly useful is breakeven analysis. Breakeven analysis would furnish management with information about the various levels of profit or loss associated with various levels of revenue. To use this tool, USAir would have to determine the total fixed costs necessary to operate the airline, the price at which flights are sold, and the variable costs associated with various flights.

For example, if management wanted to determine how many tickets had to be sold before the company would break even on a particular flight, it could arrive at this breakeven point algebraically by following three steps. First, all fixed costs attributable to operating the flight—for example, airport facility rent—would be totaled. Second, all the variable costs of furnishing a flight to a passenger would be totaled, and from this total management would subtract the revenue that a ticket will generate. Variable costs include such expenses as meal costs, fuel costs, and labor needed to furnish the flight. Finally, the answer calculated in step 2 would be divided into the answer derived in step 1, and this figure would tell management how many tickets must be sold at the projected revenue level to break even.

USAir management also could choose to determine the breakeven point by constructing a graph showing fixed costs, variable costs, and revenue per flight. Such a graph would probably give managers a more useful picture for formulating profit-oriented flight plans.

Other Broad Operations Control Tools

Some of the best-known and most commonly used operations control tools are discussed in the following sections. The primary purpose of these tools is to control the production of organizational goods and services.[21]

Decision tree analysis is a statistical and graphical multiphased decision-making technique that shows the sequence and interdependence of decisions.

Decision Tree Analysis

Decision tree analysis, as you recall from Chapter 7, is a statistical and graphical multiphase decision-making technique containing a series of steps showing the sequence and interdependence of decisions. Decision trees allow a decision maker to deal with uncertain events by determining the relative expected value of each alternative course of action. The probabilities of different possible events are known, as are the monetary payoffs that result from a particular alternative and a particular event. Decision trees are best suited to situations in which capacity

decisions involve several capacity expansion alternatives and the selection of the alternative with the highest expected profit or the lowest expected cost is necessary.

Process Control

Statistical process control, known as **process control,** is a technique that assists in monitoring production processes. Production processes must be monitored continually to ensure that the quality of their output is acceptable. The earlier the detection of a faulty production process, the better. If detection occurs late in the production process, the company may find parts that do not meet quality standards, and scrapping or reworking these is a costly proposition. If a production process results in unstable performance or is downright out of control, corrective action must be taken. Process control can be implemented with the aid of graphical charts known as control charts.

> **Process control** is a technique that assists in monitoring production processes.

Value Analysis

Value analysis is a cost control and cost reduction technique that aids managers controlling operations by focusing primarily on material costs. The goal of this analysis, which is performed by examining all the parts and materials and their functions, is to reduce costs by using cheaper components and materials in such a way that product quality or appeal is not affected. Simplification of parts—which lowers production costs—is also a goal of value analysis. Value analysis can result not only in cost savings but also in an improved product.

Value analysis requires a team effort. The team, if not companywide, should at least include personnel from operations, purchasing, engineering, and marketing.

> **Value analysis** is a cost control and cost reduction technique that examines all the parts, materials, and functions of an operation.

Computer-Aided Design

Computer-aided design (CAD) systems include several automated design technologies. *Computer graphics* is used to design geometric specifications for parts, while *computer-aided engineering (CAE)* is employed to evaluate and perform engineering analyses on a part. CAD also includes technologies used in process design. CAD functions to ensure the quality of a product by guaranteeing not only the quality of parts in the product but also the appropriateness of the product's design.

> **Computer-aided design (CAD)** is a computerized technique for designing new products or modifying existing ones.

Computer-Aided Manufacturing

Computer-aided manufacturing (CAM) employs computers to plan and program equipment used in the production and inspection of manufactured items. Linking CAM and CAD processes through a computer is very beneficial when production processes must be altered, because when CAD and CAM systems can share information easily, design changes can be implemented in a very short period of time.

> **Computer-aided manufacturing (CAM)** is a technique that employs computers to plan and program equipment used in the production and inspection of manufactured items.

In the machine-tool industry, which supplies equipment for manufacturing lines, computer-aided manufacturing now includes rapid-prototyping machines like this ultraviolet laser developed by 3D Systems of Valencia, California. These machines can fabricate parts directly from design data, in much the same way as a laser printer puts out data on a spreadsheet. This machine is building an oil pump by depositing one layer of powdered metal upon another.

BACK TO THE CASE ecision tree analysis, process control, value analysis, computer-aided design, and computer-aided manufacturing were presented in the text as broader operations tools that are highly useful to managers exercising the control function. Of all these tools, value analysis would have the most application to USAir's service-oriented operation. USAir management could use this cost control and cost reduction technique to examine the cost and worth of every component of customer service. To gain a complete picture of customer service components and their usefulness, USAir might establish a team comprising members from different customer service areas.

For instance, a team composed of a ticket agent, a flight attendant, a maintenance supervisor, and a baggage handler might explore different options for establishing comfortable cabin temperature while a plane is being loaded but before it taxis to the runway to await takeoff. If this team concludes, for example, that expediting the baggage-handling process would expose passengers to uncomfortable temperatures for shorter periods of time, management could take steps to speed up the process. Implementation of more efficient ways of handling baggage would result not only in better customer service but also in lower airline operating costs.

Action Summary

Reread the learning objectives below. Each objective is followed by questions. Answering these questions accurately will help you retain the most important concepts discussed in this chapter. After answering each question, check your answer against the answer key at the end of this chapter. (*Hint:* If you have any doubts regarding the correct response, consult the page whose number follows the answer.)

Circle: From studying this chapter, I will attempt to acquire:

1. Definitions of production, productivity, and quality.

a,b,c,d,e   **a.** Production is the transformation of organizational resources into: (a) profits; (b) plans; (c) forecasts; (d) processes; (e) products.

a,b,c,d,e   **b.** *Productivity* is the relationship between the amount of goods or services produced and: (a) profits; (b) the organizational resources needed to produce them; (c) quality; (d) operations management activities; (e) advanced manufacturing support.

T,F   **c.** Quality is the extent to which a product reliably does what it is intended to do.

2. An understanding of the importance of operations and production strategies, systems, and processes.

a,b,c,d   **a.** The flow of interrelated events moving toward a goal, purpose, or end is known as a: (a) system; (b) process; (c) strategy; (d) plan.

a,b,c,d   **b.** A particular linkage of mission, goals, strategies, policies, rules, human resources, and raw materials that facilitates carrying out a process is a: (a) system; (b) process; (c) strategy; (d) plan.

3. Insights into the role of operations management concepts in the workplace.

T,F   **a.** The criteria relevant for judging the actions taken as a result of operations management are effectiveness and efficiency.

a,b,c,d   **b.** An operations strategy is achieved in a context of objectives and policies derived from the organization's: (a) capacity strategy; (b) product strategy; (c) strategic plan; (d) human resources strategy.

a,b,c,d   **c.** The reputation of an organization is determined by: (a) its size; (b) its style of management; (c) its profits; (d) its product quality.

4. An understanding of how operations control procedures can be used to control production.

T,F   **a.** Just-in-time inventory control is an inventory control technique based on the management philosophy that products should be manufactured when customers need them.

a,b,c,d,e   **b.** Potential pitfalls of using budgets as control tools include: (a) placing too much emphasis on relatively insignificant organizational expenses; (b) changing budgets periodically;

(c) increasing budgeted expenses year after year without adequate information; (d) a and c; (e) a and b.

a,b,c,d   **c.** Managers can use ratio analysis in the following way to control an organization:
  a. Evaluate all ratios simultaneously to get a picture of the organization as a whole.
  b. Compare computed values for ratios with values of industry averages.
  c. Accumulate values for ratios for successive time periods to uncover specific organizational trends.
  d. a, b, and c.

5. Insights concerning operations control tools and how they evolve into a continual improvement approach to production management and control.

T,F   **a.** By using inspection, managers can expect to catch any problems that are built into the system.

T,F   **b.** Management by exception is a control technique that allows only significant deviations between planned and actual performance to be brought to the manager's attention.

a,b,c,d,e   **c.** The overall effect on the breakeven point of increasing costs or decreasing selling prices is that: (a) the number of products an organization must sell to break even increases; (b) the amount of profit a firm will receive at a fixed number of units sold increases; (c) the number of products an organization must sell to break even decreases; (d) a and b; (e) there is no effect on the breakeven point.

Introductory Case Wrap-Up

"The Quick Turn at USAir" (p. 476) and its related back-to-the-case sections were written to help you better understand the management concepts contained in this chapter. Answer the following discussion questions about this introductory case to enrich your understanding of the chapter content:

1. Why is USAir attempting to raise productivity through shorter turnaround times? From your personal experience with airlines,

in what other ways do you think the company could increase productivity?

2. List three concepts discussed in this chapter that could help USAir management to increase productivity. Be sure to explain how each concept could help.

3. Which concept listed in question 2 do you think would have the most positive impact on increasing productivity? Explain fully.

Issues for Review and Discussion

1. Define both *production* and *production control*.
2. Thoroughly explain the equation used to define productivity.
3. Discuss the relationship between quality and productivity.
4. What questions come to mind when you look at Deming's flow diagram for improving product quality?
5. What is quality assurance, and how is it related to statistical quality control?
6. Discuss how quality circles normally operate. What purpose do they serve?
7. Discuss the importance of automation in building productive organizations in the future.
8. Explain the term *operations management* as well as the major managerial activities involved in it.
9. List the three key concepts conveyed in the text discussion of operations management.
10. List the six operations strategies and explain how each contributes to continual increases in productivity.
11. What steps should management take to make sound strategic capacity decisions?
12. Discuss the three types of manufacturing processes.
13. Name the three basic types of layout patterns and give an example of each.
14. Discuss the two human resources strategy imperatives and the definition of a human resources strategy.

15. Discuss the management philosophy behind just-in-time inventory control.
16. Explain the difference between a pure-preventive maintenance policy and a pure-breakdown (repair) policy.
17. Explain why cost control is an important responsibility of every manager.
18. Define *budget*. How can managers use a budget to control an organization?
19. List three potential pitfalls of budgets.
20. What is ratio analysis?
21. What guidelines would you recommend to managers using ratio analysis to control an organization?
22. What is materials control, and how can it aid in production control?
23. What is a control tool?
24. Define *management by exception* and describe how it can help managers control production.
25. List and define seven major components of breakeven analysis.
26. How can managers use breakeven analysis to aid in controlling production?
27. List and define five other control tools.

Case Study

Sun Also Rises

The key to success is having a good idea and the faith to pursue it. At least that's the bedrock of Sun Microsystems' corporate beliefs. For more than a decade, Scott McNealy, CEO of Sun, has maintained that the value of computing will be based upon computers networked together, and he has put his company's resources to work in pursuit of his vision.

While the phenomenally successful Windows interface from Microsoft Corporation has often eclipsed the bright hopes of many technology companies, including PC pioneer Apple Computer, it has failed to deter Sun Microsystems from its network goals. In the 1980s, Sun workstations were easily accepted by engineers who needed the power of the network to do their work. In the early 1990s, Sun's sales faltered, but the Internet explosion refueled Sun's market. Company earnings jumped to $356 million in 1995, and revenues grew to $6 billion. Sun Microsystems now has a 35-percent market share of all computers used on the Internet. In the search for Internet standards, most large companies rely on Sun to provide them.

McNealy did not follow the usual path of engineer, or "techie," to the chief executive's suite at Sun. Instead, he came up through the ranks of manufacturing, and originally said he would have been content to own a machine shop and leave it as a legacy to his children. But in 1982, he was tapped by the president of Sun to come in and turn the manufacturing system around. The company was trying to deal with the enviable challenge of increasing production to keep up with exploding sales. (In 1984, sales jumped to $39 million, up from $9 million the year before.) McNealy did such a good job that, suddenly, production was moving ahead of sales. At this point, he moved over to marketing.

But then McNealy encountered a classical paradox: Success in sales led to a shortage of the cash needed to increase the level of production to meet the new level of sales. To raise the necessary money to expand the business, McNealy contacted a Sun Microsystems' customer, Eastman Kodak, to explore the possibility of a cash investment. Kodak executive vice president J. Philip

Samper was so taken with McNealy's boldness and vision that he agreed. An unexpected condition of the agreement, however, was that McNealy be appointed president of Sun. The company's board of directors agreed to a temporary appointment, but as soon as sales took off, McNealy was formally installed as CEO. He was only 30 years old at the time.

Not surprisingly, Sun's success has made the company the target of other technology firms looking for a piece of the Internet pie. McNealy, however, is undeterred by attacks from competitors. Besides the success of Sun workstations as Web servers, he is counting on a new product called Java to loosen the viselike grip Microsoft and Intel Corporation have on the industry. The so-called Wintel standard seems to be unshakable for stand-alone computers, but Java allows a computer to reach across the expanse of the Internet and mimic the computer at the other end. Thus, instead of creating software to run in the dominant Windows environment, a company would be free to develop software in its own way and see it used in the freedom of the Internet.

Besides waging war with other technology companies over the Internet, McNealy must protect his home turf—the workstation. Corporations like Hewlett Packard, IBM, and DEC are encroaching on that part of Sun's business. Although Sun has lost some sales to Hewlett Packard, a redoubled commitment to support the customer seems to be paying off. In order to maintain a highly visible level of support, McNealy makes it a point to regularly call on the company's customers himself. He has also increased Sun's employee base by 50 percent in little more than a year's time. The emphasis on servers instead of workstations has helped the company increase revenues.

Finally, McNealy has always tried to instill an element of fun and camaraderie into Sun's corporate culture. Each April Fool's Day, for instance, reporters descend on corporate headquarters in Mountain View, California, to record the big event. The high point one year was the construction of a golf green inside the CEO's office. McNealy believes that fun is an essential part of the Sun

equation. His hard-working employees need some amusing diversions to relieve their stress as they push to meet their CEO's ultimate goals.

Questions:

1. What parts usually make up a successful corporate equation? Using information from this case study, create the specific formula for success at Sun Microsystems.

2. What are the benefits and liabilities of being first with a new product or technology?
3. Why is "vision" crucial in creating a successful technology company? Illustrate how Sun, Apple, IBM, Microsoft, and others are examples of vision—good or bad.
4. Chart McNealy's rise in the company and describe how this experience has helped make him a successful leader of a technology company.

Skills Exercise

Create a chart of technology companies to track and compare Sun Microsystems' success or failure. Consider sales, market dominance, innovations, corporate culture, growth, etc. Rank the companies. Which company would you prefer to work for? Why?

The Internet learning materials that accompany this chapter can be found at
http://www.profcerto.com
Additional information can be found on the inside front and back covers of this text.

21 chapter

INFORMATION AND TECHNOLOGY

STUDENT LEARNING OBJECTIVES

From studying this chapter, I will attempt to acquire:

1. An understanding of the relationship between data and information.

2. Insights about the main factors that influence the value of information.

3. Knowledge of some potential steps for evaluating information.

4. An understanding of the importance of a management information system (MIS) to an organization.

5. A feasible strategy for establishing an MIS.

6. An appreciation for the roles of computers and computer networks in handling information.

7. Information about what a management decision support system is and how it operates.

CHAPTER OUTLINE

Introductory Case: Sam Walton Taught Others at Wal-Mart to Use Information

Essentials of Information

Factors Influencing the Value of Information

Information Appropriateness

Information Quality

Information Timeliness

Information Quantity

Evaluating Information

The Management Information System (MIS)

Global Spotlight: Pohang Iron & Steel Company Needs a Complex MIS

Describing the MIS

Diversity Spotlight: Target's MIS Focuses on Hispanic Workers

Establishing an MIS

Information Technology

Computer Assistance in Using Information

The Management Decision Support System (MDSS)

Computer Networks

People Perspectives: People Are the Key to Making the Network Work at Arthur Andersen

The Local Area Network

The Internet

Cutting Edge: Dell Computer Company Surfs the Internet to Service Customers and Build Its Image

Sam Walton Taught Others at Wal-Mart to Use Information

Samuel Moore Walton, who died in 1992 at 74 after a long fight with cancer, did not invent the discount department store, although it hardly seems possible that he didn't. Mr. Sam grabbed hold of the leading edge of retailing in 1962 and never let go, creating a value-powered merchandising machine that seems certain to outlive his memory. . . .

Wal-Mart is ultimately a monument to consumers: It has saved them billions. Walton's perpetual obsession with lowering the cost to consumers forced prices down elsewhere—in department stores, for example. Recalls Kurt Barnard, president of the Retail Marketing Report and a Walton friend: "He always said, 'Nothing happens until a customer walks into a store with a purpose, buys something, and walks out.' That was his philosophy. Satisfy the customer."

Once an Army intelligence officer, Walton had an insatiable hunger for information, which in turn equipped Wal-Mart for speedy decision making. He collected ideas and numbers on his famous yellow pads and converted them to merchanding action using the most rapid means available. At first this was a heavily laden, beat-up Plymouth that Walton would drive—and none too well, say all who knew him—from the Bentonville store to outlying branches.

That demand for information, and its creative use, is just as evident today. Wal-Mart is deep into information systems, and not because Walton loved computers—he didn't. His people insisted on serious crunching ability, and Mr. Pickup Truck listened—another Walton trait—and then signed the check. So, long before its rivals, Wal-Mart had enough computer and satellite capacity to track a space shuttle or towel sales in Tuscaloosa. Walton's memorial service was broadcast to every store over the company's satellite system.

Wal-Mart today converts information to action virtually immediately, a remarkable achievement for a $44-billion-a-year company. Managers suck in information from Monday to Thursday, exchange ideas on Friday and Saturday, and implement decisions in the stores on Monday. This bias toward action left a big impression on General Electric CEO Jack Welch. As he said to a *Fortune* conference: "Everybody there has a passion for an idea, and everyone's ideas count. Hierarchy doesn't matter. They get people in a room and understand how to deal with each other without structure. I have been there three times now. Every time you go to that place in Arkansas, you can fly back to New York without a plane. The place actually vibrates."

Wal-Mart's commitment to information management is evident in its Bentonville, Arkansas, "satellite room," where virtually all relationships with suppliers are conducted on a computer-to-computer basis.

what's ahead

The introductory case discusses how Sam Walton, a former army intelligence officer, had an insatiable hunger for information. In addition, the case discusses how information, the computer, and an information system are all used together at Wal-Mart to help managers make quicker and better decisions. This chapter presents material that should be useful to managers, like those at Wal-Mart, who are attempting to better use information in organizations. The major topics of the chapter are:

1. Essentials of information.
2. The management information system (MIS).
3. Information technology.

Controlling is the process of making things happen as planned. Of course, managers cannot make things happen as planned if they lack information on the manner in which various events in the organization occur. This chapter discusses the fundamental principles of handling information in an organization by first presenting the essentials of information and then examining both the management information system (MIS) and information technology.

ESSENTIALS OF INFORMATION

Data are facts or statistics.

Information is the set of conclusions derived from data analysis.

The process of developing information begins with the gathering of some type of facts or statistics, called **data.** Once gathered, data typically are analyzed in some manner. In general terms, **information** is the set of conclusions derived from data analysis. In management terms, information is the set of conclusions derived from the analysis of data that relate to the operation of an organization. As examples to illustrate the relationship between data and information, managers gather data regarding pay rates that individuals are receiving within industries in order to develop information about how to develop competitive pay rates, data regarding hazardous-materials accidents in order to gain information about how to improve worker safety, and data regarding customer demographics in order to gain information about product demand in the future.[1]

The information that managers receive heavily influences managerial decision making, which, in turn, determines the activities that will be performed within the organization, which, in turn, dictate the eventual success or failure of the organization. Some management writers consider information to be of such fundamental importance to the management process that they define *management* as the process of converting information into action through decision making.[2] The next sections discuss the following aspects of information and decision making:

1. Factors that influence the value of information.
2. How to evaluate information.
3. Computer assistance in using information.

Factors Influencing the Value of Information

Some information is more valuable than other information.[3] The value of information is defined in terms of the benefit that can accrue to the organization through the use of the information. The greater this benefit, the more valuable the information.

Four primary factors determine the value of information:

1. Information appropriateness.
2. Information quality.
3. Information timeliness.
4. Information quantity.

In 1993, Caterpillar, a maker of earthmoving vehicles based in Aurora, Illinois, returned to profitability after seven straight quarters of losses. One key was the use of computers to cut inventories by as much as 40 percent. Computers, for instance, monitor parts usage and transmit orders to suppliers on a strict as-needed basis.

In general, management should encourage the generation, distribution, and use of organizational information that is appropriate, of high quality, timely, and of sufficient quantity. Following this guideline will not necessarily guarantee sound decisions, but it will ensure that important resources necessary to make such decisions are available.[4] Each of the factors that determines information value is discussed in more detail in the paragraphs that follow.

Information Appropriateness

Information appropriateness is defined in terms of how relevant the information is to the decision-making situation the manager faces. If the information is quite relevant, then it is said to be appropriate. Generally, as the appropriateness of information increases, so does the value of that information.

Figure 21.1 shows the characteristics of information appropriate for the following common decision-making situations:[5]

1. Operational control.
2. Management control.
3. Strategic planning.

Information appropriateness is the degree to which information is relevant to the decision-making situation the manager faces.

CHARACTERISTICS OF INFORMATION	OPERATIONAL CONTROL	MANAGEMENT CONTROL	STRATEGIC PLANNING
Source	Largely internal	→	External
Scope	Well defined, narrow	→	Very wide
Level of aggregation	Detailed	→	Aggregate
Time horizon	Historical	→	Future
Currency	Highly current	→	Quite old/historical
Required accuracy	High	→	Low
Frequency of use	Very frequent	→	Infrequent

Figure 21.1   Characteristics of information appropriate for decisions related to operational control, management control, and strategic planning

Operational Control, Management Control, and Strategic Planning

Decisions   *Operational control decisions* relate to ensuring that specific organizational tasks are carried out effectively and efficiently. *Management control decisions* relate to obtaining and effectively and efficiently using the organizational resources necessary to reach organizational objectives. *Strategic planning decisons* relate to determining organizational objectives and designating the corresponding action necessary to reach them.

As Figure 21.1 shows, characteristics of appropriate information change as managers shift from making operational control decisions to making management control decisions to making strategic planning decisions. Strategic planning decision makers need information that focuses on the relationship of the organization to its external environment, emphasizes the future, is wide in scope, and presents a broad view. Appropriate information for this type of decision is generally not completely current, but more historical in nature. In addition, this information does not need to be completely accurate because strategic decisions tend to be characterized by some subjectivity and focus on areas, like customer satisfaction, that are difficult to measure.

Information appropriate for making operational control decisions has dramatically different characteristics from information appropriate for making strategic planning decisions. Operational control decision makers need information that focuses for the most part on the internal organizational environment, emphasizes the performance history of the organization, and is well defined, narrow in scope, and detailed. In addition, appropriate information for this type of decision is both highly current and highly accurate.

Information appropriate for making management control decisions generally has characteristics that fall somewhere between the extreme characteristics of appropriate operational control information and appropriate strategic planning information.

Information Quality

Information quality is the degree to which information represents reality.

The second primary factor that determines the value of information is **information quality**—the degree to which information represents reality. The more closely information represents reality, the higher the quality and the greater the value of that information. In general, the higher the quality of information available to managers, the better equipped managers are to make appropriate decisions and the greater the probability that the organization will be successful over the long term.

Perhaps the most significant factor in producing poor-quality information is *data contamination*. Inaccurate data gathering can result in information that is of very low quality—a poor representation of reality.[6]

Information Timeliness

Information timeliness is the extent to which the receipt of information allows decisions to be made and action to be taken so the organization can gain some benefit from possessing the information.

Information timeliness, the third primary factor that determines the value of information, is the extent to which the receipt of information allows decisions to be made and action to be taken so the organization can gain some benefit from possessing the information. Information received by managers at a point when it can be used to the advantage of the organization is said to be timely.

For example, a product may be selling poorly because its established market price is significantly higher than the price of competitive products. If this information is received by management after the product has been discontinued, the information will be untimely. If, however, it is received soon enough to adjust the selling price of the product and thereby significantly increase sales, it will be timely.

Information Quantity

Information quantity is the amount of decision-related information a manager possesses.

The fourth and final determinant of the value of information is **information quantity**—the amount of decision-related information managers possess. Before making a

UPS driver Kevin Smith can use a so-called "electronic clipboard" developed by McCaw Cellular Communications to track packages over a cellular network. The messages that he sends are converted into "packet-switched data" that improve upon both information timeliness and quantity.

decision, managers should assess the quantity of information they possess that relates to the decision being made. If this quantity is judged to be insufficient, more information should be gathered before the decision is made. If the amount of information is judged to be as complete as necessary, managers can feel justified in making the decision.

There is such a thing as *too* much information. According to Rick Feldcamp of Century Life of America, information overload—too much information to consider properly—can make managers afraid to make decisions and result in important decisions going unmade. Information overload is generally considered to be the major cause of indecision in organizations—commonly referred to as "paralysis by analysis."[7]

Evaluating Information

Evaluating information is the process of determining whether the acquisition of specified information is justified. As with all evaluations of this kind, the primary concern of management is to weigh the dollar value of benefit gained from using some quantity of information against the cost of generating that information.

Identifying and Evaluating Data   According to the flowchart in Figure 21.2, the first major step in evaluating organizational information is to ascertain the value of that information by pinpointing the data to be analyzed and then determining the expected value or return to be received from obtaining perfect information based on these data. Then this expected value is reduced by the amount of benefit that will not be realized because of deficiencies and inaccuracies expected to appear in the information.

Evaluating the Cost of Data   Next, the expected value of organizational information is compared with the expected cost of obtaining that information. If the expected cost does not exceed the expected value, the information should be gathered. If it does exceed the expected value, managers either must increase the information's expected value or decrease its expected cost before the information gathering can be justified. If neither of these objectives is possible, management cannot justify gathering the information.

 According to the text discussion, information at Wal-Mart can be defined as the conclusions derived from the analysis of data relating to the way in which the company operates. The case implies that managers at Wal-Mart are better able to make sound decisions, including more effective control

decisions, because of the successful data handling achieved by the company's information system.

One important factor in evaluating the overall worth of Wal-Mart's information-handling system is the overall impact of the system on the value of information that company managers receive. Sam Walton determined, probably through a process of gathering feedback from Wal-Mart managers, that investing in computers, satellites, and other data-handling devices would enhance the value of information that organization members would receive, and do so at a reasonable cost. That is, for a reasonable cost, equipment such as computers would enhance the appropriateness, quality, timeliness, and quantity of information that Wal-Mart managers would have available. Overall, Sam Walton believed that the benefits of making investments in computers and information systems would outweigh the costs of the equipment; he therefore had Wal-Mart invest in the equipment.

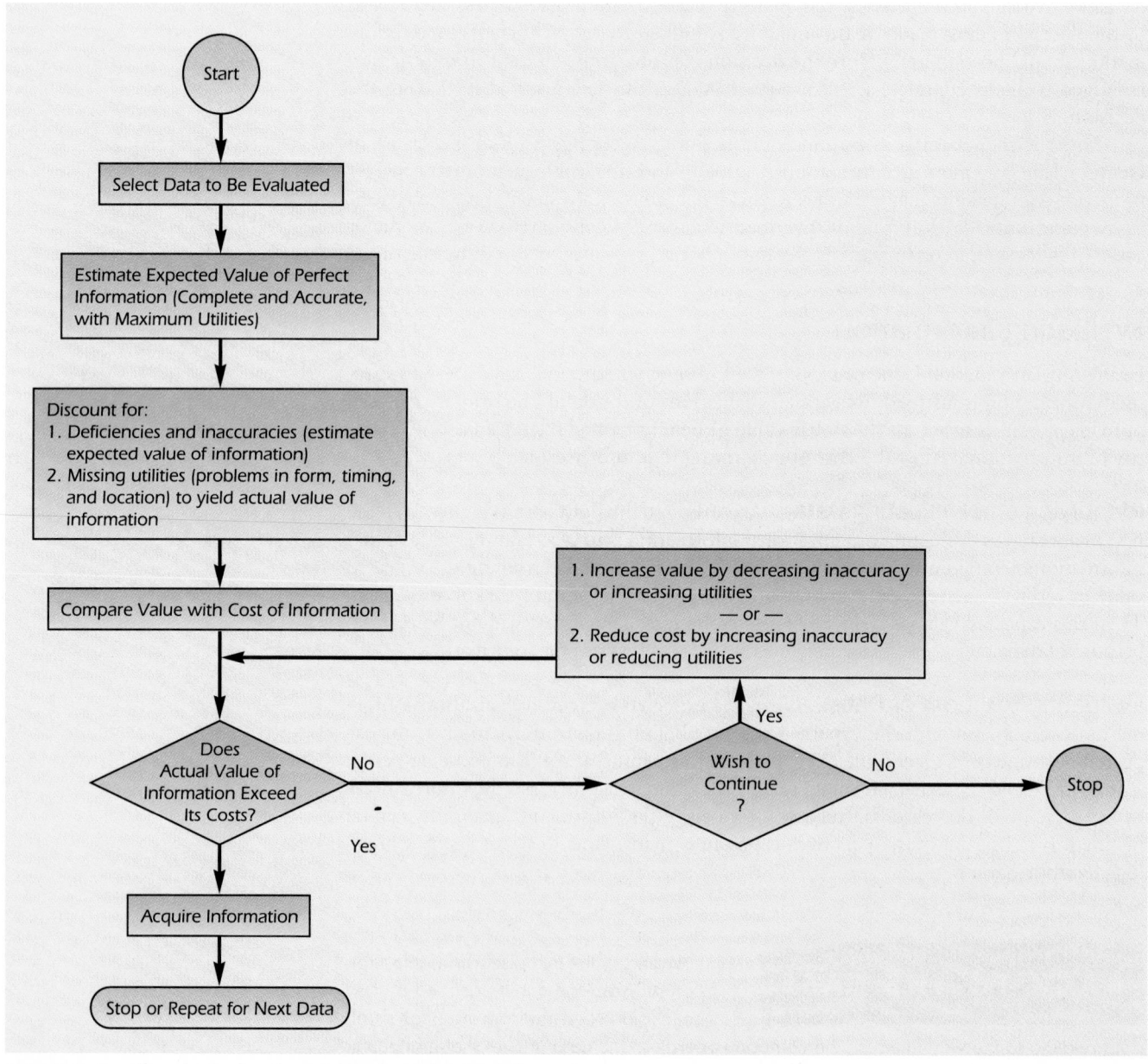

Figure 21.2   Flowchart of main activities in evaluating information

THE MANAGEMENT INFORMATION SYSTEM (MIS)

In simple terms, a **management information system (MIS)** is a network established within an organization to provide managers with information that will assist them in decision making.[8] The following, more complete definition of an MIS was developed by the Management Information System Committee of the Financial Executives Institute:

> An MIS is a system designed to provide selected decision-oriented information needed by management to plan, control, and evaluate the activities of the corporation. It is designed within a framework that emphasizes profit planning, performance planning, and control at all levels. It contemplates the ultimate integration of required business information subsystems, both financial and nonfinancial, within the company.[9]

The typical MIS is a formally established organizational network that gives managers continual access to vital information. For example, the MIS normally provides managers with ongoing reports relevant to significant organizational activities like sales, worker productivity, and labor turnover. As this example implies, the purview of an MIS is usually limited to internal organizational events. Based upon information they gain via an MIS, managers make decisions that are aimed at improving organizational performance. Because the typical MIS is characterized by computer usage, managers can use an MIS to gain online access to company records and condensed information in the form of summaries and reports. Overall, the MIS is a planned, systematic mechanism for providing managers with relevant information in a systematic fashion.[10]

The title of the specific organization member responsible for developing and maintaining an MIS varies from organization to organization. In smaller organizations, a president or vice president may have this responsibility. In larger organizations, an individual with a title such as "director of information systems" may be solely responsible for appropriately managing an entire MIS department. The term *MIS manager* is used in the sections that follow to indicate the person within the organization who has the primary responsibility for managing the MIS. The term *MIS personnel* is used to designate the nonmanagement individuals within the organization who possess the primary responsibility for actually operating the MIS. Examples of nonmanagement individuals are computer operators and computer programmers. The sections that follow describe an MIS more fully and outline the steps managers take to establish an MIS.

A **management information system (MIS)** is a network established within an organization to provide managers with information that will assist them in decision making. An MIS gets information to where it is needed.

POHANG IRON & STEEL COMPANY NEEDS A COMPLEX MIS

GLOBAL SPOTLIGHT

A management information system is used in managing activities at virtually all levels of an organization. Thus, although a given MIS may be relatively simple, managers at some organizations have to develop and use a very complex MIS, especially if their organizations are of significant size.

Management at the Pohang Iron & Steel Company in Korea faced the challenge of developing a complex MIS to manage Pohang's organizational activities efficiently and effectively. A complex MIS was needed primarily because of the large size of the company and the complexity of the activities involved in manufacturing steel. Pohang established an MIS that permits managers to monitor any phase of the steel production process. In addition, the system continually monitors about 60,000 items that are critical in controlling production costs and, at specified intervals, automatically updates the status of these items. To best interpret and react to information that flows on its MIS, management uses regularly scheduled video conferences with organization members in different locations. Pohang is the only Korean company to use reg-

ularly scheduled video conferences in this fashion. Pohang was founded in 1973 by the government of the Republic of Korea and is now the second largest and most competitive steel maker in the world. The company's success is largely credited to its development and use of its sophisticated MIS.≈

Describing the MIS

The MIS is perhaps best described by a summary of the steps necessary to properly operate it,[11] and by a discussion of the different kinds of information various managers need to make job-related decisions.

Operating the MIS   MIS personnel generally need to perform six sequential steps to properly operate an MIS.[12] (Figure 21.3 summarizes the steps and indicates the order in which they are performed.) The first step is to determine what information is needed within the organization, when it will be needed, and in what form it will be needed. Because the basic purpose of the MIS is to assist management in making decisions, one way to begin determining management information needs is to analyze the following:

1. Decision areas in which management makes decisions.
2. Specific decisions within these decision areas that management must actually make.
3. Alternatives that must be evaluated to make these specific decisions.

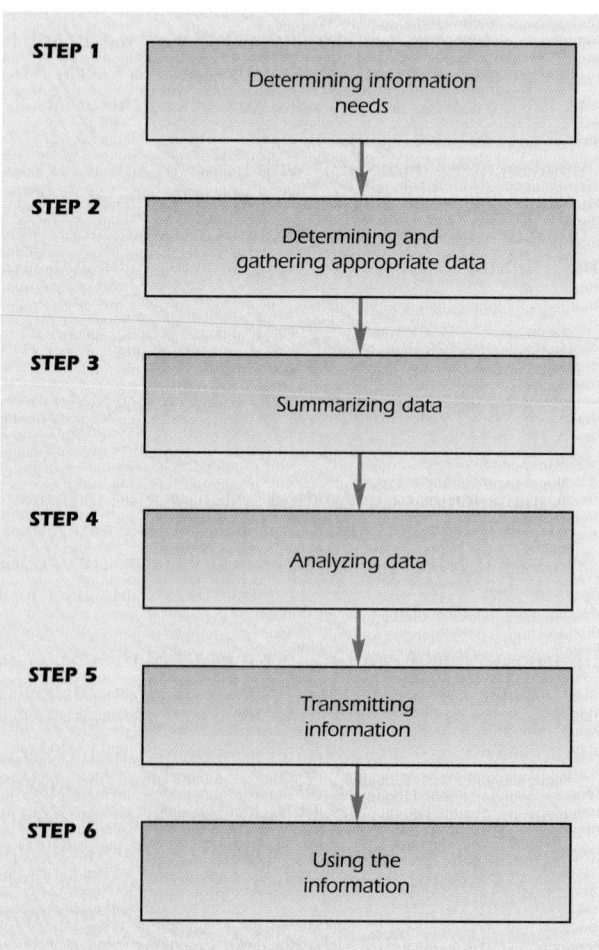

Figure 21.3   The six steps necessary to operate an MIS properly in order of their performance

For example, insights regarding what information management needs in a particular organization can be gleaned by understanding that management makes decisions in the area of plant and equipment, that a specific decision related to this area involves acquiring new equipment, and that two alternatives that must be evaluated relating to this decision are buying newly developed, high-technology equipment versus buying more standard equipment that has been around for some time in the industry.

Target's MIS Focuses on Hispanic Workers

DIVERSITY SPOTLIGHT

According to Target's vice president of public and consumer affairs, George Hite, and its president, Warren Feldberg, Target Stores is implementing aggressive expansion plans. Target, a consumer products retailer, has gained its success primarily by designing merchandise programs that reflect lifestyle trends. Company success has been significant enough to yield plans to add about 300 new stores over the next three years. Target managers are being prepared for expansion through comprehensive planning and a strong emphasis on management development.

Several MIS challenges face a company as substantial as Target. For example, management must have certain information: how competitive the company must be in order to hire an adequate number of workers; current trends in technology that might help Target become more efficient; financial results that the company is generating; the kind of continuing education necessary to build a productive workforce; international factors, such as the desirability of purchasing cheaper products abroad; and the level of workforce diversity that the company possesses and should aspire to.

The MIS at Target has provided management with a foundation of information upon which to make diversity-related decisions. For example, in southern California, the company is monitoring changing demographics of the population surrounding Target stores and attempting to build a workforce that reflects the diversity of that population. As a result, in southern California, Target is hiring a greater proportion of Hispanic workers. In order to help these workers become more productive, Target is offering them free English classes.≈

The second major step in operating the MIS is pinpointing and collecting the data that will yield needed organizational information. This step is just as important as determining the information needs of the organization. If collected data do not relate properly to information needs, it will be impossible to generate needed information.

After the information needs of the organization have been determined and appropriate data have been pinpointed and gathered, summarizing the data and analyzing the data are, respectively, the third and fourth steps MIS personnel generally should take to properly operate an MIS. It is in the performance of these steps that MIS personnel find computer assistance of great benefit.

The fifth and sixth steps are transmitting the information generated by data analysis to appropriate managers and getting the managers to actually use the information. The performance of these last two steps results in managerial decision making. Although each of the six steps is necessary if an MIS is to run properly, the time spent on performing each step will naturally vary from organization to organization.

Different Managers Need Different Kinds of Information   For maximum benefit, an MIS must collect relevant data, transform that data into appropriate information, and transmit that information to the appropriate managers. Appropriate information for one manager within an organization, however, may not be appropriate information for another. Robert G. Murdick suggests that the degree of appropri-

Organizational Level	Type of Management	Manager's Organizational Objectives	Appropriate Information from MIS	How MIS Information Is Used
1. Top management	CEO, president, vice president	Survival of the firm, profit growth, accumulation and efficient use of resources	Environmental data and trends, summary reports of operations, exception reports of problems, forecasts	Corporate objectives, policies, constraints, decisions on strategic plans, decisions on control of the total company
2. Middle management	Middle managers in such areas as marketing, production, and finance	Allocation of resources to assigned tasks, establishment of plans to meet operating objectives, control of operations	Summaries and exception reports of operating results, corporate objectives, policies, constraints, decisions on strategic plans, relevant actions and decisions of other middle managers	Operating plans and policies, exception reports, operating summaries, control procedures, decisions on resource allocations, actions and decisions related to other middle managers
3. First-line management	First-line managers whose work is closely related	Production of goods to meet marketing needs, supplying budgets, estimates of resource requirements, movement and storage of materials	Summary reports of transactions, detailed reports of problems, operating plans and policies, control procedures, actions and decisions of related first-line managers	Exception reports, progress reports, resource requests, dispatch orders, cross-functional reports

Figure 21.4   Appropriate MIS information under various sets of organizational circumstances

ateness of MIS information for a manager depends on the activities for which the manager will use the information, the organizational objectives assigned to the manager, and the level of management at which the manager functions.[13] All of these factors, of course, are closely related.

Murdick's thoughts on this matter are best summarized in Figure 21.4. As you can see from this figure, because the overall job situations of top managers, middle managers, and first-line managers are significantly different, the kinds of information these managers need to satisfactorily perform their jobs are also significantly different.

BACK TO THE CASE   In order for a company like Wal-Mart to get maximum benefit from its MIS, management must appropriately build each main ingredient of the MIS. A company's MIS is the organizational network established to provide managers with information that helps them make job-related decisions. Such a system at a major company like Wal-Mart necessitates the use of several MIS personnel, who help determine information needs at the company, help determine and collect ap-

propriate Wal-Mart data, summarize and analyze these data, transmit the analyzed data to appropriate Wal-Mart managers, and help managers to interpret the MIS information they receive.

To make sure that managers get appropriate information, MIS personnel must appreciate that different managers at a company like Wal-Mart need different kinds of information. As an example, a top manager like Sam Walton needs information that summarizes trends such as consumer tastes, competitor moves, and summary reports for the company as a whole. Middle managers at Wal-Mart need information that focuses more on specific operating divisions or units within the company—for example, all stores in the state of Alabama. Lower-level managers—perhaps store managers or department supervisors—need information such as daily sales figures by departments within a store or number of errors made in handling customers at the checkout counter.

Establishing an MIS

The process of establishing an MIS involves four stages:

1. Planning for the MIS.
2. Designing the MIS.
3. Implementing the MIS.
4. Improving the MIS.

Planning for the MIS
The planning stage is perhaps the most important stage of the process. Commonly cited factors that make planning for the establishment of an MIS an absolute necessity are the typically long periods of time needed to acquire MIS-related data-processing equipment and to integrate it into the operations of the organization, the difficulty of hiring competent equipment operators, and the major amounts of financial and managerial resources typically needed to operate an MIS.[14]

The specific types of plans for an MIS vary from organization to organization. However, a sample plan for the establishment of an MIS at a large consumer-products company is shown in Figure 21.5. This hypothetical plan, of course, is abbreviated; much more detailed outlines of each of the areas in this plan would be needed before it could be implemented. Notice that this plan includes a point (about a third of the way down the figure) at which management must decide if there is enough potential benefit to be gained from an MIS to continue the process of establishing such a system. This particular plan specifies that if management decides there is insufficient potential benefit to be gained from an MIS, given its total costs, the project should be terminated.

Designing the MIS
Although data-processing equipment is normally an important component of management information systems, the designing of an MIS should not begin with a comparative analysis of the types of such equipment available. Many MIS managers mistakenly think that data-processing equipment and an MIS are synonymous.

Analyzing Managers' Decisions.   Stoller and Van Horn indicate that because the purpose of an MIS is to provide information that will assist managers in making better decisions, the designing of an MIS should begin with an analysis of the kinds of decisions the managers actually make in a particular organization.[15] These authors suggest that designing an MIS should consist of four steps:

1. Defining various decisions that must be made to run an organization.
2. Determining the types of existing management policies that may influence the ways in which these decisions should be made.
3. Pinpointing the types of data needed to make these decisions.
4. Establishing a mechanism for gathering and appropriately processing the data to obtain needed information.

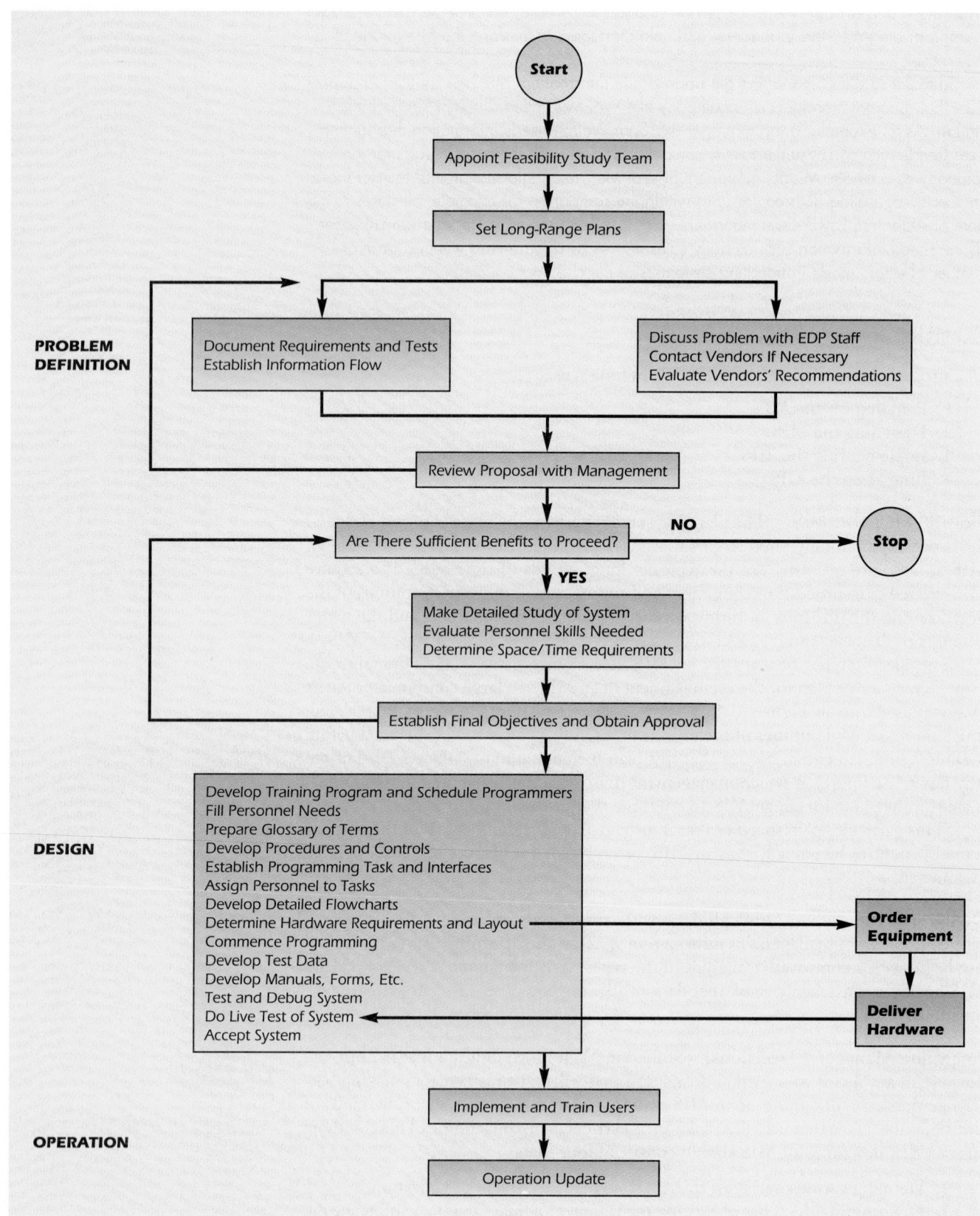

Figure 21.5   Plan for establishing a hypothetical MIS

Implementing the MIS The third stage in the process of establishing an MIS within an organization is implementation—that is, putting the planned-for and designed MIS into operation. In this stage, the equipment is acquired and integrated into the organization. Designated data are gathered, analyzed as planned, and distributed to appropriate managers within the organization. Line managers make decisions based on the information they receive from the MIS.

Making sure that the MIS is as simple as possible and serves the information needs of management is critical to a successful implementation of an MIS. If the MIS is overly complicated or does not meet management's information needs, the implementation of the system will encounter much resistance and will probably have only limited success.

Enlisting Management Support. Management of the implementation process of the MIS can determine the ultimate success or failure of the system.[16] To help ensure that this process will be successful, management can attempt to find an executive sponsor—a high-level manager who understands and supports the MIS implementation process. The support of such a sponsor will be a sign to all organization members that the MIS implementation is important to the organization and that all organization members should cooperate in making the implementation process successful.

Improving the MIS Once the MIS is operating, MIS managers should continually strive to maximize its value. The two sections that follow provide insights on how MIS improvements might be made.

Symptoms of Inadequate MIS. To improve an MIS, MIS managers must first find symptoms or signs that the existing MIS is inadequate. A list of such symptoms, developed by Bertram A. Colbert, a principal of Price Waterhouse & Company, is presented in Table 21.1.[17]

Table 21.1

Symptoms of an Inadequate MIS

OPERATIONAL	PSYCHOLOGICAL	REPORT CONTENT
Large physical inventory adjustments	Surprise at financial results	Excessive use of tabulations of figures
Capital expenditure overruns	Poor attitude of executives about usefulness of information	Multiple preparation and distribution of identical data
Inability of executives to explain changes from year to year in operating results	Lack of understanding of financial information on part of nonfinancial executives	Disagreeing information from different sources
Uncertain direction of company growth	Lack of concern for environmental changes	Lack of periodic comparative information and trends
Cost variances unexplainable	Executive homework reviewing reports considered excessive	Lateness of information
No order backlog awareness		Too little or excess detail
No internal discussion of reported data		Inaccurate information
Insufficient knowledge about competition		Lack of standards for comparison
Purchasing parts from outside vendors when internal capability and capacity to make are available		Failure to identify variances by cause and responsibility
Record of some "sour" investments in facilities, or in programs such as R&D and advertising		Inadequate externally generated information

Colbert divides the symptoms into three types:

1. Operational
2. Psychological
3. Report content

Operational symptoms and psychological symptoms relate, respectively, to the operation of the organization and the functioning of organization members. Report content symptoms relate to the actual makeup of the information generated by the MIS.

Although the symptoms listed in the table are clues that an MIS is inadequate, the symptoms, by themselves, may not actually pinpoint MIS weaknesses. Therefore, after such symptoms are detected, MIS managers usually must gather additional information to determine what MIS weaknesses exist. Answering questions such as the following helps MIS managers to determine these weaknesses:[18]

1. Where and how do managers get information?
2. Can managers make better use of their contacts to get information?
3. In what areas is managers' knowledge weakest, and how can managers be given information to minimize these weaknesses?
4. Do managers tend to act before receiving information?
5. Do managers wait so long for information that opportunities pass them by and the organization becomes bottlenecked?

Typical Improvements to an MIS. MIS inadequacies vary from situation to situation, depending on such factors as the quality of an MIS plan, the appropriateness of an MIS design, and the kinds of individuals operating an MIS. However, several activities have the potential of improving the MIS of most organizations:[19]

1. *Building cooperation among MIS personnel and line managers.* Cooperation of this sort encourages line managers to give MIS personnel honest opinions of the quality of information being received. Through this type of interaction, MIS designers and operators should be able to improve the effectivness of an MIS.
2. *Constantly stressing that MIS personnel should strive to accomplish the purpose of the MIS—providing managers with decision-related information.* In this regard, it probably would be of great benefit to hold line managers responsible for continually educating MIS personnel on the types of decisions organization members make and the corresponding steps taken to make these decisions. The better MIS personnel understand the decision situations that face operating managers, the higher the probability that MIS information will be appropriate for decisions these managers must make.

At River Hills West Healthcare Center in Pewaukee, Wisconsin, an electronic notepad called a CompuScriber is the most important piece of information technology in the war on paperwork. For example, when a nurse writes in the first three letters of a drug's name, a list of choices appears, along with check-off boxes for doses and times. Moreover, records are stored and instantly updated.

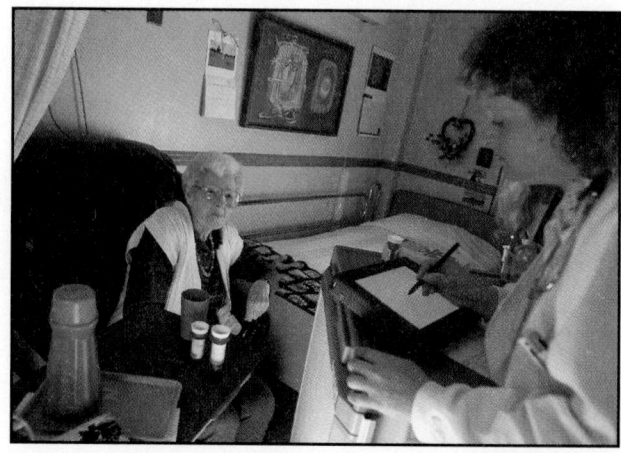

3. *Holding, wherever possible, both line managers and MIS personnel accountable for MIS activities on a cost-benefit basis.* This accountability reminds line managers and MIS personnel that the benefits the organization receives from MIS functions must exceed the costs. In effect, this accountability emphasis helps increase the cost consciousness of both line managers and MIS personnel.

4. *Operating an MIS in a "people-conscious" manner.* An MIS, like the formal pyramidal organization, is based on the assumption that organizational affairs can and should be handled in a completely logical manner. Logic, of course, is important to the design and implementation of an MIS. However, MIS activities should also take human considerations into account. After all, even when MIS activities are well-thought-out and completely logical, an MIS can be ineffective simply because people do not use it as intended.

BACK TO THE CASE

When Wal-Mart established its new MIS, it gained significantly by carefully planning the way in which the system would be established. For example, the following questions during the planning stage of Wal-Mart's MIS proved highly useful: Is an appropriate computer-based system being acquired and integrated? Does the company need new MIS personnel or will present personnel require further training in order to operate the new MIS? Will managers need additional training in order to operate the new MIS?

About the design and implementation stages of Wal-Mart's new MIS, management sought answers to such questions as: How do we design the new MIS based upon managerial decision making? How can we ensure that the new MIS as designed and implemented will be functional?

Managers as well as MIS personnel should continually try to improve the new MIS at Wal-Mart. All users of the new MIS should constantly attempt to pinpoint and eliminate weaknesses in the system. Suggestions for improving the new MIS could include: (1) building additional cooperation between MIS managers, MIS personnel, and line managers; (2) stressing that the purpose of the MIS is to provide managers with decision-related information; (3) using cost-benefit analysis to evaluate MIS activities; and (4) ensuring that the MIS operates in a people-conscious manner.

INFORMATION TECHNOLOGY

Technology consists of any type of equipment or process that organization members use in the performance of their work. This definition includes tools as old as a blacksmith's anvil and tools as new and innovative as virtual reality. This section discusses one segment of technology, **information technology,** or technology that focuses on the use of information in the performance of work. Some recent information technology introductions are covered in more detail through the following topics: computer assistance in using information, the management decision support system (MDSS), and computer networks.

Technology consists of any type of equipment or process that organization members use in the performance of their work.

Information technology is technology that focuses on the use of information in the performance of work.

Computer Assistance in Using Information

Managers have an overwhelming amount of data to gather, analyze, and transform into information before making numerous decisions. In fact, many managers in the United States as well as in the United Kingdom and other foreign countries are currently complaining that they are overloaded with information.[20] A computer is a tool managers can use to assist in the complicated and time-consuming task of generating this information.

A **computer** is an electronic tool capable of accepting data, interpreting data, performing ordered operations on data, and reporting on the outcome of these opera-

A **computer** is an electronic tool capable of accepting data, interpreting data, performing ordered operations on data, and reporting on the outcome of these operations. Computers are extremely helpful in generating information from raw data.

tions. Computers give managers the ability to store vast amounts of financial, inventory, and other data so that the data will be readily accessible for making day-to-day decisions. These decisions can be quite diverse and focus on issues like billing customers more efficiently, keeping track of receivables that are past due, ordering materials in appropriate quantities, paying vendors on a timely basis, and making sure that planned projects are on schedule.

The sections that follow discuss the main functions of computers and possible pitfalls in using computers.

Main Functions of Computers

A computer function is a computer activity that must be performed to generate organizational information. Computers perform five main functions:

1. Input
2. Storage
3. Control
4. Processing
5. Output

The relationships among these functions are shown in Figure 21.6.

Input. The **input function** consists of computer activities through which the computer enters the data to be analyzed and the instructions to be followed to analyze the data appropriately. As Figure 21.6 shows, the purpose of the input function is to provide data and instructions to be used in the performance of the storage, processing, control, and output functions.

Storage. The **storage function** consists of computer activities involved with retaining the material entered into the computer during the performance of the input function. The storage unit, or memory, of a computer is similar to the human mem-

The five main functions of computers are:

1. The **input function**—computer activities through which the computer enters the data to be analyzed and the instructions to be followed to analyze the data appropriately.

2. The **storage function**—computer activities involved with retaining the material entered into the computer during the performance of the input function.

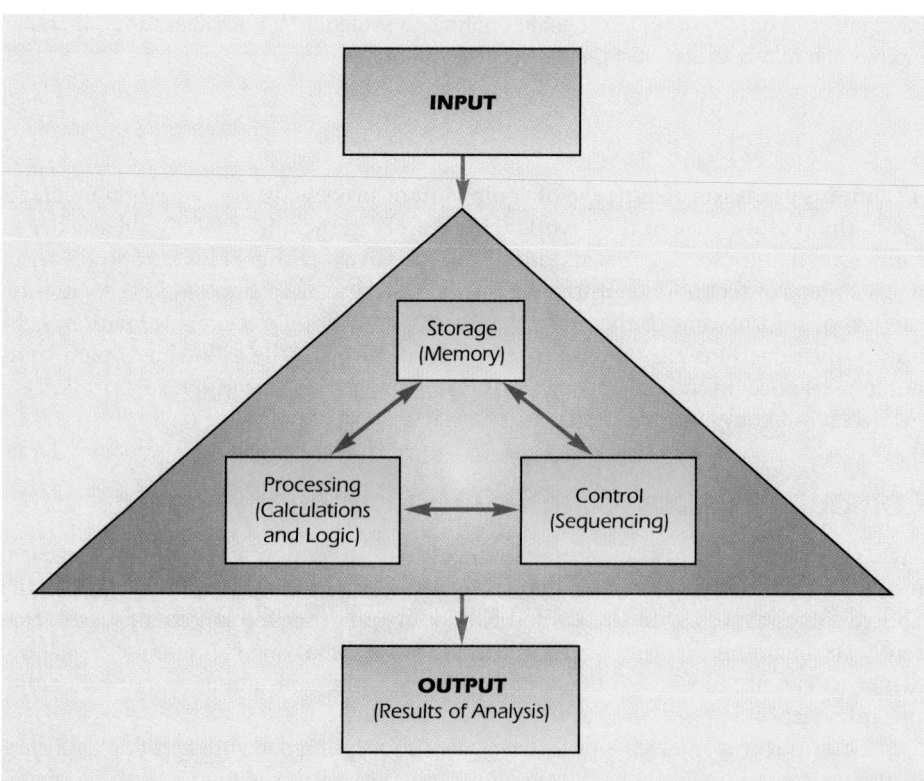

Figure 21.6 Relationships among the five main functions of a computer

ory in that various facts can be stored until they are needed for processing. In addition, facts can be stored, used in processing, and then restored as many times as necessary. As Figure 21.6 demonstrates, the storage, processing, and control activities are dependent on one another and ultimately yield computer output.

Processing.   The **processing function** consists of the computer activities involved with performing both logic and calculation steps necessary to analyze data appropriately. Calculation activities include virtually any numeric analysis. Logic activities include such analysis as comparing one number to another to determine which is larger. Data, as well as directions for processing the data, are furnished by input and storage activities.

3. The **processing function**—computer activities involved with performing the logic and calculation steps necessary to analyze data appropriately.

Control.   Computer activities that dictate the order in which other computer functions are performed compose the **control function.** Control activities indicate the following:

1. When data should be retrieved after storage
2. When and how the data should be analyzed
3. If and when the data should be restored after analysis
4. If and when additional data should be retrieved
5. When output activities (described in the next paragraph) should begin and end

4. The **control function**—computer activities that dictate the order in which other computer functions are performed.

Output.   The **output function** comprises the activities that take the results of the input, storage, processing, and control functions and transmit them outside the computer. These results can appear in such diverse forms as data on magnetic tape or characters typed on paper. Obviously, the form in which output appears is determined primarily by how the output is to be used. Output that appears on magnetic tape, for example, can be used as input for another computer analysis but is of little value for analysis by human beings.

5. The **output function**—computer activities that take the results of input, storage, processing, and control functions and transmit them outside the computer.

Possible Pitfalls in Using Computers   The computer is a sophisticated management tool with the potential to make a significant contribution to organizational

Sorry, but according to our brand-new $40,000 computer, we don't have any paintbrushes — and if we did, it wouldn't know how much to charge for one.

Orlando Sentinel (May 1, 1989).

success. For this potential to materialize, however, the following possible pitfalls should be avoided:[21]

1. *Thinking that a computer is capable of independently performing creative activities.* A computer does not lessen the organization's need for a manager's personal creative ability and professional judgment. A computer is capable only of following precise and detailed instructions provided by the computer user. The individual using the computer must tell the computer exactly what to do, how to do it, and when to do it. Computers are simply pieces of equipment that must be directed very precisely by computer users to perform some function.

2. *Spending too much money on computer assistance.* In general, computers can be of great assistance to managers. The initial cost of purchasing a computer and the costs of updating it when necessary, however, can be very high. Managers need to keep comparing the benefits obtained from computer assistance with the costs of obtaining this assistance. In essence, an investment in a computer should be expected to help the organization generate enough added revenue to not only finance the computer but also to contribute an acceptable level of net profit.

3. *Overestimating the value of computer output.* Some managers fall into the trap of assuming that they have "the answer" once they have received information generated by computer analysis. The cartoon preceding illustrates the kind of problems that can arise when organization members think that computers generate "the answer." Managers must recognize that computer output is only as good as the quality of data and directions for analyzing the data that human beings have put into the computer. Inaccurate data or inappropriate computer instructions yield useless computer output. A commonly used phrase to describe such an occurrence is "garbage in, garbage out."

BACK TO THE CASE

Sam Walton recognized the value of the computer in making management decisions. The computer at Wal-Mart can accept data from within the company, such as daily sales levels of various products; perform operations on the data, such as finding the percentage increases of various product sales on a daily or weekly basis; and quickly distribute the results of this analysis to managers. In order for such results to be distributed to management, data must be put into Wal-Mart computers, stored, and appropriately controlled and processed.

In addition to providing such valuable decision-related information as sales volume reports, computers at a company like Wal-Mart can perform many other functions. As examples, computers can generate and track bills to Wal-Mart customers, generate payroll checks to Wal-Mart employees, and write orders for products as they are needed from product wholesalers. Despite Mr. Sam's intense interest in computers, he knew very well that they, like any other management tool, have their limitations. He knew, for instance, that computer assistance at Wal-Mart, as in any company, is only as good as the people running the computers, and that managers should not expect computers to independently perform creative activities.

THE MANAGEMENT DECISION SUPPORT SYSTEM (MDSS)

Traditionally, the MIS that uses electronic assistance in gathering data and providing related information to managers has been invaluable. This MIS assistance has been especially useful in areas where programmed decisions (see Chapter 7) are necessary, because the computer continually generates the information that helps managers make these decisions. An example is using the computer to track cumulative labor costs by

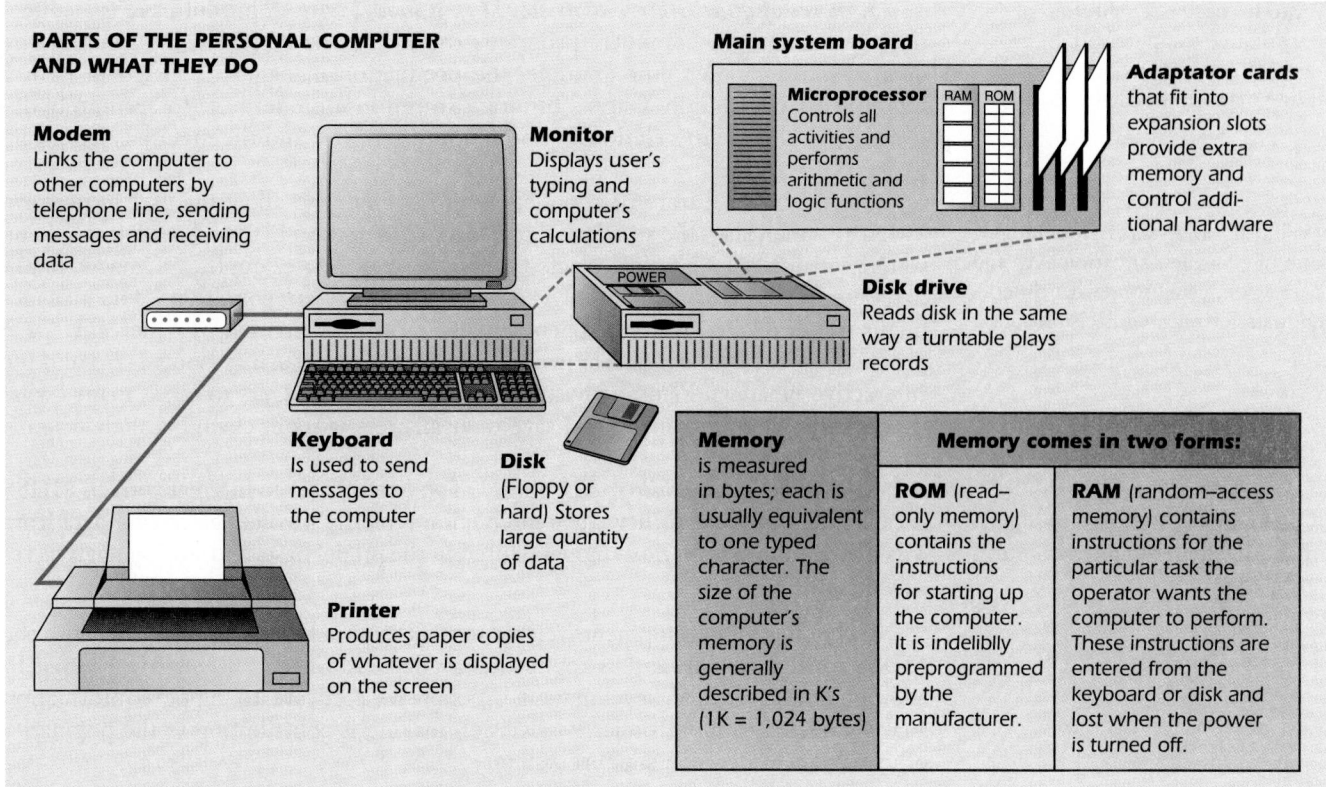

PARTS OF THE PERSONAL COMPUTER AND WHAT THEY DO

Modem
Links the computer to other computers by telephone line, sending messages and receiving data

Monitor
Displays user's typing and computer's calculations

Main system board

Microprocessor
Controls all activities and performs arithmetic and logic functions

Adaptator cards
that fit into expansion slots provide extra memory and control additional hardware

Disk drive
Reads disk in the same way a turntable plays records

Keyboard
Is used to send messages to the computer

Disk
(Floppy or hard) Stores large quantity of data

Printer
Produces paper copies of whatever is displayed on the screen

Memory is measured in bytes; each is usually equivalent to one typed character. The size of the computer's memory is generally described in K's (1K = 1,024 bytes)	**Memory comes in two forms:**	
	ROM (read–only memory) contains the instructions for starting up the computer. It is indeliblly preprogrammed by the manufacturer.	**RAM** (random–access memory) contains instructions for the particular task the operator wants the computer to perform. These instructions are entered from the keyboard or disk and lost when the power is turned off.

Figure 21.7   Possible components of a management decision support system (MDSS)

department. The computer can automatically gather and update the cumulative labor costs per department, compare these costs to corresponding annual budgets, and calculate the percentage of the budget that each department has reached to date. Such information is normally very useful in controlling department labor costs.

Closely related to the MIS is the **management decision support system (MDSS)**—an interdependent set of decision aids that help managers make nonprogrammed decisions (see Chapter 7).[22] Figure 21.7 illustrates possible components of the MDSS and describes what they do. The MDSS is typically characterized by the following:[23]

1. One or more corporate databases. A **database** is a reservoir of corporate facts consistently organized to fit the information needs of a variety of organization members. These databases (also termed *corporate databases*) tend to contain facts about all of the important facets of company operations, including both financial and nonfinancial information. These facts are used to explore issues important to the corporation. For example, a manager might find facts from the corporate databases useful for forecasting profits for each of the next three years.

2. One or more user databases. In addition to the corporate database, an MDSS usually contains several user databases. A **user database** is a database developed by an individual manager or other user. Such databases may be derived from, but are not necessarily limited to, the corporate database. They tend to address specific issues peculiar to the individual user. For example, a production manager might be interested in exploring the specific issue of lowering production costs. To do so, the manager might build a simple user database that includes departmental facts about reject rates of materials purchased from various suppliers. The manager might be able to lower production costs by eliminating the purchase of materials from suppliers with the highest reject rates.

A **management decision support system (MDSS)** is an interdependent set of computer-oriented decision aids that help managers make nonprogrammed decisions. The following characteristics are typical of an MDSS:

A **database** is a reservoir of corporate facts consistently organized to fit the information needs of a variety of organization members.

A **user database** is a database developed by an individual manager or other user.

A **model base** is a collection of quantitative computer programs that can assist MDSS users in analyzing data within databases.

3. *A set of quantitative tools stored in a model base.* A **model base** is a collection of quantitative computer programs that can assist MDSS users in analyzing data within databases. For example, the production manager discussed in item 2 might use a correlation analysis program stored in a model base to accurately determine if there is any relationship between reject rates and the materials from various suppliers.

One desirable feature of a model base is its ability to allow the user to perform **"what if" analysis**—the simulation of a business situation over and over again, using somewhat different data for selected decision areas. For example, a manager might first determine the profitability of a company under present conditions. The manager might then ask *what* would happen *if* materials costs increased by 5 percent. Or *if* products were sold at a different price. Popular programs such as Lotus 1-2-3 and the Interactive Financial Planning System (IFPS)[24] allow managers to ask as many "what if" questions as they want to and save their answers without changing their original data.

"What if" analysis is the simulation of a business situation over and over again, using somewhat different data for selected decision areas.

4. *A dialogue capability.* The ability of an MDSS user to interact with an MDSS is called **dialogue capability.** Such interaction typically involves extracting data from a database, calling up various models stored in the model base, and storing analysis results in a file.

A **dialogue capability** is the ability of an MDSS user to interact with an MDSS.

Technological developments related to microcomputers have made the use of the MDSS concept feasible and its application available to virtually all managers today. In addition, the continual development of extensive software to support information analysis related to more subjective decision making is contributing to the popularity of management decision support systems.

BACK TO THE CASE The text information about MDSS implies that Wal-Mart managers could use their own software to tap into corporate databases. In order for Wal-Mart to gain maximum advantage from an MIS, its managers should be able to use an MDSS efficiently and effectively. If Wal-Mart managers are not familiar with the MDSS concept, they can undergo training designed to give them an understanding of and ability to use the MDSS. Wal-Mart managers could employ the MDSS in making both programmed and nonprogrammed decisions.

In building and using the most advantageous MIS possible, management at a company like Wal-Mart should ensure that MIS users within the company have adequate equipment to operate and use an MDSS, have sufficient access to a corporate database, are properly employing user databases, have available appropriate model bases, and possess adequate dialogue capability within the company's MDSS. If management ensures all these things, the probability is high that the company MDSS will be properly used.

COMPUTER NETWORKS

A **computer network** is a system of two or more connected computers that allows computer users to communicate, cooperate, and share resources.

A **computer network** is a system of two or more connected computers that allows computer users to communicate, cooperate, and share resources. When working properly, a computer network is an information technology tool that encourages employees to maximize their potential and their productivity. No matter how good the network equipment, however, management has to realize that people are the key to ensuring that networks work properly, as the following PEOPLE PERSPECTIVES emphasizes.

The next sections discuss the two computer networks that have received the most attention recently from modern managers: local area networks and the Internet.

People Are the Key to Making the Network Work at Arthur Andersen

PEOPLE PERSPECTIVES

Andersen Consulting, a big purveyor of computer networks to corporate America, recently got a first-hand lesson in just how vulnerable computer networks can be: An Andersen employee made an inadvertent computer error that spread to hundreds of other computers, and suddenly thousands of Andersen employees couldn't get electronic mail.

The first sign of trouble came for managing partner Lyle Ginsburg late one Friday after he had sent a series of E-mail memos via modem from his hotel. Dialing up Andersen's computer network to check on the messages, he found his mailbox full of a repeated error message: "user . . . not found in name and address file."

That unsettling error message was showing up in mailboxes around the world because an employee—Andersen won't say who or where—unwittingly installed a new directory in the local "server" computer that stores, sends, and receives E-mail. The new directory replaced the existing one, which contained 24,000 user names and addresses. Then, the wayward computer—doing precisely what it was programmed to do—automatically contacted the other 300 or so servers around the world and had them replace their directories with the new one. Without the user names, the network didn't know where anyone was.≈

The Local Area Network

One type of computer network commonly used in modern organizations is called a **local area network (LAN).** A LAN is a computer network characterized by software that manages how information travels through cables to arrive at a number of connected single-user computer workstations. One rule of thumb recommends that when an organization reaches the use of five independent computer workstations, the computers should probably be connected as a LAN.[25] At this number of computers, the cost of networking should be outweighed by the gain of important organizational advantages—for example, allowing computer users to communicate more efficiently and effectively with one another and enabling workers to share the use of expensive software.

Figure 21.8 indicates the growth of management interest in usage of LANs by illustrating the continuing upward trend of sales of equipment used to build LANs. Although this growing enthusiasm for LANs has prompted many computer support companies to expand the array of LAN products they offer to organizations, managers should be cautious and refrain from investing in LAN products that do not satisfy a rigorous cost-benefit analysis.[26]

A **local area network (LAN)** is a computer network characterized by software that manages how information travels through cables to arrive at a number of connected single-user computer workstations.

A program called Project Hearth enables agents at Houston-based American Express Travel Services to do telephone order-entry work at home. Travel agents like Faye Compton are hooked up to the company's central datalines and can look up fares and book reservations on their own PCs. AmEx calculates that an agent handles 26 percent more calls at home than from the traditional office.

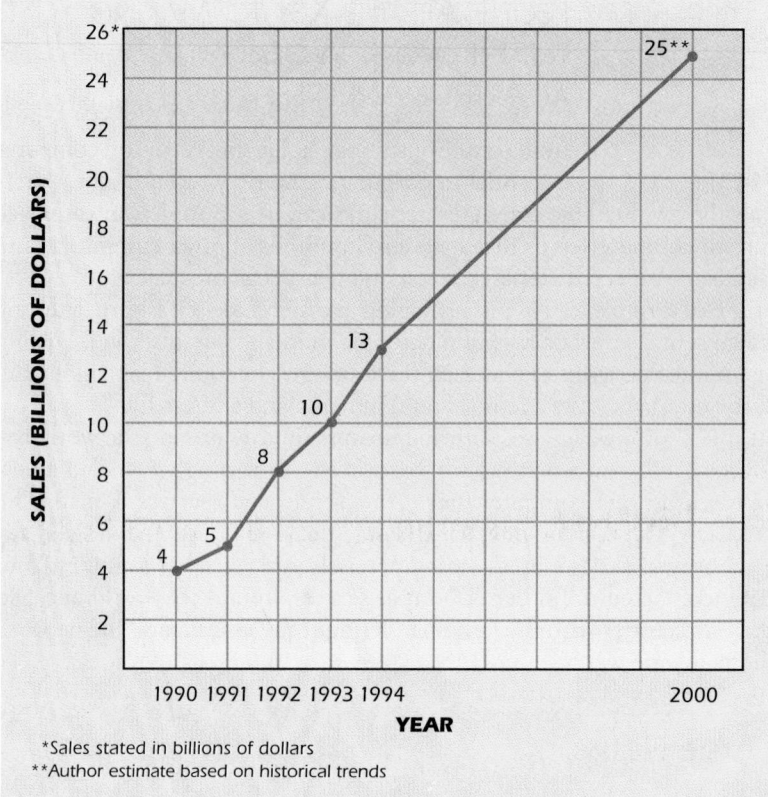

Figure 21.8   Total dollar sales of equipment used to build LANs in organizations

*Sales stated in billions of dollars
**Author estimate based on historical trends

The **Internet** is a large interconnected network of computer networks linking people and computers all over the world via phone lines, satellites, and other telecommunications systems.

The Internet

The **Internet,** an information technology tool, is a large interconnected network of computer networks linking people and computers all over the world via phone lines, satellites, and other telecommunications systems. Simply stated, the Internet is an expansive computer network linking about 1 million smaller networks worldwide.[27] The following quote contains a worthwhile description of the Internet:

> Probably the best model or analogy is that of a giant highway system that connects computers. The Internet connects all kinds of computers, no matter who made them, what programs run on them, or who they belong to—computers as large as the biggest supercomputers in the world or as small as a laptop PC. By connecting these computers, the Internet connects the poeple who use the computers. It's called the Internet because it connects not only the computers, but all the different kinds of regional and local networks that hook up these computers as well. Like the highway system, the Internet consists of interstates and state highways, and little roads. The number of computers and people linked by the Internet is now in the tens of millions and growing at an ever-faster rate.[28]

Evolving out of a project conceived and initiated by the U.S. Department of Defense in the early 1970s to allow scientists and researchers to better communicate and exchange data, today the Internet provides over 30 million users with information and the ability to communicate worldwide. Forecasts indicate that by the year 2000, more than 100 million people will be using the Internet. In addition, as Table 21.2 shows, the number of managers registering their businesses on the Internet is growing very rapidly, with no signs of slowing.

Managers are using the Internet in many different ways. Some use it to continually monitor and gather late-breaking news that can impact their organization in the short run. For example, news regarding fluctuations in interest rates and the latest moves of competitors is readily available on the Internet. Other managers use the In-

Table 21.2

The Growing Number of Businesses Registering for Use of the Internet

TYPES OF BUSINESS	1990	1991	1992	1993	1994[1]	2000[3]
Financial services	3	17	46	125	281	18,000
Law	0	4	10	38	114	7,300
Advertising	0	1	1	7	21	1,300
Publishing	1	8	27	96	212	13,500
Entertainment	0	1	2	4	16	1,024
Venture capital	0	0	1	11	23	1,600
Total[2]	93	1,044	3,054	8,412	18,245	1,180,000

(*Source:* Jared Sandberg, "Technology: The Business Plan," *The Wall Street Journal*, November 14, 1994, p. R14)
Source: Internet Info
[1]Through Aug. 15.
[2]Includes other categories.
[3]Author projection based on historical trend.

ternet to monitor and track government trends that can impact an organization's long-run viability. For example, issues like the evolving trade relationship between the United States and China or the latest turn in affirmative action legislation are easily monitored on the Internet. The following CUTTING EDGE feature describes how Dell Computer Corporation uses the Internet to reach customer service as well as company image objectives.

The following sections elaborate on the Internet by discussing the WorldWide Web and showing how this segment of the Internet helps managers achieve organizational goals.

DELL COMPUTER COMPANY SURFS THE INTERNET TO SERVICE CUSTOMERS AND BUILD ITS IMAGE

CUTTING EDGE

Avowed computer nut Jay Snyder sits all day doing what he loves to do: surf the Internet. And he gets paid for it.

Mr. Snyder and six others make up Dell Computer Corporations' Internet SWAT team. They peruse traffic for any mention of Dell products, ready to swoop into "threads" of conversations to help solve customer problems, change negative perceptions, and protect the company's reputation.

"I am having way too much fun," Mr. Snyder says.

To Dell and other computer companies, though, the Internet is more than just sport. Every day, computer users post queries about what products others recommend. Every hour, the cyberspace chatter includes complaints that can damage a company's reputation.

"People aren't shy about their opinions on that thing," says Steve Smith, Dell's director of technical support.

The Internet isn't the only place that computer-company employees are trolling and scrolling these days. Networks like CompuServe, America Online, and Prodigy have become increasingly important customer-service venues. Most major computer makers now have "forums" for questions and product information. Technical advisors offer answers and forward concerns to executives.

The electronic outlets are cheaper than phone banks, and company officials say they sometimes learn more from customers electronically than through telephone-service calls and traditional marketing surveys. "People can be pretty direct. You can

be pretty cocky when you don't have to look someone in the eye," says Mal Ransom, Packard Bell Electronics Inc.'s marketing vice president, who sometimes takes to Prodigy and CompuServe himself to answer customers.≈

The WorldWide Web

The **WorldWide Web** is a segment of the Internet that allows managers to have an information location called a **website** available continually to Internet users. Each website has a beginning page called a **home page,** and each home page generally has several supporting pages called **branch pages** that expand on the thoughts and ideas contained in the home page.

The WorldWide Web   Perhaps the fastest-growing segment of the Internet is the WorldWide Web.[29] The **WorldWide Web** is a system that allows managers to have an information location called a **website** that is available 24 hours a day, 7 days a week, to anyone who is using the Internet. Each website has a beginning page called a **home page,** and each home page generally has several supporting pages called **branch pages** that expand on the thoughts and ideas contained in the home page. Special programming features allow website visitors to quickly visit branch pages and quickly return to a home page.

For example, Figure 21.9 is the actual home page of WebSolvers, a company that provides professional website services to managers across the world. With the click of a computer mouse on any words at the bottom of the home page appearing in blue, the site visitor quickly shifts to a branch page that provides more information regarding the highlighted topic. A similar click on the branch page quickly returns the visitor to the home page. For example, clicking on "Services" on the WebSolvers home page will give the site visitor more information on a branch page about the company's offerings. Another click on the branch page will quickly return the visitor to the WebSolvers home page.

Reaching Organizational Goals via the WorldWide Web

Reaching Organizational Goals via the WorldWide Web   The number of managers establishing websites has been growing exponentially, and it is predicted that the number will continue to increase rapidly in the foreseeable future. Managers are using websites to perform a wide array of activities ranging from soliciting venture capital to making business travel arrangements.[30]

Managers should not rush into establishing websites, but rather should take great care to design and implement a website that is consistent with organizational goals. Recall that the fundamental job of the manager is to reach organizational goals

Figure 21.9   The WorldWide Web home page of WebSolvers

through the use of organizational resources. A properly designed and used website is an organizational resource that can help managers reach organizational goals like the following:

- *Marketing Products More Effectively.* Marketing is a very popular use of a website. Organizations already offer thousands of diverse products, including T-shirts, computers, books, financial services, travel advice and arrangements, and candy, on websites. An appropriately organized website can help managers promote products through an electronic brochure that is cost-efficient, easily updated, and instantaneously distributed across the world.
- *Enhancing the Quality of Recruits to the Organization.* A properly designed website enables management to recruit highly qualified people to the organization. Managers using websites appropriately can project the image of a progressive organization that keeps abreast of meaningful business trends and that uses any and all innovative tools available to ensure its success. This image should be useful in attracting the finest human resources.
- *Enhancing Product Quality.* An important part of establishing a high-quality product is the ability to offer high-quality service and to maintain communication with customers after the product is purchased. A website gives managers an effective and efficient vehicle for communicating with customers *after* an organization's product is purchased.
- *Communicating Globally.* Many modern managers need to communicate across the globe. A website enables them to reach out quickly and easily to almost anywhere in the world—and communicating globally via a website is generally less costly than using the more traditional global communication vehicles. In addition, a website can bring international communities closer together.
- *Encouraging Creativity in Organization Members.* Every successful organization maintains its success by devising creative solutions to problems. If appropriately designed and administered, a website can be a creative solution to myriad organizational problems. Perhaps more importantly, by establishing a website, management is sending a clear signal to all organization members that it is willing to provide technological tools for creatively solving problems, and also that it expects members to strive to develop their own creative solutions to their job problems.

BACK TO THE CASE

The introductory case implies that Wal-Mart makes good use of computer networking. In-store computers promptly summarize the data managers use in making decisions within individual stores. Through the network, computers in individual stores also feed data to a central location, where they are combined, summarized, and analyzed so that top management can tell how the company as a whole is doing. Such networking allows Wal-Mart to quickly translate information into action, not only for individual stores, but also for the entire chain, and this is a major competitive advantage.

Through its website on the Internet, Wal-Mart is using modern information technology to battle competitors. An inspection of the Wal-Mart website and its linked branch pages indicates that the company has purposefully designed its site both to help customers locate stores and to recruit talented career people. The site presents Wal-Mart as an employer that does not discriminate on the basis of sex, color, or age. Finally, the site provides an up-to-date profile of the company's financial performance, promotes Sam's Club (a related retail store), offers a recent Wal-Mart advertising circular, and gives site visitors an easy means to obtain additional information via electronic mail.

Action Summary

Reread the learning objectives below. Each objective is followed by questions. Answering these questions accurately will help you retain the most important concepts discussed in this chapter. After answering each question, check your answer against the answer key at the end of the chapter. (*Hint:* If you have any doubts regarding the correct response, consult the page whose number follows the answer.)

Circle: From studying this chapter, I will attempt to acquire:

1. An understanding of the relationship between data and information.

a,b,c,d,e   **a.** Data can be: (a) information; (b) opinion; (c) premises; (d) facts; (e) gossip.

a,b,c,d,e   **b.** Information can be defined as conclusions derived from: (a) data analysis; (b) opinion; (c) premises; (d) gossip; (e) none of the above.

2. Insights about the main factors that influence the value of information.

a,b,c,d,e   **a.** All of the following are primary factors determining the value of information except: (a) appropriateness; (b) expense; (c) quality; (d) timeliness; (e) quantity.

T,F   **b.** The appropriateness of the information increases as the volume of the information increases.

3. Knowledge of some potential steps for evaluating information.

a,b,c,d,e   **a.** All of the following are main activities in evaluating information except: (a) acquiring information; (b) comparing value with cost of information; (c) selecting data to be evaluated; (d) using information in decision making; (e) discounting expected value for deficiencies and inaccuracies.

T,F   **b.** The primary concern of management in evaluating information is the dollar value of the benefits gained compared to the cost of generating the information.

4. An understanding of the importance of a management information system (MIS) to an organization.

T,F   **a.** A management information system is a network established within an organization to provide managers with information that will assist them in decision making.

a,b,c,d,e   **b.** "Determining information needs" is which of the steps necessary to operate an MIS: (a) first; (b) second; (c) third; (d) fourth; (e) none of the above.

5. A feasible strategy for establishing an MIS.

a,b,c,d,e   **a.** All of the following are stages in the process of establishing an MIS except: (a) planning; (b) designing; (c) improving; (d) implementing; (e) all of the above are stages.

a,b,c,d,e   **b.** Which of the following activities has the potential of improving an MIS: (a) stressing that MIS personnel should strive to accomplish the purpose of an MIS; (b) operating an MIS in a ``people-conscious'' manner; (c) encouraging line managers to continually request additional information through the MIS; (d) a and b; (e) all of the above.

6. An appreciation for the roles of computers and computer networks in handling information.

a,b,c,d,e   **a.** All of the following are main computer functions except: (a) input; (b) storage; (c) control; (d) heuristic; (e) output.

a,b,c,d,e   **b.** All of the following are possible pitfalls in using the computer except: (a) thinking that a computer is independently capable of creative activities; (b) failing to realize that a computer is capable only of following precise and detailed instructions; (c) training and retraining all computer operating personnel; (d) spending too much money on computer assistance; (e) overestimating the value of computer output.

T,F   **c.** A LAN and the Internet are basically identical.

T,F   **d.** A website can help managers achieve many different organizational goals.

7. Information about what a management decision support system is and how it operates.

T,F   **a.** A management decision support system is a set of decision aids aimed at helping managers make nonprogrammed decisions.

T,F   **b.** There is basically no difference between a corporate database and a user database.

T,F   **c.** Dialogue capability allows the MDSS user to interact with an MIS.

Introductory Case Wrap-Up

"Sam Walton Taught Others at Wal-Mart to Use Information" (p. 507) and its related back-to-the-case sections were written to help you better understand the management concepts contained in this chapter. Answer the following discussion questions about this introductory case to further enrich your understanding of the chapter content:

1. If you were a store manager at Wal-Mart, what three functions would you use a computer to perform? Be as specific as possible.

2. List three decisions that an MDSS could help the manager of a Wal-Mart garden supplies department make. For each decision, describe the data that must be in the database in order to provide such help.

3. The main steps of the controlling process are measuring performance, comparing performance to standards, and taking corrective action. Discuss a possible role of an MIS at Wal-Mart in each of these steps.

Issues for Review and Discussion

1. What is the difference between data and information?
2. List and define four major factors that influence the value of information.
3. What are operational control decisions and strategic planning decisions? What characterizes information appropriate for making each of these decisions?
4. Discuss the major activities involved in evaluating information.
5. What factors tend to limit the usefulness of information, and how can these factors be overcome?
6. Define *MIS* and discuss its importance to management.
7. What steps must be performed to operate an MIS properly?
8. What major steps are involved in establishing an MIS?
9. Why is planning for an MIS such an important part of establishing an MIS?
10. Why does the designing of an MIS begin with analyzing managerial decision making?
11. How should managers use the symptoms of an inadequate MIS as listed in Table 21.1?
12. How could building cooperation between MIS personnel and line managers improve an MIS?
13. How can management use cost-benefit analysis to improve an MIS?
14. Describe five possible causes of resistance to using an MIS. What can managers do to ensure that these causes do not affect their organization's MIS?
15. Is a computer a flexible management tool? Explain.
16. How do the main functions of a computer relate to one another?
17. Summarize the major pitfalls managers must avoid when using a computer.
18. How does an MDSS differ from an MIS? Define *"what if" analysis* and give an illustration of how a manager might use it.
19. How are local area networks and the Internet different? How are they similar? Explain fully.
20. Define a website and explain the relationship between a home page and branch pages.
21. Discuss three different organizational goals that a website might help a manager achieve. Be sure to clearly show how a website would help.

Action Summary Answer Key

1. **a.** d, p. 508
   b. a, pp. 508–509
2. **a.** b, pp. 508–509
   b. F, pp. 509–510
3. **a.** d, pp. 511–512
   b. T, p. 511
4. **a.** T, p. 513
   b. a, pp. 514–515
5. **a.** e, pp. 519–521
   b. d, pp. 519–521
6. **a.** d, pp. 521–524
   b. c, pp. 523–524
   c. F, pp. 527–528
   d. T, pp. 530–531
7. **a.** T, pp. 524–525
   b. F, pp. 524–525
   c. F, p. 526

Case Study

The Internet Becomes a Technological Battlefield

The appearance of the Internet about 20 years ago as a U.S. Defense Department network did not foreshadow its boom as a commercial highway. Throughout the 1980s, the Internet continued to develop, connecting universities around the world—a "network of networks." Still, there was no strong commercial interest in this fast and powerful higher-ed linkup until Mosiac introduced color and graphics and point-and-click commands. Then the Internet stepped down from the towers of academia and into homes and offices all around the world. Powerful interests like Microsoft, Intel, and IBM, plus an array of start-up challengers like Netscape, Sun Microsystems, and Spyglass, got into the fray.

No wonder the stakes are high. Analysts estimate, for example, that the Internet industry will generate $13 billion in revenue by the year 2000, as companies sell the tools to make the "Net" a sound business medium. These tools will help companies and consumers buy and sell goods and services worth almost $20 billion. Meanwhile, managing the companies that guide businesses through the Internet of the future offers a challenge to both established high-tech firms and newcomers.

Netscape and Sun Microsystems have taken the lead in exploring the future, and thus have set the Internet standard. Older technology leaders—IBM, Oracle, Apple Computer, Silicon Graphics—have been forced to build Internet software compatible with Sun and Netscape platforms. Thus the industry has converged around Java, the Sun programming system that makes it possible to pull in little programs. Sun calls these programs "applets" or small applications. Why are they so valuable? They make it possible to create "active content" on a website—for instance, real-time weather radar maps or credit applications with built-in calculators. Dozens of companies are licensing JavaScript, Netscape's WorldWide Web programming language that makes creating Java applets easier.

Netscape Communications founders are Jim Clark, once head of Silicon Graphics, and Marc Andreesen, creator of the pioneering Mosiac web browser. Clark and Andreesen have followed a radical plan for the nascent Internet industry: They give away Netscape's powerful browser and make money selling software that supports companies using the Internet. Their goal is to become the "de facto standard" software for on-line commerce. Netscape's products guide the search for information across the Internet, provide companies with more viable means of building and maintaining their own WorldWide Web sites, and set up and improve security for growing online commercial enterprises. Netscape

shipped its first product in December 1994, and by December 1995 was claiming that over 8,500 companies were using its technology to develop websites and software programs and services.

Moreover, the Netscape platform is not tied to the Microsoft operating systems that are standard in most PCs. Clark believes, therefore, that "the Internet basically blew apart [Microsoft's] whole strategy" for the 1990s. Sun CEO Scott McNealy doesn't believe Microsoft can get into the fray quickly enough to dominate the Internet. Microsoft's Bill Gates admits that his company has had to play "catch-up," but insists that Microsoft stands ready to lead the newest technological advances. Right now, for example, research and development dollars are pouring into the following Microsoft Internet projects:

1. Visual Basic or VB Script, which helps companies write applications that work across the Web.
2. Internet Studio, a Web authoring language.
3. Microsoft Network, a consumer Internet service.
4. The Internet Information Server, which is included in Windows NT and manages Web information.
5. Object Linking and Embedding (OLE) technology, which allows software "objects" to communicate across the Web, much like Java's applets.

Unlike Java, OLE controls are ready-made. Thus using them does not require skilled programmers. Gates believes that ordinary businesses are more likely to want these ready-made components.

In addition, Gates doesn't worry that entering the Internet fray later than newcomers like Netscape and Sun did will matter in the end. For one thing, most new products are giveaways intended to build the market. According to Gates, the real money will come in the future, when managers reorganize their business operations around the Internet and consumers embrace online commerce. And in fact, commercial online services have begun to see the importance of Internet access to businesses and consumers. America Online, CompuServe, and Prodigy all offer gateways to the Internet in addition to their regular services. Some observers, however, believe that newer Internet service providers (ISP), such as Pipeline USA and Netcom On-Line Communication Services, offer more specialized and less expensive access.

The Internet may prove to be the computing shift of the 1990s. In the 1960s and 1970s, mainframe providers were the leaders. Ultimately, however, companies like IBM, Univac, Burroughs, and Control Data lost their

momentum when the focus shifted to minicomputers. Names like Digital Computers and Data General rose to the top. In the 1980s, Microsoft and Intel led the movement to PCs. What's in store for managers in the 1990s? Will the PC go the way of its predecessors? Will the industry shift to the Internet and new names in technology? Will government regulation affect commerce on the Internet?

Questions:

1. In the information age, how is managing a technology company different from managing other businesses? How is it similar?

2. What does all the excitement surrounding new Internet tools mean to the ordinary manager? What must a manager understand about these new products? Explain.

3. Scott McNealy (Sun Microsystems), Jim Clark (Netscape Communications), Bill Gates (Microsoft)—what do these managers have in common? How are they different? Based on the continuing commercial path of the Internet, who do you believe is the best manager? Why?

4. Dial into these home pages to keep track of the Internet competition and to find the newest information for making management decisions:
http://www.microsoft.com
http://www.netscape.com
http://www.sun.com

Skills Exercise

Find and evaluate several different business home pages on the Internet. Consider ways in which home page help managers reach organizational goals—such as marketing products or services more effectively, enhancing the quality of new recruits, improving product or service quality, communicating globally, and encouraging employee creativity. Correlate the results of your analysis with those of others in the class. Does the Web seem to be an effective management tool at this time? Why or why not? Select one home page and outline improvements that you would make on it.

The Internet learning materials that accompany this chapter can be found at
http://www.profcerto.com
Additional information can be found on the inside front and back covers of this text.

Lands' End: Getting the Product Out to the Customer

This is the sixth case in this book that explores a variety of management-related issues at the well-known direct-retailing company Lands' End. The first installment (on pp. 24–26) is designed to be a general introduction. You may want to refer to it when you are studying the cases that appear at the end of each part of the book.

Lands' End is one of the very few organizations that can get a product out to a customer within three working days of an order receipt. What makes LE so fast and efficient? According to Phil Schaecher, Sr. Vice President for Operations,

it's because LE's distribution center is staffed by the best people available working together with some of the most sophisticated technology in the industry. When I worked for a mail-order company in Baltimore, I honestly would have needed two people for every one I have here. It's just a completely different work ethic at Lands' End.

Let's take a closer look at how it all happens at the Lands' End distribution center in Dodgeville, Wisconsin. The chart on the next page provides an overview of the major operations.

Receiving is the first stop for Lands' End items. The night before scheduled receipt, a bar-coded slip is printed for each item due to be trucked in. As each carton is unloaded from the truck, a bar-coded label is attached. "If there are slips left over when the truck is empty," explains Facilities Services Supervisor Dave Burreson, "then we know we didn't get all the pieces that were to be in that order." Then, orders come upstairs via conveyor. Next, operators enter the contents of each box into the computer and compare the results to the original purchase order—a second accuracy check. Vendors are then notified of any order discrepancies. The bar code is used to track the merchandise throughout the building. "Bar code labeling has really moved us forward," says Schaecher. "It has been a significant factor in automating our operations." The process however, has not been glitch-free. "When the current system first came online," Schaecher reports,

we told operators, "Don't think—just record the number of items printed on the box." Everything went along smoothly for the first few days. Then we began getting reports that we were running low on items that should be showing large volume inventory. We soon discovered that operators had taken us at our word. You see, boxed items shipped from some of our overseas vendors are labeled in dozens—for example, twelve dozen shirts. These were recorded as 12 items. We had to go back and correct the posting error and explain to operators that they did need to multiply 12×12 and record the number in the box as 144 items, not 12.

Based upon current demand, the computer determines if a carton will be sent to reserve storage, to active bins, to quality assurance, or, for back orders, straight to packing and shipping. Most merchandise goes to reserve storage. Using a special crane, operators store cartons up to 64 feet—8 stories—high. Boxes are "organized" in reserve storage wherever they can fit in. "In other words," explains Schaecher,

a box of men's green socks may be stacked on top of a box of lady's blue sweaters, and next to a box of children's white shorts. However, when the bar-code on a box is scanned in by the crane operator, it is immediately followed by the bar-code on the shelf just below the carton. These two numbers allow the computer to keep track of the precise location of each carton. When items are needed in the active-bin area, the computer can quickly locate them in reserve storage, using these matched shelf and carton bar-codes.

A certain percentage of the merchandise received at the distribution center is inspected internally by quality-assurance people. Each inspector is given a specific flaw or problem to look for—for example, loose threads on a button or a turtleneck collar

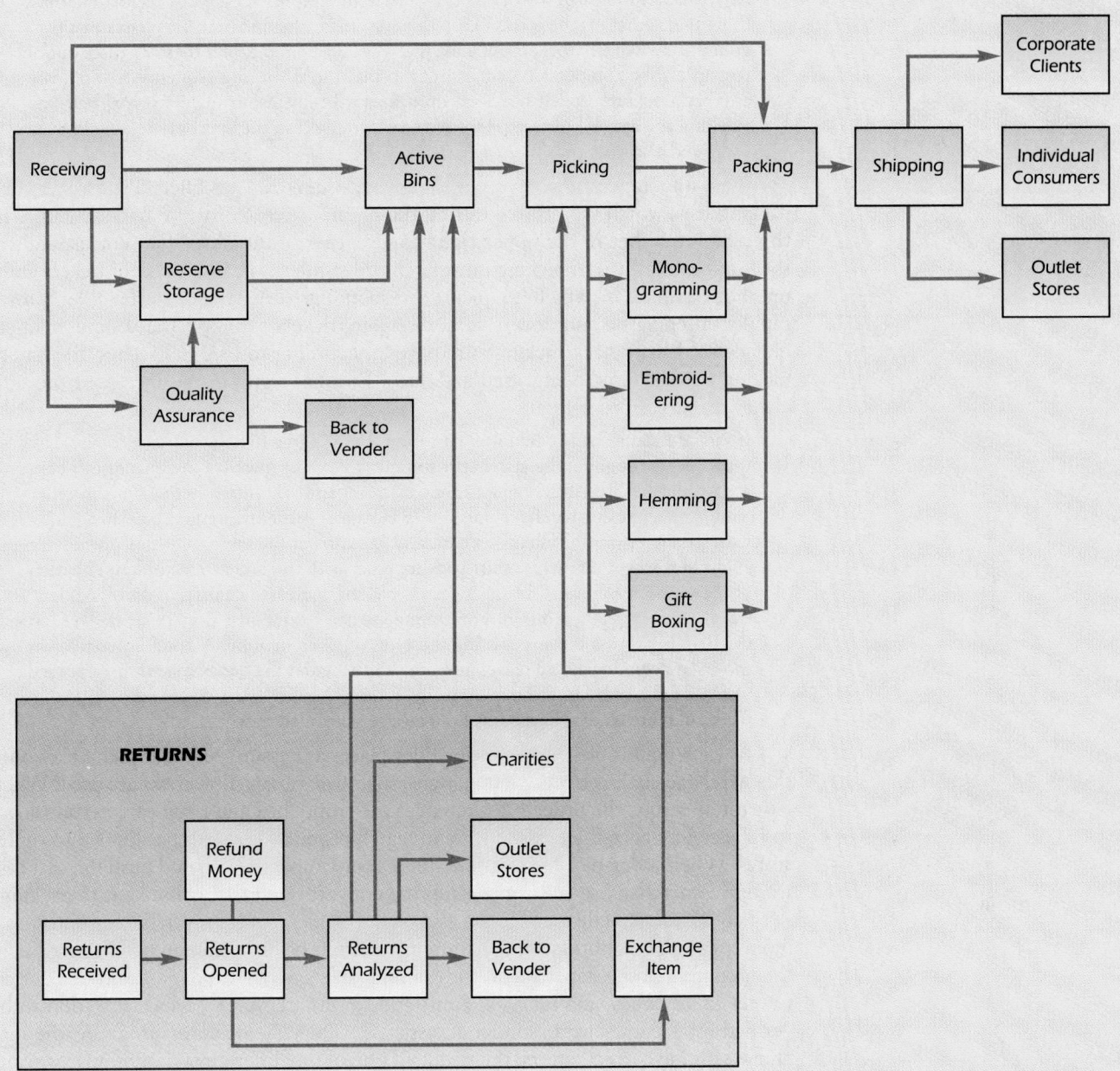

Lands' End: From Receiving to Shipping (Including Returns)

that is too tight to pull over someone's head. "If QA begins to find numerous problems," says Burreson, "they can inspect every item in the order or send the entire order back to the vendor." In all cases, inspectors chart their findings, which are then reported to both vendors and LE's quality-assurance specialists.

Some merchandise may be needed as soon as it arrives. In this case, operators route cartons to the correct aisles in the active-bin area by scanning bar codes. A stockkeeper in each area is assigned to put merchandise into correct bins. To prevent loose merchandise from being stored on shelves, vendors are required to put products in boxes with perforated panels. Because these panels can be easily removed, boxes can be put directly onto the shelves. When a bin is getting low, the computer knows to send more of that item from reserve storage. Notes Schaecher:

At 4:45 a.m., the earliest stockers arrive back in high bay (reserve storage). The first thing that comes off the computer in the morning is the first hour's replenishments to go into active bins. Stockers get a list that says, for example, pull these 27 cases out of this aisle. The computer puts the order in the proper picking sequence to eliminate any backtracking. Pulled boxes go on a forward-replenishment [conveyor] belt and ride into the active-bin area. Here they are sorted off in the appropriate aisle by bar-code, and a stocker puts them away.

Once the active bins have been stocked, orders can be filled. Pick tickets and packing lists, which are printed during the night, are ready for use by 7:30 a.m. The three-digit number in the upper right-hand corner of the pick ticket corresponds to the number assigned to picking bins. Each order-filler is given a stack of tickets and a one-hour period in which to pick corresponding orders. The order-filler moves rapidly up one aisle and down the next. Again, tickets come off the computer in sequence so that no backtracking is required. According to Phil Schaecher, the batch-picking method now being used at Lands' End has significantly increased the efficiency of today's order-filler:

> If you're picking by order, and a customer orders three items, you have to circulate that order throughout the warehouse to find those three pieces of merchandise. There are obviously three different locations in storage for the three items. On the other hand, if you're using batch picking and 78 customers order the same white shirt (along with a number of other items), we pick all 78 shirts at the same time and worry later about how to get that white shirt back together with the other items ordered by each of those 78 customers. Obviously, batch picking increases density, and order-fillers' travel time is greatly reduced. For example, when I came to LE in 1982, we were in the building across the street using the order-picking method. A good order-filler in those days could pick 150 pieces an hour. Today, under the batch system these people pick several hundred per hour. Actually, today [October 13, 1995] we'll pick 93,000 pieces of merchandise in the five hours we're scheduled to work.

As each item is picked, the order-filler places a pressure-sensitive pick ticket onto the merchandise. For large-volume items, so-called gravity-flow racks are used: When a carton is empty, the order-filler removes the empty box and a full carton rolls down to replace it. Order-fillers also pick and tag all products that will be shipped to outlet stores. When order-pickers' carts are filled, they simply unlatch and push the cart forward; the merchandise is emptied onto the conveyor belt that will take it to packing.

Not all merchandise is shipped as is; some orders require special processing—say, monogramming, embroidering, hemming, and gift boxing. As merchandise arrives in the monogramming department, for example, it is sorted into one of four categories: towels, knits, robes, and luggage. Knits and towels are sent to a special station to be verified for accuracy by a monogram assistant. Then the operator programs the machine with the correct letters, the size, and one of the different styles. Similarly, pants arriving in the hemming department are sorted by fabric, color, type of hem, and fabric weight. The pick ticket is kept in the pants pocket until cutting, hemming, and pressing are completed.

Another special service at LE is gift boxing. If this service is requested, the merchandise is removed from its poly bag, neatly folded, and placed in tissue paper with a seal. Items are then placed in an LE gift box. A ribbon and gift card are attached, and the gift box is secured in a shipping box.

As merchandise enters the packing department, each individual item is placed, bar code up, on a tilting tray. As these conveyorized trays move toward the packing-bin area, a scanner (similar to an upside-down grocery-store scanner) reads the bar-code data on the pick ticket. When the tray arrives at the proper station to meet the rest of the order, a signal is sent, the tray is tipped, and the merchandise slides into the proper packing bin. Now, says Phil Schaecher, it's fairly easy to see how the rest of the batch-picking process works: The bar code on the pick ticket is actually the number of the packing bin. So the three earlier-mentioned picked items were all given the same three-digit bar code and will all end up in the same packing bin. That is what puts the order back together.

Packing lists are then delivered to packing stations. These lists provide all the information needed to pack an order, including directions for the size of box or bag to be used and a list of items in each order. According to packer Bill Gattenbein,

bins are first hand-sorted by order. Then each order is checked off as it is placed into the designated box or bag. This is not only a number count, but also an accuracy check. For example, let's say an order includes a monogrammed sweater. We check the monogram to make sure the monogramming is correct according to the packing slip. Once the box is filled, the address label is attached and the container sealed.

Packers, says Schaecher,

catch 99.9 percent of all order-filling errors. Someone says, "Hey, this is not a white shirt, it's a blue shirt." If there's really an error, a runner is available to take care of the problem. Runners can also take care of missing items. Actually, what the packer may do is let the order "soak" for an hour or so. In other words, they just set everything that they currently have on the back shelf and wait. Maybe the missing item fell off the conveyor belt and somebody will find it and put it back on. If they don't have the item by the end of the second hour, they write out a trouble ticket and put it in the basket, and a runner will take care of it. Either the runner brings the item back and the order is completed, or the runner says, "We're out of that item" and the order is adjusted.

After merchandise is packed, packages are placed on another conveyor that takes them to shipping sorters. Once again, the computer scans the bar code on the address label and the tray tips to send the package down the appropriate chute—UPS, Parcel Post, or next-day UPS. Schaecher points out another benefit of bar-code labeling:

The bar code on each package is scanned and identified with a particular trailer. That becomes our tracking number. If you call and say, "Where is my order?" we know when it left here and what truck it went on.

Most packages go by UPS. Private trucking firms are contracted to deliver packages to UPS hubs throughout the country. "By using private trucking firms," explains Schaecher, "we make sure that packages reach the hub more quickly but reduce shipping costs."

In the mail-order business, of course, some merchandise will be returned. At LE, return openers look at each package. They will verify the correct name and address, the fact that the merchandise is being returned by the customer, and any other information needed to process the return. Merchandise is then sorted into categories and sent on to the return analyzer. This person analyses each item to determine if it should go back into stock, be returned to the vendor, be given to charity, or be sent to an outlet store. About 80 percent of all returned items are returned to stock.

Questions:

1. Applying what you have learned from your text, what can you say about controlling at Lands' End?
2. What operations management and operations control components and activities were evident in the case?
3. What reasons could you give for information systems (IS) to attach higher priority to issues other than the problem of "returns"?

22 chapter

QUALITY: BUILDING COMPETITIVE ORGANIZATIONS

STUDENT LEARNING OBJECTIVES

From studying this chapter, I will attempt to acquire:

1. An understanding of the relationship between quality and total quality management.
2. An appreciation for the importance of quality.
3. Insights about how to achieve quality.
4. An understanding of how strategic planning can be used to promote quality.
5. Knowledge about the quality improvement process and reengineering.

CHAPTER OUTLINE

Introductory Case: IOMEGA Corporation: Success Built on Continuous Improvement

Fundamentals of Quality

Defining Total Quality Management

Quality Spotlight: "Quality Is Job 1" at Ford

The Importance of Quality

Established Quality Awards
Achieving Quality

Ethics Spotlight: American Marketing Association Promotes "Zero Defects" Ethics

Cutting Edge: The Shingo Prize for Excellence in Manufacturing

Quality through Strategic Planning

Environmental Analysis and Quality
Establishing Organizational Direction and Quality
Strategy Formulation and Quality
Strategy Implementation and Quality
Strategic Control and Quality

The Quality Improvement Process

The Incremental Improvement Process

People Perspectives: Keeping People Involved in Incremental Improvement: Bearings, Inc.

Reengineering Improvements

IOMEGA Corporation: Success Built on Continuous Improvement

Many experts regard IOMEGA Corporation as one of the world's leading manufacturers of removable mass-storage devices for computers. For example, the Jaz drive (introduced in 1995) is a removable disk with enough capacity to permit desktop PC users to store large data files, including graphics, video, and audio.

In recognition of its successful commitment to quality, productivity, and customer satisfaction, IOMEGA was awarded the prestigious Shingo Prize for Excellence in American Manufacturing in 1992. It is interesting that this award came only a few years after the company's vital signs warned of impending disaster.

After some initial success following its founding in 1980, IOMEGA experienced serious difficulties in the mid-1980s. Some of these difficulties could be attributed to general conditions in the U.S. computer industry at that time. However, enough of them were directly attributable to the company's management that, in 1987, new senior managers were appointed to rescue the company.

IOMEGA's comeback strategy was to achieve customer satisfaction through the application of unique technology in the production and delivery of profitable, high-quality, leading-edge products. At the end of 1992, IOMEGA employed more than 1,100 people worldwide and by 1995, the company was shipping more than one million removable drives annually. In 1996, Micron Electronics began offering an entire line of factory-installed IOMEGA storage drives in its desktop PCs.

Examples of improvement initiatives are companywide efforts to:

- Establish a clear direction and values, being sure that every employee, customer, supplier, and shareholder clearly understands these commitments.
- Eliminate wasted effort and cost.
- Improve product quality to the point of consistent defect-free production.
- Reduce cycle time from customer order to product delivery.
- Empower spontaneous (self-appointed) quality improvement teams.

- Improve information systems and communication networks.
- Train, retrain, and cross-train employees, and take full advantage of individual employee knowledge and expertise.
- Continuously improve *everything*.

The effects of these and similar management initiatives have resulted in remarkable improvements in performance. Quantitative evidence of IOMEGA's world-class performance includes the following:

- Almost 80 percent of sales are to repeat buyers.
- Overall, almost 99 percent of customers state they would recommend IOMEGA products to a friend (the figure is 100 percent for some products and no less than 98 percent for any product).
- The overall product defect rate is less than 0.4 percent.
- Cycle time has been reduced by up to 95 percent.

Such performance, resulting from an uncompromising commitment to customer satisfaction, quality, and productivity, places IOMEGA among the elite of American manufacturers.

Companywide quality initiatives at IOMEGA have led to customer satisfaction and financial success for the company through the production and delivery of high-quality yet profitable products such as the Bernoulli Box.

The introductory case focuses on how IOMEGA has become a leading-edge U.S. company in its commitment to quality. This chapter presents useful information for managers like those at IOMEGA who are interested in emphasizing quality throughout their organizations. It does the following:

1. Defines quality and total quality management.
2. Explains the importance of quality.
3. Discusses how to achieve quality.
4. Describes how strategic planning can improve quality.
5. Outlines skills useful in achieving quality.

FUNDAMENTALS OF QUALITY

Quality is the extent to which a product does what it is supposed to do—how closely and reliably it satisfies the specifications to which it is built.

Quality was defined in Chapter 20 as how well a product does what it is supposed to do—how closely and reliably it satisfies the specifications to which it is built. In that chapter, quality was presented as the degree of excellence on which products or services can be ranked on the basis of selected features. This chapter expands on the topic of product quality.

Defining *Total Quality Management*

Total quality management (TQM) is the continuous process of involving all organization members in ensuring that every activity related to the production of goods or services has an appropriate role in establishing product quality.

Total quality management (TQM) is the continuous process of involving all organization members in ensuring that every activity related to the production of goods or services has an appropriate role in establishing product quality.[1] In other words, all organization members emphasize the appropriate performance of activities throughout the company in order to maintain the quality of products offered by the company. Under the TQM concept, organization members work both individually and collectively to maintain the quality of products offered to the marketplace.

Although the TQM movement actually began in the United States, its establishment, development, and growth throughout the world are largely credited to the Japanese. The Japanese believe that a TQM program should be companywide and must include the cooperation of all people within a company. Top managers, middle managers, supervisors, and workers throughout the company must strive together to ensure that all phases of company operations appropriately affect product quality. The company operations referred to include areas like market research, research and development, product planning, design, production, purchasing, vendor management, manufacturing, inspection, sales, after-sales customer care, financial control, personnel administration, and company training and education.

"QUALITY IS JOB 1" AT FORD

QUALITY SPOTLIGHT

Ford Motor Company has advertised for a number of years that "Quality Is Job 1" at Ford. Symbolic of that commitment is the company's refusal, a few years ago, to release its new Thunderbird model in time for *Motor Trend*'s Car of the Year competition; Ford chose to delay the Thunderbird's release because it had not yet solved certain quality problems. This decision is especially striking because the Thunderbird was the leading contender for the award that year, which would have meant millions of dollars in additional sales and some highly visible publicity for Ford.

Its commitment to quality has made Ford the leader among American automobile manufacturers in meeting the Japanese quality challenge. American automakers have been regaining market share in recent years largely because of the improved quality of their products.

The TQM concept has been adopted by a majority of Japanese firms. In fact, TQM is generally credited with being a major factor in establishing Japan as a major competitor in the world marketplace. Although U.S. firms have been moving toward accepting and implementing the TQM concept, there are still some basic differences between the traditional (U.S.) and Japanese positions on establishing and maintaining total quality.

TQM is a means to the end of product quality. The excellence or quality of all management activities (planning, organizing, influencing, and controlling) in an organization inevitably influences the quality of final goods or services offered by that organization to the marketplace. In general, the more effective its TQM program, the higher the quality of goods and services the organization can offer to the marketplace. The QUALITY SPOTLIGHT feature has been used throughout this text to illustrate how quality is related to planning, organizing, influencing, and controlling issues.≈

The Importance of Quality

Many managers and management theorists warn that U.S. organizations without high-quality products will very soon be unable to compete in the world marketplace. A 1990 book by Armand V. Feigenbaum put the problem succinctly:[2]

> Quality. Remember it? American manufacturing has slumped a long way from the glory days of the 1950s and '60s when "Made in the U.S.A." proudly stood for the best that industry could turn out.... While the Japanese were developing remarkably higher standards for a whole host of products, from consumer electronics to cars and machine tools, many U.S. managers were smugly dozing at the switch. Now, aside from aerospace and agriculture, there are few markets left where the U.S. carries its own weight in international trade. For American industry, the message is simple: Get Better or Get Beat.

Producing high-quality products is not an end in itself. Rather, successfully offering high-quality goods and services to the marketplace typically results in three important ends for the organization:

1. A positive company image.
2. Lower costs and higher market share.
3. Decreased product liability costs.

Positive Company Image   A reputation for high-quality products creates a positive image for an organization, and organizations gain many advantages from having such an image. A positive image helps a firm recruit valuable new employees, accelerate sales of its new products, and obtain needed loans from financial institutions. To summarize, high-quality products generally result in a positive company image, which leads to numerous organizational benefits.

Lower Costs and Higher Market Share   Activities that support product quality benefit the organization by yielding lower costs and greater market share. Figure 22.1 illustrates this point. As shown in the top half of this figure, greater market share or gain in product sales is a direct result of customer perception of improved product quality. As shown in the bottom half of the figure, organizational activities that contribute to product quality result in such benefits as increased productivity, lower rework and scrap costs, and lower warranty costs, which, in turn, result in lower manufacturing costs and lower costs of servicing products after they are sold. Figure 22.1 also makes the important point that both greater market share and lower costs attributed to high quality normally result in greater organizational profits.

Decreased Product Liability Costs   Product manufacturers are increasingly facing costly legal suits over damages caused by faulty products. More and more frequently, organizations that design and produce faulty products are being held liable in

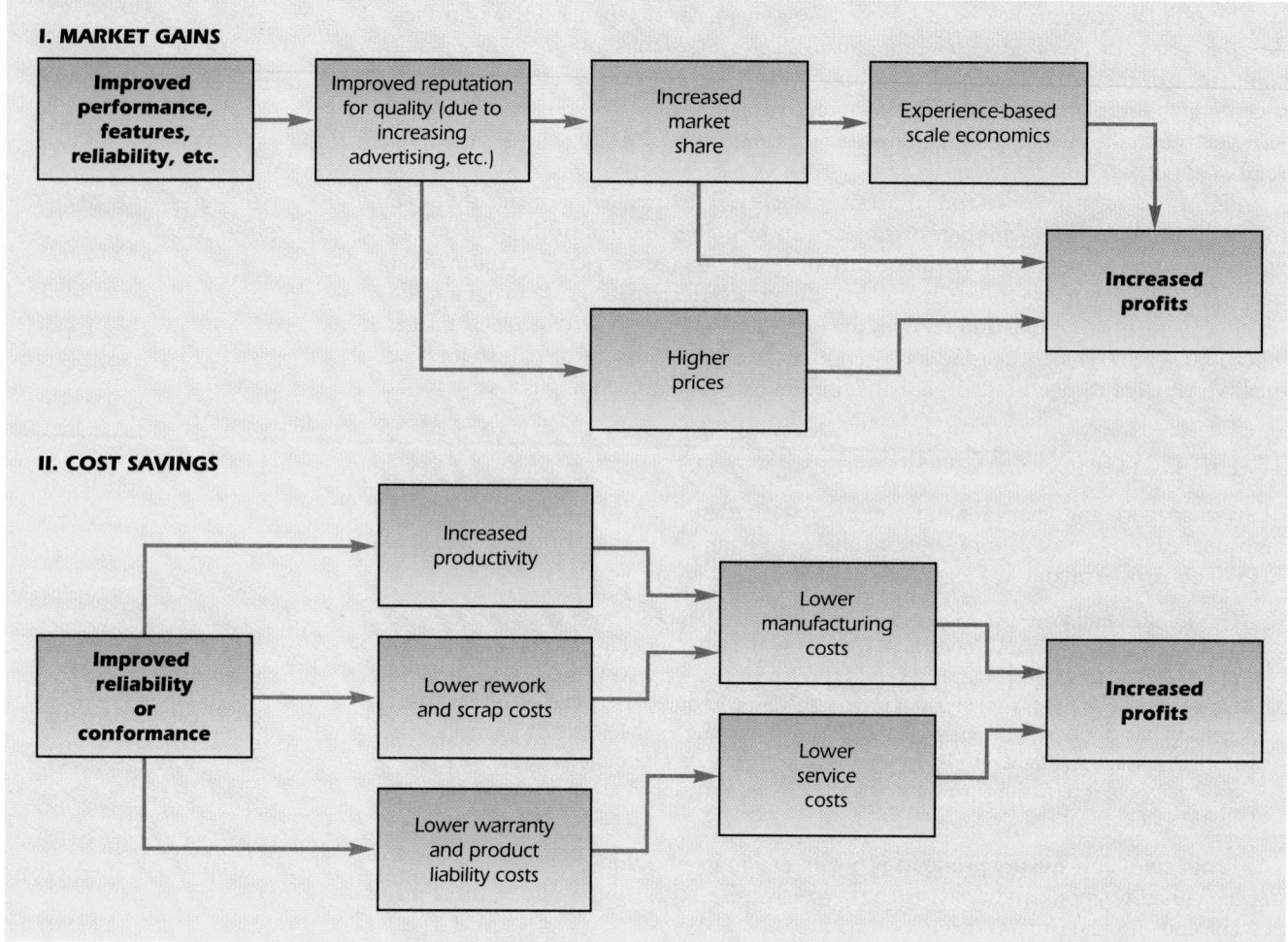

I. MARKET GAINS

- Improved performance, features, reliability, etc.
- Improved reputation for quality (due to increasing advertising, etc.)
- Increased market share
- Experience-based scale economics
- Higher prices
- **Increased profits**

II. COST SAVINGS

- Improved reliability or conformance
- Increased productivity
- Lower rework and scrap costs
- Lower warranty and product liability costs
- Lower manufacturing costs
- Lower service costs
- **Increased profits**

Figure 22.1   TQM typically results in lower costs and greater market share

the courts for damages resulting from the use of such products. To take one dramatic example, Pfizer, a company that develops mechanical heart valves, recently settled an estimated 180 lawsuits by heart-implant patients claiming that the valves used in their implants were faulty.[3] Successful TQM efforts typically result in improved products and product performance, and the normal result of improved products and product performance is lower product liability costs.

Established Quality Awards

Recognizing all these benefits of quality, U.S. companies have been placing greater emphasis on manufacturing high-quality products in recent years. Several major awards have been established in the United States and abroad to recognize those organizations that produce exceptionally high-quality products and services.

The most prestigious international award is the Deming Award, established in Japan in honor of W. Edwards Deming, who introduced Japanese firms to statistical quality control and quality improvement techniques after World War II.

The most widely known award in the United States is the Malcolm Baldrige National Quality Award, awarded by the American Society of Quality and Control. This award was established in 1988.[4]

A few major awards recognize outstanding quality in particular industries. One example is the Shingo Prize for Excellence in American Manufacturing, sponsored by

several industry groups, including the Association for Manufacturing Excellence and the National Association of Manufacturers, and administered by Utah State University. Another example, this one from the health-care industry, is the Healthcare Forum/Witt Award: Commitment to Quality.

The president of the United States and several states have established a variety of quality awards. NASA, for example, gives awards for outstanding quality to its exceptional subcontractors.

As these examples suggest, quality is an increasingly important element in an organization's ability to compete in today's global marketplace.

BACK TO THE CASE OMEGA Corporation has defined quality as "conformance to requirements." Meeting all requirements but one (even if that is only one of hundreds or thousands) still results in a defective product. The company's commitment to quality demands defect-free products and services for every customer, every time.

In company brochures and in interviews with management and employees, the statement is the same: "Quality is more than an objective. It is a way of life." All IOMEGA employees—not just production employees—are trained in total quality management and improvement techniques. Accountants, secretaries, and housekeeping employees learn similar techniques to establish and maintain world-class performance in their respective responsibilities. Many employees describe how even their personal lives have been improved by using total quality management techniques at home and in community activities.

IOMEGA's experience supports a quotation from Aristotle that "quality is a habit." A university professor stated recently, only half jokingly, that the United States will regain its preeminent economic position in the world when its highways are clear of litter.

Achieving Quality

Ensuring that all company operations play a productive role in maintaining product quality may seem like an overwhelming task. The task is indeed formidable, but several sets of valuable guidelines have been formulated to make it more achievable. Guidelines from five internationally acclaimed experts—Philip B. Crosby, W. Edwards Deming, Joseph M. Juran, Shigeo Shingo, and Armand V. Feigenbaum—on how to achieve product quality are summarized in the sections that follow.[5]

Crosby's Guidelines for Achieving Quality

Philip B. Crosby is known throughout the world as an expert in the area of quality and is considered a pioneer of the quality movement in the United States.[6] His work provides managers with valuable insights on how to achieve product quality. According to Crosby, an organization must be "injected" with certain ingredients relating to integrity, systems, communications, operations, and policies before it will be able to achieve significant progress in product quality.

Crosby calls these ingredients the "vaccination serum" that prevents the disease of low companywide quality. The ingredients of Crosby's vaccination serum are presented in Table 22.1.

Deming's Guidelines for Achieving Quality

W. Edwards Deming, who was originally trained as a statistician and began teaching statistical quality control in Japan shortly after World War II, is recognized internationally as a primary contributor to Japanese quality improvement programs. Deming advocated that the way to achieve product quality is to continuously improve the design of a product and the process used to manufacture it.[7] According to Deming, top management has the primary responsibility for achieving product quality.

Table 22.1

Crosby's Vaccination Serum for Preventing Poor Total Quality Management

Integrity

A. The chief executive officer is dedicated to having the customer receive what was promised, believes that the company will prosper only when all employees feel the same way, and is determined that neither customers nor employees will be hassled.

B. The chief operating officer believes that management performance is a complete function requiring that quality be "first among equals"—schedule and cost.

C. The senior executives, who report to those in A and B, take requirements so seriously that they can't stand deviations.

D. The managers, who work for the senior executives, know that the future rests with their abilities to get things done through people—right the first time.

E. The professional employees know that the accuracy and completeness of their work determine the effectiveness of the entire workforce.

F. The employees as a whole recognize that their individual commitments to the integrity of requirements are what make the company sound.

Systems

A. The quality management function is dedicated to measuring conformance to requirements and reporting any differences accurately.

B. The quality education system (QES) ensures that all employees of the company have a common language of quality and understand their personal roles in causing quality to be routine.

C. The financial method of measuring nonconformance and conformance costs is used to evaluate processes.

D. The use of the company's services or products by customers is measured and reported in a manner that causes corrective action to occur.

E. The companywide emphasis on defect prevention serves as a base for continual review and planning using current and past experience to keep the past from repeating itself.

Communications

A. Information about the progress of quality improvement and achievement actions is

continually supplied to all employees.

B. Recognition programs applicable to all levels of responsibility are a part of normal operations.

C. Each person in the company can, with very little effort, identify error, waste, opportunity, or any concern to top management quickly—and receive an immediate answer.

D. Each management status meeting begins with a factual and financial review of quality.

Operations

A. Suppliers are educated and supported in order to ensure that they will deliver services and products that are dependable and on time.

B. Procedures, products, and systems are qualified and proven prior to implementation and then continually examined and officially modified when the opportunity for improvement is seen.

C. Training is a routine activity for all tasks and is particularly integrated into new processes and procedures.

Policies

A. The policies on quality are clear and unambiguous.

B. The quality function reports on the same level as those functions that are being measured and has complete freedom of activity.

C. Advertising and all external communications must be completely in compliance with the requirements that the products and services must meet.

Source: © 1979. Crosby: *Quality Without Tears.* Reprinted with permission from McGraw-Hill.

Deming advised management to follow 14 points to achieve a high level of success in improving and maintaining product quality.[8]

Deming's 14 Points.

1. Create and publish to all employees a statement of the aims and purposes of the organization. Management must constantly demonstrate its commitment to this statement.
2. Learn the new philosophy—this means top management and everybody else in the organization.
3. Understand the purpose of inspection—for improvement of processes and reduction of cost.
4. End the practice of awarding business on the basis of price tag alone.
5. Improve constantly and forever the system of production and service.
6. Institute training.
7. Teach and institute leadership.
8. Drive out fear. Create trust. Create a climate for innovation.
9. Optimize the efforts of teams, groups, staff areas toward the aims and purposes of the company.
10. Eliminate exhortations to the workforce.
11. (a) Eliminate numerical quotas for production. Instead, learn and institute methods for improvement.
    (b) Eliminate management by objectives. Instead, learn the capabilities of processes and how to improve them.
12. Remove barriers that rob people of pride of workmanship.
13. Encourage education and self-improvement for everyone.
14. Take action to accomplish the transformation.

AMERICAN MARKETING ASSOCIATION PROMOTES "ZERO DEFECTS" ETHICS

ETHICS SPOTLIGHT

Deming advises that management should strive for zero defects in its production process—that is, companies should emphasize that no mistakes can be tolerated in the production of its products. Although the concept of zero defects is normally thought of as applying to manufacturing situations, the American Marketing Association (AMA) is encouraging the application of this concept in the area of ethics.

The AMA is a professional organization dedicated to meeting the needs of professional marketing managers. It recently adopted a new code of ethics that describes the responsibilities of marketing managers and the rights and duties of all individuals involved in the marketing process. Like any code of ethics, the AMA Code will have an effect only if managers understand it, become committed to it, and comply with it. If the AMA has its way, a company or person will achieve reputability only by having high standards for quality products and services and demonstrating constant emphasis on maintaining rigorous ethical practices.

The AMA's philosophy about ethics stresses that high-quality ethics should be a component of every quality program. It must be admitted that maintaining high ethical practices within an organization is not easy. One philosophy that can help managers in this area is to adopt a zero defects philosophy about ethical practices. That is, managers should strive to eliminate every unethical practice in their organizations.≈

Juran's Guidelines for Achieving Quality   Like Deming, Joseph M. Juran taught quality concepts to the Japanese and became a significant leader in the quality

movement throughout the world. Juran's philosophy emphasizes that management should pursue the mission of quality improvement and maintenance on two levels:

1. The mission of the firm as a whole to achieve and maintain high quality.
2. The mission of individual departments within the firm to achieve and maintain high quality.

Juran insists that quality improvement and maintenance are a clear process requiring managers to become involved in the study of symptoms of quality problems, the identification of quality problems implied by the symptoms, and the application of solutions to these problems. For maximum effect of a quality effort, strategic planning for quality should be similar to the organization's strategic planning for any other organizational issue, such as finance, marketing, and human resources. That is, strategic planning for quality should include setting short-term and long-term quality goals, comparing quality results with quality plans, and integrating quality plans with other corporate strategic areas.[9] More discussion on the relationship between quality and strategic planning follows.

Shingo's Guidelines for Achieving Quality   The late Shigeo Shingo served as president of Japan's Institute of Management Improvement and there distinguished himself as one of the world's leading experts on improving the manufacturing process. He and Taiichi Ohno are credited with creating the revolutionary Toyota Production Systems.

Shingo first learned quality production techniques from Americans, who advocated statistical techniques. He later broke with this approach, however, in favor of what he called "mistake-proofing," or in Japanese, *poka yoke*.

The essence of *poka yoke* is that a production system should be made so mistakeproof that it is impossible for it to produce anything except good products. Traditionally, quality efforts were largely confined to inspecting work after it was done—to catch and then fix defects, if possible. Even statistical quality control is dependent upon product inspection to diagnose problems with production systems. Recognizing the waste and cost of such inspections, Shingo developed methods to ensure that products are produced correctly the first time, every time.

Figure 22.2 shows an example of a *poka yoke* device designed to prevent errors in a brake wire clamp mounting.[10] Before the improvement, the mounting bridge would accommodate either left or right parts, regardless of which one was needed. This often caused confusion, leading to the installation of the wrong part. A *poka yoke* bridge was devised to set on mounts to ensure that only the correct part could be inserted.

This section on achieving quality discussed the work of Shigeo Shingo. The following CUTTING EDGE feature discusses a prize for excellence in manufacturing established in his honor and names some recent recipients of the award.

THE SHINGO PRIZE FOR EXCELLENCE IN MANUFACTURING

CUTTING EDGE

Established in 1988, the Shingo Prize for Excellence in Manufacturing is administered by Utah State University. The prize, named for Shigeo Shingo, stands as a testament to the importance of the work of this Japanese quality expert. The purpose of the prize is to promote world-class manufacturing in the United States and to recognize U.S. companies that excel in productivity and process improvement. The Shingo Prize also recognizes companies that excel in the areas of quality enhancement and customer satisfaction.

The philosophy behind the Shingo Prize is that world-class manufacturing status can be achieved by improving manufacturing processes, using just-in-time systems, eliminating waste and achieving zero defects, and continuously improving products and costs. In evaluating organizations applying for the prize, the Utah State Univer-

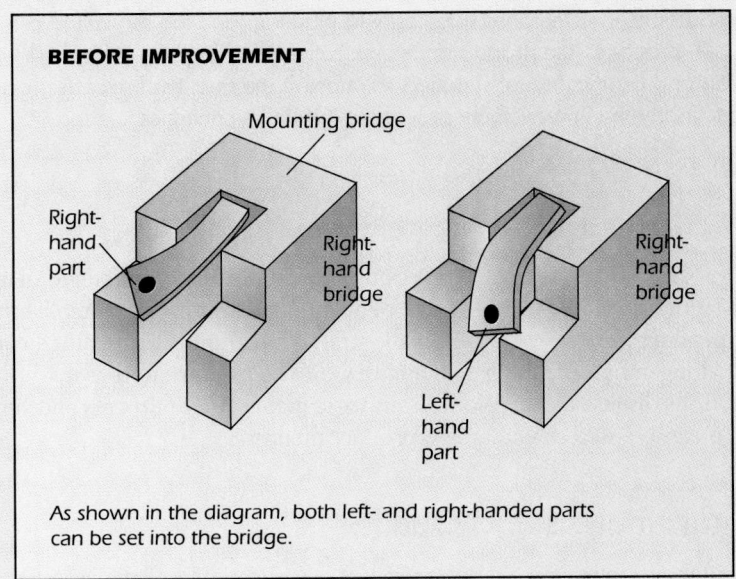
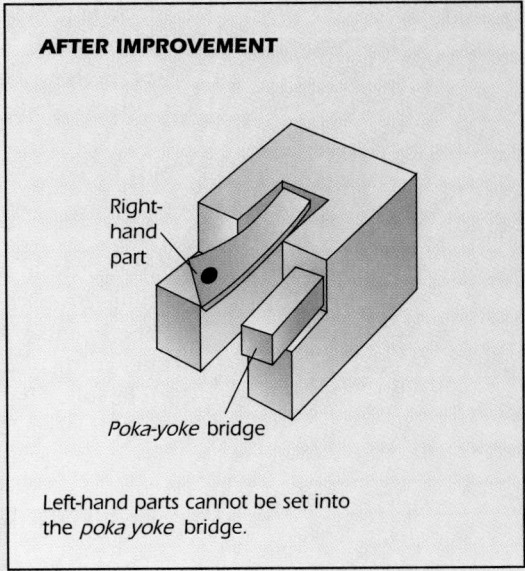

BEFORE IMPROVEMENT

Mounting bridge

Right-hand part

Right-hand bridge

Right-hand bridge

Left-hand part

As shown in the diagram, both left- and right-handed parts can be set into the bridge.

AFTER IMPROVEMENT

Right-hand part

Poka-yoke bridge

Left-hand parts cannot be set into the *poka yoke* bridge.

EFFECTS: Confusion of left and right parts was reduced to zero.

Figure 22.2   *Poka yoke* device

sity panel considers an organization's total quality and productivity culture and infra-structure, its manufacturing strategy, its measured quality and productivity results, and its measured level of customer satisfaction. Some recent recipients of the Shingo Prize are Alcatel Network Systems, Inc., AT&T Microelectronics' IC Group, Critikon, Inc., General Tire, Timken Company, and Union Carbide.≈

Feigenbaum's Guidelines for Achieving Quality   Armand V. Feigenbaum is credited with originating the term *total quality control*, today more often referred to as *total quality management*, or *TQM*. The basic idea of TQM is that every operation in an organization can benefit from the application of quality improvement principles. Defects are costly and unacceptable throughout the organization, not just on the man-ufacturing floor.[11]

BACK TO THE CASE   When asked how to achieve quality, ex-perts consistently advise making im-provements and not stopping until everything is improved, and then doing it all over and over again.

In the November 30, 1992, issue of *Business Week*, Fred Wenninger, chief executive officer of IOMEGA Corporation, responded to the question, "Where should a beginner start?" with these comments:

- Find your main bottleneck and attack it relentlessly.
- The problem and its solution should be easy for everyone to understand.
- Some improvement should show up relatively quickly.
- The problem should be "cheap" to fix.

With these criteria in mind, IOMEGA chose to attack cycle time first. In 1989, pro-duction time for a drive was 28 days. By the end of 1992, it was only $1^1/_2$ days—an almost 95 percent improvement.

Wenninger continued: "Step two is to repeat the problem-solving cycle, and keep re-peating it, until the process improves to the point where something else surfaces as the

biggest bottleneck—then go after that." This process led IOMEGA to other improvements, including: major reductions in inventories (too costly to maintain and too difficult to control defects); "mistake-proofing" the production system rather than inspecting finished products for defects; and certification of suppliers to improve the quality of materials going into production. Today the improvement process at IOMEGA continues.

QUALITY THROUGH STRATEGIC PLANNING

Managers in most organizations spend significant time and effort on strategic planning. Properly designed strategic planning can play an important role in establishing and maintaining product quality.[12] As you recall, strategic planning was defined earlier in this text as long-range planning that focuses on the organization as a whole. The following sections discuss the steps of the strategic management process and suggest how each step can be used to encourage product quality.

Environmental Analysis and Quality

The initial step in the strategic management process is environmental analysis. *Environmental analysis* was defined in Chapter 8 as the study of the organizational environment to pinpoint factors that significantly influence organizational operations. In establishing the role of environmental analysis to enhance product quality, managers should pay special attention to quality-related environmental factors. Consumer expectations about product quality, the quality of products offered by competitors, and special technology under development that will enhance the quality of organizational activities are examples of such factors.

Suppliers are often emphasized during environmental analysis by managers who stress quality. Suppliers are those companies that sell materials used in the final assembly of a product by another company. For example, General Motors has many suppliers who furnish the company with parts that are used in the final assembly of GM automobiles. Managers need to keep in mind that the satisfactory performance of a final product will be only as good as the quality of parts obtained from company suppliers. Defective parts from suppliers can result in delayed delivery schedules, reduced sales, and lower productivity. Making a special study of suppliers during the environmental analysis allows managers to identify those suppliers who will help improve product quality by furnishing high-quality parts.

At the Marriott Hotel in Schaumberg, Illinois, Tony Prsyszlak is a "guest services associate" whose job may entail checking guests in or out, fielding questions, or carrying bags. Prsyszlak's red jacket used to signify "doorman," until Marriott began redefining jobs and changing the ways that it hires, trains, and uses employees. These steps are part of a long-range strategy that is aimed at both improving service quality for customers and increasing job satisfaction among workers.

Establishing Organizational Direction and Quality

In this step of the strategic management process, the results of the environmental analysis are used to determine the path that the organization will take in the future. This path is then documented and distributed throughout the organization in the form of a mission statement and related objectives. Assuming that environmental analysis results indicate that product quality is important to the organization, a manager can use the organizational mission statement and its related objectives to give general direction to organization members regarding the focus on product quality.

The following is an example of a mission statement used to encourage total quality by Charles Steinmetz, president of All America, Inc., the largest privately owned pest control company in the United States:[13]

> All America Termite & Pest Control, Inc., operating as Sears Authorized Termite & Pest Control, was founded to provide the residential market a once-a-year pest control service as well as premium termite protection.
>
> The purpose of our company is to provide our customers the highest quality of customer service available in our industry while providing unlimited personal and financial potential to our employees.
>
> We will commit the time, energy, expertise, and resources needed to provide premier customer service. Furthermore, we realize there are no other choices, options, or alternatives in our pursuit of quality.
>
> This requires us to give each customer full value for his or her money and to provide that value the first time and every time we have an opportunity to be of service.
>
> We will resolve any customer problems quickly, whether real and apparent or hidden or imaginary. If for any reason we cannot satisfy any customer, we will stand behind our satisfaction or money-back guarantee.
>
> Our commitment to our employees is no less important. We will provide all employees with the training necessary for them to become proficient at their job as well as proper equipment, safe materials, and a safe working environment.
>
> We will provide ample personal and family benefits to provide reasonable security and offer unlimited compensation, significant opportunity for advancement, and an environment that limits success only by the limits of each employee's hard work, dedication, and capabilities.

A look at how different companies set the direction of their product quality effort reveals that different companies define product quality in very different ways. For example, some companies define it as a stronger product that will last longer, or as a heavier, more durable product. Other companies define product quality as the degree to which a product conforms to design specifications, or as product excellence at an acceptable cost to the company and an acceptable price to the consumer. In still other companies, quality is defined as the degree to which a product meets consumer requirements.

Whatever definition of product quality management decides on, this definition must be communicated to all organization members so they will work together in a focused and efficient way to achieve predetermined product quality.

Strategy Formulation and Quality

After determining organizational direction, the next step in the strategic management process is strategy formulation—deciding what actions should be taken to best deal with competitors. Incorporating product quality into the SWOT (Strengths, Weaknesses, Opportunities, Threats) analysis will help managers develop quality-based strategies. It may, for example, become apparent as a result of a SWOT analysis that organization members are not adequately trained to deal with certain product quality

issues. Obviously, a strategy based on this organizational weakness would be to improve quality-oriented training.[14]

Several management strategies have proved especially successful in improving and maintaining high-quality operations and products. Among them are the following:

- *Value Adding.* All assets and effort should, as far as possible, directly add value to the product or service. All activities, processes, and costs that do not directly add value to the product should, as far as possible, be eliminated because non–value-adding costs are wasteful and can be very costly. This particular strategy is largely responsible for the drastic reductions in staff positions in most large organizations in recent years. For instance, investment analysis does not add value to the product coming off the production line. Therefore, many companies are simplifying their investment strategies and placing greater emphasis on production processes.

- *Leadership.* The traditional vision of "The Boss," whip in hand, *driving* lazy, reluctant workers to ever-higher production goals set from on high by management, is disappearing. In quality-focused organizations, "associates" (no longer called "workers" in many quality-focused organizations) are *led.* Management sets the organizational vision and values, and then works with the associates to perfect the production process.

- *Empowerment.* Associates are organized into self-directed teams and empowered to do their jobs and even to change work processes if that will improve product quality. They are trained, retrained, and cross-trained in a variety of jobs. "Facilitators" (formerly called "supervisors") work with the associates to provide the resources necessary to meet customer needs.

- *Partnering.* The organization establishes "partnerships" with its suppliers and customers—that is, it actively works with them to find ways to improve the quality of its products and services. Management strives to reduce the number of suppliers to only those that can meet two requirements:

  1. Suppliers must prove themselves reliable and cost-effective.
  2. Suppliers must prove the sustained quality of their products.

  Many quality-focused companies formally certify their suppliers.

- *Gathering Correct and Timely Information.* The new global marketplace is exacting and unsympathetic. Managers no longer have the time to wait for indirect traditional financial reports of performance to make the decisions required to compete successfully.

Scott Rohleder is vice president of CRC Products Inc., a food-service equipment and supply distributor. Beginning in 1992, CRC initiated an electric partnering relationship with its biggest customer—the U.S. government. CRC has filed (electronically) a registration form with the government; in turn, CRC has access to government "electronic bid boards" and downloads orders from a private mailbox. CRC saves costs by filling orders earlier, combining orders, and buying inventory at lower prices.

Managers no longer have the time to wade through mountains of tables, reports, and other documents to find the right information. Consequently, in a quality management environment, information systems provide managers with immediate access to critical nonfinancial and financial information, specifically tailored to the needs of the individual manager.

Computerized information systems are especially useful here. Everyone is trained in computers, from executive management through production staff.

Computer terminals are now as commonplace on factory floors as they are in offices.

- *Continuous Improvement and Innovation.* The clarion themes of the quality movement are continuous improvement and constant innovation. Last year's best performance is not good enough today, and today's best practices will not be good enough perhaps even a month from now.

Tom Peters reported in *Thriving on Chaos: Handbook for a Management Revolution* that in 1982 Toyota, the company that established the model for quality in automobile manufacturing, was implementing an average of *5,000* employee suggestions (i.e., improvements) every day. Note that this number does not include improvements initiated by management. Peters advocated, "as a starting point," that U.S. companies target the percentage of revenues stemming from new products and services introduced in the previous 24 months at 50 percent.[15] While these numbers might seem extreme—and they almost certainly are for some companies—they suggest the urgent need to tailor strategic planning to today's rapidly changing and ruthlessly competitive marketplace.

Strategy Implementation and Quality

When the results of environmental analysis indicate that product quality is important to an organization, product quality direction has been established through the organization's mission statement and its related objectives, and a strategy has been developed for achieving or maintaining product quality, management is ready to implement its product quality strategy. Implementation, of course, is putting product quality strategy into action.

This might seem like a straightforward step, but in reality it is quite complex. To succeed at implementing product quality strategy, managers must rise to some serious challenges. First of all, they must be sensitive to the fears and frustrations of employees who have to implement the new strategy. They must then provide the organizational resources necessary to implement the strategy, monitor implementation progress, and create and effectively use a network of individuals throughout the organization who can help overcome implementation barriers.

Two tools managers commonly employ to implement product quality strategy are policies and organization structure. Each of these tools is discussed in the following sections.

Policies for Quality   A policy was defined in Chapter 9 as a standing plan that furnishes broad, general guidelines for channeling management thinking toward taking action consistent with reaching *organizational* objectives. A quality-oriented policy is a special type of policy. A **quality-oriented policy** is a standing plan that furnishes broad, general guidelines for channeling management thinking toward taking action consistent with reaching *quality* objectives.

Quality-oriented policies can be made in virtually any organizational area. They can focus on such issues as the quality of new employees recruited, the quality of plans developed within the organization, the quality of decision-related information gathered and distributed within the organization, the quality of parts purchased from suppliers to be used in the final assembly of products, and the quality of the training used to prepare employees to work in foreign subsidiaries.

A **quality-oriented policy** is a standing plan that furnishes broad, general guidelines for channeling management thinking toward taking action consistent with reaching quality objectives.

Organizing for Quality Improvement   Juran says that "to create a revolutionary rate of quality improvement requires . . . a special organization structure."[16] He suggests organizing a "quality council," consisting largely of upper managers, to direct and coordinate the company's quality improvement efforts.

The quality council's main job is to establish an appropriate infrastructure, which would include:[16]

1. A process for nominating and selecting improvement projects.
2. A process for assigning project improvement teams.
3. A process for making improvements.
4. A variety of resources, such as time for diagnosis and remedy of problems, facilitators to assist in the improvement process, diagnostic support, and training.
5. A process for review of progress.
6. A process for dissemination of results and for recognition.
7. An appropriate employee merit rating system to reward quality improvement.
8. Extension of business planning to include goals for quality improvement.

Juran points out that upper management's role in quality improvement is to get actively involved in every element of the infrastructure—even to the point of serving on some improvement project teams.

Notice also that Juran's structure involves employees at all levels. All employees, including managers, serve on quality improvement teams. True, the quality council itself comprises mostly upper management, but it, too, may include other employees.

Strategic Control and Quality

Strategic control emphasizes monitoring the strategic management process to make sure that it is operating properly. In terms of product quality, strategic control focuses on monitoring company activities to ensure that product quality strategies are operating as planned. In achieving strategic control in the area of product quality, management must measure how successful the organization has become in achieving product quality.

Philip Crosby states that in order to control product quality efforts, management needs to monitor several organizational areas. These areas include management's own understanding of and attitude toward quality, how quality efforts appear to others within the organization, how organizational problems are handled, the cost of quality as a percentage of sales, quality improvement actions taken by management, and how management summarizes the organization's quality position.

According to Crosby, organizations go through five successive stages of quality maturity as they approach the maximum level of quality in all phases of organizational activity:

1. *Uncertainty.* There is no comprehension of quality as a management tool. Problems are fought as they occur, with ad hoc methods.
2. *Awakening.* Quality management is recognized as a valuable tool, but the organization is still unwilling to provide adequate resources to attack quality problems.
3. *Enlightenment.* A quality improvement program is established. Top management becomes committed to the concept and implements all the steps necessary for the organization to face problems openly and resolve them in an orderly manner.
4. *Wisdom.* Management now thoroughly understands quality management. Quality problems are identified early, and employees are encouraged to suggest improvements to prevent defects from occurring.
5. *Certainty.* Quality management has become an essential part of the organization's system. Problems are almost always prevented, and quality improvement is a continuous activity.

BACK TO THE CASE One of the key strategies for quality improvement is the elimination, so far as possible, of every task, activity, cost, or other element of the business that does not directly add value to the product. IOMEGA Corporation discovered early in its quality improvement efforts several non–value-adding—and therefore cost- and time-adding—activities in its production process.

Storage of inventories was a particular nuisance to IOMEGA's quality improvement program. Storage costs included those for warehouse space, inventory management, warehouse employees, security, handling damage, and obsolescence. Consequently, IOMEGA began producing almost entirely products for which it had firm orders. This allowed the company to ship immediately, thereby avoiding inventory costs. In addition, by speeding up the production cycle, the company found it could further reduce its work-in-process inventories. The result was a 75 percent reduction in inventories and a 41 percent reduction in plant space.

THE QUALITY IMPROVEMENT PROCESS

Two approaches may be taken to improve quality. The first is the one advocated by most of the quality experts, including Deming, Juran, Crosby, and Feigenbaum. This process can be described as "incremental improvement"—or improve one thing at a time. Actually, many incremental improvements may be undertaken simultaneously throughout an organization; recall Toyota's average of instituting 5,000 improvements per day in 1982.

The second approach, advocated by Michael Hammer, consists of completely reengineering a process.[17] This approach requires starting with a clean slate. Management looks at operations and asks, "If we were to start over today, how would we do this?"

Each approach is discussed in detail in the following sections.

The Incremental Improvement Process

Researchers and consultants have advocated a variety of incremental approaches to achieving excellent quality in products and processes. Despite their differences, almost all of these plans bear some remarkable similarities. Although a specific improvement process may not precisely follow the outline in Figure 22.3, most such processes at least approximate it.

- *Step 1: An area of improvement is chosen, which often is called the improvement "theme."* Either management or an improvement team may choose the theme. Examples are:

  - A reduction in production cycle time.
  - An increase in the percentage of nondefective units produced.
  - A reduction in the variability of raw material going into production.
  - An increase in on-time deliveries.
  - A reduction in machine downtime.
  - A reduction in employee absenteeism.

  Many other examples are possible, of course, but these suffice to make the point that an improvement objective must be chosen.

  Consider a pizza company whose delivery business is lagging behind that of its competitors, chiefly because of slow deliveries. The improvement theme in this case may be a reduction in delivery time (i.e., cycle time).

- *Step 2: If a quality improvement team has not already been organized, one is organized.* Members of this team might include:

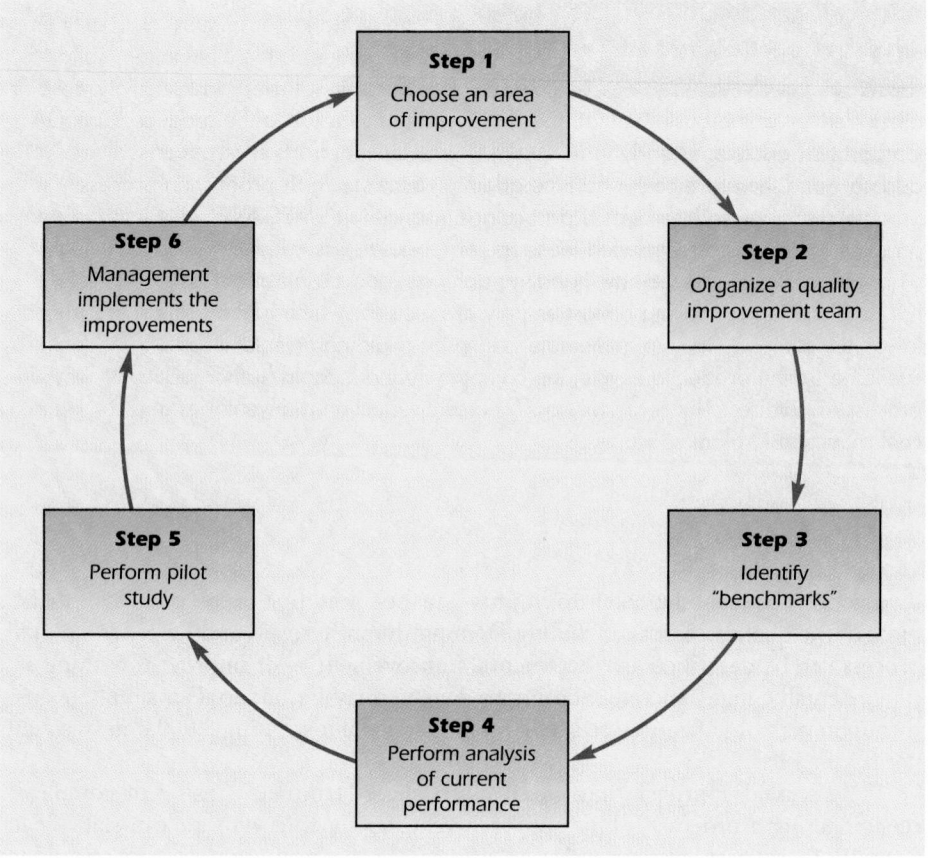

Figure 22.3   **The incremental approach to improving quality**

- One or more associates directly responsible for the work being done.
- One or more customers receiving the benefits of the work.
- One or more suppliers providing input into the work.
- A member of management.
- Perhaps one or more experts in areas particularly relevant to solving the problem and making the improvement.

    For the pizza delivery company, the team might include two pizza builders, a driver, a university student customer, a local resident customer, and a store manager.

- *Step 3: The team "benchmarks" the best performers—that is, identifies how much improvement is required in order to match the very best performance.* For example, the pizza company may discover in this step that the benchmark (i.e., the fastest average time between the moment an order is taken until the moment of front-door delivery) established by a competitor is 20 minutes.

    Suppose the company's current average delivery performance is 35 minutes. That leaves a minimum possible improvement of 15 minutes on the average.

- *Step 4: The team performs an analysis to find out how current performance can be improved to meet, or beat, the benchmark.* Factors to be analyzed here include potential problems related to equipment, materials, work methods, people, and the environmental, such as legal constraints, physical conditions, and weather. To return to the pizza delivery company, suppose the team discovered that the pizza-building process could be shortened by 4 minutes. Also suppose they found an average lag of 5 minutes between the time the pizza is ready and the time the delivery van picks it up. Finally, suppose the team discovered that a different oven could shorten cooking time by 7 minutes. Total

potential savings in delivery time, then, would be 16 minutes—which would beat the benchmark by 1 minute.

- *Step 5: The team performs a pilot study to test the selected remedies to the problem.* In the pizza case, suppose the team conducted a pilot program for a month, during which the new pizza-building process was implemented, a new driver and van were added, and a new oven was rented. At the end of the month, suppose actual improvement was 17 minutes on average.

  The question then becomes, Is the improvement worth the cost? In this case, the improved pizza-building process is improving other customer service as well, thereby increasing the company's overall sales capacity. By beating the benchmark, the company can establish a new delivery system standard—a significant marketing advantage. Suppose, then, that a cost/benefit study favors the changes.

- *Step 6: Management implements the improvements.*

Making many such incremental improvements can greatly enhance a company's competitiveness. Of course, as more and more companies achieve better and better quality, the market will become more and more demanding. The key, therefore, is to continually improve both product and process.

This section discussed the incremental improvement process in organizations in general terms. The following PEOPLE PERSPECTIVES feature provides insights about how to keep organization members involved in incremental improvement by discussing a very successful incremental improvement process at Bearings, Inc.

KEEPING PEOPLE INVOLVED IN INCREMENTAL IMPROVEMENT: BEARINGS, INC.

PEOPLE PERSPECTIVES

For over three years, operations at Bearings, Inc., have steadily improved as a result of a specially designed incremental improvement program. The program is both simple and effective. Bearings employees are asked to submit ideas for improving company operations, and ideas found to be worthwhile by management are implemented. What began as management's desire to informally solicit unedited ideas from the people who actually do the work has evolved into a program that steadily produces a swell of suggestions— one of which has trimmed $900,000 from the cost of running the program itself.

During the initial phase of the program, employees were simply invited to write down their ideas for improving company operations and to submit them to management. As the program became more formal, ideas were collected and printed in a quarterly report called *Quality Idea Briefs* and sent for review to over 4,000 organization members. Ideas presented in this report have focused on issues ranging from increasing customer satisfaction and sales to decreasing the cost of operations and the time it takes to manufacture bearings.

Submissions to *Quality Idea Briefs* have nearly tripled since the program began— in one recent year, over 8,000 ideas were submitted by workers. Bearings' success in getting workers to participate in the improvement program can probably be credited to the care management takes to inform workers of the exact status of their submitted ideas. Nearly 35 percent of all the ideas that made it into *Quality Idea Briefs* have been transformed into operating policy, and the workers who submitted the other 65 percent have been apprised of the reasons their ideas could not be implemented. Bearings workers feel proud when their ideas are accepted for implementation, and respected when management takes the time to explain to them why their ideas are inappropriate.≈

Reengineering Improvements

Hammer argues that significant improvement requires "breaking away from . . . outdated rules and . . . assumptions. . . ." It demands a complete rethinking of operations. He, too, recommends that management organize a team representing the functional units involved in the process to be reengineered, as well as other units that depend upon the process.

One important reason for reengineering instead of attempting incremental improvements is the need to integrate computerized production and information systems. This is an expensive change, and one that is very difficult to accomplish piecemeal through an incremental approach.

Hammer outlines seven principles of reengineering:

*   ***Principle 1.** Organize around outcomes, not tasks.*   Traditionally, work has been organized around different tasks, such as sawing, typing, assembling, and supervising. This first principle of reengineering would, instead, have one person or team performing all the steps in an identified process. The person or team would be responsible for the outcome of the total process.
*   ***Principle 2.** Have those who use the output of the process perform the process.*   For example, a production department may do its own purchasing, and even its own cost accounting. This principle would require a broader range of expertise from individuals and teams, and a greater integration of activities.
*   ***Principle 3.** Subsume information-processing work into the real work that produces the information.*   Modern computer technology now makes it possible for a work process to process information simultaneously. For example, scanners at checkout counters in grocery stores both process customer purchases and update accounting and inventory records at the same time.
*   ***Principle 4.** Treat geographically dispersed resources as though they were centralized.*   Hammer uses Hewlett-Packard as an example of how this principle works. Each of the company's 50 manufacturing units had its own purchasing department, which prevented the company from achieving the benefits of scale discounts. Rather than centralize purchasing, which would have reduced responsiveness to local manufacturing needs, Hewlett-Packard introduced a corporate unit to coordinate local purchases, so that scale discounts could be achieved. That way, local purchasing units retained their decentralized authority and preserved their local responsiveness.
*   ***Principle 5.** Link parallel activities instead of integrating their results.*   Several processes are often required to produce products and services. Too often, though, companies segregate these processes so that the product comes together only at the final stage. Meanwhile, problems may occur in one or more processes, and those problems may not become apparent until too late, at the final step. It is better, Hammer says, to coordinate the various processes so that such problems are avoided.
*   ***Principle 6.** Put the decision point where the work is performed and build control into the process.*   Traditional bureaucracies separate decision authority from the work. This principle suggests that the people doing the work are the ones who should make the decisions about that work. The salesperson should have the authority and responsibility to approve credit, for example. This principle saves time and allows the organization to respond more effectively and efficiently to customer needs.

    Some managers worry that this principle will reduce control over the process. However, control can be built into the process. In the example cited, criteria for credit approval can be built into a computer program, so the salesperson has guidance for every credit decision.
*   ***Principle 7.** Capture information once and at the source.*   Computerized on-line databases help make this principle achievable. It is now easy to collect information when it originates, store it, and send it to those who need it.

Since 1992, designers at Compaq Computer's Houston headquarters have participated in the company's radical change in the way it addresses its markets. Marketing information had told Compaq strategists two things: (1) its products were hard to find and (2) there were a lot of buyers for computers besides corporations. Consequently, Compaq added thousands of retailers (like Wal-Mart) and transformed itself into a maker of machines for every consumer market. Since rethinking its marketing process, Compaq has more than doubled its share of the $35 billion annual computer market.

Reengineering allows major improvements to be made all at once. While reengineering can be an expensive way to improve quality, today's rapidly changing markets sometimes demand such a drastic response.[18]

BACK TO THE CASE   OMEGA management adopted W. Edwards Deming's general approach to continuous improvement. This approach is sometimes called the Deming Cycle—although actually Deming adopted it from Walter A. Shewhart, who introduced statistical quality control techniques back in the 1930s.

The approach has four stages:

1. *Plan* what improvement needs to be made and how to do it.
2. *Do* the plan on a small scale to see if it works.
3. *Check* the results.
4. *Act*—that is, implement the indicated improvements in the process; or plan, do, and check again until such improvements are indicated.

This process is called a cycle because it is to be done over and over again. IOMEGA applies the Deming Cycle to all improvement activities, whether in production, accounting, marketing, or elsewhere in the company. Management attributes much of the company's dramatic turnaround to the "turning of the Deming Cycle."

Action Summary

Reread the learning objectives below. Each objective is followed by questions. Answering these questions accurately will help you to retain most important concepts discussed in this chapter. After answering each question, check your answer against the answer key at the end of the chapter. (*Hint:* If you have any doubts regarding the correct response, consult the page whose number follows the answer.)

Circle: From studying this chapter, I will attempt to acquire:

1. An understanding of the relationship between quality and total quality management.

T,F   **a.** Overall, product quality and total quality management are the same.

a,b,c,d,e   **b.** A TQM program is *not* characterized by: (a) a continual process; (b) efforts by all organization members; (c) a focus on only a few critical work activities; (d) a focus on the production process; (e) efforts to involve organization members.

2. An appreciation for the importance of quality.

T,F   **a.** High product quality can result in reduced costs but generally not increased market share.

T,F   **b.** Increasing product quality can reduce product liability costs for an organization.

3. Insights about how to achieve quality.

a,b,c,d,e   a. According to Crosby, in order to achieve quality, an organization must implement critical ingredients relating to: (a) integrity; (b) systems; (c) communications; (d) operations; (e) all of the above.

T,F   b. According to Deming, a company can improve its product quality by choosing suppliers based on quality rather than on price alone.

T,F   c. According to Juran, a company can improve its product quality by focusing on the quality of the organization as a whole as well as the quality of individual departments.

a,b,c,d,e   d. According to Shingo, *poka yoke* means: (a) production; (b) mistake-proofing; (c) worker commitment; (d) quality; (e) diversity.

T,F   e. According to Feigenbaum, defects are unacceptable only on the manufacturing floor.

4. An understanding of how strategic planning can be used to promote quality.

T,F   a. Establishing an appropriate mission statement is important for achieving quality.

T,F   b. Establishing and using appropriate policies and organization structure are important steps in quality-oriented strategy formulation.

5. Knowledge about the quality improvement process and reengineering.

T,F   a. The incremental improvement approach involves improving one thing at a time.

a,b,c,d,e   b. The following is a principle of the reengineering approach to improving quality: (a) organize around outcomes; (b) link parallel activities; (c) put decision points where the work is performed; (d) capture information at the source; (e) all are principles of reengineering for quality.

Introductory Case Wrap-Up

"IOMEGA Corporation: Success Built on Continuous Improvement" (p. 541) and its related back-to-the-case sections were written to help you better understand the management concepts contained in this chapter. Answer the following discussion questions about this introductory case to enrich your understanding of the chapter content:

1. Should a successful quality improvement program at IOMEGA be viewed as an improvement in the company's social performance? If not, why not? If so, how?

2. Does application of the Deming Cycle ensure IOMEGA's competitiveness in the future?

3. Given IOMEGA's success with an incremental improvement approach, what, if any, circumstances do you think would call for using a reengineering approach?

Issues for Review and Discussion

1. What is the difference between product quality and total quality management (TQM)?

2. Is a successful TQM program important to an organization? Explain.

3. Discuss three benefits resulting from the achievement of high product quality.

4. What guidelines does Crosby offer organizations that want to achieve quality?

5. What guidelines does Deming offer on achieving quality?

6. What guidelines does Juran offer on achieving quality?

7. What guidelines does Shingo offer on achieving quality?

8. Discuss how establishing organizational direction as part of the strategic management process can be used to raise the chances of success of a product quality effort.

9. Can quality be a significant component of a company's strategy? Explain.

10. Discuss the significance of policies and organization structure as components of an effort to maintain product quality.

11. Using Crosby's "five successive stages of quality maturity" as a basis, how would you control TQM efforts in an organization?

12. Discuss how the strategies of partnering and empowerment can improve quality within an organization.

13. When organizing for quality, which structural changes would you anticipate would make the greatest contributions to achieving total quality?

14. Under which circumstances would you use the incremental improvement process to improve quality?

15. Under which circumstances would you use the reengineering approach to improve quality?

16. Discuss Hammer's principles of reengineering for improvement.

17. Would you be concerned with workforce diversity in a program aimed at enhancing product quality? Why or why not? If you would be concerned, what actions would you take?

Action Summary Answer Key

1. a. F, p. 542
   b. c, pp. 542–543
2. a F, pp. 543–544
   b. T, pp. 543–544

3. a. e, p. 545
   b. T, pp. 545–547
   c. T, pp. 547–548
   d. b, p. 548
   e. F, p. 549

4. a. T, p. 551
   b. F, pp. 551–553

5. a. T, pp. 555–557
   b. e, p. 558

Case Study

Total Quality Management: Learning to Make It Work

Many U.S. companies, mostly manufacturers, adopted the total quality management (TQM) concept in the 1980s in order to compete with Japanese manufacturers. Now, however, more and more of them have begun to reassess their approach. This apparent change of heart does not mean that TQM programs have failed to show dramatic improvements in the overall quality of U.S. products and services. Rather, it means that some firms have simply reconsidered full commitment to what is often a lengthy ongoing process.

Things have changed since W. Edwards Deming and Joseph Juran first proposed their classic quality models in the 1950s. For example, although improved financial performance was not necessarily TQM's original goal, it certainly was a desirable side effect. Today's shareholders not only demand short-term results in company profitability, but also ask for a return on the firm's quality investment. "Quality management is hard to do," says Fred Smith, CEO of Federal Express, a Baldrige Quality Award winner. "It takes a long time and constant reiteration, and every kind of management effort to keep it on track."

Contemporary quality management proponents argue that company operations can and should be improved continuously and that "quality" is, by definition, a long-term, never-ending commitment. In addition, the spectrum of managerial response to TQM varies widely. While there have been hundreds of successful cases in support of TQM, there are also many documented stories in which upper management simply misunderstood the commitment needed to implement a successful program. Other managers were too engrossed in implementing TQM policies and procedures to consider either the firm's overall profitability or the real meaning of "quality management." For example, according to *Business Week* magazine, managers at Varian Associates Inc., a Silicon Valley–based scientific-equipment manufacturer, "went about virtually reinventing the way it did business. But while Varian thought it was playing quality by the book, the final chapter did not feature the happy ending the company expected." Obsessed with meeting production schedules, for instance, the staff in the vacuum equipment department did not bother to return customers' phone calls.

TQM advocates contend that Varian managers failed to commit themselves to learning how to focus on quality. Phil Scanlan, vice president for corporate quality at AT&T, agrees. He compares learning quality management with learning how to use a personal computer: "I felt like learning was a problem that takes [time] away from doing the work," he recalls. "After I learned it, I used the PC to do the work. If you see [quality] as something you have to do instead of real work, then you don't get it."

Although less well-known than Deming and Juran, brothers Val and Don Feigenbaum focus on the nitty-gritty details of making quality work. Engineers by profession, the Feigenbaums are considered TQM's hands-on implementers. Their goal, they say, is to drive "failure costs" out of operations. *Failure costs* are the aggregate costs of failing to do things right. "Eliminating one inefficiency, a defect or an excessively complex process, reduces total product costs," notes Val. "Less money is spent on inspection, complaints, and product service, for instance." Moreover, observes Feigenbaum, as you reduce failure costs, "by definition you improve customer satisfaction." The Feigenbaums estimate that failure costs average 25 percent of gross sales in most major American companies. (At world-class companies, they are no more than 10 percent.)

For example, failure costs at Tenneco Inc. were running at 22 percent or about $2.9 billion, during the 1980s. In one decision, the Feigenbaums actually found that the company wasted 20 percent to 40 percent of the material used in manufacturing auto parts. Merely changing the way raw goods were fed into the machines eliminated the waste. Since 1991, Tenneco has cut a total of $1.8 billion in failure costs, resulting in an extra $900 million in operating income.

Depending on the level of management commit-

ment, TQM may or may not satisfy upper-management and stockholder expectations of increased market share, sales, and profits. According to at least one analyst, "It is difficult to correlate TQM with those benefits. While the notion of increasing sales by offering high-quality products and services seemed reasonable, no models were developed within TQM to determine what effect, if any, improved product quality had on sales." In other areas, too, TQM was plagued by problems with management focus, and many TQM problems were simply not implemented in areas that would yield meaningful results. Invalid conclusions were often made because improvement priorities were driven by personal assumptions rather than by outside feedback.

Because many companies neglected to integrate effective customer-satisfaction research into the TQM process, managers could not identify effective customer expectations or weigh their priorities in responding to customer demands. In other words, because quality improvement was largely focused on the *product*, the intangible factors that influenced a purchase decision often went unnoticed.

The lesson, say TQM advocates, is sometimes learned the hard way, but it is worth learning: In order for companies to become successful in implementing TQM programs, managers must not only appraise operations systems but also figure out ways to meet the high expectations from two very demanding key constituencies—company shareholders and customers.

Questions:

1. Based on the information in this case study, would you argue that the failure of TQM programs is in some way inherent in the process itself? Why or why not? Is there any way to ensure successful implementation? Explain.
2. Apply Crosby's vaccination serum for preventing poor total quality management to "cure" one of the companies described. In which area(s) do you believe the company might need the greatest help? Why?

Issues for Review and Discussion

Make a plan to improve total quality in your academic work. Base your plan on either an incremental improvement process or a reengineering process. Be ready to describe and explain your plan. Specifically, what quality improvements do you want to see? Can you expect quality improvements even in areas you cannot change directly? Challenge: Implement your plan and continue to evaluate the process.

The Internet learning materials that accompany this chapter can be found at
http://www.profcerto.com
Additional information can be found on the inside front and back covers of this text.

23
chapter

MANAGEMENT AND DIVERSITY

STUDENT LEARNING OBJECTIVES

From studying this chapter, I will attempt to acquire:

1. A definition of diversity and an understanding of its importance in the corporate structure.
2. An understanding of the advantages of having a diverse workforce.
3. An awareness of the challenges facing managers within a diverse workforce.
4. An understanding of the strategies for promoting diversity in organizations.
5. Insights into the role of the manager in promoting diversity in the organization.

CHAPTER OUTLINE

Ortho Pharmaceutical: "Showcase" for Cultural Diversity

Few companies can match the cultural diversity record of Ortho Pharmaceutical. This company, part of Johnson & Johnson's $4 billion pharmaceutical manufacturing sector, produces, distributes, and markets women's health-care products, such as Ortho-Novum™ contraceptives and Retin-A™ skin ointment. Ortho is also "the most progressive client" of Elsie Cross, of Elsie Y. Cross Associates, a well-known diversity consultant. In fact, Ortho has become her diversity "showcase for the how and why of corporate culture change."

Currently, women and minorities at Ortho Pharmaceutical are being promoted in numbers representative of their numbers within the general workforce. According to a 1992 article in the *Los Angeles Times Magazine*, women hold 25 percent of management positions at Ortho, up from 22 percent in the year prior to the start of the corporate diversity program. Similarly, African-Americans in managerial positions have increased from 6 percent to 13 percent, while all minorities jumped from 10 percent representation within managerial ranks to 18 percent. Although white males still hold a significant 63 percent of top positions at the company, Ortho's record of upward mobility for women and minorities is impressive.

Ortho Pharmaceutical's move toward diversity began when the company contacted the consulting firm of Elsie Y. Cross Associates in 1986. At that time, Gary Parlin, a white male, was Ortho's president. In spite of the affirmative action policies that were in place, Ortho had difficulty retaining women and minority employees. Moreover, the financial costs of such high turnover were extensive. Parlin worked with Cross and her staff to implement an organizational development assessment of the company's systems. Their assessment revealed that white males felt comfortable about their futures in the company, while women and minorities felt stifled and ignored and saw little opportunity for advancement.

The assessment also showed that company recruiters were not seeking a diverse pool of candidates. Once hired, women and minorities received little of the feedback, mentoring, or promotions made available to their white male counterparts. After collaborating with the Cross firm and implementing an extensive planned-change effort, management has found that employees now speak very differently of their experiences in the company. After six years, a black marketing research manager at Ortho was able to say, "This is a safe harbor. . . . Here I can be myself. I can say what I like, do what I like. I can disagree with people. At other companies, just to disagree meant political suicide." The kind of qualitative cultural changes referred to by this manager would be a plus for any corporation.

Although progress has been made, only one woman and one person of color currently sit on the board of directors, the company's top policymaking body. Responding to these concerns, an Ortho spokesperson said, "What we do here isn't easy. But if you value differences among people, incorporate those differences into the team, and then reward the team, change happens. Never fast enough, but it happens nonetheless."

Diversity is valuable to an organization because it enables the organization to draw on all the rich contributions that a multicultural workforce has to offer and enlarges the pool of information available for making decisions.

what's ahead

How will the increasing diversity of the U.S. workforce affect the responsibilities of managers? Is the importance of diversity exaggerated in contemporary management writing? Or can managers expect to play an ever-increasing role in the kinds of activities already occurring at Ortho Pharmaceutical? This chapter will help managers understand the challenges that a diverse workforce poses for American businesses. It examines the following topics:

1. The definition and social implications of diversity.
2. Advantages of diversity in organizations.
3. Challenges confronting managers who work with diverse populations.
4. Managerial strategies for promoting diversity in organizations.
5. The role of the manager in promoting effective workforce diversity.

DEFINING DIVERSITY

Diversity refers to characteristics of individuals that shape their identities and the experiences they have in society. This chapter provides information about workforce diversity and discusses the strengths and problems of a diverse workforce. Understanding diversity is essential for managers today because managing diversity will undoubtedly constitute a large portion of the management agenda throughout the 1990s and well into the next century.[1]

This chapter describes some strategies for promoting social diversity in organizations. It also explains how diversity is related to the four management functions. Given the nature of this topic, you will find it necessary to integrate information you learned from other chapters into what is presented here. For example, you will need to consider the legal foundation for developing an inclusive workforce—affirmative action and Equal Employment Opportunity (EEO), discussed in Chapter 12, and ideas about organizational change, discussed in Chapter 17—as you study this chapter material.

Diversity is the degree of basic human differences among a given population. Major areas of diversity are gender, race, ethnicity, religion, social class, physical ability, sexual orientation, and age.

The Social Implications of Diversity

Workforce diversity is not a new issue in the United States. People from various other regions and cultures have been immigrating to these shores since colonial times, so the American population has always been a heterogeneous mix of races, ethnicities, religions, social classes, physical abilities, and sexual orientations.[2] These differences—along with the basic human differences of age and gender—comprise diversity. The purpose of exploring diversity issues in a management textbook is to suggest how managers might include diverse employees equally, accepting their differences and utilizing their talents.

Majority and Minority Groups

Managers must understand the relationship between two groups in organizations: majority groups and minority groups. The term **majority group** refers to that group of people in the organization who hold most of the positions that command decision-making power, control of resources and information, and access to system rewards. Note that the majority is not *always* the group with a numerical majority. The term **minority group** refers to that group of people in the organization who are smaller in number or who lack critical power, resources, acceptance, and social status. Together, the minority and majority group members form the entire social system of the organization.

Note that the minority group is not *always* lesser in number than the majority group. For example, women are seen as a minority group in most organizations because they do not have the critical power to shape organizational decisions and to control resources. Moreover, they have yet to achieve full acceptance and social status in

Majority group refers to that group of people in the organization who hold most of the positions that command decision-making power, control of resources and information, and access to system rewards.

Minority group refers to that group of people in the organization who are smaller in number or who possess fewer granted rights and lower status than the majority groups.

most workplaces. In most health-care organizations, for instance, women outnumber men. Although men are numerical minorities, however, they are seldom denied social status because white males hold most positions of power in the health-care system hierarchy, such as physician and health-care administrator.

ADVANTAGES OF DIVERSITY IN ORGANIZATIONS

Managers are becoming more dedicated to seeking a wide range of talents from every group in American culture because they now realize that there are distinct advantages to doing so.[3] For one thing, as you learned in Chapter 17, group decisions often improve the quality of decision making. For another, work groups or teams that can draw on the contributions of a multicultural membership gain the advantage of a larger pool of information and a richer array of approaches to work problems.

Ann Morrison carried out a comprehensive study of 16 private and public organizations in the United States. In the resulting book, *The New Leaders: Guidelines on Leadership Diversity in America*, she outlines the several other advantages of diversity, each of which is discussed here.[4]

Gaining and Keeping Market Share

Managers today must understand increasingly diverse markets. Failure to discern customers' preferences can cost a company business in the United States and abroad. Some people argue that one of the best ways to ensure that the organization is able to penetrate diverse markets is to include diverse managers among the organization's decision makers.[5]

Diversity in the managerial ranks has the further advantage of enhancing company credibility with customers. A manager who is of the same gender or ethnic background as customers may imply to those customers that their day-to-day experiences will be understood. One African-American female manager found that her knowledge of customers paid off when she convinced her company to change the name of a product it intended to sell at Wal-Mart. "I knew that I had shopped for household goods at Wal-Mart, whereas the CEO of this company, a white, upper-middle-class male, had not. He listened to me and we changed the name of the product."

Morrison cites a case in which one company lost an important opportunity for new business in a southwestern city's predominantly Hispanic community. The lucrative business ultimately went to a competitor that had put a Hispanic manager in charge of the project, who solicited input from the Hispanic community.

The information in this section indicates that a diverse workforce provides an organization with the potential advantage of gaining and keeping a higher market share. The following PEOPLE PERSPECTIVES feature describes how one bank encouraged minority workers to maximize their potential so that the bank could achieve better customer relations.

THE BANK OF MONTREAL ENCOURAGES MINORITY WORKERS TO MAXIMIZE POTENTIAL: GAINING ADVANTAGE WITH CUSTOMERS

PEOPLE PERSPECTIVES

The Bank of Montreal recently held comprehensive discussions to discover feasible ideas for gaining a competitive edge in its market. One idea—encouraging the hiring and promotion of employees who could relate to a diverse group of customers better than the employees of competitive banks could—quickly rose to the top of the idea list. Thus man-

agement committed the Bank of Montreal to a program designed to encourage minority employees to maximize their potential in the hope that their understanding of the bank's diverse customer base would positively influence operations at all levels.

Matthew Barrett, chairman of the bank, and Tony Comper, its president, implemented a strategic plan that committed the Bank of Montreal to give all employees an equal opportunity to reach their career potential. Specifically, the plan required that the bank define various minority employee groups that needed further development, discover and eliminate any barriers blocking their upward mobility, and change the corporate culture to one that actively encouraged the aspirations of minority employees. Initially, the bank targeted employees who were female, disabled, natives of Montreal, and members of racial and ethnic minorities. As a result of this plan, the Bank of Montreal has become a banking industry model for developing minority employees and gaining the related advantage of better customer relations.≈

Cost Savings

Companies incur high costs in recruiting, training, relocating, and replacing employees and in providing competitive compensation packages. According to Morrison, Corning Corporation's high turnover among women and people of color was costing the company an estimated $2 million to $4 million a year. Many managers questioned for her study felt that the personnel expenses associated with turnover—often totaling as much as two-thirds of an organization's budget—could be cut by instituting diversity practices that would give nontraditional managers more incentive to stay. When nontraditional managers remain with the organization, nontraditional employees at lower levels feel more committed to the company.

In addition to the personnel costs, executives are distressed by the high legal fees and staggering settlements resulting from lawsuits brought by employees who felt they had been discriminated against. For example, $17.65 million in damages was awarded to a woman employed by Texaco who claimed she had been passed over for a management promotion because of her gender. Executives are learning that such sums would be better spent on promoting diversity.

Increased Productivity and Innovation

Many executives quoted in Morrison's study believe productivity is higher in organizations that focus on diversity. These managers have found that employees who feel valued, competent, and at ease in their work setting enjoy coming to work and perform at a high level.

Morrison also cites a study by Donna Thompson and Nancy DiTomaso that concluded that a multicultural approach has a positive effect on employees' perception of equity. This, in turn, positively affects employees' morale, goal setting, effort, and performance. The managers in Morrison's study also saw innovation as a strength of a diverse workforce.

Better-Quality Management

Morrison also found that including nontraditional employees in fair competition for advancement usually improves the quality of management by providing a wider pool of talent. According to the research she cites, exposure to diverse colleagues helps managers develop breadth and openness.

The quality of management can also be improved by building more effective personnel policies and practices that, once developed, will benefit all employees in the organization, not just minorities. According to Morrison's study, many of the programs

Table 23.1

Advantages of a Diverse Workforce

- Improved ability to gain and keep market share.
- Cost savings.
- Increased productivity.
- A more innovative workforce.
- Minority and women employees who are more motivated.
- Better quality of managers.
- Employees who have internalized the message that "different" does not mean "less than."
- Employees who are accustomed to making use of differing worldviews, learning styles, and approaches in the decision-making process and in the cultivation of new ideas.
- Employees who have developed multicultural competencies, such as learning to recognize, surface, discuss, and work through work-related issues pertaining to global, cultural, or intergroup differences.
- A workforce that is more resilient when faced with change.

initially developed for nontraditional managers resulted in improvements that were later successfully applied throughout the organization. Ideas such as adding training for mentors, upgrading techniques for developing managers, and improving processes for evaluating employees for promotion—all concepts originally intended to help nontraditional managers—were later adopted for wider use. (See Table 23.1 for more information on the advantages of a diverse workforce.)

BACK TO THE CASE A company that uses the diverse talents of a multicultural workforce to its advantage benefits along with the workers. Some experts believe that one of the best ways for a company to capture diverse markets is to make sure its decision makers are a diverse group. For example, health-care products such as Ortho Pharmaceutical's contraceptives may require varied marketing strategies to sell successfully in different cultures. By promoting decision makers who are sensitive to different cultural attitudes about contraceptives, Ortho stands a better chance of establishing product and marketing strategies attractive to various groups.

Patricia Bush joined Polaroid Corporation when she graduated from college in 1979. She is now a project manager. While many companies are still working on ways to bring in more minority managers, organizations like Polaroid are focusing on ways to keep, develop, and best "utilize" those, like Patricia Bush, that they already have. For example, a team composed of senior African-American managers serves as an advocacy group, and capable minority employees are given positions with visibility and genuine authority.

As it makes progress in its diversity program, Ortho Pharmaceutical can expect its productivity to increase, because workers who feel valued, competent, and at ease in their work setting will perform better than workers who feel the organization has little respect for their efforts. Moreover, by providing training that encourages nontraditional managers to remain with the organization, Ortho Pharmaceutical can expect to lower its personnel costs for recruiting, training, and replacing nontraditional employees.

GENERAL ELECTRIC VALUES GLOBAL SENSITIVITY

DIVERSITY SPOTLIGHT

General Electric Aircraft Company has promoted specific values to indicate what management views as effective leadership. According to these guidelines, effective leaders should "have the capacity to develop global brains and global sensitivity." In keeping with this appreciation of global diversity, the company has developed diversity training sessions for all employees.

One especially innovative approach developed by General Electric Aircraft is a program titled "Leveraging Differences (Cultural Diversity)." This program, which utilizes an Interactive Video Disk (IVD), consists of the following five components:

1. An introduction explains how a company evolves from "homogeneous, to assimilative, to heterogeneous, and finally to multicultural."
2. "Walk a Mile in My Shoes" focuses on problems women face in the workplace.
3. "Something I've Always Wanted to Ask You People" gives trainees a chance to express their curiosity about members of other groups, specifically Asians, African-Americans, Hispanics, and women.
4. "You Decide" presents the trainee with a variety of problem-solving situations that have implications for diversity.
5. A summary, with closing remarks by John Rittenhouse, General Electric's senior vice president.

The strengths of this program on IVD are that the components are easily understandable by a wide range of employees, available for use on company time, and require responses from employees. "Leveraging Differences (Cultural Diversity)" reflects management's leadership values statement, which includes the following goals: selecting "the most talented team members available"; fully utilizing people "regardless of race, gender, ethnic origin, culture, or age"; and learning to see "the priority of all aspects of diversity to business success."≈

CHALLENGES THAT MANAGERS FACE IN WORKING WITH DIVERSE POPULATIONS

As you have seen, there are compelling reasons for an organization to encourage diversity in its workforce. For managers to fully appreciate the implications of promoting diversity, however, they must understand some of the challenges they face in managing a diverse workforce. Changing demographics and several issues arising out of these changes are discussed in the following sections.

Changing Demographics

Demographics, defined in Chapter 8 as the statistical characteristics of a population, are an important tool managers use to study workforce diversity. According to *Workforce 2000: Work and Workers for the Twenty-First Century*, a report done for the United States Department of Labor by the Hudson Institute, the workforce and jobs of the future will parallel changes in society and in the economy.

This report, published in 1987, projects that the following five demographic facts will be "most important" by the year 2000:[6]

1. The population and the workforce will grow more slowly than at any time since the 1930s.
2. The average age of the population and the workforce will rise, and the pool of young workers entering the labor market will shrink.
3. More women will enter the workforce.
4. Minorities will make up a larger share of new entrants into the labor force.
5. Immigrants will represent the largest share of the increase in both the general population and the workforce.

Note how this study emphasizes the growth of nonwhites, women, immigrants, and older workers within the U.S. workforce. Figure 23.1 shows the distribution of new entrants in the labor force based on these demographic patterns.

AT&T CONNECTS THE WORLD

GLOBAL SPOTLIGHT

AT&T offers five consumer services to travelers and consumers living outside the United States: AT&T USADirect, AT&T World Connect, AT&T USADirect Service In-Language, AT&T Calling Card, and AT&T TeleTicket Service. The oldest service, USADirect, introduced in 1985, allows users to save on cost when calling the United States from 113 different countries. The newest service, USADirect Service In-Language, is offered to residents in 16 countries. Consumers using this service can make calls to the United States through operators who speak their languages. Both services are drawing more

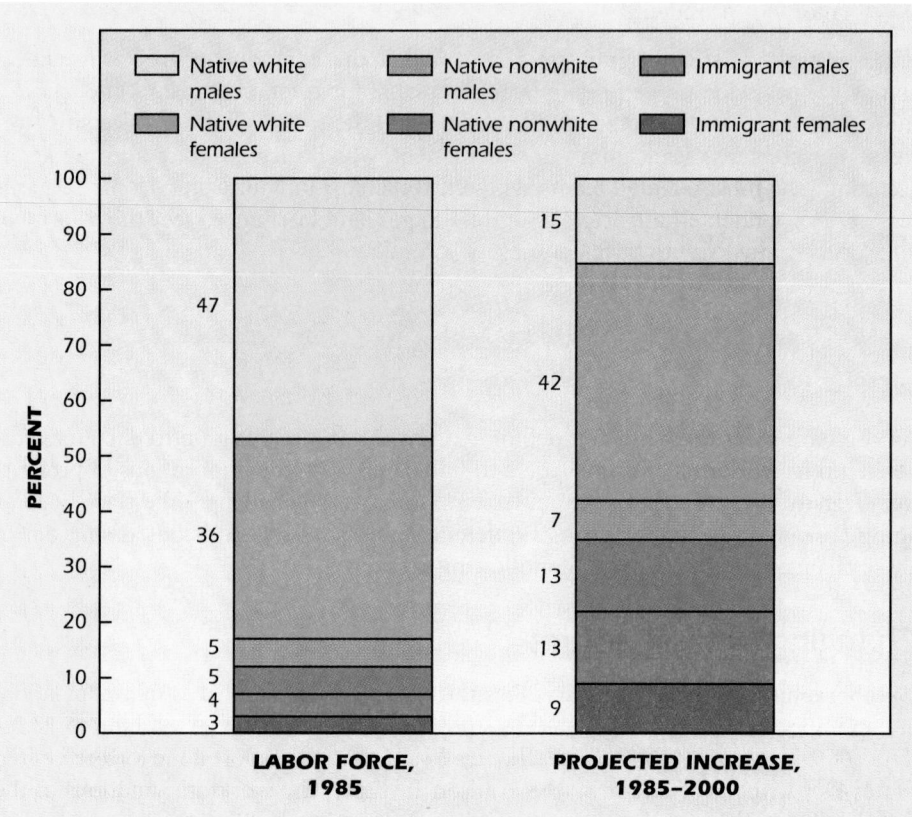

Figure 23.1   Growth of nonwhites entering the U.S. labor force

customers—and, consequently, increasing AT&T's need to hire diverse employees. Only 15 months after instituting USADirect Service In-Language, the company had to add 250 Spanish-speaking operators. Similar hiring increases occurred when the service was expanded to appeal to Polish and Hungarian speakers.

African consumers are a large market for the more established USADirect Service. According to Yaw Osei-Amoako, market development manager for Africa in Morristown, New Jersey, more than 50,000 USADirect calls are made per week from Ghana—mostly by Ghanaians calling their U.S. relatives.

With respect to global diversity, Osei-Amoako, himself a Ghanaian, says, "Patience is the key virtue here. The Europeans understand this better than the Americans because of their colonial experience. Americans want to come in, make a deal, go home. The Africans want to get to know you personally, know all about your family, what you like, what you don't like, where you come from."

In Africa, USADirect Service In-Language was initially offered only in Liberia. Now it is available in ten African countries. Africa is an emerging market that is also being pursued by Sprint and MCI. Its skills in global diversity may give AT&T a competitive edge in this market.≈

Ethnocentrism and Other Negative Dynamics

The changing demographics described in *Workforce 2000* set in motion certain social dynamics that can interfere with workforce productivity. If an organization is to be successful in diversifying, it must neutralize these dynamics.

Ethnocentrism and Stereotyping
Our natural tendency is to judge other groups less favorably than our own. This tendency is the source of **ethnocentrism,** the belief that one's own group, culture, country, or customs are superior to others'. Two related dynamics are prejudices and stereotypes. A **prejudice** is a preconceived judgment, opinion, or assumption about an issue, behavior, or group of people.[7] **Stereotype** is a positive or negative assessment of members of a group or their perceived attributes. It is important for managers to know about these negative dynamics so they can monitor their own perceptions and help their employees view diverse co-workers more accurately.

Discrimination
When verbalized or acted upon, these negative dynamics can cause discomfort and stress for the judged individual. In some cases, there is outright discrimination. **Discrimination** is the act of treating an issue, person, or behavior unjustly or inequitably on the basis of stereotypes and prejudices. Consider the disabled person who is turned down for promotion because the boss feels this employee is incapable of handling the regular travel required for this particular job. The boss' prejudgment of this employee's capabilities on the basis of "difference," and implementation of the prejudgment through differential treatment, constitutes discrimination.

Tokenism and Other Challenges
Discrimination occurs when stereotypes are acted upon in ways that affect hiring, pay, or promotion practices—for example, where older employees are steered into less visible job assignments that are unlikely to provide opportunities for advancement. Other challenges facing minorities and women include the pressure to conform to the organization's culture, high penalties for mistakes, and tokenism. **Tokenism** refers to being one of very few members of your group in the organization.[8] "Token" employees are given either very high or very low visibility in the organization. One African-American male indicated that he was "discouraged" by his white female manager from joining voluntary committees and task forces within the company—but at the same time criticized in his performance appraisal by her for being "aloof" and taking a "low-profile approach."

Ethnocentrism is the belief that one's own group, culture, country, or customs are superior to others'.

A **prejudice** is a preconceived judgment, opinion, or assumption about an issue, behavior, individual, or group of people.

A **stereotype** is a positive or negative assessment of members of a group or their perceived attributes.

Discrimination is the act of treating an issue, person, or behavior unjustly or inequitably on the basis of stereotypes or prejudices.

Tokenism refers to being one of very few members of a group in an organization.

In other cases, minorities are seen as representatives or "spokespeople" for all members of their group. As such, they are subject to high expectations and scrutiny from members of their own group. One Latino male employee described how other Latinos in the company "looked up to him" for his achievements in the organization. In general, ethnocentrism, prejudices, and stereotypes inhibit our ability to accurately process information.

Negative Dynamics and Specific Groups

The following sections more fully discuss these negative dynamics as they pertain to women, minorities, older workers, and workers with disabilities.

Women   Rosabeth Kanter has researched the pressures women managers face. In her classic study of gender dynamics in organizations, she emphasized the high expectations women have of other women as one of those pressures.[9]

Gender-role stereotypes are perceptions about the sexes based on what society believes are appropriate behaviors for men and women.

Gender Roles.   Women in organizations confront **gender-role stereotypes,** or perceptions about people based on what our society believes are appropriate behaviors for men and women. Both sexes find their self-expression constrained by gender-role stereotyping. For example, women in organizations are often assumed to be good listeners. This attribution is based on our societal view that women are nurturing. Although this is a positive assessment, it is not true of all women or of any woman all the time—hence the negative side of this stereotypical expectation for women in the workplace.

Women professionals, for instance, often remark that they are frequently sought out by colleagues who want to discuss non–work-related problems. Women managers also describe the subtle sanctions they experience from both men and women when they do not fulfill expectations that they will be nurturing managers.

The "Glass Ceiling" and Sexual Harassment.   A serious form of discrimination affecting women in organizations has been dubbed the "glass ceiling."[10] The glass ceiling refers to an invisible "ceiling," or barrier to advancement. This term, originally coined to describe the limits confronting women, is also used to describe the experiences of other minorities in organizations. Although both women and men struggle to balance work and family concerns, it is still more common for women to assume primary responsibility for household management as well as their careers, and sometimes they are denied opportunities for advancement because of this stereotype.

Sexual harassment is another form of discrimination that disproportionately affects female employees. *Sexual harassment* is defined as any unwanted sexual language, behavior, or imagery negatively affecting an employee.[11]

Minorities   Racial, ethnic, and cultural minorities also confront inhibiting stereotypes about their group. Like women, they must deal with misunderstandings and expectations based on their ethnic or cultural origins.

Bicultural stress is stress resulting from having to cope with membership in two cultures simultaneously.

Role conflict is the conflict that results when a person has to fill competing roles because of membership in two cultures.

Role overload refers to having too many expectations to comfortably fulfill.

Many members of ethnic or racial minority groups have been socialized to be members of two cultural groups—the dominant culture and their particular racial or ethnic culture. Ella Bell, professor of organizational behavior at MIT, refers to this dual membership as *biculturalism.* In her study of African-American women, she identifies the stress of coping with membership in two cultures simultaneously as **bicultural stress.**[12] She also indicates that **role conflict**—having to fill competing roles because of membership in two cultures—and **role overload**—having too many expectations to comfortably fulfill—are common characteristics of bicultural stress. Although these are problems for many minority groups, they are particularly intense for women of color. This is because this group experiences negative dynamics affecting *both* minorities and women.

Socialization in one's culture of origin can lead to misunderstandings in the workplace. This is particularly true when a manager relies solely on the cultural norms of the majority group. According to the norms of American culture, for example, it is acceptable—even positive—to publicly praise an individual for a job well done. However, in cultures that place primary value on group harmony and collective achievement, this way of rewarding an employee causes emotional discomfort because employees fear that, if praised publicly, they will "lose face" in their group.

Older Workers   Older workers are a significant and valuable component of today's labor force.[13] The "baby boomers" born in the late 1940s and 1950s are now middle aged, while the previous generation of workers is approaching retirement. Organizations need to learn how to tap the rich knowledge and experience of these workers and how to help older workers avoid the occupational stagnation of later careers. These are especially important concerns given the *Workforce 2000* predictions that the supply of younger workers is dwindling and that huge numbers of baby boomers will reach the preretirement phase of their careers simultaneously, creating fierce competition for scarce jobs.

Stereotypes and Prejudices.   Older workers present some specific challenges for managers. Stereotypes and prejudices link age with senility, incompetence, and lack of worth in the labor market.[14] Jeffrey Sonnenfeld, an expert on senior executives and older workers, compiled research findings from several studies of older employees. He found that managers view older workers as "deadwood," and seek to "weed them out" through pension incentives, biased performance appraisals, and other methods.

Actually, Sonnenfeld's compilation of research indicates that while older managers are more cautious, less likely to take risks, and less open to change than younger managers, many are high performers. Studies that tracked individuals' careers over the long term conclude that there is a peak in performance around age 45 to 50, and a second peak around 55 to 60. Performance in some fields (e.g., sales) either improves with age or does not significantly decline.

It is the manager's responsibility to value older workers for their contributions to the organization and to see to it that they are treated fairly. This requires an understanding of and sensitivity to the physiological and psychological changes that older workers are adjusting to. Supporting older workers also requires paying attention to how performance appraisal processes, retirement incentives, training programs, blocked career paths, union insurance pensions, and affirmative action goals affect this segment of the workforce.

This section of the chapter has suggested that older workers are a potentially valuable human resource for an organization. The following CUTTING EDGE feature summarizes the results of a recent study that demonstrates why older workers are valuable.

STUDY SHOWS THAT OLDER WORKERS ARE VALUABLE

CUTTING EDGE

Ongoing advances in technology and medical care are lengthening Americans' life expectancy and raising questions about the implications of this longevity for society and the individual. People are wondering, for example, what they will do with their lives in later years— how they will maintain a fulfilling and rewarding balance between work and rest. Studies show that *unretirement*—becoming reemployed after retiring—is a growing trend.

A recent survey conducted jointly by the Society for Human Resource Management and the American Association of Retired People (AARP) discovered that "unretirees" are overwhelmingly seen as valuable employees. Managers view them as a valuable resource because there is a shortage of skilled workers in younger age groups and

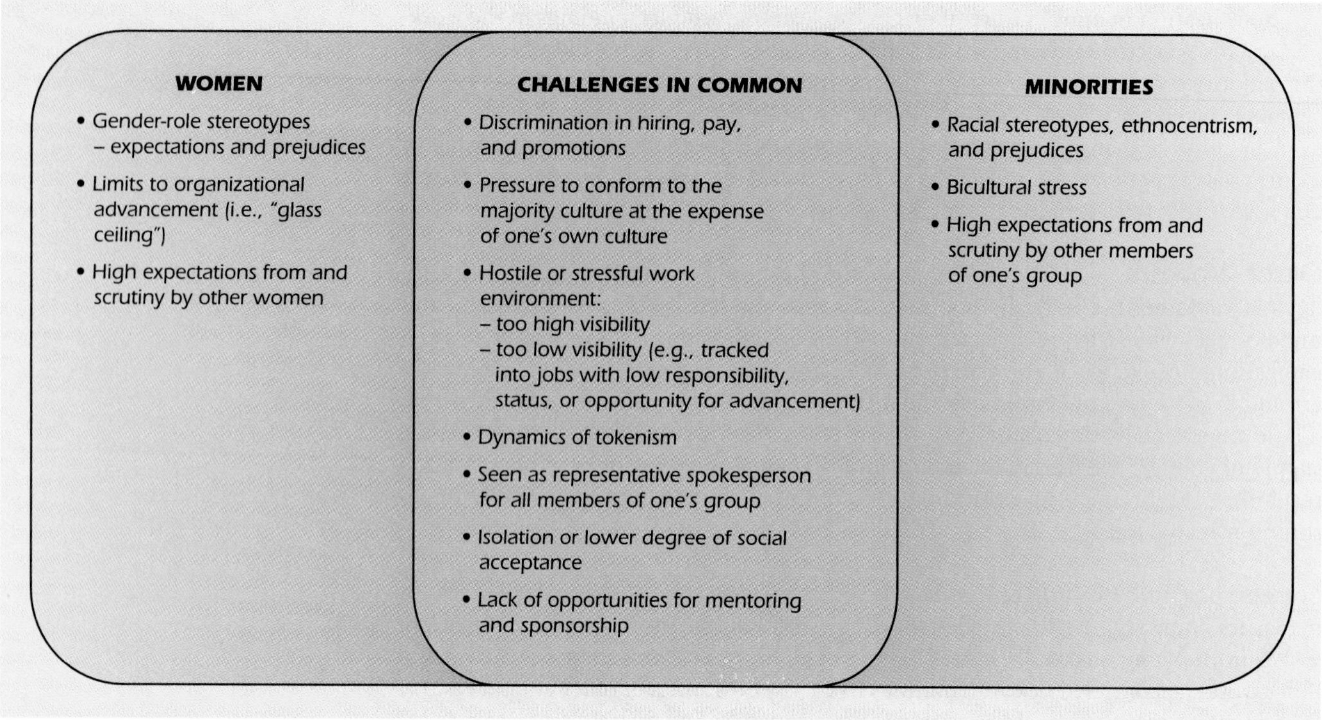

Figure 23.2   Negative dynamics confronting women and minorities in organizations

many unretirees have special skills honed over decades of work experience. Managers are also starting to realize that people in their 60s are not really that old, considering that the U.S. workforce as a whole is becoming older. Moreover, unretirees generally have a positive work ethic, and managers find them generally easier to manage than young employees.≈

Workers with Disabilities   People with disabilities are subject to the same negative dynamics that plague women, minorities, and older workers. For example, one manager confessed that before he attended diversity training sessions offered through a nearby university, he felt "uncomfortable" around disabled people. One disabled professional reported that she was always received warmly by phone and told that her background was exactly what companies were looking for, but when she showed up for job interviews, she was often rebuffed and informed that her credentials were insufficient.

The stereotyping, prejudice, and discrimination women and minorities often suffer in organizations are summarized in Figure 23.2. Managers who learn to recognize and deal with these negative dynamics will be better prepared to manage a diverse workforce.

STRATEGIES FOR PROMOTING DIVERSITY IN ORGANIZATIONS

This section looks at several approaches to diversity and strategies that managers can consider as they plan for promoting cultural diversity in their organizations. First, the six strategies for modern management offered by the Hudson Institute's *Workforce 2000* report are explored. Then the requirements of the Equal Employment Opportunity Commission, which is legally empowered to regulate organizations to ensure that management practices enhance diversity, are discussed, along with affirmative action. Finally, the wisdom of moving beyond these legal requirements and striving for pluralism is considered, and five approaches to pluralism are described.

Differently abled workers are being helped both by new laws and new technologies. For example, both the Rehabilitation Act of 1973 (which covers jobs connected with the federal government) and the Americans with Disabilities Act (which covers private-sector jobs) guarantee the right of access to training and job-performance equipment. Such laws require employers to make the reasonable accommodations *that would permit the handicapped worker to perform at the minimum level of productivity expected of a nonhandicapped worker.*

Workforce 2000

According to the authors of this Hudson Institute report, six major issues demand the full attention of U.S. business leaders and require them to take the following actions:

1. *Stimulate balanced world growth.* The United States must pay less attention to its share of world trade and more to the growth of the economies of the other nations of the world, including those nations in Europe, Latin America, and Asia with which the U.S competes.
2. *Accelerate productivity increases in service industries.* Prosperity will depend much more upon how fast output per worker increases in health care, education, retailing, government, and other services than on gains in manufacturing.
3. *Maintain the dynamism of an aging workforce.* As the age of the average American worker climbs toward 40, the nation must make sure that its workforce does not lose its adaptability and willingness to learn.
4. *Reconcile the conflicting needs of women, work, and families.* There has been a huge influx of women into the workforce in the last two decades, but organizational policies covering pay, fringe benefits, time away from work, pensions, welfare, and many other issues do not yet reflect this new reality.
5. *Fully integrate African-American and Hispanic workers into the economy.* The decline in the number of "traditional" white male workers among the young, the rapid pace of industrial change, and the rising skill requirements of the emerging economy make the full utilization of minority workers a particularly urgent challenge between now and 2000.
6. *Improve the education and skills of all workers.* Human capital—knowledge, skills, organization, and leadership—is the key to economic growth and competitiveness.[15]

As this *Workforce 2000* summary of the key strategies for modern management suggests, many of the most significant managerial challenges that lie ahead derive from dramatic demographic shifts and other complex societal issues. Organizations—and, ultimately, their leaders and managers—will need to clarify their own social values as they confront these dynamics. As you recall from Chapter 8, *social values* refer to the relative worth society places on different ways of existence and functions.

The six strategies outlined in the report strongly imply that organizations need to become more inclusive—that is, to welcome a broader mix of employees and to develop an organizational culture that maximizes the value and potential of each worker. As with any major initiative, commitment to developing an inclusive organization begins at the top of the organizational hierarchy. However, on a day-to-day operational

basis, each manager's level of commitment is a critical determinant of how well or how poorly the organization's strategies and approaches will be implemented.

Equal Employment and Affirmative Action

As you recall from Chapter 12, the Equal Employment Opportunity Commission (EEOC) is the federal agency that enforces the laws regulating recruiting and other management practices. Affirmative action was discussed in that chapter in terms of programs designed to eliminate barriers against and increase opportunities for under-utilized or disadvantaged individuals. These programs are positive steps toward promoting diversity and have created career opportunities for both women and minority groups.

Still, organizations can do much more. For example, some employees are hostile toward affirmative action programs because they feel these programs have been misused to create **reverse discrimination**—that is, they discriminate against members of the majority group in order to help groups that are underrepresented in the organization. When management implements appropriate legal approaches but stops short of developing a truly multicultural organization, intergroup conflicts are highly likely.

Reverse discrimination is the term used to describe inequities affecting members of the majority group as an outcome of programs designed to help underrepresented groups.

BACK TO THE CASE

Legal approaches alone cannot resolve all issues related to diversity. When Gary Parlin, the president of Ortho Pharmaceutical, consulted with Elsie Cross, his questions were aimed at discovering why his affirmative action policies were failing to retain minority employees. His company was investing time, energy, and money in recruiting, hiring, and training women and members of underrepresented groups only to lose them within a relatively short time. This is a common problem, and one that often goes unquestioned in organizations. Managerial monitoring of goal achievement and assessment of the effectiveness of present diversity policies are necessary to ensure that affirmative action is used to select and hire the best employees, rather than becoming simply a "paper tool" that does not lead to more effective business practices.

If a company's affirmative action policies are to be effective, managers must be held accountable for their implementation. As with any other organizational policy, these standards can be ignored, misused, or treated as a low priority. Sloppy recruitment and hiring practices are common misuses of affirmative action. Hiring women and minorities whose background, training, and personal goals are poorly matched to company needs and goals is sure to result in costly turnover. Inappropriate recruitment that emphasizes quotas rather than commitment to fair management practices damages both the company and minority employees.

Organizational Commitment to Diversity

Figure 23.3 shows the range of organizational commitment to multiculturalism. At the bottom of the continuum are organizations that have committed resources, planning, and time to the ongoing shaping and sustaining of a multicultural organization. At the top of the continuum are organizations that make no efforts whatever to achieve diversity in their workforces. Most organizations fall somewhere between the extremes depicted in the figure.

Ignoring Differences. Some organizations make no effort to promote diversity and do not even bother to comply with affirmative action and EEOC standards. They are sending a strong message to their employees that the dynamics of difference are unimportant. By ignoring EEOC policies, they are sending an even more detrimental message to their managers: that it is permissible to maintain exclusionary practices.

No diversity efforts:
- noncompliance with affirmative action and EEOC

Diversity efforts based on:
- compliance with affirmative action and EEOC policies
- inconsistent enforcement and implementation (those who breach policies may not be sanctioned unless noncompliance results in legal action)
- support of policies is not rewarded; organization relies on individual managers' interest or commitment

Diversity efforts based on:
- compliance with and enforcement of affirmative action and EEOC policies
- no organizational supports with respect to education, training
- inconsistent or poor managerial commitment

Diversity efforts based on:
- narrowly defined affirmative action and EEOC policies combined with one-shot education and/or training programs
- inconsistent managerial commitment; rewards not tied to effective implementation of diversity programs and goal achievement
- no attention directed toward organizational climate

Diversity efforts based on:
- effective implementation of affirmative action and EEOC policies
- ongoing education and training programs
- managerial commitment tied to organizational rewards
- minimal attention directed toward cultivating an inclusive and supportive organizational climate

Broad-based diversity efforts based on:
- effective implementation of affirmative action and EEOC policies
- organization-wide assessment and management's top-down commitment to diversity
- managerial commitment tied to organizational rewards
- ongoing processes of organization assessment and programs for the purpose of creating an organizational climate that is inclusive and supportive of diverse groups

FIGURE 23.3 Organizational diversity continuum

Complying with External Policies. Some organizations base their diversity strategy solely on compliance with affirmative action and EEOC policies. They make no attempt to provide education and training for employees, nor do they use the organization's reward system to reinforce managerial commitment to diversity. Managers in some companies in this category breach company affirmative action and EEOC policies with impunity. When top management does not punish them, the likelihood of costly legal action against the organization rises.

Enforcing External Policies. Some organizations go so far as to enforce affirmative action and EEOC policies, but provide no organizational supports for education or training for diversity. Managerial commitment to a diverse workforce is either weak or inconsistent.

Responding Inadequately. Other organizations fully comply with affirmative action and EEOC policies, but define these policies quite narrowly. Organizational systems and structures are inadequate to support real organizational change. Education

and training in diversity are sporadic, and managerial rewards for implementing diversity programs are inconsistent or nonexistent. Although these organizations may design some useful programs, they are unlikely to result in any long-term organizational change, so the organizational climate never becomes truly receptive to diverse groups.

Implementing Adequate Programs.   Some organizations effectively implement affirmative action and EEOC policies, provide ongoing education and training programs pertaining to diversity, and tie managerial rewards to success in meeting diversity goals and addressing diversity issues. However, such companies make only a minimal attempt to cultivate the kind of inclusive and supportive organizational climate diverse populations of employees will feel comfortable in.

Taking Effective Action.   The most effective diversity efforts are based on managerial implementation of affirmative action and EEOC policies that are developed in conjunction with an organization-wide assessment of the company's systems and structures. Such an assessment is necessary to determine how these systems and structures support or hinder diversity goals.

Generally, for such a comprehensive assessment to take place, top management must "buy" the idea that diversity is important to the company. Actually, support from the top is critical to all successful diversity efforts and underlies tying organizational rewards to managers' commitment to diversity. Ongoing assessment and continuing programs are also necessary to create an organizational climate that is inclusive and supportive of diverse groups.

BACK TO THE CASE   Managerial commitment is one of the most significant predictors of the success of company diversity initiatives. In the case of Ortho Pharmaceutical, it was Gary Parlin's interest in achieving excellence in all areas that prompted him to seek answers to a very costly company problem—high turnover among women and minority employees. Once an organizational assessment and diagnosis were made, Parlin discovered that there were serious performance breakdowns at the operational level.

He was quick to respond to the finding that recruiting problems were hindering the hiring of a diverse workforce. Having an overview and diagnosis of company strengths and weaknesses relating to diversity allowed Parlin and his staff of top managers to put in place an effective long-term plan for the company. Managerial commitment to this organizational plan resulted in a dramatic increase in upward mobility for women and minority workers at Ortho.

Pluralism

Pluralism is an environment in which cultural, group, and individual differences are acknowledged, accepted, and viewed as significant contributors to the entirety.

Pluralism refers to an environment in which differences are acknowledged, accepted, and seen as significant contributors to the entirety. A diverse workforce is most effective when managers are capable of guiding the organization toward achieving pluralism. Approaches, or strategies, to achieve effective workforce diversity have been classified into five major categories by Jean Kim of Stanford University:[16]

1. "Golden Rule" approach.
2. Assimilation approach.
3. "Righting-the-wrongs" approach.
4. Culture-specific approach.
5. Multicultural approach.

Each approach is described briefly in the following sections.

"Golden Rule" Approach

The "Golden Rule" approach to diversity relies on the biblical dictate "Do unto others as you would have them do unto you."[17] The major strength of this approach is that it emphasizes individual morality. Its major flaw is that individuals apply the Golden Rule from their own particular frame of reference without knowing the cultural expectations, traditions, and preferences of the other person.

One African-American male manager recalled a situation in which he was having difficulty scheduling a work-related event. In exasperation, he volunteered to schedule the event on Saturday. He was reminded by another employee that many of the company's Jewish employees went to religious services on Saturday. He was initially surprised—then somewhat embarrassed—that he had simply assumed that "all people" attended "church" on Sunday.

Assimilation Approach

The assimilation approach advocates shaping organization members to fit the existing culture of the organization. This approach pressures employees who do not belong to the dominant culture to conform—at the expense of renouncing their own cultures and worldviews. The end result is the creation of a homogeneous culture that suppresses the creativity and diversity of views that could benefit the organization.

One African-American woman in middle management said, "I always felt uncomfortable in very formal meetings. I tend to be very animated when I talk, and this is not the norm for the company. Until I became more comfortable with myself and my style, I felt inhibited. I was tempted to try to change my style to fit in."

"Righting-the-Wrongs" Approach

"Righting-the-wrongs" is an approach that addresses past injustices experienced by a particular group. When a group's history places its members at a disadvantage for achieving career success and mobility, policies are developed to create a more equitable set of conditions. For example, the original migration of African-Americans to the United States was forced upon them as slaves. Righting-the-wrongs approaches are designed to compensate for the damages African-Americans have suffered because of historical inequalities.

This approach most closely parallels the affirmative action policies discussed in Chapter 12. It goes beyond affirmative action, however, in that it emphasizes tapping the unique talents of each group in the service of organizational productivity.

Culture-Specific Approach

The culture-specific approach teaches employees the norms and practices of another culture to prepare them to interact with people from that culture effectively. This approach is often used to help employees prepare for international assignments. The problem with it is that it usually fails to give employees a genuine appreciation for the culture they are about to encounter.

Stewart Black and Hal Gergerson, in their study of managers on assignment in foreign countries, found that some identify much more with their parent firm than with the local operation.[18] One male manager, for instance, after spending two years opening retail outlets throughout Europe, viewed Europeans as "lazy and slow to respond to directives." Obviously, his training and preparation had failed to help him adjust to European host countries or to appreciate their peoples and cultures.

Multicultural Approach

The multicultural approach gives employees the opportunity to develop an appreciation for both differences of culture and variations in personal characteristics. This approach focuses on how interpersonal skills and attitudinal changes relate to organizational performance. One of its strengths is that it assumes the organization itself—as well as individuals working within it—will be required to change in order to accommodate the diversity of the organization's workforce.

The multicultural approach is probably the most effective approach to pluralism because it advocates change on the part of management, employees, and organization

The multicultural approach at Pitney-Bowes, the world's largest maker of postal equipment, is evident in its training programs. Nearly 20 languages are spoken at the company's Stamford, Connecticut, manufacturing plant; human resource managers also discovered that 40 percent of the plant's workers could read only at the fourth-grade level and that 65 percent needed basic-math training. Pitney-Bowes thus collaborated with a local community college to set up a seven-stage training program. Today, many employees now work on teams with engineers, order materials, and monitor product quality.

systems and structures. It has the added advantage of stressing the idea that equity demands making some efforts to "right the wrongs" so that underrepresented groups will be fairly included throughout the organization.

THE ROLE OF THE MANAGER

Managers play an essential role in tapping the potential capacities of each person within their departments. To do this requires competencies that are anchored in the four basic management functions of planning, organizing, influencing, and controlling. In this context, planning refers to the manager's role in developing programs to promote diversity, while organizing, influencing, and controlling, of course, take place in the implementation phases of those programs.

Planning   Recall from Chapter 9 that planning is a specific action proposed to help the organization achieve its objectives. It is an ongoing process that includes troubleshooting and continually defining areas where improvements can be made. Planning for diversity may involve selecting diversity training programs for the organization or setting diversity goals for employees within the department.

Setting recruitment goals for members of underrepresented groups is a key component of diversity planning. If top management has identified Hispanics as an underrepresented group within the company, every manager throughout the company will need to collaborate with the human resources department to achieve the organizational goal of higher Hispanic representation. For example, a manager might establish goals and objectives for the increased representation of this group within five years. To achieve this five-year vision, the manager will need to set benchmark goals for each year.

Organizing   Chapter 10 defined organizing as the process of establishing orderly uses for all resources within the management system. To achieve a diverse workplace, managers have to work with human resource professionals in the areas of recruitment, hiring, and retention so that the best match is made between the company and the employees it hires. Managerial responsibilities in this area may include establishing task forces or committees to explore issues and provide ideas, carefully choosing work assignments to support the career development of all employees, and evaluating the extent to which diversity goals are being achieved.

After managers have begun hiring from a diverse pool of employees, they will need to focus on retaining them. This means paying attention to the many concerns of a diverse workforce. In the case of working women and men with families, skillfully utilizing the organization's resources to support their need for day care for dependents, allowing flexible work arrangements in keeping with company policy, and as-

signing and reassigning work responsibilities equitably to accommodate family leave usage are all examples of managers applying the organizing function.

Influencing   Chapter 20 defined influencing as the process of guiding the activities of organization members in appropriate directions. Integral to this management function are an effective leadership style, good communication skills, knowledge about how to motivate others, and an understanding of the organization's culture and group dynamics. In the area of diversity, influencing organization members means that managers must not only encourage and support employees to participate constructively in a diverse work environment, but must themselves engage in the career development and training processes that will give them the skills to facilitate the smooth operation of a diverse work community.

Managers are accountable as well for informing their employees of breaches of organizational policy and etiquette. Let us assume that the diversity strategy selected by top management includes educating employees about organizational policies concerning diversity (e.g., making sure that employees understand what constitutes sexual harassment) as well as providing workshops for employees on specific cultural diversity issues. The manager's role in this case would be to hold employees accountable for learning about company diversity policies and complying with them. This could be accomplished by consulting with staff and holding regular group meetings and one-on-one meetings when necessary. To encourage participation in diversity workshops, the manager may need to communicate to employees the importance the organization places on this knowledge base. Alternatively, the manager might choose to tie organizational rewards to the development of diversity competencies. Examples of such rewards are giving employees public praise or recognition and providing workers with opportunities to use their diversity skills on desirable work assignments.

Controlling   Overseeing compliance with the legal stipulations of EEOC and affirmative action is one aspect of the controlling function in the area of diversity. Chapter 19 defines controlling as the set of activities that make something happen as planned. Hence the evaluation activities necessary to assess diversity efforts are part of the controlling role that managers play in shaping a multicultural workforce.

Managers may find this function the most difficult one of the four to execute. It is hard to evaluate planned-change approaches in general, and it is particularly hard to do so in the area of diversity. Many times the most successful diversity approaches reveal more problems as employees begin to speak openly about their concerns. Moreover, subtle attitudinal changes in one group's perception of another group are very difficult to measure. What *can* be accurately measured are the outcome variables of turnover, representation of women, minorities, and other underrepresented groups at all levels of the company, and legal problems stemming from inappropriate or illegal behaviors (e.g., discrimination and sexual harassment).

Managers engaged in the controlling function in the area of diversity need to continually monitor their units' progress with respect to diversity goals and standards. They must decide what control measures to use (e.g., indicators of productivity, turnover, absenteeism, or promotion) and how to interpret the information these measures yield in light of diversity goals and standards.

For example, a manager may need to assess whether the low rate of promotions for African-American men in her department is due to subtle biases toward this group or group members' poor performance compared to others in the department. She may find she needs to explore current organizational dynamics, as well as create effective supports for this group. Such supports might include fostering greater social acceptance of African-American men among other employees, learning more about the African-American male's bicultural experience in the company, making mentoring or other opportunities available to members of this group, and providing them with some specific job-related training.

Management Development and Diversity Training

Given the complex set of managerial skills needed to promote diversity, it is obvious that managers themselves will need organizational support if the company is to achieve its diversity goals. One important component of the diversity strategy of a large number of companies is diversity training. **Diversity training** is a learning process designed to raise managers' awareness and develop their competencies to deal with the issues endemic to managing a diverse workforce.

Basic Themes of Diversity Training   Chapter 12 refers to training as the process of developing qualities in human resources that will make them more productive and better able to contribute to organizational goal attainment. Some companies develop intensive programs for management and less intensive, more generalized programs for other employees. As stated in Chapter 12, such programs generally focus on the following five components or themes:

1. Behavioral awareness.
2. Acknowledgment of biases and stereotypes.
3. Focus on job performance.
4. Avoidance of assumptions.
5. Modification of policy and procedure manuals.

Stages in Managing a Diverse Workforce   Donaldson and Scannell, authors of *Human Resource Development: The New Trainer's Guide*, have developed a four-stage model to describe how managers progress in managing a diverse workforce.[19] In the first stage, known as "unconscious incompetence," managers are unaware of behaviors they engage in that are problematic for members of other groups. In the second stage, "conscious incompetence," managers go through a learning process in which they become conscious of behaviors that make them incompetent in their interactions with members of diverse groups.

The third stage is one of becoming "consciously competent": Managers learn how to interact with diverse groups and cultures by deliberately thinking about how to behave. In the last stage, "unconscious competence," managers have internalized these new behaviors and feel so comfortable relating to others different from themselves that they need to devote little conscious effort to doing so:

> Managers who have progressed to the "unconscious competence" stage will be the most effective with respect to interacting in a diverse workforce. Effective interaction is key to carrying out the four management functions previously discussed.

Table 23.2 summarizes our discussion of the challenges facing those who manage a diverse workforce. Managers, who are generally responsible for controlling organizational goals and outcomes, are accountable for understanding these diversity challenges and recognizing the dynamics described here. In addition to treating employees fairly, they must influence other employees to cooperate with the company's diversity goals.

Understanding and Influencing Employee Responses.   Managers cannot rise to the challenge of managing a diverse workforce unless they recognize that many employees have difficulties in coping with diversity. Among these difficulties are natural resistance to change, ethnocentrism, and lack of information and outright misinformation about other groups, as well as prejudices, biases, and stereotypes. Some employees lack the motivation to understand and cope with cultural differences—which, after all, requires time, energy, and a willingness to take some emotional risks.

Another problem is that employees often receive no social rewards (.e.g, peer support and approval) or concrete rewards (e.g., financial compensation or career opportunities) for cooperating with the organization's diversity policies.

Diversity training is a learning process designed to raise managers' awareness and develop their competencies to deal with the issues endemic to managing a diverse workforce.

Table 23.2

Organizational Challenges and Supports Related to Managing a Diverse Workforce

ORGANIZATIONAL CHALLENGES	ORGANIZATIONAL SUPPORTS
Employee Difficulties in Coping with Cultural Diversity • Resistance to change • Ethnocentrism • Lack of information and misinformation • Prejudices, biases, and stereotypes **Reasons Employees Are Unmotivated to Understand Cultural Differences** • Lack of time and energy and unwillingness to assume the emotional risk necessary to explore issues of diversity • Absence of social or concrete rewards for investing in diversity work (e.g., lack of peer support and monetary rewards, unclear linkage between multicultural competence and career mobility) • Interpersonal and intergroup conflicts arising when diversity issues are either ignored or mismanaged **Work Group Problems** • Lack of cohesiveness • Communication problems • Employee stress	**Educational Programs and Training to Assist Employees in Working Through Difficulties** **Top-Down Management Support for Diversity** • Managers who have diversity skills and competence • Education and training • Awareness raising • Peer support • Organizational climate that supports diversity • Open communication with manager about diversity issues • Recognition for employee development of diversity skills and competencies • Recognition for employee contributions to diversity goals • Organizational rewards for managers' implementation of organizational diversity goals and objectives

For all these difficulties, managers cannot afford to ignore or mismanage diversity issues because the cost of doing so is interpersonal and intergroup conflicts. These conflicts very often affect the functioning of the work group by destroying cohesiveness and causing communications problems and employee stress.

Managers who are determined to deal effectively with their diverse workforce can usually obtain organizational support. One primary support is education and training programs designed to help employees work through their difficulties in coping with diversity. Besides recommending such programs to their employees, managers may find it helpful to enroll in available programs themselves.

Getting Top-Down Support.   Another very important source of support for managers dealing with diversity issues is top management. Organizations that provide top-down support are more likely to boast the following features:

1. Managers skilled at working with a diverse workforce.
2. Effective education and diversity training programs.
3. An organizational climate that promotes diversity and fosters peer support for exploring diversity issues.
4. Open communication between employees and managers about diversity issues.
5. Recognition for employees' development of diversity skills and competencies.
6. Recognition for employee contributions to diversity goals.
7. Organizational rewards for managers' implementation of organizational diversity goals and objectives.

BACK TO THE CASE

In most organizations, managers are given more extensive diversity training than other employees because they are the key to implementing diversity initiatives. They not only need to effectively apply the four management functions to diversity-related tasks; they also have to recognize their own levels of competency in this area.

Managers who know how to interact with people of other cultures and identify groups are more effective members of the management team than those who do not have this multicultural competence. They are better able to foster the kind of culture change that organizations like Ortho Pharmaceutical are determined to implement.

One of the major benefits of cultivating diversity is that the organization becomes safer for the expression of differences and more open to the kinds of new ideas that surface through disagreement and open communication. One African-American market research manager at Ortho, for example, described the company as a place where he can disagree with others without being penalized. It is a place where he feels he can be himself—*and* be effective.

Today the distribution of women and minorities throughout Ortho Pharmaceutical is more equitable, but such improvements have not changed the company's culture very much, for this kind of subtle change takes time. To Ortho's credit, its top managers' promotion of diversity has extended beyond increasing the numerical presence of women and minorities at all organizational levels. Management seems to genuinely value difference, is willing to incorporate diverse employees into the management team, and has tied organizational rewards to diversity efforts. This complex long-term strategy is having positive results at Ortho.

Action Summary

Reread the learning objectives below. Each objective is followed by questions. Answering these questions accurately will help you retain the most important concepts discussed in this chapter. After answering each question, check your answer against the answer key at the end of this chapter. (*Hint:* If you have any doubts regarding the correct response, consult the page whose number follows the answer).

Circle: From studying this chapter, I will attempt to acquire:

1. A definition of diversity and an understanding of its importance in the corporate structure.

T,F
    a. Diversity refers to characteristics that shape people's identities and the experiences they have in society.

a,b,c,d,e
    b. The following is *not* true of workforce diversity: (a) it is a new issue; (b) it stems from workforce demographics; (c) it involves developing an inclusive organization; (d) it includes age and physical ability; (e) it is a strength that can be built on.

2. An understanding of the advantages of having a diverse workforce.

a,b,c,d,e
    a. All of the following are advantages of a diverse workforce *except:* (a) employees who develop multicultural competencies; (b) cost savings; (c) similarity in thinking and approaches; (d) increased productivity; (e) improved ability to gain and keep market share.

T,F
    b. A diverse workforce results in a "better quality of management" because managers are recruited from a wider pool of talent.

3. An awareness of the challenges facing managers within a diverse workforce.

a,b,c,d,e
    a. Challenges facing American corporations include all of the following *except:* (a) the need to look beyond traditional sources of personnel; (b) the need to assess the opportunities suggested by demographic projections; (c) the need to adapt to changes in the structure of the workforce; (d) the need to prepare for a huge influx of younger workers by the year 2000; (e) the need to improve the educational preparation of all workers.

a,b,c,d,e
    b. The following is a potential challenge facing American business leaders: (a) reconciling the conflicting needs of women, work, and families; (b) fully assimilating into the economy African-American and Hispanic workers; (c) maintaining the dynamism of an aging workforce; (d) accelerating productivity increases in service industries; (e) all of the above.

a,b,c,d,e   **c.** The dynamics of coping with diverse populations include: (a) "the glass ceiling"; (b) tokenism; (c) bicultural stress; (d) ethnocentrism; (e) all of the above.

4. An understanding of the strategies for promoting diversity in organizations.

T,F   **a.** Following the appropriate affirmative action and EEOC guidelines will resolve intergroup conflicts and result in an effectively diverse organization.

a,b,c,d,e   **b.** The following is true regarding strategies for promoting diversity in organizations: (a) organizations vary widely with respect to the strategies they employ; (b) all organizations comply with affirmative action and EEOC guidelines; (c) exclusionary practices have no effect on an organization; (d) diversity programs always result in comprehensive culture change; (e) all of the above.

5. Insights into the role of the manager in promoting diversity in the organization.

a,b,c,d,e   **a.** A manager engaged in the four functions of management with respect to diversity might take all of the following actions *except:* (a) establishing hiring goals for specific underrepresented groups; (b) granting family leave time; (c) communicating the importance of diversity training; (d) letting employees know they are not accountable for knowing diversity-related policies; (e) assessing progress toward diversity goals.

T,F   **b.** In a diverse organization, the highest level of diversity competence is described as "conscious competence."

Introductory Case Wrap-Up

"Ortho Pharmaceutical 'Showcase' for Cultural Diversity" (page 564) and its related back-to-the-case sections were written to help you better understand the management concepts contained in this chapter. Answer the following discussion questions about this introductory case to enrich your understanding of the chapter content:

1. How important to an organization such as Ortho Pharmaceutical is the implementation of workforce diversity goals? Explain.

2. On the basis of the facts discussed in the introductory case, what strengths has Ortho Pharmaceutical gained from cultivating diversity within the company?

3. On the basis of the facts discussed in the introductory case, what organizational challenges does Ortho Pharmaceutical face? Discuss the organizational supports available to managers addressing these challenges.

Issues for Review and Discussion

1. What is diversity?
2. Why is diversity an important contemporary management issue?
3. List the six challenges facing American businesses according to *Workforce 2000*.
4. Define *pluralism*.
5. Describe the five major approaches organizations can employ in responding to diversity.
6. List the advantages of a diverse workforce.
7. List the managerial challenges presented by a diverse workforce.
8. Give a detailed description of the dynamics encountered by diverse populations in the workplace.

9. Outline the organizational supports available to help managers address the challenges of a diverse workforce.
10. Describe the range of strategies organizations employ to implement workforce diversity.
11. Explain the concept of reverse discrimination.
12. What is the relationship between the four management functions and the implementation of diversity goals?
13. Why should managers undergo diversity training?
14. What is the meaning of "unconscious competence" and why is it desirable for managers?

Action Summary Answer Key

1. **a.** T, pp. 565–566
   b. a, pp. 565–566
2. **a** c, pp. 566–568
   b. T, pp. 567–568

3. **a.** d, pp. 569–574
   b. e, pp. 569–570
   c. e, pp. 572–574

4. **a.** F, p. 576
   b. a, pp. 574–580

5. **a.** d, pp. 580–581
   b. F, p. 582

Case Study

Levi Strauss: Valuing Diversity

In the 1987 study *Workforce 2000: Work and Workers for the Twenty-First Century*, an executive-shaking statistic was projected: By the year 2000, only 15 percent of the people entering the workforce will be American-born white males. Companies rushed to respond, hiring consultants and trainees to sensitize employees to racial and gender differences. Unfortunately, many of these efforts misfired—group stereotypes were rigidified, racial and gender groups were pitted against one another, or white males became workplace scapegoats for any and all inequalities.

Some companies have begun to change their approaches to the increasing diversity of the U.S. workplace. In fact, many have begun to make *diversity* the watchword for broader efforts to change corporate culture. Consider the case of Levi Strauss & Company. In 1994, instead of focusing simply on race or gender, Levi Strauss adopted a new management policy called by CEO Robert D. Haas "responsible commercial success." Under Haas' direction, a set of written corporate "aspirations" was created by top management to guide all major company decisions. According to a report in *Business Week* magazine, these guidelines describe a policy that not only "aspires" to create tangible opportunities for minority employees at Levi Strauss, but also sets out to "make each of [Strauss'] workers, from the factory floor on up, feel as if they are an integral part of the making and selling of blue jeans. [Management hoped] to ensure that all views on all issues are heard and respected."

In support of his "aspirations," Haas cited a study issued by Gordon Group, Inc., for the California Public Employees' Retirement System. According to this report, "Companies that involve employees more often in decision-making boast stronger market valuations than those that don't." However, Levi Strauss soon found that putting this idea into practice proved quite expensive. In 1985, Haas, who had become chairman and CEO the year before, decided to avert any possible takeover bids by taking Levi Strauss private in a leveraged buyout. His action saddled the company with $1.6 billion in debt, cost 6,000 jobs, and forced the closing of 26 plants. In the ensuing decade, however, Haas' action paid off. Since the buyout, profits have shaved corporate debt considerably. Record sales and earnings for the years between 1988 and 1993 culminated in a 36 percent rise in profits in 1993, and the estimated appreciation in stock values since 1985 is 1300 percent.

Implementing Haas' vision has not been easy, however. Perhaps distracted by an array of new managing techniques, Levi's has allowed its product development and customer service in the United States to slip since setting records in 1993. However, Haas believes the problem would be even worse were it not for the company's encouragement of the free exchange of ideas among its many employees. As Daniel M. Chew, Levi's director of corporate marketing, points out, "A diverse workforce, unafraid to volunteer idiosyncratic ideas and opinions, leads to better marketing decisions."

Consider Levi's "501 Blues" TV ads. They worked well with Levi's many hip, young customers. However, Levi's Hispanic employees were put off by them. They advised the company to pitch an image of family and friends—camaraderie rather than rugged individualism—to their community. These changes in the ads paid off: Sales in the Hispanic community boomed.

Many of Levi's employees view the company's new management policy changes with mixed feelings. Louis Kirtman, an African-American who has worked as an executive at Levi's since the early 1980s, sees Haas' "aspirations" as positive. Before the change, Kirtman had seen African-American executives whom he thought were highly qualified passed over for plum jobs at Levi's. In fact, his own career seemed stalled on a midlevel management plateau until 1994, when he became president of Levi's Britannia Sportswear division and stood only a step away from the company's senior management ranks.

Managing according to the new values is seen by many as a tough task, producing often contradictory results. The loss of old-boy networks, the pressure to assume new responsibilities and new ways of thinking, and the problems that result when values seem to interfere with bottom-line figures—all such changes can impose negative pressure. Empowerment and teamwork can be alien, uncomfortable concepts for those who have spent their working lives taking and giving orders.

Haas' controversial "aspirations" cannot yet be finally evaluated. Since 1984, the company has doubled the percentage of minority managers to 36 percent and has boosted the ranks of women in management from 32 to 54 percent. Recent marketing successes appear to support the belief that the cultivation of a workplace culture devoted to diversity and empowerment is making Levi's more responsive in the marketplace. Bankers are happy with the company's feat of shaving its debt to 4.6 percent of total capital. Haas admits that his company is "far from perfect. But," he insists, "the goal is out there, and it's worth striving for."

Questions:

1. According to the text, diversity is the best way for a company to gain and keep market share. How does the experience of Levi Strauss bear this out? What

kind of changes in minority management has Levi's seen in recent years? What corresponding changes in the company's marketing programs would you expect to see?

2. Levi's diverse workforce ethic could also pay off in international markets. Use information from the text to give reasons to support or refute this speculation.

3. Has Bob Haas' influence on his company's corporate community improved the company's bottom line? Explain.

Skills Exercise

According to *Business Week* magazine, Bob Haas "calls his 'grand social experiment' [in diversity] a 'responsible commercial success'." More conservative executives might call it "flaky." His own employees reflect this dichotomy. Says financial planner Margaret P. Lourenco, for example, "I found that [this policy] isn't about New Age feel-good. It's about being open and direct. It's about getting rid of hidden agendas." On the other hand, F. Warren Hellman, a San Francisco investment banker and a Levi's director, observes, "Doing the right thing is fine, but there's a danger that this [policy] will degrade into a touchy-feely, I-don't-want-to-offend-you, creativity-stifling style of management." Choose sides and use research, this textbook, and information from the case study on Levi Strauss to defend your side in a class debate.

 The Internet learning materials that accompany this chapter can be found at
http://www.profcerto.com
Additional information can be found on the inside front and back covers of this text.

Giving High-Quality Customer Service: A Focal Point at Lands' End

This is the seventh case in this book that explores a variety of management-related issues at the well-known direct-retailing company Lands' End. The first installment (on pp. 24–26) is designed to be a general introduction. You may want to refer to it when you are studying the cases that appear at the end of each part of the book.

ON LOCATION!

Reconsider for a moment both your first exposure to Lands' End in the introductory section of the text and the case at the end of the Organizing Section. It should already be obvious that Lands' End places great emphasis on quality both of product and of service. Service quality at Lands' End is the responsibility of Joan Conlin, Director of Customer Services. According to Conlin, service quality derives from the company's fundamental principles of doing business (refer again to "Lands' End—Principles of Doing Business" in the introductory section of your text), its "Customer Services Mission," and its philosophy of servicing the customer. More specifically, however, it is a function of selection, continuous training, and monitoring.

Interviewing, according to Conlin, is a primary ingredient in selecting customer sales representatives—the people primarily responsible for servicing customer needs. "Extensive interviewing," she explains,

> is an important part of the selection process for customer sales reps at Lands' End. Prospective hires first have a phone interview with a employee services representative. HR knows the qualities that we are looking for in an individual. Once the potential hire has passed the phone screening process, two additional face-to-face interviews are scheduled; one is with employee services, the second with either a supervisor or a manager in the sales division. Part of the interview always involves asking the individual about a personal experience with people and how they handled it. How they handled their own specific situation gives us a good indication of their people skills and how they would service our customers—in other words, how much they would be willing to tolerate.

If the potential hire is selected, the individual is then put through a relatively extensive training program. According to Conlin:

> Once we get a candidate that we think will service the customer in the way we believe he or she should, we put the person through 70 to 80 hours of training. We train on all of our basic products and core items. We talk about product features, how we make products, and even fabrics, so that the individual gets a basic understanding of what we sell. We also do a phone-courtesy unit to make sure that new hires know proper politeness on the phone and how we expect them to operate when assisting customers. The training that new hires receive also includes background on our computer system and how to get to different help screens. Once they have completed the initial classroom training, they work on the training phone system that is identical to our actual system and do a lot of role-playing with other trainees. They take mock catalog requests with the screens in front of them and learn to do everything that they need to do on the live system.

On-the-job-training then takes a couple of additional days. "After all that role-playing," reports Conlin,

> most new customer-service reps feel very comfortable when placed on the live phone system, but a trainer sits behind each new rep for at least a couple of days to answer questions. Once the remaining uncertainties are overcome, they are left on their own, though not without considerable assistance at hand. For example, at the push of the assist button, supervisors are always available to answer procedural or policy questions. Also, they know that if product questions arise, they can call specialty shoppers. And if any after-order problem arises (say, a package wasn't received or a customer wasn't satisfied), they can contact customer service. So they have support teams day in and day out.

But assessment of service-rep effectiveness does not stop there. Supervisors listen to at least four calls for each customer-sales representative (new and old) each month; they also complete monitoring forms related to those calls and provide written feedback on how specific components were handled in each call. For example, failure to repeat the product ordered back to the customer would be called to the attention of the service rep. Monitoring is done at random and the individual does not know when or if it is occurring.

The newest performance-monitoring and improvement tool developed at Lands' End is what is called the SOS Program. SOS, which stands for *S*trengthening *O*perator *S*kills, is a peer monitoring process in which actual operators monitor each other. According to Conlin,

> a group of six operators meets in one of our monitoring rooms and one volunteers to go out to a designated station and take calls. The room is fitted with equipment that permits those in the room to not only hear the service rep and the actual customer conducting business, but also to see on the big screen the computer screens that the rep is accessing as the actual order is being input. General observation guidelines and a much more detailed checklist for phone orders are provided to the observer group. After feedback is shared with volunteer number one, each of the other members of the peer group takes a turn on the phone and receives feedback.

Conlin admits that the announcement of the SOS Program to customer sales representatives initially met with some skepticism. "The initial reaction of operators," she recalls,

> was, "I don't want my co-workers listening to me!" But it's become a very popular means of increasing operator effectiveness. Now we try to place some of our newer people with some of our veterans so that they're both learning and exchanging ideas. Of course, the old timers have great skills, but the newer people have the fresh, unique ideas, so this combination really works well. As you can see, our whole approach is one of continuous improvement. We're always looking at ways we can do a better job at servicing our customer. You know, it's not service unless the customer thinks it is.

Lands' End customer sales representatives are explicitly instructed that they are not there to *sell:* they are there to *provide service.* According to Conlin,

> our customer sales representatives are there to help customers accomplish what they called for—to meet the customer's need; they are not there to try to market other products that the company has available. Their job is to listen and to respond to customers' needs; it's service, not sales. When they're on the phone with the customer, they have all the support they need. They can go to different resources, and they know what they are. So, they can always satisfy that customer. That's a real comforting feeling.

How service-oriented does Lands' End wants its customer sales representativs to be? As ten-year veteran Sally Kunkel puts it, they are to do whatever they can to be of assistance to the customer. "We try every way possible," she says,

> to meet the customer's need. We will look for substitutes for the item in question if the requested item is unavailable—some requests are from catalogs that are as much as three or four years old and the item can no longer be found. But if after exhausting all options and finding that what Lands' End has to offer will not satisfy the customer, I bring up the screen with the list of our competitors and their 800 numbers. I then suggest to the customer those competitors who may have what they're looking for.

The speed with which a call is answered also is an indicator of the company's ability to service customers. According to Conlin, a customer's call should be answered within 20 seconds of being placed: "Our goal," she says,

> is to answer 90 percent of our calls in 20 seconds. Most of our callers are not even hearing a ring, and our average answering speed is five seconds—maybe two rings. Because we have automatic call-distribution systems in each of our phone centers, we can monitor each center, and we have the capability of shifting more calls to any of the centers if, for example, one center has a lot of people out due to sickness.

We also monitor talk-time—the time duration of a call. We watch especially the high end, the greatest talk-times, with the idea that if the high end gets too high, it may be a systems problem and maybe we need to adjust our monthly training to bring it back into line with our standard. In such cases, the operator may have become too chatty, and we know that customers do not like that either.

We also look at what we call "aux-time," which is the time that service reps make themselves unavailable to take calls, either to do paperwork, use the restroom, or whatever. Again, if they make themselves unavailable above the standard length of time, we call it to their attention.

SEPTEMBER 1995 CUSTOMER COMMENTS

SEPTEMBER COMMENTS

TO: LANDS' END COMPANY WIDE

FROM: Rachel Powell (ext #4574) and Tami Bollant (ext #4146)

DATE: October 13, 1995

SUBJECT: SEPTEMBER CUSTOMER COMMENTS

There were 10,299 comments for the month of September—a decrease of 2,207 from August and a decrease of 2,708 from September 1994.

SEPTEMBER CUSTOMER COMMENTS		1995	1994
A.	Sizing Requests	3,203	4,099
B.	Product Requests	3,546	4,301
C.	Procedure Comments	1,320	1,865
D.	Fit and Quality	1,436	1,546
E.	Backorder and Availability	672	967
F.	Miscellaneous	122	229
	TOTALS	10,299	13,007

CUSTOMER COMMENTS SUMMARY TO DATE

	Size	Prod.	Proc.	F & Q	Avail.	Misc.
09/95	31%	34%	13%	14%	7%	1%
08/95	30%	35%	11%	13%	10%	1%
07/95	25%	36%	11%	15%	15%	1%
06/95	26%	35%	9%	13%	15%	2%
05/95	31%	35%	9%	13%	11%	1%
04/95	31%	36%	10%	15%	7%	1%
03/95	31%	34%	12%	15%	7%	1%
02/95	28%	31%	13%	19%	8%	1%
01/95	27%	32%	13%	19%	8%	1%
12/94	22%	26%	23%	16%	12%	1%
11/94	26%	32%	19%	15%	7%	1%
10/94	32%	34%	15%	12%	6%	1%
09/94	32%	33%	14%	12%	7%	2%

Our goal is to keep sales representatives working the phones 85 percent of the time. This means that expected idle time should be about 15 percent. If we get below 85 percent, then we may decide to send some of the part-timers home because we need to get call frequency higher. Conversely, if phone occupancy is at 89 percent, we know we can't meet our service goal and we'll shift calls to another center if possible, or maybe call people in.

Finally, how serious is Lands' End about customer feedback? Apparently, very serious. For example, customer phone comments made to sales representatives are logged and, on a monthly basis, reported on several different levels for the company as a whole, for each division, for the breakdowns within that division (for instance, Men's Tailored, Coed Knits), and by issues. Look, for example at the overview of September 1995 Customer Comments. From information in this inset, one can see that 10,299 comments were received in September of 1995—a decrease of 2,207 comments from August 1995 and a decrease of 2,708 comments from a year earlier (September 1994). Furthermore, you can see that 3,203 comments were related to sizing issues—issues that were reported less (by 1 percent of callers) in September than they were in August. Also worthy of note is the fact that the entire September 1995 Customer Comments document is 190 pages long. It examines customer comments in the minutest possible detail (for example, 5 comments were made on men's size S print polo shirt in the coed knit category, 1 negative comment was made that swimsuits with #1 leg openings are still cut too high).

Questions:

1. Do you believe that customer-service practices at Lands' End would qualify as total quality management (TQM)? Explain.
2. To which of Demming's 14 points would it appear that Lands' End is subscribing? Explain.
3. Which of the management strategies for quality (that is, value adding, leadership, and so forth) is Lands' End apparently implementing in its operations? Explain.
4. Do you see any example in the cases that Lands' End may have heeded Juran's advice on achieving quality? Explain.

GLOSSARY

Accountability refers to the management philosophy whereby individuals are held liable, or accountable, for how well they use their authority or live up to their responsibility of performing predetermined activities. *p. 260*

Activities are specified sets of behavior within a project. *p. 216*

Adjourning the fifth and last stage of the team development process, is the stage in which the team finishes its job and prepares to disband. *p. 419*

Affirmative action programs are organizational programs whose basic purpose is to eliminate barriers against and increase employment opportunities for underutilized or disadvantaged individuals. *p. 280*

Alderfer's ERG theory is an explanation of human needs that divides them into three basic types: existence needs, relatedness needs, and growth needs. *p. 386*

Appropriate human resources are the individuals in the organization who make a valuable contribution to management system goal attainment. *p. 274*

Argyris' maturity-immaturity continuum is a concept that furnishes insights into human needs by focusing on an individual's natural progress from immaturity to maturity. *p. 386*

Assessment center is a program in which participants engage in, and are evaluated on, a number of individual and group exercises constructed to simulate important activities at the organizational levels to which they aspire. *p. 284*

Attitude is a predisposition to react to a situation, person, or concept with a particular response. *p. 430*

Attribution is the process by which people interpret the behavior of others by assigning to it motives or causes. *p. 439*

Attribution error is the tendency to overestimate internal causes of behavior and underestimate external ones when judging other people's behavior. *p. 441*

Authority is the right to perform or command. *p. 256*

Behavior modification is a program that focuses on managing human activity by controlling the consequences of performing that activity. *p. 394*

Behavioral approach to management is a management approach that emphasizes increasing organizational success by focusing on human variables within the organization. *p. 37*

Beliefs are accepted facts or truths about an object or person that have been gained from either direct experience or a secondary source. *p. 430*

Bicultural stress is stress resulting from having to cope with membership in two cultures simultaneously. *p. 572*

Brainstorming is a group decision-making process in which negative feedback on any suggested alternative to any group member is forbidden until all group members have presented alternatives that they perceive as valuable. *p. 169*

Breakeven analysis is a control tool that summarizes the various levels of profit or loss associated with various levels of production. *p. 497*

Breakeven point is that level of production where the total revenue of an organization equals its total costs. *p. 497*

Budget is a control tool that outlines how funds in a given period will be spent, as well as how they will be obtained. *p. 206, p. 492*

Bureaucracy is the term Max Weber used to describe a management system characterized by detailed procedures and rules, a clearly outlined organizational hierarchy, and impersonal relationships among organization members. *p. 232*

Business portfolio analysis is the development of business-related strategy based primarily on the market share of businesses and the growth of markets in which businesses exist. *p. 188*

Capacity strategy is an operational plan of action aimed at providing the organization with the right facilities to produce the needed output at the right time. *p. 485*

Career is a sequence of work-related positions occupied by a person over the course of a lifetime. *p. 12*

Career plateauing is a period of little or no apparent progress in the growth of a career. *p. 13*

Centralization refers to the situation in which a minimal number of job activities and a minimal amount of authority are delegated to subordinates. *p. 265*

Change agent is an individual inside or outside the organization who tries to modify an existing organizational situation. *p. 300*

Changing is the state in which individuals begin to experiment with performing new behaviors. *p. 311*

Changing an organization is the process of modifying an existing organization to increase organizational effectiveness. *p. 298*

Classical approach to management is a management approach that emphasizes organizational efficiency to increase organizational success. *p. 29*

Classical organizing theory comprises the cumulative insights of early management writers on how organizational resources can best be used to enhance goal attainment. *p. 232*

Closed system is one that is not influenced by, and does not interact with, its environment. *p. 42*

Coaching is leadership that instructs followers on how to meet the special organizational challenges they face. *p. 368*

Code of ethics is a formal statement that acts as a guide for making decisions and acting within an organization. *p. 70*

Cognitive learning an approach theory that focuses on thought processes, assumes that human beings have a high capacity to act in a purposeful manner, and so to choose behaviors that will enable them to achieve long-run goals. *p. 443*

Command group is a formal group that is outlined in the chain of command on an organization chart. Command groups handle routine activities. *p. 405*

Commitment principle is a management guideline that advises managers to commit funds for planning only if they can anticipate, in the foreseeable future, a return on planning expenses as a result of the long-range planning analysis. *p. 177*

Committee is a task group that is charged with performing some type of specific activity. *p. 406*

Communication is the process of sharing information with other individuals. *p. 329*

Communication macrobarriers are factors hindering successful communication that relate primarily to the communication environment and the larger world in which communication takes place. *p. 331*

Communication microbarriers are factors hindering successful communication that relate primarily to such variables as the communication message, the source, and the destination. *p. 332*

Comparative management is the study of the management process in different countries to examine the potential of management action under different environmental conditions. *p. 99*

Complete certainty condition is the decision-making situation in which the decision maker knows exactly what the results of an implemented alternative will be. *p. 165*

Complete uncertainty condition is the decision-making situation in which the decision maker has absolutely no idea what the results of an implemented alternative will be. *p. 165*

Comprehensive analysis of management involves studying the management function as a whole. *p. 35*

Computer is an electronic tool capable of accepting data, interpreting data, performing ordered operations on data, and reporting on the outcome of these operations. Computers are extremely helpful in generating information from raw data. *p. 521*

Computer-aided design (CAD) is a computerized technique for designing new products or modifying existing ones. *p. 501*

Computer-aided manufacturing (CAM) is a technique that employs computers to plan and program equipment used in the production and inspection of manufactured items. *p. 501*

Computer network is a system of two or more connected computers that allows computer users to communicate, cooperate, and share resources. *p. 526*

Conceptual skills are skills involving the ability to see the organization as a whole. *p. 11*

Concurrent control is control that takes place as some unit of work is being performed. *p. 463*

Consensus is agreement on a decision by all individuals involved in making that decision. *p. 156*

Consideration behavior is leadership behavior that reflects friendship, mutual trust, respect, and warmth in the relationship between leader and followers. *p. 359*

Content theories of motivation are explanations of motivation that emphasize people's internal characteristics. *p. 380*

Contingency approach to management is a management approach that emphasizes that what managers do in practice depends on a given set of circumstances—a situation. *p. 41*

Contingency theory of leadership is a leadership concept that hypothesizes that, in any given leadership situation, success is determined primarily by (1) the degree to which the task being performed by the followers is structured, (2) the degree of position power possessed by the leader, and (3) the type of relationship that exists between the leader and the followers. *p. 362*

Control is making something happen the way it was planned to happen. *p. 456*

Control function is computer activities that dictate the order in which other computer functions are performed. *p. 523*

Controller is the staff person whose basic responsibility is to assist line managers with the controlling function by gathering appropriate information and generating necessary reports that reflect this information. *p. 465*

Controlling is the process managers go through to control. It is a systematic effort to compare performance to predetermined standards, plans, or objectives to determine whether performance is in line with those standards or needs to be corrected. *p. 456*

Control tool is a specific procedure or technique that presents pertinent organizational information in a way that helps managers to develop and implement an appropriate control strategy. *p. 495*

Coordination is the orderly arrangement of group effort to provide unity of action in the pursuit of a common purpose. It involves encouraging the completion of individual portions of a task in an appropriate, synchronized order. *p. 239*

Corporate culture is a set of shared values and beliefs that organization members have regarding the functioning and existence of their organization. *p. 422*

Corporate social responsibility is the managerial obligation to take action that protects and improves both the welfare of society as a whole and the interests of the organization. *p. 51*

Corrective action is managerial activity aimed at bringing organizational performance up to the level of performance standards. *p. 461*

Cost-benefit analysis is the process of comparing the cost of some activity with the benefit or revenue that results from the activity to determine the activity's total worth to the organization. *p. 465*

Cost leadership is a strategy that focuses on making an organization more competitive by producing products more cheaply than competitors can. *p. 191*

Critical path is the sequence of events and activities within a program evaluation and review technique (PERT) network that requires the longest period of time to complete. *p. 216*

Critical question analysis is a strategy development tool that consists of answering basic questions about the present purposes and objectives of the organization, its present direction and environment, and actions that can be taken to achieve organizational objectives in the future. *p. 187*

Cross-functional team is an organizational team composed of people from different functional areas of the organization who are all focused on a specified objective. *p. 417*

Data are facts or statistics. *p. 508*

Database is a reservoir of corporate facts consistently organized to fit the information needs of a variety of organization members. *p. 525*

Decentralization refers to the situation in which a significant number of job activities and a maximum amount of authority are delegated to subordinates. *p. 265*

Decision is a choice made between two or more available alternatives. *p. 154*

Decision tree is a graphic decision-making tool typically used to evaluate decisions involving a series of steps. *p. 167*

Decision-tree analysis is a statistical and graphical multiphased decision-making technique that shows the sequence and interdependence of decisions. *p. 500*

Decline stage is the fourth and last stage in career evolution; it occurs near retirement age, when individuals of about 65 years of age show declining productivity. *p. 13*

Decoder/destination   is the person or persons in the interpersonal communication situation with whom the source is attempting to share information. *p. 331*

Delegation   is the process of assigning job activities and related authority to specific individuals in the organization. *p. 262*

Delphi technique   is a group decision-making process that involves circulating questionnaires on a specific problem among group members, sharing the questionnaire results with them, and then continuing to recirculate and refine individual responses until a consensus regarding the problem is reached. *p. 170*

Demographics   are the statistical characteristics of a population. Organizational strategy should reflect demographics. *p. 181*

Department   is a unique group of resources established by management to perform some organizational task. *p. 234*

Departmentalization   is the process of establishing departments within the management system. *p. 234*

Dialogue capability   is the ability of an MDSS user to interact with an MDSS. *p. 526*

Differentiation   is a strategy that focuses on making an organization more competitive by developing a product or products that customers perceive as being different from products offered by competitors. *p. 191*

Direct investing   is using the assets of one company to purchase the operating assets of another company. *p. 91*

Discrimination   is the act of treating an issue, person, or behavior unjustly or inequitably on the basis of stereotypes or prejudices. *p. 571*

Diversity   is the degree of basic human differences among a given population. Major areas of diversity are gender, race, ethnicity, religion, social class, physical ability, sexual orientation, and age. *p. 565*

Diversity training   is a learning process designed to raise managers' awareness and develop their competencies to deal with the issues endemic to managing a diverse workforce. *p. 582*

Divestiture   is a strategy adopted to eliminate a strategic business unit that is not generating a satisfactory amount of business and has little hope of doing so in the future. *p. 192*

Division of labor   is the assignment of various portions of a particular task among a number of organization members. Division of labor calls for specialization. *p. 239*

Domestic organization   is a company that essentially operates within a single country. *p. 82*

Downward organizational communication   is communication that flows from any point on an organization chart downward to another point on the organization chart. *p. 338*

Economics   is the science that focuses on understanding how people of a particular community or nation produce, distribute, and use various goods and services. *p. 180*

Effectiveness   is the degree to which managers attain organizational objectives; it is doing the right things. *p. 485*

Efficiency   is the degree to which organizational resources contribute to production; it is doing things right. *p. 485*

Employee-centered behavior   is leader behavior that focuses primarily on subordinates as people. *p. 360*

Entrepreneurial leadership   is leadership that is based on the attitude that the leader is self-employed. *p. 370*

Environmental analysis   is the study of the organizational environment to pinpoint environmental factors that can significantly influence organizational operations. *p. 179*

Equal Employment Opportunity Commission (EEOC)   is an agency established to enforce federal laws regulating recruiting and other employment practices. *p. 279*

Equity theory of motivation   is an explanation of motivation that emphasizes the individual's perceived fairness of an employment situation and how perceived inequities can cause certain behaviors. *p. 382*

Establishment stage   is the second stage in career evolution; individuals of about 25 to 45 years of age typically start to become more productive, or higher performers. *p. 13*

Esteem needs   are Maslow's fourth set of human needs—including the desires for self-respect and respect from others. *p. 385*

Ethics   is our concern for good behavior; our obligation to consider not only our own personal well-being but also that of other human beings. *p. 68*

Ethnocentric attitude   reflects the belief that multinational corporations should regard home-country management practices as superior to foreign-country management practices. *p. 95*

Ethnocentrism   is the belief that one's own group, culture, country, or customs are superior to others'. *p. 571*

Events   are the completions of major project tasks. *p. 216*

Expected value (EV)   is the measurement of the anticipated value of some event, determined by multiplying the income an event would produce by its probability of producing that income (EV 5 I 3 P). *p. 166*

Exploration stage   is the first stage in career evolution; it occurs at the beginning of a career, when the individual is typically 15–25 years of age, and is characterized by self-analysis and the exploration of different types of available jobs. *p. 12*

Exporting   is selling goods or services to another country. *p. 91*

Extrinsic rewards   are rewards that are extraneous to the task accomplished. *p. 382*

Feedback   is, in the interpersonal communication situation, the destination's reaction to a message. *p. 334*

Feedback control   is control that takes place after some unit of work has been performed. *p. 463*

Financial objectives   are organizational targets relating to monetary issues. They are influenced by return on investment and financial comparisons with competitors. *p. 119*

Fixed costs   are expenses incurred by the organization regardless of the number of products produced. *p. 497*

Fixed-position layout   is a layout plan appropriate for organizations involved in a large number of different tasks that require low volumes, multipurpose equipment, and broad employee skills. *p. 488*

Flat organization chart   is an organization chart characterized by few levels and a relatively broad span of management. *p. 242*

Flextime   is a program that allows workers to complete their jobs within a workweek of a normal number of hours that they schedule themselves. *p. 393*

Focus   is a strategy that emphasizes making an organization more competitive by targeting a particular customer. *p. 191*

Forecasting   is a planning tool used to predict future environ-

mental happenings that will influence the operation of the organization. *p. 211*

Formal group   is a group that exists in an organization by virtue of management decree to perform tasks that enhance the attainment of organizational objectives. *p. 404*

Formal organizational communication   is organizational communication that follows the lines of the organization chart. *p. 337*

Formal structure   is defined as the relationships among organizational resources as outlined by management. *p. 234*

Forming   is the first stage of the team development process, during which members of the newly formed team become oriented to the team and acquainted with one another as they explore issues related to their new job situation. *p. 419*

Friendship group   is an informal group that forms in organizations because of the personal affiliation members have with one another. *p. 412*

Functional authority   consists of the right to give orders within a segment of the management system in which the right is normally nonexistent. *p. 260*

Functional objectives   are targets relating to key organizational functions. They should be consistent with financial and product-market mix objectives. *p. 121*

Functional similarity method   is a method for dividing job activities in the organization. *p. 252*

Gangplank   is a communication channel extending from one organizational division to another but not shown in the lines of communication outlined on an organization chart. Use of Fayol's gangplank may be quicker, but could prove costly in the long run. *p. 244*

Gantt chart   is a scheduling tool composed of a bar chart with time on the horizontal axis and the resource to be scheduled on the vertical axis. It is used for scheduling resources. *p. 215*

Gender-role stereotypes   are perceptions about the sexes based on what society believes are appropriate behaviors for men and women. *p. 572*

General environment   is the level of an organization's external environment that contains components normally having broad long-term implications for managing the organization; its components are economic, social, political, legal, and technological. *p. 180*

Geocentric attitude   reflects the belief that the overall quality of management recommendations, rather than the location of managers, should determine the acceptability of management practices used to guide multinational corporations. The geocentric attitude is considered most appropriate for long-term organizational success. *p. 95*

Goal integration   is compatibility between individual and organizational objectives. It occurs when organizational and individual objectives are the same. *p. 116*

Graicunas' formula   is a formula that makes the span-of-management point that as the number of a manager's subordinates increases arithmetically, the number of possible relationships between the manager and the subordinates increases geometrically. *p. 241*

Grapevine   is the network of informal organizational communication. *p. 341*

Grid organization development (grid OD)   is a commonly used organization development technique based on a theoretical model called the managerial grid. *p. 306*

Group   is any number of people who (1) interact with one another, (2) are psychologically aware of one another, and (3) perceive themselves to be a group. *p. 404*

Groupthink   is the mode of thinking that group members engage in when the desire for agreement so dominates the group that it overrides the need to realistically appraise alternate problem solutions. *p. 408*

Growth   is a strategy adopted by management to increase the amount of business that a strategic business unit is currently generating. *p. 192*

Halo effect   results from allowing one particular aspect of someone's behavior to influence one's evaluation of all other aspects of that person's behavior. *p. 440*

Hierarchy of objectives   is the overall organizational objectives and the subobjectives assigned to the various people or units of the organization. *p. 122*

Host country   is the country in which an investment is made by a foreign company. *p. 86*

Human relations movement   is a people-oriented approach to management in which the interaction of people in organizations is studied to judge its impact on organizational success. *p. 38*

Human relations skill   is the ability to work with people in a way that enhances organizational success. *p. 38*

Human resource inventory   is an accumulation of information about the characteristics of organization members; this information focuses on members' past performance as well as on how they might be trained and best used in the future. *p. 276*

Human resource planning   is input planning that involves obtaining the human resources necessary for the organization to achieve its objectives. *p. 210*

Human resources strategy   s an operational plan to use the organization's human resources effectively and efficiently while maintaining or improving the quality of work life. *p. 488*

Human skills   are skills involving the ability to build cooperation within the team being led. *p. 11*

Hygiene, or maintenance, factors   are items that influence the degree of job dissatisfaction. *p. 391*

Importing   is buying goods or services from another country. *p. 91*

Individual objectives   are personal goals that each organization member would like to reach as a result of personal activity in the organization. *p. 116*

Influencing   is the process of guiding the activities of organization members in appropriate directions. It involves the performance of four management activities: (1) leading, (2) motivating, (3) considering groups, and (4) communicating. *p. 326*

Informal group   is a collection of individuals whose common work experiences result in the development of a system of interpersonal relations that extend beyond those established by management. *p. 411*

Informal organizational communication   is organizational communication that does not follow the lines of the organization chart. *p. 340*

Informal structure   is defined as the patterns of relationships that develop because of the informal activities of organization members. *p. 234*

Information   is the set of conclusions derived from data analysis. *p. 508*

Information appropriateness is the degree to which information is relevant to the decision-making situation the manager faces. *p. 509*

Information quality is the degree to which information represents reality. *p. 510*

Information quantity is the amount of decision-related information a manager possesses. *p. 510*

Information technology is technology that focuses on the use of information in the performance of work. *p. 521*

Information timeliness is the extent to which the receipt of information allows decisions to be made and action to be taken so the organization can gain some benefit from possessing the information. *p. 510*

Input function is computer activities through which the computer enters the data to be analyzed and the instructions to be followed to analyze the data appropriately. *p. 522*

Input planning is the development of proposed action that will furnish sufficient and appropriate organizational resources for reaching established organizational objectives. *p. 207*

Interest group is an informal group that gains and maintains membership primarily because of a common concern members have about a specific issue. *p. 412*

Intermediate-term objectives are targets to be achieved within one to five years. *p. 118*

Internal environment is the level of an organization's environment that exists inside the organization and normally has immediate and specific implications for managing the organization. *p. 184*

International joint venture is a partnership formed by a company in one country with a company in another country for the purpose of pursuing some mutually desirable business undertaking. *p. 92*

International management is the performance of management activities across national borders. *p. 79*

International market agreement is an arrangement among a cluster of countries that facilitates a high level of trade among these countries. *p. 92*

International organization is a company that is primarily based within a single country but has continuing, meaningful transactions in other countries. *p. 82*

Internet is a large interconnected network of computer networks linking people and computers all over the world via phone lines, satellites, and other telecommunications systems. *p. 528*

Intrinsic rewards are rewards that come directly from performing a task. *p. 382*

Job analysis is a technique commonly used to gain an understanding of what a task entails and the type of individual who should be hired to perform that task. *p. 275*

Job-centered behavior is leader behavior that focuses primarily on the work a subordinate is doing. *p. 360*

Job description is a list of specific activities that must be performed to accomplish some task or job. *p. 251, p. 275*

Job design is an operational plan that determines who will do a specific job and how and where the job will be done. *p. 489*

Job enlargement is the process of increasing the number of operations an individual performs in a job. *p. 391*

Job enrichment is the process of incorporating motivators into a job situation. *p. 391*

Job rotation is the process of moving workers from one job to another rather than requiring them to perform only one simple and specialized job over the long term. *p. 390*

Job specification is a list of the characteristics of the individual who should be hired to perform a specific task or job. *p. 275*

Jury of executive opinion method is a method of predicting future sales levels primarily by asking appropriate managers to give their opinions on what will happen to sales in the future. *p. 212*

Just-in-time (JIT) inventory control is a technique for reducing inventories to a minimum by arranging for production components to be delivered to the production facility "just in time" to be used. *p. 490*

Lateral organizational communication is communication that flows from any point on an organization chart horizontally to another point on the organization chart. *p. 338*

Law of the situation indicates that managers must continually analyze the unique circumstances within their organizations and apply management concepts to fit those circumstances. *p. 17*

Layout is the overall arrangement of equipment, work areas, service areas, and storage areas within a facility that produces goods or provides services. *p. 488*

Layout strategy is an operational plan that determines the location and flow of organizational resources around, into, and within production and service facilities. *p. 487*

Leader flexibility is the ability to change leadership style. *p. 362*

Leadership is the process of directing the behavior of others toward the accomplishment of objectives. *p. 350*

Leadership style is the behavioral pattern a leader establishes while guiding organization members in appropriate directions. *p. 359*

Learning is a more or less permanent change in behavior resulting from practice, experience, education, or training. *p. 443*

Lecture is primarily a one-way communication situation in which an instructor trains by orally presenting information to an individual or a group. *p. 287*

Level dimension of a plan is the level of the organization at which the plan is aimed. *p. 203*

License agreement is a right granted by one company to another to use its brand name, technology, product specifications, and so on in the manufacture or sale of goods and services. *p. 91*

Life cycle theory of leadership is a leadership concept that hypothesizes that leadership styles should reflect primarily the maturity level of the followers. *p. 361*

Line authority consists of the right to make decisions and to give orders concerning the production-, sales-, or finance-related behavior of subordinates. *p. 257*

Local area network (LAN) is a computer network characterized by software that manages how information travels through cables to arrive at a number of connected single-user computer workstations. *p. 527*

Location strategy is an operational plan of action that provides the organization with a competitive location for its headquarters, manufacturing, services, and distribution activities. *p. 485*

Long-term objectives are targets to be achieved within five to seven years. *p. 118*

Loss is the amount of the total costs of producing a product that exceeds the total revenue gained from selling the product. *p. 497*

Maintenance stage is the third stage in career evolution; individuals of about 45 to 65 years of age either become more productive, stabilize, or become less productive. *p. 13*

Majority group refers to that group of people in the organization who hold most of the positions that command decision-making power, control of resources and information, and access to system rewards. *p. 565*

Management is the process of reaching organizational goals by working with and through people and other organizational resources. *p. 6*

Management by exception is a control tool that allows only significant deviations between planned and actual performance to be brought to a manager's attention. *p. 496*

Management by objectives (MBO) is a management approach that uses organizational objectives as the primary means of managing organizations. *p. 125*

Management decision support system (MDSS) is an interdependent set of computer-oriented decision aids that help managers make nonprogrammed decisions. The following characteristics are typical of an MDSS. *p. 525*

Management functions are activities that make up the management process. The four basic management activities are planning, organizing, influencing, and controlling. *p. 6*

Management information system (MIS) is a network established within an organization to provide managers with information that will assist them in decision making. An MIS gets information to where it is needed. *p. 513*

Management inventory card is a form used in compiling a human resource inventory. It contains the organizational history of an individual and indicates how that individual might be used in the organization in the future. *p. 275*

Management manpower replacement chart is a form used in compiling a human resource inventory. It is people-oriented and presents a composite view of individuals management considers significant to human resource planning. *p. 278*

Management responsibility guide is a tool that is used to clarify the responsibilities of various managers in the organization. *p. 254*

Management science approach is a management approach that emphasizes the use of the scientific method and quantitative techniques to increase organizational success. *p. 39*

Management system is an open system whose major parts are organizational input, organizational process, and organizational output. *p. 43*

Managerial effectiveness refers to management's use of organizational resources in meeting organizational goals. *p. 9*

Managerial efficiency is the degree to which organizational resources contribute to productivity. It is measured by the proportion of total organizational resources used during the production process. *p. 9*

Managerial grid is a theoretical model based on the premise that concern for people and concern for production are the two primary attitudes that influence management style. *p. 306*

Manpower planning is an operational plan that focuses on hiring the right employees for a job and training them to be productive. *p. 488*

Materials control is an operational activity that determines the flow of materials from vendors through an operations system to customers. *p. 494*

Matrix organization is a traditional organizational structure that is modified primarily for the purpose of completing some type of special project. *p. 303*

McClelland's acquired needs theory is an explanation of human needs that focuses on the desires for achievement, power, and affiliation that people develop as a result of their life experiences. *p. 387*

Means-ends analysis is the process of outlining the means by which various organizational objectives, or ends, can be achieved. *p. 124*

Message is encoded information that the source intends to share with others. *p. 330*

Message interference refers to stimuli that compete with the communication message for the attention of the destination. *p. 333*

Minority group refers to that group of people in the organization who are smaller in number or who possess fewer granted rights and lower status than the majority groups. *p. 565*

Mission statement is a written document developed by management, normally based on input by managers as well as nonmanagers, that describes and explains the organization's mission. *p. 186*

Model base is a collection of quantitative computer programs that can assist MDSS users in analyzing data within databases. *p. 526*

Motion study finds the best way to accomplish a task by analyzing the movements necessary to perform that task. *p. 31*

Motion-study techniques are operational tools that are used to improve productivity. *p. 489*

Motivating factors, or motivators are items that influence the degree of job satisfaction. *p. 391*

Motivation is the inner state that causes an individual to behave in a way that ensures the accomplishment of some goal. *p. 380*

Motivation strength is an individual's degree of desire to perform a behavior. *p. 381*

Multinational corporation (MNC) is a company that has significant operations in more than one country. *p. 82*

Needs-goal theory is a motivation model that hypothesizes that felt needs cause human behavior. *p. 380*

Negative reinforcement is a reward that consists of the elimination of an undesirable consequence of behavior. *p. 394*

Nominal group technique is a group decision-making process in which every group member is assured of equal participation in making the group decision. After each member writes down individual ideas and presents them orally to the group, the entire group discusses all the ideas and then votes for the best idea in a secret ballot. *p. 170*

Nonprogrammed decisions are typically one-shot decisions that are usually less structured than programmed decisions. *p. 154*

Nonverbal communication is the sharing of information without using words. *p. 336*

Norming the third stage of the team development process, is characterized by agreement among team members on roles, rules, and acceptable behavior while working on the team. *p. 419*

On-the-job-training is a training technique that blends job-related knowledge with experience in using that knowledge on the job. *p. 289*

Open system is one that is influenced by, and is constantly interacting with, its environment. *p. 42*

Operant learning is an approach that holds the behavior leading to positive consequences is more likely to be repeated. *p. 443*

Operating environment is the level of the organization's external environment that contains components normally having relatively specific and immediate implications for managing the organization. *p. 183*

Operational objectives are objectives that are stated in observable or measurable terms. They specify the activities or operations needed to attain them. *p. 123*

Operations control is an operational plan that specifies the operational activities of an organization. *p. 490*

Operations management is the systematic direction (strategy) and control of operations processes that transform resources into finished goods and services; it is getting things done by working with or through other people. *p. 484*

Organization chart is a graphic representation of organizational structure. *p. 232*

Organization development (OD) is the process that emphasizes changing an organization by changing organization members and bases these changes on an overview of structure, technology, and all other organizational ingredients. *p. 306*

Organizational communication is interpersonal communication within organizations. *p. 337*

Organizational mission is the purpose for which, or the reason why, an organization exists. *p. 185*

Organizational objectives are the targets toward which the open management system is directed. They flow from the organization's purpose or mission. *p. 112*

Organizational purpose is what the organization exists to do, given a particular group of customers and customer needs. *p. 112*

Organizational resources are all assets available for activation during normal operations; they include human resources, monetary resources, raw materials resources, and capital resources. *p. 8*

Organizing is the process of establishing orderly uses for all the organization's resources. *p. 228*

Output function is computer activities that take the results of input, storage, processing, and control functions and transmit them outside the computer. *p. 523*

Overlapping responsibility refers to a situation in which more than one individual is responsible for the same activity. *p. 252*

Parent company is the company investing in international operations. *p. 86*

Path-goal theory of leadership is a theory of leadership that suggests that the primary activities of a leader are to make desirable and achievable rewards available to organization members who attain organizational goals and to clarify the kinds of behavior that must be performed to earn those rewards. *p. 365*

People change is a type of organizational change that emphasizes modifying certain aspects of organization members to increase organizational effectiveness. *p. 305*

People factors are attitudes, leadership skills, communication skills, and all other characteristics of the organization's employees. *p. 301*

Perception is the interpretation of a message by an individual. *p. 333*

Perception is the psychological process of selecting stimuli, organizing the data into recognizable patterns, and interpreting the resulting information. *p. 438*

Perceptual process is the series of actions that individuals follow in order to select, organize, and interpret stimuli from the environment. *p. 438*

Performance appraisal is the process of reviewing past productive activity to evaluate the contribution individuals have made toward attaining management system objectives. *p. 290*

Performing the fourth stage of the team development process, is characterized by a focus on solving organizational problems and meeting assigned challenges. *p. 419*

Personal power is the power derived from a manager's relationships with others. *p. 467*

Physiological needs are Maslow's first set of human needs—for the normal functioning of the body, including the desires for water, food, rest, sex, and air. *p. 385*

Plan is a specific action proposed to help the organization achieve its objectives. *p. 202*

Plan for planning is a listing of all the steps that must be taken to plan for an organization. It ensures that planning gets done. *p. 142*

Planning is the process of determining how the management system will achieve its objectives. In other words, it determines how the organization can get where it wants to go. *p. 134*

Plant facilities planning is input planning that involves developing the type of work facility an organization will need to reach its objectives. *p. 207*

Planning tools are techniques managers can use to help develop plans. *p. 211*

Pluralism is an environment in which cultural, group, and individual differences are acknowledged, accepted, and viewed as significant contributors to the entirety. *p. 578*

Policy is a standing plan that furnishes broad guidelines for channeling management toward taking action consistent with reaching organizational objectives. *p. 204*

Polycentric attitude reflects the belief that because foreign managers are closer to foreign organizational units, they probably understand them better, and therefore foreign management practices should generally be viewed as more insightful than home-country management practices. *p. 95*

Porter-Lawler theory is a motivation theory that hypothesizes that felt needs cause human behavior and that motivation strength is determined primarily by the perceived value of the result of performing the behavior and the perceived probability that the behavior performed will cause the result to materialize. *p. 382*

Position power is power derived from the organizational position a manager holds. *p. 467*

Position replacement form is used in compiling a human resource inventory. It summarizes information about organization members who could fill a position should it open up. *p. 275*

Positive reinforcement is a reward that consists of a desirable consequence of behavior. *p. 394*

Power is the extent to which an individual is able to influence others so that they respond to orders. *p. 467*

Precontrol is control that takes place before some unit of work is actually performed. *p. 463*

Prejudice is a preconceived judgment, opinion, or assumption about an issue, behavior, individual, or group of people. *p. 571*

Premises are the assumptions on which an alternative to reaching an organizational objective is based. *p. 137*

Principle of the objective is a management guideline that recommends that before managers initiate any action, they should clearly determine, understand, and state organizational objectives. *p. 118*

Probability theory is a decision-making tool used in risk situations—situations in which the decision maker is not completely sure of the outcome of an implemented alternative. *p. 166*

Problems are factors within an organization that are barriers to organizational goal attainment. *p. 461*

Problem-solving team is an organizational team set up to help eliminate a specified problem within the organization. *p. 416*

Procedural justice is the perceived fairness of the process used for deciding workplace outcomes such as merit increases and promotions. *p. 442*

Procedure is a standing plan that outlines a series of related actions that must be taken to accomplish a particular task. *p. 205*

Process (functional) layout is a layout pattern based primarily on grouping together similar types of equipment. *p. 488*

Process control is a technique that assists in monitoring production processes. *p. 501*

Processing function is computer activities involved with performing the logic and calculation steps necessary to analyze data appropriately. *p. 523*

Process strategy is an operational plan of action outlining the means and methods the organization will use to transform resources into goods and services. *p. 487*

Process theories of motivation are explanations of motivation that emphasize how individuals are motivated. *p. 380*

Production is the transformation of organizational resources into products. *p. 477*

Productivity is the relationship between the total amount of goods or services being produced (output) and the organizational resources needed to produce them (input). *p. 478*

Product layout is a layout designed to accommodate a limited number of different products that require high volumes, highly specialized equipment, and narrow employee skills. *p. 488*

Product life cycle is the five stages through which most products and services pass: introduction, growth, maturity, saturation, and decline. *p. 213*

Product-market mix objectives are objectives that outline which products—and the relative number or mix of these products—the organization will attempt to sell. *p. 120*

Product strategy is an operational plan of action outlining which goods and services an organization will produce and market. *p. 487*

Processing function is computer activities involved with performing the logic and calculation steps necessary to analyze data appropriately. *p. 523*

Production control ensures that an organization produces goods and services as planned. *p. 477*

Profits are the amount of total revenue that exceeds total costs. *p. 497*

Program is a single-use plan designed to carry out a special project in an organization that, if accomplished, will contribute to the organization's long-term success. *p. 206*

Program evaluation and review technique (PERT) is a scheduling tool that is essentially a network of project activities showing estimates of time necessary to complete each activity and the sequence of activities that must be followed to complete the project. *p. 216*

Programmed decisions are decisions that are routine and repetitive and that typically require specific handling methods. *p. 154*

Programmed learning is a technique for instructing without the presence or intervention of a human instructor. Small pieces of information requiring responses are presented to individual trainees, and the trainees determine from checking their responses against provided answers whether their understanding of the information is accurate. *p. 288*

Projection is the unconscious tendency to assign one's own traits, motives, beliefs, and attitudes to others. *p. 440*

Punishment is the presentation of an undesirable behavioral consequence or the removal of a desirable one that decreases the likelihood that the behavior will continue. *p. 394*

Pure-breakdown (repair) policy is a maintenance control policy that decrees that machine adjustments, lubrication, cleaning, parts replacement, painting, and needed repairs and overhaul will be performed only after facilities or machines malfunction. *p. 491*

Pure-preventive maintenance policy is a maintenance control policy that tries to ensure that machine adjustments, lubrication, cleaning, parts replacement, painting, and needed repairs and overhauls will be performed before facilities or machines malfunction. *p. 491*

Quality is the extent to which a product does what it is supposed to do—how closely and reliably it satisfies the specifications to which it is built. *p. 479, p. 542*

Quality assurance is an operations process involving a broad group of activities that are aimed at achieving the organization's quality objectives. *p. 480*

Quality circles are small groups of workers that meet to discuss quality-related problems on a particular project and communicate their solutions to these problems to management at a formal presentation session. *p. 481*

Quality-oriented policy is a standing plan that furnishes broad, general guidelines for channeling management thinking toward taking action consistent with reaching quality objectives. *p. 553*

Ratio analysis is a control tool that summarizes the financial position of an organization by calculating ratios based on various financial measures. *p. 493*

Recruitment is the initial attraction and screening of the supply of prospective human resources available to fill a position. *p. 274*

Refreezing is the state in which an individual's experimentally performed behaviors become part of the person. *p. 311*

Relevant alternatives are alternatives that are considered feasible for solving an existing problem and for implementation. *p. 159*

Repatriation is the process of bringing individuals who have

been working abroad back to their home country and reintegrating them into the organization's home-country operations. *p. 88*

Repetitiveness dimension of a plan is the extent to which the plan is to be used over and over again. *p. 203*

Responsibility is the obligation to perform assigned activities. *p. 251*

Responsibility gap exists when certain organizational tasks are not included in the responsibility area of any individual organization member. *p. 253*

Retrenchment is a strategy adopted by management to strengthen or protect the amount of business a strategic business unit is currently generating. *p. 192*

Reverse discrimination is the term used to describe inequities affecting members of the majority group as an outcome of programs designed to help underrepresented groups. *p. 576*

Risk condition is the decision-making situation in which the decision maker has only enough information to estimate how probable the outcome of implemented alternatives will be. *p. 165*

Robotics is the study of the development and use of robots. *p. 483*

Role conflict is the conflict that results when a person has to fill competing roles because of membership in two cultures. *p. 572*

Role overload refers to having too many expectations to comfortably fulfill. *p. 572*

Rule is a standing plan that designates specific required action. *p. 205*

Salesforce estimation method predicts future sales levels primarily by asking appropriate salespeople for their opinions of what will happen to sales in the future. *p. 212*

Scalar relationships refer to the chain-of-command positioning of individuals on an organization chart. *p. 243*

Scheduling is the process of formulating a detailed listing of activities that must be accomplished to attain an objective, allocating the resources necessary to attain the objective, and setting up and following timetables for completing the objective. *p. 215*

Scientific management emphasizes the "one best way" to perform a task. *p. 30*

Scope dimension of a plan is the portion of the total management system at which the plan is aimed. *p. 203*

Scope of the decision is the proportion of the total management system that a particular decision will affect. The broader the scope of a decision, the higher the level of the manager responsible for making that decision. *p. 156*

Security, or safety, needs are Maslow's second set of human needs—reflecting the human desire to keep free from physical harm. *p. 385*

Selection is choosing an individual to hire from all those who have been recruited. *p. 282*

Selective perception is the tendency to collect information that not only supports one's own motives, beliefs, and attitudes but also minimizes the emotional distress caused by unfamiliar or troublesome stimuli. *p. 441*

Self-actualization needs are Maslow's fifth, and final, set of human needs—reflecting the human desire to maximize personal potential. *p. 385*

Self-managed team is an organizational team established to plan, organize, influence, and control its own work situation with only minimal direction from management. *p. 417*

Self-serving bias is the tendency to overestimate external causes of behavior and underestimate internal ones when judging one's own behavior. *p. 441*

Serial transmission involves the passing of information from one individual to another in a series. *p. 339*

Short-term objectives are targets to be achieved in one year or less. *p. 118*

Signal is a message that has been transmitted from one person to another. *p. 330*

Single-use plans are plans that are used only once—or, at most, several times—because they focus on unique or rare situations within the organization. *p. 204*

Site selection involves determining where a plant facility should be located. It may use a weighting process to compare site differences. *p. 207*

Situational approach to leadership is a relatively modern view of leadership that suggests that successful leadership requires a unique combination of leaders, followers, and leadership situations. *p. 352*

Social audit is the process of measuring the present social responsibility activities of an organization. It monitors, measures, and appraises all aspects of an organization's social responsibility performance. *p. 66*

Social needs are Maslow's third set of human needs—reflecting the human desire to belong, including longings for friendship, companionship, and love. *p. 385*

Social obligation approach is an approach to meeting social obligations that considers business to have primarily economic purposes and confines social responsibility activity largely to conformance to existing legislation. *p. 60*

Social responsibility approach is an approach to meeting social obligations that considers business as having both societal and economic goals. *p. 60*

Social responsiveness is the degree of effectiveness and efficiency an organization displays in pursuing its social responsibilities. *p. 58*

Social responsiveness approach is an approach to meeting social obligations that considers business to have societal and economic goals as well as the obligation to anticipate potential social problems and to work actively toward preventing them from occurring. *p. 60*

Social values are the relative degrees of worth society places on the manner in which it exists and functions. *p. 181*

Sociogram is a sociometric diagram that summarizes the personal feelings of organization members about the people in the organization with whom they would like to spend free time. *p. 413*

Sociometry is an analytical tool that can be used to determine what informal groups exist in an organization and who the members of those groups are. *p. 413*

Source/encoder is the person in the interpersonal communication situation who originates and encodes information to be shared with another person or persons. *p. 330*

Span of management is the number of individuals a manager supervises. *p. 241*

Stability is a strategy adopted by management to maintain or slightly improve the amount of business a strategic business unit is generating. *p. 192*

Staff authority consists of the right to advise or assist those who possess line authority. *p. 257*

Stakeholders are all individuals and groups that are directly or indirectly affected by an organization's decisions. *p. 58*

Standard is the level of activity established to serve as a model for evaluating organizational performance. *p. 459*

Standing plans are plans that are used over and over because they focus on organizational situations that occur repeatedly. *p. 204*

Statistical quality control is the process used to determine how many products should be inspected to calculate a probability that the total number of products will meet organizational quality standards. *p. 481*

Stereotype is a fixed, distorted generalization about members of a group. *p. 440*

Stereotype is a positive or negative assessment of members of a group or their perceived attributes. *p. 571*

Storage function is computer activities involved with retaining the material entered into the computer during the performance of the input function. *p. 522*

Storming the second stage of the team development process, is characterized by conflict and disagreement as team members try to clarify their individual roles and challenge the way the team functions. *p. 419*

Strategic business unit (SBU) is, in business portfolio analysis, a significant organizational segment that is analyzed to develop organizational strategy aimed at generating future business or revenue. SBUs vary in form, but all are a single business (or collection of businesses), have their own competitors and a manager accountable for operations, and can be independently planned for. *p. 188*

Strategic control the last step of the strategy management process, consists of monitoring and evaluating the strategy management process as a whole to ensure that it is operating properly. *p. 193*

Strategic planning is long-range planning that focuses on the organization as a whole. *p. 177*

Strategy is a broad and general plan developed to reach long-term organizational objectives; it is the end result of strategic planning. *p. 177*

Strategy formulation is the process of determining appropriate courses of action for achieving organizational objectives and thereby accomplishing organizational purpose. Strategy development tools include critical question analysis, SWOT analysis, business portfolio analysis, and Porter's Model for Industry Analysis. *p. 187*

Strategy implementation the fourth step of the strategy management process, is putting formulated strategy into action. *p. 192*

Strategy management is the process of ensuring that an organization possesses and benefits from the use of an appropriate organizational strategy. *p. 178*

Stress is the bodily strain that an individual experiences as a result of coping with some environmental factor. *p. 313*

Stressor is an environmental demand that causes people to feel stress. *p. 315*

Structural change is a type of organizational change that emphasizes modifying an existing organizational structure. *p. 303*

Structural factors are organizational controls, such as policies and procedures. *p. 301*

Structure refers to the designated relationships among resources of the management system. *p. 232*

Structure behavior is leadership activity that (1) delineates the relationship between the leader and the leader's followers or (2) establishes well-defined procedures that the followers should adhere to in performing their jobs. *p. 359*

Suboptimization is a condition wherein organizational subobjectives are conflicting or not directly aimed at accomplishing the overall organizational objectives. *p. 122*

Subsystem is a system created as part of the process of the overall management system. A planning subsystem increases the effectiveness of the overall management system. *p. 138*

Successful communication refers to an interpersonal communication situation in which the information the source intends to share with the destination and the meaning the destination derives from the transmitted message are the same. *p. 331*

Superleadership is leadership that inspires organizational success by showing followers how to lead themselves. *p. 369*

Suppliers are individuals or agencies that provide organizations with the resources they need to produce goods and services. *p. 184*

SWOT analysis is a strategy development tool that matches internal organizational strengths and weaknesses with external opportunities and threats. *p. 188*

Symptom is a sign that a problem exists. *p. 461*

System is a number of interdependent parts functioning as a whole for some purpose. *p. 42*

System approach to management is a management approach based on general system theory—the theory that to understand fully the operation of an entity, the entity must be viewed as a system. This requires understanding the interdependence of its parts. *p. 42*

Tactical planning is short-range planning that emphasizes the current operations of various parts of the organization. *p. 194*

Task group is a formal group of organization members who interact with one another to accomplish nonroutine organizational tasks. Members of any one task group can and often do come from various levels and segments of an organization. *p. 405*

Team is a group whose members influence one another toward the accomplishment of (an) organizational objective(s). *p. 415*

Technical skills are skills involving the ability to apply specialized knowledge and expertise to work-related techniques and procedures. *p. 10*

Technological change is a type of organizational change that emphasizes modifying the level of technology in the management system. *p. 303*

Technological factors are any types of equipment or processes that assist organization members in the performance of their jobs. *p. 301*

Technology consists of any type of equipment or process that organization members use in the performance of their work. *p. 521*

Testing is examining human resources for qualities relevant to performing available jobs. *p. 283*

Theory of reasoned action states that when a behavior is a mat-

ter of choice, the best predictor of the behavior is the person's intention to perform it. *p. 433*

Theory X is a set of essentially negative assumptions about human nature. *p. 389*

Theory Y is a set of essentially positive assumptions about human nature. *p. 389*

Theory Z is the effectiveness dimension that implies that managers who use either Theory X or Theory Y assumptions when dealing with people can be successful, depending on their situation. *p. 390*

Time dimension of a plan is the length of time the plan covers. *p. 203*

Time series analysis method is a method of predicting future sales levels by analyzing the historical relationship in an organization between sales and time. *p. 212*

Tokenism refers to being one of very few members of a group in an organization. *p. 571*

Total costs are the sum of fixed costs and variable costs. *p. 497*

Total power is the entire amount of power an individual in an organization possesses. It is made up of position power and personal power. *p. 467*

Total quality management (TQM) is the continuous process of involving all organization members in ensuring that every activity related to the production of goods or services has an appropriate role in establishing product quality. *p. 542*

Total revenue is all sales dollars accumulated from selling the goods or services produced by the organization. *p. 497*

Training is the process of developing qualities in human resources that will enable them to be more productive. *p. 285*

Training needs are the information or skill areas of an individual or group that require further development to increase the productivity of that individual or group. *p. 286*

Trait approach to leadership is an outdated view of leadership that sees the personal characteristics of an individual as the main determinants of how successful that individual could be as a leader. *p. 351*

Transformational leadership is leadership that inspires organizational success by profoundly affecting followers' beliefs in what an organization should be, as well as their values, such as justice and integrity. *p. 368*

Transnational organizations also called global organizations, take the entire world as their business arena. *p. 97*

Triangular management is a management approach that emphasizes using information from the classical, behavioral, and management science schools of thought to manage the open management system. *p. 44*

Unfreezing is the state in which individuals experience the ineffectiveness of their present mode of behavior and become ready to learn new behaviors. *p. 311*

Unity of command is the management principle that recommends that an individual have only one boss. *p. 243*

Universality of management means that the principles of management are applicable to all types of organizations and organizational levels. *p. 11*

Unsuccessful communication refers to an interpersonal communication situation in which the information the source intends to share with the destination and the meaning the destination derives from the transmitted message are different. *p. 331*

Upward organizational communication is communication that flows from any point on an organization chart upward to another point on the organization chart. *p. 338*

User database is a database developed by an individual manager or other user. *p. 525*

Value analysis is a cost control and cost reduction technique that examines all the parts, materials, and functions of an operation. *p. 501*

Values are the global beliefs that guide one's actions and judgments across a variety of situations. *p. 430*

Variable budget (also known as a flexible budget) is one that outlines the levels of resources to be allocated for each organizational activity according to the level of production within the organization. *p. 493*

Variable costs are expenses that fluctuate with the number of products produced. *p. 497*

Verbal communication is the sharing of information through words, either written or spoken. *p. 336*

Vroom expectancy theory is a motivation theory that hypothesizes that felt needs cause human behavior and that motivation strength depends on an individual's degree of desire to perform a behavior. *p. 381*

Vroom-Yetton-Jago (VYJ) Model of leadership is a modern view of leadership that suggests that successful leadership requires determining through a decision tree what style of leadership will produce decisions that are beneficial to the organization and accepted and committed to by subordinates. *p. 356*

"What if" analysis is the simulation of a business situation over and over again, using somewhat different data for selected decision areas. *p. 526*

Work measurement methods are operational tools that are used to establish labor standards. *p. 489*

Work methods analysis is an operational tool used to improve productivity and ensure the safety of workers. *p. 489*

Work team is a task group used in organizations to achieve greater organizational flexibility or to cope with rapid growth. *p. 408*

WorldWide Web is a segment of the Internet that allows managers to have an information location called a website available continually to Internet users. Each website has a beginning page called a home page, and each home page generally has several supporting pages called branch pages that expand on the thoughts and ideas contained in the home page. *p. 530*

Zero-base budgeting requires managers to justify their entire budget request in detail rather than simply referring to budget amounts established in previous years. *p. 493*

CHAPTER 1

1. For an interesting discussion of differences between managers and leaders, Abraham Zaleznik, "Managers and Leaders: Are They Different?" *Harvard Business Review*, March/April 1992, pp. 126–35; Peter F. Drucker, "Management's New Role," *Harvard Business Review*, November/December 1969, p. 54.

2. Geoffrey Colvin, "How to Pay the CEO Right," *Fortune*, April 6, 1992, pp. 60–69; Eric S. Hardy, "Marathon Men" *Forbes*, May 23, 1994, p. 141.

3. Robert Albanese, *Management* (Cincinnati Southwestern, 1988), p. 8.

4. Gary Hamel and C. K. Prahalad, "Seeing the Future First," *Fortune*, September 5, 1994, pp. 64–70.

5. For a discussion of efficiency of savings and loans, see Benjamin E. Hermalin and Nancy E. Wallace, "The Determinants of Efficiency and Solvency in Savings and Loans," *Rand Journal of Economics 25* (Autumn 1994): 361–81.

6. William Wiggenhorn, "Motorola U: When Training Becomes an Education," *Harvard Business Review*, July/August 1990, pp. 71–83.

7. Robert L. Katz, "Skills of an Effective Administrator," *Harvard Business Review*, January/February 1955, pp. 33–41.

8. Ruth Davidhizar, "The Two-Minute Manager," *Health Supervisor* 7 (April 1989): 25–29; for an article that demonstrates how important human skills are for middle managers, see also Philip A. Rudolph and Brian H. Kleiner, "The Art of Motivating Employees," *Journal of Managerial Psychology* 4 (1989): i–iv.

9. Henri Fayol, *General and Industrial Management* (London: Sir Isaac Pitman & Sons, 1949).

10. B.C. Forbes, *Forbes*, March 15, 1976, p. 128.

11. Don Hellriegel, John W. Slocum, Jr., and Richard W. Woodman, *Organizational Behavior*, 6th ed. (St. Paul: West Publishing Company, 1992), p. 681.

12. John Ivancevich and Michael T. Matteson, *Organizational Behavior and Management* (Homewood, Ill.: BPI/Irwin, 1990), pp. 593–95.

13. John W. Slocum, Jr., William L. Cron, and Linda C. Yows, "Whose Career Is Likely to Plateau?" *Business Horizons*, March/April 1987, pp. 31–38.

14. Joseph E. McKendrick, Jr., "What Are You Doing the Rest of Your Life?" *Management World*, September/October 1987, p. 2; Carl Anderson, *Management: Skills, Functions, and Organizational Performance*, 2d ed. (Boston: Allyn and Bacon, 1988).

15. Paul H. Thompson, Robin Zenger Baker, and Norman Smallwood, "Improving Personal Development by Applying the Four-Stage Career Model," *Organizational Dynamics*, Autumn 1986, pp. 49–62.

16. Kenneth Labich, "Take Control of Your Career," *Fortune*. November 18, 1991, pp. 87–90; Buck Blessing, "Career Planning: Five Fatal Assumptions," *Training and Development Journal*, September 1986, pp. 49–51.

17. Thomas J. Peters, Jr., "The Best New Managers Will Listen, Motivate, Support," *Working Woman*, September 1990, pp. 142–43, 216–17.

18. For an interesting discussion of conflict of interest and dual-career couples, see Owen Ullmann and Mike McNamee, "Couples, Careers, and Conflicts," *Business Week*, February 21, 1994, pp. 32–34.

19. For related information, see Colin Leinster, "The Young Exec as Superdad," *Fortune*. April 25, 1988, pp. 237–42; Uma Sekaran, *Dual-Career Families* (San Francisco: Jossey-Bass, 1986); F.S. Hall and T.D. Hall, "Dual Careers—How Do Couples and Companies Cope with the Problems?" *Organizational Dynamics 6* (1978): 57–77.

20. Carol Milano, "Reevaluating Recruitment to Better Target Top Minority Talent," *Management Review*, August 1989), pp. 29–32; Colin Leinster, "Black Executives: How They're Doing," *Fortune*. January 18, 1988, pp. 109–20.

21. James F. Wolf, "The Legacy of Mary Parker Follett," *Bureaucrat 17* (Winter 1988–89): 53–57.

22. "Hazardous Materials Disaster Management," *Environmental Manager*, October 1994, pp. 7–9.

23. Philip M. Burgess, "Making It in America's New Economy," *Vital Speeches of the Day 60* (September 15, 1994): 716–19. For a useful discussion of special training issues related to such employees, see Adrienne S. Harris, "And the Prepared Will Inherit the Future," *Black Enterprise*, February 1990, 121–28.

24. Stephen J. Harrison and Ronald Stupak, "Total Quality Management: The Organizational Equivalent of Truth in Public Administration Theory and Practice," *Public Administration Quarterly 16* (Winter 1993): 416–29.

Introductory Case: Dyan Machan and Vicki Contavespi, "Compound Interest Are Our Favorite Words," *Forbes*, December 1994, pp. 244–58.

CHAPTER 2

1. James H. Donnelly, Jr., James L. Gibson, and John M. Ivancevich, *Fundamentals of Management* (Plano, Tex.: Business Publications, 1987), pp. 6–8; Harold Koontz, Cyril O'Donnell, and Heinz Weihrich, *Management*, 8th ed. (New York: McGraw-Hill, 1984), pp. 52–69; W. Warren Haynes and Joseph L. Massie, *Management*, 2d ed. (Englewood Cliffs, N.J.: Prentice Hall, 1969), pp. 4–13.

2. David W. Hays, "Quality Improvement and Its Origin in Scientific Management," *Quality Progress*, May 5, 1994, pp. 89–90.

3. Frederick W. Taylor, *The Principles of Scientific Management* (New York: Harper & Bros., 1947), pp. 66–71.

4. For a discussion of how Taylor stressed employee relationships, see Hindy Schachter, "Taylor's Scientific Management," *Public Administration Review*, July/August 1990, pp. 471–72. For more information on the work of Frederick Taylor, see Edward Rimer, "Organization Theory and Frederick Taylor," *Public Administration Review 53* (May/June 1993): 270–72.

5. J. Michael Gotcher, "Assisting the Handicapped: The Pioneering Efforts of Frank and Lillian Gilbreth," *Journal of Management*, March 1992, pp. 5–13. See also Franz T. Lohrke, "Motion Study for the Blinded: A Review of the Gilbreths' Work with the Visually Handicapped," *International Journal of Public Administration 16* (1993): 667–68.

6. Edward A. Michaels, "Work Measurement," *Small Business Reports 14* (March 1989): 55–63.

7. Henry L. Gantt, *Industrial Leadership* (New Haven, Conn.: Yale University Press, 1916), p. 57.

8. Ralph V. Rogers, "An Interactive Graphical Aided Scheduling System," *Computers and Industrial Engineering 17* (1989): 113–18. For more information on the Gantt chart, see G. William Page, "Using Project Management Software in Planning," *Journal of the American Planning Association 55* (Autumn 1989): 494–99.

9. Doug Green and Denise Green, "MacSchedule Has Rich Features at Low Price," *InfoWorld*, July 12, 1993, p. 88.

10. Gantt, *Industrial Leadership*, p. 85.

11. Chester I. Barnard, *Organization and Management* (Cambridge, Mass.: Harvard University Press, 1952). For more current discussion of Barnard's work, see Christopher Vasillopulos, "Heroism, Self–Abnegation and the Liberal Organization," *Journal of Business Ethics 7* (August 1988): 585–91.

12. Alvin Brown, *Organization of Industry* (Englewood Cliffs, N.J.: Pren-

tice Hall, 1947; Henry S. Dennison, *Organization Engineering* (New York: McGraw-Hill, 1931); Luther Gulick and Lyndall Urwick, eds., *Papers on the Science of Administration* (New York: Institute of Public Administration, 1937); J.D. Mooney and A.C. Reiley. *Onward Industry!* (New York: Harper & Bros., 1931); Oliver Sheldon, *The Philosophy of Management* (London: Sir Isaac Pitman and Sons, 1923).

13. Henri Fayol, *General and Industrial Management* (London: Sir Isaac Pitman and Sons, 1949).

14. Charles A. Mowll, "Successful Management Based on Key Principles," *Healthcare Financial Management 43* (June 1989): 122, 124.

15. Fayol, *General and Industrial Management*, pp. 19–42. For an excellent discussion of the role of accountability and organization structure, see Elliott Jaques, "In Praise of Hierarchy," *Harvard Business Review 68* (January/February 1990): 127–133.

16. For an interesting discussion of how modern training programs are teaching managers to establish productive authority relationships in organizations, see A. Glenn Kiser, Terry Humphries, and Chip Bell, "Breaking Through Rational Leadership," *Training and Development Journal 44* (January 1990): 42–45. For an interesting discussion on how "chain of command" helps to minimize the negative impact of oil spills, see James Hunt, Bruce Carter, and Frank Kelly, "Clearly Defined Chain-of-Command Helps Mobilize Oil Spill," *Occupational Health & Safety*, June 1993, pp. 40–45. For a discussion of the impact of remuneration on an organization, see Jeffrey Bradt, "Pay for Impact," *Personnel Journal*, January 1992, pp. 76–79. For a discussion of centralization, see Paul T. Mill and Josephine Bonan, "Site-Based Management: Decentralization and Accountability," *Education Digest*, September 1991, pp. 23–25.

17. For detailed summaries of these studies, see *Industrial Worker*, 2 vols. (Cambridge, Mass.: Harvard University Press, 1938); and F.J. Roethlisberger and W.J. Dickson, *Management and the Worker* (Cambridge, Mass.: Harvard University Press, 1939). For a more recent discussion of the Hawthorne Studies, see Bev Geber, "The Hawthorne Effect: Orwell or Buscaglia? *Training 23* (November 1986): 113–114.

18. Stephen Jones, "Worker Interdependence and Output: The Hawthorne Studies Reevaluated," *American Sociological Review*, April 1990, pp. 176–90.

19. Jennifer Laabs, "Corporate Anthropologists," *Personnel Journal*, January 1992, pp. 81–91; Samuel C. Certo, *Human Relations Today: Concepts and Skills* (Burr Ridge, IL: Irwin, 1995), p. 4.

20. C. West Churchman, Russell L. Ackoff, and E. Leonard Arnoff, *Introduction to Operations Research* (New York: Wiley, 1957), p. 18.

21. Hamdy A. Taha, *Operations Research: An Introduction* (New York: Macmillan, 1988), pp. 1–2.

22. James R. Emshoff, *Analysis of Behavioral Systems* (New York: Macmillan, 1971), p. 10. For an interesting account of how the scientific method can be applied to studying management problems like information system problems, see Allen S. Lee, "A Scientific Methodology for the MIS Case Studies," *MIS Quarterly 13* (March 1989): 33–50.

23. C.C. Shumacher and B.E. Smith, "A Sample Survey of Industrial Operations Research Activities 11," *Operations Research 13* (1965): 1023–27; Catherine L. Morgan, " A Survey of MS/OR Surveys," *Interfaces 19* (November/December 1989): 95–103.

24. The discussion concerning these factors is adapted from Donnelly, Gibson, and Ivancevich, *Fundamentals of Management*, pp. 302–03; Efraim Turban and Jack R. Meredith, *Fundamentals of Management Science* (Plano, Tex.: Business Publications, 1981), pp. 15–23.

25. Harold Koontz, "The Management Theory Jungle Revisited," *Academy of Management Review 5* (1980): 175–87. For an excellent illustration of how the contingency approach might apply to developing strategies for handling competing firms, see Moonkyu Lee, "Contingency Approach to Strategies for Service Firms," *Journal of Business Research 19* (December 1989): 293–301.

26. Don Hellriegel, John W. Slocum, and Richard W. Woodman, *Organizational Behavior* (St. Paul, Minn.: West Publishing, 1986), p. 22.

27. J.W. Lorsch, "Organization Design: A Situational Perspective," *Organizational Dynamics 6* (1977): 2–4; Louis W. Fry and Deborah A. Smith, "Congruence, Contingency, and Theory Building," *Academy of Management Review*, January 1987, pp. 117–32.

28. For a more detailed development of von Bertalanffy's ideas, see "General System Theory: A New Approach to Unity of Science," *Human Biology*, December 1951, pp. 302–61.

29. L. Thomas Hopkins, *Integration: Its Meaning and Application* (New York: Appleton-Century-Crofts, 1937), pp. 36–49.

30. Joe Schwartz, "Why They Buy," *American Demographics 11* (March 1989): 40–41.

Introductory Case: Vicki Vaughn, "Disney Testing Fast-Food Recipe," *The Orlando Sentinel*, November 4, 1990, pp. D1, D2; Jim DeSimone, "It'll Be a Jungle in There at New Disney Restaurant," *The Orlando Sentinel*, September 7, 1995, pp. A1, A7.

Cutting Edge: Michelle Levander, "Unusual Schedules May Benefit Workers," *The Orlando Sentinel*, December 28, 1994, p. B–5.

People Perspectives: This highlight is based on Edward O. Welles, "Lessons of a Bottom Feeder," *Inc.*, July 1994, p. 54–62.

Case Study: John A. Byrne "The Shredder," *Business Week*, January 15, 1996; Mary Kane, "Downsizing: Profit vs. Pain," *The Atlanta Journal-Constitution*, January 14, 1996, p. C1–2; "Scott Paper Company," *Hoover's Company Profile Database* (Austin, Tex.: The Reference Press, 1995).

CHAPTER 3

1. For a good discussion of many factors involved in the modern meanings of social responsibility, see Frederick D. Sturdivant and Heidi Vernon-Wortzel, *Business and Society: A Managerial Approach*. 4th ed. (Homewood, Ill: Irwin, 1990, pp. 3–24. The definition of corporate social responsibility is adapted from Keith Davis and Robert L. Blomstrom, *Business and Society: Environment and Responsibility*, 3d. ed. (New York: McGraw-Hill, 1975), p. 6. Also see Richard A. Rodewald, "The Corporate Social Responsibility Debate: Unanswered Questions About the Consequences of Moral Reform," *American Business Law Journal*, Fall 1987, pp. 443–66. For an illustration of how social responsibility makes good economic sense, see David Woodruff, "Herman Miller; How Green Is My Factory," *Business Week*, September 16, 1992, pp. 54–56.

2. Peter L. Berger, "New Attack on the Legitimacy of Business," *Harvard Business Review*, September/October 1981, pp. 82–89.

3. Keith Davis, "Five Propositions for Social Responsibility," *Business Horizons*, June 1975, pp. 9–24.

4. For extended discussion of arguments for and against social responsibility, see William C. Frederick, Keith Davis, and James E. Post, *Business and Society: Corporate Strategy, Public Policy, Ethics*, 6th ed. (New York: McGraw-Hill), 1988, pp. 36–43.

5. K.E. Apperle, A.B. Carroll, and J.D. Hatfield, "An Empirical Examination of the Relationship Between Corporate Social Responsibility and Profitability," *Academy of Management Journal*, June 1985, pp. 446–63: J.B. McGuire, A. Sundgren, and T. Schneeweis, "Corporate Social Responsibility and Firm Financial Performance," *Academy of Management Journal*, *December 1988, pp. 854–72; Vogel, "Ethics and Profits Don't Always Go Hand in Hand." Los Angeles Times, December 28, 1988, p. 7.*

6. For Friedman's current view, see "Freedom and Philanthropy: An Interview with Milton Friedman," *Business and Society Review*, Fall 1989, pp. 11–18. See also Neil M.Brown and Paul F. Haas, "Social Responsibility: The Uncertain Hypothesis," *MSU Business Topics. Summer* 1974, p. 48.

7. Milton Friedman, "Does Business Have Social Responsibility?" *Bank Administration*, April 1971, pp. 13–14.

8. Eric J. Savitz, "The Vision Thing: Control Data Abandons It for the Bottom Line," *Barron's*, May 7, 1990, pp. 10–11, 22; and Jagannath Dubashi, "The Do-Gooder," *Financial World*, June 27, 1989, pp. 70–74.

9. Joan E. Rigdon, "The Wrist Watch: How a Plant Handles Occupational Hazard with Common Sense," *Wall Street Journal*, September 28, 1992, p. 1.

10. Sandra L. Holmes, "Executive Perceptions of Corporate Social Responsibility," *Business Horizons*, June 1976, pp. 34–40.

11. For a insights regarding SC Johnson Wax's position on social respon-

sibility involvement, see Reva A. Holmes, "At SC Johnson Wax Philanthropy Is an Investment," *Management Accounting*, August 1994, pp. 42–45.

12. Sturdivant and Vernon-Wortzel, Business and Society, pp. 9–11.

13. Samuel C. Certo and J. Paul Peter, The Strategic Management Process, 3rd ed. (Chicago: 1995), p. 219.

14. Carlo Wolff, "Living with the New Amenity," *Lodging Hospitality*, December 1994, pp. 66–68.

15. Harry A. Lipson, "Do Corporate Executives Plan for Social Responsibility?" *Business and Society Review*, Winter 1974–75, pp. 80–81.

16. S. Prakash Sethi, "Dimensions of Corporate Social Performance: An Analytical Framework," *California Management Review*, Spring 1975, pp. 58–64.

17. For information on the growing trend for business to make contributions to support education, see Joel Keehn, "How Business Helps the Schools," Fortune, October 21, 1991, pp. 161–71.

18. Frank H. Cassell, "The Social Cost of Doing Business," MSU Business Topics, Autumn 1974, pp. 19–26.

19. Donald W. Garner, "The Cigarette Industry's Escape from Liability," Business and Society Review 33 (Spring 1980): 22.

20. Meinolf Dierkes and Ariane Berthoin Antal, "Whither Corporate Social Reporting: Is It Time to Legislate?" California Management Review, Spring 1986, pp. 106–21.

21. Condensed from Jerry McAfee, "How Society Can Help Business," Newsweek, July 3, 1978, p. 15. Copyright 1978 by Newsweek, Inc. All rights reserved. Reprinted by permission.

22. "Borden Chemicals Lashes Back at EPA," Chemical Marketing Reporter, November 7, 1994, pp. 5, 19.

23. Leonard J. Brooks, Jr., "Corporate Codes of Ethics," *Journal of Business Ethics*, February/March 1989, pp. 117–29; James Strodes, "Mr. Diogenes, Call Your Office," Financial World, June 27, 1989.

24. For an interesting discussion of the ethical dilemma of fairly allocating an individual's time between work and personal life, see Paul B. Hofmann, "Balancing Professional and Personal Priorities," Healthcare Executive, May/June 1994, p. 42.

25. Archie B. Carroll, "In Search of the Moral Manager," Business Horizons, March/April 1987, pp. 7–15.

26. Sundeep Waslekar, "'Good Citizens and Reap Rewards," Asian Business, January 1994 p. 52. See also Genine Babakian, "Who Will Control Russian Advertising?" Adweek [Eastern Edit.] August 1, 1994, p. 16.

27. John F. Akers, "Ethics and Competitiveness—Putting First Things First," Sloan Management Review, Winter 1989, pp. 69–71.

28. "Helping Workers Helps Bottom Line," *Employee Benefit Plan Review*, July 1990.

29. Sandy Lutz, "Psych Hospitals Fight for Survival," *Modern Healthcare*, May 8, 1995, pp. 62–65.

30. Patrick E. Murphy, "'Creating Ethical Corporate Structures," Sloan *Management Review*, Winter 1989, pp. 81–87; Louis J. D'Amore, "A Code of Ethics and Guidelines for Socially and Environmentally Responsible Tourism," Journal of Travel Research, *Winter 1993, pp. 64–66.*

31. *Richard A. Spinell, "Lessons from the Salomon Scandal," America. December 28, 1991, pp. 476–77; Touche Ross, Ethics in American Business (New York: Touche Ross & Co., January 1988).*

32. *For additional insights on how to create an ethical workplace, see Larry L. Axline, "The Bottom Line on Ethics," Journal of Accountancy, December 1990, pp. 87–91.*

33. *Alan L. Otten, "Ethics on the Job: Companies Alert Employees to Potential Dilemmas," Wall Street Journal, July 14, 1986, p. 25.*

34. Gene R. Laczniak, "Framework for Analyzing Marketing Ethics," *Journal of Macromarketing*, Spring 1983, pp. 7–18. See also Karen L. Fernicola, "Take the Highroad . . . To Ethical Management: An Interview with Kenneth Blanchard," *Association Management*, May 1988, 60–66; Patricia Haddock and Marilyn Manning, "Ethically Speaking," Sky, March 1990, pp. 128–31.

35. Saul W. Gellerman, "Managing Ethics from the Top Down," *Sloan Management Review*, Winter 1989, pp. 73–79. For an interesting discussion of what management should do when charged with unethical actions, see John A. Byrne, "Here's What to Do Next, Dow Corning," *Business Week*, February 24, 1992, p. 33.

Introductory Case: Based on Joseph Pereira, "Toy Maker Faces Dilemmas As Water Gun Spurs Violence," *Wall Street Journal*, © June 11, 1992, pp. B1, B9. Reprinted by permission of *Wall Street Journal*, 1992 Dow Jones & Company, Inc. All Rights Reserved Worldwide. Karen Benezra, "Hardee's Hopes to Soak Mac, BK Summer Kid Promos," *Brandweek*, February 28, 1994, p. 12; Anne G. Pepper, "Deadly Toys Aren't Good Business," *Japan 21st*, December 1994, p. 15.

People Perspectives: Anita Roddick, "Corporate Responsibility: Good Works, Not Good Words," *Vital Speeches*, January 15, 1994, pp. 196–99.

Cutting Edge: John W. Collins, "Is Business Ethics on Oxymoron?" *Business Horizons*, September/October 1994, pp. 1–8.

Case Study: "Informed Consent" *Business Week*, October 2, 1995, pp. 104–16; "Fatal Litigation," *Fortune*, October 30, 1995, pp. 137–58.

CHAPTER 4

1. For additional information on this topic, see: Samuel C. Certo, *Human Relations Today: Concepts and Skills* (Chicago: Austen Press/Irwin, 1995), pp. 352–75.

2. "Dossier: Telecommunications in Asia, Malaysia, Thailand," *International Business Newsletter*, June 1993, p. 12.

3. Robert N. Lussier, Robert W. Baeder, and Joel Corman, "Measuring Global Practices: Global Strategic Planning Through Company Situational Analysis," *Business Horizons* 37 (September/October 1994): 56–63.

4. Alyssa A. Lappen, "Worldwide Connections," *Forbes*, June 27, 1988, pp. 78–82.

5. Gale Eisenstodt, "'We are happy,'" *Forbes*, May 8, 1995, pp. 44–45.

6. "Global Investment: The Smart Money Is Flowing South," *Harvard Business Review* 71 (September/October 1993): 13–14.

7. Ben J. Wattenberg, "Their Deepest Concerns," *Business Month*, January 1988, pp. 27–33; American Assembly of Collegiate Schools of Business, *Accreditation Council Policies, Procedures, and Standards, 1990–92*, St. Louis, Mo.; Sylvia Nasar, "America's Competitive Revival," *Fortune*, January 4, 1988, pp. 44–52.

8. For additional information regarding various forms of organization based on international involvement, see Arvind Phatak, *International Dimensions of Management*, (Boston: Kent, 1993).

9. "Nu Horizons Electronics," *Fortune*, June 13, 1994, p. 121.

10. U.S. Department of Commerce, *The Multinational Corporation: Studies on U.S. Foreign Investment*, Vol. 1 (Washington, D.C.: Government Printing Office).

11. Benjamin Gomes-Casseres, "Group versus Group: How Alliance Networks Compete," *Harvard Business Review* 72 (July/August 1994), 62–74.

12. Grover Starling, *The Changing Environment of Business* (Boston: Kent, 1980), p. 140.

13. This section is based primarily on Richard D. Robinson, *International Management* (New York: Holt, Rinehart & Winston, 1967), pp. 3–5.

14. 1971 Survey of National Foreign Trade Council, cited in Frederick D. Sturdivant, *Business and Society: A Managerial Approach* (Homewood, Ill.: Richard D. Irwin, 1977), p. 425. For an interesting discussion of diversification as an advantage to internationalizing, see Jeff Madura and Ann Marie Whyte, "Diversification Benefits of Direct Foreign Investment," *Management International Review* 30 (First quarter 1990):73–85.

15. Barrie James, "Reducing the Risks of Globalization," *Long Range Planning* 23 (February 1990):80–88.

16. "NCR's Standard Contract Clause," *Harvard Business Review* 72 (May/June 1994):125.

17. Roberta Maynard, "Importing Can Help a Firm Expand and Diversify," *Nation's Business*, January 1995, p. 11.

18. Karen Paul, "Fading Images at Eastman Kodak," *Business and Society Review 48* (Winter 1984):56. For a discussion of how Eastman Kodak is attempting to reduce costs associated with its exporting, see Robert J. Bowman "Cheaper by Air?" *World Trade* 7 (October 1994):88–91.

19. G. Sam Samdani, "Mobil Develops a Way to Extract Hg from Gas Streams," *Chemical Engineering 102* (April 1995):17.

20. Robert Neff, "The Japanese Are Back—But There's a Difference," *Business Week*, Industrial/Technology Edition, October 31, 1994, pp. 58–59.

21. Ken Korane, "Geo Metro: Economy Is Key" *Machine Design 67* (April 6, 1995):146–48.

22. Francisco Granell, "The European Union's Enlargement Negotiations with Austria, Finland, Norway, and Sweden," *Journal of Common Market Studies 33* (March 1995):117–41; Gwenan Roberts, "Swedish Lawyers Look South," *International Financial Law Review 14* (May 1995):12–14; Jim Rollo, "EC Enlargement and the World Trade System," *European Economic Review 39* (April 1995):467–73.

23. Jim Mele, "Mexico in '95: From Good to Better," *Fleet Owner*, January 1995, pp. 56–60; William C. Symonds, "Meanwhile, to the North, NAFTA Is a Smash," *Business Week*, February 27, 1995, p. 66; Robert Selwitz, "NAFTA Expansion Possiblities," *Global Trade & Transportation*, October 1994, p. 17.

24. N. Carroll Mohn, "Pacific Rim Prices," *Marketing Research: A Magazine of Management & Applications*, Winter 1994, pp. 22–27; Louis Kraar, "The Growing Power of Asia," *Fortune*, October 7, 1991, pp. 118–31.

25. For an interesting account of organizing to go global, see Regina Fazio Maruca, "The Right Way to Go Global: An Interview with Whirlpool CEO David Whitwam," *Harvard Business Review 72* (March/April 1994):134–45.

26. Howard V. Perlmutter, "The Tortuous Evolution of the Multinational Corporation," *Columbia Journal of World Business*, January/February 1969, pp. 9–18; Rose Knotts, "Cross-Cultural Management: Transformations and Adaptations," *Business Horizons*, January/February 1989, pp. 29–33.

27. Geert Hotstede, "Motivation, Leadership, and Organization: Do American Theories Apply Abroad?" *Organizational Dynamics 9* (Summer 1980):42–63.

28. Walter Sweet, "International Firms Strive for Uniform Nets Abroad," *Network World*, May 28, 1990, pp. 35–36.

29. To gain a feel for the broad range of activities occurring at a transnational company like Nestlé, see Joel Chernoff, "Advancing Corporate Governance in Europe," *Pensions & Investments*, June 12, 1995, pp. 3, 37; E. Guthrie McTigue and Andy Sears, "The Safety 80," *Global Finance*, May 1995, pp. 62–65; Robert W. Lear, "Whatever Happened to the Old-Fashioned Boss?" *Chief Executive*, April 1995, p. 71; Claudio Loderer and Andreas Jacobs, "The Nestlé Crash" *Journal of Financial Economics 37* (March 1995):315–39; Roberto Ceniceros, "Companies Aiding Workers, Starting to Assess Damage," *Business Insurance*, January 30, 1995, pp. 22–23.

30. R. N. Farmer, "International Management," in *Contemporary Management Issues and Viewpoints*, ed. J. W. McGuire (Englewood Cliffs, N.J.: Prentice Hall, 1974, p. 302; Frank Ching, "China's Managers Get U.S. Lessons," *Wall Street Journal*, January 23, 1981, p. 27.

31. Philip R. Catoera, *International Marketing*, 8th ed. (Homewood, Ill.: Richard D. Irwin, 1993).

32. Charles McMillan, "Is Japanese Management Really So Different?" *Business Quarterly*, Autumn 1980, pp. 26–31; Masaru Ibuka, "Management Opinion," *Administrative Management*. May 5, 1980, p. 86; "How Japan Does It," *Time*, March 30, 1981, p. 55.

33. Lane Kelly and Reginald Worthley, "The Role of Culture in Comparative Management," *Academy of Management Journal 24* (1981):164–73; Linda S. Dillon, "Adopting Japanese Management: Some Cultural Stumbling Blocks," *Personnel*, July/August 1983, pp. 73–77; Isaac Shapiro, "Second Thoughts About Japan." *Wall Street Journal*, June 5, 1981.

34. William Ouchi, *Theory Z* (Reading, Mass.: Addison Wesley, 1981).

35. Gene Koretz, "Yankees Go East—On a Scale That's Startling," *Business Week*, January 18, 1993, p. 26.

Introductory Case: Karen Benezra, "Baskin in Sara Lee's Glory," *Brandweek 35* (September 12, 1994):4; Beth Lorenzini, "Sweets Chains Bundle Up in Nontraditional Sites," *Restaurants & Institutions 104* (July 15, 1994):98–100; Richard Martin, "Baskin-Robbins Tests New Venues," *Nation's Restaurant News 28* (May 23, 1994):3, 51; "Baskin-Robbins Brings U.S. Ice Cream Back to Embargo-Free Ho Chi Minh City," *The Orlando Sentinel*, December 28, 1994, p. B-5.

People Perspectives: Howard Tu and Sherry E. Sullivan, "Preparing Yourself for an International Assignment," *Business Horizons 37* (January/February 1994):67–70.

Cutting Edge: William S. Brown, Rebecca E. Lubove, and James Kwalwasser, "Karoshi: Alternative Perspectives of Japanese Management Styles," *Business Horizons*, March/April 1994, pp. 58–60.

Case Study: "A Conversation with Roberto Goizueta and Jack Welch," Fortune, December 11, 1995, pp. 96–102; Milton Moskowitz, Michael Katz, and Robert Levering. *Everybody's Business: An Almanac* (San Francisco: Harper & Row, 1980), pp. 16–20; Chris Roush, "Coca-Colas Global Growth Takes Hit" *The Atlanta Journal-Constitution*, December 22, 1995, p. 1G; Kenneth Shea, "Top Quality Buys," The Outlook, (New York: Standard & Poor's, October 11, 1995), p. S3.

CHAPTER 5

1. James F. Lincoln, "Intelligent Selfishness and Manufacturing," Bulletin 434 (New York: Lincoln Electric Company).

2. John F. Mee, "Management Philosophy for Professional Executives," *Business Horizons*, December 1956, p. 7.

3. Paul Psarouthakis, "Getting There by Goal Setting," *Supervisory Management*, June 1989, pp. 14–15.

4. Hans Hinterhuber and Wolfgang Popp, "Are You a Strategist or Just a Manager?" *Harvard Business Review*, January/February 1992, pp. 105–13.

5. For insights on how the Compaq Computer Corporation uses objectives to evaluate performance, see Alan M. Webber, "Consensus, Continuity, and Common Sense," *Harvard Business Review*, July/August 1990, p. 120.

6. Y.K. Sherry, "New Look at Corporate Goals," *California Management Review 22* (Winter 1979): 71–79. For more recent evidence that profitability, growth, and market share continue to be the most commonly set organizational objectives, see Luiz Moutinho, "Goal Setting Process and Typologies: The Case of Professional Services," *Journal of Professional Services Marketing*, pp. 83–100.

7. For a description of how Levi Strauss attempts to keep individual objectives consistent with organizational objectives, see "Levi Strauss & Company Implements New Pay and Performance System," *Employee Benefit Plan Review*, January 1994, pp. 46–48.

8. Peter F. Drucker, *The Practice of Management* (New York: Harper & Bros., 1954), pp. 62–65, 126–29. For an interesting discussion of objectives set in the customer service area, see John Marshall, "Northwest Chain Store Enhances Customer Service and Lowers Operational Costs by Replacing Outdated POS Terminals," *Chain Store Age Executive*, June 1994, p. 92.

9. Theodore Levitt, "Marketing Myopia," *Harvard Business Review*, July/August 1960, p. 45.

10. Jay T. Knippen and Thad B. Green, "Directing Employee Efforts Through Goal-Setting," *Supervisory Management*, April 1989, pp. 32–36.

11. Tom Brown, "What You "Know" Could Be What Hurts You In Business," *Industry Week*, February 3, 1992, pp. 13–19.

12. For a successful history of a company setting and meeting financial objectives over the long run, see Charles F. Knight, "Emerson Electric: Consistent Profits, Consistently," *Harvard Business Review*, January/February 1992, pp. 57–70.

13. Joseph G. Louderback and George E. Manners, Jr., "Integrating ROI and CVP," *Management Accounting*, April 1981, pp. 33–39. For a related

discussion of financial objectives, see Gordon Donaldson, "Financial Goals and Strategic Consequences," *Harvard Business Review*, May/June 1985, pp. 56–66.

14. Adapted, by permission of the publisher, from "How to Set Company Objectives," by Charles H. Granger, *Management Review* (July 1970). © 1970 by American Management Association, Inc. All rights reserved. See also Max D. Richards, *Setting Goals and Objectives* (St. Paul, Minn.: West Publishing, 1986).

15. Charles H. Granger, "The Hierarchy of Objectives," *Harvard Business Review*, May/June 1964, pp. 64–74. See also Heinz Weihrich, *Management Excellence: Productivity Through MBO* (New York: McGraw-Hill, 1985), pp. 65–84.

16. See also Edwin A. Locke, Dong-Ok Chah, Scott Harrison, and Nancy Lustgarten, "Separating the Effects of Goal Specificity from Goal Level," *Organizational Behavior and Human Decision Processes*, April 1989, pp. 270–87; Mike Deblieux, "The Challenge and Value of Documenting Performance," *HR Focus*, March 1994, p. 3.

17. For a discussion supporting the importance of making objectives operational or measurable, see Dan Logan, "Integrated Communication Offers Competitive Edge," *Bank Marketing*, May 1994, pp. 63–67.

18. James G. March and Herbert A. Simon, Organization (New York: Wiley, 1958), p. 191.

19. Drucker, *The Practice of Management*; see also Peter Drucker, Harold Smiddy, and Ronald G. Greenwood, "Management by Objectives," *Academy of Management Review* 6 (April 1981): 225. And see Robert Rodgers and John E. Hunter, "A Foundation of Good Management Practices in Government: Management by Objectives," *Public Administration Review*, January/February 1992, pp. 27–39.

20. Robert L. Mathis and John H. Jackson, *Personnel: Human Resource Management* (St. Paul, Minn.: West Publishing, 1985), pp. 353–55.

21. Robert Rodgers and John E. Hunter, "Impact of Management by Objectives on Organizational Productivity," *Journal of Applied Psychology* 1991, pp. 322–35; Jerry L. Rostund, "Evaluating Management Objectives with the Quality Loss Function," *Quality Progress*, August 1989, pp. 45–9; William H. Franklin, Jr., "Create an Atmosphere of Positive Expectations," *Administrative Management*, April 1980, 32–34; Peter Crutchley, "Management by Objectives," *Credit Management*, May 1994, pp. 36–38; William J. Kretlow and Winford E. Holland, "Implementing Management by Objectives in Research Administration," *Journal of the Society of Research Administrators*, Summer 1988, pp. 135–41.

22. Charles H. Ford, "Manage by Decisions, Not by Objectives," *Business Horizons*, February 1980, pp. 17–18; Kretlow and Holland, "Implementing Management by Objectives in Research Administration," pp. 135–41; E.J. Seyna, "MBO: The Fad That Changed Management," *Long-Range Planning*, December 1986, pp. 116–23.

Case Study: The Atlanta Olympic Committee On-line (http://www. atlanta.olympic.org); The International Olympic Committee On-line (http://www.olympic.org); *The Atlanta-Journal Constitution* Olympic Reports On-line (http://www.ajc.com); "The Disposable Games," *The Atlanta-Journal Constitution*, December 8, 1995, p. K1.

Introductory Case: William Stern, "A Lesson Learned Early," *Forbes*, November 8, 1993, pp. 220–21.

Cutting Edge: Barbara Presley Noble, "The Bottom Line on 'People' Issues," *The New York Times*, February 19, 1995, p. 23.

People Perspectives: "Teamwork Is the Key to Successful Agent/Manufacturer Relations," *Agency Sales Magazine*, August 1994, pp. 34–36.

CHAPTER 6

1. Harry Jones, *Preparing Company Plans: A Workbook for Effective Corporate Planning* (New York: Wiley, 1974), p. 3.

2. Robert G. Reed, "Five Challenges Multiple-Line Companies Face," *Market Facts*, January/February 1990, 5–6; Brian Burrows and Ken G.B. Blakewell, "Management Functions and Librarians," *Library Management*, 1989, pp. 2–61.

3. C.W. Roney, "The Two Purposes of Business Planning," *Managerial Planning*, November/December 1976, pp. 1–6.

4. Wendy Zellner, "Moving Tofu into the Mainstream," *Business Weeks*, May 25, 1992, p. 94.

5. Harold Koontz and Cyril O'Donnell, *Management: A Systems and Contingency Analysis of Management Functions* (New York: McGraw-Hill, 1976), p. 130.

6. For an interesting discussion on how the importance of planning relates to even day-to-day operations, see Teri Lammers, "The Custom-Made Day Planner," *Inc.*, February 1992, pp. 61–62.

7. Kenneth R. Allen, "Creating and Executing a Business Plan," *American Agent & Broker*, July 1994, pp. 20–21.

8. For a discussion of U.S. shortsightedness in planning, see Michael T. Jacobs, "A Cure for America's Corporate Short-termism," *Planning Review*, January/February 1992, pp. 4–9. For a discussion of the close relationship between objectives and planning, see "Mistakes to Avoid: From a Business Owner," *Business Owner*, September/October 1994, p. 11.

9. For more detailed information on how strategic planning takes place, see Richard F. Vancil and Peter Lorange, "Strategic Planning in Diversified Companies," *Harvard Business Review*, January/February 1975, pp. 81–90.

10. Excerpted, by permission of the publisher, from *1974–75 Exploratory Planning Briefs: Planning for the Future by Corporations and Agencies, Domestic and International*, by William A. Simmons, © 1975 by AMA-COM, a division of American Management Associations, pp. 10–11. All rights reserved.

11. Henry Mintzberg, "A New Look at the Chief Executive's Job," *Organizational Dynamics*, Winter 1973, pp. 20–40.

12. For similar questions focusing on strategic planning, see Hans Hinterhuber and Wolfgang Popp, "Are You a Strategist or Just a Manager?" *Harvard Business Review*, January/February 1992, pp. 105–13.

13. James M. Hardy, *Corporate Planning for Nonprofit Organizations* (New York: Association Press, 1972), p. 37; Peter Beck, "Creating a Path to the Future," *Director*, February 1989, pp. 64–66.

14. Milton Leontiades, "The Dimensions of Planning in Large Industrialized Organizations," *California Management Review* 22 (Summer 1980): 82–86.

15. For a discussion of outside consultants who develop plans for business clients, see Donald F. Kuratko and Arnold Cirtin, "Developing a Business Plan for Your Clients," *National Public Accountant*, January 1990, pp. 24–27.

16. The section "Qualifications of Planners" is adapted from John Argenti, *Systematic Corporate Planning* (New York: Wiley, 1974), p. 126.

17. These three duties are adapted from Walter B. Schaffir, "What Have We Learned about Corporate Planning?" *Management Review*, August 1973, pp. 19–26.

18. For a discussion of how modern planners must focus more on gathering information related to the international environment, see William H. Davidson, "The Rule of Global Scanning in Business Planning," *Organizational Dynamics*, Winter 1991, pp. 4–16. For insights on how a planner can use groups to solve problems, see Andrew E. Schwartz, "Group Decision-Making," *CPA Journal*, August 1994, pp. 60–63. See also Thomas P. Houck, "Improving Efficiency in Your Audit Department," *Internal Auditing*, Winter 1994, pp. 32–37.

19. Frank Corcell, "How to Identify a Sick Company in Time to Help It," *Practical Accountant*, October 1989, pp. 90–99.

20. Michael Muckian and Mary Auestad Arnold, "Manager, Appraise Thyself," *Credit Union Management*, December 1989, pp. 26–28.

21. Edward J. Green, *Workbook for Corporate Planning* (New York: American Management Association, 1970).

22. Z.A. Malik, "Formal Long-Range Planning and Organizational Performance," Ph.D. diss. (Rensselaer Polytechnic Institute, 1974).

23. James Brian Quinn, "Managing Strategic Changes," *Sloan Management Review* 21 (Summer 1980): 3–20.

24. Kamal E. Said and Robert E. Sciler, "An Empirical Study of Long-Range Planning Systems: Strengths—Weaknesses—Outlook," *Managerial*

Planning 28 (July/August 1979): 24–28. See also John T. Sakai, "Japan as an Attractive Alliance Partner," *Directors & Boards*, Winter 1994, pp. 42–44.

25. Paul J. Stonich, "Formal Planning Pitfalls and How to Avoid Them," *Management Review*, June 1975, pp.5–6.

26. Nigel Piercy, "Diagnosing and Solving Implementation Problems in Strategic Planning," *Journal of General Management*, Autumn 1989, 19–38. Concerning the emerging role of middle management in implementing customer satisfaction and profitability plans, see David Jackson and John Humble, "Middle Managers: New Purpose, New Directions," *Journal of Management Development 13* (1994): 15–21.

27. Peter F. Drucker, *Management: Tasks, Responsibilities, Practices* (New York: Harper & Row, 1973). See also Bernard W. Taylor III and K. Roscoe David, "Implementing an Action Program via Organizational Change," *Journal of Economics and Business* Spring/Summer 1976, pp. 203–08.

28. William H. Reynolds, "The Edsel: Faulty Execution of a Sound Marketing Plan," *Business Horizons*, Fall 1967, pp. 39–46.

29. Luis MaR. Calingo, "Achieving Excellence in Strategic Planning Systems," *Advanced Management Journal*, Spring 1989, pp. 21–23. For more discussion on including the right people in the planning process, see Gary Hines, "Strategic Planning Made Easy," *Training & Development Journal*, April 1991, pp. 39–43.

Source: This case is taken from James P. Miller, "DuPont Adds Women's Clothes to Its Mix," *The Wall Street Journal*, January 9, 1995, pp. B1, B2.

Perspectives: Andrew E. Serwer, "McDonald's Conquers the World," *Fortune*, October 17, 1994, pp. 103–16.

Cutting Edge: D. Keith Denton, "The Power of Flexibility," *Business Horizons*, July, August 1994, pp. 43–46.

Case Study: The Quaker Oats Company, *Hoover's Company Profile Database* (Austin, Tex.: The Reference Press, 1996); "Business Brief—Quaker Oats Co.: Fiscal 2nd-Quarter Loss Is Reported by Company," *Wall Street Journal*, February 7, 1996, p. B6; "Will Quaker Get the Recipe Right?" *Business Week*, February 5, 1996, pp. 140–45.

CHAPTER 7

1. For an excellent discussion of various decisions that managers make, see Michael Verespej, "Gutsy Decisions of 1991," *Industry Week*, February 17, 1992, pp. 21–31.

2. Abraham Zaleznik, "What Makes a Leader?" *Success*, June 1989, pp. 42–45.

3. Mervin Kohn, *Dynamic Managing: Principles, Process, Practice* (Menlo Park, Ca.: Cummings, 1977, pp. 38–62. For an interesting discussion of how to train managers to become better decision makers by slowing down the decision-making process, see Jack Falvey, "Making Great Managers," *Small Business Reports*, February 1990, pp. 15–18. See also Herbert A. Simon, *The New Science of Management Decision* (New York: Harper & Bros., 1960), pp. 5–8.

4. William H. Miller, "Tough Decisions on the Forgotten Continent," *Industry Week*, June 6, 1994, pp. 40–44.

5. *The D of Research and Development* (Wilmington, Del.: DuPont, 1966), pp. 28–29. Apparently, DuPont's basic tenets regarding how the scope of decisions influences how decisions should be made have evolved over many years. See, for example, George J. Titus, "Forty-Year Evolution of Engineering Research: A Case Study of DuPont's Engineering Research and Development," *IEEE Transactions on Engineering Management 41* (November): 1994, 350–54.

6. Marcia V. Wilkof, "Organizational Culture and Decision Making: A Case of Consensus Management," *R&D Management*, April 1989, pp. 185–99. For tips on how to build a consensus, see Joseph D. O'Brian. "Negotiating with Peers: Consensus, Not Power," *Supervisory Management*, January 1992, p. 4.

7. Charles Wilson and Marcus Alexis, "Basic Frameworks for Decision," *Academy of Management Journal 5* (August 1962): 151–64.

8. For a discussion of the importance of understanding decision makers in organizations, see Walter D. Barndt, Jr., "Profiling Rival Decision Mak-

ers," *Journal of Business Strategy*, January, February 1991, pp. 8–11. See also Ernest Dale, *Management: Theory and Practice* (New York: McGraw-Hill, 1973, pp. 548–49.

9. "New OCC Guidelines for Appraising Management," *Issues in Bank Regulation*, Fall 1989, pp. 20–22.

10. For an extended discussion of this model, see William B. Werther, Jr., "Productivity Through People: The Decision-Making Process," *Management Decisions*, 1988, pp. 37–41.

11. These assumptions are adapted from James G. March and Herbert A. Simon, *Organizations* (New York: Wiley, 1958), pp. 137–38.

12. William C. Symonds, "There's More than Beer in Molson's Mug," *Business Week*, February 10, 1992, p. 108.

13. Chester I. Barnard, *The Function of the Executive* (Cambridge, Mass.: Harvard University Press, 1938).

14. For further elaboration on these factors, see Robert Tannenbaum, Irving R. Weschle, and Fred Massarik, *Leadership and Organization: A Behavioral Science Approach* (New York: McGraw-Hill, 1961), pp. 277–78.

15. For more discussion of these factors, see F.A. Shull, Jr., A.I. Delbecq, and L.L. Cummings, *Organizational Decision Making* (New York: Mc-Graw-Hill, 1970).

16. For a worthwhile discussion of forecasting and evaluating the outcomes of alternatives, see J.R.C. Wensley, "Effective Decision Aids in Marketing," *European Journal of Marketing*, 1989, pp. 70–79.

17. Timothy A. Park and Frances Antonovitz, "Econometric Tests of Firm Decision Making under Uncertainty: Optimal Output and Hedging Decisions," *Southern Economic Journal*, January 1992, pp. 593–609.

18. For a discussion of risk and decisions, see Sim B. Sitkin and Amy L. Pablo, "Reconceptualizing the determinants of Risk Behavior," *Academy of Management Review*, January 1992, p. 11. See also Michael J. Ryan, "Constrained Gaming Approaches to Decision Making under Uncertainty," *European Journal of Operational Research*, August 25, 1994, pp. 70–81.

19. Steven C. Harper, "What Separates Executives from Managers," *Business Horizons*, September/October 1988, pp. 13–19; Russ Holloman, "The Light and Dark Sides of Decision Making," *Supervisory Management*, (December 1989), pp. 33–34.

20. The scope of this text does not permit elaboration on these three decision-making tools. However, for an excellent discussion on how they are used in decision making, see Richard M. Hodgetts, *Management: Theory, Process and Practice* (Philadelphia: Saunders, 1975), pp. 234–66. For a discussion of the computer as a decision-making tool, see Robert Addleman, "Scientific Decision-Making," *Healthcare Forum*, March/April 1994, pp. 47–50.

21. Richard C. Mosier, "Expected Value: Applying Research to Uncertainty," *Appraisal Journal*, July 1989, pp. 293–96. See also Amartya Sen, "The Formulation of Rational Choice," *American Economic Review 84* (May 1994): 385–90.

22. Peter Boys, "Answers Grow on Decision Trees," *Accountancy*, January 1990, pp. 86–89.

23. John F. Magee, "Decision Trees for Decision Making," *Harvard Business Review*, July/August 1964. To see how decision trees can be applied to the problem of stress management, refer to Lin Grensing-Pophal, "If the Answer Is 'No,' Then 'Let It Go': Using the 'Stress Relief Decision Tree,'" *Manage*, July 1994, pp. 18–20.

24. Rakesh Sarin and Peter Wakker, "Folding Back in Decision Tree Analysis," *Management Science 40* (May 1994): 625–28.

25. This section is based on Samuel C. Certo, *Supervision: Quality and Diversity Through Leadership* (Homewood, Ill.: Austen Press/Irwin, 1994), pp. 198–202.

26. Clark Wigley, "Working Smart on Tough Business Problems," *Supervisory Management*, February 1992, p. 1.

27. Joseph Alan Redman, "Nine Creative Brainstorming Techniques," *Quality Digest*, August 1992, pp. 50–51.

28. David M. Armstrong, "Management by Storytelling," *Executive Female*, May/June 1992, pp. 38–41.

29. André, Delbecq, Andrew Van de Ven, and D. Gustafson, *Group Tech-*

niques for Program Planning (Glenview, Ill.: Scott, Foresman, 1975); Philip L. Roth, L.F. Lydia, and Fred S. Switzer, "Nominal Group Technique—An Aid for Implementing TQM," *CPA Journal*, May 1995, pp. 68–69.

30. N. Delkey, *The Delphi Method: An Experimental Study of Group Opinion* (Santa Monica, Cal.: Rand Corporation, 1969); Delia Neuman, "High School Students' Use of Databases: Results of a National Delphi Study," *Journal of the American Society for Information Science 46* (1995): 284–98; Sibylle Breiner, Kerstin Cuhls, and Hariolf Grupp, "Technology Foresight Using a Delphi Approach: A Japanese-German Cooperation," *R&D Management*, April 1994, pp. 141–53.

Introductory Case: This case is excerpted from Gabriella Stern, "Cadillac Covets the Range Rover Crowd," *Wall Street Journal*, January 17, 1995, p. B1.

Cutting Edge: Ralph L. Keeney, "Creativity in Decision Making with Value-Focused Thinking," *Sloan Management Review*, Summer 1994, pp. 33–41; and *One CFO Team: Best and Fastest Together*, AT&T company document, 1995.

People Perspectives: Kevin Kelly, "The New Soul of John Deere," *Business Week*, January 31, 1994, pp. 64–66.

CHAPTER 8

1. Tony Grundy and Dave King, "Using Strategic Planning to Drive Strategic Change," *Long-Range Planning*, February 1992, pp. 100–108; Andrall E. Pearson, "Six Basics for General Managers," *Harvard Business Review*, July/August 1989, pp. 94–101.

2. Charles R. Greer, "Counter-Cyclical Hiring as a Staffing Strategy for Managerial and Professional Personnel: Some Considerations and Issues," *Academy of Management Review 9* (April 1984):324–30; Dyan Machan, "The Strategy Thing," *Forbes*, May 23, 1994, pp. 113–14.

3. Richard B. Robinson, Jr., and John A. Pearce II, "Research Thrusts in Small Firm Strategic Planning," *Academy of Management Review 9* (January 1984):128–37; George Sawyer, "Elements of Strategy," *Managerial Planning*, May/June 1981, pp. 3–59.

4. This section is based on Samuel C. Certo and J. Paul Peter, *Strategic Management: Concepts and Applications*, (Chicago: Austin Press/Irwin, 1995), pp. 3–27.

5. Samuel C. Certo and J. Paul Peter, *The Strategic Management Process* 4th ed., (Chicago: Austen Press/Irwin, 1995), p. 32; Philip S. Thomas, "Environment Analysis for Corporate Planning," *Business Horizons*, October 1974, pp. 28–38.

6. This section is based on William F. Glueck and Lawrence R. Jauch, *Business Policy and Strategic Management* (New York: McGraw-Hill, 1984), pp. 99–110.

7. John F. Watkins, "Retirees as a New Growth Industry? Assessing the Demographic and Social Impact," *Review of Business*, Spring 1994, pp. 9–14.

8. Bruce Henderson, "The Origin of Strategy," *Harvard Business Review*, November/December 1989, pp. 139–43; R.S. Wilson, "Managing in the Competitive Environment," *Long-Range Planning 17* (1984):50–63.

9. Peter Wright, "MNC—Third World Business Unit Performance: Application of Strategic Elements," *Strategic Management Journal 5* (1984):231–40.

10. M. Klemm, S. Sanderson, and G. Luffman, "Mission Statements: Selling Corporate Values to Employees," *Long-Range Planning*, June 1991, pp. 73–78.

11. Colin Coulson-Thomas, "Strategic Vision or Strategic Cons: Rhetoric or Reality," *Long-Range Planning*, February 1992, pp. 81–89.

12. This section is based primarily on Thomas H. Naylor and Kristin Neva, "Design of a Strategic Planning Process," *Managerial Planning*, January/February 1980, pp. 2–7; Donald W. Mitchell, "Pursuing Strategic Potential," *Managerial Planning*, May/June 1980, pp. 6–10; Benton E. Gup, "Begin Strategic Planning by Asking Three Questions," *Managerial Planning*, November/December 1979, pp. 28–31, 35; L.A. Gerstner, Jr., "Can Strategic Planning Pay Offs," *Business Horizons 15* (1972):5–16.

13. For a practical example of SWOT applied in the business world, see

Robert H. Woods, "Strategic Planning: A Look at Ruby Tuesday," *Cornell Hotel & Restaurant Administration Quarterly*, June 1994, pp. 41–49.

14. Philip Kotler, *Marketing Management Analysis, Planning and Control*. 7th ed. (Englewood Cliffs, N.J.: Prentice Hall, 1991), 39–41.

15. Harold W. Fox, "The Frontiers of Strategic Planning: Intuition or Formal Models?" *Management Review*, April 1981, pp. 8–14. See also J. Scott Armstrong and Roderick J. Brodie, "Effects of Portfolio Planning Methods on Decision Making: Experimental Results," *International Journal of Research in Marketing*, January 1994, pp. 73–84; Robin Wensley, "Making Better Decisions: The Challenge of Marketing Strategy Techniques—A Comment on 'Effects of Portfolio Planning Methods on Decision Making: Experimental Results' by Armstrong and Brodie," *International Journal of Research in Marketing*, January 1994, pp. 85–90.

16. This discussion of Porter's model is based on Chapters 1 and 2 of Porter's *Competitive Strategy* (New York: The Free Press, 1980), and Chapter 1 of Porter's *Competitive Advantage: Creating and Sustaining Superior Performance* (New York: The Free Press, 1985). For an application of Porter's concepts, see William P. Munk and Barry Shane, "Using Competitive Analysis Models to Set Strategy in the Northwest Hardboard Industry," *Forest Products Journal*, July/August 1994, pp. 11–18.

17. Ian C. MacMillan, Donald C. Hambrick, and Diana L. Day, "The Product Portfolio and Profitability—A PIMS- Based Analysis of Industrial-Product Businesses," *Academy of Management Journal*, December 1982, pp. 733–55.

18. Bill Saporito, "Black & Decker's Gamble on Globalization," *Fortune*, May 14, 1984, pp. 40–48; Walecia Konrad and Bruce Einhorn, "Famous Amos Gets a Chinese Accent," *Business Week*, September 28, 1992, p. 76.

19. Doron P. Levin, "Westinghouse's New Chief Aims to Push New Lines, Revitalize Traditional Ones," *Wall Street Journal*, November 28, 1983, p. 10.

20. William Sandy, "Avoid the Breakdowns Between Planning and Implementation," *Journal of Business Strategy*, September/October 1991, pp. 30–33.

21. Thomas V. Bonoma, "Making Your Marketing Strategy Work," *Harvard Business Review*, March/April 1984, pp. 69–76.

22. For a good discussion of the importance of monitoring the progress of the strategic planning process, see William B. Carper and Terry A. Bresnick, "Strategic Planning Conferences," *Business Horizons*, September/October 1989, pp. 34–40. See also Stephen Bungay and Michael Goold, "Creating a Strategic Control System," *Long-Range Planning*, June 1991, pp. 32–39.

23. For a detailed discussion of the characteristics of strategic and tactical planning, see George A. Steiner, *Top Management Planning* (Toronto, Canada: Collier-Macmillan, 1969), pp. 37–39.

24. Russell L. Ackoff, *A Concept of Corporate Planning* (New York: Wiley, 1970), p. 4.

25. "The New Breed of Strategic Planner," *Business Week*, September 17, 1984, pp. 62–67.

Case Study: "The View from IBM," *Business Week*, October 20, 1995, pp. 142–52; "Information Week Industry Update."

Introductory Case: Susan G. Strother, "Sea World Plots Competitive Course 1st Ride." *Orlando Sentinel*, May 15, 1996, pp. C1, C6. Reprinted by permission.

Cutting Edge: Jeffrey Pfeffer, "Competitive Advantage through People," *California Management Review*, Winter 1994, pp. 9–28.

People Perspectives: Michael Schachner, "Child Care Investment Yields Excellent Returns for Wall Street Firms," *Business Insurance*, March 28, 1994, pp. 3, 6.

CHAPTER 9

1. Charles B. Ames, "Straight Talk from the New CEO" *Harvard Business Review*, November/December 1989, pp. 132–38.

2. Fremont E. Kast and James E. Rosenzweig, *Organization and Management: A Systems Approach* (New York: McGraw-Hill, 1970), pp. 443–49. For a classic discussion on expanding this list of characteristics to 13, see P. LeBreton and D.A. Henning, *Planning Theory* (Englewood Cliffs, N.J.:

Prentice Hall, 1961), pp. 320–44. These authors list the dimensions of a plan as (1) complexity, (2) significance, (3) comprehensiveness, (4) time, (5) specificity, (6) completeness, (7) flexibility, (8) frequency, (9) formality, (10) confidential nature, (11) authorization, (12) ease of implementation, and (13) ease of control.

3. Jennifer A. Knight, "Loss Control Solution to Limiting Costs of Workplace Violence," *Corporate Cashflow*, July 1994, pp. 16–17.

4Kirkland Wilcox and Richard Discenza, "The TQM Advantage," *CA Magazine*, May 1994, pp. 37–41.

5. From "Seize the Future—Make Top Trends Pay Off Now," *Success*, March 1990, pp. 39–45.

6. For an interesting article outlining how currency exchange rates complicate budgets that relate to operations in more than one country, see Paul V. Mannino and Ken Milani, "Budgeting for an International Business," *Management Accounting*, February 1992, pp. 36–41. See also J. Fred Weston and Eugene F. Brigham, *Essentials of Managerial Finance* (New York: Holt, Rinehart & Winston, 1971), p. 107; Mark M. Klein, "Questions to Ask Before You Sharpen Your Budget Knife," *Bottomline*, March 1990, pp. 32–37; Pierre Filiatrault and Jean-Charles Chebat, "How Service Firms Set Their Marketing Budgets," *Industrial Marketing Management*, (February 1990), pp. 63–67.

7. Kjell A. Ringbakk, "Why Planning Fails," *European Business*, July 1970. See also William G. Gang, "Strategic Planning and Competition: A Survival Guide for Electric Utilities," *Fortnightly*, February 1, 1994, pp. 20–23. For a good discussion on involving people in the planning process, see Margaret M. Lucas, "Business Plan Is the Key to Agency Success," *National Underwriter 94* (March 5, 1990):15, 17.

8. For information that ranks U.S. cities on the possible site selection criterion of growth, see John Case, "Where the Growth Is," *Inc.*, June 1991, pp. 66–79. See also Walt Yesberg, "Get a Grip on Building Costs," *ABA Banking Journal 82* (March 1990):90, 92; Robert Bowman, "Key Logistics Issues in Site Selection," *Distribution 88* (December 1989):56–57.

9. Douglas P. Woodward, "Locational Determinants of Japanese Manufacturing Start-Ups in the United States," *Southern Economic Journal*, January 1992, pp. 690–708.

10. Greg Nakanishi, "Building Business Through Partnerships," *HR Magazine*, June 1991, pp. 108–12; Dale S. Beach, *Personnel: The Management of People at Work* (New York: Macmillan, 1975), p. 220.

11. Charles F. Kettering, "A Glimpse at the Future," *Industry Week*, July 1, 1991, p. 34.

12. William C. House, "Environmental Analysis: Key to More Effective Dynamic Planning," *Managerial Planning*, January/February 1977, pp. 25–29. The basic components of this forecasting method, as well as of other methods, are discussed in Chaman L. Jain, "How to Determine the Approach to Forecasting," *Journal of Business Forecasting Methods & Systems*, Summer 1995, pp. 2, 28.

13. Marshall L. Fisher et al., "Making Supply Meet Demand in an Uncertain World," *Harvard Business Review*, May/June 1994, pp. 83–89.

14. Olfa Hemler, "The Uses of Delphi Techniques in Problems of Educational Innovations," no. 8499, RAND Corporation, December 1966. For an interesting illustration of how the delphi method works, see Yeong Wee Yong, Kau Ah Keng, and Tan Leng Leng, "A Delphi Forecast for the Singapore Tourism Industry," *International Marketing Review 6* (1989):35–46.

15. James E. Cox, Jr., "Approaches for Improving Salespersons' Forecasts," *Industrial Marketing Management 18* (November 1989):307–11.

16. N. Carroll Mohn, "Forecasting Sales with Trend Models—Coca-Cola's Experience," *Journal of Business Forecasting 8* (Fall 1989):6–8.

17. For elaboration on these methods, see George A. Steiner, *Top Management Planning* (London: Collier-Macmillan, 1969), pp. 223–27.

18. Willard Fazar, "The Origin of PERT," *The Controller*, December 1962. See also Harold L. Wattel, *Network Scheduling and Control Systems CAP/PERT* (Hempstead, N.Y.: Hostra University, 1964); see also Khaled A. Bushait, "The Application of Project Management Techniques to Construction and Research and Development Projects," *Project Management*

Journal 20 (June 1989):17–22. For a discussion of software packages that draw preliminary PERT and Gantt charts, see Pat Sweet, "A Planner's Best Friend?" *Accountancy*, February 1994, pp. 56, 58.

19. R.J. Schonberger, "Custom-Tailored PERT/CPM Systems," *Business Horizons 15* (1972): 64–66. See also H.M. Soroush, "The Most Critical Path in a PERT Network," *Journal of the Operational Research Society 45* (March 1994): 287–300.

20. Avraham Shrub, "The Integration of CPM and Material Management in Project Management," *Construction Management and Economics 6* (Winter 1988): 261–72.

21. For extended discussion of these steps, see Edward K. Shelmerdine, "Planning for Project Management," *Journal of Systems Management 40* (January 1989): 16–20.

Introductory Case: Guy Collins. "Fiat Will Build, Expand in Italy's Depressed South," *Wall Street Journal*. November 29, 1990, A9. Reprinted by permission of *Wall Street Journal*, © 1990 Dow Jones & Company, Inc. All Rights Reserved Worldwide, See also John Rossant, "After Gianni, There Are Mostly Questions," *Business Week*, July 10, 1995, p.55; Rob Cleveland, "European Suppliers on Fast Track," *Ward's Auto World*, July 1995, pp. 35–37; and Rossant: "The Man Who's Driving Fiat like a Ferrari," *Business Week*, January 23, 1995, pp. 82–83.

Perspectives: Linda Thornburg, "Money Is Still the Best Reward," *HR Magazine*, August 1994, pp. 58–59.

Cutting Edge: Alan David MacCormack, Lawrence James Newman III, and Donald B. Rosenfield, "The New Dynamics of Global Manufacturing Site Location," *Sloan Management Review*, Summer 1994, pp. 69–80.

CHAPTER 10

1. Douglas S. Sherwin, "Management of Objectives," *Harvard Business Review*, May/June 1976, pp. 149–60. See also Lloyd Sandelands and Robert Drazin, "On the Language of Organization Theory," *Organizational Studies 10* (1989): 457–77.

2. Henri Fayol, *General and Industrial Management* (London: Sir Isaac Pitman and Sons, 1949), pp. 53–54.

3. For a discussion emphasizing the importance of continually adapting organization structure, see Michael A. Verespej, "When Change Becomes the Norm," *Industry Week*, March 16, 1992, pp. 35–36.

4. Saul W. Gellerman, "In Organizations, as in Architecture, Form Follows Function," *Organizational Dynamics 18* (Winter 1990): 57–68. For a discussion of how evaluation can contribute to increased worker productivity, see Eugene F. Finklin, "Techniques for Making People More Productive," *Journal of Business Strategy*, March/April 1991), pp. 53–56.

5. Max Weber, *Theory of Social and Economic Organization*, trans. and ed. A.M. Henderson and Talcott Parsons (London: Oxford University Press, 1947); Stanley Vanagunas, "Max Weber's Authority Models and the Theory of X-Inefficiency: The Economic Sociologist's Analysis Adds More Structure to Leibenstein's Critique of Rationality," *American Journal of Economics and Sociology 48* (October 1989): 393–400; Foad Derakhshan and Kamal Fatehi, "Bureaucracy as a Leadership Substitute: A Review of History," *Leadership and Organization Development Journal 6* (1985): 13–16.

6. Sandra T. Gray, "Fostering Leadership for the New Millennium," *Association Management*, January 1995, pp. L-78–L-82.

7. Lyndall Urwich, *Notes on the Theory of Organization* (New York: American Management Association, 1952).

8. For an interesting discussion of a nontraditional organization structure, see John E. Tropman, "The Organizational Circle: A New Approach to Drawing an Organizational Chart," *Administration in Social Work 13* (1989): 35–44.

9. Sally Helgesen, *The Female Advantage: Women's Ways of Leadership* (New York: Doubleday/Currency, 1990); Tom Peters, "The Best New Managers Will Listen, Motivate, Support," *Working Woman*, (September 1990); pp. 142–43, 216–17.

10. Raef T. Hussein, "Informal Groups, Leadership, and Productivity," *Leadership and Organization Development Journal 10* (1989): 9–16.

11. Geary A. Rummler and Alan P. Brache, "Managing the White Space

on the Organization Chart," *Supervision*, May 1991), pp. 6–12. For an article arguing in favor of having organizations designed by function, see Jack Cohen, "Managing the Managers," *Supermarket Business 44* (September 1989): 16, 244.

12. Roderick E. White and Thomas A. Poynter, "Organizing for Worldwide Advantage," *Business Quarterly 54* (Summer 1989): 84–89.

13. Y.K. Sherry and Howard M. Carlisle, "A Contingency Model of Organization Design," *California Management Review 15* (1972): 38–45. For additional discussion of factors influencing formal structure, see Paul Dwyer, "Tearing Up Today's Organization Chart," *Business Week*, November 18, 1994, pp. 80–90.

14. For insights on how Ralph Larsen, CEO of Johnson & Johnson, views problems and how his view might influence the formal structure of his organization, see Brian Dumaine, "Is Big Still Good?" *Fortune*, April 30, 1992, pp. 50–60.

15. Carol Ann Dorn, "Einstein: Still No Equal," *Journal of Business strategy*, November/December 1994 pp. 20–23.

16. C.R. Walker and R. H. Guest, *The Man on the Assembly Line* (Cambridge, Mass.: Harvard University Press, 1952). For an excellent example of how technology can affect division of labor, see John P. Walsh, "Technological Change and the Division of Labor: The Case of Retail Meatcutters," *Work and Occupations 16* (May 1989): 165–83.

17. J. Mooney, "The Principles of Organization," in *Ideas and Issues in Public Administration*, ed. D. Waldo (New York: McGraw-Hill, 1953), p. 86. For a discussion of the importance of cooperation and coordination in division of labor, see Jason Magidson and Andrew E. Polcha, "Creating Market Economies Within Organizations," *The Planning Forum*, January/February 1992, pp. 37–40. See also Peter Jackson, "Speed versus Heed," *CA Magazine*, November 1994, pp. 56–57.

18. Bruce D. Sanders, "Making Work Groups Work," *Computerworld 24* (March 5, 1990): 85–89.

19. George D. Greenberg, "The Coordinating Roles of Management," *Midwest Review of Public Administration 10* (1976): 66–76.

20. Henry C. Metcalf and Lyndall F. Urwich, eds., *Dynamic Administration: The Collected Papers of Mary Parker Follett* (New York: Harper & Bros., 1942), pp. 297–99; James F. Wolf, "The Legacy of Mary Parker Follett," Bureaucrat Winter 1988–89, pp. 53–57.

21. Leon McKenzie, "Supervision: Learning from Experience," *Health Care Supervisor 8* (January 1990): 1–11. For an interesting discussion of how span of management impacts a manager's perceived need for additional training, see James P. Guthrie and Catherine E. Schwoerer, "Individual and Contextual Influences on Self-Assessed Training Needs," *Journal of Organizational Behavior 15* (1994): 405–22.

22. Harold Koontz, "Making Theory Operational: The Span of Management," *Journal of Management Studies*, (October 1966), pp. 229–43; see also John S. McClenahen, "Managing More People in the '90s," *Industry Week 238* (March 1989): 30–38.

23. V.A. Graicunas, "Relationships in Organization," *Bulletin of International Management Institute*, (March 1933), pp. 183–87. For more on the life of Graicunas, see Arthur C. Bedeian, "Vytautas Andrius Graicunas: A Biographical Note," *Academy of Management Journal 17* (June 1974): 347–49. See also L.F. Urwick, "V.A. Graicunas and the Span of Control," *Academy of Management Journal 17* (June 1974): 349–54.

24. John R. Brandt, "Middle Management: 'Where the Action Will Be,' " *Industry Week*, May 2, 1994, pp. 30–36.

25. Philip R. Nienstedt, "Effectively Downsizing Management Structures," *Human Resources Planning 12* (1989): 155–65; Robin Bellis-Jones and Max Hand, "Improving Managerial Spans of Control," *Management Accounting 67* (October 1989): 20–21.

26. Cass Bettinger, "The Nine Principles of War," *Bank Marketing 21* (December 1989): 32–34; Charles A. Mowll, "Successful Management Based on Key Principles," *Healthcare Financial Management 43* (June 1989): 122, 124.

27. Henri Fayol, *General and Industrial Administration* (Belmont, Cal.: Pitman, 1949).

Introductory Case: Mary Lu Carnevale, "MCI to Revamp Units, May Cut 1,500 Staffers," *Wall Street Journal*, November 16, 1990, p. A3. Reprinted by permission of *Wall Street Journal*, © *1990 Dow Jones & Company, Inc. All Rights Reserved Worldwide. See also Robin Gareiss, "Uses Rate Long-Distance Carriers,"* Data Communications, August 1995, pp. 81–88.

People Perspectives: Richard Burnett, "Aerospace Giant Prepares Cuts," *The Orlando Sentinel*, August 27, 1994, p. C1; Leon A. Danco, "Lighting the Long Fuse" *Agency Sales Magazine*, July 1994, pp. 52–57.

Cutting Edge: John R. Brandt, "Middle Management: 'Where the Action Will Be,' " *Industry Week*, May 2, 1994, pp. 30–36; M.L. Stein, "More Cost-Cutting Measures for Times Mirror," *Editor & Publisher*, July 29, 1995, pp. 20–21.

Case Study: "Divide and Conquer?" *Business Week*, October 2, 1995, pp. 56–57; "Just Three Easy Pieces," *Time*, Octobe 2, 1995, 47–48; "Strategic Restructuring for the 21st Century," remarks by Robert Allen, September 20, 1995.

CHAPTER 11

1. Andre Nelson, "Have I the Right Stuff to Be a Supervisor?" *Supervision 51* (January 1990):10–12.

2. J.E. Osborne, "Job Descriptions Do More Than Describe Duties," *Supervisory Management*, February 1992, p. 8; Stephen X. Doyle and Benson P. Shapiro, "What Counts Most in Motivating Your Sales Force?" *Harvard Business Review*, May/June 1980, pp. 133–40. See also G.F. Scollard, "Dynamic Descriptions: Job Descriptions Should Work for You," *Management World*, May 1985, pp. 34–35; Charlene Marmer Solomon, "Repatriation Planning Checklist," *Personnel Journal*, January 1995, p. 32; Bruce Shawkey, "Job Descriptions," *Credit Union Executive 29* (Winter 1989/1990):20–23.

3. Robert J. Theirauf, Robert C. Klekamp, and Daniel W. Geeding, *Management Principles and Practices: A Contingency and Questionnaire Approach* (New York: Wiley, 1977), p. 334.

4. Deborah S. Kezsbom, "Managing the Chaos: Conflict Among Project Teams," *AACE Transactions*, 1989, pp. A.4.1–A.4.8.

5. Chuck Douros, "Clear Division of Responsibility Defeats Inefficiency," *Nation's Restaurant News*, February 21, 1994, p. 20.

6. Robert D. Melcher, "Roles and Relationships: Clarifying the Manager's Job," *Personnel 44* (May/June 1967):34–41.

7. This section is based primarily on John H. Zenger, "Responsible Behavior: Stamp of the Effective Manager," *Supervisory Management*, (July 1976), pp. 18–24.

8. Stephen Bushardt, David Duhon, and Aubrey Fowler, "Management Delegation Myths and the Paradox of Task Assignment," *Business Horizons*, March/April 1991, pp. 37–43; Jack J. Phillips, "Authority: It Just Doesn't Come with Your Job," *Management Solutions 31* (August 1986):35–37.

9. Max Weber, "The Three Types of Legitimate Rule," trans. Hans Gerth, *Berkeley Journal of Sociology 4* (1953):1–11; for a current illustration of this concept, see Gail DeGeorge, "Yo, Ho, Ho, and a Battle for Bacardi," *Business Week*, April 16, 1990, pp. 47–48.

10. John Gardner, "The Anti-Leadership Vaccine," *Carnegie Foundation Annual Report*, 1965.

11. Chester I. Barnard, *The Functions of the Executive* (Cambridge, Mass.: Harvard University Press, 1938).

12. Patti Wolf, Gerald Grimes, and John Dayani, "Getting the Most out of Staff Functions," *Small Business Reports 14* (October 1989):68–70.

13. Harold Stieglitz, "On Concepts of Corporate Structure," *Conference Board Record 11* (February 1974):7–13.

14. Wendell L. French, *The Personnel Management Process: Human Resource Administration and Development* (Boston: Houghton Mifflin, 1987), pp. 66–68.

15. Derek Sheane, "When and How to Intervene in Conflict," *Personnel Management*, (November 1979), pp. 32–36; John M. Ivancevich and Michael T. Matteson, "Intergroup Behavior and Conflict," in their *Organizational Behavior and Management* (Plano, Tex.: Business Publications, 1987), pp. 305–45.

16. Robert Albanese, *Management* (Cincinnati: South-Western Publishing, 1988), p. 313. For an excellent discussion of the role of accountability and organization structure, see Elliott Jacques, "In Praise of Hierarchy," *Harvard Business Review* 68 (January/February 1990):127–33.

17. "How Ylvisaker Makes 'Produce or Else' Work," *Business Week*, October 27, 1973, p. 112. For an interesting discussion of the importance of establishing an environment of accountability in a small women's specialty retail store, see Nan Napier, "Change Is Big Even for a Little Guy," *Business Quarterly*, Winter 1994, pp. 21–27.

18. William H. Newman and E. Kirby Warren, *The Process of Management: Concepts, Behavior, and Practice*, 4th ed. (Englewood Cliffs, N.J.: Prentice Hall, 1977), pp. 39–40; these steps are also discussed in Jay T. Knippen and Thad B. Green, "Delegation," *Supervision* 51 (March 1990):7–9, 17. See also Robert Rohrer, "Does the Buck Ever Really Stop?" *Supervision*, July 1991, pp. 7–8.

19. R. S. Drever, "The Ultimate Frustration," *Supervision*, May 1991, pp. 22–23.

20. Ted Pollock, "Secrets of Successful Delegation," *Production*, December 1994, pp. 10–11; Robert B. Nelson, "Mastering Delegation," *Executive Excellence* 7 (January 1990):13–14; Jimmy Calano and Jeff Salzman, "How Delegation Can Lead Your Team to Victory," Working Woman, August 1989, pp. 86–87, 95.

21. Roz Ayres-Williams, "Mastering the Fine Art of Delegation," *Black Enterprise*, April 1992, pp. 91–93.

22. Harold Koontz, Cyril O'Donnell, and Heinz Weihrich, *Essentials of Management*, 8th ed. (New York: McGraw-Hill, 1986), pp. 231–33.

23. For an interesting discussion of whether or not to centralize the marketing function, see Richard Kitaeff, "The Great Debate: Centralized vs. Decentralized Marketing Research Function," *Marketing Research: A Magazine of Management & Applications*, Winter 1994, p. 59.

24. Steve Weinstein, "A Look at Fleming's New Look," *Progressive Grocer*, 74 (1995):47–49.

25. H. Gilman, "J.C. Penney Decentralizes Its Purchasing," *Wall Street Journal*, May 8, 1986, p. 6.

26. Donald O. Harper, "Project Management as a Control and Planning Tool in the Decentralized Company," *Management Accounting*, November 1968, pp. 29–33.

27. Information for this section is mainly from John G. Staiger, "What Cannot Be Decentralized," *Management Record* 25 (January 1963):19–21. At the time the article was written, Staiger was vice president of administration, North American Operations, Massey-Ferguson, Limited.

Introductory Case: CNN Cable News Network "Pinnacle" interview, September 24, 1988, and Dennis P. Kimbro, "Dreamers: Black Sales Heros and Their Secrets," *Success* 37 (May 1990):40–41; Fonda Marie Lloyd, "A Cookie by Any Other Name," *Black Enterprise*, January 1995, p. 22.

People Perspectives: Michael A. Verespej, "Before It's Too Late," *Industry Week*, September 19, 1994, p. 11.

Cutting Edge: Mary Ann Linsen, "Making the Big Time," *Progressive Grocer* 73, Part 1 (1994):91–100.

Case Study: "Wanted: Company Change Agents," *Fortune*, February 5, 1996, pp. 60–61; Jon R. Katzenbach, Real Change Leaders (1996).

CHAPTER 12

1. Bruce Shawkey, "Job Descriptions," *Credit Union Executive* 29 (Winter 1989/1990):20–23; Howard D. Feldman, "Why Are Similar Managerial Jobs So Different?" *Review of Business* 11 (Winter 1989):15–22. For a discussion of the legal importance of job analysis, see James P. Clifford, "Job Analysis: Why Do It, and How Should It Be Done?" *Public Personnel Management* 23 (1994):321–40.

2. "Job Analysis," *Bureau of Intergovernmental Personnel Programs*, December 1973, pp. 135–52; Gundars E. Kaupins, "Lies, Damn Lies, and Job Evaluations," *Personnel* 66 (November 1989):62–65.

3. James H. Martin, and Elizabeth B. Franz, "Attracting Applicants from a Changing Labor Market: A Strategic Marketing Framework," *Journal of Managerial Issues*, Spring 1994, pp. 33–53.

4. Fred K. Foulkes, "How Top Nonunion Companies Manage Employees," *Harvard Business Review*, September/October 1981, p. 90; John Perham, "Management Succession: A Hard Game to Play," *Dun's Review*, April 1981, pp. 54–55, 58.

5. Walter S. Wikstrom, "Developing Managerial Competence: Concepts, Emerging Practices," *Studies in Personnel Policy*, no. 189, National Industrial Conference Board (1964):95–105.

6. Patricia Panchak, "Resourceful Software Boosts HR Efficiency," *Modern Office Technology* 35 (April 1990):76–80.

7. Ray H. Hodges, "Developing an Effective Affirmative Action Program," *Journal of Intergroup Relations* 5 (November 1976):13. For a more philosophical argument supporting affirmative action, see Leo Goarke, "Affirmative Action as a Form of Restitution," *Journal of Business Ethics* 9 (March 1990):207–13.

8. R. Roosevelt Thomas, Jr., "From Affirmative Action to Affirming Diversity," *Harvard Business Review* 68 (March/April, 1990):107–17. For an argument on how using quotas to achieve affirmative action may harm business, see George Weimer, "Quotas and Other Dumb Ideas," *Industry Week*, April 6, 1992, p. 86.

9. For insights on how to select high performers, see Michael Rozek, "Can You Spot A Peak Performer?"," *Personnel Journal*, June 1991, pp. 77–78.

10. For more discussion of the stages of the selection process, see David J. Cherrington, *Personnel Management: The Management of Human Resources* (Dubuque, IA: Wm. C. Brown, 1987), pp. 186–231.

11. This section is based on Andrew F. Sikula, *Personnel Administration and Human Resource Management* (New York: Wiley, 1976), pp. 188–90. For information on various tests available, see O.K. Buros, ed., *The 8th Mental Measurements Yearbook* (Highland Park, N.J.: Gryphon Press, 1978).

12. Daniel P. O'Meara, "Personality Tests Raise Questions of Legality and Effectiveness," *HRMagazine*, January 1994, pp. 97–100.

13. For a discussion of EEOC guidelines concerning appropriate pre-employment testing for Americans with disabilities, see Melanie K. St. Clair and David W. Arnold, "Preemployment Screening: No More Test Stress," *Security Management*, February 1995, p. 73. See also Robin Inwald, "Preemployment Testing: Those Seven Deadly Sins," *Security Management* 34 (April 1990):73–76.

14. David Littlefield, "Menu for Change at Novotel," *People Management*, January 26, 1995, pp. 34–36; D.W. Bray and D.L. Grant, "The Assessment Center in the Measurement of Potential for Business Management," *Psychological Monographs 80* (1966):1–27; Susan O. Hendricks and Susan E. Ogborn, "Supervisory and Managerial Assessment Centers in Health Care," *Health Care Supervisor* 8 (April 1990):65–75.

15. Barry M. Cohen, "Assessment Centers," *Supervisory Management*, June 1975, p. 30. See also T.J. Hanson and J.C. Balestreri-Sepro, "An Alternative to Interviews: Pre-employment Assessment Process," *Personnel Journal*, June 1985, p. 114.

16. Ann Howard, "An Assessment of Assessment Centers," *Academy of Management Journal* 17 (March 1974):117.

17. William Umiker and Thomas Conlin, "Assessing the Need for Supervisory Training: Use of Performance Appraisals," *Health Care Supervisor* 8 (January 1990):40–45.

18. Bass and Vaughn, *Training in Industry*.

19. David Sutton, "Further Thoughts on Action Learning," *Journal of European Industrial Training* 13 (1989):32–35.

20. For more information on training techniques, see Cherrington, *Personnel Management*, pp. 304–36.

21. Samuel C. Certo, "The Experiential Exercise Situation: A Comment on Instructional Role and Pedagogy Evaluation," *Academy of Management Review*, July 1976, pp. 113–16. For a worthwhile discussion of the advantages of facilitation over lecturing for overcoming trainee resistance to learning, see Margaret Kaeter, "Coping with Resistant Trainees," *Training 31* (1994):110–14. For more information on instructional roles in various situations, see Bernard Keys, "The Management of Learning Grid for

Management Development," *Academy of Management Review*, April 1977, pp. 289–97.

22. "Training Program's Results Measured in Unique Way," *Supervision* Editors-Supervision, February 1992, pp. 18–19.

23. William Keenan, Jr., "Are You Overspending on Training?" *Sales and Marketing Management 142* (January 1990):56–60.

24. For a review of the literature linking performance appraisal and training needs, see Glenn Herbert and Dennis Doverspike, "Performance Appraisal in the Training Needs Analysis Process: A Review and Critique," *Public Personnel Management*, Fall, 1990, pp. 253–70. See also Mike Deblieux, "Performance Reviews Support the Quest for Quality," *HR Focus*, November 1991, pp. 3–4.

25. Douglas McGregor, "An Uneasy Look at Performance Appraisal," *Harvard Business Review*, September/October 1972, pp. 133–34. For insights on how performance appraisal can motivate employees, see Kenneth M. Dawson and Sheryl N. Dawson, "How to Motivate Your Employees," *HRMagazine 35* (April 1990):78–80.

26. Linda J. Segall, "KISS Appraisal Woes Goodbye," *Supervisory Management 34* (December 1989):23–28.

27. Robert M. Gerst, "Assessing Organizational Performance," *Quality Progress*, February 1995, pp. 85–88. See also George A. Rider, "Performance Review: A Mixed Bag," *Harvard Business Review*, July/August 1973, pp. 61–67; Robert Loo, "Quality Performance Appraisals," *Canadian Manager 14* (December 1989):24–26.

Introductory Case: Michael J. McCarthy, "Unlike Rival Airlines, United Is Setting Off on Costly Expansion," *Wall Street Journal*, March 6, 1995, pp. A1, A8.

People Perspectives: Michele Galen, "Honey, We're Cheating the Kids," *Business Week*, February 20, 1995, pp. 38–40.

Cutting Edge: Kevin Kelly, "Motorola: Training for the Millennium," *Business Week* (Industrial/Technology Edition), March 28, 1994, pp. 158–63.

Case Study: "Buy! Employee Solutions, Inc.," The Volume Investor Special Update, June 8, 1995; Blomberg Business Wire, February 5, 1996.

CHAPTER 13

1. John H. Zimmerman, "The Principles of Managing Change," *HR Focus*, February 1995, pp. 15–16.

2. Rosabeth Moss Kanter, "The New Managerial Work," *Harvard Business Review*, November/December 1989, pp. 85–92. For a review of planned change models as related to a nursing environment, see Constance Rimmer Tiffany et al., "Planned Change Theory: Survey of Nursing Periodical Literature," *Nursing Management*, July 1994, pp. 54–59.

3. John S. Morgan, *Managing Change: The Strategies of Making Change Work for You* (New York: McGraw-Hill, 1972), p. 99.

4. Bart Nooteboom, "Paradox, Identity, and Change in Management," *Human Systems Management 8* (1989):291–300. For an interesting discussion of how to handle employee stress, see Alan Farnham, "Who Beats Stress Best—And How," *Fortune*, October 7, 1991, pp. 71–86.

5. For a discussion of the value of outside change agents, see John H. Sheridan, "Careers on the Line," *Fortune*, September 16, 1991, pp. 29–30. See also John H. Zimmerman, "The Deming Approach to Construction Safety Management," *Professional Safety*, December 1994, pp. 35–37.

6. Myron Tribus, "Changing the Corporate Culture—A Roadmap for the Change Agent," *Human Systems Management 8* (1989):11–22.

7. For an interesting case illustrating the changing nature of organization structure at Procter & Gamble, see Aelita G. B. Martinsons and Maris G. Martinsons, "In Search of Structural Excellence," *Leadership & Organization Development Journal 15* (1994):24–28. See also Saul W. Gellerman, "In Organizations, as In Architecture, Form Follows Function," *Organizational Dynamics 18* (Winter 1990):57–68.

8. C. J. Middleton, "How to Set Up a Project Organization," *Harvard Business Review*, March/April 1967, p. 73. See also George J. Chambers, "The Individual in a Matrix Organization," *Project Management Journal 20* (December 1989):37–42, 50.

9. John F. Mee, "Matrix Organization," *Business Horizons*, Summer 1964.

10. Robert E. Jones, K. Michelle Jones, and Richard F. Deckro, "Strategic Decision Processes in Matrix Organizations," *European Journal of Operational Research 78* (1994):192–203. See also Middleton, "How to Set Up a Project Organization," p. 74; Deborah S. Kezsbom, "Managing the Chaos: Conflict Among Project Teams," *AACE Transactions*, 1989, pp. A.4.1–A.4.8; Harvey F. Kolodny, "Managing in a Matrix," *Business Horizons*, March/April 1981, pp. 17–24.

11. This section is based primarily on R. Blake, J. Mouton, and L. Greiner, "Breakthrough in Organization Development," *Harvard Business Review*, November/December 1964, pp. 133–55. For a discussion of other methods for implementing OD change, see William F. Glueck, *Organization Planning and Development* (New York: American Management Association, 1971).

12. Blake, Mouton, and Greiner, "Breakthrough in Organization Development."

13. W.J. Heisler, "Patterns of OD in Practice," *Business Horizons*, February 1975, pp. 77–84.

14. Martin G. Evans, "Failures in OD Programs—What Went Wrong," *Business Horizons*, April 1974, pp. 18–22.

15. David Coghlan, "OD Interventions in Catholic Religious Orders," *Journal of Managerial Psychology 4* (1989):4–6. See also Paul A. Iles and Thomas Johnston, "Searching for Excellence in Second-Hand Clothes?: A Note," *Personnel Review 18* (1989):32–35; Ewa Maslyk-Musial, "Organization Development in Poland: Stages of Growth," *Public Administration Quarterly 13* (Summer 1989):196–214.

16. For an interesting discussion of resistance to change from inherited staff, see: Margaret Russell, "Records Management Program-Directing: Inherited Staff," *ARMA Records Management Quarterly 24* (January 1990):18–22.

17. This strategy for minimizing resistance to change is based on "How Companies Overcome Resistance to Change," Management Review, November 1972, pp. 17–25. See also Hank Williams, "Learning to Manage Change," *Industrial and Commercial Training 21* (May/June 1989):17–20; John P. Kotter and Leonard A. Schlesinger, "Choosing Strategies for Change," *Harvard Business Review*, March/April 1979, pp. 106–13; Arnold S. Judson, *A Manager's Guide to Making Changes* (New York: Wiley, 1966), p. 118.

18. Kurt Lewin, "Frontiers in Group Dynamics: Concept, Method, and Reality of Social Sciences—Social Equilibria and Social Change," *Human Relations 1* (June 1947):5–14; Ivan Louis Rare, "The Three Phases of Change," *Quality Progress 19* (November 1986):47–49.

19. Edgar H. Schein, "Management Development as a Process of Influence," *Industrial Management Review*, May 1961, pp. 59–76. For a more current discussion of the phases of change, see Dottie Perlman and George J. Takacs, "The 10 Stages of Change," *Nursing Management 21* (April 1990):33–38.

20. Newton Margulies and John Wallace, *Organizational Change: Techniques and Applications* (Chicago: Scott, Foresman, 1973), p. 14.

21. Edgar C. Williams, "Changing Systems and Behavior: People's Perspectives on Prospective Changes," *Business Horizons*, August 1969, p. 53.

22. Hans Selve, *The Stress of Life* (New York: McGraw-Hill, 1956). See also James C. Quick and Jonathan D. Quick, *Organizational Stress and Preventive Management* (New York: McGraw-Hlll, 1984).

23. James D. Bodzinski, Robert F. Scherer, and Karen A. Gover, "Workplace Stress," *Personnel Administrator 34* (July 1989):76–80; Richard M. Steers, *Introduction to Organizational Behavior* (Glenview, Ill.: Scott, Foresman, 1981), pp. 340–41.

24. Corinne M. Smereka, "Outwitting, Controlling Stress for a Healthier Lifestyle," *Healthcare Financial Management 44* (March 1990):70–75.

25. J. Clifton Williams, *Human Behavior in Organizations* (Cincinnati: South-Western, 1982), pp. 212–13; Thomas L. Brown, "Are You Living in 'Quiet Desperation'?" *Industry Week*, March 16, 1992, p. 17.

26. Stewart L. Stokes, Jr., "Life after Rightsizing," *Information Systems Management*, Fall 1994, pp. 69–71. For a discussion of other stressors, see

"Workplace Stress," *HR Magazine*, Society of Human Resource Management, August 1991, pp. 75–76.

27. For an interesting article addressing how managers can handle their own stress, see Thomas Brown, "Are You Stressed Out?" *Industry Week*, September 16, 1991, p. 21.

28. Fred Luthans, *Organizational Behavior* (New York: McGraw-Hill, 1985), pp. 146–48.

29. Donald B. Miller, "Career Planning and Management in Organizations," *S.A.M. Advanced Management Journal 43* (Spring 1978):33–43.

Introductory Case: Scott McCartney, "Michael Dell—and His Company—Grow Up," *Wall Street Journal*, January 31, 1995, pp. B1, B4.

People Perspectives: Laxmi Nakarmi and Robert Neff, "Samsung's Radical Shakeup," *Business Week* (Industrial/Technology Edition), February 28, 1994, pp. 74–76.

Cutting Edge: Edmund Faltermayer, "New Ways to Foil Heart Attacks," *Fortune*, February 20, 1995, pp. 84–90.

Case Study: Robert E. Allen "Strategic Restructuring for the 21st Century," speech, September 20, 1995. AT&T On-line (http://www.att.com/news/speeches/95/950920.raa.html; John J. Keller, "AT&T Will Eliminate 40,000 Jobs and Take a Charge of $4 Billion," *Wall Street Journal*, January 3, 1996, pp. A3, A6; Deborah Lohse, "New Jersey to Be Hit Hard by Cutback at Largest Private Employer in State," *Wall Street Journal*, January 3, 1996, pp. A3, A4; "AT&T Managers Ponder Their Future for Last Day," CNNfn On-line, December 29, 1995; (http://www.cnnfn.com/news/9512/29/att.managers/index.html); "Out One Door and in Another," *Business Week*, January 22, 1996, p. 41.

CHAPTER 14

1. Derek Torrington and Jane Weightman, "Middle Management Work," *Journal of General Management 13* (Winter 1987):74–89. For a useful discussion of how to influence people, see Martin Wilding, "Win Friends and Influence People by Being Sincere," *Marketing*, February 23, 1995, p. 16; Esther Bogin, "From Staff to Dream Team," *Financial Executive*, January/February 1995, pp. 54–56.

2. Bernard Reilly and Joseph DiAngelo, Jr., "Communication: A Cultural System of Meaning and Value," *Human Relations 43* (February 1990):129–40. See also Paul Sandwith, "Effective Communication," *Training and Development*, January 1992, pp. 29–32; Christine Clements, Richard J. Wagner, and Christopher Roland, "The Ins and Outs of Experimental Training," *Training & Development*, February 1995, pp. 52–56.

3. This section is based on the following classic article on interpersonal communication: Wilbur Schramm, "How Communication Works," *The Process and Effects of Mass Communication*, ed. Wilbur Schramm (Urbana: University of Illinois Press, 1954), pp. 3–10.

4. David S. Brown, "Barriers to Successful Communication: Part I, Macrobarriers," *Management Review*, December 1975, pp. 24–29.

5. James K. Weekly and Raj Aggarwal, *International Business: Operating in the Global Economy* (New York: Dryden Press, 1987).

6. Davis S. Brown, "Barriers to Successful Communication: Part II, Microbarriers," *Management Review*, January 1976, pp. 15–21.

7. Sally Bulkley Pancrazio and James J. Pancrazio, "Better Communication for Managers," *Supervisory Management*, June 1981, pp. 31–37. See also Gene E. Burton, "Barriers to Effective Communication," *Management World*, March 1977, pp. 4–8; John S. Fielden, "Why Can't Managers Communicate?" *Business 39* (January/February/March 1989): 41–44.

8. Lydia Strong, "Do You Know How to Listen?" in *Effective Communications on the Job*, ed. M. Joseph Dooher and Vivienne Marquis (New York: American Management Association, 1956), p. 28. See also John R. White, "Some Thoughts on Lexicon and Syntax," *Appraisal Journal 57* (July 1989):417–21.

9. Robert E. Callahan, C. Patrick Fleenor, and Harry R. Knudson, *Understanding Organizational Behavior: A Managerial Viewpoint* (Columbus, Ohio: Charles E. Merrill, 1986). For a discussion of the process of generating feedback, see Elizabeth Wolfe Morrison and Robert J. Bies, "Impression Management in the Feedback-Seeking Process: Literature Review and Research Agenda," *Academy of Management Review*, July 1991, pp. 522–41.

10. For more on nonverbal issues, see I. T. Sheppard, "Silent Signals," *Supervisory Management*, March 1986, pp. 31–33.

11. Verne Burnett, "Management's Tower of Babel," *Management Review*, June 1961, pp. 4–11.

12. Reprinted, by permission of the publisher, from "Ten Commandments of Good Communication," by American Management Association AMA-COM. et al. from *Management Review*, October 1955. © 1953 American Management Association, Inc. All rights reserved. See also Robb Ware, "Communication Problems," *Journal of Systems Management*, September 1991, p. 20; "Communicating: Face-to-Face," *Agency Sales Magazine*, January 1994, pp. 22–23.

13. Ted Pollock, "Mind Your Own Business," *Supervision*, May 1994, pp. 24–26.

14. Albert Mehrabian, "Communication Without Words," *Psychology Today*, September 1968, pp. 53–55. For a practical article emphasizing the role of gestures in communication, see S. D. Gladis, "Notes Are Not Enough," *Training and Development Journal*, August 1985, pp. 35–38. See also Nicole Steckler and Robert Rosenthal, "Sex Differences in Nonverbal and Verbal Communication with Bosses, Peers, and Subordinates," *Journal of Applied Psychology*, February 1985, pp. 157–63; Andrew J. DuBrin, *Contemporary Applied Management* (Plano, Tex.: Business Publications, 1982), pp. 127–34; W. Alan Randolph, *Understanding and Managing Organizational Behavior* (Homewood, Ill.: Richard D. Irwon, 1985), pp. 349–50; Karen O. Down and Jeanne Liedtka, "What Corporations Seek in MBA Hires: A Survey," *Selections*, Winter 1994, pp. 34–39.

15. Gerald M. Goldhaber, *Organizational Communication* (Dubuque, Iowa: Wm. C. Brown, 1983).

16. Kenneth R. Van Voorhis, "Organizational Communication: Advances Made during the Period from World War II Through the 1950s," *Journal of Business Communication 11* (1974):11–18. See also Phillip J. Lewis, "The Status of 'Organizational Communication,' in Colleges of Business," *Journal of Business Communication 12* (1975):25–28.

17. Paul Preston, "The Critical 'Mix' in Managerial Communications," *Industrial Management*, March/April 1976, pp. 5–9.

18. For a discussion of how to communicate failures upward in an organization, see Jay T. Knippen, Thad B. Green and Kurt Sutton, "How to Communicate Failures to Your Boss," *Supervisory Management*, September 1991, p. 10.

19. "Upward/Downward Communication—Critical Information Channels," *Small Business Report 10* (October 1985):85–88; Anne B. Fisher, "CEOs Think That Morale is Dandy," *Fortune*, November 18, 1991, pp. 70–71.

20. William V. Haney, "Serial Communication of Information in Organizations," in *Concepts and Issues in Administrative Behavior*, ed. Sidney Mailick and Edward H. Van Ness (Englewood Cliffs, N.J.: Prentice Hall, 1962), p. 150.

21. Alex Bavelas and Ermot Barrett, "An Experimental Approach to Organizational Communication," *Personnel 27* (1951):366–71.

22. Polly LaBarre, "The Other Network," *Industry Week*, September 19, 1994, pp. 33–36.

23. George de Mare, "Communicating: The Key to Establishing Good Working Relationships," *Price Waterhouse Review 33* (1989):30–37; Alan Zaremba, "Working with the Organizational Grapevine," *Personnel Journal 67* (July 1988):38–42; Stanley J. Modic, "Grapevine Rated Most Believable," *Industry Week*, May 15, 1989, pp. 11, 14.

24. Keith Davis, "Management Communication and the Grapevine," *Harvard Business Review*, January/February 1953, pp. 43–49.

25. Linda McCallister, "The Interpersonal Side of Internal Communications," *Public Relations Journal*, February 1981, pp. 20–23. See also Joseph M. Putti, Samuel Aryee, and Joseph Phua, "Communication Relationship Satisfaction and Organizational Commitment," *Group and Organizational Studies 15* (March 1990):44–52. For an article defending the value of grapevines, see W. Kiechel, "In Praise of Office Gossip," *Fortune*, August 19, 1985, pp. 253–54.

Source: Thomas F. O'Boyle, "A Manufacturer Grows Efficient by Soliciting Ideas from Employees," *Wall Street Journal,* June 5, 1992, pp. A1, A4. Reprinted by permission of *Wall Street Journal,* © 1992 Dow Jones & Company, Inc. All Rights Reserved Worldwide.

Source: Dyan Machan, "Can I Go Home Now?" *Forbes,* October 24, 1994, pp. 250–51.

Cutting Edge: Robert D. Hof, "The Education of Andrew Grove," *Business Week,* January 1995, pp. 60–62.

Source: Mark Ashworth, manager of Communication Services at Chick-fil-A, in a telephone conversation, January 10, 1996.

CHAPTER 15

1. David Nadler and Michael L. Tushman, "Beyond the Charismatic Leader: Leadership and Organizational Change," *California Management Review 32* (Winter 1990):77–97.

2. Abraham Zaleznik, "Executives and Organizations: Real Work," *Harvard Business Review,* January/February 1989, pp. 57–64; Abraham Zaleznik, "Managers and Leaders: Are They Different?" *Harvard Business Review,* May/June 1977, pp. 67–78.

3. Theodore Levitt, "Management and the Post-Industrial Society," *Public Interest,* Summer 1976, p. 73.

4. Patrick L. Townsend and Joan E. Gebhardt, "We Have Lots of Managers . . . We Need Leaders," *Journal for Quality and Participation,* September 1989, 18–20; Craig Hickman, "The Winning Mix: Mind of a Manager, Soul of a Leader," *Canadian Business 63* (February 1990):69–72.

5. Ralph M. Stogdill, "Personal Factors Associated with Leadership: A Survey of the Literature," *Journal of Psychology 25* (January 1948):35–64.

6. Cecil A. Gibb, "Leadership," in *Handbook of Social Psychology,* ed. Gardner Lindzey, Reading, Mass.: Addison-Wesley, 1954); Eugene E. Jennings, "The Anatomy of Leadership," *Management of Personnel Quarterly 1* (Autumn 1961).

7. J. Oliver Crom, "What's New in Leadership?" *Executive Excellence 7* (January 1990):15–16.

8. For an interesting discussion of followers in a leadership situation, see Robert E. Kelly, "In Praise of Followers," *Harvard Business Review,* November/December 1988, pp. 142–48.

9. Robert Tannenbaum and Warren H. Schmidt, "How to Choose a Leadership Pattern," *Harvard Business Review,* March/April 1957, pp. 95–101.

10. William E. Zierden, "Leading Through the Follower's Point of View," *Organizational Dynamics,* Spring 1980, pp. 27–46. See also Tannenbaum and Schmidt, "How to Choose a Leadership Pattern."

11. Robert Tannenbaum and Warren H. Schmidt, "How to Choose a Leadership Pattern," *Harvard Business Review,* May/June 1973, pp. 162–80.

12. Victor H. Vroom and Philip H. Yetton, *Leadership and Decision-Making* (Pittsburgh: University of Pittsburgh Press, 1973); Victor H. Vroom and Arthur G. Jago, *The New Leadership* (Englewood Cliffs, N.J.: Prentice Hall, 1988).

13. Gary A. Yukl, *Leadership in Organizations,* 2d ed. (Englewood Cliffs, N.J.: Prentice Hall, 1989).

14. Vishwanath V. Baba and Merle E. Ace, "Serendipity in Leadership: Initiating Structure and Consideration in the Classroom," *Human Relations 42* (June 1989):509–25; Desmond Nolan, "Leadership Appraisals: Your Management Style Can Affect Productivity," *Credit Union Executive 28* (Winter 1988):36–37.

15. Rensis Likert, *New Patterns of Management* (New York: McGraw-Hill, 1961).

16. Andrew W. Halpin, *The Leadership Behavior of School Superintendents* (Chicago: University of Chicago Midwest Administration Center, 1959); Harvey A. Hornstein, Madeline E. Heilman, Edward Mone, and Ross Tartell, "Responding to Contingent Leadership Behavior," *Organizational Dynamics 15* (Spring 1987):56–65.

17. A.K. Korman, "'Consideration,' 'Initiating Structure,' and Organizational Criteria—A Review," *Personnel Psychology 19* (Winter 1966:349–61.

See also Rick Roskin, "Management Style and Achievement: A Model Synthesis," *Management Decision 27* (1989):17–22.

18. P. Hersey and K.H. Blanchard, "Life Cycle Theory of Leadership," *Training and Development Journal,* May 1969, pp. 26–34.

19. Mary J. Keenan, Joseph B. Hurst, Robert S. Dennis, and Glenna Frey, "Situational Leadership for Collaboration in Health Care Settings," *Health Care Supervisor 8* (April 1990):19–25. See also Claude L. Graeff, "The Situational Leadership Theory: A Critical View," *Academy of Management Review 8* (1983):285–91; Robert P. Vecchio, "Situational Leadership Theory: An Examination of a Prescriptive Theory," *Journal of Applied Psychology 72* (August 1987):444–51; Jane R. Goodson, Gail W. McGee, and James F. Cashman, "Situational Leadership Theory: A Test of Leadership Prescriptions," *Group and Organizational Studies 14* (December 1989):446–61.

20. Fred E. Fiedler, "Engineer the Job to Fit the Manager," *Harvard Business Review,* September/October 1965, pp. 115–22. See also Fred E. Fiedler, *A Theory of Leadership Effectiveness* (New York: McGraw-Hill, 1967).

21. From *A Theory of Leadership Effectiveness,* pp. 255–56 by F.E. Fiedler. Copyright © 1967 by McGraw-Hill, Inc. Used with permission of McGraw-Hill Company.

22. L.H. Peters, D.D. Harike, and J.T. Pohlmann, "Fiedler's Contingency Theory of Leadership: An Application of the Meta-analysis Procedures of Schmidt and Hunter," *Psychological Bulletin 97* (1985):224–85.

23. Robert J. House and Terence R. Mitchell, "Path-Goal Theory of Leadership," *Journal of Contemporary Business,* Autumn 1974; pp. 81–98; Gary A. Yukl, *Leadership in Organizations.*

24. Alan C. Filley, Robert House, and Steven Kerr, *Managerial Process and Organizational Behavior* (Glenview, Ill.: Scott, Foresman, 1976), pp. 256–60. For a worthwhile review of the path-goal theory of leadership, see Gary A. Yukl, *Leadership in Organizations.* See also F.E. Fiedler and M.M. Chemers, *Leadership and Effective Management* (Glenview, Ill.: Scott Foresman, 1974).

25. To learn how some managers are reacting to modern challenges, see Jaclyn Fierman, "Winning Ideas from Maverick Managers," *Fortune,* February 6, 1995, pp. 66–80.

26. Andrew J. DuBrin, *Reengineering Survival Guide* (Cincinnati, Ohio, Thomson Executive Press, 1996), pp. 115–29.

27. Karl W. Kuhnert and Philip Lewis, "Transactional and Transformational Leadership: A Constructive/Developmental Analysis," *Academy of Management Review,* October 1987, pp. 648–57.

28. Bernard M. Bass, *Leadership and Performance Beyond Expectations* (New York: Free Press, 1985); Noel M. Tichy and David M. Ulrich, "The Leadership Challenge: A Call for Transformational Leadership," *Sloan Management Review,* Fall 1984, 59–68.

29. For more information on empathy and leadership, see William G. Pagonis, "The Work of the Leader," *Harvard Business Review,* November/December 1992, pp. 118–26.

30. Charles C. Manz, "Helping Yourself and Others to Master Self-Leadership," *Supervisory Management,* November 1991, pp. 19–38; Manz and Henry P. Sims, Jr., "SuperLeadership: Beyond the Myth of Heroic Leadership," *Organizational Dynamics,* Spring 1991, p. 28–40.

31. S. Kerr and J.M. Jermier, "Substitutes for Leadership: Their Meaning and Measurement," *Organizational Behavior and Human Performance 22* (1978):375–403; J. Pfeffer, "The Ambiguity of Leadership," *Academy of Management Review 2* (1977):104–12; C.C. Manz and H.P. Sims, Jr., "Leading Workers to Lead Themselves: The External Leadership on Self-Managing Work Teams," *Administrative Science Quarterly,* March 1987, pp. 106–29.

32. J.R. Meindl and S.B. Ehrlich, "The Romance of Leadership and the Evaluation of Organizational Performance," *Academy of Management Journal 30*:91–109.

33. Data in this section come from the following sources: Ralph M. Stogdill, *Handbook of Leadership* (New York: Free Press, 1974); U.S. Department of Labor, Bureau of Labor Statistics, 1989. *Employment and Earnings* (Washington, D.C.: Table 1–22), p. 29; "Workforce 2000 is Wel-

come Today at Digital," *Business Ethics*, July/August 1990, pp. 5–16; Any Salzman, "Trouble at the Top," *U.S. News and World Report*, June 17, 1991; Susan B. Garland, "Throwing Stones at the Glass Ceiling," *Business Week*, August 19, 1991, p. 29.

34. See the following articles: J.B. Rosener, "Ways Women Lead," *Harvard Business Review*, May/June 1990, pp. 103–11; B.M. Bass Leadership. "Good, Better, Best," *Organizational Dynamics*, Winter 1985, pp. 26–40.

Source: Material in this case is excerpted from Leslie Doolittle, "New Disney Park Will Feature Wildlife, Exotic Gardens, Waterfalls," *The Orlando Sentinel*, June 21, 1995, p. A-6.

(*Source:* Genevieve Capowski, "Anatomy of a Leader: Where Are the Leaders of Tomorrow," *Management Review*, March, 1994, p. 12).

Source: Marshall Loeb, "Empowerment That Pays Off," *Fortune*, March 20, 1995, pp. 145–46.

Source: Adapted from Andrew J. DuBrin, *Participant Guide to Module 10: Development of Subordinates* (McGregor, Tex.: Leadership Systems Corporation, 1985), p. 11.

Sources: Andrew E. Serwer, "Paths to Wealth in the New Economy," *Fortune* February 20, 1995, pp. 56–62; Bill Walsh, "The Case for Kudos," *Forbes*, October 10, 1994, p. 17.

Sources: Steering Through Turbulence, *Atlanta Journal and Constitution*, January 14, 1996, pp. F1–F2; Morale Falters as Change Rocks Delta's Family, *Atlanta Journal and Constitution*, January 14, 1996, p. F5; Turns Out This Critter Can Fly, *Fortune*, November 27, 1995, p. 51.

CHAPTER 16

1. Philip A. Rudolph and Brian H. Kleiner, "The Art of Motivating Employees," *Journal of Managerial Psychology 4* (1989):i–iv.

2. Mike DeLuca, "Motivating Your Staff Is Key to Your Success," *Restaurant Hospitality*, February 1995, p. 20.

3. Craig Miller, "How to Construct Programs for Teams," *Reward & Recognition*, August/September 1991, pp. 4–6; Walter F. Charsley, "Management, Morale, and Motivation," *Management World 17* (July/August 1988):27–28.

4. Victor H. Vroom, *Work and Motivation* (New York: Wiley, 1964); Thomas L. Quick, "How to Motivate People," *Working Women 12* (September 1987):15, 17.

5. J. Stacy Adams, "Towards an Understanding of Inequity," *Journal of Abnormal and Social Psychology 67* (1963):422–36. For a rationale linking expectancy and equity theories, see Joseph W. Harder, "Equity Theory versus Expectancy Theory: The Case of Major League Baseball Free Agents," *Journal of Applied Psychology*, June 1991, pp. 458–64.

6. L.W. Porter and E.E. Lawler, *Managerial Attitudes and Performance* (Homewood, Ill.: Richard D. Irwin, 1968). For more information on intrinsic and extrinsic rewards, see Pat Buhler, "Rewards in the Organization," *Supervision 50* (January 1989):5–7.

7. Eric G. Flamholtz and Yvonne Randle, "The Inner Game of Management," *Management Review 77* (April 1988):24–30.

8. Abraham Maslow, *Motivation and Personality*, 2d ed. (New York: Harper & Row, 1970). For an up-to-date discussion of the value of Maslow's ideas, see Edward Hoffman, "Abraham Maslow: Father of Enlightened Management," *Training 25* (September 1988):79–82. See also Abraham Maslow, *Eupsychian Management* (Homewood, Ill.: Richard D. Irwin, 1965).

9. For critiques of Maslow, see Jack W. Duncan, *Essentials of Management* (Hinsdale, Ill.: Dryden Press, 1975), p. 105; C.P. Alderfer, "An Empirical Test of a New Theory of Human Needs," *Organizational Behavior and Human Performance 4* (1969):142–75; D.T. Hall and K. Nougaim, "An Examination of Maslow's Need Hierarchy in an Organizational Setting," *Organizational Behavior and Human Performance 3* (1968):12–35; Hoffman, "Abraham Maslow: Father of Enlightened Management;" Dale L. Mort, "Lead Your Team to the Top," *Security Management 32* (January 1988):43–45.

10. Clayton Alderfer, *Existence, Relatedness, and Growth* (New York: Free Press, 1972). For a reconstruction of Maslow's hierarchy, see Francis Heylighen, "A Cognitive-Systemic Reconstruction of Maslow's Theory of Self-Actualization," *Behavioral Science*, January 1992, pp. 39–58.

11. Chris Argyris, *Personality and Organization* (New York: Harper & Bros., 1957). See also Charles R. Davis, "The Primacy of Self-Development in Chris Argyris's Writings," *International Journal of Public Administration 10* (September 1987):177–207.

12. David C. McClelland and David G. Winter, *Motivating Economic Achievement* (New York: Free Press, 1969); David C. McClelland, "Power Is the Great Motivator," *Harvard Business Review*, March/April 1976, pp. 100–10. See also Burt K. Scanlan, "Creating a Climate for Achievement," *Business Horizons 24* (March/April 1981):5–9; Lawrence Holp, "Achievement Motivation and Kaizen," *Training and Development Journal 43* (October 1989):53–63; McClelland, *The Achieving Society* (New York: Van Nostrand, 1961); McClelland and David H. Burnham, "Power Is the Great Motivator," *Harvard Business Review*, January/February 1995, pp. 126–39.

13. Michael Sanson, "Fired Up!" *Restaurant Hospitality*, February 1995, pp. 53–64.

14. Douglas McGregor, *The Human Side of Enterprise* (New York: McGraw-Hill, 1960). For a current illustration of how Theory X–Theory Y relates to modern business, see Kenneth B. Slutsky, "Viewpoint: Why Not Theory Z?" *Security Management 33* (April 1989):110, 112. See also W.J. Reddin, "The Tri-Dimensional Grid," *Training and Development Journal*, July 1964. For a discussion of Theories X, Y, and Z as they relate to the adoption of new technology in organizations, see Richard T. Due, "Client/Server Feasibility," *Information Systems Management*, Summer 1994, pp. 79–82.

15. For more discussion on the implications of job rotation in organizations, see Alan W. Farrant, "Job Rotation Is Important," *Supervision*, August 1987, pp. 14–16.

16. L.E. Davis and E.S. Valfer, "Intervening Responses to Changes in Supervisor Job Designs," *Occupational Psychology*, July 1965, pp. 171–90; M.D. Kilbridge, "Do Workers Prefer Larger Jobs?" *Personnel*, September/October 1960, pp. 45–48.

17. This section is based on Frederick Herzberg, "One More Time: How Do You Motivate Employees?" *Harvard Business Review*, January/February 1968, pp. 53–62.

18. Scott M. Meyers, "Who Are Your Motivated Workers?" *Harvard Business Review*, January/February 1964, pp. 73–88; John M. Roach, "Why Volvo Abolished the Assembly Line," *Management Review*, September 1977, p. 50; Matt Oechsli, "Million Dollar Success Habits," *Managers Magazine 65* (February 1990):6–14; J. Barton Cunningham and Ted Eberle, "A Guide to Job Enrichment and Redesign," Personnel 67 (February 1990):56–61; Richard J. Hackman, "Is Job Enrichment Just a Fad?" *Harvard Business Review*, September/October 1975, pp. 129–38.

19. Bob Smith and Karen Matthes, "Flexibility Now for the Future," *HR Focus*, January 1992, p. 5.

20. D.A. Bratton, "Moving Away from Nine to Five," *Canadian Business Review 13* (Spring 1986):15–17.

21. Douglas L. Fleuter, "Flextime—A Social Phenomenon," *Personnel Journal*, June 1975, pp. 318–19; Lee A. Graf, "An Analysis of the Effect of Flexible Working Hours on the Management Functions of the First-Line Supervisor," Ph.D. diss., (Mississippi State University, 1976); Jill Kanin-Lovers, "Meeting the Challenge of Workforce, 2000," *Journal of Compensation and Benefits 5* (January/February 1990):233–36; William Wong, "Rather Come in Late or Go Home Earlier? More Bosses Say OK," *Wall Street Journal*, July 12, 1973, p. 1.

22. B.F. Skinner, *Contingencies of Reinforcement* (New York: Appleton-Century-Crofts, 1969). See also E.L. Thorndike, "The Original Nature of Man," *Educational Psychology 1* 1903; Fred Luthans and Robert Kreitner, *Organizational Behavior Modification and Beyond* (Glenview, Ill.: Scott, Foresman, 1985).

23. P.M. Padokaff, "Relationships Between Leader Reward and Punishment Behavior and Group Process and Productivity," *Journal of Management 11* (Spring 1985):55–73. For a practical discussion of punishment, see Bruce R. McAfee and William Poffenberger, *Productivity Strategies: Enhancing Employee Job Performance* (Englewood Cliffs, N.J.: Prentice Hall, Spectrum, 1982).

24. "New Tool: Reinforcement for Good Work," *Psychology Today*, April 1972, pp. 68–69.

25. W. Clay Hamner and Ellen P. Hamner, "Behavior Modification on the Bottom Line," *Organizational Dynamics 4* (Spring 1976):6–8.

26. James K. Hickel, "Paying Employees to Control Costs," *Human Resources Professional*, January/February 1995, pp. 21–24.

27. Rensis Likert, *New Patterns of Management* (New York: McGraw-Hill, 1961). For an interesting discussion of the worth of Likert's ideas, see Marvin R. Weisbord, "For More Productive Workplaces," *Journal of Management Consulting 4* (1988):7–14. The following descriptions are based on the table of organizational and performance characteristics of different management systems in Rensis Likert, *The Human Organization* (New York: McGraw-Hill, 1967), pp. 4–10.

28. For a discussion of a novel monetary incentive program, see Charles A. Cerami, "Special Incentives May Appeal to Valued Employees," *HR Focus*, November 1991, p. 17. See also "Incentive Pay Plan Replaces Wage Hikes: Lump Sum Bonuses, Profit-Sharing Attract and Maintain Good Workers," *Chain Store Age Executive*, February 1989, pp. 78, 79.

29. Jeffrey P. Davidson, "A Great Place to Work: Seven Strategies for Keeping Employees Committed to Your Company," *Management World*, June/August 1987, pp. 24–25.

Case Study: Joan E. Rigdon, "Using Lateral Moves to Spur Employees," *Wall Street Journal*, May 26, 1992, pp. B1, B9. Reprinted by permission of *Wall Street Journal*, © 1992 Dow Jones & Company, Inc. All Rights Reserved Worldwide.

Cutting Edge: Joshua Levine, "Lighter Than Air," *Forbes*, October 10, 1994, pp. 120–22.

People Perspectives: Dan Lavin, "Millionaires at Work," *Fortune*, April 3, 1995, pp. 20–21.

Case Study: Interview with Glenn Goldberg, Director of Human Resources, Western Pacific Airlines; "If at First You Don't Secceed . . .", *Forbes*, February 12, 1996, pp. 54–58.

CHAPTER 17

1. For an article illustrating the importance of managing groups in organizations, see Gregory E. Kaebnick, "Notes from Underground: Walter Corbitt Talks About Monitoring Paperwork for 35,000 Underground Storage Tanks," *Inform 3* (July/August 1989): 21–22, 48.

2. Edgar H. Schein, *Organizational Psychology* (Englewood Cliffs, N.J.: Prentice Hall, 1965), p. 67.

3. Dorwin Cartwright and Ronald Lippitt, "Group Dynamics and the Individual," *International Journal of Group Psychotherapy* 7 (January 1957): 86–102.

4. Edgar H. Schein, *Organizational Psychology*, 2d ed. (Englewood Cliffs, N.J.: Prentice Hall, 1970), p. 182.

5. For useful guidelines on how to make committees work, see Arthur R. Pell, "Making Committees Work," *Managers Magazine 64* (September 1989): 28.

6. Cyril O'Donnell, "Group Rules for Using Committees," *Management Review 50* (October 1961): 63–67. See also "Making Committees Work." *Infosystems*, October 1985, pp. 38–39.

7. These and other guidelines are discussed in "Applying Small-Group Behavior Dynamics to Improve Action-Team Performance," *Employment Relations Today*, Autumn 1991, pp. 343–53. For additional guidelines, see Peggy S. Williams, "Physical Fitness for Committees: Getting on Track," *Association Management 4* (June 1989): 104–11.

8. See Irving L. Janis, *Groupthink* (Boston: Houghton Mifflin, 1982). For insights on how to avoid groupthink, see Michael J. Woodruff, "Understanding—and Combatting—Groupthink," *Supervisory Management*, October 1991, p. 8.

9. Craig Cina, "Company Study: Five Steps to Service Excellence," *Journal of Services Marketing 4* (Spring 1990): 39–47. To see how teams can increase productivity, consult Jana Schilder, "Work Teams Boost Productivity," *Personnel Journal* pp. 67–71; For suggestions on how to build a team, see Edward Glassman, "Silence Is Not Consent," *Supervisory Management*,

March 1992, pp. 6–7; Robert B. Reich, "Entrepreneurship Reconsidered: The Team as a Hero," *Harvard Business Review*, May/June 1987, pp. 77–83.

10. Bernard Bass, *Organizational Psychology* (Boston: Allyn and Bacon, 1965), pp. 197–98. For more insights on characteristics of productive groups, see Edward Glassman, "Self-Directed Team Building Without a Consultant," *Supervisory Management*, March 1992, p. 6.

11. Raef T. Hussein, "Informal Groups, Leadership, and Productivity," *Leadership and Organization Development Journal 10* (1989): 9–16.

12. Keith Davis and John W. Newstrom, *Human Behavior at Work: Organizational Behavior* (New York: McGraw-Hill, 1985), pp. 310–12. See also Muhammad Jamal, "Shift Work Related to Job Attitudes, Social Participation, and Withdrawal Behavior: A Study of Nurses and Industrial Workers," *Personnel Psychology 34* (Autumn 1981): 535–47.

13. For the importance of determining such information, see Dave Day, "New Supervisors and the Informal Group," *Supervisory Management 34* (May 1989): 31–33. For a classic study illustrating sociometry and sociometric procedures, see Muzafer Sherif, "A Preliminary Experimental Study of Intergroup Relations," in *Social Psychology at the Crossroads*, ed. John H. Rohrer and Muzafer Sherif (New York: Harper & Bros., 1951).

14. Homans, *The Human Group*.

15. William G. Dyer, *Teambuilding: Issues and Alternatives* (Reading, Mass.: Addison-Wesley, 1987), p. 4. See also Dawn R. Deeter-Schmelz and Rosemary Ramsey, "A Conceptualization of the Functions and Roles of Formalized Selling and Buying Teams," *Journal of Personal Selling & Sales Management*, Spring 1995, pp. 47–60.

16. J. H. Shonk, *Team-Based Organizations* (Homewood, Ill.: Business One Irwin, 1992).

17. Jack L. Lederer and Carl R. Weinberg, "Equity-Based Pay: The Compensation Paradigm for the Re-Engineered Corporation," *Chief Executive*, April 1995, pp. 36–39.

18. Kevin R. Zuidema and Brian H. Kleiner, "Self-Directed Work Groups Gain Popularity," *Business Credit*, October 1994, pp. 21–26.

19. Sami M. Abbasi and Kenneth W. Hollman, "Self-Managed Teams: The Productivity Breakthrough of the 1990s," *Journal of Managerial Psychology 9* (1994): 25–30.

20. For more information on cross-functional teams, see D. Keith Denton, "Multi-Skilled Teams Replace Old Work Systems," *HR Magazine*, September 1992, pp. 48–56; Michael D. Hutt, Beth A. Walker, and Gary L. Frankwick, "Hurdle the Cross-Functional Barriers to Strategic Change," *Sloan Management Review*, Spring 1995, pp. 22–30; John Teresko, "Reinventing the Future," *Industry Week*, April 17, 1995, pp. 32–38; Margaret L. Gagne and Richard Discenza, "Target Costing," *Journal of Business & Industrial Marketing 10* (1995): 16–22.

21. Bruce W. Tuckman and Mary Ann C. Jensen, "Stages of Small Group Development Revisited," *Group and Organizational Studies 2* (1977): 419–27.

22. Hans J. Thamhain, "Managing Technologically Innovative Team Efforts Toward New Product Success," *Journal of Product Innovation Management*, March 1990, pp. 5–18.

23 Jerre L. Stead, "People Power: The Engine in Reengineering," *Executive Speeches*, April/May 1995, pp. 28–32.

24. Fernando Bartolome, "Nobody Trusts the Boss Completely—Now What?" *Harvard Business Review*, March/April 1989, pp. 114–131.

25. Cass Bettinger, "Use Corporate Culture to Trigger High Performance," *The Journal of Business Strategies*, March/April 1989, pp. 38–42.

26. The text discussion of these mechanisms is based on Edgar H. Schein, *Organizational Culture and Leadership* (San Francisco: Jossey-Bass, 1985), pp. 223–43. See also John Hassard and Sudi Sharifi. "Corporate Culture, and Strategic Change," *Journal of General Management 15* (Winter 1989): 4–19.

Introductory Case: "The Fall of an American Icon," *Business Week*, February 5, 1996, pp. 34–44; "New Task at Apple: First Order, Then Orders," *Wall Street Journal*, February 5, 1996, pp. A3–A4; "Inside Apple's Boardroom Coup," *Business Week*, February 19, 1996, pp. 28–30.

Case Study: Timothy Aeppel, "Rolls-Royce Tries to Restore Luster as Car Sales Fade, *Wall Street Journal,* May 26, 1992, p. B3. Reprinted by permission of *Wall Street Journal,* © 1992 Dow Jones & Company, Inc. All Rights Reserved Worldwide.

Cutting Edge: Beverly Geber, "Virtual Teams," *Training,* April 1995, pp. 36–40.

People Perspectives: W. Alan Randolph, "Navigating the Journey to Empowerment," *Organizational Dynamics,* Spring 1995, pp. 19–32.

CHAPTER 18

1. Martin Fishbein and Isek Ajyen, *Belief, Attitude, Intention and Behavior: An Introduction to Theory and Research* (Reading, Mass.: Addison-Wesley, 1975).

2. Milton Kokeach, *The Nature of Human Values* (New York: Free Press, 1973); William K. Tracey, *The Human Resources Glossary* (New York: AMACOM, 1991), p. 366.

3. John K. Schermerhorn, James G. Hunt, and Richard N. Osborn, *Managing Organizational Behavior,* 4th ed. (New York: Wiley, 1991), pp. 115–17.

4. Barry M. Staw and Jerry Ross, "Stability in the Midst of Change: A Dispositional Approach to Job Attitudes," *Journal of Applied Psychology,* August, 1985, pp. 469–80.

5. Martin Fishbein and Mark Stasson, "The Role of Desires, Self-Predictions, and Perceived Control in the Prediction of Training Session Attendance," *Journal of Applied Social Psychology 20,* (1990): 173–98; Robert P. Steel and Nestor K. Ovalle II, "A Review and Meta-Analysis of Research on the Relationship Between Behavioral Intentions and Employee Turnover," *Journal of Applied Psychology,* November 1984, pp. 873–86.

6. Staw and Ross, pp. 469–80.

7. Angelo J. Kinicki, Kenneth P. Carson, and George W. Bohlander, "Relationships Between an Organization's Actual Human Resource Efforts and Employee Attitudes," *Group & Organization Management 17,* (June 1992): 135–52.

8. Michael R. Carrell, Norbert Elbert, Robert Hatfield, *Human Resource Management,* 5th ed. (Englewood Cliffs, N.J.: Prentice Hall, 1995), pp. 699–702.

9. M. J. Martinko and W. L. Gardner, "The Leader-Member Attribution Process," *Academy of Management Review 12,* (1987): 235–49.

10. Richard M. Steers and J. Stewart Black, *Organizational Behavior* (New York: Harper Collins, 1994, pp. 80–83.

11. Jerald Greenberg, "Looking Fair vs. Being Fair: Managing Impressions of Organizational Justice," *Research in Organizational Behavior, ed. B. M. Staw and L. L. Cummings, Vol. 12 (Greenwich, Conn.: JAI Press, 1990).

12. *L. Alan Witt and Jennifer G. Myers, "Perceived Environmental Uncertainty and Participation in Decision Making in the Prediction of Perceptions of the Fairness of Personnel Decisions,"* Review of Public Personnel Administration, May/August 1993, pp. 48–55.

13. R. Karambayya, J. Brett, and A. Lytle, "Effects of Formal Authority and Experience on Third-Party Roles, Outcomes, and Perceptions of Fairness," *Academy of Management Journal 35* (1992): 426–38.

14. Carrell, Elbert, and Hatfield, pp. 780–84.

15. Edwin A. Locke and G. P. Latham, *A Theory of Goal Setting and Task Performance (Englewood Cliffs, N.J.: Prentice Hall), 1990.*

16. *Kenneth N. Wexley and Gary P. Latham,* Developing and Training Human Resources in Organizations (New York: Harper Collins, 1991).

17. Joseph B. Treasfer, "Employer Drug Testing Driving Down Use in Society," *The New York Times,* 21, 1993.

Introductory Case: Adapted from Terrence L. Johnson, "Workplace Enthusiasm Revivable," Wall Street Journal, June 4, 1995, G1, 12.

People Perspectives: Adapted from Terrence R. Gray, "A Hospital Takes Action on Employee Survey," *Personnel Journal,* March, 1995, pp. 74–77.

Cutting Edge: Adapted from Kenneth Labich, "Is Heb Kelleher America's Best CEO?" *Fortune,* May 2, 1994, pp. 44–52.

*Global Highlight: A*dapted by Michael R. Carrell, Norbert Elbert, *Human*

Resource Management (Englewood Cliffs, NJ: Prentice Hall, 1995), as adapted from James A. McCaffrey and Craig R. Hafner, "When Two Cultures Collide: Doing Business Overseas," *Training and Development Journal,* October 1985, p. 26. Copyright 1985, *Training and Development Journal,* American Society for Training and Development. Reprinted with permission. All rights reserved.

People Perspectives: Mark Maremont, "Blind Ambition" Business Week, October 23, 1995, p. 78–92; "Bad Math at Bausch & Lomb," Business Week, December 19, 1994, pp. 108–10; "Judgement Day at Bausch & Lomb," Business Week, December 25, 1995, p. 39.

CHAPTER 19

1. For an illustration of the complexity of control in an international context, see Jean-Francois Hennart, "Control in Multinational Firms: The Role of Price and Hierarchy," *Management International Review,* Special Issue 1991, pp. 71–96. See also L.R. Bittle and J.E Ramsey (eds.), *Handbook for Professional Managers* (New York: McGraw-Hill, 1985).

2. K.A. Merchant, "The Control Function of Management," *Sloan Management Review 23* (Summer 1982): 43–55. For an example of how a control system can be used with a formal planning model, see A.M. Jaeger and B.R. Baliga, "Control Systems and Strategic Adaptations: Lessons from the Japanese Experience," *Strategic Management Journal 6* (April/June 1985): 115–34.

3. Robert L. Dewelt, "Control: Key to Making Financial Strategy Work," *Management Review,* March 1977, p. 18.

4. For more discussion on Murphy's Law, see Grady W. Harris, "Living with Murphy's Law," *Research-Technology Management,* January/February 1994, pp. 10–13.

5. Robert J. Mockler, ed., *Readings in Management Control* (New York: Appleton-Century-Crofts, 1970), p. 14.

6. For insights about the process that Delta Air Lines uses to control distribution costs, Perry Flint, "Delta's `Shot Heard `round the World,' " *Air Transport World,* April 1995, pp. 61–62.

7. Francis V. McCrory and Peter Gerstberger, "The New Math of Performance Measurement," *Journal of Business Strategy,* March/April 1991, pp. 33–38.

8. James M. Bright, "A Clear Picture," *Credit Union Management,* February 1995, pp. 28–29.

9. For a discussion of how standards are set, see James B. Dilworth, *Production and Operations Management: Manufacturing and Nonmanufacturing* (New York: Random House, 1986), pp. 637–50. For more information on various facets of standards and standard setting, see the following: Len Eglo, "Save Dollars on Maintenance Management," *Chemical Engineering 97* (June 1990): 157–62; Alden M. Hayashi, "GE Says Solid State Is Here to Stay," *Electronic Business 14* (April 1, 1988): 52–56; Frank Rose, "A New Age for Business?" *Fortune,* October 8, 1990, pp. 156–64; Edward Basset, "Diamond Is Forever," *New England Business 12* (October 1990): 40–44; David Sheridan, "Getting the Big Picture," *Training,* September 1990, pp. 12–15; Thomas A. Foster and Joseph V. Barks, "The Right Chemistry for Single Sourcing," *Distribution 89* (September 1990): 44–52; Joseph Conlin, "The House That G.E. Built," *Successful Meetings 38* (August 1989): 50–58; Robert W. Mann, "A Building-Blocks Approach to Strategic Change," *Training and Development Journal 44* (August 1990); 23–25.

10. For an example of a company surpassing performance standards, see Peter Nulty, "How to Live by Your Wits," *Fortune,* April 20, 1992, pp. 119–20.

11. For an illustration of the problem/symptom relationship, see Elizabeth Dougherty, "Waste Minimization: Reduce Wastes and Reap the Benefits," *R & D 32* (April 1990); 62–68.

12. Harold Koontz, Cyril O'Donnell, and Heinz Weihrich, *Essentials of Management* (New York: McGraw-Hill, 1986), pp. 454–59.

13. For an example of concurrent control in the health-care industry, see Teri Lammers, "The Troubleshooter's Guide," *Inc.,* January 1992, pp. 65–67.

14. For a discussion of the basic concepts of feedback control, see J. Greg

Ziegler and J. Robert Connell, "For Optimum Control: Modify the Process, Not the Controls (Part 1)," *Chemical Engineering*, May 1994, pp. 132–40.

15. Vijay Sathe, *Controller Involvement in Management* (Englewood Cliffs, N.J.: Prentice Hall, 1982).

16. James D. Wilson, *Controllership: The Work of the Managerial Accountant* (New York: Wiley, 1981). For an example of individuals in organizations with more specific and limited controlling responsibilities, see the discussion by the director of production control at Nissan in John Williams, "Total Logistics—The Profit Driver," *Logistics Focus*, August 1994, pp. 20–24.

17. For other ways in which cost-benefit analysis can be used by managers, see G.S. Smith and M.S. Tseng, "Benefit-Cost-Analysis as a Performance Indicator," *Management Accounting*, June 1986, pp. 44–49; "The IS (Information System) Payoff," *Infosystems*, April 1987, pp. 18–20.

18. See Amitai Etzioni, *A Comparative Analysis of Complex Organizations* (New York: Free Press, 1961), pp. 4–6. For a study discussing the utility of various types of power to managers, see Gary Yukl and Cecilia Falbe, "Importance of Different Power Sources in Downward and Lateral Relations," *Journal of Applied Psychology*, June 1991, pp. 416–23.

19. John P. Kotter, "Power, Dependence, and Effective Management," *Harvard Business Review*, July/August 1977, p. 128.

20. Kotter, "Power, Dependence, and Effective Management," pp. 135–36. For a discussion on how empowering subordinates can increase the power of a manager, see Linda A. Hill, "Maximizing Your Influence," *Working Woman*, April 1995, pp. 21–22+.

21. Kotter, "Power, Dependence, and Effective Management," p. 131.

22. For further discussion of how to overcome the potential negative effects of control, see Ramon J. Aldag and Timothy M. Stearns, *Management* (Cincinnati, Ohio: South-Western Publishing, 1987), 653–54. See also Arnold F. Emch, "Control Means Action," *Harvard Business Review*, July/August 1954, pp. 92–98; K. Hall and L.K. Savery, "Tight Rein, More Stress," *Harvard Business Review*, January/February 1986, pp. 160–64.

23. James T. McKenna, "Eastern, Maintenance Heads Indicted by U.S. Grand Jury," *Aviation Week & Space Technology* 133 (July 1990): 84–86.

24. W. Jerome III, *Executive Control: The Catalyst* (New York: Wiley, 1961), pp. 31–34. See also William Bruns, Jr., and E. Warren McFarlan, "Information Technology Puts Power in Control Systems," *Harvard Business Review*, September/October 1987, 89–94; C. Jackson Grayson, Jr., "Management Science and Business Practice," *Harvard Business Review*, July/August 1973, pp. 41–48.

25. For an article emphasizing the importance of management understanding and being supportive of organizational control efforts, see Richard M. Morris III, "Management Support: An Underlying Premise," *Industrial Management* 31 (March/April 1989): 2–3.

Introductory Case: This case is adapted from Barbara Carton, "Polaroid to Cut Work Force by Up to 5%," *Wall Street Journal*, February 6, 1995, p. 7A.

People Perspectives: Valerie Reitman, "Toyota Names a Chief Likely to Shake Up Global Auto Business," *Wall Street Journal*, August 11, 1995, pp. A1, A4.

Cutting Edge: Drew Winter, "Special Effects," *Ward's Auto World*, November 1994, pp. 31–35.

Chapter 20

1. James B. Dilworth, *Production and Operations Management: Manufacturing and Non-Manufacturing* (New York: Random House, 1986), p. 3.

2. John W. Kendrick, *Understanding Productivity: An Introduction to the Dynamics of Productivity Change* (Baltimore: Johns Hopkins University Press, 1977), p. 114.

3. Lester C. Thurow, "Other Countries Are as Smart as We Are," *New York Times*, April 5, 1981.

4. For an example of virtual offices created to increase worker productivity, Michael K. Takagawa, "Turn Traditional Work Spaces into Virtual Offices," *Human Resources Professional*, March/April 1995, pp. 11–14.

5. W. Edwards Deming, *Out of the Crisis* (Boston: MIT Center for Advanced Engineering Study, 1986). See also Rafael Aguayo, *Dr. Deming: The American Who Taught the Japanese about Quality* (New York: Carol Publishing Group, 1990), 160–164.

6. John J. Dwyer, Jr., "Quality: Can You Prove It?" *Fleet Owner*, April 1995, p. 36.

7. Gerry Davidson, "Quality Circles Didn't Die—They Just Keep Improving," *CMA Magazine*, February 1995, p. 6. See also John B. Miner, *Organizational Behavior: Performance and Productivity* (New York: Random House, 1988), pp. 308–16.

8. John Peter Koss, "Plant Robotics and Automation," *Beverage World*, April 1995, p. 108.

9. Robert E. Kemper and Joseph Yehudai, *Experiencing Operations Management: A Walk-Through* (Boston: PWS-Kent Publishing Company, 1991), p. 48.

10. Richard B. Chase and Nicholas J. Aquilano, *Production and Operations Management: A Life Cycle Approach* (Homewood, Ill.: Richard D. Irwin, 1981), p. 4. For a worthwhile discussion of forecasting product demand as a continual operations management activity, see Jim Browne, "Forecasting Demand for Services," *Industrial Engineering*, February 1995 pp. 16–17.

11. For an example of the kinds of layout issues that concern printers in Europe, see Jill Roth, "Molto Bene," *American Printer*, March 1994, pp. 54–58.

12. Lee J. Krajewski and Larry P. Ritzman, *Operations Management: Strategy and Analysis* (Reading, Mass.: Addison-Wesley, 1987), p. 573. See also A. Ansari and Modarress Batoul, "Just-in-Time Purchasing: Problems and Solutions," *Journal of Purchasing and Materials Management*, (August 1986), 11–15; Albert F. Celley, William H. Clegg, Arthur W. Smith, and Mark A. Vonderembse, "Implementation of JIT in the United States," *Journal of Purchasing and Materials Management*, Winter 1987, pp. 9–15.

13. John D. Baxter, "Kanban Works Wonders, but Will It Work in U.S. Industry? *Iron Age*, June 7, 1982, pp. 44–48.

14. George S. Minmier, "Zero-Base Budgeting: A New Budgeting Technique for Discretionary Costs," *Mid-South Quarterly Business Review 14* (October 1976): 2–8. See also Peter A. Phyrr, "Zero-Base Budgeting," *Harvard Business Review*, November/December 1970, 111–21; E.A. Kurbis, "The Case for Zero-Base Budgeting," *CA Magazine*, April 1986, pp. 104–05; Linda J. Shinn and M. Sue Sturgeon. "Budgeting from Ground Zero," *Association Management 42* (September 1990); 45–48; Gregory E. Becwar and Jack L. Armitage, "Zero-Base Budgeting: Is It Really Dead? *Ohio CPA Journal 48* (Winter 1989): 52–54; Aaron Wildavsky and Arthur Hammann, "Comprehensive versus Incremental Budgeting in the Department of Agriculture," in *Planning Programming Budgeting: A Systems Approach to Management*, ed. Fremont J. Lyden and Ernest G. Miller (Chicago: Markham, 1968), pp. 143–44.

15. Chris argyris, "Human Problems with Budgets," *Harvard Business Review*, (January/February 1953), p. 108.

16. This section is based primarily on J. Fred Weston and Eugene F. Brigham, *Essentials of Managerial Finance*, 7th ed. (Hinsdale, Ill.: Dryden Press, 1985). See also F.L. Patrone and Donald duBois, "Financial Ratio Analysis for the Small Business," *Journal of Small Business Management*, January 1981, p.35.

17. For an excellent discussion of ratio analysis in a small business, see Patrone and duBois, "Financial Ratio Analysis," pp. 35–40.

18. Lester R. Bittle, *Management by Exception* (New York: McGraw-Hill, 1964); Frederick W. Taylor, *Shop Management* (New York: Harper & Bros., 1911), pp. 126–27.

19. These two rules are adapted from *Boardroom Reports 5* (May 1976): 4.

20. Robert J. Lambrix and Surenda S. Singhvi, "How to Set Volume-Sensitive ROI Targets," *Harvard Business Review*, March/April 1981, p. 174.

21. For a listing and discussion of quantitative tools and their appropriate uses, see Kemper and Yehudai, *Experiencing Operations Management*, pp. 341–55. For a clear discussion, illustrations, and examples of linear programming, breakeven analysis, work measurement, acceptance sampling, payoff tables, value analysis, computer-aided design (CAD), computer-aided engineering (CAE), computer-aided manufacturing (CAM), manu-

facturing resource planning, program evaluation and review technique (PERT), capacity requirements planning (CRP), and input/output control, see Jay Heizer and Barry Render, *Production and Operations Management: Strategies and Tactics* (Needham Heights, Mass.: Allyn and Bacon, 1993).

Introductory Case: This case is excerpted from Carl Quintanilla, "New Airline Fad: Faster Airport Turnarounds," *Wall Street Journal*, August 4, 1994, pp. B1, B2.

Cutting Edge: Marshall Loeb, "Empowerment That Pays Off," *Fortune*, March 20, 1995, pp. 145–46.

People Perspective: Eamonn Fingleton, "Jobs for Life: Why Japan Won't Give Them Up," *Fortune*, March 20, 1995 pp. 119–25.

Case Study: Scott McNealy's Rising Sun, *Business Week*, January 22, 1996, pp. 66–73.

CHAPTER 21

1. Garland R. Hadley and Mike C. Patterson, "Are Middle-Paying Jobs Really Declining?" *Oklahoma Business Bulletin 56* (June 1988):12–14; A. Essam Radwan and Jerome Fields, "Keeping Tabs on Toxic Spills," *Civil Engineering 60* (April 1990):70–72; Dean C. Minderman, "Marketing: Desktop Demographics." *Credit Union Management 13* (February 1990):26.

2. Henry Mintzberg, "The Myths of MIS," *California Management Review*, Fall 1972, pp. 92–97; Jay W. Forrester, "Managerial Decision Making," in *Management and the Computer of the Future*, ed. Martin Greenberger (Cambridge, Mass. and New York: MIT Press and Wiley, 1962), p. 37.

3. The following discussion is based largely on Robert H. Gregory and Richard L. VanHorn, "Value and Cost of Information." in *Systems Analysis Techniques*, ed. J. Daniel Conger and Robert W. Knapp (New York: Wiley, 1974), pp. 473–89.

4. John T. Small and William B. Lee, "In Search of MIS." *MSU Business Topics*, Autumn 1975, pp. 47–55.

5. G. Anthony Gorry and Michael S. Scott Morton, "A Framework for Management Information Systems," *Sloan Management Review 13* (Fall 1971):55–70.

6. Stephen L. Cohen, "Managing Human-Resource Data Keeping Your Data Clean," *Training & Development Journal 43* (August 1989):50–54.

7. Michael A. Verespej, "Communications Technology: Slave or Master?" *Industry Week*, June 19, 1995, pp. 48–55; John C. Scully, "Information Overload?" *Managers Magazine*, May 1995, p. 2.

8. T. Mukhapadhyay and R. B. Cooper, "Impact of Management Information Systems on Decisions," *Omega 20* (1992):37–49.

9. Robert W. Holmes, "Twelve Areas to Investigate for Better MIS," *Financial Executive*, July 1970, p. 24. A similar definition is presented and illustrated in Jeffrey A. Coopersmith, "Modern Times: Computerized Systems Are Changing the Way Todays Modern Catalog Company Is Structured," *Catalog Age 7* (June 1990):77–78. For an interesting example of how a company can decentralize an MIS, see John E. Framel and Leo F. Haas III, "Managing the Dispersed Computing Environment at Mapco, Inc., *Journal of Systems Management 43*: 6–12.

10. Kenneth C. Laudon and Jane Price Laudon, *Management Information Systems: Organization and Technology* (New York: Macmillan, 1993), p. 38.

11. For an article discussing how a well-managed MIS promotes the usefulness of information, see Albert Lederer and Veronica Gardner, "Meeting Tomorrow's Business Demands Through Strategic Information Systems Planning," *Information Strategy: The Executive's Journal*, Summer 1992, pp. 20–27.

12. This section is based on Richard A. Johnson, R. Josehp Monsen, Henry P. Knowles, and Borge O. Saxberg, *Management Systems and Society: An Introduction* (Santa Monica, Cal.: Goodyear, 1976), pp. 113–20; James Emery, "Information Technology in the 21st Century Enterprise" *MIS Quarterly*, December 1991, pp. xxi–xxiii.

13. Robert G. Murdick, "MIS for MBO," *Journal of Systems Management*, March 1977, pp. 34–40.

14. F. Warren McFarlan, "Problems in Planning the Information System," *Harvard Business Review*, March/April 1971, p. 75.

15. David S. Stoller and Richard L. Van Horn. *Design of a Management Information System* (Santa Monica, Cal: RAND Corporation, 1958).

16. Craig Barrow, "Implementing an Executive Information System: Seven Steps for Success," *Journal of Information Systems Management 7* (Spring 1990):41–46.

17. Bertram A. Colbert, "The Management Information System," *Management Services 4* (September/October 1967):15–24.

18. Adapted from Henry Mintzberg, "The Manager's Job: Folklore and Fact," *Harvard Business Review*, July/August 1975, p. 58.

19. William R. King and David I. Cleland, "Manager Analysis Teamwork in MIS," *Business Horizons 14* (April 1971):59–68; Regina Herzlinger, "Why Data Systems in Nonprofit Organizations Fail," *Harvard Business Review*, January/February 1977, pp. 81–86; John Sculley, "The Human Use of Information," *Journal for Quality and Participation*, January/February 1990, pp. 10–13; Richard Discenza and Donald G. Gardner, "Improving Productkon by Managing for Retention," *Information Strategy: The Executive's Journal*, Spring 1992, pp. 34–38.

20. David Harvey, "Making Sense of the Data Deluge," *Director 42* (April 1989):139–40.

21. Robert Chaiken, "Pitfalls of Computers in a CPA's Office," *Ohio CPA Journal 46* (Spring 1987):45–46; John E. Framel, "Managing Information Costs and Technologies as Assets," *Journal of Systems Management 41* (February 1990):12–18; Martin D. J. Buss, "Penny-wise Approach to Data Processing," *Harvard Business Review*, July/August 1981, p. 111; James A. Yardley and Parez R. Sopanwala, "Break-Even Utilization Analysis," *Journal of Commercial Bank Lending 72* (March 1990):49–56.

22. Steven L. Mandell, *Computers and Data Processing: Concepts and Applications with BASIC* (St. Paul, Minn.: West Publishing, 1982), pp. 370–91.

23. Mark G. Simkin, *Computer Information Systems for Business* (Dubuque, Iowa: Wm. C. Brown, 1987), pp. 299–301.

24. For additional information on these software packages, see *Lotus 1-2-3 Reference Manual* (Cambridge, Mass.: Lorus Development Corporation, 1985); Timothy J. O'Leary, *The Studentl Edition of Lotus 1-2-3* (Reading, Mass.: Addison-Wesley, 1989); *IFPS User's Manual* (Austin, Tex.: Execucom Systems Corporation, 1984).

25. Ron Evans, "Systems for Growing Firms," *Black Enterprise*, April 1995, pp. 44–45.

26. Kathleen Kiley, "Spin-Offs Stake Claim in LAN Rush," *Catalog Age*, May 1995, p. 24; David Reeve, "How Much Is Too Much?" *Computing Canada*, May 11, 1994, p. 47.

27. Jill Ellsworth and Matthew V. Ellsworth, *Marketing on the Internet: Multimedia Strategies for the WorldWide Web* (New York: Wiley, 1995), p. 3; James Coates, "A Mailbox in Cyberspace Brings the World to Your PC," *Chicago Tribune*, March 26, 1995, sec. 19, p. 1.

28. David Sachs and Henry Stair, *Hands-on Internet: A Beginning Guide for PC Users* (Englewood Cliffs, N.J.: Prentice Hall, 1994), p. 3.

29. Ellsworth and Ellsworth, *Marketing and the Internet*, p. xv.

30. Steve Williams, "The Internet—Exploring Its Uses for Economic Development," *Economic Development Review*, Winter 1995, pp. 64–69; Gerry Khermouch, "Holiday Inn Books in the Net; Apollo 13 Launches in Cyberspace," *Brandweek*, June 19, 1995, p. 16.

Introductory Case: Bill Saporito, "What Sam Walton Taught America," *Fortune*, May 4 1992, pp. 104–105. © 1992 Time Inc. All rights reserved. "Stores of Value, *The Economist*, March 4, 1995, p. 5.

For additional factors resulting in MIS challenges in this company, see Jie-Ae Sohn, "To Repeat POSCO's Legend? *Business Korea*, 2 August 1994, pp. 21–22; "Posco Orders an ISP Mil," *Iron Age New Steel*, 8 August 1994, p. 9.

People Perspectives: Stephen Kreider Yoder, "Technology: The Business Plan," *The Wall Street Journal*, November 14, 1994, p. R16.

Cutting Edge: Scott McCartney, "Companies Go On-line to Chat," *The Wall Street Journal*, September 15, 1994, p. B1.

Case Study: "Win '95, Lose '96," *Business Week*, December 18, 1995, pp. 34–35; "Promises of the Internet," *USA Today*, November 13, 1995, Section E; Don Clark, "Microsoft to Unveil Internet Products," *Wall Street Journal*, December 7, 1995, p. B8.

CHAPTER 22

1. "The Push for Quality," Business Week, June 8, 1987, p. 131.

2. A.V. Feigenbaum, *Total Quality Control* (New York: McGraw-Hill, 1983).

3. From Michael Schroeder, "Heart Trouble at Pfizer," *Business Week*, February 26, 1990, pp. 47–48.

4. For a discussion of companies that have recently won the Malcolm Baldrige National Award, see Karen Bemowski, "1994 Baldrige Award Recipients Share Their Expertise," *Quality Progress*, February 1995, pp. 35–40.

5. For more information on these three contributors, see Charles H. Fine and David H. Bridge, "Managing Quality Improvement," in *Quest for Quality: Managing the Total system*, ed. by M. Sepheri (Norcross, Ga.: Institute of Industrial Engineers, 1987), pp. 66–74.

6. For some of Crosby's more notable books in this area, see Philip B. Crosby, *Quality Is Free* (New York: McGraw-Hill, 1979); *Quality Without Tears* (New York: McGraw-Hill, 1984); *Let's Talk Quality: 96 Questions You Always Wanted to Ask Phil Crosby* (New York: McGraw-Hill, 1989); and *Leading* (New York: McGraw-Hill, 1990).

7. Michael J. O'Connor, "A Way of Corporate Life," *Supermarket Business*, May 1995, pp. 69–75.

8. Deming's 14 Points (January 1990 revision reprinted by permission from *Out of Crisis* by W. Edwards Deming by permission of MIT and W. Edwards Deming. Published by MIT, Center for Advanced Engineering Study, Cambridge, MA 02139. Copyright 1986 by W. Edwards Deming.

9. Tracy Benson Kirker, "The Teacher's Still a Student," *Industry Week*, May 2, 1994, pp. 37–38.

10. Alan Robinson, *Modern Approaches to Manufacturing Improvement: The Shingo System* (Productivity Press, 1990), pp. 267–68. See also Gary S. Vasilash, "On Training for Mistake-Proofing," *Production*, March 1995, pp. 42–44.

11. Tim Stevens, "Dr. Feigenbaum," *Industry Week*, July 4, 1994, pp. 12–16.

12. Ross Johnson and William O. Winchell, *Strategy and Quality* (Milwaukee, Wis.: American Society for Quality Control, 1989), pp. 1–2.

13. Company Mission Statement, All America Inc., 1991, used by permission.

14. For a discussion supporting the importance of training to a companywide quality effort, see "Dr. W. Edwards Deming," *EBS Journal*, Spring 1989, p. 3.

15. Tom Peters, *Thriving on Chaos: Handbook for a Management Revolution* (Harper & Row, 1987), pp. 88, 98, 326.

16. Joseph Juran, *Juran on Quality Leadership: How to Go from Here to There* (Juran Institute, Inc., 1987), p. 6.

17. Michael Hammer, "Reengineering Work: Don't Automate, Obliterate," *Harvard Business Review*, July/August 1990, pp. 104–12.

18. For a discussion of why some reengineering attempts fail, see Michael Hammer, "Beating the Risks of Reengineering," *Fortune*, May 15, 1995, pp. 105–14.

People Perspectives: Jeanette Rose-Preston, "Brief Ideas Enhance Quality," *Industrial Distribution*, May 1995, p. 90

Cutting Edge: Ross E. Robson, "The Shingo Prize—What It Is, and Who Won This Year," *Trapping the Network Journal*, Fall 1994/Winter 1995, pp. 23–28.

Case Study: Theresa Flanagan, "Taking the Next Step," *Marketing Tools Magazine*, September 1995; "Is TQM Dead?" *USA Today*, October 17, 1995, pp. 1b & 2b; David Greising, "Quality—How to Make It Pay," *Business Week*, August 8, 1994; John Waldes, "The Missing Link, *Marketing Tools Magazine*, March/April 1995; "Consultants, Never Mind the Buzzwords. Roll Up Your Sleeves," *Business Week*, January 22, 1996.

CHAPTER 23

1. For a discussion of diversity issues in the United Kingdom, see Ian Dodds, "Differences Can Be Strengths," *People Management*, April 20, 1995, pp. 40–43. See also Raymond Pomerleau, "A Desideratum for Managing the Diverse Workplace," *Review of Public Personnel Administration 14* (Winter 1994): 85–100.

2. Liz Winfeld and Susan Spielman, "Making Sexual Orientation Part of Diversity," *Training & Development*, April 1995, pp. 50–51.

3. Judith C. Giordan, "Valuing Diversity," *Chemical & Engineering News*, February 20, 1995, p. 40.

4. Ann M. Morrison, "Leadership Diversity as Strategy," in *The New Leaders: Guidelines on Leadership Diversity in America* (San Francisco: Jossey-Bass, 1992), pp. 11–28.

5. Prem Benimadh, "Adding Value Through Diversity," *Canadian Business Review*, Spring 1995, pp. 6–11.

6. William B. Johnston and Arnold E. Packer, "Executive Summary," *Workforce 2000: Work and Workers for the Twenty-First Century* (Indianapolis: Hudson Institute, June 1987), pp. xiii–xiv.

7. Roosevelt Thomas, "Affirmative Action or Affirming Diversity," *Harvard Business Review*, 1990, p. 110.

8. Rosabeth Moss Kanter, *Men and Women of the Corporation* (New York: Basic Books, 1977).

9. Rosabeth Moss Kanter, "Numbers: Minorities and Majorities," in *Men and Women of the Corporation* (New York: Basic Books, 1977), pp. 206–44.

10. Ann M. Morrison, *Breaking the Glass Ceiling: Can Women Reach the Top of America's Largest Corporations?* (Reading, Mass.: Addison Wesley, 1992).

11. Susan Webb, *Step Forward: Sexual Harassment in the Workplace* (New York: MasterMedia, 1991).

12. Ella Bell, "The Bicultural Life Experience of Career Oriented Black Women," *Journal of Organizational Behavior 11* (November 1990): 459–78.

13. Catherine Dorton Fyock and Anne Marrs Dorton, "Welcome to the Unretirement Generation," *HR Focus*, February 1995, pp. 22–23.

14. Jeffrey Sonnenfeld, "Dealing with the Aging Workforce," *Harvard Business Review 56* (1978): 81–92.

15. William B. Johnston and Arnold E. Packer, "Executive Summary," *Workforce 2000: Work and Workers for the Twenty-First Century* (Indianapolis: Hudson Institute, June 1987): xii–xiv.

16. Jean Kim, "Issues in Workforce Diversity," Panel Presentation at the First Annual National Diversity Conference (San Francisco, May 1991).

17. *The Holy Bible*, Authorized King James Version (Nashville: Holman Bible Publishers: 1984).

18. J. Stewart Black and Hal B. Gregersen, "Serving Two Masters: Managing the Dual Allegiance of Expatriate Employees," *Sloan Management Review*, Summer 1992, pp. 61–71.

19. Les Donaldson and Edward E. Scannell, *Human Resource Development: The New Trainer's Guide*, 2nd ed. (Reading, Mass.: Addison-Wesley, 1986), pp. 8–9.

Introductory Case: J. P. White, "Elsie Cross vs. The Suits: One Black Woman Is Teaching White Corporate America to Do the Right Thing." *Los Angeles Times Magazine*, August 9, 1992.

People Perspectives: Michelle Neely Martinez, "Equality Effort Sharpens Bank's Edge," *HRMagazine* January 1995, pp. 38–43.

Cutting Edge: Catherine Dorton Fyock and Anne Marrs Dorton, "Welcome to the Unretirement Generation," *HR Focus*, February 1995 pp. 22–23.

Case Study: "Managing by Values: Is Levi Strauss Approach Visionary—or Flaky?" *Business Week*, August 1, 1994, 46–47; "Taking Adversity Out of Diversity," *Business Week*, January 31, 1994, pp. 54–55; "Tearing Up Today's Organization Chart," *Business Week*, November 18, 1994, pp. 80–87; "Levi's Is Leaving China," *Business Horizons*,? March/April 1995, pp. 35–40.

CREDITS

CHAPTER 1

Figure 1.5: Paul Hersey and Kenneth Blanchard, *Management of Organizational Behavior: Utilizing Human Resources*, 5th ed., © 1988, p. 8 Reprinted by permission of Prentice-Hall, Inc., Englewood Cliffs, NJ. **Figure 1.6:** Douglas T. Hall, *Careers in Organizations*, © 1976 Scott, Foresman and Company. Reprinted by permission. **Table 1.3:** Reprinted, by permission of the publisher, from "Improving Professional Development by Applying the Four-Stage Career Model," by Paul H. Thompson, Robin Zenger Baker, and Norman Smallwood, *Organizational Dynamics* (Autumn/1986): 59, © 1986. American Management Association, New York. All rights reserved.

CHAPTER 2

Quality Highlight: Jeremy Main, "How to Win the Baldridge Award," *Fortune Magazine* (April 23, 1990): 101–116; Christopher W. I. Hart, Christopher Bogan, and Dan O'Brien, "When Winning Isn't Everything," *Harvard Business Review* (January/February 1990): 209.

CHAPTER 3

Global Highlight: Edgar S. Wollard, Jr. "The 'Soul' Factor in Corporate Growth and Prosperity," *Directors and Boards* (Winter 1989): 4–8. **Table 3.2:** Sandra L Holmes, "Executive Perceptions of Social Responsibility," *Business Horizons* (June 1976). Copyright, 1976, by the Foundation for the School of Business at Indiana University. Reprinted by permission. **Figure 3.1:** The Eli Broad College of Business, Michigan State University. **Figure 3.2:** Kenneth E. Newgren, "Social Forecasting: An Overview of Current Business Practices," in Archie B. Carroll, Ed., *Managing Corporate Social Responsibility*. Copyright © 1977 by Little, Brown and Company (Inc.). Reprinted by permission of the author. **Figure 3.3:** Reprinted by permission of the *Harvard Business Review*, from "How Companies Respond to Social Demands" by Robert W. Ackerman (July/August 1973): 96 Copyright © 1973 by the President and Fellows of Harvard College; all rights reserved. **Figure 3.4:** John L. Paulszek. "How Three Companies Organize for Social Responsibility." Reprinted by permission from *Business and Society Review* (Summer 1973): 18, Warren, Gorham and Lamont, Inc., 210 South St., Boston MA. All rights reserved. **Diversity Highlight:** Glenn Hasek, "Breaking Barriers: Education Erases False Perceptions of Minority Opportunities," *Hotel & Motel Management* 207 (February 24, 1992): 21–22. **Figure 3.5:** Reprinted by permission of Johnson & Johnson. **Figure 3.6:** Reprinted by permission from "Code of Ethics and Standards of Conduct" (Orlando, FL: Martin Marietta, n.d.): 3.

CHAPTER 4

Figure 4.2: "Foreign Direct Investment in the U.S.: Detail for position and Balance of Payment Flows," *Survey of Current Business* 70 (August 1990): 41–55, *Survey of Current Business* 71 (August 1991): 47–79; "Foreign Direct Investment in the U.S.: Detail for Historical Cost Position and Balance of Payment Flows, 1991" *Survey of Current Business* 72 (August 1992): 87–115. **Table 4.3:** Neil H. Jacoby, "The Multinational Corporation," reprinted by permission from *Center Magazine* 3 (May 1970): 37–55. **Ethics Highlight:** "Japanese New Earth 21 Plan," Peter Jennings on *World News Tonight*, ABC network (December 14, 1992). **Figure 4.5:** Reprinted by permission of the author from Richard D. Robinson, *International Management* (Hinsdale, IL: Dryden Press, 1967). **Diversity Highlight:** Barry Louis Rubin, "Europeans Value Diversity," *HR Magazine* 36 (January 1991): 38–41, 78.

CHAPTER 5

Figure 5.2: Jon H. Barrett, *Individual Goals and Organizational Objectives: A Study of Integration Mechanisms*, p. 5. Copyright © 1970 by the Institute for Social Research, The University of Michigan. Reprinted with permission. **Global Highlight:** Ted Agresa Asea Brown Boveri—A Model for Global Management," *R & D* 33 (December 1991): 30–34; Paul R. Sullivan, "Executive Excellence," *R&D* 33 (September 1991): 9–10. *Diversity Highlight:* Samuel K. Skinner, "Workforce Diversity." *Bureaucrat* 20 (Summer 1991): 29–31. **Figure 5.4:** Joseph L. Massie and John Douglas, *Managing*, © 1985, p. 244. Reprinted by permission of Prentice-Hall, Inc.,

Englewood Cliffs, NJ. **Table 5.2:** Howard M. Carlisle, *Management Concepts and Situations*, p. 598, © 1976. Published by Science Research Associates. Reprinted by permission of the author. **Table 5.3:** Reprinted by permission from A. N. Geller, *Executive Information Needs in Hotel Companies* (New York: Peat Marwick Main, 1984): 17. © Peat Marwick Main & Co., 1984. **Figure 5.5:** From Samuel C. Certo, Stewart T. Husted, and Max E. Douglas, *Business*, 3rd ed., p. 205. Copyright © 1990 by Allyn and Bacon. Reprinted by permission.

CHAPTER 6

Figure 6.5: William R. King and David I. Cleland, "A New Method for Strategic Systems Planning," *Business Horizons* (August 1975): 56. Copyright, 1975, by the Foundation for the School of Business Administration at Indiana University. Reprinted by permission. **Ethics Highlight:** Jean Marie Hubert van Engelshoven, "Corporate Environmental Policy in Shell, *Long -Range Planning* 24 (December 1991): 17–24. **Quality Highlight:** Bryan Siegal, "Organizing for a Successful CE Process," *Industrial Engineering* 23 (December 1991): 15–19

CHAPTER 7

Diversity Highlight: Wendell H. Joice, "Home Based Employment—A Consideration for Public Personnel Management," *Public Personnel Management* 20 (Spring 1991): 49–60. **Table 7.1:** Herbert A Simon, *The Shape of Automation* (New York: Harper & Row, 1965): 62 Used with permission of the author. **Figure 7.3:** Republished with permission of E.I. du Pont de Nemours & Company. **Global Highlight:** "United Technologies: Like Japan, but Different," Economist (UK) 317 (November 3, 1990): 76–77. **Figure 7.7:** (Copyright © 1964 by the President and Fellows of Harvard College; all rights reserved.) **Figure 7.8:** Samuel C. Certo, "Supervision: Quality and Diversity Through Leadership," (Chicago: Austen Press/Irwin), 1995, p. 202.

CHAPTER 8

Table 8.1: (a) and (b) based on E. Meadows, "How Three Companies Increased Their Productivity," *Fortune Magazine* (March 10, 1980): 92–101. (c) based on William B. Johnson, "The Transformation of a Railroad," *Long-Range Planning* 9 (December 1976): 18–23. **Figure 8.1:** Adapted from Samuel C. Certo and J. Paul Peter, *Strategic Management: Concepts and Applications* (New York: McGraw-Hill, Inc., 1991). Reprinted by permission of the authors. **Ethics Highlight:** Joshua Levine, "Locking Up the Weekend Warriors," *Forbes* (October 2, 1989): 234–235. **Table 8.2:** Adapted from Arvind V. Phatak, *International Dimensions of Management*, 2nd ed., 1989, p. 6. Copyright © 1989 by Wadsworth, Inc. Reprinted by permission of the publisher. **Quality Highlight:** Julie Johnson, "New Mission Statement Creates Unity for Health Care System," *Trustee* 45 February 1992): 10, 23. **Figure 8.3:** © 1970 The Boston Consulting Group, Inc. All rights reserved. Published by permission. **Figure 8.4:** Reprinted by permission from p. 32 of *Strategy Formulation: Analytical Concepts* by Charles W. Hofer and Dan Schendel; Copyright © 1978 by West Publishing Company. All rights reserved. **Figure 8.5:** Reprinted with the permission of The Free Press, a Division of Macmillan, Inc. from *Competitive Advantage: Creating and Sustaining Superior Performance* by Michael E. Porter.

CHAPTER 9

Ethics Highlight: Yoshihiko Shimizu, "Toyota Buckles Down to Overtake GM," *Tokyo Business Today* (Japan) 59 (February 1991): 32–34. **Tables 9.1/9.2:** Adapted from E. S. Groo, "Choosing Foreign Locations: One Company's Experience," *Columbia Journal of World Business* (September/October 1977): 77. Used with permission. **Global Highlight:** Mary B. Teagarden, Mark C. Sutler, and Mary Ann Von Glinow, "Mexico's Maquiladora Industry: Where Strategic Resource Management Makes a Difference," *Organizational Dynamics* 20 (Winter 1992): 34–47. **Figure 9.4:** Bruce Colman, "An Integrated System for Manpower Planning," *Business Horizons* (October 1970): 89–95. Copyright 1970, by the Foundation for the School of Business at Indiana University. Reprinted by permission. **Figure 9.6:** Philip Kotler, *Marketing Managing Analysis Planning and Control*, © 1967, p. 291. Adapted by permission of Prentice-Hall, Inc. Englewood Cliffs, NJ.

CHAPTER 10

Global Highlight: Tim Davis, "Crowning Achievement," *Beverage World* 111 (February 1992): 66, 78. **Quality Highlight:** Robert F. Huber, "Mercedes Manufacturing Strategy Is to Keep the Company's Market Niche Full," *Production* 103 (October 1991): 60–63.

CHAPTER 11

Table 11.1: Reprinted, by permission of the publisher, from "Roles and Relationships Clarifying the Manager's Job," by Robert D. Melcher, *Management Review* (May/June/1967): 35, 38–39, © 1967. American Management Association, New York. All rights reserved. **Ethics Highlight:** Joseph Conlin, "The House That GE Built," *Successful Meetings* 38 (August 1989): 50–58. **Diversity Highlight:** Zachary Schiller, "No More Mr. Nice Guy at P&G—Not by a Long Shot," *Business Week* (February 3, 1992): 54–56. **Figure 11.3:** David B. Starkweather, The Rationale for Decentralization in Large Hospitals," *Hospital Administration* 15 (Spring 1970): 139. Courtesy of Dr. P. N. Ghei, Secretary General Indian Hospital Association, New Delhi, India.

CHAPTER 12

Figure 12.2: Reprinted with the permission of Macmillan Publishing Company from *The Management of People at Work: Readings in Personnel*, 2nd ed. by Dale S. Beach. Copyright © 1970 Macmillan Publishing Company. **Figures 12.3, 12.4, 12.5:** Walter S. Wikstrom, "Developing Managerial Competence: Concepts, Emerging Practices," *Studies in Personnel Policy* No 189, pp. 9, 14. Used with permission. **Figure 12.6:** Reprinted by permission from L. C. Megginson, *Providing Management Talent for Small Business* (Baton Rouge, LA, Division of Research, College of Business Administration, Louisiana State University, 1961): 108. **Global Highlight:** Anne Ferguson, "Compaq's Personnel Solution," *Management Today* (May 1989): 127–128; Prabhu Guptara, "Searching the Organization for the Cross-Cultural Operators," *International Management* 41 (August 1986): 40–42. **Table 12.1:** Dale Feuer, "Where the Dollars Go." Reprinted from the October 1985 issue of *Training*, The Magazine of Human Resources Development, p. 53. Copyright 1985, Lakewood Publications, Inc., Minneapolis, MN 612-333-0471. All rights reserved. **Quality Highlight:** Kathryn W. Porter, "Tuning in to TV Training," *Training and Development Journal* 44 (April 1990): 73–77. **Table 12.2:** Compiled from Andrew F. Sikula, *Personnel Administration and Human Resource Management* (New York: John Wiley & Sons, 1976): 208–211.

CHAPTER 13

Figure 13.1: Don Hellriegel and John W Slocum, Jr. "Integrating Systems Concepts and Organizational Strategy," *Business Horizons* 15 (April 1972): 73. Copyright, 1972, by the Foundation for the School of Business at Indiana University. Reprinted by permission. **Ethics Highlight:** Jonathan Lee, *Pulp & Paper* 66 (March 1992): 198–200. **Figures 13.4, 13.5:** John F. Mee, "Matrix Organization," *Business Horizons* (Summer 1964): 71 Copyright, 1964, by the Foundation for the School of Business at Indiana University. Reprinted by permission. **Diversity Highlight:** Beverly Geber, "The Disabled: Ready, Willing and Able," *Training* 27 (December 1990): 29–36. **Figure 13.7:** Reprinted by permission of *Harvard Business Review*. From "Breakthrough in Organization Development" by Robert R. Blake, Jane S. Mouton, Louis Barnes, and Larry Greiner (November/December 1964): 136. Copyright © 1964 by the President and Fellows of Harvard College; all rights reserved.

CHAPTER 14

Table 14.1: Reprinted by permission from Stephen C. Harper, "Business Education: A View from the Top," *Business Forum* (Summer 1987): 25. **Global Highlight:** Patricia Crane and James W. Johnson, "A Bright Future for International Teleconferencing," *Satellite Communications* 13 (November 1989): 16a, 18a. **Figures 14.3, 14.4:** Wilber Schramm, *The Process and Effects of Mass Communication*, © 1954 University of Illinois Press, Champaign, IL. Reprinted by permission. **Figure 14.5:** Reprinted, by permission of the publisher, from "An Experimental Approach to Organizational Communication," by Alex Bavelas and Dermont Barrett, *Personnel* (March 1951): 370, © 1951. American Management Association, New York. All rights reserved. **Quality Highlight:** Alan Salomon, "Bass Gains Base of Confidence," *Hotel & Motel Management* 206 (November 25,

1991): 2, 42. **Figure 14.6:** Reprinted by permission of *Harvard Business Review*. An exhibit from "Management Communication and the Grapevine" by Keith Davis (September/October 1953): 45. Copyright © 1953 by the President and Fellows of Harvard College; all rights reserved. **Table 14.2:** Keith Davis, *Human Behavior at Work*, p. 396. Copyright © 1972 by McGraw-Hill, Inc. Used with permission of McGraw-Hill Book Company.

CHAPTER 15

Figure 15.2: Reprinted by permission of *Harvard Business Review*. From "How to Choose a Leadership Pattern" by Robert Tannenbaum and Warren H. Schmidt (May/June 1973). Copyright © 1973 by the President and Fellows of Harvard College; all rights reserved. **Figure 15.4:** Reprinted from *Leadership and Decision-Making* by Victor H. Vroom and Philip W. Yetton (Table 2.1, p. 13), by permission of the University of Pittsburgh Press. © 1973 by University of Pittsburgh Press. **Figure 15.5:** Reprinted from *The New Leadership: Managing Participation in Organizations* by Victor H. Vroom and Arthur G. Jago, 1988, Englewood Cliffs, NJ: Prentice-Hall. Copyright 1987 by V.H. Vroom and A. G. Jago. Used with permission of the authors. **Ethics Highlight:** Elizabeth Jensen, "NBC News President, Burned by Staged Fire and GM, Will Resign," *Wall Street Journal* (March 2, 1993): A1, A8; Douglas Lavin, "GM Accuses NBC of Rigging Test Crash of Pickup Truck on 'Dateline' Program," *Wall Street Journal* (February 9, 1993): A3, A6; Bill Loftus, "NBC Admits Forest Report Erred," *Lewiston Morning Tribune* (February 25, 1993) A1, A15; Elizabeth Jensen and Douglas Lavin, "How GM One-Upped and Embarrassed NBC on Staged News Event," *Wall Street Journal* (February 11, 1993): A1, A7; Howard Kirtz, "NBC News Credibility Crashes with GM Story," *Washington Post* (February 10, 1993): A1, A5; "A Safety Expert Under Fire," *Business Week* (March 1, 1993): 42. **Figure 15.6:** Paul Hersey and Kenneth H. Blanchard, *Management of Organizational Behavior: Utilizing Human Resources*, 3rd ed., p. 103, © 1977. Reprinted by permission of Prentice-Hall, Inc., Englewood Cliffs, NJ. **Table 15.1:** F. E. Fiedler, *A Theory of Leadership Effectiveness*, p. 34. Copyright © 1967 by McGraw-Hill, Inc. Used with permission of McGraw-Hill Book Company. **Figure 15.7:** Reprinted by permission of the *Harvard Business Review*. From "Engineer the Job to Fit the Manager" by Fred Fiedler (September/October 1965). Copyright © 1965 by the President and Fellows of Harvard College; all rights reserved. **Diversity Highlight:** Kevin D. Thompson, "Blazing New Trails," *Black Enterprise* 21 (January 1991): 54–57.

CHAPTER 16

Figure 16.3: Lyman Porter and Edward Lawler III, *Managerial Attitudes and Performance*, p. 165. Copyright © 1968 Richard D. Irwin Inc. Reprinted by permission. **Global Highlight:** Ikushi Yamaguchii, "A Mechanism of Motivational Processes in a Chinese, Japanese, and U.S. Multicultural Corporation: Presentation of 'A Contingent Motivational Model' " Management Japan 24 (Autumn 1991): 27–32. Figure 16.5: Adapted from B. Kolasa, *Introduction to Behavioral Science in Business* (New York: Wiley, 1969): 256. Used with permission. **Table 16.1:** Reprinted by permission of *Harvard Business Review*. From "One More Time: How Do You Motivate Employees?" by Frederick Herzberg (January/February 1968). Copyright © 1968 by the President and Fellows of Harvard College; all rights reserved. **Quality Highlight:** Jim Brahan, "A Rewarding Place to Work," *Industry Week* 238 (September 18, 1989): 15–19. **Table 16.2:** Edward G. Thomas, "Workers Who Set Their Own Time Clocks," (Spring 1987): 50. Reprinted by permission from *Business and Society Review*.

CHAPTER 17

Diversity Highlight: Sherri K. Lindenberg, "Managing a Multi-Ethnic Field Force," *National Underwriter* 95 (January 7, 1991): 16–18, 24. **Figure 17.2:** Reprinted by permission of *Harvard Business Review*. From "Committees on Trial" (Problems in Review) by Rollie Tillman, Jr. (May/June 1960): 163. Copyright © 1960 by the President and Fellows of Harvard College; all rights reserved. **Ethics Highlight:** Colleen Scanlon and Cornelia Fleming, "Confronting Ethical Issues: A Nursing Survey," *Nursing Management* 21 (May 1990): 63–65. **Figure 17.4:** Figure 11.5 from *Social Psychology* by Muzafer Sherif and Carolyn W. Sherif. Copyright © 1969 by Muzafer Sherif and Carolyn W. Sherif. Reprinted by permis-

sion of Harper Collins Publishers, Inc. **Figure 17.7:** Hans J. Thamhain, "Managing Technologically Innovative Team Efforts Toward New Product Success," *Journal of Product Innovation Management*, March 1990, pp. 5–18.

CHAPTER 19

Global Highlight: Sarah Grey, "Not a Mickey Mouse Organization," *Accountancy* 104 (November 1989): 16–17. **Diversity Highlight:** Lisa Lebowitz, "A Rainbow Coalition, *Working Woman* 16 (December 1991): 72–74. **Table 19.1:** Reprinted by permission from p. 13 of *Cost Accounting: A Managerial Approach*, 2/e, by Cherrington, Hubbard, and Luthy; Copyright © 1988 by West Publishing Company. All rights reserved.

CHAPTER 20

Figure 20.2: Reprinted from *Out of Crisis* by W. Edwards Deming by permission of MIT and W. Edwards Deming. Published by MIT, Center for Advanced Engineering, Cambridge, MA 02139. Copyright 1986 by W. Edwards Deming. **Quality Highlight:** Stephen Barr, "Adidas on the Rebound," *CFO: The Magazine for Senior Financial Executives* (September 1991): 48–56; Richard A. Melcher, "Now This Should Get Adidas on Its Feet," *Business Week* (July 20, 1992): 42. **Figure 20.4:** Richard B. Chase and Nicholas J. Aquilano, *Production and Operations Management: A Life Cycle Approach*, 4th ed., p. 5. © 1985 Richard D. Irwin, Inc. Reprinted by permission. **Ethics Highlight:** Mary Walton, *Deming Management at Work: Six Successful Companies that Use the Quality Principles of the World Famous W. Edwards Deming* (New York: G. P. Putnam's Sons, 1991): 185–205; Kathleen Morris, "A Bridge Far Enough: Four Years after Buying Firestone Bridgestone Finally Gets Tough," *Financial World* (June 9, 1992): 52–54.

CHAPTER 21

Figure 21.1: Reprinted by permission from G. Anthony Gorry and Michael S. Scott Morton, "A Framework for Management Information Systems," *Sloan Management Review* 13 (Fall 1971): 59. **Figure 21.2:** The Eli Broad College of Business, Michigan State University **Table 19.2:** Reprinted by permission from Alice M. Greene, "Computers Big Pay-off for Small Companies," *Iron Age* (March 30, 1972): 63–64. **Global Highlight:** Oles Gadacz, "Steel Giant Pioneers Korean IS," *Datamation* 35 (June 1, 1989): 64g–64h. **Table 21.3:** Reprinted by permission of *Harvard Business Review*. An exhibit from "Manufacturing—Missing Link in Corporate Strategy" by Wickham Skinner (May/June 1969): 141. Copyright © 1969 by the President and Fellows of Harvard College; all rights reserved. **Figure 21.4:** Adapted from Robert G. Murdick, "MIS for MBO," *Journal of Systems Management* (March 1977): 34–40. Used with permission of *Journal of Systems Management*, 24587 Bagley Road, Cleveland, OH 44138. **Diversity Highlight:** Jay L. Johnson, "Target's New Dynamics," *Discount Merchandiser* 31 (August 1991): 30–46: Terry E. Hedrick, "New Challenges for Government Managers," *Bureaucrat* 19 (Spring 1990): 17–20. **Figure 21.5:** Reprinted by permission from R. E. Breen et al., *Management Information Systems: A Subcommittee Report on Definitions* (Schenectady, NY: General Electric Co., 1969): 21. **Table 21.1:** Reprinted by permission of the Institute of Management Services from Bertram A. Colbert, "The Management Information System," *Management Services* 4 (September/October 1967): 18. **Table 21.2:** Jared Sandberg, "Technology: The Business Plan," *Wall Street Journal*, Novermbr 14, 1994, R14. **Figure 21.7:** "Parts of the Personal Computer and What They Do," *Time* (January 3, 1983): 39. Copyright 1982 Time Inc. Magazine Company. Reprinted by permission.

CHAPTER 22

Quality Highlight: Tom Peters, *Thriving on Chaos: Handbook for a Management Revolution*, Harper & Row, 1987, p. 87 **Table 22.1:** Adapted with the permission of The Free Press, a Division of Macmillan, Inc. from *Japanese Manufacturing Techniques*, p. 47–82 and *World Class Manufacturing* p. 122–143, by Richard J. Schonberger. (JMT) Copyright © 1982 by Richard J. Schonberger. (WCM) Copyright © 1986 by Schonberger & Associates, Inc. **Figure 22.1:** David A. Gavin, "What Does Product Quality Really Mean? *Sloan Management Review* 26 (Fall 1984): 37. Reprinted by permission of the publisher. Copyright 1984 by the Sloan Management Review Association. All rights reserved. **Table 22.1:** Philip B. Crosby, *Quality Without Tears*, (New York: McGraw-Hill, 1979): 8–9. Copyright

1979. Reprinted with permission of McGraw-Hill, Inc. **Ethics Highlight:** Rajendra S. Sisodia, "We Need Zero-Tolerance Ethics Violations," *Marketing News* 24 (March 5, 1990): 4, 14. **Figure 22.2:** From *Zero Quality Control: Source Inspection and the Poka Yoke System* by Shigeo Shingo. English translation copyright © 1986 by *Productivity Press, Inc.*, P.O. Box 13390, Portland, OR, 97213-0390, (800) 394-6868. Reprinted by permission.

CHAPTER 23

Table 23.1: Ann M. Morrison, *The New Leaders: Leadership Diversity in America*, adapted from pp. 18–27. Copyright 1992 by Ann M. Morrison and Jossey-Bass, Inc., Publishers. Reprinted by permission of Jossey-Bass, Inc., Publishers. **Diversity Highlight:** Parker R. Goodwin, *Laying the Groundwork for Diversity Training at CAE-LINK: Demographic and Process Issues*, (Reprinted by permission) Binghamton University (1993): 31–33. **Figure 23.1:** William B. Johnston and Arnold E. Packer, "Executive Summary," *Workforce 2000: Work and Workers for the 21st Century*. (Hudson Institute, June 1987): 95. Reprinted by permission. **Global Highlight:** "Connecting the World," *Focus For and About the People of AT&T* (September 1992).

PHOTO CREDITS

CHAPTER 1 p. 2, Kevin Larkin/AP/Wide World Photos; p. 5, Porter Gifford/Gamma-Liaison, Inc.; p. 6, Mike Greenlar; p. 7, Edward Gajdel Photography; p. 15, fX Networks; p. 17, Hoechst Celanese; **CHAPTER 2** p. 28, Andy Levin/Photo Researchers, Inc.; p. 31, Eligio Paoni/Contrasto/SABA Press Photos, Inc.; p. 33, James LukoskiPhotography; p. 36, Glentzer Photography; p. 42, Dan Bryant **CHAPTER 3** p. 50, Ira Wyman/Sygma; p 52, Steven Rubin/JB Pictures Ltd.; p. 57, Andy Freeberg Photography; p. 67, Michael Newman/PhotoEdit; p. 72, Nina Berman/SIPA Press **CHAPTER 4** p. 78, Baskin-Robbins; p. 83, Torin Boyd; p. 85, Alan Levenson; p. 91, Michael L. Abramson; p. 93, Acey Harper; p. 96, Greg Girard/Contact Press Images; p. 101, Mike Pilling **CHAPTER 5** p. 111, Comstock; p. 113, James Schnepf Photography, Inc.; p. 115, Robert Lyons; p. 120, Eli Reichman; p. 121, Chris Corsmeier Photography **CHAPTER 6** p. 133, Nancy Kaszerman/Shooting Star International Photo Agency; 137, Reid Horn; p. 141, Rex Rystedt; p. 143, Churchill and Klehr **CHAPTER 7** p. 153, Churchill and Klehr; p. 157, Michael Newman/PhotoEdit; p. 161, Molson Companies **CHAPTER 8** p. 176, Jay Clarke/Miami Herald Publishing Co.; p. 181, Kraipit Phahvut/SIPA Press; p. 181, Dilip Mehta/Contact Press Images; p. 182, Greg Girard/Contact Press Images; p. 183, Munshi Ahmed Photography **CHAPTER 9** p. 201, Eligio Paoni/Contrasto/SABA Press Photos, Inc; p. 204, Michael L. Abramson; p. 208, Peter Korniss/Black Star; p. 214, Forrest Anderson/Gamma-Liaison, Inc. **CHAPTER 10** p. 227, Peter Gregoire; p. 229, Frito-Lay, Inc.; p. 230, Rock Bottom Restaurant; p. 235, Bob Hower/Quadrant **CHAPTER 11** p. 250, Churchill and Klehr; p. 253,P. Hirth/T. Hartrich Eisenach/Transit Leipzig; p. 259, Andy Freeberg Photography; p. 266, Michael L. Abramson **CHAPTER 12** p. 273, United Airlines; p. 280, Steven Rubin/JB Pictures Ltd.; p. 280, p. 289, William Mercer McLeod; p. 280, p. 289, Steven Rubin/JB Pictures Ltd.; p. 281, Nina Barnett Photography **CHAPTER 13** p. 297, Clark Jones/AP/Wide World Photos; p. 301, Suzanne Opton; p. 303, Intel Corporation; p. 306, McIntyre Photography, Inc.; p. 310, Philip Gould; p. 316, Vincent J. Musi **CHAPTER 14** p. 325, Eaton Corporation; p. 328, Marty Lederhandler/AP/Wide World Photos; p. 330, Intel Corporation; p. 338, AT&T; p. 342, Kenneth Jarecke/Contact Press Images **CHAPTER 15** p. 349, Hiroyuki Matsumoto/Black Star; p. 354, Jack Van Antwerp/Onyx Enterprises, Inc.; p. 358, David Strick/Onyx Enterprises, Inc.; p. 360, Arnold Carbone/Ben & Jerry's; p. 372, John Abbott Photography **CHAPTER 16** p. 379, American Greetings Corporation; p. 385, Red Morgan Photography; p. 389, Wyatt McSpadden Photography; 397, Ben Van Hook Photography.**CHAPTER 17** p. 403, Brian R. Bell/ Rolls-Royce Motor Cars Limited; p. 409, Robert Holmgren Photography; p. 416, Andrew Brusso; p. 417, Doug Milner Photography; p. 422, Louis Psihoyos/Matrix International **CHAPTER 18** p. 429, Applied Communications Inc. (APCOM); p. 432, Sepp Seitz/Woodfin Camp & Associates; p. 435, Robert Holmgren Photography; p. 435, Mitsutaka Kurashina; p. 444,

INDEXES

NAME AND COMPANY

SUBJECT

Weiss Ratings'
Guide to
Life and Annuity
Insurers

Weiss Ratings' Guide to Life and Annuity Insurers

A Quarterly Compilation of Insurance
Company Ratings and Analyses

Spring 2015

GREY HOUSE PUBLISHING

Weiss Ratings
4400 Northcorp Parkway
Palm Beach Gardens, FL 33410
561-627-3300

Published by Grey House Publishing, Inc., located at 4919 Route 22, Amenia, NY 12501; telephone 518-789-8700. Grey House Publishing neither guarantees the accuracy of the data contained herein nor assumes any responsibility for errors, omissions or discrepancies. Grey House Publishing accepts no payment for listing; inclusion in the publication of any organization, agency, institution, publication, service or individual does not imply endorsement of the publisher.

4919 Route 22
PO Box 56
Amenia, NY 12501-0056

Edition No. 99, Spring 2015

ISBN: 978-1-61925-593-7
ISSN: 2158-527X

Contents

Terms and Conditions

This Document is prepared strictly for the confidential use of our customer(s). It has been provided to you at your specific request. It is not directed to, or intended for distribution to or use by, any person or entity who is a citizen or resident of or located in any locality, state, country or other jurisdiction where such distribution, publication, availability or use would be contrary to law or regulation or which would subject Weiss Ratings or its affiliates to any registration or licensing requirement within such jurisdiction.

No part of the analysts' compensation was, is, or will be, directly or indirectly, related to the specific recommendations or views expressed in this research report.

This Document is not intended for the direct or indirect solicitation of business. Weiss Ratings, LLC., and its affiliates disclaims any and all liability to any person or entity for any loss or damage caused, in whole or in part, by any error (negligent or otherwise) or other circumstances involved in, resulting from or relating to the procurement, compilation, analysis, interpretation, editing, transcribing, publishing and/or dissemination or transmittal of any information contained herein.

Weiss Ratings has not taken any steps to ensure that the securities or investment vehicle referred to in this report are suitable for any particular investor. The investment or services contained or referred to in this report may not be suitable for you and it is recommended that you consult an independent investment advisor if you are in doubt about such investments or investment services. Nothing in this report constitutes investment, legal, accounting or tax advice or a representation that any investment or strategy is suitable or appropriate to your individual circumstances or otherwise constitutes a personal recommendation to you.

The ratings and other opinions contained in this Document must be construed solely as statements of opinion from Weiss Ratings, LLC., and not statements of fact. Each rating or opinion must be weighed solely as a factor in your choice of an institution and should not be construed as a recommendation to buy, sell or otherwise act with respect to the particular product or company involved.

Past performance should not be taken as an indication or guarantee of future performance, and no representation or warranty, expressed or implied, is made regarding future performance. Information, opinions and estimates contained in this report reflect a judgment at its original date of publication and are subject to change without notice. Weiss Ratings offers a notification service for rating changes on companies you specify. For more information visit WeissRatings.com or call 1-877-934-7778. The price, value and income from any of the securities or financial instruments mentioned in this report can fall as well as rise.

This Document and the information contained herein is copyrighted by Weiss Ratings, LLC. Any copying, displaying, selling, distributing or otherwise reproducing or delivering this information or any part of this Document to any other person or entity is prohibited without the express written consent of Weiss Ratings, LLC, with the exception of a reviewer or editor who may quote brief passages in connection with a review or a news story.

Message To Insurers

All survey data received on or before January 9, 2015 has been considered or incorporated into this edition of the Directory. If there are particular circumstances which you believe could affect your rating, please use the online survey (**http://weissratings.com/survey/**) or e-mail Weiss Ratings, LLC (**insurancesurvey@weissinc.com**) with documentation to support your request. If warranted, we will make every effort to incorporate the changes in our next edition.

Welcome to Weiss Ratings'
Guide to Life and Annuity Insurers

Most people automatically assume their insurance company will survive, year after year. However, prudent consumers and professionals realize that in this world of shifting risks, the solvency of insurance companies can't be taken for granted.

If you are looking for accurate, unbiased ratings and data to help you choose life and annuity insurance for yourself, your family, your company or your clients, *Weiss Ratings' Guide to Life and Annuity Insurers* gives you precisely what you need.

In fact, it's the only source that currently provides ratings and analyses on 1,000 life and annuity insurers.

Weiss Ratings' Mission Statement

Weiss Ratings' mission is to empower consumers, professionals, and institutions with high quality advisory information for selecting or monitoring a financial services company or financial investment.

In doing so, Weiss Ratings will adhere to the highest ethical standards by maintaining our independent, unbiased outlook and approach to advising our customers.

Why rely on Weiss Ratings?

Weiss Ratings provides fair, objective ratings to help professionals and consumers alike make educated purchasing decisions.

At Weiss Ratings, integrity is number one. Weiss Ratings never takes a penny from insurance companies for its ratings. And, we publish Weiss Financial Strength Ratings without regard for insurers' preferences. However, other rating agencies like A.M. Best, Fitch, Moody's and Standard & Poor's are paid by insurance companies for their ratings and may even suppress unfavorable ratings at an insurer's request.

Our ratings are more frequently reviewed and updated than any other ratings. You can be sure that the information you receive is accurate and current – providing you with advance warning of financial vulnerability early enough to do something about it.

Other rating agencies focus primarily on a company's current claims paying ability and consider only mild economic adversity. Weiss Ratings also considers these issues, but in addition, our analysis covers a company's ability to deal with severe economic adversity and a sharp increase in claims.

Our use of more rigorous standards stems from the viewpoint that an insurance company's obligations to its policyholders should not depend on favorable business conditions. An insurer must be able to honor its policy commitments in bad times as well as good.

Our rating scale, from A to F, is easy to understand. Only a few outstanding companies receive an A (Excellent) rating, although there are many to choose from within the B (Good) category. An even larger group falls into the broad average range which receives C (Fair) ratings. Companies that demonstrate marked vulnerabilities receive either D (Weak) or E (Very Weak) ratings.

How to Use This Guide

The purpose of the *Guide to Life and Annuity Insurers* is to provide policyholders and prospective policy purchasers with a reliable source of insurance company ratings and analyses on a timely basis. We realize that the financial stength of an insurer is an important factor to consider when making the decision to purchase a policy or change companies. The ratings and analyses in this Guide can make that evaluation easier when you are considering:

- Life insurance

- Annuities

- Health insurance

- Guaranteed Investment Contracts (GICs) and other pension products

This Guide also includes ratings for some Blue Cross Blue Shield plans.

The rating for a particular company indicates our opinion regarding that company's ability to meet its commitments to the policyholder – not only under current economic conditions, but also during a declining economy or in an environment of increased liquidity demands.

To use this Guide most effectively, we recommend you follow the steps outlined below:

Step 1   To ensure you evaluate the correct company, verify the company's exact name and state of domicile as it was given to you or appears on your policy. Many companies have similar names but are not related to one another, so you want to make sure the company you look up is really the one you are interested in evaluating.

Step 2   Turn to Section I, the Index of Companies, and locate the company you are evaluating. This section contains all companies analyzed by Weiss Ratings including those that did not receive a Financial Strength Rating. It is sorted alphabetically by the name of the company and shows the state of domicile following the name for additional verification. Once you have located your specific company, the first column after the state of domicile shows its Weiss Financial Strength Rating. Turn to *About Weiss Financial Strength Ratings* for information about what this rating means. If the rating has changed since the last issue of this Guide, a downgrade will be indicated with a down triangle ▼ to the left of the company name; an upgrade will be indicated with an up triangle ▲.

Step 3   Following Weiss Financial Strength Rating are some of the various indexes that our analysts used in rating the company. Refer to the Critical Ranges In Our Indexes table for an interpretation of which index values are considered strong, good, fair or weak. You can also turn to the introduction of Section I to see what each of these factors measures. In most cases, lower rated companies will have a low index value in one or more of the factors shown. Bear in mind, however, that Weiss Financial Strength Rating is the result of a complex qualitative and quantitative analysis which cannot be reproduced using only the data provided here.

Step 4   The quality of a company's investment portfolio – bonds, mortgages and other investments – is an integral part of our analysis. So, the right hand page of Section I shows you where the company has invested its premiums. Again, refer to the introduction of Section I for a description of each investment category.

Step 5   Some insurers have a bullet ● preceding the company name on the right hand page of Section I. If the company you are evaluating is identified with a bullet, turn to Section II, the Analysis of Largest Companies, and locate it there (otherwise skip to step 8). Section II contains the largest insurers rated by Weiss Ratings, regardless of rating. It too is sorted alphabetically by the name of the company.

Step 6   Once you have identified your company in Section II, you will find its Financial Strength Rating and a description of the rating immediately to the right of the company name. Then, below the company name is a description of the various rating factors that were considered in assigning the company's rating. These factors and the information below them are designed to give you a better feel for the company and its strengths and weaknesses. See the Section II introduction, to get a better understanding of what each of these factors means.

Step 7   To the right, you will find a five-year summary of the company's Financial Strength Rating, capitialization and income. Look for positive or negative trends in this data. Below the five-year summary, we have included a graphic illustration of the most critical factor or factors impacting the company's rating. Again, the Section II introduction provides an overview of the content of each graph or table.

Step 8   If the company you are evaluating is not highly rated and you want to find an insurer with a higher rating, turn to the page in Section IV that has your state's name at the top. This section contains those Recommended Companies (rating of A+, A, A- or B+) that are licensed to underwrite insurance in your state, sorted by rating. From here you can select a company and then refer back to Sections I and II to analyze it.

Step 9   If you decide that you would like to contact one of Weiss Recommended Companies about obtaining a policy or for additional information, refer to Section III. Following each company's name is its address and phone number to assist you in making contact.

Step 10   In order to use Weiss Financial Strength Ratings most effectively, we strongly recommend you consult the Important Warnings and Cautions listed. These are more than just "standard disclaimers"; they are very important factors you should be aware of before using this Guide. If you have any questions regarding the precise meaning of specific terms used in the Guide, refer to the Glossary.

Step 11   The Appendix contains information about State Guaranty Associations and the types of coverage they provide to policyholders when an insurance company fails. Keep in mind that while guaranty funds have now been established in all states, many do not cover all types of insurance. Furthermore, all of these funds have limits on their amount of coverage. Use the table to determine whether the level of coverage is applicable to your policy and the limits are adequate for your needs. You should pay particular attention to the notes regarding whether the coverage is for residents of the state or companies domiciled in the state.

Step 12   If you want more information on your state's guaranty fund, call the State Commissioner's Office directly.

Step 13   Keep in mind that good coverage from a state guaranty association is no substitute for dealing with a financially strong company. Weiss Ratings only recommends those companies which we feel are most able to stand on their own, without regard to what might happen in case the company does fail.

Step 14   Make sure you stay up to date with the latest information available since the publication of this Guide. For information on how to set up a rating change notification service, acquire follow-up reports or receive a more in-depth analysis of an individual company, call 1-877-934-7778 or visit www.weissratings.com.

Data Sources: Annual and quarterly statutory statements filed with state insurance commissioners and data provided by the insurance companies being rated. The National Association of Insurance Commissioners has provided some of the raw data. Any analyses or conclusions are not provided or endorsed by the NAIC.

Date of data analyzed: September 30, 2014 unless otherwise noted.

About Weiss Financial Strength Ratings

Weiss Financial Strength Ratings represent a completely independent, unbiased opinion of an insurance company's financial strength. The ratings are derived, for the most part, from annual and quarterly financial statements obtained from state insurance commissioners. These data are supplemented by information that we request from the insurance companies themselves. Although we seek to maintain an open line of communication with the companies being rated, we do not grant them the right to influence the ratings or stop their publication.

Weiss Financial Strength Ratings are assigned by our analysts based on a complex analysis of hundreds of factors that are synthesized into five indexes: capitalization, investment safety, profitability, liquidity and stability. These indexes are then used to arrive at a letter grade rating. A good rating requires consistency across all indexes. A weak score on any one index can result in a low rating, as insolvency can be caused by any one of a number of factors, such as inadequate capital, unpredictable claims experience, poor liquidity, speculative investments, or operating losses.

The primary components of Weiss Financial Strength Rating are as follows:

- **Capitalization Index** gauges capital adequacy in terms of each insurer's ability to handle a variety of business and economic scenarios as they may impact investment performance, claims experience, persistency and market position.

- **Investment Safety Index** measures the exposure of the company's investment portfolio to loss of principal and/or income due to default and market risks.

- **Profitability Index** measures the soundness of the company's operations and the contribution of profits to the company's financial strength. The profitability index is a composite of five sub-factors: 1) gain or loss on operations; 2) consistency of operating results; 3) impact of operating results on surplus; 4) adequacy of investment income as compared to the needs of policy reserves; and 5) expenses in relation to industry norms for the types of policies that the company offers.

- **Liquidity Index** values a company's ability to raise the necessary cash to settle claims and honor cash withdrawal obligations. We model various cash flow scenarios, applying liquidity tests to determine how the company might fare in the event of a spike in claims or a run on policy surrenders.

- **Stability Index** integrates a number of sub-factors that affect consistency (or lack thereof) in maintaining financial strength over time. Sub-factors include 1) risk diversification in terms of company size, group size, number of policies in force, types of policies written and use of reinsurance; 2) deterioration of operations as reported in critical asset, liability, income and expense items, such as surrender rates and premium volume; 3) years in operation; 4) former problem areas where, despite recent improvement, the company has yet to establish a record of stable performance over a suitable period of time; 5) a substantial shift in the company's operations; 6) potential instabilities such as reinsurance quality, asset/liability matching, and sources of capital; and 7) relationships with holding companies and affiliates.

Each of these indexes is measured according to the following range of values.

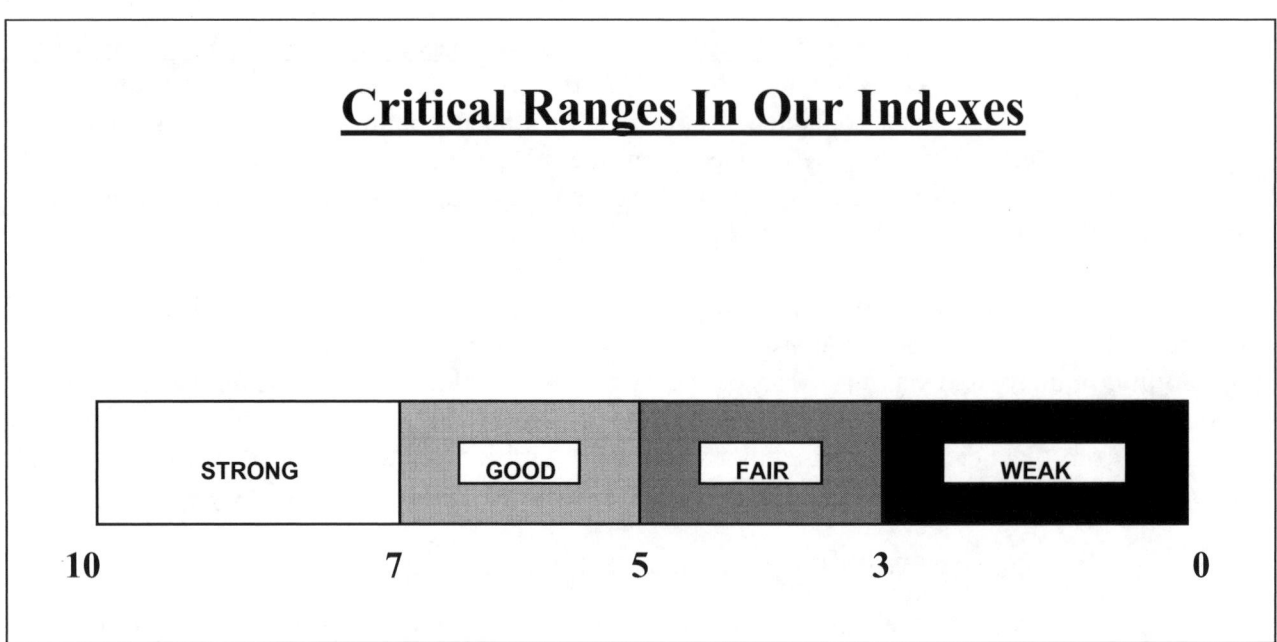

What Our Ratings Mean

A   **Excellent.**   The company offers excellent financial security. It has maintained a conservative stance in its investment strategies, business operations and underwriting commitments. While the financial position of any company is subject to change, we believe that this company has the resources necessary to deal with severe economic conditions.

B   **Good.** The company offers good financial security and has the resources to deal with a variety of adverse economic conditions. It comfortably exceeds the minimum levels for all of our rating criteria, and is likely to remain healthy for the near future. However, in the event of a *severe* recession or major financial crisis, we feel that this assessment should be reviewed to make sure that the firm is still maintaining adequate financial strength.

C   **Fair.** The company offers fair financial security and is currently stable. But during an economic downturn or other financial pressures, we feel it may encounter difficulties in maintaining its financial stability.

D   **Weak.**   The company currently demonstrates what we consider to be significant weaknesses which could negatively impact policyholders. In an unfavorable economic environment, these weaknesses could be magnified.

E   **Very Weak.** The company currently demonstrates what we consider to be significant weaknesses and has also failed some of the basic tests that we use to identify fiscal stability. Therefore, even in a favorable economic environment, it is our opinion that policyholders could incur significant risks.

F   **Failed.**   The company is deemed failed if it is either 1) under supervision of an insurance regulatory authority; 2) in the process of rehabilitation; 3) in the process of liquidation; or 4) voluntarily dissolved after disciplinary or other regulatory action by an insurance regulatory authority.

+   **The plus sign** is an indication that the company is at the upper end of the letter grade rating.

-   **The minus sign** is an indication that the company is at the lower end of the letter grade rating.

U   **Unrated Companies.** The company is unrated for one or more of the following reasons: 1) total assets are less than $1 million; 2) premium income for the current year is less than $100,000; 3) the company functions almost exclusively as a holding company rather than as an underwriter; or 4) we do not have enough information to reliably issue a rating.

How Our Ratings Differ From Those of Other Services

Weiss Financial Strength Ratings are conservative and consumer-oriented. We use tougher standards than other rating agencies because our system is specifically designed to inform risk-averse consumers about the financial strength of life and annuity insurers.

Our rating scale (A to F) is easy to understand by the general public. Users can intuitively understand that an A+ rating is at the top of the scale rather than in the middle like some of the other rating agencies.

Other rating agencies give top ratings more generously so that most companies receive excellent ratings.

More importantly, other rating agencies focus primarily on a company's *current* claims paying ability or consider only relatively mild economic adversity. We also consider these scenarios but extend our analysis to cover a company's ability to deal with severe economic adversity and potential liquidity problems. This stems from the viewpoint that an insurance company's obligations to its policyholders should not be contingent upon a healthy economy. The company must be capable of honoring its policy commitments in bad times as well.

Looking at the insurance industry as a whole, we note that several major rating firms have poor historical track records in identifying troubled companies. The 1980s saw a persistent decline in capital ratios, increased holdings of risky investments in the life and health industry as well as recurring long-term claims liabilities in the property and casualty industry. Despite these clear signs that insolvency risk was rising, other rating firms failed to downgrade at-risk insurance companies. Instead, they often rated companies by shades of excellence, understating the gravity of potential problems.

They have not issued clear warnings that the ordinary consumer can understand. Few, if any, companies receive "weak" or "poor" ratings. Surely, weak companies do exist. However, the other rating agencies apparently do not view themselves as consumer advocates with the responsibility of warning the public about the risks involved in doing business with such companies.

Additionally, these firms will at times agree *not* to issue a rating if a company denies them permission to do so. In short, too often insurance rating agencies work hand-in-glove with the companies they rate.

At Weiss Ratings, although we seek to maintain good relationships with the firms, we owe our primary obligation to the consumer, not the industry. We reserve the right to rate companies based on publicly available data and make the necessary conservative assumptions when companies choose not to provide the additional data we request.

Comparison of Insurance Company Rating Agency Scales

Weiss Ratings [a]	Best [a,b]	S&P [c]	Moody's	Fitch [d]
A+, A, A-	A++, A+	AAA	Aaa	AAA
B+, B, B-	A, A-	AA+, AA AA-	Aa1, Aa2, Aa3	AA+, AA, AA-
C+, C, C-	B++, B+,	A+, A, A-, BBB+, BBB, BBB-	A1, A2, A3, Baa1, Baa2, Baa3	A+, A, A-, BBB+, BBB, BBB-
D+, D, D-	B, B- C++, C+, C, C-	BB+, BB, BB-, B+, B, B-	Ba1, Ba2, Ba3, B1, B2, B3	BB+, BB, BB-, B+, B, B-
E+, E, E- F	D E, F	CCC R	Caa, Ca, C	CCC+, CCC, CCC- DD

[a] Weiss Ratings and Best use additional symbols to designate that they recognize an insurer's existence but do not provide a rating. These symbols are not included in this table.

[b] Best added the A++, B++ and C++ ratings in 1992. In 1994, Best classified its ratings into "secure" and "vulnerable" categories, changed the definition of its "B" and "B-" ratings from "good" to "adequate" and assigned these ratings to the "vulnerable" category. This table contains GAO's assignment of Best's ratings to bands based on our interpretation of their rating descriptions prior to 1994.

[c] S&P discontinued CCC "+" and "-" signs, CC, C and D ratings and added the R rating in 1992.
Source: 1994 GAO *Insurance Ratings* study.

[d] Duff & Phelps Credit Rating Co. merged with Fitch IBCA in 2000, and minor changes were made to the rating scale at that time. These changes were not reflected in the GAO's 1994 study, but *are* reflected in the chart.

Rate of Insurance Company Failures

Weiss Ratings provides quarterly financial strength ratings for thousands of insurance companies each year. Weiss Ratings strives for fairness and objectivity in its ratings and analyses, ensuring that each company receives the rating that most accurately depicts its current financial status, and more importantly, its ability to deal with severe economic adversity and a sharp increase in claims. Weiss Ratings has every confidence that its financial strength ratings provide an accurate representation of a company's stability.

In order for these ratings to be of any true value, it is important that they prove accurate over time. One way to determine the accuracy of a rating is to examine those insurance companies that have failed, and their respective Weiss Financial Strength Ratings. A high percentage of failed companies with "A" ratings would indicate that Weiss Ratings is not being conservative enough with its "secure" ratings, while conversely, a low percentage of failures with "vulnerable" ratings would show that Weiss Ratings is overly conservative.

Over the past 25 years (1989–2013) Weiss Ratings has rated 580 insurance companies, for all industries, that subsequently failed. The chart below shows the number of failed companies in each rating category, the average number of companies rated in each category per year, and the percentage of annual failures for each letter grade.

	Financial Strength Rating	Number of Failed Companies	Average Number of Companies Rated per year	Percentage of Failed Companies per year (by ratings category)*
Secure	A	1	154	0.03%
	B	6	1095	0.02%
	C	71	1619	0.18%
Vulnerable	D	253	753	1.34%
	E	249	213	4.68%

A=Excellent, B=Good, C=Fair, D=Weak, E=Very Weak

On average, only 0.11% of the companies Weiss Ratings rates as "secure" fail each year. On the other hand, an average of 2.08% of the companies Weiss Ratings rates as "vulnerable" fail annually. That means that a company rated by Weiss Ratings as "Vulnerable" is 19 times more likely to fail than a company rated as "Secure".

When considering a Weiss financial strength rating, one can be sure that they are getting the most fair, objective, and accurate financial rating available anywhere.

*Percentage of Failed Companies per year = (Number of Failed Companies) / [(Average Number of Companies Rated per year) x (years in study)]

Data as of December 2013 for Life and Annuity Insurers and Property and Casualty Insurers, and Health Insurers.

What Does Average Mean?

At Weiss Ratings, we consider the words average and fair to mean just that – average and fair. So when we assign our ratings to insurers, a large percentage of companies receive an average C rating. That way, you can be sure that a company receiving Weiss B or A rating is truly above average. Likewise, you can feel confident that companies with D or E ratings are truly below average. In recent years, life and health insurers have experienced consistent, solid performance resulting in a shift in the rating distribution so that more insurers than ever are rated B or better.

Percentage for Life and Annuity Insurers in Each Rating Category

2014 Weiss Ratings Distribution

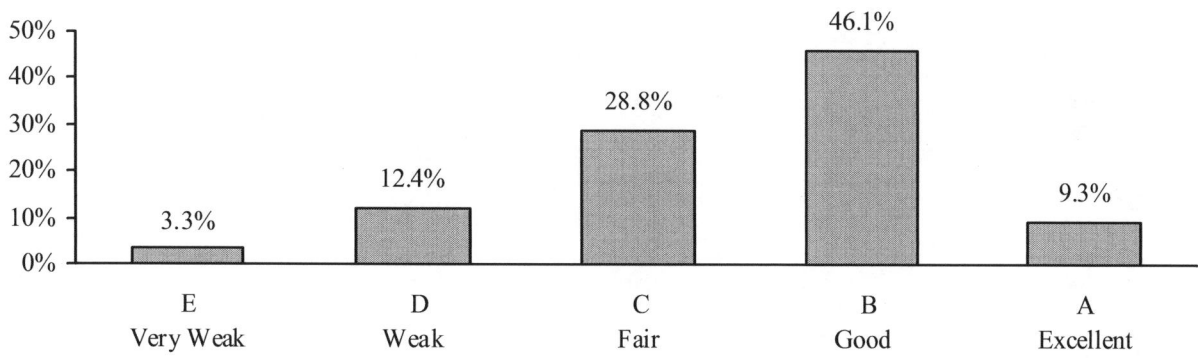

Important Warnings and Cautions

1. A rating alone cannot tell the whole story. Please read the explanatory information contained in this publication. It is provided in order to give you an understanding of our rating philosophy, as well as paint a more complete picture of how we arrive at our opinion of a company's strengths and weaknesses.

2. Weiss Financial Strength Ratings represent our opinion of a company's insolvency risk. As such, a high rating means we feel that the company has less chance of running into financial difficulties. A high rating is not a guarantee of solvency nor is a low rating a prediction of insolvency. Weiss Financial Strength Ratings are not deemed to be a recommendation concerning the purchase or sale of the securities of any insurance company that is publicly owned.

3. Company performance is only one factor in determining a rating. Conditions in the marketplace and overall economic conditions are additional factors that may affect the company's financial strength. Therefore, a rating upgrade or downgrade does not necessarily reflect changes in the company's profits, capital or other financial measures, but may be due to external factors. Likewise, changes in Weiss indexes may reflect changes in our risk assessment of business or economic conditions as well as changes in company performance.

4. All firms that have the same Financial Strength Rating should be considered to be essentially equal in strength. This is true regardless of any differences in the underlying numbers which might appear to indicate greater strengths. Weiss Financial Strength Rating already takes into account a number of lesser factors which, due to space limitations, cannot be included in this publication.

5. A good rating requires consistency. If a company is excellent on four indicators and fair on one, the company may receive a fair rating. This requirement is necessary due to the fact that fiscal problems can arise from any *one* of several causes including speculative investments, inadequate capital resources or operating losses.

6. We are an independent rating agency and do not depend on the cooperation of the companies we rate. Our data are derived, for the most part, from annual and quarterly financial statements that we obtain from federal banking regulators and state insurance commissioners. The latter may be supplemented by information insurance companies voluntarily provide upon request. Although we seek to maintain an open line of communication with the companies, we do not grant them the right to stop or influence publication of the ratings. This policy stems from the fact that this publication is designed for the protection of the consumer.

7. Affiliated companies do not automatically receive the same rating. We recognize that a troubled company may expect financial support from its parent or affiliates. Weiss Financial Strength Ratings reflect our opinion of the measure of support that may become available to a subsidiary , if the subsidiary were to experience serious financial difficulties. In the case of a strong parent and a weaker subsidiary, the affiliate relationship will generally result in a higher rating for the subsidiary than it would have on a stand-alone basis. Seldom, however, would the rating be brought up to the level of the parent. This treatment is appropriate because we do not assume the parent would have either the resources or the will to "bail out" a troubled subsidiary during a severe economic crisis. Even when there is a binding legal obligation for a parent corporation to honor the policy obligations of its subsidiaries, the possibility exists that the subsidiary could be sold and lose its parental support. Therefore, it is quite common for one affiliate to have a higher rating than another. This is another reason why it is especially important that you have the precise name of the company you are evaluating.

Section I

Index of Companies

An analysis of all rated and unrated

U.S. Life and Annuity Insurers.

Companies are listed in alphabetical order.

Section I Contents

This section contains the key rating factors and investment portfolio analysis for all rated and unrated insurers analyzed by Weiss Ratings. An explanation of each of the footnotes and stability factors appears at the end of this section.

Left Pages

1. Insurance Company Name

The legally registered name, which can sometimes differ from the name that the company uses for advertising. If you cannot find the company you are interested in, or if you have any doubts regarding the precise name, verify the information with the company before looking the name up in this Guide. Also, determine the domicile state for confirmation. (See column 2.)

2. Domicile State

The state which has primary regulatory responsibility for the company. It may differ from the location of the company's corporate headquarters. You do not have to be living in the domicile state to purchase insurance from this firm, provided it is licensed to do business in your state.

Also use this column to confirm that you have located the correct company. It is possible for two unrelated companies to have the same name if they are domiciled in different states.

3. Financial Strength Rating

Our rating is measured on a scale from A to F and considers a wide range of factors. Please see What Our Ratings Mean for specific descriptions of each letter grade. Also, refer to how our ratings differ from those of other rating agencies. Most important, when using this rating, please be sure to consider the warnings regarding the ratings' limitations and the underlying assumptions. Notes in this column refer to the date of the data included in the rating evaluation and are explained.

4. Total Assets

All assets admitted by state insurance regulators in millions of dollars. This includes investments, current business assets, and separate accounts. The year-end figure is used to correspond with the figures on the right-hand pages, some of which are only available on an annual basis.

The overall size is an important factor which affects the ability of a company to manage risk. Mortality, morbidity (sickness) and investment risks can be more effectively diversified by large companies. Because the insurance business is based on probability, the number of policies must be large enough so that actuarial statistics are valid. Life insurance policies, for example, are based on mortality tables containing the expected number of deaths per thousand at various ages.

The larger the number of policyholders, the more reliable the actuarial projections will be. A large company with a correspondingly large policy base can spread its risk and minimize the effects of claims experience that exceeds actuarial expectations.

5. **Capital and Surplus**

The company's statutory net worth in millions of dollars. Consumers may wish to limit the size of any policy so that the policyholder's maximum benefits do not exceed approximately 1% of the company's capital and surplus. For example, when buying a policy from a company with capital and surplus of $10,000,000, the 1% limit would be $100,000. (When performing this calculation, do not forget that figures in this column are expressed in millions of dollars.)

Critical Ranges In Our Indexes and Ratios

Indicators	Strong	Good	Fair	Weak
Risk-Adjusted Capital Ratio #1	—	1.0 or more	0.75 - 0.99	0.74 or less
Risk-Adjusted Capital Ratio #2	1.0 or more	0.75 - 0.99	0.5 - 0.74	0.49 or less
Capitalization Index	7 – 10	5 - 6.9	3 - 4.9	2.9 or less
5 Year Profitability Index	7 – 10	5 - 6.9	3 - 4.9	2.9 or less
Liquidity Index	7 – 10	5 - 6.9	3 - 4.9	2.9 or less
Investment Safety Index	7 – 10	5 - 6.9	3 - 4.9	2.9 or less
Stability Index	7 – 10	5 - 6.9	3 - 4.9	2.9 or less

6. **Risk-Adjusted Capital Ratio #1**

This ratio examines the adequacy of the company's capital base and whether the company has sufficient capital resources to cover potential losses which might occur in an average recession or other moderate loss scenario. Specifically, the figure cited in the table answers the question: For every dollar of capital that we feel would be needed, how many dollars in capital resources does the company actually have? (See the table above for the levels which we believe are critical.) You may find that some companies have unusually high levels of capital. This often reflects special circumstances related to the small size or unusual operations of the company.

7. **Risk-Adjusted Capital Ratio #2**

This is similar to item 6. But in this case, the question relates to whether the company has enough capital cushion to withstand a *severe* recession or other severe loss scenario.

8. **Capitalization Index**

An index that measures the adequacy of the company's capital resources to deal with a variety of business and economic scenarios. It combines Risk-Adjusted Capital Ratios #1 and #2 as well as a leverage test that examines pricing risk. (See the table above for the levels which we believe are critical.)

9. Investment Safety Index

An index that measures the exposure of the company's investment portfolio to a loss of principal and/or income due to default and market risks. It is the composite of a series of elements, some of which are shown on the right pages. Each investment area is rated by a factor that takes into consideration both quality and liquidity. (See the table on the next page for the levels which we believe are critical.)

10. 5-Year Profitability Index

An index that measures the soundness of the company's operations and the contribution of profits to the company's fiscal strength. The Profitability Index is a composite of five factors: (1) gain or loss on operations; (2) consistency of operating results; (3) impact of operating results on surplus; (4) adequacy of investment income as compared to the needs of policy reserves; and (5) expenses in relation to industry averages for the types of policies that the company offers.

This factor is especially important among health insurers including Blue Cross Blue Shield companies that rely more heavily on current earnings than do life and annuity writers. After factoring out the normal cycle, companies with stable earnings and capital growth are viewed more favorably than those whose results are erratic from year to year. (See the table for the levels which we believe are critical.)

11. Liquidity Index

An index which measures the company's ability to raise the necessary cash to meet policyholder obligations. This index includes a stress test which considers the consequences of a spike in claims or a run on policy surrenders. Sometimes a company may appear to have the necessary resources, but may be unable to sell its investments at the prices at which they are valued in the company's financial statements. (See the table for the levels which we believe are critical.)

12. Stability Index

An index which integrates a number of factors such as: (1) risk diversification in terms of company size, number of policies in force, use of reinsurance and other items related to spread of risk; (2) deterioration of operations as reported in critical asset, liability, income or expense items such as surrender rates and premium volume; (3) former problem areas where, despite recent improvement, the company has yet to establish a record of stable performance over a suitable period of time; (4) a substantial shift in the company's operations; (5) potential instabilities such as reinsurance quality, asset/liability matching and sources of capital; plus (6) relationships to holding companies and affiliates. (See the table for the levels which we believe are critical.)

| 13. | **Stability Factors** | Indicates those specific areas that have negatively impacted the company's Stability Index. |

Right Pages

| 1. | **Net Premiums** | The amount of insurance premiums received from policyholders less any premiums that have been transferred to other companies through reinsurance agreements. Generally speaking, companies with large net premium volume generally have more predictable claims experience. |

| 2. | **Invested Assets** | The value of the firm's total investment portfolio, measured in millions of dollars. The year-end figure is used to correspond with the following figures, some of which are only available on an annual basis. Use the figure in this column to determine the actual dollar amounts invested in each asset category shown in columns 3 through 11 on the right-side pages. For example, if the firm has $500 million in invested assets and column 3 shows that 10% of its portfolio is in cash, the company has $50 million in cash. |

Looking at the right-side pages, columns 3 through 11 will, unless otherwise noted, add up to approximately 100%. Column 12 (investments in affiliates) is already included in other columns (usually 4, 5 or 6) depending upon the specific investment vehicle.

| 3. | **Cash** | Cash on hand and demand deposits. A negative cash position implies checks outstanding exceed cash balances, a situation not unusual for insurance companies. |

| 4. | **CMOs (Collateralized Mortgage Obligations) and Other Structured Securities** | Mortgage-backed bonds that split the payments from mortgage pools into different classes, called tranches. The split may be based on maturity dates or a variety of other factors. For example, the owner of one type of CMO, called a PAC, receives principal and interest payments made by the mortgage holders between specific dates. The large majority of CMOs held by insurance companies are those issued by government agencies and carry very little risk of default. Virtually all of the CMOs included here are investment grade. However, they all carry some measure of risk based on the payment speed of the underlying mortgages. |

5. Other Investment Grade Bonds   All investment grade bonds other than the CMOs included in column 4. Specifically, this includes: (1) issues guaranteed by U.S. and foreign governments which are rated as "highest quality" (Class 1) by state insurance commissioners; (2) nonguaranteed obligations of governments, such as Fannie Maes, which do not carry full faith and credit guarantees; (3) obligations of governments rated as "high quality" (Class 2) by state insurance commissioners; (4) state and municipal bonds; plus (5) investment-grade corporate bonds as defined by the state insurance commissioners. The data shown in this column are based exclusively on the definition used by state insurance commissioners. However, on the companies for which a more detailed breakdown of bond ratings is available, the actual bond ratings - and not the data shown in this column - are used in our rating process to calculate the Investment Safety Index.

6. Noninvestment Grade Bonds   Low-rated issues – commonly known as "junk bonds" – which carry a high risk as defined by the state insurance commissioners. In an unfavorable economic environment, we generally assume that these will be far more subject to default than other categories of corporate bonds.

7. Common and Preferred Stock   Common and preferred equities. Although a certain amount is acceptable for the sake of diversification, excessive investment in this area is viewed as a factor that can increase the company's overall vulnerability to market declines.

8. Mortgages In Good Standing   Mortgages which are current in their payments. Mortgage-backed securities are excluded.

9. Non-performing Mortgages   Mortgages which are (a) 90 days or more past due; or (b) in process of foreclosure. If the mortgages have already been foreclosed, the asset is transferred to the next category - real estate. Clearly, a high level of nonperforming mortgages is a negative, reflecting on the quality of the entire mortgage portfolio.

10. Real Estate   Direct real estate investments including (a) property occupied by the company; and (b) properties acquired through foreclosure. A certain amount of real estate investment is considered acceptable for portfolio diversification. However, excessive amounts may subject the company to losses during a recessionary period.

11. Other Investments   Items such as premium notes, collateral loans, short-term investments, policy loans and a long list of miscellaneous items.

12. Investments in Affiliates

Bonds, preferred and common stocks, as well as other vehicles which many insurance companies use to invest in - and establish a corporate link with - affiliated companies. Since these can often be non-income-producing paper assets, they are considered less desirable than the equivalent securities of publicly traded companies. Investments in affiliates are also included in other columns (usually 4, 5 or 6). Therefore, the percentage shown here represents a duplication of some of the amounts shown in the other columns.

Footnotes:

(1)   Data items shown are from the company's 2013 annual statutory statement except for Risk-Adjusted Capital Indexes 1 and 2, Profitability Index, Investment Safety Index, Liquidity Index and Stability Index which have been updated using the company's June 2014 quarterly statutory statement. Other more recent data may have been factored into the rating when available.

(2)   Data items shown are from the company's 2013 annual statutory statement except for Risk-Adjusted Capital Indexes 1 and 2, Profitability Index, Investment Safety Index, Liquidity Index and Stability Index which have been updated using the company's March 2014 quarterly statutory statement. Other more recent data may have been factored into the rating when available.

(3)   Data items shown are from the company's 2013 annual statutory statement. Other more recent data may have been factored into the rating when available.

(4)   Data items shown are from the company's 2012 annual statutory statement except for Risk-Adjusted Capital Indexes 1 and 2, Profitability Index, Investment Safety Index, Liquidity Index and Stability Index which have been updated using the company's September 2013 quarterly statutory statement. Other more recent data may have been factored into the rating when available.

(5)   These companies have data items that are older than December 31, 2012. They will be unrated (U) if they are not failed companies (F).

(*)   Breakdown of the company's investment portfolio, shown in percentages in columns 3-11 on the right hand page, does not total to 100% due to the inclusion of non–admitted assets in the bond or mortgage figures, or due to other accounting adjustments.

Stability Factors

(A)   Stability Index was negatively impacted by the financial problems or weaknesses of a parent or **affiliate** company.

(C)   Stability Index was negatively impacted by past results on our Risk-Adjusted **Capital** tests. In general, the Stability Index of any company can be affected by past results even if current results show improvement. While such improvement is a plus, the improved results must be maintained for a period of time to assure that the improvement is not a temporary fluctuation. During a five-year period, the impact of poor past results on the Stability Index gradually diminishes.

(D)   Stability Index was negatively impacted by limited **diversification** of general business, policy, and/or investment risk. This factor especially affects smaller companies that do not issue as many policies as larger firms. It can also affect firms that specialize in only one line of business.

(E)   Stability Index was negatively impacted due to a lack of operating **experience**. The company has been in operation for less than five years. Consequently, it has not been able to establish the kind of stable track record that we believe is needed to demonstrate financial permanence and strength.

(F)   Stability Index was negatively impacted by negative cash **flow**. In other words, the company paid out more in claims and expenses than it received in premiums and investment income.

(G)   Stability Index was negatively impacted by fast asset or premium **growth**. Fast growth can pose a serious problem for insurers. It is generally achieved by offering policies with premiums that are too low, benefits that are too costly, or agents commissions that are too high. Due to the highly competitive nature of the insurance marketplace, rapid growth has been a factor in many insurance insolvencies.

(I)   Stability Index was negatively impacted by past results on our **Investment** Safety Index. This can pose a problem for insurers even after risky investments have been sold off. To illustrate, consider those companies that have sold off their junk bonds and now carry much smaller junk bond risk. For a period of time the company that had the junk bonds incorporated the expectation of higher yields into its policy design and marketing strategy. Only time will tell how the company's investment income margins and future sales will be affected by the junk bond sell off. So, while the Investment Safety Index would improve right away, the Stability Index would improve only gradually over a period of three years, if the transition to lower yielding investments is handled smoothly.

(L)   Stability Index was negatively impacted by past results on our **liquidity** tests. In general, the Stability Index of any company can be affected by past results even if current results show improvement. While such improvement is a plus, the improved results must be maintained for a period of time to assure that the improvement is not a temporary fluctuation. During a five-year period, the impact of poor past results on the Stability Index gradually diminishes.

(O)   Stability Index was negatively impacted by significant changes in the company's business **operations**. These changes can include shifts in the kinds of insurance offered by the company, a temporary or permanent freeze on the sale of new policies, or recent release from conservatorship. In these circumstances, past performance cannot be a reliable indicator of future financial strength.

(R)   Stability Index was negatively impacted by concerns about the financial strength of its **reinsurers**.

(T)   Stability Index was negatively impacted by significant **trends** in critical asset, liability, income or expense items. Examples include increasing surrender rates, increasing mortgage defaults, and shrinking premium volume.

(Z)   This company is unrated due to data, as received by Weiss Ratings, that are either incomplete in substantial ways or contain items that, in the opinion of Weiss Ratings analysts, may not be reliable.

INSURANCE COMPANY NAME	DOM. STATE	RATING	TOTAL ASSETS ($MIL)	CAPITAL & SURPLUS ($MIL)	RISK ADJUSTED CAPITAL RATIO 1	RISK ADJUSTED CAPITAL RATIO 2	CAPITAL-IZATION INDEX (PTS)	INVEST. SAFETY INDEX (PTS)	PROFIT-ABILITY INDEX (PTS)	LIQUIDITY INDEX (PTS)	STAB. INDEX (PTS)	STABILI FACTOR
4 EVER LIFE INS CO	IL	A	200.3	93.9	4.46	3.14	10.0	6.5	8.3	6.7	7.1	ADFI
AAA LIFE INS CO	MI	B	560.4	118.2	2.47	1.49	7.7	6.5	5.6	6.4	5.8	A
AAA LIFE INS CO OF NY	NY	U (3)	8.8	8.4	3.86	3.47	10.0	7.6	1.9	7.0	3.2	DEFT
ABILITY INS CO	NE	D	903.3	33.5	1.14	0.61	5.2	4.0	1.0	9.3	1.7	FGT
ACADEME INC	WA	U (3)	5.6	5.6	3.41	3.07	8.0	9.8	2.2	10.0	2.4	DFT
ACCORDIA LIFE & ANNUITY CO	IA	C-	7481.4	517.7	0.85	0.62	4.0	5.5	1.9	8.4	2.1	GT
ACE LIFE INS CO	CT	C	39.6	7.4	1.29	0.87	6.0	9.2	1.3	7.5	3.9	FT
ADVANCE INS CO OF KS	KS	B+	52.7	42.9	3.55	2.34	9.0	4.5	8.3	7.2	6.8	AI
AETNA HEALTH & LIFE INS CO	CT	B+	2221.2	306.1	3.08	1.83	8.2	6.4	7.4	7.4	6.8	AI
AETNA LIFE INS CO	CT	B+	22602.5	3679.5	1.74	1.26	7.3	6.2	7.1	6.4	6.7	AI
AGC LIFE INS CO	MO	U (3)	20893.3	15038.3	0.90	0.80	5.4	3.0	7.8	8.9	5.0	CI
ALABAMA LIFE REINS CO INC	AL	E+	28.5	11.1	2.12	1.91	8.4	7.4	1.8	7.4	0.6	DFT
ALFA LIFE INS CORP	AL	B-	1334.1	221.6	2.77	1.58	7.9	5.7	3.0	6.9	4.0	T
ALL SAVERS INS CO	IN	B-	39.0	23.1	1.34	1.11	5.8	9.0	8.5	6.2	4.9	ADG
ALL SAVERS LIFE INS CO OF CA	CA	U (3)	9.7	9.6	4.05	3.64	8.0	9.8	4.0	10.0	5.6	DT
ALLIANZ LIFE & ANNUITY CO	MN	U (3)	16.7	12.1	4.00	3.60	8.0	9.5	3.5	9.9	5.3	D
ALLIANZ LIFE INS CO OF NORTH AMERICA	MN	C+	113662.2	5035.9	1.80	1.07	7.1	6.3	2.2	6.8	4.6	G
ALLIANZ LIFE INS CO OF NY	NY	B	2833.1	143.1	4.39	2.29	8.9	7.4	5.3	9.5	5.6	AFT
ALLIED FINANCIAL INS CO	TX	U (3)	0.4	0.4	2.18	1.97	8.5	9.8	2.4	10.0	2.6	DF
ALLSTATE ASR CO	IL	A-	12.3	10.9	4.07	3.67	8.0	9.6	6.8	10.0	6.6	A
ALLSTATE LIFE INS CO	IL	B	34348.3	2721.2	1.38	0.86	5.9	4.1	4.0	5.7	4.4	CFIT
ALLSTATE LIFE INS CO OF NEW YORK	NY	B-	6580.0	588.3	2.35	1.25	7.4	5.4	4.2	6.1	5.3	FIT
▲ AMALGAMATED LIFE & HEALTH INS CO	IL	C	5.8	3.8	2.29	2.06	8.6	8.6	6.2	7.5	4.0	D
AMALGAMATED LIFE INS CO	NY	A-	110.5	50.8	3.68	2.89	9.8	8.1	8.1	6.3	6.9	
AMERICAN BANKERS LIFE ASR CO OF FL	FL	B	517.1	55.7	4.66	2.57	9.4	6.8	5.9	7.6	5.0	AFT
AMERICAN BENEFIT LIFE INS CO	OK	C-	94.2	12.8	2.03	1.64	8.0	5.8	7.8	6.5	3.2	AD
AMERICAN CENTURY LIFE INS CO	OK	D+	66.6	6.4	0.94	0.84	5.7	2.1	8.7	0.7	2.5	CDIL
AMERICAN CENTURY LIFE INS CO TX	TX	U (3)	0.6	0.4	1.56	1.41	7.6	5.1	4.0	7.2	4.2	DF
AMERICAN CLASSIC REINS CO	AZ	U	--	--	--	--	--	--	--	--	--	Z
AMERICAN COMMUNITY MUT INS CO	MI	F (5)	--	--	--	--	--	--	--	--	--	Z
AMERICAN CONTINENTAL INS CO	TN	B	151.9	63.7	1.40	1.09	5.4	8.2	1.8	5.4	5.5	DGLT
AMERICAN CREDITORS LIFE INS CO	DE	U (3)	14.3	9.9	3.50	3.15	8.0	7.3	1.3	10.0	1.5	DF
AMERICAN EQUITY INVEST LIFE INS CO	IA	B	35274.7	2067.5	2.76	1.41	7.6	6.1	8.3	5.7	6.2	I
AMERICAN EQUITY INVESTMENT LIFE NY	NY	B-	224.8	28.4	2.88	1.76	8.1	6.6	4.9	5.3	4.5	DFT
AMERICAN FAMILY LIFE ASR CO OF COLUM	NE	B+	110401.3	9775.5	3.35	2.16	8.7	7.2	6.2	7.6	6.7	IT
AMERICAN FAMILY LIFE ASR CO OF NY	NY	A-	710.2	240.9	5.25	3.68	10.0	8.0	9.3	7.7	7.3	AD
AMERICAN FAMILY LIFE INS CO	WI	A+	5200.5	866.0	4.50	2.38	9.1	6.5	8.6	6.4	7.9	AI
AMERICAN FARM LIFE INS CO	TX	B	3.6	1.7	1.61	1.45	7.7	7.9	7.6	6.9	4.0	AD
AMERICAN FARMERS & RANCHERS LIFE INS	OK	C	24.5	2.0	0.54	0.48	2.8	7.5	2.0	5.5	2.8	ACDT
AMERICAN FEDERATED LIFE INS CO	MS	C	28.1	9.4	2.25	2.03	8.5	8.6	7.8	9.0	4.3	A
AMERICAN FIDELITY ASR CO	OK	B+	4856.7	366.8	1.89	1.09	7.1	6.1	8.3	6.6	6.8	I
AMERICAN FIDELITY LIFE INS CO	FL	B-	437.3	70.1	2.38	1.58	7.9	6.1	6.3	5.8	5.3	DI
AMERICAN FINANCIAL SECURITY L I C	MO	D	5.5	4.4	2.77	2.49	9.2	7.8	2.0	7.5	1.6	DFGT
AMERICAN GENERAL LIFE INS CO	TX	B	161296.7	11201.4	3.55	1.79	8.2	5.9	7.0	6.2	5.8	AGIT
AMERICAN HEALTH & LIFE INS CO	TX	B-	996.0	180.7	2.70	1.84	8.3	5.9	6.2	8.3	5.1	T
AMERICAN HERITAGE LIFE INS CO	FL	B	1750.7	341.2	1.09	0.90	6.2	6.3	7.2	6.6	6.1	CI
AMERICAN HOME LIFE INS CO	KS	C-	239.7	19.8	2.16	1.18	7.3	5.6	3.0	4.0	3.2	DIL
AMERICAN HOME LIFE INS CO	AR	E	18.9	0.5	0.20	0.18	0.0	0.0	2.0	0.3	0.0	CIL
AMERICAN INCOME LIFE INS CO	IN	B-	2847.2	226.0	1.33	0.84	5.7	4.7	5.2	3.6	5.3	IL
AMERICAN INDEPENDENT NETWORK INS CO	NY	E	27.6	2.1	0.51	0.46	2.5	1.9	0.7	7.7	0.1	CDF
AMERICAN INTEGRITY LIFE INS CO	AR	U (3)	0.4	0.4	1.23	1.10	7.2	9.2	2.4	10.0	2.6	DFG
AMERICAN LABOR LIFE INS CO	AZ	D	8.6	6.5	3.14	2.83	9.7	7.0	8.9	9.7	2.3	D

See Page 27 for explanation of footnotes and Page 28 for explanation of stability factors.

Arrows denote recent upgrades ▲ or downgrades▼ (see Section VI for explanations)

30

www.weissratings.com

NET PREMIUM ($MIL)	IN-VESTED ASSETS ($MIL)	CASH	CMO & STRUCT. SECS.	OTH.INV. GRADE BONDS	NON-INV. GRADE BONDS	CMMON & PREF. STOCK	MORT IN GOOD STAND.	NON-PERF. MORT.	REAL ESTATE	OTHER INVEST-MENTS	INVEST. IN AFFIL	INSURANCE COMPANY NAME
120.8	162.7	3.5	34.9	46.5	5.2	6.7	0.0	0.0	0.0	3.4	0.0	● 4 EVER LIFE INS CO
82.7	472.9	2.2	20.0	64.9	8.0	4.0	0.0	0.0	0.0	1.1	1.9	● AAA LIFE INS CO
0.1	8.5	1.2	0.0	90.7	0.0	8.2	0.0	0.0	0.0	0.0	0.0	AAA LIFE INS CO OF NY
23.2	813.8	-0.5	14.7	71.5	2.1	2.3	2.2	0.1	0.0	7.7	0.0	● ABILITY INS CO
0.0	5.6	95.6	0.0	4.4	0.0	0.0	0.0	0.0	0.0	0.0	0.0	ACADEME INC
304.9	6,313.7	0.1	28.1	50.9	0.5	6.3	6.8	0.0	0.0	7.4	6.3	● ACCORDIA LIFE & ANNUITY CO
4.3	36.8	0.0	0.0	100.0	0.0	0.0	0.0	0.0	0.0	0.0	0.0	ACE LIFE INS CO
7.3	50.6	0.6	23.1	42.3	0.0	32.6	0.0	0.0	0.0	0.7	2.3	● ADVANCE INS CO OF KS
423.1	2,093.9 (*)	0.0	11.9	61.9	6.4	0.2	11.5	0.0	0.0	6.5	5.0	● AETNA HEALTH & LIFE INS CO
11,772.1	12,957.0 (*)	0.0	12.0	56.6	6.6	0.4	10.1	0.0	2.6	8.6	4.1	● AETNA LIFE INS CO
1,123.4	20,090.0	0.0	1.1	3.1	0.0	95.7	0.0	0.0	0.0	0.0	96.3	AGC LIFE INS CO
0.7	34.1	35.0	0.0	59.3	0.0	5.7	0.0	0.0	0.0	0.0	0.0	ALABAMA LIFE REINS CO INC
108.7	1,322.1	0.8	7.6	71.6	6.0	5.9	0.0	0.0	0.0	8.2	0.1	● ALFA LIFE INS CORP
75.0	21.5	74.8	0.0	25.2	0.0	0.0	0.0	0.0	0.0	0.0	0.0	ALL SAVERS INS CO
0.0	9.7	83.4	0.0	16.6	0.0	0.0	0.0	0.0	0.0	0.0	0.0	ALL SAVERS LIFE INS CO OF CA
0.0	13.1	0.5	0.0	99.5	0.0	0.0	0.0	0.0	0.0	0.0	0.0	ALLIANZ LIFE & ANNUITY CO
11,364.6	73,953.4 (*)	0.0	17.0	66.2	1.9	2.2	8.3	0.0	0.1	0.7	3.6	● ALLIANZ LIFE INS CO OF NORTH AMERICA
241.3	643.0	0.3	25.4	72.7	0.6	0.0	0.0	0.0	0.0	0.1	0.0	● ALLIANZ LIFE INS CO OF NY
0.0	0.4	100.0	0.0	0.0	0.0	0.0	0.0	0.0	0.0	0.0	0.0	ALLIED FINANCIAL INS CO
0.0	10.6	8.4	0.0	91.7	0.0	0.0	0.0	0.0	0.0	0.0	0.0	ALLSTATE ASR CO
-10,210.2	41,914.5	0.0	12.2	56.6	7.1	3.3	11.8	0.0	0.1	8.5	3.7	● ALLSTATE LIFE INS CO
111.1	5,918.8	0.0	12.0	69.7	4.1	3.6	8.1	0.0	0.0	2.8	0.0	● ALLSTATE LIFE INS CO OF NEW YORK
3.0	5.7	14.2	20.0	54.2	0.0	0.0	0.0	0.0	0.0	11.6	0.0	AMALGAMATED LIFE & HEALTH INS CO
52.2	85.6	2.3	26.3	71.2	0.1	0.0	0.0	0.0	0.0	0.1	0.0	● AMALGAMATED LIFE INS CO
59.3	428.9	5.5	9.0	64.0	1.2	0.9	8.3	0.0	8.6	2.3	0.0	● AMERICAN BANKERS LIFE ASR CO OF FL
14.6	79.4	0.5	8.6	67.2	1.3	2.6	14.6	0.7	2.0	2.6	0.0	AMERICAN BENEFIT LIFE INS CO
10.5	59.4	3.5	1.1	85.2	6.1	2.1	1.3	0.0	0.8	0.0	0.0	AMERICAN CENTURY LIFE INS CO
0.1	0.6	10.1	15.2	47.2	4.2	23.4	0.0	0.0	0.0	0.0	0.0	AMERICAN CENTURY LIFE INS CO TX
--	--	--	--	--	--	--	--	--	--	--	--	AMERICAN CLASSIC REINS CO
--	--	--	--	--	--	--	--	--	--	--	--	AMERICAN COMMUNITY MUT INS CO
281.0	116.7 (*)	0.0	11.4	95.2	0.7	0.0	0.0	0.0	0.0	0.0	0.0	● AMERICAN CONTINENTAL INS CO
0.0	14.2	8.2	0.0	82.5	0.0	9.3	0.0	0.0	0.0	0.0	0.0	AMERICAN CREDITORS LIFE INS CO
2,813.7	31,857.5	-0.1	17.9	68.0	2.1	0.4	9.1	0.0	0.0	1.9	0.4	● AMERICAN EQUITY INVEST LIFE INS CO
0.4	222.9	0.3	17.6	80.8	0.4	0.0	0.0	0.0	0.0	1.0	0.0	● AMERICAN EQUITY INVESTMENT LIFE NY
14,860.8	105,997.9	0.2	4.7	89.8	3.3	0.7	0.0	0.0	0.2	0.7	0.8	● AMERICAN FAMILY LIFE ASR CO OF COLUM
219.7	588.4	-0.5	1.0	98.2	0.9	0.0	0.0	0.0	0.0	0.4	0.0	● AMERICAN FAMILY LIFE ASR CO OF NY
254.3	4,646.4	0.4	22.0	57.0	4.5	2.2	9.1	0.0	0.0	4.8	0.0	● AMERICAN FAMILY LIFE INS CO
0.4	3.1	7.6	3.3	84.8	3.2	0.0	0.0	0.0	0.0	1.1	0.0	AMERICAN FARM LIFE INS CO
1.5	22.6	8.5	11.0	80.1	0.0	0.0	0.0	0.0	0.0	0.4	0.0	AMERICAN FARMERS & RANCHERS LIFE INS
10.0	23.2	6.8	6.8	86.4	0.0	0.0	0.0	0.0	0.0	0.0	0.0	AMERICAN FEDERATED LIFE INS CO
612.2	3,918.7	3.1	22.7	61.9	1.3	0.7	8.7	0.0	0.3	1.2	0.4	● AMERICAN FIDELITY ASR CO
8.4	438.5	0.9	0.0	78.8	0.3	5.3	5.8	0.0	7.7	1.2	8.2	● AMERICAN FIDELITY LIFE INS CO
2.9	4.7	3.7	0.0	87.3	0.0	0.1	0.0	0.0	8.9	0.0	0.0	AMERICAN FINANCIAL SECURITY L I C
10,612.4	119,021.7 (*)	-0.2	28.4	48.4	5.1	0.9	6.3	0.0	0.2	8.0	6.6	● AMERICAN GENERAL LIFE INS CO
157.2	895.5	3.2	16.7	72.7	3.4	3.9	0.0	0.0	0.0	0.3	2.3	● AMERICAN HEALTH & LIFE INS CO
562.2	1,580.9	0.0	5.3	50.1	1.1	15.5	7.5	0.0	2.3	18.8	12.3	● AMERICAN HERITAGE LIFE INS CO
17.8	226.4	2.0	27.6	54.5	2.9	2.1	4.5	0.0	0.5	5.9	0.0	AMERICAN HOME LIFE INS CO
1.7	18.1	1.4	0.0	65.7	1.8	16.9	6.3	0.0	7.1	0.9	0.0	AMERICAN HOME LIFE INS CO
557.7	2,411.6	0.0	3.5	80.5	4.2	3.6	0.0	0.0	0.0	7.3	3.6	● AMERICAN INCOME LIFE INS CO
2.0	26.5	1.5	9.0	89.5	0.0	0.0	0.0	0.0	0.0	0.0	0.0	AMERICAN INDEPENDENT NETWORK INS CO
0.0	0.4	49.8	0.0	50.2	0.0	0.0	0.0	0.0	0.0	0.0	0.0	AMERICAN INTEGRITY LIFE INS CO
1.9	7.7	53.5	0.0	32.1	0.0	13.4	0.0	0.0	0.0	1.0	0.0	AMERICAN LABOR LIFE INS CO

● Bullets denote a more detailed analysis is available in Section II.
(*) Asset category percentages do not add up to 100%

INSURANCE COMPANY NAME	DOM. STATE	RATING	TOTAL ASSETS ($MIL)	CAPITAL & SURPLUS ($MIL)	RISK ADJUSTED CAPITAL RATIO 1	RISK ADJUSTED CAPITAL RATIO 2	CAPITAL-IZATION INDEX (PTS)	INVEST. SAFETY INDEX (PTS)	PROFIT-ABILITY INDEX (PTS)	LIQUIDITY INDEX (PTS)	STAB. INDEX (PTS)	STABILITY FACTO
AMERICAN LIFE & ACC INS CO OF KY	KY	C	362.5	99.9	2.11	1.27	7.4	2.3	4.9	4.3	3.9	DIL
AMERICAN LIFE & ANNUITY CO	AR	D+	48.6	3.8	0.68	0.60	3.8	1.2	4.4	4.3	2.6	CDIL
AMERICAN LIFE & SECURITY CORP	AZ	E	17.8	3.3	0.88	0.61	4.0	4.7	1.1	4.9	0.2	CDILT
AMERICAN LIFE INS CO	DE	C	7622.5	2719.6	0.82	0.77	5.2	3.3	3.5	7.0	2.8	CFIT
AMERICAN MATURITY LIFE INS CO	CT	B	61.9	47.5	6.59	5.93	10.0	9.6	7.5	7.0	5.9	AGT
AMERICAN MEDICAL & LIFE INS CO	NY	E-	7.5	-1.3	-0.03	-0.03	0.0	9.6	0.5	6.2	0.0	CFT
AMERICAN MEMORIAL LIFE INS CO	SD	B-	2635.4	115.6	1.55	0.78	5.8	3.6	5.8	5.6	4.9	CI
AMERICAN MODERN LIFE INS CO	OH	B	49.0	27.2	1.94	1.81	8.2	8.0	2.6	8.4	4.2	DFT
AMERICAN NATIONAL INS CO	TX	B	18049.9	2843.0	1.33	1.08	7.1	5.3	7.8	6.5	6.1	FI
AMERICAN NATIONAL LIFE INS CO OF NY	NY	B	157.1	12.6	1.42	1.22	7.3	3.8	2.0	5.1	5.8	DEGII
AMERICAN NATIONAL LIFE INS CO OF TX	TX	B-	135.8	38.2	4.23	3.09	10.0	7.1	2.6	6.8	5.1	
AMERICAN PHOENIX LIFE & REASSUR CO	CT	U (3)	18.1	15.4	4.70	4.23	8.0	8.9	3.1	10.0	4.6	DT
AMERICAN PIONEER LIFE INS CO	FL	D+	76.9	11.7	1.27	0.90	6.2	7.5	1.1	6.6	2.4	FT
AMERICAN PROGRESSIVE L&H I C OF NY	NY	B	232.1	121.2	1.52	1.19	6.8	7.4	6.4	5.0	5.2	ADFT
AMERICAN PUBLIC LIFE INS CO	OK	B	82.5	23.3	2.05	1.49	7.7	7.8	8.1	7.1	6.3	T
AMERICAN REPUBLIC CORP INS CO	NE	B	26.3	8.4	1.98	1.78	8.0	8.8	4.2	6.9	5.4	
AMERICAN REPUBLIC INS CO	IA	A-	797.6	461.4	5.18	3.86	10.0	7.4	9.2	6.9	6.9	GT
AMERICAN RETIREMENT LIFE INS CO	OH	B-	56.5	31.3	2.17	1.93	8.4	8.3	2.4	7.7	3.7	DGT
AMERICAN SAVINGS LIFE INS CO	AZ	C	49.8	14.8	1.89	1.15	7.2	2.4	8.6	7.2	3.6	DGIT
AMERICAN SERVICE LIFE INS CO	AR	U (3)	0.8	0.8	2.24	2.01	8.5	9.8	9.2	9.3	8.5	D
AMERICAN UNDERWRITERS LIFE INS CO	AZ	D+	81.8	10.3	0.60	0.42	2.0	2.4	2.1	2.7	2.0	CDFII
AMERICAN UNITED LIFE INS CO	IN	B+	22778.8	1003.5	3.27	1.65	8.0	6.1	7.8	7.5	6.6	I
AMERICAN-AMICABLE LIFE INS CO OF TX	TX	C	272.0	86.0	1.39	1.22	7.3	6.2	2.4	6.4	4.1	ADT
AMERICO FINANCIAL LIFE & ANNUITY INS	TX	B-	3871.0	435.4	1.79	1.04	7.1	4.8	7.8	6.3	5.3	AGI
AMERITAS LIFE INS CORP	NE	B (1)	9678.1	1557.0	1.33	1.15	7.2	3.8	7.1	6.9	6.1	I
AMERITAS LIFE INS CORP OF NY	NY	B-	1157.3	82.9	2.26	1.21	7.3	6.3	1.8	4.2	3.6	FGLT
AMICA LIFE INS CO	RI	B	1196.2	266.8	4.88	2.79	9.7	7.0	2.9	6.7	5.6	
ANNUITY INVESTORS LIFE INS CO	OH	B	2963.6	220.3	2.87	1.44	7.7	6.5	8.5	6.1	6.2	A
ANTHEM LIFE & DISABILITY INS CO	NY	A-	23.3	19.9	5.28	4.75	10.0	8.9	6.6	9.3	5.6	AT
ANTHEM LIFE INS CO	IN	A-	559.7	98.1	2.13	1.48	7.7	7.6	7.3	6.3	7.1	A
ARKANSAS BANKERS LIFE INS CO	AR	D+	3.3	1.7	1.50	1.35	7.5	9.4	2.4	9.5	2.6	FT
ASSOCIATED MUTUAL	MI	D	10.7	7.7	2.28	2.05	8.6	8.9	1.8	6.3	2.2	DFT
ASSURITY LIFE INS CO	NE	B+	2452.3	307.9	3.21	1.71	8.1	5.5	6.9	5.8	6.6	IL
ATHENE ANNUITY & LIFE ASR CO	DE	C-	11023.3	1134.1	0.91	0.70	4.6	3.6	2.3	6.5	3.0	CFIT
ATHENE ANNUITY & LIFE ASR CO OF NY	NY	C	3420.4	176.8	1.43	0.66	5.6	2.3	5.2	10.0	2.8	CFIT
ATHENE ANNUITY & LIFE CO	IA	C+	43427.5	1013.0	1.11	0.60	4.0	2.9	5.1	5.7	3.1	CFIT
ATHENE LIFE INS CO	DE	U (3)	195.8	18.9	1.96	1.76	8.0	6.5	1.8	5.8	3.0	DE
ATHENE LIFE INS CO OF NEW YORK	NY	C	1744.3	74.8	1.94	0.91	4.0	3.8	1.3	6.7	3.5	FIT
ATLANTA LIFE INS CO	GA	D	48.7	13.8	1.35	0.96	6.7	6.3	2.0	1.6	1.6	CDFII
ATLANTIC COAST LIFE INS CO	SC	C+	127.4	12.8	1.60	1.44	7.7	4.4	4.6	6.0	4.7	I
AURIGEN REINS CO OF AMERICA	AR	D	25.1	21.0	5.76	5.18	10.0	9.1	1.9	6.8	2.2	DFGT
AURORA NATIONAL LIFE ASR CO	CA	B	3103.6	316.9	4.06	2.12	8.7	7.2	5.6	7.6	5.8	A
AUTO CLUB LIFE INS CO	MI	C+	536.5	65.5	1.21	0.84	5.7	5.7	2.0	5.3	4.5	
AUTO-OWNERS LIFE INS CO	MI	A	3592.1	347.6	2.17	1.17	7.3	5.3	5.3	6.0	6.2	IT
AUTOMOBILE CLUB OF SOUTHERN CA INS	CA	B	810.5	67.1	1.67	0.93	6.4	4.4	2.9	3.7	5.7	CIL
AXA CORPORATE SOLUTIONS LIFE REINS	DE	B-	491.4	425.6	7.21	4.38	10.0	4.9	6.4	9.8	3.8	DFIT
AXA EQUITABLE LIFE & ANNUITY CO	CO	B-	472.1	27.7	1.14	0.59	5.2	7.6	3.2	4.8	4.3	CGLT
AXA EQUITABLE LIFE INS CO	NY	B	161704.9	5428.7	2.11	1.27	7.4	6.6	6.2	6.5	6.2	
BALBOA LIFE INS CO	CA	A-	58.9	49.6	2.39	2.28	8.9	7.9	8.2	9.6	5.5	ADT
BALBOA LIFE INS CO OF NY	NY	B	19.5	18.9	5.51	4.96	10.0	8.9	5.9	10.0	5.9	T
BALTIMORE LIFE INS CO	MD	B	1129.9	76.2	2.05	1.07	7.1	5.4	4.7	3.6	5.6	IL
BANKERS CONSECO LIFE INS CO	NY	D	203.3	51.9	4.60	3.65	10.0	6.5	6.2	6.4	1.8	DIT

See Page 27 for explanation of footnotes and Page 28 for explanation of stability factors.

Arrows denote recent upgrades ▲ or downgrades▼ (see Section VI for explanations)

32

www.weissratings.com

NET PREMIUM ($MIL)	IN-VESTED ASSETS ($MIL)	CASH	CMO & STRUCT. SECS.	OTH.INV. GRADE BONDS	NON-INV. GRADE BONDS	CMMON & PREF. STOCK	MORT IN GOOD STAND.	NON-PERF. MORT.	REAL ESTATE	OTHER INVEST-MENTS	INVEST. IN AFFIL	INSURANCE COMPANY NAME
78.7	240.6	0.6	2.5	24.5	0.0	65.0	0.0	0.0	7.4	0.1	0.0	● AMERICAN LIFE & ACC INS CO OF KY
3.3	47.1	3.5	48.0	33.7	10.5	3.7	0.0	0.0	0.5	0.1	0.0	AMERICAN LIFE & ANNUITY CO
3.1	14.3	4.2	0.0	71.9	0.0	13.0	4.5	0.0	3.9	2.6	12.5	AMERICAN LIFE & SECURITY CORP
1,041.2	5,713.3	8.7	0.2	17.1	15.8	53.7	0.0	0.0	0.2	4.3	56.1	● AMERICAN LIFE INS CO
0.0	48.2	0.0	0.0	100.0	0.0	0.0	0.0	0.0	0.0	0.0	0.0	● AMERICAN MATURITY LIFE INS CO
5.1	7.1	29.4	0.0	70.7	0.0	0.0	0.0	0.0	0.0	0.0	0.0	AMERICAN MEDICAL & LIFE INS CO
377.6	2,386.5 (*)	0.0	10.2	68.9	7.8	0.9	7.6	0.0	0.0	2.5	0.0	● AMERICAN MEMORIAL LIFE INS CO
4.0	49.9	1.2	6.8	66.6	0.0	25.3	0.0	0.0	0.0	0.1	25.3	● AMERICAN MODERN LIFE INS CO
1,010.3	16,627.0	-0.1	2.4	55.0	1.8	11.2	19.4	0.0	1.9	7.5	17.1	● AMERICAN NATIONAL INS CO
27.2	134.5	0.6	0.0	95.9	0.4	1.3	1.8	0.0	0.0	0.0	0.0	AMERICAN NATIONAL LIFE INS CO OF NY
29.1	130.2	-0.8	2.9	93.1	1.5	0.0	0.0	0.0	0.0	3.3	0.0	● AMERICAN NATIONAL LIFE INS CO OF TX
0.0	17.9	19.3	8.8	71.9	0.0	0.0	0.0	0.0	0.0	0.0	0.0	AMERICAN PHOENIX LIFE & REASSUR CO
32.9	65.0 (*)	0.0	57.8	44.2	2.7	0.0	0.0	0.0	0.0	0.1	0.0	AMERICAN PIONEER LIFE INS CO
306.9	197.6 (*)	0.0	31.9	63.2	1.4	2.0	0.0	0.0	0.0	6.8	0.0	● AMERICAN PROGRESSIVE L&H I C OF NY
38.8	75.4	7.9	27.9	53.3	1.1	2.2	5.3	0.0	1.3	1.1	0.0	AMERICAN PUBLIC LIFE INS CO
0.0	12.7	10.6	12.1	77.3	0.0	0.0	0.0	0.0	0.0	0.0	0.0	AMERICAN REPUBLIC CORP INS CO
224.1	712.7	0.8	25.9	63.2	1.8	6.2	0.0	0.0	0.7	1.5	4.7	● AMERICAN REPUBLIC INS CO
82.2	17.8	-1.8	0.0	100.7	0.0	0.0	0.0	0.0	0.0	1.1	0.0	● AMERICAN RETIREMENT LIFE INS CO
1.5	47.1	11.3	0.0	6.5	0.0	1.2	64.4	4.3	9.5	2.9	0.8	AMERICAN SAVINGS LIFE INS CO
0.4	0.7	57.5	0.0	36.8	0.0	5.8	0.0	0.0	0.0	0.0	5.8	AMERICAN SERVICE LIFE INS CO
5.6	82.3	2.2	2.3	56.9	10.0	19.4	5.3	0.5	0.8	2.6	10.3	AMERICAN UNDERWRITERS LIFE INS CO
2,368.3	9,818.5	0.1	16.2	61.8	3.3	0.7	14.1	0.0	0.6	3.0	0.0	● AMERICAN UNITED LIFE INS CO
30.3	242.2 (*)	-1.9	1.4	63.2	0.2	21.8	4.2	0.0	1.1	8.6	21.5	● AMERICAN-AMICABLE LIFE INS CO OF TX
302.6	3,358.2 (*)	0.2	33.4	39.3	4.6	11.4	7.5	0.0	0.0	2.3	3.6	● AMERICO FINANCIAL LIFE & ANNUITY INS
858.6	4,100.9	0.0	8.6	40.0	1.5	30.6	12.9	0.3	1.3	4.7	24.1	● AMERITAS LIFE INS CORP
67.4	1,045.8	0.2	17.1	67.4	1.0	0.0	12.0	0.0	0.0	2.3	0.0	● AMERITAS LIFE INS CORP OF NY
46.0	1,092.0	0.1	38.4	55.4	0.4	4.8	0.0	0.0	0.0	1.0	0.0	● AMICA LIFE INS CO
171.7	2,199.2	0.0	34.1	60.4	1.9	0.3	0.0	0.0	0.0	2.7	0.0	● ANNUITY INVESTORS LIFE INS CO
4.5	22.2	42.6	0.0	57.4	0.0	0.0	0.0	0.0	0.0	0.0	0.0	ANTHEM LIFE & DISABILITY INS CO
266.8	521.5 (*)	3.5	22.6	63.1	0.2	0.3	0.0	0.0	0.0	1.4	0.0	● ANTHEM LIFE INS CO
0.6	3.5 (*)	87.0	0.0	0.0	0.0	4.4	0.0	0.0	0.0	0.0	0.0	ARKANSAS BANKERS LIFE INS CO
6.4	8.9	7.2	0.0	88.1	1.1	3.6	0.0	0.0	0.0	0.0	3.6	ASSOCIATED MUTUAL
140.5	2,353.7	0.3	16.0	58.4	1.0	2.4	13.1	0.2	2.9	5.8	0.0	● ASSURITY LIFE INS CO
96.4	8,290.8	0.6	42.7	16.4	4.3	13.1	9.0	0.0	0.0	13.1	21.7	● ATHENE ANNUITY & LIFE ASR CO
9.2	3,468.1	0.3	62.4	19.3	8.2	1.1	2.3	0.0	0.0	6.5	0.7	● ATHENE ANNUITY & LIFE ASR CO OF NY
283.9	41,593.4	0.1	12.7	66.6	3.1	0.9	11.6	0.0	0.0	4.0	2.2	● ATHENE ANNUITY & LIFE CO
0.0	180.5	9.0	60.9	27.3	0.0	2.8	0.0	0.0	0.0	0.0	0.0	ATHENE LIFE INS CO
1.6	1,657.2 (*)	0.6	2.4	84.4	0.7	0.2	8.5	0.0	0.0	2.0	0.0	● ATHENE LIFE INS CO OF NEW YORK
9.4	17.7	16.3	3.4	75.6	0.0	4.3	0.0	0.0	0.0	0.4	0.0	ATLANTA LIFE INS CO
18.3	112.0	0.3	32.5	53.7	0.9	0.4	7.4	0.0	3.3	1.5	0.0	ATLANTIC COAST LIFE INS CO
1.0	21.2	9.1	7.0	83.9	0.0	0.0	0.0	0.0	0.0	0.0	0.0	AURIGEN REINS CO OF AMERICA
0.5	3,101.6	0.6	6.6	84.8	2.5	0.0	0.0	0.0	0.0	5.5	0.0	● AURORA NATIONAL LIFE ASR CO
82.5	471.9	0.1	18.5	61.9	9.6	6.0	0.0	0.0	0.0	4.0	5.8	● AUTO CLUB LIFE INS CO
193.3	3,144.4	0.1	24.6	61.4	0.6	2.4	5.4	0.1	4.4	1.0	0.0	● AUTO-OWNERS LIFE INS CO
140.5	696.7	0.0	20.3	70.4	8.6	0.1	0.0	0.0	0.0	0.5	0.0	● AUTOMOBILE CLUB OF SOUTHERN CA INS
-534.4	955.5	0.8	0.9	96.1	2.2	0.0	0.0	0.0	0.0	0.0	0.0	● AXA CORPORATE SOLUTIONS LIFE REINS
2.4	476.9	0.1	3.5	36.1	0.4	0.0	0.0	0.0	0.0	59.9	0.0	● AXA EQUITABLE LIFE & ANNUITY CO
9,035.9	42,431.6 (*)	0.3	5.3	60.9	3.1	2.8	14.3	0.0	0.0	11.9	5.8	● AXA EQUITABLE LIFE INS CO
4.7	55.8	15.6	7.8	43.1	0.0	33.4	0.0	0.0	0.0	0.0	33.4	BALBOA LIFE INS CO
0.1	19.0	15.2	12.1	72.7	0.0	0.0	0.0	0.0	0.0	0.0	0.0	BALBOA LIFE INS CO OF NY
100.9	1,041.8	0.4	3.9	78.7	3.3	0.3	5.4	0.0	1.0	7.1	0.8	● BALTIMORE LIFE INS CO
35.2	353.6	3.0	5.8	88.4	1.8	0.0	0.0	0.0	0.0	1.0	0.0	● BANKERS CONSECO LIFE INS CO

● Bullets denote a more detailed analysis is available in Section II.
(*) Asset category percentages do not add up to 100%

INSURANCE COMPANY NAME	DOM. STATE	RATING	TOTAL ASSETS ($MIL)	CAPITAL & SURPLUS ($MIL)	RISK ADJUSTED CAPITAL RATIO 1	RISK ADJUSTED CAPITAL RATIO 2	CAPITAL-IZATION INDEX (PTS)	INVEST. SAFETY INDEX (PTS)	PROFIT-ABILITY INDEX (PTS)	LIQUIDITY INDEX (PTS)	STAB. INDEX (PTS)	STABIL FACTO
BANKERS FIDELITY ASR CO	GA	U (3)	3.4	3.4	3.08	2.77	8.0	9.3	6.9	10.0	5.6	DT
BANKERS FIDELITY LIFE INS CO	GA	B	138.7	33.9	1.42	1.00	7.0	5.7	8.8	5.6	5.7	DI
BANKERS LIFE & CAS CO	IL	D+	16389.4	1116.4	2.04	1.05	7.1	4.1	9.2	5.4	2.7	AI
BANKERS LIFE INS CO	FL	C+	324.2	22.5	2.04	0.88	4.0	2.8	7.4	7.3	3.1	AFGIT
BANKERS LIFE INS CO OF AMERICA	TX	D	5.2	0.7	0.48	0.43	2.2	4.7	2.7	5.4	1.9	CDFI
BANKERS LIFE OF LOUISIANA	LA	C	13.2	4.2	1.39	1.06	7.1	8.5	3.0	7.6	4.1	A
BANNER LIFE INS CO	MD	D	1721.0	297.9	1.15	0.87	6.0	5.9	1.9	6.8	1.4	GT
BENEFICIAL LIFE INS CO	UT	B	2942.3	608.2	5.49	2.96	9.9	7.1	4.7	6.0	5.5	FT
BERKLEY LIFE & HEALTH INS CO	IA	B-	198.6	105.0	5.75	4.45	10.0	8.6	8.3	7.5	5.2	AD
BERKSHIRE HATHAWAY LIFE INS CO OF NE	NE	C+	13999.8	3152.9	1.46	1.23	7.3	6.1	6.4	10.0	3.3	CIT
BERKSHIRE LIFE INS CO OF AMERICA	MA	A	3640.3	604.5	8.67	4.24	10.0	6.5	8.4	8.9	6.4	AIT
▲ BEST LIFE & HEALTH INS CO	TX	B-	15.6	10.8	1.49	1.21	7.3	8.4	6.9	6.1	4.9	DF
BEST MERIDIAN INS CO	FL	B-	272.0	53.3	1.87	1.21	7.3	6.5	5.3	7.2	5.3	DT
BEVERLY HILLS LIFE INS CO	AZ	U	--	--	--	--	--	--	--	--	--	Z
BLUE CROSS BLUE SHIELD OF KANSAS INC	KS	B	1592.7	777.0	2.13	1.53	7.8	4.0	7.0	6.6	6.3	I
BLUE SHIELD OF CALIFORNIA L&H INS CO	CA	A-	841.2	441.4	1.74	1.38	5.1	8.0	5.6	1.1	5.5	FL
BLUE SPIRIT INS CO	VT	U	--	--	--	--	--	--	--	--	--	Z
BLUEBONNET LIFE INS CO	MS	B+	54.6	49.4	7.24	6.52	10.0	8.1	9.3	9.7	6.5	AD
BOSTON MUTUAL LIFE INS CO	MA	B+	1230.4	155.6	2.16	1.41	7.6	6.8	6.3	4.7	6.4	IL
BROOKE LIFE INS CO	MI	C+	4937.1	4543.9	1.19	1.06	7.1	1.2	9.0	9.2	4.7	CIT
CALPERS LONG-TERM CARE PROGRAM		U	--	--	--	--	--	--	--	--	--	Z
CANADA LIFE ASSURANCE CO-US BRANCH	MI	C	4444.2	151.4	1.25	0.66	5.4	5.6	2.9	5.5	4.0	CGT
CANYON STATE LIFE INS CO	AZ	U (3)	1.8	1.0	1.68	1.52	7.8	3.7	5.7	10.0	5.7	DIT
▼ CAPITAL RESERVE LIFE INS CO	MO	E+	1.4	1.4	2.60	2.17	8.0	8.3	2.0	6.9	0.7	AFT
▲ CAPITOL LIFE INS CO	TX	C	210.6	22.7	2.47	1.38	7.6	4.5	3.0	6.5	3.6	ADFIT
CAPITOL SECURITY LIFE INS CO	TX	D-	4.6	1.3	0.91	0.82	5.6	9.3	2.2	9.2	0.9	CDF
CAREAMERICA LIFE INS CO	CA	B	29.3	25.7	6.44	5.80	10.0	8.2	6.9	9.6	4.9	DT
CARIBBEAN AMERICAN LIFE ASR CO	PR	B	41.9	13.3	2.13	1.77	8.2	8.3	5.5	8.9	5.3	AT
CARLISLE LIFE INS CO	AZ	U	--	--	--	--	--	--	--	--	--	Z
CASS COUNTY LIFE INS CO	TX	E (3)	3.2	0.3	0.37	0.34	1.1	3.3	5.7	7.2	0.1	CDFI
CATAMARAN INS OF OHIO	OH	C+	69.7	12.0	5.51	4.96	8.0	8.8	7.1	10.0	4.7	G
CATERPILLAR LIFE INS CO	MO	U (3)	158.2	61.6	4.57	2.60	8.0	4.9	4.9	10.0	6.2	DFI
CATHOLIC FINANCIAL LIFE	WI	U	--	--	--	--	--	--	--	--	--	Z
CBI INS CO	AZ	U	--	--	--	--	--	--	--	--	--	Z
CELTIC INS CO	IL	C	116.9	27.5	1.18	0.93	6.4	8.3	2.0	6.4	4.2	AFGT
CENSTAT LIFE ASR CO	AZ	C (5)	--	--	--	--	--	--	--	--	--	Z
CENTRAL RESERVE LIFE INS CO	OH	C+	25.1	22.7	1.49	1.40	7.6	4.1	7.2	8.0	3.2	DGIT
CENTRAL SECURITY LIFE INS CO	TX	B-	71.2	7.5	0.98	0.88	6.0	7.3	6.9	5.9	4.8	DF
CENTRAL STATES H & L CO OF OMAHA	NE	A-	407.1	119.1	3.90	2.77	9.7	5.8	7.9	8.0	6.9	I
CENTRAL UNITED LIFE INS CO	AR	C	303.7	78.5	0.60	0.55	3.4	5.2	6.7	6.6	3.4	CDF
CENTRE LIFE INS CO	MA	B-	1909.7	101.8	4.21	2.63	9.4	6.8	8.7	8.7	4.9	AFT
CENTURION LIFE INS CO	IA	D (2)	1211.1	406.3	4.98	2.92	9.9	6.5	1.5	6.5	1.5	GIT
CENTURY LIFE ASR CO	OK	D+	12.6	6.5	2.59	2.33	9.0	5.5	7.7	7.7	2.4	ADIT
▲ CHAMPIONS LIFE INS CO	TX	C-	35.2	3.9	0.35	0.30	0.6	5.3	6.8	6.4	1.6	CFG
CHARTER NATIONAL LIFE INS CO	IL	A-	133.2	11.6	3.71	3.34	8.0	9.6	8.4	7.0	5.9	A
CHEROKEE NATIONAL LIFE INS CO	GA	B	20.6	15.7	4.46	4.01	10.0	7.7	8.5	7.8	4.8	DFT
CHESAPEAKE LIFE INS CO	OK	C+	75.0	43.7	1.39	1.15	6.3	8.9	1.8	7.8	4.4	DGT
CHRISTIAN FIDELITY LIFE INS CO	TX	B-	79.6	35.2	2.87	2.12	8.7	7.8	7.1	7.1	5.3	AD
CHURCH LIFE INS CORP	NY	B-	287.0	50.5	3.60	1.93	8.4	6.0	7.5	6.1	5.2	D
CICA LIFE INS CO OF AMERICA	CO	C-	749.7	51.8	0.65	0.53	3.2	5.5	2.9	6.1	3.0	CD
CIGNA ARBOR LIFE INS CO	CT	C+	20.8	18.3	3.40	3.06	4.0	9.2	4.1	7.0	3.4	DFT
CIGNA HEALTH & LIFE INS CO	CT	B	5710.7	2394.6	1.89	1.48	7.1	3.7	9.6	6.5	5.6	AGIT

See Page 27 for explanation of footnotes and Page 28 for explanation of stability factors.

Arrows denote recent upgrades ▲ or downgrades▼ (see Section VI for explanations)

34

www.weissratings.com

NET PREMIUM ($MIL)	IN-VESTED ASSETS ($MIL)	% OF INVESTED ASSETS IN:									INVEST. IN AFFIL	INSURANCE COMPANY NAME
		CASH	CMO & STRUCT. SECS.	OTH.INV. GRADE BONDS	NON-INV. GRADE BONDS	CMMON & PREF. STOCK	MORT IN GOOD STAND.	NON-PERF. MORT.	REAL ESTATE	OTHER INVEST-MENTS		
0.0	3.4	5.7	0.0	94.3	0.0	0.0	0.0	0.0	0.0	0.1	0.0	BANKERS FIDELITY ASR CO
76.4	129.5	1.2	1.1	78.1	8.2	8.3	0.0	0.0	0.0	3.1	2.6 •	BANKERS FIDELITY LIFE INS CO
1,772.9	15,306.6	1.2	20.6	64.2	6.0	0.8	5.3	0.0	0.0	1.0	0.6 •	BANKERS LIFE & CAS CO
74.1	238.9	1.2	14.1	17.0	0.8	0.1	0.0	0.0	0.4	66.5	0.0	BANKERS LIFE INS CO
0.7	4.9	2.6	0.0	66.9	0.0	1.7	0.0	0.0	19.5	9.5	0.0	BANKERS LIFE INS CO OF AMERICA
9.6	12.4	0.2	6.0	87.6	0.0	6.0	0.0	0.0	0.0	0.0	0.0	BANKERS LIFE OF LOUISIANA
164.9	1,358.1	-1.0	12.0	66.4	6.1	14.4	0.0	0.0	0.0	2.1	14.4 •	BANNER LIFE INS CO
28.9	2,920.3	0.6	29.9	62.9	2.3	0.3	0.0	0.0	0.0	4.0	0.0 •	BENEFICIAL LIFE INS CO
112.5	158.9	7.5	25.0	67.2	0.3	0.0	0.0	0.0	0.0	0.0	0.0 •	BERKLEY LIFE & HEALTH INS CO
896.8	10,793.2	21.6	6.5	42.5	2.6	22.9	0.0	0.0	0.0	4.0	25.9 •	BERKSHIRE HATHAWAY LIFE INS CO OF NE
85.4	3,335.9	0.2	1.5	88.2	2.6	0.0	7.0	0.0	0.2	0.3	0.0 •	BERKSHIRE LIFE INS CO OF AMERICA
29.5	12.2	3.1	0.2	80.4	1.1	15.2	0.0	0.0	0.0	0.0	0.0	BEST LIFE & HEALTH INS CO
101.7	220.6	15.2	19.0	39.5	1.7	0.4	13.0	0.0	7.7	2.7	0.4 •	BEST MERIDIAN INS CO
--	--	--	--	--	--	--	--	--	--	--	--	BEVERLY HILLS LIFE INS CO
1,352.1	1,431.1 (*)	-3.0	15.9	42.8	1.3	35.5	0.0	0.0	2.2	3.0	2.9 •	BLUE CROSS BLUE SHIELD OF KANSAS INC
1,407.2	840.8	0.4	53.1	46.4	0.0	0.0	0.0	0.0	0.0	0.1	0.0 •	BLUE SHIELD OF CALIFORNIA L&H INS CO
--	--	--	--	--	--	--	--	--	--	--	--	BLUE SPIRIT INS CO
3.8	51.2	0.4	32.6	51.3	0.3	0.7	0.0	0.0	0.0	14.6	0.0 •	BLUEBONNET LIFE INS CO
139.8	1,074.4	0.1	5.2	62.7	0.8	3.3	13.5	0.0	0.8	13.6	2.1 •	BOSTON MUTUAL LIFE INS CO
7.2	4,777.7	0.0	1.8	7.0	0.1	91.1	0.0	0.0	0.0	0.0	91.1 •	BROOKE LIFE INS CO
--	--	--	--	--	--	--	--	--	--	--	--	CALPERS LONG-TERM CARE PROGRAM
97.7	3,373.5 (*)	1.1	18.5	62.0	0.7	0.0	6.5	0.0	0.0	8.7	0.0 •	CANADA LIFE ASSURANCE CO-US BRANCH
0.0	1.7 (*)	19.6	0.0	326.3	0.6	23.1	12.1	0.0	8.2	0.0	356.3	CANYON STATE LIFE INS CO
0.0	1.3	5.7	0.0	88.7	0.0	5.6	0.0	0.0	0.0	0.0	5.6	CAPITAL RESERVE LIFE INS CO
5.3	198.5	1.2	2.6	74.2	1.9	2.0	17.3	0.7	0.0	0.2	0.0	CAPITOL LIFE INS CO
0.9	4.1	8.8	0.0	91.2	0.0	0.0	0.0	0.0	0.0	0.0	0.0	CAPITOL SECURITY LIFE INS CO
1.2	24.1	3.5	59.3	37.1	0.0	0.0	0.0	0.0	0.0	0.1	0.0 •	CAREAMERICA LIFE INS CO
7.8	40.8	24.4	7.5	57.2	0.0	11.0	0.0	0.0	0.0	0.0	11.0	CARIBBEAN AMERICAN LIFE ASR CO
--	--	--	--	--	--	--	--	--	--	--	--	CARLISLE LIFE INS CO
0.1	3.2	3.4	0.0	53.2	9.0	5.8	9.5	0.0	0.0	19.7	0.0	CASS COUNTY LIFE INS CO
0.0	8.9	45.9	0.0	50.7	0.0	3.4	0.0	0.0	0.0	0.0	0.0	CATAMARAN INS OF OHIO
0.0	157.5	1.4	26.6	51.7	1.8	18.5	0.0	0.0	0.0	0.0	22.9	CATERPILLAR LIFE INS CO
--	--	--	--	--	--	--	--	--	--	--	--	CATHOLIC FINANCIAL LIFE
--	--	--	--	--	--	--	--	--	--	--	--	CBI INS CO
87.3	72.7 (*)	12.0	8.4	78.2	1.9	0.0	0.0	0.0	0.0	0.9	0.0 •	CELTIC INS CO
--	--	--	--	--	--	--	--	--	--	--	--	CENSTAT LIFE ASR CO
4.2	22.3	0.8	0.0	41.8	0.0	57.5	0.0	0.0	0.0	0.0	57.5	CENTRAL RESERVE LIFE INS CO
1.6	71.7	2.9	58.9	26.7	0.4	5.2	0.4	0.0	0.0	5.7	4.8	CENTRAL SECURITY LIFE INS CO
56.8	377.5	0.6	26.2	43.8	1.5	12.0	4.0	0.0	1.7	10.1	5.6 •	CENTRAL STATES H & L CO OF OMAHA
67.3	250.9	5.2	0.1	41.0	0.4	40.7	2.4	0.0	7.9	2.2	40.7 •	CENTRAL UNITED LIFE INS CO
0.0	1,901.2	0.1	15.8	84.0	0.1	0.0	0.0	0.0	0.0	0.0	0.0 •	CENTRE LIFE INS CO
64.5	1,116.1	1.3	54.9	32.9	7.8	3.1	0.0	0.0	0.0	0.0	0.0 •	CENTURION LIFE INS CO
0.9	12.0	13.8	3.9	71.6	10.3	0.0	0.0	0.4	0.0	0.1	0.0	CENTURY LIFE ASR CO
1.0	34.8	5.4	29.8	31.5	0.1	24.2	1.1	0.0	5.3	2.5	23.6	CHAMPIONS LIFE INS CO
0.0	11.8	2.8	0.0	97.2	0.0	0.0	0.0	0.0	0.0	0.0	0.0	CHARTER NATIONAL LIFE INS CO
1.7	21.4	1.9	5.7	84.1	0.0	0.0	0.0	0.0	7.8	0.5	0.0	CHEROKEE NATIONAL LIFE INS CO
86.3	39.1	-1.1	5.0	96.1	0.0	0.0	0.0	0.0	0.0	0.6	0.0 •	CHESAPEAKE LIFE INS CO
33.1	71.6	0.8	5.5	86.8	1.1	0.2	4.5	0.0	0.6	0.5	0.0 •	CHRISTIAN FIDELITY LIFE INS CO
26.6	281.9	0.2	29.1	60.2	4.7	5.4	0.0	0.0	0.0	0.2	0.0 •	CHURCH LIFE INS CORP
104.5	668.1	3.4	1.6	71.2	1.5	15.4	0.0	0.0	0.3	6.6	9.9 •	CICA LIFE INS CO OF AMERICA
0.0	37.3	0.0	0.0	100.0	0.0	0.0	0.0	0.0	0.0	0.0	0.0	CIGNA ARBOR LIFE INS CO
7,282.9	2,982.6	-2.6	2.2	59.4	9.4	7.8	13.7	0.0	0.0	10.2	15.4 •	CIGNA HEALTH & LIFE INS CO

(*) Asset category percentages do not add up to 100%

INSURANCE COMPANY NAME	DOM. STATE	RATING	TOTAL ASSETS ($MIL)	CAPITAL & SURPLUS ($MIL)	RISK ADJUSTED CAPITAL RATIO 1	RISK ADJUSTED CAPITAL RATIO 2	CAPITAL-IZATION INDEX (PTS)	INVEST. SAFETY INDEX (PTS)	PROFIT-ABILITY INDEX (PTS)	LIQUIDITY INDEX (PTS)	STAB. INDEX (PTS)	STABILI FACTO
CIGNA LIFE INS CO OF NEW YORK	NY	A-	380.6	110.7	3.79	2.38	9.1	6.6	6.4	7.3	7.0	ADI
CIGNA WORLDWIDE INS CO	DE	B	45.8	7.7	1.11	1.00	7.0	7.5	4.7	10.0	4.0	AT
CINCINNATI EQUITABLE LIFE INS CO	OH	C-	84.6	8.9	1.11	0.80	5.4	6.0	4.0	5.9	3.1	D
CINCINNATI LIFE INS CO	OH	B	3853.0	227.6	1.78	0.96	6.7	4.6	2.4	5.4	6.1	IL
CITCO LIFE INS CO	AZ	U	--	--	--	--	--	--	--	--	--	Z
CITIZENS FIDELITY INS CO	AR	C+	65.5	11.1	1.65	1.38	7.6	4.3	7.9	7.0	4.5	DI
CITIZENS NATIONAL LIFE INS CO	TX	C	12.6	2.2	3.01	2.71	9.6	8.6	1.6	6.7	3.5	ADF
CITIZENS SECURITY LIFE INS CO	KY	C	22.5	13.2	1.18	0.74	5.3	2.9	5.7	7.1	4.1	CIT
CLARIA LIFE & HEALTH INS CO	DE	D+ (4)	6.8	1.1	0.60	0.54	3.3	6.4	2.8	8.1	2.5	CEFT
CM LIFE INS CO	CT	B	8612.5	1197.0	2.66	1.62	7.9	5.3	8.9	6.2	6.0	I
CMFG LIFE INS CO	IA	B-	15616.4	1605.7	1.37	1.07	7.1	4.8	7.8	6.6	5.3	I
COLONIAL LIFE & ACCIDENT INS CO	SC	C+	2882.2	570.4	2.83	1.74	8.1	6.2	8.6	6.8	4.5	A
COLONIAL LIFE INS CO OF TX	TX	C-	17.7	13.8	4.28	3.85	10.0	7.5	6.2	8.8	3.3	D
COLONIAL PENN LIFE INS CO	PA	D+	738.8	75.6	1.18	0.68	5.3	3.7	1.9	0.2	2.2	ACFI
COLONIAL SECURITY LIFE INS CO	TX	D+	2.8	1.9	1.99	1.79	8.2	7.3	6.5	7.6	2.6	D
COLORADO BANKERS LIFE INS CO	CO	B+	280.1	30.6	2.58	1.49	7.7	7.2	2.7	5.6	6.5	DIL
COLUMBIAN LIFE INS CO	IL	C+	307.2	35.7	2.11	1.39	7.6	7.5	3.0	4.6	4.5	LR
COLUMBIAN MUTUAL LIFE INS CO	NY	B	1320.1	101.0	1.65	1.07	7.1	6.4	6.5	5.2	4.9	IT
COLUMBUS LIFE INS CO	OH	B-	3326.3	235.4	1.94	1.02	7.0	5.0	2.5	5.3	4.9	I
COMBINED INS CO OF AMERICA	IL	C+	1635.2	378.7	2.26	1.71	8.1	6.8	5.8	7.2	3.4	GT
COMBINED LIFE INS CO OF NEW YORK	NY	B	412.6	63.7	2.08	1.46	7.7	7.7	5.2	7.5	5.8	A
COMMENCEMENT BAY LIFE INS CO	WA	U (3)	7.4	7.2	3.67	3.30	8.0	9.0	8.6	10.0	8.0	D
COMMERCIAL TRAVELERS MUTUAL INS CO	NY	E+	14.9	6.7	1.18	1.06	7.1	8.3	1.6	7.5	0.8	CDFG
COMMONWEALTH ANNUITY & LIFE INS CO	MA	B-	10566.4	1534.1	1.49	1.08	4.0	4.7	6.6	9.1	4.9	AIT
COMMONWEALTH DEALERS LIFE INS CO	VA	U (3)	6.8	5.4	2.95	2.65	9.5	7.0	2.2	10.0	2.1	DT
COMPANION LIFE INS CO	NY	B-	944.6	61.8	2.03	1.06	7.1	4.6	4.1	4.3	5.3	DIL
COMPANION LIFE INS CO	SC	A-	274.9	139.7	2.82	2.21	8.8	5.7	8.7	7.4	7.2	AI
CONCERT HEALTH PLAN INS CO	IL	U (3)	2.0	1.8	1.22	1.10	7.2	9.4	0.8	8.9	1.0	CDFT
CONNECTICUT GENERAL LIFE INS CO	CT	B-	18691.4	3338.0	1.64	1.33	7.5	4.4	8.9	6.1	3.8	AFIT
▲ CONSECO LIFE INS CO	IN	C-	3763.2	215.0	1.52	0.81	5.8	3.7	4.3	0.6	2.6	CFILT
CONSECO LIFE INS CO OF TX	TX	U (3)	1059.9	990.3	0.73	0.65	4.2	1.6	8.0	10.0	3.6	CI
CONSTITUTION LIFE INS CO	TX	C+	316.1	34.3	1.71	1.13	7.2	6.8	2.9	7.3	4.5	ADG
CONSUMERS LIFE INS CO	OH	C	34.5	19.6	1.60	1.25	7.4	9.3	2.0	6.6	3.8	CFT
CONTINENTAL AMERICAN INS CO	SC	B	402.9	133.3	3.24	2.32	9.0	8.5	1.9	7.4	5.7	D
CONTINENTAL ASSURANCE CO	IL	C	2473.9	255.5	4.34	2.19	8.8	6.2	5.3	9.2	2.8	T
CONTINENTAL GENERAL INS CO	OH	C	242.0	24.3	2.63	1.50	7.8	6.0	6.4	6.7	3.5	T
CONTINENTAL LIFE INS CO	PA	D+	21.2	2.2	0.63	0.56	3.5	7.1	2.4	6.1	2.5	CDF
CONTINENTAL LIFE INS CO OF BRENTWOOD	TN	B	240.3	115.8	1.19	1.03	7.0	6.7	2.9	7.0	5.5	CDGI
COOPERATIVA DE SEGUROS DE VIDA DE PR	PR	C-	430.9	13.8	1.13	0.57	5.2	2.5	2.8	3.8	2.9	CIL
COOPERATIVE LIFE INS CO	AR	D	6.7	2.4	1.47	1.32	7.5	5.6	8.2	6.9	2.2	DF
CORVESTA LIFE INS CO	AZ	U (3)	9.2	7.7	3.60	3.24	10.0	9.1	2.1	10.0	2.3	DFT
COTTON STATES LIFE INS CO	GA	A-	330.7	61.0	3.92	2.21	8.8	6.7	7.7	6.1	7.3	DI
COUNTRY INVESTORS LIFE ASR CO	IL	A-	289.8	177.3	15.77	7.77	8.0	8.4	7.7	8.5	7.1	
COUNTRY LIFE INS CO	IL	A+	10573.7	1103.9	2.12	1.38	7.6	5.8	8.3	5.9	7.6	I
CROWN GLOBAL INS CO OF AMERICA	DE	U (3)	1.5	1.5	2.54	2.29	8.0	9.1	4.0	10.0	3.3	DEGT
CSA FRATERNAL LIFE	IL	U	--	--	--	--	--	--	--	--	--	Z
CSI LIFE INS CO	NE	B	17.7	14.6	4.44	4.00	10.0	7.9	5.9	9.1	5.5	AD
DAKOTA CAPITAL LIFE INS CO	ND	D	2.5	1.3	1.66	1.49	7.7	9.6	1.8	9.0	1.5	DEFG
DEARBORN NATIONAL LIFE INS CO	IL	A-	2183.0	492.8	2.60	1.73	8.1	6.4	5.1	6.6	5.7	FIT
DEARBORN NATIONAL LIFE INS CO OF NY	NY	B+	40.9	22.2	3.60	3.24	10.0	8.3	3.3	7.0	5.0	FT
DELAWARE AMERICAN LIFE INS CO	DE	B	150.9	82.7	5.15	3.72	10.0	7.7	8.7	7.6	6.2	AT
▲ DELAWARE LIFE INS CO	DE	C	39688.7	1519.6	1.55	0.99	6.9	4.7	2.9	7.1	3.5	CFGI

See Page 27 for explanation of footnotes and Page 28 for explanation of stability factors.
Arrows denote recent upgrades ▲ or downgrades▼ (see Section VI for explanations)

36

www.weissratings.com

NET PREMIUM ($MIL)	IN-VESTED ASSETS ($MIL)	% OF INVESTED ASSETS IN:									INVEST. IN AFFIL	INSURANCE COMPANY NAME
		CASH	CMO & STRUCT. SECS.	OTH.INV. GRADE BONDS	NON-INV. GRADE BONDS	CMMON & PREF. STOCK	MORT IN GOOD STAND.	NON-PERF. MORT.	REAL ESTATE	OTHER INVEST-MENTS		
94.1	356.0	-0.3	6.5	86.9	6.9	0.0	0.0	0.0	0.0	0.0	0.0 ●	CIGNA LIFE INS CO OF NEW YORK
0.1	47.1	-0.3	4.2	96.1	0.0	0.0	0.0	0.0	0.0	0.0	66.2	CIGNA WORLDWIDE INS CO
24.6	68.1	1.3	9.3	70.9	0.7	16.7	0.0	0.0	0.0	1.1	6.2	CINCINNATI EQUITABLE LIFE INS CO
181.7	2,866.8	1.8	3.8	86.4	4.9	0.3	0.0	0.0	0.0	2.8	0.0 ●	CINCINNATI LIFE INS CO
--	--	--	--	--	--	--	--	--	--	--	--	CITCO LIFE INS CO
2.9	65.0	2.0	0.0	84.9	3.1	6.8	0.4	0.0	2.1	0.6	0.0	CITIZENS FIDELITY INS CO
0.9	12.2	8.6	2.5	87.0	0.0	0.0	0.0	0.0	0.0	2.0	0.0	CITIZENS NATIONAL LIFE INS CO
22.5	19.0	26.1	0.0	17.9	8.4	19.2	0.0	0.0	28.4	0.4	0.0	CITIZENS SECURITY LIFE INS CO
0.1	2.7 (*)	48.5	0.0	0.0	0.0	0.0	0.0	0.0	0.0	0.0	0.0	CLARIA LIFE & HEALTH INS CO
245.7	6,982.8 (*)	-0.5	13.9	50.7	6.2	3.3	12.3	0.0	0.4	7.7	10.1 ●	CM LIFE INS CO
1,668.1	10,135.7	0.4	11.8	51.0	4.7	9.8	13.4	0.0	0.9	7.3	9.6 ●	CMFG LIFE INS CO
959.3	2,476.9	0.0	4.4	71.4	8.3	0.9	9.9	0.0	1.2	4.4	0.0 ●	COLONIAL LIFE & ACCIDENT INS CO
0.7	17.1	2.9	38.7	48.4	3.8	4.2	0.0	0.0	0.0	1.9	0.0	COLONIAL LIFE INS CO OF TX
235.2	675.9	1.2	12.8	73.7	3.5	0.4	4.4	0.0	0.9	3.1	0.3 ●	COLONIAL PENN LIFE INS CO
0.4	2.7	2.7	0.2	95.3	0.0	0.1	0.0	0.0	0.0	1.7	0.0	COLONIAL SECURITY LIFE INS CO
67.3	237.5	3.6	15.0	79.3	0.5	0.0	0.0	0.0	0.0	1.6	0.0 ●	COLORADO BANKERS LIFE INS CO
44.6	265.9	1.6	25.3	55.7	0.0	2.3	10.5	0.0	0.0	4.7	2.3	COLUMBIAN LIFE INS CO
135.5	1,193.9	0.0	23.0	56.0	0.3	2.7	11.6	0.0	0.4	6.2	2.2 ●	COLUMBIAN MUTUAL LIFE INS CO
181.4	3,001.8	-0.1	22.1	58.7	5.9	3.3	3.7	0.0	0.0	6.1	3.0 ●	COLUMBUS LIFE INS CO
328.4	1,420.7	0.7	21.9	63.5	5.5	5.6	0.0	0.0	0.0	2.9	5.6 ●	COMBINED INS CO OF AMERICA
96.3	370.3	-1.3	46.6	51.2	1.3	0.1	0.0	0.0	0.0	2.2	0.0 ●	COMBINED LIFE INS CO OF NEW YORK
0.0	7.4	0.0	21.5	78.5	0.0	0.0	0.0	0.0	0.0	0.0	0.0	COMMENCEMENT BAY LIFE INS CO
3.7	20.8	13.1	18.4	66.2	0.0	1.4	0.0	0.0	1.0	0.0	0.4	COMMERCIAL TRAVELERS MUTUAL INS CO
543.5	6,630.5	5.2	42.9	30.7	1.5	8.1	5.5	0.0	0.0	5.1	8.1 ●	COMMONWEALTH ANNUITY & LIFE INS CO
0.0	6.8	9.2	0.0	88.9	1.9	0.0	0.0	0.0	0.0	0.0	0.0	COMMONWEALTH DEALERS LIFE INS CO
71.6	791.6	2.8	28.0	55.6	2.5	0.0	7.7	0.0	0.0	3.5	0.0 ●	COMPANION LIFE INS CO
166.1	196.8	21.7	16.7	37.8	0.5	23.3	0.0	0.0	0.0	0.0	7.6 ●	COMPANION LIFE INS CO
0.0	2.0	12.8	0.0	87.2	0.0	0.0	0.0	0.0	0.0	0.0	0.0	CONCERT HEALTH PLAN INS CO
879.8	8,953.5	-0.5	5.3	31.0	11.0	20.2	6.8	0.0	1.4	24.8	23.8 ●	CONNECTICUT GENERAL LIFE INS CO
126.4	3,731.4	1.0	26.1	56.8	5.2	1.0	5.0	0.0	0.0	4.7	0.5 ●	CONSECO LIFE INS CO
0.2	1,051.4	1.0	0.0	3.4	0.0	95.5	0.0	0.0	0.0	0.1	95.5	CONSECO LIFE INS CO OF TX
73.2	302.1	-1.4	40.7	59.0	1.0	0.0	0.0	0.0	0.0	0.6	0.0 ●	CONSTITUTION LIFE INS CO
20.2	19.7 (*)	0.0	0.0	103.1	0.0	0.0	0.0	0.0	0.0	0.0	0.0	CONSUMERS LIFE INS CO
180.4	287.6	17.0	0.0	81.1	0.0	0.0	0.0	0.0	0.6	1.2	0.0 ●	CONTINENTAL AMERICAN INS CO
0.2	2,256.3	0.3	21.7	65.3	8.4	3.2	0.0	0.0	0.0	1.0	0.0 ●	CONTINENTAL ASSURANCE CO
11.0	224.3	0.1	30.3	61.0	2.7	2.2	1.3	0.0	0.0	2.4	0.0 ●	CONTINENTAL GENERAL INS CO
3.6	19.5	0.8	3.2	78.1	0.0	1.0	8.1	0.0	2.7	6.1	0.0	CONTINENTAL LIFE INS CO
244.9	187.3	28.5	14.3	29.5	0.0	27.4	0.0	0.0	0.0	0.5	27.4 ●	CONTINENTAL LIFE INS CO OF BRENTWOOD
66.6	397.0 (*)	3.6	0.1	81.8	0.0	1.7	0.7	1.2	8.7	1.1	0.0	COOPERATIVA DE SEGUROS DE VIDA DE PR
0.3	6.6	5.2	2.8	73.6	2.3	15.9	0.0	0.0	0.2	0.2	0.0	COOPERATIVE LIFE INS CO
0.0	9.2	12.2	32.8	55.0	0.0	0.0	0.0	0.0	0.0	0.0	0.0	CORVESTA LIFE INS CO
21.0	312.0	-0.1	20.9	67.5	2.4	3.7	0.0	0.0	0.0	5.5	0.0 ●	COTTON STATES LIFE INS CO
0.0	201.4	-0.3	22.1	76.8	1.2	0.0	0.0	0.0	0.0	0.1	0.0 ●	COUNTRY INVESTORS LIFE ASR CO
468.2	8,005.7 (*)	-0.1	22.1	55.3	4.2	7.1	3.5	0.0	0.5	4.7	4.0 ●	COUNTRY LIFE INS CO
0.0	1.5	7.3	0.0	92.7	0.0	0.0	0.0	0.0	0.0	0.0	0.0	CROWN GLOBAL INS CO OF AMERICA
--	--	--	--	--	--	--	--	--	--	--	--	CSA FRATERNAL LIFE
2.6	17.0	6.2	0.0	88.0	0.0	5.8	0.0	0.0	0.0	0.0	49.9	CSI LIFE INS CO
1.0	2.2	53.7	0.0	46.3	0.0	0.0	0.0	0.0	0.0	0.0	0.0	DAKOTA CAPITAL LIFE INS CO
284.1	2,239.7	0.0	29.5	61.0	6.5	2.3	0.0	0.0	0.0	0.3	2.3 ●	DEARBORN NATIONAL LIFE INS CO
2.4	44.2	2.3	31.8	65.9	0.0	0.0	0.0	0.0	0.0	0.0	0.0	DEARBORN NATIONAL LIFE INS CO OF NY
76.5	109.4	9.3	19.2	66.2	0.6	0.0	0.0	0.0	0.0	4.7	4.7 ●	DELAWARE AMERICAN LIFE INS CO
1,075.9	8,430.4 (*)	0.2	14.6	41.2	2.0	5.1	8.9	0.0	1.2	15.9	4.8 ●	DELAWARE LIFE INS CO

● Bullets denote a more detailed analysis is available in Section II.
(*) Asset category percentages do not add up to 100%

INSURANCE COMPANY NAME	DOM. STATE	RATING	TOTAL ASSETS ($MIL)	CAPITAL & SURPLUS ($MIL)	RISK ADJUSTED CAPITAL RATIO 1	RISK ADJUSTED CAPITAL RATIO 2	CAPITAL-IZATION INDEX (PTS)	INVEST. SAFETY INDEX (PTS)	PROFIT-ABILITY INDEX (PTS)	LIQUIDITY INDEX (PTS)	STAB. INDEX (PTS)	STABILI FACTO
DELAWARE LIFE INS CO OF NEW YORK	NY	C	3033.2	412.3	8.51	4.16	4.0	6.4	6.8	7.5	2.8	AT
DELTA LIFE INS CO	GA	E+	60.7	7.6	0.50	0.31	1.0	1.4	2.9	4.2	0.7	CIL
DESERET MUTUAL INS CO	UT	B	40.1	7.7	1.89	1.70	8.1	8.3	2.4	7.0	4.9	CDFT
DESTINY HEALTH INS CO	IL	U (3)	3.6	3.6	3.08	2.77	8.0	9.8	2.5	10.0	2.7	DF
DIRECT GENERAL LIFE INS CO	SC	C+	29.5	16.7	4.26	3.84	10.0	9.1	7.6	6.8	4.9	AD
DIRECTORS LIFE ASR CO	OK	E	28.8	1.9	0.31	0.27	0.2	3.0	3.0	4.4	0.1	CIL
DLE LIFE INS CO	LA	D-	39.3	7.2	1.41	0.64	5.6	0.5	2.7	6.3	1.0	CDIT
DOCTORS LIFE INS CO	CA	C	16.5	7.6	2.61	2.35	9.0	9.0	3.0	10.0	3.9	DFT
DORSEY LIFE INS CO	TX	U (3)	0.3	0.0	0.00	0.00	0.0	9.8	0.4	9.2	0.0	CDFT
DUPAGE LIFE INS CO	AZ	U	--	--	--	--	--	--	--	--	--	Z
EAGLE AMERICAN LIFE INS CO	LA	U	--	--	--	--	--	--	--	--	--	Z
EAGLE INS CO	AZ	U	--	--	--	--	--	--	--	--	--	Z
EAGLE LIFE INS CO	IA	B	206.6	42.6	4.43	3.10	10.0	6.5	2.9	6.5	4.4	DGIT
EAST ARKANSAS GEM LIFE INS CO	AZ	U	--	--	--	--	--	--	--	--	--	Z
EDUCATORS LIFE INS CO OF AMERICA	IL	U (3)	390.7	374.0	1.20	1.07	7.1	0.9	8.3	9.7	2.9	DI
▼ ELCO MUTUAL LIFE & ANNUITY	IL	C	466.9	43.4	1.83	0.94	6.5	5.9	5.3	7.3	2.2	GIT
▲ EMC NATIONAL LIFE CO	IA	B	1014.7	97.6	2.38	1.38	7.6	6.7	6.0	4.2	5.6	AFLT
EMPIRE FIDELITY INVESTMENTS L I C	NY	B+	2386.2	70.5	2.51	2.26	8.9	8.3	2.7	7.0	6.7	
EMPLOYERS REASSURANCE CORP	KS	C	11081.7	1243.4	1.59	1.26	7.4	6.6	2.8	6.9	3.9	AC
ENTERPRISE LIFE INS CO	TX	C	18.3	15.5	1.14	1.04	7.1	5.7	8.4	7.9	3.3	ADGT
EPIC LIFE INSURANCE CO	WI	B	60.8	30.9	3.50	2.35	9.0	5.3	6.6	7.1	5.9	AI
EQUITABLE LIFE & CASUALTY INS CO	UT	C+	290.5	41.0	2.61	1.77	8.2	7.7	5.5	7.2	4.4	D
EQUITRUST LIFE INS CO	IL	B-	13718.0	828.8	1.98	0.91	6.5	3.8	9.0	9.0	4.6	GIT
ERIE FAMILY LIFE INS CO	PA	A-	2077.0	297.4	3.42	1.88	8.3	5.9	7.7	5.8	7.1	AI
EVERENCE ASSN INC	IN	U	--	--	--	--	--	--	--	--	--	Z
EVERENCE INS CO	IN	C	24.1	13.7	3.40	3.06	10.0	7.8	5.1	7.1	3.7	DFT
EVERGREEN LIFE INS CO	TX	U (3)	1.6	1.6	2.61	2.35	8.0	9.8	3.0	10.0	3.2	DT
FAMILY BENEFIT LIFE INS CO	MO	C	66.3	12.3	1.74	1.57	7.9	5.7	7.8	6.2	2.9	ADFG
FAMILY HERITAGE LIFE INS CO OF AMER	OH	A-	725.3	66.0	1.82	1.26	7.4	7.2	9.5	8.2	7.3	AD
FAMILY LIBERTY LIFE INS CO	TX	D	31.7	8.6	1.99	1.42	7.6	4.9	2.4	6.0	2.2	DFI
FAMILY LIFE INS CO	TX	C	148.2	33.8	3.61	2.80	9.7	8.7	2.9	6.6	4.2	
FAMILY SECURITY LIFE INS CO INC	MS	C	6.6	1.6	0.94	0.84	5.7	6.5	2.9	7.0	3.4	
FAMILY SERVICE LIFE INS CO	TX	U (3)	393.1	27.0	2.19	1.27	7.4	4.7	2.2	4.3	4.2	DFIL
FARM BUREAU LIFE INS CO	IA	B+	8042.3	562.9	2.19	1.13	7.2	5.5	7.5	4.4	6.4	IL
FARM BUREAU LIFE INS CO OF MICHIGAN	MI	A-	2356.3	435.9	3.66	1.98	8.5	5.7	7.7	5.5	6.9	I
FARM BUREAU LIFE INS CO OF MISSOURI	MO	A-	522.5	58.8	2.08	1.32	7.5	5.8	6.7	5.8	6.9	I
FARM FAMILY LIFE INS CO	NY	B	1270.3	152.1	2.09	1.19	7.3	4.6	6.9	5.5	6.0	I
FARMERS LIFE INS CO	TN	U	--	--	--	--	--	--	--	--	--	Z
FARMERS NEW WORLD LIFE INS CO	WA	B-	7118.7	603.7	2.26	1.27	7.4	6.1	4.0	5.5	5.3	A
FEDERAL LIFE INS CO (MUTUAL)	IL	C	231.8	17.3	1.32	0.88	6.0	4.8	2.1	5.3	3.4	DI
FEDERATED LIFE INS CO	MN	A	1497.0	305.7	4.60	2.53	9.3	6.7	8.4	6.7	7.4	AI
FIDELITY & GUARANTY LIFE INS CO	IA	C+	18461.3	1134.4	1.33	0.74	5.5	3.7	8.1	6.1	4.6	ACGI
FIDELITY & GUARANTY LIFE INS CO NY	NY	B-	517.0	64.1	3.59	1.84	8.3	6.6	4.5	6.8	5.1	ADGI
FIDELITY INVESTMENTS LIFE INS CO	UT	A-	23882.2	656.2	2.98	1.78	8.2	6.6	6.8	7.0	7.2	I
FIDELITY LIFE ASSN A LEGAL RESERVE	IL	C	412.7	129.0	5.15	2.88	9.8	5.9	1.4	6.5	4.0	DFT
FIDELITY MUTUAL LIFE INS CO	PA	F (5)	--	--	--	--	--	--	--	--	--	Z
FIDELITY SECURITY LIFE INS CO	MO	B-	841.6	147.1	3.01	1.90	8.4	6.4	6.6	6.2	3.5	GT
FIDELITY SECURITY LIFE INS CO OF NY	NY	B	40.3	9.3	2.00	1.80	8.2	5.8	6.3	6.5	4.3	AFGI
FIDELITY STANDARD LIFE INS CO	AR	D+	3.3	0.5	0.80	0.72	4.8	5.2	2.7	6.4	2.5	ACDF
FINANCIAL AMERICAN LIFE INS CO	KS	D+	23.4	9.4	2.16	1.94	8.4	8.2	2.4	7.2	2.5	FT
FINANCIAL ASSURANCE LIFE INS CO	TX	U (3)	10.7	9.7	3.88	3.49	10.0	7.8	8.4	10.0	8.4	D
FIRST ALLMERICA FINANCIAL LIFE INS	MA	C-	4211.4	208.3	4.25	2.02	4.0	6.6	4.4	5.5	3.3	GT

See Page 27 for explanation of footnotes and Page 28 for explanation of stability factors.
Arrows denote recent upgrades ▲ or downgrades▼ (see Section VI for explanations)

38

www.weissratings.com

NET PREMIUM ($MIL)	IN-VESTED ASSETS ($MIL)	CASH	CMO & STRUCT. SECS.	OTH.INV. GRADE BONDS	NON-INV. GRADE BONDS	CMMON & PREF. STOCK	MORT IN GOOD STAND.	NON-PERF. MORT.	REAL ESTATE	OTHER INVEST-MENTS	INVEST. IN AFFIL	INSURANCE COMPANY NAME
25.1	1,226.7	-0.4	19.6	74.0	1.1	1.4	4.1	0.0	0.0	0.2	0.0 ●	DELAWARE LIFE INS CO OF NEW YORK
11.2	60.9	6.6	0.0	23.7	1.2	36.3	0.9	0.0	20.8	10.6	20.2	DELTA LIFE INS CO
7.8	39.3	10.3	0.0	88.6	0.1	1.0	0.0	0.0	0.0	0.0	0.0	DESERET MUTUAL INS CO
0.0	3.6	58.4	0.0	41.6	0.0	0.0	0.0	0.0	0.0	0.0	0.0	DESTINY HEALTH INS CO
15.3	13.1	2.6	21.0	76.4	0.0	0.0	0.0	0.0	0.0	0.0	0.0	DIRECT GENERAL LIFE INS CO
3.9	26.5	2.9	1.0	92.7	1.8	0.0	0.0	0.0	0.0	1.7	0.0	DIRECTORS LIFE ASR CO
2.7	40.6 (*)	2.9	0.0	45.8	0.0	0.0	8.6	0.5	41.6	14.3	0.0	DLE LIFE INS CO
0.1	16.6	1.1	13.2	85.7	0.0	0.0	0.0	0.0	0.0	0.0	0.0	DOCTORS LIFE INS CO
0.0	0.3	100.0	0.0	0.0	0.0	0.0	0.0	0.0	0.0	0.0	0.0	DORSEY LIFE INS CO
--	--	--	--	--	--	--	--	--	--	--	--	DUPAGE LIFE INS CO
--	--	--	--	--	--	--	--	--	--	--	--	EAGLE AMERICAN LIFE INS CO
--	--	--	--	--	--	--	--	--	--	--	--	EAGLE INS CO
13.5	186.7	0.9	15.9	79.5	2.7	0.0	1.0	0.0	0.0	0.0	0.0 ●	EAGLE LIFE INS CO
--	--	--	--	--	--	--	--	--	--	--	--	EAST ARKANSAS GEM LIFE INS CO
1.2	389.8	0.1	0.0	0.6	3.8	95.5	0.0	0.0	0.0	0.0	95.5	EDUCATORS LIFE INS CO OF AMERICA
55.6	348.5	4.4	0.0	87.2	0.9	4.7	1.9	0.0	1.0	0.1	0.0 ●	ELCO MUTUAL LIFE & ANNUITY
45.6	985.9	-0.2	10.0	81.2	0.2	2.8	3.6	0.0	0.2	2.3	0.0 ●	EMC NATIONAL LIFE CO
120.3	117.7	-0.9	8.3	92.6	0.0	0.0	0.0	0.0	0.0	0.0	0.0 ●	EMPIRE FIDELITY INVESTMENTS L I C
294.4	10,668.0	0.0	18.8	65.5	2.2	5.6	4.8	0.0	0.0	2.9	7.1 ●	EMPLOYERS REASSURANCE CORP
14.4	16.8	10.3	2.7	24.5	0.0	62.5	0.0	0.0	0.0	0.0	62.5	ENTERPRISE LIFE INS CO
19.6	59.8	3.4	9.2	67.2	0.0	20.2	0.0	0.0	0.0	0.0	0.0 ●	EPIC LIFE INSURANCE CO
51.4	248.4	4.5	21.5	68.7	0.3	0.0	4.9	0.0	0.1	0.1	0.0 ●	EQUITABLE LIFE & CASUALTY INS CO
1,495.9	10,830.9 (*)	1.2	32.8	30.2	5.0	1.4	13.6	0.0	0.1	8.9	10.6 ●	EQUITRUST LIFE INS CO
111.9	1,933.3	-0.3	2.8	88.6	2.0	5.3	0.1	0.0	0.1	1.6	0.0 ●	ERIE FAMILY LIFE INS CO
--	--	--	--	--	--	--	--	--	--	--	--	EVERENCE ASSN INC
0.1	24.7	4.1	5.4	85.3	0.9	0.3	4.1	0.0	0.0	0.0	3.6	EVERENCE INS CO
0.0	1.6	80.9	0.0	19.1	0.0	0.0	0.0	0.0	0.0	0.0	0.0	EVERGREEN LIFE INS CO
5.0	61.2	0.2	0.2	91.7	4.2	0.6	1.4	0.0	0.2	1.5	0.0	FAMILY BENEFIT LIFE INS CO
166.4	619.9	0.0	0.0	99.3	0.0	0.0	0.0	0.0	0.0	0.7	0.0 ●	FAMILY HERITAGE LIFE INS CO OF AMER
1.3	31.3	0.5	2.0	78.0	1.4	16.5	1.3	0.0	0.2	0.0	1.3	FAMILY LIBERTY LIFE INS CO
19.0	130.7	13.8	5.9	67.4	0.0	0.0	2.3	0.0	0.0	10.6	0.0 ●	FAMILY LIFE INS CO
0.6	6.4	0.4	0.0	90.2	2.3	2.1	0.0	0.0	4.9	0.0	0.0	FAMILY SECURITY LIFE INS CO INC
0.0	385.7	0.6	0.0	95.0	3.0	1.3	0.0	0.0	0.0	0.1	1.3	FAMILY SERVICE LIFE INS CO
496.6	6,786.9	0.1	22.8	59.6	3.7	1.7	7.4	0.0	0.0	4.7	0.0 ●	FARM BUREAU LIFE INS CO
85.0	2,204.7	-0.1	2.6	67.7	3.0	6.7	16.5	0.1	0.5	2.8	0.6 ●	FARM BUREAU LIFE INS CO OF MICHIGAN
30.6	490.6	0.1	19.6	60.5	0.3	9.9	0.0	0.0	0.0	9.7	1.6 ●	FARM BUREAU LIFE INS CO OF MISSOURI
53.2	1,221.7	0.2	3.8	72.3	2.7	10.5	5.4	0.0	0.9	4.3	0.0 ●	FARM FAMILY LIFE INS CO
--	--	--	--	--	--	--	--	--	--	--	--	FARMERS LIFE INS CO
436.9	6,199.0	-0.1	24.8	66.3	1.1	0.0	1.3	0.0	0.8	5.1	0.4 ●	FARMERS NEW WORLD LIFE INS CO
15.8	194.9	0.3	26.8	55.3	4.6	6.7	0.0	0.0	1.0	5.4	3.2	FEDERAL LIFE INS CO (MUTUAL)
119.8	1,392.9	0.0	11.2	81.9	3.5	2.0	0.0	0.0	0.0	1.5	0.0 ●	FEDERATED LIFE INS CO
1,675.5	16,493.4	2.4	21.2	65.2	6.2	3.1	0.6	0.0	0.0	0.8	3.5 ●	FIDELITY & GUARANTY LIFE INS CO
22.4	498.3	0.1	15.5	76.8	3.1	2.5	0.0	0.0	0.0	1.2	0.0 ●	FIDELITY & GUARANTY LIFE INS CO NY
1,412.2	751.8	-1.0	8.3	76.8	6.8	9.0	0.0	0.0	0.0	0.1	9.0 ●	FIDELITY INVESTMENTS LIFE INS CO
43.3	398.6	5.5	17.3	52.5	4.4	8.6	3.0	0.0	0.1	8.5	0.0 ●	FIDELITY LIFE ASSN A LEGAL RESERVE
--	--	--	--	--	--	--	--	--	--	--	--	FIDELITY MUTUAL LIFE INS CO
126.8	789.0	2.2	39.7	49.7	3.7	2.1	0.5	0.0	0.0	2.1	1.4 ●	FIDELITY SECURITY LIFE INS CO
1.1	39.9	0.6	29.1	68.1	1.3	1.0	0.0	0.0	0.0	0.0	0.0	FIDELITY SECURITY LIFE INS CO OF NY
0.1	1.7	13.2	0.0	59.0	2.5	25.0	0.0	0.0	0.0	0.3	0.0	FIDELITY STANDARD LIFE INS CO
-2.9	25.9	1.9	54.8	41.8	1.5	0.0	0.0	0.0	0.0	0.0	0.0	FINANCIAL AMERICAN LIFE INS CO
0.1	10.6	0.0	61.5	38.3	0.0	0.0	0.0	0.0	0.0	0.2	0.0	FINANCIAL ASSURANCE LIFE INS CO
60.8	2,575.7	0.4	41.9	53.1	1.5	0.0	0.0	0.0	0.0	3.2	0.0 ●	FIRST ALLMERICA FINANCIAL LIFE INS

● Bullets denote a more detailed analysis is available in Section II.
(*) Asset category percentages do not add up to 100%

INSURANCE COMPANY NAME	DOM. STATE	RATING	TOTAL ASSETS ($MIL)	CAPITAL & SURPLUS ($MIL)	RISK ADJUSTED CAPITAL RATIO 1	RISK ADJUSTED CAPITAL RATIO 2	CAPITAL- IZATION INDEX (PTS)	INVEST. SAFETY INDEX (PTS)	PROFIT- ABILITY INDEX (PTS)	LIQUIDITY INDEX (PTS)	STAB. INDEX (PTS)	STABILI FACTO
FIRST AMTENN LIFE INS CO	MS	U	--	--	--	--	--	--	--	--	--	Z
FIRST ASR LIFE OF AMERICA	LA	B	37.7	32.2	3.17	3.01	10.0	8.8	8.3	9.1	5.7	A
FIRST BANK SYSTEM LIFE INS CO	VT	U	--	--	--	--	--	--	--	--	--	Z
FIRST BERKSHIRE HATHAWAY LIFE INS CO	NY	C+	370.5	31.5	3.04	2.74	9.6	7.5	1.0	10.0	4.4	GT
FIRST COMMAND LIFE INS CO	TX	B-	32.6	11.0	2.41	2.17	8.8	6.3	7.5	6.7	4.3	DI
FIRST COMMUNITY LIFE INS CO	TN	U	--	--	--	--	--	--	--	--	--	Z
FIRST CONTINENTAL LIFE & ACC INS CO	TX	D	5.9	4.3	1.26	1.17	7.3	7.2	2.7	0.9	1.8	CDGL
FIRST DIMENSION LIFE INS CO INC	OK	U (3)	4.7	3.6	2.46	2.22	8.8	8.1	7.9	7.8	8.0	D
FIRST FINANCIAL ASSURANCE CO	AR	U (5)	--	--	--	--	--	--	--	--	--	Z
FIRST GUARANTY INS CO	LA	C	55.2	5.3	0.82	0.74	4.9	4.4	5.6	5.6	4.0	CI
FIRST HEALTH LIFE & HEALTH INS CO	TX	B	577.2	234.2	1.27	1.05	5.4	9.3	1.8	0.2	4.1	DFLT
FIRST INVESTORS LIFE INS CO	NY	B	1786.5	55.8	2.25	1.18	7.3	6.7	5.1	7.1	5.9	G
FIRST LANDMARK LIFE INS CO	NE	U (3)	2.0	2.0	2.79	2.51	8.0	9.5	2.8	10.0	3.0	DF
FIRST METLIFE INVESTORS INS CO	NY	C	6265.7	121.2	1.69	0.85	6.0	6.3	2.0	8.6	4.2	T
FIRST MICHIGAN LIFE INS CO	AZ	U	--	--	--	--	--	--	--	--	--	Z
FIRST NATIONAL LIFE INS CO OF USA	NE	C-	5.9	1.9	1.31	0.95	6.6	2.6	2.9	6.9	2.9	FI
FIRST PENN-PACIFIC LIFE INS CO	IN	B	1744.5	231.6	2.97	1.61	7.9	5.7	7.7	5.4	5.8	AFIL
FIRST RELIANCE STANDARD LIFE INS CO	NY	A	188.7	69.6	6.07	3.87	10.0	6.8	7.7	7.0	6.2	AI
FIRST SECURITY BENEFIT LIFE & ANN	NY	B	695.6	31.9	1.79	0.87	6.2	3.8	2.0	9.6	4.6	ACDC
FIRST SYMETRA NATL LIFE INS CO OF NY	NY	A-	932.2	103.2	3.93	1.95	8.4	6.7	9.1	6.3	7.0	ADGI
FIRST UNITED AMERICAN LIFE INS CO	NY	B+	191.8	36.0	2.32	1.50	7.8	5.0	6.8	5.2	6.7	ADIL
FIRST UNUM LIFE INS CO	NY	C+	2794.1	267.7	2.67	1.36	7.5	4.5	7.6	7.3	4.8	AI
FIRST VOLUNTEER INS CO	AZ	U	--	--	--	--	--	--	--	--	--	Z
▼ FIRST WYOMING LIFE INS CO	WY	D-	4.3	3.3	2.48	2.23	8.8	8.2	2.0	7.0	1.1	ADEG
FIVE STAR LIFE INS CO	LA	C+	258.8	35.2	2.60	1.62	7.9	6.7	1.9	5.9	4.3	
FLORIDA COMBINED LIFE INS CO INC	FL	B	45.7	25.0	4.76	3.76	8.0	5.3	4.2	7.7	5.4	I
FOOTHILLS LIFE INS CO	AZ	U	--	--	--	--	--	--	--	--	--	Z
FOR LIFE INS CO	AZ	U	--	--	--	--	--	--	--	--	--	Z
FORETHOUGHT LIFE INS CO	IN	B-	11568.0	757.1	3.79	1.95	8.4	6.1	7.7	6.6	5.3	AG
FORETHOUGHT NATIONAL LIFE INS CO	TX	C	210.6	23.0	2.31	1.74	4.0	8.8	2.0	0.0	2.6	DFLT
FOUNDATION LIFE INS CO OF AR	AR	D+	5.5	1.6	1.23	1.10	7.2	4.6	2.0	8.0	2.5	F
FRANDISCO LIFE INS CO	GA	A-	65.0	61.1	8.47	7.62	10.0	8.9	9.8	9.4	6.5	AD
FREEDOM LIFE INS CO OF AMERICA	TX	C	54.8	28.8	0.82	0.71	4.7	6.7	7.2	7.1	3.7	CGI
FREMONT LIFE INS CO	CA	F (5)	--	--	--	--	--	--	--	--	--	Z
FRINGE BENEFIT LIFE INS CO	TX	D+	45.4	28.6	4.63	2.43	9.1	4.3	8.2	7.0	2.5	DIT
FUNERAL DIRECTORS LIFE INS CO	TX	B-	1046.4	89.9	2.32	1.27	7.4	6.4	8.0	2.6	4.6	L
FUTURAL LIFE INS CO	AZ	D+ (3)	4.8	3.5	2.51	2.25	8.9	3.8	4.9	10.0	2.4	DFIT
GARDEN STATE LIFE INS CO	TX	A-	120.3	52.6	5.86	5.27	10.0	6.7	8.1	6.8	7.1	ADI
GENERAL AMERICAN LIFE INS CO	MO	B	12151.6	854.2	3.00	1.35	7.5	5.5	6.4	5.5	5.5	AFI
GENERAL FIDELITY LIFE INS CO	SC	C+	88.2	75.6	9.10	8.19	10.0	9.2	4.1	10.0	3.1	ADFT
GENERAL RE LIFE CORP	CT	B+	3335.8	620.1	2.14	1.34	7.5	5.0	7.6	8.4	6.7	AI
GENERATION LIFE INS CO	AZ	B	30.2	28.3	5.84	5.26	10.0	8.4	2.0	10.0	5.3	DFG
GENWORTH LIFE & ANNUITY INS CO	VA	B-	24254.6	2220.8	1.50	1.09	7.1	5.0	6.4	6.6	3.6	AIT
GENWORTH LIFE INS CO	DE	B-	37409.9	3338.1	1.03	0.81	5.5	6.5	5.2	7.4	5.1	AGT
GENWORTH LIFE INS CO OF NEW YORK	NY	B	8185.1	513.4	2.26	1.13	7.2	5.1	5.8	6.6	5.6	AI
GEORGIA PEOPLES LIFE INS CO	AZ	U	--	--	--	--	--	--	--	--	--	Z
GERBER LIFE INS CO	NY	A-	2749.8	279.8	2.03	1.24	7.4	6.4	7.7	5.5	7.2	I
GERMANIA LIFE INS CO	TX	C-	68.8	9.1	1.27	1.14	7.2	6.7	2.3	6.0	3.3	A
GERTRUDE GEDDES WILLIS LIFE INS CO	LA	F (5)	--	--	--	--	--	--	--	--	--	Z
GLOBE LIFE & ACCIDENT INS CO	NE	B	3511.4	262.1	1.82	0.98	6.8	4.6	6.5	5.2	6.0	AIL
GMHP HEALTH INS LMTD	GU	U (3)	0.9	0.8	2.11	1.90	8.0	3.2	1.3	9.2	1.5	DIT
GOLDEN GATE CAPTIVE INS CO	SC	U (5)	--	--	--	--	--	--	--	--	--	Z

See Page 27 for explanation of footnotes and Page 28 for explanation of stability factors.

Arrows denote recent upgrades ▲ or downgrades▼ (see Section VI for explanations)

40

www.weissratings.com

NET PREMIUM ($MIL)	IN-VESTED ASSETS ($MIL)	% OF INVESTED ASSETS IN:									INVEST. IN AFFIL	INSURANCE COMPANY NAME
		CASH	CMO & STRUCT. SECS.	OTH.INV. GRADE BONDS	NON-INV. GRADE BONDS	CMMON & PREF. STOCK	MORT IN GOOD STAND.	NON-PERF. MORT.	REAL ESTATE	OTHER INVEST-MENTS		
--	--	--	--	--	--	--	--	--	--	--	--	FIRST AMTENN LIFE INS CO
2.6	36.4	4.8	0.0	68.9	0.0	25.6	0.0	0.0	0.0	0.0	25.6 ●	FIRST ASR LIFE OF AMERICA
--	--	--	--	--	--	--	--	--	--	--	--	FIRST BANK SYSTEM LIFE INS CO
44.0	283.5	0.8	2.9	94.6	0.0	1.7	0.0	0.0	0.0	0.0	0.0	FIRST BERKSHIRE HATHAWAY LIFE INS CO
1.9	30.1	0.2	3.1	91.8	4.4	0.0	0.0	0.0	0.0	0.5	0.0	FIRST COMMAND LIFE INS CO
--	--	--	--	--	--	--	--	--	--	--	--	FIRST COMMUNITY LIFE INS CO
4.3	6.6	41.1	0.0	21.0	0.0	38.0	0.0	0.0	0.0	0.0	38.0	FIRST CONTINENTAL LIFE & ACC INS CO
0.0	4.6	2.9	9.2	87.5	0.0	0.5	0.0	0.0	0.0	0.4	0.0	FIRST DIMENSION LIFE INS CO INC
--	--	--	--	--	--	--	--	--	--	--	--	FIRST FINANCIAL ASSURANCE CO
4.4	53.2	2.3	12.6	72.5	0.6	2.1	8.7	0.0	1.0	0.3	0.0	FIRST GUARANTY INS CO
699.3	105.4	42.9	7.4	49.7	0.0	0.0	0.0	0.0	0.0	0.0	0.0 ●	FIRST HEALTH LIFE & HEALTH INS CO
179.3	446.0 (*)	0.5	0.0	76.6	0.8	0.0	0.0	0.0	0.0	19.8	0.0 ●	FIRST INVESTORS LIFE INS CO
0.0	2.0	0.2	0.0	99.8	0.0	0.0	0.0	0.0	0.0	0.0	242.3	FIRST LANDMARK LIFE INS CO
104.9	814.3	-0.3	18.0	60.9	7.2	0.0	11.8	0.0	0.0	2.5	0.0 ●	FIRST METLIFE INVESTORS INS CO
--	--	--	--	--	--	--	--	--	--	--	--	FIRST MICHIGAN LIFE INS CO
0.8	5.8	0.7	55.0	8.0	0.0	36.2	0.0	0.0	0.0	0.2	0.0	FIRST NATIONAL LIFE INS CO OF USA
110.5	1,620.6	-0.2	13.6	70.4	3.5	0.2	10.4	0.0	0.0	2.1	0.0 ●	FIRST PENN-PACIFIC LIFE INS CO
42.3	174.8	0.0	23.9	65.7	5.2	0.0	0.0	0.0	0.0	5.3	0.0 ●	FIRST RELIANCE STANDARD LIFE INS CO
90.8	465.8	4.8	30.9	61.6	1.4	0.1	0.0	0.0	0.0	1.2	0.0 ●	FIRST SECURITY BENEFIT LIFE & ANN
163.2	802.0	0.0	24.7	62.5	1.4	0.0	11.7	0.0	0.0	0.0	0.0 ●	FIRST SYMETRA NATL LIFE INS CO OF NY
56.0	155.8 (*)	2.6	5.9	78.7	6.1	0.0	0.0	0.0	0.0	3.9	0.0 ●	FIRST UNITED AMERICAN LIFE INS CO
270.1	2,626.3	0.0	8.8	75.6	8.8	0.0	5.7	0.0	0.0	0.8	0.0 ●	FIRST UNUM LIFE INS CO
--	--	--	--	--	--	--	--	--	--	--	--	FIRST VOLUNTEER INS CO
0.5	4.3	5.3	0.0	94.7	0.0	0.0	0.0	0.0	0.0	0.0	0.0	FIRST WYOMING LIFE INS CO
94.6	196.0	4.2	16.4	70.0	5.6	0.0	0.0	0.0	0.0	3.9	0.1 ●	FIVE STAR LIFE INS CO
0.0	34.4	16.5	1.2	25.2	0.0	0.0	0.0	0.0	0.0	57.1	57.1	FLORIDA COMBINED LIFE INS CO INC
--	--	--	--	--	--	--	--	--	--	--	--	FOOTHILLS LIFE INS CO
--	--	--	--	--	--	--	--	--	--	--	--	FOR LIFE INS CO
3,610.3	7,219.8	0.4	12.0	76.0	3.8	0.2	6.3	0.0	0.0	1.0	0.1 ●	FORETHOUGHT LIFE INS CO
0.1	14.3	43.8	13.4	42.8	0.0	0.0	0.0	0.0	0.0	0.1	0.0	FORETHOUGHT NATIONAL LIFE INS CO
0.8	5.5	31.0	0.0	41.1	10.7	15.3	0.0	0.0	0.0	2.0	0.0	FOUNDATION LIFE INS CO OF AR
10.8	58.6	0.1	0.0	99.9	0.0	0.0	0.0	0.0	0.0	0.0	0.0 ●	FRANDISCO LIFE INS CO
79.6	47.5	21.3	8.4	38.2	2.0	30.2	0.0	0.0	0.0	0.0	30.2 ●	FREEDOM LIFE INS CO OF AMERICA
--	--	--	--	--	--	--	--	--	--	--	--	FREMONT LIFE INS CO
0.1	43.9 (*)	1.9	0.9	24.0	8.1	17.9	21.7	0.0	0.0	30.8	0.0 ●	FRINGE BENEFIT LIFE INS CO
155.2	953.3	0.1	1.6	88.5	0.0	0.6	6.3	0.0	2.0	0.9	1.4 ●	FUNERAL DIRECTORS LIFE INS CO
0.2	4.8 (*)	4.5	0.0	100.1	0.0	20.3	0.0	0.0	0.0	0.0	0.0	FUTURAL LIFE INS CO
18.4	101.5	-0.8	3.5	93.3	1.0	0.0	0.0	0.0	0.0	3.0	0.0 ●	GARDEN STATE LIFE INS CO
493.3	10,538.8	0.1	18.5	45.2	5.7	0.9	7.7	0.0	0.5	20.9	2.5 ●	GENERAL AMERICAN LIFE INS CO
0.8	79.3	35.1	7.9	57.0	0.0	0.0	0.0	0.0	0.0	0.0	0.0 ●	GENERAL FIDELITY LIFE INS CO
777.8	3,098.5	0.4	0.3	66.3	8.0	8.8	0.0	0.0	0.0	16.2	16.6 ●	GENERAL RE LIFE CORP
2.2	32.3	57.9	0.0	38.0	0.0	4.1	0.0	0.0	0.0	0.0	0.0 ●	GENERATION LIFE INS CO
1,198.9	13,337.4	-0.4	24.1	48.1	3.7	7.6	11.3	0.0	0.2	4.9	7.4 ●	GENWORTH LIFE & ANNUITY INS CO
1,223.1	35,227.5 (*)	-0.1	15.4	58.7	3.3	7.8	10.0	0.0	0.0	3.8	8.5 ●	GENWORTH LIFE INS CO
380.2	6,783.7	-0.2	24.2	57.0	4.5	0.8	12.0	0.0	0.0	1.1	0.3 ●	GENWORTH LIFE INS CO OF NEW YORK
--	--	--	--	--	--	--	--	--	--	--	--	GEORGIA PEOPLES LIFE INS CO
436.8	2,360.3	0.0	16.7	73.3	2.7	2.8	0.0	0.0	0.0	4.6	0.0 ●	GERBER LIFE INS CO
5.0	62.3	0.4	35.1	57.4	5.6	0.1	0.0	0.0	0.0	1.4	0.0	GERMANIA LIFE INS CO
--	--	--	--	--	--	--	--	--	--	--	--	GERTRUDE GEDDES WILLIS LIFE INS CO
489.9	2,985.5	0.0	4.0	85.2	6.4	0.0	0.0	0.0	0.0	4.2	2.8 ●	GLOBE LIFE & ACCIDENT INS CO
0.0	0.9	27.9	0.0	0.0	0.0	0.0	0.0	0.0	72.1	0.0	0.0	GMHP HEALTH INS LMTD
--	--	--	--	--	--	--	--	--	--	--	--	GOLDEN GATE CAPTIVE INS CO

● Bullets denote a more detailed analysis is available in Section II.
(*) Asset category percentages do not add up to 100%

INSURANCE COMPANY NAME	DOM. STATE	RATING	TOTAL ASSETS ($MIL)	CAPITAL & SURPLUS ($MIL)	RISK ADJUSTED CAPITAL RATIO 1	RISK ADJUSTED CAPITAL RATIO 2	CAPITAL-IZATION INDEX (PTS)	INVEST. SAFETY INDEX (PTS)	PROFIT-ABILITY INDEX (PTS)	LIQUIDITY INDEX (PTS)	STAB. INDEX (PTS)	STABILITY FACTOR
GOLDEN GATE II CAPTIVE INS CO	SC	U (5)	--	--	--	--	--	--	--	--	--	Z
GOLDEN RULE INS CO	IN	B	736.6	314.5	1.31	1.04	5.0	8.1	8.8	6.2	5.4	A
GOVERNMENT PERSONNEL MUTUAL L I C	TX	B+	830.8	106.9	2.62	1.68	8.0	7.0	7.3	5.2	6.4	DL
GRANGE LIFE INS CO	OH	B-	366.5	54.6	2.53	1.61	7.9	7.2	2.6	6.3	5.0	D
GREAT AMERICAN LIFE INS CO	OH	B-	22140.3	1638.8	1.88	1.07	7.1	5.5	9.0	5.8	5.3	A
GREAT CENTRAL LIFE INS CO	LA	C (3)	21.4	6.5	1.32	0.87	6.0	2.9	6.1	6.9	4.0	I
GREAT FIDELITY LIFE INS CO	IN	D+	4.2	2.8	1.94	1.75	8.1	6.7	2.7	9.2	2.4	AFT
▼ GREAT PLAINS LIFE ASR CO	SD	E+	6.0	2.0	1.26	1.13	7.2	8.6	1.9	9.2	0.7	ADEG
GREAT REPUBLIC LIFE INS CO	WA	F (5)	--	--	--	--	--	--	--	--	--	Z
GREAT SOUTHERN LIFE INS CO	TX	B	225.3	42.4	4.63	2.43	9.1	6.5	9.1	7.6	5.4	AGT
GREAT WEST LIFE ASR CO	MI	B-	78.1	17.9	2.26	1.74	8.1	7.2	3.8	6.5	4.9	AFT
GREAT WESTERN INS CO	UT	B-	883.7	61.1	2.17	1.12	7.2	5.4	7.0	6.4	4.9	FGIT
GREAT WESTERN LIFE INS CO	MT	U (3)	2.1	1.6	2.09	1.88	8.3	8.7	7.4	7.8	7.6	D
GREAT-WEST LIFE & ANNUITY INS CO	CO	B-	56894.9	1120.6	1.22	0.68	5.3	5.6	6.2	6.7	5.0	CT
GREAT-WEST LIFE & ANNUITY INS OF NY	NY	B	1568.3	79.1	2.80	1.46	7.7	6.3	5.1	7.3	5.9	AI
GREATER GEORGIA LIFE INS CO	GA	B+	49.9	17.0	1.30	0.97	6.8	8.4	2.6	6.7	6.3	A
GREATER MISSOURI LIFE INS CO	AZ	U	--	--	--	--	--	--	--	--	--	Z
GREENFIELDS LIFE INS CO	CO	B	6.9	5.3	6.20	5.58	10.0	9.1	1.9	7.8	5.8	DEGT
GRIFFIN LEGGETT BURIAL INS CO	AR	U (3)	0.1	0.1	2.15	1.93	8.4	9.8	1.9	10.0	2.1	DFT
GUARANTEE TRUST LIFE INS CO	IL	B	408.5	55.7	1.44	0.99	6.9	6.3	7.7	7.4	5.9	I
GUARANTY INCOME LIFE INS CO	LA	C-	482.6	33.8	2.29	1.13	7.2	3.9	4.6	5.1	3.1	DFIT
GUARDIAN INS & ANNUITY CO INC	DE	B	15244.7	225.3	1.91	0.95	6.6	6.6	4.8	9.4	5.9	
GUARDIAN LIFE INS CO OF AMERICA	NY	A	44890.2	5759.7	2.72	1.76	8.1	6.4	7.5	5.9	7.5	I
GUGGENHEIM LIFE & ANNUITY CO	DE	B-	11992.0	585.3	1.32	0.73	5.5	4.0	7.5	8.0	5.0	CGIT
GULF GUARANTY LIFE INS CO	MS	D	15.4	8.4	1.46	1.14	7.2	4.5	2.7	7.9	2.2	F
GULF STATES LIFE INS CO INC	LA	U (3)	2.9	2.6	2.89	2.60	4.0	4.1	6.9	9.6	4.9	DFIT
HALLMARK LIFE INS CO	AZ	C	23.6	15.9	3.64	3.28	10.0	8.6	7.6	10.0	4.0	ADFG
HANNOVER LIFE REASSUR CO OF AMERICA	FL	C	4534.7	202.9	1.06	0.61	5.1	6.7	7.9	6.9	4.0	CFT
HARLEYSVILLE LIFE INS CO	PA	B	410.9	32.4	1.73	1.00	7.0	6.5	5.3	3.5	4.0	CLT
HARRIS LIFE INS CO	AZ	U	--	--	--	--	--	--	--	--	--	Z
HARTFORD INTL LIFE REASR CORP	CT	B-	1144.5	89.5	2.23	1.13	7.2	6.7	3.3	6.5	5.1	AT
HARTFORD LIFE & ACCIDENT INS CO	CT	C-	9041.5	1522.6	0.31	0.29	0.5	0.6	3.6	6.9	1.9	ACFIT
HARTFORD LIFE & ANNUITY INS CO	CT	B-	48312.7	3323.9	6.88	3.96	4.0	7.5	5.4	9.1	3.9	AFT
HARTFORD LIFE INS CO	CT	C+	124390.0	5525.3	1.41	1.10	4.0	5.5	2.9	9.3	4.1	AT
HAWKEYE LIFE INS GROUP INC	IA	C-	12.2	9.1	3.40	3.06	10.0	8.9	5.8	8.4	3.3	D
HAWTHORN LIFE INS CO	TX	D	11.7	3.3	0.27	0.26	0.1	3.4	9.0	6.5	0.4	ACDI
HCC LIFE INS CO	IN	B	885.8	516.9	3.98	3.24	10.0	7.8	9.4	6.9	6.1	AD
HEALTH NET LIFE INS CO	CA	B	618.8	279.4	1.87	1.52	7.8	8.3	3.9	5.5	5.2	ADT
HEALTHMARKETS INS CO	OK	B-	28.9	17.1	4.49	3.47	10.0	9.5	2.8	7.2	4.9	ADFG
HEARTLAND NATIONAL LIFE INS CO	IN	C	9.5	4.4	1.96	1.76	8.1	9.5	3.7	7.3	3.5	G
HERITAGE LIFE INS CO	AZ	C-	5039.7	1034.3	4.23	1.86	8.3	4.9	4.5	9.3	3.1	T
HERITAGE UNION LIFE INS CO	MN	U	11.8	8.5	3.21	2.89	4.0	9.4	1.8	7.0	4.1	AFGT
HIGGINBOTHAM BURIAL INS CO	AR	F (5)	--	--	--	--	--	--	--	--	--	Z
HM LIFE INS CO	PA	B	583.7	299.7	3.17	2.41	9.1	5.1	8.7	6.8	6.1	ADI
HM LIFE INS CO OF NEW YORK	NY	B+	72.4	32.4	2.52	1.99	8.5	8.7	6.5	7.1	6.2	AD
HOMESTEADERS LIFE CO	IA	B	2475.7	158.6	2.11	1.20	7.3	6.3	5.8	6.8	5.5	I
HORACE MANN LIFE INS CO	IL	B	7830.3	387.2	1.89	0.95	6.6	5.3	8.1	5.2	5.4	AIL
HUMANA INS CO OF KENTUCKY	KY	B-	122.2	74.2	2.40	1.84	8.3	8.1	2.9	6.7	5.1	AGIT
HUMANA INS CO OF PUERTO RICO INC	PR	B-	69.1	52.5	2.96	2.35	9.0	8.4	5.9	6.6	4.3	AT
IA AMERICAN LIFE INS CO	TX	C	236.6	136.2	1.14	1.06	7.1	5.4	2.7	6.5	3.9	CFT
IBC LIFE INS CO	TX	U (3)	3.5	3.4	3.04	2.74	9.6	9.8	8.2	10.0	5.3	DFT
IDEALIFE INS CO	CT	C+	21.0	14.9	4.16	3.74	10.0	9.6	2.3	10.0	4.6	DT

See Page 27 for explanation of footnotes and Page 28 for explanation of stability factors.
Arrows denote recent upgrades ▲ or downgrades ▼ (see Section VI for explanations)

42

www.weissratings.com

NET PREMIUM ($MIL)	IN-VESTED ASSETS ($MIL)	% OF INVESTED ASSETS IN:									INVEST. IN AFFIL	INSURANCE COMPANY NAME
		CASH	CMO & STRUCT. SECS.	OTH.INV. GRADE BONDS	NON-INV. GRADE BONDS	CMMON & PREF. STOCK	MORT IN GOOD STAND.	NON-PERF. MORT.	REAL ESTATE	OTHER INVEST-MENTS		
--	--	--	--	--	--	--	--	--	--	--	--	GOLDEN GATE II CAPTIVE INS CO
1,409.1	691.7	-0.5	18.4	78.4	0.0	0.0	0.0	0.0	0.5	3.2	0.0 ●	GOLDEN RULE INS CO
35.3	801.3	1.7	0.0	68.1	1.5	2.9	15.1	0.2	1.5	9.0	1.9 ●	GOVERNMENT PERSONNEL MUTUAL L I C
34.7	307.4 (*)	4.6	31.8	51.8	4.0	2.1	0.0	0.0	0.0	3.4	2.1 ●	GRANGE LIFE INS CO
2,555.7	19,563.2 (*)	0.2	35.2	52.4	3.0	2.9	3.4	0.0	0.4	1.2	1.2 ●	GREAT AMERICAN LIFE INS CO
2.2	21.4	5.8	0.0	22.1	0.0	39.5	20.6	0.0	12.0	0.0	10.4	GREAT CENTRAL LIFE INS CO
0.1	3.9	6.7	2.3	72.8	3.9	0.5	11.2	0.0	2.7	0.0	0.0	GREAT FIDELITY LIFE INS CO
1.5	5.3	50.5	0.0	49.5	0.0	0.0	0.0	0.0	0.0	0.0	0.0	GREAT PLAINS LIFE ASR CO
--	--	--	--	--	--	--	--	--	--	--	--	GREAT REPUBLIC LIFE INS CO
0.1	226.0	-0.5	26.6	64.5	0.4	8.6	0.4	0.0	0.0	0.2	0.0 ●	GREAT SOUTHERN LIFE INS CO
2.0	72.3	0.3	29.6	65.9	0.0	0.0	0.0	0.0	1.6	2.6	0.0	GREAT WEST LIFE ASR CO
375.5	480.6	0.2	6.1	81.1	0.9	2.5	9.2	0.0	0.0	0.1	0.7 ●	GREAT WESTERN INS CO
0.0	2.1	2.3	0.0	97.2	0.0	0.0	0.0	0.0	0.0	0.5	0.0	GREAT WESTERN LIFE INS CO
4,292.9	24,563.9	-0.1	22.1	45.0	1.6	0.7	12.3	0.0	0.2	18.1	1.0 ●	GREAT-WEST LIFE & ANNUITY INS CO
220.0	896.4 (*)	0.1	20.5	63.4	0.9	0.0	10.6	0.0	0.0	3.2	0.0 ●	GREAT-WEST LIFE & ANNUITY INS OF NY
20.8	43.9 (*)	5.8	46.1	44.4	0.5	0.0	0.0	0.0	0.0	0.7	0.0	GREATER GEORGIA LIFE INS CO
--	--	--	--	--	--	--	--	--	--	--	--	GREATER MISSOURI LIFE INS CO
1.2	2.3	2.6	30.2	67.2	0.0	0.0	0.0	0.0	0.0	0.0	0.0	GREENFIELDS LIFE INS CO
0.0	0.1	100.0	0.0	0.0	0.0	0.0	0.0	0.0	0.0	0.0	0.0	GRIFFIN LEGGETT BURIAL INS CO
159.0	339.0	0.7	33.5	51.8	3.0	0.7	7.7	0.5	0.2	2.0	1.6 ●	GUARANTEE TRUST LIFE INS CO
24.9	473.0	2.2	30.8	55.3	0.7	3.2	0.8	0.0	3.6	3.5	0.7 ●	GUARANTY INCOME LIFE INS CO
1,178.9	2,313.7	0.2	3.4	87.3	1.4	0.2	1.8	0.0	0.0	5.7	0.7 ●	GUARDIAN INS & ANNUITY CO INC
5,157.2	37,710.4	0.1	7.3	61.7	5.2	4.4	7.5	0.0	0.4	13.4	4.5 ●	GUARDIAN LIFE INS CO OF AMERICA
1,153.7	7,571.2 (*)	5.7	28.5	25.6	3.2	3.6	8.7	0.0	0.0	16.2	16.6 ●	GUGGENHEIM LIFE & ANNUITY CO
4.6	15.5	21.2	0.0	28.9	0.0	35.1	2.2	0.0	10.4	3.0	23.9	GULF GUARANTY LIFE INS CO
-0.1	2.8	18.4	0.0	43.6	0.7	33.0	0.0	0.0	4.3	0.0	0.0	GULF STATES LIFE INS CO INC
7.1	27.5	0.0	0.0	100.0	0.0	0.0	0.0	0.0	0.0	0.0	0.0	HALLMARK LIFE INS CO
209.0	2,434.0	0.2	7.0	88.8	2.4	0.0	1.2	0.0	0.1	0.3	0.0 ●	HANNOVER LIFE REASSUR CO OF AMERICA
27.1	398.8	0.4	18.1	79.5	0.5	0.0	0.0	0.0	0.0	1.6	0.0 ●	HARLEYSVILLE LIFE INS CO
--	--	--	--	--	--	--	--	--	--	--	--	HARRIS LIFE INS CO
3.3	1,108.7	0.0	14.0	24.5	2.1	1.1	6.3	0.0	0.0	52.0	0.0 ●	HARTFORD INTL LIFE REASR CORP
1,902.8	13,179.8 (*)	1.1	8.2	40.2	2.2	38.8	5.2	0.0	0.3	2.5	38.4 ●	HARTFORD LIFE & ACCIDENT INS CO
41,271.7	9,841.2 (*)	2.6	21.0	52.2	2.4	1.3	7.6	0.0	0.3	5.4	11.0 ●	HARTFORD LIFE & ANNUITY INS CO
-1,186.0	21,366.9 (*)	0.7	18.9	41.2	3.6	15.7	6.4	0.0	0.4	10.3	14.8 ●	HARTFORD LIFE INS CO
2.0	12.3	0.6	0.0	99.5	0.0	0.0	0.0	0.0	0.0	0.0	2.2	HAWKEYE LIFE INS GROUP INC
0.4	11.8	5.3	22.2	2.4	0.0	70.1	0.0	0.0	0.0	0.0	70.1	HAWTHORN LIFE INS CO
713.5	703.1	0.3	20.1	76.4	0.5	2.7	0.0	0.0	0.0	0.0	2.7 ●	HCC LIFE INS CO
775.4	370.4	-4.5	25.3	78.4	0.9	0.0	0.0	0.0	0.0	0.0	0.0 ●	HEALTH NET LIFE INS CO
10.6	11.1	9.2	0.0	90.8	0.0	0.0	0.0	0.0	0.0	0.0	0.0	HEALTHMARKETS INS CO
3.8	6.6	41.2	2.1	56.7	0.0	0.0	0.0	0.0	0.0	0.0	0.0	HEARTLAND NATIONAL LIFE INS CO
26.9	4,779.1 (*)	8.1	27.8	35.6	11.0	1.0	0.0	0.0	0.0	10.0	5.5 ●	HERITAGE LIFE INS CO
0.0	6.3 (*)	17.6	8.0	71.3	0.0	0.0	0.0	0.0	0.0	1.6	0.0	HERITAGE UNION LIFE INS CO
--	--	--	--	--	--	--	--	--	--	--	--	HIGGINBOTHAM BURIAL INS CO
488.8	504.3 (*)	7.4	14.1	59.9	11.0	1.4	0.0	0.0	0.0	0.2	1.4 ●	HM LIFE INS CO
56.9	70.3	31.7	24.0	44.3	0.0	0.0	0.0	0.0	0.0	0.0	0.0 ●	HM LIFE INS CO OF NEW YORK
304.3	2,320.0	0.3	22.2	72.3	0.4	0.0	3.8	0.3	0.5	0.3	0.0 ●	HOMESTEADERS LIFE CO
433.9	5,417.1	0.2	24.6	66.5	3.3	0.7	0.2	0.0	0.0	4.4	0.2 ●	HORACE MANN LIFE INS CO
88.1	64.5	2.9	36.2	60.8	0.0	0.0	0.0	0.0	0.0	0.0	0.0 ●	HUMANA INS CO OF KENTUCKY
71.3	64.5 (*)	0.0	58.7	42.1	1.6	0.0	0.0	0.0	0.0	0.0	0.0 ●	HUMANA INS CO OF PUERTO RICO INC
8.6	201.7	0.7	0.3	44.8	0.8	44.8	5.3	0.4	0.0	2.8	67.5	IA AMERICAN LIFE INS CO
0.1	3.4	100.0	0.0	0.0	0.0	0.0	0.0	0.0	0.0	0.0	0.0	IBC LIFE INS CO
1.5	20.0	7.8	0.0	80.1	0.0	0.0	0.0	0.0	0.0	12.1	0.0	IDEALIFE INS CO

● Bullets denote a more detailed analysis is available in Section II.
(*) Asset category percentages do not add up to 100%

INSURANCE COMPANY NAME	DOM. STATE	RATING	TOTAL ASSETS ($MIL)	CAPITAL & SURPLUS ($MIL)	RISK ADJUSTED CAPITAL RATIO 1	RISK ADJUSTED CAPITAL RATIO 2	CAPITAL-IZATION INDEX (PTS)	INVEST. SAFETY INDEX (PTS)	PROFIT-ABILITY INDEX (PTS)	LIQUIDITY INDEX (PTS)	STAB. INDEX (PTS)	STABILITY FACTOR
ILLINOIS MUTUAL LIFE INS CO	IL	A-	1368.4	195.3	3.38	1.91	8.4	6.5	7.0	6.6	6.9	I
INDEPENDENCE INS INC	DE	U (3)	1.7	1.7	2.67	2.40	8.0	9.8	3.7	10.0	3.9	D
INDEPENDENCE LIFE & ANNUITY CO	DE	C	2540.6	129.1	4.54	2.90	4.0	8.0	7.5	7.2	3.5	AFG
INDIVIDUAL ASR CO LIFE HEALTH & ACC	OK	D	17.9	8.4	2.47	2.23	8.8	4.3	2.9	7.8	1.4	IT
INDUSTRIAL ALLIANCE INS & FIN SERV	TX	C	190.2	56.9	4.57	2.68	9.5	5.0	2.0	6.4	2.9	DFGT
INSOUTH LIFE INS CO	TN	U	--	--	--	--	--	--	--	--	--	Z
INTEGRITY LIFE INS CO	OH	B-	6199.4	735.1	1.61	1.18	7.3	5.0	2.5	7.4	4.9	I
INTERNATIONAL AMERICAN LIFE INS CO	TX	D-	2.1	0.8	1.14	1.03	7.0	9.4	2.2	9.4	1.0	DG
INTRAMERICA LIFE INS CO	NY	B	34.4	9.7	1.93	1.74	8.1	9.6	7.7	10.0	4.9	GT
▲ INVESTORS GROWTH LIFE INS CO	AZ	B-	19.0	10.0	2.94	2.10	8.7	6.4	6.7	7.1	4.2	DFT
INVESTORS HERITAGE LIFE INS CO	KY	C	480.0	20.3	1.03	0.62	5.0	2.7	2.9	1.0	3.0	CILR
INVESTORS LIFE INS CO NORTH AMERICA	TX	B	680.7	52.0	2.65	1.42	4.0	4.8	8.5	6.1	6.1	AFI
INVESTORS PREFERRED LIFE INS CO	SD	U (3)	0.7	0.7	2.22	2.00	8.0	9.8	1.9	10.0	2.1	DEFT
ISLAND INS CORP	PR	U (5)	--	--	--	--	--	--	--	--	--	Z
JACKSON GRIFFIN INS CO	AR	E	11.2	0.6	0.31	0.28	0.4	0.5	0.4	0.6	0.3	CFIL
JACKSON NATIONAL LIFE INS CO	MI	B+	176820.4	4505.9	2.01	1.07	7.1	5.6	7.8	7.6	6.4	I
JACKSON NATIONAL LIFE INS CO OF NY	NY	B	9263.1	397.9	5.07	2.45	9.2	5.4	8.5	9.6	6.3	AI
JAMESTOWN LIFE INS CO	VA	B	143.7	36.5	3.96	2.91	9.9	7.3	4.3	7.8	5.5	AD
JEFF DAVIS MORTUARY BENEFIT ASSOC	LA	C (5)	--	--	--	--	--	--	--	--	--	Z
JEFFERSON LIFE INS CO	TX	D	2.7	1.7	1.84	1.66	8.0	9.4	1.6	9.3	1.7	DT
JEFFERSON NATIONAL LIFE INS CO	TX	C-	3581.0	39.1	1.39	0.69	5.6	5.3	4.1	10.0	3.2	FGT
JOHN ALDEN LIFE INS CO	WI	B	335.7	55.4	2.30	1.63	7.9	6.5	6.3	6.1	4.4	ADFT
JOHN HANCOCK LIFE & HEALTH INS CO	MA	B	10285.2	711.0	3.02	1.79	8.2	5.1	3.1	8.1	4.0	IT
JOHN HANCOCK LIFE INS CO (USA)	MI	B	241722.8	5540.7	0.99	0.63	4.9	3.1	5.6	7.2	4.9	CGIT
JOHN HANCOCK LIFE INS CO OF NY	NY	A-	17279.2	1345.7	2.96	1.76	8.1	5.0	6.3	7.3	5.5	AIT
JORDAN FUNERAL & INS CO INC	AL	U (3)	1.1	0.2	0.42	0.37	1.4	6.9	1.8	9.1	0.0	CDFI
JRD LIFE INS CO	AZ	U	--	--	--	--	--	--	--	--	--	Z
KANAWHA INS CO	SC	C	1657.2	130.5	2.18	1.33	7.5	6.6	1.5	7.8	3.5	T
KANSAS CITY LIFE INS CO	MO	B	3390.6	351.6	1.82	1.13	7.2	5.1	6.4	5.9	6.3	I
KENTUCKY FUNERAL DIRECTORS LIFE INS	KY	B-	17.3	4.9	1.59	1.43	7.6	8.0	8.0	6.4	4.5	AD
KENTUCKY HOME LIFE INS CO	KY	E+	5.7	3.5	2.94	2.64	9.5	6.4	3.5	7.2	0.6	AFT
KILPATRICK LIFE INS CO	LA	E+	181.5	5.8	0.51	0.30	1.1	0.5	2.0	2.4	0.6	CIL
KNIGHTS OF COLUMBUS	CT	U	--	--	--	--	--	--	--	--	--	Z
KSKJ LIFE	IL	U	--	--	--	--	--	--	--	--	--	Z
LAFAYETTE LIFE INS CO	OH	B	3985.3	202.6	1.67	0.85	6.0	4.9	4.0	5.2	5.7	ACIL
LANDCAR LIFE INS CO	UT	C+	22.6	13.5	1.47	1.21	7.3	3.1	6.0	9.2	4.0	ADFI
LANDMARK LIFE INS CO	TX	D	44.9	4.6	0.82	0.74	4.9	4.5	2.8	5.0	1.4	CDIT
LEADERS LIFE INS CO	OK	C+	5.9	3.1	1.79	1.56	7.8	8.2	2.4	5.1	4.1	FIT
LEWER LIFE INS CO	MO	C	29.0	9.5	2.22	1.70	8.1	5.9	4.2	6.9	3.3	D
LIBERTY BANKERS LIFE INS CO	OK	D+	1103.8	167.2	1.17	0.80	5.4	3.6	6.0	7.1	2.9	CIT
LIBERTY LIFE ASR CO OF BOSTON	NH	B	14303.2	894.9	2.17	1.26	7.4	6.4	6.6	6.9	6.2	AIT
LIBERTY NATIONAL LIFE INS CO	NE	B	7400.5	585.4	2.23	1.16	7.2	5.3	5.7	3.2	5.2	AIL
LIFE ASR CO OF AMERICA	IL	C-	6.2	2.7	1.37	1.24	7.4	6.2	3.7	7.2	2.0	DFGT
LIFE ASSURANCE CO INC	OK	C-	5.3	2.2	1.37	1.23	7.3	9.7	2.6	9.3	3.0	F
LIFE INS CO OF ALABAMA	AL	A-	112.0	36.0	3.02	2.01	8.5	6.3	9.0	6.7	6.3	I
LIFE INS CO OF BOSTON & NEW YORK	NY	A-	122.2	23.4	2.60	2.08	8.6	8.0	5.8	6.7	7.0	A
LIFE INS CO OF LOUISIANA	LA	C- (3)	8.4	3.9	2.14	1.60	7.9	3.3	2.7	6.9	2.9	DFI
LIFE INS CO OF NORTH AMERICA	PA	B	7167.4	1249.0	2.45	1.55	7.8	5.4	7.9	7.0	5.8	AI
LIFE INS CO OF THE SOUTHWEST	TX	B	12900.2	772.9	2.16	1.05	7.1	4.5	8.6	4.3	5.5	ACIL
LIFE OF AMERICA INS CO	TX	C	11.4	2.0	0.74	0.67	3.0	6.7	2.2	0.0	2.6	ACDI
LIFE OF THE SOUTH INS CO	GA	C	79.3	19.8	0.84	0.67	4.4	7.6	5.9	7.8	3.6	C
LIFE PROTECTION INS CO	TX	D+	8.7	7.9	3.45	3.11	10.0	4.4	3.3	10.0	2.3	AFIT

See Page 27 for explanation of footnotes and Page 28 for explanation of stability factors.
Arrows denote recent upgrades ▲ or downgrades▼ (see Section VI for explanations)

44

www.weissratings.com

NET PREMIUM ($MIL)	IN-VESTED ASSETS ($MIL)	% OF INVESTED ASSETS IN:									INVEST. IN AFFIL	INSURANCE COMPANY NAME
		CASH	CMO & STRUCT. SECS.	OTH.INV. GRADE BONDS	NON-INV. GRADE BONDS	CMMON & PREF. STOCK	MORT IN GOOD STAND.	NON-PERF. MORT.	REAL ESTATE	OTHER INVEST-MENTS		
75.4	1,204.3	1.1	20.5	72.5	0.7	1.6	1.0	0.0	0.2	2.5	0.1 ●	ILLINOIS MUTUAL LIFE INS CO
0.0	1.7	91.4	0.0	8.6	0.0	0.0	0.0	0.0	0.0	0.0	0.0	INDEPENDENCE INS INC
-0.3	151.2	0.3	18.7	69.7	0.0	0.0	0.0	0.0	0.0	11.2	0.0 ●	INDEPENDENCE LIFE & ANNUITY CO
1.5	16.2	38.1	0.0	19.8	0.0	0.0	0.0	0.0	22.9	19.2	0.0	INDIVIDUAL ASR CO LIFE HEALTH & ACC
41.8	182.1	2.0	0.0	75.8	0.6	0.0	6.6	2.6	5.5	6.9	0.0 ●	INDUSTRIAL ALLIANCE INS & FIN SERV
--	--	--	--	--	--	--	--	--	--	--	--	INSOUTH LIFE INS CO
260.6	3,430.5	0.0	22.6	47.1	7.3	15.4	1.3	0.0	0.0	6.2	10.2 ●	INTEGRITY LIFE INS CO
0.3	1.9	8.5	0.0	91.5	0.0	0.0	0.0	0.0	0.0	0.0	0.0	INTERNATIONAL AMERICAN LIFE INS CO
0.0	12.6	7.8	0.0	92.2	0.0	0.0	0.0	0.0	0.0	0.0	0.0	INTRAMERICA LIFE INS CO
8.4	16.6	5.7	0.0	69.9	2.0	22.5	0.0	0.0	0.0	0.0	0.0	INVESTORS GROWTH LIFE INS CO
40.0	446.2	0.5	21.3	67.4	3.7	1.3	4.2	0.0	0.1	1.5	1.1	INVESTORS HERITAGE LIFE INS CO
-0.3	448.9	0.0	29.0	55.3	5.7	5.9	0.0	0.0	0.0	4.5	1.1 ●	INVESTORS LIFE INS CO NORTH AMERICA
0.0	0.7	100.0	0.0	0.0	0.0	0.0	0.0	0.0	0.0	0.0	0.0	INVESTORS PREFERRED LIFE INS CO
--	--	--	--	--	--	--	--	--	--	--	--	ISLAND INS CORP
0.7	10.8	5.8	0.0	69.7	12.6	12.3	0.0	0.0	0.0	0.0	0.0	JACKSON GRIFFIN INS CO
18,783.0	59,115.9	-0.2	16.7	57.8	3.0	1.4	10.3	0.0	0.2	10.0	1.7 ●	JACKSON NATIONAL LIFE INS CO
1,386.0	1,770.9	-0.2	27.6	68.5	3.4	0.0	0.0	0.0	0.0	0.0	0.0 ●	JACKSON NATIONAL LIFE INS CO OF NY
3.7	139.0	1.6	57.1	40.8	0.4	0.0	0.0	0.0	0.0	0.1	0.0 ●	JAMESTOWN LIFE INS CO
--	--	--	--	--	--	--	--	--	--	--	--	JEFF DAVIS MORTUARY BENEFIT ASSOC
0.5	2.7	62.4	3.9	21.0	0.0	0.0	0.0	0.0	0.0	12.7	0.0	JEFFERSON LIFE INS CO
608.9	482.8	2.1	48.2	38.7	3.1	2.0	4.2	0.1	0.3	1.4	0.0 ●	JEFFERSON NATIONAL LIFE INS CO
137.2	339.5	-0.6	11.9	69.7	5.9	1.3	4.6	0.0	0.0	7.3	0.0 ●	JOHN ALDEN LIFE INS CO
431.0	3,491.8 (*)	0.2	5.3	65.8	1.8	0.8	9.1	0.0	4.8	6.2	0.9 ●	JOHN HANCOCK LIFE & HEALTH INS CO
9,264.8	89,961.4 (*)	0.3	7.6	48.3	2.8	3.6	13.6	0.0	6.2	11.7	4.4 ●	JOHN HANCOCK LIFE INS CO (USA)
814.3	8,281.3 (*)	0.4	8.3	64.3	2.0	0.0	14.0	0.0	3.3	2.9	0.0 ●	JOHN HANCOCK LIFE INS CO OF NY
0.0	1.1	24.0	0.0	47.0	0.0	0.0	20.9	0.0	8.0	0.1	0.0	JORDAN FUNERAL & INS CO INC
--	--	--	--	--	--	--	--	--	--	--	--	JRD LIFE INS CO
159.9	1,533.5	5.2	11.4	81.0	1.2	0.1	0.2	0.0	0.0	0.9	0.0 ●	KANAWHA INS CO
235.7	2,893.3	0.0	8.8	61.1	1.9	3.2	18.2	0.2	3.2	4.0	1.9 ●	KANSAS CITY LIFE INS CO
1.9	15.9	1.8	0.1	94.0	2.6	1.6	0.0	0.0	0.0	0.0	0.0	KENTUCKY FUNERAL DIRECTORS LIFE INS
1.2	5.6	3.7	0.0	80.2	0.0	16.1	0.0	0.0	0.0	0.0	0.0	KENTUCKY HOME LIFE INS CO
12.4	170.8	2.4	18.7	50.4	8.4	2.2	7.4	1.9	2.1	6.5	6.4	KILPATRICK LIFE INS CO
--	--	--	--	--	--	--	--	--	--	--	--	KNIGHTS OF COLUMBUS
--	--	--	--	--	--	--	--	--	--	--	--	KSKJ LIFE
398.7	3,709.9 (*)	-0.1	18.8	52.7	4.6	2.4	6.9	0.0	0.0	10.5	0.5 ●	LAFAYETTE LIFE INS CO
-0.3	22.2	8.1	0.0	25.0	0.0	65.8	1.2	0.0	0.0	0.0	31.6	LANDCAR LIFE INS CO
4.2	40.2	2.5	23.0	54.0	2.0	0.4	10.5	0.0	5.7	1.9	0.0	LANDMARK LIFE INS CO
3.2	3.8	26.2	0.5	62.4	0.0	10.8	0.0	0.0	0.0	0.1	0.0	LEADERS LIFE INS CO
5.3	28.6	4.2	11.6	72.4	1.3	9.0	0.0	0.0	0.0	1.5	0.0	LEWER LIFE INS CO
177.9	983.8	6.4	5.6	37.1	2.2	11.7	22.6	1.5	8.2	4.4	7.6 ●	LIBERTY BANKERS LIFE INS CO
1,812.7	12,719.2 (*)	0.1	12.0	77.6	2.3	0.2	2.9	0.0	0.0	2.7	0.1 ●	LIBERTY LIFE ASR CO OF BOSTON
425.8	6,064.0	-0.1	4.8	73.3	6.1	5.2	0.0	0.0	0.0	10.8	7.9 ●	LIBERTY NATIONAL LIFE INS CO
0.1	6.0	0.5	27.6	52.9	0.0	15.1	0.0	0.0	0.0	3.9	0.0	LIFE ASR CO OF AMERICA
1.2	5.1	79.9	6.5	13.6	0.0	0.0	0.0	0.0	0.0	0.0	0.0	LIFE ASSURANCE CO INC
28.3	100.6	0.8	0.0	83.9	2.9	6.7	0.0	0.0	0.6	5.1	0.0 ●	LIFE INS CO OF ALABAMA
18.5	109.1	1.4	8.5	66.8	0.5	0.0	0.0	0.0	0.0	22.8	0.0	LIFE INS CO OF BOSTON & NEW YORK
0.2	7.3	9.4	0.0	43.2	0.0	47.3	0.0	0.0	0.0	0.1	3.9	LIFE INS CO OF LOUISIANA
2,491.4	5,963.7	-0.5	4.5	61.3	10.5	0.8	17.7	0.0	0.0	5.8	4.7 ●	LIFE INS CO OF NORTH AMERICA
1,142.7	12,167.7 (*)	-0.1	25.6	46.7	4.4	0.3	13.6	0.0	0.0	2.7	0.0 ●	LIFE INS CO OF THE SOUTHWEST
0.0	3.3	24.3	0.0	53.2	6.4	0.6	15.4	0.0	0.0	0.2	0.0	LIFE OF AMERICA INS CO
47.2	67.2	1.9	13.4	62.4	0.2	18.6	0.0	0.0	0.0	4.4	9.5	LIFE OF THE SOUTH INS CO
0.0	9.7	62.9	2.4	3.4	0.0	31.3	0.0	0.0	0.0	0.0	0.0	LIFE PROTECTION INS CO

● Bullets denote a more detailed analysis is available in Section II.
(*) Asset category percentages do not add up to 100%

INSURANCE COMPANY NAME	DOM. STATE	RATING	TOTAL ASSETS ($MIL)	CAPITAL & SURPLUS ($MIL)	RISK ADJUSTED CAPITAL RATIO 1	RISK ADJUSTED CAPITAL RATIO 2	CAPITAL-IZATION INDEX (PTS)	INVEST. SAFETY INDEX (PTS)	PROFIT-ABILITY INDEX (PTS)	LIQUIDITY INDEX (PTS)	STAB. INDEX (PTS)	STABILI FACTO
LIFECARE ASSURANCE CO	AZ	B-	1899.4	95.3	1.69	0.92	6.4	4.8	5.5	9.3	5.2	I
LIFEMAP ASR CO	OR	B	84.5	42.3	1.79	1.29	7.4	4.6	2.5	6.7	5.7	I
LIFESECURE INS CO	MI	D-	215.7	25.0	2.27	1.49	7.7	7.5	1.7	8.4	1.3	D
LIFESHIELD NATIONAL INS CO	OK	B-	67.0	22.5	2.15	1.26	7.4	3.8	7.7	7.6	5.0	I
LIFEWISE ASR CO	WA	A	125.6	87.1	6.58	5.00	10.0	8.5	9.2	7.0	7.0	AD
LINCOLN BENEFIT LIFE CO	NE	B+	12911.3	733.5	2.15	0.96	6.7	4.8	8.1	10.0	6.4	CFGI
LINCOLN HERITAGE LIFE INS CO	IL	B-	794.5	114.0	4.00	2.09	8.6	7.1	2.7	6.4	5.2	D
LINCOLN LIFE & ANNUITY CO OF NY	NY	B	12543.7	634.8	2.46	1.27	7.4	5.6	5.3	5.5	5.5	AI
LINCOLN NATIONAL LIFE INS CO	IN	B	208169.3	7027.0	1.46	0.97	6.8	6.0	6.7	6.7	5.8	AI
LINCOLN REPUBLIC INS CO	ND	B	30.4	13.3	2.89	2.60	9.4	7.1	4.0	6.7	4.9	FT
LOCOMOTIVE ENGRS&COND MUT PROT ASSN	MI	B+	55.4	46.7	7.01	6.02	10.0	6.1	7.6	9.1	5.6	DI
LONDON LIFE INS CO	MI	C+	25.3	14.0	3.29	2.96	9.9	8.3	5.3	10.0	4.1	DFT
LONDON LIFE REINSURANCE CO	PA	C+	324.0	54.1	4.94	2.56	4.0	7.8	2.9	9.1	3.0	T
LONE STAR LIFE INS CO	TX	F (5)	--	--	--	--	--	--	--	--	--	Z
LONGEVITY INS CO	TX	D+	9.1	7.6	3.38	3.04	8.0	9.7	2.3	10.0	2.6	F
LOYAL AMERICAN LIFE INS CO	OH	C	251.3	74.7	1.46	1.08	7.1	6.1	4.7	6.9	3.8	CT
LOYAL CHRISTIAN BENEFIT ASSN	PA	U	--	--	--	--	--	--	--	--	--	Z
M & T LIFE INS CO	AZ	U	--	--	--	--	--	--	--	--	--	Z
M LIFE INS CO	CO	C	248.6	65.0	4.49	2.99	10.0	7.9	3.0	7.3	4.2	DT
MADISON NATIONAL LIFE INS CO INC	WI	C+	491.1	83.7	1.31	1.09	7.1	7.9	4.5	0.7	3.1	FLT
MAGNA INS CO	MS	D+	2.6	2.3	2.65	2.39	9.1	9.1	2.7	7.0	2.8	DGT
MAGNOLIA GUARANTY LIFE INS CO	MS	B	9.8	2.5	1.27	1.14	7.2	4.7	7.5	8.1	4.5	ADGI
MAJESTIC LIFE INS CO	LA	U	--	--	--	--	--	--	--	--	--	Z
MANHATTAN LIFE INS CO	NY	B	335.6	37.5	1.19	0.98	6.8	7.2	4.9	6.4	5.4	ADFG
MANHATTAN NATIONAL LIFE INS CO	OH	B	181.3	12.9	1.46	1.31	7.5	5.0	7.0	10.0	5.5	AFGI
MAPFRE LIFE INS CO	DE	C+	26.7	23.4	6.48	5.83	10.0	9.6	3.9	10.0	3.2	T
MAPFRE LIFE INS CO OF PR	PR	C+	66.0	29.0	1.43	1.14	7.2	8.3	1.9	6.9	3.6	CDFT
MARQUETTE INDEMNITY & LIFE INS CO	AZ	C	7.3	3.2	1.73	1.56	7.8	5.6	3.3	8.6	3.7	T
MARQUETTE NATIONAL LIFE INS CO	TX	C	6.7	5.6	3.02	2.71	9.6	9.2	2.4	8.2	2.8	AFT
MASSACHUSETTS MUTUAL LIFE INS CO	MA	A-	190575.4	13961.5	1.93	1.35	7.5	6.2	7.1	7.0	7.0	I
MCB LIFE INS CO	TN	U	--	--	--	--	--	--	--	--	--	Z
MCS LIFE INS CO	PR	E+	67.3	21.9	0.42	0.36	1.3	9.2	8.2	1.7	0.6	ACDF
MEDAMERICA INS CO	PA	B	878.9	38.8	2.80	2.09	8.6	2.4	2.0	9.0	6.2	CDI
MEDAMERICA INS CO OF FL	FL	C+	25.9	2.5	0.66	0.60	3.8	4.2	1.9	9.2	3.8	CDI
MEDAMERICA INS CO OF NEW YORK	NY	B	565.5	19.1	1.59	1.00	7.0	6.5	1.7	9.1	6.3	
MEDICAL BENEFITS MUTUAL LIFE INS CO	OH	D	18.3	11.2	2.13	1.48	7.7	4.3	1.8	1.8	2.3	DFLT
MEDICO CORP LIFE INS CO	NE	B+	26.0	24.5	6.04	5.43	8.0	8.4	8.4	10.0	6.5	T
MEDICO INS CO	NE	B	67.2	31.2	4.26	3.84	10.0	7.4	1.9	6.8	4.7	FIT
MEGA LIFE & HEALTH INS CO	OK	B-	271.8	118.8	2.37	1.84	8.3	6.1	7.0	7.2	4.3	T
MELANCON LIFE INS CO	LA	D (5)	--	--	--	--	--	--	--	--	--	Z
MELLON LIFE INS CO	DE	C	24.9	24.5	6.05	5.45	10.0	9.4	4.0	10.0	3.9	DT
MEMBERS LIFE INS CO	IA	C	27.3	18.4	4.80	4.32	10.0	9.4	2.0	9.2	3.4	T
MEMORIAL INS CO OF AMERICA	AR	D	1.2	1.1	2.21	1.66	8.0	5.2	4.0	9.3	1.9	AT
MEMORIAL LIFE INS CO	LA	C- (5)	--	--	--	--	--	--	--	--	--	Z
MERIT LIFE INS CO	IN	B+	584.3	173.1	5.53	3.56	10.0	6.1	5.6	9.1	6.3	GIT
METLIFE INS CO USA	DE	B	56480.8	3584.4	1.18	0.86	5.9	6.0	5.3	7.6	4.5	ACIT
METLIFE INS LTD GUAM BRANCH	GU	B-	3.1	2.0	1.98	1.78	8.2	9.8	6.2	10.0	5.2	ADFT
METROPOLITAN LIFE INS CO	NY	B-	392833.7	13925.2	1.38	0.90	6.2	4.5	6.2	7.1	5.2	I
METROPOLITAN TOWER LIFE INS CO	DE	B-	5083.2	815.0	3.21	1.41	7.6	3.1	6.9	6.4	5.1	FI
MIAMI VALLEY INS CO	AZ	U	--	--	--	--	--	--	--	--	--	Z
MID-WEST NATIONAL LIFE INS CO OF TN	TX	B-	63.2	27.5	3.77	2.95	9.9	8.8	6.0	8.2	3.7	AT
MIDLAND NATIONAL LIFE INS CO	IA	B+	40607.9	2776.8	2.21	1.15	7.2	5.0	8.9	6.8	6.5	AI

See Page 27 for explanation of footnotes and Page 28 for explanation of stability factors.
Arrows denote recent upgrades ▲ or downgrades▼ (see Section VI for explanations)

46

www.weissratings.com

NET PREMIUM ($MIL)	IN-VESTED ASSETS ($MIL)	% OF INVESTED ASSETS IN:									INVEST. IN AFFIL	INSURANCE COMPANY NAME
		CASH	CMO & STRUCT. SECS.	OTH.INV. GRADE BONDS	NON-INV. GRADE BONDS	CMMON & PREF. STOCK	MORT IN GOOD STAND.	NON-PERF. MORT.	REAL ESTATE	OTHER INVEST-MENTS		
172.0	1,710.4	0.2	39.3	57.2	2.4	0.0	0.0	0.0	0.0	0.9	0.0 ●	LIFECARE ASSURANCE CO
51.2	86.4	-0.3	20.6	53.1	0.2	26.5	0.0	0.0	0.0	0.0	1.9 ●	LIFEMAP ASR CO
31.4	178.0	0.1	0.0	99.9	0.0	0.0	0.0	0.0	0.0	0.0	0.0 ●	LIFESECURE INS CO
15.2	62.7	4.0	28.1	38.2	13.5	13.6	0.0	0.0	0.0	2.6	1.8	LIFESHIELD NATIONAL INS CO
69.6	111.1	5.3	40.0	52.9	1.8	0.0	0.0	0.0	0.0	0.0	0.0 ●	LIFEWISE ASR CO
7,021.1	280.0 (*)	0.0	10.2	111.5	0.0	0.0	0.0	0.0	0.0	0.4	0.0 ●	LINCOLN BENEFIT LIFE CO
238.4	625.6	15.7	44.2	27.4	3.1	0.2	1.1	0.0	1.9	6.2	0.0 ●	LINCOLN HERITAGE LIFE INS CO
936.5	7,743.6	0.0	10.6	73.9	4.1	0.0	6.7	0.0	0.0	4.8	0.0 ●	LINCOLN LIFE & ANNUITY CO OF NY
15,989.1	80,940.0	-0.2	7.8	71.9	3.5	3.5	8.0	0.0	0.1	4.7	4.3 ●	LINCOLN NATIONAL LIFE INS CO
0.7	29.4	0.9	7.8	89.5	0.0	0.0	0.0	0.0	0.0	1.8	0.0	LINCOLN REPUBLIC INS CO
15.0	51.8	0.7	1.2	81.2	0.7	16.2	0.0	0.0	0.0	0.0	0.0 ●	LOCOMOTIVE ENGRS&COND MUT PROT ASSN
0.8	25.3	13.8	3.9	82.4	0.0	0.0	0.0	0.0	0.0	0.0	0.0	LONDON LIFE INS CO
1.7	230.1	2.7	12.8	81.8	1.5	1.1	0.0	0.0	0.0	0.0	0.0 ●	LONDON LIFE REINSURANCE CO
--	--	--	--	--	--	--	--	--	--	--	--	LONE STAR LIFE INS CO
0.0	9.0	46.4	0.0	53.6	0.0	0.0	0.0	0.0	0.0	0.0	0.0	LONGEVITY INS CO
184.1	223.3 (*)	0.0	0.7	97.2	0.2	3.8	0.0	0.0	0.0	0.0	3.8 ●	LOYAL AMERICAN LIFE INS CO
--	--	--	--	--	--	--	--	--	--	--	--	LOYAL CHRISTIAN BENEFIT ASSN
--	--	--	--	--	--	--	--	--	--	--	--	M & T LIFE INS CO
279.9	121.4	14.9	23.1	60.3	1.3	0.0	0.0	0.0	0.0	0.4	0.0 ●	M LIFE INS CO
111.7	439.6 (*)	2.0	1.6	78.0	0.0	12.1	0.0	0.0	0.0	4.9	12.7 ●	MADISON NATIONAL LIFE INS CO INC
0.7	2.5 (*)	1.4	0.0	42.1	0.0	0.0	0.0	0.0	0.0	0.0	0.0	MAGNA INS CO
2.6	8.5	3.3	3.6	60.6	5.2	27.4	0.0	0.0	0.0	0.0	0.0	MAGNOLIA GUARANTY LIFE INS CO
--	--	--	--	--	--	--	--	--	--	--	--	MAJESTIC LIFE INS CO
39.7	298.3	0.3	4.0	66.4	1.9	11.3	7.3	0.0	0.0	8.9	11.3 ●	MANHATTAN LIFE INS CO
1.0	174.0	-0.2	18.2	75.9	1.5	0.0	0.0	0.0	0.0	4.5	0.0	MANHATTAN NATIONAL LIFE INS CO
0.0	20.2	0.4	0.0	99.6	0.0	0.0	0.0	0.0	0.0	0.0	0.0	MAPFRE LIFE INS CO
83.2	56.8 (*)	32.0	0.4	68.1	0.0	2.0	0.0	0.0	0.0	0.4	0.0 ●	MAPFRE LIFE INS CO OF PR
0.7	6.7 (*)	0.4	41.1	48.6	0.6	9.3	0.0	0.0	0.0	1.5	0.0	MARQUETTE INDEMNITY & LIFE INS CO
0.3	6.1	-9.7	7.1	102.5	0.0	0.0	0.0	0.0	0.0	0.1	0.0	MARQUETTE NATIONAL LIFE INS CO
13,481.3	120,490.3 (*)	0.4	11.0	43.9	3.9	6.5	13.7	0.0	0.7	14.8	13.2 ●	MASSACHUSETTS MUTUAL LIFE INS CO
--	--	--	--	--	--	--	--	--	--	--	--	MCB LIFE INS CO
206.7	45.5	55.6	2.5	40.3	0.4	1.2	0.0	0.0	0.0	0.0	0.0	MCS LIFE INS CO
45.8	844.7 (*)	2.2	6.4	75.9	5.0	0.3	0.0	0.0	0.0	0.0	0.3 ●	MEDAMERICA INS CO
3.4	22.8	4.1	7.0	88.0	0.9	0.0	0.0	0.0	0.0	0.0	0.0	MEDAMERICA INS CO OF FL
33.7	523.7	1.4	5.8	92.4	0.0	0.0	0.0	0.0	0.4	0.0	0.0	MEDAMERICA INS CO OF NEW YORK
5.9	17.2	0.2	12.6	42.8	0.0	30.6	0.0	0.0	13.7	0.0	8.4	MEDICAL BENEFITS MUTUAL LIFE INS CO
0.0	24.9	1.6	19.8	78.6	0.0	0.0	0.0	0.0	0.0	0.0	0.0	MEDICO CORP LIFE INS CO
0.7	41.9	7.8	25.9	56.4	1.1	1.9	0.0	0.0	0.0	6.8	0.0 ●	MEDICO INS CO
109.4	261.3	0.8	4.0	76.6	0.0	8.0	0.0	0.0	6.2	5.3	9.8 ●	MEGA LIFE & HEALTH INS CO
--	--	--	--	--	--	--	--	--	--	--	--	MELANCON LIFE INS CO
0.1	24.9	0.4	7.3	92.3	0.0	0.0	0.0	0.0	0.0	0.0	0.0	MELLON LIFE INS CO
0.1	17.4	4.4	21.5	73.4	0.0	0.0	0.0	0.0	0.0	0.7	0.0	MEMBERS LIFE INS CO
0.1	1.1	28.6	0.0	60.6	0.0	0.0	0.0	0.0	10.8	0.0	0.0	MEMORIAL INS CO OF AMERICA
--	--	--	--	--	--	--	--	--	--	--	--	MEMORIAL LIFE INS CO
112.9	508.9	0.6	15.7	60.2	3.7	0.2	19.1	0.4	0.0	0.4	0.0 ●	MERIT LIFE INS CO
-2,680.8	39,645.3 (*)	0.3	18.8	45.2	5.8	6.4	10.4	0.0	0.2	10.7	11.5 ●	METLIFE INS CO USA
0.4	0.3	100.0	0.0	0.0	0.0	0.0	0.0	0.0	0.0	0.0	0.0 ●	METLIFE INS LTD GUAM BRANCH
25,353.1	236,551.2	-0.1	19.1	40.2	7.6	3.6	18.3	0.0	1.1	9.2	6.0 ●	METROPOLITAN LIFE INS CO
22.4	4,732.0 (*)	0.0	18.1	37.3	4.0	0.2	5.1	0.0	24.2	9.7	2.9 ●	METROPOLITAN TOWER LIFE INS CO
--	--	--	--	--	--	--	--	--	--	--	--	MIAMI VALLEY INS CO
37.9	90.0	0.9	3.0	94.5	0.0	0.0	0.0	0.0	0.0	2.5	1.4	MID-WEST NATIONAL LIFE INS CO OF TN
2,434.3	33,643.3	1.1	38.5	42.3	5.0	2.4	5.7	0.0	0.1	3.9	1.2 ●	MIDLAND NATIONAL LIFE INS CO

● Bullets denote a more detailed analysis is available in Section II.
(*) Asset category percentages do not add up to 100%

INSURANCE COMPANY NAME	DOM. STATE	RATING	TOTAL ASSETS ($MIL)	CAPITAL & SURPLUS ($MIL)	RISK ADJUSTED CAPITAL RATIO 1	RISK ADJUSTED CAPITAL RATIO 2	CAPITAL-IZATION INDEX (PTS)	INVEST. SAFETY INDEX (PTS)	PROFIT-ABILITY INDEX (PTS)	LIQUIDITY INDEX (PTS)	STAB. INDEX (PTS)	STABILI FACTO
MIDWEST SECURITY LIFE INS CO	WI	U (3)	7.2	6.2	3.23	2.90	8.0	8.0	5.9	10.0	1.6	DT
MIDWESTERN UNITED LIFE INS CO	IN	A-	236.3	124.2	12.45	11.21	10.0	8.2	7.9	6.9	7.1	ADF
MILILANI LIFE INS CO	HI	U (3)	1.9	1.8	2.53	2.28	8.9	9.8	2.6	10.0	2.8	DT
MINNESOTA LIFE INS CO	MN	B+	34693.9	2537.2	2.44	1.51	7.8	5.6	7.3	6.9	6.5	I
MINNETONKA LIFE INS CO	AZ	U	--	--	--	--	--	--	--	--	--	Z
MISSISSIPPI VALLEY LIFE INS CO	AZ	U	--	--	--	--	--	--	--	--	--	Z
MISSOURI VALLEY LIFE AND HLTH INS CO	MO	B	16.0	15.2	5.07	4.56	10.0	8.1	9.4	10.0	4.9	AD
MML BAY STATE LIFE INS CO	CT	A-	4682.4	207.5	4.49	3.03	10.0	7.3	8.0	8.6	7.2	AT
MOLINA HEALTHCARE OF TEXAS INS CO	TX	C	3.4	3.4	1.42	0.91	6.3	9.3	5.3	7.9	3.5	E
MONARCH LIFE INS CO	MA	F (3)	755.0	6.6	0.50	0.26	1.0	0.3	2.8	3.3	0.0	CFILT
MONITOR LIFE INS CO OF NEW YORK	NY	B	17.3	8.6	1.60	1.26	7.4	7.4	7.5	7.6	5.0	DT
MONY LIFE INS CO	NY	B-	7686.7	440.5	2.25	1.20	7.3	6.2	5.0	3.2	5.0	ACFL
MONY LIFE INS CO OF AMERICA	AZ	B-	2829.1	382.5	4.19	2.77	4.0	5.5	2.9	8.4	4.7	FT
MOTHE LIFE INS CO	LA	E-	15.2	-5.2	-0.19	-0.16	0.0	2.7	0.7	7.0	0.0	CDFIT
MOTORISTS LIFE INS CO	OH	B	516.8	55.1	2.49	1.38	7.6	6.0	5.7	5.7	5.8	DI
MOUNTAIN LIFE INS CO	TN	C-	11.8	5.2	1.97	1.77	8.2	8.5	2.5	9.2	2.7	FT
MTL INS CO	IL	B	1921.5	132.9	2.08	1.11	7.2	5.8	5.9	4.6	5.9	IL
MULHEARN PROTECTIVE INS CO	LA	D	12.8	2.7	0.95	0.57	4.6	1.5	3.0	8.0	2.2	CDI
MULTINATIONAL LIFE INS CO	PR	D-	128.7	13.8	1.36	0.74	5.5	4.7	1.0	6.6	1.3	CFIT
MUNICH AMERICAN LIFE REINS CO	GA	C+	1270.8	25.0	1.21	0.60	5.3	7.0	8.8	9.4	4.6	CE
MUNICH AMERICAN REASSURANCE CO	GA	B-	7304.3	749.6	1.97	1.37	7.6	8.3	2.7	5.8	3.6	AT
MUTUAL OF AMERICA LIFE INS CO	NY	A-	17110.0	973.4	3.45	1.63	7.9	6.0	7.6	7.2	6.9	I
MUTUAL OF OMAHA INS CO	NE	B+	6568.9	2981.2	1.19	1.09	7.1	6.1	8.6	7.2	6.5	AI
MUTUAL SAVINGS LIFE INS CO	AL	A-	470.5	62.4	3.01	1.89	8.3	7.3	8.1	6.5	7.3	A
NAP LIFE INS CO	TX	U (3)	2.6	2.6	2.95	2.65	8.0	6.1	3.0	10.0	3.2	DF
NATIONAL BENEFIT LIFE INS CO	NY	B+	480.5	168.1	7.13	3.96	10.0	6.6	6.8	7.0	5.7	AIT
NATIONAL FAMILY CARE LIFE INS CO	TX	C	16.0	9.1	2.97	2.67	9.5	9.6	6.6	8.3	4.2	T
NATIONAL FARM LIFE INS CO	TX	B-	374.8	34.3	2.60	1.54	7.8	7.0	5.8	1.8	3.8	DL
▲ NATIONAL FARMERS UNION LIFE INS CO	TX	B+	216.9	46.1	4.32	2.28	8.9	5.6	7.2	6.3	6.7	ADFI
NATIONAL FOUNDATION LIFE INS CO	TX	C	24.2	10.8	1.26	0.98	5.9	7.3	7.0	6.4	4.2	ACFT
NATIONAL GUARDIAN LIFE INS CO	WI	B	2903.2	261.9	1.59	1.04	7.1	5.7	6.9	6.0	6.0	I
NATIONAL HEALTH INS CO	TX	C	14.1	11.6	6.62	5.96	10.0	8.8	1.9	6.7	2.3	DFGI
NATIONAL INCOME LIFE INS CO	NY	B+	142.8	31.6	3.46	2.45	9.2	7.4	5.3	7.1	6.7	A
NATIONAL INTEGRITY LIFE INS CO	NY	B-	4807.4	367.2	3.37	1.66	8.0	6.0	2.6	6.6	5.0	
NATIONAL LIFE INS CO	VT	B	9082.4	1461.9	1.55	1.20	7.3	6.1	7.5	6.4	5.9	AI
NATIONAL SECURITY INS CO	AL	B	52.1	12.3	1.98	1.58	7.9	6.1	7.9	6.8	5.0	AI
NATIONAL SECURITY LIFE & ANNUITY CO	NY	B	410.0	30.0	2.69	2.42	9.1	7.2	4.9	10.0	5.6	DG
NATIONAL TEACHERS ASSOCIATES L I C	TX	B	418.4	78.4	2.46	1.74	8.1	7.2	4.6	8.4	6.0	D
NATIONAL WESTERN LIFE INS CO	CO	B+	10164.8	1163.2	4.39	2.38	9.1	6.8	8.5	6.4	6.5	IT
NATIONWIDE LIFE & ANNUITY INS CO	OH	B-	7340.8	517.9	2.96	1.50	7.8	5.0	1.9	5.5	4.9	AFGI
▼ NATIONWIDE LIFE INS CO	OH	B-	125130.2	4103.4	2.59	1.49	7.7	5.4	6.4	8.4	3.7	AIT
NETCARE LIFE & HEALTH INS CO	GU	E+	24.7	3.9	0.77	0.69	4.5	8.1	2.0	6.2	0.6	C
NEW ENGLAND LIFE INS CO	MA	B	11281.7	692.0	4.38	2.34	9.0	5.9	6.6	6.7	4.8	AIT
NEW ERA LIFE INS CO	TX	C	395.4	63.0	0.94	0.71	4.7	5.3	6.0	6.5	3.6	CD
NEW ERA LIFE INS CO OF THE MIDWEST	TX	C	81.6	11.6	0.70	0.49	2.9	4.9	7.0	5.9	2.9	ACDI
NEW FOUNDATION LIFE INS CO	AR	U (3)	2.1	1.7	1.03	0.92	6.4	9.1	2.4	10.0	2.6	D
NEW YORK LIFE AGENTS REIN CO	AZ	U (5)	--	--	--	--	--	--	--	--	--	Z
NEW YORK LIFE INS & ANNUITY CORP	DE	B+	124994.1	7412.9	3.30	1.61	7.9	5.8	7.9	6.4	6.7	I
NEW YORK LIFE INS CO	NY	A-	143501.4	19179.4	1.64	1.27	7.4	6.4	7.2	6.5	7.0	I
NIAGARA LIFE & HEALTH INS CO	NY	B	8.8	6.3	2.80	2.52	9.3	6.7	2.4	9.6	6.3	GT
NIPPON LIFE INS CO OF AMERICA	IA	A-	211.7	139.0	3.26	2.61	9.4	8.1	9.1	6.4	6.1	D
NORTH AMERICA LIFE INS CO OF TX	TX	E-	45.1	-15.7	-0.99	-0.66	0.0	5.5	0.8	7.3	0.0	CFGT

See Page 27 for explanation of footnotes and Page 28 for explanation of stability factors.

Arrows denote recent upgrades ▲ or downgrades▼ (see Section VI for explanations)

48

www.weissratings.com

NET PREMIUM ($MIL)	IN- VESTED ASSETS ($MIL)	% OF INVESTED ASSETS IN:										INSURANCE COMPANY NAME
		CASH	CMO & STRUCT. SECS.	OTH.INV. GRADE BONDS	NON-INV. GRADE BONDS	CMMON & PREF. STOCK	MORT IN GOOD STAND.	NON- PERF. MORT.	REAL ESTATE	OTHER INVEST- MENTS	INVEST. IN AFFIL	
0.0	7.2	0.5	0.0	91.5	0.0	0.0	0.0	0.0	8.0	0.0	0.0	MIDWEST SECURITY LIFE INS CO
2.8	233.8	4.7	6.7	81.3	1.9	0.0	1.6	0.0	0.0	3.8	0.0 ●	MIDWESTERN UNITED LIFE INS CO
0.1	1.9	100.0	0.0	0.0	0.0	0.0	0.0	0.0	0.0	0.0	0.0	MILILANI LIFE INS CO
4,112.5	13,679.9 (*)	-0.6	25.2	44.6	4.7	4.1	12.8	0.1	0.1	7.4	4.1 ●	MINNESOTA LIFE INS CO
--	--	--	--	--	--	--	--	--	--	--	--	MINNETONKA LIFE INS CO
--	--	--	--	--	--	--	--	--	--	--	--	MISSISSIPPI VALLEY LIFE INS CO
0.8	15.3	0.0	55.8	44.2	0.0	0.0	0.0	0.0	0.0	0.0	0.0	MISSOURI VALLEY LIFE AND HLTH INS CO
18.5	336.3	0.1	18.2	51.0	1.2	0.0	1.4	0.0	0.0	28.2	1.1 ●	MML BAY STATE LIFE INS CO
0.0	3.4	1.2	0.0	98.8	0.0	0.0	0.0	0.0	0.0	0.0	0.0	MOLINA HEALTHCARE OF TEXAS INS CO
5.8	523.3	0.4	14.0	70.2	1.1	0.0	0.0	0.0	0.0	14.3	0.0	MONARCH LIFE INS CO
18.7	16.3	9.6	0.1	66.7	0.0	19.5	0.0	0.0	0.0	4.3	0.0	MONITOR LIFE INS CO OF NEW YORK
204.3	7,247.3	3.2	2.4	68.4	2.5	1.3	10.7	0.0	0.0	11.5	0.0 ●	MONY LIFE INS CO
211.3	559.2 (*)	1.1	5.3	67.3	6.9	9.1	4.8	0.0	0.0	3.1	7.4 ●	MONY LIFE INS CO OF AMERICA
0.7	19.2 (*)	2.5	0.0	11.0	0.0	56.9	21.9	0.0	7.4	10.6	53.7	MOTHE LIFE INS CO
49.4	463.3	0.8	25.0	64.1	3.0	4.5	0.0	0.0	0.0	2.8	0.0 ●	MOTORISTS LIFE INS CO
2.0	10.7	40.7	0.0	54.0	0.0	0.0	0.0	0.0	5.3	0.0	0.0	MOUNTAIN LIFE INS CO
128.0	1,808.1	0.2	13.8	59.0	2.0	0.4	8.6	0.2	0.7	15.1	0.0 ●	MTL INS CO
0.7	12.0	13.7	0.8	27.9	0.0	56.5	1.0	0.0	0.0	0.1	0.0	MULHEARN PROTECTIVE INS CO
20.7	119.8	9.5	32.0	45.3	0.4	0.1	0.2	0.0	10.2	2.4	0.0	MULTINATIONAL LIFE INS CO
0.0	1,199.5	0.0	5.4	94.6	0.0	0.0	0.0	0.0	0.0	0.0	0.0	MUNICH AMERICAN LIFE REINS CO
163.3	6,358.4	0.1	5.4	93.6	0.1	0.6	0.1	0.0	0.0	0.1	0.5 ●	MUNICH AMERICAN REASSURANCE CO
1,220.9	7,970.0	0.2	37.8	52.9	4.1	0.5	0.0	0.0	3.0	1.7	0.2 ●	MUTUAL OF AMERICA LIFE INS CO
1,620.7	5,196.1	1.8	16.8	29.2	2.0	37.9	4.6	0.0	0.7	6.7	42.5 ●	MUTUAL OF OMAHA INS CO
31.1	446.2	0.2	3.8	86.6	2.1	1.4	0.0	0.0	0.2	5.7	1.3 ●	MUTUAL SAVINGS LIFE INS CO
0.0	2.6	1.7	0.4	75.6	0.0	14.7	0.0	0.0	0.0	7.7	0.0	NAP LIFE INS CO
45.5	458.7 (*)	-0.2	13.1	74.4	3.6	1.5	0.0	0.0	0.0	2.8	0.0 ●	NATIONAL BENEFIT LIFE INS CO
5.6	15.5	12.9	0.0	87.1	0.0	0.0	0.0	0.0	0.0	0.0	0.0	NATIONAL FAMILY CARE LIFE INS CO
18.9	351.4	0.2	5.0	81.5	2.1	2.3	2.5	0.0	0.1	6.2	0.5 ●	NATIONAL FARM LIFE INS CO
3.8	202.8	-0.2	30.4	37.3	5.1	12.8	5.8	0.0	0.0	8.8	2.5 ●	NATIONAL FARMERS UNION LIFE INS CO
27.9	24.1	-3.3	26.9	71.5	5.0	0.0	0.0	0.0	0.0	0.0	0.0	NATIONAL FOUNDATION LIFE INS CO
365.0	2,613.7	0.1	5.5	77.5	2.3	6.0	4.2	0.1	0.2	4.0	3.1 ●	NATIONAL GUARDIAN LIFE INS CO
0.0	13.5	14.2	0.0	85.6	0.0	0.0	0.0	0.0	0.0	0.2	0.0	NATIONAL HEALTH INS CO
43.5	117.6	12.5	3.2	79.5	2.2	0.0	0.0	0.0	0.0	2.6	0.0 ●	NATIONAL INCOME LIFE INS CO
192.7	2,720.5 (*)	-0.2	31.2	53.0	8.2	1.0	1.4	0.0	0.0	4.2	0.9 ●	NATIONAL INTEGRITY LIFE INS CO
285.1	7,723.5	-0.1	25.8	40.9	3.8	9.3	7.5	0.1	0.7	11.5	9.0 ●	NATIONAL LIFE INS CO
4.9	47.7	0.2	12.3	69.6	3.5	5.4	0.5	0.2	4.6	3.7	0.0	NATIONAL SECURITY INS CO
64.3	57.7	1.6	16.2	79.7	2.5	0.0	0.0	0.0	0.0	0.0	0.0 ●	NATIONAL SECURITY LIFE & ANNUITY CO
87.5	362.3	1.4	44.4	46.1	3.2	2.3	2.2	0.0	0.0	0.4	1.9 ●	NATIONAL TEACHERS ASSOCIATES L I C
808.6	9,623.2 (*)	-0.4	18.8	73.0	2.1	2.9	1.0	0.0	0.0	0.9	3.0 ●	NATIONAL WESTERN LIFE INS CO
707.7	5,268.3	-0.1	10.8	73.8	2.8	0.0	10.2	0.0	0.0	2.1	1.3 ●	NATIONWIDE LIFE & ANNUITY INS CO
8,644.2	35,516.2 (*)	-0.2	18.8	49.2	3.5	1.7	16.0	0.0	0.0	4.8	2.0 ●	NATIONWIDE LIFE INS CO
8.0	22.2	11.5	19.2	54.1	0.3	0.1	0.0	0.0	0.0	14.9	0.0	NETCARE LIFE & HEALTH INS CO
166.4	2,170.7	0.0	16.6	45.9	9.7	1.2	5.7	0.0	0.0	21.3	2.4 ●	NEW ENGLAND LIFE INS CO
79.4	358.1	7.3	17.6	44.5	5.7	12.6	11.7	0.0	0.4	0.3	11.4 ●	NEW ERA LIFE INS CO
51.4	71.5	13.9	16.6	59.0	5.2	0.7	2.9	0.0	0.0	1.7	0.0	NEW ERA LIFE INS CO OF THE MIDWEST
0.0	2.0	55.9	0.0	43.3	0.0	0.8	0.0	0.0	0.0	0.0	0.0	NEW FOUNDATION LIFE INS CO
--	--	--	--	--	--	--	--	--	--	--	--	NEW YORK LIFE AGENTS REIN CO
8,808.8	80,141.1	-0.1	31.8	45.0	5.5	0.6	11.6	0.0	0.1	5.3	3.2 ●	NEW YORK LIFE INS & ANNUITY CORP
9,975.4	114,321.6	0.2	17.2	40.3	4.7	9.8	9.8	0.0	0.5	17.1	13.4 ●	NEW YORK LIFE INS CO
1.0	7.3	26.6	4.9	54.4	1.4	12.7	0.0	0.0	0.0	0.0	0.0	NIAGARA LIFE & HEALTH INS CO
241.1	214.9 (*)	4.6	13.0	78.3	1.0	0.8	0.0	0.0	0.0	0.0	0.0 ●	NIPPON LIFE INS CO OF AMERICA
0.3	55.1	8.0	9.6	37.9	1.3	0.5	1.0	7.7	32.6	1.5	0.0	NORTH AMERICA LIFE INS CO OF TX

● Bullets denote a more detailed analysis is available in Section II.
(*) Asset category percentages do not add up to 100%

INSURANCE COMPANY NAME	DOM. STATE	RATING	TOTAL ASSETS ($MIL)	CAPITAL & SURPLUS ($MIL)	RISK ADJUSTED CAPITAL RATIO 1	RISK ADJUSTED CAPITAL RATIO 2	CAPITAL-IZATION INDEX (PTS)	INVEST. SAFETY INDEX (PTS)	PROFIT-ABILITY INDEX (PTS)	LIQUIDITY INDEX (PTS)	STAB. INDEX (PTS)	STABILITY FACTO
NORTH AMERICAN CO FOR LIFE & H INS	IA	B	16820.8	1169.1	2.45	1.13	7.2	4.7	9.0	6.5	6.3	AI
NORTH AMERICAN INS CO	WI	C	21.7	11.2	1.47	1.14	7.2	8.5	2.4	5.6	4.2	DFT
NORTH AMERICAN NATIONAL RE INS CO	AZ	U	--	--	--	--	--	--	--	--	--	Z
▼ NORTH CAROLINA MUTUAL LIFE INS CO	NC	E+	142.9	2.7	0.35	0.29	0.5	0.8	1.1	0.1	0.5	CFGI
NORTH COAST LIFE INS CO	WA	B	146.7	8.1	0.94	0.83	5.6	1.8	3.3	2.3	4.9	CDIL
NORTHERN NATIONAL LIFE INS CO OF RI	RI	U (5)	--	--	--	--	--	--	--	--	--	Z
NORTHWESTERN LONG TERM CARE INS CO	WI	B	2556.6	232.7	1.77	0.98	6.8	4.4	1.8	9.4	6.3	I
NORTHWESTERN MUTUAL LIFE INS CO	WI	A-	223102.7	18086.7	3.67	1.86	8.3	6.1	6.9	5.8	7.3	I
NTA LIFE INS CO OF NEW YORK	NY	U (3)	7.0	6.9	3.69	3.32	8.0	9.0	2.7	10.0	2.9	DEFT
NYLIFE INS CO OF ARIZONA	AZ	B	197.3	74.2	6.89	4.53	10.0	8.2	3.0	6.9	5.9	D
OCCIDENTAL LIFE INS CO OF NC	TX	C	258.7	36.2	3.63	2.18	8.8	7.5	2.9	5.3	4.2	ADT
OCOEE LIFE INS CO	TN	U	--	--	--	--	--	--	--	--	--	Z
OHIO MOTORISTS LIFE INSURANCE CO	OH	B-	10.1	9.9	4.13	3.71	10.0	8.9	7.5	10.0	3.5	T
OHIO NATIONAL LIFE ASR CORP	OH	B+	3548.1	315.8	2.79	1.43	7.6	5.0	7.7	5.8	6.4	AIL
OHIO NATIONAL LIFE INS CO	OH	B	26677.4	1001.3	1.36	0.95	6.6	5.7	7.7	8.4	5.8	AI
OHIO STATE LIFE INS CO	TX	B-	13.2	10.2	19.22	9.53	8.0	8.1	8.2	7.0	5.4	AF
OLD AMERICAN INS CO	MO	B	249.3	22.5	2.40	1.32	7.5	4.2	3.7	4.1	5.6	DIL
OLD REPUBLIC LIFE INS CO	IL	B-	124.6	29.3	2.94	1.85	8.3	6.0	2.9	7.0	5.3	F
OLD SPARTAN LIFE INS CO INC	SC	C	21.5	14.8	1.86	1.18	7.3	2.2	6.3	9.2	3.8	IT
OLD SURETY LIFE INS CO	OK	C	25.5	11.1	0.88	0.67	4.4	7.7	9.2	6.7	3.3	CD
OLD UNITED LIFE INS CO	AZ	B	90.2	45.7	6.06	3.51	10.0	5.2	7.1	9.4	6.2	ADI
OMAHA INS CO	NE	B-	24.5	12.3	2.21	1.26	7.4	8.8	1.9	7.4	4.0	FGT
OMAHA LIFE INS CO	NE	U (3)	10.6	10.5	4.23	3.81	8.0	8.8	4.0	10.0	5.7	DT
OPTIMUM RE INS CO	TX	B-	127.0	31.8	2.52	1.60	7.9	7.3	2.6	8.6	4.9	
ORDER UNITED COMM TRAVELERS OF AMER	OH	U	--	--	--	--	--	--	--	--	--	Z
OVERTON LIFE INS CO	TN	U	--	--	--	--	--	--	--	--	--	Z
OXFORD LIFE INS CO	AZ	B-	1181.8	154.0	2.02	1.37	7.6	6.7	8.4	6.3	4.7	T
OZARK NATIONAL LIFE INS CO	MO	B-	743.3	122.9	5.04	3.01	10.0	8.2	2.7	6.5	4.9	D
PACIFIC BEACON LIFE REASSUR INC	HI	B (5)	--	--	--	--	--	--	--	--	--	Z
PACIFIC CENTURY LIFE INS CORP	AZ	B	342.4	338.2	30.50	19.74	10.0	7.4	7.1	10.0	6.1	T
PACIFIC GUARDIAN LIFE INS CO LTD	HI	A-	511.7	107.2	4.95	2.83	9.7	6.6	7.7	6.2	7.0	I
PACIFIC LIFE & ANNUITY CO	AZ	B+	6110.8	540.3	5.18	2.54	9.3	6.4	6.7	7.9	6.8	AI
PACIFIC LIFE INS CO	NE	A-	111429.1	7258.6	2.17	1.45	7.7	5.9	3.0	6.8	6.9	AI
PACIFICARE LIFE & HEALTH INS CO	IN	C+	554.1	539.3	39.64	25.83	10.0	8.4	6.4	9.3	3.4	AT
PAN AMERICAN ASR CO	LA	B	22.6	16.9	3.92	1.97	8.5	8.8	7.2	7.5	5.7	AT
PAN AMERICAN ASR CO INTL INC	FL	U (3)	1.6	1.5	2.55	2.30	8.0	9.0	7.5	7.0	7.7	D
PAN AMERICAN LIFE INS CO OF PR	PR	B	9.4	6.7	2.27	1.74	8.1	6.7	5.1	6.6	4.6	ADFT
PAN-AMERICAN LIFE INS CO	LA	B	1424.5	254.4	2.27	1.41	7.6	5.4	6.4	6.2	6.0	FI
PARAGON LIFE INS CO OF INDIANA	IN	B-	1833.4	76.2	1.04	0.62	5.1	4.5	6.8	6.5	4.9	CEIT
PARK AVENUE LIFE INS CO	DE	B+	303.3	75.7	2.10	1.66	8.0	6.2	7.8	6.2	6.7	DFI
PARKER CENTENNIAL ASR CO	WI	A	89.4	47.1	5.71	5.14	10.0	8.5	8.3	10.0	7.7	AD
PATRIOT LIFE INS CO	MI	B	17.2	16.3	4.92	4.43	10.0	8.6	2.0	7.0	4.9	DFGT
PAUL REVERE LIFE INS CO	MA	C+	4144.1	260.0	1.42	0.91	6.3	3.7	5.9	7.6	4.8	AFI
PAUL REVERE VARIABLE ANNUITY INS CO	MA	C	56.7	41.3	6.47	4.20	8.0	5.7	2.2	9.0	3.8	A
PAVONIA LIFE INS CO OF ARIZONA	AZ	U (3)	757.5	30.0	1.37	0.76	5.6	6.5	2.9	10.0	4.9	CF
PAVONIA LIFE INS CO OF DELAWARE	DE	U (3)	132.6	130.0	1.23	1.09	7.1	2.8	4.8	10.0	3.0	DIT
PAVONIA LIFE INS CO OF MICHIGAN	MI	C	389.8	79.0	1.85	1.35	7.5	7.1	1.4	7.0	3.6	AFT
▲ PAVONIA LIFE INS CO OF NEW YORK	NY	D+	35.7	13.9	2.69	2.42	9.1	8.8	2.7	7.4	2.2	DGIT
PEKIN FINANCIAL LIFE INS CO	AZ	U	--	--	--	--	--	--	--	--	--	Z
PEKIN LIFE INS CO	IL	B	1323.2	125.9	2.32	1.41	7.6	7.0	6.4	5.9	6.2	
PELLERIN LIFE INS CO	LA	D	10.4	1.3	0.58	0.52	3.2	2.6	2.8	6.6	1.4	CDI
PENN INS & ANNUITY CO	DE	B	2542.5	334.1	3.63	1.93	4.0	6.8	2.8	6.1	5.0	T

See Page 27 for explanation of footnotes and Page 28 for explanation of stability factors.
Arrows denote recent upgrades ▲ or downgrades▼ (see Section VI for explanations)

50

www.weissratings.com

NET PREMIUM ($MIL)	IN-VESTED ASSETS ($MIL)	% OF INVESTED ASSETS IN:									INVEST. IN AFFIL	INSURANCE COMPANY NAME
		CASH	CMO & STRUCT. SECS.	OTH.INV. GRADE BONDS	NON-INV. GRADE BONDS	CMMON & PREF. STOCK	MORT IN GOOD STAND.	NON-PERF. MORT.	REAL ESTATE	OTHER INVEST-MENTS		
1,231.5	14,769.5	1.1	39.9	43.2	5.2	1.1	5.5	0.0	0.0	3.3	0.2 ●	NORTH AMERICAN CO FOR LIFE & H INS
17.3	19.7	1.4	14.8	83.5	0.0	0.3	0.0	0.0	0.0	0.1	0.0	NORTH AMERICAN INS CO
--	--	--	--	--	--	--	--	--	--	--	--	NORTH AMERICAN NATIONAL RE INS CO
15.2	113.9	1.3	10.1	71.5	0.6	0.6	7.4	0.0	0.2	8.4	0.0	NORTH CAROLINA MUTUAL LIFE INS CO
4.5	141.8	0.3	0.5	82.5	3.1	2.5	0.0	0.0	0.0	11.1	0.0	NORTH COAST LIFE INS CO
--	--	--	--	--	--	--	--	--	--	--	--	NORTHERN NATIONAL LIFE INS CO OF RI
373.6	2,152.4	0.1	0.3	68.0	10.3	7.8	12.3	0.0	0.0	1.4	0.0 ●	NORTHWESTERN LONG TERM CARE INS CO
12,023.4	182,491.4	0.0	18.9	42.2	6.1	1.7	14.6	0.0	0.8	15.5	4.3 ●	NORTHWESTERN MUTUAL LIFE INS CO
0.0	6.9	3.0	63.6	33.4	0.0	0.0	0.0	0.0	0.0	0.0	0.0	NTA LIFE INS CO OF NEW YORK
25.9	154.2	-1.1	18.5	79.7	0.4	0.0	0.0	0.0	0.0	2.6	2.6 ●	NYLIFE INS CO OF ARIZONA
25.7	237.4 (*)	0.0	1.1	81.3	1.1	1.5	8.7	0.0	0.0	5.0	0.0 ●	OCCIDENTAL LIFE INS CO OF NC
--	--	--	--	--	--	--	--	--	--	--	--	OCOEE LIFE INS CO
0.0	9.8	0.2	0.0	99.8	0.0	0.0	0.0	0.0	0.0	0.0	0.0	OHIO MOTORISTS LIFE INSURANCE CO
188.0	2,841.0 (*)	0.0	17.1	58.0	4.7	0.4	13.8	0.0	0.0	3.5	0.0 ●	OHIO NATIONAL LIFE ASR CORP
2,002.2	6,612.3 (*)	3.7	16.0	50.9	3.1	6.4	12.7	0.1	0.4	5.1	5.4 ●	OHIO NATIONAL LIFE INS CO
0.0	11.9 (*)	0.0	28.6	72.6	0.0	8.9	0.0	0.0	0.0	0.0	0.0	OHIO STATE LIFE INS CO
52.8	224.5	-0.4	12.6	63.3	0.9	0.9	17.6	0.0	0.0	5.1	0.0	OLD AMERICAN INS CO
14.9	108.1	1.0	0.0	93.9	0.0	4.0	0.0	0.0	0.0	1.1	0.0 ●	OLD REPUBLIC LIFE INS CO
5.6	20.7	18.6	0.0	6.7	0.0	74.7	0.0	0.0	0.0	0.0	0.0	OLD SPARTAN LIFE INS CO INC
31.3	24.2	13.2	1.1	72.9	0.0	0.0	3.9	0.0	7.2	1.7	0.0	OLD SURETY LIFE INS CO
6.3	86.2	-0.3	16.4	58.1	7.3	18.5	0.0	0.0	0.0	0.0	0.0 ●	OLD UNITED LIFE INS CO
9.7	20.5	10.1	44.4	45.5	0.0	0.0	0.0	0.0	0.0	0.0	0.0	OMAHA INS CO
0.0	10.6	0.0	50.8	49.2	0.0	0.0	0.0	0.0	0.0	0.0	20.2	OMAHA LIFE INS CO
36.9	122.3	3.0	0.0	88.5	1.1	1.9	0.0	0.0	2.7	2.8	0.0 ●	OPTIMUM RE INS CO
--	--	--	--	--	--	--	--	--	--	--	--	ORDER UNITED COMM TRAVELERS OF AMER
--	--	--	--	--	--	--	--	--	--	--	--	OVERTON LIFE INS CO
144.9	1,074.9	1.1	4.6	75.5	2.1	3.9	10.3	0.0	0.5	1.6	3.7 ●	OXFORD LIFE INS CO
61.4	686.7	0.6	12.6	82.2	0.0	0.0	0.0	0.0	1.2	3.3	0.0 ●	OZARK NATIONAL LIFE INS CO
--	--	--	--	--	--	--	--	--	--	--	--	PACIFIC BEACON LIFE REASSUR INC
0.7	335.4	9.6	0.0	4.6	0.0	0.1	85.7	0.0	0.0	0.0	0.0 ●	PACIFIC CENTURY LIFE INS CORP
52.8	478.1	0.3	17.5	41.3	0.0	0.0	35.0	0.0	0.0	5.9	0.0 ●	PACIFIC GUARDIAN LIFE INS CO LTD
369.5	3,447.2	0.2	9.3	74.3	1.2	0.2	14.1	0.0	0.0	0.6	0.0 ●	PACIFIC LIFE & ANNUITY CO
6,202.6	48,386.2	0.0	11.2	45.6	3.6	4.2	16.4	0.0	0.4	18.0	5.5 ●	PACIFIC LIFE INS CO
28.9	601.5	-1.0	14.6	86.4	0.0	0.0	0.0	0.0	0.0	0.0	0.0 ●	PACIFICARE LIFE & HEALTH INS CO
0.0	21.3	17.8	0.4	79.9	0.0	1.9	0.0	0.0	0.0	0.0	0.0	PAN AMERICAN ASR CO
0.0	1.5	0.0	0.0	100.0	0.0	0.0	0.0	0.0	0.0	0.0	0.0	PAN AMERICAN ASR CO INTL INC
11.0	8.3	23.0	14.7	55.6	5.8	0.2	0.0	0.0	0.0	0.8	0.2	PAN AMERICAN LIFE INS CO OF PR
204.7	1,324.6	0.7	7.3	66.9	9.0	4.5	0.4	0.0	0.7	10.0	1.8 ●	PAN-AMERICAN LIFE INS CO
84.5	1,021.3 (*)	12.6	42.5	11.8	0.2	4.7	18.6	0.0	0.0	6.3	15.7 ●	PARAGON LIFE INS CO OF INDIANA
2.1	298.3	0.8	0.5	84.2	4.3	9.0	0.0	0.0	0.0	1.1	9.0 ●	PARK AVENUE LIFE INS CO
4.5	81.1	0.0	0.0	99.3	0.7	0.0	0.0	0.0	0.0	0.0	0.0 ●	PARKER CENTENNIAL ASR CO
0.4	17.8	1.0	10.6	88.4	0.0	0.0	0.0	0.0	0.0	0.0	0.0	PATRIOT LIFE INS CO
69.1	4,098.9	0.0	6.1	77.7	7.2	4.6	3.3	0.0	0.2	1.2	2.7 ●	PAUL REVERE LIFE INS CO
0.0	50.7	0.6	17.1	79.5	0.0	0.0	0.0	0.0	0.0	2.8	0.0 ●	PAUL REVERE VARIABLE ANNUITY INS CO
0.0	744.0	0.2	0.1	98.3	1.4	0.0	0.0	0.0	0.0	0.0	0.0	PAVONIA LIFE INS CO OF ARIZONA
0.2	132.3	0.1	0.0	1.7	0.0	98.2	0.0	0.0	0.0	0.0	98.1	PAVONIA LIFE INS CO OF DELAWARE
73.5	412.9	4.2	6.5	77.3	0.0	6.0	0.0	0.0	0.0	5.9	3.2 ●	PAVONIA LIFE INS CO OF MICHIGAN
3.8	32.4	6.7	0.2	93.1	0.0	0.0	0.0	0.0	0.0	0.0	0.0	PAVONIA LIFE INS CO OF NEW YORK
--	--	--	--	--	--	--	--	--	--	--	--	PEKIN FINANCIAL LIFE INS CO
155.5	1,257.9 (*)	0.4	25.1	65.5	0.0	1.1	0.0	0.0	0.1	1.3	0.0 ●	PEKIN LIFE INS CO
0.7	7.8	12.8	1.4	31.3	0.0	3.6	19.7	3.1	27.8	0.3	14.6	PELLERIN LIFE INS CO
152.0	2,184.2	0.0	19.7	53.3	2.3	0.3	0.0	0.0	0.0	24.4	2.6 ●	PENN INS & ANNUITY CO

● Bullets denote a more detailed analysis is available in Section II.
(*) Asset category percentages do not add up to 100%

INSURANCE COMPANY NAME	DOM. STATE	RATING	TOTAL ASSETS ($MIL)	CAPITAL & SURPLUS ($MIL)	RISK ADJUSTED CAPITAL RATIO 1	RISK ADJUSTED CAPITAL RATIO 2	CAPITAL- IZATION INDEX (PTS)	INVEST. SAFETY INDEX (PTS)	PROFIT- ABILITY INDEX (PTS)	LIQUIDITY INDEX (PTS)	STAB. INDEX (PTS)	STABILITY FACTO
PENN MUTUAL LIFE INS CO	PA	B	16715.6	1541.9	2.22	1.48	7.7	6.4	3.8	6.3	6.1	I
PENN OHIO LIFE INS CO	AZ	U	--	--	--	--	--	--	--	--	--	Z
PERFORMANCE LIFE OF AMERICA	LA	B-	29.9	18.4	4.16	3.74	10.0	8.8	9.4	9.3	5.1	ADT
PHARMACISTS LIFE INS CO	IA	B	91.9	7.2	1.01	0.90	6.2	5.7	3.0	2.2	4.8	ACDI
PHILADELPHIA AMERICAN LIFE INS CO	TX	B-	215.8	31.0	1.32	0.86	5.9	5.0	9.0	6.1	5.0	AGI
PHILADELPHIA FINANCIAL LIFE ASR CO	PA	E	4603.8	21.1	0.43	0.26	0.2	8.1	3.3	7.0	0.2	CT
PHILADELPHIA FINANCIAL LIFE ASR NY	NY	U (3)	4.6	4.3	3.00	2.70	9.6	8.7	5.0	10.0	5.2	DT
PHL VARIABLE INS CO	CT	C	6426.3	252.4	2.52	1.29	7.4	6.1	2.7	7.3	3.5	AI
PHOENIX LIFE & ANNUITY CO	CT	C+	45.2	21.1	3.44	3.09	10.0	7.3	3.5	9.2	3.9	AT
PHOENIX LIFE INS CO	NY	C	13326.4	619.9	1.18	0.72	5.3	4.9	5.1	5.3	4.2	ACFI
▼ PHYSICIANS BENEFITS TRUST LIFE INS	IL	C	14.2	6.5	1.88	1.52	7.8	8.8	1.8	6.7	4.6	ADFT
PHYSICIANS LIFE INS CO	NE	A-	1421.0	124.1	2.89	1.41	7.6	5.7	6.2	5.8	6.9	I
PHYSICIANS MUTUAL INS CO	NE	A+	1989.7	964.3	4.31	3.25	10.0	6.5	8.9	7.4	7.9	I
PINE BELT LIFE INS CO	MS	D-	2.1	0.5	0.68	0.61	3.9	9.8	2.0	10.0	1.0	CDT
PIONEER AMERICAN INS CO	TX	C	56.5	19.7	2.88	2.59	9.4	8.6	2.0	6.8	3.3	CDGT
PIONEER MILITARY INS CO	NV	U (3)	3.7	2.9	2.43	2.19	4.0	9.8	4.7	10.0	4.9	DT
PIONEER MUTUAL LIFE INS CO	ND	B+	510.6	43.3	2.93	1.55	7.8	6.8	6.3	5.1	6.5	ADIL
PIONEER SECURITY LIFE INS CO	TX	C+	122.2	100.7	1.20	1.16	7.2	3.6	2.4	7.0	4.8	ADI
PLATEAU INS CO	TN	B-	31.2	12.0	2.48	1.92	8.4	8.6	5.6	8.2	4.8	ART
POPULAR LIFE RE	PR	C+	55.6	28.8	4.21	3.35	10.0	5.8	6.6	9.0	4.8	T
PORT-O-CALL LIFE INS CO	AR	U (3)	0.8	0.7	1.83	1.65	8.0	6.3	4.8	10.0	4.0	DFT
PREFERRED SECURITY LIFE INS CO	TX	U (3)	3.1	0.3	0.27	0.24	0.0	3.5	0.7	0.7	0.0	CDFC
PRENEED REINS CO OF AMERICA	AZ	B	32.9	30.8	6.82	6.14	10.0	9.0	9.6	2.0	4.2	L
PRESERVATION LIFE INS CO	MO	U (3)	1.4	1.4	2.53	2.28	8.0	9.8	2.8	10.0	3.0	DFT
PRESIDENTIAL LIFE INS CO	TX	C	4.3	2.9	2.33	1.93	8.4	3.0	7.6	7.1	3.6	DIT
PRIDE OF CARROLL LIFE INS CO	LA	U	--	--	--	--	--	--	--	--	--	Z
PRIMERICA LIFE INS CO	MA	B	1474.0	651.8	1.69	1.38	7.6	4.3	7.4	6.9	5.8	IT
PRINCIPAL LIFE INS CO	IA	B+	148782.3	4050.8	2.07	1.09	7.1	5.4	5.9	7.2	6.7	I
PRINCIPAL LIFE INS CO IOWA	IA	U (3)	231.7	231.7	1.25	1.11	7.2	9.7	3.9	10.0	5.9	DG
PRINCIPAL NATIONAL LIFE INS CO	IA	B	131.2	84.9	6.66	3.29	10.0	8.5	2.5	9.2	5.7	FT
▲ PROFESSIONAL INS CO	TX	C	108.3	36.0	4.03	2.86	9.8	7.0	2.8	6.7	3.4	ADF
PROFESSIONAL LIFE & CAS CO	IL	C	153.0	35.7	2.63	1.41	7.6	3.2	9.0	5.5	4.3	DIT
PROTEC INS CO	IL	C	2.7	2.4	2.83	2.55	9.3	9.7	7.0	10.0	2.6	ADET
PROTECTIVE LIFE & ANNUITY INS CO	AL	B	2105.5	176.1	2.54	1.31	7.5	6.2	5.5	4.9	4.6	AFIL
PROTECTIVE LIFE INS CO	TN	B	41449.6	3307.6	1.41	1.05	7.1	5.7	8.0	6.4	4.9	AIT
PROVIDENT AMER LIFE & HEALTH INS CO	OH	B-	16.4	14.0	1.97	1.70	8.1	8.5	6.0	7.3	3.8	DT
PROVIDENT AMERICAN INS CO	TX	D+	21.1	10.9	0.65	0.58	3.6	7.6	9.2	2.0	2.5	CDFL
PROVIDENT LIFE & ACCIDENT INS CO	TN	C+	8316.4	688.3	2.54	1.28	7.4	4.3	6.8	7.3	4.8	AI
PROVIDENT LIFE & CAS INS CO	TN	B-	777.2	153.4	4.69	2.49	9.2	4.6	8.4	7.2	5.3	ADI
PRUCO INS CO OF IOWA	IA	U (3)	6.0	6.0	3.49	3.14	10.0	8.9	3.2	10.0	4.6	DET
PRUCO LIFE INS CO	AZ	C+	104592.5	2827.5	2.51	1.51	7.8	5.7	5.6	9.7	4.4	AT
PRUCO LIFE INS CO OF NEW JERSEY	NJ	B-	12642.3	347.8	2.70	1.36	7.5	5.5	5.4	9.1	5.2	AT
PRUDENTIAL ANNUITIES LIFE ASR CORP	AZ	C	48138.0	473.8	1.08	0.90	4.0	6.4	4.7	7.0	3.4	T
PRUDENTIAL INS CO OF AMERICA	NJ	B	306159.5	11579.9	1.50	1.02	7.0	5.6	7.6	7.0	4.3	AIT
PRUDENTIAL RETIREMENT INS & ANNUITY	CT	B-	77318.5	1098.4	1.84	0.88	6.3	3.6	5.1	7.7	5.1	AI
PURITAN LIFE INS CO	TX	D+	12.7	5.0	0.37	0.34	1.1	5.3	3.5	9.5	1.2	ACT
PURITAN LIFE INS CO OF AMERICA	TX	D+	36.8	6.7	1.17	0.96	6.7	7.2	2.2	7.3	2.2	FGT
PYRAMID LIFE INS CO	KS	C	170.6	83.8	1.65	1.30	6.0	7.5	5.9	5.8	2.9	DT
RABENHORST LIFE INS CO	LA	C- (4)	29.1	3.3	0.87	0.78	5.2	4.5	3.5	5.7	3.2	CDFI
REGAL LIFE OF AMERICA INS CO	TX	D-	10.1	6.2	0.92	0.90	6.2	3.0	2.1	8.4	0.9	DFGT
REGAL REINSURANCE COMPANY	MA	U (3)	9.1	8.7	0.66	0.66	4.3	4.4	4.0	9.2	4.2	CDI
REGIONS LIFE INS CO	AZ	U	--	--	--	--	--	--	--	--	--	Z

NET PREMIUM ($MIL)	IN- VESTED ASSETS ($MIL)	% OF INVESTED ASSETS IN:									INVEST. IN AFFIL	INSURANCE COMPANY NAME
		CASH	CMO & STRUCT. SECS.	OTH.INV. GRADE BONDS	NON-INV. GRADE BONDS	CMMON & PREF. STOCK	MORT IN GOOD STAND.	NON- PERF. MORT.	REAL ESTATE	OTHER INVEST- MENTS		
1,070.9	8,784.2	0.2	28.3	53.0	1.8	3.9	0.0	0.0	0.2	11.8	5.9 ●	PENN MUTUAL LIFE INS CO
--	--	--	--	--	--	--	--	--	--	--	--	PENN OHIO LIFE INS CO
6.6	28.3 (*)	2.2	0.0	95.7	0.0	0.0	0.0	0.0	0.0	0.0	0.0	PERFORMANCE LIFE OF AMERICA
3.0	84.7	0.6	5.6	86.2	1.5	4.4	0.0	0.0	0.0	1.7	0.0	PHARMACISTS LIFE INS CO
109.1	199.2	3.0	25.4	59.6	7.9	0.4	3.3	0.0	0.3	0.1	0.0 ●	PHILADELPHIA AMERICAN LIFE INS CO
185.8	122.9	2.3	0.1	10.7	0.0	3.8	0.0	0.0	0.0	83.1	3.8	PHILADELPHIA FINANCIAL LIFE ASR CO
0.0	4.6	2.7	0.0	97.3	0.0	0.0	0.0	0.0	0.0	0.0	0.0	PHILADELPHIA FINANCIAL LIFE ASR NY
705.6	1,937.9 (*)	6.9	27.0	54.9	3.8	0.3	0.0	0.0	0.0	4.4	0.0 ●	PHL VARIABLE INS CO
0.1	36.9	32.4	19.9	39.4	4.2	0.0	0.0	0.0	0.0	4.3	0.0	PHOENIX LIFE & ANNUITY CO
229.8	11,779.9	2.2	19.5	43.7	5.7	4.0	0.0	0.0	0.3	24.8	2.5 ●	PHOENIX LIFE INS CO
12.6	15.8	1.4	0.0	98.6	0.0	0.0	0.0	0.0	0.0	0.0	0.0	PHYSICIANS BENEFITS TRUST LIFE INS
194.1	1,348.8	0.1	21.6	66.0	7.9	1.3	0.0	0.0	0.0	2.5	0.0 ●	PHYSICIANS LIFE INS CO
317.1	1,887.3	0.0	8.3	71.8	7.5	11.8	0.0	0.0	0.5	0.0	6.5 ●	PHYSICIANS MUTUAL INS CO
0.5	2.0	100.0	0.0	0.0	0.0	0.0	0.0	0.0	0.0	0.0	0.0	PINE BELT LIFE INS CO
8.9	47.6 (*)	1.6	0.0	80.1	0.0	0.5	6.7	0.0	0.0	9.9	0.0	PIONEER AMERICAN INS CO
0.0	3.7	73.1	0.0	26.9	0.0	0.0	0.0	0.0	0.0	0.0	0.0	PIONEER MILITARY INS CO
20.5	488.4	0.9	27.1	56.1	2.3	0.0	8.2	0.0	0.0	5.5	0.0 ●	PIONEER MUTUAL LIFE INS CO
5.7	98.0	0.3	0.0	16.4	0.0	80.6	0.3	0.0	0.0	1.8	80.6 ●	PIONEER SECURITY LIFE INS CO
13.9	22.9 (*)	32.2	0.0	66.3	0.0	3.0	0.0	0.0	0.9	0.9	1.3	PLATEAU INS CO
14.6	50.9	4.8	20.2	61.6	9.8	3.6	0.0	0.0	0.0	0.0	0.0 ●	POPULAR LIFE RE
0.1	0.8	82.3	0.2	0.0	0.0	17.5	0.0	0.0	0.0	0.0	0.0	PORT-O-CALL LIFE INS CO
0.0	3.1	20.0	0.0	55.8	0.0	24.2	0.0	0.0	0.0	0.0	0.0	PREFERRED SECURITY LIFE INS CO
75.9	22.8	0.3	0.0	99.7	0.0	0.0	0.0	0.0	0.0	0.0	0.0 ●	PRENEED REINS CO OF AMERICA
0.0	1.4	57.7	0.0	42.3	0.0	0.0	0.0	0.0	0.0	0.0	0.0	PRESERVATION LIFE INS CO
0.1	4.4 (*)	14.9	4.4	7.5	2.0	50.8	0.0	0.0	0.0	3.1	0.0	PRESIDENTIAL LIFE INS CO
--	--	--	--	--	--	--	--	--	--	--	--	PRIDE OF CARROLL LIFE INS CO
219.1	1,445.4 (*)	-1.0	11.8	55.3	4.1	24.9	0.0	0.0	0.0	0.4	22.7 ●	PRIMERICA LIFE INS CO
3,840.1	57,344.9	0.6	21.7	45.8	5.2	1.3	17.4	0.0	0.5	6.5	5.7 ●	PRINCIPAL LIFE INS CO
0.0	231.4	0.3	0.0	2.1	0.0	97.6	0.0	0.0	0.0	0.0	97.6	PRINCIPAL LIFE INS CO IOWA
0.0	76.1	1.8	0.0	98.2	0.0	0.0	0.0	0.0	0.0	0.0	0.0 ●	PRINCIPAL NATIONAL LIFE INS CO
24.1	99.5	-0.5	7.9	85.5	1.0	0.0	0.0	0.0	0.0	5.7	0.0 ●	PROFESSIONAL INS CO
4.6	142.7	0.9	0.0	58.0	16.7	24.4	0.0	0.0	0.0	0.1	0.0 ●	PROFESSIONAL LIFE & CAS CO
0.0	2.4	37.2	0.0	62.8	0.0	0.0	0.0	0.0	0.0	0.0	0.0	PROTEC INS CO
39.1	1,902.4	0.4	14.9	74.5	3.0	1.1	4.1	0.0	0.0	2.1	0.0 ●	PROTECTIVE LIFE & ANNUITY INS CO
1,794.4	24,414.1	-0.2	14.4	60.0	3.7	7.4	9.8	0.0	0.2	3.8	9.6 ●	PROTECTIVE LIFE INS CO
9.3	13.8	1.0	0.0	76.8	0.0	22.2	0.0	0.0	0.0	0.0	22.2	PROVIDENT AMER LIFE & HEALTH INS CO
51.6	18.6	22.7	9.4	62.3	3.7	0.0	0.0	0.0	0.0	1.9	0.0	PROVIDENT AMERICAN INS CO
685.8	7,784.1	0.0	7.6	72.1	9.0	0.8	5.5	0.0	1.1	4.0	0.0 ●	PROVIDENT LIFE & ACCIDENT INS CO
63.6	738.8	0.0	9.1	74.0	11.4	0.0	4.3	0.0	0.0	0.8	0.0 ●	PROVIDENT LIFE & CAS INS CO
0.0	6.0	0.0	0.0	100.0	0.0	0.0	0.0	0.0	0.0	0.0	0.0	PRUCO INS CO OF IOWA
6,564.2	7,338.6	0.0	11.8	47.2	4.3	5.2	16.2	0.0	0.0	15.0	9.0 ●	PRUCO LIFE INS CO
817.3	1,407.0	0.0	14.4	47.1	3.2	0.0	20.1	0.0	0.0	15.8	2.4 ●	PRUCO LIFE INS CO OF NEW JERSEY
-104.6	2,058.9	0.0	20.4	56.7	6.5	0.3	12.5	0.0	0.0	3.5	3.0 ●	PRUDENTIAL ANNUITIES LIFE ASR CORP
12,927.8	160,819.2	-0.2	17.2	46.2	4.4	6.5	14.8	0.0	0.4	10.0	7.0 ●	PRUDENTIAL INS CO OF AMERICA
368.7	24,498.3	0.1	26.8	48.3	5.5	0.1	17.8	0.0	0.0	0.9	0.9 ●	PRUDENTIAL RETIREMENT INS & ANNUITY
2.1	9.5	3.5	0.0	36.1	0.0	60.5	0.0	0.0	0.0	0.0	63.8	PURITAN LIFE INS CO
6.0	32.3	4.9	23.8	49.2	0.0	22.1	0.0	0.0	0.0	0.0	26.7	PURITAN LIFE INS CO OF AMERICA
158.1	182.7 (*)	0.0	22.6	72.6	0.0	4.1	0.0	0.0	0.0	5.5	0.0 ●	PYRAMID LIFE INS CO
1.6	22.0	0.6	18.5	52.7	0.0	16.9	10.9	0.0	0.0	0.5	10.9	RABENHORST LIFE INS CO
1.3	11.3	9.0	0.0	32.0	0.0	56.9	0.0	0.0	0.0	2.1	56.9	REGAL LIFE OF AMERICA INS CO
0.0	9.1	0.3	0.0	27.0	0.0	72.7	0.0	0.0	0.0	0.0	72.7	REGAL REINSURANCE COMPANY
--	--	--	--	--	--	--	--	--	--	--	--	REGIONS LIFE INS CO

● Bullets denote a more detailed analysis is available in Section II.
(*) Asset category percentages do not add up to 100%

INSURANCE COMPANY NAME	DOM. STATE	RATING	TOTAL ASSETS ($MIL)	CAPITAL & SURPLUS ($MIL)	RISK ADJUSTED CAPITAL RATIO 1	RISK ADJUSTED CAPITAL RATIO 2	CAPITAL-IZATION INDEX (PTS)	INVEST. SAFETY INDEX (PTS)	PROFIT-ABILITY INDEX (PTS)	LIQUIDITY INDEX (PTS)	STAB. INDEX (PTS)	STABILI FACTO
REINSURANCE CO OF MO INC	MO	C+	1604.2	1595.8	1.01	0.91	6.3	1.4	8.8	7.0	3.4	FIT
RELIABLE LIFE INS CO	MO	B-	22.6	13.6	2.60	1.30	7.5	9.7	9.1	7.0	5.3	T
RELIABLE LIFE INS CO	LA	E+ (5)	--	--	--	--	--	--	--	--	--	Z
RELIABLE SERVICE INS CO	LA	U (5)	--	--	--	--	--	--	--	--	--	Z
RELIANCE STANDARD LIFE INS CO	IL	B	7447.4	700.3	1.67	0.92	6.4	4.5	6.5	6.7	5.9	ACI
RELIANCE STANDARD LIFE INS CO OF TX	TX	U (3)	746.4	687.0	1.15	1.15	7.2	7.9	8.1	10.0	7.1	DT
RELIASTAR LIFE INS CO	MN	C+	21234.6	1829.9	2.17	1.30	7.5	6.2	3.5	5.4	4.4	AFT
RELIASTAR LIFE INS CO OF NEW YORK	NY	B	3194.3	295.2	3.44	1.83	8.2	6.5	5.2	5.9	5.8	AT
RESERVE NATIONAL INS CO	OK	A	112.1	53.5	2.46	1.89	8.3	8.0	7.1	6.6	7.6	AD
RESOURCE LIFE INS CO	IL	C+	25.5	10.6	3.33	3.00	4.0	7.4	6.0	10.0	4.5	ADFG
RGA REINSURANCE CO	MO	B	23567.0	1502.6	1.67	0.88	6.0	5.1	6.8	5.5	4.4	ACIT
RHODES LIFE INS CO OF LA INC	LA	E	4.1	0.1	0.13	0.12	0.0	0.0	0.5	8.4	0.0	CGIT
RIVER LAKE INS CO	SC	C	1328.7	95.6	0.73	0.43	2.8	5.7	2.0	7.5	2.8	CI
RIVER LAKE INS CO II	SC	C	1117.9	115.6	1.00	0.60	5.0	5.9	1.3	7.7	4.0	CIT
RIVERMONT LIFE INS CO I	SC	C	526.0	148.6	4.48	2.47	9.2	7.2	1.6	7.9	4.0	DT
RIVERSOURCE LIFE INS CO	MN	C-	103856.3	3154.3	1.92	1.14	7.2	5.9	4.5	7.9	3.3	T
RIVERSOURCE LIFE INS CO OF NY	NY	C	6480.9	287.6	3.08	1.54	7.8	6.0	3.8	7.8	4.4	A
ROCKETT LIFE INS CO	LA	U	--	--	--	--	--	--	--	--	--	Z
ROYAL NEIGHBORS OF AMERICA	IL	U	--	--	--	--	--	--	--	--	--	Z
ROYAL STATE NATIONAL INS CO LTD	HI	B-	46.2	29.5	3.13	2.20	8.8	6.1	5.4	6.9	5.1	D
▲ S USA LIFE INS CO INC	AZ	C+	13.5	8.0	2.84	2.56	9.3	8.2	2.5	7.0	4.5	DG
SAGICOR LIFE INS CO	TX	C-	1193.0	72.5	1.38	0.72	5.6	3.6	2.0	5.0	3.1	CIT
SAVINGS BANK LIFE INS CO OF MA	MA	B+	2567.5	192.0	2.67	1.47	7.7	6.5	5.5	5.6	6.4	IL
SBLI USA MUT LIFE INS CO INC	NY	B-	1588.6	100.9	1.66	0.93	6.4	5.8	7.5	3.8	4.9	CFIL
SCOR GLOBAL LIFE AMERICAS REIN CO	DE	C-	1468.9	190.6	1.29	0.81	5.5	6.4	1.9	7.5	3.3	AFT
▲ SCOR GLOBAL LIFE REINS CO OF DE	DE	C	430.4	61.2	2.02	1.24	7.4	8.3	2.3	8.8	3.7	AT
SCOR GLOBAL LIFE USA RE CO	DE	C	800.9	429.2	7.42	4.42	10.0	8.6	2.9	7.6	3.8	ADFG
SCOTTISH RE US INC	DE	C-	1770.7	185.3	1.89	1.04	7.1	6.3	1.9	5.8	3.0	FGT
SEARS LIFE INS CO	TX	B	52.0	19.8	3.01	2.71	9.6	7.8	5.7	9.1	5.9	AT
SECU LIFE INS CO	NC	D+	25.4	24.4	6.10	5.49	10.0	7.4	2.9	10.0	2.4	DEFG
SECURIAN LIFE INS CO	MN	B	234.4	135.8	6.48	4.52	10.0	8.2	5.4	6.9	6.3	
SECURITAS FINANCIAL LIFE INS CO	NC	U (3)	5.6	5.5	3.34	3.01	8.0	9.0	3.9	10.0	4.1	D
SECURITY BENEFIT LIFE INS CO	KS	B	23360.9	1005.8	1.93	0.92	6.4	4.5	8.4	9.2	6.2	ACGI
SECURITY LIFE INS CO OF AMERICA	MN	B	71.7	19.9	1.22	0.91	6.3	7.8	5.2	5.8	5.6	CDFT
SECURITY LIFE OF DENVER INS CO	CO	C+	14195.5	1087.6	1.80	1.02	7.0	6.2	2.4	5.9	3.1	AFT
SECURITY MUTUAL LIFE INS CO OF NY	NY	B	2670.6	131.5	1.49	0.81	5.7	6.0	6.2	1.6	4.0	CIL
SECURITY NATIONAL LIFE INS CO	UT	D-	505.7	31.3	0.49	0.34	1.1	1.5	5.6	7.1	1.1	CI
SECURITY PLAN LIFE INS CO	LA	C+	321.7	52.4	2.72	1.70	8.1	6.3	5.9	6.8	4.5	AD
SENIOR HEALTH INS CO OF PENNSYLVANIA	PA	D+	2898.4	69.6	0.99	0.48	4.8	0.8	1.7	6.8	2.8	CFI
SENIOR LIFE INS CO	GA	C-	46.8	11.6	2.04	1.00	7.0	2.9	2.2	6.8	2.9	DIT
SENTINEL AMERICAN LIFE INS CO	TX	U (3)	31.9	5.0	1.59	1.43	7.6	6.8	1.9	6.9	3.2	DF
SENTINEL SECURITY LIFE INS CO	UT	D	443.7	22.1	1.18	0.56	5.3	2.1	2.2	7.8	2.1	GIT
SENTRY LIFE INS CO	WI	A	5237.9	290.6	3.97	2.28	8.9	7.4	6.2	7.4	7.4	A
SENTRY LIFE INS CO OF NEW YORK	NY	B+	76.3	10.7	1.40	1.26	7.4	7.7	6.2	6.9	6.5	DG
SEQUATCHIE LIFE INS CO	TN	U	--	--	--	--	--	--	--	--	--	Z
SERVCO LIFE INS CO	TX	C+	8.9	5.6	2.59	2.33	4.0	6.3	6.0	9.4	4.0	ADFF
SERVICE LIFE & CAS INS CO	TX	C	41.9	32.9	4.74	2.00	4.0	2.9	5.3	8.1	4.0	DFIR
SETTLERS LIFE INS CO	WI	B	394.0	55.6	3.58	1.92	8.4	6.4	6.0	6.6	6.2	AI
SHELTER LIFE INS CO	MO	A-	1108.6	187.0	3.67	2.40	9.1	7.9	6.0	6.0	7.3	A
SHELTERPOINT INS CO	FL	U (3)	7.9	7.8	4.26	3.83	4.0	9.8	5.1	10.0	5.0	DFT
SHELTERPOINT LIFE INS CO	NY	A	104.4	51.9	3.14	2.30	9.0	6.6	8.0	7.2	6.6	DI
SHENANDOAH LIFE INS CO	VA	C	1220.8	82.6	1.79	0.96	6.7	5.7	3.1	3.4	3.7	FLT

See Page 27 for explanation of footnotes and Page 28 for explanation of stability factors.
Arrows denote recent upgrades ▲ or downgrades▼ (see Section VI for explanations)

54   www.weissratings.com

NET PREMIUM ($MIL)	IN-VESTED ASSETS ($MIL)	% OF INVESTED ASSETS IN:									INVEST. IN AFFIL	INSURANCE COMPANY NAME
		CASH	CMO & STRUCT. SECS.	OTH.INV. GRADE BONDS	NON-INV. GRADE BONDS	CMMON & PREF. STOCK	MORT IN GOOD STAND.	NON-PERF. MORT.	REAL ESTATE	OTHER INVEST-MENTS		
5.0	1,643.8	0.0	1.0	4.6	0.1	94.3	0.0	0.0	0.0	0.0	94.3 ●	REINSURANCE CO OF MO INC
0.0	22.3	17.7	0.0	82.3	0.0	0.0	0.0	0.0	0.0	0.1	0.0	RELIABLE LIFE INS CO
--	--	--	--	--	--	--	--	--	--	--	--	RELIABLE LIFE INS CO
--	--	--	--	--	--	--	--	--	--	--	--	RELIABLE SERVICE INS CO
1,388.2	5,665.9	0.1	48.8	35.5	6.8	3.3	1.3	0.0	0.0	3.9	1.9 ●	RELIANCE STANDARD LIFE INS CO
0.1	664.7	0.1	0.0	9.0	0.0	90.9	0.0	0.0	0.0	0.0	98.8	RELIANCE STANDARD LIFE INS CO OF TX
-438.6	18,748.1 (*)	1.7	11.7	62.6	3.9	2.0	11.4	0.0	0.0	5.3	3.2 ●	RELIASTAR LIFE INS CO
106.0	2,094.5 (*)	1.6	9.7	72.3	2.9	0.2	6.5	0.0	0.0	5.7	0.1 ●	RELIASTAR LIFE INS CO OF NEW YORK
103.4	95.2	-0.6	5.0	92.0	0.0	0.0	0.0	0.0	0.0	3.6	0.3 ●	RESERVE NATIONAL INS CO
-0.1	15.2 (*)	0.1	0.0	99.9	0.0	0.0	0.0	0.0	0.0	8.7	0.0	RESOURCE LIFE INS CO
1,520.8	16,157.4	0.9	14.2	49.9	8.0	0.6	15.4	0.0	0.0	10.6	2.6 ●	RGA REINSURANCE CO
0.5	4.0	11.8	1.9	62.8	0.0	0.3	14.1	0.0	9.0	0.1	0.0	RHODES LIFE INS CO OF LA INC
38.2	1,309.4	0.0	36.7	62.1	0.9	0.0	0.0	0.0	0.0	0.3	0.0 ●	RIVER LAKE INS CO
45.5	1,098.5	0.0	33.8	65.8	0.4	0.0	0.0	0.0	0.0	0.0	0.0 ●	RIVER LAKE INS CO II
20.4	491.9	0.0	28.4	70.8	0.8	0.0	0.0	0.0	0.0	0.0	0.0 ●	RIVERMONT LIFE INS CO I
4,429.6	29,581.8 (*)	0.0	24.0	44.0	5.5	2.3	10.8	0.0	0.4	2.5	2.3 ●	RIVERSOURCE LIFE INS CO
304.9	1,948.6 (*)	0.0	23.9	58.7	4.9	0.0	7.8	0.0	0.0	2.2	0.0 ●	RIVERSOURCE LIFE INS CO OF NY
--	--	--	--	--	--	--	--	--	--	--	--	ROCKETT LIFE INS CO
--	--	--	--	--	--	--	--	--	--	--	--	ROYAL NEIGHBORS OF AMERICA
8.3	44.1	4.6	8.6	70.3	0.0	16.0	0.0	0.0	0.0	0.6	3.3 ●	ROYAL STATE NATIONAL INS CO LTD
0.8	12.6	2.8	42.2	51.3	0.8	0.0	0.0	0.0	0.0	2.9	0.0	S USA LIFE INS CO INC
46.6	1,143.6 (*)	0.1	17.0	72.8	1.0	2.1	1.7	0.0	0.1	3.7	0.0 ●	SAGICOR LIFE INS CO
141.5	2,358.7	0.0	25.4	62.9	2.5	3.1	0.0	0.0	0.2	5.9	0.0 ●	SAVINGS BANK LIFE INS CO OF MA
46.9	1,446.5	0.4	36.7	49.8	2.6	1.4	0.0	0.0	0.4	9.0	0.6 ●	SBLI USA MUT LIFE INS CO INC
78.7	1,144.3 (*)	1.0	21.6	61.3	8.6	4.5	0.0	0.0	0.0	1.7	4.5 ●	SCOR GLOBAL LIFE AMERICAS REIN CO
30.5	401.8 (*)	2.3	22.0	61.5	0.2	0.3	0.0	0.0	0.0	3.5	0.0 ●	SCOR GLOBAL LIFE REINS CO OF DE
160.0	652.2 (*)	0.5	0.8	87.3	0.5	0.0	0.0	0.0	0.0	1.3	0.0 ●	SCOR GLOBAL LIFE USA RE CO
184.9	1,578.9	1.0	46.9	47.3	4.6	0.1	0.0	0.0	0.0	0.0	0.0 ●	SCOTTISH RE US INC
8.5	42.4	13.1	19.3	67.6	0.0	0.0	0.0	0.0	0.0	0.0	0.0	SEARS LIFE INS CO
1.7	24.4	97.6	0.0	2.5	0.0	0.0	0.0	0.0	0.0	0.0	0.0	SECU LIFE INS CO
68.9	196.0	2.3	7.3	89.5	0.8	0.0	0.0	0.0	0.0	0.2	0.0 ●	SECURIAN LIFE INS CO
0.0	5.6	9.5	0.0	90.5	0.0	0.0	0.0	0.0	0.0	0.0	0.0	SECURITAS FINANCIAL LIFE INS CO
4,030.1	14,143.3 (*)	2.8	29.4	35.7	2.5	0.6	3.7	0.0	0.1	20.7	13.5 ●	SECURITY BENEFIT LIFE INS CO
60.8	67.5	3.7	9.7	76.9	0.0	1.5	6.6	0.0	0.0	1.9	0.0	SECURITY LIFE INS CO OF AMERICA
-81.6	12,891.7 (*)	2.0	14.1	61.6	1.7	1.2	6.3	0.0	0.0	11.5	3.4 ●	SECURITY LIFE OF DENVER INS CO
124.3	2,514.4	0.0	9.6	69.5	0.4	0.2	6.9	0.0	0.3	13.2	0.1 ●	SECURITY MUTUAL LIFE INS CO OF NY
47.0	463.9	0.1	1.0	33.4	1.4	3.4	29.1	2.7	8.0	21.2	2.4 ●	SECURITY NATIONAL LIFE INS CO
32.4	305.0	4.1	2.2	81.8	3.3	4.8	0.0	0.0	1.5	2.2	1.7 ●	SECURITY PLAN LIFE INS CO
118.6	2,943.8	0.0	15.2	71.7	5.7	3.2	2.9	0.0	0.0	1.3	0.1 ●	SENIOR HEALTH INS CO OF PENNSYLVANIA
7.6	40.1	19.4	9.0	13.2	0.3	9.8	0.0	0.0	30.4	17.9	0.0	SENIOR LIFE INS CO
0.0	31.5	6.2	0.5	93.1	0.0	0.0	0.0	0.0	0.0	0.3	0.0	SENTINEL AMERICAN LIFE INS CO
19.6	396.3	3.0	47.9	41.5	3.6	1.8	0.4	0.0	1.4	0.4	0.0	SENTINEL SECURITY LIFE INS CO
422.9	2,375.1	0.0	7.8	89.2	2.0	0.4	0.0	0.0	0.0	0.6	0.4 ●	SENTRY LIFE INS CO
6.1	33.3	0.3	2.2	91.5	3.5	0.0	0.0	0.0	0.0	2.4	0.0	SENTRY LIFE INS CO OF NEW YORK
--	--	--	--	--	--	--	--	--	--	--	--	SEQUATCHIE LIFE INS CO
-0.1	8.9	5.0	44.4	38.1	0.6	12.0	0.0	0.0	0.0	0.0	0.0	SERVCO LIFE INS CO
-0.4	39.1	2.3	6.1	13.4	0.8	0.6	17.7	0.0	55.3	3.9	0.6 ●	SERVICE LIFE & CAS INS CO
33.5	370.6	0.0	6.4	84.0	2.8	3.3	0.0	0.0	1.0	2.5	0.0 ●	SETTLERS LIFE INS CO
86.0	1,016.8	0.3	21.6	70.1	0.0	1.1	1.1	0.0	0.0	5.8	3.0 ●	SHELTER LIFE INS CO
0.0	7.9	71.4	0.0	28.6	0.0	0.0	0.0	0.0	0.0	0.0	0.0	SHELTERPOINT INS CO
68.3	86.2	3.0	13.9	78.3	4.9	0.0	0.0	0.0	0.0	0.0	0.0 ●	SHELTERPOINT LIFE INS CO
37.9	1,238.0	0.3	28.6	55.7	1.7	0.6	10.3	0.1	0.2	2.7	0.0 ●	SHENANDOAH LIFE INS CO

● Bullets denote a more detailed analysis is available in Section II.
(*) Asset category percentages do not add up to 100%

INSURANCE COMPANY NAME	DOM. STATE	RATING	TOTAL ASSETS ($MIL)	CAPITAL & SURPLUS ($MIL)	RISK ADJUSTED CAPITAL RATIO 1	RISK ADJUSTED CAPITAL RATIO 2	CAPITAL-IZATION INDEX (PTS)	INVEST. SAFETY INDEX (PTS)	PROFIT-ABILITY INDEX (PTS)	LIQUIDITY INDEX (PTS)	STAB. INDEX (PTS)	STABIL. FACTO
SHERIDAN LIFE INS CO	OK	C	2.2	2.0	2.55	2.30	9.0	9.8	4.1	10.0	3.0	ADT
SMITH BURIAL & LIFE INS CO	AR	D-	4.8	0.5	0.37	0.33	1.0	7.4	2.3	6.9	1.0	CDF
SOUTHERN FARM BUREAU LIFE INS CO	MS	A	12937.4	2403.0	4.43	2.40	9.1	6.0	8.1	6.3	7.4	I
SOUTHERN FIDELITY LIFE INS CO	AR	U (3)	0.1	0.1	1.92	1.73	8.1	7.7	2.9	10.0	3.1	DF
SOUTHERN FINANCIAL LIFE INS CO	KY	C	4.1	3.4	2.72	2.45	9.2	8.7	5.0	7.5	3.4	AFT
SOUTHERN FINANCIAL LIFE INS CO	LA	D+	102.5	27.8	2.65	1.46	7.7	2.9	8.9	6.7	2.8	DIT
SOUTHERN LIFE & HEALTH INS CO	WI	U (3)	95.0	34.9	1.96	1.78	8.2	5.7	7.4	8.1	7.3	DGI
SOUTHERN NATL LIFE INS CO INC	LA	C	15.6	11.0	1.68	1.35	7.5	5.9	1.7	3.5	3.3	FGLT
SOUTHERN PIONEER LIFE INS CO	AR	B	19.2	12.2	3.42	3.08	10.0	8.7	4.7	9.4	4.9	DFGT
SOUTHERN SECURITY LIFE INS CO INC	MS	D+	2.0	1.6	2.59	2.33	8.0	6.5	4.0	10.0	2.2	A
▼ SOUTHLAND NATIONAL INS CORP	AL	D	165.9	9.8	1.14	0.91	6.3	4.6	2.0	5.1	2.2	CFIT
SOUTHWEST CREDIT LIFE INC	NM	U (3)	0.8	0.6	1.66	1.50	7.8	9.2	1.6	9.6	1.8	DF
SOUTHWEST SERVICE LIFE INS CO	TX	D	12.6	5.4	0.91	0.81	5.5	8.2	2.0	7.5	1.4	ADFT
SPJST	TX	U	--	--	--	--	--	--	--	--	--	Z
SQUIRE REASSURANCE CO LLC	MI	U (3)	11.7	11.6	4.46	4.01	8.0	8.4	8.5	10.0	8.0	D
STANDARD INS CO	OR	B+	19885.1	1114.5	1.95	1.09	7.1	5.6	7.1	6.7	6.5	AI
STANDARD LIFE & ACCIDENT INS CO	TX	A-	523.8	251.8	5.03	3.10	10.0	4.9	8.7	6.9	6.9	AI
STANDARD LIFE & CAS INS CO	UT	D+	30.4	5.6	1.27	1.14	7.2	5.9	5.1	5.6	2.5	CDIT
STANDARD LIFE INS CO OF NY	NY	A-	272.4	74.3	3.41	2.26	8.9	7.4	7.0	6.8	7.2	A
STANDARD SECURITY LIFE INS CO OF NY	NY	B	247.0	114.8	3.34	2.70	9.6	7.2	7.2	6.8	5.9	ADGT
STARMOUNT LIFE INS CO	LA	B	56.6	24.2	1.41	1.06	7.1	7.2	3.5	6.2	5.4	
STARVED ROCK LIFE INS CO	AZ	U	--	--	--	--	--	--	--	--	--	Z
STATE FARM HEALTH INS CO	IL	U (3)	8.4	8.4	3.91	3.52	8.0	9.5	3.9	10.0	5.4	DF
STATE FARM LIFE & ACCIDENT ASR CO	IL	A+	2436.7	436.5	5.76	3.32	10.0	8.0	6.6	6.4	7.9	A
STATE FARM LIFE INS CO	IL	A+	62712.0	8910.9	4.35	2.48	9.2	6.7	6.6	6.2	7.9	AI
STATE LIFE INS CO	IN	B	5315.2	344.4	2.05	1.06	7.1	5.3	8.0	4.7	6.3	IL
STATE LIFE INS FUND	WI	B (3)	98.9	11.5	1.44	1.29	7.4	7.8	8.5	3.0	4.2	DL
STATE MUTUAL INS CO	GA	C	294.0	28.9	1.67	1.01	7.0	5.4	3.8	6.1	3.5	DF
STERLING INVESTORS LIFE INS CO	GA	C-	15.4	6.5	1.97	1.56	7.8	8.9	3.7	6.8	2.9	T
STONEBRIDGE LIFE INS CO	VT	B-	1772.2	172.6	2.13	1.17	7.3	4.6	5.4	7.3	5.3	AIT
STRUCTURED ANNUITY RE CO	IA	C-	1412.3	73.2	1.31	0.61	5.5	4.2	1.7	10.0	3.1	ET
SUN LIFE & HEALTH INS CO	CT	C-	369.9	183.4	5.21	3.46	10.0	7.2	2.4	6.9	3.3	AFG
SUN LIFE ASR CO OF CANADA	MI	D	16300.0	924.1	0.99	0.52	4.0	2.2	2.4	1.8	2.3	CFILT
SUNSET LIFE INS CO OF AMERICA	MO	B-	358.9	34.3	2.81	1.43	7.6	5.5	2.1	5.2	5.2	DFGI
SUPERIOR FUNERAL & LIFE INS CO	AR	C+	167.7	22.4	2.44	1.51	7.8	5.5	7.8	5.1	4.4	D
SURENCY LIFE & HEALTH INS CO	KS	C	8.4	7.4	3.75	3.34	10.0	5.8	2.0	9.1	3.4	DFGT
SURETY LIFE & CASUALTY INS CO	ND	C-	10.6	4.1	1.79	1.61	7.9	5.0	8.6	8.7	2.8	D
▼ SURETY LIFE INS CO	NE	C+	14.3	12.4	2.14	1.07	7.1	9.1	4.2	9.6	4.7	F
SWBC LIFE INS CO	TX	B	23.2	16.4	3.83	2.42	9.1	5.0	9.3	9.4	5.7	I
SWISS RE LIFE & HEALTH AMER INC	CT	C+	10472.4	1770.5	2.04	1.43	7.6	7.1	6.9	6.8	4.7	T
SYMETRA LIFE INS CO	IA	B+	28794.9	1951.2	2.21	1.20	7.3	5.4	7.9	6.5	6.7	GI
SYMETRA NATIONAL LIFE INS CO	IA	B	16.7	10.1	3.21	2.89	9.8	8.8	4.9	6.9	6.3	AD
SYMPHONIX HEALTH INS INC	MI	U (3)	9.8	7.6	3.16	2.84	8.0	9.1	0.6	8.8	0.8	FT
T J M LIFE INS CO	TX	D+	15.0	1.8	0.72	0.64	4.1	5.3	3.0	5.9	2.7	CD
TEACHERS INS & ANNUITY ASN OF AM	NY	A+	261389.2	33825.5	5.88	3.11	10.0	6.8	9.1	7.3	7.9	I
TEACHERS PROTV MUTUAL LIFE INS CO	PA	D	61.8	3.4	0.52	0.47	2.6	5.2	0.9	6.1	1.5	CT
TENNESSEE FARMERS LIFE INS CO	TN	A	1978.3	351.2	2.30	1.48	7.7	6.0	7.0	6.4	7.4	AI
TENNESSEE LIFE INS CO	AZ	U	--	--	--	--	--	--	--	--	--	Z
TEXAS DIRECTORS LIFE INS CO	TX	C (3)	5.9	0.9	0.54	0.49	2.9	4.9	7.6	5.6	2.9	CDFI
TEXAS IMPERIAL LIFE INS CO	TX	D	3.5	3.4	3.11	2.80	8.0	8.5	8.4	10.0	1.8	A
TEXAS LIFE INS CO	TX	B	1000.7	98.6	2.32	1.26	7.4	5.5	4.4	5.8	5.3	ADI
TEXAS SERVICE LIFE INS CO	TX	C-	43.6	6.3	1.22	1.10	7.2	7.6	2.8	7.4	3.1	D

See Page 27 for explanation of footnotes and Page 28 for explanation of stability factors.

Arrows denote recent upgrades ▲ or downgrades▼ (see Section VI for explanations)

56

www.weissratings.com

NET PREMIUM ($MIL)	IN-VESTED ASSETS ($MIL)	% OF INVESTED ASSETS IN:										INSURANCE COMPANY NAME
		CASH	CMO & STRUCT. SECS.	OTH.INV. GRADE BONDS	NON-INV. GRADE BONDS	CMMON & PREF. STOCK	MORT IN GOOD STAND.	NON-PERF. MORT.	REAL ESTATE	OTHER INVEST-MENTS	INVEST. IN AFFIL	
0.0	2.2	100.0	0.0	0.0	0.0	0.0	0.0	0.0	0.0	0.0	0.0	SHERIDAN LIFE INS CO
0.3	4.8	18.0	0.0	79.7	0.0	2.3	0.0	0.0	0.0	0.0	0.0	SMITH BURIAL & LIFE INS CO
605.1	12,187.8	0.1	15.7	57.4	1.5	5.7	10.1	0.0	0.1	9.5	0.9 ●	SOUTHERN FARM BUREAU LIFE INS CO
0.0	0.1	90.9	0.0	0.0	0.0	9.1	0.0	0.0	0.0	0.0	0.0	SOUTHERN FIDELITY LIFE INS CO
1.0	3.5	3.8	10.5	75.8	1.5	8.5	0.0	0.0	0.0	0.0	0.0	SOUTHERN FINANCIAL LIFE INS CO
6.3	95.1	0.8	0.0	51.1	16.8	26.0	0.0	0.0	0.0	5.3	0.0 ●	SOUTHERN FINANCIAL LIFE INS CO
0.1	94.2 (*)	0.2	1.5	57.3	0.0	34.0	0.0	0.0	0.0	0.9	29.4	SOUTHERN LIFE & HEALTH INS CO
10.8	15.1	9.5	10.4	48.6	0.0	31.1	0.0	0.0	0.0	0.4	15.7	SOUTHERN NATL LIFE INS CO INC
0.9	19.4 (*)	12.3	5.7	81.0	0.0	1.0	0.0	0.0	0.0	2.7	0.0	SOUTHERN PIONEER LIFE INS CO
0.0	1.6	25.7	0.0	49.5	0.0	0.0	19.5	0.0	5.3	0.0	0.0	SOUTHERN SECURITY LIFE INS CO INC
4.6	163.8	1.1	15.7	80.4	1.9	0.7	0.1	0.0	0.0	0.1	0.5	SOUTHLAND NATIONAL INS CORP
0.1	0.8	0.4	0.0	99.6	0.0	0.0	0.0	0.0	0.0	0.0	0.0	SOUTHWEST CREDIT LIFE INC
7.7	12.7	8.4	0.0	65.6	0.0	26.0	0.0	0.0	0.0	0.0	26.0	SOUTHWEST SERVICE LIFE INS CO
--	--	--	--	--	--	--	--	--	--	--	--	SPJST
0.0	11.6	0.0	15.5	84.1	0.0	0.4	0.0	0.0	0.0	0.0	0.0	SQUIRE REASSURANCE CO LLC
3,146.9	12,371.5 (*)	0.8	2.1	49.2	3.2	0.0	42.7	0.0	0.3	3.5	0.0 ●	STANDARD INS CO
90.6	510.5	-0.4	1.3	69.7	3.0	17.5	7.3	0.0	0.0	1.7	0.2 ●	STANDARD LIFE & ACCIDENT INS CO
7.0	26.8	3.4	6.0	60.2	0.0	0.0	26.1	0.0	0.7	3.6	0.0	STANDARD LIFE & CAS INS CO
71.8	253.1	2.4	0.1	47.7	1.7	0.0	48.2	0.0	0.0	0.0	0.0 ●	STANDARD LIFE INS CO OF NY
156.6	187.7 (*)	1.1	1.8	68.4	0.0	19.0	0.0	0.0	0.0	5.8	15.8 ●	STANDARD SECURITY LIFE INS CO OF NY
70.4	40.5	22.6	0.0	63.4	1.4	2.5	0.0	0.0	9.2	0.9	0.0	STARMOUNT LIFE INS CO
--	--	--	--	--	--	--	--	--	--	--	--	STARVED ROCK LIFE INS CO
0.0	8.4 (*)	0.4	0.0	80.2	0.0	0.0	0.0	0.0	0.0	0.0	19.3	STATE FARM HEALTH INS CO
164.2	2,234.8 (*)	0.0	21.0	69.9	0.3	0.0	0.0	0.0	0.0	7.0	1.8 ●	STATE FARM LIFE & ACCIDENT ASR CO
3,719.5	57,744.0 (*)	0.0	19.6	55.3	0.3	5.6	8.8	0.0	0.0	8.8	3.2 ●	STATE FARM LIFE INS CO
445.3	4,921.0	0.4	18.2	70.2	3.4	0.5	6.8	0.0	0.0	0.6	0.0 ●	STATE LIFE INS CO
1.5	97.3 (*)	0.0	0.0	93.5	1.1	0.0	0.0	0.0	0.0	3.7	0.0	STATE LIFE INS FUND
13.8	271.5	1.2	20.1	40.7	2.8	2.2	15.0	0.7	2.9	14.4	7.3 ●	STATE MUTUAL INS CO
3.4	12.7	4.7	13.2	76.0	0.0	0.0	3.8	0.0	0.0	2.4	0.0	STERLING INVESTORS LIFE INS CO
302.5	1,633.0 (*)	0.1	14.2	63.4	4.1	0.2	6.4	0.0	1.7	5.5	0.2 ●	STONEBRIDGE LIFE INS CO
-211.6	1,414.6	0.0	0.0	98.2	0.0	0.0	0.0	0.0	0.0	1.8	0.0 ●	STRUCTURED ANNUITY RE CO
126.5	241.9	0.5	46.2	41.5	0.5	0.4	10.6	0.0	0.0	0.0	0.0 ●	SUN LIFE & HEALTH INS CO
1,703.3	14,232.8 (*)	-0.2	7.3	50.2	2.0	5.4	20.4	0.0	8.2	5.1	1.7 ●	SUN LIFE ASR CO OF CANADA
13.6	349.2	0.6	13.0	62.1	2.8	0.4	17.5	0.0	0.0	3.6	0.0 ●	SUNSET LIFE INS CO OF AMERICA
11.4	164.8	1.8	10.1	78.1	4.8	4.2	0.0	0.3	0.4	0.3	0.0 ●	SUPERIOR FUNERAL & LIFE INS CO
3.0	7.3	78.1	0.0	21.6	0.0	0.3	0.0	0.0	0.0	0.0	0.0	SURENCY LIFE & HEALTH INS CO
1.1	9.6	17.1	0.0	57.1	5.1	15.7	0.0	0.0	1.1	4.1	0.0	SURETY LIFE & CASUALTY INS CO
0.0	11.8 (*)	0.0	0.0	114.7	0.0	0.0	0.0	0.0	0.0	0.0	0.0	SURETY LIFE INS CO
5.7	21.5	29.9	0.0	40.5	5.9	23.6	0.0	0.0	0.0	0.0	0.0	SWBC LIFE INS CO
1,196.0	9,063.2	0.1	15.0	72.3	1.9	4.2	4.0	0.0	0.0	2.5	9.7 ●	SWISS RE LIFE & HEALTH AMER INC
2,568.7	21,493.6	0.0	12.9	61.4	5.2	3.6	15.0	0.0	0.0	1.7	0.5 ●	SYMETRA LIFE INS CO
0.2	16.5	0.1	62.9	35.9	0.0	0.0	0.0	0.0	0.0	1.1	0.0	SYMETRA NATIONAL LIFE INS CO
0.0	8.8	4.2	0.0	95.8	0.0	0.0	0.0	0.0	0.0	0.0	0.0	SYMPHONIX HEALTH INS INC
1.0	14.2	5.4	42.7	30.6	0.0	0.0	0.0	0.0	16.5	4.9	0.0	T J M LIFE INS CO
8,304.3	222,848.7	0.5	33.9	42.1	5.5	1.2	6.4	0.0	0.8	9.7	6.9 ●	TEACHERS INS & ANNUITY ASN OF AM
10.6	63.2	1.8	0.8	90.5	0.0	6.5	0.0	0.0	0.1	0.3	0.0	TEACHERS PROTV MUTUAL LIFE INS CO
126.1	1,830.5	0.8	0.8	62.3	6.7	26.7	0.3	0.0	0.7	1.7	23.3 ●	TENNESSEE FARMERS LIFE INS CO
--	--	--	--	--	--	--	--	--	--	--	--	TENNESSEE LIFE INS CO
0.3	5.7	0.1	1.2	89.7	5.4	3.4	0.0	0.0	0.0	0.2	0.0	TEXAS DIRECTORS LIFE INS CO
0.0	3.3	8.9	65.9	25.2	0.0	0.0	0.0	0.0	0.0	0.0	0.0	TEXAS IMPERIAL LIFE INS CO
151.7	921.0	1.1	31.8	54.2	5.1	1.3	0.0	0.0	0.2	6.3	0.0 ●	TEXAS LIFE INS CO
13.4	31.6	27.3	60.7	6.9	0.0	0.3	0.0	0.0	2.7	2.0	0.0	TEXAS SERVICE LIFE INS CO

● Bullets denote a more detailed analysis is available in Section II.
(*) Asset category percentages do not add up to 100%

INSURANCE COMPANY NAME	DOM. STATE	RATING	TOTAL ASSETS ($MIL)	CAPITAL & SURPLUS ($MIL)	RISK ADJUSTED CAPITAL RATIO 1	RISK ADJUSTED CAPITAL RATIO 2	CAPITAL-IZATION INDEX (PTS)	INVEST. SAFETY INDEX (PTS)	PROFIT-ABILITY INDEX (PTS)	LIQUIDITY INDEX (PTS)	STAB. INDEX (PTS)	STABILI FACTOI
THRIVENT FINANCIAL FOR LUTHERANS	WI	U	--	--	--	--	--	--	--	--	--	Z
THRIVENT LIFE INS CO	MN	B+	3530.2	176.0	2.48	1.20	7.3	5.6	6.6	6.1	6.6	I
TIAA-CREF LIFE INS CO	NY	B	8766.7	364.0	2.41	1.25	7.4	6.4	3.9	6.1	6.3	GI
TIME INS CO	WI	B-	848.6	297.6	1.30	1.02	5.3	6.2	3.9	5.2	4.9	AT
TIPPECANOE LIFE INS CO	AZ	U	--	--	--	--	--	--	--	--	--	Z
TOWER LIFE INS CO	TX	D+	54.5	28.8	4.27	2.68	9.5	4.8	1.3	6.9	2.7	DFT
TOWN & COUNTRY LIFE INS CO	UT	C-	6.0	3.5	2.14	1.92	8.4	6.9	7.9	7.4	2.4	D
TRANS CITY LIFE INS CO	AZ	C-	19.4	9.4	3.38	3.04	10.0	7.0	2.4	9.7	2.9	D
TRANS OCEANIC LIFE INS CO	PR	A	62.9	30.5	2.69	1.80	8.2	7.2	9.0	8.7	6.4	D
TRANS WORLD ASR CO	CA	B	347.3	78.9	2.12	1.68	8.0	6.0	7.0	6.1	5.4	DI
TRANS-WESTERN LIFE INS CO	TX	U (3)	0.5	0.5	2.19	1.72	8.0	9.8	6.2	10.0	6.4	T
TRANSAM ASR CO	AZ	U (3)	4.3	3.4	2.52	2.27	8.9	9.5	3.9	10.0	4.1	DF
TRANSAMERICA ADVISORS LIFE INS CO	AR	B	9792.9	915.5	10.43	5.23	10.0	7.4	5.2	6.7	5.3	AT
TRANSAMERICA FINANCIAL LIFE INS CO	NY	B (1)	30565.9	1029.5	2.93	1.43	7.6	5.3	6.1	9.3	5.9	AFI
TRANSAMERICA LIFE INS CO	IA	B-	118208.1	5730.5	1.89	1.19	7.3	5.7	3.9	7.2	5.1	F
TRANSAMERICA PREMIER LIFE INS CO	IA	C+	32048.5	699.2	1.20	0.59	5.3	3.5	4.4	6.4	4.7	CI
TRINITY LIFE INS CO	OK	D-	127.2	8.6	0.50	0.38	1.6	3.3	5.8	4.9	0.9	CDGI
TRIPLE S VIDA INC	PR	B-	537.9	63.6	1.04	0.70	5.1	4.8	7.6	4.1	5.1	CIL
TRIPLE-S BLUE INC	PR	D-	18.7	4.8	1.59	1.44	7.7	7.1	1.1	7.2	1.2	FT
▼ TRUASSURE INS CO	IL	D+	7.7	7.4	4.09	3.68	10.0	9.6	2.2	10.0	2.5	DT
TRUSTMARK INS CO	IL	B+	1404.5	311.1	2.93	1.70	8.1	5.0	7.5	7.4	6.8	I
TRUSTMARK LIFE INS CO	IL	B+	370.8	170.4	4.54	3.10	10.0	6.5	6.4	6.7	6.6	DI
TRUSTMARK LIFE INS CO OF NEW YORK	NY	B	6.5	6.1	3.15	2.83	9.7	9.1	2.0	7.7	4.9	DFGT
UBS LIFE INS CO USA	CA	C-	41.6	39.1	6.29	5.66	10.0	9.1	5.4	7.0	3.0	DGT
ULLICO LIFE INS CO	TX	B	11.8	11.5	6.38	5.74	8.0	9.2	4.5	10.0	4.9	AFT
UNICARE LIFE & HEALTH INS CO	IN	B (1)	402.8	76.5	1.85	1.37	7.6	3.8	6.6	6.5	4.1	IT
UNIFIED LIFE INS CO	TX	B	183.7	22.8	2.28	1.32	7.5	4.8	8.3	5.8	6.3	FI
UNIMERICA INS CO	WI	B	458.7	215.0	3.10	2.47	9.2	8.5	9.1	7.0	5.8	ADG
UNIMERICA LIFE INS CO OF NY	NY	B	36.1	19.3	4.04	3.64	10.0	8.8	5.8	9.1	5.5	AGT
UNION FIDELITY LIFE INS CO	KS	D+	19466.6	492.7	1.00	0.51	5.0	3.0	1.7	8.6	2.7	CFI
UNION LABOR LIFE INS CO	MD	B-	3351.0	77.0	1.40	0.99	6.9	7.6	2.9	6.9	5.0	FT
UNION NATIONAL LIFE INS CO	LA	B	19.1	14.7	4.87	2.57	8.0	9.1	9.3	10.0	5.8	A
UNION SECURITY INS CO	KS	B	4942.9	422.9	1.84	1.19	7.3	5.4	6.4	5.0	5.6	AFIL
UNION SECURITY LIFE INS CO OF NY	NY	B+	139.8	41.5	4.50	4.05	10.0	7.0	5.9	6.8	5.0	AFT
▼ UNITED AMERICAN INS CO	NE	B-	1717.2	170.8	0.99	0.72	4.9	5.8	6.6	6.5	4.9	C
UNITED ASR LIFE INS CO	TX	D-	2.1	1.0	1.42	1.28	7.4	9.6	1.9	9.3	1.0	DG
UNITED BENEFIT LIFE INS CO	OH	U (3)	3.1	3.1	3.00	2.70	8.0	9.2	3.1	10.0	4.3	DF
UNITED BURIAL INS CO OF WINNSBORO	LA	U	--	--	--	--	--	--	--	--	--	Z
UNITED FARM FAMILY LIFE INS CO	IN	A	2129.9	285.5	3.13	1.87	8.3	6.8	6.5	5.9	7.4	I
UNITED FIDELITY LIFE INS CO	TX	C	757.1	440.1	0.72	0.70	4.6	3.6	7.5	6.9	4.3	CDI
UNITED FUNERAL BENEFIT LIFE INS CO	OK	D	48.6	7.3	0.94	0.80	5.4	7.2	7.9	6.9	1.8	ADT
▼ UNITED FUNERAL DIR BENEFIT LIC	TX	D-	103.3	5.2	0.39	0.35	1.2	3.2	8.1	6.1	1.2	CGIT
UNITED HEALTHCARE INS CO	CT	C	14592.8	4865.2	0.85	0.72	4.2	6.8	9.4	1.5	3.5	CL
UNITED HERITAGE LIFE INS CO	ID	B-	522.4	57.0	2.64	1.37	7.6	6.1	8.0	2.6	4.6	L
UNITED HOME LIFE INS CO	IN	B	76.9	18.8	2.50	2.25	8.9	7.4	6.1	6.4	6.2	D
UNITED INS CO OF AMERICA	IL	B-	3655.6	446.6	1.58	0.99	6.9	4.5	7.2	5.3	5.3	AI
UNITED INTERNATIONAL LIFE INS	OK	U (3)	3.3	0.4	0.41	0.37	1.4	7.0	1.1	1.5	1.3	CDLT
UNITED LIFE INS CO	IA	B	1640.6	164.5	2.86	1.50	7.8	6.0	6.0	6.5	6.1	AFI
UNITED NATIONAL LIFE INS CO OF AM	IL	C	14.7	3.3	0.72	0.55	3.4	8.1	5.4	7.7	3.4	CG
UNITED OF OMAHA LIFE INS CO	NE	B	18551.4	1406.6	1.99	1.15	7.2	5.1	5.4	5.9	5.4	I
UNITED SECURITY ASR CO OF PA	PA	D+	150.9	12.4	1.38	1.07	7.1	3.9	1.9	7.0	2.6	D
UNITED SECURITY LIFE & HEALTH INS CO	IL	D	4.0	2.8	1.14	1.03	5.5	8.0	1.8	1.3	1.8	ACFL

See Page 27 for explanation of footnotes and Page 28 for explanation of stability factors.
Arrows denote recent upgrades ▲ or downgrades▼ (see Section VI for explanations)

58

www.weissratings.com

NET PREMIUM ($MIL)	IN-VESTED ASSETS ($MIL)	% OF INVESTED ASSETS IN:									INVEST. IN AFFIL	INSURANCE COMPANY NAME
		CASH	CMO & STRUCT. SECS.	OTH.INV. GRADE BONDS	NON-INV. GRADE BONDS	CMMON & PREF. STOCK	MORT IN GOOD STAND.	NON-PERF. MORT.	REAL ESTATE	OTHER INVEST-MENTS		
--	--	--	--	--	--	--	--	--	--	--	--	THRIVENT FINANCIAL FOR LUTHERANS
82.9	1,793.1	1.5	25.8	64.4	6.8	0.0	0.0	0.0	0.0	1.0	0.8 ●	THRIVENT LIFE INS CO
488.2	4,247.1	0.8	10.8	86.2	1.6	0.1	0.0	0.0	0.0	0.6	0.0 ●	TIAA-CREF LIFE INS CO
1,322.2	602.5 (*)	0.0	9.0	64.8	5.4	7.5	13.1	0.0	2.0	5.1	0.0 ●	TIME INS CO
--	--	--	--	--	--	--	--	--	--	--	--	TIPPECANOE LIFE INS CO
0.4	57.0	2.2	7.5	54.8	5.3	9.9	0.8	0.0	16.8	2.8	0.0 ●	TOWER LIFE INS CO
2.6	5.6	17.5	0.0	58.4	0.0	19.2	5.0	0.0	0.0	0.0	0.0	TOWN & COUNTRY LIFE INS CO
1.5	18.2	25.6	0.0	45.5	0.0	25.2	0.0	0.0	3.6	0.0	25.6	TRANS CITY LIFE INS CO
22.4	53.1	31.8	26.7	32.0	0.0	1.2	0.0	0.0	8.3	0.1	0.0 ●	TRANS OCEANIC LIFE INS CO
8.7	342.1	1.0	0.0	74.7	2.0	9.6	8.0	0.0	4.2	0.4	8.9 ●	TRANS WORLD ASR CO
0.0	0.4	95.3	0.0	0.0	0.0	0.0	0.0	0.0	0.0	4.7	0.0	TRANS-WESTERN LIFE INS CO
0.0	4.3	50.3	0.0	31.9	0.0	17.6	0.0	0.0	0.0	0.1	37.7	TRANSAM ASR CO
9.3	2,654.4 (*)	-0.2	7.5	53.2	1.2	0.3	1.4	0.0	0.0	27.0	0.0 ●	TRANSAMERICA ADVISORS LIFE INS CO
2,773.6	8,906.3 (*)	0.1	16.0	65.4	4.8	0.1	6.2	0.0	0.0	2.4	0.9 ●	TRANSAMERICA FINANCIAL LIFE INS CO
12,170.8	51,914.1 (*)	0.3	18.6	47.2	5.9	3.4	10.9	0.0	0.2	5.8	6.1 ●	TRANSAMERICA LIFE INS CO
1,313.8	16,497.4 (*)	0.5	14.9	56.7	6.3	0.5	10.3	0.0	0.0	7.7	3.2 ●	TRANSAMERICA PREMIER LIFE INS CO
24.7	101.8	2.5	0.2	58.4	2.8	12.2	17.2	0.1	6.1	0.6	13.8	TRINITY LIFE INS CO
117.2	480.9	1.4	9.7	73.3	0.0	14.3	0.0	0.0	0.0	1.4	2.0 ●	TRIPLE S VIDA INC
2.2	13.8	30.7	3.4	55.1	0.0	0.0	0.0	0.0	0.0	10.7	0.0	TRIPLE-S BLUE INC
0.2	6.4	29.0	0.0	71.0	0.0	0.0	0.0	0.0	0.0	0.0	0.0	TRUASSURE INS CO
227.9	1,337.7	0.1	26.8	45.8	6.2	12.2	1.9	0.0	1.9	5.0	1.2 ●	TRUSTMARK INS CO
159.4	346.2	-1.3	10.0	64.2	8.2	15.8	0.0	0.0	0.0	3.2	1.9 ●	TRUSTMARK LIFE INS CO
0.6	7.3	2.1	0.0	97.9	0.0	0.0	0.0	0.0	0.0	0.0	0.0	TRUSTMARK LIFE INS CO OF NEW YORK
0.1	41.9	2.5	0.0	97.5	0.0	0.0	0.0	0.0	0.0	0.0	0.0 ●	UBS LIFE INS CO USA
0.0	11.3	0.5	23.5	76.0	0.0	0.0	0.0	0.0	0.0	0.2	0.0	ULLICO LIFE INS CO
159.0	309.0 (*)	8.5	1.8	75.2	13.1	0.1	0.0	0.0	0.0	0.0	0.0 ●	UNICARE LIFE & HEALTH INS CO
25.1	160.6	1.9	26.5	58.1	6.8	0.0	0.2	0.0	0.0	5.9	0.0	UNIFIED LIFE INS CO
440.2	376.9	-1.0	13.7	87.3	0.0	0.0	0.0	0.0	0.0	0.0	0.0 ●	UNIMERICA INS CO
5.6	34.6	9.4	21.4	69.2	0.0	0.0	0.0	0.0	0.0	0.0	0.0	UNIMERICA LIFE INS CO OF NY
209.1	19,130.3	0.0	12.5	75.3	3.8	0.3	5.5	0.0	0.0	2.6	1.7 ●	UNION FIDELITY LIFE INS CO
106.0	319.6	-0.9	28.9	55.4	1.2	7.3	6.7	0.0	0.0	1.7	7.3 ●	UNION LABOR LIFE INS CO
0.0	19.4	26.6	0.0	73.4	0.0	0.0	0.0	0.0	0.0	0.0	0.0	UNION NATIONAL LIFE INS CO
763.0	3,191.6 (*)	-0.6	3.7	64.7	4.3	3.4	17.7	0.0	0.1	5.3	0.8 ●	UNION SECURITY INS CO
18.1	129.5	-0.6	7.3	66.0	3.0	4.1	19.6	0.0	0.0	0.6	0.0 ●	UNION SECURITY LIFE INS CO OF NY
646.2	1,510.4 (*)	0.8	4.1	83.4	4.0	3.6	0.0	0.0	0.0	2.6	3.6 ●	UNITED AMERICAN INS CO
0.6	1.8	26.4	0.0	73.6	0.0	0.0	0.0	0.0	0.0	0.0	0.0	UNITED ASR LIFE INS CO
0.0	3.1	2.6	0.0	97.4	0.0	0.0	0.0	0.0	0.0	0.0	0.0	UNITED BENEFIT LIFE INS CO
--	--	--	--	--	--	--	--	--	--	--	--	UNITED BURIAL INS CO OF WINNSBORO
109.4	2,019.1	0.9	13.1	61.3	0.0	2.9	15.3	0.1	0.2	6.2	1.3 ●	UNITED FARM FAMILY LIFE INS CO
6.1	769.7	0.0	8.5	7.2	1.3	74.6	2.8	0.0	0.3	5.2	72.8 ●	UNITED FIDELITY LIFE INS CO
1.4	49.5	1.7	66.3	16.5	0.0	14.9	0.0	0.0	0.0	0.6	12.7	UNITED FUNERAL BENEFIT LIFE INS CO
5.2	107.5	3.5	71.6	18.7	0.0	5.7	0.3	0.0	0.0	0.3	4.5	UNITED FUNERAL DIR BENEFIT LIC
33,276.5	9,973.2	-0.1	17.6	58.1	5.5	16.6	0.0	0.0	0.0	2.4	14.7 ●	UNITED HEALTHCARE INS CO
48.0	500.7	0.2	8.7	80.1	4.7	0.8	3.0	0.0	1.3	1.4	0.0 ●	UNITED HERITAGE LIFE INS CO
13.6	62.1	2.3	15.3	74.7	0.0	4.3	0.0	0.0	0.0	3.4	0.0	UNITED HOME LIFE INS CO
278.2	3,397.1	0.2	4.3	62.2	7.9	6.5	0.0	0.0	4.8	14.3	4.7 ●	UNITED INS CO OF AMERICA
0.0	3.3	1.0	6.6	84.1	3.5	0.0	0.0	0.0	0.0	4.9	0.0	UNITED INTERNATIONAL LIFE INS
143.1	1,622.1	0.6	15.5	78.3	2.6	1.6	0.3	0.0	0.0	1.2	0.0 ●	UNITED LIFE INS CO
12.5	12.5	1.2	26.0	63.7	0.2	0.0	8.2	0.0	0.1	0.5	0.0	UNITED NATIONAL LIFE INS CO OF AM
1,851.6	14,356.8 (*)	0.9	25.9	49.6	3.4	1.1	13.2	0.0	0.4	4.2	2.6 ●	UNITED OF OMAHA LIFE INS CO
23.8	143.4	0.2	6.3	90.3	3.1	0.0	0.0	0.0	0.0	0.1	0.0	UNITED SECURITY ASR CO OF PA
1.8	8.3	5.9	40.6	51.2	2.3	0.0	0.0	0.0	0.0	0.0	0.0	UNITED SECURITY LIFE & HEALTH INS CO

● Bullets denote a more detailed analysis is available in Section II.
(*) Asset category percentages do not add up to 100%

INSURANCE COMPANY NAME	DOM. STATE	RATING	TOTAL ASSETS ($MIL)	CAPITAL & SURPLUS ($MIL)	RISK ADJUSTED CAPITAL RATIO 1	RISK ADJUSTED CAPITAL RATIO 2	CAPITAL-IZATION INDEX (PTS)	INVEST. SAFETY INDEX (PTS)	PROFIT-ABILITY INDEX (PTS)	LIQUIDITY INDEX (PTS)	STAB. INDEX (PTS)	STABILI FACTO
UNITED STATES LIFE INS CO IN NYC	NY	B-	28449.0	1994.7	2.62	1.29	7.4	5.1	5.9	5.7	4.6	AIT
UNITED TEACHER ASSOCIATES INS CO	TX	C	986.6	85.0	2.05	1.11	7.2	5.2	2.6	7.2	4.2	GIT
UNITED TRUST INS CO	AL	B	62.5	10.7	1.58	1.42	7.6	6.5	3.9	9.7	5.1	D
UNITED WORLD LIFE INS CO	NE	B+	114.3	48.7	4.02	1.68	8.0	7.6	6.7	7.0	6.7	AF
UNITEDHEALTHCARE LIFE INS CO	WI	B	101.5	44.1	1.32	1.06	7.1	8.4	6.4	7.2	5.8	AGT
UNITY FINANCIAL LIFE INS CO	OH	C-	185.4	11.4	1.27	1.14	7.2	4.4	3.0	7.0	3.2	D
UNIVANTAGE INS CO	UT	U (3)	1.9	1.9	2.74	2.46	8.0	9.6	4.1	10.0	4.3	D
UNIVERSAL FIDELITY LIFE INS CO	OK	D	14.5	4.1	1.41	1.10	7.2	6.1	3.4	6.7	1.7	D
▲ UNIVERSAL GUARANTY LIFE INS CO	OH	C+	345.7	40.0	1.31	0.84	5.7	3.6	7.8	4.7	4.8	CDFIL
UNIVERSAL LIFE INS CO	PR	B	740.2	40.8	1.85	1.00	7.0	4.4	8.2	9.0	5.4	ADGI
UNIVERSAL UNDERWRITERS LIFE INS CO	KS	B-	159.3	23.1	2.47	2.22	8.8	7.7	4.0	6.4	5.1	AD
UNUM LIFE INS CO OF AMERICA	ME	C+	19496.1	1504.2	2.37	1.27	7.4	4.0	6.8	7.1	4.8	AFI
US ALLIANCE LIFE & SECURITY CO	KS	D-	4.5	2.2	1.20	1.08	7.1	5.0	1.7	6.5	1.1	DEFG
US FINANCIAL LIFE INS CO	OH	B	639.7	72.3	2.40	1.28	7.4	7.1	4.8	5.6	5.7	A
USA INS CO	MS	C-	3.2	2.3	2.47	2.22	8.8	5.1	9.1	6.9	1.9	DF
USA LIFE ONE INS CO OF INDIANA	IN	B-	36.6	16.0	3.03	2.73	9.6	8.1	5.0	6.9	4.0	D
USAA LIFE INS CO	TX	A	21964.7	2161.8	4.09	2.18	8.8	6.8	8.9	5.7	7.4	AI
USAA LIFE INS CO OF NEW YORK	NY	B+	667.0	66.3	2.53	1.30	7.5	5.7	8.2	5.0	6.5	IL
USABLE LIFE	AR	B+	432.6	187.6	1.76	1.29	7.4	5.4	7.6	5.9	6.3	IT
USIC LIFE INS CO	PR	B	7.8	6.3	2.34	1.39	7.6	4.1	7.6	7.6	5.6	AI
VALUE HEALTH REINS INC	AZ	U (5)	--	--	--	--	--	--	--	--	--	Z
VANTIS LIFE INS CO	CT	B-	877.6	73.3	1.95	1.07	7.1	5.3	6.0	4.7	5.3	FIL
VANTISLIFE INS CO OF NEW YORK	NY	B-	8.6	5.2	2.52	2.27	8.9	8.3	1.9	7.0	4.5	ADGT
VARIABLE ANNUITY LIFE INS CO	TX	B	77039.3	4243.3	3.58	1.69	8.0	5.8	7.9	6.5	5.8	AI
VERSANT LIFE INS CO	MS	B-	5.5	4.5	2.79	2.51	9.3	8.9	7.1	10.0	4.2	ADG
VOYA INS & ANNUITY CO	IA	B	66208.2	2026.6	1.95	0.98	6.8	5.1	6.0	7.9	4.3	AGIT
VOYA RETIREMENT INS & ANNUITY CO	CT	B	88666.7	1983.2	2.56	1.25	7.4	5.7	7.2	9.1	5.8	AI
WASHINGTON NATIONAL INS CO	IN	D+	4769.5	319.7	1.63	0.87	6.0	3.9	6.4	6.8	2.7	AIT
WATEREE LIFE INS	SC	C-	10.4	9.2	3.73	3.36	10.0	9.0	4.2	9.7	2.9	D
WEA INS CORP	WI	C	683.2	205.9	1.94	1.37	7.6	4.4	2.0	6.7	4.0	DI
WEST COAST LIFE INS CO	NE	C+	4715.9	362.3	2.49	1.24	7.4	5.5	1.9	6.0	4.6	AFT
WESTERN & SOUTHERN LIFE INS CO	OH	B	9796.0	4450.2	1.80	1.51	7.8	3.4	7.6	7.0	5.7	AI
WESTERN AMERICAN LIFE INS CO	TX	C	31.9	3.0	0.64	0.57	3.6	7.1	3.0	5.9	3.6	ACD
WESTERN CATHOLIC UNION	IL	U	--	--	--	--	--	--	--	--	--	Z
WESTERN UNITED LIFE ASR CO	WA	B- (3)	14.8	7.4	2.59	2.33	9.0	9.5	2.8	10.0	5.0	ADF
WESTERN-SOUTHERN LIFE ASR CO	OH	B	13473.7	1254.9	2.55	1.32	7.5	5.4	8.7	5.6	5.9	AIT
WESTPORT LIFE INS CO	AZ	D (5)	--	--	--	--	--	--	--	--	--	Z
WICHITA NATIONAL LIFE INS CO	OK	C	17.8	8.0	2.44	2.20	8.8	8.8	4.4	9.4	4.3	F
WILBERT LIFE INS CO	LA	U	--	--	--	--	--	--	--	--	--	Z
WILLIAM PENN LIFE INS CO OF NEW YORK	NY	C-	1149.7	174.0	3.76	1.79	8.2	6.5	2.0	6.3	3.1	AFGT
▼ WILLIAMS PROGRESSIVE LIFE & ACC I C	LA	E+	11.1	0.5	0.32	0.29	0.5	1.9	1.2	7.0	0.5	CFIT
▼ WILTON REASSURANCE CO	MN	B-	3820.4	637.4	1.23	0.87	6.0	4.3	7.9	6.3	5.3	AGIT
▼ WILTON REASSURANCE LIFE CO OF NY	NY	B-	910.9	108.7	3.14	1.58	4.0	6.4	7.1	5.4	5.3	AIT
WINDSOR LIFE INS CO	TX	B-	3.2	2.9	2.77	2.50	9.3	7.7	4.2	10.0	3.7	ADT
WMI MUTUAL INS CO	UT	C	14.5	7.1	1.48	1.11	7.2	5.0	4.9	6.1	3.5	DF
WOODMEN OF THE WORLD/ASSURED LIFE	CO	U	--	--	--	--	--	--	--	--	--	Z
XL LIFE INS & ANNUITY CO	IL	U (3)	13.9	13.7	10.78	9.70	8.0	9.6	5.5	7.0	6.5	AT
YADKIN VALLEY LIFE INS CO	AZ	U	--	--	--	--	--	--	--	--	--	Z
ZALE LIFE INS CO	AZ	B-	11.4	9.2	3.63	3.26	10.0	6.7	7.9	9.2	4.9	A
ZURICH AMERICAN LIFE INS CO	IL	C	12655.1	147.5	1.99	1.16	4.0	8.0	1.5	7.7	2.8	FT
ZURICH AMERICAN LIFE INS CO OF NY	NY	C+	42.6	21.1	5.76	5.18	10.0	9.6	3.5	10.0	4.4	ADE

See Page 27 for explanation of footnotes and Page 28 for explanation of stability factors.

Arrows denote recent upgrades ▲ or downgrades▼ (see Section VI for explanations)

60

www.weissratings.com

NET PREMIUM ($MIL)	IN-VESTED ASSETS ($MIL)	% OF INVESTED ASSETS IN:										INSURANCE COMPANY NAME
		CASH	CMO & STRUCT. SECS.	OTH.INV. GRADE BONDS	NON-INV. GRADE BONDS	CMMON & PREF. STOCK	MORT IN GOOD STAND.	NON-PERF. MORT.	REAL ESTATE	OTHER INVEST-MENTS	INVEST. IN AFFIL	
1,455.3	23,293.1 (*)	-0.1	23.7	55.7	4.9	0.2	7.3	0.0	0.1	5.2	0.2 ●	UNITED STATES LIFE INS CO IN NYC
56.4	909.0	0.4	27.8	60.6	5.0	4.2	0.0	0.0	0.0	2.0	0.0 ●	UNITED TEACHER ASSOCIATES INS CO
3.2	53.6	5.0	1.3	89.1	0.0	4.6	0.0	0.0	0.0	0.0	0.0	UNITED TRUST INS CO
1.0	98.9 (*)	1.4	28.0	65.3	1.1	0.0	0.0	0.0	0.0	0.7	0.0 ●	UNITED WORLD LIFE INS CO
164.2	54.0	-3.3	17.4	85.9	0.0	0.0	0.0	0.0	0.0	0.0	0.0 ●	UNITEDHEALTHCARE LIFE INS CO
33.2	167.2	0.4	9.0	90.6	0.0	0.0	0.0	0.0	0.0	0.0	0.0	UNITY FINANCIAL LIFE INS CO
0.0	1.9	4.9	0.0	95.1	0.0	0.0	0.0	0.0	0.0	0.0	0.0	UNIVANTAGE INS CO
7.1	9.4	8.3	9.7	53.2	1.3	13.1	0.0	0.0	12.5	1.9	0.2	UNIVERSAL FIDELITY LIFE INS CO
5.7	341.6	4.1	0.4	44.7	6.2	15.6	5.9	2.1	5.6	15.5	10.4 ●	UNIVERSAL GUARANTY LIFE INS CO
89.4	399.1 (*)	1.0	12.4	77.3	1.5	3.5	0.0	0.0	0.0	0.1	0.0 ●	UNIVERSAL LIFE INS CO
5.1	146.5	0.5	37.3	57.0	0.3	0.0	0.0	0.0	0.0	4.8	0.0	UNIVERSAL UNDERWRITERS LIFE INS CO
2,165.5	18,124.8	0.0	7.9	76.0	8.9	0.3	4.5	0.0	0.5	2.1	0.2 ●	UNUM LIFE INS CO OF AMERICA
1.9	3.6	8.1	22.4	50.3	11.1	8.1	0.0	0.0	0.0	0.0	0.0	US ALLIANCE LIFE & SECURITY CO
29.5	560.6	0.7	0.9	88.8	4.4	0.7	0.0	0.0	0.0	4.6	0.0 ●	US FINANCIAL LIFE INS CO
0.4	2.8	9.0	0.0	0.0	0.0	0.0	57.8	0.0	31.6	1.6	5.2	USA INS CO
1.0	36.5	7.6	0.5	86.5	2.4	0.7	0.0	0.0	0.3	1.9	0.0	USA LIFE ONE INS CO OF INDIANA
1,204.1	20,607.7	0.0	29.6	64.0	2.4	1.3	0.1	0.0	0.0	1.6	1.2 ●	USAA LIFE INS CO
29.2	620.6	0.3	25.6	69.9	2.4	1.0	0.0	0.0	0.0	1.0	0.0 ●	USAA LIFE INS CO OF NEW YORK
442.8	345.7	0.6	7.3	68.1	0.4	14.9	3.9	0.0	2.3	2.6	1.9 ●	USABLE LIFE
3.3	7.2	8.3	0.0	81.2	7.7	2.9	0.0	0.0	0.0	0.0	0.0	USIC LIFE INS CO
--	--	--	--	--	--	--	--	--	--	--	--	VALUE HEALTH REINS INC
25.6	834.2	0.3	15.9	77.7	2.3	1.4	0.1	0.0	0.7	1.7	0.7 ●	VANTIS LIFE INS CO
2.0	7.5	2.9	6.8	90.2	0.0	0.0	0.0	0.0	0.0	0.1	0.0	VANTISLIFE INS CO OF NEW YORK
3,672.7	43,972.6 (*)	-0.2	38.6	39.2	3.2	0.2	9.6	0.0	0.1	7.5	9.3 ●	VARIABLE ANNUITY LIFE INS CO
0.5	5.3 (*)	9.8	0.0	85.7	0.0	0.0	0.0	0.0	0.0	0.0	0.0	VERSANT LIFE INS CO
1,977.5	25,161.2 (*)	1.2	17.0	64.8	3.0	0.3	10.7	0.0	0.1	0.9	0.4 ●	VOYA INS & ANNUITY CO
6,860.8	24,160.9 (*)	0.9	12.4	63.4	3.6	0.3	14.1	0.0	0.3	3.2	1.7 ●	VOYA RETIREMENT INS & ANNUITY CO
450.0	5,068.3	1.9	24.9	56.4	5.7	1.5	6.7	0.0	1.1	1.6	1.2 ●	WASHINGTON NATIONAL INS CO
0.7	10.2	8.5	0.0	91.0	0.0	0.4	0.0	0.0	0.0	0.0	0.4	WATEREE LIFE INS
445.8	690.8	5.2	23.2	50.7	0.1	20.8	0.0	0.0	0.0	0.0	0.0 ●	WEA INS CORP
15.5	4,104.6	1.4	6.3	70.9	3.9	2.4	14.2	0.0	0.0	0.9	0.0 ●	WEST COAST LIFE INS CO
190.2	8,312.9	0.1	11.1	27.9	2.4	44.1	0.2	0.0	0.4	13.5	34.2 ●	WESTERN & SOUTHERN LIFE INS CO
2.0	31.7	5.7	63.4	29.8	0.4	0.6	0.0	0.0	0.0	0.0	0.0	WESTERN AMERICAN LIFE INS CO
--	--	--	--	--	--	--	--	--	--	--	--	WESTERN CATHOLIC UNION
0.6	14.3	-0.1	0.0	100.1	0.0	0.0	0.0	0.0	0.0	0.0	0.0	WESTERN UNITED LIFE ASR CO
642.3	12,330.9	0.1	34.8	45.9	8.9	2.0	5.9	0.0	0.0	1.9	1.6 ●	WESTERN-SOUTHERN LIFE ASR CO
--	--	--	--	--	--	--	--	--	--	--	--	WESTPORT LIFE INS CO
2.9	17.6	76.0	6.4	0.1	0.0	10.9	0.0	0.0	1.3	5.2	10.9	WICHITA NATIONAL LIFE INS CO
--	--	--	--	--	--	--	--	--	--	--	--	WILBERT LIFE INS CO
34.6	1,069.5	-1.0	12.5	77.0	7.3	0.0	0.9	0.0	0.0	3.2	0.0 ●	WILLIAM PENN LIFE INS CO OF NEW YORK
1.1	11.2	23.3	3.1	19.8	0.2	11.2	32.6	1.5	1.9	6.4	0.9	WILLIAMS PROGRESSIVE LIFE & ACC I C
432.4	3,228.2	0.5	27.1	49.7	2.6	9.0	0.0	0.0	0.0	10.9	12.9 ●	WILTON REASSURANCE CO
13.4	874.3 (*)	0.8	33.0	55.3	5.2	1.3	0.0	0.0	0.0	3.1	0.0 ●	WILTON REASSURANCE LIFE CO OF NY
0.1	3.0	2.8	0.0	93.8	3.4	0.0	0.0	0.0	0.0	0.0	0.0	WINDSOR LIFE INS CO
14.1	12.8	1.3	1.2	69.7	0.0	27.7	0.0	0.0	0.0	0.0	2.5	WMI MUTUAL INS CO
--	--	--	--	--	--	--	--	--	--	--	--	WOODMEN OF THE WORLD/ASSURED LIFE
0.0	13.8	4.9	0.0	95.1	0.0	0.0	0.0	0.0	0.0	0.0	0.0	XL LIFE INS & ANNUITY CO
--	--	--	--	--	--	--	--	--	--	--	--	YADKIN VALLEY LIFE INS CO
1.5	11.2	5.8	0.3	79.3	0.0	13.3	0.0	0.0	0.0	1.3	0.0	ZALE LIFE INS CO
28.0	527.8	3.8	26.5	55.5	0.8	4.0	0.0	0.0	0.0	9.5	4.0 ●	ZURICH AMERICAN LIFE INS CO
20.5	21.3	1.2	0.0	98.9	0.0	0.0	0.0	0.0	0.0	0.0	0.0	ZURICH AMERICAN LIFE INS CO OF NY

● Bullets denote a more detailed analysis is available in Section II.
(*) Asset category percentages do not add up to 100%

Section II

Analysis of Largest Companies

A summary analysis of those

U.S. Life and Annuity Insurers

with capital in excess of $25 million.

Companies are listed in alphabetical order.

Section II Contents

This section contains rating factors, historical data and general information on each of the largest life and health insurers. Companies with capital and surplus of less than $25 million, Blue Cross Blue Shield plans and companies lacking year-end data do not appear in this section. You can find information on these firms in Section I.

1.	**Financial Strength Rating**	The current rating appears to the right of the company name. Our ratings are designed to distinguish levels of insolvency risk and are measured on a scale from A (Excellent) to F (Failed). Highly rated companies are, in our opinion, less likely to experience financial difficulties than lower rated firms. See *About Weiss Financial Strength Ratings* for more information.
2.	**Major Rating Factors**	A synopsis of the key indexes and sub-factors that have most influenced the rating of a particular insurer. Items are presented in the approximate order of their importance to the rating. There may be additional factors which have influenced the rating but do not appear due to space limitations or confidentiality agreements with insurers.
3.	**Other Rating Factors**	A summary of those Weiss Ratings indexes that were not included as Major Rating Factors, but nevertheless, may have had some impact on the final grade.
4.	**Principal Business**	The major types of policies written by an insurer along with the percentages for each line in relation to the entire book of business, including direct premium and deposit funds (from Exhibit 1 Part 1 of the annual statutory statement). Lines of business written by life, health and annuity insurers are individual life, individual health, individual annuities, group life, group health, group retirement contracts, credit life, credit health and reinsurance. The data used to calculate these amounts are the latest available from the National Association of Insurance Commissioners.

Note: Percentages contained in this column may not agree with similar figures displayed in Section III which are based on net premium after reinsurance. |
| **5.** | **Principal Investments** | The major investments in an insurer's portfolio. These include non CMO Bonds (debt obligations which are rated Class 1 through Class 6 based on risk of default), CMOs and other structured securities, which consist primarily of mortgage-backed bonds, real estate, mortgages in good standing, nonperforming mortgages, common and preferred stocks, policy loans (which are loans given to policyholders), miscellaneous investments and cash. |

6. Investments in Affiliates

The percentage of bonds, common and preferred stocks and other financial instruments an insurer has invested with affiliated companies. This is not a subcategory of "Principal Investments."

7. Group Affiliation

The name of the group of companies to which a particular insurer belongs.

8. Licensed in

List of the states in which an insurer is licensed to conduct business.

9. Commenced Business

The date when the company first opened for business.

10. Address

The address of an insurer's corporate headquarters. This location may differ from the company's state of domicile.

11. Phone

The telephone number of an insurer's corporate headquarters.

12. Domicile State

The state that has primary regulatory responsibility for this company. You do not have to live in the domicile state to do business with this firm, provided it is registered to do business in your state.

13. NAIC Code

The identification number assigned to an insurer by the National Association of Insurance Commissioners (NAIC).

14. Historical Data

Five years of background data for Weiss Financial Strength Rating, risk-adjusted capital ratios (moderate and severe loss scenarios), total assets, capital (including capital stock and retained earnings), net premium and net income. See the following page for more details on how to read the historical data table.

15. Customized Graph (or Table)

A graph or table depicting one of the company's major strengths or weaknesses. See the following page for more details.

How to Read the Historical Data Table

Data Date:
The quarterly or annual date of the financial statements that provide the source of the data.

RACR#1:
Ratio of the capital resources an insurer currently has to the resources that would be needed to deal with a modest loss scenario.

Total Assets:
Total admitted assets in millions of dollars, including investments and other business assets.

Net Premiums:
The total volume of premium dollars, in millions, retained by an insurer. This figure is equal to direct premiums written plus deposit funds, and reinsurance assumed, less reinsurance ceded.

Data Date	Financial Strength Rating	RACR #1	RACR #2	Total Assets ($mil)	Capital ($mil)	Net Premium ($mil)	Net Income ($mil)
9-14	A	4.46	3.14	200.3	93.9	120.8	4.8
9-13	A	4.47	3.18	195.9	83.0	108.8	3.5
2013	A	3.92	2.79	186.9	89.9	148.4	6.4
2012	A-	3.43	2.51	187.2	84.4	170.1	6.2
2011	A-	3.49	2.61	174.6	79.7	171.5	6.9
2010	B	3.49	2.63	174.5	77.8	167.5	4.4
2009	B	3.27	2.50	181.4	80.6	188.6	2.4

Financial Strength Rating:
Our opinion of the financial risk of an insurer based on data from that time period.

RACR #2:
Ratio of the capital resources an insurer currently has to the resources that would be needed to deal with a severe loss scenario.

Capital:
The equity or net worth of an insurer in millions of dollars.

Net Income:
Profit gained on operations and investments, after expenses and taxes.

Row Descriptions:

Row 1 contains the most recent quarterly data as filed with state regulators and is presented on a year-to-date basis. For example, the figure for third quarter premiums includes premiums received through the third quarter. Row 2 consists of data from the same quarter of the prior year. Compare current quarterly results to those of a year ago.

Row 3 contains data from the most recent annual statutory filing. **Rows 4-7** include data from year-end statements going back four years from the most recent annual filing. Compare current year-end results to those of the previous four years. With the exception of Total Assets and Capital, quarterly data are not comparable with annual data.

Customized Graphs

In the lower right-hand corner of each company section, a customized graph or text block highlights a key factor affecting that company's financial strength. One of fifteen types of information is found, identified by one of the following headings:

Adverse Trends in Operations lists changes in key balance sheet and income statement items which may be leading indicators of deteriorating business performance.

Exposure to Withdrawals Without Penalty answers the question: For each dollar of capital and surplus, how much does the company have in annuity and deposit funds that can be withdrawn by policyholders with minimal or no penalty? The figures do not include the effects of reinsurance or funds subject to withdrawals from cash value life insurance policies.

Group Ratings shows the group name, a composite Weiss Financial Strength Rating for the group, and a list of the largest members with their ratings. The composite Financial Strength Rating is made up of the weighted average, by assets, of the individual ratings of each company in the group (including life/health companies, property/casualty companies or HMOs) plus a factor for the financial strength of the holding company, where applicable.

High Risk Assets as a % of Capital answers the question: For each dollar of capital and surplus, how much does the company have in junk bonds, nonperforming mortgages and repossessed real estate? Accumulations in the Asset Valuation Reserve or AVR, which provide some protection against investment losses, have not been included in the figure for capital. These figures are based on year-end data.

Investment Income Compared to Needs of Reserves answers the question: Is the company earning enough investment income to meet the expectations of actuaries when they priced their policies and set reserve levels? According to state insurance regulators, it would be "unusual" if an insurer were to have less than $1.25 in actual investment income for each dollar of investment income that it projected in its actuarial forecasts. This provides an excess margin of at least 25 cents on the dollar to cover any unexpected decline in income or increase in claims. This graph shows whether or not the company is maintaining the appropriate 25% margin and is based on year-end data.

Junk Bonds as a % of Capital answers the question: For each dollar of capital and surplus, how much does the company have in junk bonds? In addition, it shows a breakdown of the junk bond portfolio by bond rating – BB, B, CCC or in default. Accumulations in the Asset Valuation Reserve or AVR, which provide some protection against investment losses, have not been included in the figure for capital. These figures are based on year-end data.

Net Income History plots operating gains and losses over the most recent five-year period.

Policy Leverage answers the question: To what degree is this insurer capable of handling an unexpected spike in claims? Low leverage indicates low exposure; high leverage is high exposure.

Premium Growth History depicts the change in the insurer's net premiums written. Such changes may be the result of issuing more policies or changes in reinsurance arrangements. In either case, growth rates above 20% per year are considered excessive. "Standard" growth is under 20%; "shrinkage" refers to net declines.

Rating Indexes illustrate the score and range – strong, good, fair or weak – on each of the five Weiss Ratings indexes. The indexes are **capitalization**, **stability**, **investment safety**, **profitability** and **liquidity**.

Risk-Adjusted Capital Ratio #1 answers the question: In each of the past five years, does the insurer have sufficient capital to cover potential losses in its investments and business operations in a *moderate* loss scenario?

Risk-Adjusted Capital Ratio #2 answers the question: In each of the past five years, does the insurer have sufficient capital to cover potential losses in its investments and business operations in a *severe* loss scenario?

Risk-Adjusted Capital Ratios answers these questions for both a moderate loss scenario (RACR #1 shown by the dark bar) and a severe loss scenario (RACR #2, light bar).

4 EVER LIFE INSURANCE COMPANY *

A Excellent

Major Rating Factors: Good quality investment portfolio (6.5 on a scale of 0 to 10) despite mixed results such as: no exposure to mortgages and substantial holdings of BBB bonds but minimal holdings in junk bonds. Good liquidity (6.7) with sufficient resources to handle a spike in claims as well as a significant increase in policy surrenders. Excellent overall results on stability tests (7.1) excellent operational trends and excellent risk diversification.

Other Rating Factors: Strong capitalization (10.0) based on excellent risk adjusted capital (severe loss scenario). Excellent profitability (8.3) with operating gains in each of the last five years.

Principal Business: Group health insurance (82%), reinsurance (12%), and group life insurance (6%).

Principal Investments: NonCMO investment grade bonds (46%), CMOs and structured securities (35%), common & preferred stock (7%), noninv. grade bonds (5%), and cash (3%).

Investments in Affiliates: None
Group Affiliation: BCS Financial Corp
Licensed in: All states, the District of Columbia and Puerto Rico
Commenced Business: November 1949
Address: 2 Mid America Plaza Suite 200, Oakbrook Terrace, IL 60181
Phone: (312) 951-7700 **Domicile State:** IL **NAIC Code:** 80985

Data Date	Rating	RACR #1	RACR #2	Total Assets ($mil)	Capital ($mil)	Net Premium ($mil)	Net Income ($mil)
9-14	A	4.46	3.14	200.3	93.9	120.8	4.8
9-13	A	4.47	3.18	195.9	83.0	108.8	3.5
2013	A	3.92	2.79	186.9	89.9	148.4	6.4
2012	A-	3.43	2.51	187.2	84.4	170.1	6.2
2011	A-	3.49	2.61	174.6	79.7	171.5	6.9
2010	B	3.49	2.63	174.5	77.8	167.5	4.4
2009	B	3.27	2.50	181.4	80.6	188.6	2.4

Adverse Trends in Operations

Decrease in premium volume from 2012 to 2013 (13%)
Increase in policy surrenders from 2011 to 2012 (33%)
Decrease in asset base during 2010 (4%)
Decrease in premium volume from 2009 to 2010 (11%)
Increase in policy surrenders from 2009 to 2010 (268%)

AAA LIFE INSURANCE COMPANY

B Good

Major Rating Factors: Good overall results on stability tests (5.8 on a scale of 0 to 10). Stability strengths include excellent operational trends and excellent risk diversification. Good quality investment portfolio (6.5) despite mixed results such as: large holdings of BBB rated bonds but moderate junk bond exposure. Good overall profitability (5.6) although investment income, in comparison to reserve requirements, is below regulatory standards.

Other Rating Factors: Good liquidity (6.4). Strong capitalization (7.7) based on excellent risk adjusted capital (severe loss scenario).

Principal Business: Individual life insurance (48%), group life insurance (28%), individual annuities (12%), group health insurance (10%), and individual health insurance (2%).

Principal Investments: NonCMO investment grade bonds (65%), CMOs and structured securities (20%), noninv. grade bonds (8%), common & preferred stock (4%), and misc. investments (3%).

Investments in Affiliates: 2%
Group Affiliation: ACLI Acquisition Co
Licensed in: All states except NY, PR
Commenced Business: July 1969
Address: 17900 N Laurel Park Dr, Livonia, MI 48152
Phone: (734) 779-2600 **Domicile State:** MI **NAIC Code:** 71854

Data Date	Rating	RACR #1	RACR #2	Total Assets ($mil)	Capital ($mil)	Net Premium ($mil)	Net Income ($mil)
9-14	B	2.47	1.49	560.4	118.2	82.7	10.6
9-13	B	2.65	1.50	533.5	103.6	88.1	4.7
2013	B	2.27	1.39	539.2	104.1	119.4	7.2
2012	B	2.19	1.20	502.8	97.5	113.7	5.6
2011	B	2.61	1.49	468.4	87.8	113.6	4.2
2010	B	2.60	1.50	437.9	83.7	108.4	2.9
2009	B	2.65	1.55	402.8	84.2	105.4	2.2

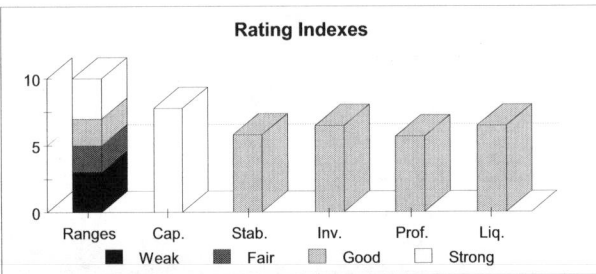

Rating Indexes

Ranges | Cap. | Stab. | Inv. | Prof. | Liq.
■ Weak ■ Fair ▨ Good □ Strong

ABILITY INSURANCE COMPANY

D Weak

Major Rating Factors: Weak profitability (1.0 on a scale of 0 to 10) with operating losses during the first nine months of 2014. Return on equity has been low, averaging -29.7%. Weak overall results on stability tests (1.7) including negative cash flow from operations for 2013. Fair quality investment portfolio (4.0).

Other Rating Factors: Good capitalization (5.2) based on good risk adjusted capital (moderate loss scenario). Excellent liquidity (9.3).

Principal Business: Individual health insurance (85%), reinsurance (14%), and individual life insurance (1%).

Principal Investments: NonCMO investment grade bonds (71%), CMOs and structured securities (15%), noninv. grade bonds (2%), common & preferred stock (2%), and mortgages in good standing (2%).

Investments in Affiliates: None
Group Affiliation: Advantage Capital Partners LLC
Licensed in: AL, AZ, AR, CA, CO, DC, DE, FL, GA, HI, ID, IL, IN, IA, KS, LA, MD, MA, MN, MS, MO, MT, NE, NM, NC, ND, OH, OK, OR, PA, SC, SD, TN, TX, UT, VA, WA, WV, WI, WY
Commenced Business: June 1968
Address: 222 S 15th St Suite 1202S, Omaha, NE 68102
Phone: (402) 218-4069 **Domicile State:** NE **NAIC Code:** 71471

Data Date	Rating	RACR #1	RACR #2	Total Assets ($mil)	Capital ($mil)	Net Premium ($mil)	Net Income ($mil)
9-14	D	1.14	0.61	903.3	33.5	23.2	-1.8
9-13	D	1.68	0.91	816.1	36.5	3.5	-10.9
2013	D	1.81	0.89	827.1	35.2	4.6	-9.6
2012	D	1.11	0.75	805.3	49.0	247.4	-15.7
2011	D	2.40	1.47	840.1	47.2	67.3	2.5
2010	D	2.93	2.04	214.1	33.0	46.0	-9.5
2009	D	2.36	1.76	195.3	21.7	22.9	-7.5

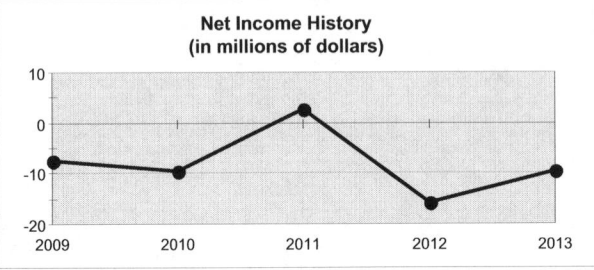

Net Income History
(in millions of dollars)

ACCORDIA LIFE & ANNUITY COMPANY   C-   Fair

Major Rating Factors: Fair capitalization for the current period (4.0 on a scale of 0 to 10) based on mixed results -- excessive policy leverage mitigated by fair risk adjusted capital (moderate loss scenario) reflecting some improvement over results in 2013. Weak profitability (1.9) with investment income below regulatory standards in relation to interest assumptions of reserves. Weak overall results on stability tests (2.1) including weak results on operational trends, weak risk adjusted capital in prior years.
Other Rating Factors: Good quality investment portfolio (5.5). Excellent liquidity (8.4).
Principal Business: Reinsurance (100%).
Principal Investments: NonCMO investment grade bonds (51%), CMOs and structured securities (28%), mortgages in good standing (7%), policy loans (6%), and common & preferred stock (6%).
Investments in Affiliates: 6%
Group Affiliation: Global Atlantic Financial Group
Licensed in: All states except CT, MA, NY, WY, PR
Commenced Business: September 1967
Address: 215 10th St Suite 1100, Des Moines, IA 50309
Phone: (800) 926-7599 **Domicile State:** IA **NAIC Code:** 62200

Data Date	Rating	RACR #1	RACR #2	Total Assets ($mil)	Capital ($mil)	Net Premium ($mil)	Net Income ($mil)
9-14	C-	0.85	0.62	7,481.4	517.7	304.9	73.9
9-13	U	N/A	N/A	10.7	10.6	0.0	-0.1
2013	D	0.64	0.48	7,059.0	382.2	4,725.1	-112.1
2012	U	3.36	3.02	5.7	5.6	0.0	0.7
2011	U	2.58	2.32	17.3	8.2	0.0	0.4
2010	U	2.35	2.11	19.0	8.0	0.0	0.1
2009	U	2.25	2.02	19.8	7.8	0.0	-0.6

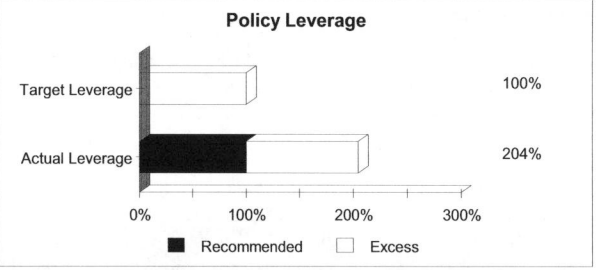

Policy Leverage

Target Leverage   100%
Actual Leverage   204%

■ Recommended   ☐ Excess

ADVANCE INSURANCE COMPANY OF KANSAS *   B+   Good

Major Rating Factors: Good overall results on stability tests (6.8 on a scale of 0 to 10). Stability strengths include excellent operational trends and excellent risk diversification. Fair quality investment portfolio (4.5). Strong capitalization (9.0) based on excellent risk adjusted capital (severe loss scenario). Moreover, capital levels have been consistently high over the last five years.
Other Rating Factors: Excellent profitability (8.3) with operating gains in each of the last five years. Excellent liquidity (7.2).
Principal Business: Group life insurance (53%), group health insurance (33%), and individual life insurance (14%).
Principal Investments: NonCMO investment grade bonds (42%), common & preferred stock (33%), CMOs and structured securities (23%), and cash (1%).
Investments in Affiliates: 2%
Group Affiliation: Blue Cross Blue Shield Kansas
Licensed in: KS
Commenced Business: July 2004
Address: 1133 SW Topeka Blvd, Topeka, KS 66629-0001
Phone: (785) 291-7052 **Domicile State:** KS **NAIC Code:** 12143

Data Date	Rating	RACR #1	RACR #2	Total Assets ($mil)	Capital ($mil)	Net Premium ($mil)	Net Income ($mil)
9-14	B+	3.55	2.34	52.7	42.9	7.3	2.0
9-13	B+	3.60	2.39	50.3	40.8	7.2	1.4
2013	B+	3.51	2.32	51.4	41.5	9.6	1.6
2012	B+	3.78	2.54	47.5	38.9	9.6	0.9
2011	B+	3.98	2.70	44.9	37.9	9.7	1.2
2010	B+	4.37	3.02	43.9	37.2	10.3	1.9
2009	B+	4.49	3.14	41.2	35.5	10.7	1.7

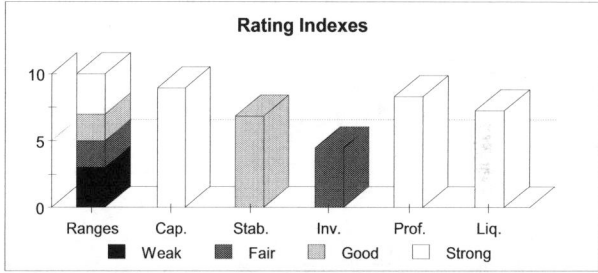

Rating Indexes

Ranges   Cap.   Stab.   Inv.   Prof.   Liq.

■ Weak   ▦ Fair   ▥ Good   ☐ Strong

AETNA HEALTH & LIFE INSURANCE COMPANY *   B+   Good

Major Rating Factors: Good overall results on stability tests (6.8 on a scale of 0 to 10). Stability strengths include excellent operational trends and excellent risk diversification. Good quality investment portfolio (6.4) despite substantial holdings of BBB bonds in addition to moderate junk bond exposure. Exposure to mortgages is significant, but the mortgage default rate has been low. Strong capitalization (8.2) based on excellent risk adjusted capital (severe loss scenario).
Other Rating Factors: Excellent profitability (7.4) with operating gains in each of the last five years. Excellent liquidity (7.4).
Principal Business: Reinsurance (100%).
Principal Investments: NonCMO investment grade bonds (62%), CMOs and structured securities (12%), mortgages in good standing (11%), and noninv. grade bonds (6%).
Investments in Affiliates: 5%
Group Affiliation: Aetna Inc
Licensed in: All states except FL, MO, NH, PR
Commenced Business: October 1971
Address: 151 Farmington Avenue, Hartford, IL 06156-0417
Phone: (708) 245-4001 **Domicile State:** CT **NAIC Code:** 78700

Data Date	Rating	RACR #1	RACR #2	Total Assets ($mil)	Capital ($mil)	Net Premium ($mil)	Net Income ($mil)
9-14	B+	3.08	1.83	2,221.2	306.1	423.1	70.9
9-13	B+	2.67	1.55	2,159.6	245.6	372.3	32.2
2013	B+	3.04	1.80	2,148.2	280.6	501.0	71.2
2012	B+	3.11	1.77	1,988.1	256.3	420.1	53.4
2011	B+	3.21	1.77	1,913.0	248.8	369.5	56.3
2010	B	3.31	1.89	1,906.1	251.7	383.1	58.5
2009	B	2.52	1.54	1,773.0	205.8	396.1	23.1

Adverse Trends in Operations

Decrease in capital during 2011 (1%)
Decrease in premium volume from 2010 to 2011 (4%)
Decrease in premium volume from 2009 to 2010 (3%)

AETNA LIFE INSURANCE COMPANY *   B+   Good

Major Rating Factors: Good quality investment portfolio (6.2 on a scale of 0 to 10) despite significant exposure to mortgages . Mortgage default rate has been low. large holdings of BBB rated bonds in addition to small junk bond holdings. Good liquidity (6.4) with sufficient resources to handle a spike in claims as well as a significant increase in policy surrenders. Good overall results on stability tests (6.7) despite excessive premium growth excellent operational trends and excellent risk diversification.

Other Rating Factors: Strong capitalization (7.3) based on excellent risk adjusted capital (severe loss scenario). Excellent profitability (7.1) with operating gains in each of the last five years.

Principal Business: Group health insurance (61%), individual health insurance (32%), group life insurance (5%), group retirement contracts (1%), and reinsurance (1%).

Principal Investments: NonCMO investment grade bonds (57%), CMOs and structured securities (12%), mortgages in good standing (10%), noninv. grade bonds (7%), and real estate (3%).

Investments in Affiliates: 4%

Group Affiliation: Aetna Inc

Licensed in: All states, the District of Columbia and Puerto Rico

Commenced Business: December 1850

Address: 151 Farmington Ave, Hartford, CT 06156

Phone: (860) 273-0123 **Domicile State:** CT **NAIC Code:** 60054

Data Date	Rating	RACR #1	RACR #2	Total Assets ($mil)	Capital ($mil)	Net Premium ($mil)	Net Income ($mil)
9-14	B+	1.74	1.26	22,602.5	3,679.5	11,772.1	1,007.9
9-13	B+	2.01	1.41	21,592.2	3,429.9	9,037.6	825.6
2013	B+	1.76	1.25	21,793.1	3,199.9	12,142.0	911.1
2012	B+	1.89	1.33	21,175.5	3,332.3	12,689.8	1,020.0
2011	B+	1.73	1.22	20,894.4	3,047.1	11,199.3	1,001.2
2010	B	2.05	1.48	21,237.4	4,182.4	13,868.7	1,193.1
2009	B	2.19	1.58	22,490.3	4,858.2	15,428.6	882.6

Adverse Trends in Operations

Increase in policy surrenders from 2012 to 2013 (336%)
Decrease in capital during 2011 (27%)
Decrease in premium volume from 2010 to 2011 (19%)
Decrease in capital during 2010 (14%)
Decrease in premium volume from 2009 to 2010 (10%)

ALFA LIFE INSURANCE CORPORATION   B-   Good

Major Rating Factors: Good quality investment portfolio (5.7 on a scale of 0 to 10) despite mixed results such as: substantial holdings of BBB bonds but moderate junk bond exposure. Good liquidity (6.9) with sufficient resources to handle a spike in claims as well as a significant increase in policy surrenders. Fair profitability (3.0) with investment income below regulatory standards in relation to interest assumptions of reserves.

Other Rating Factors: Fair overall results on stability tests (4.0). Strong capitalization (7.9) based on excellent risk adjusted capital (severe loss scenario).

Principal Business: Individual life insurance (96%), individual annuities (3%), group life insurance (1%), and individual health insurance (1%).

Principal Investments: NonCMO investment grade bonds (71%), CMOs and structured securities (8%), policy loans (6%), common & preferred stock (6%), and misc. investments (9%).

Investments in Affiliates: None

Group Affiliation: Alfa Ins Group

Licensed in: AL, AR, FL, GA, LA, MS, MO, NC, SC, TN, VA

Commenced Business: March 1955

Address: 2108 East South Blvd, Montgomery, AL 36116-2015

Phone: (334) 288-3900 **Domicile State:** AL **NAIC Code:** 79049

Data Date	Rating	RACR #1	RACR #2	Total Assets ($mil)	Capital ($mil)	Net Premium ($mil)	Net Income ($mil)
9-14	B-	2.77	1.58	1,334.1	221.6	108.7	16.4
9-13	B	2.87	1.63	1,338.4	212.6	101.5	14.0
2013	B-	3.00	1.69	1,357.2	218.0	134.1	25.8
2012	B	2.72	1.56	1,295.4	202.4	148.0	11.5
2011	B+	2.93	1.70	1,218.6	188.0	136.9	21.8
2010	B+	3.52	2.12	1,185.5	190.1	127.6	23.9
2009	B+	3.96	2.40	1,141.9	183.0	122.5	18.3

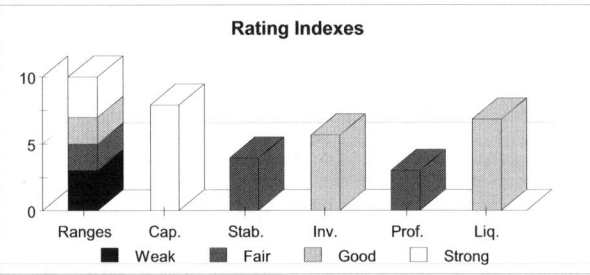

Rating Indexes

Ranges | Cap. | Stab. | Inv. | Prof. | Liq.
■ Weak   ▨ Fair   ▥ Good   ☐ Strong

ALLIANZ LIFE INSURANCE COMPANY OF NEW YORK   B   Good

Major Rating Factors: Good overall results on stability tests (5.6 on a scale of 0 to 10) despite fair financial strength of affiliated Allianz Ins Group and negative cash flow from operations for 2013. Other stability subfactors include good operational trends and excellent risk diversification. Good overall profitability (5.3) although investment income, in comparison to reserve requirements, is below regulatory standards. Strong capitalization (8.9) based on excellent risk adjusted capital (severe loss scenario).

Other Rating Factors: High quality investment portfolio (7.4). Excellent liquidity (9.5).

Principal Business: Individual annuities (98%) and individual health insurance (1%).

Principal Investments: NonCMO investment grade bonds (73%), CMOs and structured securities (25%), and noninv. grade bonds (1%).

Investments in Affiliates: None

Group Affiliation: Allianz Ins Group

Licensed in: CT, DC, IL, MN, MO, NY, ND

Commenced Business: April 1984

Address: One Chase Manhattan Plz 28 Fl, New York, NY 10005-1423

Phone: (212) 586-7733 **Domicile State:** NY **NAIC Code:** 64190

Data Date	Rating	RACR #1	RACR #2	Total Assets ($mil)	Capital ($mil)	Net Premium ($mil)	Net Income ($mil)
9-14	B	4.39	2.29	2,833.1	143.1	241.3	16.5
9-13	B	4.00	2.05	2,577.2	111.9	247.1	11.4
2013	B	3.07	1.60	2,668.0	97.8	317.4	7.4
2012	B-	4.79	2.58	2,294.7	135.4	346.7	30.4
2011	C	2.74	1.44	1,868.5	85.1	374.5	-7.8
2010	C	3.48	1.81	1,600.6	96.1	433.0	11.3
2009	C	3.15	1.66	1,139.5	64.8	191.7	16.7

Allianz Ins Group
Composite Group Rating: C+

Largest Group Members	Assets ($mil)	Rating
ALLIANZ LIFE INS CO OF NORTH AMERICA	104723	C+
FIREMANS FUND INS CO	9844	C
ALLIANZ GLOBAL RISKS US INS CO	3177	C-
ALLIANZ LIFE INS CO OF NY	2668	B
AGCS MARINE INS CO	873	D+

ALLIANZ LIFE INSURANCE COMPANY OF NORTH AMERICA   C+   Fair

Major Rating Factors: Fair overall results on stability tests (4.6 on a scale of 0 to 10) including excessive premium growth. Good quality investment portfolio (6.3) despite mixed results such as: large holdings of BBB rated bonds but moderate junk bond exposure. Good liquidity (6.8) with sufficient resources to handle a spike in claims as well as a significant increase in policy surrenders.

Other Rating Factors: Weak profitability (2.2) with investment income below regulatory standards in relation to interest assumptions of reserves. Strong capitalization (7.1) based on excellent risk adjusted capital (severe loss scenario).

Principal Business: Individual annuities (93%), individual life insurance (5%), and individual health insurance (2%).

Principal Investments: NonCMO investment grade bonds (66%), CMOs and structured securities (17%), mortgages in good standing (8%), noninv. grade bonds (2%), and common & preferred stock (2%).

Investments in Affiliates: 4%
Group Affiliation: Allianz Ins Group
Licensed in: All states except NY
Commenced Business: December 1979
Address: 5701 Golden Hills Dr, Minneapolis, MN 55416-1297
Phone: (800) 328-5601   **Domicile State:** MN   **NAIC Code:** 90611

Data Date	Rating	RACR #1	RACR #2	Total Assets ($mil)	Capital ($mil)	Net Premium ($mil)	Net Income ($mil)
9-14	C+	1.80	1.07	113,662	5,035.9	11,364.6	610.1
9-13	B	2.04	1.24	100,347	4,847.5	5,853.6	397.0
2013	C+	1.63	0.98	104,723	4,426.2	8,775.2	269.3
2012	B	2.22	1.35	94,322.9	5,332.4	8,321.2	413.0
2011	C+	1.97	1.14	89,742.0	4,993.1	9,600.9	477.7
2010	C+	1.92	1.03	84,464.2	4,595.2	9,618.6	855.4
2009	C+	1.94	0.97	75,453.9	3,923.2	8,403.3	-30.7

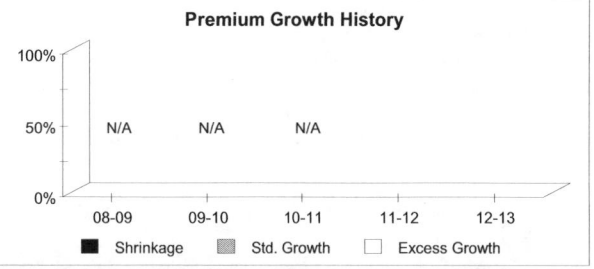

Premium Growth History

ALLSTATE LIFE INSURANCE COMPANY   B   Good

Major Rating Factors: Good current capitalization (5.9 on a scale of 0 to 10) based on good risk adjusted capital (severe loss scenario) reflecting some improvement over results in 2010. Good liquidity (5.7) with sufficient resources to cover a large increase in policy surrenders. Fair quality investment portfolio (4.1).

Other Rating Factors: Fair profitability (4.0) with investment income below regulatory standards in relation to interest assumptions of reserves. Fair overall results on stability tests (4.4) including negative cash flow from operations for 2013, fair risk adjusted capital in prior years.

Principal Business: Reinsurance (55%), individual annuities (27%), individual life insurance (15%), group life insurance (1%), and group health insurance (1%).

Principal Investments: NonCMO investment grade bonds (57%), mortgages in good standing (12%), CMOs and structured securities (12%), noninv. grade bonds (7%), and misc. investments (12%).

Investments in Affiliates: 4%
Group Affiliation: Allstate Group
Licensed in: All states, the District of Columbia and Puerto Rico
Commenced Business: September 1957
Address: 3100 Sanders Rd, Northbrook, IL 60062-7127
Phone: (847) 402-5000   **Domicile State:** IL   **NAIC Code:** 60186

Data Date	Rating	RACR #1	RACR #2	Total Assets ($mil)	Capital ($mil)	Net Premium ($mil)	Net Income ($mil)
9-14	B	1.38	0.86	34,348.3	2,721.2	-10,210.2	896.8
9-13	B	1.43	0.86	48,447.6	3,258.5	1,730.5	197.6
2013	B	1.31	0.80	47,858.5	2,875.1	2,377.5	425.1
2012	B	1.42	0.85	51,808.2	3,382.9	2,240.2	371.1
2011	B	1.33	0.78	53,978.8	3,455.7	1,976.7	-107.8
2010	B+	1.21	0.70	58,763.0	3,339.1	2,459.6	-453.3
2009	B+	1.23	0.71	63,008.5	3,467.4	3,261.8	-895.9

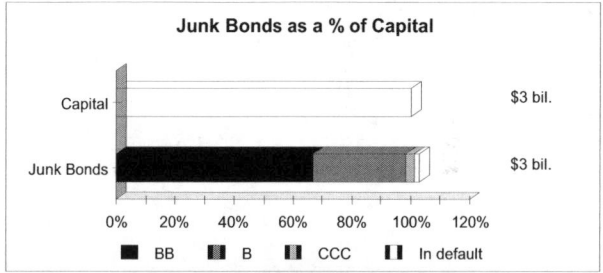

Junk Bonds as a % of Capital

ALLSTATE LIFE INSURANCE COMPANY OF NEW YORK   B-   Good

Major Rating Factors: Good quality investment portfolio (5.4 on a scale of 0 to 10) despite mixed results such as: large holdings of BBB rated bonds but moderate junk bond exposure. Good liquidity (6.1) with sufficient resources to cover a large increase in policy surrenders. Good overall results on stability tests (5.3) despite negative cash flow from operations for 2013 good operational trends, good risk adjusted capital for prior years and excellent risk diversification.

Other Rating Factors: Fair profitability (4.2) with investment income below regulatory standards in relation to interest assumptions of reserves. Strong capitalization (7.4) based on excellent risk adjusted capital (severe loss scenario).

Principal Business: Individual life insurance (80%), individual annuities (9%), individual health insurance (8%), and group retirement contracts (2%).

Principal Investments: NonCMO investment grade bonds (70%), CMOs and structured securities (12%), mortgages in good standing (8%), noninv. grade bonds (4%), and misc. investments (7%).

Investments in Affiliates: None
Group Affiliation: Allstate Group
Licensed in: CA, DC, DE, IL, MO, NE, NJ, NY, NC, PA, TX
Commenced Business: December 1967
Address: One Allstate Dr, Farmingville, NY 11738
Phone: (516) 451-5300   **Domicile State:** NY   **NAIC Code:** 70874

Data Date	Rating	RACR #1	RACR #2	Total Assets ($mil)	Capital ($mil)	Net Premium ($mil)	Net Income ($mil)
9-14	B-	2.35	1.25	6,580.0	588.3	111.1	37.1
9-13	B-	2.22	1.16	6,788.1	553.2	111.6	31.3
2013	B-	2.21	1.17	6,741.9	553.9	153.2	25.9
2012	B-	2.15	1.11	6,918.8	540.0	118.3	18.8
2011	B-	2.14	1.09	7,244.9	524.0	123.8	46.0
2010	B	1.87	0.95	7,615.1	497.0	166.9	-17.3
2009	B	1.95	1.01	7,876.0	506.3	305.2	-8.6

Adverse Trends in Operations

Decrease in asset base during 2012 (5%)
Decrease in premium volume from 2010 to 2011 (26%)
Change in premium mix from 2009 to 2010 (5.4%)
Increase in policy surrenders from 2009 to 2010 (26%)
Decrease in premium volume from 2009 to 2010 (45%)

AMALGAMATED LIFE INSURANCE COMPANY *   A-   Excellent

Major Rating Factors: Good liquidity (6.3 on a scale of 0 to 10) with sufficient resources to handle a spike in claims. Good overall results on stability tests (6.9). Strengths that enhance stability include excellent operational trends and good risk diversification. Strong capitalization (9.8) based on excellent risk adjusted capital (severe loss scenario). Moreover, capital has steadily grown over the last five years.

Other Rating Factors: High quality investment portfolio (8.1). Excellent profitability (8.1) with operating gains in each of the last five years.

Principal Business: Reinsurance (42%), group life insurance (39%), and group health insurance (18%).

Principal Investments: NonCMO investment grade bonds (72%), CMOs and structured securities (26%), and cash (2%).

Investments in Affiliates: None

Group Affiliation: ALICO Services Corp

Licensed in: All states except PR

Commenced Business: February 1944

Address: 333 Westchester Ave, White Plains, NY 10604

Phone: (914) 367-5000 **Domicile State:** NY **NAIC Code:** 60216

Data Date	Rating	RACR #1	RACR #2	Total Assets ($mil)	Capital ($mil)	Net Premium ($mil)	Net Income ($mil)
9-14	A-	3.68	2.89	110.5	50.8	52.2	2.5
9-13	A-	3.39	2.66	94.7	44.3	45.5	2.0
2013	A-	3.45	2.72	99.9	47.2	64.3	3.5
2012	A-	3.31	2.64	88.6	42.2	56.3	3.7
2011	A-	2.99	2.36	78.9	38.3	55.7	1.9
2010	A-	3.13	2.49	72.2	36.3	46.3	2.8
2009	A-	2.89	2.26	65.8	33.5	44.5	2.5

Adverse Trends in Operations

Increase in policy surrenders from 2012 to 2013 (90%)
Increase in policy surrenders from 2011 to 2012 (42%)
Increase in policy surrenders from 2009 to 2010 (28%)

AMERICAN BANKERS LIFE ASSURANCE COMPANY OF FLORID/   B   Good

Major Rating Factors: Good overall results on stability tests (5.0 on a scale of 0 to 10) despite negative cash flow from operations for 2013. Other stability subfactors include good operational trends and excellent risk diversification. Good quality investment portfolio (6.8) despite mixed results such as: minimal exposure to mortgages and large holdings of BBB rated bonds but minimal holdings in junk bonds. Good overall profitability (5.9).

Other Rating Factors: Strong capitalization (9.4) based on excellent risk adjusted capital (severe loss scenario). Excellent liquidity (7.6).

Principal Business: Credit life insurance (40%), credit health insurance (37%), reinsurance (17%), individual life insurance (2%), and other lines (4%).

Principal Investments: NonCMO investment grade bonds (64%), CMOs and structured securities (9%), real estate (9%), mortgages in good standing (8%), and misc. investments (9%).

Investments in Affiliates: None

Group Affiliation: Assurant Inc

Licensed in: All states except NY

Commenced Business: April 1952

Address: 11222 Quail Roost Dr, Miami, FL 33157

Phone: (305) 253-2244 **Domicile State:** FL **NAIC Code:** 60275

Data Date	Rating	RACR #1	RACR #2	Total Assets ($mil)	Capital ($mil)	Net Premium ($mil)	Net Income ($mil)
9-14	B	4.66	2.57	517.1	55.7	59.3	10.1
9-13	B	3.79	2.24	524.2	65.9	85.5	9.8
2013	B	4.07	2.32	521.6	50.4	114.9	11.0
2012	B	3.76	2.25	553.8	67.3	127.7	13.4
2011	B	4.20	2.48	588.1	73.8	118.9	15.4
2010	B	5.75	3.19	626.5	88.1	89.1	23.9
2009	B	6.16	3.43	671.1	116.6	100.9	27.0

Adverse Trends in Operations

Decrease in premium volume from 2012 to 2013 (10%)
Decrease in capital during 2013 (25%)
Decrease in capital during 2011 (16%)
Decrease in capital during 2010 (24%)
Decrease in premium volume from 2009 to 2010 (12%)

AMERICAN CONTINENTAL INSURANCE COMPANY   B   Good

Major Rating Factors: Good current capitalization (5.4 on a scale of 0 to 10) based on mixed results -- excessive policy leverage mitigated by excellent risk adjusted capital (severe loss scenario) reflecting significant improvement over results in 2009. Good liquidity (5.4) with sufficient resources to handle a spike in claims. Good overall results on stability tests (5.5) despite excessive premium growth and fair risk adjusted capital in prior years good operational trends and excellent risk diversification.

Other Rating Factors: Weak profitability (1.8) with operating losses during the first nine months of 2014. High quality investment portfolio (8.2).

Principal Business: Individual health insurance (90%) and individual life insurance (10%).

Principal Investments: NonCMO investment grade bonds (96%), CMOs and structured securities (11%), and noninv. grade bonds (1%).

Investments in Affiliates: None

Group Affiliation: Aetna Inc

Licensed in: AL, AZ, AR, CO, FL, GA, IL, IN, IA, KS, KY, LA, MI, MN, MS, MO, MT, NE, NV, NM, NC, ND, OH, OK, PA, SC, SD, TN, TX, UT, VA, WV, WI, WY

Commenced Business: September 2005

Address: 800 Crescent Centre Dr, Franklin, TN 37067

Phone: (800) 264-4000 **Domicile State:** TN **NAIC Code:** 12321

Data Date	Rating	RACR #1	RACR #2	Total Assets ($mil)	Capital ($mil)	Net Premium ($mil)	Net Income ($mil)
9-14	B	1.40	1.09	151.9	63.7	281.0	-12.5
9-13	B	1.30	1.01	119.6	54.3	219.4	-12.4
2013	B	1.32	1.03	127.2	51.3	300.6	-13.5
2012	B	2.02	1.56	98.2	57.5	178.7	-6.0
2011	C	2.01	1.56	84.7	49.7	133.0	-12.0
2010	C	1.53	1.16	61.3	38.6	107.1	-10.9
2009	C+	0.89	0.70	36.7	16.4	66.5	-11.6

Policy Leverage

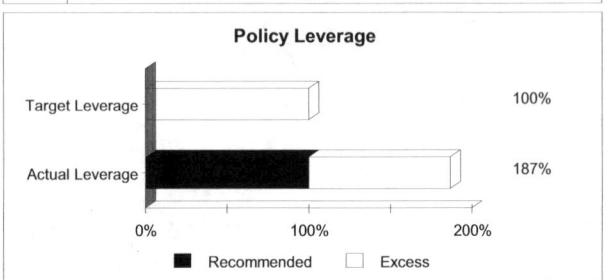

AMERICAN EQUITY INVEST LIFE INSURANCE COMPANY   B   Good

Major Rating Factors: Good quality investment portfolio (6.1 on a scale of 0 to 10) despite mixed results such as: large holdings of BBB rated bonds but moderate junk bond exposure. Good liquidity (5.7) with sufficient resources to cover a large increase in policy surrenders. Good overall results on stability tests (6.2) excellent operational trends and excellent risk diversification.

Other Rating Factors: Strong capitalization (7.6) based on excellent risk adjusted capital (severe loss scenario). Excellent profitability (8.3) with operating gains in each of the last five years.

Principal Business: Individual annuities (100%).

Principal Investments: NonCMO investment grade bonds (68%), CMOs and structured securities (18%), mortgages in good standing (9%), and noninv. grade bonds (2%).

Investments in Affiliates: None

Group Affiliation: American Equity Investment Group

Licensed in: All states except NY, PR

Commenced Business: January 1981

Address: 5000 Westown Parkway, West Des Moines, IA 50266

Phone: (888) 222-1234 **Domicile State:** IA **NAIC Code:** 92738

Data Date	Rating	RACR #1	RACR #2	Total Assets ($mil)	Capital ($mil)	Net Premium ($mil)	Net Income ($mil)
9-14	B	2.76	1.41	35,274.7	2,067.5	2,813.7	230.1
9-13	B	2.67	1.35	31,468.1	1,813.8	2,871.6	143.7
2013	B	2.63	1.36	32,435.5	1,870.7	3,876.3	205.2
2012	B	2.64	1.36	28,079.0	1,658.9	3,484.8	82.0
2011	B	3.40	1.75	24,685.6	1,597.0	4,511.6	169.4
2010	B	3.31	1.73	21,125.5	1,400.7	4,051.5	177.3
2009	B-	3.40	1.82	16,697.6	1,193.1	2,827.0	124.6

Adverse Trends in Operations

Decrease in premium volume from 2011 to 2012 (23%)

AMERICAN EQUITY INVESTMENT LIFE NEW YORK   B-   Good

Major Rating Factors: Good quality investment portfolio (6.6 on a scale of 0 to 10) despite mixed results such as: no exposure to mortgages and large holdings of BBB rated bonds but minimal holdings in junk bonds. Good liquidity (5.3) with sufficient resources to cover a large increase in policy surrenders. Fair profitability (4.9) with investment income below regulatory standards in relation to interest assumptions of reserves.

Other Rating Factors: Fair overall results on stability tests (4.5) including negative cash flow from operations for 2013. Strong capitalization (8.1) based on excellent risk adjusted capital (severe loss scenario).

Principal Business: Individual annuities (100%).

Principal Investments: NonCMO investment grade bonds (80%) and CMOs and structured securities (18%).

Investments in Affiliates: None

Group Affiliation: American Equity Investment Group

Licensed in: NY

Commenced Business: July 2001

Address: 1979 Marcus Ave Suite 210, Lake Success, NY 11042

Phone: (866) 233-6660 **Domicile State:** NY **NAIC Code:** 11135

Data Date	Rating	RACR #1	RACR #2	Total Assets ($mil)	Capital ($mil)	Net Premium ($mil)	Net Income ($mil)
9-14	B-	2.88	1.76	224.8	28.4	0.4	1.0
9-13	B-	2.73	1.62	227.2	27.2	1.0	1.6
2013	B-	2.79	1.70	226.1	27.6	1.0	2.1
2012	B-	2.61	1.53	229.3	26.2	13.7	0.1
2011	B-	2.60	1.68	215.4	26.0	45.6	1.3
2010	B-	2.65	1.99	175.2	25.2	53.6	-1.5
2009	B-	2.88	2.59	124.8	26.6	11.2	-7.4

Rating Indexes

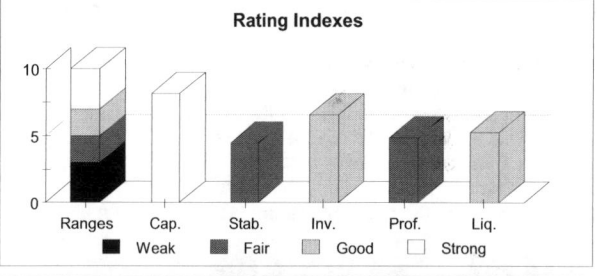

AMERICAN FAMILY LIFE ASSUR COMPANY OF NEW YORK *   A-   Excellent

Major Rating Factors: Excellent overall results on stability tests (7.3 on a scale of 0 to 10). Strengths that enhance stability include excellent operational trends and excellent risk diversification. Strong capitalization (10.0) based on excellent risk adjusted capital (severe loss scenario). Furthermore, this high level of risk adjusted capital has been consistently maintained over the last five years. High quality investment portfolio (8.0).

Other Rating Factors: Excellent profitability (9.3) with operating gains in each of the last five years. Excellent liquidity (7.7).

Principal Business: Individual health insurance (95%), individual life insurance (3%), and group health insurance (2%).

Principal Investments: NonCMO investment grade bonds (98%), CMOs and structured securities (1%), and noninv. grade bonds (1%).

Investments in Affiliates: None

Group Affiliation: AFLAC Inc

Licensed in: CT, MA, NJ, NY, ND, VT

Commenced Business: December 1964

Address: 22 Corporate Woods Blvd #2, Albany, NY 12211

Phone: (706) 660-7208 **Domicile State:** NY **NAIC Code:** 60526

Data Date	Rating	RACR #1	RACR #2	Total Assets ($mil)	Capital ($mil)	Net Premium ($mil)	Net Income ($mil)
9-14	A-	5.25	3.68	710.2	240.9	219.7	14.6
9-13	A-	4.72	3.34	612.2	210.4	215.8	34.9
2013	A-	4.96	3.49	645.3	221.8	285.5	45.4
2012	A-	4.18	2.99	555.9	176.2	271.1	40.0
2011	A-	3.17	2.29	454.0	123.4	251.8	26.5
2010	A-	2.66	1.94	383.1	95.7	232.8	20.2
2009	A-	2.32	1.71	322.6	77.0	211.9	12.9

Adverse Trends in Operations

Increase in policy surrenders from 2012 to 2013 (34%)
Increase in policy surrenders from 2011 to 2012 (92%)

AMERICAN FAMILY LIFE ASSURANCE COMPANY OF COLUMBU — B+ — Good

Major Rating Factors: Good overall profitability (6.2 on a scale of 0 to 10) although investment income, in comparison to reserve requirements, is below regulatory standards. Good overall results on stability tests (6.7). Stability strengths include excellent operational trends and excellent risk diversification. Strong capitalization (8.7) based on excellent risk adjusted capital (severe loss scenario).

Other Rating Factors: High quality investment portfolio (7.2). Excellent liquidity (7.6).

Principal Business: Individual health insurance (72%), individual life insurance (24%), individual annuities (4%), and reinsurance (1%).

Principal Investments: NonCMO investment grade bonds (89%), CMOs and structured securities (5%), noninv. grade bonds (3%), and common & preferred stock (1%).

Investments in Affiliates: 1%
Group Affiliation: AFLAC Inc
Licensed in: All states except NY
Commenced Business: April 1956
Address: 1932 Wynnton Rd, Columbus, GA 31999
Phone: (706) 323-3431 **Domicile State:** NE **NAIC Code:** 60380

Data Date	Rating	RACR #1	RACR #2	Total Assets ($mil)	Capital ($mil)	Net Premium ($mil)	Net Income ($mil)
9-14	B+	3.35	2.16	110,401	9,775.5	14,860.8	2,080.4
9-13	B+	3.25	2.06	106,478	9,667.8	15,575.4	2,347.9
2013	B+	3.23	2.09	107,913	9,630.1	20,550.2	2,360.6
2012	B+	2.77	1.74	115,347	8,891.8	23,102.5	2,337.3
2011	B+	2.45	1.44	103,582	6,371.1	20,945.0	443.6
2010	B+	2.78	1.62	89,723.3	6,739.8	18,324.8	1,468.1
2009	B+	2.44	1.40	75,798.4	5,767.9	16,829.9	1,414.1

Net Income History
(in millions of dollars)

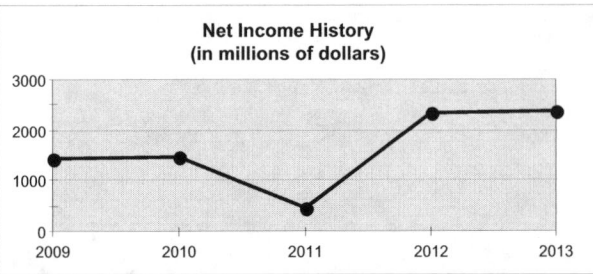

AMERICAN FAMILY LIFE INSURANCE COMPANY * — A+ — Excellent

Major Rating Factors: Good quality investment portfolio (6.5 on a scale of 0 to 10) despite mixed results such as: minimal exposure to mortgages and large holdings of BBB rated bonds but small junk bond holdings. Good liquidity (6.4) with sufficient resources to handle a spike in claims as well as a significant increase in policy surrenders. Excellent overall results on stability tests (7.9) excellent operational trends and excellent risk diversification.

Other Rating Factors: Strong capitalization (9.1) based on excellent risk adjusted capital (severe loss scenario). Excellent profitability (8.6) with operating gains in each of the last five years.

Principal Business: Individual life insurance (91%), individual annuities (6%), reinsurance (1%), and group life insurance (1%).

Principal Investments: NonCMO investment grade bonds (57%), CMOs and structured securities (22%), mortgages in good standing (9%), policy loans (5%), and misc. investments (7%).

Investments in Affiliates: None
Group Affiliation: American Family Ins Group
Licensed in: AZ, CA, CO, GA, ID, IL, IN, IA, KS, MI, MN, MO, MT, NE, NV, NM, NC, ND, OH, OR, SC, SD, TX, UT, WA, WI, WY
Commenced Business: December 1957
Address: 6000 American Parkway, Madison, WI 53783-0001
Phone: (608) 242-4100 **Domicile State:** WI **NAIC Code:** 60399

Data Date	Rating	RACR #1	RACR #2	Total Assets ($mil)	Capital ($mil)	Net Premium ($mil)	Net Income ($mil)
9-14	A+	4.50	2.38	5,200.5	866.0	254.3	58.1
9-13	A+	4.50	2.39	5,035.6	769.0	263.6	43.6
2013	A+	4.66	2.47	5,074.0	822.8	347.9	66.2
2012	A+	4.63	2.48	4,839.9	736.4	372.2	69.3
2011	A+	4.76	2.74	4,598.7	691.5	371.9	69.5
2010	A+	4.08	2.25	4,432.1	637.0	373.6	95.7
2009	A+	3.83	2.11	4,153.2	556.5	384.9	76.9

Adverse Trends in Operations

Decrease in premium volume from 2012 to 2013 (7%)
Decrease in premium volume from 2009 to 2010 (3%)

AMERICAN FIDELITY ASSURANCE COMPANY * — B+ — Good

Major Rating Factors: Good quality investment portfolio (6.1 on a scale of 0 to 10) despite mixed results such as: minimal exposure to mortgages and large holdings of BBB rated bonds but small junk bond holdings. Good liquidity (6.6) with sufficient resources to cover a large increase in policy surrenders. Good overall results on stability tests (6.8) excellent operational trends, good risk adjusted capital for prior years and excellent risk diversification.

Other Rating Factors: Strong capitalization (7.1) based on excellent risk adjusted capital (severe loss scenario). Excellent profitability (8.3) with operating gains in each of the last five years.

Principal Business: Group health insurance (45%), individual health insurance (23%), individual life insurance (13%), individual annuities (13%), and reinsurance (5%).

Principal Investments: NonCMO investment grade bonds (62%), CMOs and structured securities (23%), mortgages in good standing (9%), cash (3%), and misc. investments (4%).

Investments in Affiliates: None
Group Affiliation: Cameron Associates Inc
Licensed in: All states except NY
Commenced Business: December 1960
Address: 2000 N Classen Blvd, Oklahoma City, OK 73106
Phone: (405) 523-2000 **Domicile State:** OK **NAIC Code:** 60410

Data Date	Rating	RACR #1	RACR #2	Total Assets ($mil)	Capital ($mil)	Net Premium ($mil)	Net Income ($mil)
9-14	B+	1.89	1.09	4,856.7	366.8	612.2	54.4
9-13	B+	1.73	1.02	4,597.5	341.7	578.1	57.0
2013	B+	1.82	1.05	4,709.9	342.7	780.9	71.7
2012	B+	1.60	0.95	4,358.1	308.9	765.7	58.5
2011	B+	1.74	1.01	3,994.1	295.0	712.8	55.6
2010	A	1.82	1.06	3,780.9	287.2	681.2	55.9
2009	A	1.92	1.13	3,567.6	282.1	619.7	49.5

Adverse Trends in Operations

Increase in policy surrenders from 2009 to 2010 (28%)

AMERICAN FIDELITY LIFE INSURANCE COMPANY — B- — Good

Major Rating Factors: Good quality investment portfolio (6.1 on a scale of 0 to 10) despite mixed results such as: minimal exposure to mortgages and substantial holdings of BBB bonds but minimal holdings in junk bonds. Good overall profitability (6.3). Excellent expense controls. Return on equity has been low, averaging 4.6%. Good liquidity (5.8).

Other Rating Factors: Good overall results on stability tests (5.3) good operational trends and good risk diversification. Strong capitalization (7.9) based on excellent risk adjusted capital (severe loss scenario).

Principal Business: Individual life insurance (67%), individual annuities (20%), and reinsurance (13%).

Principal Investments: NonCMO investment grade bonds (79%), real estate (8%), mortgages in good standing (6%), common & preferred stock (5%), and misc. investments (2%).

Investments in Affiliates: 8%
Group Affiliation: AMFI Corp
Licensed in: All states except NY, VT, PR
Commenced Business: September 1956
Address: 4060 Barrancas Ave, Pensacola, FL 32507
Phone: (850) 456-7401 **Domicile State:** FL **NAIC Code:** 60429

Data Date	Rating	RACR #1	RACR #2	Total Assets ($mil)	Capital ($mil)	Net Premium ($mil)	Net Income ($mil)
9-14	B-	2.38	1.58	437.3	70.1	8.4	1.6
9-13	B-	2.57	1.66	446.2	71.8	9.0	3.1
2013	B-	2.53	1.68	445.7	71.8	11.1	4.1
2012	B-	2.59	1.70	450.5	70.0	11.6	6.0
2011	B-	2.62	1.74	455.9	70.3	13.1	2.9
2010	B-	2.59	1.80	460.7	70.7	13.5	3.3
2009	B-	2.70	1.88	460.9	71.5	14.3	-0.9

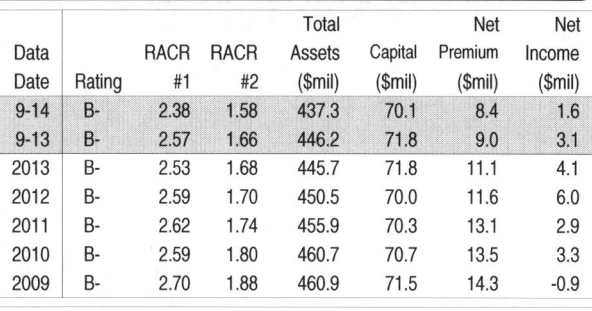

Rating Indexes

AMERICAN GENERAL LIFE INSURANCE COMPANY — B — Good

Major Rating Factors: Good overall results on stability tests (5.8 on a scale of 0 to 10). Stability strengths include good operational trends and excellent risk diversification. Good quality investment portfolio (5.9) despite mixed results such as: large holdings of BBB rated bonds but junk bond exposure equal to 54% of capital. Good liquidity (6.2).

Other Rating Factors: Strong capitalization (8.2) based on excellent risk adjusted capital (severe loss scenario). Excellent profitability (7.0).

Principal Business: Individual annuities (46%), group retirement contracts (31%), individual life insurance (21%), individual health insurance (1%), and group life insurance (1%).

Principal Investments: NonCMO investment grade bonds (49%), CMOs and structured securities (28%), mortgages in good standing (6%), noninv. grade bonds (5%), and misc. investments (9%).

Investments in Affiliates: 7%
Group Affiliation: American International Group
Licensed in: All states except NY
Commenced Business: August 1960
Address: 2727-A Allen Parkway, Houston, TX 77019
Phone: (713) 522-1111 **Domicile State:** TX **NAIC Code:** 60488

Data Date	Rating	RACR #1	RACR #2	Total Assets ($mil)	Capital ($mil)	Net Premium ($mil)	Net Income ($mil)
9-14	B	3.55	1.79	161,297	11,201.4	10,612.4	2,074.2
9-13	C	3.61	1.90	155,008	12,031.5	9,000.7	2,172.3
2013	B-	3.97	2.00	159,157	12,656.1	12,783.1	3,430.8
2012	C	3.50	1.84	149,628	11,514.5	7,937.0	3,641.2
2011	B	1.47	1.19	43,097.1	7,393.6	1,173.5	1,055.2
2010	B-	1.44	1.15	41,582.7	6,612.1	1,367.0	425.8
2009	C+	1.34	1.06	39,653.1	5,954.0	1,724.5	-100.5

Adverse Trends in Operations

Change in premium mix from 2011 to 2012 (8%)
Increase in policy surrenders from 2011 to 2012 (562%)
Decrease in premium volume from 2010 to 2011 (14%)
Decrease in premium volume from 2009 to 2010 (21%)

AMERICAN HEALTH & LIFE INSURANCE COMPANY — B- — Good

Major Rating Factors: Good quality investment portfolio (5.9 on a scale of 0 to 10) despite mixed results such as: no exposure to mortgages and large holdings of BBB rated bonds but small junk bond holdings. Good overall profitability (6.2). Excellent expense controls. Return on equity has been excellent over the last five years averaging 29.0%. Good overall results on stability tests (5.1) good operational trends and excellent risk diversification.

Other Rating Factors: Strong capitalization (8.3) based on excellent risk adjusted capital (severe loss scenario). Excellent liquidity (8.3).

Principal Business: Credit health insurance (34%), credit life insurance (32%), reinsurance (30%), group life insurance (2%), and group health insurance (2%).

Principal Investments: NonCMO investment grade bonds (72%), CMOs and structured securities (17%), common & preferred stock (4%), noninv. grade bonds (3%), and cash (3%).

Investments in Affiliates: 2%
Group Affiliation: Citigroup Inc
Licensed in: All states except NY, PR
Commenced Business: June 1954
Address: 307 West 7th Street, Ste 400, Fort Worth, TX 76102
Phone: (817) 348-7500 **Domicile State:** TX **NAIC Code:** 60518

Data Date	Rating	RACR #1	RACR #2	Total Assets ($mil)	Capital ($mil)	Net Premium ($mil)	Net Income ($mil)
9-14	B-	2.70	1.84	996.0	180.7	157.2	53.6
9-13	B-	2.82	1.93	912.2	186.0	163.1	62.9
2013	B-	3.08	2.11	941.1	208.6	221.8	84.1
2012	B-	3.52	2.39	972.0	234.7	213.5	110.0
2011	B-	2.52	2.05	1,153.2	371.7	214.8	123.8
2010	B	1.99	1.59	1,129.3	278.4	354.5	15.4
2009	B+	4.63	3.56	1,360.5	623.7	148.5	100.0

Adverse Trends in Operations

Decrease in asset base during 2012 (16%)
Decrease in capital during 2012 (37%)
Decrease in premium volume from 2010 to 2011 (39%)
Decrease in capital during 2010 (55%)
Decrease in asset base during 2010 (17%)

AMERICAN HERITAGE LIFE INSURANCE COMPANY — B — Good

Major Rating Factors: Good current capitalization (6.2 on a scale of 0 to 10) based on good risk adjusted capital (severe loss scenario), although results have slipped from the excellent range over the last two years. Good quality investment portfolio (6.3) despite mixed results such as: minimal exposure to mortgages and large holdings of BBB rated bonds but minimal holdings in junk bonds. Good liquidity (6.6).

Other Rating Factors: Good overall results on stability tests (6.1) excellent operational trends and excellent risk diversification. Excellent profitability (7.2) with operating gains in each of the last five years.

Principal Business: Group health insurance (49%), individual health insurance (33%), individual life insurance (12%), group life insurance (5%), and reinsurance (2%).

Principal Investments: NonCMO investment grade bonds (50%), policy loans (19%), common & preferred stock (16%), mortgages in good standing (7%), and misc. investments (8%).

Investments in Affiliates: 12%
Group Affiliation: Allstate Group
Licensed in: All states except NY
Commenced Business: December 1956
Address: 1776 American Heritage Life Dr, Jacksonville, FL 32224-6688
Phone: (904) 992-1776 **Domicile State:** FL **NAIC Code:** 60534

Data Date	Rating	RACR #1	RACR #2	Total Assets ($mil)	Capital ($mil)	Net Premium ($mil)	Net Income ($mil)
9-14	B	1.09	0.90	1,750.7	341.2	562.2	107.0
9-13	B	1.20	0.98	1,715.9	325.5	529.1	44.2
2013	B	1.18	0.97	1,770.2	337.7	707.7	57.0
2012	B	1.26	1.05	1,710.7	335.8	649.7	74.7
2011	B	1.24	1.02	1,650.1	293.7	639.9	41.5
2010	B	1.15	0.93	1,518.4	255.0	617.6	26.3
2009	B	1.31	1.06	1,404.5	240.9	458.3	18.2

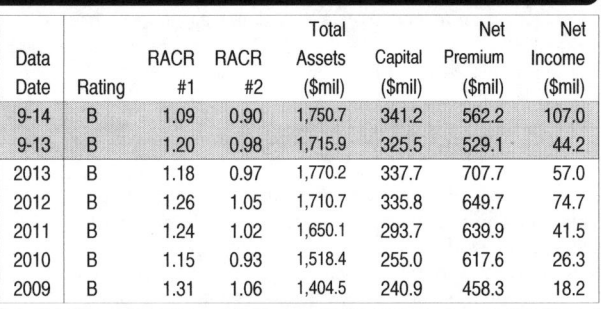

Risk-Adjusted Capital Ratio #2 (Severe Loss Scenario)

Weak ■ Fair ■ Good ■ Strong □

AMERICAN INCOME LIFE INSURANCE COMPANY — B- — Good

Major Rating Factors: Good capitalization (5.7 on a scale of 0 to 10) based on good risk adjusted capital (severe loss scenario). Capital levels have been relatively consistent over the last five years. Good overall profitability (5.2) although investment income, in comparison to reserve requirements, is below regulatory standards. Good overall results on stability tests (5.3) excellent operational trends and excellent risk diversification.

Other Rating Factors: Fair quality investment portfolio (4.7). Fair liquidity (3.6).
Principal Business: Individual life insurance (90%), individual health insurance (8%), and group health insurance (1%).
Principal Investments: NonCMO investment grade bonds (81%), policy loans (5%), common & preferred stock (4%), noninv. grade bonds (4%), and CMOs and structured securities (3%).

Investments in Affiliates: 4%
Group Affiliation: Torchmark Corp
Licensed in: All states except NY, PR
Commenced Business: August 1954
Address: 8604 Allisonville Rd Suite 151, Indianapolis, IN 46250
Phone: (254) 761-6400 **Domicile State:** IN **NAIC Code:** 60577

Data Date	Rating	RACR #1	RACR #2	Total Assets ($mil)	Capital ($mil)	Net Premium ($mil)	Net Income ($mil)
9-14	B-	1.33	0.84	2,847.2	226.0	557.7	114.7
9-13	B-	1.24	0.77	2,645.6	206.7	573.6	90.0
2013	B-	1.36	0.86	2,694.7	232.3	747.9	132.6
2012	B-	1.28	0.78	2,518.3	219.7	723.1	122.2
2011	B-	1.34	0.80	2,291.1	195.4	669.6	107.7
2010	B-	1.71	1.01	2,136.4	200.1	625.5	116.7
2009	B-	1.77	1.04	1,932.8	188.1	577.8	85.5

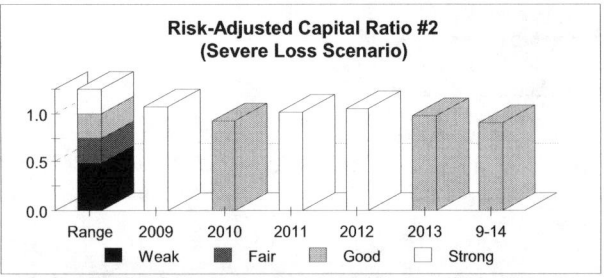

Risk-Adjusted Capital Ratio #2 (Severe Loss Scenario)

Weak ■ Fair ■ Good ■ Strong □

AMERICAN LIFE & ACCIDENT INSURANCE COMPANY OF KENTU — C — Fair

Major Rating Factors: Fair profitability (4.9 on a scale of 0 to 10). Excellent expense controls. Return on equity has been low, averaging -0.2%. Fair liquidity (4.3) as cash from operations and sale of marketable assets may not be adequate to cover a spike in claims or a run on policy withdrawals. Fair overall results on stability tests (3.9) including excessive premium growth.

Other Rating Factors: Low quality investment portfolio (2.3). Strong capitalization (7.4) based on excellent risk adjusted capital (severe loss scenario).
Principal Business: Reinsurance (100%).
Principal Investments: Common & preferred stock (65%), nonCMO investment grade bonds (25%), real estate (7%), CMOs and structured securities (2%), and cash (1%).

Investments in Affiliates: None
Group Affiliation: None
Licensed in: AR, GA, IN, KY, MD, OH, PA, TN
Commenced Business: July 1906
Address: 3 Riverfront Plaza, Louisville, KY 40202-2975
Phone: (502) 585-5347 **Domicile State:** KY **NAIC Code:** 60666

Data Date	Rating	RACR #1	RACR #2	Total Assets ($mil)	Capital ($mil)	Net Premium ($mil)	Net Income ($mil)
9-14	C	2.11	1.27	362.5	99.9	78.7	18.4
9-13	C	2.37	1.41	350.0	103.4	56.6	5.2
2013	C	2.08	1.25	358.7	95.9	83.3	-4.6
2012	C-	2.26	1.35	319.6	86.0	82.1	16.1
2011	C-	2.16	1.29	307.5	76.1	96.5	-11.4
2010	C-	2.37	1.43	325.0	97.3	81.6	-27.3
2009	C	3.69	2.13	232.0	118.6	20.5	7.8

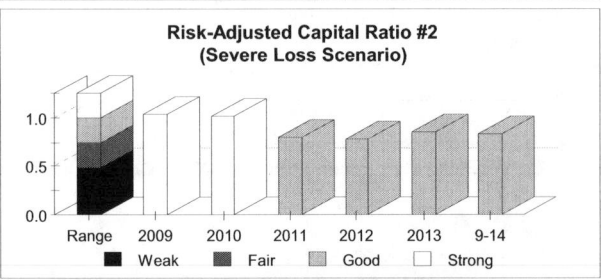

Net Income History (in millions of dollars)

AMERICAN LIFE INSURANCE COMPANY — C — Fair

Major Rating Factors: Fair quality investment portfolio (3.3 on a scale of 0 to 10). Fair profitability (3.5). Good current capitalization (5.2) based on good risk adjusted capital (severe loss scenario) reflecting some improvement over results in 2011.

Other Rating Factors: Weak overall results on stability tests (2.8) including weak results on operational trends and negative cash flow from operations for 2013. Excellent liquidity (7.0).

Principal Business: Individual life insurance (42%), reinsurance (22%), group health insurance (15%), group retirement contracts (7%), and other lines (14%).

Principal Investments: Common & preferred stock (54%), nonCMO investment grade bonds (17%), noninv. grade bonds (16%), cash (9%), and policy loans (2%).

Investments in Affiliates: 56%
Group Affiliation: MetLife Inc
Licensed in: DE
Commenced Business: August 1921
Address: One ALICO Plaza, Wilmington, DE 19801
Phone: (302) 594-2000 **Domicile State:** DE **NAIC Code:** 60690

Data Date	Rating	RACR #1	RACR #2	Total Assets ($mil)	Capital ($mil)	Net Premium ($mil)	Net Income ($mil)
9-14	C	0.82	0.77	7,622.5	2,719.6	1,041.2	38.5
9-13	C	0.97	0.90	7,096.8	2,623.7	862.0	916.9
2013	C	0.92	0.88	7,296.4	2,711.2	1,140.4	630.5
2012	C	1.01	0.93	8,224.8	3,043.6	8,991.4	317.1
2011	C-	0.80	0.57	102,198	3,309.9	15,495.3	333.8
2010	C-	1.11	0.82	94,591.6	4,320.7	16,504.5	803.4
2009	C-	N/A	N/A	91,042.8	4,146.5	12,861.0	668.6

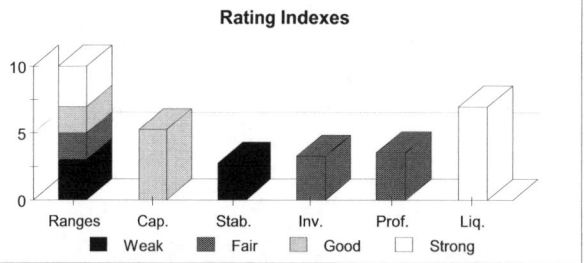

Rating Indexes

Ranges — Cap. — Stab. — Inv. — Prof. — Liq.
■ Weak ▨ Fair ▨ Good □ Strong

AMERICAN MATURITY LIFE INSURANCE COMPANY — B — Good

Major Rating Factors: Good overall results on stability tests (5.9 on a scale of 0 to 10) despite fair financial strength of affiliated Hartford Financial Services Inc. Other stability subfactors include good operational trends and excellent risk diversification. Strong capitalization (10.0) based on excellent risk adjusted capital (severe loss scenario). High quality investment portfolio (9.6).

Other Rating Factors: Excellent profitability (7.5) with operating gains in each of the last five years. Excellent liquidity (7.0).

Principal Business: Group retirement contracts (87%) and individual annuities (13%).

Principal Investments: NonCMO investment grade bonds (100%).
Investments in Affiliates: None
Group Affiliation: Hartford Financial Services Inc
Licensed in: All states except PR
Commenced Business: March 1973
Address: 200 Hopmeadow St, Simsbury, CT 06070
Phone: (860) 843-5867 **Domicile State:** CT **NAIC Code:** 81213

Data Date	Rating	RACR #1	RACR #2	Total Assets ($mil)	Capital ($mil)	Net Premium ($mil)	Net Income ($mil)
9-14	B	6.59	5.93	61.9	47.5	0.0	0.1
9-13	B	6.58	5.93	60.4	47.1	0.1	0.6
2013	B	6.55	5.89	61.2	47.2	0.1	0.7
2012	B	6.55	5.89	60.0	46.8	0.0	0.6
2011	B	6.29	5.66	63.5	46.0	0.1	0.7
2010	B	6.47	5.82	62.0	46.9	0.1	1.0
2009	B	6.31	5.68	60.9	45.4	0.0	1.5

Hartford Financial Services Inc Composite Group Rating: C+ Largest Group Members	Assets ($mil)	Rating
HARTFORD LIFE INS CO	128074	C+
HARTFORD LIFE ANNUITY INS CO	54557	B-
HARTFORD FIRE INS CO	25685	B
HARTFORD LIFE ACCIDENT INS CO	13891	C-
HARTFORD ACCIDENT INDEMNITY CO	11122	B

AMERICAN MEMORIAL LIFE INS CO — B- — Good

Major Rating Factors: Good capitalization (5.8 on a scale of 0 to 10) based on good risk adjusted capital (moderate loss scenario). Good overall profitability (5.8). Return on equity has been excellent over the last five years averaging 17.6%. Good liquidity (5.6) with sufficient resources to cover a large increase in policy surrenders.

Other Rating Factors: Fair quality investment portfolio (3.6). Fair overall results on stability tests (4.9).

Principal Business: N/A

Principal Investments: NonCMO investment grade bonds (69%), CMOs and structured securities (10%), noninv. grade bonds (8%), mortgages in good standing (8%), and common & preferred stock (1%).

Investments in Affiliates: None
Group Affiliation: Assurant Inc
Licensed in: All states except NY, PR
Commenced Business: October 1959
Address: 440 Mount Rushmore Rd, Rapid City, SD 57701
Phone: (605) 348-1262 **Domicile State:** SD **NAIC Code:** 67989

Data Date	Rating	RACR #1	RACR #2	Total Assets ($mil)	Capital ($mil)	Net Premium ($mil)	Net Income ($mil)
9-14	B-	1.55	0.78	2,635.4	115.6	377.6	18.1
9-13	B-	1.48	0.75	2,471.0	101.0	364.0	10.6
2013	B-	1.48	0.75	2,493.7	103.5	483.2	20.4
2012	B-	1.50	0.76	2,345.8	102.9	431.3	25.9
2011	B-	1.51	0.76	2,202.9	100.3	389.9	14.6
2010	B-	1.66	0.84	2,107.9	108.3	324.8	26.0
2009	B-	1.73	0.89	2,067.8	109.7	288.2	18.2

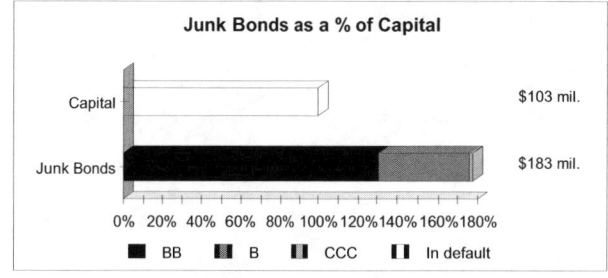

Junk Bonds as a % of Capital

Capital — $103 mil.
Junk Bonds — $183 mil.

0% 20% 40% 60% 80% 100% 120% 140% 160% 180%
■ BB ▨ B ▨ CCC ▨ In default

AMERICAN MODERN LIFE INSURANCE COMPANY   B   Good

Major Rating Factors: Fair overall results on stability tests (4.2 on a scale of 0 to 10) including negative cash flow from operations for 2013. Weak profitability (2.6) with investment income below regulatory standards in relation to interest assumptions of reserves. Strong capitalization (8.2) based on excellent risk adjusted capital (severe loss scenario).
Other Rating Factors: High quality investment portfolio (8.0). Excellent liquidity (8.4).
Principal Business: Credit life insurance (58%), credit health insurance (40%), and reinsurance (2%).
Principal Investments: NonCMO investment grade bonds (66%), common & preferred stock (25%), CMOs and structured securities (7%), and cash (1%).
Investments in Affiliates: 25%
Group Affiliation: Securian Financial Group
Licensed in: All states except NH, NJ, PR
Commenced Business: January 1957
Address: 400 Robert St N, St Paul, MN 55101-2098
Phone: (800) 543-2644 **Domicile State:** OH **NAIC Code:** 65811

Data Date	Rating	RACR #1	RACR #2	Total Assets ($mil)	Capital ($mil)	Net Premium ($mil)	Net Income ($mil)
9-14	B	1.94	1.81	49.0	27.2	4.0	1.4
9-13	B	1.76	1.63	53.5	25.8	3.5	3.0
2013	B	1.89	1.76	52.1	26.4	4.7	3.9
2012	B	1.55	1.43	58.8	23.1	8.1	1.9
2011	B	1.37	1.21	60.0	20.3	14.2	-3.6
2010	B	1.32	1.25	62.6	21.1	9.7	0.6
2009	B	1.23	1.19	63.4	20.8	11.1	2.8

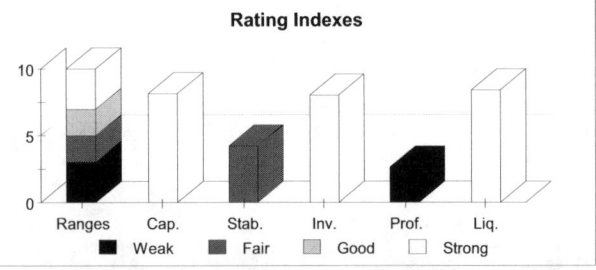

Rating Indexes

Ranges Cap. Stab. Inv. Prof. Liq.
■ Weak ■ Fair ▨ Good □ Strong

AMERICAN NATIONAL INSURANCE COMPANY   B   Good

Major Rating Factors: Good quality investment portfolio (5.3 on a scale of 0 to 10) despite significant exposure to mortgages . Mortgage default rate has been low. large holdings of BBB rated bonds in addition to small junk bond holdings. Good liquidity (6.5) with sufficient resources to handle a spike in claims as well as a significant increase in policy surrenders. Good overall results on stability tests (6.1) despite negative cash flow from operations for 2013 good operational trends, good risk adjusted capital for prior years and excellent risk diversification.
Other Rating Factors: Strong capitalization (7.1) based on excellent risk adjusted capital (severe loss scenario). Excellent profitability (7.8) with operating gains in each of the last five years.
Principal Business: Individual life insurance (36%), individual annuities (34%), group retirement contracts (13%), reinsurance (6%), and other lines (11%).
Principal Investments: NonCMO investment grade bonds (55%), mortgages in good standing (19%), common & preferred stock (11%), policy loans (2%), and misc. investments (11%).
Investments in Affiliates: 17%
Group Affiliation: American National Group Inc
Licensed in: All states except NY
Commenced Business: March 1905
Address: One Moody Plaza, Galveston, TX 77550-7999
Phone: (409) 763-4661 **Domicile State:** TX **NAIC Code:** 60739

Data Date	Rating	RACR #1	RACR #2	Total Assets ($mil)	Capital ($mil)	Net Premium ($mil)	Net Income ($mil)
9-14	B	1.33	1.08	18,049.9	2,843.0	1,010.3	119.9
9-13	B	1.33	1.06	17,875.2	2,513.6	812.0	126.2
2013	B	1.27	1.03	18,036.2	2,667.9	1,146.3	149.1
2012	B	1.23	0.99	17,787.3	2,260.3	1,340.5	193.7
2011	B	1.28	0.98	17,390.0	2,000.6	2,180.6	176.9
2010	B	1.26	0.97	16,438.2	1,954.1	2,021.0	129.9
2009	B	1.20	0.94	15,359.3	1,892.5	2,630.0	53.9

Adverse Trends in Operations

Decrease in premium volume from 2012 to 2013 (14%)
Decrease in premium volume from 2011 to 2012 (39%)
Increase in policy surrenders from 2010 to 2011 (27%)
Decrease in premium volume from 2009 to 2010 (23%)

AMERICAN NATIONAL LIFE INSURANCE COMPANY OF TEXAS   B-   Good

Major Rating Factors: Good liquidity (6.8 on a scale of 0 to 10) with sufficient resources to handle a spike in claims as well as a significant increase in policy surrenders. Good overall results on stability tests (5.1). Strengths include good financial support from affiliation with American National Group Inc, good operational trends and excellent risk diversification. Weak profitability (2.6).
Other Rating Factors: Strong capitalization (10.0) based on excellent risk adjusted capital (severe loss scenario). High quality investment portfolio (7.1).
Principal Business: Group health insurance (59%), reinsurance (31%), individual health insurance (6%), and individual life insurance (4%).
Principal Investments: NonCMO investment grade bonds (93%), CMOs and structured securities (3%), policy loans (3%), and noninv. grade bonds (2%).
Investments in Affiliates: None
Group Affiliation: American National Group Inc
Licensed in: All states except ME, NJ, NY, VT, PR
Commenced Business: December 1954
Address: One Moody Plaza, Galveston, TX 77550
Phone: (409) 763-4661 **Domicile State:** TX **NAIC Code:** 71773

Data Date	Rating	RACR #1	RACR #2	Total Assets ($mil)	Capital ($mil)	Net Premium ($mil)	Net Income ($mil)
9-14	B-	4.23	3.09	135.8	38.2	29.1	1.0
9-13	B-	4.03	2.76	135.0	37.1	34.4	1.7
2013	B-	4.55	3.17	135.1	41.4	45.1	2.1
2012	B-	4.01	2.80	133.5	39.2	52.8	-2.0
2011	B-	2.51	1.80	115.1	27.5	64.2	-0.8
2010	B-	1.87	1.36	124.5	28.5	92.5	-5.5
2009	B-	1.58	1.16	125.4	26.7	105.1	-14.5

American National Group Inc Composite Group Rating: B Largest Group Members	Assets ($mil)	Rating
AMERICAN NATIONAL INS CO	18036	B
FARM FAMILY LIFE INS CO	1248	B
AMERICAN NATIONAL PROPERTY CAS CO	1156	B
FARM FAMILY CASUALTY INS CO	1037	B+
STANDARD LIFE ACCIDENT INS CO	528	A-

AMERICAN PROGRESSIVE L&H INSURANCE COMPANY OF NY — B — Good

Major Rating Factors: Good overall results on stability tests (5.2 on a scale of 0 to 10) despite fair financial strength of affiliated Universal American Corp and negative cash flow from operations for 2013. Other stability subfactors include good operational trends and excellent risk diversification. Good current capitalization (6.8) based on excellent risk adjusted capital (severe loss scenario) reflecting improvement over results in 2010. Good overall profitability (6.4) despite operating losses during the first nine months of 2014.

Other Rating Factors: Good liquidity (5.0). High quality investment portfolio (7.4).

Principal Business: Individual health insurance (97%) and individual life insurance (3%).

Principal Investments: NonCMO investment grade bonds (63%), CMOs and structured securities (32%), common & preferred stock (2%), and noninv. grade bonds (1%).

Investments in Affiliates: None

Group Affiliation: Universal American Corp

Licensed in: AL, AR, CO, CT, DC, DE, GA, HI, IL, IN, LA, ME, MD, MA, MN, MO, NH, NJ, NY, NC, OH, OK, OR, PA, RI, SC, TX, VT, VA, WV

Commenced Business: March 1946

Address: 6 International Dr Suite 190, Rye Brook, NY 10573

Phone: (914) 934-8300 **Domicile State:** NY **NAIC Code:** 80624

Data Date	Rating	RACR #1	RACR #2	Total Assets ($mil)	Capital ($mil)	Net Premium ($mil)	Net Income ($mil)
9-14	B	1.52	1.19	232.1	121.2	306.9	-1.0
9-13	B	1.62	1.28	259.1	137.1	349.0	4.9
2013	B	1.39	1.10	235.7	122.3	469.8	13.5
2012	B	1.84	1.46	263.8	145.4	419.3	14.8
2011	C+	1.39	1.11	252.1	132.0	507.7	4.8
2010	C	1.02	0.83	288.9	140.5	744.3	35.2
2009	C	1.04	0.85	244.8	129.5	557.3	25.1

Universal American Corp
Composite Group Rating: C

Largest Group Members	Assets ($mil)	Rating
CONSTITUTION LIFE INS CO	317	C+
AMERICAN PROGRESSIVE LH I C OF NY	236	B
PYRAMID LIFE INS CO	212	C
SELECTCARE OF TEXAS LLC	133	C
AMERICAN PIONEER LIFE INS CO	77	D+

AMERICAN REPUBLIC INSURANCE COMPANY * — A- — Excellent

Major Rating Factors: Good liquidity (6.9 on a scale of 0 to 10) with sufficient resources to handle a spike in claims as well as a significant increase in policy surrenders. Good overall results on stability tests (6.9). Strengths that enhance stability include good operational trends and excellent risk diversification. Strong capitalization (10.0) based on excellent risk adjusted capital (severe loss scenario).

Other Rating Factors: High quality investment portfolio (7.4). Excellent profitability (9.2) with operating gains in each of the last five years.

Principal Business: Reinsurance (46%), individual health insurance (27%), group health insurance (21%), individual life insurance (4%), and credit life insurance (1%).

Principal Investments: NonCMO investment grade bonds (63%), CMOs and structured securities (26%), common & preferred stock (6%), noninv. grade bonds (2%), and misc. investments (3%).

Investments in Affiliates: 5%

Group Affiliation: American Enterprise Mutual Holding

Licensed in: All states except NY, PR

Commenced Business: May 1929

Address: 601 Sixth Ave, Des Moines, IA 50309

Phone: (515) 245-2000 **Domicile State:** IA **NAIC Code:** 60836

Data Date	Rating	RACR #1	RACR #2	Total Assets ($mil)	Capital ($mil)	Net Premium ($mil)	Net Income ($mil)
9-14	A-	5.18	3.86	797.6	461.4	224.1	23.8
9-13	A-	N/A	N/A	809.5	428.4	245.5	22.3
2013	A-	4.85	3.67	801.4	437.5	325.1	40.5
2012	A-	6.09	4.36	522.7	286.4	224.0	44.2
2011	A	4.60	3.35	538.6	259.3	294.5	17.1
2010	A	4.10	3.06	537.8	264.9	362.8	32.6
2009	A-	3.44	2.58	521.5	241.0	399.8	19.0

Adverse Trends in Operations

Increase in policy surrenders from 2012 to 2013 (109%)
Decrease in premium volume from 2011 to 2012 (24%)
Decrease in premium volume from 2010 to 2011 (19%)
Decrease in capital during 2011 (2%)
Decrease in premium volume from 2009 to 2010 (9%)

AMERICAN RETIREMENT LIFE INSURANCE COMPANY — B- — Good

Major Rating Factors: Fair overall results on stability tests (3.7 on a scale of 0 to 10). Weak profitability (2.4) with operating losses during the first nine months of 2014. Return on equity has been low, averaging -14.9%. Strong capitalization (8.4) based on excellent risk adjusted capital (severe loss scenario). Capital levels have been relatively consistent over the last five years.

Other Rating Factors: High quality investment portfolio (8.3). Excellent liquidity (7.7).

Principal Business: Individual health insurance (100%).

Principal Investments: NonCMO investment grade bonds (101%).

Investments in Affiliates: None

Group Affiliation: CIGNA Corp

Licensed in: AL, AZ, AR, CA, CO, DE, FL, GA, IL, IN, IA, KS, KY, LA, MD, MN, MS, MO, MT, NE, NV, NH, NM, NC, ND, OH, OK, OR, PA, RI, SC, SD, TN, TX, UT, VA, WV, WI, WY

Commenced Business: November 1978

Address: 1300 E Ninth St, Cleveland, OH 44114

Phone: (512) 451-2224 **Domicile State:** OH **NAIC Code:** 88366

Data Date	Rating	RACR #1	RACR #2	Total Assets ($mil)	Capital ($mil)	Net Premium ($mil)	Net Income ($mil)
9-14	B-	2.17	1.93	56.5	31.3	82.2	-10.5
9-13	B-	5.09	4.58	12.2	8.3	5.9	-2.4
2013	B-	1.61	1.25	18.0	8.4	16.7	-4.3
2012	B-	3.32	2.99	5.7	5.4	-0.7	0.1
2011	U	3.13	2.82	6.4	5.5	0.0	0.0
2010	U	3.14	2.82	6.4	5.5	0.0	0.0
2009	U	3.14	2.82	6.4	5.5	0.0	0.0

Rating Indexes

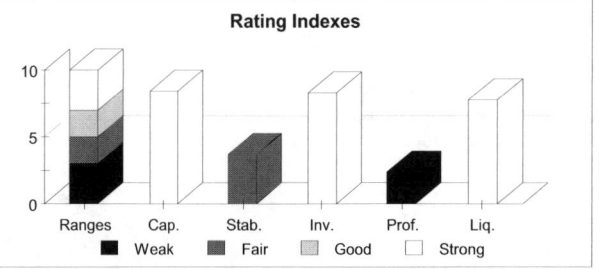

AMERICAN UNITED LIFE INSURANCE COMPANY * B+ Good

Major Rating Factors: Good quality investment portfolio (6.1 on a scale of 0 to 10) despite large holdings of BBB rated bonds in addition to moderate junk bond exposure. Exposure to mortgages is significant, but the mortgage default rate has been low. Good overall results on stability tests (6.6). Stability strengths include excellent operational trends and excellent risk diversification. Strong capitalization (8.0) based on excellent risk adjusted capital (severe loss scenario).

Other Rating Factors: Excellent profitability (7.8) with operating gains in each of the last five years. Excellent liquidity (7.5).

Principal Business: Group retirement contracts (76%), reinsurance (8%), individual life insurance (7%), individual annuities (4%), and other lines (5%).

Principal Investments: NonCMO investment grade bonds (62%), CMOs and structured securities (16%), mortgages in good standing (14%), noninv. grade bonds (3%), and misc. investments (5%).

Investments in Affiliates: None

Group Affiliation: American United Life Group

Licensed in: All states except PR

Commenced Business: November 1877

Address: One American Square, Indianapolis, IN 46204

Phone: (317) 285-1877 **Domicile State:** IN **NAIC Code:** 60895

Data Date	Rating	RACR #1	RACR #2	Total Assets ($mil)	Capital ($mil)	Net Premium ($mil)	Net Income ($mil)
9-14	B+	3.27	1.65	22,778.8	1,003.5	2,368.3	35.8
9-13	B+	3.20	1.60	21,113.3	931.1	2,174.8	57.6
2013	B+	3.28	1.66	22,267.4	980.7	3,055.8	65.7
2012	B+	3.20	1.61	19,367.7	883.6	2,763.7	58.6
2011	B+	3.03	1.52	17,342.6	835.9	2,769.9	42.5
2010	B+	3.12	1.58	16,537.5	812.2	2,353.9	69.4
2009	B+	2.97	1.52	14,839.2	758.8	2,198.2	61.3

Rating Indexes

Ranges | Cap. | Stab. | Inv. | Prof. | Liq.
■ Weak ■ Fair ▨ Good □ Strong

AMERICAN-AMICABLE LIFE INSURANCE COMPANY OF TEXAS C Fair

Major Rating Factors: Fair overall results on stability tests (4.1 on a scale of 0 to 10) including fair financial strength of affiliated Industrial Alliance Ins & Financial. Good quality investment portfolio (6.2) despite mixed results such as: minimal exposure to mortgages and substantial holdings of BBB bonds but minimal holdings in junk bonds. Good liquidity (6.4).

Other Rating Factors: Weak profitability (2.4) with investment income below regulatory standards in relation to interest assumptions of reserves. Strong capitalization (7.3) based on excellent risk adjusted capital (severe loss scenario).

Principal Business: Individual life insurance (88%), individual annuities (6%), and group life insurance (6%).

Principal Investments: NonCMO investment grade bonds (64%), common & preferred stock (22%), policy loans (6%), mortgages in good standing (4%), and misc. investments (3%).

Investments in Affiliates: 21%

Group Affiliation: Industrial Alliance Ins & Financial

Licensed in: All states except IA, MA, MI, NH, NJ, NY, RI, VT, PR

Commenced Business: December 1981

Address: 425 Austin Ave, Waco, TX 76701

Phone: (254) 297-2777 **Domicile State:** TX **NAIC Code:** 68594

Data Date	Rating	RACR #1	RACR #2	Total Assets ($mil)	Capital ($mil)	Net Premium ($mil)	Net Income ($mil)
9-14	C	1.39	1.22	272.0	86.0	30.3	6.6
9-13	C	1.45	1.18	249.8	65.9	39.6	0.2
2013	C	1.31	1.16	258.6	79.0	44.7	4.0
2012	C	1.54	1.29	235.8	64.9	52.4	7.6
2011	C+	1.23	0.91	446.4	57.4	48.9	12.0
2010	C+	1.14	1.00	394.6	58.0	46.4	-3.5
2009	B	1.12	0.97	374.4	57.7	44.1	0.3

Industrial Alliance Ins Financial Composite Group Rating: C Largest Group Members	Assets ($mil)	Rating
AMERICAN-AMICABLE LIFE INS CO OF TX	259	C
OCCIDENTAL LIFE INS CO OF NC	250	C
IA AMERICAN LIFE INS CO	221	C
INDUSTRIAL ALLIANCE INS FIN SERV	201	C
PIONEER SECURITY LIFE INS CO	110	C+

AMERICO FINANCIAL LIFE & ANNUITY INSURANCE B- Good

Major Rating Factors: Good liquidity (6.3 on a scale of 0 to 10) with sufficient resources to cover a large increase in policy surrenders. Good overall results on stability tests (5.3) despite excessive premium growth. Other stability subfactors include good operational trends, good risk adjusted capital for prior years and excellent risk diversification. Fair quality investment portfolio (4.8).

Other Rating Factors: Strong capitalization (7.1) based on excellent risk adjusted capital (severe loss scenario). Excellent profitability (7.8) with operating gains in each of the last five years.

Principal Business: Individual life insurance (46%), reinsurance (33%), individual annuities (13%), group life insurance (7%), and group retirement contracts (1%).

Principal Investments: NonCMO investment grade bonds (40%), CMOs and structured securities (33%), common & preferred stock (11%), mortgages in good standing (8%), and misc. investments (7%).

Investments in Affiliates: 4%

Group Affiliation: Americo Life Inc

Licensed in: All states except NY

Commenced Business: July 1946

Address: 500 North Akard, Dallas, TX 75201

Phone: (816) 391-2000 **Domicile State:** TX **NAIC Code:** 61999

Data Date	Rating	RACR #1	RACR #2	Total Assets ($mil)	Capital ($mil)	Net Premium ($mil)	Net Income ($mil)
9-14	B-	1.79	1.04	3,871.0	435.4	302.6	60.2
9-13	B-	2.02	1.21	3,810.9	456.8	171.5	41.6
2013	B-	1.92	1.15	3,804.4	442.3	233.4	54.7
2012	B-	1.86	1.11	3,777.8	402.3	295.5	63.3
2011	B-	1.75	1.04	3,747.5	371.1	349.7	89.2
2010	B-	1.71	1.04	3,628.3	352.6	316.3	66.5
2009	C+	1.50	0.91	3,557.8	311.3	312.3	54.1

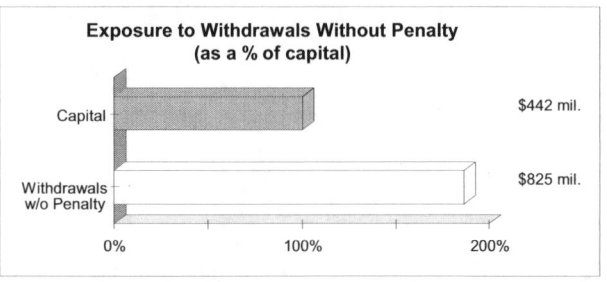

Exposure to Withdrawals Without Penalty (as a % of capital)

Capital — $442 mil.
Withdrawals w/o Penalty — $825 mil.

0%   100%   200%

AMERITAS LIFE INSURANCE CORP OF NEW YORK   B-   Good

Major Rating Factors: Good quality investment portfolio (6.3 on a scale of 0 to 10) despite significant exposure to mortgages . Mortgage default rate has been low. large holdings of BBB rated bonds in addition to small junk bond holdings. Fair liquidity (4.2) due, in part, to cash value policies that are subject to withdrawals with minimal or no penalty. Fair overall results on stability tests (3.6) including weak results on operational trends, negative cash flow from operations for 2013.

Other Rating Factors: Weak profitability (1.8) with operating losses during the first nine months of 2014. Strong capitalization (7.3) based on excellent risk adjusted capital (severe loss scenario).

Principal Business: Reinsurance (74%), individual life insurance (16%), group health insurance (7%), group retirement contracts (2%), and individual health insurance (1%).

Principal Investments: NonCMO investment grade bonds (68%), CMOs and structured securities (17%), mortgages in good standing (12%), policy loans (2%), and noninv. grade bonds (1%).

Investments in Affiliates: None

Group Affiliation: UNIFI Mutual Holding Co

Licensed in: NY

Commenced Business: May 1994

Address: 400 Rella Blvd Suite 214, Suffern, NY 10901

Phone: (914) 357-3816 **Domicile State:** NY **NAIC Code:** 60033

Data Date	Rating	RACR #1	RACR #2	Total Assets ($mil)	Capital ($mil)	Net Premium ($mil)	Net Income ($mil)
9-14	B-	2.26	1.21	1,157.3	82.9	67.4	-5.1
9-13	B-	2.51	1.39	1,048.8	71.2	251.7	-32.0
2013	B-	2.12	1.17	1,113.0	81.8	285.0	-45.8
2012	B-	3.72	3.07	122.3	33.5	71.4	-4.2
2011	B	4.09	3.50	104.6	36.6	71.6	-9.8
2010	B	6.13	5.52	71.0	46.9	29.9	-1.7
2009	B	3.42	2.62	40.5	19.3	30.2	-0.4

Adverse Trends in Operations

Increase in policy surrenders from 2012 to 2013 (76%)
Increase in policy surrenders from 2011 to 2012 (741%)
Decrease in capital during 2011 (22%)
Increase in policy surrenders from 2010 to 2011 (109%)
Increase in policy surrenders from 2009 to 2010 (54%)

AMERITAS LIFE INSURANCE CORPORATION   B   Good

Major Rating Factors: Good liquidity (6.9 on a scale of 0 to 10) with sufficient resources to handle a spike in claims as well as a significant increase in policy surrenders. Good overall results on stability tests (6.1). Stability strengths include excellent operational trends and excellent risk diversification. Fair quality investment portfolio (3.8).

Other Rating Factors: Strong capitalization (7.2) based on excellent risk adjusted capital (severe loss scenario). Excellent profitability (7.1) with operating gains in each of the last five years.

Principal Business: Group health insurance (35%), group retirement contracts (27%), individual annuities (18%), individual life insurance (15%), and other lines (5%).

Principal Investments: NonCMO investment grade bonds (40%), common & preferred stock (31%), mortgages in good standing (13%), CMOs and structured securities (9%), and misc. investments (7%).

Investments in Affiliates: 24%

Group Affiliation: UNIFI Mutual Holding Co

Licensed in: All states except NY, PR

Commenced Business: May 1887

Address: 5900 O Street, Lincoln, NE 68510

Phone: (402) 467-1122 **Domicile State:** NE **NAIC Code:** 61301

Data Date	Rating	RACR #1	RACR #2	Total Assets ($mil)	Capital ($mil)	Net Premium ($mil)	Net Income ($mil)
6-14	B	1.33	1.15	9,678.1	1,557.0	858.6	32.5
6-13	B	1.32	1.13	8,363.9	1,305.5	791.1	47.7
2013	B	1.30	1.13	9,187.8	1,501.8	1,622.4	64.9
2012	B	1.31	1.13	7,997.9	1,298.4	1,494.5	0.0
2011	B	1.41	1.23	7,278.3	1,349.1	1,265.0	26.2
2010	B+	1.51	1.30	7,124.6	1,330.9	1,154.1	77.9
2009	B+	1.46	1.26	6,529.5	1,249.0	1,227.6	49.9

Adverse Trends in Operations

Decrease in capital during 2012 (4%)
Decrease in premium volume from 2009 to 2010 (6%)

AMICA LIFE INSURANCE COMPANY   B   Good

Major Rating Factors: Good liquidity (6.7 on a scale of 0 to 10) with sufficient resources to cover a large increase in policy surrenders. Good overall results on stability tests (5.6). Strengths include good financial support from affiliation with Amica Mutual Group, excellent operational trends and excellent risk diversification. Weak profitability (2.9) with investment income below regulatory standards in relation to interest assumptions of reserves.

Other Rating Factors: Strong capitalization (9.7) based on excellent risk adjusted capital (severe loss scenario). High quality investment portfolio (7.0).

Principal Business: Individual life insurance (85%), individual annuities (12%), and group life insurance (3%).

Principal Investments: NonCMO investment grade bonds (56%), CMOs and structured securities (38%), common & preferred stock (5%), and policy loans (1%).

Investments in Affiliates: None

Group Affiliation: Amica Mutual Group

Licensed in: All states except HI, PR

Commenced Business: May 1970

Address: One Hundred Amica Way, Lincoln, RI 02867

Phone: (401) 334-6000 **Domicile State:** RI **NAIC Code:** 72222

Data Date	Rating	RACR #1	RACR #2	Total Assets ($mil)	Capital ($mil)	Net Premium ($mil)	Net Income ($mil)
9-14	B	4.88	2.79	1,196.2	266.8	46.0	6.0
9-13	B	4.02	2.33	1,127.5	205.8	45.9	1.9
2013	B	4.16	2.43	1,133.1	217.5	61.8	5.6
2012	B	4.04	2.34	1,099.5	202.1	62.2	3.8
2011	A-	4.14	2.42	1,067.0	197.0	70.3	13.0
2010	A-	4.04	2.36	1,024.0	185.7	71.2	16.0
2009	A-	3.83	2.23	989.2	167.7	87.4	8.9

Amica Mutual Group
Composite Group Rating: B+

Largest Group Members	Assets ($mil)	Rating
AMICA MUTUAL INS CO	4855	B+
AMICA LIFE INS CO	1133	B
AMICA LLOYDS OF TEXAS	93	A-
AMICA PROPERTY CASUALTY INS CO	33	C-

ANNUITY INVESTORS LIFE INSURANCE COMPANY   B   Good

Major Rating Factors: Good overall results on stability tests (6.2 on a scale of 0 to 10). Stability strengths include excellent operational trends, good risk adjusted capital for prior years and excellent risk diversification. Good quality investment portfolio (6.5) despite mixed results such as: no exposure to mortgages and large holdings of BBB rated bonds but small junk bond holdings. Good liquidity (6.1).

Other Rating Factors: Strong capitalization (7.7) based on excellent risk adjusted capital (severe loss scenario). Excellent profitability (8.5).

Principal Business: Individual annuities (88%) and group retirement contracts (12%).

Principal Investments: NonCMO investment grade bonds (60%), CMOs and structured securities (34%), policy loans (3%), and noninv. grade bonds (2%).

Investments in Affiliates: None

Group Affiliation: American Financial Group Inc

Licensed in: All states except NY, VT, PR

Commenced Business: December 1981

Address: 250 E Fifth St, Cincinnati, OH 45202

Phone: (513) 357-3300 **Domicile State:** OH **NAIC Code:** 93661

Data Date	Rating	RACR #1	RACR #2	Total Assets ($mil)	Capital ($mil)	Net Premium ($mil)	Net Income ($mil)
9-14	B	2.87	1.44	2,963.6	220.3	171.7	21.0
9-13	B	2.72	1.36	2,830.7	195.5	169.8	17.0
2013	B	2.68	1.35	2,892.9	203.2	232.4	23.2
2012	B	2.52	1.25	2,693.8	178.5	267.7	29.5
2011	B	2.34	1.16	2,520.6	157.4	300.3	20.6
2010	B	2.05	0.99	2,440.0	142.0	351.3	13.6
2009	B-	2.06	1.00	2,167.2	129.6	421.9	1.3

Adverse Trends in Operations

Decrease in premium volume from 2012 to 2013 (13%)
Decrease in premium volume from 2011 to 2012 (11%)
Decrease in premium volume from 2010 to 2011 (15%)
Increase in policy surrenders from 2010 to 2011 (28%)
Decrease in premium volume from 2009 to 2010 (17%)

ANTHEM LIFE INSURANCE COMPANY *   A-   Excellent

Major Rating Factors: Good liquidity (6.3 on a scale of 0 to 10) with sufficient resources to handle a spike in claims. Excellent overall results on stability tests (7.1). Strengths that enhance stability include excellent operational trends and excellent risk diversification. Strong capitalization (7.7) based on excellent risk adjusted capital (severe loss scenario). Furthermore, this high level of risk adjusted capital has been consistently maintained over the last five years.

Other Rating Factors: High quality investment portfolio (7.6). Excellent profitability (7.3) with operating gains in each of the last five years.

Principal Business: Reinsurance (45%), group life insurance (31%), group health insurance (23%), and individual life insurance (1%).

Principal Investments: NonCMO investment grade bonds (63%), CMOs and structured securities (23%), and cash (3%).

Investments in Affiliates: None

Group Affiliation: WellPoint Inc

Licensed in: All states except NY, RI, VT, PR

Commenced Business: June 1956

Address: 6740 N High St Suite 200, Worthington, OH 43085

Phone: (614) 438-3959 **Domicile State:** IN **NAIC Code:** 61069

Data Date	Rating	RACR #1	RACR #2	Total Assets ($mil)	Capital ($mil)	Net Premium ($mil)	Net Income ($mil)
9-14	A-	2.13	1.48	559.7	98.1	266.8	26.5
9-13	A-	2.18	1.53	571.6	100.8	259.4	25.0
2013	A-	2.17	1.51	575.3	120.4	345.1	47.1
2012	A-	1.60	1.12	565.4	87.4	336.1	13.8
2011	A-	1.46	1.03	542.7	77.8	206.6	6.4
2010	A-	1.98	1.41	326.1	71.5	168.7	24.3
2009	A-	1.70	1.24	285.2	60.8	165.1	18.3

Adverse Trends in Operations

Increase in policy surrenders from 2011 to 2012 (129%)

ASSURITY LIFE INSURANCE COMPANY *   B+   Good

Major Rating Factors: Good quality investment portfolio (5.5 on a scale of 0 to 10) despite significant exposure to mortgages . Mortgage default rate has been low. large holdings of BBB rated bonds in addition to minimal holdings in junk bonds. Good overall profitability (6.9). Return on equity has been low, averaging 4.4%. Good liquidity (5.8).

Other Rating Factors: Good overall results on stability tests (6.6) excellent operational trends and excellent risk diversification. Strong capitalization (8.1) based on excellent risk adjusted capital (severe loss scenario).

Principal Business: Individual life insurance (52%), individual health insurance (28%), group health insurance (10%), reinsurance (4%), and other lines (7%).

Principal Investments: NonCMO investment grade bonds (58%), CMOs and structured securities (16%), mortgages in good standing (13%), policy loans (5%), and misc. investments (7%).

Investments in Affiliates: None

Group Affiliation: Assurity Security Group Inc

Licensed in: All states except NY, PR

Commenced Business: March 1964

Address: 2000 Q Street, Lincoln, NE 68503

Phone: (402) 476-6500 **Domicile State:** NE **NAIC Code:** 71439

Data Date	Rating	RACR #1	RACR #2	Total Assets ($mil)	Capital ($mil)	Net Premium ($mil)	Net Income ($mil)
9-14	B+	3.21	1.71	2,452.3	307.9	140.5	12.2
9-13	B+	3.16	1.64	2,433.8	276.4	140.7	10.9
2013	B+	3.17	1.69	2,449.3	306.4	191.2	14.6
2012	B+	3.00	1.57	2,419.2	262.7	225.0	21.9
2011	B+	2.77	1.45	2,403.2	257.8	240.6	23.0
2010	B+	2.09	1.21	2,326.3	256.9	254.4	15.0
2009	B+	2.52	1.44	2,237.6	248.7	266.9	-5.8

Rating Indexes

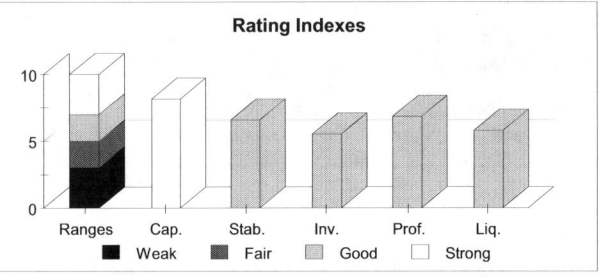

ATHENE ANNUITY & LIFE ASSURANCE COMPANY   C-   Fair

Major Rating Factors: Fair capitalization for the current period (4.6 on a scale of 0 to 10) based on fair risk adjusted capital (moderate loss scenario) reflecting some improvement over results in 2012. Fair quality investment portfolio (3.6) with substantial holdings of BBB bonds in addition to moderate junk bond exposure. Fair overall results on stability tests (3.0) including weak risk adjusted capital in prior years, negative cash flow from operations for 2013.

Other Rating Factors: Weak profitability (2.3) with investment income below regulatory standards in relation to interest assumptions of reserves. Good liquidity (6.5).

Principal Business: Individual annuities (74%), individual life insurance (14%), reinsurance (8%), group health insurance (2%), and individual health insurance (1%).

Principal Investments: CMOs and structured securities (43%), nonCMO investment grade bonds (16%), common & preferred stock (13%), mortgages in good standing (9%), and misc. investments (18%).

Investments in Affiliates: 22%

Group Affiliation: BRH Holdings GP Ltd

Licensed in: All states except NY, PR

Commenced Business: July 1909

Address: 2711 Centerville Rd Suite 400, Wilmington, DE 19808

Phone: (864) 609-1000 **Domicile State:** DE **NAIC Code:** 61492

Data Date	Rating	RACR #1	RACR #2	Total Assets ($mil)	Capital ($mil)	Net Premium ($mil)	Net Income ($mil)
9-14	C-	0.91	0.70	11,023.3	1,134.1	96.4	38.3
9-13	D+	0.67	0.42	10,755.0	275.4	145.5	28.3
2013	D+	0.87	0.66	11,775.6	1,050.1	200.1	49.5
2012	D+	0.54	0.34	10,481.2	276.9	3,166.8	11.5
2011	D+	0.46	0.25	7,482.7	142.6	2,154.6	-18.8
2010	B-	1.62	0.92	4,995.4	278.0	1,030.2	-0.5
2009	C	1.77	1.01	4,326.6	275.0	994.6	-31.9

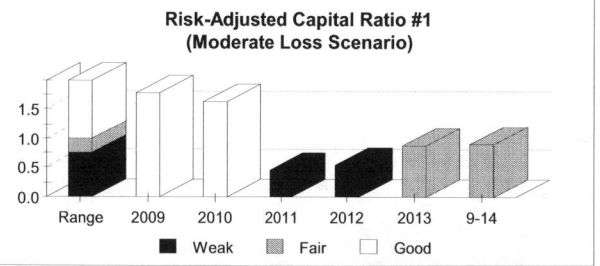

Risk-Adjusted Capital Ratio #1 (Moderate Loss Scenario)

ATHENE ANNUITY & LIFE ASSURANCE COMPANY OF NEW YOR   C   Fair

Major Rating Factors: Good capitalization (5.6 on a scale of 0 to 10) based on good risk adjusted capital (moderate loss scenario). Good overall profitability (5.2). Return on equity has been excellent over the last five years averaging 18.0%. Low quality investment portfolio (2.3) containing large holdings of BBB rated bonds in addition to significant exposure to junk bonds.

Other Rating Factors: Weak overall results on stability tests (2.8) including weak results on operational trends and negative cash flow from operations for 2013. Excellent liquidity (10.0).

Principal Business: Individual annuities (77%) and individual life insurance (22%).

Principal Investments: CMOs and structured securities (62%), nonCMO investment grade bonds (20%), noninv. grade bonds (8%), mortgages in good standing (2%), and misc. investments (8%).

Investments in Affiliates: 1%

Group Affiliation: BRH Holdings GP Ltd

Licensed in: All states except PR

Commenced Business: October 1966

Address: 69 Lydecker St, Nyack, NY 10960

Phone: (800) 926-7599 **Domicile State:** NY **NAIC Code:** 68039

Data Date	Rating	RACR #1	RACR #2	Total Assets ($mil)	Capital ($mil)	Net Premium ($mil)	Net Income ($mil)
9-14	C	1.43	0.66	3,420.4	176.8	9.2	6.4
9-13	C	2.09	0.97	3,583.8	183.5	13.4	6.4
2013	C	1.29	0.60	3,525.6	164.4	17.4	12.0
2012	C+	2.35	1.10	3,454.8	215.5	-2,478.7	125.5
2011	C+	2.39	1.19	3,561.2	345.4	62.4	51.3
2010	C	1.96	0.99	3,627.3	273.0	122.1	34.1
2009	C-	1.78	0.90	3,613.9	269.8	208.1	36.0

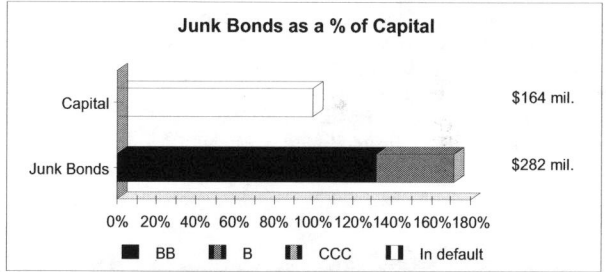

Junk Bonds as a % of Capital

Capital — $164 mil.
Junk Bonds — $282 mil.

ATHENE ANNUITY & LIFE COMPANY   C+   Fair

Major Rating Factors: Fair overall capitalization (4.0 on a scale of 0 to 10) based on mixed results -- excessive policy leverage mitigated by good risk adjusted capital (moderate loss scenario). Fair overall results on stability tests (3.1) including weak results on operational trends, negative cash flow from operations for 2013, fair risk adjusted capital in prior years. Good overall profitability (5.1).

Other Rating Factors: Good liquidity (5.7). Low quality investment portfolio (2.9).

Principal Business: N/A

Principal Investments: NonCMO investment grade bonds (66%), CMOs and structured securities (13%), mortgages in good standing (12%), noninv. grade bonds (3%), and misc. investments (5%).

Investments in Affiliates: 2%

Group Affiliation: BRH Holdings GP Ltd

Licensed in: All states except NY, PR

Commenced Business: February 1896

Address: 7700 Mills Civic Parkway, West Des Moines, IA 50266

Phone: (515) 283-2371 **Domicile State:** IA **NAIC Code:** 61689

Data Date	Rating	RACR #1	RACR #2	Total Assets ($mil)	Capital ($mil)	Net Premium ($mil)	Net Income ($mil)
9-14	C+	1.11	0.60	43,427.5	1,013.0	283.9	105.7
9-13	C+	1.70	1.00	51,049.1	3,379.8	7,187.5	506.9
2013	C+	0.95	0.51	43,841.7	978.8	-25,903.0	43.1
2012	C+	1.44	0.84	51,044.2	2,868.5	5,610.1	-1.9
2011	C+	1.24	0.72	48,504.3	2,678.6	3,048.6	148.2
2010	C+	1.39	0.78	45,603.0	2,356.1	6,465.8	106.1
2009	C+	1.44	0.78	41,990.4	2,282.9	-407.1	-95.9

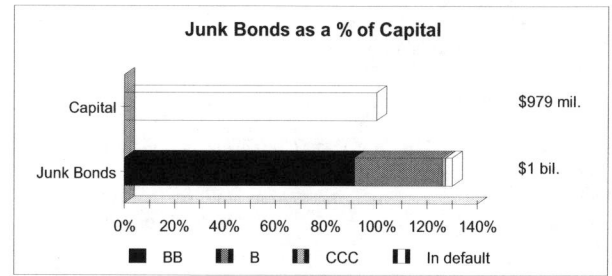

Junk Bonds as a % of Capital

Capital — $979 mil.
Junk Bonds — $1 bil.

AURORA NATIONAL LIFE ASSURANCE COMPANY   B   Good

Major Rating Factors: Good overall results on stability tests (5.8 on a scale of 0 to 10) despite fair financial strength of affiliated Swiss Reinsurance Group. Other stability subfactors include good operational trends and excellent risk diversification. Good overall profitability (5.6) although investment income, in comparison to reserve requirements, is below regulatory standards. Strong capitalization (8.7) based on excellent risk adjusted capital (severe loss scenario).

Other Rating Factors: High quality investment portfolio (7.2). Excellent liquidity (7.6).

Principal Business: Individual life insurance (97%) and group life insurance (3%).

Principal Investments: NonCMO investment grade bonds (84%), CMOs and structured securities (7%), policy loans (5%), noninv. grade bonds (3%), and cash (1%).

Investments in Affiliates: None
Group Affiliation: Swiss Reinsurance Group
Licensed in: All states except CT, ME, NH, NY, PR
Commenced Business: December 1961
Address: 2525 Colorado Ave, Bl C, Santa Monica, CA 90404-3540
Phone: (310) 264-3200 **Domicile State:** CA **NAIC Code:** 61182

Data Date	Rating	RACR #1	RACR #2	Total Assets ($mil)	Capital ($mil)	Net Premium ($mil)	Net Income ($mil)
9-14	B	4.06	2.12	3,103.6	316.9	0.5	13.0
9-13	B-	4.40	2.25	3,188.2	339.6	0.5	11.3
2013	B-	4.39	2.27	3,143.7	341.5	0.6	17.8
2012	C+	5.06	2.63	3,007.1	368.7	0.7	34.9
2011	C+	5.13	2.67	2,818.7	355.6	0.8	18.1
2010	C+	5.34	2.78	2,902.4	341.9	1.0	19.7
2009	C+	4.41	2.38	2,999.8	336.7	1.1	-1.4

Swiss Reinsurance Group
Composite Group Rating: C+

Largest Group Members	Assets ($mil)	Rating
SWISS REINSURANCE AMERICA CORP	11409	B-
SWISS RE LIFE HEALTH AMER INC	9995	C+
WESTPORT INS CORP	5454	C+
AURORA NATIONAL LIFE ASR CO	3144	B
NORTH AMERICAN SPECIALTY INS CO	514	C

AUTO CLUB LIFE INSURANCE COMPANY   C+   Fair

Major Rating Factors: Fair overall results on stability tests (4.5 on a scale of 0 to 10) including excessive premium growth. Good overall capitalization (5.7) based on good risk adjusted capital (severe loss scenario). Nevertheless, capital levels have fluctuated during prior years. Good quality investment portfolio (5.7).

Other Rating Factors: Good liquidity (5.3). Weak profitability (2.0) with operating losses during the first nine months of 2014.

Principal Business: Reinsurance (89%), individual life insurance (9%), individual annuities (1%), and group health insurance (1%).

Principal Investments: NonCMO investment grade bonds (61%), CMOs and structured securities (19%), noninv. grade bonds (10%), common & preferred stock (6%), and policy loans (2%).

Investments in Affiliates: 6%
Group Affiliation: Automobile Club of Michigan Group
Licensed in: AZ, AR, CA, CO, IL, IN, IA, KS, KY, MD, MI, MN, MO, NE, NM, NC, ND, OH, OK, PA, SC, SD, TX, VA, WA, WI
Commenced Business: August 1974
Address: 17250 Newburgh Road, Livonia, MI 48152
Phone: (734) 591-9442 **Domicile State:** MI **NAIC Code:** 84522

Data Date	Rating	RACR #1	RACR #2	Total Assets ($mil)	Capital ($mil)	Net Premium ($mil)	Net Income ($mil)
9-14	C+	1.21	0.84	536.5	65.5	82.5	-6.5
9-13	C+	1.21	0.84	496.0	58.0	62.9	-7.0
2013	C+	1.14	0.81	503.6	59.6	89.0	-6.7
2012	B-	1.32	0.92	475.8	63.7	74.4	-6.6
2011	B	1.58	1.10	453.0	68.3	63.9	1.2
2010	B-	1.54	1.05	425.6	65.9	62.4	3.5
2009	B-	1.39	0.95	450.3	63.0	64.0	4.6

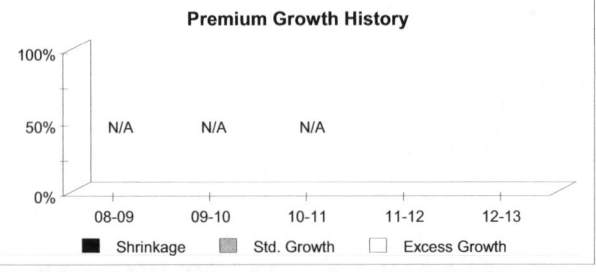

Premium Growth History

AUTO-OWNERS LIFE INSURANCE COMPANY *   A   Excellent

Major Rating Factors: Good quality investment portfolio (5.3 on a scale of 0 to 10) despite mixed results such as: minimal exposure to mortgages and substantial holdings of BBB bonds but minimal holdings in junk bonds. Good overall profitability (5.3) although investment income, in comparison to reserve requirements, is below regulatory standards. Good liquidity (6.0).

Other Rating Factors: Good overall results on stability tests (6.2) good operational trends and excellent risk diversification. Strong capitalization (7.3) based on excellent risk adjusted capital (severe loss scenario).

Principal Business: Individual life insurance (40%), individual annuities (39%), group retirement contracts (14%), individual health insurance (5%), and group health insurance (1%).

Principal Investments: NonCMO investment grade bonds (61%), CMOs and structured securities (25%), mortgages in good standing (5%), real estate (4%), and misc. investments (4%).

Investments in Affiliates: None
Group Affiliation: Auto-Owners Group
Licensed in: AL, AZ, AR, CO, FL, GA, ID, IL, IN, IA, KS, KY, MI, MN, MS, MO, NE, NV, NM, NC, ND, OH, OR, PA, SC, SD, TN, UT, VA, WA, WI
Commenced Business: January 1966
Address: 6101 Anacapri Blvd, Lansing, MI 48917
Phone: (517) 323-1200 **Domicile State:** MI **NAIC Code:** 61190

Data Date	Rating	RACR #1	RACR #2	Total Assets ($mil)	Capital ($mil)	Net Premium ($mil)	Net Income ($mil)
9-14	A	2.17	1.17	3,592.1	347.6	193.3	20.6
9-13	A	2.21	1.18	3,478.4	294.9	184.6	19.7
2013	A	2.24	1.20	3,509.2	323.5	248.4	22.7
2012	A	2.13	1.13	3,297.1	277.5	250.1	26.2
2011	A	1.97	1.05	3,106.7	257.4	406.5	14.3
2010	A	2.11	1.15	2,735.6	250.9	411.5	13.5
2009	A	2.41	1.31	2,338.8	240.5	244.7	9.2

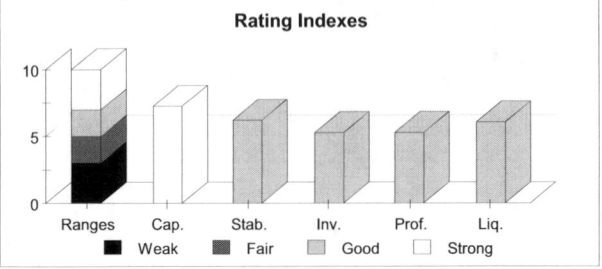

Rating Indexes

AUTOMOBILE CLUB OF SOUTHERN CALIFORNIA INSURANCE   B   Good

Major Rating Factors: Good current capitalization (6.4 on a scale of 0 to 10) based on good risk adjusted capital (severe loss scenario) reflecting some improvement over results in 2012. Good overall results on stability tests (5.7) despite excessive premium growth and fair risk adjusted capital in prior years. Strengths include potential support from affiliation with Interins Exch Automobile Club, excellent operational trends and excellent risk diversification. Fair quality investment portfolio (4.4).

Other Rating Factors: Fair liquidity (3.7). Weak profitability (2.9) with operating losses during the first nine months of 2014.

Principal Business: Reinsurance (100%).

Principal Investments: NonCMO investment grade bonds (71%), CMOs and structured securities (20%), noninv. grade bonds (9%), and policy loans (1%).

Investments in Affiliates: None

Group Affiliation: Interins Exch Automobile Club

Licensed in: CA, MI

Commenced Business: December 1999

Address: 3333 Fairview Road, Costa Mesa, CA 92625

Phone: (714) 850-5111 **Domicile State:** CA **NAIC Code:** 60256

Data Date	Rating	RACR #1	RACR #2	Total Assets ($mil)	Capital ($mil)	Net Premium ($mil)	Net Income ($mil)
9-14	B	1.67	0.93	810.5	67.1	140.5	-8.1
9-13	B	1.44	0.79	732.2	51.0	102.1	-11.3
2013	B	1.39	0.78	746.9	53.7	140.6	-15.2
2012	B	1.31	0.71	683.9	46.9	119.3	-12.0
2011	B	1.63	0.90	639.8	52.3	112.9	-3.3
2010	B	1.75	0.98	584.8	50.6	115.4	-9.0
2009	B	1.70	0.97	501.2	48.2	145.6	-3.1

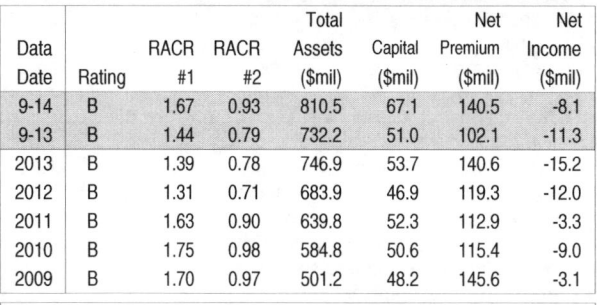

Risk-Adjusted Capital Ratio #2 (Severe Loss Scenario)

AVIVA LIFE & ANNUITY COMPANY OF NEW YORK   C   Fair

Major Rating Factors: Fair overall capitalization (4.0 on a scale of 0 to 10) based on mixed results -- excessive policy leverage mitigated by good risk adjusted capital (moderate loss scenario). Nevertheless, capital levels have fluctuated during prior years. Fair quality investment portfolio (3.8). Fair overall results on stability tests (3.5) including negative cash flow from operations for 2013.

Other Rating Factors: Good liquidity (6.7). Weak profitability (1.3).

Principal Business: Individual life insurance (93%), group life insurance (4%), reinsurance (1%), and individual health insurance (1%).

Principal Investments: NonCMO investment grade bonds (85%), mortgages in good standing (8%), policy loans (2%), CMOs and structured securities (2%), and misc. investments (2%).

Investments in Affiliates: None

Group Affiliation: BRH Holdings GP Ltd

Licensed in: CT, FL, IL, IN, IA, KS, KY, MA, MI, MS, NV, NJ, NY, NC, PA, RI, VT

Commenced Business: November 1958

Address: 324 S Service Rd Suite 200, Melville, NY 11747

Phone: (516) 364-5900 **Domicile State:** NY **NAIC Code:** 63932

Data Date	Rating	RACR #1	RACR #2	Total Assets ($mil)	Capital ($mil)	Net Premium ($mil)	Net Income ($mil)
9-14	C	1.94	0.91	1,744.3	74.8	1.6	6.5
9-13	C	1.83	0.95	1,788.4	99.5	36.7	-51.6
2013	C	1.76	0.83	1,727.8	64.0	-661.7	-114.9
2012	C	1.46	0.76	1,679.7	76.1	52.1	-85.4
2011	C+	2.09	1.09	1,588.5	116.9	28.8	22.5
2010	C	2.10	1.08	1,542.4	108.1	58.3	15.5
2009	C	1.94	1.00	1,474.8	98.2	93.6	-18.8

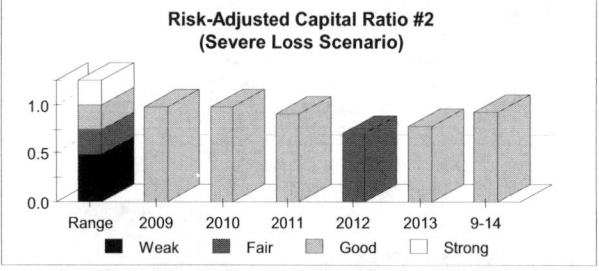

Policy Leverage

AXA CORPORATE SOLUTIONS LIFE REINSURANCE COMPANY   B-   Good

Major Rating Factors: Good overall profitability (6.4 on a scale of 0 to 10). Excellent expense controls. Despite its volitility, return on equity has been excellent over the last five years averaging 28.0%. Fair quality investment portfolio (4.9). Fair overall results on stability tests (3.8) including negative cash flow from operations for 2013.

Other Rating Factors: Strong capitalization (10.0) based on excellent risk adjusted capital (severe loss scenario). Excellent liquidity (9.8).

Principal Business: Reinsurance (100%).

Principal Investments: NonCMO investment grade bonds (96%), noninv. grade bonds (2%), CMOs and structured securities (1%), and cash (1%).

Investments in Affiliates: None

Group Affiliation: AXA Financial Inc

Licensed in: All states except FL, PR

Commenced Business: January 1983

Address: 1209 Orange St, Wilmington, DE 19801

Phone: (201) 743-7217 **Domicile State:** DE **NAIC Code:** 68365

Data Date	Rating	RACR #1	RACR #2	Total Assets ($mil)	Capital ($mil)	Net Premium ($mil)	Net Income ($mil)
9-14	B-	7.21	4.38	491.4	425.6	-534.4	91.7
9-13	B-	6.67	4.57	1,029.1	242.0	38.3	37.3
2013	B-	8.09	5.47	978.0	253.9	52.4	57.8
2012	B-	5.51	3.76	1,174.3	199.1	48.9	-43.3
2011	B-	6.94	4.51	1,387.0	279.8	72.3	-2.1
2010	B-	6.90	4.48	1,276.5	265.2	83.8	-137.9
2009	B	11.63	8.14	1,433.4	401.4	88.3	-8.3

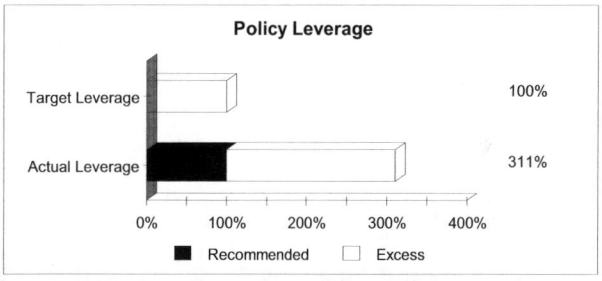

Net Income History (in millions of dollars)

AXA EQUITABLE LIFE & ANNUITY COMPANY   B-   Good

Major Rating Factors: Good capitalization (5.2 on a scale of 0 to 10) based on good risk adjusted capital (moderate loss scenario). Fair profitability (3.2) with investment income below regulatory standards in relation to interest assumptions of reserves. Fair liquidity (4.8) as cash from operations and sale of marketable assets may not be adequate to cover a spike in claims or a run on policy withdrawals.
Other Rating Factors: Fair overall results on stability tests (4.3) including fair risk adjusted capital in prior years. High quality investment portfolio (7.6).
Principal Business: Individual life insurance (100%).
Principal Investments: Policy loans (60%), nonCMO investment grade bonds (37%), and CMOs and structured securities (3%).
Investments in Affiliates: None
Group Affiliation: AXA Financial Inc
Licensed in: All states except NY, PR
Commenced Business: June 1984
Address: 135 W 50th St Location 6F, New York, NY 10020
Phone: (212) 641-8231 **Domicile State:** CO **NAIC Code:** 62880

Data Date	Rating	RACR #1	RACR #2	Total Assets ($mil)	Capital ($mil)	Net Premium ($mil)	Net Income ($mil)
9-14	B-	1.14	0.59	472.1	27.7	2.4	0.4
9-13	B	1.30	0.67	478.2	29.6	3.7	4.7
2013	B-	1.21	0.62	464.9	27.5	5.2	2.6
2012	B	2.91	1.51	526.4	64.8	3.2	3.0
2011	B	2.71	1.40	521.7	62.6	3.5	0.3
2010	B-	2.72	1.41	520.6	61.9	5.4	7.6
2009	B-	2.44	1.26	517.7	55.5	4.6	5.4

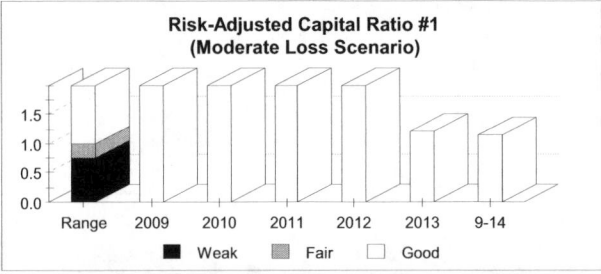

Risk-Adjusted Capital Ratio #1 (Moderate Loss Scenario)

AXA EQUITABLE LIFE INSURANCE COMPANY   B   Good

Major Rating Factors: Good quality investment portfolio (6.6 on a scale of 0 to 10) despite significant exposure to mortgages . Mortgage default rate has been low. large holdings of BBB rated bonds in addition to small junk bond holdings. Good overall profitability (6.2). Return on equity has been excellent over the last five years averaging 30.2%. Good liquidity (6.5).
Other Rating Factors: Good overall results on stability tests (6.2) despite fair risk adjusted capital in prior years excellent operational trends and excellent risk diversification. Strong capitalization (7.4) based on excellent risk adjusted capital (severe loss scenario).
Principal Business: Individual annuities (57%), group retirement contracts (21%), individual life insurance (20%), reinsurance (2%), and individual health insurance (1%).
Principal Investments: NonCMO investment grade bonds (61%), mortgages in good standing (14%), policy loans (8%), CMOs and structured securities (5%), and misc. investments (10%).
Investments in Affiliates: 6%
Group Affiliation: AXA Financial Inc
Licensed in: All states, the District of Columbia and Puerto Rico
Commenced Business: July 1859
Address: 787 Seventh Ave, New York, NY 10019
Phone: (212) 641-8231 **Domicile State:** NY **NAIC Code:** 62944

Data Date	Rating	RACR #1	RACR #2	Total Assets ($mil)	Capital ($mil)	Net Premium ($mil)	Net Income ($mil)
9-14	B	2.11	1.27	161,705	5,428.7	9,035.9	2,060.0
9-13	B	1.55	0.92	154,772	3,929.8	8,747.4	-628.5
2013	B	1.49	0.90	158,658	3,825.5	11,934.6	-28.5
2012	B	1.77	1.05	144,827	4,689.4	11,487.5	602.4
2011	C+	1.98	1.10	134,496	4,624.8	10,354.6	967.1
2010	C	1.29	0.81	135,726	3,801.3	9,678.7	-510.4
2009	C-	1.05	0.68	126,784	3,115.9	10,215.6	1,782.9

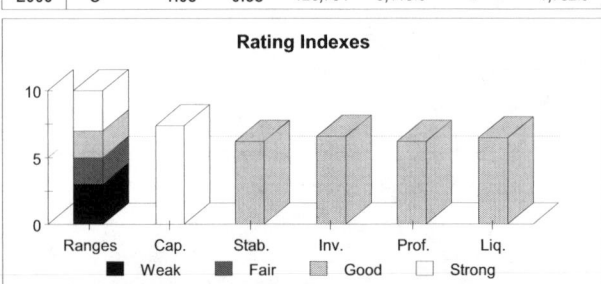

Rating Indexes

BALBOA LIFE INSURANCE COMPANY *   A-   Excellent

Major Rating Factors: Good overall results on stability tests (5.5 on a scale of 0 to 10). Strengths that enhance stability include good operational trends and excellent risk diversification. Strong capitalization (8.9) based on excellent risk adjusted capital (severe loss scenario). Moreover, capital levels have been consistently high over the last five years. High quality investment portfolio (7.9).
Other Rating Factors: Excellent profitability (8.2) with operating gains in each of the last five years. Excellent liquidity (9.6).
Principal Business: Group health insurance (81%), individual life insurance (17%), and group life insurance (1%).
Principal Investments: NonCMO investment grade bonds (43%), common & preferred stock (33%), cash (16%), and CMOs and structured securities (8%).
Investments in Affiliates: 33%
Group Affiliation: Securian Financial Group
Licensed in: All states except PR
Commenced Business: January 1969
Address: 400 Robert Street North, St Paul, MN 55101-2098
Phone: (651) 665-3500 **Domicile State:** CA **NAIC Code:** 68160

Data Date	Rating	RACR #1	RACR #2	Total Assets ($mil)	Capital ($mil)	Net Premium ($mil)	Net Income ($mil)
9-14	A-	2.39	2.28	58.9	49.6	4.7	1.7
9-13	A-	2.23	2.10	57.6	47.0	5.6	2.4
2013	A-	2.31	2.21	57.7	47.8	7.3	3.4
2012	A-	2.06	1.95	56.8	44.1	11.7	4.2
2011	B+	1.83	1.73	53.0	39.9	14.5	3.5
2010	B+	1.74	1.64	47.7	36.7	13.1	1.3
2009	B+	1.67	1.57	48.1	37.1	14.8	5.6

Adverse Trends in Operations

Decrease in premium volume from 2012 to 2013 (38%)
Decrease in premium volume from 2011 to 2012 (19%)
Decrease in premium volume from 2009 to 2010 (12%)
Change in premium mix from 2009 to 2010 (6.4%)

BALTIMORE LIFE INSURANCE COMPANY — B — Good

Major Rating Factors: Good quality investment portfolio (5.4 on a scale of 0 to 10) despite mixed results such as: large holdings of BBB rated bonds but moderate junk bond exposure. Good overall results on stability tests (5.6). Stability strengths include excellent operational trends and good risk diversification. Fair profitability (4.7).

Other Rating Factors: Fair liquidity (3.6). Strong capitalization (7.1) based on excellent risk adjusted capital (severe loss scenario).

Principal Business: Individual life insurance (79%), group life insurance (10%), individual annuities (7%), reinsurance (3%), and group health insurance (1%).

Principal Investments: NonCMO investment grade bonds (79%), mortgages in good standing (5%), policy loans (4%), CMOs and structured securities (4%), and misc. investments (8%).

Investments in Affiliates: 1%

Group Affiliation: Baltimore Life Holdings Inc

Licensed in: All states except NY, PR

Commenced Business: March 1882

Address: 10075 Red Run Blvd, Owings Mills, MD 21117-6050

Phone: (410) 581-6600 **Domicile State:** MD **NAIC Code:** 61212

Data Date	Rating	RACR #1	RACR #2	Total Assets ($mil)	Capital ($mil)	Net Premium ($mil)	Net Income ($mil)
9-14	B	2.05	1.07	1,129.9	76.2	100.9	3.7
9-13	B	2.06	1.07	1,063.6	68.5	110.7	-0.3
2013	B	2.02	1.06	1,085.7	72.8	147.8	-2.6
2012	B	2.11	1.10	1,004.6	70.4	125.1	6.5
2011	B	1.93	1.02	944.3	65.4	106.2	4.8
2010	B	2.05	1.07	917.9	71.7	105.8	7.8
2009	B	2.39	1.22	856.8	80.3	113.2	1.3

Adverse Trends in Operations

Decrease in capital during 2011 (9%)
Decrease in premium volume from 2009 to 2010 (7%)
Decrease in capital during 2010 (11%)

BANKERS CONSECO LIFE INSURANCE COMPANY — D — Weak

Major Rating Factors: Weak overall results on stability tests (1.8 on a scale of 0 to 10). Good quality investment portfolio (6.5) despite mixed results such as: no exposure to mortgages and large holdings of BBB rated bonds but small junk bond holdings. Good overall profitability (6.2). Excellent expense controls. Return on equity has been fair, averaging 6.5%.

Other Rating Factors: Good liquidity (6.4). Strong capitalization (10.0) based on excellent risk adjusted capital (severe loss scenario).

Principal Business: Individual life insurance (59%), individual health insurance (28%), individual annuities (11%), and reinsurance (2%).

Principal Investments: NonCMO investment grade bonds (88%), CMOs and structured securities (6%), cash (3%), noninv. grade bonds (2%), and policy loans (1%).

Investments in Affiliates: None

Group Affiliation: CNO Financial Group Inc

Licensed in: NY

Commenced Business: July 1987

Address: 11815 N Pennsylvania St, Carmel, IN 46032

Phone: (215) 244-1600 **Domicile State:** NY **NAIC Code:** 68560

Data Date	Rating	RACR #1	RACR #2	Total Assets ($mil)	Capital ($mil)	Net Premium ($mil)	Net Income ($mil)
9-14	D	4.60	3.65	203.3	51.9	35.2	4.2
9-13	D	2.85	1.61	364.0	30.0	38.6	2.1
2013	D	4.11	2.30	383.2	45.5	49.2	21.7
2012	D	2.16	1.29	343.6	22.6	48.7	-2.0
2011	D	2.49	1.59	323.4	26.0	44.8	0.0
2010	D	2.54	1.76	301.2	26.4	37.5	2.2
2009	D	2.36	1.80	277.1	25.0	34.8	-4.1

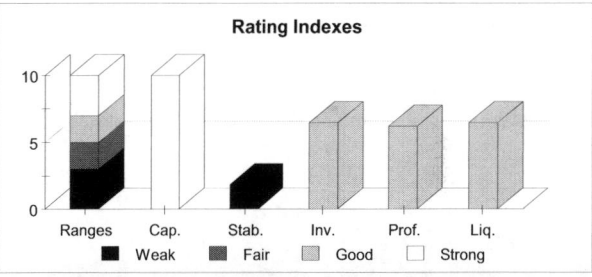

Rating Indexes

BANKERS FIDELITY LIFE INSURANCE COMPANY — B — Good

Major Rating Factors: Good quality investment portfolio (5.7 on a scale of 0 to 10) despite mixed results such as: large holdings of BBB rated bonds but moderate junk bond exposure. Good liquidity (5.6) with sufficient resources to handle a spike in claims as well as a significant increase in policy surrenders. Good overall results on stability tests (5.7) excellent operational trends and good risk diversification.

Other Rating Factors: Strong capitalization (7.0) based on excellent risk adjusted capital (severe loss scenario). Excellent profitability (8.8) with operating gains in each of the last five years.

Principal Business: Individual health insurance (89%) and individual life insurance (11%).

Principal Investments: NonCMO investment grade bonds (78%), common & preferred stock (8%), noninv. grade bonds (8%), policy loans (2%), and misc. investments (3%).

Investments in Affiliates: 3%

Group Affiliation: Atlantic American Corp

Licensed in: All states except CA, CT, NY, VT, PR

Commenced Business: November 1955

Address: 4370 Peachtree Rd NE, Atlanta, GA 30319

Phone: (404) 266-5500 **Domicile State:** GA **NAIC Code:** 61239

Data Date	Rating	RACR #1	RACR #2	Total Assets ($mil)	Capital ($mil)	Net Premium ($mil)	Net Income ($mil)
9-14	B	1.42	1.00	138.7	33.9	76.4	2.1
9-13	B	1.89	1.31	136.1	34.7	75.1	2.0
2013	B	1.58	1.14	138.8	34.5	99.6	3.0
2012	B	2.03	1.48	128.7	33.1	89.6	2.3
2011	B	2.32	1.67	122.1	32.1	70.7	3.6
2010	B	2.44	1.75	117.9	31.9	62.8	3.0
2009	B	2.73	2.01	116.0	31.5	57.2	2.5

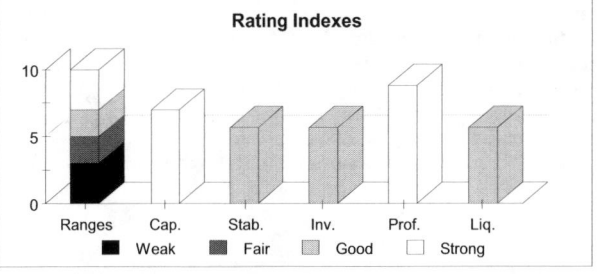

Rating Indexes

BANKERS LIFE & CASUALTY COMPANY — D+ — Weak

Major Rating Factors: Weak overall results on stability tests (2.7 on a scale of 0 to 10). Fair quality investment portfolio (4.1) with large holdings of BBB rated bonds in addition to junk bond exposure equal to 82% of capital. Good liquidity (5.4) with sufficient resources to cover a large increase in policy surrenders.

Other Rating Factors: Strong capitalization (7.1) based on excellent risk adjusted capital (severe loss scenario). Excellent profitability (9.2) with operating gains in each of the last five years.

Principal Business: Individual health insurance (41%), individual annuities (30%), individual life insurance (18%), reinsurance (9%), and group health insurance (2%).

Principal Investments: NonCMO investment grade bonds (64%), CMOs and structured securities (21%), noninv. grade bonds (6%), mortgages in good standing (5%), and misc. investments (3%).

Investments in Affiliates: 1%

Group Affiliation: CNO Financial Group Inc

Licensed in: All states except NY, PR

Commenced Business: January 1879

Address: 222 Merchandise Mart Plaza, Chicago, IL 60654

Phone: (312) 396-6000 **Domicile State:** IL **NAIC Code:** 61263

Data Date	Rating	RACR #1	RACR #2	Total Assets ($mil)	Capital ($mil)	Net Premium ($mil)	Net Income ($mil)
9-14	D+	2.04	1.05	16,389.4	1,116.4	1,772.9	151.9
9-13	D+	1.92	1.00	15,625.4	1,011.3	1,722.1	181.3
2013	D+	2.04	1.06	15,839.5	1,057.0	2,323.5	161.9
2012	D+	1.83	0.96	14,941.3	914.6	2,282.5	231.3
2011	D+	1.60	0.86	14,515.9	816.8	2,518.6	212.0
2010	D+	1.55	0.82	13,753.7	774.7	2,329.0	166.4
2009	D+	1.41	0.80	12,318.8	730.2	2,601.5	86.7

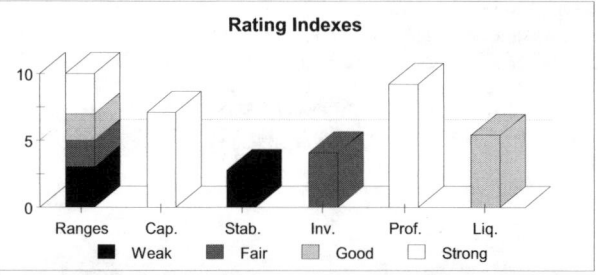

Rating Indexes

Weak · Fair · Good · Strong (Ranges, Cap., Stab., Inv., Prof., Liq.)

BANNER LIFE INSURANCE COMPANY — D — Weak

Major Rating Factors: Weak profitability (1.9 on a scale of 0 to 10) with operating losses during the first nine months of 2014. Return on equity has been low, averaging 2.0%. Weak overall results on stability tests (1.4). Good current capitalization (6.0) based on good risk adjusted capital (severe loss scenario), although results have slipped from the excellent range during the last year.

Other Rating Factors: Good quality investment portfolio (5.9). Good liquidity (6.8).

Principal Business: Individual life insurance (100%).

Principal Investments: NonCMO investment grade bonds (66%), common & preferred stock (14%), CMOs and structured securities (12%), noninv. grade bonds (6%), and misc. investments (1%).

Investments in Affiliates: 14%

Group Affiliation: Legal & General America Inc

Licensed in: All states except NY, PR

Commenced Business: October 1981

Address: 3275 Bennett Creek Ave, Frederick, MD 21704

Phone: (301) 279-4800 **Domicile State:** MD **NAIC Code:** 94250

Data Date	Rating	RACR #1	RACR #2	Total Assets ($mil)	Capital ($mil)	Net Premium ($mil)	Net Income ($mil)
9-14	D	1.15	0.87	1,721.0	297.9	164.9	-99.3
9-13	D	0.54	0.45	1,584.3	160.3	121.3	-98.4
2013	D	1.84	1.44	1,687.7	450.0	324.1	-44.0
2012	C	1.38	1.19	1,703.8	459.0	96.0	-17.9
2011	D	1.13	0.92	1,524.0	252.7	119.5	55.8
2010	D+	1.18	1.08	1,918.5	675.5	81.4	26.7
2009	D+	1.82	1.42	1,414.1	311.3	206.2	101.3

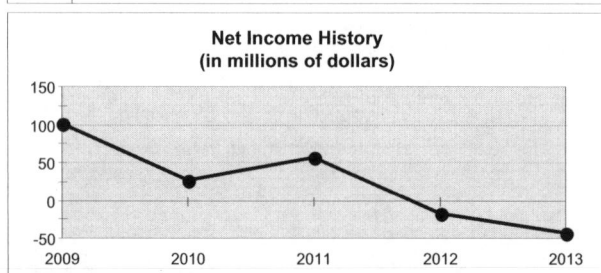

Net Income History
(in millions of dollars)

BENEFICIAL LIFE INSURANCE COMPANY — B — Good

Major Rating Factors: Good liquidity (6.0 on a scale of 0 to 10) with sufficient resources to cover a large increase in policy surrenders. Good overall results on stability tests (5.5) despite negative cash flow from operations for 2013. Other stability subfactors include good operational trends and excellent risk diversification. Fair profitability (4.7) with investment income below regulatory standards in relation to interest assumptions of reserves.

Other Rating Factors: Strong capitalization (9.9) based on excellent risk adjusted capital (severe loss scenario). High quality investment portfolio (7.1).

Principal Business: Individual life insurance (91%), individual annuities (7%), and reinsurance (3%).

Principal Investments: NonCMO investment grade bonds (63%), CMOs and structured securities (30%), policy loans (3%), noninv. grade bonds (2%), and cash (1%).

Investments in Affiliates: None

Group Affiliation: DMC Reserve Trust

Licensed in: All states except NY, PR

Commenced Business: May 1905

Address: 36 South State St, Salt Lake City, UT 84136

Phone: (801) 933-1100 **Domicile State:** UT **NAIC Code:** 61395

Data Date	Rating	RACR #1	RACR #2	Total Assets ($mil)	Capital ($mil)	Net Premium ($mil)	Net Income ($mil)
9-14	B	5.49	2.96	2,942.3	608.2	28.9	50.5
9-13	B	5.16	2.74	3,060.9	574.3	33.3	32.9
2013	B	6.14	3.22	3,011.2	579.1	43.0	44.9
2012	B-	5.42	2.85	3,090.3	546.0	47.7	15.1
2011	C+	4.37	2.23	3,185.1	511.2	50.4	-0.6
2010	C+	3.88	1.91	3,325.3	507.7	62.0	17.6
2009	C+	3.25	1.57	3,446.4	478.1	302.6	10.5

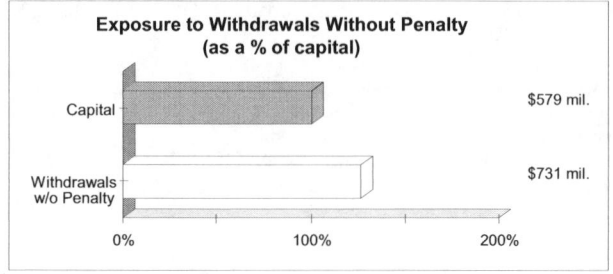

Exposure to Withdrawals Without Penalty
(as a % of capital)

Capital — $579 mil.

Withdrawals w/o Penalty — $731 mil.

BERKLEY LIFE & HEALTH INSURANCE COMPANY   B-   Good

Major Rating Factors: Good overall results on stability tests (5.2 on a scale of 0 to 10) despite fair financial strength of affiliated W R Berkley Corp and excessive premium growth. Other stability subfactors include excellent operational trends and excellent risk diversification. Strong capitalization (10.0) based on excellent risk adjusted capital (severe loss scenario). Moreover, capital levels have been consistently high over the last five years. High quality investment portfolio (8.6).

Other Rating Factors: Excellent profitability (8.3) despite modest operating losses during 2011. Excellent liquidity (7.5).

Principal Business: Group health insurance (100%).

Principal Investments: NonCMO investment grade bonds (67%), CMOs and structured securities (25%), and cash (8%).

Investments in Affiliates: None

Group Affiliation: W R Berkley Corp

Licensed in: All states except PR

Commenced Business: July 1963

Address: 200 Clarendon St, Boston, MA 02117

Phone: (203) 851-1755 **Domicile State:** IA **NAIC Code:** 64890

Data Date	Rating	RACR #1	RACR #2	Total Assets ($mil)	Capital ($mil)	Net Premium ($mil)	Net Income ($mil)
9-14	B-	5.75	4.45	198.6	105.0	112.5	10.9
9-13	B	6.13	4.71	157.4	92.3	84.5	9.1
2013	B-	6.16	4.73	166.3	94.2	117.1	11.3
2012	B	5.25	4.11	148.7	83.3	123.9	7.7
2011	B	4.59	3.60	112.0	59.5	101.1	-0.6
2010	B	5.64	5.08	31.5	26.4	4.8	0.3
2009	B	6.28	5.65	26.6	26.2	0.0	0.6

W R Berkley Corp
Composite Group Rating: C

Largest Group Members	Assets ($mil)	Rating
BERKLEY INS CO	16123	C
BERKLEY REGIONAL INS CO	681	C+
ADMIRAL INS CO	667	C-
NAUTILUS INS CO	246	C-
STARNET INS CO	203	C

BERKSHIRE HATHAWAY LIFE INSURANCE COMPANY OF NEBR   C+   Fair

Major Rating Factors: Fair overall results on stability tests (3.3 on a scale of 0 to 10) including weak risk adjusted capital in prior years. Good quality investment portfolio (6.1) with no exposure to mortgages and minimal holdings in junk bonds. Good overall profitability (6.4). Excellent expense controls. Return on equity has been low, averaging -8.6%.

Other Rating Factors: Strong capitalization (7.3) based on excellent risk adjusted capital (severe loss scenario). Excellent liquidity (10.0).

Principal Business: Reinsurance (79%), group retirement contracts (18%), and individual annuities (3%).

Principal Investments: NonCMO investment grade bonds (43%), common & preferred stock (23%), cash (22%), CMOs and structured securities (6%), and noninv. grade bonds (3%).

Investments in Affiliates: 26%

Group Affiliation: Berkshire-Hathaway

Licensed in: All states except PR

Commenced Business: June 1993

Address: 3024 Harney St, Omaha, NE 68131

Phone: (402) 536-3000 **Domicile State:** NE **NAIC Code:** 62345

Data Date	Rating	RACR #1	RACR #2	Total Assets ($mil)	Capital ($mil)	Net Premium ($mil)	Net Income ($mil)
9-14	C+	1.46	1.23	13,999.8	3,152.9	896.8	400.3
9-13	C+	1.26	1.11	13,582.7	3,120.9	3,263.3	846.0
2013	C+	1.35	1.19	13,768.3	2,701.4	4,073.2	1,527.4
2012	C+	0.95	0.85	10,938.2	2,238.4	3,452.0	-350.4
2011	C+	0.78	0.68	8,809.5	1,824.2	2,013.2	345.8
2010	C+	0.68	0.60	8,413.3	1,553.3	2,435.7	-463.2
2009	C+	0.42	0.39	7,625.0	1,032.6	2,338.9	-878.6

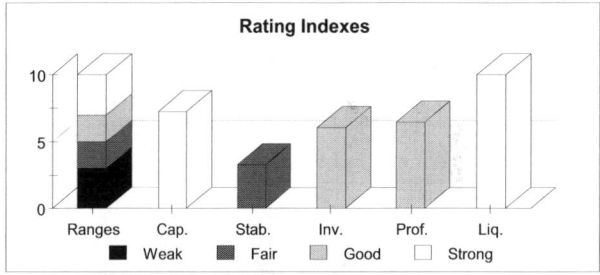

Rating Indexes

BERKSHIRE LIFE INSURANCE COMPANY OF AMERICA *   A   Excellent

Major Rating Factors: Good overall results on stability tests (6.4 on a scale of 0 to 10). Strengths that enhance stability include good operational trends and excellent risk diversification. Good quality investment portfolio (6.5) despite mixed results such as: minimal exposure to mortgages and large holdings of BBB rated bonds but small junk bond holdings. Strong capitalization (10.0) based on excellent risk adjusted capital (severe loss scenario).

Other Rating Factors: Excellent profitability (8.4) with operating gains in each of the last five years. Excellent liquidity (8.9).

Principal Business: Individual health insurance (66%), reinsurance (32%), and individual life insurance (2%).

Principal Investments: NonCMO investment grade bonds (89%), mortgages in good standing (7%), noninv. grade bonds (3%), and CMOs and structured securities (1%).

Investments in Affiliates: None

Group Affiliation: Guardian Group

Licensed in: All states except PR

Commenced Business: July 2001

Address: 700 South St, Pittsfield, MA 01201

Phone: (413) 499-4321 **Domicile State:** MA **NAIC Code:** 71714

Data Date	Rating	RACR #1	RACR #2	Total Assets ($mil)	Capital ($mil)	Net Premium ($mil)	Net Income ($mil)
9-14	A	8.67	4.24	3,640.3	604.5	85.4	21.3
9-13	A	7.83	3.89	3,417.5	583.4	89.1	55.2
2013	A	8.68	4.24	3,461.4	583.0	115.9	60.0
2012	A	5.30	3.03	3,209.2	543.4	493.9	43.9
2011	A	5.44	3.14	3,034.7	530.9	477.9	29.3
2010	A	5.33	3.11	2,814.7	493.8	458.1	50.7
2009	A	5.02	2.91	2,626.9	452.3	445.6	34.0

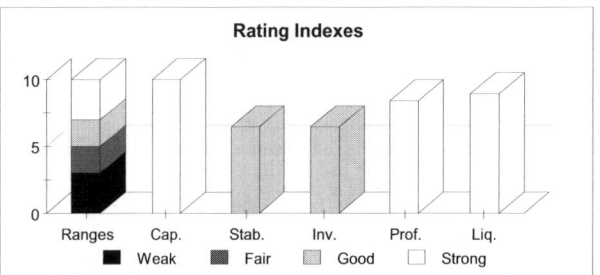

Rating Indexes

BEST MERIDIAN INSURANCE COMPANY

B- **Good**

Major Rating Factors: Good quality investment portfolio (6.5 on a scale of 0 to 10) despite significant exposure to mortgages . Mortgage default rate has been low. minimal holdings in junk bonds. Good overall profitability (5.3) although investment income, in comparison to reserve requirements, is below regulatory standards. Good overall results on stability tests (5.3) despite excessive premium growth good operational trends, good risk adjusted capital for prior years and good risk diversification.

Other Rating Factors: Strong capitalization (7.3) based on excellent risk adjusted capital (severe loss scenario). Excellent liquidity (7.2).

Principal Business: Individual health insurance (46%), individual life insurance (27%), reinsurance (25%), and group health insurance (1%).

Principal Investments: NonCMO investment grade bonds (39%), CMOs and structured securities (19%), cash (15%), mortgages in good standing (13%), and misc. investments (12%).

Investments in Affiliates: None
Group Affiliation: BMI Financial Group
Licensed in: FL
Commenced Business: August 1987
Address: 1320 S.Dixie Hwy, 6th Floor, Coral Gables, FL 33146
Phone: (305) 443-2898 **Domicile State:** FL **NAIC Code:** 63886

Data Date	Rating	RACR #1	RACR #2	Total Assets ($mil)	Capital ($mil)	Net Premium ($mil)	Net Income ($mil)
9-14	B-	1.87	1.21	272.0	53.3	101.7	5.7
9-13	B-	1.60	1.11	250.8	49.6	76.3	5.4
2013	B-	2.02	1.33	254.5	47.9	100.8	7.0
2012	B-	1.08	0.78	239.2	45.9	202.5	7.8
2011	B	2.00	1.25	216.8	41.3	69.5	3.6
2010	B	2.30	1.37	200.1	39.0	63.9	6.4
2009	B	2.16	1.36	181.8	32.9	60.7	5.8

Adverse Trends in Operations

Increase in policy surrenders from 2012 to 2013 (67%)
Decrease in premium volume from 2012 to 2013 (50%)
Change in asset mix during 2012 (4%)
Change in premium mix from 2011 to 2012 (5%)

BLUE CROSS BLUE SHIELD OF KANSAS INCORPORATED

B **Good**

Major Rating Factors: Good liquidity (6.6 on a scale of 0 to 10) with sufficient resources to handle a spike in claims. Good overall results on stability tests (6.3). Stability strengths include excellent operational trends and excellent risk diversification. Fair quality investment portfolio (4.0).

Other Rating Factors: Strong capitalization (7.8) based on excellent risk adjusted capital (severe loss scenario). Excellent profitability (7.0).

Principal Business: Group health insurance (76%) and individual health insurance (24%).

Principal Investments: NonCMO investment grade bonds (43%), common & preferred stock (35%), CMOs and structured securities (16%), real estate (2%), and misc. investments (1%).

Investments in Affiliates: 3%
Group Affiliation: Blue Cross Blue Shield Kansas
Licensed in: KS
Commenced Business: July 1942
Address: 1133 SW Topeka Blvd, Topeka, KS 66629-0001
Phone: (785) 291-7000 **Domicile State:** KS **NAIC Code:** 70729

Data Date	Rating	RACR #1	RACR #2	Total Assets ($mil)	Capital ($mil)	Net Premium ($mil)	Net Income ($mil)
9-14	B	2.13	1.53	1,592.7	777.0	1,352.1	2.7
9-13	B	2.30	1.65	1,533.3	787.7	1,262.4	53.7
2013	B	2.26	1.62	1,541.9	800.8	1,689.2	78.6
2012	B	2.23	1.62	1,433.2	762.3	1,680.3	55.9
2011	B	2.09	1.55	1,285.8	666.9	1,683.1	77.5
2010	B	2.09	1.56	1,203.4	657.1	1,712.3	72.0
2009	B	2.12	1.63	1,073.1	589.9	1,620.4	19.9

Adverse Trends in Operations

Decrease in premium volume from 2010 to 2011 (2%)

BLUE SHIELD OF CALIFORNIA LIFE & HEALTH INS COMPANY *

A- **Excellent**

Major Rating Factors: Good current capitalization (5.1 on a scale of 0 to 10) based on excellent risk adjusted capital (severe loss scenario) reflecting improvement over results in 2012. Good overall profitability (5.6). Excellent expense controls. Return on equity has been low, averaging -4.6%. Good overall results on stability tests (5.5) despite negative cash flow from operations for 2013 good operational trends and excellent risk diversification.

Other Rating Factors: Weak liquidity (1.1). High quality investment portfolio (8.0).

Principal Business: Group health insurance (75%) and individual health insurance (25%).

Principal Investments: CMOs and structured securities (53%) and nonCMO investment grade bonds (47%).

Investments in Affiliates: None
Group Affiliation: Blue Shield of California
Licensed in: CA
Commenced Business: July 1954
Address: 50 Beale St, San Francisco, CA 94105
Phone: (800) 642-5599 **Domicile State:** CA **NAIC Code:** 61557

Data Date	Rating	RACR #1	RACR #2	Total Assets ($mil)	Capital ($mil)	Net Premium ($mil)	Net Income ($mil)
9-14	A-	1.74	1.38	841.2	441.4	1,407.2	76.2
9-13	A-	1.43	1.13	914.1	408.5	1,784.3	80.8
2013	A-	1.22	0.97	890.7	367.1	2,381.3	12.3
2012	A-	1.20	0.95	802.7	297.3	1,937.3	-19.1
2011	A-	1.31	1.03	637.2	229.9	1,370.8	-41.4
2010	A-	1.58	1.25	578.8	275.5	1,348.0	6.7
2009	A-	1.57	1.25	521.0	247.9	1,214.2	-63.2

Risk-Adjusted Capital Ratio #2
(Severe Loss Scenario)

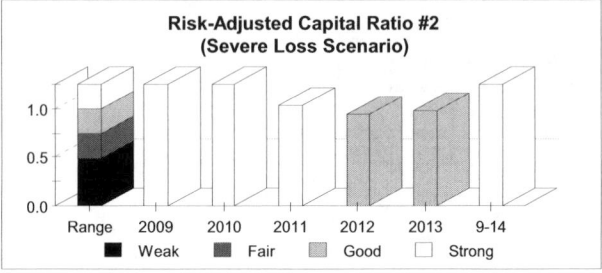

■ Weak	■ Fair	▨ Good	□ Strong

BLUEBONNET LIFE INSURANCE COMPANY *   B+   Good

Major Rating Factors: Good overall results on stability tests (6.5 on a scale of 0 to 10). Stability strengths include excellent operational trends and good risk diversification. Strong capitalization (10.0) based on excellent risk adjusted capital (severe loss scenario). Moreover, capital levels have been consistently high over the last five years. High quality investment portfolio (8.1).

Other Rating Factors: Excellent profitability (9.3) with operating gains in each of the last five years. Excellent liquidity (9.7).

Principal Business: Group life insurance (96%), individual life insurance (3%), reinsurance (1%), and group health insurance (1%).

Principal Investments: NonCMO investment grade bonds (51%), CMOs and structured securities (33%), and common & preferred stock (1%).

Investments in Affiliates: None

Group Affiliation: Bl Cross & Bl Shield of Mississippi

Licensed in: AL, AR, LA, MS, TN

Commenced Business: June 1984

Address: 3475 Lakeland Drive, Jackson, MS 39208

Phone: (601) 932-8269 **Domicile State:** MS **NAIC Code:** 68535

Data Date	Rating	RACR #1	RACR #2	Total Assets ($mil)	Capital ($mil)	Net Premium ($mil)	Net Income ($mil)
9-14	B+	7.24	6.52	54.6	49.4	3.8	1.7
9-13	B+	7.08	6.37	52.3	47.0	4.1	2.0
2013	B+	6.99	6.29	52.0	47.7	5.5	2.4
2012	B+	6.84	6.16	49.2	45.4	5.6	2.6
2011	B+	6.73	6.06	46.5	42.8	5.9	2.9
2010	B+	6.60	5.94	43.6	40.0	6.3	3.0
2009	B+	6.42	5.78	40.8	36.9	6.9	3.1

Adverse Trends in Operations

Decrease in premium volume from 2012 to 2013 (2%)
Decrease in premium volume from 2011 to 2012 (5%)
Decrease in premium volume from 2010 to 2011 (7%)
Decrease in premium volume from 2009 to 2010 (9%)

BOSTON MUTUAL LIFE INSURANCE COMPANY *   B+   Good

Major Rating Factors: Good quality investment portfolio (6.8 on a scale of 0 to 10) despite significant exposure to mortgages . Mortgage default rate has been low. substantial holdings of BBB bonds in addition to minimal holdings in junk bonds. Good overall profitability (6.3). Good overall results on stability tests (6.4) excellent operational trends and excellent risk diversification.

Other Rating Factors: Fair liquidity (4.7). Strong capitalization (7.6) based on excellent risk adjusted capital (severe loss scenario).

Principal Business: Individual life insurance (60%), group health insurance (19%), group life insurance (15%), and individual health insurance (6%).

Principal Investments: NonCMO investment grade bonds (63%), mortgages in good standing (14%), policy loans (12%), CMOs and structured securities (5%), and misc. investments (6%).

Investments in Affiliates: 2%

Group Affiliation: Boston Mutual Group

Licensed in: All states, the District of Columbia and Puerto Rico

Commenced Business: February 1892

Address: 120 Royall St, Canton, MA 02021-1098

Phone: (781) 828-7000 **Domicile State:** MA **NAIC Code:** 61476

Data Date	Rating	RACR #1	RACR #2	Total Assets ($mil)	Capital ($mil)	Net Premium ($mil)	Net Income ($mil)
9-14	B+	2.16	1.41	1,230.4	155.6	139.8	8.8
9-13	B+	2.10	1.36	1,178.0	137.8	138.6	9.2
2013	B+	2.07	1.36	1,188.8	142.5	182.6	16.0
2012	B+	1.97	1.27	1,138.4	126.0	180.4	12.8
2011	B+	1.95	1.29	1,102.7	126.3	180.1	12.1
2010	B+	2.12	1.38	1,048.9	118.8	171.2	12.4
2009	B+	2.05	1.31	995.3	108.1	170.5	10.0

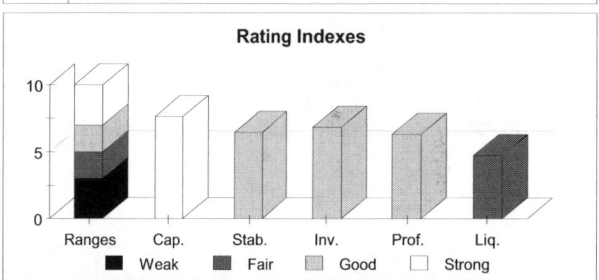

Rating Indexes

(Ranges, Cap., Stab., Inv., Prof., Liq.) — Weak, Fair, Good, Strong

BROOKE LIFE INSURANCE COMPANY   C+   Fair

Major Rating Factors: Fair overall results on stability tests (4.7 on a scale of 0 to 10) including fair risk adjusted capital in prior years. Low quality investment portfolio (1.2). Strong current capitalization (7.1) based on excellent risk adjusted capital (severe loss scenario) reflecting significant improvement over results in 2009.

Other Rating Factors: Excellent profitability (9.0) with operating gains in each of the last five years. Excellent liquidity (9.2).

Principal Business: Individual annuities (88%), group life insurance (7%), and reinsurance (5%).

Principal Investments: Common & preferred stock (91%), nonCMO investment grade bonds (7%), and CMOs and structured securities (2%).

Investments in Affiliates: 91%

Group Affiliation: Prudential plc

Licensed in: MI

Commenced Business: August 1987

Address: 5901 Executive Dr, Lansing, MI 48911

Phone: (517) 394-3400 **Domicile State:** MI **NAIC Code:** 78620

Data Date	Rating	RACR #1	RACR #2	Total Assets ($mil)	Capital ($mil)	Net Premium ($mil)	Net Income ($mil)
9-14	C+	1.19	1.06	4,937.1	4,543.9	7.2	556.2
9-13	C+	1.06	0.94	4,738.0	3,982.0	10.5	411.3
2013	C+	1.06	0.94	4,783.6	4,042.2	14.8	408.4
2012	C	0.95	0.84	4,718.2	3,576.4	16.1	300.6
2011	C	0.81	0.72	4,056.6	2,628.5	15.7	476.9
2010	C	0.81	0.72	4,763.8	3,087.3	16.5	220.2
2009	C	0.77	0.68	4,365.0	2,674.2	21.2	180.7

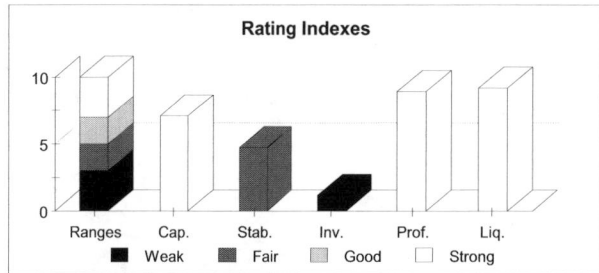

Rating Indexes

(Ranges, Cap., Stab., Inv., Prof., Liq.) — Weak, Fair, Good, Strong

CANADA LIFE ASSURANCE COMPANY-US BRANCH   C   Fair

Major Rating Factors: Fair overall results on stability tests (4.0 on a scale of 0 to 10) including fair risk adjusted capital in prior years. Good capitalization (5.4) based on good risk adjusted capital (moderate loss scenario). Good quality investment portfolio (5.6) despite mixed results such as: minimal exposure to mortgages and large holdings of BBB rated bonds but small junk bond holdings.
Other Rating Factors: Good liquidity (5.5). Weak profitability (2.9) with investment income below regulatory standards in relation to interest assumptions of reserves.
Principal Business: Reinsurance (98%) and individual life insurance (2%).
Principal Investments: NonCMO investment grade bonds (62%), CMOs and structured securities (19%), policy loans (8%), mortgages in good standing (7%), and misc. investments (3%).
Investments in Affiliates: None
Group Affiliation: Great West Life Asr
Licensed in: All states except PR
Commenced Business: August 1847
Address: 330 University Ave, Toronto Ontario, CN M5G 1R8
Phone: (770) 953-1959 **Domicile State:** MI **NAIC Code:** 80659

Data Date	Rating	RACR #1	RACR #2	Total Assets ($mil)	Capital ($mil)	Net Premium ($mil)	Net Income ($mil)
9-14	C	1.25	0.66	4,444.2	151.4	97.7	13.5
9-13	C	1.37	0.72	4,532.9	164.8	116.3	33.0
2013	C	1.15	0.61	4,318.9	135.4	141.6	36.5
2012	C	1.36	0.71	4,766.7	165.2	52.3	-75.3
2011	B-	1.49	0.74	4,340.9	173.7	126.8	37.7
2010	B-	1.39	0.69	4,269.5	124.2	61.5	-19.6
2009	B-	1.66	0.79	4,197.8	187.4	70.8	53.0

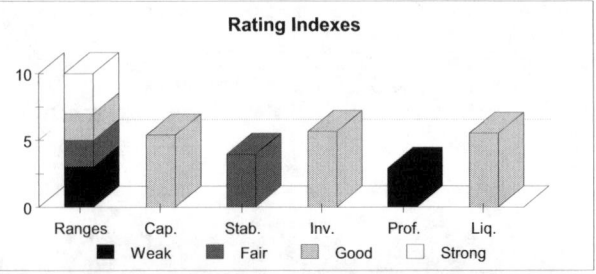

Rating Indexes

Ranges Cap. Stab. Inv. Prof. Liq.
■ Weak ■ Fair ▨ Good □ Strong

CAREAMERICA LIFE INSURANCE COMPANY   B   Good

Major Rating Factors: Good overall profitability (6.9 on a scale of 0 to 10). Excellent expense controls. Return on equity has been fair, averaging 8.4%. Fair overall results on stability tests (4.9). Strong overall capitalization (10.0) based on excellent risk adjusted capital (severe loss scenario). Nevertheless, capital levels have fluctuated during prior years.
Other Rating Factors: High quality investment portfolio (8.2). Excellent liquidity (9.6).
Principal Business: Group life insurance (88%), group health insurance (7%), individual life insurance (4%), and reinsurance (1%).
Principal Investments: CMOs and structured securities (59%), nonCMO investment grade bonds (37%), and cash (3%).
Investments in Affiliates: None
Group Affiliation: Blue Shield of California
Licensed in: AZ, CA, CT, LA, NV, NM, ND, OR
Commenced Business: August 1968
Address: 50 Beale St, San Francisco, CA 94105
Phone: (415) 229-5703 **Domicile State:** CA **NAIC Code:** 71331

Data Date	Rating	RACR #1	RACR #2	Total Assets ($mil)	Capital ($mil)	Net Premium ($mil)	Net Income ($mil)
9-14	B	6.44	5.80	29.3	25.7	1.2	4.3
9-13	B	5.41	4.87	25.1	22.3	1.6	0.7
2013	B	5.63	5.07	24.6	22.5	2.1	0.9
2012	B	5.72	5.15	25.7	23.5	2.6	1.6
2011	B	5.69	5.12	26.9	24.1	3.7	1.4
2010	B	5.76	5.18	27.8	25.0	3.1	1.5
2009	B	5.53	4.98	26.9	23.5	3.4	1.9

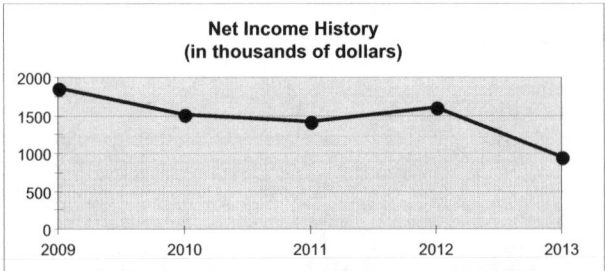

Net Income History
(in thousands of dollars)

2009   2010   2011   2012   2013

CELTIC INSURANCE COMPANY   C   Fair

Major Rating Factors: Fair overall results on stability tests (4.2 on a scale of 0 to 10) including fair financial strength of affiliated Centene Corp and negative cash flow from operations for 2013. Good current capitalization (6.4) based on good risk adjusted capital (severe loss scenario), although results have slipped from the excellent range during the last year. Good liquidity (6.4).
Other Rating Factors: Weak profitability (2.0). High quality investment portfolio (8.3).
Principal Business: Individual health insurance (57%) and group health insurance (42%).
Principal Investments: NonCMO investment grade bonds (79%), cash (12%), CMOs and structured securities (8%), and noninv. grade bonds (2%).
Investments in Affiliates: None
Group Affiliation: Centene Corp
Licensed in: All states except NY, PR
Commenced Business: January 1950
Address: 233 S Wacker Dr Suite 700, Chicago, IL 60606-6393
Phone: (312) 332-5401 **Domicile State:** IL **NAIC Code:** 80799

Data Date	Rating	RACR #1	RACR #2	Total Assets ($mil)	Capital ($mil)	Net Premium ($mil)	Net Income ($mil)
9-14	C	1.18	0.93	116.9	27.5	87.3	3.6
9-13	C	1.52	1.23	86.1	43.8	98.5	0.2
2013	C	1.82	1.45	83.5	43.8	125.1	0.3
2012	C	1.39	1.13	100.0	43.7	154.7	-19.0
2011	C+	1.25	1.01	68.8	25.5	98.2	-5.3
2010	B	1.19	0.96	57.0	20.7	81.4	0.7
2009	B	1.19	0.95	58.2	19.8	79.4	2.3

Centene Corp Composite Group Rating: C Largest Group Members	Assets ($mil)	Rating
BANKERS RESERVE LIFE INS CO OF WI	435	C-
SUPERIOR HEALTHPLAN INC	349	C
KENTUCKY SPIRIT HEALTH PLAN INC	218	C-
SUNFLOWER STATE HEALTH PLAN INC	215	D+
BUCKEYE COMMUNITY HEALTH PLAN INC	199	C+

CENTRAL STATES HEALTH & LIFE COMPANY OF OMAHA *   A-   Excellent

Major Rating Factors: Good quality investment portfolio (5.8 on a scale of 0 to 10) despite mixed results such as: minimal exposure to mortgages and substantial holdings of BBB bonds but minimal holdings in junk bonds. Good overall results on stability tests (6.9). Strengths that enhance stability include excellent operational trends and excellent risk diversification. Strong capitalization (9.7) based on excellent risk adjusted capital (severe loss scenario).

Other Rating Factors: Excellent profitability (7.9). Excellent liquidity (8.0).

Principal Business: Credit life insurance (51%), credit health insurance (33%), individual health insurance (12%), group health insurance (2%), and individual life insurance (2%).

Principal Investments: NonCMO investment grade bonds (44%), CMOs and structured securities (26%), common & preferred stock (12%), mortgages in good standing (4%), and misc. investments (15%).

Investments in Affiliates: 6%

Group Affiliation: Central States Group

Licensed in: All states except NY

Commenced Business: June 1932

Address: 1212 N 96th St, Omaha, NE 68114

Phone: (402) 397-1111 **Domicile State:** NE **NAIC Code:** 61751

Data Date	Rating	RACR #1	RACR #2	Total Assets ($mil)	Capital ($mil)	Net Premium ($mil)	Net Income ($mil)
9-14	A-	3.90	2.77	407.1	119.1	56.8	3.4
9-13	A-	3.91	2.76	390.6	113.9	59.0	-1.4
2013	A-	3.98	2.85	395.5	119.6	77.1	0.2
2012	A-	4.26	3.06	372.0	111.0	72.2	3.8
2011	A-	4.12	2.95	343.8	104.5	61.8	8.6
2010	B	4.12	2.91	331.4	102.3	65.9	5.7
2009	B	4.33	3.08	329.7	98.1	57.8	4.2

Adverse Trends in Operations

Decrease in premium volume from 2010 to 2011 (6%)

CENTRAL UNITED LIFE INSURANCE COMPANY   C   Fair

Major Rating Factors: Fair capitalization for the current period (3.4 on a scale of 0 to 10) based on fair risk adjusted capital (severe loss scenario) reflecting some improvement over results in 2009. Fair overall results on stability tests (3.4) including weak risk adjusted capital in prior years, negative cash flow from operations for 2013. Good quality investment portfolio (5.2).

Other Rating Factors: Good overall profitability (6.7). Good liquidity (6.6).

Principal Business: Individual health insurance (79%), reinsurance (12%), group health insurance (5%), and individual life insurance (4%).

Principal Investments: Common & preferred stock (41%), nonCMO investment grade bonds (41%), real estate (8%), cash (5%), and misc. investments (4%).

Investments in Affiliates: 41%

Group Affiliation: Harris Insurance Holdings Inc

Licensed in: All states except CT, NJ, NY, RI, VT, PR

Commenced Business: September 1963

Address: 2727 Allen Parkway,6th Floor, Houston, TX 77019-2115

Phone: (713) 529-0045 **Domicile State:** AR **NAIC Code:** 61883

Data Date	Rating	RACR #1	RACR #2	Total Assets ($mil)	Capital ($mil)	Net Premium ($mil)	Net Income ($mil)
9-14	C	0.60	0.55	303.7	78.5	67.3	3.1
9-13	C	0.81	0.65	307.9	74.5	67.4	3.4
2013	C	0.59	0.54	307.2	76.6	88.8	3.8
2012	C	0.77	0.67	302.0	59.7	92.0	8.8
2011	D+	0.70	0.61	312.5	56.6	97.6	3.9
2010	D+	0.67	0.59	321.8	53.9	102.6	12.1
2009	D+	0.53	0.47	332.6	44.6	98.2	4.2

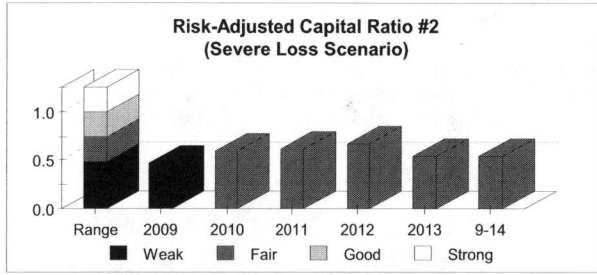

Risk-Adjusted Capital Ratio #2 (Severe Loss Scenario)

Range 2009 2010 2011 2012 2013 9-14

■ Weak ▨ Fair ▦ Good ☐ Strong

CENTRE LIFE INSURANCE COMPANY   B-   Good

Major Rating Factors: Good quality investment portfolio (6.8 on a scale of 0 to 10) with no exposure to mortgages and minimal holdings in junk bonds. Fair overall results on stability tests (4.9) including fair financial strength of affiliated Zurich Financial Services Group and negative cash flow from operations for 2013. Strong capitalization (9.4) based on excellent risk adjusted capital (severe loss scenario).

Other Rating Factors: Excellent profitability (8.7). Excellent liquidity (8.7).

Principal Business: Reinsurance (61%) and individual health insurance (39%).

Principal Investments: NonCMO investment grade bonds (84%) and CMOs and structured securities (16%).

Investments in Affiliates: None

Group Affiliation: Zurich Financial Services Group

Licensed in: All states except PR

Commenced Business: October 1927

Address: 1600 McConnor Parkway, Schaumburg, IL 60196-6801

Phone: (847) 874-7400 **Domicile State:** MA **NAIC Code:** 80896

Data Date	Rating	RACR #1	RACR #2	Total Assets ($mil)	Capital ($mil)	Net Premium ($mil)	Net Income ($mil)
9-14	B-	4.21	2.63	1,909.7	101.8	0.0	1.9
9-13	B-	4.28	2.53	1,934.3	100.6	0.0	1.3
2013	B-	4.13	2.67	1,927.7	101.2	0.0	1.9
2012	C+	4.15	2.72	1,815.1	98.8	0.0	0.3
2011	C+	4.18	2.78	1,811.6	100.5	-1.5	0.3
2010	C+	3.64	2.01	1,841.2	89.2	3.1	16.2
2009	C+	2.98	1.35	1,969.0	77.1	10.2	-4.8

Zurich Financial Services Group Composite Group Rating: C Largest Group Members	Assets ($mil)	Rating
ZURICH AMERICAN INS CO	30184	C+
ZURICH AMERICAN LIFE INS CO	12969	C
FARMERS NEW WORLD LIFE INS CO	7141	B-
CENTRE LIFE INS CO	1928	B-
FARMERS REINS CO	1400	B-

CENTURION LIFE INSURANCE COMPANY | D | Weak

Major Rating Factors: Weak profitability (1.5 on a scale of 0 to 10). Excellent expense controls. Weak overall results on stability tests (1.5) including weak results on operational trends. Good quality investment portfolio (6.5) despite mixed results such as: no exposure to mortgages and large holdings of BBB rated bonds but no exposure to junk bonds.

Other Rating Factors: Good liquidity (6.5). Strong capitalization (9.9) based on excellent risk adjusted capital (severe loss scenario).

Principal Business: Reinsurance (99%).

Principal Investments: CMOs and structured securities (55%), nonCMO investment grade bonds (33%), noninv. grade bonds (8%), common & preferred stock (3%), and cash (1%).

Investments in Affiliates: None

Group Affiliation: Wells Fargo Group

Licensed in: All states except ME, NY, VT, PR

Commenced Business: July 1956

Address: 206 Eighth Street, Des Moines, IA 50309

Phone: (515) 243-2131 **Domicile State:** IA **NAIC Code:** 62383

Data Date	Rating	RACR #1	RACR #2	Total Assets ($mil)	Capital ($mil)	Net Premium ($mil)	Net Income ($mil)
3-14	D	4.98	2.92	1,211.1	406.3	64.5	8.5
3-13	D	11.68	5.95	1,183.3	372.6	33.0	-259.3
2013	D	4.92	2.88	1,209.0	397.3	204.6	-227.0
2012	C+	20.93	10.33	1,475.0	599.9	13.7	39.4
2011	C+	16.61	8.13	1,472.9	545.1	23.8	47.0
2010	B	30.68	15.76	1,965.1	1,066.4	81.1	41.6
2009	B-	29.31	15.09	1,887.8	1,023.4	202.2	37.5

Adverse Trends in Operations

Decrease in capital during 2013 (34%)
Decrease in premium volume from 2011 to 2012 (43%)
Decrease in premium volume from 2010 to 2011 (71%)
Decrease in capital during 2011 (49%)
Decrease in premium volume from 2009 to 2010 (60%)

CHESAPEAKE LIFE INSURANCE COMPANY | C+ | Fair

Major Rating Factors: Fair overall results on stability tests (4.4 on a scale of 0 to 10) including excessive premium growth and fair risk adjusted capital in prior years. Good current capitalization (6.3) based on excellent risk adjusted capital (severe loss scenario) reflecting significant improvement over results in 2013. Weak profitability (1.8).

Other Rating Factors: High quality investment portfolio (8.9). Excellent liquidity (7.8).

Principal Business: Individual health insurance (62%), individual life insurance (35%), group health insurance (1%), and reinsurance (1%).

Principal Investments: NonCMO investment grade bonds (96%) and CMOs and structured securities (5%).

Investments in Affiliates: None

Group Affiliation: HealthMarkets

Licensed in: All states except NJ, NY, VT, PR

Commenced Business: October 1956

Address: 9151 Grapevine Highway, North Richland Hills, TX 76180

Phone: (817) 255-3100 **Domicile State:** OK **NAIC Code:** 61832

Data Date	Rating	RACR #1	RACR #2	Total Assets ($mil)	Capital ($mil)	Net Premium ($mil)	Net Income ($mil)
9-14	C+	1.39	1.15	75.0	43.7	86.3	0.7
9-13	C+	0.95	0.75	38.8	19.6	58.6	-2.9
2013	C+	0.85	0.67	42.5	20.9	82.6	-3.2
2012	C+	1.60	1.22	36.2	23.3	47.1	-2.1
2011	C+	4.46	3.22	47.0	35.7	24.4	0.1
2010	C+	6.19	4.80	60.6	44.7	18.7	2.4
2009	C+	5.42	4.87	73.4	42.3	18.1	-1.1

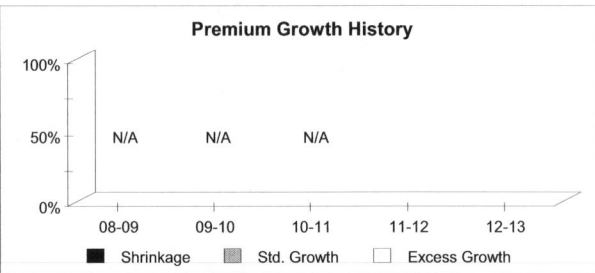

Premium Growth History

CHRISTIAN FIDELITY LIFE INSURANCE COMPANY | B- | Good

Major Rating Factors: Good overall results on stability tests (5.3 on a scale of 0 to 10) despite fair financial strength of affiliated Amerco Corp. Other stability subfactors include good operational trends and good risk diversification. Strong overall capitalization (8.7) based on excellent risk adjusted capital (severe loss scenario). Nevertheless, capital levels have fluctuated during prior years. High quality investment portfolio (7.8).

Other Rating Factors: Excellent profitability (7.1) with operating gains in each of the last five years. Excellent liquidity (7.1).

Principal Business: Individual health insurance (88%), group health insurance (9%), and individual life insurance (3%).

Principal Investments: NonCMO investment grade bonds (87%), mortgages in good standing (5%), CMOs and structured securities (5%), noninv. grade bonds (1%), and misc. investments (2%).

Investments in Affiliates: None

Group Affiliation: Amerco Corp

Licensed in: AL, AZ, AR, CO, FL, GA, ID, IL, IN, KS, KY, LA, MS, MO, MT, NE, NV, NM, ND, OH, OK, OR, SC, SD, TN, TX, UT, VA, WA, WV, WY

Commenced Business: December 1935

Address: 2721 N Central Ave, Phoenix, AZ 85004-1172

Phone: (972) 937-4420 **Domicile State:** TX **NAIC Code:** 61859

Data Date	Rating	RACR #1	RACR #2	Total Assets ($mil)	Capital ($mil)	Net Premium ($mil)	Net Income ($mil)
9-14	B-	2.87	2.12	79.6	35.2	33.1	6.4
9-13	B-	2.61	1.93	84.9	34.6	37.1	6.7
2013	B-	2.20	1.63	75.4	28.8	48.9	9.6
2012	B-	2.00	1.49	77.9	28.0	54.3	8.7
2011	B	1.64	1.34	85.3	36.2	49.1	8.5
2010	B-	1.49	1.22	83.2	32.8	52.0	4.3
2009	B-	1.87	1.52	88.1	39.8	53.9	6.4

Amerco Corp
Composite Group Rating: C
Largest Group Members

Largest Group Members	Assets ($mil)	Rating
OXFORD LIFE INS CO	1098	B-
REPWEST INS CO	285	D-
CHRISTIAN FIDELITY LIFE INS CO	75	B-
NORTH AMERICAN INS CO	22	C
ARCOA RRG INC	10	E

CHURCH LIFE INSURANCE CORPORATION   B-   Good

Major Rating Factors: Good quality investment portfolio (6.0 on a scale of 0 to 10) despite mixed results such as: large holdings of BBB rated bonds but moderate junk bond exposure. Good liquidity (6.1) with sufficient resources to cover a large increase in policy surrenders. Good overall results on stability tests (5.2) excellent operational trends and good risk diversification.
Other Rating Factors: Strong capitalization (8.4) based on excellent risk adjusted capital (severe loss scenario). Excellent profitability (7.5) with operating gains in each of the last five years.
Principal Business: Group life insurance (46%), group retirement contracts (31%), individual annuities (21%), and individual life insurance (2%).
Principal Investments: NonCMO investment grade bonds (60%), CMOs and structured securities (29%), noninv. grade bonds (5%), and common & preferred stock (5%).
Investments in Affiliates: None
Group Affiliation: Church Pension Fund
Licensed in: All states except PR
Commenced Business: July 1922
Address: 445 Fifth Ave, New York, NY 10016
Phone: (212) 592-9473 **Domicile State:** NY **NAIC Code:** 61875

Data Date	Rating	RACR #1	RACR #2	Total Assets ($mil)	Capital ($mil)	Net Premium ($mil)	Net Income ($mil)
9-14	B-	3.60	1.93	287.0	50.5	26.6	1.1
9-13	B-	3.38	1.84	281.7	47.7	30.3	2.2
2013	B-	3.69	1.98	285.3	50.3	37.9	5.5
2012	B-	3.33	1.83	279.1	43.1	42.0	3.2
2011	B-	3.24	1.79	254.6	38.5	37.6	1.0
2010	B-	3.48	1.97	237.1	38.9	36.2	4.2
2009	C+	3.45	2.02	219.5	35.3	35.0	2.3

Adverse Trends in Operations

Decrease in premium volume from 2012 to 2013 (10%)
Increase in policy surrenders from 2011 to 2012 (46%)
Decrease in capital during 2011 (1%)
Increase in policy surrenders from 2009 to 2010 (36%)

CICA LIFE INSURANCE COMPANY OF AMERICA   C-   Fair

Major Rating Factors: Fair capitalization (3.2 on a scale of 0 to 10) based on fair risk adjusted capital (severe loss scenario). Fair overall results on stability tests (3.0) including fair risk adjusted capital in prior years. Weak profitability (2.9) with investment income below regulatory standards in relation to interest assumptions of reserves.
Other Rating Factors: Good quality investment portfolio (5.5). Good liquidity (6.1).
Principal Business: Individual life insurance (96%), individual annuities (3%), and credit health insurance (1%).
Principal Investments: NonCMO investment grade bonds (71%), common & preferred stock (15%), policy loans (7%), cash (3%), and misc. investments (3%).
Investments in Affiliates: 10%
Group Affiliation: Citizens Inc
Licensed in: AL, AZ, AR, CO, DC, GA, HI, ID, IN, KS, KY, LA, MN, MS, MO, MT, NE, NV, NM, ND, OK, OR, PA, SC, SD, TN, TX, UT, WA, WV, WY
Commenced Business: June 1968
Address: 1675 Broadway, Denver, CO 80202
Phone: (512) 837-7100 **Domicile State:** CO **NAIC Code:** 71463

Data Date	Rating	RACR #1	RACR #2	Total Assets ($mil)	Capital ($mil)	Net Premium ($mil)	Net Income ($mil)
9-14	C-	0.65	0.53	749.7	51.8	104.5	4.8
9-13	C-	0.69	0.56	675.9	56.5	97.4	3.2
2013	C-	0.73	0.59	700.6	57.9	136.0	3.2
2012	C-	0.67	0.55	629.6	53.8	129.5	2.9
2011	C-	0.70	0.60	568.6	58.0	121.6	4.7
2010	C-	0.67	0.60	500.2	50.7	110.0	15.2
2009	C-	0.63	0.57	469.6	49.3	105.2	9.5

Risk-Adjusted Capital Ratio #2
(Severe Loss Scenario)

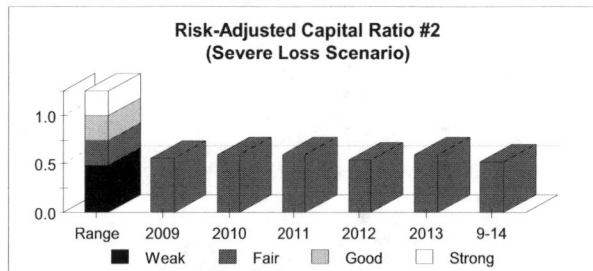

	Range	2009	2010	2011	2012	2013	9-14

■ Weak   ▨ Fair   ▤ Good   ☐ Strong

CIGNA HEALTH & LIFE INSURANCE COMPANY   B   Good

Major Rating Factors: Good overall results on stability tests (5.6 on a scale of 0 to 10) despite excessive premium growth. Other stability subfactors include good operational trends and excellent risk diversification. Good liquidity (6.5) with sufficient resources to handle a spike in claims. Fair quality investment portfolio (3.7).
Other Rating Factors: Strong capitalization (7.1) based on excellent risk adjusted capital (severe loss scenario). Excellent profitability (9.6) with operating gains in each of the last five years.
Principal Business: Group health insurance (99%) and reinsurance (1%).
Principal Investments: NonCMO investment grade bonds (60%), mortgages in good standing (14%), noninv. grade bonds (9%), common & preferred stock (8%), and misc. investments (9%).
Investments in Affiliates: 15%
Group Affiliation: CIGNA Corp
Licensed in: All states except PR
Commenced Business: February 1964
Address: 900 Cottage Grove Rd, Hartford, CT 06152
Phone: (303) 729-7462 **Domicile State:** CT **NAIC Code:** 67369

Data Date	Rating	RACR #1	RACR #2	Total Assets ($mil)	Capital ($mil)	Net Premium ($mil)	Net Income ($mil)
9-14	B	1.89	1.48	5,710.7	2,394.6	7,282.9	750.4
9-13	B	1.99	1.59	3,658.0	1,602.1	4,684.1	388.1
2013	B	1.68	1.37	4,139.3	1,713.2	6,456.2	489.1
2012	B	1.92	1.66	1,681.4	1,017.9	1,883.9	300.7
2011	B	10.20	6.05	713.4	543.4	296.6	122.8
2010	B	9.56	8.61	65.2	51.0	23.6	12.1
2009	B	9.19	8.27	50.0	42.0	26.9	17.9

Adverse Trends in Operations

Change in asset mix during 2013 (5%)
Change in asset mix during 2011 (10.1%)
Decrease in premium volume from 2009 to 2010 (12%)
Change in asset mix during 2010 (6.8%)

CIGNA LIFE INSURANCE COMPANY OF NEW YORK * | A- | Excellent

Major Rating Factors: Good quality investment portfolio (6.6 on a scale of 0 to 10) despite mixed results such as: no exposure to mortgages and large holdings of BBB rated bonds but small junk bond holdings. Good overall profitability (6.4). Return on equity has been excellent over the last five years averaging 18.6%. Excellent overall results on stability tests (7.0) excellent operational trends and excellent risk diversification.

Other Rating Factors: Strong capitalization (9.1) based on excellent risk adjusted capital (severe loss scenario). Excellent liquidity (7.3).

Principal Business: Group health insurance (66%) and group life insurance (33%).

Principal Investments: NonCMO investment grade bonds (86%), CMOs and structured securities (7%), and noninv. grade bonds (7%).

Investments in Affiliates: None

Group Affiliation: CIGNA Corp

Licensed in: AL, DC, MO, NY, PA, TN

Commenced Business: December 1965

Address: 499 Washington Blvd, Jersey City, NJ 07310-1995

Phone: (212) 618-5757 **Domicile State:** NY **NAIC Code:** 64548

Data Date	Rating	RACR #1	RACR #2	Total Assets ($mil)	Capital ($mil)	Net Premium ($mil)	Net Income ($mil)
9-14	A-	3.79	2.38	380.6	110.7	94.1	19.0
9-13	B+	3.71	2.33	383.7	103.8	89.9	11.8
2013	B+	3.21	2.03	375.9	93.5	119.9	16.9
2012	B+	3.54	2.38	376.0	93.8	115.6	15.8
2011	B	4.12	2.77	387.8	102.4	124.7	16.6
2010	B	3.94	2.71	395.5	103.4	131.6	26.7
2009	B-	3.91	2.73	388.0	97.2	124.1	15.5

Adverse Trends in Operations

Decrease in premium volume from 2011 to 2012 (7%)
Decrease in asset base during 2012 (3%)
Decrease in capital during 2012 (8%)
Decrease in asset base during 2011 (2%)
Decrease in premium volume from 2010 to 2011 (5%)

CINCINNATI LIFE INSURANCE COMPANY | B | Good

Major Rating Factors: Good current capitalization (6.7 on a scale of 0 to 10) based on good risk adjusted capital (severe loss scenario), although results have slipped from the excellent range during the last year. Good liquidity (5.4) with sufficient resources to cover a large increase in policy surrenders. Good overall results on stability tests (6.1) good operational trends, excellent risk adjusted capital for prior years and excellent risk diversification.

Other Rating Factors: Fair quality investment portfolio (4.6). Weak profitability (2.4) with operating losses during the first nine months of 2014.

Principal Business: Individual life insurance (84%), individual annuities (13%), individual health insurance (2%), and group life insurance (1%).

Principal Investments: NonCMO investment grade bonds (86%), noninv. grade bonds (5%), CMOs and structured securities (4%), cash (2%), and policy loans (1%).

Investments in Affiliates: None

Group Affiliation: Cincinnati Financial Corp

Licensed in: All states except NY, PR

Commenced Business: February 1988

Address: 6200 S Gilmore Rd, Fairfield, OH 45014-5141

Phone: (513) 870-2000 **Domicile State:** OH **NAIC Code:** 76236

Data Date	Rating	RACR #1	RACR #2	Total Assets ($mil)	Capital ($mil)	Net Premium ($mil)	Net Income ($mil)
9-14	B	1.78	0.96	3,853.0	227.6	181.7	-11.9
9-13	B	2.10	1.15	3,682.6	255.8	175.6	-17.5
2013	B	1.94	1.06	3,737.5	247.0	235.3	-19.7
2012	B	2.27	1.26	3,569.9	275.8	241.8	4.6
2011	B	2.50	1.41	3,357.3	281.2	299.7	-13.3
2010	B	2.43	1.37	3,165.2	303.0	368.7	14.9
2009	B	2.63	1.48	2,830.6	300.2	338.1	15.1

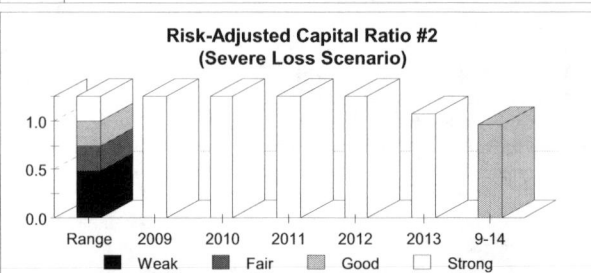

Risk-Adjusted Capital Ratio #2 (Severe Loss Scenario)

Range 2009 2010 2011 2012 2013 9-14
■ Weak ■ Fair ▦ Good □ Strong

CM LIFE INSURANCE COMPANY | B | Good

Major Rating Factors: Good quality investment portfolio (5.3 on a scale of 0 to 10) despite large holdings of BBB rated bonds in addition to moderate junk bond exposure. Exposure to mortgages is significant, but the mortgage default rate has been low. Good liquidity (6.2) with sufficient resources to cover a large increase in policy surrenders. Good overall results on stability tests (6.0) good operational trends and excellent risk diversification.

Other Rating Factors: Strong capitalization (7.9) based on excellent risk adjusted capital (severe loss scenario). Excellent profitability (8.9) with operating gains in each of the last five years.

Principal Business: Individual annuities (53%) and individual life insurance (47%).

Principal Investments: NonCMO investment grade bonds (51%), CMOs and structured securities (14%), mortgages in good standing (12%), noninv. grade bonds (6%), and misc. investments (11%).

Investments in Affiliates: 10%

Group Affiliation: Massachusetts Mutual Group

Licensed in: All states except NY

Commenced Business: May 1981

Address: 100 Bright Meadow Blvd, Enfield, CT 06082

Phone: (413) 788-8411 **Domicile State:** CT **NAIC Code:** 93432

Data Date	Rating	RACR #1	RACR #2	Total Assets ($mil)	Capital ($mil)	Net Premium ($mil)	Net Income ($mil)
9-14	B	2.66	1.62	8,612.5	1,197.0	245.7	84.3
9-13	B	2.29	1.39	8,933.0	1,043.8	266.9	102.9
2013	B	2.37	1.44	8,984.0	1,071.2	355.6	170.6
2012	B	2.16	1.32	8,594.3	960.8	383.6	94.4
2011	B	2.19	1.33	8,388.5	930.0	389.0	90.6
2010	B	2.07	1.23	8,427.8	837.2	445.3	60.1
2009	B	1.72	1.03	8,170.6	717.5	871.1	43.8

Adverse Trends in Operations

Decrease in premium volume from 2012 to 2013 (7%)
Decrease in premium volume from 2011 to 2012 (1%)
Decrease in premium volume from 2010 to 2011 (13%)
Decrease in premium volume from 2009 to 2010 (49%)

CMFG LIFE INSURANCE COMPANY   B-   Good

Major Rating Factors: Good liquidity (6.6 on a scale of 0 to 10) with sufficient resources to handle a spike in claims as well as a significant increase in policy surrenders. Good overall results on stability tests (5.3). Stability strengths include excellent operational trends, good risk adjusted capital for prior years and excellent risk diversification. Fair quality investment portfolio (4.8).

Other Rating Factors: Strong capitalization (7.1) based on excellent risk adjusted capital (severe loss scenario). Excellent profitability (7.8) with operating gains in each of the last five years.

Principal Business: Group retirement contracts (39%), credit health insurance (12%), group life insurance (12%), individual life insurance (10%), and other lines (27%).

Principal Investments: NonCMO investment grade bonds (51%), mortgages in good standing (13%), CMOs and structured securities (12%), common & preferred stock (10%), and misc. investments (13%).

Investments in Affiliates: 10%
Group Affiliation: CUNA Mutual Ins Group
Licensed in: All states, the District of Columbia and Puerto Rico
Commenced Business: August 1935
Address: 2000 Heritage Way, Waverly, IA 50677
Phone: (608) 238-5851 **Domicile State:** IA **NAIC Code:** 62626

Data Date	Rating	RACR #1	RACR #2	Total Assets ($mil)	Capital ($mil)	Net Premium ($mil)	Net Income ($mil)
9-14	B-	1.37	1.07	15,616.4	1,605.7	1,668.1	58.5
9-13	B-	1.25	0.96	15,379.7	1,503.2	1,394.1	72.5
2013	B-	1.26	0.98	15,659.8	1,553.5	1,923.4	101.9
2012	B-	1.19	0.91	14,664.2	1,458.0	1,874.0	97.0
2011	B-	1.18	0.89	13,762.3	1,401.0	2,166.0	80.6
2010	B-	1.14	0.87	13,330.4	1,354.8	2,264.3	33.4
2009	C+	1.02	0.79	12,441.2	1,201.1	2,540.5	281.6

Adverse Trends in Operations

Change in premium mix from 2011 to 2012 (5%)
Decrease in premium volume from 2011 to 2012 (13%)
Decrease in premium volume from 2010 to 2011 (4%)
Increase in policy surrenders from 2009 to 2010 (41%)
Decrease in premium volume from 2009 to 2010 (11%)

COLONIAL LIFE & ACCIDENT INSURANCE COMPANY   C+   Fair

Major Rating Factors: Fair overall results on stability tests (4.5 on a scale of 0 to 10). Good quality investment portfolio (6.2) despite mixed results such as: large holdings of BBB rated bonds but moderate junk bond exposure. Good liquidity (6.8) with sufficient resources to handle a spike in claims as well as a significant increase in policy surrenders.

Other Rating Factors: Strong capitalization (8.1) based on excellent risk adjusted capital (severe loss scenario). Excellent profitability (8.6) with operating gains in each of the last five years.

Principal Business: Individual health insurance (75%), individual life insurance (20%), group health insurance (4%), and group life insurance (1%).

Principal Investments: NonCMO investment grade bonds (72%), mortgages in good standing (10%), noninv. grade bonds (8%), CMOs and structured securities (4%), and misc. investments (6%).

Investments in Affiliates: None
Group Affiliation: Unum Group
Licensed in: All states except NY
Commenced Business: September 1939
Address: 6335 S. East Street, Suite A, Indianapolis, IN 46227
Phone: (803) 798-7000 **Domicile State:** SC **NAIC Code:** 62049

Data Date	Rating	RACR #1	RACR #2	Total Assets ($mil)	Capital ($mil)	Net Premium ($mil)	Net Income ($mil)
9-14	C+	2.83	1.74	2,882.2	570.4	959.3	118.5
9-13	C+	2.79	1.70	2,734.3	552.1	933.2	106.5
2013	C+	2.71	1.66	2,752.7	538.2	1,238.8	134.4
2012	C+	2.75	1.68	2,651.4	534.9	1,208.2	139.7
2011	C+	2.84	1.74	2,521.2	532.3	1,152.4	136.0
2010	C+	2.81	1.75	2,300.1	491.7	1,103.9	142.3
2009	C+	2.80	1.76	2,141.8	459.7	1,043.0	124.4

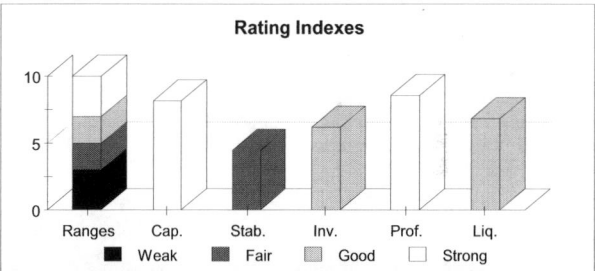

Rating Indexes

(Ranges, Cap., Stab., Inv., Prof., Liq. — Weak, Fair, Good, Strong)

COLONIAL PENN LIFE INSURANCE COMPANY   D+   Weak

Major Rating Factors: Weak profitability (1.9 on a scale of 0 to 10) with operating losses during the first nine months of 2014. Weak liquidity (0.2) as a spike in claims or a run on policy withdrawals may stretch capacity. Weak overall results on stability tests (2.2) including weak risk adjusted capital in prior years, negative cash flow from operations for 2013.

Other Rating Factors: Fair quality investment portfolio (3.7). Good capitalization (5.3) based on good risk adjusted capital (moderate loss scenario).

Principal Business: Individual health insurance (56%), individual life insurance (24%), group life insurance (20%), and reinsurance (1%).

Principal Investments: NonCMO investment grade bonds (74%), CMOs and structured securities (13%), mortgages in good standing (4%), policy loans (3%), and misc. investments (5%).

Investments in Affiliates: None
Group Affiliation: CNO Financial Group Inc
Licensed in: All states except NY
Commenced Business: September 1959
Address: 399 Market St, Philadelphia, PA 19181
Phone: (215) 928-8000 **Domicile State:** PA **NAIC Code:** 62065

Data Date	Rating	RACR #1	RACR #2	Total Assets ($mil)	Capital ($mil)	Net Premium ($mil)	Net Income ($mil)
9-14	D+	1.18	0.68	738.8	75.6	235.2	-17.6
9-13	D+	1.10	0.63	733.5	65.9	215.1	-14.7
2013	D+	1.05	0.60	740.3	62.0	277.8	-19.1
2012	D+	1.20	0.68	736.6	70.6	253.5	-3.9
2011	D+	1.41	0.78	743.9	76.7	222.8	9.2
2010	D+	1.48	0.78	733.8	73.3	194.0	0.3
2009	D+	0.88	0.46	683.6	32.7	182.3	-3.8

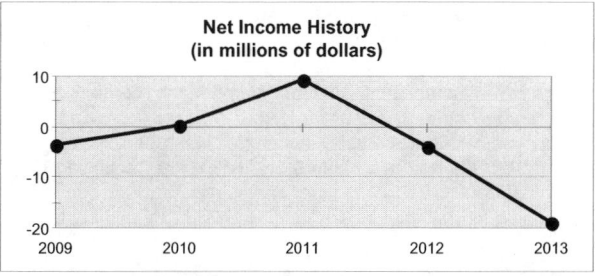

Net Income History
(in millions of dollars)

COLORADO BANKERS LIFE INSURANCE COMPANY *   B+   Good

Major Rating Factors: Good liquidity (5.6 on a scale of 0 to 10) with sufficient resources to cover a large increase in policy surrenders. Good overall results on stability tests (6.5). Strengths include potential support from affiliation with HCSC Group, excellent operational trends, good risk adjusted capital for prior years and good risk diversification. Weak profitability (2.7) with investment income below regulatory standards in relation to interest assumptions of reserves.

Other Rating Factors: Strong capitalization (7.7) based on excellent risk adjusted capital (severe loss scenario). High quality investment portfolio (7.2).

Principal Business: Individual life insurance (62%), individual annuities (29%), reinsurance (5%), individual health insurance (3%), and group health insurance (1%).

Principal Investments: NonCMO investment grade bonds (79%), CMOs and structured securities (15%), cash (4%), policy loans (2%), and noninv. grade bonds (1%).

Investments in Affiliates: None
Group Affiliation: HCSC Group
Licensed in: All states except NY, PR
Commenced Business: November 1974
Address: 5990 Greenwood Plaza Blvd, Englewood, CO 80111
Phone: (303) 220-8500 **Domicile State:** CO **NAIC Code:** 84786

Data Date	Rating	RACR #1	RACR #2	Total Assets ($mil)	Capital ($mil)	Net Premium ($mil)	Net Income ($mil)
9-14	B+	2.58	1.49	280.1	30.6	67.3	1.6
9-13	B+	2.74	1.61	251.8	30.4	67.5	2.3
2013	B+	2.49	1.46	256.9	28.9	89.4	3.2
2012	B+	2.46	1.42	232.5	27.5	87.8	-9.1
2011	B+	1.60	0.94	202.3	16.9	86.4	1.5
2010	B+	1.79	1.06	183.0	17.9	81.0	-1.3
2009	B+	1.49	1.06	154.6	14.2	68.9	-4.2

HCSC Group
Composite Group Rating: A+

Largest Group Members	Assets ($mil)	Rating
HEALTH CARE SVC CORP A MUT LEG RES	16714	A+
DEARBORN NATIONAL LIFE INS CO	2324	A-
HCSC INS SERVICES CO	300	B+
COLORADO BANKERS LIFE INS CO	257	B+
DEARBORN NATIONAL LIFE INS CO OF NY	45	B+

COLUMBIAN LIFE INSURANCE COMPANY   C+   Fair

Major Rating Factors: Fair profitability (3.0 on a scale of 0 to 10) with operating losses during the first nine months of 2014. Fair liquidity (4.6) as cash from operations and sale of marketable assets may not be adequate to cover a spike in claims or a run on policy withdrawals. Fair overall results on stability tests (4.5).

Other Rating Factors: Strong capitalization (7.6) based on excellent risk adjusted capital (severe loss scenario). High quality investment portfolio (7.5).

Principal Business: Individual life insurance (76%), group life insurance (14%), group health insurance (7%), individual annuities (3%), and reinsurance (1%).

Principal Investments: NonCMO investment grade bonds (56%), CMOs and structured securities (25%), mortgages in good standing (10%), policy loans (5%), and misc. investments (4%).

Investments in Affiliates: 2%
Group Affiliation: Columbian Life Group
Licensed in: All states except AL, AK, ME, NY, ND, VT, PR
Commenced Business: June 1988
Address: Vestal Parkway East, Binghamton, NY 13902
Phone: (607) 724-2472 **Domicile State:** IL **NAIC Code:** 76023

Data Date	Rating	RACR #1	RACR #2	Total Assets ($mil)	Capital ($mil)	Net Premium ($mil)	Net Income ($mil)
9-14	C+	2.11	1.39	307.2	35.7	44.6	-0.6
9-13	B-	1.53	1.03	287.8	25.5	45.9	-1.3
2013	C+	1.48	0.99	292.7	24.3	58.0	-2.1
2012	B-	1.24	0.83	274.8	20.2	58.6	-1.6
2011	B-	1.57	1.06	266.3	24.8	52.5	-1.6
2010	C	2.03	1.17	256.3	19.5	47.7	0.1
2009	C	1.99	1.21	248.4	19.0	42.5	-0.7

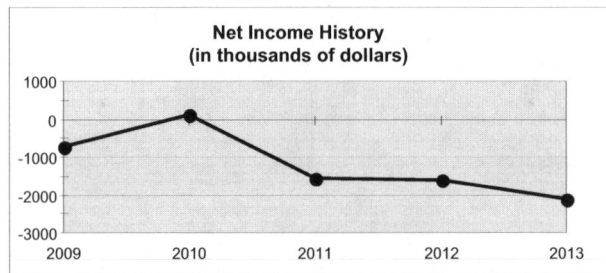

Net Income History
(in thousands of dollars)

COLUMBIAN MUTUAL LIFE INSURANCE COMPANY   B   Good

Major Rating Factors: Good quality investment portfolio (6.4 on a scale of 0 to 10) despite significant exposure to mortgages . Mortgage default rate has been low. substantial holdings of BBB bonds in addition to minimal holdings in junk bonds. Good overall profitability (6.5). Good liquidity (5.2).

Other Rating Factors: Fair overall results on stability tests (4.9). Strong capitalization (7.1) based on excellent risk adjusted capital (severe loss scenario).

Principal Business: Reinsurance (61%), individual life insurance (36%), individual health insurance (1%), individual annuities (1%), and group retirement contracts (1%).

Principal Investments: NonCMO investment grade bonds (56%), CMOs and structured securities (23%), mortgages in good standing (12%), policy loans (5%), and common & preferred stock (3%).

Investments in Affiliates: 2%
Group Affiliation: Columbian Life Group
Licensed in: All states, the District of Columbia and Puerto Rico
Commenced Business: February 1883
Address: Vestal Parkway East, Binghamton, NY 13902
Phone: (607) 724-2472 **Domicile State:** NY **NAIC Code:** 62103

Data Date	Rating	RACR #1	RACR #2	Total Assets ($mil)	Capital ($mil)	Net Premium ($mil)	Net Income ($mil)
9-14	B	1.65	1.07	1,320.1	101.0	135.5	2.7
9-13	B	1.52	0.97	1,279.6	78.8	139.0	0.7
2013	B	1.76	1.16	1,289.8	101.8	182.8	3.1
2012	B	1.71	1.10	1,251.1	89.5	-118.0	-0.9
2011	B+	1.55	1.01	1,230.4	88.5	184.3	-1.3
2010	B	2.04	1.35	914.5	88.4	164.0	3.0
2009	B	2.03	1.38	872.8	86.5	145.9	6.7

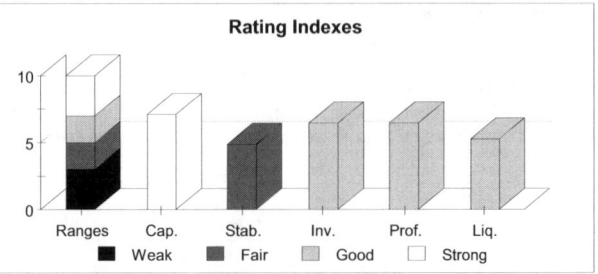

Rating Indexes

COLUMBUS LIFE INSURANCE COMPANY   B-   Good

Major Rating Factors: Good quality investment portfolio (5.0 on a scale of 0 to 10) despite mixed results such as: large holdings of BBB rated bonds but junk bond exposure equal to 75% of capital. Good liquidity (5.3) with sufficient resources to cover a large increase in policy surrenders. Fair overall results on stability tests (4.9).

Other Rating Factors: Weak profitability (2.5) with operating losses during the first nine months of 2014. Strong capitalization (7.0) based on excellent risk adjusted capital (severe loss scenario).

Principal Business: Individual life insurance (70%) and individual annuities (30%).

Principal Investments: NonCMO investment grade bonds (59%), CMOs and structured securities (22%), noninv. grade bonds (6%), mortgages in good standing (4%), and misc. investments (9%).

Investments in Affiliates: 3%

Group Affiliation: Western & Southern Group

Licensed in: All states except NY, PR

Commenced Business: July 1988

Address: 400 E 4th St, Cincinnati, OH 45202

Phone: (513) 357-4000 **Domicile State:** OH **NAIC Code:** 99937

Data Date	Rating	RACR #1	RACR #2	Total Assets ($mil)	Capital ($mil)	Net Premium ($mil)	Net Income ($mil)
9-14	B-	1.94	1.02	3,326.3	235.4	181.4	-15.2
9-13	B	1.94	0.98	3,105.7	207.0	156.7	-12.7
2013	B	2.05	1.09	3,198.9	250.8	228.6	-24.8
2012	B+	2.02	1.04	3,011.2	214.8	191.8	1.1
2011	B+	1.91	0.98	2,958.7	206.2	238.6	7.8
2010	B+	2.40	1.24	2,916.3	258.5	191.6	12.5
2009	B+	2.60	1.32	2,719.1	271.6	247.0	3.9

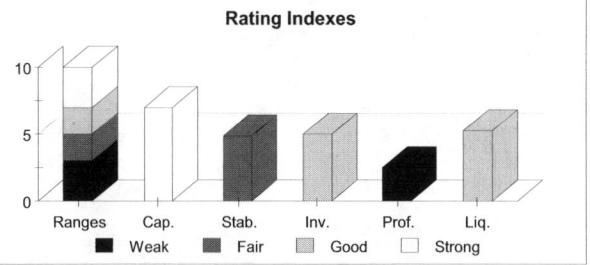

Rating Indexes

Ranges · Cap. · Stab. · Inv. · Prof. · Liq.
■ Weak ■ Fair ▨ Good □ Strong

COMBINED INSURANCE COMPANY OF AMERICA   C+   Fair

Major Rating Factors: Fair overall results on stability tests (3.4 on a scale of 0 to 10). Good quality investment portfolio (6.8) despite mixed results such as: no exposure to mortgages and substantial holdings of BBB bonds but small junk bond holdings. Good overall profitability (5.8). Return on equity has been excellent over the last five years averaging 32.6%.

Other Rating Factors: Strong capitalization (8.1) based on excellent risk adjusted capital (severe loss scenario). Excellent liquidity (7.2).

Principal Business: Individual health insurance (70%), group health insurance (20%), individual life insurance (8%), reinsurance (1%), and group life insurance (1%).

Principal Investments: NonCMO investment grade bonds (63%), CMOs and structured securities (22%), common & preferred stock (6%), noninv. grade bonds (5%), and misc. investments (4%).

Investments in Affiliates: 6%

Group Affiliation: ACE Ltd

Licensed in: All states except NY

Commenced Business: January 1922

Address: 1000 North Milwakee Ave, Glenview, IL 60025

Phone: (312) 701-3000 **Domicile State:** IL **NAIC Code:** 62146

Data Date	Rating	RACR #1	RACR #2	Total Assets ($mil)	Capital ($mil)	Net Premium ($mil)	Net Income ($mil)
9-14	C+	2.26	1.71	1,635.2	378.7	328.4	50.8
9-13	C+	1.95	1.54	1,554.2	362.4	318.8	61.1
2013	C+	1.99	1.54	1,588.9	324.6	428.1	71.8
2012	C+	2.06	1.61	1,543.6	320.7	151.5	195.8
2011	B-	1.96	1.68	1,995.5	496.6	597.2	121.4
2010	B-	3.26	2.69	2,543.8	741.7	478.9	221.9
2009	B-	2.46	2.00	2,508.2	642.7	869.2	178.9

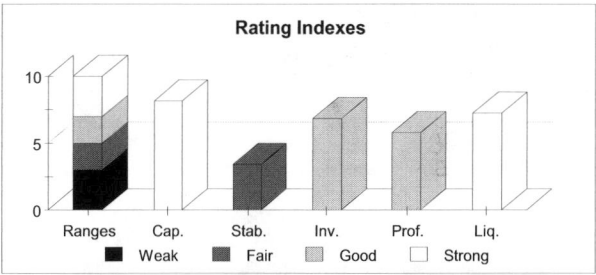

Rating Indexes

Ranges · Cap. · Stab. · Inv. · Prof. · Liq.
■ Weak ■ Fair ▨ Good □ Strong

COMBINED LIFE INSURANCE COMPANY OF NEW YORK   B   Good

Major Rating Factors: Good overall results on stability tests (5.8 on a scale of 0 to 10) despite fair financial strength of affiliated ACE Ltd. Other stability subfactors include excellent operational trends and excellent risk diversification. Good overall profitability (5.2) although investment income, in comparison to reserve requirements, is below regulatory standards. Strong capitalization (7.7) based on excellent risk adjusted capital (severe loss scenario).

Other Rating Factors: High quality investment portfolio (7.7). Excellent liquidity (7.5).

Principal Business: Individual health insurance (74%), individual life insurance (14%), group health insurance (11%), and group life insurance (1%).

Principal Investments: NonCMO investment grade bonds (51%), CMOs and structured securities (47%), policy loans (2%), and noninv. grade bonds (1%).

Investments in Affiliates: None

Group Affiliation: ACE Ltd

Licensed in: FL, IL, NY

Commenced Business: June 1971

Address: 11 British Anerican Blvd, Latham, NY 12110

Phone: (518) 220-9333 **Domicile State:** NY **NAIC Code:** 78697

Data Date	Rating	RACR #1	RACR #2	Total Assets ($mil)	Capital ($mil)	Net Premium ($mil)	Net Income ($mil)
9-14	B	2.08	1.46	412.6	63.7	96.3	6.2
9-13	B	1.82	1.27	396.4	55.6	95.0	3.1
2013	B	1.85	1.29	402.9	56.4	126.0	3.7
2012	B	2.23	1.55	398.9	67.7	126.0	7.2
2011	B	1.95	1.38	382.7	60.3	132.4	15.6
2010	B	1.97	1.41	381.6	60.7	135.2	18.6
2009	B	1.92	1.36	391.1	61.6	138.0	20.5

ACE Ltd Composite Group Rating: C+ Largest Group Members	Assets ($mil)	Rating
ACE AMERICAN INS CO	11697	B-
ACE PROPERTY CASUALTY INS CO	7214	C
PACIFIC EMPLOYERS INS CO	3309	B-
WESTCHESTER FIRE INS CO	2056	C
COMBINED INS CO OF AMERICA	1589	C+

COMMONWEALTH ANNUITY & LIFE INSURANCE COMPANY   B-   Good

Major Rating Factors: Fair overall results on stability tests (4.9 on a scale of 0 to 10) including fair financial strength of affiliated Global Atlantic Financial Group. Fair current capitalization (4.0) based on mixed results -- excessive policy leverage mitigated by excellent risk adjusted capital (severe loss scenario) reflecting improvement over results in 2012. Fair quality investment portfolio (4.7).

Other Rating Factors: Good overall profitability (6.6). Excellent liquidity (9.1).

Principal Business: Individual annuities (69%), reinsurance (20%), and individual life insurance (11%).

Principal Investments: CMOs and structured securities (43%), nonCMO investment grade bonds (31%), common & preferred stock (8%), cash (5%), and misc. investments (11%).

Investments in Affiliates: 8%

Group Affiliation: Global Atlantic Financial Group

Licensed in: All states except NY, PR

Commenced Business: January 1967

Address: 440 Lincoln St, Worcester, MA 01653

Phone: (508) 855-1000   **Domicile State:** MA   **NAIC Code:** 84824

Data Date	Rating	RACR #1	RACR #2	Total Assets ($mil)	Capital ($mil)	Net Premium ($mil)	Net Income ($mil)
9-14	B-	1.49	1.08	10,566.4	1,534.1	543.5	82.4
9-13	C	1.99	1.17	9,858.6	573.9	-938.4	-108.7
2013	C	1.10	0.86	10,211.9	723.6	-637.5	-32.6
2012	C	1.25	0.76	9,089.8	327.4	-996.0	-7.4
2011	C	1.78	1.09	7,575.0	374.6	1,519.0	122.4
2010	C-	1.57	1.17	6,755.7	411.6	41.3	161.9
2009	C-	1.75	1.24	6,929.4	455.9	1,534.0	-140.6

Global Atlantic Financial Group Composite Group Rating: C Largest Group Members	Assets ($mil)	Rating
COMMONWEALTH ANNUITY LIFE INS CO	10212	B-
FORETHOUGHT LIFE INS CO	7957	B-
ACCORDIA LIFE ANNUITY CO	7059	C-
FIRST ALLMERICA FINANCIAL LIFE INS	4206	C-
FORETHOUGHT NATIONAL LIFE INS CO	208	C

COMPANION LIFE INSURANCE COMPANY   B-   Good

Major Rating Factors: Good overall results on stability tests (5.3 on a scale of 0 to 10). Strengths include good financial support from affiliation with Mutual Of Omaha Group, excellent operational trends, good risk adjusted capital for prior years and excellent risk diversification. Fair quality investment portfolio (4.6) with large holdings of BBB rated bonds in addition to moderate junk bond exposure. Fair profitability (4.1).

Other Rating Factors: Fair liquidity (4.3). Strong capitalization (7.1) based on excellent risk adjusted capital (severe loss scenario).

Principal Business: Individual life insurance (78%), group life insurance (13%), individual annuities (5%), and group retirement contracts (4%).

Principal Investments: NonCMO investment grade bonds (56%), CMOs and structured securities (28%), mortgages in good standing (8%), policy loans (3%), and misc. investments (5%).

Investments in Affiliates: None

Group Affiliation: Mutual Of Omaha Group

Licensed in: CT, NJ, NY

Commenced Business: July 1949

Address: 303 Merrick Rd Ste 503, Lynbrook, NY 11563-2515

Phone: (800) 877-5399   **Domicile State:** NY   **NAIC Code:** 62243

Data Date	Rating	RACR #1	RACR #2	Total Assets ($mil)	Capital ($mil)	Net Premium ($mil)	Net Income ($mil)
9-14	B-	2.03	1.06	944.6	61.8	71.6	0.0
9-13	B	1.94	1.01	872.0	56.3	63.9	-3.2
2013	B-	1.61	0.84	883.2	47.0	84.5	0.3
2012	B	2.05	1.07	847.5	58.9	90.1	6.7
2011	B	2.37	1.24	809.3	65.7	78.4	-1.5
2010	B	2.48	1.30	780.2	66.8	77.2	4.2
2009	B	2.49	1.31	751.0	65.4	76.9	0.8

Mutual Of Omaha Group Composite Group Rating: B Largest Group Members	Assets ($mil)	Rating
UNITED OF OMAHA LIFE INS CO	18122	B
MUTUAL OF OMAHA INS CO	5795	B+
COMPANION LIFE INS CO	883	B-
UNITED WORLD LIFE INS CO	115	B+
OMAHA INS CO	23	B-

COMPANION LIFE INSURANCE COMPANY *   A-   Excellent

Major Rating Factors: Good quality investment portfolio (5.7 on a scale of 0 to 10) despite mixed results such as: no exposure to mortgages and substantial holdings of BBB bonds but minimal holdings in junk bonds. Excellent overall results on stability tests (7.2). Strengths that enhance stability include excellent operational trends and excellent risk diversification. Strong capitalization (8.8) based on excellent risk adjusted capital (severe loss scenario).

Other Rating Factors: Excellent profitability (8.7) with operating gains in each of the last five years. Excellent liquidity (7.4).

Principal Business: Group health insurance (91%), group life insurance (5%), reinsurance (3%), and individual health insurance (1%).

Principal Investments: NonCMO investment grade bonds (37%), common & preferred stock (23%), cash (22%), CMOs and structured securities (17%), and noninv. grade bonds (1%).

Investments in Affiliates: 8%

Group Affiliation: Blue Cross Blue Shield of S Carolina

Licensed in: All states except CA, HI, NJ, NY, PR

Commenced Business: July 1970

Address: 2501 Faraway Dr, Columbia, SC 29219

Phone: (800) 753-0404   **Domicile State:** SC   **NAIC Code:** 77828

Data Date	Rating	RACR #1	RACR #2	Total Assets ($mil)	Capital ($mil)	Net Premium ($mil)	Net Income ($mil)
9-14	A-	2.82	2.21	274.9	139.7	166.1	12.0
9-13	A-	2.88	2.29	226.8	130.2	150.8	9.7
2013	A-	2.92	2.31	251.7	138.0	202.8	14.5
2012	A-	2.75	2.19	203.8	120.7	181.8	12.5
2011	A-	2.53	2.02	186.8	110.0	177.8	8.7
2010	A-	2.86	2.20	160.1	91.8	161.5	8.4
2009	A-	3.01	2.38	140.2	84.8	152.1	7.0

Rating Indexes

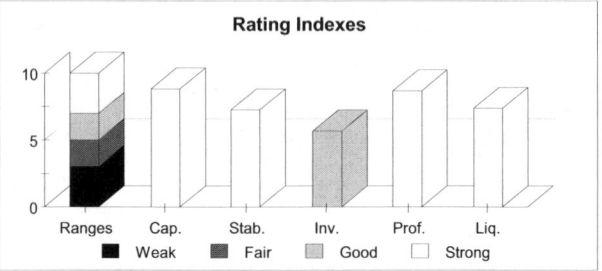

Ranges   Cap.   Stab.   Inv.   Prof.   Liq.

■ Weak   ▨ Fair   ▥ Good   ☐ Strong

CONNECTICUT GENERAL LIFE INSURANCE COMPANY   B-   Good

Major Rating Factors: Good liquidity (6.1 on a scale of 0 to 10) with sufficient resources to handle a spike in claims as well as a significant increase in policy surrenders. Fair quality investment portfolio (4.4) with substantial holdings of BBB bonds in addition to moderate junk bond exposure. Fair overall results on stability tests (3.8) including negative cash flow from operations for 2013.

Other Rating Factors: Strong capitalization (7.5) based on excellent risk adjusted capital (severe loss scenario). Excellent profitability (8.9) with operating gains in each of the last five years.

Principal Business: Group health insurance (47%), individual health insurance (36%), individual life insurance (8%), group life insurance (6%), and reinsurance (2%).

Principal Investments: NonCMO investment grade bonds (31%), common & preferred stock (20%), policy loans (16%), noninv. grade bonds (11%), and misc. investments (22%).

Investments in Affiliates: 24%
Group Affiliation: CIGNA Corp
Licensed in: All states, the District of Columbia and Puerto Rico
Commenced Business: October 1865
Address: 900 Cottage Grove Rd,S-330, Bloomfield, CT 06002
Phone: (860) 726-7234 **Domicile State:** CT **NAIC Code:** 62308

Data Date	Rating	RACR #1	RACR #2	Total Assets ($mil)	Capital ($mil)	Net Premium ($mil)	Net Income ($mil)
9-14	B-	1.64	1.33	18,691.4	3,338.0	879.8	189.1
9-13	B-	1.96	1.47	18,822.9	3,230.5	2,655.2	489.4
2013	B-	1.63	1.33	18,573.6	3,283.0	3,440.5	601.8
2012	B-	1.78	1.35	20,921.6	3,040.9	7,272.6	588.9
2011	B-	2.04	1.48	20,751.9	2,918.2	6,803.9	590.3
2010	C+	2.64	1.77	20,055.5	3,014.5	8,750.9	676.4
2009	C+	2.89	1.93	19,037.0	2,919.2	6,821.0	647.1

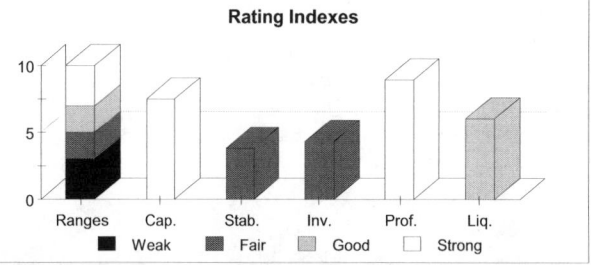

Rating Indexes — Ranges, Cap., Stab., Inv., Prof., Liq. (Weak, Fair, Good, Strong)

CONSECO LIFE INSURANCE COMPANY   C-   Fair

Major Rating Factors: Fair quality investment portfolio (3.7 on a scale of 0 to 10) with large holdings of BBB rated bonds in addition to junk bond exposure equal to 91% of capital. Fair profitability (4.3). Excellent expense controls. Return on equity has been fair, averaging 7.0%. Weak liquidity (0.6) as a spike in claims or a run on policy withdrawals may stretch capacity.

Other Rating Factors: Weak overall results on stability tests (2.6) including weak risk adjusted capital in prior years, negative cash flow from operations for 2013. Good capitalization (5.8) based on good risk adjusted capital (moderate loss scenario).

Principal Business: Individual life insurance (66%), reinsurance (23%), and individual health insurance (11%).

Principal Investments: NonCMO investment grade bonds (57%), CMOs and structured securities (26%), policy loans (5%), noninv. grade bonds (5%), and misc. investments (7%).

Investments in Affiliates: 1%
Group Affiliation: Wilton Re Holdings Ltd
Licensed in: All states except NY
Commenced Business: May 1962
Address: 11825 N Pennsylvania St, Carmel, IN 46032
Phone: (317) 817-6400 **Domicile State:** IN **NAIC Code:** 65900

Data Date	Rating	RACR #1	RACR #2	Total Assets ($mil)	Capital ($mil)	Net Premium ($mil)	Net Income ($mil)
9-14	C-	1.52	0.81	3,763.2	215.0	126.4	49.9
9-13	D	0.78	0.42	3,847.0	96.6	182.3	30.8
2013	D	1.00	0.53	3,825.5	129.7	237.1	49.7
2012	D	0.55	0.29	3,957.2	51.4	257.2	-34.5
2011	D	0.78	0.42	4,151.6	117.4	278.0	22.1
2010	D	0.64	0.34	4,272.8	103.7	294.5	1.8
2009	D	0.60	0.33	4,382.2	111.5	316.8	-21.2

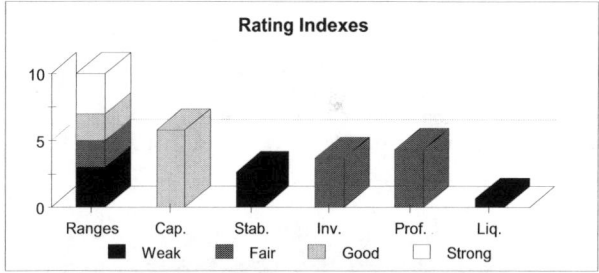

Rating Indexes — Ranges, Cap., Stab., Inv., Prof., Liq. (Weak, Fair, Good, Strong)

CONSTITUTION LIFE INSURANCE COMPANY   C+   Fair

Major Rating Factors: Fair overall results on stability tests (4.5 on a scale of 0 to 10) including fair financial strength of affiliated Universal American Corp and excessive premium growth. Good quality investment portfolio (6.8) despite mixed results such as: no exposure to mortgages and large holdings of BBB rated bonds but minimal holdings in junk bonds. Weak profitability (2.9) with investment income below regulatory standards in relation to interest assumptions of reserves.

Other Rating Factors: Strong capitalization (7.2) based on excellent risk adjusted capital (severe loss scenario). Excellent liquidity (7.3).

Principal Business: Reinsurance (50%), individual health insurance (41%), and individual life insurance (8%).

Principal Investments: NonCMO investment grade bonds (59%), CMOs and structured securities (41%), and noninv. grade bonds (1%).

Investments in Affiliates: None
Group Affiliation: Universal American Corp
Licensed in: All states except NJ, NY, PR
Commenced Business: June 1929
Address: 4211 Norbourne Blvd, Louisville, KY 40207-4048
Phone: (214) 954-7111 **Domicile State:** TX **NAIC Code:** 62359

Data Date	Rating	RACR #1	RACR #2	Total Assets ($mil)	Capital ($mil)	Net Premium ($mil)	Net Income ($mil)
9-14	C+	1.71	1.13	316.1	34.3	73.2	6.6
9-13	B	1.39	1.06	49.8	23.8	46.5	3.8
2013	C+	1.56	1.05	317.3	33.5	109.5	9.2
2012	B-	1.52	1.16	57.4	28.4	69.2	4.5
2011	C	1.66	1.26	56.7	27.1	56.0	4.9
2010	C+	2.32	1.76	62.9	37.2	54.7	11.7
2009	C+	2.08	1.59	54.7	27.5	-3.8	3.7

Universal American Corp
Composite Group Rating: C

Largest Group Members	Assets ($mil)	Rating
CONSTITUTION LIFE INS CO	317	C+
AMERICAN PROGRESSIVE LH I C OF NY	236	B
PYRAMID LIFE INS CO	212	C
SELECTCARE OF TEXAS LLC	133	C
AMERICAN PIONEER LIFE INS CO	77	D+

CONTINENTAL AMERICAN INSURANCE COMPANY — B — Good

Major Rating Factors: Good overall results on stability tests (5.7 on a scale of 0 to 10). Strengths include good financial support from affiliation with AFLAC Inc, excellent operational trends and excellent risk diversification. Weak profitability (1.9) with operating losses during the first nine months of 2014. Return on equity has been low, averaging -14.7%. Strong capitalization (9.0) based on excellent risk adjusted capital (severe loss scenario).

Other Rating Factors: High quality investment portfolio (8.5). Excellent liquidity (7.4).

Principal Business: Group health insurance (92%), group life insurance (4%), and reinsurance (3%).

Principal Investments: NonCMO investment grade bonds (81%), cash (17%), policy loans (1%), and real estate (1%).

Investments in Affiliates: None

Group Affiliation: AFLAC Inc

Licensed in: All states except NY, PR

Commenced Business: January 1969

Address: 2801 Devine St, Columbia, SC 29205

Phone: (803) 256-6265 **Domicile State:** SC **NAIC Code:** 71730

Data Date	Rating	RACR #1	RACR #2	Total Assets ($mil)	Capital ($mil)	Net Premium ($mil)	Net Income ($mil)
9-14	B	3.24	2.32	402.9	133.3	180.4	-6.1
9-13	B	3.74	2.68	375.3	139.6	176.7	15.6
2013	B	3.47	2.49	382.4	138.0	233.4	18.8
2012	B	4.36	3.13	344.0	137.4	183.7	-21.2
2011	B	1.68	1.32	167.4	36.0	162.6	-32.4
2010	A-	2.30	1.78	116.8	31.5	104.0	-2.1
2009	A-	3.08	2.36	118.0	38.5	87.3	5.8

AFLAC Inc Composite Group Rating: B+ Largest Group Members	Assets ($mil)	Rating
AMERICAN FAMILY LIFE ASR CO OF COLUM	107913	B+
AMERICAN FAMILY LIFE ASR CO OF NY	645	A-
CONTINENTAL AMERICAN INS CO	382	B

CONTINENTAL ASSURANCE COMPANY — C — Fair

Major Rating Factors: Good quality investment portfolio (6.2 on a scale of 0 to 10) despite mixed results such as: large holdings of BBB rated bonds but junk bond exposure equal to 75% of capital. Good overall profitability (5.3). Excellent expense controls. Return on equity has been fair, averaging 6.6%. Weak overall results on stability tests (2.8) including weak results on operational trends.

Other Rating Factors: Strong capitalization (8.8) based on excellent risk adjusted capital (severe loss scenario). Excellent liquidity (9.2).

Principal Business: Individual life insurance (93%), group retirement contracts (4%), and individual health insurance (2%).

Principal Investments: NonCMO investment grade bonds (65%), CMOs and structured securities (22%), noninv. grade bonds (8%), and common & preferred stock (3%).

Investments in Affiliates: None

Group Affiliation: Wilton Re Holdings Ltd

Licensed in: All states, the District of Columbia and Puerto Rico

Commenced Business: August 1911

Address: 333 S Wabash Ave, Chicago, IL 60604

Phone: (312) 822-5000 **Domicile State:** IL **NAIC Code:** 62413

Data Date	Rating	RACR #1	RACR #2	Total Assets ($mil)	Capital ($mil)	Net Premium ($mil)	Net Income ($mil)
9-14	C	4.34	2.19	2,473.9	255.5	0.2	41.9
9-13	C	7.53	3.62	2,991.3	587.6	0.4	32.6
2013	C	7.87	3.84	2,937.9	597.3	0.5	47.7
2012	C	5.81	3.10	3,094.6	556.2	0.4	43.8
2011	C	5.73	3.04	3,210.0	519.4	0.5	29.0
2010	C	6.18	3.26	3,235.4	497.6	0.9	86.0
2009	C	6.13	3.17	3,208.2	447.6	0.7	-65.1

Adverse Trends in Operations
Decrease in asset base during 2012 (4%)
Increase in policy surrenders from 2011 to 2012 (555%)
Decrease in premium volume from 2011 to 2012 (21%)
Decrease in premium volume from 2010 to 2011 (48%)
Change in premium mix from 2009 to 2010 (8.9%)

CONTINENTAL LIFE INSURANCE COMPANY OF BRENTWOOD — B — Good

Major Rating Factors: Good quality investment portfolio (6.7 on a scale of 0 to 10) with no exposure to mortgages and no exposure to junk bonds. Good overall results on stability tests (5.5) despite excessive premium growth and fair risk adjusted capital in prior years. Strengths include good financial support from affiliation with Aetna Inc, good operational trends and excellent risk diversification. Weak profitability (2.9) with operating losses during the first nine months of 2014.

Other Rating Factors: Strong capitalization (7.0) based on excellent risk adjusted capital (severe loss scenario). Excellent liquidity (7.0).

Principal Business: Individual health insurance (96%), group health insurance (3%), and individual life insurance (2%).

Principal Investments: NonCMO investment grade bonds (30%), cash (29%), common & preferred stock (27%), CMOs and structured securities (14%), and policy loans (1%).

Investments in Affiliates: 27%

Group Affiliation: Aetna Inc

Licensed in: All states except AK, CT, DC, HI, ME, MA, NY, WA, PR

Commenced Business: December 1983

Address: 800 Crescent Centre Dr, Franklin, TN 37067

Phone: (800) 264-4000 **Domicile State:** TN **NAIC Code:** 68500

Data Date	Rating	RACR #1	RACR #2	Total Assets ($mil)	Capital ($mil)	Net Premium ($mil)	Net Income ($mil)
9-14	B	1.19	1.03	240.3	115.8	244.9	-0.9
9-13	B	0.96	0.87	193.2	87.8	186.7	0.1
2013	B	1.12	1.01	205.6	97.0	256.6	3.2
2012	B	0.97	0.89	175.6	80.2	166.4	9.7
2011	C	0.71	0.65	144.3	54.2	139.0	5.7
2010	B	0.93	0.83	143.9	59.0	142.5	11.6
2009	B+	1.53	1.29	146.0	61.4	152.2	11.1

Aetna Inc Composite Group Rating: B+ Largest Group Members	Assets ($mil)	Rating
AETNA LIFE INS CO	21793	B+
AETNA HEALTH LIFE INS CO	2148	B+
COVENTRY HEALTH LIFE INS CO	1163	B+
AETNA HEALTH INC (A PA CORP)	814	B
FIRST HEALTH LIFE HEALTH INS CO	526	B

COTTON STATES LIFE INSURANCE COMPANY *   A-   Excellent

Major Rating Factors: Good quality investment portfolio (6.7 on a scale of 0 to 10) despite mixed results such as: minimal exposure to mortgages and large holdings of BBB rated bonds but small junk bond holdings. Good liquidity (6.1) with sufficient resources to handle a spike in claims as well as a significant increase in policy surrenders. Strong capitalization (8.8) based on excellent risk adjusted capital (severe loss scenario).

Other Rating Factors: Excellent profitability (7.7). Excellent overall results on stability tests (7.3) excellent operational trends and excellent risk diversification.

Principal Business: Individual life insurance (100%).

Principal Investments: NonCMO investment grade bonds (67%), CMOs and structured securities (21%), policy loans (6%), common & preferred stock (4%), and noninv. grade bonds (2%).

Investments in Affiliates: None

Group Affiliation: COUNTRY Financial

Licensed in: AL, FL, GA, KY, LA, MS, NC, SC, TN, VA

Commenced Business: December 1955

Address: 13560 Morris Rd Suite 4000, Alpharetta, GA 30004

Phone: (309) 821-3000 **Domicile State:** GA **NAIC Code:** 62537

Data Date	Rating	RACR #1	RACR #2	Total Assets ($mil)	Capital ($mil)	Net Premium ($mil)	Net Income ($mil)
9-14	A-	3.92	2.21	330.7	61.0	21.0	4.7
9-13	A-	3.83	2.15	326.5	56.6	22.6	4.0
2013	A-	3.82	2.15	329.6	58.2	29.7	5.2
2012	A-	3.67	2.05	322.3	53.1	32.4	5.2
2011	B+	3.27	1.80	315.0	48.4	35.3	4.5
2010	B+	2.82	1.56	306.2	42.9	38.4	5.1
2009	B+	2.40	1.37	291.7	34.8	42.0	-1.1

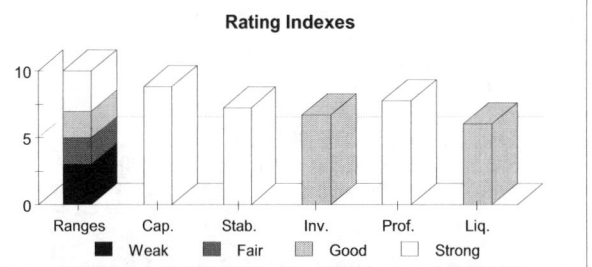

Rating Indexes

COUNTRY INVESTORS LIFE ASSURANCE COMPANY *   A-   Excellent

Major Rating Factors: Strong capitalization (8.0 on a scale of 0 to 10) based on excellent risk adjusted capital (severe loss scenario). Furthermore, this high level of risk adjusted capital has been consistently maintained over the last five years. High quality investment portfolio (8.4) despite no exposure to mortgages and substantial holdings of BBB bonds but minimal holdings in junk bonds. Excellent profitability (7.7) with operating gains in each of the last five years.

Other Rating Factors: Excellent liquidity (8.5). Excellent overall results on stability tests (7.1) excellent operational trends and excellent risk diversification.

Principal Business: Individual annuities (78%) and individual life insurance (22%).

Principal Investments: NonCMO investment grade bonds (77%), CMOs and structured securities (22%), and noninv. grade bonds (1%).

Investments in Affiliates: None

Group Affiliation: COUNTRY Financial

Licensed in: All states except CA, DC, HI, NH, NJ, NY, UT, VT, PR

Commenced Business: November 1981

Address: 1701 N Towanda Ave, Bloomington, IL 61701

Phone: (309) 821-3000 **Domicile State:** IL **NAIC Code:** 94218

Data Date	Rating	RACR #1	RACR #2	Total Assets ($mil)	Capital ($mil)	Net Premium ($mil)	Net Income ($mil)
9-14	A-	15.77	7.77	289.8	177.3	0.0	3.9
9-13	A-	14.61	7.16	269.8	172.3	0.0	3.8
2013	A-	14.95	7.35	286.9	173.4	0.0	4.8
2012	A-	15.53	7.66	260.8	169.2	0.0	4.9
2011	A-	16.08	7.96	248.3	164.7	0.0	4.7
2010	A-	16.39	8.26	244.9	160.2	0.0	4.4
2009	A-	16.44	8.53	205.4	154.9	0.0	1.8

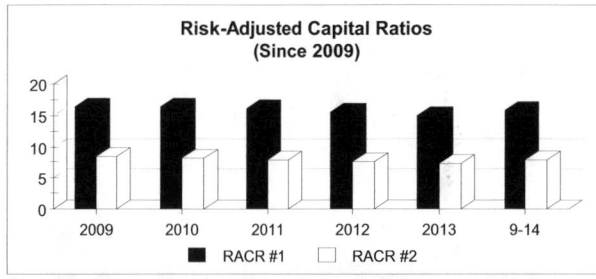

Risk-Adjusted Capital Ratios (Since 2009)

COUNTRY LIFE INSURANCE COMPANY *   A+   Excellent

Major Rating Factors: Good quality investment portfolio (5.8 on a scale of 0 to 10) despite mixed results such as: large holdings of BBB rated bonds but moderate junk bond exposure. Good liquidity (5.9) with sufficient resources to handle a spike in claims as well as a significant increase in policy surrenders. Strong capitalization (7.6) based on excellent risk adjusted capital (severe loss scenario).

Other Rating Factors: Excellent profitability (8.3). Excellent overall results on stability tests (7.6) excellent operational trends and excellent risk diversification.

Principal Business: Individual life insurance (57%), reinsurance (26%), individual health insurance (15%), group life insurance (1%), and group retirement contracts (1%).

Principal Investments: NonCMO investment grade bonds (55%), CMOs and structured securities (22%), common & preferred stock (7%), policy loans (4%), and misc. investments (8%).

Investments in Affiliates: 4%

Group Affiliation: COUNTRY Financial

Licensed in: All states except CA, DC, HI, NH, NJ, NY, VT, PR

Commenced Business: December 1928

Address: 1701 N Towanda Ave, Bloomington, IL 61701-2090

Phone: (309) 821-3000 **Domicile State:** IL **NAIC Code:** 62553

Data Date	Rating	RACR #1	RACR #2	Total Assets ($mil)	Capital ($mil)	Net Premium ($mil)	Net Income ($mil)
9-14	A+	2.12	1.38	10,573.7	1,103.9	468.2	39.5
9-13	A+	2.05	1.33	10,047.7	1,065.8	462.6	40.8
2013	A+	2.15	1.42	10,262.6	1,096.3	612.7	55.6
2012	A+	2.04	1.35	9,553.0	1,027.4	638.4	43.2
2011	A+	2.06	1.37	8,947.4	1,000.9	588.7	34.1
2010	A+	2.11	1.38	8,576.6	985.3	588.2	64.5
2009	A+	2.18	1.43	7,895.3	918.0	720.9	-38.8

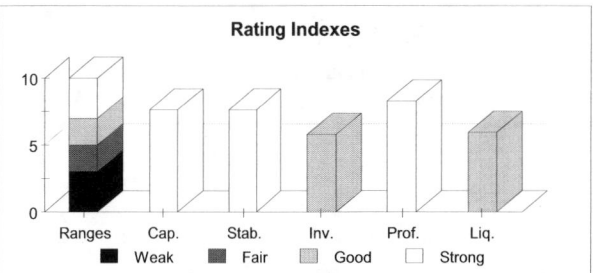

Rating Indexes

DEARBORN NATIONAL LIFE INSURANCE COMPANY *   A-   Excellent

Major Rating Factors: Good quality investment portfolio (6.4 on a scale of 0 to 10) despite mixed results such as: large holdings of BBB rated bonds but moderate junk bond exposure. Good overall profitability (5.1). Return on equity has been low, averaging 2.8%. Good liquidity (6.6) with sufficient resources to handle a spike in claims as well as a significant increase in policy surrenders.

Other Rating Factors: Good overall results on stability tests (5.7) despite negative cash flow from operations for 2013 excellent risk diversification. Strong capitalization (8.1) based on excellent risk adjusted capital (severe loss scenario).

Principal Business: Group life insurance (55%), group health insurance (43%), individual life insurance (2%), and individual annuities (1%).

Principal Investments: NonCMO investment grade bonds (62%), CMOs and structured securities (29%), noninv. grade bonds (6%), and common & preferred stock (2%).

Investments in Affiliates: 2%
Group Affiliation: HCSC Group
Licensed in: All states except NY
Commenced Business: April 1969
Address: 300 East Randolph Street, Chicago, IL 60601-5099
Phone: (800) 633-3696 **Domicile State:** IL **NAIC Code:** 71129

Data Date	Rating	RACR #1	RACR #2	Total Assets ($mil)	Capital ($mil)	Net Premium ($mil)	Net Income ($mil)
9-14	A-	2.60	1.73	2,183.0	492.8	284.1	38.9
9-13	A-	2.06	1.36	2,391.2	427.5	379.7	30.5
2013	A-	2.27	1.52	2,324.1	439.7	495.5	42.3
2012	A-	1.85	1.21	2,621.0	402.8	563.1	-6.1
2011	A-	1.75	1.10	2,895.8	399.7	694.6	-10.8
2010	A-	1.77	1.09	3,077.2	451.5	747.2	-10.3
2009	A-	1.90	1.13	3,093.1	457.4	1,142.2	-39.8

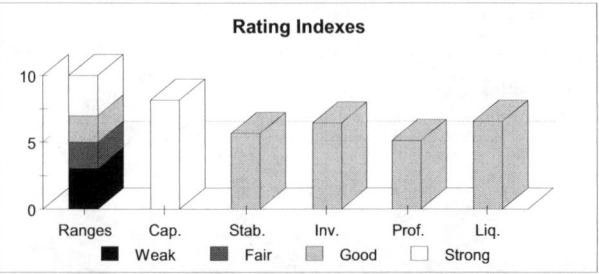

Rating Indexes
(Ranges, Cap., Stab., Inv., Prof., Liq.)
■ Weak ■ Fair ■ Good □ Strong

DELAWARE AMERICAN LIFE INSURANCE COMPANY   B   Good

Major Rating Factors: Good overall results on stability tests (6.2 on a scale of 0 to 10). Stability strengths include excellent operational trends and excellent risk diversification. Strong capitalization (10.0) based on excellent risk adjusted capital (severe loss scenario). Moreover, capital has steadily grown over the last five years. High quality investment portfolio (7.7).

Other Rating Factors: Excellent profitability (8.7) with operating gains in each of the last five years. Excellent liquidity (7.6).

Principal Business: Group health insurance (53%), reinsurance (32%), group life insurance (13%), and individual life insurance (2%).

Principal Investments: NonCMO investment grade bonds (66%), CMOs and structured securities (19%), cash (9%), and noninv. grade bonds (1%).

Investments in Affiliates: 5%
Group Affiliation: MetLife Inc
Licensed in: All states except NM, PR
Commenced Business: August 1966
Address: 600 King St, Wilmington, DE 19801
Phone: (302) 594-2000 **Domicile State:** DE **NAIC Code:** 62634

Data Date	Rating	RACR #1	RACR #2	Total Assets ($mil)	Capital ($mil)	Net Premium ($mil)	Net Income ($mil)
9-14	B	5.15	3.72	150.9	82.7	76.5	6.3
9-13	B	4.26	3.16	126.2	68.6	67.3	11.3
2013	B	4.89	3.54	137.1	74.3	91.1	17.1
2012	B	3.60	2.62	128.7	54.6	76.1	7.7
2011	B	3.08	2.23	135.8	51.4	72.4	12.6
2010	B	2.09	1.59	86.1	29.4	72.7	6.5
2009	B	3.85	2.83	65.3	25.9	-5.8	2.7

Adverse Trends in Operations

Decrease in asset base during 2012 (5%)
Change in asset mix during 2011 (4.8%)
Change in premium mix from 2009 to 2010 (117.4%)

DELAWARE LIFE INSURANCE COMPANY   C   Fair

Major Rating Factors: Fair quality investment portfolio (4.7 on a scale of 0 to 10). Fair overall results on stability tests (3.5) including negative cash flow from operations for 2013, fair risk adjusted capital in prior years. Good current capitalization (6.9) based on good risk adjusted capital (severe loss scenario) reflecting some improvement over results in 2012.

Other Rating Factors: Weak profitability (2.9). Excellent liquidity (7.1).

Principal Business: Group retirement contracts (65%), individual life insurance (34%), individual annuities (7%), and group life insurance (7%).

Principal Investments: NonCMO investment grade bonds (41%), CMOs and structured securities (15%), mortgages in good standing (9%), policy loans (6%), and misc. investments (11%).

Investments in Affiliates: 5%
Group Affiliation: Delaware Life Partners LLC
Licensed in: All states except NY
Commenced Business: January 1973
Address: 1209 Orange St, Wilmington, DE 19801
Phone: (781) 237-6030 **Domicile State:** DE **NAIC Code:** 79065

Data Date	Rating	RACR #1	RACR #2	Total Assets ($mil)	Capital ($mil)	Net Premium ($mil)	Net Income ($mil)
9-14	C	1.55	0.99	39,688.7	1,519.6	1,075.9	74.5
9-13	D+	1.25	0.81	41,859.0	1,358.1	1,498.3	682.1
2013	D+	1.43	0.93	39,279.2	1,410.4	1,559.4	682.9
2012	D	1.08	0.67	42,526.4	1,235.9	415.9	-400.8
2011	D	1.38	0.83	43,017.2	1,315.3	3,230.2	-517.1
2010	C+	1.73	1.00	48,259.1	1,879.9	3,466.7	-135.8
2009	C+	1.61	0.89	42,453.6	1,749.8	4,207.7	-44.0

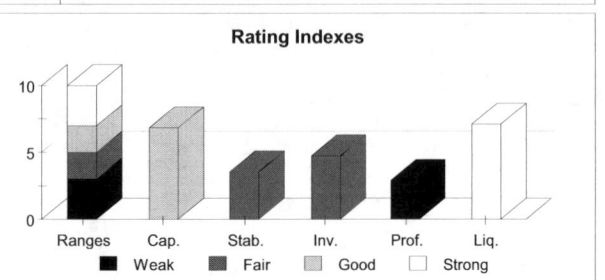

Rating Indexes
(Ranges, Cap., Stab., Inv., Prof., Liq.)
■ Weak ■ Fair ■ Good □ Strong

DELAWARE LIFE INSURANCE COMPANY OF NEW YORK | C | Fair

Major Rating Factors: Fair overall capitalization (4.0 on a scale of 0 to 10) based on mixed results -- excessive policy leverage mitigated by excellent risk adjusted capital (severe loss scenario). Moreover, capital levels have been consistently high over the last five years. Good quality investment portfolio (6.4) despite mixed results such as: minimal exposure to mortgages and large holdings of BBB rated bonds but minimal holdings in junk bonds. Good overall profitability (6.8).

Other Rating Factors: Weak overall results on stability tests (2.8) including fair financial strength of affiliated Delaware Life Partners LLC and weak results on operational trends. Excellent liquidity (7.5).

Principal Business: N/A

Principal Investments: NonCMO investment grade bonds (74%), CMOs and structured securities (20%), mortgages in good standing (4%), noninv. grade bonds (1%), and common & preferred stock (1%).

Investments in Affiliates: None

Group Affiliation: Delaware Life Partners LLC

Licensed in: CT, NY, RI

Commenced Business: August 1985

Address: 1115 Broadway 12th Floor, New York, NY 10010

Phone: (781) 237-6030 **Domicile State:** NY **NAIC Code:** 72664

Data Date	Rating	RACR #1	RACR #2	Total Assets ($mil)	Capital ($mil)	Net Premium ($mil)	Net Income ($mil)
9-14	C	8.51	4.16	3,033.2	412.3	25.1	29.4
9-13	C	5.93	3.18	3,438.5	410.4	-14.0	34.6
2013	C	7.96	3.91	3,194.6	399.9	-8.7	16.9
2012	C	4.96	2.73	3,509.7	348.6	145.0	37.6
2011	C	4.65	2.48	3,503.0	304.9	387.8	5.3
2010	C	4.14	2.25	3,426.7	295.7	433.2	55.5
2009	C	3.27	1.78	3,071.4	232.4	728.9	17.6

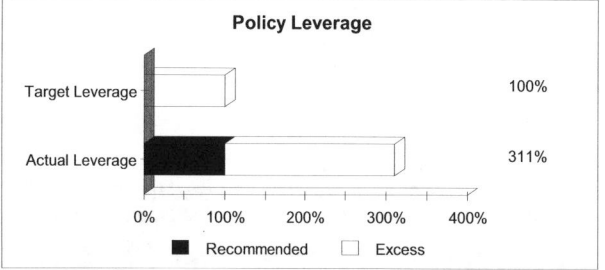

Policy Leverage

Target Leverage — 100%
Actual Leverage — 311%

■ Recommended □ Excess

EAGLE LIFE INSURANCE COMPANY | B | Good

Major Rating Factors: Good quality investment portfolio (6.5 on a scale of 0 to 10) despite mixed results such as: minimal exposure to mortgages and large holdings of BBB rated bonds but small junk bond holdings. Good liquidity (6.5) with sufficient resources to handle a spike in claims as well as a significant increase in policy surrenders. Fair overall results on stability tests (4.4).

Other Rating Factors: Weak profitability (2.9) with investment income below regulatory standards in relation to interest assumptions of reserves. Strong capitalization (10.0) based on excellent risk adjusted capital (severe loss scenario).

Principal Business: Individual annuities (52%) and reinsurance (48%).

Principal Investments: NonCMO investment grade bonds (79%), CMOs and structured securities (16%), noninv. grade bonds (3%), cash (1%), and mortgages in good standing (1%).

Investments in Affiliates: None

Group Affiliation: American Equity Investment Group

Licensed in: All states except AL, ID, MD, NY, PR

Commenced Business: August 2008

Address: 5000 Westown Pkwy, West Des Moines, IA 50266-5921

Phone: (515) 221-0002 **Domicile State:** IA **NAIC Code:** 13183

Data Date	Rating	RACR #1	RACR #2	Total Assets ($mil)	Capital ($mil)	Net Premium ($mil)	Net Income ($mil)
9-14	B	4.43	3.10	206.6	42.6	13.5	3.2
9-13	B	4.35	3.18	187.4	40.1	18.6	-1.7
2013	B	4.10	2.87	188.7	39.5	22.9	-2.2
2012	B	1.32	1.13	139.0	12.0	31.4	-2.5
2011	B	1.09	0.99	106.1	9.7	56.9	-2.7
2010	U	1.12	1.00	51.8	7.5	15.5	-3.0
2009	U	1.21	1.09	32.8	5.9	27.7	-0.4

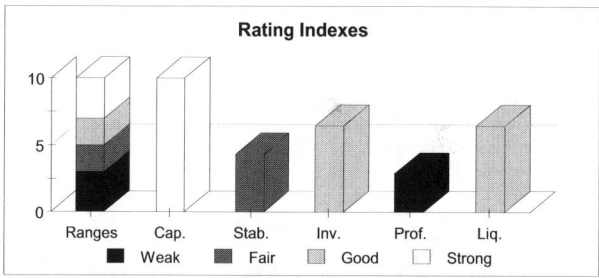

Rating Indexes

Ranges Cap. Stab. Inv. Prof. Liq.

■ Weak ▨ Fair ▧ Good □ Strong

ELCO MUTUAL LIFE & ANNUITY | C | Fair

Major Rating Factors: Good capitalization (6.5 on a scale of 0 to 10) based on good risk adjusted capital (severe loss scenario). Moreover, capital has steadily grown over the last five years. Good quality investment portfolio (5.9) despite mixed results such as: minimal exposure to mortgages and large holdings of BBB rated bonds but minimal holdings in junk bonds. Good overall profitability (5.3) although investment income, in comparison to reserve requirements, is below regulatory standards.

Other Rating Factors: Weak overall results on stability tests (2.2) including weak results on operational trends. Excellent liquidity (7.3).

Principal Business: Individual annuities (92%), individual life insurance (6%), and reinsurance (1%).

Principal Investments: NonCMO investment grade bonds (87%), common & preferred stock (5%), cash (4%), mortgages in good standing (2%), and misc. investments (2%).

Investments in Affiliates: None

Group Affiliation: None

Licensed in: All states except AK, CT, DC, HI, MA, NH, NJ, NY, RI, VT, PR

Commenced Business: May 1946

Address: 916 Sherwood Dr, Lake Bluff, IL 60044-2285

Phone: (847) 295-6000 **Domicile State:** IL **NAIC Code:** 84174

Data Date	Rating	RACR #1	RACR #2	Total Assets ($mil)	Capital ($mil)	Net Premium ($mil)	Net Income ($mil)
9-14	C	1.83	0.94	466.9	43.4	55.6	2.5
9-13	B-	1.49	0.75	647.6	39.1	13.2	3.8
2013	B-	1.72	0.88	362.8	40.8	17.3	4.3
2012	B-	1.47	0.75	553.5	35.1	20.0	6.9
2011	B-	1.73	0.91	460.1	29.1	23.4	4.7
2010	B-	2.06	1.11	384.8	25.0	122.0	1.6
2009	B	1.49	0.79	477.2	18.6	221.1	0.6

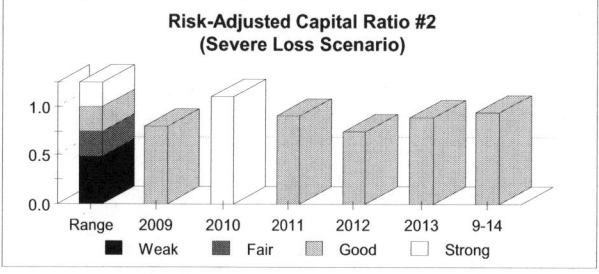

Risk-Adjusted Capital Ratio #2
(Severe Loss Scenario)

Range 2009 2010 2011 2012 2013 9-14

■ Weak ▨ Fair ▧ Good □ Strong

EMC NATIONAL LIFE COMPANY — B — Good

Major Rating Factors: Good overall results on stability tests (5.6 on a scale of 0 to 10) despite negative cash flow from operations for 2013. Other stability subfactors include good operational trends, good risk adjusted capital for prior years and excellent risk diversification. Good quality investment portfolio (6.7) despite mixed results such as: minimal exposure to mortgages and substantial holdings of BBB bonds but minimal holdings in junk bonds. Good overall profitability (6.0).

Other Rating Factors: Fair liquidity (4.2). Strong capitalization (7.6) based on excellent risk adjusted capital (severe loss scenario).

Principal Business: Individual life insurance (55%), individual annuities (32%), group life insurance (6%), reinsurance (4%), and individual health insurance (2%).

Principal Investments: NonCMO investment grade bonds (81%), CMOs and structured securities (10%), mortgages in good standing (4%), common & preferred stock (3%), and policy loans (2%).

Investments in Affiliates: None
Group Affiliation: Employers Mutual Group
Licensed in: All states except NJ, NY, PR
Commenced Business: April 1963
Address: 4095 NW Urbandale Dr, Urbandale, IA 50322
Phone: (515) 280-2511 **Domicile State:** IA **NAIC Code:** 62928

Data Date	Rating	RACR #1	RACR #2	Total Assets ($mil)	Capital ($mil)	Net Premium ($mil)	Net Income ($mil)
9-14	B	2.38	1.38	1,014.7	97.6	45.6	7.8
9-13	B-	2.04	1.19	1,038.2	84.3	45.3	4.5
2013	B-	2.14	1.24	1,030.2	87.9	60.6	5.6
2012	C	1.99	1.16	1,053.1	82.2	64.9	7.7
2011	C	2.16	1.25	1,043.3	79.9	98.2	9.1
2010	C	2.02	1.18	1,024.8	75.9	125.2	12.5
2009	C	1.35	0.81	958.7	55.0	128.7	-22.0

Adverse Trends in Operations

Decrease in asset base during 2013 (2%)
Increase in policy surrenders from 2012 to 2013 (58%)
Decrease in premium volume from 2011 to 2012 (34%)
Decrease in premium volume from 2010 to 2011 (22%)
Decrease in premium volume from 2009 to 2010 (3%)

EMPIRE FIDELITY INVESTMENTS LIFE INSURANCE COMPANY * — B+ — Good

Major Rating Factors: Good overall results on stability tests (6.7 on a scale of 0 to 10). Strengths include potential support from affiliation with FMR LLC, excellent operational trends and excellent risk diversification. Weak profitability (2.7) with investment income below regulatory standards in relation to interest assumptions of reserves. Strong capitalization (8.9) based on excellent risk adjusted capital (severe loss scenario).

Other Rating Factors: High quality investment portfolio (8.3). Excellent liquidity (7.0).

Principal Business: Individual annuities (99%) and individual life insurance (1%).

Principal Investments: NonCMO investment grade bonds (93%) and CMOs and structured securities (8%).

Investments in Affiliates: None
Group Affiliation: FMR LLC
Licensed in: NY
Commenced Business: June 1992
Address: 200 Liberty St 1 World Financl, New York, NY 10281
Phone: (212) 335-5706 **Domicile State:** NY **NAIC Code:** 71228

Data Date	Rating	RACR #1	RACR #2	Total Assets ($mil)	Capital ($mil)	Net Premium ($mil)	Net Income ($mil)
9-14	B+	2.51	2.26	2,386.2	70.5	120.3	3.1
9-13	B+	2.64	2.38	2,153.9	66.1	159.8	1.1
2013	B+	2.40	2.16	2,270.4	67.4	202.1	2.3
2012	B+	2.59	2.33	1,926.4	64.9	179.8	2.5
2011	B+	2.67	2.41	1,663.5	60.7	155.9	2.9
2010	A-	2.55	2.30	1,648.8	57.5	153.7	2.4
2009	A-	2.62	2.35	1,451.1	54.5	138.9	1.9

FMR LLC
Composite Group Rating: A-
Largest Group Members

	Assets ($mil)	Rating
FIDELITY INVESTMENTS LIFE INS CO	22477	A-
EMPIRE FIDELITY INVESTMENTS L I C	2270	B+

EMPLOYERS REASSURANCE CORPORATION — C — Fair

Major Rating Factors: Fair overall results on stability tests (3.9 on a scale of 0 to 10) including fair financial strength of affiliated GE Insurance Solutions and fair risk adjusted capital in prior years. Good quality investment portfolio (6.6) despite mixed results such as: minimal exposure to mortgages and substantial holdings of BBB bonds but small junk bond holdings. Good liquidity (6.9).

Other Rating Factors: Weak profitability (2.8). Strong capitalization (7.4) based on excellent risk adjusted capital (severe loss scenario).

Principal Business: Reinsurance (100%).

Principal Investments: NonCMO investment grade bonds (65%), CMOs and structured securities (19%), common & preferred stock (6%), mortgages in good standing (5%), and noninv. grade bonds (2%).

Investments in Affiliates: 7%
Group Affiliation: GE Insurance Solutions
Licensed in: All states except NY
Commenced Business: November 1907
Address: 5200 Metcalf Ave, Overland Park, KS 66201
Phone: (913) 676-5724 **Domicile State:** KS **NAIC Code:** 68276

Data Date	Rating	RACR #1	RACR #2	Total Assets ($mil)	Capital ($mil)	Net Premium ($mil)	Net Income ($mil)
9-14	C	1.59	1.26	11,081.7	1,243.4	294.4	127.0
9-13	C	1.01	0.79	10,861.6	799.5	335.1	118.0
2013	C	1.53	1.21	11,002.6	1,224.8	441.3	453.8
2012	C-	0.93	0.71	10,766.2	763.3	488.8	-418.0
2011	C-	0.91	0.69	10,960.8	653.9	504.1	-115.5
2010	C-	0.95	0.72	10,205.2	692.0	632.6	-95.8
2009	C-	0.79	0.64	9,604.7	724.5	671.4	-129.8

GE Insurance Solutions
Composite Group Rating: C-
Largest Group Members

	Assets ($mil)	Rating
UNION FIDELITY LIFE INS CO	19511	D+
EMPLOYERS REASSURANCE CORP	11003	C

EPIC LIFE INSURANCE COMPANY · B · Good

Major Rating Factors: Good overall results on stability tests (5.9 on a scale of 0 to 10) despite fair financial strength of affiliated Wisconsin Physicians Ins Group. Other stability subfactors include excellent operational trends and good risk diversification. Good quality investment portfolio (5.3) with no exposure to mortgages and no exposure to junk bonds. Good overall profitability (6.6) despite operating losses during the first nine months of 2014.
Other Rating Factors: Strong capitalization (9.0) based on excellent risk adjusted capital (severe loss scenario). Excellent liquidity (7.1).
Principal Business: Group health insurance (66%), group life insurance (27%), reinsurance (5%), and individual health insurance (2%).
Principal Investments: NonCMO investment grade bonds (67%), common & preferred stock (20%), CMOs and structured securities (9%), and cash (3%).
Investments in Affiliates: None
Group Affiliation: Wisconsin Physicians Ins Group
Licensed in: AZ, AR, CO, FL, IL, IN, IA, KS, KY, MD, MI, MN, MO, NE, NV, ND, OH, OK, OR, PA, SC, SD, TN, TX, VA, WV, WI
Commenced Business: August 1984
Address: 1717 W Broadway, Madison, WI 53713
Phone: (608) 221-6882 **Domicile State:** WI **NAIC Code:** 64149

Data Date	Rating	RACR #1	RACR #2	Total Assets ($mil)	Capital ($mil)	Net Premium ($mil)	Net Income ($mil)
9-14	B	3.50	2.35	60.8	30.9	19.6	-0.6
9-13	B	3.41	2.31	59.8	30.4	19.1	0.7
2013	B	2.95	1.99	61.8	31.6	25.5	1.4
2012	B+	2.55	1.73	56.9	28.2	24.5	2.4
2011	B+	2.55	1.74	54.5	26.6	21.7	2.2
2010	B+	2.82	1.89	51.5	25.9	18.2	1.1
2009	B+	2.78	1.88	47.8	23.9	18.3	1.2

Wisconsin Physicians Ins Group
Composite Group Rating: C+

Largest Group Members	Assets ($mil)	Rating
WISCONSIN PHYSICIANS SERVICE INS	345	C+
EPIC LIFE INSURANCE CO	62	B
WPS HEALTH PLAN INC	23	C

EQUITABLE LIFE & CASUALTY INSURANCE COMPANY · C+ · Fair

Major Rating Factors: Fair overall results on stability tests (4.4 on a scale of 0 to 10). Good overall profitability (5.5). Excellent expense controls. Return on equity has been low, averaging 1.6%. Strong capitalization (8.2) based on excellent risk adjusted capital (severe loss scenario). Capital levels have been relatively consistent over the last five years.
Other Rating Factors: High quality investment portfolio (7.7). Excellent liquidity (7.2).
Principal Business: Individual health insurance (88%), individual life insurance (9%), and reinsurance (3%).
Principal Investments: NonCMO investment grade bonds (68%), CMOs and structured securities (22%), mortgages in good standing (5%), and cash (4%).
Investments in Affiliates: None
Group Affiliation: Insurance Investment Co
Licensed in: All states except CA, FL, MN, NJ, NY, PR
Commenced Business: June 1935
Address: 3 Triad Center Suite 200, Salt Lake City, UT 84180
Phone: (801) 579-3400 **Domicile State:** UT **NAIC Code:** 62952

Data Date	Rating	RACR #1	RACR #2	Total Assets ($mil)	Capital ($mil)	Net Premium ($mil)	Net Income ($mil)
9-14	C+	2.61	1.77	290.5	41.0	51.4	6.8
9-13	D+	1.52	1.08	258.8	28.5	74.0	-2.2
2013	D+	2.15	1.51	275.8	39.1	91.1	-0.3
2012	C-	1.51	1.08	243.0	30.3	111.1	1.8
2011	C-	1.61	1.15	230.6	30.9	110.1	1.4
2010	C	1.55	1.08	215.8	29.5	77.4	-5.4
2009	B-	1.43	1.04	233.1	30.0	109.1	-1.5

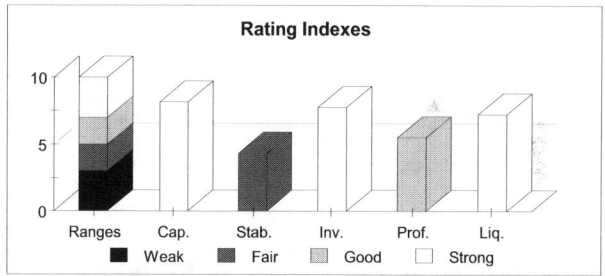

Rating Indexes

Ranges · Cap. · Stab. · Inv. · Prof. · Liq.
■ Weak ▨ Fair ▥ Good ☐ Strong

EQUITRUST LIFE INSURANCE COMPANY · B- · Good

Major Rating Factors: Good capitalization (6.5 on a scale of 0 to 10) based on good risk adjusted capital (moderate loss scenario). Capital levels have been relatively consistent over the last five years. Fair quality investment portfolio (3.8) with large holdings of BBB rated bonds in addition to junk bond exposure equal to 65% of capital. Exposure to mortgages is significant, but the mortgage default rate has been low. Fair overall results on stability tests (4.6).
Other Rating Factors: Excellent profitability (9.0) with operating gains in each of the last five years. Excellent liquidity (9.0).
Principal Business: Individual annuities (79%), group retirement contracts (14%), individual life insurance (6%), and reinsurance (1%).
Principal Investments: CMOs and structured securities (33%), nonCMO investment grade bonds (30%), mortgages in good standing (14%), noninv. grade bonds (5%), and misc. investments (10%).
Investments in Affiliates: 11%
Group Affiliation: Sammons Enterprises Inc
Licensed in: All states except NY, PR
Commenced Business: July 1967
Address: 228 W Monroe St Suite 4900, Chicago, IL 60606
Phone: (515) 225-5400 **Domicile State:** IL **NAIC Code:** 62510

Data Date	Rating	RACR #1	RACR #2	Total Assets ($mil)	Capital ($mil)	Net Premium ($mil)	Net Income ($mil)
9-14	B-	1.98	0.91	13,718.0	828.8	1,495.9	140.6
9-13	B-	1.66	0.76	12,101.9	723.1	1,593.7	147.9
2013	B-	2.33	1.07	12,615.5	846.2	2,131.9	203.6
2012	B-	1.82	0.85	11,418.6	710.0	1,391.4	185.4
2011	B-	2.31	1.04	7,238.9	437.1	647.3	19.7
2010	B-	2.10	0.95	7,360.7	451.5	390.9	37.8
2009	B-	2.11	0.97	7,163.8	435.0	602.3	57.2

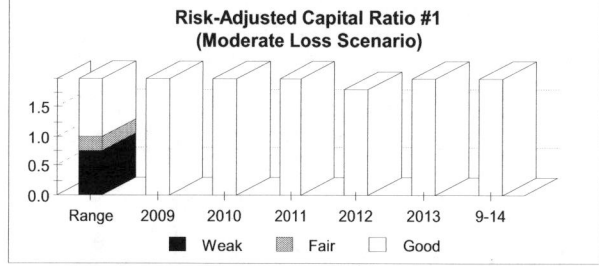

Risk-Adjusted Capital Ratio #1
(Moderate Loss Scenario)

Range · 2009 · 2010 · 2011 · 2012 · 2013 · 9-14
■ Weak ▨ Fair ☐ Good

ERIE FAMILY LIFE INSURANCE COMPANY *   A-   Excellent

Major Rating Factors: Good quality investment portfolio (5.9 on a scale of 0 to 10) despite mixed results such as: minimal exposure to mortgages and large holdings of BBB rated bonds but small junk bond holdings. Good liquidity (5.8) with sufficient resources to handle a spike in claims as well as a significant increase in policy surrenders. Excellent overall results on stability tests (7.1) excellent operational trends and excellent risk diversification.

Other Rating Factors: Strong capitalization (8.3) based on excellent risk adjusted capital (severe loss scenario). Excellent profitability (7.7) with operating gains in each of the last five years.

Principal Business: Individual life insurance (76%), individual annuities (22%), and group life insurance (2%).

Principal Investments: NonCMO investment grade bonds (88%), common & preferred stock (5%), CMOs and structured securities (3%), noninv. grade bonds (2%), and policy loans (1%).

Investments in Affiliates: None

Group Affiliation: Erie Ins Group

Licensed in: DC, IL, IN, KY, MD, MN, NC, OH, PA, TN, VA, WV, WI

Commenced Business: September 1967

Address: 100 Erie Insurance Pl, Erie, PA 16530

Phone: (800) 458-0811 **Domicile State:** PA **NAIC Code:** 70769

Data Date	Rating	RACR #1	RACR #2	Total Assets ($mil)	Capital ($mil)	Net Premium ($mil)	Net Income ($mil)
9-14	A-	3.42	1.88	2,077.0	297.4	111.9	7.0
9-13	A-	3.52	1.93	2,001.3	292.4	101.3	12.3
2013	A-	3.36	1.86	2,021.4	290.7	137.2	14.9
2012	A-	3.44	1.90	1,933.1	281.5	130.7	25.5
2011	B+	3.19	1.74	1,838.9	244.9	133.9	33.8
2010	B	2.79	1.49	1,750.3	208.2	158.0	37.7
2009	B	2.42	1.28	1,665.9	173.5	224.6	3.2

Adverse Trends in Operations

Decrease in premium volume from 2011 to 2012 (2%)
Decrease in premium volume from 2010 to 2011 (15%)
Decrease in premium volume from 2009 to 2010 (30%)

FAMILY HERITAGE LIFE INSURANCE COMPANY OF AMERICA *   A-   Excellent

Major Rating Factors: Excellent overall results on stability tests (7.3 on a scale of 0 to 10). Strengths that enhance stability include excellent operational trends and excellent risk diversification. Strong capitalization (7.4) based on excellent risk adjusted capital (severe loss scenario). Furthermore, this high level of risk adjusted capital has been consistently maintained over the last five years. High quality investment portfolio (7.2).

Other Rating Factors: Excellent profitability (9.5) with operating gains in each of the last five years. Excellent liquidity (8.2).

Principal Business: Individual health insurance (97%), group health insurance (3%), and individual life insurance (1%).

Principal Investments: NonCMO investment grade bonds (99%).

Investments in Affiliates: None

Group Affiliation: Torchmark Corp

Licensed in: All states except NY

Commenced Business: November 1989

Address: 6001 E Royalton Rd Suite 200, Cleveland, OH 44147-3529

Phone: (440) 922-5200 **Domicile State:** OH **NAIC Code:** 77968

Data Date	Rating	RACR #1	RACR #2	Total Assets ($mil)	Capital ($mil)	Net Premium ($mil)	Net Income ($mil)
9-14	A-	1.82	1.26	725.3	66.0	166.4	12.2
9-13	A-	2.52	1.80	631.6	79.3	143.2	11.6
2013	A-	2.09	1.48	641.5	66.9	192.7	17.0
2012	B+	2.15	1.57	571.1	62.1	177.0	16.5
2011	B+	2.22	1.71	488.5	55.3	161.0	15.6
2010	B+	2.19	1.72	431.9	48.3	145.9	14.0
2009	B+	2.06	1.63	365.4	41.7	132.0	13.3

Adverse Trends in Operations

Increase in policy surrenders from 2012 to 2013 (77%)
Increase in policy surrenders from 2010 to 2011 (33%)
Increase in policy surrenders from 2009 to 2010 (119%)

FAMILY LIFE INSURANCE COMPANY   C   Fair

Major Rating Factors: Fair overall results on stability tests (4.2 on a scale of 0 to 10). Good liquidity (6.6) with sufficient resources to handle a spike in claims as well as a significant increase in policy surrenders. Weak profitability (2.9) with investment income below regulatory standards in relation to interest assumptions of reserves.

Other Rating Factors: Strong capitalization (9.7) based on excellent risk adjusted capital (severe loss scenario). High quality investment portfolio (8.7).

Principal Business: Individual health insurance (71%) and individual life insurance (29%).

Principal Investments: NonCMO investment grade bonds (67%), cash (14%), policy loans (11%), CMOs and structured securities (6%), and mortgages in good standing (2%).

Investments in Affiliates: None

Group Affiliation: Harris Insurance Holdings Inc

Licensed in: All states except NY, PR

Commenced Business: June 1949

Address: 1200 6th Ave Park Place Bldg, Seattle, WA 98101

Phone: (512) 404-5284 **Domicile State:** TX **NAIC Code:** 63053

Data Date	Rating	RACR #1	RACR #2	Total Assets ($mil)	Capital ($mil)	Net Premium ($mil)	Net Income ($mil)
9-14	C	3.61	2.80	148.2	33.8	19.0	3.8
9-13	C+	3.35	2.65	151.3	31.4	19.8	3.1
2013	C	3.41	2.69	147.6	31.9	26.0	3.5
2012	C	3.39	2.63	147.4	31.7	27.9	5.8
2011	C	3.23	2.77	126.4	29.5	23.2	3.7
2010	C+	3.20	2.58	130.3	29.3	27.4	5.1
2009	C+	2.84	2.55	122.3	26.0	16.2	4.4

Rating Indexes

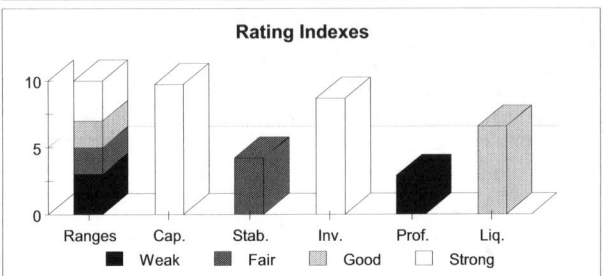

FARM BUREAU LIFE INSURANCE COMPANY *   B+   Good

Major Rating Factors: Good quality investment portfolio (5.5 on a scale of 0 to 10) despite mixed results such as: large holdings of BBB rated bonds but moderate junk bond exposure. Good overall results on stability tests (6.4). Stability strengths include excellent operational trends and excellent risk diversification. Fair liquidity (4.4).

Other Rating Factors: Strong capitalization (7.2) based on excellent risk adjusted capital (severe loss scenario). Excellent profitability (7.5) with operating gains in each of the last five years.

Principal Business: Individual life insurance (55%), individual annuities (40%), reinsurance (2%), group retirement contracts (1%), and individual health insurance (1%).

Principal Investments: NonCMO investment grade bonds (59%), CMOs and structured securities (23%), mortgages in good standing (7%), noninv. grade bonds (4%), and misc. investments (7%).

Investments in Affiliates: None

Group Affiliation: Iowa Farm Bureau

Licensed in: AZ, CO, ID, IA, KS, MN, MT, NE, NV, NM, ND, OK, OR, SD, UT, WA, WI, WY

Commenced Business: January 1945

Address: 5400 University Ave, West Des Moines, IA 50266-5997

Phone: (515) 225-5400   **Domicile State:** IA   **NAIC Code:** 63088

Data Date	Rating	RACR #1	RACR #2	Total Assets ($mil)	Capital ($mil)	Net Premium ($mil)	Net Income ($mil)
9-14	B+	2.19	1.13	8,042.3	562.9	496.6	66.9
9-13	B+	1.91	0.96	7,673.4	462.4	483.3	66.6
2013	B+	2.01	1.03	7,723.0	492.5	636.8	94.6
2012	B+	2.20	1.11	7,415.2	547.4	648.2	86.6
2011	B+	2.16	1.08	6,956.3	509.2	690.0	72.7
2010	B+	2.17	1.10	6,622.9	453.6	610.7	72.3
2009	B+	2.21	1.13	5,983.3	428.5	596.1	45.5

Adverse Trends in Operations

Decrease in premium volume from 2012 to 2013 (2%)
Decrease in capital during 2013 (10%)
Decrease in premium volume from 2011 to 2012 (6%)

FARM BUREAU LIFE INSURANCE COMPANY OF MICHIGAN *   A-   Excellent

Major Rating Factors: Good quality investment portfolio (5.7 on a scale of 0 to 10) despite significant exposure to mortgages . Mortgage default rate has been low. large holdings of BBB rated bonds in addition to small junk bond holdings. Good liquidity (5.5) with sufficient resources to cover a large increase in policy surrenders. Good overall results on stability tests (6.9) excellent operational trends and excellent risk diversification.

Other Rating Factors: Strong capitalization (8.5) based on excellent risk adjusted capital (severe loss scenario). Excellent profitability (7.7) with operating gains in each of the last five years.

Principal Business: Individual life insurance (67%), individual annuities (31%), group retirement contracts (1%), and group life insurance (1%).

Principal Investments: NonCMO investment grade bonds (67%), mortgages in good standing (17%), common & preferred stock (7%), noninv. grade bonds (3%), and misc. investments (7%).

Investments in Affiliates: 1%

Group Affiliation: Michigan Farm Bureau

Licensed in: MI

Commenced Business: September 1951

Address: 7373 West Saginaw Hwy, Lansing, MI 48909

Phone: (517) 323-7000   **Domicile State:** MI   **NAIC Code:** 63096

Data Date	Rating	RACR #1	RACR #2	Total Assets ($mil)	Capital ($mil)	Net Premium ($mil)	Net Income ($mil)
9-14	A-	3.66	1.98	2,356.3	435.9	85.0	26.1
9-13	A-	3.41	1.84	2,279.2	380.7	86.0	18.2
2013	A-	3.44	1.86	2,294.0	409.4	116.9	24.6
2012	A-	3.29	1.78	2,246.8	354.4	126.7	26.3
2011	A-	3.25	1.78	2,122.5	327.7	145.7	20.5
2010	A-	2.77	1.59	2,045.9	317.9	182.5	15.9
2009	A-	2.97	1.68	1,884.2	300.5	164.5	18.9

Rating Indexes

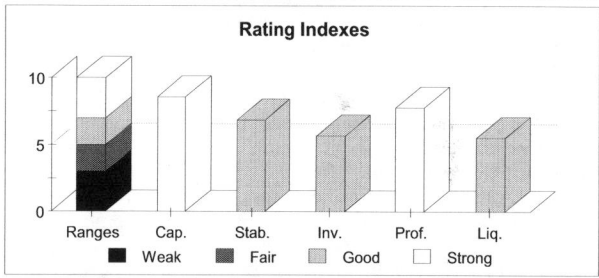

FARM BUREAU LIFE INSURANCE COMPANY OF MISSOURI *   A-   Excellent

Major Rating Factors: Good quality investment portfolio (5.8 on a scale of 0 to 10) despite mixed results such as: no exposure to mortgages and substantial holdings of BBB bonds but minimal holdings in junk bonds. Good overall profitability (6.7). Return on equity has been low, averaging 3.3%. Good liquidity (5.8).

Other Rating Factors: Good overall results on stability tests (6.9) excellent operational trends and excellent risk diversification. Strong capitalization (7.5) based on excellent risk adjusted capital (severe loss scenario).

Principal Business: Individual life insurance (75%), individual annuities (24%), group life insurance (1%), and group health insurance (1%).

Principal Investments: NonCMO investment grade bonds (60%), CMOs and structured securities (20%), common & preferred stock (10%), and policy loans (5%).

Investments in Affiliates: 2%

Group Affiliation: Missouri Farm Bureau

Licensed in: MO

Commenced Business: July 1950

Address: 701 S Country Club Dr, Jefferson City, MO 65109

Phone: (573) 893-1400   **Domicile State:** MO   **NAIC Code:** 63118

Data Date	Rating	RACR #1	RACR #2	Total Assets ($mil)	Capital ($mil)	Net Premium ($mil)	Net Income ($mil)
9-14	A-	2.08	1.32	522.5	58.8	30.6	2.6
9-13	A-	2.02	1.26	498.5	51.1	34.3	2.9
2013	A-	1.98	1.25	506.1	54.2	42.3	4.6
2012	A-	1.94	1.22	472.7	52.8	38.0	2.1
2011	A-	2.61	1.59	446.8	49.2	36.8	1.8
2010	A-	2.70	1.64	422.3	47.3	39.0	-1.3
2009	A-	2.85	1.72	391.1	45.3	42.0	1.6

Rating Indexes

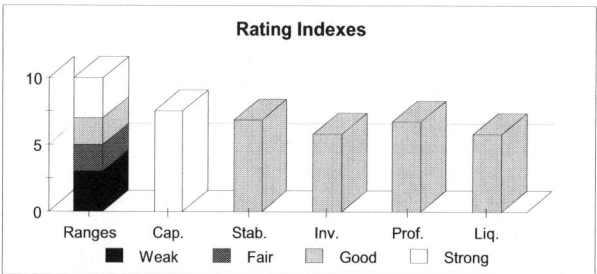

FARM FAMILY LIFE INSURANCE COMPANY — B — Good

Major Rating Factors: Good overall profitability (6.9 on a scale of 0 to 10). Return on equity has been fair, averaging 5.7%. Good liquidity (5.5) with sufficient resources to cover a large increase in policy surrenders. Good overall results on stability tests (6.0). Stability strengths include excellent operational trends and excellent risk diversification.

Other Rating Factors: Fair quality investment portfolio (4.6). Strong capitalization (7.3) based on excellent risk adjusted capital (severe loss scenario).

Principal Business: Individual life insurance (71%), individual annuities (22%), individual health insurance (7%), and group life insurance (1%).

Principal Investments: NonCMO investment grade bonds (72%), common & preferred stock (10%), mortgages in good standing (5%), policy loans (4%), and misc. investments (9%).

Investments in Affiliates: None

Group Affiliation: American National Group Inc

Licensed in: CT, DE, ME, MD, MA, NH, NJ, NY, PA, RI, VT, VA, WV

Commenced Business: January 1954

Address: 344 Route 9W, Glenmont, NY 12077

Phone: (518) 431-5000 **Domicile State:** NY **NAIC Code:** 63126

Data Date	Rating	RACR #1	RACR #2	Total Assets ($mil)	Capital ($mil)	Net Premium ($mil)	Net Income ($mil)
9-14	B	2.09	1.19	1,270.3	152.1	53.2	0.4
9-13	B	2.36	1.31	1,236.9	148.6	51.9	15.7
2013	B	2.15	1.22	1,248.4	151.9	72.2	18.6
2012	B	2.26	1.25	1,196.4	134.2	76.6	10.7
2011	B	2.22	1.22	1,149.3	124.5	82.3	15.1
2010	B	2.12	1.18	1,110.1	122.7	75.8	10.9
2009	B	2.11	1.14	1,055.4	108.7	71.5	1.9

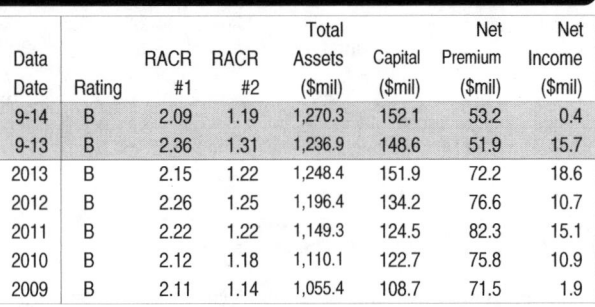

Net Income History (in millions of dollars)

FARMERS NEW WORLD LIFE INSURANCE COMPANY — B- — Good

Major Rating Factors: Good overall results on stability tests (5.3 on a scale of 0 to 10) despite fair financial strength of affiliated Zurich Financial Services Group. Other stability subfactors include good operational trends and excellent risk diversification. Good quality investment portfolio (6.1) despite mixed results such as: minimal exposure to mortgages and substantial holdings of BBB bonds but small junk bond holdings. Good liquidity (5.5).

Other Rating Factors: Fair profitability (4.0) with investment income below regulatory standards in relation to interest assumptions of reserves. Strong capitalization (7.4) based on excellent risk adjusted capital (severe loss scenario).

Principal Business: Individual life insurance (89%), individual annuities (7%), reinsurance (2%), and individual health insurance (2%).

Principal Investments: NonCMO investment grade bonds (66%), CMOs and structured securities (25%), policy loans (5%), noninv. grade bonds (1%), and misc. investments (2%).

Investments in Affiliates: None

Group Affiliation: Zurich Financial Services Group

Licensed in: All states except NY, PR

Commenced Business: May 1911

Address: 3003 77th Ave SE, Mercer Island, WA 98040-2890

Phone: (206) 232-8400 **Domicile State:** WA **NAIC Code:** 63177

Data Date	Rating	RACR #1	RACR #2	Total Assets ($mil)	Capital ($mil)	Net Premium ($mil)	Net Income ($mil)
9-14	B-	2.26	1.27	7,118.7	603.7	436.9	100.7
9-13	B-	2.58	1.44	7,081.0	622.4	442.4	129.4
2013	B-	2.39	1.33	7,141.0	566.6	469.3	79.8
2012	B-	2.40	1.33	6,995.4	578.6	609.1	209.6
2011	B-	2.46	1.38	6,859.6	601.0	630.2	137.2
2010	B-	2.50	1.34	6,858.8	671.5	610.6	124.4
2009	B-	2.54	1.38	6,739.6	674.1	600.7	-13.3

Zurich Financial Services Group
Composite Group Rating: C

Largest Group Members	Assets ($mil)	Rating
ZURICH AMERICAN INS CO	30184	C+
ZURICH AMERICAN LIFE INS CO	12969	C
FARMERS NEW WORLD LIFE INS CO	7141	B-
CENTRE LIFE INS CO	1928	B-
FARMERS REINS CO	1400	B-

FEDERATED LIFE INSURANCE COMPANY * — A — Excellent

Major Rating Factors: Good quality investment portfolio (6.7 on a scale of 0 to 10) despite mixed results such as: no exposure to mortgages and large holdings of BBB rated bonds but small junk bond holdings. Good liquidity (6.7) with sufficient resources to handle a spike in claims as well as a significant increase in policy surrenders. Excellent overall results on stability tests (7.4) excellent operational trends and excellent risk diversification.

Other Rating Factors: Strong capitalization (9.3) based on excellent risk adjusted capital (severe loss scenario). Excellent profitability (8.4) with operating gains in each of the last five years.

Principal Business: Individual life insurance (69%), individual annuities (16%), individual health insurance (13%), and group life insurance (3%).

Principal Investments: NonCMO investment grade bonds (82%), CMOs and structured securities (11%), noninv. grade bonds (4%), common & preferred stock (2%), and policy loans (1%).

Investments in Affiliates: None

Group Affiliation: Federated Mutual Ins Group

Licensed in: All states except AK, DC, HI, PR

Commenced Business: January 1959

Address: 121 E Park Square, Owatonna, MN 55060

Phone: (507) 455-5200 **Domicile State:** MN **NAIC Code:** 63258

Data Date	Rating	RACR #1	RACR #2	Total Assets ($mil)	Capital ($mil)	Net Premium ($mil)	Net Income ($mil)
9-14	A	4.60	2.53	1,497.0	305.7	119.8	13.5
9-13	A	4.44	2.41	1,395.9	287.7	125.3	8.4
2013	A	4.42	2.46	1,435.5	293.5	179.5	13.9
2012	A	4.29	2.35	1,309.3	275.9	177.0	13.8
2011	A	4.37	2.41	1,187.5	261.5	153.5	17.8
2010	A	4.61	2.53	1,099.2	247.5	143.7	18.7
2009	A	4.55	2.48	1,018.5	234.5	134.7	19.2

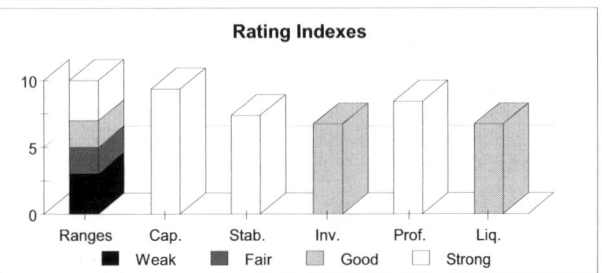

Rating Indexes

Ranges · Cap. · Stab. · Inv. · Prof. · Liq.

■ Weak ▦ Fair ▨ Good □ Strong

FIDELITY & GUARANTY LIFE INSURANCE COMPANY   C+   Fair

Major Rating Factors: Fair quality investment portfolio (3.7 on a scale of 0 to 10) with large holdings of BBB rated bonds in addition to junk bond exposure equal to 89% of capital. Fair overall results on stability tests (4.6) including fair risk adjusted capital in prior years. Good capitalization (5.5) based on good risk adjusted capital (moderate loss scenario).

Other Rating Factors: Good liquidity (6.1). Excellent profitability (8.1).

Principal Business: Individual annuities (74%), individual life insurance (24%), and reinsurance (2%).

Principal Investments: NonCMO investment grade bonds (65%), CMOs and structured securities (21%), noninv. grade bonds (6%), common & preferred stock (3%), and misc. investments (4%).

Investments in Affiliates: 3%

Group Affiliation: Harbinger Holdings LLC

Licensed in: All states except NY, PR

Commenced Business: November 1960

Address: 1001 Fleet St, Baltimore, MD 21202

Phone: (410) 895-0100 **Domicile State:** IA **NAIC Code:** 63274

Data Date	Rating	RACR #1	RACR #2	Total Assets ($mil)	Capital ($mil)	Net Premium ($mil)	Net Income ($mil)
9-14	C+	1.33	0.74	18,461.3	1,134.4	1,675.5	84.6
9-13	C+	1.43	0.81	17,184.0	1,064.3	802.6	22.4
2013	C+	1.36	0.77	17,422.5	1,108.3	1,363.8	118.2
2012	C+	1.35	0.79	16,698.7	900.5	324.8	102.2
2011	C+	1.61	0.86	15,784.8	846.4	-631.8	110.3
2010	C+	1.58	0.81	16,386.1	902.1	1,127.6	245.8
2009	C	1.36	0.69	16,742.3	816.4	775.7	-319.1

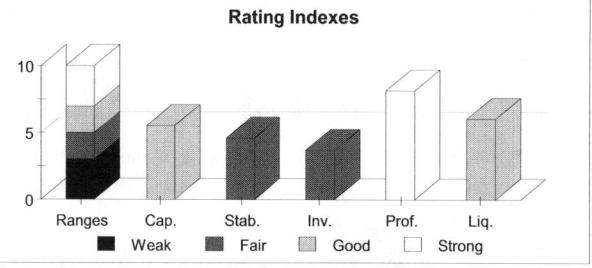

Rating Indexes

■ Weak   ■ Fair   ▨ Good   □ Strong

FIDELITY & GUARANTY LIFE INSURANCE COMPANY OF NEW Y(B-   Good

Major Rating Factors: Good overall results on stability tests (5.1 on a scale of 0 to 10) despite fair financial strength of affiliated Harbinger Holdings LLC. Other stability subfactors include excellent operational trends and excellent risk diversification. Good quality investment portfolio (6.6) despite mixed results such as: no exposure to mortgages and large holdings of BBB rated bonds but small junk bond holdings. Good liquidity (6.8).

Other Rating Factors: Fair profitability (4.5) with investment income below regulatory standards in relation to interest assumptions of reserves. Strong capitalization (8.3) based on excellent risk adjusted capital (severe loss scenario).

Principal Business: Individual annuities (92%) and individual life insurance (8%).

Principal Investments: NonCMO investment grade bonds (76%), CMOs and structured securities (16%), noninv. grade bonds (3%), and common & preferred stock (3%).

Investments in Affiliates: None

Group Affiliation: Harbinger Holdings LLC

Licensed in: NY

Commenced Business: November 1962

Address: 445 Park Ave 10th Floor, New York, NY 10022

Phone: (888) 697-5433 **Domicile State:** NY **NAIC Code:** 69434

Data Date	Rating	RACR #1	RACR #2	Total Assets ($mil)	Capital ($mil)	Net Premium ($mil)	Net Income ($mil)
9-14	B-	3.59	1.84	517.0	64.1	22.4	4.0
9-13	B-	3.81	1.96	507.3	62.2	27.9	2.6
2013	B-	3.55	1.82	504.3	61.9	33.5	1.3
2012	B-	2.49	1.27	472.7	41.1	18.9	1.0
2011	B-	2.91	1.45	471.8	44.7	9.7	4.5
2010	B-	2.53	1.24	476.9	41.9	36.8	0.9
2009	B-	2.33	1.14	461.8	39.4	17.9	-3.5

Harbinger Holdings LLC
Composite Group Rating: C+

Largest Group Members	Assets ($mil)	Rating
FIDELITY GUARANTY LIFE INS CO	17423	C+
FIDELITY GUARANTY LIFE INS CO NY	504	B-

FIDELITY INVESTMENTS LIFE INSURANCE COMPANY *   A-   Excellent

Major Rating Factors: Good quality investment portfolio (6.6 on a scale of 0 to 10) despite mixed results such as: no exposure to mortgages and large holdings of BBB rated bonds but minimal holdings in junk bonds. Good overall profitability (6.8). Excellent expense controls. Return on equity has been fair, averaging 6.8%. Strong capitalization (8.2) based on excellent risk adjusted capital (severe loss scenario).

Other Rating Factors: Excellent liquidity (7.0). Excellent overall results on stability tests (7.2) excellent operational trends and excellent risk diversification.

Principal Business: Individual annuities (99%) and individual life insurance (1%).

Principal Investments: NonCMO investment grade bonds (77%), common & preferred stock (9%), CMOs and structured securities (8%), and noninv. grade bonds (7%).

Investments in Affiliates: 9%

Group Affiliation: FMR LLC

Licensed in: All states except NY, PR

Commenced Business: December 1981

Address: 175 E 400 S 8th Floor, Salt Lake City, UT 84111

Phone: (617) 563-9106 **Domicile State:** UT **NAIC Code:** 93696

Data Date	Rating	RACR #1	RACR #2	Total Assets ($mil)	Capital ($mil)	Net Premium ($mil)	Net Income ($mil)
9-14	A-	2.98	1.78	23,882.2	656.2	1,412.2	37.9
9-13	A-	2.95	1.79	21,275.2	593.0	1,458.1	36.5
2013	A-	2.90	1.75	22,477.4	614.7	1,871.3	56.1
2012	A-	2.97	1.83	18,981.4	554.4	1,704.8	64.4
2011	A-	4.44	2.74	16,892.5	766.9	1,606.0	21.6
2010	A-	4.44	2.74	16,673.0	739.3	1,517.3	63.7
2009	A	4.46	2.78	14,513.4	669.3	1,194.0	13.3

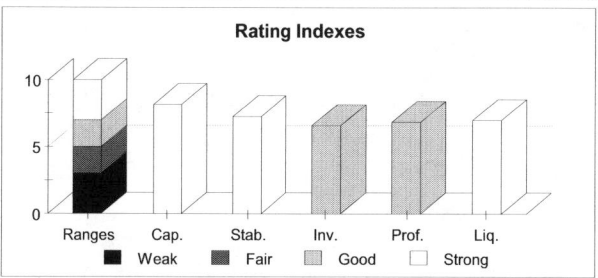

Rating Indexes

■ Weak   ■ Fair   ▨ Good   □ Strong

FIDELITY LIFE ASSOCIATION

C   **Fair**

Major Rating Factors: Fair overall results on stability tests (4.0 on a scale of 0 to 10) including negative cash flow from operations for 2013. Good quality investment portfolio (5.9) despite mixed results such as: minimal exposure to mortgages and large holdings of BBB rated bonds but small junk bond holdings. Good liquidity (6.5) with sufficient resources to handle a spike in claims.

Other Rating Factors: Weak profitability (1.4) with investment income below regulatory standards in relation to interest assumptions of reserves. Strong capitalization (9.8) based on excellent risk adjusted capital (severe loss scenario).

Principal Business: Individual life insurance (76%), group life insurance (19%), reinsurance (5%), and group health insurance (1%).

Principal Investments: NonCMO investment grade bonds (53%), CMOs and structured securities (17%), common & preferred stock (9%), cash (6%), and misc. investments (16%).

Investments in Affiliates: None

Group Affiliation: Fidelity Lifecorp Inc

Licensed in: All states except NY, WY, PR

Commenced Business: February 1896

Address: 1211 W. 22nd St., Ste 209, Oak Brook, IL 60523

Phone: (630) 522-0392   **Domicile State:** IL   **NAIC Code:** 63290

Data Date	Rating	RACR #1	RACR #2	Total Assets ($mil)	Capital ($mil)	Net Premium ($mil)	Net Income ($mil)
9-14	C	5.15	2.88	412.7	129.0	43.3	24.2
9-13	C	4.07	2.29	413.2	102.6	60.3	-28.2
2013	C	5.12	2.88	414.6	124.1	44.3	-22.8
2012	C	5.20	2.94	441.7	135.8	71.5	-30.3
2011	C+	6.56	3.71	463.7	175.3	72.0	-14.3
2010	B-	6.88	3.87	480.5	196.4	63.1	-12.7
2009	B	8.59	4.82	484.8	220.5	41.6	-19.7

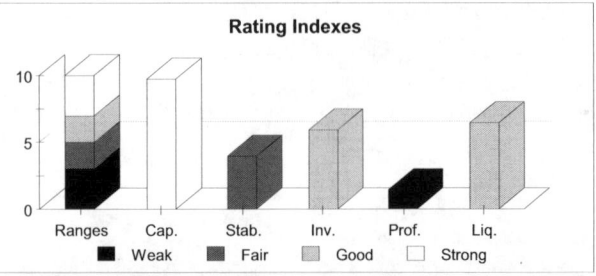

Rating Indexes

FIDELITY SECURITY LIFE INSURANCE COMPANY

B-   **Good**

Major Rating Factors: Good quality investment portfolio (6.4 on a scale of 0 to 10) despite mixed results such as: minimal exposure to mortgages and large holdings of BBB rated bonds but small junk bond holdings. Good overall profitability (6.6). Return on equity has been good over the last five years, averaging 10.3%. Good liquidity (6.2).

Other Rating Factors: Fair overall results on stability tests (3.5) including excessive premium growth and weak results on operational trends. Strong capitalization (8.4) based on excellent risk adjusted capital (severe loss scenario).

Principal Business: Group health insurance (88%), reinsurance (5%), individual annuities (2%), individual health insurance (2%), and other lines (3%).

Principal Investments: NonCMO investment grade bonds (49%), CMOs and structured securities (40%), noninv. grade bonds (4%), common & preferred stock (2%), and misc. investments (5%).

Investments in Affiliates: 1%

Group Affiliation: Fidelity Security Group

Licensed in: All states except PR

Commenced Business: July 1969

Address: 3130 Broadway, Kansas City, MO 64111

Phone: (816) 750-1060   **Domicile State:** MO   **NAIC Code:** 71870

Data Date	Rating	RACR #1	RACR #2	Total Assets ($mil)	Capital ($mil)	Net Premium ($mil)	Net Income ($mil)
9-14	B-	3.01	1.90	841.6	147.1	126.8	13.1
9-13	B	3.31	2.01	797.9	132.0	84.3	10.2
2013	B-	2.99	1.83	819.5	135.3	109.2	13.9
2012	B	2.79	1.67	789.7	123.2	202.7	2.3
2011	B+	3.01	1.85	702.7	122.8	117.3	14.9
2010	B+	2.87	1.82	664.4	109.4	207.9	16.0
2009	B+	1.74	1.24	608.5	93.9	361.9	10.4

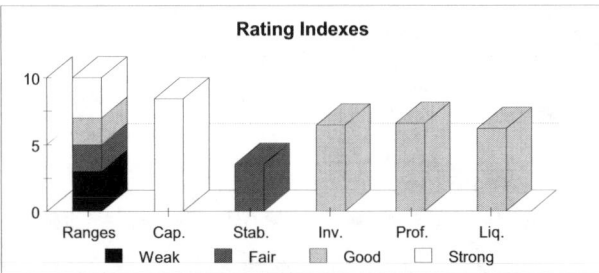

Rating Indexes

FIRST ALLMERICA FINANCIAL LIFE INSURANCE

C-   **Fair**

Major Rating Factors: Fair overall capitalization (4.0 on a scale of 0 to 10) based on mixed results -- excessive policy leverage mitigated by excellent risk adjusted capital (severe loss scenario). However, capital levels have fluctuated somewhat during past years. Fair profitability (4.4). Return on equity has been fair, averaging 9.1%. Fair overall results on stability tests (3.3).

Other Rating Factors: Good quality investment portfolio (6.6). Good liquidity (5.5).

Principal Business: Reinsurance (98%) and individual life insurance (1%).

Principal Investments: NonCMO investment grade bonds (53%), CMOs and structured securities (42%), policy loans (3%), and noninv. grade bonds (1%).

Investments in Affiliates: None

Group Affiliation: Global Atlantic Financial Group

Licensed in: All states except PR

Commenced Business: June 1845

Address: 440 Lincoln St, Worcester, MA 01653

Phone: (508) 855-1000   **Domicile State:** MA   **NAIC Code:** 69140

Data Date	Rating	RACR #1	RACR #2	Total Assets ($mil)	Capital ($mil)	Net Premium ($mil)	Net Income ($mil)
9-14	C-	4.25	2.02	4,211.4	208.3	60.8	59.9
9-13	D	2.88	1.45	3,181.9	109.9	-1,198.6	-65.8
2013	D	3.47	1.65	4,206.0	154.7	-313.6	-38.7
2012	C	2.93	1.46	2,898.3	125.4	1,632.8	19.6
2011	C	8.28	3.93	1,276.4	85.9	27.2	19.5
2010	C	9.56	4.30	1,479.6	189.0	30.9	37.1
2009	C	8.93	4.31	1,580.6	156.9	147.8	10.8

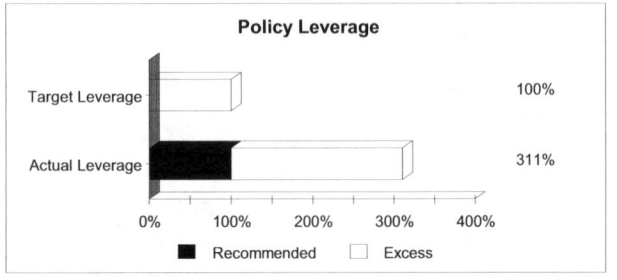

Policy Leverage

FIRST ASSURANCE LIFE OF AMERICA   B   Good

Major Rating Factors: Good overall results on stability tests (5.7 on a scale of 0 to 10). Stability strengths include good operational trends and good risk diversification. Strong capitalization (10.0) based on excellent risk adjusted capital (severe loss scenario). Moreover, capital levels have been consistently high over the last five years. High quality investment portfolio (8.8).

Other Rating Factors: Excellent profitability (8.3) with operating gains in each of the last five years. Excellent liquidity (9.1).

Principal Business: Credit life insurance (74%) and credit health insurance (26%).

Principal Investments: NonCMO investment grade bonds (69%), common & preferred stock (26%), and cash (5%).

Investments in Affiliates: 26%

Group Affiliation: LDS Group

Licensed in: AL, LA, MS, TN

Commenced Business: September 1981

Address: 9016 Bluebonnet Blvd, Baton Rouge, LA 70884-2810

Phone: (504) 769-9923 **Domicile State:** LA **NAIC Code:** 94579

Data Date	Rating	RACR #1	RACR #2	Total Assets ($mil)	Capital ($mil)	Net Premium ($mil)	Net Income ($mil)
9-14	B	3.17	3.01	37.7	32.2	2.6	0.4
9-13	B	3.14	2.99	36.6	31.5	2.8	0.4
2013	B	3.14	2.98	36.8	31.7	3.0	0.7
2012	B	3.10	2.95	35.8	31.1	3.2	0.9
2011	B	4.02	3.78	31.3	27.0	2.7	1.0
2010	B	4.15	3.93	30.9	25.6	-2.2	1.0
2009	B	3.70	3.44	30.7	24.3	4.3	0.9

Adverse Trends in Operations

Decrease in premium volume from 2012 to 2013 (4%)
Change in premium mix from 2010 to 2011 (38.2%)
Decrease in premium volume from 2009 to 2010 (150%)

FIRST BERKSHIRE HATHAWAY LIFE INSURANCE COMPANY   C+   Fair

Major Rating Factors: Fair overall results on stability tests (4.4 on a scale of 0 to 10). Weak profitability (1.0) with operating losses during the first nine months of 2014. Strong capitalization (9.6) based on excellent risk adjusted capital (severe loss scenario). Capital levels have been relatively consistent over the last five years.

Other Rating Factors: High quality investment portfolio (7.5). Excellent liquidity (10.0).

Principal Business: Group retirement contracts (100%).

Principal Investments: NonCMO investment grade bonds (95%), CMOs and structured securities (3%), common & preferred stock (2%), and cash (1%).

Investments in Affiliates: None

Group Affiliation: Berkshire-Hathaway

Licensed in: (No states)

Commenced Business: March 2003

Address: Marine Air Terminal LaGuardia, Flushing, NY 11371

Phone: (402) 536-3000 **Domicile State:** NY **NAIC Code:** 11591

Data Date	Rating	RACR #1	RACR #2	Total Assets ($mil)	Capital ($mil)	Net Premium ($mil)	Net Income ($mil)
9-14	C+	3.04	2.74	370.5	31.5	44.0	-4.3
9-13	B-	2.14	1.85	223.0	15.0	64.4	2.4
2013	C	2.48	2.23	286.6	25.5	80.1	-87.3
2012	B-	1.74	1.57	63.4	12.5	30.0	2.3
2011	C+	3.03	2.73	18.4	10.1	1.6	-1.4
2010	U	4.13	3.71	13.0	11.3	0.0	0.2
2009	U	4.20	3.78	12.5	11.3	0.0	0.4

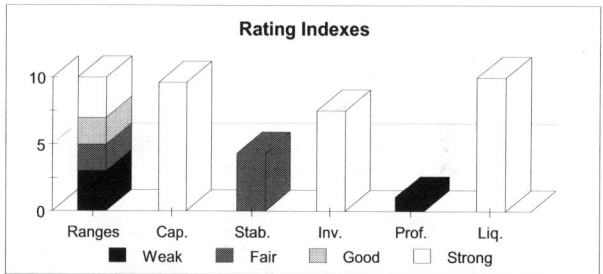

Rating Indexes

FIRST HEALTH LIFE & HEALTH INSURANCE COMPANY   B   Good

Major Rating Factors: Good current capitalization (5.4 on a scale of 0 to 10) based on mixed results -- excessive policy leverage mitigated by excellent risk adjusted capital (severe loss scenario) reflecting significant improvement over results in 2009. Fair overall results on stability tests (4.1) including negative cash flow from operations for 2013, weak risk adjusted capital in prior years. Weak profitability (1.8).

Other Rating Factors: Weak liquidity (0.2). High quality investment portfolio (9.3).

Principal Business: Individual health insurance (99%) and group health insurance (1%).

Principal Investments: NonCMO investment grade bonds (50%), cash (43%), and CMOs and structured securities (7%).

Investments in Affiliates: None

Group Affiliation: Aetna Inc

Licensed in: All states except NY, PR

Commenced Business: June 1979

Address: 300 W 11th St, Kansas City, MO 64199-3487

Phone: (816) 391-2231 **Domicile State:** TX **NAIC Code:** 90328

Data Date	Rating	RACR #1	RACR #2	Total Assets ($mil)	Capital ($mil)	Net Premium ($mil)	Net Income ($mil)
9-14	B	1.27	1.05	577.2	234.2	699.3	0.7
9-13	B	1.12	0.94	591.9	301.1	1,086.5	-108.6
2013	B	1.02	0.85	525.6	253.3	1,420.5	-175.3
2012	C+	1.46	1.22	600.2	412.2	1,494.9	48.3
2011	C+	1.19	0.99	577.0	363.5	1,156.5	28.4
2010	C+	1.61	1.33	592.4	329.3	1,125.2	64.8
2009	C+	0.59	0.49	811.1	269.5	2,729.2	-49.4

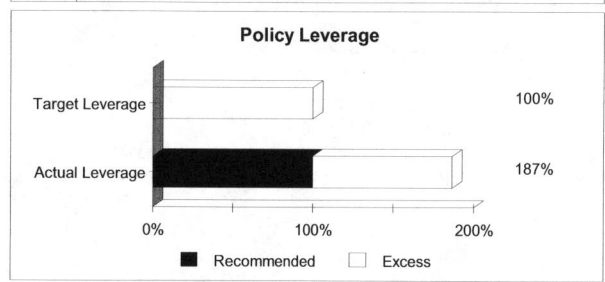

Policy Leverage

FIRST INVESTORS LIFE INSURANCE COMPANY   B   Good

Major Rating Factors: Good quality investment portfolio (6.7 on a scale of 0 to 10) despite mixed results such as: no exposure to mortgages and large holdings of BBB rated bonds but minimal holdings in junk bonds. Good overall profitability (5.1) although investment income, in comparison to reserve requirements, is below regulatory standards. Good overall results on stability tests (5.9) despite excessive premium growth excellent operational trends and good risk diversification.

Other Rating Factors: Strong capitalization (7.3) based on excellent risk adjusted capital (severe loss scenario). Excellent liquidity (7.1).

Principal Business: Individual annuities (63%) and individual life insurance (37%).

Principal Investments: NonCMO investment grade bonds (77%), policy loans (18%), and noninv. grade bonds (1%).

Investments in Affiliates: None

Group Affiliation: First Investors Consolidated Corp

Licensed in: All states except SD, PR

Commenced Business: December 1962

Address: 110 Wall Street, New York, NY 10005

Phone: (800) 832-7783 **Domicile State:** NY **NAIC Code:** 63495

Data Date	Rating	RACR #1	RACR #2	Total Assets ($mil)	Capital ($mil)	Net Premium ($mil)	Net Income ($mil)
9-14	B	2.25	1.18	1,786.5	55.8	179.3	4.4
9-13	B+	2.44	1.30	1,518.2	51.0	111.4	4.7
2013	B	2.23	1.19	1,641.4	51.8	182.1	9.9
2012	B+	2.36	1.27	1,341.1	46.5	126.6	10.3
2011	B+	2.16	1.18	1,192.2	36.5	111.6	10.2
2010	A-	1.79	1.03	1,152.9	28.5	101.6	10.1
2009	A-	6.47	3.59	1,139.2	120.0	82.1	9.7

Adverse Trends in Operations

Decrease in capital during 2010 (76%)

FIRST METLIFE INVESTORS INSURANCE COMPANY   C   Fair

Major Rating Factors: Fair overall results on stability tests (4.2 on a scale of 0 to 10). Good overall capitalization (6.0) based on good risk adjusted capital (moderate loss scenario). Nevertheless, capital levels have fluctuated during prior years. Good quality investment portfolio (6.3) despite large holdings of BBB rated bonds in addition to moderate junk bond exposure. Exposure to mortgages is significant, but the mortgage default rate has been low.

Other Rating Factors: Weak profitability (2.0) with operating losses during the first nine months of 2014. Excellent liquidity (8.6).

Principal Business: Individual annuities (75%) and individual life insurance (25%).

Principal Investments: NonCMO investment grade bonds (61%), CMOs and structured securities (18%), mortgages in good standing (12%), and noninv. grade bonds (7%).

Investments in Affiliates: None

Group Affiliation: MetLife Inc

Licensed in: NY

Commenced Business: March 1993

Address: 200 Park Avenue, New York, NY 10166-0188

Phone: (212) 766-4923 **Domicile State:** NY **NAIC Code:** 60992

Data Date	Rating	RACR #1	RACR #2	Total Assets ($mil)	Capital ($mil)	Net Premium ($mil)	Net Income ($mil)
9-14	C	1.69	0.85	6,265.7	121.2	104.9	-2.4
9-13	C	2.12	1.06	6,019.1	152.9	253.7	-19.1
2013	C	2.12	1.07	6,235.1	152.3	295.6	-23.2
2012	C	2.63	1.31	5,530.6	176.5	595.9	-22.7
2011	C	3.24	1.63	4,688.3	196.0	1,049.9	-21.1
2010	C+	4.45	2.24	3,908.8	220.2	712.8	-27.6
2009	C+	5.91	2.99	3,013.3	225.9	634.8	-8.2

Rating Indexes

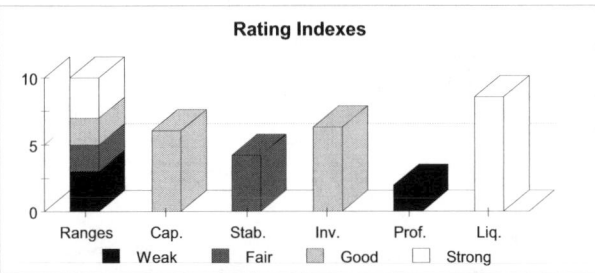

FIRST PENN-PACIFIC LIFE INSURANCE COMPANY   B   Good

Major Rating Factors: Good overall results on stability tests (5.8 on a scale of 0 to 10) despite negative cash flow from operations for 2013. Other stability subfactors include good operational trends and excellent risk diversification. Good quality investment portfolio (5.7) despite significant exposure to mortgages . Mortgage default rate has been low. large holdings of BBB rated bonds in addition to small junk bond holdings. Good liquidity (5.4).

Other Rating Factors: Strong capitalization (7.9) based on excellent risk adjusted capital (severe loss scenario). Excellent profitability (7.7) with operating gains in each of the last five years.

Principal Business: Individual life insurance (59%) and reinsurance (41%).

Principal Investments: NonCMO investment grade bonds (70%), CMOs and structured securities (14%), mortgages in good standing (10%), noninv. grade bonds (4%), and policy loans (2%).

Investments in Affiliates: None

Group Affiliation: Lincoln National Corp

Licensed in: All states except NY, PR

Commenced Business: June 1964

Address: 1300 S Clinton St, Fort Wayne, IN 46802-3518

Phone: (260) 455-2000 **Domicile State:** IN **NAIC Code:** 67652

Data Date	Rating	RACR #1	RACR #2	Total Assets ($mil)	Capital ($mil)	Net Premium ($mil)	Net Income ($mil)
9-14	B	2.97	1.61	1,744.5	231.6	110.5	18.4
9-13	B	2.59	1.39	1,818.4	217.1	93.1	2.0
2013	B	2.95	1.60	1,817.4	235.6	129.8	64.1
2012	B	2.98	1.59	1,897.3	257.5	127.0	80.4
2011	B	2.33	1.24	1,880.4	209.7	132.4	31.0
2010	B	2.22	1.19	1,894.4	204.9	174.1	2.1
2009	B	2.31	1.20	1,857.1	205.4	2.5	31.6

Adverse Trends in Operations

Decrease in asset base during 2013 (4%)
Decrease in capital during 2013 (9%)
Decrease in premium volume from 2011 to 2012 (4%)
Decrease in premium volume from 2010 to 2011 (24%)
Change in premium mix from 2009 to 2010 (4.3%)

FIRST RELIANCE STANDARD LIFE INSURANCE COMPANY *   A   Excellent

Major Rating Factors: Good overall results on stability tests (6.2 on a scale of 0 to 10). Strengths that enhance stability include excellent operational trends and excellent risk diversification. Good quality investment portfolio (6.8) despite mixed results such as: no exposure to mortgages and substantial holdings of BBB bonds but small junk bond holdings. Strong capitalization (10.0) based on excellent risk adjusted capital (severe loss scenario).

Other Rating Factors: Excellent profitability (7.7) with operating gains in each of the last five years. Excellent liquidity (7.0).

Principal Business: Group health insurance (58%) and group life insurance (42%).

Principal Investments: NonCMO investment grade bonds (66%), CMOs and structured securities (24%), and noninv. grade bonds (5%).

Investments in Affiliates: None

Group Affiliation: Tokio Marine Holdings Inc

Licensed in: DC, DE, NY

Commenced Business: October 1984

Address: 590 Madison Ave 29th Floor, New York, NY 10022

Phone: (215) 787-4000 **Domicile State:** NY **NAIC Code:** 71005

Data Date	Rating	RACR #1	RACR #2	Total Assets ($mil)	Capital ($mil)	Net Premium ($mil)	Net Income ($mil)
9-14	A	6.07	3.87	188.7	69.6	42.3	5.3
9-13	A	6.33	4.16	190.6	67.8	43.4	3.8
2013	A	5.71	3.72	182.7	64.2	56.8	5.9
2012	A	6.69	4.70	176.2	63.6	53.5	6.7
2011	B	6.47	4.93	166.3	60.5	48.3	4.1
2010	B	6.51	4.94	160.5	60.6	52.1	4.3
2009	B	4.54	3.33	147.7	56.8	58.1	6.1

Adverse Trends in Operations

Decrease in premium volume from 2010 to 2011 (7%)
Decrease in premium volume from 2009 to 2010 (10%)
Increase in policy surrenders from 2009 to 2010 (568%)

FIRST SECURITY BENEFIT LIFE & ANNUITY   B   Good

Major Rating Factors: Good current capitalization (6.2 on a scale of 0 to 10) based on good risk adjusted capital (moderate loss scenario) reflecting some improvement over results in 2012. Fair overall results on stability tests (4.6) including fair risk adjusted capital in prior years. Fair quality investment portfolio (3.8).

Other Rating Factors: Weak profitability (2.0) with investment income below regulatory standards in relation to interest assumptions of reserves. Excellent liquidity (9.6).

Principal Business: Individual annuities (92%) and group retirement contracts (7%).

Principal Investments: NonCMO investment grade bonds (62%), CMOs and structured securities (31%), cash (5%), and noninv. grade bonds (1%).

Investments in Affiliates: None

Group Affiliation: Sammons Enterprises Inc

Licensed in: KS, NY

Commenced Business: July 1995

Address: 800 Westchester Ave Ste 641 N, Rye Brook, NY 10573

Phone: (785) 431-3000 **Domicile State:** NY **NAIC Code:** 60084

Data Date	Rating	RACR #1	RACR #2	Total Assets ($mil)	Capital ($mil)	Net Premium ($mil)	Net Income ($mil)
9-14	B	1.79	0.87	695.6	31.9	90.8	2.3
9-13	B	1.17	0.69	534.6	12.7	142.5	-2.9
2013	B	1.92	0.96	617.1	30.6	216.9	-3.8
2012	B	0.88	0.69	380.6	9.8	77.1	-2.9
2011	B	1.25	1.13	158.4	11.9	4.2	0.3
2010	B	1.20	1.08	181.2	11.6	5.3	0.9
2009	B	1.11	1.00	180.2	10.7	15.6	0.8

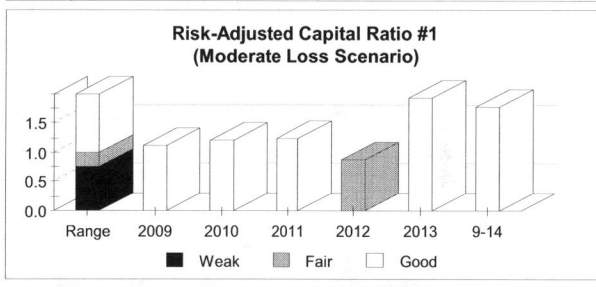

Risk-Adjusted Capital Ratio #1 (Moderate Loss Scenario)

Range 2009 2010 2011 2012 2013 9-14

■ Weak   ▨ Fair   □ Good

FIRST SYMETRA NATIONAL LIFE INSURANCE COMPANY OF NE   A-   Excellent

Major Rating Factors: Good quality investment portfolio (6.7 on a scale of 0 to 10) despite significant exposure to mortgages . Mortgage default rate has been low. large holdings of BBB rated bonds in addition to small junk bond holdings. Good liquidity (6.3) with sufficient resources to handle a spike in claims as well as a significant increase in policy surrenders. Excellent overall results on stability tests (7.0) excellent operational trends and excellent risk diversification.

Other Rating Factors: Strong capitalization (8.4) based on excellent risk adjusted capital (severe loss scenario). Excellent profitability (9.1) despite modest operating losses during 2009.

Principal Business: Individual annuities (94%) and group health insurance (6%).

Principal Investments: NonCMO investment grade bonds (62%), CMOs and structured securities (25%), mortgages in good standing (12%), and noninv. grade bonds (1%).

Investments in Affiliates: None

Group Affiliation: White Mountains Group

Licensed in: NY

Commenced Business: January 1990

Address: 260 Madison Ave 8th Floor, New York, NY 10016

Phone: (425) 256-8000 **Domicile State:** NY **NAIC Code:** 78417

Data Date	Rating	RACR #1	RACR #2	Total Assets ($mil)	Capital ($mil)	Net Premium ($mil)	Net Income ($mil)
9-14	A-	3.93	1.95	932.2	103.2	163.2	6.7
9-13	A-	3.87	1.98	794.4	95.2	107.7	10.2
2013	A-	4.03	2.02	813.2	96.7	154.6	11.9
2012	B+	3.68	1.91	727.3	85.9	110.8	12.5
2011	B	3.08	1.62	705.6	74.6	121.9	5.2
2010	B	3.42	1.78	639.3	68.6	116.4	7.9
2009	C+	3.52	1.83	538.0	62.0	232.0	-0.6

Adverse Trends in Operations

Increase in policy surrenders from 2011 to 2012 (40%)
Decrease in premium volume from 2011 to 2012 (9%)
Increase in policy surrenders from 2010 to 2011 (179%)
Increase in policy surrenders from 2009 to 2010 (51%)
Decrease in premium volume from 2009 to 2010 (50%)

FIRST UNITED AMERICAN LIFE INSURANCE COMPANY * B+ Good

Major Rating Factors: Good overall results on stability tests (6.7 on a scale of 0 to 10). Stability strengths include excellent operational trends and excellent risk diversification. Good quality investment portfolio (5.0) despite mixed results such as: large holdings of BBB rated bonds but moderate junk bond exposure. Good overall profitability (6.8). Excellent expense controls.

Other Rating Factors: Good liquidity (5.2). Strong capitalization (7.8) based on excellent risk adjusted capital (severe loss scenario).

Principal Business: Individual health insurance (58%), individual life insurance (30%), individual annuities (9%), and group health insurance (3%).

Principal Investments: NonCMO investment grade bonds (79%), CMOs and structured securities (6%), noninv. grade bonds (6%), policy loans (4%), and cash (3%).

Investments in Affiliates: None
Group Affiliation: Torchmark Corp
Licensed in: NY
Commenced Business: December 1984
Address: 1020 7th North St, Liverpool, NY 13088
Phone: (315) 451-2544 **Domicile State:** NY **NAIC Code:** 74101

Data Date	Rating	RACR #1	RACR #2	Total Assets ($mil)	Capital ($mil)	Net Premium ($mil)	Net Income ($mil)
9-14	B+	2.32	1.50	191.8	36.0	56.0	5.2
9-13	B+	2.43	1.59	182.4	34.0	60.5	2.8
2013	B+	2.18	1.42	178.0	34.2	78.7	3.1
2012	B+	2.31	1.49	165.4	34.3	88.7	9.9
2011	B+	2.46	1.60	140.4	33.5	66.2	4.4
2010	A-	2.78	1.85	132.7	38.0	65.5	9.3
2009	A-	3.02	2.03	126.8	38.4	64.5	4.9

Adverse Trends in Operations

Decrease in premium volume from 2012 to 2013 (11%)
Change in premium mix from 2011 to 2012 (5%)
Decrease in capital during 2011 (12%)

FIRST UNUM LIFE INSURANCE COMPANY C+ Fair

Major Rating Factors: Fair overall results on stability tests (4.8 on a scale of 0 to 10) including fair financial strength of affiliated Unum Group. Fair quality investment portfolio (4.5) with large holdings of BBB rated bonds in addition to junk bond exposure equal to 86% of capital. Strong capitalization (7.5) based on excellent risk adjusted capital (severe loss scenario).

Other Rating Factors: Excellent profitability (7.6) with operating gains in each of the last five years. Excellent liquidity (7.3).

Principal Business: Group health insurance (54%), individual health insurance (26%), group life insurance (18%), and individual life insurance (2%).

Principal Investments: NonCMO investment grade bonds (75%), CMOs and structured securities (9%), noninv. grade bonds (9%), and mortgages in good standing (6%).

Investments in Affiliates: None
Group Affiliation: Unum Group
Licensed in: NY
Commenced Business: January 1960
Address: Christiana Bldg Suite 100, Tarrytown, NY 10591
Phone: (914) 524-4056 **Domicile State:** NY **NAIC Code:** 64297

Data Date	Rating	RACR #1	RACR #2	Total Assets ($mil)	Capital ($mil)	Net Premium ($mil)	Net Income ($mil)
9-14	C+	2.67	1.36	2,794.1	267.7	270.1	3.5
9-13	C+	2.48	1.27	2,663.2	241.9	261.5	21.0
2013	C+	2.75	1.42	2,704.1	266.3	348.7	20.4
2012	C+	2.65	1.41	2,682.6	251.8	360.2	11.3
2011	C+	3.16	1.82	2,398.7	269.3	381.1	30.7
2010	C+	2.69	1.63	2,123.3	239.4	392.8	27.2
2009	C+	2.41	1.45	2,012.2	218.3	401.7	7.5

Unum Group
Composite Group Rating: C+
Largest Group Members

	Assets ($mil)	Rating
UNUM LIFE INS CO OF AMERICA	19079	C+
PROVIDENT LIFE ACCIDENT INS CO	8348	C+
PAUL REVERE LIFE INS CO	4302	C+
COLONIAL LIFE ACCIDENT INS CO	2753	C+
FIRST UNUM LIFE INS CO	2704	C+

FIVE STAR LIFE INSURANCE COMPANY C+ Fair

Major Rating Factors: Fair overall results on stability tests (4.3 on a scale of 0 to 10). Good quality investment portfolio (6.7) despite mixed results such as: large holdings of BBB rated bonds but moderate junk bond exposure. Good liquidity (5.9) with sufficient resources to handle a spike in claims as well as a significant increase in policy surrenders.

Other Rating Factors: Weak profitability (1.9) with operating losses during the first nine months of 2014. Strong capitalization (7.9) based on excellent risk adjusted capital (severe loss scenario).

Principal Business: Group life insurance (80%) and individual life insurance (20%).

Principal Investments: NonCMO investment grade bonds (70%), CMOs and structured securities (16%), noninv. grade bonds (6%), cash (4%), and policy loans (3%).

Investments in Affiliates: None
Group Affiliation: 5 Star Financial LLC
Licensed in: All states except NY
Commenced Business: May 1943
Address: 8440 Jefferson Hwy Ste 301, Baton Rouge, LA 70809-7652
Phone: (800) 776-2322 **Domicile State:** LA **NAIC Code:** 77879

Data Date	Rating	RACR #1	RACR #2	Total Assets ($mil)	Capital ($mil)	Net Premium ($mil)	Net Income ($mil)
9-14	C+	2.60	1.62	258.8	35.2	94.6	-8.4
9-13	B	3.41	2.14	240.4	45.1	85.6	-2.6
2013	B-	2.98	1.87	248.7	40.5	116.0	-6.2
2012	B	3.95	2.51	243.2	52.4	111.6	2.0
2011	B	2.00	1.40	218.4	54.3	107.6	1.5
2010	B-	1.99	1.38	202.9	52.8	101.6	2.8
2009	B-	1.93	1.35	188.4	51.0	98.9	0.5

Rating Indexes

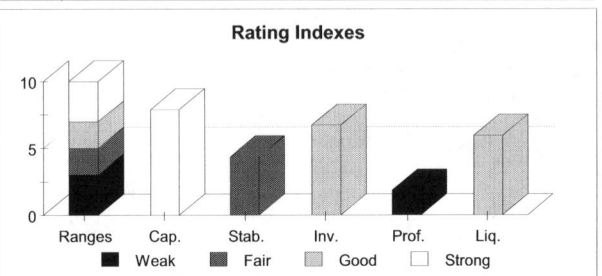

	Ranges	Cap.	Stab.	Inv.	Prof.	Liq.

■ Weak ▨ Fair ▥ Good ▢ Strong

FLORIDA COMBINED LIFE INSURANCE COMPANY INCORPORAT | B | Good

Major Rating Factors: Good quality investment portfolio (5.3 on a scale of 0 to 10) with no exposure to mortgages and no exposure to junk bonds. Good overall results on stability tests (5.4). Strengths include good financial support from affiliation with Blue Cross Blue Shield of Florida, excellent operational trends and good risk diversification. Fair profitability (4.2).

Other Rating Factors: Strong capitalization (8.0) based on excellent risk adjusted capital (severe loss scenario). Excellent liquidity (7.7).

Principal Business: Group health insurance (52%), individual health insurance (24%), group life insurance (20%), individual life insurance (2%), and reinsurance (2%).

Principal Investments: NonCMO investment grade bonds (25%), cash (16%), and CMOs and structured securities (1%).

Investments in Affiliates: 57%

Group Affiliation: Blue Cross Blue Shield of Florida

Licensed in: AL, FL, GA, NC, SC

Commenced Business: May 1988

Address: 5011 Gate Pkwy Bld 200 Ste 400, Jacksonville, FL 32256

Phone: (800) 333-3256 **Domicile State:** FL **NAIC Code:** 76031

Data Date	Rating	RACR #1	RACR #2	Total Assets ($mil)	Capital ($mil)	Net Premium ($mil)	Net Income ($mil)
9-14	B	4.76	3.76	45.7	25.0	0.0	0.0
9-13	B+	4.97	4.17	42.1	22.8	0.0	0.1
2013	B+	4.40	3.96	42.8	23.4	0.0	0.2
2012	B+	4.87	4.24	35.3	22.4	0.0	0.1
2011	B+	4.85	4.36	34.5	22.0	0.0	0.2
2010	B+	4.78	4.31	32.9	21.5	0.0	1.0
2009	B+	4.49	4.04	32.0	20.3	0.0	0.7

Blue Cross Blue Shield of Florida Composite Group Rating: B Largest Group Members	Assets ($mil)	Rating
BLUE CROSS BLUE SHIELD OF FLORIDA	6225	B+
CAPITAL HEALTH PLAN INC	451	A-
FLORIDA HEALTH CARE PLAN INC	114	A-
COMP OPTIONS INS CO INC	82	D
FLORIDA COMBINED LIFE INS CO INC	43	B

FORETHOUGHT LIFE INSURANCE COMPANY | B- | Good

Major Rating Factors: Good overall results on stability tests (5.3 on a scale of 0 to 10) despite fair financial strength of affiliated Global Atlantic Financial Group. Other stability subfactors include excellent operational trends and excellent risk diversification. Good quality investment portfolio (6.1) despite mixed results such as: large holdings of BBB rated bonds but moderate junk bond exposure. Good liquidity (6.6).

Other Rating Factors: Strong capitalization (8.4) based on excellent risk adjusted capital (severe loss scenario). Excellent profitability (7.7) with operating gains in each of the last five years.

Principal Business: Individual annuities (70%), reinsurance (10%), group life insurance (10%), group retirement contracts (5%), and other lines (4%).

Principal Investments: NonCMO investment grade bonds (76%), CMOs and structured securities (12%), mortgages in good standing (6%), and noninv. grade bonds (4%).

Investments in Affiliates: None

Group Affiliation: Global Atlantic Financial Group

Licensed in: All states except NY

Commenced Business: September 1980

Address: Forethought Center, Batesville, IN 47006

Phone: (812) 933-6600 **Domicile State:** IN **NAIC Code:** 91642

Data Date	Rating	RACR #1	RACR #2	Total Assets ($mil)	Capital ($mil)	Net Premium ($mil)	Net Income ($mil)
9-14	B-	3.79	1.95	11,568.0	757.1	3,610.3	110.3
9-13	B	2.78	1.37	7,474.2	501.9	1,603.6	61.0
2013	B	2.73	1.38	7,957.2	522.5	2,331.0	23.0
2012	B	2.93	1.49	6,256.1	461.4	1,413.8	69.0
2011	B	2.94	1.47	5,465.8	416.4	877.3	50.7
2010	C+	2.99	1.54	4,939.5	417.3	811.3	69.3
2009	C+	2.78	1.47	4,543.4	346.8	922.9	68.3

Global Atlantic Financial Group Composite Group Rating: C Largest Group Members	Assets ($mil)	Rating
COMMONWEALTH ANNUITY LIFE INS CO	10212	B-
FORETHOUGHT LIFE INS CO	7957	B-
ACCORDIA LIFE ANNUITY CO	7059	C-
FIRST ALLMERICA FINANCIAL LIFE INS	4206	C-
FORETHOUGHT NATIONAL LIFE INS CO	208	C

FRANDISCO LIFE INSURANCE COMPANY * | A- | Excellent

Major Rating Factors: Good overall results on stability tests (6.5 on a scale of 0 to 10). Strengths that enhance stability include excellent operational trends and good risk diversification. Strong capitalization (10.0) based on excellent risk adjusted capital (severe loss scenario). Moreover, capital has steadily grown over the last five years. High quality investment portfolio (8.9).

Other Rating Factors: Excellent profitability (9.8) with operating gains in each of the last five years. Excellent liquidity (9.4).

Principal Business: Reinsurance (100%).

Principal Investments: NonCMO investment grade bonds (100%).

Investments in Affiliates: None

Group Affiliation: Franklin Financial Corp

Licensed in: GA

Commenced Business: November 1977

Address: 213 E Tugalo St, Toccoa, GA 30577

Phone: (706) 886-7571 **Domicile State:** GA **NAIC Code:** 89079

Data Date	Rating	RACR #1	RACR #2	Total Assets ($mil)	Capital ($mil)	Net Premium ($mil)	Net Income ($mil)
9-14	A-	8.47	7.62	65.0	61.1	10.8	4.4
9-13	A-	7.98	7.18	59.0	55.4	10.6	3.8
2013	A-	7.86	7.07	60.5	56.7	14.5	5.0
2012	A-	7.40	6.66	54.6	51.6	13.0	4.7
2011	A-	7.00	6.30	49.3	46.7	12.0	4.3
2010	B+	6.83	6.14	43.7	41.4	11.0	4.1
2009	B+	6.69	6.02	40.3	38.1	10.8	4.4

Adverse Trends in Operations
Change in asset mix during 2011 (4.2%)

FREEDOM LIFE INSURANCE COMPANY OF AMERICA   C   Fair

Major Rating Factors: Fair overall capitalization (4.7 on a scale of 0 to 10) based on mixed results -- excessive policy leverage mitigated by fair risk adjusted capital (moderate loss scenario). Fair overall results on stability tests (3.7) including fair risk adjusted capital in prior years. Good quality investment portfolio (6.7).

Other Rating Factors: Excellent profitability (7.2) despite modest operating losses during 2009 and 2010. Excellent liquidity (7.1).

Principal Business: Group health insurance (80%), individual health insurance (14%), and individual life insurance (6%).

Principal Investments: NonCMO investment grade bonds (39%), common & preferred stock (30%), cash (21%), CMOs and structured securities (8%), and noninv. grade bonds (2%).

Investments in Affiliates: 30%

Group Affiliation: Credit Suisse Group

Licensed in: AL, AZ, AR, CO, DE, FL, GA, IL, IN, IA, KS, KY, LA, MD, MI, MN, MS, MO, NE, NV, NM, NC, OH, OK, OR, PA, SC, SD, TN, TX, UT, VA, WA, WV, WY

Commenced Business: June 1956

Address: 110 W 7th St Suite 300, Fort Worth, TX 76102

Phone: (817) 878-3300 **Domicile State:** TX **NAIC Code:** 62324

Data Date	Rating	RACR #1	RACR #2	Total Assets ($mil)	Capital ($mil)	Net Premium ($mil)	Net Income ($mil)
9-14	C	0.82	0.71	54.8	28.8	79.6	5.8
9-13	C+	0.91	0.79	50.7	28.3	71.4	7.3
2013	C	0.67	0.59	56.2	22.6	98.1	12.3
2012	C	0.73	0.65	41.5	19.6	68.8	5.9
2011	C-	0.74	0.65	34.4	13.9	44.9	0.6
2010	C-	0.90	0.79	31.4	14.0	31.9	0.0
2009	C-	1.57	1.39	31.8	17.8	19.7	-6.8

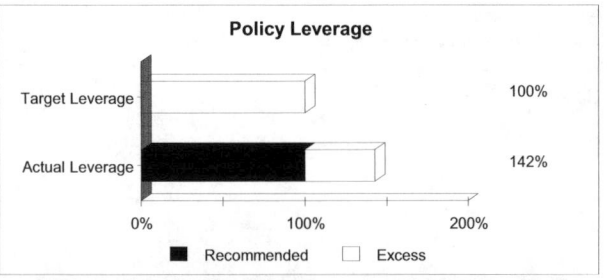

Policy Leverage

Target Leverage — 100%
Actual Leverage — 142%

0%   100%   200%

■ Recommended   □ Excess

FRINGE BENEFIT LIFE INSURANCE COMPANY   D+   Weak

Major Rating Factors: Weak overall results on stability tests (2.5 on a scale of 0 to 10). Fair quality investment portfolio (4.3) with significant exposure to mortgages . Mortgage default rate has been low. Strong capitalization (9.1) based on excellent risk adjusted capital (severe loss scenario). Moreover, capital levels have been consistently high over the last five years.

Other Rating Factors: Excellent profitability (8.2). Excellent liquidity (7.0).

Principal Business: Reinsurance (58%) and individual life insurance (42%).

Principal Investments: NonCMO investment grade bonds (24%), mortgages in good standing (22%), common & preferred stock (18%), noninv. grade bonds (8%), and misc. investments (29%).

Investments in Affiliates: None

Group Affiliation: FBH Inc

Licensed in: MN, OK, TX

Commenced Business: March 1982

Address: 2901 Morton St, Fort Worth, TX 76107

Phone: (817) 885-8223 **Domicile State:** TX **NAIC Code:** 99457

Data Date	Rating	RACR #1	RACR #2	Total Assets ($mil)	Capital ($mil)	Net Premium ($mil)	Net Income ($mil)
9-14	D+	4.63	2.43	45.4	28.6	0.1	2.1
9-13	D+	4.53	2.45	43.8	26.5	0.1	1.2
2013	D+	4.39	2.30	44.3	26.9	0.2	1.6
2012	D+	4.48	2.55	42.7	24.9	0.3	1.9
2011	D+	4.23	2.71	41.5	23.1	0.3	1.7
2010	C	N/A	N/A	41.3	21.8	-0.4	2.5
2009	C	3.69	2.83	39.8	19.6	-0.2	1.3

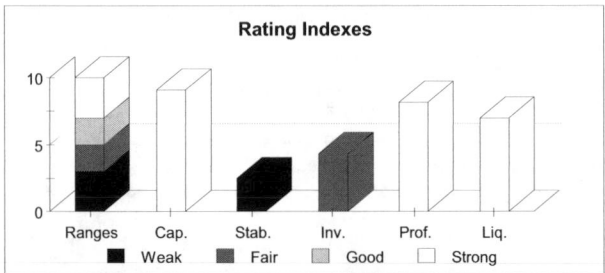

Rating Indexes

10

5

0
Ranges   Cap.   Stab.   Inv.   Prof.   Liq.

■ Weak   ▨ Fair   ▨ Good   □ Strong

FUNERAL DIRECTORS LIFE INSURANCE COMPANY   B-   Good

Major Rating Factors: Good quality investment portfolio (6.4 on a scale of 0 to 10) despite mixed results such as: minimal exposure to mortgages and large holdings of BBB rated bonds but minimal holdings in junk bonds. Fair overall results on stability tests (4.6). Weak liquidity (2.6) as a spike in claims or a run on policy withdrawals may stretch capacity.

Other Rating Factors: Strong capitalization (7.4) based on excellent risk adjusted capital (severe loss scenario). Excellent profitability (8.0) with operating gains in each of the last five years.

Principal Business: Individual annuities (63%), group life insurance (18%), individual life insurance (14%), and reinsurance (5%).

Principal Investments: NonCMO investment grade bonds (88%), mortgages in good standing (6%), real estate (2%), CMOs and structured securities (2%), and common & preferred stock (1%).

Investments in Affiliates: 1%

Group Affiliation: Directors Investment Group

Licensed in: All states except DC, ME, MA, NH, NY, WY, PR

Commenced Business: April 1981

Address: 6550 Directors Pkwy, Abilene, TX 79606

Phone: (915) 695-3412 **Domicile State:** TX **NAIC Code:** 99775

Data Date	Rating	RACR #1	RACR #2	Total Assets ($mil)	Capital ($mil)	Net Premium ($mil)	Net Income ($mil)
9-14	B-	2.32	1.27	1,046.4	89.9	155.2	5.3
9-13	B-	2.37	1.31	957.8	85.1	158.7	5.2
2013	B-	2.26	1.26	978.5	85.6	205.5	6.0
2012	B-	2.27	1.25	884.2	80.5	180.2	7.7
2011	B-	2.12	1.16	799.0	72.9	178.7	8.4
2010	B-	2.01	1.08	714.5	66.0	165.9	8.8
2009	B-	1.67	0.93	632.5	57.8	143.5	6.0

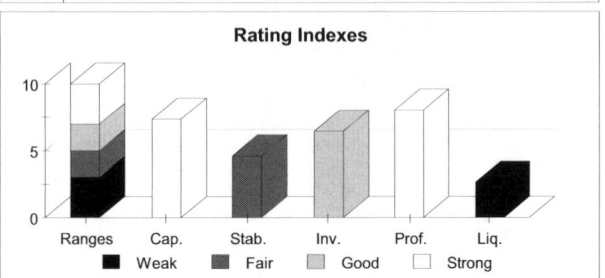

Rating Indexes

10

5

0
Ranges   Cap.   Stab.   Inv.   Prof.   Liq.

■ Weak   ▨ Fair   ▨ Good   □ Strong

GARDEN STATE LIFE INSURANCE COMPANY *   A-   Excellent

Major Rating Factors: Good quality investment portfolio (6.7 on a scale of 0 to 10) despite mixed results such as: no exposure to mortgages and large holdings of BBB rated bonds but minimal holdings in junk bonds. Good liquidity (6.8) with sufficient resources to handle a spike in claims. Excellent overall results on stability tests (7.1) excellent operational trends and excellent risk diversification.

Other Rating Factors: Strong capitalization (10.0) based on excellent risk adjusted capital (severe loss scenario). Excellent profitability (8.1) despite modest operating losses during 2009.

Principal Business: Individual life insurance (100%).

Principal Investments: NonCMO investment grade bonds (94%), CMOs and structured securities (3%), policy loans (3%), and noninv. grade bonds (1%).

Investments in Affiliates: None

Group Affiliation: American National Group Inc

Licensed in: All states except PR

Commenced Business: November 1956

Address: 2450 S Shore Blvd Suite 301, League City, TX 77573

Phone: (409) 763-4661 **Domicile State:** TX **NAIC Code:** 63657

Data Date	Rating	RACR #1	RACR #2	Total Assets ($mil)	Capital ($mil)	Net Premium ($mil)	Net Income ($mil)
9-14	A-	5.86	5.27	120.3	52.6	18.4	4.0
9-13	A-	5.41	4.87	117.6	48.3	20.1	4.3
2013	A-	5.42	4.88	117.1	48.5	26.2	5.6
2012	A-	5.04	4.54	116.5	44.9	28.5	9.1
2011	B+	4.76	3.42	115.2	41.5	30.9	8.5
2010	B	2.94	1.78	101.2	24.6	34.8	5.8
2009	B	2.18	1.34	93.2	18.7	36.4	-0.7

Adverse Trends in Operations

Decrease in premium volume from 2012 to 2013 (8%)
Decrease in premium volume from 2011 to 2012 (8%)
Increase in policy surrenders from 2010 to 2011 (26%)
Decrease in premium volume from 2010 to 2011 (11%)
Decrease in premium volume from 2009 to 2010 (4%)

GENERAL AMERICAN LIFE INSURANCE COMPANY   B   Good

Major Rating Factors: Good overall results on stability tests (5.5 on a scale of 0 to 10) despite negative cash flow from operations for 2013. Other stability subfactors include excellent operational trends and excellent risk diversification. Good quality investment portfolio (5.5) despite mixed results such as: substantial holdings of BBB bonds but junk bond exposure equal to 69% of capital. Good overall profitability (6.4).

Other Rating Factors: Good liquidity (5.5). Strong capitalization (7.5) based on excellent risk adjusted capital (severe loss scenario).

Principal Business: Reinsurance (53%), individual life insurance (46%), individual health insurance (1%), and individual annuities (1%).

Principal Investments: NonCMO investment grade bonds (45%), CMOs and structured securities (19%), policy loans (17%), mortgages in good standing (8%), and misc. investments (11%).

Investments in Affiliates: 3%

Group Affiliation: MetLife Inc

Licensed in: All states except NY

Commenced Business: September 1933

Address: 700 Market St, St Louis, MO 63101

Phone: (314) 843-8700 **Domicile State:** MO **NAIC Code:** 63665

Data Date	Rating	RACR #1	RACR #2	Total Assets ($mil)	Capital ($mil)	Net Premium ($mil)	Net Income ($mil)
9-14	B	3.00	1.35	12,151.6	854.2	493.3	59.5
9-13	B	2.66	1.19	11,983.4	789.3	427.5	27.2
2013	B	2.84	1.29	12,025.7	818.1	587.0	60.2
2012	B	2.91	1.31	11,865.7	872.9	519.7	19.1
2011	B	2.99	1.34	11,395.8	825.1	350.9	127.8
2010	B	3.14	1.47	11,178.2	944.0	342.4	63.8
2009	C+	3.37	1.58	11,049.2	995.2	382.0	65.5

Adverse Trends in Operations

Decrease in capital during 2013 (6%)
Increase in policy surrenders from 2012 to 2013 (37%)
Decrease in capital during 2011 (13%)
Decrease in capital during 2010 (5%)
Decrease in premium volume from 2009 to 2010 (10%)

GENERAL FIDELITY LIFE INSURANCE COMPANY   C+   Fair

Major Rating Factors: Fair overall results on stability tests (3.1 on a scale of 0 to 10) including fair financial strength of affiliated Bank of America Corp and weak results on operational trends, negative cash flow from operations for 2013. Fair profitability (4.1) with operating losses during the first nine months of 2014. Return on equity has been low, averaging 4.4%. Strong capitalization (10.0) based on excellent risk adjusted capital (severe loss scenario).

Other Rating Factors: High quality investment portfolio (9.2). Excellent liquidity (10.0).

Principal Business: Reinsurance (83%), credit life insurance (19%), and group life insurance (2%).

Principal Investments: NonCMO investment grade bonds (57%), cash (35%), and CMOs and structured securities (8%).

Investments in Affiliates: None

Group Affiliation: Bank of America Corp

Licensed in: All states except ME, NY, PR

Commenced Business: July 1981

Address: 150 N College St 20th Floor, Charlotte, NC 29201

Phone: (800) 456-2133 **Domicile State:** SC **NAIC Code:** 93521

Data Date	Rating	RACR #1	RACR #2	Total Assets ($mil)	Capital ($mil)	Net Premium ($mil)	Net Income ($mil)
9-14	C+	9.10	8.19	88.2	75.6	0.8	-0.9
9-13	C+	4.35	2.51	236.5	64.2	1.1	13.1
2013	C+	8.67	7.80	85.9	72.0	1.4	19.2
2012	B	14.37	8.28	230.5	205.8	25.7	6.5
2011	A-	8.96	5.68	226.9	195.7	90.8	11.2
2010	B	8.52	5.41	228.4	184.7	60.7	16.0
2009	B-	5.80	3.68	214.9	170.5	55.7	2.8

Bank of America Corp Composite Group Rating: C Largest Group Members	Assets ($mil)	Rating
BALBOA INS CO	298	C-
GENERAL FIDELITY LIFE INS CO	86	C+
MERITPLAN INS CO	81	C
NEWPORT INS CO	53	C

GENERAL RE LIFE CORPORATION *   B+   Good

Major Rating Factors: Good overall results on stability tests (6.7 on a scale of 0 to 10). Stability strengths include excellent operational trends and excellent risk diversification. Good quality investment portfolio (5.0) despite mixed results such as: substantial holdings of BBB bonds but moderate junk bond exposure. Strong capitalization (7.5) based on excellent risk adjusted capital (severe loss scenario).

Other Rating Factors: Excellent profitability (7.6) with operating gains in each of the last five years. Excellent liquidity (8.4).

Principal Business: Reinsurance (100%).

Principal Investments: NonCMO investment grade bonds (67%), common & preferred stock (9%), and noninv. grade bonds (8%).

Investments in Affiliates: 17%

Group Affiliation: Berkshire-Hathaway

Licensed in: All states except PR

Commenced Business: August 1967

Address: 30 Oak Street, Stamford, CT 06905-5339

Phone: (203) 352-3000 **Domicile State:** CT **NAIC Code:** 86258

Data Date	Rating	RACR #1	RACR #2	Total Assets ($mil)	Capital ($mil)	Net Premium ($mil)	Net Income ($mil)
9-14	B+	2.14	1.34	3,335.8	620.1	777.8	70.5
9-13	B	2.27	1.38	3,205.8	624.6	770.3	78.5
2013	B	2.31	1.44	3,337.4	667.2	1,047.7	121.2
2012	B	2.18	1.32	3,100.6	587.3	1,043.6	14.7
2011	B	2.31	1.36	2,917.2	638.2	1,020.5	87.4
2010	B+	3.03	1.92	2,911.9	702.5	1,060.3	141.5
2009	B+	2.60	1.68	2,780.9	560.8	1,072.8	99.1

Adverse Trends in Operations

Decrease in capital during 2012 (8%)
Decrease in premium volume from 2010 to 2011 (4%)
Decrease in capital during 2011 (9%)
Change in asset mix during 2011 (4.1%)
Decrease in premium volume from 2009 to 2010 (1%)

GENERATION LIFE INSURANCE COMPANY   B   Good

Major Rating Factors: Good overall results on stability tests (5.3 on a scale of 0 to 10) despite negative cash flow from operations for 2013. Strengths include good financial support from affiliation with Tennessee Farmers Ins Companies, good operational trends and excellent risk diversification. Weak profitability (2.0) with operating losses during the first nine months of 2014. Return on equity has been low, averaging -5.9%. Strong capitalization (10.0) based on excellent risk adjusted capital (severe loss scenario).

Other Rating Factors: High quality investment portfolio (8.4). Excellent liquidity (10.0).

Principal Business: Individual life insurance (100%).

Principal Investments: Cash (58%), nonCMO investment grade bonds (38%), and common & preferred stock (4%).

Investments in Affiliates: None

Group Affiliation: Tennessee Farmers Ins Companies

Licensed in: All states except CA, CT, GA, ME, MA, NH, NJ, NY, NC, PR

Commenced Business: May 1966

Address: 5025 N Central Ave #546, Phoenix, AZ 85012

Phone: (855) 436-4533 **Domicile State:** AZ **NAIC Code:** 73504

Data Date	Rating	RACR #1	RACR #2	Total Assets ($mil)	Capital ($mil)	Net Premium ($mil)	Net Income ($mil)
9-14	B	5.84	5.26	30.2	28.3	2.2	-2.9
9-13	U	N/A	N/A	23.4	22.2	0.7	-3.1
2013	B	6.40	5.76	32.6	31.1	1.1	-4.2
2012	U	6.09	5.48	26.1	25.3	0.0	-1.5
2011	U	4.47	4.02	12.8	12.2	0.0	-0.4
2010	U	4.52	4.07	13.3	12.6	0.0	-0.3
2009	C	8.13	7.31	58.7	57.9	-2.2	0.9

Tennessee Farmers Ins Companies Composite Group Rating: B+ Largest Group Members	Assets ($mil)	Rating
TENNESSEE FARMERS MUTUAL INS CO	2192	B+
TENNESSEE FARMERS LIFE INS CO	1914	A
TENNESSEE FARMERS ASR CO	1014	B+
GENERATION LIFE INS CO	33	B

GENWORTH LIFE & ANNUITY INSURANCE COMPANY   B-   Good

Major Rating Factors: Good quality investment portfolio (5.0 on a scale of 0 to 10) despite significant exposure to mortgages . Mortgage default rate has been low. large holdings of BBB rated bonds in addition to small junk bond holdings. Good overall profitability (6.4). Despite its volitility, return on equity has been excellent over the last five years averaging 15.8%. Good liquidity (6.6).

Other Rating Factors: Fair overall results on stability tests (3.6) including excessive premium growth. Strong capitalization (7.1) based on excellent risk adjusted capital (severe loss scenario).

Principal Business: Individual life insurance (43%), individual annuities (28%), reinsurance (26%), and individual health insurance (2%).

Principal Investments: NonCMO investment grade bonds (48%), CMOs and structured securities (24%), mortgages in good standing (11%), common & preferred stock (8%), and misc. investments (9%).

Investments in Affiliates: 7%

Group Affiliation: Genworth Financial

Licensed in: All states except NY, PR

Commenced Business: April 1871

Address: 6610 W Broad St, Richmond, VA 23230

Phone: (804) 662-2400 **Domicile State:** VA **NAIC Code:** 65536

Data Date	Rating	RACR #1	RACR #2	Total Assets ($mil)	Capital ($mil)	Net Premium ($mil)	Net Income ($mil)
9-14	B-	1.50	1.09	24,254.6	2,220.8	1,198.9	203.7
9-13	B-	1.30	0.98	23,940.9	2,134.3	957.9	110.9
2013	B-	1.51	1.11	24,161.7	2,235.0	1,893.8	343.9
2012	B-	1.35	1.00	24,030.7	2,255.3	-266.4	353.8
2011	B-	1.15	0.84	23,484.5	1,842.9	1,129.5	-91.1
2010	B-	1.15	0.81	25,149.4	1,776.6	943.5	53.6
2009	B-	1.24	0.88	25,113.0	1,935.7	-10.0	250.9

Rating Indexes

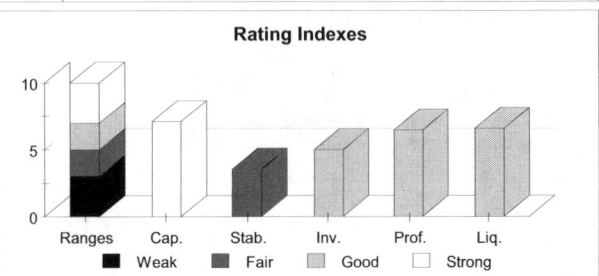

GENWORTH LIFE INSURANCE COMPANY   B-   Good

Major Rating Factors: Good overall results on stability tests (5.1 on a scale of 0 to 10). Stability strengths include good operational trends and excellent risk diversification. Good capitalization (5.5) based on good risk adjusted capital (severe loss scenario). Capital levels have been relatively consistent over the last five years. Good quality investment portfolio (6.5).

Other Rating Factors: Good overall profitability (5.2) despite operating losses during the first nine months of 2014. Excellent liquidity (7.4).

Principal Business: Individual health insurance (56%), individual annuities (15%), individual life insurance (11%), reinsurance (10%), and group health insurance (7%).

Principal Investments: NonCMO investment grade bonds (59%), CMOs and structured securities (15%), mortgages in good standing (10%), common & preferred stock (8%), and misc. investments (7%).

Investments in Affiliates: 8%

Group Affiliation: Genworth Financial

Licensed in: All states except NY

Commenced Business: October 1956

Address: 6604 West Broad St, Richmond, VA 23230

Phone: (800) 255-7836   **Domicile State:** DE   **NAIC Code:** 70025

Data Date	Rating	RACR #1	RACR #2	Total Assets ($mil)	Capital ($mil)	Net Premium ($mil)	Net Income ($mil)
9-14	B-	1.03	0.81	37,409.9	3,338.1	1,223.1	-178.9
9-13	C+	0.98	0.78	36,402.2	3,306.4	2,510.0	119.2
2013	C+	1.06	0.85	36,445.4	3,487.2	2,578.1	329.8
2012	C+	1.01	0.80	36,783.8	3,410.5	1,659.0	201.0
2011	C+	1.04	0.80	35,784.2	3,097.3	1,607.6	22.9
2010	C+	0.98	0.76	33,585.1	2,983.6	1,273.4	-137.4
2009	C+	0.99	0.76	32,974.6	3,164.8	1,252.2	-199.4

Adverse Trends in Operations

Change in premium mix from 2012 to 2013 (4.5%)
Change in premium mix from 2010 to 2011 (5.5%)
Decrease in capital during 2010 (6%)

GENWORTH LIFE INSURANCE COMPANY OF NEW YORK   B   Good

Major Rating Factors: Good overall results on stability tests (5.6 on a scale of 0 to 10). Stability strengths include good operational trends, good risk adjusted capital for prior years and excellent risk diversification. Good quality investment portfolio (5.1) despite large holdings of BBB rated bonds in addition to junk bond exposure equal to 59% of capital. Exposure to mortgages is significant, but the mortgage default rate has been low. Good overall profitability (5.8) despite operating losses during the first nine months of 2014.

Other Rating Factors: Good liquidity (6.6). Strong capitalization (7.2) based on excellent risk adjusted capital (severe loss scenario).

Principal Business: Individual annuities (52%), individual health insurance (25%), individual life insurance (12%), reinsurance (9%), and group health insurance (2%).

Principal Investments: NonCMO investment grade bonds (57%), CMOs and structured securities (24%), mortgages in good standing (12%), noninv. grade bonds (5%), and common & preferred stock (1%).

Investments in Affiliates: None

Group Affiliation: Genworth Financial

Licensed in: CT, DC, DE, FL, IL, NJ, NY, RI, VA

Commenced Business: October 1988

Address: 125 Park Ave 6th Floor, New York, NY 10017-5529

Phone: (800) 357-1066   **Domicile State:** NY   **NAIC Code:** 72990

Data Date	Rating	RACR #1	RACR #2	Total Assets ($mil)	Capital ($mil)	Net Premium ($mil)	Net Income ($mil)
9-14	B	2.26	1.13	8,185.1	513.4	380.2	-4.9
9-13	B	2.47	1.24	8,002.7	558.2	394.0	37.2
2013	B	2.29	1.15	8,139.0	527.3	610.9	13.1
2012	B	2.36	1.18	7,815.8	540.1	542.6	19.1
2011	B-	2.45	1.23	7,691.7	559.5	576.6	6.5
2010	B-	2.39	1.18	7,432.0	549.1	329.8	130.0
2009	C	1.85	0.92	7,218.4	429.5	340.0	40.9

Adverse Trends in Operations

Decrease in capital during 2013 (2%)
Decrease in capital during 2012 (3%)
Decrease in premium volume from 2011 to 2012 (6%)
Change in premium mix from 2010 to 2011 (4.9%)
Decrease in premium volume from 2009 to 2010 (3%)

GERBER LIFE INSURANCE COMPANY *   A-   Excellent

Major Rating Factors: Good quality investment portfolio (6.4 on a scale of 0 to 10) despite mixed results such as: no exposure to mortgages and large holdings of BBB rated bonds but small junk bond holdings. Good liquidity (5.5) with sufficient resources to handle a spike in claims as well as a significant increase in policy surrenders. Strong capitalization (7.4) based on excellent risk adjusted capital (severe loss scenario).

Other Rating Factors: Excellent profitability (7.7) with operating gains in each of the last five years. Excellent overall results on stability tests (7.2) excellent operational trends and excellent risk diversification.

Principal Business: Individual life insurance (40%), group health insurance (35%), individual health insurance (18%), and reinsurance (7%).

Principal Investments: NonCMO investment grade bonds (73%), CMOs and structured securities (17%), policy loans (5%), common & preferred stock (3%), and noninv. grade bonds (3%).

Investments in Affiliates: None

Group Affiliation: Nestle SA

Licensed in: All states, the District of Columbia and Puerto Rico

Commenced Business: September 1968

Address: 1311 Mamaroneck Ave, White Plains, NY 10605

Phone: (877) 778-0839   **Domicile State:** NY   **NAIC Code:** 70939

Data Date	Rating	RACR #1	RACR #2	Total Assets ($mil)	Capital ($mil)	Net Premium ($mil)	Net Income ($mil)
9-14	A-	2.03	1.24	2,749.8	279.8	436.8	16.5
9-13	A-	2.02	1.22	2,488.0	257.5	389.7	16.4
2013	A-	2.00	1.21	2,548.1	263.5	506.8	22.7
2012	A-	1.96	1.17	2,306.7	237.9	464.1	20.2
2011	A-	1.91	1.15	2,110.0	215.5	432.2	4.9
2010	A-	2.01	1.21	1,901.1	213.0	393.7	14.9
2009	A-	2.07	1.29	1,712.6	194.3	379.0	17.6

Rating Indexes

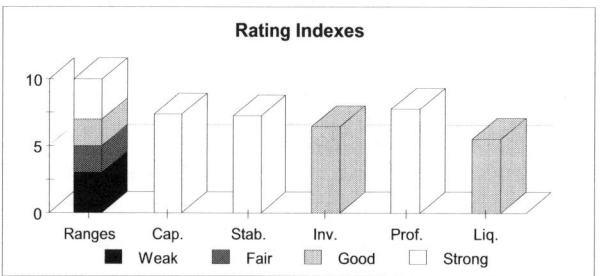

GLOBE LIFE & ACCIDENT INSURANCE COMPANY | B | Good

Major Rating Factors: Good overall results on stability tests (6.0 on a scale of 0 to 10). Stability strengths include good operational trends and excellent risk diversification. Good overall capitalization (6.8) based on good risk adjusted capital (severe loss scenario). Nevertheless, capital levels have fluctuated during prior years. Good overall profitability (6.5). Excellent expense controls.

Other Rating Factors: Good liquidity (5.2). Fair quality investment portfolio (4.6).

Principal Business: Group life insurance (55%), individual life insurance (41%), and individual health insurance (4%).

Principal Investments: NonCMO investment grade bonds (85%), noninv. grade bonds (6%), CMOs and structured securities (4%), and policy loans (2%).

Investments in Affiliates: 3%

Group Affiliation: Torchmark Corp

Licensed in: All states except NY, PR

Commenced Business: September 1980

Address: 10306 Regency Parkway Bldg, Omaha, NE 68114-3743

Phone: (405) 270-1400 **Domicile State:** NE **NAIC Code:** 91472

Data Date	Rating	RACR #1	RACR #2	Total Assets ($mil)	Capital ($mil)	Net Premium ($mil)	Net Income ($mil)
9-14	B	1.82	0.98	3,511.4	262.1	489.9	65.9
9-13	B	1.25	0.92	3,536.5	444.0	487.9	169.6
2013	B	1.74	0.95	3,363.5	258.3	618.0	314.8
2012	B	1.31	0.97	3,454.4	477.6	577.1	203.3
2011	B	1.28	0.93	3,208.3	436.8	570.7	178.8
2010	B	1.27	0.96	3,029.6	418.6	540.0	187.3
2009	B	1.52	1.13	2,899.4	479.5	498.1	225.1

Adverse Trends in Operations

Decrease in capital during 2013 (46%)
Decrease in asset base during 2013 (3%)
Decrease in capital during 2010 (13%)

GOLDEN RULE INSURANCE COMPANY | B | Good

Major Rating Factors: Good overall results on stability tests (5.4 on a scale of 0 to 10) despite fair financial strength of affiliated UnitedHealth Group Inc. Other stability subfactors include good operational trends and excellent risk diversification. Good current capitalization (5.0) based on mixed results -- excessive policy leverage mitigated by excellent risk adjusted capital (severe loss scenario) reflecting improvement over results in 2009. Good liquidity (6.2).

Other Rating Factors: High quality investment portfolio (8.1). Excellent profitability (8.8) with operating gains in each of the last five years.

Principal Business: Group health insurance (82%), individual health insurance (15%), and individual life insurance (2%).

Principal Investments: NonCMO investment grade bonds (79%), CMOs and structured securities (18%), real estate (1%), and , and misc. investments (2%).

Investments in Affiliates: None

Group Affiliation: UnitedHealth Group Inc

Licensed in: All states except NY, PR

Commenced Business: June 1961

Address: 712 Eleventh St, Lawrenceville, IL 62439-2395

Phone: (317) 290-8100 **Domicile State:** IN **NAIC Code:** 62286

Data Date	Rating	RACR #1	RACR #2	Total Assets ($mil)	Capital ($mil)	Net Premium ($mil)	Net Income ($mil)
9-14	B	1.31	1.04	736.6	314.5	1,409.1	84.6
9-13	B	1.37	1.08	793.6	338.3	1,491.4	134.6
2013	B	1.12	0.89	759.8	293.5	2,020.6	129.4
2012	B	1.19	0.94	782.5	292.3	1,879.5	127.6
2011	B	1.43	1.13	814.9	312.1	1,673.4	104.6
2010	B	1.49	1.18	694.0	304.8	1,566.3	202.0
2009	B	1.03	0.81	524.4	175.8	1,324.3	156.3

UnitedHealth Group Inc
Composite Group Rating: C+
Largest Group Members

	Assets ($mil)	Rating
UNITED HEALTHCARE INS CO	14513	C
OXFORD HEALTH INS INC	2078	C+
UNITED HEALTHCARE INS CO OF NY	1983	B-
OXFORD HEALTH PLANS (NY) INC	1820	A+
UNITEDHEALTHCARE PLAN RIVER VALLEY	1094	B+

GOVERNMENT PERSONNEL MUTUAL LIFE INSURANCE CO * | B+ | Good

Major Rating Factors: Good liquidity (5.2 on a scale of 0 to 10) with sufficient resources to cover a large increase in policy surrenders. Good overall results on stability tests (6.4). Stability strengths include excellent operational trends and excellent risk diversification. Strong capitalization (8.0) based on excellent risk adjusted capital (severe loss scenario).

Other Rating Factors: High quality investment portfolio (7.0). Excellent profitability (7.3) with operating gains in each of the last five years.

Principal Business: Individual life insurance (63%), individual health insurance (37%), group life insurance (1%), individual annuities (1%), and reinsurance (1%).

Principal Investments: NonCMO investment grade bonds (68%), mortgages in good standing (15%), policy loans (9%), common & preferred stock (3%), and misc. investments (5%).

Investments in Affiliates: 2%

Group Affiliation: GPM Life Group

Licensed in: All states except NJ, NY, PR

Commenced Business: October 1934

Address: 2211 NW Loop 410, San Antonio, TX 78217

Phone: (800) 938-9765 **Domicile State:** TX **NAIC Code:** 63967

Data Date	Rating	RACR #1	RACR #2	Total Assets ($mil)	Capital ($mil)	Net Premium ($mil)	Net Income ($mil)
9-14	B+	2.62	1.68	830.8	106.9	35.3	1.4
9-13	B+	2.63	1.69	830.5	104.1	35.6	3.1
2013	B+	2.69	1.72	830.9	109.2	46.9	4.1
2012	B+	2.64	1.69	833.7	104.8	51.1	4.9
2011	B+	3.51	1.92	834.1	97.0	54.6	6.8
2010	B+	2.98	1.71	821.2	92.0	56.5	7.2
2009	B+	2.54	1.47	801.9	87.8	55.0	0.6

Exposure to Withdrawals Without Penalty
(as a % of capital)

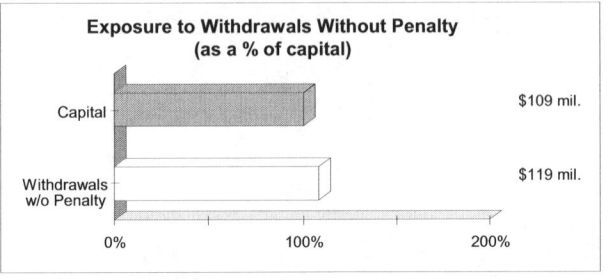

Capital — $109 mil.
Withdrawals w/o Penalty — $119 mil.

0% 100% 200%

GRANGE LIFE INSURANCE COMPANY B- Good

Major Rating Factors: Good liquidity (6.3 on a scale of 0 to 10) with sufficient resources to handle a spike in claims as well as a significant increase in policy surrenders. Good overall results on stability tests (5.0). Strengths include good financial support from affiliation with Grange Mutual Casualty Group, excellent operational trends and excellent risk diversification. Weak profitability (2.6) with investment income below regulatory standards in relation to interest assumptions of reserves.

Other Rating Factors: Strong capitalization (7.9) based on excellent risk adjusted capital (severe loss scenario). High quality investment portfolio (7.2).

Principal Business: Individual life insurance (92%), reinsurance (4%), group life insurance (2%), and individual annuities (1%).

Principal Investments: NonCMO investment grade bonds (52%), CMOs and structured securities (32%), cash (5%), noninv. grade bonds (4%), and misc. investments (5%).

Investments in Affiliates: 2%

Group Affiliation: Grange Mutual Casualty Group

Licensed in: GA, IL, IN, IA, KS, KY, MI, MN, MO, OH, PA, SC, TN, VA, WI

Commenced Business: July 1968

Address: 650 S Front St, Columbus, OH 43216

Phone: (614) 445-2820 **Domicile State:** OH **NAIC Code:** 71218

Data Date	Rating	RACR #1	RACR #2	Total Assets ($mil)	Capital ($mil)	Net Premium ($mil)	Net Income ($mil)
9-14	B-	2.53	1.61	366.5	54.6	34.7	1.2
9-13	B-	2.59	1.68	344.0	50.0	34.2	0.7
2013	B-	2.51	1.63	353.4	51.0	46.4	3.0
2012	B-	2.61	1.70	347.6	49.1	44.8	1.3
2011	B	3.06	1.80	316.6	42.4	47.7	2.2
2010	A-	3.06	1.80	291.6	39.8	49.6	2.8
2009	A-	2.99	1.76	271.9	37.9	44.8	2.9

Grange Mutual Casualty Group
Composite Group Rating: B

Largest Group Members	Assets ($mil)	Rating
GRANGE MUTUAL CAS CO	2012	B+
GRANGE LIFE INS CO	353	B-
TRUSTGARD INS CO	96	B+
GRANGE INDEMNITY INS CO	88	C
INTEGRITY MUTUAL INS CO	83	B-

GREAT AMERICAN LIFE INSURANCE COMPANY B- Good

Major Rating Factors: Good quality investment portfolio (5.5 on a scale of 0 to 10) despite mixed results such as: substantial holdings of BBB bonds but moderate junk bond exposure. Good liquidity (5.8) with sufficient resources to cover a large increase in policy surrenders. Good overall results on stability tests (5.3) excellent operational trends, good risk adjusted capital for prior years and excellent risk diversification.

Other Rating Factors: Strong capitalization (7.1) based on excellent risk adjusted capital (severe loss scenario). Excellent profitability (9.0).

Principal Business: Individual annuities (98%), individual life insurance (1%), and group retirement contracts (1%).

Principal Investments: NonCMO investment grade bonds (53%), CMOs and structured securities (35%), noninv. grade bonds (3%), common & preferred stock (3%), and misc. investments (5%).

Investments in Affiliates: 1%

Group Affiliation: American Financial Group Inc

Licensed in: All states except NY, PR

Commenced Business: August 1963

Address: 250 E Fifth St, Cincinnati, OH 45202

Phone: (800) 854-3649 **Domicile State:** OH **NAIC Code:** 63312

Data Date	Rating	RACR #1	RACR #2	Total Assets ($mil)	Capital ($mil)	Net Premium ($mil)	Net Income ($mil)
9-14	B-	1.88	1.07	22,140.3	1,638.8	2,555.7	272.2
9-13	B-	1.95	1.11	18,978.1	1,459.0	2,481.6	167.0
2013	B-	1.82	1.04	20,182.2	1,511.8	3,801.6	262.2
2012	B-	1.82	1.05	16,508.6	1,274.7	2,955.4	155.6
2011	B-	1.67	0.95	13,950.5	1,070.5	2,802.9	152.2
2010	B-	1.80	1.02	11,470.5	990.9	1,942.0	161.2
2009	B-	1.78	0.99	9,962.0	874.6	911.6	-31.6

Adverse Trends in Operations

Increase in policy surrenders from 2011 to 2012 (27%)

GREAT SOUTHERN LIFE INSURANCE COMPANY B Good

Major Rating Factors: Good overall results on stability tests (5.4 on a scale of 0 to 10). Stability strengths include good operational trends and excellent risk diversification. Good quality investment portfolio (6.5) despite mixed results such as: minimal exposure to mortgages and large holdings of BBB rated bonds but minimal holdings in junk bonds. Strong capitalization (9.1) based on excellent risk adjusted capital (severe loss scenario).

Other Rating Factors: Excellent profitability (9.1). Excellent liquidity (7.6).

Principal Business: Individual life insurance (85%), group life insurance (7%), group health insurance (3%), reinsurance (2%), and individual annuities (2%).

Principal Investments: NonCMO investment grade bonds (64%), CMOs and structured securities (27%), and common & preferred stock (9%).

Investments in Affiliates: None

Group Affiliation: Americo Life Inc

Licensed in: All states except NH, NY, RI, VT, PR

Commenced Business: November 1909

Address: 500 N Akard, Dallas, TX 75201

Phone: (214) 954-8100 **Domicile State:** TX **NAIC Code:** 90212

Data Date	Rating	RACR #1	RACR #2	Total Assets ($mil)	Capital ($mil)	Net Premium ($mil)	Net Income ($mil)
9-14	B	4.63	2.43	225.3	42.4	0.1	1.9
9-13	B	4.45	2.10	230.5	40.6	0.0	1.8
2013	B	4.43	2.29	231.9	40.3	0.8	2.3
2012	B	4.23	1.95	233.1	38.8	0.2	1.5
2011	B	4.02	1.99	242.9	37.1	0.2	2.5
2010	B-	3.85	1.86	248.2	35.8	0.3	2.0
2009	C+	3.59	1.70	254.8	34.3	0.4	0.0

Adverse Trends in Operations

Decrease in asset base during 2012 (4%)
Increase in policy surrenders from 2011 to 2012 (33%)
Decrease in premium volume from 2010 to 2011 (38%)
Decrease in asset base during 2010 (3%)
Decrease in premium volume from 2009 to 2010 (15%)

GREAT WESTERN INSURANCE COMPANY | B- | Good

Major Rating Factors: Good quality investment portfolio (5.4 on a scale of 0 to 10) despite mixed results such as: minimal exposure to mortgages and large holdings of BBB rated bonds but minimal holdings in junk bonds. Good liquidity (6.4) with sufficient resources to handle a spike in claims. Fair overall results on stability tests (4.9) including negative cash flow from operations for 2013.

Other Rating Factors: Strong capitalization (7.2) based on excellent risk adjusted capital (severe loss scenario). Excellent profitability (7.0) despite modest operating losses during 2009.

Principal Business: Group life insurance (76%), individual life insurance (21%), individual annuities (2%), and reinsurance (2%).

Principal Investments: NonCMO investment grade bonds (81%), mortgages in good standing (9%), CMOs and structured securities (6%), common & preferred stock (2%), and noninv. grade bonds (1%).

Investments in Affiliates: 1%

Group Affiliation: Great Western Co

Licensed in: All states except AK, CT, HI, NY, PR

Commenced Business: May 1983

Address: 3434 Washington Blvd, Ogden, UT 84401

Phone: (801) 621-5688 **Domicile State:** UT **NAIC Code:** 71480

Data Date	Rating	RACR #1	RACR #2	Total Assets ($mil)	Capital ($mil)	Net Premium ($mil)	Net Income ($mil)
9-14	B-	2.17	1.12	883.7	61.1	375.5	2.0
9-13	B-	2.52	1.39	508.0	57.2	25.4	8.2
2013	B-	2.78	1.54	496.5	60.6	39.0	14.2
2012	B-	2.51	1.40	503.8	52.0	54.1	13.6
2011	B-	1.86	1.01	492.2	40.2	64.0	0.8
2010	B-	1.60	0.87	494.8	38.5	94.2	5.3
2009	B-	1.66	0.83	462.1	34.3	121.0	-4.1

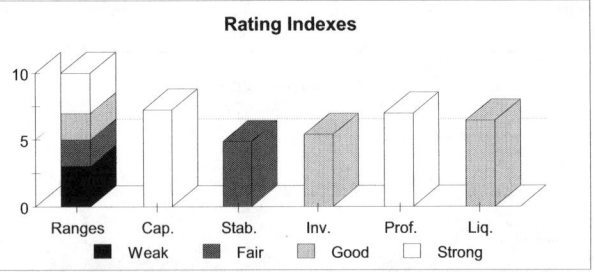

Rating Indexes — Ranges, Cap., Stab., Inv., Prof., Liq. — Weak / Fair / Good / Strong

GREAT-WEST LIFE & ANNUITY INSURANCE COMPANY | B- | Good

Major Rating Factors: Good capitalization (5.3 on a scale of 0 to 10) based on good risk adjusted capital (moderate loss scenario). Good quality investment portfolio (5.6) despite large holdings of BBB rated bonds in addition to moderate junk bond exposure. Exposure to mortgages is significant, but the mortgage default rate has been low. Good overall profitability (6.2). Return on equity has been excellent over the last five years averaging 18.2%.

Other Rating Factors: Good liquidity (6.7). Good overall results on stability tests (5.0) despite fair risk adjusted capital in prior years good operational trends and excellent risk diversification.

Principal Business: Group retirement contracts (80%), individual life insurance (15%), individual annuities (2%), group life insurance (1%), and group health insurance (1%).

Principal Investments: NonCMO investment grade bonds (45%), CMOs and structured securities (22%), policy loans (17%), mortgages in good standing (12%), and misc. investments (4%).

Investments in Affiliates: 1%

Group Affiliation: Great West Life Asr

Licensed in: All states, the District of Columbia and Puerto Rico

Commenced Business: April 1907

Address: 8515 E Orchard Rd, Englewood, CO 80111

Phone: (800) 537-2033 **Domicile State:** CO **NAIC Code:** 68322

Data Date	Rating	RACR #1	RACR #2	Total Assets ($mil)	Capital ($mil)	Net Premium ($mil)	Net Income ($mil)
9-14	B-	1.22	0.68	56,894.9	1,120.6	4,292.9	133.5
9-13	B-	1.30	0.72	53,018.7	1,167.5	4,020.9	124.9
2013	B-	1.33	0.75	52,282.0	1,200.6	5,610.4	175.3
2012	B-	1.30	0.72	49,029.5	1,109.5	5,498.0	147.7
2011	B-	1.27	0.71	45,163.1	1,069.5	-823.2	146.9
2010	B-	1.44	0.78	45,084.6	1,152.7	6,219.7	398.6
2009	B-	1.75	0.94	40,243.9	1,360.9	6,056.0	282.0

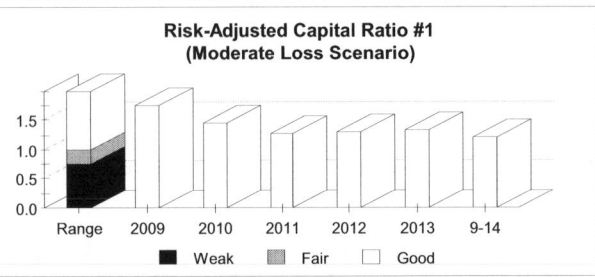

Risk-Adjusted Capital Ratio #1 (Moderate Loss Scenario) — Range, 2009, 2010, 2011, 2012, 2013, 9-14 — Weak / Fair / Good

GREAT-WEST LIFE & ANNUITY INSURANCE COMPANY OF NEW | B | Good

Major Rating Factors: Good overall results on stability tests (5.9 on a scale of 0 to 10) despite fair financial strength of affiliated Great West Life Asr. Other stability subfactors include good operational trends and excellent risk diversification. Good quality investment portfolio (6.3) despite significant exposure to mortgages . Mortgage default rate has been low. large holdings of BBB rated bonds in addition to minimal holdings in junk bonds. Good overall profitability (5.1) despite operating losses during the first nine months of 2014.

Other Rating Factors: Strong capitalization (7.7) based on excellent risk adjusted capital (severe loss scenario). Excellent liquidity (7.3).

Principal Business: Group retirement contracts (80%), individual life insurance (19%), and individual annuities (1%).

Principal Investments: NonCMO investment grade bonds (64%), CMOs and structured securities (20%), mortgages in good standing (11%), policy loans (3%), and noninv. grade bonds (1%).

Investments in Affiliates: None

Group Affiliation: Great West Life Asr

Licensed in: NY

Commenced Business: January 1972

Address: 50 Main St 9th Floor, White Plains, NY 10606

Phone: (914) 682-3611 **Domicile State:** NY **NAIC Code:** 79359

Data Date	Rating	RACR #1	RACR #2	Total Assets ($mil)	Capital ($mil)	Net Premium ($mil)	Net Income ($mil)
9-14	B	2.80	1.46	1,568.3	79.1	220.0	-1.3
9-13	B	3.08	1.59	1,367.8	82.6	188.8	-0.3
2013	B	2.91	1.52	1,456.3	79.5	248.1	-4.5
2012	B	3.34	1.75	1,213.9	83.0	237.3	4.5
2011	B	3.43	1.77	1,010.6	77.4	203.4	6.9
2010	B-	3.25	1.60	1,066.4	71.0	135.5	8.5
2009	B-	3.18	1.62	889.5	65.9	117.2	8.9

Great West Life Asr
Composite Group Rating: C+
Largest Group Members

	Assets ($mil)	Rating
GREAT-WEST LIFE ANNUITY INS CO	52282	B-
CANADA LIFE ASSURANCE CO-US BRANCH	4319	C
GREAT-WEST LIFE ANNUITY INS OF NY	1456	B
LONDON LIFE REINSURANCE CO	344	C+
GREAT WEST LIFE ASR CO	79	B-

GUARANTEE TRUST LIFE INSURANCE COMPANY   B   Good

Major Rating Factors: Good current capitalization (6.9 on a scale of 0 to 10) based on good risk adjusted capital (severe loss scenario), although results have slipped from the excellent range during the last year. Good quality investment portfolio (6.3) despite mixed results such as: minimal exposure to mortgages and substantial holdings of BBB bonds but small junk bond holdings. Good overall results on stability tests (5.9) excellent operational trends and excellent risk diversification.

Other Rating Factors: Excellent profitability (7.7) with operating gains in each of the last five years. Excellent liquidity (7.4).

Principal Business: Individual health insurance (66%), group health insurance (19%), individual life insurance (9%), reinsurance (3%), and other lines (3%).

Principal Investments: NonCMO investment grade bonds (51%), CMOs and structured securities (34%), mortgages in good standing (8%), noninv. grade bonds (3%), and misc. investments (4%).

Investments in Affiliates: 2%

Group Affiliation: Guarantee Trust

Licensed in: All states except NY

Commenced Business: June 1936

Address: 1275 Milwaukee Ave, Glenview, IL 60025

Phone: (847) 699-0600 **Domicile State:** IL **NAIC Code:** 64211

Data Date	Rating	RACR #1	RACR #2	Total Assets ($mil)	Capital ($mil)	Net Premium ($mil)	Net Income ($mil)
9-14	B	1.44	0.99	408.5	55.7	159.0	3.0
9-13	B	1.33	0.93	356.9	48.0	150.6	4.1
2013	B	1.49	1.03	366.1	54.3	196.4	7.1
2012	B	1.36	0.97	325.0	44.2	182.9	3.3
2011	B	1.38	0.98	283.7	42.1	165.2	4.9
2010	B-	1.26	0.88	258.0	40.1	164.0	3.2
2009	C+	1.29	0.91	232.5	40.4	164.6	1.6

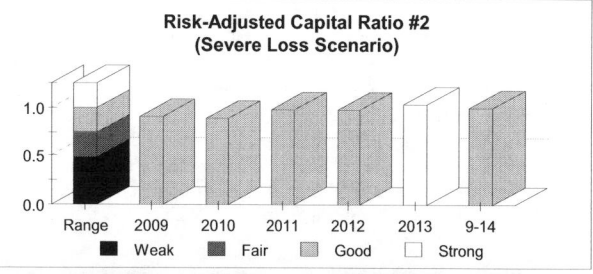

Risk-Adjusted Capital Ratio #2
(Severe Loss Scenario)

GUARANTY INCOME LIFE INSURANCE COMPANY   C-   Fair

Major Rating Factors: Fair quality investment portfolio (3.9 on a scale of 0 to 10). Fair profitability (4.6) with investment income below regulatory standards in relation to interest assumptions of reserves. Fair overall results on stability tests (3.1) including negative cash flow from operations for 2013 and excessive premium growth.

Other Rating Factors: Good liquidity (5.1). Strong capitalization (7.2) based on excellent risk adjusted capital (severe loss scenario).

Principal Business: Individual annuities (77%), individual health insurance (13%), and individual life insurance (10%).

Principal Investments: NonCMO investment grade bonds (55%), CMOs and structured securities (31%), real estate (4%), common & preferred stock (3%), and misc. investments (4%).

Investments in Affiliates: 1%

Group Affiliation: Guaranty Corp

Licensed in: AL, AZ, AR, CA, CO, FL, GA, IL, IN, IA, KS, KY, LA, MI, MS, MO, MT, NE, NV, NM, NC, ND, OH, OK, OR, SC, TN, TX, UT, WA, WY

Commenced Business: February 1926

Address: 929 Government St, Baton Rouge, LA 70802

Phone: (225) 383-0355 **Domicile State:** LA **NAIC Code:** 64238

Data Date	Rating	RACR #1	RACR #2	Total Assets ($mil)	Capital ($mil)	Net Premium ($mil)	Net Income ($mil)
9-14	C-	2.29	1.13	482.6	33.8	24.9	4.1
9-13	C-	2.02	0.96	476.5	24.9	19.9	3.5
2013	C-	2.35	1.13	477.9	31.0	26.7	5.2
2012	C-	1.85	0.86	476.7	23.2	22.6	2.7
2011	C-	1.90	1.22	488.9	21.9	30.3	0.0
2010	B-	1.85	1.18	492.0	21.1	55.8	-0.7
2009	B-	1.92	1.18	457.8	21.6	77.8	-1.6

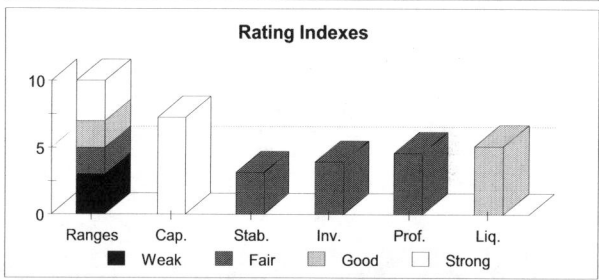

Rating Indexes

GUARDIAN INSURANCE & ANNUITY COMPANY INCORPORATED   B   Good

Major Rating Factors: Good current capitalization (6.6 on a scale of 0 to 10) based on good risk adjusted capital (severe loss scenario), although results have slipped from the excellent range over the last two years. Good quality investment portfolio (6.6) despite mixed results such as: minimal exposure to mortgages and large holdings of BBB rated bonds but small junk bond holdings. Good overall results on stability tests (5.9) good operational trends and excellent risk diversification.

Other Rating Factors: Fair profitability (4.8) with investment income below regulatory standards in relation to interest assumptions of reserves. Excellent liquidity (9.4).

Principal Business: Individual annuities (74%), group retirement contracts (23%), and individual life insurance (3%).

Principal Investments: NonCMO investment grade bonds (88%), policy loans (5%), CMOs and structured securities (3%), mortgages in good standing (2%), and noninv. grade bonds (1%).

Investments in Affiliates: 1%

Group Affiliation: Guardian Group

Licensed in: All states except PR

Commenced Business: December 1971

Address: 1209 Orange St, Wilmington, DE 19801

Phone: (212) 598-8000 **Domicile State:** DE **NAIC Code:** 78778

Data Date	Rating	RACR #1	RACR #2	Total Assets ($mil)	Capital ($mil)	Net Premium ($mil)	Net Income ($mil)
9-14	B	1.91	0.95	15,244.7	225.3	1,178.9	4.3
9-13	B	1.91	0.97	13,731.6	187.2	1,061.2	-75.4
2013	B	1.62	0.85	14,529.6	180.9	1,420.3	-82.5
2012	B	2.21	1.18	12,073.3	215.1	1,932.6	-28.9
2011	B	2.99	1.52	10,135.1	253.8	1,531.1	0.2
2010	B	2.88	1.46	10,072.5	241.2	1,116.4	15.9
2009	B	2.74	1.38	9,022.9	236.2	1,268.2	9.9

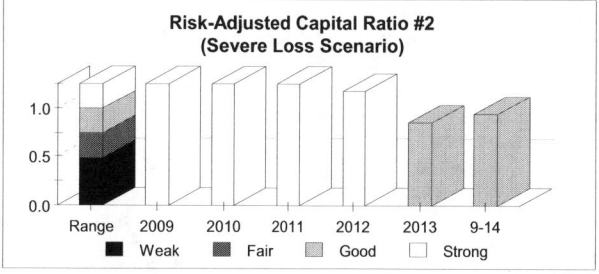

Risk-Adjusted Capital Ratio #2
(Severe Loss Scenario)

GUARDIAN LIFE INSURANCE COMPANY OF AMERICA *   A   Excellent

Major Rating Factors: Good quality investment portfolio (6.4 on a scale of 0 to 10) despite mixed results such as: large holdings of BBB rated bonds but moderate junk bond exposure. Good liquidity (5.9) with sufficient resources to handle a spike in claims as well as a significant increase in policy surrenders. Strong capitalization (8.1) based on excellent risk adjusted capital (severe loss scenario).

Other Rating Factors: Excellent profitability (7.5) with operating gains in each of the last five years. Excellent overall results on stability tests (7.5) excellent operational trends and excellent risk diversification.

Principal Business: Individual life insurance (51%), group health insurance (33%), reinsurance (6%), group life insurance (6%), and individual health insurance (3%).

Principal Investments: NonCMO investment grade bonds (62%), mortgages in good standing (8%), policy loans (8%), CMOs and structured securities (7%), and misc. investments (14%).

Investments in Affiliates: 4%

Group Affiliation: Guardian Group

Licensed in: All states except PR

Commenced Business: July 1860

Address: 7 Hanover Square, New York, NY 10004-4025

Phone: (212) 598-8000 **Domicile State:** NY **NAIC Code:** 64246

Data Date	Rating	RACR #1	RACR #2	Total Assets ($mil)	Capital ($mil)	Net Premium ($mil)	Net Income ($mil)
9-14	A	2.72	1.76	44,890.2	5,759.7	5,157.2	302.4
9-13	A	2.62	1.70	41,537.7	4,947.3	4,934.2	224.6
2013	A	2.64	1.73	42,066.0	5,011.9	6,705.6	285.5
2012	A	2.59	1.70	37,530.7	4,752.0	6,011.2	253.3
2011	A	2.63	1.70	35,130.0	4,572.6	5,874.6	195.9
2010	A	2.63	1.72	33,178.0	4,431.0	5,943.5	205.3
2009	A	2.58	1.72	30,895.2	4,188.0	5,925.4	27.7

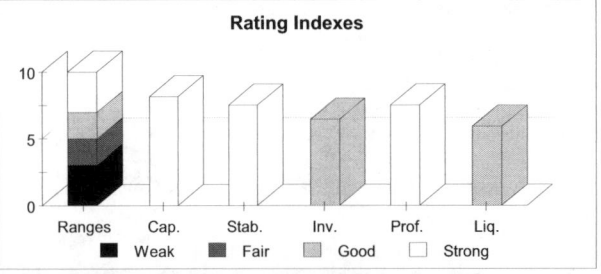

Rating Indexes

GUGGENHEIM LIFE & ANNUITY COMPANY   B-   Good

Major Rating Factors: Good capitalization (5.5 on a scale of 0 to 10) based on good risk adjusted capital (moderate loss scenario). Good overall results on stability tests (5.0) despite fair risk adjusted capital in prior years. Strengths include good financial support from affiliation with Sammons Enterprises Inc, good operational trends and excellent risk diversification. Fair quality investment portfolio (4.0).

Other Rating Factors: Excellent profitability (7.5) despite modest operating losses during 2009 and 2010. Excellent liquidity (8.0).

Principal Business: Reinsurance (62%) and individual annuities (38%).

Principal Investments: CMOs and structured securities (28%), nonCMO investment grade bonds (26%), mortgages in good standing (9%), cash (6%), and misc. investments (22%).

Investments in Affiliates: 17%

Group Affiliation: Sammons Enterprises Inc

Licensed in: All states except NJ, NY, PR

Commenced Business: October 1985

Address: 2711 Centerville Rd Suite 400, Wilmington, DE 19808-1645

Phone: (317) 396-9950 **Domicile State:** DE **NAIC Code:** 83607

Data Date	Rating	RACR #1	RACR #2	Total Assets ($mil)	Capital ($mil)	Net Premium ($mil)	Net Income ($mil)
9-14	B-	1.32	0.73	11,992.0	585.3	1,153.7	97.9
9-13	B-	1.19	0.63	10,707.6	474.1	1,360.5	78.0
2013	B-	1.34	0.75	11,101.8	550.8	1,726.0	107.4
2012	B-	1.38	0.77	9,134.0	490.3	676.8	122.0
2011	C-	1.39	0.69	5,908.2	312.8	608.2	118.4
2010	U	2.30	1.17	2,763.2	190.6	670.7	-21.4
2009	U	2.44	1.23	1,302.8	115.7	0.0	-27.9

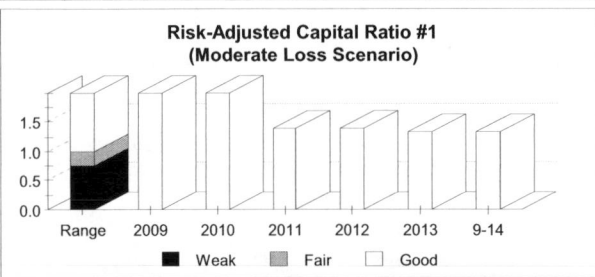

Risk-Adjusted Capital Ratio #1
(Moderate Loss Scenario)

HANNOVER LIFE REASSURANCE COMPANY OF AMERICA   C   Fair

Major Rating Factors: Fair overall results on stability tests (4.0 on a scale of 0 to 10) including negative cash flow from operations for 2013, fair risk adjusted capital in prior years. Good capitalization (5.1) based on good risk adjusted capital (moderate loss scenario). Good quality investment portfolio (6.7).

Other Rating Factors: Good liquidity (6.9). Excellent profitability (7.9) despite modest operating losses during 2009.

Principal Business: Reinsurance (100%).

Principal Investments: NonCMO investment grade bonds (89%), CMOs and structured securities (7%), noninv. grade bonds (2%), and mortgages in good standing (1%).

Investments in Affiliates: None

Group Affiliation: Talanx AG

Licensed in: All states, the District of Columbia and Puerto Rico

Commenced Business: October 1988

Address: 800 N Magnolia Ave, Ste 1000, Orlando, FL 32803-3251

Phone: (407) 649-8411 **Domicile State:** FL **NAIC Code:** 88340

Data Date	Rating	RACR #1	RACR #2	Total Assets ($mil)	Capital ($mil)	Net Premium ($mil)	Net Income ($mil)
9-14	C	1.06	0.61	4,534.7	202.9	209.0	19.3
9-13	C	1.00	0.58	5,010.7	196.6	325.4	28.3
2013	C	1.03	0.60	4,528.0	196.9	412.4	23.2
2012	C	0.87	0.50	4,617.8	181.0	399.0	9.4
2011	C	0.89	0.50	4,296.2	175.3	359.9	4.1
2010	C	0.96	0.57	3,451.4	166.6	388.9	0.2
2009	C	0.83	0.50	3,499.9	140.8	403.0	-6.1

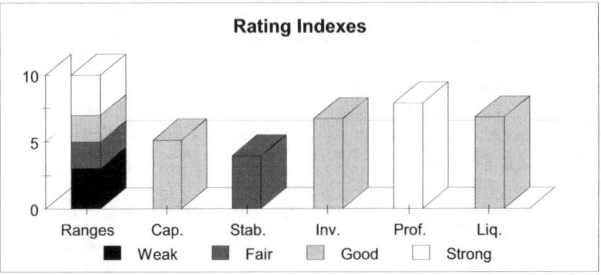

Rating Indexes

HARLEYSVILLE LIFE INSURANCE COMPANY   B   Good

Major Rating Factors: Good quality investment portfolio (6.5 on a scale of 0 to 10) despite mixed results such as: no exposure to mortgages and large holdings of BBB rated bonds but minimal holdings in junk bonds. Good overall profitability (5.3) although investment income, in comparison to reserve requirements, is below regulatory standards. Fair liquidity (3.5).

Other Rating Factors: Fair overall results on stability tests (4.0) including fair risk adjusted capital in prior years. Strong capitalization (7.0) based on excellent risk adjusted capital (severe loss scenario).

Principal Business: Individual life insurance (58%), group health insurance (18%), group life insurance (17%), and individual annuities (7%).

Principal Investments: NonCMO investment grade bonds (80%), CMOs and structured securities (18%), and policy loans (2%).

Investments in Affiliates: None

Group Affiliation: Nationwide Corp

Licensed in: AL, AZ, AR, CT, DC, DE, FL, GA, IL, IN, IA, KY, MD, MA, MI, MN, NE, NH, NJ, NM, NC, ND, OH, PA, RI, SC, SD, TN, TX, UT, VA, WV, WI

Commenced Business: June 1961

Address: 355 Maple Ave, Harleysville, PA 19438-2285

Phone: (215) 256-5000 **Domicile State:** PA **NAIC Code:** 64327

Data Date	Rating	RACR #1	RACR #2	Total Assets ($mil)	Capital ($mil)	Net Premium ($mil)	Net Income ($mil)
9-14	B	1.73	1.00	410.9	32.4	27.1	6.2
9-13	B	1.40	0.81	414.5	26.3	28.7	2.8
2013	B	1.39	0.80	415.0	26.0	37.6	3.2
2012	B	1.17	0.69	405.5	21.6	40.6	-2.5
2011	C+	1.20	0.75	392.4	20.4	51.0	-2.2
2010	C+	1.20	0.75	375.9	19.5	52.2	-2.8
2009	C+	1.21	0.76	356.5	19.0	53.1	-2.8

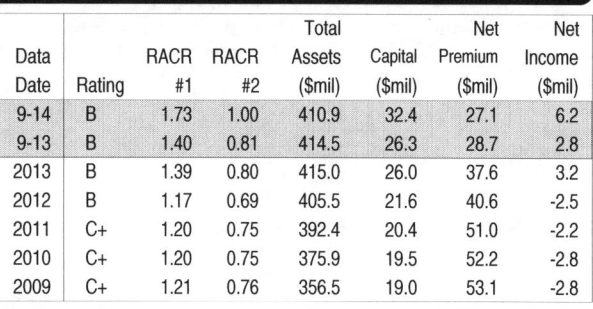

Rating Indexes

HARTFORD INTERNATIONAL LIFE REASSURANCE CORP   B-   Good

Major Rating Factors: Good overall results on stability tests (5.1 on a scale of 0 to 10) despite fair financial strength of affiliated Hartford Financial Services Inc. Other stability subfactors include good operational trends and excellent risk diversification. Good quality investment portfolio (6.7) despite mixed results such as: substantial holdings of BBB bonds but moderate junk bond exposure. Good liquidity (6.5).

Other Rating Factors: Fair profitability (3.3) with operating losses during the first nine months of 2014. Strong capitalization (7.2) based on excellent risk adjusted capital (severe loss scenario).

Principal Business: Reinsurance (100%).

Principal Investments: Policy loans (52%), nonCMO investment grade bonds (25%), CMOs and structured securities (14%), mortgages in good standing (6%), and misc. investments (3%).

Investments in Affiliates: None

Group Affiliation: Hartford Financial Services Inc

Licensed in: AK, AR, CA, CT, DC, DE, ID, IL, IN, IA, KS, KY, MD, MA, MI, MS, MT, NV, NH, NJ, NY, NC, ND, OH, PA, SC, SD, TX, UT, WA, WV, WI

Commenced Business: September 1987

Address: 200 Hopmeadow St, Simsbury, CT 06070

Phone: (860) 547-5000 **Domicile State:** CT **NAIC Code:** 93505

Data Date	Rating	RACR #1	RACR #2	Total Assets ($mil)	Capital ($mil)	Net Premium ($mil)	Net Income ($mil)
9-14	B-	2.23	1.13	1,144.5	89.5	3.3	0.0
9-13	B-	2.27	1.17	1,134.7	87.7	9.0	4.2
2013	B-	2.21	1.13	1,138.1	88.2	16.4	6.0
2012	B-	2.11	1.09	1,127.6	84.1	18.9	-8.8
2011	B	2.44	1.29	1,254.5	92.0	18.3	4.5
2010	B	2.21	1.12	1,125.4	95.9	15.9	5.4
2009	B	2.09	1.05	1,129.4	91.8	12.0	-3.3

Hartford Financial Services Inc Composite Group Rating: C+ Largest Group Members	Assets ($mil)	Rating
HARTFORD LIFE INS CO	128074	C+
HARTFORD LIFE ANNUITY INS CO	54557	B-
HARTFORD FIRE INS CO	25685	B
HARTFORD LIFE ACCIDENT INS CO	13891	C-
HARTFORD ACCIDENT INDEMNITY CO	11122	B

HARTFORD LIFE & ACCIDENT INSURANCE COMPANY   C-   Fair

Major Rating Factors: Poor current capitalization (0.5 on a scale of 0 to 10) based on weak risk adjusted capital (severe loss scenario), although results have slipped from the excellent range during the last year. Low quality investment portfolio (0.6). Weak overall results on stability tests (1.9) including excessive premium growth and negative cash flow from operations for 2013.

Other Rating Factors: Fair profitability (3.6) with operating losses during the first nine months of 2014. Good liquidity (6.9).

Principal Business: Group health insurance (53%), group life insurance (35%), reinsurance (11%), and individual life insurance (1%).

Principal Investments: NonCMO investment grade bonds (40%), common & preferred stock (39%), CMOs and structured securities (8%), mortgages in good standing (5%), and misc. investments (5%).

Investments in Affiliates: 38%

Group Affiliation: Hartford Financial Services Inc

Licensed in: All states, the District of Columbia and Puerto Rico

Commenced Business: February 1967

Address: 200 Hopmeadow St, Simsbury, CT 06070

Phone: (860) 547-5000 **Domicile State:** CT **NAIC Code:** 70815

Data Date	Rating	RACR #1	RACR #2	Total Assets ($mil)	Capital ($mil)	Net Premium ($mil)	Net Income ($mil)
9-14	C-	0.31	0.29	9,041.5	1,522.6	1,902.8	-383.3
9-13	B-	1.11	1.04	14,499.7	5,991.8	1,336.5	-259.9
2013	B-	1.05	1.00	13,890.8	5,595.2	1,974.0	-174.0
2012	B-	1.07	1.01	14,404.8	5,767.3	2,878.5	-397.8
2011	B-	1.06	1.01	15,388.3	6,737.2	3,178.7	-23.0
2010	B-	1.04	1.00	14,950.7	6,577.1	3,314.6	164.8
2009	B-	1.02	0.98	14,254.5	6,005.3	3,350.8	70.4

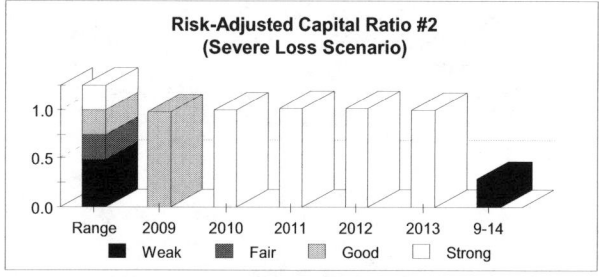

Risk-Adjusted Capital Ratio #2 (Severe Loss Scenario)

HARTFORD LIFE & ANNUITY INSURANCE COMPANY — B- — Good

Major Rating Factors: Fair overall results on stability tests (3.9 on a scale of 0 to 10) including fair financial strength of affiliated Hartford Financial Services Inc and negative cash flow from operations for 2013. Fair overall capitalization (4.0) based on mixed results -- excessive policy leverage mitigated by excellent risk adjusted capital (severe loss scenario). Nevertheless, capital levels have fluctuated during prior years. Good overall profitability (5.4).

Other Rating Factors: High quality investment portfolio (7.5). Excellent liquidity (9.1).

Principal Business: Individual life insurance (63%), individual annuities (28%), and reinsurance (9%).

Principal Investments: NonCMO investment grade bonds (52%), CMOs and structured securities (21%), mortgages in good standing (8%), cash (3%), and misc. investments (8%).

Investments in Affiliates: 11%

Group Affiliation: Hartford Financial Services Inc

Licensed in: All states except NY

Commenced Business: July 1965

Address: 200 Hopmeadow St, Simsbury, CT 06070

Phone: (860) 547-5000 **Domicile State:** CT **NAIC Code:** 71153

Data Date	Rating	RACR #1	RACR #2	Total Assets ($mil)	Capital ($mil)	Net Premium ($mil)	Net Income ($mil)
9-14	B-	6.88	3.96	48,312.7	3,323.9	41,271.7	23.7
9-13	B-	2.72	1.95	56,189.9	3,383.0	-2,986.9	773.5
2013	B-	6.35	3.36	54,556.9	3,080.6	-2,982.6	721.8
2012	B-	2.42	1.68	65,710.7	3,026.2	1,288.8	711.4
2011	C	2.76	1.98	67,758.0	3,931.4	1,401.1	-857.9
2010	B-	3.06	2.14	73,626.9	4,062.5	1,110.0	79.9
2009	B-	2.33	1.71	73,406.5	4,085.6	-55,103.3	2,408.6

Hartford Financial Services Inc
Composite Group Rating: C+

Largest Group Members	Assets ($mil)	Rating
HARTFORD LIFE INS CO	128074	C+
HARTFORD LIFE ANNUITY INS CO	54557	B-
HARTFORD FIRE INS CO	25685	B
HARTFORD LIFE ACCIDENT INS CO	13891	C-
HARTFORD ACCIDENT INDEMNITY CO	11122	B

HARTFORD LIFE INSURANCE COMPANY — C+ — Fair

Major Rating Factors: Fair current capitalization (4.0 on a scale of 0 to 10) based on mixed results -- excessive policy leverage mitigated by excellent risk adjusted capital (severe loss scenario) reflecting improvement over results in 2009. Fair overall results on stability tests (4.1). Good quality investment portfolio (5.5).

Other Rating Factors: Weak profitability (2.9) with operating losses during the first nine months of 2014. Excellent liquidity (9.3).

Principal Business: Group retirement contracts (67%), individual annuities (10%), individual life insurance (8%), group health insurance (8%), and other lines (6%).

Principal Investments: NonCMO investment grade bonds (41%), CMOs and structured securities (19%), common & preferred stock (16%), mortgages in good standing (6%), and misc. investments (15%).

Investments in Affiliates: 15%

Group Affiliation: Hartford Financial Services Inc

Licensed in: All states except PR

Commenced Business: January 1979

Address: 200 Hopmeadow St, Simsbury, CT 06070

Phone: (860) 547-5000 **Domicile State:** CT **NAIC Code:** 88072

Data Date	Rating	RACR #1	RACR #2	Total Assets ($mil)	Capital ($mil)	Net Premium ($mil)	Net Income ($mil)
9-14	C+	1.41	1.10	124,390	5,525.3	-1,186.0	-28.4
9-13	C+	1.39	1.07	129,238	5,433.6	-7,347.0	563.4
2013	C+	1.28	0.99	128,074	5,005.0	-7,168.0	549.9
2012	C+	1.22	0.92	140,501	5,015.5	3,115.8	224.3
2011	C	1.15	0.90	144,044	5,920.1	3,614.0	184.2
2010	C	1.08	0.85	148,900	5,831.5	4,112.3	122.5
2009	C-	0.99	0.77	140,232	5,365.0	5,824.5	-538.8

Policy Leverage

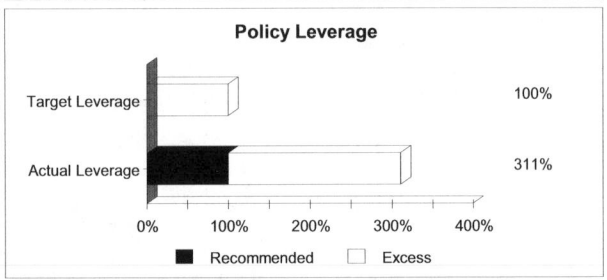

Target Leverage — 100%
Actual Leverage — 311%

0% 100% 200% 300% 400%

■ Recommended ☐ Excess

HCC LIFE INSURANCE COMPANY — B — Good

Major Rating Factors: Good overall results on stability tests (6.1 on a scale of 0 to 10). Stability strengths include excellent operational trends and excellent risk diversification. Good liquidity (6.9) with sufficient resources to handle a spike in claims. Strong capitalization (10.0) based on excellent risk adjusted capital (severe loss scenario).

Other Rating Factors: High quality investment portfolio (7.8). Excellent profitability (9.4) with operating gains in each of the last five years.

Principal Business: Group health insurance (94%), individual health insurance (4%), and reinsurance (1%).

Principal Investments: NonCMO investment grade bonds (77%), CMOs and structured securities (20%), and common & preferred stock (3%).

Investments in Affiliates: 3%

Group Affiliation: HCC Ins Holdings Inc

Licensed in: All states except PR

Commenced Business: March 1981

Address: 300 N Meridian St Ste 2700, Indianapolis, IN 46204

Phone: (713) 996-1200 **Domicile State:** IN **NAIC Code:** 92711

Data Date	Rating	RACR #1	RACR #2	Total Assets ($mil)	Capital ($mil)	Net Premium ($mil)	Net Income ($mil)
9-14	B	3.98	3.24	885.8	516.9	713.5	76.8
9-13	B	3.20	2.74	836.0	484.0	637.7	106.3
2013	B	3.61	2.96	750.2	436.9	854.6	142.1
2012	B	2.72	2.34	731.2	413.7	821.0	100.2
2011	B	2.97	2.57	655.7	400.2	686.0	89.0
2010	B	3.01	2.60	608.3	390.3	637.0	78.6
2009	B	2.81	2.43	598.0	367.7	651.8	66.0

Adverse Trends in Operations

Decrease in premium volume from 2009 to 2010 (2%)

HEALTH NET LIFE INSURANCE COMPANY   B   Good

Major Rating Factors: Good overall results on stability tests (5.2 on a scale of 0 to 10) despite fair financial strength of affiliated Health Net Inc. Other stability subfactors include good operational trends and excellent risk diversification. Good liquidity (5.5) with sufficient resources to handle a spike in claims. Fair profitability (3.9) with operating losses during the first nine months of 2014.
Other Rating Factors: Strong capitalization (7.8) based on excellent risk adjusted capital (severe loss scenario). High quality investment portfolio (8.3).
Principal Business: Group health insurance (55%) and individual health insurance (45%).
Principal Investments: NonCMO investment grade bonds (79%), CMOs and structured securities (25%), and noninv. grade bonds (1%).
Investments in Affiliates: None
Group Affiliation: Health Net Inc
Licensed in: All states except NY, PR
Commenced Business: January 1987
Address: 225 N Main St, Pueblo, CO 81003
Phone: (719) 585-8017 **Domicile State:** CA **NAIC Code:** 66141

Data Date	Rating	RACR #1	RACR #2	Total Assets ($mil)	Capital ($mil)	Net Premium ($mil)	Net Income ($mil)
9-14	B	1.87	1.52	618.8	279.4	775.4	-40.1
9-13	B	2.38	1.93	603.4	350.4	705.5	33.7
2013	B	1.88	1.52	485.1	257.2	916.1	22.9
2012	C+	2.25	1.82	632.0	365.6	1,079.4	107.7
2011	C+	1.99	1.63	548.6	352.9	1,178.4	22.6
2010	B+	2.33	1.89	680.5	414.5	1,159.6	26.9
2009	B	2.14	1.74	643.1	383.6	1,161.6	58.2

Health Net Inc Composite Group Rating: C+ Largest Group Members	Assets ($mil)	Rating
HEALTH NET OF CALIFORNIA INC	1948	C+
HEALTH NET COMMUNITY SOLUTIONS INC	578	C+
HEALTH NET LIFE INS CO	485	B
HEALTH NET OF ARIZONA INC	350	C-
HEALTH NET HEALTH PLAN OF OREGON INC	95	E

HERITAGE LIFE INSURANCE COMPANY   C-   Fair

Major Rating Factors: Fair quality investment portfolio (4.9 on a scale of 0 to 10) with large holdings of BBB rated bonds in addition to junk bond exposure equal to 51% of capital. Fair profitability (4.5). Return on equity has been low, averaging -0.7%. Fair overall results on stability tests (3.1).
Other Rating Factors: Strong capitalization (8.3) based on excellent risk adjusted capital (severe loss scenario). Excellent liquidity (9.3).
Principal Business: Reinsurance (100%).
Principal Investments: NonCMO investment grade bonds (35%), CMOs and structured securities (28%), noninv. grade bonds (11%), cash (8%), and common & preferred stock (1%).
Investments in Affiliates: 6%
Group Affiliation: HLIC Holdings Inc
Licensed in: All states except NY, PR
Commenced Business: August 1957
Address: 30851 W Agoura Rd, Agoura Hills, CA 91301
Phone: (818) 597-5962 **Domicile State:** AZ **NAIC Code:** 64394

Data Date	Rating	RACR #1	RACR #2	Total Assets ($mil)	Capital ($mil)	Net Premium ($mil)	Net Income ($mil)
9-14	C-	4.23	1.86	5,039.7	1,034.3	26.9	45.6
9-13	U	N/A	N/A	4,411.0	998.1	63.4	16.9
2013	C-	4.49	1.94	4,872.4	1,018.0	85.8	34.0
2012	U	14.27	8.59	3,893.5	1,000.1	0.0	-0.2
2011	U	9.83	8.84	8.7	8.2	0.0	-0.9
2010	U	9.43	8.48	9.1	8.0	0.0	-1.4
2009	U	9.03	8.13	30.9	28.9	0.0	5.0

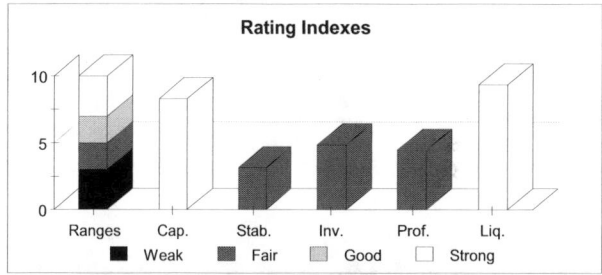

Rating Indexes

HM LIFE INSURANCE COMPANY   B   Good

Major Rating Factors: Good overall results on stability tests (6.1 on a scale of 0 to 10). Stability strengths include excellent operational trends and excellent risk diversification. Good quality investment portfolio (5.1) with no exposure to mortgages and small junk bond holdings. Good liquidity (6.8) with sufficient resources to handle a spike in claims.
Other Rating Factors: Strong capitalization (9.1) based on excellent risk adjusted capital (severe loss scenario). Excellent profitability (8.7) with operating gains in each of the last five years.
Principal Business: Group health insurance (87%) and reinsurance (13%).
Principal Investments: NonCMO investment grade bonds (60%), CMOs and structured securities (14%), noninv. grade bonds (11%), cash (7%), and common & preferred stock (1%).
Investments in Affiliates: 1%
Group Affiliation: Highmark Inc
Licensed in: All states except NY, PR
Commenced Business: May 1981
Address: 120 Fifth Avenue, Pittsburgh, PA 15222
Phone: (800) 328-5433 **Domicile State:** PA **NAIC Code:** 93440

Data Date	Rating	RACR #1	RACR #2	Total Assets ($mil)	Capital ($mil)	Net Premium ($mil)	Net Income ($mil)
9-14	B	3.17	2.41	583.7	299.7	488.8	14.8
9-13	B	2.98	2.27	569.3	272.4	473.0	23.3
2013	B	3.07	2.35	557.9	284.6	634.0	35.5
2012	B	2.87	2.20	491.3	250.0	588.8	25.4
2011	B-	2.64	2.03	471.6	219.5	568.8	27.7
2010	B-	2.69	2.04	415.2	189.2	491.9	25.8
2009	B-	2.86	2.15	346.2	157.8	394.1	12.7

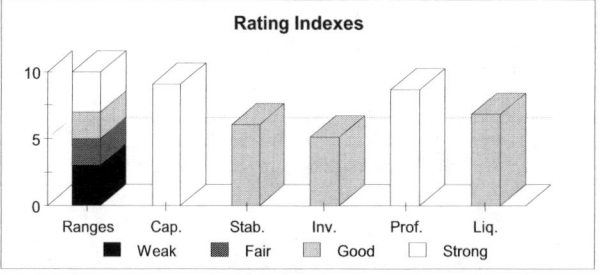

Rating Indexes

HM LIFE INSURANCE COMPANY OF NEW YORK *   B+   Good

Major Rating Factors: Good overall results on stability tests (6.2 on a scale of 0 to 10). Stability strengths include good operational trends and good risk diversification. Good overall profitability (6.5). Return on equity has been fair, averaging 5.9%. Strong capitalization (8.5) based on excellent risk adjusted capital (severe loss scenario).

Other Rating Factors: High quality investment portfolio (8.7). Excellent liquidity (7.1).

Principal Business: N/A

Principal Investments: NonCMO investment grade bonds (44%), cash (32%), and CMOs and structured securities (24%).

Investments in Affiliates: None

Group Affiliation: Highmark Inc

Licensed in: DC, NY, RI

Commenced Business: March 1997

Address: 420 Fifth Ave 3rd Floor, New York, NY 10018

Phone: (800) 328-5433 **Domicile State:** NY **NAIC Code:** 60213

Data Date	Rating	RACR #1	RACR #2	Total Assets ($mil)	Capital ($mil)	Net Premium ($mil)	Net Income ($mil)
9-14	B+	2.52	1.99	72.4	32.4	56.9	0.8
9-13	B+	2.04	1.62	75.2	32.3	65.4	0.6
2013	B+	2.28	1.81	76.1	31.9	85.4	-0.4
2012	B+	2.00	1.59	66.5	31.8	88.4	9.0
2011	B-	1.90	1.50	44.9	22.9	63.1	2.5
2010	B-	1.51	1.21	44.3	20.1	71.0	-0.3
2009	B	1.91	1.52	41.1	20.6	61.2	-1.1

Adverse Trends in Operations

Decrease in premium volume from 2012 to 2013 (3%)
Decrease in premium volume from 2010 to 2011 (11%)
Decrease in capital during 2010 (2%)

HOMESTEADERS LIFE COMPANY   B   Good

Major Rating Factors: Good quality investment portfolio (6.3 on a scale of 0 to 10) despite mixed results such as: minimal exposure to mortgages and substantial holdings of BBB bonds but minimal holdings in junk bonds. Good overall profitability (5.8). Return on equity has been good over the last five years, averaging 10.3%. Good liquidity (6.8).

Other Rating Factors: Good overall results on stability tests (5.5) excellent operational trends, good risk adjusted capital for prior years and excellent risk diversification. Strong capitalization (7.3) based on excellent risk adjusted capital (severe loss scenario).

Principal Business: Group life insurance (95%), individual annuities (3%), and individual life insurance (2%).

Principal Investments: NonCMO investment grade bonds (72%), CMOs and structured securities (22%), and mortgages in good standing (4%).

Investments in Affiliates: None

Group Affiliation: None

Licensed in: All states except NY, PR

Commenced Business: February 1906

Address: 2141 Grand Ave, Des Moines, IA 50312

Phone: (515) 288-7481 **Domicile State:** IA **NAIC Code:** 64505

Data Date	Rating	RACR #1	RACR #2	Total Assets ($mil)	Capital ($mil)	Net Premium ($mil)	Net Income ($mil)
9-14	B	2.11	1.20	2,475.7	158.6	304.3	9.5
9-13	B	2.04	1.17	2,349.0	138.8	303.1	9.9
2013	B	2.02	1.16	2,378.1	149.6	396.7	12.6
2012	B	1.97	1.13	2,249.0	132.5	413.8	15.3
2011	B-	2.06	1.14	2,093.3	119.7	397.4	15.9
2010	B-	1.94	1.07	1,937.1	106.4	389.9	14.0
2009	B-	1.72	0.95	1,762.2	94.4	358.3	10.3

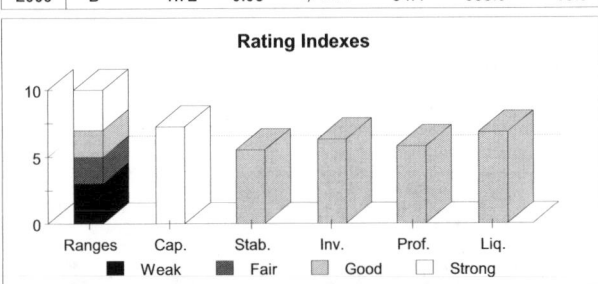

Rating Indexes

Ranges   Cap.   Stab.   Inv.   Prof.   Liq.
■ Weak   ■ Fair   ▨ Good   □ Strong

HORACE MANN LIFE INSURANCE COMPANY   B   Good

Major Rating Factors: Good capitalization (6.6 on a scale of 0 to 10) based on good risk adjusted capital (severe loss scenario). Moreover, capital levels have been consistent over the last five years. Good quality investment portfolio (5.3) despite mixed results such as: large holdings of BBB rated bonds but moderate junk bond exposure. Good liquidity (5.2).

Other Rating Factors: Good overall results on stability tests (5.4) excellent operational trends and excellent risk diversification. Excellent profitability (8.1) with operating gains in each of the last five years.

Principal Business: Individual annuities (73%), individual life insurance (19%), group retirement contracts (7%), and group life insurance (1%).

Principal Investments: NonCMO investment grade bonds (66%), CMOs and structured securities (25%), policy loans (3%), noninv. grade bonds (3%), and common & preferred stock (1%).

Investments in Affiliates: None

Group Affiliation: Horace Mann Educators Corp

Licensed in: All states except NJ, NY, PR

Commenced Business: September 1949

Address: 1 Horace Mann Plaza, Springfield, IL 62715

Phone: (800) 999-1030 **Domicile State:** IL **NAIC Code:** 64513

Data Date	Rating	RACR #1	RACR #2	Total Assets ($mil)	Capital ($mil)	Net Premium ($mil)	Net Income ($mil)
9-14	B	1.89	0.95	7,830.3	387.2	433.9	38.0
9-13	B	1.97	0.97	6,960.9	368.4	387.7	37.3
2013	B	1.90	0.96	7,281.4	372.4	520.1	54.1
2012	B	1.92	0.95	6,302.5	347.7	514.1	44.8
2011	B	2.11	1.05	5,817.2	339.7	530.7	53.7
2010	B	2.24	1.12	5,554.5	322.9	493.4	46.5
2009	B	2.21	1.13	5,087.0	307.6	448.7	39.5

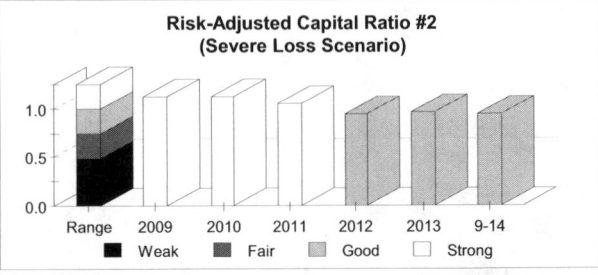

Risk-Adjusted Capital Ratio #2
(Severe Loss Scenario)

Range   2009   2010   2011   2012   2013   9-14
■ Weak   ■ Fair   ▨ Good   □ Strong

HUMANA INSURANCE COMPANY OF KENTUCKY　　　　　B-　　　Good

Major Rating Factors: Good overall results on stability tests (5.1 on a scale of 0 to 10) despite fair financial strength of affiliated Humana Inc. Other stability subfactors include good operational trends and good risk diversification. Good liquidity (6.7) with sufficient resources to handle a spike in claims. Weak profitability (2.9) with investment income below regulatory standards in relation to interest assumptions of reserves.

Other Rating Factors: Strong capitalization (8.3) based on excellent risk adjusted capital (severe loss scenario). High quality investment portfolio (8.1).

Principal Business: Reinsurance (60%), individual health insurance (20%), group life insurance (17%), and group health insurance (3%).

Principal Investments: NonCMO investment grade bonds (61%), CMOs and structured securities (36%), and cash (3%).

Investments in Affiliates: None

Group Affiliation: Humana Inc

Licensed in: KY

Commenced Business: January 2001

Address: 500 W Main St, Louisville, KY 40202

Phone: (502) 580-1000　**Domicile State:** KY　**NAIC Code:** 60219

Data Date	Rating	RACR #1	RACR #2	Total Assets ($mil)	Capital ($mil)	Net Premium ($mil)	Net Income ($mil)
9-14	B-	2.40	1.84	122.2	74.2	88.1	13.2
9-13	B-	2.13	1.67	46.0	31.4	32.8	6.6
2013	B-	2.03	1.57	108.6	61.1	111.5	15.7
2012	B-	1.73	1.35	42.3	24.8	40.8	6.4
2011	B-	1.40	1.10	35.9	18.5	36.6	-1.9
2010	B-	1.54	1.21	37.4	19.9	37.9	-0.1
2009	B-	1.74	1.37	34.2	19.6	33.7	0.1

Humana Inc
Composite Group Rating: C+

Largest Group Members	Assets ($mil)	Rating
KANAWHA INS CO	1623	C
HUMANA MEDICAL PLAN INC	1595	B
HUMANA HEALTH PLAN INC	812	C
HUMANA HEALTH BENEFIT PLAN LA	388	B
HUMANA HEALTH PLAN OF TEXAS INC	335	B

HUMANA INSURANCE COMPANY OF PUERTO RICO INCORPOR/　　B-　　Good

Major Rating Factors: Good overall profitability (5.9 on a scale of 0 to 10) despite operating losses during the first nine months of 2014. Good liquidity (6.6) with sufficient resources to handle a spike in claims. Fair overall results on stability tests (4.3) including fair financial strength of affiliated Humana Inc.

Other Rating Factors: Strong capitalization (9.0) based on excellent risk adjusted capital (severe loss scenario). High quality investment portfolio (8.4).

Principal Business: Group health insurance (78%) and individual health insurance (22%).

Principal Investments: CMOs and structured securities (59%), nonCMO investment grade bonds (42%), and noninv. grade bonds (2%).

Investments in Affiliates: None

Group Affiliation: Humana Inc

Licensed in: PR

Commenced Business: September 1971

Address: 383 F D Roosevelt Ave, San Juan, PR 00918-2131

Phone: (787) 282-7900　**Domicile State:** PR　**NAIC Code:** 84603

Data Date	Rating	RACR #1	RACR #2	Total Assets ($mil)	Capital ($mil)	Net Premium ($mil)	Net Income ($mil)
9-14	B-	2.96	2.35	69.1	52.5	71.3	-4.2
9-13	C+	3.21	2.54	72.2	57.5	69.9	5.5
2013	B-	3.20	2.52	73.3	57.0	93.2	4.7
2012	C+	2.86	2.27	70.2	52.1	98.6	4.6
2011	C	3.28	2.60	73.6	48.8	88.1	7.9
2010	C	N/A	N/A	57.5	40.9	89.2	8.1
2009	C	2.25	1.84	49.8	32.8	80.6	1.3

Humana Inc
Composite Group Rating: C+

Largest Group Members	Assets ($mil)	Rating
KANAWHA INS CO	1623	C
HUMANA MEDICAL PLAN INC	1595	B
HUMANA HEALTH PLAN INC	812	C
HUMANA HEALTH BENEFIT PLAN LA	388	B
HUMANA HEALTH PLAN OF TEXAS INC	335	B

ILLINOIS MUTUAL LIFE INSURANCE COMPANY *　　　A-　　Excellent

Major Rating Factors: Good quality investment portfolio (6.5 on a scale of 0 to 10) despite mixed results such as: minimal exposure to mortgages and large holdings of BBB rated bonds but minimal holdings in junk bonds. Good liquidity (6.6) with sufficient resources to handle a spike in claims as well as a significant increase in policy surrenders. Good overall results on stability tests (6.9) excellent operational trends, good risk adjusted capital for prior years and excellent risk diversification.

Other Rating Factors: Strong capitalization (8.4) based on excellent risk adjusted capital (severe loss scenario). Excellent profitability (7.0).

Principal Business: Individual health insurance (51%), individual life insurance (46%), individual annuities (2%), and group health insurance (1%).

Principal Investments: NonCMO investment grade bonds (72%), CMOs and structured securities (21%), common & preferred stock (2%), policy loans (1%), and misc. investments (4%).

Investments in Affiliates: None

Group Affiliation: None

Licensed in: All states except AK, DC, HI, NY, PR

Commenced Business: July 1912

Address: 300 SW Adams, Peoria, IL 61634

Phone: (309) 674-8255　**Domicile State:** IL　**NAIC Code:** 64580

Data Date	Rating	RACR #1	RACR #2	Total Assets ($mil)	Capital ($mil)	Net Premium ($mil)	Net Income ($mil)
9-14	A-	3.38	1.91	1,368.4	195.3	75.4	21.6
9-13	A-	3.42	1.99	1,313.7	160.8	78.9	15.1
2013	A-	3.57	2.05	1,329.4	173.7	104.2	26.7
2012	B	3.07	1.76	1,289.1	144.2	102.0	27.0
2011	B	2.58	1.46	1,227.9	115.6	104.3	22.3
2010	B	1.85	1.05	1,211.6	104.1	104.5	-63.5
2009	B+	1.67	0.89	1,248.0	136.4	138.4	1.0

Adverse Trends in Operations

Decrease in premium volume from 2011 to 2012 (2%)
Decrease in asset base during 2010 (3%)
Change in premium mix from 2009 to 2010 (5.4%)
Decrease in capital during 2010 (24%)
Decrease in premium volume from 2009 to 2010 (25%)

INDEPENDENCE LIFE & ANNUITY COMPANY

C   **Fair**

Major Rating Factors: Fair overall results on stability tests (3.5 on a scale of 0 to 10) including potential financial drain due to affiliation with Sun Life Assurance Group and negative cash flow from operations for 2013. Fair overall capitalization (4.0) based on mixed results -- excessive policy leverage mitigated by excellent risk adjusted capital (severe loss scenario). Moreover, capital levels have been consistently high over the last five years. High quality investment portfolio (8.0).
Other Rating Factors: Excellent profitability (7.5) with operating gains in each of the last five years. Excellent liquidity (7.2).
Principal Business: Reinsurance (100%).
Principal Investments: NonCMO investment grade bonds (69%), CMOs and structured securities (19%), and policy loans (11%).
Investments in Affiliates: None
Group Affiliation: Sun Life Assurance Group
Licensed in: All states except NY, PR
Commenced Business: November 1945
Address: 1209 Orange St, Wilmington, DE 19801
Phone: (781) 237-6030 **Domicile State:** DE **NAIC Code:** 64602

Data Date	Rating	RACR #1	RACR #2	Total Assets ($mil)	Capital ($mil)	Net Premium ($mil)	Net Income ($mil)
9-14	C	4.54	2.90	2,540.6	129.1	-0.3	1.8
9-13	C	7.14	6.42	132.9	65.1	-0.3	0.9
2013	C	4.48	2.72	2,284.3	127.3	-0.4	1.2
2012	C-	7.04	6.33	128.5	64.2	-0.4	2.4
2011	B-	6.80	6.12	126.0	61.8	-0.4	4.1
2010	B	6.43	5.79	126.5	58.6	-0.4	2.8
2009	B-	6.09	5.48	125.9	55.4	-0.5	2.6

Sun Life Assurance Group Composite Group Rating: D+ Largest Group Members	Assets ($mil)	Rating
SUN LIFE ASR CO OF CANADA	15369	D
INDEPENDENCE LIFE ANNUITY CO	2284	C
SUN LIFE HEALTH INS CO	354	C-
PROFESSIONAL INS CO	105	C-

INDUSTRIAL ALLIANCE INS & FIN SERV

C   **Fair**

Major Rating Factors: Good quality investment portfolio (5.0 on a scale of 0 to 10) despite mixed results such as: minimal exposure to mortgages and large holdings of BBB rated bonds but minimal holdings in junk bonds. Good liquidity (6.4) with sufficient resources to cover a large increase in policy surrenders. Weak profitability (2.0) with operating losses during the first nine months of 2014.
Other Rating Factors: Weak overall results on stability tests (2.9) including negative cash flow from operations for 2013 and weak results on operational trends. Strong capitalization (9.5) based on excellent risk adjusted capital (severe loss scenario).
Principal Business: Reinsurance (47%), individual annuities (39%), and individual life insurance (14%).
Principal Investments: NonCMO investment grade bonds (76%), mortgages in good standing (6%), real estate (6%), nonperforming mortgages (3%), and misc. investments (9%).
Investments in Affiliates: None
Group Affiliation: Industrial Alliance Ins & Financial
Licensed in: All states except CT, FL, MN, NY, NC, PR
Commenced Business: June 1967
Address: 425 Austin Ave, Waco, TX 76701
Phone: (480) 473-5540 **Domicile State:** TX **NAIC Code:** 14406

Data Date	Rating	RACR #1	RACR #2	Total Assets ($mil)	Capital ($mil)	Net Premium ($mil)	Net Income ($mil)
9-14	C	4.57	2.68	190.2	56.9	41.8	-2.9
9-13	C+	8.38	4.16	204.1	87.4	5.5	1.1
2013	C	5.59	3.22	200.7	73.2	31.7	-18.5
2012	C+	8.43	4.19	221.3	83.4	60.0	12.2
2011	N/A	N/A	N/A	0.0	0.0	0.0	0.0
2010	N/A	N/A	N/A	0.0	0.0	0.0	0.0
2009	N/A	N/A	N/A	0.0	0.0	0.0	0.0

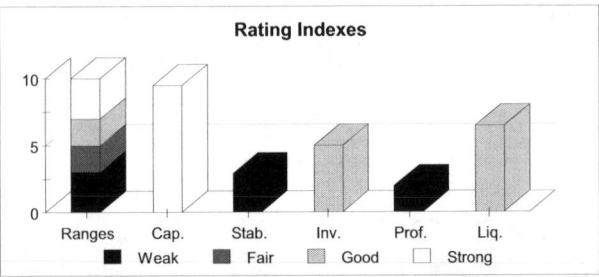

Rating Indexes

INTEGRITY LIFE INSURANCE COMPANY

B-   **Good**

Major Rating Factors: Good quality investment portfolio (5.0 on a scale of 0 to 10) despite mixed results such as: substantial holdings of BBB bonds but moderate junk bond exposure. Fair overall results on stability tests (4.9) including excessive premium growth. Weak profitability (2.5) with investment income below regulatory standards in relation to interest assumptions of reserves.
Other Rating Factors: Strong capitalization (7.3) based on excellent risk adjusted capital (severe loss scenario). Excellent liquidity (7.4).
Principal Business: Individual annuities (100%).
Principal Investments: NonCMO investment grade bonds (47%), CMOs and structured securities (23%), common & preferred stock (15%), noninv. grade bonds (7%), and misc. investments (7%).
Investments in Affiliates: 10%
Group Affiliation: Western & Southern Group
Licensed in: All states except ME, NH, NY, VT, PR
Commenced Business: May 1966
Address: 400 Broadway St, Cincinnati, OH 45202-3341
Phone: (513) 629-1800 **Domicile State:** OH **NAIC Code:** 74780

Data Date	Rating	RACR #1	RACR #2	Total Assets ($mil)	Capital ($mil)	Net Premium ($mil)	Net Income ($mil)
9-14	B-	1.61	1.18	6,199.4	735.1	260.6	44.1
9-13	B-	1.53	1.11	6,029.9	652.4	177.7	31.5
2013	B-	1.52	1.12	6,056.7	668.0	249.8	42.2
2012	B-	1.43	1.04	5,988.3	599.7	302.2	33.7
2011	B-	1.37	0.98	5,916.1	547.2	352.2	25.3
2010	B-	1.41	1.01	5,909.7	529.2	389.4	42.6
2009	C+	1.43	1.03	5,414.0	501.5	554.0	-12.4

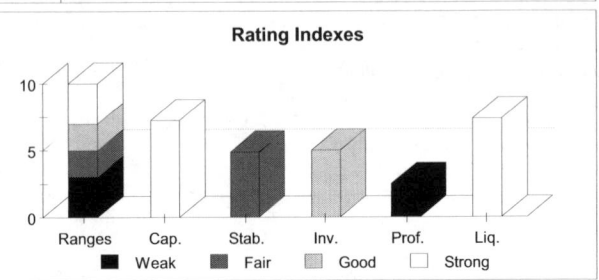

Rating Indexes

INVESTORS LIFE INSURANCE COMPANY NORTH AMERICA | B | Good

Major Rating Factors: Good overall results on stability tests (6.1 on a scale of 0 to 10) despite negative cash flow from operations for 2013. Other stability subfactors include excellent operational trends, good risk adjusted capital for prior years and excellent risk diversification. Good liquidity (6.1) with sufficient resources to cover a large increase in policy surrenders. Fair overall capitalization (4.0) based on mixed results -- excessive policy leverage mitigated by excellent risk adjusted capital (severe loss scenario).
Other Rating Factors: Fair quality investment portfolio (4.8). Excellent profitability (8.5).
Principal Business: Individual life insurance (99%) and individual annuities (1%).
Principal Investments: NonCMO investment grade bonds (55%), CMOs and structured securities (29%), noninv. grade bonds (6%), common & preferred stock (6%), and policy loans (4%).
Investments in Affiliates: 1%
Group Affiliation: Americo Life Inc
Licensed in: All states except NY, PR
Commenced Business: December 1963
Address: 6500 River Place Blvd Bldg One, Austin, TX 78730
Phone: (512) 404-5000 **Domicile State:** TX **NAIC Code:** 63487

Data Date	Rating	RACR #1	RACR #2	Total Assets ($mil)	Capital ($mil)	Net Premium ($mil)	Net Income ($mil)
9-14	B	2.65	1.42	680.7	52.0	-0.3	0.9
9-13	B-	2.35	1.21	685.5	47.4	-0.1	1.5
2013	B-	2.45	1.25	691.3	49.2	-0.1	1.9
2012	C+	2.41	1.21	691.7	45.7	-0.3	2.1
2011	C	2.06	0.98	705.8	44.0	-0.1	3.2
2010	C	N/A	N/A	741.1	41.7	-0.3	2.5
2009	C	2.11	1.13	746.1	39.5	0.0	1.9

Adverse Trends in Operations

Decrease in premium volume from 2011 to 2012 (177%)
Decrease in asset base during 2012 (2%)
Increase in policy surrenders from 2010 to 2011 (143%)
Decrease in asset base during 2011 (5%)
Decrease in premium volume from 2009 to 2010 (1295%)

IOWA AMERICAN LIFE INSURANCE COMPANY | C | Fair

Major Rating Factors: Fair overall results on stability tests (3.9 on a scale of 0 to 10) including negative cash flow from operations for 2013, fair risk adjusted capital in prior years. Good quality investment portfolio (5.4) despite mixed results such as: minimal exposure to mortgages and substantial holdings of BBB bonds but minimal holdings in junk bonds. Good liquidity (6.5).
Other Rating Factors: Weak profitability (2.7) with operating losses during the first nine months of 2014. Strong capitalization (7.1) based on excellent risk adjusted capital (severe loss scenario).
Principal Business: Individual life insurance (64%), reinsurance (29%), individual health insurance (4%), and individual annuities (3%).
Principal Investments: Common & preferred stock (45%), nonCMO investment grade bonds (45%), mortgages in good standing (6%), policy loans (3%), and misc. investments (2%).
Investments in Affiliates: 68%
Group Affiliation: Industrial Alliance Ins & Financial
Licensed in: All states except NY, PR
Commenced Business: May 1980
Address: 425 Austin Ave, Waco, TX 76701
Phone: (480) 473-5540 **Domicile State:** TX **NAIC Code:** 91693

Data Date	Rating	RACR #1	RACR #2	Total Assets ($mil)	Capital ($mil)	Net Premium ($mil)	Net Income ($mil)
9-14	C	1.14	1.06	236.6	136.2	8.6	-2.2
9-13	C-	1.11	1.04	201.9	106.8	8.0	0.7
2013	C-	0.75	0.78	221.1	112.3	10.6	0.6
2012	C-	1.10	1.03	205.5	106.3	11.5	7.2
2011	D	0.60	0.67	182.5	81.7	12.4	-2.8
2010	D	0.65	0.61	171.9	73.6	89.9	-12.6
2009	D	2.79	1.64	37.9	16.9	12.4	-9.4

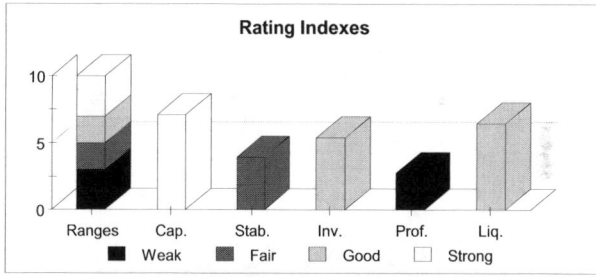

Rating Indexes

(Ranges, Cap., Stab., Inv., Prof., Liq.)
■ Weak ▨ Fair ▢ Good ☐ Strong

JACKSON NATIONAL LIFE INSURANCE CO OF NEW YORK | B | Good

Major Rating Factors: Good overall results on stability tests (6.3 on a scale of 0 to 10) despite excessive premium growth. Other stability subfactors include excellent operational trends and excellent risk diversification. Good quality investment portfolio (5.4) despite mixed results such as: no exposure to mortgages and large holdings of BBB rated bonds but small junk bond holdings. Strong capitalization (9.2) based on excellent risk adjusted capital (severe loss scenario).
Other Rating Factors: Excellent profitability (8.5) with operating gains in each of the last five years. Excellent liquidity (9.6).
Principal Business: Individual annuities (100%).
Principal Investments: NonCMO investment grade bonds (68%), CMOs and structured securities (28%), and noninv. grade bonds (3%).
Investments in Affiliates: None
Group Affiliation: Prudential plc
Licensed in: DE, MI, NY
Commenced Business: August 1996
Address: 5901 Executive Dr, Lansing, MI 48911
Phone: (517) 394-3400 **Domicile State:** NY **NAIC Code:** 60140

Data Date	Rating	RACR #1	RACR #2	Total Assets ($mil)	Capital ($mil)	Net Premium ($mil)	Net Income ($mil)
9-14	B	5.07	2.45	9,263.1	397.9	1,386.0	21.5
9-13	B	4.83	2.25	7,518.7	353.4	948.6	35.2
2013	B	4.75	2.33	8,079.2	370.9	1,317.3	57.6
2012	B-	4.74	2.20	6,335.7	317.0	1,079.4	46.2
2011	B-	4.22	1.98	5,137.0	268.5	1,103.8	15.9
2010	B	4.60	2.16	4,486.4	256.1	1,063.5	43.9
2009	B	3.75	1.69	3,398.3	212.4	784.0	44.7

Adverse Trends in Operations

Increase in policy surrenders from 2012 to 2013 (31%)
Decrease in premium volume from 2011 to 2012 (2%)
Increase in policy surrenders from 2010 to 2011 (27%)

JACKSON NATIONAL LIFE INSURANCE COMPANY *   B+   Good

Major Rating Factors: Good quality investment portfolio (5.6 on a scale of 0 to 10) despite large holdings of BBB rated bonds in addition to moderate junk bond exposure. Exposure to mortgages is significant, but the mortgage default rate has been low. Good overall results on stability tests (6.4). Stability strengths include good operational trends and excellent risk diversification. Strong capitalization (7.1) based on excellent risk adjusted capital (severe loss scenario).

Other Rating Factors: Excellent profitability (7.8) despite modest operating losses during 2011. Excellent liquidity (7.6).

Principal Business: Individual annuities (83%), group retirement contracts (12%), individual life insurance (4%), and reinsurance (1%).

Principal Investments: NonCMO investment grade bonds (57%), CMOs and structured securities (17%), mortgages in good standing (10%), policy loans (7%), and misc. investments (7%).

Investments in Affiliates: 2%

Group Affiliation: Prudential plc

Licensed in: All states except NY, PR

Commenced Business: August 1961

Address: 5901 Executive Dr, Lansing, MI 48911

Phone: (517) 394-3400 **Domicile State:** MI **NAIC Code:** 65056

Data Date	Rating	RACR #1	RACR #2	Total Assets ($mil)	Capital ($mil)	Net Premium ($mil)	Net Income ($mil)
9-14	B+	2.01	1.07	176,820	4,505.9	18,783.0	816.2
9-13	B+	2.09	1.08	154,884	4,290.7	17,122.8	541.5
2013	B+	2.00	1.06	163,834	4,353.8	22,736.2	741.3
2012	B+	2.28	1.16	136,820	4,296.2	18,356.3	847.2
2011	B+	2.21	1.15	102,932	3,645.8	19,052.6	-591.1
2010	B	2.57	1.33	93,805.0	4,361.9	16,949.9	769.6
2009	B	2.29	1.15	77,789.1	3,972.7	13,419.9	373.6

Adverse Trends in Operations

Change in premium mix from 2012 to 2013 (4.9%)
Change in premium mix from 2011 to 2012 (5%)
Decrease in premium volume from 2011 to 2012 (4%)
Decrease in capital during 2011 (16%)

JAMESTOWN LIFE INSURANCE COMPANY   B   Good

Major Rating Factors: Good overall results on stability tests (5.5 on a scale of 0 to 10). Stability strengths include good operational trends and excellent risk diversification. Fair profitability (4.3) with investment income below regulatory standards in relation to interest assumptions of reserves. Strong capitalization (9.9) based on excellent risk adjusted capital (severe loss scenario).

Other Rating Factors: High quality investment portfolio (7.3). Excellent liquidity (7.8).

Principal Business: Reinsurance (100%).

Principal Investments: CMOs and structured securities (57%), nonCMO investment grade bonds (41%), and cash (2%).

Investments in Affiliates: None

Group Affiliation: Genworth Financial

Licensed in: VA

Commenced Business: December 1982

Address: 700 Main St, Lynchburg, VA 24504

Phone: (804) 845-0911 **Domicile State:** VA **NAIC Code:** 97144

Data Date	Rating	RACR #1	RACR #2	Total Assets ($mil)	Capital ($mil)	Net Premium ($mil)	Net Income ($mil)
9-14	B	3.96	2.91	143.7	36.5	3.7	2.9
9-13	B	3.93	3.54	143.8	36.4	4.0	2.2
2013	B	3.59	2.68	141.1	33.0	5.5	2.2
2012	B	3.69	3.07	141.2	34.0	5.6	3.2
2011	B	3.87	3.08	143.3	35.6	6.7	4.6
2010	B	3.45	2.19	139.5	31.1	6.9	4.3
2009	B	5.02	3.28	154.2	47.3	7.1	9.6

Adverse Trends in Operations

Change in asset mix during 2013 (6%)
Decrease in capital during 2012 (5%)
Decrease in premium volume from 2011 to 2012 (16%)
Change in asset mix during 2011 (4.1%)
Decrease in capital during 2010 (34%)

JEFFERSON NATIONAL LIFE INSURANCE COMPANY   C-   Fair

Major Rating Factors: Fair profitability (4.1 on a scale of 0 to 10) with operating losses during the first nine months of 2014. Return on equity has been fair, averaging 5.3%. Fair overall results on stability tests (3.2) including negative cash flow from operations for 2013, fair risk adjusted capital in prior years. Good overall capitalization (5.6) based on mixed results -- excessive policy leverage mitigated by good risk adjusted capital (moderate loss scenario).

Other Rating Factors: Good quality investment portfolio (5.3). Excellent liquidity (10.0).

Principal Business: Individual annuities (97%) and individual life insurance (3%).

Principal Investments: CMOs and structured securities (48%), nonCMO investment grade bonds (39%), mortgages in good standing (4%), noninv. grade bonds (3%), and misc. investments (5%).

Investments in Affiliates: None

Group Affiliation: Jefferson National Financial Corp

Licensed in: All states except NY

Commenced Business: February 1937

Address: 350 N St Paul St, Dallas, TX 75201

Phone: (502) 587-7626 **Domicile State:** TX **NAIC Code:** 64017

Data Date	Rating	RACR #1	RACR #2	Total Assets ($mil)	Capital ($mil)	Net Premium ($mil)	Net Income ($mil)
9-14	C-	1.39	0.69	3,581.0	39.1	608.9	-3.0
9-13	D	1.50	0.75	2,757.3	38.9	511.0	-1.0
2013	C-	1.55	0.78	3,053.5	39.4	740.9	-1.1
2012	D	1.69	0.85	2,259.0	41.5	420.3	-2.9
2011	D	2.08	1.05	1,862.0	47.2	275.6	-4.8
2010	D	1.68	0.88	1,768.5	31.3	-5.5	-1.9
2009	D	1.28	0.68	1,572.6	25.9	147.5	1.4

Net Income History
(in thousands of dollars)

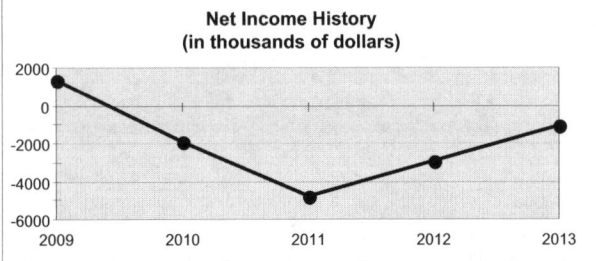

JOHN ALDEN LIFE INSURANCE COMPANY   B   Good

Major Rating Factors: Good quality investment portfolio (6.5 on a scale of 0 to 10) despite mixed results such as: large holdings of BBB rated bonds but moderate junk bond exposure. Good overall profitability (6.3). Return on equity has been excellent over the last five years averaging 21.0%. Good liquidity (6.1) with sufficient resources to handle a spike in claims.

Other Rating Factors: Fair overall results on stability tests (4.4) including negative cash flow from operations for 2013. Strong capitalization (7.9) based on excellent risk adjusted capital (severe loss scenario).

Principal Business: Group health insurance (84%), individual health insurance (13%), individual life insurance (2%), and group life insurance (1%).

Principal Investments: NonCMO investment grade bonds (70%), CMOs and structured securities (12%), policy loans (6%), noninv. grade bonds (6%), and mortgages in good standing (5%).

Investments in Affiliates: None
Group Affiliation: Assurant Inc
Licensed in: All states except NY, PR
Commenced Business: January 1974
Address: 7300 Corporate Center Dr, Miami, FL 33102-0270
Phone: (305) 715-3772 **Domicile State:** WI **NAIC Code:** 65080

Data Date	Rating	RACR #1	RACR #2	Total Assets ($mil)	Capital ($mil)	Net Premium ($mil)	Net Income ($mil)
9-14	B	2.30	1.63	335.7	55.4	137.2	12.3
9-13	B	2.02	1.45	394.1	79.8	244.5	11.7
2013	B	1.93	1.40	362.8	68.4	314.5	18.1
2012	B	1.76	1.28	410.7	82.6	410.7	30.8
2011	B	1.91	1.40	486.8	107.5	474.1	14.7
2010	B-	1.73	1.26	472.4	100.7	494.1	19.9
2009	B-	1.53	1.13	462.7	85.2	486.8	1.8

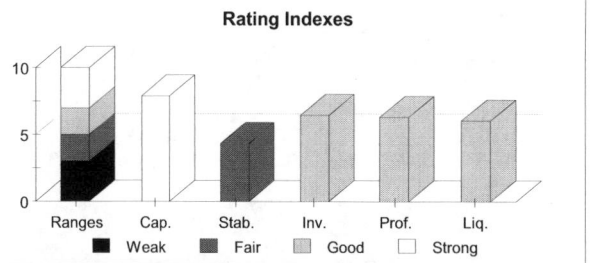

Rating Indexes

Ranges   Cap.   Stab.   Inv.   Prof.   Liq.
■ Weak   ▨ Fair   ▤ Good   ☐ Strong

JOHN HANCOCK LIFE & HEALTH INSURANCE COMPANY   B   Good

Major Rating Factors: Good quality investment portfolio (5.1 on a scale of 0 to 10) despite mixed results such as: minimal exposure to mortgages and substantial holdings of BBB bonds but minimal holdings in junk bonds. Fair profitability (3.1) with operating losses during the first nine months of 2014. Return on equity has been low, averaging -4.5%. Fair overall results on stability tests (4.0).

Other Rating Factors: Strong capitalization (8.2) based on excellent risk adjusted capital (severe loss scenario). Excellent liquidity (8.1).

Principal Business: Group health insurance (67%), individual health insurance (24%), reinsurance (8%), and group retirement contracts (1%).

Principal Investments: NonCMO investment grade bonds (66%), mortgages in good standing (9%), real estate (5%), CMOs and structured securities (5%), and misc. investments (9%).

Investments in Affiliates: 1%
Group Affiliation: Manulife Financial Group
Licensed in: All states, the District of Columbia and Puerto Rico
Commenced Business: October 1981
Address: 2711 Centerville Rd Ste 400, Wilmington, DE 19808
Phone: (617) 572-6000 **Domicile State:** MA **NAIC Code:** 93610

Data Date	Rating	RACR #1	RACR #2	Total Assets ($mil)	Capital ($mil)	Net Premium ($mil)	Net Income ($mil)
9-14	B	3.02	1.79	10,285.2	711.0	431.0	-9.7
9-13	B	3.34	1.87	10,492.2	683.5	423.2	33.7
2013	B	3.05	1.81	9,737.6	682.7	565.5	82.4
2012	B	3.50	1.94	10,039.5	664.9	562.3	12.0
2011	B	3.09	1.78	8,947.4	597.9	491.2	93.1
2010	B	2.22	1.29	7,615.6	461.8	528.4	-218.5
2009	B	1.22	0.79	6,443.0	350.9	1,149.2	-1.4

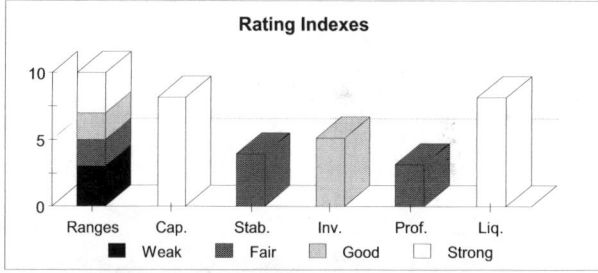

Rating Indexes

Ranges   Cap.   Stab.   Inv.   Prof.   Liq.
■ Weak   ▨ Fair   ▤ Good   ☐ Strong

JOHN HANCOCK LIFE INSURANCE COMPANY (USA)   B   Good

Major Rating Factors: Good overall profitability (5.6 on a scale of 0 to 10) despite operating losses during the first nine months of 2014. Return on equity has been fair, averaging 9.1%. Fair current capitalization (4.9) based on fair risk adjusted capital (moderate loss scenario), although results have slipped from the good range over the last two years. Fair quality investment portfolio (3.1).

Other Rating Factors: Fair overall results on stability tests (4.9) including fair risk adjusted capital in prior years. Excellent liquidity (7.2).

Principal Business: Group retirement contracts (64%), individual life insurance (23%), individual health insurance (6%), reinsurance (5%), and other lines (3%).

Principal Investments: NonCMO investment grade bonds (48%), mortgages in good standing (14%), CMOs and structured securities (8%), policy loans (6%), and misc. investments (19%).

Investments in Affiliates: 4%
Group Affiliation: Manulife Financial Group
Licensed in: All states except NY
Commenced Business: January 1956
Address: 38500 Woodward Ave, Bloomfield Hills, MI 48304
Phone: (416) 926-0100 **Domicile State:** MI **NAIC Code:** 65838

Data Date	Rating	RACR #1	RACR #2	Total Assets ($mil)	Capital ($mil)	Net Premium ($mil)	Net Income ($mil)
9-14	B	0.99	0.63	241,723	5,540.7	9,264.8	-2,054.1
9-13	B	1.06	0.67	234,846	6,088.5	9,412.2	2,448.9
2013	B	0.97	0.62	239,096	5,809.2	12,881.7	3,015.4
2012	B	1.04	0.65	227,142	5,794.1	7,546.5	221.1
2011	B	1.08	0.67	218,287	4,971.2	11,040.3	-2,887.5
2010	B	0.94	0.59	214,163	5,176.7	9,173.3	103.8
2009	B	0.83	0.55	203,396	5,018.6	12,925.2	-71.6

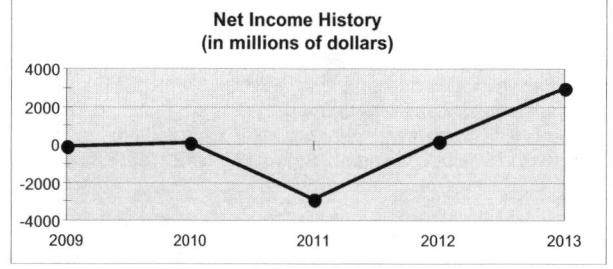

Net Income History
(in millions of dollars)

JOHN HANCOCK LIFE INSURANCE COMPANY OF NEW YORK * A- Excellent

Major Rating Factors: Good overall results on stability tests (5.5 on a scale of 0 to 10). Strengths that enhance stability include excellent risk diversification. Good quality investment portfolio (5.0) despite significant exposure to mortgages . Mortgage default rate has been low. substantial holdings of BBB bonds in addition to small junk bond holdings. Good overall profitability (6.3) despite operating losses during the first nine months of 2014.

Other Rating Factors: Strong capitalization (8.1) based on excellent risk adjusted capital (severe loss scenario). Excellent liquidity (7.3).

Principal Business: Group retirement contracts (50%), reinsurance (24%), individual life insurance (22%), and individual annuities (3%).

Principal Investments: NonCMO investment grade bonds (65%), mortgages in good standing (14%), CMOs and structured securities (8%), real estate (3%), and misc. investments (5%).

Investments in Affiliates: None

Group Affiliation: Manulife Financial Group

Licensed in: NY

Commenced Business: July 1992

Address: 100 Summit Lake Dr 2nd Floor, Valhalla, NY 10595

Phone: (800) 344-1029 **Domicile State:** NY **NAIC Code:** 86375

Data Date	Rating	RACR #1	RACR #2	Total Assets ($mil)	Capital ($mil)	Net Premium ($mil)	Net Income ($mil)
9-14	A-	2.96	1.76	17,279.2	1,345.7	814.3	-3.0
9-13	A-	4.65	2.26	16,902.6	1,256.2	775.8	376.8
2013	A-	2.77	1.62	17,315.6	1,284.3	1,043.3	465.8
2012	A-	4.06	1.98	16,677.6	1,005.1	-504.9	69.1
2011	A-	3.19	1.54	17,559.8	890.4	1,177.9	-282.5
2010	A-	2.28	1.22	17,155.1	994.6	3,803.3	-67.8
2009	A-	11.71	10.02	8,770.6	1,017.0	1,176.3	309.5

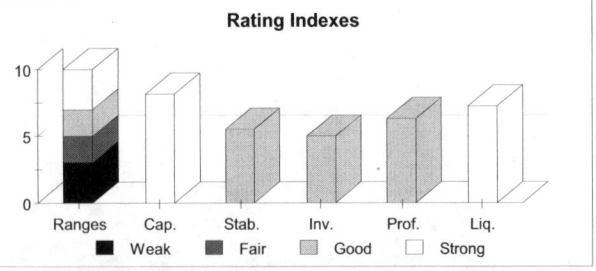

Rating Indexes

KANAWHA INSURANCE COMPANY C Fair

Major Rating Factors: Fair overall results on stability tests (3.5 on a scale of 0 to 10). Good quality investment portfolio (6.6) despite mixed results such as: minimal exposure to mortgages and large holdings of BBB rated bonds but small junk bond holdings. Weak profitability (1.5) with operating losses during the first nine months of 2014. Return on equity has been low, averaging -68.4%.

Other Rating Factors: Strong capitalization (7.5) based on excellent risk adjusted capital (severe loss scenario). Excellent liquidity (7.8).

Principal Business: Individual health insurance (40%), group health insurance (30%), group life insurance (17%), individual life insurance (12%), and reinsurance (2%).

Principal Investments: NonCMO investment grade bonds (81%), CMOs and structured securities (11%), cash (5%), noninv. grade bonds (1%), and policy loans (1%).

Investments in Affiliates: None

Group Affiliation: Humana Inc

Licensed in: All states except AK, ME, NY, PR

Commenced Business: December 1958

Address: 210 S White St, Lancaster, SC 29721

Phone: (803) 283-5300 **Domicile State:** SC **NAIC Code:** 65110

Data Date	Rating	RACR #1	RACR #2	Total Assets ($mil)	Capital ($mil)	Net Premium ($mil)	Net Income ($mil)
9-14	C	2.18	1.33	1,657.2	130.5	159.9	-27.5
9-13	C	4.35	2.74	1,505.3	268.2	176.9	12.2
2013	C	2.68	1.67	1,623.0	155.1	228.1	-174.9
2012	C	4.02	2.54	1,456.8	255.5	252.2	-112.4
2011	C	3.22	2.03	1,288.9	190.5	206.5	-77.4
2010	C	1.45	0.91	1,109.0	80.8	178.4	-87.0
2009	C	1.88	1.22	926.4	92.7	156.6	-77.1

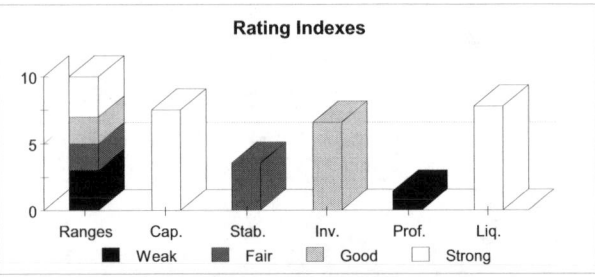

Rating Indexes

KANSAS CITY LIFE INSURANCE COMPANY B Good

Major Rating Factors: Good quality investment portfolio (5.1 on a scale of 0 to 10) despite significant exposure to mortgages . Mortgage default rate has been low. large holdings of BBB rated bonds in addition to small junk bond holdings. Good overall profitability (6.4). Return on equity has been fair, averaging 6.0%. Good liquidity (5.9).

Other Rating Factors: Good overall results on stability tests (6.3) excellent operational trends and excellent risk diversification. Strong capitalization (7.2) based on excellent risk adjusted capital (severe loss scenario).

Principal Business: Individual annuities (39%), individual life insurance (35%), group health insurance (14%), reinsurance (8%), and group life insurance (3%).

Principal Investments: NonCMO investment grade bonds (61%), mortgages in good standing (18%), CMOs and structured securities (9%), real estate (3%), and misc. investments (9%).

Investments in Affiliates: 2%

Group Affiliation: Kansas City Life Group

Licensed in: All states except NY, VT, PR

Commenced Business: May 1895

Address: 3520 Broadway, Kansas City, MO 64111-2565

Phone: (816) 753-7000 **Domicile State:** MO **NAIC Code:** 65129

Data Date	Rating	RACR #1	RACR #2	Total Assets ($mil)	Capital ($mil)	Net Premium ($mil)	Net Income ($mil)
9-14	B	1.82	1.13	3,390.6	351.6	235.7	24.5
9-13	B	1.90	1.16	3,362.7	294.7	245.9	-2.4
2013	B	1.74	1.08	3,386.4	330.6	329.4	0.3
2012	B	2.05	1.26	3,317.6	327.4	277.0	46.5
2011	B	2.00	1.18	3,224.4	307.2	265.7	22.6
2010	B	2.05	1.21	3,235.0	322.5	294.8	12.7
2009	B	2.04	1.24	3,152.6	336.6	293.6	19.5

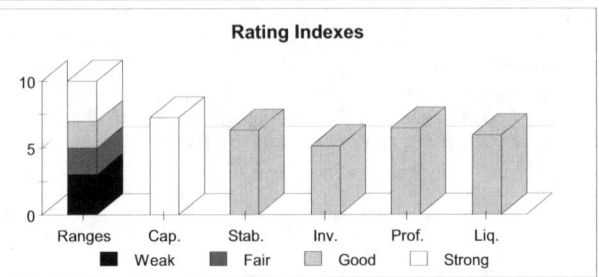

Rating Indexes

LAFAYETTE LIFE INSURANCE COMPANY   B   Good

Major Rating Factors: Good overall results on stability tests (5.7 on a scale of 0 to 10). Stability strengths include excellent operational trends and excellent risk diversification. Good capitalization (6.0) based on good risk adjusted capital (moderate loss scenario). Capital levels have been relatively consistent over the last five years. Good liquidity (5.2).

Other Rating Factors: Fair quality investment portfolio (4.9). Fair profitability (4.0).

Principal Business: Individual life insurance (70%), individual annuities (28%), and group retirement contracts (2%).

Principal Investments: NonCMO investment grade bonds (53%), CMOs and structured securities (19%), policy loans (9%), mortgages in good standing (7%), and misc. investments (7%).

Investments in Affiliates: 1%

Group Affiliation: Western & Southern Group

Licensed in: All states except AK, NY, PR

Commenced Business: December 1905

Address: 400 Broadway, Cincinnati, OH 45202

Phone: (513) 362-4900 **Domicile State:** OH **NAIC Code:** 65242

Data Date	Rating	RACR #1	RACR #2	Total Assets ($mil)	Capital ($mil)	Net Premium ($mil)	Net Income ($mil)
9-14	B	1.67	0.85	3,985.3	202.6	398.7	8.7
9-13	B	1.59	0.79	3,672.9	150.0	454.5	-5.7
2013	B	1.70	0.88	3,836.5	193.7	593.3	-7.8
2012	B	1.76	0.91	3,322.1	160.7	561.3	16.3
2011	B	1.77	0.90	2,996.1	152.3	612.9	5.7
2010	B	1.79	0.90	2,598.7	112.0	586.1	3.3
2009	B-	1.94	0.97	2,268.2	115.8	404.1	0.2

Adverse Trends in Operations

Decrease in premium volume from 2011 to 2012 (8%)
Decrease in capital during 2010 (3%)

LIBERTY BANKERS LIFE INSURANCE COMPANY   D+   Weak

Major Rating Factors: Weak overall results on stability tests (2.9 on a scale of 0 to 10) including weak risk adjusted capital in prior years. Fair quality investment portfolio (3.6) with significant exposure to mortgages . Mortgage default rate has been low. Good current capitalization (5.4) based on good risk adjusted capital (severe loss scenario) reflecting significant improvement over results in 2010.

Other Rating Factors: Good overall profitability (6.0). Excellent liquidity (7.1).

Principal Business: N/A

Principal Investments: NonCMO investment grade bonds (37%), mortgages in good standing (22%), common & preferred stock (12%), real estate (8%), and misc. investments (20%).

Investments in Affiliates: 8%

Group Affiliation: Heritage Guaranty Group

Licensed in: AZ, AR, CA, CO, DE, FL, GA, HI, ID, IL, IN, IA, KS, KY, LA, MD, MI, MS, MO, MT, NE, NV, NM, NC, ND, OH, OK, OR, PA, SC, SD, TN, TX, UT, VA, WA, WV, WI, WY

Commenced Business: February 1958

Address: 1800 Valley View Lane Ste 300, Dallas, TX 75234

Phone: (800) 745-4927 **Domicile State:** OK **NAIC Code:** 68543

Data Date	Rating	RACR #1	RACR #2	Total Assets ($mil)	Capital ($mil)	Net Premium ($mil)	Net Income ($mil)
9-14	D+	1.17	0.80	1,103.8	167.2	177.9	5.0
9-13	D+	1.05	0.75	995.5	154.5	169.1	1.6
2013	D+	1.23	0.84	1,035.3	168.0	205.5	10.3
2012	D+	1.11	0.79	952.0	160.5	-259.6	15.2
2011	D+	0.77	0.54	1,302.0	130.5	242.8	2.6
2010	D+	0.71	0.46	1,113.6	85.9	195.2	1.5
2009	D+	0.92	0.57	1,040.4	96.0	290.6	4.2

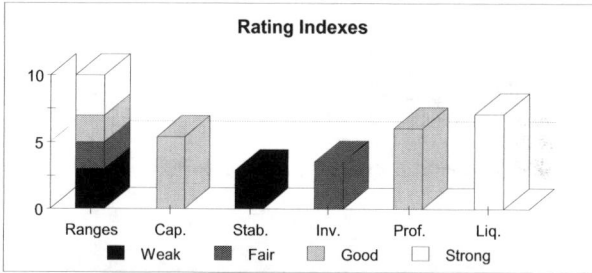

Rating Indexes

Ranges Cap. Stab. Inv. Prof. Liq.
■ Weak   ▨ Fair   ▨ Good   □ Strong

LIBERTY LIFE ASSURANCE COMPANY OF BOSTON   B   Good

Major Rating Factors: Good overall results on stability tests (6.2 on a scale of 0 to 10). Stability strengths include excellent operational trends, good risk adjusted capital for prior years and excellent risk diversification. Good quality investment portfolio (6.4) despite mixed results such as: large holdings of BBB rated bonds but moderate junk bond exposure. Good overall profitability (6.6).

Other Rating Factors: Good liquidity (6.9). Strong capitalization (7.4) based on excellent risk adjusted capital (severe loss scenario).

Principal Business: N/A

Principal Investments: NonCMO investment grade bonds (78%), CMOs and structured securities (12%), mortgages in good standing (3%), noninv. grade bonds (2%), and policy loans (1%).

Investments in Affiliates: None

Group Affiliation: Liberty Mutual Group

Licensed in: All states except PR

Commenced Business: January 1964

Address: 175 Berkeley St, Boston, MA 02117

Phone: (617) 357-9500 **Domicile State:** NH **NAIC Code:** 65315

Data Date	Rating	RACR #1	RACR #2	Total Assets ($mil)	Capital ($mil)	Net Premium ($mil)	Net Income ($mil)
9-14	B	2.17	1.26	14,303.2	894.9	1,812.7	26.4
9-13	B	1.71	1.08	12,842.2	747.6	1,570.9	157.7
2013	B	1.83	1.07	13,115.1	716.9	2,095.9	39.2
2012	B	1.63	1.03	12,403.2	688.6	1,807.1	31.3
2011	B	1.65	1.04	15,165.1	660.6	1,641.5	53.4
2010	B	1.69	1.07	14,160.7	637.7	1,390.3	40.3
2009	B-	1.58	0.96	12,983.2	597.5	1,208.7	-23.5

Adverse Trends in Operations

Increase in policy surrenders from 2012 to 2013 (38%)
Decrease in asset base during 2012 (18%)
Increase in policy surrenders from 2009 to 2010 (44%)

LIBERTY NATIONAL LIFE INSURANCE COMPANY | B | Good

Major Rating Factors: Good overall results on stability tests (5.2 on a scale of 0 to 10). Stability strengths include excellent operational trends, good risk adjusted capital for prior years and excellent risk diversification. Good quality investment portfolio (5.3) despite mixed results such as: large holdings of BBB rated bonds but junk bond exposure equal to 63% of capital. Good overall profitability (5.7) although investment income, in comparison to reserve requirements, is below regulatory standards.

Other Rating Factors: Fair liquidity (3.2). Strong capitalization (7.2) based on excellent risk adjusted capital (severe loss scenario).

Principal Business: Individual life insurance (57%), individual health insurance (19%), reinsurance (14%), group life insurance (7%), and individual annuities (4%).

Principal Investments: NonCMO investment grade bonds (73%), noninv. grade bonds (6%), common & preferred stock (5%), CMOs and structured securities (5%), and policy loans (4%).

Investments in Affiliates: 8%
Group Affiliation: Torchmark Corp
Licensed in: All states except NY, PR
Commenced Business: July 1929
Address: 10306 Regency Parkway Dr, Omaha, NE 68114
Phone: (205) 325-4918 **Domicile State:** NE **NAIC Code:** 65331

Data Date	Rating	RACR #1	RACR #2	Total Assets ($mil)	Capital ($mil)	Net Premium ($mil)	Net Income ($mil)
9-14	B	2.23	1.16	7,400.5	585.4	425.8	121.2
9-13	B	2.25	1.16	7,212.8	592.6	419.4	109.1
2013	B	2.16	1.13	7,257.9	589.7	565.9	151.1
2012	B	2.16	1.12	7,102.6	592.2	584.2	174.3
2011	B	2.26	1.17	6,802.8	622.4	538.0	175.9
2010	B	3.84	2.02	6,954.2	953.2	569.2	487.6
2009	B-	1.10	0.85	5,514.6	721.6	597.2	62.7

Adverse Trends in Operations

Decrease in premium volume from 2012 to 2013 (3%)
Decrease in premium volume from 2010 to 2011 (5%)
Decrease in asset base during 2011 (2%)
Decrease in capital during 2011 (35%)
Decrease in premium volume from 2009 to 2010 (5%)

LIFE INSURANCE COMPANY OF ALABAMA * | A- | Excellent

Major Rating Factors: Good quality investment portfolio (6.3 on a scale of 0 to 10) despite mixed results such as: no exposure to mortgages and large holdings of BBB rated bonds but minimal holdings in junk bonds. Good liquidity (6.7) with sufficient resources to handle a spike in claims. Good overall results on stability tests (6.3) excellent operational trends and good risk diversification.

Other Rating Factors: Strong capitalization (8.5) based on excellent risk adjusted capital (severe loss scenario). Excellent profitability (9.0) with operating gains in each of the last five years.

Principal Business: Individual health insurance (77%), individual life insurance (17%), and group health insurance (6%).

Principal Investments: NonCMO investment grade bonds (84%), common & preferred stock (7%), policy loans (3%), noninv. grade bonds (3%), and misc. investments (4%).

Investments in Affiliates: None
Group Affiliation: None
Licensed in: AL, AR, FL, GA, KY, LA, MS, NC, OK, SC, TN
Commenced Business: August 1952
Address: 302 Broad St, Gadsden, AL 35901
Phone: (205) 543-2022 **Domicile State:** AL **NAIC Code:** 65412

Data Date	Rating	RACR #1	RACR #2	Total Assets ($mil)	Capital ($mil)	Net Premium ($mil)	Net Income ($mil)
9-14	A-	3.02	2.01	112.0	36.0	28.3	5.9
9-13	A-	2.68	1.83	105.7	31.9	28.0	2.2
2013	A-	2.88	1.95	108.0	33.0	37.2	2.7
2012	A-	2.52	1.74	102.6	29.4	38.0	3.0
2011	A-	2.03	1.43	94.9	25.0	39.2	3.1
2010	B+	1.91	1.39	96.6	22.8	40.9	3.5
2009	B+	1.56	1.13	88.8	18.9	40.7	3.3

Adverse Trends in Operations

Decrease in premium volume from 2012 to 2013 (2%)
Decrease in premium volume from 2011 to 2012 (3%)
Decrease in asset base during 2011 (2%)
Decrease in premium volume from 2010 to 2011 (4%)

LIFE INSURANCE COMPANY OF NORTH AMERICA | B | Good

Major Rating Factors: Good overall results on stability tests (5.8 on a scale of 0 to 10). Stability strengths include excellent operational trends and excellent risk diversification. Good quality investment portfolio (5.4) despite large holdings of BBB rated bonds in addition to junk bond exposure equal to 50% of capital. Exposure to mortgages is significant, but the mortgage default rate has been low. Strong capitalization (7.8) based on excellent risk adjusted capital (severe loss scenario).

Other Rating Factors: Excellent profitability (7.9) with operating gains in each of the last five years. Excellent liquidity (7.0).

Principal Business: Group health insurance (52%), group life insurance (40%), and reinsurance (7%).

Principal Investments: NonCMO investment grade bonds (61%), mortgages in good standing (18%), noninv. grade bonds (10%), CMOs and structured securities (5%), and misc. investments (6%).

Investments in Affiliates: 5%
Group Affiliation: CIGNA Corp
Licensed in: All states, the District of Columbia and Puerto Rico
Commenced Business: September 1957
Address: 1601 Chestnut ST,2 Liberty Pl, Philadelphia, PA 19192-2235
Phone: (860) 726-7234 **Domicile State:** PA **NAIC Code:** 65498

Data Date	Rating	RACR #1	RACR #2	Total Assets ($mil)	Capital ($mil)	Net Premium ($mil)	Net Income ($mil)
9-14	B	2.45	1.55	7,167.4	1,249.0	2,491.4	199.9
9-13	B	2.14	1.35	6,706.0	983.2	2,582.7	95.8
2013	B	2.20	1.39	6,711.9	1,103.5	3,232.7	173.3
2012	B	2.10	1.34	6,089.4	884.4	2,705.9	198.7
2011	B-	2.28	1.47	5,628.9	872.4	2,474.3	202.0
2010	B-	2.31	1.50	5,815.7	841.7	2,350.8	721.7
2009	B-	1.87	1.27	5,732.7	769.4	2,304.5	215.6

Adverse Trends in Operations

Increase in policy surrenders from 2011 to 2012 (72%)
Decrease in asset base during 2011 (3%)
Change in asset mix during 2010 (8.3%)

LIFE INSURANCE COMPANY OF THE SOUTHWEST   B   Good

Major Rating Factors: Good overall results on stability tests (5.5 on a scale of 0 to 10). Stability strengths include excellent operational trends, good risk adjusted capital for prior years and excellent risk diversification. Fair quality investment portfolio (4.5) with large holdings of BBB rated bonds in addition to junk bond exposure equal to 68% of capital. Exposure to mortgages is significant, but the mortgage default rate has been low. Fair liquidity (4.3).

Other Rating Factors: Strong capitalization (7.1) based on excellent risk adjusted capital (severe loss scenario). Excellent profitability (8.6) with operating gains in each of the last five years.

Principal Business: Individual annuities (65%), individual life insurance (31%), and group retirement contracts (5%).

Principal Investments: NonCMO investment grade bonds (46%), CMOs and structured securities (26%), mortgages in good standing (14%), noninv. grade bonds (4%), and policy loans (2%).

Investments in Affiliates: None
Group Affiliation: National Life Group
Licensed in: All states except NY, PR
Commenced Business: January 1956
Address: 1300 W Mockingbird Lane, Dallas, TX 75247
Phone: (800) 579-2878 **Domicile State:** TX **NAIC Code:** 65528

Data Date	Rating	RACR #1	RACR #2	Total Assets ($mil)	Capital ($mil)	Net Premium ($mil)	Net Income ($mil)
9-14	B	2.16	1.05	12,900.2	772.9	1,142.7	71.4
9-13	B	1.93	0.95	11,924.0	697.1	962.9	102.9
2013	B	2.10	1.03	12,354.9	720.2	1,329.9	142.5
2012	B	1.67	0.83	10,952.0	625.2	1,360.6	98.7
2011	B	1.52	0.76	9,913.2	567.0	1,200.8	89.3
2010	B	1.69	0.84	9,165.3	551.5	1,385.2	95.9
2009	B	1.69	0.82	8,209.8	492.3	1,574.6	51.8

Adverse Trends in Operations

Decrease in premium volume from 2012 to 2013 (2%)
Decrease in premium volume from 2010 to 2011 (13%)
Decrease in premium volume from 2009 to 2010 (12%)

LIFECARE ASSURANCE COMPANY   B-   Good

Major Rating Factors: Good capitalization (6.4 on a scale of 0 to 10) based on good risk adjusted capital (severe loss scenario). Capital levels have been relatively consistent over the last five years. Good overall profitability (5.5) although investment income, in comparison to reserve requirements, is below regulatory standards. Good overall results on stability tests (5.2) excellent operational trends and good risk diversification.

Other Rating Factors: Fair quality investment portfolio (4.8). Excellent liquidity (9.3).

Principal Business: Reinsurance (100%).

Principal Investments: NonCMO investment grade bonds (58%), CMOs and structured securities (39%), and noninv. grade bonds (2%).

Investments in Affiliates: None
Group Affiliation: 21st Century Life & Health Co Inc
Licensed in: AK, AZ, AR, CA, CO, DC, DE, GA, HI, IL, IN, KS, KY, LA, MD, MI, MS, MO, MT, NE, NV, NJ, NM, NC, ND, OH, OK, OR, PA, TN, UT, WA, WV
Commenced Business: July 1980
Address: 8601 N Scottsdale Rd Ste 300, Scottsdale, AZ 85253
Phone: (818) 887-4436 **Domicile State:** AZ **NAIC Code:** 91898

Data Date	Rating	RACR #1	RACR #2	Total Assets ($mil)	Capital ($mil)	Net Premium ($mil)	Net Income ($mil)
9-14	B-	1.69	0.92	1,899.4	95.3	172.0	9.2
9-13	B-	1.58	0.88	1,735.9	86.3	174.7	9.4
2013	B-	1.71	0.94	1,780.0	95.7	233.9	17.7
2012	B-	1.51	0.86	1,596.7	80.8	239.7	15.4
2011	B-	1.43	0.83	1,400.7	73.2	237.5	11.7
2010	C+	1.38	0.85	1,199.5	65.4	230.7	13.2
2009	C	1.26	0.79	997.0	55.2	221.2	16.2

Risk-Adjusted Capital Ratio #2
(Severe Loss Scenario)

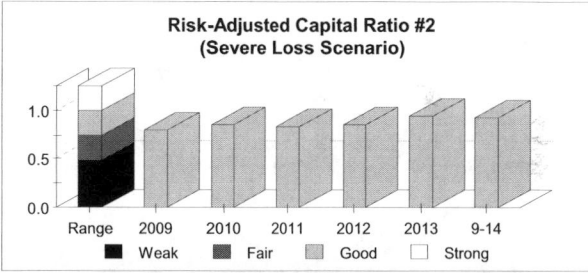

LIFEMAP ASSURANCE COMPANY   B   Good

Major Rating Factors: Good liquidity (6.7 on a scale of 0 to 10) with sufficient resources to handle a spike in claims. Good overall results on stability tests (5.7). Strengths include good financial support from affiliation with Regence Group, good operational trends and excellent risk diversification. Fair quality investment portfolio (4.6).

Other Rating Factors: Weak profitability (2.5) with operating losses during the first nine months of 2014. Strong capitalization (7.4) based on excellent risk adjusted capital (severe loss scenario).

Principal Business: Group health insurance (58%), group life insurance (30%), individual health insurance (11%), and reinsurance (1%).

Principal Investments: NonCMO investment grade bonds (53%), common & preferred stock (26%), and CMOs and structured securities (21%).

Investments in Affiliates: 2%
Group Affiliation: Regence Group
Licensed in: AK, ID, MT, OR, UT, WA, WY
Commenced Business: July 1966
Address: 100 SW Market St, Portland, OR 97201
Phone: (503) 225-6048 **Domicile State:** OR **NAIC Code:** 97985

Data Date	Rating	RACR #1	RACR #2	Total Assets ($mil)	Capital ($mil)	Net Premium ($mil)	Net Income ($mil)
9-14	B	1.79	1.29	84.5	42.3	51.2	-0.9
9-13	B+	1.97	1.41	88.9	43.9	46.9	-0.5
2013	B	1.96	1.41	89.6	45.3	64.1	-0.5
2012	B+	2.17	1.56	86.1	44.9	55.0	-1.8
2011	B+	2.38	1.71	89.5	46.8	49.5	-0.1
2010	B+	2.39	1.70	87.1	46.1	44.0	3.0
2009	B+	2.27	1.63	89.2	42.7	44.9	2.8

Regence Group
Composite Group Rating: B
Largest Group Members

Largest Group Members	Assets ($mil)	Rating
REGENCE BLUESHIELD	1692	B+
REGENCE BL CROSS BL SHIELD OREGON	1008	B+
REGENCE BLUE CROSS BLUE SHIELD OF UT	535	B
REGENCE BLUESHIELD OF IDAHO INC	274	B
ASURIS NORTHWEST HEALTH	100	B

LIFESECURE INSURANCE COMPANY   D-   Weak

Major Rating Factors: Weak profitability (1.7 on a scale of 0 to 10) with operating losses during the first nine months of 2014. Weak overall results on stability tests (1.3). Strong current capitalization (7.7) based on excellent risk adjusted capital (severe loss scenario) reflecting improvement over results in 2009.

Other Rating Factors: High quality investment portfolio (7.5). Excellent liquidity (8.4).

Principal Business: Reinsurance (54%), individual health insurance (25%), individual life insurance (17%), and individual annuities (4%).

Principal Investments: NonCMO investment grade bonds (100%).

Investments in Affiliates: None

Group Affiliation: Blue Cross Blue Shield of Michigan

Licensed in: All states except ME, MA, NH, NY, PR

Commenced Business: July 1954

Address: 1005 Congress Ave, Ste 825, Austin, TX 78701

Phone: (847) 402-5000 **Domicile State:** MI **NAIC Code:** 77720

Data Date	Rating	RACR #1	RACR #2	Total Assets ($mil)	Capital ($mil)	Net Premium ($mil)	Net Income ($mil)
9-14	D-	2.27	1.49	215.7	25.0	31.4	-7.2
9-13	E+	1.90	1.19	189.9	18.1	24.5	-6.4
2013	D-	2.10	1.34	189.7	20.2	33.4	-3.9
2012	E+	2.50	1.79	174.9	23.8	28.2	-6.2
2011	E+	2.78	2.11	148.3	26.0	25.2	-3.1
2010	E+	1.49	1.20	119.2	13.5	23.3	-7.6
2009	E	1.11	0.95	96.1	9.7	12.6	-12.0

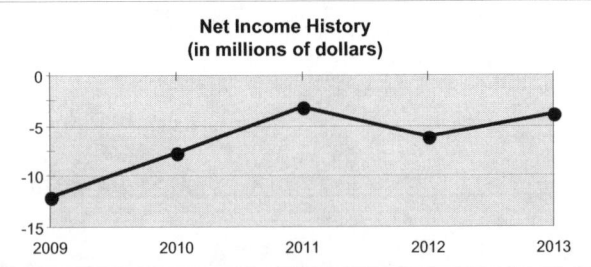

Net Income History
(in millions of dollars)

LIFEWISE ASSURANCE COMPANY *   A   Excellent

Major Rating Factors: Excellent overall results on stability tests (7.0 on a scale of 0 to 10). Strengths that enhance stability include excellent operational trends and good risk diversification. Strong capitalization (10.0) based on excellent risk adjusted capital (severe loss scenario). Furthermore, this high level of risk adjusted capital has been consistently maintained over the last five years. High quality investment portfolio (8.5).

Other Rating Factors: Excellent profitability (9.2) with operating gains in each of the last five years. Excellent liquidity (7.0).

Principal Business: Group health insurance (93%) and group life insurance (6%).

Principal Investments: NonCMO investment grade bonds (53%), CMOs and structured securities (40%), cash (5%), and noninv. grade bonds (2%).

Investments in Affiliates: None

Group Affiliation: PREMERA

Licensed in: AK, AZ, CA, CO, ID, KS, MT, NV, NM, ND, OK, OR, TX, UT, WA, WY

Commenced Business: November 1981

Address: 7007 220th SW, Mountlake Terrace, WA 98043

Phone: (206) 670-4584 **Domicile State:** WA **NAIC Code:** 94188

Data Date	Rating	RACR #1	RACR #2	Total Assets ($mil)	Capital ($mil)	Net Premium ($mil)	Net Income ($mil)
9-14	A	6.58	5.00	125.6	87.1	69.6	6.2
9-13	A	6.61	4.93	122.2	78.8	63.8	7.1
2013	A	6.19	4.70	119.4	81.1	85.4	9.5
2012	A	5.90	4.42	118.4	71.6	84.3	12.8
2011	A	2.94	2.22	94.5	57.8	89.7	4.3
2010	A	3.21	2.40	94.8	52.3	66.5	7.2
2009	A	2.82	2.02	76.4	45.4	51.6	4.4

Adverse Trends in Operations

Decrease in premium volume from 2011 to 2012 (6%)

LINCOLN BENEFIT LIFE COMPANY *   B+   Good

Major Rating Factors: Good current capitalization (6.7 on a scale of 0 to 10) based on good risk adjusted capital (severe loss scenario), although results have slipped from the excellent range during the last year. Good overall results on stability tests (6.4) despite negative cash flow from operations for 2013. Other stability subfactors include excellent operational trends, excellent risk adjusted capital for prior years and excellent risk diversification. Fair quality investment portfolio (4.8).

Other Rating Factors: Excellent profitability (8.1) with operating gains in each of the last five years. Excellent liquidity (10.0).

Principal Business: Individual life insurance (87%), individual annuities (6%), individual health insurance (5%), and group life insurance (2%).

Principal Investments: NonCMO investment grade bonds (112%) and CMOs and structured securities (10%).

Investments in Affiliates: None

Group Affiliation: Resolution Life Holdings Inc

Licensed in: All states except NY, PR

Commenced Business: October 1938

Address: 206 S 13th St, Suite 200, Lincoln, NE 68508

Phone: (800) 525-9287 **Domicile State:** NE **NAIC Code:** 65595

Data Date	Rating	RACR #1	RACR #2	Total Assets ($mil)	Capital ($mil)	Net Premium ($mil)	Net Income ($mil)
9-14	B+	2.15	0.96	12,911.3	733.5	7,021.1	45.9
9-13	B+	3.48	1.73	2,021.9	330.7	0.0	5.9
2013	B+	3.75	1.87	2,070.9	332.5	0.0	7.7
2012	B+	3.57	1.78	2,008.9	323.9	0.0	8.5
2011	B+	3.47	1.73	2,052.4	319.5	0.0	8.6
2010	B+	3.15	1.57	2,396.6	310.8	0.0	8.7
2009	B+	3.18	1.58	2,418.5	306.0	0.0	8.5

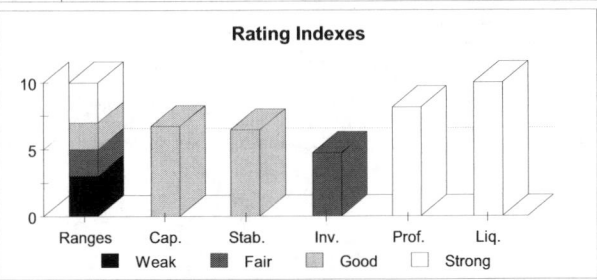

Rating Indexes

Ranges | Cap. | Stab. | Inv. | Prof. | Liq.
■ Weak   ▨ Fair   ▤ Good   □ Strong

LINCOLN HERITAGE LIFE INSURANCE COMPANY B- Good

Major Rating Factors: Good liquidity (6.4 on a scale of 0 to 10) with sufficient resources to handle a spike in claims as well as a significant increase in policy surrenders. Good overall results on stability tests (5.2). Stability strengths include excellent operational trends and excellent risk diversification. Weak profitability (2.7) with investment income below regulatory standards in relation to interest assumptions of reserves.
Other Rating Factors: Strong capitalization (8.6) based on excellent risk adjusted capital (severe loss scenario). High quality investment portfolio (7.1).
Principal Business: Individual life insurance (86%), individual health insurance (6%), reinsurance (4%), and group life insurance (4%).
Principal Investments: CMOs and structured securities (44%), nonCMO investment grade bonds (28%), cash (16%), policy loans (6%), and misc. investments (6%).
Investments in Affiliates: None
Group Affiliation: Londen Ins Group
Licensed in: All states except NY
Commenced Business: October 1963
Address: Government Ctr 200 Pleasant St, Malden, MA 02148
Phone: (602) 957-1650 **Domicile State:** IL **NAIC Code:** 65927

Data Date	Rating	RACR #1	RACR #2	Total Assets ($mil)	Capital ($mil)	Net Premium ($mil)	Net Income ($mil)
9-14	B-	4.00	2.09	794.5	114.0	238.4	7.1
9-13	B	3.99	2.15	729.0	106.3	196.3	4.2
2013	B-	3.71	1.96	740.8	101.2	259.8	3.9
2012	B	4.15	2.26	692.8	106.0	204.3	4.2
2011	B	4.01	2.15	664.8	108.3	189.0	9.6
2010	B+	3.27	1.72	762.1	100.5	249.5	-2.6
2009	B+	3.64	1.88	697.7	109.8	218.4	0.2

Adverse Trends in Operations

Decrease in capital during 2013 (5%)
Decrease in capital during 2012 (2%)
Decrease in asset base during 2011 (13%)
Decrease in premium volume from 2010 to 2011 (24%)
Decrease in capital during 2010 (8%)

LINCOLN LIFE & ANNUITY COMPANY OF NEW YORK B Good

Major Rating Factors: Good quality investment portfolio (5.6 on a scale of 0 to 10) despite mixed results such as: large holdings of BBB rated bonds but moderate junk bond exposure. Good overall profitability (5.3). Return on equity has been fair, averaging 7.5%. Good liquidity (5.5) with sufficient resources to handle a spike in claims as well as a significant increase in policy surrenders.
Other Rating Factors: Good overall results on stability tests (5.5) excellent operational trends and excellent risk diversification. Strong capitalization (7.4) based on excellent risk adjusted capital (severe loss scenario).
Principal Business: Individual annuities (48%), individual life insurance (23%), reinsurance (12%), group retirement contracts (11%), and other lines (6%).
Principal Investments: NonCMO investment grade bonds (74%), CMOs and structured securities (11%), mortgages in good standing (7%), policy loans (4%), and noninv. grade bonds (4%).
Investments in Affiliates: None
Group Affiliation: Lincoln National Corp
Licensed in: All states except PR
Commenced Business: December 1897
Address: 100 Madison St Suite 1860, Syracuse, NY 13202-2802
Phone: (336) 691-3000 **Domicile State:** NY **NAIC Code:** 62057

Data Date	Rating	RACR #1	RACR #2	Total Assets ($mil)	Capital ($mil)	Net Premium ($mil)	Net Income ($mil)
9-14	B	2.46	1.27	12,543.7	634.8	936.5	20.9
9-13	B-	2.75	1.40	11,682.0	712.6	887.3	68.2
2013	B-	2.76	1.43	12,046.4	713.0	1,229.4	161.2
2012	C	2.54	1.29	10,925.5	648.4	1,034.0	73.5
2011	C	2.34	1.18	10,160.0	586.1	959.3	-121.0
2010	B-	3.17	1.59	9,910.9	794.1	866.9	54.9
2009	B-	3.24	1.59	9,375.1	819.0	864.9	13.2

Rating Indexes

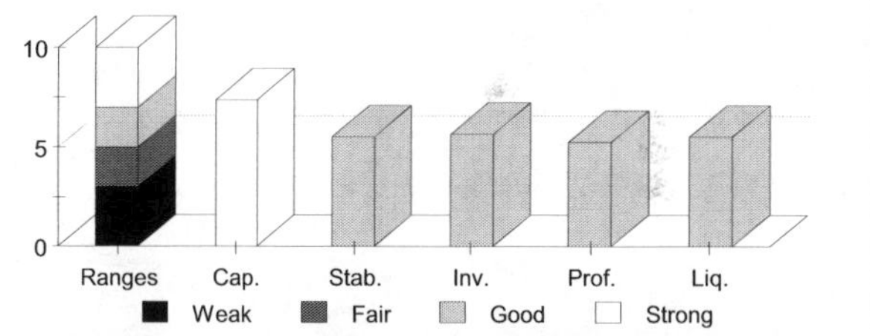
10
5
0
Ranges
Cap.
Stab.
Inv.
Prof.
Liq.
Weak
Fair
Good
Strong

LINCOLN NATIONAL LIFE INSURANCE COMPANY B Good

Major Rating Factors: Good overall capitalization (6.8 on a scale of 0 to 10) based on good risk adjusted capital (severe loss scenario). However, capital levels have fluctuated somewhat during past years. Good quality investment portfolio (6.0) despite mixed results such as: large holdings of BBB rated bonds but moderate junk bond exposure. Good overall profitability (6.7).
Other Rating Factors: Good liquidity (6.7). Good overall results on stability tests (5.8) excellent operational trends and excellent risk diversification.
Principal Business: Individual annuities (57%), individual life insurance (20%), group retirement contracts (11%), group health insurance (5%), and other lines (8%).
Principal Investments: NonCMO investment grade bonds (72%), mortgages in good standing (8%), CMOs and structured securities (8%), policy loans (3%), and misc. investments (8%).
Investments in Affiliates: 4%
Group Affiliation: Lincoln National Corp
Licensed in: All states except NY
Commenced Business: September 1905
Address: 1300 S Clinton St, Fort Wayne, IN 46802
Phone: (260) 455-2000 **Domicile State:** IN **NAIC Code:** 65676

Data Date	Rating	RACR #1	RACR #2	Total Assets ($mil)	Capital ($mil)	Net Premium ($mil)	Net Income ($mil)
9-14	B	1.46	0.97	208,169	7,027.0	15,989.1	877.2
9-13	B-	1.36	0.90	192,904	6,555.9	16,450.7	412.9
2013	B-	1.40	0.93	200,018	6,836.1	21,752.4	577.6
2012	B-	1.40	0.93	180,025	6,399.6	18,518.2	602.8
2011	B-	1.43	0.97	165,222	6,754.8	18,326.9	207.0
2010	B-	1.71	1.06	158,433	6,465.6	18,052.7	497.2
2009	B-	1.59	0.99	143,346	6,245.1	16,101.6	-116.2

Risk-Adjusted Capital Ratio #2 (Severe Loss Scenario)

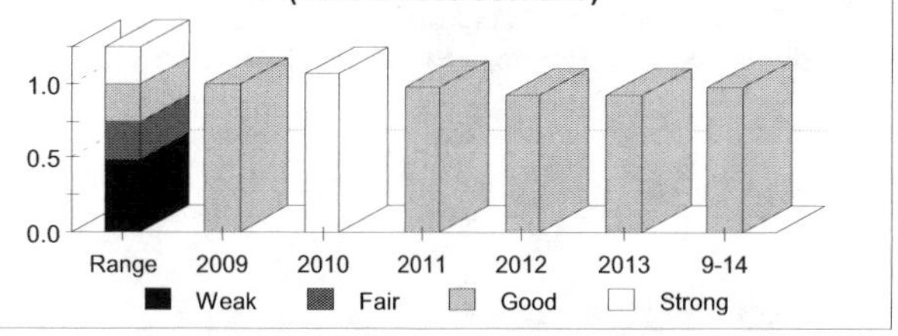
1.0
0.5
0.0
Range
2009
2010
2011
2012
2013
9-14
Weak
Fair
Good
Strong

LOCOMOTIVE ENGINEERS & CONDUCTORS MUTUAL PROTECT   B+   Good

Major Rating Factors: Good quality investment portfolio (6.1 on a scale of 0 to 10) with no exposure to mortgages and minimal holdings in junk bonds. Good overall results on stability tests (5.6). Stability strengths include excellent operational trends and good risk diversification. Strong capitalization (10.0) based on excellent risk adjusted capital (severe loss scenario).

Other Rating Factors: Excellent profitability (7.6) with operating gains in each of the last five years. Excellent liquidity (9.1).

Principal Business: Individual life insurance (100%).

Principal Investments: NonCMO investment grade bonds (81%), common & preferred stock (16%), noninv. grade bonds (1%), CMOs and structured securities (1%), and cash (1%).

Investments in Affiliates: None

Group Affiliation: None

Licensed in: MI, NE, NM, TX

Commenced Business: July 1910

Address: 535 Griswold St Suite 1210, Detroit, MI 48226-3689

Phone: (313) 962-1512 **Domicile State:** MI **NAIC Code:** 87920

Data Date	Rating	RACR #1	RACR #2	Total Assets ($mil)	Capital ($mil)	Net Premium ($mil)	Net Income ($mil)
9-14	B+	7.01	6.02	55.4	46.7	15.0	3.1
9-13	B+	6.98	6.28	49.9	42.7	14.9	5.1
2013	B+	6.50	5.85	52.1	43.2	19.9	5.5
2012	B	6.06	5.45	45.2	36.9	19.5	4.5
2011	B	5.84	5.26	39.5	32.4	18.7	5.8
2010	C+	5.30	4.77	34.5	26.7	18.1	5.7
2009	C	4.76	4.28	28.4	20.8	19.3	10.0

Adverse Trends in Operations

Decrease in premium volume from 2009 to 2010 (6%)

LONDON LIFE REINSURANCE COMPANY   C+   Fair

Major Rating Factors: Fair overall capitalization (4.0 on a scale of 0 to 10) based on mixed results -- excessive policy leverage mitigated by excellent risk adjusted capital (severe loss scenario). Nevertheless, capital levels have fluctuated during prior years. Fair overall results on stability tests (3.0) including weak results on operational trends. Weak profitability (2.9) with investment income below regulatory standards in relation to interest assumptions of reserves.

Other Rating Factors: High quality investment portfolio (7.8). Excellent liquidity (9.1).

Principal Business: Reinsurance (100%).

Principal Investments: NonCMO investment grade bonds (82%), CMOs and structured securities (13%), cash (3%), noninv. grade bonds (2%), and common & preferred stock (1%).

Investments in Affiliates: None

Group Affiliation: Great West Life Asr

Licensed in: All states, the District of Columbia and Puerto Rico

Commenced Business: December 1969

Address: 1787 Sentry Parkway, Ste 420, Blue Bell, PA 1942-22

Phone: (215) 542-7200 **Domicile State:** PA **NAIC Code:** 76694

Data Date	Rating	RACR #1	RACR #2	Total Assets ($mil)	Capital ($mil)	Net Premium ($mil)	Net Income ($mil)
9-14	C+	4.94	2.56	324.0	54.1	1.7	1.6
9-13	C+	4.55	2.30	352.5	62.0	-8.6	1.6
2013	C+	4.74	2.39	344.1	52.9	-8.1	2.3
2012	C+	4.67	2.38	424.6	67.2	29.9	1.6
2011	B-	3.85	2.06	464.4	69.9	39.2	2.0
2010	B	3.68	2.02	515.6	71.6	34.3	2.0
2009	B	3.26	1.80	704.5	74.0	51.1	6.8

Policy Leverage

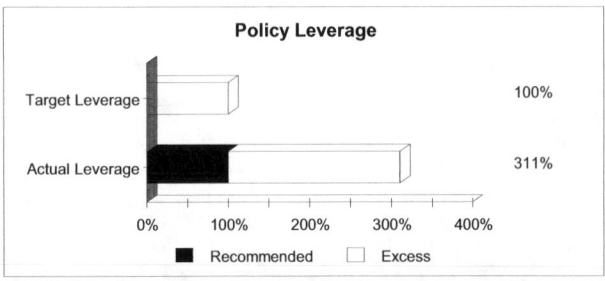

LOYAL AMERICAN LIFE INSURANCE COMPANY   C   Fair

Major Rating Factors: Fair profitability (4.7 on a scale of 0 to 10) with investment income below regulatory standards in relation to interest assumptions of reserves. Fair overall results on stability tests (3.8) including fair risk adjusted capital in prior years. Good quality investment portfolio (6.1).

Other Rating Factors: Good liquidity (6.9). Strong capitalization (7.1) based on excellent risk adjusted capital (severe loss scenario).

Principal Business: Reinsurance (54%), individual health insurance (41%), individual life insurance (2%), and group health insurance (2%).

Principal Investments: NonCMO investment grade bonds (97%), common & preferred stock (4%), and CMOs and structured securities (1%).

Investments in Affiliates: 4%

Group Affiliation: CIGNA Corp

Licensed in: All states except NY, PR

Commenced Business: July 1955

Address: 525 Vine Street,20th Floor, Cincinnati, OH 45202

Phone: (800) 633-6752 **Domicile State:** OH **NAIC Code:** 65722

Data Date	Rating	RACR #1	RACR #2	Total Assets ($mil)	Capital ($mil)	Net Premium ($mil)	Net Income ($mil)
9-14	C	1.46	1.08	251.3	74.7	184.1	13.5
9-13	C	7.52	5.94	248.1	77.4	196.5	13.0
2013	C	1.53	1.18	244.0	71.5	260.0	14.3
2012	C	1.71	1.32	282.3	78.2	-80.2	-22.2
2011	C	0.97	0.67	438.9	40.8	103.3	2.8
2010	C+	0.94	0.64	452.9	37.9	87.4	10.6
2009	C+	0.90	0.60	465.8	33.3	52.9	2.3

Net Income History
(in millions of dollars)

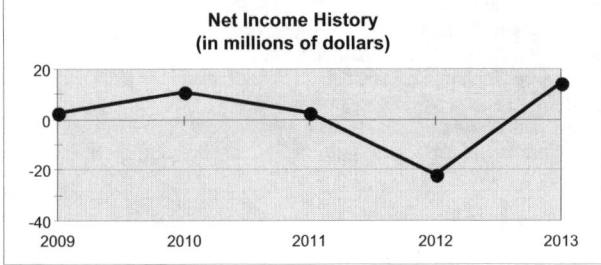

## M LIFE INSURANCE COMPANY					C			Fair

Major Rating Factors: Fair profitability (3.0 on a scale of 0 to 10) with investment income below regulatory standards in relation to interest assumptions of reserves. Fair overall results on stability tests (4.2). Strong capitalization (10.0) based on excellent risk adjusted capital (severe loss scenario).
Other Rating Factors: High quality investment portfolio (7.9). Excellent liquidity (7.3).
Principal Business: Reinsurance (100%).
Principal Investments: NonCMO investment grade bonds (60%), CMOs and structured securities (23%), cash (15%), and noninv. grade bonds (1%).
Investments in Affiliates: None
Group Affiliation: M Financial Holdings Inc
Licensed in: AZ, CO, DE, MI, NE, NJ
Commenced Business: December 1981
Address: 1290 Broaday, Denver, CO 80203-5699
Phone: (503) 232-6960 **Domicile State:** CO **NAIC Code:** 93580

Data Date	Rating	RACR #1	RACR #2	Total Assets ($mil)	Capital ($mil)	Net Premium ($mil)	Net Income ($mil)
9-14	C	4.49	2.99	248.6	65.0	279.9	16.0
9-13	C	5.92	3.96	233.9	78.4	256.3	31.0
2013	C	6.05	4.02	257.0	87.0	347.6	39.5
2012	C	5.56	3.68	284.4	74.0	322.1	27.6
2011	B-	5.14	3.62	285.1	59.8	225.4	58.0
2010	B-	5.54	3.88	206.1	80.4	270.9	24.5
2009	B-	5.29	3.61	121.7	77.2	340.6	19.2

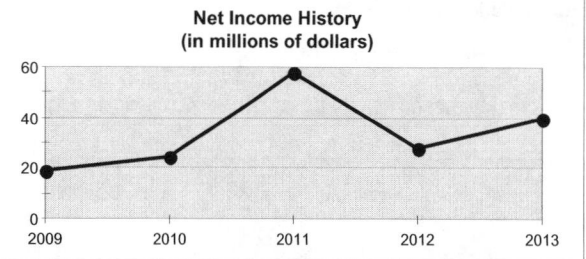

Net Income History
(in millions of dollars)

## MADISON NATIONAL LIFE INSURANCE COMPANY INCORPORA⌐		C+			Fair

Major Rating Factors: Fair profitability (4.5 on a scale of 0 to 10) with investment income below regulatory standards in relation to interest assumptions of reserves. Fair overall results on stability tests (3.1) including negative cash flow from operations for 2013. Weak liquidity (0.7) as a spike in claims or a run on policy withdrawals may stretch capacity.
Other Rating Factors: Strong capitalization (7.1) based on excellent risk adjusted capital (severe loss scenario). High quality investment portfolio (7.9).
Principal Business: Group health insurance (65%), reinsurance (11%), group life insurance (10%), individual life insurance (9%), and individual annuities (5%).
Principal Investments: NonCMO investment grade bonds (78%), common & preferred stock (12%), policy loans (2%), CMOs and structured securities (2%), and cash (2%).
Investments in Affiliates: 13%
Group Affiliation: Geneve Holdings Inc
Licensed in: All states except PR
Commenced Business: March 1962
Address: 6120 University Ave, Middleton, WI 53562
Phone: (608) 238-2691 **Domicile State:** WI **NAIC Code:** 65781

Data Date	Rating	RACR #1	RACR #2	Total Assets ($mil)	Capital ($mil)	Net Premium ($mil)	Net Income ($mil)
9-14	C+	1.31	1.09	491.1	83.7	111.7	8.3
9-13	B	1.31	1.07	492.9	82.0	126.7	16.0
2013	C+	1.20	1.00	488.6	78.0	168.8	11.7
2012	B	1.12	0.89	689.7	72.3	136.4	11.9
2011	B	1.09	0.84	686.7	70.3	140.2	15.1
2010	B	0.97	0.88	801.7	174.2	141.1	12.8
2009	C+	0.95	0.86	784.4	169.3	121.2	21.4

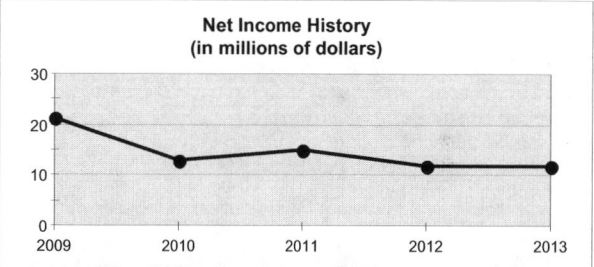

Net Income History
(in millions of dollars)

## MANHATTAN LIFE INSURANCE COMPANY			B			Good

Major Rating Factors: Good overall results on stability tests (5.4 on a scale of 0 to 10) despite fair financial strength of affiliated Harris Insurance Holdings Inc and negative cash flow from operations for 2013. Other stability subfactors include excellent operational trends, excellent risk adjusted capital for prior years and good risk diversification. Good current capitalization (6.8) based on good risk adjusted capital (severe loss scenario), although results have slipped from the excellent range during the last year. Good liquidity (6.4).
Other Rating Factors: Fair profitability (4.9) with investment income below regulatory standards in relation to interest assumptions of reserves. High quality investment portfolio (7.2).
Principal Business: Individual life insurance (78%), group health insurance (8%), reinsurance (7%), individual health insurance (6%), and individual annuities (1%).
Principal Investments: NonCMO investment grade bonds (66%), common & preferred stock (11%), policy loans (9%), mortgages in good standing (7%), and misc. investments (6%).
Investments in Affiliates: 11%
Group Affiliation: Harris Insurance Holdings Inc
Licensed in: All states except PR
Commenced Business: August 1850
Address: 111 W 57th St, New York, NY 10019
Phone: (212) 484-9300 **Domicile State:** NY **NAIC Code:** 65870

Data Date	Rating	RACR #1	RACR #2	Total Assets ($mil)	Capital ($mil)	Net Premium ($mil)	Net Income ($mil)
9-14	B	1.19	0.98	335.6	37.5	39.7	2.5
9-13	B-	1.27	1.07	312.7	37.9	9.2	3.5
2013	B	1.23	1.03	310.4	36.9	12.1	3.7
2012	C+	1.32	1.15	320.8	39.4	12.4	2.4
2011	C+	1.40	1.20	330.9	40.3	12.7	4.0
2010	C+	1.40	1.20	343.7	39.5	13.1	4.4
2009	C+	1.37	1.15	345.2	34.2	14.2	2.5

Harris Insurance Holdings Inc Composite Group Rating: C+ Largest Group Members	Assets ($mil)	Rating
MANHATTAN LIFE INS CO	310	B
CENTRAL UNITED LIFE INS CO	307	C
FAMILY LIFE INS CO	148	C
WESTERN UNITED LIFE ASR CO	15	B-

MAPFRE LIFE INSURANCE COMPANY OF PUERTO RICO C+ Fair

Major Rating Factors: Fair overall results on stability tests (3.6 on a scale of 0 to 10) including weak risk adjusted capital in prior years, negative cash flow from operations for 2013. Good liquidity (6.9) with sufficient resources to handle a spike in claims. Weak profitability (1.9). Return on equity has been low, averaging -3.4%.

Other Rating Factors: Strong capitalization (7.2) based on excellent risk adjusted capital (severe loss scenario). High quality investment portfolio (8.3).

Principal Business: Group health insurance (85%), individual health insurance (9%), credit life insurance (3%), group life insurance (2%), and reinsurance (1%).

Principal Investments: NonCMO investment grade bonds (68%), cash (32%), and common & preferred stock (2%).

Investments in Affiliates: None

Group Affiliation: MAPFRE Ins Group

Licensed in: PR

Commenced Business: February 1984

Address: 297 Ave Carlos Chardon, San Juan, PR 00918-1410

Phone: (787) 250-6500 **Domicile State:** PR **NAIC Code:** 77054

Data Date	Rating	RACR #1	RACR #2	Total Assets ($mil)	Capital ($mil)	Net Premium ($mil)	Net Income ($mil)
9-14	C+	1.43	1.14	66.0	29.0	83.2	1.3
9-13	D	0.38	0.31	43.0	8.8	67.6	4.0
2013	C+	1.61	1.29	64.0	27.9	88.4	5.5
2012	D	0.25	0.21	62.6	8.8	158.4	-11.4
2011	B-	0.57	0.47	73.8	19.5	166.3	0.8
2010	B-	0.76	0.62	74.7	22.5	149.4	3.3
2009	C	0.83	0.67	82.0	24.5	151.8	16.0

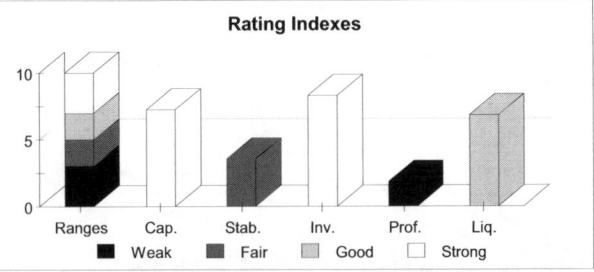

Rating Indexes

MASSACHUSETTS MUTUAL LIFE INSURANCE COMPANY * A- Excellent

Major Rating Factors: Good quality investment portfolio (6.2 on a scale of 0 to 10) despite large holdings of BBB rated bonds in addition to moderate junk bond exposure. Exposure to mortgages is significant, but the mortgage default rate has been low. Strong capitalization (7.5) based on excellent risk adjusted capital (severe loss scenario). Furthermore, this high level of risk adjusted capital has been consistently maintained over the last five years. Excellent profitability (7.1).

Other Rating Factors: Excellent liquidity (7.0). Excellent overall results on stability tests (7.0) excellent operational trends and excellent risk diversification.

Principal Business: Group retirement contracts (44%), individual life insurance (23%), individual annuities (16%), reinsurance (9%), and other lines (8%).

Principal Investments: NonCMO investment grade bonds (44%), mortgages in good standing (14%), CMOs and structured securities (11%), policy loans (9%), and misc. investments (18%).

Investments in Affiliates: 13%

Group Affiliation: Massachusetts Mutual Group

Licensed in: All states, the District of Columbia and Puerto Rico

Commenced Business: August 1851

Address: 1295 State St, Springfield, MA 01111

Phone: (413) 788-8411 **Domicile State:** MA **NAIC Code:** 65935

Data Date	Rating	RACR #1	RACR #2	Total Assets ($mil)	Capital ($mil)	Net Premium ($mil)	Net Income ($mil)
9-14	A-	1.93	1.35	190,575	13,961.5	13,481.3	413.5
9-13	A-	1.82	1.28	176,686	12,329.8	14,511.5	-38.6
2013	A-	1.80	1.28	182,776	12,524.4	20,418.8	-285.6
2012	A	1.92	1.38	155,649	12,686.9	20,309.5	755.5
2011	A	1.92	1.37	136,968	11,417.4	13,478.5	344.6
2010	A	2.08	1.41	129,290	10,352.4	11,158.5	534.9
2009	A	2.35	1.45	121,329	9,258.8	12,389.5	-289.4

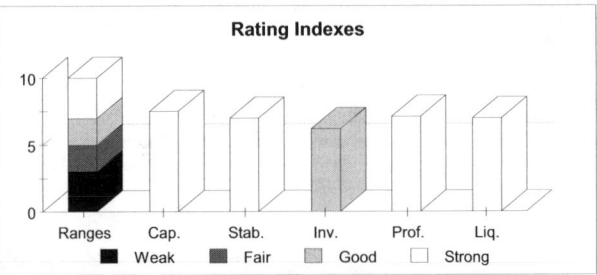

Rating Indexes

MEDAMERICA INSURANCE COMPANY B Good

Major Rating Factors: Good overall results on stability tests (6.2 on a scale of 0 to 10). Strengths include potential support from affiliation with Lifetime Healthcare Inc, excellent operational trends, good risk adjusted capital for prior years and excellent risk diversification. Low quality investment portfolio (2.4) containing large holdings of BBB rated bonds in addition to significant exposure to junk bonds. Weak profitability (2.0) with operating losses during the first nine months of 2014.

Other Rating Factors: Strong capitalization (8.6) based on excellent risk adjusted capital (severe loss scenario). Excellent liquidity (9.0).

Principal Business: Individual health insurance (60%), reinsurance (30%), and group health insurance (10%).

Principal Investments: NonCMO investment grade bonds (76%), CMOs and structured securities (6%), noninv. grade bonds (5%), and cash (2%).

Investments in Affiliates: None

Group Affiliation: Lifetime Healthcare Inc

Licensed in: All states except FL, NY, PR

Commenced Business: August 1966

Address: Foster Plaza VIII 730 Holiday, Pittsburgh, PA 15220

Phone: (410) 684-3200 **Domicile State:** PA **NAIC Code:** 69515

Data Date	Rating	RACR #1	RACR #2	Total Assets ($mil)	Capital ($mil)	Net Premium ($mil)	Net Income ($mil)
9-14	B	2.80	2.09	878.9	38.8	45.8	-3.8
9-13	B	1.12	0.60	831.9	23.7	41.1	-7.9
2013	B	1.85	1.00	866.2	43.6	54.6	1.7
2012	B	1.44	0.78	733.7	28.7	49.0	-7.7
2011	B	1.71	0.99	678.0	33.8	50.0	-8.1
2010	B	2.00	1.19	552.6	37.3	43.4	0.5
2009	B-	1.91	1.21	497.1	33.1	42.8	4.5

Lifetime Healthcare Inc Composite Group Rating: A- Largest Group Members	Assets ($mil)	Rating
EXCELLUS HEALTH PLAN INC	3044	A+
MEDAMERICA INS CO	866	B
MEDAMERICA INS CO OF NEW YORK	535	B
MEDAMERICA INS CO OF FL	23	C+

MEDICO INSURANCE COMPANY   B   Good

Major Rating Factors: Good liquidity (6.8 on a scale of 0 to 10) with sufficient resources to handle a spike in claims. Fair overall results on stability tests (4.7) including negative cash flow from operations for 2013. Weak profitability (1.9). Return on equity has been low, averaging -19.6%.

Other Rating Factors: Strong capitalization (10.0) based on excellent risk adjusted capital (severe loss scenario). High quality investment portfolio (7.4).

Principal Business: Individual health insurance (68%), group health insurance (28%), individual life insurance (2%), and reinsurance (1%).

Principal Investments: NonCMO investment grade bonds (56%), CMOs and structured securities (26%), cash (8%), common & preferred stock (2%), and misc. investments (8%).

Investments in Affiliates: None

Group Affiliation: American Enterprise Mutual Holding

Licensed in: All states except CT, NJ, NY, PR

Commenced Business: April 1930

Address: 1515 S 75th St, Omaha, NE 68124

Phone: (402) 391-6900 **Domicile State:** NE **NAIC Code:** 31119

Data Date	Rating	RACR #1	RACR #2	Total Assets ($mil)	Capital ($mil)	Net Premium ($mil)	Net Income ($mil)
9-14	B	4.26	3.84	67.2	31.2	0.7	0.1
9-13	B	4.42	3.98	63.8	30.2	0.7	1.3
2013	B	4.06	3.66	65.7	29.7	0.9	0.8
2012	B	4.07	2.82	55.1	31.5	25.4	-12.4
2011	D+	2.06	1.28	91.0	21.0	39.9	-13.7
2010	C	4.26	2.74	102.6	36.9	26.7	-5.3
2009	C+	5.03	4.27	113.1	44.7	18.6	-4.0

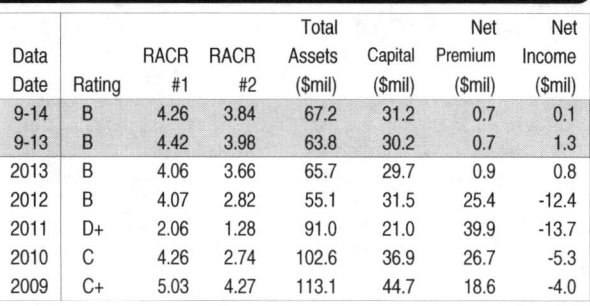

Rating Indexes

MEGA LIFE & HEALTH INSURANCE COMPANY   B-   Good

Major Rating Factors: Good quality investment portfolio (6.1 on a scale of 0 to 10) with no exposure to mortgages and no exposure to junk bonds. Fair overall results on stability tests (4.3). Strong current capitalization (8.3) based on excellent risk adjusted capital (severe loss scenario) reflecting improvement over results in 2011.

Other Rating Factors: Excellent profitability (7.0) with operating gains in each of the last five years. Excellent liquidity (7.2).

Principal Business: Group health insurance (71%), individual health insurance (25%), and individual life insurance (3%).

Principal Investments: NonCMO investment grade bonds (77%), common & preferred stock (8%), real estate (6%), CMOs and structured securities (4%), and cash (1%).

Investments in Affiliates: 10%

Group Affiliation: HealthMarkets

Licensed in: All states except NY, PR

Commenced Business: June 1982

Address: 9151 Grapevine Highway, North Richland Hills, TX 76180

Phone: (817) 255-3100 **Domicile State:** OK **NAIC Code:** 97055

Data Date	Rating	RACR #1	RACR #2	Total Assets ($mil)	Capital ($mil)	Net Premium ($mil)	Net Income ($mil)
9-14	B-	2.37	1.84	271.8	118.8	109.4	8.8
9-13	B-	1.58	1.31	280.3	102.7	174.4	21.2
2013	B-	1.95	1.57	281.0	109.2	229.2	26.8
2012	B-	1.26	1.04	289.5	90.9	289.1	27.6
2011	B-	1.15	0.96	346.0	110.5	362.7	47.1
2010	B-	2.34	1.93	590.8	291.8	489.8	119.5
2009	B-	1.62	1.32	643.8	235.1	688.5	67.6

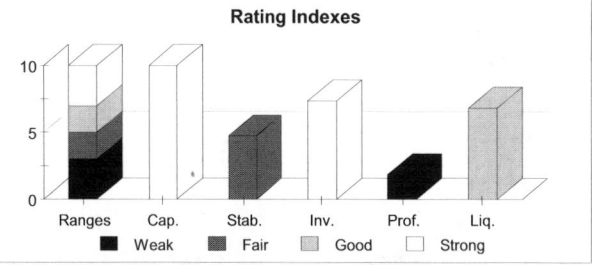

Rating Indexes

MERIT LIFE INSURANCE COMPANY *   B+   Good

Major Rating Factors: Good quality investment portfolio (6.1 on a scale of 0 to 10) despite significant exposure to mortgages . Mortgage default rate has been low. large holdings of BBB rated bonds in addition to small junk bond holdings. Good overall profitability (5.6). Excellent expense controls. Return on equity has been low, averaging 4.9%. Good overall results on stability tests (6.3) good operational trends and excellent risk diversification.

Other Rating Factors: Strong capitalization (10.0) based on excellent risk adjusted capital (severe loss scenario). Excellent liquidity (9.1).

Principal Business: Credit health insurance (37%), credit life insurance (29%), individual life insurance (18%), individual health insurance (13%), and group life insurance (2%).

Principal Investments: NonCMO investment grade bonds (60%), mortgages in good standing (20%), CMOs and structured securities (16%), noninv. grade bonds (4%), and cash (1%).

Investments in Affiliates: None

Group Affiliation: American General Finance Inc

Licensed in: All states except AK, MA, VT

Commenced Business: October 1957

Address: 601 NW Second St, Evansville, IN 47708-1013

Phone: (812) 424-8031 **Domicile State:** IN **NAIC Code:** 65951

Data Date	Rating	RACR #1	RACR #2	Total Assets ($mil)	Capital ($mil)	Net Premium ($mil)	Net Income ($mil)
9-14	B+	5.53	3.56	584.3	173.1	112.9	1.2
9-13	B+	7.28	4.29	516.8	180.7	92.0	2.9
2013	B+	6.34	4.09	532.0	184.5	128.1	3.3
2012	B+	10.53	5.92	549.0	245.4	85.9	10.1
2011	B+	13.33	7.16	630.4	334.8	79.3	8.5
2010	B	13.42	6.72	646.3	341.2	62.9	17.7
2009	B	11.74	5.72	659.6	316.1	56.9	28.0

Adverse Trends in Operations

Decrease in asset base during 2013 (3%)
Decrease in capital during 2013 (25%)
Decrease in asset base during 2012 (13%)
Decrease in capital during 2012 (27%)
Decrease in asset base during 2011 (2%)

METLIFE INSURANCE COMPANY USA

B **Good**

Major Rating Factors: Good current capitalization (5.9 on a scale of 0 to 10) based on good risk adjusted capital (severe loss scenario), although results have slipped from the excellent range during the last year. Good quality investment portfolio (6.0) despite substantial holdings of BBB bonds in addition to junk bond exposure equal to 64% of capital. Exposure to mortgages is significant, but the mortgage default rate has been low. Good overall profitability (5.3).

Other Rating Factors: Fair overall results on stability tests (4.5). Excellent liquidity (7.6).

Principal Business: Individual annuities (44%), individual life insurance (25%), reinsurance (16%), individual health insurance (12%), and group retirement contracts (3%).

Principal Investments: NonCMO investment grade bonds (45%), CMOs and structured securities (19%), mortgages in good standing (10%), noninv. grade bonds (6%), and misc. investments (17%).

Investments in Affiliates: 11%

Group Affiliation: MetLife Inc

Licensed in: All states except NY

Commenced Business: April 1864

Address: One Cityplace, Hartford, CT 06103-3415

Phone: (860) 308-7397 **Domicile State:** DE **NAIC Code:** 87726

Data Date	Rating	RACR #1	RACR #2	Total Assets ($mil)	Capital ($mil)	Net Premium ($mil)	Net Income ($mil)
9-14	B	1.18	0.86	56,480.8	3,584.4	-2,680.8	391.9
9-13	B	1.52	1.06	61,357.6	4,693.1	979.5	458.2
2013	B	1.52	1.09	60,275.2	4,794.6	1,361.1	789.5
2012	B	1.71	1.18	63,750.3	5,331.0	1,306.9	848.0
2011	B	1.66	1.15	64,781.2	5,133.3	1,436.6	46.2
2010	B	1.70	1.19	68,697.0	5,104.9	1,515.9	667.9
2009	B	1.53	1.06	67,232.7	4,928.7	2,767.4	80.5

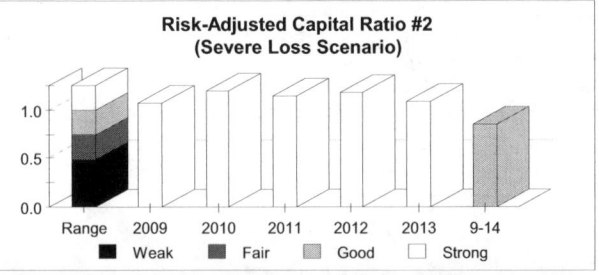

Risk-Adjusted Capital Ratio #2 (Severe Loss Scenario)

METROPOLITAN LIFE INSURANCE COMPANY

B- **Good**

Major Rating Factors: Good current capitalization (6.2 on a scale of 0 to 10) based on good risk adjusted capital (severe loss scenario) reflecting some improvement over results in 2009. Good overall profitability (6.2). Return on equity has been good over the last five years, averaging 12.0%. Good overall results on stability tests (5.2) despite fair risk adjusted capital in prior years good operational trends and excellent risk diversification.

Other Rating Factors: Fair quality investment portfolio (4.5). Excellent liquidity (7.1).

Principal Business: Group retirement contracts (35%), group life insurance (22%), group health insurance (16%), individual annuities (11%), and other lines (16%).

Principal Investments: NonCMO investment grade bonds (40%), CMOs and structured securities (19%), mortgages in good standing (18%), noninv. grade bonds (8%), and misc. investments (15%).

Investments in Affiliates: 6%

Group Affiliation: MetLife Inc

Licensed in: All states, the District of Columbia and Puerto Rico

Commenced Business: May 1867

Address: 200 Park Avenue, New York, NY 10166-0188

Phone: (212) 578-2211 **Domicile State:** NY **NAIC Code:** 65978

Data Date	Rating	RACR #1	RACR #2	Total Assets ($mil)	Capital ($mil)	Net Premium ($mil)	Net Income ($mil)
9-14	B-	1.38	0.90	392,834	13,925.2	25,353.1	1,718.1
9-13	B-	1.31	0.85	369,288	13,766.2	22,743.0	477.7
2013	B-	1.24	0.82	373,393	12,428.1	30,808.0	369.0
2012	B-	1.40	0.92	360,501	14,294.8	35,781.3	1,320.0
2011	B-	1.09	0.78	333,261	13,506.8	36,579.6	1,970.5
2010	B-	0.99	0.71	316,204	13,217.4	31,363.6	2,066.4
2009	B-	0.92	0.66	289,575	12,633.9	25,241.1	1,221.4

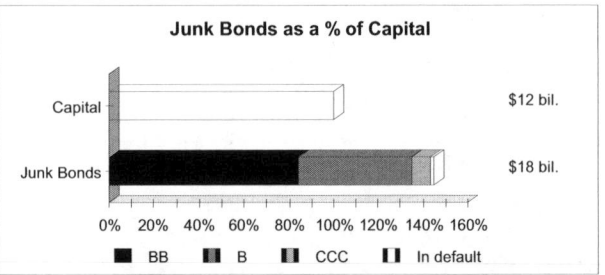

Junk Bonds as a % of Capital

METROPOLITAN TOWER LIFE INSURANCE COMPANY

B- **Good**

Major Rating Factors: Good overall profitability (6.9 on a scale of 0 to 10) despite operating losses during the first nine months of 2014. Return on equity has been fair, averaging 7.4%. Good liquidity (6.4) with sufficient resources to handle a spike in claims as well as a significant increase in policy surrenders. Good overall results on stability tests (5.1) despite negative cash flow from operations for 2013 excellent operational trends and excellent risk diversification.

Other Rating Factors: Fair quality investment portfolio (3.1). Strong capitalization (7.6) based on excellent risk adjusted capital (severe loss scenario).

Principal Business: Individual life insurance (98%) and individual annuities (2%).

Principal Investments: NonCMO investment grade bonds (37%), real estate (24%), CMOs and structured securities (18%), policy loans (6%), and misc. investments (13%).

Investments in Affiliates: 3%

Group Affiliation: MetLife Inc

Licensed in: All states except PR

Commenced Business: February 1983

Address: 200 Park Avenue, New York, NY 10166-0188

Phone: (212) 578-2211 **Domicile State:** DE **NAIC Code:** 97136

Data Date	Rating	RACR #1	RACR #2	Total Assets ($mil)	Capital ($mil)	Net Premium ($mil)	Net Income ($mil)
9-14	B-	3.21	1.41	5,083.2	815.0	22.4	-9.1
9-13	B-	2.38	1.08	5,058.7	805.4	25.3	48.6
2013	B-	2.55	1.08	4,942.8	735.5	27.6	51.5
2012	B-	2.17	1.00	5,055.6	781.3	30.7	60.9
2011	B-	2.32	1.05	5,041.7	828.5	35.9	63.0
2010	B-	2.52	1.09	4,953.8	804.5	42.4	151.4
2009	B	2.57	1.14	5,000.3	866.6	49.6	57.2

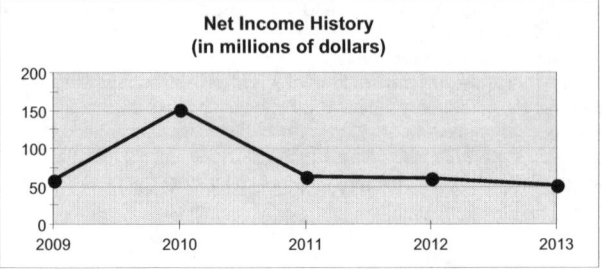

Net Income History (in millions of dollars)

MID-WEST NATIONAL LIFE INSURANCE COMPANY OF TENNES   B-   Good

Major Rating Factors: Good overall profitability (6.0 on a scale of 0 to 10). Return on equity has been excellent over the last five years averaging 24.2%. Fair overall results on stability tests (3.7) including fair financial strength of affiliated HealthMarkets. Strong capitalization (9.9) based on excellent risk adjusted capital (severe loss scenario).
Other Rating Factors: High quality investment portfolio (8.8). Excellent liquidity (8.2).
Principal Business: Group health insurance (82%), individual health insurance (12%), and individual life insurance (5%).
Principal Investments: NonCMO investment grade bonds (95%), CMOs and structured securities (3%), and cash (1%).
Investments in Affiliates: 1%
Group Affiliation: HealthMarkets
Licensed in: All states except ME, NH, NY, VT
Commenced Business: May 1965
Address: 9151 Grapevine Highway, North Richland Hills, TX 76180
Phone: (817) 255-3100   **Domicile State:** TX   **NAIC Code:** 66087

Data Date	Rating	RACR #1	RACR #2	Total Assets ($mil)	Capital ($mil)	Net Premium ($mil)	Net Income ($mil)
9-14	B-	3.77	2.95	63.2	27.5	37.9	0.0
9-13	B-	5.15	4.03	103.6	63.8	64.8	5.9
2013	B-	4.24	3.34	92.0	51.7	80.4	6.4
2012	B-	3.78	2.95	103.9	56.6	108.9	13.3
2011	B-	3.78	2.92	137.8	73.7	141.5	12.8
2010	B	3.39	2.62	177.2	96.0	206.3	48.7
2009	B	2.29	1.74	197.3	77.8	247.5	31.9

HealthMarkets
Composite Group Rating: C+

Largest Group Members	Assets ($mil)	Rating
MEGA LIFE HEALTH INS CO	281	B-
MID-WEST NATIONAL LIFE INS CO OF TN	92	B-
CHESAPEAKE LIFE INS CO	42	C+
HEALTHMARKETS INS CO	16	B-

MIDLAND NATIONAL LIFE INSURANCE COMPANY *   B+   Good

Major Rating Factors: Good overall results on stability tests (6.5 on a scale of 0 to 10). Stability strengths include excellent operational trends and excellent risk diversification. Good quality investment portfolio (5.0) despite mixed results such as: large holdings of BBB rated bonds but junk bond exposure equal to 61% of capital. Good liquidity (6.8).
Other Rating Factors: Strong capitalization (7.2) based on excellent risk adjusted capital (severe loss scenario). Excellent profitability (8.9).
Principal Business: Individual annuities (56%), individual life insurance (34%), group retirement contracts (10%), and group life insurance (1%).
Principal Investments: NonCMO investment grade bonds (43%), CMOs and structured securities (38%), mortgages in good standing (6%), noninv. grade bonds (5%), and misc. investments (7%).
Investments in Affiliates: 1%
Group Affiliation: Sammons Enterprises Inc
Licensed in: All states except NY
Commenced Business: September 1906
Address: One Midland Plaza, Sioux Falls, SD 57193
Phone: (605) 335-5700   **Domicile State:** IA   **NAIC Code:** 66044

Data Date	Rating	RACR #1	RACR #2	Total Assets ($mil)	Capital ($mil)	Net Premium ($mil)	Net Income ($mil)
9-14	B+	2.21	1.15	40,607.9	2,776.8	2,434.3	194.1
9-13	B+	2.17	1.08	36,622.5	2,224.0	2,783.6	260.4
2013	B+	2.16	1.11	37,441.0	2,563.1	3,631.9	455.7
2012	B+	2.18	1.10	32,851.3	2,124.3	2,941.7	343.8
2011	B+	2.06	1.00	30,132.9	1,854.2	2,544.4	318.2
2010	B+	2.09	1.05	28,627.8	1,639.7	2,599.9	226.7
2009	B+	2.26	1.09	26,496.9	1,391.9	2,267.3	-31.3

Adverse Trends in Operations

Decrease in premium volume from 2010 to 2011 (2%)

MIDWESTERN UNITED LIFE INSURANCE COMPANY *   A-   Excellent

Major Rating Factors: Good liquidity (6.9 on a scale of 0 to 10) with sufficient resources to handle a spike in claims as well as a significant increase in policy surrenders. Excellent overall results on stability tests (7.1). Strengths that enhance stability include excellent operational trends and excellent risk diversification. Strong capitalization (10.0) based on excellent risk adjusted capital (severe loss scenario).
Other Rating Factors: High quality investment portfolio (8.2). Excellent profitability (7.9) with operating gains in each of the last five years.
Principal Business: N/A
Principal Investments: NonCMO investment grade bonds (81%), CMOs and structured securities (7%), cash (5%), policy loans (4%), and misc. investments (4%).
Investments in Affiliates: None
Group Affiliation: Voya Financial Inc
Licensed in: All states except NY, PR
Commenced Business: August 1948
Address: 8605 Kings Mill Pl, Fort Wayne, IN 46804
Phone: (303) 860-1290   **Domicile State:** IN   **NAIC Code:** 66109

Data Date	Rating	RACR #1	RACR #2	Total Assets ($mil)	Capital ($mil)	Net Premium ($mil)	Net Income ($mil)
9-14	A-	12.45	11.21	236.3	124.2	2.8	2.2
9-13	B	12.14	10.92	239.5	121.4	2.8	1.2
2013	B	12.23	11.01	238.7	122.0	3.7	1.9
2012	B	12.01	10.81	242.1	120.1	3.7	3.5
2011	B	11.61	10.45	242.7	115.5	3.9	4.0
2010	B	11.15	8.79	241.3	111.1	4.2	7.6
2009	B	10.31	8.23	243.7	102.9	4.2	7.5

Adverse Trends in Operations

Decrease in asset base during 2013 (1%)
Decrease in premium volume from 2011 to 2012 (4%)
Decrease in premium volume from 2010 to 2011 (7%)
Decrease in premium volume from 2009 to 2010 (1%)

MINNESOTA LIFE INSURANCE COMPANY *   B+   Good

Major Rating Factors: Good quality investment portfolio (5.6 on a scale of 0 to 10) despite large holdings of BBB rated bonds in addition to moderate junk bond exposure. Exposure to mortgages is significant, but the mortgage default rate has been low. Good liquidity (6.9) with sufficient resources to handle a spike in claims as well as a significant increase in policy surrenders. Good overall results on stability tests (6.5) excellent operational trends and excellent risk diversification.

Other Rating Factors: Strong capitalization (7.8) based on excellent risk adjusted capital (severe loss scenario). Excellent profitability (7.3) with operating gains in each of the last five years.

Principal Business: Group life insurance (32%), group retirement contracts (25%), individual life insurance (22%), individual annuities (16%), and other lines (6%).

Principal Investments: NonCMO investment grade bonds (45%), CMOs and structured securities (25%), mortgages in good standing (13%), noninv. grade bonds (5%), and misc. investments (11%).

Investments in Affiliates: 4%

Group Affiliation: Securian Financial Group

Licensed in: All states, the District of Columbia and Puerto Rico

Commenced Business: August 1880

Address: 400 N Robert St, St Paul, MN 55101

Phone: (612) 665-3500 **Domicile State:** MN **NAIC Code:** 66168

Data Date	Rating	RACR #1	RACR #2	Total Assets ($mil)	Capital ($mil)	Net Premium ($mil)	Net Income ($mil)
9-14	B+	2.44	1.51	34,693.9	2,537.2	4,112.5	171.0
9-13	B+	2.38	1.48	31,572.5	2,265.8	3,795.2	93.0
2013	B+	2.29	1.44	33,154.4	2,329.7	5,261.5	118.9
2012	B+	2.39	1.50	28,415.0	2,181.8	4,574.7	129.5
2011	B	2.47	1.54	25,661.6	2,037.1	4,124.9	123.3
2010	B	2.52	1.54	25,492.6	1,939.2	4,208.0	96.6
2009	B	2.34	1.45	22,800.1	1,741.6	4,434.9	60.7

Adverse Trends in Operations

Decrease in premium volume from 2010 to 2011 (2%)
Decrease in premium volume from 2009 to 2010 (5%)

MML BAY STATE LIFE INSURANCE COMPANY *   A-   Excellent

Major Rating Factors: Excellent overall results on stability tests (7.2 on a scale of 0 to 10). Strengths that enhance stability include excellent operational trends and excellent risk diversification. Strong capitalization (10.0) based on excellent risk adjusted capital (severe loss scenario). Furthermore, this high level of risk adjusted capital has been consistently maintained over the last five years. High quality investment portfolio (7.3).

Other Rating Factors: Excellent profitability (8.0) with operating gains in each of the last five years. Excellent liquidity (8.6).

Principal Business: Individual life insurance (97%) and group life insurance (2%).

Principal Investments: NonCMO investment grade bonds (51%), policy loans (28%), CMOs and structured securities (18%), noninv. grade bonds (1%), and mortgages in good standing (1%).

Investments in Affiliates: 1%

Group Affiliation: Massachusetts Mutual Group

Licensed in: All states except NY, PR

Commenced Business: July 1894

Address: 100 Bright Meadow Blvd, Enfield, CT 06082

Phone: (413) 788-8411 **Domicile State:** CT **NAIC Code:** 70416

Data Date	Rating	RACR #1	RACR #2	Total Assets ($mil)	Capital ($mil)	Net Premium ($mil)	Net Income ($mil)
9-14	A-	4.49	3.03	4,682.4	207.5	18.5	11.1
9-13	B	4.66	3.10	4,577.0	212.1	20.9	19.3
2013	A-	4.06	2.80	4,587.9	196.0	28.5	22.3
2012	B	4.13	2.83	4,489.2	196.2	29.8	22.2
2011	A	3.76	2.66	4,411.4	176.5	29.0	29.2
2010	A	3.19	2.28	4,413.2	152.0	31.4	36.0
2009	A	3.35	2.40	4,345.1	158.1	38.0	7.7

Adverse Trends in Operations

Decrease in premium volume from 2012 to 2013 (4%)
Increase in policy surrenders from 2011 to 2012 (156%)
Change in asset mix during 2012 (5%)
Decrease in premium volume from 2009 to 2010 (17%)
Decrease in capital during 2010 (4%)

MONY LIFE INSURANCE COMPANY   B-   Good

Major Rating Factors: Good quality investment portfolio (6.2 on a scale of 0 to 10) despite large holdings of BBB rated bonds in addition to moderate junk bond exposure. Exposure to mortgages is significant, but the mortgage default rate has been low. Good profitability (5.0). Return on equity has been excellent over the last five years averaging 21.0%. Good overall results on stability tests (5.0) despite negative cash flow from operations for 2013, fair risk adjusted capital in prior years good operational trends and excellent risk diversification.

Other Rating Factors: Fair liquidity (3.2). Strong capitalization (7.3) based on excellent risk adjusted capital (severe loss scenario).

Principal Business: Individual life insurance (85%), individual health insurance (10%), and individual annuities (3%).

Principal Investments: NonCMO investment grade bonds (69%), mortgages in good standing (11%), policy loans (11%), noninv. grade bonds (3%), and misc. investments (6%).

Investments in Affiliates: None

Group Affiliation: Protective Life Group

Licensed in: All states, the District of Columbia and Puerto Rico

Commenced Business: February 1843

Address: 1740 Broadway, New York, NY 10019

Phone: (212) 708-2300 **Domicile State:** NY **NAIC Code:** 66370

Data Date	Rating	RACR #1	RACR #2	Total Assets ($mil)	Capital ($mil)	Net Premium ($mil)	Net Income ($mil)
9-14	B-	2.25	1.20	7,686.7	440.5	204.3	111.6
9-13	B-	1.00	0.74	8,206.6	598.0	217.6	-106.7
2013	B-	1.60	0.84	7,683.1	309.2	305.0	-567.1
2012	C+	1.03	0.75	8,441.1	619.6	325.5	174.4
2011	C	0.84	0.59	8,505.7	440.2	363.4	112.5
2010	C	0.90	0.65	8,795.0	567.2	387.9	54.2
2009	C	1.01	0.75	9,181.5	728.7	400.3	44.6

Adverse Trends in Operations

Decrease in asset base during 2013 (9%)
Decrease in capital during 2013 (50%)
Decrease in premium volume from 2011 to 2012 (10%)
Decrease in capital during 2011 (22%)
Decrease in capital during 2010 (22%)

MONY LIFE INSURANCE COMPANY OF AMERICA   B-   Good

Major Rating Factors: Fair current capitalization (4.0 on a scale of 0 to 10) based on mixed results -- excessive policy leverage mitigated by excellent risk adjusted capital (severe loss scenario) reflecting improvement over results in 2010. Fair overall results on stability tests (4.7) including negative cash flow from operations for 2013. Good quality investment portfolio (5.5).
Other Rating Factors: Weak profitability (2.9) with investment income below regulatory standards in relation to interest assumptions of reserves. Excellent liquidity (8.4).
Principal Business: Individual life insurance (90%), individual annuities (9%), and group life insurance (1%).
Principal Investments: NonCMO investment grade bonds (68%), common & preferred stock (9%), noninv. grade bonds (7%), mortgages in good standing (5%), and misc. investments (9%).
Investments in Affiliates: 7%
Group Affiliation: AXA Financial Inc
Licensed in: All states except NY
Commenced Business: June 1969
Address: 1740 Broadway, New York, NY 10019
Phone: (212) 708-2300 **Domicile State:** AZ **NAIC Code:** 78077

Data Date	Rating	RACR #1	RACR #2	Total Assets ($mil)	Capital ($mil)	Net Premium ($mil)	Net Income ($mil)
9-14	B-	4.19	2.77	2,829.1	382.5	211.3	9.5
9-13	B	2.24	1.35	4,108.7	296.7	288.4	13.2
2013	B-	4.02	2.70	2,794.3	356.7	-1,140.4	33.6
2012	B-	2.16	1.30	3,936.0	281.9	267.0	33.3
2011	B-	1.77	1.03	3,830.9	224.5	252.4	35.2
2010	C+	1.54	0.94	4,122.4	227.9	213.1	-18.6
2009	C+	1.72	1.06	4,276.9	273.8	216.9	11.7

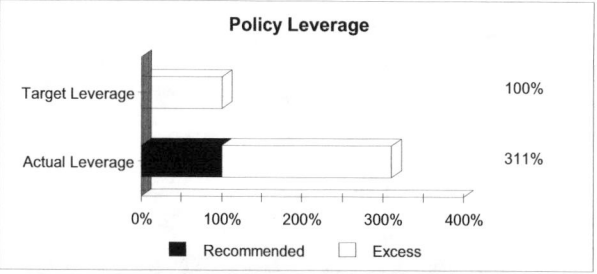

Policy Leverage

MOTORISTS LIFE INSURANCE COMPANY   B   Good

Major Rating Factors: Good quality investment portfolio (6.0 on a scale of 0 to 10) with no exposure to mortgages and small junk bond holdings. Good overall profitability (5.7) although investment income, in comparison to reserve requirements, is below regulatory standards. Good liquidity (5.7) with sufficient resources to handle a spike in claims as well as a significant increase in policy surrenders.
Other Rating Factors: Good overall results on stability tests (5.8) excellent operational trends and excellent risk diversification. Strong capitalization (7.6) based on excellent risk adjusted capital (severe loss scenario).
Principal Business: Individual life insurance (64%), individual annuities (35%), and group life insurance (1%).
Principal Investments: NonCMO investment grade bonds (64%), CMOs and structured securities (25%), common & preferred stock (5%), policy loans (3%), and misc. investments (4%).
Investments in Affiliates: None
Group Affiliation: The Motorists Group
Licensed in: FL, GA, IL, IN, IA, KY, MI, MN, NE, OH, PA, SC, TN, VA, WV, WI
Commenced Business: January 1967
Address: 471 E Broad St, Columbus, OH 43215
Phone: (888) 876-6542 **Domicile State:** OH **NAIC Code:** 66311

Data Date	Rating	RACR #1	RACR #2	Total Assets ($mil)	Capital ($mil)	Net Premium ($mil)	Net Income ($mil)
9-14	B	2.49	1.38	516.8	55.1	49.4	1.1
9-13	B	2.78	1.56	495.1	57.7	58.0	1.8
2013	B	2.54	1.42	494.7	54.6	70.0	3.5
2012	B	2.73	1.54	458.5	56.1	68.1	3.0
2011	B	3.08	1.77	418.1	53.5	59.3	1.9
2010	B	3.10	1.81	388.0	49.7	54.9	1.0
2009	B	2.99	1.75	359.3	44.5	57.5	-1.1

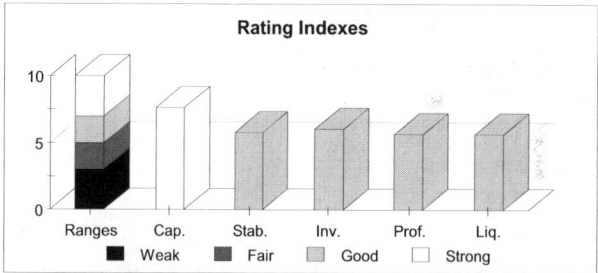

Rating Indexes

MTL INSURANCE COMPANY   B   Good

Major Rating Factors: Good quality investment portfolio (5.8 on a scale of 0 to 10) despite mixed results such as: large holdings of BBB rated bonds but moderate junk bond exposure. Good overall profitability (5.9). Return on equity has been low, averaging 2.0%. Good overall results on stability tests (5.9) good operational trends and excellent risk diversification.
Other Rating Factors: Fair liquidity (4.6). Strong capitalization (7.2) based on excellent risk adjusted capital (severe loss scenario).
Principal Business: Individual life insurance (98%) and individual annuities (2%).
Principal Investments: NonCMO investment grade bonds (59%), CMOs and structured securities (14%), policy loans (14%), mortgages in good standing (9%), and misc. investments (4%).
Investments in Affiliates: None
Group Affiliation: Mutual Trust Holding Co
Licensed in: All states except NY, PR
Commenced Business: April 1905
Address: 1200 Jorie Blvd, Oak Brook, IL 60523
Phone: (800) 323-7320 **Domicile State:** IL **NAIC Code:** 66427

Data Date	Rating	RACR #1	RACR #2	Total Assets ($mil)	Capital ($mil)	Net Premium ($mil)	Net Income ($mil)
9-14	B	2.08	1.11	1,921.5	132.9	128.0	6.9
9-13	B	1.99	1.07	1,875.1	122.1	149.1	-2.9
2013	B	2.04	1.09	1,894.9	127.8	201.2	2.0
2012	B	1.90	1.04	1,780.8	89.6	219.4	1.6
2011	B	2.31	1.21	1,652.2	96.4	228.6	0.1
2010	B	2.14	1.19	1,509.3	96.4	191.5	-0.4
2009	B	2.38	1.23	1,398.5	92.1	153.6	-2.2

Adverse Trends in Operations

Decrease in premium volume from 2012 to 2013 (8%)
Increase in policy surrenders from 2012 to 2013 (26%)
Decrease in capital during 2012 (7%)
Decrease in premium volume from 2011 to 2012 (4%)

MUNICH AMERICAN REASSURANCE COMPANY | B- | Good

Major Rating Factors: Good liquidity (5.8 on a scale of 0 to 10) with sufficient resources to handle a spike in claims as well as a significant increase in policy surrenders. Fair overall results on stability tests (3.6) including fair financial strength of affiliated Munich Re America Corp. Weak profitability (2.7) with operating losses during the first nine months of 2014.

Other Rating Factors: Strong capitalization (7.6) based on excellent risk adjusted capital (severe loss scenario). High quality investment portfolio (8.3).

Principal Business: Reinsurance (100%).

Principal Investments: NonCMO investment grade bonds (94%), CMOs and structured securities (5%), and common & preferred stock (1%).

Investments in Affiliates: 1%

Group Affiliation: Munich Re America Corp

Licensed in: All states, the District of Columbia and Puerto Rico

Commenced Business: November 1959

Address: 56 Perimeter Ctr E NE Ste 200, Atlanta, GA 30346-2290

Phone: (770) 394-5665 **Domicile State:** GA **NAIC Code:** 66346

Data Date	Rating	RACR #1	RACR #2	Total Assets ($mil)	Capital ($mil)	Net Premium ($mil)	Net Income ($mil)
9-14	B-	1.97	1.37	7,304.3	749.6	163.3	-61.6
9-13	B-	2.31	1.59	6,767.6	805.8	166.9	-14.5
2013	B-	2.05	1.43	6,981.2	789.9	261.1	-29.0
2012	B-	2.35	1.63	6,363.8	810.8	224.2	21.4
2011	B-	2.41	1.67	5,865.7	818.0	167.7	-20.6
2010	B-	2.34	1.59	6,349.9	729.4	116.0	118.1
2009	B-	2.03	1.37	5,984.4	609.7	1,073.2	46.1

Munich Re America Corp Composite Group Rating: C+ Largest Group Members	Assets ($mil)	Rating
MUNICH REINSURANCE AMERICA INC	16841	C+
MUNICH AMERICAN REASSURANCE CO	6981	B-
HARTFORD SM BOIL INSPECTION INS	1372	B
AMERICAN MODERN HOME INS CO	1256	C+
MUNICH AMERICAN LIFE REINS CO	1214	C+

MUTUAL OF AMERICA LIFE INSURANCE COMPANY * | A- | Excellent

Major Rating Factors: Good quality investment portfolio (6.0 on a scale of 0 to 10) despite mixed results such as: large holdings of BBB rated bonds but moderate junk bond exposure. Good overall results on stability tests (6.9). Strengths that enhance stability include excellent operational trends and excellent risk diversification. Strong capitalization (7.9) based on excellent risk adjusted capital (severe loss scenario).

Other Rating Factors: Excellent profitability (7.6). Excellent liquidity (7.2).

Principal Business: Group retirement contracts (70%) and individual annuities (29%).

Principal Investments: NonCMO investment grade bonds (53%), CMOs and structured securities (38%), noninv. grade bonds (4%), real estate (3%), and misc. investments (2%).

Investments in Affiliates: None

Group Affiliation: None

Licensed in: All states except PR

Commenced Business: October 1945

Address: 320 Park Ave, New York, NY 10022

Phone: (212) 224-1879 **Domicile State:** NY **NAIC Code:** 88668

Data Date	Rating	RACR #1	RACR #2	Total Assets ($mil)	Capital ($mil)	Net Premium ($mil)	Net Income ($mil)
9-14	A-	3.45	1.63	17,110.0	973.4	1,220.9	35.6
9-13	A-	3.34	1.59	15,985.2	932.7	1,262.1	33.5
2013	A-	3.41	1.62	16,666.7	951.2	1,771.8	49.4
2012	B	3.22	1.55	14,643.8	907.9	1,684.6	45.1
2011	B	3.09	1.49	13,502.3	846.2	1,552.7	40.9
2010	B	3.23	1.54	13,656.9	834.6	1,674.9	16.2
2009	B	3.19	1.53	12,427.6	796.9	1,441.5	-2.7

Adverse Trends in Operations

Decrease in premium volume from 2010 to 2011 (7%)
Decrease in asset base during 2011 (1%)
Increase in policy surrenders from 2010 to 2011 (27%)
Increase in policy surrenders from 2009 to 2010 (40%)

MUTUAL OF OMAHA INSURANCE COMPANY * | B+ | Good

Major Rating Factors: Good overall results on stability tests (6.5 on a scale of 0 to 10). Stability strengths include excellent operational trends, good risk adjusted capital for prior years and excellent risk diversification. Good quality investment portfolio (6.1) despite mixed results such as: minimal exposure to mortgages and substantial holdings of BBB bonds but minimal holdings in junk bonds. Strong capitalization (7.1) based on excellent risk adjusted capital (severe loss scenario).

Other Rating Factors: Excellent profitability (8.6) with operating gains in each of the last five years. Excellent liquidity (7.2).

Principal Business: Reinsurance (53%), individual health insurance (35%), and group health insurance (12%).

Principal Investments: Common & preferred stock (38%), nonCMO investment grade bonds (29%), CMOs and structured securities (17%), mortgages in good standing (5%), and misc. investments (9%).

Investments in Affiliates: 42%

Group Affiliation: Mutual Of Omaha Group

Licensed in: All states, the District of Columbia and Puerto Rico

Commenced Business: January 1910

Address: Mutual Of Omaha Plaza, Omaha, NE 68175

Phone: (402) 342-7600 **Domicile State:** NE **NAIC Code:** 71412

Data Date	Rating	RACR #1	RACR #2	Total Assets ($mil)	Capital ($mil)	Net Premium ($mil)	Net Income ($mil)
9-14	B+	1.19	1.09	6,568.9	2,981.2	1,620.7	30.0
9-13	B+	1.13	1.04	5,820.4	2,509.8	1,542.9	91.3
2013	B+	1.11	1.04	5,795.4	2,674.5	2,071.2	105.8
2012	B+	1.09	1.02	5,549.8	2,406.0	1,946.8	56.8
2011	B+	1.05	0.97	5,247.4	2,314.9	1,909.5	33.0
2010	B+	1.12	1.05	5,239.9	2,580.8	1,752.5	40.5
2009	B+	1.03	0.97	4,730.2	2,237.9	1,620.4	26.0

Adverse Trends in Operations

Decrease in capital during 2011 (10%)

MUTUAL SAVINGS LIFE INSURANCE COMPANY *   A-   Excellent

Major Rating Factors: Good liquidity (6.5 on a scale of 0 to 10) with sufficient resources to handle a spike in claims as well as a significant increase in policy surrenders. Excellent overall results on stability tests (7.3). Strengths that enhance stability include excellent operational trends and excellent risk diversification. Strong capitalization (8.3) based on excellent risk adjusted capital (severe loss scenario).

Other Rating Factors: High quality investment portfolio (7.3). Excellent profitability (8.1) with operating gains in each of the last five years.

Principal Business: Individual life insurance (82%), individual health insurance (13%), and reinsurance (4%).

Principal Investments: NonCMO investment grade bonds (86%), CMOs and structured securities (4%), policy loans (4%), noninv. grade bonds (2%), and common & preferred stock (1%).

Investments in Affiliates: 1%

Group Affiliation: Kemper Corporation

Licensed in: AL, FL, GA, IN, LA, MS, TN

Commenced Business: January 1927

Address: 12115 Lackland Rd, St Louis, MO 63146-4003

Phone: (205) 552-7347 **Domicile State:** AL **NAIC Code:** 66397

Data Date	Rating	RACR #1	RACR #2	Total Assets ($mil)	Capital ($mil)	Net Premium ($mil)	Net Income ($mil)
9-14	A-	3.01	1.89	470.5	62.4	31.1	4.8
9-13	B+	2.73	1.71	461.9	55.3	32.2	4.7
2013	B+	2.80	1.76	464.3	57.3	41.6	6.7
2012	B+	2.52	1.58	454.5	50.6	43.3	8.1
2011	B	2.20	1.39	446.8	42.7	44.3	10.2
2010	B	1.78	1.13	438.5	33.4	43.9	7.9
2009	B	1.79	1.13	439.5	33.8	43.7	7.2

Adverse Trends in Operations

Decrease in premium volume from 2012 to 2013 (4%)
Decrease in premium volume from 2011 to 2012 (2%)
Increase in policy surrenders from 2011 to 2012 (50%)
Decrease in capital during 2010 (1%)

NATIONAL BENEFIT LIFE INSURANCE COMPANY *   B+   Good

Major Rating Factors: Good overall results on stability tests (5.7 on a scale of 0 to 10). Stability strengths include good operational trends and excellent risk diversification. Good quality investment portfolio (6.6) despite mixed results such as: no exposure to mortgages and large holdings of BBB rated bonds but minimal holdings in junk bonds. Good overall profitability (6.8).

Other Rating Factors: Strong capitalization (10.0) based on excellent risk adjusted capital (severe loss scenario). Excellent liquidity (7.0).

Principal Business: Individual life insurance (79%), group health insurance (20%), and group life insurance (1%).

Principal Investments: NonCMO investment grade bonds (74%), CMOs and structured securities (13%), noninv. grade bonds (4%), policy loans (3%), and common & preferred stock (2%).

Investments in Affiliates: None

Group Affiliation: Primerica Inc

Licensed in: All states except PR

Commenced Business: May 1963

Address: One Court Square, Long Island City, NY 11120-0001

Phone: (718) 248-8000 **Domicile State:** NY **NAIC Code:** 61409

Data Date	Rating	RACR #1	RACR #2	Total Assets ($mil)	Capital ($mil)	Net Premium ($mil)	Net Income ($mil)
9-14	B+	7.13	3.96	480.5	168.1	45.5	13.8
9-13	B+	7.55	4.26	500.8	184.4	68.7	14.3
2013	B+	7.13	4.02	484.0	174.5	88.8	22.3
2012	B+	7.55	4.30	489.1	175.9	85.7	24.9
2011	B+	7.60	4.36	498.6	173.7	84.5	15.8
2010	B+	7.66	4.36	479.3	163.2	-81.5	23.6
2009	A-	10.59	5.71	781.3	359.0	129.6	31.3

Adverse Trends in Operations

Decrease in asset base during 2013 (1%)
Change in premium mix from 2010 to 2011 (22.7%)
Decrease in asset base during 2010 (39%)
Decrease in capital during 2010 (55%)
Decrease in premium volume from 2009 to 2010 (163%)

NATIONAL FARM LIFE INSURANCE COMPANY   B-   Good

Major Rating Factors: Good overall profitability (5.8 on a scale of 0 to 10). Excellent expense controls. Return on equity has been good over the last five years, averaging 10.3%. Fair overall results on stability tests (3.8). Weak liquidity (1.8) based on large exposure to policies that are subject to policyholder withdrawals with minimal or no penalty.

Other Rating Factors: Strong capitalization (7.8) based on excellent risk adjusted capital (severe loss scenario). High quality investment portfolio (7.0).

Principal Business: Individual life insurance (94%) and individual annuities (6%).

Principal Investments: NonCMO investment grade bonds (82%), policy loans (6%), CMOs and structured securities (5%), mortgages in good standing (3%), and misc. investments (4%).

Investments in Affiliates: None

Group Affiliation: National Farm Group

Licensed in: TX

Commenced Business: May 1946

Address: 6001 Bridge St, Fort Worth, TX 76112-2619

Phone: (817) 496-2637 **Domicile State:** TX **NAIC Code:** 66532

Data Date	Rating	RACR #1	RACR #2	Total Assets ($mil)	Capital ($mil)	Net Premium ($mil)	Net Income ($mil)
9-14	B-	2.60	1.54	374.8	34.3	18.9	2.3
9-13	B-	2.50	1.47	363.7	31.8	18.8	1.9
2013	B-	2.48	1.47	366.3	32.6	26.1	2.9
2012	B-	2.35	1.38	352.6	30.0	24.6	3.8
2011	B-	2.34	1.36	301.6	27.1	25.7	1.9
2010	B-	2.01	1.21	285.3	25.8	22.6	3.1
2009	B-	1.93	1.08	270.4	22.9	21.6	1.1

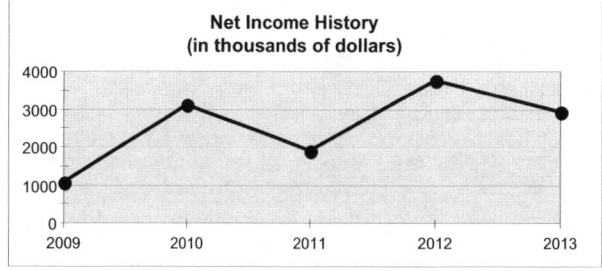

Net Income History
(in thousands of dollars)

NATIONAL FARMERS UNION LIFE INSURANCE COMPANY *   B+   Good

Major Rating Factors: Good overall results on stability tests (6.7 on a scale of 0 to 10) despite negative cash flow from operations for 2013. Other stability subfactors include good operational trends and excellent risk diversification. Good quality investment portfolio (5.6) despite mixed results such as: minimal exposure to mortgages and large holdings of BBB rated bonds but small junk bond holdings. Good liquidity (6.3).

Other Rating Factors: Strong capitalization (8.9) based on excellent risk adjusted capital (severe loss scenario). Excellent profitability (7.2) with operating gains in each of the last five years.

Principal Business: Individual life insurance (69%), reinsurance (29%), individual annuities (1%), and group life insurance (1%).

Principal Investments: NonCMO investment grade bonds (38%), CMOs and structured securities (30%), common & preferred stock (13%), mortgages in good standing (6%), and misc. investments (14%).

Investments in Affiliates: 2%

Group Affiliation: Americo Life Inc

Licensed in: AK, AZ, AR, CA, CO, DC, ID, IL, IN, IA, KS, KY, MI, MN, MS, MO, MT, NE, NV, NM, ND, OH, OK, OR, PA, SD, TX, UT, VA, WA, WI, WY

Commenced Business: April 1938

Address: 500 North Akard, Dallas, TX 75201

Phone: (816) 391-2000 **Domicile State:** TX **NAIC Code:** 66540

Data Date	Rating	RACR #1	RACR #2	Total Assets ($mil)	Capital ($mil)	Net Premium ($mil)	Net Income ($mil)
9-14	B+	4.32	2.28	216.9	46.1	3.8	3.4
9-13	B	4.17	2.18	225.2	45.5	4.7	2.7
2013	B	4.09	2.17	221.6	43.2	4.8	3.8
2012	B	4.10	2.16	225.9	42.4	5.5	4.2
2011	B	4.03	2.03	236.8	44.2	5.9	5.2
2010	B-	4.39	2.31	244.1	44.5	6.4	5.6
2009	B-	3.92	1.99	251.8	43.6	6.6	5.2

Adverse Trends in Operations

Decrease in premium volume from 2012 to 2013 (11%)
Decrease in asset base during 2013 (2%)
Decrease in capital during 2012 (4%)
Decrease in premium volume from 2009 to 2010 (3%)
Decrease in asset base during 2010 (3%)

NATIONAL GUARDIAN LIFE INSURANCE COMPANY   B   Good

Major Rating Factors: Good quality investment portfolio (5.7 on a scale of 0 to 10) despite mixed results such as: minimal exposure to mortgages and large holdings of BBB rated bonds but small junk bond holdings. Good overall profitability (6.9). Good liquidity (6.0) with sufficient resources to handle a spike in claims as well as a significant increase in policy surrenders.

Other Rating Factors: Good overall results on stability tests (6.0) excellent operational trends, good risk adjusted capital for prior years and excellent risk diversification. Strong capitalization (7.1) based on excellent risk adjusted capital (severe loss scenario).

Principal Business: Group health insurance (36%), group life insurance (32%), individual life insurance (21%), reinsurance (6%), and other lines (4%).

Principal Investments: NonCMO investment grade bonds (77%), common & preferred stock (6%), CMOs and structured securities (6%), mortgages in good standing (4%), and misc. investments (6%).

Investments in Affiliates: 3%

Group Affiliation: NGL Ins Group

Licensed in: All states except NY, PR

Commenced Business: October 1910

Address: 2 E Gilman St, Madison, WI 53703

Phone: (608) 257-5611 **Domicile State:** WI **NAIC Code:** 66583

Data Date	Rating	RACR #1	RACR #2	Total Assets ($mil)	Capital ($mil)	Net Premium ($mil)	Net Income ($mil)
9-14	B	1.59	1.04	2,903.2	261.9	365.0	14.8
9-13	B	1.51	0.97	2,683.2	224.9	318.9	17.4
2013	B	1.51	0.99	2,730.8	241.3	416.1	28.8
2012	B	1.43	0.93	2,532.8	196.4	395.8	18.9
2011	B	1.29	0.84	2,331.4	182.4	494.2	8.7
2010	B+	1.45	0.97	2,043.2	196.4	385.5	3.3
2009	B+	1.48	0.99	1,776.3	187.4	238.9	8.2

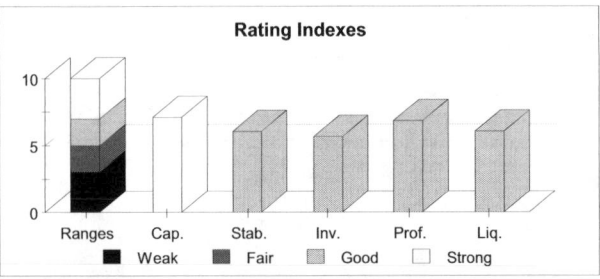

Rating Indexes

NATIONAL INCOME LIFE INSURANCE COMPANY *   B+   Good

Major Rating Factors: Good overall results on stability tests (6.7 on a scale of 0 to 10). Stability strengths include excellent operational trends and excellent risk diversification. Good overall profitability (5.3) although investment income, in comparison to reserve requirements, is below regulatory standards. Strong capitalization (9.2) based on excellent risk adjusted capital (severe loss scenario).

Other Rating Factors: High quality investment portfolio (7.4). Excellent liquidity (7.1).

Principal Business: Individual life insurance (87%) and individual health insurance (12%).

Principal Investments: NonCMO investment grade bonds (80%), cash (13%), CMOs and structured securities (3%), policy loans (3%), and noninv. grade bonds (2%).

Investments in Affiliates: None

Group Affiliation: Torchmark Corp

Licensed in: NY

Commenced Business: November 2000

Address: 1020 Seventh N St Suite 130, Liverpool, NY 13088

Phone: (315) 451-2544 **Domicile State:** NY **NAIC Code:** 10093

Data Date	Rating	RACR #1	RACR #2	Total Assets ($mil)	Capital ($mil)	Net Premium ($mil)	Net Income ($mil)
9-14	B+	3.46	2.45	142.8	31.6	43.5	4.4
9-13	B+	3.30	2.19	121.7	29.6	40.5	3.9
2013	B+	3.90	2.76	132.5	35.7	53.9	5.0
2012	B+	3.36	2.36	110.9	30.2	49.9	4.5
2011	B	2.19	1.41	81.4	17.5	42.7	5.0
2010	B	2.05	1.36	68.5	15.3	36.7	5.1
2009	B	1.66	1.18	54.2	11.3	33.9	2.0

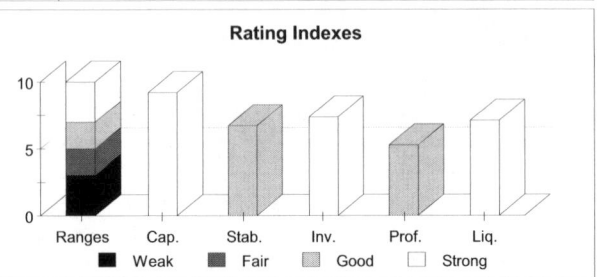

Rating Indexes

NATIONAL INTEGRITY LIFE INSURANCE COMPANY — B- — Good

Major Rating Factors: Good quality investment portfolio (6.0 on a scale of 0 to 10) despite mixed results such as: substantial holdings of BBB bonds but junk bond exposure equal to 61% of capital. Good liquidity (6.6) with sufficient resources to cover a large increase in policy surrenders. Good overall results on stability tests (5.0) despite excessive premium growth good operational trends and excellent risk diversification.

Other Rating Factors: Weak profitability (2.6) with investment income below regulatory standards in relation to interest assumptions of reserves. Strong capitalization (8.0) based on excellent risk adjusted capital (severe loss scenario).

Principal Business: Individual annuities (94%) and individual life insurance (6%).

Principal Investments: NonCMO investment grade bonds (53%), CMOs and structured securities (31%), noninv. grade bonds (8%), policy loans (2%), and misc. investments (5%).

Investments in Affiliates: 1%

Group Affiliation: Western & Southern Group

Licensed in: CT, DC, FL, ME, NH, NY, OH, RI, VT

Commenced Business: December 1968

Address: 15 Matthews St Suite 200, Goshen, NY 10924

Phone: (914) 615-1018 **Domicile State:** NY **NAIC Code:** 75264

Data Date	Rating	RACR #1	RACR #2	Total Assets ($mil)	Capital ($mil)	Net Premium ($mil)	Net Income ($mil)
9-14	B-	3.37	1.66	4,807.4	367.2	192.7	34.3
9-13	B-	3.18	1.54	4,799.0	323.1	149.0	29.3
2013	B-	3.07	1.50	4,767.1	321.0	215.3	34.4
2012	B-	3.09	1.51	4,758.8	301.7	204.1	41.3
2011	B-	2.87	1.39	4,723.3	272.5	302.0	30.6
2010	B-	3.28	1.54	4,830.6	252.0	346.3	28.4
2009	B-	3.50	1.62	4,432.4	225.6	552.5	1.1

Adverse Trends in Operations

Decrease in premium volume from 2011 to 2012 (32%)
Decrease in asset base during 2011 (2%)
Decrease in premium volume from 2010 to 2011 (13%)
Decrease in premium volume from 2009 to 2010 (37%)

NATIONAL LIFE INSURANCE COMPANY — B — Good

Major Rating Factors: Good overall results on stability tests (5.9 on a scale of 0 to 10). Stability strengths include excellent operational trends and excellent risk diversification. Good quality investment portfolio (6.1) despite mixed results such as: minimal exposure to mortgages and large holdings of BBB rated bonds but small junk bond holdings. Good liquidity (6.4).

Other Rating Factors: Strong capitalization (7.3) based on excellent risk adjusted capital (severe loss scenario). Excellent profitability (7.5).

Principal Business: Individual life insurance (86%), individual health insurance (6%), individual annuities (6%), and group retirement contracts (2%).

Principal Investments: NonCMO investment grade bonds (41%), CMOs and structured securities (26%), common & preferred stock (9%), mortgages in good standing (8%), and misc. investments (16%).

Investments in Affiliates: 9%

Group Affiliation: National Life Group

Licensed in: All states except PR

Commenced Business: January 1850

Address: 1 National Life Dr, Montpelier, VT 05604

Phone: (802) 229-3333 **Domicile State:** VT **NAIC Code:** 66680

Data Date	Rating	RACR #1	RACR #2	Total Assets ($mil)	Capital ($mil)	Net Premium ($mil)	Net Income ($mil)
9-14	B	1.55	1.20	9,082.4	1,461.9	285.1	11.5
9-13	B	1.62	1.23	8,984.6	1,381.4	284.1	57.7
2013	B	1.52	1.19	9,091.3	1,413.1	418.3	88.5
2012	B	1.54	1.17	8,855.8	1,287.1	421.1	64.6
2011	B	1.47	1.10	8,774.6	1,142.7	445.1	25.9
2010	B	1.50	1.12	8,656.5	1,136.2	465.4	20.9
2009	B	1.60	1.18	8,501.2	1,134.2	540.1	-11.4

Adverse Trends in Operations

Decrease in premium volume from 2011 to 2012 (5%)
Decrease in premium volume from 2010 to 2011 (4%)
Decrease in premium volume from 2009 to 2010 (14%)

NATIONAL SECURITY LIFE & ANNUITY COMPANY — B — Good

Major Rating Factors: Good overall results on stability tests (5.6 on a scale of 0 to 10) despite excessive premium growth. Other stability subfactors include good operational trends and excellent risk diversification. Fair profitability (4.9). Return on equity has been low, averaging 2.2%. Strong capitalization (9.1) based on excellent risk adjusted capital (severe loss scenario).

Other Rating Factors: High quality investment portfolio (7.2). Excellent liquidity (10.0).

Principal Business: Individual annuities (98%) and reinsurance (2%).

Principal Investments: NonCMO investment grade bonds (80%), CMOs and structured securities (16%), noninv. grade bonds (2%), and cash (2%).

Investments in Affiliates: None

Group Affiliation: Ohio Natonal Mutual Inc

Licensed in: AZ, AR, DC, IL, IN, IA, KS, LA, NE, NH, NJ, NY, OH, OK, OR, PA, SC, SD, TX, UT

Commenced Business: July 1975

Address: Court House Square, Bimghamton, NY 13901

Phone: (303) 860-1290 **Domicile State:** NY **NAIC Code:** 85472

Data Date	Rating	RACR #1	RACR #2	Total Assets ($mil)	Capital ($mil)	Net Premium ($mil)	Net Income ($mil)
9-14	B	2.69	2.42	410.0	30.0	64.3	1.0
9-13	B	2.72	2.44	321.6	27.9	49.6	5.5
2013	B	2.56	2.31	354.8	28.6	71.9	6.2
2012	B-	2.43	2.18	257.7	25.0	31.6	1.1
2011	B-	2.01	1.81	209.7	19.8	10.2	-6.1
2010	B	1.65	1.48	197.9	16.1	11.5	-0.6
2009	B	2.10	1.89	162.2	19.9	32.9	3.5

Adverse Trends in Operations

Increase in policy surrenders from 2011 to 2012 (104%)
Decrease in premium volume from 2010 to 2011 (11%)
Increase in policy surrenders from 2010 to 2011 (40%)
Decrease in capital during 2010 (19%)
Decrease in premium volume from 2009 to 2010 (65%)

NATIONAL TEACHERS ASSOCIATES LIFE INSURANCE COMPAN   B   Good

Major Rating Factors: Good overall results on stability tests (6.0 on a scale of 0 to 10). Stability strengths include excellent operational trends and good risk diversification. Fair profitability (4.6) with investment income below regulatory standards in relation to interest assumptions of reserves. Strong capitalization (8.1) based on excellent risk adjusted capital (severe loss scenario).

Other Rating Factors: High quality investment portfolio (7.2). Excellent liquidity (8.4).

Principal Business: Individual health insurance (98%) and individual life insurance (2%).

Principal Investments: NonCMO investment grade bonds (47%), CMOs and structured securities (44%), noninv. grade bonds (3%), common & preferred stock (2%), and misc. investments (3%).

Investments in Affiliates: 2%

Group Affiliation: Ellard Enterprises Inc

Licensed in: All states except NY, PR

Commenced Business: July 1938

Address: 4949 Keller Springs Rd, Addison, TX 75001-5910

Phone: (972) 532-2100   **Domicile State:** TX   **NAIC Code:** 87963

Data Date	Rating	RACR #1	RACR #2	Total Assets ($mil)	Capital ($mil)	Net Premium ($mil)	Net Income ($mil)
9-14	B	2.46	1.74	418.4	78.4	87.5	5.3
9-13	B+	3.24	2.19	375.1	74.4	80.4	6.0
2013	B	2.55	1.84	381.8	73.1	108.1	7.0
2012	B+	3.40	2.34	347.2	67.1	99.0	9.2
2011	B+	2.95	2.01	325.6	56.3	92.8	12.0
2010	B	2.43	1.65	309.4	44.5	88.1	8.8
2009	B	2.02	1.38	272.9	35.3	83.4	4.7

Adverse Trends in Operations

Increase in policy surrenders from 2012 to 2013 (29%)
Increase in policy surrenders from 2009 to 2010 (57%)

NATIONAL WESTERN LIFE INSURANCE COMPANY *   B+   Good

Major Rating Factors: Good quality investment portfolio (6.8 on a scale of 0 to 10) despite mixed results such as: minimal exposure to mortgages and large holdings of BBB rated bonds but small junk bond holdings. Good liquidity (6.4) with sufficient resources to handle a spike in claims as well as a significant increase in policy surrenders. Good overall results on stability tests (6.5) good operational trends and excellent risk diversification.

Other Rating Factors: Strong capitalization (9.1) based on excellent risk adjusted capital (severe loss scenario). Excellent profitability (8.5) with operating gains in each of the last five years.

Principal Business: Individual annuities (71%) and individual life insurance (28%).

Principal Investments: NonCMO investment grade bonds (73%), CMOs and structured securities (19%), common & preferred stock (3%), noninv. grade bonds (2%), and misc. investments (2%).

Investments in Affiliates: 3%

Group Affiliation: None

Licensed in: All states except NY

Commenced Business: June 1957

Address: 1675 Broadway #1200, Denver, CO 80202

Phone: (512) 836-1010   **Domicile State:** CO   **NAIC Code:** 66850

Data Date	Rating	RACR #1	RACR #2	Total Assets ($mil)	Capital ($mil)	Net Premium ($mil)	Net Income ($mil)
9-14	B+	4.39	2.38	10,164.8	1,163.2	808.6	56.6
9-13	B+	4.20	2.20	9,607.2	1,073.4	825.6	64.5
2013	B+	4.35	2.38	9,771.2	1,126.2	1,105.4	106.2
2012	B+	4.09	2.15	9,164.8	1,004.8	1,088.0	84.5
2011	B+	3.71	1.99	8,669.7	922.5	1,564.0	53.9
2010	B+	4.02	2.09	7,782.9	878.5	1,587.6	77.0
2009	B+	4.35	2.24	6,726.5	817.0	986.6	72.9

Adverse Trends in Operations

Change in premium mix from 2011 to 2012 (6%)
Decrease in premium volume from 2011 to 2012 (30%)
Decrease in premium volume from 2010 to 2011 (1%)

NATIONWIDE LIFE & ANNUITY INSURANCE COMPANY   B-   Good

Major Rating Factors: Good quality investment portfolio (5.0 on a scale of 0 to 10) despite large holdings of BBB rated bonds in addition to moderate junk bond exposure. Exposure to mortgages is significant, but the mortgage default rate has been low. Good liquidity (5.5) with sufficient resources to cover a large increase in policy surrenders. Fair overall results on stability tests (4.9) including negative cash flow from operations for 2013.

Other Rating Factors: Weak profitability (1.9) with operating losses during the first nine months of 2014. Strong capitalization (7.8) based on excellent risk adjusted capital (severe loss scenario).

Principal Business: Individual life insurance (73%) and individual annuities (26%).

Principal Investments: NonCMO investment grade bonds (74%), CMOs and structured securities (11%), mortgages in good standing (10%), noninv. grade bonds (3%), and policy loans (1%).

Investments in Affiliates: 1%

Group Affiliation: Nationwide Corp

Licensed in: All states except NY, PR

Commenced Business: May 1981

Address: One West Nationwide Blvd, Columbus, OH 43216

Phone: (614) 249-5227   **Domicile State:** OH   **NAIC Code:** 92657

Data Date	Rating	RACR #1	RACR #2	Total Assets ($mil)	Capital ($mil)	Net Premium ($mil)	Net Income ($mil)
9-14	B-	2.96	1.50	7,340.8	517.9	707.7	-91.1
9-13	B-	2.59	1.33	6,623.9	421.8	-97.4	-66.7
2013	B-	3.13	1.60	6,901.6	534.1	84.3	-103.3
2012	B-	2.03	1.04	6,243.3	311.0	404.6	-54.1
2011	B-	2.30	1.17	5,357.4	302.5	337.9	-61.2
2010	B	2.33	1.16	5,431.2	287.2	-48.5	-49.5
2009	B	1.92	0.97	5,243.4	213.5	292.5	-61.1

Rating Indexes

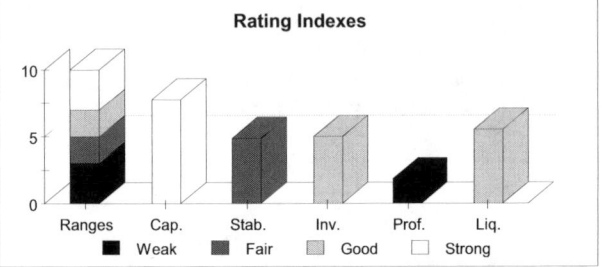

NATIONWIDE LIFE INSURANCE COMPANY   B-   Good

Major Rating Factors: Good quality investment portfolio (5.4 on a scale of 0 to 10) despite large holdings of BBB rated bonds in addition to moderate junk bond exposure. Exposure to mortgages is significant, but the mortgage default rate has been low. Good overall profitability (6.4). Return on equity has been excellent over the last five years averaging 28.5%. Fair overall results on stability tests (3.7) including weak results on operational trends.

Other Rating Factors: Strong capitalization (7.7) based on excellent risk adjusted capital (severe loss scenario). Excellent liquidity (8.4).

Principal Business: Individual annuities (57%), group retirement contracts (28%), individual life insurance (6%), group life insurance (5%), and other lines (4%).

Principal Investments: NonCMO investment grade bonds (49%), CMOs and structured securities (19%), mortgages in good standing (16%), policy loans (3%), and misc. investments (7%).

Investments in Affiliates: 2%

Group Affiliation: Nationwide Corp

Licensed in: All states, the District of Columbia and Puerto Rico

Commenced Business: January 1931

Address: One Nationwide Plaza, Columbus, OH 43215-2220

Phone: (614) 249-5227 **Domicile State:** OH **NAIC Code:** 66869

Data Date	Rating	RACR #1	RACR #2	Total Assets ($mil)	Capital ($mil)	Net Premium ($mil)	Net Income ($mil)
9-14	B-	2.59	1.49	125,130	4,103.4	8,644.2	323.0
9-13	B	2.67	1.47	115,436	3,683.3	8,533.2	179.6
2013	B	2.30	1.34	120,676	3,550.0	11,604.5	262.2
2012	B	2.91	1.60	106,578	3,836.6	10,383.7	764.4
2011	B	2.80	1.52	99,940.8	3,590.9	12,670.9	18.4
2010	B	2.87	1.53	95,838.8	3,685.5	10,087.9	560.3
2009	B	2.55	1.31	88,955.2	3,129.6	8,885.9	397.3

Adverse Trends in Operations

Decrease in capital during 2013 (7%)
Decrease in premium volume from 2011 to 2012 (18%)
Decrease in capital during 2011 (3%)

NEW ENGLAND LIFE INSURANCE COMPANY   B   Good

Major Rating Factors: Good quality investment portfolio (5.9 on a scale of 0 to 10) despite mixed results such as: large holdings of BBB rated bonds but moderate junk bond exposure. Good overall profitability (6.6). Return on equity has been excellent over the last five years averaging 16.4%. Good liquidity (6.7).

Other Rating Factors: Fair overall results on stability tests (4.8). Strong capitalization (9.0) based on excellent risk adjusted capital (severe loss scenario).

Principal Business: Individual life insurance (76%), individual annuities (22%), and individual health insurance (2%).

Principal Investments: NonCMO investment grade bonds (45%), policy loans (19%), CMOs and structured securities (17%), noninv. grade bonds (10%), and misc. investments (9%).

Investments in Affiliates: 2%

Group Affiliation: MetLife Inc

Licensed in: All states except PR

Commenced Business: December 1980

Address: 501 Boylston St, Boston, MA 02117

Phone: (617) 578-2000 **Domicile State:** MA **NAIC Code:** 91626

Data Date	Rating	RACR #1	RACR #2	Total Assets ($mil)	Capital ($mil)	Net Premium ($mil)	Net Income ($mil)
9-14	B	4.38	2.34	11,281.7	692.0	166.4	96.6
9-13	B	4.01	2.09	11,346.6	631.1	191.4	90.8
2013	B	3.73	2.01	11,640.2	571.1	260.1	102.7
2012	B	3.65	1.93	10,601.4	538.6	348.1	78.7
2011	B-	3.70	2.06	10,142.1	529.4	354.1	63.0
2010	B	4.35	2.41	11,085.5	592.0	442.2	32.6
2009	B	4.20	2.32	10,718.9	564.2	933.2	110.8

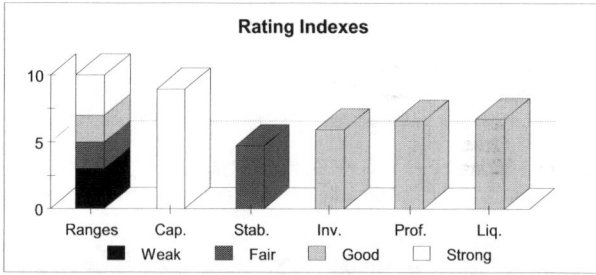

Rating Indexes

Ranges   Cap.   Stab.   Inv.   Prof.   Liq.
■ Weak   ▨ Fair   ▧ Good   ☐ Strong

NEW ERA LIFE INSURANCE COMPANY   C   Fair

Major Rating Factors: Fair capitalization (4.7 on a scale of 0 to 10) based on fair risk adjusted capital (moderate loss scenario). Fair overall results on stability tests (3.6) including fair risk adjusted capital in prior years and excessive premium growth. Good quality investment portfolio (5.3) despite large holdings of BBB rated bonds in addition to moderate junk bond exposure. Exposure to mortgages is significant, but the mortgage default rate has been low.

Other Rating Factors: Good overall profitability (6.0). Good liquidity (6.5).

Principal Business: Individual health insurance (62%), individual annuities (36%), and individual life insurance (1%).

Principal Investments: NonCMO investment grade bonds (44%), CMOs and structured securities (18%), common & preferred stock (13%), mortgages in good standing (12%), and misc. investments (13%).

Investments in Affiliates: 11%

Group Affiliation: New Era Life Group

Licensed in: AL, AZ, CA, CO, DE, FL, GA, IN, KY, LA, MS, MO, NE, NM, NC, OH, OK, PA, SC, SD, TN, TX, UT, WA, WV

Commenced Business: June 1924

Address: 200 Westlake Park Blvd, Houston, TX 77079

Phone: (713) 368-7200 **Domicile State:** TX **NAIC Code:** 78743

Data Date	Rating	RACR #1	RACR #2	Total Assets ($mil)	Capital ($mil)	Net Premium ($mil)	Net Income ($mil)
9-14	C	0.94	0.71	395.4	63.0	79.4	2.9
9-13	C	0.88	0.66	367.1	54.6	61.1	2.4
2013	C	0.90	0.69	371.3	58.0	77.3	4.6
2012	C	0.86	0.65	352.2	52.0	68.3	2.1
2011	C	0.81	0.62	353.6	47.1	67.0	-4.2
2010	C	0.86	0.64	344.3	48.2	78.6	0.8
2009	C	0.81	0.57	320.1	45.2	71.4	-3.7

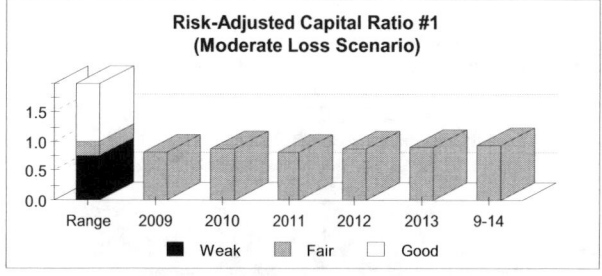

Risk-Adjusted Capital Ratio #1
(Moderate Loss Scenario)

Range   2009   2010   2011   2012   2013   9-14
■ Weak   ▨ Fair   ☐ Good

NEW YORK LIFE INSURANCE & ANNUITY CORPORATION *   B+   Good

Major Rating Factors: Good quality investment portfolio (5.8 on a scale of 0 to 10) despite large holdings of BBB rated bonds in addition to junk bond exposure equal to 59% of capital. Exposure to mortgages is significant, but the mortgage default rate has been low. Good liquidity (6.4) with sufficient resources to cover a large increase in policy surrenders. Good overall results on stability tests (6.7) excellent operational trends and excellent risk diversification.

Other Rating Factors: Strong capitalization (7.9) based on excellent risk adjusted capital (severe loss scenario). Excellent profitability (7.9) with operating gains in each of the last five years.

Principal Business: Individual annuities (80%), individual life insurance (18%), group retirement contracts (1%), and group life insurance (1%).

Principal Investments: NonCMO investment grade bonds (45%), CMOs and structured securities (32%), mortgages in good standing (12%), noninv. grade bonds (5%), and misc. investments (6%).

Investments in Affiliates: 3%

Group Affiliation: New York Life Group

Licensed in: All states except PR

Commenced Business: December 1980

Address: 200 Continental Dr, Newark, DE 19713

Phone: (212) 576-7000 **Domicile State:** DE **NAIC Code:** 91596

Data Date	Rating	RACR #1	RACR #2	Total Assets ($mil)	Capital ($mil)	Net Premium ($mil)	Net Income ($mil)
9-14	B+	3.30	1.61	124,994	7,412.9	8,808.8	592.8
9-13	B+	3.13	1.50	117,203	6,702.5	7,936.2	534.7
2013	B+	3.15	1.53	119,947	6,748.1	10,411.6	798.0
2012	B+	3.16	1.53	109,510	6,398.6	8,330.2	638.9
2011	B+	2.95	1.42	103,287	5,794.2	9,219.5	293.9
2010	A-	2.85	1.36	97,717.1	5,424.3	10,157.8	562.2
2009	A-	2.98	1.41	88,832.6	4,997.6	12,027.2	225.2

Adverse Trends in Operations

Decrease in premium volume from 2011 to 2012 (10%)
Decrease in premium volume from 2010 to 2011 (9%)
Decrease in premium volume from 2009 to 2010 (16%)

NEW YORK LIFE INSURANCE COMPANY *   A-   Excellent

Major Rating Factors: Good quality investment portfolio (6.4 on a scale of 0 to 10) despite mixed results such as: substantial holdings of BBB bonds but moderate junk bond exposure. Good liquidity (6.5) with sufficient resources to handle a spike in claims as well as a significant increase in policy surrenders. Strong capitalization (7.4) based on excellent risk adjusted capital (severe loss scenario).

Other Rating Factors: Excellent profitability (7.2) with operating gains in each of the last five years. Excellent overall results on stability tests (7.0) excellent operational trends and excellent risk diversification.

Principal Business: Individual life insurance (46%), group retirement contracts (32%), group life insurance (12%), reinsurance (4%), and other lines (6%).

Principal Investments: NonCMO investment grade bonds (41%), CMOs and structured securities (17%), common & preferred stock (10%), mortgages in good standing (10%), and misc. investments (23%).

Investments in Affiliates: 13%

Group Affiliation: New York Life Group

Licensed in: All states, the District of Columbia and Puerto Rico

Commenced Business: April 1845

Address: 51 Madison Ave, New York, NY 10010

Phone: (212) 576-7000 **Domicile State:** NY **NAIC Code:** 66915

Data Date	Rating	RACR #1	RACR #2	Total Assets ($mil)	Capital ($mil)	Net Premium ($mil)	Net Income ($mil)
9-14	A-	1.64	1.27	143,501	19,179.4	9,975.4	429.5
9-13	A-	1.54	1.19	137,460	17,130.7	9,423.9	499.4
2013	A-	1.55	1.22	139,198	17,853.8	13,049.9	520.3
2012	A-	1.51	1.18	134,727	16,568.5	13,720.8	690.5
2011	A-	1.52	1.17	130,686	15,128.9	14,107.2	262.6
2010	A-	1.51	1.16	122,008	14,716.8	12,473.5	525.6
2009	A-	1.47	1.12	117,836	13,686.3	11,161.5	455.3

Rating Indexes

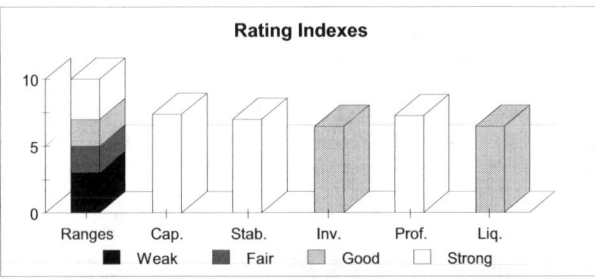

NIPPON LIFE INSURANCE COMPANY OF AMERICA *   A-   Excellent

Major Rating Factors: Good liquidity (6.4 on a scale of 0 to 10) with sufficient resources to handle a spike in claims. Good overall results on stability tests (6.1). Strengths that enhance stability include good operational trends and excellent risk diversification. Strong capitalization (9.4) based on excellent risk adjusted capital (severe loss scenario). Furthermore, this high level of risk adjusted capital has been consistently maintained over the last five years.

Other Rating Factors: High quality investment portfolio (8.1). Excellent profitability (9.1) with operating gains in each of the last five years.

Principal Business: Group health insurance (99%) and group life insurance (1%).

Principal Investments: NonCMO investment grade bonds (78%), CMOs and structured securities (13%), cash (5%), common & preferred stock (1%), and noninv. grade bonds (1%).

Investments in Affiliates: None

Group Affiliation: Nippon Life Ins Co Japan

Licensed in: All states except ME, NH, WY, PR

Commenced Business: July 1973

Address: 650 8th St, Des Moines, IA 50309

Phone: (212) 682-3992 **Domicile State:** IA **NAIC Code:** 81264

Data Date	Rating	RACR #1	RACR #2	Total Assets ($mil)	Capital ($mil)	Net Premium ($mil)	Net Income ($mil)
9-14	A-	3.26	2.61	211.7	139.0	241.1	6.0
9-13	A-	3.20	2.54	224.3	135.2	257.1	5.1
2013	A-	2.96	2.35	225.1	136.7	351.2	6.7
2012	A-	3.44	2.71	213.7	134.6	295.4	8.4
2011	A-	3.83	2.99	196.5	129.8	251.6	7.6
2010	A-	3.77	2.84	167.9	121.3	229.2	7.0
2009	A-	3.91	3.00	157.9	114.7	211.5	0.7

Rating Indexes

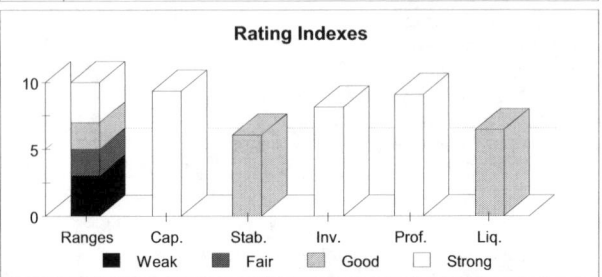

NORTH AMERICAN COMPANY FOR LIFE & HEALTH INSURANCE   B   Good

Major Rating Factors: Good overall results on stability tests (6.3 on a scale of 0 to 10). Stability strengths include excellent operational trends and excellent risk diversification. Good liquidity (6.5) with sufficient resources to handle a spike in claims as well as a significant increase in policy surrenders. Fair quality investment portfolio (4.7).

Other Rating Factors: Strong capitalization (7.2) based on excellent risk adjusted capital (severe loss scenario). Excellent profitability (9.0).

Principal Business: Individual annuities (57%), individual life insurance (32%), group retirement contracts (9%), and group life insurance (1%).

Principal Investments: NonCMO investment grade bonds (43%), CMOs and structured securities (40%), noninv. grade bonds (5%), mortgages in good standing (5%), and misc. investments (6%).

Investments in Affiliates: None
Group Affiliation: Sammons Enterprises Inc
Licensed in: All states except NY
Commenced Business: June 1886
Address: 525 W VanBuren, Chicago, IL 60607
Phone: (312) 648-7600 **Domicile State:** IA **NAIC Code:** 66974

Data Date	Rating	RACR #1	RACR #2	Total Assets ($mil)	Capital ($mil)	Net Premium ($mil)	Net Income ($mil)
9-14	B	2.45	1.13	16,820.8	1,169.1	1,231.5	110.3
9-13	B	2.29	1.05	14,715.3	925.6	1,251.5	-18.2
2013	B	2.38	1.09	15,021.7	1,065.1	1,713.6	121.9
2012	B	2.55	1.18	13,018.7	977.4	1,576.0	130.2
2011	B	2.22	1.02	11,728.9	842.9	2,064.4	135.5
2010	B	2.84	1.40	10,363.2	767.0	1,461.2	46.0
2009	B	2.48	1.27	9,117.5	647.4	1,456.6	-7.7

Adverse Trends in Operations

Decrease in premium volume from 2011 to 2012 (24%)
Increase in policy surrenders from 2009 to 2010 (37%)

NORTHWESTERN LONG TERM CARE INSURANCE COMPANY   B   Good

Major Rating Factors: Good current capitalization (6.8 on a scale of 0 to 10) based on good risk adjusted capital (severe loss scenario), although results have slipped from the excellent range over the last two years. Good overall results on stability tests (6.3). Strengths include potential support from affiliation with Northwestern Mutual Group, excellent operational trends and excellent risk diversification. Fair quality investment portfolio (4.4).

Other Rating Factors: Weak profitability (1.8) with operating losses during the first nine months of 2014. Excellent liquidity (9.4).

Principal Business: Individual health insurance (100%).

Principal Investments: NonCMO investment grade bonds (68%), mortgages in good standing (12%), noninv. grade bonds (10%), and common & preferred stock (8%).

Investments in Affiliates: None
Group Affiliation: Northwestern Mutual Group
Licensed in: All states except PR
Commenced Business: October 1953
Address: 720 E Wisconsin Ave, Milwaukee, WI 53202
Phone: (414) 299-3136 **Domicile State:** WI **NAIC Code:** 69000

Data Date	Rating	RACR #1	RACR #2	Total Assets ($mil)	Capital ($mil)	Net Premium ($mil)	Net Income ($mil)
9-14	B	1.77	0.98	2,556.6	232.7	373.6	-6.4
9-13	B	2.54	1.43	2,124.1	309.6	340.8	18.2
2013	B	1.76	0.99	2,220.1	213.8	457.3	-84.2
2012	B	2.45	1.40	1,861.6	274.7	387.1	-192.9
2011	B	2.14	1.29	1,193.9	210.1	300.6	10.5
2010	B-	1.91	1.27	926.2	149.6	338.6	-49.5
2009	B-	1.66	1.10	528.2	71.4	186.5	-17.1

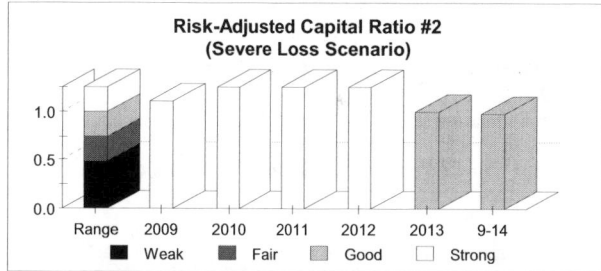

**Risk-Adjusted Capital Ratio #2
(Severe Loss Scenario)**

NORTHWESTERN MUTUAL LIFE INSURANCE COMPANY *   A-   Excellent

Major Rating Factors: Good quality investment portfolio (6.1 on a scale of 0 to 10) despite substantial holdings of BBB bonds in addition to junk bond exposure equal to 62% of capital. Exposure to mortgages is significant, but the mortgage default rate has been low. Good overall profitability (6.9). Excellent expense controls. Good liquidity (5.8).

Other Rating Factors: Strong capitalization (8.3) based on excellent risk adjusted capital (severe loss scenario). Excellent overall results on stability tests (7.3) excellent operational trends and excellent risk diversification.

Principal Business: Individual life insurance (78%), individual annuities (14%), individual health insurance (6%), group retirement contracts (1%), and group health insurance (1%).

Principal Investments: NonCMO investment grade bonds (42%), CMOs and structured securities (19%), mortgages in good standing (15%), policy loans (9%), and misc. investments (16%).

Investments in Affiliates: 4%
Group Affiliation: Northwestern Mutual Group
Licensed in: All states except PR
Commenced Business: November 1858
Address: 720 E Wisconsin Ave, Milwaukee, WI 53202
Phone: (414) 271-1444 **Domicile State:** WI **NAIC Code:** 67091

Data Date	Rating	RACR #1	RACR #2	Total Assets ($mil)	Capital ($mil)	Net Premium ($mil)	Net Income ($mil)
9-14	A-	3.67	1.86	223,103	18,086.7	12,023.4	706.2
9-13	A-	3.22	1.74	210,867	17,165.2	11,410.2	643.7
2013	A-	3.60	1.84	215,165	17,198.8	15,995.2	886.4
2012	A-	3.15	1.71	200,945	16,175.8	14,924.6	976.7
2011	A-	2.87	1.56	188,692	14,813.4	14,255.1	634.6
2010	A-	2.74	1.51	179,289	14,385.2	13,866.1	805.8
2009	A-	3.05	1.58	166,747	12,402.6	12,832.8	338.1

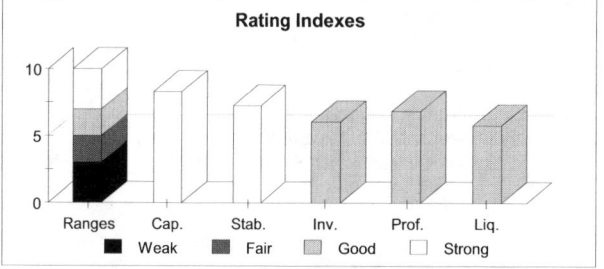

Rating Indexes

NYLIFE INSURANCE COMPANY OF ARIZONA — B — Good

Major Rating Factors: Good liquidity (6.9 on a scale of 0 to 10) with sufficient resources to handle a spike in claims. Good overall results on stability tests (5.9) despite excessive premium growth. Strengths include good financial support from affiliation with New York Life Group, excellent operational trends and excellent risk diversification. Fair profitability (3.0) with investment income below regulatory standards in relation to interest assumptions of reserves.

Other Rating Factors: Strong capitalization (10.0) based on excellent risk adjusted capital (severe loss scenario). High quality investment portfolio (8.2).

Principal Business: Individual life insurance (99%) and reinsurance (1%).

Principal Investments: NonCMO investment grade bonds (80%), CMOs and structured securities (18%), and , and , and misc. investments (2%).

Investments in Affiliates: 3%

Group Affiliation: New York Life Group

Licensed in: All states except ME, NY, PR

Commenced Business: December 1987

Address: 14850 N Scottsdale Rd Ste 400, Scottsdale, AZ 85254

Phone: (212) 576-7000 **Domicile State:** AZ **NAIC Code:** 81353

Data Date	Rating	RACR #1	RACR #2	Total Assets ($mil)	Capital ($mil)	Net Premium ($mil)	Net Income ($mil)
9-14	B	6.89	4.53	197.3	74.2	25.9	6.3
9-13	B	5.40	3.52	193.1	64.8	18.4	5.9
2013	B	6.08	3.94	194.9	68.2	24.9	8.1
2012	B	4.84	3.14	197.1	59.0	29.4	3.8
2011	B	4.48	2.93	199.7	59.5	35.2	0.8
2010	B	4.15	2.71	195.3	58.2	39.3	3.7
2009	B	3.87	2.56	193.2	54.5	38.7	2.9

New York Life Group
Composite Group Rating: B+

Largest Group Members	Assets ($mil)	Rating
NEW YORK LIFE INS CO	139198	A-
NEW YORK LIFE INS ANNUITY CORP	119947	B+
EXPRESS SCRIPTS INS CO	240	B+
NYLIFE INS CO OF ARIZONA	195	B

OCCIDENTAL LIFE INSURANCE COMPANY OF NORTH CAROLIN — C — Fair

Major Rating Factors: Fair overall results on stability tests (4.2 on a scale of 0 to 10) including fair financial strength of affiliated Industrial Alliance Ins & Financial. Good liquidity (5.3) with sufficient resources to handle a spike in claims as well as a significant increase in policy surrenders. Weak profitability (2.9) with investment income below regulatory standards in relation to interest assumptions of reserves.

Other Rating Factors: Strong capitalization (8.8) based on excellent risk adjusted capital (severe loss scenario). High quality investment portfolio (7.5).

Principal Business: Individual life insurance (86%), individual annuities (13%), and group life insurance (1%).

Principal Investments: NonCMO investment grade bonds (81%), mortgages in good standing (9%), policy loans (5%), common & preferred stock (2%), and misc. investments (2%).

Investments in Affiliates: None

Group Affiliation: Industrial Alliance Ins & Financial

Licensed in: All states except NY

Commenced Business: November 1906

Address: 425 Austin Avenue, Waco, TX 76701

Phone: (254) 297-2775 **Domicile State:** TX **NAIC Code:** 67148

Data Date	Rating	RACR #1	RACR #2	Total Assets ($mil)	Capital ($mil)	Net Premium ($mil)	Net Income ($mil)
9-14	C	3.63	2.18	258.7	36.2	25.7	3.6
9-13	C	2.88	1.68	250.9	28.4	30.7	1.0
2013	C	3.30	2.01	249.9	33.0	37.1	5.3
2012	C	2.79	1.71	246.9	28.0	41.1	1.8
2011	C	1.64	0.95	259.6	22.0	39.1	3.4
2010	B-	3.44	2.56	265.9	35.6	34.6	1.6
2009	B	3.20	2.24	261.5	32.9	31.5	3.0

Industrial Alliance Ins Financial
Composite Group Rating: C

Largest Group Members	Assets ($mil)	Rating
AMERICAN-AMICABLE LIFE INS CO OF TX	259	C
OCCIDENTAL LIFE INS CO OF NC	250	C
IA AMERICAN LIFE INS CO	221	C
INDUSTRIAL ALLIANCE INS FIN SERV	201	C
PIONEER SECURITY LIFE INS CO	110	C+

OHIO NATIONAL LIFE ASSURANCE CORPORATION * — B+ — Good

Major Rating Factors: Good overall results on stability tests (6.4 on a scale of 0 to 10). Stability strengths include excellent operational trends and excellent risk diversification. Good quality investment portfolio (5.0) despite large holdings of BBB rated bonds in addition to moderate junk bond exposure. Exposure to mortgages is significant, but the mortgage default rate has been low. Good liquidity (5.8).

Other Rating Factors: Strong capitalization (7.6) based on excellent risk adjusted capital (severe loss scenario). Excellent profitability (7.7).

Principal Business: Individual life insurance (97%) and individual health insurance (3%).

Principal Investments: NonCMO investment grade bonds (58%), CMOs and structured securities (17%), mortgages in good standing (14%), noninv. grade bonds (5%), and policy loans (3%).

Investments in Affiliates: None

Group Affiliation: Ohio Natonal Mutual Inc

Licensed in: All states except AK, HI, NY

Commenced Business: August 1979

Address: One Financial Way, Cincinnati, OH 45242

Phone: (513) 794-6100 **Domicile State:** OH **NAIC Code:** 89206

Data Date	Rating	RACR #1	RACR #2	Total Assets ($mil)	Capital ($mil)	Net Premium ($mil)	Net Income ($mil)
9-14	B+	2.79	1.43	3,548.1	315.8	188.0	13.3
9-13	B+	2.42	1.25	3,389.2	286.1	178.2	15.8
2013	B+	2.82	1.45	3,408.1	316.8	278.6	13.6
2012	B+	2.76	1.42	3,315.3	317.4	213.1	30.1
2011	B+	2.96	1.53	3,172.5	332.4	205.9	34.6
2010	B+	1.99	1.05	3,169.6	251.2	246.8	10.7
2009	B+	2.32	1.19	2,886.9	277.8	267.4	-0.6

Adverse Trends in Operations

Decrease in capital during 2012 (2%)
Decrease in premium volume from 2010 to 2011 (17%)
Decrease in capital during 2010 (10%)
Increase in policy surrenders from 2009 to 2010 (26%)
Decrease in premium volume from 2009 to 2010 (8%)

OHIO NATIONAL LIFE INSURANCE COMPANY   B   Good

Major Rating Factors: Good capitalization (6.6 on a scale of 0 to 10) based on good risk adjusted capital (severe loss scenario). Capital levels have been relatively consistent over the last five years. Good quality investment portfolio (5.7) despite significant exposure to mortgages . Mortgage default rate has been low. large holdings of BBB rated bonds in addition to small junk bond holdings. Good overall results on stability tests (5.8) excellent operational trends and excellent risk diversification.

Other Rating Factors: Excellent profitability (7.7) with operating gains in each of the last five years. Excellent liquidity (8.4).

Principal Business: Individual annuities (76%), individual life insurance (11%), reinsurance (7%), and group retirement contracts (6%).

Principal Investments: NonCMO investment grade bonds (51%), CMOs and structured securities (16%), mortgages in good standing (13%), common & preferred stock (6%), and misc. investments (12%).

Investments in Affiliates: 5%
Group Affiliation: Ohio Natonal Mutual Inc
Licensed in: All states except AK, HI, NY
Commenced Business: October 1910
Address: One Financial Way, Cincinnati, OH 45242
Phone: (513) 794-6100 **Domicile State:** OH **NAIC Code:** 67172

Data Date	Rating	RACR #1	RACR #2	Total Assets ($mil)	Capital ($mil)	Net Premium ($mil)	Net Income ($mil)
9-14	B	1.36	0.95	26,677.4	1,001.3	2,002.2	52.8
9-13	B	1.27	0.92	23,855.5	1,021.5	2,087.7	52.7
2013	B	1.38	0.97	25,384.9	1,002.7	2,830.6	61.6
2012	B	1.33	0.96	21,631.2	1,048.3	3,259.8	107.6
2011	B	1.27	0.94	18,129.0	902.5	1,948.4	73.4
2010	B	1.73	1.14	17,968.2	860.7	1,836.2	143.6
2009	B	1.52	1.02	15,785.0	816.7	2,882.3	80.8

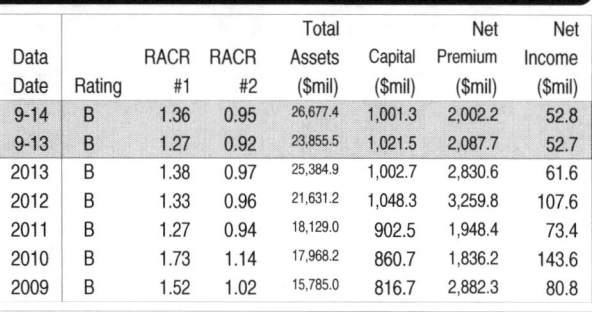

Risk-Adjusted Capital Ratio #2
(Severe Loss Scenario)

OLD REPUBLIC LIFE INSURANCE COMPANY   B-   Good

Major Rating Factors: Good quality investment portfolio (6.0 on a scale of 0 to 10) despite mixed results such as: no exposure to mortgages and large holdings of BBB rated bonds but no exposure to junk bonds. Good overall results on stability tests (5.3) despite negative cash flow from operations for 2013. Strengths include good financial support from affiliation with Old Republic Group, good operational trends and excellent risk diversification. Weak profitability (2.9) with operating losses during the first nine months of 2014.

Other Rating Factors: Strong capitalization (8.3) based on excellent risk adjusted capital (severe loss scenario). Excellent liquidity (7.0).

Principal Business: Individual life insurance (40%), group health insurance (40%), reinsurance (19%), and individual annuities (1%).

Principal Investments: NonCMO investment grade bonds (94%), common & preferred stock (4%), policy loans (1%), and cash (1%).

Investments in Affiliates: None
Group Affiliation: Old Republic Group
Licensed in: All states except NY
Commenced Business: April 1923
Address: 307 N Michigan Ave, Chicago, IL 60601
Phone: (312) 346-8100 **Domicile State:** IL **NAIC Code:** 67261

Data Date	Rating	RACR #1	RACR #2	Total Assets ($mil)	Capital ($mil)	Net Premium ($mil)	Net Income ($mil)
9-14	B-	2.94	1.85	124.6	29.3	14.9	-1.2
9-13	B	4.26	2.73	133.7	37.5	16.1	2.3
2013	B-	4.30	2.81	131.7	36.4	21.2	2.2
2012	B	4.68	3.13	138.4	40.6	21.0	1.6
2011	B+	4.69	3.12	142.3	41.0	22.4	4.8
2010	B+	4.41	2.85	149.1	40.6	26.4	4.0
2009	B+	4.45	2.90	151.9	41.0	25.5	5.1

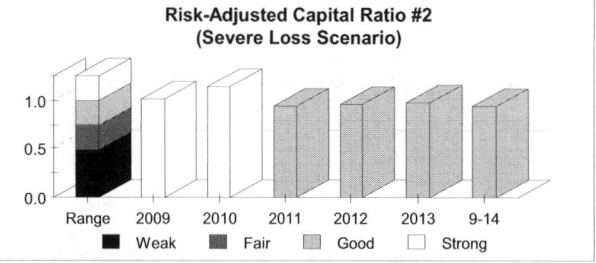

Old Republic Group
Composite Group Rating: B
Largest Group Members

Largest Group Members	Assets ($mil)	Rating
OLD REPUBLIC INS CO	2473	A-
REPUBLIC MORTGAGE INS CO	1933	F
GREAT WEST CASUALTY CO	1737	A-
OLD REPUBLIC GENERAL INS CORP	1731	A-
BITCO GENERAL INS CORP	788	A-

OLD UNITED LIFE INSURANCE COMPANY   B   Good

Major Rating Factors: Good overall results on stability tests (6.2 on a scale of 0 to 10). Stability strengths include excellent operational trends and good risk diversification. Good quality investment portfolio (5.2) despite mixed results such as: no exposure to mortgages and large holdings of BBB rated bonds but small junk bond holdings. Strong capitalization (10.0) based on excellent risk adjusted capital (severe loss scenario).

Other Rating Factors: Excellent profitability (7.1) with operating gains in each of the last five years. Excellent liquidity (9.4).

Principal Business: Credit life insurance (51%) and credit health insurance (49%).

Principal Investments: NonCMO investment grade bonds (59%), common & preferred stock (18%), CMOs and structured securities (16%), and noninv. grade bonds (7%).

Investments in Affiliates: None
Group Affiliation: Van Enterprises Group
Licensed in: All states except ME, NH, NY, PR
Commenced Business: January 1964
Address: 8500 W Shawnee Mission Pky 200, Merriam, KS 66202
Phone: (913) 432-6400 **Domicile State:** AZ **NAIC Code:** 76007

Data Date	Rating	RACR #1	RACR #2	Total Assets ($mil)	Capital ($mil)	Net Premium ($mil)	Net Income ($mil)
9-14	B	6.06	3.51	90.2	45.7	6.3	0.9
9-13	B	6.06	3.52	86.5	44.3	6.7	-0.1
2013	B	6.08	3.55	87.4	44.9	8.5	0.4
2012	B	5.95	3.86	82.3	43.9	9.8	1.0
2011	B	6.03	5.15	76.2	43.6	4.9	2.2
2010	B	5.79	5.21	75.9	41.8	5.2	1.5
2009	B-	5.57	5.02	73.5	40.2	3.4	4.2

Adverse Trends in Operations

Decrease in premium volume from 2012 to 2013 (13%)
Decrease in premium volume from 2010 to 2011 (6%)
Increase in policy surrenders from 2010 to 2011 (96%)
Change in premium mix from 2009 to 2010 (4.3%)

OPTIMUM RE INSURANCE COMPANY   B-   Good

Major Rating Factors: Fair overall results on stability tests (4.9 on a scale of 0 to 10). Weak profitability (2.6) with investment income below regulatory standards in relation to interest assumptions of reserves. Strong capitalization (7.9) based on excellent risk adjusted capital (severe loss scenario). Capital levels have been relatively consistent over the last five years.

Other Rating Factors: High quality investment portfolio (7.3). Excellent liquidity (8.6).

Principal Business: Reinsurance (100%).

Principal Investments: NonCMO investment grade bonds (88%), cash (3%), real estate (3%), common & preferred stock (2%), and noninv. grade bonds (1%).

Investments in Affiliates: None

Group Affiliation: Optimum Group Inc

Licensed in: All states except NY, VA

Commenced Business: June 1978

Address: 2505 Turtle Creek Blvd, Dallas, TX 75219-4713

Phone: (214) 528-2020 **Domicile State:** TX **NAIC Code:** 88099

Data Date	Rating	RACR #1	RACR #2	Total Assets ($mil)	Capital ($mil)	Net Premium ($mil)	Net Income ($mil)
9-14	B-	2.52	1.60	127.0	31.8	36.9	4.7
9-13	B-	2.16	1.41	111.1	28.1	34.3	1.2
2013	B-	2.36	1.51	114.9	27.9	44.3	2.0
2012	B-	2.12	1.38	103.7	26.7	45.6	2.1
2011	B-	1.81	1.18	92.5	26.2	45.0	2.6
2010	B-	1.56	1.03	84.8	25.7	42.3	3.1
2009	B-	1.61	1.07	79.0	24.2	31.9	1.4

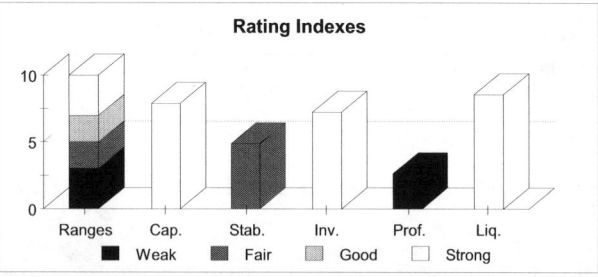

OXFORD LIFE INSURANCE COMPANY   B-   Good

Major Rating Factors: Good quality investment portfolio (6.7 on a scale of 0 to 10) despite significant exposure to mortgages . Mortgage default rate has been low. large holdings of BBB rated bonds in addition to small junk bond holdings. Good liquidity (6.3) with sufficient resources to handle a spike in claims as well as a significant increase in policy surrenders. Fair overall results on stability tests (4.7).

Other Rating Factors: Strong capitalization (7.6) based on excellent risk adjusted capital (severe loss scenario). Excellent profitability (8.4) with operating gains in each of the last five years.

Principal Business: Individual annuities (59%), individual life insurance (22%), individual health insurance (10%), and reinsurance (8%).

Principal Investments: NonCMO investment grade bonds (75%), mortgages in good standing (10%), CMOs and structured securities (5%), common & preferred stock (4%), and misc. investments (6%).

Investments in Affiliates: 4%

Group Affiliation: Amerco Corp

Licensed in: All states except NY, VT, PR

Commenced Business: June 1968

Address: 2721 N Central Ave, Phoenix, AZ 85004-1120

Phone: (602) 263-6666 **Domicile State:** AZ **NAIC Code:** 76112

Data Date	Rating	RACR #1	RACR #2	Total Assets ($mil)	Capital ($mil)	Net Premium ($mil)	Net Income ($mil)
9-14	B-	2.02	1.37	1,181.8	154.0	144.9	1.6
9-13	B-	1.99	1.37	1,080.1	137.9	152.8	2.0
2013	B-	2.05	1.42	1,097.7	148.5	197.1	11.1
2012	B-	2.04	1.45	968.6	137.7	350.9	19.7
2011	B-	1.73	1.35	693.5	129.4	188.5	4.0
2010	B-	1.92	1.55	572.3	126.8	140.3	2.3
2009	B-	1.90	1.57	501.6	133.9	68.0	3.3

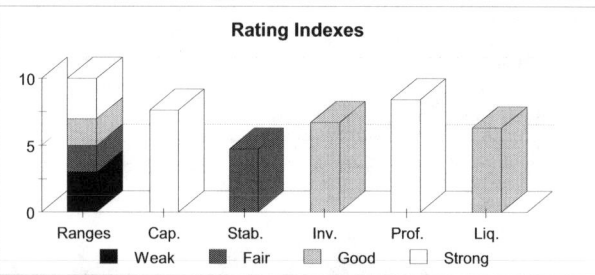

OZARK NATIONAL LIFE INSURANCE COMPANY   B-   Good

Major Rating Factors: Good liquidity (6.5 on a scale of 0 to 10) with sufficient resources to handle a spike in claims as well as a significant increase in policy surrenders. Fair overall results on stability tests (4.9). Weak profitability (2.7) with investment income below regulatory standards in relation to interest assumptions of reserves.

Other Rating Factors: Strong capitalization (10.0) based on excellent risk adjusted capital (severe loss scenario). High quality investment portfolio (8.2).

Principal Business: Individual life insurance (99%).

Principal Investments: NonCMO investment grade bonds (82%), CMOs and structured securities (13%), policy loans (3%), cash (1%), and real estate (1%).

Investments in Affiliates: None

Group Affiliation: CNS Corp

Licensed in: AL, AZ, AR, CA, CO, FL, GA, IL, IN, IA, KS, KY, LA, MI, MN, MS, MO, MT, NE, NV, NM, ND, OH, OK, SD, TN, TX, UT, WI, WY

Commenced Business: June 1964

Address: 500 E 9th St, Kansas City, MO 64106

Phone: (816) 842-6300 **Domicile State:** MO **NAIC Code:** 67393

Data Date	Rating	RACR #1	RACR #2	Total Assets ($mil)	Capital ($mil)	Net Premium ($mil)	Net Income ($mil)
9-14	B-	5.04	3.01	743.3	122.9	61.4	9.2
9-13	B-	5.05	3.00	725.4	122.3	61.2	10.4
2013	B-	5.07	3.02	730.6	123.4	82.3	14.9
2012	B-	5.05	3.00	711.4	122.1	82.0	15.4
2011	B-	5.45	3.30	690.6	118.7	82.9	16.9
2010	B	5.46	3.30	669.0	114.9	84.3	19.8
2009	B	5.00	2.99	642.9	107.3	85.8	23.2

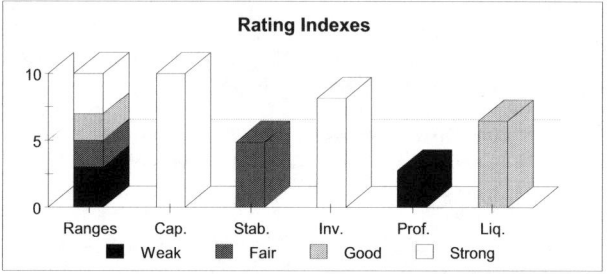

PACIFIC CENTURY LIFE INSURANCE CORPORATION   B   Good

Major Rating Factors: Good overall results on stability tests (6.1 on a scale of 0 to 10). Stability strengths include good operational trends and excellent risk diversification. Strong capitalization (10.0) based on excellent risk adjusted capital (severe loss scenario). High quality investment portfolio (7.4).

Other Rating Factors: Excellent profitability (7.1) with operating gains in each of the last five years. Excellent liquidity (10.0).

Principal Business: Reinsurance (84%), credit life insurance (15%), and credit health insurance (1%).

Principal Investments: Mortgages in good standing (86%), cash (10%), and nonCMO investment grade bonds (5%).

Investments in Affiliates: None

Group Affiliation: Bank of Hawaii Corp

Licensed in: AZ, HI

Commenced Business: February 1982

Address: 2700 N Third St Ste 2000, Phoenix, AZ 85004

Phone: (602) 200-6900 **Domicile State:** AZ **NAIC Code:** 93815

Data Date	Rating	RACR #1	RACR #2	Total Assets ($mil)	Capital ($mil)	Net Premium ($mil)	Net Income ($mil)
9-14	B	30.50	19.74	342.4	338.2	0.7	5.5
9-13	B-	29.83	21.99	334.8	330.9	0.9	5.5
2013	B	30.00	22.50	336.8	332.8	1.1	7.4
2012	B-	30.00	25.79	336.7	332.8	1.1	7.3
2011	C+	29.82	22.97	333.4	329.8	0.7	7.7
2010	C+	29.27	21.94	324.8	321.4	0.3	8.6
2009	C+	29.62	19.57	330.4	326.5	0.5	10.2

Adverse Trends in Operations

Change in premium mix from 2010 to 2011 (12.1%)
Decrease in asset base during 2010 (2%)
Decrease in capital during 2010 (2%)
Change in premium mix from 2009 to 2010 (6.4%)
Decrease in premium volume from 2009 to 2010 (35%)

PACIFIC GUARDIAN LIFE INSURANCE COMPANY LIMITED *   A-   Excellent

Major Rating Factors: Good quality investment portfolio (6.6 on a scale of 0 to 10) despite large exposure to mortgages . Mortgage default rate has been low. substantial holdings of BBB bonds in addition to no exposure to junk bonds. Good liquidity (6.2) with sufficient resources to handle a spike in claims as well as a significant increase in policy surrenders. Strong capitalization (9.7) based on excellent risk adjusted capital (severe loss scenario).

Other Rating Factors: Excellent profitability (7.7) with operating gains in each of the last five years. Excellent overall results on stability tests (7.0) excellent operational trends and excellent risk diversification.

Principal Business: Individual life insurance (42%), group health insurance (42%), and group life insurance (16%).

Principal Investments: NonCMO investment grade bonds (41%), mortgages in good standing (35%), CMOs and structured securities (18%), and policy loans (6%).

Investments in Affiliates: None

Group Affiliation: Meiji Yasuda Life Ins Co

Licensed in: AK, AZ, CA, CO, HI, ID, IA, LA, MO, MT, NE, NV, NM, OK, OR, SD, TX, UT, WA, WY

Commenced Business: June 1962

Address: 1440 Kapiolani Blvd Ste 1700, Honolulu, HI 96814

Phone: (808) 955-2236 **Domicile State:** HI **NAIC Code:** 64343

Data Date	Rating	RACR #1	RACR #2	Total Assets ($mil)	Capital ($mil)	Net Premium ($mil)	Net Income ($mil)
9-14	A-	4.95	2.83	511.7	107.2	52.8	5.8
9-13	A-	4.78	2.76	502.6	99.5	53.4	5.2
2013	A-	5.09	2.93	504.7	108.0	69.8	6.9
2012	A-	4.98	2.91	486.8	99.8	70.5	6.2
2011	A-	4.90	2.87	464.2	99.6	66.3	7.0
2010	A-	4.84	2.85	448.4	96.4	63.4	9.9
2009	A-	3.73	2.23	433.3	87.5	66.3	6.6

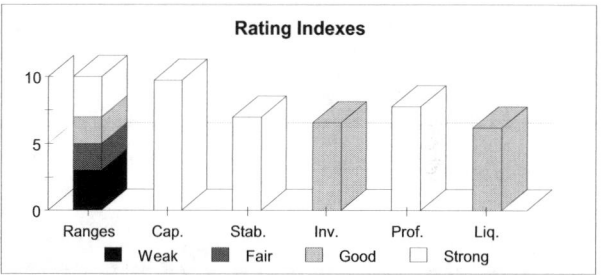

Rating Indexes

Ranges · Cap. · Stab. · Inv. · Prof. · Liq.
■ Weak ▨ Fair ▨ Good □ Strong

PACIFIC LIFE & ANNUITY COMPANY *   B+   Good

Major Rating Factors: Good quality investment portfolio (6.4 on a scale of 0 to 10) despite significant exposure to mortgages . Mortgage default rate has been low. large holdings of BBB rated bonds in addition to minimal holdings in junk bonds. Good overall profitability (6.7). Return on equity has been good over the last five years, averaging 13.4%. Good overall results on stability tests (6.8) good operational trends and excellent risk diversification.

Other Rating Factors: Strong capitalization (9.3) based on excellent risk adjusted capital (severe loss scenario). Excellent liquidity (7.9).

Principal Business: Individual annuities (93%), individual life insurance (4%), and reinsurance (2%).

Principal Investments: NonCMO investment grade bonds (75%), mortgages in good standing (14%), CMOs and structured securities (9%), and noninv. grade bonds (1%).

Investments in Affiliates: None

Group Affiliation: Pacific LifeCorp

Licensed in: All states except PR

Commenced Business: July 1983

Address: 638 N Fifth Ave, Phoenix, AZ 85003

Phone: (714) 640-3011 **Domicile State:** AZ **NAIC Code:** 97268

Data Date	Rating	RACR #1	RACR #2	Total Assets ($mil)	Capital ($mil)	Net Premium ($mil)	Net Income ($mil)
9-14	B+	5.18	2.54	6,110.8	540.3	369.5	44.2
9-13	B+	5.10	2.49	5,675.0	526.8	310.1	41.3
2013	B+	5.06	2.49	5,819.5	495.4	455.5	45.8
2012	B+	4.86	2.33	5,329.8	488.6	384.9	84.0
2011	B+	5.53	2.56	4,927.2	447.7	747.5	17.0
2010	A-	5.98	2.83	4,285.4	423.9	641.5	50.1
2009	A-	6.32	3.00	3,539.1	371.0	804.7	117.5

Adverse Trends in Operations

Decrease in premium volume from 2011 to 2012 (49%)
Decrease in premium volume from 2009 to 2010 (20%)
Increase in policy surrenders from 2009 to 2010 (75%)

PACIFIC LIFE INSURANCE COMPANY *

A-   Excellent

Major Rating Factors: Good quality investment portfolio (5.9 on a scale of 0 to 10) despite significant exposure to mortgages . Mortgage default rate has been low. large holdings of BBB rated bonds in addition to small junk bond holdings. Good liquidity (6.8) with sufficient resources to handle a spike in claims as well as a significant increase in policy surrenders. Good overall results on stability tests (6.9) excellent operational trends and excellent risk diversification.

Other Rating Factors: Fair profitability (3.0) with investment income below regulatory standards in relation to interest assumptions of reserves. Strong capitalization (7.7) based on excellent risk adjusted capital (severe loss scenario).

Principal Business: Individual annuities (65%), individual life insurance (28%), reinsurance (5%), and group retirement contracts (2%).

Principal Investments: NonCMO investment grade bonds (46%), mortgages in good standing (16%), policy loans (15%), CMOs and structured securities (11%), and misc. investments (10%).

Investments in Affiliates: 5%

Group Affiliation: Pacific LifeCorp

Licensed in: All states except NY, PR

Commenced Business: May 1868

Address: 1299 Farnam St, Omaha, NE 68102

Phone: (714) 630-3011 **Domicile State:** NE **NAIC Code:** 67466

Data Date	Rating	RACR #1	RACR #2	Total Assets ($mil)	Capital ($mil)	Net Premium ($mil)	Net Income ($mil)
9-14	A-	2.17	1.45	111,429	7,258.6	6,202.6	479.2
9-13	A-	1.96	1.29	105,898	6,279.5	6,146.3	374.2
2013	A-	2.01	1.36	109,065	6,502.9	8,702.0	521.4
2012	A-	2.02	1.33	101,001	6,175.1	7,606.7	961.8
2011	A-	2.03	1.35	95,724.4	5,577.0	5,911.2	-735.5
2010	A-	2.32	1.40	98,780.9	5,866.7	5,238.7	741.4
2009	A-	2.72	1.45	94,738.5	5,005.9	8,579.3	651.8

Adverse Trends in Operations

Decrease in capital during 2011 (5%)
Decrease in asset base during 2011 (3%)
Decrease in premium volume from 2009 to 2010 (39%)

PACIFICARE LIFE & HEALTH INSURANCE COMPANY

C+   Fair

Major Rating Factors: Fair overall results on stability tests (3.4 on a scale of 0 to 10) including fair financial strength of affiliated UnitedHealth Group Inc. Good overall profitability (6.4). Excellent expense controls. Return on equity has been fair, averaging 9.5%. Strong capitalization (10.0) based on excellent risk adjusted capital (severe loss scenario).

Other Rating Factors: High quality investment portfolio (8.4). Excellent liquidity (9.3).

Principal Business: Group health insurance (58%) and individual health insurance (42%).

Principal Investments: NonCMO investment grade bonds (86%) and CMOs and structured securities (15%).

Investments in Affiliates: None

Group Affiliation: UnitedHealth Group Inc

Licensed in: All states except NY, PR

Commenced Business: September 1967

Address: 23046 Avenida Dela Carlota 700, Laguna Hills, CA 92653-1519

Phone: (714) 226-3321 **Domicile State:** IN **NAIC Code:** 70785

Data Date	Rating	RACR #1	RACR #2	Total Assets ($mil)	Capital ($mil)	Net Premium ($mil)	Net Income ($mil)
9-14	C+	39.64	25.83	554.1	539.3	28.9	5.0
9-13	C+	26.75	17.60	619.0	592.7	81.8	13.2
2013	C+	29.46	19.62	616.2	592.6	104.7	13.2
2012	C+	23.08	15.56	622.2	582.0	139.3	18.7
2011	C+	19.76	14.03	695.3	650.6	205.8	87.4
2010	B-	20.19	14.98	848.3	677.6	225.6	117.6
2009	B-	15.23	11.50	745.7	680.5	322.1	120.7

UnitedHealth Group Inc
Composite Group Rating: C+
Largest Group Members

	Assets ($mil)	Rating
UNITED HEALTHCARE INS CO	14513	C
OXFORD HEALTH INS INC	2078	C+
UNITED HEALTHCARE INS CO OF NY	1983	B-
OXFORD HEALTH PLANS (NY) INC	1820	A+
UNITEDHEALTHCARE PLAN RIVER VALLEY	1094	B+

PAN-AMERICAN LIFE INSURANCE COMPANY

B   Good

Major Rating Factors: Good quality investment portfolio (5.4 on a scale of 0 to 10) despite mixed results such as: large holdings of BBB rated bonds but moderate junk bond exposure. Good overall profitability (6.4). Return on equity has been fair, averaging 7.0%. Good liquidity (6.2) with sufficient resources to handle a spike in claims as well as a significant increase in policy surrenders.

Other Rating Factors: Good overall results on stability tests (6.0) despite negative cash flow from operations for 2013 excellent operational trends and excellent risk diversification. Strong capitalization (7.6) based on excellent risk adjusted capital (severe loss scenario).

Principal Business: Group health insurance (65%), individual life insurance (15%), reinsurance (11%), individual health insurance (5%), and group life insurance (3%).

Principal Investments: NonCMO investment grade bonds (67%), noninv. grade bonds (9%), CMOs and structured securities (7%), policy loans (6%), and misc. investments (10%).

Investments in Affiliates: 2%

Group Affiliation: Pan-American Life

Licensed in: All states except ME, NY, VT

Commenced Business: March 1912

Address: Pan American Life Center, New Orleans, LA 70130

Phone: (504) 566-1300 **Domicile State:** LA **NAIC Code:** 67539

Data Date	Rating	RACR #1	RACR #2	Total Assets ($mil)	Capital ($mil)	Net Premium ($mil)	Net Income ($mil)
9-14	B	2.27	1.41	1,424.5	254.4	204.7	17.2
9-13	B	2.15	1.32	1,457.7	237.9	204.3	24.3
2013	B	2.29	1.43	1,425.5	244.6	270.3	27.3
2012	B	2.12	1.31	1,444.4	226.6	255.0	15.3
2011	B	2.36	1.45	1,478.2	248.4	239.3	23.0
2010	B	2.41	1.45	1,487.7	256.7	218.3	24.8
2009	B	2.48	1.47	1,515.4	259.4	190.3	9.0

Rating Indexes

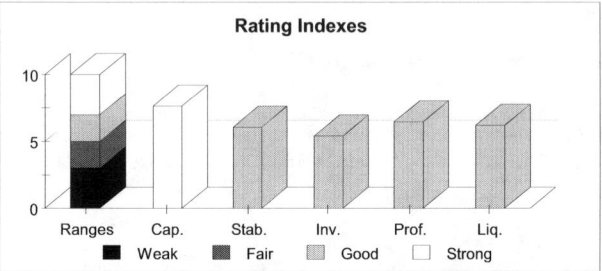

PARAGON LIFE INSURANCE COMPANY OF INDIANA   B-   Good

Major Rating Factors: Good capitalization (5.1 on a scale of 0 to 10) based on good risk adjusted capital (moderate loss scenario). Good overall profitability (6.8). Excellent expense controls. Good liquidity (6.5) with sufficient resources to cover a large increase in policy surrenders.

Other Rating Factors: Fair quality investment portfolio (4.5). Fair overall results on stability tests (4.9) including lack of operational experience, fair risk adjusted capital in prior years.

Principal Business: Reinsurance (100%).

Principal Investments: CMOs and structured securities (43%), mortgages in good standing (19%), cash (13%), nonCMO investment grade bonds (11%), and common & preferred stock (5%).

Investments in Affiliates: 16%

Group Affiliation: Sammons Enterprises Inc

Licensed in: DE, IN

Commenced Business: February 2011

Address: 8425 Woodfield Crossing #305 E, Indianapolis, IN 46240

Phone: (317) 396-9953   **Domicile State:** IN   **NAIC Code:** 14029

Data Date	Rating	RACR #1	RACR #2	Total Assets ($mil)	Capital ($mil)	Net Premium ($mil)	Net Income ($mil)
9-14	B-	1.04	0.62	1,833.4	76.2	84.5	10.6
9-13	B-	0.90	0.56	1,792.1	72.6	161.0	11.3
2013	B-	1.02	0.62	1,792.7	71.2	189.2	20.9
2012	B-	0.88	0.57	1,697.7	66.6	292.9	6.0
2011	B-	1.83	1.07	1,490.5	56.7	355.0	-1.5
2010	N/A	N/A	N/A	0.0	0.0	0.0	0.0
2009	N/A	N/A	N/A	0.0	0.0	0.0	0.0

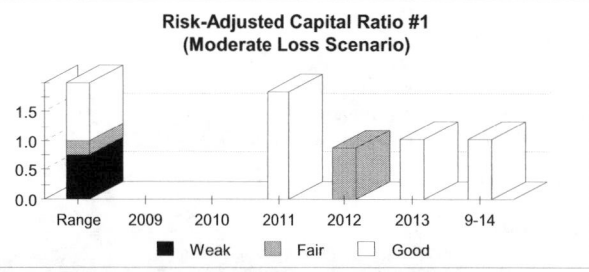

**Risk-Adjusted Capital Ratio #1
(Moderate Loss Scenario)**

Range, 2009, 2010, 2011, 2012, 2013, 9-14

■ Weak   ▨ Fair   □ Good

PARK AVENUE LIFE INSURANCE COMPANY *   B+   Good

Major Rating Factors: Good quality investment portfolio (6.2 on a scale of 0 to 10) despite mixed results such as: no exposure to mortgages and large holdings of BBB rated bonds but small junk bond holdings. Good liquidity (6.2) with sufficient resources to handle a spike in claims as well as a significant increase in policy surrenders. Good overall results on stability tests (6.7) despite negative cash flow from operations for 2013 good operational trends and excellent risk diversification.

Other Rating Factors: Strong capitalization (8.0) based on excellent risk adjusted capital (severe loss scenario). Excellent profitability (7.8) with operating gains in each of the last five years.

Principal Business: Reinsurance (74%) and individual life insurance (26%).

Principal Investments: NonCMO investment grade bonds (84%), common & preferred stock (9%), noninv. grade bonds (4%), CMOs and structured securities (1%), and misc. investments (2%).

Investments in Affiliates: 9%

Group Affiliation: Guardian Group

Licensed in: All states except HI, NY, PR

Commenced Business: April 1965

Address: 9100 Keystone Crossing Ste 600, Indianapolis, IN 46240

Phone: (212) 598-8179   **Domicile State:** DE   **NAIC Code:** 60003

Data Date	Rating	RACR #1	RACR #2	Total Assets ($mil)	Capital ($mil)	Net Premium ($mil)	Net Income ($mil)
9-14	B+	2.10	1.66	303.3	75.7	2.1	3.7
9-13	B	1.96	1.50	308.6	65.6	2.3	3.7
2013	B	1.94	1.54	305.8	67.8	3.0	6.7
2012	B	1.79	1.38	309.9	57.7	3.4	5.3
2011	B	1.56	1.25	307.0	55.4	3.9	0.7
2010	B	1.41	1.17	319.7	64.9	4.3	38.2
2009	B	1.49	1.37	419.4	156.2	4.8	6.3

Adverse Trends in Operations

Decrease in premium volume from 2012 to 2013 (11%)
Decrease in capital during 2011 (15%)
Decrease in premium volume from 2009 to 2010 (10%)
Decrease in asset base during 2010 (24%)
Decrease in capital during 2010 (58%)

PARKER CENTENNIAL ASSURANCE COMPANY *   A   Excellent

Major Rating Factors: Excellent overall results on stability tests (7.7 on a scale of 0 to 10). Strengths that enhance stability include excellent operational trends and excellent risk diversification. Strong capitalization (10.0) based on excellent risk adjusted capital (severe loss scenario). Furthermore, this high level of risk adjusted capital has been consistently maintained over the last five years. High quality investment portfolio (8.5).

Other Rating Factors: Excellent profitability (8.3) with operating gains in each of the last five years. Excellent liquidity (10.0).

Principal Business: Group retirement contracts (100%).

Principal Investments: NonCMO investment grade bonds (99%) and noninv. grade bonds (1%).

Investments in Affiliates: None

Group Affiliation: Sentry Ins Group

Licensed in: All states except NY, PR

Commenced Business: August 1973

Address: 2345 Waukegan Rd #5210, Bannockburn, IL 60015-1553

Phone: (614) 764-7000   **Domicile State:** WI   **NAIC Code:** 71099

Data Date	Rating	RACR #1	RACR #2	Total Assets ($mil)	Capital ($mil)	Net Premium ($mil)	Net Income ($mil)
9-14	A	5.71	5.14	89.4	47.1	4.5	1.3
9-13	B+	5.79	5.21	83.6	46.9	2.6	1.2
2013	A	5.55	5.00	84.4	45.8	5.0	1.6
2012	B+	5.64	5.07	81.2	45.7	5.1	1.6
2011	B	5.58	5.02	76.6	44.2	2.8	1.8
2010	B	5.47	4.92	73.0	42.4	4.3	1.4
2009	B	5.42	4.88	68.6	41.1	2.8	1.5

Adverse Trends in Operations

Decrease in premium volume from 2012 to 2013 (2%)
Decrease in premium volume from 2010 to 2011 (36%)

PAUL REVERE LIFE INSURANCE COMPANY — C+ — Fair

Major Rating Factors: Fair overall results on stability tests (4.8 on a scale of 0 to 10) including fair financial strength of affiliated Unum Group and negative cash flow from operations for 2013. Fair quality investment portfolio (3.7) with large holdings of BBB rated bonds in addition to significant exposure to junk bonds. Good capitalization (6.3) based on good risk adjusted capital (severe loss scenario).

Other Rating Factors: Good overall profitability (5.9). Excellent liquidity (7.6).
Principal Business: Individual health insurance (66%), reinsurance (28%), group health insurance (4%), and individual life insurance (3%).
Principal Investments: NonCMO investment grade bonds (78%), noninv. grade bonds (7%), CMOs and structured securities (6%), common & preferred stock (5%), and mortgages in good standing (3%).
Investments in Affiliates: 3%
Group Affiliation: Unum Group
Licensed in: All states except PR
Commenced Business: July 1930
Address: 18 Chestnut St, Worcester, MA 01608
Phone: (508) 792-6377 **Domicile State:** MA **NAIC Code:** 67598

Data Date	Rating	RACR #1	RACR #2	Total Assets ($mil)	Capital ($mil)	Net Premium ($mil)	Net Income ($mil)
9-14	C+	1.42	0.91	4,144.1	260.0	69.1	58.1
9-13	C+	1.99	1.24	4,357.0	369.1	68.7	50.7
2013	C+	1.78	1.13	4,301.8	336.1	90.4	66.5
2012	C+	1.99	1.23	4,458.2	368.3	91.9	81.7
2011	C+	2.21	1.36	4,602.4	408.0	93.4	89.8
2010	C+	2.25	1.39	4,678.4	419.5	90.4	64.9
2009	C+	2.54	1.54	4,744.8	450.5	92.0	131.4

Unum Group Composite Group Rating: C+ Largest Group Members	Assets ($mil)	Rating
UNUM LIFE INS CO OF AMERICA	19079	C+
PROVIDENT LIFE ACCIDENT INS CO	8348	C+
PAUL REVERE LIFE INS CO	4302	C+
COLONIAL LIFE ACCIDENT INS CO	2753	C+
FIRST UNUM LIFE INS CO	2704	C+

PAUL REVERE VARIABLE ANNUITY INSURANCE COMPANY — C — Fair

Major Rating Factors: Fair overall results on stability tests (3.8 on a scale of 0 to 10). Good quality investment portfolio (5.7) despite mixed results such as: no exposure to mortgages and large holdings of BBB rated bonds but no exposure to junk bonds. Weak profitability (2.2) with investment income below regulatory standards in relation to interest assumptions of reserves.

Other Rating Factors: Strong capitalization (8.0) based on excellent risk adjusted capital (severe loss scenario). Excellent liquidity (9.0).
Principal Business: Individual life insurance (100%).
Principal Investments: NonCMO investment grade bonds (80%), CMOs and structured securities (17%), and cash (1%).
Investments in Affiliates: None
Group Affiliation: Unum Group
Licensed in: All states except AK, NY, PR
Commenced Business: February 1966
Address: 18 Chestnut St, Worcester, MA 01608-0000
Phone: (508) 792-6377 **Domicile State:** MA **NAIC Code:** 67601

Data Date	Rating	RACR #1	RACR #2	Total Assets ($mil)	Capital ($mil)	Net Premium ($mil)	Net Income ($mil)
9-14	C	6.47	4.20	56.7	41.3	0.0	1.7
9-13	C	6.31	3.84	54.3	39.8	0.0	1.8
2013	C	6.30	3.80	54.8	40.1	0.0	2.2
2012	C	6.13	3.52	53.6	38.5	0.0	2.3
2011	C	5.81	3.59	55.8	36.9	0.0	2.5
2010	C	5.70	3.31	51.6	35.1	0.0	4.5
2009	C	5.32	2.69	49.1	31.8	0.0	7.1

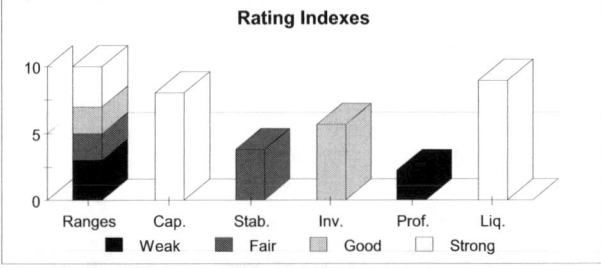

Rating Indexes

Ranges, Cap., Stab., Inv., Prof., Liq.
■ Weak ▨ Fair ▧ Good ☐ Strong

PAVONIA LIFE INSURANCE COMPANY OF MICHIGAN — C — Fair

Major Rating Factors: Fair overall results on stability tests (3.6 on a scale of 0 to 10) including fair financial strength of affiliated Enstar Group Limited and negative cash flow from operations for 2013. Weak profitability (1.4). Excellent expense controls. Return on equity has been low, averaging -4.8%. Strong capitalization (7.5) based on excellent risk adjusted capital (severe loss scenario).

Other Rating Factors: High quality investment portfolio (7.1). Excellent liquidity (7.0).
Principal Business: Credit life insurance (28%), individual life insurance (25%), reinsurance (20%), credit health insurance (13%), and other lines (14%).
Principal Investments: NonCMO investment grade bonds (78%), common & preferred stock (6%), policy loans (6%), CMOs and structured securities (6%), and cash (4%).
Investments in Affiliates: 3%
Group Affiliation: Enstar Group Limited
Licensed in: All states except NY, PR
Commenced Business: January 1981
Address: 500 Woodward Ave., Ste 4000, Detroit, MI 48226
Phone: (810) 848-7811 **Domicile State:** MI **NAIC Code:** 93777

Data Date	Rating	RACR #1	RACR #2	Total Assets ($mil)	Capital ($mil)	Net Premium ($mil)	Net Income ($mil)
9-14	C	1.85	1.35	389.8	79.0	73.5	4.2
9-13	C	1.82	1.40	429.4	78.9	84.2	8.2
2013	C	2.39	1.77	445.9	99.8	112.0	25.1
2012	C	1.51	1.17	432.1	65.5	144.7	-45.5
2011	B	6.69	5.17	707.1	356.8	171.2	7.1
2010	B	6.41	5.04	769.2	382.1	171.8	22.6
2009	B	5.49	4.27	797.4	351.7	207.1	18.7

Enstar Group Limited Composite Group Rating: C- Largest Group Members	Assets ($mil)	Rating
SEABRIGHT INS CO	714	D+
CLARENDON NATIONAL INS CO	643	C
PAVONIA LIFE INS CO OF MICHIGAN	446	C
TORUS SPECIALTY INS CO	182	C-
TORUS NATIONAL INS CO	140	C

PEKIN LIFE INSURANCE COMPANY   B   Good

Major Rating Factors: Good overall profitability (6.4 on a scale of 0 to 10). Return on equity has been low, averaging 1.1%. Good liquidity (5.9) with sufficient resources to cover a large increase in policy surrenders. Good overall results on stability tests (6.2). Stability strengths include excellent operational trends and excellent risk diversification.

Other Rating Factors: Strong capitalization (7.6) based on excellent risk adjusted capital (severe loss scenario). High quality investment portfolio (7.0).

Principal Business: Individual life insurance (29%), group health insurance (22%), group life insurance (18%), individual health insurance (12%), and other lines (19%).

Principal Investments: NonCMO investment grade bonds (66%), CMOs and structured securities (25%), policy loans (1%), and common & preferred stock (1%).

Investments in Affiliates: None

Group Affiliation: Farmers Automobile Ins Assn

Licensed in: AL, AZ, AR, IL, IN, IA, KS, KY, LA, MI, MN, MS, MO, NE, OH, PA, TN, VA, WI

Commenced Business: September 1965

Address: 2505 Court St, Pekin, IL 61558

Phone: (309) 346-1161 **Domicile State:** IL **NAIC Code:** 67628

Data Date	Rating	RACR #1	RACR #2	Total Assets ($mil)	Capital ($mil)	Net Premium ($mil)	Net Income ($mil)
9-14	B	2.32	1.41	1,323.2	125.9	155.5	5.5
9-13	B	2.18	1.35	1,291.0	118.9	171.9	2.9
2013	B	2.24	1.37	1,301.6	122.7	227.0	2.4
2012	B	2.24	1.39	1,209.2	119.2	221.1	7.6
2011	B+	2.31	1.44	1,124.2	117.9	224.4	3.1
2010	B+	2.08	1.32	1,095.9	112.9	245.8	4.2
2009	B+	2.26	1.44	926.0	111.8	245.4	-2.7

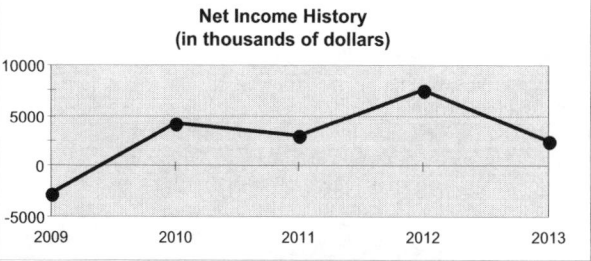

Net Income History
(in thousands of dollars)

PENN INSURANCE & ANNUITY COMPANY   B   Good

Major Rating Factors: Good quality investment portfolio (6.8 on a scale of 0 to 10) despite mixed results such as: no exposure to mortgages and substantial holdings of BBB bonds but small junk bond holdings. Good liquidity (6.1) with sufficient resources to handle a spike in claims as well as a significant increase in policy surrenders. Good overall results on stability tests (5.0) good operational trends, excellent risk adjusted capital for prior years and excellent risk diversification.

Other Rating Factors: Fair overall capitalization (4.0) based on mixed results -- excessive policy leverage mitigated by excellent risk adjusted capital (severe loss scenario). Weak profitability (2.8) with investment income below regulatory standards in relation to interest assumptions of reserves.

Principal Business: Individual life insurance (87%) and reinsurance (13%).

Principal Investments: NonCMO investment grade bonds (53%), CMOs and structured securities (20%), policy loans (19%), and noninv. grade bonds (2%).

Investments in Affiliates: 3%

Group Affiliation: Penn Mutual Group

Licensed in: All states except NH, NY, PR

Commenced Business: April 1981

Address: 1209 Orange St, Wilmington, DE 19801

Phone: (215) 956-8000 **Domicile State:** DE **NAIC Code:** 93262

Data Date	Rating	RACR #1	RACR #2	Total Assets ($mil)	Capital ($mil)	Net Premium ($mil)	Net Income ($mil)
9-14	B	3.63	1.93	2,542.5	334.1	152.0	21.0
9-13	B	2.71	1.41	2,256.9	225.5	192.6	-3.7
2013	B	2.73	1.73	2,307.3	310.7	-108.0	-2.4
2012	B	2.57	1.38	2,027.0	190.4	411.7	-24.1
2011	B	2.21	1.18	1,592.9	131.2	345.7	-15.9
2010	B	2.54	1.38	1,275.8	105.1	227.5	-34.1
2009	B+	2.98	1.61	1,092.2	103.6	97.9	-2.1

Adverse Trends in Operations

Increase in policy surrenders from 2012 to 2013 (48%)
Decrease in premium volume from 2012 to 2013 (126%)
Increase in policy surrenders from 2011 to 2012 (27%)
Increase in policy surrenders from 2010 to 2011 (45%)

PENN MUTUAL LIFE INSURANCE COMPANY   B   Good

Major Rating Factors: Good quality investment portfolio (6.4 on a scale of 0 to 10) despite mixed results such as: no exposure to mortgages and substantial holdings of BBB bonds but minimal holdings in junk bonds. Good liquidity (6.3) with sufficient resources to handle a spike in claims as well as a significant increase in policy surrenders. Good overall results on stability tests (6.1) excellent operational trends and excellent risk diversification.

Other Rating Factors: Fair profitability (3.8). Strong capitalization (7.7) based on excellent risk adjusted capital (severe loss scenario).

Principal Business: Individual life insurance (47%), individual annuities (45%), group retirement contracts (4%), reinsurance (3%), and individual health insurance (1%).

Principal Investments: NonCMO investment grade bonds (53%), CMOs and structured securities (28%), common & preferred stock (4%), policy loans (3%), and noninv. grade bonds (2%).

Investments in Affiliates: 6%

Group Affiliation: Penn Mutual Group

Licensed in: All states except PR

Commenced Business: May 1847

Address: 600 Dresher Rd, Horsham, PA 19044

Phone: (215) 956-8000 **Domicile State:** PA **NAIC Code:** 67644

Data Date	Rating	RACR #1	RACR #2	Total Assets ($mil)	Capital ($mil)	Net Premium ($mil)	Net Income ($mil)
9-14	B	2.22	1.48	16,715.6	1,541.9	1,070.9	1.1
9-13	A-	2.49	1.57	15,524.7	1,439.7	1,122.9	-27.0
2013	B	2.19	1.48	15,945.2	1,490.7	1,483.0	-34.4
2012	A-	2.67	1.70	14,330.7	1,495.4	1,616.8	-38.9
2011	A-	3.25	2.00	13,059.8	1,542.7	1,484.9	12.4
2010	A-	3.31	2.02	12,217.5	1,520.9	1,405.4	-15.2
2009	B+	3.49	2.10	10,939.5	1,364.3	1,317.5	70.8

Adverse Trends in Operations

Decrease in premium volume from 2012 to 2013 (8%)
Decrease in capital during 2012 (3%)

PHILADELPHIA AMERICAN LIFE INSURANCE COMPANY — B- — Good

Major Rating Factors: Good overall results on stability tests (5.0 on a scale of 0 to 10) despite fair financial strength of affiliated New Era Life Group. Other stability subfactors include excellent operational trends and good risk diversification. Good capitalization (5.9) based on good risk adjusted capital (severe loss scenario). Moreover, capital has steadily grown over the last five years. Good quality investment portfolio (5.0).

Other Rating Factors: Good liquidity (6.1). Excellent profitability (9.0) with operating gains in each of the last five years.

Principal Business: Individual health insurance (85%), individual annuities (11%), group health insurance (3%), and individual life insurance (1%).

Principal Investments: NonCMO investment grade bonds (60%), CMOs and structured securities (25%), noninv. grade bonds (8%), cash (3%), and mortgages in good standing (3%).

Investments in Affiliates: None

Group Affiliation: New Era Life Group

Licensed in: All states except NY, RI, PR

Commenced Business: March 1978

Address: 3121 Buffalo Speedway, Houston, TX 77098

Phone: (281) 368-7247 **Domicile State:** TX **NAIC Code:** 67784

Data Date	Rating	RACR #1	RACR #2	Total Assets ($mil)	Capital ($mil)	Net Premium ($mil)	Net Income ($mil)
9-14	B-	1.32	0.86	215.8	31.0	109.1	3.1
9-13	B-	1.32	0.84	203.9	27.1	89.2	1.5
2013	B-	1.38	0.88	205.7	29.0	120.4	3.1
2012	B-	1.68	0.99	197.6	26.1	69.5	4.3
2011	C+	1.70	0.95	194.8	24.5	62.9	3.4
2010	C	1.73	1.00	190.8	22.1	62.4	1.2
2009	C	1.71	0.96	175.2	20.9	51.3	0.2

New Era Life Group
Composite Group Rating: C

Largest Group Members	Assets ($mil)	Rating
NEW ERA LIFE INS CO	371	C
PHILADELPHIA AMERICAN LIFE INS CO	206	B-
NEW ERA LIFE INS CO OF THE MIDWEST	74	C
LIFE OF AMERICA INS CO	12	C

PHL VARIABLE INSURANCE COMPANY — C — Fair

Major Rating Factors: Fair overall results on stability tests (3.5 on a scale of 0 to 10). Good quality investment portfolio (6.1) despite mixed results such as: large holdings of BBB rated bonds but moderate junk bond exposure. Weak profitability (2.7). Return on equity has been fair, averaging 5.5%.

Other Rating Factors: Strong capitalization (7.4) based on excellent risk adjusted capital (severe loss scenario). Excellent liquidity (7.3).

Principal Business: Individual annuities (62%) and individual life insurance (37%).

Principal Investments: NonCMO investment grade bonds (55%), CMOs and structured securities (27%), cash (7%), noninv. grade bonds (4%), and policy loans (3%).

Investments in Affiliates: None

Group Affiliation: Phoenix Companies

Licensed in: All states except ME, NY

Commenced Business: July 1981

Address: 200 Park Ave 7th Floor, New York, NY 10166

Phone: (860) 403-1179 **Domicile State:** CT **NAIC Code:** 93548

Data Date	Rating	RACR #1	RACR #2	Total Assets ($mil)	Capital ($mil)	Net Premium ($mil)	Net Income ($mil)
9-14	C	2.52	1.29	6,426.3	252.4	705.6	19.7
9-13	C	3.12	1.57	5,950.9	272.2	646.4	23.4
2013	C	2.29	1.18	6,163.6	222.9	854.8	-86.1
2012	C	3.51	1.76	5,657.1	313.5	1,011.0	49.7
2011	C	2.84	1.46	5,438.3	312.8	1,168.2	61.4
2010	C	2.69	1.31	4,778.7	275.7	468.2	47.0
2009	C	2.22	1.07	4,586.3	235.7	364.2	-87.5

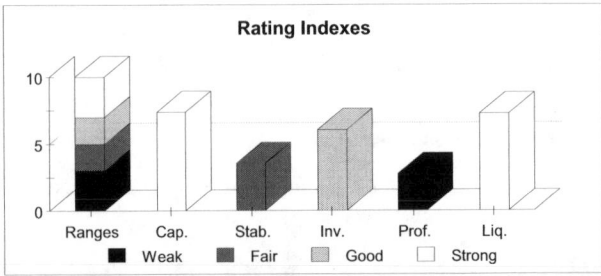

Rating Indexes
Ranges · Cap. · Stab. · Inv. · Prof. · Liq.
■ Weak ■ Fair ■ Good □ Strong

PHOENIX LIFE INSURANCE COMPANY — C — Fair

Major Rating Factors: Fair quality investment portfolio (4.9 on a scale of 0 to 10) with large holdings of BBB rated bonds in addition to significant exposure to junk bonds. Fair overall results on stability tests (4.2) including negative cash flow from operations for 2013, weak risk adjusted capital in prior years. Good capitalization (5.3) based on good risk adjusted capital (moderate loss scenario).

Other Rating Factors: Good overall profitability (5.1) although investment income, in comparison to reserve requirements, is below regulatory standards. Good liquidity (5.3).

Principal Business: Individual life insurance (92%), reinsurance (6%), individual annuities (1%), and group retirement contracts (1%).

Principal Investments: NonCMO investment grade bonds (43%), CMOs and structured securities (20%), policy loans (19%), noninv. grade bonds (6%), and misc. investments (11%).

Investments in Affiliates: 2%

Group Affiliation: Phoenix Companies

Licensed in: All states, the District of Columbia and Puerto Rico

Commenced Business: May 1851

Address: 100 Bright Meadow Blvd, Enfield, CT 06083-1900

Phone: (860) 403-1000 **Domicile State:** NY **NAIC Code:** 67814

Data Date	Rating	RACR #1	RACR #2	Total Assets ($mil)	Capital ($mil)	Net Premium ($mil)	Net Income ($mil)
9-14	C	1.18	0.72	13,326.4	619.9	229.8	85.0
9-13	C	1.06	0.67	13,583.8	643.4	238.2	-19.7
2013	C	1.12	0.68	13,564.2	597.0	330.1	-21.0
2012	C	1.20	0.74	13,837.2	793.6	366.5	156.2
2011	C	1.09	0.67	14,057.8	728.8	-2,429.2	95.0
2010	C	1.01	0.61	14,425.7	658.5	579.7	139.6
2009	C	0.82	0.49	14,654.5	517.2	647.4	-59.9

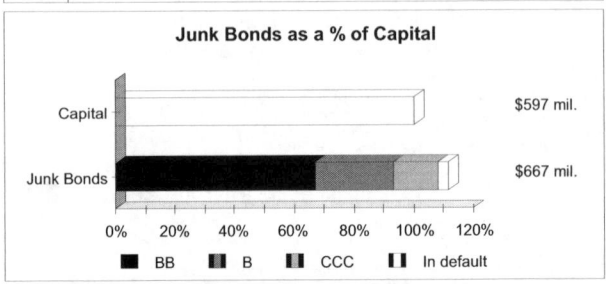

Junk Bonds as a % of Capital
Capital — $597 mil.
Junk Bonds — $667 mil.
0% 20% 40% 60% 80% 100% 120%
■ BB ■ B ■ CCC □ In default

PHYSICIANS LIFE INSURANCE COMPANY *

A-   Excellent

Major Rating Factors: Good quality investment portfolio (5.7 on a scale of 0 to 10) despite mixed results such as: large holdings of BBB rated bonds but junk bond exposure equal to 87% of capital. Good overall profitability (6.2). Return on equity has been fair, averaging 5.9%. Good liquidity (5.8).

Other Rating Factors: Good overall results on stability tests (6.9) excellent operational trends and excellent risk diversification. Strong capitalization (7.6) based on excellent risk adjusted capital (severe loss scenario).

Principal Business: Individual life insurance (47%), individual health insurance (25%), individual annuities (16%), group life insurance (11%), and reinsurance (1%).

Principal Investments: NonCMO investment grade bonds (66%), CMOs and structured securities (22%), noninv. grade bonds (8%), policy loans (2%), and common & preferred stock (1%).

Investments in Affiliates: None

Group Affiliation: Physicians Mutual Group

Licensed in: All states except NY, PR

Commenced Business: January 1970

Address: 2600 Dodge St, Omaha, NE 68131-2671

Phone: (402) 633-1000 **Domicile State:** NE **NAIC Code:** 72125

Data Date	Rating	RACR #1	RACR #2	Total Assets ($mil)	Capital ($mil)	Net Premium ($mil)	Net Income ($mil)
9-14	A-	2.89	1.41	1,421.0	124.1	194.1	5.1
9-13	A-	3.09	1.53	1,346.8	119.3	184.0	6.8
2013	A-	2.94	1.45	1,378.7	122.7	248.6	8.3
2012	A-	3.02	1.50	1,285.0	115.8	211.2	8.7
2011	A-	2.78	1.40	1,268.9	108.7	200.9	4.4
2010	A-	2.79	1.40	1,257.5	106.1	197.5	5.0
2009	A-	2.55	1.26	1,252.7	101.5	193.8	6.3

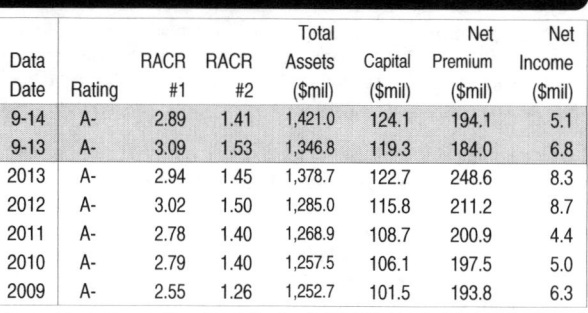

Rating Indexes

PHYSICIANS MUTUAL INSURANCE COMPANY *

A+   Excellent

Major Rating Factors: Good quality investment portfolio (6.5 on a scale of 0 to 10) despite mixed results such as: no exposure to mortgages and large holdings of BBB rated bonds but small junk bond holdings. Strong capitalization (10.0) based on excellent risk adjusted capital (severe loss scenario). Furthermore, this high level of risk adjusted capital has been consistently maintained over the last five years. Excellent profitability (8.9) with operating gains in each of the last five years.

Other Rating Factors: Excellent liquidity (7.4). Excellent overall results on stability tests (7.9) excellent operational trends and excellent risk diversification.

Principal Business: Individual health insurance (61%), reinsurance (36%), and group health insurance (4%).

Principal Investments: NonCMO investment grade bonds (72%), common & preferred stock (12%), noninv. grade bonds (8%), CMOs and structured securities (8%), and real estate (1%).

Investments in Affiliates: 7%

Group Affiliation: Physicians Mutual Group

Licensed in: All states except PR

Commenced Business: February 1902

Address: 2600 Dodge St, Omaha, NE 68131-2671

Phone: (402) 633-1000 **Domicile State:** NE **NAIC Code:** 80578

Data Date	Rating	RACR #1	RACR #2	Total Assets ($mil)	Capital ($mil)	Net Premium ($mil)	Net Income ($mil)
9-14	A+	4.31	3.25	1,989.7	964.3	317.1	35.1
9-13	A+	4.18	3.16	1,899.2	892.1	340.7	23.7
2013	A+	4.23	3.22	1,920.5	931.1	453.9	33.6
2012	A+	4.02	3.04	1,829.7	866.1	447.6	30.2
2011	A+	4.19	3.19	1,732.5	843.4	434.3	35.8
2010	A+	4.28	3.25	1,641.1	824.6	380.5	35.4
2009	A+	4.39	3.36	1,539.4	799.1	386.0	25.0

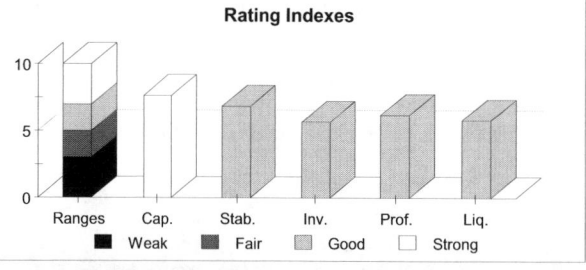

Rating Indexes

PIONEER MUTUAL LIFE INSURANCE COMPANY *

B+   Good

Major Rating Factors: Good overall results on stability tests (6.5 on a scale of 0 to 10). Stability strengths include excellent operational trends and excellent risk diversification. Good quality investment portfolio (6.8) despite mixed results such as: large holdings of BBB rated bonds but moderate junk bond exposure. Good overall profitability (6.3).

Other Rating Factors: Good liquidity (5.1). Strong capitalization (7.8) based on excellent risk adjusted capital (severe loss scenario).

Principal Business: Individual life insurance (93%) and individual annuities (6%).

Principal Investments: NonCMO investment grade bonds (56%), CMOs and structured securities (27%), mortgages in good standing (8%), policy loans (5%), and misc. investments (3%).

Investments in Affiliates: None

Group Affiliation: American United Life Group

Licensed in: All states except AK, NY, PR

Commenced Business: November 1947

Address: 203 N 10th St, Fargo, ND 58102

Phone: (701) 277-2300 **Domicile State:** ND **NAIC Code:** 67911

Data Date	Rating	RACR #1	RACR #2	Total Assets ($mil)	Capital ($mil)	Net Premium ($mil)	Net Income ($mil)
9-14	B+	2.93	1.55	510.6	43.3	20.5	3.5
9-13	B+	2.93	1.54	497.9	43.7	19.3	2.6
2013	B+	2.76	1.46	500.1	39.9	24.7	-1.4
2012	B+	2.81	1.47	492.2	41.1	26.1	1.6
2011	B	2.66	1.38	486.8	39.2	25.4	3.5
2010	B	2.54	1.34	477.5	35.5	28.1	3.9
2009	B	2.28	1.20	476.3	31.5	36.1	1.0

Adverse Trends in Operations

Decrease in premium volume from 2012 to 2013 (6%)
Decrease in capital during 2013 (3%)
Decrease in premium volume from 2010 to 2011 (10%)
Decrease in premium volume from 2009 to 2010 (22%)

PIONEER SECURITY LIFE INSURANCE COMPANY   C+   Fair

Major Rating Factors: Fair overall results on stability tests (4.8 on a scale of 0 to 10) including fair financial strength of affiliated Industrial Alliance Ins & Financial. Fair quality investment portfolio (3.6). Weak profitability (2.4) with investment income below regulatory standards in relation to interest assumptions of reserves.
Other Rating Factors: Strong capitalization (7.2) based on excellent risk adjusted capital (severe loss scenario). Excellent liquidity (7.0).
Principal Business: Individual life insurance (99%).
Principal Investments: Common & preferred stock (81%), nonCMO investment grade bonds (16%), and policy loans (1%).
Investments in Affiliates: 81%
Group Affiliation: Industrial Alliance Ins & Financial
Licensed in: AL, AR, CA, CO, DC, DE, FL, GA, HI, ID, IL, IN, KS, KY, LA, MD, MN, MS, MO, MT, NE, NM, NC, ND, OK, OR, PA, SC, SD, TN, TX, UT, VA, WA, WV, WI
Commenced Business: November 1956
Address: 425 Austin Ave, Waco, TX 76701
Phone: (254) 297-2778 **Domicile State:** TX **NAIC Code:** 67946

Data Date	Rating	RACR #1	RACR #2	Total Assets ($mil)	Capital ($mil)	Net Premium ($mil)	Net Income ($mil)
9-14	C+	1.20	1.16	122.2	100.7	5.7	5.0
9-13	C+	1.08	1.06	92.9	72.0	10.2	-2.3
2013	C+	1.11	1.10	109.7	89.3	10.1	2.0
2012	C+	1.10	1.09	89.6	73.1	9.9	6.8
2011	B-	1.06	1.04	84.3	62.6	6.8	4.0
2010	B-	1.31	1.29	96.7	77.2	4.5	0.5
2009	B-	1.29	1.27	100.0	76.5	4.8	3.1

Industrial Alliance Ins Financial Composite Group Rating: C Largest Group Members	Assets ($mil)	Rating
AMERICAN-AMICABLE LIFE INS CO OF TX	259	C
OCCIDENTAL LIFE INS CO OF NC	250	C
IA AMERICAN LIFE INS CO	221	C
INDUSTRIAL ALLIANCE INS FIN SERV	201	C
PIONEER SECURITY LIFE INS CO	110	C+

POPULAR LIFE RE   C+   Fair

Major Rating Factors: Fair overall results on stability tests (4.8 on a scale of 0 to 10). Good quality investment portfolio (5.8) with no exposure to mortgages and small junk bond holdings. Good overall profitability (6.6). Excellent expense controls. Return on equity has been good over the last five years, averaging 12.1%.
Other Rating Factors: Strong capitalization (10.0) based on excellent risk adjusted capital (severe loss scenario). Excellent liquidity (9.0).
Principal Business: Reinsurance (100%).
Principal Investments: NonCMO investment grade bonds (62%), CMOs and structured securities (20%), noninv. grade bonds (10%), cash (5%), and common & preferred stock (4%).
Investments in Affiliates: None
Group Affiliation: Popular Inc
Licensed in: PR
Commenced Business: December 2003
Address: Solar A Marginal Martinez Nada, Guaynabo, PR 00966
Phone: (787) 759-0080 **Domicile State:** PR **NAIC Code:** 11876

Data Date	Rating	RACR #1	RACR #2	Total Assets ($mil)	Capital ($mil)	Net Premium ($mil)	Net Income ($mil)
9-14	C+	4.21	3.35	55.6	28.8	14.6	1.7
9-13	C+	6.26	5.64	70.0	46.8	13.3	3.1
2013	C+	3.96	3.26	52.6	27.2	18.0	3.4
2012	C+	5.85	5.27	66.2	43.7	17.1	4.1
2011	C+	5.45	4.91	61.7	39.6	15.5	3.6
2010	C	5.06	2.80	58.3	35.6	13.4	4.1
2009	C	4.54	3.64	56.4	31.7	12.5	6.2

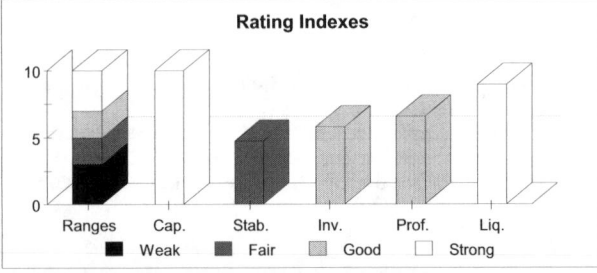

Rating Indexes

PRENEED REINSURANCE COMPANY OF AMERICA   B   Good

Major Rating Factors: Fair overall results on stability tests (4.2 on a scale of 0 to 10). Weak liquidity (2.0) as a spike in claims may stretch capacity. Strong capitalization (10.0) based on excellent risk adjusted capital (severe loss scenario). Moreover, capital has steadily grown over the last five years.
Other Rating Factors: High quality investment portfolio (9.0). Excellent profitability (9.6) with operating gains in each of the last five years.
Principal Business: Reinsurance (100%).
Principal Investments: NonCMO investment grade bonds (100%).
Investments in Affiliates: None
Group Affiliation: NGL Ins Group
Licensed in: AZ
Commenced Business: October 2001
Address: 3225 N Central Ave, Phoenix, AZ 85012
Phone: (608) 257-5612 **Domicile State:** AZ **NAIC Code:** 11155

Data Date	Rating	RACR #1	RACR #2	Total Assets ($mil)	Capital ($mil)	Net Premium ($mil)	Net Income ($mil)
9-14	B	6.82	6.14	32.9	30.8	75.9	3.8
9-13	B	6.25	5.62	27.4	25.4	76.2	3.7
2013	B	6.03	5.43	29.3	27.2	99.6	5.2
2012	B	5.58	5.02	25.1	23.1	101.4	5.8
2011	B	4.96	4.47	20.7	18.8	100.5	5.2
2010	B	4.18	3.76	16.0	14.3	97.7	3.7
2009	B	3.50	3.15	12.0	10.7	83.9	1.6

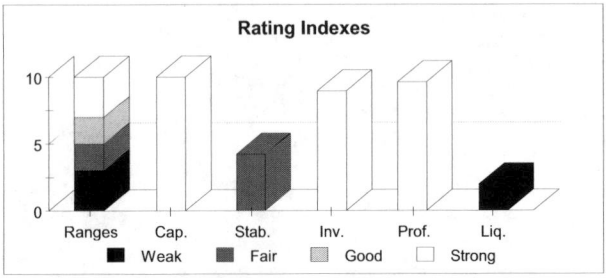

Rating Indexes

PRIMERICA LIFE INSURANCE COMPANY

B   **Good**

Major Rating Factors: Good liquidity (6.9 on a scale of 0 to 10) with sufficient resources to handle a spike in claims as well as a significant increase in policy surrenders. Good overall results on stability tests (5.8). Stability strengths include good operational trends and excellent risk diversification. Fair quality investment portfolio (4.3).

Other Rating Factors: Strong capitalization (7.6) based on excellent risk adjusted capital (severe loss scenario). Excellent profitability (7.4).

Principal Business: Individual life insurance (100%).

Principal Investments: NonCMO investment grade bonds (55%), common & preferred stock (25%), CMOs and structured securities (12%), and noninv. grade bonds (4%).

Investments in Affiliates: 23%

Group Affiliation: Primerica Inc

Licensed in: All states except NY

Commenced Business: January 1903

Address: One Federal Street, Boston, MA 02110

Phone: (770) 381-1000   **Domicile State:** MA   **NAIC Code:** 65919

Data Date	Rating	RACR #1	RACR #2	Total Assets ($mil)	Capital ($mil)	Net Premium ($mil)	Net Income ($mil)
9-14	B	1.69	1.38	1,474.0	651.8	219.1	225.4
9-13	B	1.52	1.26	1,401.2	548.7	184.0	235.4
2013	B	1.54	1.27	1,479.8	563.3	255.7	307.1
2012	B	1.80	1.49	1,569.7	670.4	230.5	257.3
2011	B	1.87	1.37	1,575.8	443.1	297.6	182.4
2010	B	2.77	2.04	1,777.6	629.8	-3,632.7	-1,766.6
2009	A-	1.56	1.32	6,805.1	1,705.6	1,193.5	125.9

Adverse Trends in Operations

Increase in policy surrenders from 2011 to 2012 (240%)
Decrease in asset base during 2011 (11%)
Decrease in capital during 2011 (30%)
Decrease in capital during 2010 (63%)
Decrease in premium volume from 2009 to 2010 (404%)

PRINCIPAL LIFE INSURANCE COMPANY *

B+   **Good**

Major Rating Factors: Good quality investment portfolio (5.4 on a scale of 0 to 10) despite large holdings of BBB rated bonds in addition to junk bond exposure equal to 73% of capital. Exposure to mortgages is significant, but the mortgage default rate has been low. Good overall profitability (5.9). Return on equity has been good over the last five years, averaging 12.3%. Good overall results on stability tests (6.7) excellent operational trends and excellent risk diversification.

Other Rating Factors: Strong capitalization (7.1) based on excellent risk adjusted capital (severe loss scenario). Excellent liquidity (7.2).

Principal Business: Individual annuities (38%), individual life insurance (19%), group health insurance (16%), reinsurance (8%), and other lines (19%).

Principal Investments: NonCMO investment grade bonds (45%), CMOs and structured securities (22%), mortgages in good standing (17%), noninv. grade bonds (5%), and misc. investments (9%).

Investments in Affiliates: 6%

Group Affiliation: Principal Financial Group

Licensed in: All states, the District of Columbia and Puerto Rico

Commenced Business: September 1879

Address: 711 High St, Des Moines, IA 50392-0420

Phone: (800) 986-3343   **Domicile State:** IA   **NAIC Code:** 61271

Data Date	Rating	RACR #1	RACR #2	Total Assets ($mil)	Capital ($mil)	Net Premium ($mil)	Net Income ($mil)
9-14	B+	2.07	1.09	148,782	4,050.8	3,840.1	292.5
9-13	B+	2.03	1.05	138,460	3,803.8	3,811.8	326.4
2013	B+	2.05	1.09	143,742	4,142.2	5,267.0	607.9
2012	B+	2.11	1.09	130,020	3,944.3	5,388.6	576.1
2011	B+	2.27	1.16	121,390	4,218.2	4,800.3	326.8
2010	B+	2.31	1.17	122,004	4,377.8	5,582.3	404.6
2009	A-	2.51	1.25	118,786	4,588.7	6,021.4	42.1

Adverse Trends in Operations

Decrease in capital during 2012 (6%)
Decrease in premium volume from 2010 to 2011 (14%)
Decrease in capital during 2011 (4%)
Decrease in capital during 2010 (5%)
Decrease in premium volume from 2009 to 2010 (7%)

PRINCIPAL NATIONAL LIFE INSURANCE CO

B   **Good**

Major Rating Factors: Good overall results on stability tests (5.7 on a scale of 0 to 10) despite negative cash flow from operations for 2013. Strengths include good financial support from affiliation with Principal Financial Group, good operational trends and excellent risk diversification. Weak profitability (2.5) with operating losses during the first nine months of 2014. Return on equity has been low, averaging -5.4%. Strong capitalization (10.0) based on excellent risk adjusted capital (severe loss scenario).

Other Rating Factors: High quality investment portfolio (8.5). Excellent liquidity (9.2).

Principal Business: Individual life insurance (100%).

Principal Investments: NonCMO investment grade bonds (98%) and cash (2%).

Investments in Affiliates: None

Group Affiliation: Principal Financial Group

Licensed in: All states except NY, PR

Commenced Business: March 1968

Address: 711 High St, Des Moines, IA 50392-0001

Phone: (515) 247-5111   **Domicile State:** IA   **NAIC Code:** 71161

Data Date	Rating	RACR #1	RACR #2	Total Assets ($mil)	Capital ($mil)	Net Premium ($mil)	Net Income ($mil)
9-14	B	6.66	3.29	131.2	84.9	0.0	-3.2
9-13	B	8.74	4.30	107.9	84.3	0.0	-5.1
2013	B	6.16	3.04	110.4	84.2	0.0	-6.4
2012	B	7.09	3.54	84.9	70.8	0.0	-6.0
2011	B	7.82	4.72	65.1	58.1	0.0	-7.0
2010	U	3.67	3.30	43.1	22.1	0.0	-0.1
2009	U	4.38	3.94	12.7	11.9	0.0	0.2

Principal Financial Group
Composite Group Rating: B+
Largest Group Members

	Assets ($mil)	Rating
PRINCIPAL LIFE INS CO	143742	B+
PRINCIPAL NATIONAL LIFE INS CO	110	B

PROFESSIONAL INSURANCE COMPANY C Fair

Major Rating Factors: Fair overall results on stability tests (3.4 on a scale of 0 to 10) including potential financial drain due to affiliation with Sun Life Assurance Group and negative cash flow from operations for 2013. Good liquidity (6.7) with sufficient resources to handle a spike in claims. Weak profitability (2.8). Excellent expense controls.

Other Rating Factors: Strong capitalization (9.8) based on excellent risk adjusted capital (severe loss scenario). High quality investment portfolio (7.0).

Principal Business: Individual health insurance (95%) and individual life insurance (5%).

Principal Investments: NonCMO investment grade bonds (85%), CMOs and structured securities (8%), policy loans (4%), noninv. grade bonds (1%), and misc. investments (1%).

Investments in Affiliates: None

Group Affiliation: Sun Life Assurance Group

Licensed in: All states except AK, DE, ME, NH, NJ, NY, RI, VT, PR

Commenced Business: September 1937

Address: 4850 Street Road, Trevose, PA 19049

Phone: (800) 730-6484 **Domicile State:** TX **NAIC Code:** 68047

Data Date	Rating	RACR #1	RACR #2	Total Assets ($mil)	Capital ($mil)	Net Premium ($mil)	Net Income ($mil)
9-14	C	4.03	2.86	108.3	36.0	24.1	1.9
9-13	D+	2.99	2.09	105.1	29.5	28.0	2.6
2013	C-	3.16	2.21	105.1	29.5	37.1	3.4
2012	D	2.61	1.84	108.6	28.6	44.6	1.1
2011	D	1.52	1.09	104.5	20.8	53.8	-9.2
2010	C	1.82	1.30	105.5	29.4	70.1	-6.8
2009	C	2.07	1.43	111.2	33.6	71.5	0.0

Sun Life Assurance Group Composite Group Rating: D+ Largest Group Members	Assets ($mil)	Rating
SUN LIFE ASR CO OF CANADA	15369	D
INDEPENDENCE LIFE ANNUITY CO	2284	C
SUN LIFE HEALTH INS CO	354	C-
PROFESSIONAL INS CO	105	C-

PROFESSIONAL LIFE & CASUALTY COMPANY C Fair

Major Rating Factors: Fair quality investment portfolio (3.2 on a scale of 0 to 10) with large holdings of BBB rated bonds in addition to junk bond exposure equal to 67% of capital. Fair overall results on stability tests (4.3) including fair risk adjusted capital in prior years. Good liquidity (5.5) with sufficient resources to handle a spike in claims as well as a significant increase in policy surrenders.

Other Rating Factors: Strong capitalization (7.6) based on excellent risk adjusted capital (severe loss scenario). Excellent profitability (9.0) with operating gains in each of the last five years.

Principal Business: Individual annuities (99%) and individual life insurance (1%).

Principal Investments: NonCMO investment grade bonds (58%), common & preferred stock (24%), noninv. grade bonds (17%), and cash (1%).

Investments in Affiliates: None

Group Affiliation: None

Licensed in: IL, IN, MT, ND, OK

Commenced Business: September 1957

Address: 20 N Wacker Dr Ste 3110, Chicago, IL 60606

Phone: (312) 220-0655 **Domicile State:** IL **NAIC Code:** 68063

Data Date	Rating	RACR #1	RACR #2	Total Assets ($mil)	Capital ($mil)	Net Premium ($mil)	Net Income ($mil)
9-14	C	2.63	1.41	153.0	35.7	4.6	2.5
9-13	C	2.68	1.42	142.1	31.9	7.5	3.8
2013	C	2.66	1.39	144.3	33.3	9.6	6.5
2012	C	2.39	1.18	129.2	25.1	13.0	3.2
2011	C	2.53	1.23	116.4	22.5	15.6	3.3
2010	C	2.48	1.12	104.3	19.9	8.2	8.0
2009	D	1.35	0.62	81.8	11.3	7.2	2.5

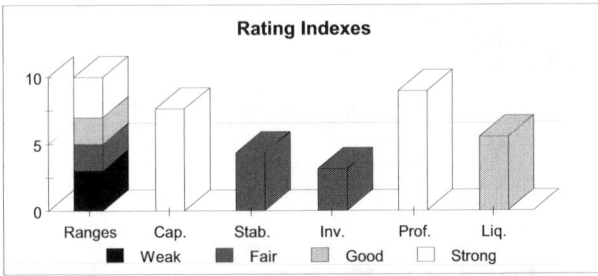

Rating Indexes

Ranges | Cap. | Stab. | Inv. | Prof. | Liq.

■ Weak ■ Fair ▨ Good □ Strong

PROTECTIVE LIFE & ANNUITY INSURANCE COMPANY B Good

Major Rating Factors: Good quality investment portfolio (6.2 on a scale of 0 to 10) despite mixed results such as: large holdings of BBB rated bonds but moderate junk bond exposure. Good overall profitability (5.5) although investment income, in comparison to reserve requirements, is below regulatory standards. Fair overall results on stability tests (4.6) including negative cash flow from operations for 2013.

Other Rating Factors: Fair liquidity (4.9). Strong capitalization (7.5) based on excellent risk adjusted capital (severe loss scenario).

Principal Business: Individual annuities (74%), individual life insurance (14%), and reinsurance (12%).

Principal Investments: NonCMO investment grade bonds (74%), CMOs and structured securities (15%), mortgages in good standing (4%), noninv. grade bonds (3%), and misc. investments (3%).

Investments in Affiliates: None

Group Affiliation: Protective Life Group

Licensed in: AL, AZ, AR, CA, CO, FL, GA, IL, IN, IA, KS, KY, LA, MA, MI, MS, MO, NE, NV, NM, NY, NC, OH, OK, OR, SC, TN, TX, UT, VA, WA

Commenced Business: December 1978

Address: 2801 Highway 280 South, Birmingham, AL 35223

Phone: (205) 268-1000 **Domicile State:** AL **NAIC Code:** 88536

Data Date	Rating	RACR #1	RACR #2	Total Assets ($mil)	Capital ($mil)	Net Premium ($mil)	Net Income ($mil)
9-14	B	2.54	1.31	2,105.5	176.1	39.1	27.0
9-13	B	2.58	1.32	2,163.0	185.6	142.4	19.7
2013	B	2.79	1.44	2,162.7	193.6	156.6	27.7
2012	B	2.86	1.45	2,133.9	206.3	290.1	27.9
2011	B	2.20	1.11	1,278.2	94.4	253.0	17.7
2010	B	2.18	1.08	1,068.0	82.2	194.6	16.9
2009	B-	2.36	1.17	927.4	78.7	185.7	13.4

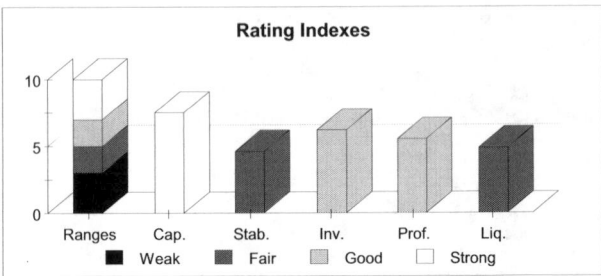

Rating Indexes

Ranges | Cap. | Stab. | Inv. | Prof. | Liq.

■ Weak ■ Fair ▨ Good □ Strong

PROTECTIVE LIFE INSURANCE COMPANY — B — Good

Major Rating Factors: Good quality investment portfolio (5.7 on a scale of 0 to 10) despite mixed results such as: large holdings of BBB rated bonds but moderate junk bond exposure. Good liquidity (6.4) with sufficient resources to cover a large increase in policy surrenders. Fair overall results on stability tests (4.9).

Other Rating Factors: Strong capitalization (7.1) based on excellent risk adjusted capital (severe loss scenario). Excellent profitability (8.0) with operating gains in each of the last five years.

Principal Business: Individual annuities (39%), reinsurance (32%), and individual life insurance (27%).

Principal Investments: NonCMO investment grade bonds (60%), CMOs and structured securities (14%), mortgages in good standing (10%), common & preferred stock (7%), and misc. investments (8%).

Investments in Affiliates: 10%

Group Affiliation: Protective Life Group

Licensed in: All states except NY

Commenced Business: September 1907

Address: 1620 Westgate Cir Suite 200, Brentwood, TN 37027-8035

Phone: (205) 879-9230 **Domicile State:** TN **NAIC Code:** 68136

Data Date	Rating	RACR #1	RACR #2	Total Assets ($mil)	Capital ($mil)	Net Premium ($mil)	Net Income ($mil)
9-14	B	1.41	1.05	41,449.6	3,307.6	1,794.4	526.4
9-13	B	1.53	1.12	38,662.2	3,301.6	2,413.6	335.6
2013	B	1.03	0.83	41,027.0	2,917.7	4,589.6	165.5
2012	B	1.31	1.01	36,355.3	2,983.9	3,963.6	376.3
2011	B	1.18	0.92	32,250.9	2,625.9	5,637.9	259.2
2010	B	1.17	0.92	28,616.4	2,621.6	3,132.1	303.6
2009	B-	1.32	0.96	26,654.7	2,616.5	2,504.6	549.9

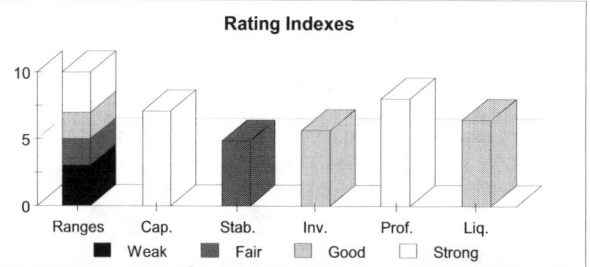

Rating Indexes

Ranges — Cap. — Stab. — Inv. — Prof. — Liq.

■ Weak ■ Fair ■ Good □ Strong

PROVIDENT LIFE & ACCIDENT INSURANCE COMPANY — C+ — Fair

Major Rating Factors: Fair overall results on stability tests (4.8 on a scale of 0 to 10) including fair financial strength of affiliated Unum Group. Fair quality investment portfolio (4.3) with large holdings of BBB rated bonds in addition to significant exposure to junk bonds. Good overall profitability (6.8). Excellent expense controls. Return on equity has been excellent over the last five years averaging 21.8%.

Other Rating Factors: Strong capitalization (7.4) based on excellent risk adjusted capital (severe loss scenario). Excellent liquidity (7.3).

Principal Business: Individual health insurance (69%), individual life insurance (28%), group health insurance (1%), reinsurance (1%), and group life insurance (1%).

Principal Investments: NonCMO investment grade bonds (72%), noninv. grade bonds (9%), CMOs and structured securities (8%), mortgages in good standing (5%), and misc. investments (6%).

Investments in Affiliates: None

Group Affiliation: Unum Group

Licensed in: All states except NY

Commenced Business: May 1887

Address: 1 Fountain Square, Chattanooga, TN 37402

Phone: (423) 755-1373 **Domicile State:** TN **NAIC Code:** 68195

Data Date	Rating	RACR #1	RACR #2	Total Assets ($mil)	Capital ($mil)	Net Premium ($mil)	Net Income ($mil)
9-14	C+	2.54	1.28	8,316.4	688.3	685.8	134.2
9-13	C+	2.40	1.21	8,383.2	653.7	684.9	133.6
2013	C+	2.55	1.28	8,347.6	699.7	898.5	166.4
2012	C+	2.30	1.16	8,452.0	642.8	960.1	168.9
2011	C+	2.35	1.19	8,417.2	653.0	924.9	170.4
2010	C+	2.47	1.25	8,271.6	654.6	887.4	130.3
2009	C+	2.26	1.16	8,004.3	567.1	862.5	113.3

Unum Group
Composite Group Rating: C+
Largest Group Members

	Assets ($mil)	Rating
UNUM LIFE INS CO OF AMERICA	19079	C+
PROVIDENT LIFE ACCIDENT INS CO	8348	C+
PAUL REVERE LIFE INS CO	4302	C+
COLONIAL LIFE ACCIDENT INS CO	2753	C+
FIRST UNUM LIFE INS CO	2704	C+

PROVIDENT LIFE & CASUALTY INSURANCE COMPANY — B- — Good

Major Rating Factors: Good overall results on stability tests (5.3 on a scale of 0 to 10) despite fair financial strength of affiliated Unum Group. Other stability subfactors include excellent operational trends and excellent risk diversification. Fair quality investment portfolio (4.6) with large holdings of BBB rated bonds in addition to junk bond exposure equal to 55% of capital. Strong capitalization (9.2) based on excellent risk adjusted capital (severe loss scenario).

Other Rating Factors: Excellent profitability (8.4) with operating gains in each of the last five years. Excellent liquidity (7.2).

Principal Business: Individual health insurance (90%), reinsurance (6%), and individual life insurance (3%).

Principal Investments: NonCMO investment grade bonds (74%), noninv. grade bonds (11%), CMOs and structured securities (9%), and mortgages in good standing (4%).

Investments in Affiliates: None

Group Affiliation: Unum Group

Licensed in: AK, AR, CO, CT, DC, DE, GA, HI, ID, IL, IA, KY, LA, MA, MS, MO, NE, NH, NJ, NM, NY, NC, ND, OH, OK, PA, RI, SC, SD, TN, VA, WA

Commenced Business: January 1952

Address: 1 Fountain Square, Chattanooga, TN 37402

Phone: (423) 755-1373 **Domicile State:** TN **NAIC Code:** 68209

Data Date	Rating	RACR #1	RACR #2	Total Assets ($mil)	Capital ($mil)	Net Premium ($mil)	Net Income ($mil)
9-14	B-	4.69	2.49	777.2	153.4	63.6	7.7
9-13	B-	4.76	2.48	775.5	162.2	64.8	18.5
2013	B-	4.65	2.46	764.1	150.9	86.2	18.3
2012	B-	4.43	2.33	777.6	145.9	87.8	17.8
2011	B-	4.45	2.37	768.3	142.0	85.3	14.5
2010	B-	4.55	2.44	747.2	142.6	84.0	13.3
2009	B-	4.20	2.29	722.0	130.2	86.6	6.1

Unum Group
Composite Group Rating: C+
Largest Group Members

	Assets ($mil)	Rating
UNUM LIFE INS CO OF AMERICA	19079	C+
PROVIDENT LIFE ACCIDENT INS CO	8348	C+
PAUL REVERE LIFE INS CO	4302	C+
COLONIAL LIFE ACCIDENT INS CO	2753	C+
FIRST UNUM LIFE INS CO	2704	C+

PRUCO LIFE INSURANCE COMPANY — C+ — Fair

Major Rating Factors: Fair overall results on stability tests (4.4 on a scale of 0 to 10). Good quality investment portfolio (5.7) despite significant exposure to mortgages . Mortgage default rate has been low. large holdings of BBB rated bonds in addition to small junk bond holdings. Good overall profitability (5.6) although investment income, in comparison to reserve requirements, is below regulatory standards.

Other Rating Factors: Strong capitalization (7.8) based on excellent risk adjusted capital (severe loss scenario). Excellent liquidity (9.7).

Principal Business: Individual annuities (52%), reinsurance (33%), and individual life insurance (15%).

Principal Investments: NonCMO investment grade bonds (47%), mortgages in good standing (16%), policy loans (12%), CMOs and structured securities (12%), and misc. investments (12%).

Investments in Affiliates: 9%

Group Affiliation: Prudential of America

Licensed in: All states except NY, PR

Commenced Business: December 1971

Address: 2999 N 44th St Suite 250, Phoenix, AZ 85018

Phone: (877) 301-1212 **Domicile State:** AZ **NAIC Code:** 79227

Data Date	Rating	RACR #1	RACR #2	Total Assets ($mil)	Capital ($mil)	Net Premium ($mil)	Net Income ($mil)
9-14	C+	2.51	1.51	104,592	2,827.5	6,564.2	16.4
9-13	C+	2.19	1.37	93,113.5	2,517.2	9,135.0	368.9
2013	C+	2.18	1.32	98,541.3	2,386.9	11,307.7	553.1
2012	C+	2.09	1.34	81,002.0	2,210.6	18,196.4	591.4
2011	C+	2.03	1.23	59,524.8	1,496.0	18,292.6	-588.6
2010	C+	1.93	1.17	46,231.6	1,218.3	15,207.4	276.8
2009	C+	1.73	1.02	29,252.5	874.8	4,727.6	106.4

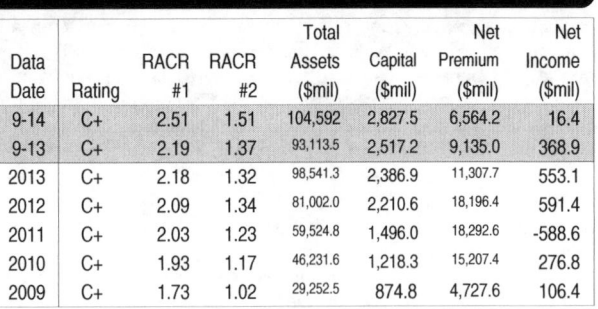

Rating Indexes

PRUCO LIFE INSURANCE COMPANY OF NEW JERSEY — B- — Good

Major Rating Factors: Good overall results on stability tests (5.2 on a scale of 0 to 10). Stability strengths include good operational trends, good risk adjusted capital for prior years and excellent risk diversification. Good quality investment portfolio (5.5) despite significant exposure to mortgages . Mortgage default rate has been low. large holdings of BBB rated bonds in addition to small junk bond holdings. Good overall profitability (5.4) although investment income, in comparison to reserve requirements, is below regulatory standards.

Other Rating Factors: Strong capitalization (7.5) based on excellent risk adjusted capital (severe loss scenario). Excellent liquidity (9.1).

Principal Business: Individual annuities (66%) and individual life insurance (34%).

Principal Investments: NonCMO investment grade bonds (47%), mortgages in good standing (20%), CMOs and structured securities (14%), policy loans (13%), and noninv. grade bonds (3%).

Investments in Affiliates: 2%

Group Affiliation: Prudential of America

Licensed in: NJ, NY

Commenced Business: December 1982

Address: 213 Washington St, Newark, NJ 07102

Phone: (877) 301-1212 **Domicile State:** NJ **NAIC Code:** 97195

Data Date	Rating	RACR #1	RACR #2	Total Assets ($mil)	Capital ($mil)	Net Premium ($mil)	Net Income ($mil)
9-14	B-	2.70	1.36	12,642.3	347.8	817.3	52.4
9-13	B-	2.99	1.51	11,074.3	360.9	758.2	60.0
2013	B-	3.11	1.57	11,810.8	379.7	1,078.5	81.2
2012	B-	4.33	2.18	9,960.2	465.3	1,696.3	65.6
2011	B	2.60	1.30	7,960.6	260.3	1,663.3	12.6
2010	B-	2.49	1.26	6,569.8	215.7	1,509.4	52.4
2009	C	1.96	0.99	4,801.5	153.4	628.0	-3.8

Adverse Trends in Operations

Increase in policy surrenders from 2012 to 2013 (27%)
Decrease in premium volume from 2012 to 2013 (36%)
Decrease in capital during 2013 (18%)
Increase in policy surrenders from 2010 to 2011 (77%)
Change in premium mix from 2009 to 2010 (6.0%)

PRUDENTIAL ANNUITIES LIFE ASSURANCE CORPORATION — C — Fair

Major Rating Factors: Fair overall capitalization (4.0 on a scale of 0 to 10) based on mixed results -- excessive policy leverage mitigated by good risk adjusted capital (severe loss scenario). Nevertheless, capital levels have fluctuated during prior years. Fair profitability (4.7). Fair overall results on stability tests (3.4).

Other Rating Factors: Good quality investment portfolio (6.4). Excellent liquidity (7.0).

Principal Business: Individual annuities (97%), group retirement contracts (2%), and individual life insurance (1%).

Principal Investments: NonCMO investment grade bonds (57%), CMOs and structured securities (20%), mortgages in good standing (12%), noninv. grade bonds (6%), and policy loans (1%).

Investments in Affiliates: 3%

Group Affiliation: Prudential of America

Licensed in: All states, the District of Columbia and Puerto Rico

Commenced Business: May 1988

Address: One Corporate Dr, 10th Floor, Shelton, CT 06484

Phone: (800) 628-6039 **Domicile State:** AZ **NAIC Code:** 86630

Data Date	Rating	RACR #1	RACR #2	Total Assets ($mil)	Capital ($mil)	Net Premium ($mil)	Net Income ($mil)
9-14	C	1.08	0.90	48,138.0	473.8	-104.6	227.2
9-13	C	0.93	0.70	49,802.3	399.4	-86.9	235.7
2013	C	1.01	0.81	50,649.1	443.5	-127.6	406.1
2012	C+	1.04	0.79	49,555.9	447.7	558.8	217.4
2011	C+	1.55	1.18	49,168.3	671.6	837.4	177.0
2010	B	2.01	1.70	54,688.2	935.9	5,368.2	348.4
2009	C+	2.07	1.73	49,616.0	881.0	11,596.2	266.6

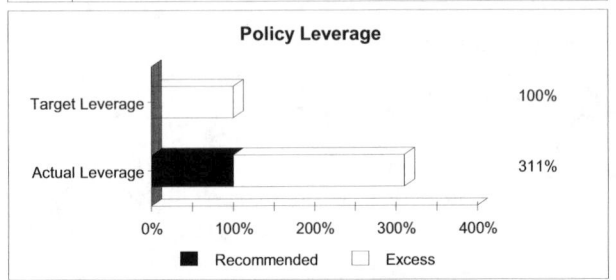

Policy Leverage

PRUDENTIAL INSURANCE COMPANY OF AMERICA | B | Good

Major Rating Factors: Good quality investment portfolio (5.6 on a scale of 0 to 10) despite large holdings of BBB rated bonds in addition to junk bond exposure equal to 60% of capital. Exposure to mortgages is significant, but the mortgage default rate has been low. Fair overall results on stability tests (4.3). Strong capitalization (7.0) based on excellent risk adjusted capital (severe loss scenario).

Other Rating Factors: Excellent profitability (7.6) with operating gains in each of the last five years. Excellent liquidity (7.0).

Principal Business: Reinsurance (43%), group retirement contracts (25%), group life insurance (15%), individual life insurance (11%), and other lines (5%).

Principal Investments: NonCMO investment grade bonds (46%), CMOs and structured securities (17%), mortgages in good standing (15%), common & preferred stock (6%), and misc. investments (14%).

Investments in Affiliates: 7%

Group Affiliation: Prudential of America

Licensed in: All states, the District of Columbia and Puerto Rico

Commenced Business: October 1875

Address: 751 Broad St, Newark, NJ 07102-3777

Phone: (973) 802-6000 **Domicile State:** NJ **NAIC Code:** 68241

Data Date	Rating	RACR #1	RACR #2	Total Assets ($mil)	Capital ($mil)	Net Premium ($mil)	Net Income ($mil)
9-14	B	1.50	1.02	306,159	11,579.9	12,927.8	995.8
9-13	B	1.31	0.89	294,755	9,624.2	15,584.3	512.1
2013	B	1.29	0.88	296,637	9,382.6	21,059.8	1,357.8
2012	B	1.21	0.83	285,087	8,698.9	52,479.2	1,382.4
2011	B	1.28	0.86	246,842	8,159.7	17,275.9	825.6
2010	B	1.30	0.87	233,141	8,364.2	16,370.8	1,622.9
2009	C+	1.55	1.00	225,788	10,041.7	17,192.7	1,100.6

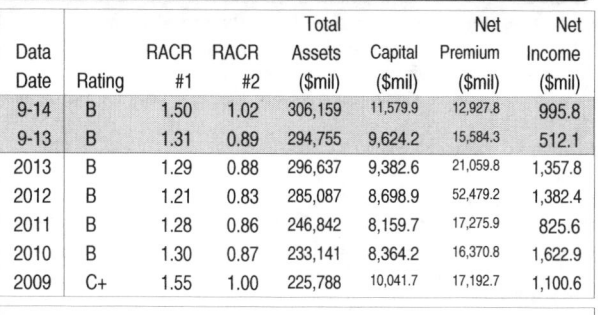

Rating Indexes

PRUDENTIAL RETIREMENT INSURANCE & ANNUITY | B- | Good

Major Rating Factors: Good overall capitalization (6.3 on a scale of 0 to 10) based on good risk adjusted capital (moderate loss scenario). Nevertheless, capital levels have fluctuated during prior years. Good overall profitability (5.1). Return on equity has been excellent over the last five years averaging 17.1%. Good overall results on stability tests (5.1) excellent operational trends and excellent risk diversification.

Other Rating Factors: Fair quality investment portfolio (3.6). Excellent liquidity (7.7).

Principal Business: Group retirement contracts (78%) and reinsurance (22%).

Principal Investments: NonCMO investment grade bonds (48%), CMOs and structured securities (27%), mortgages in good standing (18%), and noninv. grade bonds (5%).

Investments in Affiliates: 1%

Group Affiliation: Prudential of America

Licensed in: All states except PR

Commenced Business: October 1981

Address: 280 Trumbull St, Hartford, CT 06103-3509

Phone: (860) 534-2000 **Domicile State:** CT **NAIC Code:** 93629

Data Date	Rating	RACR #1	RACR #2	Total Assets ($mil)	Capital ($mil)	Net Premium ($mil)	Net Income ($mil)
9-14	B-	1.84	0.88	77,318.5	1,098.4	368.7	144.2
9-13	B-	2.13	0.92	78,494.1	1,211.5	442.2	217.7
2013	B-	1.66	0.79	78,046.5	941.0	583.1	313.0
2012	B-	2.04	0.91	69,265.3	1,072.0	451.6	231.4
2011	B-	2.10	0.90	63,442.9	1,079.4	233.1	168.4
2010	B-	2.45	1.07	65,837.8	1,278.8	109.7	277.3
2009	C+	2.15	0.91	59,982.6	1,166.4	71.6	107.0

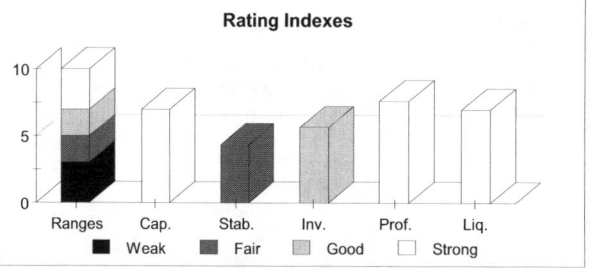

Junk Bonds as a % of Capital

PYRAMID LIFE INSURANCE COMPANY | C | Fair

Major Rating Factors: Good current capitalization (6.0 on a scale of 0 to 10) based on excellent risk adjusted capital (severe loss scenario) reflecting significant improvement over results in 2010. Good overall profitability (5.9). Excellent expense controls. Return on equity has been good over the last five years, averaging 12.8%. Good liquidity (5.8).

Other Rating Factors: Weak overall results on stability tests (2.9) including weak results on operational trends. High quality investment portfolio (7.5).

Principal Business: Individual health insurance (99%) and individual life insurance (1%).

Principal Investments: NonCMO investment grade bonds (72%), CMOs and structured securities (23%), and common & preferred stock (4%).

Investments in Affiliates: None

Group Affiliation: Universal American Corp

Licensed in: AL, AZ, AR, CA, CO, DE, FL, GA, ID, IL, IN, IA, KS, KY, LA, MD, MA, MI, MN, MS, MO, MT, NE, NV, NM, NC, ND, OH, OK, OR, PA, SC, SD, TN, TX, UT, VA, WA, WI, WY

Commenced Business: August 1914

Address: 6201 Johnson Dr, Shawnee Mission, KS 66202

Phone: (913) 722-1110 **Domicile State:** KS **NAIC Code:** 68284

Data Date	Rating	RACR #1	RACR #2	Total Assets ($mil)	Capital ($mil)	Net Premium ($mil)	Net Income ($mil)
9-14	C	1.65	1.30	170.6	83.8	158.1	3.9
9-13	C	1.08	0.87	200.7	91.6	321.2	10.2
2013	C	1.29	1.03	211.8	104.2	425.6	23.5
2012	C	1.86	1.49	307.4	187.0	532.9	12.6
2011	C	1.59	1.28	385.2	253.5	748.1	14.4
2010	C-	0.65	0.53	477.2	239.0	1,754.8	38.1
2009	C-	0.73	0.60	369.3	179.5	1,063.5	24.4

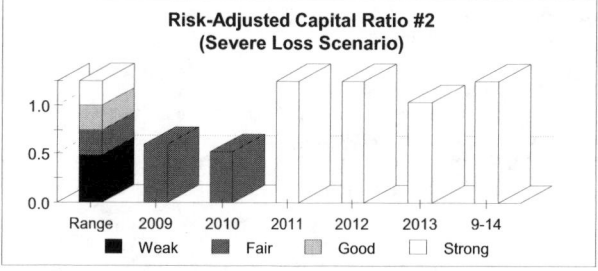

Risk-Adjusted Capital Ratio #2 (Severe Loss Scenario)

REINSURANCE COMPANY OF MISSOURI INCORPORATED — C+ — Fair

Major Rating Factors: Fair overall results on stability tests (3.4 on a scale of 0 to 10) including negative cash flow from operations for 2013. Good capitalization (6.3) based on good risk adjusted capital (severe loss scenario). Capital levels have been relatively consistent over the last five years. Low quality investment portfolio (1.4).

Other Rating Factors: Excellent profitability (8.8) despite modest operating losses during 2009. Excellent liquidity (7.0).

Principal Business: Reinsurance (100%).

Principal Investments: Common & preferred stock (94%), nonCMO investment grade bonds (5%), and CMOs and structured securities (1%).

Investments in Affiliates: 94%

Group Affiliation: RGA Inc

Licensed in: MO

Commenced Business: December 1998

Address: 1370 Timberlake Manor Pkwy, Chesterfield, MO 63017-6039

Phone: (636) 736-7368 **Domicile State:** MO **NAIC Code:** 89004

Data Date	Rating	RACR #1	RACR #2	Total Assets ($mil)	Capital ($mil)	Net Premium ($mil)	Net Income ($mil)
9-14	C+	1.01	0.91	1,604.2	1,595.8	5.0	9.9
9-13	C+	1.06	0.94	1,703.7	1,661.9	24.7	9.7
2013	C+	1.04	0.94	1,746.6	1,633.4	30.9	109.1
2012	C+	1.08	0.96	1,748.7	1,692.2	83.6	58.5
2011	C+	1.08	0.96	1,655.4	1,478.9	93.1	37.1
2010	C+	1.06	0.94	1,696.6	1,486.9	47.5	53.7
2009	C+	1.13	1.00	1,507.0	1,412.9	73.8	-16.8

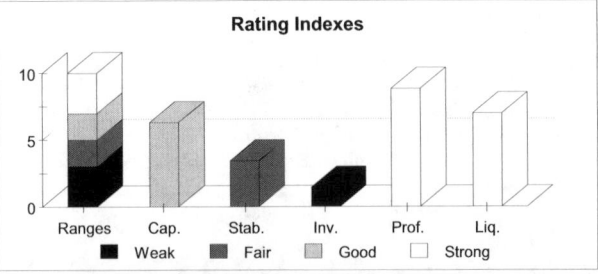

Rating Indexes

Ranges / Cap. / Stab. / Inv. / Prof. / Liq.
■ Weak ■ Fair ▨ Good □ Strong

RELIANCE STANDARD LIFE INSURANCE COMPANY — B — Good

Major Rating Factors: Good overall results on stability tests (5.9 on a scale of 0 to 10). Stability strengths include excellent operational trends, excellent risk adjusted capital for prior years and excellent risk diversification. Good current capitalization (6.4) based on good risk adjusted capital (severe loss scenario), although results have slipped from the excellent range during the last year. Good overall profitability (6.5).

Other Rating Factors: Good liquidity (6.7). Fair quality investment portfolio (4.5).

Principal Business: Group health insurance (37%), individual annuities (29%), group life insurance (22%), group retirement contracts (8%), and reinsurance (3%).

Principal Investments: CMOs and structured securities (49%), nonCMO investment grade bonds (35%), noninv. grade bonds (7%), common & preferred stock (3%), and mortgages in good standing (1%).

Investments in Affiliates: 2%

Group Affiliation: Tokio Marine Holdings Inc

Licensed in: All states, the District of Columbia and Puerto Rico

Commenced Business: April 1907

Address: 111 S Wacker Dr Suite 4400, Chicago, IL 60606-4410

Phone: (215) 787-4000 **Domicile State:** IL **NAIC Code:** 68381

Data Date	Rating	RACR #1	RACR #2	Total Assets ($mil)	Capital ($mil)	Net Premium ($mil)	Net Income ($mil)
9-14	B	1.67	0.92	7,447.4	700.3	1,388.2	118.4
9-13	B	1.92	1.16	5,697.7	637.6	1,128.8	109.1
2013	B	1.78	1.06	5,980.4	598.4	1,642.5	134.6
2012	B	1.74	1.02	5,186.9	561.5	1,386.6	88.4
2011	B-	1.72	1.04	4,618.0	522.3	1,320.9	76.9
2010	B-	1.97	1.19	4,193.8	530.6	1,148.0	64.3
2009	B-	1.78	1.12	3,821.3	541.0	1,212.9	-29.1

Adverse Trends in Operations

Increase in policy surrenders from 2012 to 2013 (50%)
Decrease in capital during 2011 (2%)
Decrease in capital during 2010 (2%)
Decrease in premium volume from 2009 to 2010 (5%)

RELIASTAR LIFE INSURANCE COMPANY — C+ — Fair

Major Rating Factors: Fair profitability (3.5 on a scale of 0 to 10). Return on equity has been low, averaging 0.8%. Fair overall results on stability tests (4.4) including negative cash flow from operations for 2013. Good quality investment portfolio (6.2) despite large holdings of BBB rated bonds in addition to moderate junk bond exposure. Exposure to mortgages is significant, but the mortgage default rate has been low.

Other Rating Factors: Good liquidity (5.4). Strong capitalization (7.5) based on excellent risk adjusted capital (severe loss scenario).

Principal Business: Individual life insurance (40%), group health insurance (22%), group life insurance (16%), individual annuities (15%), and other lines (7%).

Principal Investments: NonCMO investment grade bonds (62%), CMOs and structured securities (12%), mortgages in good standing (11%), noninv. grade bonds (4%), and misc. investments (9%).

Investments in Affiliates: 3%

Group Affiliation: Voya Financial Inc

Licensed in: All states, the District of Columbia and Puerto Rico

Commenced Business: September 1885

Address: 20 Washington Ave S, Minneapolis, MN 55401

Phone: (770) 980-5100 **Domicile State:** MN **NAIC Code:** 67105

Data Date	Rating	RACR #1	RACR #2	Total Assets ($mil)	Capital ($mil)	Net Premium ($mil)	Net Income ($mil)
9-14	C+	2.17	1.30	21,234.6	1,829.9	-438.6	110.0
9-13	C	2.08	1.25	21,228.8	1,735.4	629.2	145.9
2013	C	2.29	1.38	21,621.2	1,942.5	840.3	215.9
2012	C-	2.57	1.54	21,526.1	2,284.6	858.8	-155.3
2011	C-	2.48	1.44	20,779.6	2,104.3	886.1	-83.0
2010	C	2.29	1.35	20,811.4	2,078.1	287.3	-234.2
2009	B-	2.32	1.36	20,673.3	2,190.3	566.3	-92.5

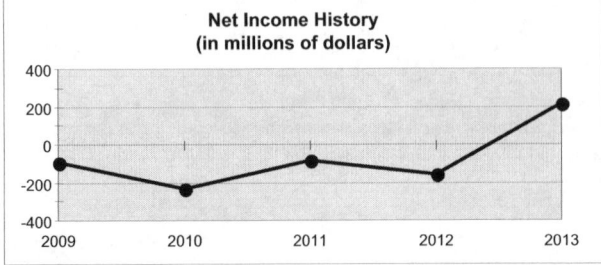

Net Income History
(in millions of dollars)

RELIASTAR LIFE INSURANCE COMPANY OF NEW YORK   B   Good

Major Rating Factors: Good overall results on stability tests (5.8 on a scale of 0 to 10). Stability strengths include good operational trends and excellent risk diversification. Good quality investment portfolio (6.5) despite mixed results such as: minimal exposure to mortgages and large holdings of BBB rated bonds but small junk bond holdings. Good overall profitability (5.2) despite operating losses during the first nine months of 2014.
Other Rating Factors: Good liquidity (5.9). Strong capitalization (8.2) based on excellent risk adjusted capital (severe loss scenario).
Principal Business: Individual life insurance (79%), group health insurance (12%), group life insurance (5%), individual annuities (3%), and individual health insurance (1%).
Principal Investments: NonCMO investment grade bonds (72%), CMOs and structured securities (10%), mortgages in good standing (6%), policy loans (5%), and misc. investments (5%).
Investments in Affiliates: None
Group Affiliation: Voya Financial Inc
Licensed in: All states except PR
Commenced Business: September 1917
Address: 1000 Woodbury Rd Suite 102, Woodbury, NY 11797
Phone: (516) 682-8700 **Domicile State:** NY **NAIC Code:** 61360

Data Date	Rating	RACR #1	RACR #2	Total Assets ($mil)	Capital ($mil)	Net Premium ($mil)	Net Income ($mil)
9-14	B	3.44	1.83	3,194.3	295.2	106.0	-41.9
9-13	B-	3.51	1.88	3,199.0	325.4	104.0	8.3
2013	B-	3.86	2.04	3,208.8	329.5	139.2	20.5
2012	B-	3.69	1.98	3,232.4	340.6	157.4	40.1
2011	C	3.31	1.77	3,307.9	281.5	114.3	-49.1
2010	C+	3.56	1.86	3,364.5	320.2	174.2	-20.0
2009	C+	3.67	1.91	3,209.4	322.6	282.6	95.2

Adverse Trends in Operations

Decrease in premium volume from 2012 to 2013 (12%)
Decrease in premium volume from 2010 to 2011 (34%)
Decrease in capital during 2011 (12%)
Change in premium mix from 2009 to 2010 (6.3%)
Decrease in premium volume from 2009 to 2010 (38%)

RESERVE NATIONAL INSURANCE COMPANY *   A   Excellent

Major Rating Factors: Good liquidity (6.6 on a scale of 0 to 10) with sufficient resources to handle a spike in claims. Excellent overall results on stability tests (7.6). Strengths that enhance stability include excellent operational trends and excellent risk diversification. Strong capitalization (8.3) based on excellent risk adjusted capital (severe loss scenario). Furthermore, this high level of risk adjusted capital has been consistently maintained over the last five years.
Other Rating Factors: High quality investment portfolio (8.0). Excellent profitability (7.1) with operating gains in each of the last five years.
Principal Business: Individual health insurance (90%), individual life insurance (8%), and group health insurance (2%).
Principal Investments: NonCMO investment grade bonds (92%), CMOs and structured securities (5%), and , and , and misc. investments (3%).
Investments in Affiliates: None
Group Affiliation: Kemper Corporation
Licensed in: All states except CA, HI, MA, MN, NH, NY, RI, PR
Commenced Business: September 1956
Address: 601 E Britton Rd, Oklahoma City, OK 73114
Phone: (405) 848-7931 **Domicile State:** OK **NAIC Code:** 68462

Data Date	Rating	RACR #1	RACR #2	Total Assets ($mil)	Capital ($mil)	Net Premium ($mil)	Net Income ($mil)
9-14	A	2.46	1.89	112.1	53.5	103.4	1.2
9-13	A	2.73	2.09	117.5	60.4	107.8	3.1
2013	A	2.27	1.76	111.2	52.4	143.6	4.9
2012	A	2.66	2.04	116.0	58.4	135.2	8.8
2011	B	2.63	1.95	118.6	60.6	135.2	9.9
2010	B	2.21	1.62	109.3	50.2	131.7	7.4
2009	B	2.09	1.52	107.9	47.3	128.0	2.7

Adverse Trends in Operations

Decrease in asset base during 2013 (4%)
Decrease in capital during 2013 (10%)
Decrease in asset base during 2012 (2%)
Decrease in capital during 2012 (4%)

RGA REINSURANCE COMPANY   B   Good

Major Rating Factors: Good capitalization (6.0 on a scale of 0 to 10) based on good risk adjusted capital (severe loss scenario). Good quality investment portfolio (5.1) despite large holdings of BBB rated bonds in addition to junk bond exposure equal to 84% of capital. Exposure to mortgages is significant, but the mortgage default rate has been low. Good overall profitability (6.8). Excellent expense controls.
Other Rating Factors: Good liquidity (5.5). Fair overall results on stability tests (4.4).
Principal Business: Reinsurance (100%).
Principal Investments: NonCMO investment grade bonds (50%), mortgages in good standing (15%), CMOs and structured securities (14%), policy loans (8%), and misc. investments (13%).
Investments in Affiliates: 3%
Group Affiliation: RGA Inc
Licensed in: All states except PR
Commenced Business: October 1982
Address: 660 Mason Ridge Center Dr, St Louis, MO 63141
Phone: (314) 453-7368 **Domicile State:** MO **NAIC Code:** 93572

Data Date	Rating	RACR #1	RACR #2	Total Assets ($mil)	Capital ($mil)	Net Premium ($mil)	Net Income ($mil)
9-14	B	1.67	0.88	23,567.0	1,502.6	1,520.8	74.3
9-13	B	1.81	0.97	23,164.2	1,605.0	1,785.4	-61.2
2013	B	1.70	0.90	23,259.8	1,550.1	2,305.6	115.8
2012	B	1.75	0.95	22,835.1	1,644.6	5,213.8	3.5
2011	B	1.97	1.13	16,913.0	1,515.9	3,176.5	129.7
2010	B	2.03	1.17	15,327.9	1,528.9	2,225.9	68.0
2009	B	1.90	1.11	14,893.4	1,416.5	2,239.6	63.2

Risk-Adjusted Capital Ratio #2
(Severe Loss Scenario)

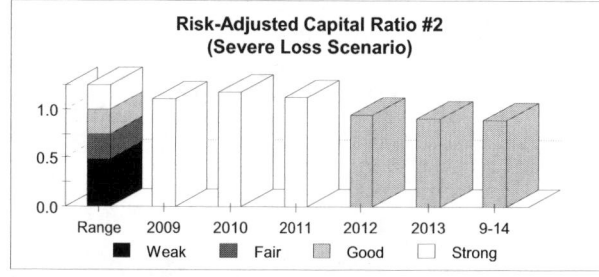

| Range | 2009 | 2010 | 2011 | 2012 | 2013 | 9-14 |

■ Weak   ▨ Fair   ▢ Good   □ Strong

RIVER LAKE INSURANCE COMPANY   C   Fair

Major Rating Factors: Good quality investment portfolio (5.7 on a scale of 0 to 10) with no exposure to mortgages and small junk bond holdings. Poor capitalization (2.8) based on weak risk adjusted capital (moderate loss scenario). Weak profitability (2.0) with investment income below regulatory standards in relation to interest assumptions of reserves.

Other Rating Factors: Weak overall results on stability tests (2.8) including weak risk adjusted capital in prior years. Excellent liquidity (7.5).

Principal Business: Reinsurance (100%).

Principal Investments: NonCMO investment grade bonds (62%), CMOs and structured securities (37%), and noninv. grade bonds (1%).

Investments in Affiliates: None

Group Affiliation: Genworth Financial

Licensed in: SC

Commenced Business: July 2003

Address: 151 Meeting St Suite 301, Charleston, SC 29401

Phone: (843) 577-1026 **Domicile State:** SC **NAIC Code:** 13215

Data Date	Rating	RACR #1	RACR #2	Total Assets ($mil)	Capital ($mil)	Net Premium ($mil)	Net Income ($mil)
9-14	C	0.73	0.43	1,328.7	95.6	38.2	39.6
9-13	D	0.75	0.44	1,363.9	104.1	43.4	29.5
2013	D	0.56	0.33	1,338.1	71.4	69.2	9.0
2012	E+	0.60	0.34	1,373.0	92.9	71.9	28.4
2011	E	0.49	0.27	1,367.7	79.5	80.7	-18.5
2010	U	0.53	0.29	1,357.0	95.1	81.1	-28.8
2009	U	0.50	0.29	1,331.0	96.6	86.4	-79.6

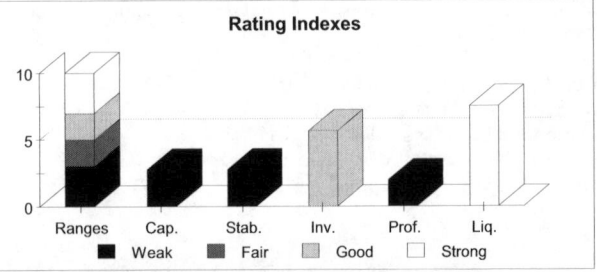

RIVER LAKE INSURANCE COMPANY II   C   Fair

Major Rating Factors: Fair overall results on stability tests (4.0 on a scale of 0 to 10) including fair risk adjusted capital in prior years. Good capitalization (5.0) based on good risk adjusted capital (moderate loss scenario). Good quality investment portfolio (5.9) with no exposure to mortgages and minimal holdings in junk bonds.

Other Rating Factors: Weak profitability (1.3) with operating losses during the first nine months of 2014. Excellent liquidity (7.7).

Principal Business: Reinsurance (100%).

Principal Investments: NonCMO investment grade bonds (66%) and CMOs and structured securities (34%).

Investments in Affiliates: None

Group Affiliation: Genworth Financial

Licensed in: SC

Commenced Business: October 2004

Address: 151 Meeting St Suite 301, Charleston, SC 29401

Phone: (843) 577-1026 **Domicile State:** SC **NAIC Code:** 13216

Data Date	Rating	RACR #1	RACR #2	Total Assets ($mil)	Capital ($mil)	Net Premium ($mil)	Net Income ($mil)
9-14	C	1.00	0.60	1,117.9	115.6	45.5	-9.4
9-13	C	1.09	0.64	1,109.1	130.7	44.4	-11.2
2013	C	1.07	0.65	1,112.0	124.7	59.6	-14.1
2012	C	1.04	0.59	1,085.6	129.4	74.2	-18.2
2011	C	1.06	0.57	1,070.9	149.1	66.7	-40.8
2010	U	1.30	0.71	1,049.3	185.9	69.8	-46.6
2009	U	1.73	0.93	1,026.4	237.4	73.8	-94.0

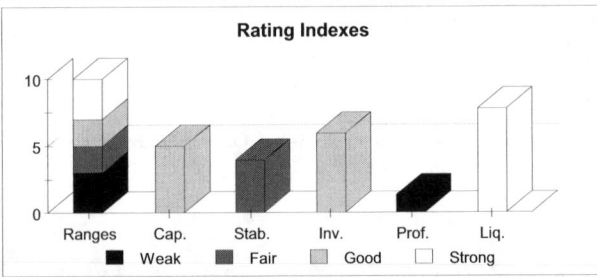

RIVERMONT LIFE INSURANCE COMPANY I   C   Fair

Major Rating Factors: Fair overall results on stability tests (4.0 on a scale of 0 to 10). Weak profitability (1.6) with operating losses during the first nine months of 2014. Strong overall capitalization (9.2) based on excellent risk adjusted capital (severe loss scenario). Nevertheless, capital levels have fluctuated during prior years.

Other Rating Factors: High quality investment portfolio (7.2). Excellent liquidity (7.9).

Principal Business: Reinsurance (100%).

Principal Investments: NonCMO investment grade bonds (71%), CMOs and structured securities (28%), and noninv. grade bonds (1%).

Investments in Affiliates: None

Group Affiliation: Genworth Financial

Licensed in: SC

Commenced Business: October 2006

Address: 151 Meeting St Suite 301, Charleston, SC 29401

Phone: (843) 577-1026 **Domicile State:** SC **NAIC Code:** 13219

Data Date	Rating	RACR #1	RACR #2	Total Assets ($mil)	Capital ($mil)	Net Premium ($mil)	Net Income ($mil)
9-14	C	4.48	2.47	526.0	148.6	20.4	-8.5
9-13	C	4.87	2.65	498.4	155.3	22.4	-10.6
2013	C	4.64	2.54	502.6	153.8	29.1	-12.5
2012	C	5.06	2.72	496.1	165.4	54.4	7.2
2011	C	5.01	2.58	460.8	163.1	19.4	-19.6
2010	U	5.95	2.97	451.1	199.6	31.9	-21.3
2009	U	7.72	3.96	437.5	226.4	37.5	-24.4

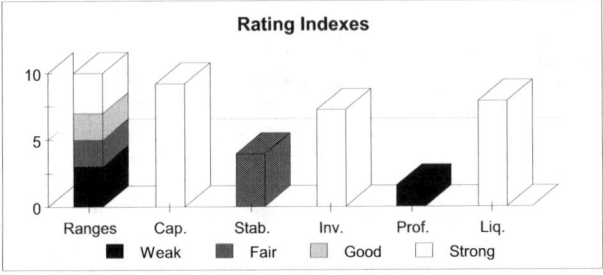

RIVERSOURCE LIFE INSURANCE COMPANY   C-   Fair

Major Rating Factors: Fair profitability (4.5 on a scale of 0 to 10) with investment income below regulatory standards in relation to interest assumptions of reserves. Fair overall results on stability tests (3.3). Good quality investment portfolio (5.9) despite large holdings of BBB rated bonds in addition to junk bond exposure equal to 51% of capital. Exposure to mortgages is significant, but the mortgage default rate has been low.
Other Rating Factors: Strong capitalization (7.2) based on excellent risk adjusted capital (severe loss scenario). Excellent liquidity (7.9).
Principal Business: Individual annuities (78%), individual life insurance (16%), individual health insurance (5%), and group retirement contracts (1%).
Principal Investments: NonCMO investment grade bonds (44%), CMOs and structured securities (24%), mortgages in good standing (11%), noninv. grade bonds (5%), and misc. investments (4%).
Investments in Affiliates: 2%
Group Affiliation: Ameriprise Financial Inc
Licensed in: All states except NY, PR
Commenced Business: October 1957
Address: 227 AXP Financial Center, Minneapolis, MN 55474
Phone: (612) 671-3131 **Domicile State:** MN **NAIC Code:** 65005

Data Date	Rating	RACR #1	RACR #2	Total Assets ($mil)	Capital ($mil)	Net Premium ($mil)	Net Income ($mil)
9-14	C-	1.92	1.14	103,856	3,154.3	4,429.6	593.4
9-13	C-	1.70	1.00	100,752	2,737.3	4,629.1	1,087.8
2013	C-	1.59	0.95	104,356	2,685.9	6,187.8	1,336.8
2012	C-	1.94	1.14	96,669.1	3,112.6	6,323.6	1,975.9
2011	C-	1.90	1.10	91,266.4	2,681.3	7,638.7	-599.3
2010	B	2.40	1.39	88,873.8	3,735.4	7,469.3	1,111.8
2009	B	2.11	1.23	81,313.1	3,370.7	9,759.2	1,886.6

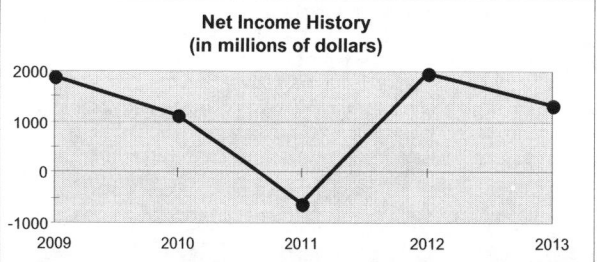

Net Income History
(in millions of dollars)

RIVERSOURCE LIFE INSURANCE COMPANY OF NEW YORK   C   Fair

Major Rating Factors: Fair overall results on stability tests (4.4 on a scale of 0 to 10) including fair financial strength of affiliated Ameriprise Financial Inc. Fair profitability (3.8) with investment income below regulatory standards in relation to interest assumptions of reserves. Good quality investment portfolio (6.0).
Other Rating Factors: Strong capitalization (7.8) based on excellent risk adjusted capital (severe loss scenario). Excellent liquidity (7.8).
Principal Business: Individual annuities (78%), individual life insurance (15%), individual health insurance (4%), and group retirement contracts (3%).
Principal Investments: NonCMO investment grade bonds (59%), CMOs and structured securities (24%), mortgages in good standing (8%), noninv. grade bonds (5%), and policy loans (2%).
Investments in Affiliates: None
Group Affiliation: Ameriprise Financial Inc
Licensed in: NY
Commenced Business: October 1972
Address: 20 Madison Avenue Extension, Albany, NY 12203
Phone: (518) 869-8613 **Domicile State:** NY **NAIC Code:** 80594

Data Date	Rating	RACR #1	RACR #2	Total Assets ($mil)	Capital ($mil)	Net Premium ($mil)	Net Income ($mil)
9-14	C	3.08	1.54	6,480.9	287.6	304.9	37.1
9-13	C	2.61	1.31	6,114.0	248.1	320.8	70.6
2013	C	2.67	1.34	6,315.7	250.3	428.1	90.4
2012	C	2.74	1.38	5,821.9	252.8	417.2	82.4
2011	B	2.70	1.36	5,503.6	235.5	482.2	-6.2
2010	B	3.15	1.60	5,473.1	287.8	452.3	63.1
2009	B-	3.05	1.55	5,048.4	284.3	589.5	86.2

Ameriprise Financial Inc Composite Group Rating: C Largest Group Members	Assets ($mil)	Rating
RIVERSOURCE LIFE INS CO	104356	C-
RIVERSOURCE LIFE INS CO OF NY	6316	C
IDS PROPERTY CASUALTY INS CO	1268	B
AMERIPRISE INS CO	46	B

ROYAL STATE NATIONAL INSURANCE COMPANY LIMITED   B-   Good

Major Rating Factors: Good quality investment portfolio (6.1 on a scale of 0 to 10) despite mixed results such as: no exposure to mortgages and substantial holdings of BBB bonds but no exposure to junk bonds. Good overall profitability (5.4). Return on equity has been low, averaging 1.9%. Good liquidity (6.9) with sufficient resources to handle a spike in claims.
Other Rating Factors: Good overall results on stability tests (5.1) good operational trends and good risk diversification. Strong capitalization (8.8) based on excellent risk adjusted capital (severe loss scenario).
Principal Business: Group life insurance (65%), group health insurance (26%), individual life insurance (6%), and reinsurance (3%).
Principal Investments: NonCMO investment grade bonds (70%), common & preferred stock (16%), CMOs and structured securities (9%), cash (5%), and policy loans (1%).
Investments in Affiliates: 3%
Group Affiliation: Royal State Group
Licensed in: HI
Commenced Business: August 1961
Address: 819 S Beretania St, Honolulu, HI 96813
Phone: (808) 539-1600 **Domicile State:** HI **NAIC Code:** 68551

Data Date	Rating	RACR #1	RACR #2	Total Assets ($mil)	Capital ($mil)	Net Premium ($mil)	Net Income ($mil)
9-14	B-	3.13	2.20	46.2	29.5	8.3	0.7
9-13	B-	3.26	2.33	45.8	29.2	8.0	0.4
2013	B-	3.29	2.33	45.6	28.9	10.6	0.4
2012	B-	3.29	2.38	44.6	28.9	10.5	-0.1
2011	B-	4.44	3.08	43.3	28.6	5.8	0.8
2010	B-	4.63	3.42	48.7	28.2	5.9	1.1
2009	B-	4.54	3.78	48.1	27.8	6.0	0.6

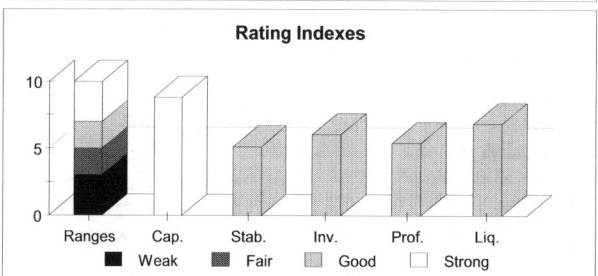

Rating Indexes

Ranges   Cap.   Stab.   Inv.   Prof.   Liq.

■ Weak   ▨ Fair   ▦ Good   □ Strong

SAGICOR LIFE INSURANCE COMPANY

C- **Fair**

Major Rating Factors: Fair quality investment portfolio (3.6 on a scale of 0 to 10). Fair overall results on stability tests (3.1) including fair risk adjusted capital in prior years. Weak profitability (2.0) with investment income below regulatory standards in relation to interest assumptions of reserves.

Other Rating Factors: Good capitalization (5.6) based on good risk adjusted capital (moderate loss scenario). Good liquidity (5.0).

Principal Business: Individual annuities (88%), individual life insurance (11%), and reinsurance (1%).

Principal Investments: NonCMO investment grade bonds (73%), CMOs and structured securities (17%), policy loans (3%), common & preferred stock (2%), and misc. investments (4%).

Investments in Affiliates: None

Group Affiliation: Sagicor Financial Corp

Licensed in: All states except AK, CT, NY, PR

Commenced Business: April 1954

Address: 2720 E Camelback Rd, Phoenix, AZ 85016

Phone: (800) 531-5067 **Domicile State:** TX **NAIC Code:** 60445

Data Date	Rating	RACR #1	RACR #2	Total Assets ($mil)	Capital ($mil)	Net Premium ($mil)	Net Income ($mil)
9-14	C-	1.38	0.72	1,193.0	72.5	46.6	4.2
9-13	C-	1.42	0.74	1,182.1	70.5	75.3	-0.7
2013	C-	1.43	0.74	1,176.2	75.8	87.4	1.1
2012	C-	1.26	0.66	1,099.9	60.1	148.8	-9.5
2011	C-	1.62	0.82	870.0	52.8	101.8	-3.8
2010	C	1.67	0.87	792.0	46.3	119.9	-20.2
2009	C	1.56	0.80	676.7	38.6	152.6	-23.8

Rating Indexes

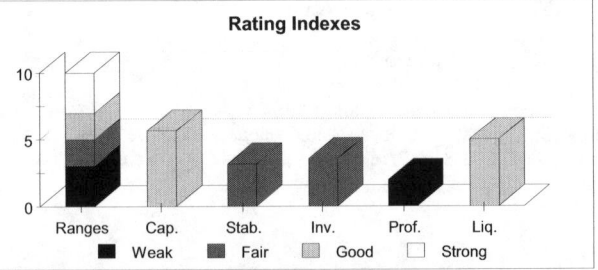

SAVINGS BANK LIFE INSURANCE COMPANY OF MASSACHUSE⸱

B+ **Good**

Major Rating Factors: Good quality investment portfolio (6.5 on a scale of 0 to 10) despite mixed results such as: large holdings of BBB rated bonds but moderate junk bond exposure. Good overall profitability (5.5) despite operating losses during the first nine months of 2014. Return on equity has been low, averaging 3.2%. Good liquidity (5.6).

Other Rating Factors: Good overall results on stability tests (6.4) excellent operational trends and excellent risk diversification. Strong capitalization (7.7) based on excellent risk adjusted capital (severe loss scenario).

Principal Business: Individual life insurance (93%) and individual annuities (7%).

Principal Investments: NonCMO investment grade bonds (63%), CMOs and structured securities (25%), policy loans (3%), common & preferred stock (3%), and noninv. grade bonds (3%).

Investments in Affiliates: None

Group Affiliation: Savings Bank Life Group

Licensed in: All states except NY, PR

Commenced Business: January 1992

Address: One Linscott Rd, Woburn, MA 01801

Phone: (781) 938-3500 **Domicile State:** MA **NAIC Code:** 70435

Data Date	Rating	RACR #1	RACR #2	Total Assets ($mil)	Capital ($mil)	Net Premium ($mil)	Net Income ($mil)
9-14	B+	2.67	1.47	2,567.5	192.0	141.5	-12.3
9-13	B+	2.83	1.57	2,463.6	205.3	124.5	9.6
2013	B+	2.90	1.60	2,534.4	213.6	169.1	17.9
2012	B+	2.93	1.65	2,406.5	202.8	207.9	22.6
2011	B+	2.92	1.65	2,396.0	193.5	187.8	17.7
2010	B+	2.43	1.40	2,562.9	159.2	214.5	12.3
2009	B+	2.76	1.64	2,203.7	162.9	214.8	-8.5

Rating Indexes

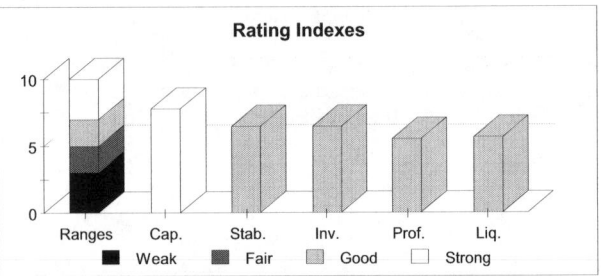

SBLI USA MUTUAL LIFE INSURANCE COMPANY INCORPORATE

B- **Good**

Major Rating Factors: Good current capitalization (6.4 on a scale of 0 to 10) based on good risk adjusted capital (severe loss scenario) reflecting some improvement over results in 2010. Good quality investment portfolio (5.8) despite mixed results such as: substantial holdings of BBB bonds but moderate junk bond exposure. Fair liquidity (3.8).

Other Rating Factors: Fair overall results on stability tests (4.9) including negative cash flow from operations for 2013, fair risk adjusted capital in prior years. Excellent profitability (7.5) despite operating losses during the first nine months of 2014.

Principal Business: Individual life insurance (70%), group life insurance (25%), reinsurance (4%), and individual health insurance (1%).

Principal Investments: NonCMO investment grade bonds (49%), CMOs and structured securities (37%), policy loans (7%), noninv. grade bonds (2%), and common & preferred stock (1%).

Investments in Affiliates: 1%

Group Affiliation: Reservoir Capital Group LLC

Licensed in: IL, IA, MI, MS, NH, NJ, NY, NC, OH, PA, SD, VT, PR

Commenced Business: January 2000

Address: 460 W 34th St Suite 800, New York, NY 10001-2320

Phone: (212) 356-0346 **Domicile State:** NY **NAIC Code:** 60176

Data Date	Rating	RACR #1	RACR #2	Total Assets ($mil)	Capital ($mil)	Net Premium ($mil)	Net Income ($mil)
9-14	B-	1.66	0.93	1,588.6	100.9	46.9	-9.0
9-13	B-	1.32	0.71	1,506.9	82.4	49.3	-2.3
2013	B-	1.44	0.79	1,479.1	89.0	65.6	-2.2
2012	C	1.22	0.65	1,486.5	81.3	68.4	-16.9
2011	C	1.11	0.59	1,486.1	76.4	72.5	-2.1
2010	C-	0.93	0.50	1,472.6	64.5	91.3	-10.3
2009	C+	1.40	0.70	1,502.8	113.1	134.3	7.0

Risk-Adjusted Capital Ratio #2
(Severe Loss Scenario)

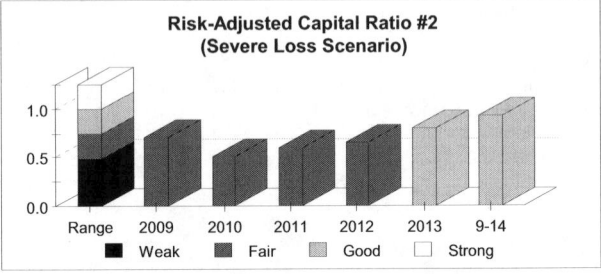

SCOR GLOBAL LIFE AMERICAS REINSURANCE COMPANY   C-   Fair

Major Rating Factors: Fair overall results on stability tests (3.3 on a scale of 0 to 10) including potential financial drain due to affiliation with SCOR Reinsurance Group, weak risk adjusted capital in prior years, negative cash flow from operations for 2013 and excessive premium growth. Weak profitability (1.9). Excellent expense controls. Good capitalization (5.5) based on good risk adjusted capital (severe loss scenario).
Other Rating Factors: Good quality investment portfolio (6.4). Excellent liquidity (7.5).
Principal Business: Reinsurance (100%).
Principal Investments: NonCMO investment grade bonds (61%), CMOs and structured securities (22%), noninv. grade bonds (9%), common & preferred stock (4%), and misc. investments (3%).
Investments in Affiliates: 4%
Group Affiliation: SCOR Reinsurance Group
Licensed in: All states except NY, OR, RI, PR
Commenced Business: April 1945
Address: 2711 Centerville Rd Suite 400, Wilmington, DE 19808
Phone: (704) 344-2700 **Domicile State:** DE **NAIC Code:** 64688

Data Date	Rating	RACR #1	RACR #2	Total Assets ($mil)	Capital ($mil)	Net Premium ($mil)	Net Income ($mil)
9-14	C-	1.29	0.81	1,468.9	190.6	78.7	0.3
9-13	C-	1.38	0.84	1,394.6	166.2	60.5	-31.0
2013	C-	1.11	0.71	1,355.3	151.8	98.1	-40.6
2012	C-	1.93	1.17	1,378.6	157.8	90.0	6.6
2011	C-	1.44	0.95	1,453.0	175.3	-852.3	-2.8
2010	D+	N/A	N/A	2,328.3	194.7	123.7	-4.3
2009	D+	0.68	0.46	2,307.9	126.2	499.1	-51.3

SCOR Reinsurance Group Composite Group Rating: D+ Largest Group Members	Assets ($mil)	Rating
SCOR REINSURANCE CO	2365	D
SCOR GLOBAL LIFE AMERICAS REIN CO	1355	C-
SCOR GLOBAL LIFE USA RE CO	949	C
SCOR GLOBAL LIFE REINS CO OF DE	470	C-
GENERAL SECURITY NATIONAL INS CO	273	C-

SCOR GLOBAL LIFE REINSURANCE COMPANY OF DELAWARE   C   Fair

Major Rating Factors: Fair overall results on stability tests (3.7 on a scale of 0 to 10) including potential financial drain due to affiliation with SCOR Reinsurance Group and fair risk adjusted capital in prior years. Weak profitability (2.3) with investment income below regulatory standards in relation to interest assumptions of reserves. Strong capitalization (7.4) based on excellent risk adjusted capital (severe loss scenario).
Other Rating Factors: High quality investment portfolio (8.3). Excellent liquidity (8.8).
Principal Business: Reinsurance (100%).
Principal Investments: NonCMO investment grade bonds (61%), CMOs and structured securities (22%), policy loans (3%), and cash (2%).
Investments in Affiliates: None
Group Affiliation: SCOR Reinsurance Group
Licensed in: All states except AL
Commenced Business: May 1977
Address: 2711 Centerville Rd Suite 400, Wilmington, DE 19808
Phone: (704) 344-2700 **Domicile State:** DE **NAIC Code:** 87017

Data Date	Rating	RACR #1	RACR #2	Total Assets ($mil)	Capital ($mil)	Net Premium ($mil)	Net Income ($mil)
9-14	C	2.02	1.24	430.4	61.2	30.5	2.9
9-13	C-	1.63	1.00	441.4	51.3	37.4	-4.0
2013	C-	1.70	1.04	470.0	51.3	37.9	-3.7
2012	D+	1.66	1.03	450.6	25.5	33.0	-17.4
2011	D	1.19	0.75	409.0	32.1	109.8	-39.4
2010	D+	N/A	N/A	328.2	47.0	17.7	15.8
2009	D+	0.88	0.56	321.0	19.9	27.2	-9.3

SCOR Reinsurance Group Composite Group Rating: D+ Largest Group Members	Assets ($mil)	Rating
SCOR REINSURANCE CO	2365	D
SCOR GLOBAL LIFE AMERICAS REIN CO	1355	C-
SCOR GLOBAL LIFE USA RE CO	949	C
SCOR GLOBAL LIFE REINS CO OF DE	470	C-
GENERAL SECURITY NATIONAL INS CO	273	C-

SCOR GLOBAL LIFE USA RE CO   C   Fair

Major Rating Factors: Fair overall results on stability tests (3.8 on a scale of 0 to 10) including potential financial drain due to affiliation with SCOR Reinsurance Group and negative cash flow from operations for 2013. Weak profitability (2.9) with investment income below regulatory standards in relation to interest assumptions of reserves. Strong capitalization (10.0) based on excellent risk adjusted capital (severe loss scenario).
Other Rating Factors: High quality investment portfolio (8.6). Excellent liquidity (7.6).
Principal Business: Reinsurance (100%).
Principal Investments: NonCMO investment grade bonds (87%) and CMOs and structured securities (1%).
Investments in Affiliates: None
Group Affiliation: SCOR Reinsurance Group
Licensed in: All states except PR
Commenced Business: October 1982
Address: 150 King St W 11th Fl, Toronto Ontario, CN M5H 1J9
Phone: (416) 979-6266 **Domicile State:** DE **NAIC Code:** 97071

Data Date	Rating	RACR #1	RACR #2	Total Assets ($mil)	Capital ($mil)	Net Premium ($mil)	Net Income ($mil)
9-14	C	7.42	4.42	800.9	429.2	160.0	6.3
9-13	B-	2.76	1.77	1,148.0	374.5	281.2	7.8
2013	C	8.20	5.04	949.3	422.6	908.2	61.6
2012	B-	2.66	1.72	1,109.1	364.0	370.0	18.7
2011	B-	2.64	1.71	1,033.1	346.8	355.4	32.2
2010	B-	2.74	1.79	987.2	342.1	315.7	23.4
2009	B-	2.69	1.78	913.1	311.4	293.0	12.4

SCOR Reinsurance Group Composite Group Rating: D+ Largest Group Members	Assets ($mil)	Rating
SCOR REINSURANCE CO	2365	D
SCOR GLOBAL LIFE AMERICAS REIN CO	1355	C-
SCOR GLOBAL LIFE USA RE CO	949	C
SCOR GLOBAL LIFE REINS CO OF DE	470	C-
GENERAL SECURITY NATIONAL INS CO	273	C-

SCOTTISH RE US INCORPORATED

C- **Fair**

Major Rating Factors: Fair overall results on stability tests (3.0 on a scale of 0 to 10) including negative cash flow from operations for 2013, fair risk adjusted capital in prior years. Weak profitability (1.9) with investment income below regulatory standards in relation to interest assumptions of reserves. Good quality investment portfolio (6.3).

Other Rating Factors: Good liquidity (5.8). Strong capitalization (7.1) based on excellent risk adjusted capital (severe loss scenario).

Principal Business: Reinsurance (100%).

Principal Investments: CMOs and structured securities (47%), nonCMO investment grade bonds (47%), noninv. grade bonds (5%), and cash (1%).

Investments in Affiliates: None

Group Affiliation: Scottish Annuity & Life Holdings Ltd

Licensed in: All states except PA, PR

Commenced Business: September 1977

Address: 15800 John J Delaney Dr #200, Charlotte, NC 28277

Phone: (704) 542-9192 **Domicile State:** DE **NAIC Code:** 87572

Data Date	Rating	RACR #1	RACR #2	Total Assets ($mil)	Capital ($mil)	Net Premium ($mil)	Net Income ($mil)
9-14	C-	1.89	1.04	1,770.7	185.3	184.9	12.2
9-13	F	N/A	N/A	1,831.1	202.6	180.1	7.2
2013	C-	1.73	0.95	1,808.2	171.7	251.2	-24.2
2012	F	1.84	1.11	1,556.9	193.5	135.5	-28.5
2011	F	2.10	1.32	1,722.6	328.6	114.1	-199.7
2010	F	1.45	0.93	1,833.9	292.3	98.1	49.4
2009	F	1.00	0.64	1,845.5	235.7	-149.3	119.1

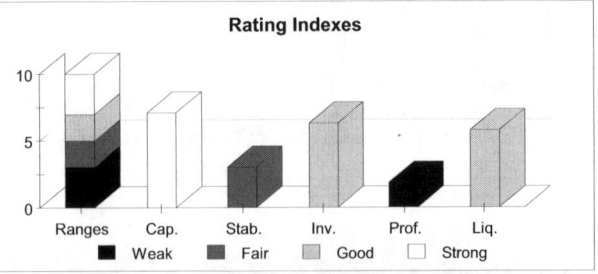

Rating Indexes

Ranges   Cap.   Stab.   Inv.   Prof.   Liq.

■ Weak   ■ Fair   ▨ Good   □ Strong

SECURIAN LIFE INSURANCE COMPANY

B **Good**

Major Rating Factors: Good overall profitability (5.4 on a scale of 0 to 10). Excellent expense controls. Return on equity has been low, averaging 1.9%. Good liquidity (6.9) with sufficient resources to handle a spike in claims. Good overall results on stability tests (6.3). Stability strengths include excellent operational trends and excellent risk diversification.

Other Rating Factors: Strong capitalization (10.0) based on excellent risk adjusted capital (severe loss scenario). High quality investment portfolio (8.2).

Principal Business: Group life insurance (37%), group health insurance (31%), reinsurance (12%), individual life insurance (11%), and other lines (9%).

Principal Investments: NonCMO investment grade bonds (90%), CMOs and structured securities (7%), cash (2%), and noninv. grade bonds (1%).

Investments in Affiliates: None

Group Affiliation: Securian Financial Group

Licensed in: All states except PR

Commenced Business: December 1981

Address: 400 Robert St N, St Paul, MN 55101

Phone: (651) 665-3500 **Domicile State:** MN **NAIC Code:** 93742

Data Date	Rating	RACR #1	RACR #2	Total Assets ($mil)	Capital ($mil)	Net Premium ($mil)	Net Income ($mil)
9-14	B	6.48	4.52	234.4	135.8	68.9	4.6
9-13	B	7.88	5.53	206.2	132.6	60.6	-2.8
2013	B	6.47	4.56	207.8	131.5	83.2	-3.0
2012	A-	8.20	5.79	190.1	134.9	72.0	0.3
2011	B+	8.60	6.17	167.6	134.2	65.5	4.7
2010	B+	10.79	7.66	155.2	129.7	50.5	3.3
2009	B+	11.07	7.70	149.7	126.5	44.6	3.9

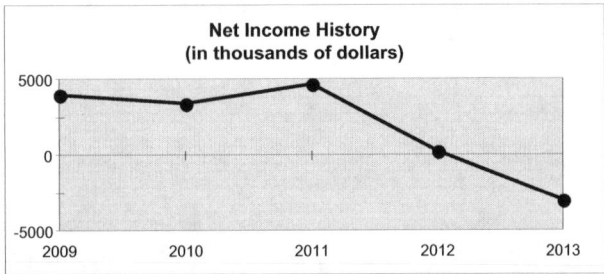

Net Income History
(in thousands of dollars)

2009   2010   2011   2012   2013

SECURITY BENEFIT LIFE INSURANCE COMPANY

B **Good**

Major Rating Factors: Good overall results on stability tests (6.2 on a scale of 0 to 10). Stability strengths include excellent operational trends and excellent risk diversification. Good current capitalization (6.4) based on good risk adjusted capital (severe loss scenario), although results have slipped from the excellent range during the last year. Fair quality investment portfolio (4.5).

Other Rating Factors: Excellent profitability (8.4). Excellent liquidity (9.2).

Principal Business: Individual annuities (98%), group retirement contracts (1%), and reinsurance (1%).

Principal Investments: NonCMO investment grade bonds (36%), CMOs and structured securities (29%), mortgages in good standing (4%), policy loans (3%), and misc. investments (15%).

Investments in Affiliates: 13%

Group Affiliation: Sammons Enterprises Inc

Licensed in: All states except NY, PR

Commenced Business: February 1892

Address: One Security Benefit Place, Topeka, KS 66636-0001

Phone: (785) 431-3000 **Domicile State:** KS **NAIC Code:** 68675

Data Date	Rating	RACR #1	RACR #2	Total Assets ($mil)	Capital ($mil)	Net Premium ($mil)	Net Income ($mil)
9-14	B	1.93	0.92	23,360.9	1,005.8	4,030.1	131.0
9-13	B	1.87	0.89	19,161.7	770.3	4,477.0	158.1
2013	B	2.31	1.12	20,702.3	1,044.8	6,191.9	163.6
2012	B	2.19	1.06	15,392.6	774.0	2,478.2	156.9
2011	B-	2.22	1.09	10,507.8	612.8	1,629.1	1.2
2010	B-	2.23	1.15	9,921.6	615.1	339.7	12.8
2009	C+	1.57	0.79	9,862.1	427.4	518.8	-21.1

Adverse Trends in Operations

Change in premium mix from 2009 to 2010 (4.1%)
Decrease in premium volume from 2009 to 2010 (35%)

SECURITY LIFE OF DENVER INSURANCE COMPANY   C+   Fair

Major Rating Factors: Fair overall results on stability tests (3.1 on a scale of 0 to 10) including weak results on operational trends, negative cash flow from operations for 2013. Good quality investment portfolio (6.2) despite mixed results such as: minimal exposure to mortgages and large holdings of BBB rated bonds but small junk bond holdings. Good liquidity (5.9).

Other Rating Factors: Weak profitability (2.4). Strong capitalization (7.0) based on excellent risk adjusted capital (severe loss scenario).

Principal Business: Reinsurance (77%) and individual life insurance (23%).

Principal Investments: NonCMO investment grade bonds (62%), CMOs and structured securities (14%), policy loans (9%), mortgages in good standing (6%), and misc. investments (8%).

Investments in Affiliates: 3%

Group Affiliation: Voya Financial Inc

Licensed in: All states, the District of Columbia and Puerto Rico

Commenced Business: May 1950

Address: 1290 Broadway, Denver, CO 80203-0000

Phone: (303) 860-1290 **Domicile State:** CO **NAIC Code:** 68713

Data Date	Rating	RACR #1	RACR #2	Total Assets ($mil)	Capital ($mil)	Net Premium ($mil)	Net Income ($mil)
9-14	C+	1.80	1.02	14,195.5	1,087.6	-81.6	24.3
9-13	B-	1.62	0.93	15,121.0	973.0	808.5	-2.7
2013	C+	1.80	1.04	15,066.6	1,034.0	910.8	-0.1
2012	B-	2.25	1.27	16,427.4	1,459.9	7,104.5	-129.8
2011	C+	2.29	1.27	17,271.3	1,519.5	5,684.7	175.2
2010	C+	2.01	1.05	19,251.3	1,457.0	2,180.1	-339.9
2009	C+	1.82	0.90	20,770.4	1,697.5	950.5	23.7

Adverse Trends in Operations

Decrease in premium volume from 2012 to 2013 (87%)
Decrease in capital during 2013 (29%)
Increase in policy surrenders from 2010 to 2011 (163%)
Decrease in asset base during 2011 (10%)
Decrease in capital during 2010 (14%)

SECURITY MUTUAL LIFE INSURANCE CO OF NEW YORK   B   Good

Major Rating Factors: Good current capitalization (5.7 on a scale of 0 to 10) based on good risk adjusted capital (moderate loss scenario) reflecting some improvement over results in 2009. Good quality investment portfolio (6.0) despite mixed results such as: minimal exposure to mortgages and large holdings of BBB rated bonds but minimal holdings in junk bonds. Good overall profitability (6.2).

Other Rating Factors: Fair overall results on stability tests (4.0) including fair risk adjusted capital in prior years. Weak liquidity (1.6).

Principal Business: Individual life insurance (88%), individual annuities (6%), group health insurance (3%), group life insurance (3%), and individual health insurance (1%).

Principal Investments: NonCMO investment grade bonds (69%), policy loans (13%), CMOs and structured securities (10%), and mortgages in good standing (7%).

Investments in Affiliates: None

Group Affiliation: None

Licensed in: All states except PR

Commenced Business: January 1887

Address: Court House Square, Bimghamton, NY 13901

Phone: (607) 723-3551 **Domicile State:** NY **NAIC Code:** 68772

Data Date	Rating	RACR #1	RACR #2	Total Assets ($mil)	Capital ($mil)	Net Premium ($mil)	Net Income ($mil)
9-14	B	1.49	0.81	2,670.6	131.5	124.3	6.1
9-13	B	1.37	0.77	2,665.5	123.8	127.2	7.5
2013	B	1.52	0.83	2,676.4	133.6	170.7	8.4
2012	B	1.35	0.76	2,625.0	120.1	170.9	5.7
2011	B	1.33	0.75	2,557.5	120.4	159.8	10.0
2010	B	1.36	0.75	2,497.4	116.2	205.7	6.9
2009	B	1.31	0.72	2,426.9	113.0	319.1	7.2

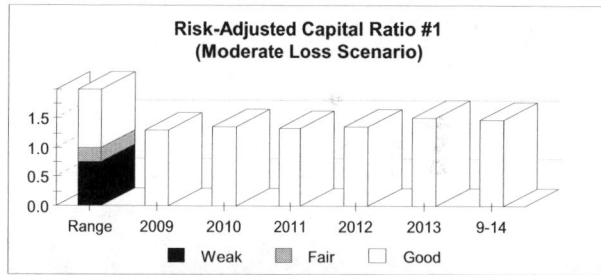

Risk-Adjusted Capital Ratio #1 (Moderate Loss Scenario)

Range 2009 2010 2011 2012 2013 9-14
■ Weak ▦ Fair ☐ Good

SECURITY NATIONAL LIFE INSURANCE COMPANY   D-   Weak

Major Rating Factors: Poor capitalization (1.1 on a scale of 0 to 10) based on weak risk adjusted capital (moderate loss scenario). Low quality investment portfolio (1.5) containing large exposure to mortgages . Mortgage default rate has been low. Weak overall results on stability tests (1.1) including weak risk adjusted capital in prior years.

Other Rating Factors: Good overall profitability (5.6) although investment income, in comparison to reserve requirements, is below regulatory standards. Excellent liquidity (7.1).

Principal Business: Individual life insurance (81%), individual annuities (12%), and reinsurance (7%).

Principal Investments: NonCMO investment grade bonds (33%), mortgages in good standing (29%), real estate (8%), common & preferred stock (3%), and misc. investments (7%).

Investments in Affiliates: 2%

Group Affiliation: Security National Life

Licensed in: AL, AK, AZ, AR, CA, CO, DC, DE, FL, GA, HI, ID, IL, IN, IA, KS, KY, LA, MD, MI, MN, MS, MO, MT, NE, NV, NM, ND, OK, OR, SC, SD, TN, TX, UT, VA, WI, WY

Commenced Business: July 1967

Address: 5300 S 360 West Ste 310, Salt Lake City, UT 84132-1047

Phone: (801) 264-1060 **Domicile State:** UT **NAIC Code:** 69485

Data Date	Rating	RACR #1	RACR #2	Total Assets ($mil)	Capital ($mil)	Net Premium ($mil)	Net Income ($mil)
9-14	D-	0.49	0.34	505.7	31.3	47.0	3.2
9-13	D	0.55	0.34	479.1	28.7	44.6	1.0
2013	D	0.51	0.35	477.6	29.6	59.3	1.3
2012	D	0.67	0.43	464.3	29.8	55.8	0.4
2011	D	0.59	0.37	422.7	24.3	55.1	0.0
2010	D	0.71	0.43	370.4	21.2	45.5	1.1
2009	D	0.53	0.31	364.2	17.1	44.4	3.2

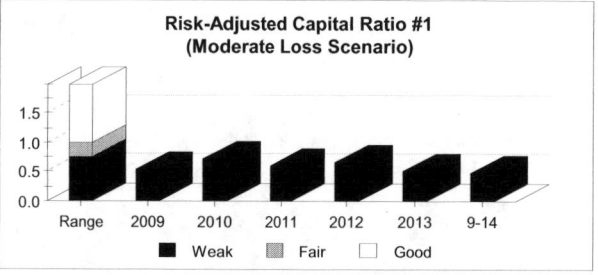

Risk-Adjusted Capital Ratio #1 (Moderate Loss Scenario)

Range 2009 2010 2011 2012 2013 9-14
■ Weak ▦ Fair ☐ Good

SECURITY PLAN INSURANCE COMPANY

C+   **Fair**

Major Rating Factors: Fair overall results on stability tests (4.5 on a scale of 0 to 10) including fair financial strength of affiliated Citizens Inc. Good quality investment portfolio (6.3) despite mixed results such as: minimal exposure to mortgages and substantial holdings of BBB bonds but small junk bond holdings. Good overall profitability (5.9). Return on equity has been low, averaging 3.6%.

Other Rating Factors: Good liquidity (6.8). Strong capitalization (8.1) based on excellent risk adjusted capital (severe loss scenario).

Principal Business: Individual life insurance (94%), individual annuities (5%), and individual health insurance (1%).

Principal Investments: NonCMO investment grade bonds (82%), common & preferred stock (5%), cash (4%), noninv. grade bonds (3%), and misc. investments (6%).

Investments in Affiliates: 2%

Group Affiliation: Citizens Inc

Licensed in: AR, LA, MS

Commenced Business: March 1996

Address: 110 Railroad Ave, Donaldsonville, LA 70346-2520

Phone: (504) 473-8654 **Domicile State:** LA **NAIC Code:** 60076

Data Date	Rating	RACR #1	RACR #2	Total Assets ($mil)	Capital ($mil)	Net Premium ($mil)	Net Income ($mil)
9-14	C+	2.72	1.70	321.7	52.4	32.4	0.9
9-13	C+	2.96	1.85	319.1	53.2	32.4	1.2
2013	C+	3.10	1.95	320.5	54.1	41.0	2.2
2012	C+	2.94	1.87	318.5	52.4	41.3	1.7
2011	C+	3.20	2.05	313.6	53.0	41.0	2.2
2010	C	3.63	2.39	300.2	48.4	40.4	0.7
2009	C	3.83	2.42	302.3	52.8	39.5	6.1

Citizens Inc Composite Group Rating: C Largest Group Members	Assets ($mil)	Rating
CICA LIFE INS CO OF AMERICA	701	C-
SECURITY PLAN LIFE INS CO	321	C+
CITIZENS NATIONAL LIFE INS CO	13	C
MAGNOLIA GUARANTY LIFE INS CO	9	B
SECURITY PLAN FIRE INS CO	6	D

SENIOR HEALTH INSURANCE COMPANY OF PENNSYLVANIA

D+   **Weak**

Major Rating Factors: Low quality investment portfolio (0.8 on a scale of 0 to 10) containing large holdings of BBB rated bonds in addition to significant exposure to junk bonds. Weak profitability (1.7) with operating losses during the first nine months of 2014. Return on equity has been low, averaging -7.2%. Weak overall results on stability tests (2.8) including negative cash flow from operations for 2013.

Other Rating Factors: Fair capitalization (4.8) based on fair risk adjusted capital (moderate loss scenario). Good liquidity (6.8).

Principal Business: Individual health insurance (92%), reinsurance (7%), and group health insurance (1%).

Principal Investments: NonCMO investment grade bonds (72%), CMOs and structured securities (15%), noninv. grade bonds (6%), common & preferred stock (3%), and mortgages in good standing (3%).

Investments in Affiliates: None

Group Affiliation: Senior Health Care Oversight Trust

Licensed in: All states except CT, NY, RI, VT, PR

Commenced Business: February 1965

Address: 11815 N Pennsylvania St, Carmel, IN 46032

Phone: (317) 817-3700 **Domicile State:** PA **NAIC Code:** 76325

Data Date	Rating	RACR #1	RACR #2	Total Assets ($mil)	Capital ($mil)	Net Premium ($mil)	Net Income ($mil)
9-14	D+	0.99	0.48	2,898.4	69.6	118.6	-16.6
9-13	D+	1.16	0.57	3,015.0	87.6	132.4	-11.6
2013	D+	1.25	0.62	2,985.9	98.2	173.7	-3.4
2012	D+	1.22	0.60	3,080.7	105.5	194.0	-4.0
2011	D+	1.22	0.60	3,161.1	114.4	213.8	-57.2
2010	D+	1.74	0.83	3,317.0	177.3	234.2	-15.0
2009	D+	1.94	0.92	3,252.0	193.4	249.9	-17.5

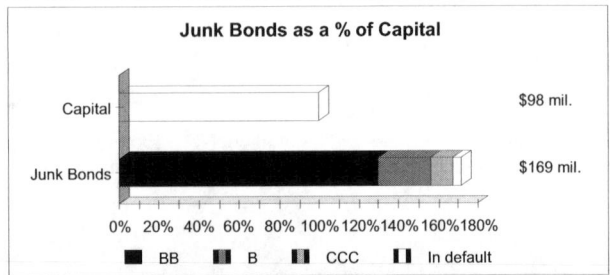

Junk Bonds as a % of Capital

Capital $98 mil.
Junk Bonds $169 mil.

0% 20% 40% 60% 80% 100%120%140%160%180%

■ BB   ▨ B   ▥ CCC   ▤ In default

SENTRY LIFE INSURANCE COMPANY *

A   **Excellent**

Major Rating Factors: Good overall profitability (6.2 on a scale of 0 to 10). Return on equity has been fair, averaging 8.4%. Excellent overall results on stability tests (7.4). Strengths that enhance stability include excellent operational trends and excellent risk diversification. Strong capitalization (8.9) based on excellent risk adjusted capital (severe loss scenario). Furthermore, this high level of risk adjusted capital has been consistently maintained over the last five years.

Other Rating Factors: High quality investment portfolio (7.4). Excellent liquidity (7.4).

Principal Business: Group retirement contracts (90%), individual life insurance (6%), group life insurance (1%), group health insurance (1%), and individual annuities (1%).

Principal Investments: NonCMO investment grade bonds (89%), CMOs and structured securities (8%), noninv. grade bonds (2%), and policy loans (1%).

Investments in Affiliates: None

Group Affiliation: Sentry Ins Group

Licensed in: All states except NY, PR

Commenced Business: November 1958

Address: 1800 North Point Dr, Stevens Point, WI 54481

Phone: (715) 346-6000 **Domicile State:** WI **NAIC Code:** 68810

Data Date	Rating	RACR #1	RACR #2	Total Assets ($mil)	Capital ($mil)	Net Premium ($mil)	Net Income ($mil)
9-14	A	3.97	2.28	5,237.9	290.6	422.9	19.9
9-13	A	4.02	2.30	4,757.2	287.7	379.6	19.1
2013	A	3.77	2.16	4,909.7	272.5	502.1	26.2
2012	A	3.90	2.26	4,364.9	269.8	466.9	20.5
2011	A	4.15	2.40	3,873.5	274.8	400.3	22.9
2010	A	4.37	2.53	3,732.0	275.6	387.9	23.9
2009	A	4.50	2.61	3,340.6	275.1	342.8	18.5

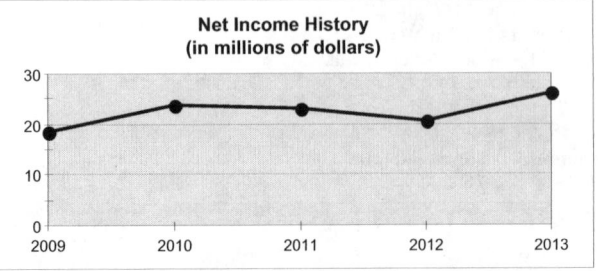

Net Income History (in millions of dollars)

30
20
10
0
2009   2010   2011   2012   2013

SERVICE LIFE & CASUALTY INSURANCE COMPANY — C — Fair

Major Rating Factors: Fair overall capitalization (4.0 on a scale of 0 to 10) based on mixed results -- excessive policy leverage mitigated by excellent risk adjusted capital (severe loss scenario). Nevertheless, capital levels have fluctuated during prior years. Fair overall results on stability tests (4.0) including negative cash flow from operations for 2013. Good overall profitability (5.3).
Other Rating Factors: Low quality investment portfolio (2.9). Excellent liquidity (8.1).
Principal Business: N/A
Principal Investments: Real estate (55%), mortgages in good standing (18%), nonCMO investment grade bonds (14%), CMOs and structured securities (6%), and misc. investments (8%).
Investments in Affiliates: 1%
Group Affiliation: Service Ins Group
Licensed in: AZ, CO, LA, NM, SC, TX
Commenced Business: January 1970
Address: 6907 Capital of Texas Hwy, Austin, TX 78731
Phone: (512) 343-0600 **Domicile State:** TX **NAIC Code:** 77151

Data Date	Rating	RACR #1	RACR #2	Total Assets ($mil)	Capital ($mil)	Net Premium ($mil)	Net Income ($mil)
9-14	C	4.74	2.00	41.9	32.9	-0.4	0.9
9-13	C	4.46	1.89	46.9	33.2	-1.0	3.1
2013	C	4.36	1.84	42.1	30.7	-1.1	2.0
2012	C	4.04	1.73	52.3	30.7	-2.5	4.8
2011	C	3.36	1.55	75.0	35.2	-4.7	3.3
2010	C	4.46	2.13	103.0	41.1	-7.0	9.7
2009	C	3.94	1.99	127.7	34.3	3.1	9.2

Policy Leverage

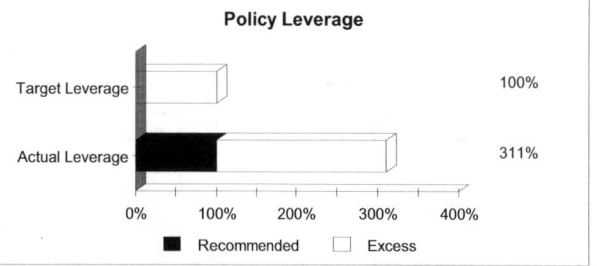

Target Leverage — 100%
Actual Leverage — 311%

■ Recommended □ Excess

SETTLERS LIFE INSURANCE COMPANY — B — Good

Major Rating Factors: Good overall results on stability tests (6.2 on a scale of 0 to 10). Stability strengths include good operational trends and good risk diversification. Good quality investment portfolio (6.4) despite mixed results such as: no exposure to mortgages and large holdings of BBB rated bonds but small junk bond holdings. Good overall profitability (6.0).
Other Rating Factors: Good liquidity (6.6). Strong capitalization (8.4) based on excellent risk adjusted capital (severe loss scenario).
Principal Business: Individual life insurance (85%), group life insurance (14%), and individual health insurance (1%).
Principal Investments: NonCMO investment grade bonds (84%), CMOs and structured securities (6%), noninv. grade bonds (3%), common & preferred stock (3%), and misc. investments (4%).
Investments in Affiliates: None
Group Affiliation: NGL Ins Group
Licensed in: All states except NY, PR
Commenced Business: September 1982
Address: 2 E Gilman St, Madison, WI 53703-1494
Phone: (608) 257-5611 **Domicile State:** WI **NAIC Code:** 97241

Data Date	Rating	RACR #1	RACR #2	Total Assets ($mil)	Capital ($mil)	Net Premium ($mil)	Net Income ($mil)
9-14	B	3.58	1.92	394.0	55.6	33.5	5.1
9-13	B	3.63	1.93	386.1	54.1	33.2	5.1
2013	B	3.41	1.84	385.6	51.5	44.0	6.9
2012	B	3.45	1.83	378.3	49.6	43.1	4.7
2011	B	3.78	1.99	378.3	55.6	42.2	6.5
2010	B	4.30	2.31	373.0	60.0	-11.2	9.4
2009	B+	3.43	1.83	414.8	53.3	41.2	6.9

Adverse Trends in Operations

Decrease in capital during 2012 (11%)
Change in premium mix from 2010 to 2011 (11.7%)
Decrease in capital during 2011 (7%)
Decrease in asset base during 2010 (10%)
Decrease in premium volume from 2009 to 2010 (127%)

SHELTER LIFE INSURANCE COMPANY * — A- — Excellent

Major Rating Factors: Good overall profitability (6.0 on a scale of 0 to 10) although investment income, in comparison to reserve requirements, is below regulatory standards. Good liquidity (6.0) with sufficient resources to handle a spike in claims as well as a significant increase in policy surrenders. Excellent overall results on stability tests (7.3) excellent operational trends and excellent risk diversification.
Other Rating Factors: Strong capitalization (9.1) based on excellent risk adjusted capital (severe loss scenario). High quality investment portfolio (7.9).
Principal Business: Individual life insurance (87%), individual annuities (6%), group health insurance (5%), group life insurance (1%), and individual health insurance (1%).
Principal Investments: NonCMO investment grade bonds (70%), CMOs and structured securities (22%), policy loans (2%), common & preferred stock (1%), and mortgages in good standing (1%).
Investments in Affiliates: 3%
Group Affiliation: Shelter Ins Companies
Licensed in: AR, CO, IL, IN, IA, KS, KY, LA, MS, MO, NE, NV, OK, TN
Commenced Business: March 1959
Address: 1817 W Broadway, Columbia, MO 65218
Phone: (573) 445-8441 **Domicile State:** MO **NAIC Code:** 65757

Data Date	Rating	RACR #1	RACR #2	Total Assets ($mil)	Capital ($mil)	Net Premium ($mil)	Net Income ($mil)
9-14	A-	3.67	2.40	1,108.6	187.0	86.0	4.5
9-13	A-	3.48	2.27	1,077.1	172.4	84.5	6.0
2013	A-	3.60	2.37	1,078.4	181.6	113.0	14.6
2012	A-	3.34	2.19	1,044.8	165.4	128.4	15.5
2011	A-	3.39	2.20	1,012.8	162.3	147.0	11.8
2010	A-	3.63	2.35	961.3	164.1	135.6	16.8
2009	A-	4.47	2.78	940.4	176.7	126.0	44.1

Net Income History
(in millions of dollars)

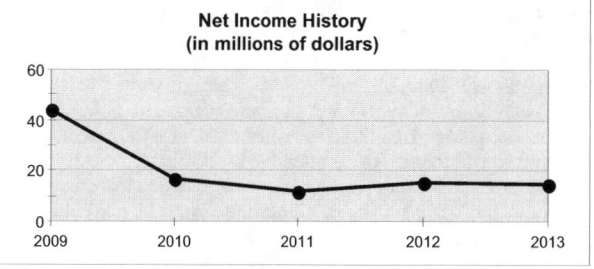

SHELTERPOINT LIFE INSURANCE COMPANY * | A | Excellent

Major Rating Factors: Good quality investment portfolio (6.6 on a scale of 0 to 10) despite mixed results such as: no exposure to mortgages and substantial holdings of BBB bonds but minimal holdings in junk bonds. Good overall results on stability tests (6.6). Strengths that enhance stability include excellent operational trends and good risk diversification. Strong capitalization (9.0) based on excellent risk adjusted capital (severe loss scenario).

Other Rating Factors: Excellent profitability (8.0) with operating gains in each of the last five years. Excellent liquidity (7.2).

Principal Business: Group health insurance (98%) and group life insurance (2%).

Principal Investments: NonCMO investment grade bonds (78%), CMOs and structured securities (14%), noninv. grade bonds (5%), and cash (3%).

Investments in Affiliates: None

Group Affiliation: Rehab Services Corp

Licensed in: CO, CT, DC, DE, IL, MD, MA, MI, MN, NJ, NY, NC, PA, RI, SC, TN

Commenced Business: November 1972

Address: 600 Northern Blvd, Great Neck, NY 11021-5202

Phone: (516) 829-8100 **Domicile State:** NY **NAIC Code:** 81434

Data Date	Rating	RACR #1	RACR #2	Total Assets ($mil)	Capital ($mil)	Net Premium ($mil)	Net Income ($mil)
9-14	A	3.14	2.30	104.4	51.9	68.3	2.0
9-13	A	3.96	3.00	99.3	51.8	63.9	4.2
2013	A	3.82	2.91	100.4	48.2	82.4	5.7
2012	A-	4.13	3.18	93.5	47.3	71.9	4.5
2011	B	3.87	3.01	87.2	43.4	69.2	4.5
2010	B-	2.87	2.26	94.3	42.4	95.2	3.5
2009	C	2.85	2.22	93.5	42.0	95.3	2.4

Adverse Trends in Operations

Decrease in asset base during 2011 (7%)
Decrease in premium volume from 2010 to 2011 (27%)

SHENANDOAH LIFE INS CO | C | Fair

Major Rating Factors: Fair profitability (3.1 on a scale of 0 to 10) with investment income below regulatory standards in relation to interest assumptions of reserves. Fair liquidity (3.4) due, in part, to cash value policies that are subject to withdrawals with minimal or no penalty. Fair overall results on stability tests (3.7) including negative cash flow from operations for 2013.

Other Rating Factors: Good capitalization (6.7) based on good risk adjusted capital (severe loss scenario). Good quality investment portfolio (5.7).

Principal Business: Individual life insurance (86%), individual health insurance (12%), group life insurance (1%), and individual annuities (1%).

Principal Investments: NonCMO investment grade bonds (55%), CMOs and structured securities (29%), mortgages in good standing (10%), policy loans (2%), and misc. investments (3%).

Investments in Affiliates: None

Group Affiliation: Reservoir Capital Group LLC

Licensed in: AL, AZ, AR, CO, DC, DE, GA, IL, IN, IA, KS, KY, LA, MD, MI, MN, MS, MO, NE, NJ, NM, NC, OH, OK, PA, SC, TN, TX, VA, WV, WI

Commenced Business: February 1916

Address: 2301 Brambleton Ave SW, Roanoke, VA 24015

Phone: (540) 985-4400 **Domicile State:** VA **NAIC Code:** 68845

Data Date	Rating	RACR #1	RACR #2	Total Assets ($mil)	Capital ($mil)	Net Premium ($mil)	Net Income ($mil)
9-14	C	1.79	0.96	1,220.8	82.6	37.9	13.8
9-13	C	1.47	0.81	1,294.5	68.8	41.5	11.1
2013	C	1.74	0.93	1,278.8	81.1	54.7	12.6
2012	D	1.45	0.78	1,379.9	87.2	61.6	28.1
2011	N/A	N/A	N/A	1,432.1	15.6	65.7	8.3
2010	N/A	N/A	N/A	1,439.2	15.0	72.6	8.9
2009	N/A	N/A	N/A	1,428.7	0.4	112.4	-15.2

Investment Income Compared to Needs of Reserves

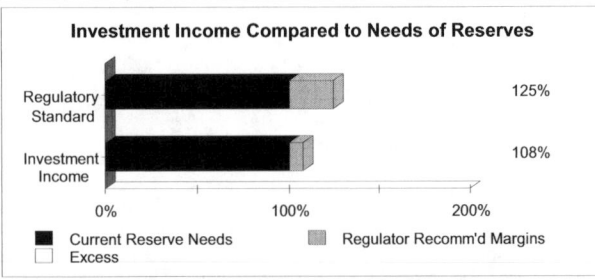

SOUTHERN FARM BUREAU LIFE INSURANCE COMPANY * | A | Excellent

Major Rating Factors: Good quality investment portfolio (6.0 on a scale of 0 to 10) despite significant exposure to mortgages . Mortgage default rate has been low. large holdings of BBB rated bonds in addition to minimal holdings in junk bonds. Good liquidity (6.3) with sufficient resources to handle a spike in claims as well as a significant increase in policy surrenders. Strong capitalization (9.1) based on excellent risk adjusted capital (severe loss scenario).

Other Rating Factors: Excellent profitability (8.1) with operating gains in each of the last five years. Excellent overall results on stability tests (7.4) excellent operational trends and excellent risk diversification.

Principal Business: Individual life insurance (79%), individual annuities (14%), individual health insurance (4%), group health insurance (3%), and group life insurance (1%).

Principal Investments: NonCMO investment grade bonds (57%), CMOs and structured securities (16%), mortgages in good standing (10%), common & preferred stock (6%), and misc. investments (10%).

Investments in Affiliates: 1%

Group Affiliation: Southern Farm Bureau Group

Licensed in: AL, AR, CO, FL, GA, KY, LA, MS, NC, SC, TN, TX, VA, PR

Commenced Business: December 1946

Address: 1401 Livingston Lane, Jackson, MS 39213

Phone: (601) 981-7422 **Domicile State:** MS **NAIC Code:** 68896

Data Date	Rating	RACR #1	RACR #2	Total Assets ($mil)	Capital ($mil)	Net Premium ($mil)	Net Income ($mil)
9-14	A	4.43	2.40	12,937.4	2,403.0	605.1	121.4
9-13	A	4.35	2.37	12,579.3	2,229.4	599.2	94.7
2013	A	4.42	2.42	12,679.3	2,327.2	785.7	149.8
2012	A	4.17	2.26	12,254.5	2,082.3	852.2	148.8
2011	A	3.92	2.14	11,673.2	1,904.2	906.9	150.0
2010	A	3.81	2.05	11,182.0	1,782.0	915.0	92.7
2009	A	3.90	2.14	10,545.7	1,669.2	796.3	10.4

Rating Indexes

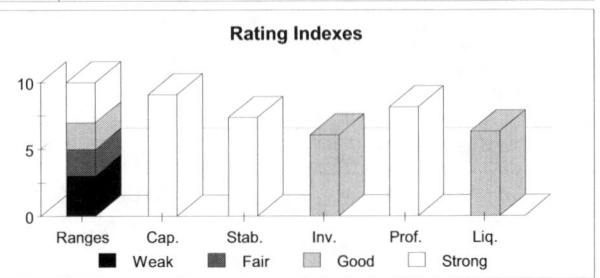

SOUTHERN FINANCIAL LIFE INSURANCE COMPANY   D+   Weak

Major Rating Factors: Low quality investment portfolio (2.9 on a scale of 0 to 10) containing large holdings of BBB rated bonds in addition to junk bond exposure equal to 57% of capital. Weak overall results on stability tests (2.8). Good liquidity (6.7) with sufficient resources to handle a spike in claims.
Other Rating Factors: Strong capitalization (7.7) based on excellent risk adjusted capital (severe loss scenario). Excellent profitability (8.9) with operating gains in each of the last five years.
Principal Business: Reinsurance (98%) and individual life insurance (2%).
Principal Investments: NonCMO investment grade bonds (51%), common & preferred stock (26%), noninv. grade bonds (17%), and cash (1%).
Investments in Affiliates: None
Group Affiliation: None
Licensed in: LA, TX
Commenced Business: June 1984
Address: 310 Heatheroak Ave, Lafayette, LA 70506
Phone: (813) 442-4084 **Domicile State:** LA **NAIC Code:** 69418

Data Date	Rating	RACR #1	RACR #2	Total Assets ($mil)	Capital ($mil)	Net Premium ($mil)	Net Income ($mil)
9-14	D+	2.65	1.46	102.5	27.8	6.3	2.9
9-13	D+	2.26	1.21	98.8	22.7	6.6	3.2
2013	D+	2.43	1.33	102.4	24.7	9.9	3.6
2012	D+	2.23	1.20	93.1	18.0	20.5	1.2
2011	D+	2.30	1.21	73.9	17.6	7.7	3.1
2010	D+	1.97	1.04	72.6	15.0	10.3	2.9
2009	D+	1.62	0.86	69.7	11.8	9.3	2.1

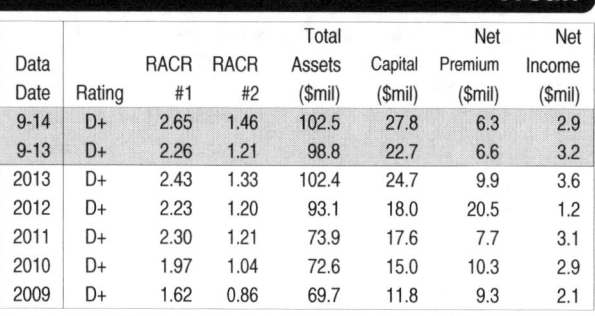

Rating Indexes

Ranges   Cap.   Stab.   Inv.   Prof.   Liq.
■ Weak   ■ Fair   ▦ Good   □ Strong

STANDARD INSURANCE COMPANY *   B+   Good

Major Rating Factors: Good quality investment portfolio (5.6 on a scale of 0 to 10) despite substantial holdings of BBB bonds in addition to moderate junk bond exposure. Exposure to mortgages is large, but the mortgage default rate has been low. Good liquidity (6.7) with sufficient resources to cover a large increase in policy surrenders. Good overall results on stability tests (6.5) excellent operational trends and excellent risk diversification.
Other Rating Factors: Strong capitalization (7.1) based on excellent risk adjusted capital (severe loss scenario). Excellent profitability (7.1) with operating gains in each of the last five years.
Principal Business: Group retirement contracts (36%), group health insurance (28%), group life insurance (19%), individual annuities (8%), and other lines (9%).
Principal Investments: NonCMO investment grade bonds (49%), mortgages in good standing (43%), noninv. grade bonds (3%), CMOs and structured securities (2%), and cash (1%).
Investments in Affiliates: None
Group Affiliation: Stancorp Financial Group
Licensed in: All states except NY, PR
Commenced Business: April 1906
Address: 1100 SW Sixth Ave, Portland, OR 97204
Phone: (503) 321-7000 **Domicile State:** OR **NAIC Code:** 69019

Data Date	Rating	RACR #1	RACR #2	Total Assets ($mil)	Capital ($mil)	Net Premium ($mil)	Net Income ($mil)
9-14	B+	1.95	1.09	19,885.1	1,114.5	3,146.9	159.1
9-13	B+	2.36	1.31	18,601.8	1,225.0	2,565.2	122.0
2013	B+	2.37	1.32	19,118.7	1,287.3	3,489.3	195.8
2012	B+	2.36	1.33	17,250.3	1,190.3	3,506.4	125.4
2011	B+	2.44	1.42	16,014.1	1,139.2	3,547.4	127.2
2010	B+	2.51	1.49	15,616.8	1,171.5	3,263.5	190.1
2009	B+	2.66	1.58	14,524.9	1,193.7	3,359.4	217.8

Adverse Trends in Operations

Decrease in capital during 2011 (3%)
Increase in policy surrenders from 2010 to 2011 (33%)
Decrease in capital during 2010 (2%)
Increase in policy surrenders from 2009 to 2010 (38%)
Decrease in premium volume from 2009 to 2010 (3%)

STANDARD LIFE & ACCIDENT INSURANCE COMPANY *   A-   Excellent

Major Rating Factors: Good overall results on stability tests (6.9 on a scale of 0 to 10). Strengths that enhance stability include excellent operational trends and excellent risk diversification. Good liquidity (6.9) with sufficient resources to handle a spike in claims as well as a significant increase in policy surrenders. Fair quality investment portfolio (4.9).
Other Rating Factors: Strong capitalization (10.0) based on excellent risk adjusted capital (severe loss scenario). Excellent profitability (8.7) with operating gains in each of the last five years.
Principal Business: Individual health insurance (38%), reinsurance (35%), group health insurance (21%), individual life insurance (6%), and individual annuities (1%).
Principal Investments: NonCMO investment grade bonds (70%), common & preferred stock (18%), mortgages in good standing (7%), noninv. grade bonds (3%), and misc. investments (3%).
Investments in Affiliates: None
Group Affiliation: American National Group Inc
Licensed in: All states except ME, NH, NJ, NY, PR
Commenced Business: June 1976
Address: One Moody Plaza, Galveston, TX 77550
Phone: (409) 763-4661 **Domicile State:** TX **NAIC Code:** 86355

Data Date	Rating	RACR #1	RACR #2	Total Assets ($mil)	Capital ($mil)	Net Premium ($mil)	Net Income ($mil)
9-14	A-	5.03	3.10	523.8	251.8	90.6	15.7
9-13	A-	5.41	3.30	521.8	251.0	80.3	12.6
2013	A-	5.22	3.20	527.6	252.2	108.7	18.0
2012	A-	5.88	3.59	527.8	255.8	106.2	22.4
2011	A-	5.71	3.50	515.1	235.5	105.2	26.5
2010	A-	5.19	3.19	512.9	222.5	111.4	21.5
2009	A-	5.29	3.24	505.9	217.7	121.0	3.2

Adverse Trends in Operations

Decrease in capital during 2013 (1%)
Decrease in premium volume from 2010 to 2011 (6%)
Decrease in premium volume from 2009 to 2010 (8%)

STANDARD LIFE INSURANCE COMPANY OF NEW YORK *   A-   Excellent

Major Rating Factors: Good liquidity (6.8 on a scale of 0 to 10) with sufficient resources to handle a spike in claims. Excellent overall results on stability tests (7.2). Strengths that enhance stability include excellent operational trends and excellent risk diversification. Strong capitalization (8.9) based on excellent risk adjusted capital (severe loss scenario). Furthermore, this high level of risk adjusted capital has been consistently maintained over the last five years.

Other Rating Factors: High quality investment portfolio (7.4). Excellent profitability (7.0) despite modest operating losses during 2011.

Principal Business: Group health insurance (56%) and group life insurance (43%).

Principal Investments: Mortgages in good standing (48%), nonCMO investment grade bonds (48%), noninv. grade bonds (2%), and cash (2%).

Investments in Affiliates: None

Group Affiliation: Stancorp Financial Group

Licensed in: NY

Commenced Business: January 2001

Address: 360 Hamilton Ave Suite 210, White Plains, NY 10601-1871

Phone: (503) 321-7859 **Domicile State:** NY **NAIC Code:** 89009

Data Date	Rating	RACR #1	RACR #2	Total Assets ($mil)	Capital ($mil)	Net Premium ($mil)	Net Income ($mil)
9-14	A-	3.41	2.26	272.4	74.3	71.8	3.1
9-13	A-	3.04	2.03	264.1	69.2	72.5	0.0
2013	A-	3.28	2.19	265.6	71.6	98.0	2.7
2012	A-	3.07	2.10	251.1	69.3	100.1	6.1
2011	A-	3.34	2.21	231.3	53.8	65.9	-1.3
2010	B+	3.50	2.34	212.1	55.3	65.0	5.4
2009	B+	3.46	2.31	196.2	49.5	61.2	6.7

Adverse Trends in Operations

Increase in policy surrenders from 2012 to 2013 (771%)
Decrease in premium volume from 2012 to 2013 (2%)
Decrease in capital during 2011 (3%)
Increase in policy surrenders from 2010 to 2011 (303%)

STANDARD SECURITY LIFE INSURANCE CO OF NEW YORK   B   Good

Major Rating Factors: Good overall results on stability tests (5.9 on a scale of 0 to 10) despite fair financial strength of affiliated Geneve Holdings Inc. Other stability subfactors include excellent operational trends and excellent risk diversification. Good liquidity (6.8) with sufficient resources to handle a spike in claims. Strong capitalization (9.6) based on excellent risk adjusted capital (severe loss scenario).

Other Rating Factors: High quality investment portfolio (7.2). Excellent profitability (7.2) with operating gains in each of the last five years.

Principal Business: Group health insurance (79%) and reinsurance (20%).

Principal Investments: NonCMO investment grade bonds (68%), common & preferred stock (19%), CMOs and structured securities (2%), and cash (1%).

Investments in Affiliates: 16%

Group Affiliation: Geneve Holdings Inc

Licensed in: All states, the District of Columbia and Puerto Rico

Commenced Business: December 1958

Address: 485 Madison Ave, New York, NY 10022-5872

Phone: (212) 355-4141 **Domicile State:** NY **NAIC Code:** 69078

Data Date	Rating	RACR #1	RACR #2	Total Assets ($mil)	Capital ($mil)	Net Premium ($mil)	Net Income ($mil)
9-14	B	3.34	2.70	247.0	114.8	156.6	7.5
9-13	B	3.49	2.85	249.8	113.8	158.1	6.4
2013	B	3.29	2.67	249.5	114.0	214.4	9.2
2012	B	4.05	3.25	239.5	116.3	148.4	15.8
2011	A-	3.38	2.63	371.6	106.5	151.6	7.7
2010	B+	3.28	2.61	363.5	109.3	141.3	3.3
2009	B+	3.03	2.45	370.8	115.1	180.2	8.8

Geneve Holdings Inc
Composite Group Rating: C+

Largest Group Members	Assets ($mil)	Rating
MADISON NATIONAL LIFE INS CO INC	489	C+
STANDARD SECURITY LIFE INS CO OF NY	250	B
INDEPENDENCE AMERICAN INS CO	102	C

STATE FARM LIFE & ACCIDENT ASSURANCE COMPANY *   A+   Excellent

Major Rating Factors: Good overall profitability (6.6 on a scale of 0 to 10). Excellent expense controls. Return on equity has been fair, averaging 6.9%. Good liquidity (6.4) with sufficient resources to handle a spike in claims as well as a significant increase in policy surrenders. Excellent overall results on stability tests (7.9) excellent operational trends and excellent risk diversification.

Other Rating Factors: Strong capitalization (10.0) based on excellent risk adjusted capital (severe loss scenario). High quality investment portfolio (8.0).

Principal Business: Individual life insurance (88%) and individual annuities (12%).

Principal Investments: NonCMO investment grade bonds (70%), CMOs and structured securities (21%), and policy loans (7%).

Investments in Affiliates: 2%

Group Affiliation: State Farm Group

Licensed in: CT, IL, NY, WI

Commenced Business: July 1961

Address: One State Farm Plaza, Bloomington, IL 61710

Phone: (309) 766-2311 **Domicile State:** IL **NAIC Code:** 69094

Data Date	Rating	RACR #1	RACR #2	Total Assets ($mil)	Capital ($mil)	Net Premium ($mil)	Net Income ($mil)
9-14	A+	5.76	3.32	2,436.7	436.5	164.2	19.3
9-13	A+	5.76	3.32	2,291.8	412.0	150.4	16.4
2013	A+	5.61	3.25	2,334.1	417.4	210.1	21.5
2012	A+	5.70	3.29	2,198.3	403.5	195.7	31.6
2011	A+	5.23	3.03	2,048.4	364.7	188.8	28.1
2010	A+	5.24	3.09	1,926.9	336.9	193.6	23.9
2009	A+	4.67	2.74	1,792.6	289.2	183.3	25.7

Net Income History
(in millions of dollars)

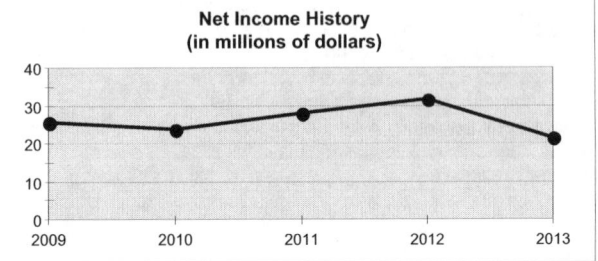

STATE FARM LIFE INSURANCE COMPANY *

A+   Excellent

Major Rating Factors: Good quality investment portfolio (6.7 on a scale of 0 to 10) despite mixed results such as: minimal exposure to mortgages and substantial holdings of BBB bonds but minimal holdings in junk bonds. Good overall profitability (6.6). Excellent expense controls. Return on equity has been fair, averaging 6.0%. Good liquidity (6.2).

Other Rating Factors: Excellent overall results on stability tests (7.9) excellent operational trends and excellent risk diversification. Strong capitalization (9.2) based on excellent risk adjusted capital (severe loss scenario).

Principal Business: Individual life insurance (85%), individual annuities (13%), and group life insurance (1%).

Principal Investments: NonCMO investment grade bonds (55%), CMOs and structured securities (20%), mortgages in good standing (9%), policy loans (7%), and common & preferred stock (6%).

Investments in Affiliates: 3%

Group Affiliation: State Farm Group

Licensed in: All states except MA, NY, WI, PR

Commenced Business: April 1929

Address: One State Farm Plaza, Bloomington, IL 61710

Phone: (309) 766-2311 **Domicile State:** IL **NAIC Code:** 69108

Data Date	Rating	RACR #1	RACR #2	Total Assets ($mil)	Capital ($mil)	Net Premium ($mil)	Net Income ($mil)
9-14	A+	4.35	2.48	62,712.0	8,910.9	3,719.5	354.3
9-13	A+	4.27	2.44	59,332.0	7,911.1	3,437.1	260.8
2013	A+	4.30	2.46	60,442.0	8,444.7	4,750.7	433.6
2012	A+	4.25	2.43	56,865.4	7,538.2	4,433.4	475.1
2011	A+	4.04	2.30	53,597.5	6,798.4	4,350.3	572.4
2010	A+	3.90	2.24	50,996.2	6,202.4	4,293.9	366.2
2009	A+	3.70	2.11	47,959.8	5,662.6	4,275.1	404.9

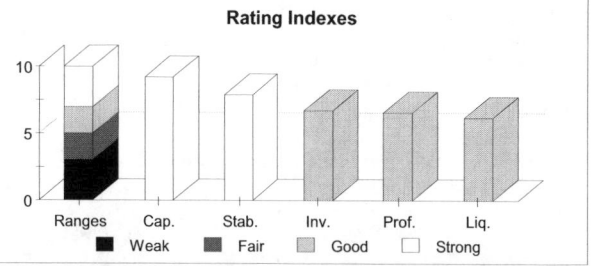

Rating Indexes

STATE LIFE INSURANCE COMPANY

B   Good

Major Rating Factors: Good quality investment portfolio (5.3 on a scale of 0 to 10) despite mixed results such as: large holdings of BBB rated bonds but moderate junk bond exposure. Good overall results on stability tests (6.3). Stability strengths include excellent operational trends, good risk adjusted capital for prior years and excellent risk diversification. Fair liquidity (4.7).

Other Rating Factors: Strong capitalization (7.1) based on excellent risk adjusted capital (severe loss scenario). Excellent profitability (8.0) with operating gains in each of the last five years.

Principal Business: Individual life insurance (45%), individual annuities (43%), reinsurance (8%), and individual health insurance (5%).

Principal Investments: NonCMO investment grade bonds (70%), CMOs and structured securities (18%), mortgages in good standing (7%), noninv. grade bonds (3%), and misc. investments (2%).

Investments in Affiliates: None

Group Affiliation: American United Life Group

Licensed in: All states except NY, PR

Commenced Business: September 1894

Address: 141 E Washington St, Indianapolis, IN 46204

Phone: (317) 285-1877 **Domicile State:** IN **NAIC Code:** 69116

Data Date	Rating	RACR #1	RACR #2	Total Assets ($mil)	Capital ($mil)	Net Premium ($mil)	Net Income ($mil)
9-14	B	2.05	1.06	5,315.2	344.4	445.3	17.6
9-13	B	2.07	1.06	4,910.7	325.7	387.6	23.0
2013	B	2.02	1.05	5,010.6	332.0	524.0	29.5
2012	B	2.00	1.03	4,597.5	306.2	531.9	35.0
2011	B	1.98	1.02	4,089.8	279.7	550.5	59.4
2010	B	1.82	0.93	3,646.7	221.7	549.8	20.9
2009	B	1.89	0.97	3,162.5	210.2	373.5	27.6

Adverse Trends in Operations

Decrease in premium volume from 2012 to 2013 (1%)
Decrease in premium volume from 2011 to 2012 (3%)

STATE MUTUAL INSURANCE COMPANY

C   Fair

Major Rating Factors: Fair profitability (3.8 on a scale of 0 to 10) with investment income below regulatory standards in relation to interest assumptions of reserves. Fair overall results on stability tests (3.5) including negative cash flow from operations for 2013, fair risk adjusted capital in prior years. Good quality investment portfolio (5.4).

Other Rating Factors: Good liquidity (6.1). Strong capitalization (7.0) based on excellent risk adjusted capital (severe loss scenario).

Principal Business: Reinsurance (47%), individual life insurance (34%), and individual health insurance (19%).

Principal Investments: NonCMO investment grade bonds (41%), CMOs and structured securities (20%), mortgages in good standing (15%), policy loans (9%), and misc. investments (16%).

Investments in Affiliates: 7%

Group Affiliation: None

Licensed in: All states except AK, CA, CT, ME, MA, MI, NH, NJ, NY, PR

Commenced Business: October 1890

Address: 210 E Second Ave Suite 301, Rome, GA 30161-1714

Phone: (706) 291-1054 **Domicile State:** GA **NAIC Code:** 69132

Data Date	Rating	RACR #1	RACR #2	Total Assets ($mil)	Capital ($mil)	Net Premium ($mil)	Net Income ($mil)
9-14	C	1.67	1.01	294.0	28.9	13.8	1.3
9-13	C	1.83	1.06	296.9	27.4	16.6	1.2
2013	C	1.73	1.04	296.8	30.0	21.5	0.8
2012	C	1.93	1.11	298.0	29.4	16.3	1.4
2011	C-	2.04	1.18	304.6	32.7	-134.3	-0.5
2010	C-	1.06	0.69	383.5	25.8	28.9	-1.3
2009	C	1.21	0.81	392.8	29.9	30.1	1.3

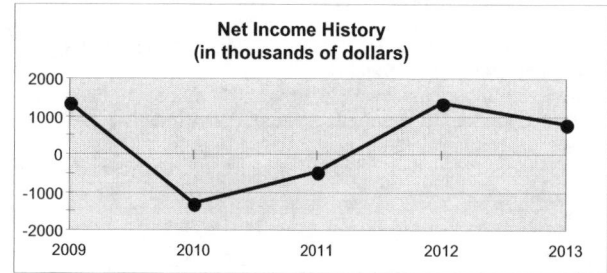

Net Income History
(in thousands of dollars)

STONEBRIDGE LIFE INSURANCE COMPANY   B-   Good

Major Rating Factors: Good overall results on stability tests (5.3 on a scale of 0 to 10). Stability strengths include good operational trends, good risk adjusted capital for prior years and excellent risk diversification. Good overall profitability (5.4). Return on equity has been excellent over the last five years averaging 104.0%. Fair quality investment portfolio (4.6).

Other Rating Factors: Strong capitalization (7.3) based on excellent risk adjusted capital (severe loss scenario). Excellent liquidity (7.3).

Principal Business: Group health insurance (46%), group life insurance (21%), individual life insurance (15%), individual health insurance (9%), and reinsurance (8%).

Principal Investments: NonCMO investment grade bonds (64%), CMOs and structured securities (14%), mortgages in good standing (6%), noninv. grade bonds (4%), and misc. investments (8%).

Investments in Affiliates: None
Group Affiliation: AEGON USA Group
Licensed in: All states except NY, PR
Commenced Business: May 1906
Address: 187 West St, Rutland, VT 05701
Phone: (319) 355-8511 **Domicile State:** VT **NAIC Code:** 65021

Data Date	Rating	RACR #1	RACR #2	Total Assets ($mil)	Capital ($mil)	Net Premium ($mil)	Net Income ($mil)
9-14	B-	2.13	1.17	1,772.2	172.6	302.5	78.0
9-13	C+	2.02	1.08	1,775.1	155.5	269.8	62.0
2013	C+	1.44	0.78	1,739.9	108.5	360.5	83.6
2012	C+	1.55	0.83	1,676.9	113.7	362.5	383.1
2011	C+	2.09	1.14	1,749.6	161.1	372.8	163.4
2010	B+	4.34	2.33	2,157.6	368.5	-297.2	136.8
2009	B+	1.87	1.05	2,024.8	182.1	509.9	135.0

Adverse Trends in Operations

Decrease in capital during 2013 (5%)
Decrease in capital during 2012 (29%)
Decrease in asset base during 2011 (19%)
Decrease in capital during 2011 (56%)
Decrease in premium volume from 2009 to 2010 (158%)

STRUCTURED ANNUITY RE CO   C-   Fair

Major Rating Factors: Fair quality investment portfolio (4.2 on a scale of 0 to 10). Fair overall results on stability tests (3.1) including weak risk adjusted capital in prior years, lack of operational experience. Weak profitability (1.7). Excellent expense controls.

Other Rating Factors: Good capitalization (5.5) based on good risk adjusted capital (moderate loss scenario). Excellent liquidity (10.0).

Principal Business: Reinsurance (100%).
Principal Investments: NonCMO investment grade bonds (98%).
Investments in Affiliates: None
Group Affiliation: BRH Holdings GP Ltd
Licensed in: IA
Commenced Business: August 2013
Address: 7700 Mills Civic Parkway, West Des Moines, IA 50266-3862
Phone: (800) 800-9882 **Domicile State:** IA **NAIC Code:** 15306

Data Date	Rating	RACR #1	RACR #2	Total Assets ($mil)	Capital ($mil)	Net Premium ($mil)	Net Income ($mil)
9-14	C-	1.31	0.61	1,412.3	73.2	-211.6	26.8
9-13	N/A	N/A	N/A	1,478.2	90.5	1,104.0	-5.0
2013	D	0.77	0.36	1,452.1	48.7	221.0	-49.4
2012	N/A	N/A	N/A	0.0	0.0	0.0	0.0
2011	N/A	N/A	N/A	0.0	0.0	0.0	0.0
2010	N/A	N/A	N/A	0.0	0.0	0.0	0.0
2009	N/A	N/A	N/A	0.0	0.0	0.0	0.0

Rating Indexes

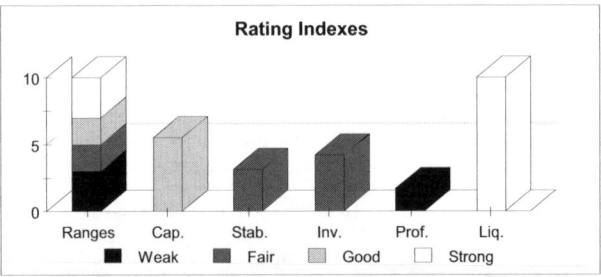

Ranges / Cap. / Stab. / Inv. / Prof. / Liq.
■ Weak ▨ Fair ▥ Good ☐ Strong

SUN LIFE & HEALTH INSURANCE COMPANY   C-   Fair

Major Rating Factors: Fair overall results on stability tests (3.3 on a scale of 0 to 10) including potential financial drain due to affiliation with Sun Life Assurance Group and negative cash flow from operations for 2013. Weak profitability (2.4) with investment income below regulatory standards in relation to interest assumptions of reserves. Good liquidity (6.9).

Other Rating Factors: Strong capitalization (10.0) based on excellent risk adjusted capital (severe loss scenario). High quality investment portfolio (7.2).

Principal Business: Reinsurance (50%), group health insurance (30%), and group life insurance (20%).

Principal Investments: CMOs and structured securities (46%), nonCMO investment grade bonds (42%), and mortgages in good standing (11%).

Investments in Affiliates: None
Group Affiliation: Sun Life Assurance Group
Licensed in: All states, the District of Columbia and Puerto Rico
Commenced Business: January 1975
Address: 100 Bright Meadow Blvd, Enfield, CT 06083-1900
Phone: (860) 403-1179 **Domicile State:** CT **NAIC Code:** 80926

Data Date	Rating	RACR #1	RACR #2	Total Assets ($mil)	Capital ($mil)	Net Premium ($mil)	Net Income ($mil)
9-14	C-	5.21	3.46	369.9	183.4	126.5	3.6
9-13	C-	9.85	4.73	315.5	140.1	130.1	-30.9
2013	C-	5.38	3.67	353.7	182.0	166.8	-35.8
2012	C-	6.10	2.98	64.6	48.1	0.0	1.8
2011	C	5.80	2.84	65.1	44.3	0.0	1.6
2010	C	5.41	2.54	65.7	42.3	0.0	2.6
2009	C	5.30	3.12	72.7	40.8	0.0	-1.1

Sun Life Assurance Group
Composite Group Rating: D+
Largest Group Members

	Assets ($mil)	Rating
SUN LIFE ASR CO OF CANADA	15369	D
INDEPENDENCE LIFE ANNUITY CO	2284	C
SUN LIFE HEALTH INS CO	354	C-
PROFESSIONAL INS CO	105	C-

SUN LIFE ASSURANCE COMPANY OF CANADA

D **Weak**

Major Rating Factors: Low quality investment portfolio (2.2 on a scale of 0 to 10) containing large holdings of BBB rated bonds in addition to moderate junk bond exposure. Exposure to mortgages is significant, but the mortgage default rate has been low. Weak profitability (2.4) with operating losses during the first nine months of 2014. Weak liquidity (1.8).

Other Rating Factors: Weak overall results on stability tests (2.3) including weak risk adjusted capital in prior years and negative cash flow from operations for 2013. Fair overall capitalization (4.0) based on mixed results -- excessive policy leverage mitigated by fair risk adjusted capital (moderate loss scenario).

Principal Business: N/A

Principal Investments: NonCMO investment grade bonds (51%), mortgages in good standing (20%), real estate (8%), CMOs and structured securities (7%), and misc. investments (12%).

Investments in Affiliates: 2%

Group Affiliation: Sun Life Assurance Group

Licensed in: All states except NY

Commenced Business: May 1871

Address: One Sun Life Executive Park, Wellesley Hills, MA 02481

Phone: (781) 237-6030 **Domicile State:** MI **NAIC Code:** 80802

Data Date	Rating	RACR #1	RACR #2	Total Assets ($mil)	Capital ($mil)	Net Premium ($mil)	Net Income ($mil)
9-14	D	0.99	0.52	16,300.0	924.1	1,703.3	-75.5
9-13	C-	0.86	0.48	15,211.4	1,157.1	329.3	327.0
2013	D	0.53	0.30	15,368.9	766.7	-919.7	234.8
2012	C-	0.79	0.45	17,403.4	1,037.6	2,283.3	119.1
2011	C-	0.77	0.44	17,348.7	1,017.6	2,397.5	-253.2
2010	C	0.80	0.45	16,039.3	890.8	2,513.6	159.1
2009	C	0.54	0.30	15,278.5	662.0	2,600.1	156.5

Rating Indexes

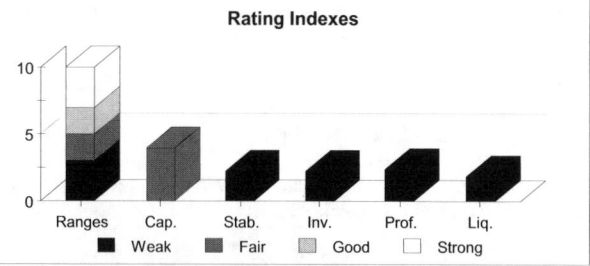

SUNSET LIFE INSURANCE COMPANY OF AMERICA

B- **Good**

Major Rating Factors: Good quality investment portfolio (5.5 on a scale of 0 to 10) despite large holdings of BBB rated bonds in addition to moderate junk bond exposure. Exposure to mortgages is significant, but the mortgage default rate has been low. Good liquidity (5.2) with sufficient resources to cover a large increase in policy surrenders. Good overall results on stability tests (5.2) despite negative cash flow from operations for 2013 excellent operational trends and good risk diversification.

Other Rating Factors: Weak profitability (2.1) with investment income below regulatory standards in relation to interest assumptions of reserves. Strong capitalization (7.6) based on excellent risk adjusted capital (severe loss scenario).

Principal Business: Individual life insurance (60%) and individual annuities (40%).

Principal Investments: NonCMO investment grade bonds (62%), mortgages in good standing (17%), CMOs and structured securities (13%), policy loans (3%), and misc. investments (5%).

Investments in Affiliates: None

Group Affiliation: Kansas City Life Group

Licensed in: All states except AL, NH, NJ, NY, TN, VT, WI, PR

Commenced Business: May 1937

Address: 3520 Broadway, Kansas City, MO 64121-9532

Phone: (816) 753-7000 **Domicile State:** MO **NAIC Code:** 69272

Data Date	Rating	RACR #1	RACR #2	Total Assets ($mil)	Capital ($mil)	Net Premium ($mil)	Net Income ($mil)
9-14	B-	2.81	1.43	358.9	34.3	13.6	5.2
9-13	B	2.60	1.32	362.9	33.2	11.4	4.2
2013	B-	2.61	1.34	355.7	31.2	15.3	4.8
2012	B	2.58	1.30	368.1	32.6	10.0	6.3
2011	B	2.54	1.26	379.2	33.7	12.4	5.4
2010	B	2.55	1.26	392.2	34.3	11.8	6.4
2009	B	2.48	1.24	402.4	34.9	13.7	5.2

Adverse Trends in Operations

Decrease in asset base during 2013 (3%)
Decrease in capital during 2012 (3%)
Decrease in premium volume from 2011 to 2012 (19%)
Decrease in premium volume from 2009 to 2010 (14%)
Decrease in asset base during 2010 (3%)

SWISS RE LIFE & HEALTH AMERICA INCORPORATED

C+ **Fair**

Major Rating Factors: Fair overall results on stability tests (4.7 on a scale of 0 to 10). Good overall profitability (6.9). Excellent expense controls. Return on equity has been fair, averaging 7.4%. Good liquidity (6.8) with sufficient resources to handle a spike in claims as well as a significant increase in policy surrenders.

Other Rating Factors: Strong capitalization (7.6) based on excellent risk adjusted capital (severe loss scenario). High quality investment portfolio (7.1).

Principal Business: Reinsurance (100%).

Principal Investments: NonCMO investment grade bonds (72%), CMOs and structured securities (15%), common & preferred stock (4%), mortgages in good standing (4%), and misc. investments (5%).

Investments in Affiliates: 10%

Group Affiliation: Swiss Reinsurance Group

Licensed in: All states, the District of Columbia and Puerto Rico

Commenced Business: September 1967

Address: 969 High Ridge Rd, Stamford, CT 06904-2060

Phone: (203) 321-3141 **Domicile State:** CT **NAIC Code:** 82627

Data Date	Rating	RACR #1	RACR #2	Total Assets ($mil)	Capital ($mil)	Net Premium ($mil)	Net Income ($mil)
9-14	C+	2.04	1.43	10,472.4	1,770.5	1,196.0	201.1
9-13	C-	1.86	1.32	9,995.7	1,640.8	1,258.5	60.2
2013	C	1.86	1.31	9,994.7	1,644.0	1,644.4	95.4
2012	D+	1.35	0.97	9,138.9	1,185.3	1,557.8	95.4
2011	D	4.69	2.13	9,006.5	1,050.2	315.6	-889.9
2010	B-	1.32	1.04	10,408.9	1,621.3	1,152.6	114.4
2009	B-	2.21	1.67	12,176.2	3,039.5	311.5	367.3

Rating Indexes

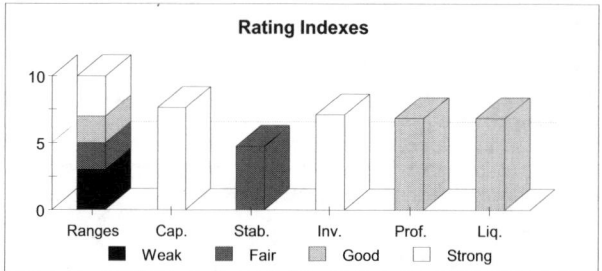

SYMETRA LIFE INSURANCE COMPANY *   B+   Good

Major Rating Factors: Good quality investment portfolio (5.4 on a scale of 0 to 10) despite large holdings of BBB rated bonds in addition to junk bond exposure equal to 58% of capital. Exposure to mortgages is significant, but the mortgage default rate has been low. Good liquidity (6.5) with sufficient resources to cover a large increase in policy surrenders. Good overall results on stability tests (6.7) excellent operational trends and excellent risk diversification.

Other Rating Factors: Strong capitalization (7.3) based on excellent risk adjusted capital (severe loss scenario). Excellent profitability (7.9) with operating gains in each of the last five years.

Principal Business: Individual annuities (72%), group health insurance (19%), individual life insurance (6%), group retirement contracts (1%), and group life insurance (1%).

Principal Investments: NonCMO investment grade bonds (61%), mortgages in good standing (15%), CMOs and structured securities (13%), noninv. grade bonds (5%), and common & preferred stock (4%).

Investments in Affiliates: 1%

Group Affiliation: White Mountains Group

Licensed in: All states except NY, PR

Commenced Business: April 1957

Address: 5550 Wild Rose Lane Suite 400, West Des Moines, IA 50266

Phone: (425) 376-8000 **Domicile State:** IA **NAIC Code:** 68608

Data Date	Rating	RACR #1	RACR #2	Total Assets ($mil)	Capital ($mil)	Net Premium ($mil)	Net Income ($mil)
9-14	B+	2.21	1.20	28,794.9	1,951.2	2,568.7	123.4
9-13	B+	2.27	1.25	26,740.0	1,940.6	2,068.2	181.3
2013	B+	2.18	1.19	27,220.0	1,869.7	2,995.6	183.6
2012	B+	2.32	1.28	25,467.8	1,912.6	1,955.3	252.3
2011	B+	2.33	1.23	24,771.5	1,822.8	2,626.7	155.8
2010	B+	2.64	1.38	23,192.4	1,752.3	3,012.2	194.5
2009	B	2.40	1.26	20,799.1	1,415.4	2,827.9	43.1

Adverse Trends in Operations

Decrease in capital during 2013 (2%)
Decrease in premium volume from 2011 to 2012 (26%)
Decrease in premium volume from 2010 to 2011 (13%)

TEACHERS INSURANCE & ANNUITY ASSOCIATION OF AMERICA   A+   Excellent

Major Rating Factors: Good quality investment portfolio (6.8 on a scale of 0 to 10) despite mixed results such as: substantial holdings of BBB bonds but moderate junk bond exposure. Strong capitalization (10.0) based on excellent risk adjusted capital (severe loss scenario). Furthermore, this high level of risk adjusted capital has been consistently maintained over the last five years. Excellent profitability (9.1).

Other Rating Factors: Excellent liquidity (7.3). Excellent overall results on stability tests (7.9) excellent operational trends and excellent risk diversification.

Principal Business: Individual annuities (55%), group retirement contracts (43%), and individual life insurance (3%).

Principal Investments: NonCMO investment grade bonds (42%), CMOs and structured securities (34%), mortgages in good standing (6%), noninv. grade bonds (5%), and misc. investments (12%).

Investments in Affiliates: 7%

Group Affiliation: TIAA Family of Companies

Licensed in: All states, the District of Columbia and Puerto Rico

Commenced Business: May 1918

Address: 730 Third Ave 7th Floor, New York, NY 10017

Phone: (212) 490-9000 **Domicile State:** NY **NAIC Code:** 69345

Data Date	Rating	RACR #1	RACR #2	Total Assets ($mil)	Capital ($mil)	Net Premium ($mil)	Net Income ($mil)
9-14	A+	5.88	3.11	261,389	33,825.5	8,304.3	809.0
9-13	A+	5.39	2.88	247,468	30,442.2	9,550.6	1,616.3
2013	A+	5.68	3.00	250,494	30,779.1	12,580.2	1,751.5
2012	A+	5.25	2.82	237,038	29,309.0	10,431.7	2,041.8
2011	A+	4.85	2.66	225,932	27,130.9	11,084.6	2,358.9
2010	A+	4.71	2.57	214,544	25,155.8	11,067.6	1,381.0
2009	A+	4.64	2.48	201,728	22,844.0	9,778.5	-452.1

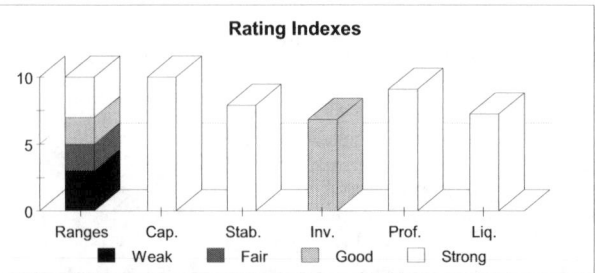

Rating Indexes

(Ranges, Cap., Stab., Inv., Prof., Liq. — Weak, Fair, Good, Strong)

TENNESSEE FARMERS LIFE INSURANCE COMPANY *   A   Excellent

Major Rating Factors: Good quality investment portfolio (6.0 on a scale of 0 to 10) despite mixed results such as: large holdings of BBB rated bonds but moderate junk bond exposure. Good liquidity (6.4) with sufficient resources to handle a spike in claims as well as a significant increase in policy surrenders. Excellent overall results on stability tests (7.4) excellent operational trends and excellent risk diversification.

Other Rating Factors: Strong capitalization (7.7) based on excellent risk adjusted capital (severe loss scenario). Excellent profitability (7.0) with operating gains in each of the last five years.

Principal Business: Individual life insurance (68%), individual annuities (31%), and reinsurance (2%).

Principal Investments: NonCMO investment grade bonds (62%), common & preferred stock (27%), noninv. grade bonds (7%), CMOs and structured securities (1%), and misc. investments (4%).

Investments in Affiliates: 23%

Group Affiliation: Tennessee Farmers Ins Companies

Licensed in: TN

Commenced Business: September 1973

Address: 147 Bear Creek Pike, Columbia, TN 38401-2266

Phone: (931) 388-7872 **Domicile State:** TN **NAIC Code:** 82759

Data Date	Rating	RACR #1	RACR #2	Total Assets ($mil)	Capital ($mil)	Net Premium ($mil)	Net Income ($mil)
9-14	A	2.30	1.48	1,978.3	351.2	126.1	29.0
9-13	A	2.34	1.50	1,882.2	318.9	139.6	25.7
2013	A	2.24	1.46	1,913.6	328.1	185.5	34.5
2012	A	2.33	1.56	1,790.6	292.7	194.5	31.9
2011	A	2.46	1.62	1,665.4	267.0	207.8	16.1
2010	A	2.38	1.60	1,528.1	256.6	183.8	39.4
2009	A	2.43	1.57	1,399.8	228.6	147.0	12.1

Adverse Trends in Operations

Decrease in premium volume from 2012 to 2013 (5%)
Decrease in premium volume from 2011 to 2012 (6%)

TEXAS LIFE INSURANCE COMPANY　　　B　　Good

Major Rating Factors: Good overall results on stability tests (5.3 on a scale of 0 to 10) despite fair financial strength of affiliated Wilton Re Holdings Ltd. Other stability subfactors include excellent operational trends, good risk adjusted capital for prior years and excellent risk diversification. Good quality investment portfolio (5.5) despite mixed results such as: large holdings of BBB rated bonds but moderate junk bond exposure. Good liquidity (5.8).

Other Rating Factors: Fair profitability (4.4) with investment income below regulatory standards in relation to interest assumptions of reserves. Strong capitalization (7.4) based on excellent risk adjusted capital (severe loss scenario).

Principal Business: Individual life insurance (100%).

Principal Investments: NonCMO investment grade bonds (54%), CMOs and structured securities (32%), noninv. grade bonds (5%), policy loans (4%), and misc. investments (4%).

Investments in Affiliates: None

Group Affiliation: Wilton Re Holdings Ltd

Licensed in: All states except NY, PR

Commenced Business: April 1901

Address: 900 Washington Ave, Waco, TX 76701

Phone: (254) 752-6521　**Domicile State:** TX　**NAIC Code:** 69396

Data Date	Rating	RACR #1	RACR #2	Total Assets ($mil)	Capital ($mil)	Net Premium ($mil)	Net Income ($mil)
9-14	B	2.32	1.26	1,000.7	98.6	151.7	28.4
9-13	B	2.30	1.24	958.3	95.9	144.1	25.2
2013	B	1.96	1.07	952.9	80.4	197.7	33.2
2012	B	1.84	1.01	878.4	69.6	148.8	1.1
2011	C+	1.71	0.93	816.5	52.3	135.5	27.6
2010	B-	2.05	1.18	779.6	53.1	117.3	14.4
2009	B-	2.20	1.30	727.0	48.4	103.3	18.1

Wilton Re Holdings Ltd
Composite Group Rating: C

Largest Group Members	Assets ($mil)	Rating
CONSECO LIFE INS CO	3825	D+
WILTON REASSURANCE CO	3471	B
CONTINENTAL ASSURANCE CO	2938	C
TEXAS LIFE INS CO	953	B
WILTON REASSURANCE LIFE CO OF NY	901	B

THRIVENT LIFE INSURANCE COMPANY *　　　B+　　Good

Major Rating Factors: Good quality investment portfolio (5.6 on a scale of 0 to 10) despite mixed results such as: large holdings of BBB rated bonds but junk bond exposure equal to 69% of capital. Good overall profitability (6.6). Excellent expense controls. Return on equity has been good over the last five years, averaging 12.1%. Good liquidity (6.1).

Other Rating Factors: Good overall results on stability tests (6.6) excellent operational trends and excellent risk diversification. Strong capitalization (7.3) based on excellent risk adjusted capital (severe loss scenario).

Principal Business: Individual annuities (93%) and individual life insurance (7%).

Principal Investments: NonCMO investment grade bonds (64%), CMOs and structured securities (26%), noninv. grade bonds (7%), policy loans (1%), and cash (1%).

Investments in Affiliates: 1%

Group Affiliation: Thrivent Financial for Lutherans Grp

Licensed in: All states except GA, ME, MA, NH, NY, NC, RI, VT, WY, PR

Commenced Business: December 1982

Address: 625 Fourth Ave S, Minneapolis, MN 55415

Phone: (612) 340-7214　**Domicile State:** MN　**NAIC Code:** 97721

Data Date	Rating	RACR #1	RACR #2	Total Assets ($mil)	Capital ($mil)	Net Premium ($mil)	Net Income ($mil)
9-14	B+	2.48	1.20	3,530.2	176.0	82.9	11.9
9-13	B+	2.71	1.28	3,443.5	183.7	116.7	7.9
2013	B+	2.35	1.13	3,468.2	162.6	147.9	25.2
2012	B+	2.53	1.20	3,283.8	167.8	145.7	26.0
2011	B+	2.63	1.23	3,132.3	169.5	157.0	21.3
2010	B+	2.75	1.29	3,182.8	172.0	184.7	21.2
2009	B+	2.74	1.27	3,035.1	172.2	154.7	12.4

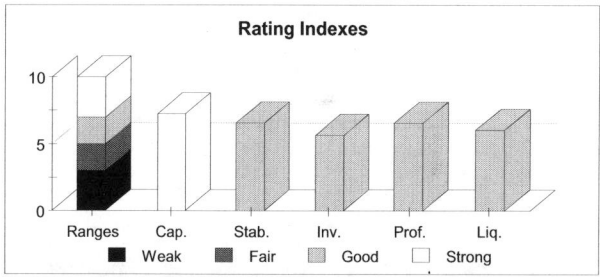

Rating Indexes

Ranges　Cap.　Stab.　Inv.　Prof.　Liq.

■ Weak　▦ Fair　▨ Good　□ Strong

TIAA-CREF LIFE INSURANCE COMPANY　　　B　　Good

Major Rating Factors: Good quality investment portfolio (6.4 on a scale of 0 to 10) despite mixed results such as: no exposure to mortgages and large holdings of BBB rated bonds but small junk bond holdings. Good liquidity (6.1) with sufficient resources to cover a large increase in policy surrenders. Good overall results on stability tests (6.3) despite excessive premium growth excellent operational trends and excellent risk diversification.

Other Rating Factors: Fair profitability (3.9) with operating losses during the first nine months of 2014. Strong capitalization (7.4) based on excellent risk adjusted capital (severe loss scenario).

Principal Business: Individual life insurance (39%), individual annuities (37%), group life insurance (23%), and individual health insurance (1%).

Principal Investments: NonCMO investment grade bonds (86%), CMOs and structured securities (11%), noninv. grade bonds (2%), and cash (1%).

Investments in Affiliates: None

Group Affiliation: TIAA Family of Companies

Licensed in: All states except PR

Commenced Business: December 1996

Address: 730 Third Ave, New York, NY 10017

Phone: (212) 916-4900　**Domicile State:** NY　**NAIC Code:** 60142

Data Date	Rating	RACR #1	RACR #2	Total Assets ($mil)	Capital ($mil)	Net Premium ($mil)	Net Income ($mil)
9-14	B	2.41	1.25	8,766.7	364.0	488.2	-3.7
9-13	A-	2.89	1.52	6,984.0	402.9	317.0	-4.6
2013	B	2.49	1.32	7,988.6	373.8	480.9	-29.3
2012	A-	3.18	1.69	5,656.3	412.9	282.5	18.1
2011	A-	3.50	1.85	4,250.1	398.4	223.8	29.5
2010	A-	3.52	1.80	3,571.0	370.6	218.9	24.9
2009	B	3.57	1.87	3,319.1	353.3	232.5	-7.0

Adverse Trends in Operations

Decrease in capital during 2013 (9%)
Decrease in premium volume from 2009 to 2010 (6%)

TIME INSURANCE COMPANY   B-   Good

Major Rating Factors: Good current capitalization (5.3 on a scale of 0 to 10) based on mixed results -- excessive policy leverage mitigated by excellent risk adjusted capital (severe loss scenario) reflecting improvement over results in 2013. Good quality investment portfolio (6.2) despite significant exposure to mortgages . Mortgage default rate has been low. large holdings of BBB rated bonds in addition to small junk bond holdings. Good liquidity (5.2).

Other Rating Factors: Fair profitability (3.9) with operating losses during the first nine months of 2014. Fair overall results on stability tests (4.9) including excessive premium growth.

Principal Business: Group health insurance (57%), individual health insurance (40%), and individual life insurance (3%).

Principal Investments: NonCMO investment grade bonds (65%), mortgages in good standing (13%), CMOs and structured securities (9%), common & preferred stock (8%), and misc. investments (6%).

Investments in Affiliates: None

Group Affiliation: Assurant Inc

Licensed in: All states except NY, PR

Commenced Business: March 1910

Address: 501 W Michigan, Milwaukee, WI 53201

Phone: (612) 738-4449 **Domicile State:** WI **NAIC Code:** 69477

Data Date	Rating	RACR #1	RACR #2	Total Assets ($mil)	Capital ($mil)	Net Premium ($mil)	Net Income ($mil)
9-14	B-	1.30	1.02	848.6	297.6	1,322.2	-22.5
9-13	B-	1.28	0.98	681.9	218.8	931.9	17.2
2013	B-	1.14	0.88	691.5	212.0	1,269.5	5.6
2012	B-	1.20	0.92	645.4	205.8	1,164.5	48.7
2011	B-	1.51	1.16	748.7	273.0	1,215.0	34.5
2010	B-	1.40	1.07	748.3	274.5	1,321.0	44.2
2009	B-	1.20	0.92	795.8	239.5	1,310.8	-43.5

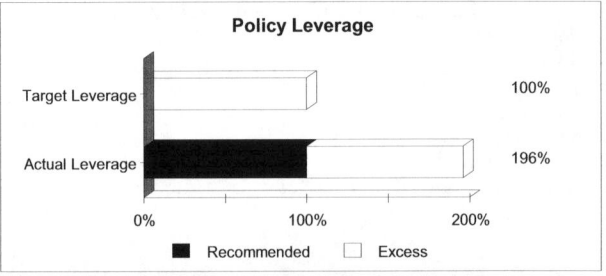

Policy Leverage

Target Leverage — 100%
Actual Leverage — 196%

■ Recommended □ Excess

TOWER LIFE INSURANCE COMPANY   D+   Weak

Major Rating Factors: Weak profitability (1.3 on a scale of 0 to 10) with operating losses during the first nine months of 2014. Weak overall results on stability tests (2.7) including negative cash flow from operations for 2013. Fair quality investment portfolio (4.8).

Other Rating Factors: Good liquidity (6.9). Strong capitalization (9.5) based on excellent risk adjusted capital (severe loss scenario).

Principal Business: Individual life insurance (70%), reinsurance (24%), group health insurance (4%), and individual annuities (2%).

Principal Investments: NonCMO investment grade bonds (54%), real estate (17%), common & preferred stock (10%), CMOs and structured securities (8%), and misc. investments (10%).

Investments in Affiliates: None

Group Affiliation: None

Licensed in: NM, OK, TX

Commenced Business: March 1955

Address: 310 St Marys, San Antonio, TX 78205

Phone: (210) 226-7151 **Domicile State:** TX **NAIC Code:** 69493

Data Date	Rating	RACR #1	RACR #2	Total Assets ($mil)	Capital ($mil)	Net Premium ($mil)	Net Income ($mil)
9-14	D+	4.27	2.68	54.5	28.8	0.4	-1.6
9-13	D+	4.41	2.69	58.9	30.9	0.8	-1.8
2013	D+	4.47	2.65	57.8	30.3	0.9	-2.1
2012	C-	4.63	3.34	62.0	32.6	1.6	-2.9
2011	C-	4.83	4.35	67.2	35.4	1.7	-1.0
2010	C	4.94	4.45	68.1	36.5	1.8	-0.3
2009	C	4.81	4.33	74.5	36.8	1.6	0.0

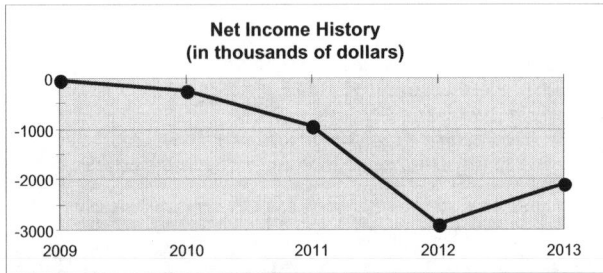

Net Income History
(in thousands of dollars)

2009 2010 2011 2012 2013

TRANS OCEANIC LIFE INSURANCE COMPANY *   A   Excellent

Major Rating Factors: Good overall results on stability tests (6.4 on a scale of 0 to 10). Strengths that enhance stability include excellent operational trends, good risk adjusted capital for prior years and good risk diversification. Strong current capitalization (8.2) based on excellent risk adjusted capital (severe loss scenario) reflecting improvement over results in 2009. High quality investment portfolio (7.2).

Other Rating Factors: Excellent profitability (9.0) with operating gains in each of the last five years. Excellent liquidity (8.7).

Principal Business: Individual health insurance (91%) and individual life insurance (8%).

Principal Investments: Cash (32%), nonCMO investment grade bonds (32%), CMOs and structured securities (27%), real estate (8%), and common & preferred stock (1%).

Investments in Affiliates: None

Group Affiliation: Trans-Oceanic Group Inc

Licensed in: FL, PR

Commenced Business: December 1959

Address: 3 Munet Court, Guaynabo, PR 00936-3467

Phone: (787) 782-2680 **Domicile State:** PR **NAIC Code:** 69523

Data Date	Rating	RACR #1	RACR #2	Total Assets ($mil)	Capital ($mil)	Net Premium ($mil)	Net Income ($mil)
9-14	A	2.69	1.80	62.9	30.5	22.4	2.2
9-13	B+	2.18	1.47	54.9	24.6	22.3	2.0
2013	B+	2.67	1.83	58.9	29.5	29.8	6.0
2012	B+	2.11	1.46	49.6	22.5	28.5	3.7
2011	B+	1.80	1.26	42.9	17.3	26.1	3.3
2010	B	1.53	1.08	38.1	13.7	24.8	2.0
2009	C-	1.06	0.78	32.1	9.0	24.9	2.4

Adverse Trends in Operations

Increase in policy surrenders from 2012 to 2013 (257%)
Increase in policy surrenders from 2009 to 2010 (594%)

TRANS WORLD ASSURANCE COMPANY   B   Good

Major Rating Factors: Good quality investment portfolio (6.0 on a scale of 0 to 10) despite mixed results such as: minimal exposure to mortgages and large holdings of BBB rated bonds but minimal holdings in junk bonds. Good liquidity (6.1) with sufficient resources to cover a large increase in policy surrenders. Good overall results on stability tests (5.4) excellent operational trends and good risk diversification.

Other Rating Factors: Strong capitalization (8.0) based on excellent risk adjusted capital (severe loss scenario). Excellent profitability (7.0) with operating gains in each of the last five years.

Principal Business: Individual life insurance (77%), reinsurance (13%), and individual annuities (9%).

Principal Investments: NonCMO investment grade bonds (75%), common & preferred stock (10%), mortgages in good standing (8%), real estate (4%), and misc. investments (3%).

Investments in Affiliates: 9%

Group Affiliation: Trans World Asr Group

Licensed in: All states except NH, NY, VT, PR

Commenced Business: December 1963

Address: 885 South El Camino Real, San Mateo, CA 94402

Phone: (850) 456-7401 **Domicile State:** CA **NAIC Code:** 69566

Data Date	Rating	RACR #1	RACR #2	Total Assets ($mil)	Capital ($mil)	Net Premium ($mil)	Net Income ($mil)
9-14	B	2.12	1.68	347.3	78.9	8.7	2.1
9-13	B	1.78	1.44	346.5	75.7	8.8	3.3
2013	B	2.06	1.62	347.8	77.1	11.0	4.9
2012	B	1.75	1.43	346.3	73.2	11.2	5.9
2011	B	1.70	1.41	345.1	72.0	11.9	2.1
2010	B	1.66	1.39	342.1	72.0	10.9	3.5
2009	B	1.81	1.53	338.4	70.0	12.4	4.0

Adverse Trends in Operations

Decrease in premium volume from 2012 to 2013 (2%)
Decrease in premium volume from 2011 to 2012 (6%)
Decrease in premium volume from 2009 to 2010 (12%)

TRANSAMERICA ADVISORS LIFE INSURANCE COMPANY   B   Good

Major Rating Factors: Good overall results on stability tests (5.3 on a scale of 0 to 10). Stability strengths include good operational trends and excellent risk diversification. Good overall profitability (5.2). Despite its volitility, return on equity has been excellent over the last five years averaging 20.8%. Good liquidity (6.7).

Other Rating Factors: Strong capitalization (10.0) based on excellent risk adjusted capital (severe loss scenario). High quality investment portfolio (7.4).

Principal Business: Individual annuities (63%) and individual life insurance (37%).

Principal Investments: NonCMO investment grade bonds (54%), policy loans (27%), CMOs and structured securities (7%), noninv. grade bonds (1%), and mortgages in good standing (1%).

Investments in Affiliates: None

Group Affiliation: AEGON USA Group

Licensed in: All states except NY, PR

Commenced Business: December 1986

Address: 425 W Capital Ave Suite 1800, Little Rock, AR 72201

Phone: (800) 535-5549 **Domicile State:** AR **NAIC Code:** 79022

Data Date	Rating	RACR #1	RACR #2	Total Assets ($mil)	Capital ($mil)	Net Premium ($mil)	Net Income ($mil)
9-14	B	10.43	5.23	9,792.9	915.5	9.3	151.2
9-13	C+	8.73	4.46	10,305.9	807.5	15.8	376.5
2013	B-	8.73	4.45	10,135.2	733.4	18.0	196.6
2012	D	7.41	3.78	10,031.8	636.2	17.9	178.2
2011	D	5.34	2.75	10,050.8	438.0	16.2	-340.2
2010	B-	8.55	4.32	11,139.7	813.1	28.3	181.2
2009	B-	6.41	3.24	11,102.8	599.0	282.7	225.3

Adverse Trends in Operations

Decrease in capital during 2011 (46%)
Decrease in asset base during 2011 (10%)
Decrease in premium volume from 2010 to 2011 (43%)
Decrease in premium volume from 2009 to 2010 (90%)

TRANSAMERICA FINANCIAL LIFE INSURANCE COMPANY   B   Good

Major Rating Factors: Good overall results on stability tests (5.9 on a scale of 0 to 10) despite negative cash flow from operations for 2013. Other stability subfactors include excellent operational trends, good risk adjusted capital for prior years and excellent risk diversification. Good quality investment portfolio (5.3) despite mixed results such as: large holdings of BBB rated bonds but moderate junk bond exposure. Good overall profitability (6.1).

Other Rating Factors: Strong capitalization (7.6) based on excellent risk adjusted capital (severe loss scenario). Excellent liquidity (9.3).

Principal Business: Group retirement contracts (75%), individual annuities (12%), reinsurance (9%), individual life insurance (2%), and other lines (2%).

Principal Investments: NonCMO investment grade bonds (65%), CMOs and structured securities (16%), mortgages in good standing (6%), noninv. grade bonds (5%), and policy loans (1%).

Investments in Affiliates: 1%

Group Affiliation: AEGON USA Group

Licensed in: All states except PR

Commenced Business: October 1947

Address: 440 Mamaroneck Ave, Harrison, NY 10528

Phone: (914) 697-8000 **Domicile State:** NY **NAIC Code:** 70688

Data Date	Rating	RACR #1	RACR #2	Total Assets ($mil)	Capital ($mil)	Net Premium ($mil)	Net Income ($mil)
6-14	B	2.93	1.43	30,565.9	1,029.5	2,773.6	67.8
6-13	B	2.52	1.23	27,741.1	883.2	2,504.6	127.1
2013	B	2.71	1.32	29,402.4	934.6	5,239.6	226.1
2012	C+	2.43	1.19	26,958.7	836.0	4,935.8	198.0
2011	C+	2.04	0.99	25,478.4	692.1	4,424.7	-266.8
2010	B	2.06	1.02	24,312.5	794.7	5,143.8	70.3
2009	B-	2.14	1.06	20,937.1	911.6	4,327.2	274.9

Adverse Trends in Operations

Decrease in capital during 2011 (13%)
Decrease in premium volume from 2010 to 2011 (14%)
Decrease in capital during 2010 (13%)
Increase in policy surrenders from 2009 to 2010 (37%)

TRANSAMERICA LIFE INSURANCE COMPANY　　　B-　　Good

Major Rating Factors: Good quality investment portfolio (5.7 on a scale of 0 to 10) despite large holdings of BBB rated bonds in addition to junk bond exposure equal to 53% of capital. Exposure to mortgages is significant, but the mortgage default rate has been low. Good overall results on stability tests (5.1) despite negative cash flow from operations for 2013 excellent operational trends, good risk adjusted capital for prior years and excellent risk diversification. Fair profitability (3.9).

Other Rating Factors: Strong capitalization (7.3) based on excellent risk adjusted capital (severe loss scenario). Excellent liquidity (7.2).

Principal Business: Individual annuities (39%), group retirement contracts (34%), individual life insurance (12%), reinsurance (8%), and other lines (6%).

Principal Investments: NonCMO investment grade bonds (47%), CMOs and structured securities (19%), mortgages in good standing (11%), noninv. grade bonds (6%), and misc. investments (8%).

Investments in Affiliates: 6%

Group Affiliation: AEGON USA Group

Licensed in: All states except NY

Commenced Business: March 1962

Address: 4333 Edgewood Rd NE, Cedar Rapids, IA 52499

Phone: (319) 398-8511 **Domicile State:** IA **NAIC Code:** 86231

Data Date	Rating	RACR #1	RACR #2	Total Assets ($mil)	Capital ($mil)	Net Premium ($mil)	Net Income ($mil)
9-14	B-	1.89	1.19	118,208	5,730.5	12,170.8	218.6
9-13	B-	1.69	1.04	109,345	4,897.4	11,561.0	-10.0
2013	B-	1.63	1.02	115,276	4,717.9	15,446.5	57.5
2012	C	1.83	1.13	105,497	5,470.6	11,782.0	791.6
2011	C	1.69	1.02	102,718	5,121.6	9,845.0	-2,459.3
2010	B-	1.70	0.92	106,887	4,298.1	9,145.4	417.7
2009	B-	2.10	1.03	101,455	5,026.8	8,085.1	-99.5

Adverse Trends in Operations

Decrease in capital during 2013 (14%)
Decrease in asset base during 2011 (4%)
Decrease in capital during 2010 (14%)

TRANSAMERICA PREMIER LIFE INSURANCE COMPANY　　　C+　　Fair

Major Rating Factors: Fair quality investment portfolio (3.5 on a scale of 0 to 10) with large holdings of BBB rated bonds in addition to significant exposure to junk bonds. Exposure to mortgages is significant, but the mortgage default rate has been low. Fair profitability (4.4) with operating losses during the first nine months of 2014. Fair overall results on stability tests (4.7) including fair risk adjusted capital in prior years.

Other Rating Factors: Good capitalization (5.3) based on good risk adjusted capital (moderate loss scenario). Good liquidity (6.4).

Principal Business: Individual life insurance (31%), individual annuities (27%), group health insurance (20%), reinsurance (7%), and other lines (14%).

Principal Investments: NonCMO investment grade bonds (57%), CMOs and structured securities (15%), mortgages in good standing (10%), noninv. grade bonds (6%), and misc. investments (9%).

Investments in Affiliates: 3%

Group Affiliation: AEGON USA Group

Licensed in: All states except NY

Commenced Business: May 1860

Address: 4333 Edgewood Rd NE, Cedar Rapids, IA 52499

Phone: (319) 355-8511 **Domicile State:** IA **NAIC Code:** 66281

Data Date	Rating	RACR #1	RACR #2	Total Assets ($mil)	Capital ($mil)	Net Premium ($mil)	Net Income ($mil)
9-14	C+	1.20	0.59	32,048.5	699.2	1,313.8	-113.1
9-13	C+	1.41	0.70	31,299.4	931.3	1,210.5	107.3
2013	C+	1.58	0.78	31,879.6	971.2	1,586.3	166.9
2012	C+	1.20	0.59	31,057.2	811.3	1,497.6	143.5
2011	C+	1.31	0.64	31,107.3	980.9	1,391.7	481.7
2010	C+	1.43	0.68	32,851.2	1,174.4	1,347.6	-0.5
2009	C+	1.62	0.77	34,728.0	1,436.6	1,846.9	191.7

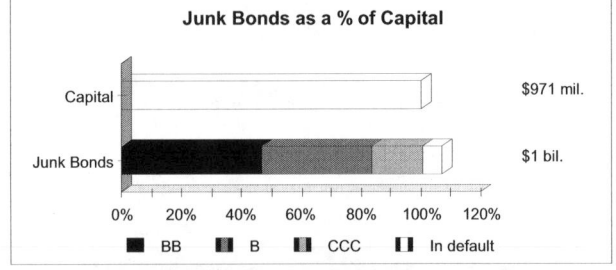

Junk Bonds as a % of Capital

TRIPLE S VIDA INCORPORATED　　　B-　　Good

Major Rating Factors: Good capitalization (5.1 on a scale of 0 to 10) based on good risk adjusted capital (moderate loss scenario). Good overall results on stability tests (5.1) despite fair risk adjusted capital in prior years. Strengths include good financial support from affiliation with Triple-S Management Corp, excellent operational trends and good risk diversification. Fair quality investment portfolio (4.8).

Other Rating Factors: Fair liquidity (4.1). Excellent profitability (7.6) despite modest operating losses during 2009.

Principal Business: Individual life insurance (53%), individual health insurance (31%), individual annuities (6%), group health insurance (6%), and group life insurance (5%).

Principal Investments: NonCMO investment grade bonds (73%), common & preferred stock (14%), CMOs and structured securities (10%), policy loans (1%), and cash (1%).

Investments in Affiliates: 2%

Group Affiliation: Triple-S Management Corp

Licensed in: PR

Commenced Business: September 1964

Address: 1052 Munoz Rivera Ave, Rio Piedras, PR 00927

Phone: (787) 758-4888 **Domicile State:** PR **NAIC Code:** 73814

Data Date	Rating	RACR #1	RACR #2	Total Assets ($mil)	Capital ($mil)	Net Premium ($mil)	Net Income ($mil)
9-14	B-	1.04	0.70	537.9	63.6	117.2	9.8
9-13	B-	1.17	0.75	506.5	57.8	110.9	3.7
2013	B-	1.00	0.69	513.0	61.7	147.3	6.0
2012	B-	1.16	0.75	480.8	57.4	172.6	4.5
2011	B-	1.21	0.78	424.9	57.6	151.5	5.5
2010	C+	1.48	0.98	380.6	54.1	122.4	5.2
2009	C+	1.26	0.82	352.5	49.3	112.1	-1.1

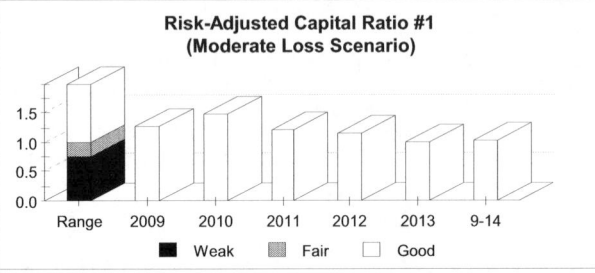

Risk-Adjusted Capital Ratio #1
(Moderate Loss Scenario)

TRUSTMARK INSURANCE COMPANY *   B+   Good

Major Rating Factors: Good quality investment portfolio (5.0 on a scale of 0 to 10) despite mixed results such as: substantial holdings of BBB bonds but moderate junk bond exposure. Good overall results on stability tests (6.8). Stability strengths include excellent operational trends and excellent risk diversification. Strong capitalization (8.1) based on excellent risk adjusted capital (severe loss scenario).

Other Rating Factors: Excellent profitability (7.5) with operating gains in each of the last five years. Excellent liquidity (7.4).

Principal Business: Group life insurance (43%), group health insurance (25%), individual health insurance (23%), individual life insurance (7%), and reinsurance (1%).

Principal Investments: NonCMO investment grade bonds (46%), CMOs and structured securities (27%), common & preferred stock (12%), noninv. grade bonds (6%), and misc. investments (9%).

Investments in Affiliates: 1%

Group Affiliation: Trustmark Group Inc

Licensed in: All states, the District of Columbia and Puerto Rico

Commenced Business: January 1913

Address: 400 Field Dr, Lake Forest, IL 60045-2581

Phone: (847) 615-1500 **Domicile State:** IL **NAIC Code:** 61425

Data Date	Rating	RACR #1	RACR #2	Total Assets ($mil)	Capital ($mil)	Net Premium ($mil)	Net Income ($mil)
9-14	B+	2.93	1.70	1,404.5	311.1	227.9	20.0
9-13	B+	2.92	1.70	1,363.6	300.8	215.4	22.7
2013	B+	3.24	1.89	1,369.8	297.8	294.0	30.0
2012	B+	3.00	1.78	1,320.0	266.5	307.6	22.3
2011	B	3.19	1.85	1,264.8	256.4	283.3	22.7
2010	B	3.16	1.84	1,234.3	237.8	270.6	27.1
2009	B	3.45	1.99	1,172.0	240.3	261.3	26.2

Adverse Trends in Operations

Decrease in premium volume from 2012 to 2013 (4%)
Decrease in capital during 2010 (1%)

TRUSTMARK LIFE INSURANCE COMPANY *   B+   Good

Major Rating Factors: Good quality investment portfolio (6.5 on a scale of 0 to 10) with no exposure to mortgages and small junk bond holdings. Good overall profitability (6.4). Return on equity has been fair, averaging 5.7%. Good liquidity (6.7) with sufficient resources to handle a spike in claims.

Other Rating Factors: Good overall results on stability tests (6.6) good operational trends and excellent risk diversification. Strong capitalization (10.0) based on excellent risk adjusted capital (severe loss scenario).

Principal Business: Group health insurance (96%) and group life insurance (4%).

Principal Investments: NonCMO investment grade bonds (64%), common & preferred stock (16%), CMOs and structured securities (10%), noninv. grade bonds (8%), and misc. investments (2%).

Investments in Affiliates: 2%

Group Affiliation: Trustmark Group Inc

Licensed in: All states except PR

Commenced Business: February 1925

Address: 400 Field Dr, Lake Forest, IL 60045-2581

Phone: (847) 615-1500 **Domicile State:** IL **NAIC Code:** 62863

Data Date	Rating	RACR #1	RACR #2	Total Assets ($mil)	Capital ($mil)	Net Premium ($mil)	Net Income ($mil)
9-14	B+	4.54	3.10	370.8	170.4	159.4	10.6
9-13	B+	3.95	2.76	380.5	177.8	203.8	14.1
2013	B+	3.61	2.53	365.5	160.6	264.5	13.9
2012	B+	3.28	2.34	367.8	165.8	320.1	15.1
2011	B+	2.99	2.25	370.2	168.2	383.3	13.2
2010	B	3.14	2.38	360.0	177.0	392.0	7.8
2009	B	4.57	3.40	362.2	184.6	380.6	2.1

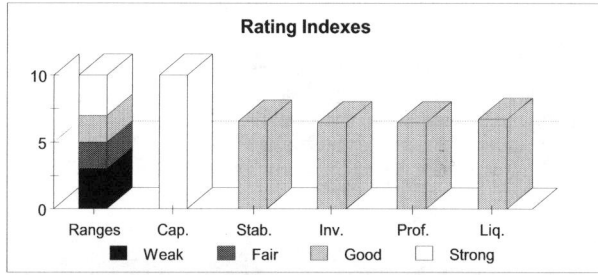

Rating Indexes
(Ranges, Cap., Stab., Inv., Prof., Liq.)
Weak — Fair — Good — Strong

UBS LIFE INSURANCE COMPANY USA   C-   Fair

Major Rating Factors: Fair overall results on stability tests (3.0 on a scale of 0 to 10). Good overall profitability (5.4). Excellent expense controls. Return on equity has been low, averaging 3.5%. Strong capitalization (10.0) based on excellent risk adjusted capital (severe loss scenario).

Other Rating Factors: High quality investment portfolio (9.1). Excellent liquidity (7.0).

Principal Business: Reinsurance (100%).

Principal Investments: NonCMO investment grade bonds (98%) and cash (2%).

Investments in Affiliates: None

Group Affiliation: UBS AG

Licensed in: All states except CT, NY, PR

Commenced Business: September 1956

Address: 601 6th Ave, Des Moines, IA 50309

Phone: (515) 245-2001 **Domicile State:** CA **NAIC Code:** 67423

Data Date	Rating	RACR #1	RACR #2	Total Assets ($mil)	Capital ($mil)	Net Premium ($mil)	Net Income ($mil)
9-14	C-	6.29	5.66	41.6	39.1	0.1	0.9
9-13	U	N/A	N/A	44.4	42.2	0.1	0.8
2013	C-	6.16	5.55	45.0	38.2	0.2	1.1
2012	U	6.73	6.06	44.5	41.5	0.1	2.1
2011	B-	6.51	5.86	43.7	39.6	0.5	4.2
2010	B-	6.08	5.48	44.1	37.2	0.5	-0.7
2009	C+	6.31	5.68	44.1	38.6	0.4	0.5

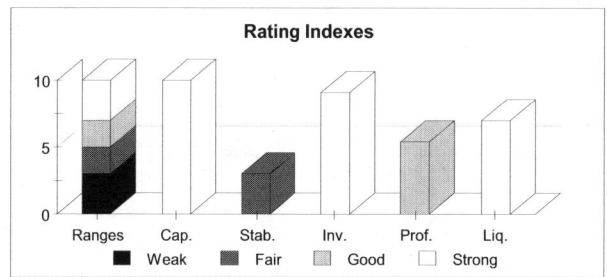

Rating Indexes
(Ranges, Cap., Stab., Inv., Prof., Liq.)
Weak — Fair — Good — Strong

UNICARE LIFE & HEALTH INSURANCE COMPANY   B   Good

Major Rating Factors: Good overall profitability (6.6 on a scale of 0 to 10). Excellent expense controls. Return on equity has been excellent over the last five years averaging 40.8%. Good liquidity (6.5) with sufficient resources to handle a spike in claims. Fair quality investment portfolio (3.8).

Other Rating Factors: Fair overall results on stability tests (4.1). Strong capitalization (7.6) based on excellent risk adjusted capital (severe loss scenario).

Principal Business: Group life insurance (33%), reinsurance (29%), individual health insurance (21%), and group health insurance (17%).

Principal Investments: NonCMO investment grade bonds (75%), noninv. grade bonds (13%), cash (9%), and CMOs and structured securities (2%).

Investments in Affiliates: None

Group Affiliation: WellPoint Inc

Licensed in: All states, the District of Columbia and Puerto Rico

Commenced Business: December 1980

Address: 1209 Orange St, Wilmington, DE 19801

Phone: (877) 864-2273 **Domicile State:** IN **NAIC Code:** 80314

Data Date	Rating	RACR #1	RACR #2	Total Assets ($mil)	Capital ($mil)	Net Premium ($mil)	Net Income ($mil)
6-14	B	1.85	1.37	402.8	76.5	159.0	12.4
6-13	B	1.94	1.39	426.1	93.6	159.9	20.9
2013	B	3.13	2.32	469.1	126.3	321.7	43.7
2012	B	2.83	2.05	554.2	158.8	439.4	74.4
2011	B	2.27	1.66	642.9	149.3	632.5	51.2
2010	B	1.43	1.04	971.9	168.9	987.0	68.2
2009	B	1.27	0.96	1,482.4	381.3	2,429.2	156.5

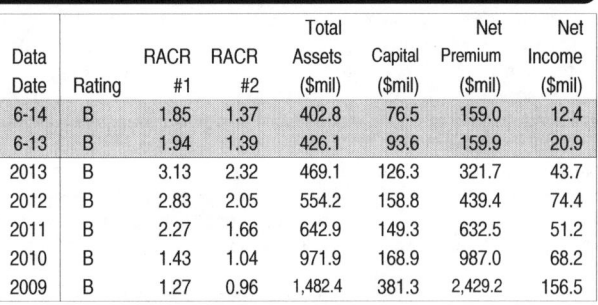

Net Income History
(in millions of dollars)

UNIMERICA INSURANCE COMPANY   B   Good

Major Rating Factors: Good overall results on stability tests (5.8 on a scale of 0 to 10) despite fair financial strength of affiliated UnitedHealth Group Inc and excessive premium growth. Other stability subfactors include excellent operational trends and excellent risk diversification. Strong capitalization (9.2) based on excellent risk adjusted capital (severe loss scenario). Capital levels have been relatively consistent over the last five years. High quality investment portfolio (8.5).

Other Rating Factors: Excellent profitability (9.1) with operating gains in each of the last five years. Excellent liquidity (7.0).

Principal Business: Group health insurance (54%), reinsurance (43%), and group life insurance (2%).

Principal Investments: NonCMO investment grade bonds (87%) and CMOs and structured securities (14%).

Investments in Affiliates: None

Group Affiliation: UnitedHealth Group Inc

Licensed in: All states except NY, PR

Commenced Business: December 1980

Address: 711 High St, Des Moines, IA 50392

Phone: (877) 832-7734 **Domicile State:** WI **NAIC Code:** 91529

Data Date	Rating	RACR #1	RACR #2	Total Assets ($mil)	Capital ($mil)	Net Premium ($mil)	Net Income ($mil)
9-14	B	3.10	2.47	458.7	215.0	440.2	53.5
9-13	B	2.98	2.33	397.7	170.0	330.8	31.6
2013	B	2.82	2.24	410.1	181.1	489.2	43.3
2012	B	3.17	2.48	326.6	153.2	319.8	32.2
2011	B	3.07	2.37	289.0	129.9	228.4	9.5
2010	B	3.34	2.57	264.2	133.1	199.3	20.5
2009	B	2.36	1.82	262.1	113.0	235.7	5.2

UnitedHealth Group Inc Composite Group Rating: C+ Largest Group Members	Assets ($mil)	Rating
UNITED HEALTHCARE INS CO	14513	C
OXFORD HEALTH INS INC	2078	C+
UNITED HEALTHCARE INS CO OF NY	1983	B-
OXFORD HEALTH PLANS (NY) INC	1820	A+
UNITEDHEALTHCARE PLAN RIVER VALLEY	1094	B+

UNION FIDELITY LIFE INSURANCE COMPANY   D+   Weak

Major Rating Factors: Weak profitability (1.7 on a scale of 0 to 10) with operating losses during the first nine months of 2014. Return on equity has been low, averaging -41.0%. Weak overall results on stability tests (2.7) including weak risk adjusted capital in prior years, negative cash flow from operations for 2013. Fair quality investment portfolio (3.0).

Other Rating Factors: Good capitalization (5.0) based on good risk adjusted capital (moderate loss scenario). Excellent liquidity (8.6).

Principal Business: Reinsurance (86%), group health insurance (6%), group life insurance (4%), individual life insurance (2%), and individual health insurance (1%).

Principal Investments: NonCMO investment grade bonds (76%), CMOs and structured securities (12%), mortgages in good standing (5%), and noninv. grade bonds (4%).

Investments in Affiliates: 2%

Group Affiliation: General Electric Corp Group

Licensed in: All states except NY, PR

Commenced Business: February 1926

Address: 7101 College Blvd Suite 1400, Overland Park, KS 66210

Phone: (913) 982-3700 **Domicile State:** KS **NAIC Code:** 62596

Data Date	Rating	RACR #1	RACR #2	Total Assets ($mil)	Capital ($mil)	Net Premium ($mil)	Net Income ($mil)
9-14	D+	1.00	0.51	19,466.6	492.7	209.1	-46.6
9-13	D+	0.96	0.50	19,563.8	512.0	224.8	-43.0
2013	D+	1.07	0.55	19,510.6	569.3	305.7	6.3
2012	D	1.01	0.52	19,585.3	560.1	316.1	-430.4
2011	D+	0.80	0.42	19,089.5	445.2	320.2	-598.5
2010	C-	0.74	0.40	18,522.5	438.9	335.4	-294.3
2009	C-	0.98	0.53	18,377.8	611.7	344.7	32.7

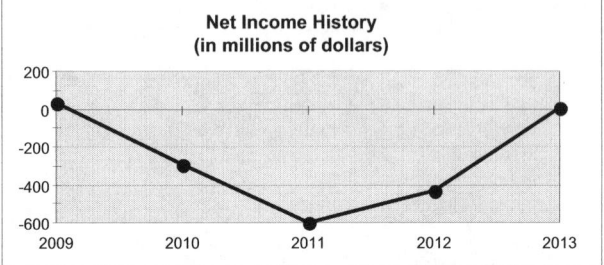

Net Income History
(in millions of dollars)

UNION LABOR LIFE INSURANCE COMPANY | B- | Good

Major Rating Factors: Good current capitalization (6.9 on a scale of 0 to 10) based on good risk adjusted capital (severe loss scenario), although results have slipped from the excellent range during the last year. Good liquidity (6.9) with sufficient resources to handle a spike in claims. Good overall results on stability tests (5.0) despite negative cash flow from operations for 2013 excellent operational trends, excellent risk adjusted capital for prior years and excellent risk diversification.

Other Rating Factors: Weak profitability (2.9) with investment income below regulatory standards in relation to interest assumptions of reserves. High quality investment portfolio (7.6).

Principal Business: Group health insurance (45%), group life insurance (31%), reinsurance (19%), group retirement contracts (4%), and individual health insurance (1%).

Principal Investments: NonCMO investment grade bonds (55%), CMOs and structured securities (29%), common & preferred stock (7%), mortgages in good standing (7%), and misc. investments (2%).

Investments in Affiliates: 7%

Group Affiliation: Union Labor Group

Licensed in: All states except PR

Commenced Business: May 1927

Address: 111 Massachusetts Ave NW, Washington, DC 20001-1625

Phone: (202) 682-6690 **Domicile State:** MD **NAIC Code:** 69744

Data Date	Rating	RACR #1	RACR #2	Total Assets ($mil)	Capital ($mil)	Net Premium ($mil)	Net Income ($mil)
9-14	B-	1.40	0.99	3,351.0	77.0	106.0	2.8
9-13	B	1.96	1.32	2,751.2	84.9	106.4	-7.7
2013	B-	1.66	1.20	2,813.7	87.7	139.5	-11.1
2012	B-	2.22	1.50	2,905.9	96.9	148.8	7.9
2011	C+	1.82	1.15	3,495.0	91.0	156.3	2.7
2010	C+	1.89	1.25	3,928.8	93.4	147.2	7.5
2009	C+	1.72	1.10	3,882.3	92.1	155.2	8.7

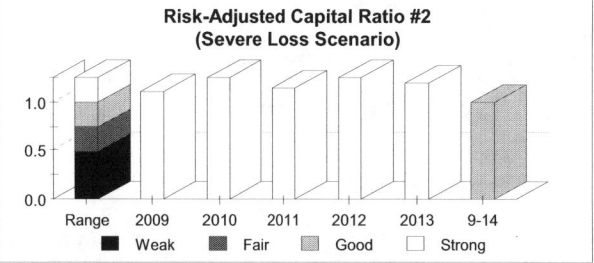

Risk-Adjusted Capital Ratio #2
(Severe Loss Scenario)

■ Weak   ■ Fair   ■ Good   □ Strong

UNION SECURITY INSURANCE COMPANY | B | Good

Major Rating Factors: Good overall results on stability tests (5.6 on a scale of 0 to 10) despite negative cash flow from operations for 2013. Other stability subfactors include good operational trends and excellent risk diversification. Good quality investment portfolio (5.4) despite large holdings of BBB rated bonds in addition to moderate junk bond exposure. Exposure to mortgages is significant, but the mortgage default rate has been low. Good overall profitability (6.4).

Other Rating Factors: Good liquidity (5.0). Strong capitalization (7.3) based on excellent risk adjusted capital (severe loss scenario).

Principal Business: Group health insurance (56%), group life insurance (16%), reinsurance (13%), individual health insurance (8%), and other lines (7%).

Principal Investments: NonCMO investment grade bonds (64%), mortgages in good standing (18%), noninv. grade bonds (4%), CMOs and structured securities (4%), and misc. investments (7%).

Investments in Affiliates: 1%

Group Affiliation: Assurant Inc

Licensed in: All states except NY, PR

Commenced Business: September 1910

Address: 500 Bielenberg Dr, Woodbury, MN 55125

Phone: (612) 738-5063 **Domicile State:** KS **NAIC Code:** 70408

Data Date	Rating	RACR #1	RACR #2	Total Assets ($mil)	Capital ($mil)	Net Premium ($mil)	Net Income ($mil)
9-14	B	1.84	1.19	4,942.9	422.9	763.0	59.8
9-13	B	2.03	1.25	5,036.1	420.3	734.6	50.9
2013	B	1.88	1.21	5,085.8	434.7	986.2	85.4
2012	B	2.10	1.28	5,015.5	438.8	986.8	95.3
2011	B	2.02	1.24	5,139.5	455.8	1,050.4	69.1
2010	B	1.89	1.15	5,529.4	449.6	1,109.5	81.0
2009	C+	1.68	1.01	5,653.2	418.4	1,103.3	59.9

Adverse Trends in Operations

Decrease in premium volume from 2011 to 2012 (6%)
Decrease in asset base during 2012 (2%)
Decrease in capital during 2012 (4%)
Decrease in premium volume from 2010 to 2011 (5%)
Decrease in asset base during 2010 (2%)

UNION SECURITY LIFE INSURANCE COMPANY OF NEW YORK * | B+ | Good

Major Rating Factors: Good overall results on stability tests (5.0 on a scale of 0 to 10) despite negative cash flow from operations for 2013. Other stability subfactors include good operational trends and excellent risk diversification. Good overall profitability (5.9). Return on equity has been good over the last five years, averaging 12.0%. Good liquidity (6.8).

Other Rating Factors: Strong capitalization (10.0) based on excellent risk adjusted capital (severe loss scenario). High quality investment portfolio (7.0).

Principal Business: Group health insurance (40%), individual health insurance (25%), reinsurance (16%), group life insurance (10%), and other lines (8%).

Principal Investments: NonCMO investment grade bonds (66%), mortgages in good standing (20%), CMOs and structured securities (7%), common & preferred stock (4%), and misc. investments (2%).

Investments in Affiliates: None

Group Affiliation: Assurant Inc

Licensed in: NY

Commenced Business: April 1974

Address: 220 Salina Meadows Pkwy #255, Syracuse, NY 13212

Phone: (315) 451-0066 **Domicile State:** NY **NAIC Code:** 81477

Data Date	Rating	RACR #1	RACR #2	Total Assets ($mil)	Capital ($mil)	Net Premium ($mil)	Net Income ($mil)
9-14	B+	4.50	4.05	139.8	41.5	18.1	4.6
9-13	B+	4.81	4.21	154.4	45.0	20.8	2.6
2013	B+	4.44	4.00	147.7	40.9	27.4	5.4
2012	B	5.02	4.21	160.6	46.9	30.1	5.5
2011	B	4.32	3.39	168.1	40.7	35.2	-0.1
2010	B	4.81	3.59	174.2	45.8	37.6	7.8
2009	B	5.32	3.60	164.5	50.5	43.5	9.6

Adverse Trends in Operations

Decrease in capital during 2013 (13%)
Increase in policy surrenders from 2012 to 2013 (769%)
Decrease in premium volume from 2011 to 2012 (14%)
Decrease in capital during 2011 (11%)
Decrease in premium volume from 2009 to 2010 (14%)

UNITED AMERICAN INSURANCE COMPANY

B-   **Good**

Major Rating Factors: Fair current capitalization (4.9 on a scale of 0 to 10) based on fair risk adjusted capital (moderate loss scenario), although results have slipped from the good range during the last year. Fair overall results on stability tests (4.9). Good quality investment portfolio (5.8).

Other Rating Factors: Good overall profitability (6.6). Good liquidity (6.5).

Principal Business: Individual health insurance (75%), group health insurance (15%), individual annuities (5%), individual life insurance (3%), and reinsurance (2%).

Principal Investments: NonCMO investment grade bonds (84%), common & preferred stock (4%), noninv. grade bonds (4%), CMOs and structured securities (4%), and misc. investments (4%).

Investments in Affiliates: 4%

Group Affiliation: Torchmark Corp

Licensed in: All states except NY, PR

Commenced Business: August 1981

Address: 10306 Regency Parkway Dr, Omaha, NE 68114

Phone: (972) 529-5085 **Domicile State:** NE **NAIC Code:** 92916

Data Date	Rating	RACR #1	RACR #2	Total Assets ($mil)	Capital ($mil)	Net Premium ($mil)	Net Income ($mil)
9-14	B-	0.99	0.72	1,717.2	170.8	646.2	11.3
9-13	B	1.20	0.86	1,713.6	197.5	562.4	30.9
2013	B	1.27	0.91	1,683.4	211.6	745.1	58.1
2012	B	1.47	1.05	1,722.8	256.1	779.2	78.8
2011	B	1.54	1.07	1,703.5	243.9	692.2	75.0
2010	B	1.57	1.12	1,698.1	266.2	749.5	93.6
2009	B	1.55	1.10	1,649.6	257.0	787.2	79.4

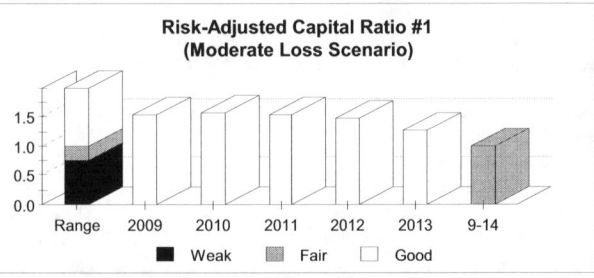

Risk-Adjusted Capital Ratio #1 (Moderate Loss Scenario)

UNITED FARM FAMILY LIFE INSURANCE COMPANY *

A   **Excellent**

Major Rating Factors: Good quality investment portfolio (6.8 on a scale of 0 to 10) despite significant exposure to mortgages . Mortgage default rate has been low. substantial holdings of BBB bonds in addition to no exposure to junk bonds. Good overall profitability (6.5). Return on equity has been fair, averaging 5.4%. Good liquidity (5.9).

Other Rating Factors: Strong capitalization (8.3) based on excellent risk adjusted capital (severe loss scenario). Excellent overall results on stability tests (7.4) excellent operational trends and excellent risk diversification.

Principal Business: Individual life insurance (81%), reinsurance (10%), individual annuities (9%), and individual health insurance (1%).

Principal Investments: NonCMO investment grade bonds (61%), mortgages in good standing (15%), CMOs and structured securities (13%), policy loans (5%), and misc. investments (5%).

Investments in Affiliates: 1%

Group Affiliation: Indiana Farm Bureau

Licensed in: AZ, CA, IL, IN, MD, MA, NH, NJ, NC, ND, OH, PA

Commenced Business: May 1964

Address: 225 S East St, Indianapolis, IN 46202

Phone: (317) 692-7200 **Domicile State:** IN **NAIC Code:** 69892

Data Date	Rating	RACR #1	RACR #2	Total Assets ($mil)	Capital ($mil)	Net Premium ($mil)	Net Income ($mil)
9-14	A	3.13	1.87	2,129.9	285.5	109.4	13.7
9-13	A	2.99	1.77	2,071.8	258.0	109.3	9.8
2013	A	3.07	1.84	2,087.0	275.2	144.3	12.8
2012	A	2.97	1.77	2,006.6	242.4	145.3	14.6
2011	A	2.97	1.77	1,923.8	235.8	155.0	12.1
2010	A	3.02	1.80	1,843.3	234.4	152.9	11.5
2009	A	2.94	1.72	1,768.0	218.8	116.1	13.3

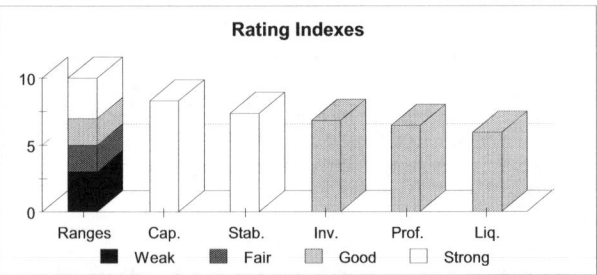

Rating Indexes

UNITED FIDELITY LIFE INSURANCE COMPANY

C   **Fair**

Major Rating Factors: Fair capitalization (4.6 on a scale of 0 to 10) based on fair risk adjusted capital (severe loss scenario). Fair quality investment portfolio (3.6). Fair overall results on stability tests (4.3) including fair risk adjusted capital in prior years.

Other Rating Factors: Good liquidity (6.9). Excellent profitability (7.5) despite modest operating losses during 2009.

Principal Business: Individual life insurance (90%), individual annuities (4%), individual health insurance (4%), and reinsurance (2%).

Principal Investments: Common & preferred stock (75%), CMOs and structured securities (9%), nonCMO investment grade bonds (7%), mortgages in good standing (3%), and misc. investments (6%).

Investments in Affiliates: 73%

Group Affiliation: Americo Life Inc

Licensed in: All states except CT, FL, HI, ME, MI, MN, NH, NJ, NY, VT, PR

Commenced Business: September 1977

Address: 500 North Akard, Dallas, TX 75201

Phone: (816) 391-2000 **Domicile State:** TX **NAIC Code:** 87645

Data Date	Rating	RACR #1	RACR #2	Total Assets ($mil)	Capital ($mil)	Net Premium ($mil)	Net Income ($mil)
9-14	C	0.72	0.70	757.1	440.1	6.1	42.5
9-13	C	0.78	0.74	778.4	452.0	6.5	-7.1
2013	C	0.74	0.72	778.2	450.2	8.6	44.2
2012	C	0.70	0.68	730.1	396.9	9.3	24.2
2011	C	0.70	0.68	717.4	376.9	10.1	27.7
2010	D+	0.71	0.69	718.9	367.1	10.7	25.8
2009	D+	0.70	0.67	690.5	328.4	11.6	-8.4

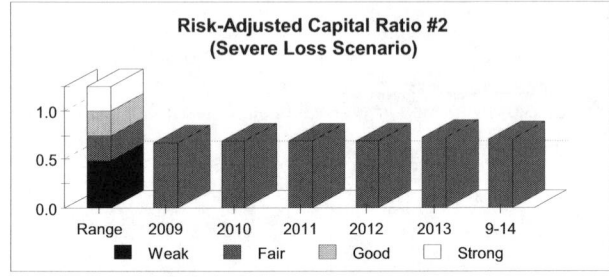

Risk-Adjusted Capital Ratio #2 (Severe Loss Scenario)

UNITED HEALTHCARE INSURANCE COMPANY   C   Fair

Major Rating Factors: Fair overall capitalization (4.2 on a scale of 0 to 10) based on mixed results -- excessive policy leverage mitigated by fair risk adjusted capital (severe loss scenario). Fair overall results on stability tests (3.5) including fair risk adjusted capital in prior years. Good quality investment portfolio (6.8).

Other Rating Factors: Weak liquidity (1.5). Excellent profitability (9.4) with operating gains in each of the last five years.

Principal Business: Group health insurance (58%), individual health insurance (31%), and reinsurance (11%).

Principal Investments: NonCMO investment grade bonds (58%), CMOs and structured securities (18%), common & preferred stock (17%), and noninv. grade bonds (5%).

Investments in Affiliates: 15%

Group Affiliation: UnitedHealth Group Inc

Licensed in: All states except NY

Commenced Business: April 1972

Address: 185 Asylum St, Hartford, CT 06103-3408

Phone: (877) 832-7734 **Domicile State:** CT **NAIC Code:** 79413

Data Date	Rating	RACR #1	RACR #2	Total Assets ($mil)	Capital ($mil)	Net Premium ($mil)	Net Income ($mil)
9-14	C	0.85	0.72	14,592.8	4,865.2	33,276.5	1,934.2
9-13	C	0.81	0.68	14,632.6	4,261.3	33,662.5	1,675.6
2013	C	0.76	0.64	14,512.6	5,039.5	44,680.4	2,384.0
2012	C	0.76	0.64	14,118.3	4,711.9	42,602.9	2,531.0
2011	C	0.73	0.62	15,022.1	4,421.6	41,956.3	2,430.1
2010	C+	0.70	0.59	13,677.4	4,022.0	39,966.2	2,259.1
2009	C+	0.66	0.56	11,899.7	3,425.8	35,846.0	1,993.9

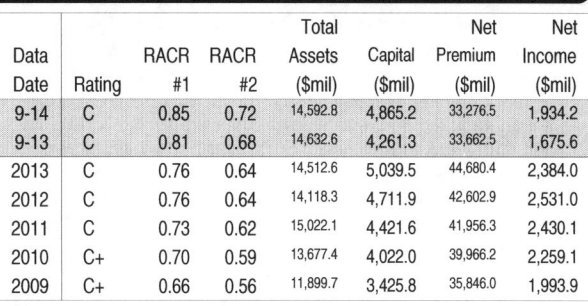

Policy Leverage

Target Leverage — 100%
Actual Leverage — 293%

■ Recommended □ Excess

UNITED HERITAGE LIFE INSURANCE COMPANY   B-   Good

Major Rating Factors: Good quality investment portfolio (6.1 on a scale of 0 to 10) despite mixed results such as: large holdings of BBB rated bonds but moderate junk bond exposure. Fair overall results on stability tests (4.6). Weak liquidity (2.6) based on large exposure to policies that are subject to policyholder withdrawals with minimal or no penalty.

Other Rating Factors: Strong capitalization (7.6) based on excellent risk adjusted capital (severe loss scenario). Excellent profitability (8.0) with operating gains in each of the last five years.

Principal Business: Individual life insurance (69%), individual annuities (20%), group life insurance (5%), group health insurance (4%), and group retirement contracts (1%).

Principal Investments: NonCMO investment grade bonds (80%), CMOs and structured securities (9%), noninv. grade bonds (5%), mortgages in good standing (3%), and misc. investments (3%).

Investments in Affiliates: None

Group Affiliation: United Heritage Mutual Holding Co

Licensed in: AK, AZ, AR, CA, CO, DC, DE, FL, GA, HI, ID, IL, IN, IA, KS, KY, LA, MI, MN, MO, MT, NE, NV, NM, NC, ND, OH, OK, OR, PA, SC, SD, TN, TX, UT, VA, WA, WI, WY

Commenced Business: September 1935

Address: 707 East United Heritage Ct, Meridian, ID 83642-3527

Phone: (208) 466-7856 **Domicile State:** ID **NAIC Code:** 63983

Data Date	Rating	RACR #1	RACR #2	Total Assets ($mil)	Capital ($mil)	Net Premium ($mil)	Net Income ($mil)
9-14	B-	2.64	1.37	522.4	57.0	48.0	4.5
9-13	B-	2.68	1.38	517.9	54.4	51.9	4.5
2013	B-	2.71	1.40	520.1	55.4	68.1	5.9
2012	B-	2.64	1.36	504.2	52.4	65.4	6.0
2011	B	2.57	1.35	486.6	49.1	58.0	5.3
2010	B	2.44	1.26	465.6	46.2	56.5	6.2
2009	B	2.09	1.05	438.3	40.8	56.0	0.6

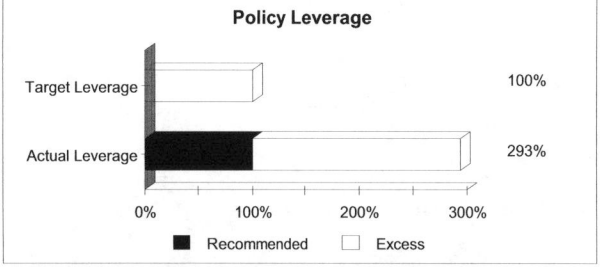

Rating Indexes

Ranges Cap. Stab. Inv. Prof. Liq.

■ Weak ▨ Fair ▧ Good □ Strong

UNITED INSURANCE COMPANY OF AMERICA   B-   Good

Major Rating Factors: Good current capitalization (6.9 on a scale of 0 to 10) based on good risk adjusted capital (severe loss scenario), although results have slipped from the excellent range over the last two years. Good liquidity (5.3) with sufficient resources to handle a spike in claims as well as a significant increase in policy surrenders. Good overall results on stability tests (5.3) despite fair risk adjusted capital in prior years excellent operational trends and excellent risk diversification.

Other Rating Factors: Fair quality investment portfolio (4.5). Excellent profitability (7.2) with operating gains in each of the last five years.

Principal Business: Reinsurance (51%), individual life insurance (47%), and individual health insurance (3%).

Principal Investments: NonCMO investment grade bonds (62%), noninv. grade bonds (8%), policy loans (8%), common & preferred stock (6%), and misc. investments (15%).

Investments in Affiliates: 5%

Group Affiliation: Kemper Corporation

Licensed in: All states except AK, NY, PR

Commenced Business: April 1928

Address: 12115 Lackland Rd, St Louis, MO 63146-4003

Phone: (312) 661-4681 **Domicile State:** IL **NAIC Code:** 69930

Data Date	Rating	RACR #1	RACR #2	Total Assets ($mil)	Capital ($mil)	Net Premium ($mil)	Net Income ($mil)
9-14	B-	1.58	0.99	3,655.6	446.6	278.2	51.4
9-13	B-	1.55	0.98	3,589.0	441.0	289.5	49.9
2013	B-	1.53	0.95	3,591.7	436.1	375.0	79.0
2012	B-	1.58	1.00	3,550.3	464.1	383.6	95.9
2011	B-	1.63	1.05	3,493.3	480.6	386.6	95.4
2010	B-	1.52	0.98	3,387.9	405.5	388.8	73.1
2009	B-	1.16	0.74	3,238.9	303.5	407.4	52.0

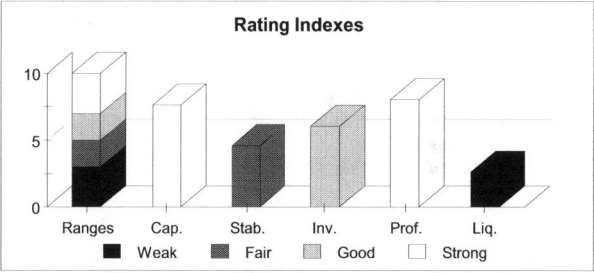

Risk-Adjusted Capital Ratio #2
(Severe Loss Scenario)

Range 2009 2010 2011 2012 2013 9-14

■ Weak ▨ Fair ▧ Good □ Strong

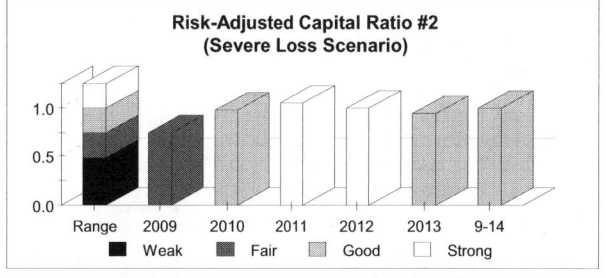

UNITED LIFE INSURANCE COMPANY   B   Good

Major Rating Factors: Good overall results on stability tests (6.1 on a scale of 0 to 10) despite negative cash flow from operations for 2013 and excessive premium growth. Other stability subfactors include excellent operational trends and excellent risk diversification. Good quality investment portfolio (6.0) despite mixed results such as: minimal exposure to mortgages and large holdings of BBB rated bonds but small junk bond holdings. Good overall profitability (6.0).

Other Rating Factors: Good liquidity (6.5). Strong capitalization (7.8) based on excellent risk adjusted capital (severe loss scenario).

Principal Business: Individual annuities (66%), individual life insurance (33%), and individual health insurance (1%).

Principal Investments: NonCMO investment grade bonds (78%), CMOs and structured securities (16%), noninv. grade bonds (3%), common & preferred stock (2%), and cash (1%).

Investments in Affiliates: None

Group Affiliation: United Fire & Casualty Group

Licensed in: AL, AZ, AR, CA, CO, DE, FL, ID, IL, IN, IA, KS, KY, LA, MD, MI, MN, MS, MO, MT, NE, NV, NJ, NM, NC, ND, OH, OK, PA, SD, TN, TX, UT, VA, WV, WI, WY

Commenced Business: October 1962

Address: 118 Second Ave SE, Cedar Rapids, IA 52401

Phone: (800) 553-7937 **Domicile State:** IA **NAIC Code:** 69973

Data Date	Rating	RACR #1	RACR #2	Total Assets ($mil)	Capital ($mil)	Net Premium ($mil)	Net Income ($mil)
9-14	B	2.86	1.50	1,640.6	164.5	143.1	2.6
9-13	B	2.81	1.46	1,661.1	164.5	107.4	2.7
2013	B	2.74	1.42	1,648.0	158.0	164.3	5.9
2012	B	2.72	1.39	1,675.7	158.7	154.2	7.4
2011	B	2.86	1.44	1,651.1	167.2	170.0	6.2
2010	B	2.81	1.40	1,554.0	158.4	136.8	13.4
2009	B	2.89	1.43	1,480.6	160.2	255.8	3.5

Adverse Trends in Operations

Decrease in asset base during 2013 (2%)
Increase in policy surrenders from 2012 to 2013 (43%)
Increase in policy surrenders from 2011 to 2012 (48%)
Decrease in capital during 2012 (5%)
Decrease in premium volume from 2009 to 2010 (47%)

UNITED OF OMAHA LIFE INSURANCE COMPANY   B   Good

Major Rating Factors: Good quality investment portfolio (5.1 on a scale of 0 to 10) despite large holdings of BBB rated bonds in addition to moderate junk bond exposure. Exposure to mortgages is significant, but the mortgage default rate has been low. Good overall profitability (5.4). Excellent expense controls. Return on equity has been low, averaging -1.2%. Good liquidity (5.9).

Other Rating Factors: Good overall results on stability tests (5.4) excellent operational trends, good risk adjusted capital for prior years and excellent risk diversification. Strong capitalization (7.2) based on excellent risk adjusted capital (severe loss scenario).

Principal Business: Individual health insurance (34%), individual life insurance (31%), group health insurance (11%), group life insurance (9%), and other lines (15%).

Principal Investments: NonCMO investment grade bonds (49%), CMOs and structured securities (26%), mortgages in good standing (13%), noninv. grade bonds (3%), and misc. investments (6%).

Investments in Affiliates: 3%

Group Affiliation: Mutual Of Omaha Group

Licensed in: All states except NY

Commenced Business: November 1926

Address: Mutual Of Omaha Plaza, Omaha, NE 68175

Phone: (402) 342-7600 **Domicile State:** NE **NAIC Code:** 69868

Data Date	Rating	RACR #1	RACR #2	Total Assets ($mil)	Capital ($mil)	Net Premium ($mil)	Net Income ($mil)
9-14	B	1.99	1.15	18,551.4	1,406.6	1,851.6	141.2
9-13	B	1.51	0.89	17,817.6	1,107.0	2,641.9	57.2
2013	B	1.71	1.00	18,122.5	1,226.9	3,428.2	69.9
2012	B	1.42	0.83	16,698.1	1,027.2	3,464.0	-31.5
2011	B	1.46	0.86	15,737.8	1,036.1	3,162.9	-207.0
2010	B	1.83	1.08	15,119.8	1,210.2	2,441.2	-110.5
2009	B+	1.95	1.13	14,037.3	1,245.1	2,416.3	-5.2

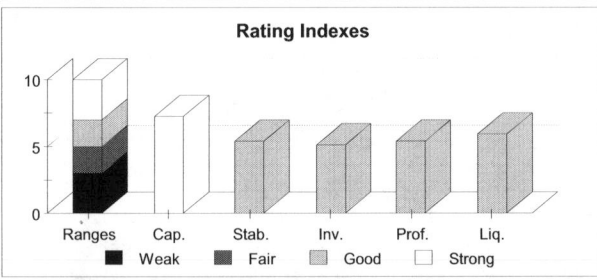

Rating Indexes

Ranges — Cap. — Stab. — Inv. — Prof. — Liq.
■ Weak   ▨ Fair   ▧ Good   ☐ Strong

UNITED STATES LIFE INSURANCE COMPANY IN NYC   B-   Good

Major Rating Factors: Good quality investment portfolio (5.1 on a scale of 0 to 10) despite mixed results such as: large holdings of BBB rated bonds but junk bond exposure equal to 57% of capital. Good overall profitability (5.9). Return on equity has been excellent over the last five years averaging 17.8%. Good liquidity (5.7).

Other Rating Factors: Fair overall results on stability tests (4.6). Strong capitalization (7.4) based on excellent risk adjusted capital (severe loss scenario).

Principal Business: Individual annuities (63%), individual life insurance (14%), group health insurance (13%), group life insurance (6%), and group retirement contracts (3%).

Principal Investments: NonCMO investment grade bonds (55%), CMOs and structured securities (24%), mortgages in good standing (7%), noninv. grade bonds (5%), and policy loans (1%).

Investments in Affiliates: None

Group Affiliation: American International Group

Licensed in: All states except PR

Commenced Business: March 1850

Address: 390 Park Ave, New York, NY 10022-4684

Phone: (212) 709-6000 **Domicile State:** NY **NAIC Code:** 70106

Data Date	Rating	RACR #1	RACR #2	Total Assets ($mil)	Capital ($mil)	Net Premium ($mil)	Net Income ($mil)
9-14	B-	2.62	1.29	28,449.0	1,994.7	1,455.3	335.1
9-13	B-	2.54	1.23	25,246.1	1,784.2	1,257.6	443.7
2013	B-	2.32	1.15	25,538.0	1,765.2	1,771.2	420.1
2012	B-	2.58	1.27	24,541.6	1,878.3	1,458.3	269.6
2011	B-	2.59	1.28	23,095.9	1,842.3	2,429.6	107.2
2010	B-	2.82	1.48	11,591.7	1,167.4	722.3	117.4
2009	C	2.56	1.34	5,318.1	488.9	491.8	193.9

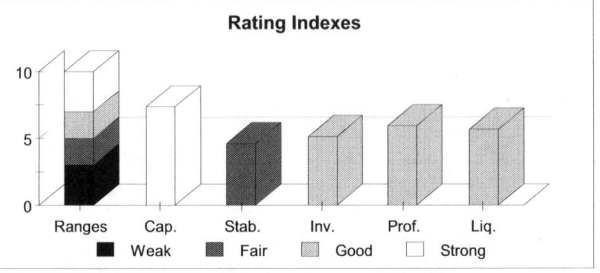

Rating Indexes

Ranges — Cap. — Stab. — Inv. — Prof. — Liq.
■ Weak   ▨ Fair   ▧ Good   ☐ Strong

UNITED TEACHER ASSOCIATES INSURANCE COMPANY   C   Fair

Major Rating Factors: Fair overall results on stability tests (4.2 on a scale of 0 to 10). Good quality investment portfolio (5.2) despite mixed results such as: substantial holdings of BBB bonds but junk bond exposure equal to 53% of capital. Weak profitability (2.6). Return on equity has been low, averaging -2.1%.
Other Rating Factors: Strong capitalization (7.2) based on excellent risk adjusted capital (severe loss scenario). Excellent liquidity (7.2).
Principal Business: Individual health insurance (79%), group health insurance (13%), individual life insurance (3%), reinsurance (3%), and group retirement contracts (2%).
Principal Investments: NonCMO investment grade bonds (60%), CMOs and structured securities (28%), noninv. grade bonds (5%), common & preferred stock (4%), and policy loans (2%).
Investments in Affiliates: None
Group Affiliation: American Financial Group Inc
Licensed in: All states except NH, NY, RI, VT
Commenced Business: January 1959
Address: 5508 Parkcrest Dr, Austin, TX 78731
Phone: (512) 451-2224 **Domicile State:** TX **NAIC Code:** 63479

Data Date	Rating	RACR #1	RACR #2	Total Assets ($mil)	Capital ($mil)	Net Premium ($mil)	Net Income ($mil)
9-14	C	2.05	1.11	986.6	85.0	56.4	2.0
9-13	C	1.76	0.90	905.0	59.3	59.0	-4.1
2013	C	2.13	1.16	940.0	84.4	77.7	3.5
2012	C	1.69	0.84	839.3	47.9	52.8	-14.7
2011	B-	1.51	0.92	847.1	66.9	205.7	7.2
2010	B-	1.48	0.92	772.0	69.1	224.0	8.3
2009	B-	1.38	0.86	736.9	66.2	235.8	-7.4

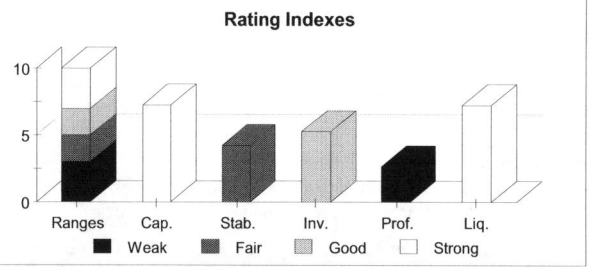

Rating Indexes

Ranges · Cap. · Stab. · Inv. · Prof. · Liq.
■ Weak   ▨ Fair   ▥ Good   □ Strong

UNITED WORLD LIFE INSURANCE COMPANY *   B+   Good

Major Rating Factors: Good overall results on stability tests (6.7 on a scale of 0 to 10) despite negative cash flow from operations for 2013. Other stability subfactors include good operational trends and excellent risk diversification. Good overall profitability (6.7). Return on equity has been low, averaging 3.3%. Strong capitalization (8.0) based on excellent risk adjusted capital (severe loss scenario).
Other Rating Factors: High quality investment portfolio (7.6). Excellent liquidity (7.0).
Principal Business: Individual health insurance (100%).
Principal Investments: NonCMO investment grade bonds (65%), CMOs and structured securities (28%), policy loans (1%), noninv. grade bonds (1%), and cash (1%).
Investments in Affiliates: None
Group Affiliation: Mutual Of Omaha Group
Licensed in: All states except CT, NY, PR
Commenced Business: April 1970
Address: Mutual Of Omaha Plaza, Omaha, NE 68175
Phone: (402) 342-7600 **Domicile State:** NE **NAIC Code:** 72850

Data Date	Rating	RACR #1	RACR #2	Total Assets ($mil)	Capital ($mil)	Net Premium ($mil)	Net Income ($mil)
9-14	B+	4.02	1.68	114.3	48.7	1.0	0.9
9-13	B+	3.79	1.58	111.1	48.1	1.1	0.7
2013	B+	4.19	1.76	114.9	48.6	1.6	1.2
2012	B+	3.89	1.63	103.1	47.3	1.7	0.1
2011	B+	3.67	1.53	106.1	47.3	1.9	1.9
2010	B+	3.44	1.44	101.0	45.4	2.0	2.3
2009	B+	3.22	1.35	92.8	43.2	2.2	2.3

Adverse Trends in Operations

Decrease in premium volume from 2012 to 2013 (7%)
Change in asset mix during 2013 (4%)
Decrease in asset base during 2012 (3%)
Increase in policy surrenders from 2010 to 2011 (36%)
Decrease in premium volume from 2009 to 2010 (9%)

UNITEDHEALTHCARE LIFE INSURANCE COMPANY   B   Good

Major Rating Factors: Good overall results on stability tests (5.8 on a scale of 0 to 10) despite fair financial strength of affiliated UnitedHealth Group Inc. Other stability subfactors include good operational trends and excellent risk diversification. Good overall profitability (6.4) despite operating losses during the first nine months of 2014. Despite its volitility, return on equity has been excellent over the last five years averaging 33.6%. Strong capitalization (7.1) based on excellent risk adjusted capital (severe loss scenario).
Other Rating Factors: High quality investment portfolio (8.4). Excellent liquidity (7.2).
Principal Business: Group health insurance (85%), individual health insurance (15%), and group life insurance (1%).
Principal Investments: NonCMO investment grade bonds (86%) and CMOs and structured securities (17%).
Investments in Affiliates: None
Group Affiliation: UnitedHealth Group Inc
Licensed in: All states except AK, ME, MA, NH, NJ, NY, RI, PR
Commenced Business: December 1982
Address: 3100 AMS Blvd, Green Bay, WI 54313
Phone: (800) 232-5432 **Domicile State:** WI **NAIC Code:** 97179

Data Date	Rating	RACR #1	RACR #2	Total Assets ($mil)	Capital ($mil)	Net Premium ($mil)	Net Income ($mil)
9-14	B	1.32	1.06	101.5	44.1	164.2	-2.1
9-13	B	1.82	1.46	52.4	29.4	65.2	6.0
2013	B	2.11	1.69	57.0	29.3	84.8	7.3
2012	B	1.50	1.21	49.0	23.8	99.9	8.9
2011	B	1.74	1.40	65.7	32.3	119.4	10.3
2010	B	1.82	1.48	70.0	41.9	142.3	24.4
2009	B	1.71	1.40	79.6	39.9	166.3	18.3

UnitedHealth Group Inc
Composite Group Rating: C+
Largest Group Members

	Assets ($mil)	Rating
UNITED HEALTHCARE INS CO	14513	C
OXFORD HEALTH INS INC	2078	C+
UNITED HEALTHCARE INS CO OF NY	1983	B-
OXFORD HEALTH PLANS (NY) INC	1820	A+
UNITEDHEALTHCARE PLAN RIVER VALLEY	1094	B+

UNIVERSAL GUARANTY LIFE INSURANCE COMPANY　　C+　　Fair

Major Rating Factors: Fair quality investment portfolio (3.6 on a scale of 0 to 10) with large holdings of BBB rated bonds in addition to junk bond exposure equal to 52% of capital. Fair liquidity (4.7) due, in part, to cash value policies that are subject to withdrawals with minimal or no penalty. Fair overall results on stability tests (4.8) including negative cash flow from operations for 2013, fair risk adjusted capital in prior years.

Other Rating Factors: Good capitalization (5.7) based on good risk adjusted capital (severe loss scenario). Excellent profitability (7.8).

Principal Business: Individual life insurance (94%), individual annuities (4%), and group life insurance (2%).

Principal Investments: NonCMO investment grade bonds (45%), common & preferred stock (16%), noninv. grade bonds (6%), mortgages in good standing (6%), and misc. investments (27%).

Investments in Affiliates: 10%

Group Affiliation: UTG Inc

Licensed in: AL, AZ, AR, CO, DE, GA, ID, IL, IN, IA, KS, KY, LA, MA, MN, MS, MO, MT, NE, NV, NM, NC, ND, OH, OK, OR, PA, RI, SC, SD, TN, TX, UT, VA, WA, WV, WI

Commenced Business: December 1966

Address: 65 E State St Suite 2100, Columbus, OH 43215-4260

Phone: (217) 241-6300　**Domicile State:** OH　**NAIC Code:** 70130

Data Date	Rating	RACR #1	RACR #2	Total Assets ($mil)	Capital ($mil)	Net Premium ($mil)	Net Income ($mil)
9-14	C+	1.31	0.84	345.7	40.0	5.7	3.4
9-13	C	1.08	0.68	348.9	33.6	6.4	3.2
2013	C	1.16	0.72	348.1	34.9	8.2	4.8
2012	C	1.06	0.68	360.6	32.2	9.0	6.9
2011	C	1.14	0.80	263.2	33.2	7.4	0.6
2010	C	0.89	0.66	272.5	30.4	7.7	4.8
2009	C-	0.82	0.62	265.0	27.3	9.0	0.2

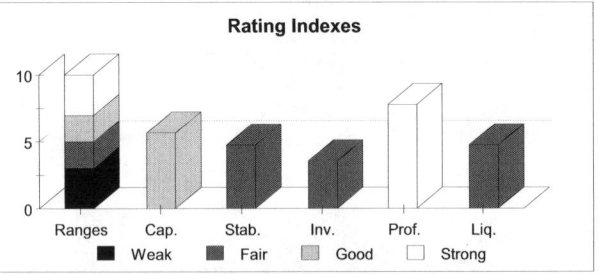

Rating Indexes

Ranges / Cap. / Stab. / Inv. / Prof. / Liq.
■ Weak　■ Fair　■ Good　□ Strong

UNIVERSAL LIFE INSURANCE COMPANY　　B　　Good

Major Rating Factors: Good overall results on stability tests (5.4 on a scale of 0 to 10) despite fair financial strength of affiliated Universal Ins Co Group. Other stability subfactors include good operational trends, good risk adjusted capital for prior years and excellent risk diversification. Fair quality investment portfolio (4.4). Strong capitalization (7.0) based on excellent risk adjusted capital (severe loss scenario).

Other Rating Factors: Excellent profitability (8.2) with operating gains in each of the last five years. Excellent liquidity (9.0).

Principal Business: Individual annuities (88%), credit life insurance (4%), group life insurance (4%), group health insurance (2%), and credit health insurance (1%).

Principal Investments: NonCMO investment grade bonds (78%), CMOs and structured securities (12%), common & preferred stock (4%), noninv. grade bonds (2%), and cash (1%).

Investments in Affiliates: None

Group Affiliation: Universal Ins Co Group

Licensed in: PR

Commenced Business: September 1994

Address: 16 Calle Mejico, San Juan, PR 00919-1899

Phone: (787) 706-7337　**Domicile State:** PR　**NAIC Code:** 60041

Data Date	Rating	RACR #1	RACR #2	Total Assets ($mil)	Capital ($mil)	Net Premium ($mil)	Net Income ($mil)
9-14	B	1.85	1.00	740.2	40.8	89.4	14.9
9-13	C+	1.43	0.80	729.8	28.6	108.4	2.8
2013	C+	1.34	0.77	773.5	29.4	140.7	3.6
2012	C+	1.58	0.91	592.0	27.6	140.2	3.8
2011	C+	2.01	1.16	429.7	23.9	137.4	1.7
2010	C+	2.18	1.64	309.1	23.4	87.2	1.5
2009	C+	2.21	1.99	217.0	22.1	64.4	1.2

Universal Ins Co Group Composite Group Rating: C+ Largest Group Members	Assets ($mil)	Rating
UNIVERSAL INS CO	803	B-
UNIVERSAL LIFE INS CO	774	B
UNIVERSAL NORTH AMERICA INS CO	173	C-
UNIVERSAL INS CO OF NORTH AMERICA	118	C-

UNUM LIFE INSURANCE COMPANY OF AMERICA　　C+　　Fair

Major Rating Factors: Fair quality investment portfolio (4.0 on a scale of 0 to 10) with large holdings of BBB rated bonds in addition to significant exposure to junk bonds. Fair overall results on stability tests (4.8) including negative cash flow from operations for 2013. Good overall profitability (6.8). Return on equity has been good over the last five years, averaging 13.6%.

Other Rating Factors: Strong capitalization (7.4) based on excellent risk adjusted capital (severe loss scenario). Excellent liquidity (7.1).

Principal Business: Group health insurance (60%), group life insurance (29%), individual health insurance (9%), reinsurance (2%), and individual life insurance (1%).

Principal Investments: NonCMO investment grade bonds (76%), noninv. grade bonds (9%), CMOs and structured securities (8%), and mortgages in good standing (5%).

Investments in Affiliates: None

Group Affiliation: Unum Group

Licensed in: All states, the District of Columbia and Puerto Rico

Commenced Business: September 1966

Address: 2211 Congress St, Portland, ME 04122

Phone: (207) 770-9306　**Domicile State:** ME　**NAIC Code:** 62235

Data Date	Rating	RACR #1	RACR #2	Total Assets ($mil)	Capital ($mil)	Net Premium ($mil)	Net Income ($mil)
9-14	C+	2.37	1.27	19,496.1	1,504.2	2,165.5	152.5
9-13	C+	2.53	1.36	19,037.6	1,578.5	2,118.3	185.6
2013	C+	2.49	1.34	19,078.5	1,557.9	2,794.2	176.2
2012	C+	2.57	1.38	18,879.8	1,573.5	2,702.0	202.9
2011	C+	2.65	1.42	18,303.5	1,548.8	2,603.1	199.0
2010	C+	2.73	1.48	17,822.8	1,539.6	2,612.5	246.3
2009	C+	2.73	1.48	17,214.8	1,541.1	2,634.5	249.4

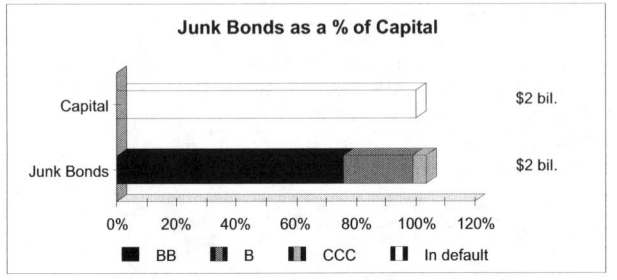

Junk Bonds as a % of Capital

Capital　$2 bil.
Junk Bonds　$2 bil.

0%　20%　40%　60%　80%　100%　120%
■ BB　▦ B　▥ CCC　▯ In default

US FINANCIAL LIFE INSURANCE COMPANY — B — Good

Major Rating Factors: Good overall results on stability tests (5.7 on a scale of 0 to 10). Stability strengths include excellent operational trends and excellent risk diversification. Good liquidity (5.6) with sufficient resources to handle a spike in claims as well as a significant increase in policy surrenders. Fair profitability (4.8) with investment income below regulatory standards in relation to interest assumptions of reserves.

Other Rating Factors: Strong capitalization (7.4) based on excellent risk adjusted capital (severe loss scenario). High quality investment portfolio (7.1).

Principal Business: Individual life insurance (100%).

Principal Investments: NonCMO investment grade bonds (89%), policy loans (5%), noninv. grade bonds (4%), common & preferred stock (1%), and misc. investments (2%).

Investments in Affiliates: None

Group Affiliation: AXA Financial Inc

Licensed in: All states except NY, PR

Commenced Business: September 1974

Address: 6 East Fourth St, Cincinnati, OH 45202

Phone: (513) 287-6805 **Domicile State:** OH **NAIC Code:** 84530

Data Date	Rating	RACR #1	RACR #2	Total Assets ($mil)	Capital ($mil)	Net Premium ($mil)	Net Income ($mil)
9-14	B	2.40	1.28	639.7	72.3	29.5	10.3
9-13	B	2.45	1.31	635.2	72.8	32.6	7.2
2013	B	2.08	1.10	638.1	62.5	43.3	8.0
2012	B	2.08	1.11	628.9	63.2	46.2	30.2
2011	B	1.98	1.05	628.4	61.9	52.5	-6.6
2010	C	2.37	1.29	621.3	71.0	53.2	13.9
2009	C	2.27	1.23	598.8	70.6	61.2	16.7

Adverse Trends in Operations

Decrease in capital during 2013 (1%)
Decrease in premium volume from 2011 to 2012 (12%)
Decrease in premium volume from 2010 to 2011 (1%)
Decrease in capital during 2011 (13%)
Decrease in premium volume from 2009 to 2010 (13%)

USAA LIFE INSURANCE COMPANY * — A — Excellent

Major Rating Factors: Good quality investment portfolio (6.8 on a scale of 0 to 10) despite mixed results such as: minimal exposure to mortgages and large holdings of BBB rated bonds but small junk bond holdings. Good liquidity (5.7) with sufficient resources to handle a spike in claims as well as a significant increase in policy surrenders. Excellent overall results on stability tests (7.4) excellent operational trends and excellent risk diversification.

Other Rating Factors: Strong capitalization (8.8) based on excellent risk adjusted capital (severe loss scenario). Excellent profitability (8.9) with operating gains in each of the last five years.

Principal Business: Individual annuities (51%), individual life insurance (40%), and individual health insurance (9%).

Principal Investments: NonCMO investment grade bonds (64%), CMOs and structured securities (30%), noninv. grade bonds (2%), common & preferred stock (1%), and policy loans (1%).

Investments in Affiliates: 1%

Group Affiliation: USAA Group

Licensed in: All states except NY, PR

Commenced Business: August 1963

Address: 9800 Fredericksburg Rd, San Antonio, TX 78288

Phone: (210) 498-8000 **Domicile State:** TX **NAIC Code:** 69663

Data Date	Rating	RACR #1	RACR #2	Total Assets ($mil)	Capital ($mil)	Net Premium ($mil)	Net Income ($mil)
9-14	A	4.09	2.18	21,964.7	2,161.8	1,204.1	204.9
9-13	A	4.15	2.28	20,909.9	1,994.8	1,378.9	181.0
2013	A	3.83	2.05	21,114.0	1,973.4	1,786.6	244.5
2012	A	3.92	2.17	19,647.1	1,834.3	1,612.0	211.0
2011	A	3.70	1.94	18,240.3	1,703.4	1,788.0	283.8
2010	A	3.68	1.93	16,815.6	1,485.5	1,951.8	240.0
2009	A	3.65	1.92	14,780.1	1,295.1	2,233.0	42.0

Adverse Trends in Operations

Decrease in premium volume from 2011 to 2012 (10%)
Decrease in premium volume from 2010 to 2011 (8%)
Increase in policy surrenders from 2010 to 2011 (38%)
Increase in policy surrenders from 2009 to 2010 (38%)
Decrease in premium volume from 2009 to 2010 (13%)

USAA LIFE INSURANCE COMPANY OF NEW YORK * — B+ — Good

Major Rating Factors: Good quality investment portfolio (5.7 on a scale of 0 to 10) despite mixed results such as: no exposure to mortgages and large holdings of BBB rated bonds but small junk bond holdings. Good liquidity (5.0) with sufficient resources to cover a large increase in policy surrenders. Good overall results on stability tests (6.5) good operational trends and excellent risk diversification.

Other Rating Factors: Strong capitalization (7.5) based on excellent risk adjusted capital (severe loss scenario). Excellent profitability (8.2) with operating gains in each of the last five years.

Principal Business: Individual life insurance (53%) and individual annuities (47%).

Principal Investments: NonCMO investment grade bonds (69%), CMOs and structured securities (26%), noninv. grade bonds (2%), common & preferred stock (1%), and policy loans (1%).

Investments in Affiliates: None

Group Affiliation: USAA Group

Licensed in: NY

Commenced Business: November 1997

Address: 529 Main Street, Highland Falls, NY 10928

Phone: (210) 498-8000 **Domicile State:** NY **NAIC Code:** 60228

Data Date	Rating	RACR #1	RACR #2	Total Assets ($mil)	Capital ($mil)	Net Premium ($mil)	Net Income ($mil)
9-14	B+	2.53	1.30	667.0	66.3	29.2	4.1
9-13	B+	2.70	1.42	631.5	62.6	29.8	3.4
2013	B+	2.41	1.25	641.1	62.9	39.3	3.8
2012	B+	2.60	1.37	599.6	59.6	46.8	5.1
2011	B+	2.31	1.17	554.7	54.5	66.3	8.8
2010	B+	2.23	1.13	489.5	45.5	64.8	4.6
2009	B+	2.30	1.17	436.6	42.0	60.1	0.8

Adverse Trends in Operations

Decrease in premium volume from 2012 to 2013 (16%)
Decrease in premium volume from 2011 to 2012 (29%)
Increase in policy surrenders from 2010 to 2011 (36%)
Increase in policy surrenders from 2009 to 2010 (76%)

USABLE LIFE *   B+   Good

Major Rating Factors: Good quality investment portfolio (5.4 on a scale of 0 to 10) despite mixed results such as: minimal exposure to mortgages and large holdings of BBB rated bonds but minimal holdings in junk bonds. Good liquidity (5.9) with sufficient resources to handle a spike in claims. Good overall results on stability tests (6.3) good operational trends and excellent risk diversification.

Other Rating Factors: Strong capitalization (7.4) based on excellent risk adjusted capital (severe loss scenario). Excellent profitability (7.6).

Principal Business: Reinsurance (55%), group health insurance (19%), group life insurance (19%), individual health insurance (5%), and individual life insurance (1%).

Principal Investments: NonCMO investment grade bonds (68%), common & preferred stock (15%), CMOs and structured securities (7%), mortgages in good standing (4%), and misc. investments (6%).

Investments in Affiliates: 2%

Group Affiliation: Arkansas Bl Cross Bl Shield Group

Licensed in: All states except NY, PR

Commenced Business: December 1980

Address: 320 W Capitol Suite 700, Little Rock, AR 72201

Phone: (501) 375-7200 **Domicile State:** AR **NAIC Code:** 94358

Data Date	Rating	RACR #1	RACR #2	Total Assets ($mil)	Capital ($mil)	Net Premium ($mil)	Net Income ($mil)
9-14	B+	1.76	1.29	432.6	187.6	442.8	20.0
9-13	B+	N/A	N/A	397.8	159.6	425.7	5.9
2013	B+	1.60	1.17	408.3	166.3	570.0	11.5
2012	B+	1.64	1.21	381.2	156.3	505.7	15.4
2011	B+	1.72	1.28	346.8	144.0	454.4	8.2
2010	B+	1.83	1.37	334.2	137.5	419.4	3.3
2009	A-	1.75	1.32	305.9	122.3	384.0	2.7

Adverse Trends in Operations

Change in asset mix during 2012 (8%)
Increase in policy surrenders from 2010 to 2011 (29%)

VANTIS LIFE INSURANCE COMPANY   B-   Good

Major Rating Factors: Good quality investment portfolio (5.3 on a scale of 0 to 10) despite mixed results such as: large holdings of BBB rated bonds but moderate junk bond exposure. Good overall profitability (6.0). Return on equity has been low, averaging 3.4%. Good overall results on stability tests (5.3) despite negative cash flow from operations for 2013 good operational trends, good risk adjusted capital for prior years and good risk diversification.

Other Rating Factors: Fair liquidity (4.7). Strong capitalization (7.1) based on excellent risk adjusted capital (severe loss scenario).

Principal Business: Individual life insurance (49%), individual annuities (43%), and group life insurance (8%).

Principal Investments: NonCMO investment grade bonds (78%), CMOs and structured securities (16%), noninv. grade bonds (2%), common & preferred stock (1%), and misc. investments (3%).

Investments in Affiliates: 1%

Group Affiliation: VantisLife Group

Licensed in: All states except NY, PR

Commenced Business: January 1964

Address: 200 Day Hill Rd, Windsor, CT 06095

Phone: (860) 298-5400 **Domicile State:** CT **NAIC Code:** 68632

Data Date	Rating	RACR #1	RACR #2	Total Assets ($mil)	Capital ($mil)	Net Premium ($mil)	Net Income ($mil)
9-14	B-	1.95	1.07	877.6	73.3	25.6	2.4
9-13	B-	1.82	1.01	897.4	69.7	26.4	0.5
2013	B-	1.89	1.04	896.3	71.7	34.4	1.8
2012	B-	1.85	1.03	899.7	70.3	33.9	2.0
2011	C+	1.76	0.97	903.0	70.5	33.4	1.3
2010	C+	1.79	0.99	898.7	71.1	48.5	3.0
2009	C+	1.81	1.00	870.8	71.1	237.2	0.3

Adverse Trends in Operations

Increase in policy surrenders from 2011 to 2012 (32%)
Decrease in premium volume from 2010 to 2011 (31%)
Change in premium mix from 2009 to 2010 (6.5%)
Decrease in premium volume from 2009 to 2010 (80%)

VARIABLE ANNUITY LIFE INSURANCE COMPANY   B   Good

Major Rating Factors: Good overall results on stability tests (5.8 on a scale of 0 to 10). Stability strengths include excellent operational trends and excellent risk diversification. Good quality investment portfolio (5.8) despite mixed results such as: large holdings of BBB rated bonds but moderate junk bond exposure. Good liquidity (6.5).

Other Rating Factors: Strong capitalization (8.0) based on excellent risk adjusted capital (severe loss scenario). Excellent profitability (7.9) with operating gains in each of the last five years.

Principal Business: Group retirement contracts (56%) and individual annuities (44%).

Principal Investments: CMOs and structured securities (39%), nonCMO investment grade bonds (39%), mortgages in good standing (10%), noninv. grade bonds (3%), and policy loans (2%).

Investments in Affiliates: 9%

Group Affiliation: American International Group

Licensed in: All states except PR

Commenced Business: May 1969

Address: 2929 Allen Parkway, Houston, TX 77019

Phone: (713) 522-1111 **Domicile State:** TX **NAIC Code:** 70238

Data Date	Rating	RACR #1	RACR #2	Total Assets ($mil)	Capital ($mil)	Net Premium ($mil)	Net Income ($mil)
9-14	B	3.58	1.69	77,039.3	4,243.3	3,672.7	851.7
9-13	B	4.12	1.98	74,586.2	4,457.9	4,138.5	826.5
2013	B	4.01	1.90	77,174.4	4,811.9	5,616.9	1,271.0
2012	B	4.02	1.95	70,614.3	4,235.5	5,409.8	703.0
2011	B	3.48	1.73	65,226.4	4,238.8	5,972.2	832.1
2010	B	3.44	1.66	63,975.4	3,800.3	5,202.8	74.4
2009	B	3.20	1.51	59,451.5	3,625.7	5,247.2	129.6

Adverse Trends in Operations

Decrease in premium volume from 2011 to 2012 (9%)

VOYA INSURANCE & ANNUITY COMPANY   B   Good

Major Rating Factors: Good current capitalization (6.8 on a scale of 0 to 10) based on good risk adjusted capital (severe loss scenario), although results have slipped from the excellent range over the last two years. Good quality investment portfolio (5.1) despite large holdings of BBB rated bonds in addition to moderate junk bond exposure. Exposure to mortgages is significant, but the mortgage default rate has been low. Good overall profitability (6.0) although investment income, in comparison to reserve requirements, is below regulatory standards.

Other Rating Factors: Fair overall results on stability tests (4.3) including fair risk adjusted capital in prior years. Excellent liquidity (7.9).

Principal Business: Group retirement contracts (71%), individual annuities (21%), reinsurance (7%), and individual life insurance (1%).

Principal Investments: NonCMO investment grade bonds (65%), CMOs and structured securities (17%), mortgages in good standing (11%), noninv. grade bonds (3%), and cash (1%).

Investments in Affiliates: None

Group Affiliation: Voya Financial Inc

Licensed in: All states except NY, PR

Commenced Business: October 1973

Address: 909 Locust St, Des Moines, IA 50309

Phone: (770) 980-5100 **Domicile State:** IA **NAIC Code:** 80942

Data Date	Rating	RACR #1	RACR #2	Total Assets ($mil)	Capital ($mil)	Net Premium ($mil)	Net Income ($mil)
9-14	B	1.95	0.98	66,208.2	2,026.6	1,977.5	260.7
9-13	C+	1.90	0.95	69,023.8	2,108.1	4,439.4	86.9
2013	B	1.86	0.93	69,266.0	1,941.6	6,164.9	-55.8
2012	C	1.99	1.00	68,101.4	2,174.1	3,344.2	-9.1
2011	C	1.91	0.95	71,509.0	2,222.0	3,859.9	386.0
2010	C	1.42	0.70	73,377.0	1,724.7	2,580.6	-384.4
2009	C	1.17	0.58	71,917.1	1,485.1	6,835.4	-638.3

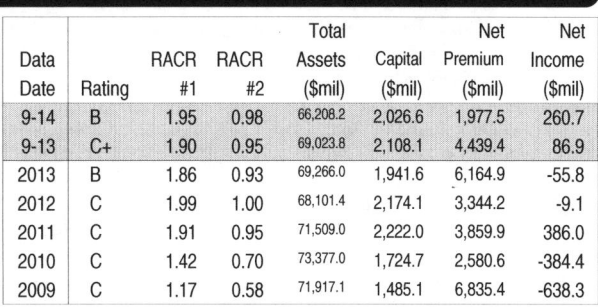

Risk-Adjusted Capital Ratio #2 (Severe Loss Scenario)

Range | 2009 | 2010 | 2011 | 2012 | 2013 | 9-14
■ Weak   ■ Fair   ▨ Good   □ Strong

VOYA RETIREMENT INSURANCE & ANNUITY COMPANY   B   Good

Major Rating Factors: Good overall results on stability tests (5.8 on a scale of 0 to 10). Stability strengths include excellent operational trends and excellent risk diversification. Good quality investment portfolio (5.7) despite large holdings of BBB rated bonds in addition to moderate junk bond exposure. Exposure to mortgages is significant, but the mortgage default rate has been low. Strong capitalization (7.4) based on excellent risk adjusted capital (severe loss scenario).

Other Rating Factors: Excellent profitability (7.2) with operating gains in each of the last five years. Excellent liquidity (9.1).

Principal Business: Group retirement contracts (98%), individual life insurance (1%), and individual annuities (1%).

Principal Investments: NonCMO investment grade bonds (64%), mortgages in good standing (14%), CMOs and structured securities (12%), noninv. grade bonds (4%), and misc. investments (4%).

Investments in Affiliates: 2%

Group Affiliation: Voya Financial Inc

Licensed in: All states, the District of Columbia and Puerto Rico

Commenced Business: April 1976

Address: One Orange Way, Windsor, CT 06095-4774

Phone: (866) 723-4646 **Domicile State:** CT **NAIC Code:** 86509

Data Date	Rating	RACR #1	RACR #2	Total Assets ($mil)	Capital ($mil)	Net Premium ($mil)	Net Income ($mil)
9-14	B	2.56	1.25	88,666.7	1,983.2	6,860.8	181.0
9-13	B	2.69	1.32	84,122.1	1,995.1	6,907.6	90.8
2013	B	2.65	1.30	85,670.1	2,010.8	9,439.7	175.2
2012	B-	2.62	1.28	78,660.1	1,921.8	8,592.0	261.6
2011	B-	2.62	1.28	69,340.0	1,931.9	9,060.2	194.4
2010	B-	2.24	1.10	68,943.2	1,667.3	8,157.5	45.0
2009	B-	2.33	1.12	62,474.6	1,762.1	8,320.2	271.6

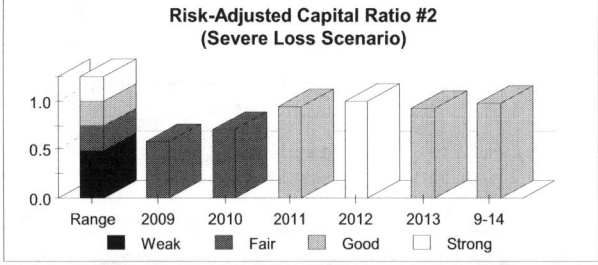

Adverse Trends in Operations

Increase in policy surrenders from 2012 to 2013 (26%)
Decrease in premium volume from 2011 to 2012 (5%)
Decrease in capital during 2010 (5%)
Decrease in premium volume from 2009 to 2010 (2%)

WASHINGTON NATIONAL INSURANCE COMPANY   D+   Weak

Major Rating Factors: Weak overall results on stability tests (2.7 on a scale of 0 to 10) including potential financial drain due to affiliation with CNO Financial Group Inc. Fair quality investment portfolio (3.9) with large holdings of BBB rated bonds in addition to junk bond exposure equal to 91% of capital. Good capitalization (6.0) based on good risk adjusted capital (severe loss scenario).

Other Rating Factors: Good overall profitability (6.4). Good liquidity (6.8).

Principal Business: Individual health insurance (66%), group health insurance (21%), individual life insurance (9%), individual annuities (2%), and reinsurance (2%).

Principal Investments: NonCMO investment grade bonds (56%), CMOs and structured securities (25%), mortgages in good standing (7%), noninv. grade bonds (6%), and misc. investments (7%).

Investments in Affiliates: 1%

Group Affiliation: CNO Financial Group Inc

Licensed in: All states except NY

Commenced Business: September 1923

Address: 11825 N Pennsylvania St, Carmel, I2 60069

Phone: (847) 793-3379 **Domicile State:** IN **NAIC Code:** 70319

Data Date	Rating	RACR #1	RACR #2	Total Assets ($mil)	Capital ($mil)	Net Premium ($mil)	Net Income ($mil)
9-14	D+	1.63	0.87	4,769.5	319.7	450.0	36.2
9-13	D+	2.00	1.09	5,204.1	421.3	406.1	49.9
2013	D+	2.20	1.15	5,286.1	431.9	540.7	59.6
2012	D+	2.28	1.23	5,247.6	469.4	522.4	58.6
2011	D+	2.22	1.20	5,335.9	500.9	523.9	71.3
2010	D+	2.30	1.23	4,911.7	491.8	637.4	-606.7
2009	D+	1.21	0.98	1,926.7	400.1	180.0	-43.3

CNO Financial Group Inc
Composite Group Rating: D+
Largest Group Members

	Assets ($mil)	Rating
BANKERS LIFE CAS CO	15840	D+
WASHINGTON NATIONAL INS CO	5286	D+
COLONIAL PENN LIFE INS CO	740	D+
BANKERS CONSECO LIFE INS CO	383	D

WEA INSURANCE CORPORATION   C   Fair

Major Rating Factors: Fair quality investment portfolio (4.4 on a scale of 0 to 10). Fair overall results on stability tests (4.0). Good liquidity (6.7) with sufficient resources to handle a spike in claims.
Other Rating Factors: Weak profitability (2.0) with operating losses during the first nine months of 2014. Return on equity has been low, averaging -6.2%. Strong capitalization (7.6) based on excellent risk adjusted capital (severe loss scenario).
Principal Business: Group health insurance (100%).
Principal Investments: NonCMO investment grade bonds (51%), CMOs and structured securities (23%), common & preferred stock (21%), and cash (5%).
Investments in Affiliates: None
Group Affiliation: WEA Inc
Licensed in: WI
Commenced Business: July 1985
Address: 45 Nob Hill Rd, Madison, WI 53713
Phone: (608) 276-4000 **Domicile State:** WI **NAIC Code:** 72273

Data Date	Rating	RACR #1	RACR #2	Total Assets ($mil)	Capital ($mil)	Net Premium ($mil)	Net Income ($mil)
9-14	C	1.94	1.37	683.2	205.9	445.8	-26.2
9-13	C	2.31	1.66	676.7	242.3	447.6	-8.1
2013	C	2.28	1.61	720.9	243.0	594.6	-15.1
2012	B-	2.19	1.59	686.8	232.1	635.9	19.1
2011	B	1.88	1.39	643.7	221.5	770.3	-0.5
2010	B+	1.84	1.37	654.4	233.2	846.5	-14.7
2009	B	1.92	1.45	596.6	240.2	863.4	2.7

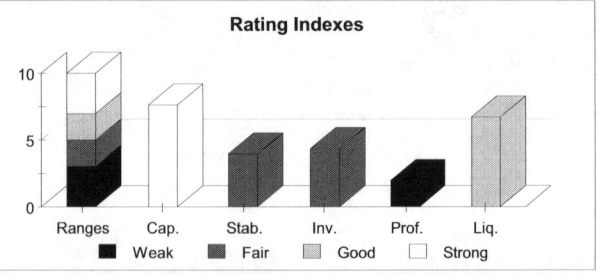

Rating Indexes

WEST COAST LIFE INSURANCE COMPANY   C+   Fair

Major Rating Factors: Fair overall results on stability tests (4.6 on a scale of 0 to 10) including negative cash flow from operations for 2013. Good quality investment portfolio (5.5) despite large holdings of BBB rated bonds in addition to moderate junk bond exposure. Exposure to mortgages is significant, but the mortgage default rate has been low. Good liquidity (6.0).
Other Rating Factors: Weak profitability (1.9) with operating losses during the first nine months of 2014. Strong capitalization (7.4) based on excellent risk adjusted capital (severe loss scenario).
Principal Business: Individual life insurance (65%) and reinsurance (35%).
Principal Investments: NonCMO investment grade bonds (71%), mortgages in good standing (14%), CMOs and structured securities (6%), noninv. grade bonds (4%), and misc. investments (4%).
Investments in Affiliates: None
Group Affiliation: Protective Life Group
Licensed in: All states except NY, PR
Commenced Business: February 1915
Address: 9140 W Dodge Rd, Omaha, NE 68114
Phone: (415) 591-8200 **Domicile State:** NE **NAIC Code:** 70335

Data Date	Rating	RACR #1	RACR #2	Total Assets ($mil)	Capital ($mil)	Net Premium ($mil)	Net Income ($mil)
9-14	C+	2.49	1.24	4,715.9	362.3	15.5	-144.4
9-13	C+	2.94	1.46	4,448.5	397.4	25.9	-56.5
2013	C+	3.24	1.62	4,516.1	450.0	24.6	12.5
2012	C+	3.47	1.72	4,210.3	471.8	-574.3	-67.0
2011	C+	2.03	1.29	4,085.2	488.3	273.7	8.2
2010	C	2.60	1.65	3,827.2	644.1	134.8	-289.2
2009	C	1.87	1.23	3,529.5	525.6	215.2	-95.9

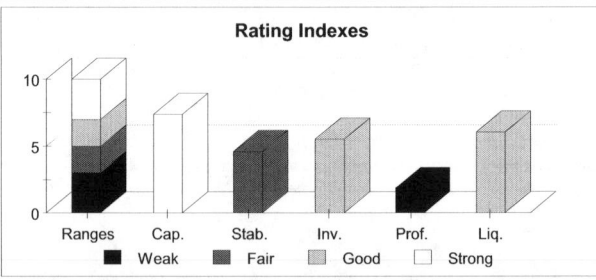

Rating Indexes

WESTERN & SOUTHERN LIFE INSURANCE COMPANY   B   Good

Major Rating Factors: Good overall results on stability tests (5.7 on a scale of 0 to 10). Stability strengths include excellent operational trends and excellent risk diversification. Fair quality investment portfolio (3.4). Strong capitalization (7.8) based on excellent risk adjusted capital (severe loss scenario). Moreover, capital levels have been consistently high over the last five years.
Other Rating Factors: Excellent profitability (7.6). Excellent liquidity (7.0).
Principal Business: Individual life insurance (87%), individual health insurance (11%), reinsurance (1%), and group life insurance (1%).
Principal Investments: Common & preferred stock (44%), nonCMO investment grade bonds (28%), CMOs and structured securities (11%), policy loans (2%), and noninv. grade bonds (2%).
Investments in Affiliates: 34%
Group Affiliation: Western & Southern Group
Licensed in: All states except AK, CT, ME, MA, NH, NY, VT, PR
Commenced Business: April 1888
Address: 400 Broadway, Cincinnati, OH 45202
Phone: (513) 357-4000 **Domicile State:** OH **NAIC Code:** 70483

Data Date	Rating	RACR #1	RACR #2	Total Assets ($mil)	Capital ($mil)	Net Premium ($mil)	Net Income ($mil)
9-14	B	1.80	1.51	9,796.0	4,450.2	190.2	135.8
9-13	B	1.82	1.51	9,227.2	4,024.6	192.0	44.1
2013	B	1.75	1.49	9,405.3	4,211.0	266.8	90.6
2012	B	1.79	1.53	8,612.3	3,728.5	279.2	11.2
2011	B	1.81	1.54	8,316.2	3,554.6	280.4	276.6
2010	B	1.73	1.48	8,484.1	3,533.6	286.1	52.3
2009	B	1.76	1.54	7,955.4	3,464.9	286.5	78.8

Adverse Trends in Operations

Decrease in premium volume from 2012 to 2013 (4%)
Decrease in asset base during 2011 (2%)
Decrease in premium volume from 2010 to 2011 (2%)
Increase in policy surrenders from 2010 to 2011 (44%)

WESTERN-SOUTHERN LIFE ASSURANCE COMPANY   B   Good

Major Rating Factors: Good overall results on stability tests (5.9 on a scale of 0 to 10). Stability strengths include good operational trends and excellent risk diversification. Good quality investment portfolio (5.4) despite mixed results such as: large holdings of BBB rated bonds but junk bond exposure equal to 88% of capital. Good liquidity (5.6).
Other Rating Factors: Strong capitalization (7.5) based on excellent risk adjusted capital (severe loss scenario). Excellent profitability (8.7).
Principal Business: Individual annuities (63%), individual life insurance (23%), and reinsurance (14%).
Principal Investments: NonCMO investment grade bonds (46%), CMOs and structured securities (35%), noninv. grade bonds (9%), mortgages in good standing (6%), and common & preferred stock (2%).
Investments in Affiliates: 2%
Group Affiliation: Western & Southern Group
Licensed in: All states except AK, ME, NH, NY, RI, PR
Commenced Business: March 1981
Address: 400 Broadway, Cincinnati, OH 45202
Phone: (513) 357-4000 **Domicile State:** OH **NAIC Code:** 92622

Data Date	Rating	RACR #1	RACR #2	Total Assets ($mil)	Capital ($mil)	Net Premium ($mil)	Net Income ($mil)
9-14	B	2.55	1.32	13,473.7	1,254.9	642.3	122.2
9-13	B-	2.41	1.21	12,887.1	1,122.4	672.7	110.5
2013	B	2.44	1.25	13,146.8	1,176.7	935.7	108.8
2012	B-	2.30	1.17	12,387.9	1,025.7	1,553.3	34.3
2011	B-	2.32	1.13	11,394.9	986.9	887.8	104.3
2010	B-	2.38	1.14	11,725.3	1,032.3	1,024.7	80.6
2009	B-	2.25	1.10	10,884.7	1,005.0	1,196.7	-57.4

Adverse Trends in Operations

Decrease in premium volume from 2012 to 2013 (40%)
Decrease in asset base during 2011 (3%)
Decrease in premium volume from 2010 to 2011 (13%)
Decrease in capital during 2011 (4%)
Decrease in premium volume from 2009 to 2010 (14%)

WILLIAM PENN LIFE INSURANCE COMPANY OF NEW YORK   C-   Fair

Major Rating Factors: Fair overall results on stability tests (3.1 on a scale of 0 to 10) including potential financial drain due to affiliation with Legal & General America Inc and negative cash flow from operations for 2013. Weak profitability (2.0) with operating losses during the first nine months of 2014. Return on equity has been low, averaging -4.5%. Good quality investment portfolio (6.5).
Other Rating Factors: Good liquidity (6.3). Strong capitalization (8.2) based on excellent risk adjusted capital (severe loss scenario).
Principal Business: Individual life insurance (100%).
Principal Investments: NonCMO investment grade bonds (77%), CMOs and structured securities (12%), noninv. grade bonds (7%), policy loans (3%), and mortgages in good standing (1%).
Investments in Affiliates: None
Group Affiliation: Legal & General America Inc
Licensed in: CT, DC, FL, ID, MD, NJ, NY, OK, OR, PA, RI, SC, SD
Commenced Business: February 1963
Address: 100 Quentin Roosevelt Blvd, Garden City, NY 11530
Phone: (516) 794-3700 **Domicile State:** NY **NAIC Code:** 66230

Data Date	Rating	RACR #1	RACR #2	Total Assets ($mil)	Capital ($mil)	Net Premium ($mil)	Net Income ($mil)
9-14	C-	3.76	1.79	1,149.7	174.0	34.6	-16.6
9-13	C-	4.32	2.10	1,119.7	183.7	32.2	-9.9
2013	C-	4.50	2.19	1,134.1	195.9	47.2	-15.2
2012	C	5.59	2.93	1,121.3	206.4	3.4	-13.4
2011	C	4.73	2.45	1,140.7	190.2	49.2	-1.3
2010	C	3.20	1.67	1,097.3	143.7	28.0	-3.1
2009	C	3.02	1.64	989.0	124.1	50.0	1.5

Legal General America Inc Composite Group Rating: D Largest Group Members	Assets ($mil)	Rating
BANNER LIFE INS CO	1688	D
WILLIAM PENN LIFE INS CO OF NEW YORK	1134	C-

WILTON REASSURANCE COMPANY   B-   Good

Major Rating Factors: Good overall results on stability tests (5.3 on a scale of 0 to 10) despite fair financial strength of affiliated Wilton Re Holdings Ltd and excessive premium growth. Other stability subfactors include good operational trends and excellent risk diversification. Good current capitalization (6.0) based on good risk adjusted capital (severe loss scenario), although results have slipped from the excellent range during the last year. Good liquidity (6.3).
Other Rating Factors: Fair quality investment portfolio (4.3). Excellent profitability (7.9) despite modest operating losses during 2011.
Principal Business: Reinsurance (100%).
Principal Investments: NonCMO investment grade bonds (50%), CMOs and structured securities (27%), common & preferred stock (9%), policy loans (3%), and misc. investments (12%).
Investments in Affiliates: 13%
Group Affiliation: Wilton Re Holdings Ltd
Licensed in: All states except NY, PR
Commenced Business: February 1901
Address: 213 Washington St, Newark, NJ 07102-2992
Phone: (201) 802-5807 **Domicile State:** MN **NAIC Code:** 66133

Data Date	Rating	RACR #1	RACR #2	Total Assets ($mil)	Capital ($mil)	Net Premium ($mil)	Net Income ($mil)
9-14	B-	1.23	0.87	3,820.4	637.4	432.4	52.7
9-13	B	1.21	0.94	3,321.4	474.0	274.6	22.9
2013	B	1.52	1.13	3,470.8	608.8	345.1	67.1
2012	B	1.12	0.87	3,260.0	427.2	691.9	141.7
2011	C	1.01	0.80	2,678.8	328.9	897.0	-5.6
2010	D	1.19	1.09	1,383.6	328.1	276.3	43.8
2009	D	0.97	0.93	1,179.6	258.3	31.3	1.6

Wilton Re Holdings Ltd Composite Group Rating: C Largest Group Members	Assets ($mil)	Rating
CONSECO LIFE INS CO	3825	D+
WILTON REASSURANCE CO	3471	B
CONTINENTAL ASSURANCE CO	2938	C
TEXAS LIFE INS CO	953	B
WILTON REASSURANCE LIFE CO OF NY	901	B

WILTON REASSURANCE LIFE COMPANY OF NEW YORK | B- | Good

Major Rating Factors: Fair current capitalization (4.0 on a scale of 0 to 10) based on mixed results -- excessive policy leverage mitigated by excellent risk adjusted capital (severe loss scenario) reflecting improvement over results in 2011. Good overall results on stability tests (5.3) despite fair financial strength of affiliated Wilton Re Holdings Ltd. Other stability subfactors include good operational trends, good risk adjusted capital for prior years and excellent risk diversification. Good quality investment portfolio (6.4).

Other Rating Factors: Good liquidity (5.4). Excellent profitability (7.1) despite modest operating losses during 2011.

Principal Business: Individual life insurance (84%), individual annuities (12%), and reinsurance (4%).

Principal Investments: NonCMO investment grade bonds (55%), CMOs and structured securities (33%), noninv. grade bonds (5%), policy loans (2%), and misc. investments (3%).

Investments in Affiliates: None

Group Affiliation: Wilton Re Holdings Ltd

Licensed in: All states except PR

Commenced Business: November 1956

Address: 320 Park Ave, New York, NY 10022

Phone: (212) 224-1879 **Domicile State:** NY **NAIC Code:** 60704

Data Date	Rating	RACR #1	RACR #2	Total Assets ($mil)	Capital ($mil)	Net Premium ($mil)	Net Income ($mil)
9-14	B-	3.14	1.58	910.9	108.7	13.4	-3.5
9-13	C+	3.35	1.69	913.4	118.3	-37.2	16.1
2013	C+	3.18	1.59	901.3	113.1	-32.5	13.7
2012	C+	3.30	1.65	884.0	118.3	-375.6	36.3
2011	C+	1.68	0.85	1,195.1	87.0	48.0	-0.7
2010	D	2.05	1.09	1,199.6	98.7	48.4	9.6
2009	D	1.97	1.05	1,182.5	95.3	53.1	28.0

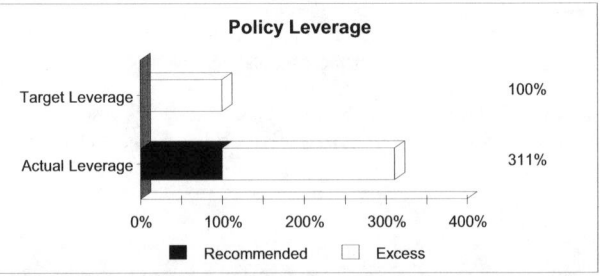

Policy Leverage

Target Leverage — 100%
Actual Leverage — 311%

■ Recommended □ Excess

ZURICH AMERICAN LIFE INSURANCE COMPANY | C | Fair

Major Rating Factors: Fair overall capitalization (4.0 on a scale of 0 to 10) based on mixed results -- excessive policy leverage mitigated by excellent risk adjusted capital (severe loss scenario). Nevertheless, capital levels have fluctuated during prior years. Weak profitability (1.5) with investment income below regulatory standards in relation to interest assumptions of reserves. Weak overall results on stability tests (2.8) including weak results on operational trends, negative cash flow from operations for 2013.

Other Rating Factors: High quality investment portfolio (8.0). Excellent liquidity (7.7).

Principal Business: Individual life insurance (49%), individual annuities (39%), group retirement contracts (7%), group life insurance (4%), and group health insurance (1%).

Principal Investments: NonCMO investment grade bonds (55%), CMOs and structured securities (27%), policy loans (10%), common & preferred stock (4%), and misc. investments (5%).

Investments in Affiliates: 4%

Group Affiliation: Zurich Financial Services Group

Licensed in: All states except NY, PR

Commenced Business: September 1947

Address: 1400 American Lane, Schaumburg, IL 60196-5452

Phone: (877) 301-5376 **Domicile State:** IL **NAIC Code:** 90557

Data Date	Rating	RACR #1	RACR #2	Total Assets ($mil)	Capital ($mil)	Net Premium ($mil)	Net Income ($mil)
9-14	C	1.99	1.16	12,655.1	147.5	28.0	13.8
9-13	C	1.78	1.00	12,954.3	125.5	-212.0	-44.2
2013	C	1.86	1.08	12,968.6	132.1	-295.0	-49.5
2012	C	2.19	1.25	12,767.4	168.6	-103.5	-5.2
2011	C	2.19	1.26	12,697.1	168.4	-137.2	-6.6
2010	C	2.24	1.42	13,208.1	184.2	-127.8	4.8
2009	C	2.24	1.45	13,324.9	187.5	-132.0	17.4

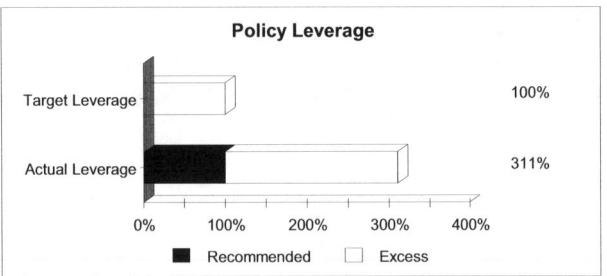

Policy Leverage

Target Leverage — 100%
Actual Leverage — 311%

■ Recommended □ Excess

Section III

Weiss Ratings
Recommended Companies

A compilation of those

U.S. Life and Annuity Insurers

receiving a Weiss Financial Strength Rating
of A+, A, A- or B+.

Companies are listed in alphabetical order.

Section III Contents

This section provides a list of recommended carriers along with additional information you should have when shopping for insurance. It contains all insurers receiving a Weiss Financial Strength Rating of A+, A, A-, or B+. If an insurer is not on this list, it should not be automatically assumed that the firm is weak. Indeed, there are many firms that have not achieved a B+ or better rating but are in relatively good condition with adequate resources to cover their risk during an average recession. Not being included in this list should not be construed as a recommendation to surrender policies.

Left Pages

1. Financial Strength Rating	Our rating is measured on a scale from A to F and considers a wide range of factors. Highly-rated companies are, in our opinion, less likely to experience financial difficulties than lower rated firms. See *About Weiss Financial Strength Ratings* for more information.
2. Insurance Company Name	The legally registered name, which can sometimes differ from the name that the company uses for advertising. An insurer's name can be very similar to the name of other companies which may not be on our Recommended List, so make sure you note the exact name before contacting your agent.
3. Address	The address of the main office where you can contact the firm for additional financial data or for the location of local branches and/or registered agents.
4. Telephone Number	The number to call for additional financial data or for the phone numbers of local branches and/or registered agents.

Right Pages

The right-side pages present the percentage of the company's business that is involved in each type of insurance. Specifically, the numbers shown are the amounts of premium (including certain annuity payments and other deposit funds not technically called premiums) for each line of business as a percent of total premiums. The amounts shown are net premiums and, therefore, include only policies for which the company carries risk.

1. Domicile State	The state which has primary regulatory responsibility for the company. It may differ from the location of the company's corporate headquarters. You do not have to be living in the domicile state to purchase insurance from this firm, provided it is licensed to do business in your state.
2. Individual Life	Life insurance policies for individual customers, as opposed to group policies.
3. Individual Health	Health insurance policies for individual customers, as opposed to group policies.

4. **Individual Annuities**   Annuity contracts for individual customers which may be fixed and/or variable annuity contracts.

5. **Group Life**   Life insurance policies for groups such as the employees of a corporation, public institution, or union.

6. **Group Health**   Health insurance policies for groups such as the employees of a corporation, public institution or union.

7. **Group Annuities**   Annuity contracts for groups such as the employees of a corporation, public institution or union. These include Guaranteed Interest Contracts (GICs) and other pension products.

8. **Credit Life**   Life insurance policies designed to protect lenders against the eventual death of the borrower. Typically, if the borrower dies, the policy guarantees repayment of the loan balance.

9. **Credit Health**   Health insurance policies designed to protect lenders against the sickness of the borrower. Typically, if the borrower becomes ill, the policy guarantees repayment of the loan balance.

10. **Supplemental Contracts**   Policies in which the premium is paid from the benefits of another contract.

Weiss Financial Strength Ratings are not deemed to be a recommendation concerning the purchase or sale of the securities of any insurance company that is publicly owned.

RATING	INSURANCE COMPANY NAME	ADDRESS	CITY	STATE	ZIP	PHONE
A	4 EVER LIFE INS CO	2 MID AMERICA PLAZA SUITE 200	OAKBROOK TERRACE	IL	60181	(888) 923-4227
B+	ADVANCE INS CO OF KS	1133 SW TOPEKA BLVD.	TOPEKA	KS	66629	(800) 530-5989
B+	AETNA HEALTH & LIFE INS CO	151 FARMINGTON AVENUE	HARTFORD	IL	06156	(800) 872-3862
B+	AETNA LIFE INS CO	151 FARMINGTON AVE	HARTFORD	CT	06156	(800) 872-3862
A-	ALLSTATE ASR CO	1 FOUNTAIN SQUARE	CHATTANOOGA	TN	37402	(800) 255-7828
A-	AMALGAMATED LIFE INS CO	333 WESTCHESTER AVE	WHITE PLAINS	NY	10604	(914) 367-5000
B+	AMERICAN FAMILY LIFE ASR CO OF COLUM	1932 WYNNTON RD	COLUMBUS	GA	31999	(800) 992-3522
A-	AMERICAN FAMILY LIFE ASR CO OF NY	22 CORPORATE WOODS BLVD #2	ALBANY	NY	12211	(800) 992-3522
A+	AMERICAN FAMILY LIFE INS CO	6000 AMERICAN PARKWAY	MADISON	WI	53783	(800) 692-6326
B+	AMERICAN FIDELITY ASR CO	2000 N CLASSEN BLVD	OKLAHOMA CITY	OK	73106	(800) 654-8489
A-	AMERICAN REPUBLIC INS CO	601 SIXTH AVE	DES MOINES	IA	50309	(800) 247-2190
B+	AMERICAN UNITED LIFE INS CO	ONE AMERICAN SQUARE	INDIANAPOLIS	IN	46204	(317) 285-1877
A-	ANTHEM LIFE & DISABILITY INS CO	1 LIBERTY PLAZA 165 BROADWAY	NEW YORK	NY	10006	(212) 476-1000
A-	ANTHEM LIFE INS CO	6740 N HIGH ST SUITE 200	WORTHINGTON	OH	43085	(800) 551-7265
B+	ASSURITY LIFE INS CO	2000 Q STREET	LINCOLN	NE	68503	(800) 869-0355
A	AUTO-OWNERS LIFE INS CO	6101 ANACAPRI BLVD	LANSING	MI	48917	(517) 323-1200
A-	BALBOA LIFE INS CO	400 ROBERT STREET NORTH	ST PAUL	MN	55101	(651) 665-3500
A	BERKSHIRE LIFE INS CO OF AMERICA	700 SOUTH ST	PITTSFIELD	MA	01201	(800) 819-2468
A-	BLUE SHIELD OF CALIFORNIA L&H INS CO	50 BEALE ST	SAN FRANCISCO	CA	94105	(800) 537-0668
B+	BLUEBONNET LIFE INS CO	3475 LAKELAND DRIVE	JACKSON	MS	39208	(800) 222-8046
B+	BOSTON MUTUAL LIFE INS CO	120 ROYALL ST	CANTON	MA	02021	(800) 669-2668
A-	CENTRAL STATES H & L CO OF OMAHA	1212 N 96TH ST	OMAHA	NE	68114	(800) 826-6587
A-	CHARTER NATIONAL LIFE INS CO	3100 SANDERS RD	NORTHBROOK	IL	60062	(847) 402-5000
A-	CIGNA LIFE INS CO OF NEW YORK	499 WASHINGTON BLVD	JERSEY CITY	NJ	07310	(212) 618-5757
B+	COLORADO BANKERS LIFE INS CO	5990 GREENWOOD PLAZA BLVD	ENGLEWOOD	CO	80111	(800) 367-7814
A-	COMPANION LIFE INS CO	2501 FARAWAY DR	COLUMBIA	SC	29219	(800) 753-0404
A-	COTTON STATES LIFE INS CO	13560 MORRIS RD SUITE 4000	ALPHARETTA	GA	30004	(866) 714-6902
A-	COUNTRY INVESTORS LIFE ASR CO	1701 N TOWANDA AVE	BLOOMINGTON	IL	61701	(866) 268-6879
A+	COUNTRY LIFE INS CO	1701 N TOWANDA AVE	BLOOMINGTON	IL	61701	(866) 268-6879
A-	DEARBORN NATIONAL LIFE INS CO	300 EAST RANDOLPH STREET	CHICAGO	IL	60601	(800) 348-4512
B+	DEARBORN NATIONAL LIFE INS CO OF NY	1250 PITTSFORD VICTOR RD # 116	PITTSFORD	NY	14534	(888) 851-9156
B+	EMPIRE FIDELITY INVESTMENTS L I C	200 LIBERTY ST 1 WORLD FINANCL	NEW YORK	NY	10281	(800) 634-9361
A-	ERIE FAMILY LIFE INS CO	100 ERIE INSURANCE PL	ERIE	PA	16530	(800) 458-0811
A-	FAMILY HERITAGE LIFE INS CO OF AMER	6001 E ROYALTON RD SUITE 200	CLEVELAND	OH	44147	(440) 922-5200
B+	FARM BUREAU LIFE INS CO	5400 UNIVERSITY AVE	WEST DES MOINES	IA	50266	(800) 247-4170
A-	FARM BUREAU LIFE INS CO OF MICHIGAN	7373 WEST SAGINAW HWY	LANSING	MI	48909	(800) 292-2680
A-	FARM BUREAU LIFE INS CO OF MISSOURI	701 S COUNTRY CLUB DR	JEFFERSON CITY	MO	65109	(800) 778-6452
A	FEDERATED LIFE INS CO	121 E PARK SQUARE	OWATONNA	MN	55060	(888) 333-4949
A-	FIDELITY INVESTMENTS LIFE INS CO	175 E 400 S 8TH FLOOR	SALT LAKE CITY	UT	84111	(800) 634-9361
A	FIRST RELIANCE STANDARD LIFE INS CO	590 MADISON AVE 29TH FLOOR	NEW YORK	NY	10022	(800) 353-3986
A-	FIRST SYMETRA NATL LIFE INS CO OF NY	260 MADISON AVE 8TH FLOOR	NEW YORK	NY	10016	(800) 796-3872
B+	FIRST UNITED AMERICAN LIFE INS CO	1020 7TH NORTH ST	LIVERPOOL	NY	13088	(315) 451-2544
A-	FRANDISCO LIFE INS CO	213 E TUGALO ST	TOCCOA	GA	30577	(706) 886-7571
A-	GARDEN STATE LIFE INS CO	2450 S SHORE BLVD SUITE 301	LEAGUE CITY	TX	77573	(800) 638-8565
B+	GENERAL RE LIFE CORP	30 OAK STREET	STAMFORD	CT	06905	(203) 352-3000
A-	GERBER LIFE INS CO	1311 MAMARONECK AVE	WHITE PLAINS	NY	10605	(800) 704-2180
B+	GOVERNMENT PERSONNEL MUTUAL L I C	2211 NE LOOP 410	SAN ANTONIO	TX	78217	(800) 938-4765
B+	GREATER GEORGIA LIFE INS CO	THREE RAVINIA DR SUITE 1700	ATLANTA	GA	30346	(888) 208-2183
A	GUARDIAN LIFE INS CO OF AMERICA	7 HANOVER SQUARE	NEW YORK	NY	10004	(800) 441-6455
B+	HM LIFE INS CO OF NEW YORK	420 FIFTH AVE 3RD FLOOR	NEW YORK	NY	10018	(800) 328-5433
A-	ILLINOIS MUTUAL LIFE INS CO	300 SW ADAMS	PEORIA	IL	61634	(800) 437-7355
B+	JACKSON NATIONAL LIFE INS CO	5901 EXECUTIVE DR	LANSING	MI	48911	(877) 565-2968
A-	JOHN HANCOCK LIFE INS CO OF NY	100 SUMMIT LAKE DR 2ND FLOOR	VALHALLA	NY	10595	(800) 743-5542
A-	LIFE INS CO OF ALABAMA	302 BROAD ST	GADSDEN	AL	35901	(800) 226-2371
A-	LIFE INS CO OF BOSTON & NEW YORK	277 NORTH AVE SUITE 200	NEW ROCHELLE	NY	10801	(800) 645-2317
A	LIFEWISE ASR CO	7007 220TH SW	MOUNTLAKE TERRACE	WA	98043	(800) 258-0394

DOM. STATE	IND. LIFE	IND. HEALTH	IND. ANNU.	GROUP LIFE	GROUP HEALTH	GROUP ANNU	CREDIT LIFE	CREDIT HEALTH	SUP. CONTR.	OTHER	INSURANCE COMPANY NAME
IL	0	0	0	4	96	0	0	0	0	0	4 EVER LIFE INS CO
KS	15	0	0	58	28	0	0	0	0	0	ADVANCE INS CO OF KS
CT	0	0	0	0	100	0	0	0	0	0	AETNA HEALTH & LIFE INS CO
CT	0	44	0	5	49	2	0	0	0	0	AETNA LIFE INS CO
IL	0	0	0	0	0	0	0	0	0	0	ALLSTATE ASR CO
NY	2	0	0	78	19	0	0	0	0	0	AMALGAMATED LIFE INS CO
NE	24	72	4	0	1	0	0	0	0	0	AMERICAN FAMILY LIFE ASR CO OF COLUM
NY	3	95	0	0	2	0	0	0	0	0	AMERICAN FAMILY LIFE ASR CO OF NY
WI	92	0	7	1	0	0	0	0	0	0	AMERICAN FAMILY LIFE INS CO
OK	9	29	18	0	43	1	0	0	0	0	AMERICAN FIDELITY ASR CO
IA	3	69	0	0	28	0	0	0	0	0	AMERICAN REPUBLIC INS CO
IN	7	0	5	3	2	84	0	0	0	0	AMERICAN UNITED LIFE INS CO
NY	0	0	0	75	25	0	0	0	0	0	ANTHEM LIFE & DISABILITY INS CO
IN	1	0	0	78	20	0	0	0	0	0	ANTHEM LIFE INS CO
NE	59	33	4	2	0	1	0	0	0	0	ASSURITY LIFE INS CO
MI	40	5	39	1	1	14	0	0	0	0	AUTO-OWNERS LIFE INS CO
CA	10	0	0	2	89	0	0	0	0	0	BALBOA LIFE INS CO
MA	1	99	0	0	0	0	0	0	0	0	BERKSHIRE LIFE INS CO OF AMERICA
CA	0	25	0	0	75	0	0	0	0	0	BLUE SHIELD OF CALIFORNIA L&H INS CO
MS	3	0	0	97	1	0	0	0	0	0	BLUEBONNET LIFE INS CO
MA	70	5	0	14	11	0	0	0	0	0	BOSTON MUTUAL LIFE INS CO
NE	3	0	0	0	0	0	56	41	0	0	CENTRAL STATES H & L CO OF OMAHA
IL	0	0	0	0	0	0	0	0	0	0	CHARTER NATIONAL LIFE INS CO
NY	0	0	0	33	67	0	0	0	0	0	CIGNA LIFE INS CO OF NEW YORK
CO	63	3	31	0	3	0	0	0	0	0	COLORADO BANKERS LIFE INS CO
SC	0	1	0	13	86	0	0	0	0	0	COMPANION LIFE INS CO
GA	100	0	0	0	0	0	0	0	0	0	COTTON STATES LIFE INS CO
IL	0	0	0	0	0	0	0	0	0	0	COUNTRY INVESTORS LIFE ASR CO
IL	59	14	16	1	9	1	0	0	0	0	COUNTRY LIFE INS CO
IL	2	0	1	57	41	0	0	0	0	0	DEARBORN NATIONAL LIFE INS CO
NY	0	0	0	39	61	0	0	0	0	0	DEARBORN NATIONAL LIFE INS CO OF NY
NY	0	0	100	0	0	0	0	0	0	0	EMPIRE FIDELITY INVESTMENTS L I C
PA	68	0	29	2	0	0	0	0	0	0	ERIE FAMILY LIFE INS CO
OH	1	97	0	0	3	0	0	0	0	0	FAMILY HERITAGE LIFE INS CO OF AMER
IA	55	0	44	0	0	1	0	0	0	0	FARM BUREAU LIFE INS CO
MI	66	0	33	0	0	1	0	0	0	0	FARM BUREAU LIFE INS CO OF MICHIGAN
MO	72	0	27	1	0	0	0	0	0	0	FARM BUREAU LIFE INS CO OF MISSOURI
MN	67	13	16	3	0	0	0	0	0	0	FEDERATED LIFE INS CO
UT	0	0	100	0	0	0	0	0	0	0	FIDELITY INVESTMENTS LIFE INS CO
NY	0	0	0	23	76	0	0	0	0	0	FIRST RELIANCE STANDARD LIFE INS CO
NY	0	0	94	0	6	0	0	0	0	0	FIRST SYMETRA NATL LIFE INS CO OF NY
NY	30	58	9	0	3	0	0	0	0	0	FIRST UNITED AMERICAN LIFE INS CO
GA	0	0	0	0	0	0	37	63	0	0	FRANDISCO LIFE INS CO
TX	100	0	0	0	0	0	0	0	0	0	GARDEN STATE LIFE INS CO
CT	58	37	0	2	2	0	0	0	0	0	GENERAL RE LIFE CORP
NY	64	3	0	0	33	0	0	0	0	0	GERBER LIFE INS CO
TX	94	6	2	-2	0	0	0	0	0	0	GOVERNMENT PERSONNEL MUTUAL L I C
GA	4	0	0	63	33	0	0	0	0	0	GREATER GEORGIA LIFE INS CO
NY	52	6	0	6	36	0	0	0	0	0	GUARDIAN LIFE INS CO OF AMERICA
NY	0	0	0	0	100	0	0	0	0	0	HM LIFE INS CO OF NEW YORK
IL	43	53	2	0	1	0	0	0	0	0	ILLINOIS MUTUAL LIFE INS CO
MI	3	0	85	0	0	12	0	0	0	0	JACKSON NATIONAL LIFE INS CO
NY	22	0	3	0	0	75	0	0	0	0	JOHN HANCOCK LIFE INS CO OF NY
AL	16	78	0	0	6	0	0	0	0	0	LIFE INS CO OF ALABAMA
NY	62	35	0	0	3	0	0	0	0	0	LIFE INS CO OF BOSTON & NEW YORK
WA	0	0	0	0	100	0	0	0	0	0	LIFEWISE ASR CO

RATING	INSURANCE COMPANY NAME	ADDRESS	CITY	STATE	ZIP	PHONE
B+	LINCOLN BENEFIT LIFE CO	206 S 13TH ST, SUITE 200	LINCOLN	NE	68508	(800) 525-9287
B+	LOCOMOTIVE ENGRS&COND MUT PROT ASSN	535 GRISWOLD ST SUITE 1210	DETROIT	MI	48226	(800) 514-0010
A-	MASSACHUSETTS MUTUAL LIFE INS CO	1295 STATE ST	SPRINGFIELD	MA	01111	(800) 272-2216
B+	MEDICO CORP LIFE INS CO	11808 GRANT ST	OMAHA	NE	68164	(800) 822-9993
B+	MERIT LIFE INS CO	601 NW SECOND ST	EVANSVILLE	IN	47708	(800) 325-2147
B+	MIDLAND NATIONAL LIFE INS CO	ONE MIDLAND PLAZA	SIOUX FALLS	SD	57193	(800) 923-3223
A-	MIDWESTERN UNITED LIFE INS CO	8605 KINGS MILL PL	FORT WAYNE	IN	46804	(800) 333-6965
B+	MINNESOTA LIFE INS CO	400 N ROBERT ST	ST PAUL	MN	55101	(651) 665-3500
A-	MML BAY STATE LIFE INS CO	100 BRIGHT MEADOW BLVD	ENFIELD	CT	06082	(800) 272-2216
A-	MUTUAL OF AMERICA LIFE INS CO	320 PARK AVE	NEW YORK	NY	10022	(800) 468-3785
B+	MUTUAL OF OMAHA INS CO	MUTUAL OF OMAHA PLAZA	OMAHA	NE	68175	(800) 228-7104
A-	MUTUAL SAVINGS LIFE INS CO	12115 LACKLAND RD	ST LOUIS	MO	63146	(205) 552-7347
B+	NATIONAL BENEFIT LIFE INS CO	ONE COURT SQUARE	LONG ISLAND CITY	NY	11120	(800) 222-2062
B+	NATIONAL FARMERS UNION LIFE INS CO	500 NORTH AKARD	DALLAS	TX	75201	(800) 366-6565
B+	NATIONAL INCOME LIFE INS CO	1020 SEVENTH N ST SUITE 130	LIVERPOOL	NY	13088	(315) 451-2544
B+	NATIONAL WESTERN LIFE INS CO	1675 BROADWAY #1200	DENVER	CO	80202	(800) 531-5442
B+	NEW YORK LIFE INS & ANNUITY CORP	200 CONTINENTAL DR	NEWARK	DE	19713	(212) 576-7000
A-	NEW YORK LIFE INS CO	51 MADISON AVE	NEW YORK	NY	10010	(212) 576-7000
A-	NIPPON LIFE INS CO OF AMERICA	650 8TH ST	DES MOINES	IA	50309	(800) 374-1835
A-	NORTHWESTERN MUTUAL LIFE INS CO	720 E WISCONSIN AVE	MILWAUKEE	WI	53202	(414) 271-1444
B+	OHIO NATIONAL LIFE ASR CORP	ONE FINANCIAL WAY	CINCINNATI	OH	45242	(800) 366-6654
A-	PACIFIC GUARDIAN LIFE INS CO LTD	1440 KAPIOLANI BLVD STE 1700	HONOLULU	HI	96814	(800) 432-3306
B+	PACIFIC LIFE & ANNUITY CO	638 N FIFTH AVE	PHOENIX	AZ	85003	(800) 800-7646
A-	PACIFIC LIFE INS CO	1299 FARNAM ST	OMAHA	NE	68102	(800) 800-7646
B+	PARK AVENUE LIFE INS CO	9100 KEYSTONE CROSSING STE 600	INDIANAPOLIS	IN	46240	(888) 600-4667
A	PARKER CENTENNIAL ASR CO	2345 WAUKEGAN RD #5210	BANNOCKBURN	IL	60015	(800) 373-6879
A-	PHYSICIANS LIFE INS CO	2600 DODGE ST	OMAHA	NE	68131	(800) 228-9100
A+	PHYSICIANS MUTUAL INS CO	2600 DODGE ST	OMAHA	NE	68131	(800) 228-9100
B+	PIONEER MUTUAL LIFE INS CO	203 N 10TH ST	FARGO	ND	58102	(877) 285-3863
B+	PRINCIPAL LIFE INS CO	711 HIGH ST	DES MOINES	IA	50392	(800) 986-3343
A	RESERVE NATIONAL INS CO	601 E BRITTON RD	OKLAHOMA CITY	OK	73114	(800) 654-9106
B+	SAVINGS BANK LIFE INS CO OF MA	ONE LINSCOTT RD	WOBURN	MA	01801	(888) 438-7254
A	SENTRY LIFE INS CO	1800 NORTH POINT DR	STEVENS POINT	WI	54481	(800) 373-6879
B+	SENTRY LIFE INS CO OF NEW YORK	251 SALINA MEADOWS PARKWAY	NORTH SYRACUSE	NY	13212	(800) 373-6879
A-	SHELTER LIFE INS CO	1817 W BROADWAY	COLUMBIA	MO	65218	(800) 743-5837
A	SHELTERPOINT LIFE INS CO	600 NORTHERN BLVD	GREAT NECK	NY	11021	(800) 365-4999
A	SOUTHERN FARM BUREAU LIFE INS CO	1401 LIVINGSTON LANE	JACKSON	MS	39213	(800) 457-9611
B+	STANDARD INS CO	1100 SW SIXTH AVE	PORTLAND	OR	97204	(503) 321-7000
A-	STANDARD LIFE & ACCIDENT INS CO	ONE MOODY PLAZA	GALVESTON	TX	77550	(888) 290-1085
A-	STANDARD LIFE INS CO OF NY	360 HAMILTON AVE SUITE 210	WHITE PLAINS	NY	10601	(503) 321-7859
A+	STATE FARM LIFE & ACCIDENT ASR CO	ONE STATE FARM PLAZA	BLOOMINGTON	IL	61710	(855) 733-7333
A+	STATE FARM LIFE INS CO	ONE STATE FARM PLAZA	BLOOMINGTON	IL	61710	(855) 733-7333
B+	SYMETRA LIFE INS CO	5550 WILD ROSE LANE SUITE 400	WEST DES MOINES	IA	50266	(800) 796-3872
A+	TEACHERS INS & ANNUITY ASN OF AM	730 THIRD AVE 7TH FLOOR	NEW YORK	NY	10017	(800) 842-2252
A	TENNESSEE FARMERS LIFE INS CO	147 BEAR CREEK PIKE	COLUMBIA	TN	38401	(931) 388-7872
B+	THRIVENT LIFE INS CO	625 FOURTH AVE S	MINNEAPOLIS	MN	55415	(800) 847-4836
A	TRANS OCEANIC LIFE INS CO	3 MUNET COURT	GUAYNABO	PR	00936	(787) 620-2680
B+	TRUSTMARK INS CO	400 FIELD DR	LAKE FOREST	IL	60045	(800) 366-6663
B+	TRUSTMARK LIFE INS CO	400 FIELD DR	LAKE FOREST	IL	60045	(800) 366-6663
B+	UNION SECURITY LIFE INS CO OF NY	220 SALINA MEADOWS PKWY #255	SYRACUSE	NY	13212	(800) 852-2244
A	UNITED FARM FAMILY LIFE INS CO	225 S EAST ST	INDIANAPOLIS	IN	46202	(800) 723-3276
B+	UNITED WORLD LIFE INS CO	MUTUAL OF OMAHA PLAZA	OMAHA	NE	68175	(800) 228-7104
A	USAA LIFE INS CO	9800 FREDERICKSBURG RD	SAN ANTONIO	TX	78288	(210) 498-8000
B+	USAA LIFE INS CO OF NEW YORK	529 MAIN STREET	HIGHLAND FALLS	NY	10928	(210) 498-8000
B+	USABLE LIFE	320 W CAPITOL SUITE 700	LITTLE ROCK	AR	72201	(800) 370-5856

DOM. STATE	IND. LIFE	IND. HEALTH	IND. ANNU.	GROUP LIFE	GROUP HEALTH	GROUP ANNU	CREDIT LIFE	CREDIT HEALTH	SUP. CONTR.	OTHER	INSURANCE COMPANY NAME
NE	0	0	0	0	0	0	0	0	0	0	LINCOLN BENEFIT LIFE CO
MI	100	0	0	0	0	0	0	0	0	0	LOCOMOTIVE ENGRS&COND MUT PROT ASSN
MA	22	3	16	5	0	54	0	0	0	0	MASSACHUSETTS MUTUAL LIFE INS CO
NE	0	0	0	0	0	0	0	0	0	0	MEDICO CORP LIFE INS CO
IN	18	13	0	2	0	0	29	37	0	0	MERIT LIFE INS CO
IA	30	0	59	1	0	10	0	0	0	0	MIDLAND NATIONAL LIFE INS CO
IN	97	0	3	0	0	0	0	0	0	0	MIDWESTERN UNITED LIFE INS CO
MN	22	0	17	28	3	28	1	1	0	0	MINNESOTA LIFE INS CO
CT	96	0	1	4	0	0	0	0	0	0	MML BAY STATE LIFE INS CO
NY	0	0	29	0	0	71	0	0	0	0	MUTUAL OF AMERICA LIFE INS CO
NE	0	88	0	0	12	0	0	0	0	0	MUTUAL OF OMAHA INS CO
AL	86	14	0	0	0	0	0	0	0	0	MUTUAL SAVINGS LIFE INS CO
NY	60	0	0	0	40	0	0	0	0	0	NATIONAL BENEFIT LIFE INS CO
TX	96	0	2	2	0	0	0	0	0	0	NATIONAL FARMERS UNION LIFE INS CO
NY	87	12	0	0	0	0	0	0	0	0	NATIONAL INCOME LIFE INS CO
CO	27	0	73	0	0	0	0	0	0	0	NATIONAL WESTERN LIFE INS CO
DE	14	0	84	1	0	1	0	0	0	0	NEW YORK LIFE INS & ANNUITY CORP
NY	46	2	2	15	2	33	0	0	0	0	NEW YORK LIFE INS CO
IA	0	0	0	1	99	0	0	0	0	0	NIPPON LIFE INS CO OF AMERICA
WI	77	6	15	0	0	1	0	0	0	0	NORTHWESTERN MUTUAL LIFE INS CO
OH	98	2	0	0	0	0	0	0	0	0	OHIO NATIONAL LIFE ASR CORP
HI	40	0	0	14	45	0	0	0	0	0	PACIFIC GUARDIAN LIFE INS CO LTD
AZ	6	0	94	0	0	0	0	0	0	0	PACIFIC LIFE & ANNUITY CO
NE	25	0	73	0	0	3	0	0	0	0	PACIFIC LIFE INS CO
DE	100	0	0	0	0	0	0	0	0	0	PARK AVENUE LIFE INS CO
WI	0	0	0	0	0	100	0	0	0	0	PARKER CENTENNIAL ASR CO
NE	64	0	22	14	0	0	0	0	0	0	PHYSICIANS LIFE INS CO
NE	0	81	0	0	19	0	0	0	0	0	PHYSICIANS MUTUAL INS CO
ND	92	0	8	0	0	0	0	0	0	0	PIONEER MUTUAL LIFE INS CO
IA	20	5	43	6	17	9	0	0	0	0	PRINCIPAL LIFE INS CO
OK	8	90	0	0	2	0	0	0	0	0	RESERVE NATIONAL INS CO
MA	86	0	14	0	0	0	0	0	0	0	SAVINGS BANK LIFE INS CO OF MA
WI	5	0	1	1	0	93	0	0	0	0	SENTRY LIFE INS CO
NY	8	0	1	2	2	87	0	0	0	0	SENTRY LIFE INS CO OF NEW YORK
MO	85	1	7	1	5	0	0	0	0	0	SHELTER LIFE INS CO
NY	0	0	0	2	98	0	0	0	0	0	SHELTERPOINT LIFE INS CO
MS	82	1	15	1	1	0	0	0	0	0	SOUTHERN FARM BUREAU LIFE INS CO
OR	0	5	9	15	32	40	0	0	0	0	STANDARD INS CO
TX	12	76	2	0	10	0	0	0	0	0	STANDARD LIFE & ACCIDENT INS CO
NY	0	0	0	44	56	0	0	0	0	0	STANDARD LIFE INS CO OF NY
IL	88	0	12	0	0	0	0	0	0	0	STATE FARM LIFE & ACCIDENT ASR CO
IL	85	0	13	1	0	0	0	0	0	0	STATE FARM LIFE INS CO
IA	5	0	74	1	19	1	0	0	0	0	SYMETRA LIFE INS CO
NY	3	0	55	0	0	43	0	0	0	0	TEACHERS INS & ANNUITY ASN OF AM
TN	66	0	32	0	2	0	0	0	0	0	TENNESSEE FARMERS LIFE INS CO
MN	7	0	93	0	0	0	0	0	0	0	THRIVENT LIFE INS CO
PR	7	92	0	0	0	0	0	0	0	0	TRANS OCEANIC LIFE INS CO
IL	5	25	1	44	25	0	0	0	0	0	TRUSTMARK INS CO
IL	0	0	0	5	95	0	0	0	0	0	TRUSTMARK LIFE INS CO
NY	1	1	0	14	80	0	2	3	0	0	UNION SECURITY LIFE INS CO OF NY
IN	89	0	11	0	0	0	0	0	0	0	UNITED FARM FAMILY LIFE INS CO
NE	100	0	0	0	0	0	0	0	0	0	UNITED WORLD LIFE INS CO
TX	26	11	63	0	0	0	0	0	0	0	USAA LIFE INS CO
NY	37	0	63	0	0	0	0	0	0	0	USAA LIFE INS CO OF NEW YORK
AR	1	14	0	26	60	0	0	0	0	0	USABLE LIFE

Section IV

Weiss Ratings
Recommended Companies
by State

A compilation of those

U.S. Life and Annuity Insurers

receiving a Weiss Financial Strength Rating
of A+, A, A- or B+.

Companies are ranked by Financial Strength Rating
in each state where they are licensed to do business.

Section IV Contents

This section provides a list of the recommended carriers licensed to do business in each state. It contains all insurers receiving a Weiss Financial Strength Rating of A+, A, A-, or B+. If an insurer is not on this list, it should not be automatically assumed that the firm is weak. Indeed, there are many firms that have not achieved a B+ or better rating but are in relatively good condition with adequate resources to cover their risk during an average recession. Not being included in this list should not be construed as a recommendation to surrender policies.

Companies are ranked within each state by their Financial Strength Rating. However, companies with the same rating should be viewed as having the same relative strength regardless of their ranking in this table. While the specific order in which they appear on the page is based upon differences in our underlying indexes, you can assume that companies with the same rating have differences that are only minor and relatively inconsequential.

1. **Financial Strength Rating**

   Our rating is measured on a scale from A to F and considers a wide range of factors. Highly-rated companies are, in our opinion, less likely to experience financial difficulties than lower rated firms. See *About Weiss Financial Strength Ratings* for more information.

2. **Insurance Company Name**

   The legally registered name, which can sometimes differ from the name that the company uses for advertising. An insurer's name can be very similar to the name of other companies which may not be on our Recommended List, so make sure you note the exact name before contacting your agent.

3. **Domicile State**

   The state which has primary regulatory responsibility for the company. It may differ from the location of the company's corporate headquarters. You do not have to be living in the domicile state to purchase insurance from this firm, provided it is licensed to do business in your state.

4. **Total Assets**

   All assets admitted by state insurance regulators in millions of dollars. This includes investments, current business assets, and separate accounts.

Weiss Financial Strength Ratings are not deemed to be a recommendation concerning the purchase or sale of the securities of any insurance company that is publicly owned.

Alabama

INSURANCE COMPANY NAME	DOM. STATE	TOTAL ASSETS ($MIL)	INSURANCE COMPANY NAME	DOM. STATE	TOTAL ASSETS ($MIL)
Rating: A+			BLUEBONNET LIFE INS CO	MS	54.6
			BOSTON MUTUAL LIFE INS CO	MA	1,230.4
COUNTRY LIFE INS CO	IL	10,573.7	COLORADO BANKERS LIFE INS CO	CO	280.1
PHYSICIANS MUTUAL INS CO	NE	1,989.7	GENERAL RE LIFE CORP	CT	3,335.8
STATE FARM LIFE INS CO	IL	62,712.0	GOVERNMENT PERSONNEL MUTUAL L I C	TX	830.8
TEACHERS INS & ANNUITY ASN OF AM	NY	261,389.2	GREATER GEORGIA LIFE INS CO	GA	49.9
			JACKSON NATIONAL LIFE INS CO	MI	176,820.4
Rating: A			LINCOLN BENEFIT LIFE CO	NE	12,911.3
			MEDICO CORP LIFE INS CO	NE	26.0
4 EVER LIFE INS CO	IL	200.3	MERIT LIFE INS CO	IN	584.3
AUTO-OWNERS LIFE INS CO	MI	3,592.1	MIDLAND NATIONAL LIFE INS CO	IA	40,607.6
BERKSHIRE LIFE INS CO OF AMERICA	MA	3,640.3	MINNESOTA LIFE INS CO	MN	34,693.9
FEDERATED LIFE INS CO	MN	1,497.0	MUTUAL OF OMAHA INS CO	NE	6,568.9
GUARDIAN LIFE INS CO OF AMERICA	NY	44,890.2	NATIONAL BENEFIT LIFE INS CO	NY	480.5
PARKER CENTENNIAL ASR CO	WI	89.4	NATIONAL WESTERN LIFE INS CO	CO	10,164.8
RESERVE NATIONAL INS CO	OK	112.1	NEW YORK LIFE INS & ANNUITY CORP	DE	124,994.1
SENTRY LIFE INS CO	WI	5,237.9	OHIO NATIONAL LIFE ASR CORP	OH	3,548.1
SOUTHERN FARM BUREAU LIFE INS CO	MS	12,937.4	PACIFIC LIFE & ANNUITY CO	AZ	6,110.8
USAA LIFE INS CO	TX	21,964.7	PARK AVENUE LIFE INS CO	DE	303.3
			PIONEER MUTUAL LIFE INS CO	ND	510.6
Rating: A-			PRINCIPAL LIFE INS CO	IA	148,782.3
			SAVINGS BANK LIFE INS CO OF MA	MA	2,567.5
ALLSTATE ASR CO	IL	12.3	STANDARD INS CO	OR	19,885.1
AMALGAMATED LIFE INS CO	NY	110.5	SYMETRA LIFE INS CO	IA	28,794.9
AMERICAN REPUBLIC INS CO	IA	797.6	THRIVENT LIFE INS CO	MN	3,530.2
ANTHEM LIFE INS CO	IN	559.7	TRUSTMARK INS CO	IL	1,404.5
BALBOA LIFE INS CO	CA	58.9	TRUSTMARK LIFE INS CO	IL	370.8
CENTRAL STATES H & L CO OF OMAHA	NE	407.1	UNITED WORLD LIFE INS CO	NE	114.3
CHARTER NATIONAL LIFE INS CO	IL	133.2	USABLE LIFE	AR	432.6
CIGNA LIFE INS CO OF NEW YORK	NY	380.6			
COMPANION LIFE INS CO	SC	274.9			
COTTON STATES LIFE INS CO	GA	330.7			
COUNTRY INVESTORS LIFE ASR CO	IL	289.8			
DEARBORN NATIONAL LIFE INS CO	IL	2,183.0			
FAMILY HERITAGE LIFE INS CO OF AMER	OH	725.3			
FIDELITY INVESTMENTS LIFE INS CO	UT	23,882.2			
GARDEN STATE LIFE INS CO	TX	120.3			
GERBER LIFE INS CO	NY	2,749.8			
ILLINOIS MUTUAL LIFE INS CO	IL	1,368.4			
LIFE INS CO OF ALABAMA	AL	112.0			
MASSACHUSETTS MUTUAL LIFE INS CO	MA	190,575.4			
MIDWESTERN UNITED LIFE INS CO	IN	236.3			
MML BAY STATE LIFE INS CO	CT	4,682.4			
MUTUAL OF AMERICA LIFE INS CO	NY	17,110.0			
MUTUAL SAVINGS LIFE INS CO	AL	470.5			
NEW YORK LIFE INS CO	NY	143,501.4			
NIPPON LIFE INS CO OF AMERICA	IA	211.7			
NORTHWESTERN MUTUAL LIFE INS CO	WI	223,102.7			
PACIFIC LIFE INS CO	NE	111,429.1			
PHYSICIANS LIFE INS CO	NE	1,421.0			
STANDARD LIFE & ACCIDENT INS CO	TX	523.8			
Rating: B+					
AETNA HEALTH & LIFE INS CO	CT	2,221.2			
AETNA LIFE INS CO	CT	22,602.5			
AMERICAN FAMILY LIFE ASR CO OF COLUM	NE	110,401.3			
AMERICAN FIDELITY ASR CO	OK	4,856.7			
AMERICAN UNITED LIFE INS CO	IN	22,778.8			
ASSURITY LIFE INS CO	NE	2,452.3			

Alaska

INSURANCE COMPANY NAME	DOM. STATE	TOTAL ASSETS ($MIL)
Rating: A+		
COUNTRY LIFE INS CO	IL	10,573.7
PHYSICIANS MUTUAL INS CO	NE	1,989.7
STATE FARM LIFE INS CO	IL	62,712.0
TEACHERS INS & ANNUITY ASN OF AM	NY	261,389.2
Rating: A		
4 EVER LIFE INS CO	IL	200.3
BERKSHIRE LIFE INS CO OF AMERICA	MA	3,640.3
GUARDIAN LIFE INS CO OF AMERICA	NY	44,890.2
LIFEWISE ASR CO	WA	125.6
PARKER CENTENNIAL ASR CO	WI	89.4
RESERVE NATIONAL INS CO	OK	112.1
SENTRY LIFE INS CO	WI	5,237.9
USAA LIFE INS CO	TX	21,964.7
Rating: A-		
ALLSTATE ASR CO	IL	12.3
AMALGAMATED LIFE INS CO	NY	110.5
AMERICAN REPUBLIC INS CO	IA	797.6
ANTHEM LIFE INS CO	IN	559.7
BALBOA LIFE INS CO	CA	58.9
CENTRAL STATES H & L CO OF OMAHA	NE	407.1
CHARTER NATIONAL LIFE INS CO	IL	133.2
COMPANION LIFE INS CO	SC	274.9
COUNTRY INVESTORS LIFE ASR CO	IL	289.8
DEARBORN NATIONAL LIFE INS CO	IL	2,183.0
FAMILY HERITAGE LIFE INS CO OF AMER	OH	725.3
FIDELITY INVESTMENTS LIFE INS CO	UT	23,882.2
GARDEN STATE LIFE INS CO	TX	120.3
GERBER LIFE INS CO	NY	2,749.8
MASSACHUSETTS MUTUAL LIFE INS CO	MA	190,575.4
MIDWESTERN UNITED LIFE INS CO	IN	236.3
MML BAY STATE LIFE INS CO	CT	4,682.4
MUTUAL OF AMERICA LIFE INS CO	NY	17,110.0
NEW YORK LIFE INS CO	NY	143,501.4
NIPPON LIFE INS CO OF AMERICA	IA	211.7
NORTHWESTERN MUTUAL LIFE INS CO	WI	223,102.7
PACIFIC GUARDIAN LIFE INS CO LTD	HI	511.7
PACIFIC LIFE INS CO	NE	111,429.1
PHYSICIANS LIFE INS CO	NE	1,421.0
STANDARD LIFE & ACCIDENT INS CO	TX	523.8
Rating: B+		
AETNA HEALTH & LIFE INS CO	CT	2,221.2
AETNA LIFE INS CO	CT	22,602.5
AMERICAN FAMILY LIFE ASR CO OF COLUM	NE	110,401.3
AMERICAN FIDELITY ASR CO	OK	4,856.7
AMERICAN UNITED LIFE INS CO	IN	22,778.8
ASSURITY LIFE INS CO	NE	2,452.3
BOSTON MUTUAL LIFE INS CO	MA	1,230.4
COLORADO BANKERS LIFE INS CO	CO	280.1
GENERAL RE LIFE CORP	CT	3,335.8
GOVERNMENT PERSONNEL MUTUAL L I C	TX	830.8
JACKSON NATIONAL LIFE INS CO	MI	176,820.4
LINCOLN BENEFIT LIFE CO	NE	12,911.3

INSURANCE COMPANY NAME	DOM. STATE	TOTAL ASSETS ($MIL)
MEDICO CORP LIFE INS CO	NE	26.0
MIDLAND NATIONAL LIFE INS CO	IA	40,607.9
MINNESOTA LIFE INS CO	MN	34,693.9
MUTUAL OF OMAHA INS CO	NE	6,568.9
NATIONAL BENEFIT LIFE INS CO	NY	480.5
NATIONAL FARMERS UNION LIFE INS CO	TX	216.9
NATIONAL WESTERN LIFE INS CO	CO	10,164.8
NEW YORK LIFE INS & ANNUITY CORP	DE	124,994.1
PACIFIC LIFE & ANNUITY CO	AZ	6,110.8
PARK AVENUE LIFE INS CO	DE	303.3
PRINCIPAL LIFE INS CO	IA	148,782.3
SAVINGS BANK LIFE INS CO OF MA	MA	2,567.5
STANDARD INS CO	OR	19,885.1
SYMETRA LIFE INS CO	IA	28,794.9
THRIVENT LIFE INS CO	MN	3,530.2
TRUSTMARK INS CO	IL	1,404.5
TRUSTMARK LIFE INS CO	IL	370.8
UNITED WORLD LIFE INS CO	NE	114.3
USABLE LIFE	AR	432.6

Arizona

INSURANCE COMPANY NAME	DOM. STATE	TOTAL ASSETS ($MIL)

Rating: A+

INSURANCE COMPANY NAME	DOM. STATE	TOTAL ASSETS ($MIL)
AMERICAN FAMILY LIFE INS CO	WI	5,200.5
COUNTRY LIFE INS CO	IL	10,573.7
PHYSICIANS MUTUAL INS CO	NE	1,989.7
STATE FARM LIFE INS CO	IL	62,712.0
TEACHERS INS & ANNUITY ASN OF AM	NY	261,389.2

Rating: A

INSURANCE COMPANY NAME	DOM. STATE	TOTAL ASSETS ($MIL)
4 EVER LIFE INS CO	IL	200.3
AUTO-OWNERS LIFE INS CO	MI	3,592.1
BERKSHIRE LIFE INS CO OF AMERICA	MA	3,640.3
FEDERATED LIFE INS CO	MN	1,497.0
GUARDIAN LIFE INS CO OF AMERICA	NY	44,890.2
LIFEWISE ASR CO	WA	125.6
PARKER CENTENNIAL ASR CO	WI	89.4
RESERVE NATIONAL INS CO	OK	112.1
SENTRY LIFE INS CO	WI	5,237.9
UNITED FARM FAMILY LIFE INS CO	IN	2,129.9
USAA LIFE INS CO	TX	21,964.7

Rating: A-

INSURANCE COMPANY NAME	DOM. STATE	TOTAL ASSETS ($MIL)
ALLSTATE ASR CO	IL	12.3
AMALGAMATED LIFE INS CO	NY	110.5
AMERICAN REPUBLIC INS CO	IA	797.6
ANTHEM LIFE INS CO	IN	559.7
BALBOA LIFE INS CO	CA	58.9
CENTRAL STATES H & L CO OF OMAHA	NE	407.1
CHARTER NATIONAL LIFE INS CO	IL	133.2
COMPANION LIFE INS CO	SC	274.9
COUNTRY INVESTORS LIFE ASR CO	IL	289.8
DEARBORN NATIONAL LIFE INS CO	IL	2,183.0
FAMILY HERITAGE LIFE INS CO OF AMER	OH	725.3
FIDELITY INVESTMENTS LIFE INS CO	UT	23,882.2
GARDEN STATE LIFE INS CO	TX	120.3
GERBER LIFE INS CO	NY	2,749.8
ILLINOIS MUTUAL LIFE INS CO	IL	1,368.4
MASSACHUSETTS MUTUAL LIFE INS CO	MA	190,575.4
MIDWESTERN UNITED LIFE INS CO	IN	236.3
MML BAY STATE LIFE INS CO	CT	4,682.4
MUTUAL OF AMERICA LIFE INS CO	NY	17,110.0
NEW YORK LIFE INS CO	NY	143,501.4
NIPPON LIFE INS CO OF AMERICA	IA	211.7
NORTHWESTERN MUTUAL LIFE INS CO	WI	223,102.7
PACIFIC GUARDIAN LIFE INS CO LTD	HI	511.7
PACIFIC LIFE INS CO	NE	111,429.1
PHYSICIANS LIFE INS CO	NE	1,421.0
STANDARD LIFE & ACCIDENT INS CO	TX	523.8

Rating: B+

INSURANCE COMPANY NAME	DOM. STATE	TOTAL ASSETS ($MIL)
AETNA HEALTH & LIFE INS CO	CT	2,221.2
AETNA LIFE INS CO	CT	22,602.5
AMERICAN FAMILY LIFE ASR CO OF COLUM	NE	110,401.3
AMERICAN FIDELITY ASR CO	OK	4,856.7
AMERICAN UNITED LIFE INS CO	IN	22,778.8
ASSURITY LIFE INS CO	NE	2,452.3
BOSTON MUTUAL LIFE INS CO	MA	1,230.4

INSURANCE COMPANY NAME	DOM. STATE	TOTAL ASSETS ($MIL)
COLORADO BANKERS LIFE INS CO	CO	280.1
FARM BUREAU LIFE INS CO	IA	8,042.3
GENERAL RE LIFE CORP	CT	3,335.8
GOVERNMENT PERSONNEL MUTUAL L I C	TX	830.8
JACKSON NATIONAL LIFE INS CO	MI	176,820.4
LINCOLN BENEFIT LIFE CO	NE	12,911.3
MEDICO CORP LIFE INS CO	NE	26.0
MERIT LIFE INS CO	IN	584.3
MIDLAND NATIONAL LIFE INS CO	IA	40,607.9
MINNESOTA LIFE INS CO	MN	34,693.9
MUTUAL OF OMAHA INS CO	NE	6,568.9
NATIONAL BENEFIT LIFE INS CO	NY	480.5
NATIONAL FARMERS UNION LIFE INS CO	TX	216.9
NATIONAL WESTERN LIFE INS CO	CO	10,164.8
NEW YORK LIFE INS & ANNUITY CORP	DE	124,994.1
OHIO NATIONAL LIFE ASR CORP	OH	3,548.1
PACIFIC LIFE & ANNUITY CO	AZ	6,110.8
PARK AVENUE LIFE INS CO	DE	303.3
PIONEER MUTUAL LIFE INS CO	ND	510.6
PRINCIPAL LIFE INS CO	IA	148,782.3
SAVINGS BANK LIFE INS CO OF MA	MA	2,567.5
STANDARD INS CO	OR	19,885.1
SYMETRA LIFE INS CO	IA	28,794.9
THRIVENT LIFE INS CO	MN	3,530.2
TRUSTMARK INS CO	IL	1,404.5
TRUSTMARK LIFE INS CO	IL	370.8
UNITED WORLD LIFE INS CO	NE	114.3
USABLE LIFE	AR	432.6

Arkansas

INSURANCE COMPANY NAME	DOM. STATE	TOTAL ASSETS ($MIL)
Rating: A+		
COUNTRY LIFE INS CO	IL	10,573.7
PHYSICIANS MUTUAL INS CO	NE	1,989.7
STATE FARM LIFE INS CO	IL	62,712.0
TEACHERS INS & ANNUITY ASN OF AM	NY	261,389.2
Rating: A		
4 EVER LIFE INS CO	IL	200.3
AUTO-OWNERS LIFE INS CO	MI	3,592.1
BERKSHIRE LIFE INS CO OF AMERICA	MA	3,640.3
FEDERATED LIFE INS CO	MN	1,497.0
GUARDIAN LIFE INS CO OF AMERICA	NY	44,890.2
PARKER CENTENNIAL ASR CO	WI	89.4
RESERVE NATIONAL INS CO	OK	112.1
SENTRY LIFE INS CO	WI	5,237.9
SOUTHERN FARM BUREAU LIFE INS CO	MS	12,937.4
USAA LIFE INS CO	TX	21,964.7
Rating: A-		
ALLSTATE ASR CO	IL	12.3
AMALGAMATED LIFE INS CO	NY	110.5
AMERICAN REPUBLIC INS CO	IA	797.6
ANTHEM LIFE INS CO	IN	559.7
BALBOA LIFE INS CO	CA	58.9
CENTRAL STATES H & L CO OF OMAHA	NE	407.1
CHARTER NATIONAL LIFE INS CO	IL	133.2
COMPANION LIFE INS CO	SC	274.9
COUNTRY INVESTORS LIFE ASR CO	IL	289.8
DEARBORN NATIONAL LIFE INS CO	IL	2,183.0
FAMILY HERITAGE LIFE INS CO OF AMER	OH	725.3
FIDELITY INVESTMENTS LIFE INS CO	UT	23,882.2
GARDEN STATE LIFE INS CO	TX	120.3
GERBER LIFE INS CO	NY	2,749.8
ILLINOIS MUTUAL LIFE INS CO	IL	1,368.4
LIFE INS CO OF ALABAMA	AL	112.0
MASSACHUSETTS MUTUAL LIFE INS CO	MA	190,575.4
MIDWESTERN UNITED LIFE INS CO	IN	236.3
MML BAY STATE LIFE INS CO	CT	4,682.4
MUTUAL OF AMERICA LIFE INS CO	NY	17,110.0
NEW YORK LIFE INS CO	NY	143,501.4
NIPPON LIFE INS CO OF AMERICA	IA	211.7
NORTHWESTERN MUTUAL LIFE INS CO	WI	223,102.7
PACIFIC LIFE INS CO	NE	111,429.1
PHYSICIANS LIFE INS CO	NE	1,421.0
SHELTER LIFE INS CO	MO	1,108.6
STANDARD LIFE & ACCIDENT INS CO	TX	523.8
Rating: B+		
AETNA HEALTH & LIFE INS CO	CT	2,221.2
AETNA LIFE INS CO	CT	22,602.5
AMERICAN FAMILY LIFE ASR CO OF COLUM	NE	110,401.3
AMERICAN FIDELITY ASR CO	OK	4,856.7
AMERICAN UNITED LIFE INS CO	IN	22,778.8
ASSURITY LIFE INS CO	NE	2,452.3
BLUEBONNET LIFE INS CO	MS	54.6
BOSTON MUTUAL LIFE INS CO	MA	1,230.4

INSURANCE COMPANY NAME	DOM. STATE	TOTAL ASSETS ($MIL)
COLORADO BANKERS LIFE INS CO	CO	280.1
GENERAL RE LIFE CORP	CT	3,335.8
GOVERNMENT PERSONNEL MUTUAL L I C	TX	830.8
JACKSON NATIONAL LIFE INS CO	MI	176,820.4
LINCOLN BENEFIT LIFE CO	NE	12,911.3
MEDICO CORP LIFE INS CO	NE	26.0
MERIT LIFE INS CO	IN	584.3
MIDLAND NATIONAL LIFE INS CO	IA	40,607.9
MINNESOTA LIFE INS CO	MN	34,693.9
MUTUAL OF OMAHA INS CO	NE	6,568.9
NATIONAL BENEFIT LIFE INS CO	NY	480.5
NATIONAL FARMERS UNION LIFE INS CO	TX	216.9
NATIONAL WESTERN LIFE INS CO	CO	10,164.8
NEW YORK LIFE INS & ANNUITY CORP	DE	124,994.1
OHIO NATIONAL LIFE ASR CORP	OH	3,548.1
PACIFIC LIFE & ANNUITY CO	AZ	6,110.8
PARK AVENUE LIFE INS CO	DE	303.3
PIONEER MUTUAL LIFE INS CO	ND	510.6
PRINCIPAL LIFE INS CO	IA	148,782.3
SAVINGS BANK LIFE INS CO OF MA	MA	2,567.5
STANDARD INS CO	OR	19,885.1
SYMETRA LIFE INS CO	IA	28,794.9
THRIVENT LIFE INS CO	MN	3,530.2
TRUSTMARK INS CO	IL	1,404.5
TRUSTMARK LIFE INS CO	IL	370.8
UNITED WORLD LIFE INS CO	NE	114.3
USABLE LIFE	AR	432.6

California

INSURANCE COMPANY NAME	DOM. STATE	TOTAL ASSETS ($MIL)

Rating: A+

INSURANCE COMPANY NAME	DOM. STATE	TOTAL ASSETS ($MIL)
AMERICAN FAMILY LIFE INS CO	WI	5,200.5
PHYSICIANS MUTUAL INS CO	NE	1,989.7
STATE FARM LIFE INS CO	IL	62,712.0
TEACHERS INS & ANNUITY ASN OF AM	NY	261,389.2

Rating: A

INSURANCE COMPANY NAME	DOM. STATE	TOTAL ASSETS ($MIL)
4 EVER LIFE INS CO	IL	200.3
BERKSHIRE LIFE INS CO OF AMERICA	MA	3,640.3
FEDERATED LIFE INS CO	MN	1,497.0
GUARDIAN LIFE INS CO OF AMERICA	NY	44,890.2
LIFEWISE ASR CO	WA	125.6
PARKER CENTENNIAL ASR CO	WI	89.4
SENTRY LIFE INS CO	WI	5,237.9
UNITED FARM FAMILY LIFE INS CO	IN	2,129.9
USAA LIFE INS CO	TX	21,964.7

Rating: A-

INSURANCE COMPANY NAME	DOM. STATE	TOTAL ASSETS ($MIL)
ALLSTATE ASR CO	IL	12.3
AMALGAMATED LIFE INS CO	NY	110.5
AMERICAN REPUBLIC INS CO	IA	797.6
ANTHEM LIFE INS CO	IN	559.7
BALBOA LIFE INS CO	CA	58.9
BLUE SHIELD OF CALIFORNIA L&H INS CO	CA	841.2
CENTRAL STATES H & L CO OF OMAHA	NE	407.1
CHARTER NATIONAL LIFE INS CO	IL	133.2
DEARBORN NATIONAL LIFE INS CO	IL	2,183.0
FAMILY HERITAGE LIFE INS CO OF AMER	OH	725.3
FIDELITY INVESTMENTS LIFE INS CO	UT	23,882.2
GARDEN STATE LIFE INS CO	TX	120.3
GERBER LIFE INS CO	NY	2,749.8
ILLINOIS MUTUAL LIFE INS CO	IL	1,368.4
MASSACHUSETTS MUTUAL LIFE INS CO	MA	190,575.4
MIDWESTERN UNITED LIFE INS CO	IN	236.3
MML BAY STATE LIFE INS CO	CT	4,682.4
MUTUAL OF AMERICA LIFE INS CO	NY	17,110.0
NEW YORK LIFE INS CO	NY	143,501.4
NIPPON LIFE INS CO OF AMERICA	IA	211.7
NORTHWESTERN MUTUAL LIFE INS CO	WI	223,102.7
PACIFIC GUARDIAN LIFE INS CO LTD	HI	511.7
PACIFIC LIFE INS CO	NE	111,429.1
PHYSICIANS LIFE INS CO	NE	1,421.0
STANDARD LIFE & ACCIDENT INS CO	TX	523.8

Rating: B+

INSURANCE COMPANY NAME	DOM. STATE	TOTAL ASSETS ($MIL)
AETNA HEALTH & LIFE INS CO	CT	2,221.2
AETNA LIFE INS CO	CT	22,602.5
AMERICAN FAMILY LIFE ASR CO OF COLUM	NE	110,401.3
AMERICAN FIDELITY ASR CO	OK	4,856.7
AMERICAN UNITED LIFE INS CO	IN	22,778.8
ASSURITY LIFE INS CO	NE	2,452.3
BOSTON MUTUAL LIFE INS CO	MA	1,230.4
COLORADO BANKERS LIFE INS CO	CO	280.1
GENERAL RE LIFE CORP	CT	3,335.8
GOVERNMENT PERSONNEL MUTUAL L I C	TX	830.8
JACKSON NATIONAL LIFE INS CO	MI	176,820.4

INSURANCE COMPANY NAME	DOM. STATE	TOTAL ASSETS ($MIL)
LINCOLN BENEFIT LIFE CO	NE	12,911.3
MERIT LIFE INS CO	IN	584.3
MIDLAND NATIONAL LIFE INS CO	IA	40,607.9
MINNESOTA LIFE INS CO	MN	34,693.9
MUTUAL OF OMAHA INS CO	NE	6,568.9
NATIONAL BENEFIT LIFE INS CO	NY	480.5
NATIONAL FARMERS UNION LIFE INS CO	TX	216.9
NATIONAL WESTERN LIFE INS CO	CO	10,164.8
NEW YORK LIFE INS & ANNUITY CORP	DE	124,994.1
OHIO NATIONAL LIFE ASR CORP	OH	3,548.1
PACIFIC LIFE & ANNUITY CO	AZ	6,110.8
PARK AVENUE LIFE INS CO	DE	303.3
PIONEER MUTUAL LIFE INS CO	ND	510.6
PRINCIPAL LIFE INS CO	IA	148,782.3
SAVINGS BANK LIFE INS CO OF MA	MA	2,567.5
STANDARD INS CO	OR	19,885.1
SYMETRA LIFE INS CO	IA	28,794.9
THRIVENT LIFE INS CO	MN	3,530.2
TRUSTMARK INS CO	IL	1,404.5
TRUSTMARK LIFE INS CO	IL	370.8
UNITED WORLD LIFE INS CO	NE	114.3
USABLE LIFE	AR	432.6

Colorado

INSURANCE COMPANY NAME	DOM. STATE	TOTAL ASSETS ($MIL)
Rating: A+		
AMERICAN FAMILY LIFE INS CO	WI	5,200.5
COUNTRY LIFE INS CO	IL	10,573.7
PHYSICIANS MUTUAL INS CO	NE	1,989.7
STATE FARM LIFE INS CO	IL	62,712.0
TEACHERS INS & ANNUITY ASN OF AM	NY	261,389.2
Rating: A		
4 EVER LIFE INS CO	IL	200.3
AUTO-OWNERS LIFE INS CO	MI	3,592.1
BERKSHIRE LIFE INS CO OF AMERICA	MA	3,640.3
FEDERATED LIFE INS CO	MN	1,497.0
GUARDIAN LIFE INS CO OF AMERICA	NY	44,890.2
LIFEWISE ASR CO	WA	125.6
PARKER CENTENNIAL ASR CO	WI	89.4
RESERVE NATIONAL INS CO	OK	112.1
SENTRY LIFE INS CO	WI	5,237.9
SHELTERPOINT LIFE INS CO	NY	104.4
SOUTHERN FARM BUREAU LIFE INS CO	MS	12,937.4
USAA LIFE INS CO	TX	21,964.7
Rating: A-		
ALLSTATE ASR CO	IL	12.3
AMALGAMATED LIFE INS CO	NY	110.5
AMERICAN REPUBLIC INS CO	IA	797.6
ANTHEM LIFE INS CO	IN	559.7
BALBOA LIFE INS CO	CA	58.9
CENTRAL STATES H & L CO OF OMAHA	NE	407.1
CHARTER NATIONAL LIFE INS CO	IL	133.2
COMPANION LIFE INS CO	SC	274.9
COUNTRY INVESTORS LIFE ASR CO	IL	289.8
DEARBORN NATIONAL LIFE INS CO	IL	2,183.0
FAMILY HERITAGE LIFE INS CO OF AMER	OH	725.3
FIDELITY INVESTMENTS LIFE INS CO	UT	23,882.2
GARDEN STATE LIFE INS CO	TX	120.3
GERBER LIFE INS CO	NY	2,749.8
ILLINOIS MUTUAL LIFE INS CO	IL	1,368.4
MASSACHUSETTS MUTUAL LIFE INS CO	MA	190,575.4
MIDWESTERN UNITED LIFE INS CO	IN	236.3
MML BAY STATE LIFE INS CO	CT	4,682.4
MUTUAL OF AMERICA LIFE INS CO	NY	17,110.0
NEW YORK LIFE INS CO	NY	143,501.4
NIPPON LIFE INS CO OF AMERICA	IA	211.7
NORTHWESTERN MUTUAL LIFE INS CO	WI	223,102.7
PACIFIC GUARDIAN LIFE INS CO LTD	HI	511.7
PACIFIC LIFE INS CO	NE	111,429.1
PHYSICIANS LIFE INS CO	NE	1,421.0
SHELTER LIFE INS CO	MO	1,108.6
STANDARD LIFE & ACCIDENT INS CO	TX	523.8
Rating: B+		
AETNA HEALTH & LIFE INS CO	CT	2,221.2
AETNA LIFE INS CO	CT	22,602.5
AMERICAN FAMILY LIFE ASR CO OF COLUM	NE	110,401.3
AMERICAN FIDELITY ASR CO	OK	4,856.7
AMERICAN UNITED LIFE INS CO	IN	22,778.8

INSURANCE COMPANY NAME	DOM. STATE	TOTAL ASSETS ($MIL)
ASSURITY LIFE INS CO	NE	2,452.3
BOSTON MUTUAL LIFE INS CO	MA	1,230.4
COLORADO BANKERS LIFE INS CO	CO	280.1
FARM BUREAU LIFE INS CO	IA	8,042.3
GENERAL RE LIFE CORP	CT	3,335.8
GOVERNMENT PERSONNEL MUTUAL L I C	TX	830.8
JACKSON NATIONAL LIFE INS CO	MI	176,820.4
LINCOLN BENEFIT LIFE CO	NE	12,911.3
MEDICO CORP LIFE INS CO	NE	26.0
MERIT LIFE INS CO	IN	584.3
MIDLAND NATIONAL LIFE INS CO	IA	40,607.9
MINNESOTA LIFE INS CO	MN	34,693.9
MUTUAL OF OMAHA INS CO	NE	6,568.9
NATIONAL BENEFIT LIFE INS CO	NY	480.5
NATIONAL FARMERS UNION LIFE INS CO	TX	216.9
NATIONAL WESTERN LIFE INS CO	CO	10,164.8
NEW YORK LIFE INS & ANNUITY CORP	DE	124,994.1
OHIO NATIONAL LIFE ASR CORP	OH	3,548.1
PACIFIC LIFE & ANNUITY CO	AZ	6,110.8
PARK AVENUE LIFE INS CO	DE	303.3
PIONEER MUTUAL LIFE INS CO	ND	510.6
PRINCIPAL LIFE INS CO	IA	148,782.3
SAVINGS BANK LIFE INS CO OF MA	MA	2,567.5
STANDARD INS CO	OR	19,885.1
SYMETRA LIFE INS CO	IA	28,794.9
THRIVENT LIFE INS CO	MN	3,530.2
TRUSTMARK INS CO	IL	1,404.5
TRUSTMARK LIFE INS CO	IL	370.8
UNITED WORLD LIFE INS CO	NE	114.3
USABLE LIFE	AR	432.6

Connecticut

INSURANCE COMPANY NAME	DOM. STATE	TOTAL ASSETS ($MIL)
Rating: A+		
COUNTRY LIFE INS CO	IL	10,573.7
PHYSICIANS MUTUAL INS CO	NE	1,989.7
STATE FARM LIFE & ACCIDENT ASR CO	IL	2,436.7
STATE FARM LIFE INS CO	IL	62,712.0
TEACHERS INS & ANNUITY ASN OF AM	NY	261,389.2
Rating: A		
4 EVER LIFE INS CO	IL	200.3
BERKSHIRE LIFE INS CO OF AMERICA	MA	3,640.3
FEDERATED LIFE INS CO	MN	1,497.0
GUARDIAN LIFE INS CO OF AMERICA	NY	44,890.2
PARKER CENTENNIAL ASR CO	WI	89.4
RESERVE NATIONAL INS CO	OK	112.1
SENTRY LIFE INS CO	WI	5,237.9
SHELTERPOINT LIFE INS CO	NY	104.4
USAA LIFE INS CO	TX	21,964.7
Rating: A-		
ALLSTATE ASR CO	IL	12.3
AMALGAMATED LIFE INS CO	NY	110.5
AMERICAN FAMILY LIFE ASR CO OF NY	NY	710.2
AMERICAN REPUBLIC INS CO	IA	797.6
ANTHEM LIFE INS CO	IN	559.7
BALBOA LIFE INS CO	CA	58.9
CENTRAL STATES H & L CO OF OMAHA	NE	407.1
CHARTER NATIONAL LIFE INS CO	IL	133.2
COMPANION LIFE INS CO	SC	274.9
COUNTRY INVESTORS LIFE ASR CO	IL	289.8
DEARBORN NATIONAL LIFE INS CO	IL	2,183.0
FAMILY HERITAGE LIFE INS CO OF AMER	OH	725.3
FIDELITY INVESTMENTS LIFE INS CO	UT	23,882.2
GARDEN STATE LIFE INS CO	TX	120.3
GERBER LIFE INS CO	NY	2,749.8
ILLINOIS MUTUAL LIFE INS CO	IL	1,368.4
MASSACHUSETTS MUTUAL LIFE INS CO	MA	190,575.4
MIDWESTERN UNITED LIFE INS CO	IN	236.3
MML BAY STATE LIFE INS CO	CT	4,682.4
MUTUAL OF AMERICA LIFE INS CO	NY	17,110.0
NEW YORK LIFE INS CO	NY	143,501.4
NIPPON LIFE INS CO OF AMERICA	IA	211.7
NORTHWESTERN MUTUAL LIFE INS CO	WI	223,102.7
PACIFIC LIFE INS CO	NE	111,429.1
PHYSICIANS LIFE INS CO	NE	1,421.0
STANDARD LIFE & ACCIDENT INS CO	TX	523.8
Rating: B+		
AETNA HEALTH & LIFE INS CO	CT	2,221.2
AETNA LIFE INS CO	CT	22,602.5
AMERICAN FAMILY LIFE ASR CO OF COLUM	NE	110,401.3
AMERICAN FIDELITY ASR CO	OK	4,856.7
AMERICAN UNITED LIFE INS CO	IN	22,778.8
ASSURITY LIFE INS CO	NE	2,452.3
BOSTON MUTUAL LIFE INS CO	MA	1,230.4
COLORADO BANKERS LIFE INS CO	CO	280.1
GENERAL RE LIFE CORP	CT	3,335.8

INSURANCE COMPANY NAME	DOM. STATE	TOTAL ASSETS ($MIL)
GOVERNMENT PERSONNEL MUTUAL L I C	TX	830.8
JACKSON NATIONAL LIFE INS CO	MI	176,820.4
LINCOLN BENEFIT LIFE CO	NE	12,911.3
MERIT LIFE INS CO	IN	584.3
MIDLAND NATIONAL LIFE INS CO	IA	40,607.9
MINNESOTA LIFE INS CO	MN	34,693.9
MUTUAL OF OMAHA INS CO	NE	6,568.9
NATIONAL BENEFIT LIFE INS CO	NY	480.5
NATIONAL WESTERN LIFE INS CO	CO	10,164.8
NEW YORK LIFE INS & ANNUITY CORP	DE	124,994.1
OHIO NATIONAL LIFE ASR CORP	OH	3,548.1
PACIFIC LIFE & ANNUITY CO	AZ	6,110.8
PARK AVENUE LIFE INS CO	DE	303.3
PIONEER MUTUAL LIFE INS CO	ND	510.6
PRINCIPAL LIFE INS CO	IA	148,782.3
SAVINGS BANK LIFE INS CO OF MA	MA	2,567.5
STANDARD INS CO	OR	19,885.1
SYMETRA LIFE INS CO	IA	28,794.9
THRIVENT LIFE INS CO	MN	3,530.2
TRUSTMARK INS CO	IL	1,404.5
TRUSTMARK LIFE INS CO	IL	370.8
USABLE LIFE	AR	432.6

Delaware

INSURANCE COMPANY NAME	DOM. STATE	TOTAL ASSETS ($MIL)
Rating: A+		
COUNTRY LIFE INS CO	IL	10,573.7
PHYSICIANS MUTUAL INS CO	NE	1,989.7
STATE FARM LIFE INS CO	IL	62,712.0
TEACHERS INS & ANNUITY ASN OF AM	NY	261,389.2
Rating: A		
4 EVER LIFE INS CO	IL	200.3
BERKSHIRE LIFE INS CO OF AMERICA	MA	3,640.3
FEDERATED LIFE INS CO	MN	1,497.0
FIRST RELIANCE STANDARD LIFE INS CO	NY	188.7
GUARDIAN LIFE INS CO OF AMERICA	NY	44,890.2
PARKER CENTENNIAL ASR CO	WI	89.4
RESERVE NATIONAL INS CO	OK	112.1
SENTRY LIFE INS CO	WI	5,237.9
SHELTERPOINT LIFE INS CO	NY	104.4
USAA LIFE INS CO	TX	21,964.7
Rating: A-		
ALLSTATE ASR CO	IL	12.3
AMALGAMATED LIFE INS CO	NY	110.5
AMERICAN REPUBLIC INS CO	IA	797.6
ANTHEM LIFE INS CO	IN	559.7
BALBOA LIFE INS CO	CA	58.9
CENTRAL STATES H & L CO OF OMAHA	NE	407.1
CHARTER NATIONAL LIFE INS CO	IL	133.2
COMPANION LIFE INS CO	SC	274.9
COUNTRY INVESTORS LIFE ASR CO	IL	289.8
DEARBORN NATIONAL LIFE INS CO	IL	2,183.0
FAMILY HERITAGE LIFE INS CO OF AMER	OH	725.3
FIDELITY INVESTMENTS LIFE INS CO	UT	23,882.2
GARDEN STATE LIFE INS CO	TX	120.3
GERBER LIFE INS CO	NY	2,749.8
ILLINOIS MUTUAL LIFE INS CO	IL	1,368.4
MASSACHUSETTS MUTUAL LIFE INS CO	MA	190,575.4
MIDWESTERN UNITED LIFE INS CO	IN	236.3
MML BAY STATE LIFE INS CO	CT	4,682.4
MUTUAL OF AMERICA LIFE INS CO	NY	17,110.0
NEW YORK LIFE INS CO	NY	143,501.4
NIPPON LIFE INS CO OF AMERICA	IA	211.7
NORTHWESTERN MUTUAL LIFE INS CO	WI	223,102.7
PACIFIC LIFE INS CO	NE	111,429.1
PHYSICIANS LIFE INS CO	NE	1,421.0
STANDARD LIFE & ACCIDENT INS CO	TX	523.8
Rating: B+		
AETNA HEALTH & LIFE INS CO	CT	2,221.2
AETNA LIFE INS CO	CT	22,602.5
AMERICAN FAMILY LIFE ASR CO OF COLUM	NE	110,401.3
AMERICAN FIDELITY ASR CO	OK	4,856.7
AMERICAN UNITED LIFE INS CO	IN	22,778.8
ASSURITY LIFE INS CO	NE	2,452.3
BOSTON MUTUAL LIFE INS CO	MA	1,230.4
COLORADO BANKERS LIFE INS CO	CO	280.1
GENERAL RE LIFE CORP	CT	3,335.8
GOVERNMENT PERSONNEL MUTUAL L I C	TX	830.8

INSURANCE COMPANY NAME	DOM. STATE	TOTAL ASSETS ($MIL)
JACKSON NATIONAL LIFE INS CO	MI	176,820.4
LINCOLN BENEFIT LIFE CO	NE	12,911.3
MEDICO CORP LIFE INS CO	NE	26.0
MERIT LIFE INS CO	IN	584.3
MIDLAND NATIONAL LIFE INS CO	IA	40,607.9
MINNESOTA LIFE INS CO	MN	34,693.9
MUTUAL OF OMAHA INS CO	NE	6,568.9
NATIONAL BENEFIT LIFE INS CO	NY	480.5
NATIONAL WESTERN LIFE INS CO	CO	10,164.8
NEW YORK LIFE INS & ANNUITY CORP	DE	124,994.1
OHIO NATIONAL LIFE ASR CORP	OH	3,548.1
PACIFIC LIFE & ANNUITY CO	AZ	6,110.8
PARK AVENUE LIFE INS CO	DE	303.3
PIONEER MUTUAL LIFE INS CO	ND	510.6
PRINCIPAL LIFE INS CO	IA	148,782.3
SAVINGS BANK LIFE INS CO OF MA	MA	2,567.5
STANDARD INS CO	OR	19,885.1
SYMETRA LIFE INS CO	IA	28,794.9
THRIVENT LIFE INS CO	MN	3,530.2
TRUSTMARK INS CO	IL	1,404.5
TRUSTMARK LIFE INS CO	IL	370.8
UNITED WORLD LIFE INS CO	NE	114.3
USABLE LIFE	AR	432.6

District Of Columbia

Rating: A+

INSURANCE COMPANY NAME	DOM. STATE	TOTAL ASSETS ($MIL)
PHYSICIANS MUTUAL INS CO	NE	1,989.7
STATE FARM LIFE INS CO	IL	62,712.0
TEACHERS INS & ANNUITY ASN OF AM	NY	261,389.2

Rating: A

INSURANCE COMPANY NAME	DOM. STATE	TOTAL ASSETS ($MIL)
4 EVER LIFE INS CO	IL	200.3
BERKSHIRE LIFE INS CO OF AMERICA	MA	3,640.3
FIRST RELIANCE STANDARD LIFE INS CO	NY	188.7
GUARDIAN LIFE INS CO OF AMERICA	NY	44,890.2
PARKER CENTENNIAL ASR CO	WI	89.4
RESERVE NATIONAL INS CO	OK	112.1
SENTRY LIFE INS CO	WI	5,237.9
SHELTERPOINT LIFE INS CO	NY	104.4
USAA LIFE INS CO	TX	21,964.7

Rating: A-

INSURANCE COMPANY NAME	DOM. STATE	TOTAL ASSETS ($MIL)
ALLSTATE ASR CO	IL	12.3
AMALGAMATED LIFE INS CO	NY	110.5
AMERICAN REPUBLIC INS CO	IA	797.6
ANTHEM LIFE INS CO	IN	559.7
BALBOA LIFE INS CO	CA	58.9
CENTRAL STATES H & L CO OF OMAHA	NE	407.1
CHARTER NATIONAL LIFE INS CO	IL	133.2
CIGNA LIFE INS CO OF NEW YORK	NY	380.6
COMPANION LIFE INS CO	SC	274.9
DEARBORN NATIONAL LIFE INS CO	IL	2,183.0
ERIE FAMILY LIFE INS CO	PA	2,077.0
FAMILY HERITAGE LIFE INS CO OF AMER	OH	725.3
FIDELITY INVESTMENTS LIFE INS CO	UT	23,882.2
GARDEN STATE LIFE INS CO	TX	120.3
GERBER LIFE INS CO	NY	2,749.8
MASSACHUSETTS MUTUAL LIFE INS CO	MA	190,575.4
MIDWESTERN UNITED LIFE INS CO	IN	236.3
MML BAY STATE LIFE INS CO	CT	4,682.4
MUTUAL OF AMERICA LIFE INS CO	NY	17,110.0
NEW YORK LIFE INS CO	NY	143,501.4
NIPPON LIFE INS CO OF AMERICA	IA	211.7
NORTHWESTERN MUTUAL LIFE INS CO	WI	223,102.7
PACIFIC LIFE INS CO	NE	111,429.1
PHYSICIANS LIFE INS CO	NE	1,421.0
STANDARD LIFE & ACCIDENT INS CO	TX	523.8

Rating: B+

INSURANCE COMPANY NAME	DOM. STATE	TOTAL ASSETS ($MIL)
AETNA HEALTH & LIFE INS CO	CT	2,221.2
AETNA LIFE INS CO	CT	22,602.5
AMERICAN FAMILY LIFE ASR CO OF COLUM	NE	110,401.3
AMERICAN FIDELITY ASR CO	OK	4,856.7
AMERICAN UNITED LIFE INS CO	IN	22,778.8
ASSURITY LIFE INS CO	NE	2,452.3
BOSTON MUTUAL LIFE INS CO	MA	1,230.4
COLORADO BANKERS LIFE INS CO	CO	280.1
GENERAL RE LIFE CORP	CT	3,335.8
GOVERNMENT PERSONNEL MUTUAL L I C	TX	830.8
HM LIFE INS CO OF NEW YORK	NY	72.4
JACKSON NATIONAL LIFE INS CO	MI	176,820.4
LINCOLN BENEFIT LIFE CO	NE	12,911.3
MEDICO CORP LIFE INS CO	NE	26.0
MERIT LIFE INS CO	IN	584.3
MIDLAND NATIONAL LIFE INS CO	IA	40,607.9
MINNESOTA LIFE INS CO	MN	34,693.9
MUTUAL OF OMAHA INS CO	NE	6,568.9
NATIONAL BENEFIT LIFE INS CO	NY	480.5
NATIONAL FARMERS UNION LIFE INS CO	TX	216.9
NATIONAL WESTERN LIFE INS CO	CO	10,164.8
NEW YORK LIFE INS & ANNUITY CORP	DE	124,994.1
OHIO NATIONAL LIFE ASR CORP	OH	3,548.1
PACIFIC LIFE & ANNUITY CO	AZ	6,110.8
PARK AVENUE LIFE INS CO	DE	303.3
PIONEER MUTUAL LIFE INS CO	ND	510.6
PRINCIPAL LIFE INS CO	IA	148,782.3
SAVINGS BANK LIFE INS CO OF MA	MA	2,567.5
STANDARD INS CO	OR	19,885.1
SYMETRA LIFE INS CO	IA	28,794.9
THRIVENT LIFE INS CO	MN	3,530.2
TRUSTMARK INS CO	IL	1,404.5
TRUSTMARK LIFE INS CO	IL	370.8
UNITED WORLD LIFE INS CO	NE	114.3
USABLE LIFE	AR	432.6

Florida

INSURANCE COMPANY NAME	DOM. STATE	TOTAL ASSETS ($MIL)	INSURANCE COMPANY NAME	DOM. STATE	TOTAL ASSETS ($MIL)
Rating: A+			COLORADO BANKERS LIFE INS CO	CO	280.1
			GENERAL RE LIFE CORP	CT	3,335.8
COUNTRY LIFE INS CO	IL	10,573.7	GOVERNMENT PERSONNEL MUTUAL L I C	TX	830.8
PHYSICIANS MUTUAL INS CO	NE	1,989.7	JACKSON NATIONAL LIFE INS CO	MI	176,820.4
STATE FARM LIFE INS CO	IL	62,712.0	LINCOLN BENEFIT LIFE CO	NE	12,911.3
TEACHERS INS & ANNUITY ASN OF AM	NY	261,389.2	MEDICO CORP LIFE INS CO	NE	26.0
Rating: A			MERIT LIFE INS CO	IN	584.3
			MIDLAND NATIONAL LIFE INS CO	IA	40,607.9
4 EVER LIFE INS CO	IL	200.3	MINNESOTA LIFE INS CO	MN	34,693.9
AUTO-OWNERS LIFE INS CO	MI	3,592.1	MUTUAL OF OMAHA INS CO	NE	6,568.9
BERKSHIRE LIFE INS CO OF AMERICA	MA	3,640.3	NATIONAL BENEFIT LIFE INS CO	NY	480.5
FEDERATED LIFE INS CO	MN	1,497.0	NATIONAL WESTERN LIFE INS CO	CO	10,164.8
GUARDIAN LIFE INS CO OF AMERICA	NY	44,890.2	NEW YORK LIFE INS & ANNUITY CORP	DE	124,994.1
PARKER CENTENNIAL ASR CO	WI	89.4	OHIO NATIONAL LIFE ASR CORP	OH	3,548.1
RESERVE NATIONAL INS CO	OK	112.1	PACIFIC LIFE & ANNUITY CO	AZ	6,110.8
SENTRY LIFE INS CO	WI	5,237.9	PARK AVENUE LIFE INS CO	DE	303.3
SOUTHERN FARM BUREAU LIFE INS CO	MS	12,937.4	PIONEER MUTUAL LIFE INS CO	ND	510.6
TRANS OCEANIC LIFE INS CO	PR	62.9	PRINCIPAL LIFE INS CO	IA	148,782.3
USAA LIFE INS CO	TX	21,964.7	SAVINGS BANK LIFE INS CO OF MA	MA	2,567.5
Rating: A-			STANDARD INS CO	OR	19,885.1
			SYMETRA LIFE INS CO	IA	28,794.9
ALLSTATE ASR CO	IL	12.3	THRIVENT LIFE INS CO	MN	3,530.2
AMALGAMATED LIFE INS CO	NY	110.5	TRUSTMARK INS CO	IL	1,404.5
AMERICAN REPUBLIC INS CO	IA	797.6	TRUSTMARK LIFE INS CO	IL	370.8
ANTHEM LIFE INS CO	IN	559.7	UNITED WORLD LIFE INS CO	NE	114.3
BALBOA LIFE INS CO	CA	58.9	USABLE LIFE	AR	432.6
CENTRAL STATES H & L CO OF OMAHA	NE	407.1			
CHARTER NATIONAL LIFE INS CO	IL	133.2			
COMPANION LIFE INS CO	SC	274.9			
COTTON STATES LIFE INS CO	GA	330.7			
COUNTRY INVESTORS LIFE ASR CO	IL	289.8			
DEARBORN NATIONAL LIFE INS CO	IL	2,183.0			
FAMILY HERITAGE LIFE INS CO OF AMER	OH	725.3			
FIDELITY INVESTMENTS LIFE INS CO	UT	23,882.2			
GARDEN STATE LIFE INS CO	TX	120.3			
GERBER LIFE INS CO	NY	2,749.8			
ILLINOIS MUTUAL LIFE INS CO	IL	1,368.4			
LIFE INS CO OF ALABAMA	AL	112.0			
MASSACHUSETTS MUTUAL LIFE INS CO	MA	190,575.4			
MIDWESTERN UNITED LIFE INS CO	IN	236.3			
MML BAY STATE LIFE INS CO	CT	4,682.4			
MUTUAL OF AMERICA LIFE INS CO	NY	17,110.0			
MUTUAL SAVINGS LIFE INS CO	AL	470.5			
NEW YORK LIFE INS CO	NY	143,501.4			
NIPPON LIFE INS CO OF AMERICA	IA	211.7			
NORTHWESTERN MUTUAL LIFE INS CO	WI	223,102.7			
PACIFIC LIFE INS CO	NE	111,429.1			
PHYSICIANS LIFE INS CO	NE	1,421.0			
STANDARD LIFE & ACCIDENT INS CO	TX	523.8			
Rating: B+					
AETNA LIFE INS CO	CT	22,602.5			
AMERICAN FAMILY LIFE ASR CO OF COLUM	NE	110,401.3			
AMERICAN FIDELITY ASR CO	OK	4,856.7			
AMERICAN UNITED LIFE INS CO	IN	22,778.8			
ASSURITY LIFE INS CO	NE	2,452.3			
BOSTON MUTUAL LIFE INS CO	MA	1,230.4			

Georgia

INSURANCE COMPANY NAME	DOM. STATE	TOTAL ASSETS ($MIL)
Rating: A+		
AMERICAN FAMILY LIFE INS CO	WI	5,200.5
COUNTRY LIFE INS CO	IL	10,573.7
PHYSICIANS MUTUAL INS CO	NE	1,989.7
STATE FARM LIFE INS CO	IL	62,712.0
TEACHERS INS & ANNUITY ASN OF AM	NY	261,389.2
Rating: A		
4 EVER LIFE INS CO	IL	200.3
AUTO-OWNERS LIFE INS CO	MI	3,592.1
BERKSHIRE LIFE INS CO OF AMERICA	MA	3,640.3
FEDERATED LIFE INS CO	MN	1,497.0
GUARDIAN LIFE INS CO OF AMERICA	NY	44,890.2
PARKER CENTENNIAL ASR CO	WI	89.4
RESERVE NATIONAL INS CO	OK	112.1
SENTRY LIFE INS CO	WI	5,237.9
SOUTHERN FARM BUREAU LIFE INS CO	MS	12,937.4
USAA LIFE INS CO	TX	21,964.7
Rating: A-		
ALLSTATE ASR CO	IL	12.3
AMALGAMATED LIFE INS CO	NY	110.5
AMERICAN REPUBLIC INS CO	IA	797.6
ANTHEM LIFE INS CO	IN	559.7
BALBOA LIFE INS CO	CA	58.9
CENTRAL STATES H & L CO OF OMAHA	NE	407.1
CHARTER NATIONAL LIFE INS CO	IL	133.2
COMPANION LIFE INS CO	SC	274.9
COTTON STATES LIFE INS CO	GA	330.7
COUNTRY INVESTORS LIFE ASR CO	IL	289.8
DEARBORN NATIONAL LIFE INS CO	IL	2,183.0
FAMILY HERITAGE LIFE INS CO OF AMER	OH	725.3
FIDELITY INVESTMENTS LIFE INS CO	UT	23,882.2
FRANDISCO LIFE INS CO	GA	65.0
GARDEN STATE LIFE INS CO	TX	120.3
GERBER LIFE INS CO	NY	2,749.8
ILLINOIS MUTUAL LIFE INS CO	IL	1,368.4
LIFE INS CO OF ALABAMA	AL	112.0
MASSACHUSETTS MUTUAL LIFE INS CO	MA	190,575.4
MIDWESTERN UNITED LIFE INS CO	IN	236.3
MML BAY STATE LIFE INS CO	CT	4,682.4
MUTUAL OF AMERICA LIFE INS CO	NY	17,110.0
MUTUAL SAVINGS LIFE INS CO	AL	470.5
NEW YORK LIFE INS CO	NY	143,501.4
NIPPON LIFE INS CO OF AMERICA	IA	211.7
NORTHWESTERN MUTUAL LIFE INS CO	WI	223,102.7
PACIFIC LIFE INS CO	NE	111,429.1
PHYSICIANS LIFE INS CO	NE	1,421.0
STANDARD LIFE & ACCIDENT INS CO	TX	523.8
Rating: B+		
AETNA HEALTH & LIFE INS CO	CT	2,221.2
AETNA LIFE INS CO	CT	22,602.5
AMERICAN FAMILY LIFE ASR CO OF COLUM	NE	110,401.3
AMERICAN FIDELITY ASR CO	OK	4,856.7
AMERICAN UNITED LIFE INS CO	IN	22,778.8

INSURANCE COMPANY NAME	DOM. STATE	TOTAL ASSETS ($MIL)
ASSURITY LIFE INS CO	NE	2,452.3
BOSTON MUTUAL LIFE INS CO	MA	1,230.4
COLORADO BANKERS LIFE INS CO	CO	280.1
GENERAL RE LIFE CORP	CT	3,335.8
GOVERNMENT PERSONNEL MUTUAL L I C	TX	830.8
GREATER GEORGIA LIFE INS CO	GA	49.9
JACKSON NATIONAL LIFE INS CO	MI	176,820.4
LINCOLN BENEFIT LIFE CO	NE	12,911.3
MEDICO CORP LIFE INS CO	NE	26.0
MERIT LIFE INS CO	IN	584.3
MIDLAND NATIONAL LIFE INS CO	IA	40,607.9
MINNESOTA LIFE INS CO	MN	34,693.9
MUTUAL OF OMAHA INS CO	NE	6,568.9
NATIONAL BENEFIT LIFE INS CO	NY	480.5
NATIONAL WESTERN LIFE INS CO	CO	10,164.8
NEW YORK LIFE INS & ANNUITY CORP	DE	124,994.1
OHIO NATIONAL LIFE ASR CORP	OH	3,548.1
PACIFIC LIFE & ANNUITY CO	AZ	6,110.8
PARK AVENUE LIFE INS CO	DE	303.3
PIONEER MUTUAL LIFE INS CO	ND	510.6
PRINCIPAL LIFE INS CO	IA	148,782.3
SAVINGS BANK LIFE INS CO OF MA	MA	2,567.5
STANDARD INS CO	OR	19,885.1
SYMETRA LIFE INS CO	IA	28,794.9
TRUSTMARK INS CO	IL	1,404.5
TRUSTMARK LIFE INS CO	IL	370.8
UNITED WORLD LIFE INS CO	NE	114.3
USABLE LIFE	AR	432.6

Hawaii

INSURANCE COMPANY NAME	DOM. STATE	TOTAL ASSETS ($MIL)
Rating: A+		
PHYSICIANS MUTUAL INS CO	NE	1,989.7
STATE FARM LIFE INS CO	IL	62,712.0
TEACHERS INS & ANNUITY ASN OF AM	NY	261,389.2
Rating: A		
4 EVER LIFE INS CO	IL	200.3
BERKSHIRE LIFE INS CO OF AMERICA	MA	3,640.3
GUARDIAN LIFE INS CO OF AMERICA	NY	44,890.2
PARKER CENTENNIAL ASR CO	WI	89.4
SENTRY LIFE INS CO	WI	5,237.9
USAA LIFE INS CO	TX	21,964.7
Rating: A-		
ALLSTATE ASR CO	IL	12.3
AMALGAMATED LIFE INS CO	NY	110.5
AMERICAN REPUBLIC INS CO	IA	797.6
ANTHEM LIFE INS CO	IN	559.7
BALBOA LIFE INS CO	CA	58.9
CENTRAL STATES H & L CO OF OMAHA	NE	407.1
CHARTER NATIONAL LIFE INS CO	IL	133.2
DEARBORN NATIONAL LIFE INS CO	IL	2,183.0
FAMILY HERITAGE LIFE INS CO OF AMER	OH	725.3
FIDELITY INVESTMENTS LIFE INS CO	UT	23,882.2
GARDEN STATE LIFE INS CO	TX	120.3
GERBER LIFE INS CO	NY	2,749.8
MASSACHUSETTS MUTUAL LIFE INS CO	MA	190,575.4
MIDWESTERN UNITED LIFE INS CO	IN	236.3
MML BAY STATE LIFE INS CO	CT	4,682.4
MUTUAL OF AMERICA LIFE INS CO	NY	17,110.0
NEW YORK LIFE INS CO	NY	143,501.4
NIPPON LIFE INS CO OF AMERICA	IA	211.7
NORTHWESTERN MUTUAL LIFE INS CO	WI	223,102.7
PACIFIC GUARDIAN LIFE INS CO LTD	HI	511.7
PACIFIC LIFE INS CO	NE	111,429.1
PHYSICIANS LIFE INS CO	NE	1,421.0
STANDARD LIFE & ACCIDENT INS CO	TX	523.8
Rating: B+		
AETNA HEALTH & LIFE INS CO	CT	2,221.2
AETNA LIFE INS CO	CT	22,602.5
AMERICAN FAMILY LIFE ASR CO OF COLUM	NE	110,401.3
AMERICAN FIDELITY ASR CO	OK	4,856.7
AMERICAN UNITED LIFE INS CO	IN	22,778.8
ASSURITY LIFE INS CO	NE	2,452.3
BOSTON MUTUAL LIFE INS CO	MA	1,230.4
COLORADO BANKERS LIFE INS CO	CO	280.1
GENERAL RE LIFE CORP	CT	3,335.8
GOVERNMENT PERSONNEL MUTUAL L I C	TX	830.8
JACKSON NATIONAL LIFE INS CO	MI	176,820.4
LINCOLN BENEFIT LIFE CO	NE	12,911.3
MEDICO CORP LIFE INS CO	NE	26.0
MERIT LIFE INS CO	IN	584.3
MIDLAND NATIONAL LIFE INS CO	IA	40,607.9
MINNESOTA LIFE INS CO	MN	34,693.9
MUTUAL OF OMAHA INS CO	NE	6,568.9

INSURANCE COMPANY NAME	DOM. STATE	TOTAL ASSETS ($MIL)
NATIONAL BENEFIT LIFE INS CO	NY	480.5
NATIONAL WESTERN LIFE INS CO	CO	10,164.8
NEW YORK LIFE INS & ANNUITY CORP	DE	124,994.1
PACIFIC LIFE & ANNUITY CO	AZ	6,110.8
PIONEER MUTUAL LIFE INS CO	ND	510.6
PRINCIPAL LIFE INS CO	IA	148,782.3
SAVINGS BANK LIFE INS CO OF MA	MA	2,567.5
STANDARD INS CO	OR	19,885.1
SYMETRA LIFE INS CO	IA	28,794.9
THRIVENT LIFE INS CO	MN	3,530.2
TRUSTMARK INS CO	IL	1,404.5
TRUSTMARK LIFE INS CO	IL	370.8
UNITED WORLD LIFE INS CO	NE	114.3
USABLE LIFE	AR	432.6

Idaho

INSURANCE COMPANY NAME	DOM. STATE	TOTAL ASSETS ($MIL)
Rating: A+		
AMERICAN FAMILY LIFE INS CO	WI	5,200.5
COUNTRY LIFE INS CO	IL	10,573.7
PHYSICIANS MUTUAL INS CO	NE	1,989.7
STATE FARM LIFE INS CO	IL	62,712.0
TEACHERS INS & ANNUITY ASN OF AM	NY	261,389.2
Rating: A		
4 EVER LIFE INS CO	IL	200.3
AUTO-OWNERS LIFE INS CO	MI	3,592.1
BERKSHIRE LIFE INS CO OF AMERICA	MA	3,640.3
FEDERATED LIFE INS CO	MN	1,497.0
GUARDIAN LIFE INS CO OF AMERICA	NY	44,890.2
LIFEWISE ASR CO	WA	125.6
PARKER CENTENNIAL ASR CO	WI	89.4
RESERVE NATIONAL INS CO	OK	112.1
SENTRY LIFE INS CO	WI	5,237.9
USAA LIFE INS CO	TX	21,964.7
Rating: A-		
ALLSTATE ASR CO	IL	12.3
AMALGAMATED LIFE INS CO	NY	110.5
AMERICAN REPUBLIC INS CO	IA	797.6
ANTHEM LIFE INS CO	IN	559.7
BALBOA LIFE INS CO	CA	58.9
CENTRAL STATES H & L CO OF OMAHA	NE	407.1
CHARTER NATIONAL LIFE INS CO	IL	133.2
COMPANION LIFE INS CO	SC	274.9
COUNTRY INVESTORS LIFE ASR CO	IL	289.8
DEARBORN NATIONAL LIFE INS CO	IL	2,183.0
FAMILY HERITAGE LIFE INS CO OF AMER	OH	725.3
FIDELITY INVESTMENTS LIFE INS CO	UT	23,882.2
GARDEN STATE LIFE INS CO	TX	120.3
GERBER LIFE INS CO	NY	2,749.8
ILLINOIS MUTUAL LIFE INS CO	IL	1,368.4
MASSACHUSETTS MUTUAL LIFE INS CO	MA	190,575.4
MIDWESTERN UNITED LIFE INS CO	IN	236.3
MML BAY STATE LIFE INS CO	CT	4,682.4
MUTUAL OF AMERICA LIFE INS CO	NY	17,110.0
NEW YORK LIFE INS CO	NY	143,501.4
NIPPON LIFE INS CO OF AMERICA	IA	211.7
NORTHWESTERN MUTUAL LIFE INS CO	WI	223,102.7
PACIFIC GUARDIAN LIFE INS CO LTD	HI	511.7
PACIFIC LIFE INS CO	NE	111,429.1
PHYSICIANS LIFE INS CO	NE	1,421.0
STANDARD LIFE & ACCIDENT INS CO	TX	523.8
Rating: B+		
AETNA HEALTH & LIFE INS CO	CT	2,221.2
AETNA LIFE INS CO	CT	22,602.5
AMERICAN FAMILY LIFE ASR CO OF COLUM	NE	110,401.3
AMERICAN FIDELITY ASR CO	OK	4,856.7
AMERICAN UNITED LIFE INS CO	IN	22,778.8
ASSURITY LIFE INS CO	NE	2,452.3
BOSTON MUTUAL LIFE INS CO	MA	1,230.4
COLORADO BANKERS LIFE INS CO	CO	280.1

INSURANCE COMPANY NAME	DOM. STATE	TOTAL ASSETS ($MIL)
FARM BUREAU LIFE INS CO	IA	8,042.3
GENERAL RE LIFE CORP	CT	3,335.8
GOVERNMENT PERSONNEL MUTUAL L I C	TX	830.8
JACKSON NATIONAL LIFE INS CO	MI	176,820.4
LINCOLN BENEFIT LIFE CO	NE	12,911.3
MEDICO CORP LIFE INS CO	NE	26.0
MERIT LIFE INS CO	IN	584.3
MIDLAND NATIONAL LIFE INS CO	IA	40,607.9
MINNESOTA LIFE INS CO	MN	34,693.9
MUTUAL OF OMAHA INS CO	NE	6,568.9
NATIONAL BENEFIT LIFE INS CO	NY	480.5
NATIONAL FARMERS UNION LIFE INS CO	TX	216.9
NATIONAL WESTERN LIFE INS CO	CO	10,164.8
NEW YORK LIFE INS & ANNUITY CORP	DE	124,994.1
OHIO NATIONAL LIFE ASR CORP	OH	3,548.1
PACIFIC LIFE & ANNUITY CO	AZ	6,110.8
PARK AVENUE LIFE INS CO	DE	303.3
PIONEER MUTUAL LIFE INS CO	ND	510.6
PRINCIPAL LIFE INS CO	IA	148,782.3
SAVINGS BANK LIFE INS CO OF MA	MA	2,567.5
STANDARD INS CO	OR	19,885.1
SYMETRA LIFE INS CO	IA	28,794.9
THRIVENT LIFE INS CO	MN	3,530.2
TRUSTMARK INS CO	IL	1,404.5
TRUSTMARK LIFE INS CO	IL	370.8
UNITED WORLD LIFE INS CO	NE	114.3
USABLE LIFE	AR	432.6

Illinois

INSURANCE COMPANY NAME	DOM. STATE	TOTAL ASSETS ($MIL)
Rating: A+		
AMERICAN FAMILY LIFE INS CO	WI	5,200.5
COUNTRY LIFE INS CO	IL	10,573.7
PHYSICIANS MUTUAL INS CO	NE	1,989.7
STATE FARM LIFE & ACCIDENT ASR CO	IL	2,436.7
STATE FARM LIFE INS CO	IL	62,712.0
TEACHERS INS & ANNUITY ASN OF AM	NY	261,389.2
Rating: A		
4 EVER LIFE INS CO	IL	200.3
AUTO-OWNERS LIFE INS CO	MI	3,592.1
BERKSHIRE LIFE INS CO OF AMERICA	MA	3,640.3
FEDERATED LIFE INS CO	MN	1,497.0
GUARDIAN LIFE INS CO OF AMERICA	NY	44,890.2
PARKER CENTENNIAL ASR CO	WI	89.4
RESERVE NATIONAL INS CO	OK	112.1
SENTRY LIFE INS CO	WI	5,237.9
SHELTERPOINT LIFE INS CO	NY	104.4
UNITED FARM FAMILY LIFE INS CO	IN	2,129.9
USAA LIFE INS CO	TX	21,964.7
Rating: A-		
ALLSTATE ASR CO	IL	12.3
AMALGAMATED LIFE INS CO	NY	110.5
AMERICAN REPUBLIC INS CO	IA	797.6
ANTHEM LIFE INS CO	IN	559.7
BALBOA LIFE INS CO	CA	58.9
CENTRAL STATES H & L CO OF OMAHA	NE	407.1
CHARTER NATIONAL LIFE INS CO	IL	133.2
COMPANION LIFE INS CO	SC	274.9
COUNTRY INVESTORS LIFE ASR CO	IL	289.8
DEARBORN NATIONAL LIFE INS CO	IL	2,183.0
ERIE FAMILY LIFE INS CO	PA	2,077.0
FAMILY HERITAGE LIFE INS CO OF AMER	OH	725.3
FIDELITY INVESTMENTS LIFE INS CO	UT	23,882.2
GARDEN STATE LIFE INS CO	TX	120.3
GERBER LIFE INS CO	NY	2,749.8
ILLINOIS MUTUAL LIFE INS CO	IL	1,368.4
MASSACHUSETTS MUTUAL LIFE INS CO	MA	190,575.4
MIDWESTERN UNITED LIFE INS CO	IN	236.3
MML BAY STATE LIFE INS CO	CT	4,682.4
MUTUAL OF AMERICA LIFE INS CO	NY	17,110.0
NEW YORK LIFE INS CO	NY	143,501.4
NIPPON LIFE INS CO OF AMERICA	IA	211.7
NORTHWESTERN MUTUAL LIFE INS CO	WI	223,102.7
PACIFIC LIFE INS CO	NE	111,429.1
PHYSICIANS LIFE INS CO	NE	1,421.0
SHELTER LIFE INS CO	MO	1,108.6
STANDARD LIFE & ACCIDENT INS CO	TX	523.8
Rating: B+		
AETNA HEALTH & LIFE INS CO	CT	2,221.2
AETNA LIFE INS CO	CT	22,602.5
AMERICAN FAMILY LIFE ASR CO OF COLUM	NE	110,401.3
AMERICAN FIDELITY ASR CO	OK	4,856.7
AMERICAN UNITED LIFE INS CO	IN	22,778.8

INSURANCE COMPANY NAME	DOM. STATE	TOTAL ASSETS ($MIL)
ASSURITY LIFE INS CO	NE	2,452.3
BOSTON MUTUAL LIFE INS CO	MA	1,230.4
COLORADO BANKERS LIFE INS CO	CO	280.1
GENERAL RE LIFE CORP	CT	3,335.8
GOVERNMENT PERSONNEL MUTUAL L I C	TX	830.8
JACKSON NATIONAL LIFE INS CO	MI	176,820.4
LINCOLN BENEFIT LIFE CO	NE	12,911.3
MEDICO CORP LIFE INS CO	NE	26.0
MERIT LIFE INS CO	IN	584.3
MIDLAND NATIONAL LIFE INS CO	IA	40,607.9
MINNESOTA LIFE INS CO	MN	34,693.9
MUTUAL OF OMAHA INS CO	NE	6,568.9
NATIONAL BENEFIT LIFE INS CO	NY	480.5
NATIONAL FARMERS UNION LIFE INS CO	TX	216.9
NATIONAL WESTERN LIFE INS CO	CO	10,164.8
NEW YORK LIFE INS & ANNUITY CORP	DE	124,994.1
OHIO NATIONAL LIFE ASR CORP	OH	3,548.1
PACIFIC LIFE & ANNUITY CO	AZ	6,110.8
PARK AVENUE LIFE INS CO	DE	303.3
PIONEER MUTUAL LIFE INS CO	ND	510.6
PRINCIPAL LIFE INS CO	IA	148,782.3
SAVINGS BANK LIFE INS CO OF MA	MA	2,567.5
STANDARD INS CO	OR	19,885.1
SYMETRA LIFE INS CO	IA	28,794.9
THRIVENT LIFE INS CO	MN	3,530.2
TRUSTMARK INS CO	IL	1,404.5
TRUSTMARK LIFE INS CO	IL	370.8
UNITED WORLD LIFE INS CO	NE	114.3
USABLE LIFE	AR	432.6

Indiana

INSURANCE COMPANY NAME	DOM. STATE	TOTAL ASSETS ($MIL)

Rating: A+

INSURANCE COMPANY NAME	DOM. STATE	TOTAL ASSETS ($MIL)
AMERICAN FAMILY LIFE INS CO	WI	5,200.5
COUNTRY LIFE INS CO	IL	10,573.7
PHYSICIANS MUTUAL INS CO	NE	1,989.7
STATE FARM LIFE INS CO	IL	62,712.0
TEACHERS INS & ANNUITY ASN OF AM	NY	261,389.2

Rating: A

INSURANCE COMPANY NAME	DOM. STATE	TOTAL ASSETS ($MIL)
4 EVER LIFE INS CO	IL	200.3
AUTO-OWNERS LIFE INS CO	MI	3,592.1
BERKSHIRE LIFE INS CO OF AMERICA	MA	3,640.3
FEDERATED LIFE INS CO	MN	1,497.0
GUARDIAN LIFE INS CO OF AMERICA	NY	44,890.2
PARKER CENTENNIAL ASR CO	WI	89.4
RESERVE NATIONAL INS CO	OK	112.1
SENTRY LIFE INS CO	WI	5,237.9
UNITED FARM FAMILY LIFE INS CO	IN	2,129.9
USAA LIFE INS CO	TX	21,964.7

Rating: A-

INSURANCE COMPANY NAME	DOM. STATE	TOTAL ASSETS ($MIL)
ALLSTATE ASR CO	IL	12.3
AMALGAMATED LIFE INS CO	NY	110.5
AMERICAN REPUBLIC INS CO	IA	797.6
ANTHEM LIFE INS CO	IN	559.7
BALBOA LIFE INS CO	CA	58.9
CENTRAL STATES H & L CO OF OMAHA	NE	407.1
CHARTER NATIONAL LIFE INS CO	IL	133.2
COMPANION LIFE INS CO	SC	274.9
COUNTRY INVESTORS LIFE ASR CO	IL	289.8
DEARBORN NATIONAL LIFE INS CO	IL	2,183.0
ERIE FAMILY LIFE INS CO	PA	2,077.0
FAMILY HERITAGE LIFE INS CO OF AMER	OH	725.3
FIDELITY INVESTMENTS LIFE INS CO	UT	23,882.2
GARDEN STATE LIFE INS CO	TX	120.3
GERBER LIFE INS CO	NY	2,749.8
ILLINOIS MUTUAL LIFE INS CO	IL	1,368.4
MASSACHUSETTS MUTUAL LIFE INS CO	MA	190,575.4
MIDWESTERN UNITED LIFE INS CO	IN	236.3
MML BAY STATE LIFE INS CO	CT	4,682.4
MUTUAL OF AMERICA LIFE INS CO	NY	17,110.0
MUTUAL SAVINGS LIFE INS CO	AL	470.5
NEW YORK LIFE INS CO	NY	143,501.4
NIPPON LIFE INS CO OF AMERICA	IA	211.7
NORTHWESTERN MUTUAL LIFE INS CO	WI	223,102.7
PACIFIC LIFE INS CO	NE	111,429.1
PHYSICIANS LIFE INS CO	NE	1,421.0
SHELTER LIFE INS CO	MO	1,108.6
STANDARD LIFE & ACCIDENT INS CO	TX	523.8

Rating: B+

INSURANCE COMPANY NAME	DOM. STATE	TOTAL ASSETS ($MIL)
AETNA HEALTH & LIFE INS CO	CT	2,221.2
AETNA LIFE INS CO	CT	22,602.5
AMERICAN FAMILY LIFE ASR CO OF COLUM	NE	110,401.3
AMERICAN FIDELITY ASR CO	OK	4,856.7
AMERICAN UNITED LIFE INS CO	IN	22,778.8
ASSURITY LIFE INS CO	NE	2,452.3

INSURANCE COMPANY NAME	DOM. STATE	TOTAL ASSETS ($MIL)
BOSTON MUTUAL LIFE INS CO	MA	1,230.4
COLORADO BANKERS LIFE INS CO	CO	280.1
GENERAL RE LIFE CORP	CT	3,335.8
GOVERNMENT PERSONNEL MUTUAL L I C	TX	830.8
JACKSON NATIONAL LIFE INS CO	MI	176,820.4
LINCOLN BENEFIT LIFE CO	NE	12,911.3
MEDICO CORP LIFE INS CO	NE	26.0
MERIT LIFE INS CO	IN	584.3
MIDLAND NATIONAL LIFE INS CO	IA	40,607.9
MINNESOTA LIFE INS CO	MN	34,693.9
MUTUAL OF OMAHA INS CO	NE	6,568.9
NATIONAL BENEFIT LIFE INS CO	NY	480.5
NATIONAL FARMERS UNION LIFE INS CO	TX	216.9
NATIONAL WESTERN LIFE INS CO	CO	10,164.8
NEW YORK LIFE INS & ANNUITY CORP	DE	124,994.1
OHIO NATIONAL LIFE ASR CORP	OH	3,548.1
PACIFIC LIFE & ANNUITY CO	AZ	6,110.8
PARK AVENUE LIFE INS CO	DE	303.3
PIONEER MUTUAL LIFE INS CO	ND	510.6
PRINCIPAL LIFE INS CO	IA	148,782.3
SAVINGS BANK LIFE INS CO OF MA	MA	2,567.5
STANDARD INS CO	OR	19,885.1
SYMETRA LIFE INS CO	IA	28,794.9
THRIVENT LIFE INS CO	MN	3,530.2
TRUSTMARK INS CO	IL	1,404.5
TRUSTMARK LIFE INS CO	IL	370.8
UNITED WORLD LIFE INS CO	NE	114.3
USABLE LIFE	AR	432.6

Iowa

INSURANCE COMPANY NAME	DOM. STATE	TOTAL ASSETS ($MIL)	INSURANCE COMPANY NAME	DOM. STATE	TOTAL ASSETS ($MIL)
Rating: A+			FARM BUREAU LIFE INS CO	IA	8,042.3
			GENERAL RE LIFE CORP	CT	3,335.8
AMERICAN FAMILY LIFE INS CO	WI	5,200.5	GOVERNMENT PERSONNEL MUTUAL L I C	TX	830.8
COUNTRY LIFE INS CO	IL	10,573.7	JACKSON NATIONAL LIFE INS CO	MI	176,820.4
PHYSICIANS MUTUAL INS CO	NE	1,989.7	LINCOLN BENEFIT LIFE CO	NE	12,911.3
STATE FARM LIFE INS CO	IL	62,712.0	MEDICO CORP LIFE INS CO	NE	26.0
TEACHERS INS & ANNUITY ASN OF AM	NY	261,389.2	MERIT LIFE INS CO	IN	584.3
			MIDLAND NATIONAL LIFE INS CO	IA	40,607.9
Rating: A			MINNESOTA LIFE INS CO	MN	34,693.9
			MUTUAL OF OMAHA INS CO	NE	6,568.9
4 EVER LIFE INS CO	IL	200.3	NATIONAL BENEFIT LIFE INS CO	NY	480.5
AUTO-OWNERS LIFE INS CO	MI	3,592.1	NATIONAL FARMERS UNION LIFE INS CO	TX	216.9
BERKSHIRE LIFE INS CO OF AMERICA	MA	3,640.3	NATIONAL WESTERN LIFE INS CO	CO	10,164.8
FEDERATED LIFE INS CO	MN	1,497.0	NEW YORK LIFE INS & ANNUITY CORP	DE	124,994.1
GUARDIAN LIFE INS CO OF AMERICA	NY	44,890.2	OHIO NATIONAL LIFE ASR CORP	OH	3,548.1
PARKER CENTENNIAL ASR CO	WI	89.4	PACIFIC LIFE & ANNUITY CO	AZ	6,110.8
RESERVE NATIONAL INS CO	OK	112.1	PARK AVENUE LIFE INS CO	DE	303.3
SENTRY LIFE INS CO	WI	5,237.9	PIONEER MUTUAL LIFE INS CO	ND	510.6
USAA LIFE INS CO	TX	21,964.7	PRINCIPAL LIFE INS CO	IA	148,782.3
			SAVINGS BANK LIFE INS CO OF MA	MA	2,567.5
Rating: A-			STANDARD INS CO	OR	19,885.1
			SYMETRA LIFE INS CO	IA	28,794.9
ALLSTATE ASR CO	IL	12.3	THRIVENT LIFE INS CO	MN	3,530.2
AMALGAMATED LIFE INS CO	NY	110.5	TRUSTMARK INS CO	IL	1,404.5
AMERICAN REPUBLIC INS CO	IA	797.6	TRUSTMARK LIFE INS CO	IL	370.8
ANTHEM LIFE INS CO	IN	559.7	UNITED WORLD LIFE INS CO	NE	114.3
BALBOA LIFE INS CO	CA	58.9	USABLE LIFE	AR	432.6
CENTRAL STATES H & L CO OF OMAHA	NE	407.1			
CHARTER NATIONAL LIFE INS CO	IL	133.2			
COMPANION LIFE INS CO	SC	274.9			
COUNTRY INVESTORS LIFE ASR CO	IL	289.8			
DEARBORN NATIONAL LIFE INS CO	IL	2,183.0			
FAMILY HERITAGE LIFE INS CO OF AMER	OH	725.3			
FIDELITY INVESTMENTS LIFE INS CO	UT	23,882.2			
GARDEN STATE LIFE INS CO	TX	120.3			
GERBER LIFE INS CO	NY	2,749.8			
ILLINOIS MUTUAL LIFE INS CO	IL	1,368.4			
MASSACHUSETTS MUTUAL LIFE INS CO	MA	190,575.4			
MIDWESTERN UNITED LIFE INS CO	IN	236.3			
MML BAY STATE LIFE INS CO	CT	4,682.4			
MUTUAL OF AMERICA LIFE INS CO	NY	17,110.0			
NEW YORK LIFE INS CO	NY	143,501.4			
NIPPON LIFE INS CO OF AMERICA	IA	211.7			
NORTHWESTERN MUTUAL LIFE INS CO	WI	223,102.7			
PACIFIC GUARDIAN LIFE INS CO LTD	HI	511.7			
PACIFIC LIFE INS CO	NE	111,429.1			
PHYSICIANS LIFE INS CO	NE	1,421.0			
SHELTER LIFE INS CO	MO	1,108.6			
STANDARD LIFE & ACCIDENT INS CO	TX	523.8			
Rating: B+					
AETNA HEALTH & LIFE INS CO	CT	2,221.2			
AETNA LIFE INS CO	CT	22,602.5			
AMERICAN FAMILY LIFE ASR CO OF COLUM	NE	110,401.3			
AMERICAN FIDELITY ASR CO	OK	4,856.7			
AMERICAN UNITED LIFE INS CO	IN	22,778.8			
ASSURITY LIFE INS CO	NE	2,452.3			
BOSTON MUTUAL LIFE INS CO	MA	1,230.4			
COLORADO BANKERS LIFE INS CO	CO	280.1			

Kansas

INSURANCE COMPANY NAME	DOM. STATE	TOTAL ASSETS ($MIL)	INSURANCE COMPANY NAME	DOM. STATE	TOTAL ASSETS ($MIL)
			COLORADO BANKERS LIFE INS CO	CO	280.1
			FARM BUREAU LIFE INS CO	IA	8,042.3
Rating: A+			GENERAL RE LIFE CORP	CT	3,335.8
			GOVERNMENT PERSONNEL MUTUAL L I C	TX	830.8
AMERICAN FAMILY LIFE INS CO	WI	5,200.5	JACKSON NATIONAL LIFE INS CO	MI	176,820.4
COUNTRY LIFE INS CO	IL	10,573.7	LINCOLN BENEFIT LIFE CO	NE	12,911.3
PHYSICIANS MUTUAL INS CO	NE	1,989.7	MEDICO CORP LIFE INS CO	NE	26.0
STATE FARM LIFE INS CO	IL	62,712.0	MERIT LIFE INS CO	IN	584.3
TEACHERS INS & ANNUITY ASN OF AM	NY	261,389.2	MIDLAND NATIONAL LIFE INS CO	IA	40,607.9
			MINNESOTA LIFE INS CO	MN	34,693.9
Rating: A			MUTUAL OF OMAHA INS CO	NE	6,568.9
			NATIONAL BENEFIT LIFE INS CO	NY	480.5
4 EVER LIFE INS CO	IL	200.3	NATIONAL FARMERS UNION LIFE INS CO	TX	216.9
AUTO-OWNERS LIFE INS CO	MI	3,592.1	NATIONAL WESTERN LIFE INS CO	CO	10,164.8
BERKSHIRE LIFE INS CO OF AMERICA	MA	3,640.3	NEW YORK LIFE INS & ANNUITY CORP	DE	124,994.1
FEDERATED LIFE INS CO	MN	1,497.0	OHIO NATIONAL LIFE ASR CORP	OH	3,548.1
GUARDIAN LIFE INS CO OF AMERICA	NY	44,890.2	PACIFIC LIFE & ANNUITY CO	AZ	6,110.8
LIFEWISE ASR CO	WA	125.6	PARK AVENUE LIFE INS CO	DE	303.3
PARKER CENTENNIAL ASR CO	WI	89.4	PIONEER MUTUAL LIFE INS CO	ND	510.6
RESERVE NATIONAL INS CO	OK	112.1	PRINCIPAL LIFE INS CO	IA	148,782.3
SENTRY LIFE INS CO	WI	5,237.9	SAVINGS BANK LIFE INS CO OF MA	MA	2,567.5
USAA LIFE INS CO	TX	21,964.7	STANDARD INS CO	OR	19,885.1
			SYMETRA LIFE INS CO	IA	28,794.9
Rating: A-			THRIVENT LIFE INS CO	MN	3,530.2
			TRUSTMARK INS CO	IL	1,404.5
ALLSTATE ASR CO	IL	12.3	TRUSTMARK LIFE INS CO	IL	370.8
AMALGAMATED LIFE INS CO	NY	110.5	UNITED WORLD LIFE INS CO	NE	114.3
AMERICAN REPUBLIC INS CO	IA	797.6	USABLE LIFE	AR	432.6
ANTHEM LIFE INS CO	IN	559.7			
BALBOA LIFE INS CO	CA	58.9			
CENTRAL STATES H & L CO OF OMAHA	NE	407.1			
CHARTER NATIONAL LIFE INS CO	IL	133.2			
COMPANION LIFE INS CO	SC	274.9			
COUNTRY INVESTORS LIFE ASR CO	IL	289.8			
DEARBORN NATIONAL LIFE INS CO	IL	2,183.0			
FAMILY HERITAGE LIFE INS CO OF AMER	OH	725.3			
FIDELITY INVESTMENTS LIFE INS CO	UT	23,882.2			
GARDEN STATE LIFE INS CO	TX	120.3			
GERBER LIFE INS CO	NY	2,749.8			
ILLINOIS MUTUAL LIFE INS CO	IL	1,368.4			
MASSACHUSETTS MUTUAL LIFE INS CO	MA	190,575.4			
MIDWESTERN UNITED LIFE INS CO	IN	236.3			
MML BAY STATE LIFE INS CO	CT	4,682.4			
MUTUAL OF AMERICA LIFE INS CO	NY	17,110.0			
NEW YORK LIFE INS CO	NY	143,501.4			
NIPPON LIFE INS CO OF AMERICA	IA	211.7			
NORTHWESTERN MUTUAL LIFE INS CO	WI	223,102.7			
PACIFIC LIFE INS CO	NE	111,429.1			
PHYSICIANS LIFE INS CO	NE	1,421.0			
SHELTER LIFE INS CO	MO	1,108.6			
STANDARD LIFE & ACCIDENT INS CO	TX	523.8			
Rating: B+					
ADVANCE INS CO OF KS	KS	52.7			
AETNA HEALTH & LIFE INS CO	CT	2,221.2			
AETNA LIFE INS CO	CT	22,602.5			
AMERICAN FAMILY LIFE ASR CO OF COLUM	NE	110,401.3			
AMERICAN FIDELITY ASR CO	OK	4,856.7			
AMERICAN UNITED LIFE INS CO	IN	22,778.8			
ASSURITY LIFE INS CO	NE	2,452.3			
BOSTON MUTUAL LIFE INS CO	MA	1,230.4			

Kentucky

INSURANCE COMPANY NAME	DOM. STATE	TOTAL ASSETS ($MIL)

Rating: A+

INSURANCE COMPANY NAME	DOM. STATE	TOTAL ASSETS ($MIL)
COUNTRY LIFE INS CO	IL	10,573.7
PHYSICIANS MUTUAL INS CO	NE	1,989.7
STATE FARM LIFE INS CO	IL	62,712.0
TEACHERS INS & ANNUITY ASN OF AM	NY	261,389.2

Rating: A

INSURANCE COMPANY NAME	DOM. STATE	TOTAL ASSETS ($MIL)
4 EVER LIFE INS CO	IL	200.3
AUTO-OWNERS LIFE INS CO	MI	3,592.1
BERKSHIRE LIFE INS CO OF AMERICA	MA	3,640.3
FEDERATED LIFE INS CO	MN	1,497.0
GUARDIAN LIFE INS CO OF AMERICA	NY	44,890.2
PARKER CENTENNIAL ASR CO	WI	89.4
RESERVE NATIONAL INS CO	OK	112.1
SENTRY LIFE INS CO	WI	5,237.9
SOUTHERN FARM BUREAU LIFE INS CO	MS	12,937.4
USAA LIFE INS CO	TX	21,964.7

Rating: A-

INSURANCE COMPANY NAME	DOM. STATE	TOTAL ASSETS ($MIL)
ALLSTATE ASR CO	IL	12.3
AMALGAMATED LIFE INS CO	NY	110.5
AMERICAN REPUBLIC INS CO	IA	797.6
ANTHEM LIFE INS CO	IN	559.7
BALBOA LIFE INS CO	CA	58.9
CENTRAL STATES H & L CO OF OMAHA	NE	407.1
CHARTER NATIONAL LIFE INS CO	IL	133.2
COMPANION LIFE INS CO	SC	274.9
COTTON STATES LIFE INS CO	GA	330.7
COUNTRY INVESTORS LIFE ASR CO	IL	289.8
DEARBORN NATIONAL LIFE INS CO	IL	2,183.0
ERIE FAMILY LIFE INS CO	PA	2,077.0
FAMILY HERITAGE LIFE INS CO OF AMER	OH	725.3
FIDELITY INVESTMENTS LIFE INS CO	UT	23,882.2
GARDEN STATE LIFE INS CO	TX	120.3
GERBER LIFE INS CO	NY	2,749.8
ILLINOIS MUTUAL LIFE INS CO	IL	1,368.4
LIFE INS CO OF ALABAMA	AL	112.0
MASSACHUSETTS MUTUAL LIFE INS CO	MA	190,575.4
MIDWESTERN UNITED LIFE INS CO	IN	236.3
MML BAY STATE LIFE INS CO	CT	4,682.4
MUTUAL OF AMERICA LIFE INS CO	NY	17,110.0
NEW YORK LIFE INS CO	NY	143,501.4
NIPPON LIFE INS CO OF AMERICA	IA	211.7
NORTHWESTERN MUTUAL LIFE INS CO	WI	223,102.7
PACIFIC LIFE INS CO	NE	111,429.1
PHYSICIANS LIFE INS CO	NE	1,421.0
SHELTER LIFE INS CO	MO	1,108.6
STANDARD LIFE & ACCIDENT INS CO	TX	523.8

Rating: B+

INSURANCE COMPANY NAME	DOM. STATE	TOTAL ASSETS ($MIL)
AETNA HEALTH & LIFE INS CO	CT	2,221.2
AETNA LIFE INS CO	CT	22,602.5
AMERICAN FAMILY LIFE ASR CO OF COLUM	NE	110,401.3
AMERICAN FIDELITY ASR CO	OK	4,856.7
AMERICAN UNITED LIFE INS CO	IN	22,778.8
ASSURITY LIFE INS CO	NE	2,452.3
BOSTON MUTUAL LIFE INS CO	MA	1,230.4
COLORADO BANKERS LIFE INS CO	CO	280.1
GENERAL RE LIFE CORP	CT	3,335.8
GOVERNMENT PERSONNEL MUTUAL L I C	TX	830.8
JACKSON NATIONAL LIFE INS CO	MI	176,820.4
LINCOLN BENEFIT LIFE CO	NE	12,911.3
MEDICO CORP LIFE INS CO	NE	26.0
MERIT LIFE INS CO	IN	584.3
MIDLAND NATIONAL LIFE INS CO	IA	40,607.9
MINNESOTA LIFE INS CO	MN	34,693.9
MUTUAL OF OMAHA INS CO	NE	6,568.9
NATIONAL BENEFIT LIFE INS CO	NY	480.5
NATIONAL FARMERS UNION LIFE INS CO	TX	216.9
NATIONAL WESTERN LIFE INS CO	CO	10,164.8
NEW YORK LIFE INS & ANNUITY CORP	DE	124,994.1
OHIO NATIONAL LIFE ASR CORP	OH	3,548.1
PACIFIC LIFE & ANNUITY CO	AZ	6,110.8
PARK AVENUE LIFE INS CO	DE	303.3
PIONEER MUTUAL LIFE INS CO	ND	510.6
PRINCIPAL LIFE INS CO	IA	148,782.3
SAVINGS BANK LIFE INS CO OF MA	MA	2,567.5
STANDARD INS CO	OR	19,885.1
SYMETRA LIFE INS CO	IA	28,794.9
THRIVENT LIFE INS CO	MN	3,530.2
TRUSTMARK INS CO	IL	1,404.5
TRUSTMARK LIFE INS CO	IL	370.8
UNITED WORLD LIFE INS CO	NE	114.3
USABLE LIFE	AR	432.6

Louisiana

INSURANCE COMPANY NAME	DOM. STATE	TOTAL ASSETS ($MIL)

Rating: A+

INSURANCE COMPANY NAME	DOM. STATE	TOTAL ASSETS ($MIL)
COUNTRY LIFE INS CO	IL	10,573.7
PHYSICIANS MUTUAL INS CO	NE	1,989.7
STATE FARM LIFE INS CO	IL	62,712.0
TEACHERS INS & ANNUITY ASN OF AM	NY	261,389.2

Rating: A

INSURANCE COMPANY NAME	DOM. STATE	TOTAL ASSETS ($MIL)
4 EVER LIFE INS CO	IL	200.3
BERKSHIRE LIFE INS CO OF AMERICA	MA	3,640.3
FEDERATED LIFE INS CO	MN	1,497.0
GUARDIAN LIFE INS CO OF AMERICA	NY	44,890.2
PARKER CENTENNIAL ASR CO	WI	89.4
RESERVE NATIONAL INS CO	OK	112.1
SENTRY LIFE INS CO	WI	5,237.9
SOUTHERN FARM BUREAU LIFE INS CO	MS	12,937.4
USAA LIFE INS CO	TX	21,964.7

Rating: A-

INSURANCE COMPANY NAME	DOM. STATE	TOTAL ASSETS ($MIL)
ALLSTATE ASR CO	IL	12.3
AMALGAMATED LIFE INS CO	NY	110.5
AMERICAN REPUBLIC INS CO	IA	797.6
ANTHEM LIFE INS CO	IN	559.7
BALBOA LIFE INS CO	CA	58.9
CENTRAL STATES H & L CO OF OMAHA	NE	407.1
CHARTER NATIONAL LIFE INS CO	IL	133.2
COMPANION LIFE INS CO	SC	274.9
COTTON STATES LIFE INS CO	GA	330.7
COUNTRY INVESTORS LIFE ASR CO	IL	289.8
DEARBORN NATIONAL LIFE INS CO	IL	2,183.0
FAMILY HERITAGE LIFE INS CO OF AMER	OH	725.3
FIDELITY INVESTMENTS LIFE INS CO	UT	23,882.2
GARDEN STATE LIFE INS CO	TX	120.3
GERBER LIFE INS CO	NY	2,749.8
ILLINOIS MUTUAL LIFE INS CO	IL	1,368.4
LIFE INS CO OF ALABAMA	AL	112.0
MASSACHUSETTS MUTUAL LIFE INS CO	MA	190,575.4
MIDWESTERN UNITED LIFE INS CO	IN	236.3
MML BAY STATE LIFE INS CO	CT	4,682.4
MUTUAL OF AMERICA LIFE INS CO	NY	17,110.0
MUTUAL SAVINGS LIFE INS CO	AL	470.5
NEW YORK LIFE INS CO	NY	143,501.4
NIPPON LIFE INS CO OF AMERICA	IA	211.7
NORTHWESTERN MUTUAL LIFE INS CO	WI	223,102.7
PACIFIC GUARDIAN LIFE INS CO LTD	HI	511.7
PACIFIC LIFE INS CO	NE	111,429.1
PHYSICIANS LIFE INS CO	NE	1,421.0
SHELTER LIFE INS CO	MO	1,108.6
STANDARD LIFE & ACCIDENT INS CO	TX	523.8

Rating: B+

INSURANCE COMPANY NAME	DOM. STATE	TOTAL ASSETS ($MIL)
AETNA HEALTH & LIFE INS CO	CT	2,221.2
AETNA LIFE INS CO	CT	22,602.5
AMERICAN FAMILY LIFE ASR CO OF COLUM	NE	110,401.3
AMERICAN FIDELITY ASR CO	OK	4,856.7
AMERICAN UNITED LIFE INS CO	IN	22,778.8
ASSURITY LIFE INS CO	NE	2,452.3

INSURANCE COMPANY NAME	DOM. STATE	TOTAL ASSETS ($MIL)
BLUEBONNET LIFE INS CO	MS	54.6
BOSTON MUTUAL LIFE INS CO	MA	1,230.4
COLORADO BANKERS LIFE INS CO	CO	280.1
GENERAL RE LIFE CORP	CT	3,335.8
GOVERNMENT PERSONNEL MUTUAL L I C	TX	830.8
JACKSON NATIONAL LIFE INS CO	MI	176,820.4
LINCOLN BENEFIT LIFE CO	NE	12,911.3
MEDICO CORP LIFE INS CO	NE	26.0
MERIT LIFE INS CO	IN	584.3
MIDLAND NATIONAL LIFE INS CO	IA	40,607.9
MINNESOTA LIFE INS CO	MN	34,693.9
MUTUAL OF OMAHA INS CO	NE	6,568.9
NATIONAL BENEFIT LIFE INS CO	NY	480.5
NATIONAL WESTERN LIFE INS CO	CO	10,164.8
NEW YORK LIFE INS & ANNUITY CORP	DE	124,994.1
OHIO NATIONAL LIFE ASR CORP	OH	3,548.1
PACIFIC LIFE & ANNUITY CO	AZ	6,110.8
PARK AVENUE LIFE INS CO	DE	303.3
PIONEER MUTUAL LIFE INS CO	ND	510.6
PRINCIPAL LIFE INS CO	IA	148,782.3
SAVINGS BANK LIFE INS CO OF MA	MA	2,567.5
STANDARD INS CO	OR	19,885.1
SYMETRA LIFE INS CO	IA	28,794.9
THRIVENT LIFE INS CO	MN	3,530.2
TRUSTMARK INS CO	IL	1,404.5
TRUSTMARK LIFE INS CO	IL	370.8
UNITED WORLD LIFE INS CO	NE	114.3
USABLE LIFE	AR	432.6

Maine

INSURANCE COMPANY NAME	DOM. STATE	TOTAL ASSETS ($MIL)
Rating: A+		
COUNTRY LIFE INS CO	IL	10,573.7
PHYSICIANS MUTUAL INS CO	NE	1,989.7
STATE FARM LIFE INS CO	IL	62,712.0
TEACHERS INS & ANNUITY ASN OF AM	NY	261,389.2
Rating: A		
4 EVER LIFE INS CO	IL	200.3
BERKSHIRE LIFE INS CO OF AMERICA	MA	3,640.3
FEDERATED LIFE INS CO	MN	1,497.0
GUARDIAN LIFE INS CO OF AMERICA	NY	44,890.2
PARKER CENTENNIAL ASR CO	WI	89.4
RESERVE NATIONAL INS CO	OK	112.1
SENTRY LIFE INS CO	WI	5,237.9
USAA LIFE INS CO	TX	21,964.7
Rating: A-		
ALLSTATE ASR CO	IL	12.3
AMALGAMATED LIFE INS CO	NY	110.5
AMERICAN REPUBLIC INS CO	IA	797.6
ANTHEM LIFE INS CO	IN	559.7
BALBOA LIFE INS CO	CA	58.9
CENTRAL STATES H & L CO OF OMAHA	NE	407.1
CHARTER NATIONAL LIFE INS CO	IL	133.2
COMPANION LIFE INS CO	SC	274.9
COUNTRY INVESTORS LIFE ASR CO	IL	289.8
DEARBORN NATIONAL LIFE INS CO	IL	2,183.0
FAMILY HERITAGE LIFE INS CO OF AMER	OH	725.3
FIDELITY INVESTMENTS LIFE INS CO	UT	23,882.2
GARDEN STATE LIFE INS CO	TX	120.3
GERBER LIFE INS CO	NY	2,749.8
ILLINOIS MUTUAL LIFE INS CO	IL	1,368.4
MASSACHUSETTS MUTUAL LIFE INS CO	MA	190,575.4
MIDWESTERN UNITED LIFE INS CO	IN	236.3
MML BAY STATE LIFE INS CO	CT	4,682.4
MUTUAL OF AMERICA LIFE INS CO	NY	17,110.0
NEW YORK LIFE INS CO	NY	143,501.4
NORTHWESTERN MUTUAL LIFE INS CO	WI	223,102.7
PACIFIC LIFE INS CO	NE	111,429.1
PHYSICIANS LIFE INS CO	NE	1,421.0
Rating: B+		
AETNA HEALTH & LIFE INS CO	CT	2,221.2
AETNA LIFE INS CO	CT	22,602.5
AMERICAN FAMILY LIFE ASR CO OF COLUM	NE	110,401.3
AMERICAN FIDELITY ASR CO	OK	4,856.7
AMERICAN UNITED LIFE INS CO	IN	22,778.8
ASSURITY LIFE INS CO	NE	2,452.3
BOSTON MUTUAL LIFE INS CO	MA	1,230.4
COLORADO BANKERS LIFE INS CO	CO	280.1
GENERAL RE LIFE CORP	CT	3,335.8
GOVERNMENT PERSONNEL MUTUAL L I C	TX	830.8
JACKSON NATIONAL LIFE INS CO	MI	176,820.4
LINCOLN BENEFIT LIFE CO	NE	12,911.3
MEDICO CORP LIFE INS CO	NE	26.0
MERIT LIFE INS CO	IN	584.3

INSURANCE COMPANY NAME	DOM. STATE	TOTAL ASSETS ($MIL)
MIDLAND NATIONAL LIFE INS CO	IA	40,607.9
MINNESOTA LIFE INS CO	MN	34,693.9
MUTUAL OF OMAHA INS CO	NE	6,568.9
NATIONAL BENEFIT LIFE INS CO	NY	480.5
NATIONAL WESTERN LIFE INS CO	CO	10,164.8
NEW YORK LIFE INS & ANNUITY CORP	DE	124,994.1
OHIO NATIONAL LIFE ASR CORP	OH	3,548.1
PACIFIC LIFE & ANNUITY CO	AZ	6,110.8
PARK AVENUE LIFE INS CO	DE	303.3
PIONEER MUTUAL LIFE INS CO	ND	510.6
PRINCIPAL LIFE INS CO	IA	148,782.3
SAVINGS BANK LIFE INS CO OF MA	MA	2,567.5
STANDARD INS CO	OR	19,885.1
SYMETRA LIFE INS CO	IA	28,794.9
TRUSTMARK INS CO	IL	1,404.5
TRUSTMARK LIFE INS CO	IL	370.8
UNITED WORLD LIFE INS CO	NE	114.3
USABLE LIFE	AR	432.6

Maryland

INSURANCE COMPANY NAME	DOM. STATE	TOTAL ASSETS ($MIL)
Rating: A+		
COUNTRY LIFE INS CO	IL	10,573.7
PHYSICIANS MUTUAL INS CO	NE	1,989.7
STATE FARM LIFE INS CO	IL	62,712.0
TEACHERS INS & ANNUITY ASN OF AM	NY	261,389.2
Rating: A		
4 EVER LIFE INS CO	IL	200.3
BERKSHIRE LIFE INS CO OF AMERICA	MA	3,640.3
FEDERATED LIFE INS CO	MN	1,497.0
GUARDIAN LIFE INS CO OF AMERICA	NY	44,890.2
PARKER CENTENNIAL ASR CO	WI	89.4
RESERVE NATIONAL INS CO	OK	112.1
SENTRY LIFE INS CO	WI	5,237.9
SHELTERPOINT LIFE INS CO	NY	104.4
UNITED FARM FAMILY LIFE INS CO	IN	2,129.9
USAA LIFE INS CO	TX	21,964.7
Rating: A-		
ALLSTATE ASR CO	IL	12.3
AMALGAMATED LIFE INS CO	NY	110.5
AMERICAN REPUBLIC INS CO	IA	797.6
ANTHEM LIFE INS CO	IN	559.7
BALBOA LIFE INS CO	CA	58.9
CENTRAL STATES H & L CO OF OMAHA	NE	407.1
CHARTER NATIONAL LIFE INS CO	IL	133.2
COMPANION LIFE INS CO	SC	274.9
COUNTRY INVESTORS LIFE ASR CO	IL	289.8
DEARBORN NATIONAL LIFE INS CO	IL	2,183.0
ERIE FAMILY LIFE INS CO	PA	2,077.0
FAMILY HERITAGE LIFE INS CO OF AMER	OH	725.3
FIDELITY INVESTMENTS LIFE INS CO	UT	23,882.2
GARDEN STATE LIFE INS CO	TX	120.3
GERBER LIFE INS CO	NY	2,749.8
ILLINOIS MUTUAL LIFE INS CO	IL	1,368.4
MASSACHUSETTS MUTUAL LIFE INS CO	MA	190,575.4
MIDWESTERN UNITED LIFE INS CO	IN	236.3
MML BAY STATE LIFE INS CO	CT	4,682.4
MUTUAL OF AMERICA LIFE INS CO	NY	17,110.0
NEW YORK LIFE INS CO	NY	143,501.4
NIPPON LIFE INS CO OF AMERICA	IA	211.7
NORTHWESTERN MUTUAL LIFE INS CO	WI	223,102.7
PACIFIC LIFE INS CO	NE	111,429.1
PHYSICIANS LIFE INS CO	NE	1,421.0
STANDARD LIFE & ACCIDENT INS CO	TX	523.8
Rating: B+		
AETNA HEALTH & LIFE INS CO	CT	2,221.2
AETNA LIFE INS CO	CT	22,602.5
AMERICAN FAMILY LIFE ASR CO OF COLUM	NE	110,401.3
AMERICAN FIDELITY ASR CO	OK	4,856.7
AMERICAN UNITED LIFE INS CO	IN	22,778.8
ASSURITY LIFE INS CO	NE	2,452.3
BOSTON MUTUAL LIFE INS CO	MA	1,230.4
COLORADO BANKERS LIFE INS CO	CO	280.1
GENERAL RE LIFE CORP	CT	3,335.8

INSURANCE COMPANY NAME	DOM. STATE	TOTAL ASSETS ($MIL)
GOVERNMENT PERSONNEL MUTUAL L I C	TX	830.8
JACKSON NATIONAL LIFE INS CO	MI	176,820.4
LINCOLN BENEFIT LIFE CO	NE	12,911.3
MEDICO CORP LIFE INS CO	NE	26.0
MERIT LIFE INS CO	IN	584.3
MIDLAND NATIONAL LIFE INS CO	IA	40,607.9
MINNESOTA LIFE INS CO	MN	34,693.9
MUTUAL OF OMAHA INS CO	NE	6,568.9
NATIONAL BENEFIT LIFE INS CO	NY	480.5
NATIONAL WESTERN LIFE INS CO	CO	10,164.5
NEW YORK LIFE INS & ANNUITY CORP	DE	124,994.1
OHIO NATIONAL LIFE ASR CORP	OH	3,548.1
PACIFIC LIFE & ANNUITY CO	AZ	6,110.8
PARK AVENUE LIFE INS CO	DE	303.3
PIONEER MUTUAL LIFE INS CO	ND	510.6
PRINCIPAL LIFE INS CO	IA	148,782.3
SAVINGS BANK LIFE INS CO OF MA	MA	2,567.5
STANDARD INS CO	OR	19,885.1
SYMETRA LIFE INS CO	IA	28,794.9
THRIVENT LIFE INS CO	MN	3,530.2
TRUSTMARK INS CO	IL	1,404.5
TRUSTMARK LIFE INS CO	IL	370.8
UNITED WORLD LIFE INS CO	NE	114.3
USABLE LIFE	AR	432.6

Massachusetts

INSURANCE COMPANY NAME	DOM. STATE	TOTAL ASSETS ($MIL)

Rating: A+

INSURANCE COMPANY NAME	DOM. STATE	TOTAL ASSETS ($MIL)
COUNTRY LIFE INS CO	IL	10,573.7
PHYSICIANS MUTUAL INS CO	NE	1,989.7
TEACHERS INS & ANNUITY ASN OF AM	NY	261,389.2

Rating: A

INSURANCE COMPANY NAME	DOM. STATE	TOTAL ASSETS ($MIL)
4 EVER LIFE INS CO	IL	200.3
BERKSHIRE LIFE INS CO OF AMERICA	MA	3,640.3
FEDERATED LIFE INS CO	MN	1,497.0
GUARDIAN LIFE INS CO OF AMERICA	NY	44,890.2
PARKER CENTENNIAL ASR CO	WI	89.4
SENTRY LIFE INS CO	WI	5,237.9
SHELTERPOINT LIFE INS CO	NY	104.4
UNITED FARM FAMILY LIFE INS CO	IN	2,129.9
USAA LIFE INS CO	TX	21,964.7

Rating: A-

INSURANCE COMPANY NAME	DOM. STATE	TOTAL ASSETS ($MIL)
ALLSTATE ASR CO	IL	12.3
AMALGAMATED LIFE INS CO	NY	110.5
AMERICAN FAMILY LIFE ASR CO OF NY	NY	710.2
AMERICAN REPUBLIC INS CO	IA	797.6
ANTHEM LIFE INS CO	IN	559.7
BALBOA LIFE INS CO	CA	58.9
CENTRAL STATES H & L CO OF OMAHA	NE	407.1
CHARTER NATIONAL LIFE INS CO	IL	133.2
COMPANION LIFE INS CO	SC	274.9
COUNTRY INVESTORS LIFE ASR CO	IL	289.8
DEARBORN NATIONAL LIFE INS CO	IL	2,183.0
FAMILY HERITAGE LIFE INS CO OF AMER	OH	725.3
FIDELITY INVESTMENTS LIFE INS CO	UT	23,882.2
GARDEN STATE LIFE INS CO	TX	120.3
GERBER LIFE INS CO	NY	2,749.8
ILLINOIS MUTUAL LIFE INS CO	IL	1,368.4
MASSACHUSETTS MUTUAL LIFE INS CO	MA	190,575.4
MIDWESTERN UNITED LIFE INS CO	IN	236.3
MML BAY STATE LIFE INS CO	CT	4,682.4
MUTUAL OF AMERICA LIFE INS CO	NY	17,110.0
NEW YORK LIFE INS CO	NY	143,501.4
NIPPON LIFE INS CO OF AMERICA	IA	211.7
NORTHWESTERN MUTUAL LIFE INS CO	WI	223,102.7
PACIFIC LIFE INS CO	NE	111,429.1
PHYSICIANS LIFE INS CO	NE	1,421.0
STANDARD LIFE & ACCIDENT INS CO	TX	523.8

Rating: B+

INSURANCE COMPANY NAME	DOM. STATE	TOTAL ASSETS ($MIL)
AETNA HEALTH & LIFE INS CO	CT	2,221.2
AETNA LIFE INS CO	CT	22,602.5
AMERICAN FAMILY LIFE ASR CO OF COLUM	NE	110,401.3
AMERICAN FIDELITY ASR CO	OK	4,856.7
AMERICAN UNITED LIFE INS CO	IN	22,778.8
ASSURITY LIFE INS CO	NE	2,452.3
BOSTON MUTUAL LIFE INS CO	MA	1,230.4
COLORADO BANKERS LIFE INS CO	CO	280.1
GENERAL RE LIFE CORP	CT	3,335.8
GOVERNMENT PERSONNEL MUTUAL L I C	TX	830.8
JACKSON NATIONAL LIFE INS CO	MI	176,820.4

INSURANCE COMPANY NAME	DOM. STATE	TOTAL ASSETS ($MIL)
LINCOLN BENEFIT LIFE CO	NE	12,911.3
MIDLAND NATIONAL LIFE INS CO	IA	40,607.9
MINNESOTA LIFE INS CO	MN	34,693.9
MUTUAL OF OMAHA INS CO	NE	6,568.9
NATIONAL BENEFIT LIFE INS CO	NY	480.5
NATIONAL WESTERN LIFE INS CO	CO	10,164.8
NEW YORK LIFE INS & ANNUITY CORP	DE	124,994.1
OHIO NATIONAL LIFE ASR CORP	OH	3,548.1
PACIFIC LIFE & ANNUITY CO	AZ	6,110.8
PARK AVENUE LIFE INS CO	DE	303.3
PIONEER MUTUAL LIFE INS CO	ND	510.6
PRINCIPAL LIFE INS CO	IA	148,782.3
SAVINGS BANK LIFE INS CO OF MA	MA	2,567.5
STANDARD INS CO	OR	19,885.1
SYMETRA LIFE INS CO	IA	28,794.9
TRUSTMARK INS CO	IL	1,404.5
TRUSTMARK LIFE INS CO	IL	370.8
UNITED WORLD LIFE INS CO	NE	114.3
USABLE LIFE	AR	432.6

Michigan

INSURANCE COMPANY NAME	DOM. STATE	TOTAL ASSETS ($MIL)

Rating: A+

INSURANCE COMPANY NAME	DOM. STATE	TOTAL ASSETS ($MIL)
AMERICAN FAMILY LIFE INS CO	WI	5,200.5
COUNTRY LIFE INS CO	IL	10,573.7
PHYSICIANS MUTUAL INS CO	NE	1,989.7
STATE FARM LIFE INS CO	IL	62,712.0
TEACHERS INS & ANNUITY ASN OF AM	NY	261,389.2

Rating: A

INSURANCE COMPANY NAME	DOM. STATE	TOTAL ASSETS ($MIL)
4 EVER LIFE INS CO	IL	200.3
AUTO-OWNERS LIFE INS CO	MI	3,592.1
BERKSHIRE LIFE INS CO OF AMERICA	MA	3,640.3
FEDERATED LIFE INS CO	MN	1,497.0
GUARDIAN LIFE INS CO OF AMERICA	NY	44,890.2
PARKER CENTENNIAL ASR CO	WI	89.4
RESERVE NATIONAL INS CO	OK	112.1
SENTRY LIFE INS CO	WI	5,237.9
SHELTERPOINT LIFE INS CO	NY	104.4
USAA LIFE INS CO	TX	21,964.7

Rating: A-

INSURANCE COMPANY NAME	DOM. STATE	TOTAL ASSETS ($MIL)
ALLSTATE ASR CO	IL	12.3
AMALGAMATED LIFE INS CO	NY	110.5
AMERICAN REPUBLIC INS CO	IA	797.6
ANTHEM LIFE INS CO	IN	559.7
BALBOA LIFE INS CO	CA	58.9
CENTRAL STATES H & L CO OF OMAHA	NE	407.1
CHARTER NATIONAL LIFE INS CO	IL	133.2
COMPANION LIFE INS CO	SC	274.9
COUNTRY INVESTORS LIFE ASR CO	IL	289.8
DEARBORN NATIONAL LIFE INS CO	IL	2,183.0
FAMILY HERITAGE LIFE INS CO OF AMER	OH	725.3
FARM BUREAU LIFE INS CO OF MICHIGAN	MI	2,356.3
FIDELITY INVESTMENTS LIFE INS CO	UT	23,882.2
GARDEN STATE LIFE INS CO	TX	120.3
GERBER LIFE INS CO	NY	2,749.8
ILLINOIS MUTUAL LIFE INS CO	IL	1,368.4
MASSACHUSETTS MUTUAL LIFE INS CO	MA	190,575.4
MIDWESTERN UNITED LIFE INS CO	IN	236.3
MML BAY STATE LIFE INS CO	CT	4,682.4
MUTUAL OF AMERICA LIFE INS CO	NY	17,110.0
NEW YORK LIFE INS CO	NY	143,501.4
NIPPON LIFE INS CO OF AMERICA	IA	211.7
NORTHWESTERN MUTUAL LIFE INS CO	WI	223,102.7
PACIFIC LIFE INS CO	NE	111,429.1
PHYSICIANS LIFE INS CO	NE	1,421.0
STANDARD LIFE & ACCIDENT INS CO	TX	523.8

Rating: B+

INSURANCE COMPANY NAME	DOM. STATE	TOTAL ASSETS ($MIL)
AETNA HEALTH & LIFE INS CO	CT	2,221.2
AETNA LIFE INS CO	CT	22,602.5
AMERICAN FAMILY LIFE ASR CO OF COLUM	NE	110,401.3
AMERICAN FIDELITY ASR CO	OK	4,856.7
AMERICAN UNITED LIFE INS CO	IN	22,778.8
ASSURITY LIFE INS CO	NE	2,452.3
BOSTON MUTUAL LIFE INS CO	MA	1,230.4
COLORADO BANKERS LIFE INS CO	CO	280.1

INSURANCE COMPANY NAME	DOM. STATE	TOTAL ASSETS ($MIL)
GENERAL RE LIFE CORP	CT	3,335.8
GOVERNMENT PERSONNEL MUTUAL L I C	TX	830.8
JACKSON NATIONAL LIFE INS CO	MI	176,820.4
LINCOLN BENEFIT LIFE CO	NE	12,911.3
LOCOMOTIVE ENGRS&COND MUT PROT ASSN	MI	55.4
MEDICO CORP LIFE INS CO	NE	26.0
MERIT LIFE INS CO	IN	584.3
MIDLAND NATIONAL LIFE INS CO	IA	40,607.9
MINNESOTA LIFE INS CO	MN	34,693.9
MUTUAL OF OMAHA INS CO	NE	6,568.9
NATIONAL BENEFIT LIFE INS CO	NY	480.5
NATIONAL FARMERS UNION LIFE INS CO	TX	216.9
NATIONAL WESTERN LIFE INS CO	CO	10,164.8
NEW YORK LIFE INS & ANNUITY CORP	DE	124,994.1
OHIO NATIONAL LIFE ASR CORP	OH	3,548.1
PACIFIC LIFE & ANNUITY CO	AZ	6,110.8
PARK AVENUE LIFE INS CO	DE	303.3
PIONEER MUTUAL LIFE INS CO	ND	510.6
PRINCIPAL LIFE INS CO	IA	148,782.3
SAVINGS BANK LIFE INS CO OF MA	MA	2,567.5
STANDARD INS CO	OR	19,885.1
SYMETRA LIFE INS CO	IA	28,794.9
THRIVENT LIFE INS CO	MN	3,530.2
TRUSTMARK INS CO	IL	1,404.5
TRUSTMARK LIFE INS CO	IL	370.8
UNITED WORLD LIFE INS CO	NE	114.3
USABLE LIFE	AR	432.6

Minnesota

INSURANCE COMPANY NAME	DOM. STATE	TOTAL ASSETS ($MIL)	INSURANCE COMPANY NAME	DOM. STATE	TOTAL ASSETS ($MIL)
			GENERAL RE LIFE CORP	CT	3,335.8
			GOVERNMENT PERSONNEL MUTUAL L I C	TX	830.8
Rating: A+			JACKSON NATIONAL LIFE INS CO	MI	176,820.4
			LINCOLN BENEFIT LIFE CO	NE	12,911.3
AMERICAN FAMILY LIFE INS CO	WI	5,200.5	MEDICO CORP LIFE INS CO	NE	26.0
COUNTRY LIFE INS CO	IL	10,573.7	MERIT LIFE INS CO	IN	584.3
PHYSICIANS MUTUAL INS CO	NE	1,989.7	MIDLAND NATIONAL LIFE INS CO	IA	40,607.9
STATE FARM LIFE INS CO	IL	62,712.0	MINNESOTA LIFE INS CO	MN	34,693.9
TEACHERS INS & ANNUITY ASN OF AM	NY	261,389.2	MUTUAL OF OMAHA INS CO	NE	6,568.9
			NATIONAL BENEFIT LIFE INS CO	NY	480.5
Rating: A			NATIONAL FARMERS UNION LIFE INS CO	TX	216.9
			NATIONAL WESTERN LIFE INS CO	CO	10,164.8
4 EVER LIFE INS CO	IL	200.3	NEW YORK LIFE INS & ANNUITY CORP	DE	124,994.1
AUTO-OWNERS LIFE INS CO	MI	3,592.1	OHIO NATIONAL LIFE ASR CORP	OH	3,548.1
BERKSHIRE LIFE INS CO OF AMERICA	MA	3,640.3	PACIFIC LIFE & ANNUITY CO	AZ	6,110.8
FEDERATED LIFE INS CO	MN	1,497.0	PARK AVENUE LIFE INS CO	DE	303.3
GUARDIAN LIFE INS CO OF AMERICA	NY	44,890.2	PIONEER MUTUAL LIFE INS CO	ND	510.6
PARKER CENTENNIAL ASR CO	WI	89.4	PRINCIPAL LIFE INS CO	IA	148,782.3
SENTRY LIFE INS CO	WI	5,237.9	SAVINGS BANK LIFE INS CO OF MA	MA	2,567.5
SHELTERPOINT LIFE INS CO	NY	104.4	SENTRY LIFE INS CO OF NEW YORK	NY	76.3
USAA LIFE INS CO	TX	21,964.7	STANDARD INS CO	OR	19,885.1
			SYMETRA LIFE INS CO	IA	28,794.9
Rating: A-			THRIVENT LIFE INS CO	MN	3,530.2
			TRUSTMARK INS CO	IL	1,404.5
ALLSTATE ASR CO	IL	12.3	TRUSTMARK LIFE INS CO	IL	370.8
AMALGAMATED LIFE INS CO	NY	110.5	UNITED WORLD LIFE INS CO	NE	114.3
AMERICAN REPUBLIC INS CO	IA	797.6	USABLE LIFE	AR	432.6
ANTHEM LIFE INS CO	IN	559.7			
BALBOA LIFE INS CO	CA	58.9			
CENTRAL STATES H & L CO OF OMAHA	NE	407.1			
CHARTER NATIONAL LIFE INS CO	IL	133.2			
COMPANION LIFE INS CO	SC	274.9			
COUNTRY INVESTORS LIFE ASR CO	IL	289.8			
DEARBORN NATIONAL LIFE INS CO	IL	2,183.0			
ERIE FAMILY LIFE INS CO	PA	2,077.0			
FAMILY HERITAGE LIFE INS CO OF AMER	OH	725.3			
FIDELITY INVESTMENTS LIFE INS CO	UT	23,882.2			
GARDEN STATE LIFE INS CO	TX	120.3			
GERBER LIFE INS CO	NY	2,749.8			
ILLINOIS MUTUAL LIFE INS CO	IL	1,368.4			
MASSACHUSETTS MUTUAL LIFE INS CO	MA	190,575.4			
MIDWESTERN UNITED LIFE INS CO	IN	236.3			
MML BAY STATE LIFE INS CO	CT	4,682.4			
MUTUAL OF AMERICA LIFE INS CO	NY	17,110.0			
NEW YORK LIFE INS CO	NY	143,501.4			
NIPPON LIFE INS CO OF AMERICA	IA	211.7			
NORTHWESTERN MUTUAL LIFE INS CO	WI	223,102.7			
PACIFIC LIFE INS CO	NE	111,429.1			
PHYSICIANS LIFE INS CO	NE	1,421.0			
STANDARD LIFE & ACCIDENT INS CO	TX	523.8			
Rating: B+					
AETNA HEALTH & LIFE INS CO	CT	2,221.2			
AETNA LIFE INS CO	CT	22,602.5			
AMERICAN FAMILY LIFE ASR CO OF COLUM	NE	110,401.3			
AMERICAN FIDELITY ASR CO	OK	4,856.7			
AMERICAN UNITED LIFE INS CO	IN	22,778.8			
ASSURITY LIFE INS CO	NE	2,452.3			
BOSTON MUTUAL LIFE INS CO	MA	1,230.4			
COLORADO BANKERS LIFE INS CO	CO	280.1			
FARM BUREAU LIFE INS CO	IA	8,042.3			

Mississippi

INSURANCE COMPANY NAME	DOM. STATE	TOTAL ASSETS ($MIL)

Rating: A+

INSURANCE COMPANY NAME	DOM. STATE	TOTAL ASSETS ($MIL)
COUNTRY LIFE INS CO	IL	10,573.7
PHYSICIANS MUTUAL INS CO	NE	1,989.7
STATE FARM LIFE INS CO	IL	62,712.0
TEACHERS INS & ANNUITY ASN OF AM	NY	261,389.2

Rating: A

INSURANCE COMPANY NAME	DOM. STATE	TOTAL ASSETS ($MIL)
4 EVER LIFE INS CO	IL	200.3
AUTO-OWNERS LIFE INS CO	MI	3,592.1
BERKSHIRE LIFE INS CO OF AMERICA	MA	3,640.3
FEDERATED LIFE INS CO	MN	1,497.0
GUARDIAN LIFE INS CO OF AMERICA	NY	44,890.2
PARKER CENTENNIAL ASR CO	WI	89.4
RESERVE NATIONAL INS CO	OK	112.1
SENTRY LIFE INS CO	WI	5,237.9
SOUTHERN FARM BUREAU LIFE INS CO	MS	12,937.4
USAA LIFE INS CO	TX	21,964.7

Rating: A-

INSURANCE COMPANY NAME	DOM. STATE	TOTAL ASSETS ($MIL)
ALLSTATE ASR CO	IL	12.3
AMALGAMATED LIFE INS CO	NY	110.5
AMERICAN REPUBLIC INS CO	IA	797.6
ANTHEM LIFE INS CO	IN	559.7
BALBOA LIFE INS CO	CA	58.9
CENTRAL STATES H & L CO OF OMAHA	NE	407.1
CHARTER NATIONAL LIFE INS CO	IL	133.2
COMPANION LIFE INS CO	SC	274.9
COTTON STATES LIFE INS CO	GA	330.7
COUNTRY INVESTORS LIFE ASR CO	IL	289.8
DEARBORN NATIONAL LIFE INS CO	IL	2,183.0
FAMILY HERITAGE LIFE INS CO OF AMER	OH	725.3
FIDELITY INVESTMENTS LIFE INS CO	UT	23,882.2
GARDEN STATE LIFE INS CO	TX	120.3
GERBER LIFE INS CO	NY	2,749.8
ILLINOIS MUTUAL LIFE INS CO	IL	1,368.4
LIFE INS CO OF ALABAMA	AL	112.0
MASSACHUSETTS MUTUAL LIFE INS CO	MA	190,575.4
MIDWESTERN UNITED LIFE INS CO	IN	236.3
MML BAY STATE LIFE INS CO	CT	4,682.4
MUTUAL OF AMERICA LIFE INS CO	NY	17,110.0
MUTUAL SAVINGS LIFE INS CO	AL	470.5
NEW YORK LIFE INS CO	NY	143,501.4
NIPPON LIFE INS CO OF AMERICA	IA	211.7
NORTHWESTERN MUTUAL LIFE INS CO	WI	223,102.7
PACIFIC LIFE INS CO	NE	111,429.1
PHYSICIANS LIFE INS CO	NE	1,421.0
SHELTER LIFE INS CO	MO	1,108.6
STANDARD LIFE & ACCIDENT INS CO	TX	523.8

Rating: B+

INSURANCE COMPANY NAME	DOM. STATE	TOTAL ASSETS ($MIL)
AETNA HEALTH & LIFE INS CO	CT	2,221.2
AETNA LIFE INS CO	CT	22,602.5
AMERICAN FAMILY LIFE ASR CO OF COLUM	NE	110,401.3
AMERICAN FIDELITY ASR CO	OK	4,856.7
AMERICAN UNITED LIFE INS CO	IN	22,778.8
ASSURITY LIFE INS CO	NE	2,452.3

INSURANCE COMPANY NAME	DOM. STATE	TOTAL ASSETS ($MIL)
BLUEBONNET LIFE INS CO	MS	54.6
BOSTON MUTUAL LIFE INS CO	MA	1,230.4
COLORADO BANKERS LIFE INS CO	CO	280.1
GENERAL RE LIFE CORP	CT	3,335.8
GOVERNMENT PERSONNEL MUTUAL L I C	TX	830.8
GREATER GEORGIA LIFE INS CO	GA	49.9
JACKSON NATIONAL LIFE INS CO	MI	176,820.4
LINCOLN BENEFIT LIFE CO	NE	12,911.3
MEDICO CORP LIFE INS CO	NE	26.0
MERIT LIFE INS CO	IN	584.3
MIDLAND NATIONAL LIFE INS CO	IA	40,607.9
MINNESOTA LIFE INS CO	MN	34,693.9
MUTUAL OF OMAHA INS CO	NE	6,568.9
NATIONAL BENEFIT LIFE INS CO	NY	480.5
NATIONAL FARMERS UNION LIFE INS CO	TX	216.9
NATIONAL WESTERN LIFE INS CO	CO	10,164.8
NEW YORK LIFE INS & ANNUITY CORP	DE	124,994.1
OHIO NATIONAL LIFE ASR CORP	OH	3,548.1
PACIFIC LIFE & ANNUITY CO	AZ	6,110.8
PARK AVENUE LIFE INS CO	DE	303.3
PIONEER MUTUAL LIFE INS CO	ND	510.6
PRINCIPAL LIFE INS CO	IA	148,782.3
SAVINGS BANK LIFE INS CO OF MA	MA	2,567.5
STANDARD INS CO	OR	19,885.1
SYMETRA LIFE INS CO	IA	28,794.9
THRIVENT LIFE INS CO	MN	3,530.2
TRUSTMARK INS CO	IL	1,404.5
TRUSTMARK LIFE INS CO	IL	370.8
UNITED WORLD LIFE INS CO	NE	114.3
USABLE LIFE	AR	432.6

Missouri

INSURANCE COMPANY NAME	DOM. STATE	TOTAL ASSETS ($MIL)
Rating: A+		
AMERICAN FAMILY LIFE INS CO	WI	5,200.5
COUNTRY LIFE INS CO	IL	10,573.7
PHYSICIANS MUTUAL INS CO	NE	1,989.7
STATE FARM LIFE INS CO	IL	62,712.0
TEACHERS INS & ANNUITY ASN OF AM	NY	261,389.2
Rating: A		
4 EVER LIFE INS CO	IL	200.3
AUTO-OWNERS LIFE INS CO	MI	3,592.1
BERKSHIRE LIFE INS CO OF AMERICA	MA	3,640.3
FEDERATED LIFE INS CO	MN	1,497.0
GUARDIAN LIFE INS CO OF AMERICA	NY	44,890.2
PARKER CENTENNIAL ASR CO	WI	89.4
RESERVE NATIONAL INS CO	OK	112.1
SENTRY LIFE INS CO	WI	5,237.9
USAA LIFE INS CO	TX	21,964.7
Rating: A-		
ALLSTATE ASR CO	IL	12.3
AMALGAMATED LIFE INS CO	NY	110.5
AMERICAN REPUBLIC INS CO	IA	797.6
ANTHEM LIFE INS CO	IN	559.7
BALBOA LIFE INS CO	CA	58.9
CENTRAL STATES H & L CO OF OMAHA	NE	407.1
CHARTER NATIONAL LIFE INS CO	IL	133.2
CIGNA LIFE INS CO OF NEW YORK	NY	380.6
COMPANION LIFE INS CO	SC	274.9
COUNTRY INVESTORS LIFE ASR CO	IL	289.8
DEARBORN NATIONAL LIFE INS CO	IL	2,183.0
FAMILY HERITAGE LIFE INS CO OF AMER	OH	725.3
FARM BUREAU LIFE INS CO OF MISSOURI	MO	522.5
FIDELITY INVESTMENTS LIFE INS CO	UT	23,882.2
GARDEN STATE LIFE INS CO	TX	120.3
GERBER LIFE INS CO	NY	2,749.8
ILLINOIS MUTUAL LIFE INS CO	IL	1,368.4
MASSACHUSETTS MUTUAL LIFE INS CO	MA	190,575.4
MIDWESTERN UNITED LIFE INS CO	IN	236.3
MML BAY STATE LIFE INS CO	CT	4,682.4
MUTUAL OF AMERICA LIFE INS CO	NY	17,110.0
NEW YORK LIFE INS CO	NY	143,501.4
NIPPON LIFE INS CO OF AMERICA	IA	211.7
NORTHWESTERN MUTUAL LIFE INS CO	WI	223,102.7
PACIFIC GUARDIAN LIFE INS CO LTD	HI	511.7
PACIFIC LIFE INS CO	NE	111,429.1
PHYSICIANS LIFE INS CO	NE	1,421.0
SHELTER LIFE INS CO	MO	1,108.6
STANDARD LIFE & ACCIDENT INS CO	TX	523.8
Rating: B+		
AETNA LIFE INS CO	CT	22,602.5
AMERICAN FAMILY LIFE ASR CO OF COLUM	NE	110,401.3
AMERICAN FIDELITY ASR CO	OK	4,856.7
AMERICAN UNITED LIFE INS CO	IN	22,778.8
ASSURITY LIFE INS CO	NE	2,452.3
BOSTON MUTUAL LIFE INS CO	MA	1,230.4

INSURANCE COMPANY NAME	DOM. STATE	TOTAL ASSETS ($MIL)
COLORADO BANKERS LIFE INS CO	CO	280.1
GENERAL RE LIFE CORP	CT	3,335.8
GOVERNMENT PERSONNEL MUTUAL L I C	TX	830.8
JACKSON NATIONAL LIFE INS CO	MI	176,820.4
LINCOLN BENEFIT LIFE CO	NE	12,911.3
MEDICO CORP LIFE INS CO	NE	26.0
MERIT LIFE INS CO	IN	584.3
MIDLAND NATIONAL LIFE INS CO	IA	40,607.9
MINNESOTA LIFE INS CO	MN	34,693.9
MUTUAL OF OMAHA INS CO	NE	6,568.9
NATIONAL BENEFIT LIFE INS CO	NY	480.5
NATIONAL FARMERS UNION LIFE INS CO	TX	216.9
NATIONAL WESTERN LIFE INS CO	CO	10,164.8
NEW YORK LIFE INS & ANNUITY CORP	DE	124,994.1
OHIO NATIONAL LIFE ASR CORP	OH	3,548.1
PACIFIC LIFE & ANNUITY CO	AZ	6,110.8
PARK AVENUE LIFE INS CO	DE	303.3
PIONEER MUTUAL LIFE INS CO	ND	510.6
PRINCIPAL LIFE INS CO	IA	148,782.3
SAVINGS BANK LIFE INS CO OF MA	MA	2,567.5
STANDARD INS CO	OR	19,885.1
SYMETRA LIFE INS CO	IA	28,794.9
THRIVENT LIFE INS CO	MN	3,530.2
TRUSTMARK INS CO	IL	1,404.5
TRUSTMARK LIFE INS CO	IL	370.8
UNITED WORLD LIFE INS CO	NE	114.3
USABLE LIFE	AR	432.6

Montana

INSURANCE COMPANY NAME	DOM. STATE	TOTAL ASSETS ($MIL)

Rating: A+

INSURANCE COMPANY NAME	DOM. STATE	TOTAL ASSETS ($MIL)
AMERICAN FAMILY LIFE INS CO	WI	5,200.5
COUNTRY LIFE INS CO	IL	10,573.7
PHYSICIANS MUTUAL INS CO	NE	1,989.7
STATE FARM LIFE INS CO	IL	62,712.0
TEACHERS INS & ANNUITY ASN OF AM	NY	261,389.2

Rating: A

INSURANCE COMPANY NAME	DOM. STATE	TOTAL ASSETS ($MIL)
4 EVER LIFE INS CO	IL	200.3
BERKSHIRE LIFE INS CO OF AMERICA	MA	3,640.3
FEDERATED LIFE INS CO	MN	1,497.0
GUARDIAN LIFE INS CO OF AMERICA	NY	44,890.2
LIFEWISE ASR CO	WA	125.6
PARKER CENTENNIAL ASR CO	WI	89.4
RESERVE NATIONAL INS CO	OK	112.1
SENTRY LIFE INS CO	WI	5,237.9
USAA LIFE INS CO	TX	21,964.7

Rating: A-

INSURANCE COMPANY NAME	DOM. STATE	TOTAL ASSETS ($MIL)
ALLSTATE ASR CO	IL	12.3
AMALGAMATED LIFE INS CO	NY	110.5
AMERICAN REPUBLIC INS CO	IA	797.6
ANTHEM LIFE INS CO	IN	559.7
BALBOA LIFE INS CO	CA	58.9
CENTRAL STATES H & L CO OF OMAHA	NE	407.1
CHARTER NATIONAL LIFE INS CO	IL	133.2
COMPANION LIFE INS CO	SC	274.9
COUNTRY INVESTORS LIFE ASR CO	IL	289.8
DEARBORN NATIONAL LIFE INS CO	IL	2,183.0
FAMILY HERITAGE LIFE INS CO OF AMER	OH	725.3
FIDELITY INVESTMENTS LIFE INS CO	UT	23,882.2
GARDEN STATE LIFE INS CO	TX	120.3
GERBER LIFE INS CO	NY	2,749.8
ILLINOIS MUTUAL LIFE INS CO	IL	1,368.4
MASSACHUSETTS MUTUAL LIFE INS CO	MA	190,575.4
MIDWESTERN UNITED LIFE INS CO	IN	236.3
MML BAY STATE LIFE INS CO	CT	4,682.4
MUTUAL OF AMERICA LIFE INS CO	NY	17,110.0
NEW YORK LIFE INS CO	NY	143,501.4
NIPPON LIFE INS CO OF AMERICA	IA	211.7
NORTHWESTERN MUTUAL LIFE INS CO	WI	223,102.7
PACIFIC GUARDIAN LIFE INS CO LTD	HI	511.7
PACIFIC LIFE INS CO	NE	111,429.1
PHYSICIANS LIFE INS CO	NE	1,421.0
STANDARD LIFE & ACCIDENT INS CO	TX	523.8

Rating: B+

INSURANCE COMPANY NAME	DOM. STATE	TOTAL ASSETS ($MIL)
AETNA HEALTH & LIFE INS CO	CT	2,221.2
AETNA LIFE INS CO	CT	22,602.5
AMERICAN FAMILY LIFE ASR CO OF COLUM	NE	110,401.3
AMERICAN FIDELITY ASR CO	OK	4,856.7
AMERICAN UNITED LIFE INS CO	IN	22,778.8
ASSURITY LIFE INS CO	NE	2,452.3
BOSTON MUTUAL LIFE INS CO	MA	1,230.4
COLORADO BANKERS LIFE INS CO	CO	280.1
FARM BUREAU LIFE INS CO	IA	8,042.3

INSURANCE COMPANY NAME	DOM. STATE	TOTAL ASSETS ($MIL)
GENERAL RE LIFE CORP	CT	3,335.8
GOVERNMENT PERSONNEL MUTUAL L I C	TX	830.8
JACKSON NATIONAL LIFE INS CO	MI	176,820.4
LINCOLN BENEFIT LIFE CO	NE	12,911.3
MEDICO CORP LIFE INS CO	NE	26.0
MERIT LIFE INS CO	IN	584.3
MIDLAND NATIONAL LIFE INS CO	IA	40,607.9
MINNESOTA LIFE INS CO	MN	34,693.9
MUTUAL OF OMAHA INS CO	NE	6,568.9
NATIONAL BENEFIT LIFE INS CO	NY	480.5
NATIONAL FARMERS UNION LIFE INS CO	TX	216.9
NATIONAL WESTERN LIFE INS CO	CO	10,164.8
NEW YORK LIFE INS & ANNUITY CORP	DE	124,994.1
OHIO NATIONAL LIFE ASR CORP	OH	3,548.1
PACIFIC LIFE & ANNUITY CO	AZ	6,110.8
PARK AVENUE LIFE INS CO	DE	303.3
PIONEER MUTUAL LIFE INS CO	ND	510.6
PRINCIPAL LIFE INS CO	IA	148,782.3
SAVINGS BANK LIFE INS CO OF MA	MA	2,567.5
STANDARD INS CO	OR	19,885.1
SYMETRA LIFE INS CO	IA	28,794.9
THRIVENT LIFE INS CO	MN	3,530.2
TRUSTMARK INS CO	IL	1,404.5
TRUSTMARK LIFE INS CO	IL	370.8
UNITED WORLD LIFE INS CO	NE	114.3
USABLE LIFE	AR	432.6

Nebraska

INSURANCE COMPANY NAME	DOM. STATE	TOTAL ASSETS ($MIL)	INSURANCE COMPANY NAME	DOM. STATE	TOTAL ASSETS ($MIL)
Rating: A+			FARM BUREAU LIFE INS CO	IA	8,042.3
			GENERAL RE LIFE CORP	CT	3,335.8
AMERICAN FAMILY LIFE INS CO	WI	5,200.5	GOVERNMENT PERSONNEL MUTUAL L I C	TX	830.8
COUNTRY LIFE INS CO	IL	10,573.7	JACKSON NATIONAL LIFE INS CO	MI	176,820.4
PHYSICIANS MUTUAL INS CO	NE	1,989.7	LINCOLN BENEFIT LIFE CO	NE	12,911.3
STATE FARM LIFE INS CO	IL	62,712.0	LOCOMOTIVE ENGRS&COND MUT PROT ASSN	MI	55.4
TEACHERS INS & ANNUITY ASN OF AM	NY	261,389.2	MEDICO CORP LIFE INS CO	NE	26.0
			MERIT LIFE INS CO	IN	584.3
Rating: A			MIDLAND NATIONAL LIFE INS CO	IA	40,607.9
			MINNESOTA LIFE INS CO	MN	34,693.9
4 EVER LIFE INS CO	IL	200.3	MUTUAL OF OMAHA INS CO	NE	6,568.9
AUTO-OWNERS LIFE INS CO	MI	3,592.1	NATIONAL BENEFIT LIFE INS CO	NY	480.5
BERKSHIRE LIFE INS CO OF AMERICA	MA	3,640.3	NATIONAL FARMERS UNION LIFE INS CO	TX	216.9
FEDERATED LIFE INS CO	MN	1,497.0	NATIONAL WESTERN LIFE INS CO	CO	10,164.8
GUARDIAN LIFE INS CO OF AMERICA	NY	44,890.2	NEW YORK LIFE INS & ANNUITY CORP	DE	124,994.1
PARKER CENTENNIAL ASR CO	WI	89.4	OHIO NATIONAL LIFE ASR CORP	OH	3,548.1
RESERVE NATIONAL INS CO	OK	112.1	PACIFIC LIFE & ANNUITY CO	AZ	6,110.8
SENTRY LIFE INS CO	WI	5,237.9	PARK AVENUE LIFE INS CO	DE	303.3
USAA LIFE INS CO	TX	21,964.7	PIONEER MUTUAL LIFE INS CO	ND	510.6
			PRINCIPAL LIFE INS CO	IA	148,782.3
Rating: A-			SAVINGS BANK LIFE INS CO OF MA	MA	2,567.5
			STANDARD INS CO	OR	19,885.1
ALLSTATE ASR CO	IL	12.3	SYMETRA LIFE INS CO	IA	28,794.9
AMALGAMATED LIFE INS CO	NY	110.5	THRIVENT LIFE INS CO	MN	3,530.2
AMERICAN REPUBLIC INS CO	IA	797.6	TRUSTMARK INS CO	IL	1,404.5
ANTHEM LIFE INS CO	IN	559.7	TRUSTMARK LIFE INS CO	IL	370.8
BALBOA LIFE INS CO	CA	58.9	UNITED WORLD LIFE INS CO	NE	114.3
CENTRAL STATES H & L CO OF OMAHA	NE	407.1	USABLE LIFE	AR	432.6
CHARTER NATIONAL LIFE INS CO	IL	133.2			
COMPANION LIFE INS CO	SC	274.9			
COUNTRY INVESTORS LIFE ASR CO	IL	289.8			
DEARBORN NATIONAL LIFE INS CO	IL	2,183.0			
FAMILY HERITAGE LIFE INS CO OF AMER	OH	725.3			
FIDELITY INVESTMENTS LIFE INS CO	UT	23,882.2			
GARDEN STATE LIFE INS CO	TX	120.3			
GERBER LIFE INS CO	NY	2,749.8			
ILLINOIS MUTUAL LIFE INS CO	IL	1,368.4			
MASSACHUSETTS MUTUAL LIFE INS CO	MA	190,575.4			
MIDWESTERN UNITED LIFE INS CO	IN	236.3			
MML BAY STATE LIFE INS CO	CT	4,682.4			
MUTUAL OF AMERICA LIFE INS CO	NY	17,110.0			
NEW YORK LIFE INS CO	NY	143,501.4			
NIPPON LIFE INS CO OF AMERICA	IA	211.7			
NORTHWESTERN MUTUAL LIFE INS CO	WI	223,102.7			
PACIFIC GUARDIAN LIFE INS CO LTD	HI	511.7			
PACIFIC LIFE INS CO	NE	111,429.1			
PHYSICIANS LIFE INS CO	NE	1,421.0			
SHELTER LIFE INS CO	MO	1,108.6			
STANDARD LIFE & ACCIDENT INS CO	TX	523.8			
Rating: B+					
AETNA HEALTH & LIFE INS CO	CT	2,221.2			
AETNA LIFE INS CO	CT	22,602.5			
AMERICAN FAMILY LIFE ASR CO OF COLUM	NE	110,401.3			
AMERICAN FIDELITY ASR CO	OK	4,856.7			
AMERICAN UNITED LIFE INS CO	IN	22,778.8			
ASSURITY LIFE INS CO	NE	2,452.3			
BOSTON MUTUAL LIFE INS CO	MA	1,230.4			
COLORADO BANKERS LIFE INS CO	CO	280.1			

Nevada

INSURANCE COMPANY NAME	DOM. STATE	TOTAL ASSETS ($MIL)
Rating: A+		
AMERICAN FAMILY LIFE INS CO	WI	5,200.5
COUNTRY LIFE INS CO	IL	10,573.7
PHYSICIANS MUTUAL INS CO	NE	1,989.7
STATE FARM LIFE INS CO	IL	62,712.0
TEACHERS INS & ANNUITY ASN OF AM	NY	261,389.2
Rating: A		
4 EVER LIFE INS CO	IL	200.3
AUTO-OWNERS LIFE INS CO	MI	3,592.1
BERKSHIRE LIFE INS CO OF AMERICA	MA	3,640.3
FEDERATED LIFE INS CO	MN	1,497.0
GUARDIAN LIFE INS CO OF AMERICA	NY	44,890.2
LIFEWISE ASR CO	WA	125.6
PARKER CENTENNIAL ASR CO	WI	89.4
RESERVE NATIONAL INS CO	OK	112.1
SENTRY LIFE INS CO	WI	5,237.9
USAA LIFE INS CO	TX	21,964.7
Rating: A-		
ALLSTATE ASR CO	IL	12.3
AMALGAMATED LIFE INS CO	NY	110.5
AMERICAN REPUBLIC INS CO	IA	797.6
ANTHEM LIFE INS CO	IN	559.7
BALBOA LIFE INS CO	CA	58.9
CENTRAL STATES H & L CO OF OMAHA	NE	407.1
CHARTER NATIONAL LIFE INS CO	IL	133.2
COMPANION LIFE INS CO	SC	274.9
COUNTRY INVESTORS LIFE ASR CO	IL	289.8
DEARBORN NATIONAL LIFE INS CO	IL	2,183.0
FAMILY HERITAGE LIFE INS CO OF AMER	OH	725.3
FIDELITY INVESTMENTS LIFE INS CO	UT	23,882.2
GARDEN STATE LIFE INS CO	TX	120.3
GERBER LIFE INS CO	NY	2,749.8
ILLINOIS MUTUAL LIFE INS CO	IL	1,368.4
MASSACHUSETTS MUTUAL LIFE INS CO	MA	190,575.4
MIDWESTERN UNITED LIFE INS CO	IN	236.3
MML BAY STATE LIFE INS CO	CT	4,682.4
MUTUAL OF AMERICA LIFE INS CO	NY	17,110.0
NEW YORK LIFE INS CO	NY	143,501.4
NIPPON LIFE INS CO OF AMERICA	IA	211.7
NORTHWESTERN MUTUAL LIFE INS CO	WI	223,102.7
PACIFIC GUARDIAN LIFE INS CO LTD	HI	511.7
PACIFIC LIFE INS CO	NE	111,429.1
PHYSICIANS LIFE INS CO	NE	1,421.0
SHELTER LIFE INS CO	MO	1,108.6
STANDARD LIFE & ACCIDENT INS CO	TX	523.8
Rating: B+		
AETNA HEALTH & LIFE INS CO	CT	2,221.2
AETNA LIFE INS CO	CT	22,602.5
AMERICAN FAMILY LIFE ASR CO OF COLUM	NE	110,401.3
AMERICAN FIDELITY ASR CO	OK	4,856.7
AMERICAN UNITED LIFE INS CO	IN	22,778.8
ASSURITY LIFE INS CO	NE	2,452.3
BOSTON MUTUAL LIFE INS CO	MA	1,230.4

INSURANCE COMPANY NAME	DOM. STATE	TOTAL ASSETS ($MIL)
COLORADO BANKERS LIFE INS CO	CO	280.1
FARM BUREAU LIFE INS CO	IA	8,042.3
GENERAL RE LIFE CORP	CT	3,335.8
GOVERNMENT PERSONNEL MUTUAL L I C	TX	830.8
JACKSON NATIONAL LIFE INS CO	MI	176,820.4
LINCOLN BENEFIT LIFE CO	NE	12,911.3
MEDICO CORP LIFE INS CO	NE	26.0
MERIT LIFE INS CO	IN	584.3
MIDLAND NATIONAL LIFE INS CO	IA	40,607.9
MINNESOTA LIFE INS CO	MN	34,693.9
MUTUAL OF OMAHA INS CO	NE	6,568.9
NATIONAL BENEFIT LIFE INS CO	NY	480.5
NATIONAL FARMERS UNION LIFE INS CO	TX	216.9
NATIONAL WESTERN LIFE INS CO	CO	10,164.8
NEW YORK LIFE INS & ANNUITY CORP	DE	124,994.1
OHIO NATIONAL LIFE ASR CORP	OH	3,548.1
PACIFIC LIFE & ANNUITY CO	AZ	6,110.8
PARK AVENUE LIFE INS CO	DE	303.3
PIONEER MUTUAL LIFE INS CO	ND	510.6
PRINCIPAL LIFE INS CO	IA	148,782.3
SAVINGS BANK LIFE INS CO OF MA	MA	2,567.5
STANDARD INS CO	OR	19,885.1
SYMETRA LIFE INS CO	IA	28,794.9
THRIVENT LIFE INS CO	MN	3,530.2
TRUSTMARK INS CO	IL	1,404.5
TRUSTMARK LIFE INS CO	IL	370.8
UNITED WORLD LIFE INS CO	NE	114.3
USABLE LIFE	AR	432.6

New Hampshire

INSURANCE COMPANY NAME	DOM. STATE	TOTAL ASSETS ($MIL)
Rating: A+		
PHYSICIANS MUTUAL INS CO	NE	1,989.7
STATE FARM LIFE INS CO	IL	62,712.0
TEACHERS INS & ANNUITY ASN OF AM	NY	261,389.2
Rating: A		
4 EVER LIFE INS CO	IL	200.3
BERKSHIRE LIFE INS CO OF AMERICA	MA	3,640.3
FEDERATED LIFE INS CO	MN	1,497.0
GUARDIAN LIFE INS CO OF AMERICA	NY	44,890.2
PARKER CENTENNIAL ASR CO	WI	89.4
SENTRY LIFE INS CO	WI	5,237.9
UNITED FARM FAMILY LIFE INS CO	IN	2,129.9
USAA LIFE INS CO	TX	21,964.7
Rating: A-		
ALLSTATE ASR CO	IL	12.3
AMALGAMATED LIFE INS CO	NY	110.5
AMERICAN REPUBLIC INS CO	IA	797.6
ANTHEM LIFE INS CO	IN	559.7
BALBOA LIFE INS CO	CA	58.9
CENTRAL STATES H & L CO OF OMAHA	NE	407.1
CHARTER NATIONAL LIFE INS CO	IL	133.2
COMPANION LIFE INS CO	SC	274.9
DEARBORN NATIONAL LIFE INS CO	IL	2,183.0
FAMILY HERITAGE LIFE INS CO OF AMER	OH	725.3
FIDELITY INVESTMENTS LIFE INS CO	UT	23,882.2
GARDEN STATE LIFE INS CO	TX	120.3
GERBER LIFE INS CO	NY	2,749.8
ILLINOIS MUTUAL LIFE INS CO	IL	1,368.4
MASSACHUSETTS MUTUAL LIFE INS CO	MA	190,575.4
MIDWESTERN UNITED LIFE INS CO	IN	236.3
MML BAY STATE LIFE INS CO	CT	4,682.4
MUTUAL OF AMERICA LIFE INS CO	NY	17,110.0
NEW YORK LIFE INS CO	NY	143,501.4
NORTHWESTERN MUTUAL LIFE INS CO	WI	223,102.7
PACIFIC LIFE INS CO	NE	111,429.1
PHYSICIANS LIFE INS CO	NE	1,421.0
Rating: B+		
AETNA LIFE INS CO	CT	22,602.5
AMERICAN FAMILY LIFE ASR CO OF COLUM	NE	110,401.3
AMERICAN FIDELITY ASR CO	OK	4,856.7
AMERICAN UNITED LIFE INS CO	IN	22,778.8
ASSURITY LIFE INS CO	NE	2,452.3
BOSTON MUTUAL LIFE INS CO	MA	1,230.4
COLORADO BANKERS LIFE INS CO	CO	280.1
GENERAL RE LIFE CORP	CT	3,335.8
GOVERNMENT PERSONNEL MUTUAL L I C	TX	830.8
JACKSON NATIONAL LIFE INS CO	MI	176,820.4
LINCOLN BENEFIT LIFE CO	NE	12,911.3
MERIT LIFE INS CO	IN	584.3
MIDLAND NATIONAL LIFE INS CO	IA	40,607.9
MINNESOTA LIFE INS CO	MN	34,693.9
MUTUAL OF OMAHA INS CO	NE	6,568.9
NATIONAL BENEFIT LIFE INS CO	NY	480.5

INSURANCE COMPANY NAME	DOM. STATE	TOTAL ASSETS ($MIL)
NATIONAL WESTERN LIFE INS CO	CO	10,164.8
NEW YORK LIFE INS & ANNUITY CORP	DE	124,994.1
OHIO NATIONAL LIFE ASR CORP	OH	3,548.1
PACIFIC LIFE & ANNUITY CO	AZ	6,110.8
PARK AVENUE LIFE INS CO	DE	303.3
PIONEER MUTUAL LIFE INS CO	ND	510.6
PRINCIPAL LIFE INS CO	IA	148,782.3
SAVINGS BANK LIFE INS CO OF MA	MA	2,567.5
STANDARD INS CO	OR	19,885.1
SYMETRA LIFE INS CO	IA	28,794.9
TRUSTMARK INS CO	IL	1,404.5
TRUSTMARK LIFE INS CO	IL	370.8
UNITED WORLD LIFE INS CO	NE	114.3
USABLE LIFE	AR	432.6

New Jersey

INSURANCE COMPANY NAME	DOM. STATE	TOTAL ASSETS ($MIL)
Rating: A+		
PHYSICIANS MUTUAL INS CO	NE	1,989.7
STATE FARM LIFE INS CO	IL	62,712.0
TEACHERS INS & ANNUITY ASN OF AM	NY	261,389.2
Rating: A		
4 EVER LIFE INS CO	IL	200.3
BERKSHIRE LIFE INS CO OF AMERICA	MA	3,640.3
FEDERATED LIFE INS CO	MN	1,497.0
GUARDIAN LIFE INS CO OF AMERICA	NY	44,890.2
PARKER CENTENNIAL ASR CO	WI	89.4
RESERVE NATIONAL INS CO	OK	112.1
SENTRY LIFE INS CO	WI	5,237.9
SHELTERPOINT LIFE INS CO	NY	104.4
UNITED FARM FAMILY LIFE INS CO	IN	2,129.9
USAA LIFE INS CO	TX	21,964.7
Rating: A-		
ALLSTATE ASR CO	IL	12.3
AMALGAMATED LIFE INS CO	NY	110.5
AMERICAN FAMILY LIFE ASR CO OF NY	NY	710.2
AMERICAN REPUBLIC INS CO	IA	797.6
ANTHEM LIFE INS CO	IN	559.7
BALBOA LIFE INS CO	CA	58.9
CENTRAL STATES H & L CO OF OMAHA	NE	407.1
CHARTER NATIONAL LIFE INS CO	IL	133.2
DEARBORN NATIONAL LIFE INS CO	IL	2,183.0
FAMILY HERITAGE LIFE INS CO OF AMER	OH	725.3
FIDELITY INVESTMENTS LIFE INS CO	UT	23,882.2
GARDEN STATE LIFE INS CO	TX	120.3
GERBER LIFE INS CO	NY	2,749.8
ILLINOIS MUTUAL LIFE INS CO	IL	1,368.4
MASSACHUSETTS MUTUAL LIFE INS CO	MA	190,575.4
MIDWESTERN UNITED LIFE INS CO	IN	236.3
MML BAY STATE LIFE INS CO	CT	4,682.4
MUTUAL OF AMERICA LIFE INS CO	NY	17,110.0
NEW YORK LIFE INS CO	NY	143,501.4
NIPPON LIFE INS CO OF AMERICA	IA	211.7
NORTHWESTERN MUTUAL LIFE INS CO	WI	223,102.7
PACIFIC LIFE INS CO	NE	111,429.1
PHYSICIANS LIFE INS CO	NE	1,421.0
Rating: B+		
AETNA HEALTH & LIFE INS CO	CT	2,221.2
AETNA LIFE INS CO	CT	22,602.5
AMERICAN FAMILY LIFE ASR CO OF COLUM	NE	110,401.3
AMERICAN FIDELITY ASR CO	OK	4,856.7
AMERICAN UNITED LIFE INS CO	IN	22,778.8
ASSURITY LIFE INS CO	NE	2,452.3
BOSTON MUTUAL LIFE INS CO	MA	1,230.4
COLORADO BANKERS LIFE INS CO	CO	280.1
GENERAL RE LIFE CORP	CT	3,335.8
JACKSON NATIONAL LIFE INS CO	MI	176,820.4
LINCOLN BENEFIT LIFE CO	NE	12,911.3
MERIT LIFE INS CO	IN	584.3
MIDLAND NATIONAL LIFE INS CO	IA	40,607.9

INSURANCE COMPANY NAME	DOM. STATE	TOTAL ASSETS ($MIL)
MINNESOTA LIFE INS CO	MN	34,693.9
MUTUAL OF OMAHA INS CO	NE	6,568.9
NATIONAL BENEFIT LIFE INS CO	NY	480.5
NATIONAL WESTERN LIFE INS CO	CO	10,164.8
NEW YORK LIFE INS & ANNUITY CORP	DE	124,994.1
OHIO NATIONAL LIFE ASR CORP	OH	3,548.1
PACIFIC LIFE & ANNUITY CO	AZ	6,110.8
PARK AVENUE LIFE INS CO	DE	303.3
PIONEER MUTUAL LIFE INS CO	ND	510.6
PRINCIPAL LIFE INS CO	IA	148,782.3
SAVINGS BANK LIFE INS CO OF MA	MA	2,567.5
STANDARD INS CO	OR	19,885.1
SYMETRA LIFE INS CO	IA	28,794.9
THRIVENT LIFE INS CO	MN	3,530.2
TRUSTMARK INS CO	IL	1,404.5
TRUSTMARK LIFE INS CO	IL	370.8
UNITED WORLD LIFE INS CO	NE	114.3
USABLE LIFE	AR	432.6

New Mexico

INSURANCE COMPANY NAME	DOM. STATE	TOTAL ASSETS ($MIL)

Rating: A+

INSURANCE COMPANY NAME	DOM. STATE	TOTAL ASSETS ($MIL)
AMERICAN FAMILY LIFE INS CO	WI	5,200.5
COUNTRY LIFE INS CO	IL	10,573.7
PHYSICIANS MUTUAL INS CO	NE	1,989.7
STATE FARM LIFE INS CO	IL	62,712.0
TEACHERS INS & ANNUITY ASN OF AM	NY	261,389.2

Rating: A

INSURANCE COMPANY NAME	DOM. STATE	TOTAL ASSETS ($MIL)
4 EVER LIFE INS CO	IL	200.3
AUTO-OWNERS LIFE INS CO	MI	3,592.1
BERKSHIRE LIFE INS CO OF AMERICA	MA	3,640.3
FEDERATED LIFE INS CO	MN	1,497.0
GUARDIAN LIFE INS CO OF AMERICA	NY	44,890.2
LIFEWISE ASR CO	WA	125.6
PARKER CENTENNIAL ASR CO	WI	89.4
RESERVE NATIONAL INS CO	OK	112.1
SENTRY LIFE INS CO	WI	5,237.9
USAA LIFE INS CO	TX	21,964.7

Rating: A-

INSURANCE COMPANY NAME	DOM. STATE	TOTAL ASSETS ($MIL)
ALLSTATE ASR CO	IL	12.3
AMALGAMATED LIFE INS CO	NY	110.5
AMERICAN REPUBLIC INS CO	IA	797.6
ANTHEM LIFE INS CO	IN	559.7
BALBOA LIFE INS CO	CA	58.9
CENTRAL STATES H & L CO OF OMAHA	NE	407.1
CHARTER NATIONAL LIFE INS CO	IL	133.2
COMPANION LIFE INS CO	SC	274.9
COUNTRY INVESTORS LIFE ASR CO	IL	289.8
DEARBORN NATIONAL LIFE INS CO	IL	2,183.0
FAMILY HERITAGE LIFE INS CO OF AMER	OH	725.3
FIDELITY INVESTMENTS LIFE INS CO	UT	23,882.2
GARDEN STATE LIFE INS CO	TX	120.3
GERBER LIFE INS CO	NY	2,749.8
ILLINOIS MUTUAL LIFE INS CO	IL	1,368.4
MASSACHUSETTS MUTUAL LIFE INS CO	MA	190,575.4
MIDWESTERN UNITED LIFE INS CO	IN	236.3
MML BAY STATE LIFE INS CO	CT	4,682.4
MUTUAL OF AMERICA LIFE INS CO	NY	17,110.0
NEW YORK LIFE INS CO	NY	143,501.4
NIPPON LIFE INS CO OF AMERICA	IA	211.7
NORTHWESTERN MUTUAL LIFE INS CO	WI	223,102.7
PACIFIC GUARDIAN LIFE INS CO LTD	HI	511.7
PACIFIC LIFE INS CO	NE	111,429.1
PHYSICIANS LIFE INS CO	NE	1,421.0
STANDARD LIFE & ACCIDENT INS CO	TX	523.8

Rating: B+

INSURANCE COMPANY NAME	DOM. STATE	TOTAL ASSETS ($MIL)
AETNA HEALTH & LIFE INS CO	CT	2,221.2
AETNA LIFE INS CO	CT	22,602.5
AMERICAN FAMILY LIFE ASR CO OF COLUM	NE	110,401.3
AMERICAN FIDELITY ASR CO	OK	4,856.7
AMERICAN UNITED LIFE INS CO	IN	22,778.8
ASSURITY LIFE INS CO	NE	2,452.3
BOSTON MUTUAL LIFE INS CO	MA	1,230.4
COLORADO BANKERS LIFE INS CO	CO	280.1
FARM BUREAU LIFE INS CO	IA	8,042.3
GENERAL RE LIFE CORP	CT	3,335.8
GOVERNMENT PERSONNEL MUTUAL L I C	TX	830.8
JACKSON NATIONAL LIFE INS CO	MI	176,820.4
LINCOLN BENEFIT LIFE CO	NE	12,911.3
LOCOMOTIVE ENGRS&COND MUT PROT ASSN	MI	55.4
MEDICO CORP LIFE INS CO	NE	26.0
MERIT LIFE INS CO	IN	584.3
MIDLAND NATIONAL LIFE INS CO	IA	40,607.9
MINNESOTA LIFE INS CO	MN	34,693.9
MUTUAL OF OMAHA INS CO	NE	6,568.9
NATIONAL BENEFIT LIFE INS CO	NY	480.5
NATIONAL FARMERS UNION LIFE INS CO	TX	216.9
NATIONAL WESTERN LIFE INS CO	CO	10,164.8
NEW YORK LIFE INS & ANNUITY CORP	DE	124,994.1
OHIO NATIONAL LIFE ASR CORP	OH	3,548.1
PACIFIC LIFE & ANNUITY CO	AZ	6,110.8
PARK AVENUE LIFE INS CO	DE	303.3
PIONEER MUTUAL LIFE INS CO	ND	510.6
PRINCIPAL LIFE INS CO	IA	148,782.3
SAVINGS BANK LIFE INS CO OF MA	MA	2,567.5
STANDARD INS CO	OR	19,885.1
SYMETRA LIFE INS CO	IA	28,794.9
THRIVENT LIFE INS CO	MN	3,530.2
TRUSTMARK INS CO	IL	1,404.5
TRUSTMARK LIFE INS CO	IL	370.8
UNITED WORLD LIFE INS CO	NE	114.3
USABLE LIFE	AR	432.6

New York

INSURANCE COMPANY NAME	DOM. STATE	TOTAL ASSETS ($MIL)
Rating: A+		
PHYSICIANS MUTUAL INS CO	NE	1,989.7
STATE FARM LIFE & ACCIDENT ASR CO	IL	2,436.7
TEACHERS INS & ANNUITY ASN OF AM	NY	261,389.2
Rating: A		
4 EVER LIFE INS CO	IL	200.3
BERKSHIRE LIFE INS CO OF AMERICA	MA	3,640.3
FEDERATED LIFE INS CO	MN	1,497.0
FIRST RELIANCE STANDARD LIFE INS CO	NY	188.7
GUARDIAN LIFE INS CO OF AMERICA	NY	44,890.2
SHELTERPOINT LIFE INS CO	NY	104.4
Rating: A-		
ALLSTATE ASR CO	IL	12.3
AMALGAMATED LIFE INS CO	NY	110.5
AMERICAN FAMILY LIFE ASR CO OF NY	NY	710.2
ANTHEM LIFE & DISABILITY INS CO	NY	23.3
BALBOA LIFE INS CO	CA	58.9
CIGNA LIFE INS CO OF NEW YORK	NY	380.6
FIRST SYMETRA NATL LIFE INS CO OF NY	NY	932.2
GARDEN STATE LIFE INS CO	TX	120.3
GERBER LIFE INS CO	NY	2,749.8
JOHN HANCOCK LIFE INS CO OF NY	NY	17,279.2
LIFE INS CO OF BOSTON & NEW YORK	NY	122.2
MASSACHUSETTS MUTUAL LIFE INS CO	MA	190,575.4
MUTUAL OF AMERICA LIFE INS CO	NY	17,110.0
NEW YORK LIFE INS CO	NY	143,501.4
NIPPON LIFE INS CO OF AMERICA	IA	211.7
NORTHWESTERN MUTUAL LIFE INS CO	WI	223,102.7
STANDARD LIFE INS CO OF NY	NY	272.4
Rating: B+		
AETNA HEALTH & LIFE INS CO	CT	2,221.2
AETNA LIFE INS CO	CT	22,602.5
AMERICAN UNITED LIFE INS CO	IN	22,778.8
BOSTON MUTUAL LIFE INS CO	MA	1,230.4
DEARBORN NATIONAL LIFE INS CO OF NY	NY	40.9
EMPIRE FIDELITY INVESTMENTS L I C	NY	2,386.2
FIRST UNITED AMERICAN LIFE INS CO	NY	191.8
GENERAL RE LIFE CORP	CT	3,335.8
HM LIFE INS CO OF NEW YORK	NY	72.4
MERIT LIFE INS CO	IN	584.3
MINNESOTA LIFE INS CO	MN	34,693.9
MUTUAL OF OMAHA INS CO	NE	6,568.9
NATIONAL BENEFIT LIFE INS CO	NY	480.5
NATIONAL INCOME LIFE INS CO	NY	142.8
NEW YORK LIFE INS & ANNUITY CORP	DE	124,994.1
PACIFIC LIFE & ANNUITY CO	AZ	6,110.8
PRINCIPAL LIFE INS CO	IA	148,782.3
SENTRY LIFE INS CO OF NEW YORK	NY	76.3
TRUSTMARK INS CO	IL	1,404.5
TRUSTMARK LIFE INS CO	IL	370.8
UNION SECURITY LIFE INS CO OF NY	NY	139.8
USAA LIFE INS CO OF NEW YORK	NY	667.0

North Carolina

INSURANCE COMPANY NAME	DOM. STATE	TOTAL ASSETS ($MIL)
Rating: A+		
AMERICAN FAMILY LIFE INS CO	WI	5,200.5
COUNTRY LIFE INS CO	IL	10,573.7
PHYSICIANS MUTUAL INS CO	NE	1,989.7
STATE FARM LIFE INS CO	IL	62,712.0
TEACHERS INS & ANNUITY ASN OF AM	NY	261,389.2
Rating: A		
4 EVER LIFE INS CO	IL	200.3
AUTO-OWNERS LIFE INS CO	MI	3,592.1
BERKSHIRE LIFE INS CO OF AMERICA	MA	3,640.3
FEDERATED LIFE INS CO	MN	1,497.0
GUARDIAN LIFE INS CO OF AMERICA	NY	44,890.2
PARKER CENTENNIAL ASR CO	WI	89.4
RESERVE NATIONAL INS CO	OK	112.1
SENTRY LIFE INS CO	WI	5,237.9
SHELTERPOINT LIFE INS CO	NY	104.4
SOUTHERN FARM BUREAU LIFE INS CO	MS	12,937.4
UNITED FARM FAMILY LIFE INS CO	IN	2,129.9
USAA LIFE INS CO	TX	21,964.7
Rating: A-		
ALLSTATE ASR CO	IL	12.3
AMALGAMATED LIFE INS CO	NY	110.5
AMERICAN REPUBLIC INS CO	IA	797.6
ANTHEM LIFE INS CO	IN	559.7
BALBOA LIFE INS CO	CA	58.9
CENTRAL STATES H & L CO OF OMAHA	NE	407.1
CHARTER NATIONAL LIFE INS CO	IL	133.2
COMPANION LIFE INS CO	SC	274.9
COTTON STATES LIFE INS CO	GA	330.7
COUNTRY INVESTORS LIFE ASR CO	IL	289.8
DEARBORN NATIONAL LIFE INS CO	IL	2,183.0
ERIE FAMILY LIFE INS CO	PA	2,077.0
FAMILY HERITAGE LIFE INS CO OF AMER	OH	725.3
FIDELITY INVESTMENTS LIFE INS CO	UT	23,882.2
GARDEN STATE LIFE INS CO	TX	120.3
GERBER LIFE INS CO	NY	2,749.8
ILLINOIS MUTUAL LIFE INS CO	IL	1,368.4
LIFE INS CO OF ALABAMA	AL	112.0
MASSACHUSETTS MUTUAL LIFE INS CO	MA	190,575.4
MIDWESTERN UNITED LIFE INS CO	IN	236.3
MML BAY STATE LIFE INS CO	CT	4,682.4
MUTUAL OF AMERICA LIFE INS CO	NY	17,110.0
NEW YORK LIFE INS CO	NY	143,501.4
NIPPON LIFE INS CO OF AMERICA	IA	211.7
NORTHWESTERN MUTUAL LIFE INS CO	WI	223,102.7
PACIFIC LIFE INS CO	NE	111,429.1
PHYSICIANS LIFE INS CO	NE	1,421.0
STANDARD LIFE & ACCIDENT INS CO	TX	523.8
Rating: B+		
AETNA HEALTH & LIFE INS CO	CT	2,221.2
AETNA LIFE INS CO	CT	22,602.5
AMERICAN FAMILY LIFE ASR CO OF COLUM	NE	110,401.3
AMERICAN FIDELITY ASR CO	OK	4,856.7

INSURANCE COMPANY NAME	DOM. STATE	TOTAL ASSETS ($MIL)
AMERICAN UNITED LIFE INS CO	IN	22,778.8
ASSURITY LIFE INS CO	NE	2,452.3
BOSTON MUTUAL LIFE INS CO	MA	1,230.4
COLORADO BANKERS LIFE INS CO	CO	280.1
GENERAL RE LIFE CORP	CT	3,335.8
GOVERNMENT PERSONNEL MUTUAL L I C	TX	830.8
GREATER GEORGIA LIFE INS CO	GA	49.9
JACKSON NATIONAL LIFE INS CO	MI	176,820.4
LINCOLN BENEFIT LIFE CO	NE	12,911.3
MEDICO CORP LIFE INS CO	NE	26.0
MERIT LIFE INS CO	IN	584.3
MIDLAND NATIONAL LIFE INS CO	IA	40,607.9
MINNESOTA LIFE INS CO	MN	34,693.9
MUTUAL OF OMAHA INS CO	NE	6,568.9
NATIONAL BENEFIT LIFE INS CO	NY	480.5
NATIONAL WESTERN LIFE INS CO	CO	10,164.8
NEW YORK LIFE INS & ANNUITY CORP	DE	124,994.1
OHIO NATIONAL LIFE ASR CORP	OH	3,548.1
PACIFIC LIFE & ANNUITY CO	AZ	6,110.8
PARK AVENUE LIFE INS CO	DE	303.3
PIONEER MUTUAL LIFE INS CO	ND	510.6
PRINCIPAL LIFE INS CO	IA	148,782.3
SAVINGS BANK LIFE INS CO OF MA	MA	2,567.5
STANDARD INS CO	OR	19,885.1
SYMETRA LIFE INS CO	IA	28,794.9
TRUSTMARK INS CO	IL	1,404.5
TRUSTMARK LIFE INS CO	IL	370.8
UNITED WORLD LIFE INS CO	NE	114.3
USABLE LIFE	AR	432.6

North Dakota

INSURANCE COMPANY NAME	DOM. STATE	TOTAL ASSETS ($MIL)

Rating: A+

INSURANCE COMPANY NAME	DOM. STATE	TOTAL ASSETS ($MIL)
AMERICAN FAMILY LIFE INS CO	WI	5,200.5
COUNTRY LIFE INS CO	IL	10,573.7
PHYSICIANS MUTUAL INS CO	NE	1,989.7
STATE FARM LIFE INS CO	IL	62,712.0
TEACHERS INS & ANNUITY ASN OF AM	NY	261,389.2

Rating: A

INSURANCE COMPANY NAME	DOM. STATE	TOTAL ASSETS ($MIL)
4 EVER LIFE INS CO	IL	200.3
AUTO-OWNERS LIFE INS CO	MI	3,592.1
BERKSHIRE LIFE INS CO OF AMERICA	MA	3,640.3
FEDERATED LIFE INS CO	MN	1,497.0
GUARDIAN LIFE INS CO OF AMERICA	NY	44,890.2
LIFEWISE ASR CO	WA	125.6
PARKER CENTENNIAL ASR CO	WI	89.4
RESERVE NATIONAL INS CO	OK	112.1
SENTRY LIFE INS CO	WI	5,237.9
UNITED FARM FAMILY LIFE INS CO	IN	2,129.9
USAA LIFE INS CO	TX	21,964.7

Rating: A-

INSURANCE COMPANY NAME	DOM. STATE	TOTAL ASSETS ($MIL)
ALLSTATE ASR CO	IL	12.3
AMALGAMATED LIFE INS CO	NY	110.5
AMERICAN FAMILY LIFE ASR CO OF NY	NY	710.2
AMERICAN REPUBLIC INS CO	IA	797.6
ANTHEM LIFE INS CO	IN	559.7
BALBOA LIFE INS CO	CA	58.9
CENTRAL STATES H & L CO OF OMAHA	NE	407.1
CHARTER NATIONAL LIFE INS CO	IL	133.2
COMPANION LIFE INS CO	SC	274.9
COUNTRY INVESTORS LIFE ASR CO	IL	289.8
DEARBORN NATIONAL LIFE INS CO	IL	2,183.0
FAMILY HERITAGE LIFE INS CO OF AMER	OH	725.3
FIDELITY INVESTMENTS LIFE INS CO	UT	23,882.2
GARDEN STATE LIFE INS CO	TX	120.3
GERBER LIFE INS CO	NY	2,749.8
ILLINOIS MUTUAL LIFE INS CO	IL	1,368.4
MASSACHUSETTS MUTUAL LIFE INS CO	MA	190,575.4
MIDWESTERN UNITED LIFE INS CO	IN	236.3
MML BAY STATE LIFE INS CO	CT	4,682.4
MUTUAL OF AMERICA LIFE INS CO	NY	17,110.0
NEW YORK LIFE INS CO	NY	143,501.4
NIPPON LIFE INS CO OF AMERICA	IA	211.7
NORTHWESTERN MUTUAL LIFE INS CO	WI	223,102.7
PACIFIC LIFE INS CO	NE	111,429.1
PHYSICIANS LIFE INS CO	NE	1,421.0
STANDARD LIFE & ACCIDENT INS CO	TX	523.8

Rating: B+

INSURANCE COMPANY NAME	DOM. STATE	TOTAL ASSETS ($MIL)
AETNA HEALTH & LIFE INS CO	CT	2,221.2
AETNA LIFE INS CO	CT	22,602.5
AMERICAN FAMILY LIFE ASR CO OF COLUM	NE	110,401.3
AMERICAN FIDELITY ASR CO	OK	4,856.7
AMERICAN UNITED LIFE INS CO	IN	22,778.8
ASSURITY LIFE INS CO	NE	2,452.3
BOSTON MUTUAL LIFE INS CO	MA	1,230.4

INSURANCE COMPANY NAME	DOM. STATE	TOTAL ASSETS ($MIL)
COLORADO BANKERS LIFE INS CO	CO	280.1
FARM BUREAU LIFE INS CO	IA	8,042.3
GENERAL RE LIFE CORP	CT	3,335.8
GOVERNMENT PERSONNEL MUTUAL L I C	TX	830.8
JACKSON NATIONAL LIFE INS CO	MI	176,820.4
LINCOLN BENEFIT LIFE CO	NE	12,911.3
MEDICO CORP LIFE INS CO	NE	26.0
MERIT LIFE INS CO	IN	584.3
MIDLAND NATIONAL LIFE INS CO	IA	40,607.9
MINNESOTA LIFE INS CO	MN	34,693.9
MUTUAL OF OMAHA INS CO	NE	6,568.9
NATIONAL BENEFIT LIFE INS CO	NY	480.5
NATIONAL FARMERS UNION LIFE INS CO	TX	216.9
NATIONAL WESTERN LIFE INS CO	CO	10,164.8
NEW YORK LIFE INS & ANNUITY CORP	DE	124,994.1
OHIO NATIONAL LIFE ASR CORP	OH	3,548.1
PACIFIC LIFE & ANNUITY CO	AZ	6,110.8
PARK AVENUE LIFE INS CO	DE	303.3
PIONEER MUTUAL LIFE INS CO	ND	510.6
PRINCIPAL LIFE INS CO	IA	148,782.3
SAVINGS BANK LIFE INS CO OF MA	MA	2,567.5
SENTRY LIFE INS CO OF NEW YORK	NY	76.3
STANDARD INS CO	OR	19,885.1
SYMETRA LIFE INS CO	IA	28,794.9
THRIVENT LIFE INS CO	MN	3,530.2
TRUSTMARK INS CO	IL	1,404.5
TRUSTMARK LIFE INS CO	IL	370.8
UNITED WORLD LIFE INS CO	NE	114.3
USABLE LIFE	AR	432.6

Ohio

INSURANCE COMPANY NAME	DOM. STATE	TOTAL ASSETS ($MIL)
Rating: A+		
AMERICAN FAMILY LIFE INS CO	WI	5,200.5
COUNTRY LIFE INS CO	IL	10,573.7
PHYSICIANS MUTUAL INS CO	NE	1,989.7
STATE FARM LIFE INS CO	IL	62,712.0
TEACHERS INS & ANNUITY ASN OF AM	NY	261,389.2
Rating: A		
4 EVER LIFE INS CO	IL	200.3
AUTO-OWNERS LIFE INS CO	MI	3,592.1
BERKSHIRE LIFE INS CO OF AMERICA	MA	3,640.3
FEDERATED LIFE INS CO	MN	1,497.0
GUARDIAN LIFE INS CO OF AMERICA	NY	44,890.2
PARKER CENTENNIAL ASR CO	WI	89.4
RESERVE NATIONAL INS CO	OK	112.1
SENTRY LIFE INS CO	WI	5,237.9
UNITED FARM FAMILY LIFE INS CO	IN	2,129.9
USAA LIFE INS CO	TX	21,964.7
Rating: A-		
ALLSTATE ASR CO	IL	12.3
AMALGAMATED LIFE INS CO	NY	110.5
AMERICAN REPUBLIC INS CO	IA	797.6
ANTHEM LIFE INS CO	IN	559.7
BALBOA LIFE INS CO	CA	58.9
CENTRAL STATES H & L CO OF OMAHA	NE	407.1
CHARTER NATIONAL LIFE INS CO	IL	133.2
COMPANION LIFE INS CO	SC	274.9
COUNTRY INVESTORS LIFE ASR CO	IL	289.8
DEARBORN NATIONAL LIFE INS CO	IL	2,183.0
ERIE FAMILY LIFE INS CO	PA	2,077.0
FAMILY HERITAGE LIFE INS CO OF AMER	OH	725.3
FIDELITY INVESTMENTS LIFE INS CO	UT	23,882.2
GARDEN STATE LIFE INS CO	TX	120.3
GERBER LIFE INS CO	NY	2,749.8
ILLINOIS MUTUAL LIFE INS CO	IL	1,368.4
MASSACHUSETTS MUTUAL LIFE INS CO	MA	190,575.4
MIDWESTERN UNITED LIFE INS CO	IN	236.3
MML BAY STATE LIFE INS CO	CT	4,682.4
MUTUAL OF AMERICA LIFE INS CO	NY	17,110.0
NEW YORK LIFE INS CO	NY	143,501.4
NIPPON LIFE INS CO OF AMERICA	IA	211.7
NORTHWESTERN MUTUAL LIFE INS CO	WI	223,102.7
PACIFIC LIFE INS CO	NE	111,429.1
PHYSICIANS LIFE INS CO	NE	1,421.0
STANDARD LIFE & ACCIDENT INS CO	TX	523.8
Rating: B+		
AETNA HEALTH & LIFE INS CO	CT	2,221.2
AETNA LIFE INS CO	CT	22,602.5
AMERICAN FAMILY LIFE ASR CO OF COLUM	NE	110,401.3
AMERICAN FIDELITY ASR CO	OK	4,856.7
AMERICAN UNITED LIFE INS CO	IN	22,778.8
ASSURITY LIFE INS CO	NE	2,452.3
BOSTON MUTUAL LIFE INS CO	MA	1,230.4
COLORADO BANKERS LIFE INS CO	CO	280.1

INSURANCE COMPANY NAME	DOM. STATE	TOTAL ASSETS ($MIL)
GENERAL RE LIFE CORP	CT	3,335.8
GOVERNMENT PERSONNEL MUTUAL L I C	TX	830.8
JACKSON NATIONAL LIFE INS CO	MI	176,820.4
LINCOLN BENEFIT LIFE CO	NE	12,911.3
MEDICO CORP LIFE INS CO	NE	26.0
MERIT LIFE INS CO	IN	584.3
MIDLAND NATIONAL LIFE INS CO	IA	40,607.9
MINNESOTA LIFE INS CO	MN	34,693.9
MUTUAL OF OMAHA INS CO	NE	6,568.9
NATIONAL BENEFIT LIFE INS CO	NY	480.5
NATIONAL FARMERS UNION LIFE INS CO	TX	216.9
NATIONAL WESTERN LIFE INS CO	CO	10,164.8
NEW YORK LIFE INS & ANNUITY CORP	DE	124,994.1
OHIO NATIONAL LIFE ASR CORP	OH	3,548.1
PACIFIC LIFE & ANNUITY CO	AZ	6,110.8
PARK AVENUE LIFE INS CO	DE	303.3
PIONEER MUTUAL LIFE INS CO	ND	510.6
PRINCIPAL LIFE INS CO	IA	148,782.3
SAVINGS BANK LIFE INS CO OF MA	MA	2,567.5
STANDARD INS CO	OR	19,885.1
SYMETRA LIFE INS CO	IA	28,794.9
THRIVENT LIFE INS CO	MN	3,530.2
TRUSTMARK INS CO	IL	1,404.5
TRUSTMARK LIFE INS CO	IL	370.8
UNITED WORLD LIFE INS CO	NE	114.3
USABLE LIFE	AR	432.6

Oklahoma

INSURANCE COMPANY NAME	DOM. STATE	TOTAL ASSETS ($MIL)	INSURANCE COMPANY NAME	DOM. STATE	TOTAL ASSETS ($MIL)
			FARM BUREAU LIFE INS CO	IA	8,042.3
			GENERAL RE LIFE CORP	CT	3,335.8
Rating: A+			GOVERNMENT PERSONNEL MUTUAL L I C	TX	830.8
			JACKSON NATIONAL LIFE INS CO	MI	176,820.4
COUNTRY LIFE INS CO	IL	10,573.7	LINCOLN BENEFIT LIFE CO	NE	12,911.3
PHYSICIANS MUTUAL INS CO	NE	1,989.7	MEDICO CORP LIFE INS CO	NE	26.0
STATE FARM LIFE INS CO	IL	62,712.0	MERIT LIFE INS CO	IN	584.3
TEACHERS INS & ANNUITY ASN OF AM	NY	261,389.2	MIDLAND NATIONAL LIFE INS CO	IA	40,607.9
			MINNESOTA LIFE INS CO	MN	34,693.9
Rating: A			MUTUAL OF OMAHA INS CO	NE	6,568.4
			NATIONAL BENEFIT LIFE INS CO	NY	480.5
4 EVER LIFE INS CO	IL	200.3	NATIONAL FARMERS UNION LIFE INS CO	TX	216.9
BERKSHIRE LIFE INS CO OF AMERICA	MA	3,640.3	NATIONAL WESTERN LIFE INS CO	CO	10,164.8
FEDERATED LIFE INS CO	MN	1,497.0	NEW YORK LIFE INS & ANNUITY CORP	DE	124,994.1
GUARDIAN LIFE INS CO OF AMERICA	NY	44,890.2	OHIO NATIONAL LIFE ASR CORP	OH	3,548.1
LIFEWISE ASR CO	WA	125.6	PACIFIC LIFE & ANNUITY CO	AZ	6,110.8
PARKER CENTENNIAL ASR CO	WI	89.4	PARK AVENUE LIFE INS CO	DE	303.3
RESERVE NATIONAL INS CO	OK	112.1	PIONEER MUTUAL LIFE INS CO	ND	510.6
SENTRY LIFE INS CO	WI	5,237.9	PRINCIPAL LIFE INS CO	IA	148,782.3
USAA LIFE INS CO	TX	21,964.7	SAVINGS BANK LIFE INS CO OF MA	MA	2,567.5
			STANDARD INS CO	OR	19,885.1
Rating: A-			SYMETRA LIFE INS CO	IA	28,794.9
			THRIVENT LIFE INS CO	MN	3,530.2
ALLSTATE ASR CO	IL	12.3	TRUSTMARK INS CO	IL	1,404.5
AMALGAMATED LIFE INS CO	NY	110.5	TRUSTMARK LIFE INS CO	IL	370.8
AMERICAN REPUBLIC INS CO	IA	797.6	UNITED WORLD LIFE INS CO	NE	114.3
ANTHEM LIFE INS CO	IN	559.7	USABLE LIFE	AR	432.6
BALBOA LIFE INS CO	CA	58.9			
CENTRAL STATES H & L CO OF OMAHA	NE	407.1			
CHARTER NATIONAL LIFE INS CO	IL	133.2			
COMPANION LIFE INS CO	SC	274.9			
COUNTRY INVESTORS LIFE ASR CO	IL	289.8			
DEARBORN NATIONAL LIFE INS CO	IL	2,183.0			
FAMILY HERITAGE LIFE INS CO OF AMER	OH	725.3			
FIDELITY INVESTMENTS LIFE INS CO	UT	23,882.2			
GARDEN STATE LIFE INS CO	TX	120.3			
GERBER LIFE INS CO	NY	2,749.8			
ILLINOIS MUTUAL LIFE INS CO	IL	1,368.4			
LIFE INS CO OF ALABAMA	AL	112.0			
MASSACHUSETTS MUTUAL LIFE INS CO	MA	190,575.4			
MIDWESTERN UNITED LIFE INS CO	IN	236.3			
MML BAY STATE LIFE INS CO	CT	4,682.4			
MUTUAL OF AMERICA LIFE INS CO	NY	17,110.0			
NEW YORK LIFE INS CO	NY	143,501.4			
NIPPON LIFE INS CO OF AMERICA	IA	211.7			
NORTHWESTERN MUTUAL LIFE INS CO	WI	223,102.7			
PACIFIC GUARDIAN LIFE INS CO LTD	HI	511.7			
PACIFIC LIFE INS CO	NE	111,429.1			
PHYSICIANS LIFE INS CO	NE	1,421.0			
SHELTER LIFE INS CO	MO	1,108.6			
STANDARD LIFE & ACCIDENT INS CO	TX	523.8			
Rating: B+					
AETNA HEALTH & LIFE INS CO	CT	2,221.2			
AETNA LIFE INS CO	CT	22,602.5			
AMERICAN FAMILY LIFE ASR CO OF COLUM	NE	110,401.3			
AMERICAN FIDELITY ASR CO	OK	4,856.7			
AMERICAN UNITED LIFE INS CO	IN	22,778.8			
ASSURITY LIFE INS CO	NE	2,452.3			
BOSTON MUTUAL LIFE INS CO	MA	1,230.4			
COLORADO BANKERS LIFE INS CO	CO	280.1			

Oregon

INSURANCE COMPANY NAME	DOM. STATE	TOTAL ASSETS ($MIL)
Rating: A+		
AMERICAN FAMILY LIFE INS CO	WI	5,200.5
COUNTRY LIFE INS CO	IL	10,573.7
PHYSICIANS MUTUAL INS CO	NE	1,989.7
STATE FARM LIFE INS CO	IL	62,712.0
TEACHERS INS & ANNUITY ASN OF AM	NY	261,389.2
Rating: A		
4 EVER LIFE INS CO	IL	200.3
AUTO-OWNERS LIFE INS CO	MI	3,592.1
BERKSHIRE LIFE INS CO OF AMERICA	MA	3,640.3
FEDERATED LIFE INS CO	MN	1,497.0
GUARDIAN LIFE INS CO OF AMERICA	NY	44,890.2
LIFEWISE ASR CO	WA	125.6
PARKER CENTENNIAL ASR CO	WI	89.4
RESERVE NATIONAL INS CO	OK	112.1
SENTRY LIFE INS CO	WI	5,237.9
USAA LIFE INS CO	TX	21,964.7
Rating: A-		
ALLSTATE ASR CO	IL	12.3
AMALGAMATED LIFE INS CO	NY	110.5
AMERICAN REPUBLIC INS CO	IA	797.6
ANTHEM LIFE INS CO	IN	559.7
BALBOA LIFE INS CO	CA	58.9
CENTRAL STATES H & L CO OF OMAHA	NE	407.1
CHARTER NATIONAL LIFE INS CO	IL	133.2
COMPANION LIFE INS CO	SC	274.9
COUNTRY INVESTORS LIFE ASR CO	IL	289.8
DEARBORN NATIONAL LIFE INS CO	IL	2,183.0
FAMILY HERITAGE LIFE INS CO OF AMER	OH	725.3
FIDELITY INVESTMENTS LIFE INS CO	UT	23,882.2
GARDEN STATE LIFE INS CO	TX	120.3
GERBER LIFE INS CO	NY	2,749.8
ILLINOIS MUTUAL LIFE INS CO	IL	1,368.4
MASSACHUSETTS MUTUAL LIFE INS CO	MA	190,575.4
MIDWESTERN UNITED LIFE INS CO	IN	236.3
MML BAY STATE LIFE INS CO	CT	4,682.4
MUTUAL OF AMERICA LIFE INS CO	NY	17,110.0
NEW YORK LIFE INS CO	NY	143,501.4
NIPPON LIFE INS CO OF AMERICA	IA	211.7
NORTHWESTERN MUTUAL LIFE INS CO	WI	223,102.7
PACIFIC GUARDIAN LIFE INS CO LTD	HI	511.7
PACIFIC LIFE INS CO	NE	111,429.1
PHYSICIANS LIFE INS CO	NE	1,421.0
STANDARD LIFE & ACCIDENT INS CO	TX	523.8
Rating: B+		
AETNA HEALTH & LIFE INS CO	CT	2,221.2
AETNA LIFE INS CO	CT	22,602.5
AMERICAN FAMILY LIFE ASR CO OF COLUM	NE	110,401.3
AMERICAN FIDELITY ASR CO	OK	4,856.7
AMERICAN UNITED LIFE INS CO	IN	22,778.8
ASSURITY LIFE INS CO	NE	2,452.3
BOSTON MUTUAL LIFE INS CO	MA	1,230.4
COLORADO BANKERS LIFE INS CO	CO	280.1

INSURANCE COMPANY NAME	DOM. STATE	TOTAL ASSETS ($MIL)
FARM BUREAU LIFE INS CO	IA	8,042.3
GENERAL RE LIFE CORP	CT	3,335.8
GOVERNMENT PERSONNEL MUTUAL L I C	TX	830.8
JACKSON NATIONAL LIFE INS CO	MI	176,820.4
LINCOLN BENEFIT LIFE CO	NE	12,911.3
MEDICO CORP LIFE INS CO	NE	26.0
MERIT LIFE INS CO	IN	584.3
MIDLAND NATIONAL LIFE INS CO	IA	40,607.9
MINNESOTA LIFE INS CO	MN	34,693.9
MUTUAL OF OMAHA INS CO	NE	6,568.9
NATIONAL BENEFIT LIFE INS CO	NY	480.5
NATIONAL FARMERS UNION LIFE INS CO	TX	216.9
NATIONAL WESTERN LIFE INS CO	CO	10,164.8
NEW YORK LIFE INS & ANNUITY CORP	DE	124,994.1
OHIO NATIONAL LIFE ASR CORP	OH	3,548.1
PACIFIC LIFE & ANNUITY CO	AZ	6,110.8
PARK AVENUE LIFE INS CO	DE	303.3
PIONEER MUTUAL LIFE INS CO	ND	510.6
PRINCIPAL LIFE INS CO	IA	148,782.3
SAVINGS BANK LIFE INS CO OF MA	MA	2,567.5
STANDARD INS CO	OR	19,885.1
SYMETRA LIFE INS CO	IA	28,794.9
THRIVENT LIFE INS CO	MN	3,530.2
TRUSTMARK INS CO	IL	1,404.5
TRUSTMARK LIFE INS CO	IL	370.8
UNITED WORLD LIFE INS CO	NE	114.3
USABLE LIFE	AR	432.6

Pennsylvania

INSURANCE COMPANY NAME	DOM. STATE	TOTAL ASSETS ($MIL)
Rating: A+		
COUNTRY LIFE INS CO	IL	10,573.7
PHYSICIANS MUTUAL INS CO	NE	1,989.7
STATE FARM LIFE INS CO	IL	62,712.0
TEACHERS INS & ANNUITY ASN OF AM	NY	261,389.2
Rating: A		
4 EVER LIFE INS CO	IL	200.3
AUTO-OWNERS LIFE INS CO	MI	3,592.1
BERKSHIRE LIFE INS CO OF AMERICA	MA	3,640.3
FEDERATED LIFE INS CO	MN	1,497.0
GUARDIAN LIFE INS CO OF AMERICA	NY	44,890.2
PARKER CENTENNIAL ASR CO	WI	89.4
RESERVE NATIONAL INS CO	OK	112.1
SENTRY LIFE INS CO	WI	5,237.9
SHELTERPOINT LIFE INS CO	NY	104.4
UNITED FARM FAMILY LIFE INS CO	IN	2,129.9
USAA LIFE INS CO	TX	21,964.7
Rating: A-		
ALLSTATE ASR CO	IL	12.3
AMALGAMATED LIFE INS CO	NY	110.5
AMERICAN REPUBLIC INS CO	IA	797.6
ANTHEM LIFE INS CO	IN	559.7
BALBOA LIFE INS CO	CA	58.9
CENTRAL STATES H & L CO OF OMAHA	NE	407.1
CHARTER NATIONAL LIFE INS CO	IL	133.2
CIGNA LIFE INS CO OF NEW YORK	NY	380.6
COMPANION LIFE INS CO	SC	274.9
COUNTRY INVESTORS LIFE ASR CO	IL	289.8
DEARBORN NATIONAL LIFE INS CO	IL	2,183.0
ERIE FAMILY LIFE INS CO	PA	2,077.0
FAMILY HERITAGE LIFE INS CO OF AMER	OH	725.3
FIDELITY INVESTMENTS LIFE INS CO	UT	23,882.2
GARDEN STATE LIFE INS CO	TX	120.3
GERBER LIFE INS CO	NY	2,749.8
ILLINOIS MUTUAL LIFE INS CO	IL	1,368.4
MASSACHUSETTS MUTUAL LIFE INS CO	MA	190,575.4
MIDWESTERN UNITED LIFE INS CO	IN	236.3
MML BAY STATE LIFE INS CO	CT	4,682.4
MUTUAL OF AMERICA LIFE INS CO	NY	17,110.0
NEW YORK LIFE INS CO	NY	143,501.4
NIPPON LIFE INS CO OF AMERICA	IA	211.7
NORTHWESTERN MUTUAL LIFE INS CO	WI	223,102.7
PACIFIC LIFE INS CO	NE	111,429.1
PHYSICIANS LIFE INS CO	NE	1,421.0
STANDARD LIFE & ACCIDENT INS CO	TX	523.8
Rating: B+		
AETNA HEALTH & LIFE INS CO	CT	2,221.2
AETNA LIFE INS CO	CT	22,602.5
AMERICAN FAMILY LIFE ASR CO OF COLUM	NE	110,401.3
AMERICAN FIDELITY ASR CO	OK	4,856.7
AMERICAN UNITED LIFE INS CO	IN	22,778.8
ASSURITY LIFE INS CO	NE	2,452.3
BOSTON MUTUAL LIFE INS CO	MA	1,230.4

INSURANCE COMPANY NAME	DOM. STATE	TOTAL ASSETS ($MIL)
COLORADO BANKERS LIFE INS CO	CO	280.1
GENERAL RE LIFE CORP	CT	3,335.8
GOVERNMENT PERSONNEL MUTUAL L I C	TX	830.8
JACKSON NATIONAL LIFE INS CO	MI	176,820.4
LINCOLN BENEFIT LIFE CO	NE	12,911.3
MEDICO CORP LIFE INS CO	NE	26.0
MERIT LIFE INS CO	IN	584.3
MIDLAND NATIONAL LIFE INS CO	IA	40,607.9
MINNESOTA LIFE INS CO	MN	34,693.9
MUTUAL OF OMAHA INS CO	NE	6,568.9
NATIONAL BENEFIT LIFE INS CO	NY	480.5
NATIONAL FARMERS UNION LIFE INS CO	TX	216.9
NATIONAL WESTERN LIFE INS CO	CO	10,164.8
NEW YORK LIFE INS & ANNUITY CORP	DE	124,994.1
OHIO NATIONAL LIFE ASR CORP	OH	3,548.1
PACIFIC LIFE & ANNUITY CO	AZ	6,110.8
PARK AVENUE LIFE INS CO	DE	303.3
PIONEER MUTUAL LIFE INS CO	ND	510.6
PRINCIPAL LIFE INS CO	IA	148,782.3
SAVINGS BANK LIFE INS CO OF MA	MA	2,567.5
STANDARD INS CO	OR	19,885.1
SYMETRA LIFE INS CO	IA	28,794.9
THRIVENT LIFE INS CO	MN	3,530.2
TRUSTMARK INS CO	IL	1,404.5
TRUSTMARK LIFE INS CO	IL	370.8
UNITED WORLD LIFE INS CO	NE	114.3
USABLE LIFE	AR	432.6

Puerto Rico

INSURANCE COMPANY NAME	DOM. STATE	TOTAL ASSETS ($MIL)
Rating: A+		
TEACHERS INS & ANNUITY ASN OF AM	NY	261,389.2
Rating: A		
4 EVER LIFE INS CO	IL	200.3
SOUTHERN FARM BUREAU LIFE INS CO	MS	12,937.4
TRANS OCEANIC LIFE INS CO	PR	62.9
Rating: A-		
CENTRAL STATES H & L CO OF OMAHA	NE	407.1
DEARBORN NATIONAL LIFE INS CO	IL	2,183.0
FAMILY HERITAGE LIFE INS CO OF AMER	OH	725.3
GERBER LIFE INS CO	NY	2,749.8
MASSACHUSETTS MUTUAL LIFE INS CO	MA	190,575.4
NEW YORK LIFE INS CO	NY	143,501.4
Rating: B+		
AETNA LIFE INS CO	CT	22,602.5
AMERICAN FAMILY LIFE ASR CO OF COLUM	NE	110,401.3
AMERICAN FIDELITY ASR CO	OK	4,856.7
BOSTON MUTUAL LIFE INS CO	MA	1,230.4
MERIT LIFE INS CO	IN	584.3
MIDLAND NATIONAL LIFE INS CO	IA	40,607.9
MINNESOTA LIFE INS CO	MN	34,693.9
MUTUAL OF OMAHA INS CO	NE	6,568.9
NATIONAL WESTERN LIFE INS CO	CO	10,164.8
OHIO NATIONAL LIFE ASR CORP	OH	3,548.1
PRINCIPAL LIFE INS CO	IA	148,782.3
TRUSTMARK INS CO	IL	1,404.5

INSURANCE COMPANY NAME	DOM. STATE	TOTAL ASSETS ($MIL)

Rhode Island

INSURANCE COMPANY NAME	DOM. STATE	TOTAL ASSETS ($MIL)
MERIT LIFE INS CO	IN	584.3
MIDLAND NATIONAL LIFE INS CO	IA	40,607.9
MINNESOTA LIFE INS CO	MN	34,693.9
MUTUAL OF OMAHA INS CO	NE	6,568.9
NATIONAL BENEFIT LIFE INS CO	NY	480.5
NATIONAL WESTERN LIFE INS CO	CO	10,164.8
NEW YORK LIFE INS & ANNUITY CORP	DE	124,994.1
OHIO NATIONAL LIFE ASR CORP	OH	3,548.1
PACIFIC LIFE & ANNUITY CO	AZ	6,110.8
PARK AVENUE LIFE INS CO	DE	303.3
PIONEER MUTUAL LIFE INS CO	ND	510.6
PRINCIPAL LIFE INS CO	IA	148,782.3
SAVINGS BANK LIFE INS CO OF MA	MA	2,567.5
STANDARD INS CO	OR	19,885.1
SYMETRA LIFE INS CO	IA	28,794.9
TRUSTMARK INS CO	IL	1,404.5
TRUSTMARK LIFE INS CO	IL	370.8
UNITED WORLD LIFE INS CO	NE	114.3
USABLE LIFE	AR	432.6

Rating: A+

INSURANCE COMPANY NAME	DOM. STATE	TOTAL ASSETS ($MIL)
COUNTRY LIFE INS CO	IL	10,573.7
PHYSICIANS MUTUAL INS CO	NE	1,989.7
STATE FARM LIFE INS CO	IL	62,712.0
TEACHERS INS & ANNUITY ASN OF AM	NY	261,389.2

Rating: A

INSURANCE COMPANY NAME	DOM. STATE	TOTAL ASSETS ($MIL)
4 EVER LIFE INS CO	IL	200.3
BERKSHIRE LIFE INS CO OF AMERICA	MA	3,640.3
FEDERATED LIFE INS CO	MN	1,497.0
GUARDIAN LIFE INS CO OF AMERICA	NY	44,890.2
PARKER CENTENNIAL ASR CO	WI	89.4
SENTRY LIFE INS CO	WI	5,237.9
SHELTERPOINT LIFE INS CO	NY	104.4
USAA LIFE INS CO	TX	21,964.7

Rating: A-

INSURANCE COMPANY NAME	DOM. STATE	TOTAL ASSETS ($MIL)
ALLSTATE ASR CO	IL	12.3
AMALGAMATED LIFE INS CO	NY	110.5
AMERICAN REPUBLIC INS CO	IA	797.6
BALBOA LIFE INS CO	CA	58.9
CENTRAL STATES H & L CO OF OMAHA	NE	407.1
CHARTER NATIONAL LIFE INS CO	IL	133.2
COMPANION LIFE INS CO	SC	274.9
COUNTRY INVESTORS LIFE ASR CO	IL	289.8
DEARBORN NATIONAL LIFE INS CO	IL	2,183.0
FAMILY HERITAGE LIFE INS CO OF AMER	OH	725.3
FIDELITY INVESTMENTS LIFE INS CO	UT	23,882.2
GARDEN STATE LIFE INS CO	TX	120.3
GERBER LIFE INS CO	NY	2,749.8
ILLINOIS MUTUAL LIFE INS CO	IL	1,368.4
MASSACHUSETTS MUTUAL LIFE INS CO	MA	190,575.4
MIDWESTERN UNITED LIFE INS CO	IN	236.3
MML BAY STATE LIFE INS CO	CT	4,682.4
MUTUAL OF AMERICA LIFE INS CO	NY	17,110.0
NEW YORK LIFE INS CO	NY	143,501.4
NIPPON LIFE INS CO OF AMERICA	IA	211.7
NORTHWESTERN MUTUAL LIFE INS CO	WI	223,102.7
PACIFIC LIFE INS CO	NE	111,429.1
PHYSICIANS LIFE INS CO	NE	1,421.0
STANDARD LIFE & ACCIDENT INS CO	TX	523.8

Rating: B+

INSURANCE COMPANY NAME	DOM. STATE	TOTAL ASSETS ($MIL)
AETNA HEALTH & LIFE INS CO	CT	2,221.2
AETNA LIFE INS CO	CT	22,602.5
AMERICAN FAMILY LIFE ASR CO OF COLUM	NE	110,401.3
AMERICAN FIDELITY ASR CO	OK	4,856.7
AMERICAN UNITED LIFE INS CO	IN	22,778.8
ASSURITY LIFE INS CO	NE	2,452.3
BOSTON MUTUAL LIFE INS CO	MA	1,230.4
COLORADO BANKERS LIFE INS CO	CO	280.1
GENERAL RE LIFE CORP	CT	3,335.8
GOVERNMENT PERSONNEL MUTUAL L I C	TX	830.8
HM LIFE INS CO OF NEW YORK	NY	72.4
JACKSON NATIONAL LIFE INS CO	MI	176,820.4
LINCOLN BENEFIT LIFE CO	NE	12,911.3

South Carolina

INSURANCE COMPANY NAME	DOM. STATE	TOTAL ASSETS ($MIL)
Rating: A+		
AMERICAN FAMILY LIFE INS CO	WI	5,200.5
COUNTRY LIFE INS CO	IL	10,573.7
PHYSICIANS MUTUAL INS CO	NE	1,989.7
STATE FARM LIFE INS CO	IL	62,712.0
TEACHERS INS & ANNUITY ASN OF AM	NY	261,389.2
Rating: A		
4 EVER LIFE INS CO	IL	200.3
AUTO-OWNERS LIFE INS CO	MI	3,592.1
BERKSHIRE LIFE INS CO OF AMERICA	MA	3,640.3
FEDERATED LIFE INS CO	MN	1,497.0
GUARDIAN LIFE INS CO OF AMERICA	NY	44,890.2
PARKER CENTENNIAL ASR CO	WI	89.4
RESERVE NATIONAL INS CO	OK	112.1
SENTRY LIFE INS CO	WI	5,237.9
SHELTERPOINT LIFE INS CO	NY	104.4
SOUTHERN FARM BUREAU LIFE INS CO	MS	12,937.4
USAA LIFE INS CO	TX	21,964.7
Rating: A-		
ALLSTATE ASR CO	IL	12.3
AMALGAMATED LIFE INS CO	NY	110.5
AMERICAN REPUBLIC INS CO	IA	797.6
ANTHEM LIFE INS CO	IN	559.7
BALBOA LIFE INS CO	CA	58.9
CENTRAL STATES H & L CO OF OMAHA	NE	407.1
CHARTER NATIONAL LIFE INS CO	IL	133.2
COMPANION LIFE INS CO	SC	274.9
COTTON STATES LIFE INS CO	GA	330.7
COUNTRY INVESTORS LIFE ASR CO	IL	289.8
DEARBORN NATIONAL LIFE INS CO	IL	2,183.0
FAMILY HERITAGE LIFE INS CO OF AMER	OH	725.3
FIDELITY INVESTMENTS LIFE INS CO	UT	23,882.2
GARDEN STATE LIFE INS CO	TX	120.3
GERBER LIFE INS CO	NY	2,749.8
ILLINOIS MUTUAL LIFE INS CO	IL	1,368.4
LIFE INS CO OF ALABAMA	AL	112.0
MASSACHUSETTS MUTUAL LIFE INS CO	MA	190,575.4
MIDWESTERN UNITED LIFE INS CO	IN	236.3
MML BAY STATE LIFE INS CO	CT	4,682.4
MUTUAL OF AMERICA LIFE INS CO	NY	17,110.0
NEW YORK LIFE INS CO	NY	143,501.4
NIPPON LIFE INS CO OF AMERICA	IA	211.7
NORTHWESTERN MUTUAL LIFE INS CO	WI	223,102.7
PACIFIC LIFE INS CO	NE	111,429.1
PHYSICIANS LIFE INS CO	NE	1,421.0
STANDARD LIFE & ACCIDENT INS CO	TX	523.8
Rating: B+		
AETNA HEALTH & LIFE INS CO	CT	2,221.2
AETNA LIFE INS CO	CT	22,602.5
AMERICAN FAMILY LIFE ASR CO OF COLUM	NE	110,401.3
AMERICAN FIDELITY ASR CO	OK	4,856.7
AMERICAN UNITED LIFE INS CO	IN	22,778.8
ASSURITY LIFE INS CO	NE	2,452.3

INSURANCE COMPANY NAME	DOM. STATE	TOTAL ASSETS ($MIL)
BOSTON MUTUAL LIFE INS CO	MA	1,230.4
COLORADO BANKERS LIFE INS CO	CO	280.1
GENERAL RE LIFE CORP	CT	3,335.8
GOVERNMENT PERSONNEL MUTUAL L I C	TX	830.8
GREATER GEORGIA LIFE INS CO	GA	49.9
JACKSON NATIONAL LIFE INS CO	MI	176,820.4
LINCOLN BENEFIT LIFE CO	NE	12,911.3
MEDICO CORP LIFE INS CO	NE	26.0
MERIT LIFE INS CO	IN	584.3
MIDLAND NATIONAL LIFE INS CO	IA	40,607.9
MINNESOTA LIFE INS CO	MN	34,693.9
MUTUAL OF OMAHA INS CO	NE	6,568.9
NATIONAL BENEFIT LIFE INS CO	NY	480.5
NATIONAL WESTERN LIFE INS CO	CO	10,164.8
NEW YORK LIFE INS & ANNUITY CORP	DE	124,994.1
OHIO NATIONAL LIFE ASR CORP	OH	3,548.1
PACIFIC LIFE & ANNUITY CO	AZ	6,110.8
PARK AVENUE LIFE INS CO	DE	303.3
PIONEER MUTUAL LIFE INS CO	ND	510.6
PRINCIPAL LIFE INS CO	IA	148,782.3
SAVINGS BANK LIFE INS CO OF MA	MA	2,567.5
STANDARD INS CO	OR	19,885.1
SYMETRA LIFE INS CO	IA	28,794.9
THRIVENT LIFE INS CO	MN	3,530.2
TRUSTMARK INS CO	IL	1,404.5
TRUSTMARK LIFE INS CO	IL	370.8
UNITED WORLD LIFE INS CO	NE	114.3
USABLE LIFE	AR	432.6

South Dakota

INSURANCE COMPANY NAME	DOM. STATE	TOTAL ASSETS ($MIL)

Rating: A+

INSURANCE COMPANY NAME	DOM. STATE	TOTAL ASSETS ($MIL)
AMERICAN FAMILY LIFE INS CO	WI	5,200.5
COUNTRY LIFE INS CO	IL	10,573.7
PHYSICIANS MUTUAL INS CO	NE	1,989.7
STATE FARM LIFE INS CO	IL	62,712.0
TEACHERS INS & ANNUITY ASN OF AM	NY	261,389.2

Rating: A

INSURANCE COMPANY NAME	DOM. STATE	TOTAL ASSETS ($MIL)
4 EVER LIFE INS CO	IL	200.3
AUTO-OWNERS LIFE INS CO	MI	3,592.1
BERKSHIRE LIFE INS CO OF AMERICA	MA	3,640.3
FEDERATED LIFE INS CO	MN	1,497.0
GUARDIAN LIFE INS CO OF AMERICA	NY	44,890.2
PARKER CENTENNIAL ASR CO	WI	89.4
RESERVE NATIONAL INS CO	OK	112.1
SENTRY LIFE INS CO	WI	5,237.9
USAA LIFE INS CO	TX	21,964.7

Rating: A-

INSURANCE COMPANY NAME	DOM. STATE	TOTAL ASSETS ($MIL)
ALLSTATE ASR CO	IL	12.3
AMALGAMATED LIFE INS CO	NY	110.5
AMERICAN REPUBLIC INS CO	IA	797.6
ANTHEM LIFE INS CO	IN	559.7
BALBOA LIFE INS CO	CA	58.9
CENTRAL STATES H & L CO OF OMAHA	NE	407.1
CHARTER NATIONAL LIFE INS CO	IL	133.2
COMPANION LIFE INS CO	SC	274.9
COUNTRY INVESTORS LIFE ASR CO	IL	289.8
DEARBORN NATIONAL LIFE INS CO	IL	2,183.0
FAMILY HERITAGE LIFE INS CO OF AMER	OH	725.3
FIDELITY INVESTMENTS LIFE INS CO	UT	23,882.2
GARDEN STATE LIFE INS CO	TX	120.3
GERBER LIFE INS CO	NY	2,749.8
ILLINOIS MUTUAL LIFE INS CO	IL	1,368.4
MASSACHUSETTS MUTUAL LIFE INS CO	MA	190,575.4
MIDWESTERN UNITED LIFE INS CO	IN	236.3
MML BAY STATE LIFE INS CO	CT	4,682.4
MUTUAL OF AMERICA LIFE INS CO	NY	17,110.0
NEW YORK LIFE INS CO	NY	143,501.4
NIPPON LIFE INS CO OF AMERICA	IA	211.7
NORTHWESTERN MUTUAL LIFE INS CO	WI	223,102.7
PACIFIC GUARDIAN LIFE INS CO LTD	HI	511.7
PACIFIC LIFE INS CO	NE	111,429.1
PHYSICIANS LIFE INS CO	NE	1,421.0
STANDARD LIFE & ACCIDENT INS CO	TX	523.8

Rating: B+

INSURANCE COMPANY NAME	DOM. STATE	TOTAL ASSETS ($MIL)
AETNA HEALTH & LIFE INS CO	CT	2,221.2
AETNA LIFE INS CO	CT	22,602.5
AMERICAN FAMILY LIFE ASR CO OF COLUM	NE	110,401.3
AMERICAN FIDELITY ASR CO	OK	4,856.7
AMERICAN UNITED LIFE INS CO	IN	22,778.8
ASSURITY LIFE INS CO	NE	2,452.3
BOSTON MUTUAL LIFE INS CO	MA	1,230.4
COLORADO BANKERS LIFE INS CO	CO	280.1
FARM BUREAU LIFE INS CO	IA	8,042.3

INSURANCE COMPANY NAME	DOM. STATE	TOTAL ASSETS ($MIL)
GENERAL RE LIFE CORP	CT	3,335.8
GOVERNMENT PERSONNEL MUTUAL L I C	TX	830.8
JACKSON NATIONAL LIFE INS CO	MI	176,820.4
LINCOLN BENEFIT LIFE CO	NE	12,911.3
MEDICO CORP LIFE INS CO	NE	26.0
MERIT LIFE INS CO	IN	584.3
MIDLAND NATIONAL LIFE INS CO	IA	40,607.9
MINNESOTA LIFE INS CO	MN	34,693.9
MUTUAL OF OMAHA INS CO	NE	6,568.9
NATIONAL BENEFIT LIFE INS CO	NY	480.5
NATIONAL FARMERS UNION LIFE INS CO	TX	216.9
NATIONAL WESTERN LIFE INS CO	CO	10,164.8
NEW YORK LIFE INS & ANNUITY CORP	DE	124,994.1
OHIO NATIONAL LIFE ASR CORP	OH	3,548.1
PACIFIC LIFE & ANNUITY CO	AZ	6,110.8
PARK AVENUE LIFE INS CO	DE	303.3
PIONEER MUTUAL LIFE INS CO	ND	510.6
PRINCIPAL LIFE INS CO	IA	148,782.3
SAVINGS BANK LIFE INS CO OF MA	MA	2,567.5
STANDARD INS CO	OR	19,885.1
SYMETRA LIFE INS CO	IA	28,794.9
THRIVENT LIFE INS CO	MN	3,530.2
TRUSTMARK INS CO	IL	1,404.5
TRUSTMARK LIFE INS CO	IL	370.8
UNITED WORLD LIFE INS CO	NE	114.3
USABLE LIFE	AR	432.6

Tennessee

INSURANCE COMPANY NAME	DOM. STATE	TOTAL ASSETS ($MIL)

Rating: A+

INSURANCE COMPANY NAME	DOM. STATE	TOTAL ASSETS ($MIL)
COUNTRY LIFE INS CO	IL	10,573.7
PHYSICIANS MUTUAL INS CO	NE	1,989.7
STATE FARM LIFE INS CO	IL	62,712.0
TEACHERS INS & ANNUITY ASN OF AM	NY	261,389.2

Rating: A

INSURANCE COMPANY NAME	DOM. STATE	TOTAL ASSETS ($MIL)
4 EVER LIFE INS CO	IL	200.3
AUTO-OWNERS LIFE INS CO	MI	3,592.1
BERKSHIRE LIFE INS CO OF AMERICA	MA	3,640.3
FEDERATED LIFE INS CO	MN	1,497.0
GUARDIAN LIFE INS CO OF AMERICA	NY	44,890.2
PARKER CENTENNIAL ASR CO	WI	89.4
RESERVE NATIONAL INS CO	OK	112.1
SENTRY LIFE INS CO	WI	5,237.9
SHELTERPOINT LIFE INS CO	NY	104.4
SOUTHERN FARM BUREAU LIFE INS CO	MS	12,937.4
TENNESSEE FARMERS LIFE INS CO	TN	1,978.3
USAA LIFE INS CO	TX	21,964.7

Rating: A-

INSURANCE COMPANY NAME	DOM. STATE	TOTAL ASSETS ($MIL)
ALLSTATE ASR CO	IL	12.3
AMALGAMATED LIFE INS CO	NY	110.5
AMERICAN REPUBLIC INS CO	IA	797.6
ANTHEM LIFE INS CO	IN	559.7
BALBOA LIFE INS CO	CA	58.9
CENTRAL STATES H & L CO OF OMAHA	NE	407.1
CHARTER NATIONAL LIFE INS CO	IL	133.2
CIGNA LIFE INS CO OF NEW YORK	NY	380.6
COMPANION LIFE INS CO	SC	274.9
COTTON STATES LIFE INS CO	GA	330.7
COUNTRY INVESTORS LIFE ASR CO	IL	289.8
DEARBORN NATIONAL LIFE INS CO	IL	2,183.0
ERIE FAMILY LIFE INS CO	PA	2,077.0
FAMILY HERITAGE LIFE INS CO OF AMER	OH	725.3
FIDELITY INVESTMENTS LIFE INS CO	UT	23,882.2
GARDEN STATE LIFE INS CO	TX	120.3
GERBER LIFE INS CO	NY	2,749.8
ILLINOIS MUTUAL LIFE INS CO	IL	1,368.4
LIFE INS CO OF ALABAMA	AL	112.0
MASSACHUSETTS MUTUAL LIFE INS CO	MA	190,575.4
MIDWESTERN UNITED LIFE INS CO	IN	236.3
MML BAY STATE LIFE INS CO	CT	4,682.4
MUTUAL OF AMERICA LIFE INS CO	NY	17,110.0
MUTUAL SAVINGS LIFE INS CO	AL	470.5
NEW YORK LIFE INS CO	NY	143,501.4
NIPPON LIFE INS CO OF AMERICA	IA	211.7
NORTHWESTERN MUTUAL LIFE INS CO	WI	223,102.7
PACIFIC LIFE INS CO	NE	111,429.1
PHYSICIANS LIFE INS CO	NE	1,421.0
SHELTER LIFE INS CO	MO	1,108.6
STANDARD LIFE & ACCIDENT INS CO	TX	523.8

Rating: B+

INSURANCE COMPANY NAME	DOM. STATE	TOTAL ASSETS ($MIL)
AETNA HEALTH & LIFE INS CO	CT	2,221.2
AETNA LIFE INS CO	CT	22,602.5

INSURANCE COMPANY NAME	DOM. STATE	TOTAL ASSETS ($MIL)
AMERICAN FAMILY LIFE ASR CO OF COLUM	NE	110,401.3
AMERICAN FIDELITY ASR CO	OK	4,856.7
AMERICAN UNITED LIFE INS CO	IN	22,778.8
ASSURITY LIFE INS CO	NE	2,452.3
BLUEBONNET LIFE INS CO	MS	54.6
BOSTON MUTUAL LIFE INS CO	MA	1,230.4
COLORADO BANKERS LIFE INS CO	CO	280.1
GENERAL RE LIFE CORP	CT	3,335.8
GOVERNMENT PERSONNEL MUTUAL L I C	TX	830.8
GREATER GEORGIA LIFE INS CO	GA	49.9
JACKSON NATIONAL LIFE INS CO	MI	176,820.4
LINCOLN BENEFIT LIFE CO	NE	12,911.3
MEDICO CORP LIFE INS CO	NE	26.0
MERIT LIFE INS CO	IN	584.3
MIDLAND NATIONAL LIFE INS CO	IA	40,607.9
MINNESOTA LIFE INS CO	MN	34,693.9
MUTUAL OF OMAHA INS CO	NE	6,568.9
NATIONAL BENEFIT LIFE INS CO	NY	480.5
NATIONAL WESTERN LIFE INS CO	CO	10,164.8
NEW YORK LIFE INS & ANNUITY CORP	DE	124,994.1
OHIO NATIONAL LIFE ASR CORP	OH	3,548.1
PACIFIC LIFE & ANNUITY CO	AZ	6,110.8
PARK AVENUE LIFE INS CO	DE	303.3
PIONEER MUTUAL LIFE INS CO	ND	510.6
PRINCIPAL LIFE INS CO	IA	148,782.3
SAVINGS BANK LIFE INS CO OF MA	MA	2,567.5
STANDARD INS CO	OR	19,885.1
SYMETRA LIFE INS CO	IA	28,794.9
THRIVENT LIFE INS CO	MN	3,530.2
TRUSTMARK INS CO	IL	1,404.5
TRUSTMARK LIFE INS CO	IL	370.8
UNITED WORLD LIFE INS CO	NE	114.3
USABLE LIFE	AR	432.6

Texas

INSURANCE COMPANY NAME	DOM. STATE	TOTAL ASSETS ($MIL)

Rating: A+

INSURANCE COMPANY NAME	DOM. STATE	TOTAL ASSETS ($MIL)
AMERICAN FAMILY LIFE INS CO	WI	5,200.5
COUNTRY LIFE INS CO	IL	10,573.7
PHYSICIANS MUTUAL INS CO	NE	1,989.7
STATE FARM LIFE INS CO	IL	62,712.0
TEACHERS INS & ANNUITY ASN OF AM	NY	261,389.2

Rating: A

INSURANCE COMPANY NAME	DOM. STATE	TOTAL ASSETS ($MIL)
4 EVER LIFE INS CO	IL	200.3
BERKSHIRE LIFE INS CO OF AMERICA	MA	3,640.3
FEDERATED LIFE INS CO	MN	1,497.0
GUARDIAN LIFE INS CO OF AMERICA	NY	44,890.2
LIFEWISE ASR CO	WA	125.6
PARKER CENTENNIAL ASR CO	WI	89.4
RESERVE NATIONAL INS CO	OK	112.1
SENTRY LIFE INS CO	WI	5,237.9
SOUTHERN FARM BUREAU LIFE INS CO	MS	12,937.4
USAA LIFE INS CO	TX	21,964.7

Rating: A-

INSURANCE COMPANY NAME	DOM. STATE	TOTAL ASSETS ($MIL)
ALLSTATE ASR CO	IL	12.3
AMALGAMATED LIFE INS CO	NY	110.5
AMERICAN REPUBLIC INS CO	IA	797.6
ANTHEM LIFE INS CO	IN	559.7
BALBOA LIFE INS CO	CA	58.9
CENTRAL STATES H & L CO OF OMAHA	NE	407.1
CHARTER NATIONAL LIFE INS CO	IL	133.2
COMPANION LIFE INS CO	SC	274.9
COUNTRY INVESTORS LIFE ASR CO	IL	289.8
DEARBORN NATIONAL LIFE INS CO	IL	2,183.0
FAMILY HERITAGE LIFE INS CO OF AMER	OH	725.3
FIDELITY INVESTMENTS LIFE INS CO	UT	23,882.2
GARDEN STATE LIFE INS CO	TX	120.3
GERBER LIFE INS CO	NY	2,749.8
ILLINOIS MUTUAL LIFE INS CO	IL	1,368.4
MASSACHUSETTS MUTUAL LIFE INS CO	MA	190,575.4
MIDWESTERN UNITED LIFE INS CO	IN	236.3
MML BAY STATE LIFE INS CO	CT	4,682.4
MUTUAL OF AMERICA LIFE INS CO	NY	17,110.0
NEW YORK LIFE INS CO	NY	143,501.4
NIPPON LIFE INS CO OF AMERICA	IA	211.7
NORTHWESTERN MUTUAL LIFE INS CO	WI	223,102.7
PACIFIC GUARDIAN LIFE INS CO LTD	HI	511.7
PACIFIC LIFE INS CO	NE	111,429.1
PHYSICIANS LIFE INS CO	NE	1,421.0
STANDARD LIFE & ACCIDENT INS CO	TX	523.8

Rating: B+

INSURANCE COMPANY NAME	DOM. STATE	TOTAL ASSETS ($MIL)
AETNA HEALTH & LIFE INS CO	CT	2,221.2
AETNA LIFE INS CO	CT	22,602.5
AMERICAN FAMILY LIFE ASR CO OF COLUM	NE	110,401.3
AMERICAN FIDELITY ASR CO	OK	4,856.7
AMERICAN UNITED LIFE INS CO	IN	22,778.8
ASSURITY LIFE INS CO	NE	2,452.3
BOSTON MUTUAL LIFE INS CO	MA	1,230.4
COLORADO BANKERS LIFE INS CO	CO	280.1

INSURANCE COMPANY NAME	DOM. STATE	TOTAL ASSETS ($MIL)
GENERAL RE LIFE CORP	CT	3,335.8
GOVERNMENT PERSONNEL MUTUAL L I C	TX	830.8
JACKSON NATIONAL LIFE INS CO	MI	176,820.4
LINCOLN BENEFIT LIFE CO	NE	12,911.3
LOCOMOTIVE ENGRS&COND MUT PROT ASSN	MI	55.4
MEDICO CORP LIFE INS CO	NE	26.0
MERIT LIFE INS CO	IN	584.3
MIDLAND NATIONAL LIFE INS CO	IA	40,607.9
MINNESOTA LIFE INS CO	MN	34,693.9
MUTUAL OF OMAHA INS CO	NE	6,568.9
NATIONAL BENEFIT LIFE INS CO	NY	480.5
NATIONAL FARMERS UNION LIFE INS CO	TX	216.9
NATIONAL WESTERN LIFE INS CO	CO	10,164.9
NEW YORK LIFE INS & ANNUITY CORP	DE	124,994.1
OHIO NATIONAL LIFE ASR CORP	OH	3,548.1
PACIFIC LIFE & ANNUITY CO	AZ	6,110.8
PARK AVENUE LIFE INS CO	DE	303.3
PIONEER MUTUAL LIFE INS CO	ND	510.6
PRINCIPAL LIFE INS CO	IA	148,782.3
SAVINGS BANK LIFE INS CO OF MA	MA	2,567.5
STANDARD INS CO	OR	19,885.1
SYMETRA LIFE INS CO	IA	28,794.9
THRIVENT LIFE INS CO	MN	3,530.2
TRUSTMARK INS CO	IL	1,404.5
TRUSTMARK LIFE INS CO	IL	370.8
UNITED WORLD LIFE INS CO	NE	114.3
USABLE LIFE	AR	432.6

Utah

INSURANCE COMPANY NAME	DOM. STATE	TOTAL ASSETS ($MIL)	INSURANCE COMPANY NAME	DOM. STATE	TOTAL ASSETS ($MIL)
			GENERAL RE LIFE CORP	CT	3,335.8
			GOVERNMENT PERSONNEL MUTUAL L I C	TX	830.8

Rating: A+

INSURANCE COMPANY NAME	DOM. STATE	TOTAL ASSETS ($MIL)
AMERICAN FAMILY LIFE INS CO	WI	5,200.5
COUNTRY LIFE INS CO	IL	10,573.7
PHYSICIANS MUTUAL INS CO	NE	1,989.7
STATE FARM LIFE INS CO	IL	62,712.0
TEACHERS INS & ANNUITY ASN OF AM	NY	261,389.2

Rating: A

INSURANCE COMPANY NAME	DOM. STATE	TOTAL ASSETS ($MIL)
4 EVER LIFE INS CO	IL	200.3
AUTO-OWNERS LIFE INS CO	MI	3,592.1
BERKSHIRE LIFE INS CO OF AMERICA	MA	3,640.3
FEDERATED LIFE INS CO	MN	1,497.0
GUARDIAN LIFE INS CO OF AMERICA	NY	44,890.2
LIFEWISE ASR CO	WA	125.6
PARKER CENTENNIAL ASR CO	WI	89.4
RESERVE NATIONAL INS CO	OK	112.1
SENTRY LIFE INS CO	WI	5,237.9
USAA LIFE INS CO	TX	21,964.7

Rating: A-

INSURANCE COMPANY NAME	DOM. STATE	TOTAL ASSETS ($MIL)
ALLSTATE ASR CO	IL	12.3
AMALGAMATED LIFE INS CO	NY	110.5
AMERICAN REPUBLIC INS CO	IA	797.6
ANTHEM LIFE INS CO	IN	559.7
BALBOA LIFE INS CO	CA	58.9
CENTRAL STATES H & L CO OF OMAHA	NE	407.1
CHARTER NATIONAL LIFE INS CO	IL	133.2
COMPANION LIFE INS CO	SC	274.9
DEARBORN NATIONAL LIFE INS CO	IL	2,183.0
FAMILY HERITAGE LIFE INS CO OF AMER	OH	725.3
FIDELITY INVESTMENTS LIFE INS CO	UT	23,882.2
GARDEN STATE LIFE INS CO	TX	120.3
GERBER LIFE INS CO	NY	2,749.8
ILLINOIS MUTUAL LIFE INS CO	IL	1,368.4
MASSACHUSETTS MUTUAL LIFE INS CO	MA	190,575.4
MIDWESTERN UNITED LIFE INS CO	IN	236.3
MML BAY STATE LIFE INS CO	CT	4,682.4
MUTUAL OF AMERICA LIFE INS CO	NY	17,110.0
NEW YORK LIFE INS CO	NY	143,501.4
NIPPON LIFE INS CO OF AMERICA	IA	211.7
NORTHWESTERN MUTUAL LIFE INS CO	WI	223,102.7
PACIFIC GUARDIAN LIFE INS CO LTD	HI	511.7
PACIFIC LIFE INS CO	NE	111,429.1
PHYSICIANS LIFE INS CO	NE	1,421.0
STANDARD LIFE & ACCIDENT INS CO	TX	523.8

Rating: B+

INSURANCE COMPANY NAME	DOM. STATE	TOTAL ASSETS ($MIL)
AETNA HEALTH & LIFE INS CO	CT	2,221.2
AETNA LIFE INS CO	CT	22,602.5
AMERICAN FAMILY LIFE ASR CO OF COLUM	NE	110,401.3
AMERICAN FIDELITY ASR CO	OK	4,856.7
AMERICAN UNITED LIFE INS CO	IN	22,778.8
ASSURITY LIFE INS CO	NE	2,452.3
BOSTON MUTUAL LIFE INS CO	MA	1,230.4
COLORADO BANKERS LIFE INS CO	CO	280.1
FARM BUREAU LIFE INS CO	IA	8,042.3

INSURANCE COMPANY NAME	DOM. STATE	TOTAL ASSETS ($MIL)
GENERAL RE LIFE CORP	CT	3,335.8
GOVERNMENT PERSONNEL MUTUAL L I C	TX	830.8
JACKSON NATIONAL LIFE INS CO	MI	176,820.4
LINCOLN BENEFIT LIFE CO	NE	12,911.3
MEDICO CORP LIFE INS CO	NE	26.0
MERIT LIFE INS CO	IN	584.3
MIDLAND NATIONAL LIFE INS CO	IA	40,607.9
MINNESOTA LIFE INS CO	MN	34,693.9
MUTUAL OF OMAHA INS CO	NE	6,568.9
NATIONAL BENEFIT LIFE INS CO	NY	480.5
NATIONAL FARMERS UNION LIFE INS CO	TX	216.9
NATIONAL WESTERN LIFE INS CO	CO	10,164.8
NEW YORK LIFE INS & ANNUITY CORP	DE	124,994.1
OHIO NATIONAL LIFE ASR CORP	OH	3,548.1
PACIFIC LIFE & ANNUITY CO	AZ	6,110.8
PARK AVENUE LIFE INS CO	DE	303.3
PIONEER MUTUAL LIFE INS CO	ND	510.6
PRINCIPAL LIFE INS CO	IA	148,782.3
SAVINGS BANK LIFE INS CO OF MA	MA	2,567.5
STANDARD INS CO	OR	19,885.1
SYMETRA LIFE INS CO	IA	28,794.9
THRIVENT LIFE INS CO	MN	3,530.2
TRUSTMARK INS CO	IL	1,404.5
TRUSTMARK LIFE INS CO	IL	370.8
UNITED WORLD LIFE INS CO	NE	114.3
USABLE LIFE	AR	432.6

Vermont

Rating: A+

INSURANCE COMPANY NAME	DOM. STATE	TOTAL ASSETS ($MIL)
PHYSICIANS MUTUAL INS CO	NE	1,989.7
STATE FARM LIFE INS CO	IL	62,712.0
TEACHERS INS & ANNUITY ASN OF AM	NY	261,389.2

Rating: A

INSURANCE COMPANY NAME	DOM. STATE	TOTAL ASSETS ($MIL)
4 EVER LIFE INS CO	IL	200.3
BERKSHIRE LIFE INS CO OF AMERICA	MA	3,640.3
FEDERATED LIFE INS CO	MN	1,497.0
GUARDIAN LIFE INS CO OF AMERICA	NY	44,890.2
PARKER CENTENNIAL ASR CO	WI	89.4
RESERVE NATIONAL INS CO	OK	112.1
SENTRY LIFE INS CO	WI	5,237.9
USAA LIFE INS CO	TX	21,964.7

Rating: A-

INSURANCE COMPANY NAME	DOM. STATE	TOTAL ASSETS ($MIL)
ALLSTATE ASR CO	IL	12.3
AMALGAMATED LIFE INS CO	NY	110.5
AMERICAN FAMILY LIFE ASR CO OF NY	NY	710.2
AMERICAN REPUBLIC INS CO	IA	797.6
BALBOA LIFE INS CO	CA	58.9
CENTRAL STATES H & L CO OF OMAHA	NE	407.1
CHARTER NATIONAL LIFE INS CO	IL	133.2
COMPANION LIFE INS CO	SC	274.9
DEARBORN NATIONAL LIFE INS CO	IL	2,183.0
FAMILY HERITAGE LIFE INS CO OF AMER	OH	725.3
FIDELITY INVESTMENTS LIFE INS CO	UT	23,882.2
GARDEN STATE LIFE INS CO	TX	120.3
GERBER LIFE INS CO	NY	2,749.8
ILLINOIS MUTUAL LIFE INS CO	IL	1,368.4
MASSACHUSETTS MUTUAL LIFE INS CO	MA	190,575.4
MIDWESTERN UNITED LIFE INS CO	IN	236.3
MML BAY STATE LIFE INS CO	CT	4,682.4
MUTUAL OF AMERICA LIFE INS CO	NY	17,110.0
NEW YORK LIFE INS CO	NY	143,501.4
NIPPON LIFE INS CO OF AMERICA	IA	211.7
NORTHWESTERN MUTUAL LIFE INS CO	WI	223,102.7
PACIFIC LIFE INS CO	NE	111,429.1
PHYSICIANS LIFE INS CO	NE	1,421.0
STANDARD LIFE & ACCIDENT INS CO	TX	523.8

Rating: B+

INSURANCE COMPANY NAME	DOM. STATE	TOTAL ASSETS ($MIL)
AETNA HEALTH & LIFE INS CO	CT	2,221.2
AETNA LIFE INS CO	CT	22,602.5
AMERICAN FAMILY LIFE ASR CO OF COLUM	NE	110,401.3
AMERICAN FIDELITY ASR CO	OK	4,856.7
AMERICAN UNITED LIFE INS CO	IN	22,778.8
ASSURITY LIFE INS CO	NE	2,452.3
BOSTON MUTUAL LIFE INS CO	MA	1,230.4
COLORADO BANKERS LIFE INS CO	CO	280.1
GENERAL RE LIFE CORP	CT	3,335.8
GOVERNMENT PERSONNEL MUTUAL L I C	TX	830.8
JACKSON NATIONAL LIFE INS CO	MI	176,820.4
LINCOLN BENEFIT LIFE CO	NE	12,911.3
MEDICO CORP LIFE INS CO	NE	26.0
MIDLAND NATIONAL LIFE INS CO	IA	40,607.9
MINNESOTA LIFE INS CO	MN	34,693.9
MUTUAL OF OMAHA INS CO	NE	6,568.9
NATIONAL BENEFIT LIFE INS CO	NY	480.5
NATIONAL WESTERN LIFE INS CO	CO	10,164.8
NEW YORK LIFE INS & ANNUITY CORP	DE	124,994.1
OHIO NATIONAL LIFE ASR CORP	OH	3,548.1
PACIFIC LIFE & ANNUITY CO	AZ	6,110.8
PARK AVENUE LIFE INS CO	DE	303.3
PIONEER MUTUAL LIFE INS CO	ND	510.6
PRINCIPAL LIFE INS CO	IA	148,782.3
SAVINGS BANK LIFE INS CO OF MA	MA	2,567.5
STANDARD INS CO	OR	19,885.1
SYMETRA LIFE INS CO	IA	28,794.9
TRUSTMARK INS CO	IL	1,404.5
TRUSTMARK LIFE INS CO	IL	370.8
UNITED WORLD LIFE INS CO	NE	114.3
USABLE LIFE	AR	432.6

Virginia

INSURANCE COMPANY NAME	DOM. STATE	TOTAL ASSETS ($MIL)	INSURANCE COMPANY NAME	DOM. STATE	TOTAL ASSETS ($MIL)
Rating: A+			GENERAL RE LIFE CORP	CT	3,335.8
			GOVERNMENT PERSONNEL MUTUAL L I C	TX	830.8
COUNTRY LIFE INS CO	IL	10,573.7	GREATER GEORGIA LIFE INS CO	GA	49.9
PHYSICIANS MUTUAL INS CO	NE	1,989.7	JACKSON NATIONAL LIFE INS CO	MI	176,820.4
STATE FARM LIFE INS CO	IL	62,712.0	LINCOLN BENEFIT LIFE CO	NE	12,911.3
TEACHERS INS & ANNUITY ASN OF AM	NY	261,389.2	MEDICO CORP LIFE INS CO	NE	26.0
Rating: A			MERIT LIFE INS CO	IN	584.3
			MIDLAND NATIONAL LIFE INS CO	IA	40,607.9
4 EVER LIFE INS CO	IL	200.3	MINNESOTA LIFE INS CO	MN	34,693.9
AUTO-OWNERS LIFE INS CO	MI	3,592.1	MUTUAL OF OMAHA INS CO	NE	6,568.9
BERKSHIRE LIFE INS CO OF AMERICA	MA	3,640.3	NATIONAL BENEFIT LIFE INS CO	NY	480.5
FEDERATED LIFE INS CO	MN	1,497.0	NATIONAL FARMERS UNION LIFE INS CO	TX	216.9
GUARDIAN LIFE INS CO OF AMERICA	NY	44,890.2	NATIONAL WESTERN LIFE INS CO	CO	10,164.8
PARKER CENTENNIAL ASR CO	WI	89.4	NEW YORK LIFE INS & ANNUITY CORP	DE	124,994.1
RESERVE NATIONAL INS CO	OK	112.1	OHIO NATIONAL LIFE ASR CORP	OH	3,548.1
SENTRY LIFE INS CO	WI	5,237.9	PACIFIC LIFE & ANNUITY CO	AZ	6,110.8
SOUTHERN FARM BUREAU LIFE INS CO	MS	12,937.4	PARK AVENUE LIFE INS CO	DE	303.3
USAA LIFE INS CO	TX	21,964.7	PIONEER MUTUAL LIFE INS CO	ND	510.6
Rating: A-			PRINCIPAL LIFE INS CO	IA	148,782.3
			SAVINGS BANK LIFE INS CO OF MA	MA	2,567.5
ALLSTATE ASR CO	IL	12.3	STANDARD INS CO	OR	19,885.1
AMALGAMATED LIFE INS CO	NY	110.5	SYMETRA LIFE INS CO	IA	28,794.9
AMERICAN REPUBLIC INS CO	IA	797.6	THRIVENT LIFE INS CO	MN	3,530.2
ANTHEM LIFE INS CO	IN	559.7	TRUSTMARK INS CO	IL	1,404.5
BALBOA LIFE INS CO	CA	58.9	TRUSTMARK LIFE INS CO	IL	370.8
CENTRAL STATES H & L CO OF OMAHA	NE	407.1	UNITED WORLD LIFE INS CO	NE	114.3
CHARTER NATIONAL LIFE INS CO	IL	133.2	USABLE LIFE	AR	432.6
COMPANION LIFE INS CO	SC	274.9			
COTTON STATES LIFE INS CO	GA	330.7			
COUNTRY INVESTORS LIFE ASR CO	IL	289.8			
DEARBORN NATIONAL LIFE INS CO	IL	2,183.0			
ERIE FAMILY LIFE INS CO	PA	2,077.0			
FAMILY HERITAGE LIFE INS CO OF AMER	OH	725.3			
FIDELITY INVESTMENTS LIFE INS CO	UT	23,882.2			
GARDEN STATE LIFE INS CO	TX	120.3			
GERBER LIFE INS CO	NY	2,749.8			
ILLINOIS MUTUAL LIFE INS CO	IL	1,368.4			
MASSACHUSETTS MUTUAL LIFE INS CO	MA	190,575.4			
MIDWESTERN UNITED LIFE INS CO	IN	236.3			
MML BAY STATE LIFE INS CO	CT	4,682.4			
MUTUAL OF AMERICA LIFE INS CO	NY	17,110.0			
NEW YORK LIFE INS CO	NY	143,501.4			
NIPPON LIFE INS CO OF AMERICA	IA	211.7			
NORTHWESTERN MUTUAL LIFE INS CO	WI	223,102.7			
PACIFIC LIFE INS CO	NE	111,429.1			
PHYSICIANS LIFE INS CO	NE	1,421.0			
STANDARD LIFE & ACCIDENT INS CO	TX	523.8			
Rating: B+					
AETNA HEALTH & LIFE INS CO	CT	2,221.2			
AETNA LIFE INS CO	CT	22,602.5			
AMERICAN FAMILY LIFE ASR CO OF COLUM	NE	110,401.3			
AMERICAN FIDELITY ASR CO	OK	4,856.7			
AMERICAN UNITED LIFE INS CO	IN	22,778.8			
ASSURITY LIFE INS CO	NE	2,452.3			
BOSTON MUTUAL LIFE INS CO	MA	1,230.4			
COLORADO BANKERS LIFE INS CO	CO	280.1			

Washington

INSURANCE COMPANY NAME	DOM. STATE	TOTAL ASSETS ($MIL)

Rating: A+

INSURANCE COMPANY NAME	DOM. STATE	TOTAL ASSETS ($MIL)
AMERICAN FAMILY LIFE INS CO	WI	5,200.5
COUNTRY LIFE INS CO	IL	10,573.7
PHYSICIANS MUTUAL INS CO	NE	1,989.7
STATE FARM LIFE INS CO	IL	62,712.0
TEACHERS INS & ANNUITY ASN OF AM	NY	261,389.2

Rating: A

INSURANCE COMPANY NAME	DOM. STATE	TOTAL ASSETS ($MIL)
4 EVER LIFE INS CO	IL	200.3
AUTO-OWNERS LIFE INS CO	MI	3,592.1
BERKSHIRE LIFE INS CO OF AMERICA	MA	3,640.3
FEDERATED LIFE INS CO	MN	1,497.0
GUARDIAN LIFE INS CO OF AMERICA	NY	44,890.2
LIFEWISE ASR CO	WA	125.6
PARKER CENTENNIAL ASR CO	WI	89.4
RESERVE NATIONAL INS CO	OK	112.1
SENTRY LIFE INS CO	WI	5,237.9
USAA LIFE INS CO	TX	21,964.7

Rating: A-

INSURANCE COMPANY NAME	DOM. STATE	TOTAL ASSETS ($MIL)
ALLSTATE ASR CO	IL	12.3
AMALGAMATED LIFE INS CO	NY	110.5
AMERICAN REPUBLIC INS CO	IA	797.6
ANTHEM LIFE INS CO	IN	559.7
BALBOA LIFE INS CO	CA	58.9
CENTRAL STATES H & L CO OF OMAHA	NE	407.1
CHARTER NATIONAL LIFE INS CO	IL	133.2
COMPANION LIFE INS CO	SC	274.9
COUNTRY INVESTORS LIFE ASR CO	IL	289.8
DEARBORN NATIONAL LIFE INS CO	IL	2,183.0
FAMILY HERITAGE LIFE INS CO OF AMER	OH	725.3
FIDELITY INVESTMENTS LIFE INS CO	UT	23,882.2
GARDEN STATE LIFE INS CO	TX	120.3
GERBER LIFE INS CO	NY	2,749.8
ILLINOIS MUTUAL LIFE INS CO	IL	1,368.4
MASSACHUSETTS MUTUAL LIFE INS CO	MA	190,575.4
MIDWESTERN UNITED LIFE INS CO	IN	236.3
MML BAY STATE LIFE INS CO	CT	4,682.4
MUTUAL OF AMERICA LIFE INS CO	NY	17,110.0
NEW YORK LIFE INS CO	NY	143,501.4
NIPPON LIFE INS CO OF AMERICA	IA	211.7
NORTHWESTERN MUTUAL LIFE INS CO	WI	223,102.7
PACIFIC GUARDIAN LIFE INS CO LTD	HI	511.7
PACIFIC LIFE INS CO	NE	111,429.1
PHYSICIANS LIFE INS CO	NE	1,421.0
STANDARD LIFE & ACCIDENT INS CO	TX	523.8

Rating: B+

INSURANCE COMPANY NAME	DOM. STATE	TOTAL ASSETS ($MIL)
AETNA HEALTH & LIFE INS CO	CT	2,221.2
AETNA LIFE INS CO	CT	22,602.5
AMERICAN FAMILY LIFE ASR CO OF COLUM	NE	110,401.3
AMERICAN FIDELITY ASR CO	OK	4,856.7
AMERICAN UNITED LIFE INS CO	IN	22,778.8
ASSURITY LIFE INS CO	NE	2,452.3
BOSTON MUTUAL LIFE INS CO	MA	1,230.4
COLORADO BANKERS LIFE INS CO	CO	280.1

INSURANCE COMPANY NAME	DOM. STATE	TOTAL ASSETS ($MIL)
FARM BUREAU LIFE INS CO	IA	8,042.3
GENERAL RE LIFE CORP	CT	3,335.8
GOVERNMENT PERSONNEL MUTUAL L I C	TX	830.8
JACKSON NATIONAL LIFE INS CO	MI	176,820.4
LINCOLN BENEFIT LIFE CO	NE	12,911.3
MEDICO CORP LIFE INS CO	NE	26.0
MERIT LIFE INS CO	IN	584.3
MIDLAND NATIONAL LIFE INS CO	IA	40,607.9
MINNESOTA LIFE INS CO	MN	34,693.9
MUTUAL OF OMAHA INS CO	NE	6,568.9
NATIONAL BENEFIT LIFE INS CO	NY	480.5
NATIONAL FARMERS UNION LIFE INS CO	TX	216.9
NATIONAL WESTERN LIFE INS CO	CO	10,164.8
NEW YORK LIFE INS & ANNUITY CORP	DE	124,994.1
OHIO NATIONAL LIFE ASR CORP	OH	3,548.1
PACIFIC LIFE & ANNUITY CO	AZ	6,110.8
PARK AVENUE LIFE INS CO	DE	303.3
PIONEER MUTUAL LIFE INS CO	ND	510.6
PRINCIPAL LIFE INS CO	IA	148,782.3
SAVINGS BANK LIFE INS CO OF MA	MA	2,567.5
STANDARD INS CO	OR	19,885.1
SYMETRA LIFE INS CO	IA	28,794.9
THRIVENT LIFE INS CO	MN	3,530.2
TRUSTMARK INS CO	IL	1,404.5
TRUSTMARK LIFE INS CO	IL	370.8
UNITED WORLD LIFE INS CO	NE	114.3
USABLE LIFE	AR	432.6

West Virginia

INSURANCE COMPANY NAME	DOM. STATE	TOTAL ASSETS ($MIL)
Rating: A+		
COUNTRY LIFE INS CO	IL	10,573.7
PHYSICIANS MUTUAL INS CO	NE	1,989.7
STATE FARM LIFE INS CO	IL	62,712.0
TEACHERS INS & ANNUITY ASN OF AM	NY	261,389.2
Rating: A		
4 EVER LIFE INS CO	IL	200.3
BERKSHIRE LIFE INS CO OF AMERICA	MA	3,640.3
FEDERATED LIFE INS CO	MN	1,497.0
GUARDIAN LIFE INS CO OF AMERICA	NY	44,890.2
PARKER CENTENNIAL ASR CO	WI	89.4
RESERVE NATIONAL INS CO	OK	112.1
SENTRY LIFE INS CO	WI	5,237.9
USAA LIFE INS CO	TX	21,964.7
Rating: A-		
ALLSTATE ASR CO	IL	12.3
AMALGAMATED LIFE INS CO	NY	110.5
AMERICAN REPUBLIC INS CO	IA	797.6
ANTHEM LIFE INS CO	IN	559.7
BALBOA LIFE INS CO	CA	58.9
CENTRAL STATES H & L CO OF OMAHA	NE	407.1
CHARTER NATIONAL LIFE INS CO	IL	133.2
COMPANION LIFE INS CO	SC	274.9
COUNTRY INVESTORS LIFE ASR CO	IL	289.8
DEARBORN NATIONAL LIFE INS CO	IL	2,183.0
ERIE FAMILY LIFE INS CO	PA	2,077.0
FAMILY HERITAGE LIFE INS CO OF AMER	OH	725.3
FIDELITY INVESTMENTS LIFE INS CO	UT	23,882.2
GARDEN STATE LIFE INS CO	TX	120.3
GERBER LIFE INS CO	NY	2,749.8
ILLINOIS MUTUAL LIFE INS CO	IL	1,368.4
MASSACHUSETTS MUTUAL LIFE INS CO	MA	190,575.4
MIDWESTERN UNITED LIFE INS CO	IN	236.3
MML BAY STATE LIFE INS CO	CT	4,682.4
MUTUAL OF AMERICA LIFE INS CO	NY	17,110.0
NEW YORK LIFE INS CO	NY	143,501.4
NIPPON LIFE INS CO OF AMERICA	IA	211.7
NORTHWESTERN MUTUAL LIFE INS CO	WI	223,102.7
PACIFIC LIFE INS CO	NE	111,429.1
PHYSICIANS LIFE INS CO	NE	1,421.0
STANDARD LIFE & ACCIDENT INS CO	TX	523.8
Rating: B+		
AETNA HEALTH & LIFE INS CO	CT	2,221.2
AETNA LIFE INS CO	CT	22,602.5
AMERICAN FAMILY LIFE ASR CO OF COLUM	NE	110,401.3
AMERICAN FIDELITY ASR CO	OK	4,856.7
AMERICAN UNITED LIFE INS CO	IN	22,778.8
ASSURITY LIFE INS CO	NE	2,452.3
BOSTON MUTUAL LIFE INS CO	MA	1,230.4
COLORADO BANKERS LIFE INS CO	CO	280.1
GENERAL RE LIFE CORP	CT	3,335.8
GOVERNMENT PERSONNEL MUTUAL L I C	TX	830.8
JACKSON NATIONAL LIFE INS CO	MI	176,820.4

INSURANCE COMPANY NAME	DOM. STATE	TOTAL ASSETS ($MIL)
LINCOLN BENEFIT LIFE CO	NE	12,911.3
MEDICO CORP LIFE INS CO	NE	26.0
MERIT LIFE INS CO	IN	584.3
MIDLAND NATIONAL LIFE INS CO	IA	40,607.9
MINNESOTA LIFE INS CO	MN	34,693.9
MUTUAL OF OMAHA INS CO	NE	6,568.9
NATIONAL BENEFIT LIFE INS CO	NY	480.5
NATIONAL WESTERN LIFE INS CO	CO	10,164.8
NEW YORK LIFE INS & ANNUITY CORP	DE	124,994.1
OHIO NATIONAL LIFE ASR CORP	OH	3,548.1
PACIFIC LIFE & ANNUITY CO	AZ	6,110.8
PARK AVENUE LIFE INS CO	DE	303.3
PIONEER MUTUAL LIFE INS CO	ND	510.6
PRINCIPAL LIFE INS CO	IA	148,782.3
SAVINGS BANK LIFE INS CO OF MA	MA	2,567.5
STANDARD INS CO	OR	19,885.1
SYMETRA LIFE INS CO	IA	28,794.9
THRIVENT LIFE INS CO	MN	3,530.2
TRUSTMARK INS CO	IL	1,404.5
TRUSTMARK LIFE INS CO	IL	370.8
UNITED WORLD LIFE INS CO	NE	114.3
USABLE LIFE	AR	432.6

Wisconsin

INSURANCE COMPANY NAME	DOM. STATE	TOTAL ASSETS ($MIL)

Rating: A+

INSURANCE COMPANY NAME	DOM. STATE	TOTAL ASSETS ($MIL)
AMERICAN FAMILY LIFE INS CO	WI	5,200.5
COUNTRY LIFE INS CO	IL	10,573.7
PHYSICIANS MUTUAL INS CO	NE	1,989.7
STATE FARM LIFE & ACCIDENT ASR CO	IL	2,436.7
TEACHERS INS & ANNUITY ASN OF AM	NY	261,389.2

Rating: A

INSURANCE COMPANY NAME	DOM. STATE	TOTAL ASSETS ($MIL)
4 EVER LIFE INS CO	IL	200.3
AUTO-OWNERS LIFE INS CO	MI	3,592.1
BERKSHIRE LIFE INS CO OF AMERICA	MA	3,640.3
FEDERATED LIFE INS CO	MN	1,497.0
GUARDIAN LIFE INS CO OF AMERICA	NY	44,890.2
PARKER CENTENNIAL ASR CO	WI	89.4
RESERVE NATIONAL INS CO	OK	112.1
SENTRY LIFE INS CO	WI	5,237.9
USAA LIFE INS CO	TX	21,964.7

Rating: A-

INSURANCE COMPANY NAME	DOM. STATE	TOTAL ASSETS ($MIL)
ALLSTATE ASR CO	IL	12.3
AMALGAMATED LIFE INS CO	NY	110.5
AMERICAN REPUBLIC INS CO	IA	797.6
ANTHEM LIFE INS CO	IN	559.7
BALBOA LIFE INS CO	CA	58.9
CENTRAL STATES H & L CO OF OMAHA	NE	407.1
CHARTER NATIONAL LIFE INS CO	IL	133.2
COMPANION LIFE INS CO	SC	274.9
COUNTRY INVESTORS LIFE ASR CO	IL	289.8
DEARBORN NATIONAL LIFE INS CO	IL	2,183.0
ERIE FAMILY LIFE INS CO	PA	2,077.0
FAMILY HERITAGE LIFE INS CO OF AMER	OH	725.3
FIDELITY INVESTMENTS LIFE INS CO	UT	23,882.2
GARDEN STATE LIFE INS CO	TX	120.3
GERBER LIFE INS CO	NY	2,749.8
ILLINOIS MUTUAL LIFE INS CO	IL	1,368.4
MASSACHUSETTS MUTUAL LIFE INS CO	MA	190,575.4
MIDWESTERN UNITED LIFE INS CO	IN	236.3
MML BAY STATE LIFE INS CO	CT	4,682.4
MUTUAL OF AMERICA LIFE INS CO	NY	17,110.0
NEW YORK LIFE INS CO	NY	143,501.4
NIPPON LIFE INS CO OF AMERICA	IA	211.7
NORTHWESTERN MUTUAL LIFE INS CO	WI	223,102.7
PACIFIC LIFE INS CO	NE	111,429.1
PHYSICIANS LIFE INS CO	NE	1,421.0
STANDARD LIFE & ACCIDENT INS CO	TX	523.8

Rating: B+

INSURANCE COMPANY NAME	DOM. STATE	TOTAL ASSETS ($MIL)
AETNA HEALTH & LIFE INS CO	CT	2,221.2
AETNA LIFE INS CO	CT	22,602.5
AMERICAN FAMILY LIFE ASR CO OF COLUM	NE	110,401.3
AMERICAN FIDELITY ASR CO	OK	4,856.7
AMERICAN UNITED LIFE INS CO	IN	22,778.8
ASSURITY LIFE INS CO	NE	2,452.3
BOSTON MUTUAL LIFE INS CO	MA	1,230.4
COLORADO BANKERS LIFE INS CO	CO	280.1
FARM BUREAU LIFE INS CO	IA	8,042.3

INSURANCE COMPANY NAME	DOM. STATE	TOTAL ASSETS ($MIL)
GENERAL RE LIFE CORP	CT	3,335.8
GOVERNMENT PERSONNEL MUTUAL L I C	TX	830.8
JACKSON NATIONAL LIFE INS CO	MI	176,820.4
LINCOLN BENEFIT LIFE CO	NE	12,911.3
MEDICO CORP LIFE INS CO	NE	26.0
MERIT LIFE INS CO	IN	584.3
MIDLAND NATIONAL LIFE INS CO	IA	40,607.9
MINNESOTA LIFE INS CO	MN	34,693.9
MUTUAL OF OMAHA INS CO	NE	6,568.9
NATIONAL BENEFIT LIFE INS CO	NY	480.5
NATIONAL FARMERS UNION LIFE INS CO	TX	216.9
NATIONAL WESTERN LIFE INS CO	CO	10,164.8
NEW YORK LIFE INS & ANNUITY CORP	DE	124,994.1
OHIO NATIONAL LIFE ASR CORP	OH	3,548.1
PACIFIC LIFE & ANNUITY CO	AZ	6,110.8
PARK AVENUE LIFE INS CO	DE	303.3
PIONEER MUTUAL LIFE INS CO	ND	510.6
PRINCIPAL LIFE INS CO	IA	148,782.3
SAVINGS BANK LIFE INS CO OF MA	MA	2,567.5
STANDARD INS CO	OR	19,885.1
SYMETRA LIFE INS CO	IA	28,794.9
THRIVENT LIFE INS CO	MN	3,530.2
TRUSTMARK INS CO	IL	1,404.5
TRUSTMARK LIFE INS CO	IL	370.8
UNITED WORLD LIFE INS CO	NE	114.3
USABLE LIFE	AR	432.6

Wyoming

INSURANCE COMPANY NAME	DOM. STATE	TOTAL ASSETS ($MIL)

Rating: A+

INSURANCE COMPANY NAME	DOM. STATE	TOTAL ASSETS ($MIL)
AMERICAN FAMILY LIFE INS CO	WI	5,200.5
COUNTRY LIFE INS CO	IL	10,573.7
PHYSICIANS MUTUAL INS CO	NE	1,989.7
STATE FARM LIFE INS CO	IL	62,712.0
TEACHERS INS & ANNUITY ASN OF AM	NY	261,389.2

Rating: A

INSURANCE COMPANY NAME	DOM. STATE	TOTAL ASSETS ($MIL)
4 EVER LIFE INS CO	IL	200.3
BERKSHIRE LIFE INS CO OF AMERICA	MA	3,640.3
FEDERATED LIFE INS CO	MN	1,497.0
GUARDIAN LIFE INS CO OF AMERICA	NY	44,890.2
LIFEWISE ASR CO	WA	125.6
PARKER CENTENNIAL ASR CO	WI	89.4
RESERVE NATIONAL INS CO	OK	112.1
SENTRY LIFE INS CO	WI	5,237.9
USAA LIFE INS CO	TX	21,964.7

Rating: A-

INSURANCE COMPANY NAME	DOM. STATE	TOTAL ASSETS ($MIL)
ALLSTATE ASR CO	IL	12.3
AMALGAMATED LIFE INS CO	NY	110.5
AMERICAN REPUBLIC INS CO	IA	797.6
ANTHEM LIFE INS CO	IN	559.7
BALBOA LIFE INS CO	CA	58.9
CENTRAL STATES H & L CO OF OMAHA	NE	407.1
CHARTER NATIONAL LIFE INS CO	IL	133.2
COMPANION LIFE INS CO	SC	274.9
COUNTRY INVESTORS LIFE ASR CO	IL	289.8
DEARBORN NATIONAL LIFE INS CO	IL	2,183.0
FAMILY HERITAGE LIFE INS CO OF AMER	OH	725.3
FIDELITY INVESTMENTS LIFE INS CO	UT	23,882.2
GARDEN STATE LIFE INS CO	TX	120.3
GERBER LIFE INS CO	NY	2,749.8
ILLINOIS MUTUAL LIFE INS CO	IL	1,368.4
MASSACHUSETTS MUTUAL LIFE INS CO	MA	190,575.4
MIDWESTERN UNITED LIFE INS CO	IN	236.3
MML BAY STATE LIFE INS CO	CT	4,682.4
MUTUAL OF AMERICA LIFE INS CO	NY	17,110.0
NEW YORK LIFE INS CO	NY	143,501.4
NORTHWESTERN MUTUAL LIFE INS CO	WI	223,102.7
PACIFIC GUARDIAN LIFE INS CO LTD	HI	511.7
PACIFIC LIFE INS CO	NE	111,429.1
PHYSICIANS LIFE INS CO	NE	1,421.0
STANDARD LIFE & ACCIDENT INS CO	TX	523.8

Rating: B+

INSURANCE COMPANY NAME	DOM. STATE	TOTAL ASSETS ($MIL)
AETNA HEALTH & LIFE INS CO	CT	2,221.2
AETNA LIFE INS CO	CT	22,602.5
AMERICAN FAMILY LIFE ASR CO OF COLUM	NE	110,401.3
AMERICAN FIDELITY ASR CO	OK	4,856.7
AMERICAN UNITED LIFE INS CO	IN	22,778.8
ASSURITY LIFE INS CO	NE	2,452.3
BOSTON MUTUAL LIFE INS CO	MA	1,230.4
COLORADO BANKERS LIFE INS CO	CO	280.1
FARM BUREAU LIFE INS CO	IA	8,042.3
GENERAL RE LIFE CORP	CT	3,335.8

INSURANCE COMPANY NAME	DOM. STATE	TOTAL ASSETS ($MIL)
GOVERNMENT PERSONNEL MUTUAL L I C	TX	830.8
JACKSON NATIONAL LIFE INS CO	MI	176,820.4
LINCOLN BENEFIT LIFE CO	NE	12,911.3
MEDICO CORP LIFE INS CO	NE	26.0
MERIT LIFE INS CO	IN	584.3
MIDLAND NATIONAL LIFE INS CO	IA	40,607.9
MINNESOTA LIFE INS CO	MN	34,693.9
MUTUAL OF OMAHA INS CO	NE	6,568.9
NATIONAL BENEFIT LIFE INS CO	NY	480.5
NATIONAL FARMERS UNION LIFE INS CO	TX	216.9
NATIONAL WESTERN LIFE INS CO	CO	10,164.8
NEW YORK LIFE INS & ANNUITY CORP	DE	124,994.1
OHIO NATIONAL LIFE ASR CORP	OH	3,548.1
PACIFIC LIFE & ANNUITY CO	AZ	6,110.8
PARK AVENUE LIFE INS CO	DE	303.3
PIONEER MUTUAL LIFE INS CO	ND	510.6
PRINCIPAL LIFE INS CO	IA	148,782.3
SAVINGS BANK LIFE INS CO OF MA	MA	2,567.5
STANDARD INS CO	OR	19,885.1
SYMETRA LIFE INS CO	IA	28,794.9
TRUSTMARK INS CO	IL	1,404.5
TRUSTMARK LIFE INS CO	IL	370.8
UNITED WORLD LIFE INS CO	NE	114.3
USABLE LIFE	AR	432.6

Section V

All Companies
Listed by Rating

A list of all rated and unrated

U.S. Life and Annuity Insurers

Companies are ranked by Weiss Financial Strength Rating and then listed alphabetically within each rating category.

Section V Contents

This section sorts all companies by their Weiss Financial Strength Rating and then lists them alphabetically within each rating category. The purpose of this section is to provide in one place all of those companies receiving a given rating. Companies with the same rating should be viewed as having the same relative risk regardless of their order in this table.

1. Financial Strength Rating Our rating is measured on a scale from A to F and considers a wide range of factors. Highly rated companies are, in our opinion, less likely to experience financial difficulties than lower rated firms. See *About Weiss Financial Strength Ratings* for more information.

2. Insurance Company Name The legally registered name, which can sometimes differ from the name that the company uses for advertising. An insurer's name can be very similar to that of another, so verify the company's exact name and state of domicile to make sure you are looking at the correct company.

3. Domicile State The state which has primary regulatory responsibility for the company. It may differ from the location of the company's corporate headquarters. You do not have to be living in the domicile state to purchase insurance from this firm, provided it is licensed to do business in your state.

4. Total Assets All assets admitted by state insurance regulators in millions of dollars. This includes investments, current business assets and separate accounts.

INSURANCE COMPANY NAME	DOM. STATE	TOTAL ASSETS ($MIL)
Rating: A+		
AMERICAN FAMILY LIFE INS CO	WI	5,200.5
COUNTRY LIFE INS CO	IL	10,573.7
PHYSICIANS MUTUAL INS CO	NE	1,989.7
STATE FARM LIFE & ACCIDENT ASR CO	IL	2,436.7
STATE FARM LIFE INS CO	IL	62,712.0
TEACHERS INS & ANNUITY ASN OF AM	NY	261,389.2
Rating: A		
4 EVER LIFE INS CO	IL	200.3
AUTO-OWNERS LIFE INS CO	MI	3,592.1
BERKSHIRE LIFE INS CO OF AMERICA	MA	3,640.3
FEDERATED LIFE INS CO	MN	1,497.0
FIRST RELIANCE STANDARD LIFE INS CO	NY	188.7
GUARDIAN LIFE INS CO OF AMERICA	NY	44,890.2
LIFEWISE ASR CO	WA	125.6
PARKER CENTENNIAL ASR CO	WI	89.4
RESERVE NATIONAL INS CO	OK	112.1
SENTRY LIFE INS CO	WI	5,237.9
SHELTERPOINT LIFE INS CO	NY	104.4
SOUTHERN FARM BUREAU LIFE INS CO	MS	12,937.4
TENNESSEE FARMERS LIFE INS CO	TN	1,978.3
TRANS OCEANIC LIFE INS CO	PR	62.9
UNITED FARM FAMILY LIFE INS CO	IN	2,129.9
USAA LIFE INS CO	TX	21,964.7
Rating: A-		
ALLSTATE ASR CO	IL	12.3
AMALGAMATED LIFE INS CO	NY	110.5
AMERICAN FAMILY LIFE ASR CO OF NY	NY	710.2
AMERICAN REPUBLIC INS CO	IA	797.6
ANTHEM LIFE & DISABILITY INS CO	NY	23.3
ANTHEM LIFE INS CO	IN	559.7
BALBOA LIFE INS CO	CA	58.9
BLUE SHIELD OF CALIFORNIA L&H INS CO	CA	841.2
CENTRAL STATES H & L CO OF OMAHA	NE	407.1
CHARTER NATIONAL LIFE INS CO	IL	133.2
CIGNA LIFE INS CO OF NEW YORK	NY	380.6
COMPANION LIFE INS CO	SC	274.9
COTTON STATES LIFE INS CO	GA	330.7
COUNTRY INVESTORS LIFE ASR CO	IL	289.8
DEARBORN NATIONAL LIFE INS CO	IL	2,183.0
ERIE FAMILY LIFE INS CO	PA	2,077.0
FAMILY HERITAGE LIFE INS CO OF AMER	OH	725.3
FARM BUREAU LIFE INS CO OF MICHIGAN	MI	2,356.3
FARM BUREAU LIFE INS CO OF MISSOURI	MO	522.5
FIDELITY INVESTMENTS LIFE INS CO	UT	23,882.2
FIRST SYMETRA NATL LIFE INS CO OF NY	NY	932.2
FRANDISCO LIFE INS CO	GA	65.0
GARDEN STATE LIFE INS CO	TX	120.3
GERBER LIFE INS CO	NY	2,749.8
ILLINOIS MUTUAL LIFE INS CO	IL	1,368.4
JOHN HANCOCK LIFE INS CO OF NY	NY	17,279.2
LIFE INS CO OF ALABAMA	AL	112.0

INSURANCE COMPANY NAME	DOM. STATE	TOTAL ASSETS ($MIL)
LIFE INS CO OF BOSTON & NEW YORK	NY	122.2
MASSACHUSETTS MUTUAL LIFE INS CO	MA	190,575.4
MIDWESTERN UNITED LIFE INS CO	IN	236.3
MML BAY STATE LIFE INS CO	CT	4,682.4
MUTUAL OF AMERICA LIFE INS CO	NY	17,110.0
MUTUAL SAVINGS LIFE INS CO	AL	470.5
NEW YORK LIFE INS CO	NY	143,501.4
NIPPON LIFE INS CO OF AMERICA	IA	211.7
NORTHWESTERN MUTUAL LIFE INS CO	WI	223,102.7
PACIFIC GUARDIAN LIFE INS CO LTD	HI	511.7
PACIFIC LIFE INS CO	NE	111,429.1
PHYSICIANS LIFE INS CO	NE	1,421.0
SHELTER LIFE INS CO	MO	1,108.6
STANDARD LIFE & ACCIDENT INS CO	TX	523.8
STANDARD LIFE INS CO OF NY	NY	272.4
Rating: B+		
ADVANCE INS CO OF KS	KS	52.7
AETNA HEALTH & LIFE INS CO	CT	2,221.2
AETNA LIFE INS CO	CT	22,602.5
AMERICAN FAMILY LIFE ASR CO OF COLUM	NE	110,401.3
AMERICAN FIDELITY ASR CO	OK	4,856.7
AMERICAN UNITED LIFE INS CO	IN	22,778.8
ASSURITY LIFE INS CO	NE	2,452.3
BLUEBONNET LIFE INS CO	MS	54.6
BOSTON MUTUAL LIFE INS CO	MA	1,230.4
COLORADO BANKERS LIFE INS CO	CO	280.1
DEARBORN NATIONAL LIFE INS CO OF NY	NY	40.9
EMPIRE FIDELITY INVESTMENTS L I C	NY	2,386.2
FARM BUREAU LIFE INS CO	IA	8,042.3
FIRST UNITED AMERICAN LIFE INS CO	NY	191.8
GENERAL RE LIFE CORP	CT	3,335.8
GOVERNMENT PERSONNEL MUTUAL L I C	TX	830.8
GREATER GEORGIA LIFE INS CO	GA	49.9
HM LIFE INS CO OF NEW YORK	NY	72.4
JACKSON NATIONAL LIFE INS CO	MI	176,820.4
LINCOLN BENEFIT LIFE CO	NE	12,911.3
LOCOMOTIVE ENGRS&COND MUT PROT ASSN	MI	55.4
MEDICO CORP LIFE INS CO	NE	26.0
MERIT LIFE INS CO	IN	584.3
MIDLAND NATIONAL LIFE INS CO	IA	40,607.9
MINNESOTA LIFE INS CO	MN	34,693.9
MUTUAL OF OMAHA INS CO	NE	6,568.9
NATIONAL BENEFIT LIFE INS CO	NY	480.5
NATIONAL FARMERS UNION LIFE INS CO	TX	216.9
NATIONAL INCOME LIFE INS CO	NY	142.8
NATIONAL WESTERN LIFE INS CO	CO	10,164.8
NEW YORK LIFE INS & ANNUITY CORP	DE	124,994.1
OHIO NATIONAL LIFE ASR CORP	OH	3,548.1
PACIFIC LIFE & ANNUITY CO	AZ	6,110.8
PARK AVENUE LIFE INS CO	DE	303.3
PIONEER MUTUAL LIFE INS CO	ND	510.6
PRINCIPAL LIFE INS CO	IA	148,782.3
SAVINGS BANK LIFE INS CO OF MA	MA	2,567.5

INSURANCE COMPANY NAME	DOM. STATE	TOTAL ASSETS ($MIL)	INSURANCE COMPANY NAME	DOM. STATE	TOTAL ASSETS ($MIL)
Rating: B+ (Continued)			DESERET MUTUAL INS CO	UT	40.1
SENTRY LIFE INS CO OF NEW YORK	NY	76.3	EAGLE LIFE INS CO	IA	206.6
STANDARD INS CO	OR	19,885.1	EMC NATIONAL LIFE CO	IA	1,014.7
SYMETRA LIFE INS CO	IA	28,794.9	EPIC LIFE INSURANCE CO	WI	60.8
THRIVENT LIFE INS CO	MN	3,530.2	FARM FAMILY LIFE INS CO	NY	1,270.3
TRUSTMARK INS CO	IL	1,404.5	FIDELITY SECURITY LIFE INS CO OF NY	NY	40.3
TRUSTMARK LIFE INS CO	IL	370.8	FIRST ASR LIFE OF AMERICA	LA	37.7
UNION SECURITY LIFE INS CO OF NY	NY	139.8	FIRST HEALTH LIFE & HEALTH INS CO	TX	577.2
UNITED WORLD LIFE INS CO	NE	114.3	FIRST INVESTORS LIFE INS CO	NY	1,786.5
USAA LIFE INS CO OF NEW YORK	NY	667.0	FIRST PENN-PACIFIC LIFE INS CO	IN	1,744.5
USABLE LIFE	AR	432.6	FIRST SECURITY BENEFIT LIFE & ANN	NY	695.6
Rating: B			FLORIDA COMBINED LIFE INS CO INC	FL	45.7
AAA LIFE INS CO	MI	560.4	GENERAL AMERICAN LIFE INS CO	MO	12,151.6
ALLIANZ LIFE INS CO OF NY	NY	2,833.1	GENERATION LIFE INS CO	AZ	30.2
ALLSTATE LIFE INS CO	IL	34,348.3	GENWORTH LIFE INS CO OF NEW YORK	NY	8,185.1
AMERICAN BANKERS LIFE ASR CO OF FL	FL	517.1	GLOBE LIFE & ACCIDENT INS CO	NE	3,511.4
AMERICAN CONTINENTAL INS CO	TN	151.9	GOLDEN RULE INS CO	IN	736.6
AMERICAN EQUITY INVEST LIFE INS CO	IA	35,274.7	GREAT SOUTHERN LIFE INS CO	TX	225.3
AMERICAN FARM LIFE INS CO	TX	3.6	GREAT-WEST LIFE & ANNUITY INS OF NY	NY	1,568.3
AMERICAN GENERAL LIFE INS CO	TX	161,296.7	GREENFIELDS LIFE INS CO	CO	6.9
AMERICAN HERITAGE LIFE INS CO	FL	1,750.7	GUARANTEE TRUST LIFE INS CO	IL	408.5
AMERICAN MATURITY LIFE INS CO	CT	61.9	GUARDIAN INS & ANNUITY CO INC	DE	15,244.7
AMERICAN MODERN LIFE INS CO	OH	49.0	HARLEYSVILLE LIFE INS CO	PA	410.9
AMERICAN NATIONAL INS CO	TX	18,049.9	HCC LIFE INS CO	IN	885.8
AMERICAN NATIONAL LIFE INS CO OF NY	NY	157.1	HEALTH NET LIFE INS CO	CA	618.8
AMERICAN PROGRESSIVE L&H I C OF NY	NY	232.1	HM LIFE INS CO	PA	583.7
AMERICAN PUBLIC LIFE INS CO	OK	82.5	HOMESTEADERS LIFE CO	IA	2,475.7
AMERICAN REPUBLIC CORP INS CO	NE	26.3	HORACE MANN LIFE INS CO	IL	7,830.3
AMERITAS LIFE INS CORP	NE	9,678.1	INTRAMERICA LIFE INS CO	NY	34.4
AMICA LIFE INS CO	RI	1,196.2	INVESTORS LIFE INS CO NORTH AMERICA	TX	680.7
ANNUITY INVESTORS LIFE INS CO	OH	2,963.6	JACKSON NATIONAL LIFE INS CO OF NY	NY	9,263.1
AURORA NATIONAL LIFE ASR CO	CA	3,103.6	JAMESTOWN LIFE INS CO	VA	143.7
AUTOMOBILE CLUB OF SOUTHERN CA INS	CA	810.5	JOHN ALDEN LIFE INS CO	WI	335.7
AXA EQUITABLE LIFE INS CO	NY	161,704.9	JOHN HANCOCK LIFE & HEALTH INS CO	MA	10,285.2
BALBOA LIFE INS CO OF NY	NY	19.5	JOHN HANCOCK LIFE INS CO (USA)	MI	241,722.8
BALTIMORE LIFE INS CO	MD	1,129.9	KANSAS CITY LIFE INS CO	MO	3,390.6
BANKERS FIDELITY LIFE INS CO	GA	138.7	LAFAYETTE LIFE INS CO	OH	3,985.3
BENEFICIAL LIFE INS CO	UT	2,942.3	LIBERTY LIFE ASR CO OF BOSTON	NH	14,303.2
BLUE CROSS BLUE SHIELD OF KANSAS INC	KS	1,592.7	LIBERTY NATIONAL LIFE INS CO	NE	7,400.5
CAREAMERICA LIFE INS CO	CA	29.3	LIFE INS CO OF NORTH AMERICA	PA	7,167.4
CARIBBEAN AMERICAN LIFE ASR CO	PR	41.9	LIFE INS CO OF THE SOUTHWEST	TX	12,900.2
CHEROKEE NATIONAL LIFE INS CO	GA	20.6	LIFEMAP ASR CO	OR	84.5
CIGNA HEALTH & LIFE INS CO	CT	5,710.7	LINCOLN LIFE & ANNUITY CO OF NY	NY	12,543.7
CIGNA WORLDWIDE INS CO	DE	45.8	LINCOLN NATIONAL LIFE INS CO	IN	208,169.3
CINCINNATI LIFE INS CO	OH	3,853.0	LINCOLN REPUBLIC INS CO	ND	30.4
CM LIFE INS CO	CT	8,612.5	MAGNOLIA GUARANTY LIFE INS CO	MS	9.8
COLUMBIAN MUTUAL LIFE INS CO	NY	1,320.1	MANHATTAN LIFE INS CO	NY	335.6
COMBINED LIFE INS CO OF NEW YORK	NY	412.6	MANHATTAN NATIONAL LIFE INS CO	OH	181.3
CONTINENTAL AMERICAN INS CO	SC	402.9	MEDAMERICA INS CO	PA	878.9
CONTINENTAL LIFE INS CO OF BRENTWOOD	TN	240.3	MEDAMERICA INS CO OF NEW YORK	NY	565.5
CSI LIFE INS CO	NE	17.7	MEDICO INS CO	NE	67.2
DELAWARE AMERICAN LIFE INS CO	DE	150.9	METLIFE INS CO USA	DE	56,480.8
			MISSOURI VALLEY LIFE AND HLTH INS CO	MO	16.0
			MONITOR LIFE INS CO OF NEW YORK	NY	17.3

INSURANCE COMPANY NAME	DOM. STATE	TOTAL ASSETS ($MIL)
Rating: B (Continued)		
MOTORISTS LIFE INS CO	OH	516.8
MTL INS CO	IL	1,921.5
NATIONAL GUARDIAN LIFE INS CO	WI	2,903.2
NATIONAL LIFE INS CO	VT	9,082.4
NATIONAL SECURITY INS CO	AL	52.1
NATIONAL SECURITY LIFE & ANNUITY CO	NY	410.0
NATIONAL TEACHERS ASSOCIATES L I C	TX	418.4
NEW ENGLAND LIFE INS CO	MA	11,281.7
NIAGARA LIFE & HEALTH INS CO	NY	8.8
NORTH AMERICAN CO FOR LIFE & H INS	IA	16,820.8
NORTH COAST LIFE INS CO	WA	146.7
NORTHWESTERN LONG TERM CARE INS CO	WI	2,556.6
NYLIFE INS CO OF ARIZONA	AZ	197.3
OHIO NATIONAL LIFE INS CO	OH	26,677.4
OLD AMERICAN INS CO	MO	249.3
OLD UNITED LIFE INS CO	AZ	90.2
PACIFIC BEACON LIFE REASSUR INC	HI	--
PACIFIC CENTURY LIFE INS CORP	AZ	342.4
PAN AMERICAN ASR CO	LA	22.6
PAN AMERICAN LIFE INS CO OF PR	PR	9.4
PAN-AMERICAN LIFE INS CO	LA	1,424.5
PATRIOT LIFE INS CO	MI	17.2
PEKIN LIFE INS CO	IL	1,323.2
PENN INS & ANNUITY CO	DE	2,542.5
PENN MUTUAL LIFE INS CO	PA	16,715.6
PHARMACISTS LIFE INS CO	IA	91.9
PRENEED REINS CO OF AMERICA	AZ	32.9
PRIMERICA LIFE INS CO	MA	1,474.0
PRINCIPAL NATIONAL LIFE INS CO	IA	131.2
PROTECTIVE LIFE & ANNUITY INS CO	AL	2,105.5
PROTECTIVE LIFE INS CO	TN	41,449.6
PRUDENTIAL INS CO OF AMERICA	NJ	306,159.5
RELIANCE STANDARD LIFE INS CO	IL	7,447.4
RELIASTAR LIFE INS CO OF NEW YORK	NY	3,194.3
RGA REINSURANCE CO	MO	23,567.0
SEARS LIFE INS CO	TX	52.0
SECURIAN LIFE INS CO	MN	234.4
SECURITY BENEFIT LIFE INS CO	KS	23,360.9
SECURITY LIFE INS CO OF AMERICA	MN	71.7
SECURITY MUTUAL LIFE INS CO OF NY	NY	2,670.6
SETTLERS LIFE INS CO	WI	394.0
SOUTHERN PIONEER LIFE INS CO	AR	19.2
STANDARD SECURITY LIFE INS CO OF NY	NY	247.0
STARMOUNT LIFE INS CO	LA	56.6
STATE LIFE INS CO	IN	5,315.2
STATE LIFE INS FUND	WI	98.9
SWBC LIFE INS CO	TX	23.2
SYMETRA NATIONAL LIFE INS CO	IA	16.7
TEXAS LIFE INS CO	TX	1,000.7
TIAA-CREF LIFE INS CO	NY	8,766.7
TRANS WORLD ASR CO	CA	347.3
TRANSAMERICA ADVISORS LIFE INS CO	AR	9,792.9

INSURANCE COMPANY NAME	DOM. STATE	TOTAL ASSETS ($MIL)
TRANSAMERICA FINANCIAL LIFE INS CO	NY	30,565.9
TRUSTMARK LIFE INS CO OF NEW YORK	NY	6.5
ULLICO LIFE INS CO	TX	11.8
UNICARE LIFE & HEALTH INS CO	IN	402.8
UNIFIED LIFE INS CO	TX	183.7
UNIMERICA INS CO	WI	458.7
UNIMERICA LIFE INS CO OF NY	NY	36.1
UNION NATIONAL LIFE INS CO	LA	19.1
UNION SECURITY INS CO	KS	4,942.9
UNITED HOME LIFE INS CO	IN	76.9
UNITED LIFE INS CO	IA	1,640.6
UNITED OF OMAHA LIFE INS CO	NE	18,551.4
UNITED TRUST INS CO	AL	62.5
UNITEDHEALTHCARE LIFE INS CO	WI	101.5
UNIVERSAL LIFE INS CO	PR	740.2
US FINANCIAL LIFE INS CO	OH	639.7
USIC LIFE INS CO	PR	7.8
VARIABLE ANNUITY LIFE INS CO	TX	77,039.3
VOYA INS & ANNUITY CO	IA	66,208.2
VOYA RETIREMENT INS & ANNUITY CO	CT	88,666.7
WESTERN & SOUTHERN LIFE INS CO	OH	9,796.0
WESTERN-SOUTHERN LIFE ASR CO	OH	13,473.7
Rating: B-		
ALFA LIFE INS CORP	AL	1,334.1
ALL SAVERS INS CO	IN	39.0
ALLSTATE LIFE INS CO OF NEW YORK	NY	6,580.0
AMERICAN EQUITY INVESTMENT LIFE NY	NY	224.8
AMERICAN FIDELITY LIFE INS CO	FL	437.3
AMERICAN HEALTH & LIFE INS CO	TX	996.0
AMERICAN INCOME LIFE INS CO	IN	2,847.2
AMERICAN MEMORIAL LIFE INS CO	SD	2,635.4
AMERICAN NATIONAL LIFE INS CO OF TX	TX	135.8
AMERICAN RETIREMENT LIFE INS CO	OH	56.5
AMERICO FINANCIAL LIFE & ANNUITY INS	TX	3,871.0
AMERITAS LIFE INS CORP OF NY	NY	1,157.3
AXA CORPORATE SOLUTIONS LIFE REINS	DE	491.4
AXA EQUITABLE LIFE & ANNUITY CO	CO	472.1
BERKLEY LIFE & HEALTH INS CO	IA	198.6
BEST LIFE & HEALTH INS CO	TX	15.6
BEST MERIDIAN INS CO	FL	272.0
CENTRAL SECURITY LIFE INS CO	TX	71.2
CENTRE LIFE INS CO	MA	1,909.7
CHRISTIAN FIDELITY LIFE INS CO	TX	79.6
CHURCH LIFE INS CORP	NY	287.0
CMFG LIFE INS CO	IA	15,616.4
COLUMBUS LIFE INS CO	OH	3,326.3
COMMONWEALTH ANNUITY & LIFE INS CO	MA	10,566.4
COMPANION LIFE INS CO	NY	944.6
CONNECTICUT GENERAL LIFE INS CO	CT	18,691.4
EQUITRUST LIFE INS CO	IL	13,718.0
FARMERS NEW WORLD LIFE INS CO	WA	7,118.7
FIDELITY & GUARANTY LIFE INS CO NY	NY	517.0
FIDELITY SECURITY LIFE INS CO	MO	841.6

INSURANCE COMPANY NAME	DOM. STATE	TOTAL ASSETS ($MIL)	INSURANCE COMPANY NAME	DOM. STATE	TOTAL ASSETS ($MIL)
Rating: B- (Continued)			STONEBRIDGE LIFE INS CO	VT	1,772.2
			SUNSET LIFE INS CO OF AMERICA	MO	358.9
FIRST COMMAND LIFE INS CO	TX	32.6	TIME INS CO	WI	848.6
FORETHOUGHT LIFE INS CO	IN	11,568.0	TRANSAMERICA LIFE INS CO	IA	118,208.1
FUNERAL DIRECTORS LIFE INS CO	TX	1,046.4	TRIPLE S VIDA INC	PR	537.9
GENWORTH LIFE & ANNUITY INS CO	VA	24,254.6	UNION LABOR LIFE INS CO	MD	3,351.0
GENWORTH LIFE INS CO	DE	37,409.9	UNITED AMERICAN INS CO	NE	1,717.2
GRANGE LIFE INS CO	OH	366.5	UNITED HERITAGE LIFE INS CO	ID	522.4
GREAT AMERICAN LIFE INS CO	OH	22,140.3	UNITED INS CO OF AMERICA	IL	3,655.6
GREAT WEST LIFE ASR CO	MI	78.1	UNITED STATES LIFE INS CO IN NYC	NY	28,449.0
GREAT WESTERN INS CO	UT	883.7	UNIVERSAL UNDERWRITERS LIFE INS CO	KS	159.3
GREAT-WEST LIFE & ANNUITY INS CO	CO	56,894.9	USA LIFE ONE INS CO OF INDIANA	IN	36.6
GUGGENHEIM LIFE & ANNUITY CO	DE	11,992.0	VANTIS LIFE INS CO	CT	877.6
HARTFORD INTL LIFE REASR CORP	CT	1,144.5	VANTISLIFE INS CO OF NEW YORK	NY	8.6
HARTFORD LIFE & ANNUITY INS CO	CT	48,312.7	VERSANT LIFE INS CO	MS	5.5
HEALTHMARKETS INS CO	OK	28.9	WESTERN UNITED LIFE ASR CO	WA	14.8
HUMANA INS CO OF KENTUCKY	KY	122.2	WILTON REASSURANCE CO	MN	3,820.4
HUMANA INS CO OF PUERTO RICO INC	PR	69.1	WILTON REASSURANCE LIFE CO OF NY	NY	910.9
INTEGRITY LIFE INS CO	OH	6,199.4	WINDSOR LIFE INS CO	TX	3.2
INVESTORS GROWTH LIFE INS CO	AZ	19.0	ZALE LIFE INS CO	AZ	11.4
KENTUCKY FUNERAL DIRECTORS LIFE INS	KY	17.3	**Rating: C+**		
LIFECARE ASSURANCE CO	AZ	1,899.4	ALLIANZ LIFE INS CO OF NORTH AMERICA	MN	113,662.2
LIFESHIELD NATIONAL INS CO	OK	67.0	ATHENE ANNUITY & LIFE CO	IA	43,427.5
LINCOLN HERITAGE LIFE INS CO	IL	794.5	ATLANTIC COAST LIFE INS CO	SC	127.4
MEGA LIFE & HEALTH INS CO	OK	271.8	AUTO CLUB LIFE INS CO	MI	536.5
METLIFE INS LTD GUAM BRANCH	GU	3.1	BANKERS LIFE INS CO	FL	324.2
METROPOLITAN LIFE INS CO	NY	392,833.7	BERKSHIRE HATHAWAY LIFE INS CO OF NE	NE	13,999.8
METROPOLITAN TOWER LIFE INS CO	DE	5,083.2	BROOKE LIFE INS CO	MI	4,937.1
MID-WEST NATIONAL LIFE INS CO OF TN	TX	63.2	CATAMARAN INS OF OHIO	OH	69.7
MONY LIFE INS CO	NY	7,686.7	CENTRAL RESERVE LIFE INS CO	OH	25.1
MONY LIFE INS CO OF AMERICA	AZ	2,829.1	CHESAPEAKE LIFE INS CO	OK	75.0
MUNICH AMERICAN REASSURANCE CO	GA	7,304.3	CIGNA ARBOR LIFE INS CO	CT	20.8
NATIONAL FARM LIFE INS CO	TX	374.8	CITIZENS FIDELITY INS CO	AR	65.5
NATIONAL INTEGRITY LIFE INS CO	NY	4,807.4	COLONIAL LIFE & ACCIDENT INS CO	SC	2,882.2
NATIONWIDE LIFE & ANNUITY INS CO	OH	7,340.8	COLUMBIAN LIFE INS CO	IL	307.2
NATIONWIDE LIFE INS CO	OH	125,130.2	COMBINED INS CO OF AMERICA	IL	1,635.2
OHIO MOTORISTS LIFE INSURANCE CO	OH	10.1	CONSTITUTION LIFE INS CO	TX	316.1
OHIO STATE LIFE INS CO	TX	13.2	DIRECT GENERAL LIFE INS CO	SC	29.5
OLD REPUBLIC LIFE INS CO	IL	124.6	EQUITABLE LIFE & CASUALTY INS CO	UT	290.5
OMAHA INS CO	NE	24.5	FIDELITY & GUARANTY LIFE INS CO	IA	18,461.3
OPTIMUM RE INS CO	TX	127.0	FIRST BERKSHIRE HATHAWAY LIFE INS CO	NY	370.5
OXFORD LIFE INS CO	AZ	1,181.8	FIRST UNUM LIFE INS CO	NY	2,794.1
OZARK NATIONAL LIFE INS CO	MO	743.3	FIVE STAR LIFE INS CO	LA	258.8
PARAGON LIFE INS CO OF INDIANA	IN	1,833.4	GENERAL FIDELITY LIFE INS CO	SC	88.2
PERFORMANCE LIFE OF AMERICA	LA	29.9	HARTFORD LIFE INS CO	CT	124,390.0
PHILADELPHIA AMERICAN LIFE INS CO	TX	215.8	IDEALIFE INS CO	CT	21.0
PLATEAU INS CO	TN	31.2	LANDCAR LIFE INS CO	UT	22.6
PROVIDENT AMER LIFE & HEALTH INS CO	OH	16.4	LEADERS LIFE INS CO	OK	5.9
PROVIDENT LIFE & CAS INS CO	TN	777.2	LONDON LIFE INS CO	MI	25.3
PRUCO LIFE INS CO OF NEW JERSEY	NJ	12,642.3	LONDON LIFE REINSURANCE CO	PA	324.0
PRUDENTIAL RETIREMENT INS & ANNUITY	CT	77,318.5	MADISON NATIONAL LIFE INS CO INC	WI	491.1
RELIABLE LIFE INS CO	MO	22.6	MAPFRE LIFE INS CO	DE	26.7
ROYAL STATE NATIONAL INS CO LTD	HI	46.2	MAPFRE LIFE INS CO OF PR	PR	66.0
SBLI USA MUT LIFE INS CO INC	NY	1,588.6			

INSURANCE COMPANY NAME	DOM. STATE	TOTAL ASSETS ($MIL)
Rating: C+ (Continued)		
MEDAMERICA INS CO OF FL	FL	25.9
MUNICH AMERICAN LIFE REINS CO	GA	1,270.8
PACIFICARE LIFE & HEALTH INS CO	IN	554.1
PAUL REVERE LIFE INS CO	MA	4,144.1
PHOENIX LIFE & ANNUITY CO	CT	45.2
PIONEER SECURITY LIFE INS CO	TX	122.2
POPULAR LIFE RE	PR	55.6
PROVIDENT LIFE & ACCIDENT INS CO	TN	8,316.4
PRUCO LIFE INS CO	AZ	104,592.5
REINSURANCE CO OF MO INC	MO	1,604.2
RELIASTAR LIFE INS CO	MN	21,234.6
RESOURCE LIFE INS CO	IL	25.5
S USA LIFE INS CO INC	AZ	13.5
SECURITY LIFE OF DENVER INS CO	CO	14,195.5
SECURITY PLAN LIFE INS CO	LA	321.7
SERVCO LIFE INS CO	TX	8.9
SUPERIOR FUNERAL & LIFE INS CO	AR	167.7
SURETY LIFE INS CO	NE	14.3
SWISS RE LIFE & HEALTH AMER INC	CT	10,472.4
TRANSAMERICA PREMIER LIFE INS CO	IA	32,048.5
UNIVERSAL GUARANTY LIFE INS CO	OH	345.7
UNUM LIFE INS CO OF AMERICA	ME	19,496.1
WEST COAST LIFE INS CO	NE	4,715.9
ZURICH AMERICAN LIFE INS CO OF NY	NY	42.6
Rating: C		
ACE LIFE INS CO	CT	39.6
AMALGAMATED LIFE & HEALTH INS CO	IL	5.8
AMERICAN FARMERS & RANCHERS LIFE INS	OK	24.5
AMERICAN FEDERATED LIFE INS CO	MS	28.1
AMERICAN LIFE & ACC INS CO OF KY	KY	362.5
AMERICAN LIFE INS CO	DE	7,622.5
AMERICAN SAVINGS LIFE INS CO	AZ	49.8
AMERICAN-AMICABLE LIFE INS CO OF TX	TX	272.0
ATHENE ANNUITY & LIFE ASR CO OF NY	NY	3,420.4
ATHENE LIFE INS CO OF NEW YORK	NY	1,744.3
BANKERS LIFE OF LOUISIANA	LA	13.2
CANADA LIFE ASSURANCE CO-US BRANCH	MI	4,444.2
CAPITOL LIFE INS CO	TX	210.6
CELTIC INS CO	IL	116.9
CENSTAT LIFE ASR CO	AZ	--
CENTRAL UNITED LIFE INS CO	AR	303.7
CITIZENS NATIONAL LIFE INS CO	TX	12.6
CITIZENS SECURITY LIFE INS CO	KY	22.5
CONSUMERS LIFE INS CO	OH	34.5
CONTINENTAL ASSURANCE CO	IL	2,473.9
CONTINENTAL GENERAL INS CO	OH	242.0
DELAWARE LIFE INS CO	DE	39,688.7
DELAWARE LIFE INS CO OF NEW YORK	NY	3,033.2
DOCTORS LIFE INS CO	CA	16.5
ELCO MUTUAL LIFE & ANNUITY	IL	466.9
EMPLOYERS REASSURANCE CORP	KS	11,081.7

INSURANCE COMPANY NAME	DOM. STATE	TOTAL ASSETS ($MIL)
ENTERPRISE LIFE INS CO	TX	18.3
EVERENCE INS CO	IN	24.1
FAMILY BENEFIT LIFE INS CO	MO	66.3
FAMILY LIFE INS CO	TX	148.2
FAMILY SECURITY LIFE INS CO INC	MS	6.6
FEDERAL LIFE INS CO (MUTUAL)	IL	231.8
FIDELITY LIFE ASSN A LEGAL RESERVE	IL	412.7
FIRST GUARANTY INS CO	LA	55.2
FIRST METLIFE INVESTORS INS CO	NY	6,265.7
FORETHOUGHT NATIONAL LIFE INS CO	TX	210.6
FREEDOM LIFE INS CO OF AMERICA	TX	54.8
GREAT CENTRAL LIFE INS CO	LA	21.4
HALLMARK LIFE INS CO	AZ	23.6
HANNOVER LIFE REASSUR CO OF AMERICA	FL	4,534.7
HEARTLAND NATIONAL LIFE INS CO	IN	9.5
IA AMERICAN LIFE INS CO	TX	236.6
INDEPENDENCE LIFE & ANNUITY CO	DE	2,540.6
INDUSTRIAL ALLIANCE INS & FIN SERV	TX	190.2
INVESTORS HERITAGE LIFE INS CO	KY	480.0
JEFF DAVIS MORTUARY BENEFIT ASSOC	LA	--
KANAWHA INS CO	SC	1,657.2
LEWER LIFE INS CO	MO	29.0
LIFE OF AMERICA INS CO	TX	11.4
LIFE OF THE SOUTH INS CO	GA	79.3
LOYAL AMERICAN LIFE INS CO	OH	251.3
M LIFE INS CO	CO	248.6
MARQUETTE INDEMNITY & LIFE INS CO	AZ	7.3
MARQUETTE NATIONAL LIFE INS CO	TX	6.7
MELLON LIFE INS CO	DE	24.9
MEMBERS LIFE INS CO	IA	27.3
MOLINA HEALTHCARE OF TEXAS INS CO	TX	3.4
NATIONAL FAMILY CARE LIFE INS CO	TX	16.0
NATIONAL FOUNDATION LIFE INS CO	TX	24.2
NATIONAL HEALTH INS CO	TX	14.1
NEW ERA LIFE INS CO	TX	395.4
NEW ERA LIFE INS CO OF THE MIDWEST	TX	81.6
NORTH AMERICAN INS CO	WI	21.7
OCCIDENTAL LIFE INS CO OF NC	TX	258.7
OLD SPARTAN LIFE INS CO INC	SC	21.5
OLD SURETY LIFE INS CO	OK	25.5
PAUL REVERE VARIABLE ANNUITY INS CO	MA	56.7
PAVONIA LIFE INS CO OF MICHIGAN	MI	389.8
PHL VARIABLE INS CO	CT	6,426.3
PHOENIX LIFE INS CO	NY	13,326.4
PHYSICIANS BENEFITS TRUST LIFE INS	IL	14.2
PIONEER AMERICAN INS CO	TX	56.5
PRESIDENTIAL LIFE INS CO	TX	4.3
PROFESSIONAL INS CO	TX	108.3
PROFESSIONAL LIFE & CAS CO	IL	153.0
PROTEC INS CO	IL	2.7
PRUDENTIAL ANNUITIES LIFE ASR CORP	AZ	48,138.0
PYRAMID LIFE INS CO	KS	170.6
RIVER LAKE INS CO	SC	1,328.7
RIVER LAKE INS CO II	SC	1,117.9

INSURANCE COMPANY NAME	DOM. STATE	TOTAL ASSETS ($MIL)
Rating: C (Continued)		
RIVERMONT LIFE INS CO I	SC	526.0
RIVERSOURCE LIFE INS CO OF NY	NY	6,480.9
SCOR GLOBAL LIFE REINS CO OF DE	DE	430.4
SCOR GLOBAL LIFE USA RE CO	DE	800.9
SERVICE LIFE & CAS INS CO	TX	41.9
SHENANDOAH LIFE INS CO	VA	1,220.8
SHERIDAN LIFE INS CO	OK	2.2
SOUTHERN FINANCIAL LIFE INS CO	KY	4.1
SOUTHERN NATL LIFE INS CO INC	LA	15.6
STATE MUTUAL INS CO	GA	294.0
SURENCY LIFE & HEALTH INS CO	KS	8.4
TEXAS DIRECTORS LIFE INS CO	TX	5.9
UNITED FIDELITY LIFE INS CO	TX	757.1
UNITED HEALTHCARE INS CO	CT	14,592.8
UNITED NATIONAL LIFE INS CO OF AM	IL	14.7
UNITED TEACHER ASSOCIATES INS CO	TX	986.6
WEA INS CORP	WI	683.2
WESTERN AMERICAN LIFE INS CO	TX	31.9
WICHITA NATIONAL LIFE INS CO	OK	17.8
WMI MUTUAL INS CO	UT	14.5
ZURICH AMERICAN LIFE INS CO	IL	12,655.1
Rating: C-		
ACCORDIA LIFE & ANNUITY CO	IA	7,481.4
AMERICAN BENEFIT LIFE INS CO	OK	94.2
AMERICAN HOME LIFE INS CO	KS	239.7
ATHENE ANNUITY & LIFE ASR CO	DE	11,023.3
CHAMPIONS LIFE INS CO	TX	35.2
CICA LIFE INS CO OF AMERICA	CO	749.7
CINCINNATI EQUITABLE LIFE INS CO	OH	84.6
COLONIAL LIFE INS CO OF TX	TX	17.7
CONSECO LIFE INS CO	IN	3,763.2
COOPERATIVA DE SEGUROS DE VIDA DE PR	PR	430.9
FIRST ALLMERICA FINANCIAL LIFE INS	MA	4,211.4
FIRST NATIONAL LIFE INS CO OF USA	NE	5.9
GERMANIA LIFE INS CO	TX	68.8
GUARANTY INCOME LIFE INS CO	LA	482.6
HARTFORD LIFE & ACCIDENT INS CO	CT	9,041.5
HAWKEYE LIFE INS GROUP INC	IA	12.2
HERITAGE LIFE INS CO	AZ	5,039.7
JEFFERSON NATIONAL LIFE INS CO	TX	3,581.0
LIFE ASR CO OF AMERICA	IL	6.2
LIFE ASSURANCE CO INC	OK	5.3
LIFE INS CO OF LOUISIANA	LA	8.4
MEMORIAL LIFE INS CO	LA	--
MOUNTAIN LIFE INS CO	TN	11.8
RABENHORST LIFE INS CO	LA	29.1
RIVERSOURCE LIFE INS CO	MN	103,856.3
SAGICOR LIFE INS CO	TX	1,193.0
SCOR GLOBAL LIFE AMERICAS REIN CO	DE	1,468.9
SCOTTISH RE US INC	DE	1,770.7
SENIOR LIFE INS CO	GA	46.8

INSURANCE COMPANY NAME	DOM. STATE	TOTAL ASSETS ($MIL)
STERLING INVESTORS LIFE INS CO	GA	15.4
STRUCTURED ANNUITY RE CO	IA	1,412.3
SUN LIFE & HEALTH INS CO	CT	369.9
SURETY LIFE & CASUALTY INS CO	ND	10.6
TEXAS SERVICE LIFE INS CO	TX	43.6
TOWN & COUNTRY LIFE INS CO	UT	6.0
TRANS CITY LIFE INS CO	AZ	19.4
UBS LIFE INS CO USA	CA	41.6
UNITY FINANCIAL LIFE INS CO	OH	185.4
USA INS CO	MS	3.2
WATEREE LIFE INS	SC	10.4
WILLIAM PENN LIFE INS CO OF NEW YORK	NY	1,149.7
Rating: D+		
AMERICAN CENTURY LIFE INS CO	OK	66.6
AMERICAN LIFE & ANNUITY CO	AR	48.6
AMERICAN PIONEER LIFE INS CO	FL	76.9
AMERICAN UNDERWRITERS LIFE INS CO	AZ	81.8
ARKANSAS BANKERS LIFE INS CO	AR	3.3
BANKERS LIFE & CAS CO	IL	16,389.4
CENTURY LIFE ASR CO	OK	12.6
CLARIA LIFE & HEALTH INS CO	DE	6.8
COLONIAL PENN LIFE INS CO	PA	738.8
COLONIAL SECURITY LIFE INS CO	TX	2.8
CONTINENTAL LIFE INS CO	PA	21.2
FIDELITY STANDARD LIFE INS CO	AR	3.3
FINANCIAL AMERICAN LIFE INS CO	KS	23.4
FOUNDATION LIFE INS CO OF AR	AR	5.5
FRINGE BENEFIT LIFE INS CO	TX	45.4
FUTURAL LIFE INS CO	AZ	4.8
GREAT FIDELITY LIFE INS CO	IN	4.2
LIBERTY BANKERS LIFE INS CO	OK	1,103.8
LIFE PROTECTION INS CO	TX	8.7
LONGEVITY INS CO	TX	9.1
MAGNA INS CO	MS	2.6
PAVONIA LIFE INS CO OF NEW YORK	NY	35.7
PROVIDENT AMERICAN INS CO	TX	21.1
PURITAN LIFE INS CO	TX	12.7
PURITAN LIFE INS CO OF AMERICA	TX	36.8
SECU LIFE INS CO	NC	25.4
SENIOR HEALTH INS CO OF PENNSYLVANIA	PA	2,898.4
SOUTHERN FINANCIAL LIFE INS CO	LA	102.5
SOUTHERN SECURITY LIFE INS CO INC	MS	2.0
STANDARD LIFE & CAS INS CO	UT	30.4
T J M LIFE INS CO	TX	15.0
TOWER LIFE INS CO	TX	54.5
TRUASSURE INS CO	IL	7.7
UNION FIDELITY LIFE INS CO	KS	19,466.6
UNITED SECURITY ASR CO OF PA	PA	150.9
WASHINGTON NATIONAL INS CO	IN	4,769.5
Rating: D		
ABILITY INS CO	NE	903.3
AMERICAN FINANCIAL SECURITY L I C	MO	5.5

INSURANCE COMPANY NAME	DOM. STATE	TOTAL ASSETS ($MIL)
Rating: D (Continued)		
AMERICAN LABOR LIFE INS CO	AZ	8.6
ASSOCIATED MUTUAL	MI	10.7
ATLANTA LIFE INS CO	GA	48.7
AURIGEN REINS CO OF AMERICA	AR	25.1
BANKERS CONSECO LIFE INS CO	NY	203.3
BANKERS LIFE INS CO OF AMERICA	TX	5.2
BANNER LIFE INS CO	MD	1,721.0
CENTURION LIFE INS CO	IA	1,211.1
COOPERATIVE LIFE INS CO	AR	6.7
DAKOTA CAPITAL LIFE INS CO	ND	2.5
FAMILY LIBERTY LIFE INS CO	TX	31.7
FIRST CONTINENTAL LIFE & ACC INS CO	TX	5.9
GULF GUARANTY LIFE INS CO	MS	15.4
HAWTHORN LIFE INS CO	TX	11.7
INDIVIDUAL ASR CO LIFE HEALTH & ACC	OK	17.9
JEFFERSON LIFE INS CO	TX	2.7
LANDMARK LIFE INS CO	TX	44.9
MEDICAL BENEFITS MUTUAL LIFE INS CO	OH	18.3
MELANCON LIFE INS CO	LA	--
MEMORIAL INS CO OF AMERICA	AR	1.2
MULHEARN PROTECTIVE INS CO	LA	12.8
PELLERIN LIFE INS CO	LA	10.4
SENTINEL SECURITY LIFE INS CO	UT	443.7
SOUTHLAND NATIONAL INS CORP	AL	165.9
SOUTHWEST SERVICE LIFE INS CO	TX	12.6
SUN LIFE ASR CO OF CANADA	MI	16,300.0
TEACHERS PROTV MUTUAL LIFE INS CO	PA	61.8
TEXAS IMPERIAL LIFE INS CO	TX	3.5
UNITED FUNERAL BENEFIT LIFE INS CO	OK	48.6
UNITED SECURITY LIFE & HEALTH INS CO	IL	4.0
UNIVERSAL FIDELITY LIFE INS CO	OK	14.5
WESTPORT LIFE INS CO	AZ	--
Rating: D-		
CAPITOL SECURITY LIFE INS CO	TX	4.6
DLE LIFE INS CO	LA	39.3
FIRST WYOMING LIFE INS CO	WY	4.3
INTERNATIONAL AMERICAN LIFE INS CO	TX	2.1
LIFESECURE INS CO	MI	215.7
MULTINATIONAL LIFE INS CO	PR	128.7
PINE BELT LIFE INS CO	MS	2.1
REGAL LIFE OF AMERICA INS CO	TX	10.1
SECURITY NATIONAL LIFE INS CO	UT	505.7
SMITH BURIAL & LIFE INS CO	AR	4.8
TRINITY LIFE INS CO	OK	127.2
TRIPLE-S BLUE INC	PR	18.7
UNITED ASR LIFE INS CO	TX	2.1
UNITED FUNERAL DIR BENEFIT LIC	TX	103.3
US ALLIANCE LIFE & SECURITY CO	KS	4.5
Rating: E+		
ALABAMA LIFE REINS CO INC	AL	28.5
CAPITAL RESERVE LIFE INS CO	MO	1.4

INSURANCE COMPANY NAME	DOM. STATE	TOTAL ASSETS ($MIL)
COMMERCIAL TRAVELERS MUTUAL INS CO	NY	14.9
DELTA LIFE INS CO	GA	60.7
GREAT PLAINS LIFE ASR CO	SD	6.0
KENTUCKY HOME LIFE INS CO	KY	5.7
KILPATRICK LIFE INS CO	LA	181.5
MCS LIFE INS CO	PR	67.3
NETCARE LIFE & HEALTH INS CO	GU	24.7
NORTH CAROLINA MUTUAL LIFE INS CO	NC	142.9
RELIABLE LIFE INS CO	LA	--
WILLIAMS PROGRESSIVE LIFE & ACC I C	LA	11.1
Rating: E		
AMERICAN HOME LIFE INS CO	AR	18.9
AMERICAN INDEPENDENT NETWORK INS CO	NY	27.6
AMERICAN LIFE & SECURITY CORP	AZ	17.8
CASS COUNTY LIFE INS CO	TX	3.2
DIRECTORS LIFE ASR CO	OK	28.8
JACKSON GRIFFIN INS CO	AR	11.2
PHILADELPHIA FINANCIAL LIFE ASR CO	PA	4,603.8
RHODES LIFE INS CO OF LA INC	LA	4.1
Rating: E-		
AMERICAN MEDICAL & LIFE INS CO	NY	7.5
MOTHE LIFE INS CO	LA	15.2
NORTH AMERICA LIFE INS CO OF TX	TX	45.1
Rating: F		
AMERICAN COMMUNITY MUT INS CO	MI	--
FIDELITY MUTUAL LIFE INS CO	PA	--
FREMONT LIFE INS CO	CA	--
GERTRUDE GEDDES WILLIS LIFE INS CO	LA	--
GREAT REPUBLIC LIFE INS CO	WA	--
HIGGINBOTHAM BURIAL INS CO	AR	--
LONE STAR LIFE INS CO	TX	--
MONARCH LIFE INS CO	MA	755.0
Rating: U		
AAA LIFE INS CO OF NY	NY	8.8
ACADEME INC	WA	5.6
AGC LIFE INS CO	MO	20,893.3
ALL SAVERS LIFE INS CO OF CA	CA	9.7
ALLIANZ LIFE & ANNUITY CO	MN	16.7
ALLIED FINANCIAL INS CO	TX	0.4
AMERICAN CENTURY LIFE INS CO TX	TX	0.6
AMERICAN CLASSIC REINS CO	AZ	--
AMERICAN CREDITORS LIFE INS CO	DE	14.3
AMERICAN INTEGRITY LIFE INS CO	AR	0.4
AMERICAN PHOENIX LIFE & REASSUR CO	CT	18.1
AMERICAN SERVICE LIFE INS CO	AR	0.8
ATHENE LIFE INS CO	DE	195.8
BANKERS FIDELITY ASR CO	GA	3.4
BEVERLY HILLS LIFE INS CO	AZ	--
BLUE SPIRIT INS CO	VT	--
CALPERS LONG-TERM CARE PROGRAM		--
CANYON STATE LIFE INS CO	AZ	1.8

INSURANCE COMPANY NAME	DOM. STATE	TOTAL ASSETS ($MIL)	INSURANCE COMPANY NAME	DOM. STATE	TOTAL ASSETS ($MIL)
Rating: U (Continued)			KSKJ LIFE	IL	--
			LOYAL CHRISTIAN BENEFIT ASSN	PA	--
CARLISLE LIFE INS CO	AZ	--	M & T LIFE INS CO	AZ	--
CATERPILLAR LIFE INS CO	MO	158.2	MAJESTIC LIFE INS CO	LA	--
CATHOLIC FINANCIAL LIFE	WI	--	MCB LIFE INS CO	TN	--
CBI INS CO	AZ	--	MIAMI VALLEY INS CO	AZ	--
CITCO LIFE INS CO	AZ	--	MIDWEST SECURITY LIFE INS CO	WI	7.2
COMMENCEMENT BAY LIFE INS CO	WA	7.4	MILILANI LIFE INS CO	HI	1.9
COMMONWEALTH DEALERS LIFE INS CO	VA	6.8	MINNETONKA LIFE INS CO	AZ	--
CONCERT HEALTH PLAN INS CO	IL	2.0	MISSISSIPPI VALLEY LIFE INS CO	AZ	--
CONSECO LIFE INS CO OF TX	TX	1,059.9	NAP LIFE INS CO	TX	2.6
CORVESTA LIFE INS CO	AZ	9.2	NEW FOUNDATION LIFE INS CO	AR	2.1
CROWN GLOBAL INS CO OF AMERICA	DE	1.5	NEW YORK LIFE AGENTS REIN CO	AZ	--
CSA FRATERNAL LIFE	IL	--	NORTH AMERICAN NATIONAL RE INS CO	AZ	--
DESTINY HEALTH INS CO	IL	3.6	NORTHERN NATIONAL LIFE INS CO OF RI	RI	--
DORSEY LIFE INS CO	TX	0.3	NTA LIFE INS CO OF NEW YORK	NY	7.0
DUPAGE LIFE INS CO	AZ	--	OCOEE LIFE INS CO	TN	--
EAGLE AMERICAN LIFE INS CO	LA	--	OMAHA LIFE INS CO	NE	10.6
EAGLE INS CO	AZ	--	ORDER UNITED COMM TRAVELERS OF AMER	OH	--
EAST ARKANSAS GEM LIFE INS CO	AZ	--	OVERTON LIFE INS CO	TN	--
EDUCATORS LIFE INS CO OF AMERICA	IL	390.7	PAN AMERICAN ASR CO INTL INC	FL	1.6
EVERENCE ASSN INC	IN	--	PAVONIA LIFE INS CO OF ARIZONA	AZ	757.5
EVERGREEN LIFE INS CO	TX	1.6	PAVONIA LIFE INS CO OF DELAWARE	DE	132.6
FAMILY SERVICE LIFE INS CO	TX	393.1	PEKIN FINANCIAL LIFE INS CO	AZ	--
FARMERS LIFE INS CO	TN	--	PENN OHIO LIFE INS CO	AZ	--
FINANCIAL ASSURANCE LIFE INS CO	TX	10.7	PHILADELPHIA FINANCIAL LIFE ASR NY	NY	4.6
FIRST AMTENN LIFE INS CO	MS	--	PIONEER MILITARY INS CO	NV	3.7
FIRST BANK SYSTEM LIFE INS CO	VT	--	PORT-O-CALL LIFE INS CO	AR	0.8
FIRST COMMUNITY LIFE INS CO	TN	--	PREFERRED SECURITY LIFE INS CO	TX	3.1
FIRST DIMENSION LIFE INS CO INC	OK	4.7	PRESERVATION LIFE INS CO	MO	1.4
FIRST FINANCIAL ASSURANCE CO	AR	--	PRIDE OF CARROLL LIFE INS CO	LA	--
FIRST LANDMARK LIFE INS CO	NE	2.0	PRINCIPAL LIFE INS CO IOWA	IA	231.7
FIRST MICHIGAN LIFE INS CO	AZ	--	PRUCO INS CO OF IOWA	IA	6.0
FIRST VOLUNTEER INS CO	AZ	--	REGAL REINSURANCE COMPANY	MA	9.1
FOOTHILLS LIFE INS CO	AZ	--	REGIONS LIFE INS CO	AZ	--
FOR LIFE INS CO	AZ	--	RELIABLE SERVICE INS CO	LA	--
GEORGIA PEOPLES LIFE INS CO	AZ	--	RELIANCE STANDARD LIFE INS CO OF TX	TX	746.4
GMHP HEALTH INS LMTD	GU	0.9	ROCKETT LIFE INS CO	LA	--
GOLDEN GATE CAPTIVE INS CO	SC	--	ROYAL NEIGHBORS OF AMERICA	IL	--
GOLDEN GATE II CAPTIVE INS CO	SC	--	SECURITAS FINANCIAL LIFE INS CO	NC	5.6
GREAT WESTERN LIFE INS CO	MT	2.1	SENTINEL AMERICAN LIFE INS CO	TX	31.9
GREATER MISSOURI LIFE INS CO	AZ	--	SEQUATCHIE LIFE INS CO	TN	--
GRIFFIN LEGGETT BURIAL INS CO	AR	0.1	SHELTERPOINT INS CO	FL	7.9
GULF STATES LIFE INS CO INC	LA	2.9	SOUTHERN FIDELITY LIFE INS CO	AR	0.1
HARRIS LIFE INS CO	AZ	--	SOUTHERN LIFE & HEALTH INS CO	WI	95.0
HERITAGE UNION LIFE INS CO	MN	11.8	SOUTHWEST CREDIT LIFE INC	NM	0.8
IBC LIFE INS CO	TX	3.5	SPJST	TX	--
INDEPENDENCE INS INC	DE	1.7	SQUIRE REASSURANCE CO LLC	MI	11.7
INSOUTH LIFE INS CO	TN	--	STARVED ROCK LIFE INS CO	AZ	--
INVESTORS PREFERRED LIFE INS CO	SD	0.7	STATE FARM HEALTH INS CO	IL	8.4
ISLAND INS CORP	PR	--	SYMPHONIX HEALTH INS INC	MI	9.8
JORDAN FUNERAL & INS CO INC	AL	1.1	TENNESSEE LIFE INS CO	AZ	--
JRD LIFE INS CO	AZ	--	THRIVENT FINANCIAL FOR LUTHERANS	WI	--
KNIGHTS OF COLUMBUS	CT	--	TIPPECANOE LIFE INS CO	AZ	--

INSURANCE COMPANY NAME	DOM. STATE	TOTAL ASSETS ($MIL)
Rating: U (Continued)		
TRANS-WESTERN LIFE INS CO	TX	0.5
TRANSAM ASR CO	AZ	4.3
UNITED BENEFIT LIFE INS CO	OH	3.1
UNITED BURIAL INS CO OF WINNSBORO	LA	--
UNITED INTERNATIONAL LIFE INS	OK	3.3
UNIVANTAGE INS CO	UT	1.9
VALUE HEALTH REINS INC	AZ	--
WESTERN CATHOLIC UNION	IL	--
WILBERT LIFE INS CO	LA	--
WOODMEN OF THE WORLD/ASSURED LIFE	CO	--
XL LIFE INS & ANNUITY CO	IL	13.9
YADKIN VALLEY LIFE INS CO	AZ	--

Section VI

Rating Upgrades
and Downgrades

A list of all

U.S. Life and Annuity Insurers

receiving a rating upgrade or downgrade
during the current quarter.

Section VI Contents

This section identifies those companies receiving a rating change since the previous edition of this publication, whether it be a rating upgrade, rating downgrade, newly-rated company or the withdrawal of a rating. A rating may be withdrawn due to a merger, dissolution, liquidation or lack of information. A rating upgrade or downgrade may entail a change from one letter grade to another, or it may mean the addition or deletion of a plus or minus sign within the same letter grade previously assigned to the company. Each rating upgrade and downgrade is accompanied by a brief explanation of why the rating was changed. Ratings are normally updated once each quarter of the year. In some instances, however, a company's rating may be downgraded outside of the normal updates due to overriding circumstances. The tables for new and withdrawn ratings will contain some or all of the following information:

1. **Insurance Company Name**

   The legally registered name, which can sometimes differ from the name that the company uses for advertising. An insurer's name can be very similar to that of another, so verify the company's exact name and state of domicile to make sure you are looking at the correct company.

2. **Domicile State**

   The state which has primary regulatory responsibility for the company. It may differ from the location of the company's corporate headquarters. You do not have to be living in the domicile state to purchase insurance from this firm, provided it is licensed to do business in your state.

3. **Total Assets**

   All assets admitted by state insurance regulators in millions of dollars. This includes investments, current business assets, and separate accounts.

4. **New Financial Strength Rating**

   The rating assigned to the company as of the date of this Guide's publication. Our rating is measured on a scale from A to F and considers a wide range of factors. Highly rated companies are, in our opinion, less likely to experience financial difficulties than lower-rated firms. See *About Weiss Financial Strength Ratings* for more information.

5. **Previous Financial Strength Rating**

   The rating assigned to the company prior to its most recent change.

6. **Date of Change**

   The date that the rating upgrade or downgrade officially occurred. Normally, all rating changes are put into effect on a single day each quarter of the year. In some instances, however, a rating may have been changed outside of this normal update.

New Ratings

INSURANCE COMPANY NAME	DOM. STATE	TOTAL ASSETS ($MIL)	NEW RATING	PREVIOUS RATING	DATE OF CHANGE

No new ratings are being released in this edition.

Withdrawn Ratings

INSURANCE COMPANY NAME	DOM. STATE	TOTAL ASSETS ($MIL)	NEW RATING	PREVIOUS RATING	DATE OF CHANGE
HERITAGE UNION LIFE INS CO	MN	11.8	U	B	10/09/14
METLIFE INVESTORS INS CO	MO	14,911.3	U	B-	10/09/14
METLIFE INVESTORS USA INS CO	DE	101,588.9	U	C+	10/09/14
TANDY LIFE INS CO	TX	4.5	U	D	10/09/14
WESTERN RESERVE LIFE ASR CO OF OHIO	OH	9,540.1	U	B	10/09/14

Rating Upgrades

AMALGAMATED LIFE & HEALTH INS CO was upgraded to C from C- in January 2015 based on an improved capitalization index and a markedly improved five-year profitability index.

BEST LIFE & HEALTH INS CO was upgraded to B- from C in January 2015 based on a greatly improved five-year profitability index and a greatly improved stability index.

CAPITOL LIFE INS CO was upgraded to C from C- in January 2015 based on a markedly improved stability index.

CHAMPIONS LIFE INS CO was upgraded to C- from D+ in January 2015 based on a higher stability index. enhanced financial strength of affiliates in Maximum Corporation Group.

CONSECO LIFE INS CO was upgraded to C- from D+ in January 2015 based on a higher capitalization index, an improved investment safety index and a higher five-year profitability index. composite rating for affiliated Wilton Re Holdings Ltd Group rose to C from D+.

DELAWARE LIFE INS CO was upgraded to C from C- in January 2015 based on a markedly improved capitalization index and a higher stability index.

EMC NATIONAL LIFE CO was upgraded to B from B- in January 2015 based on an improved capitalization index, an improved investment safety index, a higher five-year profitability index and a markedly improved stability index.

INVESTORS GROWTH LIFE INS CO was upgraded to B- from C+ in January 2015 based on a markedly improved investment safety index and a higher stability index.

NATIONAL FARMERS UNION LIFE INS CO was upgraded to B+ from B in January 2015 based on an improved capitalization index.

PAVONIA LIFE INS CO OF NEW YORK was upgraded to D+ from D in January 2015 based on a higher stability index.

PROFESSIONAL INS CO was upgraded to C from C- in January 2015 based on a markedly improved capitalization index, a higher five-year profitability index and a higher stability index.

S USA LIFE INS CO INC was upgraded to C+ from C in January 2015 based on a higher five-year profitability index.

SCOR GLOBAL LIFE REINS CO OF DE was upgraded to C from C- in January 2015 based on a higher capitalization index, an improved investment safety index and a higher five-year profitability index.

UNIVERSAL GUARANTY LIFE INS CO was upgraded to C+ from C in January 2015 based on a higher capitalization index, a higher investment safety index, a greatly improved five-year profitability index and a markedly improved stability index.

Rating Downgrades

CAPITAL RESERVE LIFE INS CO was downgraded to E+ from D- in January 2015 due to capitalization index and a significant decline in its investment safety index. In addition, the composite rating for affiliated Midwest Holding Inc Group fell to E+ from D-, as exemplified by recent downgrade of affiliates: GREAT PLAINS LIFE ASR CO to E+ from D-. FIRST WYOMING LIFE INS CO to D- from D.

ELCO MUTUAL LIFE & ANNUITY was downgraded to C from B- in January 2015 due to a declining investment safety index and a substantially lower stability index.

FIRST WYOMING LIFE INS CO was downgraded to D- from D in January 2015 due to a significant decline in its stability index. In addition, the composite rating for affiliated Midwest Holding Inc Group fell to E+ from D-, per the recent downgrade of affiliated company GREAT PLAINS LIFE ASR CO to E+ from D-.

GREAT PLAINS LIFE ASR CO was downgraded to E+ from D- in January 2015 due to a significant decline in its investment safety index. In addition, the composite rating for affiliated Midwest Holding Inc Group fell to E+ from D-.

NATIONWIDE LIFE INS CO was downgraded to B- from B in January 2015 due to a substantially lower stability index.

NORTH CAROLINA MUTUAL LIFE INS CO was downgraded to E+ from D- in January 2015 due to a significant decline in its capitalization index, a significant decline in its investment safety index, a lower five-year profitability index and a significant decline in its stability index.

PHYSICIANS BENEFITS TRUST LIFE INS was downgraded to C from B- in January 2015 due to a significant decline in its capitalization index, a substantially lower five-year profitability index and a declining stability index.

SOUTHLAND NATIONAL INS CORP was downgraded to D from C in January 2015 due to a substantially lower stability index. In addition, termination of affiliation with Collateral Holdings Ltd Group rated C.

SURETY LIFE INS CO was downgraded to C+ from B+ in January 2015 due to a substantially lower five-year profitability index.

TRUASSURE INS CO was downgraded to D+ from C- in January 2015 due to a lower investment safety index and a declining five-year profitability index.

UNITED AMERICAN INS CO was downgraded to B- from B in January 2015 due to a substantially lower capitalization index, a declining five-year profitability index and a substantially lower stability index.

UNITED FUNERAL DIR BENEFIT LIC was downgraded to D- from D in January 2015 due to a significant decline in its capitalization index, a declining investment safety index, a declining five-year profitability index and a significant decline in its stability index.

WILLIAMS PROGRESSIVE LIFE & ACC I C was downgraded to E+ from D- in January 2015 due to a significant decline in its capitalization index, a lower five-year profitability index and a significant decline in its stability index.

WILTON REASSURANCE CO was downgraded to B- from B in January 2015 due to a substantially lower capitalization index and a substantially lower investment safety index. In addition, the composite rating for affiliated Wilton Re Holdings Ltd Group fell to C from B.

WILTON REASSURANCE LIFE CO OF NY was downgraded to B- from B in January 2015 due to capitalization index and a declining stability index. In addition, the composite rating for affiliated Wilton Re Holdings Ltd Group fell to C from B.

Appendix

State Guaranty Associations

The states have established insurance guaranty associations to help pay claims to policyholders of failed insurance companies. However, there are several cautions which you must be aware of with respect to this coverage:

1. Most of the guaranty associations do not set aside funds in advance. Rather, states assess contributions from other insurance companies after an insolvency occurs.

2. There can be an unacceptably long delay before claims are paid.

3. Each state is governed by its own legislation, providing a wide range of coverage and conditions that may apply. According to the National Organization of Life and Health Guaranty Associations (NOLHGA), the issues are extremely complex with unique variables for each individual state.

4. The table on the following page is designed to help you sort out these issues. However, it is not intended to handle all of them. If your carrier has failed and you need a complete answer, we recommend you contact your State Insurance Official or NOLHGA at 703-481-5206.

State guaranty associations are set up to cover policyholders residing in their own state. This essentially means that each individual state is responsible for policyholders residing in that state, no matter where the insolvent insurer is domiciled.

Non-resident coverage is provided only under certain circumstances listed in the state's statutes. The general conditions are typically as follows:

a) The insurer of the policyholder must be domiciled and licensed in the state in which the non-resident is seeking coverage;

b) When the contracts were sold, the insurers that issued the policies were not licensed in the state in which the policyholder resides;

c) The non-resident policyholder is not eligible for coverage from his or her state of residence;

d) The state where the policyholder resides must have a guaranty association similar to that of the state in which he or she is seeking non-resident coverage.

Warning: Be sure to contact the specific state guaranty association for information in that state's laws. Conditions and limitations are subject to individual state statutes and can change.

Following is a brief explanation of each of the columns in the table.

1. **Maximum Aggregate Benefits for All Lines of Insurance**

   The maximum amount payable by the State Guaranty Fund to cover all types of insurance including life insurance, health insurance, disability and annuities.

2. **Maximum Death Benefit with Respect to Any One Life**

   The maximum amount payable by the State Guaranty Fund for a death claim on a single life. If the policy benefits are higher than the Guaranty Fund's coverage limits, policyholders may typically be able to file a claim with the court-appointed Liquidator of the insolvent insurance company to try to recover the difference. But success is uncertain.

3. **Liability for Cash or Withdrawal Value of Life Insurance Policy**

   The maximum cash value or withdrawal value the Guaranty Fund will assume responsibility for related to an individual life insurance policy.

4. **Maximum Liability for Present Value of an Annuity Contract**

   The maximum cash value or withdrawal value the Guaranty Fund will assume responsibility for related to an individual annuity contract. The coverage may be higher if the annuity is in the payout phase.

Coverage of State Guaranty Funds

State	Max. Aggregate Benefits for All Lines of Insurance	Max. Death Benefit with Respect to Any One Life	Max. Liability for Cash or Withdrawal Value of Life Insurance Policy	Max. Liability for Present Value of an Annuity Contract	State Guaranty Association Phone Numbers	State Guaranty Web Address
Alabama	$300,000	$300,000	$100,000	$100,000	(205) 879-2202	www.allifega.org
Alaska	$300,000	$300,000	$100,000	$100,000	(907) 243-2311	www.aklifega.org
Arizona	$300,000	$300,000	$100,000	$100,000	(602) 364-3863	www.id.state.az.us
Arkansas	$300,000	$300,000	$300,000	$300,000	(501) 375-9151	www.arlifega.org
California	80% not to exceed $300,000	80% not to exceed $300,000	80% not to exceed $100,000	80% not to exceed $250,000	(323) 782-0182	www.califega.org
Colorado	$300,000	$300,000	$100,000	$250,000	(303) 292-5022	colorado.lhiga.com
Connecticut	$500,000	$500,000	$500,000	$500,000	(860) 647-1054	www.ctlifega.org
Delaware	$300,000	$300,000	$100,000	$250,000	(302) 456-3656	www.delifega.org
Dist. of Col.	$300,000	$300,000	$100,000	$300,000	(202) 434-8771	www.dclifega.org
Florida	$300,000	$300,000	$100,000	$250,000	(904) 398-3644	www.flahiga.org
Georgia	$300,000	$300,000	$100,000	$100,000	(770) 621-9835	www.gaiga.org
Hawaii	$300,000	$300,000	$100,000	$100,000	(808) 528-5400	www.hilifega.org
Idaho	$300,000	$300,000	$100,000	$250,000	(208) 378-9510	www.idlifega.org
Illinois	$300,000	$300,000	$100,000	$250,000	(773) 714-8050	www.ilhiga.org
Indiana	$300,000	$300,000	$100,000	$100,000	(317) 692-0574	www.inlifega.org
Iowa	$300,000	$300,000	$100,000	$250,000	(515) 248-5712	www.ialifega.org
Kansas	$300,000	$300,000	$100,000	$250,000	(785) 271-1199	www.kslifega.org
Kentucky	$300,000	$300,000	$100,000	$250,000	(502) 895-5915	www.klhiga.org
Louisiana	$500,000	$300,000	$100,000	$250,000	(225) 381-0656	www.lalifega.org
Maine	$300,000	$300,000	$100,000	$250,000	(207) 633-1090	www.melifega.org
Maryland	$300,000	$300,000	$100,000	$250,000	(410) 248-0407	www.mdlifega.org
Massachusetts	$300,000	$300,000	$100,000	$100,000	(413) 744-8483	www.malifega.org
Michigan	$300,000	$300,000	$100,000	$250,000	(517) 339-1755	www.milifega.org
Minnesota	$500,000	$500,000	$130,000	$250,000	(651) 407-3149	www.mnlifega.org
Mississippi	$300,000	$300,000	$100,000	$100,000	(601) 981-0755	www.mslifega.org
Missouri	$300,000	$300,000	$100,000	$100,000	(573) 634-8455	www.mo-iga.org
Montana	$300,000	$300,000	$100,000	$250,000	(262) 965-5761	www.mtlifega.org
Nebraska	$300,000	$300,000	$100,000	$100,000	(402) 474-6900	www.nelifega.org
Nevada	$300,000	$300,000	$100,000	$100,000	(775) 329-8387	www.nvlifega.org
New Hampshire	$300,000	$300,000	$100,000	$100,000	(603) 472-3734	www.nhlifega.org
New Jersey	$500,000	$500,000	$100,000	$100,000	(732) 345-5200	www.njlifega.org
New Mexico	$300,000	$300,000	$100,000	$100,000	(505) 820-7355	www.nmlifega.org
New York	$500,000	$500,000	$500,000	$500,000	(212) 202-4243	www.nylifega.org
No. Carolina	$300,000	$300,000	$300,000	$300,000	(877) 833-6831	www.nclifega.org
North Dakota	$300,000	$300,000	$100,000	$100,000	(701) 235-4108	www.ndlifega.org
Ohio	$300,000	$300,000	$100,000	$250,000	(614) 442-6601	www.olhiga.org
Oklahoma	$300,000	$300,000	$100,000	$300,000	(405) 272-9221	www.oklifega.org
Oregon	$300,000	$300,000	$100,000	$250,000	(855) 378-9510	www.orlifega.org
Pennsylvania	$300,000	$300,000	$100,000	$100,000	(610) 975-0572	www.palifega.org
Puerto Rico	$300,000	$300,000	$100,000	$100,000	(787) 765-2095	www.ocs.gobierno.pr
Rhode Island	$300,000	$300,000	$100,000	$250,000	(401) 273-2921	www.rilifega.org
So. Carolina	$300,000	$300,000	$300,000	$300,000	(803) 783-4947	www.sclifega.org
South Dakota	$300,000	$300,000	$100,000	$100,000	(605) 336-0177	www.sdlifega.org
Tennessee	$300,000	$300,000	$100,000	$250,000	(615) 242-8758	www.tnlifega.org
Texas	$300,000	$300,000	$100,000	$250,000	(512) 476-5101	www.txlifega.org
Utah	$500,000	$500,000	$200,000	$200,000	(801) 302-9955	www.utlifega.org
Vermont	$300,000	$300,000	$100,000	$250,000	(802) 249-0284	www.vtlifega.org
Virginia	$350,000	$300,000	$100,000	$250,000	(804) 282-2240	www.valifega.org
Washington	$500,000	$500,000	$500,000	$500,000	(360) 426-6744	www.walifega.org
West Virginia	$300,000	$300,000	$100,000	$250,000	(304) 733-6904	www.wvlifega.org
Wisconsin	$300,000	$300,000	$300,000	$300,000	(608) 242-9473	www.wilifega.org
Wyoming	$300,000	$300,000	$100,000	$100,000	(303) 292-5022	wyoming.lhiga.com

State Insurance Commissioners'
Departmental Phone Numbers

State	Official's Title	Website Address	Phone Number
Alabama	Commissioner	www.aldoi.org	(334) 269-3550
Alaska	Director	http://commerce.alaska.gov/dnn/ins/Home.aspx	(800) 467-8725
Arizona	Director	http://www.azinsurance.gov/	(800) 325-2548
Arkansas	Commissioner	www.insurance.arkansas.gov	(800) 282-9134
California	Commissioner	www.insurance.ca.gov	(800) 927-4357
Colorado	Commissioner	www.dora.state.co.us/insurance/	(800) 886-7675
Connecticut	Commissioner	www.ct.gov/cid/	(800) 203-3447
Delaware	Commissioner	http://delawareinsurance.gov/	(800) 282-8611
Dist. of Columbia	Commissioner	http://disb.dc.gov/	(202) 727-8000
Florida	Commissioner	www.floir.com/	(850) 413-3140
Georgia	Commissioner	www.oci.ga.gov/	(800) 656-2298
Hawaii	Commissioner	http://hawaii.gov/dcca/ins/	(808) 586-2790
Idaho	Director	www.doi.idaho.gov	(800) 721-3272
Illinois	Director	www.insurance.illinois.gov/	(877) 527-9431
Indiana	Commissioner	www.in.gov/idoi/	(317) 232-2385
Iowa	Commissioner	www.iid.state.ia.us	(877) 955-1212
Kansas	Commissioner	www.ksinsurance.org	(800) 432-2484
Kentucky	Commissioner	http://insurance.ky.gov/	(800) 595-6053
Louisiana	Commissioner	www.ldi.la.gov/	(800) 259-5300
Maine	Superintendent	www.maine.gov/pfr/insurance/	(800) 300-5000
Maryland	Commissioner	www.mdinsurance.state.md.us	(800) 492-6116
Massachusetts	Commissioner	www.mass.gov/ocabr/government/oca-agencies/doi-lp/	(877) 563-4467
Michigan	Director	www.michigan.gov/cis/	(877) 999-6442
Minnesota	Commissioner	http://mn.gov/commerce/insurance/	(651) 539-1500
Mississippi	Commissioner	www.mid.state.ms.us/	(601) 359-3569
Missouri	Director	www.insurance.mo.gov	(800) 726-7390
Montana	Commissioner	www.csi.mt.gov/	(800) 332-6148
Nebraska	Director	www.doi.nebraska.gov/	(402) 471-2201
Nevada	Commissioner	www.doi.nv.gov/	(888) 872-3234
New Hampshire	Commissioner	www.nh.gov/insurance/	(800) 852-3416
New Jersey	Commissioner	www.state.nj.us/dobi/	(800) 446-7467
New Mexico	Superintendent	www.osi.state.nm.us/	(855) 427-5674
New York	Superintendent	www.dfs.ny.gov/	(800) 342-3736
North Carolina	Commissioner	www.ncdoi.com	(800) 546-5664
North Dakota	Commissioner	www.nd.gov/ndins/	(800) 247-0560
Ohio	Lieutenant Governor	www.insurance.ohio.gov/	(800) 686-1526
Oklahoma	Commissioner	www.ok.gov/oid/	(800) 522-0071
Oregon	Insurance Administrator	www.oregon.gov/dcbs/insurance/Pages/index.aspx	(888) 877-4894
Pennsylvania	Commissioner	www.insurance.pa.gov/	(877) 881-6388
Puerto Rico	Commissioner	www.ocs.gobierno.pr	(787) 304-8686
Rhode Island	Director	www.dbr.state.ri.us/divisions/insurance/	(401) 462-9500
South Carolina	Director	www.doi.sc.gov	(803) 737-6160
South Dakota	Director	http://dlr.sd.gov/insurance/default.aspx	(605) 773-3563
Tennessee	Commissioner	www.tn.gov/insurance/	(800) 342-4029
Texas	Commissioner	www.tdi.texas.gov/	(800) 252-3439
Utah	Commissioner	www.insurance.utah.gov	(800) 439-3805
Vermont	Commissioner	www.dfr.vermont.gov/	(802) 828-3301
Virgin Islands	Lieutenant Governor	www.ltg.gov.vi	(340) 774-7166
Virginia	Commissioner	www.scc.virginia.gov/boi	(804) 371-9741
Washington	Commissioner	www.insurance.wa.gov	(800) 562-6900
West Virginia	Commissioner	www.wvinsurance.gov	(888) 879-9842
Wisconsin	Commissioner	oci.wi.gov	(800) 236-8517
Wyoming	Commissioner	http://doi.wyo.gov/	(800) 438-5768

Risk-Adjusted Capital for Life and Annuity Insurers in Weiss Rating Model

Among the most important indicators used in the analysis of an individual company are our two risk-adjusted capital ratios, which are useful tools in determining exposure to investment, liquidity and insurance risk in relation to the capital the company has to cover those risks.

The first risk-adjusted capital ratio evaluates the company's ability to withstand a moderate loss scenario. The second ratio evaluates the company's ability to withstand a severe loss scenario.

In order to calculate these risk-adjusted capital ratios, we follow these steps:

1. Capital Resources

First, we add up all of the company's resources which could be used to cover losses. These include capital, surplus, the Asset Valuation Reserve (AVR), and a portion of the provision for future policyholders' dividends, where appropriate. Additional credit may also be given for the use of conservative reserving assumptions and other "hidden capital" when applicable.

2. Target Capital

Next, we determine the company's target capital. This answers the question: Based upon the company's level of risk in both its insurance business and its investment portfolio, how much capital would it need to cover potential losses during a moderate loss scenario? In other words, we determine how much capital we believe this company *should* have.

3. Risk-Adjusted Capital Ratio #1

We compare the results of step 1 with those of step 2. Specifically, we divide the "capital resources" by the "target capital" and express it in terms of a ratio. This ratio is called RACR #1. (See next page for more detail on methodology.)

If a company has a Risk-Adjusted Capital Ratio of 1.0 or more, it means the company has all of the capital we believe it requires to withstand potential losses which could be inflicted by a moderate loss scenario. If the company has less than 1.0, it does not currently have all of the basic capital resources we think it needs. During times of financial distress, companies often have access to additional capital through contributions from a parent company, current profits or reductions in policyholder dividends. Therefore, an allowance is made in our rating system for firms with somewhat less than 1.0 Risk-Adjusted Capital Ratios.

4. Risk-Adjusted Capital Ratio #2

We repeat steps 2 and 3, but now assuming a severe loss scenario. This ratio is called RACR #2.

5. Capitalization Index

We convert RACR #1 and #2 into an index. It is measured on a scale of zero to ten, with ten being the best and seven or better considered strong. A company whose capital, surplus and AVR equal its target capital will have a Risk-Adjusted Capital Ratio of 1.0 and a Risk-Adjusted Capital Index of 7.0.

How We Determine Target Capital

The basic procedure for determining target capital is to ask these questions:

1.   What is the breakdown of the company's investment portfolio and types of business?

2.   For each category, what are the potential losses which could be incurred in the loss scenario?

3.   In order to cover those potential losses, how much in capital resources does the company need? It stands to reason that more capital is needed as a cushion for losses on high-risk investments, such as junk bonds, than would be necessary for low-risk investments, such as AAA-rated utility bonds.

Unfortunately, the same questions we have raised about Wall Street rating systems with respect to how they rate insurance companies can be asked about the way they rate bonds. However, we do not rate bonds ourselves. Therefore, we must rely upon the bond ratings of other rating agencies. This is another reason why we have stricter capital requirements for the insurance companies. It accounts for the fact that they may need some extra protection in case an AAA-rated bond may not be quite as good as it appears to be.

Finally, target capital is adjusted for the company's spread of risk in the diversification of its investment portfolio, the size and number of the policies it writes and the diversification of its business.

Table 1 on the next page shows target capital percentages used by the National Association of Insurance Commissioners (NAIC) in relation to Weiss Risk-Adjusted Capital Ratios #1 and #2 (RACR #1 and RACR #2).

The percentages shown in the table answer the question: How much should the firm hold in capital resources for every $100 it has committed to each category? Several of the items in Table 1 are expressed as ranges. The actual percentages used in the calculation of target capital for an individual company may vary due to the levels of risks in the operations, investments or policy obligations of that specific company.

Table 1. Target Capital Percentages

Asset Risk	Weiss Ratings		NAIC
	RACR#1 (%)	RACR#2 (%)	
Bonds			
Government guaranteed bonds	0	0	0
Class 1	.5-.75	1-1.5	0.4
Class 2	2	5	1.3
Class 3	5	15	4.6
Class 4	10	30	10
Class 5	20	60	23
Class 6	20	60	30
Mortgages			
In good standing	0.5	1	0
90 days overdue	1.7-20	3.8-25	0.1-18
In process of foreclosure	25-33	33-50	1.4-23
Real Estate			
Class 1	20	50	15
Class 2	10	33	23
Preferred Stock			
Class 1	3	5	1.1
Class 2	4	6	3.0
Class 3	7	9	7.2
Class 4	12	15	15
Class 5	22	29	20
Class 6	30	39	15
Class 7	3-30	5-39	22.5-45
Common Stock			
Unaffiliated	25	33	22.5-45
Affiliated	25-100	33-100	22.5-45
Short-term investment	0.5	1	0.4
Premium notes	2	5	6.8
Collateral loans	2	5	6.8
Separate account equity	25	33	11 **
Other invested assets	5	10	6.8
Insurance Risk			
Individual life reserves*	.06-.15	.08-.21	.09-.23
Group life reserves*	.05-.12	.06-.16	.08-.18
Individual Health Premiums			
Class 1	12-20	15-25	10-16.5
Class 2	9.6	12	6.7-12
Class 3	6.4	8	3.5/$50,000
Class 4	12-28	15-35	23.1-53.9
Class 5	12-20	15-25	10.8-38.5
Group Health Premiums			
Class 1	5.6-12	7-15	9-15
Class 2	20	25	25
Class 3	9.6	12	6.7-12
Class 4	6.4	8	3.5/$50,000
Class 5	12-20	15-25	4.6-23.1
Managed care credit	5-40	6-50	NAIC calculation
Premiums subject to rate guarantees	100-209	120-250	2.4-6.4
Individual claim reserves	4	5	5-7.7
Group claim reserves	4	5	5-7.7
Reinsurance	0-2	0-5	0.8
Interest Rate Risk			
Policy loans	0-2	0-5	1.1
Life reserves	1-2	1-3	0.7-1.1
Individual annuity reserves	1-3	1-5	0.7-1.1
Group annuity reserves	1-2	1-3	0.7-1.1
Guaranteed interest contract reserves	1-2	1-3	0.7-1.1

All numbers are shown for illustrative purposes. Figures actually used in the formula vary annually based on industry experience.

*Based on net amount at risk.

**Risk-based capital for separate account assets that are not tied to an index = 100% of the risk-based capital of assets in the accounts.

Investment Class   ## Descriptions

Investment Class		Descriptions
Government guaranteed bonds		Guaranteed bonds issued by U.S. and other governments which receive the top rating of state insurance commissioners.
Bonds	Class 1	Investment grade bonds rated AAA, AA or A by Moody's or Standard & Poor's or deemed AAA - A equivalent by state insurance commissioners.
	Class 2	Investment grade bonds with some speculative elements, rated BBB or equivalent.
	Class 3	Noninvestment grade bonds, rated BB or equivalent.
	Class 4	Noninvestment grade bonds, rated B or equivalent.
	Class 5	Noninvestment grade bonds, rated CCC, CC or C or equivalent.
	Class 6	Noninvestment grade bonds, in or near default.
Mortgages		Mortgages in good standing
		Mortgages 90 days past due
		Mortgages in process of foreclosure
Real Estate	Class 1	Properties acquired in satisfaction of debt.
	Class 2	Company occupied and other investment properties.
Preferred stock	Class 1	Highest quality unaffiliated preferred stock.
	Class 2	High quality unaffiliated preferred stock.
	Class 3	Medium quality unaffiliated preferred stock.
	Class 4	Low quality unaffiliated preferred stock.
	Class 5	Lowest quality unaffiliated preferred stock.
	Class 6	Unaffiliated preferred stock, in or near default.
	Class 7	Affiliated preferred stock.
Common stock		Unaffiliated common stock.
		Affiliated common stock.
Short-term investments		All investments whose maturities at the time of acquisition were one year or less.
Premium Notes		Loans for payment of premiums.
Collateral loans		Loans made to a company or individual where the underlying security is in the form of bonds, stocks, or other marketable securities.
Separate account assets		Investments held in an account segregated from the general assets of the company, generally used to provide variable annuity benefits.
Other invested assets		Any invested assets that do not fit under the main categories above.
Individual life reserves		Funds set aside for payment of life insurance benefits under an individual contract rather than a company or group, underwriting based on individual profile.
Group life reserves		Funds set aside for payment of life insurance benefits under a contract with at least 10 people whereby all members have a common interest and are joined for a reason other than to obtain insurance.
Individual health premiums	Class 1	Usual and customary hospital and medical premiums which include traditional medical reimbursement plans that are subject to annual rate increases based on the company's claims experience.
	Class 2	Medicare supplement, dental, and other limited benefits anticipating rate increases.
	Class 3	Hospital indemnity plans, accidental death and dismemberment policies, and other limited benefits not anticipating rate increases.
	Class 4	Noncancellable disability income.
	Class 5	Guaranteed renewable disability income.

Group health premiums	Class 1	Usual and customary hospital and medical premiums which include traditional medical reimbursement plans that are subject to annual rate increases based on the company's claims experience.
	Class 2	Stop loss and minimum premium where a known claims liability is minimal or nonexistent.
	Class 3	Medicare supplement, dental, and other limited benefits anticipating rate increases.
	Class 4	Hospital indemnity plans, accidental death and dismemberment policies, and other limited benefits not anticipating rate increases.
	Class 5	Disability Income.
Managed care credit		Premiums for HMO and PPO business which carry less risk than traditional indemnity business. Included in this credit are provider compensation arrangements such as salary, capitation and fixed payment per service.
Premiums subject to rate guarantees		Health insurance premiums from policies where the rate paid by the policyholder is guaranteed for a period of time, such as one year, 15 months, 27 months or 37 months.
Individual claim reserves		Accident and health reserves for claims on individual policies.
Group claim reserves		Accident and health reserves for claims on group policies.
Reinsurance		Amounts recoverable on paid and unpaid losses for all reinsurance ceded; unearned premiums on accident and health reinsurance ceded; and funds held with unauthorized reinsurers.
Policy loans		Loans against the cash value of a life insurance policy.
Life reserves		Reserves for life insurance claims net of reinsurance and policy loans.
Individual annuity reserves		Reserves held in order to pay off maturing individual annuities or those surrendered before maturity.
Group annuity reserves		Reserves held in order to pay off maturing group annuities or those surrendered before maturity.
GIC reserves		Reserves held to pay off maturing guaranteed interest contracts.

Table 2. Bond Default Rates - potential losses as a percent of bond portfolio

| | (1) | (2) | (3) | (4) | (5) Weiss | (6) | (7) | (8) |
Bond Rating	Moody's 15 Yr Rate (%)	Moody's 12 Yr Rate (%)	Worst Year (%)	3 Cum. Recession Years (%)	15 Year Rate (%)	Assumed Loss Rate (%)	Losses as % of Holdings (%)	RACR #2 Rate (%)
Aaa	2.80	1.60	0.10	0.30	1.89	50	0.95	1.00
Aa	2.00	1.60	0.20	0.60	2.19	50	1.09	1.00
A	3.30	2.50	0.40	1.20	3.67	55	2.02	1.00
Baa	7.20	5.50	1.10	3.26	8.58	60	5.15	5.00
Ba	20.10	17.90	8.40	23.08	36.47	65	23.71	15.00
B	33.70	32.50	21.60	50.80	62.24	70	43.57	30.00

Comments On Target Capital Percentages

The factors that are chiefly responsible for the conservative results of our Risk-Adjusted Capital Ratios are the investment risks of bond Classes 2 - 6, mortgages, real estate and affiliate common stock as well as the interest rate risk for annuities and GICs. Comments on the basis of these figures are found below. Additional comments address factors that vary, based on particular performance or risk characteristics of the individual company.

Bonds

Target capital percentages for bonds are derived from a model that factors in historical cumulative bond default rates from the last 20 years and the additional loss potential during a prolonged economic decline. The continuance of post-World War II prosperity is by no means certain. Realistic analysis of potential losses must factor in the possibility of severe economic reversal. **Table 2** shows how this was done for each bond rating classification. A 15-year cumulative default rate is used (column 1), due to the 15-year average maturity at issue of bonds held by life insurance companies. These are historical default rates for 1970-1990 for each bond class, taken from *Moody's Studies Loss Potential of Life Insurance Assets*.

To factor in the additional loss potential of a severe three-year-long economic decline, we reduced the base to Moody's 12-year rate (column 2), determined the worst single year experience (column 3), spread that experience over three years (column 4), and added the historical 12-year rate to the 3-year projection to derive Weiss Ratings 15-year default rate (column 5). Note: Due to the shrinking base of nondefaulted bonds in each year, column 4 may be somewhat less than three times column 3, and column 5 may be somewhat less than the sum of column 2 and column 4.

The next step was to determine the losses that could be expected from these defaults. This would be equivalent to the capital a company should have to cover those losses. Loss rates were assigned for each bond class (column 6), based on the fact that higher-rated issues generally carry less debt and the fact that the debt is also better secured, leading to higher recovery rates upon default. Column 7 shows losses as a percent of holdings for each bond class.

Column 8 shows the target capital percentages that are used in RACR #2 (Table 1, RACR #2 column, Bonds - classes 1 to 6).

Regulations limiting junk bond holdings of insurers to a set percent of assets are a tacit acknowledgement that the 10% and 20% maximum reserve requirements used by State Insurance Commissioners (Table 1, NAIC column, Bonds-classes 4, 5 and 6) are inadequate. If the figure adequately represented full loss potential, there would be no need to limit holdings through legislation since an adequate loss reserve would provide sufficient capital to absorb potential losses.

Mortgages

Mortgage default rates for the Risk-Adjusted Capital Ratios are derived from historical studies of mortgage and real estate losses in selected depressed markets. The rate for RACR #2 (Table 1, RACR #2 column, Mortgages – 90 days overdue) will vary between 3.8 and 25%, based on the performance of the company's mortgage portfolio in terms of mortgage loans 90 days or more past due, in process of foreclosure and foreclosed during the previous year.

Real Estate

The 33% rate (Table 1, RACR #2 column, Real Estate – Class 2) used for potential real estate losses in Weiss ratios is based on historical losses in depressed markets. It avoids the commonly made assumption that the continuous appreciation of property values experienced since World War II must inevitably continue.

Affiliate Common Stock

The target capital rate on affiliate common stock for RACR #2 can vary between 33% and 100% (Table 1, RACR #2 column, Common stock - Affiliate) depending on the financial strength of the affiliate and the prospects for obtaining capital from the affiliate should the need arise.

Insurance Risk

Calculations of target capital for insurance risk vary according to categories. For individual and group life insurance, target capital is a percentage of net amount at risk (total amount of insurance in force less reserves). Individual and group health insurance risk is calculated as a percentage of premium. Categories vary from "usual and customary hospital and medical premiums" where risk is relatively low, because losses from one year are recouped by annual rate increases to "noncancellable disability income" where the risk of loss is greater because disability benefits are paid in future years without the possibility of recovery.

Reinsurance

This factor varies with the quality of the reinsuring companies and the type of reinsurance being used (e.g. co-insurance, modified co-insurance, yearly renewable term, etc.).

Interest Rate Risk On Annuities

The 1 - 5% rate on individual annuities as a percentage of reserves (Table 1, RACR #2 column 3, Individual annuity reserves) and the 1 - 3% rate for group annuities as a percentage of reserves (Table 1, RACR #2 column 3, Group annuity reserves and GICs) are derived from studies of potential losses that can occur when assets and liabilities are not properly matched.

Companies are especially prone to losses in this area for one of two reasons: (1) They promise high interest rates on their annuities and have not locked in corresponding yields on their investments. If interest rates fall, the company will have difficulties earning the promised rate. (2) They lock in high returns on their investments but allow policy surrenders without market value adjustments. If market values decline and surrenders increase, liquidity problems can result in substantial losses.

The target capital figure used for each company is based on the surrender characteristics of its policies, the interest rate used in calculating reserves and the actuarial analysis found in New York Regulation 126 filing or similar studies where applicable.

RECENT INDUSTRY FAILURES
2014

Institution	Headquarters	Industry	Date of Failure	At Date of Failure Total Assets ($Mil)	Financial Strength Rating
Union Mutual Ins Co	Oklahoma	P&C	01/24/14	5.1	E+ (Very Weak)
Commonwealth Ins Co	Pennsylvania	P&C	03/20/14	1.1	E (Very Weak)
LEMIC Ins Co	Louisiana	P&C	03/31/14	51.6	D (Weak)
Interstate Bankers Casualty Co	Illinois	P&C	04/16/14	16.2	D+ (Weak)
Freestone Ins Co	Delaware	P&C	04/28/14	421.2	D- (Weak)
Alameda Alliance For Health	California	Health	05/05/14	176.3	D (Weak)
National Guaranty Ins Co	Nevada	P&C	05/06/14	10.4	N/A
Physicians Ben. Resources RRG	Nevada	P&C	05/09/14	0.6	U (Unrated)
Sunshine State Ins Co	Florida	P&C	06/03/14	22.9	E+ (Very Weak)
Physicians United Plan Inc	Florida	Health	06/09/14	110.7	E (Very Weak)
Professional Aviation Ins Co	Nevada	P&C	07/03/14	N/A	N/A
Red Rock Ins Co	Oklahoma	P&C	08/01/14	28.5	E+ (Very Weak)
UHAB Mutual Ins Co	New York	P&C	09/26/14	N/A	E+ (Very Weak)
First Keystone RRG Inc	S. Carolina	P&C	10/21/14	13.6	N/A
SeeChange Health Ins Co	California	Health	11/19/14	23.4	D (Weak)
Florida Healthcare Plus, Inc	Florida	Health	12/10/14	11.1	U (Unrated)
CoOportunity Health, Inc	Iowa	Health	12/23/14	195.7	U (Unrated)

2013

Institution	Headquarters	Industry	Date of Failure	At Date of Failure Total Assets ($Mil)	At Date of Failure Financial Strength Rating
Partnership Health Plan Inc	Wisconsin	Health	01/18/13	27.1	D (Weak)
Driver's Insurance Co	Oklahoma	P&C	02/21/13	33.1	D+ (Weak)
Lewis & Clark LTC RRG	Nevada	P&C	02/28/13	16.4	E (Very Weak)
Pride National Ins Co	Oklahoma	P&C	03/08/13	17.1	E+ (Very Weak)
Santa Fe Auto	Texas	P&C	03/08/13	22.9	E (Very Weak)
Ullico Casualty Co	Delaware	P&C	03/11/13	327.7	D (Weak)
Builders Ins Co Inc	Nevada	P&C	03/15/13	15.0	U (Unrated)
Nevada Contractors Ins Co Inc	Nevada	P&C	03/15/13	49.0	U (Unrated)
Universal Health Care Ins Co Inc	Florida	Health	03/22/13	106.1	C (Fair)
Universal Health Care Inc	Florida	Health	03/25/13	109.0	D (Weak)
Universal HMO of Texas	Texas	Health	04/18/13	15.3	C- (Fair)
Universal Health Care of NV Inc	Nevada	Health	06/03/13	1.9	D+ (Weak)
Liberty First RRG Ins Co	Utah	P&C	08/06/13	2.5	E (Very Weak)
United Contractors Ins Co Inc, RRG	Delaware	P&C	08/22/13	17.0	E (Very Weak)
Georgia Mutual Ins Co	Georgia	P&C	09/10/13	3.3	D (Weak)
Ocean Risk Retention Group	D. C.	P&C	09/6/13	7.9	E (Very Weak)
Gertrude Geddes Willis LIC	Louisiana	L&H	10/24/13	4.9	U (Unrated)
San Antonio Indemnity Co	Texas	P&C	10/31/13	2.8	E+ (Very Weak)
Higginbotham Burial Ins Co	Arkansas	L&H	11/04/13	1.3	U (Unrated)
Indemnity Ins Corp RRG	Delaware	P&C	11/07/13	83.2	D- (Weak)
Concert Health Plan Ins Co	Illinois	L&H	12/10/13	1.8	D- (Weak)
ICM Insurance Co	New York	P&C	12/23/13	5.0	E+ (Very Weak)

2012

Institution	Headquarters	Industry	Date of Failure	At Date of Failure Total Assets ($Mil)	At Date of Failure Financial Strength Rating
Autoglass Ins Co	New York	P&C	01/09/12	N/A	U (Unrated)
Health Facilities of CA Mut I C RRG	Nevada	P&C	01/10/12	1.9	U (Unrated)
Republic Mortgage Ins Co	N. Carolina	P&C	01/19/12	1.41	E (Very Weak)
CAGC Ins Co	N. Carolina	P&C	01/26/12	11.8	U (Unrated)
First Sealord Surety Inc.	Pennsylvania	P&C	02/08/12	15.2	U (Unrated)
Scaffold Industry Ins Co RRG, Inc	D. C.	P&C	05/01/12	5.1	E+ (Very Weak)
Financial Guaranty Ins Co	New York	P&C	06/11/12	2054.0	E- (Very Weak)
Global Health Plan & Ins Co	Puerto Rico	Health	06/13/12	1.1	U (Unrated)
Garden State Indemnity Co, Inc	New Jersey	P&C	06/22/12	2.93	E- (Very Weak)
AvaHealth Inc	Florida	HMO	06/27/12	3.3	E (Very Weak)
Lumbermens Mutual Casualty Co	Illinois	P&C	07/02/12	798.0	E (Very Weak)
American Manufacturers Mutual	Illinois	P&C	07/02/12	10.0	E+ (Very Weak)
Millers First Ins Co	Illinois	P&C	07/24/12	23.0	E (Very Weak)
American Motorists Ins Co	Illinois	P&C	08/16/12	19.7	D (Weak)
Home Value Ins Co	Ohio	P&C	08/31/12	3.5	U (Unrated)
Northern Plains Ins Co	S. Dakota	P&C	09/18/12	1.4	D (Weak)
Jamestown Ins Co RRG	S. Carolina	P&C	09/24/12	5.9	E+ (Very Weak)
Interstate Auto Ins Co	Maryland	P&C	10/11/12	4.6	D (Weak)
Regional Health Ins Co, RRG	D. C.	P&C	10/18/12	0.6	U (Unrated)
DC Chartered Health Plan Inc	D. C.	HMO	10/19/12	65.4	E- (Very Weak)
American Fellowship Mut Ins Co	Michigan	P&C	10/29/12	50.0	D (Weak)
Gramercy Ins Co	Texas	P&C	12/04/12	41.8	D (Weak)
Triad Guaranty ASR Corp	Illinois	P&C	12/11/12	16.1	B (Good)
Triad Guaranty Ins Corp	Illinois	P&C	12/11/12	766.7	E (Very Weak)

2011

Institution	Headquarters	Industry	Date of Failure	At Date of Failure Total Assets ($Mil)	At Date of Failure Financial Strength Rating
Comm. Ins Alliance Reciprocal	Florida	P&C	01/26/11	N/A	N/A
Aequicap Ins Co	Florida	P&C	02/28/11	29.7	E+ (Very Weak)
US Rail Ins Co a RRG	Vermont	P&C	03/04/11	3.2	E (Very Weak)
Seminole Casualty Ins Co	Florida	P&C	03/15/11	35.6	D (Weak)
Majestic Insurance Co	California	P&C	04/21/11	313.1	D- (Weak)
Reinsurance Co of America Inc	Illinois	P&C	04/27/11	7.1	D (Weak)
National Insurance Co	Puerto Rico	P&C	05/24/11	79.4	D+ (Weak)
Argus Fire & Casualty Ins Co	Florida	P&C	05/27/11	33.8	D (Weak)
Security Pacific Ins Co	Delaware	P&C	06/15/11	N/A	N/A
Great Republic Life Ins Co	Washington	L&H	07/07/11	16.9	E+ (Very Weak)
National Group Ins Co	Florida	P&C	08/01/11	9.53	E- (Very Weak)
Federal Motors Carriers RRG Inc	Delaware	P&C	08/18/11	11.9	E (Very Weak)
PMI Insurance Co	Arizona	P&C	08/19/11	436.9	D (Weak)
PMI Mortgage Ins Co	Arizona	P&C	08/19/11	2841.2	D (Weak)
Western Insurance Co	Utah	P&C	08/25/11	21.7	U (Unrated)
Homewise Preferred Ins Co	Florida	P&C	09/02/11	11.1	E (Very Weak)
American Sterling Ins Co	California	P&C	09/26/11	15.4	D (Weak)
Quality Health Plans Inc	Florida	HMO	10/17/11	45.0	E+ (Very Weak)
HomeWise Ins Co	Florida	P&C	11/18/11	84.7	D (Weak)
Southern Eagle Ins Co	Florida	P&C	12/06/11	18.6	D (Weak)
Minnesota Surety & Trust Co	Minnesota	P&C	12/02/11	1.5	E (Very Weak)

2010

Institution	Headquarters	Industry	Date of Failure	Total Assets ($Mil)	Financial Strength Rating
				At Date of Failure	
First American Life Ins Co	Texas	L&H	02/18/10	9.4	E- (Very Weak)
Northern Capital Ins Co	Florida	P&C	02/25/10	78.2	E+ (Very Weak)
Colonial Cooperative Ins Co	New York	P&C	02/25/10	7.0	E (Very Weak)
Gibraltar National Ins Co	Arkansas	P&C	03/11/10	4.9	E+ (Very Weak)
Imperial Casualty & Indemnity Co	Oklahoma	P&C	03/18/10	39.6	C- (Fair)
National States Ins Co	Missouri	L&H	04/01/10	70.5	E (Very Weak)
Amer. Community Mutual Ins Co	Michigan	L&H	04/08/10	128.7	B (Good)
Financial Adv. Assurance Select RRG	Nevada	P&C	04/26/10	0.9	E (Very Weak)
Prof. Liability Ins Co of America	New York	P&C	04/28/10	39.5	D- (Weak)
Pegasus Insurance Co Inc	Oklahoma	P&C	06/18/10	9.9	C- (Fair)
Gulf Builders RRG, Inc	S. Carolina	P&C	08/02/10	N/A	U (Unrated)
Carrier Solutions Risk Retention Grp	Delaware	P&C	08/09/10	N/A	N/A
GA Restaurant Mut. Captive Ins Co	Georgia	P&C	08/26/10	1.2	U (Unrated)
Atlantic Mutual Ins Co	New York	P&C	09/16/10	205.4	E- (Very Weak)
Centennial Ins Co	New York	P&C	09/16/10	74.9	E- (Very Weak)
GA Timber Harvesters Mut.Captive	Georgia	P&C	09/21/10	N/A	N/A
Peoples Assd. Family Life Ins Co	Mississippi	L&H	09/23/10	N/A	N/A
Southern Casualty Ins	Georgia	P&C	09/29/10	6.3	D (Weak)
Guardian HealthCare Inc	S. Carolina	HMO	10/12/10	11.0	U (Unrated)
Long Island Insurance Co	New York	P&C	10/19/10	6.7	E- (Very Weak)
Constitutional Casualty Co.	Illinois	P&C	11/04/10	15.6	E+ (Very Weak)

2009

Institution	Headquarters	Industry	Date of Failure	Total Assets ($Mil)	Financial Strength Rating
				At Date of Failure	
Scottish RE US Inc	Delaware	L&H	01/05/09	2950.6	D (Weak)
American Network Ins Co	Pennsylvania	L&H	01/06/09	125.8	D+ (Weak)
Penn Treaty Network Am Ins Co	Pennsylvania	L&H	01/06/09	1037.6	C- (Fair)
Shenandoah Life Ins Co	Virginia	L&H	02/12/09	1735.0	B (Good)
NSA Rrg Inc	Vermont	P&C	03/09/09	23.4	N/A
Trnsportation Liability Ins Co, The	S. Carolina	P&C	03/16/09	0.8	E- (Very Weak)
Cosmopolitan Life Ins Co	Arkansas	L&H	03/19/09	2.6	E+ (Very Weak)
Wonder State Life Ins Co	Arkansas	L&H	03/23/09	N/A	U (Unrated)
Coral Ins Co	Florida	P&C	04/09/09	15.4	E+ (Very Weak)
Consumer First Ins Co	New Jersey	P&C	04/22/09	10.7	D- (Weak)
Universal Life Insurance Co	Alabama	L&H	04/24/09	13.1	E (Very Weak)
Continental Life Ins Co of SC	S. Carolina	L&H	04/27/09	2.2	E (Very Weak)
Eastern Casualty Ins Co	Massachusetts	P&C	04/27/09	28.2	U (Unrated)
Escude Life Ins Co	Louisiana	L&H	04/27/09	3.0	E- (Very Weak)
Texas Memorial Life Ins Co	Texas	L&H	06/10/09	3.80	E- (Very Weak)
Insurance Corp of New York	New York	P&C	06/29/09	87.3	E (Very Weak)
Old Am Cnty Mutual Fire Ins Co	Texas	P&C	07/02/09	82.8	E+ (Very Weak)
First Commercial Insurance Co	Florida	P&C	07/10/09	87.1	E+ (Very Weak)
First Comm. Transp & Prop Ins Co	Florida	P&C	07/10/09	19.6	E+ (Very Weak)
Newburyport Mutual Fire Ins Co	Massachusetts	P&C	07/26/09	N/A	U (Unrated)
Medicore HP	California	HMO	07/30/09	5.5	D (Weak)
Preferred Health	Puerto Rico	HMO	07/30/09	16.2	D- (Weak)
Physicians Assurance Corp	Ohio	HMO	08/18/09	3.4	D+ (Weak)
Golden State Mutual Life Ins Co	California	L&H	09/30/09	90.0	D (Weak)
American Keystone Ins Co	Florida	P&C	10/09/09	24.1	C- (Fair)
Southeastern U.S. Ins Co	Georgia	P&C	10/28/09	42.5	E (Very Weak)
Inmerica Life & Health Ins Co	Arkansas	HMO	11/18/09	8.4	D (Weak)
Park Ave Prprty & Casualty Ins Co	Oklahoma	P&C	11/18/09	92.0	C- (Fair)
Magnolia Ins	Florida	P&C	12/14/09	N/A	N/A
SDM HealthCare	Puerto Rico	HMO	12/17/09	N/A	U (Unrated)

ProSalud HMO Care	Puerto Rico	HMO	12/21/09	N/A	U (Unrated)
Astraea Risk Retention Group, Inc.	Arizona	P&C	12/30/09	3.5	E+ (Very Weak)

Astraea Risk Retention Group, Inc.	Arizona	P&C	12/30/09	3.5	E+ (Very Weak)

Glossary

This glossary contains the most important terms used in this publication.

Admitted Assets	The total of all investments and business interests that are acceptable under statutory accounting rules.
Asset/Liability Matching	The designation of particular investments (assets) to particular policy obligations (liabilities) so that investments mature at the appropriate times and with appropriate yields to meet policy obligations as they come due.
Asset Valuation Reserve (AVR)	A liability established under statutory accounting rules whose purpose is to protect the company's surplus from the effects of defaults and market value fluctuation on stocks, bonds, mortgages and real estate. This replaces the Mandatory Securities Valuation Reserve (MSVR) and is more comprehensive in that it includes a mortgage loss reserve, whereas the MSVR did not.
Average Recession	A recession involving a decline in real GDP which is approximately equivalent to the average of the postwar recessions of 1957-58, 1960, 1970, 1974-75, 1980 and 1981-82. It is assumed, however, that in today's market, the financial losses suffered from a recession of that magnitude would be greater than those experienced in previous decades. (See also "Severe Recession.")
Capital	Strictly speaking, capital refers to funds raised through the sale of common and preferred stock. Mutual companies have capital in the form of retained earnings. In a more general sense, the term capital is commonly used to refer to a company's equity or net worth, that is, the difference between assets and liabilities (i.e., capital and surplus as shown on the balance sheet).
Capital Resources	The sum of various resources which serve as a capital cushion to losses, including capital, surplus and Asset Valuation Reserve (AVR).
Capitalization Index	An index, expressed on a scale of zero to ten, with seven or higher considered excellent, that measures the adequacy of the company's capital resources to deal with a variety of business and economic scenarios. It combines Risk-Adjusted Capital Ratios #1 and #2 as well as a leverage test that examines pricing risk.
Cash and Demand Deposits	Includes cash on hand and on deposit. A negative figure indicates that the company has more checks outstanding than current funds to cover those checks. This is not an unusual situation for an insurance company.

Collateralized Mortgage Obligation (CMO)	Mortgage-backed bond that splits the payments from mortgage pools into different classes, called tranches. The investor may purchase a bond or tranche that passes through to him or her the principal and interest payments made by the mortgage holders in that specific maturity class (usually two, five, 10 or 20 years). The risk associated with a CMO is in the variation of the payment speed on the mortgage pool which, if different than originally assumed, can cause the total return to vary greatly.
Common and Preferred Stocks	See "Stocks".
Deposit Funds	Accumulated contributions of a group out of which immediate annuities are purchased as the individual members of the group retire.
Direct Premiums Written	Total gross premiums derived from policies issued directly by the company. This figure excludes the impact of reinsurance.
Financial Strength Rating	Weiss Financial Strength Ratings grade insurers on a scale from A (Excellent) to F (Failed). Ratings are based on five major factors: investment safety, policy leverage, capitalization, profitability and stability of operations.
Five-Year Profitability Index	See "Profitability Index."
Government Securities	Securities issued and/or guaranteed by U.S. and foreign governments which are rated as highest quality (Class 1) by state insurance commissioners. Included in this category are bonds issued by governmental agencies and guaranteed with the full faith and credit of the government. Regardless of the issuing entity, they are viewed as being relatively safer than the other investment categories. See "Investment Grade Bonds" to determine which items are excluded from this category.
Health Claims Reserve	Funds set aside from premiums for the eventual payment of health benefits after the end of the statement year.
Insurance Risk	The risk that the level of claims and related expenses will exceed current premiums plus reserves allocated for their payment.
Interest Rate Risk	The risk that, due to changes in interest rates, investment income will not meet the needs of policy commitments. This risk can be reduced by effective asset/liability matching.
Invested Assets	The total size of the firm's investment portfolio.
Investment Grade Bonds	This covers all investment grade bonds other than those listed in "Government Securities" (above). Specifically, this includes: (1) nonguaranteed obligations of governments; (2) obligations of governments rated as Class 2 by state insurance commissioners; (3) state and municipal bonds; plus (4) investment grade corporate bonds.

Investment Safety Index	Measured on a scale of zero to ten, with ten being the best and seven or better considered strong. Each investment area is rated as to quality and vulnerability during an unfavorable economic environment (updated using quarterly data when available).
Investments in Affiliates	Includes bonds, preferred stocks and common stocks, as well as other vehicles which many insurance companies use to invest in—and establish a corporate link with—affiliated companies
Life and Annuity Claims Reserve	Funds set aside from premiums for the eventual payment of life and annuity claims.
Liquidity Index	An index, expressed on a scale from zero to ten, with seven or higher considered excellent, which measures the company's ability to raise the necessary cash to meet policyholder obligations. This index includes a stress test which considers the consequences of a spike in claims or a run on policy surrenders. Sometimes a company may appear to have the necessary resources, but may be unable to sell its investments at the prices at which they are valued in the company's financial statements.
Mandatory Security Valuation Reserve (MSVR)	Reserve for investment losses and asset value fluctuation mandated by the state insurance commissioners for companies registered as life and health insurers. As of December 31, 1992, this was replaced by the Asset Valuation Reserve.
Moderate Loss Scenario	An economic decline from current levels approximately equivalent to that of the average postwar recession.
Mortgages in Good Standing	Mortgages which are current in their payments (excludes mortgage-backed securities).
Net Premiums Written	The total dollar volume of premiums retained by the company. This figure is equal to direct premiums written, plus reinsurance assumed less reinsurance ceded.
Noninvestment Grade Bonds	Low-rated issues, commonly known as "junk bonds," which carry a high risk as defined by the state insurance commissioners. These include bond Classes 3 - 6.
Nonperforming Mortgages	Mortgages which are (a) 90 days or more past due or (b) in process of foreclosure.
Other Investments	Items not included in any of the other categories such as premium notes, collateral loans, short-term investments and other miscellaneous items.
Other Structured Securities	Nonresidential mortgage related and other securitized loan-backed or asset-backed securities. This category also includes CMOs with noninvestment grade ratings.

Policy Leverage	A measure of insurance risk based on the relationship of net premiums to capital resources.
Policy Loans	Loans to policyholders under insurance contracts.
Profitability Index	Measured on a scale of zero to ten, with ten being the best and seven or better considered strong. A composite of five factors: (1) gain or loss on operations; (2) consistency of operating results; (3) impact of operating results on surplus; (4) adequacy of investment income as compared to the needs of policy reserves; and (5) expenses in relation to industry averages. Thus, the overall index is an indicator of the health of a company's current and past operations.
Purchase Money Mortgages	Mortgages written by an insurance company to facilitate the sale of property owned by the company.
Real Estate	Direct real estate investments including property (a) occupied by the company; (b) acquired through foreclosure and (c) purchased as an investment.
Reinsurance Assumed	Insurance risk acquired by taking on partial or full responsibility for claims on policies written by other companies. (See "Reinsurance Ceded.")
Reinsurance Ceded	Insurance risk sold to another company.
Risk-Adjusted Capital	The capital resources that would be needed in a worsening economic environment (same as "Target Capital").
Risk-Adjusted Capital Ratio #1	The capital resources which a company currently has, in relation to the resources that would be needed to deal with a moderate loss scenario. This scenario is based on historical experience during an average recession and adjusted to reflect current conditions and vulnerabilities (updated using quarterly data when available).
Risk-Adjusted Capital Ratio #2	The capital resources which a company currently has, in relation to the resources that would be needed to deal with a severe loss scenario. This scenario is based on historical experience of the postwar period and adjusted to reflect current conditions and the potential impact of a severe recession (updated using quarterly data when available).
Separate Accounts	Funds segregated from the general account and valued at market. Used to fund indexed products, such as variable life and variable annuity products.
Severe Loss Scenario	An economic decline from current levels in which the loss experience of the single worst year of the postwar period is extended for a period of three years. (See also "Moderate Loss Scenario".)
Severe Recession	A prolonged economic slowdown in which the single worst year of the postwar period is extended for a period of three years. (See also "Average Recession".)

Stability Index

Measured on a scale of zero to ten. This integrates a wide variety of factors that reflects the company's financial stability and diversification of risk.

State of Domicile

Although most insurance companies are licensed to do business in many states, they have only one state of domicile. This is the state which has primary regulatory responsibility for the company. Use the state of domicile to make absolutely sure that you have the correct company. Bear in mind, however, that this need not be the state where the company's main offices are located.

State Guaranty Funds

Funds that are designed to raise cash from existing insurance carriers to cover policy claims of bankrupt insurance companies.

Stocks

Common and preferred equities, including ownership in affiliates.

Surplus

The difference between assets and liabilities, including paid-in contributed surplus, plus the statutory equivalent of "retained earnings" in non-insurance business corporations.

Target Capital

See "Risk-Adjusted Capital."

Total Assets

Total admitted assets, including investments and other business assets. See "Admitted Assets."